MATERIALS FOR A BASIC COURSE IN

CIVIL PROCEDURE

TENTH EDITION

by

RICHARD H. FIELD
Late Story Professor of Law Emeritus, Harvard University

BENJAMIN KAPLAN
Royall Professor of Law Emeritus, Harvard University
Retired Associate Justice, Supreme Judicial Court of Massachusetts

KEVIN M. CLERMONT
Ziff Professor of Law, Cornell University

2010

195 Broadway, 9th Floor

New York, NY 10007

Phone Toll Free 1–877–888–1330

Fax (212) 367–6799

foundation–press.com

Printed in the United States of America

ISBN 978–1–59941–778–3

Mat #40893927

PREFACE

This Tenth Edition represents another updating and a thorough rewriting. Nevertheless, the revision also reflects a basic satisfaction with the objectives, with the methods, and generally with the depth and range of coverage that have characterized this casebook since its beginnings. Therefore, I appropriately begin with the words that Professor Field and Justice Kaplan used to describe their trailblazing First Edition:

"Traditional courses in Civil Procedure suffered from being too much concerned with detail and too diffuse. These defects were perhaps due to an overscrupulous regard for the obligations which Procedure was thought to owe to other courses in the curriculum; in all events Procedure often seemed to underplay the fact that it had distinctive missions of its own. And in straining either for omnibus coverage or for the satisfactions that came from historical exposition, the traditional courses dwelt too long on the common law and older code systems and gave less than adequate attention to current practice.

"We have sought to avoid these errors even if we have succeeded only in committing others. A basic course should, we think, lay stress on the fundamental and recurrent problems of litigative procedure as against particular procedural devices. To be sure, the course should insist on the mastery of specifics, but the larger picture should be kept in view. As a second objective, not antithetical but rather intrinsic to the first, the course should give a rounded understanding of a single, modern system of procedure. The choice naturally falls on the Federal system. The common law and older codes may come in by way of comparison and as a reading of the minutes of yesterday's meeting, but the Federal Rules should be a principal theme.

"The belief that the course should deal in a large way with the litigative process has impelled us at various points to deal explicitly with the general attitudes that underlie and characterize current procedural modes. It has also induced us to draw in some elementary materials on proof and division of functions between judge and jury which are usually reserved for the course in Evidence. With the adoption of Federal procedure as a center of study we have been led into a number of problems of Federal jurisdiction and into questions arising when Federal courts apply State law and State courts apply Federal law. No examination of a modern system could fail to concern itself with multi-party litigation which has so far increased in frequency and importance that it demands attention even of beginning students. We therefore deal with the subject of parties. This and some other topics of equitable flavor seem to have proper place in Procedure, and especially so when, as in our school, Equity is abolished as a separate course and distributed on a functional basis to other parts of the curriculum.

"On the side of method, we set much store by the pedagogical device which will be found early in this book in Part One, Topic B, entitled 'Phases of a Lawsuit.' Here we have about 150 pages of text interspersed with cases, statutes and questions, describing and analyzing the conduct of litigation in the Federal courts from the institution of suit through appeal. We have sought here to convey bedrock information and to locate and expose significant questions which provide the basis for much of the rest of the book. This initial survey makes considerable demands on students but it seems to us to have the virtues of giving them a sense of procedure as a whole, of raising at the threshold and keeping steadily before them the fundamental and recurrent problems of adjudication, and of enabling them to proceed thereafter on a more profound level than they might otherwise attain. Perhaps we should add that after this survey we have felt less than the usual scruples of conscience about making some omissions later in the course as pressure of time has compelled it.

"Treating a number of passages in the materials as background reading for students requiring little if any classroom discussion, we have still been unable to cover the whole book in a course given three times a week for a year. We have followed respectable precedent in leaving in rather more than can be comfortably handled, remitting to individual taste and need some choices that we have not had the fortitude to make firmly between ourselves. We regret especially that on no allocation of space which seemed to us reasonable have we been able to provide the kind of bridge we would like to make between court procedure and the procedure of administrative agencies.

"Teachers of Procedure have differed widely about the route to be travelled, but they have not differed much about the ultimate goal. They have sought in their separate ways to turn out lawyers who will not approach a practice question as just an exercise in using the index to the practice act or the rule book, but who will go about the job with a lively awareness of the importance of farsighted procedural strategy, a sense of the total procedural resources of the law, and a feeling of personal responsibility for the fair and efficient running of procedural machinery. We have hoped in this book to help students toward the vital skills and attitudes."

Those words still stand as a statement of our views on what a Civil Procedure course should try to do. Also, we continue to rely on the concentric series of three increasingly broad and deep surveys of the whole in Topics A, B, and C of Part One. These give the student a solid grounding in the subject and thereby free the teacher to pick and choose among the theoretical and practical problem areas explored in the subsequent Parts of the current edition. Indeed, the technique of an initial but substantial survey seems more and more appropriate as many Procedure courses have effectively shrunk in credit hours just when the subject itself has expanded and diversified. An efficient and systematic survey provides a way of delivering the essentials, while reserving enough time to reach the more significant and palatable.

Each succeeding edition has altered the emphases and refined the techniques, of course. In recent editions, for example, we have further attempted to foster diverse teaching by facilitating digression during the surveys at one or more points to the more advanced subsequent materials. Moreover, we rely ever more on excerpted commentary to convey a sense of the intellectual richness of Procedure.

The law persists in its refusal to stand still, fortunately. So the contents of this latest edition—as opposed to its structure—are again new-fashioned. We undertook this unavoidable part of the rewriting task with a renewed determination to integrate rather than append new developments. Although Congress and the rulemakers introduced new Rules, the prime example of recontoured terrain lies in the Supreme Court's major new cases on pleading. Yet our regard for earlier editions of this casebook has not constrained alterations in coverage to those forced upon us by legislators, rulemakers, and courts. Thus, we have tried to keep the focus moving to the significant new ideas in the field. The result of this enrichment of subject is a very slightly longer casebook. Nevertheless, this increase in length should not diminish the casebook's teachability—thanks to its structure, which permits the instructor to convey an effective compendium and then to select among problem areas according to tastes and needs.

In summary, the Tenth Edition represents growth along lines consistent with the First Edition's conception of stressing the current and pursuing Procedure's own distinctive and evolving missions. Yet concerned with methodology, we pruned and trained that growth within the casebook's proven structure. Also wary of letting the new growth obscure the basics, we did not forget the abiding importance of typical litigation in American courts today as a locus of lawmaking and value-articulation as well as of dispute resolution, nor did we abolish among Procedure's missions its supporting role in the law-school curriculum as a source of illumination.

Now for some miscellanea:

We strive to reproduce the original materials as accurately as possible. Thus, what may appear to be a typographic error is more likely a faithful reproduction of an official court document.

"It's downright embarrassing. Thirty years on the bench and just today I find out judgment is spelled without an 'E'."

We continue our practice of using the original numbers for footnotes by judges in judicial opinions and by authors in quoted materials, when we retain such footnotes; we omit other such footnotes without any statement to that effect. Editors' footnotes are lettered rather than numbered.

In some of the cases the editors' bracketed statement of the facts includes information culled from the record. We specifically indicate any such supplementation in our version of the case only when the original omission of information by the opinion-writer could conceivably have had some significance.

We do not advise the student to turn regularly to treatises or law review articles in preparing for class discussion, but we do indicate their availability for research and other special purposes. In our text we make frequent reference to the two major multivolume works—Federal Practice and Procedure by Professors Charles Alan Wright and Arthur R. Miller and others, and James Wm. Moore's Federal Practice—which we simply cite respectively by the authors' last names and as Moore. We also often cite Charles Alan Wright & Mary Kay Kane, Law of Federal Courts (6th ed. 2002), a single-volume hornbook on the jurisdiction and practice of the federal courts, and Fleming James, Jr., Geoffrey C. Hazard, Jr. & John

Leubsdorf, Civil Procedure (5th ed. 2001), a single volume dealing with procedure more generally. We cite other treatises and law review articles on a highly selective basis, usually when we think they are especially useful adjuncts to our cases and text.

For the final note, I should explain why I use "we" in writing this preface even though Professor Field died in 1978 and Justice Kaplan's absorption in judging precluded active participation after the Second Edition in 1968. My reason lies in their original conception and their powers to convey it, which give me the sensation of a continuing collaboration that prevails over the bounds of time.

K.M.C.

March 2010

FEDERAL RULES BOOKLET

The Federal Rules of Civil Procedure (together with the Advisory Committee's notes on the major amendments), many of the Federal Rules of Appellate Procedure, selected provisions of the Constitution of the United States and title 28 of the United States Code and other procedural statutes, and the Federal Rules of Evidence are integral to this book. They are printed in a separate booklet by Foundation Press.

ACKNOWLEDGMENTS

We gratefully acknowledge the permission extended by the following publishers and authors to reprint excerpts from the works indicated: American Bar Association Journal: Joint Conference on Professional Responsibility, Report, 44 A.B.A.J. 1159 (1958) ("Reprinted with permission from American Bar Association Journal"), and ABA Comm. on Professional Ethics and Grievances, Formal Op. 280, 35 A.B.A.J. 876 (1949); Foundation Press, Inc.: L. Fuller, The Problems of Jurisprudence (1949), and J. Maguire, Evidence: Common Sense and Common Law (1947); American Bar Association Reports: Pound, The Causes of Popular Dissatisfaction with the Administration of Justice, 29 A.B.A.Rep. 395 (1906); Princeton University Press: J. Frank, Courts on Trial (1949) ("Reprinted by permission of Princeton University Press"); West Publishing Co.: Schaefer, Is the Adversary System Working in Optimal Fashion?, 70 F.R.D. 159 (1976), Clark, Simplified Pleading, 2 F.R.D. 456 (1943), B. Shipman, Handbook of Common–Law Pleading (3d ed. 1923), and P. Carrington, D. Meador & M. Rosenberg, Justice on Appeal (1976); Notre Dame Lawyer: Barrett, The Adversary System and the Ethics of Advocacy, 37 Notre Dame Law. 479 (1962) ("Reprinted with permission. © by the Notre Dame Lawyer, University of Notre Dame.") (We bear responsibility for any errors which have occurred in reprinting or editing.); American Law Institute: Morgan, Foreword to Model Code of Evidence (1942) ("Copyright 1942 by The American Law Institute. Reprinted with the permission of The American Law Institute."), Restatement of Judgments (1942), Restatement (Second) of Conflict of Laws (1971) (revised 1988) ("Copyright 1971 by The American Law Institute. Reprinted with the permission of The American Law Institute."), and Restatement (Second) of Judgments (1982) ("Copyright 1982 by The American Law Institute. Reprinted with the permission of The American Law Institute."); Stanford Law Review: Curtis, The Ethics of Advocacy, 4 Stan.L.Rev. 3 (1951) ("Copyright 1951 by the Board of Trustees of the Leland Stanford Junior University"), and Scott, Two Models of the Civil Process, 27 Stan.L.Rev. 937 (1975) ("Copyright 1975 by the Board of Trustees of the Leland Stanford Junior University"); New York University School of Law: Simpson, "The Problem of Trial," in David Dudley Field Centenary Essays 141 (A. Reppy ed., 1949); Yale Law Journal: Smith, Components of Proof in Legal Proceedings, 51 Yale L.J. 537 (1942) ("Reprinted by permission of The Yale Law Journal Company and Fred B. Rothman & Company from The Yale Law Journal, Vol. 51, pp. 537, 575"), and Crick, The Final Judgment as a Basis for Appeal, 41 Yale L.J. 539 (1932); Harcourt, Brace & Co.: G. Joughin & E. Morgan, The Legacy of Sacco and Vanzetti (1948); Abram Chayes: The Role of the Judge in Public

Law Litigation, 89 Harv.L.Rev. 1281 (1976); Columbia University Press: N.Y. County Lawyers' Ass'n Comm. on Professional Ethics, Op. 309 (1933); Marvin E. Frankel: The Search for Truth: An Umpireal View, 123 U.Pa. L.Rev. 1031 (1975); Buffalo Law Review: Kaplan, Civil Procedure—Reflections on the Comparison of Systems, 9 Buff. L.Rev. 409 (1960); Cambridge University Press: F. Maitland, The Forms of Action at Common Law (1936), F. Maitland, The Constitutional History of England (1908), and F. Maitland, Equity (1909); Harvard Law Review Association: Morgan, Some Observations Concerning Presumptions, 44 Harv.L.Rev. 906 (1931), Morgan, Instructing the Jury upon Presumptions and Burden of Proof, 47 Harv.L.Rev. 59 (1933), Henderson, The Background of the Seventh Amendment, 80 Harv.L.Rev. 289 (1966), and Note, Appealability in the Federal Courts, 75 Harv.L.Rev. 351 (1961); Stevens & Sons, Ltd.: C. Fifoot, History and Sources of the Common Law (1949); Columbia Law Review: Adams, The Origin of English Equity, 16 Colum.L.Rev. 87 (1916); Methuen & Co., Ltd.: W. Holdsworth, A History of English Law (7th ed. 1956); University of Michigan Law School: Z. Chafee, Some Problems of Equity (1950); Little, Brown and Company: Bowen, "Progress in the Administration of Justice During the Victorian Period," in 1 Select Essays in Anglo–American Legal History 516 (1907), F. James, G. Hazard & J. Leubsdorf, Civil Procedure (4th ed. 1992), F. James & G. Hazard, Civil Procedure (3d ed. 1985), and F. James, Civil Procedure (1965); Macmillan Co.: The Diary of George Templeton Strong (A. Nevins & M. Thomas eds., 1952); Georgia Law Review: Wright, Procedural Reform: Its Limitations and Its Future, 1 Ga.L.Rev. 563 (1967); Minnesota Law Review: Wolfram, The Constitutional History of the Seventh Amendment, 57 Minn.L.Rev. 639 (1973); Houghton Mifflin Co.: A. Beveridge, The Life of John Marshall (1919); and Michigan Law Review: Reed, Compulsory Joinder of Parties in Civil Actions (pt. 1), 55 Mich.L.Rev. 327 (1957).

Also: Greenwood Press, Inc.: Golding, "On the Adversary System and Justice," in Philosophical Law 98 R. Bronaugh ed., 1978); West Publishing Co.: Sander, Varieties of Dispute Processing, 70 F.R.D. 111 (1976), and Current Developments in Judicial Administration: Papers Presented at the Plenary Session of the American Association of Law Schools, December, 1977, 80 F.R.D. 147 (1979); Buffalo Law Review: Landsman, The Decline of the Adversary System: How the Rhetoric of Swift and Certain Justice Has Affected Adjudication in American Courts, 29 Buff.L.Rev. 487 (1980); National Clearinghouse for Legal Services, Inc.: Singer, Nonjudicial Dispute Resolution Mechanisms: The Effects on Justice for the Poor, 13 Clearinghouse Rev. 569 (1979); American Judicature Society: Luskin, Building a Theory of Case Processing Time, 62 Judicature 115 (1978); Joseph W. Bartlett: The Law Business: A Tired Monopoly (1982); American Bar Foundation Research Journal: Brazil, Improving Judicial Controls over the Pretrial Development of Civil Actions: Model Rules for Case Management and Sanctions, 1981 Am.B.Found.Res.J. 873; Harvard Law Review Association: Resnik, Managerial Judges, 96 Harv.L.Rev. 374 (1982) ("Copyright © 1982 by the Harvard Law Review Association."), Chayes, The Supreme Court, 1981 Term—Foreword: Public Law Litigation and the Burger Court, 96 Harv.L.Rev. 4 (1982) ("Copyright © 1982 by the Harvard Law Review Association."), and Miller, Of Frankenstein Monsters and Shining Knights: Myth, Reality, and the "Class Action Problem," 92 Harv.L.Rev. 664 (1979) ("Copyright © 1979 by the Harvard Law Review Association."); American Bar Association: Ebersole, "Discovery and Pretrial Procedures," in The Improvement of the Administration of Justice 137 (F. Klein ed., 6th ed. 1981); Michigan Law Review: Note, A Probabilistic Analysis of the Doctrine of Mutuality of Collateral Estoppel, 76 Mich.L.Rev. 612 (1978); Frank M. Coffin: The Frontier of Remedies: A Call for Exploration, 67 Cal.L.Rev. 983 (1979); Stanford Law Review: Rhode, Class Conflicts in Class Actions, 34 Stan.L.Rev. 1183 (1982) ("Copyright 1982 by the Board of Trustees of the Leland Stanford Junior University"); Harvard Civil Rights–Civil Liberties Law Review: Jones, Litigation Without Representation: The Need for Intervention to Affirm Affirmative Action, 14 Harv.C.R.-C.L.L.Rev. 31 (1979); and U.C. Davis Law Review: Friedenthal, Increased Participation by Non–Parties: The Need for Limitations and Conditions, 13 U.C.Davis L.Rev. 259 (1980).

More recently: American Bar Association: Model Rules of Professional Conduct (1983) ("Excerpted from the Model Rules of Professional Conduct, copyright by the American Bar Association. All rights reserved. Reprinted with permission."); Minnesota Law Review: Shapiro, Some Problems of Discovery in an Adversary System, 63 Minn.L.Rev. 1055 (1979); Academic Press: Hans & Vidmar, "Jury Selection," in The Psychology of the Courtroom 39 (N. Kerr & R. Bray eds., 1982); Van Nostrand Reinhold: M. Saks & R. Hastie, Social Psychology in Court (1978); Journal of Legal Education: Spiegelman, Integrating Doctrine, Theory and Practice in the Law School Curriculum: The Logic of Jake's Ladder in the Context of Amy's Web, 38 J.Legal Educ. 243 (1988); Texas Law Review: Abel, Why Does the ABA Promulgate Ethical Rules?, 59 Tex.L.Rev. 639 (1981) ("Published originally in 59 Texas Law Review 639–88 (1981). Copyright © 1981 by the Texas Law Review. Reprinted by permission."); University of Florida Law Review: Sander, Alternative Methods of Dispute Resolution: An Overview, 37 U.Fla.L.Rev. 1 (1985); Little, Brown and Company: S. Goldberg, F. Sander & N. Rogers, Dispute Resolution (2d ed. 1992); National Clearinghouse for Legal Services, Inc.: Simon, Legal Informality and Redistributive Politics, 19 Clearinghouse Rev. 384 (1985); Wisconsin Law Review: Bush, Dispute Resolution Alternatives and the Goals of Civil Justice: Jurisdictional Principles for Process Choice, 1984 Wis.L.Rev. 893; Stephen N. Subrin: How Equity Conquered Common Law: The Federal Rules of Civil Procedure in Historical Perspective, 135 U.Pa.L.Rev. 909 (1987); Columbia Law Review: Marcus, The Revival of Fact Pleading Under the Federal Rules of Civil Procedure, 86 Colum.L.Rev. 433 (1986) ("Copyright © 1986 by the Directors of the Columbia Law Review Association, Inc. All Rights Reserved.

This article originally appeared at 86 Colum.L.Rev. 433 (1986). Reprinted by permission."); UCLA Law Review: Menkel–Meadow, For and Against Settlement: Uses and Abuses of the Mandatory Settlement Conference, 33 UCLA L.Rev. 485 (1985); Jeffrey W. Stempel: A Distorted Mirror: The Supreme Court's Shimmering View of Summary Judgment, Directed Verdict, and the Adjudication Process, 49 Ohio St.L.J. 95 (1988); The Michie Company: J. Frederick, The Psychology of the American Jury (1987); Kentucky Law Journal: Stephens, Controlling the Civil Jury: Towards a Functional Model of Justification, 76 Ky.L.J. 81 (1988); Plenum Publishing Corp.: V. Hans & N. Vidmar, Judging the Jury (1986); Cornell Law Review: Idleman, The Emergence of Jurisdictional Resequencing in the Federal Courts, 87 Cornell L.Rev. 1 (2001); North Carolina Law Review: Tobias, Rule 19 and the Public Rights Exception to Party Joinder, 65 N.C.L.Rev. 745 (1987) ("Reprinted with permission from 65 N.C.L.Rev. 745 (1987). Copyright © 1987 by the North Carolina Law Review Association."); American Law Institute: Complex Litigation (1994) ("Copyright 1994 by The American Law Institute. Reprinted with the permission of The American Law Institute."); Roger H. Trangsrud: Joinder Alternatives in Mass Tort Litigation, 70 Cornell L.Rev. 779 (1985); Indiana Law Journal: Rosenberg, Class Actions for Mass Torts: Doing Individual Justice by Collective Means, 62 Ind.L.J. 561 (1987); and South Carolina Law Review: Carrington, The Function of the Civil Appeal: A Late–Century View, 38 S.C.L.Rev. 411 (1987).

SUMMARY OF CONTENTS

TABLE OF CONTENTS

TOPIC B. State Courts—Continued

TABLE OF CASES

Principal cases are in bold type. Non-principal cases are in roman type. References are to Pages.

TABLE OF FEDERAL PROVISIONS

UNITED STATES

UNITED STATES CONSTITUTION

UNITED STATES CODE ANNOTATED

5 U.S.C.A.—Government Organization and Employees

9 U.S.C.A.—Arbitration

15 U.S.C.A.—Commerce and Trade

UNITED STATES CODE ANNOTATED

15 U.S.C.A.—Commerce and Trade

Sec.	This Work Page
1051—1127	740
1671—1677	122

28 U.S.C.A.—Judiciary and Judicial Procedure

Sec.	This Work Page
41	14
133	13
133	14
144	158
331	22
455	158
471—482	1307
636	108
636(b)	1250
651—658	310
652(a)	1308
1253	205
1254	18
1254	211
1254	229
1254(1)	839
1257	229
1257	1553
1291	18
1291	205
1291	689
1291	1263
1291	1545
1291	1546
1291	1548
1291	1549
1291	1551
1291	1552
1292	1552
1292(a)	206
1292(a)(1)	205
1292(a)(1)	206
1292(a)(1)	922
1292(a)(1)	1263
1292(a)(1)	1559
1292(a)(1)	1560
1292(a)(1)	1563
1292(a)(1)	1564
1292(b)	206
1292(b)	208
1292(b)	377
1292(b)	433
1292(b)	1210
1292(b)	1263
1292(b)	1511
1292(b)	1522
1292(b)	1523
1292(b)	1549
1292(b)	1565
1292(b)	1566
1292(b)	1567
1292(b)	1576

UNITED STATES CODE ANNOTATED

28 U.S.C.A.—Judiciary and Judicial Procedure

Sec.	This Work Page
1292(e)	990
1292(e)	1542
1292(e)	1551
1295	14
1304(c)	470
1312(a)(3)	470
1331	13
1331	214
1331	216
1331	403
1331	422
1331	423
1331	430
1332	214
1332	217
1332	221
1332	226
1332	236
1332	237
1332	242
1332(a)	13
1332(a)	16
1332(a)	218
1332(a)	451
1332(b)	461
1332(c)(1)	223
1332(c)(1)	225
1332(c)(1)	234
1332(c)(2)	464
1332(d)	992
1335	13
1335	225
1335	242
1335	1010
1335(a)(2)	1016
1335(b)	1017
1337	214
1337(a)	13
1338	214
1338(a)	13
1338(b)	430
1343	214
1343(3)	439
1345	13
1345	399
1345	400
1345	838
1346	13
1346(b)	444
1346(b)	1183
1359	465
1367	445
1367	447
1367	448
1367	450
1367	1003
1367(b)	447
1367(b)	448
1367(b)	459

UNITED STATES CODE ANNOTATED

28 U.S.C.A.—Judiciary and Judicial Procedure

Sec.	This Work Page
1367(c)	450
1367(c)	471
1369	225
1369	237
1369	868
1391	233
1391	234
1391	238
1391	242
1391(a)	233
1391(a)	234
1391(a)	644
1391(b)	233
1391(b)	234
1391(c)	234
1391(d)	234
1391(g)	868
1397	234
1397	242
1397	1010
1401	234
1401	249
1404(a)	235
1404(a)	378
1404(a)	637
1404(a)	638
1404(a)	641
1404(a)	642
1404(a)	643
1404(a)	644
1404(a)	683
1404(a)	858
1406(a)	643
1406(a)	644
1406(a)	645
1406(a)	655
1406(a)	683
1407	858
1441	226
1441	227
1441	237
1441	465
1441	469
1441	1181
1441(a)	234
1441(a)	469
1441(a)	470
1441(a)	471
1441(a)	472
1441(c)	470
1441(c)	471
1441(c)	472
1441(e)	868
1445(a)	227
1445(a)	471
1445(c)	471
1446—1450	226
1447(c)	472
1448	616

UNITED STATES CODE ANNOTATED

28 U.S.C.A.—Judiciary and Judicial Procedure

Sec.	This Work Page
1453	992
1631	645
1651	92
1651(a)	209
1651(a)	210
1651(a)	1568
1651(a)	1569
1652	8
1652	342
1652	344
1653	218
1653	1180
1655	504
1655	505
1655	635
1658	403
1695	249
1697	868
1712	992
1738	509
1738	801
1738	803
1738	805
1738	806
1746	166
1746	1184
1785	868
1861—1869	151
1870	151
1915	1172
1915(d)	1171
1915(d)	1172
1915(d)	1173
1915(e)(2)(B)(i)	1171
1915A	1173
1920	192
1963	507
1963	510
1963	511
2071	23
2071	208
2071	1129
2071(a)	23
2071(a)	1308
2072	23
2072	24
2072	171
2072	340
2072	1552
2072(c)	1551
2072—2074	23
2073	25
2074	25
2074	26
2074(b)	170
2074(b)	171
2077	23
2106	208

UNITED STATES CODE ANNOTATED

28 U.S.C.A.—Judiciary and Judicial Procedure

29 U.S.C.A.—Labor

33 U.S.C.A.—Navigation and Navigable Waters

42 U.S.C.A.—The Public Health and Welfare

UNITED STATES CODE ANNOTATED

45 U.S.C.A.—Railroads

46 U.S.C.A.—Shipping

STATUTES AT LARGE

POPULAR NAME ACTS

CIVIL JUSTICE REFORM ACT

CIVIL RIGHTS ACT OF 1964

CLAYTON ANTITRUST ACT

CONSUMER CREDIT PROTECTION ACT

LABOR MANAGEMENT RELATIONS ACT

NORRIS–LaGUARDIA ACT

RULES ENABLING ACT

UNITED STATES ARBITRATION ACT

FEDERAL RULES OF CIVIL PROCEDURE

FEDERAL RULES OF CIVIL PROCEDURE

FEDERAL RULES OF CIVIL PROCEDURE

FEDERAL RULES OF CIVIL PROCEDURE

FEDERAL RULES OF CIVIL PROCEDURE

FEDERAL RULES OF CIVIL PROCEDURE

FEDERAL RULES OF CIVIL PROCEDURE

FEDERAL RULES OF CIVIL PROCEDURE

MATERIALS FOR A BASIC COURSE IN

CIVIL PROCEDURE

PART ONE

A FIRST VIEW OF THE SUBJECT

TOPIC A

OPENING STATEMENTS

This course treats "Civil Procedure." For the purpose of putting general boundaries to the course, what meanings do we ascribe to these words? We shall not attempt here to define them in any formal way, but shall rather begin at this point to convey a general sense of the meanings we attach to them.

Nature of civil controversies.—The word "civil" appears in the present context in contradistinction to "criminal." The typical criminal case is one that the government initiates for the purpose of securing obedience to its laws by the punishment, correction, or incapacitation of a lawbreaker. In a civil case, ordinarily the government is not seeking a sanction against a lawbreaker, nor is it even a party in the proceedings. The typical civil case is one initiated and carried on by a person who seeks redress for some wrong alleged to have been committed against him by another. The redress he seeks is commonly, although by no means always, the payment of money to him by the wrongdoer.[a]

Wrongs can arise when people interact. People living together in organized society are bound in their interactions by rules governing their day-to-day conduct, imposed in one way or another by the government. These are rules of substance, or of substantive law. A rule of substantive law may be embodied in a legislative enactment—an act of Congress, an act of a state legislature, or a municipal ordinance. Often it finds its source in the "common law," the decisions and opinions of the courts.[b] Whatever the source of a rule of substantive law, one may cast it in the form of a proposition such as the following:

---

[a] What cases suggest themselves where the payment of money would not be a satisfactory form of redress? What other forms of redress might be appropriate? After considering these questions, see infra p. 190.

[*Note:* Editor's footnotes throughout this casebook are lettered. Footnotes by the court in judicial opinions and by authors in quoted materials, when retained, will bear the numbers of the originals; we shall omit the other footnotes without any statement to that effect.]

[b] "With the common law, unlike the [European] civil law and its Roman law precursor, the formulation of general principles has not preceded decision. In its origin it is the law of the practitioner rather than the philosopher. Decision has drawn its inspiration and its strength from the very facts which frame the issues for decision. Once made, the decision controls the future judgments of courts in like or analogous cases. General rules, underlying principles, and finally legal doctrine, have successively emerged only as the precedents, accumulated through the centuries, have been seen to follow a pattern, characteristically not without distortion and occasional broken threads, and seldom conforming consistently to principle." Harlan F. Stone, The Common Law in the United States, 50 Harv.L.Rev. 4, 6 (1936).

If *B* knowingly strikes *A*, and . . . , then, unless *A* consented, or . . . , *A* is entitled to a judgment of a court that he recover money damages from *B*.

This particular proposition refers to an event that the law calls a battery. Rules of this sort state the rights and duties among people and suggest the circumstances in which a person may seek redress against another.

The government establishes and maintains a system of courts to which a person may resort, if the person chooses to do so, to obtain such redress. Predominantly, then, the task of courts in civil cases is to decide specific cases brought before them by people who cannot or will not follow the usual course of settling their disagreements by themselves. True, in deciding a case a court may generate general rules that will guide other people later involved in similar disagreements. Much of the law student's work entails the appraisal and use of past decisions, and judicial opinions explaining these decisions, as precedents to aid in predicting how courts would likely decide future cases. These decisions and opinions are tools of the lawyer's trade. They help him or her, as adviser, to resolve the client's difficulties short of litigation and, as advocate, to further the client's cause if litigation comes. This constant resort to precedents tends, however, to becloud the proposition that the traditional purpose of a typical lawsuit is to decide a very real dispute between flesh-and-blood people and, where possible, to resolve it once and for all.[c] What, then, is the nature of these disputes with which the courts have to deal in civil cases?

In many cases that come to the courts there is dispute over what the rule of substantive law is. Legislation may be of doubtful meaning, or precedents may not speak with a clear voice. New sets of circumstances arise to pose problems for which neither existing legislation nor the precedents afford a ready answer. A court must nevertheless decide the case before it and will do so with a view to existing rules of substantive law and upon some consideration of historical continuity, of institutional competence, of prevailing morals, of policy goals, and of other factors.

In other cases the substantive law will be pretty clear, and the contest will be over what happened. The parties may agree that the pertinent rule of substantive law is the one given schematically above, but they may differ as to whether *B* struck *A*, whether she did so knowingly, or whether *A* consented.

In still other cases there will be a contest both as to what occurred and as to what the applicable rule is. In lawyers' language, such a dispute presents both questions of fact ("What happened?") and questions of law ("What is the substantive rule?").

A first word of warning is in order here. Although we have spoken of the "typical civil case," the student should not let this focus create blinders. Of late, interest in several quarters has shifted toward complex

[c] There are elaborate rules designed to prevent the relitigation of disputes once disposed of by a court. Reference to these rules, which cluster under the banner of "res judicata," recurs throughout this book. We treat them in detail in Part Four.

litigation, prototypified by desegregation cases and characterized by vastly intensified public concern and participation. Concomitantly, interest has also shifted toward alternatives to litigation, whereby almost all grievances conclude short of judicial adjudication. In some significant senses, so-called public law litigation and alternative dispute resolution both are more important than the typical civil case. Accordingly, this book will eventually turn to those matters, and the student should meanwhile bear them in mind. Nevertheless, we begin our study with so-called ordinary litigation, partly because it has abiding importance, and partly because one must begin somewhere, but mainly because we view this as the pedagogically sound place to begin.

Nature of procedural rules.—In statutes enacted by the legislature, in general rules promulgated by the courts, and in specific judicial rulings having the force of precedent, the government prescribes the procedures by which persons may bring disputes before its courts, by which they must unfold and conduct those disputes once in the courts, and by which they can enforce the resulting decisions of the courts. The scope of procedural rules may be roughly gauged by examining the table of contents of the "Federal Rules of Civil Procedure." This course deals with all such procedures, which you may think of as constituting the mechanics of litigation.

Rules of procedure provide among other things the means of laying bare what the contest is about. The court, in theory at least, knows nothing of the state of affairs between the contestants until one of them formally presents a claim to it. The rules of procedure regulate how he must do this, and also how his adversary must present the adverse side of the matter, so that the court can judge between them and grant or refuse redress. One aim of the rules is to disclose the real dispute in a minimum of time and with least expense, and thus to avoid the vexatious and wasteful business of dealing with questions on which the parties are actually not in disagreement. Another aim is to confine the parties to presenting only materials relevant to the real dispute and helpful in its resolution. Yet another is to give neither side an undeserved forensic advantage in persuading the court.

Litigation could perhaps proceed without general procedures established in advance. The parties or the court could conceivably determine as an original matter, case by case, the procedures that they consider appropriate to the particular dispute to be resolved. In out-of-court arbitration, procedures are in fact frequently improvised for the particular case. But this has not been the mode of our courts' litigation. The conduct of litigation follows existing rules of more or less general application.

Nevertheless, there remains room within the rules for a certain amount of individualized treatment of cases, and room also for discretion, experimentation, and invention as well as for argument. Perhaps procedural rules ought to be so definite and clear-cut as always to furnish a sure guide for the behavior of the parties and the courts. Whether or not this would be the ideal situation, one can say at the outset that it has not been attained, and one may doubt whether it ever could be attained.

Moreover, the rules are subject to change, have changed from time to time, and will undergo change in the future. Some of the rules look principally to preserving a settled order of proceeding, and the system could radically alter them without important consequence. In respect to other rules, there are powerful reasons of policy why they should be as they are or should not be as they are. The competing considerations in such areas of procedure will absorb much of our attention in this course.

So, it is mainly by this apparatus of malleable and changeable procedural rules, and their application by parties and courts, that society seeks to ensure that litigation will be accurately resolved in a fair and orderly way and as expeditiously and economically as may be practicable. We must approach the study of this procedure with full awareness that we shall be bedeviled by many of the same doubts and difficulties about what the rule is, or ought to be, that characterize the study of substantive law.

Therefore, although the rules of procedure aim to isolate and sharpen the issues in controversy and thus to simplify the dispute, the uncertainties in the procedural law may serve to inject a further disputatious ingredient into a lawsuit. Procedural problems are more obtrusive in our law than a beginner is likely to suppose, and perhaps more obtrusive than they ought to be.[d]

The substance/procedure distinction.—It may already be apparent that there will be difficulties in assigning particular rules to the category of substance or the category of procedure. These difficulties will sometimes defy the most careful and circumspect attempts to delineate the categories. For example, take a "statute of limitations" laying it down that a plaintiff must commence an action for battery within two years after the event. One might say that this is a rule of substance, for it expresses a firm condition on the plaintiff's right to recover. Yet, another might say that this is a rule of procedure, for it regulates a step in a lawsuit, the first step, the time within which the plaintiff must sue. We shall see many instances, and many more poignant instances, where classification will be difficult. But why should we be concerned with mere classification?

Certainly difficulties of classification are of small consequence if the aim is merely the lowly one of assigning subject matter to courses in a law school, so that if we conceive the statute of limitations to be a rule of procedure, its study would fall within Civil Procedure, but if conceived to be a rule of substance, it would be dealt with elsewhere. We shall be casual about course boundaries; if a problem arises in the heartland of Civil

---

[d] Compare the following statement: "It is characteristic of the prevailing rationalistic systems of legal philosophy that they minimize the importance of procedure by calling it adjective law, etc. But the tendency of all modern scientific and philosophic thought is to weaken the distinction between substance and attribute . . . and to emphasize the importance of method, process, or procedure." Morris R. Cohen, "The Process of Judicial Legislation," in Law and the Social Order 112, 128 (1933). Or, "The history of American freedom is, in no small measure, the history of procedure." Malinski v. New York, 324 U.S. 401, 414, 65 S.Ct. 781, 787 (1945) (Frankfurter, J., concurring). Or, "I'll let you write the substance . . . and you let me write the procedure, and I'll screw you every time." Regulatory Reform Act: Hearings on H.R. 2327 Before the Subcomm. on Admin. Law and Gov'tal Relations of the House Comm. on the Judiciary, 98th Cong. 312 (1983) (statement of Rep. John Dingell).

Procedure and takes us beyond that field, we shall follow it; and we shall often trespass on other courses without even that excuse. It is, indeed, one of our main tasks to observe how a legal problem may cut across many conventional departments of the law, and extend beyond the law.

There is, however, another and graver matter. It happens that legislatures and courts constantly use such titles as "civil procedure" or "civil practice," and they also constantly use the words "procedure" and "substance" and cognate words. Moreover, they attach serious consequences to these labels. Thus, the matter of classification may become important.

Our first case, Sibbach v. Wilson & Co., raises a question of the meaning of "practice and procedure" and "substantive rights" as those words appear in the very Act of Congress that originally empowered the Supreme Court of the United States to promulgate the Federal Rules of Civil Procedure.

Sibbach v. Wilson & Co.

Supreme Court of the United States, 1941.
312 U.S. 1, 61 S.Ct. 422.

Certiorari to the Circuit Court of Appeals for the Seventh Circuit.

■ MR. JUSTICE ROBERTS delivered the opinion of the Court.

This case calls for decision as to the validity of Rules 35 and 37 of the Rules of Civil Procedure for District Courts of the United States.

In an action brought by the petitioner[e] in the District Court for Northern Illinois to recover damages for bodily injuries, inflicted in Indiana, respondent answered denying the allegations of the complaint, and moved for an order requiring the petitioner to submit to a physical examination by one or more physicians appointed by the court to determine the nature and extent of her injuries. The court ordered that the petitioner submit to such an examination by a physician so appointed.

Compliance having been refused, the respondent obtained an order to show cause why the petitioner should not be punished for contempt. In response the petitioner challenged the authority of the court to order her to submit to the examination, asserting that the order was void. It appeared that the courts of Indiana, the state where the cause of action arose, hold such an order proper [citing Indiana precedents], whereas the courts of Illinois, the state in which the trial court sat, hold that such an order cannot be made [citing Illinois precedents]. Neither state has any statute governing the matter.

[e] The petitioner is the party who seeks review in the Supreme Court by writ of certiorari; the respondent is her adversary. The name of the petitioner appears first in the caption of the case in the Supreme Court. In this case the petitioner and the respondent happened to be the plaintiff and the defendant, respectively.

The court adjudged the petitioner guilty of contempt, and directed that she be committed until she should obey the order for examination or otherwise should be legally discharged from custody. The petitioner appealed.

The Circuit Court of Appeals decided that Rule 35, which authorizes an order for a physical examination in such a case, is valid, and affirmed the judgment. The writ of certiorari was granted because of the importance of the question involved.

The Rules of Civil Procedure were promulgated under the authority of the Act of June 19, 1934, which is:

"Be it enacted [Sec. 1.] That the Supreme Court of the United States shall have the power to prescribe, by general rules, for the district courts of the United States and for the courts of the District of Columbia, the forms of process, writs, pleadings, and motions, and the practice and procedure in civil actions at law. Said rules shall neither abridge, enlarge, nor modify the substantive rights of any litigant. They shall take effect six months after their promulgation, and thereafter all laws in conflict therewith shall be of no further force or effect.

"Sec. 2. The court may at any time unite the general rules prescribed by it for cases in equity with those in actions at law so as to secure one form of civil action and procedure for both: *Provided, however,* That in such union of rules the right of trial by jury as at common law and declared by the seventh amendment to the Constitution shall be preserved to the parties inviolate. Such united rules shall not take effect until they shall have been reported to Congress by the Attorney General at the beginning of a regular session thereof and until after the close of such session."[f]

[The Supreme Court here quoted the relevant portions of Rules 35 and 37.[g]]

The contention of the petitioner, in final analysis, is that Rules 35 and 37 are not within the mandate of Congress to this court. This is the limit of permissible debate, since argument touching the broader questions of Congressional power and of the obligation of federal courts to apply the substantive law of a state is foreclosed.

---

[f] The Rules Enabling Act of 1934 has since undergone amendment and now primarily appears as § 2072 of title 28 of the United States Code, which is cited as 28 U.S.C. § 2072.

Title 28 contains most of the statutes dealing with procedure in the courts of the United States, as distinguished from the courts of the states. It was revised and recodified in 1948.

The Rules booklet that accompanies this casebook sets out portions of title 28, along with selected provisions of the Constitution of the United States.

[g] Both of these Rules underwent heavy amendment in 1970. Rule 37(b)(2)(iv), which is now Rule 37(b)(2)(A)(vii), formerly read: "In lieu of any of the foregoing orders or in addition thereto, an order directing the arrest of any party or agent of a party for disobeying any of such orders except an order to submit to a physical or mental examination." None of the other changes bears on the Sibbach problem.

The original and amended texts of Rule 37 appear in the Rules booklet. See the section of the Rules booklet containing the amendments and the Advisory Committee's notes thereon.

Congress has undoubted power to regulate the practice and procedure of federal courts [citing Wayman v. Southard, 23 U.S. (10 Wheat.) 1, 21 (1825), among other cases,] and may exercise that power by delegating to this or other federal courts authority to make rules not inconsistent with the statutes or constitution of the United States; but it has never essayed to declare the substantive state law, or to abolish or nullify a right recognized by the substantive law of the state where the cause of action arose, save where a right or duty is imposed in a field committed to Congress by the Constitution. On the contrary it has enacted that the state law shall be the rule of decision in the federal courts.[8]

Hence we conclude that the Act of June 19, 1934, was purposely restricted in its operation to matters of pleading and court practice and procedure. Its two provisos or caveats emphasize this restriction. The first is that the court shall not "abridge, enlarge, nor modify substantive rights," in the guise of regulating procedure. The second is that if the rules are to prescribe a single form of action for cases at law and suits in equity, the constitutional right to jury trial inherent in the former must be preserved. There are other limitations upon the authority to prescribe rules which might have been, but were not mentioned in the Act; for instance, the inability of a court, by rule, to extend or restrict the jurisdiction conferred by a statute.

Whatever may be said as to the effect of the Conformity Act[h] while it remained in force, the rules, if they are within the authority granted by Congress, repeal that statute, and the District Court was not bound to follow the Illinois practice respecting an order for physical examination. On the other hand if the right to be exempt from such an order is one of substantive law, the Rules of Decision Act required the District Court, though sitting in Illinois, to apply the law of Indiana, the state where the cause of action arose, and to order the examination. To avoid this dilemma[i] the petitioner admits, and, we think, correctly, that Rules 35 and 37 are rules of procedure. She insists, nevertheless, that by the prohibition against abridging substantive rights, Congress has banned the rules here challenged. In order to reach this result she translates "substantive" into "important" or "substantial" rights. And she urges that if a rule affects such a right, albeit the rule is one of procedure merely, its prescription is not within the statutory grant of power embodied in the Act of June 19, 1934. She contends that our decisions and recognized principles require us so to hold.

8 [In a footnote here the Court cited the Rules of Decision Act of 1789, now embodied in 28 U.S.C. § 1652. We consider this important statute more extensively in connection with Erie Railroad Co. v. Tompkins, infra p. 342.]

h The Conformity Act of 1872, old 28 U.S.C. § 724, provided: "*Conformity to practice in State courts.* The practice, pleadings, and forms and modes of proceedings in civil causes, other than equity and admiralty causes, in the district courts, shall conform, as near as may be, to the practice, pleadings, and forms and modes of proceedings existing at the time in like causes in the courts of record of the State within which such district courts are held, any rule of court to the contrary notwithstanding."

i Assume for the present that the petitioner's dilemma was as stated by the Court. Later cases will shed a different light upon the problem.

[After discussing a number of prior decisions relied on by the petitioner, the Court continued:]

We are thrown back, then, to the arguments drawn from the language of the Act of June 19, 1934. Is the phrase "substantive rights" confined to rights conferred by law to be protected and enforced in accordance with the adjective law of judicial procedure? It certainly embraces such rights. One of them is the right not to be injured in one's person by another's negligence, to redress infraction of which the present action was brought. The petitioner says the phrase connotes more; that by its use Congress intended that in regulating procedure this court should not deal with important and substantial rights theretofore recognized. Recognized where and by whom? The state courts are divided as to the power in the absence of statute to order a physical examination. In a number such an order is authorized by statute or rule. The rules in question accord with the procedure now in force in Canada and England.

The asserted right, moreover, is no more important than many others enjoyed by litigants in District Courts sitting in the several states, before the Federal Rules of Civil Procedure altered and abolished old rights or privileges and created new ones in connection with the conduct of litigation. The suggestion that the rule offends the important right to freedom from invasion of the person ignores the fact that, as we hold, no invasion of freedom from personal restraint attaches to refusal so to comply with its provisions. If we were to adopt the suggested criterion of the importance of the alleged right we should invite endless litigation and confusion worse confounded. The test must be whether a rule really regulates procedure,—the judicial process for enforcing rights and duties recognized by substantive law and for justly administering remedy and redress for disregard or infraction of them. That the rules in question are such is admitted.

Finally, it is urged that Rules 35 and 37 work a major change of policy and that this was not intended by Congress. Apart from the fact already stated, that the policy of the states in this respect has not been uniform, it is to be noted that the authorization of a comprehensive system of court rules was a departure in policy, and that the new policy envisaged in the enabling act of 1934 was that the whole field of court procedure be regulated in the interest of speedy, fair and exact determination of the truth. The challenged rules comport with this policy. Moreover, in accordance with the Act, the rules were submitted to the Congress so that that body might examine them and veto their going into effect if contrary to the policy of the legislature.

The value of the reservation of the power to examine proposed rules, laws and regulations before they become effective is well understood by Congress. It is frequently, as here, employed to make sure that the action under the delegation squares with the Congressional purpose. Evidently the Congress felt the rule was within the ambit of the statute as no effort was made to eliminate it from the proposed body of rules, although this specific rule was attacked and defended before the committees of the two Houses.[18] . . . We conclude that the rules under attack are within the authority granted.

The District Court treated the refusal to comply with its order as a contempt and committed the petitioner therefor. Neither in the Circuit Court of Appeals nor here was this action assigned as error. We think, however, that in the light of the provisions of Rule 37 it was plain error of such a fundamental nature that we should notice it. Section (b)(2)(iv) of Rule 37 exempts from punishment as for contempt the refusal to obey an order that a party submit to a physical or mental examination. The District Court was in error in going counter to this express exemption. The remedies available under the rule in such a case are those enumerated in [today's (b)(2)(A)(i)–(vi)]. For this error we reverse the judgment and remand the cause to the District Court for further proceedings in conformity to this opinion.

Reversed.

■ [JUSTICE FRANKFURTER, in an opinion concurred in by Justices Black, Douglas, and Murphy, took issue with the reasoning of Justice Roberts, who had been joined by Chief Justice Hughes and Justices McReynolds, Stone, and Reed.

[Justice Frankfurter, as part of his opening, said that "it does not seem to me that the answer to our question is to be found by an analytical determination whether the power of examination here claimed is a matter of procedure or a matter of substance, even assuming that the two are mutually exclusive categories with easily ascertainable contents." To be sure, there is no constitutional immunity from the examination here sought; the matter is "amenable to statutory change." Still we should remember that the rule in question affects the "inviolability of a person" having "historic roots in Anglo–American law." Justice Frankfurter went on to say:]

So far as national law is concerned, a drastic change in public policy in a matter deeply touching the sensibilities of people or even their prejudices as to privacy, ought not to be inferred from a general authorization to formulate rules for the more uniform and effective dispatch of business on the civil side of the federal courts. I deem a requirement as to the invasion of the person to stand on a very different footing from questions pertaining to the discovery of documents, pre-trial procedure and other devices for the expeditious, economic and fair conduct of litigation. That disobedience of an

[18] Hearings before the Committee on the Judiciary, House of Representatives, 75th Cong., 3rd Sess., pp. 117, 141; Hearings before a Subcommittee of the Committee on the Judiciary, U.S. Senate, 75th Cong., 3rd Sess., pp. 36, 37, 39, 51. [A few witnesses in the hearings briefly testified that Rule 35 was substantive and otherwise troublesome, thus aggravating concerns among some senators at least.—Ed.]

order under Rule 35 cannot be visited with punishment as for contempt does not mitigate its intrusion into an historic immunity of the privacy of the person. Of course the Rule is compulsive in that the doors of the federal courts otherwise open may be shut to litigants who do not submit to such a physical examination.

In this view little significance attaches to the fact that the Rules, in accordance with the statute, remained on the table of two Houses of Congress without evoking any objection to Rule 35 and thereby automatically came into force. Plainly the Rules are not acts of Congress and can not be treated as such. Having due regard to the mechanics of legislation and the practical conditions surrounding the business of Congress when the Rules were submitted, to draw any inference of tacit approval from non-action by Congress is to appeal to unreality. And so I conclude that to make the drastic change that Rule 35 sought to introduce would require explicit legislation.

In reading any case in this course, the student should seek to visualize the successive steps taken by the parties and the courts. Topic B of this Part, "Phases of a Lawsuit," should facilitate understanding of the scenario. Briefing of the cases will aid in this process of visualization and comprehension, as the following sample brief and accompanying notes and questions illustrate.

Sample Brief

Facts: Mrs. Sibbach claimed to have received bodily injuries in Indiana, presumably caused by an employee of Wilson & Co.

Notes and Questions

(1) In this part of your brief you should state who the parties are and what happened to them before reaching the courthouse. Limit yourself to the legally relevant facts. For example, Hertha J. Sibbach's case actually arose from a serious automobile accident occurring on September 3, 1937, on a country highway near Gary, Indiana, and involving the defendant's truck. These facts are not relevant to the issue and so should be omitted from your brief, just as they were omitted from the Supreme Court opinion itself. Sometimes, however, judicial opinions will include a great many irrelevant facts, and you must sift through them for the essence. Moreover, write the "Facts" (and the other entries) in your own words. Nothing is gained by transcribing the opinion.

Sample Brief

Notes and Questions

In briefing a case, you should follow a logical and set format. As to choice of format, many possibilities are defensible. We choose to begin with the out-of-court facts in the interest of chronology and as an indication of their enormous importance in shaping decision. However, we do not here record the fruits of some abstract historical inquiry. Instead, we record the facts as they are accepted by the court for the purpose of decision. These emerge from the procedural maneuvers in the case, and the condition of the facts depends on the procedural posture of the case at the time of decision. For example, in Sibbach the facts rest upon the plaintiff's allegations, because the issues arose at the case's beginnings. Given this legalistic meaning of facts, your job of fixing the facts will prove difficult, meaning that you cannot write this first part of your brief until you have thought about the rest of your brief. This warning reflects the view that competent briefing serves as a record of thorough reading and study, as well as a stimulus to further reading and study.

Prior Proceedings: Plaintiff Sibbach (*P*) sued the corporate defendant (*D*) in the United States District Court for the Northern District of Illinois, alleging negligence and seeking money damages.

(2) This portion of your brief should be detailed, covering everything that happens from crossing the threshold of the trial court to the moment as of which the opinion before you speaks. This is especially important for this course because detailed briefing here can be very helpful in mastering procedure and also because the issues presented by a procedure case always arise here. Yet even in your other courses, you should give attention to this aspect of the brief, because it is often impossible to know precisely what or why a court is deciding without knowing the procedural background of the case. To put it better: "Now a case never reaches a court of review until it has first been through a tribunal of trial—else there would be nothing to review. But the cases, so-called, in your case-books are almost exclusively chosen from courts of review. To understand them, therefore, you must get at least some quick picture of what has gone on before they got there." Karl N. Llewellyn, The Bramble Bush 20 (7th printing 1981).

Sample Brief

Notes and Questions

(3) There is a considerable amount of learning between the lines of the sample brief's first short entry concerning "Prior Proceedings." We shall attempt to sketch it out, previewing material you will soon study and also using some information concerning the case that appears in the record but does not appear in the opinion itself.

First, Sibbach's suit was one of the sort that can be brought in either state or federal court. An essential concept here is that federal courts, unlike many state courts, are courts of limited jurisdiction. This means that federal courts normally have the power to hear only those kinds of cases that are within the constitutional grant of federal judicial power (see Article III, Section 2 of the Constitution) and that are also within some congressional enactment entrusting jurisdiction to the federal courts. There are three classes of these statutes that embrace the largest numbers of federal lawsuits. The first class comprises "federal question" cases—actions arising under the Constitution, laws, or treaties of the United States. A good many statutes confer jurisdiction over specific kinds of such cases. See, e.g., 28 U.S.C. §§ 1337(a) and 1338(a). And there is a residual statute conferring jurisdiction over such cases in general terms. See 28 U.S.C. § 1331. The second class comprises "diversity" cases—actions where there is diversity of citizenship between the parties, of which the most important category is actions between citizens of different states. See 28 U.S.C. §§ 1332(a) and 1335. A statutory requirement that the matter in controversy exceed some sum of money, in order that the case be cognizable in a federal district court, applies to a very few actions in the first class and to all actions in the second class. The third class comprises cases to which the United States itself is a party. See §§ 1345 and 1346. To come back to the present case, Sibbach based her suit in federal district court on 28 U.S.C. § 1332(a). She could do this because there was diversity of citizenship (*P* was a citizen of Illinois; *D* was a Delaware corporation, making it a citizen of that state for diversity purposes)

Sample Brief **Notes and Questions**

and her claimed damages exceeded the jurisdictional amount (she claimed $10,000 in damages, but at the time of suit the jurisdictional amount was $3000—Congress raised the jurisdictional amount under the relevant statute from $500 to $2000 in 1887, to $3000 in 1911, to $10,000 in 1958, to $50,000 in 1988, and to $75,000 in 1996).

Second, Sibbach sued in a United States District Court. The ninety-one United States District Courts are the trial courts of the federal system. A district is coterminous with a state or constitutes part of a state; thus, there is a United States District Court for the District of Delaware, and United States District Courts for the Southern, Central, and Northern Districts of Illinois. See 28 U.S.C. § 133.[j] On the next higher level of the federal court system, twelve United States Courts of Appeals (formerly called Circuit Courts of Appeals) each cover a circuit comprising a number of districts. See 28 U.S.C. § 41.[k] The primary function of the courts of appeals is to hear appeals from decisions of the district courts in their respective circuits. At the summit of this pyramid of courts is the Supreme Court of the United States.

---

[j] However, the District of Hawaii includes certain Pacific islands not part of that state, and the District of Wyoming includes those portions of Yellowstone National Park situated in Montana and Idaho.

The District of Columbia is a judicial district, and the District Court for the District of Columbia is a United States District Court. (Prior to 1970, it had a combined federal and local jurisdiction. It now exercises only federal jurisdiction like the other United States District Courts; Congress has vested local jurisdiction in local courts.)

The Commonwealth of Puerto Rico is also one of the ninety-one judicial districts, and the District Court for the District of Puerto Rico is a United States District Court (exercising federal jurisdiction).

Additionally, the Federal Rules are applicable by statute to the three so-called territorial district courts of the Virgin Islands, Guam, and the Northern Mariana Islands (exercising both federal and at least some local jurisdiction).

[k] However, the United States Court of Appeals for the District of Columbia Circuit covers only a single district.

Additionally, there is a thirteenth court of appeals—the United States Court of Appeals for the Federal Circuit—which hears appeals from a number of specialized tribunals and also hears appeals from all of the nation's district courts in cases involving certain special areas such as patents or certain claims against the United States. See 28 U.S.C. § 1295.

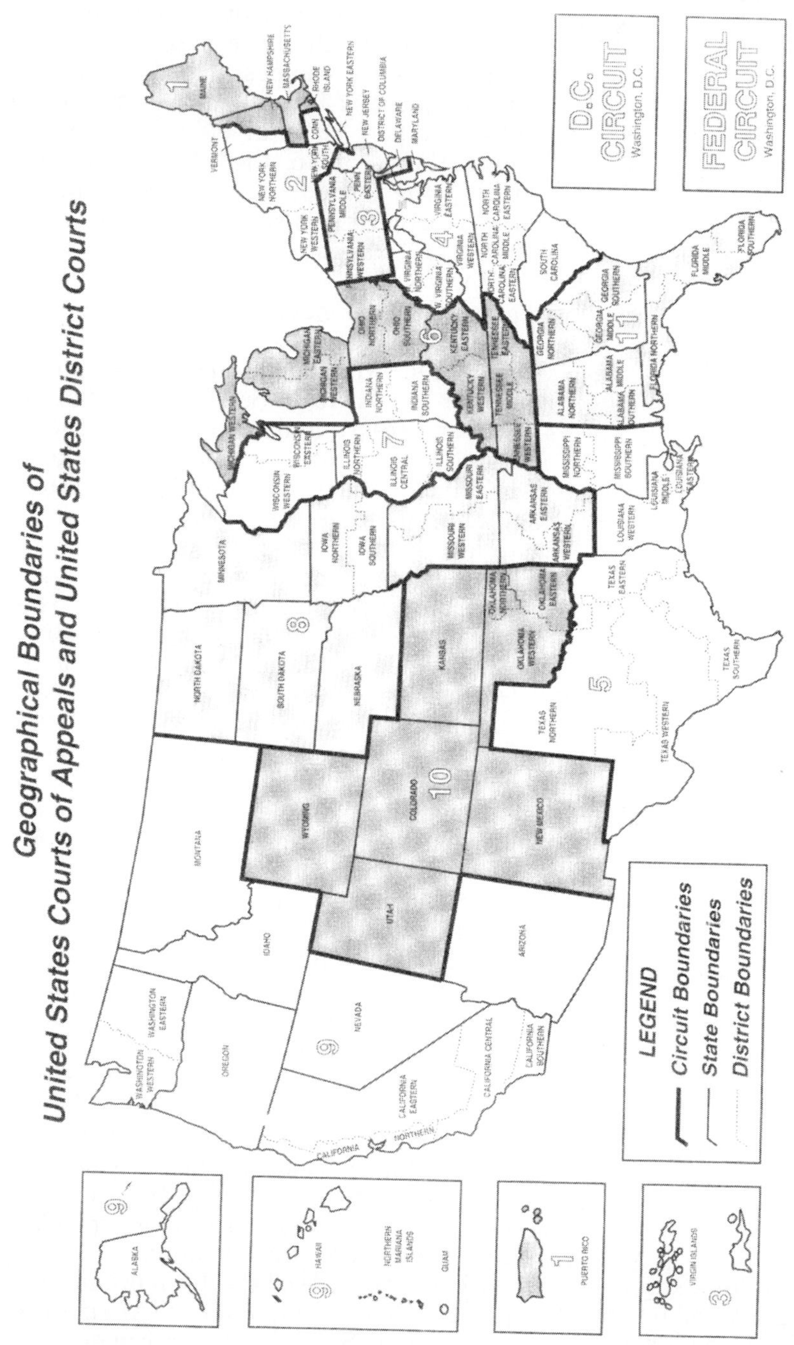
Geographical Boundaries of
United States Courts of Appeals and United States District Courts
LEGEND
Circuit Boundaries
State Boundaries
District Boundaries
D.C.
CIRCUIT
Washington, D.C.
FEDERAL
CIRCUIT
Washington, D.C.

Sample Brief | **Notes and Questions**

Third, she sued in the Northern District of Illinois, where she lived and where the defendant did some business. She had had a choice on the place of federal suit. Under the choice-of-forum law then in effect, she could have sued there, or in the District of Delaware where the defendant was incorporated, or in the Northern District of Indiana where the accident had taken place.

Fourth, when we say that she "sued," we mean that she made her grievance and request for redress known to the court by filing a complaint with the court, which she did on November 24, 1937. See Rules 3, 10(a) and (b), 8(a) and (d)(1), and 11. Following these Rules would yield a result looking much like Federal Form 11 (which is in the Appendix of Forms after the Federal Rules in the Rules booklet). In fact, Sibbach's complaint was a bit unnecessarily flamboyant, as compared to that Form. Her complaint alleged in part: "As a direct and proximate result of said acts of negligence of the defendant, the plaintiff Hertha J. Sibbach was greatly cut, wounded, lacerated, and contused in and about the head, body, arms, and legs, and divers bones in plaintiff's body were broken and fractured, and plaintiff became and was and has so remained from thence hitherto sick, sore, lame, diseased, and disordered, and has suffered great pain; all of which injuries are permanent and lasting."

Fifth, it is not enough to file the complaint: the defendant must be notified. This is done by serving the complaint, and a summons issued by the clerk of the court, in conformance with Rule 4. See Form 3.

D answered by denial.

(4) Again, a lot is buried here. Various responses are available to a defendant served with process. In this case, *D* filed an answer containing a denial of the allegations in the complaint. See Rule 8(b). Its answer looked much like the first part of Form 30, with a suitable heading and signature.

D moved for an order requiring *P* to submit to a Rule 35 physical exam, and the court granted that motion.

(5) *D* proceeded here by motion, as the express terms of Rule 35(a)(2)(A) require. What is a motion? See Rule 7(b); Form 40.

(6) An order is simply a command of the court. It may be oral or written; it may be rather formal or may be simply the words "so ordered" written at the foot of the motion; it may be accompanied by an opinion explaining

Sample Brief

P refused to comply, so D obtained an order to show cause, which required P to prove why the court should not hold her in contempt under Rule 37.

In response to the order to show cause, P argued that the court had no authority to order a physical exam. The court rejected P's argument, found her

Notes and Questions

the court's reasoning or, as in this case, it may not be. Selected district court opinions are printed in reporters, usually either in Federal Supplement or in Federal Rules Decisions.

(7) An order to show cause serves the same purpose as a motion, but the court handles it more expeditiously. It is actually an order of the court, usually drafted by the attorney for one side and submitted to the court for signature, directing the other side to appear as specified and present to the court such reasons as it has to offer that some consequence (in this case, a finding of contempt) should not ensue. The court usually grants an order to show cause only on a showing of urgency or of special need (as here, where *D* was seeking to force compliance with a court order, for which *D* had already once gone through the slower motion procedure).

(8) Contempt is a disregard or disobedience of public authority, such as a court order. There are two types of contempt proceedings, criminal and civil. The difference, it should be noted, is not necessarily in the nature of the contemptuous act but in the proceedings consequent thereto—the same contemptuous act might give rise to either or both types of proceedings. For the time being, distinguish the two as follows. Criminal contempt proceedings serve the interests of society by punishing and deterring deliberate disrespect of public authority; accordingly, the procedure is relatively protective of the defendant's rights, but an unconditional fine or prison term is the form of sanction. Civil contempt proceedings more directly help the party who would benefit from the contemnor's obedience; accordingly, the form of sanction either is a compensatory payment to such party or is a conditional fine or imprisonment that need not be paid or further suffered by the contemnor if he obeys (thus the maxim that these contemnors "carry the keys of their prison in their own pockets"). In short, the design of criminal contempt proceedings is to punish and deter, and that of civil contempt proceedings is to compensate or compel.

(9) Was this a civil or criminal contempt sanction?

Sample Brief

in contempt, and ordered her imprisoned until she submitted to a physical exam.

P appealed to the United States Court of Appeals for the Seventh Circuit.

The Seventh Circuit affirmed.

P petitioned the Supreme Court of the United States for a writ of certiorari, and the Court granted the writ because her case involved an unsettled, important question of federal law.

Notes and Questions

(10) In the federal system, the first level of appeal is a matter of right, not judicial discretion. Sibbach had the right, at some time, to appeal to the appropriate court of appeals.

As to the timing of appeal, a party can normally take one appeal at the conclusion of the case. See 28 U.S.C. § 1291. Here, however, *P* took an interlocutory appeal before the case proceeded. Possibly she was not then entitled to appeal, but the question was not raised by the parties or the courts.

There are provisions for staying a lower court's order pending appeal. So chances are that Sibbach never saw the inside of "the common jail of Cook County," to which the court had ordered her committed.

(11) The courts of appeals normally act by written decision and opinion, and many of these are printed. They appear in Federal Reporter. In this case, the affirmance appears in volume 108 of Federal Reporter, Second Series, at page 415. The Seventh Circuit handed down the affirmance on December 13, 1939. The citation is therefore 108 F.2d 415 (7th Cir.1939).

(12) There are a couple of routes from a court of appeals to the Supreme Court. See 28 U.S.C. § 1254.

The most common route is by writ of certiorari. Review thereby is not of right, but is discretionary. The party seeking review must petition the Supreme Court for the writ, and hence that party is called the petitioner. The Supreme Court decides whether to review the case pursuant to United States Supreme Court Rule 10, which provides in part: "A petition for a writ of certiorari will be granted only for compelling reasons. The following, although neither controlling nor fully measuring the Court's discretion, indicate the character of the reasons the Court considers: . . . a United States court of appeals has entered a decision in conflict with the decision of another United States court of appeals on the same important matter; . . . a United States court of appeals has decided an important question of federal law that has not been, but should be, settled by this Court, or has decided an important

Sample Brief

Notes and Questions

federal question in a way that conflicts with relevant decisions of this Court."

Sibbach told the Supreme Court in her petition that her case presented this question: "Does Rule 35 of the Federal Rules of Civil Procedure abridge or modify the substantive rights of the petitioner contrary to the provisions of the Rules Enabling Act?" You should ask yourself why the Supreme Court bothered to hear this case. What sense does it make to have the Supreme Court review the validity of rules it itself promulgated? Assuming that the Supreme Court would not have promulgated rules it thought invalid, how could this case present "an important question of federal law that has not been, but should be, settled by" the Supreme Court?

At any rate, on April 8, 1940, the Court did grant the writ. Actions by the Supreme Court are reported officially in United States Reports. The grant of the petition for a writ of certiorari in this case appears in volume 309 of United States Reports, at page 650. It also appears in volume 60 of the parallel, unofficial Supreme Court Reporter, at page 809. The citation is therefore 309 U.S. 650 (1940) or, more expansively, 309 U.S. 650, 60 S.Ct. 809 (1940).

Statutes and Rules Involved: Rules Enabling Act; Rules 35 and 37.

(13) This entry in your brief serves only as a handy reference, so at a glance you can later recall what the case was about. But we shall take this opportunity to give you some historical background on the statute and Rules here involved. For greater detail, reference should be made to Charles Alan Wright & Mary Kay Kane, Law of Federal Courts §§ 61–63 (6th ed. 2002).

(14) To understand the Rules Enabling Act, one must go back to the Process Act of 1789. This Act, and the subsequent Process Acts, required the procedural practices in the federal courts to conform in each and every state to the practices "as are now used or allowed in the supreme courts of the same." Conformity to state procedure flowed, in contemporary phraseology, from a fear of an "injurious clashing" with the procedure of the states. What the statutes called for, however, was a *static* conformity; a federal court in, say, 1850 had to apply the state procedure of 1789. Moreover, the early statutes did not cover the problem of new states; federal courts in the new states were at first free to apply any

Sample Brief **Notes and Questions**

procedure they wished; later statutes forced the procedure of federal courts in those states to conform to the state procedure of 1828, 1842, or the date of admission, the choice among these base dates depending on when the state in question had been admitted. The situation was even more complicated than this description suggests, because there were exceptions, and exceptions to exceptions. However, the basic idea here is that of static conformity, meaning that the federal courts had to ignore recent developments and reforms in state procedure and instead follow an outmoded and abandoned version of the state procedure.

Congress reworked all this by the Conformity Act of 1872, which instituted *dynamic* conformity. From then on, in theory, the same procedure prevailed in state and federal court, and the practitioner could switch courts without relearning procedure. The first question one might ask is why it took Congress almost a century to make this obvious change. One reason was that it was not until the mid-nineteenth century that state procedural reform started snowballing, leaving the procedure applied in federal courts far behind. Another reason might have been that Congress feared that such a change constituted an unconstitutional delegation of federal rulemaking power to the states, as the Supreme Court itself had suggested in Wayman v. Southard, 23 U.S. (10 Wheat.) 1 (1825); after the change in 1872 this issue of constitutionality never came up for decision in this procedural context, although the Court upheld dynamic conformity to state law in a different context in United States v. Sharpnack, 355 U.S. 286, 78 S.Ct. 291 (1958). The second question one might ask is whether dynamic conformity worked. The answer would be that the simplicity of theory was never realized in practice. Instead, the Conformity Act became riddled with exceptions, both judge-made and statutory (note the phrasing "conform, as near as may be" in the Conformity Act itself, quoted in a footnote to the Sibbach case). Federal courts in the course of a litigation consequently used some state procedure and some home-brewed procedure to create a rampantly confusing federal practice: "To the average lawyer it is Sanskrit; to the experienced federal practitioner it is monopoly; to the author of text

Sample Brief

Notes and Questions

books on federal practice it is a golden harvest." Report of the Committee on Uniform Judicial Procedure, 46 A.B.A.Rep. 461, 466 (1921).

It is against this backdrop that one can best view the Rules Enabling Act of 1934. This Act again seems the obvious answer, but it actually represented reformist agitation by the bar and bench dating back to the previous century. Finally, in 1934, reform secured the support of the national administration, and quickly Congress enacted the Rules Enabling Act. See generally Stephen B. Burbank, The Rules Enabling Act of 1934, 130 U.Pa.L.Rev. 1015 (1982).

Even after that statute passed, it took the Supreme Court a year to act on it; but when the Court eventually did act, it acted in grand style, appointing a highly distinguished Advisory Committee to assist in drafting the rules. The Advisory Committee prepared three drafts for debate and discussion in the legal community. The first draft was circulated in May 1936. The third draft was submitted in November 1937 to the Supreme Court, which promulgated it with minor changes the following month. Congress having taken no action, the Federal Rules of Civil Procedure became effective on September 16, 1938. (For the curious: although as we have seen the Sibbach complaint was filed in 1937 before the Rules were promulgated, the defendant's motion for a physical exam was filed on May 6, 1939, and was thus subject to the new Rules. See Rule 86(a)(2).) Thus ended the long reign of the Conformity Act, which was apparently superseded in toto by the new Rules and which was in any case formally repealed by Congress in 1948.

The success of the Federal Rules has been, in Professor Wright's words, "quite phenomenal," creating "a uniform procedure that is flexible, simple, clear, and efficient" and that has had a tremendous impact on the development of procedure in other jurisdictions. A less restrained commentator wrote that the Rules were "one of the greatest contributions to the free and unhampered administration of law and justice ever struck off by any group of men since the dawn of civilized law." B.H. Carey, In Favor of Uniformity, 3 F.R.D. 507, 507 (1944).

Sample Brief

Notes and Questions

Of course the Rules have not proved perfect or timeless, and so they have undergone a continuing review. The old Advisory Committee was discharged in 1956; and in 1958 the Judicial Conference of the United States, a body of federal judges headed by the Chief Justice that has long been charged with improving the administration of federal courts, took over the advisory function with respect to the Supreme Court's rulemaking power. See 28 U.S.C. § 331. There were important amendments to the Rules in 1948, 1961, 1963, 1966, 1970, 1980, 1983, 1985, 1991, 1993, 2000, 2003, and 2006. Additionally, in 2007 the rulemakers "restyled" the Rules and Forms by rewriting every single one to make it clearer and simpler, but supposedly without alteration to its meaning, and in the process redesignated some of the Rules' lettered or numbered subdivisions.

More change surely lies in the future, and you should not infer that this change will be merely in the nature of further refinement. Indeed, citing increasing dissatisfaction, some commentators have been predicting the imminent end of the Federal Rules' era itself. One of their major arguments is that the Federal Rules' preference for transsubstantive rules, or very general rules that apply to all sorts of cases, has worn out, and the time has come for returning explicitly to specialized rules tailored to particular subsets of cases.

This background allows you to focus in on the Rules involved in Sibbach. Rules 35 and 37 are part of the so-called discovery Rules, which run from Rule 26 to Rule 37. The rulemakers heavily redid the discovery Rules in 1970.

(15) This brings us to an important point. When reading an older case, it is important to know how any rule or statute in question read at the time of decision; you have to know this in order to know what the court is referring to and often what it is deciding. For example, the Sibbach Court refers to Rule 37(b)(2)(iv). Today there is no such numbered Rule. You will find the old version of the Rule in the Rules booklet.

(16) There is also the converse problem. An old case might quote an obsolete version of a statute or rule. You should look up the current version, and ask yourself how and why it has changed. For example, the Sibbach Court quotes the Rules Enabling Act. This is now 28

U.S.C. §§ 2072–2074. Comparison shows that Congress has changed the original statute in several important ways.

First, there is now a reference in § 2072 to the courts of appeals. This extension of the Supreme Court's rulemaking power came in 1966, and the eventual result thereof was the Federal Rules of Appellate Procedure (portions of which appear in the Rules booklet). Prior to the adoption of those Appellate Rules in 1968, each court of appeals had a fairly wide power to make its own rules. (To complete the procedural rulemaking picture, note that under 28 U.S.C. § 2071(a) the Supreme Court can make its own rules; recall S.Ct. Rule 10 above. Note further that all federal courts have the power under § 2071 to promulgate interstitial rules for themselves; see Rule 83 and App. Rule 47; see also 28 U.S.C. § 2077.)

Second, there is no longer a reference in § 2072 to the courts of the District of Columbia. Although the Federal Rules apply to the District Court for the District of Columbia because it is a United States District Court, the Supreme Court never used the statutory authorization to make rules for the *local* courts of the District of Columbia. Today Congress handles directly the matter of rules for the District of Columbia's local courts.

Third, current § 2072 omits the term "at law." This omission is profoundly significant, but to understand it you must appreciate the important distinction between law and equity, two historically distinct systems of courts, of remedies, and of procedures. Again for purposes of introduction, and at the price of oversimplification, law courts in old England typically gave relief only in the form of money damages. Old England's equity courts, on the other hand, typically gave relief only in the form of an order commanding the defendant to do or not to do something, such as to convey land he had promised to sell ("specific performance") or to remove a dam he had wrongfully constructed ("injunction"). The procedures of the two court systems were very different, but one of the more salient differences was that law courts offered trial by jury while equity courts did not.

The equity system was transported to the infant United States. In the federal system, parties instituted and litigated equity and law cases separately in different divisions, or

Sample Brief **Notes and Questions**

sides, of the lower federal courts, although the same judges sat on both sides. The history of federal procedure on the equity side was quite distinct from that of the procedure used on the law side. (The history imparted under (14) above concerned actions at law, not suits in equity.) Congress never required federal equity procedure to conform to state equity procedure, largely because some of the newly independent states had not developed formally any such procedure. Instead, Congress instructed the federal courts to follow generally the procedure of English equity, but gave rulemaking power to the Supreme Court. The Court did not exercise that power until 1822, but thereafter it promulgated successive sets of equity rules for use in the federal courts. The last set of these was the modernizing Equity Rules of 1912, which served as one of the models for the Federal Rules of Civil Procedure.

As we have already noted, throughout this long period the Supreme Court, while making rules in equity, was doing nothing with respect to rulemaking for the separate realm of actions at law. The Rules Enabling Act was the legislative response. Section 1 thereof authorized the Supreme Court to do for law as it had been doing for equity all along, and section 2 permitted the Supreme Court to unite the two procedures. The Supreme Court did exercise its section 2 powers right away, so that the new Federal Rules united equity and law, this being the greatest single achievement of the Rules. See Rules 1 and 2. In summary, it is by reason of this union that § 2072 can now omit "at law."

A related change in § 2072 is the omission of old section 2. Congress could omit this from the current statute because the union of equity and law under the Rules had been achieved. Yet with regard to other matters—especially the extent of the right to trial by jury in civil actions—the equity/law distinction remains very important.

Fourth, § 2072 now refers broadly to "cases" rather than to "civil actions." This change encapsulates the long-term trend toward a broader scope of the Rules Enabling Act.

The Federal Rules of Civil Procedure themselves have broadened to cover "admiralty and maritime" cases. Again, this broadening is significant, but complex in meaning. A leading

Sample Brief

Notes and Questions

text in this area explains that "the terms 'admiralty' and 'maritime law' are virtually synonymous in this country today, though the first derives from the connection of our modern law with the system administered in a single English court, while the second makes a wider and more descriptive reference." Grant Gilmore & Charles L. Black, The Law of Admiralty 1 (2d ed. 1975). We essay only the general statement, itself oversimplified, that admiralty and maritime cases comprehend torts occurring upon, or contracts having to do with commerce or navigation upon, the high seas or the navigable waters of the United States. The history of federal procedure in this realm is analogous to that in equity. Congress never required conformity to state practice. Instead, federal courts followed English admiralty practice, with rulemaking power having been given to the Supreme Court. The Court exercised this power by promulgating successive sets of admiralty rules, starting in 1844. Finally, in 1966, the Court brought admiralty and maritime cases within the coverage of the Federal Rules of Civil Procedure, with certain minor special treatment. See Rule 9(h) and the Supplemental Rules (which appear after the Appendix of Forms in the Rules booklet).

This extension of the Federal Rules of Civil Procedure leads to the question of what cases are not covered by those Rules. Most importantly, criminal cases are not so covered. These cases were handled in the federal courts by uncodified procedure until 1946, and since then by the Federal Rules of Criminal Procedure. Several other special kinds of proceedings are not covered by the Federal Rules of Civil Procedure. See Rule 81(a).

Fifth, the Rules Enabling Act has undergone changes with respect to the process for composing the rules, § 2073, and the mechanism by which promulgated rules take effect, § 2074. Under § 2073, the Judicial Conference—directed to carry on a continuous study of the rules of practice prescribed by the Court for the inferior federal courts and to make recommendations to the Court—works through a standing committee, appointed by the Chief Justice, and advisory committees, also appointed by the Chief Justice, which report to the standing committee. There are now five advisory committees respectively for Civil, Criminal, Evidence, Bankruptcy, and Ap-

Sample Brief | **Notes and Questions**

pellate Rules, each assisted by a reporter who is usually a law professor. The advisory committees draft new or amended rules with explanatory notes, circulate them under the aegis of the standing committee to the bench and bar and public for comment, rework the rules in the light of the comments, and transmit them to the standing committee. The standing committee in turn makes recommendations to the Judicial Conference, which finally advises the Court. At this point the specific procedure of the Rules Enabling Act, in § 2074, takes over with respect to submission of the rules to Congress.

Issues:

(17) In this part of the brief you should list the precise questions the court is to decide. Often the issues are far from obvious, and so this entry in the brief requires digging and careful analysis on your part.

1. Are Rules 35 and 37 valid, insofar as being within the congressional delegation to the Supreme Court expressed in the Rules Enabling Act?

An unavoidable difficulty lies in stating an issue neither too broadly nor too narrowly. There is no foolproof approach or unarguable resolution. You must tie your statement of the issue to the facts of the case, but you must also suggest any resultant rule of law that will be applicable to future cases. Try to state that legal point narrowly enough to exclude future cases not covered by the ruling but broadly enough to include all those cases within it. Obviously, room for argument exists about the scope of precedent, and arguing about that is one thing lawyers do. So, your statement of the issue can represent only your best judgment on a difficult matter. At any rate, by the time you complete studying the Sibbach case, you might be able to come up with a formulation of the first issue better than this sample brief's entry.

2. If so, was the contempt sanction imposed by the district court proper under Rule 37? (N.B.: This second issue was raised by the Supreme Court, not by *P*.)

(18) In appellate cases, the issues normally center on those lower-court actions that the appealing party designates as improper in his papers on appeal, i.e., the points assigned as error. The appellate court generally does not "notice" other errors on its own, because ours is a party-propelled adversary system. It is generally for the aggrieved parties, through their lawyers, to specify those lower-court actions with which they are dissatisfied, and so to shape the issues for resolution by the appellate court.

What are the reasons behind this policy that allows the parties to select the issues? If such a policy is generally a good one, why did the

Sample Brief

Notes and Questions

Supreme Court by noticing the error here reach out to decide this second issue? That is, why did the Supreme Court consider the propriety of the contempt finding and the commitment order if, as the Supreme Court noted, "[n]either in the Circuit Court of Appeals nor here was this action assigned as error" by Sibbach? What special circumstances were present to prompt the Court to decide the issue? Incidentally, the Supreme Court's attention was first drawn to this second issue by William D. Mitchell, who was Chairman of the Advisory Committee that had drafted the Federal Rules and who filed a brief as amicus curiae in this case when it reached the Supreme Court.

Decisions:

1. Yes (5–4).

2. No.

(19) Here you should give the decision on each one of the above-listed issues. Incidentally, were they issues of fact, substantive law, or procedural law?

(20) Note that the first decision was five to four, with Justice Frankfurter writing for the minority. So this was a very close vote in a very important case, one that was to determine the vitality of the new Federal Rules. However, no one dissented on the second issue.

Judgment reversed and case remanded to the district court, because the district court had imposed an improper sanction on *P*.

(21) Also indicate the court's disposition of the case. (Afterwards, this case disappeared on remand, there being no reported lower-court action in the case after these decisions on January 13, 1941. What do you think happened?)

In fact, the district court vacated its contempt order on April 9, 1941. The next day, that court dismissed the action, "this cause having been settled."

Reasons: As to the Court's first decision, Justice Roberts uses deductive reasoning to come to the conclusion that Rules 35 and 37 are valid. The major premise of his syllogism is that all rules that deal with procedure are valid, because Congress in the Rules Enabling Act delegated to the Supreme Court the power to make rules throughout the whole realm of procedure;

(22) In this part of your brief you should state the gist of the court's reasoning, probably even more briefly than we have. Needless to say, sometimes a great deal of work is necessary in order to perceive the court's reasoning, especially if the opinion is expressed in the form of free association. After all, Justice Owen Roberts himself seemed unable to state his own reasoning simply (but note how Justice Felix Frankfurter immediately grasped, and attacked, Roberts' major premise). When you are processing the court's reasoning, another difficult and important task is separating, as well as possible, statements of law directly involved in and necessary to the deci-

Sample Brief

thus, the Court reads narrowly the Act's limitation on the Court's power, reading the reference to "substantive rights" to mean only substantive law, i.e., things other than procedure. His minor premise is that Rules 35 and 37 deal with procedure. So, because all procedural rules are valid, and because Rules 35 and 37 are procedural, the conclusion is that Rules 35 and 37 are valid. Q.E.D.

Derivation of Roberts' major premise essentially entails divining congressional will. Roberts offers three arguments in support of his reading of the Rules Enabling Act. First, in demarking the Supreme Court's authority Congress must have meant to draw the line between substantive law and procedure, because any other division would "invite endless litigation and confusion worse confounded." Second, Congress intended that a comprehensive system of court rules be adopted, and therefore envisaged that "the whole field of court procedure be regulated." Third, the Federal Rules as promulgated by the Court did in fact cover the whole field of procedure, and Congress took no action to "veto their going into effect."

The primary support for Roberts' minor premise is that Sibbach conceded that Rules 35 and 37 are procedural. Other support comes from Roberts' defi-

Notes and Questions

sion ("holdings") from asides unnecessary to the decision ("dicta").

Why have we not included in the sample brief Roberts' observations on the importance of the particular right here involved?

Of course, this sample brief is not intended to be definitive. The entry here represents only one way of distilling and analyzing the supposed holdings. Do you see another way?

Sometimes, in uncovering the issues and the court's essential reasoning, it is helpful to reconstruct what the parties were arguing. What precisely was Mrs. Sibbach's dilemma, as stated by the Court? What did she argue in order to refute that dilemma? What did the defendant argue in response?

(23) Under Roberts' reading of the Rules Enabling Act, exactly what does the Act's limitation on the Court's power, located in the second sentence of section 1, add to the meaning of the Act? What of the canon of statutory construction that "every word and clause must be given effect"? Karl N. Llewellyn, Remarks on the Theory of Appellate Decision and the Rules or Canons About How Statutes Are to Be Construed, 3 Vand.L.Rev. 395, 404 (1950); see Jonathan R. Macey & Geoffrey P. Miller, The Canons of Statutory Construction and Judicial Preferences, 45 Vand.L.Rev. 647 (1992).

Does the Act's proviso regarding the jury right cut against Roberts' reading, in that Congress was thereby specifically telling the Court not to affect an important procedural right? But would that proviso be necessary if the caveat in the Act's second sentence had already instructed the Court not to affect important rights?

(24) Do you find Roberts' definitions useful or satisfying?

Sample Brief

nitions of procedure ("the judicial process for enforcing rights and duties recognized by substantive law and for justly administering remedy and redress for disregard or infraction of them") and substantive law ("rights conferred by law to be protected and enforced in accordance with the adjective law of judicial procedure").

As to the Court's second decision, Roberts holds the sanction improper as being simply contrary to the express provisions of the former version of Rule 37(b)(2).

Separate Opinions: Justice Frankfurter likewise argues deductively. His major premise is that only rules affecting unimportant rights are valid, because in his view Congress in the Rules Enabling Act did not intend to empower the Supreme Court to make rules in derogation of important rights. His minor premise is that Rule 35 affects an important right, the inviolability of person. Because all rules affecting important rights are invalid, and because Rule 35 affects an important right, Rule 35 is invalid.

Remarks:

Notes and Questions

(25) Is it really so clear under old Rule 37(b)(2)(iv) that the sanction imposed was improper? What is the definition of "arrest" in your legal dictionary? Assuming contempt and commitment were not permissible, what kind of order might the district court have properly made in this case?

(26) Here you should sketch out in briefest form the reasoning of the minority. You might omit supporting arguments. But think about those arguments. How did Frankfurter support his major premise? his minor premise? Do you agree? Do you see that Frankfurter may possibly have been right as to his minor premise, but that the correctness of his minor premise is rendered irrelevant if Roberts' major premise is accepted? Do you also see that Frankfurter's major premise may very well have been closer to specific congressional intent, but that Roberts' major premise may have been superior from a policy viewpoint? Should such policy notions play a role in a court's decision?

(27) Here you should jot down your comments on and criticisms of the case. You might make a preliminary attempt before class, but you should certainly supplement this during and after class. There should be special emphasis on the significance of the decision and the validity of the reasoning. For example, what is the significance of Sibbach v. Wilson & Co.? Surely it represents more than a mere "Rule 35 case."

Sample Brief

Notes and Questions

What kind of job do you think Justice Roberts did? It may seem a bit premature in your career to judge Justices. But they are only human, and some more than others. As one scholar said of Roberts, "There was an almost terpsichorean quality about this benign, conscientious jurist who established a record of inconsistency probably difficult to equal in his voting on the bench." Henry J. Abraham, Justices, Presidents, and Senators 152 (1999).

What kind of job did Sibbach's lawyer do? Why did he not assign as error the improper sanction? Why, in the first place, did he not sue in Illinois state court, instead of federal court, and thus avoid the whole problem of a physical exam? Possible explanations include mistake, or perhaps this was a test case. Do you see any more subtle explanations?

Does it affect your theorizing to know that, prior to Rule 35, the federal courts had shown hostility to the idea of physical examinations? See, e.g., Union Pac. Ry. Co. v. Botsford, 141 U.S. 250, 11 S.Ct. 1000 (1891). That case was one for negligence, brought by Clara Botsford against a railroad. She complained of head injuries, caused when an upper berth in a sleeping car fell and hit her in the head. Although there were only head injuries, and although the defendant proposed that the physical examination "should be made in manner not to expose the person of the plaintiff in any indelicate manner," the Court denied the defendant's request for a physical examination, observing: "The inviolability of the person is as much invaded by a compulsory stripping and exposure as by a blow. To compel any one, and especially a woman, to lay bare the body, or to submit it to the touch of a stranger, without lawful authority, is an indignity, an assault and a trespass; and no order or process, commanding such an exposure or submission, was ever known to the common law in the administration of justice between individuals, except in a very small number of cases, based upon special reasons, and upon ancient practice, coming down from ruder ages, now mostly obsolete in England, and never, so far as we are aware, introduced into this country." Botsford ended up with $10,000 for her troubles.

Times do change. All the states now provide for physical and mental examinations, with Mississippi in 2003 being the final state to fall

Sample Brief **Notes and Questions**

into line. Does this trend represent progress? Is Rule 35 a good rule? What makes for a "good" procedure? Why are we raising such basic questions only at the end of this treatment of Sibbach v. Wilson & Co., almost as an afterthought?

We shall have many more occasions to observe how legislatures and courts go about this business of classification with which the Sibbach case was concerned—and to observe whether a rule is uniformly assigned to the same category, such as substance or procedure, or whether it may be assigned to one category when the classification's aims and consequences are such-and-such and to another category when they are thus-and-so.

On attitudes toward the subject and the course.—We shall confine our consideration mainly to procedure in civil cases in courts. Such an initial focus on courts is not nonsensical. One reason is that early mastery of the official procedural system helps in comprehending the cases read in other law courses. The primary reason, however, is that litigation remains so extremely important to society and to citizens. The courts thereby act, when other mechanisms default to them, as the last-line enforcer of law and resolver of disputes. Litigation not only produces singular decisions that restructure society but also serves as a major vehicle for lawmaking in our government and for articulation of societal values. Meanwhile, the courts' adjudications enunciate the law that sets the standards under which potential litigants resolve their disputes alternatively, "bargaining in the shadow of the law" by nonlitigation processes to reach outcomes that generally conform to the law and thereby further the law's purposes.

Nevertheless, we should observe at the outset that there is in fact a great volume of controversies adjudicated outside the courts. The modes of operation of tribunals like workers' compensation boards, the National Labor Relations Board, and the Federal Communications Commission, to name but a few of them, will be beyond our scope, except that we shall note some interrelations between courts and administrative agencies. Nor shall we do more than touch upon adjudicative procedures within corporations, labor unions, clubs, associations, or churches—or do much more than describe procedures for arbitration, mediation, and other alternative dispute-resolution mechanisms.

This notice of exclusion leads to another caveat. The stress laid on court procedure in the first year of law school sometimes leads to an unhappy insularity or provincialism among some students. They get the notion that the general style of procedure used in the courts is the only really viable one for the resolution of controversies and that other styles, being different and being studied later, are necessarily inferior. But students should suspend judgment on this matter until they have examined the other procedures. They may find that procedure relates to setting, structure, and purpose. Although it is likely that certain fundamentals must be observed in handling any civil controversy if the handling is to be accurate and fair and efficient, it is also likely that various rules of procedure appropriate to the regular grist of court business would be quite unsuitable for resolving a controversy over collective bargaining before the NLRB or a question of licensing before the FCC. It may even be that the courts have something to learn in the way of procedural finesse from administrative agencies and other bodies that deal with civil controversies.

Another common superstition is that the particular rules making up the court procedure of one's own time and place are the only rules that would really work in courts. A possible corrective for this kind of intransigence lies in the realization that court procedures have undergone drastic changes in this country without cataclysm. Another lies in realizing that today significant differences exist among federal and various states' procedures; moreover, foreign countries have procedures very different from our own, and many of them appear to work fairly well. A proposal for change certainly deserves consideration on the merits without any arbitrary assumption that sudden doom will attend change. It is, indeed, part of the purpose of this course to evolve meritorious proposals for change, some of which we shall suggest by means that include looking at other times and places.

By the way, we have been talking of "court procedure." Do not let this mode of expression seduce you into error. One kind of error is to think of "court" entirely in the abstract as the equivalent of a disembodied law and to assume that steps of "procedure" somehow are taken without any human actors at all. A more common kind of error is to think that it is the court (that is, the judge, or perhaps some parajudge or clerk) that alone initiates the procedural steps. The fact is that under the current system, as under the traditional Anglo–American scheme, it is typically the contending parties through their lawyers who take most of the initiative in the court process.

The judge's role is predominantly that of deciding the issues put before the judge by the lawyers in their procedural thrusts and parries. All this has lent to the entire court process an air of battle or strife in which the lawyers play the part of combatant champions and the judge (and jury) the part of passive umpire. However, modern complex lawsuits, often of considerable social significance, and other modern developments seem destined to demand increased judicial initiative and control. The extent to which the judge currently plays a more active role varies from jurisdiction to jurisdiction and from judge to judge and especially from case to case. We shall consider what the judicial role ought to be.

Just as it is true that court procedure is not self-propelled but is for the most part propelled on the initiative of the lawyers, so it is true that the lawyers may exercise this initiative in a variety of ways. The lawyer at various stages of a lawsuit may have a choice whether to make one or another move. Now we must add the notable fact that success or failure in the lawsuit may well turn on the wisdom, ingenuity, and skill with which the lawyer makes those moves. Although it is indeed the object of rules of procedure to facilitate the just resolution of controversies, there is no avoiding the fact that good claims are sometimes lost, and bad claims sometimes won, because of the quality of counsel's use of procedural rules—and it is implausible that any now foreseeable improvement in the rules themselves could altogether eliminate these miscarriages. It is part of the task of a course in procedure to give you training in the strategy and tactics of controversy so that missteps by you will not contribute to such miscarriages. Another part of the task is to impress upon you that, with the lawyer's freedom of motion, comes a personal responsibility for the fair and efficient running of the procedural machinery. It will help if you constantly ask this question as you read the following materials, just as we asked about Sibbach's attorney: why did the lawyer make this particular move rather than another that was open to him or her?

TOPIC B

PHASES OF A LAWSUIT

Our purpose in this Topic is to describe the major phases in the conduct of a lawsuit. Procedure too often appears to the student to be a maze of unrelated rules to be painfully mastered. We hope in the sketch that follows to give a sense of the subject as a whole and to point out some fundamental problems. In taking a look at the entire organism before examining the separate parts, we have not allowed to deter us the knowledge that later amplification will throw a different light on many of the matters here discussed.

Focus on procedure in the United States District Courts.—Our sketch focuses on the current procedures in civil actions in the United States District Courts. The Federal Rules regulate these procedures to a large extent. See Rules 1 and 81.

Our reasons for selecting these procedures as the basis not only for the sketch but for much of the course will appear more plainly as the course develops. Some of them may, however, be worth noting here. (1) Focusing on a single procedural system most efficiently presents the essential, while spotlighting a complete system enables the student to reach those problems of theory and practice that require consideration of a system in its entirety. (2) The Federal Rules are a concise corpus, from the study of which the student can grasp rather quickly how a going system of procedure functions in a general way. (3) Although the federal procedural system created by the Rules differs in various respects from the systems of procedure prevailing in the various other times and places, which of course differ among themselves, it provides a model by reference to which the student can later study and evaluate those systems. (4) The Federal Rules' system is generally considered to be a fairly successful, but by no means perfect, representative of modern procedure.[a] (5) A majority of the state systems are now based in substantial part on the Federal Rules, and still others adopt particular features of the Rules.[b] (6) Although litigants commence the

---

[a] We shall not often interrupt the sketch by contrasting the terminology and provisions of the Federal Rules with those of predecessor procedure. Of course, some provisions of the Federal Rules will become more meaningful when considered in the light of what they superseded, so we shall later treat some of the predecessors. In the meantime, it would be helpful to the student, who in his or her substantive law courses will encounter cases involving common-law, equitable, or so-called code procedure, to know that he or she can find materials on old law equity and on the Field Code in the index's entries under common law, equity, and code.

[b] Nor shall we often interrupt this presentation by contrasting the terminology and provisions of the Federal Rules with those of the state systems of procedure. However, it would be useful for the student to examine the procedural statutes and rules of his or her

vastly greater percentage of this country's civil cases in state courts, the United States District Courts are important courts that handle a large volume of cases, many of which are of major significance.

Selection of a proper forum.—The first step in instituting a lawsuit is to select a proper court to hear the case. Each state has its own set of courts exerting the judicial power of the state, and there is an overlay of United States courts exerting the judicial power of the nation. Sometimes there is only one proper court for a particular controversy, but often two or more are available. Then a choice must be made, and that initially is the plaintiff's. However, situations exist where a suit properly lodged by the plaintiff in one court can be moved to a different one by the defendant at his option or with the court's permission.

We shall not now undertake the survey of the judicial systems of the states and the United States that would be necessary in order to determine which court or courts may properly be selected to hear a given case. (We instead defer such a survey to Sections 6 and 7 of this Topic.) Rather we shall assume during the following discussion, except when we specially raise the question, that a plaintiff has properly instituted a case in a United States District Court—that the case is of a type that such a court has the authority to adjudicate, and that the particular district court has authority over the particular case through the proper filing of a complaint with it (see Rule 3) and the proper service of papers upon the defendant (see Rule 4).

SECTION 1. PRETRIAL

(a) STATING THE CLAIM[c]

[Rules 8(a), (c), (d), and (e), 9(b), 11; Form 11]

So, according to Rule 3, the plaintiff has commenced an action by filing a complaint with the court. What is a complaint, how is it to be written, and what are its purposes?

Rule 8(a) indicates that a complaint shall contain "a short and plain statement of the claim showing that the pleader is entitled to relief" (as well as a statement of the grounds for the court's jurisdiction, and a demand for the relief sought). Here, then, is the first step in laying bare

home state, or the state where he or she expects to practice, to see the extent to which they are comparable to the Federal Rules. There is no state that remains wholly unaffected by the federal reform, but some populous states remain importantly distinctive. See John B. Oakley & Arthur F. Coon, The Federal Rules in State Courts: A Survey of State Court Systems of Civil Procedure, 61 Wash.L.Rev. 1367 (1986); John B. Oakley, A Fresh Look at the Federal Rules in State Courts, 3 Nev.L.J. 354 (2003).

[c] Immediately under this and later captions we shall give references to the most important relevant Federal Rules and Forms. Students should each of read these Rules and Forms with particular care. Other Rule and Form references in text and questions are less important, but still students should examine those Rules and Forms.

what the dispute is about. By his complaint the plaintiff is to inform his adversary and the court of the basis of his contention that he can invoke the court's aid in redressing a grievance.

Rule 8(a) by itself, however, does not go far in describing what the form of the complaint should be or just what the complaint should set forth. Other Rules are helpful on these matters. But perhaps the way to begin is to look at Forms 10 to 21, inclusive, which are illustrations of proper complaints in various kinds of lawsuits.

Who has the burden of allegation?—Surely the plaintiff need assert only relevant matters, but by reference to what is the plaintiff to determine relevancy? Doubtless the rule of substantive law that the plaintiff seeks to invoke establishes the contours of relevancy.

Examine with special care Form 11, a "Complaint for Negligence." You will observe that the plaintiff has here given a somewhat particularized statement within the compass of a rule of substantive law regarding liability for negligence—a proposition of the type shown schematically in the earlier example of battery:

> If *B* knowingly strikes *A*, and . . . , then, unless *A* consented, or . . . , *A* is entitled to a judgment . . . .

The complaint for negligence does not explicitly state the comparable substantive rule, but it implicitly invokes it.

Question: (1) Can you phrase schematically the rule of substantive law that the plaintiff is probably seeking to invoke in the Forms' Complaint for Negligence?

After putting into words the rule of law that the plaintiff is probably seeking to invoke in the Forms' Complaint for Negligence, you will notice that he appears to have limited himself in the complaint to a somewhat particularized statement of the "if" part of the rule; he has not concerned himself with negating the "unless" part. To put the matter more concretely, plaintiff may also have been negligent at the time, which would normally bar his recovery at least in part; yet plaintiff does not in his complaint assert that he was himself free of negligence or, equivalently, that he was exercising due care. It thus appears that a plaintiff need not allege in his complaint all the conditions of the defendant's liability. He may confine himself to the "ifs" and omit any reference to the "unlesses."

Unfortunately, the "if, unless" form of statement is not the only meaningful one that someone could employ. Someone could state a substantive rule—the conditions under which a court will grant a remedy—altogether in "if" fashion, without any "unless" clauses, simply by altering the form of the statement thus:

> If *B* knowingly strikes *A*, and if *A* has not consented, and . . . , then *A* is entitled to a judgment . . . .

So why do we use the "if, unless" form? Because it is a convenient way to make the point that indeed the law divides the burden of allegation between the parties. The plaintiff must assert the matters in the "if" clauses, and the defendant must assert such of the matters in the "unless" clauses as she proposes to raise. As we shall see later, an omitted matter that the plaintiff need not assert and that the defendant chooses not to assert is ordinarily not in issue in the case.

But then which matters belong on the "if" side and which on the "unless"? The law's placing of the dividing line, and the corresponding assignment of the respective burdens of allegation to the parties, does not follow from an exercise of pure logic.[d] Reconsider the Complaint for Negligence. The law might well require the plaintiff to assert that he was using due care for his own safety when the defendant drove a motor vehicle against him. Indeed, as we shall see, in some state judicial systems the law did cast the burden on the plaintiff to assert his due care rather than on the defendant to assert the contrary.

Question: (2) What are the considerations that ought to govern the allocation between the parties of the burdens of allegation?

The Federal Rules provide a guide, although not a complete one, to the way in which the law actually allocates these burdens in the United States District Courts. Rule 8(c), entitled "Affirmative Defenses," is a catalogue of certain matters that the defendant must assert in her answer, if she chooses to put them in issue, and that the plaintiff need not assert in the complaint. Note that "contributory negligence" of the plaintiff is such an affirmative defense. Beyond Rule 8(c), statutes and precedents and form books provide further guidance to the pleader.

All this gives at least an idea of what elements the parties respectively must plead. Generally, a pleader is well advised to avoid saying much more than the minimum required. We shall see later that any excess does risk causing eventual problems—such as putting into issue matters that otherwise would not be in the case or boxing the pleader in—even though the Federal Rules try to mitigate most of such risks.

How particularized must allegations be?—We have said that the plaintiff's statement of claim appears to be a somewhat particularized rendering of the "if" part of a rule of law. This leaves at large, however, the question of the degree to which the plaintiff must carry particularization. Within the contours of relevancy, how much detail is necessary?

This is the big problem. There is no easy or simple answer, but the Rules and Forms throw some light upon it. The statement of the claim is, according to Rule 8(a), to be "short" as well as "plain." And Rule 8 goes on, in its subdivisions applicable to all pleadings, to prescribe, for example, that each allegation of a pleading shall be "simple, concise, and direct."

Question: (3) Does a negligence plaintiff really need to plead the amount of his medical expenses, as Form 11 does?

Rule 9, "Pleading Special Matters," gives a number of further directions. Consider Rule 9(b). On the one hand, it tells us that in all

[d] For the logical involvements of the scheme here presented, see H.L.A. Hart, "The Ascription of Responsibilities and Rights," in Essays on Logic and Language 145 (Antony Flew ed., 1951). But see H.L.A. Hart, Punishment and Responsibility, at v & n.1 (1968). See generally Richard A. Epstein, Pleadings and Presumptions, 40 U.Chi.L.Rev. 556 (1973).

allegations of fraud or mistake, the pleader must state "with particularity" the circumstances constituting fraud or mistake. On the other hand, it says that the pleader may allege generally malice, intent, knowledge, and other conditions of mind.

Question: (4) What is the reason for the distinction that Rule 9(b) draws? Is it not becoming plain that to answer such a question you must first decide what the system intends to accomplish by the pleadings? For example, would it not be desirable to know whether the pleadings will serve any purpose during the course of the trial?

If you were now asked to draft a complaint in a battery case, would these Rules and illustrative Forms provide enough light to go by? Your client has given you, probably very volubly, a detailed account of what happened. It is your task to cull from this account a properly particularized statement of claim invoking the pertinent rule of substantive law. Should you state in your complaint when and where the attack took place? how your client happened to be there at the time? who witnessed the incident? what were the dimensions of the stick with which the defendant beat your client? the nature and extent of your client's injuries? the conversation between the parties before the attack? what the police officer who arrived on the scene said and did? Let us see what the courts have told us.

Plaintiff's Amended Statement of Claim

Filed Nov. 17, 1938, amending complaint of Sept. 13, 1938.

Martin Sierocinski, also known as Martin Selensky, the plaintiff above named, brings this action in trespass against E.I. DuPont DeNemours & Company upon a cause of action whereof the following is a statement:

1. The plaintiff is a resident of the City and County of Philadelphia.

2. The defendant, E.I. DuPont DeNemours & Company, is and was at the time of the occurrences hereinafter described, a corporation duly organized and existing under the laws of the State of Delaware, and duly authorized to transact business in the Commonwealth of Pennsylvania, in accordance with the Business Corporation Law, having its registered office at 3500 Gray's Ferry Road, Philadelphia.

3. The defendant is engaged in the business of manufacturing and distributing, and does manufacture and distribute, inter alia, blasting caps for use by the public.

4. On or about September 24, 1936, and for a long period of time prior thereto, the plaintiff was an employee of Ehret Magnesia Manufacturing Company, which has and had its principal place of business located in the vicinity of Valley Forge, Pa.

5. The plaintiff, in the course of his duties as servant, agent or employee of the said Ehret Magnesia Manufacturing Company, was charged with the responsibility and duty of handling, preparing and explod-

ing the explosives used by the said Ehret Magnesia Manufacturing Company in certain of its quarrying operations, and had occupied this position and performed these duties for a long period of time prior to September 24, 1936, as well as on said date.

6. The Ehret Magnesia Manufacturing Company furnished to the plaintiff dynamite caps manufactured by the defendant, which dynamite caps were in the same condition as they were when distributed by the said defendant.

7. On or about September 24, 1936, the plaintiff was engaged in crimping a dynamite cap, manufactured and distributed by the defendant, when it prematurely exploded causing the injuries hereinafter set forth.

8. In the crimping of the said dynamite cap, the plaintiff acted in the usual and customary manner, the process being a necessary one in the using of the said dynamite cap for the purpose for which it was manufactured and distributed, and such action on his part having been anticipated by defendant.

9. The aforementioned premature explosion, and the injuries resulting therefrom, were caused solely by the carelessness and negligence of the defendant, in:

(a) manufacturing a dynamite cap in such a fashion that it was unable to withstand the crimping which defendant knew it would be subjected to,

(b) distributing a dynamite cap which was so constructed that it was unable to withstand the crimping which defendant knew it would be subjected to,

(c) distributing a dynamite cap which was so constructed that it would explode, upon being crimped, without warning or in any fashion indicating that the said dynamite cap would explode upon being crimped,

(d) distributing a dynamite cap which it knew would be crimped when the said dynamite cap would explode upon said crimping, and such fact was known or should have been known to defendant.

10. By reason of the said premature explosion of the said dynamite cap, manufactured and distributed by the defendant, the plaintiff did suffer the following injuries: Loss of great toe of left foot; loss of sight of both eyes; lacerations of the legs, arms, shoulders, thighs, face and neck; gravel and grit were driven into various and sundry portions of his body, including his face, legs, arms, shoulders, thighs, trunk and torso; a severe shock to his nerves and nervous system; and various and sundry other injuries of a serious and permanent nature.

11. As the result of the aforesaid occurrence, the plaintiff has undergone and will undergo great pain and suffering. He was confined to his bed for a long period of time and will be blind for the rest of his life. He has required and will require medical attention and treatment, thereby incur-

ring great expenses. He has been deprived of his sole means of livelihood, and he is otherwise greatly injured and damaged.

Wherefore, the plaintiff claims to recover from the defendant the sum of Two Hundred Thousand Dollars ($200,000) as damages for the aforesaid injuries caused directly by the negligence of the defendant as aforesaid.

(s) RAYMOND A. WHITE, JR.,
Attorney for Plaintiff.

Sierocinski v. E.I. Du Pont De Nemours & Co.

United States Circuit Court of Appeals, Third Circuit, 1939.
103 F.2d 843.

■ Before MARIS, BIDDLE, and BUFFINGTON, CIRCUIT JUDGES.

■ BIDDLE, CIRCUIT JUDGE. The plaintiff's "statement of claim" (complaint), amended under an order of court [25 F.Supp. 706 (E.D.Pa. Nov. 10, 1938) (Kalodner, J.)] granting defendant's motion for a more definite statement under Rule 12(e), Rules of Civil Procedure for District Courts . . . , alleged that he was injured by the premature explosion of a dynamite cap. Specifically the plaintiff claimed as negligent acts the manufacturing and distributing of the cap "in such a fashion that it was unable to withstand the crimping which defendant knew it would be subjected to"; and distributing a cap so constructed that it would explode upon being crimped, without warning, the defendant knowing it would be crimped. Judge Kalodner granted the defendant's motion to strike this amended statement, as failing to set forth any specific act of negligence, and dismissed the action. [His unpublished opinion explained: "The allegations as amended in Paragraph 9 . . . are not sufficiently specific and do not afford the Defendant opportunity to know what issue or issues it might have to meet upon trial in regard to negligence. In brief, the amended statement of claim still fails to set forth any specific act of negligence. The allegations consist of conclusions and not facts."] From his order the plaintiff appealed to this court.

The plaintiff, as alleged, was injured while "crimping" a dynamite cap manufactured by the defendant and supplied to him by his employer. "Crimping" is a necessary and anticipated process in using the cap.

Appellee, admitting that a manufacturer is liable for injuries to a person from the use of a defectively manufactured article, argues that it is not put on notice by the complaint as to whether it must meet a claim of warranty, of misrepresentation, of the use of improper ingredients, or of faulty inspection.

But there is a specific averment of negligent manufacture and distribution of the cap in such a fashion as to make it explode when crimped. A plaintiff need not plead evidence. He "sets forth a claim for relief" when he makes "a short and plain statement of the claim showing that the pleader is entitled to relief (Rule 8(a)(2))." The same rule [Rule 8(d)(1)] requires that "each averment of a pleading shall be simple, concise, and direct. No technical forms of pleading or motions are required"; and ([e]) "all pleadings shall be so construed as to do substantial justice". Form [11] in the Appendix of Forms attached to the Rules, "intended to indicate . . . the simplicity and brevity of statement which the rules contemplate [Rule 84]",[e] contains this concise allegation of negligence: "defendant negligently drove a motor vehicle against plaintiff who was then crossing said highway". If defendant needs further information to prepare its defense, it can obtain it by interrogatories (Rule 33).

The judgment is reversed, and the cause remanded for further proceedings.

Question: (5) How convincing are Judge Biddle's arguments drawn from (a) the proposition that the plaintiff need not plead evidence, (b) the style of Form 11, and (c) the fact that the defendant might resort to Rule 33?

Upon remand, the Sierocinski case went to trial before a new judge and a jury. The jury brought in a verdict for the plaintiff. Denying the defendant's motions for a directed verdict and for judgment notwithstanding the verdict, the judge entered judgment for the plaintiff. From this judgment, the defendant took an appeal to the circuit court of appeals. The appellate court reversed the judgment, 118 F.2d 531 (3d Cir.1941), on the ground that the judge should have taken the case away from the jury. The appellate court said: "No proof, . . . either direct or circumstantial, was adduced to support a finding of any of the specific acts of negligence alleged." The appellate court also rejected the plaintiff's attempt on appeal to switch to a theory of breach of warranty.

Questions: (6) Does this subsequent history demonstrate that the decision on the first appeal was wrong?

(7) After decision on the second appeal, should it be open to the plaintiff to commence a new action, basing his claim on a legal theory not exploited before, for example, on a theory of breach of warranty?

CONLEY v. GIBSON, 355 U.S. 41, 78 S.Ct. 99 (1957). African-American members of the Brotherhood of Railway and Steamship Clerks brought suit under the Railway Labor Act to compel the union to represent them in collective bargaining without discrimination because of race. There were in the complaint allegations that the union had not done so, mainly concerning when it stood by after the employer, the Texas & New Orleans Railroad, replaced 45 plaintiff-jobholders with white hires. On motion to

[e] At the date of this decision, Rule 84 read: "The forms contained in the Appendix of Forms are intended to indicate, subject to the provisions of these rules, the simplicity and brevity of statement which the rules contemplate." Compare the present text of Rule 84.

dismiss, defendants' principal contention was that the National Railroad Adjustment Board had exclusive jurisdiction of the dispute, but defendants also moved to dismiss on the ground that the complaint was defective for failure to state a claim upon which relief could be granted.

Ultimately the Supreme Court upheld the jurisdiction of the district court. See Emily Sherwin, "The Story of Conley: Precedent by Accident," in Civil Procedure Stories 295 (Kevin M. Clermont ed., 2d ed. 2008). On the pleading point, the Court made two significant pronouncements, albeit without a lot of thought.

First, before addressing the factual detail required, the Court addressed the test of legal sufficiency. It looked to see if any legal claim existed that would be consistent with the words of the complaint. The Court said the complaint must encompass a legal claim without including allegations that would defeat it.

Second, after the Court held that the plaintiffs passed the legal test, it disposed of any contention that dismissal was proper for the complaint's failure to set forth enough specific facts to support the general allegations of discrimination. The Court said: "The decisive answer to this is that the Federal Rules of Civil Procedure do not require a claimant to set out in detail the facts upon which he bases his claim. To the contrary, all the Rules require is 'a short and plain statement of the claim' that will give the defendant fair notice of what the plaintiff's claim is and the grounds upon which it rests. The illustrative forms appended to the Rules plainly demonstrate this. Such simplified 'notice pleading' is made possible by the liberal opportunity for discovery and the other pretrial procedures established by the Rules to disclose more precisely the basis of both claim and defense and to define more narrowly the disputed facts and issues. Following the simple guide of Rule 8([e]) that 'all pleadings shall be so construed as to do substantial justice,' we have no doubt that [the] complaint adequately set forth a claim and gave the [defendants] fair notice of its basis. The Federal Rules reject the approach that pleading is a game of skill in which one misstep by counsel may be decisive to the outcome and accept the principle that the purpose of pleading is to facilitate a proper decision on the merits."

BELL ATLANTIC CORP. v. TWOMBLY, 550 U.S. 544, 127 S.Ct. 1955 (2007). Telephone and internet subscribers brought a class action against the telecommunications giants, claiming an illegal conspiracy in restraint of trade. Under antitrust law, however, parallel and even consciously identical conduct unfavorable to competition is not illegal if it comprises only independent acts by competitors without any agreement. The complaint alleged parallel conduct in great detail, explaining how each company sought to inhibit upstarts in its own region and refrained from entering the other major companies' regions. But the complaint alleged an agreement in conclusory terms upon information and belief, because the plaintiffs had no proof yet in hand.

The obvious concern in this big complex case was with opening the door to the plaintiffs' expensive discovery. So, the Court upheld dismissal on a pre-answer motion, holding that the complaint failed to show agreement to be plausible. According to the Court, the defendants' behavior was what each company would naturally have done in pursuit of its own interests. The plaintiffs needed to give factual detail to make their complaint plausible, yet they "mentioned no specific time, place, or person involved in the alleged conspiracies." Dismissal followed for these plaintiffs who "have not nudged their claims across the line from conceivable to plausible."

In so ruling, the Court added a plausibility test for claimants to pass at the pleading stage. This move represented the Court's first unmistakable step backward from the modern conception of notice pleading blessed in Conley. The Court did not step in the direction of simply reverting to a requirement of heightened detail in factual allegations, but instead it instituted a judicial inquiry into the pleading's convincingness. Such an innovation—testing factual strength at the pleading stage—would prove momentous *if* it were not limited to antitrust cases. Justice Souter for the Court explained the new test, but did so in generally applicable wording:

"This case presents the antecedent question of what a plaintiff must plead in order to state a claim under § 1 of the Sherman Act. Federal Rule of Civil Procedure 8(a)(2) requires only 'a short and plain statement of the claim showing that the pleader is entitled to relief,' in order to 'give the defendant fair notice of what the . . . claim is and the grounds upon which it rests,' Conley v. Gibson, 355 U.S. 41, 47, 78 S.Ct. 99 (1957). While a complaint attacked by a Rule 12(b)(6) motion to dismiss does not need detailed factual allegations, ibid.; Sanjuan v. American Bd. of Psychiatry and Neurology, Inc., 40 F.3d 247, 251 (C.A.7 1994), a plaintiff's obligation to provide the 'grounds' of his 'entitle[ment] to relief' requires more than labels and conclusions, and a formulaic recitation of the elements of a cause of action will not do, see Papasan v. Allain, 478 U.S. 265, 286, 106 S.Ct. 2932 (1986) (on a motion to dismiss, courts 'are not bound to accept as true a legal conclusion couched as a factual allegation'). Factual allegations must be enough to raise a right to relief above the speculative level, see 5 C. Wright & A. Miller, Federal Practice and Procedure § 1216, pp. 235–236 (3d ed. 2004) . . . ('[T]he pleading must contain something more . . . than . . . a statement of facts that merely creates a suspicion [of] a legally cognizable right of action'), on the assumption that all the allegations in the complaint are true (even if doubtful in fact), see, e.g., Swierkiewicz v. Sorema N.A., 534 U.S. 506, 508, n. 1, 122 S.Ct. 992 (2002); Neitzke v. Williams, 490 U.S. 319, 327, 109 S.Ct. 1827 (1989) ('Rule 12(b)(6) does not countenance . . . dismissals based on a judge's disbelief of a complaint's factual allegations'); Scheuer v. Rhodes, 416 U.S. 232, 236, 94 S.Ct. 1683 (1974) (a well-pleaded complaint may proceed even if it appears 'that a recovery is very remote and unlikely').

"In applying these general standards to a § 1 claim, we hold that stating such a claim requires a complaint with enough factual matter (taken as true) to suggest that an agreement was made. Asking for plausible grounds to infer an agreement does not impose a probability requirement at the pleading stage; it simply calls for enough fact to raise a reasonable expectation that discovery will reveal evidence of illegal agreement. . . . It makes sense to say, therefore, that an allegation of parallel conduct and a bare assertion of conspiracy will not suffice. Without more, parallel conduct does not suggest conspiracy, and a conclusory allegation of agreement at some unidentified point does not supply facts adequate to show illegality. Hence, when allegations of parallel conduct are set out in order to make a § 1 claim, they must be placed in a context that raises a suggestion of a preceding agreement, not merely parallel conduct that could just as well be independent action.

"The need at the pleading stage for allegations plausibly suggesting (not merely consistent with) agreement reflects the threshold requirement of Rule 8(a)(2) that the 'plain statement' possess enough heft to 'sho[w] that the pleader is entitled to relief.' A statement of parallel conduct, even conduct consciously undertaken, needs some setting suggesting the agreement necessary to make out a § 1 claim; without that further circumstance pointing toward a meeting of the minds, an account of a defendant's commercial efforts stays in neutral territory. An allegation of parallel conduct is thus much like a naked assertion of conspiracy in a § 1 complaint: it gets the complaint close to stating a claim, but without some further factual enhancement it stops short of the line between possibility and plausibility of 'entitle[ment] to relief.' Cf. DM Research, Inc. v. College of Am. Pathologists, 170 F.3d 53, 56 (C.A.1 1999) ('[T]erms like "conspiracy," or even "agreement," are border-line: they might well be sufficient in conjunction with a more specific allegation—for example, identifying a written agreement or even a basis for inferring a tacit agreement, . . . but a court is not required to accept such terms as a sufficient basis for a complaint')."

Thus, in this case the Court ignored the conclusory allegation of agreement. It had to accept as true the allegations of parallel conduct, but it could still treat them as an inadequate "showing" of entitlement to relief because they did not make plausible the existence of an agreement.

Justice Stevens, joined in relevant part by Justice Ginsburg, dissented. He saw the decision as a "dramatic departure from settled procedural law," and an unjustified one because it should have come if at all by amendment of the Federal Rules or by statute. He lamented that by imposing a plausibility test on pleadings, "the Court succumbs to the temptation that previous Courts have steadfastly resisted. . . . Here, the failure the majority identifies is not a failure of notice—which 'notice pleading' rightly condemns—but rather a failure to satisfy the Court that the agreement alleged might plausibly have occurred. That being a question not of *notice* but of *proof*," courts will now have "to engage in armchair economics at the pleading stage" in order to ascertain somehow whether the complaint's pleaded facts adequately show liability.

Justice Stevens noted the inconsistency of the majority's holding with the simple reference to "negligently" in Form 11. "Whether the Court's actions will benefit only defendants in antitrust treble-damages cases, or whether its test for the sufficiency of a complaint will inure to the benefit of all civil defendants, is a question that the future will answer."

Perhaps the answer to his question came only two weeks later, when the Court overturned a pleading dismissal in Erickson v. Pardus, 551 U.S. 89, 127 S.Ct. 2197 (2007). In that case, the pro se plaintiff brought a civil rights claim against prison officials for their wrongfully terminating his medical treatment for hepatitis C, alleging that this action endangered his life. The Tenth Circuit affirmed the dismissal, on the ground that the plaintiff had pleaded the substantial-harm element in a "conclusory" fashion. The Supreme Court vacated because that "holding departs in so stark a manner from the pleading standard mandated by the Federal Rules of Civil Procedure." It cited Twombly for the propositions that notice pleading does not require allegations of "specific facts" and that the "judge must accept as true all of the factual allegations contained in the complaint," but it did not reach and made no reference to any plausibility test. The Court's summary action was per curiam, with Justices Scalia and Thomas dissenting on other grounds. Later the lower court found the pleading sufficient, in Erickson v. Pardus, 238 F.App'x 335 (10th Cir.2007).

The real answer, however, came two years later in Ashcroft v. Iqbal, 129 S.Ct. 1937 (2009), when on interlocutory appeal the Court ruled that Twombly applied to all federal complaints and then overturned the lower courts' approval of the complaint before it. Here the civil rights plaintiff, a Pakistani Muslim arrested post–9/11 in the United States, sued high federal officials upon allegations of harsh conditions of confinement on account of his race, religion, or national origin. The Court ignored conclusory allegations of the cause of action's elements, such as that the defendants knowingly condoned a discriminatory policy. The Court then said the remaining allegations did not suffice to make plausible that the Attorney General and the FBI Director subjected the plaintiff to harsh confinement *because of* his race, religion, or national origin. Such a determination of plausibility is "a context-specific task that requires the reviewing court to draw on its judicial experience and common sense," with the issue being whether the content of the nonconclusory factual allegations "allows the court to draw the reasonable inference that the defendant is liable for the misconduct alleged." Now, Justice Souter was in dissent, joined by Justices Stevens, Ginsburg, and Breyer. The case appears infra p. 1164.

Questions: (8) In first embracing notice pleading and then inventing nonconclusory-and-plausible pleading fifty years later, the Court was interpreting the same Rule 8(a). Should the Court's activism in interpreting a Federal Rule substantially differ from its role in interpreting a statute like the Rules Enabling Act? See Catherine T. Struve, The Paradox of Delegation: Interpreting the Federal Rules of Civil Procedure, 150 U.Pa.L.Rev. 1099 (2002) (arguing forcefully in the negative).

(9) Could Mr. Conley pass the Twombly–Iqbal test? Could Mr. Sierocinski?

Statement of claim in the alternative.—Rule 8(d)(2) says that a party may set out two or more statements of a claim or defense "alternatively" (either-or) or "hypothetically" (if-then), whether in a single count or defense or in separate ones. As applied to the complaint, the main function of this provision appears to be to assist a plaintiff who is genuinely uncertain about the facts that he will be able to prove or the substantive law that will apply. The Rule permits that plaintiff to take advantage of whatever pleaded version of the claim he may eventually establish to the satisfaction of the adjudicator.

It may seem obvious to you that statements of claim in the alternative should be permissible, but it is worth pointing out that the Rule represents a departure from the practice permitted at common law. Does this not tell us more about the purposes of federal pleading?

Definition of "claim."—Throughout Rule 8, the word "claim" appears. This word is analogous to the phrase "cause of action" as it appears in various state codes of procedure, but one should not assume that "claim" and "cause of action" necessarily mean the same thing. Nor should one assume that either "claim" or "cause of action" necessarily means the same thing whenever and wherever it is used, irrespective of context.

In all events, what does "claim" mean as it appears in Rule 8's provision for alternative statements of claim? We can say at least that the drafters of the Rule thought that a plaintiff may in some cases state a *single claim* in different ways. Yet how far can the statements vary before they produce not alternative statements of a single claim, but a *multiple claims*?

Consider here that the differing statements may all invoke the same rule of substantive law, or they may each allege a violation of a distinct legal right and thereby invoke a distinct rule of substantive law (say, negligence and warranty). Does this have a bearing on whether the statements are alternative statements of one claim or constitute a number of distinct claims? Shall we say narrowly that the "legal theory," or the substantive right, is the measure of what is a claim?

Consider further that a single, straightforward statement of an episode may invoke a number of rules of substantive law, each casting liability on the defendant. Thus, if *B* sells to *A* a machine negligently constructed, and by reason of the defect it injures *A* in the course of operation, *B* may be liable by reference to a rule of tort law (negligence) or by reference to a rule of contract law (warranty). When *A* sets forth an account of the accident in her complaint, is she alleging one claim or two? Shall we say broadly that the "transaction or occurrence," or the natural grouping or congeries of events, is the measure of what is a claim?

The importance of this question—what is the distinction between alternative statements of a single claim, on the one hand, and multiple claims, on the other hand—may be minimal in the present context, because Rule 18(a) complements Rule 8(d)(2) by permitting the plaintiff to join in the complaint, either as independent or as alternative claims, as many claims as he has against the defendant. Nevertheless, we put the question here to call attention to a problem that later appears in various guises in other contexts and can sometimes be highly significant: what is the meaning of "claim"? of "cause of action"?

Consistency and truth in pleading.—Rule 8(d)(3) goes on to provide that a party may state as many separate claims or defenses as the party has against the opponent, "regardless of consistency."

Nevertheless, all statements in pleadings are subject to the obligations of Rule 11. Note thereunder that the pleader ordinarily need not verify or swear to the pleading, but presenting a pleading constitutes a certification that there is good ground to support it and that it is not interposed for improper purpose. The Rule sets forth sanctions for violations of its obligations.

Questions: (10) What obligation does Rule 11 impose on an attorney to investigate, before signing the complaint, the motivation and the legal and factual bases for the client's claim? See the section of the Rules booklet containing the 1983 and 1993 amendments to Rule 11 and the Advisory Committee's notes thereon.

(11) Considering the state of knowledge, information, and belief of Mr. Sierocinski's lawyer as to the cause of the accident, did he violate his duty under original Rule 11 when he signed the amended complaint in that action? Would Mr. White's signature have violated new Rule 11?

MURPHY v. CUOMO, 913 F.Supp. 671 (N.D.N.Y.1996). Murphy brought suit in February 1994 against a variety of defendants for injuries arising from an incident in which a New York State Police officer had sprayed Murphy with a pepper spray called CAP–STUN. The police argued that during post-arrest processing, while Murphy was intoxicated and belligerent, he had lunged at one of the officers and so prompted the spraying.

Murphy named as one of the defendants Zarc International, the manufacturer of CAP–STUN. Murphy alleged in detail that Zarc had conspired with the police to spray innocent people for testing the spray and then to forward the results to Zarc. Murphy further alleged that he had been one of those innocent people and that the incident had violated his federal statutory and constitutional rights. He sought $20 million in compensatory and punitive damages.

With the trial date fast approaching, Zarc moved for summary judgment under Rule 56 and sought sanctions pursuant to Rule 11. In granting the defendant's motion for summary judgment, the court determined that the "plaintiff has offered absolutely no evidence that Zarc conspired with the New York State Police to conduct an illegal experiment whereby officers would subject innocent and unwitting citizens to CAP–STUN in order to study the spray's effects. . . .

"The Pilot Study undertaken by the State Police appears to have been properly intended 'to evaluate the use of chemical agents [that] could be used as a non-lethal, alternative weapon to the issue side arm and the baton,' (Def.'s Mem.Supp.Summ.J. at 11), and plaintiff has presented no evidence to the contrary. In other words, the Court has no reason to believe that the Pilot Study was intended to test the effects of CAP–STUN on innocents, rather than to test whether CAP–STUN met the State Police's needs in situations where the use of some force was justified. Moreover, even if the State Police were involved in some kind of diabolical experiment, no evidence has been put forth that defendant Zarc had anything at all to do with the experiment, or with the officer's decision to use CAP–STUN on plaintiff as opposed to someone else.

"As late as his deposition in August, 1995, when discovery was supposed to be complete, plaintiff was unable to clarify the basis for his claim of conspiracy:

> Q. Do you have any information that Zarc did anything other than provide the product Cap–Stun to the New York State police department?
>
> A. I personally don't have any knowledge of that.
>
> Q. Do you know of anyone who does have any knowledge of that?
>
> A. No.
>
> Q. Do you plan on calling any witnesses at the trial of this action to testify that Zarc did anything other than provide the New York State police with Cap–Stun?
>
> A. We may.
>
> Q. Who would that be?
>
> A. I'm not sure right now.

. . . Now that discovery is complete and plaintiff has another opportunity to proffer evidence of an illegal plan to test CAP–STUN on innocent citizens, he does not fare much better. Plaintiff argues in his opposition memorandum that '[i]t is undisputed that Zarc provided the [pepper spray] for the State Police test.' (Pl.'s Mem.Opp.Summ.J. at 6.) Furthermore, '[t]o the extent that Zarc knowingly provided the State Police with training in the application of Cap–Stun . . . it helped to create the experimental protocol.' (Id.) Lastly, Zarc 'was informed of the results of the pilot study . . . and uses the results . . . as part of its advertising.' (Id. at 11.)

"The Court simply believes that, based on plaintiff's evidence, no reasonable jury could find that defendant Zarc was significantly involved in the Pilot Study. Nor could a reasonable jury find that the Pilot Study was intended to do anything but evaluate a chemical agent that could be used by police as a non-lethal, alternative weapon when the use of some force was justified."

Because no reasonable jury could find for the plaintiff, the court granted summary judgment for Zarc. It then moved on to Zarc's separate motion for sanctions.

"The objective of Rule 11 is to deter dilatory and abusive tactics in litigation, and to streamline the litigation process by lessening frivolous claims or defenses. . . . Imposition of Rule 11 sanctions does not require a finding of bad faith. Rather, '[t]he test as to whether an attorney made a reasonable inquiry prior to signing a pleading is an objective standard of reasonableness under the circumstances at the time the attorney acted.' EEOC v. Tandem Computers, Inc., 158 F.R.D. 224, 227 (D.Mass.1994).

"Rule 11 requires attorneys to take responsibility for the claims they present by requiring them to make a reasonable inquiry to assure that the claims represented by them are well-grounded in both law and fact. Id. At its simplest, Rule 11 'continues to require litigants to "stop-and-think" before initially making legal or factual contentions.' Fed.R.Civ.P. 11, Advisory Committee Notes (1993 Amendment). However, under the 1993 revisions to the rule the imposition of sanctions is always discretionary with the Court rather than mandatory. See Fed.R.Civ.P. 11(c); Knipe v. Skinner, 19 F.3d 72, 78 (2d Cir.1994). As a procedural matter, Rule 11 forbids the imposition of sanctions unless the challenged pleading has not been withdrawn or corrected within 21 days of service of the motion for sanctions. . . .

"The Court realizes that Rule 11 sanctions must be imposed with caution, so as not to chill the prosecution of meritorious claims. Knipe, 19 F.3d at 78; MacDraw, Inc. v. CIT Group Equip. Fin., Inc., 73 F.3d 1253, 1258–59 (2d Cir.1996). Furthermore, a district court must 'articulate with specificity the sanctionable conduct and the reasons supporting the sanctions.' MacDraw, 73 F.3d at 1258–59.

"[In applying these generalities, first the court concluded that plaintiff's counsel had failed to make a reasonable inquiry into the legal viability of one of his causes based on a federal drug statute, a statute that creates no private cause of action—as would have been shown by] a mere cursory review of the applicable caselaw . . . . Defendant's counsel seems to have notified plaintiff's counsel of this reality on numerous occasions, but with no effect.

"Second, in regard to plaintiff's claims against defendant Zarc for other violations of his statutory and constitutional rights, plaintiff's counsel knew at the time he signed the Complaint that plaintiff had no basis in fact for his allegations. Another perusal of plaintiff's deposition, taken 20 months after plaintiff's counsel signed a document in which he seeks $20 million, makes this fact abundantly clear . . . . Thus even 20 months after the Complaint was signed, neither plaintiff nor his counsel knew if any facts existed that would support the serious allegations they had made in the Complaint.

"It is true that the law does not require a plaintiff to be able to prove his case prior to discovery. However, . . . a complaint must always be based 'on more than pure speculation and fantasy.' In re Keegan Management Co., 154 F.R.D. 237, 241 (N.D.Cal.1994). [After discovery] plaintiff's complaint is still based on mere speculation and fantasy. In sum, federal courts 'cannot tolerate complaints grounded solely on metaphysical inferences nor those filed without an informed basis for the allegations.' Id. at 242. Plaintiff and his counsel have taken a colorable claim of excessive force against certain police officers and turned it into a conspiratorial burlesque. Monetary sanctions against plaintiff's counsel are warranted under Rule 11.

"The only question that remains is the amount of sanctions the Court should assess. Monetary sanctions must be reasonable as well as consistent with the purpose of Rule 11—to deter baseless filings and dilatory or abusive pretrial tactics. Cooter & Gell v. Hartmarx Corp., 496 U.S. 384, 393, 110 S.Ct. 2447, 2454 (1990). In determining the amount, the district court must strike a balance that furthers the purpose of the rule without chilling meritorious litigation. See id. To this end, a court may consider not only the conduct itself, but also the offending party's ability to pay. The Court will reserve on this issue pending its receipt of submissions from the parties concerning a proper amount that is consistent with the objectives of Rule 11, the egregiousness of Mr. Ballan's conduct, and the burden this suit has imposed on defendant Zarc."

Questions: (12) Rule 11 prescribes a different type of cure for the problem of a plaintiff's getting a foot in the federal courthouse door too easily. It requires knowing more, rather than pleading more. Although in place from the beginning and later tightened, it now seems a necessary requirement—if only to avoid a plaintiff's circumvention of Twombly–Iqbal by pleading factual details without any basis. Would you expect Rule 11 to be effective in regulating behavior? What are the drawbacks of Rule 11?

(13) Does Rule 11 affect substantive rights in violation of the Rules Enabling Act? Does Rule 8(a)(2), as interpreted by Twombly–Iqbal (or by Conley)?

(b) INTERPOSING DEFENSES AND OBJECTIONS

[Rules 7(b), 8(b), 12; Forms 30, 40]

A defendant who has been served with a summons and complaint pursuant to Rule 4 must make known his defenses—the grounds upon which he resists the relief demanded against him in the complaint—and must do so within certain time limits.[f] So also he has opportunity to object to the complaint for vices such as undue vagueness.

Questions: (14) Suppose the defendant does nothing during the prescribed time period. What should the plaintiff do to take advantage of the default? See Rule 55(a) and (b).

(15) What steps may the defendant take to cure such a default? See Rule 55(c). What sort of showing should he have to make? Compare Tesillo v. Emergency Physician Assocs., 230 F.R.D. 287 (W.D.N.Y.2005) (granting motion to set aside default, where defendant "forgot" to answer but plaintiff suffered no prejudice and defendant had a meritorious defense), with In re Hein, 341 B.R. 903, 905 (Bankr. N.D.Ind.2006) ("Stupidity—acting without sufficient forethought—is a legitimate basis for imposing sanctions upon an attorney. . . . An empty head but a pure heart is no defense.").

Types of defenses and objections.—Let us consider the kinds of defenses and objections that may be available to a defendant. Imagine that the defendant faces the complaint of a single plaintiff attempting to state a single claim.

1. In the first place, there may be reasons why the court should not proceed with the case that have no bearing on the intrinsic merits of the plaintiff's claim. The defendant may wish to contend that the case is of a type the plaintiff cannot maintain in any federal district court (see Rule 12(b)(1)), that the particular district court selected by the plaintiff as the place of trial—the venue—is wrong (see Rule 12(b)(3)), or that there is another party who ought to be joined before the action goes forward (see Rule 12(b)(7)). We shall consider later the possible bases for such defenses (as well as for the defenses referred to in Rule 12(b)(2), (4), and (5), which involve failure to get the defendant properly before the court).

2. The defendant may take the position that, assuming for the sake of argument the truth of the basic allegations in the complaint, they do not invoke any rule of substantive law that casts liability on the defendant. For example, plaintiff alleges merely that defendant gave him a dirty look, or plaintiff follows Form 11 but omits any charge of negligence. Here, in the language of the common-law pleader, is ground for "demurrer" or, in the words of Rule 12(b)(6), a defense of "failure to state a claim upon which relief can be granted." It is plainly desirable that there should be some procedural device for exposing the futility of the plaintiff's claim without further inquiry as to whether his allegations are true.

3. Assuming for the sake of argument that the plaintiff's statement of claim does invoke a rule of substantive law casting liability on the defendant, the defendant may wish to challenge the truth of one or more of the allegations corresponding to the "if" clauses in the rule. See Rule 8(b), regarding defense by way of denial.

4. A further possibility is that, assuming without granting that all of the plaintiff's basic allegations are true and do invoke a rule of substantive

[f] Ordinarily the time limit is twenty-one days after service of the summons and complaint. See Rules 12(a)(1) and 6(a). May the parties stipulate, i.e., agree, to enlarge this time? See Rule 6(b).

law casting liability on the defendant, there are additional matters that will avoid that liability. In other words, the defendant may wish to activate one or more of the "unless" clauses in the relevant rule of law, such as the plaintiff's contributory negligence, the running of the period of limitations before the commencement of suit, or some other affirmative defense listed in Rule 8(c).

5. A complaint may be so vague or ambiguous that the defendant cannot reasonably prepare a responsive pleading. In that case it is open to the defendant to object and require the plaintiff to give "a more definite statement." See Rule 12(e) and the Sierocinski case. Or the complaint may be objectionable because it contains "redundant, immaterial, impertinent, or scandalous matter" that causes prejudice to the defendant. In that case Rule 12(f) permits the defendant to have the court strike that matter out.

Question: (16) Is there any other position that a defendant might conceivably want to take?

The defendant may wish to take two or more of the positions outlined above. For example, suppose the plaintiff claims damages for mental anguish suffered by him by reason of the defendant's negligence. The defendant's counsel knows that according to the law of some states there exists a right of action for mental anguish inflicted in the alleged circumstances; that other states recognize no such right; and that the courts of the state in which the event occurred have not yet spoken on the question. Further, her investigation of the facts indicates considerable likelihood that the plaintiff cannot prove negligence. Further still, she wishes to challenge the venue, and also to argue that the plaintiff was contributorily negligent. In what manner should she present these defenses to the court? That is, should the defendant's counsel set up multiple defenses successively or simultaneously—and, indeed, may she set up all these defenses or do the Rules limit her to some lesser number?

Manner of presenting defenses and objections.—The pattern starts with Rule 12(b). It is, incidentally, very much at odds with the practice at common law.

1. It is clear from Rule 12(b) that the defendant may raise all defenses to a claim in the answer.

Form 30 is an example of an answer. There the answer denies certain allegations of the complaint, and it also raises the defenses that the complaint fails to state a claim and that the plaintiff has failed to join a required party. Its fourth defense asserts additional matter, namely, the affirmative defense that the applicable period of limitations had expired. Note that defenses are to be stated "in short and plain terms," the aim being to give notice. Rule 8(b)(1)(A).

Defendant serves the answer by delivering or transmitting a copy to plaintiff's attorney. Within a reasonable time after service on plaintiff's attorney, defendant files the answer in court, along with a certificate of service. See Rules 5 and 6(d). A similar pattern of service and filing normally applies to other papers subsequent to the complaint.

2. Rule 12(b) states that the defendant can instead choose to assert any of seven enumerated defenses by motion, before answer.[g] Most of these seven go to matters not affecting the merits of the claim, the obvious exception being Rule 12(b)(6)'s defense of failure to state a claim.

"Motion" receives no formal definition in the Rules, but Rule 7(b)(1) suggests that it is a request for a court order. (What order does the defendant seek when presenting each of the seven enumerated defenses by motion?) Unless made during a hearing or a trial, which is not the present circumstance, a motion must be in writing, must state with particularity its grounds, and must set forth the relief sought. Read Form 40, which is a form of motion, and then match the defenses presented there with the terms of Rule 12(b).

When a moving party wishes to bring up matters of fact in support of his motion, he may do so by affidavits. The opposing party then has an opportunity to serve and file counteraffidavits. The court may either hear and decide the motion on the affidavits or proceed to take oral testimony. See Rules 6(c) and 43(c). On disputes over the relevant law, the lawyers will usually support their respective positions by filing memoranda of law, and the court will sometimes entertain oral argument. See David F. Herr, Roger S. Haydock & Jeffrey W. Stempel, Motion Practice (3d ed. 1998).

Rule 12(i) provides with respect to the seven enumerated defenses that, whether raised in an answer or by a motion, the court will hear and determine them before trial on application by any party, unless the court orders a deferral until trial. Why does the Rule single out these enumerated defenses for preliminary hearing? Consider with respect to each of the enumerated defenses whether it is likely to involve only a question of law resolvable on memoranda and arguments of counsel, or whether it is likely to involve disputed issues of fact. Is the circumstance that a defense will involve only a question of law a sufficient reason for seeking to dispose of it at an early stage before trial? Consider with respect to each of the enumerated defenses whether it is likely to spell the end of the lawsuit.

3. We can deal summarily with the objections under Rule 12(e) and (f) of vagueness or redundancy or the like. These objections are not frequent, and they should rarely succeed. In the nature of things, the defendant makes them by motion before answer.

Consolidation and waiver of defenses and objections.—We shall now mention some consequences that attach to the defendant's actions and failures to act at the answer-or-move stage.

---

1. Consider the seven defenses listed in Rule 12(b). The effects of Rule 12(g) and (h) are as follows:

[g] See Rule 12(a)(4), which prescribes when to serve the answer if the defendant makes such a motion and the court denies it. Why does it make this extension?

First. If the defendant makes a pre-answer motion based on any of the seven defenses but omits another of those defenses then available to him, he may not make a further pre-answer motion based on the defense omitted. In other words, Rule 12(g) contemplates that the defendant will consolidate defenses in his initial motion if he chooses to make a motion.

Example: Defendant moves before answer on the ground of improper venue. The court denies the motion. She may not move again before answer to assert the defense of failure to state a claim (assuming that this defense was available to her when she first moved).

There is one exception to the consolidation requirement: the defendant may raise the defense of lack of subject-matter jurisdiction (Rule 12(b)(1)) by a second motion—indeed, Rule 12(h)(3) implies that anyone may suggest this defense at any time in any manner and that the court ought to raise it even if the defendant does not.

Second. By contrast, if the available defense omitted from the pre-answer motion was lack of jurisdiction over the person, improper venue, insufficiency of process, or insufficiency of service of process (Rule 12(b)(2)–(5)), not only can the defense not be the subject of a second pre-answer motion, but also it is waived, i.e., lost altogether. See Rule 12(h)(1)(A).

Example: Defendant moves before answer on the ground of failure to state a claim. Motion denied. Defendant loses any defense of improper venue (assuming that this defense was available to her when she moved).

If the defendant makes no pre-answer motion, defenses under Rule 12(b)(2)–(5) are nevertheless waived if the defendant does not include them in the answer or in an amendment thereof permitted to be made under Rule 15(a)(1) "as a matter of course," i.e., without applying to the court for permission. See Rule 12(h)(1)(B).

Example: Defendant makes no motion; she answers without making any reference to venue; and the time expires to amend the answer without the court's permission. The defense of improper venue is no longer open to the defendant.

Third. Notwithstanding any omission otherwise to assert the defenses of failure to state a claim upon which relief can be granted and of failure to join a party under Rule 19 (Rule 12(b)(6) and (7)), they are preserved and may be included in the answer or made the subject of a post-answer motion for judgment on the pleadings under Rule 12(c) or presented at trial. See Rule 12(h)(2).

Questions: (17) What does "available" mean as used in Rule 12(g)(2)?

(18) Why are the defenses enumerated in Rule 12(b)(2)–(5) disfavored in this way? Why are those in Rule 12(b)(6) and (7) carefully preserved? Why is the Rule 12(b)(1) defense treated with unique solicitude?

---

2. The proper way for the defendant to raise other defenses is by answer. So, suppose the defendant serves and files an answer. The effects of the Rules are as follows:

First. To the extent that the answer, after any amendment "of course" under Rule 15(a)(1), fails to deny allegations of the complaint, those allegations stand admitted for purposes of the litigation. This follows from Rule 8(b)(6), which states that allegations in a pleading to which a responsive pleading is required are admitted if the responsive pleading does not deny them.[h]

Second. Any affirmative defenses omitted from the answer, after any amendment "of course," are lost. This waiver is not explicit in the Rules, but follows from the pattern of the Rules, including Rules 8(c) and 12(b).

Example: *A* for consideration releases his claim against *B*, thus giving *B* a perfect defense to *A*'s suit. *A* can nevertheless proceed with his action and possibly get judgment, if *B* fails to present this defense in her answer or by an amendment "of course."

Third. Amendments of the answer allowed to the defendant by leave of court under Rule 15(a)(2) may, however, alleviate the described waivers as to denials and affirmative defenses. But this somewhat uncertain step will entail, like any extra step, extra expense in attorney's fees.

Questions: (19) Can Rule 15(a) on amendments, either as a matter of course or by leave of court, furnish any escape from the other waivers, for example, a waiver under Rule 12(h)(1)(A)?

(20) Take the case of alleged mental anguish set out above in this subsection and, on behalf of the defendant, describe the manner and sequence in which you might present your defenses. Mention any strategic or tactical considerations that would affect your choices.

---

3. The defendant should raise objections under Rule 12(e) and (f), dealing with vagueness or redundancy or the like, in the initial pre-answer motion. The defendant may not interpose an objection under Rule 12(e) if he has omitted it from such motion (see Rule 12(g)) or if he has answered (see Rule 12(e)). The same is true of a Rule 12(f) objection to redundancy or the like, although the Rule allows the court to act on its own initiative and so gives the court discretion to entertain a later request to strike.

Questions: (21) Assume that on Day 1, a Wednesday, a summons and complaint are served; on Day 15 defendant serves a 12(f) motion to strike scandalous matter from the complaint; and on Day 42 defendant receives notice that the court granted the 12(f) motion and thereby struck the scandalous passage. Assume further that defendant was a private party and that the manner of all service was ordinary in-hand service within the state. How much time does defendant have to serve an answer?

[h] There is one exception: allegations as to the amount of damages, although not denied in the answer, are not taken as admitted. Why this exception?

(22) Assume that on Day 0, the first Monday in October, a summons and complaint are served; on Day 15 defendant serves a 12(e) motion for a more definite statement; on Day 43 the court grants the 12(e) motion; on Day 56 plaintiff serves the more definite statement, revealing for the first time possible grounds for a 12(b)(6) motion; on Day 60 defendant serves a 12(b)(6) motion; and on Day 74 defendant receives notice that the court denied the 12(b)(6) motion. Assume further that defendant was a private party and that the manner of all service was ordinary in-hand service within the state. How much time does defendant have to serve an answer?

When learning the mechanics of the Rules, you should give thought to the policies behind them. A general policy underlying many of the Rules is the facilitation of deciding cases on their merits, rather than on procedural points. Another is the elimination of traps for the unwary or, often equivalently, the protection of clients from the effects of their lawyers' mistakes. Yet Rule 12 bristles with notions of waiver. What countervailing policies account for this?

Coleman v. Frierson

United States District Court, Northern District of Illinois, 1985.
607 F.Supp. 1566, aff'd sub nom. Coleman v. Smith, 814 F.2d 1142 (7th Cir.1987).

■ SHADUR, DISTRICT JUDGE.

[In late 1982 Samuel Coleman sued the Village of Robbins, its mayor, and its police chief under 42 U.S.C. § 1983, a very important civil rights statute that appears in the Rules booklet. Coleman alleged, among much else, that he had been a special investigator for that suburb of Chicago, authorized to investigate police corruption; that his investigation had led to the mayor's office; and that then Coleman had been summarily fired as part of a cover-up. He sought two million dollars in damages for lost wages and for injuries that allegedly included mental, emotional, and ultimately physical harm resulting from the defendants' so depriving him of property or liberty without due process of law in violation of the Fourteenth Amendment.

[The defendants' answer denied many allegations. However, the defendants were willfully delinquent during the discovery phase, and eventually the judge imposed a sanction of default as to liability.

[A jury then tried the issue of damages, giving the plaintiff a verdict for more than a half million dollars in compensatory and punitive damages. The judge entered judgment on the verdict. The defendants promptly made several motions to set aside the judgment.

[One of these motions] asserts three grounds:

1. Coleman's claims are barred by res judicata principles because they could have been raised in the context of his lawsuit against Robbins for unpaid wages, filed in the Circuit Court of Cook County in March 1980. There, claiming to have served as Special Investigator for a period of 107 weeks at a salary of $225 per week, Coleman sought a judgment of $24,000. That action was terminated January 29, 1982 when the parties filed a stipulation to dismiss the cause with prejudice.

2. Coleman's factual allegations in the Complaint, deemed admitted as a consequence of the default judgment, are insufficient to state a claim upon which relief can be granted.

3. Coleman had no property or liberty interest in his employment . . . . Robbins was therefore not required to afford him a pre-termination hearing. Under prevailing law, his due process rights were adequately guarded by the availability of an adequate state remedy.

But the short answer is that this Court need not consider the merits of those contentions at this late stage of the litigation, though different reasons for that answer attach to the differing attacks.

Defendants' first argument is an affirmative defense to liability, essentially asserting defendants (though otherwise liable) are not subject to suit because of facts outside the Complaint. Ordinarily such a defense must be pleaded in a defendant's answer to the complaint. At the least it must be raised by motion [to amend] at trial. See 5 Wright & Miller § 1277, at 328–29, 332; id. at § 1278. In any event such a defense may not be raised for the first time after judgment has been entered and the record in the case established. See Johnson v. Rogers, 621 F.2d 300, 305 (8th Cir.1980) (defense of res judicata may not be raised for the first time in a motion for judgment n.o.v.). Clearly the strong policy in favor of certain and final judgments on the merits compels such a rule.

Defendants' second argument is of the variety normally and properly raised in a Rule 12(b)(6) motion. In that regard Judge Weinfeld said . . . in Snead v. Department of Social Services of the City of New York, 409 F.Supp. 995, 1000 (S.D.N.Y.1975) (emphasis in original):

> If, as stated in Bell v. Hood, [327 U.S. 678, 682, 66 S.Ct. 773, 776 (1946),] "the failure to state a proper cause of action calls for a judgment on the merits," then a litigant should not be permitted to raise such a failure after a determination on the merits. This view finds support in Rule 12(h)(2) of the Federal Rules of Civil Procedure, which provides that "[a] defense of failure to state a claim upon which relief can be granted. . . may be made in any pleading. . . or by motion for judgment on the pleadings, or at trial on the merits." The clear thrust of the Rule is that a failure to state a claim may be raised at any time *before* a disposition on the merits but not *after*. Any other construction would not only add to intolerable delay, but create uncertainty as to the validity of a final judgment on the merits.

See also 5 Wright & Miller § 1392, at 861–62 (1969 & Supp.1984).

Defendants' third argument is not technically an affirmative defense (for it challenges one of the elements of Coleman's cause of action, rather than acknowledging the validity of the claim as pleaded by plaintiff but urging its defeat because of other factors; see Rule 8(c)), nor is it strictly speaking a Rule 12(b)(6) contention (for it asserts facts outside the Complaint itself . . .). But the same reasoning applies. See Breuer Electric Manufacturing Co. v. Toronado Systems of America, Inc., 687 F.2d 182, 186 (7th Cir.1982). Once the record in the case has been made at or before the trial on the merits, every principle of orderly jurisprudence forbids an assault on the judgment for reasons dehors the record—unless of course any of the bases for post-judgment attack under Rule 60(b) applies. Defendants do not even hint at a right to relief under that Rule, so far as the three grounds discussed in this section are concerned.

In both legal and practical contemplation a default judgment is the equivalent of a trial on the merits. That makes all the foregoing reasoning fully applicable here. Between the time Coleman filed the Complaint and the time the default. . . was entered nearly a year and a half elapsed, affording defendants ample time to have raised the arguments they only now put forward. If defendants could not with reasonable diligence have discovered the factual predicate for those arguments, the principles embodied in Rule 60(b) might perhaps compel a different analysis. But in the absence of such a showing—and defendants have made none—the default. . . as to liability must be seen as the analogue of a judgment on the merits. Its entry foreclosed arguments challenging the sufficiency of Coleman's claim for relief. Any other result would effectively allow defendants the opportunity now to press arguments they wholly neglected to advance, for no excusable reason, when they should have. Doing justice between litigants, after all, hinges as much on respect for the procedural rules governing the progress of the lawsuit as on affording parties liberal scope in making their arguments on the merits.

[The other sections of the opinion, denying the defendants' other motions, are omitted.]

Question: (23) There is in the folklore of the common law the famous Case of the Kettle. The plaintiff claimed damages for a kettle that assertedly the defendant had borrowed and had allowed to become cracked while in his possession. The defendant is supposed to have pleaded (a) that he did not borrow the kettle, (b) that it was never cracked, and (c) that it was cracked when he borrowed it. Would this pleading be permissible today under the Federal Rules?

ABA, Model Rules of Professional Conduct

(2008).

Preamble: A Lawyer's Responsibilities

A lawyer, as a member of the legal profession, is a representative of clients, an officer of the legal system and a public citizen having special responsibility for the quality of justice.

As a representative of clients, a lawyer performs various functions. As advisor, a lawyer provides a client with an informed understanding of the client's legal rights and obligations and explains their practical implications. As advocate, a lawyer zealously asserts the client's position under the rules of the adversary system. As negotiator, a lawyer seeks a result advantageous to the client but consistent with requirements of honest dealing with others. . . .

. . . .

A lawyer's responsibilities as a representative of clients, an officer of the legal system and a public citizen are usually harmonious. Thus, when an opposing party is well represented, a lawyer can be a zealous advocate on behalf of a client and at the same time assume that justice is being done. . . .

In the nature of law practice, however, conflicting responsibilities are encountered. Virtually all difficult ethical problems arise from conflict between a lawyer's responsibilities to clients, to the legal system and to the lawyer's own interest in remaining an ethical person while earning a satisfactory living. The Rules of Professional Conduct often prescribe terms for resolving such conflicts. Within the framework of these Rules, however, many difficult issues of professional discretion can arise. Such issues must be resolved through the exercise of sensitive professional and moral judgment guided by the basic principles underlying the Rules. These principles include the lawyer's obligation zealously to protect and pursue a client's legitimate interests, within the bounds of the law, while maintaining a professional, courteous and civil attitude toward all persons involved in the legal system.

. . . .

Scope

The Rules of Professional Conduct are rules of reason. They should be interpreted with reference to the purposes of legal representation and of the law itself. Some of the Rules are imperatives, cast in the terms "shall" or "shall not." These define proper conduct for purposes of professional discipline. Others, generally cast in the term "may," are permissive and define areas under the Rules in which the lawyer has discretion to exercise professional judgment. No disciplinary action should be taken when the lawyer chooses not to act or acts within the bounds of such discretion. Other Rules define the nature of relationships between the lawyer and others. The Rules are thus partly obligatory and disciplinary and partly constitutive and descriptive in that they define a lawyer's professional role. Many of the Comments use the term "should." Comments do not add obligations to the Rules but provide guidance for practicing in compliance with the Rules.

. . . .

RULE 3.1 Meritorious Claims and Contentions

A lawyer shall not bring or defend a proceeding, or assert or controvert an issue therein, unless there is a basis in law and fact for doing so that is not frivolous, which includes a good faith argument for an extension, modification or reversal of existing law. A lawyer for the defendant in a criminal proceeding, or the respondent in a proceeding that could result in incarceration, may nevertheless so defend the proceeding as to require that every element of the case be established.

COMMENT:

[1] The advocate has a duty to use legal procedure for the fullest benefit of the client's cause, but also a duty not to abuse legal procedure. The law, both procedural and substantive, establishes the limits within which an advocate may proceed. However, the law is not always clear and never is static. Accordingly, in determining the proper scope of advocacy, account must be taken of the law's ambiguities and potential for change.

[2] The filing of an action or defense or similar action taken for a client is not frivolous merely because the facts have not first been fully substantiated or because the lawyer expects to develop vital evidence only by discovery. What is required of lawyers, however, is that they inform themselves about the facts of their clients' cases and the applicable law and determine that they can make good faith arguments in support of their clients' positions. Such action is not frivolous even though the lawyer believes that the client's position ultimately will not prevail. The action is frivolous, however, if the lawyer is unable either to make a good faith argument on the merits of the action taken or to support the action taken by a good faith argument for an extension, modification or reversal of existing law.

. . . .

RULE 3.2 Expediting Litigation

A lawyer shall make reasonable efforts to expedite litigation consistent with the interests of the client.

COMMENT:

[1] Dilatory practices bring the administration of justice into disrepute. Although there will be occasions when a lawyer may properly seek a postponement for personal reasons, it is not proper for a lawyer to routinely fail to expedite litigation solely for the convenience of the advocates. Nor will a failure to expedite be reasonable if done for the purpose of frustrating an opposing party's attempt to obtain rightful redress or repose. It is not a justification that similar conduct is often tolerated by the bench and bar. The question is whether a competent lawyer acting in good faith would regard the course of action as having some substantial purpose other

than delay. Realizing financial or other benefit from otherwise improper delay in litigation is not a legitimate interest of the client.

(c) REPLYING TO DEFENSES

[Rule 7(a)]

If the defendant's answer includes only denials, there is no occasion for a response by the plaintiff, because the matters in dispute appear on the face of the complaint and the answer.

Suppose, however, that the answer sets up an affirmative defense. May the plaintiff respond to it? Must he respond to it or have it taken as admitted? Rule 7(a)(7)—differing sharply from the practice at common law and under many state codes of procedure—not only does not require the plaintiff to plead, but does not permit him to do so unless the court orders a reply. The court ordinarily will not order a reply unless it is the defendant who moves for such an order, and there are relatively few cases in which it will order a reply even on the defendant's motion.

Questions: (24) What is the purpose of the general prohibition on replies to defenses?

(25) In what circumstances should the court order a reply?

Rule 8(b)(6) is the necessary complement of Rule 7(a)(7). Its second sentence provides that allegations in a pleading to which no responsive pleading is required will be considered *denied* or *avoided*.

If, then, plaintiff makes allegations 1, 2, 3, and 4, and defendant in her answer denies 1 and asserts 5, 6, and 7 by way of affirmative defense, and there is no order that plaintiff reply, what are the matters in dispute? Allegation 1 is in dispute because the plaintiff asserts the affirmative and the defendant the negative of it. Allegations 2, 3, and 4 stand admitted under the first sentence of Rule 8(b)(6).

Allegations 5, 6, and 7 are in dispute by reason of that Rule's second sentence. Defendant asserts the affirmative on 5, 6, and 7. The pleadings do not disclose plaintiff's position with respect to these allegations. At the trial, or otherwise, he may (a) assert the negative (denial), (b) assert that, granting for the sake of argument the truth of the allegations, there are further matters that vitiate their effect (avoidance), or (c) take both such positions. For instance, if defendant alleges the affirmative defense that plaintiff for consideration released his claim against defendant, plaintiff without filing a reply is free at trial to deny that he received consideration for the release; or he can assert that defendant procured the release by fraud; or both.

Furthermore, by a motion to strike under Rule 12(f), the plaintiff may raise the point that a defense in an answer is "insufficient"—a point that Rule 12(h)(2) preserves through the stage of trial. This is the plaintiff's analogue of a defendant's Rule 12(b)(6) motion addressed to the complaint.

Finally, under Rule 12(f), the plaintiff may move to strike matter from an answer as being redundant or the like, much as a defendant can object to a complaint.

(d) INTERPOSING COUNTERCLAIMS

[Rule 13]

Defendant, whether or not he asserts defenses or objections to plaintiff's statement of claim, may desire to assert one or more claims against plaintiff. Must he resort to a separate action against plaintiff, or may (or must) he assert such claims as "counterclaims" in his answer to plaintiff's complaint?

You may first wonder whether we are repeating ourselves. Did we not consider counterclaims already in our discussion of contributory negligence? In a word, no. That discussion involved an affirmative defense, not a counterclaim. Imagine that *A* sues *B* for negligence, based on a two-car accident. *B* can (1) deny *B*'s negligence and (2) affirmatively defend by alleging that *A*'s contributory negligence helped to cause the accident. Her aim in pleading the second defense, as well as the first defense, is to defeat *A*'s suit that seeks damages for *A*'s injuries. Yet in that accident, *B* might have suffered injuries too. *B* might then want to counterclaim by alleging that *A*'s negligence caused the injurious accident. Her aim in counterclaiming would be to recover damages for *B*'s injuries, which are of course a thing different from *A*'s injuries. Although beginning students always confuse affirmative defenses and counterclaims, the two are not the same. Here, the same acts characterizable as *A*'s lack of due care constitute both contributory negligence and also negligence, but the former is an affirmative defense to *A*'s claim that is completely distinguishable from a counterclaim seeking *B*'s damages caused by *A*'s negligence.

Rule 13 deals with this new question of counterclaims. Rule 13(a) covers "compulsory counterclaims" and Rule 13(b) "permissive counterclaims." It is important to examine the differences between the two.

Compulsory counterclaims.—*A* sues *B* for slander during a different incident. *B* wishes to contend (1) that she has a good defense to *A*'s claim, because she did not use the slanderous words alleged, and (2) that at the time and place of the alleged slander *A* struck her, so that she has a claim against *A* for battery. The events involved in these two claims are closely interwoven. If it were necessary for *B* to bring a separate action, the same witnesses might well have to be brought to court again, and much of the same testimony would have to be repeated. There is a generally recognized wisdom in permitting enlargement of plaintiff's action to encompass defendant's claim when the latter arises out of the same "transaction or occurrence" that is the subject matter of plaintiff's claim. The Federal Rules, however, go further, making enlargement in those circumstances compulsory and not merely permissive. Note that the plaintiff can thus choose the forum for the defendant's claim, a choice that can constitute a significant advantage.

The language of Rule 13(a) is mandatory, so that the defendant must state the counterclaim. Of course, this does not mean that the defendant is jailed or fined for failing to assert a compulsory counterclaim. It does suggest that if she fails to assert the claim in her answer or an amendment to her answer, she is thereafter precluded from asserting it against the plaintiff in an independent action. This preclusion involves an application of the principle of finality in litigation. If a person who has failed to assert a compulsory counterclaim later sues on that claim, the opponent can then plead res judicata or the like as a defense.

Question: (26) *P* sues *D*, who moves under Rule 12(b)(6) for failure to state a claim upon which relief can be granted. The court grants the motion and dismisses the case, *D* never having filed an answer. There is no appeal. Then *D* sues *P* on a claim arising out of the same transaction or occurrence as *P*'s earlier attempted claim. *P* defends solely on the ground that *D*'s claim is precluded by *D*'s failure to interpose it as a counterclaim in the first action. What judgment? Does the word "pleading" as used in the first sentence of Rule 13(a) include a motion? Consider Rule 7. See Lawhorn v. Atlantic Ref. Co., 299 F.2d 353 (5th Cir.1962) (judgment for *D*). (Always herein, when a cited case or other authority seems to provide the law's answer, you should think further to construct reasons for that outcome and to question its soundness.)

Permissive counterclaims.—*A* and *B* have a troubled relationship. Suppose now that when *A* sues *B* for breach of a contract, *B* has a claim against *A* for another battery arising out of a transaction or occurrence wholly unrelated to the subject matter of *A*'s contract claim. Rule 13(b) permits but does not compel *B* to assert such an unrelated claim by way of counterclaim in her answer in *A*'s action. If *B* chooses not to assert the counterclaim, she is free to bring an independent action for this battery.

We should mention here that, in furtherance of convenience or to avoid prejudice, the court may order a separate trial of any claim, counterclaim, or issue in an action. See Rule 42(b). There will naturally be more frequent occasion to apply Rule 42(b) to permissive than to compulsory counterclaims.

Furthermore, Rule 42(a) allows the court to combine separate actions pending before it if they involve a common question of law or fact. Thus, the two parts of Rule 42 provide the court with a means to take into account the peculiarities of particular cases, by appropriately peeling off compulsory counterclaims or piling on separate claims, without having to twist Rule 13's definition of compulsoriness completely out of shape.

Definition of "transaction or occurrence."—Having been warned that words like "procedure" and "claim" are legal chameleons that may change their meaning as the context changes, you may nevertheless wonder whether the key phrase of Rule 13(a) and (b), "transaction or occurrence," has proven to be a chameleon.

There are relatively few cases in which a party has invoked Rule 13(a) in an attempt to bar a later suit, and hence there is a dearth of judicial decisions defining "transaction or occurrence" for purposes of Rule 13 in those circumstances.

Question: (27) What probably accounts for the dearth of case law on this point?

A minority of states make no provision for a compulsory counterclaim. Indeed, a code of procedure might permit the defendant to interpose only certain kinds of counterclaims. In such a code, the definition of permitted kinds of counterclaims is commonly this: "a cause of action arising out of the contract or transaction set forth in the complaint as the foundation of the plaintiff's claim, or connected with the subject of the action." This code language has generated case law defining "transaction."

Question: (28) Consider whether the defendant may interpose his counterclaim in the following cases under that code language. Then consider whether the counterclaim would be compulsory under Federal Rule 13(a).

(a) Lyric Piano Co. v. Purvis, 194 Ky. 826, 241 S.W. 69 (1922): *P* sues *D* for the balance due on an installment contract for the sale of a piano. *D* seeks to counterclaim for a battery by *P*'s representative while engaged in collecting the sum due.

(b) Mulcahy v. Duggan, 67 Mont. 9, 214 P. 1106 (1923): *P* sues *D* for a battery occurring on May 17. *D* seeks to counterclaim for a libel published by *P* about *D* on May 8, with *D* alleging that the subsequent altercation was the result of the publication of the libel.

Obviously, the question posed by the state code is different from the question of compulsoriness under Rule 13, and so the definitions given in answer do differ. But you must also bear in mind that the meaning of "transaction or occurrence," even only for the purposes of a particular Rule such as Rule 13, does in fact vary with the broad type of circumstances of the case and the consequent effects on the parties and the public. As Justice Oliver Wendell Holmes, Jr., put it in Towne v. Eisner, 245 U.S. 418, 425, 38 S.Ct. 158, 159 (1918): "A word is not a crystal, transparent and unchanged, it is the skin of a living thought and may vary greatly in color and content according to the circumstances and the time in which it is used." Thus, you will certainly find it wise, in seeking the meaning of a phrase in a certain type of circumstances under a particular Rule, to bear steadily in mind what the purposes of the Rule may be.

For example, in regard to compulsory counterclaims and their consequences, contrast res judicata with the statute of limitations. Although the limitation period's application to counterclaims is a complicated subject that we shall treat later in some detail, one popular approach allows assertion of a counterclaim on which the statute of limitations expired between the filing of the complaint and the filing of the counterclaim, provided that the counterclaim arises out of the same transaction or occurrence as the main claim. (That approach may seem to address a bizarrely rare scenario, but some plaintiffs have an inclination to wait until the last moment to file.)

Question: (29) Now imagine the facts of the Mulcahy case arising recently in Montana, which adopted a replica of Federal Rule 13 way back in 1962. Would the court, facing this timing scenario and applying that popular approach, uphold or reject a statute of limitations attack by the plaintiff on the counterclaim?

Williams v. Robinson

United States District Court, District of Columbia, 1940.
1 F.R.D. 211.

■ LETTS, JUSTICE. By way of background it may be stated that the following matters transpired in sequence as related; the defendant's wife filed a suit for maintenance; the defendant filed his answer with a cross-complaint[i] seeking an absolute divorce upon the ground of adultery, [joining in accordance with the old practice] this plaintiff as co-respondent; in his answer to such cross-complaint this plaintiff contented himself with denying the acts of adultery with which he was charged; such maintenance cause is identified as Civil Action No. 5224, and is pending in this court.

Plaintiff brings this suit entitling his complaint as one for libel and slander. He alleges that he was libeled and slandered by the matters set up by the defendant in the cross-complaint wherein the defendant falsely and maliciously charged that this plaintiff had been guilty of adultery with the defendant's wife.

The defendant has filed no answer but moves to dismiss the complaint upon the ground that plaintiff has failed to assert his claim, if any he has, in his answer to the cross-complaint in the maintenance suit. Defendant invokes Rule 13(a) of the Federal Rules of Civil Procedure. . . and insists that plaintiff was obliged thereunder to then assert the claim which he now brings as an independent action. It is the defendant's position that since plaintiff failed so to do by way of counterclaim he is now precluded from asserting it here.

Rule 13(a) relates to compulsory counterclaims and clearly required this plaintiff in the maintenance suit to state as a counterclaim any claim which at the time of filing his answer in the maintenance case he had against this defendant if such claim arose out of the transaction or occurrence that was the subject matter of the defendant's cross-complaint in the maintenance suit.

But one question arises for consideration: was the slander and libel of which plaintiff complains part and parcel of the transaction or occurrence that was the subject matter of the defendant's cross-complaint in the maintenance suit? The question may be otherwise stated; the defendant in his cross-complaint charged this plaintiff with specific acts of adultery; these charges were in response to the wife's complaint for maintenance; can it be said that the acts of adultery alleged and relied upon by defendant and his subsequent accusations respecting such adultery may be grouped

[i] In the terminology of the Federal Rules, this cross-complaint would properly be called a counterclaim. Note, incidentally, Rule 13(h).

together as one and the same transaction or the same occurrence within the meaning of the rule?

The word "transaction" has abundant use in many statutes as; requiring or permitting joinder of causes of action growing out of the same transaction; making it necessary or optional for a defendant to plead as a counterclaim a cause of action arising out of the transaction which is the subject matter of the plaintiff's suit; relating to the admissibility of evidence pertaining to personal transactions with persons since deceased; statutes of limitation and many others which the courts have had occasion to construe. As a result of judicial determination the word "transaction" as so used has acquired a well defined meaning which, if applied to Rule 13(a), will give to it the intended sense and meaning.

The decided cases indicate that the word "transaction" denotes something done; a completed action; an affair as a whole; in Craft Refrigerating Mach. Co. v. Quinnipiac Brewing Co., 63 Conn. 551, 29 A. 76, 25 L.R.A. 856, the word "transaction" is defined to mean something which has been acted out to the end. In Cheatham v. Bobbitt, 118 N.C. 343, 24 S.E. 13, it is said the word "transaction" as found in the North Carolina Code in reference to the joinder of actions is used in the sense of the conduct of finishing up an affair, which constitutes as a whole the subject of an action. A right of action for slander and one for false imprisonment of plaintiff at the time the words were uttered cannot be united in one action, under the New York Code of Civil Procedure, as being causes arising out of the same transaction; DeWolfe v. Abraham, 151 N.Y. 186, 45 N.E. 455 [(1896)].

The use of the word "occurrence" in the rule in connection with the word "transaction" can serve no other purpose than to make clear the meaning of the word "transaction". An "occurrence" is defined to be a happening; an incident; or event. The word "transaction" is somewhat broader in its scope than the word "occurrence". The word "transaction" commonly indicates an act of transacting or conducting business but in the rule under consideration it is not restricted to such sense. It is broad enough to include an occurrence. It seems apt to say that the words "transaction" and "occurrence" as used in Rule 13(a) include the facts and circumstances out of which a cause of action may arise; Scarborough v. Smith, 18 Kan. 399. The words "transaction" and "occurrence" probably mean, whatever may be done by one person which affects another's rights and out of which a cause of action may arise. Whether the subject matter of opposing claims is the same requires an examination into the basic facts underlying each of them. A familiar test may be applied by inquiring whether the same evidence will support or refute the opposing claims.

It is clear that the use of the defamatory language of which plaintiff complains constituted no portion of the facts or circumstances alleged and relied on by this defendant in his cross-complaint filed in his wife's maintenance suit. There is no common point between the causes of action. The rule is in accordance with modern trend and the general prevailing policy to have the whole subject matter of any controversy settled in one action. It does not apply to causes growing out of separate transactions.

To sustain defendant's motion to dismiss would be in effect to require plaintiff to admit that there was a transaction or occurrence within the meaning of the rule, and as alleged by defendant in his cross-complaint in the maintenance suit. He makes no such admission but specifically denies the acts of adultery with which he is charged.

It follows that defendant's motion to dismiss the complaint must be overruled.

Questions: (30) Some have suggested that the test of compulsoriness should be whether there is a "logical relationship" between claim and counterclaim. What do you think of this possible criterion?

(31) Is there an undesirable inconsistency between Rule 18(a), which states that a plaintiff *may* join his claims, and Rule 13(a), which states that a defendant *must* assert her claims arising from the same transaction or occurrence as the plaintiff's claim?

Response to counterclaim.—A counterclaim, whether compulsory or permissive, is treated very much like a complaint for pleading purposes, with the counterclaiming defendant assuming to that extent the role of a plaintiff, and the original plaintiff the role of a defendant. See Rules 7(a) and 12(a). Note that the plaintiff must file an answer (formerly called a reply) to the counterclaim in much the same way as a defendant must answer a complaint. And, reading the remainder of Rule 12, you will see that the plaintiff may make motions in respect to the counterclaim in much the same way that a defendant may move in respect to a complaint.

Questions: (32) What would be the consequence if the plaintiff failed to answer or to move with respect to the counterclaim? See Rule 55.

(33) *P* sues *D* on a contract. *D* sets up in her answer a counterclaim on an unrelated contract. *P* answers, denying that he committed any breach of the second contract. The court eventually gives judgment on the merits of the action, including the counterclaim. Thereafter *P* sues *D* for a breach of the second contract occurring before he interposed his answer to *D*'s counterclaim in the first suit. *D* sets up a defense based upon *P*'s failure to counterclaim in the first suit. Is *P*'s second suit precluded? See 5 Wright & Miller § 1188. Why were we careful to say that the breach of the second contract occurred before the interposition of *P*'s answer?

Recovery on claim and counterclaim.—In an action that involves a counterclaim, the plaintiff may prevail on his claim and the defendant on the counterclaim. If the defendant's recovery is for a smaller sum than the plaintiff's, the result is a judgment in favor of the plaintiff for the difference, unless some special statute or contract provides against offset. Likewise, if the defendant's recovery is for a larger amount than the plaintiff's, there will be an affirmative judgment in favor of the defendant for the difference. See Rule 13(c). An affirmative judgment for the defendant will also follow where the plaintiff fails on his claim and the defendant succeeds on the counterclaim.

(e) AMENDING THE PLEADINGS

[Rule 15]

Rule 15 reflects the idea that a party ought not to be irretrievably bound to stand by his first formulation of a pleading of either claim or defense—that the contours of the controversy should not become frozen beyond change too soon. A party may commit an innocent mistake in framing his pleading; or he may see the need for altering it in the light of his opponent's subsequent pleading; or the investigation of the facts, carried on privately or by means of the discovery methods soon to be described, may show that the matters in dispute are not as the party first supposed. A party who finds himself in such a situation will naturally want to amend his pleading.

The question of the degree of freedom of amendment that the system should permit turns on the answer to the general question already posed: what are the purposes of the pleading process? In this light consider why Rule 15 attaches importance to the stage of the lawsuit at which the party seeks to amend.

Amendments before trial.—Rule 15(a)(1) permits a party to amend his pleading once as a matter of course during a certain limited time. The length of this period of grace turns on whether his pleading requires a responsive pleading.

Afterwards, unless the party obtains his opponent's written consent, the allowance of an amendment rests in the discretion of the court. Rule 15(a)(2) says that the trial-court judge "should freely give leave when justice so requires." Courts have interpreted this to mean that the judge should balance the equities, although it is up to the amendment's opponent to convince the judge to disallow the amendment. Because the equities involve a series of offsetting factors that fall on either side of the balance, the amendment's opponent must show (a) [the *fault* of the other side in delaying his motion to amend, minus the *prejudice* to that movant's presentation interests (i.e., detriment to a full presentation of the merits attributable to the pleading misstep) that would be unavoidably caused by denying the amendment] outweighs (b) [any *fault* of the amendment's opponent in inducing the delay in moving, minus the *prejudice* to that opponent's reliance interests (i.e., disadvantage attributable to the delay) that would be unavoidably caused by allowing the amendment]. Then the court must also throw onto the scales of the balance the considerations of *public interest* (which usually favor amendment).

Question: (34) Under that approach, should a court generally be more ready to allow amendment of an answer than of a complaint?

The party seeks leave to amend by a motion made in accordance with Rule 7(b). The party should present the proposed amendment with the motion. As a general rule the court on such a motion will not pass on the sufficiency of the proposed amended pleading, and clearly the granting of the motion is not an adjudication on this point. If, however, it is obvious that the proposed amended pleading is insufficient, the court is likely in the exercise of its discretion to disallow the amendment.

Question: (35) Are there still other factors that should influence the court in granting or refusing amendment?

An amended pleading supersedes the original pleading, which drops out of the case. Note the time that Rule 15(a)(3) gives the opposing party to respond to an amended pleading.

Beeck v. Aquaslide 'N' Dive Corp.

United States Court of Appeals, Eighth Circuit, 1977.
562 F.2d 537.

■ Before BRIGHT and HENLEY, CIRCUIT JUDGES,% SAND Benson, District Judge.*

■ BENSON, DISTRICT JUDGE.

This case is an appeal from the trial court's exercise of discretion on procedural matters in a diversity personal injury action.

Jerry A. Beeck was severely injured. . . while using a water slide. He and his wife, Judy A. Beeck, sued Aquaslide 'N' Dive Corporation (Aquaslide), a Texas corporation, alleging it manufactured the slide involved in the accident, and sought to recover substantial damages on theories of negligence, strict liability and breach of implied warranty.

Aquaslide initially admitted manufacture of the slide, but later moved to amend its answer to deny manufacture; the motion was resisted. The district court granted leave to amend. On motion of the defendant [under Federal Rule 42(b)], a separate trial was held on the issue of "whether the defendant designed, manufactured or sold the slide in question." This motion was also resisted by the plaintiffs. The issue was tried to a jury, which returned a verdict for the defendant, after which the trial court entered summary judgment of dismissal of the case. Plaintiffs took this appeal. . . .

A brief review of the facts found by the trial court in its order granting leave to amend, and which do not appear to have been in dispute, is essential to a full understanding of appellants' claims.

In 1971 Kimberly Village Home Association of Davenport, Iowa, ordered an Aquaslide product from one George Boldt, who was a local distributor handling defendant's products. The order was forwarded by Boldt to Sentry Pool and Chemical Supply Co. in Rock Island, Illinois, and Sentry forwarded the order to Purity Swimming Pool Supply in Hammond, Indiana. A slide was delivered from a Purity warehouse to Kimberly Village, and was installed by Kimberly employees. On July 15, 1972, Jerry A. Beeck was injured while using the slide at a social gathering sponsored

* The Honorable Paul Benson, Chief Judge, United States District Court for the District of North Dakota, sitting by designation.

at Kimberly Village by his employer, Harker Wholesale Meats, Inc. Soon after the accident investigations were undertaken by representatives of the separate insurers of Harker and Kimberly Village. On October 31, 1972, Aquaslide first learned of the accident through a letter sent by a representative of Kimberly's insurer to Aquaslide, advising that "one of your Queen Model #Q–3D slides" was involved in the accident. Aquaslide forwarded this notification to its insurer. Aquaslide's insurance adjuster made an on-site investigation of the slide in May, 1973, and also interviewed persons connected with the ordering and assembly of the slide. An inter-office letter dated September 23, 1973, indicates that Aquaslide's insurer was of the opinion the "Aquaslide in question was definitely manufactured by our insured." The complaint was filed [in the Southern District of Iowa on] October 15, 1973. Investigators for three different insurance companies, representing Harker, Kimberly and the defendant, had concluded that the slide had been manufactured by Aquaslide, and the defendant, with no information to the contrary, answered the complaint on December 12, 1973, and admitted that it "designed, manufactured, assembled and sold" the slide in question.

The statute of limitations on plaintiff's personal injury claim expired on July 15, 1974. About six and one-half months later Carl Meyer, president and owner of Aquaslide, visited the site of the accident prior to the taking of his deposition by the plaintiff.[5] From his on-site inspection of the slide, he determined it was not a product of the defendant [but instead a counterfeit slide]. Thereafter, [on February 26, 1975,] Aquaslide moved the court for leave to amend its answer to deny manufacture of the slide.

. . . .

It is evident from the order of the district court that in the exercise of its discretion in ruling on defendant's motion for leave to amend, it searched the record for evidence of bad faith, prejudice and undue delay which might be sufficient to overbalance the mandate of Rule 15(a). . . that leave to amend should be "freely given." Plaintiffs had not at any time conceded that the slide in question had not been manufactured by the defendant, and at the time the motion for leave to amend was at issue, the court had to decide whether the defendant should be permitted to litigate a material factual issue on its merits.

In inquiring into the issue of bad faith, the court noted the fact that the defendant, in initially concluding that it had manufactured the slide, relied upon the conclusions of three different insurance companies, each of which had conducted an investigation into the circumstances surrounding the accident. This reliance upon investigations of three insurance companies, and the fact that "no contention has been made by anyone that the defendant influenced this possibly erroneous conclusion," persuaded the court that "defendant has not acted in such bad faith as to be precluded from contesting the issue of manufacture at trial." The court further found

[5] Plaintiffs apparently requested Meyer to inspect the slide prior to the taking of his deposition to determine whether it was defectively installed or assembled.

"[t]o the extent that 'blame' is to be spread regarding the original identification, the record indicates that it should be shared equally."

In considering the issue of prejudice that might result to the plaintiffs from the granting of the motion for leave to amend, the trial court held that the facts presented to it did not support plaintiffs' assertion that, because of the running of the two year Iowa statute of limitations on personal injury claims, the allowance of the amendment would sound the "death knell" of the litigation. In order to accept plaintiffs' argument, the court would have had to assume that the defendant would prevail at trial on the factual issue of manufacture of the slide, and further that plaintiffs would be foreclosed, should the amendment be allowed, from proceeding against other parties if they were unsuccessful in pressing their claim against Aquaslide. On the state of the record before it, the trial court was unwilling to make such assumptions, and concluded "[u]nder these circumstances, the Court deems that the possible prejudice to the plaintiffs is an insufficient basis on which to deny the proposed amendment." The court reasoned that the amendment would merely allow the defendant to contest a disputed factual issue at trial, and further that it would be prejudicial to the defendant to deny the amendment.

The court also held that defendant and its insurance carrier, in investigating the circumstances surrounding the accident, had not been so lacking in diligence as to dictate a denial of the right to litigate the factual issue of manufacture of the slide.

On this record we hold that the trial court did not abuse its discretion in allowing the defendant to amend its answer.[j]

. . . .

The judgment of the district court is affirmed.

Amendments during or after trial.—Rule 15(a) imposes no absolute time limit on seeking amendment. Rule 15(b) shows that a motion to amend made during the course of the trial is not necessarily too late, and indeed that there are circumstances in which a party may seek and a court may allow an amendment even after the conclusion of trial and the entry of judgment.

Question: (36) Why would a party ever seek amendment of the pleadings after judgment, and why would a court ever allow it?

Rule 15(b) specially handles two late situations within the general scope of Rule 15(a). Rule 15(b)(1) makes provision for allowing amendment

[j] The reference here is to a deferential standard of review called abuse of discretion. For a decision that depends on the presence of the judge upon the trial-court scene to hear evidence and get a feel for the case, an appellate court will not overturn the decision unless clearly convinced there was error. This contrasts with the de novo standard of review for a decision on pure law, where the appellate court will substitute its view whenever it thinks the decision was wrong.

in this situation: where a party seeks to amend after the opposing side has successfully objected to trial evidence as going beyond the pleadings. Rule 15(b)(2) provides for treating the pleadings as amended in this situation: where the opposing side, having failed to object fully to trial evidence unambiguously going beyond the pleadings, thereby consented to try those new issues.

Questions: (37) How does an objecting party show, under Rule 15(b)(1), that she will suffer adequate "prejudice" by the admission of evidence not within the issues made by the pleadings? How does the standard of decision here compare with the standard applicable under Rule 15(a)(2)?

(38) What is a "continuance," referred to in Rule 15(b)(1)? Is this device feasible in jury trials?

Relation back of amendments.—What is the purpose of Rule 15(c)?

Blair v. Durham

United States Circuit Court of Appeals, Sixth Circuit, 1943.
134 F.2d 729.

■ Before HICKS, SIMONS, and HAMILTON, CIRCUIT JUDGES.

■ HAMILTON, CIRCUIT JUDGE. Appellant, Algernon Blair,[k] doing business as the Algernon Blair Construction Company, was general contractor for the repair of and improvements on, the United States Post Office, Customs House and United States Court Building in the city of Nashville, Tennessee, and appellant, C.W. Roberts, was the Superintendent and Manager for his co-appellant. The work was being done while the building was occupied and in use by officers and employees of the United States.

On or about August 17, 1938, appellee, Nelle B. Durham, a stenographic clerk in the Social Security Division in the office of the Collector of Internal Revenue, while at work in one of the rooms where the rebuilding under appellant's contract was going on, was struck in the head and injured by a heavy piece of timber falling from a scaffold.

Appellee originally filed this action [in the Middle District of Tennessee] on January 14, 1939, and alleged in her complaint that "by reason of the negligence and carelessness of defendants, their agents and servants in handling certain heavy timbers on and about the scaffolding that was

---

[k] Blair was a defendant.

In the district court, the caption of the case is, of course, in the form of Plaintiff v. Defendant; if there are several parties on either side, only the first is named in citing the case. Cf. Rule 10(a). In the courts of appeals, it was long the usual practice to reformulate the caption as Appellant v. Appellee; but since 1968, when the Federal Rules of Appellate Procedure were adopted, the title given to the action in the district court is retained on appeal. See App. Rule 12(a). In the Supreme Court, the practice is still to caption the case thus: party who seeks review versus adverse party.

So in this case from a court of appeals in 1943, because defendants were appealing plaintiff's victory in the district court, the caption of the case is Appellant (i.e., defendant) v. Appellee (i.e., plaintiff).

erected in the office in which the plaintiff was working, a large and heavy piece of board approximately 2 x 4 inches in width and thickness and about 3 feet long was permitted to fall from said scaffolding, which was about 10 feet above the floor, and onto plaintiff's head with great force and violence injuring her."

Issue was joined on this complaint and the cause came on for trial before a jury. In the course of the trial on August 15, 1940, appellee with the consent of the court filed an amended complaint alleging the same facts with the following revision: "The defendants had erected said scaffolding and provided it for the use of persons engaged in the installation of air-conditioning equipment in said building and said scaffold was erected in such a manner that it did not protect persons, including the plaintiff, who were required to work thereunder, but was erected in such a manner that the defendants might have reasonably anticipated that heavy objects would be likely to fall therefrom."

At the time the amendment was filed, the empanelling of the jury was set aside and the cause continued. Thereupon appellants moved to dismiss the amended complaint on the ground it stated a new cause of action and was barred by the Tennessee Statute of Limitations of one year. (Code of Tennessee, Sec. 8595.) Said motion was overruled by the court.

On retrial, the jury returned a verdict on behalf of plaintiff for $6,500. Appellants assign the following points:

1. Appellee's amended complaint was barred by the one-year statutory period of limitation.

[Two other assignments of error are omitted.]

Rule 15(a) of the Rules of Civil Procedure. . . provides that a party may amend his pleadings by leave of court, which leave shall be freely given when justice so requires at any time during the proceedings, and subsection (c) of the rule provides that whenever the amended pleading arose out of the conduct, transaction or occurrence set forth or attempted to be set forth in the original pleadings, the amendment relates back to the date of the original pleading. The issue here as to whether the statute of limitations was tolled by the original complaint depends upon whether the amendment stated a new cause of action.

A cause of action is the unlawful violation of a right or failure to discharge a duty which the facts show. The variety of facts alleged does not establish more than one cause of action so long as their result, whether they be considered severally or in combination, is the violation of but one right by a single legal wrong. A multiplicity of grounds of negligence alleged as causing the same injury does not result in pyramiding as many causes of action as separate allegations of actual negligence.

An amendment does not set up a new cause of action so long as the cause of action alleged grows out of the same transaction and is basically the same or is identical in the essential elements upon which the right to sue is based and upon which defendant's duty to perform is alleged to have arisen. As long as a plaintiff adheres to a legal duty breached or an injury originally declared on, an alteration of the modes in which defendant has breached the legal duty or caused the injury is not an introduction of a new cause of action. The true test is whether the proposed amendment is a different matter or the same matter more fully or differently laid.

A comparison between the appellee's original complaint and the amendment leaves no room for doubt that in both she relies on the same unlawful violation of a duty which appellants owed her at the place and in the position where she worked.

The original complaint which alleged that appellee's injuries were due to the negligence of appellant's employees in the use of the scaffold states no different cause of action as respects limitation than the amended complaint which stated that her injuries were due to the negligent manner in which the scaffold was constructed, because the two acts alleged were but different invasions of appellee's primary right and different breaches of the same duty. There was but one injury and it is immaterial whether it resulted from the negligence of the users of the scaffold or from its construction, since in either case it was a violation of the same obligation. [Citations omitted.]

[The remainder of the opinion, dealing with the other assignments of error, is omitted. However, in the course of its discussion the court did mention this: the evidence at trial had shown that at the time of the accident, the scaffold was being used solely by employees of a subcontractor.]

. . . Judgment affirmed.

Questions: (39) How could the plaintiff have pleaded originally to avoid all this trouble?

(40) It does not appear that the defendants objected to the making of the amendment itself. Why did they not do so?

(41) Some state codes prohibit amendments that would have the effect of changing or substantially changing the "cause of action" or "defense." Do you find a comparable limitation in Rule 15? So, do you agree with the court's statement in Blair v. Durham that "[t]he issue here . . . depends upon whether the amendment stated a new cause of action"?

"Cause of action" and "claim."—Of "cause of action" the Supreme Court has said: "One of the most theory-ridden of legal concepts is a 'cause of action.' This Court has recognized its 'shifting meanings' and the danger of determining rights based upon definitions of 'a cause of action' unrelated to the function which the concept serves in a particular situation." United States v. Dickinson, 331 U.S. 745, 748, 67 S.Ct. 1382, 1385 (1947) (quoting United States v. Memphis Cotton Oil Co., 288 U.S. 62, 67, 53 S.Ct. 278, 280 (1933)). The Federal Rules avoid use of "cause of action," but do use the word "claim" in a number of places. We shall have to observe how far the avoidance of the former phrase actually obviates the difficulties to which the Court referred.

Definition of "conduct, transaction, or occurrence."—Federal courts today read the transactional test of Rule 15(c)(1)(B) in light of its putting-on-notice function and therefore usually read the test loosely to require for relation back no more than "a common core of operative facts." 6A Wright, Miller & Kane § 1497, at 85. For example, a mere switch in a complaint's legal theory from negligence to warranty will relate back. Hood v. P. Ballantine & Sons, 38 F.R.D. 502 (S.D.N.Y.1965). So also, there should be relation back for an amendment adding a count of false imprisonment to a complaint alleging battery in the very same incident.

Questions: (42) An associate professor brings a federal civil rights action against her college and its president based on the failure to renew her contract of employment. Much later, her amended complaint also alleges defamation by the college's president near the time of and in connection with her termination. Does the defamation count relate back? See Pendrell v. Chatham College, 386 F.Supp. 341 (W.D.Pa.1974) (Teitelbaum, J., holding no and saying, "A more reasonable interpretation of F.R.Civ.P. 15(c) does not permit lawyers to endlessly answer the question: How many causes of action can you find in this fact situation? much as they might have done years earlier in law school examinations.").

(43) Do you see any disadvantages in the prevailing functional reading of certain malleable terms in the Federal Rules?

(f) DISCLOSURES AND DISCOVERY

[Rules 26, 30–37]

General purposes.—The pleadings, as well as the motions attacking the pleadings, serve among other things to acquaint the parties with the character and scope of the controversy. But the pleadings contain limited detail on facts or contentions (for example, Form 11 does no more than identify the accident and charge the defendant with negligence: the plaintiff does not describe the accident with precision, nor does the plaintiff state in what way the defendant was negligent). Moreover, even when the pleadings do go into detail, they do not often disclose the witnesses, documents, or other evidence by which the parties propose to make their proof.

If, apart from the pleadings, the parties knew all about the relevant facts and contentions and how the proof would be made by both sides at the trial, the pretrial exchange of information might stop with the pleadings. But this is rarely the situation in practice. The parties are often quite in the dark about the facts and about each other's positions and sources of proof. Indeed, they may not know precisely what detailed positions they themselves will ultimately take or how they will prove their own claims or defenses.

Private investigation is possible for those with means. But no one is bound to talk or display papers to an investigator, and an adverse party or a person friendly to an adverse party is unlikely to cooperate voluntarily.

When the time for trial comes, a party may compel by subpoena any person, including an adverse party, to attend court and testify; and the person may also be commanded by subpoena duces tecum to bring with him and produce designated documents and the like. See Rule 45. Knowledge acquired through such trial testimony or evidence, however, may well not come in time for effective use. It may, for instance, point to a new line of inquiry, revealed too late to undertake. Moreover, in the event of unexpected and unfavorable testimony, the surprised party may suffer seriously from lack of opportunity for further investigation to rebut it. And counsel's decision whether to call a given witness may quite properly turn on advance knowledge of what the witness will say—the practical hazard in calling a witness whose testimony may boomerang is obvious.

The Federal Rules on "disclosures and discovery" add another machinery, much of which is a striking departure from tradition, for sifting of facts and exploration of positions and evidence before trial. As a result of disclosures and by the use of the discovery devices, a party may learn facts or sources of proof not hitherto known to him that will aid him in establishing his own contentions, or he may obtain leads that will help him to search out and uncover such facts or sources of proof for himself. He may also uncover to a considerable extent what his adversary will seek to prove in support of a claim or defense and how his adversary expects to prove it. He may simply discover what a particular witness will say in court. Or, by the skillful use of the discovery devices he may eliminate from the trial issues on which there is no real dispute.

A major motive behind these Rules is to prevent the trial from being a drama of surprises with the happy ending for the side with the more extensive facilities for private investigation or the more agile court performer. Accordingly, the disclosure and discovery provisions not only shape the preparation for trial but also profoundly affect the strategy and tactics of the trial itself.

The disclosure and discovery provisions affect other aspects of procedure as well. For example, as the Sierocinski case suggested, the availability of discovery devices might influence decision on how much detail the pleadings must supply. Indeed, as Twombly suggested, the whole problem of pleading under the Federal Rules is bound up with the discovery provisions and ultimately cannot be fruitfully considered apart from them. All this implies that another major motive behind the disclosure and discovery Rules is to facilitate the efficient presentation and resolution of controversies.

General provisions governing disclosure (Rule 26(a), (f), and (g)).—In 1993, amid much controversy, the rulemakers introduced a new phase of procedure called disclosure. Elaborating on the pleaded facts, parties now must disclose certain core information, without awaiting a discovery request.

Disclosure aims at achieving some savings in time and expense, and also at moderating litigants' adversary behavior in the pretrial process. At least intuitively, this innovation makes some sense. Opponents find the core information useful in virtually all cases. Almost all the information would be discoverable anyway. Disclosure essentially makes the obvious interrogatories automatic, so that parties just hand over the information without awaiting a discovery request.

According to Federal Rule 26(a), there are three distinct types of disclosure. However, the judge by order, or the parties by stipulation, may alter these disclosure obligations.

1. Rule 26(a)(1) requires disclosure, at the outset, of routine evidentiary and insurance matters, except in certain special categories of cases. These initial disclosures comprise (i) witnesses likely to have discoverable information that the disclosing party may use to support its claims or defenses, unless solely for impeachment, (ii) documents, electronically stored information, and other things that the disclosing party has in its possession, custody, or control and may use to support its claims or defenses, unless solely for impeachment, (iii) computation of claimed damages, and (iv) insurance agreements that might cover part or all of an eventual judgment.

2. Rule 26(a)(2) requires a party to disclose, at a specified time, information regarding any expert whom it may call at trial. Most of these experts must also deliver a detailed report, which must include all opinions the witness will express and the underlying reasons, as well as details about qualifications, compensation, and previous experience as a witness.

3. Rule 26(a)(3) requires disclosure, shortly before trial, of trial witness lists and the like regarding nonimpeachment evidence. In particular, the party must disclose trial exhibits, which allows airing evidentiary disputes in advance of trial.

Disclosure under the Federal Rules is meant to proceed in an atmosphere of cooperation. Still, there are rules. First, all disclosures are to be in writing, signed, and served. See Rule 26(a)(4). Second, an attorney, or if there is no attorney then the party, must sign each disclosure under (a)(1) or (a)(3); the signature is a certification, to the best of the signer's knowledge, information, and belief formed after reasonable inquiry, that the disclosure is complete and correct as of the time it is made; the court must punish violations. See Rule 26(g), which for each *discovery* request or response likewise imposes a certification requirement analogous to the provision for pleadings and motions in Rule 11. Third, the disclosing party must promptly file pretrial disclosures under (a)(3) with the court. See Rule 5(d), which provides that the other disclosures, like most *discovery* items too, must not be filed until used in the proceeding.

An increasingly key feature of the disclosure and *discovery* schemes lies in Rule 26(f): very early on, the attorneys and unrepresented parties normally must confer to consider the case and the disclosures, as well as attempt in good faith to develop a proposed discovery plan and promptly submit a written report to the court along the lines of Form 52. Under Rule 26(d)(1), discovery normally cannot proceed until this conference takes place. Under Rule 26(a)(1)(C), initial disclosures are normally due within fourteen days after the conference.

General provisions governing discovery (Rule 26(b), (c), and (d)).—Disclosure conveys only basic or core information about the case. A great deal more information is discoverable through the various discovery devices introduced in 1938.

What may a discovering party inquire into? The scope of discovery is wide. Fundamental is Rule 26(b)(1). As a general proposition,[l] the party may obtain discovery regarding any *nonprivileged*[m] matter that is *relevant* to the claim or defense of any party. Moreover, for good cause shown on a party's motion, the court may extend the scope of discovery to any matter that is relevant not merely to a "claim or defense" but to the slightly broader "subject matter involved in the action" (and thus perhaps relevant only to unasserted but possible claims or defenses).

Relevance embraces, among much else, the existence and location of documents or other things and the identity and whereabouts of persons having knowledge of any discoverable matter. "Relevant information need not be admissible at the trial if the discovery appears reasonably calculated to lead to the discovery of admissible evidence." Thus, in an action based on alleged negligence of the defendant in maintaining a skylight through which the plaintiff fell, the plaintiff can discover from the defendant what repairs it made to the skylight following the accident. See Caulk v. Baltimore & Ohio R.R., 306 F.Supp. 1171 (D.Md.1969). This is true even though evidence law makes evidence of such subsequent remedial measures inadmissible at trial, in order not to discourage persons from making repairs. See Federal Rule of Evidence 407, which is in the Rules booklet.

Question: (44) In an action for alleged violation of the federal antitrust laws, plaintiff during discovery refuses to answer (a) questions concerning the circumstances surrounding the bringing of the suit, including possibly unethical financial arrangements between plaintiff and his counsel for bearing the costs of this litigation, and (b) questions concerning plaintiff's net worth, including his ability to satisfy a judgment for costs if defendant were to prevail in the action. Defendant moves to compel answers. What should be the decision? See Bogosian v. Gulf Oil Corp., 337 F.Supp. 1228 (E.D.Pa.1971) (discovery disallowed); 6 Moore § 26.41[8].

Rule 26 follows these general formulae with specific provisions not only authorizing case-by-case judicial supervision of duplicative or disproportionate discovery (see Rule 26(b)(2)), but also limiting the discovery of so-called work product (see Rule 26(b)(3) on discovery of these critically useful materials prepared by or for a party or his representative in anticipation of litigation or for trial) and the discovery of expert information (see Rule 26(b)(4) on discovery regarding these players who have become so important in modern litigation) in ways that we save for later study.

Question: (45) What if the defendants in a suit for sexual harassment during state-police training sought discovery of the plaintiffs' sexual history? their sexual

[l] The introductory clause of Rule 26(b) provides a significant exception for contrary orders of the court. See, e.g., Rule 26(c) (protective orders).

[m] The reference is to such limitations as the attorney-client privilege. We shall soon consider the law of privileges in connection with the trial, infra p. 169, as part of a general treatment of the admissibility of evidence.

behavior during the training period? See Mitchell v. Hutchings, 116 F.R.D. 481 (D.Utah 1987) (allowing discovery, but only for contemporaneous work-environment behavior); Herchenroeder v. Johns Hopkins Univ. Applied Physics Lab., 171 F.R.D. 179 (D.Md.1997) (further subjecting such discovery to a confidentiality order). Do such restrictions rest on privilege, irrelevance, or something else? Where do the current Federal Rules impose such restrictions on discovery? What if the plaintiffs seek to discover the defendants' sexual history or behavior?

Theory expects discovery to work almost wholly by action of the parties without intervention by the court. Physical or mental examination under Rule 35, already considered in Sibbach v. Wilson & Co., is the only discovery device that the discovering party must initiate by motion addressed to the court. The five other devices—depositions by oral examination, depositions by written questions, interrogatories to parties, production of documents and things, and requests for admission—generally start and move along by party initiative alone. A party makes application to the court only in special situations or when something goes awry, as when a request for discovery is resisted or a misuse of discovery is threatened. Incidentally, the six devices may proceed in any sequence according to Rule 26(d)(2), unless a party gets the court to step in and order otherwise.

Question: (46) Why should a request for a physical or mental examination require an order made only on motion for good cause?

In practice, much of discovery proceeds in accordance with negotiated agreement between the parties, as Rule 29 recognizes. A litigator should beware of pursuing a defiant or aggressive tactic without contacting the other counsel informally. And the litigator should certainly hesitate before involving the court.

Depositions by oral examination (Rule 30).—This method of discovery comprises oral examination of anyone, party or nonparty, thought to have information within the scope of discovery as set out in Rule 26. In considering this surprisingly awesome power bestowed on parties, it may be well to begin by asking why a party might want to take a deposition. Here are some possible reasons, which in a sense particularize the purposes of discovery discussed above:

1. The discovering party may know or suspect that some person has information that would aid him in his own investigation and preparation for trial. For example, under Rule 26(b)(1) he can force the person deposed to reveal the names and addresses of other witnesses to the events in suit.

2. He may be left genuinely in the dark by his adversary's pleadings and disclosures, and so may want to take the adversary's deposition to uncover the nature of the claim or defense that he must prepare to meet in settlement negotiations or at trial.

3. He may have a witness with whose story he is fully familiar, so there is no occasion to "discover" it. But the witness may be old and likely to die before trial, or she may be young and about to join the armed forces, or she simply may live far from the place of trial, or there may be some other danger that she will be unavailable to testify at trial. A deposition

serves to record testimony and, as we shall see, may be used at trial upon a proper showing that the witness is unavailable.

4. He may know the story some other witness will tell well enough for purposes of his own preparation. But he nevertheless may want a deposition to pin the witness down by sworn testimony in advance of trial. If, as sometimes happens, the witness tells a different story at trial, he may use the deposition to discredit the witness.

5. He may hope that he can by a deposition expose a fatal weakness in his adversary's claim or defense, and thus be able to avoid a trial altogether by a motion for summary judgment pursuant to Rule 56.

To follow the main features of the oral-deposition process, read these provisions in order: Rules 30(a) and (b); 45(a), (b), and (e); 28(a); and 30(c), (e), and (f).

In the usual case, leave of court is not necessary to initiate the deposition procedure.[n] The discovering party gives reasonable notice in writing to the other parties to the action, specifying the time and place of the deposition and naming the person to be examined ("deponent"). On the one hand, service of a subpoena upon a nonparty deponent officially summons her to appear at the deposition. Under Rule 45(a)(1), a subpoena duces tecum may command the nonparty deponent to bring with her and produce documents and other things. On the other hand, if the deponent is a party, a subpoena is not necessary, because the notice of examination itself suffices as a command. Under Rule 30(b)(2), a request under Rule 34 to produce documents and other things at the taking of the deposition may accompany the notice to the party deponent.

Question: (47) With regard to the place specified by the discovering party for taking the deposition, what is the effect of the geographical limits set by Rule 45(b)(2)?

The actual taking of the deposition resembles the taking of testimony at a trial.[o] The deponent is sworn, interrogated by counsel for the discovering party, cross-examined by counsel for the other party or parties, and so on, the questions and answers being taken down stenographically or otherwise recorded.

There is, however, no judge present as at a trial. The person presiding at the deposition does not have judicial powers. This difference becomes important upon an objection to a question. At a trial, the judge would rule on the objection and the witness would answer or not, depending on the ruling. At the deposition, no one is on hand to make the ruling. How, then, is the objection disposed of?

Consider the possible reasons for objection: (1) A question put at deposition may be within the scope of discovery described in Rule 26, but

---

[n] Reread Rule 30(a)(2), describing the situations in which leave of court is necessary, and consider why. Cf. Rule 27 (discovery to perpetuate testimony, in anticipation of an action's commencement or after judgment pending appeal).

[o] But see again Rule 30(b)(4), which permits a stipulation or order that a deposition be taken by telephone or by other remote electronic means.

would be objectionable at trial under the rules of evidence. (2) A question may be objectionable as not falling within the scope of discovery (in such case, it would in all likelihood also be objectionable at the trial proper).

In situation (1)—where the examining party puts a question at deposition that is within the scope of discovery—the Rules contemplate that the deponent will answer the question and that the objection will simply be recorded. See again Rule 30(c)(2). Then, if the deposition is offered in evidence at trial, the objection will in effect be renewed and the trial judge will pass on it as if the deponent were testifying orally. (In fact, when a deposition is offered at trial, a party may ordinarily object under the rules of evidence to deposition questions even without an objection during the deposition. However, if the ground for objection is one that might have been obviated if presented at the taking of the deposition, the party cannot raise the objection for the first time at trial. It would be patently unfair to exclude deposition testimony at trial if the examining party, upon alert, could have remedied the error during the deposition. For example, a leading question on direct examination is objectionable in form, but a rephrasing of the question provides a ready corrective; yet the error would be fatal if the opponent could object for the first time at trial, and if the deponent was then unavailable to answer the rephrased question. See Rule 32(b) and (d)(3)(A) and (B). But see Rule 26(a)(3)(B). Other problems are more difficult. Suppose at deposition a party asks a doctor a question calling for an expert opinion on a medical question, and at trial the opponent objects on the ground that her expert qualifications were not sufficiently shown: is the objection untimely because the ground for it was obviable? Uncertainty in the few precedents in this area often leads lawyers either to attempt to protect themselves by excessive objections at the deposition or to stipulate at the time of the deposition that all objections except as to form may be first made at the trial.)

Even in situation (2)—where the examining party puts a question at deposition that is not within the scope of discovery—the deponent and the other parties may be willing to have it answered if the answer would not prove damaging or offensive. But suppose the question is thought to enter the field of privilege. Here there may be strong reason to decline to give an answer unless the court actually orders one, for the answer may be harmful in itself, and ruling the question improper at the subsequent trial would not cure that harm. The system indulges such reasons.

In summary, the deponent should answer, under any appropriate objection, all questions, except for particular questions thought to fall outside the scope of discovery and to call for an answer that would infringe on privilege in a damaging or offensive fashion.

If the examining party is unhappy regarding a deponent who refuses to answer or who has accepted advice by an opposing party not to answer, the examining party can complete or adjourn the deposition and then seek an enforceable court order to answer. See Rule 37(a). Note that the examining party may request payment of expenses for proceedings occasioned by unreasonable failure to answer a proper question, and the deponent or opposing party may make a corresponding request in case of unreasonable insistence on an answer to an improper question. The court may oblige counsel advising unreasonable action to pay these expenses personally.

UMPHRES v. SHELL OIL CO., 15 Fed.R.Serv.2d (Callaghan) 1116 (S.D.Tex.1971). This case involved a Rule 37(a) motion to compel the plaintiff, who was formerly a Shell retailer in the Houston area, to answer certain questions asked of him during the taking of his oral deposition by the defendant.

"Apparently, defendant commenced plaintiff's deposition as scheduled, on August 30, 1971. As pointed out by the defendant in its memorandum in support of its motion to compel answers, counsel for the defendant commenced interrogating the plaintiff with regard to an alleged conspiracy [with other oil companies to fix prices in violation of the antitrust laws] pleaded by him. Plaintiff's counsel advised his client not to answer any questions about conspiracy, to which the attorney for the defendant observed, in effect, that conspiracy is a question of fact and the proper subject for interrogation, and the defendant should be entitled 'to inquire of him what he thinks the conspiracy was.' Plaintiff's counsel, Mr. Conde Anderson, replied, 'Well, you know full well, Mr. Kingdon, that I prepared the complaint and that Mr. Umphres didn't. And I attempted to prepare it, keeping in mind what I understood the law to be, and I don't think this is a proper line of inquiry and I'm going to instruct him not to answer.'

"Mr. Kingdon then continued with his next question, being, 'Mr. Umphres, do you have any information regarding the allegation in the complaint that Shell exercised control of numerous retail dealers with whom it contracted in areas elsewhere in the state of Texas other than Harris County, Texas, and in many other states, do you have any information to support that claim that there was a conspiracy in areas other than Harris County, Texas?' The plaintiff did not answer this question under instructions from his counsel.

"The court is of the opinion that the oral interrogatory may very well ask for plaintiff's conclusion as to the legal meaning of conspiracy, and, if so, since plaintiff is not an experienced man in the field and the subject matter which is involved in such question, he should not be required to answer the question as asked. However, it seems to the court that defendant is certainly entitled to interrogate plaintiff about the facts upon which the claim of conspiracy was based. But, up to now, defendant's counsel has not asked Mr. Anderson for the details upon which he relied to plead conspiracy.

"This court considers any motion relating to discovery to be premature until the party making such request has first explored all reasonable avenues of agreement as to discovery problems by conference with counsel for the other side. Therefore, counsel for the plaintiff and counsel for the defendant are here directed to sit down, face to face, and in good faith discuss the question of conspiracy as alleged by the plaintiff, and the attorney for the plaintiff is to detail for the benefit of the defendant those facts which he took into account in making his allegations of conspiracy. Upon the furnishing of such factual information to the defendant, then the deposition of plaintiff should resume and the defendant's counsel is at liberty to interrogate the plaintiff with regard to the particular facts which his counsel has divulged, or which may be developed during the interrogation."

Note that the court ordered such a conference long before the rulemakers imposed duties to confer under Rules 26(f) and 37(a) in 1993. Note further that at trial the plaintiff eventually lost by directed verdict because of lack of evidence, a result affirmed at 512 F.2d 420 (5th Cir.), cert. denied, 423 U.S. 929, 96 S.Ct. 278 (1975).

BRANDENBERG v. EL AL ISRAEL AIRLINES, 79 F.R.D. 543 (S.D.N.Y.1978). Plaintiff sued two airlines for $900,000, alleging negligent and reckless treatment that had caused physical stress and mental injuries. Mrs. Brandenberg's position was "that in view of her age and physical condition (she suffered from diabetes), the airlines were obligated to treat her with particular care, and that they failed in that obligation, on the contrary, 'abandoning' her in times of need."

Defendants deposed the 72–year-old plaintiff. Counsel for British Airways questioned her concerning the events of its leg of the flight that had carried her abroad to visit her daughter. "It is fair to say that the plaintiff . . . had some difficulty in remembering the sequence of events." The court further noted: "It is also fair to say that, having studied her account of the events involving British Airways, the precise complaint or complaints which the plaintiff makes concerning her treatment at the hands of that defendant are not clear." Contrariwise, her criticism of the other airline had been "entirely clear."

"In these circumstances, counsel for British Airways posed, or attempted to pose, the following questions to plaintiff at the end of the deposition:

'Q. Do you know of any factual basis to support the allegations in your complaints against British—'

'Q. Do you know of anything that British Airways did that was not proper treatment of you at Heathrow Airport in March of 1976?'

'Q. Mrs. Brandenberg, can you tell me in your own words what the basis of your claim against British Airways—'

'Q. Do you know of anything that British Airways did to you that was not in accordance with the way you thought you should be treated by them?'

'Q. What facts do you contend show that British Airways did not properly treat you?'

"On direction of her attorney, the plaintiff declined to answer any of these questions. British Airways now moves for an order under Rule 37(a) compelling answers. Plaintiff resists on the ground that the questions call for legal conclusions of a lay witness."

The court concluded that such contentions were discoverable: "British Airways is understandably left in the dark, on the present deposition record, as to the factual basis perceived by plaintiff for the charge of negligence against it. British Airways is entitled to inquire on that score, and plaintiff is directed to respond to such questions, at a continuation of her deposition at a place and time to be mutually agreed or, failing such agreement, as directed by the Court."

The Rules give a party (or the deponent) certain opportunities to take the initiative against the examining party, halt the examination, and obtain a court order to limit the deposition if it is going too far afield or becoming abusive or to furnish other kinds of protection. See Rule 30(d)(3); cf. Rule 26(c), which in certain circumstances allows seeking court protection against the deposition before its stated starting time. Again, the court may order an offending person to pay expenses.

Moreover, recall that Rule 26(b)(2)(C) encourages district courts on their own to curb discovery overuse. Thus, the court can limit duplicative or disproportionate discovery. Here again, by the way, is explicit recognition that there are significant limitations on the scope of discovery other than privilege and irrelevance.

After examination of the deponent and upon prior request, the deponent has a chance to review the transcript or recording, and then append any changes with the deponent's reasons. Finally, the person who presided at the deposition certifies and delivers the transcript or recording to the deposing attorney.

Depositions by written questions (Rule 31).—The typical notice to take a deposition by oral examination does not specify the particular matters to be inquired into, but rather might at most refer generally to some matters involved in the action. The notice for taking a deposition by written questions, however, comes with the questions to be put to the deponent, who may be a nonparty or party and who is summoned to appear in the same way as for a Rule 30 deposition. Within 14 days after being served with the notice and questions, any party may serve questions for cross-examination, and then questions for redirect and recross may follow. The deposing party delivers all questions to the person designated to preside at the deposition. He swears the deponent, and he reads the questions one by one, with the deponent responding orally. As for an oral deposition, the testimony is recorded, reviewed, certified, and delivered.

Again consult Rule 37(a) to see when and how an examining party may secure an order directing a deponent to answer a written question, and see

Rule 26(c) as to when and how a party or deponent may secure a protective order in respect to a deposition by written questions.

Questions: (48) Why is there no equivalent in Rule 31 of Rule 30(d)(3)'s motion to terminate or limit?

(49) Is it proper for counsel, who has received the Rule 31 questions from her opponent in advance, to rehearse her client or a friendly nonparty deponent by reading the questions to him? Compare 7 Moore § 31.02, with 8A Wright, Miller & Marcus § 2133.

Rule 31 depositions by written questions are typically much cheaper than Rule 30 depositions by oral examination. The saving under Rule 31 arises from the fact that counsel can with reasonable safety absent themselves from the examination. Yet depositions by written questions are rare. One reason is that counsel labor under the handicap of having to frame questions without knowing what answers the deponent will have given to the previous questions. Hence they must frame questions on predictions or on alternative assumptions about the content of the prior answers. This procedure is uncertain and cumbersome. And if the deponent is unfriendly to the examining side, it may be harder to pin him down by written questions than by oral examination.

Question: (50) What may a party do in an effort to save the expense of attending another party's oral deposition of, say, a nonparty deponent of peripheral importance who lives far away? See Rule 30(c)(3). What difficulties can you foresee?

Interrogatories to parties (Rule 33).—This method of discovery is relatively simple and inexpensive. The discovering party can serve a limited number of written questions, each of which is called an interrogatory and is similar to a written question in a Rule 31 deposition, upon any other party to the action. The responding party and his lawyer, on their own, sit down to prepare responses. They have to answer each interrogatory separately and fully in writing under oath—unless they object to the particular interrogatory, in which event they have to state the reasons for objection with specificity. Answers are signed by the person making them, but objections are signed by the attorney.

Questions: (51) Give some typical reasons why the attorney might fairly object to an interrogatory.

(52) What may an interrogating party do to compel an answer when she considers an objection insufficient? when she considers an answer, unaccompanied by an objection, insufficient?

(53) May a responding party seek any protection against the interrogatories otherwise than by written objections in lieu of answers?

(54) So the general provisions governing discovery extend to interrogatories much as they do to depositions. But may a responding party serve cross-interrogatories, i.e., interrogatories directed to himself? Compare that negative answer to the affirmative answers to the following questions: May a party who is being deposed by oral examination have his own counsel cross-examine him? Might any useful purpose be so achieved? Indeed, may a party initiate a deposition by oral examination in which he himself is the deponent? Might any useful purpose be achieved by

such a deposition? In a deposition by written questions, may a deposed party direct cross-questions to himself? May a party depose himself by written questions?

Under Rule 33(d), instead of actually answering interrogatories involving business records, the responding party sometimes may invite the interrogating party to inspect the records from which answers can be derived. The very extensive 1970 discovery amendments added this subdivision. See the Advisory Committee's notes thereon in the Rules booklet.

O'Brien v. International Brotherhood of Electrical Workers

United States District Court, Northern District of Georgia, 1977.
443 F.Supp. 1182.

■ EDENFIELD, DISTRICT JUDGE.

This action was brought pursuant to the Labor Management Reporting and Disclosure Act, 29 U.S.C. §§ 401, et seq., against a local union and its parent international union. . . .

Plaintiff was charged by a fellow union member with violating certain sections of the IBEW constitution when he distributed certain information which was allegedly detrimental to the union. Local 613's executive board heard the charges on January 27, 1976 and found plaintiff guilty, fining him $2,725.00 and temporarily suspending him from local union activities. The decision of Local 613 was rescinded when it was discovered that defendant IBEW, not Local 613, had jurisdiction over the charges pursuant to the IBEW constitution. On March 15, 1976 plaintiff was notified of a new hearing to be held before the International Executive Council of IBEW on May 6, 1976. At this hearing, plaintiff was found guilty and fined $100. Thereafter, plaintiff filed this action.

Plaintiff has alleged that the charges, trials and disciplinary measures violated plaintiff's rights of free speech and assembly as guaranteed by the LMRDA in 29 U.S.C. § 411(a)(2).*. . .

[The court first disposed of a number of other motions.]

Lastly, the court must concern itself with plaintiff's motion to compel answers to interrogatories from Local 613. Plaintiff's interrogatories, filed May 18, 1977, seek to have defendants explain why they found plaintiff guilty of the union charges. Local 613 has registered a general objection to plaintiff's interrogatories which may be readily disposed of. Local 613

---

* Section 411(a)(2) of Title 29, U.S.C., provides:

"Every member of any labor organization shall have the right to meet and assemble freely with other members; and to express any views, arguments, or opinions; and to express at meetings of the labor organization his views, upon candidates in an election of the labor organization or upon any business properly before the meeting, subject to the organization's established and reasonable rules pertaining to the conduct of meetings: *Provided*, That nothing herein shall be construed to impair the right of a labor organization to adopt and enforce reasonable rules as to the responsibility of every member toward the organization as an institution and to his refraining from conduct that would interfere with its performance of its legal or contractual obligations." [Footnote by court.—Ed.]

claims that since its decision to fine and suspend [plaintiff] was rescinded, its reasons for trying plaintiff and finding him guilty are now irrelevant. However, plaintiff is charging that both defendants in their respective actions taken against plaintiff violated plaintiff's free speech rights under the LMRDA. Plaintiff seeks, among other relief, the expenses incurred in defending and appealing Local 613's decision. While the decision may have been rescinded, the expenses were not.

A second objection listed by Local 613 is that plaintiff has not sought to compel discovery as against IBEW. While that is a matter for plaintiff to decide, it must be noted that plaintiff cannot expect the local union to answer interrogatories that are within the distinct knowledge of the international union, specifically interrogatories numbered 1(c) and (d), 2(2), and 5.

Interrogatory numbers 1(a) and (b) ask for the specific statements allegedly made by plaintiff for which he was tried. The court sees no reason why defendant should not be required to set out these statements, despite the fact that plaintiff might be able to cull this information from the hearing transcript. The same may be said with respect to interrogatory number 2, wherein plaintiff asks that defendant Local 613 state which provisions of the IBEW constitution were violated by which statements.

Interrogatory number 3 seeks an explanation as to why these statements violated these constitutional provisions. While defendant Local 613 argues that this question seeks a legal theory which is not discoverable, when the constitutional provisions presumably involved are examined, the interrogatory appears to be one that Local 613 should answer. All but one of the provisions proscribe false statements. Plaintiff is entitled to know the facts which render his utterances untrue. One constitutional provision deals with conduct which causes dissension and dissatisfaction among union members. Plaintiff is entitled to know the facts which, in Local 613's view, constituted dissension caused by plaintiff's statements.

Interrogatory number 4 provides as follows:

> In respect to each act and/or utterance listed in response to Interrogatory 1. above, explain the manner in which each said act and/or utterance (a) violated plaintiff's responsibility toward Local 613, IBEW and IBEW as institutions, and (b) interfered with Local 613, IBEW's, and IBEW's performance of their respective legal or contractual obligations. (If any of said acts/utterances violated neither standard, please indicate which did not.)

Clearly this question seeks to discover defendant's legal theory based on the facts elicited from the other interrogatories. Interrogatory number 4 is based on the exceptions in the free speech section of the LMRDA [the court here quoted again the proviso of 29 U.S.C. § 411(a)(2)]. Anticipating that defendant will rely on this language as a defense to this action, plaintiff asks defendant to explain its application to the communications made by the plaintiff.

Rule 33. . . makes clear that such discovery is in fact permissible [the court here quoted what is now Rule 33(a)(2) treating opinion and contention interrogatories]. This rule cuts against many older cases which imposed a strict rule against opinions, contentions and conclusions. The Advisory Committee Note only excludes those interrogatories which "extend to issues of 'pure law,' i.e., legal issues unrelated to the facts of the case." Note to 1970 Amendment of Rule 33 . . . , 48 F.R.D. 485, 524 (1970), see Wright & Miller, Federal Practice and Procedure, § 2167 at 513. Interrogatory number 4 seeks an application of law to the central facts of the case, and accordingly is permissible under Rule 33 . . . . Since the discovery period is nearly complete, there is no danger of tying defendant to a legal theory before he has had an opportunity to fully explore the case, see Wright & Miller, supra, at 514.

Interrogatory number 6 reads as follows:

> In respect to each and every constitutional provision listed in response to Interrogatory 2., state and explain the reasons why each provision is *not* deprived of force and effect by operation of 29 U.S.C. § 411(b)[p] in respect to plaintiff and the acts and utterances listed in response to Interrogatory 1.

In contrast to the interrogatory previously discussed, this question seeks pure legal conclusions which are related not to the facts, but to the law of the case. While the line demarcating permissible discovery under Rule 33 . . . may be obscure, the court concludes that this interrogatory exceeds the bounds of permissible discovery under the rule.

For these reasons, plaintiff's motion to compel discovery is DENIED as to interrogatories numbered 1(c) and (d), 2(2), 5 and 6, but is GRANTED as to the balance of the interrogatories in dispute. The court further concludes that each party should bear the cost incurred in bringing and opposing these discovery motions.

. . . .

Questions: (55) In the Sierocinski case, would it be proper under present Rule 33(a)(2) for the defendant to put to the plaintiff the interrogatory: "What specific acts or omissions by the defendant do you contend constituted negligence?" How about the interrogatory: "Do you intend to rely on the doctrine of res ipsa loquitur?" How about: "What do you contend are the contours of the doctrine of res ipsa loquitur in this state?"

(56) If Mr. Sierocinski were to answer any such interrogatory, how binding on him should his answer be?

(57) Would it be proper for the defendant instead to put those same questions when deposing Mr. Sierocinski? when deposing Mr. White, the plaintiff's lawyer?

---

[p] That statute provides: "(b) Any provision of the constitution and bylaws of any labor organization which is inconsistent with the provisions of [29 U.S.C. § 411(a)] shall be of no force or effect."

A most significant point is that, unlike depositions, interrogatories cannot be used to question nonparties. But both devices serve to question parties.

So, what is the difference between depositions by written questions, when addressed to parties, and interrogatories to parties? In the former case, the party as deponent is at least formally on his own when he testifies and gives answers to the written questions read out to him. In the latter case, the party answering can and commonly does sit down with his attorney, examine the questions at leisure, and make use of his attorney's advice in framing the answers. Despite the often studied and artful answers consequently returned to Rule 33 interrogatories, this discovery method is a good and relatively cheap means of obtaining evidence or leads to evidence, or of obliging one's adversary to specify positions on the issues arising in the case. Indeed, interrogatories are so much cheaper than a written deposition that one would employ the latter only when interrogatories just cannot do the job, as when the desired respondent is a nonparty (and there is insufficient need for the very expensive effectiveness of an oral deposition).

More generally, the expenses incurred in discovery can sometimes be enormous. Normally, they fall ultimately on the party who initially incurred them; for example, the discovering party pays the small cost of preparing interrogatories, and the responding party pays the potentially huge cost of answering them. However, the court may eventually award certain, relatively insignificant discovery expenses as costs to the party who prevails in the lawsuit, as we shall see. More significantly, as we have suggested, the Rules have ample provisions for shifting reasonable discovery expenses (including attorney's fees) as a condition of approving discovery; for ordering parties, deponents, or counsel to reimburse anyone's reasonable expenses incurred in successfully invoking the court's assistance in a discovery dispute or resisting such an attempt; and for requiring reimbursement of reasonable expenses as a discovery sanction.

Requests for admission (Rule 36).—A party may serve upon any other party a written request to admit the truth of matters separately set forth in the request or to admit the genuineness of described documents. See Form 51. Observe what action or inaction by the requested party may result in an admission, what the requesting party may do about inadequate answers or improper objections, and what the effect of an admission is.

Question: (58) Prior to 1970, a party could seek Rule 36 admissions only as to genuineness of described documents and as to matters of "fact." Compare present Rule 36(a)(1)(A), and see Booth Oil Site Admin. Group v. Safety–Kleen Corp., 194 F.R.D. 76 (W.D.N.Y.2000) ("where the question of the meaning of the document is at issue in the case, a request directed to another party seeking an admission or denial of a document's meaning or intent . . . is authorized by Rule 36"). Was the earlier version preferable?

A denial defeats the attempt to obtain an admission. But consider the sanctions contained in Rule 37(c)(2), which aim to discourage capricious denials.

Questions: (59) What is the meaning of "fails to admit" and "proves" in Rule 37(c)(2)? But what, in your opinion, is the practical likelihood of securing a Rule 37(c)(2) order?

(60) How do Rule 36 requests for admission differ from Rule 33 interrogatories, and wherein do the functions of these devices differ?

Production of documents and things (Rule 34).—Witnesses, including parties, may be compelled to produce documents and other things during trial, but this may be too late for effective use. Rule 34(a)(1) enables a party to anticipate trial and compel any other party to produce any designated documents, electronically stored information, or tangible things within his possession, custody, or control, so that the discovering party may inspect, copy, and (in the case of things) test or sample them. (Also, Rule 34(a)(2) provides for securing entry on any other party's land or property for the purposes of inspection, measuring, or the like.) All this must of course be within the scope of Rule 26.

In modern litigation, this discovery device receives heavy use, and ever more so with the advent of e-discovery. The Rule 34 process begins by service of a request in writing. See Form 50. The requested party serves a written response either acquiescing in the request or objecting with reasons. The discovering party has a remedy under Rule 37(a) for an insufficient response.

Questions: (61) Rule 34(a)(1)(A) refers to "designated documents." What should a party do if she does not know enough to identify the documents she wants?

(62) A party can address requests under Rule 34 only to other parties. Suppose a document or thing is under the control of a nonparty. How can the party compel its production? See Rule 34(c).

Physical and mental examinations (Rule 35).—Physical or mental condition is frequently in question in lawsuits, and almost invariably in actions for personal injuries. In a personal-injury case, the defendant will generally want his physician to conduct an examination of the plaintiff. Otherwise he will be at a disadvantage in meeting an exaggerated or fraudulent claim by the plaintiff, and in evaluating a valid claim for purposes of settlement.

The plaintiff will often agree to examination by the defendant's physician because she also has interest in settlement. Moreover, she is aware that the trier might draw unfavorable inferences from revelation at trial that she had refused an examination. But when for any reason a person declines to allow an examination, Rule 35 is useful.

Question: (63) The Rule reaches only a party (or a person in the custody or legal control of a party). How, then, does a litigant prepare on the condition of a nonparty, e.g., the eyesight of a witness to the accident in suit?

The discovering party initiates the Rule 35 procedure by a motion. The physical or mental condition must be "in controversy" in the action, and the movant must show "good cause." In the Schlagenhauf case below, the Supreme Court said this about these requirements of "in controversy" and "good cause": "They are not met by mere conclusory allegations of the pleadings—nor by mere relevance to the case—but require an affirmative showing by the movant that each condition as to which the examination is sought is really and genuinely in controversy and that good cause exists for ordering each particular examination. Obviously, what may be good cause for one type of examination may not be so for another. The ability of the movant to obtain the desired information by other means is also relevant. Rule 35, therefore, requires discriminating application by the trial judge . . . ."

Question: (64) The Court further noted: "Of course, there are situations where the pleadings alone are sufficient to meet these requirements. A plaintiff in a negligence action who asserts mental or physical injury, cf. Sibbach v. Wilson & Co., supra, places that mental or physical injury clearly in controversy and provides the defendant with good cause for an examination to determine the existence and extent of such asserted injury." In what circumstances would it be necessary in a personal-injury case to establish "in controversy" and "good cause" otherwise than by the pleadings?

SCHLAGENHAUF v. HOLDER, 379 U.S. 104, 85 S.Ct. 234 (1964). In a diversity action involving a collision between a bus and the rear of a tractor-trailer, the plaintiff bus passengers named as defendants the bus owner, bus driver, tractor owner, tractor driver, and trailer owner. Bus owner crossclaimed against tractor owner, tractor driver, and trailer owner for damage to the bus, alleging that the tractor-trailer was driven at a dangerously low speed; alleging that it had not remained in lane; and alleging that it was not equipped with proper rear lights. Tractor owner and driver, answering the crossclaim, denied their own negligence; alleged contributory negligence on the part of the bus driver, one Schlagenhauf; and further alleged that Schlagenhauf was "not mentally or physically capable" of driving a bus at the time of the accident.

Tractor owner, tractor driver, and trailer owner together moved for an order directing Schlagenhauf to submit to mental and physical examinations by one specialist each in the fields of internal medicine, ophthalmology, neurology, and psychiatry. They accompanied the motion with an affidavit of counsel stating that Schlagenhauf admitted on deposition that he had seen the red lights of the trailer 10 to 15 seconds prior to the collision and yet had driven on without change of speed or course; stating that the only eyewitness testified that he also had been approaching the trailer from the rear and had seen the lights from three-quarters to one-half mile away; and stating that Schlagenhauf also admitted in his deposition that he had been involved in a prior rear-end collision of a similar type.

While the motion was pending, trailer owner answered the crossclaim and included a counterclaim against bus owner and Schlagenhauf for damage to the trailer caused by his negligence when both knew he had defective vision.

The district court granted the requested examinations, and the court of appeals refused to vacate this order upon a petition for mandamus.[q] The denial of mandamus reached the Supreme Court upon its granting Schlagenhauf's petition for certiorari.

After considering the threshold problem whether mandamus was a proper avenue for review and deciding that it was, the Supreme Court dealt with Schlagenhauf's contentions that application of Rule 35 to defendants was a violation of the Rules Enabling Act and an unconstitutional invasion of privacy. (Although no federal court had previously applied Rule 35 to a defendant, how could Schlagenhauf argue that these issues remained open after Sibbach v. Wilson & Co.?) The Court also considered Schlagenhauf's contentions that he was not an opposing party vis-à-vis the discovering parties, that his physical and mental condition was not "in controversy," and that the movants had not shown "good cause."

How should the Court decide the case?

Question: (65) Justice Douglas dissented, with the thought that the Court should refer the problem to the Civil Rules Advisory Committee so that, if the Rule were to be apply to defendants, the rulemakers might make the standards and conditions discriminating and precise. He referred to the need to safeguard "against the awful risks of blackmail." What do you think he meant by "blackmail"? What standards and conditions would you prescribe to safeguard against those "risks"?

The party against whom an order is made has the right upon request to receive from the discovering party a detailed written report of the examination made under Rule 35(a) and also like reports of earlier examinations of the same condition to which the latter may have access.

Questions: (66) If a discovering party delivers these reports, to what does he become entitled? See Rule 35(b)(3) and (4).

(67) Should an examined party hold the right to have her attorney present during the physical or mental examination? See Brandenberg v. El Al Israel Airlines, 79 F.R.D. 543 (S.D.N.Y.1978) (no, with respect to a court-ordered psychiatric examination of Mrs. Brandenberg).

Sanctions for failure to make disclosures or to cooperate in discovery (Rule 37).—We have referred at a number of points to a party's motion under Rule 37(a) for a directive order, that is, an order compelling disclosure or discovery. Note the court to which the party addresses such a motion; the use of the motion to enforce various duties under Rules 26(a), 30, 31, 33, and 34; and the possibilities of securing reimbursement of expenses incurred in making or opposing the motion. Although it may be open to another party or a deponent to seek a protective order under Rule 26(c) in anticipation of an application for a directive order, this is an

[q] Petitioning for the extraordinary remedy of mandamus sometimes functions as a kind of irregular means of securing review of district-court action by the court of appeals. See 28 U.S.C. § 1651 and Topic D of Part Nine.

optional route and is not a condition of that person's resisting and avoiding a directive order.

In general, when the party encounters recalcitrance, he must assume the burden: first, of conferring with the recalcitrant person; second, in case of nonagreement, of going to court to get a directive order; and, third, in case of continued recalcitrance, of going to court to obtain a sanction. Rule 37(b) states the sanctions for refusals to obey such directive orders. But some qualifications are needed here.

As to disclosure, a less elaborate procedure must additionally be available to allow disclosure to work. So, Rule 37(c)(1) provides that a party who without substantial justification fails to make a mandatory disclosure, unless such failure was harmless, is subject to appropriate sanctions, which will usually prohibit use of the undisclosed evidence.

As to discovery, first, Rule 37(d) provides that in certain cases of gross failure of a party to comply with the process for giving discovery, the discovering party need not apply for a directive order but instead may move for a sanction forthwith; and the party from whom discovery is sought cannot excuse his failure on the ground that the discovery sought was objectionable unless he has an already pending motion for a protective order. The gross failures referred to are failure to appear to be deposed, to serve any answers or objections to interrogatories, or to serve any written response to a request for inspection. Consider also the contempt sanction that Rule 45(e) provides for nonparties.

Second, because Rule 35 requires a preliminary court order, Rule 37(a) and (d) has no application. The discovering party may proceed immediately to seek sanctions for disobedience under Rule 37(b), as in the Sibbach case.

Third, as already mentioned, orders and sanctions for failure to make discovery under Rule 36 receive special treatment in Rules 36(a) and 37(c)(2).

Supplementing disclosures and discovery responses (Rule 26(e)).—If a party's disclosures or discovery responses that were actually or presumably correct and complete when given come to be revealed as incorrect or incomplete by reason of later events or newly acquired knowledge, they may seriously mislead other parties who rely upon them. But a full obligation to supplement would be extremely onerous because it would force the disclosing or responding party's lawyer to keep checking for new bits of information and matching them against the prior documents.

Rule 26(e) now deals with the problem, in a way designed to limit the burden on the disclosing or responding party and at the same time to protect the other parties. It provides that the party has a duty to supplement disclosures under Rule 26(a) and responses under Rules 33, 34, and 36 if the party learns that they are in some material respect incomplete or incorrect, unless the other parties are aware of the additional information.

Questions: (68) Apart from any provision by Rule, is an attorney ethically justified in standing silently by and letting answers that the attorney knows are no longer true mislead an opponent? Cf. N.Y. County Lawyers' Ass'n Comm. on

Professional Ethics, Op. 309 (1933), which appears infra p. 287 and which suggests that, although the attorney has an ethical duty of truthfulness, there is no general duty of candor.

(69) What might a federal trial judge appropriately do if a party calls at trial a witness whose identity the party had not revealed despite a Rule 26(e)(1) duty to do so? See Rule 37(c)(1).

(70) Suppose you are counsel in a personal-injury case in which, during the disclosure and discovery phases, you have fully complied with a duty to identify all known witnesses with knowledge of the facts in litigation. When the trial is nearly over, a witness previously unknown to you appears and tells you that she read of the case in the newspaper and that she was an eyewitness to the accident. Her story is favorable to your client's case. What should you do? Suppose instead her story is very unfavorable to your client's case. What, if anything, should you do?

David L. Shapiro, Some Problems of Discovery in an Adversary System

63 Minn.L.Rev. 1055, 1055–58, 1073–75, 1090 (1979).

[I]n a recent article, Professor [now Magistrate Judge] Brazil has argued that the present adversary character of civil discovery systematically encourages obstruction of the goals of discovery and that substantial changes in the pretrial environment must be made if those goals are to be achieved.[3] He would "curtail substantially" the role of the adversary system at the pretrial stage, preserving it in its present form primarily for the "dialectical evaluation of the relevant evidence" at the trial itself.

He may be right. Surely, there is considerable tension between the apparent duty of the lawyer, in response to discovery requests, to reveal information, opinion, and even belief, and the duty and desire of that same lawyer to represent his client zealously and effectively. Perhaps such tension may be found in every corner of litigation, both civil and criminal. But it may well be more acute in the civil arena, where the client is not entitled to stand mute in the dock, and especially in the realm of discovery, where the lawyer may be asked to act as investigator, counselor, advocate, witness, and officer of the court all at the same time.

. . . .

But a drastic change in the nature of litigation of the sort suggested by Professor Brazil would be hard to legislate and even harder to implement. Is it possible, then, that at least some of the difficulty may be due not to

---

[3] Brazil, The Adversary Character of Civil Discovery: A Critique and Proposals for Change, 31 Vand.L.Rev. 1295 (1978). . . . The core of his proposed changes includes shifting the lawyer's obligation before trial away from the client's interest and "toward the court"; imposing a duty on counsel to investigate thoroughly the factual background of disputes; imposing a "duty" on counsel and client to disclose "voluntarily" all relevant information and evidence (how can there be a duty to volunteer?); narrowing the scope of the attorney-client privilege and the work product doctrine; expanding the role of the court in supervising discovery; and requiring "judicial review of, or participation in, all settlements that exceed a specified dollar amount." Id. at 1349.

the inevitability of conflict between the goals of discovery and the nature of the adversary system, but rather to a gap between the theory and practice of discovery? Is it also possible that the present rules . . . do not speak to practitioners and judges with a sufficiently clear voice? If so, there may be hope for reducing the conflict without so thorough an overhaul of the system itself.

[Professor Shapiro surveyed litigators with a questionnaire that included the following hypothetical case:]

1. You represent *A*, executor of *B*, in a Superior Court action for negligence arising out of an automobile accident at a highway intersection in the state. The intersection contained a stop sign at all access roads. *B* died in the accident and *C*, a passenger in the car *B* was driving, stated to you in an interview that *B* did not come to a full stop before entering the intersection. *C* too has since died, from causes unrelated to the accident, and none of the other witnesses you have spoken to claims to have seen *B* enter the intersection. You have no reason to doubt the correctness of *C*'s statement. *D*, the defendant in the action, has alleged contributory negligence as a defense and has submitted the following interrogatory to *A* under Rule 33 of the state rules of civil procedure:

"Did *B* come to a full stop before entering the intersection where the accident in suit occurred?"

What should be the response to this interrogatory?

[Eighty to ninety percent of the respondents said that they would have their client in effect refuse to answer such an interrogatory, most by saying something like: "I do not know." Is such a response proper?]

I think not. In the first place, there is substantial authority for the view that if the party interrogated does not know the answer to a question, he must specify in some detail the effort he has made to find out.[67] Such detail in this case should probably include a reference to *C*'s [inadmissible] statement and its contents, though it might also add that *C* is dead and that other witnesses interviewed were unable to corroborate or refute that statement.

Moreover, failure to disclose information relevant to the question is, in my view, a failure to answer the question. Every interrogatory of this type—which asks directly about the fact and not for information relating to the fact—is in substance a two-part question: (1) what information do you have that relates to this fact? and (2) what is your evaluation of that information? Assuming that the discoveree is unable or for some proper reason unwilling to answer the second part of the question with a clear statement, that should not shield him from answering the first. The purpose of an interrogatory is not simply to determine a party's position with respect to a fact, or to extract an admission, but to get information.

[67] See, e.g., Miller v. Doctor's Gen. Hosp., 76 F.R.D. 136, 140 (W.D.Okla.1977); Cohn v. Dart Industries, Inc., 21 Fed.R.Serv.2d 792, 793 (D.Mass.1976); Breeland v. Bethlehem Steel Co., 179 F.Supp. 464, 467 (S.D.N.Y.1959); 4A Moore's Federal Practice ¶ 33.26, at 33–140 (2d ed. 1979).

Nor should the discoveror be required to break the question down into its components to get that information. The failure to break down into components an interrogatory seeking disclosure of the existence of a fact may result in the discoveror receiving an answer to only the second implicit part when the discoveree is willing to swear to an unqualified "yes" or "no." I do not think it should have this result, however, if the answer falls short of an unqualified response.

The matter was well put in Riley v. United Air Lines, Inc.,[68] where the plaintiff served interrogatories asking the defendant to state in detail how the accident in suit occurred. In holding insufficient the defendant's response that it had "no knowledge sufficient to answer the said interrogatories because all the crew members died in the accident," the court said:

> It is apparent from the opposing affidavit that the defendant has already obtained certain information from third persons relating to some of the interrogatories . . . . In this situation, defendant should furnish whatever information it now has, regardless of when or from whom it acquired it. . . .
>
> Defendant may state in its answers what the source of the information is, if it so desires, [but when] the information has been obtained by persons under defendant's control solely from [questions they have addressed to] third persons, defendant is not required to admit its accuracy. If no one under defendant's control now has any information from any source as to a particular interrogatory, defendant may so state under oath, and such a statement shall be a sufficient answer.

While the suggestion in Riley that the discoveree has no duty to investigate is contrary to my own view as well as to respectable authority,[70] the Riley court's statement of the obligation to disclose information a party does have, regardless of its reliability or credibility, seems eminently sound. The fact that so many respondents to question 1 took a different and less forthcoming approach can perhaps be explained by the failure of rule 33 to make this obligation sufficiently clear. It may also, as Professor Brazil might argue, be attributable to the bias against disclosure inherent in the adversary system. But before that conclusion is reached and its implications explored, the less drastic remedy of writing a clarifying amendment to rule 33 should be considered.

. . . .

One would be hard pressed to deny the tension between the tenets of the adversary system and the goals of pretrial discovery. Certainly it is difficult to square some expansive theories of discovery expressed or implicit in the rules and supported by commentators with the protective attitudes of litigating lawyers.

---

[68] 32 F.R.D. 230 (S.D.N.Y.1962). See, e.g., Coyne v. Monongahela Connecting R.R., 24 F.R.D. 357, 359 (W.D.Pa.1959); Stom v. Pennsylvania R.R., 15 F.R.D. 284, 285 (E.D.Pa.1953).

[70] See note 67 supra and accompanying text.

But tension is not always evil. A system of adjudication single-mindedly dedicated to total pretrial disclosure, or to maximum pretrial secrecy, might be found more wanting than the present uneasy compromise. If things are now more confused than they need to be, it is possible that some clarifying changes in the rules—here in the direction of disclosure and there in the direction of protecting the lawyer in his function as advocate—may improve matters and render unnecessary more drastic remedies.

Question: (71) In the Sierocinski case, would it be improper under the present Rule 11(b) for the plaintiff's lawyer to continue to pursue the case if discovery revealed to him that there had been no good ground to support the complaint?

Using disclosures and discovery products in court proceedings (Rule 32).—The mere presence of, say, a deposition in an attorney's files or even in the court's files does not mean that the court will consider it in deciding the action. Usually the court will ignore a deposition unless a party elects to offer it in evidence. Indeed, the use by the court of a deposition that a party has not introduced into evidence is often improper and may amount to reversible error.

Rule 32 deals with the use by parties of depositions. The big barrier to introducing a deposition at a hearing or trial is the hearsay rule, which as we shall soon see is a rule of evidence that in general renders out-of-court statements inadmissible and thus would tend to exclude all depositions. So Rule 32(a) lists a series of circumstances—such as some situations when the deponent is presently unavailable to testify—in which the hearsay rule should not apply to exclude a deposition simply because it embodies out-of-court statements. In those circumstances, a party may use a deposition so far as admissible under the rules of evidence applied as though the deponent were then present and testifying.

Questions: (72) Rule 32(a)(4)(E) overrides the hearsay rule if the court finds "exceptional circumstances," but in making its finding the court is to give due regard to the importance of presenting witnesses' testimony orally in open court. See also Rule 43(a). Why the preference for live testimony? See John Leubsdorf, Presuppositions of Evidence Law, 91 Iowa L.Rev. 1209, 1234–44 (2006).

(73) What explains the special treatment in Rule 32(a)(3) of the deposition of a party?

Rule 32 regulates the use in court proceedings only of depositions, and it exists mainly to facilitate admission of these rather formal records of testimony. What about the use in court proceedings of disclosures and the products of other discovery methods—answers to interrogatories, documents, etc.? In general, it is correct to say simply that a party may use these items so far as admissible under all the usual rules of evidence. See, e.g., Rule 33(c). Thus, the plaintiff in the Freed case below could introduce at trial the defendant's answer to an interrogatory under the rule that relevant out-of-court statements by the party-opponent are admissible in evidence, as we shall soon explain.

Freed v. Erie Lackawanna Railway Co.

United States Court of Appeals, Sixth Circuit, 1971.
445 F.2d 619, cert. denied, 404 U.S. 1017, 92 S.Ct. 678 (1972).

■ Before PECK, BROOKS and KENT, CIRCUIT JUDGES.

■ BROOKS, CIRCUIT JUDGE. Plaintiff-appellant, Floyd W. Freed, III, brought this action under the Federal Employers' Liability Act against defendant-appellee, Erie Lackawanna Railway Company, for personal injuries sustained when he was struck by a train. This appeal follows a jury verdict for the defendant [in 1969].

At the time plaintiff was injured, he was the head brakeman on a freight train running from Cleveland to Youngstown, Ohio. The accident occurred in the North Randall switching area where there were numerous sets of tracks and switching operations were frequent. The plaintiff and the fireman, a fellow crewman, had just dropped off their train and had started walking down a right-of-way adjacent to a side track on their way to lunch when plaintiff was struck by a caboose, which was the lead car of a switching train that was slowly backing in performance of its switching assignment. Seconds before getting in the path of the train, plaintiff's attention was diverted when the fireman turned and called to the engineer of the freight train to throw him his cigarettes which he had forgotten and left in the cab of the locomotive.

The principal issue raised by plaintiff on appeal is whether an answer made by the defendant to an interrogatory is binding on it although contradicted by other evidence adduced by the defendant. In response to one of plaintiff's interrogatories, defendant stated that the location of the switch train at the time of the accident was not within the yard limits. A train that is not within yard limits was subject to road rule Number 103 which requires cars being pushed by engines in an area outside the yard limits to have a lookout posted on the lead car. There was no such lookout on the car of the switch train that injured the plaintiff. At trial the defendant produced testimony that the switch train was actually operating within the yard limits and, therefore, no lookout on the lead car was required, thus contradicting the answer given in the interrogatory as to the location of the train at the time of the accident.

While the jury was deliberating, the jury foreman submitted a question to the court asking if the switch train was within the yard limits at the time of the accident. The court declined to answer the question on the grounds that it involved a question of fact which it was the duty of the jury to resolve. Plaintiff argues that the answer to the interrogatory, when introduced in evidence, was . . . binding on the defendant, and therefore the court should have answered the jury's question in accordance with the answer given in the interrogatory. . . . As stated in Victory Carriers, Inc. v. Stockton Stevedoring Company, [388 F.2d 955 (9th Cir.1968)]:

> "An answer to an interrogatory is comparable to answers, which may be mistaken, given in deposition testimony or during the course of the trial itself. Answers to interrogatories must often be supplied before investigation is completed and can rest only upon knowledge which is available at the time. When there is conflict between answers supplied in response to interrogatories and answers obtained through other questioning, either in deposition or trial, the finder of fact must weigh all of the answers and resolve the conflict."

The court properly declined to answer the question dealing with the location of the switch train at the time of the accident.

. . . .

Affirmed.

■ [The concurring opinion of JUDGE PECK is omitted.]

Questions: (74) Would the result in the Freed case have been different given Rule 26(e)(1), which was added in 1970 and amended in 1993? Assume that the defendant had discovered the error and chose not to supplement, but then at trial tried to contradict its discovery response.

(75) Would the decision in the Freed case have been different if the plaintiff had utilized Rule 36 rather than Rule 33? Assume that the defendant had admitted the point, and then at trial tried to contradict it.

General problems.—Gradually the bar came generally to accept discovery on the broad scale envisaged by the Federal Rules, but not universally and not without some lingering doubts and second thoughts. Thus, some critics of discovery have suggested that compliant or unscrupulous witnesses, having gone through the informing experience of testifying on deposition, or having learned about the results of other discovery, can contrive to manipulate their stories to meet all exigencies when they finally testify at trial. Some view "surprise" at trial—at least up to a point—as a promoter of truth rather than the opposite.

Apart from that dispute over the value of discovery, there is the risk of discovery abuse and recalcitrance. Thus, for example, all would agree that if carried on without decent restraint, discovery could give wealthy litigants excellent opportunities to browbeat their weaker adversaries. Lawyers can make discovery very expensive, or embarrassing. And, of course, the oppressive sword of discovery cuts both ways. Plaintiffs may use nuisance suits to extort unjust settlements from wealthy litigants, who realize it is sometimes cheaper to buy off opponents than to defend. Empirical surveys have tended to indicate that discovery has generally kept within reasonable bounds of expense. The typical case sees little discovery. But the possibility that a party will attempt through discovery to price a lawsuit out of the market for his adversary—and might succeed despite the protections offered by such provisions as Rule 26(c)—must be real in many cases.

Added to these truth and fairness costs are simple laments over the time and expense consumed even by proper discovery, especially in those occasional cases where that consumption mounts to almost unimaginable heights. Ultimately, one could argue, albeit without real empirical support, that together all these different kinds of costs outweigh any benefits of discovery. At the least, no one could deny that the system must make an effort to lower those costs.

During the 1970s these complaints about the burdens of discovery grew more intense. Various proposals to limit and control discovery circulated. In response, the Supreme Court in 1980 and 1983 adopted a series of amendments to the discovery Rules, changes that were relatively modest but may have succeeded in changing emphasis and the resultant atmosphere. See the section of the Rules booklet containing those amendments and the Advisory Committee's notes thereon. Innovations such as Rule 26(b)(2)(C) should to some degree facilitate a more active but selective case-by-case supervision of discovery by the court—such supervision (despite its serious shortcomings) being the most effective of feasible remedies for discovery abuse, and explicit amendments to the Rules arguably being necessary to overcome longstanding judicial reluctance to use existing powers of control.

In 1993, however, the Supreme Court made significant Rule amendments, the most dramatic of which was the addition of the disclosure requirements in Rule 26(a). Because the notion of lessening the burdens of discovery by overlaying a whole new system of mandatory disclosure is, at least on first impression, bizarre, the result was torrid controversy.

Question: (76) In dissenting from the promulgation of the disclosure Rules, Justice Scalia's big argument was the increase in direct costs that would accompany this new system of disclosure. See Order of April 22, 1993, 507 U.S. 1089, 1099. Moreover, the reform would impose these costs even in the majority of cases where there was currently no discovery or at least no real dispute over discovery, and also in the many cases where disclosure currently occurred on a voluntary basis between cooperative lawyers. Meanwhile, the costs of the discovery system itself would largely persist. How could the rulemakers have responded to this argument? See the 1993 Advisory Committee's note on Rule 26(a) in the Rules booklet.

Unsurprisingly, the controversy surrounding the disclosure and discovery provisions did not end with the 1993 changes. A new round of amendments became effective in 2000, making several changes aimed at achieving cost reduction: the rulemakers sharply reduced the scope of initial disclosures in recognition of that provision's ineffectiveness, so that the disclosing party now has to initially disclose only *favorable* witnesses, documents, and things; the usual scope of discovery, which had been information relevant to the subject matter, now became information relevant to claims and defenses only; and a presumptive one-day limit came to apply to depositions. In 2006, the rulemakers moved to control the fire ignited by the astounding upswing in e-discovery. See the section of the

Rules booklet containing those amendments and the Advisory Committee's notes thereon. One must still wonder whether this tinkering with the Rules will have the desired effects.

In addition, a basic controversy remains that is as old as the Federal Rules themselves: whether downplayed pleading with the consequently broad scope of discovery is the best allocation of issue-narrowing and fact-alleging functions, or whether the barriers at the pleading stage should be higher even than those Twombly has erected. One academic has pointed out that, "[w]hether we like it or not, whether we admit it or not, the harsher reality is that procedural rules allocate power and advantage. . . . It is no secret that the anti-discovery pressure has come from defendants, especially defendants in product liability, securities, and antitrust cases." Elizabeth G. Thornburg, Giving the "Haves" a Little More: Considering the 1998 Discovery Proposals, 52 SMU L.Rev. 229, 230, 243 (1999). Can the rulemakers allocate functions between the pleading stage and the discovery stage in a value-neutral way? Indeed, should they?

(g) PRETRIAL CONFERENCES

[Rule 16]

Playing in with pleadings and with disclosure and discovery—serving some of the same functions and also having the distinct missions of *propelling* and *focusing* the case—are the pretrial conferences under Rule 16. Note the objectives and range of this procedure as given in Rule 16(a) and (c).

The original Rule 16 was a brief and relatively simple Rule. Practice thereunder, although highly variable in response to obvious tensions of policy, was generally rather *informal, uncomplicated, noncoercive, and nonbinding*. See McCargo v. Hedrick, 545 F.2d 393 (4th Cir.1976). The court could call the attorneys for a talk and typically would do so once late in the litigation to consider with them what the points in controversy were and how together they might facilitate the trial of the action.

In 1983, however, the rulemakers rewrote Rule 16 in expansive form, certainly changing the tone thereof if not the practice thereunder. Case management by the judge from the institution of suit was the new emphasis, motivated by the "widespread feeling" that modern litigation demanded a move in that direction. See the lengthy 1983 Advisory Committee's note on the amended Rule in the Rules booklet. The empirical and theoretical bases for this change were, respectively, quite scanty and disputed. Moreover, it was not clear that such detailed rulemaking, rather than some form of more tentative and flexible experimentation, was the most desirable route to reform. Yet in 1993, the rulemakers chose to make Rule 16 even more detailed.

The initial step in the current procedure is the scheduling order of Rule 16(b). In most cases, within about one hundred days of commencement, the court *must* after consultation fix time limits for settling pleadings, filing motions, and completing discovery. In actuality, however, the court often finds a way not to do so.

Then there *may* be one or more pretrial conferences. (Indeed, a scheduling conference may have preceded the scheduling order under Rule 16(b).) The court may hold one or more pretrial conferences relatively early in the litigation to address some of the pretrial concerns listed in Rule 16(c). A final pretrial conference, which can be especially useful when the parties have obtained substantial discovery, may occur shortly before trial to formulate a plan for trial, as prescribed in Rule 16(e). The use of the pretrial conference is optional with the court.

The actual practice varies from district to district. In some districts the judges hold a conference in each case, in other districts they confine conferences to selected cases, and in still others they resort to Rule 16 perfunctorily if at all.

The degree to which particular judges actively employ the pretrial conference also varies considerably. It depends not only upon the temperaments of the judges but also upon their views of what their role is or should be in the litigation process.

The use of the pretrial conference likewise varies from case to case. A small, simple case may not warrant the expense and effort entailed in a conference. In an average case there might be a single, "final" pretrial conference. And in large or complex litigation, such as antitrust cases and class actions, judges find extensive use of conferences nearly indispensable. (The Manual for Complex Litigation gives elaborate advice about how to employ multiple conferences at intervals to elucidate the issues, organize and control discovery, and otherwise prepare the "big case" for trial. More generally, that semi-official Manual, which is the product of the drafting and revising efforts of a committee of judges over the last few decades, serves as a tracking mechanism by suggesting specialized guidelines for handling complex actions.)

If held, a pretrial conference culminates in an order that, according to Rule 16(d) and (e), controls the subsequent course of the action unless modified. The order may articulate in a convenient and helpful way the remaining controverted issues. Even though the order does not in terms amend the pleadings (as it may do), in practice the order has the effect of superseding the pleadings. And because the order is binding on the parties, they need not offer evidence at the trial to prove a proposition established in the order, nor will the court admit contrary evidence.

Question: (77) Should the court permit a party to offer evidence on a proposition established in her favor in the pretrial order? Why might she want to do so?

Finally, Rule 16(f) expressly provides for sanctions that the court might impose for certain violations of the Rule.

In summary, the changes from the original to the current Rule 16 are massive, but still the practice remains variegated. To the extent any generalizations are meaningful, what can we say about how *informal, uncomplicated, noncoercive, and nonbinding* today's pretrial conferences remain? Not too much.

First, as a marker of informality, consider whether courts should hold pretrial conferences in chambers or in open court, and off the record or on a record taken down by some means. The fact is that there is still no consensus on such practices.

Second, although Rule 16 does not in terms provide for it, most courts now require the attorneys for both sides to meet prior to a pretrial conference and to agree if possible upon a joint pretrial statement, or to file separate pretrial statements indicating their respective positions. Many districts have complicated local rules on this subject, some of which at least literally require fairly extensive and detailed preparation by counsel. (More generally, throughout the phases of a lawsuit, counsel must keep a sharp eye on local rules, which are often surprisingly and unfortunately voluminous, restrictive, and demanding.)

Third, Rule 16 does not well specify the appropriate coerciveness of a pretrial conference, and so the result is considerable disagreement. For example, judges differ in their views about the propriety and wisdom of introducing the subject of settlement or urging it on the parties. Perhaps settlement talk should arise, if at all, only as a natural by-product of a businesslike pretrial conference aimed at shaping the litigation. Or perhaps judges should take an active role in pushing for settlement. There has in fact been a wide range of judicial practice regarding settlement, but in recent decades there has been a noticeable shift toward activism. Since 1983, Rule 16(a)(5) and (c)(2)(I) expressly mentions settlement and the note thereon even suggests the possibility of a settlement conference. The amended Rule's emphasis would only accelerate that shift toward activism. The following case explores the appropriate limits on activism.

Identiseal Corp. v. Positive Identification Systems, Inc.

United States Court of Appeals, Seventh Circuit, 1977.
560 F.2d 298.

■ Before SWYGERT and BAUER, CIRCUIT JUDGES, and JAMESON, SENIOR DISTRICT JUDGE.[1]

■ SWYGERT, CIRCUIT JUDGE. The outcome of this appeal turns on whether the district court, in presiding over the pretrial phase of the case, had the power to compel plaintiff to conduct discovery instead of permitting it to litigate the entire suit at trial. We conclude that the district court lacked the authority to compel involuntary discovery and we reverse the court's order dismissing the complaint.

. . . .

---

[1] The Honorable William J. Jameson, Senior District Judge for the District of Montana, is sitting by designation.

On April 26, 1973, plaintiff Identiseal Corporation of Wisconsin filed a complaint against defendant Positive Identification Systems, Inc. in the district court for the Eastern District of Wisconsin. The complaint charged that defendant induced plaintiff to enter into a franchising agreement for the sale of a product known as "Identiseal"; that defendant represented to plaintiff that defendant was successful in the promotion of its products, causing plaintiff to invest $15,000 in defendant's products; and that in fact defendant was not successful in the promotion of its products. Plaintiff sought relief under a common law theory of misrepresentation and under Wisconsin statutes relating to franchising. Jurisdiction was based on diversity of citizenship.

After a delay caused by the death of plaintiff's attorney, the litigation proceeded and a final pretrial conference was held on February 26, 1976. On March 8, 1976, the district court issued an order in which it concluded "that the pretrial work necessary to efficiently try this action had not been done." It ordered that the action be dismissed for want of prosecution, but stayed the order until June 4, 1976 and stated that the order would be vacated if plaintiff's counsel had conducted specified discovery . . . by that date.[2]

. . . Plaintiff's counsel [subsequently argued to no avail] that he had "made a considered judgment that discovery would in no way be beneficial to the plaintiff's interest and would at most be of some significant support or assistance to the defendant." He also asserted that the court had exceeded its authority under the Federal Rules of Civil Procedure in ordering plaintiff to conduct discovery or suffer dismissal of the complaint.

[Pursuant to the March 8 order the district court ultimately dismissed the action without prejudice, and the plaintiff appealed. The defendant had not moved for the March 8 order, but was willing to ride that order to judgment rather than pursue its own discovery.]

Discovery in lawsuits in the federal courts is governed by Rules 26 to 37 of the Federal Rules of Civil Procedure. Although these rules provide for judicial intervention to settle disputes about the scope of discovery and to enforce a legitimate request by one party for information or documents from the other party, they do not give district judges the authority to compel a litigant to engage in discovery in the first place.

---

[2] The court held that its order of dismissal would be vacated if plaintiff's counsel satisfied the following conditions:

1. Counsel shall, by means of discovery such as written interrogatories, requests for production of documents, or requests for admissions, ascertain the identity of those persons who have knowledge of the facts relevant or material to the issues of this action and those documents containing information relevant or material to the issues of this action.

2. Counsel shall then, by means of further discovery such as oral depositions or deposition on written questions, determine the actual knowledge of such persons disclosed as having knowledge of the facts. Counsel shall also, by means of requests for production of documents or requests for admissions, obtain copies of relevant documents not already within their possession.

. . . .

Therefore, the district court's March 8 order can only be upheld if the court had the power, under its general authority over the pretrial phase of a lawsuit, to compel plaintiff to conduct discovery. Pretrial procedure in the district courts is governed by Fed.R.Civ.P. 16, which states in relevant part that "the court may in its discretion direct the attorneys for the parties to appear before it for a conference to consider . . . [t]he possibility of obtaining admissions of fact and of documents which will avoid unnecessary proof." Under the rule, "the court has wide discretion and power to advance the cause and simplify the procedure before the cause is presented to the jury." O'Malley v. Chrysler Corp., 160 F.2d 35, 36 (7th Cir.1947).

This discretion, however, is not unlimited. The language of the rule does not, by its terms, confer upon the court the power to *compel* the litigants to obtain admissions of fact and of documents even if it is clear that such admissions would simplify the trial of the case. Instead, the rule requires the parties to appear and *consider the possibility* of admissions which would lessen their task at trial.

We have recently decided a case in which we made clear that there are limitations on the district court's power at the pretrial conference. In J.F. Edwards Construction Co. v. Anderson Safeway Guard Rail Corp., 542 F.2d 1318 (7th Cir.1976) (per curiam), we held that a district court lacks the authority under Rule 16 to dismiss an action because one of the parties would not agree to a stipulation of facts. We noted that Rule 16 was noncoercive in nature, and we concluded that a dismissal based on a party's refusal to follow the trial judge's wishes expressed at the pretrial conference could only be upheld if that refusal could be characterized as a "failure to prosecute." Because the party that would not agree to the stipulation of facts was clearly not attempting to avoid trial, the district court's order could not stand.

In our judgment this appeal is controlled by J.F. Edwards. Like the appellant in J.F. Edwards, plaintiff in the case at bar did not engage in conduct that could be characterized as a failure to prosecute. Plaintiff was ready to go to trial, and simply disagreed with the district court about the desirability of eliminating the need to develop all of the facts at trial. Although we recognize that its order was based on a commendable desire to simplify the lawsuit, the court had no more authority under Rule 16 to command discovery than the district court in J.F. Edwards had to require a stipulation of facts. The limit of the court's power was to compel plaintiff to consider the possibility of conducting discovery,[7] and there is no evidence in the record that plaintiff's attorney rejected the district court's preferred method of litigating the action without giving it serious consideration.

Our decision is predicated on more than the absence of express authority in Rule 16 authorizing compulsory discovery. It is also based on the traditional principle that the parties, rather than the court, should determine litigation strategy. See Chayes, The Role of the Judge in Public

[7] We note that our resolution of this issue is in conflict with the Third Circuit's decision in Buffington v. Wood, 351 F.2d 292 (3d Cir.1965). . . .

Law Litigation, 89 Harv.L.Rev. 1281, 1283 (1976); Developments in the Law—Class Actions, 89 Harv.L.Rev. 1318, 1414 (1976). It was the judgment of plaintiff's attorney that his client's chances of prevailing would be maximized if he did not conduct discovery but instead developed his entire case at trial. We cannot say whether this decision was correct. We can say, however, that the decision was for plaintiff's attorney, and not the district court, to make.

The judgment of the district court is reversed and the cause is remanded for further proceedings consistent with this opinion.

Questions: (78) Is Identiseal still good law under amended Rule 16? Is J.F. Edwards? Compare Strandell v. Jackson County, Ill., 838 F.2d 884 (7th Cir.1987) (in holding that Rule 16 does not permit district judge to compel a nonbinding summary jury trial as a pretrial device for encouraging settlement, the Seventh Circuit relied on Identiseal and J.F. Edwards), with G. Heileman Brewing Co. v. Joseph Oat Corp., 871 F.2d 648 (7th Cir.1989) (6–5 en banc decision) (while acknowledging Identiseal and J.F. Edwards, the Seventh Circuit held that district court has inherent power to order represented litigant itself to attend settlement conference). Are Identiseal and J.F. Edwards still good law despite other Rule amendments, such as the continuing obligation under amended Rule 11 to make reasonable inquiry into the facts?

(79) Can a question of propriety ever arise as to whether the pretrial judge should preside at the trial? For context, you should be aware that the now prevailing "individual assignment system" randomly assigns a case to a federal judge for all purposes; thus as a usual matter under the typical local scheme, the same judge will sit in pretrial and at trial, unless that judge decides that it would be proper to delegate a pretrial task to a parajudge or shift the case itself to another judge.

Fourth, as to bindingness, there is the usual tension between freezing things and allowing amendments. The following case considers whether to modify what was the final pretrial order.

SHUBER v. S.S. KRESGE CO., 458 F.2d 1058 (3d Cir.1972), aff'g, 55 F.R.D. 52 (W.D.Pa.1970). Wife-plaintiff brought a diversity action against Kresge in federal court for personal injuries, in which her husband joined with a claim for her medical expenses and the loss of her services. The theory of recovery was that defendant had been negligent in installing or having installed a light fixture that fell upon wife-plaintiff while she was working for an independent concessionaire in defendant's store in 1965. As required by the local rule for pretrial procedure, plaintiffs set forth this theory in a narrative pretrial statement and also listed therein "plaintiff" (not "plaintiffs") as a witness on the issue of liability. There was no indication that husband-plaintiff, an electrician by trade, was to testify concerning the fixture.

At trial around the beginning of 1970, plaintiffs' evidence, including wife-plaintiff's testimony, pointed to the contention that the fixture had been negligently installed by an electrical subcontractor to the construction company employed by Kresge's landlord. But the evidence failed to connect Kresge with the negligence. Kresge moved for judgment as a matter of law at the close of plaintiffs' case. After argument on the motion, plaintiffs moved for leave to reopen to call a witness not listed in the pretrial statement. Their counsel announced that he intended to call husband-plaintiff to testify that Kresge itself installed the ceiling tiles and, in doing so, disconnected the light fixtures and reinstalled them negligently. Defendant objected to the complete change of the theory of liability. Wife-plaintiff had testified on deposition that her husband had no knowledge of the facts of the accident, and he had been present throughout the trial without any suggestion that he had such evidence to offer.

The trial judge referred to the statement in Washington Hospital Center v. Cheeks, 394 F.2d 964, 965 (D.C.Cir.1968) (Burger, J., who became U.S. Chief Justice in 1969), that liberal modification of pretrial orders encourages careless preparation but that an unbending attitude may work grave injustice. In that case, a medical malpractice action against a hospital, the testimony as to causation on defendant's cross-examination of plaintiff's attending physician genuinely surprised plaintiff's counsel, who sought leave the next day to offer an expert medical witness not on the pretrial list. The district court modified the final pretrial order and let the expert testify the following day, first giving defendant a chance to depose him. Defendant did not request a longer continuance or mistrial, but took the deposition and sought only to exclude the new testimony. The expert's testimony supported plaintiff's claim, and verdict and judgment were for plaintiff. The Court of Appeals for the District of Columbia Circuit held that there had been no abuse of discretion by the district judge, who was in a superior position to evaluate the situation.

Nevertheless, the trial judge here refused to allow the Shubers to reopen their case and granted defendant's motion for judgment, saying that the "Court has an interest to support the integrity of its pretrial procedures. The Pretrial Order in the case binds and limits the parties to what they have presented and revealed in their Pretrial Narratives and at the Pretrial Conference. Neither at the Pretrial Conference, nor in the trial was this new line of evidence suggested. We must either require adherence to our Pretrial Rules or abandon them utterly in this case. We think that the interests of the efficient administration of justice require their enforcement."

The Court of Appeals for the Third Circuit affirmed, expressing itself as thoroughly in accord with the trial judge's quoted statement. The court of appeals commented that counsel's inadequate prosecution of his clients' cause "would appear to be in violation of the Code of Professional Responsibility of the American Bar Association requiring a lawyer to represent his client competently and zealously within the bounds of the law."

Question: (80) A complaint alleged that *P* and *D* had entered into an oral partnership to sell certain oil-well drilling equipment on commission, that they were to divide equally any commission, and that *D* had received a commission of over $39,000 but had paid *P* only $3000. The answer denied any partnership, and stated that *P* had demanded a portion of the commission for services performed in the sale and that *D* had paid *P* $3000 in full settlement of *P*'s claim. The final pretrial order included agreement as to the amount of the commission and the amount paid to *P*, and it recited that the only matter of controversy for determination by the jury was whether a partnership existed. At trial the judge charged the jury on the question of partnership without any objection, but at the end of the charge the judge refused a request to instruct on the issue of compromise settlement on the ground that it was not within the pretrial order. Should the appellate court sustain *D*'s appeal from this refusal? See Case v. Abrams, 352 F.2d 193 (10th Cir.1965) (no). Should it matter that *D*'s proof in support of the compromise settlement had been admitted without objection? Of what relevance is Rule 15(b)(2)? See Monod v. Futura, Inc., 415 F.2d 1170 (10th Cir.1969) (suggesting that Rule 15(b)(2) applies by analogy, if amender makes adequate showing of issue's trial by consent).

MAGISTRATE JUDGES AND MASTERS

Rule 16(c) mentions the two principal kinds of parajudges in the federal system.

Congress created the corps of magistrates in 1968 and has since expanded their jurisdiction several times. See 28 U.S.C. § 636 and Rules 72 and 73. Magistrate judges are salaried judicial officers appointed for a term, a number being appointed for each district by the district judges of that district. They number more than 500 nationwide. In addition to a good deal of criminal work, magistrate judges exercise the following civil jurisdiction:

1. a district judge may designate a magistrate judge to hear and determine any so-called nondispositive pretrial matter, examples being discovery disputes and pretrial conferences; the district judge will consider any party's objections to the magistrate judge's determination, setting aside any portion shown to be clearly erroneous or to be contrary to law;

2. a district judge may designate a magistrate judge to conduct hearings, make proposed findings of fact when appropriate, and recommend disposition with respect to a so-called dispositive pretrial matter, an example being a motion for summary judgment; the district judge must make a de novo determination (upon the record or after additional evidence) on those portions of the magistrate judge's findings and recommendation that any party objects to;

3. a district judge may designate a magistrate judge to serve as a special master, a role explained below;

4. upon consent of all the parties, the court clerk may refer to a specially designated magistrate judge all proceedings in any case, including trial of a jury or nonjury case and entry of judgment; appeal

from the magistrate judge's judgment goes to the appropriate court of appeals; and

5. district judges may assign to a magistrate judge "such additional duties as are not inconsistent with the Constitution and laws of the United States."

Although this procedural innovation has enjoyed heavy use and proved generally successful, the broad extent of the magistrate judges' jurisdiction raises some unsettled constitutional questions of due process and separation of powers. See generally Tim A. Baker, The Expanding Role of Magistrate Judges in the Federal Courts, 39 Val.U.L.Rev. 661 (2005).

The use of masters has ancient roots, and Rule 53 continues to authorize that use while limiting and regulating it. Today the only kind of master is what was formerly called a special master, i.e., someone specially appointed by the district judge to help handle a particular action. The judge supposedly can appoint a master only upon the parties' consent or in complicated cases where there is exceptional need, and the master must assist rather than displace the judge. The judge gives the master specific assignments, traditionally most often involving ascertainment of facts in nonjury cases but today also involving an impressive range of pretrial and post-trial tasks. Ultimately, the master files a report with the judge, and the master's factual findings as well as his legal conclusions are normally subject to de novo review by the judge. The master's compensation, fixed by the judge, falls on the parties upon terms directed by the judge. See generally Wayne D. Brazil, Special Masters in Complex Cases: Extending the Judiciary or Reshaping Adjudication?, 53 U.Chi.L.Rev. 394 (1986).

(h) DEVICES FOR TERMINATING LITIGATION WITHOUT TRIAL

[Rules 12(c), 56]

We have already seen a number of ways in which a case may terminate short of trial. For example, if defendant presents by motion under Rule 12(b)(6) the defense that the complaint fails to state a claim, and the court grants the motion, and plaintiff does not thereafter amend the complaint, then the case is ripe for a judgment for defendant.

Question: (81) In what other ways may a case terminate short of trial? See Rules 41 and 55.

Motion for judgment on the pleadings.—We call attention now to another device that may conclude the case without trial. Rule 12(c) provides for a motion for judgment on the pleadings. A party can make this motion after the pleadings are closed, and it asserts that upon the pleadings the moving party is entitled to judgment in his favor. In deciding it, the court can resolve only questions of law, never disputes as to facts.

Suppose the complaint adequately alleges a claim, and the answer admits the allegations of the complaint but sets up two purported affirmative defenses. If one but not both of the defenses is insufficient as a matter of law, a timely motion by plaintiff lies under Rule 12(f) to strike that defense; the court's grant of that motion will eliminate the insufficient defense, but the case will then stand for trial on the other defense. If, however, both defenses are insufficient as matters of law, plaintiff may move for judgment on the pleadings.

For purposes of the Rule 12(c) motion, the moving party admits his adversary's allegations, but his own allegations stand as true only if his adversary's pleading has admitted them. Thus, in the example last given, if defendant, besides setting up the two insufficient defenses, had denied in her answer material allegations of the complaint, the court would have had to deny plaintiff's motion for judgment on the pleadings, although it would grant a motion under Rule 12(f) to strike the affirmative defenses.

A motion by defendant for judgment on the pleadings ordinarily challenges the sufficiency of the complaint only, just as does a motion under Rule 12(b)(6). It takes on no added strength by reason of one or more affirmative defenses in the answer. For, as we have seen, the allegations of such defenses are taken as denied or avoided under Rule 8(b)(6).

Questions: (82) *P* files a complaint attempting to allege defamation. *D* answers, admitting *P*'s factual allegations as to the statement in question and attempting to assert the defense of immunity on the ground that the statement was pertinently uttered in the course of judicial proceedings. *D* moves for judgment on the pleadings. What are the facts for purposes of the motion? What legal issues does the motion raise? *P* also moves for judgment on the pleadings at the same point. What are the facts for purposes of this motion? What legal issues does this motion raise?

(83) Suppose that, instead of admitting *P*'s factual allegations, *D* denies them and also attempts to assert the defense of immunity. *D*'s motion is unaffected. But what relief can *P* get if the immunity defense is insufficient as a matter of law? In what manner may *P* pursue that relief? Does it matter how much time has elapsed since service of *D*'s answer?

Motion for summary judgment.—The motion for judgment on the pleadings is available where a pleading is legally insufficient. But must there necessarily be a trial whenever the pleadings show a disputed issue of fact, either by an actual denial of an adversary's allegation or through the operation of Rule 8(b)(6)?

If so, the system could not deliver the "just, speedy, and inexpensive determination of every action" set forth as the ideal in Rule 1. In certain district courts, the trial list for civil cases is in such a congested condition that the median lapse of time between the filing of an answer and a trial on the merits is over two years. A defendant against whom the plaintiff has asserted a just claim is likely to want to put off the day of reckoning as long as possible: there is thus a temptation, despite Rule 11, to file an answer with denials or affirmative defenses for purposes of delay, even though the defendant knows that certain defeat awaits at the trial. Similarly, a plaintiff may assert a baseless claim in vain hope or in order to harass.

To prevent such behavior, Rule 56 on "summary judgment" provides a means of going behind the pleadings to see whether there really is a genuine dispute as to any material fact. If there is not, there is no occasion for a trial, and so the case is ripe for a successful motion for summary judgment. Such a motion may be filed by either a plaintiff or a defendant in any type of case. The motion may be made even before the pleadings are closed, but ordinarily only until thirty days after the close of all discovery. On a summary judgment motion, the movant maintains that there is no genuine issue of material fact and that, upon resolution of any disputed questions of law, he is entitled to judgment.

The court may grant a summary judgment on the entire case or on only a part of it. For example, the court may grant summary judgment on the issue of liability alone, although a genuine dispute on the amount of damages remains. Furthermore, upon motion for summary judgment the court may specify that certain facts are not genuinely at issue, thus narrowing the issues for trial in a way somewhat similar to the pretrial procedure under Rule 16.

Ordinarily the movant will accompany the motion with affidavits (of the movant or of others) in support of the contention that there is no genuine dispute over fact. The affidavits may incorporate exhibits; the affidavits must be on the personal knowledge of the affiants; and the contents of the affidavits must be such as would be admissible in evidence. The opposing party may file like counter-affidavits. On the motion the court will also consider the pleadings—and normally will consider depositions, answers to interrogatories, documents, admissions, and similar material on file, to the extent they represent admissible evidence.

Question: (84) Recall that Rule 32(a)(1) speaks of the use of a deposition not only at trial, but also upon the hearing of a motion. Can the court apply Rule 32 according to its terms when it uses depositions upon a motion for summary judgment under Rule 56(c)? (You should renew this question after reading the next case.)

If the movant's affidavits convincingly maintain that there is no genuine factual dispute but the opponent then contests that point, the judge faces a subtlety. This subtlety has generated the following standard of decision: the judge can agree with the movant that no genuine issue exists as to a particular factual matter only if a reasonable trier of fact could not find for the opponent on that matter.

Under this standard of decision, in a medical malpractice case where the plaintiff is contending that under the law the claim accrued on the date of discovery of the harm and the defendant is contending that it accrued on the date of the surgery, a defendant could obtain summary judgment on a statute-of-limitations defense if the judge decides that legally the time of accrual is the date of the surgery and if, given the detailed affidavits for the defendant and given the plaintiff's lack of any statement as to the date of surgery, a trier could not reasonably find that the operation took place within the thirty-month statutory limitations period preceding the action's commencement.

Bear in mind, however, that a motion for summary judgment is not a means of trying questions of fact upon conflicting affidavits. The function of the court on this motion is to determine whether there is a genuine factual dispute, not to resolve a genuine factual dispute found to exist. Hence, if on the motion the judge encounters a genuine factual dispute, he must deny the motion even though he has strong ground for the belief that one set of affidavits is true and the other false.

Thus, the defendant in the medical malpractice case could not obtain summary judgment on a statute-of-limitations defense if under the law the time of accrual was the date of the discovery of the harm and if, given conflicting affidavits, a trier operating within the outer bounds of reason could go either way on whether that discovery date came within the thirty-month statutory limitations period preceding the action's commencement. Likewise, the plaintiff could not obtain summary judgment.

Question: (85) May a judge ever grant summary judgment when the case is of a type in which trial by jury is constitutionally guaranteed and proper demand for a jury has been made?

American Airlines v. Ulen

United States Court of Appeals, District of Columbia Circuit, 1949.
186 F.2d 529.

■ Before [BENNETT] CLARK, WILBUR K. MILLER, and PRETTYMAN, JUDGES.

■ CLARK, JUDGE. Appellant, American Airlines, Inc., a certified carrier engaged in the business of transporting passengers for hire, separately appeals from two final judgments of the District Court. The appeal in No. 9921 attacks the judgment based upon a jury verdict for $25,000 in favor of appellee, Violet Ulen, for personal injuries and property damage. The appeal in No. 9922 was taken from a judgment based on a jury verdict for $2,500 in favor of appellee, Francis Graeme Ulen, husband of Violet Ulen, for medical and other expenses resulting from his wife's injuries and for loss of her services. These two appeals were consolidated for the purpose of filing briefs and for hearing and decision by order of this court dated July 24, 1948. Accordingly, this opinion shall dispose of both appeals.

At about midnight on February 22–23, 1945, Violet Ulen boarded appellant's plane at Washington National Airport with a ticket entitling her to transportation to Mexico City, Mexico. The plane took off from Washington at 12:15 A.M. on February 23, 1945. At approximately 2:25 A.M. that morning, appellant's plane, with Violet Ulen aboard, crashed close to the summit of Glade Mountain near the town of Rural Retreat in Southwest Virginia. The crash, in which both the pilot and the co-pilot of the plane lost their lives, resulted, admittedly, in very serious and aggravated injury to Violet Ulen and in her permanent partial disability.

On January 11, 1946, the Ulens both filed complaints in the District Court alleging that their injuries and losses directly resulted from the negligence of agents of the appellant in carelessly planning and approving the flight and in unskillfully operating the plane. The complaint filed by Violet Ulen sought recovery in the amount of $257,500. Mr. Ulen's complaint asked for $50,000 in damages. Appellant carrier answered both complaints by admitting the facts alleged but denying that the injuries were caused by its negligence and disclaiming any knowledge of the extent of Violet Ulen's injuries. Thereupon the Ulens served a set of 55 interrogatories on appellant and these were answered in detail by appellant. The Ulens then filed motions for summary judgment in their favor and to impanel a jury for the purpose of determining damages. As grounds for these motions the Ulens asserted that the pleadings together with the carrier's answers to the interrogatories demonstrated that there was no genuine issue as to any material fact except as to damages. After these motions for summary judgment came on for oral argument in the court below, appellant carrier filed a motion for leave to amend its answers to the complaints by including additional defenses. At the same time appellant filed its opposition to the motions for summary judgment. On July 14, 1947, Judge Morris entered a memorandum opinion in which he indicated his intention of granting the motions for summary judgment in favor of the Ulens, but in which he also indicated that decision on the motions would be continued in order to allow the filing by the carrier of an amended answer. A court order to that effect was entered below and appellant filed its amended answer which added the additional [affirmative] defense that Violet Ulen was a passenger in international transportation within the purview of the Warsaw Convention,[1] and hence that total recovery, if any, is limited thereby to the sum of $8,291.87.[2]

On November 12, 1947, the motions for summary judgment were granted and the cases were assigned for inquisition by a jury as to the amount of damages. The court expressly reserved the defense based upon the Warsaw Convention for disposition by the court at the time of such inquisition. In April, 1948, the two cases were tried together before a jury. Defendant-appellant moved for directed verdicts both at the close of plaintiffs' case and at the close of all the evidence, but said motions were overruled. The jury then returned verdicts for Violet Ulen in the amount of $25,000 and for her husband in the amount of $2,500 and judgments thereon were entered. Following the denial of various other motions of the carrier, separate appeals were taken from those judgments.

Appellant raises two major issues on these appeals which shall be dealt with separately herein. First, appellant asserts that plaintiff-appellees were not entitled to summary judgment. Second, it is vigorously urged that, if there is any liability at all, it is definitely limited in amount by the applicable provisions of the Warsaw Convention.

---

[1] 49 Stat. (Part 2) 3000 (1929).

[2] Under Article 22 of the Warsaw Convention the liability of the carrier for each passenger was limited to the sum of 125,000 francs. It is agreed by the parties to this appeal that the figure above is the equivalent, in United States currency, of $8,291.87.

Appellant's first point is that summary judgment was erroneously granted and to its great prejudice, because the *pleadings* (that is, the complaint alleging negligence and the answer as amended denying any negligence) raised genuine issues as to material facts which could only have been properly determined by a trial on the merits. Thus far, we have no difficulty in agreeing with appellant and, in fact, appellees concede that this contention, so far as it goes, is correct. However, it is vitally significant that *before* summary judgment was granted the trial judge had before him not only the complaint and the answer as amended but also the 55 interrogatories of plaintiffs and all of defendant's detailed, sworn answers thereto as well as a lengthy "Defendant's Brief in Opposition to Motion for Summary Judgment." . . .

The answers to the interrogatories which Judge Morris had before him in this case show undeniably that appellant was negligent. The answers show that appellant's authorized and experienced agents planned, agreed upon, and were in the process of executing, a flight plan which called for the plane to fly at an altitude of 4000 feet on the leg of the flight on which the accident occurred (Pulaski to Tri–City). From the flight log kept by the pilot during this particular flight it is clear that he was following this flight plan up to the time of his last entry. The last radio contact with the plane while in flight was received at 2:05 A.M. (about 20 minutes before the crash) when the pilot reported his altitude as 4000 feet. At the time this flight was planned and flown there was in effect a Civil Air Regulation [No. 61.7401] promulgated by the Civil Aeronautics Board which read as follows:

"No scheduled air carrier aircraft shall be flown at an altitude of less than 1000 feet above the highest obstacle located within a horizontal distance of 5 miles from the center of the course intended to be flown . . . ."

The answers to the interrogatories show further that appellant's plane crashed at an elevation of 3910 feet near the summit of Glade Mountain which was located near the center of Green Airway No. 5, a strip ten miles wide over which the plane was scheduled to, and did, fly. The answers admit that a certain chart apparently in appellant's possession indicates that "the terrain [Glade Mountain] is more than 3500 ft. high but less than 4000 ft. above sea level."

We have no difficulty in finding, as did the lower court, that negligence and proximate cause were sufficiently established so as to justify entry of summary judgment in favor of appellees subject only to a determination of the amount of damages and the applicability of the Warsaw Convention.

Appellant's second major contention is that, because of the applicability of the Warsaw Convention, appellant's liability is limited to the sum of $8,291.87. This Convention, to which the United States was not a signatory but to which, pursuant to Presidential Proclamation, this country adheres, applies to "all international transportation of persons, baggage, or goods performed by aircraft for hire." In the view which we take of this case it is unnecessary for this court to decide whether or not the Convention applies since the result would be the same either way. Assuming, without deciding, that the Convention does apply here, we are of the opinion that one of the Articles of the Convention itself precludes appellant's claim of limited liability in this case. Article 25(1) of the Convention as it appears in the official translation from the original French reads as follows:

"The carrier shall not be entitled to avail himself of the provisions of this convention which exclude or limit his liability, *if the damage is caused by his wilful misconduct or by such default on his part as, in accordance with the law of the court to which the case is submitted, is considered to be equivalent to wilful misconduct.*" (Emphasis supplied.)

The words "wilful misconduct" as they twice appear in the language quoted above were represented in the original French of the Convention by the word "dol." Appellant vigorously urges that the word "dol" was improperly translated and that properly translated it means "fraud" or "deceit." As we understand appellant's argument, the carrier must be guilty of well-nigh criminal intent before Article 25(1) has application. Stated somewhat differently, it is appellant's claim that its liability, if any, is limited unless it can be successfully shown that the pilot, or other agents of appellant, with malicious or felonious intent, planned to fly the plane into the mountain to the injury of its passengers. We cannot agree that the language of Article 25 quoted above goes, or was intended to go, this far.

Appellant has gone to the trouble of having translated (by a translator of its own selection) a portion of the official minutes of the Conference which later formulated the Convention. We see nothing in these minutes which would justify a holding that the official translation of "dol" into "wilful misconduct" is incorrect. Those minutes show little more than that the delegates were at the time in disagreement as to what terms would express their intent when translated into various languages. In fact, one statement by an English delegate to the Conference lends force to appellees' claim that the term is properly translated. That delegate said: "We have in English the expression 'wilful misconduct'. I think that it covers all that you want to say; it covers not only the acts accomplished deliberately, but also of insouciance, without concern for the consequences."

We, therefore, see no basis for questioning the correctness of the official translation as quoted above. The problem thus becomes one of deciding whether the trial judge properly applied the "law of the court to which the case is submitted" when, in his charge to the jury he said as follows:

"Now, wilful misconduct is not, as I have said, merely misconduct, but wilful misconduct. So if the carrier, or its employees or agents, wilfully performed any act with the knowledge that the performance of that act was likely to result in injury to a passenger, or performed that act with reckless and wanton disregard of its probable consequences, then that would constitute wilful misconduct; and if the result of that wilful misconduct was injury to Mrs. Ulen, then her recovery would not be limited by this sum of some eight thousand dollars.

. . . .

"Now, the mere violation of those [safety rules and regulations], . . . even if intentional, would not necessarily constitute wilful misconduct, but if the violation was intentional with knowledge that the violation was likely to cause injury to a passenger, then that would be wilful misconduct, and likewise, if it was done with a wanton and reckless disregard of the consequences."

We are of the opinion that this charge to the jury was substantially correct and that there was ample evidence upon which the jury could base its verdict, finding appellant guilty of wilful misconduct. One recent federal court decision defines the term as follows: " 'Wilful misconduct' means a deliberate purpose not to discharge some duty necessary to safety."[15] This definition squarely fits the facts in the instant case. The obvious and sole purpose of Civil Air Regulation 61.7401, supra, is safety. It imposed a duty upon all scheduled carriers which appellant deliberately, knowingly and intentionally violated. Appellant attempts to excuse itself by stating that the "center of the course intended to be flown" is not the same as the center of the airway and by arguing that it was possible for the airplane, by zigzagging first to the right of the airlane and then to the left, to fly at 4000 feet and still more than five miles distant from and 1000 feet above the highest obstacle and thereby comply, appellant says, with Regulation 61.7401. We need not pass upon the technical distinction between "center of the course" and "center of the airway," because, even adopting appellant's theory, the evidence clearly establishes a deliberate violation of the safety regulation.

The flight plan, drawn up, approved, and partially executed by appellant's admittedly experienced and otherwise qualified personnel, indicates that the "course intended to be flown" by this plane from Pulaski to Tri–City (the leg of the flight on which the accident occurred) was 246 degrees magnetic. The aeronautical chart introduced in evidence at the trial shows Glade Mountain to be 4080 feet in elevation and lying very close to the center of the *airway* over which this plane was to fly. That chart also shows clearly that a plane proceeding at an altitude of 4000 feet from Pulaski toward Tri–City on a magnetic bearing of 246 degrees—*the course intended to be flown*—would pass *within 1½ miles, or at most 2 miles, from Glade Mountain, a mountain 4080 feet high!* Under these circumstances, it requires no stretch of the imagination whatever to visualize what *could* happen and what *did* happen in this case. Appellant's case is only weakened by its proof that the same pilot had flown this same route in the same manner several times before. This is only evidence of deliberateness and full knowledge which renders appellant's actions the more reprehensible. One further fact of record cannot escape note. In appellant's answers to the interrogatories it made the astonishing admission that "we do not know the official elevation of Glade Mountain." From the foregoing it is evident that wilful misconduct in planning and executing this flight has been

[15] Circuit Judge Minton in Rowe v. Gatke Corporation, 7 Cir., 1942, 126 F.2d 61, 66. [A later and more complete definition of wilful misconduct's dual requirements in this particular context comes from Bayer Corp. v. British Airways, LLC, 210 F.3d 236, 238 (4th Cir.2000): "Negligence will not suffice, nor even recklessness judged objectively. Rather, a plaintiff must show that a defendant either intended to cause the damage or acted recklessly with *subjective* knowledge that the damage would probably result."—Ed.]

completely and conclusively shown in this case. Finally, there is nothing in either the flight plan or the flight log of this plane to show that the zigzag course, which appellant now argues would safely carry the plane through the mountains in compliance with Regulation 61.7401, was ever contemplated or attempted in the case of this flight. The fact that there might have been a safe way to fly this flight over this route cannot help this appellant where all the evidence of record shows indisputably that an obviously unsafe method was employed and planned.

It follows that the Warsaw Convention, by its own terms, is inapplicable and does not operate to limit appellant's liability in these cases.[r] Both judgments appealed from in these cases must be, and are hereby

Affirmed.

---

[r] On or after September 28, 1955, a good number of countries including the United States signed the Hague Protocol. This was a new treaty incorporating important amendments to the Warsaw Convention. The Protocol doubled the Convention's limitation on liability for personal injury or death to passengers. However, the Protocol eliminated the Convention's reference to "dol" or "wilful misconduct," and instead provided that the limitation on liability was not to apply "if it is proved that the damage resulted from an act or omission of the carrier, his servants or agents, done with intent to cause damage or recklessly and with knowledge that damage would probably result." Although in force elsewhere, the Protocol was not ratified by the United States.

On November 15, 1965, the United States gave notice of "denunciation" of the Warsaw Convention (meaning withdrawal in accordance with the terms of the Convention), emphasizing that such action was solely because of the Convention's low limitation on liability. The notice was to become effective six months later. Within that period, the International Air Transport Association made efforts to effect an arrangement among domestic and foreign air carriers that would raise the limitation and provide a basis upon which the United States could rescind its notice of denunciation. The result was the so-called Montreal Agreement among numerous carriers by which they bound themselves to include in their tariffs a special contract providing for liability regardless of fault up to $75,000 per passenger. There was no change in the wilful misconduct exception to limited liability. This contract was to be applicable to international transportation that included a place in the United States as a point of origin, point of destination, or agreed stopping place. Thereupon, the United States officially rescinded its notice of denunciation of the Convention.

Since then, on March 8, 1971, in Guatemala City and on September 25, 1975, in Montreal, the United States and other countries signed controversial new treaties in an attempt to amend further the Warsaw Convention. These treaties provided for no-fault liability of the airline up to approximately $100,000 per passenger, with the possibility of a country's imposing supplemental mandatory insurance coverage. However, there was to be no exception, on wilful misconduct or other grounds, to this limited liability. Of these treaties, the United States ratified only Montreal Protocol No. 4, by which, as of March 4, 1999, the United States finally adhered to the old Hague Protocol and its defined exception to limited liability.

Meanwhile, the IATA was taking steps to get the airlines unilaterally to eliminate the cap on liability. It adopted the Intercarrier Agreement on Passenger Liability on October 31, 1995, in Malaysia, by which the airlines would "take action to waive the limitation on liability." By subsequent agreements, effective January 1, 1997, there was strict liability of the airline up to about $140,000 per passenger and, further, there was full compensation unless the airline could prove the absence of fault on its part.

Finally, activity shifted back to the treaty front, culminating in the Montreal Convention of May 28, 1999. It replaces the Warsaw Convention and adopts the above-stated terms of the IATA Intercarrier Agreements. After the United States ratified it, it went into force on November 4, 2003. See Devendra Pradhan, The Fifth Jurisdiction Under the Montreal Liability Convention: Wandering American or Wandering Everybody?, 68 J.Air L. & Com. 717 (2003).

AMERICAN AIRLINES AND VIOLET ULEN

One could disagree with the appellate court's view of the record. American Airlines had a decent argument, although its counsel failed to express it very clearly even on appeal. The argument ran that the evidence showed the pilot was probably flying not on instruments but by Contact Flight Rules, whereby the pilot would maneuver the plane by simple adjustments of direction to maintain the appropriate five-mile distance from terrestrial obstacles as the pilot flew visually from flight beacon to flight beacon; that the bearing given in the flight plan, which contemplated a CFR flight, properly was only an indication of the general direction of the flight, and therefore the center of the airway was not "the course intended to be flown"; that it was for the pilot in flight to decide whether circumstances warranted sticking with CFR, which was a routine and acceptable practice and, under certain higher-altitude weather conditions, would be the most prudent course for this particular flight; and that the crash could have resulted from a nonnegligent cause such as the unexpected squall that blew through the area that night at the right time and in the right direction and could have pushed the airplane miles off course. Actually, the airline's interrogatory answers implied this argument and its witnesses so testified explicitly at trial, and the plaintiffs offered no evidence to refute this theory of how *the appellant had not violated the Civil Air Regulation.* If the appellate court had so understood the appellant's argument, would its decision have changed on either of the two issues before it?

In any event, Mrs. Ulen died in 1979. Her obituary in the Washington Post, Sept. 24, 1979, at C4, recounted the crash:

"Mrs. Ulen later recalled for reporters that it was snowing, and she did not move for some time because when she first tried to move she had disturbed a badly injured Marine Corps colonel. 'He begged me to shoot him,' Mrs. Ulen said. 'The colonel died about daybreak,' she went on, 'then I dug myself out of the wreckage.'

"After trying to find her shoes, she gave up, and began a barefoot seven-hour trek over mountainous terrain in an effort to find aid for the other survivors. She was discovered by a farmer who helped her to a phone to call for help.

"According to newspaper accounts at the time, Mrs. Ulen accomplished this even though she herself was suffering from a fractured collar bone, broken ribs, and assorted cuts as a result of the crash.

"Her search for help resulted in additional injuries, including frostbitten hands and feet, and torn ankle ligaments. During the three months she spent in the hospital, it also was discovered that she had a brain concussion, according to later newspaper stories.

"Mrs. Ulen was awarded a bronze medal by the Carnegie Hero Fund Commission of Pittsburgh and honored by the Commission for 'risking her life to save others.' She was one of five persons to survive the crash."

Questions: (86) How did the plaintiffs in the American Airlines case go about proving to the jury the defendant's "wilful misconduct"? Could they have relied simply on the answers to interrogatories?

(87) Would you expect courts often to grant summary judgment in favor of plaintiffs in actions based on charges of negligence?

(88) What did the district court in the American Airlines case accomplish by granting summary judgment as to liability?

SCOTT v. HARRIS, 550 U.S. 372, 127 S.Ct. 1769 (2007). Just three weeks before Bell Atlantic Corp. v. Twombly, the Supreme Court stepped in to encourage use of summary judgment as another way for judges to short-circuit litigation, with the Court taking a very activist role in drawing inferences from the record in order to reverse a denial of summary judgment.

The case was a civil rights action complaining of the conduct of a police officer in pursuing an automobile, which he had clocked at 73 mph in a 55–mph zone. The officer ultimately bumped the car, causing it to crash and thereby grievously injuring the plaintiff driver. The Fourth Amendment required the police behavior to be objectively reasonable, and so the summary judgment question boiled down to whether the defendant could, as a matter of law, defeat a finding of violation of the Fourth Amendment. The Supreme Court, after viewing a videotape of the chase (available at http://www.youtube.com/watch?v=DBY2y2YsmN0), held that the plaintiff's conduct posed a risk of imminent harm to others substantial enough to justify the police conduct. That is, the plaintiff's "version of events is so utterly discredited by the record that no reasonable jury could have believed him."

Justice Stevens, the sole dissenter, objected to "this unprecedented departure from our well-settled standard." He contended that the videotape "surely does not provide a principled basis for depriving the [plaintiff] of his right to have a jury evaluate the question whether the police officers' decision to use deadly force to bring the chase to an end was reasonable." Indeed, he found the video ambiguous, and also pointed out that the majority was purely speculating as to matters such as what would have happened if the police had simply ceased their pursuit. "In my judgment, jurors in Georgia should be allowed to evaluate the reasonableness of the decision to ram respondent's speeding vehicle in a manner that created an obvious risk of death and has in fact made him a quadriplegic at the age of 19."

The Court seemed to rely on logic and anecdote when reining in the perceived excesses of today's litigation, rather than on an accurate sense of how often parties were making and winning summary judgment motions. By contrast, the Federal Judicial Center has recently released the premier published study of summary judgment. Joe S. Cecil, Rebecca N. Eyre, Dean Miletich & David Rindskopf, A Quarter–Century of Summary Judgment

Practice in Six Federal District Courts, 4 J.Empirical Legal Stud. 861 (2007). That study looked at a sample of federal civil cases (excluding prisoner, Social Security, and benefit repayment cases) in six districts from 1975 to 2000. While emphasizing that summary judgment practice varies considerably with locale and case type, it found overall that the percentage of cases involving one or more summary judgment motions increased from 12% in fiscal year 1975 to 20% in calendar year 2000; the court granted such a motion in full or in part in 6% and 12%, in those respective years, of all cases in the sample; and grant of summary judgment resulted in termination of 3.7% and 7.8%, respectively, of all cases. It suggested that the modern ascendancy of summary judgment dates from the upswing in the late 1970s of judicial case management and its emphasis on motion practice. Incidentally, among all the summary judgment motions over the whole time period studied, viewed on a motion level rather than a case level, 72% were motions by defendants (with a 49% rate of granting in full or in part in 2000), while 28% were plaintiffs' motions (with a 36% success rate in 2000).

Interchangeability of motion for summary judgment and motion for judgment on the pleadings.—It is clear under Rule 56 that if the moving party is legally entitled to judgment solely based on the pleadings, unassisted by affidavits or other factual materials, the court should give summary judgment in his favor. Correspondingly, Rule 12(d) states that if on a motion for judgment on the pleadings the court chooses to receive factual materials outside the pleadings, the court must treat the motion as one for summary judgment, which includes giving the parties an opportunity to present any further material they may have pertinent to a summary judgment motion. There is no point in insistence on mere form—here the names of the motions.

Questions: (89) Why, then, would a party ever use Rule 12(c) in preference to Rule 56?

(90) What can be said of the interchangeability of a motion for summary judgment and a motion under Rule 12(b)(6) for failure to state a claim upon which relief can be granted or a motion under Rule 12(f) to strike an insufficient defense?

(i) PROVISIONAL REMEDIES

[Rules 64, 65]

It is worth pausing to make the point that although we are canvassing the "phases of a lawsuit"—a phrase that might suggest a set order of proceedings—modern lawsuits do not exhibit a fixed or invariant pattern. They are fluid affairs. It is true that under the Rules certain moves necessarily precede other moves, and in this sense any lawsuit has a certain sequential order. The complaint precedes the answer, and a motion for a more definite statement necessarily follows the pleading that it addresses, and so on. But a lawsuit is not a cotillion in which the litigants invariably take the same steps according to a definite routine. In a particular litigation, the litigants will make only some of the large variety of moves that are theoretically available under the Rules; they will not make those moves in an absolutely fixed order; they may carry out a number of moves more or less simultaneously; and they may respond to a given move in one or more of a variety of ways.

Law.—It is the mark of the first-class litigating lawyer to be able to hold the entire litigation in view while considering particular steps. One of the things he or she must bear in mind is that the adversary will sometimes not remain in a condition of repose while the lawsuit is taking its course. Suppose plaintiff begins an action for a money judgment. If he wins, he can then take steps to have defendant's property in the court's jurisdiction seized and sold to satisfy the judgment. But what is to prevent defendant from concealing her property or removing it from the jurisdiction so that plaintiff cannot reach it? Or, for that matter, what is to prevent her from dissipating her property? In either case, plaintiff's victory might be a hollow one, leaving him with an uncollectible judgment.

State legislatures have provided various devices designed to secure a plaintiff against these hazards, and Federal Rule 64 makes available in the district court whatever remedies of this sort are available under the law of the state in which the district court sits. There are considerable differences in the remedies available to plaintiff from state to state, in the circumstances where plaintiff can use them, and in the types of property that plaintiff can reach thereby. Because the district courts follow the local state practice, the result is a divergence in practice among the district courts. Note, however, that Rule 64's adoption of state law by reference is subject to the qualification that any statute of the United States governs in federal court as far as applicable.

Speaking generally, the most important of the state remedies are attachment and garnishment. Attachment is the seizure of defendant's property in advance of judgment, commonly at a very early stage in the proceedings, to give security to plaintiff that the judgment he hopes to obtain will be collectible. Garnishment is a process that makes a debt owed by a third person to defendant, or more generally property in the hands of a third person but belonging to defendant, similarly subject to plaintiff's claim. A typical example of a garnishable debt is defendant's bank deposit: the service of proper process upon the bank warns it not to pay defendant the amount deposited and garnished, but to hold that amount for application to plaintiff's judgment if he gets one; the garnishment excuses the bank from paying defendant in the meantime; indeed, if the bank nevertheless does pay defendant, the successful plaintiff can make it pay again.[s]

[s] Similarly, state statutes have long provided for garnishment of wages by service of proper process upon the employer. However, over the years, varying but increasing statutory restrictions have come to regulate this power to garnish wages.

These remedies are drastic ones, particularly if the seizure takes effect upon plaintiff's say-so, thus depriving defendant of control of property before there has been any sort of impartial adjudication that plaintiff's claim is sound or even prima facie sound. Accordingly, in recent decades lawsuits have repeatedly challenged, and often with success, the fundamental fairness of these remedies and therefore their constitutional validity. Of course, much turns on the details of the attachment or garnishment procedure provided by the particular state, the kinds of claims and the classes of creditors and debtors covered by the procedure, the type of property involved, and the like. We shall examine this question later, in Topic C of Part Three. In any event, we can summarize here that the district courts follow the local statutes unless those statutes are determined to be unconstitutional.

Equity.—Attachment and garnishment are possible provisional remedies when plaintiff is seeking a money judgment. But the ultimate relief sought may be a judgment directing defendant to do or to refrain from doing particular acts. In appropriate circumstances, the court will issue such ultimate relief, denominated a final injunction, after a decision for plaintiff on the merits of the dispute. Defendant's disobedience of such an order will result in severe action by the court. Yet here again intervening events may frustrate the effectiveness of this final relief. Suppose defendant is about to conduct blasting operations in dangerous proximity to plaintiff's property, and plaintiff seeks an injunction directing defendant to desist. Defendant may inflict the harm feared by plaintiff before the court can hear and decide the case.

Rule 65 shows that plaintiff is not helpless in this situation. On a sufficient showing of urgency and irreparable harm, the court may issue a "temporary restraining order" without a hearing and, in particularly exigent cases, even without notice to the adverse party. But plaintiff should promptly follow up on such an order with an application for a "preliminary injunction," which requires notice and hearing under Rule 65(a)(1).

Note the strict limitations imposed by Rule 65(b), (c), and (d) on the issuance and duration of a temporary restraining order. Why did the rulemakers deem them necessary? It is hard at this point of your study to appreciate just how much is at stake. Perhaps the best we can do for you is to allude to the dark history of federal labor injunctions, wherein broad temporary injunctions against strikes proved so effective at busting unions that in 1932 Congress had to step in to impose procedural and substantive limits on the federal-court injunctive power in labor disputes. More broadly, we can merely pronounce that temporary injunctive relief is a breathtak-

---

Most significantly, in 1970 by Title III of the Consumer Credit Protection Act, Congress greatly restricted this device not only in the federal courts but in the state courts as well. Title III overrode state law except to the extent that state law imposes more stringent restrictions on wage garnishment. Title III generally provides that the maximum amount subject to garnishment is the lesser of (1) 25% of the defendant's weekly disposable earnings or (2) the amount by which those earnings exceed 30 times the federal minimum hourly wage. Title III also makes it a criminal offense to discharge an employee because of a single garnishment of the employee's wages. See 15 U.S.C. §§ 1671–1677.

ingly effective remedy, enforceable as it is by the unignorable power of contempt. Furthermore, in practical terms, the grant or refusal of this provisional remedy often spells the outcome of the dispute, as many parties cannot persevere until trial. Accordingly, the law must concern itself with how a judge is to decide on this remedy, knowing that the judge must decide without all the procedural safeguards of a trial.

In particular, the working of the security requirement is a bit tricky. The court must require security, which comes usually in the form of a bond. However, the court can discretionarily fix the amount at a nominal level for a poor but deserving plaintiff. The defendant who ultimately prevails on the propriety of injunctive relief, by any means from a full-blown trial down to a voluntary dismissal without her consent, can recover her actual economic losses resulting from obeying the wrongfully imposed injunction. She can ordinarily recover these losses up to the amount of the bond, but not beyond. This limitation follows from the proposition that a plaintiff is ordinarily not liable for the harm that a defendant suffers from litigation.

Question: (91) Most importantly, what should be the standard for granting a preliminary injunction? Begin by considering the standard stated in Sonesta International Hotels Corp. v. Wellington Associates, 483 F.2d 247, 250 (2d Cir.1973): "The settled rule is that a preliminary injunction should issue only upon a clear showing of either (1) probable success on the merits *and* possible irreparable injury, *or* (2) sufficiently serious questions going to the merits to make them a fair ground for litigation *and* a balance of hardships tipping decidedly toward the party requesting the preliminary relief." But the standard for granting a preliminary injunction is worth worrying about some more.

American Hospital Supply Corp. v. Hospital Products Ltd.

United States Court of Appeals, Seventh Circuit, 1986.
780 F.2d 589.

■ Before POSNER, CIRCUIT JUDGE, and SWYGERT and PELL, SENIOR CIRCUIT JUDGES.

■ POSNER, CIRCUIT JUDGE.

A supplier terminated a distributor, who sued for breach of contract and got a preliminary injunction. The supplier has appealed under 28 U.S.C. § 1292(a)(1). The appeal raises issues of procedure and contract law.

The supplier, Hospital Products (as we shall call the affiliated corporations that are the defendants), a small firm now undergoing reorganization in bankruptcy, is one of the world's two principal manufacturers of "reusable surgical stapling systems for internal surgical procedures" ("surgical stapling systems," for short). The terminated distributor, American Hospital Supply Corporation, the world's largest distributor of medical and surgical supplies, in 1982 became the exclusive distributor in the United States of Hospital Products' surgical stapling systems. The contract of distribution was for three years initially, but provided that it would be renewed automatically for successive one-year periods (to a limit of ten years) unless American Hospital Supply notified Hospital Products at least 90 days before the three years were up [on September 1, 1985] (or any successive one-year period for which the contract had been renewed) that it wanted to terminate the contract, and this meant, by June 3, 1985.

On that day Hospital Products hand-delivered a letter to American Hospital Supply demanding to know whether it intended to renew the contract and reminding it that if it failed to respond by the end of the day this would mean that the contract had been renewed. American Hospital Supply responded the same day in a letter which pointed out that since it wasn't terminating, the contract was, indeed, renewed. But on the next day Hospital Products announced that it was going to treat the contract as having been terminated, and on June 7 it sent a telegram to American Hospital Supply's dealers informing them that effective June 3 American Hospital Supply was "no longer the authorized distributor of [Hospital Products'] stapling products."

American Hospital Supply forthwith brought this diversity breach of contract suit against Hospital Products and moved for a preliminary injunction, which was granted on July 8 after an evidentiary hearing. The injunction forbids Hospital Products to take any action in derogation of American Hospital Supply's contract rights so long as the injunction is in force (i.e., pending the outcome of the trial). It also requires Hospital Products to notify American Hospital Supply's dealers that American Hospital Supply is still Hospital Products' authorized distributor, and this has been done. Hospital Products counterclaimed, alleging breach of contract, fraud, and unfair competition.

Two months after the entry of the injunction, Hospital Products, which had been in parlous financial state even before this litigation began, filed a petition for bankruptcy under Chapter 11 of the Bankruptcy Act (reorganization). . . .

A district judge asked to decide whether to grant or deny a preliminary injunction must choose the course of action that will minimize the costs of being mistaken. Because he is forced to act on an incomplete record, the danger of a mistake is substantial. And a mistake can be costly. If the judge grants the preliminary injunction to a plaintiff who it later turns out is not entitled to any judicial relief—whose legal rights have not been violated—the judge commits a mistake whose gravity is measured by the irreparable harm, if any, that the injunction causes to the defendant while it is in effect. If the judge denies the preliminary injunction to a plaintiff who it later turns out is entitled to judicial relief, the judge commits a mistake whose gravity is measured by the irreparable harm, if any, that the denial of the preliminary injunction does to the plaintiff.

These mistakes can be compared, and the one likely to be less costly can be selected, with the help of a simple formula: grant the preliminary injunction if but only if $P \times H_p > (1 - P) \times H_d$, or, in words, only if the harm to the plaintiff if the injunction is denied, multiplied by the probability that the denial would be an error (that the plaintiff, in other words, will win at trial), exceeds the harm to the defendant if the injunction is granted, multiplied by the probability that granting the injunction would be an error. That probability is simply one minus the probability that the plaintiff will win at trial; for if the plaintiff has, say, a 40 percent chance of winning, the defendant must have a 60 percent chance of winning (1.00 − .40 = .60). The left-hand side of the formula is simply the probability of an erroneous denial weighted by the cost of denial to the plaintiff, and the right-hand side simply the probability of an erroneous grant weighted by the cost of grant to the defendant.

This formula, a procedural counterpart to Judge Learned Hand's famous negligence formula, see United States v. Carroll Towing Co., 159 F.2d 169, 173 (2d Cir.1947); [other citation omitted], is not offered as a new legal standard; it is intended not to force analysis into a quantitative straitjacket but to assist analysis by presenting succinctly the factors that the court must consider in making its decision and by articulating the relationship among the factors. It is actually just a distillation of the familiar four (sometimes five) factor test that courts use in deciding whether to grant a preliminary injunction. The court asks whether the plaintiff will be irreparably harmed if the preliminary injunction is denied (sometimes also whether the plaintiff has an adequate remedy at law), whether the harm to the plaintiff if the preliminary injunction is denied will exceed the harm to the defendant if it is granted, whether the plaintiff is reasonably likely to prevail at trial, and whether the public interest will be affected by granting or denying the injunction (i.e., whether third parties will be harmed—and these harms can then be added to H_p or H_d as the case may be). See, e.g., Palmer v. City of Chicago, 755 F.2d 560, 576 (7th Cir.1985). The court undertakes these inquiries to help it figure out whether granting the injunction would be the error-minimizing course of action, which depends on the probability that the plaintiff is in the right and on the costs to the plaintiff, the defendant, or others of granting or denying the injunction. All this is explained at length in Roland Machinery Co. v. Dresser Industries, Inc., 749 F.2d 380, 382–88 (7th Cir.1984) [(Posner, J.)], where a panel of this court applied the verbal counterpart to our algebraic formula, as did a different panel in Maxim's Ltd. v. Badonsky, 772 F.2d 388, 391 (7th Cir.1985). See also Leubsdorf, The Standard for Preliminary Injunctions, 91 Harv.L.Rev. 525 (1978). The formula is new; the analysis it capsulizes is standard.

The formula does not depend on the legal basis of the plaintiff's claim, whether it is antitrust law (Roland) or trademark law (Badonsky) or, as here, the common law of contract, although the nature of the right asserted by the plaintiff may affect the weighting of the harms, see, e.g., Shondel v. McDermott, 775 F.2d 859, 866–67 (7th Cir.1985). So may the nature of the permanent remedy to which the plaintiff would be entitled if he prevailed at trial. For example, prevailing parties in breach of contract cases normally are not awarded specific performance, that is, a mandatory injunction to perform. Since many breaches of contract are involuntary, implying that performance would be very costly, routinely ordering specific performance would create situations where the defendant was forced to bargain desperately to buy his way out of the injunction. The high bargaining costs that would result are a dead-weight cost of equitable relief. To the extent that those costs attend a preliminary injunction, they are of course relevant to the decision whether to issue such an injunction. But the formula takes account of this; the case we have described would be one where the harm to the defendant from granting the injunction would be very great. Thus the fact that a plaintiff might have no hope of getting specific performance ordered at the conclusion of the trial need not prevent him from obtaining a preliminary injunction. Cf. Roland v. Dresser Industries, Inc., supra, 749 F.2d at 386. The premise of the preliminary injunction is that the remedy available at the end of trial will not make the plaintiff whole; and, in a sense, the more limited that remedy, the stronger the argument for a preliminary injunction—provided that the remedy is not limited for reasons that would make a preliminary injunction equally inappropriate.

As explained in Roland, the scope of judicial review of a district judge's decision to grant or deny a preliminary injunction is limited. See 749 F.2d at 384–85, 388–91. The usual formulation is that the decision will be reversed only if it is found to be an "abuse of discretion." Unfortunately this phrase covers a family of review standards rather than a single standard, and a family whose members differ greatly in the actual stringency of review. See, e.g., id. at 388–91; Metlyn Realty Corp. v. Esmark, Inc., 763 F.2d 826, 831–32 (7th Cir.1985); Friendly, Indiscretion About Discretion, 31 Emory L.J. 747 (1982). For example, when we review an order granting or denying a preliminary injunction, we do not do so with as much deference (virtually complete deference) as when reviewing a criminal sentence that is within legal limits but is challenged as too harsh; we do "not simply engage in a perfunctory rubber-stamping of the district court's decision." Olin Water Services v. Midland Research Laboratories, Inc., 774 F.2d 303, 307 n. 7 (8th Cir.1985). But we do give that decision substantial deference, bearing in mind that the district judge had to act in haste, that he had to balance factors which, though they can be related in a neat formula, usually cannot be quantified, and that in dealing with the parties and their witnesses and counsel in the hectic atmosphere of a preliminary-injunction proceeding the judge may have developed a feel for the facts and the equities that remote appellate judges cannot obtain from a transcript. To reverse an order granting or denying a preliminary injunction, therefore, it is not enough that we think we would have acted differently in the district judge's shoes; we must have a strong conviction that he exceeded the permissible bounds of judgment. And although recognizing that the order granting such an injunction must set forth the judge's reasons, see Fed.R.Civ.P. 65(d), we also recognize that the haste with which the judge must act precludes as full a statement of reasons as could reasonably be demanded of a final decision.

We have now to apply these precepts, and we begin with the balance of harms. . . .

[The appellate court saw a threat of substantial irreparable harm to the plaintiff, in its being stuck with excess inventory upon the loss of distributorship status and likely being unable eventually to recover damages from the insolvent defendant for breach of contract. The court saw harm to the defendant from the preliminary injunction in the increased risk of bankruptcy, but this harm was offset at least in part by the $5 million bond that the plaintiff posted under Rule 65(c). The court remained unpersuaded "that the district judge erred in concluding that the balance of harms inclined in favor of granting the preliminary injunction."]

. . . Even if there were no clear basis for differentiating between the irreparable harms to American Hospital Supply from denying and to Hospital Products from granting a preliminary injunction, in which event those harms would have to be treated as equal, Hospital Products' appeal would fail. If the harms to the plaintiff and the defendant of denying and granting the injunction, respectively, are equal, the injunction must be granted if the plaintiff has a better than 50 percent chance of winning the case, for then P in our preliminary-injunction formula must exceed $1 - P$, and therefore $P \times H_p$ must exceed $(1 - P) \times H_d$ from the assumption that $H_p = H_d$.

The district judge was persuaded that Hospital Products, not American Hospital Supply, had broken the contract, implying a very high P. He undoubtedly was correct if the contract was renewed on June 3 and in force the next day when Hospital Products announced that the contract was terminated. But we must consider as did he whether American Hospital Supply repudiated the contract before this announcement. That would make this a case of anticipatory breach of contract . . . .

[The appellate court, by lengthy discussion, concluded that "as nearly as we can determine, the able and experienced district judge who resolved the uncertainty in American Hospital Supply's favor was on solid ground in doing so." The appellate court indicated that findings of fact were subject to a clearly erroneous standard of review, while conclusions of law were subject to nondeferential review.]

. . . In thus commenting on the merits, however, as we must do to review the district court's action in granting the injunction, we do not mean to prejudge the outcome of the full trial, which may cast the facts in a different light from how they appeared in the preliminary injunction proceeding. This caveat applies to all the discussion of the merits of the case in this opinion.

. . . .

We comment briefly on the term of the preliminary injunction. Since federal litigation is sometimes protracted and since the contract entitles American Hospital Supply to renew the contract annually for six more years after this year, there is a theoretical possibility that the injunction will remain in effect for many years. Over such a period the balance of harms and impact on the public interest may of course change. We trust that the district judge will bear this in mind in considering any requests to modify the injunction.

. . . .

Affirmed.

■ SWYGERT, SENIOR CIRCUIT JUDGE, dissenting.

[Among other lines of attack, the dissenting judge argued that "the district court clearly erred in finding that the balance of harms weighed in AHS's favor" and argued that there was an insufficient showing of likelihood of success on the merits.]

I would have preferred to avoid commenting on the majority's attempt to reduce the well-developed and complex law of preliminary injunctions to a "simple" mathematical formula. But because of the potentially far-reaching and baneful consequences of today's decision, I must regretfully voice my concerns.

Henceforth, the district courts of this circuit should grant a preliminary injunction if, "but only if," $P \times H_p > (1 - P) \times H_d$ . . . .

The majority describes its formula as a procedural counterpart to Judge Hand's negligence formula first appearing in United States v. Carroll Towing, 159 F.2d 169, 173 (2d Cir.1947). Carroll Towing was an admiralty case in which a shipowner's duty to provide against injuries resulting from the breaking of a vessel's moorings was expressed in algebraic terms. In Hand's formula the liability of the shipowner depends on whether $B < PL$, where P is the probability that the ship will break away; where L is the gravity of the resulting injury if she does; and where B is the burden of adequate precautions. . . . My quarrel, however, is not with Carroll Towing but rather with the majority's attempt today to create its equitable analogue. A quantitative approach may be an appropriate and useful heuristic device in determining negligence in tort cases, but it has limited value in determining whether a preliminary injunction should issue. Proceedings in equity and cases sounding in tort demand entirely different responses of a district judge. The judgment of the district judge in a tort case must be definite; the judgment of the district judge in an injunction proceeding cannot, by its very nature, be as definite. The judgment of a district judge in an injunction proceeding must be flexible and discretionary—within the bounds of the now settled four-prong test.

I question the necessity and the wisdom of the court's adoption of a mathematical formula as the governing law of preliminary injunctions. The majority claims that its formula is merely a distillation of the traditional four-prong test. But if nothing is added to the substantive law, why bother? The standard four-prong test for determining whether a preliminary injunction should issue has survived for so many years because it has proven to be a workable summation of the myriad factors a district court must consider in deciding whether to grant an injunction. The test articulated in Technical Publishing v. Lebhar–Friedman, 729 F.2d 1136, 1138 (7th Cir. 1984), and in countless other cases, may not exhibit the "precision" the majority seems to demand, but such "precision" is antithetical to the underlying principles of injunctive relief. Equity, as the majority concedes, involves the assessment of factors that cannot be quantified. A district court faced with the task of deciding whether to issue a preliminary injunction must to some extent, the majority concedes, rely on the "feel" of the case. See generally my discussion in Roland, 749 F.2d at 396 [(dissenting opinion)]. The majority's formula will not assist the district courts in their assessment of this aspect of the decision to grant a preliminary injunction. The traditional element of discretion residing in the decision of a trial court to grant a preliminary injunction has been all but eliminated by today's decision.

Ironically, the majority never attempts to assign a numerical value to the variables of its own formula. We are never told how to measure P or H_p or H_d. I believe, and the majority appears to concede, that a numerical value could never be assigned to these variables. Who can say, for instance, what *exactly* the probability is that the granting of the injunction was an error? How then will the majority's formula ease in a meaningful way the responsibilities of the district courts? Judges asked to issue a preliminary injunction must, in large part, rely on their own judgment, not on mathematical quanta.

We must, of course, be mindful not to vest too much imprecision in the preliminary injunction standard, for law implies a system of known and generally applicable rules. See Fiss & Rendleman, Injunctions 104 (2d ed. 1984). The existing four-prong test, however, represents the historical balance struck by the courts between the rigidity of law and the flexibility of equity.

The majority disavows any effort to force the district courts into a "quantitative straitjacket," but I suspect that today's decision may lead to just that. District judges operate under enormous pressure to be decisive and precise. Much rides on their smallest decisions. Like a Homeric Siren the majority's formula offers a seductive but deceptive security. Moreover, the majority's formula invites members of the Bar to dust off their calculators and dress their arguments in quantitative clothing. The resulting spectacle will perhaps be entertaining, but I do not envy the district courts of this circuit and I am not proud of the task we have given them.

I would reverse the district court's issuance of the preliminary injunction.

. . . .[t]

---

[t] Compare Linz Audain, Of Posner, and Newton, and Twenty-first Century Law: An Economic and Statistical Analysis of the Posner Rule for Granting Preliminary Injunctions, 23 Loy.L.A.L.Rev. 1215 (1990), with Linda S. Mullenix, Burying (with Kindness) the Felicific Calculus of Civil Procedure, 40 Vand.L.Rev. 541 (1987). For a startlingly different economic approach, taking as its premise that the purpose of preliminary injunctions is mere efficiency rather than the minimization of the interim loss of legal rights, see Richard R.W. Brooks & Warren F. Schwartz, Legal Uncertainty, Economic Efficiency, and the Preliminary Injunction Doctrine, 58 Stan.L.Rev. 381 (2005). For a psychological approach to this sort of problem, see Hal R. Arkes & Victoria A. Shaffer, "Should We Use Decision Aids or Gut Feelings," in Heuristics and the Law 411 (C. Gigerenzer & C. Engel eds., 2006).

The American Hospital formula has enjoyed only a smattering of judicial support. For later treatment of the formula by other panels of the same court of appeals, see, e.g., Lawson

COUNTRY FLOORS, INC. v. A PARTNERSHIP COMPOSED OF CHARLEY GEPNER AND GARY FORD, 930 F.2d 1056 (3d Cir.1991). Country Floors, a manufacturer of upscale ceramic tiles, brought a suit for trademark infringement against a partnership selling tiles under the name Country Tiles. At the outset, the district court denied plaintiff's motion for a preliminary injunction, which plaintiff supported by its employees' testimony of customer confusion between the tile products, with the court ruling in part that plaintiff had not made a sufficient showing of a likelihood of confusion. Later, after complete discovery, the court granted defendant's motion for summary judgment, relying in part on credibility determinations that it had made in connection with the preliminary injunction motion.

The court of appeals reversed, on the ground that the court could not so use such determinations and that indeed a genuine issue of fact existed as to the likelihood of confusion. It wrote:

"[C]redibility evaluations are inappropriate in deciding a motion for summary judgment. It is error to rely on the previous resolution of credibility issues in deciding a motion for summary judgment because such reliance cannot co-exist with the requirement of Rule 56(c) that no genuine issues of material fact remain outstanding.

. . . .

". . . [O]n a motion for summary judgment the responsibility of the district court is to determine if there are triable issues, rather than to try those issues and make findings based on the affidavits and other materials accompanying the motion.

"Accordingly, inferences concerning credibility that were previously made in ruling on the Corporation's motion for a preliminary injunction cannot determine the Partnership's Rule 56(c) motion and should not be

---

Prods., Inc. v. Avnet, Inc., 782 F.2d 1429 (7th Cir.1986) (Flaum, J.) (politely but explicitly endorsing the circuit's traditional approach). Abbott Lab. v. Mead Johnson & Co., 971 F.2d 6, 11–12 (7th Cir.1992) (Flaum, J.) (some citations omitted), ruled:

"As a threshold matter, a party seeking a preliminary injunction must demonstrate (1) some likelihood of succeeding on the merits, and (2) that it has 'no adequate remedy at law' and will suffer 'irreparable harm' if preliminary relief is denied. If the moving party cannot establish either of these prerequisites, a court's inquiry is over and the injunction must be denied. If, however, the moving party clears both thresholds, the court must then consider: (3) the irreparable harm the non-moving party will suffer if preliminary relief is granted, balancing that harm against the irreparable harm to the moving party if relief is denied; and (4) the public interest, meaning the consequences of granting or denying the injunction to non-parties.

"The court, sitting as would a chancellor in equity, then 'weighs' all four factors in deciding whether to grant the injunction, seeking at all times to 'minimize the costs of being mistaken.' American Hosp. Supply, 780 F.2d at 593. We call this process the 'sliding scale' approach: the more likely it is the plaintiff will succeed on the merits, the less the balance of irreparable harms need weigh towards its side; the less likely it is the plaintiff will succeed, the more the balance need weigh towards its side. This weighing process, as noted, also takes into consideration the consequences to the public interest of granting or denying preliminary relief. While we have at times framed the sliding scale approach in mathematical terms, see American Hosp. Supply, 780 F.2d at 593–94, it is more properly characterized as subjective and intuitive, one which permits district courts to 'weigh the competing considerations and mold appropriate relief.' Lawson Prods., 782 F.2d at 1436."

used to support propositions that underpin the decision to grant the motion for summary judgment. . . .

. . . .

"Additionally, in the context of this case, we note that the considerations that determine a motion for a preliminary injunction are foreign to those that govern decision on a motion for summary judgment."

SECTION 2. SETTLEMENT

(a) INCIDENCE

Most lawsuits do not make it all the way through the pretrial practice we have studied. Indeed, most disputes do not even become lawsuits. Aggrieved persons abandon or settle the overwhelming majority of grievances at some point along the line.

A useful image is the so-called grievance pyramid:

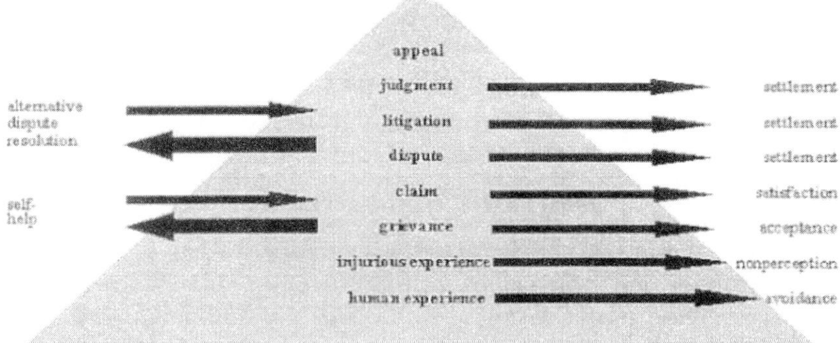

This image represents, as one progresses up the steps of the pyramid, how the whole realm of experiences narrows to disputes, a subset that produces in turn those selected cases we study in law school. Infinite experiences produce countless disputes, which yield few cases. For example, only a small percentage of grievances ripen into claims, by the aggrieved's voicing the grievance to the injurer; most aggrieved persons accept their injury as part of life or just figure that there is no remedy available; tellingly, the theorists in this subject sometimes refer to acceptance as "lumping it." Similarly, most disputants never make it to a lawyer, much less to a courthouse. So this image of a pyramid suggests another image: in this book we have thus far focused on the tiny tip of a huge iceberg.

The slope of the sides of the pyramid is quite gentle. That is, a huge percentage of situations leaves the pyramid at each step upward. A survey of more than five thousand households indicated that during the previous three years just over a third of them had perceived one or more grievances of certain litigable types; 71.8% of those grievances produced a claim informally; 62.6% of those claims met an initial rebuff to produce a dispute; and 11.2% of those disputes resulted in filing a lawsuit. See David M. Trubek, Austin Sarat, William L.F. Felstiner, Herbert M. Kritzer & Joel B. Grossman, The Costs of Ordinary Litigation, 31 UCLA L.Rev. 72, 86–87 (1983). Indeed, these percentages are exaggeratedly high, because the survey limited its inquiries to grievances involving $1000 or more. But even for such substantial grievances, litigation is by no means a knee-jerk or common reaction in the United States, because these numbers mean that overall only about 5% of those grievances ultimately resulted in a court filing.

In the world of litigation at the top of the pyramid, the slope remains gentle. Of the relatively few filed cases, only a small percentage make it through the procedural system to a contested judgment. We can look at all the 271,753 federal civil cases terminated during fiscal year 2005. Of these, at least 67.7% were settled in one way or another; approximately 20.7% were adjudicated at the pretrial stage, as by a motion under Rule 12 or 56; about 1.3% were adjudicated at the trial stage; and the other 10.3% of the cases fell into a welter of other disposition method codes, such as remand or transfer to another court, whereby most result in an eventual settlement rather than a final adjudication.

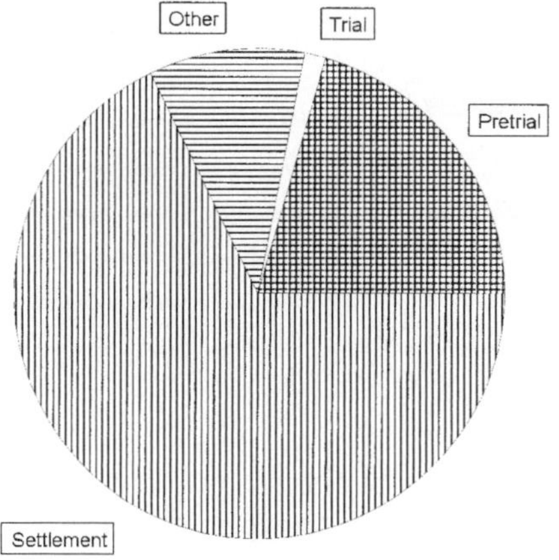

We can combine all these rough numbers with the visual presentation of the grievance pyramid. From the experiential infinitude, imagine that 1000 sizable grievances arise. This typical thousand will decrease to 718 claims, 449 disputes, 50 filed cases, 12 litigated judgments, and 1 decided appeal. Thus, we advisedly described the pyramid's sides by saying that their slope is gentle.

Merely stating such numbers, as rough as they are, constitutes a major step forward for students as well as for proceduralists. A new wave of empirical research is giving a fresh sense of reality to the field of procedure.

Moreover, there is a growing need for such study, because in recent years anecdotal evidence has created a frenzy about the current state of litigation and led to a host of ill-conceived reform efforts. Before undertaking reform, one should know whether and to what extent there really is a problem.

Although these new empirical studies are a step in the right direction, one of course needs to be careful. Interpreting them can be difficult, risky, and subjective. Looking at actual court statistics is far from a controlled experiment, which means that it is hard to interpret court output when the cases entering the system vary. Indeed, interpretation ends up being almost as much art as science. See generally Kevin M. Clermont & Theodore Eisenberg, Litigation Realities, 88 Cornell L.Rev. 119 (2002) (also explaining how to gain access to raw court data on the Internet); Kevin M. Clermont, Litigation Realities Redux, 84 Notre Dame L.Rev. 1919 (2009).

(b) IMPORTANCE

From the viewpoint of the civil justice system, settlement is a critical need. Ours is a slow and expensive procedure. The system simply would not be able to adjudicate all cases filed. We depend on the parties' finding alternatives to using the system. Accordingly, reformers are constantly seeking ways to increase the settlement rate (which is a loose term that measures the percentage of cases leaving the sides of the grievance pyramid, whether by abandonment, concession, or privately negotiated settlement or by alternative dispute resolution such as arbitration, mediation, and conciliation).

Nevertheless, the system must adjudicate some cases in order to pronounce the law. These cases set the standards under which the parties negotiate settlement of their disputes. The parties "bargain in the shadow of the law" to reach outcomes that generally conform to the law and thereby further the law's purposes. Thus, the settlement rate could conceivably become too high. If parties settled all cases, there would be big gaps in the law that is supposed to be setting the standards for settlement. If courts adjudicated some cases, but still too few, the gaps might be smaller but the law would remain not only inefficiently fuzzy but also insufficiently conformed to social purposes. But at some lower settlement rate, the law would be optimally set so that further adjudication would be wasteful.

Reformers might nonetheless contend that the settlement rate in America today lies below that optimum. In reality, however, they would not find it easy to raise, or for that matter lower, the settlement rate. Almost all reform attempts to enhance settlement will be largely offset by increases in the amount of litigation. See George L. Priest, Private Litigants and the Court Congestion Problem, 69 B.U.L.Rev. 527 (1989).

Shifting from the viewpoint of the system to that of the disputants, settlement is also of critical importance. For them in the usual course, settlement *is* our system of justice. (For their "trial" lawyers, negotiating settlements—and pursuing other alternatives to litigation—is what their profession primarily comprises.) All those alternatives usually offer procedural and substantive advantages to the disputants. Again, however, some optimal settlement rate exists, above which the increases in external pressure to settle would impose undesirable costs on party autonomy. See Stephen McG. Bundy, The Policy in Favor of Settlement in an Adversary System, 44 Hastings L.J. 1 (1992).

So why are we postponing focused study of all these important alternative dispute-resolution mechanisms until Topic C, which treats generally the characteristics of a procedural system? We have already explained that early mastery of the official procedural system helps in comprehending the cases read in other law courses. More importantly, litigation remains extremely important to society and to citizens. By it, courts act as the default enforcer of law and resolver of disputes. Litigation not only produces singular decisions that restructure society but also serves as a major vehicle for lawmaking in our government and for articulation of societal values. And the legal system's adjudication enunciates the law, in the shadow of which the grievance pyramid lies and the potential litigants operate those nonlitigation processes.

However, negotiating settlements, which constitutes the preeminent alternative dispute-resolution process, is too essential an appendage of the litigation process to ignore even temporarily. Indeed, some theorists propose renaming litigation as "litigotiation." Accordingly, we find it necessary to pause here and consider settlement itself in some detail.

MARC GALANTER, THE EMERGENCE OF THE JUDGE AS A MEDIATOR IN CIVIL CASES, 69 Judicature 257, 257 (1986). "Most civil cases filed in American courts are settled by an agreement between the parties rather than resolved by a decision of the court. 'Bargaining in the shadow of the law' is the prevalent means of resolving civil cases in American courts. Typically, settlement negotiations involve only counsel for the respective parties. But in many instances the negotiations are encouraged, brokered, or actively mediated by the judge. Most American judges participate to some extent in the settlement of some of the cases before them. Indeed, this has become a respectable, even esteemed, feature of judicial work.

"There have always been a lot of settlements in American civil courts. It remains unclear whether the percentage of cases terminated by settlement has increased in recent years. And, if there has been an increase, it is unclear whether it is caused by the increased intervention of judges. There has been a sea change, however, in the way judges talk about settlement and think about their roles as judges."

There are "two recurrent themes that impel and justify judicial involvement in the settlement process. We might call these the 'warm' theme and the 'cool' theme. The 'warm' theme refers to the impulse to replace adversary conflict by [for example] a process of conciliation to bring the parties into a mutual accord that expresses and produces community among them. The 'cool' theme emphasizes not a more admirable process but efficient institutional management: clearing dockets, reducing delay, eliminating expense, unburdening the courts."

Question: (1) With our focus now squarely on settlement, consider again how actively should the judge push for it. What would be the effect of activism on the direct costs of operating the legal system, taking into account the time and expense of public judges and officers as well as private lawyers and parties, and subtracting litigation savings but only to the extent that settlement would not have occurred anyway? What would be the other costs, taking into account the negative impact on a range of values regarding fair process and accurate outcome, some of which are not obvious as the next excerpt will illustrate, but all of which offset the gains in the "warm" values served? Bear in mind that the costs vary with different kinds of settlement techniques, different kinds of cases, and different courts and judges.

OWEN M. FISS, AGAINST SETTLEMENT, 93 Yale L.J. 1073, 1075, 1085 (1984). "I do not believe that settlement as a generic practice is preferable to judgment or should be institutionalized on a wholesale and indiscriminate basis. It should be treated instead as a highly problematic technique for streamlining dockets. Settlement is for me the civil analogue of plea bargaining: Consent is often coerced; the bargain may be struck by someone without authority; the absence of a trial and judgment renders subsequent judicial involvement troublesome; and although dockets are trimmed, justice may not be done. Like plea bargaining, settlement is a capitulation to the conditions of mass society and should be neither encouraged nor praised."

Adjudication employs *public* officials, whose "job is not to maximize the ends of private parties, nor simply to secure the peace, but to explicate and give force to the values embodied in authoritative texts such as the Constitution and statutes: to interpret those values and to bring reality into accord with them. This duty is not discharged when the parties settle."

CARRIE MENKEL-MEADOW, FOR AND AGAINST SETTLEMENT: USES AND ABUSES OF THE MANDATORY SETTLEMENT CONFERENCE, 33 UCLA L.Rev. 485, 504–05, 507–11, 513–14 (1985). "I will not repeat the often stated assertion that settlement is a 'docket-clearing' device. We have examined the efficiency argument and found it wanting. What settlement offers is a substantive justice that may be more responsive to the parties needs than adjudication. Settlement can be particularized to the needs of the parties, it can avoid win/lose, binary results, provide richer remedies than the commodification or monetarization of all claims, and achieve legitimacy through consent. In addition, settlement offers a different substantive process by allowing participation by the parties as well as the lawyers. Settlement fosters a communication process that can be more direct and less stylized than litigation, and affords greater flexibility of procedure and remedy.

. . . .

"For those who seek to use the settlement conference as a docket-clearing device, the conference becomes most problematic in terms of the substantive and process values (i.e., *quality* of solution) previously discussed. . . .

"A much touted settlement technique is the use of the 'Lloyds of London' formula: The settlement judge asks the parties to assess the probabilities of liability and damages and, if the figures are within reasonable range, to split the difference. The difficulty with such settlement techniques is that they tend to monetarize and compromise all the issues in the case. Although some cases are reducible to monetary issues, an approach to case evaluation on purely monetary grounds may decrease the likelihood of settlement by making fewer issues available for trade-offs. Furthermore, a wider definition of options may make compromise unnecessary. As the recent outpouring of popular and scholarly literature on negotiation illustrates, the greater the number of issues in controversy between the parties, the greater the likelihood of achieving a variety of solutions. Parties may place complementary values on different items. The irony is that settlement managers, who think they are making settlement easier by reducing the issues, may in fact be increasing the likelihood of deadlock by reducing the issues to one. Furthermore, [their approach] may thwart the possibilities for . . . mutual gain.

"In addition to foreclosing a number of possible settlements, the efficiency-minded settlement officer seems prone to use coercive techniques such as suggesting a particular result, making threats about taking the case off the docket, directing meetings with clients or parties. Lawyers find these techniques problematic. Thus, the quest for efficiency may in fact be counterproductive.

"Some recent data seem to indicate that greater satisfaction can be achieved with a different settlement management role—the facilitator of good settlements. [Examples included] judges who analyzed the particular facts of the case (as opposed to those who used formulas like 'Lloyds of London'), offered explicit suggestions and assessments of the parties' positions, occasionally spoke directly to recalcitrant clients, and expressed views about the unfairness of particular results. . . .

. . . .

"Judges who perform these functions are not necessarily mediators, though they are frequently called that by themselves and others. Strictly speaking, a mediator facilitates communication between the parties and helps them to reach their own solution. As a mediator becomes more directly involved in suggesting the substantive solution, his or her role can change and he or she can become an arbitrator or adjudicator. It appears that the role judges and magistrates assume in many settlement conferences is this hybrid form of med-arb. Med-arb uses all the techniques associated with mediation and arbitration—caucusing (meeting with the parties separately), making suggestions to the parties, allowing closed or best-offer bidding, and meeting with principals (clients) who have authority to settle or to reconsider and reconceive the problem. As the med-arb process moves toward arbitration, 'settlements' may closely resemble adjudication with rationalized, normative, or law-based solutions.

. . . .

"We might ask the procedural question: Who should bear the burden of proof on success? Critics like Fiss . . . assume that adjudication is the preferred process and challenge the 'settlors' to prove up their claims. Judges and judicial administrators argue vehemently that settlement devices speed cases along and provide better settlements, and assert that adjudication be used only when a strong need for it can be shown. My own view is that settlement is now the norm. The pertinent question is how can it be used most effectively (for the parties and for other users of the system) when traditional adjudicators are brought into the process. . . . Thus, on balance I support the movements toward mandatory settlement conferences, as long as they are 'properly' conducted by settlement officers sensitive to the efficiency-quality problem."

Kothe v. Smith

United States Court of Appeals, Second Circuit, 1985.
771 F.2d 667.

■ Before LUMBARD, VAN GRAAFEILAND and PIERCE, CIRCUIT JUDGES.

■ VAN GRAAFEILAND, CIRCUIT JUDGE:

Dr. James Smith appeals from a judgment of the United States District Court for the Southern District of New York (Sweet, J.), which directed him to pay $1,000 to plaintiff-appellee's attorney, $1,000 to plaintiff-appellee's medical witness, and $480 to the Clerk of the Court. For the reasons hereinafter discussed, we direct that the judgment be vacated.

Patricia Kothe brought this suit for medical malpractice against . . . Dr. Smith . . . , seeking $2 million in damages. . . .

Three weeks prior [to trial], Judge Sweet held a pretrial conference, during which he directed counsel for the parties to conduct settlement negotiations. Although it is not clear from the record, it appears that Judge Sweet recommended that the case be settled for between $20,000 and $30,000. He also warned the parties that, if they settled for a comparable figure after trial had begun, he would impose sanctions against the dilatory party. Smith, whose defense has been conducted throughout this litigation by his malpractice insurer, offered $5,000 on the day before trial, but it was rejected.

Although Kothe's attorney had indicated to Judge Sweet that his client would settle for $20,000, he had requested that the figure not be disclosed to Smith. Kothe's counsel conceded at oral argument that the lowest pretrial settlement demand communicated to Smith was $50,000. Nevertheless, when the case was settled for $20,000 after one day of trial, the district court proceeded to penalize Smith alone. In imposing the penalty, the court stated that it was "determined to get the attention of the carrier" and that "the carriers are going to have to wake up when a judge tells them that they want [sic] to settle a case and they don't want to settle it." Under the circumstances of this case, we believe that the district court's imposition of a penalty against Smith was an abuse of the sanction power given it by Fed.R.Civ.P. 16(f).

Although the law favors the voluntary settlement of civil suits, ABKCO Music, Inc. v. Harrisongs Music, Ltd., 722 F.2d 988, 997 (2d Cir.1983), it does not sanction efforts by trial judges to effect settlements through coercion. Del Rio v. Northern Blower Co., 574 F.2d 23, 26 (1st Cir.1978) (citing Wolff v. Laverne, Inc., 17 A.D.2d 213, 233 N.Y.S.2d 555 (1962)); see MacLeod v. D.C. Transit System, Inc., 283 F.2d 194, 195 n. 1 (D.C.Cir. 1960); 89 C.J.S., Trial, § 577 at 355. In the Wolff case, cited with approval in Del Rio, supra, the Court said:

> We view with disfavor all pressure tactics whether directly or obliquely, to coerce settlement by litigants and their counsel. Failure to concur in what the Justice presiding may consider an adequate settlement should not result in an imposition upon a litigant or his counsel, who reject it, of any retributive sanctions not specifically authorized by law.

17 A.D.2d at 215, 233 N.Y.S.2d 555. In short, pressure tactics to coerce settlement simply are not permissible. [Citations omitted.] "The judge must not compel agreement by arbitrary use of his power and the attorney must not meekly submit to a judge's suggestion, though it be strongly urged." Brooks v. Great Atlantic & Pacific Tea Co., 92 F.2d 794, 796 (9th Cir.1937).

Rule 16 of the Fed.R.Civ.P. was not designed as a means for clubbing the parties—or one of them—into an involuntary compromise. See Padovani v. Bruchhausen, 293 F.2d 546, 548 (2d Cir.1961); Clark, To An Understanding Use of Pre–Trial, 1961, 29 F.R.D. 454, 456; Smith, Pretrial Conference—A Study of Methods, 1961, 29 F.R.D. 348, 353; Moskowitz, Glimpses of Federal Trials and Procedure, 1946, 4 F.R.D. 216, 218. Although subsection [(c)(2)(I)] of Rule 16, added in the 1983 amendments of the Rule, was designed to encourage pretrial settlement discussions, it was not its purpose to "impose settlement negotiations on unwilling litigants." See Advisory Committee Note, 1983, 97 F.R.D. 205, 210.

We find the coercion in the instant case especially troublesome because the district court imposed sanctions on Smith alone. Offers to settle a claim are not made in a vacuum. They are part of a more complex process which includes "conferences, informal discussions, offers, counterdemands, more discussions, more haggling, and finally, in the great majority of cases, a compromise." J. & D. Sindell, Let's Talk Settlement 300 (1963). In other words, the process of settlement is a two-way street, and a defendant should not be expected to bid against himself. In the instant case, Smith never received a demand of less than $50,000. Having received no indication from Kothe that an offer somewhere in the vicinity of $20,000 would at least be given careful consideration, Smith should not have been required to make an offer in this amount simply because the court wanted him to.

Smith's attorney should not be condemned for changing his evaluation of the case after listening to Kothe's testimony during the first day of trial. As every experienced trial lawyer knows, the personalities of the parties and their witnesses play an important role in litigation. It is one thing to have a valid claim; it is quite another to convince a jury of this fact. It is not at all unusual, therefore, for a defendant to change his perception of a case based on the plaintiff's performance on the witness stand. We see nothing about that occurrence in the instant case that warranted the imposition of sanctions against the defendant alone.

Although we commend Judge Sweet for his efforts to encourage settlement negotiations, his excessive zeal leaves us no recourse but to remand the matter with instructions to vacate the judgment.[a]

JEFFREY A. PARNESS, IMPROVING JUDICIAL SETTLEMENT CONFERENCES, 39 U.C.Davis L.Rev. 1891, 1908 (2006). Professor Fiss, among others, has "expressed concerns about the unbounded, unchecked, unbridled, and virtually unfettered judicial discretion of trial judges who preside over civil case settlement conferences. I, too, am concerned. But the best response is not to abolish or severely restrict judicial settlement conferences. Rather, it is to add more formality and more written guidelines. . . . These guidelines should involve . . . both more adversary control and more detailed and written criteria. In addition, new guidelines should expressly recognize that the claims and interests that might be discussed at judicial settlement conferences are far more expansive than the justiciable claims that might be discussed at trial preparation conferences. Thus, civil case settlements subject to same-case judicial enforcement can involve many more claims, interests, and people than would have been involved in any adversarial proceedings in the same case."

---

[a] In a later case Judge Sweet imposed a $1000 fine on defendant for criminal contempt of a pretrial conference order to submit a "bonafide" settlement offer. In an opinion by Judge Van Graafeiland, another panel of the Second Circuit reversed, finding the order too vague and imprecise. Hess v. N.J. Transit Rail Operations, 846 F.2d 114, 104 A.L.R.Fed. 455 (2d Cir.1988). But cf., e.g., White v. Raymark Indus., Inc., 783 F.2d 1175 (4th Cir.1986) (upholding assessment of juror costs on defendant, upon notice and hearing and pursuant to local rule, for delaying settlement until morning of trial).

WAYNE D. BRAZIL, EFFECTIVE LAWYERING IN JUDICIALLY HOSTED SETTLEMENT CONFERENCES, 1988 J.Disp.Resol. 1, 54. "Lawyers who are good settlement negotiators understand clearly that the hat they wear during negotiations is very different from the hat they might wear at an adversarial hearing or during a trial. They know that effectiveness in the settlement dynamic requires careful preparation (by them and of their clients), tight reasoning, unusual levels of candor about strengths and weaknesses, calm and open-minded exchanges of views, a quiet, understated confidence, flexibility, and the capacity to make controlled concessions. Good settlement lawyers pay attention to the needs (economic and psychological) of others and know that they have an advantage if, by the reasonableness and professionalism of their presentations, they can convert the settlement judge to an advocate of a solution that they can recommend to their client."

(c) MODEL

The "law and economics" movement has enjoyed great success as an analytic aid since its birth around 1960, and it promises to continue to do so. See generally Richard A. Posner, Economic Analysis of Law (7th ed. 2007). We have already seen an example in the American Hospital Supply case, and we can further demonstrate its usefulness by constructing a simple explanatory model of the disputants' settlement decision.

The aim is to construct the condition for litigation under a number of simplifying assumptions, including known recovery, equal costs, risk neutrality, rational decisionmaking by lawyers acting in their clients' best interests, and absence of impediments to bargaining. In that situation, settlement negotiations will collapse and litigation will proceed only if the minimum amount that the potential plaintiff will accept in settlement exceeds the maximum amount that the potential defendant will pay. The plaintiff's minimum is the eventually recoverable judgment (J) discounted by his estimated probability of winning (P_p), minus his future cost of litigating (L), which he would save by settling, plus his transaction cost of settling (S), which he would incur in arranging a settlement. The defendant will pay up to the eventual judgment times her estimate of the probability of the plaintiff's winning (P_d), plus litigation cost, minus settlement cost. That is to say, the necessary condition for litigation is

$$P_p J - L + S > P_d J + L - S.$$

The lessons become clearer upon rewriting the inequality as

$$(P_p - P_d) J > 2 (L - S).$$

Thus, if the two disputants agree on the probability of the outcome, and given that litigation is normally more expensive than settlement, then the left side of the second inequality is zero and the right side is positive, so that the condition for litigation will never be met—or, in other words, a settlement range between the plaintiff's minimum demand and the defendant's maximum offer will always exist, and the parties will negotiate a settlement amount that divides the range between themselves somehow. Conversely, litigation should ensue only when each disputant persists in viewing his or her chance more favorably than the opponent does. That represents a significant insight.

Questions: (2) Create a numerical example in which the condition for litigation is met. Now, what changes to J, L, and S will produce a settlement range?

(3) If a critical condition for litigation is that each side be relatively optimistic about its chances, what effect would you expect a robust discovery scheme to have on the settlement rate? But what if psychologists are correct in teaching that humans tend to assimilate information in a self-serving way, so that each side interprets new information in a way that is relatively favorable to its position? See Samuel Issacharoff, The Content of Our Casebooks: Why Do Cases Get Litigated?, 29 Fla.St.U.L.Rev. 1265, 1284–86 (2002) (discussing self-serving assessments of fairness in pretrial bargaining).

To proceed much further in analysis with assurance, one would obviously have to relax the simplifying assumptions, such as damages known by both sides to be a certain amount. Also, one would have to supplement this economic technique with other methods, such as game theory or behavioral decision theory. See Robert G. Bone, Civil Procedure: The Economics of Civil Procedure (2003). Nevertheless, simple modeling, even if based on somewhat unrealistic assumptions, can prove quite helpful to the student.

Consider, for example, the problem of frivolous litigation. The right side of the first of the two inequalities suggests why a defendant facing expensive litigation might be willing to make an offer, even if P_d is near zero. The right side is still positive, which means that the defendant can save her cost of litigating by settling. But if the legal system shifts the defendant's cost of litigating to the plaintiff, which is an indemnification that Rule 11 permits, then the plaintiff's cost of litigating goes to $2L$ and the defendant's cost of litigating falls to zero. Making frivolous litigation costless for the defendant would be a way for the system to remove the frivolous plaintiff's ability to threaten litigation in order to extort a nuisance settlement from the defendant.

Nonetheless, a glance at the left side of the first inequality suggests that the real world of frivolous litigation is a complex one. The left side should be negative, in that a straightforwardly frivolous suit has a negative expected value for the plaintiff, rendering mysterious why a rational plaintiff would file suit, and why a rational defendant would offer to settle. As a matter of strategy, the defendant, especially if concerned about her reputation for fighting frivolous lawsuits, would be tempted to call the plaintiff's bluff. The plaintiff, facing an out-of-pocket loss, would then cave. For frivolous litigation to be frequent enough to constitute a social problem, which it seems to be, it therefore must often involve asymmetric information. That is, either the plaintiff or the defendant wrongly thinks that the plaintiff has a decent chance of winning. Then the plaintiff will be willing to file a suit, and the defendant will be willing to offer a settlement. Such situations of asymmetric information therefore call for regulation that goes beyond cost-shifting—perhaps regulation both to require prefiling investigation, as Rule 11 does, and to provide for early judicial screening, as Rule 56 does to some extent. See Robert G. Bone, Modeling Frivolous Suits, 145 U.Pa.L.Rev. 519 (1997). But cf. Chris Guthrie, Framing Frivolous Litigation: A Psychological Theory, 67 U.Chi.L.Rev. 163 (2000) (supplementing rational-actor model with law-and-psychology's framing theory, which predicts litigants' overvaluing of low-probability litigation).

SECTION 3. TRIAL

If the case has survived the pretrial maneuvers and has not been settled by the parties or otherwise accelerated to termination, a trial is in order. Bear in mind that fewer and fewer trials take place each year. Nevertheless, the vanishing civil trial retains importance because it is the last-line resolver of factual disputes. Settlement will proceed in reflection of the trial's potential outcome.

Rule 40 directs each district court to provide by local rule for the placing of cases upon the calendar for trial. These local rules vary. In some districts, one of the parties must take the initiative in order to secure a trial; in others, the court exclusively handles the matter. One way or another, the case is set for trial, with or without a jury. About two-thirds of federal civil trials are jury trials.

(a) JURY

[Rules 38, 39, 47, 48]

Jury right.—Will the trial be to a judge alone or to a jury (under the supervision of a judge)? For the answer, begin by reading the Seventh Amendment to the Constitution of the United States. Until fairly recently, we could have said with a fair amount of accuracy that the measure of the jury right preserved by the Constitution was whether the case was of a type that was triable by jury in a superior court of common law in England[a] when the United States adopted the Seventh Amendment in 1791. Although that historical test is still of central importance, it no longer tells the whole story. Complications arise primarily from the fact that under the Federal Rules the federal courts hear cases in a procedural context unknown to the English courts, with the Rules' merger of law and equity

[a] The superior courts of common law were the Court of Common Pleas, the Court of King's Bench, and the Court of Exchequer. These courts generally utilized trial by jury. Actions at law typically were those that sought relief in the form of money damages.

The Court of Chancery, which had jurisdiction of suits in equity, did not use the jury method of trial, except that the chancellor sometimes referred a case to a jury for advisory purposes. Suits in equity typically sought relief in the form of an order commanding the defendant to do or not to do some act.

being particularly significant here. The question is a difficult one. We reach it at Topic E of Part Eight.

The fact that a case falls into a category making it triable by jury as a matter of right does not necessarily mean that a jury will ultimately render a verdict upon it. The parties waive the jury right unless a party makes timely demand for it in accordance with Rule 38(b) and (c). At any rate, even if a jury is impanelled, it may never be given anything to decide, for the jury's sole function is to pass upon contested questions of fact. If, for instance, the judge has reserved until trial the question whether the plaintiff has stated a claim upon which relief can be granted, the judge's determination of this question of law adversely to the plaintiff may dispose of the case without the intervention of the jury. Similarly, a ruling of law that the proof is insufficient to warrant a reasonable jury in finding that a claim or defense has been established may result in withdrawal of the case from the jury.

Jury characteristics.—A common-law jury numbered twelve, and its verdict had to be unanimous. Until recently it was accepted without question that the jury right preserved by the Seventh Amendment entitled a party in a federal civil case to a unanimous verdict of twelve jurors. See Maxwell v. Dow, 176 U.S. 581, 586, 20 S.Ct. 448, 450 (1900). But does the Seventh Amendment actually preserve these incidents of a civil jury trial?

Consider first the *number* of jurors. It was long the common assumption that the Seventh Amendment entitled a party in federal court to a twelve-person jury. Some states, on the other hand, had provided in certain civil cases for juries of fewer than twelve persons, as the Seventh Amendment itself does not restrict the states.[b] A few states had gone further, prescribing juries of fewer than twelve in certain criminal cases, even though here the Sixth Amendment does restrict the states. Yet, in Williams v. Florida, 399 U.S. 78, 90 S.Ct. 1893 (1970), the Supreme Court rejected precedent to hold that a six-person jury, acting unanimously, in a state criminal trial does not constitute a violation of the Federal Constitution. Encouraged by these developments on the criminal side, most federal district courts came to provide by local rule for six-person civil juries.[c]

---

[b] By interpretation of the Fourteenth Amendment, the Supreme Court has held most of the rights in the Bill of Rights to be fundamental enough to be guaranteed against invasion by the states, but the Seventh Amendment right to a civil jury has not been one of those. E.g., Walker v. Sauvinet, 92 U.S. 90 (1876); Melancon v. McKeithen, 345 F.Supp. 1025 (E.D.La.), aff'd mem. sub nom. Mayes v. Ellis, 409 U.S. 943, 93 S.Ct. 289, 290 (1972), Davis v. Edwards, 409 U.S. 1098, 93 S.Ct. 908 (1973). That is to say, the Seventh Amendment applies to actions in the federal courts, but not to state-court actions. State constitutions, however, most often contain provisions similar to the Seventh Amendment.

In contrast, the Sixth Amendment right to a criminal jury does apply to the states through the Fourteenth Amendment. Why this distinction?

[c] Federal district courts could not experiment with the criminal jury, because the Federal Rules of Criminal Procedure, independently of the Constitution, did and still do require normally a twelve-person jury that acts unanimously in federal criminal cases.

Colgrove v. Battin

Supreme Court of the United States, 1973.
413 U.S. 149, 93 S.Ct. 2448.

■ MR. JUSTICE BRENNAN delivered the opinion of the Court.

Local Rule 13(d)(1) of the Revised Rules of Procedure of the United States District Court for the District of Montana provides that a jury for the trial of civil cases shall consist of six persons.[1] When respondent District Court Judge set this diversity case for trial before a jury of six in compliance with the Rule, petitioner sought mandamus from the Court of Appeals for the Ninth Circuit to direct respondent to impanel a 12–member jury. Petitioner contended that the local Rule (1) violated the Seventh Amendment; (2) violated the statutory provision, 28 U.S.C. § 2072, [which until 1988 provided] that rules "shall preserve the right of trial by jury as at common law and as declared by the Seventh Amendment . . ."; and (3) was rendered invalid by Fed.Rule Civ.Proc. 83 because "inconsistent with" Fed.Rule Civ.Proc. 48 [which until 1991 provided in its entirety: "The parties may stipulate that the jury shall consist of any number less than twelve or that a verdict or a finding of a stated majority of the jurors shall be taken as the verdict or finding of the jury."] The Court of Appeals found no merit in these contentions, sustained the validity of local Rule 13(d)(1), and denied the writ, 456 F.2d 1379 (1972). We granted certiorari, 409 U.S. 841, 93 S.Ct. 44 (1972). We affirm.

I

In Williams v. Florida, 399 U.S. 78, 90 S.Ct. 1893 (1970), the Court sustained the constitutionality of a Florida statute providing for six-member juries in certain criminal cases. The constitutional challenge rejected in that case relied on the guarantees of jury trial secured the accused by Art. III, § 2, cl. 3, of the Constitution and by the Sixth Amendment. We expressly reserved, however, the question whether "additional references to the 'common law' that occur in the Seventh Amendment might support a different interpretation" with respect to jury trial in civil cases. Id., at 92 n. 30, 90 S.Ct., at 1901 n. 30. We conclude that they do not.

The pertinent words of the Seventh Amendment are: "In Suits at common law . . . the right of trial by jury shall be preserved . . . ." On its face, this language is not directed to jury characteristics, such as size, but rather defines the kind of cases for which jury trial is preserved, namely, "suits at common law." And while it is true that "[w]e have almost no direct evidence concerning the intention of the framers of the seventh amendment itself,"[7] the historical setting in which the Seventh Amend-

---

[1] Rule 13(d)(1) provides:

"A jury for the trial of civil cases shall consist of six persons plus such alternate jurors as may be impaneled."

Similar local rules have been adopted by 54 other federal district courts, at least as to some civil cases. . . .

[7] Henderson, The Background of the Seventh Amendment, 80 Harv.L.Rev. 289, 291 (1966).

ment was adopted highlighted a controversy that was generated, not by concern for preservation of jury characteristics at common law, but by fear that the civil jury itself would be abolished unless protected in express words. Almost a century and a half ago, this Court recognized that "[o]ne of the strongest objections originally taken against the constitution of the United States, was the want of an express provision securing the right of trial by jury in civil cases." Parsons v. Bedford, 3 Pet. 433, 445 (1830). But the omission of a protective clause from the Constitution was not because an effort was not made to include one. On the contrary, a proposal was made to include a provision in the Constitution to guarantee the right of trial by jury in civil cases but the proposal failed because the States varied widely as to the cases in which civil jury trial was provided, and the proponents of a civil jury guarantee found too difficult the task of fashioning words appropriate to cover the different state practices. The strong pressures for a civil jury provision in the Bill of Rights encountered the same difficulty. Thus, it was agreed that, with no federal practice to draw on and since state practices varied so widely, any compromising language would necessarily have to be general. As a result, although the Seventh Amendment achieved the primary goal of jury trial adherents to incorporate an explicit constitutional protection of the right of trial by jury in civil cases, the right was limited in general words to "suits at common law." We can only conclude, therefore, that by referring to the "common law," the Framers of the Seventh Amendment were concerned with preserving the *right* of trial by jury in civil cases where it existed at common law, rather than the various incidents of trial by jury. In short, what was said in Williams with respect to the criminal jury is equally applicable here: constitutional history reveals no intention on the part of the Framers "to equate the constitutional and common-law characteristics of the jury." 399 U.S., at 99, 90 S.Ct., at 1905.

Consistently with the historical objective of the Seventh Amendment, our decisions have defined the jury right preserved in cases covered by the Amendment, as "the substance of the common-law right of trial by jury, as distinguished from mere matters of form or procedure . . . ." Baltimore & Carolina Line, Inc. v. Redman, 295 U.S. 654, 657, 55 S.Ct. 890, 891 (1935). The Amendment, therefore, does not "bind the federal courts to the exact procedural incidents or details of jury trial according to the common law in 1791," Galloway v. United States, 319 U.S. 372, 390, 63 S.Ct. 1077, 1087 (1943); see also Ex parte Peterson, 253 U.S. 300, 309, 40 S.Ct. 543, 546 (1920); Walker v. New Mexico & S.P.R. Co., 165 U.S. 593, 596, 17 S.Ct. 421, 422 (1897), and "[n]ew devices may be used to adapt the ancient institution to present needs and to make of it an efficient instrument in the administration of justice. . . ." Ex parte Peterson, supra, 253 U.S., at 309–310, 40 S.Ct., at 546; Funk v. United States, 290 U.S. 371, 382, 54 S.Ct. 212, 215 (1933).

Our inquiry turns, then, to whether a jury of 12 is of the substance of the common-law right of trial by jury. Keeping in mind the purpose of the jury trial in criminal cases to prevent government oppression, Williams, 399 U.S., at 100, 90 S.Ct., at 1905, and, in criminal and civil cases, to assure a fair and equitable resolution of factual issues, Gasoline Products Co. v. Champlin Refining Co., 283 U.S. 494, 498, 51 S.Ct. 513, 514 (1931), the question comes down to whether jury performance is a function of jury size. In Williams, we rejected the notion that "the reliability of the jury as a factfinder . . . [is] a function of its size," 399 U.S., at 100–101, 90 S.Ct., at 1906, and nothing has been suggested to lead us to alter that conclusion. Accordingly, we think it cannot be said that 12 members is a substantive aspect of the right of trial by jury.

It is true, of course, that several earlier decisions of this Court have made the statement that "trial by jury" means "a trial by a jury of 12 . . . ." Capital Traction Co. v. Hof, 174 U.S. 1, 13, 19 S.Ct. 580, 585 (1899); see also American Publishing Co. v. Fisher, 166 U.S. 464, 17 S.Ct. 618 (1897); Maxwell v. Dow, 176 U.S. 581, 586, 20 S.Ct. 448, 450 (1900). But in each case, the reference to "a jury of twelve" was clearly dictum and not a decision upon a question presented or litigated. . . . Insofar as the Hof statement implied that the Seventh Amendment required a jury of 12, it was at best an assumption. And even if that assumption had support in common-law doctrine, our canvass of the relevant constitutional history, like the history canvassed in Williams concerning the criminal jury, "casts considerable doubt on the easy assumption in our past decisions that if a given feature existed in a jury at common law . . . then it was necessarily preserved in the Constitution." 399 U.S., at 92–93, 90 S.Ct., at 1902. We cannot, therefore, accord the unsupported dicta of these earlier decisions the authority of decided precedents.

There remains, however, the question whether a jury of six satisfies the Seventh Amendment guarantee of "trial by jury." We had no difficulty reaching the conclusion in Williams that a jury of six would guarantee an accused the trial by jury secured by Art. III and the Sixth Amendment. Significantly, our determination that there was "no discernible difference between the results reached by the two different-sized juries," 399 U.S., at 101, 90 S.Ct., at 1906, drew largely upon the results of studies of the operations of juries of six in civil cases. Since then, much has been written about the six-member jury, but nothing that persuades us to depart from the conclusion reached in Williams.[15] Thus, while we express no view as to whether any number less than six would suffice,[16] we conclude that a jury of six satisfies the Seventh Amendment's guarantee of trial by jury in civil cases.

---

[15] Arguments, pro and con, on the effectiveness of a jury of six compared to a jury of 12 will be found in Devitt, [The Six Man Jury in the Federal Court, 53 F.R.D. 273 (1971)]; . . . Zeisel, . . . And Then There Were None: The Diminution of the Federal Jury, 38 U.Chi.L.Rev. 710 (1971) . . . . [On the dangers of the use by courts of social science research, see Jeffrey J. Rachlinski, "The Story of Colgrove: Social Science on Trial," in Civil Procedure Stories 389 (Kevin M. Clermont ed., 2d ed. 2008).—Ed.]

[16] What is required for a "jury" is a number large enough to facilitate group deliberation combined with a likelihood of obtaining a representative cross section of the community. Williams v. Florida, 399 U.S., at 100, 90 S.Ct., at 1905. It is undoubtedly true that at some point the number becomes too small to accomplish these goals, but, on the basis of presently available data, that cannot be concluded as to the number six. [Citations omitted.]

[Parts II and III of the Court's opinion dealt with those of the petitioner's arguments based on § 2072 and on Rules 48 and 83, and are omitted.]

Affirmed.

. . . .

■ MR. JUSTICE MARSHALL, with whom MR. JUSTICE STEWART joins, dissenting.

Some 30 years ago, Mr. Justice Black warned his Brethren against the "gradual process of judicial erosion which . . . has slowly worn away a major portion of the essential guarantee of the Seventh Amendment." Galloway v. United States, 319 U.S. 372, 397, 63 S.Ct. 1077, 1090 (1943) (dissenting opinion). Today, the erosion process reaches bedrock. . . .

. . . No one need be fooled by reference to the six-man trier of fact utilized in the District Court for the District of Montana as a "jury." . . . We deal here not with some minor tinkering with the role of the civil jury, but with its wholesale abolition and replacement with a different institution which functions differently, produces different results, and was wholly unknown to the Framers of the Seventh Amendment.

. . . .

When a historical approach is applied to the issue at hand, it cannot be doubted that the Framers envisioned a jury of 12 when they referred to trial by jury. . . .

. . . .

The Court today elects to abandon the certainty of this historical test, as well as the many cases which support it, in favor of a vaguely defined functional analysis which asks not what the Framers meant by "trial by jury" but rather whether some substitute for the common-law jury performs the same functions as a jury and serves as an adequate substitute for one. . . .

. . . But the composition of the jury itself is a matter of arbitrary, a priori definition. As Mr. Justice Harlan argued "[t]he right to a trial by jury . . . has no enduring meaning apart from historical form." Williams v. Florida, 399 U.S., at 125, 90 S.Ct., at 1919 (separate opinion).

It is senseless, then, to say that a panel of six constitutes a "jury" without first defining what one means by a jury, and that initial definition must, in the nature of things, be arbitrary. One could, of course, define the term "jury" as being a body of six or more laymen. But the line between five and six would then be just as arbitrary as the line between 11 and 12. There is no way by reference to abstract principle or "function" that one can determine that six is "enough," five is "too small," and 30 "too large."[8] These evaluations can only be made by reference to a hypothetical

[8] The Court asserts that "[w]hat is required for a 'jury' is a number large enough to facilitate group deliberation combined with a likelihood of obtaining a representative cross section of the community." See ante, at . . . n. 16. We can bypass for the moment the intriguing question of where the majority finds this requirement in the words of the Seventh Amendment. For our purposes, it is sufficient to note that, upon examination, this "test"

ideal jury of some arbitrarily chosen size. All one can say is that a jury of six functions less like a jury of 12 than would a jury of, say eight, but more like a jury of 12 than would a jury of three.[9] Although I think it clear that my Brethren would reject, for example, a jury of one, the Court does not begin to tell us how it would go about drawing a line in a nonarbitrary fashion, and it is obvious that in matters of degree of this kind, nonarbitrary line drawing is a logical impossibility.

Of course, there is nothing intrinsically wrong with drawing arbitrary lines and, indeed, . . . in order to resolve certain problems they are essential. Thus, this Court has not hesitated in the past to rely on arbitrary demarcations in cases where constitutional rights depend on matters of degree. See, e.g., Burns v. Fortson, 410 U.S. 686, 93 S.Ct. 1209 (1973) [(upholding fifty-day pre-election cutoff on voter registration, while saying this approaches constitutional limit)]. But in cases where arbitrary lines are necessary, I would have thought it more consonant with our limited role in a constitutional democracy to draw them with reference to the fixed bounds of the Constitution rather than on a wholly ad hoc basis.

I think history will bear out the proposition that when constitutional rights are grounded in nothing more solid than the intuitive, unexplained sense of five Justices that a certain line is "right" or "just," those rights are certain to erode and, eventually, disappear altogether. Today, a majority of this Court may find six-man juries to represent a proper balance between competing demands of expedition and group representation. But as dockets become more crowded and pressures on jury trials grow, who is to say that some future Court will not find three, or two, or one a number large enough to satisfy its unexplicated sense of justice? It should be clear that constitutional rights which are so vulnerable to pressures of the moment are not really protected by the Constitution at all. . . .

. . . It may well be that the number 12 is no more than a "historical accident" and is "wholly without significance 'except to mystics.'" Williams v. Florida, supra, 399 U.S., at 102, 90 S.Ct., at 1907. But surely there is nothing more significant about the number six, or three, or one. The line must be drawn somewhere, and the difference between drawing it in the light of history and drawing it on an ad hoc basis is, ultimately, the difference between interpreting a constitution and making it up as one goes along.

. . . .

turns out to be no test at all. It may be that the ideal jury would provide "enough" group deliberation and community representation. But the question in this case is how much is "enough." Obviously, the larger the jury the more group representation it will provide. . . . Merely observing that a certain level of group representation is constitutionally required fails to tell us what that level is. And, more significantly, it fails to tell us how to go about deciding what that level is.

[9] It thus will not do to argue, as has my Brother White, that one "can get off the 'slippery slope' before he reaches the bottom. . . ." Williams v. Florida, 399 U.S. 78, 91 n. 28, 90 S.Ct. 1893, 1901 n. 28 (1970). This begs the question how one knows at what point to get off—a question for which the Court apparently has no answer.

■ [JUSTICES DOUGLAS and POWELL dissented on other grounds, allowing them to avoid reaching the constitutional issue. Their opinions are omitted.]

A strong majority of states have since moved to juries smaller than twelve. However, in Ballew v. Georgia, 435 U.S. 223, 98 S.Ct. 1029 (1978), the Supreme Court held that in a state criminal trial a five-person jury, even though acting unanimously, constitutes a violation of the Federal Constitution. All the Justices supported this holding, although the case produced five opinions. Justice Blackmun, through a lengthy review of the numerous post-Williams empirical studies on the jury, explained that reducing the jury below six members would adversely affect group deliberation and cross-sectional representation. Among other points, he observed that the smaller the jury, the less likely is the group to remember accurately, to overcome the biases of its members, and to exhibit self-criticism; also, "the data now raise doubts about the accuracy of the results achieved by smaller and smaller panels," as well as about the consistency thereof. Furthermore, reducing jury size erects barriers to "the representation of minority groups in the community." Meanwhile, he argued, reducing the jury below six members would offer only minimal savings in court time and financial costs. Accordingly, the Court drew the line.

In the meantime, a roughly similar scenario is working itself out on the *unanimity* front. It has long been the general assumption that the Seventh Amendment entitles a party in federal court to a unanimous verdict. Indeed, here it is more than assumption, the Supreme Court having in fact so held in Springville v. Thomas, 166 U.S. 707, 17 S.Ct. 717 (1897), and apparently also in American Publishing Co. v. Fisher, 166 U.S. 464, 17 S.Ct. 618 (1897). Some states, on the other hand, abolished the unanimity requirement for certain civil and criminal cases. When the issue finally arose, in Apodaca v. Oregon, 406 U.S. 404, 92 S.Ct. 1628 (1972), and Johnson v. Louisiana, 406 U.S. 356, 92 S.Ct. 1620 (1972), a sharply divided Supreme Court held that a nonunanimous verdict, by a twelve-person jury, in a state criminal trial passes federal constitutional muster. There was some indication by the Court, however, that a "substantial majority of the jury" is necessary and that a 9–3 verdict is at or very near the constitutional floor for twelve-person state criminal juries.

Questions: (1) The winds of change are obviously buffeting Springville and American Publishing. Do you see any way that their constitutional requirement of unanimity for federal civil juries could survive the trend of the modern cases, if somehow a challenge were to arise? Is there an argument in the fact that the Court here faces actual holdings directly in point, unlike the situation confronting the Court in Colgrove? If not, is there an argument you can build on the fact (a) that Apodaca and Johnson are criminal cases, as contrasted to civil cases governed by the Seventh Amendment, or (b) that Apodaca and Johnson are state cases, thus leaving open the question whether unanimity is still a requirement for federal juries? Or is there an argument tied to the belief that unanimity is a more important concern than is the number of jurors, thus allowing Colgrove to be distinguished?

(2) Assuming nonunanimous verdicts by federal civil juries are authorized, what combinations of reduced numbers of jurors and majority verdicts would you deem constitutionally permissible? Eight-out-of-nine?

In Burch v. Louisiana, 441 U.S. 130, 99 S.Ct. 1623 (1979), the Court held that in a state criminal trial a nonunanimous verdict, by a six-person jury, violates the Federal Constitution. All the Justices were in agreement that a 5–1 verdict is invalid. Writing for the Court, Justice Rehnquist addressed this "'close'" question "at the intersection of our decisions concerning jury size and unanimity" by first noting that "having already departed from the strictly historical requirements of jury trial, it is inevitable that lines must be drawn somewhere if the substance of the jury trial right is to be preserved." He then quickly concluded that "much the same reasons that led us in Ballew to decide that use of a five-member jury threatened the fairness of the proceeding and the proper role of the jury, lead us to conclude now that conviction for a nonpetty offense by only five members of a six-person jury presents a similar threat to preservation of the substance of the jury trial guarantee and justifies our requiring verdicts rendered by six-person juries to be unanimous."

However, well more than half of the states permit a less than unanimous verdict in a civil case. In some states, three-quarters or even two-thirds of the jurors are sufficient for a verdict. In New York, under NYCPLR § 4113, a verdict may be rendered by five-sixths of the six jurors. See generally Hans Zeisel, The Verdict of Five out of Six Civil Jurors: Constitutional Problems, 1982 Am.B.Found.Res.J. 141, 155.

On December 1, 1991, Rule 48 took on essentially its present form, expressly specifying the key characteristics of the federal civil jury and thus restricting further experimentation by any federal district court's local rule. The new Rule 48 invoked the Colgrove holding to provide for juries of at least six persons, who act unanimously, unless the parties otherwise stipulate. The drafters of new Rule 48 envisaged as the normal course the seating of juries somewhat larger than six members, but not more than twelve, to insure against attrition during the trial. If the judge excused one or more jurors pursuant to Rule 47(c), as for illness, there should then still be at least six persons to render verdict. So today, eight-person federal civil juries are most commonly impanelled.

Interestingly, the rulemakers worked this reform soon after the American Bar Association, upon a weighing of the evidence and values, had called for returning to a federal civil jury of twelve but allowing 10–2 verdicts. 58 U.S.L.W. 2474, 2478 (Feb. 20, 1990). More recently, the ABA, in its Principles for Juries & Jury Trials princs. 3–4 (2005), threw its support to twelve-person juries acting unanimously.

Still more interestingly, after the 1991 amendment of Rule 48, the civil rulemaking committees proposed amending it to require the seating of twelve-person juries that act unanimously. But the Judicial Conference in

1996 rejected this proposal as inefficient. The Advisory Committee's note had explained its purpose:

"Rule 48 [would be] amended to restore the core of the twelve-member body that has constituted the definition of a civil jury for centuries. Local rules setting smaller jury sizes [would be] invalid because inconsistent with Rule 48.

"The rulings that the Seventh Amendment permits six-member juries, and that former Rule 48 permitted local rules establishing six-member juries, do not speak to the question whether six-member juries are desirable. Much has been learned since 1973 about the advantages of twelve-member juries. Twelve-member juries substantially increase the representative quality of most juries, greatly improving the probability that most juries will include members of minority groups. The sociological and psychological dynamics of jury deliberation also are strongly influenced by jury size. Members of a twelve-person jury are less easily dominated by an aggressive juror, better able to recall the evidence, more likely to rise above the biases and prejudices of individual members, and enriched by a broader base of community experience. The wisdom enshrined in the twelve-member tradition is increasingly demonstrated by contemporary social science."

Jury selection.—The Jury Selection and Service Act of 1968, 28 U.S.C. §§ 1861–1869, aims at ensuring selection of federal jurors at random from a fair cross section of the community without discrimination on account of race, color, religion, sex, national origin, or economic status. Each district court must adopt a selection plan, normally tied to voter lists.

The Act otherwise leaves the selection of the actual jury largely to local rule and practice. Still, some general description is possible. From the list of available citizens, the statutory officials summon to the courtroom a panel of jurors. From that panel, they draw by lot the tentative jurors for the particular trial. These jurors then undergo the questioning process referred to in Rule 47(a), which is called the voir dire examination and which in federal court is usually conducted by the judge. Its purpose is to determine whether good reason exists why any of them should not serve in the case.

If, for example, a juror is related to a party, or if she has a financial interest in the outcome of the case, or if she is prejudiced against a party, she may be challenged "for cause." The court will exclude the juror if it finds that the cause exists. In addition, at some point in the process, each side can exercise a limited number of "peremptory challenges": 28 U.S.C. § 1870 provides each party in a civil case with three peremptory challenges, but when there are multiple plaintiffs or defendants, the court in its discretion may treat each side as a single party or may allow additional peremptory challenges. A party may exercise peremptory challenges at the party's mainly uncontrolled pleasure.

Jurors who have been excluded by either type of challenge are replaced by other persons similarly drawn by lot from the panel and similarly subjected to questioning and challenge. When the process of selection is completed, the jury is sworn. The trial proceeds.

VALERIE P. HANS & NEIL VIDMAR, "JURY SELECTION", in The Psychology of the Courtroom 39, 63–64, 68 (Norbert L. Kerr & Robert M. Bray eds., 1982). "Trial tactics handbooks used in the training of lawyers provide us with some indirect evidence about the theories of 'good' jurors and 'bad' jurors that guide selection practices. The handbooks . . . consist of a mixture of legal lore, streamlined social science findings, and common sense. Some of the advice extended to lawyers betrays an obvious trafficking in stereotypes. A case in point is provided by Bailey and Rothblatt[, Successful Techniques for Criminal Trials] (1971), who suggest that defense lawyers choose women for the jury if the principal witness against the defendant is female, since women are 'somewhat distrustful' of other women; they also caution that the occupation of a prospective woman juror's husband is of importance, since generally a woman 'will feel and think in the same manner as her husband [p. 105].' Given that the information about jurors is often minimal, the trial tactics manuals do display a remarkable ingenuity in developing generalizations about those characteristics typically available to lawyers, such as occupation. For example, Bailey and Rothblatt maintain that salesmen, actors, artists, and writers are highly desirable as defense jurors, reasoning that because their occupations have exposed them to varied aspects of life, these individuals are not so easily shocked by crime as are people in less adventuresome occupations. [Another manual] warns defense lawyers to beware of individuals who are employees of large bureaucratic organizations, since these persons are less inclined to sympathize with the nonconforming behavior of the defendant. Also of note in the trial tactics manuals is an emphasis on fitting juror characteristics to the details of the specific case (e.g., women jurors for an attractive male defendant but male jurors when the offense is rape).

"In addition to providing a wealth of information about demographic predictors of the sympathetic juror (information that is of dubious value), trial manuals also suggest strategies for the conduct of the voir dire. Lawyers are advised [for example] to use the voir dire not only to ferret out those who are unfavorable to their case but also to ingratiate themselves with the jury. . . .

. . . .

"There is, therefore, scanty concrete information about the effectiveness of lawyers' selection techniques although what we do know indicates that generally selection strategies may be only minimally effective. From a psychological perspective, it seems unlikely that future studies of lawyer effectiveness would substantially alter the current conclusion that attorney strategies have minimal impact on the jury's verdict. . . . In real jury trials, the voir dire may be effective in eliminating openly prejudiced persons, but we cannot expect too much more.

"On the other hand, the most useful function of the voir dire may be its ability to indoctrinate and sensitize jurors about the need to set aside prejudices and participate in the trial with an impartial mind. This function of the voir dire . . . awaits systematic empirical examination.

. . . .

"In the late 1960s and early 1970s, social scientists became directly involved in jury selection in a series of political trials evolving out of racial protests and the Vietnam War. Variously labeled 'scientific' or 'systematic' jury selection, the techniques provide the defense with an alternative to traditional jury selection [and include community opinion surveys, investigation of jury panel members, and courtroom observation of prospective jurors]."

MICHAEL J. SAKS & REID HASTIE, SOCIAL PSYCHOLOGY IN COURT 49, 66–71 (1978). "The theory underlying the core hypothesis, that the characteristics of jurors affect the decision they reach, can be stated fairly simply. A person's demographic background (socioeconomic class, race, religion, sex, age, education, and so forth) denotes a particular kind of socializing history for that person. If you are poor, young, black, and female, you will have been conditioned to view the world differently, to react to it differently, and to hold different attitudes compared with a person who is wealthy, old, white, and male. These perceptions, attitudes, and values, in turn, help determine the decision you make as a juror. In addition to demographic characteristics, personality type (whether personality arises through genetics, psychodynamic development, or conditioning history) is thought to predispose a juror to a particular decision. If you are highly dependent on order, for example, you might be conviction-prone. It is unclear whether the theory holds that personality type determines the substantive preference one has (e.g., always wanting to be punitive) or whether it influences the way one processes the evidence (giving more weight to the government's evidence than to the defense's). Thus, juror demographic characteristics, personality, and attitudes are thought to have substantial impact on their decisions.

. . . .

"Despite a good deal of excitement about scientific jury selection . . . , and despite the apparently widely held assumption that the kind of person making a decision affects the decision made, the evidence consistently indicates that a jury's composition is a relatively minor determinant of the verdict. In the face of such enthusiastic countervailing belief, this conclusion may seem surprising. However, it should not. Small-group researchers have long recognized that individual difference variables account for little of the variation in group performance . . . . Juries are merely a special case of small-group decision making and are not exempt from the principles that apply to small groups generally. Nor should small-group researchers be surprised by the lack of impact of personality and attitude variables. The relative unimportance of personality . . . and attitudes . . . as determinants of behavior has become increasingly evident in the study of human behavior generally. What, then, does determine the verdict a jury will render if it is not the characteristics of the group members? . . .

. . . .

"In another study [Michael J. Saks, Carol M. Werner & Thomas M. Ostrom, The Presumption of Innocence and the American Juror, 2 J.Contemp.L. 46 (1975)], a sample of former jurors from Columbus, Ohio, were asked to indicate their certainty of a defendant's guilt or innocence in a series of brief hypothetical cases, each consisting of a set of evidentiary statements. They were given cases in which the crime alleged differed, where the amount of evidence against the defendant differed, and in which the strength of the evidence varied; it was either moderately (prescaled to reflect a .44 probability of guilt) or highly (.77) incriminating. Jurors were also tested with a scale of defendant-related attitudes in order to classify them as favorable or unfavorable to the defense. The attitude scale did predict how the jurors would respond. Jurors designated 'antidefendant' gave an average rating of guilt of 58 while 'prodefendant' jurors gave ratings that averaged −20. (A score of zero would indicate a juror thought it was equally likely that the defendant was guilty as not guilty; positive scores are in the guilty direction; negative scores in the not guilty direction.) That is a spread of 78 points. But the point spread between average certainty of guilt in response to one item of evidence compared to six items of evidence was 143 points. And presenting moderately incriminating evidence compared to highly incriminating evidence produced a spread of 172 points. In terms of the proportion of variance accounted for by each of the independent variables, the amount of evidence was more than three times as powerful, and the strength of evidence was more than seven times as powerful as attitudes were in determining the jurors' verdicts. Juror characteristics made a difference, but not nearly so much of a difference as characteristics of the trial evidence.

. . . .

"The studies are unanimous in showing that evidence is a substantially more potent determinant of jurors' verdicts than the individual characteristics of jurors. Indeed, the power of evidence is so well recognized by jury researchers that when studying processes other than evidence, they must calibrate the evidence to be moderate so that it leaves some variance to be influenced by the variables under study. Manipulating the evidence powerfully influences the verdict the group renders. This finding also is consistent with findings from elsewhere in psychological research. However important personality and attitudes may be in determining overt behavior, they generally are not as important as stimulus features of the situation . . . . What this implies about human behavior, on juries or off, is that while we are unique individuals, our differences are vastly overshadowed by our similarities. Moreover, the range of situations we are likely to encounter is far more varied than the range of human beings who will encounter them.

. . . .

"From the viewpoint of the jury system, [all the research] findings mean that jurors [especially] are much more responsive to the evidence placed before them than to their own personalities and attitudes. Our educated speculation is that this may well be due to the special social situation created by the court. Through learning outside of court and by the court's atmosphere, the judge's charges, and the rules of the game, jurors adopt a role of 'fairness' and 'objectivity' which may be as extreme as they ever have had or will have in their lives. That jurors are selected who do not have ongoing relationships with the parties or interests at stake in the case further enhances the success of the 'objective factfinders' role. Common-sense assumptions that the personal politics and prejudice which characterize much of human life invade the jury box ignore the special situational characteristics of the court and the human relationships constructed there.

. . . .

"From the viewpoint of attorneys and social scientists, working to serve a particular side of a particular case, these findings mean that while jury selection will have some impact on the outcome of the case, it is not as effective as directing their efforts at building and structuring the evidence to be presented to the jury."

KEVIN M. CLERMONT & THEODORE EISENBERG, TRIAL BY JURY OR JUDGE: TRANSCENDING EMPIRICISM, 77 Cornell L.Rev. 1124, 1151–55 (1992) (footnotes omitted). "Indeed, one of the more remarkable lessons that empirical study has to offer the law is that virtually no evidence exists to support the prevailing ingrained intuitions about juries [as biased and incompetent, relative to judges]. In fact, existing evidence is to the contrary.

"Admittedly, not much effective empirical work exists on the quality of the jury's performance, and there is even less on juries' performance as compared to that of judges. Studies on broad questions regarding the jury are difficult to do, and correspondingly shaky to interpret. But the evidence, such as it is, consistently supports a view of the jury as generally unbiased and competent, or at least so compared to a judge. The fact that jury and judge show a high degree of agreement is better supported.

"Research, for example, indicates that the strength of the trial evidence is the most important determinant of the verdict. Evaluated over the run of cases, juries are good factfinders. More specifically, research does not support a view of the jury as overly generous on awards, frequently ignoring the law, or institutionally unable to handle complex cases. Related research indeed suggests that a jury could even outperform a judge, because the judge is also human and groups typically outperform individuals by virtue of superiority in such tasks as recall of facts and correction of errors.

"The classic work in this area by Kalven and Zeisel[, The American Jury 63–64 (2d ed. 1971),] addressed reliability (the ability to treat like cases alike) rather than the validity or correctness of jury decisionmaking. Their questionnaires to presiding judges in some 4000 actual civil jury trials in the 1950's yielded data showing a 78% agreement between judge and jury on liability. When judge and jury disagreed, they exhibited no distinct pattern other than the juries' very small tendency to favor plaintiffs relative to judges.

"When compared to other human decisionmakers, the rate of agreement is more impressive than it first appears. This 78% agreement rate is better than the rate of agreement [on dichotomous decisions] between scientists doing peer review, employment interviewers ranking applicants, and psychiatrists and physicians diagnosing patients, and almost as good as the 79% or 80% rate of agreement between judges making sentencing decisions [of custody or no custody] in an experimental setting. So although theory plausibly suggests some judge/jury differences—such as that juries, because of a need for compromise to produce a unanimous verdict, would tend to give plaintiffs more wins but less money—the significance of any such differences seems to fade in actuality. Apparently, judge trial and jury trial combine to operate a decisionmaking system that is, at least in one sense, highly reliable.

"Much of the recent research has focused on jury verdicts, revealing trends such as the average award markedly increasing in recent years. Even if accurate, these observations do not bear on the issue of jury performance versus judge performance. Judges, who go wholly unobserved in this research, might be responding similarly to similar forces. For a specific example, [the graph] presents from our data, in millions of 1989 dollars, the mean recovery in judge and jury trials of successful product liability cases over the calendar years covered by this study. The similarity of the recovery trends suggests that the explanation for trends in awards lies somewhere other than in peculiarities of the jury system."

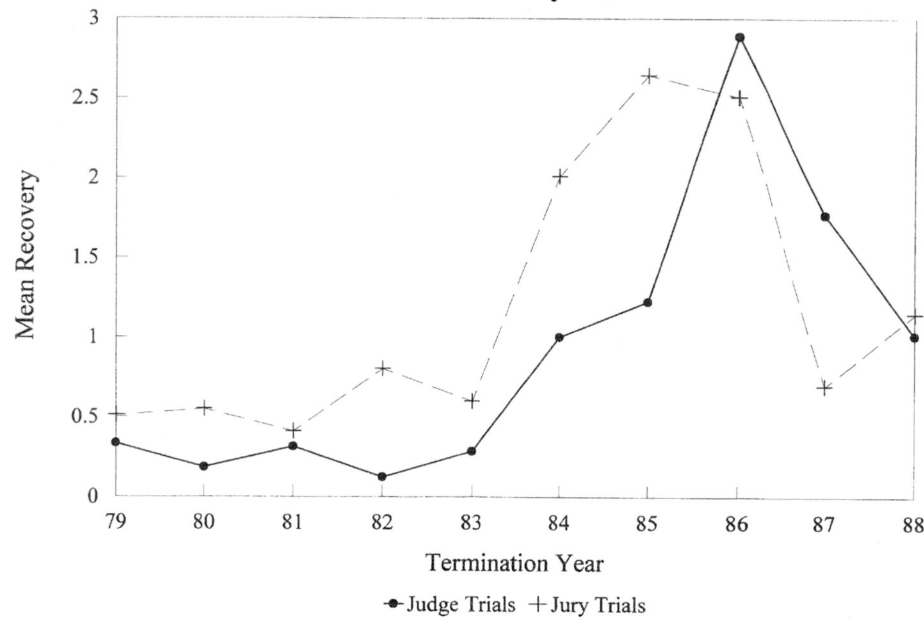

Source: Administrative Office Data, 1979-1989

PEREMPTORY CHALLENGES

Amidst this swirl of deleterious, negligible, and beneficial effects, one might presume that the permissibility of peremptory challenges has little net effect on outcome. Then why should the law permit this questionable type of challenge, which comes into play only when the court does not find cause to excuse? What are the benefits and costs of peremptory challenges?

Could one defend permitting these challenges on the ground that, all else being equal, we have a better process, as a process, when people have a say in selecting their own adjudicator?

But even if this is true, counter-values would seem also to be at stake. Most obviously, parties can surely misuse peremptory challenges of jurors. Although recent cases prohibit their use on invidious bases such as race, that imperfect regulation obviously increases the costs of administration. See Minetos v. CUNY, 925 F.Supp. 177, 183 (S.D.N.Y.1996) (dictum) ("All peremptory challenges should now be banned as an unnecessary waste of time and an obvious corruption of the judicial process."). But cf. Mary R. Rose, A Voir Dire of Voir Dire: Listening to Jurors' Views Regarding the Peremptory Challenge, 78 Chi.-Kent L.Rev. 1061 (2003).

Perhaps those counter-values explain why no equivalent of the peremptory challenge exists under 28 U.S.C. §§ 144 and 455, which provide the standards for disqualification of federal district judges.

KEVIN M. CLERMONT, ROBERT A. HILLMAN, SHERI LYNN JOHNSON & ROBERT S. SUMMERS, LAW FOR SOCIETY: NATURE, FUNCTIONS, AND LIMITS 101 (2010). "[Process-oriented] law, if well designed, will reflect a variety of important values. These values generate standards or criteria for judging the goodness or badness of processes such as adjudication, legislation, and administration. The important point here is that one has not exhaustively accounted for the total significance of such values merely by stressing their relationship to quality of outcome. Some processes have significance quite apart from their impact on outcome, and some indeed lead to a negative impact on outcome. This point is overlooked by some contemporary reformers who have their tunnel vision focused on result and result alone.

"There is independent worth, for example, in having processes in which those most vitally affected can be meaningfully heard and in having processes free of the taint of undue influence. The kinds of values reflected thereby, in contrast to *outcome values,* we shall call *process values.* To speak somewhat more carefully, then, we shall use the phrase 'process values' to refer to values by which we can judge a legal process to be good as a process, apart from any good outcome it may yield in the case at hand. We might use the phrase 'outcome-value efficacy' to refer to the tendency of a legal process to favor the desired winner.

"We do not mean to suggest that process values are beyond argument. Indeed, the word 'value' suggests just the opposite. They are latent and subtle. Moreover, much room remains for debate as to what they mean precisely (think particularly of equality) and how much weight they deserve relatively (think generally of process versus outcome values) and also as to whose values they are and how they come into play. Nevertheless, process values do seem to exist, independent of outcome values. One proof of the independent importance of process values is that we all know from experience that we would condemn public processes that did not reflect such values even if the processes' decisional output were invariably good. That is, for reasons independent of outcome, we want processes in which affected parties are heard and in which decision makers are free of undue influence. All that ends well is not well after all."

Question: (3) What would be an example of a rule that serves process values while not serving, or while even undercutting, outcome values?

(b) ORDER AND METHOD OF PROOF

[Rules 50(a), 52(c)]

The law largely confides the conduct of a trial to the trial judge's discretion, rather than governing it by specific Rules. Therefore we resort in much of the following description to an account of the traditional course of a usual trial. For the purpose of this account, we assume that the trial includes a jury. But the main elements of that traditional course are much the same whether the trial is by jury and judge or by the judge alone.

Burden of proof.—Who must prove what? What happens if no evidence is presented on a disputed issue, or not enough evidence to persuade the jury?[d]

Speaking broadly, the law allots between the parties the burden of persuading the jury on particular disputed issues in the same way that the rules of pleading assign the burden of allegation.[e] Thus, plaintiff will lose if the jury is not persuaded of the truth of the allegations of the complaint that defendant has denied in the answer. So also, defendant's affirmative defenses will fail if the jury is not persuaded of their truth. The party who thus suffers the consequences of nonpersuasion on an issue is said to have the "burden of proof" with respect to it.

Ordinarily, plaintiff has the initial obligation to bring forward the evidence in support of the disputed elements of his claim.

Question: (4) Why is this ordinarily so? Suggest cases where it is not so.

Opening statements.—Before calling his witnesses, plaintiff's attorney customarily makes an opening statement in which he tells the jury what the issues in the action are and what he proposes to prove. The purpose of the opening is to explain the case in such a way that the jury will be better able to follow the testimony. Commonly, defendant's attorney follows immediately with a comparable opening statement, although defendant's attorney sometimes can choose to postpone this until the beginning of defendant's case.

Plaintiff's case.—Then plaintiff's first witness is called to the stand, sworn to tell the truth, and questioned first by plaintiff's attorney (direct examination) and next by defendant's attorney (cross-examination), following which there may be redirect examination, recross-examination, and so on. Other witnesses for plaintiff are called and subjected to the same process of examination until plaintiff's attorney is satisfied that he has done all that he feasibly can to establish the elements of the claim. In theory he is not supposed at this stage of the case to anticipate defenses

---

[d] We pass over at this point the question of the degree of persuasion to which the evidence must bring the minds of the jurors before they can properly accept a proposition as established. Suffice it now to say that in a civil case the required degree of persuasion, or standard of proof, is normally "preponderance of the evidence," which requires a showing of more-probable-than-not.

[e] This is not invariably so. For example, the defendant is to plead contributory negligence as an affirmative defense under Rule 8(c)(1), but we shall see that the law sometimes cast upon the plaintiff the burden of proving the absence of contributory negligence.

and rebut them; but matters of claim and defense are frequently so interwoven that it is not practicable to try to separate them, and so the trial judge usually allows considerable leeway. Upon the completion of the testimony in support of his "case in chief," plaintiff's attorney announces that he rests his case.

Motion at the close of plaintiff's case.—When plaintiff rests, he may have failed to present any evidence on an issue upon which he has the burden of proof, or his evidence on it may be so insufficient that it could not persuade any reasonable trier of fact. In such a situation, defendant may move for judgment as a matter of law pursuant to Rule 50(a), a motion formerly called a motion for a directed verdict. If the judge grants such a motion, the judge will withdraw the case from the jury. Judgment will be entered for defendant.

Question: (5) The corresponding motion by the defendant where the action is being tried without a jury is a motion for a judgment on partial findings under Rule 52(c). However, here the standard that the defendant must meet is the much less stringent one that "the court finds against" the plaintiff on a dispositive issue. Do you see why such very different standards should prevail under Rules 50(a) and 52(c)?

Defendant does not risk all by making a motion at the close of plaintiff's case. If the judge does not grant the motion, defendant may proceed with his case just as if he had not made the motion.

Defendant's case.—If plaintiff has presented evidence sufficient to permit a reasonable trier to find in plaintiff's favor, defendant's motion would be futile because the judge will not withdraw such a case from the jury. Yet defendant may still cut short the scenario—by resting without offering proof.

Why would defendant rest right away? After plaintiff rests, the condition of the evidence may be such that reasonable triers could differ as to whether plaintiff has sustained the burden of proof. For example, the situation may be that plaintiff has sustained the burden only if the jury believes a given piece of evidence, and a reasonable jury might either believe or disbelieve it. By resting, defendant stakes his chances upon argument to the jury that they should not accept plaintiff's story as true. Defendant would do so where he has little evidence to offer or a lot of confidence, or perhaps where defendant's only evidence would entail great expense or risk backfiring.

Ordinarily, however, defendant will proceed to offer his own evidence. Defendant may design this evidence to disprove one or more of the disputed issues on which plaintiff has the burden of proof. Or defendant's evidence may break new ground, being designed to prove matters of affirmative defense upon which defendant has the burden of proof. The process of direct examination by defendant's attorney and cross-examination by plaintiff's attorney is the same as that already described. Upon completion of his presentation of evidence, defendant's attorney rests.

Motion at the close of defendant's case.—When defendant rests, plaintiff may move for judgment as a matter of law pursuant to Rule 50(a), without waiving his right to put in rebuttal evidence if the judge does not grant his motion.

Questions: (6) May plaintiff make a corresponding motion at this point if the case is being tried without a jury? See Rule 52(c).

(7) May defendant, at this point, make a motion for judgment as a matter of law or a motion for a judgment on partial findings? See Rules 50(a) and 52(c).

Rebuttal and rejoinder.—Assuming that plaintiff has not moved for judgment as a matter of law, or that the judge has not granted his motion, he now has the chance to offer rebuttal evidence. Properly speaking, plaintiff should limit rebuttal to evidence that meets new facts put in evidence by defendant. On the one hand, rebuttal can nevertheless go beyond evidence designed to meet an affirmative defense. For instance, defendant may have presented a supposed eyewitness to an automobile accident whose testimony contradicted that of plaintiff's witnesses. It would be proper rebuttal on the part of plaintiff to put on a witness to testify that defendant's witness was elsewhere at the time of the accident. On the other hand, mere reiteration of plaintiff's own evidence for the purpose of giving it added emphasis so as to overcome the effect of contradictory testimony is improper rebuttal.

It is also improper to reserve for rebuttal material that was properly a part of the case in chief, as defendant may have supposed that the case in chief was the entire case to meet. However, the trial judge has a wide discretion in these matters. The judge is likely, for example, to permit testimony in rebuttal that plaintiff inadvertently omitted earlier. Indeed, even after both parties have rested at the end of all the evidence, the court has some discretion in the interests of justice to permit the introduction of evidence to repair the damage of an inadvertent omission in a party's proof.

Again, examination of rebuttal witnesses is the same as that already described. After presenting all his evidence in rebuttal, plaintiff rests. And again, defendant may move for judgment as a matter of law.

After the rebuttal, the defendant may present evidence in rejoinder, as to which the same general principles apply. And there may be still further stages until finally both parties rest.

In Subsection (d) we shall pick up with the motions that are available at the stage when both parties have rested. But first we should digress to consider what all this evidence coming to the trier of fact comprises.

(c) RULES OF EVIDENCE

The process of proof that we have described in general terms is subject throughout to the rules of evidence. These rules originated in the decisions of common-law judges and changed over the years by the traditional common-law method of case-by-case adjudication. Progress was inevitably sporadic, uncertain, and unsystematic, with the result that accidents of history hampered the administration of justice.

The rules of evidence developed differently from jurisdiction to jurisdiction, just as did the rules of substantive law. The original Federal Rules of Civil Procedure contained only minimal provisions about evidence, not a detailed set of evidence rules for actions in federal courts. Rule 43(a) provided for admissibility of evidence if it fell in any one of three categories: (1) evidence admissible under federal statutes, of which there were few; (2) evidence admissible under the rules "heretofore" applied in federal courts in suits in equity; or (3) evidence admissible under the rules applied in the courts of the state in which the federal court sat. This was a rule of admissibility, not a rule of exclusion, so that the statute or rule favoring reception of the evidence governed.

On November 20, 1972, the Supreme Court prescribed Federal Rules of Evidence, to be effective on July 1, 1973, that would govern civil and criminal cases in federal courts; this was the culmination of years of study by an advisory committee, publication of two drafts, revision in light of comments from bench and bar, and approval by the standing committee and the Judicial Conference of the United States. However, taking into account serious objections that had arisen concerning some of those rules, Congress enacted a statute, signed by the President on March 30, 1973, as Pub.L. No. 93–12, 87 Stat. 9, providing that those rules should have no force or effect without express congressional approval. A two-year redrafting project produced a substantially revised and less revolutionary House bill (see H.R.Rep. No. 93–650), Senate amendments that moved back toward the Court-proposed rules (see S.Rep. No. 93–1277), and a compromise conference bill (see H.R.Conf.Rep. No. 93–1597), which was finally passed and signed into law on January 2, 1975, as Pub.L. No. 93–595, 88 Stat. 1926. That law (1) adopted the redrafted Federal Rules of Evidence, as a statute, (2) amended the Rules Enabling Act specifically to treat rules of evidence in the future, and (3) made minor conforming changes to the Federal Rules of Civil Procedure and the Federal Rules of Criminal Procedure. The effective date for the new Federal Rules of Evidence[f] and the conforming changes was July 1, 1975.

The following pages constitute a brief survey of the law of evidence.[g] Focus will center on the Evidence Rules, not only because they are controlling in the federal courts but also because to an extent they reflect current thinking as to what modern rules of evidence should be—they have already spurred most states to adopt similar rules, and other states are likely to follow, just as was the case with the Federal Rules of Civil Procedure. Nevertheless, for the purpose of contrast, we shall make fre-

[f] Hereinafter cited as Evidence Rules. This set of provisions is in the Rules booklet.

[g] Certainly, the brevity will raise some questions without answering them. Answers are often readily available, however. Many are available by reading the Evidence Rules themselves; where the text or footnotes refer to particular Evidence Rules, it is meant that you should read them. In further study of a particular Evidence Rule, the original Advisory Committee's notes, together with the above-cited legislative reports, are often invaluable; a multivolume work, keyed to the Evidence Rules and including the notes and the legislative history, is Weinstein's Federal Evidence (Joseph M. McLaughlin gen. ed., 2d ed. 2009). If you desire further information of a more general nature, an excellent compact treatise is McCormick on Evidence (Kenneth S. Broun gen. ed., 6th ed. 2006).

quent reference to the practice at common law and to the practices prevailing in the several states.

Kinds of evidence.—Testimony does not always consist of the simple narration by a witness of what he observed. Sometimes a witness may give *opinion evidence*.

When the evaluation of evidence calls for specialized knowledge not possessed by the ordinary juror, a qualified expert may testify to assist the jury. On a given point, the needed expert may be a doctor, a chemist, a fingerprint specialist, a musician, a carpenter, or anyone with a specialty. The expert may express reliable opinions in his field of expertness. See Evidence Rules 702, 703, and 705. Determination of an expert's qualifications is in the first instance for the judge. See Evidence Rule 104(a) and (c). Counsel examine and cross-examine experts much as they examine and cross-examine lay witnesses. The testimony of experts is of course often in sharp conflict. The credibility of experts and the weight to be given their testimony are for the jury. See Evidence Rule 104(e).

How about opinion evidence from a lay witness? Clearly he cannot give an opinion upon a matter as to which he is not qualified, but there are many matters upon which an ordinary adult is capable of giving a valid opinion. Indeed, it is perhaps already obvious that what we above called "the simple narration by a witness of what he observed" necessarily embodies a certain quantum of inference and hence in a sense is opinion evidence. "I saw *B*" is a product of inference and hence an opinion. "*B* was drunk" is more obviously a matter of opinion, and a useful one. Nevertheless, the jury is presumably equally capable of forming its own opinion if it has before it the data on which the witness bases his opinion. Is not the forming of such opinions precisely what the jury's job is? If the witness is allowed to express his opinion, is he not usurping the jury's function? Shall we then confine the non-expert witness to matters of "fact"? See Evidence Rules 701, 704(a), and 602.

Question: (8) Consider the admissibility under the Evidence Rules of the following statements by an ordinary witness, who was a bystander to the automobile accident at issue in a personal-injury suit: (a) "The road was very slippery." (b) "The defendant's automobile was going very fast" (or "too fast"). (c) "The defendant's automobile was going 30 miles per hour" (or "about 30 miles per hour"). (d) "The defendant was driving the automobile in a very negligent manner."

We have so far spoken of testimony given in court by witnesses. There is also, as it is sometimes rather uninformatively called, *real evidence*: a person or thing shown to the jury for use of the jurors' own powers of direct observation. A jury might be shown a scarred face, a bloodstained garment, a sample of seized narcotics, or a document. If an object cannot be produced in court, the jury may at the court's discretion be taken elsewhere to view it. For example, the jury might be taken to the scene of an automobile accident to observe how the roads intersect. Before the jury views real evidence, the introducing party must authenticate that evidence. See Evidence Rule 901(a). Authentication in the first instance is a question for the judge, not the jury. However, the jury again has the ultimate say, because it has the option of giving no weight to the evidence offered.

A word on the best-evidence rule should suffice to drive home the point that the choice of the kind of evidence is not entirely free. Suppose a defendant wishes to prove payment by means of proving the content of a written receipt given by the plaintiff. The defendant can prove payment otherwise than through the content of the receipt, even if the plaintiff in fact gave a receipt. But suppose that the defendant intends to rely on showing the content of the receipt. The "best evidence" of the content consists of the original paper, which the judge will admit upon sufficient authentication. May the defendant prove the content not by means of the original paper but by means of a copy of the paper, or by means of oral testimony regarding the content by a witness who read it? Evidence Rules 1001 and 1002 tell us that the defendant usually may not do this. But exceptions exist, as explained in Evidence Rules 1003, 1004, and 1007.

Experiments performed in the presence of the jury fall into the same general category as real evidence. So do charts, models, and diagrams. These items, which have not played a part in the events in suit but which are offered to illustrate or explain testimony, are sometimes called *demonstrative evidence*.

Finally, *judicial notice* may appear to be another medium of presenting evidence at a trial, but it is actually a means of dispensing with proof. When the judge can safely assume that a matter to be proved is indisputably true as a matter of public knowledge (not his own private knowledge), he may "notice" it, that is, instruct the jury that it is true. The judge may have to inform himself of the fact before "noticing" it. For example, he may consult a calendar to ascertain that August 29, 2010, fell on a Sunday, or an almanac to ascertain that the sun set at 4:43 p.m. on December 31, 1977. The object of judicial notice is to save the time and expense of proving matters not subject to reasonable dispute. See Evidence Rule 201.

Relevance.—With regard to admissibility of evidence, regardless of kind, we take it as our starting point that the judge will allow evidence only if it is relevant, that is, only if it has some rational tendency to make more or less probable any proposition of fact that is of consequence to the action. See Evidence Rules 401 and 402.

First, to determine what propositions are of consequence, we look to the issues shown by the pleadings as narrowed and clarified by the pretrial techniques already considered. When proof of a proposition of fact could have no proper effect on the outcome of the case, either because the parties have not chosen to put it in issue or because as a matter of substantive law it makes no difference whether it is true or false, evidence bearing only on that proposition is inadmissible.

Accordingly, what is in appearance a ruling on evidence is often actually a ruling on substantive law. Sherrod v. Berry, 856 F.2d 802 (7th Cir.1988) (en banc), provides an example. A police officer stopped a robbery suspect and then fatally shot him when, according to the officer's testimony, the suspect made a quick hand movement into his coat as if going for a weapon. The resultant civil rights action turned on the objective reasonableness of using deadly force under the circumstances then known by the policeman. The divided appellate court overturned a $1.6 million award because of error in admitting irrelevant evidence, namely, the later discovery that the suspect had been unarmed.

Second, relevant evidence may be probative of propositions of consequence with varying degrees of directness or persuasiveness. For illustration, imagine that *A* sues *B* on a promissory note and that the genuineness of *B*'s signature on the note is in dispute. On the one hand, *W–1*'s testimony for *A*, "I saw *B* sign the note," bears directly on the disputed issue, and if the jury believes *W–1*'s testimony the jury may so determine. On the other hand, *W–2*'s testimony for *B*, "I saw *B* in bed in a Boston hospital on the morning of July 1, 2010" (the day the note was allegedly signed in Los Angeles), bears more remotely on the disputed issue. In each case the witness is testifying to what she observed, but in the latter case what she observed is significant only if the jury takes account of certain general propositions and infers that *B* did not sign the note in Los Angeles. The general propositions are that a flight to Los Angeles takes a certain number of hours, that a man in a hospital bed is probably sick and unable or unwilling to fly, and so on. In order to introduce evidence thus inferentially connected—lawyers often term such evidence "circumstantial"—the inference need not be a necessary one. *W–2*'s testimony is admissible although the possibility has not been excluded that *B* left his hospital bed and went by plane to Los Angeles in time to sign the note. It is open to *A* to attempt to overcome *W–2*'s testimony by proving these facts.

Question: (9) There may of course be several links in the chain of inference between the evidence and the proposition to be proved. Suppose the proposition for the plaintiff to prove is that *Y* killed *X*, and the plaintiff offers in evidence a love letter from *Y* to *X*'s wife.[h] Spell out the series of inferences that the plaintiff is asking the jury to make.

Thus, not all relevant evidence deserves the same amount of weight. The weight of a piece of evidence depends upon the number of successive inferences necessary to connect it with the proposition to be proved and upon the probability of each inference. Sometimes a single piece of evidence will be enough to induce the jury to infer the proposition. Often the party must present many pieces of evidence before their cumulative effect is such as to induce the jury so to conclude. (And remember, of course, that the testimony may be subject to an initial discount if there is a question whether the witness correctly and truthfully reported her observation. The man in the hospital bed may not have been *B*, but *Z*. The witness may be mistaken or lying.)

Third, here is a procedural note on relevance. Often a party offers a piece of evidence that will become relevant only after or in connection with other evidence not yet presented. Practical necessities prevent excluding it.

---

[h] The illustration comes from Edmund M. Morgan, Introduction to Evidence, in Austin W. Scott & Sidney P. Simpson, Cases and Other Materials on Civil Procedure 941, 943 (1950).

A party must start somewhere, and the connecting evidence would very likely be subject to the same infirmity if presented first. The judge resolves the dilemma by admitting the piece of evidence conditionally on the assurance of counsel that it will be "connected up" later. If it turns out not to be, the judge will strike it on motion and instruct the jury to disregard it. See Evidence Rule 104(b). (But is it realistic to assume that the jurors can or will eliminate from their minds evidence that they have heard or seen, merely because the judge instructs them to do so? "Indeed, instructions to disregard seemingly important, damaging evidence may be like telling someone to ignore the elephant that is in the room with them." Paul F. Rothstein, Myrna S. Raeder & David Crump, Evidence in a Nutshell 14 (5th ed. 2007); see J. Alexander Tanford, The Law and Psychology of Jury Instructions, 69 Neb.L.Rev. 71 (1990).)

Rules excluding relevant evidence.—So, to be admissible, evidence must be relevant. It is not true, however, that all relevant evidence is admissible. The rules of evidence sometimes have the effect of excluding relevant evidence. Some persons who could give relevant testimony cannot testify at all; some witnesses cannot give certain kinds of testimony although relevant; and some kinds of relevant evidence are inadmissible no matter who the witness is. To return to the case of the promissory note, testimony tending to show that *B* signed the note is relevant. Yet the judge may not permit an insane person, prepared to swear that he saw *B* sign, to testify (a question of *incompetency*). Nor can *B*'s attorney testify that *B* told her the signature was genuine (a question of *privilege*). Nor can any witness, *W*, testify that *X* told him that she, *X*, saw *B* sign (a question of *hearsay*).

As we examine these three major rules that prevent relevant evidence from being presented to the jury, you should ask yourself whether the claimed justification for each is valid.

Incompetency.—We have said that some persons cannot testify at all. For example, some states have the rule that a person may be so lacking in mental capacity that he is unfit to be a witness. The judge would therefore not allow a two-year-old child or a wildly insane person to testify. But how about a four-year-old, six-year-old, or eight-year-old child? How about a patient in a mental hospital who although "of unsound mind" has sufficient mental capacity to observe an event, remember it, and narrate what he saw?

Question: (10) Of what effect is lack of understanding of the nature and meaning of an oath? What about an atheist who says that the oath means nothing to her? See Evidence Rule 603; Federal Rule 43(b); 28 U.S.C. § 1746; cf. Evidence Rule 610.

How does the judge go about determining whether a person is incompetent to be a witness? In some instances, such as extreme infancy or insanity, mere observation may be enough. In others, preliminary questioning of the prospective witness may satisfy the judge. But it may become necessary to supplement these methods by calling witnesses to testify about the mental capacity of the witness in question. Suppose instead that the incapacity appears for the first time in the course of the direct examination or cross-examination of the witness: the judge may then strike out the testimony already given and tell the jury to disregard it.

It is well to remember that although the judge has the first word as to the competency of a witness, the jury will have the last as to his worth if the judge allows him to testify. The judge may decide that a six-year-old child has sufficient mental capacity to testify, but the jury may give no weight or credence to what he says. Does this suggest that in a doubtful case the judge should allow the testimony to come in and leave it to the jury to appraise it?

Some other competency rules persist in the several states. For a first example, a very few states still hold to an old common-law rule rendering a person incompetent as a witness if he has been convicted of a serious crime.

Questions: (11) What justification could exist for this rule? Is the rule a sound one?

(12) Assuming that a state has no such rule rendering incompetent a person convicted of a crime, to what extent if any should it be permissible to inform the jury of the witness's conviction? Cf. Evidence Rule 609.

A second type of incompetency demands a word. Until the middle of the nineteenth century the common-law courts took the cynical view that a party's interest in the outcome of the litigation rendered him so unreliable that he should not testify at all. This rule frequently produced the bizarre result of silencing those who knew most about the controversy. Nowadays the states have entirely abolished this disqualification in its broad form. Instead, the judge warns the jurors to take into account the interest of the party when they come to appraise the credibility of his testimony.

A vestige of party incompetency remains, however, in the many states that have a so-called Dead Man's Act. The various states' statutes vary widely in scope, and their interpretation has given rise to much litigation. But generally, in suits prosecuted or defended by an executor or administrator on behalf of the decedent, these statutes render the surviving opponent-party incompetent as a witness against the estate concerning some or all matters in issue. Note that this incompetency question arises only with respect to a survivor in actions with an executor or administrator. Thus, there is no general rule silencing a party where the only person who could have contradicted him has died before trial.

Question: (13) Do these statutes reflect merely the same purpose as the old disqualification of parties for interest? Do you think the statutes are wise?

Enough examples of state law: how do the rules of incompetency work in federal court? Against the patchwork background of the states' incompetency rules, Evidence Rule 601 as originally proposed by the Supreme Court represented a major advance. It simply provided that "[e]very person is competent to be a witness except as otherwise provided in these rules," thus virtually abolishing the concept of incompetency in federal court because the Evidence Rules "otherwise provided" in only the very special circumstances of Evidence Rules 605 and 606. Included among the grounds of incompetency to be abolished were mental incapacity, conviction of crime, and party status; also, state Dead Man's Acts would become ineffective in federal court. The common law's total exclusion of testimony from a doubtful witness, the reformers thought, was a rather inept and primitive manner of handling the problem. Instead, the reformers said, the judge should let in the testimony of almost all witnesses, and the jury could appraise its weight and credibility. Their rationale was that it is generally better to let a witness testify and then—in order to counter the effects of mental incapacity, moral turpitude, and interest—to rely on cross-examination, extrinsic evidence, and warnings by the judge to the jury. Judges, however, could still exclude testimony from witnesses so mentally deficient that no reasonable juror could believe them, using Evidence Rule 403 to invoke the requirement of personal knowledge and capacity for truthfulness embodied in Evidence Rules 602 and 603.

The congressional redrafting of Evidence Rule 601 cut back the extent of this proposed advance. The redraft added a second sentence providing that in civil cases "with respect to an element of a claim or defense as to which State law supplies the rule of decision, the competency of a witness shall be determined in accordance with State law." You will not fully understand this change until you have studied Part Two of this book. However, in very gross terms, we can describe the new rule, its significance, and its rationale respectively as follows.

As you have already seen in several cases, federal courts sometimes apply state substantive law; that is to say, state law sometimes supplies the rule of decision. For example, if a New Jersey driver runs down a New Yorker in New York City and if the New Yorker sues in the United States District Court for the Southern District of New York, that court will apply New York State's negligence law, not some uniform federal law of negligence. Evidence Rule 601 now says that as to testimony tending to support or defeat a finding of negligence in such a suit, New York State's rules as to competency will control. The federal court will apply not only state substantive law, but also state evidence law dealing with competence.

What this signifies in practical terms is that the Evidence Rules do not provide for uniform practice in federal district courts on the subject of competency. The federal court will treat the competency of some witnesses under the uniform federal rule embodied in the first sentence of Evidence Rule 601, while the judge will determine the competency of others under diverse state rules incorporated by the second sentence thereof. So, in the area of testimonial competency, the federal practitioner must be the master of both federal and state evidence law.

The legislators' rationale for introducing this note of confusion into the Evidence Rules was, in part, that the federal interest in a uniform law of evidence for federal courts is not strong enough to override the state policies embodied in the states' competency rules. The states had no strong policies wrapped up in rules of, say, judicial notice, but Congress thought that competency rules such as the Dead Man's Acts might involve more important state policies.

Privilege.—There are various rules protecting certain persons from disclosure of particular matters. To take a familiar example: if a party calls *L*, a lawyer, as a witness and asks about what *B*, her client, confidentially told her in the course of seeking legal advice, *B* may prevent *L* from responding. Assuming, as we shall see may be the case, that if *B* told the same things to a layperson, the layperson could testify to what *B* said, why does the law deal differently with statements to a lawyer? The law also commonly privileges confidential communications between husband and wife, patient and physician, and penitent and clergyman. What are the reasons for and against each of these privileges?

What would you say about confidential communications to an accountant by her client? How about confidential communications between parent and child? How about a communication made to any person on a pledge of secrecy? The communications just listed are commonly not privileged. Should they be?

Would you compel a newspaper reporter to disclose the source of information given to her in confidence? See the absorbing case of Branzburg v. Hayes, 408 U.S. 665, 92 S.Ct. 2646 (1972) (regarding newspaper reporters' obligation to testify before grand juries), which held that the First Amendment does not give rise to a general journalists' privilege but which left plenty of room for distinguishing the holding. And, of course, the absence of a privilege of constitutional origin does not preclude a judge-made or statutory privilege. Thus, most of the federal circuits have molded some degree of qualified privilege for journalists, and more than half the states have enacted shield legislation that accords reporters some form of privilege as to their confidential sources. See also Herbert v. Lando, 441 U.S. 153, 99 S.Ct. 1635 (1979). See generally 23 Wright & Graham § 5426.

In addition to privileged communications and sources, there are topics privileged from disclosure. For example, the public interest may require that state secrets be privileged. Within limits, too, trade secrets important to the existence of a particular business may be privileged. Here also falls the familiar privilege against self-incrimination. A witness can claim this constitutional privilege in all kinds of proceedings: criminal and civil actions, administrative hearings, and legislative investigations. Although a witness in a civil action is thereby privileged not to reveal facts appreciably tending to subject himself to criminal liability, he has no such privilege as to facts incriminating someone else.

We might mention here as well the restrictions on use in criminal cases of confessions and evidence illegally obtained. Under "privilege" we would also class the question of whether the President, a state governor, or a foreign ambassador can claim immunity from compulsory process to testify as a witness.

However, we do not here attempt to draw a logically satisfying distinction between incompetency and privilege. We shall just observe that the key to it would lie in the differing purposes of the two doctrines. Incompetency rules centrally concern the reliability of evidence, whereas privilege rules foster social policies extrinsic to the courtroom. That is, privilege does not aim at the ascertainment of truth, but rather at some other goal often pursued at the price of shutting out the truth.

A telling contrast lies in the common-law rule that husband and wife were incompetent to testify either for or against each other in any case, civil or criminal. Today in the states this rule has largely disappeared, eroding and transmuting into a privilege in criminal cases whereby the accused may elect to keep his or her spouse off the stand, except when the charge is the commission of a crime against the spouse, and whereby the accused's spouse may refuse to testify adversely, and most often eroding still further to some narrower version of this privilege that is even more readily distinguishable from the old rule of incompetency. (Note that both the dying rule of spousal incompetency and the eroding criminal privilege to avoid adverse spousal testimony are distinguishable from the above-mentioned privilege against disclosure of confidential communications between husband and wife.)

Questions: (14) If a judge erroneously upholds a witness's privilege and excludes testimony, should the party damaged by the ruling be able to attack it on appeal?

(15) What if the judge erroneously denies the privilege and admits the testimony? See McCormick on Evidence § 73.1 (Kenneth S. Broun gen. ed., 6th ed. 2006).

Each particular privilege, being tied to a certain extrinsic social policy, requires individual consideration as to how broad it is in scope, as to who may claim it, and as to how it may be waived. It is worth thinking about the answer the law should give to these three questions for each of the privileges mentioned above.

As to privilege in general, we again need to consider separately the situation in federal court. Against the background of the states' accepted rules regarding privilege, the Evidence Rules as originally proposed by the Supreme Court represented another major change. Proposed Evidence Rules 501 to 513 codified the rules of privilege for federal courts in accordance with modern thinking on the subject. Thus, their effect was, in general, to restrict the realm of privilege, eliminating some common-law privileges and modifying others. However, these privilege provisions generated more controversy in Congress than did any other aspect of the Evidence Rules, and the result was the enactment of a redrafted version of Evidence Rule 501 and the passage of 28 U.S.C. § 2074(b).

Evidence Rule 501, as enacted, is similar in effect to Evidence Rule 601. It provides for the application of federal privilege rules in certain circumstances and state privilege rules in others. Thus, just as for competence, the federal practitioner must be the master of both federal and state privilege law. But there is an important difference between Evidence Rules 501 and 601. The first sentence of Evidence Rule 601 represents a codification of federal competence law. In contrast, the first sentence of Evidence Rule 501, along with the congressional deletion of the codification attempted by the rulemakers in their proposed Evidence Rules, leaves federal privilege rules to a continuing case-by-case development. This change was a reflection of the furor that the proposed privilege provisions generated in Congress.

Section 2074(b) was a further reflection of that controversy. This statutory provision specifically restricted the Supreme Court's rulemaking power in the area of privilege. The congressional concern expressed here was more with separation of powers than with federalism.

Question: (16) Would the codification of privilege rules as proposed by the Supreme Court have been within the terms of 28 U.S.C. § 2072?

Hearsay.—We have already given one example of hearsay: in the suit on the promissory note, *W* testifies that *X* told him that *X* saw *B* sign the note. This testimony is objectionable as hearsay. See Evidence Rule 802. Why is it objectionable? Because *W* may be mistaken in his memory as to what *X* said? Suppose then that *W* produces in court a written statement that *X* prepared. The testimony is still objectionable. Is this because *X* was not under oath? Suppose then that *W* is a notary public and has taken *X*'s oath that the statement is true. Even this does not cure the hearsay difficulty. Why all this squeamishness about hearsay? Responsible persons daily make important decisions in their own lives in reliance upon patent hearsay—indeed, normal life could hardly go on if this were not so. Why should courts reject a type of evidence so commonly relied upon outside the courtroom?

The heart of the objection to hearsay is the absence of an opportunity for cross-examination of the declarant (the person who made the out-of-court statement offered in evidence by the testimony of another). Cross-examination may lay falsehood bare; it may expose errors in observation, memory, or narration; it may bring out important matters omitted from the original statement; or it may at least raise doubts as to the credence and weight the jury should give to the testimony. Often, of course, cross-examination fails of its purposes and, particularly if it is unskillful, may serve only to reinforce the original story. But the law regards the chance for cross-examination as such an essential check on the reliability of testimony that where cross-examination is not possible the testimony is ordinarily not admissible. For example, if the witness dies immediately after direct examination, thus defeating the opportunity for cross-examination, the judge may strike the testimony already given under oath in open court.

The concern generated by lack of an opportunity for cross-examination largely explains the hearsay rule, but not entirely. The rule may apply even when the declarant is sitting in court, readily available for cross-examination. Indeed, testimony in a previous trial or hearing where the declarant was in fact subject to cross-examination may in certain circumstances run afoul of the hearsay rule. In such situations the hearsay rule applies simply because calling the declarant to the stand to testify as to what she has to say, as a method of proof, is usually superior to letting some witness testify as to what the declarant previously said. If the party calls the declarant, the fact-finder can consider her demeanor on the stand along with her in-court statements.

How sound is the hearsay rule? Granting that there is a risk of error or falsehood that cross-examination and demeanor might expose, does this risk so overcome the probative value of the testimony that the fact-finder should not get the chance to hear and appraise it, while making what the fact-finder thinks is due allowance for its infirmity? Basic to the rule excluding hearsay and to some other exclusionary rules is a distrust of the capacity of the jury to appraise the evidence properly. You will find that such rules frequently do not apply when the trier of fact is an expert administrative tribunal, even though this contrary practice likewise rests on untested empirical assumptions.

Question: (17) Should the hearsay rule apply when the trier of fact is a judge sitting in a nonjury case? See McCormick on Evidence § 60 (Kenneth S. Broun gen. ed., 6th ed. 2006).

Do not fall into the error of assuming that repetition in court of an out-of-court statement of another person invariably raises a hearsay problem. Assume that *A* is suing *B* for slander, alleging that *B* called her a thief, and *B* by answer has denied that he made such a statement. *W* testifies that at the time and place in question he heard *B* say that *A* was a thief. In this case, although *W* is testifying to what he heard *B* say, *W*'s testimony is admissible. No question of hearsay is involved. What is the difference between this case and the one where *W* testified as to what *X* had said about seeing *B* sign the note? There the purpose of the testimony was to prove that *B* had signed the note, and the credibility and weight of *X*'s out-of-court statement were therefore important. In the present case, the purpose of offering *W*'s testimony is simply to prove that *B* made the slanderous statement that *W* says he made, and for that purpose the credibility and weight of *B*'s statement are unimportant. The credibility and weight of *W*'s testimony are important, but *W* is on the stand and subject to cross-examination. We can generalize and say that it is only when the statement of the declarant is offered to prove the truth of the statement—when, in effect, testimony by the declarant is being offered through the mouth of another—that a question of hearsay arises. See Evidence Rule 801(c).

Question: (18) *P* sued Dr. *D* for negligence in leaving a sponge in the incision after an operation on *P*'s spine. Several doctors had operated on *P*'s spine at various times prior to the discovery of the sponge. To establish liability it was necessary to prove (a) that a sponge was left in the incision by Dr. *D* and (b) that it was left there as the result of Dr. *D*'s failure to exercise proper skill and care. Among other evidence, *P* offered testimony by an assisting physician, *W*, that in the operating room an unidentified nurse had told Dr. *D* that "the sponge count did not come out right." The judge excluded this testimony on the ground that it was hearsay. There was a verdict and a judgment for Dr. *D*, and *P* appealed. The question on appeal was the propriety of excluding the proffered testimony. What argument would you make for *P*, and what do you think the decision should be? See Smedra v. Stanek, 187 F.2d 892 (10th Cir.1951) (reversal).

Exceptions to the hearsay rule.—The rule excluding hearsay is riddled with exceptions. We shall not catalogue them all or probe the refinements of any of them. Were we to do so, you would quickly see that the pattern is haphazard rather than logical. Not only does the law differ greatly from state to state, but the law of any one state is likely to be shifting, uncertain, and abounding in inconsistencies; on the federal level, the thirty exceptions listed in Evidence Rules 803 and 804 suggest a similar complexity. Rather we shall consider in a general way why the rejection of hearsay has not been complete and what conditions must exist before making an exception to the rule.

In the first place, it is apparent that not all forms of hearsay are inherently unreliable, and a rational system would attempt to segregate and admit hearsay evidence that falls high on the reliability scale. In the second place, although an out-of-court utterance might be a less desirable method of proof than in-court testimony, it is further apparent that a rigorous exclusion of all hearsay, or of all but the most reliable hearsay, would sometimes block effective proof of an essential issue. Because of these two considerations, courts have always admitted some types of hearsay.

Accordingly, exceptions to the hearsay rule have arisen where there is something about the out-of-court utterance that justifies trusting that evidence even in the absence of accompanying demeanor evidence and cross-examination. In other words, the circumstances in which the declarant made the statement must be such as to make it seem reliable. See Evidence Rule 803. Absolute trustworthiness is not, of course, the test—even the testimony of a witness on the stand and subjected to cross-examination does not approach that ideal.

For certain hearsay exceptions, circumstances surrounding the declarant's statement that suggest some degree of reliability do not constitute a sufficient condition for admission, and so the law imposes the additional requirement that the declarant be unavailable to testify (for example, because she is dead or absent from the jurisdiction). In other words, there is an explicit notion of need linked to the hearsay exception. See Evidence Rule 804. However, careful examination of most hearsay exceptions, including those that apply whether or not the declarant is unavailable, will reveal implicit notions of need or at least of practicality.

With these generalities in mind, consider the following examples of major exceptions to the hearsay rule.

1. Our first illustration comes originally from the criminal law. *A* is charged with the murder of *B*. Testimony of *W* is offered to the effect that *B*, knowing that death was imminent, said, "*A* shot me," or, for that matter, "*C* shot me." *W*'s testimony is clearly hearsay, but the likelihood that *B* told the truth under the circumstances set forth is supposedly strong enough to justify admitting *W*'s account. Of course, *B* may have been mistaken or may have lied to get revenge upon *A* or *C*, to protect someone, or for some other reason; but these considerations will go only to the credit to be given to the evidence.

You may well ask how much scientific support there is for the supposition upon which this "dying declaration" exception rests.[i] Indeed, distrust of its scientific support perhaps explains the fact that the common law and many states have construed this exception narrowly. Traditionally, for it to apply, (a) the case has to be a criminal prosecution for homicide, (b) the declarant has to have died, a victim of that homicide, (c) the declarant had to make the utterance while believing that the declarant's own death was imminent, and (d) the utterance had to concern the circumstances of that impending death. In many states, then, *W*'s testimony of *B*'s dying declaration, admissible in a murder trial, is oddly not admissible in a civil action for *B*'s wrongful death.

Evidence Rule 804(b)(2) significantly expands the exception by modifying requirements (a) and (b), although the drafters based that expansion not on a belief in the reliability of dying declarations, but rather on a feeling that the traditional requirements were illogical and arbitrary. You should specially note that the dying declaration exception to the hearsay rule is now available in civil cases in federal court.

2. *A*, injured by a hit-and-run driver, civilly sues *B* as the alleged driver. The identity of the driver remains in dispute. *B* offers the testimony of *W* that *C*, now dead, said to *W*, "I ran over *A* and was lucky enough to get away." Should the court admit it? How is the requirement of reliability satisfied? The theory is that a person is unlikely to make a statement against the person's own interest unless it is true.

This "declaration against interest" exception to the hearsay rule is well recognized. It is, however, narrowly limited. Traditionally, (a) the declarant had to be unavailable and (b) the statement had to have been against a *proprietary* or a *pecuniary* interest. Some state courts still say that a statement that would inferentially subject the declarant to tort liability is not sufficiently against pecuniary interest to be admissible, and such courts would therefore exclude the statement of the hit-and-run driver given above. Is there any rational basis for this limitation?

Evidence Rule 804(b)(3) extends the exception to cover a statement of a declarant unavailable as a witness that "so far tended to subject the declarant to civil or criminal liability, or to render invalid a claim by the declarant against another, that a reasonable person . . . would not have made the statement unless believing it to be true."

3. "Admissions" form another traditional exception, and an extremely important one. These are out-of-court statements by a party or the

[i] "The existing rule, with its strict limitations, has been introduced into India where it appears to have worked badly, according to Mr. Justice Stephen, who says: 'I have heard that in the Punjab the effect of it is that a person mortally wounded frequently makes a statement bringing all his hereditary enemies on to the scene at the time of his receiving his wound, thus using his last opportunity to do them an injury. A remark made on the policy of the rule by a native of Madras shows how differently such matters are viewed in different parts of the world. "Such evidence," he said, "ought never to be admitted in any case. What motive for telling the truth can any man possibly have when he is at the point of death." ' (1 Stephen's Hist. Crim. Law of England, 448, 449.)" People v. Becker, 215 N.Y. 126, 147, 109 N.E. 127, 133 (1915).

party's representative offered by an opponent as evidence of their content.[j] They were usually against interest when made, but they need not have been so. *A* is suing *B* for negligently inflicted injuries; *A* can introduce testimony of *W* that *B* said, "It was all my fault," or, "I had only one drink before the accident, but I didn't see *A* until after I hit her." Dean McCormick cited this example: someone has stated that a note is a forgery, but then buys the note and sues on it; the statement can come in against him as an admission. McCormick on Evidence § 254 (Kenneth S. Broun gen. ed., 6th ed. 2006).

Admissions and declarations against interest are frequently confused. But note: (a) admissions are utterances attributable to parties, while a declaration against interest can be uttered by anyone; (b) admissions need not be against interest when made, while a declaration against interest obviously must be; and (c) for admissions availability of the declarant is immaterial, while for a declaration against interest the declarant must be unavailable.

Question: (19) What is the justification for the exception regarding admissions?

Admissions receive similar treatment under the Evidence Rules, in that they are still admissible. However, the analytic approach differs. As just explained, courts have traditionally treated admissions as an exception to the hearsay rule, but the Evidence Rules treat admissions as simply not hearsay in the first place. See Evidence Rule 801(d)(2). The Advisory Committee's note thereto says: "Admissions by a party-opponent are excluded from the category of hearsay on the theory that their admissibility in evidence is the result of the adversary system rather than satisfaction of the conditions of the hearsay rule."

4. Courts have also created a hearsay exception for statements relating to a startling event made while the declarant was under the stress of excitement caused by the event. This is one of several hearsay exceptions often lumped together under the label "res gestae" without serious analysis.[k]

Questions: (20) What is the voucher of trustworthiness for this "excited utterance" exception?

(21) Should it make any difference whether the declarant is available?

---

[j] Contrast these "evidential" admissions with binding "judicial" admissions such as those made under Federal Rule 36. See Freed v. Erie Lackawanna Ry. Co., supra p. 98.

[k] "The marvelous capacity of a Latin phrase to serve as a substitute for reasoning, and the confusion of thought inevitably accompanying the use of inaccurate terminology, are nowhere better illustrated than in the decisions dealing with the admissibility of evidence as 'res gestae.' It is probable that this troublesome expression owes its existence and persistence in our law of evidence to an inclination of judges and lawyers to avoid the toilsome exertion of exact analysis and precise thinking." Edmund M. Morgan, A Suggested Classification of Utterances Admissible as Res Gestae, 31 Yale L.J. 229, 229 (1922).

Handel v. New York Rapid Transit Corp.

Supreme Court of New York, Appellate Division, Second Department, 1937.
252 App.Div. 142, 297 N.Y.S. 216, aff'd mem., 277 N.Y. 548, 13 N.E.2d 468 (1938).

■ TAYLOR, J. In an action to recover damages for the death of plaintiff-appellant's intestate alleged to have resulted from the negligence of the defendant-respondent, judgment dismissing the complaint, entered upon a nonsuit, affirmed, with costs. The plaintiff's proofs failed to establish, prima facie, a cause of action. The claimed declaration of the intestate after the happening of the accident, to wit, "Save me. Help me—why did that conductor close the door on me," was incompetent as evidence and properly excluded by the trial court. The declaration was not admissible as part of the res gestae. [Citations omitted.] It was narrative of a past event and within the hearsay rule.

■ DAVIS, ADEL and TAYLOR, JJ., concur; CLOSE, J., with whom HAGARTY, J., concurs, dissents and votes for reversal of the judgment and for a new trial, with opinion.

■ CLOSE, J. (dissenting). In my opinion the evidence, offered in behalf of the plaintiff, of a statement made by the decedent after the accident was admissible as a part of the res gestae, and the trial court erred in excluding it. A recital of the circumstances under which the statement was made will serve to define the point of law.

The decedent was a police officer attached to Precinct 60, located at West Eighth street, Brooklyn. At some time between three-forty and four o'clock in the morning of April 22, 1934, Timothy Downing, another policeman, saw him coming from a nearby lunch wagon. Handel was off duty, having finished at midnight, and was not due back at the station house until the following afternoon. After a brief conversation, the two policemen crossed the street to the West Eighth Street station of the defendant's elevated railroad, located almost opposite the precinct station house. Handel passed through the door, and Downing last saw him as he was going up the stairs toward the elevated platform. As Downing walked back across the street he heard the rumble of an approaching train. It was then about four o'clock.

Mrs. Ida Pfeifer lived on the top floor of an apartment house on West Third street, with her bedroom window directly facing the elevated structure. She slept with the window open. She testified that at about four o'clock in the morning she was awakened by the sound of someone screaming. Looking out the window, she saw a train come to a stop and something that looked like "a big bundle" fall from the side door of the last car down to Park place. The screaming continued. Mrs. Pfeifer put on a bathrobe and slippers, ran down three flights of stairs to the front entrance of her house, and proceeded from there to Park place, a distance of about seventy feet. There she found the body of Handel. He was moaning, and made a statement to the witness which was excluded from evidence on the defendant's objection. The record shows that the witness would have testified, if permitted, that Handel said, "Save me. Help me—why did that conductor close the door on me."

John Leyton also lived in the vicinity of West Third street and Park place. A little before four o'clock in the morning he had taken his dog out for a walk. When he returned it was "Pretty near four o'clock." As he approached the house he heard the noise of an elevated train, and looking up he saw a train stop near West Third street. Leyton put the dog in the house and stepped out again. As he did so he heard someone moaning under the elevated structure. He estimated that it took him about half a minute to get to where Handel lay, and that about two and one-half minutes elapsed between the time when he heard the train and his arrival at the place where the deceased lay. Mrs. Pfeifer was already there. Leyton would also have testified to Handel's statement if permitted to do so. One of Handel's shoes was missing, and his pants were torn off from the hips down.

Officer Downing testified that he received word of the accident about three-quarters of an hour after he had left Handel at the station entrance. In company with a detective named Fitzsimmons, he went up to the station platform, walked to the end of the platform, and then proceeded along a "catwalk" beside the tracks. The "catwalk" ended about fifty feet from West Third street. The two men then walked on the ties between the rails to a point just over the curb of West Third street, about 1,000 feet distant from the station entrance. There they found a shoe, with the laces broken out of it, wedged between the rail and a wooden beam. The toe of the shoe pointed back toward West Eighth street.

Downing returned and examined the station platform. He found two dark marks running parallel with the edge of the platform for a distance of about 125 to 150 feet, increasing in width as they approached the end of the platform. The inference is that the marks were made by the rubber heels of Handel's shoes as he was dragged along by a moving train. Beyond the end of the platform no marks were visible.

When the decedent was examined by a doctor it was found that, in addition to numerous lacerations and contusions, he had suffered a concussion of the brain, a broken right hand, a fracture of the right femur, a broken pelvis, and a ruptured bladder. He was also in profound shock. Of course, this must have been his condition at the time when he made his statement to Mrs. Pfeifer and Leyton. Apparently, he died later in the day.

The foregoing is substantially all the evidence offered by the plaintiff. At the close of the plaintiff's case, the trial court dismissed the complaint. We are all agreed that the dismissal was proper if the declaration of the decedent was properly excluded; because without that declaration the record is wholly lacking in proof of negligence on the part of the defendant. From the drag marks on the platform, the broken shoe wedged between the rails, and the fact that the deceased was seen to fall from the car door at just about the point where the shoe was found, it might reasonably be inferred that the deceased had, in some manner, been caught in the door at the station platform; that he had been dragged along with his body hanging outside the train as far as West Third street; that his foot had then become caught between the ties or the rails; and that his shoe had been torn off and his body jerked from the train at the same time. But the circumstances throw no light on how the deceased came to be trapped in the door, and the proof is therefore insufficient to warrant an inference of negligence.

However, the declaration of the deceased, if admissible, would constitute some evidence of negligence. . . . The question to be determined is whether this evidence was competent as a part of the res gestae. The trial court concluded . . . that the evidence was not admissible under that exception to the hearsay rule. A majority of this court are of the same opinion. With that conclusion I disagree.

. . . .

. . . We must answer two questions: (1) Was the declaration "spontaneously expressive of the injured person's observation" of the occurrence? (2) Was the utterance made "within such limit of time as presumably to preclude fabrication?"

Handel's statement was of a spontaneous character. It was not made in response to any question . . . . The spontaneous nature of the utterance is shown by the words "Save me. Help me," which preceded the reference to the action of the conductor. . . . The statement about the conductor took the form of a question, "why did that conductor close the door on me," which in itself is an indication of spontaneity. A construction which holds this declaration merely a narrative of a past event ignores the language used and its plain implications.

The other element is that of time. We are asked to consider the fact that the deceased had traveled from West Eighth street to West Third street before he fell. I would disregard that entirely. On a journey so perilous, one has little leisure for plotting fiction. The only material period of time is that which elapsed after the deceased fell to the street. The best estimate of the interval is that given by the witness Leyton, who said that about two and one-half minutes elapsed between the time when he heard the train and his arrival at the place where Handel was found. . . . But it is not a question of precisely how many seconds or minutes elapsed. The question is whether "the utterance is made within such limit of time as presumably to preclude fabrication."

My conclusion is that Handel's utterance came within the confines of the rule. It seems to me incredible that a man so broken in body and so profoundly shocked in mind could have spent the slight interval before aid arrived in manufacturing a false explanation of the extremity in which he was found.

If there is a "spontaneous exclamation exception to the hearsay rule," here is a case for its application. In my opinion the evidence was wrongly excluded, and the error requires a reversal of the judgment and a new trial.

Questions: (22) Assuming that the Handel case arose today in federal court, would the evidence be admissible under Evidence Rule 803(2)? under Evidence Rule 803(1)?

(23) Adopting the same assumption, would Handel's statement be admissible as a dying declaration under Evidence Rule 804(b)(2)? See Shepard v. United States, 290 U.S. 96, 54 S.Ct. 22 (1933) (Cardozo, J.) ("There must be a 'settled hopeless expectation' [citation omitted] that death is near at hand, and what is said must have been spoken in the hush of its impending presence.").

5. Entries contemporaneously made in books and records in the ordinary course of business generally may come into evidence without producing the persons who actually made the entries.

For the contours of the business records exception under federal law, see Evidence Rule 803(6), as well as the subsequent subdivisions of that Evidence Rule.

This "business records" exception serves to point up again the important fact that writings may present hearsay problems, e.g., where a party offers a document in evidence to prove the facts it relates. See Evidence Rule 801(a)(1). In order to get such evidence in, the introducing party must authenticate the document, and also find an applicable hearsay exception (such as business records).

Incidentally, nonverbal conduct may similarly present hearsay problems, e.g., where a witness testifies that someone nodded his head to show assent. See Evidence Rule 801(a)(2). Was there a hearsay problem with Mrs. Pfeifer testifying that she had heard someone scream?

6. We close with some brief observations on other illustrative exceptions to the hearsay rule. (a) *Testimony given at another hearing of the same or a different proceeding by a witness now unavailable.* This is an easy exception to justify when the parties to the former hearing were the same and the issues substantially identical. But suppose the testimony is now offered against a person not a party before. Should the opportunity for cross-examination by someone else with similar motive and interest suffice as a voucher of reliability? See Evidence Rule 804(b)(1). Apparently, Federal Rule 32(a) provides alternative exceptions to the hearsay rule, so that a deposition satisfying an exception under either the Federal Rules or the Evidence Rules is admissible. See Evidence Rule 802. (b) *Declarations concerning family history.* See Evidence Rule 804(b)(4); cf. Evidence Rule 803(13). If it were not for this exception, proof of matters of pedigree might be extremely difficult. But what is the basis for holding such declarations reliable? (c) *Statements in ancient writings.* The party introducing an ancient document may satisfy the usual requirement of authentication of documents by a showing that its condition is such as to create no suspicion concerning its authenticity and that it was in a place where, if authentic, it would likely be. See Evidence Rule 901(b)(8). But as usual there is a separate requirement of admissibility as against a hearsay objection, if the party is offering the document for the truth of statements made in it. See Evidence Rule 803(16). (d) *Other exceptions.* Consider the potential of

Evidence Rule 807. Do you think that this residual exception portends the demise of the hearsay rule?

Multiple hearsay.—Finally, there is the problem of, as Evidence Rule 805 puts it, "hearsay within hearsay." The rule here is that when testimony includes multiple levels of hearsay, each level must come within a hearsay exception in order for the testimony to be admissible.

Question: (24) In a civil wrongful-death action brought in federal court by *X*'s wife against *K*, plaintiff calls *W* to testify that *W* saw *X* and his wife walking together, that *X* fell, that *W* ran over, that *X* was then dead, and that *W* heard *X*'s wife cry, "*X* just groaned that *K* wasn't joking in telling him that *K* had poisoned him." Can the quoted testimony come in, over objection?

Remote, confusing, and prejudicial evidence.—The fact that a piece of relevant evidence does not run afoul of any of the three foregoing exclusionary rules does not necessarily mean that the judge will admit it. The judge has discretion to exclude evidence of comparatively slight probative value when the judge believes that it is not worth the time required to hear it. See Evidence Rule 403. Thus, to prevent the piling up of merely cumulative testimony, the judge has discretion to limit the number of witnesses on a particular issue, a discretion frequently exercised with respect to the number of expert witnesses and often specified in a pretrial order under Federal Rule 16.

A similar discretion exists when the confusion or the prejudice that evidence would produce substantially outweighs its probative value. For example, will the plaintiff suing for injuries from an allegedly defective condition on the defendant's premises be permitted to prove that other accidents occurred there, for the purpose of showing that the situation was dangerous? Generally yes. Will the defendant be allowed to show an absence of other accidents, as evidence of nonexistence of danger? Generally not. Why the distinction? Should this plaintiff be permitted to prove that liability insurance covers the defendant, as the basis for an inference that he had nothing to lose by his carelessness and hence was less likely to be careful? See Evidence Rule 411.

Still in that suit for injuries allegedly due to a defective condition on the defendant's premises, should the plaintiff's evidence that the defendant made repairs after the accident be admissible, as some proof of negligence? See Evidence Rule 407. Should the defendant's pretrial offer to make a compromise settlement be admissible, as evidence for the plaintiff? See Evidence Rule 408. Are your conclusions with respect to these last two questions tied exclusively to notions of remoteness, confusion, and prejudice?

Objecting to inadmissible evidence.—When a party offers evidence that the opponent believes to be inadmissible, the opponent should object specifically, with grounds. Examine Federal Rule 46, and you will find that a formal "exception" is not also necessary. This is a reference to the old requirement of such ritualistic words as, "I except," or, "Please note my exception," in order for a party to have the right to appeal eventually an adverse ruling. Although in some states the old ritual still prevails, in the federal courts it is now necessary only to state an objection.

The objection should come immediately, as soon as possible after the ground for objection appears. Indeed, pretrial disclosures under Federal Rule 26(a)(3)(A) should trigger the opponent's listing of objections under Rule 26(a)(3)(B) and, possibly, the court's advance evidential rulings. More generally, the opponent can make a motion to exclude evidence in advance of trial, which is called a motion in limine and which the court in its discretion can choose to decide immediately or to postpone until trial. Usually, however, the opponent can wait to object upon evidence's offering at trial.

The objection has a two-fold purpose: (1) to keep the evidence out, or to have it stricken; and (2) to lay the foundation for a later appeal if the judge admits the evidence. The jury may give any evidence admitted without objection such weight as the jury thinks it deserves, and usually the opponent has waived any error in its admission. See Evidence Rule 103(a)(1) and (d). For instance, the jury may properly base a finding upon hearsay testimony to which no objection was made. In any such case, of course, the jury may nevertheless discount or disregard the testimony because of the inherent weakness that gave rise to the exclusionary rule in question.

It will often happen that offered evidence is properly admissible for one purpose but inadmissible for another. The risk that the jury might improperly apply it to the inadmissible purpose does not ordinarily require its exclusion. But the opponent may acquire some protection by asking the judge to instruct the jury as to the limited purpose for which it is being admitted. See Evidence Rule 105. If the judge gives no such instruction, the jury may properly give the evidence its natural probative force for any purpose.

Question: (25) In the case in the earlier question involving the statement that the sponge count did not come out right, if the judge admitted the proffered testimony over objection, what should the objecting party then do?

If the judge erroneously admits proffered evidence over objection, the record is clear for purposes of appeal. If, however, the judge sustains the objection and excludes the evidence, the proffering party should make known to the judge by "offer of proof" the substance of the proffered evidence (for example, the answer the party expected from the witness), unless the substance is apparent from the context. If not, the party cannot predicate error on the exclusion, for it is only in this way that the appellate court can appraise the seriousness of the error. See Evidence Rule 103(a)(2) and (b). For obvious reasons the party should make the offer of proof out of the hearing of the jury. See Evidence Rule 103(c).

Question: (26) Suppose the opponent does not agree that the witness would answer the objectionable question as the proffering party expected. How can this difficulty be resolved?

Combating admissible evidence.—Let us assume that a party has called a witness whose direct testimony, if believed, will be damaging to the opponent. What may the opponent do to combat it?

The opponent may try in various ways to impeach (that is, discredit) the witness. See, e.g., Evidence Rules 608 and 609. His first chance is on cross-examination, when he may ask questions designed to bring out bias; prior inconsistent statements; weakness of observation, of memory, or of narration; bad character; or the like. The opponent has a second chance, in that he may wait until he puts on his own case, and then impeach the witness by the testimony of other witnesses or documentary evidence bringing out similar defects. However, to prevent unreasonable excursions, the rules limit such impeachment by extrinsic evidence to the more significant defects, and so on lesser matters the opponent must "take the witness's answer" on cross-examination. See, e.g., Evidence Rule 608(b). (The other side may attempt the counterstep of rehabilitating an impeached witness. See, e.g., Evidence Rule 608(a)(2).)

In addition to impeaching the witness in these ways, the opponent may introduce other evidence to contradict (that is, disprove) the story of the witness. In line with the constant objective of keeping a trial within bounds, there are again limitations on the extent to which the judge will permit contradiction of "collateral" matters in a witness's testimony.

Now let us assume instead that a witness has unexpectedly given testimony damaging to the party who called her. The combination of Evidence Rules 607 and 801(d)(1)(A) turns out to be especially helpful in dealing with the turncoat witness, who changes her story and deprives the party calling her of essential testimony.

That party may of course contradict the witness through other evidence, but the traditional rule has been that a party cannot "impeach his own witness," that is, discredit a witness he himself has called. This rule has long been subject to criticism. It was rejected in a few states, and inroads upon it by way of limitations and exceptions were made in others. Evidence Rule 607 abandons it entirely. The Advisory Committee's note thereto says that the traditional rule was "based on false premises. A party does not hold out his witnesses as worthy of belief, since he rarely has a free choice in selecting them."

An especially effective form of impeachment is a prior statement inconsistent with the testimony of the witness on the stand. The statement has traditionally been admissible for the purpose of discrediting her court testimony, but normally not for the purpose of proving the truth of what she previously said. For the former purpose, it is not hearsay, because the point is just to show she earlier uttered an inconsistent statement. For the latter purpose, the great majority of courts, including the Supreme Court of the United States, Bridges v. Wixon, 326 U.S. 135, 65 S.Ct. 1443 (1945), have considered it hearsay. However, Evidence Rule 801(d)(1)(A) alters the definition of hearsay somewhat so that when a declarant testifies and is subject to cross-examination concerning a prior inconsistent statement made under certain formal circumstances, that statement is not hearsay and can therefore be used for its truth. The argument for this Rule is that the trier of fact, being able to observe demeanor and consider the nature of the testimony, is in as good a position to determine the truth or falsity of such a prior statement as it is to determine the truth or falsity of the inconsistent testimony given in court.

Cross-examining witnesses.—A conventional method of cross-examination is to put "leading questions," that is, questions that suggest the desired answer. One such type is, "Isn't it a fact that . . . ?" Leading questions are usually improper on direct examination, although they generally pass without objection on routine matters of a preliminary nature, and also the judge may permit them in specified situations including interrogation of a hostile witness. See Evidence Rule 611(c); cf. Evidence Rule 611(a).

Question: (27) Why are leading questions ordinarily objectionable on direct but permissible on cross-examination?

How far does the scope of cross-examination extend beyond impeaching a witness? That is, how far may the cross-examining party go in seeking to support his own case out of the mouth of the witness? Not far, according to the rule in most states and in the federal courts. See Evidence Rule 611(b). Accordingly, the party may cross-examine the witness only as to facts and circumstances connected with the matters covered in direct examination, in addition to matters affecting credibility. Departures from this rule are, however, permissible in the discretion of the trial judge, but then direct examination's predisposition against leading questions will apply to the cross-examiner.

Given the restricted scope of cross-examination, a party who has cross-examined may find it necessary to recall the witness at a later stage of the trial to get additional testimony. In doing so the party is held to "make the witness his own," thus subjecting the questioning on recall to the rules governing direct rather than cross-examination.

By contrast, in some states the scope of proper cross-examination extends to all aspects of the case, so that the cross-examining party may interrogate as to matters on which he has the burden of proof and may even use leading questions thereon. Evidence Rule 611(b) as originally proposed by the Court adopted this minority "wide-open" position. However, in the final version of the Evidence Rules enacted as a statute, Congress had redrafted the Rule to return to the traditional "restrictive" practice.

Question: (28) What reasons can you advance for and against the majority rule of limiting the scope of cross-examination?

(d) Motions at the Close of All the Evidence

We resume our consideration of the course of a jury trial. When all the evidence is in, either party may move for judgment as a matter of law. See Rule 50(a). Note that the motion must state specific grounds. The granting of this motion results in the withdrawal of the case from the jury. When may the judge take this drastic step without impinging upon the constitutional right to trial by jury? This brings us to examine in greater detail the difficult question of the standard for granting judgment as a matter of law.

Suppose that plaintiff has the burden of proof on propositions *A*, *B*, and *C*, all essential to his case, and defendant has the burden on defensive propositions *D* and *E*. When the evidence is closed, no evidence bearing on *A* has been offered by either party. The judge should grant defendant's motion for judgment as a matter of law. It is immaterial that there may be a conflict in the evidence as to *B, C, D,* and *E*, because the jury's resolution of these conflicts could make no difference in the result. There is no more infringement of the right to trial by jury here than there would be if plaintiff failed to allege *A* and the judge dismissed his complaint for failure to state a claim upon which relief could be granted.

Next let us assume that there is some evidence bearing on *A* but so little that the judge is satisfied that, looking only to the evidence favorable to the plaintiff, a reasonable jury would not be justified in finding *A*. Conceding that it is the function of the jury and not of the judge to resolve disputed issues of fact, is it not wholly proper to say that here there is no basis for a genuine dispute as to *A*? The almost universal answer to this question, and the answer given by the federal courts, is that judgment as a matter of law is proper in these circumstances.

Suppose, however, that there is testimony that, standing alone, would warrant a finding of *A*, but there is overwhelming evidence to the contrary. If the judge is satisfied that no jury reasonably considering the evidence could find *A*, must the judge nevertheless submit the case to the jury? This is a debated question. It is argued, on the one hand, that to grant judgment as a matter of law here would be an invasion of the jury's authority to determine the credibility of witnesses and, on the other hand, that the judge ought not to permit a jury to act unreasonably.

Now let us assume that the plaintiff has offered highly persuasive testimony as to *A, B,* and *C* and that the defendant has rested without impeaching the testimony and without putting in any evidence of her own.[1] We know that in a courtroom, as well as outside, people sometimes lie and honest people are sometimes mistaken. It could be argued, then, that the credibility of the testimony is necessarily at issue and, because this is a matter for the jury to decide, the defendant has the right to argue to the jury that it should disbelieve the unimpeached and uncontradicted evidence of the plaintiff's witnesses. So, can the party with the burden of proof ever obtain judgment as a matter of law when highly persuasive testimony in support of all of his essential allegations is unimpeached and uncontradicted? The usual answer to this question, and the answer given by the federal courts, is that such a judgment is theoretically available in such circumstances.

[1] The same problems are raised if the defendant offers highly persuasive evidence as to *D* and *E*, constituting a complete defense if believed, and the plaintiff offers nothing to counteract it.

Finally, suppose that defendant has offered only some slight impeachment or contradiction of highly persuasive testimony tending to establish *A*, *B*, and *C* and that the testimony in support of plaintiff's essential allegations is still overwhelming. If the judge is satisfied that no jury reasonably considering the evidence could find for defendant, must the judge nevertheless submit the case to the jury? This is also a much debated question.

How can one generalize? There is some formula to be applied that is tied to a notion of whether reasonable minds could not differ. But this formula is applied only to a certain portion of the evidence, including all evidence that is favorable to the opponent of the motion and also apparently including unquestionable evidence (such as unimpeached and uncontradicted testimony from disinterested witnesses) that is favorable to the movant. How does the standard for granting judgment as a matter of law compare with the standard for granting summary judgment? May judgment as a matter of law ever properly be granted when summary judgment for the same movant has properly been denied?

Question: (29) Is there, in an action tried without a jury, any motion analogous to a motion for judgment as a matter of law at the close of all the evidence? Is there a need for one?

(e) SUBMISSION TO JURY AND RETURN OF VERDICT

[Rules 49, 51, 52]

If a motion for judgment as a matter of law at the close of all the evidence is not made, or is made but not granted, the disputed issues of fact will be submitted to the jury for decision (at least in the first place). The jury will announce its decision in the form of a verdict.

Closing arguments and jury instructions.—Before the judge gives the case to the jury, however, counsel for the plaintiff and the defendant will make closing arguments to the jury that the proof is with their respective side. Normally, the party who could make the first opening statement can now make both initial and final closing argument.

Then, typically, the judge will instruct, or charge, the jury as to the law. This subject is treated in Rule 51, which leaves the timing to the judge's discretion.

Question: (30) In some states, instructions to the jury precede closing arguments. What are the advantages and disadvantages of the traditionally contrary federal practice?

The judge in his instructions to the jury will customarily state the issues that are in dispute and the contentions of the parties with respect to them; state who has the burden of proof on which issues, and what degree of persuasion the jury must reach before it decides that a party has successfully carried a burden of proof; and analyze or at least summarize the evidence. A federal judge may also, if he chooses, express his views on the facts, provided he makes clear to the jury that matters of fact are for its determination and that his views are not binding.

Question: (31) Despite this acknowledged power to "comment on the evidence," including the power to indicate who in their judgment should prevail on the facts, many federal judges refrain from expressing their views. In the majority of state courts, the judges do not have the power. What arguments can be made for and against the federal position of allowing comment?

What is the lawyers' role in connection with the judge's instructions? In the first place, Rule 51(a) gives the parties the right to file written requests for specific instructions. But the lawyers have other opportunities to urge on the judge what the instructions should include.

Question: (32) *P* sues *D* for damage to *P*'s truck allegedly caused by *D*'s negligence. Because of industry-wide shortages *P* cannot obtain the requisite repair parts for some time, nor can *P* obtain a substitute truck. As a result, *P* loses the anticipated profit from a trucking contract. *P*'s attorney wants the jury to award as an element of damages the loss of this profit. Suppose: (a) *P*'s attorney requests an instruction that the jury may properly consider the loss of profit as an element of damages, and the judge refuses so to instruct; (b) *P*'s attorney makes no such request, and the judge's charge expressly excludes from the jury's consideration every element of damages except the diminution in value of the truck caused by the accident; or (c) *P*'s attorney makes no such request, and the judge's charge makes no specific reference to the matter. In case (a), what must *P*'s attorney next do if she thinks the judge is in error on the law and if she wants to preserve the point for appeal? Has she lost appeal rights in case (b) or (c) by not requesting an instruction?

Verdict.—Because the nature of the attorneys' arguments and the judge's instructions is affected by the kind of verdict that the jury will be asked to return, it is appropriate concurrently to ponder the kinds of verdict authorized by the Rules. This subject is treated in Rule 49.

The verdict may be a general one, for example, "The jury find for the plaintiff and assess damages in the sum of $_______," or, "The jury find for the defendant." Or the verdict may be a general one accompanied by written questions upon one or more issues of fact necessary to decision. Rule 49(b). Or the verdict may be special, in the form of a special written finding upon each issue of fact. Rule 49(a).

Questions: (33) Who determines which kind of verdict will be used, and when is the determination made?

(34) On what basis should the determination be made?

(35) How would the kind of verdict affect the nature of the attorneys' arguments?

Whenever the jury has to return a general verdict, whether or not accompanied by written questions, the judge must determine and then instruct the jury on the rules of substantive law that govern the case. For the jurors cannot rationally find a verdict "for the plaintiff" or "for the defendant" without applying the rules of substantive law to the facts as they find them, and they do not and should not know these rules except as the judge states them. The rules of substantive law that the judge imparts to the jury may be rather vague or general, leaving a considerable range of judgment to the jury (instructions on the standard of due care in most negligence cases are perforce general), or they may be fairly specific. In all events, the judge's instructions on the law will usually be a good deal more particularized than the legal rubrics that the pleadings invoked or implied. For example, in an action for battery the defendant may have pleaded self-defense in a general way, but the judge may have to explain to the jury in detail the factors that should go into a determination of whether a defendant can justifiably strike a plaintiff in response to what appears to be a threatened attack.

If the jury is to return only a special verdict, the judge may reduce in scope his instructions on the applicable rules of substantive law, because the judge will himself apply those rules to the jury's special findings on the issues of fact.

Whatever the kind of verdict, the jury, after hearing arguments and receiving instructions, retires to deliberate in private. The jury is occasionally kept sequestered the entire time from when it retires until the judge finally discharges it. If the jurors are unable to reach a verdict, the judge will discharge the jury; and the case may have to be retried. If the jurors reach decision, the foreman of the jury will appropriately complete and sign a given form of verdict; the verdict will be returned in open court with the jury present and will then be recorded; and the jury will be discharged.

Questions: (36) In an action tried without a jury, should the parties have a right to make closing argument to the judge?

(37) Our discussion of instructions and verdict is obviously inapplicable in an action tried without a jury. In a nonjury case, "the court must find the facts specially" and state separately its conclusions of law. Rule 52(a)(1); see Rule 52(c). Why should the judge be required to find the facts specially when the jury is not required to do so (at least when it returns a general verdict)?

(f) MOTIONS AFTER VERDICT

[Rules 50, 59]

Suppose the jury has come in with a verdict for one of the parties. Will the result of the litigation in the district court necessarily conform to the verdict? No. Judgment is normally entered (at least in the first place) in accordance with the verdict. But even after that judgment has been entered, the party against whom the judgment went still has two motions available to him that may change the result.[m]

Renewed motion for judgment as a matter of law.—You will note that Rule 50(b) permits a party, whose motion for judgment as a matter of law under Rule 50(a) has been denied or not granted, to move to have the verdict and any judgment entered on the verdict set aside and to have judgment entered in his favor despite the adverse verdict. This later motion for judgment as a matter of law was formerly called a motion for judgment notwithstanding the verdict, a name often shortened to judgment n.o.v. from the Latin *non obstante veredicto*. The verdict-loser must file it not

---

[m] Besides the renewed motion for judgment as a matter of law (Rule 50(b)) and the motion for a new trial (Rule 59(a)(1)) discussed in the text, see Rule 59(e) (motion to amend judgment) and Rule 60 (motion for relief from judgment).

later than the twenty-eighth day after entry of judgment on the verdict. Note carefully that it is a condition of a party's making an effective *renewed* motion for judgment as a matter of law that he previously moved for judgment as a matter of law.

Indeed, as the text of Rule 50(b) suggests, the standard for granting a renewed motion for judgment as a matter of law is in theory the same as the standard for granting a motion for judgment as a matter of law, say, one made at the close of all the evidence. What hope is there, then, that the judge will grant a renewed motion for judgment as a matter of law when the judge has previously declined to grant the same party's motion for judgment as a matter of law at the close of all the evidence? Will not the jury's verdict against that party fortify the judge in the view supposedly expressed in ruling on the earlier motion?

In seeking an answer to these questions, consider a situation where defendant moves for judgment as a matter of law in his favor at the close of all the evidence, and the judge inclines to the belief that the motion is well-founded but she is not certain and wants time to reflect. Will she perhaps deny the motion, or refrain from granting it, and pass the case to the jury believing that the jury will probably find for defendant, thus rendering it unnecessary to deal further with the difficulty posed by the motion for judgment as a matter of law? And if the jury does find for defendant, has not the judge avoided the appearance of intruding into the sphere of the jury and obviated the appellate court's close scrutiny of judgment as a matter of law? But if the jury returns a verdict for plaintiff, may she not grant defendant's renewed motion for judgment as a matter of law in accordance with her original inclination?

The value of this judicial approach will be more apparent if we anticipate the course of later proceedings on appeal.

Questions: (38) Suppose the judge grants defendant's motion for judgment as a matter of law at the close of all the evidence. The appellate court later decides that she was wrong and that the case should have gone to the jury. What happens after that?

(39) Suppose the judge instead denies defendant's motion, submits the case to the jury, and, after a verdict for plaintiff, grants judgment as a matter of law on defendant's renewed motion. The appellate court later finds her in error in granting that motion. What then happens?

(40) So there are excellent reasons for a judge to deny a motion for judgment as a matter of law even though the judge would feel bound to grant the same party's renewed motion, if necessary. Then why would judges ever grant judgment as a matter of law before a verdict, as they sometimes do?

Motion for a new trial.—A party dissatisfied with a verdict has yet another motion—the motion for a new trial under Rule 59(a)(1)—that the party may file not later than twenty-eight days after entry of judgment on the verdict. A new trial motion asks that the verdict and any judgment entered on the verdict be set aside and that the case be retried. The judge may grant such a motion on any of numerous grounds.

1. One possible ground is that the verdict is, as is said, "against the weight of the evidence." The jury by its verdict will have decided one or more disputed factual issues. If the judge, looking at all the evidence, is clearly convinced that the jury was wrong in deciding as it did—that is, if the judge is convinced that the jury grossly misjudged the credibility of the testimony or misconceived where the weight of the evidence lay—the judge should order a new trial.

Here we touch upon a difficult problem. On the one hand, the judge should not order a new trial merely because the judge disagrees with the jury's resolution of the issues. On the other hand, there are cases where the verdict is so far against the general current of the evidence that to let it stand would be to countenance injustice. In the latter situation, the judge may properly set aside the verdict and order a new trial.

Questions: (41) What is the difference in practical result between (a) granting the defendant's renewed motion for judgment as a matter of law and (b) setting aside a verdict for the plaintiff and ordering a new trial?

(42) How does the standard for ordering a new trial on the ground that the verdict is against the weight of the evidence compare with the standard applied under Rule 50(a) and (b)? May a party's new trial motion on such ground ever properly be granted when the same party's motions for judgment as a matter of law have properly been denied?

(43) Suppose the jury returns a verdict, but the judge sets aside the verdict as against the weight of the evidence and orders a new trial. On the second trial before a new jury and possibly before a new judge, the same verdict is returned. May a new trial be ordered? Should there be a limit to the number of times a new trial may be ordered?

2. Sometimes the judge will order a new trial because it is clear that the jury has failed to follow her instructions.

Question: (44) Can you imagine a situation where it would be manifest from a general verdict that such error has occurred?

A similar reason for granting a new trial is that the judge believes that she herself committed an error, for example, in instructing the jury or ruling on the admissibility of evidence. The motion for a new trial in a sense gives the judge a chance to reconsider her own actions; if she believes they need correction, she may order a new trial. Indeed, Rule 59(d) provides that "the court, on its own, may order a new trial for any reason that would justify granting one on a party's motion."

The list of such irregularities that might occur during the course of a trial, and on the basis of which the court could justifiably grant a new trial after verdict and judgment to prevent injustice, is a lengthy one. But see Rule 61.

3. The judge may also grant a new trial on the ground of newly discovered evidence.

Joinder of motions.—The verdict-loser may, and usually does, make a motion for a new trial together with any renewed motion for judgment as a matter of law. See Rule 50(b). If the judge denies both the renewed motion for judgment and the motion for a new trial, judgment on the verdict will stand. If the judge denies the renewed motion for judgment but grants the motion for a new trial, the judge will set aside the verdict and any judgment entered thereon, and the case will again stand for trial. If the judge grants the renewed motion for judgment, the judge will set aside the verdict and any judgment entered thereon, and the contrary judgment will be entered; in such case, the judge will also rule on the new trial motion, either *conditionally* granting or *conditionally* denying it pursuant to Rule 50(c)(1). We shall explore the detailed interplay of these motions in Section 5 of Topic D of Part Eight.

Question: (45) Is there, in an action tried without a jury, any motion analogous to a renewed motion for judgment as a matter of law? Cf. Rule 52(b). Is there any motion analogous to a motion for a new trial? Cf. Rule 59(a).

SECTION 4. JUDGMENT

(a) ENTRY OF JUDGMENT

[Rule 58]

The upshot of litigation in the district court is a judgment that sets out any relief the parties have won. This may come about short of, or after, completed trial.

Where the judgment is a simple one—a jury has returned a general verdict, or in a nonjury case the court has decided that a party shall recover a sum of money or has denied all relief—the clerk prepares, signs, and enters the judgment immediately. In the more complicated cases, the court promptly approves the form of judgment and the clerk enters it. See Rule 58(b); Forms 70 and 71.

(b) KINDS OF RELIEF AFFORDED BY JUDGMENT

[Rules 54, 57]

It is worth pausing on the kinds of relief that a judgment may afford. We should perhaps have dealt with this subject at the outset of our discussion of the phases of a lawsuit, for the questions, "What kinds of relief are available in this type of case?" and, "Which should I choose if I have a choice?" are often of first importance to an intending plaintiff, and he will consider them before he frames his complaint. Observe, however, that under Rule 54(c), every final judgment should grant the relief to which the party is entitled, even if the party has not demanded such relief in the pleadings—except that a judgment by default must not be different in kind from or exceed in amount what the party requested in the demand for relief.

Question: (1) What are the reasons for these provisions of Rule 54(c)?

Coercive relief.—A common type of judgment for a successful plaintiff is one for money damages designed to compensate him for the defendant's wrong. Thus, an ordinary measure of damages for breach of contract is the difference between what the defendant promised and what the plaintiff got. In an action for personal injuries, the measure of damages is the sum that will supposedly restore the plaintiff as nearly as possible to the position he would have been in had the defendant not committed the tort, even though the difficulties in putting a dollar figure on such things as pain and suffering or facial disfigurement are obvious. In other kinds of cases the provision of nominal damages, which is a trifling sum given in recognition of the plaintiff's legal right, or a restitutionary measure of damages, which prevents the defendant's unjust enrichment, may be appropriate. In some kinds of cases the judgment may give the plaintiff punitive damages, designed to punish or make an example of the defendant. Additionally, the judgment may award interest, accruing after and in some kinds of cases before judgment.

Another type of judgment may award the restoration of property wrongfully withheld by the defendant from the plaintiff, as where the defendant has wrongfully appropriated the plaintiff's watch and retains it, or where the defendant has wrongfully entered upon the plaintiff's land and occupies it.

The foregoing types of judgment trace historically from the courts of common law. There is another type of judgment, historically associated only with the courts of equity, that orders the losing party to do or to refrain from doing some act. Orders in suits in equity were called decrees, while actions at law resulted in judgments. Note that Rule 54(a) now defines "judgment" as including a decree.

For an equitable example, in proper cases the judge may direct a party in default under a contract to carry out the contract according to its terms (specific performance). In some situations the judgment will not go so far as to order the party to carry out her promise, but it will order her to refrain from acting inconsistently with her promise (injunction). So, if the defendant, a famous opera singer, has promised to sing exclusively for the plaintiff over a certain period of time and wrongfully refuses to perform, the judgment may order the defendant not to sing for the plaintiff's competitors during the time in question.

An equitable judgment may order the defendant to refrain from committing some other kind of wrong. If the defendant is wrongfully selling chewing gum packaged so as to imitate plaintiff Wrigley's, the judgment may order it to desist from this unfair competition. Or if the defendant has wrongfully constructed a dam that floods the plaintiff's land, the judge may order her to tear it down.

A judgment may combine one kind of relief with another. Thus, a judgment for plaintiff ordering defendant to perform a promise may also award damages to plaintiff for past breaches by defendant.

RITTER v. RITTER, 381 Ill. 549, 46 N.E.2d 41 (1943). Joseph Ritter agreed with defendant, a relative named Louis Ritter, that they would buy two pieces of real estate upon foreclosure sale, taking title in their names as joint tenants; and that if there was no redemption, Joseph would take the "Nixon property" and defendant the "brick building." After the purchase Joseph became critically ill; he asked defendant whether, in case of his death, his wife and daughter would have any trouble securing the Nixon property; and defendant assured him they would not. Nevertheless, after Joseph had died and the redemption period had passed, defendant procured a master's deed to both properties in his own name. Thus, Joseph's widow and daughter had to start a chancery suit against defendant in order to impose a constructive trust upon the Nixon property in their favor. They succeeded in the suit.

The widow and daughter then sued Louis to recover the expenses of the chancery suit that had not been assessed therein as costs. After trial without jury, judgment was entered in plaintiffs' favor for $2007, representing primarily counsel fees paid in prosecuting the prior suit. On appeal, the intermediate appellate court affirmed.

But the Supreme Court of Illinois reversed, holding that the subsequent action would not lie. Among the reasons given were the following: (1) Under Illinois law recovery of litigation expenses depends on statute, and here there is none in point. (2) As defendant had the "right" to resist plaintiffs' claim, on general principles he should not be liable for the consequences of his conduct in refusing to convey the property. (3) It is true that cases exist where *A* has been liable to *B* for wrongful conduct that involved *B* in litigation with a third party, and that there the measure of damages has included *B*'s expenses of litigation with the third party, but those cases are not relevant to an attempt by successful litigants to recover their expenses against their immediate adversary. (4) The rule urged by plaintiffs would involve endless litigation, because if plaintiffs recover here, they could institute another action for expenses of the present action, and so on in an infinite series. (5) True, some jurisdictions consider litigation expenses in situations where they allow punitive damages, but that is different from recovery in a separate action. (6) Because Illinois has permitted an action for "malicious prosecution of a civil suit without probable cause" only if arrest, seizure of property, or other special injury accompanied the wrong (in refusing to extend this tort, this court has stressed the need to leave the courts "open to every citizen"), the converse must be true, namely, that a plaintiff cannot bring an action against a defendant who made a "groundless and causeless defense."

COSTS

"Costs" are normally awarded to the prevailing party, either plaintiff or defendant, as a part of any judgment. See 28 U.S.C. § 1920. After decision in the case, the clerk "taxes" these costs, subject to the judge's review and to the judge's possible refusal to award costs. See Rule 54(d)(1).

Taxable costs may include certain direct expenses incurred in conducting the litigation, such as fees of clerk and marshal, statutory fees and disbursements for witnesses, docket fees, some deposition expenses, and like items. Defining the bounds on such costs is a complicated and variable matter, but suffice it to say that such costs certainly do not reimburse even total out-of-pocket expenditures. Of crucial importance is the precept that costs in American courts (other than in Alaska) ordinarily cannot include counsel fees, so that each party ordinarily pays his own lawyer. Thus, although sometimes rather significant in absolute terms, costs represent only a small percentage of the total expenses of litigation.

In most of the rest of the Western world, including England, the losing party also pays the attorney's fees of the prevailing party. Indeed, the so-called American rule against fee-shifting might be better termed the "American exception." But using comparative law to leap to conclusions of heresy must be resisted. It is true that the historical reasons for our early departure from the English rule are murky and largely obsolete. Nevertheless, the reasons behind the persistence of the difference in practice may well lie in profound societal differences, especially in differing views on the nature of law, the role of courts, and the desirability of litigation.

Here and today, the American rule appears firmly entrenched. See Alyeska Pipeline Serv. Co. v. Wilderness Soc'y, 421 U.S. 240, 95 S.Ct. 1612 (1975). Yet academic criticism of that rule remains high, and exceptions to it are slowly multiplying on both federal and state levels. Therefore, the complexities of adopting the English rule in America deserve consideration.

Considering the effects of a change to fee-shifting on the litigants' economic incentives, there has been little effective empirical work. There has been some theoretical work, but it is surprisingly inconclusive. See generally James W. Hughes & Edward A. Snyder, Litigation and Settlement Under the English and American Rules: Theory and Evidence, 38 J.Law & Econ. 225 (1995). For purposes of illustration, picture the Ritter plaintiffs' initial chancery suit under a regime that would require the loser to pay, in addition to his own counsel fees, the winning side's counsel fees as costs; so victory will be more complete, but the risk of loss is greater. First—on the decision to pursue the claim—probably the English rule relatively encourages small meritorious suits, while somewhat discouraging larger dubious suits and nuisance suits; however, risk aversion discourages the middle class from resorting to litigation under the English rule. Second—on the subsequent decision whether to settle—although the effects of implementing the English rule on the likelihood and timing of settlement are rather unclear, strong claims would tend to be settled for more and weak claims for less than under the American rule. Third—on the conduct of litigation—although the English rule might relatively encourage the litigants to escalate expenditures, its influence on the overall economic costs of the litigation system is unknown and arguably unknowable. Fourth—on the incentive to comply with substantive law—the comparison between English and American rules gets really complex, because the interaction or interplay of effects on these various incentives can no longer be ignored. In any event, predicting the direction of an effect tells us nothing of the size of the effect or the importance of side effects. The lesson seems to be this: beware of simplistic analysis of the English–American dispute.

There are many considerations other than these economic concerns, of course. In a perspicacious article, Professor Rowe lists five other common rationales for fee-shifting: "The first is a sense of simple fairness: the idea that it is only just for the loser to have to pay, at least in considerable part, the winner's legal costs appears to be a major underpinning of the English indemnity rule. The second, the theme of making a litigant financially whole for a legal wrong suffered, is probably most familiar as the idea of compensation in the substantive law of remedies. A punitive emphasis on fee shifting to deter and punish misconduct, either in litigation or in the underlying transaction, is a third rationale. Fourth, the 'private attorney general' theory justifies a fee award on the basis of the public usefulness of advancing a particular type of claim. A fifth justification is a desire to affect the relative strengths of the parties, a theme that appears in discussion of schemes for fee shifting against government, particularly when the private party involved is an individual or a small concern." Thomas D. Rowe, Jr., The Legal Theory of Attorney Fee Shifting: A Critical Overview, 1982 Duke L.J. 651, 653. But as he goes on to demonstrate, the validity or at least the reach of each of these arguments is open to serious question or qualification. And counterarguments remain, including an effective claim that the weak rationales for the English rule fail generally to justify the undeniably substantial transaction costs of adopting and then operating a system of fee-shifting. Moreover, all these conflicting policies must be considered in a broader context, which would take into account at least the presence or absence of contingent fees, legal aid, legal insurance, small-claims courts, other alternative dispute-resolution mechanisms, class actions, and other representative litigation and also the effects of any security-for-costs or offer-of-judgment provisions. See, e.g., Rule 68. The lesson here seems to be this: beware of thinking too narrowly.

One should recognize that neither the English rule nor the American rule exists in pure form anywhere. There are exceptions on whether to shift fees; and given shifting, there are variations on how much of the fees should shift in the particular case. One should also recognize that the English and American rules do not exhaust the possible fee-shifting regimes. An obvious alternative is one-way fee-shifting, such as shifting only in favor of a prevailing plaintiff. Indeed, Professor Rowe apparently supported a one-way pro-prevailing-plaintiff scheme, although he would have allowed a shift in favor of any prevailing defendant who had faced a truly baseless action. Very importantly, because of the interplay of policies, the chosen rules for fee-shifting should probably differ according to the type or size of the case or the characteristics or behavior of the litigants. See Phillip J. Mause, Winner Takes All: A Re-examination of the Indemnity System, 55 Iowa L.Rev. 26 (1969). The lesson here seems to be this: beware of thinking too generally.

In summary, the English–American dispute raises very complex issues. In all likelihood, we shall retain the American rule; but the courts and especially the legislatures will continue to move cautiously by a sort of common-law incremental method away from that polar position, adopting numerous targeted exceptions such as the federal ones that currently allow discretionary shifting of reasonable fees, under the case law, when the opponent has litigated in bad faith; or, under 42 U.S.C. § 1988(b), when in a civil rights action a plaintiff has prevailed or a prevailing defendant has faced a truly baseless suit; or, under 28 U.S.C. § 2412, when certain private parties have prevailed against the federal government. Perhaps by now this approach does not appear as inappropriate as it might at first have seemed to you. See generally Attorney Fee Shifting, Law & Contemp.Probs., Winter 1984, at 1; Dan B. Dobbs, Awarding Attorney Fees Against Adversaries: Introducing the Problem, 1986 Duke L.J. 435.

Declaratory relief.—The judgments so far considered are plainly coercive. The power of government is behind them, as we shall see shortly.

A judgment for the defendant is less plainly coercive, because the result of the litigation is a denial rather than a grant of the relief sought. The force of government may, however, secure, by execution against the defeated plaintiff, the recovery of the costs awarded to the prevailing defendant. More importantly, such a judgment for the defendant is a determination of rights and other legal relations, which the principle of res judicata may make conclusive.

Finally, Rule 57 speaks of declaratory judgments and refers to 28 U.S.C. § 2201. See also § 2202. The action for a declaratory judgment differs from the usual action in that the plaintiff instituting it need not seek the imposition of any sanction apart from a declaration of rights and other legal relations. He may, for example, seek a declaration as to whether a particular act that he proposes to commit will be tortious, by suing in a situation where the defendant, a person whom the act would affect, has asserted that she will so regard it.

Questions: (2) Rule 57 says that the "existence of another adequate remedy" does not preclude a judgment for declaratory relief in cases where it is otherwise appropriate. What does Rule 57 mean thereby? Why does Rule 57 so provide?

(3) What is the "further relief" that is mentioned in § 2201, and what is the "further relief" mentioned in § 2202? Why do these statutes so provide?

American Machine & Metals, Inc. v. De Bothezat Impeller Co.

United States Circuit Court of Appeals, Second Circuit, 1948.
166 F.2d 535.

■ Before SWAN, CHASE and FRANK, CIRCUIT JUDGES.

■ SWAN, CIRCUIT JUDGE. This appeal presents a question under the Declaratory Judgment Act, 28 U.S.C.A. § 400,[a] which authorizes the courts of the United States "in cases of actual controversy" to declare "rights and other legal relations of any interested party petitioning for such declaration," without regard to whether further relief is or could be sought. . . . From the judgment of dismissal the plaintiff [American Machine] has appealed.

In summary the allegations of the complaint are the following:

In 1934 the parties entered into a contract under which the defendant conveyed to the plaintiff certain patents and certain physical equipment for the making of fans and other products and the plaintiff agreed to pay the defendant license fees (not less than $5,000 annually) based on the "net sales" of its products. So long as the contract continued the fees were to be paid on "net sales" regardless of whether the plaintiff's products were covered by the patents or whether the patents had expired. The contract contained no expiration date but could be terminated at any time by the plaintiff on six months' notice. In the event of such termination the plaintiff was to transfer the patents back to the defendant and to cease using the name "De Bothezat," which it agreed to use in its literature and sales promotion while the contract continued. Since February 19, 1946, the plaintiff has neither manufactured nor sold any product for which possession of the patents is essential. The plaintiff "desires and intends" to exercise its right of termination under the contract and "desires and intends" to continue in the business of selling fans and ventilating equipment. The defendant at various times has made claims and assertions to the plaintiff and other persons to the effect that upon termination of the contract the plaintiff will no longer have the right to continue the manufacture of fans and ventilating equipment, and "has led plaintiff to believe" that upon termination of the contract defendant will sue plaintiff if it does not cease the manufacture and sale of fans and ventilating equipment. Said claims and assertions by defendant "are without basis and an actual controversy exists between the parties," and plaintiff seeks a declaration of the rights of the parties in order to avoid the possible accrual of avoidable damages. The prayer [in this diversity action] requests a declaration "particularly with respect to the proper interpretation and effect of the agreement" and that the court declare the right of plaintiff to continue to manufacture and sell fans and other noninfringing products after termination of the agreement and without the payment of further sums to defendant.

In concluding that no controversy exists the district judge noted that the plaintiff has not yet given notice of termination of the contract and may never do so; the opinion states [75 F.Supp. 421, 424]:

"In this case, if the court should decide that plaintiff might terminate and continue its manufacture and sale of products other than those covered by patents, plaintiff might and probably would terminate. If the court should decide otherwise, plaintiff would probably continue under the agree-

[a] With changes this section, originally enacted in 1934, now appears as 28 U.S.C. § 2201.

ment until its termination and no controversy such as now claimed to exist might ever be present. In other words, plaintiff has not elected what it wishes to do and its action might and could render academic the very declaration which it seeks.

"The complaint is, therefore, dismissed because no justiciable controversy exists which would justify the maintenance of an action under the Declaratory Judgment Statute. The relief prayed for should not be granted at this time either as a matter of discretion or otherwise."

We think the judge construed the statute too narrowly. . . . After [giving notice of termination] it will be too late to avoid an action for damages if the plaintiff acts as he intends by continuing the business. The very purpose of the declaratory judgment procedure is to prevent the accrual of such avoidable damages. . . .

. . . .

Judgment reversed and cause remanded for trial on the merits.[b]

PRASCO, LLC v. MEDICIS PHARMACEUTICAL CORP., 537 F.3d 1329 (Fed.Cir.2008). Prasco, the eventual plaintiff, makes a generic benzoyl peroxide cleansing product called OSCION. Defendant Medicis makes another such product called TRIAZ, which it marks as covered by four patents owned by the defendants. Medicis earlier sued Prasco in an unrelated patent suit. Prasco asked the defendants to agree not to sue on the basis of OSCION, but the defendants declined.

Prasco then brought an action for a declaration that OSCION does not infringe those four patents. The U.S. District Court for the Southern District of Ohio dismissed for lack of jurisdiction because of the absence of an "actual controversy."

The court of appeals, on appeal under 28 U.S.C. § 1295(a)(1), began by explaining the context: "The Declaratory Judgment Act is not an independent basis for subject matter jurisdiction. Skelly Oil Co. v. Phillips Petroleum Co., 339 U.S. 667, 671–72, 70 S.Ct. 876 (1950). Rather, it provides a remedy available only if the court has jurisdiction from some other source. [Citation omitted.] Such jurisdiction is limited by Article III of the Constitution, which restricts federal judicial power to the adjudication of 'Cases' or 'Controversies.' [Citations omitted.] The Declaratory Judgment Act's requirement of 'a case of actual controversy' simply affirms this Constitu-

[b] After the decision set out in the text, defendant again moved to dismiss the complaint and to obtain other relief, this time presenting affidavits to show that there was no controversy. The motion was denied, 8 F.R.D. 324 (S.D.N.Y.1948). Later reported steps in the case will be found at 8 F.R.D. 306; 8 F.R.D. 459; 82 F.Supp. 556; and 173 F.2d 890. Finally, plaintiff obtained a declaration that it could terminate the contract and continue to sell "any and all fans, ventilating equipment and other products, not infringing upon valid patents owned by defendant after such termination." This judgment was affirmed, 180 F.2d 342 (2d Cir.), cert. denied, 339 U.S. 979, 70 S.Ct. 1025 (1950).

tional requirement, having long been interpreted as referring to any case and controversy that is justiciable under Article III. . . .

"For there to be a case or controversy under Article III, the dispute must be 'definite and concrete, touching the legal relations of parties having adverse legal interests,' 'real and substantial,' and 'admi[t] of specific relief through a decree of a conclusive character, as distinguished from an opinion advising what the law would be upon a hypothetical state of facts.' MedImmune, [Inc. v. Genentech, Inc., 549 U.S. 118, 127, 127 S.Ct. 764, 771 (2007)] (quoting Aetna Life [Ins. Co. v. Haworth, 300 U.S. 227, 240–41, 57 S.Ct. 461, 464 (1937)]). As the Supreme Court has recently reiterated, however, there is no bright-line rule for determining whether an action satisfies the case or controversy requirement. Id. To the contrary, '[t]he difference between an abstract question and a "controversy" contemplated by the Declaratory Judgment Act is necessarily one of degree, and it would be difficult, if it would be possible, to fashion a precise test for determining in every case whether there is such a controversy.' Md. Cas. Co. v. Pac. Coal & Oil Co., 312 U.S. 270, 273, 61 S.Ct. 510 (1941). Instead of a bright-line rule, 'the analysis must be calibrated to the particular facts of each case,' Cat Tech LLC [v. TubeMaster, Inc., 528 F.3d 871, 879 (Fed.Cir. 2008)], with the basic standard being whether 'the facts alleged, under all the circumstances, show that there is a substantial controversy, between parties having adverse legal interests, of sufficient immediacy and reality to warrant the issuance of a declaratory judgment,' MedImmune, 127 S.Ct. at 771 (quoting Md. Cas. Co., 312 U.S. at 273); see also Caraco Pharms. Labs. Ltd. v. Forest Labs., 527 F.3d 1278, 1290 (Fed.Cir.2008)."

The Federal Circuit court affirmed: "Considering the totality of the circumstances, Prasco has not alleged a controversy of sufficient 'immediacy and reality' to create a justiciable controversy. . . . Absent an injury-in-fact fairly traceable to the patentee, there can be no immediate and real controversy.

". . . The mere existence of a potentially adverse patent does not cause an injury nor create an imminent risk of an injury; absent action by the patentee, 'a potential competitor . . . is legally free to market its product in the face of an adversely-held patent.' [Teva Pharms. USA, Inc. v. Novartis Pharms. Corp., 482 F.3d 1330, 1345 (Fed.Cir.2007).]

"Prasco argues that a case and controversy has nevertheless been created because Medicis has caused Prasco to suffer an actual harm—namely, 'paralyzing uncertainty' from fear that Medicis will bring an infringement suit against it. Appellant's Br. 23. As Prasco admitted at oral argument, however, any uncertainty has not been paralyzing. To the contrary, notwithstanding this lawsuit, Prasco has launched its OSCION product. . . . [T]he bedrock rule [remains] that a case or controversy must be based on a real and immediate injury or threat of future injury that is caused by the defendants—an objective standard that cannot be met by a purely subjective or speculative fear of future harm. . . .

"Rather than a purely subjective fear or the mere existence of a potentially adverse patent alone, the alleged injury at the root of most justiciable declaratory judgment controversies in the patent context is a 'restraint on the free exploitation of non-infringing goods,' or an imminent threat of such restraint. Caraco, 527 F.3d at 1291 (quoting Red Wing Shoe Co., Inc. v. Hockerson–Halberstadt, Inc., 148 F.3d 1355, 1360 (Fed.Cir. 1998)).

"A patentee can cause such an injury in a variety of ways, for example, by creating a reasonable apprehension of an infringement suit, [citation omitted], demanding the right to royalty payments, [citation omitted], or creating a barrier to the regulatory approval of a product that is necessary for marketing, [citation omitted]." But here the court noted by contrast that "the defendants have not accused Prasco of infringement or asserted any rights to OSCION, nor have they taken any actions which imply such claims. Instead, all we have before us is Prasco's allegation that its product does not infringe the defendants' patents."

In sum, "where Prasco has suffered no actual present injury traceable to the defendants, and the defendants have not asserted any rights against Prasco related to the patents nor taken any affirmative actions concerning Prasco's current product, one prior suit concerning unrelated patents and products and the defendants' failure to sign a covenant not to sue are simply not sufficient to establish that Prasco is at risk of imminent harm from the defendants and that there is an actual controversy between the parties of sufficient immediacy and reality to warrant declaratory judgment jurisdiction. Although we understand Prasco's desire to have a definitive answer on whether its products infringe defendants' patents, were the district court to reach the merits of this case, it would merely be providing an advisory opinion. This is impermissible under Article III."

International Longshoremen's Local 37 v. Boyd

Supreme Court of the United States, 1954.
347 U.S. 222, 74 S.Ct. 447.

■ MR. JUSTICE FRANKFURTER delivered the opinion of the Court.

This is an action by Local 37 of the International Longshoremen's and Warehousemen's Union and several of its [permanent resident] alien members to enjoin the District Director of Immigration and Naturalization at Seattle from so construing § 212(d)(7) of the Immigration and Nationality Act of 1952* as to treat aliens domiciled in the continental United States returning from temporary work in Alaska as if they were aliens entering the United States for the first time. Declaratory relief to the same effect is also sought. Since petitioners asserted in the alternative that such a construction of the challenged statute would be unconstitutional, a three-

* This section states that the exclusionary provisions of § 212(a) shall, with exceptions not here relevant, "be applicable to any alien who shall leave Hawaii, Alaska, Guam, Puerto Rico, or the Virgin Islands of the United States, and who seeks to enter the continental United States . . . ." 8 U.S.C. § 1182(d)(7). [Footnote by Court.—Ed.]

judge district court was convened.[c] The case came before it on stipulated facts and issues of law, from which it appeared that the union has over three thousand members who work every summer in the herring and salmon canneries of Alaska, that some of these are aliens, and that if alien workers going to Alaska for the 1953 canning season were excluded on their return, their "contract and property rights [would] be jeopardized and forfeited." The District Court entertained the suit but dismissed it on the merits. 111 F.Supp. 802 [(W.D.Wash. Apr. 10, 1953)]. . . .

On this appeal, appellee contends [inter alia] that the District Court should not have reached the statutory and constitutional questions—that it should have dismissed the suit for want of a "case or controversy" . . . .

Appellants in effect asked the District Court to rule that a statute the sanctions of which had not been set in motion against individuals on whose behalf relief was sought, because an occasion for doing so had not arisen, would not be applied to them if in the future such a contingency should arise. That is not a lawsuit to enforce a right; it is an endeavor to obtain a court's assurance that a statute does not govern hypothetical situations that may or may not make the challenged statute applicable. Determination of the scope and constitutionality of legislation in advance of its immediate adverse effect in the context of a concrete case involves too remote and abstract an inquiry for the proper exercise of the judicial function. United Public Workers v. Mitchell, 330 U.S. 75, 67 S.Ct. 556; see Muskrat v. United States, 219 U.S. 346, 31 S.Ct. 250, and Alabama State Federation of Labor v. McAdory, 325 U.S. 450, 65 S.Ct. 1384. Since we do not have on the record before us a controversy appropriate for adjudication, the judgment of the District Court must be vacated, with directions to dismiss the complaint.

It is so ordered.

■ MR. JUSTICE BLACK, with whom MR. JUSTICE DOUGLAS concurs, dissenting.

This looks to me like the very kind of "case or controversy" courts should decide. With the abstract principles of law relied on by the majority for dismissing the case, I am not in disagreement. Of course federal courts do not pass on the meaning or constitutionality of statutes as they might be thought to govern mere "hypothetical situations . . . ." Nor should courts entertain such statutory challenges on behalf of persons upon whom adverse statutory effects are "too remote and abstract an inquiry for the proper exercise of the judicial function." But as I read the record it shows that judicial action is absolutely essential to save a large group of wage

---

[c] For the three-judge district court referred to, see 28 U.S.C. § 2284.

Prior to 1976, federal law required three-judge district courts not infrequently. Most importantly, a district court composed of three judges had to hear federal actions seeking injunctive relief against the enforcement of a federal or state statute on the ground that the statute in question was contrary to the Federal Constitution.

Now, the three-judge requirement is much more limited in scope, applying primarily to reapportionment suits and to certain cases under the 1964 Civil Rights and 1965 Voting Rights Acts. See generally Charles Alan Wright & Mary Kay Kane, Law of Federal Courts § 50 (6th ed. 2002).

earners on whose behalf this action is brought from irreparable harm due to alleged lawless enforcement of a federal statute. My view makes it necessary for me to set out the facts with a little more detail than they appear in the Court's opinion.

Every summer members of the appellant union go from the west coast of continental United States to Alaska to work in salmon and herring canneries under collective-bargaining agreements. As the 1953 canning season approached the union and its members looked forward to this Alaska employment. A troublesome question arose, however, on account of the Immigration and Nationality Act of 1952, 66 Stat. 163. Section 212(d)(7) of this new Act has language that given one construction provides that all aliens seeking admission to continental United States from Alaska, even those previously accepted as permanent United States residents, shall be examined as if entering from a foreign country with a view to excluding them on any of the many grounds applicable to aliens generally. This new law created an acute problem for the union and its numerous members who were lawful alien residents, since aliens generally can be excluded from this country for many reasons which would not justify deporting aliens lawfully residing here. The union and its members insisted on another construction. They denied that Congress intended to require alien workers to forfeit their right to live in this country for no reason at all except that they went to Alaska, territory of the United States, to engage in lawful work under a lawfully authorized collective-bargaining contract. The defendant immigration officer announced that the union's interpretation was wrong and that workers going to Alaska would be subject to examination and exclusion. This is the controversy.

It was to test the right of the immigration officer to apply § 212(d)(7) to make these workers subject to exclusion that this suit was filed by the union and two of its officers on behalf of themselves and all union members who are aliens and permanent residents. True, the action was begun before the union members went to Alaska for the 1953 canning season. But it is not only admitted that the Immigration official intended to enforce § 212(d)(7) as the union and these workers feared. It is admitted here that he has since done precisely that. All 1953 alien cannery workers have actually been subjected to the wearisome routine of immigration procedure as though they had never lived here. And some of the union members are evidently about to be denied the right ever to return to their homes on grounds that could not have been legally applied to them had they stayed in California or Washington instead of going to Alaska to work for an important American industry.

Thus the threatened injury which the Court dismisses as "remote" and "hypothetical" has come about. For going to Alaska to engage in honest employment many of these workers may lose the home this country once afforded them. This is a strange penalty to put on productive work. Maybe this is what Congress meant by passing § 212(d)(7). And maybe in these times such a law would be held constitutional. But even so, can it be that a challenge to this law on behalf of those whom it hits the hardest is so frivolous that it should be dismissed for want of a controversy that courts should decide? Workers threatened with irreparable damages, like others, should have their cases tried.[d]

Question: (4) Four years after the International Longshoremen's case, an appeal came to the Supreme Court from dismissal of an action on the ground that there was no "actual controversy." The plaintiff's complaint sought a declaration that a Tennessee statute requiring segregated seating arrangements in transportation facilities on account of race was unconstitutional, and also sought an injunction against enforcement of this statute. The three-judge district court found that the plaintiff had boarded a bus in Memphis, Tennessee, and seated himself in the front; that the driver told him that he must move to the rear, the driver stating that the law required it because of his color; that the plaintiff refused; that two police officers shortly thereafter boarded the bus and ordered the plaintiff to go to the back of the bus or get off, or he would be arrested; and that thereupon the plaintiff left the bus. The record further showed that the defendants, who were officials and officers of the City of Memphis and of the company operating the bus, intended to enforce the Tennessee statute until final adjudication of unconstitutionality. The Supreme Court decided the appeal in a per curiam opinion without hearing argument. What would you expect the decision to be? Is the case distinguishable from the International Longshoremen's case? Should it matter that the plaintiff boarded the bus for the purpose of instituting this litigation? See Evers v. Dwyer, 358 U.S. 202, 79 S.Ct. 178 (1958).

(c) ENFORCEMENT OF JUDGMENT

[Rule 69]

Do not make the mistake of thinking that an unappealed judgment concludes the scenario. The maneuvering may have just begun. An unsatisfied judgment often does the victor little good, and the losing party is not always a good sport about compliance. In short, there are frequently extensive post-judgment proceedings.

An equitable judgment is in the form and nature of a court order to the defendant. If he disobeys, the judge could imprison the defendant until he complies (or fine him unless he complies), and thus coerce him into compliance. This enforcement would derive from the court's civil contempt powers. Criminal contempt is not, strictly speaking, a means of enforcement, but the possibility of criminal contempt incidentally benefits the plaintiff by encouraging compliance with the judgment.

A legal judgment, by contrast, typically does not express its relief as an order to the defendant to pay or to restore, but rather as a statement that the plaintiff shall recover a sum of money or certain property from the

---

[d] Eventually, United States ex rel. Alcantra v. Boyd, 222 F.2d 445 (9th Cir.1955) (habeas corpus case by person held for deportation after the 1953 cannery season), held § 212(d)(7) inapplicable to any permanent resident alien who went from the continental United States to work temporarily in Alaska, and so who was not using the territories as stepping stones to "enter" the continental United States from a foreign land.

defendant. This signifies more than a matter of form or a historical oddity. A legal judgment is not an order to the defendant, and so it is up to the plaintiff to enforce the judgment.

Take as an example a judgment for money damages, and assume that the defendant does not voluntarily pay it. The initial step for the plaintiff is to identify and locate the defendant's assets. This sometimes requires extensive investigation. The plaintiff can utilize the discovery devices of the Federal Rules for this purpose; state law may provide other means of discovery, which the plaintiff can use in connection with the enforcement of a federal judgment. See Rule 69(a)(2).

The plaintiff is then in a position to invoke the force of government in order to obtain the relief to which the court has found the plaintiff entitled. In federal court the procedure for this generally conforms to the local state law. The interplay of federal and state law here is similar to that prevailing under Rule 64 for provisional remedies. See Rule 69(a)(1).

Question: (5) What are the advantages and disadvantages of such incorporation by the Rules of state procedure?

Typically, the plaintiff will obtain from the federal court a writ of execution addressed to the district's federal marshal. Pursuant to this writ and with information from the plaintiff, the marshal (or deputy marshal) will levy on, or seize, so much of the defendant's nonexempt property within the state (state laws provide many and varied exemptions) as is necessary to pay the judgment. See Rule 4.1. If the defendant still does not pay, the marshal will sell that property, use the proceeds to cover the marshal's own fees and expenses and to satisfy the plaintiff's judgment, and then give any remainder to the defendant.

If execution is less than fully successful, there are other remedies available to the plaintiff by permission of the federal court, namely, state-law devices called supplementary proceedings. For example, state statutes commonly provide a means for compelling the judgment debtor to appear for sworn examination before the court as to his assets and his ability to pay the judgment; if the court finds that he has property not exempt from execution, the court may order him to turn over the property so that the marshal may take it on execution. For another example, under the law of some states, the court may order the debtor to make installment payments on the judgment debt, from time to time out of future income; the court will fix the payment schedule after taking into account the reasonable requirements of the debtor and his dependents. Now the defendant is the subject of a court order, and failure to obey an order of the court in supplementary proceedings is punishable as contempt.

As is the case with provisional remedies, some of the more pro-plaintiff enforcement mechanisms may be quite drastic in effect. Consequently, some have of late been attacked in lawsuits, and a few struck down, on the ground of fundamental unfairness. As a matter of constitutional law, then, the state legislatures must carefully draw their remedial procedure, while according with the dictates of procedural due process that we shall explore in Topic C of Part Three.

GABOVITCH v. LUNDY, 584 F.2d 559 (1st Cir.1978). A federal-court judgment creditor of appellee Lundy obtained a writ of execution from the clerk for the District of Massachusetts. "The writ was returned on May 5, 1976, certifying a levy on appellee Taunton Co–Operative Bank in the amount of $3000, representing Lundy's deposits in the bank. The bank ignored appellant's numerous demands that it pay over the $3000. On February 24, 1978, appellant petitioned the district court" to enforce the writ. The district court denied relief, holding the writ ineffective because of the creditor's failure to comply with state procedure. The creditor appealed.

The court of appeals affirmed. The appellant had argued that Rule 69(a) makes state law applicable to procedures in aid of execution but not to the mere issuance of process. "Unfortunately for appellant, the legislative history and judicial application of Rule 69(a) make clear that the first sentence of the Rule expresses a limitation on the means of enforcement of money judgments and does not create a general power to issue writs of execution in disregard of the state law incorporated by the rest of the Rule."

Rule 69(a) was meant only (1) to adopt a prior practice of following state law on both the procedure for obtaining process and the effect of such writs and (2) to extend this practice to purely monetary equitable judgments.

"Finally, the courts have consistently read Rule 69(a) as limiting all federal process on money judgments to the type of process available under state law. This court held in First National Bank of Boston v. Antonio Santisteban & Co., Inc., 285 F.2d 855 (1st Cir.1961), that a federal writ of execution did not reach unearned wages of a Puerto Rican judgment debtor because Puerto Rican law gave no effect to such a writ. See Travelers Insurance Co. v. Lawrence, 509 F.2d 83, 86–88 (9th Cir.1974) (Rule 69 makes availability and effect of federal process subject to state law); United States ex rel. Marcus v. Lord Elec. Co., 43 F.Supp. 12 (W.D.Pa.1942) (bank deposits affected by writ of execution because state law so provides). Thus, we have no difficulty concluding that the writ of execution issued by the clerk had no effect. Under Massachusetts law, attachment of bank accounts takes place by trustee process. Mass.Gen.Laws Ann. ch. 246. Attachment on trustee process requires court approval. Mass.Rules Civ.Proc. 4.2(c). Because a writ issued solely on the authority of a court clerk has no effect on a bank account under Massachusetts law, it has no effect under Rule 69(a).[3]"

---

[3] Although the forms of the process would, of course, be federal, the essential elements of state procedure for obtaining the writ must be followed. Mass.Gen.Laws Ann. ch. 246 § 5 and

Question: (6) In a state where a plaintiff's lawyer can issue the documents for execution, as under NYCPLR § 5230(b), must the holder of a federal-court judgment go to the court clerk for a writ of execution?

SECTION 5. APPEAL

(a) APPEAL TO THE COURT OF APPEALS

Avenues of appeal.—According to 28 U.S.C. § 1291, a party, claiming that a "final decision"[a] of a district court is erroneous, has a right to appeal to the appropriate circuit's United States Court of Appeals[b] for correction of the error, that is, for reversal or modification of the decision. What a final decision is within the meaning of § 1291 may become a serious question, but the basic design is to accord an appeal of right when the court below has fully treated the case, save for award of costs and enforcement of judgment.

Question: (1) What are the arguments for and against generally limiting the right of appeal to final decisions?

When the Federal Rules came in to permit the inclusion in a single action of a number of claims to be litigated among a number of parties—a condition that could exist in the prior practice but was now to become more common—the rulemakers thought it desirable to permit appeal from the disposition of a clearly divisible part of a complicated case. Under Rule 54(b), the district court must make an express determination that "there is no just reason for delay" before it directs the entry of a final decision as to one or more of several claims or parties, which in effect releases a part of the case for appeal under § 1291.

There is also a right of appeal from certain "interlocutory decisions" of the district court, that is, nonfinal decisions. The most important class is described in 28 U.S.C. § 1292(a)(1) as interlocutory orders that grant, refuse, modify, or otherwise affect injunctions. By interpretation, prelimi-

---

Mass.Rules Civ.Proc. 4.2(a) provide for trustee process to attach the "credits" of a defendant. Receipt of a trustee summons notifies a bank of attachment of a depositor's credits. Mass.Gen. Laws Ann. ch. 246 § 20; Mass.Rules Civ.Proc. 4.2(b). But a trustee summons cannot issue without a prior court approval of the attachment. Mass.Rules Civ.Proc. 4.2(c). Under the same rule, the attachment usually will not be approved without a prior adversary hearing. Once the trustee process issues, the trustee must answer specifying the property subjected to the attachment. Mass.Gen.Laws Ann. ch. 246 § 10. If the court then adjudges the bank to be a trustee, it must pay over to the creditor or be subject to a trustee writ of execution. Mass.Gen.Laws Ann. ch. 246 § 45. Because appellant failed to obtain court approval of his process, it could not be effective to attach the property held by the bank.

[a] We shift here from the word "judgment" because the appeals statutes usually do not use that term, which is more inclusive than final decision. Note again the wording of Rule 54(a).

[b] There are special situations in which decisions of the district courts, final or interlocutory, are subject to direct review by the Supreme Court. See 17 Wright, Miller, Cooper & Amar §§ 4039–4040 (citing and summarizing these few statutes). For example, 28 U.S.C. § 1253 gives any party a right of direct appeal from an order granting or denying an interlocutory or permanent injunction in an action required to be heard by a three-judge district court.

nary injunctions are within § 1292(a)(1)—the statute allowed the appeal in the American Hospital case—but temporary restraining orders are generally not.

Question: (2) Why has Congress singled out these particular interlocutory orders for appeal of right?

Section 1292(b) permits appeal of an interlocutory order other than one covered by § 1292(a) when, first, the district judge states that it "involves a controlling question of law as to which there is substantial ground for difference of opinion" and that immediate appeal "may materially advance the ultimate termination of the litigation" and, second, the court of appeals in its discretion agrees to hear the appeal. Because of these multiple requirements, appeals under § 1292(b) are not at all common.

Dilly v. S.S. Kresge

United States Court of Appeals, Fourth Circuit, 1979.
606 F.2d 62.

■ Before RUSSELL and WIDENER, CIRCUIT JUDGES, and HOFFMAN, DISTRICT JUDGE.*

■ WIDENER, CIRCUIT JUDGE:

The plaintiffs, Bernard and Eleanor Dilly, brought this action against her employer, S.S. Kresge Co., for injuries she received during the course of employment. The uncontested facts are that an assistant manager of Kresge came to the soda fountain area of the store, where Eleanor Dilly worked, and ordered a cup of hot chocolate. After he was told that they had no hot chocolate, the assistant manager grabbed Mrs. Dilly, shook her and said "What the hell do you mean running out of hot chocolate?" Eleanor Dilly stated in her deposition that she thought the assistant manager was serious and angry. The assistant manager contends that he was joking. As a result of the assistant manager's action, Mrs. Dilly claims her neck was injured.

The parties filed cross-motions for summary judgment. The district court granted summary judgment for the plaintiffs on the issue of liability and set a hearing to ascertain the amount of damages, if any, due the plaintiffs. Kresge filed a motion to set aside the district court's order pursuant to FRCP 59. This motion was denied. A notice of appeal was then filed and an appeal was taken to the order granting summary judgment in favor of the plaintiffs.

The defendant takes the position that the appeal from the grant of summary judgment for the plaintiffs and the denial of its Rule 59 motion is an appeal from a final order. We do not agree. The notice of appeal was filed and the appeal was taken prior to the ascertainment of damages; therefore, it was not a final order within the meaning of 28 U.S.C. § 1291. Neither has an interlocutory appeal been perfected as provided for in

* U.S. District Court for the Eastern District of Virginia, sitting by designation.

§ 1292(b). Thus, we are without jurisdiction to hear this appeal. "A 'final decision' generally is one which ends the litigation on the merits and leaves nothing for the court to do but execute the judgment." Catlin v. United States, 324 U.S. 229, 233, 65 S.Ct. 631, 633, 89 L.Ed. 911 (1945). In the case at bar, the district court found the defendant liable but delayed awarding damages until a hearing was held to determine their existence and amount. There is obviously something else for the district court to do but execute the judgment. . . .

Accordingly, the appeal is dismissed.[1]

Question: (3) Would the Dilly result on appealability change if the district court had entered judgment after granting summary judgment in favor of the defendant? if there had been two defendants and if it had granted summary judgment in favor of one of the defendants?

An appellant takes an appeal from and formally attacks the "final decision" or "interlocutory decision," but what the appellant really claims in many appeals is that some action of the district court taken prior to the entry of the final or interlocutory decision, and objected to at the time, was erroneous and that this error has infected the final or interlocutory decision with substantial error. The district court during the course of the litigation may have ruled on a variety of questions—motions attacking a pleading, objections to the admission and exclusion of evidence, motions for judgment as a matter of law, and so on. On appeal the losing party may be urging that one or more of these rulings were wrong and, hence, that the final or interlocutory decision appealed from is wrong. For example, a losing plaintiff may be urging on appeal that the judgment for the defendant is wrong, and that the appellate court must reverse the judgment and

---

[1] The question concerning the dismissal of the appeal and the jurisdiction of the court was initiated by the court at oral argument. The briefs did not address that subject. The subject briefed, however, and also argued was the question of whether or not summary judgment for the plaintiffs was appropriate.

While what follow are dicta, the case must be reconsidered by the district court, so what we say may not be too far a departure from appropriate judicial restraint. Perhaps another appeal on the same record can be avoided.

West Virginia law exempts employers, who pay into the workmen's compensation fund, from liability for injuries to employees which occur in the course of their employment unless the injury results "from the deliberate intention of [the] employer to produce such injury." West Virginia Code §§ 23–2–6, 23–4–2.

The West Virginia court recently held that these provisions meant that "an employer loses immunity from common law actions where such employer's conduct constitutes an intentional tort or willful, wanton, or reckless misconduct." Mandolidis v. Elkins Industries, Inc., 246 S.E.2d 907, 914 (W.Va.1978).

In view of the fact that the testimony of the assistant manager was that his touching of the plaintiff, Eleanor Dilly, was in a joking manner, and the testimony of her that his touching of her was not in a joking manner, rather serious or angry, we think the district court should carefully reconsider its grant of summary judgment. It recognized this very conflict in its opinion. The key and essential evidence in the case appears to be in direct conflict, and if that be true, as the record before us now indicates, the entry of summary judgment is open to serious question.

order a new trial, because the district court erroneously excluded evidence offered by the plaintiff that, had it been received and considered, might have caused the jury to bring in a different verdict. It is of the utmost importance to our understanding of any case in an appellate court to single out the precise act or acts of the lower court that the appellant complains of as having been erroneous.

This is a convenient point to ask whether it makes sense to have any system of appeals and, if so, what limits should exist on appellate review. It would seem that there is no constitutional right to appeal. See National Union of Marine Cooks & Stewards v. Arnold, 348 U.S. 37, 43, 75 S.Ct. 92, 95 (1954) ("While a statutory review is important and must be exercised without discrimination, such a review is not a requirement of due process."). In all events, why do we have the particular arrangements set out in the current statutes with their emphasis on the distinction between final decisions and interlocutory decisions and their peculiar mix of appeals of right and discretionary appeals? These fundamental questions we shall explore in Part Nine.

Appellate procedure.—The Federal Rules of Appellate Procedure outline the procedure for taking appeals. We do not recount this procedure here, but students should familiarize themselves with it in a general way, especially App. Rules 3 and 4 (appeal of right), 5 (appeal under § 1292(b)), 7 (bond for costs), 10 and 11 (record on appeal), 12 (docketing appeal; required filings), 28 and 30–32 (briefs), 34 (oral argument), and 35 (possibility of en banc hearing). For detail, see 16A & 16AA Wright, Miller, Cooper & Struve §§ 3945–3994.

In addition to the uniform provisions of the Federal Rules of Appellate Procedure, the courts of appeals may severally adopt their own rules of procedure not inconsistent with them. See 28 U.S.C. § 2071; App. Rule 47.

Despite local variations, the courts of appeals conduct their chief business in much the same way throughout the country, and it is largely the way traditional to our appellate courts. The appellate court hears the appeal on the record and on the briefs of counsel, and often there is also oral argument. The appellate court applies to the alleged reviewable errors the appropriate standard of review, which might be a nondeferential redetermination by the appellate judges or might involve some or much deference to the trial judge's view. By majority vote of the usual three-judge panel, the appellate court affirms, reverses, or modifies the decision appealed from. If it follows from the view of the case adopted by the appellate court that further testimony should be taken, this will not be done by the appellate court, but rather by the lower court on remand. See 28 U.S.C. § 2106.

Stay of proceedings to enforce a judgment.—What happens to an appealable decision before the appellate court can dispose of any appeal? Does it remain effective or rest in abeyance until the court of appeals finishes? The arrangements are rather complex.

Where the judgment is an ordinary one, such as the usual one for money, there is an automatic stay of enforcement for fourteen days after entry of judgment under Rule 62(a). If a party makes a post-judgment motion, the district court may stay enforcement until the disposition of that motion, this being done under Rule 62(b) as a matter of discretion and on appropriate conditions for the security of the adverse party.

If a party takes an appeal, the party has a right to a stay upon giving a supersedeas bond that meets the approval of the district court. Normally such a bond is in an amount sufficient to cover the judgment, costs on appeal, interest, and damages for delay consequent to the stay. See Rule 62(d) and (e); see also Rule 62(f) and (h).

Question: (4) The plaintiff you represent won, on Day 0, a money judgment of a type to which neither Rule 62(f) nor Rule 62(h) applies. The defendant made no post-judgment motions, but she did file a notice of appeal in accordance with App. Rule 4(a) on the thirtieth day after entry of the judgment. On that same day, the defendant gave a supersedeas bond and the district court approved it. The appeal is still pending. When could you have executed? What could the defendant have done to foreclose such possibility?

Consider now an interlocutory or final judgment in an action for an injunction. There is no provision for an automatic stay. However, the district court in its discretion may order a stay (or modify, restore, or grant an injunction) in the period prior to appeal, see Rule 62(a) and (b), or after an appeal is taken, see Rule 62(c), always upon such terms as to bond or otherwise as it considers proper for the security of the adverse party's rights.

Matters regarding stays of enforcement are, in the first instance, within the purview of the district court. But if a party could not there obtain a stay, and if an appeal has been taken, the party can seek relief in the court of appeals. See Rule 62(g); App. Rule 8(a); 28 U.S.C. § 1651(a). In exceptional situations where a hearing by a panel of the court of appeals would be impracticable because of the requirements of time, the party may apply for a stay to a single judge of that court. See App. Rule 8(a)(2)(D). Again, the appellate "court may condition relief on a party's filing a bond or other appropriate security in the district court." App. Rule 8(a)(2)(E).

LONG v. ROBINSON, 432 F.2d 977 (4th Cir.1970). In a class action a federal district court declared unconstitutional a Maryland statute and the corresponding local ordinance exempting Baltimore City from the uniform state definition of juvenile age as under 18 years and providing that a person in Baltimore City ceases to be a juvenile at the age of 16. (The age for determining who is a juvenile is important because the criminal justice system treats accused juveniles differently from accused adults.) The order required the authorities to turn over to the juvenile system as expeditiously as possible all persons between 16 and 18 years of age currently in jail in

Baltimore City awaiting trial. It was on August 6, 1970, that the district court handed down this judgment, 316 F.Supp. 22 (D.Md.1970).

The district judge refused a stay. The defendants applied to a single judge of the court of appeals, Circuit Judge Winter, for a stay pending appeal. They asserted that the district judge's legal conclusions were incorrect and that the administrative and economic burdens in complying with the order would be very heavy. They estimated that the order would double the yearly caseload of juvenile cases in the city and would require expansion of detention facilities, training schools, courts and court personnel, social workers, and other personnel. They said that until these facilities and personnel became available, the treatment program for juveniles under 16 would suffer adverse effects. Finally, they argued that the unavailability of sufficient funds to meet the costs of the additional juvenile cases might necessitate a special session of the General Assembly of Maryland to make the needed appropriations.

Judge Winter stated the legal principles governing such an application: "a party seeking a stay must show (1) that he will likely prevail on the merits of the appeal, (2) that he will suffer irreparable injury if the stay is denied, (3) that other parties will not be substantially harmed by the stay, and (4) that the public interest will be served by granting the stay." He found: (1) that the defendants' probability of success on appeal was not substantial; (2) that the principal irreparable injury that the defendants claimed they would suffer was of their own making (the state legislature had abolished the lower age for juveniles in Baltimore City in 1966, to be effective in 1969, but nothing had been done to effectuate the change; the legislature had twice postponed the effective date for a year, but still no steps beyond some preliminary planning had been taken; and it "would seem elementary that a party may not claim equity in his own defaults"); (3) that a stay's deleterious consequences to the 16– and 17–year-old members of the plaintiff class by reason of their incarceration with older persons were clear; and (4) that the public interest lay in the immediate implementation of the order.

Judge Winter denied the stay on August 11, 1970, but ordered an expedited hearing of the appeal. The court of appeals heard argument on September 17, 1970. It affirmed the district court's decision on the merits on January 18, 1971, 436 F.2d 1116 (4th Cir.1971).

If the court of appeals denies a stay of enforcement of the district court's judgment, a party may seek immediate relief in the Supreme Court. See 28 U.S.C. § 1651(a). The party makes application to the single Justice assigned to the particular circuit from which the case comes. If the Justice grants the stay, he or she may condition it upon the giving of adequate security. If the Justice denies the stay, the applicant may (with scant hope of success) renew the request to any other Justice, and so on. Any Justice may refer a request for a stay to the entire Court for action.

If the party obtains a stay somewhere along this line, the adverse party may seek to modify or vacate the stay, on good grounds shown, by pursuing relief up the line in similar manner.

If no stay issues, the party who prevailed in the district court may proceed to enforce his money judgment or take the benefit of an injunction in his favor.

Question: (5) What then is the situation if the court of appeals ultimately reverses on the merits?

(b) Review by the Supreme Court

After appeal, the litigant disappointed by an adverse decision of the court of appeals has still another chance. See 28 U.S.C. § 1254, which provides for review by the Supreme Court of cases in the courts of appeals by certiorari or by certified questions. Review via certification of questions by a court of appeals is extremely unusual, on the order of once per decade. The usual avenue to the Supreme Court is the petition for certiorari.

Review on certiorari is not a matter of right, but of discretion, and "will be granted only for compelling reasons." S.Ct. Rule 10, further quoted supra p. 18. A showing of a conflict in decisions of the courts of appeals on a point involved in the case is likely to weigh strongly with the Court as a factor favoring review, but the fact that it is strongly arguable that the decision below was wrong is not in itself a compelling reason for review. So a denial of certiorari, theoretically, says nothing as to the merits of the case.

Question: (6) Is certiorari available to review a decision of the court of appeals that is nonfinal? Is it actually necessary to await a decision by the court of appeals before applying for certiorari? At what point, precisely, can certiorari be sought, and by whom?

The Rules of the Supreme Court of the United States prescribe the procedure for review by the Court. Return your focus to certiorari. The petition for a writ of certiorari must contain the questions presented for review, a concise statement of the case, and an argument regarding the reasons for allowance of the writ. The Court denies or grants certiorari upon consideration of the petition and any brief in opposition and reply brief, there being no oral argument at this stage. If the Court grants the petition, a step that requires the vote of only four of the nine Justices, the Court has thereby agreed to consider the merits. The case is normally then briefed on the merits and heard on oral argument. Ultimately, the Supreme Court—by majority vote, with six Justices constituting a quorum—affirms, reverses, or modifies the decision being reviewed, possibly remanding to a court below for further proceedings.

A stay with respect to the adverse decision of the court of appeals is available from that court or a judge thereof, or from a Justice or the Supreme Court, under circumstances and in a manner analogous to the stay procedure described above for a district court's judgment.

Final decision in the Supreme Court brings the federal court case to the end of the line, and to the end of this survey of the conduct of a lawsuit. As Justice Jackson observed in Brown v. Allen, 344 U.S. 443, 540, 73 S.Ct. 397, 427 (1953) (concurring opinion), "We are not final because we are infallible, but we are infallible only because we are final."

SECTION 6. SELECTION OF A PROPER FORUM: LIMITATIONS ON JURISDICTION OVER SUBJECT MATTER

Having described the conduct of lawsuits in the district courts and their review in the courts of appeals and the Supreme Court, we shall now return to a question put at the beginning of the survey: in which courts may the plaintiff institute a particular action? Our concern therewith shifts to jurisdiction or, as it is called more specifically, jurisdiction over the subject matter. We start with a consideration of the division of business between the state court systems, on the one hand, and the federal court system, on the other hand.

(a) THE JUDICIAL POWER OF THE STATES

The Tenth Amendment to the Constitution of the United States, which is largely declaratory of the relationships created by the Constitution proper, declares: "The powers not delegated to the United States by the Constitution, nor prohibited by it to the States, are reserved to the States respectively, or to the people." The Constitution nowhere expressly prohibits any judicial power to the states.

First, as we shall see, Article III declares that the federal judicial power shall extend to various enumerated "cases" and "controversies," but these constitute only a small fraction of all the disputes that require adjudication. The rest of those disputes constitutionally can proceed in the state courts exclusively.

Second, the states may handle even the Article III "cases" and "controversies," except as Congress decides that the states shall not. In other words, although Article III gives a limited judicial power to the federal government, the Constitution does not provide that the states may not exercise that power also. The states are free to exercise it, unless Congress steps in and says no, and Congress seldom does so. Much of the jurisdiction of the federal courts is thus *concurrent* with that of the state courts. That is, a plaintiff instituting a particular action often has a choice between a federal court and a state court.

Third, there are indeed a few acts of Congress that declare the federal courts must exclusively handle certain classes of Article III "cases" and "controversies." Examples of this *exclusive* federal jurisdiction are bankruptcy proceedings and actions under the federal antitrust laws.

The net result is that the states are free to handle a very large amount of business. A state may choose not to exert its full judicial power: subject to some vague but slight constitutional limitations not of immediate concern, a state may by provisions in its constitution or statutes restrict the kinds of disputes that its courts will handle. Nevertheless, state courts handle a very large percentage of this nation's judicial business, indeed well over 99% of the civil cases.

Of course, a state may set up a hierarchy of courts as it wishes and allocate business among its courts as it sees fit. There is no uniformity of pattern among the states in these respects.

(b) THE JUDICIAL POWER OF THE UNITED STATES

Article III of the Constitution fixes the outer bound on the judicial power of the United States. After reading the entire Article, consider Section 2, Paragraph 1;[a] Section 1, first sentence; and Section 2, Paragraph 2. Try to get a sense of what is meant by the statement that the federal courts are courts of *limited* jurisdiction, as opposed to *general* jurisdiction.

Questions: (1) What importance attaches to the use of the words "cases" and "controversies"? See Charles Alan Wright & Mary Kay Kane, Law of Federal Courts § 12 (6th ed. 2002).

(2) To what extent can you classify the "cases" and "controversies" enumerated in Article III, Section 2, Paragraph 1 as dependent on the nature of the claim asserted? as dependent on the types of parties involved?

(3) Is it constitutionally required that federal courts have jurisdiction over all or any of the enumerated "cases" or "controversies"?

---

[a] You should read this provision in conjunction with the Eleventh Amendment. The Supreme Court in Chisholm v. Georgia, 2 U.S. (2 Dall.) 419 (1793), allowed an action in a federal court by a citizen of South Carolina against the State of Georgia. Dissatisfaction with that decision led to the adoption of the Eleventh Amendment, providing that the federal judicial power should not be construed to extend to any action brought against one of the states by citizens of another state or by citizens or subjects of any foreign state.

The language of the Eleventh Amendment indicates that involvement of a federal-law question makes no difference. But on other matters of construction, you cannot determine the scope of the Amendment solely by reference to its wording. On the theory that the Amendment intended simply to overturn the Chisholm holding and return thereby to the original understanding of Article III, and that the original understanding was that no one other than a sister state or the United States could sue a nonconsenting state in federal trial court, the Supreme Court has far departed from the wording of the Amendment. On the one hand, it has broadly read the states' immunity, as in Hans v. Louisiana, 134 U.S. 1, 10 S.Ct. 504 (1890), where it held that a federal court could not entertain a suit by a citizen against his *own* state although the suit involved a question of federal law. On the other hand, the Court has sometimes narrowed the immunity, as in Petty v. Tennessee–Missouri Bridge Comm'n, 359 U.S. 275, 79 S.Ct. 785 (1959), where it decided not to read the Amendment as a bar to an otherwise proper federal suit by an out-of-state citizen against a state if the state consents to such suit.

With that background, note now exactly what language the Eleventh Amendment affected in Article III, Section 2, Paragraph 1.

(4) Is it constitutionally required that there be a Supreme Court? that there be inferior federal courts such as the district courts and the courts of appeals?

The federal government may choose not to exert its full judicial power: again apart from fairly slight but vague constitutional limitations not of immediate concern, although potentially of great political import, Congress appears to have a free hand in allocating to the inferior federal courts that it establishes,[b] and consequently in withholding from them, *original* jurisdiction over the enumerated "cases" and "controversies" within the federal judicial power. Thus, when the problem is whether such a federal court is authorized to hear a particular "case" or "controversy," resort must be had to federal statutes.

Questions: (5) Examine, as examples of how Congress has vested original jurisdiction in the district courts, 28 U.S.C. §§ 1331 (federal question), 1332 (diversity of citizenship), 1337 (commerce), 1338 (patents and the like), and 1343 (civil rights) and 15 U.S.C. §§ 15(a) and 15a (antitrust). With respect to each of these statutory provisions: (a) Can you relate it to one of the classes of "cases" or "controversies" enumerated in Article III, Section 2, Paragraph 1? (b) Does it comprehend the entire class or only a portion of the class? (c) Is the jurisdiction conferred exclusive or concurrent? (d) Is the jurisdiction dependent upon the amount in controversy?

(6) What is the relation between § 1331 and § 1337? between § 1331 and § 1338? between § 1331 and § 1343?

Similarly, the Constitution appears to confide the *appellate* jurisdiction of the federal courts largely to congressional control. So, when considering an issue of federal jurisdiction, one should refer first to congressional enactment and then to Article III. Generally, for such jurisdiction to exist, the particular action must fall within the bounds of both.

(c) "Federal Question" Provision

Congress could constitutionally have given the district courts jurisdiction over all civil actions arising under the Constitution, laws, or treaties of the United States and made such jurisdiction exclusive. It has not done so. The basic federal question statute is 28 U.S.C. § 1331.

---

[b] The most important "inferior Courts" established by Congress are the district courts and the courts of appeals. Congress has also established certain other Article III courts of specialized jurisdiction—currently including most significantly the United States Court of International Trade, which handles certain civil actions relating to import transactions. Distinguishably, Congress has established certain Article I bodies that are called legislative courts but are not part of the judicial branch itself—such as the United States Court of Federal Claims, the United States Tax Court, and each district's bankruptcy court.

In fact, the United States has long shown a strong preference for Article III courts of nonspecialized and broad jurisdiction, with judges who necessarily have life tenure and salary protection and who tend to be diverse generalists and independent actors. An incidental benefit of thus putting most cases into one set of courts is the minimization of boundary problems regarding which courts hear which cases or parts of cases.

Louisville & Nashville Railroad Co. v. Mottley

Supreme Court of the United States, 1908.
211 U.S. 149, 29 S.Ct. 42.

The appellees (husband and wife), being residents and citizens of Kentucky, brought this suit in equity in the Circuit Court of the United States for the Western District of Kentucky[c] against the appellant, a railroad company and a citizen of the same State. The object of the suit was to compel the specific performance of the following contract:

"Louisville, Ky., Oct. 2nd, 1871.

"The Louisville & Nashville Railroad Company in consideration that E.L. Mottley and wife, Annie E. Mottley, have this day released Company from all damages or claims for damages for injuries received by them on the 7th of September, 1871, in consequence of a collision of trains on the railroad of said Company at Randolph's Station, Jefferson County, Ky., hereby agrees to issue free passes on said Railroad and branches now existing or to exist, to said E.L. & Annie E. Mottley for the remainder of the present year, and thereafter, to renew said passes annually during the lives of said Mottley and wife or either of them."

The bill alleged that in September, 1871, plaintiffs, while passengers upon the defendant railroad, were injured by the defendant's negligence, and released their respective claims for damages in consideration of the agreement for transportation during their lives, expressed in the contract. It is alleged that the contract was performed by the defendant up to January 1, 1907, when the defendant declined to renew the passes. The bill then alleges that the refusal to comply with the contract was based solely upon that part of the act of Congress of June 29, 1906, 34 Stat. 584, which forbids the giving of free passes or free transportation. The bill further alleges: First, that the act of Congress referred to does not prohibit the giving of passes under the circumstances of this case; and, second, that if the law is to be construed as prohibiting such passes, it is in conflict with the Fifth Amendment of the Constitution, because it deprives the plaintiffs of their property without due process of law. The defendant demurred to the bill. The judge of the Circuit Court overruled the demurrer, entered a decree [in 1907] for the relief prayed for, and the defendant appealed directly to this court.

■ MR. JUSTICE MOODY, after making the foregoing statement, delivered the opinion of the court.

Two questions of law were raised by the demurrer to the bill, were brought here by appeal, and have been argued before us. They are, first, whether that part of the act of Congress of June 29, 1906 (34 Stat. 584), which forbids the giving of free passes or the collection of any different compensation for transportation of passengers than that specified in the tariff filed, makes it unlawful to perform a contract for transportation of

[c] Congress has since abolished these circuit courts. Do not confuse them with the present United States Courts of Appeals, formerly called United States Circuit Courts of Appeals.

persons who in good faith, before the passage of the act, had accepted such contract in satisfaction of a valid cause of action against the railroad; and, second, whether the statute, if it should be construed to render such a contract unlawful, is in violation of the Fifth Amendment of the Constitution of the United States. We do not deem it necessary, however, to consider either of these questions, because, in our opinion, the court below was without jurisdiction of the cause. Neither party has questioned that jurisdiction, but it is the duty of this court to see to it that the jurisdiction of the Circuit Court, which is defined and limited by statute, is not exceeded. This duty we have frequently performed of our own motion. [Citations omitted.]

There was no diversity of citizenship and it is not and cannot be suggested that there was any ground of jurisdiction, except that the case was a "suit . . . arising under the Constitution and laws of the United States." [Citation to predecessor of § 1331.] It is the settled interpretation of these words, as used in this statute, conferring jurisdiction, that a suit arises under the Constitution and laws of the United States only when the plaintiff's statement of his own cause of action shows that it is based upon those laws or that Constitution. It is not enough that the plaintiff alleges some anticipated defense to his cause of action and asserts that the defense is invalidated by some provision of the Constitution of the United States. Although such allegations show that very likely, in the course of the litigation, a question under the Constitution would arise, they do not show that the suit, that is, the plaintiff's original cause of action, arises under the Constitution. In Tennessee v. Union & Planters' Bank, 152 U.S. 454, 14 S.Ct. 654, the plaintiff, the State of Tennessee, brought suit in the Circuit Court of the United States to recover from the defendant certain taxes alleged to be due under the laws of the State. The plaintiff alleged that the defendant claimed an immunity from the taxation by virtue of its charter, and that therefore the tax was void, because in violation of the provision of the Constitution of the United States, which forbids any State from passing a law impairing the obligation of contracts. The cause was held to be beyond the jurisdiction of the Circuit Court, the court saying, by Mr. Justice Gray (p. 464), "a suggestion of one party, that the other will or may set up a claim under the Constitution or laws of the United States, does not make the suit one arising under that Constitution or those laws." Again, in Boston & Montana Consolidated Copper & Silver Mining Company v. Montana Ore Purchasing Company, 188 U.S. 632, 23 S.Ct. 434, the plaintiff brought suit in the Circuit Court of the United States for the conversion of copper ore and for an injunction against its continuance. The plaintiff then alleged, for the purpose of showing jurisdiction, in substance, that the defendant would set up in defense certain laws of the United States. The cause was held to be beyond the jurisdiction of the Circuit Court, the court saying, by Mr. Justice Peckham (pp. 638, 639):

"It would be wholly unnecessary and improper in order to prove complainant's cause of action to go into any matters of defence which the defendants might possibly set up and then attempt to reply to such defence, and thus, if possible, to show that a Federal question might or probably would arise in the course of the trial of the case. To allege such defence and then make an answer to it before the defendant has the opportunity to itself plead or prove its own defence is inconsistent with any known rule of pleading so far as we are aware, and is improper.

"The rule is a reasonable and just one that the complainant in the first instance shall be confined to a statement of its cause of action, leaving to the defendant to set up in his answer what his defence is and, if anything more than a denial of complainant's cause of action, imposing upon the defendant the burden of proving such defence.

"Conforming itself to that rule the complainant would not, in the assertion or proof of its cause of action, bring up a single Federal question. The presentation of its cause of action would not show that it was one arising under the Constitution or laws of the United States.

"The only way in which it might be claimed that a Federal question was presented would be in the complainant's statement of what the defence of defendants would be and complainant's answer to such defence. Under these circumstances the case is brought within the rule laid down in Tennessee v. Union & Planters' Bank, 152 U.S. 454, 14 S.Ct. 654. That case has been cited and approved many times since."

[The Court here cited sixteen more of its cases applying the rule.] The application of this rule to the case at bar is decisive against the jurisdiction of the Circuit Court.

It is ordered that the

Judgment be reversed and the case remitted to the Circuit Court with instructions to dismiss the suit for want of jurisdiction.

Question: (7) Suppose the action were instead one for a declaratory judgment under a statute analogous to present 28 U.S.C. § 2201, with the railroad as plaintiff seeking a declaration of its obligation in light of the statute prohibiting free passes. Would federal question jurisdiction then exist?

(d) "Diversity of Citizenship" Provision

Congress could constitutionally have given the district courts jurisdiction over all civil actions comprehended in Article III's Diversity and Alienage Clauses and made such jurisdiction exclusive. It has not done so. The basic diversity statute is 28 U.S.C. § 1332.

Question: (8) Does the required diversity under § 1332 exist in each of the following cases? Imagine each case is for an alleged vehicular tort occurring in Kansas City, Mo. The matter in controversy exceeds $75,000 in each case.

(a) *A*, a citizen of New York, sues *B*, a citizen of Missouri.

(b) *A*, a citizen of New York, sues *B*, a citizen and resident of England.

(c) *A*, a citizen and resident of Canada, sues *B*, a citizen and resident of England. See Hodgson v. Bowerbank, 9 U.S. (5 Cranch) 303 (1809) (Marshall, C.J.) (outside Article III bound).

(d) *A*, a citizen of Canada and legal permanent resident of the United States domiciled in New York, sues *B*, a citizen and resident of England. See Saadeh v. Farouki, 107 F.3d 52 (D.C.Cir.1997) (outside § 1332(a) bound, because the amendment that added the subsection's last sentence intended only to narrow jurisdiction).

The general rule with respect to federal jurisdiction is to determine it as of the time it was invoked. Although jurisdiction can be saved by certain corrective steps (which comprise the party's amendment of defective jurisdictional allegations under 28 U.S.C. § 1653 or, in compelling circumstances, the court's dropping of jurisdiction-impeding parties under Federal Rule 21), jurisdiction is not ordinarily ousted by subsequent events.

So, suppose that *A*, a citizen of New York, sues *B*, a citizen of Missouri, in a United States District Court. While the suit is pending, *A* becomes a citizen of Missouri. That change does not destroy diversity. For a named party, it is normally citizenship at the time of the federal action's commencement that controls, and so any change thereafter is immaterial.

In the ordinary case there is little difficulty in determining the citizenship of a litigant. At times, however, the parties seriously dispute the facts regarding citizenship, and the court must determine it.

Baker v. Keck

United States District Court, Eastern District of Illinois, 1936.
13 F.Supp. 486.

■ LINDLEY, DISTRICT JUDGE. Plaintiff has filed herein his suit against various individuals and the Progressive Miners of America charging a conspiracy, out of which grew certain events and in the course of which, it is averred, he was attacked by certain of the defendants and his arm shot off. This, it is said, resulted from a controversy between the United Mine Workers and the Progressive Miners of America.

Plaintiff avers that he is a citizen of the state of Oklahoma. Defendants filed a motion to dismiss, one ground of which is that plaintiff is not a citizen of the state of Oklahoma, but has a domicile in the state of Illinois, and that therefore there is no diversity of citizenship. To this motion plaintiff filed a response, with certain affidavits in support thereof.

Upon presentation of the motion, the court set the issue of fact arising upon the averments of the complaint, the motion to dismiss, and the response thereto for hearing. A jury was waived. Affidavits were received and parol evidence offered.

It appears that plaintiff formerly resided in Saline county, Ill., that he was not a member of United Mine Workers, but was in sympathy with their organization. The averment of the declaration is that he was attacked by members of, or sympathizers with, the [rival union] Progressive Mine Workers of America. He was a farmer, owning about 100 acres of land. After his injury, he removed to the state of Oklahoma, taking with him his family and all of his household goods, except two beds and some other small items. His household furniture was carried to Oklahoma by truck, and the truckman was paid $100 for transportation. Near Ulan, Okl., he rented 20 acres and a house for $150 per year, and began occupancy thereof October, 1934. He testified that he had arrangements with another party and his own son, living with him, to cultivate the ground, but that farming conditions were not satisfactory, and that it was impossible, therefore, to produce a crop in 1935. He produced potatoes, sweet corn, and other garden products used in the living of the family. He had no horses or other livestock in Oklahoma. He was unable to do any extensive work himself because of the loss of his arm. In the summer of 1935 he leased for the year 1936 the same 20 acres and an additional 20 acres at a rental of $150.

At the first opportunity to register as a qualified voter in Oklahoma after he went there, he complied with the statute in that respect and was duly registered. This was not until after he had been in the state for over a year, as, under the state statute [then in effect], a qualified voter must have resided within the state for twelve months prior to registration. He has not voted, but he testified that the only election at which he could have voted after he registered was on a day when he had to be in Illinois to give attention to his lawsuit. He has returned to Illinois for short visits three or four times.

He testified that he moved to Oklahoma for the purpose of residing there, with the intention of making it his home and that he still intends to reside there. He testified that the family started out to see if they could find a new location in 1934. Upon cross-examination it appeared that the funds for traveling and removal had been paid by the United Mine Workers or their representative; that he left his livestock on the Illinois farm, but no chickens; that he had about 60 chickens on his farm in Oklahoma; that, when he removed to Oklahoma, he rented his Illinois farm for a period of five years; that the tenant has recently defaulted upon the same.

In the affidavits it appears that plaintiff's house in Illinois was completely destroyed by fire shortly after he left. It was not insured and was a total loss. Witnesses for the defense testified that he had told them that he intended to move back to Illinois after he got his case settled; that he had told one witness in 1935 that he was going to Oklahoma but did not know for how long. Plaintiff denies that he told these witnesses that he expected to return to Illinois as soon as his litigation was completed.

I think it is a fair conclusion from all the evidence that at the time plaintiff removed to Oklahoma one of his motives was to create diversity of citizenship so that he might maintain a suit in the United States courts. But that conclusion is not of itself decisive of the question presented. There remains the further question of whether there was at the time this suit was begun an intention upon his part to become a citizen of Oklahoma. One may change his citizenship for the purpose of enabling himself to maintain a suit in the federal court, but the change must be an actual legal change made with the intention of bringing about actual citizenship in the state to which the removal is made.

Citizenship and domicile are substantially synonymous. Residency and inhabitance are too often confused with the terms and have not the same significance. Citizenship implies more than residence.[d] It carries with it the idea of identification with the state and a participation in its functions. As a citizen, one sustains social, political, and moral obligation to the state and possesses social and political rights under the Constitution and laws thereof. . . . Change of domicile arises when there is a change of abode with the absence of any present intention not to reside permanently or indefinitely in the new abode. This is the holding of the Supreme Court in Gilbert v. David, 235 U.S. 561, 35 S.Ct. 164, 167, 59 L.Ed. 360, where the court said: "As Judge Story puts it in his work on 'Conflict of Laws' (7th Ed.) § 46, page 41, 'If a person has actually removed to another place, with an intention of remaining there for an indefinite time, and as a place of fixed present domicil, it is to be deemed his place of domicil, notwithstanding he may entertain a floating intention to return at some future period.' 'The requisite animus is the present intention of permanent or indefinite residence in a given place or country, or, negatively expressed, the absence of any present intention of not residing there permanently or indefinitely.' "

It will be observed that, if there is an intention to remain, even though it be for an indefinite time, but still with the intention of making the location a place of present domicile, this latter intention will control, even though the person entertains a floating intention to return at some indefinite future period. In this respect the court in Gilbert v. David, supra, further said: "Plaintiff may have had, and probably did have, some floating intention of returning to Michigan after the determination of certain litigation. . . . But, as we have seen, a floating intention of that kind was not enough to prevent the new place, under the circumstances shown, from becoming his domicil. It was his place of abode, which he had no present intention of changing; that is the essence of domicil."

. . . .

The statement of the Restatement of the Law, Conflict of Laws, § 15, Domicil of Choice, is as follows:

"(1) A domicil of choice is a domicil acquired, through the exercise of his own will, by a person who is legally capable of changing his domicil.

"(2) To acquire a domicil of choice, a person must establish a dwelling-place with the intention of making it his home.

"(3) The fact of physical presence at a dwelling-place and the intention to make it a home must concur; if they do so, even for a moment, the change of domicil takes place."[e]

---

[d] The Fourteenth Amendment defines citizenship in terms of residence. However, that definition is not controlling for diversity-jurisdiction purposes.

[e] Among the changes in § 15 made by Restatement (Second) of Conflict of Laws § 15 (1971) is the omission of the phrase "through the exercise of his own will," this being omitted

In Holt v. Hendee, 248 Ill. 288, 93 N.E. 749, 752, 21 Ann.Cas. 202, the court said: "The intention is not necessarily determined from the statements or declarations of the party but may be inferred from the surrounding circumstances, which may entirely disprove such statements or declarations. On the question of domicile less weight will be given to the party's declaration than to his acts."

Though it must be confessed that the question is far from free of doubt, I conclude that, under the facts as they appear in the record, despite the fact that one of the plaintiff's motives was the establishment of citizenship so as to create jurisdiction in the federal court, there was at the time of his removal a fixed intention to become a citizen of the state of Oklahoma. He testified that he worked on a community project in that state without compensation. It appears that he registered as a voter; he thus became a participant in the political activities of the state. Such action is inconsistent with any conclusion other than that of citizenship, and in view of his sworn testimony that it was his intention to reside in Oklahoma and to continue to do so, it follows that the elements constituting the status of citizenship existed.

True, there is some evidence that he had said he might return to Illinois as soon as his case was settled. The language of the cases above indicates that such a floating intention is insufficient to bar citizenship, where active participation in the obligations and enjoyment of the rights of citizenship exist.

Defendants contend that the fact that the costs of plaintiff's transportation and maintenance were paid by the United Mine Workers is of decisive weight upon this issue. I cannot agree. It seems to me immaterial what motives may have inspired the United Mine Workers to help him, and the court is not now concerned with their alleged charitable and philanthropic practices.

I conclude, therefore, that plaintiff was at the time of the commencement of the suit, and is now, a citizen of the state of Oklahoma. The findings herein embraced will be adopted as findings of fact of the court and entered as such. It is ordered that the motion to dismiss because of lack of diversity of citizenship be, and the same is hereby, denied. An exception is allowed to defendants.

. . . .

Question: (9) Does the required diversity under § 1332 exist in each of the following cases? The matter in controversy exceeds the jurisdictional amount in each case.

---

to avoid any implication that the significant intention is one to acquire a domicile rather than one to make a home. Section 18, "Requisite Intention," now provides: "To acquire a domicil of choice in a place, a person must intend to make that place his home for the time at least."

(a) The soprano Felice Lyne, born in Missouri, abandoned her home there and took up residence in London, England, declaring it to be her home and that it was her intention to remain there indefinitely. She has taken no steps toward naturalization in England. Oscar Hammerstein, a citizen of New York, sues her in a Missouri federal court while she is on a temporary visit to her former home in Missouri. In the course of reaching decision, the court finds that she is domiciled in England. See Hammerstein v. Lyne, 200 F. 165 (W.D.Mo.1912) (not within jurisdictional statute, although possibly within Article III bound).

(b) *A*, a citizen of New York, sues *B*, a Cuban refugee domiciled in Florida with the status of stateless and undocumented alien.

(c) *A*, a citizen of New York, sues *B*, a Cuban citizen domiciled in Florida with the status of undocumented alien.

Domicile of students.—An unemancipated minor normally has the same domicile as the parent on whom he or she is dependent, but the student who is emancipated or who is not a minor may acquire a domicile of choice. See ConnectU LLC v. Zuckerberg, 482 F.Supp.2d 3 (D.Mass.2007) (finding the California-based, multimillionaire founder of Facebook was still domiciled with his parents in New York, which destroyed diversity jurisdiction), rev'd on other grounds, 522 F.3d 82 (1st Cir.2008); cf. Restatement (Second) of Conflict of Laws § 22 (1971).

Question: (10) Should students be free to select either their parent's home or their college residence as their domicile? If not, what should be the standards for determining domicile? Should it matter whether a student lives in a dormitory or rented apartment or buys a house? whether the student returns to his or her parent's home during vacations? Should the student's present intention regarding post-educational residence matter: what if he or she intends to return to the parent's home? intends to remain in the college community? intends to move elsewhere? does not know? Cf. Restatement (Second) of Conflict of Laws § 18 cmt. f, illus. 13–14 (1971).

Although the issue of interest here is jurisdiction, the determination of a student's domicile may carry with it other consequences. For instance, domicile may affect voting rights, state income tax liability, and automobile registration and insurance premiums. For these different purposes, a student may have different domiciles. Restatement (Second) of Conflict of Laws § 11(2) (1971) (amended 1988) recognized this possibility by providing: "Every person has a domicil at all times and, at least for the same purpose, no person has more than one domicil at a time." The conventional learning, reflected in Restatement of Conflict of Laws § 11 (1934), had been simply that every person has one and only one domicile at a time.

Domicile of wives.—At common law, a wife was not able to acquire a domicile of choice, but instead received the domicile of her husband by operation of law. This rule is close to expiration. Today a wife, particularly when she lives apart from her husband, may acquire a separate domicile of choice. Cf. Restatement (Second) of Conflict of Laws § 21 (1971) (amended 1988).

"Citizenship" of corporations.—What about diversity of citizenship with respect to corporations? The Constitution does not mention corporations, and for various constitutional purposes a corporation is not a citizen.

For instance, a corporation cannot claim the benefits of Article IV, Section 2 of the Constitution, which provides: "The Citizens of each State shall be entitled to all Privileges and Immunities of Citizens in the several States." So, does this imply that corporations are excluded from diversity jurisdiction?

The Supreme Court of the United States avoided this result by deciding that the citizenship of the stockholders effectively determined the citizenship of a corporation, and the Court then blandly laid down the conclusive presumption that for diversity purposes all the stockholders were citizens of the state of incorporation. Marshall v. Baltimore & Ohio R.R. Co., 57 U.S. (16 How.) 314 (1853). Thus courts would treat the General Motors Corporation as though it and all its stockholders were citizens of Delaware, the state of incorporation. Here is one of the many instances where the law achieved results thought desirable through the use of transparent fictions.

By statute since 1958, a corporation is for diversity purposes "deemed to be a citizen of any State by which it has been incorporated and of the State where it has its principal place of business." 28 U.S.C. § 1332(c)(1). The preferred interpretation of this language is that an American corporation is deemed a citizen of each and every state by which it has been incorporated (a corporation may be incorporated by more than one state), and also of any state in which it has its principal place of business (there can be at most one in the United States). Given the intention of the statute, the more states of which a corporation is a citizen, the less likely diversity jurisdiction is to exist.

Some other problems of interpreting § 1332(c)(1) should be becoming apparent. As for a foreign corporation, the tide is shifting toward deeming it a citizen of the country of incorporation and also of any state in which it has its principal place of business (so precluding diversity jurisdiction if its opponent is a citizen of the same state), but this remains a matter of considerable dispute.

The narrow direct-action exception to § 1332(c)(1), added in 1964, aimed at preventing the exercise of diversity jurisdiction where it would exist only because under local law the injured plaintiff can sue the liability insurer directly without joining the insured.

KELLY v. UNITED STATES STEEL CORP., 284 F.2d 850 (3d Cir. 1960). The plaintiffs, Pennsylvania citizens, sought to invoke diversity jurisdiction. The question for determination was whether USX Corp., then called United States Steel Corp. and incorporated in New Jersey, had its principal place of business in New York or Pennsylvania.

The plaintiffs urged that the test should be where the "nerve center" of the corporation's business was, that the nerve center was in New York, and hence that diversity of citizenship existed. The court did not find the "pleasant and alluring figure of speech" helpful, and turned therefore "to a consideration of the facts of the Steel Corporation's life" in order to apply a "place of activity" test.

These facts include the following activities in New York: the Board of Directors regularly meets there (although it can choose its own place of meeting and has met in Pittsburgh); the Chairman of the Board is there, spending one day a week in Pittsburgh; the Executive Committee and the Finance Committee meet regularly there; the Secretary, the Treasurer, the Comptroller, and the General Counsel have their offices there; the dividends are declared, the income tax returns filed, and the annual report mailed there; the center of the Public Relations Department is there; and the major banking and financing activities are there. To the court this adds up to the conclusion that if the test of principal place of business is where the corporation makes final decisions on corporate policy, including its financing, the principal place is New York.

The activities in Pennsylvania include the following: the Operation Policy Committee, to which the Board of Directors has delegated the duty of conducting the manufacturing, mining, transportation, and general operation of the corporation, sits and conducts its affairs there (this Committee comprises the Chairman of the Board, the President, the Chairman of the Finance Committee, the General Counsel, and the seven Executive Vice Presidents, and it makes policy decisions subject to the Board of Directors); the Executive Vice Presidents, one heading each of the seven great branches of the corporation, have headquarters and staffs there; and 34 percent of the management personnel work there, fourteen times as many as in New York. All this points, the court says, to "the conclusion that business by way of activities is centered in Pennsylvania."

The court then adds some other facts "of lesser importance" but having "some significance": Pennsylvania has 32 percent of employee personnel (twenty-five times as many as New York); more than 33 percent of the tangible property is there (with less than one percent in New York); and about 35 percent of the total productive capacity is there (New York has none). "These facts," the court concludes, "added to what we have found to be the headquarters of day-to-day corporate activity and management, add up to the irresistible conclusion that the principal place of business of this giant corporation is in Pennsylvania."

Questions: (11) American Airlines, a Delaware corporation, had its overall business policy prescribed in and directed from New York, where its activities were substantial but represented only a modest fraction of the company's total. In states with a greater volume of activity, however, its local officers handled mostly local activities. The company repaired and serviced most of its aircraft in Oklahoma; it flew more miles in Texas and carried more passengers in California than it did in New York. Was New York then its principal place of business? See Egan v. American Airlines, 211 F.Supp. 292 (E.D.N.Y.1962) (yes, in suit brought by New Yorkers), aff'd, 324 F.2d 565 (2d Cir.1963).

(12) Central Foundry Company, a Maine corporation, manufactures soil pipe and fittings, which it sells throughout the United States and abroad. All of its production is in Holt, Alabama. Its executive offices are in New York, and all its officers are there except one in Alabama who has the title of vice president and plant manager—but he works under the director of Holt operations, who works out of New York and who spends only fifteen percent of his time in Alabama. The sales staff is in New York, where the company makes all sales policy and oversees all sales activity. The company directs all invoices to be paid in New York, keeps its books and records there, and conducts its financial affairs there. New York has 55 employees; Alabama has 1890. Annual payroll in New York is $500,000; that in Alabama is $9,200,000. Physical assets in New York have a book value of $60,000; those in Alabama have a book value of $5,695,000. Is New York its principal place of business? See Anniston Soil Pipe Co. v. Central Foundry Co., 216 F.Supp. 473 (N.D.Ala.1963) (no, in suit brought by Alabaman), aff'd on opinion below, 329 F.2d 313 (5th Cir.1964); see also J.A. Olson Co. v. City of Winona, Miss., 818 F.2d 401 (5th Cir.1987) (following Anniston on similar facts and constructing "total activity" test that implements purpose of § 1332(c)(1) by fully and flexibly considering both nerve-center factors and, somewhat more heavily, place-of-activity factors).

"Citizenship" of unincorporated associations.—Unincorporated associations include partnerships, fraternal benefit societies, trade associations, and labor unions. For diversity purposes, neither the judicial fiction extended to corporations nor their legislative treatment covers unincorporated associations. Hence, courts treat an unincorporated association like a group of individuals, and so deem it a citizen of each and every state and country of which one of its members is actually a citizen. The Supreme Court reconsidered this rule in United Steelworkers v. R.H. Bouligny, Inc., 382 U.S. 145, 86 S.Ct. 272 (1965), but there decided that change was a task for Congress and not for the courts.

Question: (13) Consider the case of a dual citizen, a man who is a citizen of both the United States and Ireland, and who is a party in a lawsuit against either a citizen of an American state or a citizen or subject of a foreign country. His treatment for diversity purposes is not clear. The leading approach concludes that only any American state citizenship is attributed to him: thus, if domiciled in New York, he could bring a big case in federal court against a citizen of Ireland for an alleged vehicular tort occurring in Kansas City, Mo. Do you agree that this is the proper approach?

Desirability of diversity jurisdiction.—It is not too early to ask whether Congress has been wise in its allocation of diversity of citizenship cases to the federal courts. Compare § 1332 to 28 U.S.C. §§ 1335 and 1369, the latter being more recent utilizations of the Diversity Clause for a special function. In forming a judgment on this question you should consider the following: What were the possible purposes of the Founders in extending the federal judicial power to diversity cases? Have any changes come about since 1789 that have any bearing on the general problem? What are the current costs and benefits of having federal courts entertain numerous state-law cases?

These questions were among the many considered by the American Law Institute before it proposed rather drastic restrictions on the scope of diversity jurisdiction. See ALI Study of the Division of Jurisdiction Between

State and Federal Courts 99–110 (1969) (recommending "that the right of a plaintiff to institute a diversity action in the federal court of his home state be abrogated"). More recently—and primarily in an effort to lessen congestion in federal court—numerous commentators, judges, legislators, and others have called for virtually complete abolition of federal jurisdiction based solely on diversity of citizenship. But see Adrienne J. Marsh, Diversity Jurisdiction: Scapegoat of Overcrowded Federal Courts, 48 Brook.L.Rev. 197 (1982). Congress has so far taken only the traditional step of raising the jurisdictional amount requirement of § 1332, increasing it in 1988 to $50,000 and in 1996 to $75,000.

As you read the next Subsection, ask yourself what difference there is between original and removal jurisdiction so far as concerns the parties' right of access to a federal court for a case involving diverse citizens. Is the difference a logical one?

(e) "REMOVAL" PROVISION

Suppose the plaintiff commences in a state court an action that he could instead have commenced in one of the federal district courts. Are there circumstances in which either party may remove the case from the state system into the federal system of courts? What reasons of policy suggest that such a course should at least in some situations be open? The basic removal statute is 28 U.S.C. § 1441.

Questions: In the following questions, assume that the matter in controversy exceeds any jurisdictional amount.

(14) *A*, a citizen of New York, sues *B*, a citizen of Pennsylvania, in a New York state court. The only possible basis of federal jurisdiction is diversity of citizenship. Can *B* properly remove to the United States District Court?

(15) *A*, a citizen of New York, sues *B*, a citizen of Pennsylvania, in a Pennsylvania state court. The only possible basis of federal jurisdiction is diversity of citizenship. Can *B* properly remove?

(16) A corporation incorporated in Delaware and having its principal place of business in New York commences a trademark action based on federal statute in a Massachusetts state court against a New York corporation having its principal place of business in Massachusetts. Can defendant properly remove?

(17) Suppose the Mottleys had instead brought the Louisville & Nashville Railroad Co. v. Mottley litigation originally in Kentucky state court. Could defendant railroad have properly removed the action to federal court under a statute analogous to present 28 U.S.C. § 1441?

The mechanics of removal appear in 28 U.S.C. §§ 1446–1450. The defendant must seek removal promptly, normally within thirty days of receipt of the complaint. In the United States District Court sitting in the same locality as the state court, the defendant files a notice of removal, subject to Rule 11 and setting forth the grounds that justify removal. The defendant then gives the plaintiff and the state court notification of the filing. By this activity solely on the part of the defendant, removal is complete. The state court can proceed no further with the action unless and until the United States District Court remands it to the state court, as upon a finding that it was by law not removable. See also Federal Rule 81(c).

There are exceptions to § 1441's general rule on removability, as is indeed suggested by the opening clause of the statute. For example, 28 U.S.C. § 1445(a) provides that a civil action arising under the Federal Employers' Liability Act (45 U.S.C. §§ 51–60) and commenced in a state court may not be removed to a federal district court. The FELA is a statute designed to make it easier for an injured railroad worker engaged in interstate commerce to recover damages from the employer. Substantively, it abrogates the common-law rule that prevented an employee from recovering from the employer for injuries sustained through the negligence of a fellow servant; and it provides that the plaintiff's contributory negligence is not a complete defense, but works only to reduce damages on a comparative-negligence basis. Procedurally, it gives the injured worker a choice between a state court and a federal district court that the defendant employer cannot frustrate.

We note parenthetically that the Jones Act (46 U.S.C. § 30104) gives to seamen the same substantive benefits in actions against their employers for injuries suffered in the course of their employment that the FELA gives to railroad workers. It also gives seamen the same procedural benefits by allowing them the choice between state and federal court and forbidding removal by the employer. Indeed, the Jones Act incorporates by reference all laws of the United States regulating recovery in cases of personal injury or death to railway employees.

CHOICE OF FORUM

The existence of federal jurisdiction often gives a litigant's lawyer a choice between federal and state court. There are many considerations that might affect the choice, according to empirical studies of attorneys' preferences. See Kevin M. Clermont & Theodore Eisenberg, Do Case Outcomes Really Reveal Anything About the Legal System? Win Rates and Removal Jurisdiction, 83 Cornell L.Rev. 581, 599 (1998). Most of these considerations group under four general headings: expected bias against a litigant; logistical and practical concerns; perceived disparity in quality and other characteristics between federal and state judges and between federal and state juries; and the different procedures offered by one or the other court system.

First, the importance of these considerations can vary with the situation. An out-of-state defendant insurance company, for example, would expect more bias in an action brought by a resident individual plaintiff in state court than would an out-of-state individual defendant being sued by a resident insurance company in state court. A resident litigant from a city sued in a rural county court could conceivably expect as much bias as a litigant from another state. Whether or not all these kinds of prejudices still exist, many litigants think they do.

Second, logistical concerns include the parties' relative distances from the courthouse or the place where most of the legal action will take place. Sometimes a litigant's lawyer may choose a court far from the opponent's residence to increase leverage in settlement. Very importantly, a litigant's lawyer may be more familiar with the practices of a local state court, where also there may be less expense involved. Likely one's purposes would be served by a longer or shorter docket.

Third, federal judges often are seen as being of higher quality and greater independence than are state judges. Federal juries are drawn from a wider geographical area than are state juries.

Fourth, the different procedures offered by the court systems require a lawyer to consider many other variables when choosing a court. Many preferences regarding federal court turn on its pleading practices, discovery devices, pretrial conferences, summary judgment, and judicial activism in procedural matters. The state courts' trial rules of evidence might differ. The two systems' effectiveness of appellate review might affect choice.

Whatever lawyers' reasons might be, and no matter how intangible those reasons might seem, the choice of forum apparently makes a significant difference. In recent years, the plaintiffs' win rate in nonprisoner federal question cases brought as original actions in federal court has been 52%; for such cases removed to federal court, the plaintiffs' win rate was only 25%. In diversity jurisdiction, the plaintiffs' win rate in original actions has been 71%; for removed cases, it was 34%. One must be wary in analyzing win rates because the groups of compared cases comprise different cases, which may differ in many respects. But here when the statistician controls for as many variables as possible, that robust result survives: removal seems seriously to affect case outcome. After all, that result accords with removal's purpose of protecting defendants.

For a consistent anecdote, consider Finding the Forum for a Victory, Nat'l L.J., Feb. 11, 1991, at S3:

"Choosing the right forum for a lawsuit can mean the difference between winning and losing.

"In his hate-crimes civil lawsuit against [pro se] white supremacist Tom Metzger, [plaintiffs'] attorney Morris Dees feels his selection of Oregon state court over federal court was critical.

" 'When we filed this lawsuit, we had a choice between state and federal court. We chose state court because Oregon discovery rules are quite different than the federal rules. You can do trial by ambush in Oregon. You have no interrogatories, no production of evidence; you don't have to give the names of witnesses or give the other side your documents.' As a result, Mr. Metzger had no idea how much evidence Mr. Dees had, and this ignorance would prove fatal."

(f) REVIEW OF STATE-COURT ACTIONS BY THE SUPREME COURT

If an action is properly commenced in or removed to a federal district court, it will normally remain in the federal court system to the end. There is no such thing as removal from a federal court to a state court.

But can an action that the plaintiff commenced in a state court appear in the federal court system at any later stage if it was not removable to a federal court, or if it was removable but was not in fact removed? Congress treated this matter in 28 U.S.C. § 1257, which you should read in contrast to 28 U.S.C. § 1254, discussed supra p. 211.

Questions: (18) What are the purposes, in a state/federal arrangement of courts, of § 1257?

(19) Why does § 1257 confine review by the Supreme Court of state-court decisions to "[*f*]*inal* judgments or decrees rendered by the *highest* court of a State in which a decision could be had" (emphasis added)?

Consider the subsequent history of Louisville & Nashville Railroad Co. v. Mottley, that 1908 decision you read. After the federal court dismissed their suit for want of jurisdiction, the Mottleys brought a new action in a state circuit court in Kentucky seeking the same relief. The railroad company again based its defense upon the federal statute prohibiting free passes. By its judgment granting the relief requested, the state circuit court required the railroad company to issue annual passes over its lines to the plaintiffs during their respective lives. On appeal, the Kentucky Court of Appeals, the highest court of the state, affirmed the judgment by construing the federal statute as nonretroactive and hence inapplicable. Then the railroad company put the case before the Supreme Court of the United States again, for determination of the same federal issue that the Mottleys had unsuccessfully relied upon to give the federal court original jurisdiction in the first suit. And the Supreme Court, viewing the federal statute applicable and constitutional, now reversed on the ground that the railroad company had rightly refused further to comply with its agreement to issue passes to the plaintiffs and that judicially requiring performance of the agreement was erroneous. Louisville & Nashville R.R. Co. v. Mottley, 219 U.S. 467, 31 S.Ct. 265 (1911).

Question: (20) Was Supreme Court review in the second Mottley suit constitutionally within the Court's jurisdiction?

SECTION 7. SELECTION OF A PROPER FORUM: LIMITATIONS ON TERRITORIAL AUTHORITY TO ADJUDICATE

Suppose a person has a case that fits within Article III as well as within one of the sections of the United States Code vesting original jurisdiction in the United States District Courts, so that she may (if the jurisdiction is concurrent) or must (if it is exclusive) commence her action in one of those courts. Is she free to select any federal district court in any state? Manifestly she should not be altogether free to do so.

Question: (1) What are the factors that should enter rationally into a solution of the general problem here posed? (When you complete your study of this Section, try to make a tentative determination of how well the federal scheme takes these factors into account.)

For a court properly to undertake a civil adjudication, the law says that the court must have territorial authority to adjudicate. This requirement confines the place of litigation, putting restrictions on the court's authority to entertain litigation with nonlocal elements. The scope of territorial authority to adjudicate is defined in terms of the geographic relationship among the parties, the forum, and the litigation.

In fact, territorial authority breaks down into two types of regulation that control the plaintiff's choice of a district court in which to commence the lawsuit, if the defendant objects. That is to say, territorial authority to adjudicate comprises both territorial jurisdiction and venue as requirements.

(a) TERRITORIAL JURISDICTION AS A LIMITATION

The concept of territorial jurisdiction includes the more important rules of territorial authority to adjudicate. Indeed, territorial jurisdiction rests heavily on the Due Process Clause of the Federal Constitution as its outer limit. That limit demands a connection between the sovereign's court and the target of the action that is adequately strong to justify imposing the judicial relief sought. Thus, in the typical case, adequate connections include the defendant's being served with process in the sovereign's territory, being domiciled there, consenting to suit there, or committing certain acts there such as a tort. These connections will fairly support "jurisdiction over the person" of the defendant.

But within the outer limit, federal courts generally exercise territorial jurisdiction only where authorized by Congress or its rulemaker. Congress and the Supreme Court, the latter acting as Congress's rulemaker, have implicitly or explicitly authorized varying degrees of federal-court territorial jurisdiction in the confusing complex of statutes and Rules that treat service of process. So, we must give some initial attention to that topic.

Service of process.—Service of process is the means (1) of officially informing the defendant that an action has been brought against him and that he must defend himself or suffer the entry of judgment by default and (2) of formally subjecting the defendant to the adjudicatory authority of the sovereign. The first function of giving notice reflects an obvious fairness concern. The second function reflects the underlying requirement that the court have territorial jurisdiction. Fulfillment of the two functions is enforceable by, among other means, Rules 12(b)(5) and 12(b)(2), respectively.

You already know Rule 3 of the Federal Rules, which tells us that a plaintiff commences a civil action by filing a complaint with the court.

Further now, Rule 4(b) says that, upon or after the filing of the complaint, the clerk must issue a summons, which is called process. Rule 4(a) states the formal requirements, and you should note how Form 3, the form of summons, carries out these requirements, which are enforceable under Rule 12(b)(4). Rule 4(c) provides that a copy of the summons must be served together with a copy of the complaint, and then it goes on to specify who can serve—ordinarily any nonparty at least eighteen years old. Incidentally, note that Rule 4(*l*) treats proof of service and that Rule 4(m) sets a time limit for service.

Question: (2) Consider the likely reaction of an inexperienced layperson when confronted with these formidable documents. Would it be desirable to couch the summons in simpler language? Or can something be said for the more formidable style? Why not require the use of both styles, as suggested by Oregon Rule of Civil Procedure 7C?

Manner of service.—Rule 4(e)–(j) describes the manner of service, i.e., the mechanics of delivering process to different kinds of defendants. Take a typical lawsuit for a money recovery against an individual in the United States who is neither a minor nor an incompetent. Rule 4(e)(2) says that the service may be made by delivering a copy of the summons and of the complaint to the defendant personally, or by leaving these papers at his dwelling or usual place of abode with some person of suitable age and discretion residing there, or by delivering them to an agent authorized to receive them. According to Rule 4(e)(1), it is also sufficient if the papers are served in the manner prescribed by the law of the state in which the district court is held or in which service is made.

Question: (3) How is service to be made on a corporation? on an unincorporated association?

Rule 4(d) provides that a plaintiff suing an individual (who is neither a minor nor an incompetent), a corporation, or an unincorporated association can opt to mail or transmit to the defendant a notice requesting a waiver of service. See Forms 5 and 6. If the defendant complies, the suit can proceed without need for the rather expensive formality of service. If the defendant fails to comply, the plaintiff needs to arrange for service of process, but the defendant normally will have to pay the expenses of that service. As the Advisory Committee explained: "The aims of the provision are to eliminate the costs of service of a summons on many parties and to foster cooperation among adversaries and counsel." In actuality, however, the waiver provision may not be that useful. See David D. Siegel, The New (Dec. 1, 1993) Rule 4 of the Federal Rules of Civil Procedure: Changes in Summons Service and Personal Jurisdiction (pt. 1), 151 F.R.D. 441, 457 (1994) ("the waiver procedure may be seen as toothless by canny defendants," because costs are small and because refusal to cooperate may produce timing advantages).

Circumstances of service.—Rule 4(k) regulates the circumstances of service, i.e., the "Territorial Limits of Effective Service." Its essential premise is that service will be effective only if territorial jurisdiction exists. It accordingly provides how far the federal court's territorial jurisdiction reaches for each type of service. Its approach is ordinarily to adopt the local state's law (so that a federal court reaches only as far as a state court could), but federal lawmakers have implicitly or explicitly extended the federal court's reach for certain special service types.

For a readily generalizable example, consider the familiar "nonresident motorist" statute as a law picked up by Rule 4(k)(1)(A): where *A* suffers injuries on a State *X* highway through the alleged negligence of a nonresident motorist *B*, a State *X* statute says that *A* may start her action in State *X* and serve effective process upon *B* in his home state. So, a federal court in State *X* could reach B. But if State *X* had not chosen to stretch its territorial jurisdiction to get nonresident motorists, then the federal court in State *X* could not reach *B*.

For a more specialized example, consider the federal "bulge" provision in Rule 4(k)(1)(B), which is very narrowly available but may be useful in a metropolitan area spanning more than one state: when a pending federal action is enlarged to bring in certain kinds of additional parties that we shall study in the next Section ("third-party defendants" under Rule 14 or "persons needed for just adjudication" under Rule 19), effective service upon those parties may be made at any place in the United States within the sweep of a radius of 100 miles from the courthouse. Here the federal lawmakers have promulgated an extension of the federal court's territorial jurisdiction, expressing that extension through the service provision of Rule 4(k).

Rule 4(n) supplements Rule 4(k). An example of a law within Rule 4(n)(2) is a State *X* statute permitting *A*, who claims as a creditor of a nonresident debtor *B*, to commence an action against *B* in State *X* by attaching property of *B* located in State *X* and providing some form of reasonable notice to *B* as prescribed in the statute. Such an attempt to base a suit on the attachment of property is called a nonpersonal action. The study of such actions, and the question of their constitutional validity, we put off until Part Three.

Rule 4 is somewhat intricate because, by the nature of its historical growth, it combines specific federal regulations with adopted features of state law. But the basic idea is that the federal authorities use it to specify the extent of the federal courts' territorial jurisdiction, either by incorporating federal extensions or by adopting the necessarily restrictive state law.

Effect of requiring territorial jurisdiction.—To go back to the heading of this Subsection, it is clear that the place-restrictions of territorial jurisdiction impose limits on the plaintiff's choice of a district court in which to commence the action.

Thus, for simple illustration, in a diversity action for breach of contract, the territorial jurisdiction requirement might disable a plaintiff from suing in a district court where a part of the events occurred and oblige the plaintiff to sue in the district court at the defendant's home (or wherever else personal jurisdiction exists and venue is proper). We are not at the moment intimating any opinion that this result is bad or regrettable, although we shall have to come finally to the question whether the territorial limitations of Rule 4 do make sense. Here we are simply noting the fact that the result comes about through the current rules regarding service of process.

We should further note that those rules do not seem to follow from any constitutional requirement. One purpose of service of process, already explained, is to provide notice. Because the Due Process Clause requires adequate notification to the defendant for the exercise by any American court of the authority to adjudicate, the power to loosen the service of process is not unlimited. Nevertheless, this consideration creates no constitutional barrier to obliterating *territorial limitations* on service of process. The other purpose of service of process is to subject the defendant to the adjudicatory authority of the sovereign. Because the Due Process Clause also requires an adequate connection between sovereign and defendant, it does place limits on the power to extend effective service of process. However, again there is no constitutional barrier to obliterating, for service of process in federal actions, the territorial limitations of Rule 4 adopted from state law and hence related to *state boundaries.*

All this goes to support the proposition that Congress has the power to provide generally for nationwide service of process issuing from federal courts, as indeed it has done in infrequent instances such as in the Federal Securities Exchange Act.

But all this is not to say that a federal court anywhere in the United States could conduct a particular federal action against a particular defendant consistently with the Fifth Amendment. Due process may prohibit the place of federal suit from being basically unfair for the defendant. This constitutional constraint would be not so much a restriction on territorial jurisdiction, however, as one on venue.

(b) VENUE AS A LIMITATION

Rules of venue specify where the sovereign will exercise its authority to adjudicate, i.e., in what place it will exercise its jurisdiction. The place-restrictions of venue pursue primarily the lower-level concerns of convenience and efficiency, and find expression mainly in statutes that do not employ the language of service of process.

General provision.—The general precepts regarding venue in the federal system appear in 28 U.S.C. § 1391. Under § 1391(a) or (b), which by statutory amendment have become equivalent, venue lies in a district where (1) any defendant resides if all defendants reside in the same state or (2) where a substantial part of the events or omissions giving rise to the claim occurred or a substantial part of property that is the subject of the action is situated; however, (3) the statute effectively waives this venue requirement in the rare circumstance when it would block suit in every federal court, and it then requires satisfaction of only the requirement of personal jurisdiction.

Question: (4) In which United States District Courts would venue be proper in each of the following cases? The matter in controversy exceeds any jurisdictional amount in each case.

(a) *A*, a resident of the Southern District of New York, wishes to sue *B*, a resident of Vermont, the only possible basis of jurisdiction being diversity of citizenship. The claim arose solely in Buffalo in the Western District of New York.

(b) Same as the preceding case, except that this case presents a federal question that would support jurisdiction and the claim arose solely in Quebec.

(c) Same as the just preceding case, except that *B* is a citizen and resident of Canada.

Note the use of the word "reside" in § 1391(a) and (b). Strangely, the case law generally equates this term with "citizenship" as used in the diversity statute. Congress mitigated the restrictive consequences with respect to venue by its 1966 amendment, which made the place where the claim arose a proper venue.

Question: (5) Is there any policy that should prevent a person from having more than one residence for venue purposes?

Special provisions.—Read carefully § 1391(c), which currently defines the residence of a corporate defendant by tying it to the requirement of personal jurisdiction. This means that as to a corporate defendant, the venue requirement does not place a substantial additional limitation on the plaintiff's choice of a district court. Compare § 1391(c) to 28 U.S.C. § 1332(c)(1).

For venue purposes, the Supreme Court analogized unincorporated associations to corporations and constructed a rule comparable to the statute then applicable to corporations. Hence, such an association as defendant is deemed to reside at least in each district in which it is doing business. See Denver & Rio Grande W.R.R. Co. v. Brotherhood of R.R. Trainmen, 387 U.S. 556, 87 S.Ct. 1746 (1967). Compare this rule to the treatment of unincorporated associations for diversity purposes.

As for an alien defendant, either individual or corporate, § 1391(d) means that venue lies in any district. So, as to that defendant, the venue requirement places no limitation on the plaintiff's choice of a district court.

There are various statutes and a few judge-made doctrines that lay down special venue rules for particular classes of cases. The courts have interpreted most of these special rules to supplement § 1391, thus broadening the choice of venue. E.g., 28 U.S.C. § 1401. But the courts have read some of these special rules to override § 1391(a) and (b), thus exclusively controlling venue for the particular class of cases. E.g., 28 U.S.C. § 1397.

One such exclusive provision is unique and deserves special mention: when a defendant removes a case from a state court to a federal district court, it passes "to the district court of the United States for the district and division embracing the place where such action is pending." 28 U.S.C. § 1441(a). Incidentally, Congress has subdivided many districts into divisions, but these divisions have significance only for local judicial administration.

Question: (6) Assume that the defendant properly removes a case from state court to the district court sitting in the same locality. Is that district court necessarily a court in which, under venue requirements for actions originally brought in the district courts, the plaintiff might initially have commenced the action?

Transfer of cases from one proper district court to another.— Operation of the ordinary rules will often result in a case being commenced in or removed to a federal district court that is constitutionally fair but nevertheless is not the most convenient for the conduct of the action. Congress has sought to meet this shortcoming principally by 28 U.S.C. § 1404(a).

Question: (7) What problems of interpretation are raised by the language of § 1404(a)?

(c) ADDENDUM ON ALLOCATION OF COURT BUSINESS AMONG THE STATES

A word is in order about the allocation of court business among the states. With fifty states, each having a court system, the country would seem to require some allocation among the states. The Constitution of the United States most importantly provides it, particularly through the Due Process Clause of the Fourteenth Amendment as interpreted. The control is largely negative: a defendant who has no adequate connection with a particular state is beyond that state's adjudicatory authority.

1. A highway accident occurs in Nebraska, both parties are domiciled there, the defendant has never gone outside the state and has no property outside the state, and all the witnesses reside in the state. It would seem that Nebraska is a proper state in which to conduct any resulting lawsuit. If Wyoming or some other state purports to handle the case at the plaintiff's request and to give judgment upon the defendant's default, its judgment should be open to attack or denied recognition.

2. But suppose the defendant wanders into Wyoming and is there handed summons and complaint in an action commenced in a Wyoming court based on the Nebraska accident. Does Wyoming now have constitutional authority to adjudicate? Yes.

The broad question later considered in detail is this: what must be the relation between a given state and the defendant, in light of the nature of the particular matter in dispute, so that the state will have the constitutional authority to render a judgment?

Again, we should note that a state may, by statute or otherwise, decline to exert its utmost constitutional powers of adjudication. For example, even though service of process on the defendant in the state would be sufficient, constitutionally, to support a valid default judgment, Wyoming law might say that there are reasons of convenience and efficiency for declining to entertain the action, and so its court would dismiss the action.

Parenthetically, you should note that much of the law on territorial jurisdiction applicable to the state courts is relevant to the federal litigator. Remember that by Rule 4, the federal courts can reach only as far as the forum state court could, except when some specialized federal provision has extended their reach.

Each state naturally makes its own internal arrangements for allocating business on a territorial basis among the various courts in its court system. For instance, in personal-injury cases between residents, a state may provide by its venue statute that the plaintiff must bring the action in the county of residence of the plaintiff or of the defendant.

SECTION 8. MORE COMPLEX LITIGATION: MULTIPLE PARTIES AND MULTIPLE CLAIMS

Thus far we have spoken of lawsuits mostly in terms of two parties—one plaintiff and one defendant. Even within this two-party framework, litigation may become ramified by the assertion of a considerable number of claims. Rule 18 permits a plaintiff to join in a single proceeding as many claims as he may have against the defendant, however unrelated they may be. Similarly, the defendant may by counterclaim under Rule 13 expand the lawsuit so as to include whatever claims she may have against the plaintiff. And of course, in such multiclaim litigation, each claim may generate a number of defenses.

Further complication of a lawsuit may follow from the presence in it of more than two parties and also from the parties' assertion of various claims among themselves. The number of these multiparty actions in the courts has increased markedly in modern times. This has been due not only to the adoption of rules and statutes liberalizing the joinder of parties and claims, but also to the increased complexity of financial and other transactions in our society.

The subject of multiple parties and multiple claims is a large and difficult one, as even a casual reading of Rule 14 and Rules 19 through 24 (and a rereading of Rules 13 and 18) will indicate. We shall survey the field in a very general and necessarily superficial way. But first we must refer back to jurisdiction and venue.

There is a certain fitness in dealing with this subject of complex litigation after the Sections on subject-matter jurisdiction, territorial jurisdiction, and venue, for among the major difficulties is that of finding a proper court for the multiparty, multiclaim lawsuit. We shall illustrate this point by touching upon three problems of federal jurisdiction and venue in actions involving more than one plaintiff or defendant.

First, the diversity of citizenship required to satisfy 28 U.S.C. § 1332 is complete diversity (that is, no two opposing parties can be citizens of the same state). Here is an illustration: a plaintiff who is a citizen of New York cannot invoke § 1332 when joining as defendants a citizen of Missouri and another citizen of New York, because the presence of a New Yorker on each side of the controversy destroys the required diversity.

We are speaking here only about the general diversity statute. Courts have not so narrowly interpreted the Diversity and Alienage Clauses of Article III. Thus, Congress has considerable constitutional power to bestow jurisdiction based on minimal diversity (that is, any two opposing parties are of diverse citizenship). Indeed, Congress has done so for complex actions under 28 U.S.C. § 1369.

The alignment of the parties as plaintiffs and defendants in the pleadings is not conclusive in determining diversity jurisdiction. The court will realign the parties for such purpose according to their ultimate interests. For a frequently cited statement of the principles involved in determining ultimate interests, see Indianapolis v. Chase National Bank, 314 U.S. 63, 62 S.Ct. 15 (1941) (realignment to defeat jurisdiction in that case). Realignment may either defeat or create jurisdiction.

Question: (1) Does the required diversity under § 1332 exist in each of the following cases? The matter in controversy exceeds the jurisdictional amount in each case.

(a) *A*, a citizen of New York, and *B*, a citizen of Ohio, sue *C*, a citizen of Missouri.

(b) *A*, a citizen of New York, and *B*, a citizen of Ohio, sue *C*, a citizen and domiciliary of France.

(c) *A*, a citizen of New York, and *B*, a citizen and domiciliary of France, sue *C*, a citizen of Ohio.

(d) *A*, a citizen of New York, and *B*, a citizen and domiciliary of France, sue *C*, a citizen of Ohio, and *D*, a citizen and domiciliary of France.

(e) *A*, a citizen of New York, and *B*, a citizen and domiciliary of France, sue *C*, a citizen and domiciliary of France.

(f) A partnership of *A*, a citizen of New York, and *B*, a citizen and domiciliary of France, doing business in New York, sues *C*, a citizen and domiciliary of Germany.

Second, the basic removal statute, 28 U.S.C. § 1441, provides that "the defendant or the defendants" have the right, under the conditions there prescribed, to remove an action to the federal court. Courts read this to mean that all served defendants normally must join in the notice of removal.

Questions: In the following questions, assume that the matter in controversy exceeds any jurisdictional amount.

(2) *A*, a citizen of California, sues *B*, a citizen of Connecticut, and *C* Company, a Connecticut corporation with its principal place of business in Connecticut, in a California state court, seeking joint relief. *B* is content with the state court. Can *C* Company alone properly remove the action to the local United States District Court?

(3) *A*, a citizen of California, sues *B*, a citizen of California, and *C* Company, a Connecticut corporation with its principal place of business in Connecticut, in a

California state court, seeking joint relief. Can *B* and *C* Company together properly remove?

(4) *A*, a citizen of California, sues *B*, a citizen of California, in a California state court, seeking damages for personal injuries. *C* Ins. Co., *B*'s liability insurer, refuses to defend, contending that its policy does not cover the kind of accident in question. Thereupon *B* brings an action in the same state court for a declaratory judgment of coverage, naming as defendants *A* and *C* Ins. Co., a Connecticut corporation with its principal place of business in Connecticut. Can *C* Ins. Co. properly remove? See Bonell v. General Accident Fire & Life Assur. Corp., 167 F.Supp. 384 (N.D.Cal.1958) (yes).

Third, multiparty actions also create problems with reference to venue. Note that the general venue statute, 28 U.S.C. § 1391, refers to "all defendants."

Question: (5) In which United States District Courts would venue be proper in each of the following cases? The matter in controversy exceeds any jurisdictional amount in each case.

(a) *A*, a resident of Maine, wishes to sue *B*, a resident of Vermont, and *C*, a resident of New Hampshire, the only possible basis of jurisdiction being diversity of citizenship. The claim arose solely in Maine.

(b) *A*, a resident of Maine, wishes to sue *B*, a resident of Buffalo in the Western District of New York, and *C*, a resident of Manhattan in the Southern District of New York, the only possible basis of jurisdiction being diversity of citizenship. The claim arose solely in Maine.

(c) *A*, a resident of Buffalo, and *B*, a resident of Manhattan, wish to sue *C*, a resident of Vermont, and *D*, a resident of New Hampshire, the only possible basis of jurisdiction being diversity of citizenship. The claim arose solely in Quebec. (Would it matter that *D* works in a factory in Vermont?)

We have couched the foregoing cases in terms of the plaintiff or plaintiffs "wishing" to sue. Insofar as the venue requirement—especially when taken together with the limitations on territorial jurisdiction—imposes obstacles to a *permissive* joinder of parties, the consequence is merely that the federal plaintiff must content himself with suing fewer defendants than he would like, or that several intending coplaintiffs will have to sue separately. But we shall see shortly that there is a graver problem. Sometimes party joinder is *required* (that is, the action cannot go forward in the absence of certain parties plaintiff or defendant). When this situation exists, the requirements of territorial authority to adjudicate may result in closing the door of the federal courts to a meritorious claim cognizable there in point of subject-matter jurisdiction. Indeed, it may also turn out to be impossible to find a suitable state court for the action because no state is in a position to issue process that will be effective to bring in all the required defendants.

For the most part we shall postpone until Part Three further study of the interplay between these Rules and the law of subject-matter jurisdiction, territorial jurisdiction, and venue. Such problems rapidly become much thornier and require extensive treatment. So, with this introduction on jurisdiction and venue behind us, we turn to a consideration of the Federal Rules dealing with multiple parties and multiple claims. For the moment, your task is primarily to understand how the mechanics of these particular Rules work.

(a) PERMISSIVE JOINDER OF PROPER PARTIES

[Rule 20]

There are numerous situations where a group of plaintiffs, each of whom would be free to sue separately, may consider it desirable to pool their resources and join in a single action. Rule 20(a)(1) permits them to do this, subject only to the requirements that their rights grow out of the same transaction, occurrence, or series of transactions or occurrences and that some question of law or fact common to all of them will arise in the action. Thus, for instance, ten passengers in a bus may join in suing the bus company for personal injuries sustained by them in a collision. On the one hand, such joinder may not only be advantageous to the parties, but also serve the public interest by preventing relitigation of the same facts in a succession of actions—and with a possibility of inconsistent results. On the other hand, if passengers in a series of bus accidents join in a single suit, they could be seeking an unfair advantage by suggesting gross wrongdoing by the defendant or by confusing the factfinder. Overall, the tests for permissive joinder receive flexible, but rather generous, interpretation.

Correspondingly liberal provisions allow a plaintiff (or several plaintiffs) to join a number of defendants in one action. Here are some examples of situations in which a plaintiff may join all persons claimed to be liable to him: plaintiff *A* suffers injuries in a collision of three cars owned and negligently driven by *B*, *C*, and *D* respectively; or plaintiff *T* suffers injuries through the negligence of employee *S* for which employer *M* is also responsible by the rule of respondeat superior. In situations of these concurrent-negligence and employee-employer types, the plaintiff may select his targets—he may sue all or any of those liable. Form 12 is illustrative of a claim for relief against defendants "in the alternative," which Rule 20(a)(2)(A) also expressly allows for a plaintiff who is in doubt as to which of two or more defendants is liable to him.

Questions: (6) *A* sues *C* and *D* for libel, alleging that *C* falsely wrote of her on May 1 that she was a thief and that *D* did the same on July 1. Is the joinder proper under Rule 20?

(7) *A* and *B* sue *C* and *D* for libel, alleging that *C* falsely wrote of *A* on May 1 that she was a thief and that *D* wrote the same of *B* on July 1. Is the joinder proper under Rule 20? See Wynn v. National Broad. Co., 234 F.Supp.2d 1067, 1078 (C.D. Cal. 2002) (holding that Rule 20 does not allow joinder of a plaintiff-versus-defendant claim with a different-plaintiff-versus-different-defendant claim).

(8) What is the Federal Rules' remedy for an attempted joinder that is improper under Rule 20?

The territorial limitations on effective service of process impose practical restrictions on joinder of defendants. Moreover, any joinder proper under Rule 20 may be prevented by requirements of subject-matter jurisdiction or venue, of course.

Suppose a defendant to an action wishes to assert a counterclaim that involves persons not already joined. Think of Mr. Robinson and see again Rule 13(h).

(b) REQUIRED JOINDER OF PERSONS NEEDED FOR JUST ADJUDICATION

[Rule 19]

The party-structure of a lawsuit is in the first instance a determination by the plaintiff (or plaintiffs) instituting the action. But he is not entirely free to do as he pleases. As we have just seen, there are outer limits on who *may* be joined as proper parties. And inner limits exist to tell the plaintiff who *must* be joined, limits enforceable by the defendant or the court: there are occasions when he must enlist other persons who should have joined him as plaintiffs, and there are also occasions when he must bring in certain additional persons to defend the lawsuit.

Rule 19(a)(1) declares that persons sustaining certain relationships to the action must be joined as parties if their joinder is feasible, that is, if effective service of process can reach them and if their joinder will not deprive the court of subject-matter jurisdiction. Ultimately, venue will also have to be satisfied unless the point is waived.

Rule 19(a)(1) expresses the relationships necessitating joinder in terms of, first, whether the court can give "complete relief" to those already parties if the particular person is not joined and remains outside the action and, second, whether the disposition of the action in the absence of the particular person either may as a practical matter impair the person's ability to protect a claimed interest relating to the subject of the action[a] or may leave those already parties exposed to a substantial risk of incurring double liability as the result of a later suit by that person. These relationships, as described, are rather broadly inclusive. So, for example, if *P* sues *D* for specific performance on a contract, *P*'s joint obligee is a necessary party.

Rule 19(a)(1) is not so broad, however, as to take in the concurrent-negligence and employee-employer cases hypothesized above in connection with Rule 20(a)(2). Rule 19 does not require joinder of defendants in those cases, even if feasible. Joinder is entirely optional with the plaintiff, who can select targets under Rule 20. The explanation lies in the character of

---

[a] Ordinarily the judgment in an action between *A* and *B* cannot affect *C in a legal sense.* The law ordinarily dictates that no judgment can go against *C* or alter her legal position unless she has been summoned as a party and has had an opportunity to present her side of the case.

An action between *A* and *B* may, however, affect *C in a practical sense.* Here is a simple example: *B* is holding a certain amount of money for *A* and *C* in disputed shares, and *A* recovers the whole sum from *B* by an action in which *C* has not been joined; the judgment does not preclude *C* from suit—she is unaffected legally—but as a practical matter she may be left without an adequate remedy against either *B* or *A* once the money is spent.

the substantive rights and duties of the persons involved. The traditional version of the substantive law here is often summed up as "joint-and-several" liability, but that term really represents the joinder conclusion that the plaintiff can sue the defendants together or separately. The better description of that substantive law is "entire" liability, meaning that *each* defendant is liable for *all* of the plaintiff's damages. The plaintiff who has sued and won against a number of defendants can recover the whole judgment from any judgment debtor, although the plaintiff of course cannot recover more than the amount of the judgment by going after other of the judgment debtors. The substantive policy is to make the plaintiff whole, and to leave the defendants to squabble among themselves about relative overpayment of their shares by invoking whatever law of contribution happens to exist. Because the absence or presence of other potential defendants has no legal effect on the joined defendants vis-à-vis the plaintiff, and because the substantive law intends the practical effect of disadvantaging defendants, the Rules leave it up to the plaintiff whom to sue. As usual, then, much is left to party autonomy.

Now suppose instead that some missing person is within the net of subdivision (a) of Rule 19 and thus termed "necessary," but joinder is not feasible. The court then faces the alternatives of dismissing the action or of continuing it without the full cast of characters that we would prefer to have as parties. Subdivision (b) sets out a series of factors to consider in deciding between these alternatives. Examine the statement of factors. Sometimes the case should continue: try to imagine situations in which the second and fourth factors would tend to the conclusion that the action should go forward notwithstanding the absence of a person embraced by the definition of subdivision (a). But sometimes the factors counsel dismissal: if upon consideration of the terms of Rule 19, including the factors of subdivision (b), the court finds that the person whose joinder is not feasible is so urgently needed for just adjudication that the court should dismiss the case, the person is labeled "indispensable."

Question: (9) Under the Federal Rules, how and when does the defendant raise the defense of a failure to join persons as required by Rule 19?

(c) Interpleader

[Rule 22]

As stated above, Rule 20 makes provision for a plaintiff who is doubtful which of two or more defendants is liable to him. But what of the prospective defendant who is in doubt as to which of two or more claimants has the right to payment of a debt admittedly owed to one of them?

Assume, for example, that the *A* Life Insurance Co. insured *B*'s life. *B* has died, and *C* and *D* each claim to be the sole beneficiary under the policy. There is the uncomfortable possibility that *C* might sue *A* Co. and recover, and that *D* might thereafter sue *A* Co. and likewise recover. The imposition of such a double recovery is unjust to *A* Co., but it can easily happen if each claimant sues separately. The parties might present different evidence in the two cases, or different fact-finders might take different views of substantially identical evidence. And *A* Co. cannot defend in *D*'s action by saying, "We do not have to pay you because we have already been held liable to *C* on this policy." (Why is this not a defense?)

Rule interpleader.—Rule 22(a) provides an escape from this quandary. *A* Co. may commence a suit against *C* and *D* and require them to make their respective claims in the same action, thus avoiding the hazard of double liability. Moreover, suppose *A* Co. contends that it is not liable to either *C* or *D* because *B* had procured the policy by false representations. The interpleader machinery is still available, because an admission of liability to one of the claimants is not a prerequisite to its use. See Form 20.

If one of the claimants sues *A* Co., it may still interplead. The Rule provides that a defendant in such a position may interplead the other claimant and say in effect to the two of them, "Fight it out and we'll pay the winner," or, "We'll pay the winner unless it is held that we don't have to pay either." See Form 31.

If jurisdiction for interpleader in federal court rests only on a federal question, the procedure of Rule 22(a) must be utilized, and the usual rules of subject-matter jurisdiction, venue, and service apply. Venue for such an interpleader action initiated by the stakeholder generally must satisfy 28 U.S.C. § 1391. And process runs within the usual territorial limits of Rule 4.

But most interpleader cases in federal court rest on diversity of citizenship. When the interpleader action rests on diversity jurisdiction and proceeds under Rule 22(a), the general diversity statute (28 U.S.C. § 1332) is applicable, so that the stake must exceed $75,000 and the diversity of citizenship must be complete diversity between the stakeholder on the one side and the adverse claimants on the other.

Statutory interpleader.—When diverse citizenship exists, the stakeholder may have a choice between two devices: rule interpleader under Rule 22(a) or the statutory interpleader that is cross-referenced in Rule 22(b). The cross-reference is to the federal statute providing for interpleader (see 28 U.S.C. §§ 1335, 1397, and 2361).

Here the jurisdictional amount is "$500 or more," and the required diversity has a special definition—the statute looks to diversity of citizenship among the claimants, and the Supreme Court has held that minimal as distinguished from complete diversity suffices. State Farm Fire & Cas. Co. v. Tashire, infra p. 1010. Venue for such an interpleader action initiated by the stakeholder lies in any district in which any claimant resides. Also, process runs nationwide. In other words, Congress has appropriately invoked its broad constitutional authority to handle cases that were beyond the state courts' reach.

(d) THIRD-PARTY PRACTICE

[Rule 14]

A defendant may wish to extend the lawsuit in another way. He may want to reach a third person, not joined in the action, who he believes is or may contingently be liable to him for all or part of the claim that the plaintiff is making against him. In our economy and society, such a situation is common.

Assume, for example, that *A* sues *B*, a restaurant proprietor, claiming damage as a result of eating contaminated food. *B*'s contention is that if *A* can hold him liable, then the loss ought to fall on *C*, his supplier, who furnished the food. If *B* waits until *A* has recovered a judgment against him and he has paid it, and then brings a separate action against *C*, *B* may find himself in a position not dissimilar to that of the insurance company in the interpleader situation described above. *C* is not bound by what occurred in the *A* versus *B* litigation in her absence; and the two fact-finders may arrive at inconsistent conclusions on the facts. Even if this does not happen, there will remain the wasteful business of reworking the ground already covered in the first action.

Rule 14(a) permits such a defendant to bring the third person into the case as a party, if effective service of process can reach her. (Note when the Rule requires leave of court, and see Forms 4, 16, and 41.) This device, called impleader, is optional with the defendant, so that he is free to wait and bring a separate action if he chooses. For instance, the defendant may not wish yet to arouse the third person's hostility, and inspire possibly more adverse testimony, by suing her now.

If the defendant uses Rule 14(a), the result is a kind of lawsuit within a lawsuit. The defendant becomes a "third-party plaintiff" and the impleaded newcomer becomes a "third-party defendant" with respect to the claim between them. The premise of the claim between them is not that the third-party defendant might be liable to the original plaintiff, but rather that the third-party defendant should cover part or all of the third-party plaintiff's liability to the original plaintiff. The substantive theory of the claim might be indemnity, contribution, subrogation, or warranty. So the focus of this lawsuit within a lawsuit will be on whether, under the substantive law and the actual facts, such secondary liability exists.

What then is the strategic structure of the *A–B–C* litigation above sketched, after *B* has impleaded *C*? *A* wants to establish the primary case against *B*. *B* wants to defeat *A*'s claim against him, especially if he lacks confidence in his claim against *C* or in *C*'s ability to satisfy a judgment; *B* also wants to establish *C*'s liability to him if *A*'s claim succeeds. *C* wants to see *A*'s claim against *B* defeated; *C* also wants to prove that in no event does *B* have a right of reimbursement from her, *C*.

Question: (10) Referring to Rule 14(a)(2), how should *C* plead?

The original plaintiff may have a related claim of his own against the impleaded newcomer, but originally elected not to press it. Injection of the third-party defendant into the case cannot of itself force the plaintiff to sue an unwanted adversary. Nevertheless, a plaintiff who finds a potential adversary injected into the case may well change his mind. See Rule 14(a)(3). Likewise, the third-party defendant may wish to assert a related claim against the original plaintiff. See Rule 14(a)(2)(D). Once a two-party lawsuit has become a three-cornered affair through a Rule 14 impleader, the whole matter of claims and counterclaims among the parties requires careful examination. See generally 6 Wright, Miller & Kane §§ 1455–1459.

Questions: (11) *S*, driving her employer *M*'s car on *M*'s business, collides with an automobile owned and operated by *T*. Both cars receive damage, and both *T* and *S* suffer injuries. It is a matter of doubt whether *T* or *S* or both were negligent. Under the applicable substantive law of contributory negligence: (a) *if S was negligent and T was not, T* can recover from *S* and can recover also from *M*, although *T* of course cannot actually collect from *M* and *S* more than the total amount of his damages; if *M* has to pay because of *S*'s negligence, *M* is entitled to repayment from *S*; *M* is also entitled to recover against *S* for the damage to *M*'s car; (b) *if S was not negligent and T was, S* can recover against *T* for *S*'s personal injuries, and *M* can recover against *T* for the damage to *M*'s car; and (c) *if both S and T were negligent, M* can recover against *S* for the damage to *M*'s car but cannot recover against *T* for that damage. Furthermore, under that traditional law, there is no doctrine of comparative negligence, no right to contribution among concurrent tortfeasors, and no workers' compensation law. Assume that *T*, who might sue *M* or *S* or both, elects to sue *M* only; and *M* brings in *S* as a third-party defendant. Further assume no problems of subject-matter jurisdiction, venue, or service exist. If the three parties wish to assert all the claims that they may assert under Rule 14, how should they plead? And how should they respond to the claims made against them? What claims will be foreclosed from presentation in a later lawsuit if they are not asserted here?

(12) Suppose *M*, more than fourteen days after serving its answer to *T*'s complaint, had sought leave to implead *S* under Rule 14(a)(1); *T* had opposed the impleader on the ground that *S* is impecunious and without personal-liability insurance and would be unable to reimburse *M* to any substantial extent; and *T* had also argued that the jurors would likely render a smaller verdict if they knew that *S* is ultimately responsible for payment. What action should the court have taken on leave to implead? Would your answer be different if *M* had impleaded *S* at the time it served its answer and *T* had moved to strike the third-party claim under Rule 14(a)(4)?

Now suppose a plaintiff against whom a counterclaim has been asserted wishes to reach a third person who is or may be liable to him for the counterclaim. See Rule 14(b); cf. Rule 14(a)(5).

(e) CROSSCLAIMS

[Rule 13(g)]

Once you recognize that there may be several plaintiffs, several defendants, and several third-party defendants in an action, the possibility of conflict among the coparties (meaning any parties who are not opposing parties) should become apparent. The effect of Rule 13(g) is to permit, but not to compel, coparties to assert against one another claims that bear certain prescribed relations to the rest of the controversy—such claims are called crossclaims. This provision is but another reflection of the general aim of the Rules to allow the court to dispose of related quarrels under the umbrella of a single action.

To illustrate with a simple example, assume that *A* sues *B* and *C*. *B* has a claim against *C* arising out of the same transaction. *B* may proceed by crossclaim against *C*, or he may instead elect to bring a separate action against *C*.

Questions: (13) Why should a counterclaim arising out of the same transaction be compulsory while a crossclaim against a coparty is merely permissive?

(14) Why must a crossclaim bear a certain prescribed relation to the rest of the controversy while a permissive counterclaim may be entirely unrelated?

Rule 13(g) specifies no time limit for asserting crossclaims, leaving it to judicial discretion.

Now suppose *A* and *B* sue *C* for breach of contract. *C* pleads a permissive counterclaim against *A* and *B* for negligence. According to the second sentence of Rule 13(g), *A* may plead a crossclaim against *B* to establish that *B* is liable over to *A* in respect to *C*'s counterclaim. If *A* pleads this crossclaim against *B* and if *B* has a claim against *A* arising out of the transaction or occurrence that is the subject matter of that crossclaim, *B* must assert his claim as a compulsory counterclaim under Rule 13(a), because *A* has become an opposing party within the Rule.

HENZ v. SUPERIOR TRUCKING CO., 96 F.R.D. 219 (M.D.Pa.1982). Husband and wife sued for the wife's personal injuries. Defendant sought to implead the husband, who was allegedly at fault. But Rule 14(a)(1) was unavailable because the husband was not a "nonparty"; Rule 13(g) was unavailable because the husband was not the defendant's "coparty"; and Rule 13(a) and (b) was unavailable because the contribution or indemnity claim was not a mature claim.

"The parties have suggested alternative ways of proceeding. The actions of the plaintiffs might be severed under Rule 21 and then the defendant could join Mr. Henz as a third party defendant in the action by Mrs. Henz. At this point, the action of Mr. Henz against the defendants could be left for a separate trial or Mr. Henz might raise his claims for loss of association and medical expenses as counterclaims."

The court accepted the suggestion of severance, while observing that any separate actions might be consolidated or joined for trial.

(f) CLASS ACTIONS

[Rules 23, 23.1, 23.2]

We have thus far considered who may and who must be included in an action as parties plaintiff, parties defendant, and third-party defendants, and what claims may be tried out among the parties. Rule 23 opens up a different concept, the class action, by which persons may sue or defend not merely on their own behalf but also on behalf of others not before the court as parties.

The law knows a variety of people who as parties in litigation are "stand-ins" for, or represent, others not joined as parties, just as they may represent those others in ordinary transactions. Thus a trustee sues or defends on behalf of the beneficiaries in respect to the trust property; a guardian stands in for the ward; an executor represents the estate or those interested in it. And similarly an adjudication in an action by or against a person owning an interest in land may inure to the benefit of or limit the rights of successors to that interest in the land by purchase or devolution—the predecessor may be thought of as representing those who follow her in ownership. Class actions also involve a version of representation, but of a somewhat different order.

Suppose a large number of persons have similar claims (or similar liabilities) arising from the same matrix of facts. If each person had to commence his own individual action (or defend an action brought against him alone), we would have repetitious proceedings with a large expenditure of time, money, and effort. We would also run into the possible embarrassment of inconsistent results, and this would be especially painful where the party opposing the numerous claimants (or defenders) would find himself unable or very hard put to carry out the conflicting commands comprised in the inconsistent judgments. The inability to hear from all interested persons, or indeed the practical inability to maintain small individual actions, might have deleterious effects on the full realization of substantive policies.

The operation of Rules 19 and 20 might result in a joinder of the claimants (or defenders) in a single action, which would be helpful as far as it went; but joinder under either Rule encounters obstacles of subject-matter jurisdiction, venue, and service; as the group reaches a certain size, presence of all the members makes the action unmanageable; furthermore, Rule 19 is narrow in scope, and Rule 20 joinder depends heavily on cooperative action. So, to meet the unmet problems, the class action envisaged by Rule 23 invoked the justificatory principle of adequate representation: under stated conditions and subject to certain safeguards, one or a few members may sue (or defend) on behalf of the class.

Plainly, the rulemakers had to delimit and control such a class device lest it run roughshod over the "represented" absentee members of the class or abuse the parties or overwhelm the court. Moreover, the rulemakers had to keep an eye on the inevitable substantive effects of enabling a lawsuit in situations where practicalities previously prohibited the lawsuit.

Subdivision (a) of Rule 23 sets out prerequisites for maintaining any class action: the class must be so numerous as to make joinder of all members impracticable; there must be questions of law or fact common to the class; the claims or defenses of the representative parties must be typical of the class; and there must be assurance that the representatives will be vigorous and competent champions of the class objectives. These are necessary conditions for maintaining a class action, but they are not sufficient. The case must also satisfy the provisions of subdivision (b), in that it must fit into one of the categories of that subdivision. Those categories require the absentees to be related to the representative party in a certain way, either that the absentees share common and thus aligned substantive interests with their representative or that the former somehow consented to representation by the latter. The aim of both (a) and (b) is to ensure that class treatment promises considerable benefits and acceptable costs.

Subdivision (b)(1) contemplates the evident inconveniences or absurdities or unfairnesses involved in individual adjudications. Illustrative of (1)(A) is a taxpayers' suit against a municipality to declare a bond issue invalid; and (1)(B) would include an action involving numerous persons claiming against a fund insufficient to satisfy all the claims.

Subdivision (b)(2) takes in cases where a defendant has made the characteristics of the class a basis for his own conduct, and final class-wide injunctive or corresponding declaratory relief is thus appropriate. The prime example is a desegregation case.

Coming to subdivision (b)(3), we find situations that are not as readily amenable to class treatment as those in (b)(1) and (b)(2), but in which that procedure may yet have definite advantages. For example, hypothesize false statements in a stock prospectus: any element of reliance may vary among the purchasers making up the class, and the amount of damages certainly will vary; there may, in addition, be quite legitimate reasons why the individual defrauded purchasers would want to institute and control their own lawsuits. Note that (b)(3) permits a class action only upon findings, first, that the questions common to the class "predominate" over those affecting individual members and, second, that a class action is "superior" to other methods of handling the controversy. Examine the factors listed in (b)(3) as pertinent to these findings. But even when the court is prepared to make the findings favorable to maintaining a class action, the individual member may "opt out" of the class and proceed on his own. Under subdivision (c)(2)(B), the court must give the best notice practicable to the members of a (b)(3) class of the right of any member to withdraw from the class by simply informing the court.[b] If the member does not inform the court of his desire to withdraw from the class, he remains tied into the class. He then has the option of entering an appearance in the action through counsel, which would ensure his being kept currently informed about the case. Beyond that, he may be in a position to intervene under Rule 24, as we discuss in the next Subsection.

Question: (15) Why did the drafters of Rule 23 not prescribe this notice and opting-out procedure for (b)(1) and (b)(2) cases?

Soon after commencement of the proposed class action, the court must determine under subdivision (c)(1) the propriety of allowing maintenance as a class action. Under (c)(4), class treatment may be possible or advisable

[b] The best notice practicable might consist of notice by mail to reasonably identifiable individuals together with published notice in newspapers or trade magazines or the like addressed to the class as a whole. The plaintiff must initially bear the cost of this notice.

only as to certain issues in a case, while the other issues would receive individual treatment. Similarly, under (c)(5), the court may deem class treatment proper only for certain subclasses of a proposed class.

Apart from any (c)(2) notice, Rule 23 has ample provision for discretionary notices as part of the process of the court's running any class action. See the variety of "management" provisions in subdivision (d).

A class action, when carried out to the end (note subdivision (e) on dismissal and settlement), results in a judgment extending by its terms to the class, but excluding in (b)(3) cases the opters-out. The judgment so extends whether it is favorable to the class or not. See subdivision (c)(3). The design is that the judgment will receive respect according to its terms as res judicata in subsequent litigation, but the system cannot assure that result until the subsequent litigation occurs and a plea of res judicata is made and decided. If, for instance, a (b)(3) plaintiff-class action is sloppily handled and no reasonable effort is made to notify class members, a member who got no notice of the class action may pursue his separate action and therein attack the prior class-action judgment that nominally included him.

When jurisdiction turns on an amount in controversy, that requirement applies to the claim of each class member, and in its usual complicated way. As to satisfying the usual diversity of citizenship requirement, however, the court considers only the citizenships of the named parties, not the citizenships of all the members of the class—if it instead considered the citizenships of the absentee members, the federal court would of course more often lack jurisdiction. Similarly, for purposes of venue and service, the court considers only the named parties. Topic A of Part Three on subject-matter jurisdiction and Topic C of Part Five on class actions will develop these rules in detail.

Actions relating to unincorporated associations.—The preceding paragraph leads to a mention of Rule 23.2 governing actions involving unincorporated associations, such as labor unions. Instead of joining all the association's members, lawyers have used a class action naming a few members as representatives as a device for satisfying any diversity requirement and for easing venue and service requirements. Because of the special reasons for utilizing the class device here, the rulemakers added the specifically tailored Rule 23.2 in 1966, with references where appropriate therein to Rule 23.

Derivative actions by shareholders.—A derivative action allows one or more persons to sue for the benefit of similarly situated persons on a claim that their common fiduciary refuses to assert. Imagine that a shareholder of a corporation (or a member of an unincorporated association), believing that the corporation should be asserting a right of action against another person (who may be a wrongdoing director or officer of the corporation), makes demand on the directors, and if necessary on the shareholders, to sue. The demand is refused. A right to sue upon the corporation's claim may then accrue to the shareholder. If she succeeds in the suit, the recovery goes into the treasury of the corporation to be shared (in a manner of speaking) by all the shareholders.

These derivative actions have their place even when there are few shareholders. When the number of shareholders is large, the derivative action has the character of a class action, with one or several shareholders suing on behalf of all. See Rule 23.1, also added in 1966 but having antecedents in the original Rule 23.

Only the corporation's claim need satisfy any jurisdictional amount requirement. Although the corporation must be joined as a defendant with the alleged wrongdoer, the court very occasionally realigns it with the plaintiff-shareholder for diversity of citizenship purposes. Note also the special supplementary provisions for venue and service in these actions: 28 U.S.C. §§ 1401 and 1695.

(g) INTERVENTION

[Rule 24]

Rule 19(a)(1)(B)(i) requires that persons claiming interests in the subject of an action that risk being practically impaired must be joined as parties, if feasible; and if joinder is not feasible, Rule 19(b) indeed puts the question whether the court should not dismiss the action. Rule 24(a) takes the plausible position that when such a person, instead of waiting to be forced into the action, applies to the court by timely motion to intervene, the court must allow him to do so—assuming that one of the parties does not adequately represent his interest already. This is "intervention of right."

There is also "permissive intervention," that is, intervention in the discretion of the court under the terms of Rule 24(b). This subdivision echoes Rule 20 in part.

Rule 24(c) prescribes the procedure for intervention. See also Form 42. Intervention normally means that the intervenor becomes a full party on the appropriate side of the action, but the court may impose some conditions or restrictions on an intervenor's participation.

Intervention is common in class actions. The intervening class member is typically claiming that for one reason or another the representative parties do not adequately represent his particular interest. You will notice that Rule 23(d)(1)(B)(iii) reminds the court that it may on occasion decide to give notice to class members of their opportunity to intervene.

(h) GENERAL OBSERVATIONS

Even taking into account the practical restrictions imposed by territorial limitations on effective service, by the venue requirement, and by limits on the kinds of cases that the federal courts may entertain, it is clear that an action under the Federal Rules may abundantly proliferate.

The issues of fact and law may of course be highly complex even when the action involves few claims and few parties. An antitrust case by a single plaintiff against a single defendant, for instance, may produce issues of vast difficulty. But multiclaim actions sometimes pose peculiarly perplexing problems of both planning for the parties and management for the court. And multiparty actions raise even more intense problems of planning and management. How far, for a minor example, may a court justifiably limit examination and cross-examination of a particular witness by the several parties to a lawsuit, and may the court require that parties aligned in interest speak through one lawyer only? Often problems of this order are solved by informal arrangements. Multiparty actions may also aggravate the strategic problems of counsel. The tactic of divide and conquer, for example, is not unknown in the courtroom. Plaintiff may join two defendants for the very purpose of driving between them.

Criticism of the Rules has been made on this account: it is said that they allow litigation to get "too big" in terms of claims and parties. On the one hand, the Rules themselves recognize the dangers of delay, expense, confusion, and prejudice that spring from attempting to handle too many claims and parties as a bundle. Accordingly, the Rules give the court certain discretionary powers to reshape the litigation. That is, even for a case properly pleaded between the limits of required and permissive joinder, the court can reduce the bundle in the interests of fairness and efficiency. See Rules 42(b) (separate trials in general), 21 (severance in general), 13(i) (separate trials of counterclaims and crossclaims), 14(a) (discretion in allowing third-party claims; severance and separate trials of third-party claims), 20(b) (protective orders and separate trials in relation to permissive joinder of parties), 23(c) (effective discretion in allowing class actions), and 24(b) (discretion in allowing permissive intervention). On the other hand, the court also has discretion to make the bundle larger when this will avoid inconvenience or reduce costs. See Rule 42(a) (joint trials and consolidation).

More on all this, and on grander themes and deeper concerns, appears in Part Five.

TOPIC C

CLOSING ARGUMENTS

SECTION 1. THE ADVERSARY SYSTEM

Lon L. Fuller, The Problems of Jurisprudence

706–07 (1949).

Adjudication involves a complex of factors that may appear in various combinations and that may be present in varying degrees. We may, however, say that the moral force of a judgment or decision will be at a maximum when the following conditions are satisfied: 1) The judge does not act on his own initiative, but on the application of one or both of the disputants. 2) The judge has no direct or indirect interest (even emotional) in the outcome of the case. 3) The judge confines his decision to the controversy before him and attempts no regulation of the parties' relations going beyond that controversy. 4) The case presented to the judge involves an existing controversy, and not merely the prospect of some future disagreement. 5) The judge decides the case solely on the basis of the evidence and arguments presented to him by the parties. 6) Each disputant is given ample opportunity to present his case.

It is seldom that all of these conditions can be realized in practice, and it is not here asserted that it is always wise to observe all of them. What is asserted is merely that adjudication as a principle of order achieves its maximum force when all of these conditions are satisfied. Some of this moral or persuasive force may wisely be sacrificed when other considerations dictate a departure from the conditions enumerated above, and where the tribunal, as an agent of legitimated power, has the capacity to compel respect for its decision.

The connection between the conditions enumerated above and the moral force of the judgment rendered is not something irrational and fortuitous. The key to it is found in the fact that men instinctively seek to surround the process of adjudication with those conditions that will tend to insure that the decision rendered is the closest possible approximation of the common need. This obviously explains the conditions of disinterestedness on the part of the judge and the opportunity for a full hearing of both sides, that is, conditions 2 and 6 in the enumeration above. Underlying the other four conditions is a single insight, namely, that men's interests and desires form a complex network, and that to discover the most effective and least disruptive pattern of order within this network requires an intimate acquaintance with the network itself and the interests and desires of which it is composed. In other words, these conditions are designed to obviate an evil that may be broadly called "absentee management." The judge must stick to the case before him (condition 3), because if he ventures beyond it he may attempt to regulate affairs on which he is inadequately informed. The judge must work within the framework of the parties' arguments and proof (condition 5), because if he goes beyond these he will lack the guidance given him by the parties and may not understand the interests that are affected by a decision rendered outside that framework. The case must involve a present controversy (condition 4), because neither the parties nor the judge can be sure that they fully understand the implications of a possible, future controversy or the precise interests that may be affected by it when it arises. The first condition (that the judge should act on the application of the parties) is perhaps the most difficult to justify. It arises from the fact that the judge who calls the parties in and himself sets the framework of the hearing lays himself open to the suspicion of planning a general regulation in which the controversy on which he hears evidence and arguments appears as a mere detail. Thus a violation of condition 1 tends to carry with it a strong suspicion that condition 3 is being violated.

If this discussion seems abstract, it may perhaps be given a more concrete meaning by recurring to an example . . . , that of the father who decides a dispute between two of his children. If, implored by the disputants to hear their arguments, such a father, at the conclusion of the evidence and arguments and without rendering any decision on the case before him, were to declare, "Well, now that I see what's going on around here, I announce that the following rule must be observed . . ." it is fairly obvious that he would be sacrificing his moral position as judge for that of legislator. If he were then to decide the case before him, his ruling would not seem like a decision but an order. If he wishes to preserve his moral position as judge, he would be well advised to proceed by first deciding the controversy submitted to him, and to postpone for a day or so any legislation based on the information gained through his adjudicative activities.[a]

Joint Conference on Professional Responsibility, Report

44 A.B.A.J. 1159, 1160–61 (1958).

The lawyer appearing as an advocate before a tribunal presents, as persuasively as he can, the facts and the law of the case as seen from the standpoint of his client's interest. It is essential that both the lawyer and the public understand clearly the nature of the role thus discharged. Such an understanding is required not only to appreciate the need for an adversary presentation of issues, but also in order to perceive truly the limits partisan advocacy must impose on itself if it is to remain wholesome and useful.

---

[a] See also Lon L. Fuller, The Forms and Limits of Adjudication, 92 Harv.L.Rev. 353 (1978) (elaborating his views on adjudication). See generally Robert S. Summers, Lon L. Fuller 74–109 (1984). Professor Fuller was also the primary author of the Report next set out in the text.

In a very real sense it may be said that the integrity of the adjudicative process itself depends upon the participation of the advocate. This becomes apparent when we contemplate the nature of the task assumed by any arbiter who attempts to decide a dispute without the aid of partisan advocacy.

Such an arbiter must undertake, not only the role of judge, but that of representative for both of the litigants. Each of these roles must be played to the full without being muted by qualifications derived from the others. When he is developing for each side the most effective statement of its case, the arbiter must put aside his neutrality and permit himself to be moved by a sympathetic identification sufficiently intense to draw from his mind all that it is capable of giving,—in analysis, patience and creative power. When he resumes his neutral position, he must be able to view with distrust the fruits of this identification and be ready to reject the products of his own best mental efforts. The difficulties of this undertaking are obvious. If it is true that a man in his time must play many parts, it is scarcely given to him to play them all at once.

It is small wonder, then, that failure generally attends the attempt to dispense with the distinct roles traditionally implied in adjudication. What generally occurs in practice is that at some early point a familiar pattern will seem to emerge from the evidence; an accustomed label is waiting for the case and, without awaiting further proofs, this label is promptly assigned to it. It is a mistake to suppose that this premature cataloguing must necessarily result from impatience, prejudice or mental sloth. Often it proceeds from a very understandable desire to bring the hearing into some order and coherence, for without some tentative theory of the case there is no standard of relevance by which testimony may be measured. But what starts as a preliminary diagnosis designed to direct the inquiry tends, quickly and imperceptibly, to become a fixed conclusion, as all that confirms the diagnosis makes a strong imprint on the mind, while all that runs counter to it is received with diverted attention.

An adversary presentation seems the only effective means for combatting this natural human tendency to judge too swiftly in terms of the familiar that which is not yet fully known. The arguments of counsel hold the case, as it were, in suspension between two opposing interpretations of it. While the proper classification of the case is thus kept unresolved, there is time to explore all of its peculiarities and nuances.

These are the contributions made by partisan advocacy during the public hearing of the cause. When we take into account the preparations that must precede the hearing, the essential quality of the advocate's contribution becomes even more apparent. Preceding the hearing, inquiries must be instituted to determine what facts can be proved or seem sufficiently established to warrant a formal test of their truth during the hearing. There must also be a preliminary analysis of the issues, so that the hearing may have form and direction. These preparatory measures are indispensable whether or not the parties involved in the controversy are represented by advocates.

Where that representation is present there is an obvious advantage in the fact that the area of dispute may be greatly reduced by an exchange of written pleadings or by stipulations of counsel. Without the participation of someone who can act responsibly for each of the parties, this essential narrowing of the issues becomes impossible. But here again the true significance of partisan advocacy lies deeper, touching once more the integrity of the adjudicative process itself. It is only through the advocate's participation that the hearing may remain in fact what it purports to be in theory: a public trial of the facts and issues. Each advocate comes to the hearing prepared to present his proofs and arguments, knowing at the same time that his arguments may fail to persuade and that his proofs may be rejected as inadequate. It is a part of his role to absorb these possible disappointments. The deciding tribunal, on the other hand, comes to the hearing uncommitted. It has not represented to the public that any fact can be proved, that any argument is sound, or that any particular way of stating a litigant's case is the most effective expression of its merits.

The matter assumes a very different aspect when the deciding tribunal is compelled to take into its own hands the preparations that must precede the public hearing. In such a case the tribunal cannot truly be said to come to the hearing uncommitted, for it has itself appointed the channels along which the public inquiry is to run. If an unexpected turn in the testimony reveals a miscalculation in the design of these channels, there is no advocate to absorb the blame. The deciding tribunal is under a strong temptation to keep the hearing moving within the boundaries originally set for it. The result may be that the hearing loses its character as an open trial of the facts and issues, and becomes instead a ritual designed to provide public confirmation for what the tribunal considers it has already established in private. When this occurs adjudication acquires the taint affecting all institutions that become subject to manipulation, presenting one aspect to the public, another to knowing participants.

These, then, are the reasons for believing that partisan advocacy plays a vital and essential role in one of the most fundamental procedures of a democratic society. But if we were to put all of these detailed considerations to one side, we should still be confronted by the fact that, in whatever form adjudication may appear, the experienced judge or arbitrator desires and actively seeks to obtain an adversary presentation of the issues. Only when he has had the benefit of intelligent and vigorous advocacy on both sides can he feel fully confident of his decision.

Viewed in this light, the role of the lawyer as a partisan advocate appears not as a regrettable necessity, but as an indispensable part of a larger ordering of affairs. The institution of advocacy is not a concession to the frailties of human nature, but an expression of human insight in the design of a social framework within which man's capacity for impartial judgment can attain its fullest realization.

When advocacy is thus viewed, it becomes clear by what principle limits must be set to partisanship. The advocate plays his role well when zeal for his client's cause promotes a wise and informed decision of the case. He plays his role badly, and trespasses against the obligations of professional responsibility, when his desire to win leads him to muddy the headwaters of decision, when, instead of lending a needed perspective to the controversy, he distorts and obscures its true nature.[b]

IMPLEMENTATION

At the outset, one must ask what is the aim of our system of justice. But, to say the very least, justice is not a concept that lends itself readily to definition.

If we could intuit some aim of justice, the next question would be how effective is the adversarial method in accomplishing that aim. The answer to this question is of critical importance, because here public opinion becomes concerned, and it is to the public that the system of justice must ultimately look for support.

There is no public debate on the aim of the system, which people unthinkingly take for granted. But on the implementation everyone has an opinion. As David Mellinkoff, The Conscience of a Lawyer 10 (1973), explained: "Unlike abstract principle, a system of justice calls for rules to make it work, rules that take a principle off the shelf and dirty it up with people. The rules need explaining to those who don't know them, and they have got to be explained in terms more earthy than truth and beauty and empyrean harmonies. It takes a bit of explaining, for example, to have it understood why under our system of justice a lawyer is not a scoundrel when he pleads the statute of limitations to defeat an honest debt. It is not self-evident even to a dishonest man. It is insufficient and misleading to lace fingers and gravely assure everyone that 'We are searching for truth as much as you do if not more so.' "

Roscoe Pound, The Causes of Popular Dissatisfaction with the Administration of Justice

29 A.B.A.Rep. 395, 404–06 (1906).

A no less potent source of irritation lies in our American exaggerations of the common law contentious procedure. The sporting theory of justice, the "instinct of giving the game fair play,"[2] as Professor Wigmore has put it, is so rooted in the profession in America that most of us take it for a fundamental legal tenet. But it is probably only a survival of the days when

---

[b] See also Ted Finman & Theodore Schneyer, The Role of Bar Association Ethics Opinions in Regulating Lawyer Conduct: A Critique of the Work of the ABA Committee on Ethics and Professional Responsibility, 29 UCLA L.Rev. 67, 156–67 (1981) (arguing that the ABA Committee's own procedures should be more adversarial). See generally Stephan Landsman, Readings on Adversarial Justice: The American Approach to Adjudication (1988).

[2] 1 Wigmore, Evidence, 127.

a lawsuit was a fight between two clans in which change of venue had been taken to the forum. So far from being a fundamental fact of jurisprudence, it is peculiar to Anglo–American law; and it has been strongly curbed in modern English practice. With us, it is not merely in full acceptance, it has been developed and its collateral possibilities have been cultivated to the furthest extent. Hence in America we take it as a matter of course that a judge should be a mere umpire, to pass upon objections and hold counsel to the rules of the game, and that the parties should fight out their own game in their own way without judicial interference. We resent such interference as unfair, even when in the interests of justice. The idea that procedure must of necessity be wholly contentious disfigures our judicial administration at every point. It leads the most conscientious judge to feel that he is merely to decide the contest, as counsel present it, according to the rules of the game, not to search independently for truth and justice. It leads counsel to forget that they are officers of the court and to deal with the rules of law and procedure exactly as the professional football coach with the rules of the sport. It leads to exertion to "get error into the record" rather than to dispose of the controversy finally and upon its merits. It turns witnesses, and especially expert witnesses, into partisans pure and simple. It leads to sensational cross-examinations "to affect credit," which have made the witness stand "the slaughter house of reputations."[1] It prevents the trial court from restraining the bullying of witnesses and creates a general dislike, if not fear, of the witness function which impairs the administration of justice. . . .

The effect of our exaggerated contentious procedure is not only to irritate parties, witnesses and jurors in particular cases, but to give to the whole community a false notion of the purpose and end of law. Hence comes, in large measure, the modern American race to beat the law. If the law is a mere game, neither the players who take part in it nor the public who witness it can be expected to yield to its spirit when their interests are served by evading it. And this is doubly true in a time which requires all institutions to be economically efficient and socially useful. We need not wonder that one part of the community strain their oaths in the jury box and find verdicts against unpopular litigants in the teeth of law and evidence, while another part retain lawyers by the year to advise how to evade what to them are unintelligent and unreasonable restrictions upon necessary modes of doing business. Thus the courts, instituted to administer justice according to law, are made agents or abettors of lawlessness.

WARREN E. BURGER, AGENDA FOR 2000 A.D.—A NEED FOR SYSTEMATIC ANTICIPATION, 70 F.R.D. 83, 91 (1976), reprinted in The Pound Conference: Perspectives on Justice in the Future 23 (1979). At the National Conference on the Causes of Popular Dissatisfaction with the Administration of Justice, held to commemorate the seventieth anniversary

1 2 Wigmore, Evidence, 1112.

of Roscoe Pound's address to the American Bar Association excerpted above, Chief Justice Burger delivered the keynote address. He said: "Nor should we be surprised at the loss of public confidence caused by lawyers' using the courts for their own ends rather than with a consideration of the public interest. If Pound was correct in his analysis that excessive contentiousness was an impediment to fair administration of justice in 1906, I doubt that anyone could prove it is less so today. Correct or not, there is also a widespread feeling that the legal profession and judges are overly tolerant of lawyers who exploit the inherently contentious aspects of the adversary system to their own private advantage at public expense."

Jerome Frank, Courts on Trial

80–81 (1949).

When we say that present-day trial methods are "rational," presumably we mean this: The men who compose our trial courts, judges and juries, in each law-suit conduct an intelligent inquiry into all the practically available evidence, in order to ascertain, as near as may be, the truth about the facts of that suit. That might be called the "investigatory" or "truth" method of trying cases. Such a method can yield no more than a guess, nevertheless an educated guess.

. . . .

. . . Our mode of trials is commonly known as "contentious" or "adversary." It is based on what I would call the "fight" theory, a theory which derives from the origin of trials as substitutes for private out-of-court brawls.

Many lawyers maintain that the "fight" theory and the "truth" theory coincide. They think that the best way for a court to discover the facts in a suit is to have each side strive as hard as it can, in a keenly partisan spirit, to bring to the court's attention the evidence favorable to that side. Macaulay said that we obtain the fairest decision "when two men argue, as unfairly as possible, on opposite sides," for then "it is certain that no important consideration will altogether escape notice."

Unquestionably that view contains a core of good sense. The zealously partisan lawyers sometimes do bring into court evidence which, in a dispassionate inquiry, might be overlooked. Apart from the fact element of the case, the opposed lawyers also illuminate for the court niceties of the legal rules which the judge might otherwise not perceive. The "fight" theory, therefore, has invaluable qualities with which we cannot afford to dispense.

But frequently the partisanship of the opposing lawyers blocks the uncovering of vital evidence or leads to a presentation of vital testimony in a way that distorts it.

Question: (1) To what extent does the Constitution dictate an adversary system, as for example by its case-or-controversy requirement? Cf. John Leubsdorf, Constitutional Civil Procedure, 63 Tex.L.Rev. 579 (1984).

Lassiter v. Department of Social Services

Supreme Court of the United States, 1981.
452 U.S. 18, 101 S.Ct. 2153.

■ JUSTICE STEWART delivered the opinion of the Court.

I

In the late spring of 1975, after hearing evidence that the petitioner, Abby Gail Lassiter, had not provided her infant son William with proper medical care, the District Court of Durham County, N.C., adjudicated him a neglected child and transferred him to the custody of the Durham County Department of Social Services, the respondent here. A year later, Ms. Lassiter was charged with first-degree murder, was convicted of second-degree murder, and began a sentence of 25 to 40 years of imprisonment.[1] In 1978 the Department petitioned the court to terminate Ms. Lassiter's parental rights because, the Department alleged, she "has not had any contact with the child since December of 1975" and "has willfully left the child in foster care for more than two consecutive years without showing that substantial progress has been made in correcting the conditions which led to the removal of the child, or without showing a positive response to the diligent efforts of the Department of Social Services to strengthen her relationship to the child, or to make and follow through with constructive planning for the future of the child."

Ms. Lassiter was served with the petition and with notice that a hearing on it would be held. Although her mother had retained counsel for her in connection with an effort to invalidate the murder conviction, Ms. Lassiter never mentioned the forthcoming hearing to him (or, for that matter, to any other person except, she said, to "someone" in the prison).

---

[1] The North Carolina Court of Appeals, in reviewing the petitioner's conviction, indicated that the murder occurred during an altercation between Ms. Lassiter, her mother, and the deceased:

> "Defendant's mother told [the deceased] to 'come on.' They began to struggle and deceased fell or was knocked to the floor. Defendant's mother was beating deceased with a broom. While deceased was still on the floor and being beaten with the broom, defendant entered the apartment. She went into the kitchen and got a butcher knife. She took the knife and began stabbing the deceased who was still prostrate. The body of deceased had seven stab wounds . . . ." State v. Lassiter, No. 7614SC1054 (June 1, 1977).

After her conviction was affirmed on appeal, Ms. Lassiter sought to attack it collaterally. Among her arguments was that the assistance of her trial counsel had been ineffective because he had failed to "seek to elicit or introduce before the jury the statement made by [Ms. Lassiter's mother,] 'And I did it, I hope she dies.' " Ms. Lassiter's mother had, like Ms. Lassiter, been indicted on a first-degree murder charge; however, the trial court granted the elder Ms. Lassiter's motion for a nonsuit. The North Carolina General Court of Justice, Superior Court Division, denied Ms. Lassiter's motion for collateral relief. File No. 76–CR–3102 (Mar. 20, 1979).

At the behest of the Department of Social Services' attorney, she was brought from prison to the hearing, which was held August 31, 1978. The hearing opened, apparently at the judge's instance, with a discussion of whether Ms. Lassiter should have more time in which to find legal assistance. Since the court concluded that she "has had ample opportunity to seek and obtain counsel prior to the hearing of this matter, and [that] her failure to do so is without just cause," the court did not postpone the proceedings. Ms. Lassiter did not aver that she was indigent, and the court did not appoint counsel for her.

A social worker from the respondent Department was the first witness. She testified that in 1975 the Department "received a complaint from Duke Pediatrics that William had not been followed in the pediatric clinic for medical problems and that they were having difficulty in locating Ms. Lassiter . . . ." She said that in May 1975 a social worker had taken William to the hospital, where doctors asked that he stay "because of breathing difficulties [and] malnutrition and [because] there was a great deal of scarring that indicated that he had a severe infection that had gone untreated." The witness further testified that, except for one "prearranged" visit and a chance meeting on the street, Ms. Lassiter had not seen William after he had come into the State's custody, and that neither Ms. Lassiter nor her mother had "made any contact with the Department of Social Services regarding that child." When asked whether William should be placed in his grandmother's custody, the social worker said he should not, since the grandmother "has indicated to me on a number of occasions that she was not able to take responsibility for the child" and since "I have checked with people in the community and from [Lucille] Lassiter's church who also feel that this additional responsibility would be more than she can handle." The social worker added that William "has not seen his grandmother since the chance meeting in July of '76 and that was the only time."

After the direct examination of the social worker, the judge said:

> "I notice we made extensive findings in June of '75 that you were served with papers and called the social services and told them you weren't coming; and the serious lack of medical treatment. And, as I have said in my findings of the 16th day of June '75, the Court finds that the grandmother, Ms. Lucille Lassiter, mother of Abby Gail Lassiter, filed a complaint on the 8th day of May, 1975, alleging that the daughter often left the children, Candina, Felicia and William L. with her for days without providing money or food while she was gone."

Ms. Lassiter conducted a cross-examination of the social worker, who firmly reiterated her earlier testimony. The judge explained several times, with varying degrees of clarity, that Ms. Lassiter should only ask questions at this stage; many of her questions were disallowed because they were not really questions, but arguments.

Ms. Lassiter herself then testified, under the judge's questioning, that she had properly cared for William. Under cross-examination, she said that she had seen William more than five or six times after he had been taken from her custody and that, if William could not be with her, she wanted him to be with her mother since "He knows us. Children know they family. . . . They know they people, they know they family and that child knows us anywhere. . . . I got four more other children. Three girls and a boy and they know they little brother when they see him."

Ms. Lassiter's mother was then called as a witness. She denied, under the questioning of the judge, that she had filed the complaint against Ms. Lassiter, and on cross-examination she denied both having failed to visit William when he was in the State's custody and having said that she could not care for him.

The court found that Ms. Lassiter "has not contacted the Department of Social Services about her child since December, 1975, has not expressed any concern for his care and welfare, and has made no efforts to plan for his future." Because Ms. Lassiter thus had "wilfully failed to maintain concern or responsibility for the welfare of the minor," and because it was "in the best interests of the minor," the court terminated Ms. Lassiter's status as William's parent.[2]

On appeal, Ms. Lassiter argued only that, because she was indigent, the Due Process Clause of the Fourteenth Amendment entitled her to the assistance of counsel, and that the trial court had therefore erred in not requiring the State to provide counsel for her. The North Carolina Court of Appeals decided that "[w]hile this State action does invade a protected area of individual privacy, the invasion is not so serious or unreasonable as to compel us to hold that appointment of counsel for indigent parents is constitutionally mandated." In re Lassiter, 43 N.C.App. 525, 527, 259 S.E.2d 336, 337. The Supreme Court of North Carolina summarily denied Ms. Lassiter's application for discretionary review, 299 N.C. 120, 262 S.E.2d 6, and we granted certiorari to consider the petitioner's claim under the Due Process Clause of the Fourteenth Amendment, 449 U.S. 819, 101 S.Ct. 70.

II

For all its consequence, "due process" has never been, and perhaps can never be, precisely defined. "[U]nlike some legal rules," this Court has said, due process "is not a technical conception with a fixed content unrelated to time, place and circumstances." Cafeteria Workers v. McElroy, 367 U.S. 886, 895, 81 S.Ct. 1743, 1748. Rather, the phrase expresses the requirement of "fundamental fairness," a requirement whose meaning can be as opaque as its importance is lofty. Applying the Due Process Clause is therefore an uncertain enterprise which must discover what "fundamental fairness" consists of in a particular situation by first considering any

[2] The petition had also asked that the parental rights of the putative father, William Boykin, be terminated. Boykin was not married to Ms. Lassiter, he had never contributed to William's financial support, and indeed he denied that he was William's father. The court granted the petition to terminate his alleged parental status.

relevant precedents and then by assessing the several interests that are at stake.

A

The pre-eminent generalization that emerges from this Court's precedents on an indigent's right to appointed counsel is that such a right has been recognized to exist only where the litigant may lose his physical liberty if he loses the litigation. Thus, when the Court overruled the principle of Betts v. Brady, 316 U.S. 455, 62 S.Ct. 1252, that counsel in criminal trials need be appointed only where the circumstances in a given case demand it, the Court did so in the case of a man sentenced to prison for five years. Gideon v. Wainwright, 372 U.S. 335, 83 S.Ct. 792. And thus Argersinger v. Hamlin, 407 U.S. 25, 92 S.Ct. 2006, established that counsel must be provided before any indigent may be sentenced to prison, even where the crime is petty and the prison term brief.

That it is the defendant's interest in personal freedom, and not simply the special Sixth and Fourteenth Amendments right to counsel in criminal cases, which triggers the right to appointed counsel is demonstrated by the Court's announcement in In re Gault, 387 U.S. 1, 87 S.Ct. 1428, that "the Due Process Clause of the Fourteenth Amendment requires that in respect of proceedings to determine delinquency *which may result in commitment to an institution in which the juvenile's freedom is curtailed,*" the juvenile has a right to appointed counsel even though proceedings may be styled "civil" and not "criminal." Id., at 41, 87 S.Ct., at 1451 (emphasis added). . . .

Significantly, as a litigant's interest in personal liberty diminishes, so does his right to appointed counsel. In Gagnon v. Scarpelli, 411 U.S. 778, 93 S.Ct. 1756, the Court gauged the due process rights of a previously sentenced probationer at a probation-revocation hearing. In Morrissey v. Brewer, 408 U.S. 471, 480, 92 S.Ct. 2593, 2599, which involved an analogous hearing to revoke parole, the Court had said: "Revocation deprives an individual, not of the absolute liberty to which every citizen is entitled, but only of the conditional liberty properly dependent on observance of special parole restrictions." Relying on that discussion, the Court in Scarpelli declined to hold that indigent probationers have, per se, a right to counsel at revocation hearings, and instead left the decision whether counsel should be appointed to be made on a case-by-case basis.

Finally, the Court has refused to extend the right to appointed counsel to include prosecutions which, though criminal, do not result in the defendant's loss of personal liberty. . . .

In sum, the Court's precedents speak with one voice about what "fundamental fairness" has meant when the Court has considered the right to appointed counsel, and we thus draw from them the presumption that an indigent litigant has a right to appointed counsel only when, if he loses, he may be deprived of his physical liberty. It is against this presumption that all the other elements in the due process decision must be measured.

B

The case of Mathews v. Eldridge, 424 U.S. 319, 335, 96 S.Ct. 893, 903 [(1976)], propounds three elements to be evaluated in deciding what due process requires, viz., the private interests at stake, the government's interest, and the risk that the procedures used will lead to erroneous decisions. We must balance these elements against each other, and then set their net weight in the scales against the presumption that there is a right to appointed counsel only where the indigent, if he is unsuccessful, may lose his personal freedom.

This Court's decisions have by now made plain beyond the need for multiple citation that a parent's desire for and right to "the companionship, care, custody, and management of his or her children" is an important interest that "undeniably warrants deference and, absent a powerful countervailing interest, protection." Stanley v. Illinois, 405 U.S. 645, 651, 92 S.Ct. 1208, 1212. Here the State has sought not simply to infringe upon that interest but to end it. If the State prevails, it will have worked a unique kind of deprivation. [Citations omitted.] A parent's interest in the accuracy and justice of the decision to terminate his or her parental status is, therefore, a commanding one.

Since the State has an urgent interest in the welfare of the child, it shares the parent's interest in an accurate and just decision. For this reason, the State may share the indigent parent's interest in the availability of appointed counsel. If, as our adversary system presupposes, accurate and just results are most likely to be obtained through the equal contest of opposed interests, the State's interest in the child's welfare may perhaps best be served by a hearing in which both the parent and the State acting for the child are represented by counsel, without whom the contest of interests may become unwholesomely unequal. North Carolina itself acknowledges as much by providing that where a parent files a written answer to a termination petition, the State must supply a lawyer to represent the child. N.C.Gen.Stat. § 7A–289.29 (Supp.1979).

The State's interests, however, clearly diverge from the parent's insofar as the State wishes the termination decision to be made as economically as possible and thus wants to avoid both the expense of appointed counsel and the cost of the lengthened proceedings his presence may cause. But though the State's pecuniary interest is legitimate, it is hardly significant enough to overcome private interests as important as those here, particularly in light of the concession in the respondent's brief that the "potential costs of appointed counsel in termination proceedings . . . is [sic] admittedly de minimis compared to the costs in all criminal actions."

Finally, consideration must be given to the risk that a parent will be erroneously deprived of his or her child because the parent is not represented by counsel. North Carolina law now seeks to assure accurate decisions by establishing the following procedures: A petition to terminate parental rights may be filed only by a parent seeking the termination of the other parent's rights, by a county department of social services or licensed child-placing agency with custody of the child, or by a person with whom the child has lived continuously for the two years preceding the petition. § 7A–289.24. A petition must describe facts sufficient to warrant a finding that one of the grounds for termination exists, § 7A–289.25(6), and the parent must be notified of the petition and given 30 days in which to file a written answer to it, § 7A–289.27. If that answer denies a material allegation, the court must, as has been noted, appoint a lawyer as the child's guardian ad litem and must conduct a special hearing to resolve the issues raised by the petition and the answer. § 7A–289.29. If the parent files no answer, "the court shall issue an order terminating all parental and custodial rights . . . ; provided the court shall order a hearing on the petition and may examine the petitioner or others on the facts alleged in the petition." § 7A–289.28. Findings of fact are made by a court sitting without a jury and must "be based on clear, cogent, and convincing evidence." § 7A–289.30. Any party may appeal who gives notice of appeal within 10 days after the hearing. § 7A–289.34.[4]

The respondent argues that the subject of a termination hearing—the parent's relationship with her child—far from being abstruse, technical, or unfamiliar, is one as to which the parent must be uniquely well informed and to which the parent must have given prolonged thought. The respondent also contends that a termination hearing is not likely to produce difficult points of evidentiary law, or even of substantive law, since the evidentiary problems peculiar to criminal trials are not present and since the standards for termination are not complicated. In fact, the respondent reports, the North Carolina Departments of Social Services are themselves sometimes represented at termination hearings by social workers instead of by lawyers.[5]

Yet the ultimate issues with which a termination hearing deals are not always simple, however commonplace they may be. Expert medical and psychiatric testimony, which few parents are equipped to understand and fewer still to confute, is sometimes presented. The parents are likely to be people with little education, who have had uncommon difficulty in dealing with life, and who are, at the hearing, thrust into a distressing and disorienting situation. That these factors may combine to overwhelm an uncounseled parent is evident from the findings some courts have made.

---

[4] The respondent also points out that parental termination hearings commonly occur only after a custody proceeding in which the child has judicially been found to be abused, neglected, or dependent, and that an indigent parent has a right to be represented by appointed counsel at the custody hearing. § 7A–587.

Ms. Lassiter's hearing occurred before some of these provisions were enacted. She did not, for instance, have the benefit of the "clear, cogent, and convincing" evidentiary standard, nor did she have counsel at the hearing in which William was taken from her custody.

[5] Both the respondent and the Columbia Journal of Law and Social Problems, 4 Colum.J.L. & Soc.Prob. 230 (1968), have conducted surveys purporting to reveal whether the presence of counsel reduces the number of erroneous determinations in parental termination proceedings. Unfortunately, neither survey goes beyond presenting statistics which, standing alone, are unilluminating. The Journal note does, however, report that it questioned the New York Family Court judges who preside over parental termination hearings and found that 72.2% of them agreed that when a parent is unrepresented, it becomes more difficult to conduct a fair hearing (11.1% of the judges disagreed); 66.7% thought it became difficult to develop the facts (22.2% disagreed).

[Citations omitted.] Thus, courts have generally held that the State must appoint counsel for indigent parents at termination proceedings. [Citations omitted.] The respondent is able to point to no presently authoritative case, except for the North Carolina judgment now before us, holding that an indigent parent has no due process right to appointed counsel in termination proceedings.

C

The dispositive question, which must now be addressed, is whether the three Eldridge factors, when weighed against the presumption that there is no right to appointed counsel in the absence of at least a potential deprivation of physical liberty, suffice to rebut that presumption and thus to lead to the conclusion that the Due Process Clause requires the appointment of counsel when a State seeks to terminate an indigent's parental status. To summarize the above discussion of the Eldridge factors: the parent's interest is an extremely important one (and may be supplemented by the dangers of criminal liability inherent in some termination proceedings); the State shares with the parent an interest in a correct decision, has a relatively weak pecuniary interest, and, in some but not all cases, has a possibly stronger interest in informal procedures; and the complexity of the proceeding and the incapacity of the uncounseled parent could be, but would not always be, great enough to make the risk of an erroneous deprivation of the parent's rights insupportably high.

If, in a given case, the parent's interests were at their strongest, the State's interests were at their weakest, and the risks of error were at their peak, it could not be said that the Eldridge factors did not overcome the presumption against the right to appointed counsel, and that due process did not therefore require the appointment of counsel. But since the Eldridge factors will not always be so distributed, and since "due process is not so rigid as to require that the significant interests in informality, flexibility and economy must always be sacrificed," Gagnon v. Scarpelli, 411 U.S., at 788, 93 S.Ct., at 1762, neither can we say that the Constitution requires the appointment of counsel in every parental termination proceeding. We therefore adopt the standard found appropriate in Gagnon v. Scarpelli, and leave the decision whether due process calls for the appointment of counsel for indigent parents in termination proceedings to be answered in the first instance by the trial court, subject, of course, to appellate review. See, e.g., Wood v. Georgia, 450 U.S. 261, 101 S.Ct. 1097.

III

Here, as in Scarpelli, "[i]t is neither possible nor prudent to attempt to formulate a precise and detailed set of guidelines to be followed in determining when the providing of counsel is necessary to meet the applicable due process requirements," since here, as in that case, "[t]he facts and circumstances . . . are susceptible of almost infinite variation . . . ." 411 U.S., at 790, 93 S.Ct., at 1764. Nevertheless, because child-custody litigation must be concluded as rapidly as is consistent with fairness,[7] we decide today whether the trial judge denied Ms. Lassiter due process of law when he did not appoint counsel for her.

The respondent represents that the petition to terminate Ms. Lassiter's parental rights contained no allegations of neglect or abuse upon which criminal charges could be based, and hence Ms. Lassiter could not well have argued that she required counsel for that reason. The Department of Social Services was represented at the hearing by counsel, but no expert witnesses testified and the case presented no specially troublesome points of law, either procedural or substantive. While hearsay evidence was no doubt admitted, and while Ms. Lassiter no doubt left incomplete her defense that the Department had not adequately assisted her in rekindling her interest in her son, the weight of the evidence that she had few sparks of such interest was sufficiently great that the presence of counsel for Ms. Lassiter could not have made a determinative difference. True, a lawyer might have done more with the argument that William should live with Ms. Lassiter's mother—but that argument was quite explicitly made by both Lassiters, and the evidence that the elder Ms. Lassiter had said she could not handle another child, that the social worker's investigation had led to a similar conclusion, and that the grandmother had displayed scant interest in the child once he had been removed from her daughter's custody was, though controverted, sufficiently substantial that the absence of counsel's guidance on this point did not render the proceedings fundamentally unfair.[8] Finally, a court deciding whether due process requires the appointment of counsel need not ignore a parent's plain demonstration that she is not interested in attending a hearing. Here, the trial court had previously found that Ms. Lassiter had expressly declined to appear at the 1975 child custody hearing, Ms. Lassiter had not even bothered to speak to her retained lawyer after being notified of the termination hearing, and the court specifically found that Ms. Lassiter's failure to make an effort to contest the termination proceeding was without cause. In view of all these circumstances, we hold that the trial court did not err in failing to appoint counsel for Ms. Lassiter.

IV

In its Fourteenth Amendment, our Constitution imposes on the States the standards necessary to ensure that judicial proceedings are fundamentally fair. A wise public policy, however, may require that higher standards be adopted than those minimally tolerable under the Constitution. . . . The Court's opinion today in no way implies that the standards increasing-

[7] According to the respondent's brief, William Lassiter is now living "in a pre-adoptive home with foster parents committed to formal adoption to become his legal parents." He cannot be legally adopted, nor can his status otherwise be finally clarified, until this litigation ends.

[8] Ms. Lassiter's argument here that her mother should have been given custody of William is hardly consistent with her argument in the collateral attack on her murder conviction that she was innocent because her mother was guilty. See n.1, supra.

ly urged by informed public opinion and now widely followed by the States are other than enlightened and wise.

For the reasons stated in this opinion, the judgment is affirmed.

It is so ordered.

■ CHIEF JUSTICE BURGER, concurring.

I join the Court's opinion and add only a few words to emphasize a factor I believe is misconceived by the dissenters. The purpose of the termination proceeding at issue here was not "punitive." . . . On the contrary, its purpose was *protective* of the child's best interests. . . .

■ JUSTICE BLACKMUN, with whom JUSTICE BRENNAN and JUSTICE MARSHALL join, dissenting.

The Court today denies an indigent mother the representation of counsel in a judicial proceeding initiated by the State of North Carolina to terminate her parental rights with respect to her youngest child. The Court most appropriately recognizes that the mother's interest is a "commanding one," . . . and it finds no countervailing state interest of even remotely comparable significance . . . . Nonetheless, the Court avoids what seems to me the obvious conclusion that due process requires the presence of counsel for a parent threatened with judicial termination of parental rights, and, instead, revives an ad hoc approach thoroughly discredited nearly 20 years ago in Gideon v. Wainwright, 372 U.S. 335, 83 S.Ct. 792 (1963). Because I believe that the unique importance of a parent's interest in the care and custody of his or her child cannot constitutionally be extinguished through formal judicial proceedings without the benefit of counsel, I dissent.

I

. . . .

It is not disputed that state intervention to terminate the relationship between petitioner and her child must be accomplished by procedures meeting the requisites of the Due Process Clause. Nor is there any doubt here about the kind of procedure North Carolina has prescribed. North Carolina law requires notice and a trial-type hearing before the State on its own initiative may sever the bonds of parenthood. The decisionmaker is a judge, the rules of evidence are in force, and the State is represented by counsel. The question, then, is whether proceedings in this mold, that relate to a subject so vital, can comport with fundamental fairness when the defendant parent remains unrepresented by counsel. As the Court today properly acknowledges, our consideration of the process due in this context, as in others, must rely on a balancing of the competing private and public interests, an approach succinctly described in Mathews v. Eldridge, 424 U.S. 319, 335, 96 S.Ct. 893, 903 (1976). . . .

A

At stake here is "the interest of a parent in the companionship, care, custody, and management of his or her children." Stanley v. Illinois, 405

U.S. 645, 651, 92 S.Ct. 1208, 1212 (1972). This interest occupies a unique place in our legal culture, given the centrality of family life as the focus for personal meaning and responsibility. . . . Accordingly, although the Constitution is verbally silent on the specific subject of families, freedom of personal choice in matters of family life long has been viewed as a fundamental liberty interest worthy of protection under the Fourteenth Amendment. . . .

In this case, the State's aim is not simply to influence the parent-child relationship but to *extinguish* it. A termination of parental rights is both total and irrevocable. Unlike other custody proceedings, it leaves the parent with no right to visit or communicate with the child, to participate in, or even to know about, any important decision affecting the child's religious, educational, emotional, or physical development. . . .

. . . .

Rather than opting for the insensitive presumption that incarceration is the only loss of liberty sufficiently onerous to justify a right to appointed counsel, I would abide by the Court's enduring commitment to examine the relationships among the interests on both sides, and the appropriateness of counsel in the specific type of proceeding. The fundamental significance of the liberty interest at stake in a parental termination proceeding is undeniable, and I would find this first portion of the due process balance weighing heavily in favor of refined procedural protections. The second Eldridge factor, namely, the risk of error in the procedure provided by the State, must then be reviewed with some care.

B

The method chosen by North Carolina to extinguish parental rights resembles in many respects a criminal prosecution. Unlike the probation revocation procedure reviewed in Gagnon v. Scarpelli, on which the Court so heavily relies, the termination procedure is distinctly formal and adversarial. . . .

In addition, the proceeding has an obvious accusatory and punitive focus. In moving to terminate a parent's rights, the State has concluded that it no longer will try to preserve the family unit, but instead will marshal an array of public resources to establish that the parent-child separation must be made permanent.[10] The State has legal representation through the county attorney. This lawyer has access to public records concerning the family and to professional social workers who are empowered to investigate the family situation and to testify against the parent. The State's legal representative may also call upon experts in family relations, psychology, and medicine to bolster the State's case. And, of course, the State's counsel himself is an expert in the legal standards and

[10] Significantly, the parent's rights and interests are not mentioned at all under the statement of purpose for the North Carolina termination statute. See N.C.Gen.Stat. § 7A–289.22 (Supp.1979). In contrast, in abuse, neglect, and dependency proceedings the State has a statutory obligation to keep a family together whenever possible. § 7A–542. . . .

. . . .

techniques employed at the termination proceeding, including the methods of cross-examination.

In each of these respects, the procedure devised by the State vastly differs from the informal and rehabilitative probation revocation decision in Scarpelli . . . . Indeed, the State here has prescribed virtually all the attributes of a formal trial as befits the severity of the loss at stake in the termination decision—every attribute, that is, except counsel for the defendant parent. The provision of counsel for the parent would not alter the character of the proceeding, which is already adversarial, formal, and quintessentially legal. It, however, would diminish the prospect of an erroneous termination, a prospect that is inherently substantial, given the gross disparity in power and resources between the State and the uncounseled indigent parent.

The prospect of error is enhanced in light of the legal standard against which the defendant parent is judged. As demonstrated here, that standard commonly adds another dimension to the complexity of the termination proceeding. Rather than focusing on the facts of isolated acts or omissions, the State's charges typically address the nature and quality of complicated ongoing relationships among parent, child, other relatives, and even unrelated parties. In the case at bar, the State's petition accused petitioner of two of the several grounds authorizing termination of parental rights under North Carolina law:

> "That [petitioner] has *without cause,* failed to establish or maintain *concern or responsibility* as to the child's welfare.
>
> . . . .
>
> "That [petitioner] has *willfully* left the child in foster care for more than two consecutive years without showing that *substantial progress has been made* in correcting the conditions which led to the removal of the child [for neglect], or without showing a *positive response* to the *diligent efforts of the Department of Social Services* to strengthen her relationship to the child, or *to make and follow through with constructive planning* for the future of the child." (Emphasis supplied.) Juvenile Petition ¶¶ 6, 7, App. 3.

The legal issues posed by the State's petition are neither simple nor easily defined. The standard is imprecise and open to the subjective values of the judge.[13] A parent seeking to prevail against the State must be prepared to adduce evidence about his or her personal abilities and lack of fault, as well as proof of progress and foresight as a parent that the State would deem adequate and improved over the situation underlying a previous adverse judgment of child neglect. The parent cannot possibly succeed

[13] Under North Carolina law, there is a further stage to the termination inquiry. Should the trial court determine that one or more of the conditions authorizing termination has been established, it then must consider whether the best interests of the child require maintenance of the parent-child relationship. N.C.Gen.Stat. § 7A–289.31(a) (Supp.1979).

This Court more than once has adverted to the fact that the "best interests of the child" standard offers little guidance to judges, and may effectively encourage them to rely on their own personal values. . . .

without being able to identify material issues, develop defenses, gather and present sufficient supporting nonhearsay evidence, and conduct cross-examination of adverse witnesses.

The Court, of course, acknowledges . . . that these tasks "may combine to overwhelm an uncounseled parent." I submit that that is a profound understatement. Faced with a formal accusatory adjudication, with an adversary—the State—that commands great investigative and prosecutorial resources, with standards that involve ill-defined notions of fault and adequate parenting, and with the inevitable tendency of a court to apply subjective values or to defer to the State's "expertise," the defendant parent plainly is outstripped if he or she is without the assistance of " 'the guiding hand of counsel.' " In re Gault, 387 U.S., at 36, 87 S.Ct., at 1448, quoting Powell v. Alabama, 287 U.S. 45, 69, 53 S.Ct. 55, 64 (1932). When the parent is indigent, lacking in education, and easily intimidated by figures of authority, the imbalance may well become insuperable.

The risk of error thus is severalfold. The parent who actually has achieved the improvement or quality of parenting the State would require may be unable to establish this fact. The parent who has failed in these regards may be unable to demonstrate cause, absence of willfulness, or lack of agency diligence as justification. And errors of fact or law in the State's case may go unchallenged and uncorrected.[15] Given the weight of the interests at stake, this risk of error assumes extraordinary proportions. By intimidation, inarticulateness, or confusion, a parent can lose forever all contact and involvement with his or her offspring.

C

The final factor to be considered, the interests claimed for the State, do not tip the scale against providing appointed counsel in this context. The State hardly is in a position to assert here that it seeks the informality of a rehabilitative or educative proceeding into which counsel for the parent would inject an unwelcome adversarial edge. As the Assistant Attorney General of North Carolina declared before this Court, once the State moves for termination, it "has made a decision that the child cannot go home and should not go home. It no longer has an obligation to try and restore that family." Tr. of Oral Arg. 40.

---

[15] See Parent Representation Study, [4 Colum.J.L. & Soc.Probs.] at 241 (parents appearing in Kings County, N.Y., Family Court, charged with neglect and represented by counsel, had higher rate of dismissed petitions, 25% to 7.9%, and lower rate of neglect adjudications, 62.5% to 79.5%, than similarly charged parents appearing without counsel); Brief for Respondent 38–39, 25a–31a (study of state-initiated termination actions in 73 North Carolina counties; parent prevailed in 5.5% of proceedings where represented by counsel, and in 0.15% of proceedings where unrepresented).

While these statistics hardly are dispositive, I do not share the Court's view, ante, at . . . n.5, that they are "unilluminating." Since no evidence in either study indicates that the defendant parent who can retain or is offered counsel is less culpable than the one who appears unrepresented, it seems reasonable to infer that a sizable number of cases against unrepresented parents end in termination solely because of the absence of counsel. In addition, as the Court acknowledges . . . , the judges who preside over termination hearings perceive them as less fair when the parent is without counsel.

The State may, and does, properly assert a legitimate interest in promoting the physical and emotional well-being of its minor children. But this interest is not served by terminating the rights of any concerned, responsible parent. Indeed, because North Carolina is committed to "protect[ing] all children from the unnecessary severance of a relationship with biological or legal parents," § 7A–289.22(2), "the State spites its own articulated goals when it needlessly separates" the parent from the child. Stanley v. Illinois, 405 U.S., at 653, 92 S.Ct., at 1213.

The State also has an interest in avoiding the cost and administrative inconvenience that might accompany a right to appointed counsel. But, as the Court acknowledges, the State's fiscal interest "is hardly significant enough to overcome private interests as important as those here." . . . The State's financial concern indeed is a limited one, for the right to appointed counsel may well be restricted to those termination proceedings that are instituted by the State. Moreover, no difficult line-drawing problem would arise with respect to other types of civil proceedings. The instant due process analysis takes full account of the fundamental nature of the parental interest, the permanency of the threatened deprivation, the gross imbalance between the resources employed by the prosecuting State and those available to the indigent parent, and the relatively insubstantial cost of furnishing counsel. An absence of any one of these factors might yield a different result. But where, as here, the threatened loss of liberty is severe and absolute, the State's role is so clearly adversarial and punitive, and the cost involved is relatively slight, there is no sound basis for refusing to recognize the right to counsel as a requisite of due process in a proceeding initiated by the State to terminate parental rights.

II

A

The Court's analysis is markedly similar to mine; it, too, analyzes the three factors listed in Mathews v. Eldridge, and it, too, finds the private interest weighty, the procedure devised by the State fraught with risks of error, and the countervailing governmental interest insubstantial. Yet, rather than follow this balancing process to its logical conclusion, the Court abruptly pulls back and announces that a defendant parent must await a case-by-case determination of his or her need for counsel. . . . The flexibility of due process . . . requires case-by-case consideration of different decisionmaking *contexts,* not of different *litigants* within a given context. . . . [The result should be] a rule that has general application to similarly situated cases.

. . . .

There are sound reasons for this. Procedural norms are devised to ensure that justice may be done in every case, and to protect litigants against unpredictable and unchecked adverse governmental action. Through experience with decisions in varied situations over time, lessons emerge that reflect a general understanding as to what is minimally necessary to assure fair play. Such lessons are best expressed to have general application which guarantees the predictability and uniformity that underlie our society's commitment to the rule of law. By endorsing, instead, a retrospective review of the trial record of each particular defendant parent, the Court today undermines the very rationale on which this concept of general fairness is based.

Moreover, the case-by-case approach advanced by the Court itself entails serious dangers for the interests at stake and the general administration of justice. The Court assumes that a review of the record will establish whether a defendant, proceeding without counsel, has suffered an unfair disadvantage. But in the ordinary case, this simply is not so. The pleadings and transcript of an uncounseled termination proceeding at most will show the obvious blunders and omissions of the defendant parent. Determining the difference legal representation would have made becomes possible only through imagination, investigation, and legal research focused on the particular case. Even if the reviewing court can embark on such an enterprise in each case, it might be hard pressed to discern the significance of failures to challenge the State's evidence or to develop a satisfactory defense. Such failures, however, often cut to the essence of the fairness of the trial, and a court's inability to compensate for them effectively eviscerates the presumption of innocence. Because a parent acting pro se is even more likely to be unaware of controlling legal standards and practices, and unskilled in garnering relevant facts, it is difficult, if not impossible, to conclude that the typical case has been adequately presented. [Citation omitted.][19]

Assuming that this ad hoc review were adequate to ensure fairness, it is likely to be both cumbersome and costly. And because such review involves constitutional rights implicated by state adjudications, it necessarily will result in increased federal interference in state proceedings. . . .

B

The problem of inadequate representation is painfully apparent in the present case. Petitioner, Abby Gail Lassiter, is the mother of five children. The State moved to remove the fifth child, William, from petitioner's care on the grounds of parental neglect. Although petitioner received notice of the removal proceedings, she did not appear at the hearing and was not represented. In May 1975, the State's District Court adjudicated William to be neglected under North Carolina law and placed him in the custody of the Durham County Department of Social Services. At some point, petitioner evidently arranged for the other four children to reside with and be cared for by her mother, Mrs. Lucille Lassiter. They remain under their grandmother's care at the present time.

---

[19] Of course, the case-by-case approach announced by the Court today places an even heavier burden on the trial court, which will be required to determine in advance what difference legal representation might make. A trial judge will be obligated to examine the State's documentary and testimonial evidence well before the hearing so as to reach an informed decision about the need for counsel in time to allow adequate preparation of the parent's case.

As the Court notes . . . , petitioner did not visit William after July 1976. She was unable to do so, for she was imprisoned as a result of her conviction for second-degree murder. In December 1977, she was visited in prison by a Durham County social worker who advised her that the Department planned to terminate her parental rights with respect to William. Petitioner immediately expressed strong opposition to that plan and indicated a desire to place the child with his grandmother . . . . After receiving a summons, a copy of the State's termination petition, and notice that a termination hearing would be held in August 1978, petitioner informed her prison guards about the legal proceeding. They took no steps to assist her in obtaining legal representation . . . , nor was she informed that she had a right to counsel.[21] Under these circumstances, it scarcely would be appropriate, or fair, to find that petitioner had knowingly and intelligently waived a right to counsel.

At the termination hearing, the State's sole witness was the county worker who had met petitioner on the one occasion at the prison. This worker had been assigned to William's case in August 1977, yet much of her testimony concerned events prior to that date; she represented these events as contained in the agency record. . . . Petitioner failed to uncover this weakness in the worker's testimony. That is hardly surprising, for there is no indication that an agency record was introduced into evidence or was present in court, or that petitioner or the grandmother ever had an opportunity to review any such record. The social worker also testified about her conversations with members of the community. In this hearsay testimony, the witness reported the opinion of others that the grandmother could not handle the additional responsibility of caring for the fifth child. . . . There is no indication that these community members were unavailable to testify, and the County Attorney did not justify the admission of the hearsay. Petitioner made no objection to its admission.

The court gave petitioner an opportunity to cross-examine the social worker . . . , but she apparently did not understand that cross-examination required questioning rather than declarative statements. At this point, the judge became noticeably impatient with petitioner.[22] Petitioner then

---

[21] During her imprisonment, petitioner had spoken with an attorney concerning her criminal conviction. She did not discuss the termination proceeding with this lawyer, and he has stated under oath that in view of her indigency he would not have been interested in representing her at that proceeding even had she asked him to do so. . . .

[22] Hearing Tr. 19–20:

"THE COURT: All right. Do you want to ask her any questions?

"[PETITIONER]: About what? About what she—

"THE COURT: About this child.

"[PETITIONER]: Oh, yes.

"THE COURT: All right. Go ahead.

"[PETITIONER]: The only thing I know is that when you say—

"THE COURT: I don't want you to testify.

"[PETITIONER]: Okay.

"THE COURT: I want to know whether you want to cross-examine her or ask any questions.

took the stand, and testified that she wanted William to live with his grandmother and his siblings. The judge questioned her for a brief period, and expressed open disbelief at one of her answers.[23] The final witness was the grandmother. Both the judge and the County Attorney questioned her. She denied having expressed unwillingness to take William into her home, and vehemently contradicted the social worker's statement that she had complained to the Department about her daughter's neglect of the child.[24] Petitioner was not told that she could question her mother, and did not do so.[25] The County Attorney made a closing argument . . . , and the judge

---

"[PETITIONER]: Yes, I want to. Well, you know, the only thing I know about is my part that I know about it. I know—

"THE COURT: I am not talking about what you know. I want to know if you want to ask her any questions or not.

"[PETITIONER]: About that?

"THE COURT: Yes. Do you understand the nature of this proceeding?

"[PETITIONER]: Yes.

"THE COURT: And that is to terminate any rights you have to the child and place it for adoption, if necessary.

"[PETITIONER]: Yes, I know.

"THE COURT: Are there any questions you want to ask her about what she has testified to?

"[PETITIONER]: Yes.

"THE COURT: All right. Go ahead.

"[PETITIONER]: I want to know why you think you are going to turn my child over to a foster home? He knows my mother and he knows all of us. He knows her and he knows all of us.

"THE COURT: Who is he?

"[PETITIONER]: My son, William.

"[SOCIAL WORKER]: Ms. Lassiter, your son has been in foster care since May of 1975 and since that time—

"[PETITIONER]: Yeah, yeah and I didn't know anything about it either."

23 Id., at 30:

"[THE COURT]: Did you know that your mother filed a complaint on the 8th day of May, 1975 . . . ?

"A: No, 'cause she said she didn't file no complaint.

"[THE COURT]: That was some ghost who came up here and filed it I suppose."

The judge concluded his questioning by saying to the County Attorney: "All right, Mr. Odom, see what you can do." Id., at 36.

24 This latter denial produced the following reaction from the court, id., at 55:

"Q [from respondent]: Did you tell Ms. Mangum on the 8th day of May, 1975, that when your daughter was in the hospital having William that she left the children in the cold house with no heat?

"A: No, sir, no, sir, unh unh, no, sir.

"[PETITIONER]: That's a lie.

"A: No, sir, no, sir. God knows, I'll raise my right hand to God and die saying that. Somebody else told that.

"[THE COURT]: I wish you wouldn't talk like that it scares me to be in the same room with you."

25 The judge had initiated the examination of Mrs. Lassiter; subsequently he expressed exasperation with the rambling quality of her answers, id., at 52:

then asked petitioner if she had any final remarks. She responded: "Yes. I don't think it's right." [Hearing Tr.] 61.

It is perhaps understandable that the District Court Judge experienced difficulty and exasperation in conducting this hearing. But both the difficulty and the exasperation are attributable in large measure, if not entirely, to the lack of counsel. An experienced attorney might have translated petitioner's reaction and emotion into several substantive legal arguments. The State charged petitioner with failing to arrange a "constructive plan" for her child's future or to demonstrate a "positive response" to the Department's intervention. A defense would have been that petitioner had arranged for the child to be cared for properly by his grandmother, and evidence might have been adduced to demonstrate the adequacy of the grandmother's care of the other children. [Citations omitted.] The Department's own "diligence" in promoting the family's integrity was never put in issue during the hearing, yet it is surely significant in light of petitioner's incarceration and lack of access to her child. [Citations omitted.] Finally, the asserted willfulness of petitioner's lack of concern could obviously have been attacked since she was physically unable to regain custody or perhaps even to receive meaningful visits during 21 of the 24 months preceding the action. [Citation omitted.]

III

Petitioner plainly has not led the life of the exemplary citizen or model parent. It may well be that if she were accorded competent legal representation, the ultimate result in this particular case would be the same. But the issue before the Court is not petitioner's character; it is whether she was given a meaningful opportunity to be heard when the State moved to terminate absolutely her parental rights.[26] In light of the unpursued avenues of defense, and of the experience petitioner underwent at the hearing, I find virtually incredible the Court's conclusion today that her termination proceeding was fundamentally fair. . . .

. . . .

■ JUSTICE STEVENS, dissenting.

. . . .

"THE COURT: I tell you what, let's just stop all this. You question her, please. Just answer his questions. We'll be here all day at this rate. I mean, we are just wasting time, we're skipping from one subject to another—

"CROSS EXAMINATION BY [RESPONDENT]: . . . ."

[26] Unfortunately, the Court does not confine itself to the issue at hand. By going outside the official record of this case . . . to unearth and recite details of petitioner's second-degree murder conviction set forth in an unpublished state appellate opinion, [citations omitted], the Court apparently believes it has contributed evidence relevant to petitioner's fitness as a parent, and perhaps to the fitness of petitioner's mother as well. But while some States retain statutes permitting parental rights to be terminated upon a parent's criminal conviction, North Carolina is not among them. [Citations omitted.] Reliance on such evidence is likely to encourage the kind of subjective value judgments that an adversarial judicial proceeding is meant to avoid. [Does the context matter? For the background story of the Lassiter case, see Elizabeth G. Thornburg, "The Story of Lassiter: The Importance of Counsel in an Adversary System," in Civil Procedure Stories 509 (Kevin M. Clermont ed., 2d ed. 2008).—Ed.]

In my opinion the reasons supporting the conclusion that the Due Process Clause of the Fourteenth Amendment entitles the defendant in a criminal case to representation by counsel apply with equal force to a case of this kind. The issue is one of fundamental fairness, not of weighing the pecuniary costs against the societal benefits. Accordingly, even if the costs to the State were not relatively insignificant but rather were just as great as the costs of providing prosecutors, judges, and defense counsel to ensure the fairness of criminal proceedings, I would reach the same result in this category of cases. For the value of protecting our liberty from deprivation by the State without due process of law is priceless.

AIMS

By now it should be apparent that one cannot responsibly attack or defend the adversary system without first facing the question of what is the aim of our system of justice. As reexamination will suggest, Professor Fuller, Dean Pound, and Judge Frank all faced this question, although arriving perhaps at different answers. The Lassiter case at least presented that question. Others further explore the question in the following excerpts.

WALTER V. SCHAEFER, IS THE ADVERSARY SYSTEM WORKING IN OPTIMAL FASHION?, 70 F.R.D. 159, 159–60 (1976). "The assigned question, whether the adversary system is operating in optimal fashion, immediately prompts another: What is the purpose of the adversary system. The fundamental purpose of that system, as I see it, is the ascertainment of the truth with respect, most frequently, to an event which took place in the past. All aspects of the adversary system must be measured, in my opinion, against that objective. There are peripheral considerations, but the ultimate question is whether the adversary system as we know it today is doing the best that it can to determine the truth with respect to litigated controversies."

SIDNEY POST SIMPSON, "THE PROBLEM OF TRIAL," in David Dudley Field Centenary Essays 141, 141–42 (Alison Reppy ed., 1949). "Of course, even in the most primitive societies, it has been important that some heed be paid to such moral sentiments and ideas of justice as may have received common acceptance. This was essential to the maintenance of group morale even in the early despotisms which so often emerged from expanding groups of kindred. But the fact remains that originally the essential factor in the judicial settlement of disputes has been that those disputes be settled definitely and finally, rather than that they be settled on the basis of an accurate determination of the facts.

"In considerable measure this is still true. Finality in adjudication is as essential now as it was in more primitive times. But the purpose of the legal order has changed. It is no longer merely to keep the peace. The law is now a principal means whereby mankind seeks consciously to control its collective social destiny. The accent has therefore shifted from the mere settlement of disputes to their just settlement—and by just settlement I mean the decision of controversies not only finally, and not only in a way which does not give major offense to the beliefs and moral standards of the mass of the community, but in a manner which takes account of the reality of the controversies presented and seeks to adjudicate them according to standards which the law consciously lays down. Indeed in most of the civilized world it is not too much to say that continued failure to adjudicate controversies on the basis of their real nature and in accordance with established legal standards would of itself, if that failure became a matter of public notoriety, produce a revulsion of popular feeling against the established legal and political order."

KENNETH E. SCOTT, TWO MODELS OF THE CIVIL PROCESS, 27 Stan.L.Rev. 937, 937–39 (1975). "One possible view of the civil process is a Conflict Resolution Model that sees civil process primarily as a method of achieving peaceful settlement of private disputes. . . . So in the interests of preserving the peace, society offers through the courts a mechanism for the impartial judgment of personal grievances, as an alternative to retaliation or forcible self-help. . . .

"This model has only weak implications for the precise content of the legal rules whereby judgment is rendered. To facilitate acceptance of the outcome and resort to the process, the rules should be seen as 'fair' in terms of prevailing community values, but notions of what is fair may vary a great deal from one era or society to another. Such variations are of only secondary importance; it is more important for society that the dispute be settled peaceably than that it be settled in any particular way. . . .

. . . .

"A Behavior Modification Model, on the other hand, sees the courts and civil process as a way of altering behavior by imposing costs on a person. Not the resolution of the immediate dispute but its effect on the future conduct of others is the heart of the matter. Consistency and predictability of outcome, therefore, assume an importance that they do not possess in the Conflict Resolution Model.

"The implications of the Behavior Modification Model are at their most powerful if coupled with a view of the substantive rules of civil liability as designed to contribute to economic efficiency. If a person negligently injures another, the law of torts requires him to pay for the damages he has caused; if he breaches his agreement, contract law requires him to make whole the person who has relied on it. As a result he is led to take appropriate precautions to avoid injury and to make appropriate judgments about honoring agreements; and consequently, the social loss from such conduct is minimized.[2] The imposition of legal liability is, in economists' jargon, a way of making a person 'internalize' or take into account the costs of his actions, thereby inducing appropriate levels of care and performance toward others. . . . Whatever their actual merits may be, if legal rules are

[2] This assumes that social costs and the private damages to the plaintiff are the same, which is not always the case.

seen as attempts to alter public behavior in ways that have been deemed desirable, the civil sanction contributes toward that end by depriving one who violates them of his gains or by imposing on him the costs occasioned by his violation."

MARTIN P. GOLDING, "ON THE ADVERSARY SYSTEM AND JUSTICE," in Philosophical Law 98, 107 (Richard Bronaugh ed., 1978). "The truth-finding conception of the trial process rests on the connection it perceives between legal justice and truth. It argues that the disposition of a case according to the applicable law of a system presupposes that correct answers are given to the disputed questions of fact. If a case is decided on wrong answers, the case is (legally speaking) wrongly decided, with the result that one of the parties is not given his legal due. A finding of correct answers to the disputed questions of fact is therefore a necessary condition for doing legal justice. A similar connection holds between truth and justice in the moral sense. Thus, if the applicable law in a case is also a just law according to some moral standard, then a decision made on wrong answers to the disputed questions of fact is also morally unjust, and one of the parties is not being given what moral justice requires."

EDWARD F. BARRETT, THE ADVERSARY SYSTEM AND THE ETHICS OF ADVOCACY, 37 Notre Dame Law. 479, 479 (1962). " 'The purpose of a lawsuit is,' indeed, 'to arrive at the truth of the controversy, in order that justice may be done.'[2] Undoubtedly the courts of the Spanish Inquisition and the Supreme Court of the United States would alike assent to this. It is at least another of those 'decencies of civilization that no one would dispute.'[3] However, given the ideal and given also the inescapably human features of a lawsuit, how can the truth of the matter in dispute between the parties be most practically arrived at in order that justice (not justice in the abstract but justice according to law) may be done? We have no archangel on the bench. The jury is not drawn from a venire of Cherubim or Seraphim. The litigants, their lawyers and their witnesses are not saints. The trial of a lawsuit is a very human thing."

EDMUND M. MORGAN, FOREWORD to Model Code of Evidence 3–4 (1942). "Thoughtful lawyers realize that a lawsuit is not, and cannot be made, a scientific investigation for the discovery of truth. The matter to be investigated is determined by the parties. They may eliminate many elements which a scientist would insist upon considering. The court has no machinery for discovering sources of information unknown to the parties or undisclosed by them. It must rely in the main upon data furnished by interested persons. The material event or condition may have been observed by only a few. The capacities and stimuli of each of these few for accurately observing and remembering will vary. The ability and desire to narrate truly may be slight or great. The trier of fact can get no more than the adversaries are able and willing to present. The rules governing the acceptable content of the data and the methods and forms of presenting them must be almost instantly applied in the heat and hurry of the trial.

[2] McCarty, Psychology & the Law 223 (1960).

[3] Holmes, J., in Michigan Trust v. Ferry, 228 U.S. 346, 353, 33 S.Ct. 550, 552 (1913).

Prompt decision on the merits is imperative, for justice delayed is often justice denied. Sometimes a wrong decision quickly made is better than a right decision after undue procrastination. 'Some concession must be made to the shortness of human life'. The trier must assume that the data presented are complete, and the litigants must be satisfied with a determination of the preponderance of probability. If the data leave the mind of the trier in equilibrium, the decision must be against the party having the burden of persuasion. No scientist would think of basing a conclusion upon such data so presented. The court is not a scientific body. It is composed of one or more persons skilled in the law, skilled in the general art of investigation, but not necessarily skilled in the field which the dispute concerns, acting either alone or with a body of men not necessarily trained in investigation of any kind. Its final determination is binding only between the parties and their privies. It does not pronounce upon the facts for any purpose other than the adjustment of the controversy before it. Consequently there must be a recognition at the outset that nicely accurate results cannot be expected; that society and the litigants must be content with a rather rough approximation of what a scientist might demand. And it must never be forgotten that in the settlement of disputes in a court room, as in all other experiences of individuals in our society, the emotions of the persons involved—litigants, counsel, witnesses, judge and jurors—will play a part. A trial cannot be a purely intellectual performance."

CHARLES P. CURTIS, THE ETHICS OF ADVOCACY, 4 Stan.L.Rev. 3, 12 (1951). " 'I must be cruel only to be kind,' said Hamlet, on his way to his mother. And so likewise a lawyer has to tell himself strange things on his way to court. But they are strange only to those who do not distinguish between truth and justice. Justice is something larger and more intimate than truth. Truth is only one of the ingredients of justice. . . . The administration of justice is no more designed to elicit the truth than the scientific approach is designed to extract justice from the atom."

HUBERT W. SMITH, COMPONENTS OF PROOF IN LEGAL PROCEEDINGS, 51 Yale L.J. 537, 575 (1942). "In trial by battle we see the primitive concept of letting the best man win by 'might and main,' using all the strength and means at his command short of actual foul play. This combat aspect of litigation has psychological connotations running deeper than self vindication of one's cause by valor or might. It expresses the animosity factor in litigation, the desire to be at one's assailant and 'have it out.' Later we see the more primitive arrangement giving way to combat by proxy in the form of bilateral litigation. Each party still fends for himself under rules of diligence but aided by a lawyer as his paid champion. The law suit here still retains a dual character, on the one hand being a means of settling disputes with approximate justice, and on the other a sublimation mechanism for combat feelings and expression of grudges."

CHARLES P. CURTIS, IT'S YOUR LAW (1954). "There are some subjects of litigation in which the adversary proceeding is an admirable way of administering justice. One wise judge implied as much when Charles E. Wyzanski said, 'A political libel suit is the modern substitute for ordeal by battle. It is the means which society has chosen to induce bitter partisans to wager money instead of exchanging bloody noses.'[5] But litigation by an adversary proceeding is the way we cut the knot of many disputes in which it is disastrously inappropriate. Divorces, the custody of children, will contests, almost any kind of dispute which springs from family or equally intimate dissension—there a broken bone is more easily mendable. And it is intolerably too often true that a criminal trial turns into an adversary proceeding. . . .

"What, then, is the justification for this approach to justice, other than the fact we are several centuries used to it and aside from the fact that spectators in small communities and newspaper readers in cities enjoy the spectacle? It seems to me that the justification of the adversary proceeding is the satisfaction of the parties, and not our satisfaction, except as we too are prospective litigants. This is a rational justification of the adversary approach to justice. Along this line, what the law is trying to do is give the algebraic maximum of satisfaction to both parties. This is a crude, but indeed it is not a bad, definition of the justice which the adversary proceeding provides. The law is trying to do justice between the parties for the parties rather than for us, trying to give them their own justice so far as possible and so far as compatible with what may be distinguished as our justice.

"It is necessary, to be sure, to apply the general terms of what we regard as justice to their particular case. For we too must be satisfied. We are prospective customers. But the difference is not great. They are some of us, and they are much influenced by what we regard as just. The law pays more attention to the satisfaction of the needs of the parties in the particular case than it does to our ideas about justice in general. The law takes the position that we ought to be satisfied if the parties are; and it believes that the best way to get that done is to encourage them to fight it out, and dissolve their differences in dissension. We are still a combative people, not yet so civilized and sophisticated as to forget that combat is one way to justice."[c]

J.A. JOLOWICZ, ON CIVIL PROCEDURE 70–71 (2000). "It is appropriate that the interests of the parties, as defined by law, should be seen as paramount when attention is directed to proceedings in an individual case. It does not follow, however, that procedural law as such can be based on the single hypothesis that its business is no more than to provide for the resolution of a sequence of disputes, one after the other. The importance of achieving justice between individual litigants is in no way diminished by

[5] [Charles E. Wyzanski, Jr., A Trial Judge's Freedom and Responsibility, 65 Harv.L.Rev. 1281, 1283 (1952)].

[c] Compare John W. Thibaut & Laurens Walker, Procedural Justice: A Psychological Analysis (1975) (experiments tending to prove that adversary system maximizes satisfaction), with Austin Sarat, Studying American Legal Culture: An Assessment of Survey Evidence, 11 Law & Soc'y Rev. 427, 438–41 (1977) (surveys tending to show that experience with courts disillusions parties). See generally E. Allan Lind & Tom R. Tyler, The Social Psychology of Procedural Justice (1988); Donna Shestowsky, Procedural Preferences in Alternative Dispute Resolution: A Closer, Modern Look at an Old Idea, 10 Psychol., Pub.Pol'y & L. 211 (2004).

recognition that the process of litigation, considered as a whole, serves at least two other ends, connected but distinct, and that their attainment should be included in the purposes of procedural law. First, civil proceedings serve to demonstrate the effectiveness of the law; secondly they provide the opportunity for the judges to perform their function of interpreting, clarifying, developing and, of course, applying the law."

KEVIN M. CLERMONT, ROBERT A. HILLMAN, SHERI LYNN JOHNSON & ROBERT S. SUMMERS, LAW FOR SOCIETY: NATURE, FUNCTIONS, AND LIMITS 100–01 (2010). "Yet something more profound is afoot: Truth is not the only aim. Consider the following from Sir Frederick Pollock's Essays in the Law 275 (1922): 'Perhaps the greatest of all the fallacies entertained by lay people about the law is one which, though seldom expressed in terms, an observant lawyer may quite commonly find lurking not far below the surface. This is that the business of a court of justice is to discover the truth. Its real business is to pronounce upon the justice of particular claims, and incidentally to test the truth of the assertions of fact made in support of the claim in law, provided that those assertions are relevant in law to the establishment of the desired conclusion; and this is by no means the same thing.'

"Surely a reader could ask, 'How can there be any inconsistency between truth and justice? Indeed, justice can only be done on the basis of the facts. Justice cannot be done in the dark.' But Pollock may have been considering procedural justice. For example, giving each side an equal chance to present his case may, in a particular case, lead to substantive injustice—one side, the weaker side factually, may be able to demonstrate a better case factually than can the other side. Nonetheless, recognition of this risk has not induced courts to deny each side an equal opportunity to be heard.

"Pollock's remark can be generalized: Society makes and applies laws in a way to maximize the net total of its deepest underlying values, and so society may, in an adjudicative process, subordinate the pursuit of truth to other social aims. One of these aims is that of offering the parties a day in court, a forum in which to have it out. In the end, the court may lose sight of the truth, but the parties will have had their say against each other, and this will have served as a substitute for disorderly forms of self-help. For another example, any society would favor a process that saves time and money. For yet another example, an adjudicator may have to apply rules of evidence that limit or close off relevant lines of factual inquiry altogether. Evidentiary privileges, like the husband-wife privilege, may frustrate the pursuit of truth. A rule that privileges a witness not to testify because her testimony would violate a confidential relation may operate to keep the adjudicator in the dark in the particular case. When this happens, society has sacrificed substantive justice, insofar as it is necessarily premised on truth, to the aim of inducing and protecting confidential relations. That aim is not so much procedural justice as a conflicting substantive aim.

. . . .

"A way to summarize is to say that the remedial instrument, with its elaborate procedures for resolving disputes over the factual premises of particular remedies, is a multipurpose institutional scheme, only one of the purposes of which is the pursuit of truth, with other purposes thereof either cooperatively or antagonistically involving themselves in the combined pursuit of justice."

RICHARD A. POSNER, ECONOMIC ANALYSIS OF LAW 593 (7th ed. 2007). "We must not ignore the cost of operating the procedural system. Suppose that to reduce the rate of erroneous failures to impose liability from 15 percent to below 10 percent would require an additional investment in procedure of $20 per accident. Then we should tolerate the 15 percent probability of error [if] the cost of error [to society from those erroneous judicial decisions] is less than the cost necessary to eliminate it . . . ."

VALUES

The multiple and conflicting aims of our adversary system of justice, as well as their implementation, reflect underlying values. The ultimate values comprise both a complex variety of outcome values, because we care about the substantive resolution of disputes, and also a broad set of process values, because we care about how the system handles disputes and our care extends beyond the procedure's outcome-value efficacy. Your study of civil procedure should have already convinced you of the subtle latency of some of these values. Our current search for values should be convincing you of the contestable nature of all of these values—both as to what they mean precisely (think particularly of equality) and how much weight they deserve relatively (think generally of outcome and process values) and also as to whose values they are and how they come into play. Yet despite their latency and contestability, exploring and explicating values can be surprisingly practical, as for example when lawyers argue and judges decide a case such as Lassiter. Other commentators pursue the debate on values in the two following excerpts.

PAUL J. SPIEGELMAN, INTEGRATING DOCTRINE, THEORY AND PRACTICE IN THE LAW SCHOOL CURRICULUM: THE LOGIC OF JAKE'S LADDER IN THE CONTEXT OF AMY'S WEB, 38 J.Legal Educ. 243, 247–50 (1988). "The images of Jake's ladder and Amy's web are very useful devices . . . . The images come from Carol Gilligan's description of the responses of two eleven-year-olds, Jake and Amy, to the 'Heinz dilemma,' one of a series of hypotheticals designed by Lawrence Kohlberg to measure moral development.[19] Heinz is married to a women suffering from a fatal disease that can be cured by an expensive drug. He does not have the money to pay for the drug, and the druggist refuses to give him the drug without payment. The moral dilemma presented is 'Should Heinz

---

[19] [Carol Gilligan, In a Different Voice: Psychological Theory and Women's Development 25–32 (1982)].

steal the drug?' Jake's clear and unequivocal answer is 'yes,' because 'human life is worth more than money.' Jake enjoys the problem as 'sort of like a math problem with humans.' By abstracting the issues from the individuals and situation involved and deducing the answer logically from a hierarchical ladder of values, Jake comfortably finds the 'correct' solution to the problem.

"Amy responds very differently to the hypothetical. She feels that 'he really shouldn't steal the drug—but his wife shouldn't die either.' She is uncomfortable with viewing the situation as static, wants more context, and seeks alternatives to the yes-or-no options presented by Jake's reading of the dilemma. For her the problem is not a conflict of rights but rather the druggist's failure to respond to Heinz's wife's need. Amy suggests that Heinz talk more with the druggist to help the druggist understand the seriousness of the wife's situation and to explore other payment possibilities. Amy seeks to resolve the situation contextually, by personal communication, and is frustrated by the fixed, hypothetical setting in which the dilemma is locked.

"From the two responses, Gilligan develops and describes two very different ways of looking at the world. Jake's world is one governed by rules, principles, hierarchy, and the logic of justification. He sees the moral dilemma in the Heinz hypothetical as a conflict between the druggist's property rights and Heinz's wife's right to life. His method of resolving the conflict is to look for abstract rules that determine which interest is more important. He has little trouble in ranking life over property. Beneath the surface of Jake's response is a view of the world that sees people as isolated individuals competing with each other. In his world the primary responsibility to others is to avoid interfering with their autonomy, and the function of law is to assure that the competition between individuals is conducted fairly. The image for Jake's world is the ladder both because he views human interaction as a competition for position on the socioeconomic ladder and because he resolves conflicts hierarchically, by deciding which principles or interests rank higher than competing ones.

"Amy's world is one of relationship, interdependence, cooperation, and the ethic of care. For her the moral crux in the Heinz hypothetical is the druggist's detachment from Heinz's wife's needs. Her method of resolving the problem is to explore ways in which the druggist and Heinz could cooperate so that the wife obtains her medication and the druggist his payment. Her view is in many ways more practical than Jake's because unlike Jake (who sees the situation as an isolated math problem with an instantaneous solution that conclusively resolves it), she sees the connection between present action and future consequences. When asked why Heinz should not steal the drug, Amy replies that, even if successful, the theft might not solve the problem because Heinz might not know how to administer the drug and because additional doses might be necessary. If Heinz were caught, moreover, his wife might die alone. Unlike Jake, who sees responsibility as negative (refraining from injuring others), Amy sees responsibility as positive (responding to the needs of others). Gilligan uses the image of the web to describe Amy's world because Amy sees the world as a complex of interconnections between people, time, and events.

"Gilligan's imagery provokes a consideration of the approaches to the world of legal education each of the two perspectives implies. The values and structure of traditional legal education are extraordinarily compatible with Jake's ladder. Like Jake, traditional legal education exalts the protection of legal rights and even-handed justice as the goals of the legal system and condemns interference with rights of others and unequal treatment (i.e., treatment that cannot be justified by the statement of a neutral principle that explains any difference in treatment) as evils to be avoided. Such value judgments are linked to a view of human interaction that is atomistic and competitive; they are designed not to promote cooperative interaction between people but to protect people from intrusions by others and to provide rules of fair competition. The form of dispute resolution best adapted to such a world is adjudication, for it provides the mechanism by which to define, rank, and apply the rules and principles that govern the dispute.

. . . .

"A law school education compatible with Amy's world view would look very different. Her strongest positive values are care and concern for others; to her the greatest evils are detachment from others and indifference to their needs. She views people as interconnected and their interaction as basically cooperative. She prefers nonadjudicatory modes of dispute resolution such as negotiation and mediation—modes that emphasize cooperative problem solving and achieve 'win-win' rather than 'win-lose' solutions—for settling disputes.

. . . .

"Table 1 summarizes the kind of legal education that best characterizes Jake's ladder and Amy's web."

TABLE 1

Category	Jake's Ladder	Amy's Web
Goods:	Rights, justice	Care, concern
Evils:	Interference with rights of others; inequality	Indifference to others; detachment
View of human interaction:	Atomistic, competitive	Interconnected, cooperative
Ordering devices:	Rules, principles, hierarchies	Relationships, responsibilities
Method of dispute resolution:	Adjudication	Negotiation, mediation
Educational objectives:	Knowledge, adversarial skills, analytic and critical abilities, skepticism	Understanding, cooperative skills, synthetic and integrative abilities, reflective values
Teaching methods:	Formal discussions, hypotheticals with given facts, debates	Simulations, clinics, conversations and reflections
Role of student:	Detached observer	Involved participant
Mode of thought:	Logical	Experiential
Reasoning process:	Self-contained, vertical	Interactive, lateral
Role of emotion:	Negative; excluded from rational discourse	Positive; assists in interpretation
Focus:	Abstractions	Context

Category	Jake's Ladder	Amy's Web
Role of evaluation:	Ranking based on comparative mastery	To convey degree of competence
Potentially hidden agenda:	Individualism, amorality, professionalism, cynicism	Community, personal responsibility, trust
Role of scholarship:	Arrive at truth	Communicate ideas

RICHARD L. ABEL, WHY DOES THE ABA PROMULGATE ETHICAL RULES?, 59 Tex.L.Rev. 639, 686–88 (1981). "The Rules of Professional Conduct purport to resolve the ethical dilemmas of lawyers. They do so in order that those who draft, discuss, and consult them may be reassured that their conduct is morally correct. But the Rules do not resolve those dilemmas; they merely restate them in mystifying language that obscures the issues through ambiguity, vagueness, qualification, and hypocrisy. The capacity of these precepts to legitimate is constantly being eroded as internal inconsistencies, the meaninglessness of the language, and the empirical falsity and impossibility of their claims and prescriptions become apparent or are exposed by criticism. Hence, the Rules must constantly be rewritten in a vain effort to renew their legitimating force.

"The Rules cannot resolve the ethical dilemmas of lawyers because those dilemmas are inherent in the structure of the lawyer's role. First, legal representation, like all other goods and services under capitalism, has become a commodity. This means that clients *can* buy loyalty, which should be given freely out of a sense of social and political commitment. It means that clients *must* buy justice, which should be theirs by right, and will obtain only as much justice as they can afford. And it means that lawyers *must* seek to maximize their profits (especially as competition within the market for legal services intensifies), with the result that they must sell their services to the highest bidder and withhold them from those who cannot pay the price. In a capitalist society, the highest bidders will necessarily be those who own large amounts of capital and, within that group, those who wield monopoly power. Lawyers are, therefore, partisans in the class conflict that capitalism generates and cannot resolve, and virtually all lawyers are enlisted on the side of capital and against the numerous groups it oppresses, disenfranchises, and exploits—workers, the nonworking poor, women, minorities, citizens of the Third World, and all those who must live in a polluted environment and suffer the depletion of its resources.

. . . .

"Finally, the Rules cannot resolve the contradictions inherent in liberalism, which denies the existence of any truth other than the process of pursuing truth. This denial is essential if lawyers are to claim to be morally unaccountable for their clients' aims. But it requires a faith in process—judicial, legislative, electoral, administrative, even market—that few, if any, honestly maintain. Clients know they are interested in outcome, not process. Lawyers know they are striving to manipulate the process instrumentally. And society sees case after case in which it knows that the process is corrupt and the result is wrong."

ECONOMIC ANALYSIS

To weigh procedural changes, an analytic framework is helpful. A framework that has come to enjoy wide acceptance is cost-minimization. Here is the description from a pioneering article by then Professor and now Judge Richard A. Posner, An Economic Approach to Legal Procedure and Judicial Administration, 2 J.Legal Stud. 399, 400–02 (1973):

"An important purpose of substantive legal rules (such as the rules of tort and criminal law) is to increase economic efficiency [in the sense of maximizing economic value]. It follows . . . that mistaken imposition of legal liability, or mistaken failure to impose liability, will reduce efficiency. Judicial error is therefore a source of social costs and the reduction of error is a goal of the procedural system. . . .

"Even when the legal process works flawlessly, it involves costs—the time of lawyers, litigants, witnesses, jurors, judges, and other people, plus paper and ink, law office and court house maintenance, telephone service, etc. These costs are just as real as the costs resulting from error: in general we would not want to increase the direct costs of the legal process by one dollar in order to reduce error costs by 50 (or 99) cents. The economic goal is thus to minimize the sum of error and direct costs.

"Despite its generality, this formulation provides a useful framework in which to analyze the problems and objectives of legal procedure. It is usable even when the purpose of the substantive law is to transfer wealth or to bring about some other noneconomic goal, rather than to improve efficiency. All that is necessary is that it be possible, in principle, to place a price tag on the consequences of failing to apply the substantive law in all cases in which it was intended to apply, so that our two variables, error cost and direct cost, remain commensurable.

". . . The cost inquiries required by the economic approach are not simple and will rarely yield better than crude approximations, but at the very least they serve to place questions of legal policy in a framework of rational inquiry."

This framework owes its success to its usefulness. To illustrate how well his approach worked, Posner considered the question whether to entitle the defendant to a trial-type hearing in an administrative action such as deportation or license revocation. He contrasted the traditional legal approach, which tended "to invoke either a purely visceral sense of fairness [Justice Stevens?] or a purely formal distinction between penal and nonpenal sanctions [Justice Stewart?]," with his economic approach: "We begin by asking, what is the cost of withholding a trial-type hearing in a particular type of case? This inquiry has two branches: first, how is the probability of an error likely to be affected by a trial-type hearing? If the legally dispositive issues are factual issues of the kind most reliably determined in trial-type hearings, the probability of error if such a hearing is denied may be high. Second, what is the cost of an error if one occurs? As a first approximation, if the stakes in the case are large, the cost of error in an individual case will be large, so if in addition the probability of error is high, total error costs will be very high. Having established the costs of error, we then inquire into the costs of measures—a trial-type hearing or whatever—that would reduce the error costs. If those direct costs are low . . . then adoption can be expected to reduce the sum of error and direct costs and thus increase efficiency.[2]"

For a further example of such a framework's usefulness, think still of the Lassiter case. Broadly conceived and properly utilized, economics insightfully suggests, first, that most process values played a negligibly small role in the prevailing formula and, second, that complex outcome values received a peculiarly fuzzy treatment in the clash of majority and dissent. Lack of openness and rigor allowed Justices Stewart and Blackmun to state analyses that seemed essentially to differ only in conclusion.

Indeed, such a framework is useful enough to suggest consideration of its own costs. Among other drawbacks, it tends to distort analysis by ignoring or devaluing certain values, such as those hard to quantify, while injecting or exaggerating others, such as efficiency. See Robert A. Baruch Bush, Dispute Resolution Alternatives and the Goals of Civil Justice: Jurisdictional Principles for Process Choice, 1984 Wis.L.Rev. 893, 929–32. Perhaps the Lassiter Court's very use of such a framework contributed to the opinions' inadequacies.

The best response to such a criticism is the simple but profound one that cost-minimization need not affect values. In a procedural system built on multiple and conflicting values, some analytic framework is necessary for weighing them against one another, and thus for evaluating procedural methods. Cost-minimization can play that role. It then is merely a tool for optimizing value, while the values can and should come from elsewhere. If used with careful thought about the inputted values, it does not have to denigrate or elevate any value. In other words, one can adopt a descriptive tool of economics without accepting any prescriptive baggage of economics.

SECTION 2. CHANGING OUR SYSTEM

Even if one can identify the values and aims of our system of justice, there remains the still open question of how well the adversary system implements them and at what cost. One cannot answer such a question in a vacuum. One can best gauge the effectiveness of the current adversary system relative to other methods of striving to accomplish those aims. In

[2] [Although his 1973 article contained basically the same illustration, this last quotation comes from Richard A. Posner, Economic Analysis of Law 430 (2d ed. 1977), which here appended this footnote:] The Supreme Court has recently adopted essentially this approach as the standard guiding scrutiny of administrative hearing procedures for conformity with the requirements of due process. See Mathews v. Eldridge, 424 U.S. 319, 96 S.Ct. 893 (1976), and, for criticism of the Court's approach, Jerry L. Mashaw, The Supreme Court's Due Process Calculus for Administrative Adjudication in Mathews v. Eldridge: Three Factors in Search of a Theory of Value, 44 U.Chi.L.Rev. 28, 47–49 (1976).

other words, the remaining question is not simply how effective is the adversarial method in implementing those aims, but rather what is the most effective way available to find truth, ensure fairness, and achieve a variety of secondary aims such as party satisfaction, while simultaneously pursuing economies.

In considering a change to other methods, it is necessary to distinguish the need for tinkering from the need for a totally new direction. There are many problems (e.g., access of the poor to our system of justice) and abuses (e.g., excesses of cross-examination) that we might alleviate or eliminate without endangering or abandoning the adversary system itself. But some remedies—including some that might appear quite minor—would have unavoidably broad and profound repercussions. Thus, we must consider both alterations and alternatives.

(a) Changing the Advocate's Role

New York County Lawyers' Association Committee on Professional Ethics, Opinions

Op. 309 (1933).

Question. In an action on behalf of an infant three years of age, for injuries sustained by falling off a porch owned by the defendant, due to the alleged negligence of the defendant, where there is no eye-witness known to the plaintiff's attorney, and thereafter when the case came to trial, the infant's case was dismissed on motion of the defendant's attorney on the ground that the infant plaintiff was unable to make out a sufficient case of circumstantial evidence. During the presentation of the plaintiff's case, said attorney for the defendant had an eyewitness to said accident actually present in court, and did not mention said fact, either to the plaintiff's attorney or to the Court and kept the Court in ignorance of the fact that a person did exist who actually saw said accident, and was present in court. Was the failure of the defendant's attorney to disclose said information to the Court improper professional conduct?

Answer. In the opinion of the Committee the conduct of the defendant's attorney is not professionally improper. The fact of infancy does not call for a different reply.[d]

ADVERSE FACT AND ADVERSE LAW

At the time of the foregoing opinion, the relevant provisions of the ABA's Canons of Professional Ethics (1908) were: (1) "The lawyer owes

[d] The soundness of the New York opinion is "queried" (without further comment) in Henry S. Drinker, Legal Ethics 77 n.42 (1953) (the author was for many years Chairman of the ABA Committee on Professional Ethics and Grievances). It is cited in support of a "general operating principle for American litigators" in Charles W. Wolfram, Modern Legal Ethics 639, 640 n.31 (1986). But it is implicitly questioned anew in Deborah L. Rhode, Professional Responsibility: Ethics by the Pervasive Method 443 (2d ed. 1998).

'entire devotion to the interest of the client, warm zeal in the maintenance and defense of his rights and the exertion of his utmost learning and ability,' to the end that nothing be taken or be withheld from him, save by the rules of law, legally applied," Canon 15; and (2) "The conduct of the lawyer before the Court and with other lawyers should be characterized by candor and fairness," Canon 22.

The newer Code of Professional Responsibility (1969) was no more informative, with DR 7–102(A)(3) providing that in representation of a client the lawyer shall not "[c]onceal or knowingly fail to disclose that which he is required by law to reveal." Incidentally, "disclose" is used in the present context to mean "reveal," and does not refer to disclosure in the technical sense of Federal Rule 26(a).

The succeeding Model Rules of Professional Conduct (1983) were not much clearer. Today, under the current version of the Model Rules, what is clear is that a lawyer need not disclose adverse facts in many circumstances. Indeed, a lawyer normally has a duty not to "reveal information relating to representation of a client unless the client gives informed consent" expressly or impliedly. Model Rule 1.6(a); accord, Restatement of the Law Governing Lawyers § 60 (1998). But there are exceptions, situations where the lawyer may or must disclose. Here are some suggestive provisions:

1. Model Rule 1.6(b) goes on to provide: "A lawyer may reveal information relating to the representation of a client to the extent the lawyer reasonably believes necessary: (1) to prevent reasonably certain death or substantial bodily harm; (2) to prevent the client from committing a crime or fraud that is reasonably certain to result in substantial injury to the financial interests or property of another and in furtherance of which the client has used or is using the lawyer's services; (3) to prevent, mitigate or rectify substantial injury to the financial interests or property of another that is reasonably certain to result or has resulted from the client's commission of a crime or fraud in furtherance of which the client has used the lawyer's services; (4) to secure legal advice about the lawyer's compliance with these Rules; (5) to establish a claim or defense on behalf of the lawyer in a controversy between the lawyer and the client, to establish a defense to a criminal charge or civil claim against the lawyer based upon conduct in which the client was involved, or to respond to allegations in any proceeding concerning the lawyer's representation of the client; or (6) to comply with other law or a court order."

2. Model Rule 3.3(d) provides: "In an ex parte proceeding, a lawyer shall inform the tribunal of all material facts known to the lawyer that will enable the tribunal to make an informed decision, whether or not the facts are adverse." Does this exception tell us something about the reasons for the rule against disclosing adverse facts?

3. Model Rule 3.8(d) provides that a prosecutor shall "make timely disclosure to the defense of all evidence or information known to the prosecutor that tends to negate the guilt of the accused or mitigates the

offense." Does this exception suggest more generally when the rule against disclosing adverse facts should not apply?

4. Model Rule 3.3(a)(1) and (3) provides that a lawyer shall not knowingly "make a false statement of fact or law to a tribunal," "offer evidence that the lawyer knows to be false," or leave unremedied any such statement made or evidence offered. So, regardless of any obligation of the advocate to disclose, which would constitute a so-called *duty of candor*, there is a so-called *duty of truthfulness*. Moreover, a comment accompanying the Model Rule says without elaboration: "There are circumstances where failure to make a disclosure is the equivalent of an affirmative misrepresentation."

5. The attorney's duty of truthfulness extends not only to a tribunal, but to third persons generally, according to Model Rule 4.1. Indeed, that Model Rule goes on to provide that the attorney must "disclose a material fact when disclosure is necessary to avoid assisting a criminal or fraudulent act by a client," unless disclosure falls within the prohibition of above-quoted Model Rule 1.6.

In his autobiography, Life and Law 271–72 (1941), Professor Samuel Williston tells of an incident in his brief practice when, in preparing the defense in a financial matter, he went carefully over his client's file of correspondence between the parties. The opposing lawyer did not demand production of this correspondence. Williston did not feel bound to disclose it. It included some unfavorable letters. At the end of the trial the judge gave judgment orally, citing as one reason for his decision a supposed fact that Williston knew to be unfounded. Williston says: "I had in front of me a letter that showed his error. Though I have no doubt of the propriety of my behavior in keeping silent, I was somewhat uncomfortable at the time." He explains that "doing something intrinsically regrettable, because the only alternative involves worse consequences, is a necessity in every profession," and: "One of the troublesome ethical questions which a young trial lawyer is confronted with is the extent to which he is bound to disclose to the court facts which are injurious to his client's case. The answer is not doubtful. The lawyer must decide when he takes a case whether it is a suitable one for him to undertake and after this decision is made, he is not justified in turning against his client by exposing injurious evidence entrusted to him. If that evidence was unknown to him when he took the case, he may sometimes withdraw from it, but while he is engaged as counsel he is not only not obliged to disclose unfavorable evidence, but it is a violation of his duty to his client if he does so."

Questions: (2) Should the ethical duty to disclose an adverse fact, such as an eyewitness, be any different in a jurisdiction with extensive discovery procedures, like the Federal Rules, from what it is in one permitting only limited discovery?

(3) Presumably Professor Williston would have pursued the same course of nondisclosure had the plaintiff early on sought to settle for a negligible amount, and this behavior would not violate the Model Rules. But see Nathan M. Crystal, The Lawyer's Duty to Disclose Material Facts in Contract or Settlement Negotiations, 87 Ky.L.J. 1055 (1999). But what if corporate counsel knows that a toxic-tort

victim's untreatable injuries are probably far more serious than the potential plaintiff believes them to be when asking only a small sum in settlement? Compare David Luban, The Adversary System Excuse, in The Good Lawyer 83, 115 (David Luban ed., 1983), with Stephen Gillers, Can a Good Lawyer Be a Bad Person?, 84 Mich.L.Rev. 1011, 1018–19 (1986) (reviewing Luban's book).

By contrast, Model Rule 3.3(a)(2) provides that a lawyer shall not knowingly "fail to disclose to the tribunal legal authority in the controlling jurisdiction known to the lawyer to be directly adverse to the position of the client and not disclosed by opposing counsel." Accord, Restatement of the Law Governing Lawyers § 111(2) (1998). The Code of Professional Responsibility had essentially the same provision, but the Canons of Professional Ethics had not specifically addressed this matter. See generally Commentary—The Advocate's Duty, 16 Ga.L.Rev. 821 (1982). This duty to disclose adverse legal authorities to the tribunal does not, however, extend to making the opponent's arguments or asserting his rights, and does not apply to private negotiations.

Questions: (4) Must an attorney disclose to a federal district court an adverse legal ruling of a federal court for another district or circuit? See Ass'n of the Bar of the City of N.Y. Comm. on Professional Ethics, Op. 80–4 (1980) (usually no). What of legal authority that appears adverse and comes from the federal court in which the attorney's case pends, but that the attorney believes he can distinguish? What of legal authority that is adverse, but was merely dicta?

(5) By itself, does a violation of Model Rule 3.3(a)(2), in some paper signed as part of a federal district court proceeding, constitute also a violation of Federal Rule 11? Compare Golden Eagle Distrib. Corp. v. Burroughs Corp., 801 F.2d 1531 (9th Cir.1986), and Melissa L. Nelken, Sanctions Under Amended Federal Rule 11—Some "Chilling" Problems in the Struggle Between Compensation and Punishment, 74 Geo.L.J. 1313, 1347–52 (1986), with Jorgenson v. County of Volusia, 846 F.2d 1350 (11th Cir.1988), and Judith L. Maute, Sporting Theory of Justice: Taming Adversary Zeal with a Logical Sanctions Doctrine, 20 Conn.L.Rev. 7, 88–90 (1987).

ABA Committee on Professional Ethics and Grievances, Formal Op. 280 (1949), had gone further with reference to disclosure of adverse legal authorities than the language of the Model Rules seems to require, saying:

"We would not confine the Opinion[e] to 'controlling authorities'—i.e., those decisive of the pending case—but, in accordance with the tests hereafter suggested, would apply it to a decision directly adverse to any proposition of law on which the lawyer expressly relies, which would reasonably be considered important by the judge sitting on the case.

"Of course, if the court should ask if there are any adverse decisions, the lawyer should make such frank disclosure as the question seems to warrant. Close cases can obviously be suggested, particularly in the case of

[e] The reference was to ABA Committee on Professional Ethics and Grievances, Formal Op. 146 (1935), which had ruled that a lawyer should disclose a decision adverse to the client's contentions but unknown to the adversary. This opinion had received criticism from Robert B. Tunstall, Ethics in Citation: A Plea for Re-interpretation of a Canon, 35 A.B.A.J. 5, 6 (1949) (The lawyer "is not called upon to volunteer detractions from the force of his own authorities. His march to a conclusion need not be interrupted by self-sought skirmishes, nor continued to the accompaniment of dubitandos. He is an advocate, not an umpire. He is participating in an argument, not a speculative inquiry; a trial, not a confessional.").

decisions from other states where there is no local case in point.[1] A case of doubt should obviously be resolved in favor of disclosure, or by a statement disclaiming the discussion of all conflicting decisions.

"Canon 22 should be interpreted sensibly, to preclude the obvious impropriety at which the Canon is aimed. In a case involving a right angle collision or a vested or contingent remainder, there would seem to be no necessity whatever of citing even all the relevant decisions in the jurisdiction, much less those from other states or by inferior courts. Where the question is a new or novel one, such as the constitutionality or construction of a statute, on which there is a dearth of authority, the lawyer's duty may be broader. The test in every case should be, is the decision which opposing counsel has overlooked one which the court should clearly consider in deciding the case? Would a reasonable judge properly feel that a lawyer who advances, as the law, a proposition adverse to the undisclosed decision, was lacking in candor and fairness to him? Might the judge consider himself misled by an implied representation that the lawyer knew of no adverse authority?"

Nevertheless, ABA Committee on Ethics and Professional Responsibility, Informal Op. 84–1505 (1984), affirmed the applicability of old Opinion 280 under the Code of Professional Responsibility and the new Model Rules. So, 2 Geoffrey C. Hazard, Jr., W. William Hodes & Peter R. Jarvis, The Law of Lawyering § 29.11 (3d ed. 2007), can sum up by saying, "the more unhappy a lawyer is that he found an adverse precedent, the clearer it is that he must reveal it."

Questions: (6) Is the position that a lawyer must disclose adverse legal authorities reconcilable with the position that a lawyer must not disclose adverse facts? Which is the court more likely to discover for itself? Which is the lawyer more likely to disclose for practical reasons?

(7) You are attorney for the defendant, and a contract action has just been decided by the judge against your client (although you believe wrongfully). In computing the damages, both the plaintiff's counsel and the judge err, so that the computed damages are nearly $5000 less than they should be under the judge's decision. Should you inform the court or opposing counsel of this error? See Ass'n of the Bar of the City of N.Y. Comm. on Professional Ethics, Op. 477 (1939) (yes). What if the same mistake were solely that of the plaintiff's counsel in writing up a settlement agreement? See ABA Comm. on Ethics & Professional Responsibility, Informal Op. 86–1518 (1986) (yes). In either event, was this an error of fact or law?

Marvin E. Frankel, The Search for Truth: An Umpireal View

123 U.Pa.L.Rev. 1031, 1055–58 (1975).

We should consider whether the paramount commitment of counsel concerning matters of fact should be to the discovery of truth rather than to the advancement of the client's interest. . . .

---

[1] See Glebe Company v. Trustees, 37 T.L.R. 436 (1921 A.C. 66) where the dicta of Lord Birkenhead are very broad [in favor of a duty to disclose "any authority which might throw light upon the matters under debate"—Ed.]. [Other citations omitted.]

We should face the fact that the quality of "hired gun" is close to the heart and substance of the litigating lawyer's role. As is true always of the mercenary warrior, the litigator has not won the highest esteem for his scars and his service. Apart from our image, we have had to reckon for ourselves in the dark hours with the knowledge that "selling" our stories rather than striving for the truth cannot always seem, because it is not, such noble work as befits the practitioner of a learned profession. The struggle to win, with its powerful pressures to subordinate the love of truth, is often only incidentally, or coincidentally, if at all, a service to the public interest.

We have been bemused through the ages by the hardy (and somewhat appealing) notion that we are to serve rather than judge the client. Among the implications of this theme is the idea that lawyers are not to place themselves above others and that the client must be equipped to decide for himself whether or not he will follow the path of truth and justice. . . .

It is impossible to guess closely how prevalent this view may be as a practical matter. Nor am I clear to what degree, if any, received canons of legal ethics give it sanction. My submission is in any case that it is a crass and pernicious idea, unworthy of a public profession. It is true that legal training is a source of power, for evil as well as good, and that a wicked lawyer is capable of specially skilled wrongdoing. It is likewise true that a physician or pharmacist knows homicidal devices hidden from the rest of us. Our goals must include means for limiting the numbers of crooked and malevolent people trained in the vital professions. We may be certain, notwithstanding our best efforts, that some lawyers and judges will abuse their trust. But this is no reason to encourage or facilitate wrongdoing by everyone.

Professional standards that placed truth above the client's interests would raise more perplexing questions. The privilege for client's confidences might come in for reexamination and possible modification. We have all been trained to know without question that the privilege is indispensable for effective representation. The client must know his confidences are safe so that he can tell all and thus have fully knowledgeable advice. We may want to ask, nevertheless, whether it would be an excessive price for the client to be stuck with the truth rather than having counsel allied with him for concealment and distortion. . . .

If the lawyer is to be more truth-seeker than combatant, troublesome questions of economics and professional organization may demand early confrontation. How and why should the client pay for loyalties divided between himself and the truth? Will we not stultify the energies and resources of the advocate by demanding that he judge the honesty of his cause along the way? Can we preserve the heroic lawyer shielding his client against all the world—and not least against the State—while demanding that he honor a paramount commitment to the elusive and ambiguous truth? It is strongly arguable, in short, that a simplistic preference for the truth may not comport with more fundamental ideals—including notably the ideal that generally values individual freedom and dignity above order and efficiency in government. Having stated such issues too broadly, I leave them in the hope that their refinement and study may seem worthy endeavors for the future.

. . . .

The rules of professional responsibility should compel disclosures of material facts and forbid material omissions rather than merely proscribe positive frauds. This final suggestion is meant to implement the broad and general proposition that precedes it. In an effort to be still more specific, I submit a draft of a new disciplinary rule . . . . The draft says:

> (1) In his representation of a client, unless prevented from doing so by a privilege reasonably believed to apply, a lawyer shall:
>
> > (a) Report to the court and opposing counsel the existence of relevant evidence or witnesses where the lawyer does not intend to offer such evidence or witnesses.
> >
> > (b) Prevent, or when prevention has proved unsuccessful, report to the court and opposing counsel the making of any untrue statement by client or witness or any omission to state a material fact necessary in order to make statements made, in the light of the circumstances under which they were made, not misleading.
> >
> > (c) Question witnesses with a purpose and design to elicit the whole truth, including particularly supplementary and qualifying matters that render evidence already given more accurate, intelligible, or fair than it otherwise would be.
>
> (2) In the construction and application of the rules in subdivision (1), a lawyer will be held to possess knowledge he actually has or, in the exercise of reasonable diligence, should have.[f]

(b) CHANGING THE ADJUDICATOR'S ROLE

G. Louis Joughin & Edmund M. Morgan, The Legacy of Sacco and Vanzetti

184–85, 189–91 (1948).

Ours is an adversary system of litigation. In civil litigation the parties must overcome the inertia of the courts. The parties must frame the issues to be tried; they must make the necessary investigations, discover the

[f] Mr. Frankel apparently would now abandon the privilege exception in his draft rule. See Marvin E. Frankel, The Search for Truth Continued: More Disclosure, Less Privilege, 54 U.Colo.L.Rev. 51 (1982). For a more radical restructuring of the advocate's role, see William H. Simon, The Ideology of Advocacy: Procedural Justice and Professional Ethics, 1978 Wis.L.Rev. 29. For a defense of giving the advocate an extremely adversarial role, see Monroe H. Freedman, Lawyers' Ethics in an Adversary System (1975). For an analytic framework applied to this dispute, see Stephen McG. Bundy & Einer Richard Elhauge, Do Lawyers Improve the Adversary System? A General Theory of Litigation Advice and Its Regulation, 79 Cal.L.Rev. 313, 401–13 (1991).

pertinent data, locate the necessary witnesses, and see that steps are taken to procure their attendance. The court has no duty to make an independent investigation and no facilities for doing so. At the trial the parties present the testimony and other evidence. Neither has any obligation to bring forward material which will aid his adversary or will weaken his own case. The theory of the system is that each party will discover and present everything that will favor his own cause and disclose the weaknesses of his adversary. Thus the truth will emerge to the view of the impartial tribunal. This, it will be noted, assumes that each side will be equally intelligent, equally diligent, and equally fortunate in investigation and discovery of pertinent data, that there will be no fortuitous circumstances to deprive one party of an available witness or to make any of his relevant and important evidence inaccessible or inadmissible without a corresponding disadvantage to the other, and that both parties will be equally skillful in presenting the material and equally able and persuasive in expounding its bearing upon the issues. No argument is necessary to convince the most unobserving that these assumptions are without any basis in fact. Rarely, if ever, in a contested case do they even approximate the truth. With our system of pleading and evidence, a layman is incapable of handling his own litigation. From a bar, whose membership includes men of every degree of learning, skill, and experience, to say nothing of awareness of moral responsibility, it is difficult for the average person to select competent conscientious counsel; for the ignorant and inexperienced, it is well-nigh impossible. Thorough investigation is often costly. Proper preparation for trial on the law and the facts involves expenditures of time and money. Persuasive presentation requires skill beyond the capacity of many practicing lawyers. Indeed, many lawsuits are what popular opinion believes all lawsuits to be, a battle of wits between the advocates of the parties.

. . . .

Some of the most distressing effects of our adversary system appear in its application to the rules governing evidence and witnesses. They are more than ordinarily harmful where matters in issue require special skill in observation or in drawing deductions from observed data. Judicial experience has made it abundantly clear that in numerous cases, both civil and criminal, the testimony of experts is not merely desirable; it is essential. As early as the fourteenth century courts called experts to their aid. These men, learned in arts and in science, were originally called not as witnesses for a party but as assistants to the court. As the form of trial by jury changed and the jury came to rely principally upon matter offered in court rather than upon matter within their own knowledge or learned by private inquiry, these helpers of the court took on the functions of witnesses to the jury. As witnesses they were and are selected by the parties. It is true that as to ordinary data a party can offer from among the persons having relevant information those whose observation and recollection are favorable to his cause. But they will speak about things familiar to jurors. Their testimony can be valued in the light of common experience. Their perception, memory and sincerity can be adequately tested by cross-examination in terms understandable by the ordinary man. Such inferences or conclusions as they may express will carry no undue weight because of their superior capacities for making relevant observations and drawing sound deductions. The subject of expert testimony, however, is generally beyond the ken of the layman. It calls for special skill, knowledge, experience, or training in the perception of data or in the process of drawing accurate inferences, or in both. Where experts who are equally skillful in exposition disagree, the jury is practically helpless.

Consequently it is of the highest importance that the expert witnesses should be properly qualified, honest, and impartial. So long as they were helpers of the court, these qualities could be assured in most cases. When they became witnesses in an adversary system, the temptation to make them partisans became great; and it has not been resisted. Indeed in the majority of instances they have deserted their role as witnesses and have become expert advocates. Even this would be sufferable, if they were competent and honest. The ugly truth is, however, that in many fields the most incompetent is the most glib and persuasive in presenting his views and the most positive in his statements. He can also adjust his opinions to suit the necessities of the party who retains him. He acquires skill in the use of obscure and misleading phrasing. Expert testimony as to mental responsibility in criminal cases, as to diagnosis and prognosis in personal-injury litigation, has become a scandal. . . .

. . . The conduct of the experts in this [Sacco–Vanzetti] case should cause no surprise:[g] so long as experts are chosen by the parties and are willing to lend their services as advocates, so long will the jury be at their mercy and the decision or verdict will rest on nothing much better than conjecture. Even the honest expert, if he conceives himself an advocate, will follow the recognized attitude of the lawyer; he will emphasize the data which favor his client and minimize those which favor the opponent. He will have the hypothetical questions so framed as to enable him to give an apparently favorable opinion and convince himself that it is for the adverse expert to do a corresponding job for his client. The vices of the adversary system carried to this extent, especially in criminal cases, are outrageous

---

[g] The conduct to which the authors were alluding included that of Captain Proctor, ballistics expert called by the prosecution, part of whose direct examination was as follows:

"Q. Have you an opinion as to whether bullet 3 was fired from the Colt Automatic [Sacco's pistol] which is in evidence?

"A. I have.

"Q. And what is your opinion?

"A. My opinion is that it is consistent with being fired by that pistol." 1 The Sacco–Vanzetti Case: Transcript of the Record of the Trial of Nicola Sacco and Bartolomeo Vanzetti in the Courts of Massachusetts and Subsequent Proceedings 1920–7, at 896 (1928). Cross-examination sought no clarification.

In connection with post-trial proceedings, Captain Proctor explained by affidavit what he actually meant, and what the prosecution knew he meant: "At no time was I able to find any evidence whatever which tended to convince me that the particular model [mortal?] bullet found in Berardelli's body, which came from a Colt automatic pistol, . . . came from Sacco's pistol and I so informed the District Attorney and his assistant before the trial. . . . Had I been asked the direct question: whether I had found any affirmative evidence whatever that this so-called mortal bullet had passed through this particular Sacco's pistol, I should have answered then, as I do now without hesitation, in the negative." 4 id. at 3642–43.

and intolerable. In this situation also the trial judge should hold the key. He should be given power to select impartial, competent experts wherever expert assistance will be helpful. The jury should be informed that these experts have been chosen by the court. It is probably impossible to prevent the parties from calling other experts, but their testimony will be subject to discount on account of their partisanship.[h]

JUDGES CALLING AND INTERROGATING WITNESSES

Read Evidence Rules 614 and 706, which allow the court to interrogate witnesses and even to call its own witnesses. The Advisory Committee's notes thereto make clear that these judicial powers are well established. But judges do not extensively use the power to interrogate, and they even more rarely use the power to call witnesses.

Moreover, these are powers and not duties. Extremely few cases, involving very special circumstances, can be found holding it to be reversible error for the judge to fail to question or call a witness.

In Johnson v. United States, 333 U.S. 46, 68 S.Ct. 391 (1948), Johnson, a seaman on a tanker owned and operated by the United States, brought an action under the Jones Act for injuries sustained when a block being held by Dudder, a shipmate, fell and hit Johnson on the head. Plaintiff's version of the episode was the only evidence as to how the injury occurred. He testified that the block, which Dudder had the job to hold, was permitted to fall on him as he was bending over to coil the line that ran through the block. Although available, Dudder was not called as a witness by either party. The issue before the Supreme Court was whether the rule of res ipsa loquitur applied. The majority, in an opinion by Justice Douglas reversing the court below, held that there was no reason why res ipsa loquitur was inapplicable to acts of a fellow servant and that the block's falling was sufficient basis alone for an inference of Dudder's negligence.

Justice Frankfurter, dissenting in part, did not believe that res ipsa loquitur was applicable, viewing it is a rule of necessity to be invoked only when necessary evidence is absent and not readily available. He took the position that when neither party saw fit to call Dudder, the person who actually knew what happened, it was the trial judge's duty to call him as the court's witness. "Federal judges are not referees at prize-fights but functionaries of justice," he said. "As such they have a duty of initiative to see that the issues are determined within the scope of the pleadings, not left to counsel's chosen argument." He further explained: "While a court

---

[h] Charging that the nonexpert courts with their adversary system cannot effectively handle high-technology cases, Joel Yellin, High Technology and the Courts: Nuclear Power and the Need for Institutional Reform, 94 Harv.L.Rev. 489 (1981), argued for a much broader use of masters by the courts. Considering the inherent judicial power to appoint "technical advisors," the court in Reilly v. United States, 863 F.2d 149 (1st Cir.1988), approved appointment of an economist to act somewhat like a law clerk in assisting the judge to deal with the evidence on calculation of damages in a tort case. See generally Ellen E. Deason, Managing the Managerial Expert, 1998 U.Ill.L.Rev. 341.

room is not a laboratory for the scientific pursuit of truth, a trial judge is surely not confined to an account, obviously fragmentary, of the circumstances of a happening, here the meagre testimony of Johnson, when he has at his command the means of exploring them fully, or at least more fully, before passing legal judgment. A trial is not a game of blind man's buff; and the trial judge—particularly in a case where he himself is the trier of the facts upon which he is to pronounce the law—need not blindfold himself by failing to call an available vital witness simply because the parties, for reasons of trial tactics, choose to withhold his testimony."

Questions: (8) Why do you suppose the plaintiff did not call Dudder? Why did not the defendant do so? See Note, Trial Judge's Duty to Call Witnesses in Res Ipsa Loquitur Cases, 58 Yale L.J. 183 (1948).

(9) If generally the judge's failure to call a key witness were reversible error, how would this affect the trial tactics of the parties?

Indeed, a Canadian court has held it reversible error in an uncontested divorce case for the trial judge to call the defendants (wife and co-respondent) as witnesses. The judge had been skeptical of the evidence as to the alleged adultery; when he called both defendants to the stand, they denied adultery; and so he dismissed the action. The appellate court ordered a new trial because the trial judge had thus "assumed the functions of counsel rather than of judge." Fowler v. Fowler, [1949] Ont.W.N. 244. See generally Stephen A. Saltzburg, The Unnecessarily Expanding Role of the American Trial Judge, 64 Va.L.Rev. 1, 52–80 (1978).

RESERVE MINING CO. v. LORD, 529 F.2d 181 (8th Cir.1976). In a major environmental action against a mining company that was allegedly polluting Lake Superior, District Judge Lord in November 1975 ruled against the defendant on a certain motion. Upon petition for a writ of mandamus, the Eighth Circuit undid that defeat, citing various irregularities that occurred when the trial judge, in his own words, "dispensed with the usual adversary proceeding." Furthermore, the court of appeals sua sponte ordered the recusal of the district judge, observing:

"It is urged that the district court's actions were nothing more than a judge acting upon his deep convictions formed after nine and one-half months of [bench] trial [resulting in an injunction]. No one can doubt that Judge Lord does have deep convictions in this matter or that such convictions largely influenced his actions. However, the record reveals more than a trial judge merely acting in accord with his prior judgment. In the November proceeding Judge Lord called and examined the witnesses and interspersed testimony of his own; the trial judge announced on the record that witnesses called by Reserve could not be believed, 'that in every instance Reserve Mining Company hid the evidence, misrepresented, delayed and frustrated the ultimate conclusions;' and that he did not have 'any faith' in witnesses to be called by Reserve. Transcript of November 14, 1975 hearing at 2–5, 56, 109. He further announced that the court would have to take depositions since the lawyers opposing Reserve 'did not know anything about it.' Transcript of November 19, 1975 hearing at 25.

"Judge Lord seems to have shed the robe of the judge and to have assumed the mantle of the advocate. The court thus becomes lawyer, witness and judge in the same proceeding, and abandons the greatest virtue of a fair and conscientious judge—impartiality.

"A judge best serves the administration of justice by remaining detached from the conflict between the parties. As Justice McKenna stated long ago, '[T]ribunals of the country shall not only be impartial in the controversies submitted to them but shall give assurance that they are impartial . . . .' Berger v. United States, 255 U.S. 22, 35–36, 41 S.Ct. 230, 235, 65 L.Ed. 481 (1921). When the judge joins sides, the public as well as the litigants become overawed, frightened and confused."[i]

Question: (10) Justice Jackson, concurring in Youngstown Sheet & Tube Co. v. Sawyer, 343 U.S. 579, 635, 72 S.Ct. 863, 870 (1952), said: "And court decisions are indecisive because of the judicial practice of dealing with the largest questions in the most narrow way." Should this judicial practice be changed? If so, how? Note that Justice Stevens in a speech criticized his 'present colleagues' enthusiastic attempts to codify the law instead of merely performing the judicial task of deciding the cases that come before them." 53 U.S.L.W. 2082, 2082 (Aug. 14, 1984).

Webster Eisenlohr, Inc. v. Kalodner

United States Circuit Court of Appeals, Third Circuit, 1944.
145 F.2d 316, cert. denied, 325 U.S. 867, 65 S.Ct. 1404 (1945).

■ Before BIGGS, MARIS, JONES, GOODRICH, and MCLAUGHLIN, CIRCUIT JUDGES.

■ GOODRICH, CIRCUIT JUDGE. The proceedings at bar are upon a petition to this court for writs of mandamus and prohibition to be directed to the Honorable Harry E. Kalodner, one of the Judges of the District Court of the United States for the Eastern District of Pennsylvania, and David Bortin, Esq., a Special Master appointed pursuant to his order.

[The underlying case was a class action brought by Andrew Speese on behalf of the preferred stockholders against their company, with the plaintiff class claiming exclusive voting power as a consequence of dividend

---

[i] For an account of the unrepentant Judge Lord's handling of certain Dalkon Shield litigation, in a manner reminiscent of Judge Kalodner's handling of the case next set out in the text, see Book Note, 99 Harv.L.Rev. 875 (1986) (reviewing Sheldon Engelmayer & Robert Wagman, Lord's Justice (1985)).

The student should consider how far Rule 16, dealing with pretrial conferences, authorizes or obligates the judge to join actively in readying the case for trial or in pushing for settlement. On that particular problem, see Topic C of Part Seven. Generally on the role of the trial judge, compare Marvin E. Frankel, The Search for Truth: An Umpireal View, 123 U.Pa.L.Rev. 1031 (1975), with Charles E. Wyzanski, Jr., A Trial Judge's Freedom and Responsibility, 65 Harv.L.Rev. 1281 (1952).

defaults. The certificate of incorporation provided that the preferred stock had no right to vote unless two quarterly dividends were in arrears, whereupon "full voting power" would vest in the preferred stock until the company paid the arrearages. The dispute in this case was whether "full voting power" meant exclusive voting power or only the power in the preferred stock to vote along with the common stock.]

Between hearings upon the matter before the District Court the company sent to its stockholders copies of its annual report for the year 1942. Following the sending of the report the company also wrote its preferred stockholders, offering to purchase their interests. Copies of these documents were supplied to the District Judge upon his request although not introduced in evidence in the litigation. At one of the hearings Judge Kalodner indicated his belief that the financial statement sent by the corporation to stockholders was misleading and he criticized the letter sent to preferred stockholders for failure to state facts which he deemed material. Then, at a hearing on April 24, 1943, counsel for Speese stated to the court that he had no client since the shares of Speese and other stockholders which he had represented had been purchased. Judge Kalodner again expressed his dissatisfaction with the actions of the company and stated: "I will advise you gentlemen that I am going to appoint an examiner to look into this matter." Subsequently the court did appoint Mr. Bortin as Special Master under Rule 53 of the Rules of Civil Procedure . . . . The Special Master was directed "to investigate: the acts, conduct, property, liabilities, financial condition, books, records and assets . . . [of Webster Eisenlohr, Inc.]; all the circumstances relating to an Offer made March 26, 1943 to the Holders of 7% Cumulative Preferred Stock . . . ; the arrangement made by and between . . . [Webster Eisenlohr, Inc.] with White, Weld & Co. of New York and Bertram K. Wolfe, Esq. with reference to the Offer made to the Preferred Stockholders; the conduct of the Board of Directors . . . with reference to the making of said Offer to the Preferred Stockholders; the propriety, reasonableness and adequacy of the said Offer to the Preferred Stockholders; the question as to whether or not there was any violation of Rule X–10B–5 'Employment of Manipulative and Deceptive Devices' of the Securities and Exchange Commission, and any other matters which may be referred to the Special Master by the Court as relevant to these proceedings."

Counsel for Webster Eisenlohr, Inc., sought vacation of the order in the District Court and, failing that, asks a writ of mandamus directing the District Court to vacate this appointment and a writ of prohibition directed to the Special Master to prevent him from carrying out his commission. A majority of the court believe the company's position to be well taken.

The fundamental proposition which probably no one would dispute is that a court's power is judicial only, not administrative nor investigative. A judgment may only be properly given for something raised in the course of a litigation between the parties. Now, what was the litigation in this case? The complaint presents the question of the legal effect of the provision that preferred stockholders, under given circumstances, shall have full voting power. . . .

If the plaintiff's contentions on voting rights are upheld as a matter of law, the preferred stockholders are entitled to determine who shall manage the corporation, and other questions which may be determined by stockholders. They are entitled to court help to get those rights if they need it. On the other hand, if the plaintiff's contentions as to the meaning of the phrase are incorrect, they have alleged no legal grounds for complaint. . . .

The directions given the Master went far beyond anything involved in the issues presented in the litigation, as will be seen from the reading of the order appointing him.

. . . .

. . . If the court is limited in its judicial duties, to deciding the issues presented in the litigation before it, the master's function can go no further than to aid in the court's discharge of its duties.

In this case the report made by the company to its stockholders and the circumstances under which some of the preferred stockholders disposed of their interests were not before the court in the then pending lawsuit. The District Judge felt that there were indications that the company had not been entirely aboveboard in the matter. The company, through its counsel, earnestly contended that it had been entirely fair. This court refused to hear counsel on that point, for we thought the matter not relevant. None of these stockholders was under guardianship; all had the full legal power to sell their shares under such circumstances as it pleased them to sell. If any one felt that he had been deceived, he could take the steps necessary to protect his rights. There was no indication that any party to the transaction was complaining. We think that neither the report to the stockholders nor the sale of their stock was involved in the litigation. It was therefore outside the scope of investigation both by the Special Master and the court itself.

We do not think this view imposes unduly restrictive limitations upon courts. The judicial power is limited to deciding controversies. That has been its function historically; that is its function under the Constitution of the United States. No doubt a great deal goes on in the world which ought not to go on. If courts had general investigatory powers, they might discover some of these things and possibly right them. Whether they would do as well in this respect as officers or bodies expressly set up for that purpose may be doubted, but until the concept of judicial power is widened to something quite different from what it now is courts will better serve their public function in limiting themselves to the controversies presented by parties in litigation.

[The court here observed that the class action remained pending, meaning that Rule 23(e) was not in play and also that any remaining preferred stockholders had an opportunity to intervene.]

In view of the above discussion we think it unlikely that the formal issuing of the writs prayed for will be necessary. The applicant may later apply to this court if the need presents itself. No order for costs will be made.

■ [The strong dissenting opinion of JUDGE BIGGS, with whom Judge McLaughlin joined, is omitted.]

Question: (11) Professor James distinguished between "party-presentation" and "party-prosecution." The former represents the principle that the parties are to decide what is submitted for decision, and the latter the principle that the parties are to move the case along. Assumption of responsibility by judges, he thought, is more readily justifiable with respect to the latter than with respect to the former. Fleming James, Jr., Civil Procedure 3–8 (1965). Does this suggest a way of reconciling the foregoing materials on the role of the judge?

ABRAM CHAYES, THE ROLE OF THE JUDGE IN PUBLIC LAW LITIGATION, 89 Harv.L.Rev. 1281, 1284 (1976). After arguing that the traditional view of a lawsuit as a vehicle for settling disputes between private parties about private rights was invalid as a description of much current civil litigation in the federal district courts, Professor Chayes sketched the emerging conception of "public law litigation":

"The characteristic features of the public law model are very different from those of the traditional model. The party structure is sprawling and amorphous, subject to change over the course of the litigation. The traditional adversary relationship is suffused and intermixed with negotiating and mediating processes at every point. The judge is the dominant figure in organizing and guiding the case, and he draws for support not only on the parties and their counsel, but on a wide range of outsiders—masters, experts, and oversight personnel. Most important, the trial judge has increasingly become the creator and manager of complex forms of ongoing relief, which have widespread effects on persons not before the court and require the judge's continuing involvement in administration and implementation. School desegregation, employment discrimination, and prisoners' or inmates' rights cases come readily to mind as avatars of this new form of litigation. But it would be mistaken to suppose that it is confined to these areas. Antitrust, securities fraud and other aspects of the conduct of corporate business, bankruptcy and reorganizations, union governance, consumer fraud, housing discrimination, electoral reapportionment, environmental management—cases in all these fields display in varying degrees the features of public law litigation."[j]

---

[j] This excerpt merely suggests the important transformation of the role of the judge in certain types of cases. You should be aware that some commentators take a negative view thereof, e.g., Donald L. Horowitz, The Judiciary: Umpire or Empire?, 6 Law & Hum.Behav.

UNITED STATES v. MICROSOFT CORP., 56 F.3d 1448 (D.C.Cir. 1995). "Section 16(e) of the Antitrust Procedures and Penalties Act, known as the Tunney Act, requires the district court to determine whether entry of an antitrust consent decree is 'in the public interest.' 15 U.S.C. § 16(e) (1988). In this case, the district court refused to enter a proposed consent decree the Antitrust Division of the Department of Justice negotiated with Microsoft Corporation. We conclude that the proposed consent decree is in the public interest, and that the district court exceeded its authority in concluding to the contrary. We therefore reverse and remand with instructions to enter an order approving the decree.

. . . .

"The key anticompetitive practice against which the complaint is aimed is Microsoft's use of contract terms requiring original equipment manufacturers ('OEMs') to pay Microsoft a royalty for each computer the OEM sells containing a particular microprocessor (in this case, an x86 class microprocessor), whether or not the OEM has included a Microsoft operating system with that computer. . . .

. . . .

"At the first substantive status conference on September 29, 1994, the district judge [Stanley Sporkin] informed the parties that over the summer he had read a book about Microsoft—[James Wallace & Jim Erickson, Hard Drive: Bill Gates and the Making of the Microsoft Empire (1992)]—because he 'thought it would be a good idea maybe to know as much about Microsoft as probably they're going to know about me.' Much of the ensuing discussion focused on accusations against Microsoft contained in the book. The district judge asked whether the government's lawyers had read the book and whether they had investigated the allegations made by its authors. In particular, the judge focused on the allegation that Microsoft engages in 'vaporware,' which he described in differing terms but ultimately defined as 'the public announcement of a computer product before it is ready for market for the sole purpose of causing consumers not to purchase a competitor's product that has been developed and is either currently available for sale or momentarily about to enter the market.' . . .

. . . .

"At a subsequent status hearing on November 2, 1994, the district judge again referred to Hard Drive and its 'vaporware' allegations, noting that the book 'does allege some very serious practices,' and telling the government that he wanted to be satisfied that the allegations in the book

---

129, 134–35 (1982) (arguing that adjudicative process is ill-suited to social reform because traditionally and optimally "(1) access is voluntary; (2) participation is narrow; (3) decision is mandatory; (4) the decision maker is isolated from the environment in which the decision must operate; (5) enforcement is largely private"). For development of the implications and evaluations of public law litigation, see Topics C and D of Part Five.

For a subsequent reconceptualization of the role of the judge, see William B. Rubenstein, A Transactional Model of Adjudication, 89 Geo.L.J. 371 (2001) (arguing that the judge's role in modern complex private litigation is akin to brokering a business deal). See generally Chris H. Miller, The Adaptive American Judiciary: From Classical Adjudication to Class Action Litigation, 72 Alb.L.Rev. 117 (2009) (presenting various reconceptualizations).

were not true. The Department was instructed to inform interested persons that they had until December 5, 1994 to seek leave to participate in the court's hearing on the consent decree. Only I.D.E. Corporation, which had participated in the comment process, sought leave to participate in the hearing. But on January 10, 1995, (over a month late and over the objection of both the government and Microsoft), the law firm of Wilson, Sonsini, Goodrich & Rosati, on behalf of three computer industry companies ('Doe Companies'), filed a 96–page memorandum (plus a 215–page appendix) arguing that the proposed consent decree was inadequate because it would not result in increased competition in the operating systems market, nor prevent Microsoft from monopolizing the rest of the software industry. The Doe Companies claimed that because of the unusual 'increasing returns' nature of Microsoft's market position, it would be extremely difficult to dislodge Microsoft from its dominant status and return the market to a state of equilibrium, or competition. Moreover, they claimed that Microsoft had the capacity to leverage its installed base in the operating systems market so as to dominate the related markets for applications and other software products. The Doe Companies also attached two documents purporting to show that Microsoft had engaged in 'vaporware.' Wilson, Sonsini's brief was accompanied by a motion requesting that the district court permit the late filing, and also permit the purported computer industry companies to remain anonymous, asserting 'fear' that they would be subject to unexplained retaliation from Microsoft. The district court, without a hearing on the need for or propriety of the Doe Companies' proceeding anonymously, granted the motion over the government's and Microsoft's objections.

. . . .

"Appellants contend that the district judge misinterpreted the Tunney Act—indeed interpreted that statute so as to raise serious questions regarding its constitutionality—by basing his rejection of the decree on considerations which implicate the executive branch's prosecutorial discretion. The thrust of the judge's concerns were directed to his dissatisfaction with the framework of the complaint fashioned by the Department. He thought it much too modest to deal with the imperfections in the relevant market and their cause—at least as he perceived them. Appellants contend that the judge did not simply make the proper inquiry into whether the decree was appropriate to the complaint, but instead asked whether the complaint itself was adequate. By doing so, it is argued, the judge improperly intruded on the government's prosecutorial role. The judge's demand that he be informed of the contours of the investigation, the settlement discussions, and the government's future investigative plans, indicates that the judge impermissibly arrogated to himself the President's role 'to take care that the laws be faithfully executed.'

. . . .

"At the heart of this case, then, is the proper scope of the district court's inquiry into the 'public interest.' Is the district judge entitled to seize hold of the matter—the investigation into the putative defendant's business practices—and decide for himself the appropriate combined response of the executive and judicial branches to those practices? . . .

. . . .

"When the government and a putative defendant present a proposed consent decree to a district court for review under the Tunney Act, the court can and should inquire, in the manner we have described, into the purpose, meaning, and efficacy of the decree. If the decree is ambiguous, or the district judge can foresee difficulties in implementation, we would expect the court to insist that these matters be attended to. And, certainly, if third parties contend that they would be positively injured by the decree, a district judge might well hesitate before assuming that the decree is appropriate. But, when the government is challenged for not bringing as extensive an action as it might, a district judge must be careful not to exceed his or her constitutional role. A decree, even entered as a pretrial settlement, is a judicial act, and therefore the district judge is not obliged to accept one that, on its face and even after government explanation, appears to make a mockery of judicial power. Short of that eventuality, the Tunney Act cannot be interpreted as an authorization for a district judge to assume the role of Attorney General."[k]

(c) CHANGING THE SYSTEM

Questions: (12) Judge Frank proposed a different idea. Rather than change the roles of lawyer and judge, he would have enlarged the role of the government. After observing that a court's judgment is a solemn governmental act with potentially grave consequences and that courts are alone among governmental bodies in not accepting any responsibility for establishing the facts upon which they act, he suggested for many civil cases "that we should consider whether it is not feasible to provide impartial government officials—who are not court employees, and who act on their own initiative—to dig up, and present to the courts, significant evidence which one or the other of the parties may overlook or be unable to procure. No court would be bound to accept that evidence as true. Nor would any of the parties be precluded from trying to show the unreliability of such evidence (by cross-examination or otherwise) or from introducing additional evidence. Trials would still remain adversary." Jerome Frank, Courts on Trial 98 (1949). Are you impressed by this suggestion?

(13) Mr. Frankel instead suggested a "lawyerless tribunal" for many civil cases. The aggrieved person would complain directly to a judge. "The putative claimant may be persuaded at this stage that the claim is not worth pursuing. If

---

[k] The appellate court ordered the case assigned to a different district judge. That new judge, Thomas Penfield Jackson, quickly approved the consent decree. But it was the DOJ's 1997 allegation of the decree's violation that led to the legendary and lengthy proceedings against Microsoft. During these, the appellate court disqualified Judge Jackson for the appearance of partiality against Microsoft, 253 F.3d 34, 116–17 (D.C.Cir.), cert. denied, 534 U.S. 952, 122 S.Ct. 350 (2001). The new judge, Colleen Kollar–Kotelly, approved a new consent decree, 231 F.Supp.2d 144 (D.D.C.2002), aff'd, 373 F.3d 1199 (D.C.Cir.2004), which required ongoing supervision. See William H. Page & John E. Lopatka, The Microsoft Case, at ix (2007) ("the defining antitrust case, of our era").

that does not happen, the opposed party is summoned. Efforts to settle may follow. If there is no early compromise, the judge will assign staff to investigate, to examine and cross-examine witnesses, to collect other evidence—to do, in short, whatever is necessary to reconstruct as accurately as possible the events giving rise to the dispute. Similarly, the law will be researched, perhaps by subordinates assigned to develop the best adversary stance for each of the disputants. The end of the researches, with both parties having had a chance to contest witnesses or other evidence against them, will be a decision more or less of the familiar kind our courts render." Marvin E. Frankel, Partisan Justice 116 (1980). Are you impressed by this suggestion?

KEVIN M. CLERMONT, ROBERT A. HILLMAN, SHERI LYNN JOHNSON & ROBERT S. SUMMERS, LAW FOR SOCIETY: NATURE, FUNCTIONS, AND LIMITS 136 (2010). "In the preceding passages, we offered a variety of criticisms of adversarial adjudication. It may be, though, that if a social thinker really wanted to justify abandonment of adversarial adjudication, she ought to urge abandonment of adjudication. *Adjudication*—referral of two-sided disputes to an impartial third person for decision—begets adversarial adjudication, does it not? But how could the need for adjudication itself be eliminated and aggrieved citizens still be left with something resembling a remedial instrument? This is not impossible, at least for some types of claims.

"In the Swimming Pool case [a negligence case against the operator of a swimming pool for injuries sustained from diving into the pool], the relevant rule of law might have provided that 'any person suffering personal injuries caused by another in the course of leisure activity shall be entitled to compensation therefor from public funds upon application to the appropriate public official. Satisfactory proof of such injuries, of causation by another, and of nature of activity must be submitted.'

"Observe that an arrangement of this kind would not, in the first instance, call for adjudication at all. It would not even require the loss causer to be present at the official determination of loss and causation and activity, let alone pay out of its own pocket (or that of its insurer). Indeed, there would be no reason to permit the loss causer itself to demand an elaborate day in court, for it does not risk bearing the loss and it is not being branded a wrongdoer. The proceeding would involve the loss causer only indirectly. However, the taxpayers would have to pay, and the loss causer would feel less deterrence.

"In short, here we do not have a two-sided dispute for reference to a third person. The public official would operate by unilateral inquiry, discussion, and disposition. A dispute could arise between the aggrieved and the relevant public official over facts of loss and causation and activity or over law, and *this* dispute would be of a two-sided kind that perhaps the law would then allow to be referred to a third-party adjudicative body for resolution. But absent this, no need for adjudication would arise.

"Now consider the feasibility and desirability of a system of this kind to handle personal injury claims arising from automobile accidents. One such system is the no-fault insurance scheme."

Frank E.A. Sander, Varieties of Dispute Processing

70 F.R.D. 111, 111–17, 130–31 (1976), reprinted in The Pound Conference: Perspectives on Justice in the Future 65 (1979).

Thus one concern to which we ought to address ourselves here is how we might escape from the specter [of exploding caseloads]. This might be accomplished in various ways. First, we can try to prevent disputes[4] from arising in the first place through appropriate changes in the substantive law, such as the adoption of a no-fault principle for automobile injuries or the removal of a criminal sanction for certain conduct. A less obvious substantive law issue that may have a bearing on the extent of litigation that arises is whether we opt for a discretionary rule or for one that aims to fix more or less firmly the consequences that will follow upon certain facts. For example, if a statute says that marital property on divorce will be divided in the court's discretion there is likely to be far more litigation than if the rule is, as in the community property states, that such property will normally be divided 50–50. I wonder whether legislatures and law revision commissions are sufficiently aware of this aspect of their work.

Another method of minimizing disputes is through greater emphasis on preventive law. Of course lawyers have traditionally devoted a large part of their time to anticipating various eventualities and seeking, through skillful drafting and planning, to provide for them in advance. But so far this approach has been resorted to primarily by the well-to-do. I suspect that with the advent of prepaid legal services this type of practice will be utilized more widely, resulting in a probable diminution of litigation.

A second way of reducing the judicial caseload is to explore alternative ways of resolving disputes outside the courts, and it is to this topic that I wish to devote my primary attention. By and large we lawyers and law teachers have been far too single-minded when it comes to dispute resolution. Of course, as pointed out earlier, good lawyers have always tried to prevent disputes from coming about, but when that was not possible, we have tended to assume that the courts are the natural and obvious dispute resolvers. In point of fact there is a rich variety of different processes, which, I would submit, singly or in combination, may provide far more "effective" conflict resolution.[7]

---

[4] For present purposes I use the word "dispute" to describe a matured controversy, as distinguished, for example, from a "grievance" which may be inchoate and unexpressed.

[7] I would suggest the following criteria for determining the effectiveness of a dispute resolution mechanism: cost, speed, accuracy, credibility (to the public and the parties), and workability. In some cases, but not in all, predictability may also be important.

Let me turn now to the two questions with which I wish to concern myself:

1) What are the significant characteristics of various alternative dispute resolution mechanisms (such as adjudication by courts, arbitration, mediation, negotiation, and various blends of these and other devices)?

2) How can these characteristics be utilized so that, given the variety of disputes that presently arise, we can begin to develop some rational criteria for allocating various types of disputes to different dispute resolution processes?

. . .

. . . .

The chart reproduced below attempts to depict a spectrum of some of the available processes arranged on a scale of decreasing external involvement.[12]

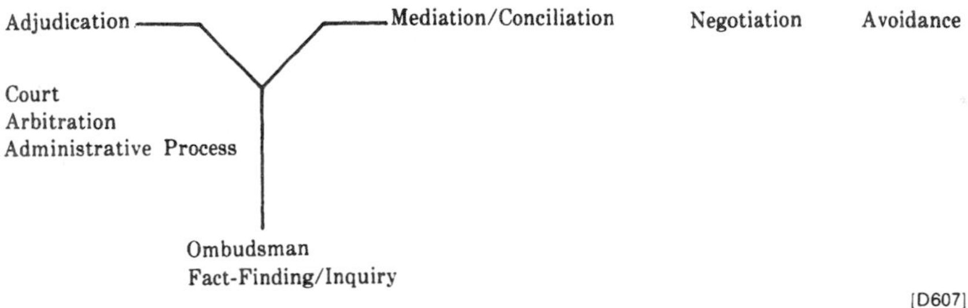

At the extreme left is adjudication, the one process that so instinctively comes to the legal mind that I suspect if we asked a random group of law students how a particular dispute might be resolved, they would invariably say "file a complaint in the appropriate court." Professor Lon Fuller, one of the few scholars who has devoted attention to an analysis of the adjudicatory process, has defined adjudication as "a social process of decision which assures to the affected party a particular form of participation, that of presenting proofs and arguments for a decision in his favor."[13] Although he places primary emphasis on process, I would like for present purposes to stress a number of other aspects—the use of a third party with coercive power, the usually "win or lose" nature of the decision, and the tendency of

[12] I have selected this factor as one that seems to me rather critical, but there are obviously other aspects in which the various processes differ and which must be considered (e.g., method and cost of selection of third party, qualifications and tenure of third party, formality of proceedings, role of advocates, number of disputants, etc.). Some of these are referred to interstitially in the ensuing discussion. Another factor that is often said to play a differing part in the various processes is the relevance of norms. But see M. Eisenberg, Private Ordering Through Negotiation: Dispute–Settlement and Rulemaking, 89 Harv.L.Rev. 637 (1976), suggesting that dispute settlement negotiation closely resembles adjudication in its frequent recourse to norms. See also A. Sarat & J. Grossman, Courts and Conflict Resolution: Problems in the Mobilization of Adjudication, 69 Am.Pol.Sci.Rev. 1200 (1975).

[13] L. Fuller, Collective Bargaining and the Arbitrator, 1963 Wis.L.Rev. 1, 19. . . .

the decision to focus narrowly on the immediate matter in issue as distinguished from a concern with the underlying relationship between the parties. Although mediation or conciliation[14] also involves the use of a third party facilitator (and is distinguished in that regard from pure negotiation), a mediator or conciliator usually has no coercive power and the process in which he engages also differs from adjudication in the other two respects just mentioned. Professor Fuller puts this point well when he refers to "the central quality of mediation, namely, its capacity to reorient the parties toward each other, not by imposing rules on them, but by helping them to achieve a new and shared perception of their relationship, a perception that will redirect their attitudes and dispositions toward one another."[15]

Of course quite a variety of procedures fit under the label of adjudication. Aside from the familiar judicial model, there is arbitration, and the administrative process. Even within any one of these, there are significant variations. Obviously there are substantial differences between the Small Claims Court and the Supreme Court. Within arbitration, too, although the version used in labor relations is generally very similar to a judicial proceeding in that there is a written opinion and an attempt to rationalize the result by reference to general principles, in some forms of commercial arbitration the judgment resembles a Solomonic pronouncement and written opinions are often not utilized. Another significant variant is whether the parties have any choice in selecting the adjudicator, as they typically do in arbitration. Usually a decision rendered by a person in whose selection the parties have played some part will, all things being equal, be less subject to later criticism by the parties.

There are important distinctions, too, concerning the way in which the case came to arbitration. There may be a statute (as in New York and Pennsylvania) requiring certain types of cases to be initially submitted to arbitration (so-called compulsory arbitration). More commonly arbitration is stipulated as the exclusive dispute resolution mechanism in a contract entered into by the parties (as is true of the typical collective bargaining agreement and some modern medical care agreements). In this situation the substantive legal rules are usually also set forth in the parties' agreement, thus giving the parties control not only over the process and the adjudicator but also over the governing principles.

As is noted on the chart, if we focus on the indicated distinctions between adjudication and mediation, there are a number of familiar hybrid processes. An inquiry, for example, in many respects resembles the typical adjudication, but the inquiring officer (or fact finder as he is sometimes called) normally has no coercive power; indeed, according to Professor Fuller's definition, many inquiries would not be adjudication at all since

[14] For present purposes the terms mediation and conciliation will be used interchangeably, although in some settings conciliation refers to the more unstructured process of facilitating communication between the parties, while mediation is reserved for a more formal process of meeting first with both parties and then with each of them separately, etc.

[15] L. Fuller, Mediation—Its Forms and Functions, 44 So.Cal.L.Rev. 305, 325 (1971).

the parties have no right to any agreed-upon form of presentation and participation.

But a fact finding proceeding may be a potent tool for inducing settlement. Particularly if the fact finder commands the respect of the parties, his independent appraisal of their respective positions will often be difficult to reject. This is especially true of the Ombudsman who normally derives his power solely from the force of his position. These considerations have particular applicability where there is a disparity of bargaining power between the disputants (e.g., citizen and government, consumer and manufacturer, student and university). Although there may often be a reluctance in these situations to give a third person power to render a binding decision, the weaker party may often accomplish the same result through the use of a skilled fact finder.

There are of course a number of other dispute resolution mechanisms which one might consider. Most of these (e.g., voting, coin tossing, self-help) are not of central concern here because of their limited utility or acceptability. But one other mechanism deserves brief mention. Professor William Felstiner[, Influences of Social Organization on Dispute Processing, 9 Law & Soc'y Rev. 63 (1974),] pointed out that in a "technologically complex rich society" avoidance becomes an increasingly common form of handling controversy. He describes avoidance as "withdrawal from or contraction of the dispute-producing relationship" (e.g., a child leaving home, a tenant moving to another apartment, or a businessman terminating a commercial relationship). . . .

[Professor Sander explores criteria that may help determine how particular disputes might best be resolved, including nature of dispute, relationship between disputants, and cost and speed of available processes. He goes on to advocate] a flexible and diverse panoply of dispute resolution processes, with particular types of cases being assigned to differing processes (or combinations of processes), according to some of the criteria previously mentioned. Conceivably such allocation might be accomplished for a particular class of cases at the outset by the legislature; that in effect is what was done by the Massachusetts legislature for malpractice cases. Alternatively one might envision by the year 2000 not simply a court house but a Dispute Resolution Center, where the grievant would first be channelled through a screening clerk who would then direct him to the process (or sequence of processes) most appropriate to his type of case. The room directory in the lobby of such a Center might look as follows:

Screening Clerk	Room 1
Mediation	Room 2
Arbitration	Room 3
Fact Finding	Room 4
Malpractice Screening Panel	Room 5
Superior Court	Room 6
Ombudsman	Room 7

Of one thing we can be certain: once such an eclectic method of dispute resolution is accepted there will be ample opportunity for everyone to play a part. Thus a court might decide of its own to refer a certain type of problem to a more suitable tribunal. Or a legislature might, in framing certain substantive rights, build in an appropriate dispute resolution process. Institutions such as prisons, schools, or mental hospitals also could get into the act by establishing indigenous dispute resolution processes.

FRANK E.A. SANDER, ALTERNATIVE METHODS OF DISPUTE RESOLUTION: AN OVERVIEW, 37 U.Fla.L.Rev. 1, 8–11 (1985). "Most of the mechanisms discussed thus far are primarily found in the private dispute resolution sector and are not a part of the formal court structure. In an attempt to make courts more responsive to the emerging alternatives movement, ADRMs have been incorporated in one way or another into the court system. In that respect, these developments represent a partial foreshadowing of the 'multi-door courthouse' [or dispute resolution center] notion . . . .

1. Small Claims Adjudication and Mediation

"Over fifty years ago courts were recognized as too elaborate and expensive for simple cases involving only small claims. This led to the creation of small claims court, where litigants themselves, without lawyers, can present their disputes. These actions normally involve claims of not more than $1,000 and result in a type of quick, rough justice. Some scholars have recently raised serious questions about the efficacy of small claims courts. Nevertheless, the institution appears to be an essentially durable one that has carved a place in the catalog of useful dispute settlement mechanisms. An interesting recent variant has been utilization of mediation in small claims court.

2. Compulsory Arbitration

"Following a 1950's experiment in Philadelphia a number of jurisdictions have recently passed legislation requiring all monetary claims cases up to a certain limit (generally around $10,000–$15,000) to be initially processed by arbitration. In view of the prevailing right to trial by jury, a right to de novo review must then be accorded in the courts. However, such recourse to the courts might be subjected to cost sanctions if the petitioner does not prevail in court. Absent such a sanction, the net result might be to substitute two proceedings for the previous one. A similar program was begun on an experimental basis in three federal district courts [and since expanded[1]]. Preliminary data from these experiments are encouraging, and

[1] "The most important statutory development to date, the Alternative Dispute Resolution Act (ADRA) of 1998 [codified at 28 U.S.C. §§ 651–658], mandates that every federal district court implement an ADR program because ADR 'has the potential to provide a variety of benefits, including greater satisfaction of the parties, innovative methods of resolving disputes, and greater efficiency in achieving settlements.' The Act requires federal civil litigants to consider ADR at appropriate stages in litigation and instructs each district court to offer at least one ADR alternative. Significantly, the Act authorizes courts to compel participation in mediation or early neutral evaluation processes but requires consent for court-annexed

show that even where a sizeable percentage of the cases are appealed to court, very few proceed to trial.

3. Malpractice Screening

"Following the malpractice 'crisis' in the mid-seventies, a number of states set up special procedures for malpractice actions. Often the parties are initially required to arbitrate their differences. In other jurisdictions, such as Massachusetts, a screening panel is established, consisting of a doctor, lawyer and judge. The panel determines whether a prima facie case is established. If not, the plaintiff may proceed only by putting up a bond for the defendant's costs. The success of these experiments has varied. In some states, the special procedures have been abandoned or declared unconstitutional. In others, the mechanisms have worked well to screen out spurious claims.

4. Large Litigation

"Many of the devices discussed above are applicable only to what has sometimes been referred to as 'minor disputes.' Some devices have also been developed to deal specifically with large and complex litigation.

a. Rent-a-Judge

"Arbitration often employs experienced individuals such as retired judges to arbitrate difficult cases. Such use of arbitration, by consent of the parties, is quite different from that discussed in Section 2 above, where reference to arbitration is compulsory rather than consensual.

"A variant of this practice has developed in some jurisdictions, notably California. It calls for parties to select a retired judge to hear the case, much as an arbitrator would. The procedures applied are the same as those that would apply in court, except as otherwise modified by the parties. Most notably, the judge's decision has the same force and effect as a judgment entered by a regular court.

"The Rent-a-Judge procedure raises important policy questions. For example, should parties be able to hire the best available judges under circumstances where their decision has the full force of law, just as if the case had been decided in court? How does this practice square with the notion of equal access to the courts regardless of means? What will be the impact of such a practice on the regular judiciary? These questions and others deserve more discussion than they have received thus far.

---

arbitration. Although the judicialization of ADR may itself raise threshold questions, the most troubling aspect of the statute is the lack of procedural guidelines provided for courts required to implement ADR programs. The ADRA directs each court to establish its own rules concerning confidentiality and disqualification of neutrals. The discretion afforded individual courts to determine the nature and extent of annexed ADR programs may encourage helpful evolution of ADR, but it may also lead to undesirable variety in procedure and practice. Furthermore, the Act appropriates no funding to implement programs, rendering impotent hopes of significant innovations in courts already struggling to cover basic expenses. More congressional support is needed before courts can properly implement and evaluate the ADRA." Developments in the Law—The Paths of Civil Litigation, 113 Harv.L.Rev. 1752, 1861–62 (2000).

b. Mini–Trial

"Ten years ago some imaginative litigants in the federal district court in California developed an innovative extrajudicial mechanism to aid in the settlement of complex and protracted litigation. The procedure calls for the parties to select an experienced individual to preside at a two-day information exchange. Each party has one day to present its case in any form it desires, including questions for the opposing side. The highest official of each party, assuming a corporate litigant, must attend this hearing. At the end of the proceeding, the two top officials confer, without their lawyers, to evaluate the case. In the seminal case utilizing this innovative procedure, the parties promptly settled. If an agreement is not reached, then the presiding official will give his view concerning how the case would be resolved in court. The parties then use this additional information to discuss settlement. If settlement is not achieved, the procedure has no evidentiary effect and the case returns to court. In virtually all cases which have utilized this procedure, however, settlement has been achieved. The procedure has the additional virtue that it can be readily adapted to different situations (e.g., the presider can be dispensed with, more or less time can be allowed for the presentations)."

STEVEN B. GOLDBERG, FRANK E.A. SANDER, NANCY H. ROGERS & SARAH RUDOLPH COLE, DISPUTE RESOLUTION 4–5 (5th ed. 2007). This coursebook offers a summary of its new subject:

"Primary" Dispute Resolution Processes

Characteristics	***Adjudication***	***Arbitration****	***Mediation***	***Negotiation***
Voluntary/Involuntary	Involuntary	Voluntary	Voluntary†	Voluntary
Binding/Nonbinding	Binding; subject to appeal	Binding, subject to review on limited grounds	If agreement, enforceable as contract; sometimes agreement embodied in court decree	If agreement, enforceable as contract
Third party	Imposed, third-party neutral decision-maker, generally with no specialized expertise in dispute subject	Party-selected third-party decision-maker, often with specialized subject expertise	Party-selected outside facilitator	No third-party facilitator
Degree of formality	Formalized and highly structured by predetermined, rigid rules	Procedurally less formal; procedural rules and substantive law may be set by parties	Usually informal, unstructured	Usually informal, unstructured
Nature of proceeding	Opportunity to present proofs and arguments	Opportunity for each party to present proofs and arguments	Unbounded presentation of evidence, arguments and interests	Unbounded presentation of evidence, arguments and interests
Outcome	Principled decision, supported by reasoned opinion	Sometimes principled decision supported by reasoned opinion; sometimes compromise without opinion	Mutually acceptable agreement sought	Mutually acceptable agreement sought
Private/Public	Public	Private, unless judicial review sought	Private †	Private

* Court-annexed arbitration is involuntary, nonbinding, and public.

† In some jurisdictions, mediation is mandatory for certain kinds of cases or if a court so orders. In such cases meditation may not be private.

"Hybrid" Dispute Resolution Processes

Characteristics	***Private Judging***	***Neutral Expert Fact-Finding***	***MiniTrial***	***Ombudsman***	***Summary Jury Trial***
Voluntary/Involuntary	Voluntary	Voluntary or involuntary under FRE 706	Voluntary	Voluntary	Voluntary or involuntary
Binding/Nonbinding	Binding, subject to appeal	Nonbinding but results may be admissible	Nonbinding; if agreement, enforceable as contract	Nonbinding	Nonbinding; if agreement, enforceable as contract
Third party	Party-selected third-party decision-maker, may have to be former judge or lawyer	Third-party neutral with specialized subject matter expertise; may be selected by the parties or the court	Party-selected neutral advisor, sometimes with specialized subject expertise	Third-party selected by institution	Mock jury impaneled by court
Degree of formality	Statutory procedure but highly flexible as to timing, place and procedures	Informal	Less formal than adjudication; procedural rules may be set by parties	Informal	Procedural rules fixed; less formal than adjudication
Nature of proceeding	Opportunity to present proofs and arguments	Investigatory	Opportunity to present summary proofs and arguments	Investigatory	Opportunity to present summary proofs and arguments
Outcome	Principled decision, sometimes supported by findings of fact and conclusions of law	Report or testimony	Mutually acceptable agreement sought	Report	Advisory verdict to facilitate settlement
Private/Public	Private, unless judicial enforcement sought	Private, unless disclosed in court	Usually Private	Private	Usually public

---

RICHARD A. POSNER, THE SUMMARY JURY TRIAL AND OTHER METHODS OF ALTERNATIVE DISPUTE RESOLUTION: SOME CAUTIONARY OBSERVATIONS, 53 U.Chi.L.Rev. 366, 367 (1986). "I am unconvinced by anecdotes, glowing testimonials, confident assertions, appeals to intuition. Lawyers, including judges and law professors, have been lazy about subjecting their hunches—which in honesty we should admit are often little better than prejudices—to systematic empirical testing. Judicial opinions and law review articles alike are full of assertions . . . that have no demonstrable factual basis. Not that the authors of these articles and opinions must be wrong on any of these assertions; they may be right on all. But they have only impressions; they have no verified knowledge. If we are to experiment with alternatives to trials, let us really experiment; let us propose testable hypotheses, and test them."

STEPHAN LANDSMAN, THE DECLINE OF THE ADVERSARY SYSTEM: HOW THE RHETORIC OF SWIFT AND CERTAIN JUSTICE HAS AFFECTED ADJUDICATION IN AMERICAN COURTS, 29 Buff.L.Rev. 487, 488, 528–30 (1980). "Pound's remarks have served as a manifesto for those championing judicial efficiency and celerity. Their goal has been to secure the adoption of what they deem to be the speediest methods of resolving disputes. In pursuit of this goal the architects of change have ignored the aims and values of those aspects of the adversary process they seek to alter. They have substituted the rhetoric of swift and certain justice for a reasoned assessment of the impact of change on the court system and society.

. . . .

"The adversary method is not of equal utility in resolving all types of disputes. . . . [S]everal situations can be identified in which the adversary process would seem particularly useful. The most outstanding of these is litigation involving a dispute between a citizen and the government. In such a dispute, whether it be a civil rights case, a criminal matter, or a contract action, the adversary [system's] judge and jury serve as a vital counterbalance to the power of the state.

"On the other hand, there are a number of settings in which adversary procedure does not seem appropriate. When the parties must continue to work or live together in intimate contact or in a cooperative relationship, the adversary method may not be the best means of resolving their dispute. Adversary procedure may exacerbate rather than resolve tensions and may not foster the kind of compromise essential to the restoration of harmony. For this reason, disputes like those between labor and management, or between family members in an intact family unit should usually be resolved in nonadversarial proceedings.

"It is also sensible to utilize nonadversarial methods when *all the parties* strongly desire speed, simplicity, and economy in adjudication. In such settings adversary process will tend to intrude undesired deliberation and expense. The labor grievance process provides an example of the type of case in which certain adversary procedures are avoided for reasons of economy and celerity. Finally, where there is no dispute, adversary machinery is not needed. In situations like the uncontested divorce, adoption, or name change, there is little call for the panoply of procedures built into the adversary process.

"While it is possible to list types of cases that seem more or less suited to adversarial adjudication, any a priori designation threatens to unfairly exclude some litigants from access to procedures they view essential to the proper consideration of their cases. An arbitrary ban on adversarial consideration of 'repetitious' cases, or cases involving small sums of money, or cases involving some 'institutional relationship' raises serious problems of social and political judgment as well as accusations of unequal treatment. A better approach than categorical exclusion may be a system that allows the parties to choose the type of process best suited to their needs. Where all the parties make an *uncoerced* choice to avoid adversarial process it seems eminently sensible to honor their decision. Use of an election mechanism may ease the burden on the adversarial courts, while protecting the rights of those who believe they cannot obtain redress outside the adversarial framework.

"Only when the nature of the adversary process and the values it vindicates are clearly understood and considered is it possible to determine the extent nonadversary processes should be utilized by American courts to resolve disputes. If these issues are ignored, intelligent change is impossible. Arguments like that concerning swift and certain justice, which tend to obscure the fundamental issues, must be rejected as a basis upon which to premise change."

JUDITH RESNIK, MANY DOORS? CLOSING DOORS? ALTERNATIVE DISPUTE RESOLUTION AND ADJUDICATION, 10 Ohio St.J. on Disp.Resol. 211, 250–52 (1995). "I turn now from claims of ADR as responsive to systemic problems, such as that of a workload crisis, [lack of access], and incivility, to clarify a sometimes overlapping claim, that ADR's responsiveness to the needs of the disputants makes ADR a better means of resolving disputes (and hence good for the system as well). This thesis comes from participants with different perspectives and varies to some extent with the kind of ADR at issue.

"For those forms of ADR that are focused on settlement, three assumptions result in efficiency: first, settlements by parties are voluntary; second, the parties have better information than adjudicators; third, with information and volition, parties have the control to achieve outcomes that are better than those imposed by adjudicators. Settlement-oriented ADR thus becomes a more efficient way to resolve disputes than adjudication. . . .

"Consent is also assumed to have benefits beyond the immediate resolution of the problem. The premise is that if parties agree to and craft a resolution, long term compliance will result. Indeed, for some ADR proponents, volition is so central to ADR that ADR is at risk if it becomes a mandatory part of the state's apparatus.

"Efficiency claims on behalf of ADR forms that are quasi-adjudicatory rest not on consent as much as on speed, accessibility, and on the quantum of procedure provided. Court-annexed arbitration is described as a quicker, shorter, less formal trial. Because efficiency is not simply equated with economy but also entails accuracy (or sufficient accuracy in light of reduced costs), claims made for scaled-down adjudication embody a serious critique of adjudication. The point made is that the outcomes are just as good, or good enough, with less process, less cost, less delay.

. . . .

"The efficiency arguments for ADR are sometimes turned into or related to arguments about fairness. Both arguments (ADR as more efficient and ADR as fairer than adjudication) share a view that parties have superior access to and actual possession of information than do third party decision makers. From this vantage point, adjudication is seen as a technique that can both distract and confuse. Legal rules operate to frame debates in a fashion that obscures parties' goals and that results in either wins or losses, rather than a richer set of possible resolutions. In contrast,

ADR is seen as focusing on issues, relaxing the law, and thus providing more 'just' results."

Current Developments in Judicial Administration: Papers Presented at the Plenary Session of the American Association of Law Schools, December, 1977

80 F.R.D. 147, 167–68, 173–74, 179–84 (1979).

Remarks of Earl Johnson, Jr. as Presentor

. . . .

Though there are some differences in analysis and emphasis in these various articles and speeches, they share a common theme: we have become too dependent upon an over-legalized, over-formalized method of resolving disputes in the U.S. . . .

There is less consensus about the cures. Nonetheless, one does often hear about the four de's: de-legalize, de-lawyer, de-formalize and de-judicialize. In other words, let's reduce the number of laws. Let's make them simple enough so that it isn't necessary for a citizen to hire a lawyer before he takes any major step or every time he attempts to resolve any dispute. Let's take some of the time-consuming, confounding formalities out of the judicial process itself. And finally, let's take as many disputes as possible completely out of the judicial framework and resolve them through other means.

. . . .

But why consider using any of these alternative forums. What is wrong with our tried and tested centuries old Anglo–American judicial model? That is an important threshold question that is related intimately to the issue of which criteria one might employ in allocating different categories of disputes to different kinds of forums.

Nor is there a single answer to this question. I suspect that different reformers would provide this audience with different answers. It is, however, possible to detect at least three independent rationales for diverting civil cases away from the traditional judicial forum. For some, the primary goal is to relieve the court workload. For a second, the primary purpose is to improve access for disputes and disputants that cannot economically reach the judicial forum. A third group of reformers feels that the judicial mode is at best an inferior way of resolving at least some kinds of disputes and furthermore that it is a socially and psychologically disruptive approach to such controversies. For convenience, I will label the first motive for channelling disputes to alternative forums as the "judicial overload" rationale, the second as the "access to justice" rationale, and the third as the "superior process" rationale.

This is not to say that a given forum must be supported by only one of these rationales. Some alternative forums are seen as contributing to two or more of these purposes. Nonetheless they are very distinct rationales. Deciding which one is the predominant motive will largely determine which kinds of disputes should be allocated to the non-judicial forum and the criteria which should be applied in judging the performance of that alternative forum.

. . . .

Whichever rationale is under consideration, it is apparent we do not yet have all the answers as to what forums work or which disputes should be channeled to which tribunals. In fact we are just beginning to ask the right questions.

The next decade is apt to see an enormous amount of activity in this field. New forums will be devised, experiments will be undertaken, evaluations will be conducted, debates will rage. In one way or another, through careful planning or confused groping I submit American society will move toward a new justice system: one in which the courts as we know them will still occupy an important position but alongside a variety of alternative forums offering disputants other methods of resolving disputes, other types of dispute resolvers and even other aspirations. It is also a justice system where non-lawyers will have a prominent role.

The entire enterprise offers both challenge and opportunity to the law schools. The chances for creative scholarship and particularly for empirical research are exciting. Meanwhile, there will be need to be flexible in our educational programs to adjust them to the needs of a rapidly evolving and probably dramatically restructured justice system. Who is to train the lay arbitrators, the mediators and other dispute resolvers, both professional and amateur? And how do we equip law students to function effectively in a multi-faceted justice system where they may be called upon to be neutral mediators as often as they are expected to be partisan advocates?

I'm sure there are many in this audience who are skeptical that anything nearly so dramatic as I have suggested will happen ever, to say nothing of within the next decade. But I submit that the three rationales I discussed today are each supported by different but very powerful constituencies. These constituencies range from right to left across the political spectrum, and are found within and without legal profession. Pushing from different directions and for different reasons I suggest they will thrust what might be viewed as revolutionary change upon the judiciary and the legal profession. It may be the historic role of the law schools not only to respond to that change but to help shape it.

Remarks of Paul D. Carrington as Commentator

. . . .

. . . I have some doubts about a complex system of alternative procedures for dispute resolution. My doubts are of two kinds. First, I find the task of measuring the supposed benefits and the apparent risks of the proposal to be very troubling. And, secondly, I am not clear to whom the benefits would flow.

[Professor Carrington first observes that the necessary cost-benefit analysis is extremely complex and elusive. Given current understanding, "[w]e are in a very poor position to give guidance to the officer who would match disputes with procedures according to the degree of adversariness appropriate." In particular, there is the risk of encouraging "overuse of legal institutions" and giving "too little reinforcement to the virtue of forbearance."]

Let me now proceed to a brief discussion of my second level of concern. My question here is not whether there is a cost or benefit to be measured, but who receives it. This question is more political and less economic. But it appears that Professor Johnson and I share a common premise that judicial reform should serve the interests of those who are generally least advantaged by the legal system.

There is a lesson to be learned from our relatively recent experience in creating small claims courts to serve as forums for the poor. That reform is about 50 years old. What happened to the small claims courts is that they were quickly captured by institutional litigants. Institutions have employees who quickly gain the experience needed to make effective lay presentations; [these] lay persons can usually be expected to roll over the beleaguered poor who appear to contest their claims as tenants or consumers. It is a rare tenant or consumer who leaves the small claims court with the warm feeling that he has secured justice at a low price. The lesson to be learned from this experience is this: Do not underestimate the ability of those who seem to exploit the present system to exploit its substitute or alternative even more effectively.

. . . .

Similarly, we might ask: who benefits from the complexity of a system of alternatives? Rarely, I suspect, will it be those citizens who are disadvantaged by the flaws in the present system of justice. The one group that is generally advantaged by complexity is the professional class who learn to manipulate the complexity and turn it to their own profit. Again, we have experience to draw on. Perhaps the most notable contribution of Roscoe Pound was his leadership in the unification movement. For decades, efforts proceeded under his guidance to simplify the judicial hierarchy and to consolidate courts and jurisdictions. This movement was intended to serve those who might be disadvantaged by the complexity of the law, who would be burdened by the costs of jurisdictional squabbling. Let us not draw more costly jurisdictional lines without a good purpose clearly in mind. As we populate our courthouses with various levels of para-judges, including such figures as magistrates, referees, court-appointed arbitrators, and other retainers, we are likely to be increasing the value of the professional lawyer's skill. We may well be making justice more of a game to be won by the side who has the best champion. And so it is by no means clear that the beneficiaries of alternative dispute-resolving processes will be those who are intended to benefit.

WILLIAM H. SIMON, LEGAL INFORMALITY AND REDISTRIBUTIVE POLITICS, 19 Clearinghouse Rev. 384, 384–85 (1985). "Until recently, one of the most consistent themes in both right and left critiques of the legal system has been the repudiation of procedural formality, that is, of specialized, rule-bound procedures. The left critique portrayed formality as facilitating the manipulation of the legal system by the privileged to the disadvantage of others. Both right and left critiques portrayed formality as expressing and fostering alienation and antagonism.

"In recent years, however, attitudes toward formality on the left have become increasingly complex and ambivalent. This development may be partly a reaction to the rising prominence of a conservative rhetoric that links proposals for informalization with conservative substantive goals, such as reduction in civil rights or welfare rights enforcement. . . . And it may be partly a reflection of the studies in the two volumes of The Politics of Informal Justice, edited by Richard Abel [1982]. No one is likely to come away from these remarkable volumes with the idea that informalization per se invariably or even presumptively serves the interests of the disadvantaged. The Abel studies illustrate again and again how broader social inequalities can be reproduced and exacerbated in informal dispute resolution procedures ostensibly designed to enhance access of the disadvantaged.

"In these circumstances, a few critics, including Abel and some of his collaborators, appear to be attracted to a notion diametrically opposed to the traditional presumption that informality benefits the disadvantaged. This is the notion that, at least in the general conditions of contemporary America (or contemporary advanced capitalism), informalism tends to worsen the situation of the disadvantaged. . . .

. . . .

"The anti-informalists raise two general concerns. First, they fear that informalization will deprive the poor of strategic advantages that arise from formal procedural rules. Anti-informalists recognize that formal rules can be designed to serve the interests of the privileged; indeed they insist that most rules are so designed. But they emphasize that the inflexibility of formal rules means that these rules serve their purposes imperfectly. The over-and under-inclusiveness of formal rules with regard to their purposes means that such rules, even when designed to serve the privileged, create pockets of leverage that are potentially available to the disadvantaged. Informalization can eliminate this leverage and turn procedure into a more flexible and precise instrument of the goals of the privileged.

"Second, the anti-informalists fear that informal procedures will induce resignation to or contentment with oppressive relationships. They argue that the alienation of which the traditional left critique complains can sometimes be a good (or at least second best) thing. The tendency of procedural formality to distance the parties from each other and to legitimate antagonistic behavior may encourage the disadvantaged to challenge oppressive relationships. Conversely, informal procedures may undercut alienation only to promote a false sense of integration with hierarchy."

LINDA R. SINGER, NONJUDICIAL DISPUTE RESOLUTION MECHANISMS: THE EFFECTS ON JUSTICE FOR THE POOR, 13 Clearinghouse Rev. 569, 571–72 (1979). "The supporters of nonjudicial forums . . . have different, sometimes unstated, objectives. Judicial endorsement of informal dispute resolution, for example, frequently proceeds from the desire to make the courts more efficient by reducing caseloads, costs and delays. Government sponsorship of community dispute centers generally is based on the hypothesis that the centers are faster and less expensive to operate than courts and that the courts themselves can be made to operate more efficiently if congestion is reduced by diverting minor disputes to other forums. A different, and possibly conflicting, objective is to augment the access of citizens to a variety of tribunals which can resolve their complaints. Achievement of this objective would bring a large number of disputes into some forum, whether judicial or nonjudicial, and thus, presumably, increase the total resources devoted to dispute resolution.

"A third objective of alternative forums is to reduce conflict by settling individual disputes that, if unresolved, might fester, recur or escalate into violent confrontations. In this regard, supporters of mediation frequently cite its superiority to formal adjudication in addressing the 'root causes,' as opposed to the most recent symptoms, of ongoing conflicts.

"On the other hand, the achievement of a fourth objective—the use of the legal system to further social, economic and political conceptions of equal justice—sometimes may result in the escalation of conflict. For the past generation legal efforts to achieve equal justice have frequently been concentrated on class action litigation. Recently, some scholars and practitioners have begun to question such heavy reliance on the courts to enforce rights and deter unfair practices. They advocate a variety of forums and procedures to redress the grievances of members of underrepresented constituencies, ranging from prisoners to consumers. Such advocates are sometimes vocal supporters of nonjudicial forums.

"Many advocates of nonjudicial dispute resolution are motivated by still other objectives such as increased fairness of both legal processes and their results, increased satisfaction with the legal system on the part of participants, and increased ability of various segments of society to govern their own affairs without having to resort regularly to judicial intervention. The last objective has been expressed quite differently in different contexts. In institutional contexts, the objective is expressed as one of self-governance or avoidance of the imposition of rules by outsiders. In neighborhoods or, occasionally, in tightly knit ethnic communities, it may be expressed as community empowerment or neighborhood justice. Finally, on an individual level, the objective is one of increased self-sufficiency or the capacity to manage one's own affairs without heavy reliance on representatives of the legal system."

"SUPERIOR PROCESS"

As explained in Edward Brunet, Questioning the Quality of Alternate Dispute Resolution, 62 Tul.L.Rev. 1 (1987), the 1970s saw the beginnings of an evangelic First Wave of systematic thinking and writing on ADR. The pioneers crystallized the subject and diversified the mechanisms, championing ADR with a heavy emphasis on reducing direct costs. However, the savings turned out to be problematic, and other values turned out to be at stake.

These realizations generated a more skeptical Second Wave that produced a more balanced view. But as some of the foregoing excerpts reveal, the political aspect proved complicated. And so did any supposedly more neutral attempt to examine the other process and outcome values at stake. Linda Singer's excerpt reinforces the point that ADR pursues multiple and conflicting aims in its attempt to deliver a "superior" procedure. A few of the resulting complications are suggested anew by the following quotations.

On the one hand, consider Jethro K. Lieberman & James F. Henry, Lessons from the Alternative Dispute Resolution Movement, 53 U.Chi. L.Rev. 424, 429 (1986), who argued that "adjudication is characterized by a 'winner-take-all' outcome. This cannot be wholly true, for jury damage awards can work compromises, and the parties can shape consent decrees through bargaining. Nevertheless, in many cases, the fundamental issue of liability can be resolved only by holding for the plaintiff or the defendant. ADR, by contrast, is not bound by the zero-sum game of adjudication. While we have defined ADR as concerned with 'legal disputes,' participants in ADR are free to go beyond the legal definition of the scope of their dispute. They can search for creative solutions to the problem that *gave rise* to the dispute, and those solutions may be far more novel than any remedy a court has the power to provide. In a mini-trial held by Texaco and Borden, for example, the parties resolved a breach-of-contract claim and antitrust counterclaim totaling in the hundreds of millions of dollars by renegotiating the entire contract for the supply of natural gas. Both parties claimed a net gain. No court could have ordered the parties to renegotiate; at best a judge or jury could only have compromised on the amount of damages it awarded the 'winner.' "

On the other hand, Richard Delgado, Chris Dunn, Pamela Brown, Helena Lee & David Hubbert, Fairness and Formality: Minimizing the Risk of Prejudice in Alternative Dispute Resolution, 1985 Wis.L.Rev. 1359, 1400, argued on the basis of social science that informality opens the door to majority group members' exhibiting biased behavior toward "minority disputants, women and the poor." Moreover, Harry T. Edwards, Alternative Dispute Resolution: Panacea or Anathema?, 99 Harv.L.Rev. 668, 679 (1986), while expressing broad concern about pushing disputes of public concern out of the courts, gave these specific examples:

"We must also be concerned lest ADR becomes a tool for diminishing the judicial development of legal rights for the disadvantaged. . . . The decisionmakers may not understand the values at stake and parties to disputes do not always possess equal power and resources. . . . Additionally, by diverting particular types of cases away from adjudication, we may stifle the development of law in certain disfavored areas of law. Imagine, for example, the impoverished nature of civil rights law that would have resulted had all race discrimination cases in the sixties and seventies been mediated rather than adjudicated. The wholesale diversion of cases involving the legal rights of the poor may result in the definition of these rights by the powerful in our society rather than by the application of fundamental societal values reflected in the rule of law.

"Family law offers one example of this concern that ADR will lead to 'second-class justice.' In the last ten years, women have belatedly gained many new rights, including new laws to protect battered women and new mechanisms to ensure the enforcement of child-support awards. There is a real danger, however, that these new rights will become simply a mirage if all 'family law' disputes are blindly pushed into mediation. The issues presented extend beyond questions of unequal bargaining power. For example, battered women often need the batterer ordered out of the home or arrested—goals fundamentally inconsistent with mediation."

Perhaps we are now riding a more mature, if somewhat disillusioned, Third Wave, according to Developments in the Law—The Paths of Civil Litigation, 113 Harv.L.Rev. 1752, 1855–57 (2000):

"Even as jurists debated the merits of the budding ADR movement, contractual arbitration and, later, mediation developed as preferred methods of dispute resolution in major areas of law practice, especially commercial and employment law . . . . ADR mechanisms nurtured in the neighborhood justice centers of the 1960s emerged by the late 1990s as the darlings of the business world for their cost efficiency and facilitation of continuing business relationships . . . .

". . . ADR is proving significant in the resolution of environmental and other public policy disputes, and mediation techniques are increasingly used in community fora addressing juvenile justice and violence in schools. ADR is also apt for disputes involving online commerce between geographically disparate parties, and a rapidly developing area of ADR is on the Internet itself, where an array of dispute resolution services are available online. Finally, increased international exchange has led to the widespread adoption of ADR in international arenas that lack a uniform set of legal and cultural expectations regarding the management of disputes. . . .

". . . The practice of ADR has coalesced into two realms: the private (or 'contractual') sphere, in which parties agree to submit disputes to nonjudicial fora of resolution, and the judicial (or 'court-annexed') sphere, in which litigants engage in ADR through the court system, sometimes at their option and sometimes as mandated by statute or local rule. Private ADR receives only limited judicial review, as courts presume that participation in arbitration is consensual and as mediated settlements are consensual by definition. In contrast, the results of court-annexed arbitration are rarely binding, and though good-faith participation in court-annexed mediation may be compelled, parties are not required to reach agreement."

What does the future hold? Robert C. Bordone, Michael L. Moffitt & Frank E.A. Sander, The Next Thirty Years: Directions and Challenges in Dispute Resolution, in The Handbook of Dispute Resolution 507, 508, 510–11 (Michael L. Moffitt & Robert C. Bordone eds., 2005), reflected on the thirty years since the modern ADR movement began at the 1976 Pound Conference with Professor Sander's address on the "Varieties of Dispute Processing," and they envisioned the next thirty years. "We have great hope that dispute resolution—both as an academic discipline *and* as a growing career opportunity for professionals—is here to stay." But "the field's evolution is not complete." Among its "important opportunities and challenges," they list:

"Part of what we need is an improved dialogue about dispute resolution processes, their promise, and their pitfalls. We need conversations, rather than polemics. We need nuanced analyses, careful examinations of real-world experiences, and a welcoming of a range of perspectives into what should be an ongoing collective effort to find the best ways to manage our differences. . . .

"Another piece of the puzzle lies with educators. Quality instruction about dispute resolution processes must also include an appreciation for how one *diagnoses* a dispute. A surgeon who knows how to operate on kidney stones, but who cannot diagnose when this surgery is appropriate, is more dangerous than helpful.

"We should situate our field, working to clarify that dispute resolution is an umbrella that encompasses the full range of mechanisms for resolving differences. A thorough study of dispute resolution must include an appreciation for traditional rights-based models (such as litigation or arbitration) in addition to models focused on nonadversarial approaches. And it should recognize that disputes do not take place against a blank slate. It is not enough to imagine what processes *should* exist, if no background processes were already in place. Early efforts simply to graft dispute resolution onto existing rights-based structures have produced as many challenges as successes. These challenges mount as one considers the myriad cultures and contexts into which dispute resolution mechanisms have been thrust. A complete understanding of dispute resolution requires knowing what processes work best *in the context* faced by the disputants."

Robert A. Baruch Bush, Dispute Resolution Alternatives and the Goals of Civil Justice: Jurisdictional Principles for Process Choice

1984 Wis.L.Rev. 893, 901–05, 908, 921–22, 934, 940–41, 948–51, 953, 960–61, 1034.

To the extent that the discussion has, implicitly or explicitly, raised questions about the goals of the civil justice system, the debate has threatened to come to a grinding halt. This is so, because after the participants assume or articulate two or more distinct goals of civil justice, the question often simply becomes one of ideological preference. That is, the wide divergence of approaches to and proposals for reform stems from a wide divergence of views as to what are the goals of civil justice to begin with, with each proponent fixing upon a different goal and then upon an approach that furthers that goal, with little use for subsequent dialogue or analysis. . . .

In fact, it is often the case that divergent—even contradictory—goals are incorporated into the operation of a single system according to coherent principles. Indeed, few systems of any significant size are uni-directional. Thus, my primary aims in this Article are: to bring the goals of civil justice, which have thus far lain in the background of the debate, into the forefront; to show how they can and must be seen as interrelated elements in an integrated conception of the civil justice system's purpose; and to show how this conception—and the goals themselves—can and must be used as the basis for developing analytically sound jurisdictional principles to guide and evaluate civil justice reform—especially as concerns proposals on process choice.

. . . .

What are the goals of the civil justice system? What is it that is to be accomplished, what is important to achieve, through the handling of a civil dispute? Without some agreement about the answers to such first order questions it is difficult to formulate policy for or evaluate civil justice reform, because it is not even clear whether any need for reform exists. Without goals, one lacks criteria for evaluation, and hence direction (and justification) for reform. Without goals, one lacks any basis for comparing dispute resolution alternatives or responding to specific process choice proposals, since there has been no determination of the ends to be achieved. . . .

. . . .

. . . In the following sections a number of such goals will be identified as underlying the views taken in the debate: resource allocation, social justice, . . . public order, human relations, legitimacy, [fundamental rights protection,] and administration. . . .

. . . .

First, the various goals mentioned . . . are not instrumental, but ultimate goals. That is, each is important in itself and not as a means to one of the others, or some further goal. As such, these goals are conceptually and practically distinct from one another. That is, the fulfillment of one, while important for its own sake, does not necessarily guarantee that of another. Because the goals are ultimate and distinct, each can and must be considered in its own right and not as a subset of another goal.

Second, while . . . different "constituencies" emphasized different goals, there are probably few who would maintain that one goal should be pursued, by society or by the civil justice system, to the exclusion of the others. This point is probably most familiar in the context of the "efficiency-equity" balance, but it applies equally to the other goals discussed. In each case, the stress placed on that goal by its advocates does not mean that they would demand its pursuit "at all costs," including ignoring all other goals.

Third, while the goals defined are distinct, they are nevertheless not always totally unrelated to or independent of one another. That is, while the fulfillment of one does not automatically assure the fulfillment of another (they are not practically identical), it may sometimes affect, positively or negatively, the furtherance of that other (they are not practically independent). . . .

The above summarizes the problem of goal competition in the civil justice system. The most important consequence of goal competition is that wherever the present operation of the system is evaluated or reform considered, positions and proposals cannot be justified by reference to present or expected furtherance (or obstruction) of one goal alone, without consideration of the present status or expected effects on other goals. For, given the multi-goal character of the system, a single-goal focus in evaluation or reform always poses the risk of inadvertently choosing a gain for one goal at the cost of even greater losses for other goals, and thus suffering an ultimately counterproductive result.

. . . .

. . . [My] model is based on the articulation and analysis of the private and social costs generated by the frustration of each of the goals described above. These costs may take the form of monetary losses or some other type of resource depletion. The main point is that, if they are incurred, the society as a whole is poorer than it would have been if the goal were attained. Thus, each goal of civil justice is related to an analogous cost associated with failure to achieve the goal. The relationship is obviously an inverse one: the cost rises as the level of goal attainment falls, and vice versa. Therefore, the goals can be stated in terms of such costs. The goal in each case becomes to avoid the associated cost as much as possible, i.e., to minimize that cost. The interrelationship and competition among goals can then be embodied in the model, by stating the overall goal of the civil justice system in terms of total cost minimization: the goal is to minimize the sum of all the different costs associated with failure to achieve different civil justice goals.

. . . .

. . . In particular, the goal is to minimize the sum of: activity costs, disparity costs, disorder costs, enmity costs, disaffection costs, oppression costs, and administrative costs. Symbolically this can be expressed as follows:

$$\text{Goal} = \text{Min}\ \Sigma C = \text{Min}[C_{AC} + C_{DP} + C_{DO} + C_{EN} + C_{DA} + C_{OP} + C_{AD}].$$ [104]

104 In this formulation, some goals are reflected in one term. For example, the resource allocation goal is reflected in activity costs. Other goals are reflected in more than one term.

This symbolic formulation demonstrates graphically the primary value of the cost-minimization approach as applied to civil justice goals. The essential step in evaluating system performance or reform proposals is to include in consideration *every* goal, and to recognize its *interrelationship* with other goals. By its very character, the cost-minimization formulation ensures that each cost (goal) is considered, for if even one is omitted, the summation simply cannot be made. Also, the structure of the formulation makes plain the essential point that the goals cannot be viewed in isolation, but must be seen in relation to one another. It is easy to see and grasp from the cost format that if a drop in one cost is accompanied by an even greater rise in another, the game is simply not worth the candle. All of this may appear overly simple-minded. However, without a discipline such as that imposed by the cost-minimization structure, it is only too easy to overlook these "simple-minded" points.

. . . .

Finally, and most important, the approach taken herein lays the basis for overcoming another serious weakness of previous analyses of dispute handling alternatives and civil justice reform. It allows for the development of *coherent principles* showing *how* to use process choice to better achieve the goals of civil justice—i.e. jurisdictional principles for process choice. . . .

The crucial practical question, in using dispute handling alternatives as a means of reform, is always the jurisdictional question—*which* process to use in *which* type of case, which "match" will be cost-minimizing? . . .

. . . .

Thus the basic assertion—that different types of cases require different processes—can and should be broken down into logically separate assertions: 1) furtherance of a range of social goals is desired; 2) in different types of cases, different goals are important in differing degrees; 3) with different dispute handling processes, different goals are affected in differing degrees. Now it can be seen much more clearly that to use process choice as a policy tool, several questions must be answered: 1) Which goals are to be furthered, and to what degree? 2) What determines which goals are important, and in what degree, in different types of cases? 3) What determines which goals are furthered, and in what degree, by different dispute handling processes? . . . Answers can be found . . . in terms of the approach developed here. Moreover, answering questions 2) and 3) can provide a set of factors that determine goal importance (cost potential) and goal furtherance (cost reduction) in different cases and through different processes; and these determining factors constitute the kind of criteria or principles, for exercising and evaluating process choice, that are being called for in the civil justice debate.

For example, the social justice goal is reflected in disparity costs, disorder costs, and enmity costs. In fact, once the costs have been adequately specified, it is not necessary to refer constantly to the goals represented and to know which is which. The significance and importance of goal and cost definition is to assure that the catalogue of costs is not incomplete or imprecise, a major weakness noted in earlier cost-minimization models. . . .

. . . .

. . . As for step 1), it has already been elaborated . . . and does not require further detail here. However, it is important to recognize that there may be disagreements about the way in which civil justice goals, and related costs, have been defined above. Others might include additional goals, or differentiate in another manner among goals included above. The point of this Article, however, is not to define categorically the goals/costs of civil justice, but rather to illustrate their legitimate diversity and to develop an analytical model that ties process choice as a means of civil justice reform to that diversity in a consistent and logical way. Therefore, disagreement about the goal definitions offered here by no means undermines the analytical approach. Indeed the approach invites, as its first step, a vigorous discussion of goals and costs. The same proviso applies to the following analysis of steps 2) and 3). . . .

. . . .

[The proposed analysis creates, in summary, the picture on the next page.]

. . . .

By reference to the whole range of case-type factors recognized in the model, it can be determined in any given case what costs are potentially significant, and in what degree relative to one another, without inadvertently overlooking (or erroneously dismissing) one or more costs. This comprehensive cost-potential configuration establishes the practical meaning of cost-minimization for that case—it "targets" fully and accurately the key costs to be addressed in order to bring down total costs in that type of case. At the same time, by reference to the whole range of process factors recognized in the model, it can be determined, for any dispute handling process, what costs can (and cannot) actually be reduced by that process, and in what degree relative to one another, thus establishing an accurate cost-reduction configuration for each process. Process alternatives can now be evaluated and selected logically and coherently, with due attention to the entire complex of civil justice goals, by examining how closely the cost-potential configuration presented by a given type of case is matched by the cost-reduction configuration presented by a given process. Even though a perfect match may be impossible, the result is nevertheless to use process choice purposefully to minimize total costs in each type of case, and ultimately in the system as a whole.[131]

---

[131] The approach could be viewed as a series of practical analytical steps: 1) identify the goals of civil justice and associated concrete costs; 2) identify case-type factors determinative of cost potentials for each of the cost/goals; 3) identify process factors determinative of actual realization of cost potentials for each cost/goal; 4) define classes of cases homogeneous with respect to case-type factors; 5) in each class of cases defined, establish the potential for occurrence of different civil justice costs, by reference to the presence and strength, in that class of cases, of the case-type factors associated with each cost; 6) for each class of cases defined and with cost potentials established as above, predict the effect of a given dispute handling process on the actual occurrence of each cost, by reference to the presence and strength, in that process, of the process factors associated with each cost; 7) repeat the previous step with reference to each different dispute handling process subject to consideration; and 8) for each class of cases choose that dispute handling process which presents the lowest predicted total cost level (subject to debate on non-quantifiable values).

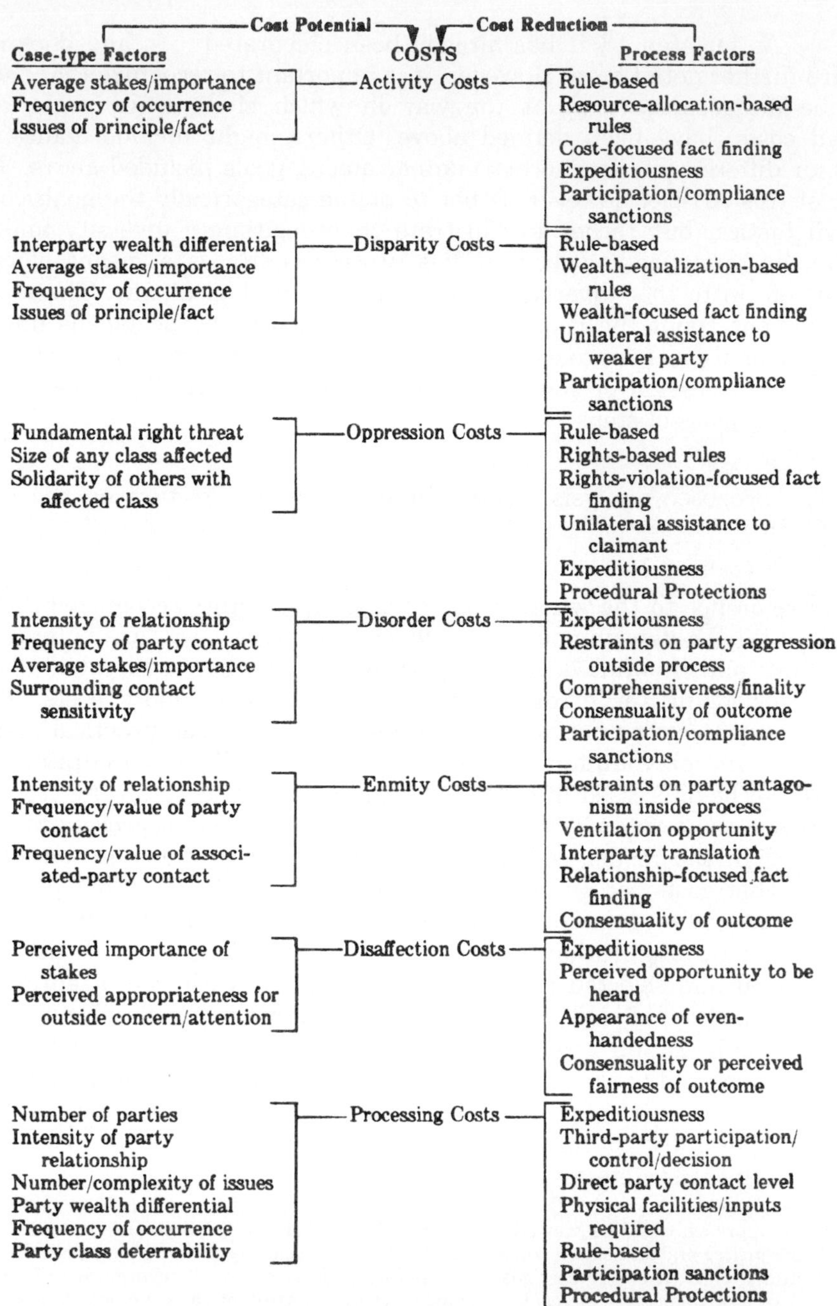
Cost Potential
Cost Reduction
Case-type Factors
COSTS
Process Factors
Average stakes/importance
Frequency of occurrence
Issues of principle/fact
Activity Costs
Rule-based
Resource-allocation-based rules
Cost-focused fact finding
Expeditiousness
Participation/compliance sanctions
Interparty wealth differential
Average stakes/importance
Frequency of occurrence
Issues of principle/fact
Disparity Costs
Rule-based
Wealth-equalization-based rules
Wealth-focused fact finding
Unilateral assistance to weaker party
Participation/compliance sanctions
Fundamental right threat
Size of any class affected
Solidarity of others with affected class
Oppression Costs
Rule-based
Rights-based rules
Rights-violation-focused fact finding
Unilateral assistance to claimant
Expeditiousness
Procedural Protections
Intensity of relationship
Frequency of party contact
Average stakes/importance
Surrounding contact sensitivity
Disorder Costs
Expeditiousness
Restraints on party aggression outside process
Comprehensiveness/finality
Consensuality of outcome
Participation/compliance sanctions
Intensity of relationship
Frequency/value of party contact
Frequency/value of associ-ated-party contact
Enmity Costs
Restraints on party antago-nism inside process
Ventilation opportunity
Interparty translation
Relationship-focused fact finding
Consensuality of outcome
Perceived importance of stakes
Perceived appropriateness for outside concern/attention
Disaffection Costs
Expeditiousness
Perceived opportunity to be heard
Appearance of even-handedness
Consensuality or perceived fairness of outcome
Number of parties
Intensity of party relationship
Number/complexity of issues
Party wealth differential
Frequency of occurrence
Party class deterrability
Processing Costs
Expeditiousness
Third-party participation/control/decision
Direct party contact level
Physical facilities/inputs required
Rule-based
Participation sanctions
Procedural Protections

[In omitted parts of this lengthy article, Professor Bush "shows that previous discussions of process choice have systematically and unduly tended, whether because of inadequate analysis or some sort of underlying bias, to favor using adjudicative processes and to disfavor the use of mediation and related processes." And "it is shown that some public intervention in the dispute-handling 'market' is necessary to encourage process choices that reflect the interests of not only the parties to the dispute but also the society of which they are a part."]

Thus, the conception of disputes and dispute handling that emerges from the goal-oriented analysis stresses most emphatically that the constructive aspect of disputes can be realized, and the goals of civil justice thereby furthered, only when questions of process choice are addressed and answered consciously, clearly and responsibly—i.e., according to consistent principles based on the very goals which such choices can so profoundly affect, both for good and for ill. Formulating and applying suitable analytical tools for this task is an essential part of the responsibility of the legal profession, and all those who are associated with the larger civil justice system. The present analysis offers some initial steps toward the development of such tools—jurisdictional principles for process choice—and thus, ultimately, toward the achievement in increasingly greater degree of the goals of civil justice.

Question: (14) Think about a dispute that recently you personally endured, and cast yourself in the hypothetical role of your lawyer. If it had been possible to provide in advance for an appropriate dispute-resolution mechanism, how would you have proposed to draft a dispute-resolution agreement or clause? If not, what kind of dispute-resolution mechanism would you have advocated after the fact "to fit the forum to the fuss" and why? See generally 1 Jay E. Grenig, Alternative Dispute Resolution ch. 2 (3d ed. 2005) (treatise); Leonard L. Riskin, James E. Westbrook, Chris Guthrie, Richard C. Reuben, Jennifer K. Robbennolt & Nancy Welsh, Dispute Resolution and Lawyers ch. VII–B (4th ed. 2009) (coursebook).

SECTION 3. COMPARING OUR SYSTEM

Benjamin Kaplan, Civil Procedure—Reflections on the Comparison of Systems

9 Buff.L.Rev. 409, 409–14 (1960).

To begin, the rules governing civil procedure in Germany today are laid down by legislative enactment stemming from the famous code of 1877; judicial rule-making plays virtually no part. There is no jury. The courts, at least those concerned in the regular proceedings for cases of consequence, are collegial in structure, acting through benches of three or—in the court of final review—five judges. To some extent, however, the plural bench may use a single judge as a representative or helper.

One of the leitmotifs of the German process is sounded by the Siegfried horn of the summons in the action. This invites appearance at a *Termin zur mündlichen Verhandlung,* a court-session for oral-argument, or rather for conference, since the ideal style of proceeding is less that of a contentious confrontation than a cooperative discussion. The conference is set perhaps three to four weeks after initial service of the papers—which by the way is usually accomplished by mail—and it is commonly attended by the parties as well as counsel. Now the point to be made is that the whole procedure up to judgment may be viewed as being essentially a series of such conferences, the rest of the process having a sort of dependent status. Prooftaking occurs to the extent necessary in the spaces, as it were, between conferences. Intermediate decisions are made along the way. But the conferences are the heart of the matter. Very promptly, then, the litigants are brought under the eye of the court and the case begins to be shaped; and this treatment is applied to the action at intervals until it is fully opened and finally broken. "Conference" betokens informality and this characterizes the entire German procedure. "Conference" also suggests what is the fact, that possibilities of settlement are openly, vigorously, and continually exploited.

I must relate German pleadings to the conference method—I shall use the word "pleadings" although these writings are quite different from the American variety. The action starts with a complaint served together with the summons, but beyond this there is no prescribed number or sequence of pleadings. Pleadings are to be put in in such numbers and at such times as to prepare for, strengthen, and expedite the conferences and thereby the general movement of the case. They have no position independent of the conferences. Indeed the framers of the code of 1877 looked to a free, oral restatement of the pleadings at conference. Such oral recapitulation no longer occurs: the court reads the pleadings in advance and the lawyers are assumed to adopt the pleadings except as they speak up to the contrary. Still no question arises as to the sufficiency of the pleadings as such, nor is there any motion practice directed to the pleadings themselves. In short, pleadings merge into, are an ingredient of the conferences. What is wanted from the pleadings as adopted and perhaps revised at conference is a narrative of the facts as the parties see them at the time, with offers of proof—mainly designated witnesses and documents—and demands for relief. There is no insistence on niceties of form, and legal argumentation, though strictly out of place, is common in today's pleadings. Amendments, even drastic amendments, of the statements can be made until the end of the case, normally without any penalty for late change. This malleability of the pleadings flows from the realization and expectation that a case may change its content and color as it is repeatedly discussed and as proof is from time to time adduced.

Returning to the conduct of the conferences, we find the presiding judge highly vocal and dominant, the parties themselves often voluble, the lawyers relatively subdued. To understand the judicial attitude and contribution at conference, we must take account of two related concepts. First, there is the principle jura novit curia, the court knows and applies the law without relying on the parties to bring it forward. Second, article 139 of the code, as strengthened in recent years, imposes a duty on all courts to clarify the cause and lead the parties toward full development of their respective positions. Thus with awareness of the law implicit in the case, the court is obliged to discuss it freely with the litigants, and in that light to indicate what will be material to decision. By discussion with counsel and the parties the court completes the picture of the controversy as presented by the litigants, throwing light upon obscurities, correcting misunderstandings, marking out areas of agreement and disagreement. It spurs and guides the parties to any necessary further exploration of facts and theories, and may suggest appropriate allegations, proof offers, and demands. The court, however, is not bound to take over and commandeer the litigation, nor does it have the power to do so in an ultimate sense. To some degree—the power is greater in "family" matters than in ordinary cases—the court may call up evidence and background information. The calling of experts is basically a matter for the court. But, in general, allegations, proof offers, and demands can be made only by the parties and so in the last analysis major control of the cause-materials remains with them. Nevertheless, as the parties are likely to follow the court's suggestions, we have here a significant potential in the court which imparts a special quality to the procedure; and this is so despite the fact that clarification and leading are hardly noticeable in simpler cases where the lawyers seem to be providing competent representation. The role of the court not only at conference but throughout the proceedings is envisioned as being both directive and protective. The court as vigorous chairman is to move the case along at a good pace, stirring the parties to action on their own behalf, exercising its limited sua sponte powers where necessary, conscious of a duty to strive for the right solution of the controversy regardless of faults of advocacy.

Conferences propel the lawsuit. Most dates are set by the court in open session. It acts in discretion with due regard to the convenience of the parties: few "iron" time provisions are laid down in the code, and the parties cannot control the pace by stipulation. When discussions disclose ripe questions of law, a time will be set for decision. If they show up disputed issues of fact, there will be an order and a time set for prooftaking.

To understand German prooftaking, we have first to ask what investigation of the facts a German lawyer customarily makes. He consults his client and his client's papers. But he has substantially no coercive means of "discovering" material for the purpose of preparing his proof offers or readying himself for prooftaking. Moreover he is by no means at liberty to go out and talk informally with prospective witnesses. He is hobbled by the principle that he is to avoid all suspicion of influencing those who may be later called to give evidence in court. I shall not attempt to mark the exact boundaries of this inhibition or to dredge up the possible evasive contrivances. I shall simply say that German lawyers are not prime movers with respect to the facts. The régime just described does make for unrehearsed witnesses. It begins to explain why a party in German litigation is not charged with any "proprietorship" over the witnesses whom he has nominated and neither "vouches" for them nor is "bound" by their testimony.

The court draws up the order for prooftaking, the *Beweisbeschluss*, from the nominations set out in the pleadings as they may have been revised at conference. Prooftaking need not be concentrated at a single session, and is in fact not often so concentrated. Accordingly the court may pick and choose what it wants to hear at particular sessions. It can take proof in any order—evidence on a defense ahead of evidence on the main case, even evidence on the negative of an issue ahead of the affirmative.

Witnesses are sequestered, kept out of the courtroom until called. The court asks the witness to state what he knows about the proof theme on which he has been summoned. When the witness has done that in narrative without undue interruption, the court interrogates him, and this is the principal interrogation. Counsel put supplemental questions. Lawyers' participation is likely to be meager. If a lawyer puts too many questions he is implying that the court does not know its business, and that is a dubious tactic. A full stenographic transcript is not kept. Instead the court dictates a summary of the witness' testimony for the minutes which is then read back and perhaps corrected.

German law has few rules excluding relevant evidence. In general relevant evidence is admissible and when admitted is freely evaluated: thus there is no bar to the admission of hearsay. But a few qualifications must be made. German law recognizes a series of privileges. It is somewhat irresolute in compelling production in court of various kinds of documentary proof. Testimony will be received from the parties themselves only in particular circumstances defined by law, and in no event may a party be compelled to testify. Party-testimony is viewed as a kind of last resort. This raises a quiddity, for parties are regularly heard in conference, nominally for purposes of clarification, not proof. I say "nominally" because German law tends to blur the line between evidence stricto sensu and other happenings in the courtroom.

Prooftaking is succeeded by conference, conference by prooftaking, and so on to the end of the regular proceedings in the first-instance court; and now we naturally ask, are there any shortcuts, any special devices for closing a case out promptly when it appears that there is overwhelming strength on one side and corresponding weakness on the other? The answer is no. The German system relies on the succession of conferences and prooftakings to show up strength or weakness with reasonable dispatch. Nor is there much in the way of stage-preclusion, that is, rules intended to discourage delaying afterthoughts by requiring that particular offers or objections be made at fixed points in the proceeding on pain of being otherwise lost to the party. The German action is not segmented into clear-cut stages—recall how pleadings may be thrown in late in the day—and it has in general a quality of "wholeness" or unity. But we do need to say here that the German system makes interestingly brisk provision for handling defaults; and we should also call attention to certain special speed-up devices: "dunning" proceedings, *Mahnverfahren,* available for "collection" cases and carried on regardless of amount in the inferior one-judge court; and "documentary-process," *Urkundenprozess,* used chiefly in suits on commercial paper, with proof initially limited to documents and party-testimony.

We come now to appellate review. The most notable fact about it is that on appeal to the court of second instance from final judgment, or from the important type of intermediate judgment which determines liability but leaves damages to be ascertained, the parties are entitled to a redoing of the case. The record made below, so far as it is thought to be free of error, stands as part of the proceedings, but the parties may add new proofs and invoke new legal theories, and the conduct of the cause is quite similar to that in the court below. Remember that article 139 on clarification and leading, with related duties and powers, continues to apply. The final court of review hears "revisions" on questions of law. As to matters of substance as distinguished from procedure, the court is not confined to the grounds urged by counsel. It seems a mark of the reality of the principle jura novit curia that this national court, dealing with a very large number of revisions coming up from the lower courts administered by the states, the *Länder*, is served by a bar limited by law to less than a score of lawyers.

The German court system is manned by a quite sizeable number of judges. They are career men, appointed on the basis of government examinations, modestly paid, of good but not exalted social prestige, looking primarily to ministerial departments of justice for advancement. In normal times men customarily enter into judicial service at an early age, generally without substantial experience in practice. Judges have traditionally been chided for *Lebensfremdheit*, undue detachment from the rough-and-tumble of life. We have caught a hint of their paternalistic role in the court procedure. This is not far distant from, indeed it comprises, an element of the bureaucratic. Working, many of them, in collegial courts whose judgments, stiffly authoritative in style, disclose neither individual authorship nor individual dissent, German judges live rather anonymous lives. And they are desk-bound through a large part of their working time, for files must be read in preparation for court sessions, and most decisions in actions large and small must be compendiously written up.

As to the German lawyers, I must avoid leaving the impression that their contribution to litigation is unimportant, or that their attitude is flaccid. Despite the court's capacity for active interposition, the frame of the case is made by the lawyers and there is room for contentious striving. Still the procedural system we have outlined does not make for notably vigorous performance by counsel. Moreover the education of lawyers tends against their full identification with clients as combatants: a significant part of their post-University required training is as apprentice-judges. Most important, we must notice some economic facts. Lawyers' fees for litigation, generally corresponding with statutory scales fixed in relation to the amount in controversy, are low.

Court costs are also fixed by statute in relation to the amount in suit, so that a litigant is on the one hand prompted to moderate his demand for judgment, and can on the other hand make a reasonably accurate advance estimate of the expense of litigation. Taking all elements of expense into consideration, German litigation is cheap by comparison with the American brand. But on the threshold a German litigant must conjure with the fact that if as plaintiff or defendant he turns out loser in the lawsuit, he will have to reimburse his opponent's expenses—counsel fees and court costs at the statutory rates together with ordinary disbursements. Let us note here that contingent-fee arrangements—agreements for quota litis—are proscribed in German practice. A comprehensive system of state-provided legal aid aims to enable not only downright paupers but any citizens of insufficient means to prosecute or defend civil cases upon a plausible showing of a prospect of success.

Lastly I must respond to the nervous question which any American lawyer would surely want to ask: Does the German system get over its court business without undue delay? German court statistics—at least those publicly available and not held in subterranean tunnels by the ministries—are curiously sparse; but these figures combine with the opinion of German lawyers familiar with the scene to indicate that the courts, although handling a very considerable volume of cases, are disposing of their calendars with fair speed. However, the court of final review—the *Bundesgerichtshof* sitting in Karlsruhe, successor to the famous *Reichsgericht* which used to reside in Leipzig—has had a hard time in recent years overcoming a serious backlog.[m]

Exercise: Set out below is a series of notes and catch phrases intended to remind you of the characteristics of American civil procedure. With respect to each item, try to describe the analogous or contrasting feature of Germanic civil procedure.

I. *Lack of nationwide uniformity*

51 systems

Abundance of detailed procedural legislation in older state systems, but spread of rulemaking and increasing adoption of Federal Rules pattern

Style of Federal Rules, leaving significant room for local rules and for judicial discretion

---

[m] Obviously, since the time of this account—which serves nicely, but merely, to describe an archetype—there have been changes in actual German procedure. See generally Peter L. Murray & Rolf Stürner, German Civil Justice (2004). Most significantly, there has been a movement, based on efficiency concerns, toward greater concentration of the proceedings in a single hearing. See Arthur T. von Mehren, Some Comparative Reflections on First Instance Civil Procedure: Recent Reforms in German Civil Procedure and in the Federal Rules, 63 Notre Dame L.Rev. 609 (1988).

Recent times have seen comparable movement toward convergence from the U.S. side too. See Edward F. Sherman, The Evolution of American Civil Trial Process Towards Greater Congruence with Continental Trial Practice, 7 Tul.J.Int'l & Comp.L. 125 (1999).

Query how far there is or should be functional adaptation of procedure to the type of case

II. *Inherent problems in allocation of cases to courts*

Federal-state cleavage

State-state divisions

Persistence of artificial determinants of case-allocation, e.g., continued importance of place of service of process

Cf. search for proper law to be applied

III. *Emphasis on full exploration of facts by parties before trial*

Importance of facts in the system of justice

Three sorties into facts: unsanctioned, discovery, trial

Free recourse to prospective witnesses

Influence of strong adversary spirit of litigation

No ex officio investigation

Single-episode trial as compelling exploration of facts beforehand

IV. *Pretrial effort to frame issues by pleadings and pleading-motions*

Generalized style of pleadings: no legal argumentation, no recital of evidence or nomination of sources of proof

Effect of disclosure (relation to discovery)

Single-episode trial as compelling formal definition of issues beforehand

V. *Mechanisms for disposition of cases before trial*

Use of pleadings and pleading-motions to secure summary disposition

Motion for summary judgment (relation to discovery)

Failure to prosecute; default; voluntary dismissal; settlement

VI. *Growing use of pretrial conferences as corrective*

Use of conferences to facilitate trial proper

To rationalize factual materials (relation to discovery)

To sharpen issues

To produce early disposition

Emergent tendency to center regulation of all pretrial activities in conferences

Tendency toward assumption by judge of greater management power and protective responsibility

Extent to which conferences (and discovery) soften adversary climate of litigation

VII. *Characteristics of trial*

Single-episode; relatively dramatic; oral and "immediate"

Fixed order of proceeding

Parties as combatants

Judge as umpire administering exclusionary rules of evidence

Question-and-answer and the verbatim transcript

Jury as centerpiece, which affects rest of procedure

Interaction of judge and jury

VIII. *Characteristics of appeal*

Three-level system, with only appellate courts collegial

Confinement of appealability substantially to final decisions

Confinement of reviewability substantially to rulings of law by trial court challenged by party when made

Simplicity of appellate procedure

IX. *Access to courts as related to expenses of litigation*

Court costs controlled, low, reimbursed to winner

Other expenses uncontrolled, high, not reimbursed

Role of the contingent fee

Actions in forma pauperis; legal aid; legal insurance plans; ADR; class actions

X. *Condition of calendars as related to number of judges and character of cases*

XI. *Image of the judge*

XII. *Image of the lawyer*

In doing this exercise, consider the following from the above-excerpted article (9 Buff.L.Rev. at 422):

"Possibilities of lifting pieces from a foreign system and incorporating them in the domestic must be approached with a sense of the interdependencies, the syndromes, so to speak, within the system a quo and the system ad quem. This is not to say that it is no use trying to import mechanisms for domestic use unless the foreign system is brought over entire. For some procedural devices can stand up pretty well in isolation from the rest of the system. I put as possible examples the special 'dunning' and documentary processes successfully employed in many cases in Germany. Another example which may make the point is service by mail, a traditional usage in Germany and elsewhere, much admired by Bentham. This has in fact been progressively adopted in our country, although its original parentage may not always have been recognized. . . . Consider the feasibility of introducing here the German practice of having witnesses give their testimony in narrative, followed by interrogation by the court; this to be followed in turn by interrogation in our conventional way by counsel for both sides. This may seem a simple change that could be commended on various imaginable grounds, but I would ask you to reflect on whether it could be effectively or safely engrafted on our present system without other profound changes."

For further words of caution from both sides of the Atlantic on legal transplants, see Konstanze Plett, Civil Justice and Its Reform in West Germany and the United States, 13 Just.Sys.J. 186 (1989), and John C. Reitz, Why We Probably Cannot Adopt the German Advantage in Civil Procedure, 75 Iowa L.Rev. 987 (1990). But see Bradley Bryant, Justice and Advantage in Civil Procedure: Langbein's Conception of Comparative Law and Procedural Justice in Question, 11 Tul.J.Int'l & Comp.L. 521 (2004). Caution should not mean paralysis, however. For an example of comparatively inspired and carefully argued reform, see Stephan Landsman, Reforming Adversary Procedure: A Proposal Concerning the Psychology of Memory and the Testimony of Disinterested Witnesses, 45 U.Pitt.L.Rev. 547 (1984) (arguing for U.S. adoption of the Germanic restriction on attorneys' pretrial contacts with witnesses).

A firestorm of controversy has raged over the more general lessons to draw from the German comparison. The best route into the literature, which is rather adversarial in tone, lies through Ronald J. Allen, Stefan Köck, Kurt Riechenberg & D. Toby Rosen, The German Advantage in Civil Procedure: A Plea for More Details and Fewer Generalities in Comparative Scholarship, 82 Nw.U.L.Rev. 705 (1988).

For a comparative look in the opposite direction, see Konstantinos D. Kerameus, A Civilian Lawyer Looks at Common Law Procedure, 47 La.L.Rev. 493 (1987).

Of course, any serious attempt at comparative civil procedure demands a wide perspective. Speaking more generally, then, Germany is a civil-law country, the adjectival reference being to the major legal system that descended from Roman law, came to dominate continental Europe, and spread widely elsewhere. It differs fundamentally from our common-law system, developed in old England.

Yet most statements about the differences between systems turn out to be overstatements. For example, supposedly the procedure here is adversarial, while in Germany it is inquisitorial with the judge actively searching for the truth. But on the one hand, as we have seen, our system is far from purely adversarial. And on the other hand, civil-law procedure for ordinary noncriminal cases in today's practice is largely adversarial.

A better differentiation lies in the observation that the common law grew inductively out of judge-made case-based law, while the civil law depends on comprehensive and coherent codes from which judges deduce their judgments. Consequently, in theory the only real law in a civil-law country comes from legislative pronouncement, and court decisions have no binding effect via stare decisis. Legislatures are supreme, and judges are functionaries. The civil-law court facing a dispute looks afresh to the general principle expressed in legislation and often reaches decision by bare syllogism. Accordingly, the French word "loi," often translated as "law," actually means only authoritative law such as legislation and not case law.

Again, however, the difference is not all that stark in practice, and it has been decreasing with time. Stare decisis is hardly a straightjacket for common-law judges, who often are left free to reason from general principles; moreover, legislation abounds in any modern country. In the civil-law system, the codes express principles that are very general indeed, leaving much to interpretation ("Any act whatever of man, which causes damage to another, obliges the one by whose fault it occurred, to compensate it," reads in its entirety the French *Code civil* article 1382, which created tort law); moreover, judicial decisions and academic commentary thereon can have a powerful persuasive effect on future decisions.

So, one might conclude that it is a small world after all. There is still reason to hesitate, though. Most statements about the similarities between common law and civil law turn out to be overstatements too!

T.S. Eliot, Little Gidding

14–15 (1942).

What we call the beginning is often the end
And to make an end is to make a beginning.

. . . .

We shall not cease from exploration
And the end of all our exploring
Will be to arrive where we started
And know the place for the first time.

PART TWO

GOVERNING LAW

TOPIC A

FEDERAL COURTS

SECTION 1. STATE LAW

We follow the preliminary overviews of litigation in the federal courts by now considering what law applies in particular federal actions. We know that the Federal Rules are the principal body of law governing matters of "practice and procedure" but that the Rules may not "abridge, enlarge or modify any substantive right." 28 U.S.C. § 2072. We have seen, too, that to draw the line between "procedure" and "substance," for this or any other purpose, is sometimes a difficult task. But assuming that we can classify a matter as one of substance, what then? Does federal or state substantive law apply in federal courts?

It comes as no surprise to the student by this time that not all courts arrive at the same answer to a given question of substantive law. The substantive law, both statutory and common, differs from state to state. But further: suppose that because diversity of citizenship exists and the jurisdictional amount is met, a plaintiff has a choice between bringing his action in the United States District Court for the Southern District of New York and instituting it in a state court of New York. Can he gain an advantage by examining the federal and state precedents and selecting the forum where the decisions on the relevant points of substantive law are more favorable to his case?

In the early years of our nation, the answer to this question was somewhat unclear. But for nearly a century after the unanimous decision in Swift v. Tyson, 41 U.S. (16 Pet.) 1 (1842) (Story, J.), the answer was clearly yes.

In the background of that classic case lay a land-fraud scheme, which had unraveled as a consequence of the Panic of 1837. In the foreground was a bill of exchange or, in other words, a negotiable instrument by which one or more drawers (acting as a sort of check-writer) instruct a drawee (playing the role that a bank would play in the case of a check) to pay a certain sum to a payee or to the payee's designee by indorsement. Here the shady Norton and Keith were drawers of a bill of exchange for $1540.30, Tyson was the drawee, and Norton the payee. Tyson accepted, or agreed to pay, the bill to Norton (or his indorsee) as part of the payment for land in Maine sold to him by Norton and Keith. Then Norton indorsed the bill to Swift in partial satisfaction of a prior, unrelated debt owing to Swift from Norton and Keith.

Confusing? Maybe this will help. The bill in essence might have looked like the following. On this bill, Tyson later might have written "Accepted at N.Y., N.Y." and signed his name. Still later, on the back of the bill, Norton might have indorsed it by writing "Pay to the order of John Swift" and signing his name.

Date: May 1, 1836

To: George W. Tyson,

Pay to the order of Nathaniel Norton $ 1540.30

Signed: *Nathaniel Norton & Jairus S. Keith*

Now, however, Tyson refused to pay Swift, asserting that the original land sale had been induced by fraudulent representations on the part of the since bankrupt Norton and Keith. Consequently Swift, the indorsee from Maine, sued Tyson, the drawee-acceptor from New York, upon the bill of exchange in the federal court for the Southern District of New York. Jurisdiction rested on diversity of citizenship, with the claim exceeding the then jurisdictional amount of $500. Tyson's defense was that he had accepted the bill as the result of the drawers' fraud.

In certain circumstances—where the indorsee was a "bona fide holder without notice for valid consideration"—the indorsee took a negotiable instrument free of most defenses otherwise available to the drawee-acceptor against the other original parties, such as the drawers' fraud. Swift, supposedly acting in good faith without notice of the alleged fraud, had taken the bill of exchange in satisfaction of a pre-existing debt. Did this make him a "bona fide holder without notice for valid consideration," so that Tyson's defense of fraud would be cut off as against him? Swift so contended, but Tyson countered that discharging a pre-existing debt was not a valid consideration under commercial law.

The issue thus narrowed to whether what the indorsee had given in exchange for the indorsement was an invalid consideration in the eyes of the law. And the outcome turned on which sovereign's law should answer that purely legal issue.

It was assumed that under the common (that is, nonstatutory) law of New York (in this case, the place of acceptance of the bill), discharging a pre-existing debt would not serve as a valid consideration. The apparent purpose of this questionable New York law was to help prevent someone holding a note subject to defenses from signing the note over to someone in cahoots, who could then enforce it free from those defenses. Nevertheless, the Supreme Court of the United States ultimately held that pre-existing debt would serve as a valid consideration under commercial law. Therefore Mr. Swift prevailed.

In explaining what was in effect a choice of federal law to govern the consideration issue, the Supreme Court said that the issue was one of general commercial law as to which the state-court decisions were not controlling. The Court conceded that if the New York rule had been laid down by statute rather than developed through judicial decisions, or if the rule were a long-established local custom having the force of law, the Rules of Decision Act of 1789, now 28 U.S.C. § 1652, would have required the opposite result.

The essential holding of Swift, then, was that "upon its true intendment and construction" the phrase "laws of the several states" in § 1652 included, as being binding, only state statutes and local usages, not the state's general common law—and therefore, in this absence of a congressional directive, that the federal courts had the power to come to an independent conclusion as to the "true" general common law. Justice Story elaborated: "In the ordinary use of language, it will hardly be contended, that the decisions of courts constitute laws. They are, at most, only evidence of what the laws are, and are not, of themselves, laws. They are often re-examined, reversed and qualified by the courts themselves, whenever they are found to be either defective, or ill-founded, or otherwise incorrect. The laws of a state are more usually understood to mean the rules and enactments promulgated by the legislative authority thereof, or long-established local customs having the force of laws." The true interpretation and effect of contracts and other commercial instruments lay "not in the decisions of the local tribunals, but in the general principles and doctrines of commercial jurisprudence."

What more detailed arguments could you marshal in favor of the Swift holding? What happened in the ensuing century to undercut those arguments? You can derive some answers to these two questions from a careful reading of the following case, which will allow you to flesh out Swift's above-sketched line of reasoning, its background jurisprudence regarding the nature of law and role of courts, and especially its motivating policies such as inducing legal uniformity, asserting federal authority, and ensuring a better commercial law. See also Richard H. Fallon, Jr., John F. Manning, Daniel J. Meltzer & David L. Shapiro, Hart and Wechsler's The Federal Courts and the Federal System 553–58 (6th ed. 2009).

Erie Railroad Co. v. Tompkins

Supreme Court of the United States, April 25, 1938.
304 U.S. 64, 58 S.Ct. 817.

■ Mr. Theodore Kiendl, with whom Messrs. William C. Cannon and Harold W. Bissell were on the brief, for petitioner.

. . . .

We do not question the finality of the holding of this Court in Swift v. Tyson . . . .

. . . .

The Pennsylvania decisions denying permissive rights on longitudinal pathways, as distinguished from crossings, declare a Pennsylvania rule sufficiently local in nature to be controlling . . . .

. . . .

■ MR. JUSTICE BRANDEIS delivered the opinion of the Court.

The question for decision is whether the oft-challenged doctrine of Swift v. Tyson shall now be disapproved.

Tompkins, a citizen of Pennsylvania, was injured on a dark night by a passing freight train of the Erie Railroad Company while walking along its right of way at Hughestown in that state. He claimed that the accident occurred through negligence in the operation, or maintenance, of the train; that he was rightfully on the premises as licensee because on a commonly used beaten footpath which ran for a short distance alongside the tracks; and that he was struck by something which looked like a door projecting from one of the moving cars. To enforce that claim he brought an action in the federal court for Southern New York, which had jurisdiction because the company is a corporation of that state. It denied liability; and the case was tried by a jury.

Erie accident scene, in a trial exhibit—photographed from 150 feet southwest of the point of impact, which is marked with a small white *x*

The Erie insisted that its duty to Tompkins was no greater than that owed to a trespasser. It contended, among other things, that its duty to

Tompkins, and hence its liability, should be determined in accordance with the Pennsylvania law; that under the law of Pennsylvania, as declared by its highest court, persons who use pathways along the railroad right of way—that is, a longitudinal pathway as distinguished from a crossing—are to be deemed trespassers; and that the railroad is not liable for injuries to undiscovered trespassers resulting from its negligence, unless it be wanton or willful. Tompkins denied that any such rule had been established by the decisions of the Pennsylvania courts; and contended that, since there was no statute of the state on the subject, the railroad's duty and liability is to be determined in federal courts as a matter of general law.

The trial judge refused to rule that the applicable law precluded recovery. The jury brought in a verdict of $30,000; and the judgment entered thereon was affirmed by the Circuit Court of Appeals, which held (2 Cir., 90 F.2d 603, 604), that it was unnecessary to consider whether the law of Pennsylvania was as contended, because the question was one not of local, but of general, law, and that "upon questions of general law the federal courts are free, in absence of a local statute, to exercise their independent judgment as to what the law is; and it is well settled that the question of the responsibility of a railroad for injuries caused by its servants is one of general law. . . . Where the public has made open and notorious use of a railroad right of way for a long period of time and without objection, the company owes to persons on such permissive pathway a duty of care in the operation of its trains. . . . It is likewise generally recognized law that a jury may find that negligence exists toward a pedestrian using a permissive path on the railroad right of way if he is hit by some object projecting from the side of the train."

The Erie had contended that application of the Pennsylvania rule was required, among other things, by § 34 of the Federal Judiciary Act of September 24, 1789, c. 20, U.S.C. § 725, which provides: "The laws of the several States, except where the Constitution, treaties, or statutes of the United States otherwise require or provide, shall be regarded as rules of decision in trials at common law, in the courts of the United States, in cases where they apply."[a]

Because of the importance of the question whether the federal court was free to disregard the alleged rule of the Pennsylvania common law, we granted certiorari. 302 U.S. 671, 58 S.Ct. 50.

First. Swift v. Tyson, 16 Pet. 1, 18, held that federal courts exercising jurisdiction on the ground of diversity of citizenship need not, in matters of general jurisprudence, apply the unwritten law of the state as declared by its highest court; that they are free to exercise an independent judgment as to what the common law of the state is—or should be; and that, as there stated by Mr. Justice Story, "the true interpretation of the 34th section limited its application to state laws strictly local, that is to say, to the positive statutes of the state, and the construction thereof adopted by the

[a] With minor changes this section now appears as 28 U.S.C. § 1652. The words "in civil actions" were substituted for "in trials at common law" in the 1948 revision of title 28, but this change was intended only to conform the statute to the existing judicial interpretation.

local tribunals, and to rights and titles to things having a permanent locality, such as the rights and titles to real estate, and other matters immovable and intraterritorial in their nature and character. It never has been supposed by us, that the section did apply, or was designed to apply, to questions of a more general nature, not at all dependent upon local statutes or local usages of a fixed and permanent operation, as, for example, to the construction of ordinary contracts or other written instruments, and especially to questions of general commercial law, where the state tribunals are called upon to perform the like functions as ourselves, that is, to ascertain, upon general reasoning and legal analogies, what is the true exposition of the contract or instrument, or what is the just rule furnished by the principles of commercial law to govern the case."

The Court in applying the rule of § 34 to equity cases, in Mason v. United States, 260 U.S. 545, 559, 43 S.Ct. 200, 204 [(1923)], said: "The statute, however, is merely declarative of the rule which would exist in the absence of the statute." The federal courts assumed, in the broad field of "general law," the power to declare rules of decision which Congress was confessedly without power to enact as statutes. Doubt was repeatedly expressed as to the correctness of the construction given § 34, and as to the soundness of the rule which it introduced. But it was the more recent research of a competent scholar, who examined the original document, which established that the construction given to it by the Court was erroneous; and that the purpose of the section was merely to make certain that, in all matters except those in which some federal law is controlling, the federal courts exercising jurisdiction in diversity of citizenship cases would apply as their rules of decision the law of the state, unwritten as well as written.[5]

Criticism of the doctrine became widespread after the decision of Black & White Taxicab & Transfer Co. v. Brown & Yellow Taxicab & Transfer Co., 276 U.S. 518, 48 S.Ct. 404 [(1928)]. There, Brown & Yellow, a Kentucky corporation owned by Kentuckians, and the Louisville & Nashville Railroad, also a Kentucky corporation, wished that the former should have the exclusive privilege of soliciting passenger and baggage transportation at the Bowling Green, Ky., railroad station; and that the Black & White, a competing Kentucky corporation, should be prevented from interfering with that privilege. Knowing that such a contract would be void under the common law of Kentucky, it was arranged that the Brown & Yellow reincorporate under the law of Tennessee, and that the contract with the railroad should be executed there. The suit was then brought by the Tennessee corporation in the federal court for Western Kentucky to enjoin competition by the Black & White; an injunction issued by the District Court was sustained by the Court of Appeals; and this Court, citing many decisions in which the doctrine of Swift v. Tyson had been applied, affirmed the decree.

[5] Charles Warren, New Light on the History of the Federal Judiciary Act of 1789 (1923) 37 Harv.L.Rev. 49, 51–52, 81–88, 108. [See 19 Wright, Miller & Cooper § 4502, at 13–14 & n.30 (discussing, in their volume on Erie doctrine, the weakness of Warren's conclusion).—Ed.]

Second. Experience in applying the doctrine of Swift v. Tyson, had revealed its defects, political and social; and the benefits expected to flow from the rule did not accrue. Persistence of state courts in their own opinions on questions of common law prevented uniformity;[7] and the impossibility of discovering a satisfactory line of demarcation between the province of general law and that of local law developed a new well of uncertainties.

On the other hand, the mischievous results of the doctrine had become apparent. Diversity of citizenship jurisdiction was conferred in order to prevent apprehended discrimination in state courts against those not citizens of the state. Swift v. Tyson introduced grave discrimination by noncitizens against citizens. It made rights enjoyed under the unwritten "general law" vary according to whether enforcement was sought in the state or in the federal court; and the privilege of selecting the court in which the right should be determined was conferred upon the noncitizen. Thus, the doctrine rendered impossible equal protection of the law. In attempting to promote uniformity of law throughout the United States, the doctrine had prevented uniformity in the administration of the law of the state.

The discrimination resulting became in practice far-reaching. This resulted in part from the broad province accorded to the so-called "general law" as to which federal courts exercised an independent judgment. In addition to questions of purely commercial law, "general law" was held to include the obligations under contracts entered into and to be performed within the state, the extent to which a carrier operating within a state may stipulate for exemption from liability for his own negligence or that of his employee, the liability for torts committed within the state upon persons resident or property located there, even where the question of liability depended upon the scope of a property right conferred by the state, and the right to exemplary or punitive damages. Furthermore, state decisions construing local deeds, mineral conveyances, and even devises of real estate were disregarded.

In part the discrimination resulted from the wide range of persons held entitled to avail themselves of the federal rule by resort to the diversity of citizenship jurisdiction. Through this jurisdiction individual citizens willing to remove from their own state and become citizens of another might avail themselves of the federal rule. And, without even change of residence, a corporate citizen of the state could avail itself of the federal rule by reincorporating under the laws of another state, as was done in the Taxicab Case.

The injustice and confusion incident to the doctrine of Swift v. Tyson have been repeatedly urged as reasons for abolishing or limiting diversity of citizenship jurisdiction. Other legislative relief has been proposed. If only a question of statutory construction were involved, we should not be pre-

---

[7] [The Court's footnote cited, among other writings, Felix Frankfurter, Distribution of Judicial Power Between United States and State Courts, 13 Cornell L.Q. 499, 524–30 (1928).]

pared to abandon a doctrine so widely applied throughout nearly a century. But the unconstitutionality of the course pursued has now been made clear, and compels us to do so.

Third. Except in matters governed by the Federal Constitution or by acts of Congress, the law to be applied in any case is the law of the state. And whether the law of the state shall be declared by its Legislature in a statute or by its highest court in a decision is not a matter of federal concern. There is no federal general common law. Congress has no power to declare substantive rules of common law applicable in a state whether they be local in their nature or "general," be they commercial law or a part of the law of torts. And no clause in the Constitution purports to confer such a power upon the federal courts. As stated by Mr. Justice Field when protesting in Baltimore & Ohio R. Co. v. Baugh, 149 U.S. 368, 401, 13 S.Ct. 914, 927 [(dissenting opinion)], against ignoring the Ohio common law of fellow-servant liability: "I am aware that what has been termed the general law of the country—which is often little less than what the judge advancing the doctrine thinks at the time should be the general law on a particular subject—has been often advanced in judicial opinions of this court to control a conflicting law of a state. I admit that learned judges have fallen into the habit of repeating this doctrine as a convenient mode of brushing aside the law of a state in conflict with their views. And I confess that, moved and governed by the authority of the great names of those judges, I have, myself, in many instances, unhesitatingly and confidently, but I think now erroneously, repeated the same doctrine. But, notwithstanding the frequency with which the doctrine has been reiterated, there stands, as a perpetual protest against its repetition, the constitution of the United States, which recognizes and preserves the autonomy and independence of the states—independence in their legislative and independence in their judicial departments. Supervision over either the legislative or the judicial action of the states is in no case permissible except as to matters by the constitution specifically authorized or delegated to the United States. Any interference with either, except as thus permitted, is an invasion of the authority of the state and, to that extent, a denial of its independence."

The fallacy underlying the rule declared in Swift v. Tyson is made clear by Mr. Justice Holmes.[23] The doctrine rests upon the assumption that there is "a transcendental body of law outside of any particular State but obligatory within it unless and until changed by statute," that federal courts have the power to use their judgment as to what the rules of common law are; and that in the federal courts "the parties are entitled to an independent judgment on matters of general law":

"But law in the sense in which courts speak of it today does not exist without some definite authority behind it. The common law so far as it is enforced in a State, whether called common law or not, is not the common law generally but the law of that State existing by the authority of that

---

[23] Kuhn v. Fairmont Coal Co., 215 U.S. 349, 370–72, 30 S.Ct. 140, 147–48; Black & White Taxicab & Transfer Co. v. Brown & Yellow Taxicab & Transfer Co., 276 U.S. 518, 532–36, 48 S.Ct. 404, 408–10. [The citations are both to dissenting opinions.—Ed.]

State without regard to what it may have been in England or anywhere else. . . .

"The authority and only authority is the State, and if that be so, the voice adopted by the State as its own [whether it be of its Legislature or of its Supreme Court] should utter the last word."

Thus the doctrine of Swift v. Tyson is, as Mr. Justice Holmes said, "an unconstitutional assumption of powers by the courts of the United States which no lapse of time or respectable array of opinion should make us hesitate to correct." In disapproving that doctrine we do not hold unconstitutional § 34 of the Federal Judiciary Act of 1789 or any other act of Congress. We merely declare that in applying the doctrine this Court and the lower courts have invaded rights which in our opinion are reserved by the Constitution to the several states.

Fourth. The defendant contended that by the common law of Pennsylvania as declared by its highest court in Falchetti v. Pennsylvania R. Co., 307 Pa. 203, 160 A. 859, the only duty owed to the plaintiff was to refrain from willful or wanton injury. The plaintiff denied that such is the Pennsylvania law. In support of their respective contentions the parties discussed and cited many decisions of the Supreme Court of the state. The Circuit Court of Appeals ruled that the question of liability is one of general law; and on that ground declined to decide the issue of state law. As we hold this was error, the judgment is reversed and the case remanded to it for further proceedings in conformity with our opinion.

Reversed.[b]

■ MR. JUSTICE CARDOZO took no part in the consideration or decision of this case.

■ [JUSTICE BUTLER filed a separate opinion concurred in by Justice McReynolds. In the course of arguing that Swift v. Tyson should not be overruled, Justice Butler gave attention to the Court's manner of proceeding:]

This Court has often emphasized its reluctance to consider constitutional questions and that legislation will not be held invalid as repugnant to the fundamental law if the case may be decided upon any other ground. In view of grave consequences liable to result from erroneous exertion of its power to set aside legislation, the Court should move cautiously, seek

---

[b] On remand to the circuit court of appeals, the railroad's view prevailed regarding the content of Pennsylvania law, 98 F.2d 49 (2d Cir.), cert. denied, 305 U.S. 637, 59 S.Ct. 108 (1938). Thus Harry Tompkins, a young one-armed unemployed laborer and father, lost his sizable judgment.

From this obvious human tragedy emerged a critical legal holding. "It is impossible to overstate the importance of the Erie decision. It announces no technical doctrine of procedure or jurisdiction, but goes to the heart of the relations between the federal government and the states . . . . [T]here has hardly been a civil case since Erie was decided that has not felt the effect of that decision." Charles Alan Wright & Mary Kay Kane, Law of Federal Courts § 55, at 378 (6th ed. 2002). And Erie has spawned an immense literature. Nevertheless, probably the best place to begin outside reading on this legal doctrine is the human story recounted by Edward A. Purcell, Jr., "The Story of Erie: How Litigants, Lawyers, Judges, Politics, and Social Change Reshape the Law," in Civil Procedure Stories 21 (Kevin M. Clermont ed., 2d ed. 2008).

assistance of counsel, act only after ample deliberation, show that the question is before the Court, that its decision cannot be avoided by construction of the statute assailed or otherwise, indicate precisely the principle or provision of the Constitution held to have been transgressed, and fully disclose the reasons and authorities found to warrant the conclusion of invalidity. . . .

. . . Against the protest of those joining in this opinion, the Court declines to assign the case for reargument. It may not justly be assumed that the labor and argument of counsel for the parties would not disclose the right conclusion and aid the Court in the statement of reasons to support it. . . .

The course pursued by the Court in this case is repugnant to the Act of Congress of August 24, 1937, 50 Stat. 751.[c] . . .

. . . [N]ear the end of the last page the Court states that it does not hold § 34 unconstitutional, but merely that, in applying the doctrine of Swift v. Tyson construing it, this Court and the lower courts have invaded rights which are reserved by the Constitution to the several states. But, plainly through the form of words employed, the substance of the decision appears; it strikes down as unconstitutional § 34 as construed by our decisions; it divests the Congress of power to prescribe rules to be followed by federal courts when deciding questions of general law. In that broad field it compels this and the lower federal courts to follow decisions of the courts of a particular state.

I am of opinion that the constitutional validity of the rule need not be considered, because under the law, as found by the courts of Pennsylvania and generally throughout the country, it is plain that the evidence required a finding that plaintiff was guilty of negligence that contributed to cause his injuries and that the judgment below should be reversed upon that ground.

■ MR. JUSTICE REED. I concur in the conclusion reached in this case, in the disapproval of the doctrine of Swift v. Tyson, and in the reasoning of the majority opinion except in so far as it relies upon the unconstitutionality of the "course pursued" by the federal courts.

The "doctrine of Swift v. Tyson," as I understand it, is that the words "the laws," as used in § 34, line one, of the Federal Judiciary Act of September 24, 1789, did not include in their meaning "the decisions of the local tribunals." Mr. Justice Story, in deciding that point, said, 16 Pet. 1, 19: "Undoubtedly, the decisions of the local tribunals upon such subjects are entitled to, and will receive, the most deliberate attention and respect of this Court; but they cannot furnish positive rules, or conclusive authority, by which our judgments are to be bound up and governed."

---

[c] This Act (with changes now 28 U.S.C. § 2403(a)) required, "whenever the constitutionality of any Act of Congress affecting the public interest is drawn in question in any court of the United States," that the court give notice to the Attorney General and allow intervention by the United States. This Act was not followed in this case, the majority apparently feeling that the Act did not apply. Why did it not apply?

To decide the case now before us and to "disapprove" the doctrine of Swift v. Tyson requires only that we say that the words "the laws" include in their meaning the decisions of the local tribunals. As the majority opinion shows, by its reference to Mr. Warren's researches and the first quotation from Mr. Justice Holmes, that this Court is now of the view that "laws" includes "decisions," it is unnecessary to go further and declare that the "course pursued" was "unconstitutional," instead of merely erroneous.

The "unconstitutional" course referred to in the majority opinion is apparently the ruling in Swift v. Tyson that the supposed omission of Congress to legislate as to the effect of decisions leaves federal courts free to interpret general law for themselves. I am not at all sure whether, in the absence of federal statutory direction, federal courts would be compelled to follow state decisions. There was sufficient doubt about the matter in 1789 to induce the first Congress to legislate. No former opinions of this Court have passed upon it. Mr. Justice Holmes evidently saw nothing "unconstitutional" which required the overruling of Swift v. Tyson, for he said in the very opinion quoted by the majority, "I should leave Swift v. Tyson undisturbed, as I indicated in Kuhn v. Fairmont Coal Co., but I would not allow it to spread the assumed dominion into new fields." Black & White Taxicab & Transfer Co. v. Brown & Yellow Taxicab & Transfer Co., 276 U.S. 518, 535, 48 S.Ct. 404, 409. If the opinion commits this Court to the position that the Congress is without power to declare what rules of substantive law shall govern the federal courts, that conclusion also seems questionable. The line between procedural and substantive law is hazy but no one doubts federal power over procedure. Wayman v. Southard, 10 Wheat. 1. The Judiciary Article and the "necessary and proper" clause of Article One may fully authorize legislation, such as this section of the Judiciary Act.

In this Court, stare decisis, in statutory construction, is a useful rule, not an inexorable command. Burnet v. Coronado Oil & Gas Co., 285 U.S. 393, dissent, page 406, note 1, 52 S.Ct. 443, 447 n. 1. Compare Read v. Bishop of Lincoln, [1892] A.C. 644, 655; London Street Tramways Co. v. London County Council, [1898] A.C. 375, 379. It seems preferable to overturn an established construction of an act of Congress, rather than, in the circumstances of this case, to interpret the Constitution. Cf. United States v. Delaware & Hudson Co., 213 U.S. 366, 29 S.Ct. 527.

There is no occasion to discuss further the range or soundness of these few phrases of the opinion. It is sufficient now to call attention to them and express my own non-acquiescence.

Questions: (1) What exactly did the Erie Court hold unconstitutional? Is that holding a restriction on the federal legislative power, or only on the federal judicial power?

(2) Why did the Court expect a lower federal court sitting in New York to apply the law of Pennsylvania?

(3) According to Justice Brandeis, how should the federal court determine what the law of Pennsylvania is?

(4) According to Justice Brandeis, in diversity and other cases, what matters will be decided under state law and what matters will be governed by federal law? Where would Justice Reed apparently draw that line?

BURDEN OF PROOF IN DIVERSITY ACTIONS

In Cities Service Oil Co. v. Dunlap, 308 U.S. 208, 60 S.Ct. 201 (1939), the plaintiff sued in diversity jurisdiction to remove a cloud on its title to certain Texas land that its deed covered. The defendants alleged in a counterclaim that the deed had included the land by mistake. The plaintiff replied that it had purchased the land in good faith, without notice of mistake, and for value. No evidence was offered by either side on the question raised by the plaintiff's reply. The district court and the circuit court of appeals found for the defendants by taking the view that the burden of proving bona fide purchase without notice for value was on the plaintiff, with the circuit court explaining that a federal court could ignore the recognized Texas rule to the contrary because burden of proof in a diversity case like this was "a matter of practice or procedure and not a matter of substantive law." The Supreme Court reversed, briefly explaining: "We cannot accept the view that the question presented was only one of practice in courts of equity. Rather we think it relates to a substantial right upon which the holder of recorded legal title to Texas land may confidently rely."

In Palmer v. Hoffman, 318 U.S. 109, 63 S.Ct. 477 (1943), the Court peremptorily disposed of the contention that an instruction to the jury, to the effect that the burden of persuasion as to contributory negligence in federal court is on the defendant, was proper because of Rule 8(c)(1). The Court said: "Rule 8(c) covers only the manner of pleading. The question of the burden of establishing contributory negligence is a question of local law which federal courts in diversity of citizenship cases . . . must apply." The Court cited Cities Service in support of this conclusion.

CHOICE OF LAW

Imagine a Pennsylvania railroad accident giving rise to a lawsuit in a New York *state* court. Which state's tort law should apply? What law governs burden of proof? As you undoubtedly perceive, a pervasive problem in litigation that involves nonlocal elements is choosing which sovereign's law to apply.

Generally, as between coequal sovereigns such as states (or countries), it is the forum court's task to choose the governing law under some technique for choice of law. The technique followed in any particular state's courts has typically evolved from (1) a traditional set of wooden and crude rules that pointed with relative certainty to the law of a particular place where some particular event occurred (e.g., the rule of lex loci delicti, or the law of the place of the wrong, controlled the choice for substantive issues in tort cases; but the lex fori, or the law of the forum, applied on all issues that the forum court characterized as procedural) to (2) a very flexible and sensitive but quite uncertain approach of comparing as to each issue the interests of the involved sovereigns in having their own law applied and then applying the law of the sovereign whose policies would be most impaired by nonapplication (so-called interest analysis). Nevertheless, this is a subject dominated today by competing subtheories that elaborate or alter interest analysis, and these subtheories conflict sharply at least on the verbal level. Many of these modern differences of opinion have arisen as theorists have worked to reinject some degree of practical certainty into the theoretical precision of interest analysis. For example, one might use interest analysis to create a new series of general rules to cover common situations. Such matters are the subject of study in the upperclass course of Conflict of Laws.

American states are under some constitutional restraint on their choice-of-law process. The Supreme Court has, however, interpreted the Federal Constitution in a way that gives state courts a very free hand in choosing the governing law and, in particular, in choosing to apply their own law. The Court summarized the constitutional restriction in Allstate Insurance Co. v. Hague, 449 U.S. 302, 308, 101 S.Ct. 633, 637–38 (1981) (plurality opinion): "In deciding constitutional choice-of-law questions, whether under the Due Process Clause or the Full Faith and Credit Clause, this Court has traditionally examined the contacts of the State, whose law was applied, with the parties and with the occurrence or transaction giving rise to the litigation. [Citation omitted.] In order to ensure that the choice of law is neither arbitrary nor fundamentally unfair, [citation omitted], the Court has invalidated the choice of law of a State which has had no significant contact or significant aggregation of contacts, creating state interests, with the parties and the occurrence or transaction."

Cases such as Erie, Cities Service, and Palmer treat a "vertical" choice of law that is similar to but distinguishable from this interstate and international, or "horizontal," choice of law. Those three cases concern a choice of law in the special sense that the federal authority is deciding whether federal law should be generated to apply to a given issue, such as burden of proof, or whether state law should be left to govern.

Now imagine a Pennsylvania railroad accident giving rise to a lawsuit in a New York *federal* court. Here the two types of choice of law intersect. There must be a vertical choice of law regarding the issue of horizontal choice of law. That is, does federal or state law decide which state's tort law to apply?

KLAXON CO. v. STENTOR ELECTRIC MANUFACTURING CO., 313 U.S. 487, 61 S.Ct. 1020 (1941). Plaintiff brought a diversity action for breach of contract in the United States District Court for the District of Delaware and obtained a verdict for $100,000. The court, applying the law of New York (the place of performance of the contract), added prejudgment interest to that sum. The Third Circuit affirmed this addition of interest, saying: (1) that the right to prejudgment interest is a matter of substance, not procedure, and so is governed by state law; (2) that such right "should be settled by reference to the law of the appropriate state according to the type of case being tried"; and (3) that in this contract case, under general principles of conflict-of-laws doctrine, the "appropriate" state is the place of performance.

On certiorari, the Supreme Court reversed. Justice Reed, for a unanimous Court, said in part:

"The principal question in this case is whether in diversity cases the federal courts must follow conflict of laws rules prevailing in the states in which they sit. We left this open in Ruhlin v. New York Life Insurance Company, 304 U.S. 202, 208, note 2, 58 S.Ct. 860, 862 n. 2. The frequent recurrence of the problem, as well as the conflict of approach to the problem between the Third Circuit's opinion here and that of the First Circuit in Sampson v. Channell, 110 F.2d 754, 759–762, led us to grant certiorari.

. . . .

"We are of opinion that the prohibition declared in Erie R. Co. v. Tompkins, 304 U.S. 64, 58 S.Ct. 817, against such independent determinations by the federal courts extends to the field of conflict of laws. The conflict of laws rules to be applied by the federal court in Delaware must conform to those prevailing in Delaware's state courts. Otherwise, the accident of diversity of citizenship would constantly disturb equal administration of justice in coordinate state and federal courts sitting side by side. See Erie R. Co. v. Tompkins, supra, 304 U.S. at 74–77, 58 S.Ct. at 820–822. Any other ruling would do violence to the principle of uniformity within a state upon which the Tompkins decision is based. Whatever lack of uniformity this may produce between federal courts in different states is attributable to our federal system, which leaves to a state, within the limits permitted by the Constitution, the right to pursue local policies diverging from those of its neighbors. It is not for the federal courts to thwart such local policies by enforcing an independent 'general law' of conflict of laws. Subject only to review by this Court on any federal question that may arise, Delaware is free to determine whether a given matter is to be governed by the law of the forum or some other law. Cf. Milwaukee County v. M.E. White Co., 296 U.S. 268, 272, 56 S.Ct. 229, 231. This Court's views are not the decisive factor in determining the applicable conflicts rule. Cf. Funkhouser v. J.B. Preston Co., 290 U.S. 163, 54 S.Ct. 134. And the proper function of the Delaware federal court is to ascertain what the state law is, not what it ought to be."

The Court remanded the case for determination of which state's law would be applied by Delaware state courts on the question of prejudgment interest. On remand, the circuit court of appeals found that Delaware would apply New York law, 125 F.2d 820 (3d Cir.), cert. denied, 316 U.S. 685, 62 S.Ct. 1284 (1942).

Question: (5) Reexamine Justice Roberts' statement of the plaintiff's dilemma in Sibbach v. Wilson & Co., supra p. 8. How did he handle the conflict-of-laws problem there? How is the plaintiff's "dilemma" affected by the Court's later decision in Klaxon? (You should periodically renew this question—how to pose properly Sibbach's "dilemma" under prevailing doctrine—as you progress through this study of Erie's progeny.)

Guaranty Trust Co. v. York

Supreme Court of the United States, 1945.
326 U.S. 99, 65 S.Ct. 1464.

■ MR. JUSTICE FRANKFURTER delivered the opinion of the Court.

[In a class action brought in the United States District Court for the Southern District of New York on diversity-of-citizenship jurisdiction, noteholders of Van Sweringen Corporation sued Guaranty Trust Company, the noteholders' trustee, for its alleged breach of trust. The court granted the defendant's motion for summary judgment. The Second Circuit reversed (2–1), holding inter alia that the state statute of limitations did not apply in this federal-court case in the face of a federal tolling doctrine. On certiorari, the Supreme Court reversed the decision of the circuit court of appeals, saying: "Our only concern is with the holding that the federal courts in a suit like this are not bound by local law."]

Our starting point must be the policy of federal jurisdiction which Erie R. Co. v. Tompkins, 304 U.S. 64, 58 S.Ct. 817, embodies. In overruling Swift v. Tyson, 16 Pet. 1, Erie R. Co. v. Tompkins did not merely overrule a venerable case. It overruled a particular way of looking at law which dominated the judicial process long after its inadequacies had been laid bare. [Citations omitted.] Law was conceived as a "brooding omnipresence" of Reason, of which decisions were merely evidence and not themselves the controlling formulations. Accordingly, federal courts deemed themselves free to ascertain what Reason, and therefore Law, required wholly independent of authoritatively declared State Law, even in cases where a legal right as the basis for relief was created by State authority and could not be created by federal authority and the case got into a federal court merely because it was "between Citizens of different States" under Art. III, § 2 of the Constitution of the United States.

. . . .

In relation to the problem now here, the real significance of Swift v. Tyson lies in the fact that it did not enunciate novel doctrine. Nor was it restricted to its particular situation. It summed up prior attitudes and expressions in cases that had come before this Court and lower federal courts for at least thirty years, at law as well as in equity. The short of it is that the doctrine was congenial to the jurisprudential climate of the time. Once established, judicial momentum kept it going. Since it was conceived that there was "a transcendental body of law outside of any particular State but obligatory within it unless and until changed by statute," [Black & White Taxicab & Transfer Co. v. Brown & Yellow Taxicab & Transfer Co.,] 276 U.S. 518, 532, 533, 48 S.Ct. 404, 408, 409, State court decisions were not "the law" but merely someone's opinion—to be sure an opinion to be respected—concerning the content of this all-pervading law. Not unnaturally, the federal courts assumed power to find for themselves the content of such a body of law. The notion was stimulated by the attractive vision of a uniform body of federal law. . . .

. . . .

Matters of "substance" and matters of "procedure" are much talked about in the books as though they defined a great divide cutting across the whole domain of law. But, of course, "substance" and "procedure" are the same key-words to very different problems. Neither "substance" nor "procedure" represents the same invariants. Each implies different variables depending upon the particular problem for which it is used. See Home Ins. Co. v. Dick, 281 U.S. 397, 409, 50 S.Ct. 338, 341. And the different problems are only distantly related at best, for the terms are in common use in connection with situations turning on such different considerations as those that are relevant to questions pertaining to ex post facto legislation, the impairment of the obligations of contract, the enforcement of federal rights in the State courts and the multitudinous phases of the conflict of laws. [Citations omitted.]

Here we are dealing with a right to recover derived not from the United States but from one of the States. When, because the plaintiff happens to be a non-resident, such a right is enforceable in a federal as well as in a State court, the forms and mode of enforcing the right may at times, naturally enough, vary because the two judicial systems are not identic. But since a federal court adjudicating a State-created right solely because of the diversity of citizenship of the parties is for that purpose, in effect, only another court of the State, it cannot afford recovery if the right to recover is made unavailable by the State nor can it substantially affect the enforcement of the right as given by the State.

And so the question is not whether a statute of limitations is deemed a matter of "procedure" in some sense. The question is whether such a statute concerns merely the manner and the means by which a right to recover, as recognized by the State, is enforced, or whether such statutory limitation is a matter of substance in the aspect that alone is relevant to our problem, namely, does it significantly affect the result of a litigation for a federal court to disregard a law of a State that would be controlling in an action upon the same claim by the same parties in a State court?

It is therefore immaterial whether statutes of limitation are characterized either as "substantive" or "procedural" in State court opinions in any use of those terms unrelated to the specific issue before us. Erie R. Co. v. Tompkins was not an endeavor to formulate scientific legal terminology. It expressed a policy that touches vitally the proper distribution of judicial power between State and federal courts. In essence, the intent of that decision was to insure that, in all cases where a federal court is exercising jurisdiction solely because of the diversity of citizenship of the parties, the outcome of the litigation in the federal court should be substantially the same, so far as legal rules determine the outcome of a litigation, as it would be if tried in a State court. The nub of the policy that underlies Erie R. Co. v. Tompkins is that for the same transaction the accident of a suit by a non-resident litigant in a federal court instead of in a State court a block away should not lead to a substantially different result. And so, putting to one side abstractions regarding "substance" and "procedure," we have held that in diversity cases the federal courts must follow the law of the State as to burden of proof, Cities Service Oil Co. v. Dunlap, 308 U.S. 208, 60 S.Ct. 201, as to conflict of laws, Klaxon Co. v. Stentor Electric Mfg. Co., 313 U.S. 487, 61 S.Ct. 1020, as to contributory negligence, Palmer v. Hoffman, 318 U.S. 109, 117, 63 S.Ct. 477, 482. And see Sampson v. Channell, 110 F.2d 754. Erie R. Co. v. Tompkins has been applied with an eye alert to essentials in avoiding disregard of State law in diversity cases in the federal courts. A policy so important to our federalism must be kept free from entanglements with analytical or terminological niceties.

Plainly enough, a statute that would completely bar recovery in a suit if brought in a State court bears on a State-created right vitally and not merely formally or negligibly. As to consequences that so intimately affect recovery or non-recovery a federal court in a diversity case should follow State law. . . .

. . . .

Diversity jurisdiction is founded on assurance to non-resident litigants of courts free from susceptibility to potential local bias. The Framers of the Constitution, according to Marshall, entertained "apprehensions" lest distant suitors be subjected to local bias in State courts, or, at least, viewed with "indulgence the possible fears and apprehensions" of such suitors. Bank of the United States v. Deveaux, 5 Cranch 61, 87. And so Congress afforded out-of-State litigants another tribunal, not another body of law. The operation of a double system of conflicting laws in the same State is plainly hostile to the reign of law. Certainly, the fortuitous circumstance of residence out of a State of one of the parties to a litigation ought not to give rise to a discrimination against others equally concerned but locally resident. The source of substantive rights enforced by a federal court under diversity jurisdiction, it cannot be said too often, is the law of the States. Whenever that law is authoritatively declared by a State, whether its voice be the legislature or its highest court, such law ought to govern in litigation founded on that law, whether the forum of application is a State or a federal court and whether the remedies be sought at law or may be had in equity.

■ [JUSTICES ROBERTS and DOUGLAS did not participate. JUSTICE RUTLEDGE, joined by Justice Murphy, dissented, and in passing observed:]

Applicable statutes of limitations in state tribunals are not always the ones which would apply if suit were instituted in the courts of the state which creates the substantive rights for which enforcement is sought. The state of the forum is free to apply its own period of limitations, regardless of whether the state originating the right has barred suit upon it. Whether or not *the action* will be held to be barred depends therefore not upon the law of the state which creates the substantive right, but upon the law of the state where suit may be brought.

Consider the following cases (all decided by the Supreme Court on the same day, June 20, 1949) in the light of the Erie Railroad Co. v. Tompkins doctrine as further spelled out in the Guaranty Trust case. The basis of jurisdiction in each case is diversity of citizenship.

RAGAN v. MERCHANTS TRANSFER & WAREHOUSE CO., 337 U.S. 530, 69 S.Ct. 1233 (1949). *P* sues *D* in the District Court for the District of Kansas for personal injuries arising out of a highway accident on October 1, 1943. The applicable state statute of limitations is two years. The complaint is filed with the court on September 4, 1945, and the summons and complaint are served on December 28, 1945. Rule 3 provides that a "civil action is commenced by filing a complaint with the court." A Kansas statute says that for statute-of-limitations purposes an action shall be deemed commenced on the date of the service of the summons. *D* pleads the statute of limitations and moves for summary judgment. Is the action barred? (8–1 decision.)

WOODS v. INTERSTATE REALTY CO., 337 U.S. 535, 69 S.Ct. 1235 (1949). *P*, a Tennessee corporation, sues *D*, a citizen of Mississippi, in the District Court for the Northern District of Mississippi for a broker's commission. A Mississippi statute requires a foreign corporation doing business in the state to file a written power of attorney designating an agent for service of process and provides that any foreign corporation not complying with this requirement "shall not be permitted to bring or maintain any action or suit in any of the courts of this state." The effect of the statute, as construed by the highest court of the state, is not to make the contracts of such a corporation void but only to make them unenforceable in the Mississippi state courts. Prior to the Erie case, in David Lupton's Sons v. Automobile Club of America, 225 U.S. 489, 32 S.Ct. 711 (1912), the Supreme Court had held that such a state statute was not a bar to a diversity suit by such a corporation, saying: "The State could not prescribe the qualifications of suitors in the courts of the United States, and could not deprive of their privileges those who were entitled under the Constitution and laws of the United States to resort to the Federal courts for the enforcement of a valid contract." Note, although the Woods Court did not advert to it, Rule 17(b)(2). *P* has not complied with the state statute. *D* moves for summary judgment on that ground. Should the motion be granted? (6–3 decision.)

COHEN v. BENEFICIAL INDUSTRIAL LOAN CORP., 337 U.S. 541, 69 S.Ct. 1221 (1949). A small stockholder, *P*, brings a shareholders' derivative action in the District Court for the District of New Jersey, the defendants being the corporation and certain of its managers and directors who are alleged to have wasted or diverted corporate assets through mismanagement and fraud. A New Jersey statute provides that when stockholders whose holdings amount to less than 5% of the total stock outstanding and not more than $50,000 in market value bring an action of this type, the corporation can require the plaintiffs to give security for the reasonable expenses, including counsel fees, that it may incur in connection with the action, and against that security the corporation shall have recourse in such amount as the court may determine upon termination of the action. Compare Rule 23.1. The corporation moves to require *P* to give security as provided by the state statute, in the amount of $125,000. Is the statute applicable in the federal court? The Supreme Court divided on this question. One of the opinions said: "We see no reason why the policy stated in Guaranty Trust . . . should not apply." Another said: "The measure of the cause of action is the claim . . . against the alleged wrongdoers. This New Jersey statute does not add one iota to nor subtract one iota from that cause of action. . . . [It] regulates only the procedure for instituting a particular cause of action and hence need not be applied in this diversity suit in the federal court." Which do you think was the majority opinion and which a dissent? (6–3 decision.)

FEDERAL DETERMINATION OF STATE LAW

Questions as to scope of state-law applicability are not the only problem that Erie has intensified for the federal courts. What is to be done when a state's law clearly governs but the state has no clear law on the point in issue?

What if the only state-court decision is a very old one by the state's highest court but one that is wholly out of line with the modern trend of authority elsewhere? What if the highest court of the state has not passed upon the point but there is a decision of an intermediate state court of appeals? (The Supreme Court said in an early case that such a decision "is not to be disregarded by a federal court unless it is convinced by other persuasive data that the highest court of the state would decide otherwise," West v. AT & T, 311 U.S. 223, 237, 61 S.Ct. 179, 183 (1940), but where would a federal judge look for such "persuasive data"?) What if there is a recent decision of an intermediate state court that is inconsistent with an old decision of the state's highest court? What if, instead of any such decisions, there are only state-court dicta? What if there is no state law of any kind on the particular point in issue?

BERNHARDT v. POLYGRAPHIC CO. OF AMERICA, 350 U.S. 198, 76 S.Ct. 273 (1956). An employment contract made in New York between the plaintiff, an individual then residing in New York, and the defendant, a New York corporation, called in case of dispute for arbitration under the law of New York by the American Arbitration Association. The plaintiff subsequently moved to Vermont where he was to carry out the contract. In this action for wrongful discharge, removed on the basis of diversity of citizenship from the Vermont state court to the District Court for the District of Vermont, the defendant corporation applied for a stay pending resort to arbitration. The district court denied the application, on the ground that Vermont law controlled and provided for no stay, because agreements to arbitrate were not enforceable according to Mead v. Owen, 83 Vt. 132, 74 A. 1058 (1910). On appeal, the federal court of appeals reversed, holding that state law did not govern this matter, because it was not "substantive" in the Erie sense, and that federal law required a stay by the United States Arbitration Act, 9 U.S.C. § 3, which the court construed to apply in any federal action with respect to any agreement to arbitrate.

On certiorari, the Supreme Court by Justice Douglas said that section 3 should be narrowly read and limited to arbitration agreements in maritime transactions and in interstate or foreign commerce transactions. Otherwise, "a constitutional question might be presented" in light of the Erie decision. (The student should attempt to formulate that question.)

With the Arbitration Act thus considered inapplicable to this particular contract, the Court next decided that state law applied to the issue of enforceability. "If the federal court allows arbitration where the state court would disallow it, the outcome of litigation might depend on the courthouse where suit is brought. For the remedy by arbitration, whatever its merits or shortcomings, substantially affects the cause of action created by the State. The nature of the tribunal where suits are tried is an important part of the parcel of rights behind a cause of action. The change from a court of law to an arbitration panel may make a radical difference in ultimate result."

As to what Vermont law was, Justice Douglas said: "That [Mead] case was decided in 1910. But it was agreed on oral argument that there is no later authority from the Vermont courts, that no fracture in the rules announced in those cases has appeared in subsequent rulings or dicta, and that no legislative movement is under way in Vermont to change the result of those cases. . . . Were the question in doubt or deserving further canvass, we would of course remand the case to the Court of Appeals to pass on this question of Vermont law. But, as we have indicated, there appears to be no confusion in the Vermont decisions, no developing line of authorities that casts a shadow over the established ones, no dicta, doubts or ambiguities in the opinions of Vermont judges on the question, no legislative development that promises to undermine the judicial rule. We see no reason, therefore, to remand the case to the Court of Appeals to pass on this question of local law."

The Court, citing Klaxon, instead remanded the case to the district court with authority to consider whether, as a matter of conflict of laws, the Vermont Supreme Court would apply New York rather than Vermont law to the enforcement of this agreement to arbitrate. (It was not clear that the district court had considered that question in rendering its decision. On remand, the district court did decide to apply the Vermont law.)

Justices Frankfurter and Harlan, concurring separately, agreed that state law controlled, but they would have remanded to the court of appeals to consider whether the Vermont Supreme Court would not now change its attitude toward the enforcement of agreements to arbitrate. Justice Frankfurter said:

"As long as there is diversity jurisdiction, 'estimates' are necessarily often all that federal courts can make in ascertaining what the state court would rule to be its law. . . . The Supreme Court of Vermont last spoke on this matter in 1910. The doctrine that it referred to was not a peculiar indigenous Vermont rule. The attitude reflected by that decision nearly half a century ago was the current traditional judicial hostility against ousting courts, as the phrase ran, of their jurisdiction. . . . To be sure, a vigorous legislative movement got under way in the 1920's expressive of a broadened outlook of view on this subject. But courts do not always wait for legislation to find a judicial doctrine outmoded. . . .

"Surely in the light of all that has happened since 1910 in the general field of the law of arbitration, it is not for us to assume that the Court of Appeals, if it had that question for consideration, could not have found that the law of Vermont today does not require disregard of a provision of a contract made in New York, with a purposeful desire to have the law of New York govern, to accomplish a result that today may be deemed to be a general doctrine of the law. Of course, if the Court of Appeals, versed in the general jurisprudence of Vermont and having among its members a Vermont lawyer, should find that the Vermont court would, despite the New York incidents of the contract, apply Vermont law and that it is the habit of the Vermont court to adhere to its precedents and to leave changes to the legislature, it would not be for the federal court to gainsay that policy."

Justice Burton dissented, viewing arbitration as merely a "form of trial" as to which the federal courts were not bound to follow state law under Erie or Guaranty Trust.

These incidental problems of federal determination of state law persist to the present time. Consider this installment of the curious case of Factors

Etc., Inc. v. Pro Arts, Inc., 701 F.2d 11 (2d Cir.1983), in which the majority opinion was as follows:

"On June 29, 1981, this panel of the Court, by a divided vote, issued an opinion reversing the District Court's grant of summary judgment in favor of the plaintiffs-appellees and the issuance of a permanent injunction barring the defendants-appellants from marketing a poster depicting Elvis Presley. Factors, Etc., Inc. v. Pro Arts, Inc., 652 F.2d 278 (2d Cir.1981). The basis for that ruling . . . was that in the absence of authoritative guidance from the courts of Tennessee, we would deem controlling in this diversity case the decision of the Sixth Circuit in Memphis Development Foundation v. Factors, Etc., Inc., 616 F.2d 956 (6th Cir.), cert. denied, 449 U.S. 953, 101 S.Ct. 358, 66 L.Ed.2d 217 (1980). Memphis Development, also a diversity case requiring application of Tennessee law, had held that Tennessee does not recognize a descendible right of publicity. Upon the return of the instant case to the District Court for the Southern District of New York, plaintiffs called to Judge Tenney's attention a decision of the Tennessee Chancery Court, issued October 2, 1981, which held that Tennessee law does recognize a descendible right of publicity. Commerce Union Bank v. Coors of the Cumberland, Inc., 7 Media L.Rptr. 2204 (Chan.Ct.Davidson Cty.Tenn.1981). That decision, not officially reported, was issued prior to the issuance of our mandate in the instant case.

"Judge Tenney thereupon stayed entry of judgment for the defendants pending an application by the plaintiffs to petition this Court to recall its mandate and consider an untimely petition for rehearing in light of the alleged intervening change in state law. [Citation omitted. (The mandate is the appellate court's clerical act that returns jurisdiction to the lower court. The appellate court retains a narrow power to recall its mandate, usually to correct what would otherwise be a miscarriage of justice in a still-pending case.)] Plaintiffs diligently sought such relief, and we granted leave to file their petition for rehearing to assess the significance of the Chancery Court's decision in Commerce Union Bank. Supplemental briefs have been received.

"Fortunately, a recent development in the Tennessee Chancery Court has made it unnecessary for us to determine whether Commerce Union Bank is of sufficient authoritativeness to warrant our disregard of the Sixth Circuit's decision in Memphis Development. On November 24, 1982, the Chancery Court, acting through a different judge from the one who rendered the decision in Commerce Union Bank, ruled that Tennessee does not recognize a descendible right of publicity. Lancaster v. Factors, Etc., Inc., [9 Media L.Rptr. 1109] (Chan.Ct.Shelby Cty.Tenn.1982). The Lancaster decision is surely entitled to no less weight than the decision in Commerce Union Bank and may even have a special pertinence since it involves a claim by the same parties who are plaintiffs in the instant litigation with respect to a descendible right of publicity concerning Elvis Presley. Whatever the weight to be given an unreported decision of the Tennessee Chancery Court by a diversity court at any stage of litigation, much less at the point where a mandate is sought to be recalled on the basis of an alleged intervening change of state law, we have no doubt that the appearance of two conflicting decisions of the Chancery Court on the precise point at issue affords us no basis for considering the law of Tennessee to have authoritatively been changed since our June 29, 1981, decision. The motion to recall the mandate and the petition for rehearing are denied."

Judge Mansfield dissented, saying that "the internal Tennessee state court conflict provides an additional reason for our following the usual practice, where we disagree with the reasoning of another circuit on an issue, of deciding a case according to what we believe to be the more rational basis."

Questions: (6) The general rule is that any federal court should use the latest available data in deciding what the state law is. Vandenbark v. Owens–Illinois Glass Co., 311 U.S. 538, 61 S.Ct. 347 (1941). Thus, a federal court of appeals should consider fresh state decisional law; this Elvis Presley case illustrates that even on a petition for rehearing, any cutoff for considering state-law changes has not yet kicked in. However, after the federal case finally ends, a cutoff has kicked in so that any change of state law, or discovered error in determining state law, is not by itself a ground for relief from judgment; the defendants' eventual victory, 562 F.Supp. 304 (S.D.N.Y.1983), should therefore survive the development several years later when Tennessee recognized a descendible right of publicity, Tennessee ex rel. Elvis Presley Int'l Memorial Found. v. Crowell, 733 S.W.2d 89 (Tenn.Ct.App.1987). But exactly when in-between should the cutoff occur?

(7) In a typical diversity case, assuming there are no last-minute changes in state law, to what degree should a federal appellate court defer to the lower federal court's presumably more expert view on what the local state law is? See Salve Regina College v. Russell, 499 U.S. 225, 111 S.Ct. 1217 (1991) (ordering nondeferential review by the courts of appeals, because such review "best serves the dual goals of doctrinal coherence and economy of judicial administration," even in the Erie setting), criticized in Jonathan Remy Nash, Resuscitating Deference to Lower Federal Court Judges' Interpretations of State Law, 77 S.Cal.L.Rev. 975 (2004) (arguing that courts of appeal do, and should, continue to afford some deference).

(8) The excerpted Elvis Presley case involves the oddity of the Second Circuit's bowing to a coordinate court (given that the Sixth Circuit covers Tennessee and so is the "home circuit"). Rather than doing so, should not the Second Circuit have been asking what consideration New York's highest state court grants to a Sixth Circuit decision when determining and applying Tennessee law? See 19 Wright, Miller & Cooper § 4507, at 218–20.

STATE DETERMINATION OF STATE LAW

To sum up, Erie imposes on the federal courts the duty of, "in effect, sitting as a state court" when deciding certain issues of law. Commissioner v. Estate of Bosch, 387 U.S. 456, 465, 87 S.Ct. 1776, 1783 (1967). So, when facing unclear state law, the federal trial or appellate court should enunciate whatever state law governs as if it were then sitting as the forum state's highest court, taking into account all the latest precedent and other data that court would. The various burdens attendant upon such duty should now be obvious. Is there any way for the federal court to shift those burdens?

A possibility is abstention, a complex doctrine under which a federal court, in deference to a state's interests, declines to exercise the federal jurisdiction. There are a number of circumstances where a federal court might abstain. Along with a few other situations, the Supreme Court has indicated: "Abstention is also appropriate where there have been presented difficult questions of state law bearing on policy problems of substantial public import whose importance transcends the result in the case then at bar. Louisiana Power & Light Co. v. City of Thibodaux, 360 U.S. 25, 79 S.Ct. 1070 (1959), for example, involved such a question. In particular, the concern there was with the scope of the eminent domain power of municipalities under state law." Colorado River Water Conservation Dist. v. United States, 424 U.S. 800, 814, 96 S.Ct. 1236, 1244–45 (1976) (dictum). Accordingly, a district court faced under the Erie doctrine with an unsettled but publicly significant state-law issue might dismiss or stay the federal diversity case, leaving the parties to pursue a coercive or declaratory remedy in the state-court system.

There is a less drastic course that in this context is more broadly applicable, viz., a process of certification of the unsettled question of state law by the federal court directly to the highest court of the state, if the state is willing. By this device the federal court retains jurisdiction, eventually handling the case in accordance with the state court's answer. The first state provision for answering certified questions was a Florida statute, which had never been used until the Supreme Court gave its blessing to the procedure in Clay v. Sun Insurance Office Ltd., 363 U.S. 207, 80 S.Ct. 1222 (1960). Almost all states have since by statute or rule authorized their highest court to answer certified questions. The National Conference of Commissioners on Uniform State Laws in 1967 approved, and recommended for adoption by the states, a Uniform Certification of Questions of Law Act—and revised it in 1995. The Supreme Court emphatically restated its approval of certification in Lehman Brothers v. Schein, 416 U.S. 386, 94 S.Ct. 1741 (1974) (instructing the Second Circuit, in a diversity case, to reconsider the possibility of certifying a question of Florida law to the Florida Supreme Court).

Certification does offer a neat means of avoiding the anomaly of different answers to the same question of law from a state and a federal court. (Is this anomaly more of a reproach to the judicial process than the anomaly of different juries coming to opposite factual findings on the same evidence?) But this neat solution comes at a stiff price.

First, certification inevitably causes some delay and increased expense for the parties. At the least, this requires the federal court to balance the interests involved, taking into account the type of question and the circumstances of the particular case. Lehman Brothers v. Schein involved a question of corporate fiduciary obligation arising in a shareholders' derivative suit. By contrast, Clay v. Sun Insurance Office Ltd. involved an individual's suit against his insurance company seeking reimbursement for lost personal property, although other considerations pushed for certification of a statute-of-limitations point. But compare Thompson v. Johns–Manville Sales Corp., 714 F.2d 581 (5th Cir.1983) (2–1 decision) (holding in asbestosis action that state would not recognize market-share or enterprise liability, over colorful dissent urging certification), with Hatfield v. Bishop Clarkson Memorial Hosp., 701 F.2d 1266 (8th Cir.1983) (4–3 en banc decision) (setting aside panel's decision in favor of plaintiff and certifying statute-of-limitations point in infant's medical-malpractice action, over dissent that includes a fable).

Second, certification imposes a burden on the state court. The unavoidably abstract nature of the question may make it difficult to answer. Indeed, a state certification provision may run aground if the state has a constitutional prohibition against giving advisory opinions. These problems are lessened by allowing certification, as Florida does, only from a federal appellate court, but most state provisions and the Uniform Act allow a federal district court to certify as well.

Third, certification poses a possible threat to the judicial function of the federal courts in diversity cases, diminishing their authority and their sense of responsibility. See generally Jonathan Remy Nash, The Uneasy Case for Transjurisdictional Adjudication, 94 Va.L.Rev. 1869 (2008).

Byrd v. Blue Ridge Rural Electric Cooperative

Supreme Court of the United States, 1958.
356 U.S. 525, 78 S.Ct. 893.

■ MR. JUSTICE BRENNAN delivered the opinion of the Court.

[This was a diversity action in a federal district court in South Carolina for injuries allegedly caused by the defendant's negligence. The plaintiff was employed as a lineman by a contractor, which held a construction contract with the defendant. The plaintiff had suffered injury while performing work under that contract.

[One of the defenses was that the South Carolina Workmen's Compensation Act imposed upon the plaintiff—because the work contracted to be done by his employer was allegedly work of the kind also done by the defendant's own construction and maintenance crews—the status of a "statutory employee" of the defendant. That classification would mean that the defendant was immune from an action at law, and the plaintiff had to accept workers' compensation benefits as his exclusive remedy.

[The Supreme Court on certiorari considered, among other things, whether the question raised by this defense—whether the work of the plaintiff's employer was work of the kind done by the defendant's crews—should be decided by the trial judge, as held in a South Carolina decision, Adams v. Davison–Paxon Co., 230 S.C. 532, 96 S.E.2d 566 (1957), or by a jury, in line with federal practice.]

First. It was decided in Erie R. Co. v. Tompkins that the federal courts in diversity cases must respect the definition of state-created rights and obligations by the state courts. We must, therefore, first examine the rule in Adams v. Davison–Paxon Co. to determine whether it is bound up with these rights and obligations in such a way that its application in the federal court is required. Cities Service Oil Co. v. Dunlap, 308 U.S. 208, 60 S.Ct. 201.

The Workmen's Compensation Act is administered in South Carolina by its Industrial Commission. The South Carolina courts hold that, on judicial review of actions of the Commission . . . , the question whether the claim of an injured workman is within the Commission's jurisdiction is a matter of law for decision by the court, which makes its own findings of fact relating to that jurisdiction. The South Carolina Supreme Court states no reasons in Adams v. Davison–Paxon Co. why [when such a question arises instead as a defense in an original court action], although the jury decides all other factual issues raised by the cause of action and defenses, the jury is displaced as to the factual issue raised by the affirmative defense . . . . The conclusion is inescapable that the Adams holding is grounded in the practical consideration that the question had theretofore come before the South Carolina courts from the Industrial Commission and the courts had become accustomed to deciding the factual issue of immunity without the aid of juries. We find nothing to suggest that this rule was announced as an integral part of the special relationship created by the statute. Thus the requirement appears to be merely a form and mode of enforcing the immunity, Guaranty Trust Co. v. York, 326 U.S. 99, 108, 65 S.Ct. 1464, 1469, and not a rule intended to be bound up with the definition of the rights and obligations of the parties. The situation is therefore not analogous to that in Dice v. Akron, C. & Y.R. Co., 342 U.S. 359, 72 S.Ct. 312 . . . .

Second. But cases following Erie have evinced a broader policy to the effect that the federal courts should conform as near as may be—in the absence of other considerations—to state rules even of form and mode where the state rules may bear substantially on the question whether the litigation would come out one way in the federal court and another way in the state court if the federal court failed to apply a particular local rule. E.g., Guaranty Trust Co. v. York, supra; Bernhardt v. Polygraphic Co., 350 U.S. 198, 76 S.Ct. 273. Concededly the nature of the tribunal which tries issues may be important in the enforcement of the parcel of rights making up a cause of action or defense, and bear significantly upon achievement of uniform enforcement of the right. It may well be that in the instant personal-injury case the outcome would be substantially affected by whether the issue of immunity is decided by a judge or a jury. Therefore, were "outcome" the only consideration, a strong case might appear for saying that the federal court should follow the state practice.

But there are affirmative countervailing considerations at work here. The federal system is an independent system for administering justice to litigants who properly invoke its jurisdiction. An essential characteristic of that system is the manner in which, in civil common-law actions, it distributes trial functions between judge and jury and, under the influence—if not the command[10]—of the Seventh Amendment, assigns the decisions of disputed questions of fact to the jury. Jacob v. City of New York, 315 U.S. 752, 62 S.Ct. 854.[11] The policy of uniform enforcement of state-created rights and obligations, see, e.g., Guaranty Trust Co. v. York, supra, cannot in every case exact compliance with a state rule[12]—not bound up with rights and obligations—which disrupts the federal system of allocating functions between judge and jury. Herron v. Southern Pacific Co., 283 U.S. 91, 51 S.Ct. 383 [(1931)]. Thus the inquiry here is whether the federal policy favoring jury decisions of disputed fact questions should yield to the state rule in the interest of furthering the objective that the litigation should not come out one way in the federal court and another way in the state court.

We think that in the circumstances of this case the federal court should not follow the state rule. It cannot be gainsaid that there is a strong federal policy against allowing state rules to disrupt the judge-jury relationship in the federal courts. In Herron v. Southern Pacific Co., supra, the trial judge in a personal-injury negligence action brought in the District Court for Arizona on diversity grounds directed a verdict for the defendant when it appeared as a matter of law that the plaintiff was guilty of contributory negligence. The federal judge refused to be bound by a provision of the Arizona Constitution which made the jury the sole arbiter of the question of contributory negligence. This Court sustained the action of the trial judge, holding that "state laws cannot alter the essential character or function of a federal court" because that function "is not in any sense a local matter, and state statutes which would interfere with the appropriate performance of that function are not binding upon the federal court under either the Conformity Act or the 'Rules of Decision' Act." Id., 283 U.S. at page 94, 51 S.Ct. at page 384. Perhaps even more clearly in light of the influence of the Seventh Amendment, the function assigned to the jury "is an essential factor in the process for which the Federal Constitution provides." Id., 283 U.S. at page 95, 51 S.Ct. at page 384. Concededly the Herron case was decided before Erie R. Co. v. Tompkins, but even when Swift v. Tyson, 16 Pet. 1, was governing law and allowed federal courts sitting in diversity cases to disregard state decisional law, it was never thought that state statutes or constitutions were similarly to be disregarded. Green v. Neal's Lessee, 6 Pet. 291. Yet Herron held that state statutes and constitutional provisions could not disrupt or alter the essential character or function of a federal court.[14]

---

[10] Our conclusion makes unnecessary the consideration of—and we intimate no view upon—the constitutional question whether the right of jury trial protected in federal courts by the Seventh Amendment embraces the factual issue of statutory immunity when asserted, as here, as an affirmative defense in a common-law negligence action.

[11] The Courts of Appeals have expressed varying views about the effect of Erie R. Co. v. Tompkins on judge-jury problems in diversity cases. [Citations omitted.]

[12] This Court held in Sibbach v. Wilson & Co., 312 U.S. 1, 61 S.Ct. 422, that Federal Rules of Civil Procedure 35 should prevail over a contrary state rule.

[14] Diederich v. American News Co., 10 Cir., 128 F.2d 144 [(1942)], decided after Erie R. Co. v. Tompkins, held that an almost identical provision of the Oklahoma Constitution was not binding on a federal judge in a diversity case.

Third. We have discussed the problem upon the assumption that the outcome of the litigation may be substantially affected by whether the issue of immunity is decided by a judge or a jury. But clearly there is not present here the certainty that a different result would follow, cf. Guaranty Trust Co. v. York, supra, or even the strong possibility that this would be the case, cf. Bernhardt v. Polygraphic Co., supra. There are factors present here which might reduce that possibility. The trial judge in the federal system has powers denied the judges of many States to comment on the weight of evidence and credibility of witnesses, and discretion to grant a new trial if the verdict appears to him to be against the weight of the evidence. We do not think the likelihood of a different result is so strong as to require the federal practice of jury determination of disputed factual issues to yield to the state rule in the interest of uniformity of outcome.

■ [JUSTICE WHITTAKER dissented from the ruling that the plaintiff was entitled to a jury determination of his status, arguing that Guaranty Trust required the application of state law. JUSTICES FRANKFURTER and HARLAN also dissented, but they did not reach the jury-trial point.]

Question: (9) Reexamine Woods v. Interstate Realty Co. Do you think its decision to apply state law is still sound after Byrd?

Hanna v. Plumer

Supreme Court of the United States, 1965.
380 U.S. 460, 85 S.Ct. 1136.

■ MR. CHIEF JUSTICE WARREN delivered the opinion of the Court.

The question to be decided is whether, in a civil action where the jurisdiction of the United States district court is based upon diversity of citizenship between the parties, service of process shall be made in the manner prescribed by state law or that set forth in Rule 4(d)(1) of the Federal Rules of Civil Procedure [which is now Rule 4(e)(2)].

On February 6, 1963, petitioner, a citizen of Ohio, filed her complaint in the District Court for the District of Massachusetts, claiming damages in excess of [the then jurisdictional amount of] $10,000 for personal injuries resulting from an automobile accident in South Carolina, allegedly caused by the negligence of one Louise Plumer Osgood, a Massachusetts citizen deceased at the time of the filing of the complaint. Respondent, Mrs. Osgood's executor and also a Massachusetts citizen, was named as defendant. On February 8, service was made by leaving copies of the summons and the complaint with respondent's wife at his residence, concededly in compliance with Rule 4(d)(1) [the Court here quoted the Rule]. Respondent filed his answer on February 26, alleging, inter alia, that the action could not be maintained because it had been brought "contrary to and in violation of the provisions of Massachusetts General Laws (Ter.Ed.) Chapter 197, Section 9." That section provides:

> "Except as provided in this chapter, an executor or administrator shall not be held to answer to an action by a creditor of the deceased which is not commenced within one year from the time of his giving bond for the performance of his trust, or to such an action which is commenced within said year unless before the expiration thereof the writ in such action has been served by delivery in hand upon such executor or administrator or service thereof accepted by him or a notice stating the name of the estate, the name and address of the creditor, the amount of the claim and the court in which the action has been brought has been filed in the proper registry of probate. . . ." Mass.Gen.Laws Ann., c. 197, § 9 (1958).

On October 17, 1963, the District Court granted respondent's motion for summary judgment, citing Ragan v. Merchants Transfer & Warehouse Co., 337 U.S. 530, 69 S.Ct. 1233, and Guaranty Trust Co. v. York, 326 U.S. 99, 65 S.Ct. 1464, in support of its conclusion that the adequacy of the service was to be measured by § 9, with which, the court held, petitioner had not complied. On appeal, petitioner admitted noncompliance with § 9, but argued that Rule 4(d)(1) defines the method by which service of process is to be effected in diversity actions. The Court of Appeals for the First Circuit, finding that "[r]elatively recent amendments [to § 9] evince a clear legislative purpose to require personal notification within the year,"[1] concluded that the conflict of state and federal rules was over "a substantive rather than a procedural matter," and unanimously affirmed. 331 F.2d 157. Because of the threat to the goal of uniformity of federal procedure posed by the decision below, we granted certiorari, 379 U.S. 813, 85 S.Ct. 52.

We conclude that the adoption of Rule 4(d)(1), designed to control service of process in diversity actions, neither exceeded the congressional mandate embodied in the Rules Enabling Act nor transgressed constitu-

[1] Section 9 is in part a statute of limitations, providing that an executor need not "answer to an action . . . which is not commenced within one year from the time of his giving bond . . . ." This part of the statute, the purpose of which is to speed the settlement of estates, Spaulding v. McConnell, 307 Mass. 144, 146, 29 N.E.2d 713, 715 (1940); Doyle v. Moylan, 141 F.Supp. 95 (D.C.Mass.1956), is not involved in this case, since the action clearly was timely commenced. (Respondent filed bond on March 1, 1962; the complaint was filed February 6, 1963; and the service—the propriety of which is in dispute—was made on February 8, 1963.) 331 F.2d, at 159. Cf. Guaranty Trust Co. v. York, supra; Ragan v. Merchants Transfer & Warehouse Co., supra.

Section 9 also provides for the manner of service. Generally, service of process must be made by "delivery in hand," although there are two alternatives: acceptance of service by the executor, or filing of a notice of claim, the components of which are set out in the statute, in the appropriate probate court. The purpose of this part of the statute, which *is* involved here, is, as the court below noted, to insure that executors will receive actual notice of claims. Parker v. Rich, 297 Mass. 111, 113–114, 8 N.E.2d 345, 347 (1937). Actual notice is of course also the goal of Rule 4(d)(1); however, the Federal Rule reflects a determination that this goal can be achieved by a method less cumbersome than that prescribed in § 9. In this case the goal seems to have been achieved; although the affidavit filed by respondent in the District Court asserts that he had not been served in hand nor had he accepted service, it does not allege lack of actual notice. [Incidentally, Massachusetts also had a general service provision similar to former Federal Rule 4(d)(1).—Ed.]

tional bounds, and that the Rule is therefore the standard against which the District Court should have measured the adequacy of the service. Accordingly, we reverse the decision of the Court of Appeals.

. . . Under the cases construing the scope of the Enabling Act, Rule 4(d)(1) clearly passes muster. Prescribing the manner in which a defendant is to be notified that a suit has been instituted against him, it relates to the "practice and procedure of the district courts." Cf. New York Life Insurance Co. v. Bangs, 103 U.S. 435, 439.

> "The test must be whether a rule really regulates procedure,—the judicial process for enforcing rights and duties recognized by substantive law and for justly administering remedy and redress for disregard or infraction of them." Sibbach v. Wilson & Co., 312 U.S. 1, 14, 61 S.Ct. 422, 426.[4]

In Mississippi Pub. Corp. v. Murphree, 326 U.S. 438, 66 S.Ct. 242, this Court upheld [former] Rule 4(f), which permits service of a summons anywhere within the State (and not merely the district) in which a district court sits:

> "We think that Rule 4(f) is in harmony with the Enabling Act . . . . Undoubtedly most alterations of the rules of practice and procedure may and often do affect the rights of litigants. Congress' prohibition of any alteration of substantive rights of litigants was obviously not addressed to such incidental effects as necessarily attend the adoption of the prescribed new rules of procedure upon the rights of litigants who, agreeably to rules of practice and procedure, have been brought before a court authorized to determine their rights. Sibbach v. Wilson & Co., 312 U.S. 1, 11–14, 61 S.Ct. 422, 425–427. The fact that the application of Rule 4(f) will operate to subject petitioner's rights to adjudication by the district court for northern Mississippi will undoubtedly affect those rights. But it does not operate to abridge, enlarge or modify the rules of decision by which that court will adjudicate its rights." Id., at 445–446, 66 S.Ct. at 246.

Thus were there no conflicting state procedure, Rule 4(d)(1) would clearly control. National Equipment Rental v. Szukhent, 375 U.S. 311, 316, 84 S.Ct. 411, 414. However, respondent, focusing on the contrary Massachusetts rule, calls to the Court's attention another line of cases, a line which—like the Federal Rules—had its birth in 1938. Erie R. Co. v. Tompkins, 304 U.S. 64, 58 S.Ct. 817, overruling Swift v. Tyson, 16 Pet. 1, held that federal courts sitting in diversity cases, when deciding questions of "substantive" law, are bound by state court decisions as well as state statutes. The broad command of Erie was therefore identical to that of the Enabling Act: federal courts are to apply state substantive law and federal procedural law. However, as subsequent cases sharpened the distinction between substance and procedure, the line of cases following Erie diverged markedly from the line construing the Enabling Act. Guaranty Trust Co. v. York, 326 U.S. 99, 65 S.Ct. 1464, made it clear that Erie-type problems

[4] See also Schlagenhauf v. Holder, 379 U.S. 104, 112–114, 85 S.Ct. 234, 239–240.

were not to be solved by reference to any traditional or common-sense substance-procedure distinction:

> "And so the question is not whether a statute of limitations is deemed a matter of 'procedure' in some sense. The question is . . . does it significantly affect the result of a litigation for a federal court to disregard a law of a State that would be controlling in an action upon the same claim by the same parties in a State court?" 326 U.S. at 109, 65 S.Ct. at 1470.[5]

Respondent, by placing primary reliance on York and Ragan, suggests that the Erie doctrine acts as a check on the Federal Rules of Civil Procedure, that despite the clear command of Rule 4(d)(1), Erie and its progeny demand the application of the Massachusetts rule. Reduced to essentials, the argument is: (1) Erie, as defined in York, demands that federal courts apply state law whenever application of federal law in its stead will alter the outcome of the case. (2) In this case, a determination that the Massachusetts service requirements obtain will result in immediate victory for respondent. If, on the other hand, it should be held that Rule 4(d)(1) is applicable, the litigation will continue, with possible victory for petitioner. (3) Therefore, Erie demands application of the Massachusetts rule. The syllogism possesses an appealing simplicity, but is for several reasons invalid.

In the first place, it is doubtful that, even if there were no Federal Rule making it clear that in-hand service is not required in diversity actions, the Erie rule would have obligated the District Court to follow the Massachusetts procedure. "Outcome-determination" analysis was never intended to serve as a talisman. Byrd v. Blue Ridge Rural Elec. Cooperative, 356 U.S. 525, 537, 78 S.Ct. 893, 900. Indeed, the message of York itself is that choices between state and federal law are to be made not by application of any automatic, "litmus paper" criterion, but rather by reference to the policies underlying the Erie rule. Guaranty Trust Co. v. York, supra, 326 U.S. at 108–112, 65 S.Ct. at 1469–1471.

The Erie rule is rooted in part in a realization that it would be unfair for the character or result of a litigation materially to differ because the suit had been brought in a federal court.

> "Diversity of citizenship jurisdiction was conferred in order to prevent apprehended discrimination in state courts against those not citizens of the state. Swift v. Tyson introduced grave discrimination by noncitizens against citizens. It made rights enjoyed under the unwritten 'general law' vary according to whether enforcement was sought in the state or in the federal court; and the privilege of selecting the court in which the right should be determined was conferred upon the noncitizen. Thus, the doctrine rendered impossible equal protection of the

[5] See also Ragan v. Merchants Transfer Co., supra; Woods v. Interstate Realty Co., 337 U.S. 535, 69 S.Ct. 1235; Bernhardt v. Polygraphic Co., 350 U.S. 198, 203–204, 207–208, 76 S.Ct. 273, 276, 278–279; cf. Byrd v. Blue Ridge Rural Elec. Cooperative, 356 U.S. 525, 78 S.Ct. 893.

law." Erie R. Co. v. Tompkins, supra, 304 U.S. at 74–75, 58 S.Ct. at 820–821.[7]

The decision was also in part a reaction to the practice of "forum-shopping" which had grown up in response to the rule of Swift v. Tyson. 304 U.S. at 73–74, 58 S.Ct. at 819–820.[8] That the York test was an attempt to effectuate these policies is demonstrated by the fact that the opinion framed the inquiry in terms of "substantial" variations between state and federal litigation. 326 U.S. at 109, 65 S.Ct. at 1469. Not only are nonsubstantial, or trivial, variations not likely to raise the sort of equal protection problems which troubled the Court in Erie; they are also unlikely to influence the choice of a forum. The "outcome-determination" test therefore cannot be read without reference to the twin aims of the Erie rule: discouragement of forum-shopping and avoidance of inequitable administration of the laws.[9]

The difference between the conclusion that the Massachusetts rule is applicable, and the conclusion that it is not, is of course at this point "outcome-determinative" in the sense that if we hold the state rule to apply, respondent prevails, whereas if we hold that Rule 4(d)(1) governs, the litigation will continue. But in this sense *every* procedural variation is "outcome-determinative." For example, having brought suit in a federal court a plaintiff cannot then insist on the right to file subsequent pleadings in accord with the time limits applicable in the state courts, even though enforcement of the federal timetable will, if he continues to insist that he must meet only the state time limit, result in determination of the controversy against him. So it is here. Though choice of the federal or state rule will at this point have a marked effect upon the outcome of the litigation, the difference between the two rules would be of scant, if any, relevance to the choice of a forum. Petitioner, in choosing her forum, was not presented with a situation where application of the state rule would wholly bar recovery;[10] rather, adherence to the state rule would have

[7] See also Klaxon Co. v. Stentor Electric Mfg. Co., 313 U.S. 487, 496, 61 S.Ct. 1020, 1021; Woods v. Interstate Realty Co., supra, note 5, 337 U.S. at 538, 69 S.Ct. at 1237.

[8] Cf. Black & White Taxicab & Transfer Co. v. Brown & Yellow Taxicab & Transfer Co., 276 U.S. 518, 48 S.Ct. 404.

[9] The Court of Appeals seemed to frame the inquiry in terms of how "important" § 9 is to the State. In support of its suggestion that § 9 serves some interest the State regards as vital to its citizens, the court noted that something like § 9 has been on the books in Massachusetts a long time, that § 9 has been amended a number of times, and that § 9 is designed to make sure that executors receive actual notice. See note 1, supra. The apparent lack of relation among these three observations is not surprising, because it is not clear to what sort of question the Court of Appeals was addressing itself. One cannot meaningfully ask how important something is without first asking "important for what purpose?" Erie and its progeny make clear that when a federal court sitting in a diversity case is faced with a question of whether or not to apply state law, the importance of a state rule is indeed relevant, but only in the context of asking whether application of the rule would make so important a difference to the character or result of the litigation that failure to enforce it would unfairly discriminate against citizens of the forum State, or whether application of the rule would have so important an effect upon the fortunes of one or both of the litigants that failure to enforce it would be likely to cause a plaintiff to choose the federal court.

[10] See Guaranty Trust Co. v. York, supra, 326 U.S. at 108–109, 65 S.Ct. at 1469; Ragan v. Merchants Transfer Co., supra, 337 U.S. at 532, 69 S.Ct. at 1234; Woods v. Interstate Realty Co., supra, note 5, 337 U.S. at 538, 69 S.Ct. at 1237.

resulted only in altering the way in which process was served.[11] Moreover, it is difficult to argue that permitting service of defendant's wife to take the place of in-hand service of defendant himself alters the mode of enforcement of state-created rights in a fashion sufficiently "substantial" to raise the sort of equal protection problems to which the Erie opinion alluded.

There is, however, a more fundamental flaw in respondent's syllogism: the incorrect assumption that the rule of Erie R. Co. v. Tompkins constitutes the appropriate test of the validity and therefore the applicability of a Federal Rule of Civil Procedure. The Erie rule has never been invoked to void a Federal Rule. It is true that there have been cases where this Court has held applicable a state rule in the face of an argument that the situation was governed by one of the Federal Rules. But the holding of each such case was not that Erie commanded displacement of a Federal Rule by an inconsistent state rule, but rather that the scope of the Federal Rule was not as broad as the losing party urged, and therefore, there being no Federal Rule which covered the point in dispute, Erie commanded the enforcement of state law.

> "Respondent contends, in the first place, that the charge was correct because of the fact that Rule 8(c) of the Rules of Civil Procedure makes contributory negligence an affirmative defense. We do not agree. Rule 8(c) covers only the manner of pleading. The question of the burden of establishing contributory negligence is a question of local law which federal courts in diversity of citizenship cases (Erie R. Co. v. Tompkins, 304 U.S. 64, 58 S.Ct. 817) must apply." Palmer v. Hoffman, 318 U.S. 109, 117, 63 S.Ct. 477, 482.[12]

(Here, of course, the clash is unavoidable; Rule 4(d)(1) says—implicitly, but with unmistakable clarity—that in-hand service is not required in federal courts.) At the same time, in cases adjudicating the validity of Federal Rules, we have not applied the York rule or other refinements of Erie, but have to this day continued to decide questions concerning the scope of the Enabling Act and the constitutionality of specific Federal Rules in light of the distinction set forth in Sibbach. E.g., Schlagenhauf v. Holder, 379 U.S. 104, 85 S.Ct. 234.

Nor has the development of two separate lines of cases been inadvertent. The line between "substance" and "procedure" shifts as the legal context changes. "Each implies different variables depending upon the

---

Similarly, a federal court's refusal to enforce the New Jersey rule involved in Cohen v. Beneficial Indus. Loan Corp., 337 U.S. 541, 69 S.Ct. 1221, requiring the posting of security by plaintiffs in stockholders' derivative actions, might well impel a stockholder to choose to bring suit in the federal, rather than the state, court.

[11] Cf. Monarch Insurance Co. of Ohio v. Spach, 281 F.2d 401, 412 (C.A.5th Cir. 1960). We cannot seriously entertain the thought that one suing an estate would be led to choose the federal court because of a belief that adherence to Rule 4(d)(1) is less likely to give the executor actual notice than § 9, and therefore more likely to produce a default judgment. Rule 4(d)(1) is well designed to give actual notice, as it did in this case. See note 1, supra.

[12] To the same effect, see Ragan v. Merchants Transfer Co., supra; Cohen v. Beneficial Indus. Loan Corp., supra, note 10, 337 U.S. at 556, 69 S.Ct. at 1230; id., at 557, 69 S.Ct. at 1230 (Douglas, J., dissenting); cf. Bernhardt v. Polygraphic Co., supra, note 5, 350 U.S. at 201–202, 76 S.Ct. at 275; see generally Iovino v. Waterson, [274 F.2d 41, 47–48 (2d Cir.1959)].

particular problem for which it is used." Guaranty Trust Co. v. York, supra, 326 U.S. at 108, 65 S.Ct. at 1469; Cook, The Logical and Legal Bases of the Conflict of Laws, pp. 154–183 (1942). It is true that both the Enabling Act and the Erie rule say, roughly, that federal courts are to apply state "substantive" law and federal "procedural" law, but from that it need not follow that the tests are identical. For they were designed to control very different sorts of decisions. When a situation is covered by one of the Federal Rules, the question facing the court is a far cry from the typical, relatively unguided Erie choice: the court has been instructed to apply the Federal Rule, and can refuse to do so only if the Advisory Committee, this Court, and Congress erred in their prima facie judgment that the Rule in question transgresses neither the terms of the Enabling Act nor constitutional restrictions.

We are reminded by the Erie opinion[14] that neither Congress nor the federal courts can, under the guise of formulating rules of decision for federal courts, fashion rules which are not supported by a grant of federal authority contained in Article I or some other section of the Constitution; in such areas state law must govern because there can be no other law. But the opinion in Erie, which involved no Federal Rule and dealt with a question which was "substantive" in every traditional sense (whether the railroad owed a duty of care to Tompkins as a trespasser or a licensee), surely neither said nor implied that measures like Rule 4(d)(1) are unconstitutional. For the constitutional provision for a federal court system (augmented by the Necessary and Proper Clause) carries with it congressional power to make rules governing the practice and pleading in those courts, which in turn includes a power to regulate matters which, though falling within the uncertain area between substance and procedure, are rationally capable of classification as either. Cf. M'Culloch v. Maryland, 4 Wheat. 316, 421. Neither York nor the cases following it ever suggested that the rule there laid down for coping with situations where no Federal Rule applies is coextensive with the limitation on Congress to which Erie had adverted. Although this Court has never before been confronted with a case where the applicable Federal Rule is in direct collision with the law of the relevant State,[15] courts of appeals faced with such clashes have rightly discerned the implications of our decisions.

> "One of the shaping purposes of the Federal Rules is to bring about uniformity in the federal courts by getting away from local rules. This is especially true of matters which relate to the administration of legal proceedings, an area in which federal courts have traditionally

[14] Erie R. Co. v. Tompkins, supra, 304 U.S. at 77–79, 58 S.Ct. at 822–823; cf. Bernhardt v. Polygraphic Co., supra, note 5, 350 U.S. at 202, 76 S.Ct. at 275; Sibbach v. Wilson & Co., supra, 312 U.S. at 10, 61 S.Ct. at 424; Guaranty Trust Co. v. York, supra, 326 U.S. at 105, 65 S.Ct. at 1467.

[15] In Sibbach v. Wilson & Co., supra, the law of the forum State (Illinois) forbade the sort of order authorized by Rule 35. However, Sibbach was decided before Klaxon Co. v. Stentor Electric Mfg. Co., supra, note 7, and the Sibbach opinion makes clear that the Court was proceeding on the assumption that if the law of any State was relevant, it was the law of the State where the tort occurred (Indiana), which, like Rule 35, made provision for such orders. 312 U.S. at 6–7, 10–11, 61 S.Ct. at 423, 424–425.

> exerted strong inherent power, completely aside from the powers Congress expressly conferred in the Rules. The purpose of the Erie doctrine, even as extended in York and Ragan, was never to bottle up federal courts with 'outcome-determinative' and 'integral-relations' stoppers—when there are 'affirmative countervailing [federal] considerations' and when there is a Congressional mandate (the Rules) supported by constitutional authority." Lumbermen's Mutual Casualty Co. v. Wright, 322 F.2d 759, 764 (C.A.5th Cir.1963).

Erie and its offspring cast no doubt on the long-recognized power of Congress to prescribe housekeeping rules for federal courts even though some of those rules will inevitably differ from comparable state rules. Cf. Herron v. Southern Pacific Co., 283 U.S. 91, 51 S.Ct. 383. "When, because the plaintiff happens to be a non-resident, such a right is enforceable in a federal as well as in a State court, the forms and mode of enforcing the right may at times, naturally enough, vary because the two judicial systems are not identic." Guaranty Trust Co. v. York, supra, 326 U.S. at 108, 65 S.Ct. at 1469; Cohen v. Beneficial Indus. Loan Corp., 337 U.S. 541, 555, 69 S.Ct. 1221, 1229. Thus, though a court, in measuring a Federal Rule against the standards contained in the Enabling Act and the Constitution, need not wholly blind itself to the degree to which the Rule makes the character and result of the federal litigation stray from the course it would follow in state courts, Sibbach v. Wilson & Co., supra, 312 U.S. at 13–14, 61 S.Ct. at 426–427, it cannot be forgotten that the Erie rule, and the guidelines suggested in York, were created to serve another purpose altogether. To hold that a Federal Rule of Civil Procedure must cease to function whenever it alters the mode of enforcing state-created rights would be to disembowel either the Constitution's grant of power over federal procedure or Congress' attempt to exercise that power in the Enabling Act. Rule 4(d)(1) is valid and controls the instant case.

Reversed.

■ MR. JUSTICE BLACK concurs in the result.

■ MR. JUSTICE HARLAN, concurring.

It is unquestionably true that up to now Erie and the cases following it have not succeeded in articulating a workable doctrine governing choice of law in diversity actions. I respect the Court's effort to clarify the situation in today's opinion. However, in doing so I think it has misconceived the constitutional premises of Erie and has failed to deal adequately with those past decisions upon which the courts below relied.

Erie was something more than an opinion which worried about "forum-shopping and avoidance of inequitable administration of the laws," ante, . . . although to be sure these were important elements of the decision. I have always regarded that decision as one of the modern cornerstones of our federalism, expressing policies that profoundly touch the allocation of judicial power between the state and federal systems. . . .

. . . .

. . . Whereas the unadulterated outcome and forum-shopping tests may err too far toward honoring state rules, I submit that the Court's [Federal Rules] test moves too fast and far in the other direction.

The courts below relied upon this Court's decisions in Ragan v. Merchants Transfer & Warehouse Co., 337 U.S. 530, 69 S.Ct. 1233, and Cohen v. Beneficial Indus. Loan Corp., 337 U.S. 541, 69 S.Ct. 1221. Those cases deserve more attention than this Court has given them, particularly Ragan which, if still good law, would in my opinion call for affirmance of the result reached by the Court of Appeals. Further, a discussion of these two cases will serve to illuminate the ["primary activity"] thesis I am advocating.

In Ragan a Kansas statute of limitations provided that an action was deemed commenced when service was made on the defendant. Despite Federal Rule 3 which provides that an action commences with the filing of the complaint, the Court held that for purposes of the Kansas statute of limitations a diversity tort action commenced only when service was made upon the defendant. The effect of this holding was that although the plaintiff had filed his federal complaint within the state period of limitations, his action was barred because the federal marshal did not serve a summons on the defendant until after the limitations period had run. I think that the decision was wrong. At most, application of the Federal Rule would have meant that potential Kansas tort defendants would have to defer for a few days the satisfaction of knowing that they had not been sued within the limitations period. The choice of the Federal Rule would have had no effect on the primary stages of private activity from which torts arise, and only the most minimal effect on behavior following the commission of the tort. In such circumstances the interest of the federal system in proceeding under its own rules should have prevailed.

Cohen v. Beneficial Indus. Loan Corp. held that a federal diversity court must apply a state statute requiring a small stockholder in a stockholder derivative suit to post a bond securing payment of defense costs as a condition to prosecuting an action. Such a statute is not "outcome determinative"; the plaintiff can win with or without it. The Court now rationalizes the case on the ground that the statute might affect the plaintiff's choice of forum (ante . . . n. 10), but as has been pointed out, a simple forum-shopping test proves too much. The proper view of Cohen is, in my opinion, that the statute was meant to inhibit small stockholders from instituting "strike suits," and thus it was designed and could be expected to have a substantial impact on private primary activity. Anyone who was at the trial bar during the period when Cohen arose can appreciate the strong state policy reflected in the statute. I think it wholly legitimate to view Federal Rule [23.1] as not purporting to deal with the problem. But even had the Federal Rules purported to do so, and in so doing provided a substantially less effective deterrent to strike suits, I think the state rule should still have prevailed. That is where I believe the Court's view differs from mine; for the Court attributes such overriding force to the Federal Rules that it is hard to think of a case where a conflicting state rule would be allowed to operate, even though the state rule reflected policy considerations which, under Erie, would lie within the realm of state legislative authority.

It remains to apply what has been said to the present case. The Massachusetts rule provides that an executor need not answer suits unless in-hand service was made upon him or notice of the action was filed in the proper registry of probate within one year of his giving bond. The evident intent of this statute is to permit an executor to distribute the estate which he is administering without fear that further liabilities may be outstanding for which he could be held personally liable. If the Federal District Court in Massachusetts applies Rule 4(d)(1) of the Federal Rules of Civil Procedure instead of the Massachusetts service rule, what effect would that have on the speed and assurance with which estates are distributed? As I see it, the effect would not be substantial. It would mean simply that an executor would have to check at his own house or the federal courthouse as well as the registry of probate before he could distribute the estate with impunity. As this does not seem enough to give rise to any real impingement on the vitality of the state policy which the Massachusetts rule is intended to serve, I concur in the judgment of the Court.

Questions: (10) Consider once again Woods v. Interstate Realty Co. Would you expect its result to be affected by Hanna? What of Rule 17(b)? See 6A Wright, Miller & Kane § 1569. Assuming that Rule 17(b) does not extend to the situation in Woods (as the Supreme Court apparently assumed, knowingly or unknowingly, when it decided Woods itself, and also when it referred to Woods in Hanna), then reference must be made not to the portion of Hanna that deals with the applicability of the Federal Rules but rather to the discussion in Hanna of the more general Erie problem. So, under Hanna's refined outcome-determinative test, was Woods rightly decided?

(11) What exactly should be the meaning given "the twin aims of the Erie rule: discouragement of forum-shopping and avoidance of inequitable administration of the laws"? The former factor seems to focus on the systemic costs of the plaintiff or the defendant selecting federal or state court because of a difference in law. Under post-Hanna cases, the latter factor apparently refers to the unfairness of treating in a substantially different way any similarly situated individuals, given that certain classes of people have a choice of court systems. This latter factor, however, renders those forum-shopping concerns in large part redundant, and seemingly insignificant as to any remaining part. Should, then, the forum-shopping factor be seen instead to stand for the otherwise missing federalism factor expressed by Byrd or by Justice Harlan in Hanna, so recognizing that the "attempt to make the federal court function like the state court 'a block away' serves federalism goals of allocating regulatory power [while it] deters shopping"? George D. Brown, The Ideologies of Forum Shopping—Why Doesn't a Conservative Court Protect Defendants?, 71 N.C.L.Rev. 649, 693 (1993).

SZANTAY v. BEECH AIRCRAFT CORP., 349 F.2d 60 (4th Cir.1965). Szantay bought a Beech aircraft in Nebraska and flew it to Florida and thence to South Carolina, where it was serviced by Dixie Aviation Co. during a brief stopover. Szantay and his passengers then left for Illinois, where they lived, but the plane crashed in Tennessee, killing all its occupants.

The Illinois personal representatives of the decedents each brought a diversity action in a federal district court in South Carolina against Beech and Dixie, alleging negligent design and manufacture on the part of Beech and negligent servicing by Dixie. The requirements for diversity jurisdiction were satisfied, as Beech was a Delaware corporation with its principal place of business in Kansas, Dixie was a South Carolina corporation doing business only in that state, and the amount in controversy exceeded the jurisdictional amount. By virtue of Beech's doing business in South Carolina, venue requirements were met and in-state service of process was properly effected.

Beech moved to dismiss the actions on the ground that a South Carolina "door-closing" statute. It provided that a foreign corporation could be sued in a South Carolina court only by (1) any South Carolina resident for any cause of action or (2) a nonresident plaintiff when the cause of action arose in South Carolina. So, a South Carolina state court could not entertain a suit brought by a nonresident against a foreign corporation on a foreign cause of action. Beech maintained that this statute should likewise bar suit in the federal court. But the court denied the motion to dismiss.

On interlocutory appeal pursuant to 28 U.S.C. § 1292(b), the court of appeals, after discussing prior decisions that included the Erie, Guaranty Trust, Woods, Byrd, and Hanna cases, generalized:

"The spirit of these decisions makes it appropriate for a court attempting to resolve a federal-state conflict in a diversity case to undertake the following analysis:

1. If the state provision, whether legislatively adopted or judicially declared, is the substantive right or obligation at issue, it is constitutionally controlling.

2. If the state provision is a procedure intimately bound up with the state right or obligation, it is likewise constitutionally controlling.[5]

3. If the state procedural provision is not intimately bound up with the right being enforced but its application would substantially affect the outcome of the litigation, the federal diversity court must still apply it unless there are affirmative countervailing federal considerations. This is not deemed a constitutional requirement but one dictated by comity."

Deciding that the case before it fell into its third category, the appellate court proceeded with the necessary further analysis by first considering the outcome-determinative factor. Rejection of the South Carolina statute

---

[5] [In a footnote here the court gave Cohen, Ragan, and Guaranty Trust as examples.]

in the federal court would have a forum-shopping effect. However, rejection of state law would not result in discrimination against South Carolina residents; indeed, such rejection would do no more than give to nonresidents what residents enjoyed anyway, viz., a South Carolina forum for a case such as this one.

The court next explored the state policies underlying the door-closing statute. Faced with a total absence of legislative history and prior judicial discussion, the court concluded that the state interests were uncertain and that the conceivable ones appeared weak. Among other possibilities, the statute could be viewed as a formulation of the doctrine of forum non conveniens or as a measure to relieve state docket congestion, but such interests would be irrelevant for Erie purposes "since federal cognizance of the case would in no way frustrate state policy."

The court then found the "countervailing federal considerations explicit, and they are numerous." The list included: (1) avoidance of discrimination against nonresidents, the very purpose of the Diversity Clause itself; (2) maximum enforcement in each state of the rights and duties created by sister states, the consideration underlying the Full Faith and Credit Clause; (3) the policy that a federal court sitting in diversity should hear and adjudicate the issues before it, citing Meredith v. Winter Haven, 320 U.S. 228, 64 S.Ct. 7 (1943); (4) encouragement of efficient joinder in multiparty actions, an interest otherwise threatened because Dixie was then subject to service only in South Carolina; and (5) the interest in providing a convenient forum for federal litigants, as expressed in provisions such as 28 U.S.C. § 1404(a).

After a final word distinguishing Woods, the court of appeals affirmed the decision below.

DAY & ZIMMERMANN, INC. v. CHALLONER, 423 U.S. 3, 96 S.Ct. 167 (1975). In May of 1970, in the midst of combat in Cambodia between American and North Vietnamese forces, a 105 mm. howitzer round prematurely exploded in the gun's barrel. The blast killed one of the gun's operators, a soldier named Daniel Nelms from Tennessee. It seriously wounded another soldier, Ken Challoner of Wisconsin. The round had been manufactured in Texas by Day & Zimmermann, a major military contractor incorporated in Maryland with its principal place of business in Pennsylvania.

Nelms's parents and Challoner brought a diversity action against the manufacturer in the United States District Court for the Eastern District of Texas. The district judge submitted the case to the jury under the strict liability principles of Texas law, as the plaintiffs had hoped it would. The jury returned sizable verdicts for the plaintiffs.

On appeal from judgment, the defendant contended that Klaxon compelled the district court to apply the Texas conflict-of-laws rule and that, because Texas then had a law-of-the-place-of-the-injury rule and because Cambodian law required proof of fault, the judgment based on a strict liability standard had to fall. The court of appeals nevertheless affirmed, 512 F.2d 77 (5th Cir.1975).

The court of appeals began by acknowledging that Klaxon "held, as a general rule," that the conflict-of-laws rules of the forum state apply in diversity cases. The court next conceded that a Texas state court would certainly look to Cambodian tort law in the wrongful-death action, and perhaps in the personal-injury action as well. Yet the Fifth Circuit went on to hold that a federal court in this situation could make an independent choice of law, thus permitting the district court here to look to the tort law of Texas rather than that of Cambodia.

The reasoning of the court of appeals in support of its assumed power to apply a federal conflict-of-laws rule was somewhat obscure. Yet its approach was unmistakably ad hoc, with the court weighing the federal interests at stake in this particular case against the forum state's interests in having its conflict-of-laws rule applied in this federal case. The federal interests predominated, and hence federal law applied.

In a per curiam opinion, the Supreme Court ruled:

"The Court of Appeals . . . supported its decision on the grounds that the rationale for applying the traditional conflicts rule applied by Texas 'is not operative under the present facts'; and that it was 'a Court of the United States, an instrumentality created to effectuate the laws and policies of the United States.'

"We believe that the Court of Appeals either misinterpreted our longstanding decision in Klaxon Co. v. Stentor Electric Mfg. Co., 313 U.S. 487, 61 S.Ct. 1020 (1941), or else determined for itself that it was no longer of controlling force in a case such as this. We are of the opinion that Klaxon is by its terms applicable here and should have been adhered to by the Court of Appeals. In Klaxon, supra, at 496, 61 S.Ct., at 1021, this Court said:

> 'The conflict of laws rules to be applied by the federal court in Delaware must conform to those prevailing in Delaware's state courts. Otherwise, the accident of diversity of citizenship would constantly disturb equal administration of justice in coordinate state and federal courts sitting side by side. See Erie R. Co. v. Tompkins . . . .'

"By parity of reasoning, the conflict-of-laws rules to be applied by a federal court in Texas must conform to those prevailing in the Texas state courts. A federal court in a diversity case is not free to engraft onto those state rules exceptions or modifications which may commend themselves to the federal court, but which have not commended themselves to the State in which the federal court sits. The Court of Appeals in this case should identify and follow the Texas conflicts rule. What substantive law will govern when Texas' rule is applied is a matter to be determined by the Court of Appeals.

"The petition for certiorari is granted, the judgment of the Court of Appeals is vacated, and the case is remanded for further proceedings in conformity with this opinion."

The court of appeals on remand ruled that Texas would apply Cambodian law, 546 F.2d 26 (5th Cir.1977) (per curiam), and so the plaintiffs would lose for inability to show negligence. Since then Texas has changed its conflicts approach, but too late for these plaintiffs.

WALKER v. ARMCO STEEL CORP., 446 U.S. 740, 100 S.Ct. 1978 (1980). This case from the United States District Court for the Western District of Oklahoma presented anew, on similar facts, the legal issue of Ragan v. Merchants Transfer & Warehouse Co. The district court and the Tenth Circuit barred suit by following Ragan, but the Supreme Court granted certiorari to resolve a conflict among the circuits. Justice Marshall, writing for a unanimous Supreme Court, ruled:

"The present case is indistinguishable from Ragan. The statutes in both cases require service of process to toll the statute of limitations, and in fact the predecessor to the Oklahoma statute in this case was derived from the predecessor to the Kansas statute in Ragan. See Dr. Koch Vegetable Tea Co. v. Davis, 48 Okl. 14, 22, 145 P. 337, 340 (1914). Here as in Ragan the complaint was filed in federal court under diversity jurisdiction within the two-year statute of limitations, but service of process did not occur until after the two-year period . . . had run. In both cases the suit would concededly have been barred in the applicable state court, and in both instances the state service statute was held to be an integral part of the statute of limitations by the lower court more familiar than we with state law. Accordingly, as the Court of Appeals held below, the instant action is barred by the statute of limitations unless Ragan is no longer good law.

"Petitioner argues that the analysis and holding of Ragan did not survive our decision in Hanna [v. Plumer, 380 U.S. 460, 85 S.Ct. 1136 (1965)]. Petitioner's position is that Okla.Stat., Tit. 12, § 97 (1971) is in direct conflict with the federal rule. Under Hanna, petitioner contends, the appropriate question is whether Rule 3 is within the scope of the Rules Enabling Act and, if so, within the constitutional power of Congress. In petitioner's view, the federal rule is to be applied unless it violates one of those two restrictions. This argument ignores both the force of stare decisis and the specific limitations that we carefully placed on the Hanna analysis.

"We note at the outset that the doctrine of stare decisis weighs heavily against petitioner in this case. Petitioner seeks to have us overrule our decision in Ragan. Stare decisis does not mandate that earlier decisions be enshrined forever, of course, but it does counsel that we use caution in rejecting established law. In this case, the reasons petitioner asserts for overruling Ragan are the same factors which we concluded in Hanna did not undermine the validity of Ragan. A litigant who in effect asks us to reconsider not one but two prior decisions bears a heavy burden of supporting such a change in our jurisprudence. Petitioner here has not met that burden.

"This Court in Hanna distinguished Ragan rather than overruled it, and for good reason. Application of the Hanna analysis is premised on a 'direct collision' between the federal rule and the state law. 380 U.S., at 472, 85 S.Ct., at 1143. In Hanna itself the 'clash' between Rule 4(d)(1) and the state in-hand service requirement was 'unavoidable.' Id., at 470, 85 S.Ct., at 1143. The first question must therefore be whether the scope of the federal rule in fact is sufficiently broad to control the issue before the Court. It is only if that question is answered affirmatively that the Hanna analysis applies.[9]

". . . [W]e recognized in Hanna that the present case is an instance where 'the scope of the Federal Rule [is] not as broad as the losing party urge[s], and therefore, there being no Federal Rule which cover[s] the point in dispute, Erie command[s] the enforcement of state law.' Ibid. Rule 3 simply states that '[a] civil action is commenced by filing a complaint with the court.' There is no indication that the Rule was intended to toll a state statute of limitations,[10] much less that it purported to displace state tolling rules for purposes of state statutes of limitations. In our view, in diversity actions[11] Rule 3 governs the date from which various timing requirements of the federal rules begin to run, but does not affect state statutes of

---

[9] This is not to suggest that the Federal Rules of Civil Procedure are to be narrowly construed in order to avoid a "direct collision" with state law. The Federal Rules should be given their plain meaning. If a direct collision with state law arises from that plain meaning, then the analysis developed in Hanna v. Plumer applies.

[10] "Rule 3 simply provides that an action is commenced by filing the complaint and has as its primary purpose the measuring of time periods that begin running from the date of commencement; the rule does not state that filing tolls the statute of limitations." 4 C. Wright & A. Miller, Federal Practice and Procedure, § 1057, at 191 (1969) (footnote omitted).

The Note of the Advisory Committee on the Rules states that

> "[w]hen a Federal or State statute of limitations is pleaded as a defense, a question may arise under this rule whether the mere filing of the complaint stops the running of the statute, or whether any further step is required, such as, service of the summons and complaint or their delivery to the marshal for service. The answer to this question may depend on whether it is competent for the Supreme Court, exercising the power to make rules of procedure without affecting substantive rights, to vary the operation of statutes of limitations. The requirement of Rule 4(a) that the clerk shall forthwith issue the summons and deliver it to the marshal for service will reduce the chances of such a question arising." 28 U.S.C.App., pp. 394–395.

This Note establishes that the Advisory Committee predicted the problem which arose in Ragan and arises again in the instant case. It does not indicate, however, that Rule 3 was *intended* to serve as a tolling provision for statute of limitations purposes; it only suggests that the Advisory Committee thought the Rule *might* have that effect.

[11] The Court suggested in Ragan that in suits to enforce rights under a federal statute Rule 3 means that filing of the complaint tolls the applicable statute of limitations. 337 U.S., at 533, 69 S.Ct., at 1234, distinguishing Bomar v. Keyes, 162 F.2d 136, 140–141 (CA2), cert. denied, 332 U.S. 825, 68 S.Ct. 166 (1947). [Other citations omitted.] We do not here address the role of Rule 3 as a tolling provision for a statute of limitations, whether set by federal law or borrowed from state law, if the cause of action is based on federal law. [See West v. Conrail, 481 U.S. 35, 39, 107 S.Ct. 1538, 1541 (1987) ("we now hold that when the underlying cause of action is based on federal law . . . the action is not barred if it has been 'commenced' in compliance with Rule 3 within the [limitations] period"), criticized in Stephen B. Burbank, Of Rules and Discretion: The Supreme Court, Federal Rules and Common Law, 63 Notre Dame L.Rev. 693 (1988).—Ed.]

limitations. Cf. 4 C. Wright & A. Miller, Federal Practice and Procedure, § 1057, at 190–191 (1969); id., § 1051, at 165–166.

"In contrast to Rule 3, the Oklahoma statute is a statement of a substantive decision by that State that actual service on, and accordingly actual notice by, the defendant is an integral part of the several policies served by the statute of limitations. See C & C Tile Co. v. Independent School District No. 7 of Tulsa County, 503 P.2d 554, 559 (Okl.1972). The statute of limitations establishes a deadline after which the defendant may legitimately have peace of mind; it also recognizes that after a certain period of time it is unfair to require the defendant to attempt to piece together his defense to an old claim. A requirement of actual service promotes both of those functions of the statute. See generally ibid.; Seitz v. Jones, 370 P.2d 300, 302 (Okl.1961). See also Ely, The Irrepressible Myth of Erie, 87 Harv.L.Rev. 693, 730–731 (1974). It is these policy aspects which make the service requirement an 'integral' part of the statute of limitations both in this case and in Ragan. As such, the service rule must be considered part and parcel of the statute of limitations.[13] Rule 3 does not replace such policy determinations found in state law. Rule 3 and Okla.Stat., Tit. 12, § 97 (1971) can exist side-by-side, therefore, each controlling its own intended sphere of coverage without conflict.

"Since there is no direct conflict between the federal rule and the state law, the Hanna analysis does not apply. Instead, the policies behind Erie and Ragan control the issue whether, in the absence of a federal rule directly on point, state service requirements which are an integral part of the state statute of limitations should control in an action based on state law which is filed in federal court under diversity jurisdiction. The reasons for the application of such a state service requirement in a diversity action in the absence of a conflicting federal rule are well explained in Erie and Ragan . . . and need not be repeated here. It is sufficient to note that although in this case failure to apply the state service law might not create any problem of forum shopping,[15] the result would be an 'inequitable administration' of the law. Hanna v. Plumer, supra, 380 U.S., at 468, 85 S.Ct., at 1142. There is simply no reason why, in the absence of a controlling federal rule, an action based on state law which concededly would be barred in the state courts by the state statute of limitations should proceed through litigation to judgment in federal court solely because of the fortuity that there is diversity of citizenship between the

[13] The substantive link of § 97 to the statute of limitations is made clear as well by another provision of Oklahoma law. Under Okla.Stat., Tit. 12, § 151 (1971), "[a] civil action is deemed commenced by filing in the office of the court clerk of the proper court a petition and by the clerk's issuance of summons thereon." This is the state law corollary to Rule 3. However, § 97, not § 151, controls the commencement of the lawsuit for statute of limitations purposes. See Tyler v. Taylor, 578 P.2d 1214 (Okl.App.1977). Just as § 97 and § 151 can both apply in state court for their separate purposes, so too § 97 and Rule 3 may both apply in federal court in a diversity action.

[15] There is no indication that when petitioner filed his suit in federal court he had any reason to believe that he would be unable to comply with the service requirements of Oklahoma law or that he chose to sue in federal court in an attempt to avoid those service requirements.

litigants. The policies underlying diversity jurisdiction do not support such a distinction between state and federal plaintiffs, and Erie and its progeny do not permit it.

"The judgment of the Court of Appeals is affirmed."

Question: (12) In a prolonged diversity action, would the federal court apply a state statute that requires dismissal of actions not tried within five years of filing? See Olympic Sports Prods., Inc. v. Universal Athletic Sales Co., 760 F.2d 910 (9th Cir.1985) (2–1 decision) (no).

BURLINGTON NORTHERN RAILROAD v. WOODS, 480 U.S. 1, 107 S.Ct. 967 (1987). After removal to the Northern District of Alabama on the basis of diversity jurisdiction, plaintiffs recovered $305,000 for personal injuries.

The defendant railroad obtained a stay pending appeal, but the Eleventh Circuit affirmed on the merits and then assessed a penalty against the railroad in accordance with an Alabama statute. This statute provided that upon any affirmance of a stayed money judgment, the appellate court must award a penalty equal to 10% of the judgment. Incidentally, Alabama also had a rule similar to Federal Rule of Appellate Procedure 38, a discretionary provision for frivolous appeals.

On certiorari, Justice Marshall, writing for a unanimous Supreme Court, concluded that the state statute did not apply in federal court. He explained that the Federal Rules of Appellate Procedure were within the Hanna holding on federal rulemaking. Then, quoting Walker, he decided that, "when fairly construed, the scope of Federal Rule 38 is 'sufficiently broad' to cause a 'direct collision' with the state law or, implicitly, to 'control the issue' before the court, thereby leaving no room for the operation of that law."

Gasperini v. Center for Humanities, Inc.

Supreme Court of the United States, 1996.
518 U.S. 415, 116 S.Ct. 2211.

■ JUSTICE GINSBURG delivered the opinion of the Court.

Under the law of New York, appellate courts are empowered to review the size of jury verdicts and to order new trials when the jury's award "deviates materially from what would be reasonable compensation." N.Y.Civ.Prac.Law and Rules (CPLR) § 5501(c) (McKinney 1995). Under the Seventh Amendment, which governs proceedings in federal court, but not in state court, "the right of trial by jury shall be preserved, and no fact tried by a jury, shall be otherwise re-examined in any Court of the United States, than according to the rules of the common law." U.S.Const., Amdt. 7. The compatibility of these provisions, in an action based on New York law but tried in federal court by reason of the parties' diverse citizenship, is the issue we confront in this case. We hold that New York's law controlling compensation awards for excessiveness or inadequacy can be given effect, without detriment to the Seventh Amendment, if the review standard set out in CPLR § 5501(c) is applied by the federal trial court judge, with appellate control of the trial court's ruling limited to review for "abuse of discretion."

I

Petitioner William Gasperini, a journalist for CBS News and the Christian Science Monitor, began reporting on events in Central America in 1984. He earned his living primarily in radio and print media and only occasionally sold his photographic work. During the course of his seven-year stint in Central America, Gasperini took over 5,000 slide transparencies, depicting active war zones, political leaders, and scenes from daily life. In 1990, Gasperini agreed to supply his original color transparencies to The Center for Humanities, Inc. (Center) for use in an educational videotape, Conflict in Central America. Gasperini selected 300 of his slides for the Center; its videotape included 110 of them. The Center agreed to return the original transparencies, but upon the completion of the project, it could not find them.

Gasperini commenced suit in the United States District Court for the Southern District of New York, invoking the court's diversity jurisdiction pursuant to 28 U.S.C. § 1332. He alleged several state-law claims for relief, including breach of contract, conversion, and negligence. . . . The Center conceded liability for the lost transparencies and the issue of damages was tried before a jury.

At trial, Gasperini's expert witness testified that the "industry standard" within the photographic publishing community valued a lost transparency at $1,500. . . . This industry standard, the expert explained, represented the average license fee a commercial photograph could earn over the full course of the photographer's copyright, i.e., in Gasperini's case, his lifetime plus 50 years. . . . Gasperini estimated that his earnings from photography totaled just over $10,000 for the period from 1984 through 1993. He also testified that he intended to produce a book containing his best photographs from Central America. . . .

After a three-day trial, the jury awarded Gasperini $450,000 in compensatory damages. This sum, the jury foreperson announced, "is [$]1500 each, for 300 slides." . . . Moving for a new trial under Federal Rule of Civil Procedure 59, the Center attacked the verdict on various grounds, including excessiveness. Without comment, the District Court denied the motion. . . .

The Court of Appeals for the Second Circuit vacated the judgment entered on the jury's verdict. 66 F.3d 427 (1995). Mindful that New York law governed the controversy, the Court of Appeals endeavored to apply CPLR § 5501(c), which instructs that, when a jury returns an itemized verdict, as the jury did in this case, the New York Appellate Division "shall determine that an award is excessive or inadequate if it deviates materially from what would be reasonable compensation." The Second Circuit's application of § 5501(c) as a check on the size of the jury's verdict followed Circuit precedent elaborated two weeks earlier in Consorti v. Armstrong World Industries, Inc., 64 F.3d 781, superseded, 72 F.3d 1003 (1995). Surveying Appellate Division decisions that reviewed damage awards for lost transparencies, the Second Circuit concluded that testimony on industry standard alone was insufficient to justify a verdict; prime among other factors warranting consideration were the uniqueness of the slides' subject matter and the photographer's earning level.

Guided by Appellate Division rulings, the Second Circuit held that the $450,000 verdict "materially deviates from what is reasonable compensation." 66 F.3d, at 431. Some of Gasperini's transparencies, the Second Circuit recognized, were unique, notably those capturing combat situations in which Gasperini was the only photographer present. Id., at 429. But others "depicted either generic scenes or events at which other professional photojournalists were present." Id., at 431. No more than 50 slides merited a $1,500 award, the court concluded, after "[g]iving Gasperini every benefit of the doubt." Ibid. Absent evidence showing significant earnings from photographic endeavors or concrete plans to publish a book, the court further determined, any damage award above $100 each for the remaining slides would be excessive. Remittiturs "presen[t] difficult problems for appellate courts," the Second Circuit acknowledged, for court of appeals judges review the evidence from "a cold paper record." Ibid. Nevertheless, the Second Circuit set aside the $450,000 verdict and ordered a new trial, unless Gasperini agreed to an award of $100,000 [as the maximum amount recoverable without being improperly excessive].

This case presents an important question regarding the standard a federal court uses to measure the alleged excessiveness of a jury's verdict in an action for damages based on state law. We therefore granted certiorari. 516 U.S. 1086, 116 S.Ct. 805 (1996).

II

Before 1986, state and federal courts in New York generally invoked the same judge-made formulation in responding to excessiveness attacks on jury verdicts: courts would not disturb an award unless the amount was so exorbitant that it "shocked the conscience of the court." See Consorti, 72 F.3d, at 1012–1013 (collecting cases). . . .

In both state and federal courts, trial judges made the excessiveness assessment in the first instance, and appellate judges ordinarily deferred to the trial court's judgment. [Citations omitted.]

In 1986, as part of a series of tort reform measures, New York codified a standard for judicial review of the size of jury awards. Placed in CPLR § 5501(c), the prescription reads:

"In reviewing a money judgment . . . in which it is contended that the award is excessive or inadequate and that a new trial should have been granted unless a stipulation is entered to a different award, the appellate division shall determine that an award is excessive or inadequate if it deviates materially from what would be reasonable compensation."

As stated in Legislative Findings and Declarations accompanying New York's adoption of the "deviates materially" formulation, the lawmakers found the "shock the conscience" test an insufficient check on damage awards; the legislature therefore installed a standard "invit[ing] more careful appellate scrutiny." Ch. 266, 1986 N.Y.Laws 470 (McKinney). At the same time, the legislature instructed the Appellate Division, in amended § 5522, to state the reasons for the court's rulings on the size of verdicts, and the factors the court considered in complying with § 5501(c). In his signing statement, then-Governor Mario Cuomo emphasized that the CPLR amendments were meant to rachet up the review standard: "This will assure greater scrutiny of the amount of verdicts and promote greater stability in the tort system and greater fairness for similarly situated defendants throughout the State." [Citation omitted.]

New York state-court opinions confirm that § 5501(c)'s "deviates materially" standard calls for closer surveillance than "shock the conscience" oversight. [Citations omitted.]

Although phrased as a direction to New York's intermediate appellate courts, § 5501(c)'s "deviates materially" standard, as construed by New York's courts, instructs state trial judges as well. [Citations omitted.] Application of § 5501(c) at the trial level is key to this case.

To determine whether an award "deviates materially from what would be reasonable compensation," New York state courts look to awards approved in similar cases. . . .

III

In cases like Gasperini's, in which New York law governs the claims for relief, does New York law also supply the test for federal court review of the size of the verdict? The Center answers yes. The "deviates materially" standard, it argues, is a substantive standard that must be applied by federal appellate courts in diversity cases. The Second Circuit agreed. See 66 F.3d, at 430; see also Consorti, 72 F.3d, at 1011 ("[CPLR § 5501(c)] is the substantive rule provided by New York law."). Gasperini, emphasizing that § 5501(c) trains on the New York Appellate Division, characterizes the provision as procedural, an allocation of decisionmaking authority regarding damages, not a hard cap on the amount recoverable. Correctly comprehended, Gasperini urges, § 5501(c)'s direction to the Appellate Division cannot be given effect by federal appellate courts without violating the Seventh Amendment's re-examination clause.

As the parties' arguments suggest, CPLR § 5501(c), appraised under Erie R. Co. v. Tompkins, 304 U.S. 64, 58 S.Ct. 817 (1938), and decisions in

Erie's path, is both "substantive" and "procedural": "substantive" in that § 5501(c)'s "deviates materially" standard controls how much a plaintiff can be awarded; "procedural" in that § 5501(c) assigns decisionmaking authority to New York's Appellate Division. Parallel application of § 5501(c) at the federal appellate level would be out of sync with the federal system's division of trial and appellate court functions, an allocation weighted by the Seventh Amendment. The dispositive question, therefore, is whether federal courts can give effect to the substantive thrust of § 5501(c) without untoward alteration of the federal scheme for the trial and decision of civil cases.

A

Federal diversity jurisdiction provides an alternative forum for the adjudication of state-created rights, but it does not carry with it generation of rules of substantive law. As Erie read the Rules of Decision Act: "Except in matters governed by the Federal Constitution or by Acts of Congress, the law to be applied in any case is the law of the State." 304 U.S., at 78, 58 S.Ct., at 822. Under the Erie doctrine, federal courts sitting in diversity apply state substantive law and federal procedural law.

Classification of a law as "substantive" or "procedural" for Erie purposes is sometimes a challenging endeavor.[7] Guaranty Trust Co. v. York, 326 U.S. 99, 65 S.Ct. 1464 (1945), an early interpretation of Erie, propounded an "outcome-determination" test: "[D]oes it significantly affect the result of a litigation for a federal court to disregard a law of a State that would be controlling in an action upon the same claim by the same parties in a State court?" 326 U.S., at 109, 65 S.Ct., at 1470. Ordering application of a state statute of limitations to an equity proceeding in federal court, the Court said in Guaranty Trust: "[W]here a federal court is exercising jurisdiction solely because of the diversity of citizenship of the parties, the outcome of the litigation in the federal court should be substantially the same, so far as legal rules determine the outcome of a litigation, as it would be if tried in a State court." Ibid; see also Ragan v. Merchants Transfer & Warehouse Co., 337 U.S. 530, 533, 69 S.Ct. 1233, 1235 (1949) (when local law that creates the cause of action qualifies it, "federal court must follow suit," for "a different measure of the cause of action in one court than in the other [would transgress] the principle of

[7] Concerning matters covered by the Federal Rules of Civil Procedure, the characterization question is usually unproblematic: It is settled that if the Rule in point is consonant with the Rules Enabling Act, 28 U.S.C. § 2072, and the Constitution, the Federal Rule applies regardless of contrary state law. See Hanna v. Plumer, 380 U.S. 460, 469–474, 85 S.Ct. 1136, 1142–1145 (1965); Burlington Northern R. Co. v. Woods, 480 U.S. 1, 4–5, 107 S.Ct. 967, 969–970 (1987). Federal courts have interpreted the Federal Rules, however, with sensitivity to important state interests and regulatory policies. See, e.g., Walker v. Armco Steel Corp., 446 U.S. 740, 750–752, 100 S.Ct. 1978, 1985–1986 (1980) (reaffirming decision in Ragan v. Merchants Transfer & Warehouse Co., 337 U.S. 530, 69 S.Ct. 1233 (1949), that state law rather than Rule 3 determines when a diversity action commences for the purposes of tolling the state statute of limitations; Rule 3 makes no reference to the tolling of state limitations, the Court observed, and accordingly found no "direct conflict"); S.A. Healy Co. v. Milwaukee Metropolitan Sewerage Dist., 60 F.3d 305, 310–312 (C.A.7 1995) (state provision for offers of settlement by plaintiffs is compatible with Federal Rule 68, which is limited to offers by defendants).

Erie"). A later pathmarking case, qualifying Guaranty Trust, explained that the "outcome-determination" test must not be applied mechanically to sweep in all manner of variations; instead, its application must be guided by "the twin aims of the Erie rule: discouragement of forum-shopping and avoidance of inequitable administration of the laws." Hanna v. Plumer, 380 U.S. 460, 468, 85 S.Ct. 1136, 1142 (1965).

Informed by these decisions, we address the question whether New York's "deviates materially" standard, codified in CPLR § 5501(c), is outcome-affective in this sense: Would "application of the [standard] . . . have so important an effect upon the fortunes of one or both of the litigants that failure to [apply] it would [unfairly discriminate against citizens of the forum State, or] be likely to cause a plaintiff to choose the federal court"? Id., at 468, n. 9, 85 S.Ct., at 1142, n. 9.

We start from a point the parties do not debate. Gasperini acknowledges that a statutory cap on damages would supply substantive law for Erie purposes. See Reply Brief for Petitioner 2 ("[T]he state as a matter of its substantive law may, among other things, eliminate the availability of damages for a particular claim entirely, limit the factors a jury may consider in determining damages, or place an absolute cap on the amount of damages available, and such substantive law would be applicable in a federal court sitting in diversity."); see also Tr. of Oral Arg. 4–5, 25; Consorti, 72 F.3d, at 1011.[9] Although CPLR § 5501(c) is less readily classified, it was designed to provide an analogous control.

New York's Legislature codified in § 5501(c) a new standard, one that requires closer court review than the common law "shock the conscience" test. . . . More rigorous comparative evaluations attend application of § 5501(c)'s "deviates materially" standard. . . . To foster predictability, the legislature required the reviewing court, when overturning a verdict under § 5501(c), to state its reasons, including the factors it considered relevant. See CPLR § 5522(b) . . . . We think it a fair conclusion that CPLR § 5501(c) differs from a statutory cap principally "in that the maximum amount recoverable is not set by statute, but rather is determined by case law." Brief for City of New York as Amicus Curiae 11. In sum, § 5501(c) contains a procedural instruction, . . . but the State's objective is manifestly substantive. Cf. S.A. Healy Co. v. Milwaukee Metropolitan Sewerage Dist., 60 F.3d 305, 310 (C.A.7 1995).

It thus appears that if federal courts ignore the change in the New York standard and persist in applying the "shock the conscience" test to damage awards on claims governed by New York law, " 'substantial' variations between state and federal [money judgments]" may be expected. See Hanna, 380 U.S., at 467–468, 85 S.Ct., at 1142. We therefore agree with the Second Circuit that New York's check on excessive damages implicates what we have called Erie's "twin aims." . . . Just as the Erie principle precludes a federal court from giving a state-created claim "longer

[9] While we have not specifically addressed the issue, courts of appeals have held that district court application of state statutory caps in diversity cases, post verdict, does not violate the Seventh Amendment. [Citations omitted.]

life . . . than [the claim] would have had in the state court," Ragan, 337 U.S., at 533–534, 69 S.Ct., at 1235, so Erie precludes a recovery in federal court significantly larger than the recovery that would have been tolerated in state court.

B

CPLR § 5501(c), as earlier noted, . . . is phrased as a direction to the New York Appellate Division. Acting essentially as a surrogate for a New York appellate forum, the Court of Appeals reviewed Gasperini's award to determine if it "deviate[d] materially" from damage awards the Appellate Division permitted in similar circumstances. The Court of Appeals performed this task without benefit of an opinion from the District Court, which had denied "without comment" the Center's Rule 59 motion. 66 F.3d, at 428. Concentrating on the authority § 5501(c) gives to the Appellate Division, Gasperini urges that the provision shifts fact-finding responsibility from the jury and the trial judge to the appellate court. Assigning such responsibility to an appellate court, he maintains, is incompatible with the Seventh Amendment's re-examination clause, and therefore, Gasperini concludes, § 5501(c) cannot be given effect in federal court. Brief for Petitioner 19–20. Although we reach a different conclusion than Gasperini, we agree that the Second Circuit did not attend to "[a]n essential characteristic of [the federal-court] system," Byrd v. Blue Ridge Rural Elec. Cooperative, Inc., 356 U.S. 525, 537, 78 S.Ct. 893, 901 (1958), when it used § 5501(c) as "the standard for [federal] appellate review," Consorti, 72 F.3d, at 1013; see also 66 F.3d, at 430.

That "essential characteristic" was described in Byrd, a diversity suit for negligence in which a pivotal issue of fact would have been tried by a judge were the case in state court. The Byrd Court held that, despite the state practice, the plaintiff was entitled to a jury trial in federal court. In so ruling, the Court said that the Guaranty Trust "outcome-determination" test was an insufficient guide in cases presenting countervailing federal interests. See Byrd, 356 U.S., at 537, 78 S.Ct., at 901. The Court described the countervailing federal interests present in Byrd this way:

> "The federal system is an independent system for administering justice to litigants who properly invoke its jurisdiction. An essential characteristic of that system is the manner in which, in civil common-law actions, it distributes trial functions between judge and jury and, under the influence—if not the command—of the Seventh Amendment, assigns the decisions of disputed questions of fact to the jury." Ibid. (footnote omitted).

The Seventh Amendment, which governs proceedings in federal court, but not in state court, bears not only on the allocation of trial functions between judge and jury, the issue in Byrd; it also controls the allocation of authority to review verdicts, the issue of concern here. . . .

Byrd involved the first clause of the Amendment, the "trial by jury" clause. This case involves the second, the "re-examination" clause. In keeping with the historic understanding, the re-examination clause does not inhibit the authority of trial judges to grant new trials "for any of the reasons for which new trials have heretofore been granted in actions at law in the courts of the United States." Fed.Rule Civ.Proc. 59(a). That authority is large. See 6A Moore's Federal Practice ¶ 59.05[2], pp. 59–44 to 59–46 (2d ed. 1996) ("The power of the English common law trial courts to grant a new trial for a variety of reasons with a view to the attainment of justice was well established prior to the establishment of our Government."); see also Aetna Casualty & Surety Co. v. Yeatts, 122 F.2d 350, 353 (C.A.4 1941) ("The exercise of [the trial court's power to set aside the jury's verdict and grant a new trial] is not in derogation of the right of trial by jury but is one of the historic safeguards of that right."); Blunt v. Little, 3 F.Cas. 760, 761–762 (Case No. 1,578) (C.C.Mass.1822) (Story, J.) ("[I]f it should clearly appear that the jury have committed a gross error, or have acted from improper motives, or have given damages excessive in relation to the person or the injury, it is as much the duty of the court to interfere, to prevent the wrong, as in any other case."). "The trial judge in the federal system," we have reaffirmed, "has . . . discretion to grant a new trial if the verdict appears to [the judge] to be against the weight of the evidence." Byrd, 356 U.S., at 540, 78 S.Ct., at 902. This discretion includes overturning verdicts for excessiveness and ordering a new trial without qualification, or conditioned on the verdict winner's refusal to agree to a reduction (remittitur). See Dimick v. Schiedt, 293 U.S. 474, 486–487, 55 S.Ct. 296, 301 (1935) (recognizing that remittitur withstands Seventh Amendment attack, but rejecting additur as unconstitutional).

In contrast, appellate review of a federal trial court's denial of a motion to set aside a jury's verdict as excessive is a relatively late, and less secure, development. Such review was once deemed inconsonant with the Seventh Amendment's re-examination clause. See, e.g., Lincoln v. Power, 151 U.S. 436, 437–438, 14 S.Ct. 387, 388 (1894); Williamson v. Osenton, 220 F. 653, 655 (C.A.4 1915); see also 6A Moore's Federal Practice ¶ 59.08[6], at 59–167 (collecting cases). We subsequently recognized that, even in cases in which the Erie doctrine was not in play—cases arising wholly under federal law—the question was not settled; we twice granted certiorari to decide the unsettled issue, but ultimately resolved the cases on other grounds. See Grunenthal v. Long Island R. Co., 393 U.S. 156, 158, 89 S.Ct. 331, 333 (1968); Neese v. Southern R. Co., 350 U.S. 77, 77, 76 S.Ct. 131, 131–132 (1955).

Before today, we have not "expressly [held] that the Seventh Amendment allows appellate review of a district court's denial of a motion to set aside an award as excessive." Browning–Ferris Industries of Vt., Inc. v. Kelco Disposal, Inc., 492 U.S. 257, 279, n. 25, 109 S.Ct. 2909, 2922, n. 25 (1989). But in successive reminders that the question was worthy of this Court's attention, we noted, without disapproval, that courts of appeals engage in review of district court excessiveness determinations, applying "abuse of discretion" as their standard. See Grunenthal, 393 U.S., at 159, 89 S.Ct., at 333. We noted the Circuit decisions in point, id., at 157, n. 3, 89 S.Ct., at 332, n. 3, and, in Browning–Ferris, we again referred to appellate court abuse-of-discretion review:

"[T]he role of the district court is to determine whether the jury's verdict is within the confines set by state law, and to determine, by reference to federal standards developed under Rule 59, whether a new trial or remittitur should be ordered. The court of appeals should then review the district court's determination under an abuse-of-discretion standard." 492 U.S., at 279, 109 S.Ct., at 2922.

As the Second Circuit explained, appellate review for abuse of discretion is reconcilable with the Seventh Amendment as a control necessary and proper to the fair administration of justice: "We must give the benefit of every doubt to the judgment of the trial judge; but surely there must be an upper limit, and whether that has been surpassed is not a question of fact with respect to which reasonable men may differ, but a question of law." Dagnello v. Long Island R. Co., 289 F.2d 797, 806 (C.A.2 1961) (quoted in Grunenthal, 393 U.S., at 159, 89 S.Ct., at 333). All other Circuits agree. [Citations omitted]. We now approve this line of decisions, and thus make explicit what Justice Stewart thought implicit in our Grunenthal disposition: "[N]othing in the Seventh Amendment . . . precludes appellate review of the trial judge's denial of a motion to set aside [a jury verdict] as excessive." 393 U.S., at 164, 89 S.Ct., at 336 (Stewart, J., dissenting) (internal quotation marks and footnote omitted).

C

In Byrd, the Court faced a one-or-the-other choice: trial by judge as in state court, or trial by jury according to the federal practice.[21] In the case before us, a choice of that order is not required, for the principal state and federal interests can be accommodated. The Second Circuit correctly recognized that when New York substantive law governs a claim for relief, New York law and decisions guide the allowable damages. See 66 F.3d, at 430; see also Consorti, 72 F.3d, at 1011. But that court did not take into account the characteristic of the federal-court system that caused us to reaffirm: "The proper role of the trial and appellate courts in the federal system in reviewing the size of jury verdicts is . . . a matter of federal law." Donovan v. Penn Shipping Co., 429 U.S. 648, 649, 97 S.Ct. 835, 837 (1977) (per curiam); [other citation omitted].

New York's dominant interest can be respected, without disrupting the federal system, once it is recognized that the federal district court is capable of performing the checking function, i.e., that court can apply the State's "deviates materially" standard in line with New York case law evolving under CPLR § 5501(c).[22] We recall, in this regard, that the

---

[21] The two-trial rule posited by Justice Scalia . . . surely would be incompatible with the existence of "[t]he federal system [as] an independent system for administering justice," Byrd v. Blue Ridge Rural Elec. Cooperative, Inc., 356 U.S. 525, 537, 78 S.Ct. 893, 901 (1958). We discern no disagreement on such examples among the many federal judges who have considered this case.

[22] Justice Scalia finds in Federal Rule of Civil Procedure 59 a "federal standard" for new trial motions in " 'direct collision' " with, and " 'leaving no room for the operation of,' " a state law like CPLR § 5501(c). . . . The relevant prescription, Rule 59(a), has remained unchanged since the adoption of the Federal Rules by this Court in 1937. 302 U.S. 783. Rule

"deviates materially" standard serves as the guide to be applied in trial as well as appellate courts in New York. . . .

Within the federal system, practical reasons combine with Seventh Amendment constraints to lodge in the district court, not the court of appeals, primary responsibility for application of § 5501(c)'s "deviates materially" check. Trial judges have the "unique opportunity to consider the evidence in the living courtroom context," Taylor v. Washington Terminal Co., 409 F.2d 145, 148 (C.A.D.C.1969), while appellate judges see only the "cold paper record," 66 F.3d, at 431.

District court applications of the "deviates materially" standard would be subject to appellate review under the standard the Circuits now employ when inadequacy or excessiveness is asserted on appeal: abuse of discretion. [Citations omitted.] In light of Erie's doctrine, the federal appeals court must be guided by the damage-control standard state law supplies,[23] but as the Second Circuit itself has said: "If we reverse, it must be because of an abuse of discretion. . . . The very nature of the problem counsels restraint. . . . We must give the benefit of every doubt to the judgment of the trial judge." Dagnello, 289 F.2d, at 806.

IV

It does not appear that the District Court checked the jury's verdict against the relevant New York decisions demanding more than "industry standard" testimony to support an award of the size the jury returned in this case . . . . Accordingly, we vacate the judgment of the Court of Appeals and instruct that court to remand the case to the District Court so that the trial judge, revisiting his ruling on the new trial motion, may test the jury's verdict against CPLR § 5501(c)'s "deviates materially" standard.

It is so ordered.[d]

■ JUSTICE STEVENS, dissenting.

While I agree with most of the reasoning in the Court's opinion, I disagree with its disposition of the case. I would affirm the judgment of the

---

59(a) is as encompassing as it is uncontroversial. It is indeed "Hornbook" law that a most usual ground for a Rule 59 motion is that "the damages are excessive." See C. Wright, Law of Federal Courts 676–677 (5th ed. 1994). Whether damages are excessive for the claim-in-suit must be governed by some law. And there is no candidate for that governance other than the law that gives rise to the claim for relief—here, the law of New York. See 28 U.S.C. § 2072(a) and (b) ("Supreme Court shall have the power to prescribe general rules of . . . procedure"; "[s]uch rules shall not abridge, enlarge or modify any substantive right"); [other citations omitted].

[23] If liability and damage-control rules are split apart here, as Justice Scalia says they must be to save the Seventh Amendment, then Gasperini's claim and others like it would be governed by a most curious "law." The sphinx-like, damage-determining law he would apply to this controversy has a state forepart, but a federal hindquarter. The beast may not be brutish, but there is little judgment in its creation.

[d] On remand, the district court followed state law to order a new trial. Strangely, it followed federal law, not state law, on the amount of remittitur to provide that Gasperini could avoid the new trial by agreeing to a reduction of the award to the maximum amount recoverable without being improperly excessive, which the court set at $375,000 and which he accepted. 972 F.Supp. 765 (S.D.N.Y.1997), modified, 149 F.3d 137 (2d Cir.1998).

Court of Appeals. I would also reject the suggestion that the Seventh Amendment limits the power of a federal appellate court sitting in diversity to decide whether a jury's award of damages exceeds a limit established by state law.

. . . .

■ JUSTICE SCALIA, with whom the CHIEF JUSTICE [REHNQUIST] and JUSTICE THOMAS join, dissenting.

. . . .

The Court's holding that federal courts of appeals may review district court denials of motions for new trials for error of fact is not the only novel [and, according to Justice Scalia, incorrect] aspect of today's decision. The Court also directs that the case be remanded to the District Court, so that it may "test the jury's verdict against CPLR § 5501(c)'s 'deviates materially' standard" . . . . This disposition contradicts the principle that "[t]he proper role of the trial and appellate courts in the federal system in reviewing the size of jury verdicts is . . . a matter of federal law." Donovan v. Penn Shipping Co., 429 U.S. 648, 649, 97 S.Ct. 835, 837 (1977) (per curiam).

The Court acknowledges that state procedural rules cannot, as a general matter, be permitted to interfere with the allocation of functions in the federal court system . . . . Indeed, it is at least partly for this reason that the Court rejects direct application of § 5501(c) at the appellate level as inconsistent with an " 'essential characteristic' " of the federal court system—by which the Court presumably means abuse-of-discretion review of denials of motions for new trials . . . . But the scope of the Court's concern is oddly circumscribed. The "essential characteristic" of the federal jury, and, more specifically, the role of the federal trial court in reviewing jury judgments, apparently counts for little. The Court approves the "accommodat[ion]" achieved by having district courts review jury verdicts under the "deviates materially" standard, because it regards that as a means of giving effect to the State's purposes "without disrupting the federal system" . . . . But changing the standard by which trial judges review jury verdicts *does* disrupt the federal system, and is plainly inconsistent with "the strong federal policy against allowing state rules to disrupt the judge-jury relationship in federal court." Byrd v. Blue Ridge Rural Elec. Cooperative, Inc., 356 U.S. 525, 538, 78 S.Ct. 893, 901 (1958).[9] The Court's opinion does not even acknowledge, let alone address, this dislocation.

We discussed precisely the point at issue here in Browning–Ferris Industries of Vt., Inc. v. Kelco Disposal, Inc., 492 U.S. 257, 109 S.Ct. 2909 (1989), and gave an answer altogether contrary to the one provided today. Browning–Ferris rejected a request to fashion a federal common-law rule limiting the size of punitive-damages awards in federal courts, reaffirming the principle of Erie R. Co. v. Tompkins, 304 U.S. 64, 58 S.Ct. 817 (1938),

---

[9] Since I reject application of the New York standard on other grounds, I need not consider whether it constitutes "reexamination" of a jury's verdict in a manner "otherwise . . . than according to the rules of the common law."

that "[i]n a diversity action, or in any other lawsuit where state law provides the basis of decision, the propriety of an award of punitive damages . . . and the factors the jury may consider in determining their amount, are questions of state law." 492 U.S., at 278, 109 S.Ct., at 2921–2922. But the opinion expressly stated that "[f]ederal law . . . will control on those issues involving the proper review of the jury award by a federal district court and court of appeals." Id., at 278–279, 109 S.Ct., at 2922. "In reviewing an award of punitive damages," it said, "the role of the district court is to determine whether the jury's verdict is within the confines of state law, and to determine, by reference to federal standards developed under Rule 59, whether a new trial or remittitur should be ordered." Id., at 279, 109 S.Ct., at 2922. The same distinction necessarily applies where the judgment under review is for compensatory damages: State substantive law controls what injuries are compensable and in what amount; but federal standards determine whether the award exceeds what is lawful to such degree that it may be set aside by order for new trial or remittitur.

The Court does not disavow those statements in Browning–Ferris (indeed, it does not even discuss them), but it presumably overrules them, at least where the state rule that governs "whether a new trial or remittitur should be ordered" is characterized as "substantive" in nature. That, at any rate, is the reason the Court asserts for giving § 5501(c) dispositive effect. The objective of that provision, the Court states, "is manifestly substantive," . . . since it operates to "contro[l] how much a plaintiff can be awarded" by "tightening the range of tolerable awards" . . . . Although "less readily classified" as substantive than "a statutory cap on damages," it nonetheless "was designed to provide an analogous control," . . . by making a new trial mandatory when the award "deviat[es] materially" from what is reasonable . . . .

I do not see how this can be so. It seems to me quite wrong to regard this provision as a "substantive" rule for Erie purposes. The "analog[y]" to "a statutory cap on damages" . . . fails utterly. There is an absolutely fundamental distinction between a *rule of law* such as that, which would ordinarily be imposed upon the jury in the trial court's instructions, and a *rule of review*, which simply determines how closely the jury verdict will be scrutinized for compliance with the instructions. A tighter standard for reviewing jury determinations can no more plausibly be called a "substantive" disposition than can a tighter appellate standard for reviewing trial-court determinations. The one, like the other, provides additional assurance *that the law has been complied with*; but the other, like the one, *leaves the law unchanged*.

The Court commits the classic Erie mistake of regarding whatever changes the outcome as substantive . . . . That is not the only factor to be considered. See Byrd, 356 U.S., at 537, 78 S.Ct., at 900 ("[W]ere 'outcome' the only consideration, a strong case might appear for saying that the federal court should follow the state practice. But there are affirmative countervailing considerations at work here"). Outcome-determination "was never intended to serve as a talisman," Hanna v. Plumer, 380 U.S. 460,

466–467, 85 S.Ct. 1136, 1141 (1965), and does not have the power to convert the most classic elements of the *process* of assuring that the law is observed into the substantive law itself. The right to have a jury make the findings of fact, for example, is generally thought to favor plaintiffs, and that advantage is often thought significant enough to be the basis for forum selection. But no one would argue that Erie confers a right to a jury in federal court wherever state courts would provide it; or that, were it not for the Seventh Amendment, Erie would require federal courts to dispense with the jury whenever state courts do so.

In any event, the Court exaggerates the difference that the state standard will make. . . . What seems to me far more likely to produce forum-shopping is the consistent difference between the state and federal *appellate* standards, which the Court leaves untouched. Under the Court's disposition, the Second Circuit reviews only for abuse of discretion, whereas New York's appellate courts engage in a de novo review for material deviation, giving the defendant a double shot at getting the damages award set aside. The only result that would produce the conformity the Court erroneously believes Erie requires is the one adopted by the Second Circuit and rejected by the Court: de novo federal appellate review under the § 5501(c) standard.

To say that application of § 5501(c) in place of the federal standard will not consistently produce disparate results is not to suggest that the decision the Court has made today is not a momentous one. The *principle* that the state standard governs is of great importance, since it bears the potential to destroy the uniformity of federal practice and the integrity of the federal court system. Under the Court's view, a state rule that directed courts "to determine that an award is excessive or inadequate if it deviates *in any degree* from *the proper measure of compensation*" would have to be applied in federal courts, effectively requiring federal judges to determine the amount of damages de novo, and effectively taking the matter away from the jury entirely. Cf. Byrd, 356 U.S., at 537–538, 78 S.Ct., at 901. Or consider a state rule that allowed the defendant a second trial on damages, with judgment ultimately in the amount of the lesser of two jury awards. [Citation omitted.] Under the reasoning of the Court's opinion, even such a rule as that would have to be applied in the federal courts.

The foregoing describes why I think the Court's Erie analysis is flawed. But in my view, one does not even reach the Erie question in this case. The standard to be applied by a district court in ruling on a motion for a new trial is set forth in Rule 59 of the Federal Rules of Civil Procedure, which provides that "[a] new trial may be granted . . . for any of the reasons for which new trials have heretofore been granted in actions at law *in the courts of the United States*" (emphasis added). That is undeniably a federal standard.[12] Federal district courts in the Second Circuit have interpreted

---

[12] I agree with the Court's entire progression of reasoning in its footnote 22, . . . leading to the conclusion that state law must determine "[w]hether damages are excessive." But the question of whether damages are excessive is quite separate from the question of when a jury award may be set aside for excessiveness. . . It is the latter that is governed by Rule 59; as

that standard to permit the granting of new trials where " 'it is quite clear that the jury has reached a seriously erroneous result' " and letting the verdict stand would result in a " 'miscarriage of justice.' " Koerner v. Club Mediterranee, S.A., 833 F.Supp. 327 (S.D.N.Y.1993) (quoting Bevevino v. Saydjari, 574 F.2d 676, 684 (C.A.2 1978)). Assuming (as we have no reason to question) that this is a correct interpretation of what Rule 59 requires, it is undeniable that the federal rule is " 'sufficiently broad' to cause a 'direct collision' with the state law or, implicitly, to 'control the issue' before the court, thereby leaving no room for the operation of that law." Burlington Northern R. Co. v. Woods, 480 U.S. 1, 4–5, 107 S.Ct. 967, 969 (1987). It is simply not possible to give controlling effect both to the federal standard and the state standard in reviewing the jury's award. That being so, the court has no choice but to apply the Federal Rule, which is an exercise of what we have called Congress's "power to regulate matters which, though falling within the uncertain area between substance and procedure, are rationally capable of classification as either," Hanna, 380 U.S., at 472, 85 S.Ct., at 1144.

. . . .

Questions: (13) How does Justice Ginsburg meet Justice Scalia's point that statutory caps on damages are not analogous to standards for new trial, one being a rule of substantive law and the other a rule of review—his point being that the jury as the federal fact-finder and law-applier must apply the New York tort damages law including any cap, but the trial judge as the federal reviewer should scrutinize the jury award for compliance in accordance with the federal standard for new trial? How does she meet his argument that strong federal interests are at stake in controlling the judge/jury relationship in the federal district courts—does she acknowledge those interests other than in footnote 21?

(14) Does the Court's decision to respect the federal interests in controlling the standard of appellate review in the federal courts of appeals prove that Byrd lives—that is, does the majority reach its trial/appeal holding by invoking Byrd's view that state interests can be outweighed by countervailing federal interests, such as those in not disrupting the federal courts' essentially characteristic allocation of trial and appellate functions? If so, did the majority perhaps reach its judge/jury holding by the same ad hoc balancing process, implicitly finding that the state interests in its own new trial standard outweigh the net of federal interests minus the refined outcome-determinative effect—and thus, despite some loose language, the majority did not in fact resurrect the substance/procedure test or preserve a bare outcome-determinative test?

(15) Perhaps Gasperini throws some old answers back into doubt. What result in a converse-Byrd situation in a federal diversity case, where the state law would give a factual issue to the jury but the federal court would give it to the judge? Also,

---

Browning–Ferris said, district courts are "to determine, by reference to *federal standards developed under Rule 59*, whether a new trial or remittitur should be ordered," 492 U.S., at 279, 109 S.Ct., at 2922 (emphasis added).

does federal or state law govern the directed-verdict standard in a federal diversity case?

ROLE OF CONGRESS

Recall that in 1972 the Supreme Court, as article V of its proposed rules on evidence, sought to create uniform rules of privilege for the federal courts. Congress in 1975 provided instead for the application of state privilege rules in certain circumstances. It did so in Evidence Rule 501, a statute that receives insightful criticism by Earl C. Dudley, Jr., Federalism and Federal Rule of Evidence 501: Privilege and Vertical Choice of Law, 82 Geo.L.J. 1781 (1994). The House Committee on the Judiciary, in H.R.Rep. No. 93–650, explained Evidence Rule 501:

"The rationale underlying the proviso is that federal law should not supersede that of the States in substantive areas such as privilege absent a compelling reason. The Committee believes that in civil cases in the federal courts where an element of a claim or defense is not grounded upon a federal question, there is no federal interest strong enough to justify departure from State policy. In addition, the Committee considered that the Court's proposed Article V would have promoted forum shopping in some civil actions, depending upon differences in the privilege law applied as among the State and federal courts. The Committee's proviso, on the other hand, under which the federal courts are bound to apply the State's privilege law in actions founded upon a State-created right or defense, removes the incentive to 'shop'."

Question: (16) A diversity action is brought in a federal court in State *A*, based on an automobile accident in State *B*. During a deposition being taken in State *C* and bearing on the issue of negligence, the physician-patient privilege is asserted with respect to a consultation that took place in State *D*. A motion for an order compelling an answer is made in the federal court for State *C*. Which state's privilege law applies?

By way of contrast to Evidence Rule 501, Congress by Evidence Rule 407 apparently chose federal law to govern admissibility of subsequent remedial measures and then formulated an appropriate rule. So, in federal court, that rule should apply despite contrary state law. See Flaminio v. Honda Motor Co., 733 F.2d 463 (7th Cir.1984) (noting that the only limits on congressional choice of law are constitutional). But cf. 2 Christopher B. Mueller & Laird C. Kirkpatrick, Federal Evidence § 4:55 (3d ed. 2007).

In summary, if Congress chooses the applicable law, the only choice-of-law question remaining is whether that choice was constitutionally valid, because the Constitution imposes the only bounds on the congressional power. Within those constitutional limits Congress can expressly or impliedly make the choice between state and federal law, and its choice will bind the federal courts. So, Congress is the senior partner in the cooperative venture of drawing the appropriate line between state and federal law in federal court.

Ideally, Congress would use a technique similar to the federal courts' Erie approach when it legislates a choice between state and federal law. However, Congress may properly opt for federal law more often than the federal courts would, because under our constitutional structure Congress should be the more active articulator of federal interests, while the courts must steer clear of blatantly formulating policies. And, of course, in practice Congress may be less systematic and rational than the courts.

If Congress chooses federal law, it can specify the content of that federal law, although it sometimes delegates to the federal courts the task of generating part or all of that federal law. It is important to keep clear this distinction between choosing the applicable law and specifying its content.

With this background, now reconsider each of the two sentences of Evidence Rule 501, and then contrast them with Evidence Rule 601.

SECTION 2. FEDERAL LAW

The Federal Constitution can dictate a choice in favor of federal law in federal courts, and of course this is binding. An example is the Seventh Amendment's guarantee of trial by jury. But most often, the Constitution does not so dictate. In many of these circumstances, Congress can validly make a choice by statute in favor of federal law, and that choice will bind the federal courts, as we have just seen in the discussion of the Evidence Rules.

What of federal common law? Justice Brandeis in Erie wrote: "There is no federal general common law." But have we not already seen post-Erie examples of federal common law being created and applied in federal courts?

CLEARFIELD TRUST CO. v. UNITED STATES, 318 U.S. 363, 63 S.Ct. 573 (1943). Justice Douglas for a unanimous Court stated the facts as follows:

"On April 28, 1936, a check was drawn on the Treasurer of the United States through the Federal Reserve Bank of Philadelphia to the order of Clair A. Barner in the amount of $24.20. It was dated at Harrisburg, Pennsylvania and was drawn for services rendered by Barner to the Works Progress Administration. The check was placed in the mail addressed to Barner at his address in Mackeyville, Pa. Barner never received the check. Some unknown person obtained it in a mysterious manner and presented it to the J.C. Penney Co. store in Clearfield, Pa., representing that he was the payee and identifying himself to the satisfaction of the employees of J.C. Penney Co. He endorsed the check in the name of Barner and transferred it to J.C. Penney Co. in exchange for cash and merchandise. Barner never authorized the endorsement nor participated in the proceeds of the check. J.C. Penney Co. endorsed the check over to the Clearfield Trust Co. which accepted it as agent for the purpose of collection and endorsed it as follows: 'Pay to the order of Federal Reserve Bank of Philadelphia, Prior Endorsements Guaranteed.'[1] Clearfield Trust Co. collected the check from the United States through the Federal Reserve Bank of Philadelphia and paid the full amount thereof to J.C. Penney Co. Neither the Clearfield Trust Co. nor J.C. Penney Co. had any knowledge or suspicion of the forgery. Each acted in good faith. On or before May 10, 1936, Barner advised the timekeeper and the foreman of the W.P.A. project on which he was employed that he had not received the check in question. This information was duly communicated to other agents of the United States and on November 30, 1936, Barner executed an affidavit alleging that the endorsement of his name on the check was a forgery. No notice was given the Clearfield Trust Co. or J.C. Penney Co. of the forgery until January 12, 1937, at which time the Clearfield Trust Co. was notified. The first notice received by Clearfield Trust Co. that the United States was asking reimbursement was on August 31, 1937.

"This suit was instituted in 1939 by the United States against the Clearfield Trust Co., the jurisdiction of the federal District Court being invoked pursuant to the provisions of § 24(1) of the Judicial Code, 28 U.S.C. § 41(1).[e] The cause of action was based on the express guaranty of prior endorsements made by the Clearfield Trust Co. J.C. Penney Co. intervened as a defendant. The case was heard on complaint, answer and stipulation of facts. The District Court held that the rights of the parties were to be determined by the law of Pennsylvania and that since the United States unreasonably delayed in giving notice of the forgery to the Clearfield Trust Co., it was barred from recovery under the rule of Market St. Title & Trust Co. v. Chelten Tr. Co., 296 Pa. 230, 145 A. 848. It accordingly dismissed the complaint. On appeal the Circuit Court of Appeals reversed. 3 Cir., 130 F.2d 93."

Justice Douglas then said: "We agree with the Circuit Court of Appeals that the rule of Erie R. Co. v. Tompkins . . . does not apply to this action. The rights and duties of the United States on commercial paper which it issues are governed by federal rather than local law." Accordingly, the Court affirmed the application of old federal case law, under which mere delay in giving notice did not bar suit.

Questions: (17) Why did the Erie rule not apply to this action? Why did the Rules of Decision Act not require application of state law?

---

[1] Guarantee of all prior indorsements on presentment for payment of such a check to Federal Reserve banks or member bank depositories is required by Treasury Regulations. 31 Code of Federal Regulations § 202.32, § 202.33.

[e] Jurisdiction rested on that part of § 24(1) vesting original jurisdiction in the district courts over civil actions in which the United States is plaintiff, now 28 U.S.C. § 1345.

(18) Reconsider yet once again Woods v. Interstate Realty Co. Would that state door-closing statute apply in a federal question action asserting a patent claim? See Kinetic Concepts, Inc. v. Kinetic Concepts, Inc., 601 F.Supp. 496 (N.D.Ga.1985) (no). Would it apply in a diversity action to compel arbitration under a foreign-commerce contract pursuant to the United States Arbitration Act? See Grand Bahama Petroleum Co. v. Asiatic Petroleum Corp., 550 F.2d 1320 (2d Cir.1977) (no).

(19) In a federal action under 28 U.S.C. § 1345 in the Western District of Texas, the United States sought to collect from Mrs. Yazell of Texas on a federal disaster loan. An issue arose as to the capacity of the defendant to bind herself personally by the loan contract. Under the peculiar Texas law of coverture that then existed, a wife could not so bind herself in the circumstances of this case. In the absence of a congressional directive, did that Texas law apply? See United States v. Yazell, 382 U.S. 341, 86 S.Ct. 500 (1966) (yes).

(20) In a diversity action, between two private parties, based on an alleged conversion of United States bonds, two issues arise: (a) who has the burden of proof on whether the defendant took the bonds in good faith; and (b) were the bonds, which had been called but were not yet mature, "overdue" at that time. Should these issues be governed by state law or federal common law? See Bank of America Nat'l Trust & Sav. Ass'n v. Parnell, 352 U.S. 29, 77 S.Ct. 119 (1956).

UNITED STATES v. KIMBELL FOODS, INC., 440 U.S. 715, 99 S.Ct. 1448 (1979). The two cases decided under this caption, both of which came from the Fifth Circuit, required a choice between federal and state law on "whether contractual liens arising from certain federal loan programs take precedence over private liens, in the absence of a federal statute setting priorities."

The first case, coming from Texas, involved a loan guaranteed by the Small Business Administration (SBA) and a debt to a private party, both obligations being secured by competing liens on the same collateral. The second case from a Georgia federal court arose in Georgia and involved loans from the Farmers Home Administration (FHA) to a farmer, secured in part by a lien on his tractor; when the farmer later brought the tractor to a private repairman but then could not pay for the repairs, the repairman retained the tractor and thus asserted a lien thereon; when still later the farmer defaulted on the federal loans, the United States sued the repairman to obtain the tractor, with jurisdiction invoked under 28 U.S.C. § 1345. State law concerning the relative priority of competing liens would have favored the private lienholders on the facts of these two cases, so the government argued for a more favorable federal common law.

On the choice-of-law problem, Justice Marshall for a unanimous Supreme Court wrote:

"This Court has consistently held that federal law governs questions involving the rights of the United States arising under nation-wide federal programs. As the Court explained in Clearfield Trust Co. v. United States, [318 U.S. 363, 366–67, 63 S.Ct. 573, 575 (1943)]:

'When the United States disburses its funds or pays its debts, it is exercising a constitutional function or power. . . . The authority [to do so] had its origin in the Constitution and the statutes of the United States and was in no way dependent on the laws [of any State]. The duties imposed upon the United States and the rights acquired by it . . . find their roots in the same federal sources. In absence of an applicable Act of Congress it is for the federal courts to fashion the governing rule of law according to their own standards.' (Citations and footnote omitted.)

"Guided by these principles, we think it clear that the priority of liens stemming from federal lending programs must be determined with reference to federal law. The SBA and FHA unquestionably perform federal functions within the meaning of Clearfield. Since the agencies derive their authority to effectuate loan transactions from specific acts of Congress passed in the exercise of a 'constitutional function or power,' Clearfield Trust Co. v. United States, supra, at 366, 63 S.Ct., at 575, their rights, as well, should derive from a federal source. When Government activities 'aris[e] from and bea[r] heavily upon a federal . . . program,' the Constitution and Acts of Congress ' "require" otherwise than that state law govern of its own force.' United States v. Little Lake Misere Land Co., 412 U.S. 580, 592, 593, 93 S.Ct. 2389, 2396, 2397 (1973). In such contexts, federal interests are sufficiently implicated to warrant the protection of federal law.[19]

"That the statutes authorizing these federal lending programs do not specify the appropriate rule of decision in no way limits the reach of federal law. It is precisely when Congress has not spoken ' "in an area comprising issues substantially related to an established program of government operation," ' id., at 593, 93 S.Ct., at 2397, quoting Mishkin, supra, n. 19, at 800, that Clearfield directs federal courts to fill the interstices of federal legislation 'according to their own standards.' Clearfield Trust Co. v. United States, supra, at 367, 63 S.Ct., at 575.

"Federal law therefore controls the Government's priority rights. The more difficult task, to which we turn, is giving content to this federal rule.

. . . .

"Controversies directly affecting the operations of federal programs, although governed by federal law, do not inevitably require resort to uniform federal rules. See Clearfield Trust Co. v. United States, supra, at 367, 63 S.Ct., at 575; United States v. Little Lake Misere Land Co., supra, at 594–595, 93 S.Ct., at 2397–2398. Whether to adopt state law or to fashion a nationwide federal rule is a matter of judicial policy 'dependent upon a variety of considerations always relevant to the nature of the

---

[19] See [citation omitted]; Mishkin, The Variousness of "Federal Law": Competence and Discretion in the Choice of National and State Rules for Decision, 105 U.Pa.L.Rev. 797, 800, and n. 15 (1957) (hereinafter Mishkin); Comment, Adopting State Law as the Federal Rule of Decision: A Proposed Test, 43 U.Chi.L.Rev. 823, 825 (1976); see also Bank of America National Trust & Savings Assn. v. Parnell, 352 U.S. 29, 33–34, 77 S.Ct. 119, 121–122 (1956); Miree v. DeKalb County, 433 U.S. 25, 29, 31–32, 97 S.Ct. 2490, 2493, 2494–2495 (1977).

specific governmental interests and to the effects upon them of applying state law.' United States v. Standard Oil Co., 332 U.S. 301, 310, 67 S.Ct. 1604, 1609 (1947).[21]

"Undoubtedly, federal programs that 'by their nature are and must be uniform in character throughout the Nation' necessitate formulation of controlling federal rules. United States v. Yazell, 382 U.S. 341, 354, 86 S.Ct. 500, 507 (1966); see Clearfield Trust Co. v. United States, supra, at 367, 63 S.Ct., at 575; United States v. Standard Oil Co., supra, at 311, 67 S.Ct., at 1609; Illinois v. City of Milwaukee, 406 U.S. 91, 105 n. 6, 92 S.Ct. 1385, 1393 n. 6 (1972). Conversely, when there is little need for a nationally uniform body of law, state law may be incorporated as the federal rule of decision. Apart from considerations of uniformity, we must also determine whether application of state law would frustrate specific objectives of the federal programs. If so, we must fashion special rules solicitous of those federal interests. Finally, our choice of law inquiry must consider the extent to which application of a federal rule would disrupt commercial relationships predicated on state law."

The Court decided "to reject generalized pleas for uniformity as substitutes for concrete evidence":

"We are unpersuaded that in the circumstances presented here, nationwide standards favoring claims of the United States are necessary to ease program administration or to safeguard the federal treasury from defaulting debtors. Because the state commercial codes 'furnish convenient solutions in no way inconsistent with adequate protection of the federal interest[s],' United States v. Standard Oil Co., supra, at 309, 67 S.Ct., at 1609, we decline to override intricate state laws of general applicability on which private creditors base their daily commercial transactions.

. . . .

"Because the ultimate consequences of altering settled commercial practices are so difficult to foresee, we hesitate to create new uncertainties, in the absence of careful legislative deliberation. Of course, formulating special rules to govern the priority of the federal consensual liens in issue here would be justified if necessary to vindicate important national interests. But neither the Government nor the Court of Appeals advanced any concrete reasons for rejecting well-established commercial rules which have proven workable over time. Thus, the prudent course is to adopt the readymade body of state law as the federal rule of decision until Congress strikes a different accommodation.

. . . .

---

[21] As explained by one commentator:

"Whether state law is to be incorporated as a matter of federal common law . . . involves the . . . problem of the relationship of a particular issue to a going federal program. The question of judicial incorporation can only arise in an area which is sufficiently close to a national operation to establish competence in the federal courts to choose the governing law, and yet not so close as clearly to require the application of a single nationwide rule of substance." Mishkin, supra, n. 19, at 805.

"Accordingly, we hold that absent a congressional directive, the relative priority of private liens and consensual liens arising from these Government lending programs is to be determined under nondiscriminatory state laws." The Court decided here to look at Texas and Georgia law, respectively, as being the appropriate states to provide the law.

The government had also argued that a federal rule was "needed to prevent States from 'undercutting' the agencies' liens by creating 'arbitrary' rules." The Court met this by noting: "Adopting state law as an appropriate federal rule does not preclude federal courts from excepting [particular] local laws that prejudice federal interests." The Court then cited again the Little Lake Misere Land Co. case, in which the Court had declined to borrow a recent Louisiana statute, which would have specially preserved private interests, when interpreting an earlier-consummated federal land contract.

Question: (21) In 1990, when 28 U.S.C. § 1658 came into effect but only for future enactments, there were over two hundred federal statutes that had created causes of action but had failed to provide a limitations period. In such cases, federal courts ordinarily adopt the forum state's statute of limitations for the most closely analogous state cause of action. See, e.g., Owens v. Okure, 488 U.S. 235, 109 S.Ct. 573 (1989) (civil rights action subjected to state's general personal-injury limitations period). How does this rule mesh with the Erie–Clearfield doctrine? When federal interests dictate, however, federal courts will instead choose to extend some analogous federal limitations provision to cover the federal cause of action. See, e.g., Agency Holding Corp. v. Malley–Duff & Assocs., 483 U.S. 143, 107 S.Ct. 2759 (1987) (civil RICO action subjected to Clayton Act's four-year limitations period). How does this exception mesh with the Erie–Clearfield doctrine? See generally Special Project, Time Bars in Specialized Federal Common Law: Federal Rights of Action and State Statutes of Limitations, 65 Cornell L.Rev. 1011 (1980).

ILLINOIS v. CITY OF MILWAUKEE, 406 U.S. 91, 92 S.Ct. 1385 (1972). The State of Illinois brought a federal action against four cities and two local sewerage commissions in Wisconsin, seeking to abate the public nuisance allegedly caused by the defendants' pollution of the interstate waters of Lake Michigan. The Court held that here the federal court should, in the absence of applicable federal statutes, apply a uniform federal common law of nuisance (and further held that such an action founded on federal common law would arise under the "laws" of the United States within the meaning of 28 U.S.C. § 1331).[f]

After the lower courts gave injunctive relief under the federal common law, the parties once again came before the Supreme Court for review. City

[f] The Fourth Circuit refused to extend the reach of the federal common law to a suit by private citizens to enjoin intrastate stream pollution. Committee for Jones Falls Sewage Sys. v. Train, 539 F.2d 1006 (4th Cir.1976) (in banc).

of Milwaukee v. Illinois, 451 U.S. 304, 101 S.Ct. 1784 (1981). In the meantime, however, Congress had enacted the Federal Water Pollution Control Act Amendments of 1972, "a comprehensive regulatory program supervised by an expert administrative agency." The Supreme Court concluded that here no remedy under the federal common law was still available, the enactment having implicitly displaced the federal common law. The Court explained that "when Congress addresses a question previously governed by a decision rested on federal common law the need for such an unusual exercise of lawmaking by federal courts disappears."[g]

[g] The Supreme Court later decided that the Act itself preserved some law of the pollution-source state even in the interstate setting. International Paper Co. v. Ouellette, 479 U.S. 481, 107 S.Ct. 805 (1987).

TOPIC B

STATE COURTS

HINDERLIDER v. LA PLATA RIVER & CHERRY CREEK DITCH CO., 304 U.S. 92, 58 S.Ct. 803 (1938). A Colorado corporation brought suit in a Colorado state court against the State Engineer of Colorado to enjoin him from depriving the plaintiff of the use of the water of the La Plata River, which runs from Colorado into New Mexico. An issue arose as to the relative rights of the two states to its water. On the very day that Erie was decided, a unanimous Court, again speaking through Justice Brandeis, held that "whether the water of an interstate stream must be apportioned between the two States is a question of 'federal common law' upon which neither the statutes nor the decisions of either State can be conclusive." This federal common law was applicable and binding in the state court, apparently by virtue of the Supremacy Clause of Article VI of the Constitution.

DICE v. AKRON, CANTON & YOUNGSTOWN RAILROAD, 342 U.S. 359, 72 S.Ct. 312 (1952). Plaintiff brought an FELA action in an Ohio state court. The railroad's defenses included a release of all claims signed by plaintiff. Plaintiff contended that the purported release was void because he had relied on the defendant's deliberately false statement that the document was merely a receipt for back wages. The Ohio Supreme Court, reversing the intermediate appellate court, sustained the trial court's entry of judgment for the defendant notwithstanding the verdict, holding that (1) Ohio, not federal, law governed the validity of the release; (2) under that Ohio law, the release bound plaintiff, a man of ordinary intelligence who could read, even though he had been induced to sign it by a deliberately false statement; and (3) under controlling Ohio law, all issues as to fraud in the execution of this release were properly decided by the judge rather than by the jury. Certiorari was granted.

The Supreme Court, in an opinion by Justice Black, held that federal common law controlled the validity of the release, that the correct federal rule was that a release of rights under the Act was void when induced by a deliberately false statement as to the contents of the release, and that the "factual" issues as to fraud had to be determined by the jury. On the last point, the Court said:

"*Third.* Ohio provides and has here accorded petitioner the usual jury trial of factual issues relating to negligence. But Ohio treats factual questions of fraudulent releases differently. It permits the judge trying a negligence case to resolve all factual questions of fraud [where the fraud is one of those kinds that constitute equitable defenses]. The factual issue of fraud is thus split into fragments, some to be determined by the judge, others by the jury.

"It is contended that since a state may consistently with the Federal Constitution provide for trial of cases under the Act by a nonunanimous verdict, Minneapolis & St. Louis R. Co. v. Bombolis, 241 U.S. 211, 36 S.Ct. 595,[a] Ohio may lawfully eliminate trial by jury as to one phase of fraud while allowing jury trial as to all other issues raised. The Bombolis case might be more in point had Ohio abolished trial by jury in all negligence cases including those arising under the federal Act. But Ohio has not done this. It has provided jury trials for cases arising under the federal Act but seeks to single out one phase of the question of fraudulent releases for determination by a judge rather than by a jury. Compare Testa v. Katt, 330 U.S. 386, 67 S.Ct. 810.

"We have previously held that 'The right to trial by jury is "a basic and fundamental feature of our system of federal jurisprudence" ' and that it is 'part and parcel of the remedy afforded railroad workers under the Employers Liability Act.' Bailey v. Central Vermont R. Co., 319 U.S. 350, 354, 63 S.Ct. 1062, 1064. We also recognized in that case that to deprive railroad workers of the benefit of a jury trial where there is evidence to support negligence 'is to take away a goodly portion of the relief which Congress has afforded them.' It follows that the right to trial by jury is too substantial a part of the rights accorded by the Act to permit it to be classified as a mere 'local rule of procedure' for denial in the manner that Ohio has here used. Brown v. Western R. of Ala., 338 U.S. 294, 70 S.Ct. 105."

Justice Frankfurter, with whom Justices Reed, Jackson, and Burton joined, dissented from that portion of the opinion requiring a jury determination of those fraud issues. He said:

"To require Ohio to try a particular issue before a different fact-finder in negligence actions brought under the Employers' Liability Act from the fact-finder on the identical issue in every other negligence case disregards the settled distribution of judicial power between Federal and State courts where Congress authorizes concurrent enforcement of federally-created rights.

. . . .

". . . The fact that Congress authorized actions under the Federal Employers' Liability Act to be brought in State as well as in Federal courts seems a strange basis for the inference that Congress overrode State procedural arrangements controlling all other negligence suits in a State, by imposing upon State courts to which plaintiffs choose to go the rules

[a] This 1916 FELA case allowed the jury in state court, over the defendant's objection, to return a five-sixths verdict after at least twelve hours of deliberation, as permitted by the constitution and statutes of Minnesota. Although no one then questioned that the Seventh Amendment required a unanimous verdict in federal court, the Court did not view this requirement as controlling in a state-court action to enforce a right created by Congress.

prevailing in the Federal courts regarding juries. Such an inference is admissible, so it seems to me, only on the theory that Congress included as part of the right created by the Employers' Liability Act an assumed likelihood that trying all issues to juries is more favorable to plaintiffs. At least, if a plaintiff's right to have all issues decided by a jury rather than the court is 'part and parcel of the remedy afforded railroad workers under the Employers Liability Act,' the Bombolis case should be overruled explicitly instead of left as a derelict bound to occasion collisions on the waters of the law. . . . It is one thing not to borrow trouble from the morrow. It is another thing to create trouble for the morrow."

BROWN v. WESTERN RAILWAY, 338 U.S. 294, 70 S.Ct. 105 (1949). Plaintiff brought an FELA action in a Georgia state court. He alleged that he had suffered injury while working when he stepped on a large clinker lying within the railroad yards, but did not allege the clinker's circumstances in a way to constitute negligence by the railroad and to exclude alternative causes. The railroad filed a general demurrer on the ground that the complaint failed to "set forth a cause of action and is otherwise insufficient in law." The trial court sustained the demurrer and dismissed the action, applying a Georgia rule to construe pleading allegations "most strongly against the pleader." The intermediate appellate court affirmed, and the Georgia Supreme Court denied review. Under Georgia law, this was a final adjudication barring recovery in any future state proceedings. Certiorari was granted.

The Supreme Court reversed in an opinion by Justice Black. He said:

"Strict local rules of pleading cannot be used to impose unnecessary burdens upon rights of recovery authorized by federal laws. 'Whatever springes the State may set for those who are endeavoring to assert rights that the State confers, the assertion of federal rights, when plainly and reasonably made, is not to be defeated under the name of local practice.' Davis v. Wechsler, 263 U.S. 22, 24, 44 S.Ct. 13, 14. Cf. Maty v. Grasselli Chemical Co., 303 U.S. 197, 58 S.Ct. 507. Should this Court fail to protect federally created rights from dismissal because of over-exacting local requirements for meticulous pleadings, desirable uniformity in adjudication of federally created rights could not be achieved. See Brady v. Southern R. Co., 320 U.S. 476, 479, 64 S.Ct. 232, 234.

"Upon trial of this case the evidence offered may or may not support inferences of negligence. We simply hold that under the facts alleged it was error to dismiss the complaint and that petitioner should be allowed to try his case."

Justice Frankfurter, with whom Justice Jackson joined, dissented. He said:

"States have varying systems of pleading and practice. One State may cherish formalities more than another, one State may be more responsive than another to procedural reforms. If a litigant chooses to enforce a Federal right in a State court, he cannot be heard to object if he is treated exactly as are plaintiffs who press like claims arising under State law with regard to the form in which the claim must be stated—the particularity, for instance, with which a cause of action must be described. . . .

. . . .

"The crucial question for this Court is whether the Georgia courts have merely enforced a local requirement of pleading, however finicky, applicable to all such litigation in Georgia without qualifying the basis of recovery under the Federal Employers' Liability Act or weighting the scales against the plaintiff. Compare Norfolk, Southern R. Co. v. Ferebee, 238 U.S. 269, 35 S.Ct. 781, with Central Vermont R. Co. v. White, 238 U.S. 507, 35 S.Ct. 865. Georgia may adhere to its requirements of pleading, but it may not put 'unreasonable obstacles in the way' of a plaintiff who seeks its courts to obtain what the Federal Act gives him. Davis v. Wechsler, 263 U.S. 22, 25, 44 S.Ct. 13, 14.

"These decisive differences are usually conveyed by the terms 'procedure' and 'substance.' The terms are not meaningless even though they do not have fixed undeviating meanings. They derive content from the functions they serve here in precisely the same way in which we have applied them in reverse situations—when confronted with the problem whether the Federal courts respected the substance of State-created rights, as required by the rule in Erie R. Co. v. Tompkins, 304 U.S. 64, 58 S.Ct. 817, or impaired them by professing merely to enforce them by the mode in which the Federal courts do business. Review on this aspect of State court judgments in Federal Employers' Liability cases presents essentially the same kind of problem as that with which this Court dealt in Guaranty Trust Co. v. York, 326 U.S. 99, 65 S.Ct. 1464, applied at the last Term in Ragan v. Merchants Transfer & Warehouse Co., 337 U.S. 530, 69 S.Ct. 1233, and Cohen v. Beneficial Industrial Loan Corp., 337 U.S. 541, 555, 69 S.Ct. 1221, 1229. Congress has authorized State courts to enforce Federal rights, and Federal courts State-created rights, but both may have their own requirements for stating claims (pleading) and conducting litigation (practice).

"In the light of these controlling considerations, I cannot find that the Court of Appeals of Georgia has either sought to evade the law of the United States or did so unwittingly."

NORFOLK & WESTERN RAILWAY v. LIEPELT, 444 U.S. 490, 100 S.Ct. 755 (1980). Plaintiff brought an FELA action in an Illinois state court for wrongful death. The trial court refused the defendant's request to instruct the jury that "your award will not be subject to any income taxes, and you should not consider such taxes in fixing the amount of your award." On appeal from verdict and judgment for plaintiff, the intermediate appellate court affirmed, and the Illinois Supreme Court denied review. Certiorari was granted.

The Supreme Court reversed in an opinion by Justice Stevens. He said, inter alia, that this was a matter governed by a uniform federal common law that called for such an instruction. "It would not be prejudicial to either party, but would merely eliminate an area of doubt or speculation that might have an improper [inflating] impact on the computation of the amount of damages."

Justice Blackmun, with whom Justice Marshall joined, dissented. He said:

"This Court, to be sure, has asserted federal control over a number of incidents of state trial practice that might appear to be procedural, and has done so out of concern, apparently, for protecting the rights of FELA plaintiffs. [Omitted citations included Dice and Brown.] I agree, of course, that state rules that interfere with federal policy are to be rejected, even if they might be characterized as 'procedural.' [Citations omitted.] I cannot conclude, however, that a purely cautionary instruction to the jury not to misbehave implicates any federal interest. This issue truly can be characterized as one of the 'ordinary incidents of state procedure,' Dickinson v. Stiles, 246 U.S. 631, 633, 38 S.Ct. 415, 416 (1918), which should be governed by state law.

"Since the law of Illinois, where this case arose, is that it is not error to refuse to instruct the jury as to the nontaxability of the award, . . . I would affirm the judgment of the Appellate Court of Illinois."

The dissent also argued that the required instruction was unnecessary and potentially misleading and that it opened the door to cautionary instructions on many other extraneous matters.

Felder v. Casey

Supreme Court of the United States, 1988.
487 U.S. 131, 108 S.Ct. 2302.

■ JUSTICE BRENNAN delivered the opinion of the Court.

[Alleging racially motivated police brutality, an arrestee named Bobby Felder brought a civil rights action under 42 U.S.C. § 1983 in a Wisconsin state court against Milwaukee and certain of its police officers. Although the plaintiff had satisfied Wisconsin's three-year statute of limitations for general personal-injury actions, the officers moved to dismiss for failure to comply with Wisconsin's notice-of-claim statute, which provides additionally that, before any suit may be brought in state court against a municipality or its officer, the plaintiff must give notice of the claim to the defendant within 120 days of the injury; that the municipality then has 120 days to act on the requested relief; and that the plaintiff must bring the suit within six months after notice of the claim's disallowance. The motion ultimately succeeded in state court. Certiorari was granted.]

No one disputes the general and unassailable proposition relied upon by the Wisconsin Supreme Court below that States may establish the rules of procedure governing litigation in their own courts. By the same token, however, where state courts entertain a federally created cause of action, the "federal right cannot be defeated by the forms of local practice." Brown v. Western Railway of Alabama, 338 U.S. 294, 296, 70 S.Ct. 105, 106 (1949). . . . Because the notice-of-claim statute at issue here conflicts both in its purpose and effects with the remedial objectives of § 1983, and because its enforcement in such actions will frequently and predictably produce different outcomes in § 1983 litigation based solely on whether the claim is asserted in state or federal court, we conclude that the state law is pre-empted when the § 1983 action is brought in a state court.

[In the course of a long opinion, the Court noted that for suits under § 1983 the federal common law adopts the state's limitations period. The Court further explained that both federal and state courts would apply the same limitations period and, moreover, that in a § 1983 lawsuit a federal court would not apply a state notice-of-claim statute. Most states have such statutes, which might encourage prompt investigation of claims, according to the Court, but which benefit governmental defendants as their primary purpose and thus discriminate against the precise type of claim that Congress created.]

Respondents and their supporting amici urge that we approve the application of the notice-of-claim statute to § 1983 actions brought in state court as a matter of equitable federalism. They note that " '[t]he general rule, bottomed deeply in belief in the importance of state control of state judicial procedure, is that federal law takes the state courts as it finds them.' " Brief for Amici Curiae 8 (quoting Hart, The Relations Between State and Federal Law, 54 Colum.L.Rev. 489, 508 (1954)). Litigants who choose to bring their civil rights actions in state courts presumably do so in order to obtain the benefit of certain procedural advantages in those courts, or to draw their juries from urban populations. Having availed themselves of these benefits, civil rights litigants must comply as well with those state rules they find less to their liking.

However equitable this bitter-with-the-sweet argument may appear in the abstract, it has no place under our Supremacy Clause analysis. Federal law takes state courts as it finds them only insofar as those courts employ rules that do not "impose unnecessary burdens upon rights of recovery authorized by federal laws." Brown v. Western R. Co. of Alabama, 338 U.S., at 298–299, 70 S.Ct., at 108; see also Monessen Southwestern R. Co. v. Morgan, 486 U.S. 330, 336, 108 S.Ct. 1837, 1842–1843 (1988) (state [prejudgment interest] rule designed to encourage settlement cannot limit recovery in federally created action). States may make the litigation of federal rights as congenial as they see fit—not as a quid pro quo for compliance with other, incongenial rules, but because such congeniality does not stand as an obstacle to the accomplishment of Congress' goals. As we have seen, enforcement of the notice-of-claim statute in § 1983 actions brought in state court so interferes with and frustrates the substantive right Congress created that, under the Supremacy Clause, it must yield to the federal interest. This interference, however, is not the only consequence of the statute that renders its application in § 1983 cases invalid. In a State that demands compliance with such a statute before a § 1983 action may be brought or maintained in its courts, the outcome of federal civil rights litigation will frequently and predictably depend on whether it is brought in state or federal court. Thus, the very notions of federalism upon which respondents rely dictate that the State's outcome-determinative law must give way when a party asserts a federal right in state court.

Under Erie R. Co. v. Tompkins, 304 U.S. 64, 58 S.Ct. 817 (1938), when a federal court exercises diversity or pendent jurisdiction over state-law claims, "the outcome of the litigation in the federal court should be substantially the same, so far as legal rules determine the outcome of a litigation, as it would be if tried in a State court." Guaranty Trust Co. v. York, 326 U.S. 99, 109, 65 S.Ct. 1464, 1470 (1945). Accordingly, federal courts entertaining state-law claims against Wisconsin municipalities are obligated to apply the notice-of-claim provision. See Orthmann v. Apple River Campground, Inc., 757 F.2d 909, 911 (C.A.7 1985). Just as federal courts are constitutionally obligated to apply state law to state claims, see Erie, supra, 304 U.S., at 78–79, 58 S.Ct., at 822–823, so too the Supremacy Clause imposes on state courts a constitutional duty "to proceed in such manner that all the substantial rights of the parties under controlling federal law [are] protected." Garrett v. Moore–McCormack Co., 317 U.S. 239, 245, 63 S.Ct. 246, 251 (1942).

. . . Wisconsin . . . may not alter the outcome of federal claims it chooses to entertain in its courts by demanding compliance with outcome-determinative rules that are inapplicable when such claims are brought in federal court, for " '[w]hatever spring[s] [sic] the State may set for those who are endeavoring to assert rights that the State confers, the assertion of federal rights, when plainly and reasonably made, is not to be defeated under the name of local practice.' " Brown v. Western R. Co. of Alabama, 338 U.S., at 299, 70 S.Ct., at 108 (quoting Davis v. Wechsler, 263 U.S. 22, 24, 44 S.Ct. 13, 14 (1923)). . . . State courts simply are not free to vindicate the substantive interests underlying a state rule of decision at the expense of the federal right.

[Accordingly, the Supreme Court reversed and remanded.]

■ [JUSTICE WHITE concurred. JUSTICE O'CONNOR, with whom Chief Justice Rehnquist joined, dissented. Their opinions are omitted.]

PREEMPTION

Although the Felder Court expressed an overtly Erie-like analysis for judicial choice of law, it also threw into the mix the terminology of preemption. Analysts frequently so draw on the preemption doctrine, hoping to get more of a handle on judicial choice between federal and state law. They look to preemption because it is the most closely related doctrine in the task of determining the reach of federal law. It is in some senses a more important doctrine than judicial choice of law, with big consequences in both federal and state litigation as well as out in the real world.

Preemption, in brief, is an ill-bounded constitutional doctrine that invalidates state law if it interferes with federal law. See Erwin Chemerinsky, Constitutional Law: Principles and Policies § 5.2 (3d ed. 2006); Christopher R. Drahozal, The Supremacy Clause 89–125 (2004). Although preemption tends to focus on displacement of state substantive law by congressional statute, judges and commentators recognize that it can occur by federal administrative act or even by the effect of federal common law, and that it can extend its effect to state procedural law. Preemption can be express or implied; and implied preemption can trump a state provision that conflicts by discrimination against or contradiction to federal law[b] or stands as an obstacle to federal law,[c] or can authorize federal law to occupy exclusively a whole field,[d] although of course all these categories are blurry.

Express preemption can follow from constitutional or congressional action. The Due Process Clause of the Fourteenth Amendment illustrates the former. For a congressional example, we can stick with the evidence area by referring to Evidence Rule 502(f), a statute enacted in 2008.

In further exploring preemption, when one gets into implied preemption by conflict and turns toward possible preemption of state procedural law otherwise applicable in state court, one encounters cases like Dice and Brown, which treatises often treat as sui generis under some heading like "State Court Procedures and Federal Law Claims" but which others see as ordinary preemption cases. When one pushes still further into judicial decisions like Norfolk or even Felder that on their own federalize some

---

[b] See Barnett Bank of Marion County v. Nelson, 517 U.S. 25, 31, 116 S.Ct. 1103, 1108 (1996) (dictum saying that state law would be preempted if laws "impose directly conflicting duties on national banks—as they would, for example, if the federal law said, 'you must sell insurance,' while the state law said, 'you may not' "); Florida Lime & Avocado Growers, Inc. v. Paul, 373 U.S. 132, 142–43, 83 S.Ct. 1210, 1217 (1963) (saying that state law would be preempted "where compliance with both federal and state regulations is a physical impossibility").

[c] See Barnett Bank of Marion County v. Nelson, 517 U.S. 25, 31, 116 S.Ct. 1103, 1108 (1996) (saying that state law would be preempted where "the Federal Statute authorizes national banks to engage in activities that the State Statute expressly forbids"); Hines v. Davidowitz, 312 U.S. 52, 67, 61 S.Ct. 399, 404 (1941) (saying that state law would be preempted where it "stands as an obstacle to the accomplishment and execution of the full purposes and objectives of Congress").

[d] See Pacific Gas & Elec. Co. v. State Energy Res. Conservation & Dev. Comm'n, 461 U.S. 190, 212–13, 103 S.Ct. 1713, 1726–27 (1983) (saying that state law would be preempted when "the Federal Government completely occupies a given field or an identifiable portion of it"); Rice v. Santa Fe Elevator Corp., 331 U.S. 218, 230, 67 S.Ct. 1146, 1152 (1947) ("The scheme of federal regulation may be so pervasive as to make reasonable the inference that Congress left no room for the States to supplement it. . . . Or the Act of Congress may touch a field in which the federal interest is so dominant that the federal system will be assumed to preclude enforcement of state laws on the same subject.").

point of law for state courts, without any semblance of a search for actual congressional intent, one starts to see the wider scope of this subject that concerns the realms of federal and state law in state court. Then, if one perceives complementary methodologies at work in these two doctrines of implied preemption and judicial choice of law, one should begin sensing the significance of the subject.

In other words, implied preemption requires more attention at this stage of your study of the Erie doctrine. Preemption obviously constitutes an important part of a broadly conceived Erie doctrine in federal court, calling for the application of much federal law without any resort to judicial balancing. Even more obviously, it is at work in state court too. Implied preemption works in favor of federal law by rejecting not only any state law that openly discriminates against or contradicts federal law but also any state law that otherwise imposes unnecessary burdens upon federal rights, as in Brown. It does so regardless of the outcome of any balancing methodology. Valid federal law that directly collides with state law simply displaces that state law.

Preemption provides the explanation of why federal law spills down into state court more than state law applies in federal court, or why state courts must apply federal procedural law to federally created claims more extensively than federal courts must apply state procedural law to state-created claims. To explain that Brown example, the state's anti-plaintiff pleading rule fell because the Court saw it as directly colliding with the pro-plaintiff FELA. The result was preemption that rejected any state interests. In the converse-Brown setting, when the question would be whether a state pro-plaintiff procedural law applies in a diversity case, the Erie balance manages to tilt in favor of federal pleading law. That is, federal procedural interests overcome the interests in favor of applying state law, even to the extent of establishing Hanna's blanket approach to the Federal Rules. In Brown the Supremacy Clause causes federal procedure to preempt state procedure, but in converse-Brown the Supremacy Clause obviously plays no comparable role to cause the state sovereign's law to trump any conflicting rules of the home court.

JOHNSON v. FANKELL, 520 U.S. 911, 117 S.Ct. 1800 (1997). Kristine Fankell brought a federal civil rights action in an Idaho state court, alleging that she had been fired from her state-government job without due process. The defendant officials unsuccessfully moved for dismissal on the ground of qualified immunity for governmental officials, and then tried to appeal immediately. The state supreme court dismissed the appeal under its finality rule, even though federal law would have allowed an interlocutory appeal. Certiorari was granted.

The Supreme Court unanimously affirmed in an opinion by Justice Stevens. After noting "our normal presumption against pre-emption," it sequentially found (1) that the "dismissal of the appeal rested squarely on a neutral state rule regarding the administration of the state courts," (2) that the federal interests at stake lay in the procedural appealability doctrine rather than in the substantive qualified-immunity doctrine, and (3) that application of the state rule was not "outcome-determinative" in the Felder sense. It then balanced the state's "countervailing considerations" regarding "the operation of its courts" against the relatively weak federal interests, at least as the Court viewed them. Thus, the Court drew a limit on federal intrusion into state-court procedure.

REVERSE–ERIE

This, then, is the reverse-Erie doctrine: federal law—be it constitutional, statutory, or common law—will apply pursuant to the Supremacy Clause in state court, subject to the Constitution or Congress having already chosen the applicable law, whenever it preempts state law *or* whenever it prevails by an Erie-like judicial choice of law.

The reverse-Erie question is a relatively simple one if the Constitution or Congress actually chose to displace state law in state court. If the Constitution or Congress expressly or impliedly made federal law applicable in state court, that choice to preempt is binding on the state courts under the Supremacy Clause, provided that any such statutory choice was constitutionally valid. However, in the absence of such a constitutional or congressional directive, and in the absence of binding precedent, the state courts and ultimately the U.S. Supreme Court must decide whether the existing federal law applies in state court.

If the state and federal laws directly collide, then the state court must recognize that federal law preempts; if not, then the state court must perform the federally mandated accommodation of interests to choose the applicable law. This judicial choice-of-law methodology complementarily smooths, while it explains, the outer reaches of preemption. On the one hand, in the setting that involves a matter more of inference by judge than of implication by statute, when state law would merely frustrate federal law, those Erie-like ideas provide refinement of how obstacle and field preemption should work: whenever federal interests outweigh state interests in an Erie sense, there should be preemption. On the other hand, as one gets into more independent judicial choice of law under reverse-Erie, the direct application of Erie-like ideas makes the precise location of the outer boundary of preemption unimportant, as that boundary becomes merely a transitional zone somewhere in the middle of the broad subject of reverse-Erie.

The reverse-Erie doctrine, comprising preemption and judicial choice of law, tells the state court when to apply existing federal law to displace state law under the command of the Supremacy Clause. If the state court thereby determines that federal law governs, then the state court applies it. The state court may have to envisage a federal court's Erie analysis to determine the reach of federal law, but the state court is merely a federal-law-applier and will never act as a federal lawmaker in the true sense.

That is, the state court will decide in accordance with existing federal law, but never create federal law. At the time, the federal law might be fully formulated or more incipient. Sometimes the state court has to be the very first to enunciate the federal law. It has this authority to enunciate federal law, as long as it decides in accordance with existing federal law by trying to discern what the federal courts would decide is the law—and not by undertaking to formulate federal law either in pursuit of strictly forward-looking policies that might guide a legislature or in accordance with general nonpositivist principles that might guide a law-creating court. That is, the state court should act as federal courts do when applying state law under Erie. In both the Erie setting and the reverse-Erie setting, the court's job is to apply the other sovereign's existing law, not to create law for it.

If the content of the governing federal law is really unclear, how should the state court determine that content? No undisputed answer exists to this pervasive and fundamental question, illustrating how unexplored all reverse-Erie matters remain. Specifically, the question of whether state courts are bound by lower federal courts on the federal law's content remains open. The better view—mainly trying to effectuate the constitutional status of state courts, while accepting some local disuniformity in the short term—is that the state court should try to determine what the U.S. Supreme Court has ruled or would rule. On the one hand, the state court should not consider itself actually bound, rather than merely informed, by the local federal courts' rulings. On the other hand, the state court would naturally be bound under stare decisis by decisions within the state's hierarchy of courts as to the federal law's content. Note the profound implication of this view: it makes the state courts into judicial hierarchies that can independently enunciate federal law, parallel to the lower federal courts and subject only to rare U.S. Supreme Court review. See generally Donald H. Zeigler, Gazing into the Crystal Ball: Reflections on the Standards State Judges Should Use to Ascertain Federal Law, 40 Wm. & Mary L.Rev. 1143 (1999).

This all seems terribly complicated, in a way so typical of American law. But in fact there is nothing peculiarly American here. The complications come from federalism itself, which is a common form of political organization. See Ronald L. Watts, Comparing Federal Systems 5 (3d ed. 2008) (40% of the world's population live under federalism, broadly defined). Because federalism involves the people living under the authority of more than one sovereign, a problem of choosing between state and federal law is inevitably ubiquitous in any federal system. See Kevin M. Clermont, Book Review, 57 Am.J.Comp.L. 258 (2009).

PART THREE

AUTHORITY TO ADJUDICATE

TOPIC A

JURISDICTION OVER SUBJECT MATTER

SECTION 1. GENERAL OBSERVATIONS

Restatement of Judgments (1942) used the expression "competency of the court" more or less interchangeably with "the court's jurisdiction over the subject matter." We propose to use these two catch phrases interchangeably. We can convey the general notion underlying both, although imperfectly, by this single question: has the sovereign properly given this court power to entertain this type of action?

As examples of lack of competence, Restatement of Judgments § 7 cmt. b (1942) gave the following: "There are many situations in which a court lacks competency to render a judgment. Thus, although a State has jurisdiction to grant a divorce of parties domiciled within the State, a decree of divorce rendered by a court which is not empowered to entertain suits for divorce is void. Similarly, a judgment rendered by a justice of the peace is void if under the law of the State such justices are not empowered to deal with the subject matter of the action; as, for example, where the action is one for tort and justices of the peace are given no power except in actions of contract. So also, where a court is given power to deal with actions involving no more than a designated amount, the statute limiting the amount is ordinarily construed not merely to make erroneous a judgment rendered by such a court in excess of its power, but to make such judgment void."

The last example suggests that, in a particular court, the failure to satisfy a minimum amount-in-controversy requirement might be a mere error, rather than a defect of competency rendering any judgment void. In fact, any particular court might have given varying treatment to the scope of competency in different situations. There seems to be no all-purpose clear-cut definition as to which legal requirements the concept of competency encompasses. Lack of competency shades off into other kinds of defects, either procedural or on the merits.

To the extent that such other defects entail the same consequences to the litigants as lack of competency, it may be unimportant to make sharp distinctions. But under current law there are situations where the court's categorization of a defect as one of competency becomes crucial.

Going beyond matters of definition, Restatement (Second) of Judgments § 11 cmt. b (1982) further elaborates subject-matter jurisdiction: "The rules of subject matter jurisdiction of a court are generally prescribed by the political authority that has created the court. (However, a superior political authority may impose limits on that authority. Thus, state law rather than federal law invests a state's courts with authority to adjudicate particular types of controversies, but federal law through preemption may supersede that authority). The prescriptions of subject matter jurisdiction express divisions of functions among the organs of that government, separating courts from other branches of government and differentiating one court from another."

The federal courts are particularly sensitive to questions of their own competency. Thus, it is possible at any stage of the federal litigation for either party to raise, or for the court on its own motion to consider, a question of jurisdiction over the subject matter. Rule 12(h)(3) in its original form made the explicit statement that "*whenever* it appears by suggestion of the parties *or otherwise* that the court lacks jurisdiction of the subject matter, the court shall dismiss the action." (Emphasis added.) That is still the law.

Dismissal for want of such jurisdiction might come in the trial court or in an appellate court. Recall Louisville & Nashville Railroad v. Mottley, supra p. 215, where the Supreme Court itself dismissed the federal suit, even though the federal issue in the case might reappear on review of an action on the same claim initiated in a state court (as indeed it did, supra p. 229).

The proposition that a federal court is bound to consider its own jurisdiction, regardless of the attitude or conduct of the parties, opens the door to strategic manipulations and wasted resources. Nevertheless, according to Mansfield, Coldwater & Lake Michigan Railway v. Swan, 111 U.S. 379, 382, 4 S.Ct. 510, 511 (1884), the proposition springs from the limited nature of the judicial power of the United States under Article III, Section 2 of the Constitution. In that case the Supreme Court, noting that the record showed lack of diversity jurisdiction, ordered the action remanded to state court, although the only asserted grounds of appeal were alleged errors at trial. This worked to the benefit of the defendants-appellants, who had themselves invoked federal jurisdiction by removal from state court.

Many cases declare that the parties cannot confer jurisdiction over the subject matter by *consent* or *collusion*. For instance, in Jackson v. Ashton, 33 U.S. (8 Pet.) 148 (1834), the Supreme Court dismissed for lack of diversity jurisdiction where both sides were eager for the Court to hear the appeal, and where counsel for the plaintiffs-appellants argued that jurisdiction existed and counsel for the defendant-appellee expressly renounced any objection to jurisdiction.

Similarly, any party—even the party who invoked federal jurisdiction in the first place—will even at a late stage be heard to say that the case should be dismissed for want of competency. In American Fire & Casualty Co. v. Finn, 341 U.S. 6, 71 S.Ct. 534 (1951), a defendant who had invoked federal jurisdiction by removal and had resisted a motion to remand was allowed to challenge subject-matter jurisdiction on appeal from an adverse judgment. That is to say, there is no general doctrine of *waiver* in connection with objections to federal jurisdiction.

Next suppose that *A* sues *B* in federal court, alleging herself to be a citizen of State *X* and *B* to be a citizen of State *Y*. *B*'s answer admits these allegations. After the running of the statute of limitations so as to bar a new action, *B* moves to dismiss for lack of subject-matter jurisdiction and satisfies the court that the parties were in fact both citizens of State *X* when suit was brought. Is the court bound to dismiss for lack of competency? Yes, as there seems to be no doctrine of equitable *estoppel* in connection with objections to federal jurisdiction. Cf. Itel Containers Int'l Corp. v. P.R. Marine Management, 108 F.R.D. 96 (D.N.J.1985) (imposing monetary sanctions for such behavior, payable to the court and to the plaintiff by the defendant and its counsel).

Questions: (1) What would you think of the constitutionality and desirability of a federal statute allowing any claim, if timely brought in federal court but dismissed for lack of subject-matter jurisdiction, to be asserted in a new action in a proper state court if the now applicable statute of limitations would not have barred the original action and if the new action is commenced within thirty days after the dismissal or within such longer period as might be available under applicable state law? See ALI Study of the Division of Jurisdiction Between State and Federal Courts § 1386(b) commentary at 373–74, 453–57 (1969); cf. Jinks v. Richland County, S.C., 538 U.S. 456, 123 S.Ct. 1667 (2003) (upholding similar federal tolling statute for certain state-law claims).

(2) What would you think of a federal statute setting up a cutoff date in any federal action after which the court could not consider, on its own motion or at the instance of any party, a newly raised question of jurisdiction over the subject matter, unless (a) a party is raising the issue and is relying upon facts the party did not know, and could not be expected to have discovered in the exercise of reasonable diligence, at an earlier stage in the proceedings, or is relying on a change in jurisdictional law, or (b) there was collusion between opposing parties in concealing a known jurisdictional defect? Would it be permissible for a federal court so to proceed to adjudication of a case for which there was in fact no subject-matter jurisdiction under the congressional grants of jurisdiction? for which there was no subject-matter jurisdiction under the Constitution? See ALI Study of the Division of Jurisdiction Between State and Federal Courts § 1386(a) commentary at 366–73 (1969).

COLLATERAL ATTACK

Under current law, federal or state, lack of competency may be raised not only in the ordinary course of review in the trial and appellate courts but even sometimes in subsequent litigation, as by collateral attack. What is a collateral attack? To take as examples some situations we shall soon explore, if a party uses a prior judgment in a new action as the basis for a claim (as where, in enforcing a judgment, the plaintiff brings suit upon the judgment in another state) or as the basis for a defense (as where a defendant pleads res judicata), and if the other party in turn attacks the prior judgment to prevent its use, we have a collateral attack.

The rule is that collateral attack will succeed only if the prior judgment contains certain, very serious errors. So, suppose an action in federal court has proceeded to final judgment upon default, and the plaintiff has brought suit upon the judgment elsewhere. The defendant now contends that the court that rendered the judgment lacked competency. If she can establish that such a defect indeed existed, the collateral-attack court generally will refuse to enforce the judgment.

Change the problem to this extent: suppose an action in federal court has proceeded to final judgment, but in that action the question of the court's competency was raised and litigated and the court decided that it had competency. In a suit upon the judgment, is it open to the second court to reexamine the question of the first court's competency and refuse to enforce the judgment, assuming it is convinced that the first court erred in its decision on its own competency? Generally not, because res judicata works to foreclose relitigation of a prior determination of subject-matter jurisdiction. This question we shall treat in Topic E of Part Four.

Questions: (3) Which law should govern the question of whether there was competency in the court that rendered judgment, upon a collateral attack in a court of a different sovereign? Should it be the law of the first court's sovereign or that of the second court's sovereign? See Restatement (Second) of Conflict of Laws § 105 cmt. b (1971) (first court's sovereign).

(4) To what extent should one be able to go beyond the record and look to extrinsic evidence establishing a lack of competency, on either appeal or collateral attack? See Restatement (Second) of Judgments § 77 (1982) (liberal admissibility). Should we say that here the governing law on evidence shifts to that of the second court's sovereign?

(5) Who should have the burden of proof on competency, in either the rendering court or the collateral-attack court? Should we say that the burden of production shifts to the attacker when the scene changes to collateral attack or to some similar procedure for relief from a rendered judgment?

MEANS AND ENDS

"The mechanism of law—what courts are to deal with which causes and subject to what conditions—cannot be dissociated from the ends that law subserves. So-called jurisdictional questions treated in isolation from the purposes of the legal system to which they relate become barren pedantry. After all, procedure is instrumental; it is the means of effectuating policy. Particularly true is this of the federal courts. The Judiciary Acts, the needs which urged their enactment, the compromises which they embodied, the consequences which they entailed, the changed conditions which in turn modified them, are the outcome of continuous interaction of traditional, political, social, and economic forces. In common with other courts, the federal courts are means for securing justice through law. But in addition and transcending this in importance, the legislation governing the structure and function of the federal judicial system is one means of providing the accommodations necessary to the operation of a federal government. The happy relation of States to Nation—constituting as it does our central political problem—is to no small extent dependent upon the wisdom with which the scope and limits of the federal courts are determined." Felix Frankfurter & James M. Landis, The Business of the Supreme Court 2 (1927).

"The law of federal courts in general, and judicial federalism in particular, is especially vulnerable to the charge that law is merely politics by another name. It is an area where decisions often have substantive implications, yet those implications are oblique, indirect, and uncertain. In addition, the rulings can readily be explained in neutral terms, no matter what their real motivation. Furthermore, much of the doctrine is so recondite that the average person, even the average lawyer, is never quite sure what is going on in a federal courts opinion. For many judges of all political stripes, the temptation to manipulate jurisdictional principles to serve substantive ends, while concealing the dirty deed behind a cloud of Federalist or Nationalist rhetoric, is too great to resist. This happens often enough to justify the assertion that naked politics explains most of the law of judicial federalism." Michael Wells, Rhetoric and Reality in the Law of Federal Courts: Professor Fallon's Faulty Premise, 6 Const. Comment. 367, 381–82 (1989).

SECTION 2. FEDERAL QUESTIONS

Federal question jurisdiction rests on the first clause of Article III, Section 2 of the Constitution. What is the meaning of the term "arising under" that there appears? The Supreme Court, early on, sweepingly construed it to cover all cases of which a federal question forms an "ingredient." Osborn v. Bank of the United States, 22 U.S. (9 Wheat.) 738 (1824) (Marshall, C.J.) (holding that the "arising under" language of Article III authorized a then-existing statute bestowing jurisdiction on the federal courts over all actions brought by the federally chartered bank, because any such action would have as an ingredient the minor federal question of whether the bank under its charter has the power to sue).

Congress for the most part tracked the constitutional language in the Act of March 3, 1875, ch. 137, § 1, 18 Stat. 470, 470, the statute that really for the first time gave the federal courts general original jurisdiction over federal question cases. That Act, with no changes of true substance, now appears as 28 U.S.C. § 1331. What is the meaning of the term "arising under" that there appears? Courts have construed it much more narrowly than the identical constitutional language. The courts have read a series of restrictions into the statutory language. In fact, we have already seen one such restriction, the well-pleaded complaint rule, in the first Louisville & Nashville Railroad v. Mottley case.

On the one hand, reading Article III expansively is desirable, because Congress thereby retains the power to bestow original jurisdiction over special kinds of cases that present a need for federal jurisdiction but possess merely a federal ingredient, and because the appellate jurisdiction of the Supreme Court thereby remains broad enough to cover all state cases that finally turn upon an issue of federal law. On the other hand, reading § 1331 narrowly is defensible, because Congress probably did not intend to inundate the lower federal courts with all the cases having a mere federal ingredient. At any rate, there is an accepted difference in scope between the constitutional and the statutory language. Indeed, we have already observed that difference in the second Louisville & Nashville Railroad v. Mottley case, when the Supreme Court ultimately reviewed an issue of federal law decided in state court, even though it had earlier held that there was no original federal question jurisdiction.

What are those other restrictions that the courts have read into "arising under" in § 1331? One critical restriction deals with the relationship of the case to its federal element. It is clear, as already suggested, that to satisfy the statute the federal element must be more than a mere ingredient. But beyond that, it is difficult to be precise—no single definition that would encompass all the decided cases is evident. The American Law Institute, faced with the jumble of cases, did not attempt definition but instead retained the "arising under" term.[a] Others have attempted a formulation. A famous one is that of Justice Holmes, who argued: "A suit arises under the law that creates the cause of action."[b] This test yields many correct answers; for an important example, an action for patent infringement does arise under federal law, but an action to recover contractual royalties for use of a patent does not. However, there are problem cases, such as Smith v. Kansas City Title & Trust Co., 255 U.S. 180, 41 S.Ct. 243 (1921) (federal jurisdiction exists for suit by a trust company shareholder to enjoin the trust company from investing in certain federal bonds; state law limited permissible investment to legal securities, but plaintiff claimed that the federal statute authorizing the bonds' issuance was unconstitutional), and Shoshone Mining Co. v. Rutter, 177 U.S. 505, 20 S.Ct. 726 (1900) (federal jurisdiction does not exist for suit to determine right to possession of mining claim; a federal statute authorized this type of suit, but directed that local law should govern the rights involved). A more accurate formulation is necessarily fuzzier. Professor Mishkin's definition in the leading article on the subject is a "claim founded 'directly' upon federal law."[c]

Question: (6) It has been argued that this absence of a precise definition is an advantage, because it frees the courts to determine the jurisdictional point on the basis of pragmatic considerations, such as: "the extent of the caseload increase for

[a] See ALI Study of the Division of Jurisdiction Between State and Federal Courts § 1311(a) commentary at 178–79 (1969).

[b] American Well Works Co. v. Layne & Bowler Co., 241 U.S. 257, 260, 36 S.Ct. 585, 586 (1916).

[c] Paul J. Mishkin, The Federal "Question" in the District Courts, 53 Colum.L.Rev. 157, 168 (1953).

federal trial courts if jurisdiction is recognized; the extent to which cases of this class will, in practice, turn on issues of state or federal law; the extent of the necessity for an expert federal tribunal to handle issues of federal law that do arise; the extent of the necessity for a sympathetic federal tribunal in cases of this class." William Cohen, The Broken Compass: The Requirement That a Case Arise "Directly" Under Federal Law, 115 U.Pa.L.Rev. 890, 916 (1967). The Supreme Court now seems receptive to some version of this argument. See Grable & Sons Metal Prods., Inc. v. Darue Eng'g & Mfg., 545 U.S. 308, 312, 125 S.Ct. 2363, 2367 (2005) (justifying "resort to the experience, solicitude, and hope of uniformity that a federal forum offers" on important federal issues). What do you think of such an approach?

Bell v. Hood

Supreme Court of the United States, 1946.
327 U.S. 678, 66 S.Ct. 773.

■ MR. JUSTICE BLACK delivered the opinion of the Court.

Petitioners brought this suit in a federal district court to recover damages in excess of [the then jurisdictional amount for federal question cases of] $3,000 from the respondents who are agents of the Federal Bureau of Investigation. The complaint alleges that the Court's jurisdiction is founded upon federal questions arising under the Fourth and Fifth Amendments. It is alleged that the damages were suffered as a result of the respondents imprisoning the petitioners in violation of their Constitutional right to be free from deprivation of their liberty without due process of law, and subjecting their premises to search and their possessions to seizure, in violation of their Constitutional right to be free from unreasonable searches and seizures.[1]

---

[1] The complaint stated in part:

"That on or about the 17th day of December, 1942, defendant R.B. Hood and each of the other defendants, unlawfully conspired with each other to act beyond their authority as said Federal Bureau of Investigation agents and police officers respectively, and agreed that they would abridge the Constitutional rights of the plaintiffs as guaranteed by the Fourth and Fifth Amendments to the Constitution of the United States to be free from the deprivation of liberty and property without due process of law, and to be free from unreasonable searches and seizures, and agreed unlawfully to simultaneously, in the early morning of December 18th, 1942, search the homes of the individual plaintiffs herein without any warrants of search or seizure, and unlawfully to seize the papers, documents and effects of said plaintiffs and of 'Mankind United,' and falsely to imprison the individual plaintiffs by unlawfully arresting some of the individual plaintiffs without a warrant of arrest and unreasonably to delay the taking of all the individual plaintiffs before a committing officer, in order to effectuate the unlawful searches and seizures aforesaid.

"That thereafter, and on the 18th day of December, 1942, . . . the defendants and each of them, in order to carry out the terms and conditions of the illegal conspiracy aforesaid, and solely for the purpose of carrying out said terms and conditions, did arrest and imprison the individual plaintiffs herein, and did search the homes of said plaintiffs, and seize and carry away books, papers and effects of said individual plaintiffs and of said 'Mankind United.' "

. . . .

". . . by reason of the deprivation of . . . [their] Constitutional rights . . . [plaintiffs had] suffered damages." [For further development of the factual background, see United States v.

Respondents moved to dismiss the complaint for failure to state a cause of action for which relief could be granted and for summary judgment on the grounds that the federal agents acted within the scope of their authority as officers of the United States and that the searches and seizures were incidental to lawful arrests and were therefore valid. Respondents filed affidavits in support of their motions and petitioners filed counter-affidavits. After hearing the motions the district judge did not pass on them but, on his own motion, dismissed the suit for want of federal jurisdiction on the ground that this action was not one that ". . . arises under the Constitution or laws of the United States . . ." as required by 28 U.S.C. § 41(1).[d] The Circuit Court of Appeals affirmed on the same ground. 9 Cir., 150 F.2d 96 [(June 7, 1945)]. At the same time it denied a motion made by petitioners asking it to direct the district court to give petitioners leave to amend their complaint in order to make it still more clearly appear that the action was directly grounded on violations of rights alleged to stem from the Fourth and Fifth Amendments. We granted certiorari because of the importance of the jurisdictional issue involved.

Respondents make the following argument in support of the district court's dismissal of the complaint for want of federal jurisdiction. First, they urge that the complaint states a cause of action for the common law tort of trespass made actionable by state law and that it therefore does not raise questions arising "under the Constitution or laws of the United States." Second, to support this contention, respondents maintain that petitioners could not recover under the Constitution or laws of the United States, since the Constitution does not expressly provide for recovery in money damages for violations of the Fourth and Fifth Amendments and Congress has not enacted a statute that does so provide. A mere reading of the complaint refutes the first contention and, as will be seen, the second one is not decisive on the question of jurisdiction of the federal court.

Whether or not the complaint as drafted states a common law action in trespass made actionable by state law, it is clear from the way it was drawn that petitioners seek recovery squarely on the ground that respondents violated the Fourth and Fifth Amendments. It charges that the respondents conspired to do acts prohibited by these amendments and alleges that respondents' conduct pursuant to the conspiracy resulted in damages in excess of $3,000. It cannot be doubted therefore that it was the pleaders' purpose to make violation of these Constitutional provisions the basis of this suit. Before deciding that there is no jurisdiction, the district court must look to the way the complaint is drawn to see if it is drawn so as to claim a right to recover under the Constitution and laws of the United States. For to that extent "the party who brings a suit is master to decide what law he will rely upon, and . . . does determine whether he will bring a 'suit arising under' the . . . [Constitution or laws] of the United States by his declaration or bill." The Fair v. Kohler Die & Specialty Co., 228 U.S. 22,

---

Bell, 48 F.Supp. 986 (S.D.Cal.1943) (related criminal case involving this pacifist religious cult).—Ed.]

[d] Now 28 U.S.C. § 1331.

25, 33 S.Ct. 410, 411. Though the mere failure to set out the federal or Constitutional claims as specifically as petitioners have done would not always be conclusive against the party bringing the suit, where the complaint, as here, is so drawn as to seek recovery directly under the Constitution or laws of the United States, the federal court, but for two possible exceptions later noted, must entertain the suit. . . . The reason for this is that the court must assume jurisdiction to decide whether the allegations state a cause of action on which the court can grant relief as well as to determine issues of fact arising in the controversy.

Jurisdiction, therefore, is not defeated as respondents seem to contend, by the possibility that the averments might fail to state a cause of action on which petitioners could actually recover. For it is well settled that the failure to state a proper cause of action calls for a judgment on the merits and not for a dismissal for want of jurisdiction. Whether the complaint states a cause of action on which relief could be granted is a question of law and just as issues of fact it must be decided after and not before the court has assumed jurisdiction over the controversy. If the court does later exercise its jurisdiction to determine that the allegations in the complaint do not state a ground for relief, then dismissal of the case would be on the merits, not for want of jurisdiction. Swafford v. Templeton, 185 U.S. 487, 493, 494, 22 S.Ct. 783, 785, 786; Binderup v. Pathe Exchange, 263 U.S. 291, 305–308, 44 S.Ct. 96, 98–99. The previously carved out exceptions are that a suit may sometimes be dismissed for want of jurisdiction where the alleged claim under the Constitution or federal statutes clearly appears to be immaterial and made solely for the purpose of obtaining jurisdiction or where such a claim is wholly insubstantial and frivolous. The accuracy of calling these dismissals jurisdictional has been questioned. The Fair v. Kohler Die & Specialty Co., supra, 228 U.S. at page 25, 33 S.Ct. at page 411. But cf. Swafford v. Templeton, supra.

But as we have already pointed out the alleged violations of the Constitution here are not immaterial but form rather the sole basis of the relief sought. Nor can we say that the cause of action alleged is so patently without merit as to justify, even under the qualifications noted, the court's dismissal for want of jurisdiction. The Circuit Court of Appeals correctly stated that "the complaint states strong cases, and if the allegations have any foundation in truth, the plaintiffs' legal rights have been ruthlessly violated." Petitioners' complaint asserts that the Fourth and Fifth Amendments guarantee their rights to be free from unauthorized and unjustified imprisonment and from unreasonable searches and seizures. They claim that respondents' invasion of these rights caused the damages for which they seek to recover and point further to 28 U.S.C. § 41(1), which authorizes the federal district courts to try "suits of a civil nature" where the matter in controversy "arises under the Constitution or laws of the United States," whether these are suits in "equity" or at "law."[e] Petitioners argue that this statute authorizes the Court to entertain this action at law and to grant recovery for the damages allegedly sustained. Respondents contend

[e] Compare the language of the present provision, § 1331.

that the Constitutional provisions here involved are prohibitions against the federal government as a government and that 28 U.S.C. § 41(1) does not authorize recovery in money damages in suits against unauthorized officials who according to respondents are in the same position as individual trespassers.

Respondents' contention does not show that petitioners' cause is insubstantial or frivolous, and the complaint does in fact raise serious questions, both of law and fact, which the district court can decide only after it has assumed jurisdiction over the controversy. The issue of law is whether federal courts can grant money recovery for damages said to have been suffered as a result of federal officers violating the Fourth and Fifth Amendments. That question has never been specifically decided by this Court. That the issue thus raised has sufficient merit to warrant exercise of federal jurisdiction for purposes of adjudicating it can be seen from the cases where this Court has sustained the jurisdiction of the district courts in suits brought to recover damages for depriving a citizen of the right to vote in violation of the Constitution. And it is established practice for this Court to sustain the jurisdiction of federal courts to issue injunctions to protect rights safeguarded by the Constitution and to restrain individual state officers from doing what the 14th Amendment forbids the state to do. Moreover, where federally protected rights have been invaded, it has been the rule from the beginning that courts will be alert to adjust their remedies so as to grant the necessary relief. And it is also well settled that where legal rights have been invaded, and a federal statute provides for a general right to sue for such invasion, federal courts may use any available remedy to make good the wrong done. Whether the petitioners are entitled to recover depends upon an interpretation of 28 U.S.C. § 41(1), and on a determination of the scope of the Fourth and Fifth Amendments' protection from unreasonable searches and deprivations of liberty without due process of law. Thus, the right of the petitioners to recover under their complaint will be sustained if the Constitution and laws of the United States are given one construction and will be defeated if they are given another. For this reason the district court has jurisdiction. Gully v. First National Bank, 299 U.S. 109, 112, 113, 57 S.Ct. 96, 97; Smith v. Kansas City Title & Trust Co., 255 U.S. 180, 199, 200, 41 S.Ct. 243, 244, 245.

Reversed.

■ [The concurring opinion of JUSTICE REED is omitted.]

■ MR. JUSTICE JACKSON took no part in the consideration or decision of this case.

■ MR. CHIEF JUSTICE STONE and MR. JUSTICE BURTON, dissenting.

The district court is without jurisdiction as a federal court unless the complaint states a cause of action arising under the Constitution or laws of the United States. Whether the complaint states such a cause of action is for the court, not the pleader, to say. When the provision of the Constitution or federal statute affords a remedy which may in some circumstances be availed of by a plaintiff, the fact that his pleading does not bring him within that class as one entitled to the remedy, goes to the sufficiency of the pleading and not to the jurisdiction. The Fair v. Kohler Die & Specialty Co., 228 U.S. 22, 25, 33 S.Ct. 410, 411; Binderup v. Pathe Exchange, 263 U.S. 291, 306–308, 44 S.Ct. 96, 98–99, and cases cited. But where as here, neither the constitutional provision nor any act of Congress affords a remedy to any person, the mere assertion by a plaintiff that he is entitled to such a remedy cannot be said to satisfy jurisdictional requirements. Hence we think that the courts below rightly decided that the district court was without jurisdiction because no cause of action under the Constitution or laws of the United States was stated.

The only effect of holding, as the Court does, that jurisdiction is conferred by the pleader's unfounded assertion that he is one who can have a remedy for damages arising under the Fourth and Fifth Amendments is to transfer to the federal court the trial of the allegations of trespass to person and property, which is a cause of action arising wholly under state law. For even though it be decided that petitioners have no right to damages under the Constitution, the district court will be required to pass upon the question whether the facts stated by petitioners give rise to a cause of action for trespass under state law. See Hurn v. Oursler, 289 U.S. 238, 53 S.Ct. 586.

Questions: (7) A building contractor brings an action in federal district court against certain unions, alleging that their strike aimed at compelling him to employ union labor is a conspiracy to restrain interstate commerce in violation of the antitrust laws. This legal contention, once an open question, has been squarely rejected by two prior Supreme Court cases. The plaintiff invokes jurisdiction on the ground that the case arises under federal antitrust law, but the defendants move for dismissal under Rule 12(b)(1). What decision on the motion? See Levering & Garrigues Co. v. Morrin, 289 U.S. 103, 53 S.Ct. 549 (1933) (grant).

(8) In a case such as Bell v. Hood, what difference does it make whether a defendant faced with a meritless federal claim wins on Rule 12(b)(1) grounds or by means of Rule 12(b)(6)?

SECTION 3. SUPPLEMENTAL JURISDICTION

Federal district courts can hear some state claims that are related to pending claims within the federal jurisdiction. Because the pertinent doctrines thus allow a federal court to hear a claim that would otherwise be only a state claim, they effectively constitute a head of federal jurisdiction. But they require as a hook some pending claim that comes within a more traditional head of federal jurisdiction, such as federal question or diversity jurisdiction.

PENDENT JURISDICTION

Backing up a bit, it is clear that if federal question jurisdiction exists for a "claim," the district court has the power to decide not only the federal question but also any other questions, be they federal or state in nature, the resolution of which is necessary to decision on the claim. After all, a court of original jurisdiction must have this power to function practically, because such a court decides whole cases and not just isolated questions (as recognized in the constitutional reference to "cases" and in the statutory references to "civil actions"). So, for example, the Osborn case indicated that if the Bank of the United States brought a claim on an ordinary contract, federal question jurisdiction would exist, and moreover the federal court would be empowered to decide all state-law questions it ran into when disposing of the contract claim on the merits.

According to a thorough researcher, old English cases had recognized the need for this judicial power. Indeed, the old cases built on it to allow, say, a plaintiff already in court to assert an additional claim against the defendant that would otherwise be beyond the court's subject-matter jurisdiction but that should be entertained in the interests of fairness. Such notions migrated to our young country and emerged in numerous American cases. See Mary Brigid McManamon, Dispelling the Myths of Pendent and Ancillary Jurisdiction: The Ramifications of a Revised History, 46 Wash. & Lee L.Rev. 863 (1989).

Hurn v. Oursler, 289 U.S. 238, 53 S.Ct. 586 (1933), crystallized from these cases the federal doctrine called pendent jurisdiction. The plaintiffs in that case joined three claims in the same complaint: (1) for infringement of the copyright in a play entitled "The Evil Hour," a claim arising under a federal statute; (2) for unfair competition in unauthorized use of the same play, a claim arising under state law; and (3) for unfair competition through interference with the plaintiffs' rights in an uncopyrighted, revised version of the play, a claim also arising under state law. At the close of the evidence in a bench trial, the trial court dismissed that first claim for failure of proof of infringement and the other two claims for lack of jurisdiction. The Supreme Court held that it was error so to dismiss the second claim, saying: "The distinction to be observed is between a case where two distinct grounds in support of a single cause of action are alleged, one only of which presents a federal question, and a case where two separate and distinct causes of action are alleged, one only of which is federal in character." On this test, the Court held that the claim of unfair competition with regard to the copyrighted play constituted the same cause of action as the copyright infringement claim and hence required decision on the merits, but the claim as to the uncopyrighted revision of the play was a separate and distinct cause of action and hence properly dismissed for lack of jurisdiction.

Question: (9) Upon remand, the district court in Bell v. Hood granted defendants' motion to dismiss the complaint on the ground that it failed to state a claim upon which relief could be granted, 71 F.Supp. 813 (S.D.Cal.1947). In doing so, it first decided that no federal claim was stated,[f] and it then concluded that consequently the pendent state trespass claim now being urged should be dismissed for lack of jurisdiction. Was this latter holding consistent with Hurn v. Oursler?

The lower courts had trouble in applying the Hurn "single cause of action" test, especially after the liberal joinder provisions of the Federal Rules came onto the scene. Although the desirability of the Hurn extension of jurisdiction seemed fairly apparent, some courts would take jurisdiction of the state claim only when there was a virtually complete identity of facts in the two claims.

In 1948 Congress purportedly codified the Hurn holding in § 1338(b) of title 28. The codification aggravated the difficulties instead of solving them. In the first place, the statute refers to a state "claim . . . when joined with a substantial and related [federal] claim." So the statute, like the Federal Rules, avoids the term "cause of action," which was the touchstone of the Hurn test. But does "claim" in the statute mean the same as "cause of action"? What meaning is to be given to "substantial"? to "related"? The statutory formulation is broader than Hurn's, but how much broader? In the second place, the statute refers only to a claim of unfair competition joined to a claim under certain federal laws. Here, the subsequent cases were clear in recognizing that the statute did not abolish pendent jurisdiction in other areas of law.

UNITED MINE WORKERS v. GIBBS, 383 U.S. 715, 86 S.Ct. 1130 (1966). Plaintiff sued the union in a federal district court, alleging that the union improperly interfered in his contractual relations with the coal company that employed him. He claimed damage from secondary boycotts under § 303 of the Labor Management Relations Act, 29 U.S.C. § 187, and also damage from the same unlawful acts under the common law of the state. The trial court dismissed the federal claim on judgment n.o.v., but it allowed the plaintiff's verdict on the state claim to stand. The court of appeals affirmed.

In holding that the court had properly entertained jurisdiction over the pendent state claim, Justice Brennan for the Supreme Court first characterized the prevailing approach of lower courts to pendent jurisdiction as "unnecessarily grudging." Rephrasing the inquiry as whether the relationship between the federal question claim and the state claim was close

---

[f] The Supreme Court has since decided, contrary to the district court in Bell v. Hood, that violation of the Fourth Amendment by federal agents acting under the color of their authority does give rise to a federal cause of action within 28 U.S.C. § 1331 for damages resulting from their unconstitutional conduct. Bivens v. Six Unknown Named Agents of Fed. Bureau of Narcotics, 403 U.S. 388, 91 S.Ct. 1999 (1971) (federal action). Justice Black, who wrote the opinion in Bell v. Hood, dissented, along with Chief Justice Burger and Justice Blackmun.

More recently, the Supreme Court decided that violation of the Due Process Clause of the Fifth Amendment similarly gives rise to a federal cause of action for damages within § 1331. Davis v. Passman, 442 U.S. 228, 99 S.Ct. 2264 (1979) (federal action).

enough to permit "the conclusion that the entire action before the court comprises but one constitutional 'case,' " he then explained:

"The state and federal claims must derive from a common nucleus of operative fact. But if, considered without regard for their federal or state character, a plaintiff's claims are such that he would ordinarily be expected to try them all in one judicial proceeding, then, assuming substantiality of the federal issues, there is *power* in federal courts to hear the whole.

"That power need not be exercised in every case in which it is found to exist. It has consistently been recognized that pendent jurisdiction is a doctrine of discretion, not of plaintiff's right. Its justification lies in considerations of judicial economy, convenience and fairness to litigants; if these are not present a federal court should hesitate to exercise jurisdiction over state claims, even though bound to apply state law to them, Erie R. Co. v. Tompkins, 304 U.S. 64, 58 S.Ct. 817. Needless decisions of state law should be avoided both as a matter of comity and to promote justice between the parties, by procuring for them a surer-footed reading of applicable law. . . . [I]f it appears that the state issues substantially predominate, whether in terms of proof, of the scope of the issues raised, or of the comprehensiveness of the remedy sought, the state claims may be dismissed without prejudice and left for resolution to state tribunals. There may, on the other hand, be situations in which the state claim is so closely tied to questions of federal policy that the argument for exercise of pendent jurisdiction is particularly strong. In the present case, for example, the allowable scope of the state claim implicates the federal doctrine of pre-emption; while this interrelationship does not create statutory federal question jurisdiction, Louisville & N.R. Co. v. Mottley, 211 U.S. 149, 29 S.Ct. 42, its existence is relevant to the exercise of discretion. Finally, there may be reasons independent of jurisdictional considerations, such as the likelihood of jury confusion in treating divergent legal theories of relief, that would justify separating state and federal claims for trial, Fed.Rule Civ.Proc. 42(b). If so, jurisdiction should ordinarily be refused.

"The question of power will ordinarily be resolved on the pleadings. But the issue whether pendent jurisdiction has been properly assumed is one which remains open throughout the litigation."

Questions: (10) Considering the *power* of a federal court under Gibbs to hear a state claim pendent to a claim arising under federal law, what constitutional arguments could have been made against the existence of such power? What arguments could have been made on the basis of the various congressional grants of federal question jurisdiction?

(11) Considering the role of *discretion* in choosing under Gibbs whether or not to hear such a state claim, is it desirable that the federal courts should have discretion so to define their own jurisdiction? See generally Gene R. Shreve,

Pragmatism Without Politics—A Half Measure of Authority for Jurisdictional Common Law, 1991 B.Y.U.L.Rev. 767.

ANCILLARY JURISDICTION

Having the same historical roots as pendent jurisdiction, ancillary jurisdiction was another judge-made doctrine under which a district court could, as an incident to deciding a claim within its jurisdiction, decide other claims that, if separately presented, would not be within the court's jurisdiction.

Ancillary jurisdiction was classically a doctrine of necessity. A federal court of original jurisdiction must have the power to handle certain incidental matters in order to function as a court of justice. For example, in Freeman v. Howe, 65 U.S. (24 How.) 450 (1861), the Supreme Court said that a federal court had jurisdiction over a claim by mortgagees to the mortgaged property in the form of railroad cars—where that property had previously been brought under the court's control by attachment in a diversity action to which the mortgagees were not parties—even though there was no independent jurisdictional ground for the mortgagees' claim. The reasoning was that a state court could not interfere with the federal control of the property, and this in turn necessitated a federal forum for the mortgagees in order not to leave them remediless. Accordingly, the federal court would hear their claim under the theory that it was "ancillary and dependent, supplementary merely to the original suit."

The doctrine perceptibly shifted gears in Moore v. New York Cotton Exchange, 270 U.S. 593, 46 S.Ct. 367 (1926), where the Court seemed to embrace a doctrine of convenience. It there held that in a federal antitrust suit complaining of the Exchange's restrictions on access to cotton price quotations, the federal court had jurisdiction over the Exchange's counterclaim seeking an injunction against the plaintiff's wrongfully obtaining those quotations. Although there was no independent jurisdictional ground for that counterclaim, it fell within the compulsory counterclaim provision of the Equity Rules of 1912.

This embrace of convenient jurisdiction for procedurally permissible claims expanded the doctrine of ancillary jurisdiction. Its scope further increased, albeit to an uncertain extent, with the broadening of provisions for joinder of claims and parties under the Federal Rules of Civil Procedure. Thus, the doctrine's historical point of departure and the subsequent accommodation to expansionist pressures justified calling ancillary jurisdiction a "child of necessity and sire of confusion." Jay C. Baker, Note, Federal Practice: Jurisdiction of Third–Party Claims, 11 Okla.L.Rev. 326, 329 (1958).

REVERE COPPER & BRASS INC. v. AETNA CASUALTY & SURETY CO., 426 F.2d 709 (5th Cir.1970). Revere Copper & Brass, a Maryland corporation, brought suit in federal court against Aetna, surety on performance bonds on construction contracts, alleging that Aetna's principal, a Maryland corporation named Fuller, had failed to perform its obligations under the contracts. There was diversity of citizenship between Revere and Aetna, and Revere sought to recover $2,045,000. Aetna denied Revere's allegations and impleaded Fuller under Rule 14(a), alleging that Fuller had agreed to indemnify Aetna for all losses from its suretyship. Fuller admitted Aetna's allegations, but Fuller denied the allegations in Revere's complaint and made claim against Revere, seeking to recover $1,328,880 on the basis of the same disputed contracts.

Revere moved to dismiss Fuller's claim against it on the ground that there was no diversity of citizenship between them. The district court found the claim to be within its ancillary jurisdiction, and it therefore denied Revere's motion. An interlocutory appeal under 28 U.S.C. § 1292(b) followed, and the court of appeals affirmed:

"The theoretical basis which underlies the modern doctrine of ancillary jurisdiction appears to be fairly well settled. . . .

"The exact criteria to be used to detect the presence of ancillary jurisdiction, however, is more elusive. The leading case on the modern doctrine of ancillarity is Moore v. New York Cotton Exchange, 270 U.S. 593, 46 S.Ct. 367, 70 L.Ed. 750 (1926), which held that a compulsory counterclaim under old Equity Rule 30 need not be supported by an independent basis of federal jurisdiction, but was ancillary to the main cause of action since it arose out of the transaction which was the subject matter of the original suit. In defining what it meant by the word 'transaction', the Court said:

> 'Transaction' is a word of flexible meaning. It may comprehend a series of many occurrences, depending not so much upon the immediateness of their connection as upon their *logical relationship*.

. . . .

"It would be fair to say, therefore, that a claim is ancillary when it bears a logical relationship to the aggregate core of operative facts which constitutes the main claim over which the court has an independent basis of federal jurisdiction. However, the type of relationship contemplated by the phrase 'logical relationship' remains somewhat clouded. Perhaps the simplest way to determine the type of the nexus that must necessarily exist between the main claim and another claim for the other claim to be considered ancillary is to examine the present extent of the application of the doctrine to the various devices of the Federal Rules allowing joinder of claims.

"While it is well established that a compulsory counterclaim under Rule 13(a) is within the ancillary jurisdiction since it necessarily arises out of the same transaction or occurrence as the original claim, Moore v. New York Cotton Exchange, supra, a permissive counterclaim under Rule 13(b) requires an independent ground of federal jurisdiction since it does not arise out of the same transaction or occurrence as the original claim, Camper & Nicholsons, Ltd. v. Yacht 'Fontainebleau II' S.D.Fla., 1968, 292 F.Supp. 734, except where a setoff is involved. Fraser v. Astra Steamship Corp., S.D.N.Y., 1955, 18 F.R.D. 240; [other citation omitted]. Contra, Robinson Bros. & Co. v. Tygart Steel Products Co., W.D.Pa., 1949, 9 F.R.D. 468.[7] Crossclaims under Rule 13(g) are considered ancillary since, under the Rule, they must arise 'out of the transaction or occurrence that is the subject matter either of the original action or of a counterclaim therein or relating to any property that is the subject matter of the original action.' Childress v. Cook, 5 Cir., 1957, 245 F.2d 798. An impleader action under Rule 14(a) is considered ancillary even though such an action does not, as a general rule, directly involve the aggregate of operative facts upon which the original claim is based, but arises out of that claim in the sense that the impleader action, such as the action for indemnity here brought by Aetna against Fuller, would not exist without the threat of liability arising out of the original claim. Waylander–Peterson Co. v. Great Northern Ry. Co., 8 Cir., 1953, 201 F.2d 408; Lesnik v. Public Industrials Corp., 2 Cir., 1944, 144 F.2d 968. Likewise, intervention as of right under Rule 24(a), available 'when the applicant claims an interest relating to the property or transaction which is the subject of the action and he is so situated that the disposition of the action may as a practical matter impair or impede his ability to protect that interest, unless the applicant's interest is adequately represented by existing parties,' is regarded as ancillary to the original claim and need not be supported by an independent ground of federal jurisdiction. Formulabs, Incorporated v. Hartley Pen Company, 9 Cir., 1963, 318 F.2d 485, 492, cert. den. 375 U.S. 945, 84 S.Ct. 352, 11 L.Ed.2d 275.

"From the application of the doctrine of ancillary jurisdiction to these joinder devices, it appears that a claim has a logical relationship to the original claim if it *arises* out of the same aggregate of operative facts as the original claim in two senses: (1) that the same aggregate of operative facts serves as the basis of both claims; or (2) that the aggregate core of facts upon which the original claim rests activates additional legal rights in a party defendant that would otherwise remain dormant.

"Before proceeding, another aspect of the Moore decision, supra, must be mentioned, and that is the Court's concern with the need to provide complete relief to the counterclaiming defendant. 270 U.S. at 610, 46 S.Ct. 367, 70 L.Ed. 750. A cursory review of the joinder situations to which ancillary jurisdiction is applied reveals that, generally, it is made available to litigants in a defensive posture, who would otherwise be prevented or greatly burdened in adequately protecting their interests. There is much to

[7] The treatment of permissive counterclaims involving set-offs is an exception to the logical relationship test in that they are independent from the original claim and can be said to be ancillary only in the sense that they are limited by the amount of the original claim. The ancillary status given set-offs is best explained historically from their source in English statute, 2 Geo. 2, c. 22, § 13 (1729). See, Note "Diversity Requirements In Multi–Party Litigation", [58 Colum.L.Rev. 548, 553–55 (1958)].

be said for allowing parties who are involuntarily brought into federal court to defend against a claim, or who must be allowed to intervene in a federal action as a defendant to secure their interests, to assert all their claims arising out of the controversy in one proceeding and that this is, or ought to be, one of the factors to be considered in determining the existence of ancillary jurisdiction. See, Note, 'Diversity Requirements in Multiparty Litigation', supra, n.[7], at 561.

"It is easily seen that Fuller's claim arises out of the aggregate of operative facts which forms the basis of Revere's claim in such a way to put their logical relationship beyond doubt. The two claims are but two sides of the same coin. The construction was not completed before the time provided in the two contracts. If Revere is not responsible for the delay, as Fuller alleges, Fuller must at least be guilty of breach of contract, not to mention the other allegations of fault in Revere's complaint. To paraphrase the Supreme Court in Moore v. New York Cotton Exchange, supra: so close is the connection between the case sought to be stated in Revere's complaint and that set up in Fuller's Rule 14(a) counterclaim that it only needs the failure of the former to establish the foundation for the latter.

"Not only is the parallel between a Rule 14(a) counterclaim and a compulsory counterclaim under Rule 13(a) so close as to be persuasive on the question of ancillarity, the parallel between the instant case and cases dealing with the ability of an intervenor of right under Rule 24(a) to counterclaim against the original plaintiff without an independent basis of federal jurisdiction removes any substantial doubt. It is well established that a contractor who has agreed to indemnify his surety on a performance bond can intervene as a party defendant as of right in a suit on the performance bond against the surety and then assert his counterclaim against the plaintiff, even in the absence of an independent ground of federal jurisdiction. United States, to Use and Benefit of Foster Wheeler Corp. v. American Surety Co., 2 Cir., 1944, 142 F.2d 726; Coleman Capital Corp. v. Fidelity & Deposit Co. of Md., S.D.N.Y., 1967, 43 F.R.D. 407. It would be anomalous to hold that Fuller could have asserted its counterclaim against Revere free of any jurisdictional impediment if it had taken the initiative of intervening, and yet hold that since Fuller was brought into this action involuntarily as a third-party defendant, its counterclaim must satisfy the requirements of strict diversity and thus fail.

. . . .

"Revere also argues that the recognition of ancillary jurisdiction in the present situation would be an unwarranted extension of federal diversity jurisdiction in contravention of Rule 82, F.R.C.P., and the general trend to restrict this head [of] jurisdiction. See, ALI, Study of the Division of Jurisdiction between State and Federal Courts (Proposed Final Draft No. 1, 1965); Field, 'Proposals on Federal Diversity Jurisdiction', 17 S.Car.L.R. 685 (1965). In answer to this argument, it should be noted that the Federal Rules do not expand ancillary jurisdiction, but provide opportunities for involving the doctrine, which, as has been seen, was already well established when the rules became effective, in additional situations."

Question: (12) What should happen to an ancillary claim if the original claim on which federal jurisdiction is based is disposed of by settlement? by summary judgment? by dismissal for failure to state a claim upon which relief can be granted? See Stamford Bd. of Educ. v. Stamford Educ. Ass'n, 697 F.2d 70, 72–73 (2d Cir.1982) (recognizing role for discretion). What if the dismissal of the original claim is for lack of subject-matter jurisdiction? See Estate of Harshman v. Jackson Hole Mountain Resort Corp., 379 F.3d 1161 (10th Cir.2004) (requiring dismissal of ancillary claim).

Owen Equipment & Erection Co. v. Kroger

Supreme Court of the United States, 1978.
437 U.S. 365, 98 S.Ct. 2396.

■ MR. JUSTICE STEWART delivered the opinion of the Court.

In an action in which federal jurisdiction is based on diversity of citizenship, may the plaintiff assert a claim against a third-party defendant when there is no independent basis for federal jurisdiction over that claim? The Court of Appeals for the Eighth Circuit held in this case that such a claim is within the ancillary jurisdiction of the federal courts. We granted certiorari, 434 U.S. 1008, 98 S.Ct. 715, because this decision conflicts with several recent decisions of other Courts of Appeals.

I

On January 18, 1972, James Kroger was electrocuted when the boom of a steel crane next to which he was walking came too close to a high tension electric power line. The respondent (his widow, who is the administratrix of his estate) filed a wrongful death action in the United States District Court for the District of Nebraska against the Omaha Public Power District (OPPD). Her complaint alleged that OPPD's negligent construction, maintenance and operation of the power line had caused Kroger's death. Federal jurisdiction was based on diversity of citizenship, since the respondent was a citizen of Iowa and OPPD was a Nebraska corporation.

OPPD then filed a third-party complaint pursuant to Fed.Rule Civ. Proc. 14(a) against the petitioner, Owen Equipment and Erection Company (Owen), alleging that the crane was owned and operated by Owen, and that Owen's negligence had been the proximate cause of Kroger's death.[3] OPPD

---

[3] Under Rule 14(a), a third-party defendant may not be impleaded merely because he may be liable to the *plaintiff*. [Citations omitted.] While the third-party complaint in this case alleged merely that Owen's negligence caused Kroger's death, and the basis of Owen's alleged liability *to OPPD* is nowhere spelled out, OPPD evidently relied upon the state common-law

later moved for summary judgment on the respondent's complaint against it. While this motion was pending, the respondent was granted leave to file an amended complaint naming Owen as an additional defendant. Thereafter, the District Court granted OPPD's motion for summary judgment in an unreported opinion. The case thus went to trial between the respondent and the petitioner alone.

The respondent's amended complaint alleged that Owen was "a Nebraska corporation with its principal place of business in Nebraska." Owen's answer admitted that it was "a corporation organized and existing under the Laws of the State of Nebraska," and denied every other allegation of the complaint. On the third day of trial, however, it was disclosed that the petitioner's principal place of business was in Iowa, not Nebraska,[5] and that the petitioner and the respondent were thus both citizens of Iowa. The petitioner then moved to dismiss the complaint for lack of jurisdiction. The District Court reserved decision on the motion, and the jury thereafter returned a verdict in favor of the respondent. In an unreported opinion issued after the trial, the District Court denied the petitioner's motion to dismiss the complaint.

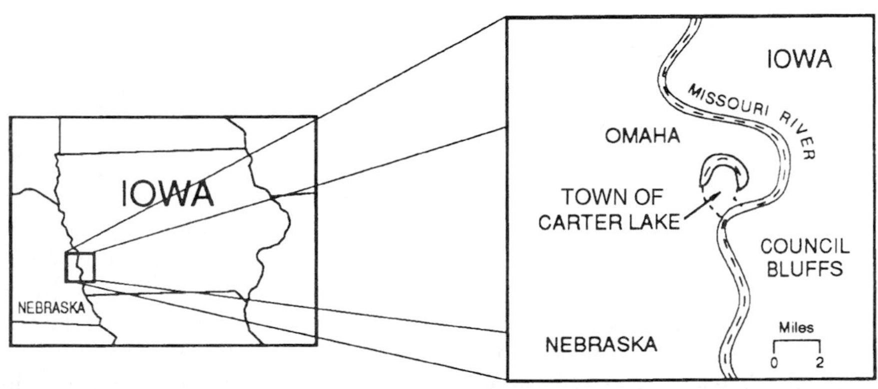

The judgment was affirmed on appeal. 558 F.2d 417. The Court of Appeals held that under this Court's decision in Mine Workers v. Gibbs, 383 U.S. 715, 86 S.Ct. 1130, the District Court had jurisdictional power, in its discretion, to adjudicate the respondent's claim against the petitioner because that claim arose from the "core of 'operative facts' giving rise to both [respondent's] claim against OPPD and OPPD's claim against Owen." 558 F.2d at 424. It further held that the District Court had properly exercised its discretion in proceeding to decide the case even after summary

right of contribution among joint tortfeasors. See Dairyland Ins. Co. v. Mumert, 212 N.W.2d 436, 438 (Iowa); Best v. Yerkes, 247 Iowa 800, 77 N.W.2d 23. The petitioner has never challenged the propriety of the third-party complaint as such.

[5] The problem apparently was one of geography. Although the Missouri River generally marks the boundary between Iowa and Nebraska, Carter Lake, Iowa, where the accident occurred and where Owen had its main office, lies west of the river, adjacent to Omaha, Neb. Apparently the river once avulsed at one of its bends, cutting Carter Lake off from the rest of Iowa.

judgment had been granted to OPPD, because the petitioner had concealed its Iowa citizenship from the respondent. . . .

II

It is undisputed that there was no independent basis of federal jurisdiction over the respondent's state-law tort action against the petitioner, since both are citizens of Iowa. And although Fed.Rule Civ.Proc. 14(a) permits a plaintiff to assert a claim against a third-party defendant, . . . it does not purport to say whether or not such a claim requires an independent basis of federal jurisdiction. Indeed, it could not determine that question, since it is axiomatic that the Federal Rules of Civil Procedure do not create or withdraw federal jurisdiction.

In affirming the District Court's judgment, the Court of Appeals relied upon the doctrine of ancillary jurisdiction, whose contours it believed were defined by this Court's holding in Mine Workers v. Gibbs, supra. The Gibbs case differed from this one in that it involved pendent jurisdiction, which concerns the resolution of a plaintiff's federal and state law claims against a single defendant in one action. By contrast, in this case there was no claim based upon substantive federal law, but rather state-law tort claims against two different defendants. Nonetheless, the Court of Appeals was correct in perceiving that Gibbs and this case are two species of the same generic problem: Under what circumstances may a federal court hear and decide a state-law claim arising between citizens of the same State?[8] But we believe that the Court of Appeals failed to understand the scope of the doctrine of the Gibbs case.

. . . .

It is apparent that Gibbs delineated the constitutional limits of federal judicial power. But even if it be assumed that the District Court in the present case had constitutional power to decide the respondent's lawsuit against the petitioner,[10] it does not follow that the decision of the Court of Appeals was correct. Constitutional power is merely the first hurdle that must be overcome in determining that a federal court has jurisdiction over a particular controversy. For the jurisdiction of the federal courts is limited not only by the provisions of Art. III of the Constitution, but by Acts of Congress. [Citations omitted.]

That statutory law as well as the Constitution may limit a federal court's jurisdiction over nonfederal claims[11] is well illustrated by . . .

---

[8] No more than in Aldinger v. Howard, 427 U.S. 1, 96 S.Ct. 2413, is it necessary to determine here "whether there are any 'principled' differences between pendent and ancillary jurisdiction; or, if there are, what effect Gibbs had on such differences." Id., at 13, 96 S.Ct., at 2420.

[10] Federal jurisdiction in Gibbs was based upon the existence of a question of federal law. The Court of Appeals in the present case believed that the "common nucleus of operative fact" test also determines the outer boundaries of constitutionally permissible federal jurisdiction when that jurisdiction is based upon diversity of citizenship. We may assume without deciding that the Court of Appeals was correct in this regard. See also n. 13, infra.

[11] As used in this opinion, the term "nonfederal claim" means one as to which there is no independent basis for federal jurisdiction. Conversely, a "federal claim" means one as to which an independent basis for federal jurisdiction exists.

Aldinger v. Howard, 427 U.S. 1, 96 S.Ct. 2413 . . . . In Aldinger the Court held that a federal district court lacked jurisdiction over a state-law claim against a county, even if that claim was alleged to be pendent to one against county officials under 42 U.S.C. § 1983. . . . [D]espite the fact that federal and nonfederal claims arose from a "common nucleus of operative fact," the Court held that the statute [28 U.S.C. § 1343(3)] conferring jurisdiction over the federal claim did not allow the exercise of jurisdiction over the nonfederal claim.

. . . Aldinger . . . thus make[s] clear that a finding that federal and nonfederal claims arise from a "common nucleus of operative fact," the test of Gibbs, does not end the inquiry into whether a federal court has power to hear the nonfederal claims along with the federal ones. Beyond this constitutional minimum, there must be an examination of the posture in which the nonfederal claim is asserted and of the specific statute that confers jurisdiction over the federal claim, in order to determine whether "Congress in [that statute] has . . . expressly or by implication negated" the exercise of jurisdiction over the particular nonfederal claim. Aldinger v. Howard, supra, 427 U.S., at 18, 96 S.Ct., at 2422.

III

The relevant statute in this case, 28 U.S.C. § 1332(a)(1), confers upon federal courts jurisdiction over "civil actions where the matter in controversy exceeds the sum or value of [the then jurisdictional amount for diversity cases of] $10,000 . . . and is between . . . citizens of different States." This statute and its predecessors have consistently been held to require complete diversity of citizenship.[13] That is, diversity jurisdiction does not exist unless *each* defendant is a citizen of a different State from *each* plaintiff. Over the years Congress has repeatedly re-enacted or amended the statute conferring diversity jurisdiction, leaving intact this rule of complete diversity. Whatever may have been the original purposes of diversity of citizenship jurisdiction, this subsequent history clearly demonstrates a congressional mandate that diversity jurisdiction is not to be available when any plaintiff is a citizen of the same State as any defendant. Cf. Snyder v. Harris, 394 U.S. 332, 338–339, 89 S.Ct. 1053, 1057–1058.[16]

Thus it is clear that the respondent could not originally have brought suit in federal court naming Owen and OPPD as codefendants, since

---

[13] E.g., Strawbridge v. Curtiss, 3 Cranch 267; Coal Company v. Blatchford, 11 Wall. 172; Indianapolis v. Chase National Bank, 314 U.S. 63, 69, 62 S.Ct. 15, 16; American Fire & Cas. Co. v. Finn, 341 U.S. 6, 17, 71 S.Ct. 534, 541. It is settled that complete diversity is not a constitutional requirement. State Farm Fire & Cas. Co. v. Tashire, 386 U.S. 523, 530–531, 87 S.Ct. 1199, 1203–1204.

[16] Notably, Congress enacted § 1332 as part of the Judicial Code of 1948, 62 Stat. 930, shortly after Rule 14 was amended in 1946. When the Rule was amended, the Advisory Committee noted that "in any case where the plaintiff could not have joined the third party originally because of jurisdictional limitations such as lack of diversity of citizenship, the majority view is that any attempt by the plaintiff to amend his complaint and assert a claim against the impleaded third party would be unavailing." 28 U.S.C.App., p. 7752. The subsequent re-enactment without relevant change of the diversity statute may thus be seen as evidence of congressional approval of that "majority view."

citizens of Iowa would have been on both sides of the litigation. Yet the identical lawsuit resulted when she amended her complaint. Complete diversity was destroyed just as surely as if she had sued Owen initially. In either situation, in the plain language of the statute, the "matter in controversy" could not be "between . . . citizens of different States."

It is a fundamental precept that federal courts are courts of limited jurisdiction. The limits upon federal jurisdiction, whether imposed by the Constitution or by Congress, must be neither disregarded nor evaded. Yet under the reasoning of the Court of Appeals in this case, a plaintiff could defeat the statutory requirement of complete diversity by the simple expedient of suing only those defendants who were of diverse citizenship and waiting for them to implead nondiverse defendants.[17] If, as the Court of Appeals thought, a "common nucleus of operative fact" were the only requirement for ancillary jurisdiction in a diversity case, there would be no principled reason why the respondent in this case could not have joined her cause of action against Owen in her original complaint as ancillary to her claim against OPPD. Congress' requirement of complete diversity would thus have been evaded completely.

It is true, as the Court of Appeals noted, that the exercise of ancillary jurisdiction over nonfederal claims has often been upheld in situations involving impleader, cross-claims or counterclaims. But in determining whether jurisdiction over a nonfederal claim exists, the context in which the nonfederal claim is asserted is crucial. See Aldinger v. Howard, 427 U.S., at 14, 96 S.Ct., at 2420. And the claim here arises in a setting quite different from the kinds of nonfederal claim that have been viewed in other cases as falling within the ancillary jurisdiction of the federal courts.

First, the nonfederal claim in this case was simply not ancillary to the federal one in the same sense that, for example, the impleader by a defendant of a third-party defendant always is. A third-party complaint depends at least in part upon the resolution of the primary lawsuit. See n. 3, supra. Its relation to the original complaint is thus not mere factual similarity but logical dependence. Cf. Moore v. New York Cotton Exchange, 270 U.S. 593, 610, 46 S.Ct. 367, 371. The respondent's claim against the petitioner, however, was entirely separate from her original claim against OPPD, since the petitioner's liability to her depended not at all upon whether or not OPPD was also liable. Far from being an ancillary and dependent claim, it was a new and independent one.

---

[17] This is not an unlikely hypothesis, since a defendant in a tort suit such as this one would surely try to limit his liability by impleading any joint tortfeasors for indemnity or contribution. Some commentators have suggested that the possible abuse of third-party practice could be dealt with under 28 U.S.C. § 1359, which forbids collusive attempts to create federal jurisdiction. See, e.g., 3 Moore's Federal Practice ¶ 14.27[1], at 14–571 (2d ed. 1974); 6 C. Wright & A. Miller, Federal Practice and Procedure § 1444, at 231–232 (1971); Note, Rule 14 Claims and Ancillary Jurisdiction, 57 Va.L.Rev. 265, 274–275 (1971). The dissenting opinion today also expresses this view. . . . But there is nothing necessarily collusive about a plaintiff selectively suing only those tortfeasors of diverse citizenship, or about the named defendants' desire to implead joint tortfeasors. Nonetheless, the requirement of complete diversity would be eviscerated by such a course of events.

Second, the nonfederal claim here was asserted by the plaintiff, who voluntarily chose to bring suit upon a state-law claim in a federal court. By contrast, ancillary jurisdiction typically involves claims by a defending party haled into court against his will, or by another person whose rights might be irretrievably lost unless he could assert them in an ongoing action in a federal court. A plaintiff cannot complain if ancillary jurisdiction does not encompass all of his possible claims in a case such as this one, since it is he who has chosen the federal rather than the state forum and must thus accept its limitations. "[T]he efficiency plaintiff seeks so avidly is available without question in the state courts." Kenrose Mfg. Co. v. Fred Whitaker Co., 512 F.2d 890, 894 (CA4).[20]

It is not unreasonable to assume that, in generally requiring complete diversity, Congress did not intend to confine the jurisdiction of federal courts so inflexibly that they are unable to protect legal rights or effectively to resolve an entire, logically entwined lawsuit. Those practical needs are the basis of the doctrine of ancillary jurisdiction. But neither the convenience of litigants nor considerations of judicial economy can suffice to justify extension of the doctrine of ancillary jurisdiction to a plaintiff's cause of action against a citizen of the same State in a diversity case. Congress has established the basic rule that diversity jurisdiction exists under 28 U.S.C. § 1332 only when there is complete diversity of citizenship. "The policy of the statute calls for its strict construction." Healy v. Ratta, 292 U.S. 263, 270, 54 S.Ct. 700, 703; [other citations omitted]. To allow the requirement of complete diversity to be circumvented as it was in this case would simply flout the congressional command.[21]

Accordingly, the judgment of the Court of Appeals is reversed.

It is so ordered.

■ MR. JUSTICE WHITE, with whom MR. JUSTICE BRENNAN joins, dissenting.

The Court today states that "[i]t is not unreasonable to assume that, in generally requiring complete diversity, Congress did not intend to confine the jurisdiction of federal courts so inflexibly that they are unable . . . effectively to resolve an entire, logically entwined lawsuit." . . . In spite of this recognition, the majority goes on to hold that in diversity suits federal courts do not have the jurisdictional power to entertain a claim asserted by a plaintiff against a third-party defendant, no matter how

---

20 Whether Iowa's statute of limitations would now bar an action by the respondent in an Iowa court is, of course, entirely a matter of state law. See Iowa Code § 614.10. Compare 558 F.2d, at 420, with id., at 432 n. 42 (Bright, J., dissenting); cf. Burnett v. New York Central R. Co., 380 U.S. 424, 431–432, and n. 9, 85 S.Ct. 1050, 1056–1057, and n. 9. [In fact, despite this uncertainty that the Supreme Court was willing to accept when ordering dismissal, the widow sued again in state court and overcame the statute of limitations, eventually settling the case on favorable terms. For the background story of the Owen Equipment case, see John B. Oakley, "The Story of Owen Equipment v. Kroger: A Change in the Weather of Federal Jurisdiction," in Civil Procedure Stories 81 (Kevin M. Clermont ed., 2d ed. 2008).—Ed.]

21 Our holding is that the District Court lacked power to entertain the respondent's lawsuit against the petitioner. Thus, the asserted inequity in the respondent's alleged concealment of its citizenship is irrelevant. Federal judicial power does not depend upon "prior action or consent of the parties." American Fire & Cas. Co. v. Finn, 341 U.S. 6, 18, 71 S.Ct. 534, 542.

entwined it is with the matter already before the court, unless there is an independent basis for jurisdiction over that claim. Because I find no support for such a requirement in either Art. III of the Constitution or in any statutory law, I dissent from the Court's "unnecessarily grudging"[1] approach.

. . . .

. . . [Gibbs'] language and reasoning were broad enough to cover the instant factual situation. . . . Accordingly, as far as Art. III of the Constitution is concerned, the District Court had power to entertain Mrs. Kroger's claim against Owen.

The majority correctly points out, however, that the analysis cannot stop here. As Aldinger v. Howard, 427 U.S. 1, 96 S.Ct. 2413 (1976), teaches, the jurisdictional power of the federal courts may be limited by Congress, as well as by the Constitution. In Aldinger, . . . the Court held that the District Court did not have pendent jurisdiction over the state claim, for, under the Court's precedents at that time, it was thought that Congress had specifically determined not to confer on the federal courts jurisdiction over civil rights claims against cities and counties. . . .

In the present case, the only indication of congressional intent that the Court can find is that contained in the diversity jurisdictional statute . . . . Because this statute has been interpreted as requiring complete diversity of citizenship between each plaintiff and each defendant, Strawbridge v. Curtiss, 3 Cranch 267 (1806), the Court holds that the District Court did not have ancillary jurisdiction over Mrs. Kroger's claim against Owen. In so holding, the Court unnecessarily expands the scope of the complete-diversity requirement while substantially limiting the doctrine of ancillary jurisdiction.

The complete-diversity requirement, of course, could be viewed as meaning that in a diversity case, a federal district court may adjudicate only those claims that are between parties of different States. Thus, in order for a defendant to implead a third-party defendant, there would have to be diversity of citizenship; the same would also be true for cross-claims between defendants and for a third-party defendant's claim against a plaintiff. Even the majority, however, refuses to read the complete-diversity requirement so broadly; it recognizes with seeming approval the exercise of ancillary jurisdiction over nonfederal claims in situations involving impleader, cross-claims and counterclaims. . . . Given the Court's willingness to recognize ancillary jurisdiction in these contexts, despite the requirements of § 1332(a), I see no justification for the Court's refusal to approve the District Court's exercise of ancillary jurisdiction in the present case.

It is significant that a plaintiff who asserts a claim against a third-party defendant is not seeking to add a new party to the lawsuit. In the present case, for example, Owen had already been brought into the suit by OPPD, and, that having been done, Mrs. Kroger merely sought to assert against Owen a claim arising out of the same transaction that was already

[1] See Mine Workers v. Gibbs, 383 U.S. 715, 725, 86 S.Ct. 1130, 1138 (1966).

before the court. Thus the situation presented here is unlike that in Aldinger, supra . . . .

Because in the instant case Mrs. Kroger merely sought to assert a claim against someone already a party to the suit, considerations of judicial economy, convenience, and fairness to the litigants—the factors relied upon in Gibbs, supra—support the recognition of ancillary jurisdiction here. Already before the court was the whole question of the cause of Mr. Kroger's death. Mrs. Kroger initially contended that OPPD was responsible; OPPD in turn contended that Owen's negligence had been the proximate cause of Mr. Kroger's death. In spite of the fact that the question of Owen's negligence was already before the District Court, the majority requires Mrs. Kroger to bring a separate action in state court in order to assert that very claim. Even if the Iowa Statute of Limitations will still permit such a suit, . . . considerations of judicial economy are certainly not served by requiring such duplicative litigation.

The majority, however, brushes aside such considerations of convenience, judicial economy, and fairness because it concludes that recognizing ancillary jurisdiction over a plaintiff's claim against a third-party defendant would permit the plaintiff to circumvent the complete-diversity requirement and thereby "flout the congressional command." Since the plaintiff in such a case does not bring the third-party defendant into the suit, however, there is no occasion for deliberate circumvention of the diversity requirement, absent collusion with the defendant. In the case of such collusion, of which there is absolutely no indication here,[5] the court can dismiss the action under the authority of 28 U.S.C. § 1359. In the absence of such collusion, there is no reason to adopt an absolute rule prohibiting the plaintiff from asserting those claims that he may properly assert against the third-party defendant pursuant to Fed.Rule Civ.Proc. 14(a). The plaintiff in such a situation brings suit against the defendant only with absolutely no assurance that the defendant will decide or be able to implead a particular third-party defendant. Since the plaintiff has no control over the defendant's decision to implead a third party, the fact that he could not have originally sued that party in federal court should be irrelevant. Moreover, the fact that a plaintiff in some cases may be able to foresee the subsequent chain of events leading to the impleader does not seem to me to be a sufficient reason to declare that a district court does not have the *power* to exercise ancillary jurisdiction over the plaintiff's claims against the third-party defendant.[7]

---

[5] When Mrs. Kroger brought suit, it was believed that Owen was a citizen of Nebraska, not Iowa. Therefore, had she desired at that time to make Owen a party to the suit, she would have done so directly by naming Owen as a defendant.

[7] Under the Gibbs analysis, recognition of the District Court's power to hear a plaintiff's nonfederal claim against a third-party defendant in a diversity suit would not mean that the court would be required to entertain such claims in all cases. The District Court would have the discretion to dismiss the nonfederal claim if it concluded that the interests of judicial economy, convenience, and fairness would not be served by the retention of the claim in the federal lawsuit. See Gibbs, 383 U.S., at 726, 86 S.Ct., at 1139. Accordingly, the majority's concerns that lead it to conclude that ancillary jurisdiction should not be recognized in the

We have previously noted that "[s]ubsequent decisions of this Court indicate that Strawbridge is not to be given an expansive reading." State Farm Fire & Cas. Co. v. Tashire, 386 U.S. 523, 531 n. 6, 87 S.Ct. 1199, 1203 n. 6 (1967). In light of this teaching, it seems to me appropriate to view § 1332 as requiring complete diversity only between the plaintiff and those parties he actually brings into the suit. Beyond that, I would hold that in a diversity case the District Court has power, both constitutional and statutory, to entertain all claims among the parties arising from the same nucleus of operative fact as the plaintiff's original, jurisdiction-conferring claim against the defendant. Accordingly, I dissent from the Court's disposition of the present case.

ORTIZ v. UNITED STATES GOVERNMENT, 595 F.2d 65 (1st Cir. 1979). Puerto Rican plaintiffs sued the United States in a federal district court for medical malpractice under the Federal Tort Claims Act, 28 U.S.C. § 1346(b), a claim within exclusive federal jurisdiction. The United States impleaded a Puerto Rican hospital. Then plaintiffs attempted to assert a nonfederal claim against the hospital under Rule 14(a). On interlocutory appeal, the court of appeals held that "pendent" jurisdiction could be exercised over such a claim.

CODIFICATION

Suppose *P* sues *D–1* in a federal district court on a claim for which there is federal question jurisdiction. Does the federal court have discretion to hear a closely related state-law claim that *P* has against *D–2*?

The lower federal courts were embracing an affirmative answer when the Supreme Court blustered in with Finley v. United States, 490 U.S. 545, 109 S.Ct. 2003 (1989). In that case, plaintiff's family died in an airplane crash while landing. She sued the United States in a federal district court for negligence in the airport's operation, invoking exclusive jurisdiction under 28 U.S.C. § 1346(b). She tried to join nonfederal claims against a municipality and a corporation that were also involved in the airport's operation. In holding against the exercise of this form of pendent jurisdiction, Justice Scalia for the Supreme Court attempted to explain:

"Analytically, petitioner's case is fundamentally different from Gibbs in that it brings into question what has become known as pendent-*party* jurisdiction, that is, jurisdiction over parties not named in any claim that is independently cognizable by the federal court. We may assume, without deciding, that the constitutional criterion for pendent-party jurisdiction is analogous to the constitutional criterion for pendent-claim jurisdiction, and

---

present situation could be met on a case-by-case basis, rather than by the absolute rule it adopts.

that petitioner's state-law claims pass that test. Our cases show, however, that with respect to the addition of parties, as opposed to the addition of only claims, we will not assume that the full constitutional power has been congressionally authorized, and will not read jurisdictional statutes broadly. . . .

. . . .

". . . [O]ur cases do not display an entirely consistent approach with respect to the necessity that jurisdiction be explicitly conferred. The Gibbs line of cases was a departure from prior practice, and a departure that we have no intent to limit or impair. But Aldinger indicated that the Gibbs approach would not be extended to the pendent-party field, and we decide today to retain that line. Whatever we say regarding the scope of jurisdiction conferred by a particular statute can of course be changed by Congress. What is of paramount importance is that Congress be able to legislate against a background of clear interpretive rules, so that it may know the effect of the language it adopts."

Justice Blackmun dissented, as did Justice Stevens, with whom Justices Brennan and Marshall joined. They stressed the widely recognized desirability of jurisdiction here, the proposition that Aldinger stood for presuming congressional intent to favor pendent jurisdiction unless Congress indicated otherwise in a specific context, and the confusion that the Finley opinion would sow with regard to additional parties under ancillary jurisdiction.

The upshot was that Congress enacted a new provision on so-called supplemental jurisdiction. Judicial Improvements Act of 1990, Pub.L. No. 101–650, tit. III, § 310, 104 Stat. 5089, 5113. This provision, now 28 U.S.C. § 1367, overturned Finley v. United States by combining and codifying the doctrines of pendent and ancillary jurisdiction. Congress explained its statute, drafted quickly in subcommittee with some academic input, in H.R.Rep. No. 101–734:

"This section would authorize jurisdiction in a case like Finley, as well as essentially restore the pre-Finley understandings of the authorization for and limits on other forms of supplemental jurisdiction. In federal question cases, it broadly authorizes the district courts to exercise supplemental jurisdiction over additional claims, including claims involving the joinder of additional parties. In diversity cases, the district courts may exercise supplemental jurisdiction, except when doing so would be inconsistent with the jurisdictional requirements of the diversity statute. In both cases, the district courts, as under current law, would have discretion to decline supplemental jurisdiction in appropriate circumstances.

"Subsection [(a)] generally authorizes the district court to exercise jurisdiction over a supplemental claim whenever it forms part of the same constitutional case or controversy as the claim or claims that provide the basis of the district court's original jurisdiction.[15] In providing for supple-

[15] In so doing, subsection (a) codifies the scope of supplemental jurisdiction first articulated by the Supreme Court in United Mine Workers v. Gibbs, 383 U.S. 715, 86 S.Ct. 1130 (1966).

mental jurisdiction over claims involving the addition of parties, subsection (a) explicitly fills the statutory gap noted in Finley v. United States.

"Subsection [(b)] prohibits a district court in a case over which it has jurisdiction founded solely on the general diversity provision, 28 U.S.C. § 1332, from exercising supplemental jurisdiction in specified circumstances.[16] In diversity-only actions the district courts may not hear plaintiffs' supplemental claims when exercising supplemental jurisdiction would encourage plaintiffs to evade the jurisdictional requirement of 28 U.S.C. § 1332 by the simple expedient of naming initially only those defendants whose joinder satisfies section 1332's requirements and later adding claims not within original federal jurisdiction against other defendants who have intervened or been joined on a supplemental basis. In accord with case law, the subsection also prohibits the joinder or intervention of persons as plaintiffs if adding them is inconsistent with section 1332's requirements. The section is not intended to affect the jurisdictional requirements of 28 U.S.C. § 1332 in diversity-only class actions, as those requirements were interpreted prior to Finley.[17]

"Subsection (b) makes one small change in pre-Finley practice. Anomalously, under current practice, the same party might intervene as of right under Federal Rule of Civil Procedure 24(a) and take advantage of supplemental jurisdiction, but not come within supplemental jurisdiction if parties already in the action sought to effect the joinder under Rule 19. Subsection (b) would eliminate this anomaly, excluding Rule 24(a) plaintiff-intervenors to the same extent as those sought to be joined as plaintiffs under Rule 19.

"If this exclusion threatened unavoidable prejudice to the interests of the prospective intervenor if the action proceeded in its absence, the district court should be more inclined not merely to deny the intervention but to dismiss the whole action for refiling in state court under the criteria of Rule 19(b).

"Subsection [(c)] codifies the factors that the Supreme Court has recognized as providing legitimate bases upon which a district court may decline jurisdiction over a supplemental claim, even though it is empowered to hear the claim. Subsection (c)(1)–(3) codifies the factors recognized as relevant under current law. Subsection (c)(4) acknowledges that occasionally there may exist other compelling reasons for a district court to decline supplemental jurisdiction, which the subsection does not foreclose a court from considering in exceptional circumstances. As under current law, subsection (c) requires the district court, in exercising its discretion, to undertake a case-specific analysis."

Question: (13) *P* of State *A* sues *D* of State *B* in a federal district court on a $101,000 claim for which diversity of citizenship is the only basis of jurisdiction. Assume that *D* impleads *T–1* of State *A*. Then *T–1* asserts a nonfederal claim

[16] The net effect of subsection (b) is to implement the principal rationale of Owen Equipment & Erection Co. v. Kroger, 437 U.S. 365, 98 S.Ct. 2396 (1978).

[17] See Supreme Tribe of Ben Hur v. Cauble, 255 U.S. 356, 41 S.Ct. 338 (1921); Zahn v. International Paper Co., 414 U.S. 291, 94 S.Ct. 505 (1973).

against *P* under Rule 14(a), which prompts a nonfederal counterclaim by *P* against *T–1* under Rule 13(a). Is supplemental jurisdiction authorized for this counterclaim? See Denis F. McLaughlin, The Federal Supplemental Jurisdiction Statute—A Constitutional and Statutory Analysis, 24 Ariz.St.L.J. 849, 942–49 (1992). Compare Evra Corp. v. Swiss Bank Corp., 673 F.2d 951 (7th Cir.1982) (yes), and Thomas D. Rowe, Jr., Stephen B. Burbank & Thomas M. Mengler, Compounding or Creating Confusion About Supplemental Jurisdiction? A Reply to Professor Freer, 40 Emory L.J. 943, 959–61 (1991), with Home Ins. Co. v. Ballenger Corp., 74 F.R.D. 93, 100 n.3 (N.D.Ga.1977) (no), and Thomas C. Arthur & Richard D. Freer, Grasping at Burnt Straws: The Disaster of the Supplemental Jurisdiction Statute, 40 Emory L.J. 963, 983–84 (1991).

While overturning Finley was an excellent idea, the execution of drafting § 1367 was not an unqualified success. Consequently, the American Law Institute moved quickly to propose a complete overhaul of that statute. ALI Federal Judicial Code Revision Project pt. I (2004). Here is its proposed amendment to the particularly troublesome § 1367(b):

> *Restriction of supplemental jurisdiction in diversity litigation.* When the jurisdiction of a district court over a supplemental claim depends upon a freestanding claim that is asserted in the same pleading and that qualifies as a freestanding claim solely on the basis of the jurisdiction conferred by section 1332 of this title, the court shall have jurisdiction of the supplemental claim . . . only if it—
>
> (1) is asserted representatively by or against a class of additional unnamed parties; or
>
> (2) would be a freestanding claim on the basis of section 1332 of this title but for the value of the claim; or
>
> (3) has been joined to the action by the intervention of a party whose joinder is not indispensable to the litigation of the action.
>
> ["Asserted in the same pleading" means that the relevant claims have been asserted in one or more of the following ways: (1) by the pleading as originally filed with the court, (2) by amendment of the pleading, (3) by order of the court reformulating the pleading to compel joinder of parties, (4) by the pleader's assertion of a claim (other than a counterclaim or a claim for indemnity or contribution) against a third party impleaded previously in response to the pleading, or (5) by the assertion of the claim or defense of an intervenor who seeks to be treated as if the pleading had asserted a claim by or against that intervenor.]

Question: (14) *P* of State *A* sues *D* of State *B* in a federal district court on a $101,000 claim for which diversity of citizenship is the only basis of jurisdiction. Assume that *D* asserts a small compulsory counterclaim against *P*, which prompts *P* to implead *T–2* of State *A*. Is there supplemental jurisdiction for the impleader under § 1367? See Guaranteed Sys., Inc. v. American Nat'l Can Co., 842 F.Supp. 855 (M.D.N.C.1994) (no, because of the wording of § 1367, even when the case had initially arrived in federal court by *D*'s removal); Peter Raven–Hansen, The Forgotten Proviso of § 1367(b) (and Why We Forgot), 74 Ind.L.J. 197 (1998). Would there be under the ALI's proposed statute?

EXECUTIVE SOFTWARE NORTH AMERICA, INC. v. UNITED STATES DISTRICT COURT, 24 F.3d 1545 (9th Cir.1994) (2–1 decision). Donna Page, as an African–American woman formerly employed by an allegedly Scientology-dominated company, brought federal and state discrimination claims in a California state-court case. Defendants removed. The federal district court chose not to retain jurisdiction over the state-law claims, the court possibly concerned about mere docket congestion but simply citing to its Gibbs discretion. The federal court of appeals granted mandamus.

The court of appeals ordered reconsideration, after taking a position in a statutory-construction dispute that has since seriously split the circuits. The court explained its view that 28 U.S.C. § 1367 had narrowed the scope of Gibbs discretion:

"Therefore, under the regime established by Gibbs . . . and . . . progeny, whether pendent jurisdiction should be exercised in a given circumstance depended on the district court assessing whether doing so 'would most sensibly accommodate' the values of 'economy, convenience, fairness, and comity.' Although the specific examples given in Gibbs informed the determination of when the particular balance of these factors was likely to point against (or in favor) of retaining jurisdiction, courts by no means found these specific illustrations to exhaust Gibbs's underlying values.

. . . .

"Section 1367 retains the basic division, reflected in Gibbs, between the power of a court to entertain a pendent claim and the authority of a court, in its discretion, to decline to exercise that power. However, Congress, in codifying supplemental jurisdiction, has chosen to codify as well the discretionary factors that warrant declining jurisdiction. Section 1367(a), providing that 'the district courts shall have supplemental jurisdiction over all other claims that are so related to claims in the action within such original jurisdiction that they form part of the same case or controversy under Article III of the United States Constitution,' . . . confers power to entertain supplemental jurisdiction in mandatory terms. By use of the word 'shall,' the statute makes clear that if power is conferred under section 1367(a), and its exercise is not prohibited by section 1367(b), a court can decline to assert supplemental jurisdiction over a pendent claim only if one of the four categories specifically enumerated in section 1367(c) applies. . . .

". . . Not only is this conclusion supported by the legislative history, see H.R. No. 734, 101st Cong., 2d Sess. 29 (1990), . . . but a contrary reading of the statute would appear to render section 1367(c) superfluous. . . .

"A consequence of the statutory structure chosen by Congress is that section 1367(c) somewhat changes the nature of the Gibbs discretionary inquiry. . . .

"The statute . . . channels the application of the underlying values to a greater degree than the Gibbs regime, although section 1367(c) continues to recognize the doctrine's dynamic aspects. Subsections (c)(1)–(c)(3) appear to codify concrete applications of the underlying Gibbs values recognized in preexisting case law. . . .

"By codifying [most of the] preexisting applications of Gibbs in subsections (c)(1)–(3), however, it is clear that Congress intended the exercise of discretion to be triggered by the court's identification of a factual predicate that corresponds to one of the section 1367(c) categories. Once that factual predicate is identified, the exercise of discretion, of course, still is informed by whether remanding the pendent state claims comports with the underlying objective of 'most sensibly accommodat[ing]' the values of 'economy, convenience, fairness, and comity.' [Citations omitted, including Carnegie–Mellon Univ. v. Cohill, 484 U.S. 343, 108 S.Ct. 614 (1988).]

"We believe that the 'catchall,' Palmer v. Schwan's Sales Enters., Inc., 1993 WL 390053 1993 U.S. Dist. LEXIS 14069, at *7 (D.Kan. Sep. 27, 1993), provided by subsection (c)(4) should be interpreted in a similar manner. Subsection (c)(4) permits a discretionary remand of pendent claims when 'in exceptional circumstances, there are other compelling reasons for declining jurisdiction.' . . . Congress's use of the word 'other' to modify 'compelling reasons' indicates that what ought to qualify as 'compelling reasons' for declining jurisdiction under subsection (c)(4) should be of the same nature as the reasons that gave rise to the categories listed in subsections (c)(1)–(3). Because, as discussed above, the subsection (c)(1)–(3) fact patterns constitute situations in which the underlying Gibbs values ordinarily will 'point toward' declining jurisdiction, Carnegie–Mellon, 484 U.S. at 350 n. 7, 108 S.Ct. at 619 n. 7, we believe that 'compelling reasons' for the purposes of subsection (c)(4) similarly should be those that lead a court to conclude that declining jurisdiction 'best accommodate[s] the values of economy, convenience, fairness, and comity.' Carnegie–Mellon, 484 U.S. at 351, 108 S.Ct. at 619.

"We do not believe, however, that Congress has replicated unaltered the command of the Carnegie–Mellon Court that the 'Judicial Branch is to shape and apply [the doctrine of pendent jurisdiction] in [light of this objective].' Id. By providing that an exercise of discretion under subsection 1367(c)(4) ought to be made only in 'exceptional circumstances' Congress has sounded a note of caution that the bases for declining jurisdiction should be extended beyond the circumstances identified in subsections (c)(1)–(3) only if the circumstances are quite unusual. In short, although we find that 'other compelling reasons' clearly refers the district court back to the subsection (c)(1)–(3) categories, and thus requires the court to balance the underlying values that they embody, we think 'exceptional circumstances' requires an additional inquiry.

"Of course, when the balance of the Gibbs values indicates that there are 'compelling reasons' to decline jurisdiction, the underlying circumstances that inform this calculus usually will demonstrate how the circumstances confronted are 'exceptional.' We do not believe, however, this always will be the case. Even when a court's balancing of the Gibbs values provides, in its judgment, 'compelling reasons' for declining jurisdiction, it might still be the case that the differences between the case it is confronting and the case in which supplemental jurisdiction is appropriate are not sufficient to justify the conclusion that the court would, in fact, be applying subsection (c)(4) properly. We think it clear from the language chosen by Congress, however, that declining jurisdiction outside of subsection (c)(1)–(3) should be the exception, rather than the rule. Courts therefore must ensure that the reasons identified as 'compelling' are not deployed in circumstances that threaten this principle. The inquiry is not particularly burdensome. A court simply must articulate why the circumstances of the case are exceptional [that is, "factual circumstances that truly are unusual"] in addition to inquiring whether the balance of the Gibbs values provide compelling reasons for declining jurisdiction in such circumstances.

. . . .

"Therefore, to the extent that Gibbs and Carnegie–Mellon were interpreted as permitting courts to extend the doctrine's underlying values beyond previously recognized applications whenever doing so was consistent with those values, [citation omitted], we believe that section 1367(c)(4) more carefully channels courts' discretion by requiring the court to identify how the circumstances that it confronts, and in which it believes the balance of the Gibbs values provides 'compelling reasons' for declining jurisdiction, are 'exceptional.' "

Question: (15) Henceforth, is supplemental jurisdiction to be measured according to a Revere-like set of wooden rules or to a Gibbs-like flexible standard? For example, imagine typical impleader claims by defendant: will all such claims automatically fall within § 1367, or might some upon a case-by-case analysis fail the common-nucleus-of-operative-fact test? Almost all courts extend supplemental jurisdiction to any such impleader claim, although some of those courts act with knowledge that § 1367(c) usually could get rid of an inappropriate extension. For a converse example, imagine permissive counterclaims by defendant: will all of them fall outside supplemental jurisdiction, or could some have a sufficiently close logical relationship to qualify? Here the courts proceed with more flexibility. See, e.g., Jones v. Ford Motor Credit Co., 358 F.3d 205, 213 (2d Cir.2004) (extending supplemental jurisdiction for debt-collection counterclaims to an Equal Credit Opportunity Act class action, the court observed: "Whether or not the Gibbs 'common nucleus' standard provides the outer limit of an Article III 'case,' and is therefore a requirement for entertaining a permissive counterclaim that otherwise lacks a jurisdictional basis, the facts of Ford Credit's counterclaims and those of the Plaintiffs' ECOA claims satisfy that standard, even though the relationship is not such as would make the counterclaims compulsory.").

SECTION 4. JURISDICTIONAL AMOUNT

Various statutes impose a jurisdictional amount requirement, but by far the most important is the requirement in 28 U.S.C. § 1332(a) that "the matter in controversy exceeds the sum or value of $75,000, exclusive of interest and costs." The purpose of such a requirement is to keep petty controversies out of the federal courts. However, what this statutory creation seems to do best is to create litigation over how it should be applied.

Snyder v. Harris
(Gas Service Co. v. Coburn)

Supreme Court of the United States, 1969.
394 U.S. 332, 89 S.Ct. 1053.

[In order to resolve a conflict among the courts of appeals, the Supreme Court granted certiorari in two cases.

[In Snyder, 390 F.2d 204 (8th Cir.1968), plaintiff brought a class action, grounded on diversity of citizenship, for herself and all others similarly situated, against members of the board of directors of Missouri Fidelity Union Trust Life Insurance Co., alleging that the defendants had sold their shares of the company's stock far in excess of fair market value, the excess representing payment to obtain control of the company, and that under Missouri law this excess should be distributed among all the shareholders. Plaintiff's own claim was for $8740 in damages; the total claim of all the 4000–odd shareholders would be about $1,200,000. The district court and the court of appeals refused to permit aggregation.

[In Gas Service Co., 389 F.2d 831 (10th Cir.1968), also a diversity action, Coburn brought a class action alleging that Gas Service Co. had billed and illegally collected a city franchise tax from him and others living outside city limits. Plaintiff alleged damages to himself of $7.81; the total claim of about 18,000 customers living outside city limits was allegedly over the then jurisdictional amount of $10,000. The district court and the court of appeals permitted aggregation, relying on the 1966 amendment to Rule 23.]

■ MR. JUSTICE BLACK delivered the opinion of the Court.

. . . The issue presented by these two cases is whether separate and distinct claims presented by and for various claimants in a class action may be added together to provide the $10,000 jurisdictional amount in controversy.

. . . .

The first congressional grant to district courts to take suits between citizens of different States fixed the requirement for the jurisdictional amount in controversy at $500. In 1887 this jurisdictional amount was increased to $2,000; in 1911 to $3,000; and in 1958 to $10,000. The traditional judicial interpretation under all of these statutes has been from the beginning that the separate and distinct claims of two or more plaintiffs cannot be aggregated in order to satisfy the jurisdictional amount requirement. Aggregation has been permitted only (1) in cases in which a single plaintiff seeks to aggregate two or more of his own claims against a single defendant and (2) in cases in which two or more plaintiffs unite to enforce a single title or right in which they have a common and undivided interest. It is contended, however, that the adoption of a 1966 amendment to Rule 23 effectuated a change in this jurisdictional doctrine. . . .

The doctrine that separate and distinct claims could not be aggregated was never, and is not now, based upon . . . any rule of procedure. That doctrine is based rather upon this Court's interpretation of the statutory phrase "matter in controversy." . . . Nothing in the amended Rule 23 changes this doctrine. The class action plaintiffs in the two cases before us argue that since the new Rule will include in the judgment all members of the class who do not ask to be out by a certain date, the "matter in controversy" now encompasses all the claims of the entire class. But it is equally true that where two or more plaintiffs join their claims under the joinder provisions of Rule 20, each and every joined plaintiff is bound by the judgment. And it was in joinder cases of this very kind that the doctrine that distinct claims could not be aggregated was originally enunciated. Troy Bank v. G.A. Whitehead & Co., 222 U.S. 39, 32 S.Ct. 9 (1911); Pinel v. Pinel, 240 U.S. 594, 36 S.Ct. 416 (1916).[g] . . .

. . . .

. . . It is urged, however, that this Court should now overrule its established statutory interpretation and hold that "matter in controversy" encompasses the aggregation of all claims that can be brought together in a single suit, regardless of whether any single plaintiff has a claim that exceeds the required jurisdictional amount. It is argued in behalf of this

---

[g] Pinel held that there could be no aggregation of claims by two children seeking to establish their interests in their father's estate, when the children were alleging that he had unintentionally omitted them from his will. Contrast this with the holding of Shields v. Thomas, 58 U.S. (17 How.) 3 (1855), that an estate's distributees, such as children of the decedent, could aggregate their claims against the person who allegedly converted the estate, because they had a common and undivided interest in a single title or right.

Thus, common and undivided interests represent a small category of ancient lineage that is virtually undefinable. One can delineate it only by such precedential examples. See 14AA Wright, Miller & Cooper § 3704 on cases concerning the obscure but narrow category of common and undivided interests. Nevertheless, one can say that fitting within this category requires much more than relatedness among the claims. Usually, it requires a dispute over a single indivisible thing. For an attempt at further generalizing, see Durant v. Servicemaster Co., 109 Fed.Appx. 27, 30 (6th Cir.2004), which posited that a necessary, but not sufficient, condition for determining that plaintiffs have a common and undivided interest is a situation such that if one plaintiff cannot or does not collect a share, the shares of the remaining plaintiffs increase—as opposed to a situation where a group of plaintiffs litigate individual claims that would be unaffected by the results obtained by fellow plaintiffs.

position that (1) the determination of whether claims are "separate and distinct" is a troublesome question that breeds uncertainty and needless litigation, and (2) the inability of parties to aggregate numerous small claims will prevent some important questions from being litigated in federal courts. And both of these factors, it is argued, will tend to undercut the attempt of the Judicial Conference to promulgate efficient and modernized class action procedures. We think that whatever the merit of these contentions, they are not sufficient to justify our abandonment of a judicial interpretation of congressional language that has stood for more than a century and a half.

. . . .

. . . Moreover, while the class action device serves a useful function across the entire range of legal questions, the jurisdictional amount requirement applies almost exclusively to controversies based upon diversity of citizenship. A large part of those matters involving federal questions can be brought, by way of class actions or otherwise, without regard to the amount in controversy. Suits involving issues of state law and brought on the basis of diversity of citizenship can often be most appropriately tried in state courts. . . . There is no compelling reason for this Court to overturn a settled interpretation of an important congressional statute in order to add to the burdens of an already overloaded federal court system. Nor can we overlook the fact that the Congress that permitted the federal rules to go into effect was assured before doing so that none of the rules would either expand or contract the jurisdiction of federal courts. If there is a present need to expand the jurisdiction of those courts we cannot overlook the fact that the Constitution specifically vests that power in the Congress, not in the courts.

. . . .

■ MR. JUSTICE FORTAS, with whom MR. JUSTICE DOUGLAS joins, dissenting.

The Court today refuses to conform the judge-made formula for computing the amount in controversy in class actions with the 1966 amendment to Rule 23 of the Federal Rules of Civil Procedure. The effect of this refusal is substantially to undermine a generally welcomed and long-needed reform in federal procedure.

. . . .

Permitting aggregation in class action cases does not involve any violation of the principle, expressed in Rule 82 and inherent in the whole procedure for the promulgation and amendment of the Federal Rules, that the courts cannot by rule expand their own jurisdictions. While the Rules cannot change subject-matter jurisdiction, changes in the forms and practices of the federal courts through changes in the Rules frequently and necessarily will affect the occasions on which subject-matter jurisdiction is exercised because they will in some cases make a difference in what cases the federal courts will hear and who will be authoritatively bound by the judgment. For example, the development of the law of joinder and ancillary jurisdiction under the Federal Rules has influenced the "jurisdiction" of the federal courts in this broader sense. . . . Making judicial rules for calculating jurisdictional amount responsive to the new structure of class actions is not an extension of the jurisdiction of the federal courts, but a recognition that the procedural framework in which the courts operate has been changed by a provision having the effect of law.

. . . .

The new Rule 23, by redefining the law of class actions, has, with the effect of statute, provided for a decision by the district courts that the nominally separate and legally "several" claims of individuals may be so much alike that they can be tried all at once, as if there were just one claim, in a single proceeding in which most members of the class asserting the claim will not be personally present at all. When that determination has been made in accordance with the painstaking demands of Rule 23, there is authorized to be brought in the federal courts a single litigation, in which, both practically and in legal theory, the thing at stake, the "matter in controversy," is the total, combined, aggregated claim of the whole class. When that happens the courts do not obey, but violate, the jurisdictional statutes if they continue to impose an ancient and artificial judicial doctrine to fragment what is in every other respect a single claim, which the courts are commanded to stand ready to hear.

For these reasons, I would measure the value of the "matter in controversy" in a class action found otherwise proper under the amended Rule 23 by the monetary value of the claim of the whole class.

Question: (16) Does it seem wise to you to allow *P* of State *A* to sue *D* of State *B* in federal court upon two wholly unrelated claims for \$37,000 and \$39,000 respectively, but not to allow *P–1* and *P–2* of State *A* to aggregate their separate and distinct claims against *D* for \$37,000 and \$39,000 respectively arising out of the same transaction or occurrence, such as an automobile accident?

ZAHN v. INTERNATIONAL PAPER CO., 414 U.S. 291, 94 S.Ct. 505 (1973). Plaintiffs brought a class action, grounded on diversity of citizenship, on behalf of certain lake-front property owners and lessees, against an alleged polluter. The named plaintiffs' claims each exceeded the jurisdictional amount of \$10,000. However, the district court and the court of appeals ruled that jurisdiction did not extend to absentees whose claims did not individually satisfy the jurisdictional amount requirement.

On certiorari, the Supreme Court affirmed. Justice White explained that the aggregation rules require "dismissal of those litigants whose [separate and distinct] claims do not satisfy the jurisdictional amount, even though other litigants assert claims sufficient to invoke the jurisdiction of the federal court."

Justice Brennan, joined by Justices Douglas and Marshall, dissented. He argued that ancillary jurisdiction should apply here.

Exxon Mobil Corp. v. Allapattah Services, Inc. (Ortega v. Star–Kist Foods, Inc.)

Supreme Court of the United States, 2005.
545 U.S. 546, 125 S.Ct. 2611.

[In order to resolve a sharp conflict among the courts of appeals, the Supreme Court granted certiorari in two cases.

[In Exxon, 333 F.3d 1248 (11th Cir.2003), several representatives of 10,000 gasoline dealers brought a diversity class action under Rule 23, alleging that Exxon had overcharged them all. The court of appeals affirmed the verdict and judgment for plaintiffs, upholding the exercise of supplemental jurisdiction over the claims of all class members, even though some of absentees' claims did not reach the jurisdictional amount.

[In Ortega, 370 F.3d 124 (1st Cir.2004), also a diversity action, a nine-year-old girl sued a food company, seeking damages for severe injuries from slicing her finger on a tuna can. Her family joined as plaintiffs under Rule 20, seeking damages for emotional distress and certain medical expenses. The court of appeals affirmed the summary judgment for defendant as to the family members, by rejecting the exercise of supplemental jurisdiction over their claims, which did not reach the jurisdictional amount.]

■ JUSTICE KENNEDY delivered the opinion of the Court.

These consolidated cases present the question whether a federal court in a diversity action may exercise supplemental jurisdiction over additional plaintiffs whose claims do not satisfy the minimum amount-in-controversy requirement, provided the claims are part of the same case or controversy as the claims of plaintiffs who do allege a sufficient amount in controversy. Our decision turns on the correct interpretation of 28 U.S.C. § 1367. . . .

We hold that, where the other elements of jurisdiction are present and at least one named plaintiff in the action satisfies the amount-in-controversy requirement, § 1367 does authorize supplemental jurisdiction over the claims of other plaintiffs in the same Article III case or controversy, even if those claims are for less than the jurisdictional amount specified in the statute setting forth the requirements for diversity jurisdiction. . . .

. . . .

. . . No sound canon of interpretation requires Congress to speak with extraordinary clarity in order to modify the rules of federal jurisdiction within appropriate constitutional bounds. Ordinary principles of statutory construction apply. In order to determine the scope of supplemental jurisdiction authorized by § 1367, then, we must examine the statute's text in light of context, structure, and related statutory provisions.

. . . The single question before us, therefore, is whether a diversity case in which the claims of some plaintiffs satisfy the amount-in-controversy requirement, but the claims of other plaintiffs do not, presents a "civil action of which the district courts have original jurisdiction." . . .

We now conclude the answer must be yes. When the well-pleaded complaint contains at least one claim that satisfies the amount-in-controversy requirement, and there are no other relevant jurisdictional defects, the district court, beyond all question, has original jurisdiction over that claim. The presence of other claims in the complaint, over which the district court may lack original jurisdiction, is of no moment. If the court has original jurisdiction over a single claim in the complaint, it has original jurisdiction over a "civil action" within the meaning of § 1367(a), even if the civil action over which it has jurisdiction comprises fewer claims than were included in the complaint. Once the court determines it has original jurisdiction over the civil action, it can turn to the question whether it has a constitutional and statutory basis for exercising supplemental jurisdiction over the other claims in the action.

. . . The terms of § 1367 do not acknowledge any distinction between pendent jurisdiction and the doctrine of so-called ancillary jurisdiction. Though the doctrines of pendent and ancillary jurisdiction developed separately as a historical matter, the Court has recognized that the doctrines are "two species of the same generic problem," [Owen Equip. & Erection Co. v. Kroger, 437 U.S. 365, 370, 98 S.Ct. 2396, 2401 (1978)]. Nothing in § 1367 indicates a congressional intent to recognize, preserve, or create some meaningful, substantive distinction between the jurisdictional categories we have historically labeled pendent and ancillary.

. . . While § 1367(b) qualifies the broad rule of § 1367(a), it does not withdraw supplemental jurisdiction over the claims of the additional parties at issue here. The specific exceptions to § 1367(a) contained in § 1367(b), moreover, provide additional support for our conclusion that § 1367(a) confers supplemental jurisdiction over these claims. Section 1367(b), which applies only to diversity cases, withholds supplemental jurisdiction over the claims of plaintiffs proposed to be joined as indispensable parties under Federal Rule of Civil Procedure 19, or who seek to intervene pursuant to Rule 24. Nothing in the text of § 1367(b), however, withholds supplemental jurisdiction over the claims of plaintiffs permissively joined under Rule 20 (like the additional plaintiffs in [Ortega]) or certified as class-action members pursuant to Rule 23 (like the additional plaintiffs in [Exxon]). The natural, indeed the necessary, inference is that § 1367 confers supplemental jurisdiction over claims by Rule 20 and Rule 23 plaintiffs. This inference, at least with respect to Rule 20 plaintiffs, is strengthened by the fact that § 1367(b) explicitly excludes supplemental jurisdiction over claims against defendants joined under Rule 20.

We cannot accept the view, urged by some of the parties, commentators, and Courts of Appeals, that a district court lacks original jurisdiction over a civil action unless the court has original jurisdiction over every claim in the complaint. As we understand this position, it requires assuming either that all claims in the complaint must stand or fall as a single, indivisible "civil action" as a matter of definitional necessity—what we will refer to as the "indivisibility theory"—or else that the inclusion of a claim or party falling outside the district court's original jurisdiction somehow contaminates every other claim in the complaint, depriving the court of original jurisdiction over any of these claims—what we will refer to as the "contamination theory."

The indivisibility theory is easily dismissed, as it is inconsistent with the whole notion of supplemental jurisdiction. . . .

. . . .

The contamination theory . . . can make some sense in the special context of the complete diversity requirement because the presence of nondiverse parties on both sides of a lawsuit eliminates the justification for providing a federal forum. The theory, however, makes little sense with respect to the amount-in-controversy requirement, which is meant to ensure that a dispute is sufficiently important to warrant federal-court attention. The presence of a single nondiverse party may eliminate the fear of bias with respect to all claims, but the presence of a claim that falls short of the minimum amount in controversy does nothing to reduce the importance of the claims that do meet this requirement.

It is fallacious to suppose, simply from the proposition that § 1332 imposes both the diversity requirement and the amount-in-controversy requirement, that the contamination theory germane to the former is also relevant to the latter. There is no inherent logical connection between the amount-in-controversy requirement and § 1332 diversity jurisdiction. . . .

. . . .

. . . The omission of Rule 20 plaintiffs from the list of exceptions in § 1367(b) may have been an "unintentional drafting gap," Meritcare [Inc. v. St. Paul Mercury Ins. Co., 166 F.3d 214, 221 & n.6 (3d Cir.1999)]. If that is the case, it is up to Congress rather than the courts to fix it. The omission may seem odd, but it is not absurd. . . .

. . . .

And so we circle back to the original question. When the well-pleaded complaint in district court includes multiple claims, all part of the same case or controversy, and some, but not all, of the claims are within the court's original jurisdiction, does the court have before it "any civil action of which the district courts have original jurisdiction"? It does. Under § 1367, the court has original jurisdiction over the civil action comprising the claims for which there is no jurisdictional defect. No other reading of § 1367 is plausible in light of the text and structure of the jurisdictional statute. Though the special nature and purpose of the diversity requirement mean that a single nondiverse party can contaminate every other claim in the lawsuit, the contamination does not occur with respect to jurisdictional defects that go only to the substantive importance of individual claims.

It follows from this conclusion that the threshold requirement of § 1367(a) is satisfied in cases, like those now before us, where some, but not all, of the plaintiffs in a diversity action allege a sufficient amount in controversy. We hold that § 1367 by its plain text overruled . . . Zahn and authorized supplemental jurisdiction over all claims by diverse parties arising out of the same Article III case or controversy, subject only to enumerated exceptions not applicable in the cases now before us.

. . . .

The proponents of the alternative view of § 1367 insist that the statute is at least ambiguous and that we should look to other interpretive tools, including the legislative history of § 1367, which supposedly demonstrate Congress did not intend § 1367 to overrule Zahn. We can reject this argument at the very outset simply because § 1367 is not ambiguous. . . .

. . . .

■ [JUSTICE STEVENS, joined by Justice Breyer, wrote a dissent, which is omitted. He urged greater reliance on the legislative history.]

■ JUSTICE GINSBURG, with whom JUSTICE STEVENS, JUSTICE O'CONNOR, and JUSTICE BREYER join, dissenting.

. . . .

The Court adopts a plausibly broad reading of § 1367, a measure that is hardly a model of the careful drafter's art. There is another plausible reading, however, one less disruptive of our jurisprudence regarding supplemental jurisdiction. If one reads § 1367(a) to instruct, as the statute's text suggests, that the district court must first have "original jurisdiction" over a "civil action" before supplemental jurisdiction can attach, then [cases such as] Zahn are preserved, and supplemental jurisdiction does not open the way for joinder of plaintiffs, or inclusion of class members, who do not independently meet the amount-in-controversy requirement. For the reasons that follow, I conclude that this narrower construction is the better reading of § 1367.

. . . .

. . . § 1367(a) addresses "civil action[s] of which the district courts have original jurisdiction," a formulation that, in diversity cases, is sensibly read to incorporate the rules on joinder and aggregation tightly tied to § 1332 at the time of § 1367's enactment. On this reading, a complaint must first meet that "original jurisdiction" measurement. If it does not, no supplemental jurisdiction is authorized. If it does, § 1367(a) authorizes "supplemental jurisdiction" over related claims. In other words, § 1367(a) would preserve undiminished, as part and parcel of § 1332 "original jurisdiction" determinations, both the "complete diversity" rule and the decisions restricting aggregation to arrive at the amount in controversy. Section 1367(b)'s office, then, would be "to prevent the erosion of the complete diversity [and amount-in-controversy] requirement[s] that might otherwise result from an expansive application of what was once termed the doctrine of ancillary jurisdiction." See Pfander, Supplemental Jurisdiction and Section 1367: The Case for a Sympathetic Textualism, 148 U.Pa.L.Rev. 109, 114 (1999) . . . .

. . .

The less disruptive view I take of § 1367 also accounts for the omission of Rule 20 plaintiffs and Rule 23 class actions in § 1367(b)'s text. . . . [P]laintiffs who do not meet the amount-in-controversy requirement would fail at the § 1367(a) threshold. Congress would have no reason to resort to a § 1367(b) exception to turn such plaintiffs away from federal court, given that their claims, from the start, would fall outside the court's § 1332 jurisdiction. See Pfander, 148 U.Pa.L.Rev., at 148.

. . . .

Question: (17) *P–1* of State *A* sues *D–1* of State *B* and *D–2* of State *B* in a federal district court on a $101,000 claim for which diversity of citizenship is the only basis of jurisdiction. Does the federal court have discretion to hear a related nonfederal claim for $4000 that *P–2* of State *A,* joining under Rule 20, has against *D–1* and *D–2*? In other words, would the presence of multiple defendants put the Ortega situation within the reach of § 1367(b)?

MEASURING THE JURISDICTIONAL AMOUNT

How is the district court to determine whether the case meets any applicable jurisdictional amount requirement? Why not wait until the end of trial to see how much the plaintiff recovers? If instead it is deemed desirable to apply the test at the outset of the case, why not have a hearing to determine the probable recovery? If instead it is deemed desirable to avoid holding a hearing, why not take the plaintiff at his word, as spoken in his ad damnum clause?

SAINT PAUL MERCURY INDEMNITY CO. v. RED CAB CO., 303 U.S. 283, 58 S.Ct. 586 (1938). Red Cab Co. sued St. Paul Mercury Indemnity Co. for failure to pay workers' compensation claims as required by its contract of insurance with Red Cab covering injuries to Red Cab's employees, as a result of which Red Cab allegedly had to pay or obligate itself to pay the sum of $4000. St. Paul removed the case to the federal district court on the basis of diversity of citizenship. Thereafter Red Cab filed an amended complaint still claiming $4000 in damages, but with an attached exhibit that listed the names of the injured employees and the amounts claimed totaling $1380.89. On a trial without jury, the court entered judgment for Red Cab in the amount of $1162.98.

St. Paul appealed on the merits. The court of appeals on its own refused to decide the merits, saying that, as the record showed Red Cab's claim did not exceed the jurisdictional amount of $3000, the district court should have remanded the case to the state court. On certiorari, the Supreme Court reversed. Justice Roberts said:

"The intent of Congress drastically to restrict federal jurisdiction in controversies between citizens of different states has always been rigorously enforced by the courts. The rule governing dismissal for want of jurisdiction in cases brought in the federal court is that, unless the law gives a different rule, the sum claimed by the plaintiff controls if the claim is apparently made in good faith. It must appear to a legal certainty that the claim is really for less than the jurisdictional amount to justify dismissal. The inability of plaintiff to recover an amount adequate to give the court jurisdiction does not show his bad faith or oust the jurisdiction. Nor does the fact that the complaint discloses the existence of a valid defense to the claim. But if, from the face of the pleadings, it is apparent, to a legal certainty, that the plaintiff cannot recover the amount claimed, or if, from the proofs, the court is satisfied to a like certainty that the plaintiff never was entitled to recover that amount, and that his claim was therefore colorable for the purpose of conferring jurisdiction, the suit will be dismissed. Events occurring subsequent to the institution of suit which reduce the amount recoverable below the statutory limit do not oust jurisdiction.

. . . .

"The present case well illustrates the propriety of the rule that subsequent reduction of the amount claimed cannot oust the district court's jurisdiction. Suit was instituted in the state court June 5, 1934. The lump sum claimed was largely in excess of $3,000, exclusive of interest and costs. The items which went to make up the respondent's demand for indemnity were numerous and each, in turn, was itself the total of several items of expenditure or liability. There is nothing to indicate that all of the sums for which reimbursement was claimed had actually been expended prior to the beginning of suit or that the sums thereafter to be expended had been ascertained. Not until the . . . amended complaint was filed in the United States court, in November 1934, did the respondent furnish a statement of the particulars of its claim. That statement is not inconsistent with the making of a claim in good faith for over $3,000 when the suit was instituted."

The much-quoted words of Justice Roberts, and subsequent decisions of the courts pursuant thereto,[h] have made it clear that the "legal certainty" test poses little problem for the plaintiff seeking to invoke federal jurisdiction. Because the jurisdictional amount and the merits overlap, courts ask for no more than a very modest factual showing to establish

[h] For example, "The test of the plaintiff's 'good faith' is not his subjective state of mind but a very strict objective standard. . . . Thus, there is but one test; good faith and legal certainty are equivalents rather than two separate tests." Jones v. Landry, 387 F.2d 102, 104 (5th Cir.1967).

jurisdiction. To satisfy the jurisdictional amount requirement in a diversity case where the plaintiff has pleaded a claim for more than $75,000 against the defendant, the plaintiff needs to be able only to show a legal possibility that the judgment could exceed $75,000 under the applicable *law*. Plaintiffs can pass this test very easily, especially in unliquidated tort cases involving pain and suffering, because jurisdiction will exist even though a recovery over $75,000 is on the *facts* highly unlikely. In order to rebut legal certainty, the plaintiff need establish only that a reasonable fact finder could award more than the jurisdictional amount or, in other words, a reasonable possibility.

Accordingly, given that the amount claimed by the plaintiff will be controlling except in flagrant circumstances, plaintiffs have often greatly inflated their claims for relief in order to circumvent the jurisdictional amount requirement. When Congress increased the amount for diversity cases from $3000 to $10,000 in 1958, it also provided a costs sanction giving the court discretionary power to deny costs to the plaintiff and in addition to impose costs upon him, if he recovered less than $10,000. 28 U.S.C. § 1332(b) (now reflecting later increases of jurisdictional amount). Because courts have used this power very rarely and because costs are not likely to be sizable anyway, this sanction has plainly not deterred plaintiffs' lawyers from making excessive claims in order to get into a federal forum. "The records of the Administrative Office of judgments after trial in diversity cases terminated in the fiscal year 1961 (some few of which were probably filed before the 1958 increase in jurisdictional amount from $3,000 to $10,000 became effective) show that 614 out of 1,268 reported judgments [for plaintiff], 48 per cent of the total, were for less than $10,000, and that the amount of the median judgment in these cases was $3,793. The amount of the median claim in these same cases was $32,200. While it is obvious that there are a good many cases where counsel might reasonably hope for a judgment over $10,000 and obtain one for substantially less than that, it seems clear that the jurisdiction is being abused." ALI Study of the Division of Jurisdiction Between State and Federal Courts 120 (1969).

Question: (18) Would you expect Rule 11 to be effective in this regard?

The case below reflects the widely held concern over the inflation of the claimed amount in controversy. Although it is not an isolated example, we should emphasize that it applies the St. Paul test with much more rigor than the general run of personal-injury actions. It raises the bar, in effect by nudging the standard of proof from a reasonable possibility up to a substantial possibility. The relevant question is whether its approach is desirable and workable.

Nelson v. Keefer

United States Court of Appeals, Third Circuit, 1971.
451 F.2d 289.

■ Before VAN DUSEN, ALDISERT and GIBBONS, CIRCUIT JUDGES.

■ ALDISERT, CIRCUIT JUDGE. These appeals question the propriety of dismissing a personal injury diversity action at pre-trial because the district court concluded that it appeared "to a legal certainty" that the claims were "really for less than the jurisdictional amount" of $10,000.

[The court summarized the damage claims of the three plaintiffs, husband, wife, and minor son, based on the automobile accident. The claims were mostly for injuries such as whiplash, the most substantial claim being the husband's which included questionably related medical bills of $603.50 and also property damage of $727.69.]

It is our intention to require removal from the trial list of those "flagrant" cases where it can be determined in advance "with legal certainty" that the congressional mandate of a $10,000 minimum was not satisfied. . . .

We are not persuaded by the argument that a termination prior to trial deprives a "plaintiff of his present statutory right to a jury trial." See Deutsch v. Hewes Street Realty Corp., [359 F.2d 96, 100 (2d Cir.1966)]. Indeed, such an argument begs the question, for the precise issue is whether plaintiff has a statutory right to enter the courtroom for any trial, jury or otherwise. The corollary suggestion that the remedy lies with Congress is similarly specious, for the reality is that Congress *did* act in 1958 in raising the amount in controversy from $3,000 to $10,000.

. . . .

Given the congressional intention to eliminate trials of unsubstantial diversity cases, and mindful that personal injury actions comprise a majority—at least 60 per cent—of diversity controversies, and that the intangible factor of pain, suffering, and inconvenience usually constitutes the largest single item of damages in personal injury claims, we have no difficulty in concluding that Congress intended that trial judges exercise permissible discretion prior to trial in adjudicating challenges to jurisdiction.

. . . .

Analogizing the authority of the court to reject a jury's verdict [by giving a new trial for its being excessive], we have no difficulty in recognizing a corollary power in that same court to evaluate a case prior to trial where sufficient information has been made available through pre-trial discovery and comprehensive pre-trial narrative statements which disclose medical reports. Assuming that claimed tangible items of damage legally related to the cause of action will be taken as true, the court should be able to determine . . . the "upper limit" of a permissible award that includes tangible recoverable items such as medical special and lost wages damage items as well as the intangibles of pain, suffering, and inconvenience. . . .

. . . .

Our scope of review under these circumstances is similar to that which is utilized in review of a trial court's determination that a verdict is "excessive" or "capricious." [Citations omitted.] Accordingly, although we must "give the benefit of every doubt to the judgment of the trial judge," we must "make a detailed appraisal of the evidence bearing on damages." Having done so, we find that the district court gave plaintiffs ample opportunity, at the pre-trial stage, to justify their jurisdictional claim. Convinced to a legal certainty that the evidence would not permit it to sustain a verdict for plaintiffs of $10,000 or more, the district court did not—and indeed could not—allow the case to proceed to trial.

. . . And since plaintiffs' legally recoverable ceiling did not at its apex reach the federal jurisdictional floor, the judgment of the district court will be affirmed.

Question: (19) *P* seeks an injunction against *D* in a federal district court on the basis of diversity of citizenship. Normally, the amount in controversy in such an action is the value of the relief requested. But what if it is stipulated that the benefit to *P* will be worth less than the jurisdictional amount, but the cost to *D* of complying with the requested relief will be greatly in excess of that figure: is the jurisdictional amount requirement met? What if the benefit to the plaintiff is more than the jurisdictional amount, but the cost to the defendant less? Should it matter whether *P* institutes the action in federal court or *D* brings it there by removal? See Charles Alan Wright & Mary Kay Kane, Law of Federal Courts § 34 (6th ed. 2002).

SECTION 5. DIVERSE CITIZENSHIP

Kramer v. Caribbean Mills, Inc.

Supreme Court of the United States, 1969.
394 U.S. 823, 89 S.Ct. 1487.

■ MR. JUSTICE HARLAN delivered the opinion of the Court.

The sole question presented by this case is whether the Federal District Court in which it was brought had jurisdiction over the cause, or whether that court was deprived of jurisdiction by 28 U.S.C. § 1359. . . .

The facts were these. Respondent Caribbean Mills, Inc. ("Caribbean") is a Haitian corporation. In May 1959 it entered into a contract with an individual named Kelly and the Panama and Venezuela Finance Company ("Panama"), a Panamanian corporation. The agreement provided that Caribbean would purchase from Panama 125 shares of corporate stock, in return for payment of $85,000 down and an additional $165,000 in 12 annual installments.

No installment payments ever were made, despite requests for payment by Panama. In 1964, Panama assigned its entire interest in the 1959 contract to petitioner Kramer, an attorney in Wichita Falls, Texas. The stated consideration was $1. By a separate agreement dated the same day, Kramer promised to pay back to Panama 95% of any net recovery on the assigned cause of action, "solely as a Bonus."

Kramer soon thereafter brought suit against Caribbean for $165,000 in the United States District Court for the Northern District of Texas, alleging diversity of citizenship between himself and Caribbean. The District Court denied Caribbean's motion to dismiss for want of jurisdiction. The case proceeded to trial, and a jury returned a $165,000 verdict in favor of Kramer.

On appeal, the Court of Appeals for the Fifth Circuit reversed, holding that the assignment was "improperly or collusively made" within the meaning of 28 U.S.C. § 1359, and that in consequence the District Court lacked jurisdiction. We granted certiorari, 393 U.S. 819, 89 S.Ct. 99 (1968). For reasons which follow, we affirm the judgment of the Court of Appeals.

[A discussion of statutory predecessors and judicial precedent is omitted.]

. . . When the assignment to Kramer is considered together with his total lack of previous connection with the matter and his simultaneous reassignment of a 95% interest back to Panama, there can be little doubt that the assignment was for purposes of collection, with Kramer to retain 5% of the net proceeds "for the use of his name and his trouble in collecting."[9] If the suit had been unsuccessful, Kramer would have been out only $1, plus costs. Moreover, Kramer candidly admits that "the assignment was in substantial part motivated by a desire by [Panama's] counsel to make diversity jurisdiction available . . . ."

The conclusion that this assignment was "improperly or collusively made" within the meaning of § 1359 is supported not only by precedent but by consideration of the statute's purpose. If federal jurisdiction could be created by assignments of this kind, which are easy to arrange and involve few disadvantages for the assignor, then a vast quantity of ordinary contract and tort litigation could be channeled into the federal courts at the will of one of the parties. Such "manufacture of Federal jurisdiction" was the very thing which Congress intended to prevent when it enacted § 1359 and its predecessors.

Kramer nevertheless argues that the assignment to him was not "improperly or collusively made" within the meaning of § 1359, for two main reasons. First, he suggests that the undisputed legality of the assignment under Texas law necessarily rendered it valid for purposes of federal jurisdiction. We cannot accept this contention. The existence of federal jurisdiction is a matter of federal, not state, law. See, e.g., Missouri P.R. Co. v. Fitzgerald, 160 U.S. 556, 582, 16 S.Ct. 389, 396 (1896). Nothing in the language or legislative history of § 1359 suggests that an assignment

[9] Hence, we have no occasion to re-examine the cases in which this Court has held that where the transfer of a claim is absolute, with the transferor retaining no interest in the subject matter, then the transfer is not "improperly or collusively made," regardless of the transferor's motive. . . .

Nor is it necessary to consider whether, in cases in which suit is required to be brought by an administrator or guardian, a motive to create diversity jurisdiction renders the appointment of an out-of-state representative "improper" or "collusive." . . . [Congress solved this latter, difficult problem in 1988 by enacting § 1332(c)(2).—Ed.]

cannot be "improperly or collusively made" even though binding under state law, and this Court several times has held to the contrary under [a predecessor of § 1359]. Moreover, to accept this argument would render § 1359 largely incapable of accomplishing its purpose; this very case demonstrates the ease with which a party may "manufacture" federal jurisdiction by an assignment which meets the requirements of state law.

Second, Kramer urges that this case is significantly distinguishable from earlier decisions because it involves diversity jurisdiction under 28 U.S.C. § 1332(a)(2), arising from the alienage of one of the parties, rather than the more common diversity jurisdiction based upon the parties' residence in different States. We can perceive no substance in this argument: by its terms, § 1359 applies equally to both types of diversity jurisdiction, and there is no indication that Congress intended them to be treated differently.

In short, we find that this assignment not only falls within the scope of § 1359 but within its very core. It follows that the District Court lacked jurisdiction to hear this action, and that petitioner must seek his remedy in the state courts. The judgment of the Court of Appeals is affirmed.

■ MR. JUSTICE FORTAS took no part in the consideration or decision of this case.

Questions: (20) Recall the Black & White Taxicab case, supra p. 345. Why did the Supreme Court not avoid, by application of the predecessor of § 1359, that unpopular decision upholding diversity jurisdiction? See 14 Wright, Miller & Cooper § 3638.

(21) *P*, a citizen of Maine, sued *D*, an Oregon citizen, in a Maine state court for breach of contract. Before bringing his action *P* had assigned 1/100 of his claim to an Oregon citizen, a law-school classmate of *P*'s attorney, for a consideration of $9. The potential value of the claim was about $300,000. The Oregon assignee joined with *P* as co-plaintiff. *P*'s attorney conceded that the sole purpose of the assignment was to defeat an anticipated removal by destroying . . . diversity of citizenship. *D* removes under 28 U.S.C. § 1441. *P* moves to remand. What decision on that motion? How is this different from the Kramer case? See Ridgeland Box Mfg. Co. v. Sinclair Ref. Co., 82 F.Supp. 274 (E.D.S.C.1949) (remand). But see Grassi v. Ciba–Geigy, Ltd., 894 F.2d 181 (5th Cir.1990) (invoking inherent power to create a kind of converse § 1359 that rejects artificial devices for defeating jurisdiction and that extends beyond the fraudulent joinder doctrine, which traditionally required the defendant to show that the claim involving the party impeding removal was factually or legally frivolous and also was pretextual with intent to deceive).

ROSE v. GIAMATTI, 721 F.Supp. 906 (S.D.Ohio 1989). Pete Rose, manager of the Cincinnati Reds, sued Commissioner of Baseball A. Bartlett Giamatti and two unincorporated associations, Major League Baseball and the Cincinnati Reds. He initiated the suit in Ohio state court upon state law on June 19, 1989, to prevent Giamatti from conducting a hearing into suspicions of Rose's gambling on baseball, with Rose contending that he would otherwise be denied a right to a fair hearing by an unbiased decisionmaker. Defendants removed. Rose moved to remand. On the basis of memoranda and oral argument, with the essential facts not being in dispute, District Judge Holschuh denied that motion on July 31, saying in part:

"Because plaintiff Rose and the defendants Major League Baseball and the Cincinnati Reds are all citizens of Ohio, if either Major League Baseball or the Cincinnati Reds is a party properly joined in this action and whose citizenship, for diversity purposes, cannot be ignored, the lack of diversity of citizenship between plaintiff and all defendants would require the Court to conclude that the removal of the case to this Court was improper. Consequently, the Court must determine whether, as the Commissioner [a citizen of New York] contends, the citizenship of these defendants should be ignored for the purpose of determining whether the removal of this case to this Court was proper.

"It is fundamental law that a plaintiff cannot confer jurisdiction upon the federal court, nor prevent a defendant from removing a case to the federal court on diversity grounds, by plaintiff's own determination as to who are proper plaintiffs and defendants to the action. As Justice Frankfurter said:

> Litigation is the pursuit of practical ends, not a game of chess. Whether the necessary "collision of interests," Dawson v. Columbia Trust Co., [197 U.S. 178,] 181, exists, is therefore not to be determined by mechanical rules. It must be ascertained from the "principal purpose of the suit," East Tennessee, V. & G.R. v. Grayson, 119 U.S. 240, 244, and the "primary and controlling matter in dispute," Merchants' Cotton–Press Co. v. Insurance Co., 151 U.S. 368, 385.

Indianapolis v. Chase National Bank, 314 U.S. 63, 69–70, 62 S.Ct. 15 (1941).

"In considering whether diversity of citizenship exists with respect to the 'principal purpose of the suit,' certain doctrines are well established. First, a plaintiff cannot defeat a defendant's right of removal on the basis of diversity of citizenship by the 'fraudulent joinder' of a non-diverse defendant against whom the plaintiff has no real cause of action. [Citations omitted.]

> The joinder of a resident defendant against whom no cause of action is stated is a patent sham, Parks v. New York Times Co., 5 Cir., 308 F.2d 474, and though a cause of action be stated, the joinder is similarly fraudulent if in fact no cause of action exists, Lobato v. Pay Less Drug Stores, Inc., 10 Cir., 261 F.2d 406.

Dodd v. Fawcett Publications, Inc., 329 F.2d 82, 85 (10th Cir.1964); Roe v. General American Life Ins. Co., 712 F.2d 450, 452 (10th Cir.1983). With respect to this doctrine, the Sixth Circuit has stated:

> In fraudulent joinder cases the underlying reason for removal is that there is no factual basis upon which it can be claimed that the resident defendant is jointly liable or where there is such liability there is no purpose to prosecute the action against the resident defendant in good faith. Wilson v. Republic Iron & Steel Co., 257 U.S. 92, 42 S.Ct. 35, 66 L.Ed. 144. In such cases the assertion of the cause of action against the resident defendant is treated as a sham.

Brady v. Indemnity Ins. Co. of North America, 68 F.2d 302, 303 (6th Cir.1933). Other courts have held that the party opposing remand has the burden of establishing either that there is no possibility that the plaintiff can establish a valid cause of action under state law against the non-diverse defendant, or that there has been an outright fraud in the plaintiff's pleading of jurisdictional facts. E.g., B., Inc. v. Miller Brewing Co., 663 F.2d 545, 549 (5th Cir. Unit A 1981).

"In many cases, removability may be determined from the original pleadings, and normally an allegation of a cause of action against the resident defendant will be sufficient to prevent removal. But when a defendant alleges that there has been fraudulent joinder, the court 'may pierce the pleadings, consider the entire record, and determine the basis of joinder by any means available.' Dodd v. Fawcett Publications, Inc., 329 F.2d at 85 (citations omitted).

"Used in this sense, the term 'fraudulent joinder' is a term of art and is not intended to impugn the integrity of a plaintiff or plaintiff's counsel. Nobers v. Crucible, Inc., 602 F.Supp. 703, 706 (W.D.Pa.1985). Although the doctrine of fraudulent joinder applies to situations in which there has been actual fraud committed in the plaintiff's pleading of jurisdictional facts for the purpose of defeating federal court jurisdiction, the Court emphasizes that there is no allegation of any fraud and no evidence of any fraud on the part of plaintiff or plaintiff's counsel in this case. To the contrary, plaintiff's counsel are highly distinguished attorneys of great integrity who have sincerely and vigorously argued that both the Cincinnati Reds and Major League Baseball are properly joined as defendants and whose citizenship cannot be ignored under any applicable rule of law.

"Second, it is also a long-established doctrine that a federal court, in its determination of whether there is diversity of citizenship between the parties, must disregard nominal or formal parties to the action and determine jurisdiction based only upon the citizenship of the real parties to the controversy. Navarro Savings Ass'n v. Lee, 446 U.S. 458 (1980).

> Early in its history, [the Supreme Court] established that the "citizens" upon whose diversity a plaintiff grounds jurisdiction must be real and substantial parties to the controversy. McNutt v. Bland, 2 How. 9, 15 (1844) . . . .

Id. at 460–61; Salem Trust Co. v. Manufacturers' Finance Co., 264 U.S. 182, 190 (1924). . . . [A] formal or nominal party is one who, in a genuine legal sense, has no interest in the result of the suit, Grant County Deposit Bank v. McCampbell, 194 F.2d 469, 472 (6th Cir.1952); Bedell v. H.R.C.

Ltd., 522 F.Supp. 732, 736 (E.D.Ky.1981), or no actual interest or control over the subject matter of the litigation. Stonybrook Tenants Ass'n, Inc. v. Alpert, 194 F.Supp. 552, 556 (D.Conn.1961).

"While these related governing principles of federal court jurisdiction are clear and not in dispute, the parties strongly disagree as to their application in the present case. But, as Justice Frankfurter stated in the Chase National Bank case:

> As is true of many problems in the law, the answer is to be found not in legal learning but in the realities of the record.

Indianapolis v. Chase National Bank, 314 U.S. at 69. The Court turns, then, to the realities of the record in this case to determine the real parties to this controversy."

The district judge saw the controversy as actually being between Rose and Giamatti, based on Giamatti's conduct. As to the Reds:

"In essence, Rose asserts that the Commissioner's rules of procedure concerning fair disciplinary hearings are incorporated as a part of his employment contract with the Cincinnati Reds, and that any action by Commissioner Giamatti in violation of his own rules of procedure would constitute a breach of Rose's contract with the Cincinnati Reds. It is Rose's position that the Cincinnati Reds owes him a contractual duty to see that the procedural rules are not violated, and that if Giamatti violates these rules by holding an unfair hearing and, as a result, sanctions Rose, the Reds will have failed in its duty and will have breached his contract. . . .

. . . .

". . . [T]here is nothing in the Major League Agreement, the Major League Rules, or in Rose's contract with the Cincinnati Reds which gives the Reds any right to prevent the Commissioner from holding a disciplinary hearing or to interfere with proceedings within the jurisdiction of the Commissioner. . . .

". . . Rose's argument that any violation by Giamatti of the Commissioner's own procedural rules would somehow constitute an automatic breach of Rose's contract with the Cincinnati Reds is without legal basis.

"It is undeniable that the Cincinnati Reds has, as a practical matter, an interest in the outcome of these proceedings, but not in the legal sense that requires its joinder as a defendant in this action. . . . [T]here is no real controversy between these parties. The Court concludes that, for the purpose of determining diversity of citizenship, the defendant Cincinnati Reds was, in a legal sense, fraudulently joined as a defendant and that it is, at best, a nominal party in this action."

As to Major League Baseball, the district judge likewise found no legal basis for suit. Here this defendant could not control and was not responsible for the acts of the highly independent Commissioner, who had broad delegated authority to investigate any activity not in the best interests of baseball. The judge added that any involvement of the major league clubs in enforcing any sanction imposed by the Commissioner lay in the future, and was not the subject of this action.

Therefore, this case was to stay in federal court. That result prompted Rose and Giamatti to settle on August 23, 1989, on terms providing for Rose's lifetime ban from baseball but with opportunity to apply for reinstatement.

Question: (22) *P* of State *A* sues *D* of State *B* in a court of State *A* on a state-law claim for $70,000. *D* removes to the federal court under 28 U.S.C. § 1441, believing that P seeks big damages and knowing that state law permits recovery in excess of the amount demanded except in default cases. *P* moves to remand. What decision on that motion? See Kevin M. Clermont & Theodore Eisenberg, CAFA Judicata: A Tale of Waste and Politics, 156 U.Pa.L.Rev. 1553, 1569–79 (2008).

SECTION 6. REMOVAL JURISDICTION

Question: (23) *P* of Delaware sues *D* of Texas in a Delaware state court on a state-law claim for $4000. *D* counterclaims for $101,000. *D* removes to the federal court under 28 U.S.C. § 1441. *P* moves to remand. What decision on that motion? Should it matter whether or not *D*'s counterclaim arises out of the same transaction or occurrence as *P*'s claim? If so, should it matter whether or not Delaware has a compulsory counterclaim provision like Rule 13(a)? See Kevin M. Clermont, Principles of Civil Procedure 208 (2d ed. 2009).

SHAMROCK OIL & GAS CORP. v. SHEETS, 313 U.S. 100, 61 S.Ct. 868 (1941). *P* of Delaware sued *D* of Texas in a Texas state court on a contract claim for more than the federal jurisdictional amount. As was permitted by Texas law, *D* counterclaimed on a wholly unrelated contract claim also in excess of the jurisdictional amount. *P* immediately removed to the federal district court on the basis of diversity of citizenship. *D* moved to remand. The district court denied that motion, and after trial it gave judgment for *P* on the claim and the counterclaim. The Fifth Circuit reversed, ordering the case remanded to state court.

On certiorari the Supreme Court affirmed the court of appeals' decision, on the basis that 28 U.S.C. § 1441(a) speaks of removal "by the defendant or the defendants" and it means what it says. The Court implied that it was irrelevant whether the counterclaim was compulsory or permissive under state law, and whether or not the counterclaim was factually related to the main claim. Indeed, the Court went out of its way to say that its conclusion that plaintiffs cannot remove was independent of whether the main claim was for more or less than the jurisdictional amount.

Questions: (24) Does the Shamrock reading of § 1441(a) make any sense? See ALI Study of the Division of Jurisdiction Between State and Federal Courts §§ 1304(c), 1312(a)(3) commentary at 147–48, 196–97 (1969).

(25) Could *P* instead have promptly dismissed the initial claim voluntarily, then quickly removed the remaining counterclaim as a defendant, and finally repleaded the initial claim as a counterclaim in federal court?

REMOVAL UNDER 28 U.S.C. § 1441(c)

This narrow and difficult statute allows removal of a claim within the general federal question statute, when joined with a separate and independent claim that would otherwise be nonremovable. That is, the defendants to the original plaintiffs' federal question claim can remove even though the plaintiffs have joined a claim completely unrelated on the facts that those defendants could not have removed if it stood by itself.

Given such joinder, the entire case becomes removable. For example, if *P* sues *D* in a state court on a federal civil rights claim and joins a completely unrelated contract claim against *D*, *D* can remove the whole case. So, § 1441(c) provides a slim opportunity to remove a case not removable under § 1441(a) because the whole case is not within the federal district court's original jurisdiction.

Question: (26) If *P* of State *A* sues *D–1* of State *B* in a court of State *A* on a federal civil rights claim and joins a completely unrelated contract claim for $200,000 against *D–1* and *D–2,* also of State *B,* and if *D–1* but not *D–2* wishes to remove, can *D–1* properly do so? See Fravel v. Stankus, 936 F.Supp. 474, 479 (N.D.Ill.1996) (yes).

Once the entire case comes before it via § 1441(c), the federal district court may remand those matters as to which state law predominates. Indeed, in the usual situation of a completely unrelated state claim not within the court's original jurisdiction, the district court must remand that claim and thus avoid any constitutional problem of entertaining a claim otherwise outside Article III—at least, this is the view expressed in the 1990 amendment's legislative history, which brushed aside many of the theoretical hesitancies generated during the long and convoluted history of § 1441(c). 136 Cong.Rec. S17,581 (daily ed. Oct. 27, 1990) (section-by-section analysis of Sen. Grassley); accord, Fullin v. Martin, 34 F.Supp.2d 726, 729–35 (E.D.Wis.1999).

The wording of the statute's current version nevertheless presents numerous other difficulties. Think, for example, of *P* suing *D* in a state court on a FELA claim and joining a completely unrelated small contract claim against *D*. Although § 1441(c) literally applies, its application would contravene 28 U.S.C. § 1445(a). Thus, § 1441(c) must mean that the entire case is removable only if the federal question claim "would be removable if sued upon alone," as the statute provided before the 1990 amendment.

Questions: (27) *P* sues *D* in a state court on a federal civil rights claim and joins a completely unrelated FELA claim against *D*. Can *D* properly remove despite § 1445(a)? See Dibble v. Grand Trunk W.R.R., 699 F.Supp. 123 (E.D.Mich.1988) (yes). If so, can the district court remand the FELA claim under § 1441(c)?

(28) *P* sues *D* in a state court on a federal civil rights claim and joins a completely unrelated workers' compensation claim against *D* under that state's law. Can *D* properly remove the case despite § 1445(c)? If so, must the district court remand the state-law claim?

Difficulties of a different type lie in who may invoke § 1441(c). Think, for example, of *P* suing *D* in a state court on a small contract claim and *D* counterclaiming with a completely unrelated federal civil rights claim. Can *P* now avoid the Shamrock rule by invoking § 1441(c)? The cases hold in the negative, although the statute does not obviously require that result. More generally, despite a close policy call in the circumstances of some additional claims, courts tend to read § 1441(c) narrowly as not applying to claims other than those joined by original plaintiffs against original defendants, even when the counterclaim, crossclaim, or third-party claim is arguably separate and independent. See 14C Wright, Miller & Cooper § 3724, at 33–34, 40–50.

Question: (29) *P* sues *D* in a state court on a small contract claim. *D* impleads *T* on an indemnity claim and, under the state equivalent of Rule 18(a), joins a completely unrelated federal civil rights claim against *T*. Can *T* properly remove? See Haden P. Gerrish, Note, Third–Party Removal Under Section 1441(c), 52 Fordham L.Rev. 133, 156–58 (1983) (arguing yes, but only in this most extreme setting).

Finally, § 1441(c) apparently now interlocks with supplemental, or pendent, jurisdiction to provide for removal of almost any federal question case. Consider a plaintiff's federal question claim that would be removable if sued upon alone, joined with an ordinary state claim against the defendant who is nondiverse. On the one hand, if the state claim falls within pendent jurisdiction, the federal and state claims being factually related, then the defendant can remove the whole case under § 1441(a). On the other hand, if the state claim does not come within pendent jurisdiction, then § 1441(c) should kick in. And, under the best view, if the plaintiff joins (1) the federal question claim, (2) the pendent state claim, and (3) the separate and independent state claim, the defendant can remove under § 1441(c), although the court must remand the third claim and, pursuant to § 1441(c), it may remand the second claim for relief with its discretion guided by the standards of 28 U.S.C. § 1367(c).

This statute is enough of a mess that the American Law Institute has proposed a rewrite, which "parallels" current law. ALI Federal Judicial Code Revision Project § 1441(c) (2004) would provide: "If a civil action is not removable under subsection (a) solely because a claim that is removable on the basis of the jurisdiction conferred by section 1331 of this title has been joined to a nonremovable claim that is not part of the same case or controversy under Article III of the Constitution, any such nonremovable claim shall be disregarded and the entire action may be removed as provided by subsection (a). Upon such removal the district court shall sever from the action all claims that are not part of the same case or controversy as the claim that is removable under section 1331, and shall remand the severed claims to the State court from which the action was removed."

CARNEGIE–MELLON UNIVERSITY v. COHILL, 484 U.S. 343, 108 S.Ct. 614 (1988). Based on an allegedly wrongful termination of employment, plaintiffs sued co-citizen defendants in Pennsylvania state court under federal and state age-discrimination laws and on various contract and tort theories. Defendants properly removed under § 1441(a), utilizing the doctrine of pendent jurisdiction. Plaintiffs did not contest removal, but six months later they (1) moved to amend their complaint by deleting certain untenable allegations, including age discrimination, and (2) moved, conditional upon that amendment, to remand. The district court granted both motions. The sharply divided Third Circuit denied a petition for mandamus.

On certiorari to resolve a conflict among circuits, the Supreme Court affirmed, upholding the power to remand. Justice Marshall for the Court acknowledged that neither 28 U.S.C. § 1447(c) nor § 1441(c) applied to give that power, but he explained that pendent jurisdiction itself entails discretion to decline jurisdiction by *dismissing* the removed case in some circumstances and hence implies the discretionary power to *remand* in such circumstances. Thus, when the federal claim that justifies removal is eliminated, the district court can remand the remaining pendent state claims to the state court in pursuit of "economy, convenience, fairness, and comity."

Justice White, joined by Chief Justice Rehnquist and Justice Scalia, dissented by arguing in support of the general rule that Congress must have statutorily authorized remand.

Borough of West Mifflin v. Lancaster

United States Court of Appeals, Third Circuit, 1995.
45 F.3d 780.

■ Before STAPLETON, GARTH, and PRATT,* CIRCUIT JUDGES.

■ PRATT, CIRCUIT JUDGE:

* Honorable George C. Pratt, United States Circuit Judge for the Second Circuit, sitting by designation.

FACTS AND BACKGROUND

The operative facts giving rise to this mandamus application are set forth in the civil complaint of respondents Alan D. Lindsey and Randall Coughanour. In September 1991 Lindsey and Coughanour were involved in disputes with security guards at an indoor shopping mall on Route 51 in West Mifflin Borough, just south of Pittsburgh, Pa. They had travelled to the mall to shop, but upon their arrival, they were "harassed, threatened, and assaulted" by the security guards. When the guards refused their request that the police be summoned, Lindsey and Coughanour themselves telephoned the West Mifflin Police Department requesting assistance. West Mifflin Police Officer Evan, one of the petitioners in this mandamus application, responded to the call. Evan refused to arrest or admonish any of the guards, but told Lindsey and Coughanour to leave the mall and never come back; otherwise, they would be arrested.

The following day, Lindsey returned to the mall in an attempt to talk to someone from the DeBartolo organization, which owned the mall, to find out why he had been accosted and why he was not permitted on the mall without permission. During the next three weeks Lindsey repeatedly and unsuccessfully attempted to contact Sam Vindovich, the mall manager, one of the defendants in the underlying action, to find out why he and Coughanour were banned from the mall. Lindsey finally consulted his present counsel, who advised him that the law permitted his entrance to the mall as long as the mall was open to the public.

On September 27, 1991, Lindsey and Coughanour returned to the mall to shop, but were accosted and handcuffed in the mall men's room, and then dragged through the mall corridor to mall offices to await the arrival of Officer Evan.

Evan then wrote out summary offense citations for disorderly conduct and defiant trespass. Lindsey and Coughanour were photographed by a Polaroid camera, and the photographs were attached to printed forms that said "DEFIANT TRESPASS". These paper forms contained, among other things a warning that, if Lindsey and Coughanour came onto the mall property again, they would be arrested. These preprinted forms were then displayed on a bulletin board in the mall at the security offices for everyone passing in front of the board to see.

The handcuffs were then removed, and Lindsey and Coughanour were ordered to leave the mall, separately, which they did. They were prosecuted and convicted in Common Pleas Court on charges stemming from the incidents at the mall, but on February 26, 1993, a three judge panel of the Superior Court of Pennsylvania vacated the convictions and discharged them.

Lindsey and Coughanour then filed a seven count complaint in the Court of Common Pleas of Allegheny County, Pennsylvania, claiming that they had committed no crimes while at the mall and that they had been maliciously abused and prosecuted. As defendants, they named the Borough of West Mifflin and Officer Evan ("the municipal defendants"), . . . as well as the owners, supervisors, and security officers of the mall ("the DeBartolo defendants"). Specifically, Lindsey and Coughanour alleged: (1) state law claims of malicious prosecution, malicious abuse of process, assault, and conspiracy against all defendants; (2) a negligence claim against the municipal defendants; (3) a negligence claim against the DeBartolo defendants; and (4) a federal claim under 42 U.S.C. § 1983 which alleged that the municipal defendants and the DeBartolo defendants conspired to deprive Lindsey and Coughanour of their civil rights through harassment, assault, false arrest, malicious prosecution, and abuse of process in violation of the 4th, 5th, and 14th amendments.

Relying on the federal civil rights claim, the . . . defendants filed a notice of removal from the state court to the United States District Court for the Western District of Pennsylvania. Lindsey and Coughanour then moved to remand the case back to state court. Magistrate Judge Kenneth J. Benson recommended a remand under 28 U.S.C. § 1441(c) of the entire case, including the § 1983 claim. He found that

> [t]he issues of state law clearly predominate in this matter. Not only do they predominate with respect to the state law claims, but there is also a predominance of state law issues with respect to the single claim pursuant to § 1983.

United States District Judge Gary L. Lancaster adopted the report and recommendation "as the opinion of the court" and entered a two page Memorandum and Order granting Lindsey and Coughanour's motion to remand the entire case.

The . . . defendants now seek in this court a writ of mandamus to compel Judge Lancaster to accept jurisdiction of this action, which, they contend, was properly removed under § 1441(a) and (b). They argue that by remanding the entire case under § 1441(c), Judge Lancaster exceeded his authority.

DISCUSSION

. . . .

The dispute on this mandamus application focuses on the effect of subdivision (c) of § 1441. . . .

. . . .

In the present case, the district court relied upon the [1990] addition which reads "the district court may . . . remand all matters in which State law predominates" to remand the entire case, including the § 1983 claim, to state court. It did so without regard for the requirement, which the Congress left unchanged when it amended § 1441(c), that the federal cause of action removed by the municipal defendants had to be "separate and independent" from the state causes of action.

Thus, § 1441(c) provides for removal or remand *only* where the federal question claims are "separate and independent" from the state law claims with which they are joined in the complaint. However, where there is a single injury to plaintiff for which relief is sought, arising from an interrelated series of events or transactions, there is no separate or independent claim or cause of action under § 1441(c). American Fire & Casualty Co. v. Finn, 341 U.S. 6, 71 S.Ct. 534, 95 L.Ed. 702 (1951). Suits involving pendent (now "supplemental") state claims that "derive from a common nucleus of operative fact", see United Mine Workers v. Gibbs, 383 U.S. 715, 725, 86 S.Ct. 1130, 1138, 16 L.Ed.2d 218 (1966), do not fall within the scope of § 1441(c), since pendent claims are not "separate and independent". Carnegie–Mellon University v. Cohill, 484 U.S. 343, 354, 108 S.Ct. 614, 621, 98 L.Ed.2d 720 (1988).

It is apparent, then, that "§ 1441(c) grants the district court only a limited authority to remand a case." Kabealo v. Davis, 829 F.Supp. 923, 926 (S.D.Ohio 1993) (citing to Buchner v. F.D.I.C., 981 F.2d 816 (5th Cir.1993)). . . .

. . . Other district courts have apparently read the 1990 amendments as broadening rather than narrowing the scope of their discretion to remand. We cannot agree.

. . . .

. . . Lindsey and Coughanour rely on the same series of events for all counts of their complaint, including the federal § 1983 count; therefore, the federal claim is not separate and independent under § 1441(c), and the district court had no authority to remand the case under that section.

. . . .

The plaintiffs insist that, even if the district court was not authorized to remand this entire case under § 1441(c), its action should be sustained under the authority of 28 U.S.C. § 1367(c) which gives a district court discretion to decline to hear certain state claims it would have supplemental jurisdiction to entertain under § 1367(a). We disagree for two reasons. First, nothing in § 1367(c) authorizes a district court to decline to entertain a claim over which it has original jurisdiction and, accordingly, that section clearly does not sanction the district court's remand of this entire case, including the civil rights claims, to the state court.

Further, § 1367(c) cannot legitimately be invoked to affirm even the district court's remand of the state claims to the state court. While we agree with plaintiffs that the discretion bestowed by § 1367(c) exists with respect to removed claims as well as claims filed initially in the district court, it is apparent that the district court has not exercised that discretion in this case. The magistrate judge's opinion, adopted by the district court, refers only to § 1441(c) and it is apparent from that opinion that the court remanded the entire case based solely on the authority of that section. Moreover, the result of an exercise of discretion under § 1367(c) in circumstances like those before the district court would have been two parallel proceedings, one in federal court and one in the state system, and a district court cannot properly exercise its discretion under § 1367(c) without taking that fact into account. The district court's § 1441(c) analysis accordingly cannot serve as a surrogate for a § 1367(c) analysis that was not conducted.

. . . .

As we have noted, the "substantially predominates" standard of § 1367(c)(2) comes from Gibbs. It is important to recognize that this standard was fashioned as a limited exception to the operation of the doctrine of pendent jurisdiction—a doctrine that seeks to promote judicial economy, convenience, and fairness to litigants by litigating in one case all claims that arise out of the same nucleus of operative fact. When a district court exercises its discretion not to hear state claims under § 1367(c)(2), the advantages of a single suit are lost. For that reason, § 1367(c)(2)'s authority should be invoked only where there is an important countervailing interest to be served by relegating state claims to the state court. This will normally be the case only where "a state claim constitutes the real body of a case, to which the federal claim is only an appendage," Gibbs, 383 U.S. at 727, 86 S.Ct. at 1140—only where permitting litigation of all claims in the district court can accurately be described as allowing a federal tail to wag what is in substance a state dog.

. . . .

In short, while we do not foreclose the parties from hereafter arguing, and the district court from hereafter considering, the issue posed by § 1367(c)(2), we think it unlikely that either will be able to point to a countervailing interest that would justify bifurcating this case into a federal and a state suit that will essentially duplicate each other.

. . . .

Accordingly, the petition for a writ of mandamus is granted.

SECTION 7. HYPOTHETICAL JURISDICTION

Ruhrgas AG v. Marathon Oil Co.

Supreme Court of the United States, 1999.
526 U.S. 574, 119 S.Ct. 1563.

■ JUSTICE GINSBURG delivered the opinion of the Court.

This case concerns the authority of the federal courts to adjudicate controversies. Jurisdiction to resolve cases on the merits requires both authority over the category of claim in suit (subject-matter jurisdiction) and authority over the parties (personal jurisdiction), so that the court's decision will bind them. In Steel Co. v. Citizens for Better Environment, 523 U.S. 83, 118 S.Ct. 1003 (1998), this Court adhered to the rule that a federal court may not hypothesize subject-matter jurisdiction for the purpose of deciding the merits. Steel Co. rejected a doctrine, once approved by several Courts of Appeals, that allowed federal tribunals to pretermit jurisdictional objections "where (1) the merits question is more readily resolved, and (2) the prevailing party on the merits would be the same as the prevailing party were jurisdiction denied." Id., at 93, 118 S.Ct. 1003. Recalling "a long and venerable line of our cases," id., at 94, 118 S.Ct. 1003, Steel Co. reiterated: "The requirement that jurisdiction be established as a threshold matter . . . is 'inflexible and without exception,' " id., at 94–95, 118 S.Ct. 1003 (quoting Mansfield, C. & L.M.R. Co. v. Swan, 111 U.S. 379, 382, 4 S.Ct. 510 (1884)); for "[j]urisdiction is power to declare the law," and " '[w]ithout jurisdiction the court cannot proceed at all in any cause,' " 523 U.S., at 94, 118 S.Ct. 1003 (quoting Ex parte McCardle, 7 Wall. 506, 514 (1868)). The Court, in Steel Co., acknowledged that "the absolute purity" of the jurisdiction-first rule had been diluted in a few extraordinary cases, 523 U.S., at 101, 118 S.Ct. 1003, and Justice O'Connor, joined by Justice Kennedy, joined the majority on the understanding that the Court's opinion did not catalog "an exhaustive list of circumstances" in which exceptions to the solid rule were appropriate, id., at 110, 118 S.Ct. 1003.

Steel Co. is the backdrop for the issue now before us: If, as Steel Co. held, jurisdiction generally must precede merits in dispositional order, must subject-matter jurisdiction precede personal jurisdiction on the decisional line? Or, do federal district courts have discretion to avoid a difficult question of subject-matter jurisdiction when the absence of personal jurisdiction is the surer ground? The particular civil action we confront was commenced in state court and removed to federal court. The specific question on which we granted certiorari asks "[w]hether a federal district court is absolutely barred in all circumstances from dismissing a removed case for lack of personal jurisdiction without first deciding its subject-matter jurisdiction." Pet. for Cert. i.

We hold that in cases removed from state court to federal court, as in cases originating in federal court, there is no unyielding jurisdictional hierarchy. Customarily, a federal court first resolves doubts about its jurisdiction over the subject matter, but there are circumstances in which a district court appropriately accords priority to a personal jurisdiction inquiry. The proceeding before us is such a case.

I

The underlying controversy stems from a venture to produce gas in the Heimdal Field of the Norwegian North Sea. In 1976, respondents Marathon Oil Company and Marathon International Oil Company acquired Marathon Petroleum Company (Norway) (MPCN) and respondent Marathon Petroleum Norge (Norge). See App. 26.[1] Before the acquisition, Norge held a license to produce gas in the Heimdal Field; following the transaction, Norge assigned the license to MPCN. . . . In 1981, MPCN contracted to

[1] Ruhrgas is a German corporation; Norge is a Norwegian corporation. See App. 21, 22. Marathon Oil Company, an Ohio corporation, and Marathon International Oil Company, a Delaware corporation, moved their principal places of business from Ohio to Texas while the venture underlying this case was in formation. . . . [As a signatory to the Heimdal Gas Agreement, MPCN's claims were subject to binding arbitration in Europe.—Ed.]

sell 70% of its share of the Heimdal gas production to a group of European buyers, including petitioner Ruhrgas AG. . . .

II

Marathon Oil Company, Marathon International Oil Company, and Norge (collectively, Marathon) filed this lawsuit against Ruhrgas in Texas state court on July 6, 1995, asserting state-law claims of fraud, tortious interference with prospective business relations, participation in breach of fiduciary duty, and civil conspiracy. See App. 33–40. Marathon Oil Company and Marathon International Oil Company alleged that Ruhrgas and the other European buyers induced them with false promises of "premium prices" and guaranteed pipeline tariffs to invest over $300 million in MPCN for the development of the Heimdal Field and the erection of a pipeline to Ruhrgas' plant in Germany. . . . Norge alleged that Ruhrgas' effective monopolization of the Heimdal gas diminished the value of the license Norge had assigned to MPCN. . . . Marathon asserted that Ruhrgas had furthered its plans at three meetings in Houston, Texas, and through a stream of correspondence directed to Marathon in Texas. . . .

Ruhrgas removed the case to the District Court for the Southern District of Texas. See 145 F.3d 211, 214 (C.A.5 1998). In its notice of removal, Ruhrgas asserted three bases for federal jurisdiction: diversity of citizenship, see 28 U.S.C. § 1332 (1994 ed. and Supp. III), on the theory that Norge, the only nondiverse plaintiff, had been fraudulently joined; federal question, see § 1331, because Marathon's claims "raise[d] substantial questions of foreign and international relations, which are incorporated into and form part of the federal common law," App. 274; and 9 U.S.C. § 205, which authorizes removal of cases "relat[ing] to" international arbitration agreements. . . . Ruhrgas moved to dismiss the complaint for lack of personal jurisdiction. Marathon moved to remand the case to the state court for lack of federal subject-matter jurisdiction. . . .

After permitting jurisdictional discovery, the District Court dismissed the case for lack of personal jurisdiction [on the ground that Ruhrgas had constitutionally insufficient contacts with Texas].

A panel of the Court of Appeals for the Fifth Circuit concluded that "respec[t]" for "the proper balance of federalism" impelled it to turn first to "the formidable subject matter jurisdiction issue presented." 115 F.3d [315, 318 (5th Cir.1997)]. After examining and rejecting each of Ruhrgas' asserted bases of federal jurisdiction . . . , the Court of Appeals vacated the judgment of the District Court and ordered the case remanded to the state court . . . . This Court denied Ruhrgas' petition for a writ of certiorari, which was limited to the question whether subject-matter jurisdiction existed under 9 U.S.C. § 205. See 522 U.S. 967, 118 S.Ct. 413 (1997).

The Fifth Circuit, on its own motion, granted rehearing en banc, thereby vacating the panel decision. See 129 F.3d 746 (C.A.5 1997). In a 9–to–7 decision, the en banc court held that, in removed cases, district courts must decide issues of subject-matter jurisdiction first, reaching issues of personal jurisdiction "only if subject-matter jurisdiction is found to exist." 145 F.3d, at 214. . . .

We granted certiorari, 525 U.S. 1039, 119 S.Ct. 589 (1998), to resolve a conflict between the Circuits and now reverse.

III

Steel Co. held that Article III generally requires a federal court to satisfy itself of its jurisdiction over the subject matter before it considers the merits of a case. "For a court to pronounce upon [the merits] when it has no jurisdiction to do so," Steel Co. declared, "is . . . for a court to act ultra vires." 523 U.S., at 101–102, 118 S.Ct. 1003. The Fifth Circuit incorrectly read Steel Co. to teach that subject-matter jurisdiction must be found to exist, not only before a federal court reaches the merits, but also before personal jurisdiction is addressed. See 145 F.3d, at 218.

A

The Court of Appeals accorded priority to the requirement of subject-matter jurisdiction because it is nonwaivable and delimits federal-court power, while restrictions on a court's jurisdiction over the person are waivable and protect individual rights. See id., at 217–218. The character of the two jurisdictional bedrocks unquestionably differs. Subject-matter limitations on federal jurisdiction serve institutional interests. They keep the federal courts within the bounds the Constitution and Congress have prescribed. Accordingly, subject-matter delineations must be policed by the courts on their own initiative even at the highest level. See Steel Co., 523 U.S., at 94–95, 118 S.Ct. 1003; Fed.Rule Civ.Proc. 12(h)(3) ("Whenever it appears . . . that the court lacks jurisdiction of the subject matter, the court shall dismiss the action."); 28 U.S.C. § 1447(c) (1994 ed., Supp. III) ("If at any time before final judgment [in a removed case] it appears that the district court lacks subject matter jurisdiction, the case shall be remanded.").

Personal jurisdiction, on the other hand, "represents a restriction on judicial power . . . as a matter of individual liberty." Insurance Corp. of Ireland v. Compagnie des Bauxites de Guinee, 456 U.S. 694, 702, 102 S.Ct. 2099 (1982). Therefore, a party may insist that the limitation be observed, or he may forgo that right, effectively consenting to the court's exercise of adjudicatory authority. See Fed.Rule Civ.Proc. 12(h)(1) (defense of lack of jurisdiction over the person waivable); Insurance Corp. of Ireland, 456 U.S., at 703, 102 S.Ct. 2099 (same).

These distinctions do not mean that subject-matter jurisdiction is ever and always the more "fundamental." Personal jurisdiction, too, is "an essential element of the jurisdiction of a district . . . court," without which the court is "powerless to proceed to an adjudication." Employers Reinsurance Corp. v. Bryant, 299 U.S. 374, 382, 57 S.Ct. 273 (1937). In this case, indeed, the impediment to subject-matter jurisdiction on which Marathon relies—lack of complete diversity—rests on statutory interpretation, not constitutional command. Marathon joined an alien plaintiff (Norge) as well as an alien defendant (Ruhrgas). If the joinder of Norge is legitimate, the . . . diversity required by 28 U.S.C. § 1332 (1994 ed. and Supp. III), but not by Article III, see State Farm Fire & Casualty Co. v. Tashire, 386 U.S. 523, 530–531, 87 S.Ct. 1199 (1967), is absent. In contrast, Ruhrgas relies on the constitutional safeguard of due process to stop the court from proceeding to the merits of the case. See Insurance Corp. of Ireland, 456 U.S., at 702, 102 S.Ct. 2099 ("The requirement that a court have personal jurisdiction flows . . . from the Due Process Clause.").

While Steel Co. reasoned that subject-matter jurisdiction necessarily precedes a ruling on the merits, the same principle does not dictate a sequencing of jurisdictional issues. "[A] court that dismisses on . . . non-merits grounds such as . . . personal jurisdiction, before finding subject-matter jurisdiction, makes no assumption of law-declaring power that violates the separation of powers principles underlying Mansfield and Steel Company." In re Papandreou, 139 F.3d 247, 255 (C.A.D.C.1998). It is hardly novel for a federal court to choose among threshold grounds for denying audience to a case on the merits. Thus, as the Court observed in Steel Co., district courts do not overstep Article III limits when they decline jurisdiction of state-law claims on discretionary grounds without determining whether those claims fall within their pendent jurisdiction, see Moor v. County of Alameda, 411 U.S. 693, 715–716, 93 S.Ct. 1785 (1973), or abstain under Younger v. Harris, 401 U.S. 37, 91 S.Ct. 746 (1971), without deciding whether the parties present a case or controversy, see Ellis v. Dyson, 421 U.S. 426, 433–434, 95 S.Ct. 1691 (1975). See Steel Co., 523 U.S., at 100–101, n. 3, 118 S.Ct. 1003; cf. Arizonans for Official English v. Arizona, 520 U.S. 43, 66–67, 117 S.Ct. 1055 (1997) (pretermitting challenge to appellants' standing and dismissing on mootness grounds).

B

Maintaining that subject-matter jurisdiction must be decided first even when the litigation originates in federal court . . . , Marathon sees removal as the more offensive case, on the ground that the dignity of state courts is immediately at stake. If a federal court dismisses a removed case for want of personal jurisdiction, that determination may preclude the parties from relitigating the very same personal jurisdiction issue in state court. See Baldwin v. Iowa State Traveling Men's Assn., 283 U.S. 522, 524–527, 51 S.Ct. 517 (1931) (personal jurisdiction ruling has issue-preclusive effect).

Issue preclusion in subsequent state-court litigation, however, may also attend a federal court's subject-matter determination. . . .

Most essentially, federal and state courts are complementary systems for administering justice in our Nation. Cooperation and comity, not competition and conflict, are essential to the federal design. A State's dignitary interest bears consideration when a district court exercises discretion in a case of this order. If personal jurisdiction raises "difficult questions of [state] law," and subject-matter jurisdiction is resolved "as eas[ily]" as personal jurisdiction, a district court will ordinarily conclude that "federalism concerns tip the scales in favor of initially ruling on the motion to remand." Allen v. Ferguson, 791 F.2d 611, 616 (C.A.7 1986). In other cases, however, the district court may find that concerns of judicial economy and restraint are overriding. See, e.g., Asociacion Nacional de Pescadores v. Dow Quimica, 988 F.2d 559, 566–567 (C.A.5 1993) (if removal is nonfrivolous and personal jurisdiction turns on federal constitutional issues, "federal intrusion into state courts' authority . . . is minimized"). The federal design allows leeway for sensitive judgments of this sort. . . .

The Fifth Circuit and Marathon posit that state-court defendants will abuse the federal system with opportunistic removals. A discretionary rule, they suggest, will encourage manufactured, convoluted federal subject-matter theories designed to wrench cases from state court. . . . This specter of unwarranted removal, we have recently observed, "rests on an assumption we do not indulge—that district courts generally will not comprehend, or will balk at applying, the rules on removal Congress has prescribed. . . . The well-advised defendant . . . will foresee the likely outcome of an unwarranted removal—a swift and nonreviewable remand order, see 28 U.S.C. §§ 1447(c), (d), attended by the displeasure of a district court whose authority has been improperly invoked." Caterpillar Inc. v. Lewis, 519 U.S. 61, 77–78, 117 S.Ct. 467 (1996).

C

. . . [W]e recognize that in most instances subject-matter jurisdiction will involve no arduous inquiry. See 145 F.3d, at 229 ("engag[ing]" subject-matter jurisdiction "at the outset of a case . . . [is] often . . . the most efficient way of going"). In such cases, both expedition and sensitivity to state courts' coequal stature should impel the federal court to dispose of that issue first. See Cantor Fitzgerald, L.P. v. Peaslee, 88 F.3d 152, 155 (C.A.2 1996) (a court disposing of a case on personal jurisdiction grounds "should be convinced that the challenge to the court's subject-matter jurisdiction is not easily resolved"). Where, as here, however, a district court has before it a straightforward personal jurisdiction issue presenting no complex question of state law, and the alleged defect in subject-matter jurisdiction raises a difficult and novel question, the court does not abuse its discretion by turning directly to personal jurisdiction.

* * *

For the reasons stated, the judgment of the Court of Appeals is reversed, and the case is remanded for proceedings consistent with this opinion.

It is so ordered.[i]

SCOTT C. IDLEMAN, THE EMERGENCE OF JURISDICTIONAL RESEQUENCING IN THE FEDERAL COURTS, 87 Cornell L.Rev. 1, 31–35, 97–98 (2001). "[O]ne of the most critical premises in Ruhrgas is that personal jurisdiction is materially as *essential* as subject-matter jurisdiction

[i] On remand, the court of appeals affirmed the district court's finding of a lack of personal jurisdiction, 182 F.3d 291 (5th Cir.1999). Under res judicata law, a finding of no jurisdiction does not produce a valid judgment and so should not be binding in another action, except to defeat jurisdiction in any attempt to sue again in a court where the same jurisdictional issue arises. The court has authority to determine its lack of authority, and so for that latter limited purpose the judgment is a valid one. See Michael J. Edney, Comment, Preclusive Abstention:

to a court's power to decide cases. Yet the Court arrives at this premise—and the conclusion that personal jurisdiction can be decided first—not by unearthing and comparing the theoretical elements of each type of jurisdiction, but simply by proclaiming it to be true. . . .

"Consider again, however, the starkness of these distinctions between subject-matter and personal jurisdiction. The former is a nonwaivable, structural limitation on a court's power to act at all; the latter, a waivable, personal liberty interest that merely limits a court's ability to bind a particular defendant with the otherwise valid exercise of judicial power. . . . Thus, while '[a] judge has no power to decide a case over which he lacks subject-matter jurisdiction, . . . he *can* decide a case though he lacks personal jurisdiction over the defendant, if the defendant waives the issue of personal jurisdiction.' To be sure, courts regularly describe their relationship to subject-matter jurisdiction in hortatory terms—noting 'their nondelegable duty to police the limits of federal jurisdiction with meticulous care,' their 'independent, constitutional obligation to protect the jurisdictional limits of the federal courts,' and 'the duty of the federal courts to assure themselves that their jurisdiction is not being exceeded'—while characterizing the requirements of personal jurisdiction as 'merely the[] personal privileges' of the parties, or collectively as 'an individual right,' or as 'procedural requirements' or 'affirmative defenses' akin to the interposition of a statute of limitations. In turn, one would think that the Court might be interested in *why* each type of jurisdiction bears different characteristics and whether these reasons indicate anything about their respective importance.

"Perhaps the most significant consideration in this regard, which the Ruhrgas Court neither noted nor explored, is the respective constitutional source of each jurisdictional requirement. Subject-matter jurisdiction ultimately derives from Article III, although its affirmation, particularly in the lower courts, is typically by statute. As such, subject-matter jurisdiction is properly characterized as an *internal* limitation on the existence of federal judicial power and thus the sovereignty of the federal government. In turn, without subject-matter jurisdiction, a federal court is entirely without power to adjudicate a dispute, irrespective of the parties' wishes. Personal jurisdiction, by comparison, is essentially the exercise of jurisdiction over a particular defendant as long as such exercise complies with the Fifth Amendment Due Process Clause. Personal jurisdiction, accordingly, is best characterized as an *external* limitation on the exercise of federal judicial power, without which a court is simply precluded from binding the defendant absent some form of consent. Personal jurisdiction, in other words, 'represents a restriction on judicial power not as a matter of sovereignty, but as a matter of individual liberty.'

"This distinction is important in at least two respects, one of judicial practice, the other of constitutional theory. First, as a matter of standard

---

Issue Preclusion and Jurisdictional Dismissals After Ruhrgas, 68 U.Chi.L.Rev. 193, 216–20 (2001) (addressing the preclusive effect of a federal court's dismissal for lack of jurisdiction). Accordingly, the federal judgment in Ruhrgas's favor would preclude later suit in a Texas state court, just as Justice Ginsburg suggested.

judicial practice, challenges premised on the internal limits on federal power ought, analytically, to precede challenges premised on the external limits on the same, assuming that the parties have presented both and that the court must address at least one. The more fundamental question, after all, is whether the federal government has the power to act in the first place, not whether its exercise of this alleged power, if it even exists, happens to transgress an external limitation. Second, this respective sequencing of internal and external power issues reflects the more basic principle that maintaining the limited nature of federal authority is, along with federalism and the separation of powers, more theoretically central to American constitutionalism than the imposition of external limits, such as due process, on the exercise of federal power otherwise delegated. In the day-to-day existence of citizens, of course, the latter is no less important and often may seem to be the Constitution's raison d'être. By their office and tenure, however, judges are obligated to view the Constitution in its architectural totality, drawing upon the historical events and philosophical understandings that gave rise to it and that have sustained its integrity over time. This is particularly true where, as in Ruhrgas, the ultimate question is not one of individual liberty as such, but rather of federal judicial power. And from this architectural perspective, it is clear not only that structural features—such as the principles of internally limited federal power, the separation of powers, and federalism—are at the core of American constitutionalism, but that the protection of liberty is, in the first instance, very much tied to their maintenance.

"To be sure, it is primarily the different constitutional sources underlying the two jurisdictional forms that explain the distinctive characteristics of each form, characteristics which the Court itself noted but inexplicably deemed irrelevant. . . .

. . . .

"The emerging power of federal courts to resequence threshold inquiries equips these tribunals with a relatively novel and potentially useful means of dispatching ill-fated lawsuits without becoming entangled in difficult jurisdictional questions, thereby promising a facilitated and more efficient use of judicial resources. In theory, the resequencing option may apply to any threshold inquiry that satisfies the initial condition of equivalence with subject-matter jurisdiction, based on a finding that the inquiry is both an essential and a constitutional prerequisite to the exercise of judicial power.[j] If a court finds equivalence, then the final resequencing decision is largely within its discretion, contingent on the relative difficulty of the resequencible issues and informed by the values of economy, restraint, and federalism.

"To embrace this doctrine at face value, however, would be to ignore the fact that the resequencing power itself raises many serious questions about the sources, nature, and limits of federal jurisdictional authority."

[j] The resequencing option extends to reach some lower-level inquiries. See Sinochem Int'l Co. v. Malay. Int'l Shipping Corp., 549 U.S. 422, 127 S.Ct. 1184 (2007) (forum non conveniens); In re LimitNone, LLC, 551 F.3d 572 (7th Cir.2008) (transfer of venue).

TOPIC B

TERRITORIAL AUTHORITY TO ADJUDICATE

SECTION 1. THE FRAMEWORK

Pennoyer v. Neff

Supreme Court of the United States, 1878.
95 U.S. 714.

[Marcus Neff, an illiterate young settler, reached Oregon by wagon train in 1848. He homesteaded a 320–acre plot in what is now Portland. For some reason, perhaps in connection with perfecting his title to the land, he consulted a Portland attorney during 1862–1863. Neff moved on to California, and prosperity, sometime thereafter.

[That attorney was John H. Mitchell. Suffice it to say that this was a man of scandalous private life and questionable professional ethics. Neither trait impeded his election in 1872 to the United States Senate, where he was again serving at the time of his 1905 conviction for corruption. For intriguing detail on the dramatis personae, see Wendy C. Perdue, Sin, Scandal, and Substantive Due Process: Personal Jurisdiction and Pennoyer Reconsidered, 62 Wash.L.Rev. 479 (1987).

[At any rate, Mitchell sued Neff in Oregon state court, claiming $253.14 as allegedly unpaid fees for those legal services. He commenced suit by filing his complaint on November 3, 1865. He properly laid venue in the Circuit Court of the State of Oregon for the County of Multnomah.

[Service presented an obvious problem, as Neff was apparently an absent nonresident who would not be voluntarily appearing. Mitchell reasonably read Oregon's ambiguous statutory scheme as authorizing his action upon service by publication. So on November 13, 1865, Mitchell applied for an order of service by publication, with the required supporting affidavit stating in its entirety:

> I, J.H. Mitchell, plaintiff, being first duly sworn, say that the defendant, Marcus Neff, is a non-resident of this state; that he resides somewhere in the State of California, at what place affiant knows not, and he cannot be found in this state. That plaintiff has a just cause of action against defendant for a money demand on account. That this court has jurisdiction of such action. That the defendant has property in this county and state.

On that same date, the court ordered service of the summons by publication for six weeks successively in the Pacific Christian Advocate, a weekly newspaper published in Multnomah County with a denominational circulation inside Oregon and practically none outside Oregon. Mitchell complied, and he filed the required proof of service in the form of an affidavit by the paper's editor.

[Naturally enough, Neff defaulted. The result, without further evidence, was a judgment for Mitchell on February 19, 1866, in the amount of $294.98, which reflected the demand plus interest and costs. Mitchell now had a judgment, but no remedy as yet. So he went after Neff's Portland land by a writ of execution. At the resulting execution sale on August 7, 1866, Mitchell himself bought the land for $341.60.

[On August 10, 1866, Mitchell assigned his interest in the land to one Sylvester Pennoyer "for value received." Pennoyer, Harvard Law School '54, was another Portland resident. Incidentally, he went on in 1886 to become a populist Governor of Oregon, widely and somewhat charitably characterized as an eccentric one.

[The bottom line here was that by Mitchell's lawsuit for under $300—a lawsuit of which Neff had no idea—a very valuable piece of property came into Pennoyer's hands. So much for Action #1, and on to Action #2 concerning that land.

[Much later and in Oregon federal court, Neff sued Pennoyer in ejectment. On September 10, 1874, he filed his complaint, which alleged diversity jurisdiction in this action by a California citizen against an Oregon citizen to recover possession of wrongfully withheld land worth $15,000. He sued in the Circuit Court of the United States for the District of Oregon, which was then the appropriate federal trial court and which sat in Portland. Its distinguished judge was Matthew P. Deady, who had been the primary author of the Oregon Code of Civil Procedure and who despised Mitchell.

[On September 12, 1874, the deputy marshal served summons and complaint by personal delivery on Pennoyer in Portland. Pennoyer promptly answered, denying Neff's title and right to possession and alleging his own good title and right to possession. Neff replied by denying Pennoyer's title and right to possession, and hence by implication collaterally attacking the earlier judgment.

[The parties having stipulated to a nonjury trial, the court tried the case on September 24–25, 1874. Neff proved his patent to the land, and then he rested. Pennoyer, over Neff's objections, established the basics as to the earlier case by showing complaint, summons, order of publication, editor's affidavit, judgment, execution, assignment, and title documents, and then he rested. Neff, over Pennoyer's objection, introduced Mitchell's affidavit from that earlier case, and then both rested.

[Upon this evidence, the outcome turned on the success of the collateral attack. Here Neff argued most fervently that the state court had been exercising neither personal jurisdiction over him nor nonpersonal jurisdiction over his land, and he also argued that Mitchell's and the editor's affidavits had been faulty. The parties thereafter submitted briefs. Therein, on the key jurisdictional point, Neff argued that pre-judgment seizure of the property had been necessary for judicial power, while Pennoyer argued that Mitchell's procedural steps had been adequate to give jurisdiction over the land.

[In 1875, Judge Deady decided the case. His opinion quickly agreed with Pennoyer that jurisdiction over the land had been available, on the theory that Oregon could and did choose to exercise nonpersonal jurisdiction with only a post-judgment seizure of in-state property. Nevertheless, he ruled for Neff because of defects in the affidavits, after lengthy exposition along the following lines. Mitchell's affidavit had violated the Oregon Code's required method of showing due diligence, in that it offered no evidence at all that Mitchell had exercised any diligence in ascertaining Neff's residence, knowledge of which would have facilitated notice. The editor's affidavit had likewise violated the Code, in that proof of publication had to be made by someone literally involved in the printing process, who would likely have had personal knowledge of the fact of actual publication. Collateral attack on these grounds would have been possible in an Oregon court, and therefore the Oregon federal court did not owe full faith and credit to this judgment of a state court lacking jurisdiction. Mitchell's judgment and Pennoyer's title were accordingly void. Therefore, Judge Deady ruled, Neff was entitled to recover possession from Pennoyer, plus costs.]

■ [In 1877, Pennoyer proceeded to the Supreme Court by writ of error. JUSTICE STEPHEN J. FIELD, a champion of substantive due process, delivered the opinion of the Court. After a very brief rendition of the facts and prior proceedings, he continued:]

The Code of Oregon provides for such service [by publication] when an action is brought against a non-resident and absent defendant, who has property within the State. It also provides, where the action is for the recovery of money or damages, for the attachment of the property of the non-resident. And it also declares that no natural person is subject to the jurisdiction of a court of the State, "unless he appear in the court, or be found within the State, or be a resident thereof, or have property therein; and, in the last case, only to the extent of such property at the time the jurisdiction attached." Construing this latter provision to mean, that, in an action for money or damages where a defendant does not appear in the court, and is not found within the State, and is not a resident thereof, but has property therein, the jurisdiction of the court extends only over such property, the declaration expresses a principle of general, if not universal, law. The authority of every tribunal is necessarily restricted by the territorial limits of the State in which it is established. Any attempt to exercise authority beyond those limits would be deemed in every other forum, as has been said by this court, an illegitimate assumption of power, and be resisted as mere abuse. D'Arcy v. Ketchum et al., 11 How. 165. In the case against the plaintiff, the property here in controversy sold under the judgment rendered was not attached nor in any way brought under the jurisdiction of the court. Its first connection with the case was caused by a levy of the execution. It was not, therefore, disposed of pursuant to any adjudication, but only in enforcement of a personal judgment, having no relation to the property, rendered against a non-resident without service of process upon him in the action, or his appearance therein. The court below did not consider that an attachment of the property was essential to its jurisdiction or to the validity of the sale, but held that the judgment was invalid from defects in the affidavit upon which the order of publication was obtained, and in the affidavit by which the publication was proved.

There is some difference of opinion among the members of this court as to the rulings upon these alleged defects. The majority are of opinion that inasmuch as the statute requires, for an order of publication, that certain facts shall appear by affidavit *to the satisfaction of the court or judge,* defects in such affidavit can only be taken advantage of on appeal, or by some other direct proceeding, and cannot be urged to impeach the judgment collaterally. The majority of the court are also of opinion that the provision of the statute requiring proof of the publication in a newspaper to be made by the "affidavit of the printer, or his foreman, or his principal clerk," is satisfied when the affidavit is made by the editor of the paper. The term "printer," in their judgment, is there used not to indicate the person who sets up the type . . . .

If, therefore, we were confined to the rulings of the court below upon the defects in the affidavits mentioned, we should be unable to uphold its decision. But it was also contended in that court, and is insisted upon here, that the judgment in the State court against the plaintiff was void for want of personal service of process on him, or of his appearance in the action in which it was rendered, and that the premises in controversy could not be subjected to the payment of the demand of a resident creditor except by a proceeding in rem; that is, by a direct proceeding against the property for that purpose. If these positions are sound, the ruling of the Circuit Court as to the invalidity of that judgment must be sustained, notwithstanding our dissent from the reasons upon which it was made. And that they are sound would seem to follow from two well-established principles of public law respecting the jurisdiction of an independent State over persons and property. The several States of the Union are not, it is true, in every respect independent, many of the rights and powers which originally belonged to them being now vested in the government created by the Constitution. But, except as restrained and limited by that instrument, they possess and exercise the authority of independent States, and the principles of public law to which we have referred are applicable to them. One of these principles is, that every State possesses exclusive jurisdiction and sovereignty over persons and property within its territory. As a consequence, every State has the power to determine for itself the civil status and capacities of its inhabitants; to prescribe the subjects upon which they may contract, the forms and solemnities with which their contracts shall be executed, the rights and obligations arising from them, and the mode in which their validity shall be determined and their obligations enforced; and also to regulate the manner and conditions upon which property situated within such territory, both personal and real, may be acquired, enjoyed, and transferred. The other principle of public law referred to follows from the one mentioned; that is, that no State can exercise direct jurisdiction and authority over persons or property without its territory. Story, Confl.Laws, c. 2; Wheat, Int.Law, pt. 2, c. 2. . . .

But as contracts made in one State may be enforceable only in another State, and property may be held by non-residents, the exercise of the jurisdiction which every State is admitted to possess over persons and property within its own territory will often affect persons and property without it. To any influence exerted in this way by a State affecting persons resident or property situated elsewhere, no objection can be justly taken; whilst any direct exertion of authority upon them, in an attempt to give ex-territorial operation to its laws, or to enforce an ex-territorial jurisdiction by its tribunals, would be deemed an encroachment upon the independence of the State in which the persons are domiciled or the property is situated, and be resisted as usurpation.

Thus the State, through its tribunals, may compel persons domiciled within its limits to execute, in pursuance of their contracts respecting property elsewhere situated, instruments in such form and with such solemnities as to transfer the title, so far as such formalities can be complied with; and the exercise of this jurisdiction in no manner interferes with the supreme control over the property by the State within which it is situated. [Citations omitted.]

So the State, through its tribunals, may subject property situated within its limits owned by non-residents to the payment of the demand of its own citizens against them; and the exercise of this jurisdiction in no respect infringes upon the sovereignty of the State where the owners are domiciled. Every State owes protection to its own citizens; and, when non-residents deal with them, it is a legitimate and just exercise of authority to hold and appropriate any property owned by such non-residents to satisfy the claims of its citizens. It is in virtue of the State's jurisdiction over the property of the non-resident situated within its limits that its tribunals can inquire into that non-resident's obligations to its own citizens, and the inquiry can then be carried only to the extent necessary to control the disposition of the property. If the non-resident have no property in the State, there is nothing upon which the tribunals can adjudicate.

. . . .

. . . If, without personal service, judgments in personam, obtained ex parte against non-residents and absent parties, upon mere publication of process, which, in the great majority of cases, would never be seen by the parties interested, could be upheld and enforced, they would be the constant instruments of fraud and oppression. Judgments for all sorts of claims upon contracts and for torts, real or pretended, would be thus obtained, under which property would be seized, when the evidence of the transactions upon which they were founded, if they ever had any existence, had perished.

Substituted service by publication, or in any other authorized form, may be sufficient to inform parties of the object of proceedings taken where property is once brought under the control of the court by seizure or some equivalent act. The law assumes that property is always in the possession of its owner, in person or by agent; and it proceeds upon the theory that its seizure will inform him, not only that it is taken into the custody of the court, but that he must look to any proceedings authorized by law upon such seizure for its condemnation and sale. Such service may also be sufficient in cases where the object of the action is to reach and dispose of property in the State, or of some interest therein, by enforcing a contract or a lien respecting the same, or to partition it among different owners, or, when the public is a party, to condemn and appropriate it for a public purpose. In other words, such service may answer in all actions which are substantially proceedings in rem. . . . Process from the tribunals of one State cannot run into another State, and summon parties there domiciled to leave its territory and respond to proceedings against them. Publication of process or notice within the State where the tribunal sits cannot create any greater obligation upon the non-resident to appear. . . .

The want of authority of the tribunals of a State to adjudicate upon the obligations of non-residents, where they have no property within its limits, is not denied by the court below; but the position is assumed, that, where they have property within the State, it is immaterial whether the property is in the first instance brought under the control of the court by attachment or some other equivalent act, and afterwards applied by its judgment to the satisfaction of demands against its owner; or such demands be first established in a personal action, and the property of the non-resident be afterwards seized and sold on execution. But the answer to this position has already been given in the statement, that the jurisdiction of the court to inquire into and determine his obligations at all is only incidental to its jurisdiction over the property. Its jurisdiction in that respect cannot be made to depend upon facts to be ascertained after it has tried the cause and rendered the judgment. If the judgment be previously void, it will not become valid by the subsequent discovery of property of the defendant, or by his subsequent acquisition of it. The judgment, if void when rendered, will always remain void: it cannot occupy the doubtful position of being valid if property be found, and void if there be none. Even if the position assumed were confined to cases where the non-resident defendant possessed property in the State at the commencement of the action, it would still make the validity of the proceedings and judgment depend upon the question whether, before the levy of the execution, the defendant had or had not disposed of the property. If before the levy the property should be sold, then, according to this position, the judgment would not be binding. This doctrine would introduce a new element of uncertainty in judicial proceedings. The contrary is the law: the validity of every judgment depends upon the jurisdiction of the court before it is rendered, not upon what may occur subsequently. . . .

The force and effect of judgments rendered against non-residents without personal service of process upon them, or their voluntary appearance, have been the subject of frequent consideration in the courts of the United States and of the several States, as attempts have been made to enforce such judgments in States other than those in which they were rendered, under the provision of the Constitution requiring that "full faith and credit shall be given in each State to the public acts, records, and judicial proceedings of every other State;" and the act of Congress providing for the mode of authenticating such acts, records, and proceedings, and declaring that, when thus authenticated, "they shall have such faith and credit given to them in every court within the United States as they have by law or usage in the courts of the State from which they are or shall be taken."[a] In the earlier cases, it was supposed that the act gave to all judgments the same effect in other States which they had by law in the State where rendered. But this view was afterwards qualified so as to make the act applicable only when the court rendering the judgment had jurisdiction of the parties and of the subject-matter, and not to preclude an inquiry into the jurisdiction of the court in which the judgment was rendered, or the right of the State itself to exercise authority over the person or the subject-matter. . . .

. . . In all the cases brought in the State and Federal courts, where attempts have been made under the act of Congress to give effect in one State to personal judgments rendered in another State against non-residents, without service upon them, or upon substituted service by publication, or in some other form, it has been held, without an exception, so far as we are aware, that such judgments were without any binding force, except as to property, or interests in property, within the State, to reach and affect which was the object of the action in which the judgment was rendered, and which property was brought under control of the court in connection with the process against the person. The proceeding in such cases, though in the form of a personal action, has been uniformly treated, where service was not obtained, and the party did not voluntarily appear, as effectual and binding merely as a proceeding in rem, and as having no operation beyond the disposition of the property, or some interest therein. . . .

. . . In several of the cases, the decision has been accompanied with the observation that a personal judgment thus recovered has no binding force without the State in which it is rendered, implying that in such State it may be valid and binding. But if the court has no jurisdiction over the person of the defendant by reason of his non-residence, and, consequently, no authority to pass upon his personal rights and obligations; if the whole proceeding, without service upon him or his appearance, is coram non judice and void; if to hold a defendant bound by such a judgment is contrary to the first principles of justice,—it is difficult to see how the judgment can legitimately have any force within the State. The language used can be justified only on the ground that there was no mode of directly reviewing such judgment or impeaching its validity within the State where rendered; and that, therefore, it could be called in question only when its

[a] Now 28 U.S.C. § 1738.

enforcement was elsewhere attempted. In later cases, this language is repeated with less frequency than formerly, it beginning to be considered, as it always ought to have been, that a judgment which can be treated in any State of this Union as contrary to the first principles of justice, and as an absolute nullity, because rendered without any jurisdiction of the tribunal over the party, is not entitled to any respect in the State where rendered. [State citations omitted.]

Be that as it may, the courts of the United States are not required to give effect to judgments of this character when any right is claimed under them. Whilst they are not foreign tribunals in their relations to the State courts, they are tribunals of a different sovereignty, exercising a distinct and independent jurisdiction, and are bound to give to the judgments of the State courts only the same faith and credit which the courts of another State are bound to give to them.

Since the adoption of the Fourteenth Amendment to the Federal Constitution,[b] the validity of such judgments may be directly questioned, and their enforcement in the State resisted, on the ground that proceedings in a court of justice to determine the personal rights and obligations of parties over whom that court has no jurisdiction do not constitute due process of law. Whatever difficulty may be experienced in giving to those terms a definition which will embrace every permissible exertion of power affecting private rights, and exclude such as is forbidden, there can be no doubt of their meaning when applied to judicial proceedings. They then mean a course of legal proceedings according to those rules and principles which have been established in our systems of jurisprudence for the protection and enforcement of private rights. To give such proceedings any validity, there must be a tribunal competent by its constitution—that is, by the law of its creation—to pass upon the subject-matter of the suit; and, if that involves merely a determination of the personal liability of the defendant, he must be brought within its jurisdiction by service of process within the State, or his voluntary appearance.

Except in cases affecting the personal status of the plaintiff [such as marital status], and cases in which that mode of service may be considered to have been assented to in advance [as where a non-resident doing business in the state actually or constructively appoints an in-state agent to receive service], . . . the substituted service of process by publication, allowed by the law of Oregon and by similar laws in other States, where actions are brought against non-residents, is effectual only where, in connection with process against the person for commencing the action, property in the State is brought under the control of the court, and subjected to its disposition by a process adapted to that purpose, or where the judgment is sought as a means of reaching such property or affecting some interest therein; in other words, where the action is in the nature of a proceeding in rem. . . .

---

[b] The date of the concurrent resolution of Congress declaring the Fourteenth Amendment a part of the Constitution, following its ratification by the state legislatures, was July 21, 1868.

It is true that, in a strict sense, a proceeding in rem is one taken directly against property, and has for its object the disposition of the property, without reference to the title of individual claimants; but, in a larger and more general sense, the terms are applied to actions between parties, where the direct object is to reach and dispose of property owned by them, or of some interest therein. Such are cases commenced by attachment against the property of debtors, or instituted to partition real estate, foreclose a mortgage, or enforce a lien. So far as they affect property in the State, they are substantially proceedings in rem in the broader sense which we have mentioned.

It is hardly necessary to observe, that in all we have said we have had reference to proceedings in courts of first instance, and to their jurisdiction, and not to proceedings in an appellate tribunal to review the action of such courts. The latter may be taken upon such notice, personal or constructive, as the State creating the tribunal may provide. They are considered as rather a continuation of the original litigation than the commencement of a new action. [Citation omitted.]

It follows from the views expressed that the personal judgment recovered in the State court of Oregon against the plaintiff herein, then a non-resident of the State, was without any validity, and did not authorize a sale of the property in controversy.

. . . .

Judgment affirmed.

■ [The dissenting opinion of JUSTICE HUNT is omitted. He argued that, as recognized in existing statutory and case law, a state could constitutionally allow a plaintiff to sue any defendant for damages and then levy on any of the latter's property in the state, as long as the defendant received reasonable notice and opportunity to be heard.]

CLOSSON v. CHASE, 158 Wis. 346, 149 N.W. 26 (1914). In an action on promissory notes, where the plaintiff claimed no pre-existing lien on or interest in any property of the nonresident defendant, the plaintiff proceeded by an action against the defendant's Wisconsin land. The relevant Wisconsin statute provided: "Service of the summons may be made without the state or by publication upon a defendant against whom a cause of action appears to exist . . . on obtaining an order therefor . . . in . . . the following cases: (1) When such defendant is a nonresident of this state . . . and . . . has property within the state . . . ." The attorney's affidavit supporting such service stated "that the defendant was the owner of real estate within this state" and then described the land. The court ordered service by publication upon the defendant.

Upon the defendant's subsequent challenge to this procedure, the appellate court said in part:

"The issuance of a writ of attachment and levy upon property thereunder is not essential to competency to make service on a defendant by publication. Gallun v. Weil, 116 Wis. 236, 92 N.W. 1091. The statutory requisite of property of the defendant within this state, existing and duly brought to the attention of the court, is all that is necessary in respect to the property feature. Such an action is regarded as one in rem. The judgment when rendered is good only against the property described in the moving papers. . . . It is the res within the jurisdiction of the court that is essential to jurisdiction, not actual seizure of it, or even constructive seizure, unless description of the property in the [action's] moving papers and [the therein] recorded purpose of the plaintiff to burden it with payment of the debt should be regarded as such seizure. Jarvis v. Barrett, 14 Wis. 591; Winner v. Fitzgerald, 19 Wis. 393; Disconto Gesellschaft v. Terlinden, 127 Wis. 651, 106 N.W. 821.

"The foregoing sufficiently answers, if any be necessary, after express and implied approval of the statute in question for more than sixty years, the suggestion that it is unconstitutional under the doctrine of Pennoyer v. Neff, 95 U.S. 714."

SECTION 2. JURISDICTION OVER THINGS—TRADITIONAL THEORY

(a) NATURE OF SUCH JURISDICTION

Tyler v. Judges of the Court of Registration

Supreme Judicial Court of Massachusetts, 1900.
175 Mass. 71, 55 N.E. 812, writ of error dismissed, 179 U.S. 405, 21 S.Ct. 206 (1900).

■ HOLMES, C.J. This is a petition for a writ of prohibition against the judges of the Court of Registration established by St.1898, c. 562, and is brought to prevent their proceeding upon an application [In re Application of Gould] concerning land in which the petitioner claims an interest. The ground of the petition is that the act establishing the court is unconstitutional. Two reasons are urged against the act, both of which are thought to go to the root of the statute and to make action under it impossible. The first and most important is that the original registration deprives all persons except the registered owner of any interest in the land without due process of law. There is no dispute that the object of the system, expressed in § 38, is that the decree of registration "shall bind the land and quiet the title thereto," and "shall be conclusive upon and against all persons," whether named in the proceedings or not, subject to few and immaterial exceptions. And this being admitted, it is objected that there is no sufficient process against, or notice to, persons having adverse claims, in a proceeding intended to bar their possible rights.

The application for registration is to be in writing and signed and sworn to. It is to contain an accurate description of the land, to set forth clearly other outstanding estates or interests known to the petitioner, to identify the deed by which he obtained title, to state the name and address of the occupant if there is one, and also to give the names and addresses so far as known of the [owners and] occupants of all lands adjoining. § 21. As soon as it is filed, a memorandum containing a copy of the description of the land concerned is to be filed in the registry of deeds. § 20. The case is immediately referred to an examiner (appointed by the judge, § 12), who makes as full an investigation as he can and reports to the court. § 29. If in the opinion of the examiner the applicant has a good title as alleged, or if the applicant after an adverse opinion elects to proceed further, the recorder is to publish a notice by order of the court in some newspaper published in the district where any portion of the land lies. This notice is to be addressed by name to all persons known to have an adverse interest, and to the adjoining owners and occupants so far as known, and to all whom it may concern. It is to contain a description of the land, the name of the applicant, and the time and place of the hearing. § 31. A copy is to be mailed to every person named in the notice whose address is known, and a duly attested copy is to be posted in a conspicuous place on each parcel of land included in the application, by a sheriff or deputy sheriff, fourteen days at least before the return day. Further notice may be ordered by the court. § 32.

It will be seen that the notice is required to name all persons known to have an adverse interest, and this of course includes any adverse claim, whether admitted or denied, that may have been discovered by the examiner, or in any way found to exist. Taking this into account, we should construe the requirement in § 21 concerning the application, as calling upon the applicant to mention not merely outstanding interests which he admits, but equally all claims of interest set up although denied by him. We mention this here to dispose of an objection of detail urged by the petitioner, and we pass to the general objection that, however construed, the mode of notice does not satisfy the Constitution . . . .

If it does not satisfy the Constitution, a judicial proceeding to clear titles against all the world hardly is possible, for the very meaning of such a proceeding is to get rid of unknown as well as known claims,—indeed certainty against the unknown may be said to be its chief end,—and unknown claims cannot be dealt with by personal service upon the claimant. It seems to have been the impression of the Supreme Court of Ohio, in the case most relied upon by the petitioner, that such a judicial proceeding is impossible in this country. State v. Guilbert, 56 Ohio St. 575, 629, 47 N.E. 551. But we cannot bring ourselves to doubt that the Constitutions of the United States and of Massachusetts at least permit it as fully as did the common law. Prescription or a statute of limitations may give a title good against the world and destroy all manner of outstanding claims without any notice or judicial proceeding at all. Time and the chance which it gives the owner to find out that he is in danger of losing rights are due process of law in that case. . . .

. . . .

Looked at either from the point of view of history or of the necessary requirements of justice, a proceeding in rem dealing with a tangible res may be instituted and carried to judgment without personal service . . . and not encounter any provision of either Constitution. Jurisdiction is secured by the power of the court over the res. As we have said, such a proceeding would be impossible, were this not so, for it hardly would do to make a distinction between the constitutional rights of claimants who were known and those who were not known to the plaintiff, when the proceeding is to bar all. Pennoyer v. Neff, 95 U.S. 714, 727. [Other citations omitted.] In Hamilton v. Brown, 161 U.S. 256, 16 S.Ct. 585, a judgment of escheat was held conclusive upon persons notified only by advertisement to all persons interested. It is true that the statute under consideration required the petition to name all known claimants, and personal service to be made on those so named. But that did the plaintiffs no good, as they were not named. So a decree allowing or disallowing a will binds everybody, although the only notice of the proceedings given be a general notice to all persons interested. And in this case, as in that of escheat just cited, the conclusive effect of the decree is not put upon the ground that the State has an absolute power to determine the persons to whom a man's property shall go at his death, but upon the characteristics of a proceeding in rem. Bonnemort v. Gill, 167 Mass. 338, 340, 45 N.E. 768. See 161 U.S. 256, 263, 274, 16 S.Ct. 585. Admiralty proceedings need only to be mentioned in this connection, and further citation of cases seems unnecessary.

Speaking for myself, I see no reason why what we have said as to proceedings in rem in general should not apply to such proceedings concerning land. [Chief Justice Oliver Wendell Holmes suggested that for proceedings in rem, notice by publication sufficed.]

But it is said that this is not a proceeding in rem. It is certain that no phrase has been more misused. In the past it has had little more significance than that the right alleged to have been violated was a right in rem. Austin thinks it necessary to quote Leibnitz for the sufficiently obvious remark that every right to restitution is a right in personam. So as to actions. If the technical object of the suit is to establish a claim against some particular person, with a judgment which generally, in theory at least, binds his body, or to bar some individual claim or objection, so that only certain persons are entitled to be heard in defence, the action is in personam, although it may concern the right to or possession of a tangible thing. Mankin v. Chandler, 2 Brock. 125, 127, Fed.Cas. No. 9,030. If, on the other hand, the object is to bar indifferently all who might be minded to make an objection of any sort against the right sought to be established, and if any one in the world has a right to be heard on the strength of alleging facts which, if true, show an inconsistent interest, the proceeding is in rem. Freem. Judgments, (4th ed.) § 606 ad fin. All proceedings, like all rights, are really against persons. Whether they are proceedings or rights in rem depends on the number of persons affected. Hence the res need not be personified and made a party defendant, as happens with the ship in the admiralty; it need not even be a tangible thing at all, as sufficiently appears by the case of the probate of wills. Personification and naming the res as defendant are mere symbols, not the essential matter. They are fictions, conveniently expressing the nature of the process and the result, nothing more.

. . . .

Then as to seizure of the res. It is convenient in the case of a vessel, in order to secure its being on hand to abide judgment, although in the case of a suit against a man jurisdiction is regarded as established by service without the need of keeping him in prison to await judgment. It is enough that the personal service shows that he could have been seized and imprisoned. Seizure, to be sure, is said to be notice to the owner. Scott v. Shearman, 2 W.Bl. 977, 979. Mankin v. Chandler, 2 Brock. 125, 127, Fed.Cas. No. 9,030. But fastening the process or a copy to the mast would seem not necessarily to depend for its effect upon the continued custody of the vessel by the marshal. However this may be, when we come to deal with immovables there would be no sense whatever in declaring seizure to be a constitutional condition of the power of the Legislature to make a proceeding against land a proceeding in rem. Hamilton v. Brown, 161 U.S. 256, 274, 16 S.Ct. 585. The land cannot escape from the jurisdiction, and, except as security against escape, seizure is a mere form, of no especial sanctity, and of much possible inconvenience.

I do not wish to ignore the fact that seizure, when it means real dispossession, is another security for actual notice. But when it is considered how purely formal such an act may be, and that even adverse possession is possible without ever coming to the knowledge of a reasonably alert owner, I cannot think that the presence or absence of the form makes a constitutional difference; or rather, to express my view still more cautiously, I cannot but think that the immediate recording of the claim is entitled to equal effect from a constitutional point of view. I am free to confess, however, that, with the rest of my brethren, I think the act ought to be amended in the direction of still further precautions to secure actual notice before a decree is entered, and that, if it is not amended, the judges of the court ought to do all that is in their power to satisfy themselves that there has been no failure in this regard before they admit a title to registration.[c]

The quotations which we have made show the intent of the statute to bind the land, and to make the proceedings adverse to all the world, even if it were not stated in § 35, or if the amendment of 1899 did not expressly provide that they should be proceedings in rem. St.1899, c. 131, § 1. Notice is to be posted on the land just as admiralty process is fixed to the mast. Any person claiming an interest may appear and be heard. § 34.

But perhaps the classification of the proceeding is not so important as the course of the discussion thus far might seem to imply. I have pursued

[c] The present statute, Mass.Gen.Laws Ann. ch. 185, § 39, enlarges on § 32 of the 1898 Act by adding: "The court shall, so far as it considers it possible, require proof of actual notice to all adjoining owners and to all persons who appear to have any interest in or claim to the land included in the complaint. Notice to such persons by mail shall be by registered letter."

that course as one which is satisfactory to my own mind, but for the purposes of decision a majority of the court prefer to assume that in cases in which, under the constitutional requirements of due process of law, it heretofore has been necessary to give to parties interested actual notice of the pending proceeding by personal service or its equivalent in order to render a valid judgment against them, it is not in the power of the Legislature, by changing the form of the proceeding from an action in personam to a suit in rem, to avoid the necessity of giving such a notice, and to assume that under this statute personal rights in property are so involved and may be so affected that effectual notice and an opportunity to be heard should be given to all claimants who are known or who by reasonable effort can be ascertained.

. . . With regard to claimants . . . remaining undiscovered, notice by publication must suffice of necessity. As to claimants . . . known, the question seems to come down to whether we can say that there is a constitutional difference between sending notice of a suit by a messenger and sending it by the post office beside publishing in a newspaper, recording in the registry, and posting on the land. It must be remembered that there is no constitutional requirement that the summons, even in a personal action, shall be served by an officer, or that the copy served shall be officially attested. Apart from local practice, it may be served by any indifferent person. It may be served on residents by leaving a copy at the last and usual place of abode. When we are considering a proceeding of this kind, it seems to us within the power of the Legislature to say that the mail . . . is a sufficient messenger to convey the notice, when other means of notifying the party, like publishing and posting, also are required. We agree that such an act as this is not to be upheld without anxiety. But the difference in degree between the case at bar and one in which the constitutionality of the act would be unquestionable seems to us too small to warrant a distinction. If the statute is within the power of the Legislature, it is not for us to criticise the wisdom or expediency of what the Legislature has done.

. . . .

Petition denied.[d]

■ [The dissenting opinion of JUSTICE LORING, with whom Justice Lathrop joined, is omitted.]

Garfein v. McInnis

Court of Appeals of New York, 1928.
248 N.Y. 261, 162 N.E. 73.

■ LEHMAN, J. In an action for the specific performance of an alleged contract to convey real estate in the State of New York, service of the summons and

---

[d] The Supreme Court later dismissed a writ of error because "the plaintiff in error has not the requisite interest to draw in question" the validity of the statute, 179 U.S. 405, 21 S.Ct. 206 (1900). Tyler was an owner of land adjoining, along a disputed boundary, the parcel to be registered; but he had actual notice of the registration proceedings.

complaint has been made in the State of Connecticut, upon a resident of that State. The motion of the defendant to set aside such service has been denied.

In an action "where the complaint demands judgment that the defendant be excluded from a vested or contingent interest in or lien upon specific real or personal property within the State or that such an interest or lien in favor of either party be enforced, regulated, defined or limited, or otherwise affecting the title to such property," the summons may be served out of the State. (Sections 232 and 235, Civ.Prac.Act.) The language of the statute is sufficiently broad to cover an action for specific performance. Service without the State is sufficient to give the court jurisdiction to grant a judgment in rem binding upon a non-resident defendant so served. It does not, however, bring the non-resident defendant's person within the jurisdiction of the court. A decree in personam can be supported against a person who is not a citizen or resident of the State in which it is rendered only by actual service upon him within its jurisdiction. (Hart v. Sansom, 110 U.S. 151, 3 S.Ct. 586.) The question presented by this appeal is whether a judgment in an action for specific performance is only a decree in personam against the party who has agreed to convey property, or whether the court in such an action may grant a judgment which will operate upon the property itself and result in a transfer of the title to a successful party though the defendant fail or refuse to obey a command of the judgment directed to him.

That a court of chancery acts only upon the person is a recognized maxim of equity jurisprudence. [Citations omitted.] "A decree of chancery spoke in terms of personal command to the defendant, but its directions could only be carried into effect by his personal act. . . . The decree never stood as a title in the place of an actual conveyance by the defendant; nor was it ever carried into effect by any officer acting in the defendant's name." (Pomeroy on Equity Jurisprudence, § 428.) In jurisdictions where the decrees of a court of equity still retain the traditional form and effect of a mere command, a court of equity cannot obtain jurisdiction over a non-resident by service without the State. [Citations omitted.]

It has been doubted whether the jurisdiction of courts of equity was ever subject to any inherent limitation that its decrees must operate solely in personam, though the early chancellors adopted the "method of acting, as they said, upon the conscience of defendants." In this country "the statutes of the several states have virtually abolished the ancient doctrine that the decrees in equity can only act upon the person of a party, and have generally provided that in all cases where the ends of justice require such an effect, and where it is possible, a decree shall either operate ex proprio vigore to create, transfer, or vest the intended right, title, estate, or interest, or else that the acts required to be done in order to accomplish the object of the decree shall be performed by an officer of the court acting for and in the name of the party against whom the adjudication is made." (Pomeroy's Equity Jurisprudence, § 135.) "A bill for the specific execution of a contract to convey real estate is not strictly a proceeding in rem, in ordinary cases; but where such a procedure is authorized by statute, on publication, without personal service of process, it is, substantially, of that character." (Boswell's Lessee v. Otis, 50 U.S. 336.)

[The court explained that although some states' equity courts have found quasi in rem remedies to be within their inherent powers, New York need not face that question because it has a statute of the appointive type.]

In this State the Legislature has provided in section 979 of the Civil Practice Act that where a "judgment directs a party . . . to convey real property, if the direction is disobeyed, the court, by order, besides punishing the disobedience as a contempt, may require the sheriff . . . to convey the real property, in conformity with the direction of the court." A decree of the court is enforceable not merely by punishment of a disobedient party but may be carried into effect by action of the sheriff operating directly upon the property. It may be that the primary purpose of the Legislature was to grant additional force to a decree in a case where the court had acquired jurisdiction of the person of a disobedient party. Its effect extends beyond such a case. It has changed the nature of the action from an action in personam, to an action substantially in rem. Though the court cannot by [out-of-state] service obtain jurisdiction of the person of a non-resident defendant and cannot compel such a defendant to obey its decree, where the court has the power to make a decree which will affect the interests of a party in property within the State, whether that party obeys the decree or not, the action is not purely in personam. The court's decree acts upon the property as well as the person of the non-resident defendant. In such case the objection that the court by [out-of-state] service obtains no jurisdiction over the person of a non-resident is without force. The Legislature has expressly provided that in an action for specific performance a court may enforce its decree by other means than direction to the defendant.

The order should be affirmed, with costs . . . .

■ CARDOZO, CH. J., POUND, CRANE, ANDREWS and O'BRIEN, JJ., concur; KELLOGG, J., dissents.

Questions: (1) *B*, a resident of North Carolina, entered into a contract with *S*, a resident of South Carolina, by which *S* undertook to convey to *B* certain real estate situated in North Carolina. *S* refused to perform. What, if any, equitable relief can *B* obtain from a South Carolina court, *S* having been personally served in South Carolina and having actively contested the suit there?

(2) The decree of the South Carolina court orders *S* to convey the North Carolina land, and *S* fails to do so. Can the South Carolina court, given the existence of a South Carolina statute of either the "appointive" or the "vesting" type, give *B* title to the land? See Fall v. Eastin, 215 U.S. 1, 30 S.Ct. 3 (1909) (no).

(3) The South Carolina court enters a decree simply ordering *S* to convey the North Carolina land, and *S* leaves the Carolinas without doing so. Thereafter *B* brings an action against *S* in North Carolina for enforcement of the South Carolina decree. What should be the result of the action?

(4) Now assume instead that *B* agreed to buy and *S* agreed to sell certain real estate situated in South Carolina. *B* refused to perform. *B* is not subject to personal jurisdiction in South Carolina and has no other property there. What, if any, relief can *S* obtain from a South Carolina court? See Prudential Ins. Co. v. Berry, 153 S.C. 496, 151 S.E. 63 (1930) (cutting off *B*'s equitable interest in the land).

Harris v. Balk

Supreme Court of the United States, 1905.
198 U.S. 215, 25 S.Ct. 625.

The plaintiff in error brings the case here in order to review the judgment of the Supreme Court of North Carolina, affirming a judgment of a lower court against him for $180, with interest, as stated therein. The case has been several times before the Supreme Court of that State, and is reported in 122 N.Car. 64; again, 124 N.Car. 467; the opinion delivered at the time of entering the judgment now under review, is to be found in 130 N.Car. 381; see also 132 N.Car. 10.

The facts are as follows: The plaintiff in error, Harris, was a resident of North Carolina at the time of the commencement of this action in 1896, and prior to that time was indebted to the defendant in error, Balk, also a resident of North Carolina, in the sum of $180, for money borrowed from Balk by Harris during the year 1896, which Harris verbally promised to repay, but there was no written evidence of the obligation. During the year above mentioned one Jacob Epstein, a resident of Baltimore, in the State of Maryland, asserted that Balk was indebted to him in the sum of [$344 for the wholesale purchase of general merchandise]. In August, 1896, Harris visited Baltimore for the purpose of purchasing merchandise, and while he was in that city temporarily on August 6, 1896, Epstein caused to be issued out of a proper court in Baltimore a foreign or non-resident writ of attachment against Balk, attaching the debt due Balk from Harris, which writ the sheriff at Baltimore laid in the hands of Harris, with a summons to appear in the court at a day named. With that attachment, a writ of summons and a short declaration against Balk (as provided by the Maryland statute), were also delivered to the sheriff and by him set up at the court house door, as required by the law of Maryland. Before the return day of the attachment writ Harris left Baltimore and returned to his home in North Carolina. He did not contest the garnishee process, which was issued to garnish the debt which Harris owed Balk. After his return Harris made an affidavit on August 11, 1896, that he owed Balk $180, and stated that the amount had been attached by Epstein of Baltimore, and by his counsel in the Maryland proceeding Harris consented therein to an order of condemnation against him as such garnishee for $180, the amount of his debt to Balk. Judgment was thereafter entered against the garnishee and in favor of the plaintiff, Epstein, for $180. After the entry of the garnishee judgment, condemning the $180 in the hands of the garnishee, Harris paid the amount of the judgment to one Warren, an attorney of Epstein, residing in North Carolina. On August 11, 1896, Balk commenced an action against Harris before a justice of the peace in North Carolina, to recover the $180 which he averred Harris owed him. The plaintiff in error, by way of answer to the suit, pleaded in bar the recovery of the Maryland judgment and his payment thereof, and contended that it was conclusive against the defendant in error in this action, because that judgment was a valid judgment in Maryland, and was therefore entitled to full faith and credit in the courts of North Carolina. This contention was not allowed by the trial court, and judgment was accordingly entered against Harris for the amount of his indebtedness to Balk, and that judgment was affirmed by the Supreme Court of North Carolina.[e] The ground of such judgment was that the Maryland court obtained no jurisdiction to attach or garnish the debt due from Harris to Balk, because Harris was but temporarily in the State, and [therefore] the situs of the debt [remained] in North Carolina.

■ MR. JUSTICE PECKHAM, after making the foregoing statement, delivered the opinion of the court.

The state court of North Carolina has refused to give any effect in this action to the Maryland judgment; and the Federal question is, whether it did not thereby refuse the full faith and credit to such judgment which is required by the Federal Constitution. If the Maryland court had jurisdiction to award it, the judgment is valid and entitled to the same full faith and credit in North Carolina that it has in Maryland as a valid domestic judgment.

The defendant in error contends that the Maryland court obtained no jurisdiction to award the judgment of condemnation, because the garnishee, although at the time in the State of Maryland, and personally served with process therein, was a non-resident of that State, only casually or temporarily within its boundaries; that the situs of the debt due from Harris, the garnishee, to the defendant in error herein was in North Carolina, and did not accompany Harris to Maryland; that, consequently, Harris, though within the State of Maryland, had not possession of any property of Balk, and the Maryland state court therefore obtained no jurisdiction over any property of Balk in the attachment proceedings, and the consent of Harris to the entry of the judgment was immaterial. The plaintiff in error, on the contrary, insists that, though the garnishee were but temporarily in Maryland, yet the laws of that State provide for an attachment of this nature, if the debtor, the garnishee, is found in the State and the court obtains jurisdiction over him by the service of process therein; that the judgment, condemning the debt from Harris to Balk, was a valid judgment, provided Balk could himself have sued Harris for the debt in Maryland. This it is asserted, he could have done, and the judgment was therefore entitled to full faith and credit in the courts of North Carolina.

. . . .

[e] It seems that Epstein was financing Harris's litigation, for the reason that "the legal question is of considerable importance to the mercantile and business world." Brief for Plaintiff in Error at 5.

We regard the contention of the plaintiff in error as the correct one. . . .

Attachment is the creature of the local law; that is, unless there is a law of the State providing for and permitting the attachment it cannot be levied there. If there be a law of the State providing for the attachment of the debt, then if the garnishee be found in that State, and process be personally served upon him therein, we think the court thereby acquires jurisdiction over him, and can garnish the debt due from him to the debtor of the plaintiff and condemn it, provided the garnishee could himself be sued by his creditor in that State. We do not see how the question of jurisdiction vel non can properly be made to depend upon the so-called original situs of the debt, or upon the character of the stay of the garnishee, whether temporary or permanent, in the State where the attachment is issued. . . .

. . . .

It thus appears that Balk could have sued Harris in Maryland to recover his debt . . . ; it also appears that the municipal law of Maryland permits the debtor of the principal debtor to be garnished, and therefore if the court of the State where the garnishee is found obtains jurisdiction over him, through the service of process upon him within the State, then the judgment entered is a valid judgment. . . .

. . . The importance of the fact of the right of the original creditor to sue his debtor in the foreign State, as affecting the right of the creditor of that creditor to sue the debtor or garnishee, lies in the nature of the attachment proceeding. The plaintiff, in such proceeding in the foreign State is able to sue out the attachment and attach the debt due from the garnishee to his (the garnishee's) creditor, because of the fact that the plaintiff is really in such proceeding a representative of the creditor of the garnishee, and therefore if such creditor himself had the right to commence suit to recover the debt in the foreign State his representative has the same right, as representing him, and may garnish or attach the debt, provided the municipal law of the State where the attachment was sued out permits it.

It seems to us, therefore, that the judgment against Harris in Maryland, condemning the $180 which he owed to Balk, was a valid judgment, because the court had jurisdiction over the garnishee by personal service of process within the State of Maryland.

It ought to be and it is the object of courts to prevent the payment of any debt twice over. Thus, if Harris owing a debt to Balk, paid it under a valid judgment against him, to Epstein, he certainly ought not to be compelled to pay it a second time, but should have the right to plead his payment under the Maryland judgment. . . .

[The Court further ruled that Balk had received adequate notice of the attachment proceeding.]

Reversed.

■ MR. JUSTICE HARLAN and MR. JUSTICE DAY dissented.

(b) PROCEDURE FOR SUCH JURISDICTION

Consideration of some of the procedural incidents of jurisdiction over things may help to clarify the nature of such jurisdiction, whether of the in rem variety as in Tyler or the quasi in rem varieties of Garfein and Harris.

For example, consider the implications of Restatement (Second) of Judgments § 32 cmt. c, illus. 1 (1982): "A brings an action against B to recover damages for breach of contract. Personal jurisdiction over B is not established, but an automobile worth $500 belonging to him is attached and he is personally notified of the proceeding. Judgment by default is rendered in favor of A for his damages to be assessed. The jury impanelled to assess the damages gives a verdict of $500 and judgment is rendered for A for $500 and $50 costs, to be paid out of the proceeds of the sale of the automobile. The automobile is sold for $500, which sum is paid to A. Of this sum $50 is applicable to the payment of the costs and $450 toward the payment of A's claim. B is not liable for the deficiency. However, in a new action brought by A against B on the original claim, A will be entitled, if successful, to recover whatever damages may be awarded in that action, which may be more or less than $500, less the sum of $450, plus the costs of the new action." On the other hand, if B successfully defends the second action on the ground that he did not breach the contract, that outcome will not affect the prior proceeding and the court will not direct A to restore his earlier recovery.

Now consider the implications of CME Media Enterprises B.V. v. Zelezny, 2001 WL 1035138 (S.D.N.Y.2001). In Amsterdam, CME obtained an arbitration award against Dr. Vladimir Zelezny in the principal amount of $23.35 million. Then in the United States, with representation by a major law firm, CME petitioned a federal court for a judgment confirming and enforcing the award. Counsel did not contend that the court had personal jurisdiction over Zelezny, who was a citizen and resident of the Czech Republic, but that the court had jurisdiction because Zelezny had assets in New York—funds in an account at Citibank. "At the time this action was commenced, however, Zelezny's Citibank account had a balance of only $69.65. Moreover, because Citibank thereafter deducted certain charges from the account, there is now a balance of only $0.05. . . . For the reasons that follow, Zelezny's motion to dismiss is denied and the petition is granted, but only to the extent of the assets that form the basis for quasi in rem jurisdiction—the $0.05 in the Account. The Court does not have jurisdiction to confirm an award in the amount of $23.35 million; CME may enforce the award only against the assets of $0.05." Incidentally, CME argued that Zelezny "may have other assets in New York. But quasi in rem jurisdiction cannot be based on speculation about the possible existence of other property. . . . Zelezny is not before the Court; only the limited assets in the Account—$0.05—are before the Court. For these reasons, petitioner's request for discovery to locate other assets in this jurisdiction is denied."

FEDERAL ACTIONS UNDER 28 U.S.C. § 1655

For in rem and some quasi in rem cases, § 1655 works to authorize territorial jurisdiction. Courts gave long held this statute to apply only to a lien or title existing prior to the suit—and not to one created by the institution of the suit itself, as for example through attachment or garnishment. The real or personal property must be present within the district.

A defendant receives notice sufficient to satisfy procedural due process. There must in addition be subject-matter jurisdiction—ordinarily, diversity of citizenship or a federal question.

If the absent defendant does not appear, the judgment affects only the property that is the subject of the action. The defendant can make the equivalent of a "special appearance" for the purpose of challenging the court's jurisdiction over the property without submitting himself to a personal judgment. Whether he can make a "limited appearance" for the purpose of defending on the merits the claim involving the property without subjecting himself to personal jurisdiction is a question addressed in the upcoming Campbell case.

FEDERAL ACTIONS UNDER RULE 4(n)(2)

For many years there was no provision for commencing an original federal action on the basis only of attachment or garnishment, that is, without personal jurisdiction over the defendant and without a pre-existing lien or title as under § 1655. See Big Vein Coal Co. v. Read, 229 U.S. 31, 33 S.Ct. 694 (1913).[f] The case of Davis v. Ensign–Bickford Co., 139 F.2d 624 (8th Cir.1944), held that Rule 64 did not effect any change, because it deals with security rather than jurisdiction; and Rosenthal v. Frankfort Distillers Corp., 193 F.2d 137 (5th Cir.1951), rejected the contention that Erie required a different result to accord with state law.

In 1963, however, the federal rulemakers closed the lacuna by amending Rule 4 to allow original quasi in rem and in rem jurisdiction to the extent authorized in the courts of the state where the federal court sits. Of course, adequate notice must be given, and jurisdiction over the subject matter must exist.

By a 1993 amendment, the rulemakers limited the use of nonpersonal jurisdiction under Rule 4(n)(2) to circumstances where personal jurisdiction

---

[f] Removal was a different matter. A suit in a state court with attachment or garnishment as the sole basis of territorial jurisdiction was removable if the usual requirements for removal were met. Incidentally, removal by itself is not a general appearance, so the removing defendant lost no rights to special and limited appearances.

(the ordinary type of jurisdiction, which we shall soon study in depth) is not available. However, as should eventually become clear to you, this change had a relatively minor effect, really affecting only those few plaintiffs who in their selected federal court had a choice between attachment-variety quasi in rem jurisdiction and long-arm personal jurisdiction and who had preferred the former.

The amended Rule 4(n)(2) will present its problems of interpretation, but these too should be minor. For example, who has to make the required showing with respect to the unavailability of personal jurisdiction, and by what standard of proof—and how does the scheme work in case of default? Probably the courts will work these problems out by following the usual and soon-to-be-studied practice on personal jurisdiction challenges and showings.

Campbell v. Murdock

United States District Court, Northern District of Ohio, 1950.
90 F.Supp. 297.

■ JONES, CHIEF JUDGE. This is an action to foreclose a mechanic's lien on land owned by defendant Murdock and for other relief.

It appears from the complaint that plaintiff expended considerable labor and materials in the improvement of Murdock's land pursuant to a contract between plaintiff and defendant McMahon, the duly authorized agent of Murdock. Plaintiff, even though he has joined McMahon as a party defendant, does not pray for relief as against him.

Plaintiff, Murdock and McMahon are respectively residents of Pennsylvania, South Carolina and Ohio. This Court has jurisdiction because of the diversity of citizenship and the provisions of 28 U.S.C.A. § 1655, formerly 28 U.S.C.A. § 118.

. . . Murdock, appearing specially and for the purpose of challenging this court's jurisdiction moves to dismiss the action against her, in so far as it asks for personal judgment and, appearing solely for the purpose of defending her interest in the property, moves for a more definite statement of the complaint.

. . . .

[Section 1655] provides in actions to enforce liens on property within the district for service on non-resident defendants by personal service where possible or by publication. The defendant is ordered to appear but if he does not, the final judgment can affect only the property which is the subject of the action.

Murdock claims that this section does not authorize a personal judgment against a non-resident defendant who does not make a general appearance, and she appears specially to move to dismiss the action insofar as it asks for personal judgment. The ultimate question to be decided, then, is whether Section 1655 permits personal judgments when jurisdiction is based solely on the fact that the property in controversy is located within the District.

We have been able to find only one case where the question has been squarely presented. In Bede Steam Shipping Co. v. New York Trust Co., 2 Cir., 54 F.2d 658, the court held that the non-resident defendant has but two choices. He could elect not to appear or he could make a general appearance and subject himself to the general jurisdiction of the court on all claims against him. The court specifically held that the defendant could not appear only for the purpose of defending his interest in the property.

This ruling seems reasonable and correct. The statute, it is true, limits the situations in which the court has in rem jurisdiction. But the statute does not prohibit the taking of personal judgments if the defendant appears, and it also provides, if the defendant does not appear, that the court's adjudication shall affect only the property before it. This leaves the inference that if the defendant does appear, the court may try the entire controversy between the parties.

There has been some suggestion that the personal judgment must be limited to such relief as is related to the in rem feature of the action which originally gives the court jurisdiction. The Bede case lends itself to such an interpretation. (See also 2 Cylo.Fed.Pro. 620–621) Even with this limitation a personal judgment may be had in this action. A personal judgment on the debt which gives rise to the lien in this action does not seem so incidental to the foreclosure of the lien as to defeat the jurisdiction of the court under section 1655. It is not necessary to decide what types of personal relief cannot be coupled with the actions listed in 1655, for the personal relief here is too closely related to the in rem feature of this case . . . .

. . . .

In the circumstances, the defendant Murdock's motion to dismiss will be overruled.

The motion for a more definite statement will be granted. It is unopposed and failure to oppose may be taken as implied consent to the court's favorable ruling on the motion.

LIMITED APPEARANCE

The same difficult problem of whether to allow a limited appearance arises in state actions, removed actions, and federal actions under Rule 4(n)(2). See generally I. Daniel Stewart, Jr., Note, Limited Appearances, 7 Utah L.Rev. 369 (1961). In drafting Rule 4(n)(2), the rulemakers decided not to resolve the problem, but instead to remit it to "the molecular process of litigation." Benjamin Kaplan, Amendments of the Federal Rules of Civil Procedure, 1961–63 (I), 77 Harv.L.Rev. 601, 628 (1964).

The Campbell approach seems efficient. But contrast with Campbell the following situation: in state court, plaintiff brings a contract claim against a foreigner not subject to personal jurisdiction, with territorial jurisdiction based on the attachment of unrelated property belonging to defendant and worth less than the claim. One leading decision held that defendant on these facts could choose to (1) sacrifice his property by default, (2) make a limited appearance, or (3) enter a general appearance that would convert the jurisdiction to in personam. Cheshire Nat'l Bank v. Jaynes, 224 Mass. 14, 112 N.E. 500 (1916). Here the wider choice seems fair, because the contract claim is unrelated to the attached property. The Campbell decision itself recognized this difference, at its second reference to the Bede precedent.

Putting Cheshire together with Campbell would suggest allowing a limited appearance if but only if it would be unreasonable for the forum to exercise personal jurisdiction with respect to the additional claim concurrently with hearing the nonpersonal action.

Question: (5) Note that the Campbell decision seems to have proceeded on the assumption that federal law governed the limited-appearance question. Some commentators disagree, and they would look instead in the circumstances of that case to state law. See 4B Wright & Miller § 1123. What arguments can you make each way?

In an action commenced on a basis other than personal jurisdiction, the defendant in federal court need not plead any counterclaims that he might happen to have. See Rule 13(a)(2)(B), which was added by amendment in 1963. This apparently holds true even if the defendant makes a general appearance; but if the defendant chooses to assert any of his counterclaims, then the compulsory counterclaim Rule comes back into normal operation.

JURISDICTIONAL AMOUNT

Suppose the plaintiff's underlying claim in a quasi in rem case is for $101,000, but territorial jurisdiction exists only over a piece of property known to be worth $5000. Should any jurisdictional amount that is required by the federal statute governing subject-matter jurisdiction be measured by the total claim or by the value of the property? Such case authority as there is indicates that the amount of the total claim is controlling. But the question really must be regarded as an open one. See 4B Wright & Miller § 1122; 14 Wright, Miller & Cooper § 3632, at 33 n.7 (arguing lesser of total claim and value of the property should control).

Questions: (6) What arguments can you make each way?

(7) Which solution is more responsive to current attitudes toward federal jurisdiction?

(8) Would your answer be different if the basis of territorial jurisdiction was an attachment of real estate, the value of which would not be known until it was sold to satisfy judgment?

SECTION 3. JURISDICTION OVER PERSONS—EVOLVING THEORY

(a) PRESENCE AS BASIS FOR JURISDICTION

DARRAH v. WATSON, 36 Iowa 116 (1873). Darrah sued Watson in Iowa upon a judgment of a Virginia state court. Watson contended that the Virginia court had not acquired jurisdiction over him for that prior judgment because, when he had received in-hand service of process in Virginia, he was a citizen and resident of Pennsylvania and was in Virginia only for a few hours on business; and after that service Watson had left Virginia, before rendition of the default judgment against him. The Iowa court held that the Virginia court had acquired jurisdiction over Watson's person, and that the Virginia judgment was therefore entitled to full faith and credit under the Constitution and the laws of the United States.

ENFORCEMENT OF JUDGMENTS IN OTHER STATES

A money judgment for the plaintiff (or a judgment for the defendant for costs) may be enforced in the state where it is rendered. In addition, a party with a personal judgment of this kind may wish to enforce it in another state, as did Darrah. But Darrah could not simply request an Iowa sheriff to levy execution on Watson's property in Iowa in order to satisfy the Virginia judgment. The Iowa sheriff would have no authority to do so, and he would be guilty of conversion if he seized the property on bare faith in a Virginia judgment. So what could Darrah do?

Testing jurisdiction of the judgment-rendering court.—The traditional way to enforce a personal judgment in another state has been to bring there an action upon the judgment, with the aim being to obtain a new judgment and then to enforce that new, domestic judgment. In such an action, the forum court will, on collateral attack as in Darrah v. Watson, inquire into the possible lack of validity of the judgment of the rendering court. If the Iowa court had decided that the Virginia judgment was not valid, it would not have allowed recovery thereon. But the Iowa court could not, and did not, look into the merits of the underlying claim for mere error by the Virginia court.

Some broad generalizations on validity are helpful here. Generally, for a judgment to be valid and hence enforceable, first, it must have been rendered by a court with competency to render it;[g] second, the court must

[g] See Section 1 of Topic A of this Part, treating competency or subject-matter jurisdiction.

have had a sufficient basis for exercising adjudicatory authority over the defendant or other target of the action;[h] and, third, the persons to be legally affected must have received an opportunity to be heard.[i] So, for example, a personal judgment rendered by a court of a state with no basis for exercising jurisdiction over the defendant is not valid, and this is what Watson was contending.

Question: (9) Do not be led into thinking that such an issue can be raised only on collateral attack. Suppose that in the original action Watson, instead of defaulting, had challenged Virginia's jurisdiction over him. (As we shall see later, the Virginia court would have permitted him to appear specially for the purpose of raising the defense of lack of jurisdiction over his person without submitting himself generally to the jurisdiction of that state.) If the trial court had rejected the challenge and given judgment for Darrah, and the highest court of the state had affirmed, would Watson have a basis for review of the jurisdictional point by the Supreme Court of the United States? What of the argument that it is only the enforcement and not the rendition of the judgment that violates Watson's constitutional rights?

However, the Iowa court did find that the Virginia judgment was valid. It held that in-hand service of process in Virginia had authorized the exercise of jurisdiction over Watson (while also satisfying the demands of procedural due process). The contention of Watson thus being overcome, Iowa had to give the Virginia judgment full faith and credit. Subject only to rare exception, the mandate of the Full Faith and Credit Clause in Article IV, Section 1 of the U.S. Constitution and of its implementing statute at 28 U.S.C. § 1738 is that a state give the same effect to a valid judgment that it has in the state that rendered the judgment.[j] This general principle of retroversion applies to all judgments as between state and federal courts. If the first judgment is from a state court and the second action is in a federal court, § 1738 ("every court within the United States") compels the same result. If the first judgment is from a federal court and the second action is in a state court, the analogous result of looking to the judgment's effect in the rendering court follows because federal law, including the federal common law of res judicata, is applicable and binding in the state court under the Supremacy Clause of Article VI. Finally, if both actions are in federal courts, the second court must give like respect to the judgment of the first because both courts are arms of the same sovereign and that sovereign respects res judicata.

---

[h] The principal concern here has been substantive due process, which permeates the doctrine called territorial jurisdiction, judicial jurisdiction, nexus, or amenability. This is the main focus of study for this Topic.

[i] The concern here is procedural due process. We deal with this concern in passing throughout this Part and will give it detailed study in Topic C of this Part. At this stage, the student should make an effort to distinguish the concept of procedural due process from competency and especially from substantive due process.

[j] In Mills v. Duryee, 11 U.S. (7 Cranch) 481 (1813), Francis Scott Key, as counsel, contended plausibly that full faith and credit required only that the judgment be weighed along with the evidence, but the Court held that at least the implementing statute required giving it a binding effect. It remains possible that the constitutional clause means merely to ensure that the judgment be admissible in another state, leaving the effect of the judgment to congressional legislation.

In an action upon a judgment, the law to be applied by the forum court in determining the validity of the judgment is the law of the judgment-rendering sovereign, but that law is subject to some very real constitutional limitations. Thus, Iowa had to look to Virginia law to see if Virginia had acquired jurisdiction over Watson, and then inquire whether this acquisition had been consistent with the Due Process Clause of the Fourteenth Amendment to the U.S. Constitution. Similarly, in deciding the effect to give a judgment that the forum court has determined to be valid, the forum court must apply the res judicata law that the rendering court would apply, again a law that includes any externally imposed constraints. However, with respect to the method of enforcement, the forum court will apply its own law, subject to the constitutional requirement that the method not be so complex or expensive as to burden unduly the enforcement of nondomestic judgments.

Acquiring jurisdiction in the judgment-enforcing court.—To bring an action upon a judgment, the plaintiff must satisfy the usual requirements for suit, including acquisition of territorial jurisdiction. The plaintiff with a money judgment could go to where the defendant has any assets and then proceed by quasi in rem jurisdiction of the attachment variety; or when the judgment targets specific property, the plaintiff can go to where the property is and proceed quasi in rem to assert his interest in that property. Alternatively, the plaintiff can go to where personal jurisdiction exists over the defendant and get a fresh personal judgment to enforce; and the enforcement could lead to orders against the defendant personally and enforceable by contempt, such as an order that the defendant turn over assets that might be located anywhere.

There have been attempts to facilitate enforcement of nondomestic judgments by creating alternative methods of enforcement. In 1948, on the federal level, Congress enacted 28 U.S.C. § 1963. This statute dispensed with the necessity of an action upon a judgment by providing for registration of a district-court judgment "for the recovery of money or property" in any other district court, with the effect of automatically converting the judgment so registered into a judgment of the court where it was registered and thus making it enforceable in like manner. In addition to saving time and expense, this statute avoids the venue requirement for an action upon the judgment. It avoids as well the jurisdictional problems of an action upon the judgment: no need exists to acquire territorial jurisdiction, and the judgment may be registered even though an action upon the judgment would have failed for lack of subject-matter jurisdiction in the registering court.[k] Finally, it removes the availability of a collateral attack by the defendant, who must instead take the initiative to seek any desired relief from the judgment by making a Rule 60(b) motion or by instituting an independent action. See 18 Moore § 130.35.

---

[k] Subject-matter jurisdiction is otherwise a serious concern because an action upon a federal judgment does not arise under the Constitution or laws of the United States, despite the fact that there was federal subject-matter jurisdiction for rendering the judgment in the original action. See Metcalf v. Watertown, 128 U.S. 586, 9 S.Ct. 173 (1888).

Question: (10) What methods of enforcement can the plaintiff invoke to enforce a registered judgment—those associated with legal judgments or those associated with equitable decrees?

The National Conference of Commissioners on Uniform State Laws in 1948 approved a Uniform Enforcement of Foreign Judgments Act providing for registration in the enacting state of federal or sister-state judgments. In 1964 the Commissioners approved a revision that further facilitated enforcement of such judgments by providing a procedure very similar to that in the federal § 1963. The later Uniform Act has been adopted in almost all states.

GRACE v. MacARTHUR, 170 F.Supp. 442 (E.D.Ark.1959). Arkansas citizens brought a diversity action in the Eastern District of Arkansas against three defendants on a claim arising in Arkansas. A marshal served one of the defendants, who was from Tennessee, by handing him the papers on a nonstop flight from Memphis, Tennessee, to Dallas, Texas, at a time when the plane was flying directly over the Eastern District of Arkansas. The defendant moved to quash the service because at the time of service he was not within the territorial limits of Arkansas as required by Federal Rule 4(k)(1)(A). The motion was denied.

WYMAN v. NEWHOUSE, 93 F.2d 313 (2d Cir.1937), cert. denied, 303 U.S. 664, 58 S.Ct. 831 (1938). Mr. N, a resident of New York, had had meretricious relations over a period of years with Mrs. W, a widow resident in Florida. Mrs. W wrote Mr. N stating that her mother was dying in Ireland, that she was leaving the United States to go to her mother and would not return, and that she wanted to see him once more before she left; she wrote also that she loved him and entreated him to come to Florida for a last visit. These statements were essentially false. Upon his arrival at the Miami airport, Mr. N was served with process in Mrs. W's Florida state-court action for money loaned to him and for seduction under promise of marriage. Mr. N did not appear in the action, and the court entered a judgment against him on his default.

In the present action upon the Florida judgment in a federal court in New York, Mr. N set up the foregoing matter as a defense. Was the defense valid? The court thought it was. The court indicated that Florida law generally governed. The facts showed that Mr. N had been fraudulently enticed into the Florida jurisdiction for the sole purpose of service of process. This made the judgment invalid, and subject to collateral attack, in the state of rendition. But Mr. N did not need to assert his defense of fraud in the Florida action or to attack the judgment in Florida. The judgment was open to collateral attack when sued upon it in another jurisdiction.

Moreover, in the present action, Mr. N did not need to show that he had a defense on the merits to the Florida action.

FRAUD AND FORCE

Restatement (Second) of Conflict of Laws § 82 (1971) says: "A state will not exercise judicial jurisdiction, which has been obtained by fraud or unlawful force, over a defendant or his property."

Comment f to that section states that this prevailing rule is "not jurisdictional," that is, the rule represents only a self-imposed limitation on the state's exercise of its utmost constitutional powers. Accordingly, if a state instead chooses to exercise judicial jurisdiction in such circumstances involving fraud or unlawful force, other states must honor its choice.

Questions: (11) New York follows the rule of § 82. See, e.g., Terlizzi v. Brodie, 38 A.D.2d 762, 329 N.Y.S.2d 589 (1972) (New Jersey defendants were telephoned at home and falsely told that they had been chosen to receive two Broadway tickets as a promotional venture to get their opinion of the new 7:30 p.m. curtain time; they were served in the theater by the man sitting behind them; motion to vacate service granted). But the prevailing rule, in New York and elsewhere, is that it is permissible to resort to subterfuge in order to serve a person who is voluntarily in the state. See, e.g., Gumperz v. Hofmann, 245 A.D. 622, 283 N.Y.S. 823 (1935), aff'd, 271 N.Y. 544, 2 N.E.2d 687 (1936) (defendant, an Argentine doctor sojourning in a New York City hotel, was telephoned by a process server who falsely represented himself to be a Dr. Goldman with a letter from the president of the New York County Medical Society to be personally delivered; they arranged to meet in the hotel lobby, where service was made; motion to vacate service denied). What difference accounts for the two rules?

(12) It has also been held that service is invalid in the following circumstances. Husband, an attorney, accompanied his wife to a New York dockside, whence she was to sail to California to visit her mother. During an affectionate farewell, he gave her a wrapped box, telling her it contained a present for her mother, but in reality it contained process for a divorce action. She sailed without opening it, and she consequently defaulted. Bulkley v. Bulkley, 6 Abb.Pr. 307 (N.Y.Sup.Ct.1858). How can you reconcile this case with Gumperz?

(13) Prospective defendant is in New York only for settlement negotiations with potential plaintiff. Negotiations break down. Plaintiff continues the conference for a few hours, not to conduct good-faith negotiations but rather as an artifice to make service on defendant in a New York state-court action by awaiting the arrival of the process server. Now there is a motion to vacate service. What decision?

IMMUNITY FROM SERVICE OF PROCESS

The customary doctrine has long been that a nonresident party, witness, or counsel is immune from service of process when present in a state for attendance at litigation and for a reasonable time to go to and fro. The rule has been criticized in its entirety, see, e.g., Arthur J. Keeffe &

John J. Roscia, Immunity and Sentimentality, 32 Cornell L.Q. 471 (1947), and has been qualified or given restrictive application, see, e.g., Wangler v. Harvey, 41 N.J. 277, 196 A.2d 513 (1963).

Again, the immunity rule is in the nature of a self-imposed limitation, which the state may choose not to adopt. See Restatement (Second) of Conflict of Laws § 83 cmt. b (1971).

Questions: (14) Are the considerations different as between a witness and a party? as between counsel and party? as between a plaintiff and a defendant?

(15) Should it matter whether the two actions involve related facts? whether the pending action for which the person comes in is criminal or civil? whether presence is for attending trial or some other phase of litigation?

(16) What, if any, effect on the immunity rule should there be if the person who claims immunity is subjectable to personal jurisdiction on some basis other than her presence in the state? (Renew consideration of this question after studying the rest of this Section.)

(b) DOMICILE AS BASIS FOR JURISDICTION

MILLIKEN v. MEYER, 311 U.S. 457, 61 S.Ct. 339 (1940). Milliken sued Meyer in a Wyoming state court to recover profits from certain Colorado oil properties. Meyer was domiciled in Wyoming at all relevant times. He received in-hand service of process in Colorado pursuant to a Wyoming statute. He did not appear in the action, and the court rendered judgment against him.

Subsequently Meyer sued Milliken in a Colorado state court to enjoin Milliken from enforcing the Wyoming judgment and to obtain a decree that the Wyoming judgment was invalid for want of jurisdiction over Meyer. Milliken appeared and defended. The Colorado Supreme Court eventually granted Meyer relief. On certiorari, the Supreme Court of the United States reversed, holding that the Wyoming judgment was valid and entitled to full faith and credit in Colorado. The Court, by Justice Douglas, said: "Domicile in the state is alone sufficient to bring an absent defendant within the reach of the state's jurisdiction for purposes of a personal judgment by means of appropriate substituted service."

The Court first discussed notice: "Substituted service in such cases has been quite uniformly upheld where the absent defendant was served at his usual place of abode in the state [citations omitted] as well as where he was personally served without the state. [Citation omitted.] That such substituted service may be wholly adequate to meet the requirements of due process was recognized by this Court in McDonald v. Mabee, 243 U.S. 90, 37 S.Ct. 343,[1] despite earlier intimations to the contrary. See Pennoyer v.

[1] This 1917 case is much cited, chiefly for the statement of Justice Holmes: "The foundation of jurisdiction is physical power . . . ." It held that service by publication would not yield a valid personal judgment against a person who, although technically domiciled in the state, had left it intending to establish his home elsewhere. The Court apparently believed

Neff, 95 U.S. 714, 733; [other citation omitted]. Its adequacy so far as due process is concerned is dependent on whether or not the form of the substituted service provided for such case and employed is reasonably calculated to give him actual notice of the proceedings and an opportunity to be heard. If it is, the traditional notions of fair play and substantial justice (McDonald v. Mabee, supra) implicit in due process are satisfied. Here there can be no question on that score."

The Court then addressed nexus: "Certainly then Meyer's domicile in Wyoming was a sufficient basis for that extraterritorial service. As in case of the authority of the United States over its absent citizens (Blackmer v. United States, 284 U.S. 421, 52 S.Ct. 252), the authority of a state over one of its citizens is not terminated by the mere fact of his absence from the state. The state which accords him privileges and affords protection to him and his property by virtue of his domicile may also exact reciprocal duties."

The old common law generally did not recognize domicile as a basis for personal jurisdiction, and state courts have therefore usually held that they cannot exercise jurisdiction on this basis unless authorized to do so by the legislature. See, e.g., Duncan v. McDonough, 105 N.H. 308, 199 A.2d 104 (1964). But again, if a state's courts were authoritatively to decide that such statutory authorization was unnecessary, their judgments on this basis would be entitled to full faith and credit.

Questions: (17) What if the defendant was a domiciliary of the forum state when the claim arose and when the action was commenced, but ceased to be before service was made? See Allen v. Superior Court, 41 Cal.2d 306, 259 P.2d 905 (1953) (jurisdiction exists pursuant to statute, for claim arising in state).

(18) What if the defendant was a domiciliary when the claim arose, but ceased to be before the action was commenced and service was made? See Owens v. Superior Court, 52 Cal.2d 822, 345 P.2d 921 (1959) (jurisdiction exists pursuant to statute, for claim arising in state).

(19) What if, at all relevant times, the defendant was a resident but not a domiciliary? See Restatement (Second) of Conflict of Laws § 30 (1971).

(c) CONSENT AS BASIS FOR JURISDICTION

Consent to personal jurisdiction before any action is brought is generally effective. It typically comes as part of a contract the breach of which is the subject of the action.[m]

---

that the notice "substituted" for personal delivery of notice, and not necessarily the nexus, was fatally defective. In this connection, Justice Holmes for the Court said: "To dispense with personal service the substitute that is most likely to reach the defendant is the least that ought to be required if substantial justice is to be done."

[m] Sometimes such consent poses serious problems—turning in part on whether the defendant voluntarily, intelligently, and knowingly consented—but we reserve these problems for consideration in Topic C of this Part.

A defendant may also effectively consent to personal jurisdiction after the action is brought. This may be done by accepting or waiving service, even though he would not otherwise be subject to jurisdiction and even though he is physically outside the state when he does the acts constituting the acceptance or waiver.[n] Or the defendant may confer jurisdiction over the person by the entry of a general appearance in the action, doing so by the defendant in person or by his authorized attorney.

Question: (20) What other action by the defendant or his authorized attorney would be effective in a federal court to confer jurisdiction over his person?

HESS v. PAWLOSKI, 274 U.S. 352, 47 S.Ct. 632 (1927). In 1923 Massachusetts enacted a statute, the material parts of which were these: "[T]he operation by a non-resident of a motor vehicle on a public way in the commonwealth . . . shall be deemed equivalent to an appointment by such non-resident of the registrar [of motor vehicles], or his successor in office, to be his true and lawful attorney upon whom may be served all lawful processes in any action or proceeding against him, growing out of any accident or collision in which said non-resident may be involved while operating a motor vehicle on such a way, and said . . . operation shall be a signification of his agreement that any such process against him which is so served shall be of the same legal force and validity as if served on him personally. Service of such process shall be made by leaving a copy of the process with a fee of two dollars in the hands of the registrar, or in his office, and such service shall be sufficient service upon the said non-resident; provided, that notice of such service and a copy of the process are forthwith sent by registered mail by the plaintiff to the defendant, and the defendant's return receipt and the plaintiff's affidavit of compliance herewith are appended to the [summons] and entered with the [complaint]. The court in which the action is pending may order such continuances as may be necessary to afford the defendant reasonable opportunity to defend the action."

In a later lawsuit, the defendant challenged, as violative of due process, service made in compliance with this statute. The Supreme Judicial Court of Massachusetts held the statute to be a valid exercise of the police power. On writ of error the Supreme Court of the United States affirmed. After citing Pennoyer v. Neff, McDonald v. Mabee, and other decisions, Justice Butler continued:

---

[n] There may be a question of interpretation whether the defendant has consented to something or has merely admitted that process has been served upon him. For instance, if he writes on the summons, "I acknowledge that this summons was handed to me in State *Y*," this is not a consent to jurisdiction in an action commenced in State *X*. In contrast, writing "I acknowledge due and personal service of this summons upon me and waive further service upon me" would be such a consent. See Restatement (Second) of Conflict of Laws § 32 cmt. d, illus. 7–8 (1971).

Given consent, another level of distinction exists between consenting to personal jurisdiction and merely agreeing not to contest the form of summons or the manner of transmitting notice.

"Motor vehicles are dangerous machines; and, even when skillfully and carefully operated, their use is attended by serious dangers to persons and property. In the public interest the State may make and enforce regulations reasonably calculated to promote care on the part of all, residents and non-residents alike, who use its highways. The measure in question operates to require a non-resident to answer for his conduct in the State where arise causes of action alleged against him, as well as to provide for a claimant a convenient method by which he may sue to enforce his rights. Under the statute the implied consent is limited to proceedings growing out of accidents or collisions on a highway in which the non-resident may be involved. It is required that he shall actually receive and receipt for notice of the service and a copy of the process. And it contemplates such continuances as may be found necessary to give reasonable time and opportunity for defense. It makes no hostile discrimination against non-residents but tends to put them on the same footing as residents. Literal and precise equality in respect of this matter is not attainable; it is not required. Canadian Northern Ry. Co. v. Eggen, 252 U.S. 553, 561–562, 40 S.Ct. 402. The State's power to regulate the use of its highways extends to their use by non-residents as well as by residents. Hendrick v. Maryland, 235 U.S. 610, 622, 35 S.Ct. 140. And, in advance of the operation of a motor vehicle on its highway by a non-resident, the State may require him to appoint one of its officials as his agent on whom process may be served in proceedings growing out of such use. Kane v. New Jersey, 242 U.S. 160, 167, 37 S.Ct. 30.[o] That case recognizes power of the State to exclude a non-resident until the formal appointment is made. And, having the power so to exclude, the State may declare that the use of the highway by the non-resident is the equivalent of the appointment of the registrar as agent on whom process may be served. [Citations omitted.] The difference between the formal and implied appointment is not substantial so far as concerns the application of the due process clause of the Fourteenth Amendment."

Questions: (21) Suppose Massachusetts amended the statute in Hess v. Pawloski so that, instead of calling for service of process upon a public official within the state and for notice by registered mail to the defendant, it required only service by registered mail to the out-of-state defendant. Would that statute be constitutional?

(22) Suppose Massachusetts amended the statute in Hess v. Pawloski by changing the operative words "on a public way in the commonwealth" to "within the commonwealth." Would it be valid as applied to a nonresident involved in an accident on private property? See Sipe v. Moyers, 353 Pa. 75, 44 A.2d 263 (1945) (yes). Why?

---

[o] The New Jersey statute required a nonresident motorist on entering the state to sign a document appointing a state official as his agent for service of process in proceedings arising out of his use of the highway. The statute was enacted in 1906, so one need not visualize traffic on the New Jersey Turnpike.

FLEXNER v. FARSON, 248 U.S. 289, 39 S.Ct. 97 (1919). In Jefferson County, Kentucky, Bernard Flexner entered into a contract to purchase bonds from Farson, Son & Company, a partnership engaged in the business of trading in securities; one Washington Flexner acted as the agent of the partnership during the negotiations. Bernard Flexner later commenced suit in a Kentucky state court against the partners for breach of the contract. The partners being domiciled and residing outside Kentucky, he made service in Jefferson County upon Washington Flexner as their agent, in attempted compliance with the following Kentucky statute: "In actions against an individual residing in another state, or a partnership, association, or joint stock company, the members of which reside in another state, engaged in business in this state, the summons may be served on the manager, or agent of, or person in charge of, such business in this state, in the county where the business is carried on, or in the county where the cause of action occurred." Defendants defaulted, and plaintiff obtained a money judgment.

In an action upon the judgment against one of the partners in an Illinois state court, the defendant partner urged that the Kentucky judgment was invalid for want of jurisdiction over the partners' persons. The plaintiff argued that the quoted statute had been implicitly incorporated into the contract and that the partners had thereby effectively consented to service in actions arising from business conducted in Kentucky. The Illinois courts denied effect to the Kentucky judgment. On writ of error the Supreme Court of the United States affirmed. The entire legal discussion in the opinion by Justice Holmes for the Court follows:

"It is argued that the pleas tacitly admit that Washington Flexner was agent of the firm at the time of the transaction sued upon in Kentucky,[p] and the Kentucky statute is construed as purporting to make him agent to receive service in suits arising out of the business done in that State. On this construction it is said that the defendants by doing business in the State consented to be bound by the service prescribed. The analogy of suits against insurance companies based upon such service is invoked. Mutual Reserve Fund Life Association v. Phelps, 190 U.S. 147, 23 S.Ct. 707. But the consent that is said to be implied in such cases is a mere fiction, founded upon the accepted doctrine that the States could exclude foreign corporations altogether, and therefore could establish this obligation as a condition to letting them in. Lafayette Ins. Co. v. French, 18 How. 404. Pennsylvania Fire Ins. Co. v. Gold Issue Mining & Milling Co., 243 U.S. 93, 96, 37 S.Ct. 344. The State had no power to exclude the defendants[q] and on

---

[p] Plaintiff alleged in the Illinois action that Washington Flexner was the partners' agent at the time of the transaction and at the time of service upon him. The defendant partner's plea, to which plaintiff demurred, alleged that Washington Flexner was not their agent at the time of service upon him, but did not allege that Washington Flexner was not their agent at the time of the transaction.

[q] The Court elaborated the distinction between nonresident individuals and foreign corporations in Hess v. Pawloski, where it explained that a state's constitutional power to exclude from doing intrastate business is lesser for individuals than for corporations because the Privileges and Immunities Clause of Article IV, Section 2 applies to individuals but not to corporations.

that ground without going farther the Supreme Court of Illinois rightly held that the analogy failed, and that the Kentucky judgment was void. If the Kentucky statute purports to have the effect attributed to it, it cannot have that effect in the present case. New York Life Ins. Co. v. Dunlevy, 241 U.S. 518, 522, 523, 36 S.Ct. 613."

(d) ACTS AS BASIS FOR JURISDICTION

HENRY L. DOHERTY & CO. v. GOODMAN, 294 U.S. 623, 55 S.Ct. 553 (1935). In Des Moines, Iowa, Goodman entered into a contract to purchase stock from Henry L. Doherty, trading as Henry L. Doherty & Company and engaged in the securities business; a salesman operating from the defendant's Des Moines office negotiated the contract. Goodman later brought suit in an Iowa state court against Mr. Doherty for damages arising out of the contract. Doherty being a citizen and resident of New York, service was made on King, the district manager in charge of the Des Moines office, in attempted compliance with Iowa Code § 11079 (in effect since 1851), which provided: "When a corporation, company, or individual has, for the transaction of any business, an office or agency in any county other than that in which the principal resides, service may be made on any agent or clerk employed in such office or agency, in all actions growing out of or connected with the business of that office or agency."

Doherty appeared specially and challenged on constitutional grounds the jurisdiction over his person. The Iowa court upheld the service, and Doherty made no further defense. The Iowa Supreme Court affirmed, pointing out that the statute did not violate the Privileges and Immunities Clause because it applied equally to residents of other counties in Iowa and to nonresidents of Iowa. On appeal the Supreme Court of the United States affirmed. Justice McReynolds said in part:

"Iowa treats the business of dealing in corporate securities as exceptional and subjects it to special regulation. Laws 1913, c. 137; Laws 1921, c. 189; Laws 1929, c. 10, approved Mar. 19, 1929. . . . Doherty voluntarily established an office in Iowa and there carried on this business. Considering this fact, and accepting the construction given to § 11079, we think to apply it as here proposed will not deprive him of any right guaranteed by the Federal Constitution.

"Flexner v. Farson, 248 U.S. 289, 39 S.Ct. 97, much relied upon, does not sustain appellant's position. There the service was made upon one not then agent for the defendants; here the situation is different. King was manager of the appellant's office when the sale contract was made; also when process was served upon him. Moreover, under the laws of Iowa, neither her citizens nor non-residents could freely engage in the business of selling securities.

"The power of the States to impose terms upon non-residents, as to activities within their borders, recently has been much discussed. Hess v. Pawloski, 274 U.S. 352, 47 S.Ct. 632; Wuchter v. Pizzutti, 276 U.S. 13, 48 S.Ct. 259; Young v. Masci, 289 U.S. 253, 53 S.Ct. 599. Under these opinions it is established doctrine that a State may rightly direct that non-residents who operate automobiles on her highways shall be deemed to have appointed the Secretary of State as agent to accept service of process, provided there is some 'provision making it reasonably probable that notice of the service on the Secretary will be communicated to the non-resident defendant who is sued.'

"So far as it affects appellant, the questioned statute goes no farther than the principle approved by those opinions permits. Only rights claimed upon the present record are determined. The limitations of § 11079 under different circumstances we do not consider."

Question: (23) What vitality remained in Flexner v. Farson after the decision in the Doherty case?

DUBIN v. CITY OF PHILADELPHIA, 34 Pa.D. & C. 61 (C.P.1939). A Pennsylvania statute provided that a nonresident owner or user of real estate and the footways and curbs adjacent thereto, by the ownership and use thereof, made the Secretary of the Commonwealth the nonresident's agent for service of process in any civil action arising out of any accident or injury involving such real estate, footways, or curbs. In addition to the service upon the Secretary, there was a provision for registered-mail notice to the defendant at its last known address.

The plaintiff sued in a Pennsylvania court for injuries from a fall on a broken sidewalk in Philadelphia. The owner of the abutting property was served in accordance with the statute. That owner, who lived in New Jersey, appeared specially to challenge on constitutional grounds the jurisdiction over her person. Presiding Judge Bok said that the statute created "another exception to the rule of personal service in personal actions" and was "a reasonable procedural requirement of a nonresident" who elected to own real estate in Pennsylvania. He therefore held it constitutional.

ADAM v. SAENGER, 303 U.S. 59, 58 S.Ct. 454 (1938). *X* brought an action against *Y* in a California state court for goods sold and delivered. *X* had no connection with California other than institution of the action against *Y*. In accordance with the California Code of Civil Procedure, *Y* chose to bring a permissive "cross-action" against *X*, alleging conversion by repossession of the goods in dispute and serving the "cross-complaint" upon *X*'s attorney of record in the pending action. Judgment in the cross-action went by default against *X*; subsequently the court dismissed the main action by *X* for want of prosecution.

Y then brought an action in a Texas state court to enforce his judgment. The Texas court dismissed, holding that the California judgment was invalid because California had not acquired jurisdiction over *X* for the purposes of the cross-action. Appeal within the state system resulted in the dismissal's affirmance. On certiorari the United States Supreme Court reversed. Justice Stone said on the jurisdictional point:

"There is nothing in the Fourteenth Amendment to prevent a state from adopting a procedure by which a judgment in personam may be rendered in a cross-action against a plaintiff in its courts, upon service of process or of appropriate pleading upon his attorney of record. The plaintiff having, by his voluntary act in demanding justice from the defendant, submitted himself to the jurisdiction of the court, there is nothing arbitrary or unreasonable in treating him as being there for all purposes for which justice to the defendant requires his presence. It is the price which the state may exact as the condition of opening its courts to the plaintiff."

Questions: (24) Why would the doctrine of supplemental jurisdiction not suffice to reach the Adam v. Saenger holding?

(25) Why would physical presence, as a basis for personal jurisdiction, not suffice to reach the Adam v. Saenger holding?

(26) *P–1* and *P–2* bring an action against *D* in a court of State *A*, which has rules concerning counterclaims and crossclaims identical with those found in the Federal Rules. *D* asserts a permissive counterclaim against *P–1*. *P–1* then brings a crossclaim, arising out of the transaction that is the subject matter of the counterclaim, against *P–2*. *P–2* has no connection with State *A* other than her institution of the action against *D*. Is there jurisdiction over *P–2* for the purposes of the crossclaim?

APPEARANCE AS DEFENDANT

If the defendant does not want to submit to personal jurisdiction, he plainly would not enter, or authorize his attorney to enter, a general appearance. If he is confident that jurisdiction over his person is lacking, he may, in theory at least, simply ignore the lawsuit entirely. Here is an illustration. Seeking money damages, *P* commences an action against *D* in a court of State *X* for an alleged tort committed by *D* in State *Y*. *D* resides in State *Y*, and he has never set foot in nor had any other connection with State *X*. *P* delivers process to *D* in State *Y*. In short, State *X* has not acquired jurisdiction over *D*'s person. If the court enters judgment on *D*'s default against him, and *P* attempts to enforce the judgment in State *Y* or elsewhere, it is generally thought that *D* can then set up the lack of jurisdiction in a collateral attack.

But *D* may wish to contest State *X*'s jurisdiction over his person in the original action. He may be in genuine doubt whether State *X* has acquired jurisdiction over him, or he may not relish the prospect of an overhanging judgment against him even though he is convinced it is invalid. And note that if *D* chooses to stay away, he may on collateral attack argue only the invalidity of the default judgment (defective competency, nexus, or notice), not the merits of the underlying claim. So, intuition suggests that, instead of staying away, *D* may come into the original action to challenge the jurisdiction. In doing so, what procedural problems might he encounter?

A state apparently, at least under hoary case law, has the power to treat *any* appearance by the defendant or his authorized attorney as a conferral of jurisdiction over his person. On this idea, a Texas statute built a particularly cruel trapdoor, which was not dismantled until fairly recently. Under the statute, an appearance carefully denominated as special for the purpose of challenging the jurisdiction would nevertheless constitute a submission to the jurisdiction and thus nullify what might have been a perfectly good objection to the jurisdiction. If the defendant had stayed away, however, he could have challenged the judgment as invalid if the plaintiff sought to enforce it in Texas or elsewhere. Accordingly, in a Texas action the defendant had to choose between (1) coming in and fighting the action on the merits and (2) staying away entirely and later challenging personal jurisdiction. The Supreme Court refused to hold that the state's imposition of this dilemma violated the Fourteenth Amendment. York v. Texas, 137 U.S. 15, 11 S.Ct. 9 (1890).

Despite the acquiescence of the Supreme Court, the Texas approach found little favor in other states.[r] Other states permitted the device of a special appearance. The defendant, at the outset, would file a notice that he was appearing solely for the purpose of challenging the jurisdiction and not submitting generally to the jurisdiction. Moreover, he had to be careful to take no action looking like a general appearance, for the court might well treat such action as evidence of waiver.[s] The details of state practice in making jurisdictional objections varied widely, and still do. Costly and even irretrievable mistakes may result from failure to master local procedure.

Under the Federal Rules and the numerous state rules patterned upon them, there is no provision for a so-called special appearance. But the rules achieve a similar result. See Rule 12(b)(2) (reading "personal" broadly to mean "territorial"); see also Rule 12(b)(4) (covering defects in the form of summons) and (5) (covering defects in the manner of transmitting notice). A defendant may raise a jurisdictional defense by including it in a motion in advance of answer or by including it in his answer along with other defenses. As Judge Maris said in Orange Theatre Corp. v. Rayherstz

[r] Texas abrogated its statute in 1962, doing so by Tex.R.Civ.P. 120a. Mississippi, the only other state to build that trapdoor, has since given it up, doing so in Mladinich v. Kohn, 250 Miss. 138, 164 So.2d 785 (1964).

[s] An ironic example lies in Jackson v. National Grange Mut. Liab. Co., 299 N.Y. 333, 87 N.E.2d 283 (1949), where the defendant urged both lack of jurisdiction over his person and lack of jurisdiction over the subject matter. The court held that the challenge to subject-matter jurisdiction, which was unsuccessful, constituted a waiver of the objection to personal jurisdiction, which would have been good. New York undid this result by statute two years later, but some states might still adhere to it.

Amusement Corp., 139 F.2d 871, 874 (3d Cir.1944): "He is no longer required at the door of the federal courthouse to intone that ancient abracadabra of the law, de bene esse,[t] in order by its magic power to enable himself to remain outside even while he steps within." This is not, of course, to say that a defendant may not still waive a jurisdictional defense by failure to present it in timely fashion. See Rule 12(g) and (h).

Questions: (27) *P* sues *D* in federal district court. *D* moves successfully under Rule 6(b)(1) for an extension of time to answer or move before the original time expired, and then within the extended time moves to dismiss under Rule 12(b)(2). Has *D* waived this jurisdictional defense?

(28) *P* sues *D* in federal district court to enjoin appropriation of trade secrets and to recover damages. *P* moves for a preliminary injunction. *D* participates in four days of contested hearing on this motion. *D* then files a motion to dismiss under Rule 12(b)(2), within the time prescribed by Rule 12(a). *P* argues that participation in the hearing on the preliminary injunction waived this jurisdictional defense. Should this argument prevail? See Wyrough & Loser, Inc. v. Pelmor Labs., 376 F.2d 543 (3d Cir.1967) (yes).

Thus, a special appearance or a Rule 12(b) defense enables the defendant to circumvent the dilemma involved in York v. Texas. But there may be another dilemma lurking down the road. Suppose the defendant has properly challenged personal jurisdiction in the original action, but the court has overruled his challenge. If he then defends on the merits, does he waive his right to renew the jurisdictional challenge on appeal?

On the one hand, a few states have answered this question in the affirmative. Unless such a state permits an interlocutory appeal, a defendant faces a hard choice between (1) defending on the merits and thereby forgoing any appeal as to personal jurisdiction and (2) standing on his jurisdictional objection alone, submitting to an adverse judgment, and then appealing the jurisdictional ruling. It appears that a state's imposition of this dilemma does not offend due process. See Western Life Indem. Co. v. Rupp, 235 U.S. 261, 35 S.Ct. 37 (1914). In justification of this approach, it has been said that a defendant who insists he is not properly before the court should not be able to do anything inconsistent with his contention. Moreover, allowing a defense on the merits to be followed by reversal for lack of personal jurisdiction upon the defendant's appeal from a final decision, an appeal that comes after much time and litigation have elapsed, could work severe hardship on the plaintiff.

On the other hand, the federal courts and most states have removed this dilemma as well. They allow the defendant to challenge the jurisdiction, defend on the merits, and then appeal the adverse decisions on the jurisdiction and on the merits. Thus, the dominant American rule is the quite pro-defendant one prescribed for the federal courts in Harkness v. Hyde, 98 U.S. 476, 479 (1879): "The right of the defendant to insist upon the objection to the illegality of the service was not waived by the special

[t] The reference was to a practice peculiar to the courts of Pennsylvania. "The legitimate purpose of the appearance de bene esse is to enable the defendant to deny the jurisdiction of the court without submitting to it." 1 Standard Pennsylvania Practice 410 (1935).

appearance of counsel for him to move the dismissal of the action on that ground, or what we consider as intended, that the service be set aside; nor, when that motion was overruled, by their answering for him to the merits of the action. Illegality in a proceeding by which jurisdiction is to be obtained is in no case waived by the appearance of the defendant for the purpose of calling the attention of the court to such irregularity; nor is the objection waived when being urged it is overruled, and the defendant is thereby compelled to answer. He is not considered as abandoning his objection because he does not submit to further proceedings without contestation. It is only where he pleads to the merits in the first instance, without insisting upon the illegality, that the objection is deemed to be waived."

Question: (29) *P* sues *D* in federal district court. *D* moves to dismiss under Rule 12(b)(2), but the trial court overrules his challenge. *D* then answers, including a counterclaim for which there is independent subject-matter jurisdiction. Claim and counterclaim are litigated and decided. If *D* loses on the main claim, may he on appeal from that judgment still assert lack of jurisdiction over his person or has he waived the jurisdictional defense? Does it matter whether the counterclaim was compulsory or permissive? A permissive counterclaim bestows jurisdiction over the defendant, and most courts rule the same for a compulsory counterclaim even though that puts the defendant in somewhat of a bind. But if *D* is in a court that allows appellate review on the jurisdictional defense and if the appellate court reversed the judgment on the main claim for lack of jurisdiction, what consequence if any should this have for the judgment on the counterclaim? Does it matter whether *D* won or lost on the counterclaim? See Dragor Shipping Corp. v. Union Tank Car Co., 378 F.2d 241 (9th Cir.1967).

In summary, just as intuition suggested, the defendant usually has a choice between (1) coming into the original action to challenge personal jurisdiction and (2) staying away to await raising the point on collateral attack. But he cannot raise jurisdiction both ways. If he loses his challenge in the original action and fails to upset the result by appeal, then the doctrine of res judicata will preclude his relitigating the point on collateral attack. This rule is further explored in Topic E of Part Four.

Question: (30) *P* brings an action against *D–1* and *D–2* in a court of State *A*, which has rules concerning crossclaims identical with those found in the Federal Rules. *D–2* makes a general appearance. *D–1* then appears, and she brings a crossclaim against *D–2*. *D–2* has no connection with State *A* other than his general appearance in *P*'s action against him. Is there jurisdiction over *D–2* for the purposes of the crossclaim? See Restatement (Second) of Judgments § 9 (1982) (providing that a state has power over anyone who has appeared as a party in a pending action in a court of the state, and that it can exercise this power with respect to an additional claim related to the original action unless determining it concurrently would be unreasonable).

HESS v. PAWLOSKI, 274 U.S. 352, 47 S.Ct. 632 (1927). The Hess case was included in the preceding Subsection because the Massachusetts legislature drew the statute in terms of implied consent. This transparent fiction was a useful first step in escaping the rigors of Pennoyer, but it proved troublesome in other contexts. For instance, some cases held that "consent" to suit in a state under a nonresident motorist statute was a waiver of objection to improper venue in the local federal court. (This was before Congress amended the general venue statute to make the district in which the claim arose a proper venue.) Finally, in Olberding v. Illinois Central Railroad, 346 U.S. 338, 340–41, 74 S.Ct. 83, 85 (1953), Justice Frankfurter, observing that this venue problem "is a horse soon curried,"[u] put the fiction to rest in these words:

"It is true that in order to ease the process by which new decisions are fitted into pre-existing modes of analysis there has been some fictive talk to the effect that the reason why a non-resident can be subjected to a state's jurisdiction is that the non-resident has 'impliedly' consented to be sued there. In point of fact, however, jurisdiction in these cases does not rest on consent at all. See Scott, Jurisdiction over Nonresident Motorists, 39 Harv.L.Rev. 563. The defendant may protest to high heaven his unwillingness to be sued and it avails him not. The liability rests on the inroad which the automobile has made on the decision of Pennoyer v. Neff, 95 U.S. 714, as it has on so many aspects of our social scene. The potentialities of damage by a motorist, in a population as mobile as ours, are such that those whom he injures must have opportunities of redress against him provided only that he is afforded an opportunity to defend himself. . . . But to conclude from [Hess v. Pawloski] that the motorist, who never consented to anything and whose consent is altogether immaterial, has actually agreed to be sued and has thus waived his federal venue rights is surely to move in the world of Alice in Wonderland."

(e) JURISDICTION OVER CORPORATIONS

DOMESTIC CORPORATIONS: SUING IN PLACE OF INCORPORATION

Having examined four bases of personal jurisdiction, we now consider how these bases translate into the corporate setting. To begin, we are talking about jurisdiction over the corporate entity. This differs from jurisdiction over its officials and workers, as the Supreme Court made clear in Riverside & Dan River Cotton Mills v. Menefee, 237 U.S. 189, 35 S.Ct. 579 (1915).

Menefee, a citizen of North Carolina, sued defendant, a Virginia corporation, in a North Carolina state court for injuries sustained while working as defendant's employee in its Virginia cotton mill. Defendant had never transacted any business in North Carolina and had no property there. In-hand service was made in North Carolina on one of defendant's directors, who resided in North Carolina but had never transacted any business in that state for defendant. The North Carolina state courts overruled the corporation's challenge to the propriety of the jurisdiction.

[u] For a metric comment on Justice Frankfurter's fondness for unusual words and phrases, see Richard H. Field, Frankfurter, J., Concurring . . . , 71 Harv.L.Rev. 77 (1957).

On writ of error the U.S. Supreme Court reversed, holding that any judgment based on such service entailed a denial of substantive due process. (Incidentally, the Court expressly rejected the argument that it was only the enforcement of judgment, and not the exercise of jurisdiction or the rendition of judgment, that would violate the Due Process Clause.)

Instead, Menefee should have gone to the corporation's Virginia home to sue. Jurisdiction always exists over a domestic corporation. Incorporation in a state gives that state a basis for the exercise of jurisdiction over the corporation in any action brought against it there, regardless of where the claim arose. This basis of jurisdiction thus assures that there is always a place at which a corporation is amenable to suit. (Procedural due process requires, of course, employing an adequate method to give the corporation notice of the action.)

FOREIGN CORPORATIONS: BACKGROUND OF THE INTERNATIONAL SHOE CASE

Introduction.—Originally no action looking to a personal judgment lay against a corporation outside the place of its incorporation—unless, perhaps, the corporation actually consented. The notion on which this doctrine went appears from Chief Justice Taney's statement in Bank of Augusta v. Earle, 38 U.S. (13 Pet.) 519, 588 (1839): "It is very true that a corporation can have no legal existence out of the boundaries of the sovereignty by which it is created." But bear in mind that back then corporations were very few and primarily localized in operation. Subsequently, corporate activities steadily increased and broadened because of the many advantages of the corporate form. Meanwhile, public and judicial attitudes toward nondomestic corporations oscillated between favor and disfavor, causing an ebb and flow in the law of jurisdiction over corporations.

Actual consent.—Taney's restrictive doctrine failed to meet evolving needs and protectionist attitudes, and so courts had to overcome it. They first managed this in the nineteenth century by manipulating the idea of "consent." If a state could exclude a foreign corporation from doing local, as distinguished from interstate, business in the state, why could it not authorize the foreign corporation to do local business on the condition that the corporation explicitly consent to personal jurisdiction in the courts of the state? This device, a kind of forced consent, worked, and still works at the present time, like this: if the state requires the foreign corporation, as a condition of doing local business in the state, to appoint an agent upon whom service of process may be made, and if the corporation does appoint such an agent, this consent provides a basis for the state's rendering valid personal judgments against the corporation. This consent is no less effective because somewhat coerced. Nor is it material that the agent so appointed is a public official, such as the Secretary of State or Commissioner of Corporations, as long as the corporation itself receives due process notice of the lawsuit. There may be a question of statutory interpretation as to whether this consent, and hence jurisdiction over the corporation, comprehends only those actions arising from business done within the state or is broad enough to cover all personal actions. On familiar principles, the highest court of the state is the final authority on this question of interpretation. If the state adopts the latter statutory construction, it might not be exceeding constitutionally permissible limits, see Pennsylvania Fire Ins. Co. v. Gold Issue Mining & Milling Co., 243 U.S. 93, 37 S.Ct. 344 (1917), although this particular question is still not settled, see Ratliff v. Cooper Laboratories, 444 F.2d 745 (4th Cir.1971).

Fictitious consent.—The foreign corporation might refuse to signify its consent in an explicit manner, however. The next step was to provide that if the foreign corporation did local business within the state, plaintiffs might bring personal actions against it (by service of process in a prescribed manner) irrespective of any explicit indication of consent. The cases held that this provided a basis for the state's assuming jurisdiction at least in actions on claims arising from business done within the state. Thus the consent idea became attenuated. Suppose now that the foreign corporation in question was doing only interstate business in the state. The cases held that jurisdiction existed for actions growing out of that business done in the state. Here the courts were pushing the implied consent fiction to the breaking point, for the state did not have the constitutional power to exclude the corporation from doing interstate business within the state. Reconsider Flexner v. Farson.

Corporate presence.—In the face of these difficulties, courts formulated a nominally different idea, that of corporate "presence." In Philadelphia & Reading Railway v. McKibbin, 243 U.S. 264, 265, 37 S.Ct. 280, 280 (1917), Justice Brandeis for the Court said: "A foreign corporation is amenable to process to enforce a personal liability, in the absence of consent, only if it is doing business within the State in such manner and to such extent as to warrant the inference that it is present there." Again, this theory presented the promise of providing nexus at least in actions on claims arising from business done in the state. But yet again, fiction had its costs.

Unrelated claims.—The cases still had not clearly answered the question of how far a foreign corporation doing business in a state would be subject, in the absence of explicit and complete consent, to personal actions on claims not arising from business done in the state. On the one hand, courts frequently cited Old Wayne Mutual Life Ass'n v. McDonough, 204 U.S. 8, 27 S.Ct. 236 (1907), and Simon v. Southern Railway, 236 U.S. 115, 35 S.Ct. 255 (1915), for the proposition that it was not constitutionally permissible for the courts of a state to hold a foreign corporation amenable to suit, without its actual consent, on a cause of action unconnected with the business done in the state. Both of these cases involved statutes providing that if a foreign corporation doing some business in the state failed to designate an agent for service of process, service might be made upon a public official. In each case, no designation of an agent having been made, the Court held service upon a public official insufficient to subject the corporation to suit on a claim arising elsewhere. However, it was not wholly clear whether the decisions turned upon statutory interpretation or constitutional power. Moreover, mention was made in both cases of the fact that no notice to the corporation was required or given. On the other hand, Tauza v. Susquehanna Coal Co., 220 N.Y. 259, 115 N.E. 915 (1917) (Cardozo, J.), as well as some U.S. Supreme Court cases, tended to affirm a state's authority over a foreign corporation doing business in the state, even as to a claim unconnected with that business, if service of process was made with statutory authorization upon an appropriate corporate official or agent. In Tauza, the defendant coal company was incorporated in Pennsylvania, but it had a branch office in New York City headed by a sales agent who had under him eight salesmen and also other stenographic and clerical personnel; sales in New York were subject to confirmation by the home office in Pennsylvania, customer payments were made to the treasurer in Pennsylvania, and shipments were made from Pennsylvania. The court held this activity to constitute doing business in New York and to make the corporation amenable to suit in New York on a cause of action having no relation to its New York business, and so it therefore upheld service on the sales agent in accordance with New York law.

Summary.—So, although the limits imposed by substantive due process were unclear, the consent and presence theories seemed to be running up against those limits. Indeed, in the early twentieth century the growing tendency to look directly at the acts of "doing business" as the relevant due process test facilitated the conservative courts' restricting the states' powers over foreign corporations, a restriction that the courts could tighten simply by raising the threshold of in-state activity necessary for jurisdiction. But then, a depression and another war set the stage for abandoning the pro-business, laissez-faire attitudes that had come to dominate. Once again, it became evident that social, economic, political, and other such forces shape jurisdictional law. See generally Joseph J. Kalo, Jurisdiction as an Evolutionary Process: The Development of Quasi In Rem and In Personam Principles, 1978 Duke L.J. 1147.

International Shoe Co. v. Washington

Supreme Court of the United States, 1945.
326 U.S. 310, 66 S.Ct. 154.

■ MR. CHIEF JUSTICE STONE delivered the opinion of the Court.

The questions for decision are (1) whether, within the limitations of the due process clause of the Fourteenth Amendment, appellant, a Delaware corporation, has by its activities in the State of Washington rendered itself amenable to proceedings in the courts of that state to recover unpaid contributions to the state unemployment compensation fund exacted by state statutes, Washington Unemployment Compensation Act, Washington Revised Statutes, § 9998–103a through § 9998–123a, 1941 Supp., and (2) whether the state can exact those contributions consistently with the due process clause of the Fourteenth Amendment.

The statutes in question set up a comprehensive scheme of unemployment compensation, the costs of which are defrayed by contributions required to be made by employers to a state unemployment compensation fund. The contributions are a specified percentage of the wages payable annually by each employer for his employees' services in the state. The assessment and collection of the contributions and the fund are administered by appellees. Section 14(c) of the Act . . . authorizes appellee Commissioner to issue an order and notice of assessment of delinquent contributions upon prescribed personal service of the notice upon the employer if found within the state, or, if not so found, by mailing the notice to the employer by registered mail at his last known address.[v] That section also authorizes the Commissioner to collect the assessment by distraint if it is not paid within ten days after service of the notice. By §§ 14e and 6b the order of assessment may be administratively reviewed by an appeal tribunal within the office of unemployment upon petition of the employer, and this determination is by § 6i made subject to judicial review on questions of law by the state Superior Court, with further right of appeal in the state Supreme Court as in other civil cases.

In this case notice of assessment for the years in question was personally served upon a sales solicitor employed by appellant in the State of Washington, and a copy of the notice was mailed by registered mail to appellant at its address in St. Louis, Missouri. Appellant appeared specially before the office of unemployment and moved to set aside the order and notice of assessment on the ground that the service upon appellant's salesman was not proper service upon appellant; that appellant was not a corporation of the State of Washington and was not doing business within the state; that it had no agent within the state upon whom service could be made; and that appellant is not an employer and does not furnish employment within the meaning of the statute.

The motion was heard on evidence and stipulation of facts by the appeal tribunal which denied the motion and ruled that appellee Commissioner was entitled to recover the unpaid contributions. That action was affirmed by the Commissioner; both the Superior Court and the Supreme Court affirmed. 22 Wash.2d 146, 154 P.2d 801. Appellant in each of these courts assailed the statute as applied, as a violation of the due process clause of the Fourteenth Amendment, and as imposing a constitutionally prohibited burden on interstate commerce. The cause comes here on appeal

---

[v] Section 14(c) of the Act stated: "At any time after the Commissioner shall find that any contribution or the interest thereon have become delinquent, the Commissioner may issue a notice of assessment specifying the amount due, which notice of assessment shall be served upon the delinquent employer in the manner prescribed for the service of summons in a civil action, except that if the employer cannot be found within the state, said notice will be deemed served when mailed to the delinquent employer at his last known address by registered mail." The Washington statute governing service of summons in a civil action upon a foreign corporation doing business in the state provided that the summons be served by delivery of a copy to any in-state agent, cashier, or secretary thereof. The state here used both the in-state and the out-of-state methods of service referred to in § 14(c). See International Shoe Co. v. State, 22 Wash.2d 146, 151, 154 P.2d 801, 803 (1945). For more factual background on this case, see Christopher D. Cameron & Kevin R. Johnson, Death of a Salesman? Forum Shopping and Outcome Determination Under International Shoe, 28 U.C. Davis L. Rev. 769 (1995).

under § 237(a) of the Judicial Code, 28 U.S.C. § 344(a),[w] appellant assigning as error that the challenged statutes as applied infringe the due process clause of the Fourteenth Amendment and the commerce clause.

The facts as found by the appeal tribunal and accepted by the state Superior Court and the Supreme Court, are not in dispute. Appellant is a Delaware corporation, having its principal place of business in St. Louis, Missouri, and is engaged in the manufacture and sale of shoes and other footwear. It maintains places of business in several states, other than Washington, at which its manufacturing is carried on and from which its merchandise is distributed interstate through several sales units or branches located outside the State of Washington.

Appellant has no office in Washington and makes no contracts either for sale or purchase of merchandise there. It maintains no stock of merchandise in that state and makes there no deliveries of goods in intrastate commerce. During the years from 1937 to 1940, now in question, appellant employed eleven to thirteen salesmen under direct supervision and control of sales managers located in St. Louis. These salesmen resided in Washington; their principal activities were confined to that state; and they were compensated by commissions based upon the amount of their sales. The commissions for each year totaled more than $31,000. Appellant supplies its salesmen with a line of samples, each consisting of one shoe of a pair, which they display to prospective purchasers. On occasion they rent permanent sample rooms, for exhibiting samples, in business buildings, or rent rooms in hotels or business buildings temporarily for that purpose. The cost of such rentals is reimbursed by appellant.

The authority of the salesmen is limited to exhibiting their samples and soliciting orders from prospective buyers, at prices and on terms fixed by appellant. The salesmen transmit the orders to appellant's office in St. Louis for acceptance or rejection, and when accepted the merchandise for filling the orders is shipped f.o.b. from points outside Washington to the purchasers within the state. All the merchandise shipped into Washington is invoiced at the place of shipment from which collections are made. No salesman has authority to enter into contracts or to make collections.

The Supreme Court of Washington was of opinion that the regular and systematic solicitation of orders in the state by appellant's salesmen, resulting in a continuous flow of appellant's product into the state, was sufficient to constitute doing business in the state so as to make appellant amenable to suit in its courts. But it was also of opinion that there were sufficient additional activities shown to bring the case within the rule frequently stated, that solicitation within a state by the agents of a foreign corporation plus some additional activities there are sufficient to render the corporation amenable to suit brought in the courts of the state to enforce an obligation arising out of its activities there. International Harvester Co. v. Kentucky, 234 U.S. 579, 587, 34 S.Ct. 944, 946; People's Tobacco Co. v. American Tobacco Co., 246 U.S. 79, 87, 38 S.Ct. 233, 235; Frene v.

[w] The current version appears as 28 U.S.C. § 1257.

Louisville Cement Co., 77 U.S.App.D.C. 129, 134 F.2d 511, 516. The court found such additional activities in the salesmen's display of samples sometimes in permanent display rooms, and the salesmen's residence within the state, continued over a period of years, all resulting in a substantial volume of merchandise regularly shipped by appellant to purchasers within the state. The court also held that the statute as applied did not invade the constitutional power of Congress to regulate interstate commerce and did not impose a prohibited burden on such commerce.

Appellant's argument, renewed here, that the statute imposes an unconstitutional burden on interstate commerce need not detain us. For 53 Stat. 1391, 26 U.S.C. § 1606(a) provides that "No person required under a State law to make payments to an unemployment fund shall be relieved from compliance therewith on the ground that he is engaged in interstate or foreign commerce, or that the State law does not distinguish between employees engaged in interstate or foreign commerce and those engaged in intrastate commerce." It is no longer debatable that Congress, in the exercise of the commerce power, may authorize the states, in specified ways, to regulate interstate commerce or impose burdens upon it. [Citations omitted.]

Appellant also insists that its activities within the state were not sufficient to manifest its "presence" there and that in its absence the state courts were without jurisdiction, that consequently it was a denial of due process for the state to subject appellant to suit. It refers to those cases in which it was said that the mere solicitation of orders for the purchase of goods within a state, to be accepted without the state and filled by shipment of the purchased goods interstate, does not render the corporation seller amenable to suit within the state. See Green v. Chicago, B. & Q.R. Co., 205 U.S. 530, 533, 27 S.Ct. 595, 596; International Harvester Co. v. Kentucky, supra, 234 U.S. 586, 587, 34 S.Ct. 946; Philadelphia & Reading R. Co. v. McKibbin, 243 U.S. 264, 268, 37 S.Ct. 280; People's Tobacco Co. v. American Tobacco Co., supra, 246 U.S. 87, 38 S.Ct. 235. And appellant further argues that since it was not present within the state, it is a denial of due process to subject it to taxation or other money exaction. It thus denies the power of the state to lay the tax or to subject appellant to a suit for its collection.

Historically the jurisdiction of courts to render judgment in personam is grounded on their de facto power over the defendant's person. Hence his presence within the territorial jurisdiction of a court was prerequisite to its rendition of a judgment personally binding him. Pennoyer v. Neff, 95 U.S. 714, 733. But now that the capias ad respondendum has given way to personal service of summons or other form of notice, due process requires only that in order to subject a defendant to a judgment in personam, if he be not present within the territory of the forum, he have certain minimum contacts with it such that the maintenance of the suit does not offend "traditional notions of fair play and substantial justice." Milliken v. Meyer, 311 U.S. 457, 463, 61 S.Ct. 339, 343. See Holmes, J., in McDonald v. Mabee, 243 U.S. 90, 91, 37 S.Ct. 343. Compare Hoopeston Canning Co. v. Cullen,

318 U.S. 313, 316, 319, 63 S.Ct. 602, 604, 606. See Blackmer v. United States, 284 U.S. 421, 52 S.Ct. 252; Hess v. Pawloski, 274 U.S. 352, 47 S.Ct. 632; Young v. Masci, 289 U.S. 253, 53 S.Ct. 599.

Since the corporate personality is a fiction, although a fiction intended to be acted upon as though it were a fact, Klein v. Board of Supervisors, 282 U.S. 19, 24, 51 S.Ct. 15, 16, it is clear that unlike an individual its "presence" without, as well as within, the state of its origin can be manifested only by activities carried on in its behalf by those who are authorized to act for it. To say that the corporation is so far "present" there as to satisfy due process requirements, for purposes of taxation or the maintenance of suits against it in the courts of the state, is to beg the question to be decided. For the terms "present" or "presence" are used merely to symbolize those activities of the corporation's agent within the state which courts will deem to be sufficient to satisfy the demands of due process. L. Hand, J., in Hutchinson v. Chase & Gilbert, 45 F.2d 139, 141. Those demands may be met by such contacts of the corporation with the state of the forum as make it reasonable, in the context of our federal system of government, to require the corporation to defend the particular suit which is brought there. An "estimate of the inconveniences" which would result to the corporation from a trial away from its "home" or principal place of business is relevant in this connection. Hutchinson v. Chase & Gilbert, supra, 45 F.2d 141.

"Presence" in the state in this sense has never been doubted when the activities of the corporation there have not only been continuous and systematic, but also give rise to the liabilities sued on, even though no consent to be sued or authorization to an agent to accept service of process has been given. St. Clair v. Cox, 106 U.S. 350, 355, 1 S.Ct. 354, 359; Connecticut Mutual Life Ins. Co. v. Spratley, 172 U.S. 602, 610–11, 19 S.Ct. 308, 311–12; Pennsylvania Lumbermen's Mut. Fire Ins. Co. v. Meyer, 197 U.S. 407, 414–415, 25 S.Ct. 483, 484–85; Commercial Mutual Accident Co. v. Davis, 213 U.S. 245, 255–256, 29 S.Ct. 445, 448; International Harvester Co. v. Kentucky, supra; cf. St. Louis S.W.R. Co. v. Alexander, 227 U.S. 218, 33 S.Ct. 245. Conversely it has been generally recognized that the casual presence of the corporate agent or even his conduct of single or isolated items of activities in a state in the corporation's behalf are not enough to subject it to suit on causes of action unconnected with the activities there. St. Clair v. Cox, supra, 106 U.S. 359, 360, 1 S.Ct. 362, 363; Old Wayne Mut. Life Ass'n v. McDonough, 204 U.S. 8, 21, 27 S.Ct. 236, 240; Frene v. Louisville Cement Co., supra, 134 F.2d 515, and cases cited. To require the corporation in such circumstances to defend the suit away from its home or other jurisdiction where it carries on more substantial activities has been thought to lay too great and unreasonable a burden on the corporation to comport with due process.

While it has been held, in cases on which appellant relies, that continuous activity of some sort within a state is not enough to support the demand that the corporation be amenable to suits unrelated to that activity, Old Wayne Mut. Life Ass'n v. McDonough, supra; Green v.

Chicago, B. & Q.R. Co., supra; Simon v. Southern R. Co., 236 U.S. 115, 35 S.Ct. 255; People's Tobacco Co. v. American Tobacco Co., supra; cf. Davis v. Farmers' Co-operative Co., 262 U.S. 312, 317, 43 S.Ct. 556, 558, there have been instances in which the continuous corporate operations within a state were thought so substantial and of such a nature as to justify suit against it on causes of action arising from dealings entirely distinct from those activities. See Missouri, K. & T.R. Co. v. Reynolds, 255 U.S. 565, 41 S.Ct. 446; Tauza v. Susquehanna Coal Co., 220 N.Y. 259, 115 N.E. 915; cf. St. Louis S.W.R. Co. v. Alexander, supra.

Finally, although the commission of some single or occasional acts of the corporate agent in a state sufficient to impose an obligation or liability on the corporation has not been thought to confer upon the state authority to enforce it, Rosenberg Bros. & Co. v. Curtis Brown Co., 260 U.S. 516, 43 S.Ct. 170, other such acts, because of their nature and quality and the circumstances of their commission, may be deemed sufficient to render the corporation liable to suit. Cf. Kane v. New Jersey, 242 U.S. 160, 37 S.Ct. 30; Hess v. Pawloski, supra; Young v. Masci, supra. True, some of the decisions holding the corporation amenable to suit have been supported by resort to the legal fiction that it has given its consent to service and suit, consent being implied from its presence in the state through the acts of its authorized agents. Lafayette Insurance Co. v. French, 18 How. 404, 407; St. Clair v. Cox, supra, 106 U.S. 356, 1 S.Ct. 359; Commercial Mutual Co. v. Davis, supra, 213 U.S. 254, 29 S.Ct. 447; Washington v. Superior Court, 289 U.S. 361, 364–365, 53 S.Ct. 624, 626–627. But more realistically it may be said that those authorized acts were of such a nature as to justify the fiction. Smolik v. Philadelphia & Reading Co., 222 F. 148, 151. Henderson, The Position of Foreign Corporations in American Constitutional Law, 94–95.

It is evident that the criteria by which we mark the boundary line between those activities which justify the subjection of a corporation to suit, and those which do not, cannot be simply mechanical or quantitative. The test is not merely, as has sometimes been suggested, whether the activity, which the corporation has seen fit to procure through its agents in another state, is a little more or a little less. St. Louis S.W.R. Co. v. Alexander, supra, 227 U.S. 228, 33 S.Ct. 248; International Harvester Co. v. Kentucky, supra, 234 U.S. 587, 34 S.Ct. 946. Whether due process is satisfied must depend rather upon the quality and nature of the activity in relation to the fair and orderly administration of the laws which it was the purpose of the due process clause to insure. That clause does not contemplate that a state may make binding a judgment in personam against an individual or corporate defendant with which the state has no contacts, ties, or relations. Cf. Pennoyer v. Neff, supra; Minnesota Commercial Ass'n v. Benn, 261 U.S. 140, 43 S.Ct. 293.

But to the extent that a corporation exercises the privilege of conducting activities within a state, it enjoys the benefits and protection of the laws of that state. The exercise of that privilege may give rise to obligations, and, so far as those obligations arise out of or are connected with the activities within the state, a procedure which requires the corporation to respond to a suit brought to enforce them can, in most instances, hardly be said to be undue. Compare International Harvester Co. v. Kentucky, supra, with Green v. Chicago, B. & Q.R. Co., supra, and People's Tobacco Co. v. American Tobacco Co., supra. Compare Connecticut Mutual Life Ins. Co. v. Spratley, supra, 172 U.S. 619, 620, 19 S.Ct. 314, 315 and Commercial Mutual Accident Co. v. Davis, supra, with Old Wayne Life Ass'n v. McDonough, supra. See 29 Columbia Law Review, 187–195.

Applying these standards, the activities carried on in behalf of appellant in the State of Washington were neither irregular nor casual. They were systematic and continuous throughout the years in question. They resulted in a large volume of interstate business, in the course of which appellant received the benefits and protection of the laws of the state, including the right to resort to the courts for the enforcement of its rights. The obligation which is here sued upon arose out of those very activities. It is evident that these operations establish sufficient contacts or ties with the state of the forum to make it reasonable and just, according to our traditional conception of fair play and substantial justice, to permit the state to enforce the obligations which appellant has incurred there. Hence we cannot say that the maintenance of the present suit in the State of Washington involves an unreasonable or undue procedure.

We are likewise unable to conclude that the service of the process within the state upon an agent whose activities establish appellant's "presence" there was not sufficient notice of the suit, or that the suit was so unrelated to those activities as to make the agent an inappropriate vehicle for communicating the notice. It is enough that appellant has established such contacts with the state that the particular form of substituted service adopted there gives reasonable assurance that the notice will be actual. [Citations omitted.] Nor can we say that the mailing of the notice of suit to appellant by registered mail at its home office was not reasonably calculated to apprise appellant of the suit. [Citations omitted.]

Only a word need be said of appellant's liability for the demanded contributions to the state unemployment fund. The Supreme Court of Washington, construing and applying the statute, has held that it imposes a tax on the privilege of employing appellant's salesmen within the state measured by a percentage of the wages, here the commissions payable to the salesmen. This construction we accept for purposes of determining the constitutional validity of the statute. The right to employ labor has been deemed an appropriate subject of taxation in this country and England, both before and since the adoption of the Constitution. [Citation omitted.] And such a tax imposed upon the employer for unemployment benefits is within the constitutional power of the states. [Citation omitted.]

Appellant having rendered itself amenable to suit upon obligations arising out of the activities of its salesmen in Washington, the state may maintain the present suit in personam to collect the tax laid upon the exercise of the privilege of employing appellant's salesmen within the state. For Washington has made one of those activities, which taken together establish appellant's "presence" there for purposes of suit, the taxable event by which the state brings appellant within the reach of its taxing power. The state thus has constitutional power to lay the tax and to subject appellant to a suit to recover it. The activities which establish its "presence" subject it alike to taxation by the state and to suit to recover the tax. [Citations omitted.]

Affirmed.

■ MR. JUSTICE JACKSON took no part in the consideration or decision of this case.

■ MR. JUSTICE BLACK delivered the following opinion.

. . . Nor is the further ground advanced on this appeal, that the State of Washington has denied appellant due process of law, any less devoid of substance [than the claim that imposition of the tax violates the commerce clause]. It is my view, therefore, that we should dismiss the appeal as unsubstantial, Seaboard Air Line R. Co. v. Watson, 287 U.S. 86, 90, 92, 53 S.Ct. 32, 34, 35, and decline the invitation to formulate broad rules as to the meaning of due process, which here would amount to deciding a constitutional question "in advance of the necessity for its decision." Alabama State Federation of Labor v. McAdory, 325 U.S. 450, 461, 65 S.Ct. 1384, 1389.

Certainly appellant cannot in the light of our past decisions meritoriously claim that notice by registered mail and by personal service on its sales solicitors in Washington did not meet the requirements of procedural due process. And the due process clause is not brought in issue any more by appellant's further conceptualistic contention that Washington could not levy a tax or bring suit against the corporation because it did not honor that State with its mystical "presence." For it is unthinkable that the vague due process clause was ever intended to prohibit a State from regulating or taxing a business carried on within its boundaries simply because this is done by agents of a corporation organized and having its headquarters elsewhere. To read this into the due process clause would in fact result in depriving a State's citizens of due process by taking from the State the power to protect them in their business dealings within its boundaries with representatives of a foreign corporation. Nothing could be more irrational or more designed to defeat the function of our federative system of government. Certainly a State, at the very least, has power to tax and sue those dealing with its citizens within its boundaries, as we have held before. Hoopeston Canning Co. v. Cullen, 318 U.S. 313, 63 S.Ct. 602. Were the Court to follow this principle, it would provide a workable standard for cases where, as here, no other questions are involved. The Court has not chosen to do so, but instead has engaged in an unnecessary discussion in the course of which it has announced vague Constitutional criteria applied for the first time to the issue before us. It has thus introduced uncertain elements confusing the simple pattern and tending to curtail the exercise of State powers to an extent not justified by the Constitution.

The criteria adopted insofar as they can be identified read as follows: Due Process does permit State courts to "enforce the obligations which appellant has incurred" if it be found "reasonable and just according to our traditional conception of fair play and substantial justice." And this in turn means that we will "permit" the State to act if upon "an 'estimate of the inconveniences' which would result to the corporation from a trial away from its 'home' or principal place of business," we conclude that it is "reasonable" to subject it to suit in a State where it is doing business.

It is true that this Court did use the terms "fair play" and "substantial justice" in explaining the philosophy underlying the holding that it could not be "due process of law" to render a personal judgment against a defendant without notice and an opportunity to be heard. Milliken v. Meyer, 311 U.S. 457, 61 S.Ct. 339. In McDonald v. Mabee, 243 U.S. 90, 91, 37 S.Ct. 343, cited in the Milliken case, Mr. Justice Holmes, speaking for the Court, warned against judicial curtailment of this opportunity to be heard and referred to such a curtailment as a denial of "fair play," which even the common law would have deemed "contrary to natural justice." And previous cases had indicated that the ancient rule against judgments without notice had stemmed from "natural justice" concepts. These cases, while giving additional reasons why notice under particular circumstances is inadequate, did not mean thereby that all legislative enactments which this Court might deem to be contrary to natural justice ought to be held invalid under the due process clause. None of the cases purport to support or could support a holding that a State can tax and sue corporations only if its action comports with this Court's notions of "natural justice." I should have thought the Tenth Amendment settled that.

I believe that the Federal Constitution leaves to each State, without any "ifs" or "buts," a power to tax and to open the doors of its courts for its citizens to sue corporations whose agents do business in those States. Believing that the Constitution gave the States that power, I think it a judicial deprivation to condition its exercise upon this Court's notion of "fair play," however appealing that term may be. Nor can I stretch the meaning of due process so far as to authorize this Court to deprive a State of the right to afford judicial protection to its citizens on the ground that it would be more "convenient" for the corporation to be sued somewhere else.

There is a strong emotional appeal in the words "fair play," "justice,"[x] and "reasonable." But they were not chosen by those who wrote the original Constitution or the Fourteenth Amendment as a measuring rod for the Court to use in invalidating State or Federal laws passed by elected legislative representatives. No one, not even those who most feared a democratic government, ever formally proposed that courts should be given power to invalidate legislation under any such elastic standards. Express prohibitions against certain types of legislation are found in the Constitu-

[x] Justice Holmes wrote to Dr. Wu on July 1, 1929, "I have said to my brethren many times that I hate justice, which means that I know if a man begins to talk about that, for one reason or another he is shirking thinking in legal terms." Justice Oliver Wendell Holmes: His Book Notices and Uncollected Letters and Papers 201 (Harry C. Shriver ed., 1936).

tion, and under the long-settled practice, courts invalidate laws found to conflict with them. This requires interpretation, and interpretation, it is true, may result in extension of the Constitution's purpose. But that is no reason for reading the due process clause so as to restrict a State's power to tax and sue those whose activities affect persons and businesses within the State, provided proper service can be had. Superimposing the natural justice concept on the Constitution's specific prohibitions could operate as a drastic abridgment of democratic safeguards they embody, such as freedom of speech, press and religion, and the right to counsel. This has already happened. Betts v. Brady, 316 U.S. 455, 62 S.Ct. 1252. Compare Feldman v. United States, 322 U.S. 487, 494–503, 64 S.Ct. 1082, 1085–1089. For application of this natural law concept, whether under the terms "reasonableness," "justice," or "fair play," makes judges the supreme arbiters of the country's laws and practices. Polk Co. v. Glover, 305 U.S. 5, 17–18, 59 S.Ct. 15, 20–21; Federal Power Commission v. Natural Gas Pipeline Co., 315 U.S. 575, 600, n. 4, 62 S.Ct. 736, 750, n. 4. This result, I believe, alters the form of government our Constitution provides. I cannot agree.

True, the State's power is here upheld. But the rule announced means that tomorrow's judgment may strike down a State or Federal enactment on the ground that it does not conform to this Court's idea of natural justice. I therefore find myself moved by the same fears that caused Mr. Justice Holmes to say in 1930:

"I have not yet adequately expressed the more than anxiety that I feel at the ever increasing scope given to the Fourteenth Amendment in cutting down what I believe to be the constitutional rights of the States. As the decisions now stand, I see hardly any limit but the sky to the invalidating of those rights if they happen to strike a majority of this Court as for any reason undesirable." Baldwin v. Missouri, 281 U.S. 586, 595, 50 S.Ct. 436, 439.

ADDITIONAL CONSTITUTIONAL LIMITATIONS: COMMERCE CLAUSE AND FIRST AMENDMENT

As suggested by the International Shoe case, constitutional bounds on a state's exercise of judicial authority over a foreign corporation may exist quite apart from the Due Process Clause. In Davis v. Farmers' Co-operative Equity Co., 262 U.S. 312, 43 S.Ct. 556 (1923), a Kansas plaintiff sued a Kansas railroad corporation in a Minnesota state court for a cause of action arising in Kansas. The railroad did not own or operate any lines in Minnesota, but it did maintain an agent there solely for the solicitation of traffic. The Supreme Court, without reaching the due process question, held that a statute authorizing service on the agent "imposes upon interstate commerce a serious and unreasonable burden which renders the statute obnoxious to the commerce clause." A district court more recently so relied on the Commerce Clause as an alternative ground for dismissal in Bryson v. Northlake Hilton, 407 F.Supp. 73 (M.D.N.C.1976). Otherwise, courts have very rarely invoked the Commerce Clause for such purpose, and its continuing vitality as an independent limitation on a state's exercise of judicial authority is in doubt. It seems unlikely that the Commerce Clause could work so to dismiss in a situation satisfying the current interpretation of the Due Process Clause.

The First Amendment also has sometimes been thought to place a limitation on a state's exercise of territorial jurisdiction over a foreign corporation, this limitation helping, for example, to ensure the free flow of information throughout the country. In New York Times Co. v. Connor, 365 F.2d 567, 572 (5th Cir.1966), which was a libel case against a newspaper, the Fifth Circuit described its view of the way in which the First Amendment restricts a state in its exercise of territorial jurisdiction: "First Amendment considerations surrounding the law of libel require a greater showing of contact to satisfy the due process clause than is necessary in asserting jurisdiction over other types of tortious activity." While agreeing that the First Amendment has a role in this area, the Second Circuit, in Buckley v. New York Post Corp., 373 F.2d 175 (2d Cir.1967), took a slightly different approach by suggesting that, with respect to a state's authority to entertain a libel case, the First Amendment imposed a restriction independent of the usual one imposed by the Due Process Clause. Cf. Lamb v. Turbine Design, Inc., 273 Ga. 154, 538 S.E.2d 437 (2000) (holding that mere dealings with a federal regulatory agency do not expose defendant to a related private tort action brought at the agency's site, in view of First Amendment right to petition for redress of grievances); Hilaire H. Butler, Note, The Government Contacts Exception to the District of Columbia Long–Arm Statute: Portrait of a Legal Morass, 36 Cath.U.L.Rev. 745 (1987). However, the Supreme Court now has put a halt to such approaches, at least in libel cases. Calder v. Jones, 465 U.S. 783, 104 S.Ct. 1482 (1984) ("We . . . reject the suggestion that First Amendment concerns enter into the jurisdictional analysis. The infusion of such considerations would needlessly complicate an already imprecise inquiry. [Citation omitted.] Moreover, the potential chill on protected First Amendment activity stemming from libel and defamation actions is already taken into account in the constitutional limitations on the substantive law governing such suits."); see also Keeton v. Hustler Magazine, Inc., 465 U.S. 770, 104 S.Ct. 1473 (1984) (holding that a nonresident individual can seek damages suffered throughout the country in a libel action against nondomestic magazine in New Hampshire, where there was a uniquely long statute of limitations but where sales of magazine were only ten to fifteen thousand per month).

To summarize the current but unclear law, the policies underlying the Commerce Clause and some First Amendment concerns might occasionally work to restrict state jurisdiction, but probably only doing so indirectly by weighing on the due process balance.

Perkins v. Benguet Consolidated Mining Co.

Supreme Court of the United States, 1952.
342 U.S. 437, 72 S.Ct. 413.

■ MR. JUSTICE BURTON delivered the opinion of the Court.

This case calls for an answer to the question whether the Due Process Clause of the Fourteenth Amendment to the Constitution of the United States precludes Ohio from subjecting a foreign corporation to the jurisdiction of its courts in this action in personam. The corporation has been carrying on in Ohio a continuous and systematic, but limited, part of its general business. Its president, while engaged in doing such business in Ohio, has been served with summons in this proceeding. The cause of action sued upon did not arise in Ohio and does not relate to the corporation's activities there. For the reasons hereafter stated, we hold that the Fourteenth Amendment leaves Ohio free to take or decline jurisdiction over the corporation.

After extended litigation elsewhere petitioner, Idonah Slade Perkins, a non-resident of Ohio, filed two actions in personam in the Court of Common Pleas of Clermont County, Ohio, against the several respondents. Among those sued is the Benguet Consolidated Mining Company, here called the mining company. It is styled a "sociedad anonima" under the laws of the Philippine Islands, where it owns and has operated profitable gold and silver mines. In one action petitioner seeks approximately $68,400 in dividends claimed to be due her as a stockholder. In the other she claims $2,500,000 damages largely because of the company's failure to issue to her certificates for 120,000 shares of its stock.[y]

In each case the trial court sustained a motion to quash the service of summons on the mining company. Ohio Com.Pl., 99 N.E.2d 515. The Court of Appeals of Ohio affirmed that decision, 88 Ohio App. 118, 95 N.E.2d 5, as did the Supreme Court of Ohio, 155 Ohio St. 116, 98 N.E.2d 33. The cases were consolidated and we granted certiorari . . . . 342 U.S. 808, 72 S.Ct. 33.

We start with the holding of the Supreme Court of Ohio, not contested here, that, under Ohio law, the mining company is to be treated as a foreign corporation. Actual notice of the proceeding was given to the corporation in the instant case through regular service of summons upon its president while he was in Ohio acting in that capacity. Accordingly, there can be no jurisdictional objection based upon a lack of notice to a responsible representative of the corporation.

The answer to the question of whether the state courts of Ohio are open to a proceeding in personam, against an amply notified foreign corporation, to enforce a cause of action not arising in Ohio and not related to the business or activities of the corporation in that State rests entirely

[y] The briefs explain that behind these two actions lay a marital dispute. Essentially, Mrs. Perkins was claiming that the mining company should have paid certain cash and stock dividends, when declared before World War II, to her rather than to her husband.

upon the law of Ohio, unless the Due Process Clause of the Fourteenth Amendment compels a decision either way.

The suggestion that federal due process *compels* the State to open its courts to such a case has no substance.

> "Provisions for making foreign corporations subject to service in the state is a matter of legislative discretion, and a failure to provide for such service is not a denial of due process. Still less is it incumbent upon a state in furnishing such process to make the jurisdiction over the foreign corporation wide enough to include the adjudication of transitory actions not arising in the state." Missouri P.R. Co. v. Clarendon Boat Oar Co., 257 U.S. 533, 535, 42 S.Ct. 210, 211.

. . .

A more serious question is presented by the claim that the Due Process Clause of the Fourteenth Amendment *prohibits* Ohio from granting such relief against a foreign corporation. The . . . report of the case below, while denying the relief sought, does not indicate whether the Supreme Court of Ohio rested its decision on Ohio law or on the Fourteenth Amendment. . . .

. . . .

. . . Accordingly, for us to allow the judgment to stand as it is would risk an affirmance of a decision which might have been decided differently if the court below had felt free, under our decisions, to do so.

. . . .

The essence of the issue here, at the constitutional level, is . . . general fairness to the corporation. Appropriate tests for that are discussed in International Shoe Co. v. Washington, [326 U.S. 310, 317–20, 66 S.Ct. 154, 158–60 (1945)]. The amount and kind of activities which must be carried on by the foreign corporation in the state of the forum so as to make it reasonable and just to subject the corporation to the jurisdiction of that state are to be determined in each case. The corporate activities of a foreign corporation which, under state statute, make it necessary for it to secure a license and to designate a statutory agent upon whom process may be served provide a helpful but not a conclusive test. For example, the state of the forum may by statute require a foreign mining corporation to secure a license in order lawfully to carry on there such functional intrastate operations as those of mining or refining ore. On the other hand, if the same corporation carries on, in that state, other continuous and systematic corporate activities as it did here—consisting of directors' meetings, business correspondence, banking, stock transfers, payment of salaries, purchasing of machinery, etc.—those activities are enough to make it fair and reasonable to subject that corporation to proceedings in personam in that state, at least insofar as the proceedings in personam seek to enforce causes of action relating to those very activities or to other activities of the corporation within the state.

. . . .

It remains only to consider, in more detail, the issue of whether, as a matter of federal due process, the business done in Ohio by the respondent mining company was sufficiently substantial and of such a nature as to *permit* Ohio to entertain a cause of action against a foreign corporation, where the cause of action arose from activities entirely distinct from its activities in Ohio. See International Shoe Co. v. Washington, supra, 326 U.S. at page 318, 66 S.Ct. at page 159.

The Ohio Court of Appeals summarized the evidence on the subject. 88 Ohio App. at pages 119–125, 95 N.E.2d at pages 6–9. From that summary the following facts are substantially beyond controversy: The company's mining properties were in the Philippine Islands. Its operations there were completely halted during the occupation of the Islands by the Japanese. During that interim the president, who was also the general manager and principal stockholder of the company, returned to his home in Clermont County, Ohio. There he maintained an office in which he conducted his personal affairs and did many things on behalf of the company. He kept there office files of the company. He carried on there correspondence relating to the business of the company and to its employees. He drew and distributed there salary checks on behalf of the company, both in his own favor as president and in favor of two company secretaries who worked there with him. He used and maintained in Clermont County, Ohio, two active bank accounts carrying substantial balances of company funds. A bank in Hamilton County, Ohio, acted as transfer agent for the stock of the company. Several directors' meetings were held at his office or home in Clermont County. From that office he supervised policies dealing with the rehabilitation of the corporation's properties in the Philippines and he dispatched funds to cover purchases of machinery for such rehabilitation. Thus he carried on in Ohio a continuous and systematic supervision of the necessarily limited wartime activities of the company. He there discharged his duties as president and general manager, both during the occupation of the company's properties by the Japanese and immediately thereafter. While no mining properties in Ohio were owned or operated by the company, many of its wartime activities were directed from Ohio and were being given the personal attention of its president in that State at the time he was served with summons [in 1947]. Consideration of the circumstances which, under the law of Ohio, ultimately will determine whether the courts of that State will choose to take jurisdiction over the corporation is reserved for the courts of that State. Without reaching that issue of state policy, we conclude that, under the circumstances above recited, it would not violate federal due process for Ohio either to take or decline jurisdiction of the corporation in this proceeding. This relieves the Ohio courts of the restriction . . . which may have influenced the judgment of the court below.

Accordingly, the judgment of the Supreme Court of Ohio is vacated and the cause is remanded to that court for further proceedings in the light of this opinion.

It is so ordered.[z]

■ MR. JUSTICE BLACK concurs in the result.

■ [The dissenting opinion of JUSTICE MINTON, with whom Chief Justice Vinson joined, is omitted.]

Question: (31) *P* of Florida sues *D*, a drug manufacturer incorporated in Delaware with its principal place of business in Connecticut, in a South Carolina federal court for over $100,000 on account of alleged injuries suffered from *D*'s drugs, which *D* manufactured outside South Carolina and which *P* purchased and consumed in Florida. *D*'s activities in South Carolina are only the solicitation by mail to South Carolina dealers and wholesalers and the mailing of promotional literature to about 650 South Carolina doctors on its mailing lists. South Carolina has a six-year statute of limitations, which has not expired, while the shorter statutes of all other states having any connection with the claim have run. *P* utilizes Federal Rule 4(k)(1)(A) to serve process pursuant to the South Carolina long-arm statute, which its highest court has held to go to the outer limits of due process. *D* moves to set aside the service and dismiss the complaint for lack of personal jurisdiction. What should the decision be? See Ratliff v. Cooper Laboratories, 444 F.2d 745 (4th Cir.1971) (grant motion).

GENERAL JURISDICTION: THE HELICOPTEROS CASE

Within the category of personal jurisdiction, the kind invoked in Perkins (and denied in Ratliff) is called general jurisdiction. It gives the state the power to adjudicate any personal claim whether or not arising from, or even related to, the defendant's contacts with the forum state. The distinction is to specific jurisdiction, by which lesser contacts give the state power to adjudicate only those personal claims related to the contacts.

You will recall that the domicile basis yields general jurisdiction. Also, an individual's physical presence in the state when served with process works that way. So, Perkins (and International Shoe) said that if a corporation's in-state business activities are, when served with process, extensively continuous and systematic—which courts phrase as "doing business" rather than merely "transacting business"—then the corporation is subject to jurisdiction even for claims wholly unrelated to the in-state business activities.

More recently, this kind of "doing business" jurisdiction came before the Supreme Court in the potentially significant case of Helicopteros Nacionales de Colombia, S.A. v. Hall, 466 U.S. 408, 104 S.Ct. 1868 (1984). The facts of this Texas state court wrongful-death action involved American pipeline workers killed when the Colombian defendant's helicopter crashed in Peru. The defendant was providing transportation services there

---

[z] On remand, the court denied defendant's motion to quash the service of summons, 158 Ohio St. 145, 107 N.E.2d 203 (1952).

pursuant to a contract negotiated with Texans in Texas, and it received payment from Texas. It had bought its helicopters and parts in Texas, and its helicopter pilots and workers had received training in Texas. These Texan contacts were substantial, but not substantial enough for general jurisdiction according to the Supreme Court's view of the Due Process Clause. Therefore, the level of activities required to produce general jurisdiction, which would allow suit on any claim whatsoever, is very high indeed. Think General Motors in Michigan. See generally B. Glenn George, In Search of General Jurisdiction, 64 Tul.L.Rev. 1097 (1990).

The frustrating thing about the Helicopteros opinion, however, is that the Court expressly decided not to reach the more difficult question of whether nongeneral jurisdiction existed. The case thus leaves unclear whether it mattered that the particular claim was at least somewhat related to the Texan contacts.

McGee v. International Life Insurance Co.

Supreme Court of the United States, 1957.
355 U.S. 220, 78 S.Ct. 199.

■ MR. JUSTICE BLACK delivered the opinion of the Court.

Petitioner, Lulu B. McGee, recovered a judgment in a California state court against respondent, International Life Insurance Company, on a contract of insurance. Respondent was not served with process in California but by registered mail at its principal place of business in Texas. The California court based its jurisdiction on a state statute which subjects foreign corporations to suit in California on insurance contracts with residents of that State even though such corporations cannot be served with process within its borders.[1]

Unable to collect the judgment in California petitioner went to Texas where she filed suit on the judgment in a Texas court. But the Texas courts refused to enforce her judgment holding it was void under the Fourteenth Amendment because service of process outside California could not give the courts of that State jurisdiction over respondent. Since the case raised important questions, not only to California but to other States which have similar laws, we granted certiorari. 352 U.S. 924, 77 S.Ct. 239. It is not controverted that if the California court properly exercised jurisdiction over respondent the Texas courts erred in refusing to give its judgment full faith and credit. 28 U.S.C. § 1738.

The material facts are relatively simple. In 1944, Lowell Franklin, a resident of California, purchased a life insurance policy from the Empire Mutual Insurance Company, an Arizona corporation. In 1948 the respondent agreed with Empire Mutual to assume its insurance obligations. Respondent then mailed a reinsurance certificate to Franklin in California

[1] Cal.Insurance Code, West's Anno. §§ 1610–1620.

offering to insure him in accordance with the terms of the policy he held with Empire Mutual. He accepted this offer and from that time until his death in 1950 paid premiums by mail from his California home to respondent's Texas office. Petitioner, Franklin's mother, was the beneficiary under the policy.[a] She sent proofs of his death to the respondent but it refused to pay claiming that he had committed suicide. It appears that neither Empire Mutual nor respondent has ever had any offices or agents in California. And so far as the record before us shows, respondent has never solicited or done any insurance business in California apart from the policy involved here.

Since Pennoyer v. Neff, 95 U.S. 714, this Court has held that the Due Process Clause of the Fourteenth Amendment places some limit on the power of state courts to enter binding judgments against persons not served with process within their boundaries. But just where this line of limitation falls has been the subject of prolific controversy, particularly with respect to foreign corporations. . . . More recently in International Shoe Co. v. State of Washington, 326 U.S. 310, 66 S.Ct. 154, the Court decided that "due process requires only that in order to subject a defendant to a judgment in personam, if he be not present within the territory of the forum, he have certain minimum contacts with it such that the maintenance of the suit does not offend 'traditional notions of fair play and substantial justice.'" Id., 326 U.S. at page 316, 66 S.Ct. at page 158.

Looking back over this long history of litigation a trend is clearly discernible toward expanding the permissible scope of state jurisdiction over foreign corporations and other nonresidents. In part this is attributable to the fundamental transformation of our national economy over the years. Today many commercial transactions touch two or more States and may involve parties separated by the full continent. With this increasing nationalization of commerce has come a great increase in the amount of business conducted by mail across state lines. At the same time modern transportation and communication have made it much less burdensome for a party sued to defend himself in a State where he engages in economic activity.

Turning to this case we think it apparent that the Due Process Clause did not preclude the California court from entering a judgment binding on respondent. It is sufficient for purposes of due process that the suit was based on a contract which had substantial connection with that State. Cf. Hess v. Pawloski, 274 U.S. 352, 47 S.Ct. 632; Henry L. Doherty & Co. v. Goodman, 294 U.S. 623, 55 S.Ct. 553; Pennoyer v. Neff, 95 U.S. 714, 735. The contract was delivered in California, the premiums were mailed from there and the insured was a resident of that State when he died. It cannot be denied that California has a manifest interest in providing effective means of redress for its residents when their insurers refuse to pay claims. These residents would be at a severe disadvantage if they were forced to follow the insurance company to a distant State in order to hold it legally

[a] She was a California resident. See McGee v. Int'l Life Ins. Co., 288 S.W.2d 579, 580 (Tex.Civ.App.1956).

accountable. When claims were small or moderate individual claimants frequently could not afford the cost of bringing an action in a foreign forum—thus in effect making the company judgment proof. Often the crucial witnesses—as here on the company's defense of suicide—will be found in the insured's locality. Of course there may be inconvenience to the insurer if it is held amenable to suit in California where it had this contract but certainly nothing which amounts to a denial of due process. Cf. Travelers Health Ass'n v. Commonwealth of Virginia ex rel. State Corporation Comm., 339 U.S. 643, 70 S.Ct. 927. There is no contention that respondent did not have adequate notice of the suit or sufficient time to prepare its defense and appear.

The California statute became law in 1949, after respondent had entered into the agreement with Franklin to assume Empire Mutual's obligation to him. Respondent contends that application of the statute to this existing contract improperly impairs the obligation of the contract. We believe that contention is devoid of merit. The statute was remedial, in the purest sense of that term, and neither enlarged nor impaired respondent's substantive rights and obligations under the contract. It did nothing more than to provide petitioner with a California forum to enforce whatever substantive rights she might have against respondent. At the same time respondent was given a reasonable time to appear and defend on the merits after being notified of the suit. Under such circumstances it had no vested right not to be sued in California. [Citations omitted.]

The judgment is reversed and the cause is remanded to the Court of Civil Appeals of the State of Texas, First Supreme Judicial District, for further proceedings not inconsistent with this opinion.

It is so ordered.

■ THE CHIEF JUSTICE [WARREN, Governor of California 1943–1953,] took no part in the consideration or decision of this case [leaving Justice Black, as the senior Justice, to designate the opinion-writer].

Question: (32) *P*, a seaman from New York City, was discharged before his ship's voyage ended, having signed on at Beaumont, Texas, on May 16, 1970, and having been discharged at Houston, Texas, on May 18, 1970. Seeking lost wages protected by federal statute, he sues *D*, the shipowner, in a Pennsylvania federal court. *P* chooses the place of suit for reasons of personal convenience. *D*, a corporation foreign to Pennsylvania, has its offices in New York City, and its only contact with Pennsylvania was when another one of its ships took on a substantial cargo in Philadelphia during June 1972. In November 1973 *P* utilizes the predecessor of Federal Rule 4(k)(1)(A) to serve process pursuant to the Pennsylvania long-arm statute, construed to go to the outer limits of due process. Upon *D*'s motion to quash service and to dismiss for lack of personal jurisdiction, what decision? See Mackensworth v. American Trading Transp. Co., 367 F.Supp. 373, 1974 A.M.C. 237 (E.D.Pa.1973) (statement of facts here supplemented by reference to the record and letters from Judge Edward R. Becker and from counsel for plaintiff, Harry Lore, Esq., which reveal that thereafter the case soon settled for $550), noted in Jerry J.

Phillips, "Minimum Contacts" Reviewed or Poetic Justice Pursued, 41 Tenn.L.Rev. 683 (1974); Seymour I. Toll, Scratch a Lawyer, Find a Poet, 37 Shingle 74 (1974); 12 Duq.L.Rev. 717 (1974); 15 Harv.Int'l L.J. 365 (1974).

ESSENTIAL CONSTITUTIONAL LIMITATIONS: DUE PROCESS

The major focus of the preceding cases was the constitutional limits on state jurisdiction. Subsequent cases will further specify due process. But already apparent is that an idea of power (whether the defendant committed sufficient acts directed at the state, given the relatedness or unrelatedness of the cause of action to those acts) interplays with an idea of reasonableness (more of an all-interests-considered inquiry into fairness).

Certainly, these ideas add up to mean that some limits exist. A state cannot reach just anyone, even in the absence of minimal contacts of defendant with the state. For example, imagine that the McGee facts were that Lowell Franklin lived in Arizona and conducted all his insurance affairs there, but his alleged suicide occurred while visiting Lulu McGee in California: there would be no jurisdiction in California, because defendant did not do enough in California, even though both plaintiff and California have plenty of interests in going forward there. Moreover, even if defendant has contacts, they presumably do not suffice. Imagine on the actual McGee facts that the insurance company instead sued the beneficiary in Texas for a declaration of nonliability: there should be no jurisdiction in Texas, because of the burden on Lulu and the presence of all the evidence in California, even though Lulu through Lowell as her "agent" had contacts with Texas related to the insurance policy. If that last example seems too complicated, an alternative might be the commonsense rule you could intuit from your own life: we should not allow a mail-order seller of clothes suing for nonpayment to exert jurisdiction over the consumer in the seller's state, simply on the basis of that one-shot sale.

These hypotheticals also raise the question of the kinds of defendants reachable by the state. The International Shoe case speaks primarily in terms of foreign corporations, although its reasoning seems equally applicable to nonresident individuals. The same is true of the Perkins case. The defendant in McGee was an insurance company, but Justice Black refers to the clearly discernible trend "toward expanding the permissible scope of state jurisdiction over foreign corporations and other nonresidents."

(f) MODERN JURISDICTIONAL STATUTES

For separation-of-powers reasons, the states generally hold that a state court must be authorized by state statute to exercise the various bases of jurisdictional power, except for the bases of presence and consent which were recognized at common law. Accordingly, once International Shoe and its immediate progeny suggested the possible extent of state reach, all the states enacted statutes, often called long-arm statutes, to extend their territorial jurisdiction.

However, a state is certainly not required to extend its jurisdiction all the way to constitutionally permissible limits. Of great practical importance is the fact that to the extent a state long-arm statute falls short of authorizing all the jurisdiction permitted by the Constitution, the statute serves in effect to restrict the state court's jurisdiction. Many assertions of jurisdiction fail because the situation in suit does not come within the statute.

As to defendants reached, most modern jurisdictional statutes in fact cover individuals as well as corporations, and no case suggests that the standards are different in substance. In Forbes v. Wells Beach Casino, Inc., 219 A.2d 542 (Me.1966), an action for specific performance of a contract in which the movant (defendant Elias Loew of Massachusetts) had been served with process in Massachusetts pursuant to the Maine long-arm statute, he argued that, at least in the case of a "human nonresident," recent Supreme Court decisions did not go to the length of upholding personal jurisdiction in respect to "activities of a kind which the State of Maine has not regarded as exceptional and has not subjected to special and unique regulation." This contention the Maine court rejected.

ILLINOIS REVISED STATUTES CHAPTER 110

§ 17. *Act submitting to jurisdiction—Process*[b]

(1) Any person, whether or not a citizen or resident of this State, who in person or through an agent does any of the acts hereinafter enumerated, thereby submits said person, and, if an individual, his personal representative, to the jurisdiction of the courts of this State as to any cause of action arising from the doing of any of said acts:

(a) The transaction of any business within this State;

(b) The commission of a tortious act within this State;

(c) The ownership, use, or possession of any real estate situated in this State;

(d) Contracting to insure any person, property or risk located within this State at the time of contracting.

(2) Service of process upon any person who is subject to the jurisdiction of the courts of this State, as provided in this section, may be made by personally serving the summons upon the defendant outside this State, as provided in this Act, with the same force and effect as though summons had been personally served within this State.

(3) Only causes of action arising from acts enumerated herein may be asserted against a defendant in an action in which jurisdiction over him is based upon this section.

[b] This is the original version of the statute, enacted in 1955 as the first comprehensive long-arm statute in the nation. The statute has since been amended, and recently in major ways, as we shall see shortly.

(4) Nothing herein contained limits or affects the right to serve any process in any other manner now or hereafter provided by law.

NELSON v. MILLER, 11 Ill.2d 378, 143 N.E.2d 673 (1957). In this action involving alleged negligence in unloading a truck in Illinois during a delivery by an out-of-state defendant, the Illinois Supreme Court upheld the Illinois jurisdictional statute. The court said sweepingly that the entire statute reflected "a conscious purpose to assert jurisdiction over nonresident defendants to the extent permitted by the due-process clause."

The defendant had argued that jurisdiction under the words "commission of a tortious act within this State" depended upon proof of all the facts necessary to spell out ultimate liability in tort. The Illinois Supreme Court rejected this construction, holding the jurisdictional requirement satisfied "when the defendant, personally or through an agent, is the author of acts or omissions within the State, and when the complaint states a cause of action in tort arising from such conduct."

The rejected construction of the statute would have produced anomalous results, as explained in detail by Kevin M. Clermont, Jurisdictional Fact, 91 Cornell L.Rev. 973 (2006). A preliminary hearing on jurisdiction would entail a full-dress trial on the merits as to all issues of liability, with troublesome problems regarding jury right and res judicata—and if the defendant won, he would get not a conclusive judgment on the merits but only a threshold dismissal for lack of jurisdiction, at the cost of having relinquished his right not to have to litigate the merits in that forum. If he instead defaulted, he could force a trial on all the issues of liability in his home state because these would be jurisdictional facts subject to collateral attack—and thus the statutory objective of forcing the defendant, when appropriate, to defend his conduct in the state where it took place would be nullified.

GRAY v. AMERICAN RADIATOR & STANDARD SANITARY CORP., 22 Ill.2d 432, 176 N.E.2d 761 (1961). The explosion in Illinois of a hot-water heater injured the plaintiff. She sued the American Radiator & Standard Sanitary Corp. and the Titan Valve Manufacturing Co. Her claim was that Titan had negligently constructed a safety valve in Ohio and sold it to American Radiator, which manufactured the heater and attached the safety valve thereto in Pennsylvania. The heater was sold to an Illinois purchaser in the course of commerce. There was no showing that Titan had had any other contact with Illinois, directly or indirectly, nor that it had any agent there. American Radiator set up a crossclaim against Titan for indemnification by reason of certain warranties made by Titan.

Titan moved to dismiss the complaint and the crossclaim for lack of jurisdiction. The trial court granted the motion, and the plaintiff appealed.

The questions presented were (1) whether a tortious act was committed in Illinois within the meaning of the Illinois statute and (2) whether the statute, if so construed, was consistent with due process of law.

On the first question, the Illinois Supreme Court said:

"The first aspect to which we must direct our attention is one of statutory construction. Under section 17(1)(b) jurisdiction is predicated on the committing of a tortious act in this State. It is not disputed, for the purpose of this appeal, that a tortious act was committed. The issue depends on whether it was committed in Illinois, so as to warrant the assertion of personal jurisdiction by service of summons in Ohio.

"The wrong in the case at bar did not originate in the conduct of a servant physically present here, but arose instead from acts performed at the place of manufacture. Only the consequences occurred in Illinois. It is well established, however, that in law the place of wrong is where the last event takes place which is necessary to render the actor liable. (Restatement, Conflict of Laws, sec. 377.) A second indication that the place of injury is the determining factor is found in rules governing the time within which an action must be brought. In applying statutes of limitation our court has computed the period from the time when the injury is done. [Citations omitted.] We think it is clear that the alleged negligence in manufacturing the valve cannot be separated from the resulting injury; and that for present purposes, like those of liability and limitations, the tort was committed in Illinois.

"Titan seeks to avoid this result by arguing that instead of using the word 'tort,' the legislature employed the term 'tortious act'; and that the latter refers only to the act or conduct, separate and apart from any consequences thereof. We cannot accept the argument. To be tortious an act must cause injury. The concept of injury is an inseparable part of the phrase. In determining legislative intention courts will read words in their ordinary and popularly understood sense. [Citations omitted.] We think the intent should be determined less from technicalities of definition than from considerations of general purpose and effect. To adopt the criteria urged by defendant would tend to promote litigation over extraneous issues concerning the elements of a tort and the territorial incidence of each, whereas the test should be concerned more with those substantial elements of convenience and justice presumably contemplated by the legislature. As we observed in Nelson v. Miller . . . , the statute contemplates the exertion of jurisdiction over nonresident defendants to the extent permitted by the due-process clause."

The court likewise answered the second question in the affirmative, after observing: "In the case at bar defendant does not claim that the present use of its product in Illinois is an isolated instance. While the record does not disclose the volume of Titan's business or the territory in which appliances incorporating its valves are marketed, it is a reasonable inference that its commercial transactions, like those of other manufacturers, result in substantial use and consumption in this State."

The court concluded: "We construe section 17(1)(b) as providing for jurisdiction under the circumstances shown in this case, and we hold that as so construed the statute does not violate due process of law."

Question: (33) If this case had come before the Supreme Court of the United States for review, what arguments would you have made for reversal? What, if any, facts in addition to those summarized above would you have considered relevant?

LONGINES–WITTNAUER WATCH CO. v. BARNES & REINECKE, INC., 15 N.Y.2d 443, 209 N.E.2d 68, 261 N.Y.S.2d 8 (1965). The court decided three cases under this caption. In one of these, Feathers v. McLucas, the plaintiffs had suffered injury by the explosion of a tractor-drawn propane gas tank, en route from Pennsylvania to Vermont, on a highway near their home in New York. They sued, among others, the Darby Corporation, which had manufactured the tank in Kansas and sold it, through an intermediary, to a Pennsylvania corporation that was an interstate carrier licensed by several states including New York. The plaintiffs charged Darby with negligence and breach of warranty in the manufacture of the tank. There was no showing that Darby had had any other contact with New York, directly or indirectly, nor that it had any agent there.

The plaintiffs asserted jurisdiction over Darby by NYCPLR § 302(a)(2), which like the Illinois statute says that jurisdiction extends to a defendant who "commits a tortious act within the state."[c] Darby contended that no jurisdiction existed.

Reversing the court below, the Court of Appeals of New York sided with Darby. It rejected the view that the legislature had intended to go to the limits of the Due Process Clause. Looking to the wording of the statute, the court said: "The language of paragraph 2 . . . is too plain and precise to permit it to be read, as has the Appellate Division, as if it were synonymous with 'commits a tortious act *without* the state which causes injury within the state.' " The court found further support for its reading in the legislative history, before concluding that expansion of the statute's scope "is a matter for the Legislature rather than the courts."

Question: (34) *P* of Illinois has brought a paternity action against *D* of Ohio in an Illinois court. *P* alleges, in essence, that *D* sired her child out of wedlock and has failed in his duty to provide support. More specifically, she alleges that "during the

---

[c] The current New York long-arm statute, along with service provisions, appears in the statutory section of the Rules booklet. You should note that the New York legislature added § 302(a)(3) in 1966, which is effectively the same as § 1.03(a)(4) of the upcoming Uniform Act.

time biologically certain to have been the instant of conception, your Plaintiff had sexual intercourse with your Defendant in Cook County, Illinois, and with no other person." *P* alleges no other connection of *D* to Illinois. *D* received in-hand service of process in Ohio pursuant to the Illinois long-arm statute reprinted above. He has now, by his attorney, submitted a motion to dismiss for lack of personal jurisdiction. *D*'s papers in support deny those allegations of the complaint and further argue that, even if they were true, such facts would not sustain jurisdiction over the person. *P*'s papers take the opposite positions. How should the motion be decided? Compare Poindexter v. Willis, 87 Ill.App.2d 213, 231 N.E.2d 1 (1967), enforced, 23 Ohio Misc. 199, 256 N.E.2d 254 (C.P.1970), with Anonymous v. Anonymous, 49 Misc.2d 675, 268 N.Y.S.2d 710 (Fam.Ct.1966). Note that many state statutes would seem to reach this kind of case, including the special provision that New York enacted in 1997 as N.Y.Fam.Ct.Act § 580–201(6) ("the individual engaged in sexual intercourse in this state and the child may have been conceived by that act of intercourse").

UNIFORM INTERSTATE AND INTERNATIONAL PROCEDURE ACT[d]

§ 1.03. [*Personal Jurisdiction Based upon Conduct*]

(a) A court may exercise personal jurisdiction over a person, who acts directly or by an agent, as to a [cause of action] [claim for relief] arising from the person's

(1) transacting any business in this state;

(2) contracting to supply services or things in this state;

(3) causing tortious injury by an act or omission in this state;

(4) causing tortious injury in this state by an act or omission outside this state if he regularly does or solicits business or engages in any other persistent course of conduct in this state or derives substantial revenue from goods or services used or consumed in this state; [or]

(5) having an interest in, using, or possessing real property in this state[; or

(6) contracting to insure any person, property, or risk located within this state at the time of contracting].

---

[d] This Uniform Act—approved by the National Conference of Commissioners on Uniform State Laws in 1962 but withdrawn in 1977 because all states had gone at least as far—presented a comprehensive code treating state litigation with interstate or international incidents. In addition to these provisions extending personal jurisdiction over persons not within the forum state, it supplanted earlier Uniform Acts for the taking of depositions outside the state, the determination of foreign law, and the proof of official records. A number of states adopted it.

The brackets generally suggest to state legislatures a choice in the form of words to conform to state usage. Section 1.03(a)(6) is in brackets because many states have similar and more explicit provisions in their insurance laws, as illustrated in McGee v. International Life Ins. Co.

. . . .

Questions: (35) What differences do you see between the Uniform Act and subsection (1) of the above-reprinted Illinois statute? What is the significance of these differences? What would have been the result if the Gray case (or Feathers v. McLucas) had arisen under the Uniform Act?

(36) Defendant makes false representations outside the state communicated by mail or telephone to plaintiff within the state, intending that they should be relied on there to plaintiff's injury. Defendant has no other connection with the state. Is there sufficient basis for jurisdiction under the above-reprinted Illinois statute? Cf. Southeast Guar. Trust Co. v. Rodman & Renshaw, Inc., 358 F.Supp. 1001 (N.D.Ill. 1973) (yes). Is there sufficient basis for jurisdiction under NYCPLR § 302(a)(2)? Cf. Bauer Indus., Inc. v. Shannon Luminous Materials Co., 52 A.D.2d 897, 383 N.Y.S.2d 80 (1976) (no). Is there sufficient basis for jurisdiction under a statute derived from the Uniform Act? See Murphy v. Erwin–Wasey, Inc., 460 F.2d 661 (1st Cir.1972) (yes, in case from Massachusetts).

(37) Defendant by his out-of-state website misleads plaintiff (or defames her—or infringes her trademark). Defendant has no other connection with plaintiff's home state. Does it have sufficient constitutional basis for jurisdiction? Is a passive home page, which merely provides information, any different from defendant's having a telephone with a recorded message in defendant's home? Or is this internet situation more like defendant's mailing a letter to plaintiff's home as part of a mass mailing? Are such analogies useful? What, if any, additional information would you consider relevant? See Kevin M. Clermont, Principles of Civil Procedure 230–33 (2d ed. 2009) (treating internet jurisdiction).

PENGUIN GROUP (USA) INC. v. AMERICAN BUDDHA, No. 09 Civ. 528, 2009 WL 1069158 (S.D.N.Y. Apr. 21, 2009). A Delaware corporation, with its principal place of business in New York, sued a nonprofit Oregon corporation for copyright infringement through its publishing complete copies of four of the plaintiff's books on the defendant's website. The plaintiff did not allege any viewing or downloading in New York, other than by the plaintiff's attorney.

The plaintiff asserted jurisdiction by NYCPLR § 302(a)(3), which required "injury" in New York. The defendant contended that no jurisdiction existed.

The court dismissed the action. It construed the statute to require a direct injury caused by the alleged tort, not merely a derivative financial loss suffered at home by a New Yorker. Thus, "in cases of injury caused by infringement of intellectual property, the intellectual property owner suffers injury where the infringement occurs,"which would be Oregon, in the absence of any alleged infringement in New York.

CALIFORNIA CODE OF CIVIL PROCEDURE

§ 410.10 *Basis*

A court of this state may exercise jurisdiction on any basis not inconsistent with the Constitution of this state or of the United States.

Question: (38) A California plaintiff brings an action in a California court against a Nebraska defendant for damages arising out of a vehicular accident, occurring in Nevada near the California border and involving plaintiff's car and defendant's truck. Defendant, an interstate trucker, was en route to California to deliver and receive cargo when the accident occurred; during the seven years preceding the accident he made about 20 trips per year into California; and he was licensed to haul freight by several states including California. Is there sufficient basis for personal jurisdiction under the California statute? See Cornelison v. Chaney, 16 Cal.3d 143, 545 P.2d 264, 127 Cal.Rptr. 352 (1976) (yes).

Cook Associates v. Lexington United Corp.

Supreme Court of Illinois, 1981.
87 Ill.2d 190, 429 N.E.2d 847.

■ WARD, JUSTICE:

This appeal arises out of an action for breach of contract brought in the circuit court of Cook County. The plaintiff, Cook Associates, an Illinois corporation, brought the action against Lexington United Corporation, a Delaware corporation not licensed to do business in Illinois. Lexington is a dinnerware manufacturer whose principal place of business is St. Louis, Missouri. Lexington filed a special appearance to contest the court's in personam jurisdiction (Ill.Rev.Stat.1977, ch. 110, par. 20), but its motion to quash service of process was denied. Thereafter, Lexington answered, discovery was taken, and subsequently summary judgment was granted in favor of Cook. The appellate court reversed the judgment (86 Ill.App.3d 909, 407 N.E.2d 944), holding that the circuit court lacked personal jurisdiction over Lexington. Because of the disposition it made, the appellate court did not consider the propriety of the summary judgment. We granted Cook's petition for leave to appeal.

Cook is an employment agency whose offices are in Chicago. From July 1973 to July 1976, it also maintained a branch office in Massachusetts, which was operated by Edith McIntosh. Cook specializes in the placement of executive and professional employees with employers who pay Cook a fee if a person referred by Cook is hired. On May 12, 1976, Joseph Runza, a Lexington executive, phoned McIntosh, with whom he had done business before, at Cook's Massachusetts office. He requested assistance in filling a sales management position at Lexington. The record is unclear as to the title of the position discussed. It appears that Runza had first described it as "national sales manager" but later changed the description to "field sales manager."

On May 13, 1976, McIntosh sent Runza the names and resumes of some prospective employees, one of whom was Gregg Hoegemeir. Her accompanying letter stated: "As you know from our previous correspondence, these men, like all of our candidates, are being submitted to you upon the understanding that if they are employed, our fee will be paid by you in accordance with the enclosed schedule." Cook's fee schedule indicated its Chicago address on the letterhead, and stated that the fee would be 20% of one year's salary for positions paying $15,000 per year or more. The schedule also stated: "A fee will be due from you as to any applicant you hire within two years of our disclosure of his identity, or of our submission or referral of him, to you."

Runza communicated with Hoegemeir and arranged to meet him in Chicago. Hoegemeir's resume discloses that he was then a regional sales manager for a Chicago manufacturer and that he resided in Ballwin, Missouri. At the meeting, Runza offered Hoegemeir the position of "field sales manager" at an annual salary of $22,000. Hoegemeir rejected the offer, and the record reflects that there were no further contacts between Lexington and him for several months.

McIntosh's employment by Cook terminated in July 1976. About three months later, she opened her own employment search and placement service in Massachusetts. It appears that soon thereafter, Runza communicated with McIntosh at her home and advised he was seeking a sales manager for Lexington. This time, it appears, the position would be that of "national sales manager" at a salary in excess of $22,000. McIntosh, acting for her own agency, submitted the names of a number of candidates, including that of Hoegemeir. After several interviews with Hoegemeir, Runza offered him the position at a salary of $25,000 and Hoegemeir accepted. The record does not show whether any of the negotiations which led to Hoegemeir's employment took place in Illinois, nor does it make clear where the contract for his employment was made.

Hoegemeir began working for Lexington in December 1976, and Lexington paid McIntosh a $5,000 fee for her services. Cook later became aware of the hiring of Hoegemeir, and it demanded a $5,000 fee, representing 20% of Hoegemeir's starting salary. When Lexington refused to pay the commission, Cook filed the action for breach of contract in July 1977.

Process was served on Lexington's president, Frank Ivitch, when he was attending a trade show in Chicago. Ivitch and several other company officials were appearing in a week-long housewares exhibit of Lexington. Exhibitors were prohibited from selling merchandise at the exhibition. Less than $50,000 in orders was taken by Lexington at the exhibit, according to the answer to an interrogatory, and were later accepted at Lexington's St. Louis office. Officials of Lexington had attended two other trade shows in Chicago in 1976 and 1977. At each of them, a similar volume of orders was received and later accepted.

Lexington's other contacts with Illinois were listed in an affidavit of Ivitch, and in Lexington's answers to interrogatories. Lexington did not have an office or an employee in this State. It had no Illinois telephone number. It did not advertise in Illinois, except in connection with the trade shows held in Chicago. Lexington merchandise was sold by an independent manufacturer's representative in Illinois to his Illinois accounts. The record does not reflect the volume of those sales. The representative sold merchandise of other manufacturers as well. Working strictly on a commission basis, he received no salary from Lexington. In the year preceding the filing of this action an employee of Lexington accompanied the representative on three or four occasions, but the employee did not make any sales.

The appellate court held, on due process grounds, that the circuit court of Cook County lacked personal jurisdiction over Lexington.

When arguing before the appellate court the parties were not in agreement as to the test or standard to be applied for determining whether there was personal jurisdiction. Lexington submitted that our long-arm statute provides the only means of acquiring jurisdiction over a nonresident corporate defendant. . . . Lexington contended that the requirements of the statute were not satisfied, because the action did not arise from "the transaction of any business" by Lexington in Illinois.

Cook, on the other hand, contended that the long-arm statute does not prohibit the acquiring of jurisdiction according to the doing-business doctrine. Under that doctrine, a foreign corporation is deemed to have submitted to our jurisdiction by doing business in Illinois. . . . Cook urged that Lexington's contacts with Illinois rendered the corporation subject to the jurisdiction of the circuit court of Cook County under the "doing business" view, or under the due process standard of "minimum contacts."

. . . .

Under the due process clause of the fourteenth amendment there are limits to which a State is confined in asserting in personam jurisdiction over a nonresident corporate defendant. . . .

It is important to recognize that this due process standard represents only the outer limits beyond which a State may not go to acquire jurisdiction over nonresidents. A State is free to set its own limits in acquiring this jurisdiction within the perimeters allowed by the due process clause. [Citations omitted.] We recently stressed that the boundaries or limits under our statute are not to be equated with the "minimum contacts" test under the due process clause. In Green v. Advance Ross Electronics Corp. (1981), 86 Ill.2d 431, 436, 427 N.E.2d 1203, 1206, we stated, in reference to the Illinois long-arm statute:

> "In Nelson v. Miller (1957), 11 Ill.2d 378, 389 [143 N.E.2d 673], this court said that the Illinois long-arm statute reflects a conscious purpose to assert jurisdiction over nonresidents to the extent permitted by the due process clause. We do not, however, regard this observation as the equivalent of declaring that the construction and application of section 17(1)(b) depend entirely upon decisions determining in what

circumstances due process requirements would permit long-arm jurisdiction. Neither do we read Nelson to say that in applying section 17(1)(b) we should not construe the meaning and intent of our own statute irrespective of the due process limitations generally applicable to State long-arm statutes. *A statute worded in the way ours is should have a fixed meaning without regard to changing concepts of due process*, except, of course, that an interpretation which renders the statute unconstitutional should be avoided, if possible. Thus, instead of turning to the array of tests which have been articulated to assist in determining whether long-arm statutes as applied exceed permissible constitutional boundaries, we prefer to resolve this appeal by looking to the meaning of our statute." (Emphasis added.)

We conclude that Lexington is not amenable to the jurisdiction of our courts under either the Illinois long-arm statute or under the doctrine of submitting to jurisdiction by virtue of doing business in Illinois.

Lexington is not amenable to service under the long-arm statute because the cause of action did not arise from the transaction of business in Illinois. Cook argues, however, that a contract between Lexington and Cook was formed in Illinois at the time of Hoegemeir's interview with Lexington. Alternatively, it says that this action arose out of Lexington's activities in Illinois because the interview with Hoegemeir in Chicago was an essential first step in a process of negotiations that culminated in the hiring of Hoegemeir. The contentions do not persuade. Hoegemeir rejected the offer of employment when he was interviewed in Illinois, and of course no contract was formed. Too, it cannot be said that the Chicago interview was any part in the negotiations that led to the hiring of Hoegemeir. The positions involved were different. Hoegemeir rejected the position of field sales manager. He later was hired as national sales manager, but there is no indication whatever in the record that the interview had any influence on his hiring. It was in the fall of 1976 that Runza asked McIntosh, who was then operating her own agency, for prospects to fill the position of national sales manager. There was no communication between Runza and Hoegemeir until McIntosh referred his name to Lexington in behalf of her own agency.

. . . .

The doing-business standard, of course, continues to be used in determining questions of jurisdiction over foreign corporations not licensed in Illinois (e.g., St. Louis–San Francisco Ry. v. Gitchoff (1977), 68 Ill.2d 38, 369 N.E.2d 52), as it was early recognized that the doctrine was not preempted by the long-arm statute. (See Lindley v. St. Louis–San Francisco Ry. Co. (7th Cir.1968), 407 F.2d 639.) In fact, it complements the long-arm statute because if a foreign, unlicensed corporation is found to be doing business in this State, it is amenable to the jurisdiction of courts of Illinois even for causes of action not arising from the defendant's transactions of business in Illinois. See Hertz Corp. v. Taylor (1959), 15 Ill.2d 552, 155 N.E.2d 610.

In Green v. Advance Ross Electronics Corp., from which we have quoted above, we held that the long-arm statute was not to be equated with the standard of due process. Here we will not equate the doing-business standard with the mere satisfaction of the minimum-contacts requirement for due process. To do so would render the long-arm statute and the doing-business standard meaningless to many corporate defendants, and it would tie our jurisdictional rules to the changing standards for due process. . . . .

There is no all-inclusive test for determining whether a foreign corporation is doing business in this State. In Pembleton v. Illinois Commercial Men's Association (1919), 289 Ill. 99, 104, 124 N.E. 355, appeal dismissed (1919), 253 U.S. 499, 40 S.Ct. 483, 64 L.Ed. 1032, this court stated that, in general, the term means that the corporation is conducting business in Illinois "of such a character and extent as to warrant the inference that the corporation has subjected itself to the jurisdiction and laws of the district in which it is served and in which it is bound to appear when a proper agent has been served with process." . . .

. . . .

More recently, in Connelly v. Uniroyal, Inc. (1979), 75 Ill.2d 393, 389 N.E.2d 155, cert. denied and appeal dismissed (1980), 444 U.S. 1060, 100 S.Ct. 992, 62 L.Ed.2d 738, an alien corporation was held to be amenable to Illinois jurisdiction in a product liability action, because the defendant's products regularly entered Illinois in substantial amounts. . . .

In the foregoing cases, there was a regularity of activities in Illinois that is absent in the case of Lexington. [Citations omitted.] Mr. Justice Cardozo, while serving on the New York Court of Appeals, defined "doing business" for jurisdictional purposes as the corporation's operating within the State "not occasionally or casually, but with a fair measure of permanence and continuity." Tauza v. Susquehanna Coal Co. (1917), 220 N.Y. 259, 267, 115 N.E. 915, 917. [Other New York citations omitted.]

We consider that Lexington was not doing business in Illinois through having an exhibit at three trade shows in Chicago, and its fruitless interview. We note that while Lexington received orders totaling less than $50,000 during each of those trade shows, the record does not show the size of the individual orders. There is no indication whether the persons who ordered merchandise were Illinois residents and that Lexington merchandise was introduced into Illinois. The independent manufacturer's representative resides in Illinois. The scant references to him in the record are inadequate for us to conclude that because of its association with him Lexington should be deemed to have submitted itself to our jurisdiction for all causes of action which might arise in Illinois. In essence, the record contains a statement that the representative sells Lexington's merchandise along with products of other manufacturers. The record does not show how much has been sold through him, and there is no indication of whether the representative is authorized to contract for Lexington or whether he merely transfers orders to Lexington for acceptance. There is no indication of the control, if any, Lexington has over this representative. A Lexington employee accompanied him a few times, but for what purpose the record fails to show. Nor does it disclose what the Lexington employee did on those occasions.

. . . .

Judgment affirmed.

IMPUTED CONTACTS

All these statutes expose the fundamental problem of when to attribute another's acts to the defendant for jurisdictional purposes. A general proposition is that to justify personal jurisdiction over a principal, the court can attribute the state-directed acts of the principal's agent. To determine whether an agent-principal relationship exists, the court looks to the ordinary law of agency, asking whether the defendant has empowered an agent and whether the agent has acted within the scope of that authority. To establish jurisdiction, then, the plaintiff must make a prima facie showing of the principal's vicarious liability under the applicable substantive law. The rationale is that if the principal would be substantively liable for the agent's acts, then those acts can contribute to a finding of jurisdiction over the principal.

Indeed, that rationale extends to a variety of contexts where a jurisdictional argument exists for attributing another's acts to the defendant. See generally Lea Brilmayer & Kathleen Paisley, Personal Jurisdiction and Substantive Legal Relations: Corporations, Conspiracies, and Agency, 74 Cal.L.Rev. 1 (1986). Of those contexts, the one giving the courts the greatest difficulty is the attribution of state-directed acts by a validly incorporated and formally separate corporation that, along with the defendant, constitutes part of a modern multistate or multinational enterprise. If the affiliate corporation has an agent-principal relationship to the defendant corporation, then the courts will attribute the affiliate's contacts to the defendant. But some courts have gone perceptibly beyond the "agency" standard, coming up with tests that ask, for example, whether the state-directed acts are sufficiently important to the defendant that it would have performed them itself in the affiliate's absence. Such tests, however, seem to be confused stabs at a standard that would conform to the rationale of tying jurisdictional attribution to substantive liability. The proper "alter ego" standard would take the courts into corporate law, asking whether the defendant would be liable for all of the affiliate's activities under the doctrine of piercing the corporate veil, which, in special situations of common control, overcomes the usual limited liability of corporations and merges the corporate entities. If so, then those activities of the affiliate can contribute to a finding of jurisdiction over the defendant.

ILLINOIS UPDATE

The Cook result would not necessarily prevail today. The court there was applying an Illinois long-arm statute basically the same as the one reprinted at the beginning of this Subsection. On September 7, 1989, Illinois amended its long-arm statute. See generally Keith H. Beyler, The Illinois Long Arm Statute: Background, Meaning, and Needed Repairs, 12 S.Ill.U.L.J. 293 (1988). With the major changes shown below, it now appears as Ill.Comp.Stat.Ann. ch. 735, § 5/2–209 (the somewhat redundant new clauses (a)(6) and (a)(8) derived from separate but almost simultaneous bills):

> (a) Any person, whether or not a citizen or resident of this State, who in person or through an agent does any of the acts hereinafter enumerated, thereby submits such person, and, if an individual, his or her personal representative, to the jurisdiction of the courts of this State as to any cause of action arising from the doing of any of such acts:
>
> (1) The transaction of any business within this State;
>
> (2) The commission of a tortious act within this State;
>
> (3) The ownership, use, or possession of any real estate situated in this State;
>
> (4) Contracting to insure any person, property or risk located within this State at the time of contracting;
>
> (5) With respect to actions of dissolution of marriage, *declaration of invalidity of marriage* and legal separation, the maintenance in this State of a matrimonial domicile at the time this cause of action arose or the commission in this State of any act giving rise to the cause of action;
>
> (6) With respect to actions brought under the Illinois Parentage Act of 1984, as now or hereafter amended, the performance of an act of sexual intercourse within this State during the possible period of conception*;*
>
> *(7) The making or performance of any contract or promise substantially connected with this State;*
>
> *(8) The performance of sexual intercourse within this State which is claimed to have resulted in the conception of a child who resides in this State;*
>
> *(9) The failure to support a child, spouse or former spouse who has continued to reside in this State since the person either formerly resided with them in this State or directed them to reside in this State;*
>
> *(10) The acquisition of ownership, possession or control of any asset or thing of value present within this State when ownership, possession or control was acquired;*
>
> *(11) The breach of any fiduciary duty within this State;*

(12) The performance of duties as a director or officer of a corporation organized under the laws of this State or having its principal place of business within this State;

(13) The ownership of an interest in any trust administered within this State; or

(14) The exercise of powers granted under the authority of this State as a fiduciary.

(b) A court may exercise jurisdiction in any action arising within or without this State against any person who:

(1) Is a natural person present within this State when served;

(2) Is a natural person domiciled or resident within this State when the cause of action arose, the action was commenced, or process was served;

(3) Is a corporation organized under the laws of this State; or

(4) Is a natural person or corporation doing business within this State.

. . . .

(c) A court may also exercise jurisdiction on any other basis now or hereafter permitted by the Illinois Constitution and the Constitution of the United States.

(d)~~(b)~~ Service of process upon any person who is subject to the jurisdiction of the courts of this State, as provided in this Section, may be made by personally serving the summons upon the defendant outside this State, as provided in this Act, with the same force and effect as though summons had been personally served within this State.

(e)~~(c)~~ . . . .

(f)~~(d)~~ Only causes of action arising from acts enumerated herein may be asserted against a defendant in an action in which jurisdiction over him or her is based upon *subsection (a)* ~~this Section~~.

(g)~~(e)~~ Nothing herein contained limits or affects the right to serve any process in any other manner now or hereafter provided by law.

Incidentally, on November 30, 1990, the Supreme Court of Illinois decided Rollins v. Ellwood, 141 Ill.2d 244, 565 N.E.2d 1302 (1990). In that case, Illinois police had arrested Sylvester Rollins for speeding and then detained him on a Maryland fugitive warrant for child abuse. John Ellwood, a Baltimore police sergeant, then went to Illinois and took him back to Maryland, where a judge found that all this had been a matter of mistaken identity. So, back in Illinois, Rollins sued Ellwood in tort. The defendant moved to quash service for lack of personal jurisdiction. The lower courts denied the motion. The Illinois Supreme Court reversed. It explained that jurisdiction over Ellwood existed under subsection (a)(2) of the state long-arm statute and under the Federal Due Process Clause, but not under the state constitution's due process clause. In the "fair, just, and reasonable" standard implicit in the latter provision, the court found a "fiduciary shield doctrine," which protected an employee from personal jurisdiction based on the employee's acts taken on behalf of the employer and not out of personal interest. Thus, the Illinois court could not exercise personal jurisdiction over this defendant.

Questions: (39) Plaintiff brings an action in her home state of Illinois against a New York lawyer for damages from alleged malpractice while representing her in prior litigation arising and conducted outside the state. Plaintiff solicited that representation from her state. Defendant briefly visited plaintiff's state in the course of discovery and frequently communicated by mail, telephone, and e-mail with her at home and periodically received billed fees from her, but had no other contacts with her state. Is there sufficient basis for personal jurisdiction? What, if any, additional information would you consider relevant?

(40) Back in the lawyer's state, would there be a sufficient basis for personal jurisdiction over the client for owed fees? What, if any, additional information would you consider relevant?

SECTION 4. A RONDEL

(a) COMPLEX PROBLEMS OF RELATIONSHIP TO THE FORUM STATE

Mullane v. Central Hanover Bank & Trust Co.

Supreme Court of the United States, 1950.
339 U.S. 306, 70 S.Ct. 652.

■ MR. JUSTICE JACKSON delivered the opinion of the Court.

This controversy questions the constitutional sufficiency of notice to beneficiaries on judicial settlement of accounts by the trustee of a common trust fund established under the New York Banking Law, Consol. Laws, c. 2. The New York Court of Appeals considered and overruled objections that the statutory notice contravenes requirements of the Fourteenth Amendment and that by allowance of the account beneficiaries were deprived of property without due process of law. The case is here on appeal under 28 U.S.C. § 1257.

Common trust fund legislation is addressed to a problem appropriate for state action. Mounting overheads have made administration of small trusts undesirable to corporate trustees. In order that donors and testators of moderately sized trusts may not be denied the service of corporate fiduciaries, the District of Columbia and some thirty states other than New York have permitted pooling small trust estates into one fund for investment administration. The income, capital gains, losses and expenses of the collective trust are shared by the constituent trusts in proportion to their contribution. By this plan, diversification of risk and economy of management can be extended to those whose capital standing alone would not obtain such advantage.

Statutory authorization for the establishment of such common trust funds is provided in the New York Banking Law, § 100–c, c. 687, L.1937, as amended by c. 602, L.1943, and c. 158, L.1944. Under this Act a trust company may, with approval of the State Banking Board, establish a common fund and, within prescribed limits, invest therein the assets of an unlimited number of estates, trusts or other funds of which it is trustee. Each participating trust shares ratably in the common fund, but exclusive management and control is in the trust company as trustee, and neither a fiduciary nor any beneficiary of a participating trust is deemed to have ownership in any particular asset or investment of this common fund. The trust company must keep fund assets separate from its own, and in its fiduciary capacity may not deal with itself or any affiliate. Provisions are made for accountings twelve to fifteen months after the establishment of a fund and triennially thereafter. The decree in each such judicial settlement of accounts is made binding and conclusive as to any matter set forth in the account upon everyone having any interest in the common fund or in any participating estate, trust or fund.

In January, 1946, Central Hanover Bank and Trust Company established a common trust fund in accordance with these provisions, and in March, 1947, it petitioned the Surrogate's Court for settlement of its first account as common trustee. During the accounting period a total of 113 trusts, approximately half inter vivos and half testamentary, participated in the common trust fund, the gross capital of which was nearly three million dollars. The record does not show the number or residence of the beneficiaries, but they were many and it is clear that some of them were not residents of the State of New York.

The only notice given beneficiaries of this specific application was by publication in a local newspaper in strict compliance with the minimum requirements of N.Y. Banking Law § 100–c(12): "After filing such petition [for judicial settlement of its account] the petitioner shall cause to be issued by the court in which the petition is filed and shall publish not less than once in each week for four successive weeks in a newspaper to be designated by the court a notice or citation addressed generally without naming them to all parties interested in such common trust fund and in such estates, trusts or funds mentioned in the petition, all of which may be described in the notice or citation only in the manner set forth in said petition and without setting forth the residence of any such decedent or donor of any such estate, trust or fund." Thus the only notice required, and the only one given, was by newspaper publication setting forth merely the name and the date of establishment of the common trust fund, and a list of all participating estates, trusts or funds.

At the time the first investment in the common fund was made on behalf of each participating estate, however, the trust company, pursuant to the requirements of § 100–c(9), had notified by mail each person of full age and sound mind whose name and address was then known to it and who was "entitled to share in the income therefrom . . . [or] . . . who would be entitled to share in the principal if the event upon which such estate, trust or fund will become distributable should have occurred at the time of sending such notice." Included in the notice was a copy of those provisions of the Act relating to the sending of the notice itself and to the judicial settlement of common trust fund accounts.

Upon the filing of the petition for the settlement of accounts, appellant was, by order of the court pursuant to § 100–c(12), appointed special guardian and attorney for all persons known or unknown not otherwise appearing who had or might thereafter have any interest in the income of the common trust fund; and appellee Vaughan was appointed to represent those similarly interested in the principal. There were no other appearances on behalf of any one interested in either interest or principal.

Appellant appeared specially, objecting that notice and the statutory provisions for notice to beneficiaries were inadequate to afford due process under the Fourteenth Amendment, and therefore that the court was without jurisdiction to render a final and binding decree. Appellant's objections were entertained and overruled, the Surrogate holding that the notice required and given was sufficient. 75 N.Y.S.2d 397. A final decree accepting the accounts has been entered, affirmed by the Appellate Division of the Supreme Court, In re [Accounting of] Central Hanover Bank & Trust Co., 275 App.Div. 769, 88 N.Y.S.2d 907, and by the Court of Appeals of the State of New York, 299 N.Y. 697, 87 N.E.2d 73.

The effect of this decree, as held below, is to settle "all questions respecting the management of the common fund." We understand that every right which beneficiaries would otherwise have against the trust company, either as trustee of the common fund or as trustee of any individual trust, for improper management of the common trust fund during the period covered by the accounting is sealed and wholly terminated by the decree. [Citations omitted.]

We are met at the outset with a challenge to the power of the State—the right of its courts to adjudicate at all as against those beneficiaries who reside without the State of New York. It is contended that the proceeding is one in personam in that the decree affects neither title to nor possession of any res, but adjudges only personal rights of the beneficiaries to surcharge their trustee for negligence or breach of trust. Accordingly, it is said, under the strict doctrine of Pennoyer v. Neff, 95 U.S. 714, the Surrogate is without jurisdiction as to nonresidents upon whom personal service of process was not made.

Distinctions between actions in rem and those in personam are ancient and originally expressed in procedural terms what seems really to have been a distinction in the substantive law of property under a system quite unlike our own. Buckland and McNair, Roman Law and Common Law, 66; Burdick, Principles of Roman Law and Their Relation to Modern Law, 298. The legal recognition and rise in economic importance of incorporeal or intangible forms of property have upset the ancient simplicity of property law and the clarity of its distinctions, while new forms of proceedings have confused the old procedural classification. American courts have sometimes classed certain actions as in rem because personal service of process was not required, and at other times have held personal service of process not required because the action was in rem. See cases collected in Freeman on Judgments, § 1517 et seq. (5th ed.).

Judicial proceedings to settle fiduciary accounts have been sometimes termed in rem, or more indefinitely quasi in rem, or more vaguely still, "in the nature of a proceeding in rem." It is not readily apparent how the courts of New York did or would classify the present proceeding, which has some characteristics and is wanting in some features of proceedings both in rem and in personam. But in any event we think that the requirements of the Fourteenth Amendment to the Federal Constitution do not depend upon a classification for which the standards are so elusive and confused generally and which, being primarily for state courts to define, may and do vary from state to state. Without disparaging the usefulness of distinctions between actions in rem and those in personam in many branches of law, or on other issues, or the reasoning which underlies them, we do not rest the power of the State to resort to constructive service in this proceeding upon how its courts or this Court may regard this historic antithesis. It is sufficient to observe that, whatever the technical definition of its chosen procedure, the interest of each state in providing means to close trusts that exist by the grace of its laws and are administered under the supervision of its courts is so insistent and rooted in custom as to establish beyond doubt the right of its courts to determine the interests of all claimants, resident or nonresident, provided its procedure accords full opportunity to appear and be heard.

■ [The portion of the majority's opinion reversing for inadequacy of notice, and JUSTICE BURTON's dissent with respect thereto, are reprinted in the next Topic. JUSTICE DOUGLAS did not participate.]

Hanson v. Denckla

Supreme Court of the United States, 1958.
357 U.S. 235, 78 S.Ct. 1228.

[In 1935 Mrs. Dora Browning Donner, a Pennsylvania domiciliary, purported to create a trust in Delaware naming the Wilmington Trust Co., a Delaware corporation, as trustee. The corpus consisted of securities. The trust instrument reserved a life estate to Mrs. Donner and empowered her to appoint the remainder interest either by will or by inter vivos instrument. In 1944 she established her domicile in Florida, and there on December 3, 1949, she executed a will and separately exercised her power of appointment under the trust. She died domiciled in Florida in 1952, and her will was probated there, with her daughter Elizabeth Hanson as executrix.

[The issue presented by this litigation was whether the trust assets passed in accordance with the residuary clause of the will or pursuant to the appointment. This in turn depended upon whether Mrs. Donner had reserved such extensive powers over the trust assets as to make the trust invalid. If the trust were valid, the appointment would be effective, and trust assets totaling $400,000 would pass to trusts of which the Delaware Trust Co., a Delaware corporation, was trustee and of which Mrs. Hanson's children, Donner Hanson and Joseph Winsor, were the beneficiaries; several other appointees would receive minor amounts of the trust assets. If the trust were invalid, on the other hand, all these assets would pass under the will to Mrs. Donner's two other daughters, Katherine Denckla and Dorothy Stewart, who were Mrs. Hanson's half-sisters and who as residuary legatees had already received over $500,000 each.

[Mrs. Denckla and Mrs. Stewart, both residents of Florida, brought a declaratory judgment action in Florida for the purpose of establishing that the assets passed under the will. The plaintiffs secured jurisdiction over Mrs. Hanson, Donner Hanson, and Joseph Winsor, all Florida residents, by personal service in Florida. The plaintiffs named as defendants the Wilmington Trust Co., the Delaware Trust Co., and certain of the other appointees; notice was given to these nonresidents by ordinary mail, and publication was made in a Palm Beach newspaper pursuant to Florida law; none of these nonresidents appeared. The Florida trial court held that the assets passed pursuant to the will.

[Meanwhile, Mrs. Hanson instituted a declaratory judgment action in Delaware to determine the persons who were entitled to the assets. The parties were substantially the same as in Florida. The nonresident defendants, including Mrs. Denckla and Mrs. Stewart, were notified by registered mail; only Mrs. Denckla did not appear. After the Florida decree, a guardian ad litem for Mrs. Stewart unsuccessfully urged it as res judicata. The Delaware trial court held that the assets passed pursuant to the appointment.

[Next the Supreme Court of Florida and then the Supreme Court of Delaware sustained on the merits the determinations of their lower courts. The Florida Supreme Court also held that the Florida courts could exercise "substantive" jurisdiction over the absent defendants; but, as the Supreme Court of the United States was later to note, "[w]hether this meant jurisdiction over the person of the defendants or jurisdiction over the trust assets is open to doubt." The Delaware Supreme Court also rejected the contention that it was bound to give full faith and credit to the Florida decree.

[These inconsistent judgments came before the Supreme Court of the United States.]

■ MR. CHIEF JUSTICE WARREN delivered the opinion of the Court.

. . . .

The issues for our decision are, first, whether Florida erred in holding that it had jurisdiction over the nonresident defendants, and second, whether Delaware erred in refusing full faith and credit to the Florida decree. . . .

No. 107, The Florida Appeal. [The Court first ruled that the proper mode of review here was by petition for certiorari, but that it would treat the appeal as such. The Court then granted certiorari.]

Relying upon the principle that a person cannot invoke the jurisdiction of this Court to vindicate the right of a third party, appellees urge that appellants lack standing to complain of a defect in jurisdiction over the nonresident trust companies, who have made no appearance in this action. Florida adheres to the general rule that a trustee is an indispensable party to litigation involving the validity of the trust. In the absence of such a party a Florida court may not proceed to adjudicate the controversy. Since state law required the acquisition of jurisdiction over the nonresident trust company[8] before the court was empowered to proceed with the action, any defendant affected by the court's judgment has that "direct and substantial personal interest in the outcome" that is necessary to challenge whether that jurisdiction was in fact acquired. Chicago v. Atchison, T. & S.F.R. Co., 357 U.S. 77, 78 S.Ct. 1063.

Appellants charge that this judgment is offensive to the Due Process Clause of the Fourteenth Amendment because the Florida court was without jurisdiction. There is no suggestion that the court failed to employ a means of notice reasonably calculated to inform nonresident defendants of the pending proceedings, or denied them an opportunity to be heard in defense of their interests. The alleged defect is the absence of those "affiliating circumstances"[11] without which the courts of a State may not enter a judgment imposing obligations on persons (jurisdiction in personam) or affecting interests in property (jurisdiction in rem or quasi in rem).[12] While the in rem and in personam classifications do not exhaust all the situations that give rise to jurisdiction,[13] they are adequate to describe the affiliating circumstances suggested here, and accordingly serve as a useful means of approach to this case.

---

[8] Hereafter the terms "trust," "trust company" and "trustee" have reference to the trust established in 1935 with the Wilmington Trust Co., the validity of which is at issue here. It is unnecessary to determine whether the Delaware Trust Co., to which the $400,000 remainder interest was appointed and was paid after Mrs. Donner's death, is also an indispensable party to this proceeding.

[11] Sunderland, The Problem of Jurisdiction, Selected Essays on Constitutional Law, 1270, 1272.

[12] A judgment in personam imposes a personal liability or obligation on one person in favor of another. A judgment in rem affects the interests of all persons in designated property. A judgment quasi in rem affects the interests of particular persons in designated property. The latter is of two types. In one the plaintiff is seeking to secure a pre-existing claim in the subject property and to extinguish or establish the nonexistence of similar interests of particular persons. In the other the plaintiff seeks to apply what he concedes to be the property of the defendant to the satisfaction of a claim against him. Restatement, Judgments, 5–9. For convenience of terminology this opinion will use "in rem" in lieu of "in rem and quasi in rem."

[13] E.g., Mullane v. Central Hanover Bank & Trust Co., 339 U.S. 306, 312, 70 S.Ct. 652, 656; Williams v. North Carolina, 317 U.S. 287, 297, 63 S.Ct. 207, 212 [(divorce)]. Fraser, Jurisdiction by Necessity, 100 U. of Pa.L.Rev. 305.

In rem jurisdiction. Founded on physical power, McDonald v. Mabee, 243 U.S. 90, 91, 37 S.Ct. 343, the in rem jurisdiction of a state court is limited by the extent of its power and by the coordinate authority of sister States. The basis of the jurisdiction is the presence of the subject property within the territorial jurisdiction of the forum State. Rose v. Himely, 4 Cranch 241, 277; Overby v. Gordon, 177 U.S. 214, 221–222, 20 S.Ct. 603, 606. Tangible property poses no problem for the application of this rule, but the situs of intangibles is often a matter of controversy. In considering restrictions on the power to tax, this Court has concluded that "jurisdiction" over intangible property is not limited to a single State. State Tax Commission of Utah v. Aldrich, 316 U.S. 174, 62 S.Ct. 1008; Curry v. McCanless, 307 U.S. 357, 59 S.Ct. 900. Whether the type of "jurisdiction" with which this opinion deals may be exercised by more than one State we need not decide. The parties seem to assume that the trust assets that form the subject matter of this action[16] were located in Delaware and not in Florida. We can see nothing in the record contrary to that assumption, or sufficient to establish a situs in Florida.[17]

The Florida court held that the presence of the subject property was not essential to its jurisdiction. Authority over the probate and construction of its domiciliary's will, under which the assets might pass, was thought sufficient to confer the requisite jurisdiction. But jurisdiction cannot be predicated upon the contingent role of this Florida will. Whatever the efficacy of a so-called "in rem" jurisdiction over assets admittedly passing under a local will, a State acquires no in rem jurisdiction to adjudicate the validity of inter vivos dispositions simply because its decision might augment an estate passing under a will probated in its courts. If such a basis of jurisdiction were sustained, probate courts would enjoy nationwide service of process to adjudicate interests in property with which neither the State nor the decedent could claim any affiliation. The settlor-decedent's Florida domicile is equally unavailing as a basis for jurisdiction over the trust assets. For the purpose of jurisdiction in rem the maxim that personalty has its situs at the domicile of its owner[19] is a fiction of limited utility. Green v. Van Buskirk, 7 Wall. 139, 150. The maxim is no less suspect when the domicile is that of a decedent. In analogous cases, this Court has

---

[16] This case does not concern the situs of a beneficial interest in trust property. These appellees were contesting the validity of the trust. Their concern was with the legal interest of the trustee or, if the trust was invalid, the settlor. Therefore, the relevant factor here is the situs of the stocks, bonds, and notes that make up the corpus of the trust. Properly speaking such assets are intangibles that have no "physical" location. But their embodiment in documents treated for most purposes as the assets themselves makes them partake of the nature of tangibles. Cf. Wheeler v. Sohmer, 233 U.S. 434, 439, 34 S.Ct. 607.

[17] The documents evidencing ownership of the trust property were held in Delaware, cf. Bank of Jasper v. First Nat. Bank, 258 U.S. 112, 119, 42 S.Ct. 202, 204, by a Delaware trustee who was the obligee of the credit instruments and the record owner of the stock. The location of the obligors and the domicile of the corporations do not appear. The trust instrument was executed in Delaware by a settlor then domiciled in Pennsylvania. Without expressing any opinion on the significance of these or other factors unnamed, we note that none relates to Florida.

[19] We assume arguendo for the purpose of this discussion that the trust was invalid so that Mrs. Donner was the "owner" of the subject property.

rejected the suggestion that the probate decree of the State where decedent was domiciled has an in rem effect on personalty outside the forum State that could render it conclusive on the interests of nonresidents over whom there was no personal jurisdiction. Riley v. New York Trust Co., 315 U.S. 343, 353, 62 S.Ct. 608, 614; Baker v. Baker, Eccles & Co., 242 U.S. 394, 401, 37 S.Ct. 152, 154; Overby v. Gordon, 177 U.S. 214, 20 S.Ct. 603. The fact that the owner is or was domiciled within the forum State is not a sufficient affiliation with the property upon which to base jurisdiction in rem. . . .

. . . .

In personam jurisdiction. Appellees' stronger argument is for in personam jurisdiction over the Delaware trustee. They urge that the circumstances of this case amount to sufficient affiliation with the State of Florida to empower its courts to exercise personal jurisdiction over this nonresident defendant. Principal reliance is placed upon McGee v. International Life Ins. Co., 355 U.S. 220, 78 S.Ct. 199. In McGee the Court noted the trend of expanding personal jurisdiction over nonresidents. As technological progress has increased the flow of commerce between States, the need for jurisdiction over nonresidents has undergone a similar increase. At the same time, progress in communications and transportation has made the defense of a suit in a foreign tribunal less burdensome. In response to these changes, the requirements for personal jurisdiction over nonresidents have evolved from the rigid rule of Pennoyer v. Neff, 95 U.S. 714, to the flexible standard of International Shoe Co. v. Washington, 326 U.S. 310, 66 S.Ct. 154. But it is a mistake to assume that this trend heralds the eventual demise of all restrictions on the personal jurisdiction of state courts. See Vanderbilt v. Vanderbilt, 354 U.S. 416, 418, 77 S.Ct. 1360, 1362. Those restrictions are more than a guarantee of immunity from inconvenient or distant litigation. They are a consequence of a territorial limitations on the power of the respective States. However minimal the burden of defending in a foreign tribunal, a defendant may not be called upon to do so unless he has had the "minimal contacts" with that State that are a prerequisite to its exercise of power over him. See International Shoe Co. v. Washington, 326 U.S. 310, 319, 66 S.Ct. 154, 159.

We fail to find such contacts in the circumstances of this case. The defendant trust company has no office in Florida, and transacts no business there. None of the trust assets has ever been held or administered in Florida, and the record discloses no solicitation of business in that State either in person or by mail. Cf. International Shoe Co. v. Washington, 326 U.S. 310, 66 S.Ct. 154; McGee v. International Life Ins. Co., 355 U.S. 220, 78 S.Ct. 199; Travelers Health Ass'n v. Virginia ex rel. State Corporation Comm., 339 U.S. 643, 70 S.Ct. 927.

The cause of action in this case is not one that arises out of an act done or transaction consummated in the forum State. In that respect, it differs from McGee v. International Life Ins. Co., 355 U.S. 220, 78 S.Ct. 199, and the cases there cited. In McGee, the nonresident defendant solicited a reinsurance agreement with a resident of California. The offer was accepted in that State, and the insurance premiums were mailed from there until the insured's death. Noting the interest California has in providing effective redress for its residents when nonresident insurers refuse to pay claims on insurance they have solicited in that State, the Court upheld jurisdiction because the suit "was based on a contract which had substantial connection with that State." In contrast, this action involves the validity of an agreement that was entered without any connection with the forum State. The agreement was executed in Delaware by a trust company incorporated in that State and a settlor domiciled in Pennsylvania. The first relationship Florida has to the agreement was years later when the settlor became domiciled there, and the trustee remitted the trust income to her in that State. From Florida Mrs. Donner carried on several bits of trust administration that may be compared to the mailing of premiums in McGee. But the record discloses no instance in which the *trustee* performed any acts in Florida that bear the same relationship to the agreement as the solicitation in McGee. Consequently, this suit cannot be said to be one to enforce an obligation that arose from a privilege the defendant exercised in Florida. Cf. International Shoe Co. v. Washington, 326 U.S. 310, 319, 66 S.Ct. 154, 159. This case is also different from McGee in that there the State had enacted special legislation (Unauthorized Insurers Process Act, West's Ann.Cal.Insurance Code § 1610 et seq.) to exercise what McGee called its "manifest interest" in providing effective redress for citizens who had been injured by nonresidents engaged in an activity that the State treats as exceptional and subjects to special regulation. Cf. Travelers Health Ass'n v. Virginia ex rel. State Corporation Comm., 339 U.S. 643, 647–649, 70 S.Ct. 927, 929–930; Doherty & Co. v. Goodman, 294 U.S. 623, 627, 55 S.Ct. 553, 554; Hess v. Pawloski, 274 U.S. 352, 47 S.Ct. 632.

The execution in Florida of the powers of appointment under which the beneficiaries and appointees claim does not give Florida a substantial connection with the contract on which this suit is based. It is the validity of the trust agreement, not the appointment, that is at issue here. For the purpose of applying its rule that the validity of a trust is determined by the law of the State of its creation, Florida ruled that the appointment amounted to a "republication" of the original trust instrument in Florida. For choice-of-law purposes such a ruling may be justified, but we think it an insubstantial connection with the trust agreement for purposes of determining the question of personal jurisdiction over a nonresident defendant. The unilateral activity of those who claim some relationship with a nonresident defendant cannot satisfy the requirement of contact with the forum State. The application of that rule will vary with the quality and nature of the defendant's activity, but it is essential in each case that there be some act by which the defendant purposefully avails itself of the privilege of conducting activities within the forum State, thus invoking the benefits and protections of its laws. International Shoe Co. v. Washington, 326 U.S. 310, 319, 66 S.Ct. 154, 159. The settlor's execution in Florida of her power of appointment cannot remedy the absence of such an act in this case.

It is urged that because the settlor and most of the appointees and beneficiaries were domiciled in Florida the courts of that State should be able to exercise personal jurisdiction over the nonresident trustees. This is a non-sequitur. With personal jurisdiction over the executor, legatees, and appointees, there is nothing in federal law to prevent Florida from adjudicating concerning the respective rights and liabilities of those parties. But Florida has not chosen to do so. As we understand its law, the trustee is an indispensable party over whom the court must acquire jurisdiction before it is empowered to enter judgment in a proceeding affecting the validity of a trust. It does not acquire that jurisdiction by being the "center of gravity" of the controversy, or the most convenient location for litigation. The issue is personal jurisdiction, not choice of law. It is resolved in this case by considering acts of the trustee. As we have indicated, they are insufficient to sustain the jurisdiction.

Because it sustained jurisdiction over the nonresident trustees, the Florida Supreme Court found it unnecessary to determine whether Florida law made those defendants indispensable parties in the circumstances of this case. Our conclusion that Florida was without jurisdiction over the Delaware trustee, or over the trust corpus held in that State, requires that we make that determination in the first instance. As we have noted earlier, the Florida Supreme Court has repeatedly held that a trustee is an indispensable party without whom a Florida court has no power to adjudicate controversies affecting the validity of a trust. For that reason the Florida judgment must be reversed not only as to the nonresident trustees but also as to appellants, over whom the Florida court admittedly had jurisdiction.

No. 117, The Delaware Certiorari. The same reasons that compel reversal of the Florida judgment require affirmance of the Delaware one. Delaware is under no obligation to give full faith and credit to a Florida judgment invalid in Florida because offensive to the Due Process Clause of the Fourteenth Amendment. . . .

. . . .

The judgment of the Delaware Supreme Court is affirmed, and the judgment of the Florida Supreme Court is reversed and the cause is remanded for proceedings not inconsistent with this opinion.

It is so ordered.

■ MR. JUSTICE BLACK, whom MR. JUSTICE BURTON and MR. JUSTICE BRENNAN join, dissenting.

I believe the courts of Florida had power to adjudicate the effectiveness of the appointment made in Florida by Mrs. Donner with respect to all those who were notified of the proceedings and given an opportunity to be heard without violating the Due Process Clause of the Fourteenth Amendment. If this is correct, it follows that the Delaware courts erred in refusing to give the prior Florida judgment full faith and credit. U.S.Const., Art. IV, § 1; 28 U.S.C. § 1738.

. . . .

. . . [I]t seems quite clear to me that there is nothing in the Due Process Clause which denies Florida the right to determine whether Mrs. Donner's appointment was valid . . . . This disposition, which was designed to take effect after her death, had very close and substantial connections with that State. Not only was the appointment made in Florida by a domiciliary of Florida, but the primary beneficiaries also lived in that State. In my view it could hardly be denied that Florida had sufficient interest so that a court with jurisdiction might properly apply Florida law, if it chose, to determine whether the appointment was effectual. Watson v. Employers Liability Assurance Corp., 348 U.S. 66, 75 S.Ct. 166; Osborn v. Ozlin, 310 U.S. 53, 60 S.Ct. 758. True, the question whether the law of a State can be applied to a transaction is different from the question whether the courts of that State have jurisdiction to enter a judgment, but the two are often closely related and to a substantial degree depend upon similar considerations. It seems to me that where a transaction has as much relationship to a State as Mrs. Donner's appointment had to Florida its courts ought to have power to adjudicate controversies arising out of that transaction, unless litigation there would impose such a heavy disproportionate burden on a nonresident defendant that it would offend what this Court has referred to as "traditional notions of fair play and substantial justice." Milliken v. Meyer, 311 U.S. 457, 463, 61 S.Ct. 339, 342, 343; International Shoe Co. v. Washington, 326 U.S. 310, 316, 66 S.Ct. 154, 158. So far as the nonresident defendants here are concerned I can see nothing which approaches that degree of unfairness. Florida, the home of the principal contenders for Mrs. Donner's largess, was a reasonably convenient forum for all.[3] Certainly there is nothing fundamentally unfair in subjecting the corporate trustee to the jurisdiction of the Florida courts. It chose to maintain business relations with Mrs. Donner in that State for eight years regularly communicating with her with respect to the business of the trust including the very appointment in question.

Florida's interest in the validity of Mrs. Donner's appointment is made more emphatic by the fact that her will is being administered in that State. It has traditionally been the rule that the State where a person is domiciled at the time of his death is the proper place to determine the validity of his will, to construe its provisions and to marshal and distribute his personal property. Here Florida was seriously concerned with winding up Mrs. Donner's estate and with finally determining what property was to be distributed under her will. In fact this suit was brought for that very purpose.

The Court's decision that Florida did not have jurisdiction over the trustee (and inferentially the nonresident beneficiaries) stems from principles stated the better part of a century ago in Pennoyer v. Neff, 95 U.S. 714. That landmark case was decided in 1878, at a time when business affairs were predominantly local in nature and travel between States was difficult, costly and sometimes even dangerous. There the Court laid down

[3] The suggestion is made that Delaware was a more suitable forum, but the plain fact is that none of the beneficiaries or legatees has ever resided in that State.

the broad principle that a State could not subject nonresidents to the jurisdiction of its courts unless they were served with process within its boundaries or voluntarily appeared, except to the extent they had property in the State. But as the years have passed the constantly increasing ease and rapidity of communication and the tremendous growth of interstate business activity have led to a steady and inevitable relaxation of the strict limits on state jurisdiction announced in that case. In the course of this evolution the old jurisdictional landmarks have been left far behind so that in many instances States may now properly exercise jurisdiction over nonresidents not amenable to service within their borders. Yet further relaxation seems certain. Of course we have not reached the point where state boundaries are without significance, and I do not mean to suggest such a view here. There is no need to do so. For we are dealing with litigation arising from a transaction that had an abundance of close and substantial connections with the State of Florida.

Perhaps the decision most nearly in point is Mullane v. Central Hanover Bank & Trust Co., 339 U.S. 306, 70 S.Ct. 652. In that case the Court held that a State could enter a personal judgment in favor of a trustee against nonresident beneficiaries of a trust even though they were not served with process in that State. So far as appeared, their only connection with the State was the fact that the trust was being administered there.[5] In upholding the State's jurisdiction the Court emphasized its great interest in trusts administered within its boundaries and governed by its laws. Id., 339 U.S. at page 313, 70 S.Ct. at page 656. Also implicit in the result was a desire to avoid the necessity for multiple litigation with its accompanying waste and possibility of inconsistent results. It seems to me that the same kind of considerations are present here supporting Florida's jurisdiction over the nonresident defendants.

. . . .

■ MR. JUSTICE DOUGLAS, dissenting.

. . . .

. . . Florida has such a plain and compelling relation to these out-of-state intangibles (cf. Curry v. McCanless, 307 U.S. 357, 59 S.Ct. 900), and the nexus between the settlor and trustee is so close, as to give Florida the right to make the controlling determination even without personal service over the trustee and those who claim under it. We must remember this is not a suit to impose liability on the Delaware trustee or on any other absent person. It is merely a suit to determine interests in those intangibles. Cf. Mullane v. Central Hanover Trust Co., supra, 339 U.S. at page 313, 70 S.Ct. at page 656. Under closely analogous facts the California Supreme Court held in Atkinson v. Superior Court, 49 Cal.2d 338, 316 P.2d 960, that California had jurisdiction over an absent trustee. I would hold the same here. . . .

---

[5] There was no basis for in rem jurisdiction since the litigation concerned the personal liability of the trustee and did not involve the trust property.

Shaffer v. Heitner

Supreme Court of the United States, 1977.
433 U.S. 186, 97 S.Ct. 2569.

■ MR. JUSTICE MARSHALL delivered the opinion of the Court.

The controversy in this case concerns the constitutionality of a Delaware statute that allows a court of that State to take jurisdiction of a lawsuit by sequestering any property of the defendant that happens to be located in Delaware. Appellants contend that the sequestration statute as applied in this case violates the Due Process Clause of the Fourteenth Amendment both because it permits the state courts to exercise jurisdiction despite the absence of sufficient contacts among the defendants, the litigation, and the State of Delaware and because it authorizes the deprivation of defendants' property without providing adequate procedural safeguards. We find it necessary to consider only the first of these contentions.

I

Appellee Heitner, a nonresident of Delaware, is the owner of one share of stock in the Greyhound Corporation, a business incorporated under the laws of Delaware with its principal place of business in Phoenix, Ariz. On May 22, 1974, he filed a [multimillion dollar] shareholder's derivative suit in the Court of Chancery for New Castle County, Del., in which he named as defendants Greyhound . . . and 28 present or former officers or directors of [Greyhound].[e] In essence, Heitner alleged that the individual defendants had violated their duties to Greyhound by causing it . . . to engage in actions that resulted in [its] being held liable for substantial damages in a private antitrust suit and a large fine in a criminal contempt action. The activities which led to these penalties took place in Oregon.

Simultaneously with his complaint, Heitner filed a motion for an order of sequestration of the Delaware property of the individual defendants pursuant to 10 Del.C. § 366.[4] This motion was accompanied by a support-

[e] A subsidiary of Greyhound was also involved in this action, but nothing in the case turns on this. For the story of the Shaffer case, see Wendy Collins Perdue, "The Story of Shaffer: Allocating Jurisdictional Authority Among the States," in Civil Procedure Stories 135 (Kevin M. Clermont ed., 2d ed. 2008).

[4] 10 Del.C. § 366 provides:

"(a) If it appears in any complaint filed in the Court of Chancery that the defendant or any one or more of the defendants is a nonresident of the State, the Court may make an order directing such nonresident defendant or defendants to appear by a day certain to be designated. Such order shall be served on such nonresident defendant or defendants by mail or otherwise, if practicable, and shall be published in such manner as the Court directs, not less than once a week for 3 consecutive weeks. The Court may compel the appearance of the defendant by the seizure of all or any part of his property, which property may be sold under the order of the Court to pay the demand of the plaintiff, if the defendant does not appear, or otherwise defaults. Any defendant whose property shall have been so seized and who shall have entered a general appearance in the cause may, upon notice to the plaintiff, petition the Court for an order releasing such property or any part thereof from the seizure. The Court shall release such property unless the plaintiff shall satisfy the Court that because of other circumstances there is a reasonable possibility that such release may render it substantially less likely that plaintiff will obtain satisfaction of any judgment secured. If such petition shall not be granted, or if no such petition shall be filed, such property shall remain subject to

ing affidavit of counsel which stated that the individual defendants were nonresidents of Delaware.[f] . . . The requested sequestration order was signed the day the motion was filed. Pursuant to that order, the sequestrator "seized" approximately 82,000 shares of Greyhound common stock belonging to 19 of the defendants,[7] and options belonging to another two defendants.[8] These seizures were accomplished by placing "stop transfer" orders or their equivalents on the books of the Greyhound Corporation. So far as the record shows, none of the certificates representing the seized property was physically present in Delaware. The stock was considered to be in Delaware, and so subject to seizure, by virtue of 8 Del.C. § 169, which makes Delaware the situs of ownership of all stock in Delaware corporations.

All 28 defendants were notified of the initiation of the suit by certified mail directed to their last known addresses and by publication in a New Castle County newspaper. The 21 defendants whose property was seized (hereafter referred to as appellants) responded by entering a special appearance for the purpose of moving to quash service of process and to vacate the sequestration order. They contended that the ex parte sequestration procedure did not accord them due process of law and that the property seized was not capable of attachment in Delaware. In addition, appellants asserted that under the rule of International Shoe Co. v. Washington, 326 U.S. 310, 66 S.Ct. 154 (1945), they did not have sufficient contacts with Delaware to sustain the jurisdiction of that State's courts.

The Court of Chancery rejected these arguments . . . .

On appeal, the Delaware Supreme Court affirmed the judgment of the Court of Chancery. Greyhound Corp. v. Heitner, 361 A.2d 225 (1976). . . .

Appellants' claim that the Delaware courts did not have jurisdiction to adjudicate this action received . . . cursory treatment. The court's analysis of the jurisdictional issue is contained in two paragraphs:

> "There are significant constitutional questions at issue here but we say at once that we do not deem the rule of International Shoe to be one of them. . . . The reason, of course, is that jurisdiction under § 366 remains . . . quasi in rem founded on the presence of capital stock here, not on prior contact by defendants with this forum. Under 8 Del.C. § 169 the 'situs of the ownership of the capital stock of all corporations existing under the laws of this State . . . [is] in this

---

seizure and may be sold to satisfy any judgment entered in the cause. The Court may at any time release such property or any part thereof upon the giving of sufficient security. . . . ."

[f] Nine states appeared in the affidavit's list of the individual defendants' last known addresses. However, nine of those addresses were in Arizona and eight in California.

[7] The closing price of Greyhound stock on the day the sequestration order was issued was \$14⅜. New York Times, May 23, 1974, at 62. Thus, the value of the sequestered stock was approximately \$1.2 million.

[8] . . . .

The remaining defendants apparently owned no property subject to the sequestration order.

State,' and that provides the initial basis for jurisdiction. Delaware may constitutionally establish situs of such shares here, . . . it has done so and the presence thereof provides the foundation for § 366 in this case. . . .

"We hold that seizure of the Greyhound shares is not invalid because plaintiff has failed to meet the prior contacts tests of International Shoe." 361 A.2d, at 229.

We noted probable jurisdiction. 429 U.S. 813, 97 S.Ct. 52.[12] We reverse.

II

The Delaware courts rejected appellants' jurisdictional challenge by noting that this suit was brought as a quasi in rem proceeding. Since quasi in rem jurisdiction is traditionally based on attachment or seizure of property present in the jurisdiction, not on contacts between the defendant and the State, the courts considered appellants' claimed lack of contacts with Delaware to be unimportant. This categorical analysis assumes the continued soundness of the conceptual structure founded on the century-old case of Pennoyer v. Neff, 95 U.S. 714 (1878).

. . . .

From our perspective, the importance of Pennoyer is not its result, but the fact that its principles and corollaries derived from them became the basic elements of the constitutional doctrine governing state-court jurisdiction. See, e.g., Hazard, A General Theory of State–Court Jurisdiction, 1965 Sup.Ct.Rev. 241. . . . [U]nder Pennoyer state authority to adjudicate was based on the jurisdiction's power over either persons or property. This fundamental concept is embodied in the very vocabulary which we use to describe judgments. If a court's jurisdiction is based on its authority over the defendant's person, the action and judgment are denominated "in personam" and can impose a personal obligation on the defendant in favor of the plaintiff. If jurisdiction is based on the court's power over property within its territory, the action is called "in rem" or "quasi in rem." The effect of a judgment in such a case is limited to the property that supports jurisdiction and does not impose a personal liability on the property owner, since he is not before the court.[17] In Pennoyer's terms, the owner is affected only "indirectly" by an in rem judgment adverse to his interest in the property subject to the court's disposition.

. . . .

The Pennoyer rules generally favored nonresident defendants by making them harder to sue. This advantage was reduced, however, by the ability of a resident plaintiff to satisfy a claim against a nonresident

[12] Under Delaware law, defendants whose property has been sequestered must enter a general appearance, thus subjecting themselves to in personam liability, before they can defend on the merits. See Greyhound Corp. v. Heitner, supra, at 235–236 . . . .

[17] [The Court here quoted from footnote 12 of Hanson v. Denckla, 357 U.S. 235, 78 S.Ct. 1228 (1958), and adopted the convention that "we will for convenience generally use the term 'in rem' in place of 'in rem and quasi in rem.' "]

defendant by bringing into court any property of the defendant located in the plaintiff's State. See, e.g., Zammit, Quasi–In–Rem Jurisdiction: Outmoded and Unconstitutional?, 49 St. John's L.Rev. 668, 670 (1975). For example, . . . Harris v. Balk, 198 U.S. 215, 25 S.Ct. 625 (1905). . . .

[The Court here traced developments from Pennoyer to International Shoe, closing with extensive quotations from the latter.[g]]

. . . Thus, the relationship among the defendant, the forum, and the litigation, rather than the mutually exclusive sovereignty of the States on which the rules of Pennoyer rest, became the central concern of the inquiry into personal jurisdiction.[20] The immediate effect of this departure from Pennoyer's conceptual apparatus was to increase the ability of the state courts to obtain personal jurisdiction over nonresident defendants. See, e.g., [citations omitted]; Developments [in the Law—State–Court Jurisdiction, 73 Harv.L.Rev. 909, 1000–08 (1960)].

No equally dramatic change has occurred in the law governing jurisdiction in rem. There have, however, been intimations that the collapse of the in personam wing of Pennoyer has not left that decision unweakened as a foundation for in rem jurisdiction. Well-reasoned lower court opinions have questioned the proposition that the presence of property in a State gives that State jurisdiction to adjudicate rights to the property regardless of the relationship of the underlying dispute and the property owner to the forum. See, e.g., U.S. Industries, Inc. v. Gregg, 540 F.2d 142 (C.A.3 1976), cert. pending, No. 76–359[, cert. denied, 433 U.S. 908, 97 S.Ct. 2972 (1977)]; Jonnet v. Dollar Savings Bank, 530 F.2d 1123, 1130–1143 (C.A.3 1976) (Gibbons, J., concurring); Camire v. Scieszka, 116 N.H. 281, 358 A.2d 397 (1976); Bekins v. Huish, 1 Ariz.App. 258, 401 P.2d 743 (1965); Atkinson v. Superior Court, 49 Cal.2d 338, 316 P.2d 960 (1957), appeal dismissed and cert. denied sub nom. Columbia Broadcasting System v. Atkinson, 357 U.S. 569, 78 S.Ct. 1381 (1958). The overwhelming majority of commentators have also rejected Pennoyer's premise that a proceeding "against" property is not a proceeding against the owners of that property. Accordingly, they urge that the "traditional notions of fair play and substantial justice" that govern a State's power to adjudicate in personam should also govern its power to adjudicate personal rights to property located in the State. See, e.g., Von Mehren & Trautman, Jurisdiction to Adjudicate: A Suggested Analysis, 79 Harv.L.Rev. 1121 (1966); Traynor, Is This Conflict Really Necessary?, 37 Tex.L.Rev. 657 (1959); Ehrenzweig, The Transient Rule of

---

[g] In the course of its discussion, the Court noted that "the International Shoe Court believed that the standard it was setting forth governed actions against natural persons as well as corporations, and we see no reason to disagree. . . . The differences between individuals and corporations may, of course, lead to the conclusion that a given set of circumstances establishes state jurisdiction over one type of defendant but not over the other."

[20] Nothing in Hanson v. Denckla, supra, is to the contrary. The Hanson Court's statement that restrictions on state jurisdiction "are a consequence of territorial limitations on the power of the respective States," id., 357 U.S., at 251, 78 S.Ct., at 1238, simply makes the point that the States are defined by their geographical territory. After making this point, the Court in Hanson determined that the defendant over which personal jurisdiction was claimed had not committed any acts sufficiently connected to the State to justify jurisdiction under the International Shoe standard.

Personal Jurisdiction: The "Power" Myth and Forum Conveniens, 65 Yale L.J. 289 (1956); Developments, supra; Hazard, supra.

. . . Moreover, in Mullane [v. Central Hanover Bank & Trust Co., 339 U.S. 306, 70 S.Ct. 652 (1950),] we held that Fourteenth Amendment rights cannot depend on the classification of an action as in rem or in personam, since that is

> "a classification for which the standards are so elusive and confused generally and which, being primarily for state courts to define, may and do vary from state to state." 339 U.S., at 312, 70 S.Ct., at 656.

It is clear, therefore, that the law of state-court jurisdiction no longer stands securely on the foundation established in Pennoyer. We think that the time is ripe to consider whether the standard of fairness and substantial justice set forth in International Shoe should be held to govern actions in rem as well as in personam.

III

The case for applying to jurisdiction in rem the same test of "fair play and substantial justice" as governs assertions of jurisdiction in personam is simple and straightforward. It is premised on recognition that "[t]he phrase, 'judicial jurisdiction over a thing,' is a customary elliptical way of referring to jurisdiction over the interests of persons in a thing." Restatement (Second) of Conflict of Laws § 56, Introductory Note (1971).[22] This recognition leads to the conclusion that in order to justify an exercise of jurisdiction in rem, the basis for jurisdiction must be sufficient to justify exercising "jurisdiction over the interests of persons in a thing."[23] The standard for determining whether an exercise of jurisdiction over the interests of persons is consistent with the Due Process Clause is the minimum-contacts standard elucidated in International Shoe.

This argument, of course, does not ignore the fact that the presence of property in a State may bear on the existence of jurisdiction by providing contacts among the forum State, the defendant, and the litigation. For example, when claims to the property itself are the source of the underlying controversy between the plaintiff and the defendant,[24] it would be unusual for the State where the property is located not to have jurisdiction. In such cases, the defendant's claim to property located in the State would normally[25] indicate that he expected to benefit from the State's protection of his

---

22 "All proceedings, like all rights, are really against persons. Whether they are proceedings or rights in rem depends on the number of persons affected." Tyler v. Court of Registration, 175 Mass. 71, 76, 55 N.E. 812, 814 (Holmes, C.J.), appeal dismissed, 179 U.S. 405, 21 S.Ct. 206 (1900).

23 It is true that the potential liability of a defendant in an in rem action is limited by the value of the property, but that limitation does not affect the argument. The fairness of subjecting a defendant to state-court jurisdiction does not depend on the size of the claim being litigated. . . .

24 This category includes true in rem actions and the first type of quasi in rem proceedings. See n. 17, supra.

25 In some circumstances the presence of property in the forum State will not support the inference suggested in text. Cf., e.g., Restatement (Second) of Conflict of Laws § 60, Com-

interest. The State's strong interests in assuring the marketability of property within its borders and in providing a procedure for peaceful resolution of disputes about the possession of that property would also support jurisdiction, as would the likelihood that important records and witnesses will be found in the State. The presence of property may also favor jurisdiction in cases, such as suits for injury suffered on the land of an absentee owner, where the defendant's ownership of the property is conceded but the cause of action is otherwise related to rights and duties growing out of that ownership.[29]

It appears, therefore, that jurisdiction over many types of actions which now are or might be brought in rem would not be affected by a holding that any assertion of state-court jurisdiction must satisfy the International Shoe standard. For the type of quasi in rem action typified by Harris v. Balk and the present case, however, accepting the proposed analysis would result in significant change. These are cases where the property which now serves as the basis for state-court jurisdiction is completely unrelated to the plaintiff's cause of action. Thus, although the presence of the defendant's property in a State might suggest the existence of other ties among the defendant, the State, and the litigation, the presence of the property alone would not support the State's jurisdiction. If those other ties did not exist, cases over which the State is now thought to have jurisdiction could not be brought in that forum.

Since acceptance of the International Shoe test would most affect this class of cases, we examine the arguments against adopting that standard as they relate to this category of litigation. Before doing so, however, we note that this type of case also presents the clearest illustration of the argument in favor of assessing assertions of jurisdiction by a single standard. For in cases such as Harris and this one, the only role played by the property is to provide the basis for bringing the defendant into court. Indeed, the express purpose of the Delaware sequestration procedure is to compel the defendant to enter a personal appearance. In such cases, if a direct assertion of personal jurisdiction over the defendant would violate the Constitution, it would seem that an indirect assertion of that jurisdiction should be equally impermissible.

The primary rationale for treating the presence of property as a sufficient basis for jurisdiction to adjudicate claims over which the State would not have jurisdiction if International Shoe applied is that a wrongdoer

> "should not be able to avoid payment of his obligations by the expedient of removing his assets to a place where he is not subject to an in personam suit." Restatement (Second) of Conflict of Laws § 66, Comment a.

---

ments c, d; Traynor, supra, at 672–673; Note, The Power of a State to Affect Title in a Chattel Atypically Removed to It, 47 Colum.L.Rev. 767 (1947).

[29] Cf. Dubin v. City of Philadelphia, 34 Pa.D. & C. 61 (1938). If such an action were brought under the in rem jurisdiction rather than under a long-arm statute, it would be a quasi in rem action of the second type. See n. 17, supra.

Accord, Developments, supra, at 955. This justification, however, does not explain why jurisdiction should be recognized without regard to whether the property is present in the State because of an effort to avoid the owner's obligations. Nor does it support jurisdiction to adjudicate the underlying claim. At most, it suggests that a State in which property is located should have jurisdiction to attach that property, by use of proper procedures, as security for a judgment being sought in a forum where the litigation can be maintained consistently with International Shoe. See, e.g., Von Mehren & Trautman, supra, at 1178; Hazard, supra, at 284–285; [other citation omitted]. Moreover, we know of nothing to justify the assumption that a debtor can avoid paying his obligations by removing his property to a State in which his creditor cannot obtain personal jurisdiction over him. The Full Faith and Credit Clause, after all, makes the valid in personam judgment of one State enforceable in all other States.[36]

It might also be suggested that allowing in rem jurisdiction avoids the uncertainty inherent in the International Shoe standard and assures a plaintiff of a forum.[37] See Folk & Moyer, [Sequestration in Delaware: A Constitutional Analysis, 73 Colum.L.Rev.] 749, 767 (1973). We believe, however, that the fairness standard of International Shoe can be easily applied in the vast majority of cases. Moreover, when the existence of jurisdiction in a particular forum under International Shoe is unclear, the cost of simplifying the litigation by avoiding the jurisdictional question may be the sacrifice of "fair play and substantial justice." That cost is too high.

We are left, then, to consider the significance of the long history of jurisdiction based solely on the presence of property in a State. Although the theory that territorial power is both essential to and sufficient for jurisdiction has been undermined, we have never held that the presence of property in a State does not automatically confer jurisdiction over the owner's interest in that property. This history must be considered as supporting the proposition that jurisdiction based solely on the presence of property satisfies the demands of due process, [citation omitted], but it is not decisive. "[T]raditional notions of fair play and substantial justice" can be as readily offended by the perpetuation of ancient forms that are no longer justified as by the adoption of new procedures that are inconsistent with the basic values of our constitutional heritage. [Citations omitted.] The fiction that an assertion of jurisdiction over property is anything but an assertion of jurisdiction over the owner of the property supports an ancient form without substantial modern justification. Its continued acceptance would serve only to allow state-court jurisdiction that is fundamentally unfair to the defendant.

---

[36] Once it has been determined by a court of competent jurisdiction that the defendant is a debtor of the plaintiff, there would seem to be no unfairness in allowing an action to realize on that debt in a State where the defendant has property, whether or not that State would have jurisdiction to determine the existence of the debt as an original matter. . . .

[37] This case does not raise, and we therefore do not consider, the question whether the presence of a defendant's property in a State is a sufficient basis for jurisdiction when no other forum is available to the plaintiff.

We therefore conclude that all assertions of state-court jurisdiction must be evaluated according to the standards set forth in International Shoe and its progeny.[39]

IV

The Delaware courts based their assertion of jurisdiction in this case solely on the statutory presence of appellants' property in Delaware. Yet that property is not the subject matter of this litigation, nor is the underlying cause of action related to the property. Appellants' holdings in Greyhound do not, therefore, provide contacts with Delaware sufficient to support the jurisdiction of that State's courts over appellants. If it exists, that jurisdiction must have some other foundation.

Appellee Heitner did not allege and does not now claim that appellants have ever set foot in Delaware. Nor does he identify any act related to his cause of action as having taken place in Delaware. Nevertheless, he contends that appellants' positions as directors and officers of a corporation chartered in Delaware provide sufficient "contacts, ties, or relations," International Shoe Co. v. Washington, supra, 326 U.S., at 319, 66 S.Ct., at 160, with that State to give its courts jurisdiction over appellants in this stockholder's derivative action. This argument is based primarily on what Heitner asserts to be the strong interest of Delaware in supervising the management of a Delaware corporation. That interest is said to derive from the role of Delaware law in establishing the corporation and defining the obligations owed to it by its officers and directors. In order to protect this interest, appellee concludes, Delaware's courts must have jurisdiction over corporate fiduciaries such as appellants.

This argument is undercut by the failure of the Delaware Legislature to assert the state interest appellee finds so compelling. Delaware law bases jurisdiction not on appellants' status as corporate fiduciaries, but rather on the presence of their property in the State. Although the sequestration procedure used here may be most frequently used in derivative suits against officers and directors, Hughes Tool Co. v. Fawcett Publications, Inc., 290 A.2d 693, 695 (Del.Ch.1972), the authorizing statute evinces no specific concern with such actions. Sequestration can be used in any suit against a nonresident, see., e.g., U.S. Industries, Inc. v. Gregg, supra (breach of contract); Hughes Tool Co. v. Fawcett Publications, Inc., supra (same), and reaches corporate fiduciaries only if they happen to own interests in a Delaware corporation, or other property in the State. But as Heitner's failure to secure jurisdiction over seven of the defendants named in his complaint demonstrates, there is no necessary relationship between holding a position as a corporate fiduciary and owning stock or other interests in the corporation. If Delaware perceived its interest in securing jurisdiction over corporate fiduciaries to be as great as Heitner suggests, we

---

[39] It would not be fruitful for us to re-examine the facts of cases decided on the rationales of Pennoyer and Harris to determine whether jurisdiction might have been sustained under the standard we adopt today. To the extent that prior decisions are inconsistent with this standard, they are overruled.

would expect it to have enacted a statute more clearly designed to protect that interest.

Moreover, even if Heitner's assessment of the importance of Delaware's interest is accepted, his argument fails to demonstrate that Delaware is a fair forum for this litigation. The interest appellee has identified may support the application of Delaware law to resolve any controversy over appellants' actions in their capacities as officers and directors. But we have rejected the argument that if a State's law can properly be applied to a dispute, its courts necessarily have jurisdiction over the parties to that dispute.

> "[The State] does not acquire . . . jurisdiction by being the 'center of gravity' of the controversy, or the most convenient location for litigation. The issue is personal jurisdiction, not choice of law. It is resolved in this case by considering the acts of the [appellants]." Hanson v. Denckla, supra, 357 U.S., at 254, 78 S.Ct., at 1240.

Appellee suggests that by accepting positions as officers or directors of a Delaware corporation, appellants performed the acts required by Hanson v. Denckla. He notes that Delaware law provides substantial benefits to corporate officers and directors, and that these benefits were at least in part the incentive for appellants to assume their positions. It is, he says, "only fair and just" to require appellants, in return for these benefits, to respond in the State of Delaware when they are accused of misusing their powers. Brief, at 15.

But like Heitner's first argument, this line of reasoning establishes only that it is appropriate for Delaware law to govern the obligations of appellants to Greyhound and its stockholders. It does not demonstrate that appellants have "purposefully avail[ed themselves] of the privilege of conducting activities within the forum State," Hanson v. Denckla, supra, 357 U.S., at 253, 78 S.Ct., at 1240, in a way that would justify bringing them before a Delaware tribunal. Appellants have simply had nothing to do with the State of Delaware. Moreover, appellants had no reason to expect to be haled before a Delaware court. Delaware, unlike some States, has not enacted a statute that treats acceptance of a directorship as consent to jurisdiction in the State. And "[i]t strains reason . . . to suggest that anyone buying securities in a corporation formed in Delaware 'impliedly consents' to subject himself to Delaware's . . . jurisdiction on any cause of action." Folk & Moyer, supra, at 785. Appellants, who were not required to acquire interests in Greyhound in order to hold their positions, did not by acquiring those interests surrender their right to be brought to judgment only in States with which they had had "minimum contacts."

The Due Process Clause

> "does not contemplate that a state may make binding a judgment . . . against an individual or corporate defendant with which the state has no contacts, ties, or relations." International Shoe Co. v. Washington, supra, 326 U.S., at 319, 66 S.Ct., at 160.

Delaware's assertion of jurisdiction over appellants in this case is inconsistent with that constitutional limitation on state power. The judgment of the Delaware Supreme Court must, therefore, be reversed.

It is so ordered.

■ MR. JUSTICE REHNQUIST took no part in the consideration or decision of this case.

■ MR. JUSTICE POWELL, concurring.

. . . .

I would explicitly reserve judgment . . . on whether the ownership of some forms of property whose situs is indisputably and permanently located within a State may, without more, provide the contacts necessary to subject a defendant to jurisdiction within the State to the extent of the value of the property. In the case of real property, in particular, preservation of the common law concept of quasi in rem jurisdiction arguably would avoid the uncertainty of the general International Shoe standard without significant cost to " 'traditional notions of fair play and substantial justice.' " . . .

Subject to the foregoing reservation, I join the opinion of the Court.

■ MR. JUSTICE STEVENS, concurring in the judgment.

The Due Process Clause affords protection against "judgments without notice." International Shoe Co. v. Washington, 326 U.S. 310, 324, 66 S.Ct. 154, 162 (opinion of Black, J.). . . .

The requirement of fair notice also, I believe, includes fair warning that a particular activity may subject a person to the jurisdiction of a foreign sovereign. If I visit another State, or acquire real estate or open a bank account in it, I knowingly assume some risk that the State will exercise its power over my property or my person while there. My contact with the State, though minimal, gives rise to predictable risks.

. . . .

One who purchases shares of stock on the open market can hardly be expected to know that he has thereby become subject to suit in a forum remote from his residence and unrelated to the transaction. . . . I therefore agree with the Court that on the record before us no adequate basis for jurisdiction exists and that the Delaware statute is unconstitutional on its face.

How the Court's opinion may be applied in other contexts is not entirely clear to me. I agree with Mr. Justice Powell that it should not be read to invalidate quasi in rem jurisdiction where real estate is involved. I would also not read it as invalidating other long-accepted methods of acquiring jurisdiction over persons with adequate notice of both the particular controversy and the fact that their local activities might subject them to suit. My uncertainty as to the reach of the opinion, and my fear that it purports to decide a great deal more than is necessary to dispose of this case, persuade me merely to concur in the judgment.

■ MR. JUSTICE BRENNAN, concurring in part and dissenting in part.

I join Parts I–III of the Court's opinion. I fully agree that the minimum contacts analysis developed in International Shoe Co. v. Washington, 326 U.S. 310, 66 S.Ct. 154 (1945), represents a far more sensible construct for the exercise of state court jurisdiction than the patchwork of legal and factual fictions that has been generated from the decision in Pennoyer v. Neff, 95 U.S. 714 (1878). It is precisely because the inquiry into minimum contacts is now of such overriding importance, however, that I must respectfully dissent from Part IV of the Court's opinion.

[Justice Brennan thought that the Court did not need to reach and should not have reached the issue in Part IV.]

Nonetheless, because the Court rules on the minimum contacts question, I feel impelled to express my view. While evidence derived through discovery might satisfy me that minimum contacts are lacking in a given case, I am convinced that as a general rule a state forum has jurisdiction to adjudicate a shareholder derivative action centering on the conduct and policies of the directors and officers of a corporation chartered by that State. Unlike the Court, I therefore would not foreclose Delaware from asserting jurisdiction over appellants were it persuaded to do so on the basis of minimum contacts.

It is well settled that a derivative lawsuit as presented here does not inure primarily to the benefit of the named plaintiff. Rather, the primary beneficiaries are the corporation and its owners, the shareholders. "The cause of action which such a plaintiff brings before the court is not his own but the corporation's. . . . Such a plaintiff often may represent an important public and stockholder interest in bringing faithless managers to book." Koster v. Lumbermens Mutual Casualty Co., 330 U.S. 518, 522, 524, 67 S.Ct. 828, 831, 832 (1947).

Viewed in this light, the chartering State has an unusually powerful interest in insuring the availability of a convenient forum for litigating claims involving a possible multiplicity of defendant fiduciaries and for vindicating the State's substantive policies regarding the management of its domestic corporations. I believe that our cases fairly establish that the State's valid substantive interests are important considerations in assessing whether it constitutionally may claim jurisdiction over a given cause of action.

In this instance, Delaware can point to at least three interrelated public policies that are furthered by its assertion of jurisdiction. First, the State has a substantial interest in providing restitution for its local corporations that allegedly have been victimized by fiduciary misconduct, even if the managerial decisions occurred outside the State. . . . Second, state courts have legitimately read their jurisdiction expansively when a cause of action centers in an area in which the forum State possesses a manifest regulatory interest. . . . Finally, a State like Delaware has a recognized interest in affording a convenient forum for supervising and overseeing the affairs of an entity that is purely the creation of that State's law. . . .

To be sure, the Court is not blind to these considerations. It notes that the State's interests "may support the application of Delaware law to resolve any controversy over appellants' actions in their capacities as officers and directors." . . . But this, the Court argues, pertains to choice of law, not jurisdiction. I recognize that the jurisdictional and choice-of-law inquiries are not identical. Hanson v. Denckla, 357 U.S. 235, 254, 78 S.Ct. 1228, 1240 (1958). But I would not compartmentalize thinking in this area quite so rigidly as it seems to me the Court does today, for both inquiries "are often closely related and to a substantial degree depend upon similar considerations." Id., at 258, 78 S.Ct., at 1242 (Black, J., dissenting). In either case an important linchpin is the extent of contacts between the controversy, the parties, and the forum State. While constitutional limitations on the choice of law are by no means settled, see, e.g., Home Ins. Co. v. Dick, 281 U.S. 397, 50 S.Ct. 338 (1930), important considerations certainly include the expectancies of the parties and the fairness of governing the defendants' acts and behavior by rules of conduct created by a given jurisdiction. See, e.g., Restatement (Second) of Conflict of Laws § 6. These same factors bear upon the propriety of a State's exercising jurisdiction over a legal dispute. At the minimum, the decision that it is fair to bind a defendant by a State's laws and rules should prove to be highly relevant to the fairness of permitting that same State to accept jurisdiction for adjudicating the controversy.

Furthermore, I believe that practical considerations argue in favor of seeking to bridge the distance between the choice-of-law and jurisdictional inquiries. Even when a court would apply the law of a different forum, as a general rule it will feel less knowledgeable and comfortable in interpretation, and less interested in fostering the policies of that foreign jurisdiction, than would the courts established by the State that provides the applicable law. [Citations omitted.] Obviously, such choice-of-law problems cannot entirely be avoided in a diverse legal system such as our own. Nonetheless, when a suitor seeks to lodge a suit in a State with a substantial interest in seeing its own law applied to the transaction in question, we could wisely act to minimize conflicts, confusion, and uncertainty by adopting a liberal view of jurisdiction, unless considerations of fairness or efficiency strongly point in the opposite direction.

This case is not one where, in my judgment, this preference for jurisdiction is adequately answered. Certainly nothing said by the Court persuades me that it would be unfair to subject appellants to suit in Delaware. The fact that the record does not reveal whether they "set foot" or committed "act[s] related to [the] cause of action" in Delaware . . . is not decisive, for jurisdiction can be based strictly on out-of-state acts having foreseeable effects in the forum State. [Citations, including Gray v. American Radiator & Standard Sanitary Corp., omitted.] I have little difficulty in applying this principle to nonresident fiduciaries whose alleged breaches of trust are said to have substantial damaging effect on the financial posture of a resident corporation. Further, I cannot understand how the existence of minimum contacts in a constitutional sense is at all affected by Delaware's failure statutorily to express an interest in controlling corporate fiduciaries. . . . To me this simply demonstrates that Delaware did not elect to assert jurisdiction to the extent the Constitution would allow.[5] Nor would I view as controlling or even especially meaningful Delaware's failure to exact from appellants their consent to be sued. . . . Once we have rejected the jurisdictional framework created in Pennoyer v. Neff, I see no reason to rest jurisdiction on a fictional outgrowth of that system such as the existence of a consent statute, expressed or implied.[6]

I, therefore, would approach the minimum contacts analysis differently than does the Court. Crucial to me is the fact that appellants voluntarily associated themselves with the State of Delaware, "invoking the benefits and protections of its laws," Hanson v. Denckla, supra, 357 U.S., at 253, 78 S.Ct., at 1240; International Shoe Co. v. Washington, supra, 326 U.S., at 319, 66 S.Ct., at 159, by entering into a long-term and fragile relationship with one of its domestic corporations. They thereby elected to assume powers and to undertake responsibilities wholly derived from that State's rules and regulations, and to become eligible for those benefits that Delaware law makes available to its corporations' officials. E.g., 8 Del.C. § 143 (interest-free loans); § 145 (indemnification). While it is possible that countervailing issues of judicial efficiency and the like might clearly favor a different forum, they do not appear on the meager record before us; and, of course, we are concerned solely with "minimum" contacts, not the "best" contacts. I thus do not believe that it is unfair to insist that appellants make themselves available to suit in a competent forum that Delaware might create for vindication of its important public policies directly pertaining to appellants' fiduciary associations with the State.

Question: (41) Thirteen days after the Shaffer decision the Delaware legislature had passed and the Governor had signed a bill providing that henceforth a nonresident's accepting a directorship or continuing in the position of director of a Delaware corporation would be deemed consent to the appointment of the registered agent of such corporation as his agent for service of process in connection with suits such as Shaffer; the statute also required direct notice of suit to the nonresident by registered mail. See Del.Code Ann. tit. 10, § 3114 (now covering

[5] In fact, it is quite plausible that the Delaware Legislature never felt the need to assert direct jurisdiction over corporate managers precisely because the sequestration statute heretofore has served as a somewhat awkward but effective basis for achieving such personal jurisdiction. . . .

[6] Admittedly, when one consents to suit in a forum, his expectation is enhanced that he may be haled into that State's courts. To this extent, I agree that consent may have bearing on the fairness of accepting jurisdiction. But whatever is the degree of personal expectation that is necessary to warrant jurisdiction should not depend on the formality of establishing a consent law. Indeed, if one's expectations are to carry such weight, then appellants here might be fairly charged with the understanding that Delaware would decide to protect its substantial interests through its own courts, for they certainly realized that in the past the sequestration law has been employed primarily as a means of securing the appearance of corporate officials in the State's courts. Supra, at n. 5. Even in the absence of such a statute, however, the close and special association between a state corporation and its managers should apprise the latter that the state may seek to offer a convenient forum for addressing claims of fiduciary breach of trust.

corporate officers too). Is this jurisdictional statute constitutional? See Armstrong v. Pomerance, 423 A.2d 174 (Del.1980) (yes). (Shortly after the enactment, Greyhound reincorporated in Arizona to avoid the new statute. See David L. Ratner & Donald E. Schwartz, The Impact of Shaffer v. Heitner on the Substantive Law of Corporations, 45 Brooklyn L.Rev. 641, 653–54 (1979) (noting, however, "that, while Delaware makes it easy for a minority shareholder to sue, it makes it very difficult to recover").)

ATKINSON v. SUPERIOR COURT, 49 Cal.2d 338, 316 P.2d 960 (1957), appeals dismissed and cert. denied, 357 U.S. 569, 78 S.Ct. 1381 (1958). Class actions were brought in a California state court on behalf of the employees of various motion picture and phonograph record companies, attacking the validity of the collective bargaining agreements between their employers and the American Federation of Musicians, and also attacking certain related trust agreements. The gist of the complaints was that the A.F. of M., in violation of its duty as the employees' collective bargaining agent, had agreed with the employers that the latter should periodically turn over certain royalty payments to a New York trustee for named trust purposes, instead of to the employees who claimed the payments as wages earned in California; they further alleged that the employers were willing to make payment to the employees but for their agreements with the A.F. of M. to make payment to the trustee, and that the officers of the A.F. of M. had wrongfully negotiated the arrangement for the selfish purpose of perpetuating themselves in office. The complaints sought a declaration of the collective bargaining agreements' invalidity and of the employees' right to the payments, and also damages from the A.F. of M.; they further asked for the appointment of a receiver to collect future royalty payments and for a preliminary injunction to prevent the employers from making payment to the trustee.

The plaintiffs named as defendants the employers, the A.F. of M., and the trustee. They obtained personal jurisdiction over the employers and the A.F. of M. in California. The trustee was served in New York, but did not appear. The trial court ruled the trustee an indispensable party and dismissed for lack of personal jurisdiction over the trustee. The Supreme Court of California, speaking through Justice Traynor, reversed, concluding that "service upon the trustee in New York was sufficient to give the court jurisdiction to adjudicate his right to receive payments under the contracts here involved."

Questions: (42) Appraise the Atkinson decision sequentially in the light of Mullane v. Central Hanover Bank & Trust Co., Hanson v. Denckla, and Shaffer v. Heitner.

(43) If the Atkinson case were to arise for the first time today, what position would you advise the defendant employers to take on the jurisdictional question?

(b) THE FRAMEWORK—RESTRUCTURED OR RESURRECTED?

KULKO v. SUPERIOR COURT, 436 U.S. 84, 98 S.Ct. 1690 (1978). Some time after a woman and first one and later the other of her children had moved to California, she sued her former husband for child support in a California court. The defendant still lived in New York City but had consented to the children's living in California. Upon Dr. Kulko's special appearance, the California courts, just before the Shaffer decision, upheld personal jurisdiction as "reasonable."

On certiorari, the Supreme Court of the United States held that here jurisdiction violated due process because the defendant lacked minimum contacts with California, even though he had visited the state a couple of times. Justice Marshall, writing for the Court, cited Hanson v. Denckla liberally. He generalized that personal jurisdiction demands "a sufficient connection between the defendant and the forum State to make it fair to require defense of the action in the forum. . . . While the interests of the forum State and of the plaintiff in proceeding with the cause in the plaintiff's forum of choice are, of course, to be considered, see McGee v. International Life Insurance Co., . . . an essential criterion in all cases is whether the 'quality and nature' of the defendant's activity is such that it is 'reasonable' and 'fair' to require him to conduct his defense in that State. International Shoe Co. v. Washington . . . ." The defendant's purposeful availment as to the forum state, apparently a sort of tacit consent, could make jurisdiction fair in this sense, but here the defendant "did not purposefully derive benefit from any activities relating to the State" and "lacks any other relevant contact with the State."

Justice Brennan, joined by Justices White and Powell, dissented.

RUSH v. SAVCHUK, 444 U.S. 320, 334, 100 S.Ct. 571, 580 (1980). In January 1972 Rush, who was the driver from Indiana, and Savchuk, the passenger also from Indiana, were in a single-car accident in Indiana. However, Indiana's guest statute would have barred a claim by the injured Savchuk.

In June 1973 Savchuk moved with his parents to Minnesota. In May 1974 he brought a $125,000 negligence action against Rush in Minnesota, which would apply its more favorable tort law. State Farm Mutual Automobile Insurance Company insured the car, owned by Rush's father, under a policy issued in Indiana. Savchuk invoked quasi in rem jurisdiction by garnishing State Farm's contractual obligation to defend and indemnify Rush, and he arranged service upon Rush in Indiana. State Farm, an insurer operating nationwide, was licensed to do and was doing business in Minnesota. Rush moved to dismiss for lack of territorial jurisdiction. The trial court denied the motion, and the state supreme court affirmed the existence of quasi in rem jurisdiction.

Savchuk's jurisdictional gambit was authorized by a specific Minnesota statute, which in turn had been based on the jurisdictional theory generated in Seider v. Roth, 17 N.Y.2d 111, 216 N.E.2d 312, 269 N.Y.S.2d 99 (1966). So-called Seider jurisdiction conceptually reified the insurer's obligation to the insured as an in-state debt that would support quasi in rem jurisdiction, given authorization to garnish and given the insurer's amenability to suit—somewhat oddly, however, the plaintiff had to be a forum-state resident, and the liability of even an appearing defendant-insured could not exceed the policy's liability limit.

On appeal, the Supreme Court of the United States reversed for lack of territorial jurisdiction. Justice Marshall, writing for the Court, cited Shaffer v. Heitner liberally. He apparently felt that Minnesota was not reasonable in categorizing this action as quasi in rem and thus evading the restrictions on personal jurisdiction. At any rate, he applied a constitutional test for personal jurisdiction, under which Rush lacked minimum contacts with the forum state. Irrelevant were, on the one hand, the marginal reasonableness of Seider's conceptual reification and, on the other hand, the possible overall fairness of going forward with this suit in Minnesota.

The Court also refused to treat this suit as being essentially against State Farm and hence the functional equivalent of a so-called direct action, whereby under a few states' law an injured plaintiff can sue the liability insurer directly without joining the insured. The Court observed that Minnesota formally required suit to be against the insured. Moreover, the insured was more than a merely nominal defendant, as the Court noted that the insured's reputation, insurability, and other interests could suffer detriment.

Justices Brennan and Stevens dissented. Excerpts from Justice Brennan's opinion appear after World–Wide Volkswagen Corp. v. Woodson, which follows below.

Question: (44) As part of its enforcement scheme, available even for registered out-of-state judgments, New York now allows the judgment creditor to utilize personal jurisdiction over a third party, if such jurisdiction otherwise exists in New York, to institute a proceeding for an order that the third party turn over money or property located outside New York and owned by the judgment debtor but possessed by the third party—without regard to the existence of connections between New York and the judgment creditor, the judgment debtor, their dispute, or the asset. See Koehler v. Bank of Bermuda Ltd., 12 N.Y.3d 533, 911 N.E.2d 825, 883 N.Y.S.2d 763 (2009). This innovation by New York uses personal jurisdiction during the enforcement process to extend the ordinary reach of quasi in rem jurisdiction against in-state assets. The policy of such aggressive enforcement is questionable, but is it even constitutional? Given that Shaffer and Rush held that a state cannot unreasonably substitute quasi in rem jurisdiction for personal jurisdiction, can New York so use personal jurisdiction as a substitute for quasi in rem jurisdiction?

World–Wide Volkswagen Corp. v. Woodson

Supreme Court of the United States, 1980.
444 U.S. 286, 100 S.Ct. 559, 580.

■ MR. JUSTICE WHITE delivered the opinion of the Court.

The issue before us is whether, consistently with the Due Process Clause of the Fourteenth Amendment, an Oklahoma court may exercise in personam jurisdiction over a nonresident automobile retailer and its wholesale distributor in a products liability action, when the defendants' only connection with Oklahoma is the fact that an automobile sold in New York to New York residents became involved in an accident in Oklahoma.

I

Respondents Harry and Kay Robinson purchased a new Audi automobile from petitioner Seaway Volkswagen, Inc. (Seaway) in Massena, N.Y., in 1976. The following year the Robinson family, who resided in New York, left that State for a new home in Arizona. As they passed through [Creek County in] the State of Oklahoma, another car struck their Audi in the rear, causing a fire which severely burned Kay Robinson and her two children.

The Robinsons subsequently brought a products liability action in the District Court for Creek County, Okla., claiming that their injuries resulted from defective design and placement of the Audi's gas tank and fuel system. They joined as defendants the automobile's manufacturer, Audi NSU Auto Union Aktiengesellschaft (Audi); its importer, Volkswagen of America, Inc. (Volkswagen); its regional distributor, petitioner World–Wide Volkswagen Corporation (World–Wide); and its retail dealer, petitioner Seaway. Seaway and World–Wide entered special appearances,[3] claiming that Oklahoma's exercise of jurisdiction over them would offend the limitations on the State's jurisdiction imposed by the Due Process Clause of the Fourteenth Amendment.

The facts presented to the District Court showed that World–Wide is incorporated and has its business office in New York. It distributes vehicles, parts, and accessories, under contract with Volkswagen, to retail dealers in New York, New Jersey, and Connecticut. Seaway, one of these retail dealers, is incorporated and has its place of business in New York. Insofar as the record reveals, Seaway and World–Wide are fully independent corporations whose relations with each other and with Volkswagen and Audi are contractual only. Respondents adduced no evidence that either World–Wide or Seaway does any business in Oklahoma, ships or sells any products to or in that State, has an agent to receive process there, or purchases advertisements in any media calculated to reach Oklahoma. In fact, as respondents' counsel conceded at oral argument, Tr. of Oral Arg.

---

[3] Volkswagen also entered a special appearance in the District Court, but unlike World–Wide and Seaway did not seek review in the Supreme Court of Oklahoma and is not a petitioner here. Both Volkswagen and Audi remain as defendants in the litigation pending before the District Court in Oklahoma. [The latter two were, respectively, New Jersey and German citizens.—Ed.]

32, there was no showing that any automobile sold by World–Wide or Seaway has ever entered Oklahoma with the single exception of the vehicle involved in the present case.

Despite the apparent paucity of contacts between petitioners and Oklahoma, the District Court rejected their constitutional claim and reaffirmed that ruling in denying petitioners' motion for reconsideration. Petitioners then sought a writ of prohibition in the Supreme Court of Oklahoma to restrain the District Judge, respondent Charles S. Woodson, from exercising in personam jurisdiction over them. They renewed their contention that because they had no "minimal contacts," App. 32, with the State of Oklahoma, the actions of the District Judge were in violation of their rights under the Due Process Clause.

The Supreme Court of Oklahoma denied the writ, 585 P.2d 351 (1978), holding that personal jurisdiction over petitioners was authorized by Oklahoma's "Long–Arm" Statute, Okla.Stat., Tit. 12, § 1701.03(a)(4) (1971).[7] Although the Court noted that the proper approach was to test jurisdiction against both statutory and constitutional standards, its analysis did not distinguish these questions, probably because § 1701.03(a)(4) has been interpreted as conferring jurisdiction to the limits permitted by the United States Constitution. The Court's rationale was contained in the following paragraph, 585 P.2d, at 354:

> "In the case before us, the product being sold and distributed by the petitioners is by its very design and purpose so mobile that petitioners can foresee its possible use in Oklahoma. This is especially true of the distributor, who has the exclusive right to distribute such automobile [sic] in New York, New Jersey and Connecticut. The evidence presented below demonstrated that goods sold and distributed by the petitioners were used in the State of Oklahoma, and under the facts we believe it reasonable to infer, given the retail value of the automobile, that the petitioners derive substantial income from automobiles which from time to time are used in the State of Oklahoma. This being the case, we hold that under the facts presented, the trial court was justified in concluding that the petitioners derive substantial revenue from goods used or consumed in this State."

We granted certiorari, 440 U.S. 907, 99 S.Ct. 1212 (1979), to consider an important constitutional question with respect to state-court jurisdiction and to resolve a conflict between the Supreme Court of Oklahoma and the highest courts of at least four other States. We reverse.

---

[7] This subsection provides:

"A court may exercise personal jurisdiction over a person, who acts directly or by an agent, as to a cause of action or claim for relief arising from the person's . . . causing tortious injury in this state by an act or omission outside this state if he regularly does or solicits business or engages in any other persistent course of conduct, or derives substantial revenue from goods used or consumed or services rendered, in this state. . . ."

The State Supreme Court rejected jurisdiction based on § 1701.03(a)(3), which authorizes jurisdiction over any person "causing tortious injury in this state by an act or omission in this state." Something in addition to the infliction of tortious injury was required.

II

The Due Process Clause of the Fourteenth Amendment limits the power of a state court to render a valid personal judgment against a nonresident defendant. Kulko v. Superior Court, 436 U.S. 84, 91, 98 S.Ct. 1690, 1696 (1978). A judgment rendered in violation of due process is void in the rendering State and is not entitled to full faith and credit elsewhere. Pennoyer v. Neff, 95 U.S. 714, 732–733 (1878). Due process requires that the defendant be given adequate notice of the suit, Mullane v. Central Hanover Trust Co., 339 U.S. 306, 313–314, 70 S.Ct. 652, 657 (1950), and be subject to the personal jurisdiction of the court, International Shoe Co. v. Washington, 326 U.S. 310, 66 S.Ct. 154 (1945). In the present case, it is not contended that notice was inadequate; the only question is whether these particular petitioners were subject to the jurisdiction of the Oklahoma courts.

As has long been settled, and as we reaffirm today, a state court may exercise personal jurisdiction over a nonresident defendant only so long as there exist "minimum contacts" between the defendant and the forum State. International Shoe Co. v. Washington, supra, at 316, 66 S.Ct., at 158. The concept of minimum contacts, in turn, can be seen to perform two related, but distinguishable, functions. It protects the defendant against the burdens of litigating in a distant or inconvenient forum. And it acts to ensure that the States, through their courts, do not reach out beyond the limits imposed on them by their status as coequal sovereigns in a federal system.

The protection against inconvenient litigation is typically described in terms of "reasonableness" or "fairness." We have said that the defendant's contacts with the forum State must be such that maintenance of the suit "does not offend 'traditional notions of fair play and substantial justice.' " International Shoe Co. v. Washington, supra, at 316, 66 S.Ct., at 158, quoting Milliken v. Meyer, 311 U.S. 457, 463, 61 S.Ct. 339, 342 (1940). The relationship between the defendant and the forum must be such that it is "reasonable . . . to require the corporation to defend the particular suit which is brought there." 326 U.S., at 317, 66 S.Ct., at 158. Implicit in this emphasis on reasonableness is the understanding that the burden on the defendant, while always a primary concern, will in an appropriate case be considered in light of other relevant factors, including the forum State's interest in adjudicating the dispute, see McGee v. International Life Ins. Co., 355 U.S. 220, 223, 78 S.Ct. 199, 201 (1957); the plaintiff's interest in obtaining convenient and effective relief, see Kulko v. Superior Court, supra, at 92, 98 S.Ct., at 1697, at least when that interest is not adequately protected by the plaintiff's power to choose the forum, cf. Shaffer v. Heitner, 433 U.S. 186, 211, n. 37, 97 S.Ct. 2569, 2583, n. 37 (1977); the interstate judicial system's interest in obtaining the most efficient resolution of controversies; and the shared interest of the several States in furthering fundamental substantive social policies, see Kulko v. Superior Court, supra, at 93, 98, 98 S.Ct., at 1697, 1700.

The limits imposed on state jurisdiction by the Due Process Clause, in its role as a guarantor against inconvenient litigation, have been substantially relaxed over the years. As we noted in McGee v. International Life Ins. Co., supra, at 222–223, 78 S.Ct., at 201, this trend is largely attributable to a fundamental transformation in the American economy:

> "Today many commercial transactions touch two or more States and may involve parties separated by the full continent. With this increasing nationalization of commerce has come a great increase in the amount of business conducted by mail across state lines. At the same time modern transportation and communication have made it much less burdensome for a party sued to defend himself in a State where he engages in economic activity."

The historical developments noted in McGee, of course, have only accelerated in the generation since that case was decided.

Nevertheless, we have never accepted the proposition that state lines are irrelevant for jurisdictional purposes, nor could we and remain faithful to the principles of interstate federalism embodied in the Constitution. The economic interdependence of the States was foreseen and desired by the Framers. In the Commerce Clause, they provided that the Nation was to be a common market, a "free trade unit" in which the States are debarred from acting as separable economic entities. H.P. Hood & Sons, Inc. v. Du Mond, 336 U.S. 525, 538, 69 S.Ct. 657, 665 (1949). But the Framers also intended that the States retain many essential attributes of sovereignty, including, in particular, the sovereign power to try causes in their courts. The sovereignty of each State, in turn, implied a limitation on the sovereignty of all of its sister States—a limitation express or implicit in both the original scheme of the Constitution and the Fourteenth Amendment.

Hence, even while abandoning the shibboleth that "[t]he authority of every tribunal is necessarily restricted by the territorial limits of the State in which it is established," Pennoyer v. Neff, supra, at 720, we emphasized that the reasonableness of asserting jurisdiction over the defendant must be assessed "in the context of our federal system of government," International Shoe Co. v. Washington, supra, at 317, 66 S.Ct., at 158, and stressed that the Due Process Clause ensures, not only fairness, but also the "orderly administration of the laws," id., at 319, 66 S.Ct., at 159. As we noted in Hanson v. Denckla, 357 U.S. 235, 250–251, 78 S.Ct. 1228, 1238 (1958):

> ". . . But it is a mistake to assume that this trend [from Pennoyer to International Shoe] heralds the eventual demise of all restrictions on the personal jurisdiction of state courts. [Citation omitted.] Those restrictions are more than a guarantee of immunity from inconvenient or distant litigation. They are a consequence of territorial limitations on the power of the respective States."

Thus, the Due Process Clause "does not contemplate that a state may make binding a judgment in personam against an individual or corporate defendant with which the state has no contacts, ties, or relations." International Shoe Co. v. Washington, supra, at 319, 66 S.Ct., at 159. Even if the defendant would suffer minimal or no inconvenience from being forced to litigate before the tribunals of another State; even if the forum State has a strong interest in applying its law to the controversy; even if the forum State is the most convenient location for litigation, the Due Process Clause, acting as an instrument of interstate federalism, may sometimes act to divest the State of its power to render a valid judgment. Hanson v. Denckla, supra, at 251, 254, 78 S.Ct., at 1238, 1240.

III

Applying these principles to the case at hand, we find in the record before us a total absence of those affiliating circumstances that are a necessary predicate to any exercise of state-court jurisdiction. Petitioners carry on no activity whatsoever in Oklahoma. They close no sales and perform no services there. They avail themselves of none of the privileges and benefits of Oklahoma law. They solicit no business there either through salespersons or through advertising reasonably calculated to reach the State. Nor does the record show that they regularly sell cars at wholesale or retail to Oklahoma customers or residents or that they indirectly, through others, serve or seek to serve the Oklahoma market. In short, respondents seek to base jurisdiction on one, isolated occurrence and whatever inferences can be drawn therefrom: the fortuitous circumstance that a single Audi automobile, sold in New York to New York residents, happened to suffer an accident while passing through Oklahoma.

It is argued, however, that because an automobile is mobile by its very design and purpose it was "foreseeable" that the Robinsons' Audi would cause injury in Oklahoma. Yet "foreseeability" alone has never been a sufficient benchmark for personal jurisdiction under the Due Process Clause. In Hanson v. Denckla, supra, it was no doubt foreseeable that the settlor of a Delaware trust would subsequently move to Florida and seek to exercise a power of appointment there; yet we held that Florida courts could not constitutionally exercise jurisdiction over a Delaware trustee that had no other contacts with the forum State. In Kulko v. Superior Court, supra, it was surely "foreseeable" that a divorced wife would move to California from New York, the domicile of the marriage, and that a minor daughter would live with the mother. Yet we held that California could not exercise jurisdiction in a child-support action over the former husband who had remained in New York.

If foreseeability were the criterion, a local California tire retailer could be forced to defend in Pennsylvania when a blowout occurs there, see Erlanger Mills, Inc. v. Cohoes Fibre Mills, Inc., 239 F.2d 502, 507 (C.A.4 1956); a Wisconsin seller of a defective automobile jack could be haled before a distant court for damage caused in New Jersey, Reilly v. Phil Tolkan Pontiac, Inc., 372 F.Supp. 1205 (NJ 1974); or a Florida soft drink concessionaire could be summoned to Alaska to account for injuries happening there, see Uppgren v. Executive Aviation Services, Inc., 304 F.Supp. 165, 170–171 (Minn.1969). Every seller of chattels would in effect appoint the chattel his agent for service of process. His amenability to suit would travel with the chattel. We recently abandoned the outworn rule of Harris v. Balk, 198 U.S. 215, 25 S.Ct. 625 (1905), that the interest of a creditor in a debt could be extinguished or otherwise affected by any State having transitory jurisdiction over the debtor. Shaffer v. Heitner, supra, 433 U.S. 186, 97 S.Ct. 2569 (1977). Having interred the mechanical rule that a creditor's amenability to a quasi in rem action travels with his debtor, we are unwilling to endorse an analogous principle in the present case.[11]

This is not to say, of course, that foreseeability is wholly irrelevant. But the foreseeability that is critical to due process analysis is not the mere likelihood that a product will find its way into the forum State. Rather, it is that the defendant's conduct and connection with the forum State are such that he should reasonably anticipate being haled into court there. See Kulko v. Superior Court, supra, at 97–98, 98 S.Ct., at 1699–1700; Shaffer v. Heitner, supra, at 216, 97 S.Ct., at 2586; and see id., at 217–219, 97 S.Ct., at 2586–2587 (Stevens, J., concurring in judgment). The Due Process Clause, by ensuring the "orderly administration of the laws," International Shoe Co. v. Washington, 326 U.S., at 319, 66 S.Ct., at 159, gives a degree of predictability to the legal system that allows potential defendants to structure their primary conduct with some minimum assurance as to where that conduct will and will not render them liable to suit.

When a corporation "purposefully avails itself of the privilege of conducting activities within the forum State," Hanson v. Denckla, supra, at 253, 78 S.Ct., at 1240, it has clear notice that it is subject to suit there, and can act to alleviate the risk of burdensome litigation by procuring insurance, passing the expected costs on to customers, or, if the risks are too great, severing its connection with the State. Hence if the sale of a product of a manufacturer or distributor such as Audi or Volkswagen is not simply an isolated occurrence, but arises from the efforts of the manufacturer or distributor to serve, directly or indirectly, the market for its product in other States, it is not unreasonable to subject it to suit in one of those States if its allegedly defective merchandise has there been the source of injury to its owner or to others. The forum State does not exceed its powers under the Due Process Clause if it asserts personal jurisdiction over a corporation that delivers its products into the stream of commerce with the expectation that they will be purchased by consumers in the forum State. Compare Gray v. American Radiator & Standard Sanitary Corp., 22 Ill.2d 432, 176 N.E.2d 761 (1961).

---

[11] Respondents' counsel, at oral argument, see Tr. of Oral Arg. 19–22, 29, sought to limit the reach of the foreseeability standard by suggesting that there is something unique about automobiles. It is true that automobiles are uniquely mobile, see Tyson v. Whitaker & Son, Inc., 407 A.2d 1, 6, and n. 11 (Me.1979) (McKusick, C.J.), that they did play a crucial role in the expansion of personal jurisdiction through the fiction of implied consent, e.g., Hess v. Pawloski, 274 U.S. 352, 47 S.Ct. 632 (1927), and that some of the cases have treated the automobile as a "dangerous instrumentality." But today, under the regime of International Shoe, we see no difference for jurisdictional purposes between an automobile and any other chattel. The "dangerous instrumentality" concept apparently was never used to support personal jurisdiction; and to the extent it has relevance today it bears not on jurisdiction but on the possible desirability of imposing substantive principles of tort law such as strict liability.

But there is no such or similar basis for Oklahoma jurisdiction over World–Wide or Seaway in this case. Seaway's sales are made in Massena, N.Y. World–Wide's market, although substantially larger, is limited to dealers in New York, New Jersey, and Connecticut. There is no evidence of record that any automobiles distributed by World–Wide are sold to retail customers outside this tri-State area. It is foreseeable that the purchasers of automobiles sold by World–Wide and Seaway may take them to Oklahoma. But the mere "unilateral activity of those who claim some relationship with a nonresident defendant cannot satisfy the requirement of contact with the forum State." Hanson v. Denckla, supra, at 253, 78 S.Ct., at 1239–1240.

In a variant on the previous argument, it is contended that jurisdiction can be supported by the fact that petitioners earn substantial revenue from goods used in Oklahoma. The Oklahoma Supreme Court so found, 585 P.2d, at 354–355, drawing the inference that because one automobile sold by petitioners had been used in Oklahoma, others might have been used there also. While this inference seems less than compelling on the facts of the instant case, we need not question the Court's factual findings in order to reject its reasoning.

This argument seems to make the point that the purchase of automobiles in New York, from which the petitioners earn substantial revenue, would not occur *but for* the fact that the automobiles are capable of use in distant States like Oklahoma. Respondents observe that the very purpose of an automobile is to travel, and that travel of automobiles sold by petitioners is facilitated by an extensive chain of Volkswagen service centers throughout the country, including some in Oklahoma. However, financial benefits accruing to the defendant from a collateral relation to the forum State will not support jurisdiction if they do not stem from a constitutionally cognizable contact with that State. See Kulko v. Superior Court, supra, at 94–95, 98 S.Ct., at 1698–1699. In our view, whatever marginal revenues petitioners may receive by virtue of the fact that their products are capable of use in Oklahoma is far too attenuated a contact to justify that State's exercise of in personam jurisdiction over them.

Because we find that petitioners have no "contacts, ties, or relations" with the State of Oklahoma, International Shoe Co. v. Washington, supra, at 319, 66 S.Ct., at 159, the judgment of the Supreme Court of Oklahoma is

Reversed.

■ MR. JUSTICE BRENNAN, dissenting [in this case and in Rush v. Savchuk, which precedes this case].

The Court holds that the Due Process Clause of the Fourteenth Amendment bars the States from asserting jurisdiction over the defendants in these two cases. In each case the Court so decides because it fails to find the "minimum contacts" that have been required since International Shoe Co. v. Washington, 326 U.S. 310, 316, 66 S.Ct. 154, 158 (1945). Because I believe that the Court reads International Shoe and its progeny too narrowly, and because I believe that the standards enunciated by those cases may already be obsolete as constitutional boundaries, I dissent.

I

The Court's opinions focus tightly on the existence of contacts between the forum and the defendant. . . .

Surely International Shoe contemplated that the significance of the contacts necessary to support jurisdiction would diminish if some other consideration helped establish that jurisdiction would be fair and reasonable. The interests of the State and other parties in proceeding with the case in a particular forum are such considerations. McGee v. International Life Insurance Co., 355 U.S. 220, 223, 78 S.Ct. 199, 201 (1957) . . . .

Another consideration is the actual burden a defendant must bear in defending the suit in the forum. McGee, supra. Because lesser burdens reduce the unfairness to the defendant, jurisdiction may be justified despite less significant contacts. . . .

. . . .

II

In each of these cases, I would find that the forum State has an interest in permitting the litigation to go forward, the litigation is connected to the forum, the defendant is linked to the forum, and the burden of defending is not unreasonable. Accordingly, I would hold that it is neither unfair nor unreasonable to require these defendants to defend in the forum State.

. . . .

In [the World–Wide case], the interest of the forum State and its connection to the litigation is strong. The automobile accident underlying the litigation occurred in Oklahoma. The plaintiffs were hospitalized in Oklahoma when they brought suit. Essential witnesses and evidence were in Oklahoma. [Citation omitted.] The State has a legitimate interest in enforcing its laws designed to keep its highway system safe, and the trial can proceed at least as efficiently in Oklahoma as anywhere else.

The petitioners are not unconnected with the forum. Although both sell automobiles within limited sales territories, each sold the automobile which in fact was driven to Oklahoma where it was involved in an accident.[8] It may be true, as the Court suggests, that each sincerely intended to limit its commercial impact to the limited territory, and that each intended to accept the benefits and protection of the laws only of those States within the territory. But obviously these were unrealistic hopes that cannot be treated as an automatic constitutional shield.[9]

---

[8] On the basis of this fact the state court inferred that the petitioners derived substantial revenue from goods used in Oklahoma. The inference is not without support. Certainly, were use of goods accepted as a relevant contact, a plaintiff would not need to have an exact count of the number of petitioners' cars that are used in Oklahoma.

[9] Moreover, imposing liability in this case would not so undermine certainty as to destroy an automobile dealer's ability to do business. According jurisdiction does not expand liability

An automobile simply is not a stationary item or one designed to be used in one place. An automobile is *intended* to be moved around. Someone in the business of selling large numbers of automobiles can hardly plead ignorance of their mobility or pretend that the automobiles stay put after they are sold. It is not merely that a dealer in automobiles foresees that they will move. . . . The dealer actually intends that the purchasers will use the automobiles to travel to distant States where the dealer does not directly "do business." The sale of an automobile does *purposefully* inject the vehicle into the stream of interstate commerce so that it can travel to distant States. [Citations omitted.]

This case is similar to Ohio v. Wyandotte Chemicals Corp., 401 U.S. 493, 91 S.Ct. 1005 (1971). There we indicated, in the course of denying leave to file an original jurisdiction case, that corporations having no direct contact with Ohio could constitutionally be brought to trial in Ohio because they dumped pollutants into streams outside Ohio's limits which ultimately, through the action of the water, reach Lake Erie and affected Ohio. No corporate acts, only their consequences, occurred in Ohio. The stream of commerce is just as natural a force as a stream of water, and it was equally predictable that the cars petitioners released would reach distant States.

The Court accepts that a State may exercise jurisdiction over a distributor which "serves" that State "indirectly" by "deliver[ing] its products into the stream of commerce with the expectation that they will be purchased by consumers in the forum State." . . . It is difficult to see why the Constitution should distinguish between a case involving goods which reach a distant State through a chain of distribution and a case involving goods which reach the same State because a consumer, using them as the dealer knew the customer would, took them there. In each case the seller purposefully injects the goods into the stream of commerce and those goods predictably are used in the forum State.[12]

Furthermore, an automobile seller derives substantial benefits from States other than its own. A large part of the value of automobiles is the extensive, nationwide network of highways. Significant portions of that network have been constructed by and are maintained by the individual States, including Oklahoma. The States, through their highway programs, contribute in a very direct and important way to the value of petitioners' businesses. Additionally, a network of other related dealerships with their service departments operate throughout the country under the protection of the laws of the various States, including Oklahoma, and enhance the value of petitioners' businesses by facilitating their customers' traveling.

---

except in the marginal case where a plaintiff cannot afford to bring an action except in the plaintiff's own State. In addition, these petitioners are represented by insurance companies. They not only could, but did, purchase insurance to protect them should they stand trial and lose the case. The costs of the insurance no doubt are passed on to customers.

[12] The manufacturer in the case cited by the Court, Gray v. American Radiator & Standard Sanitary Corp., 22 Ill.2d 432, 176 N.E.2d 761 (1961), had no more control over which States its goods would reach than did the petitioners in this case.

Thus, the Court errs in its conclusion, . . . (emphasis added), that "petitioners have *no* 'contacts, ties, or relations' " with Oklahoma. There obviously are contacts, and, given Oklahoma's connection to the litigation, the contacts are sufficiently significant to make it fair and reasonable for the petitioners to submit to Oklahoma's jurisdiction.

III

It may be that affirmance of the judgments in these cases would approach the outer limits of International Shoe's jurisdictional principle. But that principle, with its almost exclusive focus on the rights of defendants, may be outdated. . . .

International Shoe inherited its defendant focus from Pennoyer v. Neff, 95 U.S. 714 (1878), and represented the last major step this Court has taken in the long process of liberalizing the doctrine of personal jurisdiction. Though its flexible approach represented a major advance, the structure of our society has changed in many significant ways since International Shoe was decided in 1945. . . . The model of society on which the International Shoe Court based its opinion is no longer accurate. Business people, no matter how local their businesses, cannot assume that goods remain in the business' locality. Customers and goods can be anywhere else in the country usually in a matter of hours and always in a matter of a very few days.

In answering the question whether or not it is fair and reasonable to allow a particular forum to hold a trial binding on a particular defendant, the interests of the forum State and other parties loom large in today's world and surely are entitled to as much weight as are the interests of the defendant. The "orderly administration of the laws" provides a firm basis for according some protection to the interests of plaintiffs and States as well as of defendants. Certainly, I cannot see how a defendant's right to due process is violated if the defendant suffers no inconvenience. . . .

The conclusion I draw is that constitutional concepts of fairness no longer require the extreme concern for defendants that was once necessary. Rather, as I wrote in dissent from Shaffer v. Heitner, . . . (emphasis added), minimum contacts must exist "among the *parties*, the contested transaction, and the forum State." The contacts between any two of these should not be determinative. . . .

The Court's opinion . . . suggests that the defendant ought to be subject to a State's jurisdiction only if he has contacts with the State "such that he should reasonably anticipate being haled into court there."[18] . . . There is nothing unreasonable or unfair, however, about recognizing commercial reality. Given the tremendous mobility of goods and people, and the inability of businessmen to control where goods are taken by customers (or retailers), I do not think that the defendant should be in complete control of the geographical stretch of his amenability to suit. Jurisdiction is no

[18] The Court suggests that this is the critical foreseeability rather than the likelihood that the product will go to the forum State. But the reasoning begs the question. A defendant cannot know if his actions will subject him to jurisdiction in another State until we have declared what the law of jurisdiction is.

longer premised on the notion that nonresident defendants have somehow impliedly consented to suit. People should understand that they are held responsible for the consequences of their actions and that in our society most actions have consequences affecting many States. When an action in fact causes injury in another State, the actor should be prepared to answer for it there unless defending in that State would be unfair for some reason other than that a state boundary must be crossed.[19]

In effect the Court is allowing defendants to assert the sovereign rights of their home States. The expressed fear is that otherwise all limits on personal jurisdiction would disappear. But the argument's premise is wrong. I would not abolish limits on jurisdiction or strip state boundaries of all significance, [citation omitted]; I would still require the plaintiff to demonstrate sufficient contacts among the parties, the forum, and the litigation to make the forum a reasonable State in which to hold the trial.[20]

I would also, however, strip the defendant of an unjustified veto power over certain very appropriate fora—a power the defendant justifiably enjoyed long ago when communication and travel over long distances was slow and unpredictable and when notions of state sovereignty were impractical and exaggerated. But I repeat that that is not today's world. If a plaintiff can show . . . sufficient contacts . . . , then the defendant who cannot show some real injury to a constitutionally protected interest, see O'Connor v. Lee–Hy Paving Corp., 579 F.2d 194, 201 (C.A.2 1978), should have no constitutional excuse not to appear.[21]

. . . .

■ [The dissenting opinions of JUSTICES MARSHALL and BLACKMUN, not taking issue with the majority's approach but arguing that Seaway and World–Wide had sufficient contacts with Oklahoma to satisfy International Shoe, are omitted. Interestingly, however, Justice Blackmun began his opinion with this paragraph: "I confess that I am somewhat puzzled why the plaintiffs in this litigation are so insistent that the regional distributor and the retail dealer, the petitioners here, who handled the ill-fated Audi automobile involved in this litigation, be named defendants. It would appear that the manufacturer and the importer, whose subjectability to Oklahoma jurisdiction is not challenged before this Court, ought not to be judgment-proof. It may, of course, ultimately amount to a contest between insurance companies that, once begun, is not easily brought to a termination. Having made this much of an observation, I pursue it no further."][h]

---

[19] One consideration that might create some unfairness would be if the choice of forum also imposed on the defendant an unfavorable substantive law which the defendant could justly have assumed would not apply. . . .

[20] . . . I might reach a different result if the accident had not occurred in Oklahoma.

[21] Frequently, of course, the defendant will be able to influence the choice of forum through traditional doctrines, such as venue or forum non conveniens, permitting the transfer of litigation. [Citation omitted.]

[h] Soon after the Court's decision, the remaining defendants removed to a federal district court from a state court known for high verdicts. The Robinsons then lost at trial. They made

Questions: (45) How are all the Court's jurisdictional cases to be read together?

(a) To start with the case you just read, World–Wide seemed to make the following argument: The restriction that emerges from the early progeny of International Shoe, especially Mullane, rests on a concept of venue in a loose sense—the multifactor determination of "reasonableness" with respect to the litigation, a standard that was pro-plaintiff in the early days but is ultimately more party-neutral, puts the emphasis on *fairness* in selecting the forum. However, the restriction that re-emerges from the later progeny of International Shoe, beginning with Hanson, represents the current law of territorial jurisdiction in a strict sense—the conceptual concern with "power" over the target of the action, now seemingly pro-defendant in effect, puts the emphasis on governmental *structure* in limiting the states' power.

(b) In fact, Shaffer had earlier seemed to apply that same scheme: The two constitutional restrictions of reasonableness and power apply cumulatively, as the Shaffer Court showed by suggesting in part III of its opinion that the exercise of in rem or quasi in rem power must also be reasonable, and then by holding in part IV of its opinion that even a reasonable forum must have power in order to exercise personal jurisdiction (previously the cumulative relation of the two restrictions had sometimes gone unrecognized, as perhaps exemplified by Mullane). Incidentally, Shaffer also demonstrated by this treatment that the Pennoyer tripartite construct of in rem, quasi in rem, and in personam jurisdiction is alive and well (this despite the Shaffer Court's lip service to the Mullane heresy, or reform, that would have abolished the tripartite categorization as a constitutional matter).

(46) How should the Court further shape the doctrine now? Are the reasonableness and power tests bound eventually to coalesce, leaving some sort of reasonableness test as the survivor? Is the tripartite categorization then doomed?

BURGER KING CORP. v. RUDZEWICZ, 471 U.S. 462, 105 S.Ct. 2174 (1985). Burger King is a Florida corporation whose principal offices are in Miami. This huge restaurant organization operates primarily through a franchise system, which entails a twenty-year contract whereby the company lends its name, restaurant facility, and advice in exchange for an initial fee, monthly payments, and submission to exacting regulation. Burger King sets corporate policy and makes significant decisions in Miami, while its ten district offices conduct day-to-day monitoring of franchisees.

---

numerous further attempts to recover from Audi, including trying to reopen the judgment by alleging Audi's fraud in the initial litigation, but none was successful. For a heart-rending description of the accident and the litigation, see Charles W. Adams, World–Wide Volkswagen v. Woodson—The Rest of the Story, 72 Neb.L.Rev. 1122 (1993). According to later newspaper accounts, when the Robinsons lost their bid for review by the Supreme Court of that fraud suit in January 1996, almost twenty years after the accident, see Robinson v. Audi Aktiengesellschaft, 516 U.S. 1045, 116 S.Ct. 705 (1996), denying cert. to 56 F.3d 1259, 1268 (10th Cir.1995), they decided to give up. Instead of living in the home they originally purchased in Tucson near a golf course, they were living in a mobile home on the other side of town. Sadly, they say that their original attorney never told them that Audi had offered to settle the case for $1 million. See Hipolito R. Corella, Tucsonans Lose Battle Against Audi, Ariz. Daily Star, Jan. 9, 1996, at 1A, available at 1996 WL 4979662.

John Rudzewicz, an accountant from Michigan, wanted to invest by opening a Burger King restaurant in Michigan. He applied for a franchise to Burger King's district office in Michigan. Protracted negotiations followed, mainly with the district office but also with the Miami headquarters. Although Rudzewicz obtained limited concessions in the final contract, he did obligate himself to pay amounts to headquarters exceeding a million dollars over the twenty-year relationship and agreed to the standard provisions, including submission to regulation by Burger King and application of Florida law in construing the contract.

Rudzewicz's restaurant soon foundered, and he fell behind in payments. Unsuccessful negotiations led to Burger King's terminating the franchise and ordering him to vacate. Rudzewicz refused and continued to operate the facility as a Burger King restaurant until well into the ensuing lawsuit.

Burger King brought that lawsuit as a diversity action in the Southern District of Florida, including a claim against Rudzewicz for breach of the obligation to make required payments. Burger King served him by invoking, under the predecessor of Federal Rule 4(k)(1)(A), the provision of Florida's long-arm statute that specifically treats causes of action arising from a breach of contract in Florida by failure to perform acts required by the contract to be performed in Florida. Rudzewicz moved unsuccessfully to dismiss for lack of personal jurisdiction. He then answered, with a counterclaim for violations of Michigan's franchise investment law. The court found him liable for $228,875 in contract damages and found for Burger King on the counterclaim. On appeal, a divided panel of the Eleventh Circuit reversed the whole judgment on the ground that exercise of personal jurisdiction offended fundamental fairness.

On certiorari, the Supreme Court in turn reversed, concluding there was no offense to due process. Justice Brennan delivered the opinion of the Court, following a narration of the facts and prior proceedings with an explanation of the relevant principles:

"The Due Process Clause protects an individual's liberty interest in not being subject to the binding judgments of a forum with which he has established no meaningful 'contacts, ties, or relations.' International Shoe Co. v. Washington, 326 U.S. [310, 319, 66 S.Ct. 154, 160 (1945)].[13] By

[13] Although this protection operates to restrict state power, it "must be seen as ultimately a function of the individual liberty interest preserved by the Due Process Clause" rather than as a function "of federalism concerns." Insurance Corp. of Ireland, Ltd. v. Compagnie des Bauxites de Guinee, 456 U.S. 694, 702–703, n. 10, 102 S.Ct. 2099, 2104–2105, n. 10 (1982). [This case held that a federal court could establish personal jurisdiction as a discovery sanction against foreign defendants who had asserted the defense of lack of personal jurisdiction but then had resisted discovery on that issue. In the course of a murky opinion for the Court, Justice White declared that personal jurisdiction "represents a restriction on judicial power not as a matter of sovereignty, but as a matter of individual liberty." There he dropped the notorious footnote 10: "It is true that we have stated that the requirement of personal jurisdiction, as applied to state courts, reflects an element of federalism and the character of state sovereignty vis-à-vis other states. For example, in World–Wide Volkswagen Corp. v. Woodson, 444 U.S. 286, 291–293, 100 S.Ct. 559, 564–565 (1980), we stated [that the due process requirement, as one of its two functions, 'acts to ensure that the States, through their

requiring that individuals have 'fair warning that a particular activity may subject [them] to the jurisdiction of a foreign sovereign,' Shaffer v. Heitner, 433 U.S. 186, 218, 97 S.Ct. 2569, 2587 (1977) (Stevens, J., concurring in judgment), the Due Process Clause 'gives a degree of predictability to the legal system that allows potential defendants to structure their primary conduct with some minimum assurance as to where that conduct will and will not render them liable to suit,' World–Wide Volkswagen Corp. v. Woodson, 444 U.S. 286, 297, 100 S.Ct. 559, 567 (1980).

"Where a forum seeks to assert specific jurisdiction over an out-of-state defendant who has not consented to suit there, this 'fair warning' requirement is satisfied if the defendant has 'purposefully directed' his activities at residents of the forum, Keeton v. Hustler Magazine, Inc., 465 U.S. 770, 774, 104 S.Ct. 1473, 1478 (1984), and the litigation results from alleged injuries that 'arise out of or relate to' those activities, Helicopteros Nacionales de Colombia, S.A. v. Hall, 466 U.S. 408, 414, 104 S.Ct. 1868, 1872 (1984). Thus '[t]he forum State does not exceed its powers under the Due Process Clause if it asserts personal jurisdiction over a corporation that delivers its products into the stream of commerce with the expectation that they will be purchased by consumers in the forum State' and those products subsequently injure forum consumers. World–Wide Volkswagen Corp. v. Woodson, supra, at 297–298, 100 S.Ct., at 567–568. Similarly, a publisher who distributes magazines in a distant State may fairly be held accountable in that forum for damages resulting there from an allegedly defamatory story. Keeton v. Hustler Magazine, Inc., supra; see also Calder v. Jones, 465 U.S. 783, 104 S.Ct. 1482 (1984) (suit against author and editor).[i] And with respect to interstate contractual obligations, we have emphasized that parties who 'reach out beyond one state and create continuing relationships and obligations with citizens of another state' are subject to regulation and sanctions in the other State for the consequences of their activities. Travelers Health Assn. v. Virginia, 339 U.S. 643, 647, 70 S.Ct. 927, 929 (1950). See also McGee v. International Life Insurance Co., 355 U.S. 220, 222–223, 78 S.Ct. 199, 200–201 (1957).

"We have noted several reasons why a forum legitimately may exercise personal jurisdiction over a nonresident who 'purposefully directs' his

---

courts, do not reach out beyond the limits imposed on them by their status as coequal sovereigns in a federal system.'] The restriction on state sovereign power described in World–Wide Volkswagen Corp., however, must be seen as ultimately a function of the individual liberty interest preserved by the Due Process Clause. That clause is the only source of the personal jurisdiction requirement and the clause itself makes no mention of federalism concerns. Furthermore, if the federalism concept operated as an independent restriction on the sovereign power of the court, it would not be possible to waive the personal jurisdiction requirement: Individual actions cannot change the powers of sovereignty, although the individual can subject himself to powers from which he may otherwise be protected."—Ed.]

[i] Recall the Keeton and Calder cases, which raised First Amendment concerns. In particular, the Court in Calder allowed the entertainer Shirley Jones to sue for libel in her home state of California against the National Enquirer's writer and editor living and working in Florida. The Court stressed that the defendants had "intentionally directed" their Florida acts at California while knowing that their conduct would have "effects" there. See C. Douglas Floyd & Shima Baradaran–Robison, Toward a Unified Test of Personal Jurisdiction in an Era of Widely Diffused Wrongs: The Relevance of Purpose and Effects, 81 Ind.L.J. 601 (2006).

activities toward forum residents. A State generally has a 'manifest interest' in providing its residents with a convenient forum for redressing injuries inflicted by out-of-state actors. Id., at 223, 78 S.Ct., at 201; [other citation omitted]. Moreover, where individuals 'purposefully derive benefit' from their interstate activities, Kulko v. California Superior Court, 436 U.S. 84, 96, 98 S.Ct. 1690, 1699 (1978), it may well be unfair to allow them to escape having to account in other States for consequences that arise proximately from such activities; the Due Process Clause may not readily be wielded as a territorial shield to avoid interstate obligations that have been voluntarily assumed. And because 'modern transportation and communication have made it much less burdensome for a party sued to defend himself in a State where he engages in economic activity,' it usually will not be unfair to subject him to the burdens of litigating in another forum for disputes relating to such activity. McGee v. International Life Insurance Co., supra, at 223, 78 S.Ct., at 201.

"Notwithstanding these considerations, the constitutional touchstone remains whether the defendant purposefully established 'minimum contacts' in the forum State. International Shoe Co. v. Washington, supra, at 316, 66 S.Ct., at 158. Although it has been argued that foreseeability of causing *injury* in another State should be sufficient to establish such contacts there when policy considerations so require, the Court has consistently held that this kind of foreseeability is not a 'sufficient benchmark' for exercising personal jurisdiction. World–Wide Volkswagen Corp. v. Woodson, 444 U.S., at 295, 100 S.Ct., at 566. Instead, 'the foreseeability that is critical to due process analysis . . . is that the defendant's conduct and connection with the forum State are such that he should reasonably anticipate being haled into court there.' Id., at 297, 100 S.Ct., at 567. In defining when it is that a potential defendant should 'reasonably anticipate' out-of-state litigation, the Court frequently has drawn from the reasoning of Hanson v. Denckla, 357 U.S. 235, 253, 78 S.Ct. 1228, 1239–1240 (1958):

> 'The unilateral activity of those who claim some relationship with a nonresident defendant cannot satisfy the requirement of contact with the forum State. The application of that rule will vary with the quality and nature of the defendant's activity, but it is essential in each case that there be some act by which the defendant purposefully avails itself of the privilege of conducting activities within the forum State, thus invoking the benefits and protections of its laws.'

"This 'purposeful availment' requirement ensures that a defendant will not be haled into a jurisdiction solely as a result of 'random,' 'fortuitous,' or 'attenuated' contacts, Keeton v. Hustler Magazine, Inc., supra, at 774, 104 S.Ct., at 1478; World–Wide Volkswagen Corp. v. Woodson, 444 U.S., at 299, 100 S.Ct., at 568, or of the 'unilateral activity of another party or a third person,' Helicopteros Nacionales de Colombia, S.A. v. Hall, supra, at 417, 104 S.Ct., at 1873. Jurisdiction is proper, however, where the contacts proximately result from actions by the defendant *himself* that create 'a substantial connection' with the forum State. McGee v. International Life Insurance Co., supra, at 223, 78 S.Ct., at 201; [other citation omitted]. Thus where the defendant 'deliberately' has engaged in significant activities within a State, Keeton v. Hustler Magazine, Inc., 465 U.S., at 781, 104 S.Ct., at 1481, or has created 'continuing obligations' between himself and residents of the forum, Travelers Health Assn. v. Virginia, 339 U.S., at 648, 70 S.Ct., at 929, he manifestly has availed himself of the privilege of conducting business there, and because his activities are shielded by 'the benefits and protections' of the forum's laws it is presumptively not unreasonable to require him to submit to the burdens of litigation in that forum as well."

After so treating power, Justice Brennan explained reasonableness:

"Once it has been decided that a defendant purposefully established minimum contacts within the forum State, these contacts may be considered in light of other factors to determine whether the assertion of personal jurisdiction would comport with 'fair play and substantial justice.' International Shoe Co. v. Washington, 326 U.S., at 320, 66 S.Ct., at 160. Thus courts in 'appropriate case[s]' may evaluate 'the burden on the defendant,' 'the forum State's interest in adjudicating the dispute,' 'the plaintiff's interest in obtaining convenient and effective relief,' 'the interstate judicial system's interest in obtaining the most efficient resolution of controversies,' and the 'shared interest of the several States in furthering fundamental substantive social policies.' World–Wide Volkswagen Corp. v. Woodson, supra, at 292, 100 S.Ct., at 564. These considerations sometimes serve to establish the reasonableness of jurisdiction upon a lesser showing of minimum contacts than would otherwise be required. See, e.g., Keeton v. Hustler Magazine, Inc., supra, at 780, 104 S.Ct., at 1481; Calder v. Jones, supra, 465 U.S., at 788–89, 104 S.Ct., at 1486–87; McGee v. International Life Insurance Co., supra, at 223–224, 78 S.Ct., at 201–202. On the other hand, where a defendant who purposefully has directed his activities at forum residents seeks to defeat jurisdiction, he must present a compelling case that the presence of some other considerations would render jurisdiction unreasonable. Most such considerations usually may be accommodated through means short of finding jurisdiction unconstitutional. For example, the potential clash of the forum's law with the 'fundamental substantive social policies' of another State may be accommodated through application of the forum's choice-of-law rules. Similarly, a defendant claiming substantial inconvenience may seek a change of venue. Nevertheless, minimum requirements inherent in the concept of 'fair play and substantial justice' may defeat the reasonableness of jurisdiction even if the defendant has purposefully engaged in forum activities. World–Wide Volkswagen Corp. v. Woodson, 444 U.S., at 292, 100 S.Ct., at 564; see also Restatement (Second) of Conflict of Laws §§ 36–37 (1971). As we previously have noted, jurisdictional rules may not be employed in such a way as to make litigation 'so gravely difficult and inconvenient' that a party unfairly is at a 'severe disadvantage' in comparison to his opponent. The Bremen v. Zapata Off–Shore Co., 407 U.S. 1, 18, 92 S.Ct. 1907, 1917 (1972) (re forum-selection provisions); McGee v. International Life Insurance Co., supra, at 223–224, 78 S.Ct., at 201–202."

Applying those principles to this case, the Court noted that John Rudzewicz had reached out to negotiate with a Florida corporation and agreed by long-term contract to be regulated from Florida, to make payments to Florida, and to have disputes governed by the laws of Florida. The Court thus held that the record and the law supported the district court's determination that the defendant had purposefully established minimum contacts with Florida.

Similarly, the Court upheld the district court's findings and conclusions to the effect that jurisdiction was not so unfair as to be unconstitutionally unreasonable, at least in this particular case.

However, Justice Stevens, with whom Justice White joined, dissented on the ground that "there is a significant element of unfairness in requiring a franchisee to defend a case of this kind in the forum chosen by the franchisor." Justice Powell did not participate in the case.

Question: (47) In what ways does Burger King reflect alterations of the World–Wide formulae, both as to the constitutional source of the power test and the burden of proof on the reasonableness test?

ASAHI METAL INDUSTRY CO. v. SUPERIOR COURT, 480 U.S. 102, 107 S.Ct. 1026 (1987). Gary Zurcher was severely injured and his wife killed in a motorcycle accident in California, allegedly caused by the explosion of the cycle's defective rear tire. There he sued among others Cheng Shin, allegedly the Taiwanese manufacturer of the tube. Cheng Shin impleaded Asahi, allegedly the Japanese manufacturer of the tube's valve assembly. The main claims were eventually settled, leaving only Cheng Shin's indemnity claim against Asahi.

Before that settlement, Asahi had moved unsuccessfully to quash service. Asahi made its valves in Japan and sold some of them to Cheng Shin in Taiwan, where Cheng Shin made its tubes with valves by Asahi or other suppliers and then sold them throughout the world, with Cheng Shin selling a fair number in California, perhaps including the one in suit. Other Asahi valves in other manufacturers' tubes similarly came into California. Asahi apparently had no other contacts with California. The California courts ultimately upheld personal jurisdiction over Asahi as being within the state's long-arm statute and consistent with due process.

On certiorari, the Supreme Court reversed because jurisdiction here violated due process. On the one hand, five Justices suggested that power would exist over this defendant, which put its goods into the stream of commerce flowing into the forum state. On the other hand, eight Justices held that exercising jurisdiction would be unreasonable, considering the severe burdens on Asahi of defending in a foreign legal system, the slight interests of Cheng Shin and California in the exercise of jurisdiction, and the international interests in not subjecting this alien corporation to an indemnification offshoot of a product liability action in an American court. In short, here is one of those rare cases where personal jurisdiction is held unconstitutional because, even though it might pass the power test, it fails the unreasonableness test.

The complex breakdown of the Justices' opinions is perhaps telling, as indicated by this schema:

	O'Connor Rehnquist Powell	**Scalia**	**Brennan White Marshall Blackmun**	**Stevens White Blackmun**
(i)	no power, under standard requiring that defendant had purpose to serve California market	no power, applying O'Connor standard	power exists, under standard requiring only defendant's actual awareness that product was being regularly sold in California	power seemingly exists, regardless of whether Brennan's mere-awareness standard or O'Connor's awareness-plus standard governs
(ii)	unreasonable	no opinion on unreasonableness	unreasonable	unreasonable

---

Question: (48) Now what do you think would be the result if Gray v. American Radiator & Standard Sanitary Corp., supra p. 547, came before the Supreme Court of the United States? See Wiles v. Morita Iron Works Co., 125 Ill.2d 144, 530 N.E.2d 1382 (1988) (saying no power over foreign supplier unaware of Illinois destination of machines, but distinguishing Gray's facts).

BURNHAM v. SUPERIOR COURT, 495 U.S. 604, 110 S.Ct. 2105 (1990). A New Jersey couple separated by agreement, with the wife and the two children moving to California. Six months later, the husband visited California for three days on business and to see his children. The wife had him served with process for a California suit seeking divorce and monetary relief. He returned to New Jersey.

He then tried to quash service for lack of personal jurisdiction. The California courts refused, relying on his transient physical presence. The United States Supreme Court unanimously affirmed, but the Justices split so badly in their opinions as to rob the case of precedential significance.

Justice Scalia, writing only for Chief Justice Rehnquist and Justice Kennedy, opined that any basis of territorial jurisdiction accepted at the time of the Fourteenth Amendment's adoption in 1868 and still generally accepted by the states today is valid, without any regard to its possible unreasonableness. That is, although newer bases can pass muster only if the power is not unreasonable, the "traditional" bases are per se constitutional. His theoretically radical approach, however, would have little practical impact on jurisdiction. Seemingly, physical presence is the only traditional basis that so qualifies for automatic validity. Apparently, Justice Scalia's ultimately unsuccessful mission was to establish a historical approach to due process that would affect the rest of constitutional law.

Justice White wrote an obscure opinion concurring in part with Justice Scalia, but reserving some backup test of unreasonableness for the basis of physical presence.

Justice Brennan, joined by Justices Marshall, Blackmun, and O'Connor, agreed that personal jurisdiction existed in this case, as well as in most cases founded on physical presence. Usually when physical presence is intentional, the defendant is on notice of amenability to suit; the defendant gets some benefits while in the state; and the burdens of returning to defend are slight, in modern times. But Justice Brennan argued that under International Shoe and Shaffer, all bases of "jurisdiction, even ancient ones, must satisfy contemporary notions of due process." Thus, a defendant in a particular case founded on transient jurisdiction could attempt to show that jurisdiction would be unreasonable.

Justice Stevens wrote an insignificant concurrence in the judgment, refusing to take any broad position in disposing of this "easy" case.

So, the big battle was between the minority opinions of Justices Scalia and Brennan. The following extracts convey the flavor of their sharp exchange. We begin with Justice Scalia's reply, in part III of his opinion, to Justice Brennan:

"The difference between us and Justice Brennan has nothing to do with whether 'further progress [is] to be made' in the 'evolution of our legal system.' Post . . . . It has to do with whether changes are to be adopted as progressive by the American people or decreed as progressive by the Justices of this Court. Nothing we say today prevents individual States from limiting or entirely abandoning the in-state-service basis of jurisdiction. And nothing prevents an overwhelming majority of them from doing so, with the consequence that the 'traditional notions of fairness' that this Court applies may change. But the states have overwhelmingly declined to adopt such limitation or abandonment, evidently not considering it to be progress. The question is whether, armed with no authority other than individual Justices' perceptions of fairness that conflict with both past and current practice, this Court can compel the states to make such a change on the ground that 'due process' requires it. We hold that it cannot."

Justice Brennan's opinion rejoined in his footnotes 7 and 14:

"I do not propose that the 'contemporary notions of due process' to be applied are no more than 'each Justice's subjective assessment of what is fair and just.' Ante . . . . Rather, the inquiry is guided by our decisions beginning with International Shoe Co. v. Washington, 326 U.S. 310, 66 S.Ct. 154 (1945), and the specific factors that we have developed to ascertain whether a jurisdictional rule comports with 'traditional notions of fair play and substantial justice.' See, e.g., Asahi Metal Industry Co. v. Superior Court of California, Solano County, 480 U.S. 102, 113, 107 S.Ct. 1026, 1033 (1987) (noting 'several factors,' including 'the burden on the defendant, the interests of the forum State, and the plaintiff's interest in obtaining relief'). This analysis may not be 'mechanical or quantitative,' International Shoe, 326 U.S., at 319, 66 S.Ct., at 159, but neither is it 'freestanding,' ante . . . , or dependent on personal whim. Our experience with this approach demonstrates that it is well within our competence to employ.

"I note, moreover, that the dual conclusions of Justice Scalia's opinion [that tradition *alone* is completely dispositive and that no showing of unfairness can ever serve to invalidate a traditional jurisdictional practice] create a singularly unattractive result. Justice Scalia suggests that when and if a jurisdictional rule becomes substantively unfair or even 'unconscionable,' this Court is powerless to alter it. Instead, he is willing to rely on individual States to limit or abandon bases of jurisdiction that have become obsolete. . . . This reliance is misplaced, for States have little incentive to limit rules such as transient jurisdiction that make it *easier* for their own citizens to sue out-of-state defendants. That States are more likely to expand their jurisdiction is illustrated by the adoption by many States of long-arm statutes extending the reach of personal jurisdiction to the limits established by the Federal Constitution. [Citations omitted.] Out-of-staters do not vote in state elections or have a voice in state government. We should not assume, therefore, that States will be motivated by 'notions of fairness' to curb jurisdictional rules like the one at issue here. The reasoning of Justice Scalia's opinion today is strikingly oblivious to the raison d'être of various constitutional doctrines designed to protect out-of-staters, such as the Art. IV Privileges and Immunities Clause and the Commerce Clause."

Justice Scalia's opinion surrejoined in his footnote 5:

"I find quite unacceptable as a basis for this Court's decisions Justice Brennan's view that 'the raison d'être of various constitutional doctrines designed to protect out-of-staters . . .' . . . entitles this Court to brand as 'unfair,' and hence unconstitutional, the refusal of all fifty states 'to limit or abandon bases of jurisdiction that have become obsolete' . . . . 'Due process' (which is the constitutional text at issue here) does not mean that process which shifting majorities of this Court feel to be 'due'; but that process which American society—self-interested American society, which expresses its judgments in the laws of self-interested states—has traditionally considered 'due.' The notion that the Constitution, through some penumbra emanating from the Privileges and Immunities Clause and the Commerce Clause, establishes this Court as a platonic check upon the society's greedy adherence to its traditions can only be described as imperious."

Question: (49) Now what do you think would be the result if Grace v. MacArthur, supra p. 511, came before the Supreme Court of the United States? See Sarieddine v. Moussa, 820 S.W.2d 837, 840 (Tex.Ct.App.1991) (suggesting weakly that transient jurisdiction is constitutional only where its application is not so outlandish as to be unreasonable in the particular circumstances).

SECTION 5. ACTIONS IN FEDERAL COURT

We have considered statutory and constitutional limitations on the exercise of territorial jurisdiction, and in doing so we have dealt with both state cases and federal cases (such as Burger King). The time has come, however, to examine with a finer focus this issue of amenability to suit in the context of actions in federal court.

The federal courts can constitutionally reach much farther than can the state courts in exercising territorial jurisdiction.[j] Nevertheless, the federal courts have decided that ordinarily they are not to assert their utmost constitutional powers of adjudication, but instead they are to act within certain limits specified by Rule 4.

DeJames v. Magnificence Carriers

United States District Court, District of New Jersey, 1980.
491 F.Supp. 1276, aff'd, 654 F.2d 280 (3d Cir.), cert. denied, 454 U.S. 1085, 102 S.Ct. 642 (1981).

■ COHEN, SENIOR JUDGE:

Plaintiff, Joseph DeJames, a New Jersey citizen, has brought suit under the admiralty jurisdiction of the court, 28 U.S.C. § 1333, to recover damages for personal injuries suffered while working aboard the vessel M.V. Magnificence Venture. The injuries allegedly occurred on January 26, 1977, while the vessel was moored at a pier in Camden, New Jersey.

According to the pleadings defendant, Hitachi Shipbuilding and Engineering Company, Ltd. (Hitachi), entered into a contract in Japan with defendants Magnificence Carriers, Inc., Venture Shipping (Managers Ltd.), and Nippon Yusen Kaisha, the charterers of the vessel, M.V. Magnificence Venture, whereby Hitachi agreed to convert the vessel into an automobile

[j] See supra pp. 33–230.

carrier. Plaintiff alleges in his complaint that the conversion work performed by Hitachi was defective and was the direct cause of his injuries.

Presently before the court is a motion by Hitachi to dismiss the complaint against it for insufficiency of service and for lack of in personam jurisdiction.[k] Hitachi contends that it does not maintain the requisite contacts with New Jersey to enable this court to render a binding personal judgment against it. In support thereof, Hitachi has submitted an affidavit from Kiyoshi Ohno, manager of its ship repair business department located in Tokyo, Japan. According to the affidavit, Hitachi completed all work on the vessel at issue in its Japanese shipyard and had no further contact or involvement with the ship once it left Osaka, Japan. The affidavit further states that Hitachi does not maintain an office in New Jersey, nor does it have an agent of any type there or transact any business in the State.

At the outset it should be noted that when a federal court is asked to exercise personal jurisdiction over a defendant sued on a claim arising out of federal law, federal law under the due process clause of the fifth amendment is controlling. See Honeywell, Inc. v. Metz Apparatewerke, [509] F.2d 1137, 1143 (7th Cir.1975); Fraley v. Chesapeake and Ohio Railway Company, 397 F.2d 1, 3–4 (3d Cir.1968); Alco Standard Corp. v. Benalal, 345 F.Supp. 14, 24–25 (E.D.Pa.1972). That is not to say, however, that the analysis employed in diversity jurisdiction cases arising under the fourteenth amendment has no bearing on our decision in this case. In this regard, the Court of Appeals for the Third Circuit has remarked that the standard of due process set forth by the Supreme Court in International Shoe Co. v. Washington, 326 U.S. 310, 66 S.Ct. 154, 90 L.Ed. 95 (1945) and its progeny is equally applicable in cases grounded on a federal claim. See Fraley, 397 F.2d at 3; [other citations omitted].

In response to Hitachi's motion to dismiss, plaintiff argues first, that Hitachi's contacts with New Jersey are sufficient for the purposes of jurisdiction, and second, that where, as here, the court is to determine whether it has jurisdiction over a defendant who is being sued on a federal claim, it may consider not only the defendant's contacts with the forum state, but also the aggregate contacts of the defendant with the United States as a whole. We take up these arguments in turn.

[The court concluded that under the International Shoe and World–Wide cases, Hitachi lacked minimum contacts with New Jersey.]

The earliest case adopting the national contacts approach is First Flight Co. v. National Carloading Corp., 209 F.Supp. 730 (E.D.Tenn.1962). That court held that the proper inquiry in determining personal jurisdiction in a case involving federal rights is one related to the contacts with the sovereignty in question, the United States. Id. at 738. The theoretical basis behind this approach is that the restrictions of the fourteenth amendment upon state jurisdiction have no application to a cause of action arising under federal law. Instead, the argument runs, the fifth amendment due process clause controls, and a defendant's national contacts may be aggre-

[k] Hitachi was served in Japan.

gated to satisfy that standard. [Citations omitted.] As described by one court, "it is not the territory in which a court sits that determines the extent of its jurisdiction, but rather the geographical limits of the unit of government of which the court is a part." Cryomedics, Inc. v. Spembly, Ltd., 397 F.Supp. 287, 291 (D.Conn.1975); accord, Holt v. Klosters Rederi A/S, 355 F.Supp. 354, 357 (W.D.Mich.1973); [other citations omitted].

Although the fifth amendment test is sometimes expressed in more general "fairness" terms, see, e.g., Honeywell, Inc., 509 F.2d at 1143 (citing Galvan v. Press, 347 U.S. 522, 530, 74 S.Ct. 737, 742, 98 L.Ed. 911 (1954)), the International Shoe line of cases . . . provides the foundation for the test, and the analysis is substantially similar. See Honeywell, Inc., 509 F.2d at 1143; First Flight, 209 F.Supp. at 738 (E.D.Tenn.1962). Accordingly, the standard which has been applied by those courts adopting the national contacts approach is whether defendant "has such minimum contacts with the United States that the exercise of jurisdiction does not offend traditional notions of fair play and substantial justice." Holt v. Klosters Rederi A/S, 355 F.Supp. at 357 n. 2 (quoting First Flight, 209 F.Supp. at 738); [other citations omitted].

. . . .

Since the First Flight opinion discussed the national contacts theory in 1962, several jurisdictions have considered the approach in federal question cases. But most courts which have analyzed the theory have refused to apply it and have instead looked solely to state contacts as a basis for jurisdiction. While these courts generally acknowledge the logic of inquiring into a defendant's contacts with the United States where the suit is based upon a federally created right, they reason that they must have a federal rule or statute authorizing nationwide or worldwide service of process before doing so. See, e.g., Wells Fargo & Co. v. Wells Fargo Exp. Co., 556 F.2d 406, 418 (9th Cir.1977) (refused to aggregate national contacts since Lanham Act did not grant the court broad service of process powers); [other citations omitted].

A review of the pertinent case law reveals that the overwhelming majority of courts which have considered the national contacts approach have rejected its application in the absence of statutory authority for service of process. After careful analysis of the rationale underlying these decisions, the court finds that it must join their ranks. We, therefore, reject plaintiff's contention in the instant matter that defendant Hitachi's national contacts may be aggregated as a basis for the exercise of jurisdiction over Hitachi.

The court's opinion in the case at bar, however, should not be construed as a total rejection of the national contacts theory. On the contrary, the court believes that it is not unfair nor unreasonable as a matter of due process to consider the nationwide contacts of an alien defendant in determining whether jurisdiction exists. As noted by Judge Wilson in his opinion in First Flight,

> One fundamental principle of the Anglo–American law of jurisdiction is that a sovereignty has personal jurisdiction over any defendant within its territorial limits, and that it may exercise that jurisdiction by any of its courts able to obtain service upon the defendant.

209 F.Supp. at 736. This court also believes that many good policy reasons exist for applying the national contacts theory, particularly in those federal question cases involving alien defendants. . . .

We also recognize, however, that the United States has by the enactment of the Federal Rules of Civil Procedure imposed restrictions upon the exercise of personal jurisdiction by its courts. One such restriction, relevant to the case at bar, is that imposed by Rule 4(e), which provides that when substituted service is made pursuant to a state's long-arm statute, the service be made "under the circumstances and in the manner prescribed in the statute." Fed.R.Civ.P. 4(e)(2).[1] That portion of the Rule has been interpreted to mean that service under a valid state long-arm statute in a federal court is only possible in those situations where the in-state activities of the defendant would be sufficient to invoke the long-arm statute had the defendant been sued in state court. See, e.g., Hydraulics Unlimited Mfg. Co. v. B/J Manufacturing Co., 449 F.2d 775, 777 (10th Cir.1971); [other citations omitted]; see generally 4 C. Wright & A. Miller, Federal Practice and Procedure, § 1075, at 313 (2d ed. 1969). Thus, where service of process is effected by means of a state statute, a federal court is forced to look to the state in which the district is located to determine whether jurisdiction may be asserted over an out-of-state defendant.

. . . .

Plaintiff has urged the court to exercise jurisdiction on the ground that New Jersey's long-arm rule, R. 4:4–4, N.J.Court Rules (the rule employed in the case at bar) has been construed as extending New Jersey's jurisdictional reach to its constitutional limits. See Avdel v. Mecure, 58 N.J. 264, 268, 277 A.2d 207, 209 (1971). The power of the State of New Jersey, however, is still limited by the due process requirements of the fourteenth amendment. There must still be some contact of a defendant with the forum state.

It is important to note that our rejection of the national contacts approach in the instant matter is limited to those factual situations where service of process must be made pursuant to a state statute. We believe that where service can be effected through wholly federal means, a defendant's national contacts may still be a viable basis for jurisdiction in a federal question case. Thus, for instance, where Congress has provided for nationwide service of process, we can perceive of no impediment to the application of the national contacts theory with the exception of the fifth amendment's "fairness" standard. There would be no need to make reference to any state law in making service, . . . and concomitantly, no need to consider any fourteenth amendment or state restrictions on that service. See, e.g., Alco Standard Corp. v. Benalal, 345 F.Supp. 14, 25 (E.D.Pa.1972)

---

[1] The operative part of this provision now lies in Rule 4(k)(1)(A).

(In action brought under [1934 Securities] Exchange Act, which provides for nationwide service of process, court ruled that since the Act is national in scope, the court's jurisdictional inquiry should focus on a defendant's national contacts.) . . .

Since Congress has not enacted a federal statute authorizing nationwide service of process in admiralty actions, and since the district court's power in the present matter is therefore limited by the Federal Rules of Civil Procedure and, through them, the laws of New Jersey, we find the relevant jurisdictional inquiry to be the extent of the defendant Hitachi's contacts with New Jersey. And since we have determined that Hitachi lacks sufficient contacts with New Jersey to satisfy the jurisdictional standards set forth in International Shoe and its progeny, defendant Hitachi's Motion to Dismiss must be granted.[m]

As you have just seen, Rule 4(k)(1)(A) provides that a party is amenable to federal suit whenever the party would be amenable to suit in the courts of the state in which the district court sits. That is, this provision authorizes the federal court to reach only as far as the forum state could under the Fourteenth Amendment and the state's long-arm provisions. See Cofield v. Randolph County Commission, 844 F.Supp. 1499 (M.D.Ala.1994).

The rest of Rule 4(k) comprises federal-law extensions of the federal courts' reach, but these are available only in special situations. Recall, for example, the 100–mile "bulge" provision of Rule 4(k)(1)(B).

Questions: (50) Plaintiff brings suit on a state-created claim in a federal court located in State *A*. There is an attempt to bring in an additional corporate defendant under Rule 19, with service being made on one of its officers in State *B* in accordance with the "bulge" provision of Rule 4(k). The additional defendant is transacting business in the "bulge" located in State *B,* but it has no connection at all with State *A.* May the "bulge" provision operate at all in this situation? If so, should federal or state law govern amenability? (If state law is to control, should the federal court look to the law of State *A* or State *B*? If the law of State *B* is to control, what happens if the facts are changed so that the additional defendant is transacting business in State *B* but is not transacting business in and has no other

---

[m] This decision was affirmed, 654 F.2d 280 (3d Cir.), cert. denied, 454 U.S. 1085, 102 S.Ct. 642 (1981). The Third Circuit made this observation of particular interest:

"We will accept for purposes of this appeal DeJames' position that if service can be made by wholly federal means all of Hitachi's contacts with the United States may be aggregated to support jurisdiction in the District of New Jersey, even if these contacts are limited exclusively to Hawaii, to Alaska, or to a few states on the west coast. . . . [W]e are not sure that some geographic limit short of the entire United States might not be incorporated into the 'fairness' component of the fifth amendment. For a discussion of possible fifth amendment limitations, see Oxford First Corp. v. PNC Liquidating Corp., 372 F.Supp. 191, 198–204 (E.D.Pa.1974)."

This additional limitation, which would allow the defendant to defeat jurisdiction by showing unreasonableness, has been adopted in later cases. E.g., Peay v. BellSouth Med. Assistance Plan, 205 F.3d 1206 (10th Cir.2000) ("Accordingly, we hold that in a federal question case where jurisdiction is invoked based on nationwide service of process, the Fifth Amendment requires the plaintiff's choice of forum to be fair and reasonable to the defendant.").

connection with that part of State *B* constituting the "bulge," except the presence of its officer in the "bulge" when served?)

(51) Change the facts of the preceding question so that the suit is on a federally created claim. Should federal or state law govern amenability? (If a federal standard is to control, how should that standard be defined? See Benjamin Kaplan, Amendments of the Federal Rules of Civil Procedure, 1961–1963 (I), 77 Harv.L.Rev. 601, 632–33 (1964).)

Rule 4(k)(1)(C) picks up the relatively rare federal statutes that extend the federal courts' reach. The particular federal service statute prescribes amenability to the federal suit. For example, under 28 U.S.C. § 2361 an interpleader claimant may be served anywhere in the United States, and then the federal court can exercise personal jurisdiction to the limits of the Fifth Amendment Due Process Clause. Another example would be the federal securities act mentioned in the DeJames case.

Question: (52) Try finally to formulate explicitly the ultimate constitutional constraints on federal courts' territorial authority to adjudicate, working in the context of the following hypothetical case:

> Consider a small business in Hawaii that produces a small amount of toxic waste as a by-product of its operations. This firm maintains its headquarters in Hawaii and does business in both Hawaii and California. It maintains no adequate disposal facilities of its own, so it has contracted with a California waste disposal firm over the past ten years for disposal of its wastes. The California disposal firm maintains its headquarters in California and engages in waste disposal throughout most of the United States. It owns a number of advanced disposal sites, including one in California and one in New Jersey. The Hawaiian firm's contract has always required that its waste be safely disposed of at the California site. In the first year of the contract, though, the wastes were shipped to the New Jersey site because the California waste disposal site was temporarily inactive. It is now discovered that the New Jersey site is leaking wastes into the environment.
>
> The EPA responds by using "Superfund" to fund the cleanup operations necessitated by the toxic waste spill, and sues to recover its cleanup costs under section 107 of CERCLA, which imposes liability for these costs on both the generator and disposer of the toxic waste. Under CERCLA, venue for this action lies in "any district in which the release or damages occurred, or in which the defendant resides, may be found, or has his principal office." The EPA follows its usual practice of initiating suit at the site of the waste spill, and brings the action in New Jersey federal court, naming the California waste-disposal firm and the Hawaiian corporation as defendants. [CERCLA also provides for nationwide service of process, and so the Federal Environmental Protection Agency serves the defendants at their home offices.] The Hawaiian firm appears specially to challenge personal jurisdiction.

James J. Connors, II, Note, Nationwide Service of Process Under the Comprehensive Environmental Response, Compensation, and Liability Act: The Need for Effective Fairness Constraints, 73 Va.L.Rev. 631, 653–54 (1987). What result?

OMNI CAPITAL INTERNATIONAL v. RUDOLF WOLFF & CO., 484 U.S. 97, 108 S.Ct. 404 (1987). Fairly complex proceedings essentially involved disgruntled Louisiana investors suing New York financial managers (collectively referred to as "Omni") under the Federal Commodity Exchange Act for fraud in connection with a trading program on the London Metals Exchange, and Omni then impleading by out-of-state service its London traders (Wolff and Gourlay) on the basis of allegedly improper trading activities. The latter two individuals moved to dismiss for lack of personal jurisdiction. The United States District Court for the Eastern District of Louisiana at first denied the motion, but on reconsideration dismissed the claims against Wolff and Gourlay. The en banc Fifth Circuit affirmed (9–6).

In the Supreme Court on certiorari, Omni argued that in this sort of case the only limits on the district court's exercise of personal jurisdiction derive from the Due Process Clause of the Fifth Amendment. Wolff and Gourlay countered that, additionally, a statute or rule must authorize service. Omni responded that, if necessary, federal courts should fashion a gap-filling service provision.

The unanimous Supreme Court decided that personal jurisdiction was lacking and therefore affirmed. Justice Blackmun's opinion for the Court addressed the three points raised by the parties' contentions.

First, although the Court agreed that the requirement of personal jurisdiction flows from that Due Process Clause, it rejected Omni's argument that due process is the sole concern: "Before a federal court may exercise personal jurisdiction over a defendant, the procedural requirement of service of summons must be satisfied. '[S]ervice of summons is the procedure by which a court having venue and jurisdiction of the subject matter of the suit asserts jurisdiction over the person of the party served.' Mississippi Publishing Corp. v. Murphree, 326 U.S. 438, 444–445, 66 S.Ct. 242, 245–246 (1946). Thus, before a court may exercise personal jurisdiction over a defendant, there must be more than notice to the defendant and a constitutionally sufficient relationship between the defendant and the forum. There also must be a basis for the defendant's amenability to service of summons. Absent consent, this means there must be authorization for service of summons on the defendant."

Second, the Court ruled that the predecessor of Rule 4(k)(1) governed and that it required either a federal statute or a forum-state law authorizing out-of-state service in the circumstances of the case. However, the Commodity Exchange Act did not itself authorize long-arm service explicitly or implicitly. Moreover, as held below and as conceded by Omni, Wolff and Gourlay were beyond Louisiana's long-arm statute, because they had no statutorily sufficient connection to Louisiana. Thus, even for federally created claims such as these, and despite the third-party defendants' extensive contacts with the United States, "neither part of [the] Rule . . . authorizes the service of summons on Wolff and Gourlay."

Third, the Court decided against any practice of judicial ad hoc authorization of service, even to fill a possibly inadvertent gap by "authorizing service on an alien in a federal-question case when the alien is not amenable to service under the applicable state long-arm statute." Such a practice would be unwise, as well as possibly beyond the courts' power. The solution should instead come by congressional act or "from those who propose the Federal Rules of Civil Procedure."

Question: (53) Would the resultant Rule 4(k)(2) have changed the outcome in DeJames or in the Omni case itself? Note that it was unclear in both cases whether the defendants' contacts were substantial with respect to any state. See United States v. Swiss Am. Bank, 191 F.3d 30, 35 (1st Cir.1999) (in avoiding Rule, defendant has the burden of production in showing that some specific state had personal jurisdiction), dismissed on remand, 116 F.Supp.2d 217 (D.Mass.2000), aff'd, 274 F.3d 610 (1st Cir.2001).

FURTHER ON FEDERAL/STATE LAW

As we said back in Part One, with understatement, "Rule 4 is somewhat intricate because, by the nature of its historical growth, it combines specific federal regulations with adopted features of state law."

Before its 1993 rewriting, Rule 4 was even more intricate. It failed to specify the governing law on amenability in some circumstances. It thereby sometimes posed the Erie issue of whether federal or state law governed amenability in a federal suit based on a state-created claim. The cases held for state law. E.g., Arrowsmith v. UPI, 320 F.2d 219, 226 (2d Cir.1963) (in banc) ("State statutes determining what foreign corporations may be sued, for what, and by whom, are not mere whimsy; like most legislation they represent a balancing of various considerations—for example, affording a forum for wrongs connected with the state and conveniencing resident plaintiffs, while avoiding the discouragement of activity within the state by foreign corporations.").

On some issues closely related to the one involved in Arrowsmith, the Erie balance seems to come out the other way. For example, federal law determines which acts committed in the course of litigating will confer jurisdiction over the person, so that federal law will determine whether a defendant has made a general appearance.

Similarly, the cases have generally held federal law to govern in all actions in federal court the questions both of immunity from service of process and of the effect of fraud or force in the attempted acquisition of territorial jurisdiction. However, recent developments on the Erie front make some of these results now seem doubtful. There are a number of other issues where it is difficult to determine which law governs. We touch upon a few of these issues in the following questions.

Questions: (54) Plaintiff brings suit against a foreign corporation in state court on a federally created claim, service being made within the state on an officer of the defendant. The defendant removes the case to federal court and then moves to dismiss under Rule 12(b)(2), as is permissible. Should federal or state law govern this jurisdictional issue? Does it matter whether the defendant is served again after removal under 28 U.S.C. § 1448 and in accordance with a federal nationwide-service provision? See 4A Wright & Miller § 1082.

(55) Change the facts of the preceding question so that there was no removal. In what circumstances, if any, would the state court have to apply federal amenability law under the reverse-Erie doctrine? See David S. Welkowitz, Beyond Burger King: The Federal Interest in Personal Jurisdiction, 56 Fordham L.Rev. 1, 49–51 (1987).

One further aspect of the interplay between federal and state law on amenability may merit mention. Consider as an example the situation in which the plaintiff joins a nonfrivolous federal claim with a state claim in a federal action, service being made in accordance with a federal statute providing nationwide service for the federal claim. Assuming that subject-matter jurisdiction exists for the state claim, but that the nationwide-service provision is the sole basis for exercising jurisdiction over the defendant, is there personal jurisdiction for the purposes of the state claim? A careful reading of the applicable statutes reveals no congressional intent to extend nationwide service of process to state claims. However, the policies of judicial economy, convenience, and fairness underlying the exercise of supplemental jurisdiction suggest that some degree of "pendent personal jurisdiction," or "supplemental service," should exist. The courts over time have split on this problem. The trend toward reaching the state claim should accelerate, however, given the Advisory Committee's allusion to the approach in its note on the 1993 amendment to Rule 4(k)(2). See Action Embroidery Corp. v. Atlantic Embroidery, Inc., 368 F.3d 1174 (9th Cir.2004); Linda Sandstrom Simard, Exploring the Limits of Specific Personal Jurisdiction, 62 Ohio St.L.J. 1619 (2001).

SECTION 6. INTERNATIONAL LITIGATION

We have considered statutory and constitutional limitations on the exercise of territorial jurisdiction, and in doing so we have dealt with both domestic cases and international cases. The international cases came from both state court (Perkins, Helicopteros, and Asahi) and federal court (DeJames and Omni). The basic lesson was that international cases are not so special jurisdictionally. The time has come, however, to examine with a still finer focus this issue of amenability to suit in the context of international litigation.

Kadic v. Karadžić

United States Court of Appeals, Second Circuit, 1995.
70 F.3d 232, cert. denied, 518 U.S. 1005, 116 S.Ct. 2524 (1996).

■ Before NEWMAN, CHIEF JUDGE, FEINBERG and WALKER, CIRCUIT JUDGES.

■ JON O. NEWMAN, CHIEF JUDGE:

Most Americans would probably be surprised to learn that victims of atrocities committed in Bosnia are suing the leader of the insurgent Bosnian–Serb forces in a United States District Court in Manhattan. Their claims seek to build upon the foundation of this Court's decision in Filártiga v. Peña-Irala, 630 F.2d 876 (2d Cir.1980), which recognized the important principle that the venerable Alien Tort Act, 28 U.S.C. § 1350 (1988), enacted in 1789 but rarely invoked since then, validly creates federal court jurisdiction for suits alleging torts committed anywhere in the world against aliens in violation of the law of nations. The pending appeals pose additional significant issues as to the scope of the Alien Tort Act: whether some violations of the law of nations may be remedied when committed by those not acting under the authority of a state; if so, whether genocide, war crimes, and crimes against humanity are among the violations that do not require state action; and whether a person, otherwise liable for a violation of the law of nations, is immune from service of process because he is present in the United States as an invitee of the United Nations.

These issues arise on appeals by two groups of plaintiffs-appellants from the November 19, 1994, judgment of the United States District Court for the Southern District of New York (Peter K. Leisure, Judge), dismissing, for lack of subject-matter jurisdiction, their suits against defendant-appellee Radovan Karadžić, President of the self-proclaimed Bosnian–Serb republic of "Srpska." . . . For the reasons set forth below, we hold that subject-matter jurisdiction exists, that Karadžić may be found liable for genocide, war crimes, and crimes against humanity in his private capacity and for other violations in his capacity as a state actor, and that he is not immune from service of process. We therefore reverse and remand.

Background

The plaintiffs-appellants are Croat and Muslim citizens of the internationally recognized nation of Bosnia–Herzegovina, formerly a republic of Yugoslavia. Their complaints, which we accept as true for purposes of this appeal, allege that they are victims, and representatives of victims, of various atrocities, including brutal acts of rape, forced prostitution, forced impregnation, torture, and summary execution, carried out by Bosnian–Serb military forces as part of a genocidal campaign conducted in the course of the Bosnian civil war. Karadžić, formerly a citizen of Yugoslavia and now a citizen of Bosnia–Herzegovina, is the President of a three-man presidency of the self-proclaimed Bosnian–Serb republic within Bosnia–Herzegovina, sometimes referred to as "Srpska," which claims to exercise lawful authority, and does in fact exercise actual control, over large parts of the territory of Bosnia–Herzegovina. In his capacity as President, Karadžić possesses ultimate command authority over the Bosnian–Serb military forces, and the injuries perpetrated upon plaintiffs were committed as part of a pattern of systematic human rights violations that was directed by Karadžić and carried out by the military forces under his command. The complaints allege that Karadžić acted in an official capacity either as the titular head of Srpska or in collaboration with the government of the recognized nation of the former Yugoslavia and its dominant constituent republic, Serbia.

The two groups of plaintiffs asserted causes of action for genocide, rape, forced prostitution and impregnation, torture and other cruel, inhuman, and degrading treatment, assault and battery, sex and ethnic inequality, summary execution, and wrongful death. They sought compensatory and punitive damages, attorney's fees, and, in one of the cases, injunctive relief. . . .

In early 1993, Karadžić was admitted to the United States on three separate occasions as an invitee of the United Nations. According to affidavits submitted by the plaintiffs, Karadžić was personally served with the summons and complaint in each action during two of these visits while he was physically present in Manhattan. . . .

In the District Court, Karadžić moved for dismissal of both actions on the grounds of insufficient service of process, lack of personal jurisdiction, lack of subject-matter jurisdiction, and nonjusticiability of plaintiffs' claims. . . .

. . . .

Appellants aver that Karadžić was personally served with process while he was physically present in the Southern District of New York. In the Doe action, the affidavits detail that on February 11, 1993, process servers approached Karadžić in the lobby of the Hotel Intercontinental at 111 East 48th St. in Manhattan, called his name and identified their purpose, and attempted to hand him the complaint from a distance of two feet, that security guards seized the complaint papers, and that the papers fell to the floor. Karadžić submitted an affidavit of a State Department security officer, who generally confirmed the episode, but stated that the process server did not come closer than six feet of the defendant. In the Kadic action, the plaintiffs obtained from Judge Owen an order for alternate means of service, directing service by delivering the complaint to a member of defendant's State Department security detail, who was ordered to hand the complaint to the defendant. The security officer's affidavit states that he received the complaint and handed it to Karadžić outside the Russian Embassy in Manhattan. Karadžić's statement confirms that this occurred during his second visit to the United States, sometime between February 27 and March 8, 1993. Appellants also allege that during his visits to New York City, Karadžić stayed at hotels outside the "headquarters district" of the United Nations and engaged in non-United Nations-related activities such as fund-raising.

[Federal Rule 4] authorizes personal service of a summons and complaint upon an individual physically present within [the state], and such personal service comports with the requirements of due process for the assertion of personal jurisdiction. See Burnham v. Superior Court of California, 495 U.S. 604, 110 S.Ct. 2105, 109 L.Ed.2d 631 (1990).

Nevertheless, Karadžić maintains that his status as an invitee of the United Nations during his visits to the United States rendered him immune from service of process. He relies on both the Agreement Between the United Nations and the United States of America Regarding the Headquarters of the United Nations, reprinted at 22 U.S.C. § 287 note (1988) ("Headquarters Agreement"), and a claimed federal common law immunity. We reject both bases for immunity from service.

A. Headquarters Agreement

The Headquarters Agreement provides for immunity from suit only in narrowly defined circumstances. First, "service of legal process . . . may take place within the headquarters district only with the consent of and under conditions approved by the Secretary–General." Id. § 9(a). This provision is of no benefit to Karadžić, because he was not served within the well-defined confines of the "headquarters district," which is bounded by Franklin D. Roosevelt Drive, 1st Avenue, 42nd Street, and 48th Street, see id. annex 1. Second, certain representatives of members of the United Nations, whether residing inside or outside of the "headquarters district," shall be entitled to the same privileges and immunities as the United States extends to accredited diplomatic envoys. Id. § 15. This provision is also of no benefit to Karadžić, since he is not a designated representative of any member of the United Nations.

A third provision of the Headquarters Agreement prohibits federal, state, and local authorities of the United States from "impos[ing] any impediments to transit to or from the headquarters district of . . . persons invited to the headquarters district by the United Nations . . . on official business." Id. § 11. Karadžić maintains that allowing service of process upon a United Nations invitee who is on official business would violate this section, presumably because it would impose a potential burden—exposure to suit—on the invitee's transit to and from the headquarters district. However, this Court has previously refused "to extend the immunities provided by the Headquarters Agreement beyond those explicitly stated." See Klinghoffer v. S.N.C. Achille Lauro, 937 F.2d 44, 48 (2d Cir.1991). We therefore reject Karadžić's proposed construction of section 11, because it would effectively create an immunity from suit for United Nations invitees where none is provided by the express terms of the Headquarters Agreement.[9]

The parties to the Headquarters Agreement agree with our construction of it. In response to a letter from plaintiffs' attorneys opposing any grant of immunity to Karadžić, a responsible State Department official wrote: "Mr. Karadžić's status during his recent visits to the United States has been solely as an 'invitee' of the United Nations, and as such he enjoys no immunity from the jurisdiction of the courts of the United States."

[9] Conceivably, a narrow immunity from service of process might exist under section 11 for invitees who are in *direct* transit between an airport (or other point of entry into the United States) and the Headquarters District. Even if such a narrow immunity did exist—which we do not decide—Karadžić would not benefit from it since he was not served while traveling to or from the Headquarters District.

Letter from Michael J. Habib, Director of Eastern European Affairs, U.S. Dept. of State, to Beth Stephens (Mar. 24, 1993) ("Habib Letter"). Counsel for the United Nations has also issued an opinion stating that although the United States must allow United Nations invitees access to the Headquarters District, invitees are not immune from legal process while in the United States at locations outside of the Headquarters District. See In re Galvao, [1963] U.N.Jur.Y.B. 164 (opinion of U.N. legal counsel); see also Restatement (Third) [of the Foreign Relations Law of the United States] § 469 reporter's note 8 (U.N. invitee "is not immune from suit or legal process outside the headquarters district during his sojourn in the United States").

B. Federal common law immunity

Karadžić nonetheless invites us to fashion a federal common law immunity for those within a judicial district as a United Nations invitee. He contends that such a rule is necessary to prevent private litigants from inhibiting the United Nations in its ability to consult with invited visitors. Karadžić analogizes his proposed rule to the "government contacts exception" to the District of Columbia's long-arm statute, which has been broadly characterized to mean that "mere entry [into the District of Columbia] by non-residents for the purpose of contacting federal government agencies cannot serve as a basis for in personam jurisdiction," Rose v. Silver, 394 A.2d 1368, 1370 (D.C.1978); [other citation omitted]. He also points to a similar restriction upon assertion of personal jurisdiction on the basis of the presence of an individual who has entered a jurisdiction in order to attend court or otherwise engage in litigation. See generally 4 Charles A. Wright & Arthur R. Miller, Federal Practice and Procedure § 1076 (2d ed. 1987).

Karadžić also endeavors to find support for a common law immunity in our decision in Klinghoffer. Though, as noted above, Klinghoffer declined to extend the immunities of the Headquarters Agreement beyond those provided by its express provisions, the decision applied immunity considerations to its construction of New York's long-arm statute, N.Y.Civ.Prac.L. & R. 301 (McKinney 1990), in deciding whether the Palestine Liberation Organization (PLO) was doing business in the state. Klinghoffer construed the concept of "doing business" to cover only those activities of the PLO that were not United Nations-related. See 937 F.2d at 51.

Despite the considerations that guided Klinghoffer in its narrowing construction of the general terminology of New York's long-arm statute as applied to United Nations activities, we decline the invitation to create a federal common law immunity as an extension of the precise terms of a carefully crafted treaty that struck the balance between the interests of the United Nations and those of the United States.

Finally, we note that the mere possibility that Karadžić might at some future date be recognized by the United States as the head of state of a friendly nation and might thereby acquire head-of-state immunity does not transform the appellants' claims into a nonjusticiable request for an advisory opinion, as the District Court intimated. Even if such future recognition, determined by the Executive Branch, [citation omitted], would create head-of-state immunity, [citation omitted], it would be entirely inappropriate for a court to create the functional equivalent of such an immunity based on speculation about what the Executive Branch *might* do in the future. See Mexico v. Hoffman, 324 U.S. 30, 35, 65 S.Ct. 530, 532, 89 L.Ed. 729 (1945) ("[I]t is the duty of the courts, in a matter so intimately associated with our foreign policy . . . , not to enlarge an immunity to an extent which the government . . . has not seen fit to recognize.").

In sum, if appellants personally served Karadžić with the summons and complaint while he was in New York but outside of the U.N. headquarters district, as they are prepared to prove, he is subject to the personal jurisdiction of the District Court.

. . . .[n]

Suits in U.S. Courts.—The U.S. Supreme Court has largely elaborated the country's law of territorial jurisdiction by deciding cases that arose on the interstate level, and in fact it has decided only four international jurisdiction cases (Perkins, Helicopteros, Asahi, and Omni). The United States has no general treaties on international jurisdiction.

Consider a suit against a Frenchwoman in a court here. In the absence of a specific treaty, international law imposes no significant restrictions on state-court territorial jurisdiction beyond those restrictions already imposed by the Due Process Clause of the Fourteenth Amendment. Likewise, in the absence of a specific treaty, international law imposes no significant restrictions on federal-court territorial jurisdiction beyond those restrictions already imposed by the Due Process Clause of the Fifth Amendment.

Thus, the Frenchwoman is treated just like anyone else, with no special international protections. Indeed, one might instead wonder why she can even invoke the U.S. constitutional protections. But the Supreme Court has always assumed that a person subject to suit in our courts can demand treatment in accord with the Constitution. Accordingly, the lower courts extend to foreign defendants all the jurisdictional protections given to U.S. defendants.

Suits in Foreign Courts.—A quick look at the European approach to territorial jurisdiction serves to show how the law can work out differently, given different origins.

Roman law, enjoying unlimited power, embraced the idea of venue restrained with at least some spirit of fairness. *Actor sequitur forum rei*, or the plaintiff follows the defendant's forum. Generally, then, the plaintiff

---

[n] Default followed by jury trials on compensatory and punitive damages in 2000 resulted in unappealed, but unenforced, judgments for $745 million and an injunction in Kadic and $4.5 billion in Doe. Nat'l L.J., Feb. 19, 2001, at C25. For background, see Maria T. Vullo, Prosecuting Genocide, 2 Chi.J.Int'l L. 495 (2001).

had to go to the defendant's domicile, where the courts could entertain any cause of action against the defendant. Eventually, there was additional provision for long-arm-like jurisdiction in actions of tort, contract, and property, so that, for example, a plaintiff could sue for a tort at the place of wrongful conduct. In other words, the Roman law and its direct descendant, the civil law, generated a decent scheme that avoided the headaches of the U.S. territorial power dogma.

Ordinary International Cases.—The civil-law courts long ago developed these jurisdictional rules for international cases, usually by the method of extending the venue rules that they applied to domestic cases. Modern French law, for example, builds on the Roman restraint idea. Domicile is thus the foundation of French jurisdiction. But socio-economic-political pressures similar to those prevailing in the United States, as well as the usual procedural policies of accuracy, fairness, and efficiency, have pushed France to reach foreign defendants whose acts have caused harm in France.

The territorial power idea was absent from France, with telling implications. On the one hand, without the impulses of that power idea, France has not produced such excesses as tag or attachment jurisdiction. On the other hand, without the restraints of that power idea, France has succumbed even more blatantly to parochial impulses, so that as construed article 14 of its Civil Code authorizes territorial jurisdiction over virtually any action brought by a plaintiff of French nationality. Thus, a French person can sue at home on any cause of action, whether or not the events in suit related to France and regardless of the defendant's connections and interests. This French approach to jurisdiction has emigrated with French law to other countries. The forum-shopping potential of jurisdiction based on the plaintiff's nationality is evident, even though in practice this exorbitant jurisdiction is not abused all that often.

A different example, from the German system, further shows that foreign is not always better than American when it comes to jurisdiction. Germany follows the usual civil-law approach, which makes no distinction between jurisdiction over things and jurisdiction over persons, but gets to a similar result through the notion of exclusive local jurisdiction for certain kinds of suits that intrinsically involve things. Nevertheless, article 23 of Germany's Code of Civil Procedure authorizes ordinary *personal jurisdiction* given only the presence in Germany of a tangible or intangible thing belonging to the defendant, thus going considerably further than the U.S. authorization in certain circumstances of *jurisdiction over a thing* based upon presence of the thing. Recovery in a German case founded on presence of goods is not limited to the value of the goods, although obviously the plaintiff might have trouble enforcing the judgment outside Germany. Traditionally, the cause of action did not have to relate to the thing or even to Germany, but the German Supreme Court has recently invented a vague requirement that the plaintiff be domiciled in Germany or the cause of action be linked to Germany. The forum-shopping potential here too is frightening, as many enterprises have assets in countries with German-based law.

Still, when all is said and done, the civil law of today is not so different from the common law of territorial jurisdiction, at least if one ignores the exorbitant bases of jurisdiction on both sides. This evolution demonstrates how different legal systems tend toward so-called convergence, given similar influences.

Even in the doctrinal details of exorbitant jurisdiction, where national peculiarities peak, the differences are smaller than they first appear. French nationality-based jurisdiction or German property-based jurisdiction may not look much like U.S. tag or attachment jurisdiction, but in fact they share a common core: all nations tend to disregard defendants' interests in order to give their own people a way to sue at home, if the home country will be able to enforce the resulting judgment locally. See Kevin M. Clermont & John R.B. Palmer, Exorbitant Jurisdiction, 58 Me.L.Rev. 473 (2006).

Brussels Regime Cases.—More recently European lawmakers, acting from above, have partially preempted these rules for international cases. They did so by an enlightened, albeit far from perfect, treaty dating from 1968. That treaty was the Brussels Convention on Jurisdiction and the Enforcement of Judgments in Civil and Commercial Matters, which morphed into a European Union regulation on March 1, 2002. The European Court of Justice has supranational authority to decide questions arising thereunder.

By the Brussels Convention, the member states agreed to provide virtually automatic recognition and enforcement of the judgments of the other member states. This provision was like the Full Faith and Credit Clause of the U.S. Constitution. In order to make this agreement on judgments acceptable, the Brussels Convention was a "double convention" that also defined the bases of territorial jurisdiction—jurisdiction being the doctrine that must, in any judgment-respecting agreement, serve almost alone in ensuring adjudicative restraint. That is, the European member states could give respect to the others' judgments because they knew that the Brussels Convention restricted the others to appropriately limited jurisdictional reach. This latter restriction worked as the Due Process Clause does in the United States.

Today, the Brussels Regulation's jurisdictional bases follow the civil-law approach. The defendant's domicile is the usual place for suit. There is additionally long-arm-like jurisdiction for tort and contract actions; tort actions can be brought "where the harmful event occurred or may occur," and contract actions at "the place of performance of the obligation in question." Certain disadvantaged plaintiffs, such as consumers, often can sue at home. Moreover, there is authorization for forum selection clauses, and there is exclusive local jurisdiction in actions concerning real property and the like.

Further on the prohibited side, each member state gave up its exorbitant jurisdiction, so that for example France gave up its personal jurisdiction based on the plaintiff's French nationality, and Germany gave up its property-based jurisdiction. The United Kingdom gave up tag jurisdiction and attachment jurisdiction. The Brussels Regulation not only prohibits exorbitant jurisdiction, but also makes mandatory the permissible bases of jurisdiction. So, the United Kingdom abandoned its judicial practice of sometimes declining jurisdiction on expressly discretionary grounds such as forum non conveniens.

Comparative Evaluation.—As already said, the Brussels Regulation is enlightened but imperfect. For one thing, it applies only to defendants domiciled in another member state. Indeed, it openly discriminates against outsiders. Accordingly, although France cannot use its exorbitant jurisdiction in a suit by a French person against an English person, it can still use it when the defendant is an American instead. Moreover, the resulting French judgment gets recognition and enforcement in England, Germany, and elsewhere in the European Union against the American or the American's assets there. Admittedly, this example is an extreme one, without much actual use in practice to date, but it works to illustrate the legal context.

Moreover, any suggestion that European Union law on jurisdiction has achieved markedly greater certainty than U.S. law seems unfounded and even naive. This suggestion is improbable on its face. The Brussels regime attempts to satisfy and reconcile the needs of a variety of different countries and legal systems, using vague and simple formulas sometimes foggily drafted and always in multiple languages. It necessitates the complicated interplay of European and national laws, raising many Erie-like problems. In actual application, the picture is no prettier. The Brussels regime operates without the benefit of a great deal of authoritative clarifying case law. There is consequently a lot of litigating throughout the European Union about where to litigate. So the European Union is nowhere close to the perfect-certainty end of the spectrum running from uncertainty to certainty. It may be that the European Union enjoys somewhat greater certainty in its jurisdictional law, but in fact the United States is not really that far behind.

After all, jurisdictional problems remain problems because they are hard problems. A nice way to demonstrate this point is to reconsider comparatively two of the classically unclear cases from the U.S. Supreme Court: World–Wide Volkswagen Corp. v. Woodson and Asahi Metal Industry Co. v. Superior Court.

In World–Wide, which supposedly engendered a jurisdictional law that is "a hopeless mess," Patrick J. Borchers, Comparing Personal Jurisdiction in the United States and the European Community: Lessons for American Reform, 40 Am.J.Comp.L. 121, 143 (1992), the Court made the close call that Oklahoma did not have constitutional power over New York car dealers if the plaintiffs drove the car to Oklahoma and had a horrific accident there, because the defendants had not conducted sufficient Oklahoma-directed activities. The European result, imagining analogous facts subject to the Brussels Regulation, would apparently be different under its provision for tort jurisdiction "where the harmful event occurred." But the European Union achieved that "clear" result only after suffering through judicial creation of redundant jurisdiction at the places of act and of injury, as well as having addressed such questions as whether product liability actions involve tort or contract, whether such harm is sufficiently direct, and whether supranational or national law governs such issues. Incidentally, without the power test, the U.S. Constitution, like the European Union's law, would allow jurisdiction in the World–Wide setting (and properly so).

The European Union's relative clarity starts disappearing as one wades deeper into stream-of-commerce cases, such as Asahi. In that case brought by an injured motorcyclist, the U.S. Supreme Court made the close call that California's exercise of jurisdiction was constitutionally unreasonable in the peculiar circumstances involving a third-party claim by a Taiwanese manufacturer against a Japanese supplier. Curiously, on analogous facts involving a claim that happened to arrive by third-party procedure, jurisdiction would clearly exist in a European Union country by virtue of Brussels Regulation article 6(2)'s strange *juridiction dérivée*, which by simple fiat reaches *additional* defendants including third-party defendants; but that result is clarity by circumstantial fluke, and it is not necessarily a desirable outcome. Consider instead the more general circumstances of the motorcyclist as tort victim suing the foreign supplier. Although jurisdiction at the place of a sufficiently direct tortious harm would seem to exist under the construed words of the Brussels Regulation, it is hard to know what the European Court of Justice would actually do with regard to the stream of commerce as it dilutes in this way. For what it is worth, the national law of some European Union countries would likely view such jurisdiction, without any sort of foreseeability condition, as impermissibly exorbitant. The current U.S. approach seems about as clear as the European Union approach, while both stumble toward permitting foreseeable, and only foreseeable, jurisdiction in the general stream-of-commerce situation (and properly so).

SECTION 7. VENUE

Recall Part One's discussion of the rules of venue, which specify where the sovereign will exercise its territorial jurisdiction. By now the nature of venue, and its pursuit of convenience and efficiency, should reappear to you with considerably greater clarity. A few additional observations should consolidate and expand your understanding.

FEDERAL PROVISIONS

Federal venue is a personal privilege of the defendant, so only the defendant as to whom venue appears improper may raise the point. See

Camp v. Gress, 250 U.S. 308, 39 S.Ct. 478 (1919) (holding that resident defendant may not pursue point that another defendant is nonresident of district). The defendant may choose to waive a defect in venue and, in any event, will waive one not asserted in timely fashion. See Rule 12(g) and (h). Unlike some defects in subject-matter jurisdiction, territorial jurisdiction, and opportunity to be heard, defective venue does not render a judgment invalid and subject to collateral attack.

Question: (56) How can this last sentence, stating traditional doctrine, be explained?

When a plaintiff brings an action, the plaintiff waives in advance any venue objection to counterclaims—even permissive ones. See General Elec. Co. v. Marvel Rare Metals Co., 287 U.S. 430, 53 S.Ct. 202 (1932). Reading the venue statutes' restrictions on where an action "may be brought" to refer only to the original main action, subsequent case law more broadly holds that those already parties cannot block counterclaims or crossclaims on venue grounds. As to new parties, there may be an emergent doctrine of "supplemental" venue, which thus far is understood to mean that if a claim is within the supplemental jurisdiction of the federal court, then there is no ground for objection to venue with respect to that claim. See generally 14D Wright, Miller & Cooper § 3808.

STATE PROVISIONS

The place of trial of civil actions in state courts within each state is governed very largely by statute, and the statutes of the several states do not exhibit any uniform pattern. Professor George N. Stevens, in Venue Statutes: Diagnosis and Proposed Cure, 49 Mich.L.Rev. 307 (1951), listed some thirteen items that appear in various statutory schemes as grounds of venue, including the following: where the subject of action is situated; where the cause of action arose; where "some fact" is present or happened; where defendant resides; where defendant is doing business; where defendant has a place of business; where plaintiff resides; where plaintiff is doing business; where defendant may be found; where defendant may be summoned or served; and where the seat of government is located. Indeed, provisions exist that allow plaintiff to lay venue in any county designated in the complaint or, more simply, in any county. Professor Stevens criticized the existing confused situation and proposed a model venue code.

To concretize your vision of state venue, you should examine NYCPLR art. 5, most of which appears in the statutory section of the Rules booklet.

Question: (57) What is, after all, the difference between territorial jurisdiction and venue? See Kevin M. Clermont, Civil Procedure: Territorial Jurisdiction and Venue 27–30 (1999).

(a) LOCAL ACTIONS

Livingston v. Jefferson

Circuit Court of the United States, District of Virginia, 1811.
15 F.Cas. 660 (No. 8411).

This was an action of trespass [for $100,000], brought in the circuit court of the United States, for the district of Virginia, by Edward Livingston, a citizen of the state of New York, against Thomas Jefferson, a citizen of the state of Virginia, . . . for a trespass alleged to have been committed by the defendant whilst he was president, in removing him from the batture, in the city of New–Orleans, in the then territory of Orleans . . . . The suit was commenced in 1810, after the expiration of Mr. Jefferson's last term of office.

The declaration contained eight counts. The first count charged that the defendant, on the 25th day of January, 1808, at the city of New–Orleans, in the district of Orleans, to wit, at Richmond, in the county of Henrico, and district of Virginia, with force and arms, a certain messuage or dwelling-house, and a close or parcel of land thereto adjoining, . . . did break and enter, and 200 spades, (and various other tools, planks, rails, nails, &c., specifying the number and kind,) of the proper goods and chattels of the said plaintiff, of the value of ten thousand dollars, then and there being found, did break, cut in pieces, and utterly destroy, and 20,000 cart loads of earth, (sand and clay,) of the soil of the said close, with spades, &c., did dig and raise, the said soil so dug and raised being of the value of $50,000, and with carts, &c., did carry away and convert to his own use, by which digging, the soil of the said close was greatly injured, and the said plaintiff wholly lost the said parcel thereof so dug and raised, &c. All the other counts laid the venue in the same way, "at the city of New–Orleans, &c., to wit, at Richmond, &c., &c." . . .

The defendant demurred to the second, fifth, sixth, seventh, and eighth counts. He also pleaded the general issue, and four several pleas of justification. He justified the act as being done under a law of congress, and in his character of president of the United States, without malice. It is unnecessary to say more of these pleadings, since the question before the court turned on the third plea, which was a plea to the jurisdiction of the court. That plea was as follows: "And the said defendant in his proper person, comes and defends the force and injury, and saith that the mes-

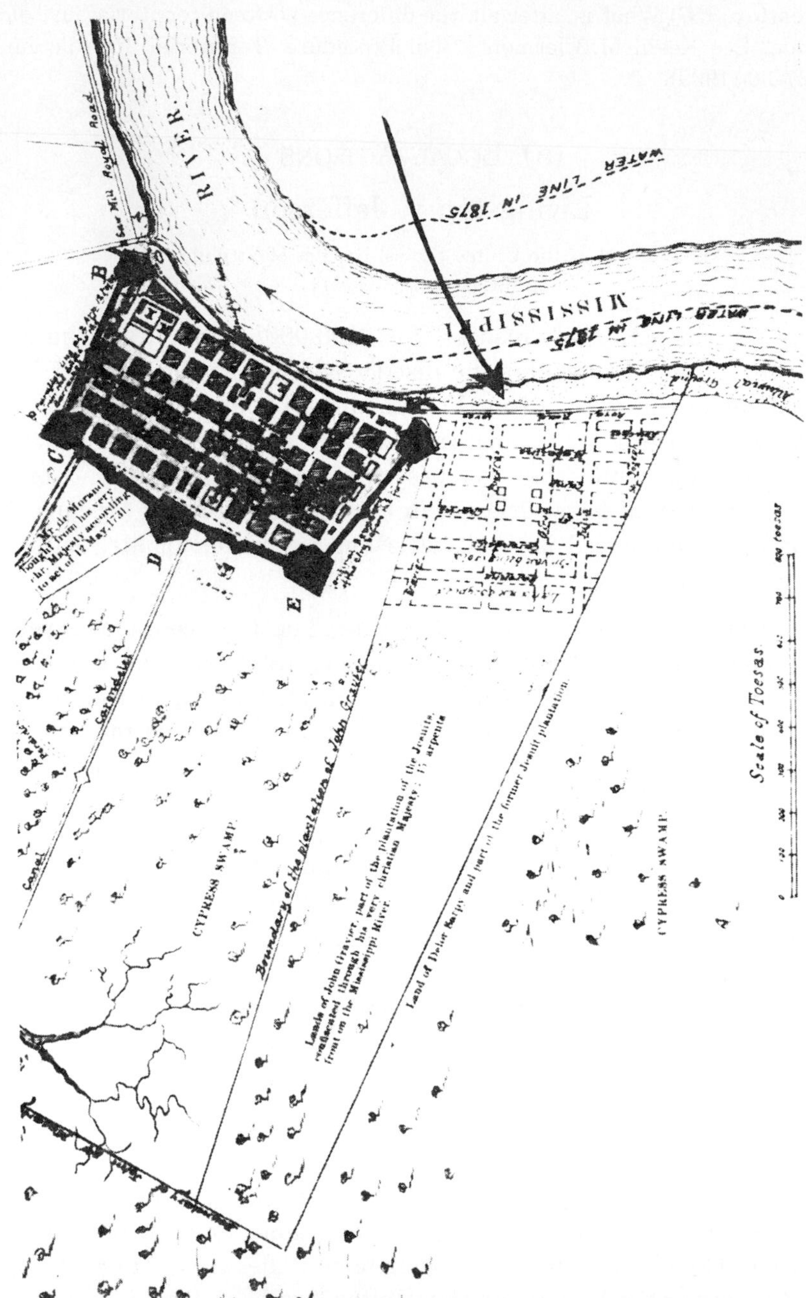

Livingston's batture—located by the long arrow drawn on an 1875 edition of a 1798 Spanish map of New Orleans' fortifications and environs

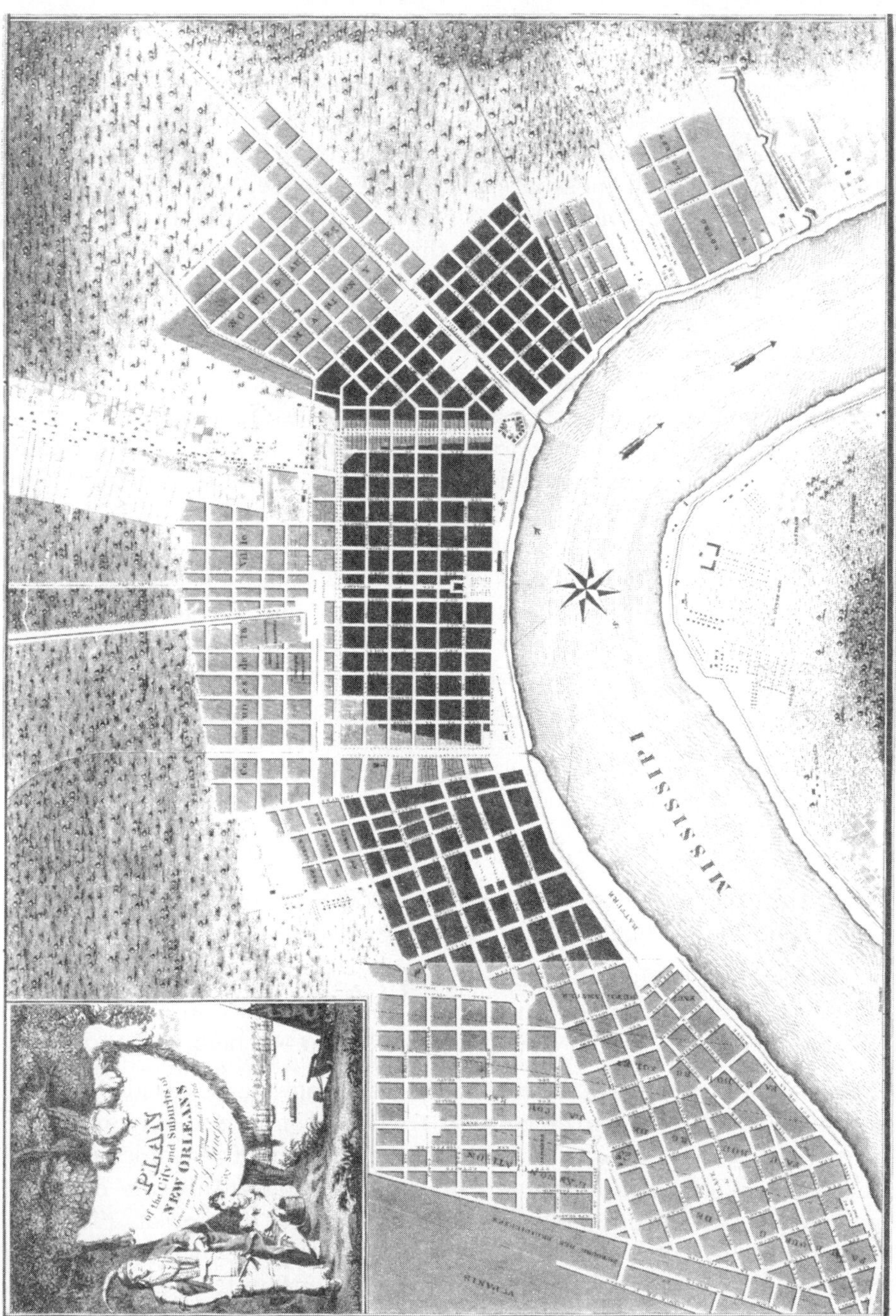

Livingston's batture—shown on an 1815 map of the fast-developing New Orleans

suage, or dwelling-house, and close or parcel of land, being a part of a parcel of land known by the name of the 'Batture of the Suburb St. Mary,' in the first and fifth counts of the plaintiff's declaration mentioned, and the several closes in the second, third, fourth, sixth, seventh, and eighth counts of the plaintiff's declaration mentioned, for the supposed breaking and entering of which said messuage, or dwelling-house, and closes, the said action is brought, are not situate, lying, and being within the Virginia district, or within the jurisdiction of this court, but are situate, lying and being in the territory of the United States of America, called the 'Territory of Orleans,' in which said territory there was, at the time of the said supposed trespasses, and long before, and at the time of the institution of the plaintiff's said action, and yet is, a court of competent jurisdiction to try and decide upon all pleas of trespass, and all causes of action arising within the said territory, wherefore since the house and lands in the declaration mentioned are not within the Virginia district, and the jurisdiction of this court, but in the said territory, the defendant prays judgment, if the court here will, or ought to have further conusance of the plea aforesaid, &c." To this plea the plaintiff replied, that ever since his cause of action, against the said defendant, accrued, "the said defendant has resided without the jurisdiction of the courts of the territory of Orleans aforesaid, to wit, within the district of Virginia, and within the jurisdiction of this court, where he now resides, by reason whereof he is not amenable to the jurisdiction of the courts of the territory of Orleans aforesaid, for the trespasses in the declaration set forth, wherefore he prays judgment, &c." To this replication the defendant demurred generally, and the plaintiff joined in demurrer.

■ Before MARSHALL, CIRCUIT JUSTICE, and TYLER, DISTRICT JUDGE.

[At the time, circuit courts sat as trial courts with two judges: the local district judge and the Supreme Court Justice assigned to that circuit.

[The opinion by JUDGE TYLER is omitted. "About the kindest thing that can be said is to attribute his entire opinion to an unhappy physical condition." 17 Moore § 110App.104[2], at 110App.–44 n.14.]

■ MARSHALL, CIRCUIT JUSTICE. The sole question now to be decided is this— Can this court take cognizance of a trespass committed on lands lying within the United States, and without the district of Virginia, in a case where the trespasser is a resident of, and is found within the district? I concur with my brother judge in the opinion that it cannot. [That sole question distilled to whether trespass on land was a local or transitory action. Why? Justice Marshall provided the background. Local actions have to be tried where the events occurred. In very old England all actions were local, because the court had to possess the power to convene a jury drawn from the events' locality. Judges therefore required every plaintiff to allege the place of events in suit. But later as the constraints on the royal courts loosened, the complaint's allegations often described the events as taking place where the plaintiff wished trial to take place. Judges sometimes permitted this practice by refusing to allow the defendant to deny, or traverse, those allegations for the purpose of defeating the action's siting—thereby permitting the plaintiff to allege in a "to wit" clause that the actual place of the events fictionally lies in any county in England. Transitory action was the name for those kinds of cases in which the judges would accept the fiction and thus let the plaintiff choose the venue. With time, the class of transitory actions grew to its currently broad but illogical dimensions. In sum, if Livingston's trespass case fell within the now narrow class of local actions, then the denial in Jefferson's third plea would be good and so he would win on demurrer.]

In the case at bar, it is traversed for that purpose, and the question is, whether this be a case in which such traverse is sustainable; or, in other words, whether courts have so far extended their fiction as, by its aid, to take cognizance of trespasses on lands not lying within those limits which bound their process. They have, without legislative aid, applied this fiction to all personal torts, and to all contracts wherever executed. To this general rule, contracts respecting lands form no exception. It is admitted, that on a contract respecting lands, an action is sustainable wherever the defendant may be found: yet, in such a case, every difficulty may occur which presents itself in an action of trespass. An investigation of title may become necessary. A question of boundary may arise, and a survey may be essential to the full merits of the cause: yet these difficulties have not prevailed against the jurisdiction of the court. They have been countervailed, and more than countervailed by the opposing consideration, that if the action be disallowed, the injured party may have a clear right without a remedy in a case where the person who has done the wrong, and who ought to make the compensation, is within the power of the court. That this consideration should lose its influence, where the action pursues a thing not within the reach of the court, is of inevitable necessity; but for the loss of its influence where the remedy is against the person and can be afforded by the court, I have not yet discerned a reason, other than a technical one, which can satisfy my judgment. If, however, this technical distinction be firmly established, if all other judges respect it, I cannot venture to disregard it.

The distinction taken is, that actions are deemed transitory, where transactions on which they are founded, might have taken place anywhere; but are local where their cause is in its nature necessarily local. If this distinction be established; if judges have determined to carry their innovation on the old rule, no further; if, for a long course of time, under circumstances which have not changed, they have determined this to be the limit of their fiction, it would require a hardihood which I do not possess, to pass this limit. This distinction has been repeatedly taken in the books, and recognized by the best elementary writers, especially Judge Blackstone, from whose authority no man will lightly dissent. 3 Bl. Comm. 294. . . . From the cases which support this distinction, no exception, I believe, is to be found among those that have been decided in court, on solemn argument. One of the greatest judges who ever sat on any bench, and who has done more than any other to remove those technical impediments which grew out of a different state of society, and too long continued to obstruct the course of substantial justice, was so struck with the weakness of the distinction, between taking jurisdiction in cases of contract respecting lands, and of torts committed on the same lands, that he attempted to abolish it. In the case of Mostyn v. Fabrigas, 1 Cowp. 166, Lord Mansfield stated the true distinction between proceedings which are in rem, in which the effect of a judgment cannot be had, unless the thing lie within the reach of the court, and proceedings against the person where damages only are demanded. But this opinion was given in an action for a personal wrong which is admitted to be transitory. It has not, therefore, the authority to which it would be entitled, had this distinction been laid down in an action deemed local. It may be termed an obiter dictum. . . .

. . . .

According to the common law of England then, the distinction taken by the defendant's counsel, between actions local and transitory, is the true distinction, and an action of quare clausum fregit, is a local action. This common law has been adopted by the legislature of Virginia. Had it not been adopted, I should have thought it in force. When our ancestors migrated to America, they brought with them the common law of their native country, so far as it was applicable to their new situation; and I do not conceive that the Revolution would, in any degree, have changed the relations of man to man, or the law which regulated those relations. In breaking our political connection with the parent state, we did not break our connection with each other. It remained subsequent to the ancient rules, until those rules should be changed by the competent authority. But it has been said, that this rule of the common law is impliedly changed by the act of [the state's] assembly, which directs that a jury shall be summoned from the bystanders. Were I to discuss the effect of this act in the courts of the state, the inquiry, whether the fiction already noticed was not equivalent to it in giving jurisdiction, would present itself. There are also other regulations, as, that the jurors should be citizens, which would deserve to be taken into view. But I pass over these considerations, because I am decidedly of opinion, that the jurisdiction of the courts of the United States depends, exclusively, on the constitution and laws of the United States.

In considering the jurisdiction of the circuit courts, as defined in the judicial act [1 Stat. 73], and in the constitution which that act carries into execution, it is worthy of observation, that the jurisdiction of the court depends on the character of the parties, and that only the court of that district in which the defendant resides, or is found, can take jurisdiction of the cause.[o] In a court so constituted, the argument drawn from the total failure of justice, should a trespasser be declared to be only amenable to the

[o] The Judiciary Act of September 24, 1789, ch. 20, § 11, 1 Stat. 73, 78–79, declared that "the circuit courts shall have original cognizance, concurrent with the courts of the several States, of all suits of a civil nature at common law or in equity, where the matter in dispute exceeds, exclusive of costs, the sum or value of five hundred dollars, and . . . the suit is between a citizen of the State where the action is brought, and a citizen of another State. . . . And no civil suit shall be brought before . . . said courts against an inhabitant of the United

court of that district in which the land lies, and in which he will never be found, appeared to me to be entitled to peculiar weight. But according to the course of the common law, the process of the court must be executed in order to give it the right to try the cause, and consequently the same defect of justice might occur. Other judges have felt the weight of this argument, and have struggled ineffectually against the distinction, which produces the inconvenience of a clear right without a remedy. I must submit to it. The law upon the demurrer is in favor of the defendant.[p]

Question: (58) On the basis of the opinion itself, why did Justice Marshall take the questionable step of injecting the local action doctrine into American law?

States, by any original process in any other district than that whereof he is an inhabitant, or in which he shall be found at the time of serving the writ . . . ."

[p] The facts out of which this case arose appear in 4 Albert J. Beveridge, The Life of John Marshall 100–16 (1919).

After commencement of the action by Livingston, Jefferson wrote to President Madison urging the appointment of Judge Tyler to a vacancy in the court that would hear the suit. After referring to the "rancorous hatred which Marshall bears to the government of his country" and "the cunning & sophistry within which he is able to enshroud himself," Jefferson wrote: "It will be difficult to find a character of firmness enough to preserve his independence on the same bench with Marshall. Tyler, I am certain, would do it. . . . A milk & water character . . . would be seen as a calamity." He concluded what Beveridge calls "this astounding letter" in these words: "It is a little doubted that his [Livingston's] knolege [sic] of Marshall's character has induced him to bring this action. His twistifications of the law in the case of Marbury, in that of Burr, & the late Yazoo case shew how dexterously he can reconcile law to his personal biasses: and nobody seems to doubt that he is ready prepared to decide that Livingston's right to the batture is unquestionable, and that I am bound to pay for it with my private fortune."

The next day Jefferson wrote Tyler that he had "laid it down as a law" to himself "never to embarrass the President with any solicitations." Yet, in Tyler's case, wrote Jefferson, "I . . . have done it with all my heart, and in the full belief that I serve him and the public in urging the appointment." Jefferson warned, "In the hands of one [Marshall] the law is nothing more than an ambiguous text, to be explained by his sophistry into any meaning which may subserve his personal malice."

A sequel appears in 1 Lyon G. Tyler, The Letters and Times of the Tylers 263 (1884). Jefferson prepared, supposedly for the use of his attorneys, an exhaustive brief covering his version of the facts and his views of the law. After the decision, Tyler wrote to Jefferson as follows: "Judge Roane [of the Virginia Supreme Court of Appeals] had perused it [the Jefferson brief] in manuscript and gave me some of the outlines of it, which heightened my desire to get hold of it, although I well knew you had probed the subject to its bottom. But as soon as I had received the appointment . . . (which I owe to your favor in great measure), it became my duty to shut the door against every observation which might in any way be derived from either side, lest the impudent British faction, who had enlisted on Livingston's side, might suppose an undue influence had seized upon me. It is true, I never did regard that part of the community, yet it was as well to avoid suspicion even of the devil and his imps. I wished very much to have heard the merits of the cause, but the question of jurisdiction precluded any enquiry on that part of the cause."

A view of the events that treats Jefferson more favorably is given in 3 Henry S. Randall, The Life of Thomas Jefferson 266–69, 500, 523–24 (1858). But see George Dargo, Jefferson's Louisiana 74–101 (1975); William B. Hatcher, Edward Livingston 137–66, 317–18 (1940).

The case is put into a broad social context by George Dargo, Public Power and Privatization 114–70 (1980), revised in George Dargo, Law in the New Republic 107–36 (1983). Finally, the case is helpfully examined from a legal perspective in Ronan E. Degnan, Livingston v. Jefferson—A Freestanding Footnote, 75 Cal.L.Rev. 115 (1987).

Reading between the lines, do you think that his opinion likely represented a demonstration of admirable albeit reluctant deference to stare decisis, as Beveridge argued, or reflected a situation in which "the great Federalist must have welcomed the common-law doctrine as an expedient to avoid deciding on the merits a case which was so full of political gunpowder" but still a vehicle to permit both a bit of righteous tongue-lashing without having heard the merits and also a demonstration of his and Jefferson's relative devotions to the rule of law, as suggested by Robert B. Looper, Jurisdiction over Immovables: The Little Case Revisited After Sixty Years, 40 Minn.L.Rev. 191, 193 (1956)?

CASEY v. ADAMS, 102 U.S. 66 (1880). The Supreme Court here held that a special venue statute for commencement of suits against national banks did not apply to local actions, thus permitting commencement of this suit where the property was located even though the special statute was not satisfied. Chief Justice Waite explained for the Court that "no one has ever supposed that laws which prescribed generally where one should be sued, included such suits as were local in their character, either by statute or the common law, unless it was expressly so declared. Local actions are in the nature of suits in rem, and are to be prosecuted where the thing on which they are founded is situated."

ELLENWOOD v. MARIETTA CHAIR CO., 158 U.S. 105, 15 S.Ct. 771 (1895). A New Jersey citizen brought an action in only one count against an Ohio citizen in the United States Circuit Court for the Southern District of Ohio for a continuing trespass upon the plaintiff's land in West Virginia and the cutting and conversion of timber growing thereon. The defendant answered, denying the allegations of the petition. The lower court ordered the case stricken from its docket on an incidental procedural point. The Supreme Court, by Justice Gray, affirmed on a different ground: "Various grounds taken by the defendant in error in support of the judgment below need not be considered, because there is one decisive reason against the maintenance of the action. . . . The entire cause of action was local. The land alleged to have been trespassed upon being in West Virginia, the action could not be maintained in Ohio. The Circuit Court of the United States, sitting in Ohio, had no jurisdiction of the cause of action, and for this reason, if for no other, rightly ordered the case stricken from its docket, although no question of jurisdiction had been made by demurrer or plea."

Question: (59) If, on the facts of Livingston v. Jefferson, the federal court sitting in Virginia rendered a default judgment for the plaintiff, would the judgment be subject to collateral attack?

STONE v. UNITED STATES, 167 U.S. 178, 17 S.Ct. 778 (1897). The United States brought suit in the United States District Court for the District of Washington to recover the reasonable value of lumber and ties manufactured from trees cut by defendant from plaintiff's land in Idaho. The Court held that the action could be maintained outside Idaho because the gravamen was conversion, not trespass, and no judgment was sought for the trespass.

Question: (60) On the facts of Livingston v. Jefferson, would a statute like 28 U.S.C. § 1655 be of any assistance to the plaintiff seeking recovery in the federal court sitting in Louisiana where the land lay, still assuming that the defendant was not subject to personal jurisdiction? Instead, would Livingston have been able to invoke Louisiana's legal tradition by asserting in a Louisiana local court its French-style article 14 personal jurisdiction, which allowed the plaintiff to sue at home, and then enforcing the default judgment in Virginia?

LOCAL ACTIONS IN STATE COURTS

Livingston v. Jefferson, although frequently criticized, has been followed in almost every state where the question has arisen. "Among various actions that have been held to be local . . . are those to set aside a preferential transfer of property, to foreclose or cancel a mortgage, for trespass to land, to abate a nuisance, to try title to land, and a number of other types of proceedings." 14D Wright, Miller & Cooper § 3822, at 461–63. The precise scope of the doctrine, however, varies from state to state.

Indeed, a few states have drastically curtailed or even eliminated the Livingston doctrine, either by decision as in Minnesota in 1896 or by statute as in New York in 1913. See 17 Moore § 110.20[2]. (Incidentally, the American Law Institute has recently recommended abolishing it statutorily for the federal courts. See ALI Federal Judicial Code Revision Project § 1391(a)(2) (2004).)

Question: (61) Thus, a state court of New York today would presumptively permit a trespass action to be maintained on the facts of Livingston v. Jefferson, assuming personal service during a visit to New York City (which Jefferson actually called "a sewer filled with all the depravities of human nature"). Should the United States District Court for the Southern District of New York today permit an action to be maintained in such circumstances? What if the case had reached the federal court by removal from the state court of New York?

(b) DISMISSAL OR TRANSFER

THE INAPPROPRIATE FORUM

In Gulf Oil Corp. v. Gilbert, 330 U.S. 501, 67 S.Ct. 839 (1947), a diversity action in the Southern District of New York, a Virginia plaintiff sued a Pennsylvania corporation, which had qualified to do business in New York, for alleged negligence in causing to burn the plaintiff's warehouse in Lynchburg, Virginia. Defendant sought dismissal under the doctrine of forum non conveniens, claiming that Virginia was the appropriate place for trial because plaintiff lived there, defendant did some business there, and all the events giving rise to the suit occurred there. The doctrine thus invoked is a discretionary one, coming into play when jurisdiction and venue are proper but the court decides that it should not hear the case because of the serious inappropriateness of the chosen forum and because of the availability of a substantially more appropriate forum.[q]

The district court dismissed, considering itself bound under Erie by New York law. The court of appeals reversed, disagreeing as to the controlling effect of New York law and taking a restrictive view of the entire doctrine. On certiorari, the Supreme Court, with four dissents, reversed the court of appeals and ordered dismissal. Finding no difference between New York and federal law, it did not pursue the Erie question. Justice Jackson for the majority continued:

"Wisely, it has not been attempted to catalogue the circumstances which will justify or require either grant or denial of remedy. The doctrine leaves much to the discretion of the court to which plaintiff resorts, and experience has not shown a judicial tendency to renounce one's own jurisdiction so strong as to result in many abuses.

"If the combination and weight of factors requisite to given results are difficult to forecast or state, those to be considered are not difficult to name. An interest to be considered, and the one likely to be most pressed, is the private interest of the litigant. Important considerations are the relative ease of access to sources of proof; availability of compulsory process for attendance of unwilling, and the cost of obtaining attendance of willing, witnesses; possibility of view of premises, if view would be appropriate to the action; and all other practical problems that make trial of a case easy, expeditious and inexpensive. There may also be questions as to the enforcibility of a judgment if one is obtained. The court will weigh relative advantages and obstacles to fair trial. It is often said that the plaintiff may not, by choice of an inconvenient forum, 'vex,' 'harass,' or 'oppress' the defendant by inflicting upon him expense or trouble not necessary to his own right to pursue his remedy. But unless the balance is strongly in favor of the defendant, the plaintiff's choice of forum should rarely be disturbed.

"Factors of public interest also have place in applying the doctrine. Administrative difficulties follow for courts when litigation is piled up in congested centers instead of being handled at its origin. Jury duty is a burden that ought not to be imposed upon the people of a community

---

[q] This usual formulation of forum non conveniens obviously has some play in it, and sometimes courts outright modify it, either by restricting or by expanding its scope. For example, New York has held that existence of an alternative forum is not an absolute prerequisite for applying the doctrine. Islamic Republic of Iran v. Pahlavi, 62 N.Y.2d 474, 467 N.E.2d 245, 478 N.Y.S.2d 597, 57 A.L.R.4th 955 (1984), discussed in Ann Alexander, Note, Forum Non Conveniens in the Absence of an Alternative Forum, 86 Colum.L.Rev. 1000 (1986).

which has no relation to the litigation. In cases which touch the affairs of many persons, there is reason for holding the trial in their view and reach rather than in remote parts of the country where they can learn of it by report only. There is a local interest in having localized controversies decided at home. There is an appropriateness, too, in having the trial of a diversity case in a forum that is at home with the state law that must govern the case, rather than having a court in some other forum untangle problems in conflict of laws, and in law foreign to itself."

THE § 1404(a) TRANSFER PROVISION

In 1948 Congress enacted 28 U.S.C. § 1404(a). The reviser's note explained the provision by saying: "Subsection (a) was drafted in accordance with the doctrine of forum non conveniens, permitting transfer to a more convenient forum, even though the venue is proper." But the statute changed the remedy from dismissal of the federal action to transfer of the action to a convenient federal forum.

Because prior to 1948 the Supreme Court had indicated that the special venue act for FELA cases precluded dismissal on the basis of forum non conveniens, Baltimore & Ohio Railroad v. Kepner, 314 U.S. 44, 62 S.Ct. 6 (1941), the question soon arose whether a federal court could transfer an FELA case under § 1404(a). The Supreme Court held that such transfer was allowable, Ex parte Collett, 337 U.S. 55, 69 S.Ct. 944 (1949).

Then, in Norwood v. Kirkpatrick, 349 U.S. 29, 75 S.Ct. 544 (1955), while declining to set aside transfer of three FELA cases, the Supreme Court held that § 1404(a) permits transfer upon a lesser showing of inconvenience than forum non conveniens had required for its remedy of dismissal. The Court added: "This is not to say that the relevant factors have changed or that the plaintiff's choice of forum is not to be considered, but only that the discretion to be exercised is broader." This sentence appeared to give an emphasis different from Justice Jackson's statement in the Gilbert case: "But unless the balance is strongly in favor of the defendant, the plaintiff's choice of forum should rarely be disturbed." The three dissenters took the view that the Court's interpretation did violence to the intent of Congress and was inconsistent with the reviser's note.

The statute worked other changes. Forum non conveniens had been a defendant's remedy. With transfer substituted for dismissal, § 1404(a) became attractive to plaintiffs as well. After some early authority that "Section 1404(a) is not available to plaintiffs who voluntarily choose their own forum," Barnhart v. John B. Rogers Producing Co., 86 F.Supp. 595 (N.D.Ohio 1949), the federal courts came to accept that transfer was available to any plaintiff in a proper case. (Forum non conveniens could be invoked on the court's own motion, and apparently the same is now true for § 1404(a) in rare circumstances.)

Questions: (62) What would be a proper case for transfer upon plaintiff's motion?

(63) What remains of the doctrine of forum non conveniens in federal court, after the enactment of § 1404(a)?

The hottest controversy under § 1404(a) concerned limiting transfer of a case to districts "where it might have been brought." Could a plaintiff obtain a transfer to a district where venue would have been improper or where service of process on the defendant would have been impossible? No. But since venue is a personal privilege of the defendant and since the defendant may consent to service, could a defendant waive any restriction implicit in the "where it might have been brought" requirement and obtain a transfer to a district where venue or service would otherwise be improper as to her?

HOFFMAN v. BLASKI, 363 U.S. 335, 80 S.Ct. 1084 (1960). In two cases the district courts ordered transfer to a more convenient district on defendants' motion. The Seventh Circuit granted mandamus, ruling that § 1404(a) did not authorize these transfers. On certiorari, the Supreme Court affirmed. Justice Whittaker explained for the Court:

"Petitioners concede that these actions were properly brought in the respective transferor forums; that statutory venue did not exist over either of these actions in the respective transferee districts, and that the respective defendants were not within the reach of the process of the respective transferee courts. . . .

"Petitioners' 'thesis' and sole claim is that § 1404(a), being remedial, Ex parte Collett, 337 U.S. 55, 71, 69 S.Ct. 944, 946, should be broadly construed, and, when so construed, the phrase 'where it might have been brought' should be held to relate not only to the time of the bringing of the action, but also to the time of the transfer; and that 'if at such time the transferee forum has the power to adjudicate the issues of the action, it is a forum in which the action might *then* have been brought.' (Emphasis added.) They argue that in the interim between the bringing of the action and the filing of a motion to transfer it, the defendants may move their residence to, or, if corporations, may begin the transaction of business in, some other district, and if such is done, the phrase 'where it might have been brought' should be construed to empower the District Court to transfer the action, on motion of the defendants, to such other district; and that, similarly, if, as here, the defendants move to transfer the action to some other district and consent to submit to the jurisdiction of such other district, the latter district should be held one 'in which the action might *then* have been brought.' (Emphasis added.)

"We do not agree. We do not think the § 1404(a) phrase 'where it might have been brought' can be interpreted to mean, as petitioners' theory would require, 'where it may now be rebrought, with defendants' consent.' This Court has said, in a different context, that § 1404(a) is 'unambiguous, direct [and] clear,' Ex parte Collett, 337 U.S. at page 58, 69 S.Ct. at page 946, and that the 'unequivocal words of § 1404(a) and the legislative history . . . [establish] that Congress indeed meant what it said.' United States v. National City Lines, Inc., 337 U.S. 78, 84, 69 S.Ct. 955, 958. Like the Seventh Circuit, . . . we think the dissenting opinion of Judges Hastie and McLaughlin in Paramount Pictures, Inc. v. Rodney, 3 Cir., 186 F.2d 111, 119, correctly answered this contention:

> 'But we do not see how the conduct of a defendant after suit has been instituted can add to the forums where "it might have been brought." In the normal meaning of words this language of Section 1404(a) directs the attention of the judge who is considering a transfer to the situation which existed when suit was instituted.'

. . . .

"The thesis urged by petitioners would not only do violence to the plain words of § 1404(a), but would also inject gross discrimination. That thesis, if adopted, would empower a District Court, upon a finding of convenience, to transfer an action to any district desired by the *defendants* and in which they were willing to waive their statutory defenses as to venue and jurisdiction over their persons, regardless of the fact that such transferee district was not one in which the action 'might have been brought' by the plaintiff. Conversely, that thesis would not permit the court, upon motion of the *plaintiffs* and a like showing of convenience, to transfer the action to the same district, without the consent and waiver of venue and personal jurisdiction defenses by the defendants. Nothing in § 1404(a), or in its legislative history, suggests such a unilateral objective and we should not, under the guise of interpretation, ascribe to Congress any such discriminatory purpose."

Justice Frankfurter in dissent, joined by Justices Harlan and Brennan, explained:

"One would have to be singularly unmindful of the treachery and versatility of our language to deny that as a mere matter of English the words 'where it might have been brought,' may carry more than one meaning. For example, under Rule 3 of the Federal Rules of Civil Procedure, civil actions are 'commenced' by filing a complaint with the court. As a matter of English there is no reason why 'commenced' so used should not be thought to be synonymous with 'brought' as used in § 1404(a), so that an action 'might have been brought' in any district where a complaint might have been filed, or perhaps only in districts with jurisdiction over the subject matter of the litigation. As a matter of English alone, the phrase might just as well be thought to refer either to those places where the defendant 'might have been' served with process, or to those places where the action 'might have been brought' in light of the applicable venue provision, for those provisions speak generally of where actions 'may be brought.' Or the phrase may be thought as a matter of English alone to refer to those places where the action 'might have been brought' in light of the applicable statute of limitations, or other provisions preventing a court from reaching the merits of the litigation. On the face of its words alone the phrase may refer to any one of these considerations, i.e., venue, amenability to service, or period of limitations, to all of them or to none of them, or to others as well. And to the extent that these are matters which may or may not be raised at the defendant's election, the English of the phrase surely does not tell whether the defendant's actual or potential waiver or failure to raise such objections is to be taken into account in determining whether a district is one in which the action 'might have been brought,' or whether the phrase refers only to those districts where the plaintiff 'might have brought' the action even over a timely objection on the part of the defendant, that is, where he had 'a right' to bring it.

. . . .

"Surely, the Court creates its own verbal prison in holding that 'the plain words' of § 1404(a) dictate that transfer may not be made in this case although transfer concededly was in the interest of 'convenience' and 'justice.' Moreover, the Court, while finding the statutory words 'plain,' decided the case by applying, not the statutory language, but a formula of words found nowhere in the statute, namely, whether plaintiffs had 'a right to bring these actions in the respective transferee districts.' This is the Court's language, not that of Congress. Although it is of course a grammatically plausible interpretation of the phrase 'where it might have been brought,' it has been, I submit, established that it is not by any means the only plausible interpretation. . . .

. . . .

"In summary, then, the 'plain meaning' of § 1404(a) does not conclude the present case against the transfer, for the statute, as applied in this case, is not 'plain' in meaning one way or another, but contains ambiguities which must be resolved by considerations relevant to the problem with which the statute deals. Moreover, the most obvious significance for the set of words here in question, considered as self-contained words, is that they have regard for the limitations contained in the regular statutory rules of venue. Those rules, it is beyond dispute, take into account the consent of the defendant to proceed in the forum, even if it is not a forum designated by statute. And the doctrine of forum non conveniens 'in accordance with' which § 1404(a) was drafted, also took into account the defendant's consent to proceed in another forum to which he was not obligated to submit. Nor can a decision against transfer be rested upon notions of 'discrimination' or of unfairness to the plaintiff in wrenching him out of the forum of his choice to go forward in a place to which he objects. In the proper administration of § 1404(a), such consequences cannot survive the necessity to find transfer to be in the interests of 'convenience' and 'justice,' before it can be made. On the other hand, to restrict transfer as the Court does to those very few places where the defendant was originally amenable to process and could have had no objection to the venue is drastically to restrict the number of situations in which § 1404(a) may serve the interests of justice by relieving the parties from a vexatious forum. And it is to restrict the operation of the section capriciously, for such a drastic limitation is not counseled by any legitimate interest of the plaintiff, or by any interest of the federal courts in their jurisdiction. The defendant's interest of course is not involved because he is the movant for transfer."

Questions: (64) Do you think Congress should rewrite § 1404(a)? If so, how?[r]

(65) Does the Hoffman reading of § 1404(a) prevent the transfer of in rem and quasi in rem actions? See 15 Wright, Miller & Cooper § 3843, at 20–22 (saying, surprisingly enough, no).

VAN DUSEN v. BARRACK, 376 U.S. 612, 84 S.Ct. 805 (1964). A large number of plaintiffs separately sued in the District Court for the Eastern District of Pennsylvania for wrongful deaths resulting from an air crash in Boston Harbor on takeoff of a flight to Philadelphia. (Many others brought similar actions in the District Court for the District of Massachusetts.) The defendants moved to transfer the Pennsylvania federal actions to Massachusetts under § 1404(a), and the court ordered the transfer.

The plaintiffs brought mandamus proceedings in the Court of Appeals for the Third Circuit, in which they successfully contended that the appellate court should vacate the district court's order because Massachusetts, although venue and jurisdiction were proper there, was not a district where the actions "might have been brought": the plaintiffs, being the decedents' personal representatives who had not obtained the appointments necessary to qualify them to initiate actions in Massachusetts, did not have an unqualified right to bring suit there. On certiorari, the Supreme Court reversed and remanded, holding "that the words 'where it might have been brought' must be construed with reference to the federal laws delimiting the districts in which such an action 'may be brought,' " without regard to laws concerning the capacity of fiduciaries to sue.

Another critical issue was what the applicable choice-of-law rule would be upon transfer. A possible difference in substantive law was at stake: Massachusetts based recovery in wrongful-death cases on the degree of the defendant's culpability and limited recovery to a $20,000 maximum, while Pennsylvania allowed compensatory damages without limitation as to amount.[s] On this issue, the Supreme Court said that the transferee district

---

[r] Curiously, the American Law Institute, after considerable study, has recently proposed amending it only thus: "For the convenience of parties and witnesses or in the interest of justice, a district court may transfer any civil action to any other district where it might have been brought." ALI Federal Judicial Code Revision Project § 1404(a) (2004). The commentary thereto notes that substantial sentiment exists for eliminating the last six words, but concludes, "For fear of the bugs beneath, this stone is here left unturned."

[s] On the one hand, the federal court sitting in Pennsylvania would of course apply the Pennsylvania choice-of-law rule. At that time, however, it was unclear what choice-of-law rule Pennsylvania would adopt in such an action arising in another state; but shortly after the Supreme Court's decision, Pennsylvania held that it would apply its own rule of compensatory damages without limitation as to amount, Griffith v. United Air Lines, 416 Pa. 1, 203 A.2d 796 (1964).

court, after transfer on defendants' motion, would have to apply the state law that would have been applied if there had been no change of venue, thus closing the door to any defendants' shopping for favorable law.[t] The explanation in part was that there is nothing "in the language or policy of § 1404(a) to justify its use by defendants to defeat the advantages accruing to plaintiffs who have chosen a forum which, although it was inconvenient, was a proper venue." Moreover, "our interpretation of that statute fully accords with and is supported by the policy underlying Erie," in that the result in federal court will conform to what would have been the result in the filing state. A change of venue in pursuit of convenience, concluded Justice Goldberg for the unanimous Court, "generally should be, with respect to state law, but a change of courtrooms.[40]"

Question: (66) *P* properly brings a diversity action against *D* for injuries to *P,* a guest passenger in *D*'s automobile, in a federal court of State *X,* which is *D*'s residence. The court properly transfers it to a federal court of State *Y, P*'s residence, pursuant to § 1404(a) upon *P*'s motion. The law of State *X* holds that a host driver is liable to his guest passenger for lack of ordinary care, regardless of where the accident occurred. The law of State *Y* holds that the duty of care is measured by the law of the place where the accident occurred, in this case State *Y,* where a guest passenger may recover only upon proof of gross negligence. What should be the governing law as to standard of care in this case?

FERENS v. JOHN DEERE CO., 494 U.S. 516, 110 S.Ct. 1274 (1990). A Pennsylvania man working on his farm lost his hand allegedly in a combine harvester manufactured by defendant, which is incorporated in Delaware with its principal place of business in Illinois but which does business widely. Three years later, he and his wife brought a diversity action, sounding in contract and warranty, in the Western District of Pennsylvania. They then properly brought another diversity action in the Southern District of Mississippi, sounding in negligence and product liability, because that court would apply Mississippi's six-year statute of limitations rather than Pennsylvania's two-year statute for torts. The plaintiffs next moved to

---

On the other hand, the plaintiffs feared and the defendants hoped that the transferee federal court sitting in Massachusetts would, under Klaxon Co. v. Stentor Electric Manufacturing Co., 313 U.S. 487, 61 S.Ct. 1020 (1941), apply the Massachusetts choice-of-law rule and hence the Massachusetts law on damages, which, according to the plaintiffs, would be highly prejudicial to them and not "in the interest of justice."

[t] Do you think this rule would make transfer generally more likely or less likely? At any rate, after remand and the further consideration ordered by the Supreme Court in the light of its decision, the district court denied transfer of these cases. Popkin v. Eastern Air Lines, 253 F.Supp. 244 (E.D.Pa.1966). See also Rapp v. Van Dusen, 350 F.2d 806 (3d Cir.1965) (holding by a divided court that Judge Van Dusen should disqualify himself as a result of the earlier mandamus proceedings in which he was a named party defendant).

[40] Of course the transferee District Court may apply its own rules governing the conduct and dispatch of cases in its court. We are only concerned here with those state laws of the transferor State which would significantly affect the outcome of the case.

transfer the second case to the Western District of Pennsylvania under § 1404(a), the defendant put up no opposition, and the court granted the motion.

The transferee court, however, dismissed the tort case by applying the Pennsylvania statute of limitations. The court of appeals affirmed. On certiorari, the Supreme Court reversed, adopting the simple rule that transferor law applies regardless of who moves to transfer under § 1404(a). Justice Kennedy for the majority argued that the core reasons behind the Van Dusen decision carried over to the context of the plaintiffs' motion. Anticipating Justice Scalia's dissent, which Justices Brennan, Marshall, and Blackmun joined, the Court's opinion further argued that the plaintiffs' opportunity to forum-shop by this file-and-transfer ploy results from our federal system, and not from § 1404(a).

Question: (67) If a transferred case involves disputed questions of federal law, should the transferee court apply the transferor court's interpretation of federal law or exercise independent judgment as to federal law? Cases are split, but most are now going the latter route. Why? See Richard L. Marcus, Conflicts Among Circuits and Transfers Within the Federal Judicial System, 93 Yale L.J. 677, 720 (1984) ("transferee court is fully competent to decide issues of federal law"). But what if the federal law is meant to be geographically nonuniform, as are some statutes of limitations? See McMasters v. United States, 260 F.3d 814 (7th Cir.2001) (dictum to effect that transferor law applies).

THE § 1406(a) TRANSFER PROVISION

A quite different statute came before the Court in Goldlawr, Inc. v. Heiman, 369 U.S. 463, 82 S.Ct. 913 (1962). Plaintiff had sued several defendants in the Eastern District of Pennsylvania for treble damages and other relief under the antitrust laws, doing so within the federal statute of limitations. On motion by two of the corporate defendants to dismiss for improper venue and lack of personal jurisdiction, the district court, passing only on the venue contention, found venue improper as to them. By this time, the statute of limitations had run. Refusing to dismiss, the court ordered transfer of the action as against the two defendants to the Southern District of New York, where venue would be proper and personal jurisdiction would be obtainable.

The transferee court, however, granted dismissal on the ground that the transferor court, lacking personal jurisdiction, had not had power under 28 U.S.C. § 1406(a) to transfer. The Court of Appeals for the Second Circuit affirmed. On certiorari, the Supreme Court reversed (5–2).

Justice Black for the majority said: "The language of § 1406(a) is amply broad enough to authorize the transfer of cases, however wrong the plaintiff may have been in filing his case as to venue, whether the court in which it was filed had personal jurisdiction over the defendants or not. The section is thus in accord with the general purpose which has prompted many of the procedural changes of the past few years—that of removing whatever obstacles may impede an expeditious and orderly adjudication of cases and controversies on their merits. When a lawsuit is filed, that filing shows a desire on the part of the plaintiff to begin his case and thereby toll whatever statutes of limitation would otherwise apply."

Justice Harlan in dissent, joined by Justice Stewart, said: "The notion that a District Court may deal with an in personam action in such a way as possibly to affect a defendant's substantive rights without first acquiring jurisdiction over him is not a familiar one in federal jurisprudence. No one suggests that Congress was aware that 28 U.S.C. § 1406(a) might be so used when it enacted that statute."

Question: (68) *P* brings a diversity action against *D* for injuries to *P,* a guest passenger in *D*'s automobile, in a federal court of State *X,* which *P* alleges to be *D*'s residence. The court properly transfers it to a federal court of State *Y, P*'s residence, pursuant to § 1406(a) when it appears that *D* is not a resident of State *X.* The law of State *X* holds that the duty of care is measured by the law of the defendant's residence, in this case State *Z,* where a guest passenger may recover only upon proof of gross negligence. The law of State *Y* holds that the duty of care is measured by the law of the place where the accident occurred, in this case State *Y,* where a host driver is liable to his guest passenger for lack of ordinary care. What should be the governing law?

MARTIN v. STOKES, 623 F.2d 469 (6th Cir.1980). In March 1975 a Virginia personal-injury plaintiff filed a diversity action against Kentucky and California defendants in her home district, the Western District of Virginia, which was a proper venue under the then-current version of § 1391(a). After personal service in their home districts, defendants moved to quash process. The district court without explanation refused to quash and ordered transfer to the Western District of Kentucky, where the automobile accident had occurred in August 1973.

The transferee court, however, granted defendants' request to dismiss on the basis of Kentucky's one-year statute of limitations, even though the transferor court would have applied Virginia's two-year statute. Plaintiff appealed.

The court of appeals ruled that (1) on state-law questions transferor law applies after a § 1404(a) transfer (which would defeat the limitations defense), but transferee law applies after a § 1406(a) transfer (which would sustain the limitations defense); (2) the two statutes being mutually exclusive but complementary, § 1404(a) operates only where the transferor court is a proper forum, but § 1406(a) can operate where the transferor court cannot acquire personal jurisdiction although venue is proper; and (3) this case should be remanded to the Western District of Kentucky to make the critical determination of whether the Virginia court could have obtained personal jurisdiction.

Questions: (69) Suppose that a federal court of State *X* would apply a one-year statute of limitations to a particular action if commenced there, while a federal court of State *Y* would apply a two-year statute if the same case were commenced there. Can plaintiff, after transfer from an improper forum under § 1406(a), maintain that action over a statute-of-limitations defense in the following situations? (a) Federal suit is brought in forum *X* nineteen months after accrual of the cause of action; transfer to forum *Y* is made one month later. (b) Federal suit is brought in forum *X* six months after accrual; transfer to forum *Y* is made nineteen months later. (c) Federal suit is brought in forum *X* nineteen months after accrual; transfer to forum *Y* is made six months later. See generally John D. Currivan, Note, Choice of Law in Federal Court After Transfer of Venue, 63 Cornell L.Rev. 149 (1977); Roberto Finzi, Note, The 28 U.S.C. § 1406(a) Transfer of Time-barred Claims, 79 Cornell L.Rev. 975 (1994).

(70) Can plaintiff transfer from a federal court lacking subject-matter jurisdiction to a federal court with subject-matter jurisdiction? See 28 U.S.C. § 1631; Jeffrey W. Tayon, The Federal Transfer Statute: 28 U.S.C. § 1631, 29 S.Tex.L.Rev. 189 (1987).

Piper Aircraft Co. v. Reyno

Supreme Court of the United States, 1981.
454 U.S. 235, 102 S.Ct. 252.

■ JUSTICE MARSHALL delivered the opinion of the Court.

These cases arise out of an air crash that took place in Scotland. Respondent, acting as representative of the estates of several Scottish citizens killed in the accident, brought wrongful-death actions against petitioners that were ultimately transferred to the United States District Court for the Middle District of Pennsylvania. Petitioners moved to dismiss on the ground of forum non conveniens. After noting that an alternative forum existed in Scotland, the District Court granted their motions. 479 F.Supp. 727 (M.D.Pa.1979). The United States Court of Appeals for the Third Circuit reversed. 630 F.2d 149 (C.A.3 1980). The Court of Appeals based its decision, at least in part, on the ground that dismissal is automatically barred where the law of the alternative forum is less favorable to the plaintiff than the law of the forum chosen by the plaintiff. Because we conclude that the possibility of an unfavorable change in law should not, by itself, bar dismissal, and because we conclude that the District Court did not otherwise abuse its discretion, we reverse.

I

A

In July 1976, a small commercial aircraft crashed in the Scottish highlands during the course of a charter flight from Blackpool to Perth. The pilot and five passengers were killed instantly. The decedents were all Scottish subjects and residents, as are their heirs and next of kin. There were no eyewitnesses to the accident. At the time of the crash the plane was subject to Scottish air traffic control.

The aircraft, a twin-engine Piper Aztec, was manufactured in Pennsylvania by petitioner Piper Aircraft Company ("Piper"). The propellers were manufactured in Ohio by petitioner Hartzell Propeller, Inc. ("Hartzell"). At the time of the crash the aircraft was registered in Great Britain and was owned and maintained by Air Navigation and Trading Co., Ltd. ("Air Navigation"). It was operated by McDonald Aviation, Ltd. ("McDonald"), a Scottish air taxi service. Both Air Navigation and McDonald were organized in the United Kingdom. The wreckage of the plane is now in a hangar in Farnsborough, England.

The British Department of Trade investigated the accident several months after it occurred. A preliminary report found that the plane crashed after developing a spin, and suggested that mechanical failure in the plane or the propeller was responsible. At Hartzell's request, this report was reviewed by a three-member Review Board, which held a nine-day adversary hearing attended by all interested parties. The Review Board found no evidence of defective equipment and indicated that pilot error may have contributed to the accident. The pilot, who had obtained his commercial pilot's license only three months earlier, was flying over high ground at an altitude considerably lower than the minimum height required by his company's operations manual.

In July 1977, a California probate court appointed respondent Gaynell Reyno administratrix of the estates of the five passengers. Reyno is not related to and does not know any of the decedents or their survivors; she was a legal secretary to the attorney who filed this lawsuit. Several days after her appointment, Reyno commenced separate wrongful death actions against Piper and Hartzell in the Superior Court of California, claiming negligence and strict liability. Air Navigation, McDonald, and the estate of the pilot are not parties to this litigation. The survivors of the five passengers whose estates are represented by Reyno filed a separate action in the United Kingdom against Air Navigation, McDonald, and the pilot's estate. Reyno candidly admits that the action against Piper and Hartzell was filed in the United States because its laws regarding liability, capacity to sue, and damages are more favorable to her position than are those of Scotland. Scottish law does not recognize strict liability in tort. Moreover, it permits wrongful-death actions only when brought by a decedent's relatives. The relatives may sue only for "loss of support and society."

On petitioners' motion, the suit was removed to the United States District Court for the Central District of California. Piper then moved for transfer to the United States District Court for the Middle District of Pennsylvania, pursuant to 28 U.S.C. § 1404(a). Hartzell moved to dismiss for lack of personal jurisdiction, or in the alternative, to transfer.[5] In December 1977, the District Court quashed service on Hartzell and transferred the case to the Middle District of Pennsylvania. Respondent then properly served process on Hartzell.

B

In May 1978, after the suit had been transferred, both Hartzell and Piper moved to dismiss the action on the ground of forum non conveniens.[u] The District Court granted these motions in October 1979. It relied on the balancing test set forth by this Court in Gulf Oil Corporation v. Gilbert, 330 U.S. 501, 67 S.Ct. 839 (1947), and its companion case, Koster v. Lumbermens Mut. Cas. Co., 330 U.S. 518, 67 S.Ct. 828 (1947). . . .

After describing our decisions in Gilbert and Koster, the District Court analyzed the facts of this case. It began by observing that an alternative forum existed in Scotland; Piper and Hartzell had agreed to submit to the jurisdiction of the Scottish courts and to waive any statute of limitations defense that might be available. It then stated that plaintiff's choice of forum was entitled to little weight. The court recognized that a plaintiff's choice ordinarily deserves substantial deference. It noted, however, that Reyno "is a representative of foreign citizens and residents seeking a forum in the United States because of the more liberal rules concerning products liability law," and that "the courts have been less solicitous when the plaintiff is not an American citizen or resident, and particularly when the foreign citizens seek to benefit from the more liberal tort rules provided for the protection of citizens and residents of the United States." 479 F.Supp. at 731.

The District Court next examined several factors relating to the private interests of the litigants, and determined that these factors strongly pointed towards Scotland as the appropriate forum. Although evidence concerning the design, manufacture, and testing of the plane and propeller is located in the United States, the connections with Scotland are otherwise "overwhelming." Id., at 732. The real parties in interest are citizens of Scotland, as were all the decedents. Witnesses who could testify regarding the maintenance of the aircraft, the training of the pilot, and the investigation of the accident—all essential to the defense—are in Great Britain. Moreover, all witnesses to damages are located in Scotland. Trial would be aided by familiarity with Scottish topography, and by easy access to the wreckage.

---

[5] The District Court concluded that it could not assert personal jurisdiction over Hartzell consistent with due process. However, it decided not to dismiss Hartzell because the corporation would be amenable to process in Pennsylvania.

[u] The defendants attributed their delay in pushing this point to delay in acquiring full knowledge of the relevant facts. In view of all the circumstances, both the Pennsylvania district court and the court of appeals refused to hold the defendants equitably estopped. For the background story of the Piper case, see Kevin M. Clermont, "The Story of Piper: Forum Matters," in Civil Procedure Stories 199 (Kevin M. Clermont ed., 2d ed. 2008).

The District Court reasoned that because crucial witnesses and evidence were beyond the reach of compulsory process, and because the defendants would not be able to implead potential Scottish third-party defendants, it would be "unfair to make Piper and Hartzell proceed to trial in this forum." Id., at 733. The survivors had brought separate actions in Scotland against the pilot, McDonald, and Air Navigation. "[I]t would be fairer to all parties and less costly if the entire case was presented to one jury with available testimony from all relevant witnesses." Ibid. Although the court recognized that if trial were held in the United States, Piper and Hartzell could file indemnity or contribution actions against the Scottish defendants, it believed that there was a significant risk of inconsistent verdicts.[7]

The District Court concluded that the relevant public interests also pointed strongly towards dismissal. The court determined that Pennsylvania law would apply to Piper and Scottish law to Hartzell if the case were tried in the Middle District of Pennsylvania.[8] As a result, "trial in this forum would be hopelessly complex and confusing for a jury." Id., at 734. In addition, the court noted that it was unfamiliar with Scottish law and thus would have to rely upon experts from that country. The court also found that the trial would be enormously costly and time-consuming; that it would be unfair to burden citizens with jury duty when the Middle District of Pennsylvania has little connection with the controversy; and that Scotland has a substantial interest in the outcome of the litigation.

In opposing the motions to dismiss, respondent contended that dismissal would be unfair because Scottish law was less favorable. The District Court explicitly rejected this claim. It reasoned that the possibility that dismissal might lead to an unfavorable change in the law did not deserve significant weight; any deficiency in the foreign law was a "matter to be dealt with in the foreign forum." Id., at 738.

C

On appeal, the United States Court of Appeals for the Third Circuit reversed and remanded for trial. The decision to reverse appears to be based on two alternative grounds. First, the Court held that the District Court abused its discretion in conducting the Gilbert analysis. Second, the

---

7 The District Court explained that inconsistent verdicts might result if petitioners were held liable on the basis of strict liability here, and then required to prove negligence in an indemnity action in Scotland. Moreover, even if the same standard of liability applied, there was a danger that different juries would find different facts and produce inconsistent results.

8 Under Klaxon v. Stentor Electric Manufacturing Co., 313 U.S. 487, 61 S.Ct. 1020 (1941), a court ordinarily must apply the choice-of-law rules of the state in which it sits. However, where a case is transferred pursuant to 28 U.S.C. § 1404(a), it must apply the choice-of-law rules of the state from which the case was transferred. Van Dusen v. Barrack, 376 U.S. 612, 84 S.Ct. 805 (1964). Relying on these two cases, the District Court concluded that California choice-of-law rules would apply to Piper, and Pennsylvania choice-of-law rules would apply to Hartzell. It further concluded that California applied a "governmental interests" analysis in resolving choice-of-law problems, and that Pennsylvania employed a "significant contacts" analysis. The court used the "governmental interests" analysis to determine that Pennsylvania liability rules would apply to Piper, and the "significant contacts" analysis to determine that Scottish liability rules would apply to Hartzell.

Court held that dismissal is never appropriate where the law of the alternative forum is less favorable to the plaintiff.

The Court of Appeals began its review of the District Court's Gilbert analysis by noting that the plaintiff's choice of forum deserved substantial weight, even though the real parties in interest are nonresidents. It then rejected the District Court's balancing of the private interests. . . . The Court of Appeals gave little weight to the fact that Piper and Hartzell would not be able to implead potential Scottish third-party defendants, reasoning that this difficulty would be "burdensome" but not "unfair," 639 F.2d at 162. Finally, the court stated that resolution of the suit would not be significantly aided by familiarity with Scottish topography, or by viewing the wreckage.

The Court of Appeals also rejected the District Court's analysis of the public interest factors. It found that the District Court gave undue emphasis to the application of Scottish law: "the mere fact that the court is called upon to determine and apply foreign law does not present a legal problem of the sort which would justify the dismissal of a case otherwise properly before the court." Id., at 163. In any event, it believed that Scottish law need not be applied. After conducting its own choice-of-law analysis, the Court of Appeals determined that American law would govern the actions against both Piper and Hartzell.[10] The same choice-of-law analysis apparently led it to conclude that Pennsylvania and Ohio, rather than Scotland, are the jurisdictions with the greatest policy interests in the dispute, and that all other public interest factors favored trial in the United States.

In any event, it appears that the Court of Appeals would have reversed even if the District Court had properly balanced the public and private interests. . . . In other words, the court decided that dismissal is automatically barred if it would lead to a change in the applicable law unfavorable to the plaintiff.

We granted certiorari in these cases to consider the questions they raise concerning the proper application of the doctrine of forum non conveniens. 450 U.S. 909, 101 S.Ct. 1346 (1981).

II

The Court of Appeals erred in holding that plaintiffs may defeat a motion to dismiss on the ground of forum non conveniens merely by showing that the substantive law that would be applied in the alternative forum is less favorable to the plaintiffs than that of the present forum. The possibility of a change in substantive law should ordinarily not be given conclusive or even substantial weight in the forum non conveniens inquiry.

---

[10] The Court of Appeals agreed with the District Court that California choice-of-law rules applied to Piper, and that Pennsylvania choice-of-law rules applied to Hartzell, see n. 8, supra. It did not agree, however, that California used a "governmental interests" analysis and that Pennsylvania used a "significant contacts" analysis. Rather, it believed that both jurisdictions employed the "false conflicts" test. Applying this test, it concluded that Ohio and Pennsylvania had a greater policy interest in the dispute than Scotland, and that American law would apply to both Piper and Hartzell.

We expressly rejected the position adopted by the Court of Appeals in our decision in Canada Malting Co. v. Paterson Steamships, Ltd., 285 U.S. 413, 52 S.Ct. 413 (1932). . . .

It is true that Canada Malting was decided before Gilbert, and that the doctrine of forum non conveniens was not fully crystallized until our decision in that case.[13] However, Gilbert in no way affects the validity of Canada Malting. Indeed, by holding that the central focus of the forum non conveniens inquiry is convenience, Gilbert implicitly recognized that dismissal may not be barred solely because of the possibility of an unfavorable change in law. Under Gilbert, dismissal will ordinarily be appropriate where trial in the plaintiff's chosen forum imposes a heavy burden on the defendant or the court, and where the plaintiff is unable to offer any specific reasons of convenience supporting his choice.[15] If substantial weight were given to the possibility of an unfavorable change in law, however, dismissal might be barred even where trial in the chosen forum was plainly inconvenient.

The Court of Appeals' decision is inconsistent with this Court's earlier forum non conveniens decisions in another respect. Those decisions have repeatedly emphasized the need to retain flexibility. . . . If central emphasis were placed on any one factor, the forum non conveniens doctrine would lose much of the very flexibility that makes it so valuable.

In fact, if conclusive or substantial weight were given to the possibility of a change in law, the forum non conveniens doctrine would become virtually useless. Jurisdiction and venue requirements are often easily satisfied. As a result, many plaintiffs are able to choose from among several forums. Ordinarily, these plaintiffs will select that forum whose choice-of-

---

13 The doctrine of forum non conveniens has a long history. It originated in Scotland, see Braucher, The Inconvenient Federal Forum, 60 Harv.L.Rev. 908, 909–911 (1947), and became part of the common law of many states, see id., at 911–912; Blair, The Doctrine of Forum Non Conveniens in Anglo–American Law, 29 Colum.L.Rev. 1 (1929). The doctrine was also frequently applied in federal admiralty actions. See, e.g., Canada Malting Co. v. Paterson Steamships, Ltd., 285 U.S. 413, 52 S.Ct. 413 (1932); see also Bickel, The Doctrine of Forum Non Conveniens As Applied in the Federal Courts in Matters of Admiralty, 35 Cornell L.Q. 12 (1949). In Williams v. Green Bay & Western R., 326 U.S. 549, 66 S.Ct. 284 (1946), the Court first indicated that motions to dismiss on grounds of forum non conveniens could be made in federal diversity actions. The doctrine became firmly established when Gilbert and Koster were decided one year later.

In previous forum non conveniens decisions, the Court has left unresolved the question whether under Erie R. v. Tompkins, 304 U.S. 64, 58 S.Ct. 817 (1938), state or federal law of forum non conveniens applies in a diversity case. Gilbert, supra, 330 U.S. at 509, 67 S.Ct., at 843; Koster, supra, 330 U.S. at 529, 67 S.Ct., at 834; Williams v. Green Bay & Western R., supra, 326 U.S. at 551, 558–559, 66 S.Ct., at 288–89 (1946). The Court did not decide this issue because the same result would have been reached in each case under federal or state law. The lower courts in this case reached the same conclusion: Pennsylvania and California law on forum non conveniens dismissals are virtually identical to federal law. See 630 F.2d at 158. Thus, here also, we need not resolve the Erie question. [By its way of settling a disputed point of forum non conveniens law, as opposed to merely applying the law, did not the Piper Court necessarily resolve the Erie question? At any rate, the trend in the lower federal courts favors applying the federal doctrine of forum non conveniens.—Ed.]

15 In other words, Gilbert held that dismissal may be warranted where a plaintiff chooses a particular forum, not because it is convenient, but solely in order to harass the defendant or take advantage of favorable law. This is precisely the situation in which the Court of Appeals' rule would bar dismissal.

law rules are most advantageous. Thus, if the possibility of an unfavorable change in substantive law is given substantial weight in the forum non conveniens inquiry, dismissal would rarely be proper.

. . . .

The Court of Appeals' approach is not only inconsistent with the purpose of the forum non conveniens doctrine, but also poses substantial practical problems. If the possibility of a change in law were given substantial weight, deciding motions to dismiss on the ground of forum non conveniens would become quite difficult. Choice-of-law analysis would become extremely important, and the courts would frequently be required to interpret the law of foreign jurisdictions. First, the trial court would have to determine what law would apply if the case were tried in the chosen forum, and what law would apply if the case were tried in the alternative forum. It would then have to compare the rights, remedies, and procedures available under the law that would be applied in each forum. Dismissal would be appropriate only if the court concluded that the law applied by the alternative forum is as favorable to the plaintiff as that of the chosen forum. The doctrine of forum non conveniens, however, is designed in part to help courts avoid conducting complex exercises in comparative law. As we stated in Gilbert, the public interest factors point towards dismissal where the court would be required to "untangle problems in conflict of laws, and in law foreign to itself." Gilbert, supra, 330 U.S. at 509, 67 S.Ct., at 843.

Upholding the decision of the Court of Appeals would result in other practical problems. . . . The American courts, which are already extremely attractive to foreign plaintiffs,[18] would become even more attractive. The flow of litigation into the United States would increase and further congest already crowded courts.[19]

---

[18] First, all but six of the 50 American states—Delaware, Massachusetts, Michigan, North Carolina, Virginia, and Wyoming—offer strict liability. 1 CCH Prod.Liab.Rep. § 4016. Rules roughly equivalent to American strict liability are effective in France, Belgium, and Luxembourg. West Germany and Japan have a strict liability statute for pharmaceuticals. However, strict liability remains primarily an American innovation. Second, the tort plaintiff may choose, at least potentially, from among 50 jurisdictions if he decides to file suit in the United States. Each of these jurisdictions applies its own set of malleable choice-of-law rules. Third, jury trials are almost always available in the United States, while they are never provided in civil law jurisdictions. G. Gloss, Comparative Law 12 (1979); J. Merryman, The Civil Law Tradition 121 (1969). Even in the United Kingdom, most civil actions are not tried before a jury. 1 G. Keeton, The United Kingdom: The Development of its Laws and Constitutions 309 (1955). Fourth, unlike most foreign jurisdictions, American courts allow contingent attorney's fees, and do not tax losing parties with their opponents' attorney's fees. R. Schlesinger, Comparative Law: Cases, Text, Materials 275–277 (3d ed. 1970); [other citation omitted]. Fifth, discovery is more extensive in American than in foreign courts. R. Schlesinger, supra, at 307, 310, and n. 33.

[19] In holding that the possibility of a change in law unfavorable to the plaintiff should not be given substantial weight, we also necessarily hold that the possibility of a change in law favorable to defendant should not be considered. Respondent suggests that Piper and Hartzell filed the motion to dismiss, not simply because trial in the United States would be inconvenient, but also because they believe the laws of Scotland are more favorable. She argues that this should be taken into account in the analysis of the private interests. We recognize, of course, that Piper and Hartzell may be engaged in reverse forum-shopping. However, this possibility ordinarily should not enter into a trial court's analysis of the private interests. If

The Court of Appeals based its decision, at least in part, on an analogy between dismissals on grounds of forum non conveniens and transfers between federal courts pursuant to § 1404(a). In Van Dusen v. Barrack, 376 U.S. 612, 84 S.Ct. 805 (1964), this Court ruled that a § 1404(a) transfer should not result in a change in the applicable law. . . . However, § 1404(a) transfers are different than dismissals on the ground of forum non conveniens.

Congress enacted § 1404(a) to permit change of venue between federal courts. Although the statute was drafted in accordance with the doctrine of forum non conveniens, [citations omitted], it was intended to be a revision rather than a codification of the common law. Norwood v. Kirkpatrick, 349 U.S. 29, 75 S.Ct. 544 (1955). District courts were given more discretion to transfer under § 1404(a) than they had to dismiss on grounds of forum non conveniens. Id., at 31–32, 75 S.Ct., at 546.

The reasoning employed in Van Dusen v. Barrack is simply inapplicable to dismissals on grounds of forum non conveniens. That case did not discuss the common-law doctrine. Rather, it focused on "the construction and application" of § 1404(a). 376 U.S. at 613, 84 S.Ct., at 807–08. Emphasizing the remedial purpose of the statute, Barrack concluded that Congress could not have intended a transfer to be accompanied by a change in law. Id., at 622, 84 S.Ct., at 812. The statute was designed as a "federal housekeeping measure," allowing easy change of venue within a unified federal system. Id., at 613, 84 S.Ct., at 807–08. The Court feared that if a change in venue were accompanied by a change in law, forum-shopping parties would take unfair advantage of the relaxed standards for transfer. The rule was necessary to ensure the just and efficient operation of the statute.

We do not hold that the possibility of an unfavorable change in law should *never* be a relevant consideration in a forum non conveniens inquiry. Of course, if the remedy provided by the alternative forum is so clearly inadequate or unsatisfactory that it is no remedy at all, the unfavorable change in law may be given substantial weight; the district court may conclude that dismissal would not be in the interests of justice.[22]

---

the defendant is able to overcome the presumption in favor of plaintiff by showing that trial in the chosen forum would be unnecessarily burdensome, dismissal is appropriate—regardless of the fact that defendant may also be motivated by a desire to obtain a more favorable forum. Cf. Kloeckner Reederei und Kohlenhandel v. A/S Hakedal, 210 F.2d 754, 757 (CA2), cert. dismissed by stipulation, 348 U.S. 801, 75 S.Ct. 17 (1954) (defendant not entitled to dismissal on grounds of forum non conveniens solely because the law of the original forum is less favorable to him than the law of the alternative forum).

[22] At the outset of any forum non conveniens inquiry, the court must determine whether there exists an alternative forum. Ordinarily, this requirement will be satisfied when the defendant is "amenable to process" in the other jurisdiction. Gilbert, supra, 330 U.S. at 506–507, 67 S.Ct., at 842. In rare circumstances, however, where the remedy offered by the other forum is clearly unsatisfactory, the other forum may not be an adequate alternative, and the initial requirement may not be satisfied. Thus, for example, dismissal would not be appropriate where the alternative forum does not permit litigation of the subject matter of the dispute. Cf. Phoenix Canada Oil Co. Ltd. v. Texaco, Inc., 78 F.R.D. 445 (D.C.Del.1978) (court refuses to dismiss, where alternative forum is Ecuador, it is unclear whether Ecuadorean tribunal will

In these cases, however, the remedies that would be provided by the Scottish courts do not fall within this category. Although the relatives of the decedents may not be able to rely on a strict liability theory, and although their potential damages award may be smaller, there is no danger that they will be deprived of any remedy or treated unfairly.

III

The Court of Appeals also erred in rejecting the District Court's Gilbert analysis. The Court of Appeals stated that more weight should have been given to the plaintiff's choice of forum, and criticized the District Court's analysis of the private and public interests. However, the District Court's decision regarding the deference due plaintiff's choice of forum was appropriate. Furthermore, we do not believe that the District Court abused its discretion in weighing the private and public interests.

A

The District Court acknowledged that there is ordinarily a strong presumption in favor of the plaintiff's choice of forum, which may be overcome only when the private and public interest factors clearly point towards trial in the alternative forum. It held, however, that the presumption applies with less force when the plaintiff or real parties in interest are foreign.

The District Court's distinction between resident or citizen plaintiffs and foreign plaintiffs is fully justified. In Koster, the Court indicated that a plaintiff's choice of forum is entitled to greater deference when the plaintiff has chosen the home forum. Koster, supra, 330 U.S. at 524, 67 S.Ct., at 831–832.[23] When the home forum has been chosen, it is reasonable to assume that this choice is convenient. When the plaintiff is foreign, however, this assumption is much less reasonable. Because the central purpose of any forum non conveniens inquiry is to ensure that the trial is convenient, a foreign plaintiff's choice deserves less deference.

B

The forum non conveniens determination is committed to the sound discretion of the trial court. It may be reversed only when there has been a clear abuse of discretion; where the court has considered all relevant public and private interest factors, and where its balancing of these factors is reasonable, its decision deserves substantial deference. Gilbert, supra, 330 U.S. at 511–512, 67 S.Ct., at 844–45; Koster, supra, 330 U.S. at 531, 67 S.Ct., at 835. Here, the Court of Appeals expressly acknowledged that the

---

hear the case, and there is no generally codified Ecuadorean legal remedy for the unjust enrichment and tort claims asserted).

23 . . . .

A citizen's forum choice should not be given dispositive weight, however. [Citations omitted.] Citizens or residents deserve somewhat more deference than foreign plaintiffs, but dismissal should not be automatically barred when a plaintiff has filed suit in his home forum. As always, if the balance of conveniences suggests that trial in the chosen forum would be unnecessarily burdensome for the defendant or the court, dismissal is proper.

standard of review was one of abuse of discretion. In examining the District Court's analysis of the public and private interests, however, the Court of Appeals seems to have lost sight of this rule, and substituted its own judgment for that of the District Court.

(1)

In analyzing the private interest factors, the District Court stated that the connections with Scotland are "overwhelming." 479 F.Supp. at 732. This characterization may be somewhat exaggerated. Particularly with respect to the question of relative ease of access to sources of proof, the private interests point in both directions. As respondent emphasizes, records concerning the design, manufacture, and testing of the propeller and plane are located in the United States. She would have greater access to sources of proof relevant to her strict liability and negligence theories if trial were held here.[25] However, the District Court did not act unreasonably in concluding that fewer evidentiary problems would be posed if the trial were held in Scotland. A large proportion of the relevant evidence is located in Great Britain.

. . . .

The District Court correctly concluded that the problems posed by the inability to implead potential third-party defendants clearly supported holding the trial in Scotland. Joinder of the pilot's estate, Air Navigation, and McDonald is crucial to the presentation of petitioners' defense. If Piper and Hartzell can show that the accident was caused not by a design defect, but rather by the negligence of the pilot, the plane's owners, or the charter company, they will be relieved of all liability. It is true, of course, that if Hartzell and Piper were found liable after a trial in the United States, they could institute an action for indemnity or contribution against these parties in Scotland. It would be far more convenient, however, to resolve all claims in one trial. The Court of Appeals rejected this argument. Forcing petitioners to rely on actions for indemnity or contributions would be "burdensome" but not "unfair." 630 F.2d at 162. Finding that trial in the plaintiff's chosen forum would be burdensome, however, is sufficient to support dismissal on grounds of forum non conveniens.

(2)

The District Court's review of the factors relating to the public interest was also reasonable. . . . The Court of Appeals found that the District Court's choice-of-law analysis was incorrect, and that American law would apply to both Hartzell and Piper. . . . Even if the Court of Appeals' conclusion is correct, however, all other public interest factors favored trial in Scotland.

. . . Respondent argues that American citizens have an interest in ensuring that American manufacturers are deterred from producing defec-

[25] In the future, where similar problems are presented, district courts might dismiss subject to the condition that defendant corporations agree to provide the records relevant to the plaintiff's claims.

tive products, and that additional deterrence might be obtained if Piper and Hartzell were tried in the United States, where they could be sued on the basis of both negligence and strict liability. However, the incremental deterrence that would be gained if this trial were held in an American court is likely to be insignificant. The American interest in this accident is simply not sufficient to justify the enormous commitment of judicial time and resources that would inevitably be required if the case were to be tried here.

IV

. . . Thus, the judgment of the Court of Appeals is

Reversed.

■ [JUSTICE POWELL took no part in the decision of this case, and JUSTICE O'CONNOR took no part in its consideration or decision.]

■ [JUSTICE WHITE partly concurred in the majority opinion and partly dissented. JUSTICE STEVENS, joined by Justice Brennan, dissented. These opinions—which agreed with Part II of the Court's opinion, but maintained for reasons not relevant here that the Court should not have considered the issues addressed in Part III—are omitted.]

Questions: (71) Courts still often condition a forum non conveniens dismissal on the defendant's effective waiver of the statute of limitations. See, e.g., In re Union Carbide Corp. Gas Plant Disaster at Bhopal, India in Dec., 1984, 809 F.2d 195 (2d Cir.1987) (dismissal also conditioned on submission to personal jurisdiction of Indian court), discussed in John Bies, Comment, Conditioning Forum Non Conveniens, 67 U.Chi.L.Rev. 489 (2000). Have the courts thereby created an analogue of § 1406(a) for forum non conveniens?

(72) If a substantive defense would otherwise block the suit elsewhere, *must* a district court condition dismissal in order to create an alternative forum and thus satisfy a threshold requirement, or is this merely a situation where the court *may* so act in its discretion and as an incident to its balancing of interests? If the latter, as Piper might suggest, what should be the district court's approach on when to impose such a condition (or exact other concessions on procedural matters, such as discovery)?

FORUM NON CONVENIENS

A good case can be made for transfer of venue between federal courts, as it efficiently and fairly works to remove unjust forum advantage. See Kevin M. Clermont & Theodore Eisenberg, Exorcising the Evil of Forum–Shopping, 80 Cornell L.Rev. 1507 (1995). But forum non conveniens in the federal courts, which applies primarily when the preferred court is foreign, is quite a different doctrine.

This doctrine tends to be fatal in application. In a survey of the plaintiffs' lawyers in the 180 reported transnational cases that the federal courts dismissed on forum non conveniens grounds from 1947 to 1984, responses covered 85 cases; of those 85, not one resulted in a plaintiff's win in the foreign court; most cases were abandoned or settled for little. David W. Robertson, Forum Non Conveniens in America and England: "A Rather Fantastic Fiction," 103 Law Q.Rev. 398, 418–20 (1987); see also David W. Robertson, The Federal Doctrine of Forum Non Conveniens: "An Object Lesson in Uncontrolled Discretion," 29 Tex.Int'l L.J. 353 (1994) (arguing for reliable rules to temper judicial discretion and otherwise to narrow forum non conveniens).

With such a stark effect on outcome, is it fair then for Piper in large part both to ignore change in law and to dismiss on the basis of mere inconvenience? Should forum non conveniens instead be applied as a doctrine of abuse, with dismissal only when the plaintiff has so abused the privilege of forum-selection that, all things considered, going forward would be a miscarriage of justice?

The lower federal courts seldom grant forum non conveniens dismissals, and the judge commonly conditions a dismissal on the defendant's varied concessions to offset an unfair change in procedural or substantive law sufficiently to keep the dismissal from being its own miscarriage of justice. Thus, perhaps forum non conveniens is in practice a doctrine of abuse, and Piper just works to remove its rigidities so that it can be an all-things-considered doctrine. See, e.g., Tuazon v. R.J. Reynolds Tobacco Co., 433 F.3d 1163 (9th Cir.2006) (affirming the Western District of Washington's finding of general jurisdiction over tobacco company and its denying of forum non conveniens dismissal, in a product-liability action brought by a Philippine smoker). But see, e.g., In re Factor VIII or IX Concentrate Blood Prods. Litig., 484 F.3d 951 (7th Cir.2007) (affirming dismissal of action against American manufacturers of blood-clotting products, brought by infected hemophiliac foreigners).

Yet, if forum non conveniens becomes merely a doctrine of abuse, what would it contribute beyond territorial jurisdiction's unreasonableness test—besides multiplying costs, increasing uncertainty, and facilitating discrimination against foreigners? Perhaps the desirable course of narrowing territorial reach should be approached openly and directly by legislative reform of jurisdiction and venue, rather than surreptitiously and dangerously by a judicial embrace of forum non conveniens.

Question: (73) Forum non conveniens obviously remains an important doctrine in almost all state courts. But what of allowing transfer between courts of different states? Think of the various ways we could implement and design such a system. One method that does not necessitate federal involvement would have states enact uniform transfer laws. In fact, the Uniform Transfer of Litigation Act, approved by the National Conference of Commissioners on Uniform State Laws in 1991, provides that the enacting state's courts may make or receive a transfer in cooperation with any other sovereign's court; the Act permits transfer by a court with jurisdiction to a consenting court that has subject-matter jurisdiction, and also permits transfer by a court lacking jurisdiction to a consenting court that has subject-matter and territorial jurisdiction; and the Act contains provisions regularizing some subsidiary concerns such as appellate review and statute of limitations. See also Leonard J. Feldman, The Interstate Compact: A Cooperative Solution to Complex Litigation in State Courts, 12 Rev.Litig. 137 (1992).

TOPIC C

OPPORTUNITY TO BE HEARD

SECTION 1. GENERAL OBSERVATIONS

Mullane v. Central Hanover Bank & Trust Co.

Supreme Court of the United States, 1950.
339 U.S. 306, 70 S.Ct. 652.

■ [The facts appear in the portion of the majority's opinion reprinted supra p. 560. After finding adequate nexus, JUSTICE JACKSON proceeded to the question of notice:]

Quite different from the question of a state's power to discharge trustees is that of the opportunity it must give beneficiaries to contest. Many controversies have raged about the cryptic and abstract words of the Due Process Clause but there can be no doubt that at a minimum they require that deprivation of life, liberty or property by adjudication be preceded by notice and opportunity for hearing appropriate to the nature of the case.

In two ways this proceeding does or may deprive beneficiaries of property. It may cut off their rights to have the trustee answer for negligent or illegal impairment of their interests. Also, their interests are presumably subject to diminution in the proceeding by allowance of fees and expenses to one who, in their names but without their knowledge, may conduct a fruitless or uncompensatory contest. Certainly the proceeding is one in which they may be deprived of property rights and hence notice and hearing must measure up to the standards of due process.

Personal service of written notice within the jurisdiction is the classic form of notice always adequate in any type of proceeding. But the vital interest of the State in bringing any issues as to its fiduciaries to a final settlement can be served only if interests or claims of individuals who are outside of the State can somehow be determined. A construction of the Due Process Clause which would place impossible or impractical obstacles in the way could not be justified.

Against this interest of the State we must balance the individual interest sought to be protected by the Fourteenth Amendment. This is defined by our holding that "The fundamental requisite of due process of law is the opportunity to be heard." Grannis v. Ordean, 234 U.S. 385, 394, 34 S.Ct. 779, 783. This right to be heard has little reality or worth unless one is informed that the matter is pending and can choose for himself whether to appear or default, acquiesce or contest.

The Court has not committed itself to any formula achieving a balance between these interests in a particular proceeding or determining when constructive notice may be utilized or what test it must meet. Personal service has not in all circumstances been regarded as indispensable to the process due to residents, and it has more often been held unnecessary as to nonresidents. We disturb none of the established rules on these subjects. No decision constitutes a controlling or even a very illuminating precedent for the case before us. But a few general principles stand out in the books.

An elementary and fundamental requirement of due process in any proceeding which is to be accorded finality is notice reasonably calculated, under all the circumstances, to apprise interested parties of the pendency of the action and afford them an opportunity to present their objections. Milliken v. Meyer, 311 U.S. 457, 61 S.Ct. 339; Grannis v. Ordean, 234 U.S. 385, 34 S.Ct. 779; Priest v. Board of Trustees of Town of Las Vegas, 232 U.S. 604, 34 S.Ct. 443; Roller v. Holly, 176 U.S. 398, 20 S.Ct. 410. The notice must be of such nature as reasonably to convey the required information, Grannis v. Ordean, supra, and it must afford a reasonable time for those interested to make their appearance, Roller v. Holly, supra, and cf. Goodrich v. Ferris, 214 U.S. 71, 29 S.Ct. 580. But if with due regard for the practicalities and peculiarities of the case these conditions are reasonably met, the constitutional requirements are satisfied. "The criterion is not the possibility of conceivable injury, but the just and reasonable character of the requirements, having reference to the subject with which the statute deals." American Land Co. v. Zeiss, 219 U.S. 47, 67, 31 S.Ct. 200, 207; and see Blinn v. Nelson, 222 U.S. 1, 7, 32 S.Ct. 1, 2.

But when notice is a person's due, process which is a mere gesture is not due process. The means employed must be such as one desirous of actually informing the absentee might reasonably adopt to accomplish it. The reasonableness and hence the constitutional validity of any chosen method may be defended on the ground that it is in itself reasonably certain to inform those affected, compare Hess v. Pawloski, 274 U.S. 352, 47 S.Ct. 632, with Wuchter v. Pizzutti, 276 U.S. 13, 48 S.Ct. 259, or, where conditions do not reasonably permit such notice, that the form chosen is not substantially less likely to bring home notice than other of the feasible and customary substitutes.

It would be idle to pretend that publication alone, as prescribed here, is a reliable means of acquainting interested parties of the fact that their rights are before the courts. It is not an accident that the greater number of cases reaching this Court on the question of adequacy of notice have been concerned with actions founded on process constructively served through local newspapers. Chance alone brings to the attention of even a local resident an advertisement in small type inserted in the back pages of a newspaper, and if he makes his home outside the area of the newspaper's normal circulation the odds that the information will never reach him are large indeed. The chance of actual notice is further reduced when, as here, the notice required does not even name those whose attention it is supposed to attract, and does not inform acquaintances who might call it to attention. In weighing its sufficiency on the basis of equivalence with actual notice we are unable to regard this as more than a feint.

Nor is publication here reinforced by steps likely to attract the parties' attention to the proceeding. It is true that publication traditionally has been acceptable as notification supplemental to other action which in itself may reasonably be expected to convey a warning. The ways of an owner with tangible property are such that he usually arranges means to learn of any direct attack upon his possessory or proprietary rights. Hence, libel of a ship, attachment of a chattel or entry upon real estate in the name of law may reasonably be expected to come promptly to the owner's attention. When the state within which the owner has located such property seizes it for some reason, publication or posting affords an additional measure of notification. A state may indulge the assumption that one who has left tangible property in the state either has abandoned it, in which case proceedings against it deprive him of nothing, [citations omitted], or that he has left some caretaker under a duty to let him know that it is being jeopardized. [Citations omitted.] As phrased long ago by Chief Justice Marshall in The Mary, 9 Cranch 126, 144, "It is the part of common prudence for all those who have any interest in [a thing], to guard that interest by persons who are in a situation to protect it."

In the case before us there is, of course, no abandonment. On the other hand these beneficiaries do have a resident fiduciary as caretaker of their interest in this property. But it is their caretaker who in the accounting becomes their adversary. Their trustee is released from giving notice of jeopardy, and no one else is expected to do so. Not even the special guardian is required or apparently expected to communicate with his ward and client, and, of course, if such a duty were merely transferred from the trustee to the guardian, economy would not be served and more likely the cost would be increased.

This Court has not hesitated to approve of resort to publication as a customary substitute in another class of cases where it is not reasonably possible or practicable to give more adequate warning. Thus it has been recognized that, in the case of persons missing or unknown, employment of an indirect and even a probably futile means of notification is all that the situation permits and creates no constitutional bar to a final decree foreclosing their rights. [Citations omitted.]

Those beneficiaries represented by appellant whose interests or whereabouts could not with due diligence be ascertained come clearly within this category. As to them the statutory notice is sufficient. However great the odds that publication will never reach the eyes of such unknown parties, it is not in the typical case much more likely to fail than any of the choices open to legislators endeavoring to prescribe the best notice practicable.

Nor do we consider it unreasonable for the State to dispense with more certain notice to those beneficiaries whose interests are either conjectural or future or, although they could be discovered upon investigation, do not in due course of business come to knowledge of the common trustee. Whatever searches might be required in another situation under ordinary standards of diligence, in view of the character of the proceedings and the nature of the interests here involved we think them unnecessary. We recognize the practical difficulties and costs that would be attendant on frequent investigations into the status of great numbers of beneficiaries, many of whose interests in the common fund are so remote as to be ephemeral; and we have no doubt that such impracticable and extended searches are not required in the name of due process. The expense of keeping informed from day to day of substitutions among even current income beneficiaries and presumptive remaindermen, to say nothing of the far greater number of contingent beneficiaries, would impose a severe burden on the plan, and would likely dissipate its advantages. These are practical matters in which we should be reluctant to disturb the judgment of the state authorities.

Accordingly we overrule appellant's constitutional objections to published notice insofar as they are urged on behalf of any beneficiaries whose interests or addresses are unknown to the trustee.

As to known present beneficiaries of known place of residence, however, notice by publication stands on a different footing. Exceptions in the name of necessity do not sweep away the rule that within the limits of practicability notice must be such as is reasonably calculated to reach interested parties. Where the names and post office addresses of those affected by a proceeding are at hand, the reasons disappear for resort to means less likely than the mails to apprise them of its pendency.

The trustee has on its books the names and addresses of the income beneficiaries represented by appellant, and we find no tenable ground for dispensing with a serious effort to inform them personally of the accounting, at least by ordinary mail to the record addresses. Cf. Wuchter v. Pizzutti, supra. Certainly sending them a copy of the statute months and perhaps years in advance does not answer this purpose. The trustee periodically remits their income to them, and we think that they might reasonably expect that with or apart from their remittances word might come to them personally that steps were being taken affecting their interests.

We need not weigh contentions that a requirement of personal service of citation on even the large number of known resident or nonresident beneficiaries would, by reasons of delay if not of expense, seriously interfere with the proper administration of the fund. Of course personal service even without the jurisdiction of the issuing authority serves the end of actual and personal notice, whatever power of compulsion it might lack. However, no such service is required under the circumstances. This type of trust presupposes a large number of small interests. The individual interest does not stand alone but is identical with that of a class. The rights of each in the integrity of the fund and the fidelity of the trustee are shared by many other beneficiaries. Therefore notice reasonably certain to reach most of those interested in objecting is likely to safeguard the interests of all, since any objections sustained would inure to the benefit of all. We think that under such circumstances reasonable risks that notice might not actually reach every beneficiary are justifiable. "Now and then an extraordinary case may turn up, but constitutional law like other mortal contrivances has to take some chances, and in the great majority of instances no doubt justice will be done." Blinn v. Nelson, supra, 222 U.S. at page 7, 32 S.Ct. at page 2.

The statutory notice to known beneficiaries is inadequate not because in fact it fails to reach everyone, but because under the circumstances it is not reasonably calculated to reach those who could easily be informed by other means at hand. However it may have been in former times, the mails today are recognized as an efficient and inexpensive means of communication. Moreover, the fact that the trust company has been able to give mailed notice to known beneficiaries at the time the common trust fund was established is persuasive that postal notification at the time of accounting would not seriously burden the plan.

In some situations the law requires greater precautions in its proceedings than the business world accepts for its own purposes. In few, if any, will it be satisfied with less. Certainly it is instructive, in determining the reasonableness of the impersonal broadcast notification here used, to ask whether it would satisfy a prudent man of business, counting his pennies but finding it in his interest to convey information to many persons whose names and addresses are in his files. We are not satisfied that it would. Publication may theoretically be available for all the world to see, but it is too much in our day to suppose that each or any individual beneficiary does or could examine all that is published to see if something may be tucked away in it that affects his property interests. We have before indicated in reference to notice by publication that, "Great caution should be used not to let fiction deny the fair play that can be secured only by a pretty close adhesion to fact." McDonald v. Mabee, 243 U.S. 90, 91, 37 S.Ct. 343.

We hold that the notice of judicial settlement of accounts required by the New York Banking Law § 100–c(12) is incompatible with the requirements of the Fourteenth Amendment as a basis for adjudication depriving known persons whose whereabouts are also known of substantial property rights. Accordingly the judgment is reversed and the cause remanded for further proceedings not inconsistent with this opinion.

Reversed.

■ MR. JUSTICE DOUGLAS took no part in the consideration or decision of this case.

■ MR. JUSTICE BURTON, dissenting.

These common trusts are available only when the instruments creating the participating trusts permit participation in the common fund. Whether or not further notice to beneficiaries should supplement the notice and representation here provided is properly within the discretion of the State. The Federal Constitution does not require it here.

Question: (1) What changes in the statute would you, as counsel to the appropriate committee of the New York legislature, recommend for adoption? See N.Y. Banking Law § 100–c(6), as amended by 1951 N.Y. Laws ch. 778, § 3, by which New York sought to meet the defects revealed by the Mullane case.

MENNONITE BOARD OF MISSIONS v. ADAMS, 462 U.S. 791, 103 S.Ct. 2706 (1983). In the course of lengthy proceedings to sell certain real property consequent to the owner's nonpayment of taxes, notice was posted in the county courthouse and published a number of times. Also, the county sent notice by certified mail to the owner. After title had passed, cutting off a recorded mortgage on the property, the mortgagee learned of the proceedings. The tax-sale purchaser then brought suit to quiet title, during which the mortgagee challenged the adequacy of notice of the tax sale. The Indiana courts upheld the prescribed procedure that had been employed.

On appeal, the United States Supreme Court reversed. Justice Marshall for the Court began by discussing Mullane and continued:

"In subsequent cases, this Court has adhered unwaveringly to the principle announced in Mullane. In Walker v. City of Hutchinson, 352 U.S. 112, 77 S.Ct. 200 (1956), for example, the Court held that notice of condemnation proceedings published in a local newspaper was an inadequate means of informing a landowner whose name was known to the city and was on the official records. Similarly, in Schroeder v. City of New York, 371 U.S. 208, 83 S.Ct. 279 (1962), the Court concluded that publication in a newspaper and posted notices were inadequate to apprise a property owner of condemnation proceedings when his name and address were readily ascertainable from both deed records and tax rolls. Most recently, in Greene v. Lindsey, 456 U.S. 444, 102 S.Ct. 1874 (1982), we held that posting a summons on the door of a tenant's apartment was an inadequate means of providing notice of forcible entry and detainer actions. [Citations omitted.]

"This case is controlled by the analysis in Mullane. To begin with, a mortgagee possesses a substantial property interest that is significantly affected by a tax sale. . . .

"Since a mortgagee clearly has a legally protected property interest, he is entitled to notice reasonably calculated to apprise him of a pending tax sale. [Citation omitted.] When the mortgagee is identified in a mortgage that is publicly recorded, constructive notice by publication must be supplemented by notice mailed to the mortgagee's last known available address, or by personal service. But unless the mortgagee is not reasonably identifiable, constructive notice alone does not satisfy the mandate of Mullane.

. . . .

"Personal service or mailed notice is required even though sophisticated creditors have means at their disposal to discover whether property taxes have not been paid and whether tax sale proceedings are therefore likely to be initiated. . . . It is true that particularly extensive efforts to provide notice may often be required when the State is aware of a party's inexperience or incompetence. [Citations omitted.] But it does not follow that the State may forgo even the relatively modest administrative burden of providing notice by mail to parties who are particularly resourceful. [Citation omitted.] Notice by mail or other means as certain to ensure actual notice is a minimum constitutional precondition to a proceeding which will adversely affect the liberty or property interests of *any* party, whether unlettered or well versed in commercial practice, if its name and address are reasonably ascertainable."

Justice O'Connor, joined by Justices Powell and Rehnquist, dissented. She argued that the Court was departing from Mullane by adopting a rigid rule against constructive notice, rather than using a balancing approach in circumstances where the mortgagee could have protected its own interest.[a]

PROCEDURAL DUE PROCESS

Procedural due process normally requires that a person or his representative receive notice and opportunity to be heard before governmental action unduly impairs his property or liberty interests. The Fourteenth Amendment extends these protections to action by a state government, while the Fifth Amendment covers action by the federal government.

In order to satisfy this constitutional prerequisite for civil adjudication, fair notice of the pendency of the lawsuit must go to any person whose interests are to be so affected or to his representative, unless waived. Fair notice must be suitably formal in tenor and informative in content. Also, fair notice must be either actual notice or notice that is reasonably calculated to result in actual notice.

A fair opportunity to be heard is also critical to procedural due process. Notice to a defendant of a claim being made against him is of no value to him if he gets no opportunity to defend the action. See Roller v. Holly, 176 U.S. 398, 20 S.Ct. 410 (1900). Indeed, it would seem that the real concern of procedural due process here is opportunity to be heard. Notice is merely the means to make possible the exercise of that right.

If the person entitled to notice and opportunity to be heard duly challenges their adequacy, the court will pass on the constitutional requirements. The typical setting where such a challenge might succeed is the defendant's attack after a default judgment. Here the Constitution generally requires the courts to provide relief from judgment if there was a violation of procedural due process, whether or not the defendant has a

---

[a] Interestingly, in a decision five days after Mennonite, its dissenters joined Chief Justice Burger and Justices Brennan and Stevens to form a new majority ruling that a known putative father who had never established any relationship with his child was not entitled to any notice of adoption proceedings. Lehr v. Robertson, 463 U.S. 248, 103 S.Ct. 2985 (1983) (Stevens, J.).

meritorious defense on the merits. Peralta v. Heights Med. Ctr., Inc., 485 U.S. 80, 108 S.Ct. 896 (1988).

On the one hand, if a reasonable method of notification was employed, mere failure to achieve actual notice will not undermine the validity of a default judgment. See Restatement (Second) of Judgments § 2 (1982). However, if the plaintiff chooses an otherwise reasonable means of notice that is substantially less likely to give actual notice than another reasonable means, the failure to give actual notice will invalidate the resulting default judgment.

On the other hand, authority persists for the somewhat surprising proposition that if the method of notification prescribed by statute, rule, or order is not reasonably calculated to result in actual notice, then notice by that method in the particular case is constitutionally defective even if the person in one way or another received actual notice. See 1 Robert C. Casad & William B. Richman, Jurisdiction in Civil Actions § 2–7[2][a] (3d ed. 1998). The idea is that we care about the steps that the government prescribes officially.

SERVICE OF PROCESS

Descending from the constitutional level, one encounters the regulations for serving process. State law lays out these regulations for state court, while Federal Rule 4 does so for federal court.

How inflexible are the prescribed procedures for service? NYCPLR § 308(5) provides for so-called expedient service in cases where service cannot practicably be made in these specified ways: service in hand; delivering process to a person of suitable age and discretion at defendant's abode or place of business, plus mailing to last known residence or to place of business; or affixing process to the door of defendant's abode or place of business, plus mailing. Pursuant to this subsection, expedient service may be made "in such manner as the court, upon motion without notice, directs."

In Dobkin v. Chapman, 21 N.Y.2d 490, 236 N.E.2d 451, 289 N.Y.S.2d 161 (1968), the New York Court of Appeals unanimously upheld the constitutionality of service in three automobile-accident cases against the contention that the methods provided by court order did not give the absent defendants sufficient chance of receiving actual notice of the commencement of the actions (incidentally, the uninsured motorist fund and the insurance company involved had challenged the service). The manner of notice ordered in the first case was ordinary mail to the address from which registered mail had been returned unclaimed; in the second case, one publication in a designated newspaper after registered mail had been returned unclaimed; and in the third case, where the defendant was known to be insured, delivery of copies of summons and complaint to the insurance carrier plus ordinary mail to the defendant's last known New York address. The court pointed out that in these cases it was the conduct of the defendants themselves—their removal without informing anyone of their whereabouts—that prevented service of process by the usual means. Chief Judge Fuld for the court said: "Indeed, in an automobile case, no defendant need be without notice unless he chooses and wants to be; many an injured plaintiff, however, will go without recompense if, in a proper case, the standards of informative notice may not be relaxed." The court relied upon Mullane, among other cases. It also referred to NYCPLR § 317, which gives a defendant served other than by personal delivery one year after learning of entry of judgment, but in no event more than five years after such entry, to come in and defend upon a finding that he did not actually receive timely notice and has a meritorious defense on the merits. See also Federal Rules 4(f)(3) and 55(c); Rio Props., Inc. v. Rio Int'l Interlink, 284 F.3d 1007 (9th Cir.2002) (approving court-ordered service by e-mail on an elusive Costa Rican defendant).

Local law may strictly enforce some of the nonconstitutional requirements of giving notice. For example, a defendant may succeed in attacking notice if the summons inaccurately named her or if the manner of service did not precisely comply with the statutes and rules. However, the trend is away from an overly strict approach, with courts now tending to ignore service irregularities where there was actual notice of suitable tenor and content and where the manner of transmitting and form of notice substantially complied with the prescribed procedure. See Restatement (Second) of Judgments §§ 2–3 (1982). Indeed, local law may dispense altogether with the requirement of formal service of process, as is done for example in connection with jurisdiction over plaintiffs for counterclaims.

SECTION 2. NOTICE BEFORE SEIZING PROPERTY

SNIADACH v. FAMILY FINANCE CORP., 395 U.S. 337, 89 S.Ct. 1820 (1969). Plaintiff finance company sued on a $420 promissory note in a Wisconsin state court, garnishing defendant's employer in order to secure any judgment that it might win. The garnishee answered, stating that it had $63.18 of the defendant's wages, earned and unpaid, and that it would pay the defendant one-half thereof as a subsistence allowance and hold the other half subject to the order of the court, as provided in a Wisconsin statute. Under that statute, the court clerk issues the garnishment summons at the request of the plaintiff's lawyer, who by serving the garnishee can then freeze the wages; the defendant must be served with the summons and complaint within ten days of service on the garnishee; if the defendant wins the main suit on the merits, the wages are restored to him, but in the interim he is deprived of them. The defendant moved to dismiss the garnishment proceedings for failure to provide procedural due process. The Wisconsin courts approved the garnishment procedure.

On certiorari, the Supreme Court reversed. After noting that wages are "a specialized type of property presenting distinct problems in our economic system," Justice Douglas for the Court held that the Wisconsin procedure violated the Fourteenth Amendment by failure to provide notice and opportunity to be heard before the garnishment. Justice Black was the lone dissenter.

FUENTES v. SHEVIN, 407 U.S. 67, 92 S.Ct. 1983 (1972). In Florida, Mrs. Fuentes purchased a stove and a stereo under conditional sales contracts that provided for monthly payments and for repossession by the seller in case of any default in payment by the buyer. Under the contracts, the seller retained a U.C.C. security interest in the goods pending full payment, but the buyer was entitled to possession absent default. The total cost of the stove and stereo was about $500, plus a financing charge of over $100. More than a year later, after a dispute over servicing the stove, Fuentes stopped making payments while still owing about $200 under the contracts. The seller initiated an action for repossession in small-claims court, simultaneously obtaining a writ of replevin ordering state agents to seize the stove and stereo. The same day a deputy sheriff went with the seller's employee to Fuentes' home, served her, and seized the disputed goods. The relevant Florida statute provides for summary issuance of a writ of replevin upon ex parte application to the court clerk by someone suing on a claim to possession of "wrongfully detained" property and upon the plaintiff's posting a bond for double the value of the property; the agent who makes the seizure holds the property for three days, during which time the defendant may regain possession of the property upon posting his own bond for double the property's value; if the defendant does not so act, the property then passes to the plaintiff, pending the final disposition of the underlying repossession action. Shortly after the seizure, Fuentes sued in federal court, challenging the replevin proceedings on procedural due process grounds.[b] Relief was denied.

On appeal, the Supreme Court reversed, holding by Justice Stewart, joined by Justices Douglas, Brennan, and Marshall, that the Florida procedure (and the similar Pennsylvania procedure involved in a companion case) violated the Fourteenth Amendment by failure to provide notice and opportunity to be heard before deprivation of a possessory interest in property. The required hearing would aim at establishing at least the probable validity of the underlying claim. Justice White, joined by Chief Justice Burger and Justice Blackmun, filed a dissenting opinion. He argued that due process calls for a more flexible approach, that the process and outcome values served by pre-seizure notice and opportunity to be heard should be weighed against other interests, and that in the real world the illusory benefits of such procedure do not match the considerable costs to

[b] For background on this important case, see C. Michael Abbott & Donald C. Peters, Fuentes v. Shevin: A Narrative of Federal Test Litigation in the Legal Services Program, 57 Iowa L.Rev. 955 (1972).

the public, creditors, consumers, and even debtors. Newly appointed Justices Powell and Rehnquist did not participate.

MITCHELL v. W.T. GRANT CO., 416 U.S. 600, 94 S.Ct. 1895 (1974). In Louisiana, W.T. Grant sold a refrigerator, range, stereo, and washer to Mr. Mitchell under installment sales contracts. About a year later, Grant sued in city court for the overdue and unpaid balance of $574.17, Mitchell having paid less than one-quarter of his total principal obligation; Grant alleged having a vendor's lien on the goods securing the unpaid balance, which lien would under state law expire if Mitchell transferred possession. Grant simultaneously obtained a writ of sequestration ordering state agents to seize the goods. Soon thereafter the constable served Mitchell at home and, at the same time, seized the disputed goods. The relevant Louisiana statute allows sequestration if the plaintiff claims ownership or right to possession of property or a lien thereon and if it would otherwise be within the defendant's power to dispose of or remove the property during the pendency of the action; the plaintiff must state specific facts by affidavit supporting issuance of the writ and must file a bond sufficient to protect the defendant against any damage resulting from wrongful issuance; ex parte application to a judge accomplishes issuance; the defendant may immediately seek dissolution of the writ, which the court must then order unless the plaintiff proves the grounds upon which the writ issued—the existence of the debt, lien, and delinquency; the defendant may also regain possession upon posting his own bond for 125% of the lesser of the value of the property or the amount of the claim. Mitchell moved to dissolve the writ of sequestration for failure to provide procedural due process. The Louisiana courts approved the sequestration procedure.

On certiorari, the Supreme Court affirmed, with Justices Powell and Rehnquist joining the three Fuentes dissenters to form a new majority. Justice White delivered the opinion of the Court, which declared in part: "In our view, this statutory procedure effects a constitutional accommodation of the conflicting interests of the parties. We cannot accept petitioner's broad assertion that the Due Process Clause of the Fourteenth Amendment guaranteed to him the use and possession of the goods until all issues in the case were judicially resolved after full adversary proceedings had been completed." Justice Powell issued a concurring opinion. The former majority in Fuentes was now in dissent, arguing that the Fuentes decision controlled.

NORTH GEORGIA FINISHING, INC. v. DI–CHEM, INC., 419 U.S. 601, 95 S.Ct. 719 (1975). Di–Chem filed suit against the corporate defendant in a Georgia state court for goods sold and delivered in the amount of $51,279.17, simultaneously obtaining process for garnishing the defendant's bank account. The relevant Georgia statute provides for garnishment upon the plaintiff's or his attorney's submitting to the court clerk an affidavit stating the amount claimed and reason to apprehend loss; the plaintiff must file a bond for double the amount claimed to protect the defendant against any damage resulting from wrongful issuance; the defendant may dissolve the garnishment by filing a bond for the amount claimed. Right after service of process, the defendant filed a bond to dissolve the garnishment. Then it moved to dismiss the garnishment proceedings and discharge its bond, arguing violation of procedural due process. The Georgia courts approved the garnishment procedure.

On certiorari, the Supreme Court reversed on Fourteenth Amendment grounds. Justice White switched sides to join the Mitchell dissenters and delivered the opinion of the Court. His opinion seemed to resuscitate Fuentes. He distinguished Mitchell by noting the Louisiana statute's requirement of a plaintiff's affidavit going beyond mere conclusory allegations and setting out clearly the facts entitling the plaintiff to seizure, its requirement of issuance by a judge, and its provision of a hearing immediately after seizure where the plaintiff must prove the grounds for the writ's issuance. In this Georgia case, the affidavit asserted the debt and "reason to apprehend the loss of said sum or some part thereof unless process of Garnishment issues," a court clerk issued the writ, and there was no provision for an early hearing where the plaintiff had "to demonstrate at least probable cause for the garnishment. . . . It may be that consumers deprived of household appliances will more likely suffer irreparably than corporations deprived of bank accounts, but the probability of irreparable injury in the latter case is sufficiently great so that some procedures are necessary to guard against the risk of initial error. We are no more inclined now than we have been in the past to distinguish among different kinds of property in applying the Due Process Clause. Fuentes v. Shevin, 407 U.S., at 89–90, 92 S.Ct., at 1998–1999." He concluded his brief opinion: "Enough has been said, we think, to require the reversal of the judgment of the Georgia Supreme Court."

Justice Powell concurred in the judgment, incidentally arguing that issuance by a court clerk would suffice under a Mitchell-type statute.

Justice Blackmun, joined by Justice Rehnquist and Chief Justice Burger, observed in dissent: "Neither do I conclude that, because this is a garnishment case, rather than a lien or vendor-vendee case, it is automatically controlled by Sniadach. Sniadach, as has been noted, concerned and reeks of wages. North Georgia Finishing is no wage earner. It is a corporation engaged in business. It was protected (a) by the fact that the garnishment procedure may be instituted in Georgia only after the primary suit has been filed or judgment obtained by the creditor, thus placing on the creditor the obligation to initiate the proceedings and the burden of proof, and assuring a full hearing to the debtor; (b) by the respondent's statutorily required and deposited double bond; and (c) by the requirement of the respondent's affidavit of apprehension of loss. It was in a position to dissolve the garnishment by the filing of a single bond. These are transactions of a day-to-day type in the commercial world. They are not situations involving contracts of adhesion or basic unfairness, imbalance, or inequality. See D.H. Overmyer Co. v. Frick Co., 405 U.S. 174, 92 S.Ct. 775 (1972); Swarb v. Lennox, 405 U.S. 191, 92 S.Ct. 767 (1972). The clerk-judge distinction, relied on by the Court, surely is of little significance so long as the court officer is not an agent of the creditor. The Georgia system, for me, affords commercial entities all the protection that is required by the Due Process Clause of the Fourteenth Amendment."

Questions: (2) What would Di–Chem have to show in the hearing required by the Supreme Court?

(3) If Georgia had had an applicable Mitchell-type statute, with which Di–Chem had complied, would the result have been different (even though Di–Chem had no pre-existing interest in the bank account)?

Connecticut v. Doehr

Supreme Court of the United States, 1991.
501 U.S. 1, 111 S.Ct. 2105.

■ JUSTICE WHITE delivered an opinion, Parts I, II, and III of which are the opinion of the Court.

This case requires us to determine whether a state statute that authorizes prejudgment attachment of real estate without prior notice or hearing, without a showing of extraordinary circumstances, and without a requirement that the person seeking the attachment post a bond, satisfies the Due Process Clause of the Fourteenth Amendment. We hold that, as applied to this case, it does not.

I

On March 15, 1988, petitioner John F. DiGiovanni submitted an application to the Connecticut Superior Court for an attachment in the amount of $75,000 on respondent Brian K. Doehr's home in Meriden, Connecticut. DiGiovanni took this step in conjunction with a civil action for assault and battery that he was seeking to institute against Doehr in the same court. The suit did not involve Doehr's real estate nor did DiGiovanni have any pre-existing interest either in Doehr's home or any of his other property.

Connecticut law authorizes prejudgment attachment of real estate without affording prior notice or the opportunity for a prior hearing to the individual whose property is subject to the attachment. The State's prejudgment remedy statute provides, in relevant part:

> "The court or a judge of the court may allow the prejudgment remedy to be issued by an attorney without hearing as provided in sections 52–278c and 52–278d upon verification by oath of the plaintiff or of some

> competent affiant, that there is probable cause to sustain the validity of the plaintiff's claim and (1) that the prejudgment remedy requested is for an attachment of real property[; or (2) that there is reasonable likelihood that the defendant (A) neither resides in nor maintains an office or place of business in this state and is not otherwise subject to jurisdiction over his person by the court, or (B) has hidden or will hide himself so that process cannot be served on him or (C) is about to remove himself or his property from this state or (D) is about to fraudulently dispose of or has fraudulently disposed of any of his property with intent to hinder, delay, or defraud his creditors or (E) has fraudulently hidden or withheld money, property, or effects which should be liable to the satisfaction of his debts or (F) has stated he is insolvent or has stated he is unable to pay his debts as they mature.] . . ." Conn.Gen.Stat. § 52–278e(a) (1991).[c]

The statute does not require the plaintiff to post a bond to insure the payment of damages that the defendant may suffer should the attachment prove wrongfully issued or the claim prove unsuccessful.

As required, DiGiovanni submitted an affidavit in support of his application. In five one-sentence paragraphs, DiGiovanni stated that the facts set forth in his previously submitted complaint were true; that "I was willfully, wantonly and maliciously assaulted by the defendant, Brian K. Doehr"; that "[s]aid assault and battery broke my left wrist and further caused an ecchymosis to my right eye, as well as other injuries"; and that "I have further expended sums of money for medical care and treatment." The affidavit concluded with the statement, "In my opinion, the foregoing facts are sufficient to show that there is probable cause that judgment will be rendered for the plaintiff."

On the strength of these submissions the Superior Court judge, by an order dated March 17, found "probable cause to sustain the validity of the plaintiff's claim" and ordered the attachment on Doehr's home "to the value of $75,000." The sheriff attached the property four days later, on March 21. Only after this did Doehr receive notice of the attachment. He also had yet to be served with the complaint, which is ordinarily necessary for an action to commence in Connecticut. [Citation omitted.] As the statute further required, the attachment notice informed Doehr that he had the right to a hearing: (1) to claim that no probable cause existed to sustain the claim; (2) to request that the attachment be vacated, modified, or that a bond be substituted; or (3) to claim that some portion of the property was exempt from execution. Conn.Gen.Stat. § 52–278e(b) (1991).

Rather than pursue these options, Doehr filed suit against DiGiovanni in Federal District Court, claiming [with similarly situated joined parties] that § 52–278e(a)(1) was unconstitutional under the Due Process Clause of the Fourteenth Amendment. The District Court upheld the statute and granted summary judgment in favor of DiGiovanni. Pinsky v. Duncan, 716

[c] As a consequence of this decision by the U.S. Supreme Court, Connecticut rewrote this statute, so that today it preserves only (2)(B)–(E) as "exigent circumstances" excusing pre-seizure notice and hearing.

F.Supp. 58 (Conn.1989). On appeal, a divided panel of the United States Court of Appeals for the Second Circuit reversed. Pinsky v. Duncan, 898 F.2d 852 (1990).[3] Judge Pratt, who wrote the opinion for the court, concluded that the Connecticut statute violated due process in permitting ex parte attachment absent a showing of extraordinary circumstances. "The rule to be derived from Sniadach and its progeny, therefore, is not that postattachment hearings are generally acceptable provided that the plaintiff files a factual affidavit and that a judicial officer supervises the process, but that a prior hearing may be postponed where exceptional circumstances justify such a delay, *and where* sufficient additional safeguards are present." Id., at 855. This conclusion was deemed to be consistent with our decision in Mitchell v. W.T. Grant Co., 416 U.S. 600, 94 S.Ct. 1895 (1974), because the absence of a preattachment hearing was approved in that case based on the presence of extraordinary circumstances.

A further reason to invalidate the statute, the court ruled, was the highly factual nature of the issues in this case. In Mitchell, there were "uncomplicated matters that len[t] themselves to documentary proof" and "[t]he nature of the issues at stake minimize[d] the risk that the writ [would] be wrongfully issued by a judge." Id., at 609–610, 94 S.Ct., at 1901. Similarly, in Mathews v. Eldridge, 424 U.S. 319, 343–344, 96 S.Ct. 893, 907 (1976), where an evidentiary hearing was not required prior to the termination of disability benefits, the determination of disability was "sharply focused and easily documented." Judge Pratt observed that in contrast the present case involved the fact-specific event of a fist fight and the issue of assault. He doubted that the judge could reliably determine probable cause when presented with only the plaintiff's version of the altercation. "Because the risk of a wrongful attachment is considerable under these circumstances, we conclude that dispensing with notice and opportunity for a hearing until after the attachment, without a showing of extraordinary circumstances, violates the requirements of due process." 898 F.2d at 856. . . .

. . . .

The dissent's conclusion accorded with the views of Connecticut Supreme Court, which had previously upheld § 52–278e in Fermont Division, Dynamics Corp. of America v. Smith, 178 Conn. 393, 423 A.2d 80 (1979). We granted certiorari to resolve the conflict of authority. 498 U.S. 809, 111 S.Ct. 42 (1990).

II

With this case we return to the question of what process must be afforded by a state statute enabling an individual to enlist the aid of the State to deprive another of his or her property by means of the prejudgment attachment or similar procedure. Our cases reflect the numerous

[3] The Court of Appeals invited Connecticut to intervene pursuant to 28 U.S.C. § 2403(b) after oral argument. The State elected to intervene in the appeal, and has fully participated in the proceedings before this Court.

variations this type of remedy can entail. [The Court here described the Sniadach, Fuentes, Mitchell, and Di–Chem cases.]

These cases "underscore the truism that '[d]ue process, unlike some legal rules, is not a technical conception with a fixed content unrelated to time, place and circumstances.' " Mathews v. Eldridge, supra, 424 U.S., at 334, 96 S.Ct., at 902 (quoting Cafeteria Workers v. McElroy, 367 U.S. 886, 895, 81 S.Ct. 1743, 1748 (1961)). In Mathews, we drew upon our prejudgment remedy decisions to determine what process is due when the government itself seeks to effect a deprivation on its own initiative. Mathews, 424 U.S., at 334, 96 S.Ct., at 902. That analysis resulted in the now familiar threefold inquiry requiring consideration of "the private interest that will be affected by the official action"; "the risk of an erroneous deprivation of such interest through the procedures used, and the probable value, if any, of additional or substitute safeguards"; and lastly "the Government's interest, including the function involved and the fiscal and administrative burdens that the additional or substitute procedural requirement would entail." Id., at 335, 96 S.Ct., at 903.

Here the inquiry is similar but the focus is different. Prejudgment remedy statutes ordinarily apply to disputes between private parties rather than between an individual and the government. Such enactments are designed to enable one of the parties to "make use of state procedures with the overt, significant assistance of state officials," and they undoubtedly involve state action "substantial enough to implicate the Due Process Clause." Tulsa Professional Collection Services, Inc. v. Pope, 485 U.S. 478, 486, 108 S.Ct. 1340, 1345 (1988). Nonetheless, any burden that increasing procedural safeguards entails primarily affects not the government, but the party seeking control of the other's property. See Fuentes v. Shevin, supra, 407 U.S., at 99–101, 92 S.Ct., at 2003–2005 (White, J., dissenting). For this type of case, therefore, the relevant inquiry requires, as in Mathews, first, consideration of the private interest that will be affected by the prejudgment measure; second, an examination of the risk of erroneous deprivation through the procedures under attack and the probable value of additional or alternative safeguards; and third, in contrast to Mathews, principal attention to the interest of the party seeking the prejudgment remedy, with, nonetheless, due regard for any ancillary interest the government may have in providing the procedure or forgoing the added burden of providing greater protections.

We now consider the Mathews factors in determining the adequacy of the procedures before us, first with regard to the safeguards of notice and a prior hearing, and then in relation to the protection of a bond.

III

We agree with the Court of Appeals that the property interests that attachment affects are significant. For a property owner like Doehr, attachment ordinarily clouds title; impairs the ability to sell or otherwise alienate the property; taints any credit rating; reduces the chance of obtaining a home equity loan or additional mortgage; and can even place an existing mortgage in technical default where there is an insecurity clause. Nor does Connecticut deny that any of these consequences occurs.

Instead, the State correctly points out that these effects do not amount to a complete, physical, or permanent deprivation of real property; their impact is less than the perhaps temporary total deprivation of household goods or wages. See Sniadach, supra, 395 U.S., at 340, 89 S.Ct., at 1822; Mitchell, supra, 416 U.S., at 613, 94 S.Ct., at 1903. But the Court has never held that only such extreme deprivations trigger due process concern. [Citation omitted.] To the contrary, our cases show that even the temporary or partial impairments to property rights that attachments, liens, and similar encumbrances entail are sufficient to merit due process protection. Without doubt, state procedures for creating and enforcing attachments, as with liens, "are subject to the strictures of due process." Peralta v. Heights Medical Center, Inc., 485 U.S. 80, 85, 108 S.Ct. 896, 899 (1988) (citing Mitchell, supra, 416 U.S., at 604, 94 S.Ct., at 1898; [other citation omitted]).[4]

We also agree with the Court of Appeals that the risk of erroneous deprivation that the State permits here is substantial. By definition, attachment statutes premise a deprivation of property on one ultimate factual contingency—the award of damages to the plaintiff which the defendant may not be able to satisfy. See Ownbey v. Morgan, 256 U.S. 94, 104–105, 41 S.Ct. 433, 435–436 (1921); [other citation omitted]. For attachments before judgment, Connecticut mandates that this determination be made by means of a procedural inquiry that asks whether "there is probable cause to sustain the validity of the plaintiff's claim." Conn.Gen. Stat. § 52–278e(a). The statute elsewhere defines the validity of the claim in terms of the likelihood "that judgment will be rendered in the matter in favor of the plaintiff." Conn.Gen.Stat. § 52–278c(a)(2) (1991) . . . .

. . . .

. . . As the record shows, and as the State concedes, only a skeletal affidavit need be and was filed. The State urges that the reviewing judge normally reviews the complaint as well, but concedes that the complaint may also be conclusory. It is self-evident that the judge could make no realistic assessment concerning the likelihood of an action's success based upon these one-sided, self-serving, and conclusory submissions. And as the Court of Appeals said, in a case like this involving an alleged assault, even a detailed affidavit would give only the plaintiff's version of the confrontation. Unlike determining the existence of a debt or delinquent payments,

[4] Our summary affirmance in Spielman–Fond, Inc. v. Hanson's Inc., 417 U.S. 901, 94 S.Ct. 2596 (1974), does not control. In Spielman–Fond, the District Court held that the filing of a mechanic's lien did not amount to the taking of a significant property interest. 379 F.Supp. 997, 999 (Ariz.1973) (three-judge court) (per curiam). A summary disposition does not enjoy the full precedential value of a case argued on the merits and disposed of by a written opinion. Edelman v. Jordan, 415 U.S. 651, 671, 94 S.Ct. 1347, 1359 (1974). The facts of Spielman–Fond presented an alternative basis for affirmance in any event. Unlike the case before us, the mechanic's lien statute in Spielman–Fond required the creditor to have a pre-existing interest in the property at issue. 379 F.Supp., at 997. As we explain below, a heightened plaintiff interest in certain circumstances can provide a ground for upholding procedures that are otherwise suspect. . . .

the issue does not concern "ordinarily uncomplicated matters that lend themselves to documentary proof." Mitchell, 416 U.S., at 609, 94 S.Ct., at 1901. The likelihood of error that results illustrates that "fairness can rarely be obtained by secret, one-sided determination of facts decisive of rights. . . . [And n]o better instrument has been devised for arriving at truth than to give a person in jeopardy of serious loss notice of the case against him and an opportunity to meet it." Joint Anti–Fascist Refugee Committee v. McGrath, 341 U.S. 123, 170–172, 71 S.Ct. 624, 647–649 (1951) (Frankfurter, J., concurring).

What safeguards the State does afford do not adequately reduce this risk. Connecticut points out that the statute also provides an "expeditiou[s]" postattachment adversary hearing, § 52–278e(c); notice for such a hearing, § 52–278e(b); judicial review of an adverse decision, § 52–278*l*(a); and a double damages action if the original suit is commenced without probable cause, § 52–568(a)(1). Similar considerations were present in Mitchell where we upheld Louisiana's sequestration statute despite the lack of predeprivation notice and hearing. But in Mitchell, the plaintiff had a vendor's lien to protect, the risk of error was minimal because the likelihood of recovery involved uncomplicated matters that lent themselves to documentary proof, Mitchell, supra, 416 U.S., at 609–610, 94 S.Ct., at 1901, and plaintiff was required to put up a bond. None of these factors diminishing the need for a predeprivation hearing is present in this case. It is true that a later hearing might negate the presence of probable cause, but this would not cure the temporary deprivation that an earlier hearing might have prevented. "The Fourteenth Amendment draws no bright lines around three-day, 10–day or 50–day deprivations of property. Any significant taking of property by the State is within the purview of the Due Process Clause." Fuentes, 407 U.S., at 86, 92 S.Ct., at 1997.

Finally, we conclude that the interests in favor of an ex parte attachment, particularly the interests of the plaintiff, are too minimal to supply such a consideration here. Plaintiff had no existing interest in Doehr's real estate when he sought the attachment. His only interest in attaching the property was to ensure the availability of assets to satisfy his judgment if he prevailed on the merits of his action. Yet there was no allegation that Doehr was about to transfer or encumber his real estate or take any other action during the pendency of the action that would render his real estate unavailable to satisfy a judgment. Our cases have recognized such a properly supported claim would be an exigent circumstance permitting postponing any notice or hearing until after the attachment is effected. See Mitchell, supra, 416 U.S., at 609, 94 S.Ct., at 1901; Fuentes, supra, 407 U.S., at 90–92, 92 S.Ct., at 1999–2000; Sniadach, 395 U.S., at 339, 89 S.Ct., at 1821. Absent such allegations, however, the plaintiff's interest in attaching the property does not justify the burdening of Doehr's ownership rights without a hearing to determine the likelihood of recovery.

No interest the government may have affects the analysis. The State's substantive interest in protecting any rights of the plaintiff cannot be any more weighty than those rights themselves. Here the plaintiff's interest is de minimis. Moreover, the State cannot seriously plead additional financial or administrative burdens involving predeprivation hearings when it already claims to provide an immediate postdeprivation hearing. [Citations omitted.]

. . . .

IV

. . . .

Although a majority of the Court does not reach the issue, Justices Marshall, Stevens, O'Connor, and I deem it appropriate to consider whether due process also requires the plaintiff to post a bond or other security in addition to requiring a hearing or showing of some exigency.

As noted, the impairments to property rights that attachments affect merit due process protection. Several consequences can be severe, such as the default of a homeowner's mortgage. In the present context, it need only be added that we have repeatedly recognized the utility of a bond in protecting property rights affected by the mistaken award of prejudgment remedies. Di–Chem, 419 U.S., at 610, 611, 95 S.Ct., at 724, 725 (Powell, J., concurring in judgment); id., at 619, 95 S.Ct., at 728 (Blackmun, J., dissenting); Mitchell, 416 U.S., at 606, n. 8, 94 S.Ct., at 1899, n. 8.

Without a bond, at the time of attachment, the danger that these property rights may be wrongfully deprived remains unacceptably high even with such safeguards as a hearing or exigency requirement. The need for a bond is especially apparent where extraordinary circumstances justify an attachment with no more than the plaintiff's ex parte assertion of a claim. We have already discussed how due process tolerates, and the States generally permit, the otherwise impermissible chance of erroneously depriving the defendant in such situations in light of the heightened interest of the plaintiff. Until a postattachment hearing, however, a defendant has no protection against damages sustained where no extraordinary circumstance in fact existed or the plaintiff's likelihood of recovery was nil. Such protection is what a bond can supply. Both the Court and its individual members have repeatedly found the requirement of a bond to play an essential role in reducing what would have been too great a degree of risk in precisely this type of circumstance. Mitchell, supra, at 610, 619, 94 S.Ct., at 1901, 1906; Di–Chem, supra, 419 U.S., at 613, 95 S.Ct., at 725 (Powell, J., concurring in judgment); id., at 619, 95 S.Ct., at 728 (Blackmun, J., dissenting); Fuentes, 407 U.S., at 101, 92 S.Ct., at 2005 (White, J., dissenting).

But the need for a bond does not end here. A defendant's property rights remain at undue risk even when there has been an adversarial hearing to determine the plaintiff's likelihood of recovery. At best, a court's initial assessment of each party's case cannot produce more than an educated prediction as to who will win. This is especially true when, as here, the nature of the claim makes any accurate prediction elusive. See Mitchell, supra, 416 U.S., at 609–610, 94 S.Ct., at 1901. In consequence, even a full hearing under a proper probable-cause standard would not prevent many defendants from having title to their homes impaired during the pendency of suits that never result in the contingency that ultimately justifies such impairment, namely, an award to the plaintiff. Attachment measures currently on the books reflect this concern. All but a handful of States require a plaintiff's bond despite also affording a hearing either before, or (for the vast majority, only under extraordinary circumstances) soon after, an attachment takes place. . . . Bonds have been a similarly common feature of other prejudgment remedy procedures that we have considered, whether or not these procedures also included a hearing. See Ownbey, 256 U.S., at 101–102 n. 1, 41 S.Ct., at 435 n. 1; Fuentes, supra, 407 U.S., at 73, n. 6, 75–76, n. 7, 81–82, 92 S.Ct., at 1990, n. 6, 1991–1992, n. 7, 1994–1995; Mitchell, supra, 416 U.S., at 606, and n. 6, 94 S.Ct., at 1899, and n. 6; Di–Chem, supra, 419 U.S., at 602–603, n. 1, 608, 95 S.Ct., at 721, n. 1, 723.

. . . .

Nor is there any appreciable interest against a bond requirement. . . .

. . . .

V

Because Connecticut's prejudgment remedy provision, Conn.Gen.Stat. § 52–278e(a)(1), violates the requirements of due process by authorizing prejudgment attachment without prior notice or a hearing, the judgment of the Court of Appeals is affirmed, and the case is remanded to that court for further proceedings consistent with this opinion.

It is so ordered.

. . . .

■ [CHIEF JUSTICE REHNQUIST and JUSTICES BLACKMUN, KENNEDY, and SOUTER joined only Parts I, II, and III, and JUSTICE SCALIA joined only Parts I and III. Chief Justice Rehnquist, joined by Justice Blackmun, wrote a concurring opinion, which is omitted; he explained that the Court did not have to reach the issue of Part IV in order to decide this case; nevertheless, by way of an aside he offered his view that in the Spielman–Fond situation, with the heightened plaintiff's interest implicit in a mechanic's lien, due process required neither pre-seizure notice and hearing nor a plaintiff's bond. Justice Scalia's concurrence, which did not specifically address the bond issue, is also omitted. For the background story of the Doehr case, see Robert G. Bone, "The Story of Connecticut v. Doehr: Balancing Costs and Benefits in Defining Procedural Rights," in Civil Procedure Stories 159 (Kevin M. Clermont ed., 2d ed. 2008).]

Question: (4) If DiGiovanni were suing on some other cause of action to protect a pre-existing interest in the real estate (imagine his filing a mechanic's lien without notice or hearing, but without exigent circumstances, while trying to recover for repairs he made to the Doehrs' house), would the constitutional result have been different? See Shaumyan v. O'Neill, 987 F.2d 122 (2d Cir.1993) (yes).

SCOPE OF SNIADACH'S PROGENY

The foregoing cases deal with the extension of procedural due process standards to regulate pre-judgment seizures of property for security. In this context and in others, the general requirement that fair notice and opportunity to be heard must be given before the government unduly impairs a person's property interest—or that at least the procedures of a Mitchell-type or Mitchell-like statute must be followed in the case of a pre-judgment seizure for security where plaintiff has a pre-existing interest in the property or where exigent circumstances endanger security—raises several more problems of definition.

For example, what kind of impaired property interest will trigger this protection? These cases show an expansive view of the impairment of property interest that is regulated by the Due Process Clauses. The property involved certainly need not be a necessity of life, and the interest may be only possessory. The deprivation might be only temporary or partial.

Sniadach and its progeny are immediately concerned only with pre-judgment seizures of property for security. It is obvious, however, that they should have an influence in many other contexts—such as termination of welfare benefits, loss of driver's license, and suspension from school—although the strength of that influence will not always be clear. Compare Goldberg v. Kelly, 397 U.S. 254, 90 S.Ct. 1011 (1970), discussed by Judith Resnik, "The Story of Goldberg: Why This Case Is Our Shorthand," in Civil Procedure Stories 473 (Kevin M. Clermont ed., 2d ed. 2008), with Mathews v. Eldridge, 424 U.S. 319, 96 S.Ct. 893 (1976), discussed in Topic C of Part One.

For a particular context, courts had in the past treated pre-judgment attachments and garnishments of property to obtain in rem or quasi in rem jurisdiction as not being subject to the procedural due process dictates of the foregoing cases. They grounded such treatment on the theory that there is strong public interest in obtaining jurisdiction and that this consideration colors the seizure as an "extraordinary situation" beyond the reach of Sniadach's progeny. Cf. Calero–Toledo v. Pearson Yacht Leasing Co., 416 U.S. 663, 94 S.Ct. 2080 (1974) (seizure of a drug-running yacht for forfeiture proceedings is such an "extraordinary situation"). But more recent cases have held that a general exception of this sort is illogical and unwise, and they have applied the Sniadach line of cases to run-of-the-mill seizures for jurisdictional purposes. Cf. United States v. James Daniel Good Real Property, 510 U.S. 43, 114 S.Ct. 492 (1993) (seizure of a drug dealer's house for forfeiture proceedings is invalid without showing of "exigent circumstances"). See generally Karen Nelson Moore, Procedural Due Process in Quasi In Rem Actions After Shaffer v. Heitner, 20 Wm. & Mary L.Rev. 157 (1978).

Another context in which the Sniadach line might have an impact is that of seizures of property to enforce judgments. Here a leading case has held, however, that a wage garnishment for enforcement need not be preceded by notice and opportunity to be heard on the propriety of the garnishment; the court reasoned that the state's interest in facilitating the enforcement of its judgments and the creditor's interest in satisfying his judgment outweighed the debtor's interests, given that the debtor had had notice and opportunity to be heard before judgment and given that the debtor would under the state law have the opportunity of a prompt post-garnishment hearing. Brown v. Liberty Loan Corp., 539 F.2d 1355 (5th Cir.1976). Yet, more recent cases have emphasized that due process generally does require prompt post-seizure notice and opportunity to be heard. E.g., Finberg v. Sullivan, 634 F.2d 50 (3d Cir.1980) (en banc). See generally Virginia C. Patterson, Commentary, Due Process and Postjudgment Enforcement Procedures: Where Do We Stand?, 37 Ala.L.Rev. 759 (1986).

Question: (5) What protection does due process afford in connection with seizure of property to obtain quasi in rem jurisdiction when the purpose of exercising that jurisdiction is to enforce an out-of-state personal judgment?

GOVERNMENTAL ACTION

Impairments of property interests invoke the Due Process Clauses only when they result from governmental action. However, such action need not involve direct action by government officials. Action by private persons that the government compels or significantly encourages may qualify as governmental action. See Reitman v. Mulkey, 387 U.S. 369, 87 S.Ct. 1627 (1967). And action by private persons that is taken under authority delegated by the government and is traditionally an exclusively public function may constitute governmental action. See Marsh v. Alabama, 326 U.S. 501, 66 S.Ct. 276 (1946). Nevertheless, to attribute private action to the government, there must be significant governmental involvement, something more than mere neutral enforcement of laws. See generally Laurence H. Tribe, American Constitutional Law 1688–720 (2d ed. 1988). At any rate, state action was clearly present in the foregoing cases of pre-judgment seizures of property for security. See Lugar v. Edmondson Oil Co., 457 U.S. 922, 102 S.Ct. 2744 (1982).

Question: (6) U.C.C. § 9–503 provides that upon default a secured party may repossess collateral in the debtor's possession without judicial process, as long as this can be done without breach of the peace. Would such repossession under § 9–503 constitute state action for the purposes of the Fourteenth Amendment? See Flagg Bros. v. Brooks, 436 U.S. 149, 98 S.Ct. 1729 (1978) (holding that a sale under U.C.C. § 7–210 does not constitute state action for the purposes of the Fourteenth Amendment (§ 7–210 provides that a warehouseman may enforce his lien on stored goods—which lien the law gives him for charges due for that storage—by selling the goods in a commercially reasonable manner without judicial process)).

Self-help thus opens an end-run on Sniadach's progeny. But it should be noted that constitutional provisions other than the Federal Due Process Clauses may contribute to the regulation of seizure procedures. For example, in Blair v. Pitchess, 5 Cal.3d 258, 486 P.2d 1242, 96 Cal.Rptr. 42 (1971), the California Supreme Court found that the warrantless seizure of property by state agents, in a Fuentes-type situation, violated the Search and Seizure Clause of the Fourth Amendment. More pertinently, in Svendsen v. Smith's Moving & Trucking Co., 54 N.Y.2d 865, 429 N.E.2d 411, 444 N.Y.S.2d 904 (1981), the New York Court of Appeals found U.C.C. § 7–210 unconstitutional under the due process clause of the state's constitution, thanks to a broader view of state action. Most importantly, federal and state legislative and administrative provisions may, of course, further restrict seizure procedures. The courts stand ready to enforce all this law, sometimes even by awarding damages in a tort action, say, for unlawful attachment. See Thomas D. Crandall, Richard B. Hagedorn & Frank W. Smith, Jr., Debtor–Creditor Law Manual ¶ 6.04[5][b] (1985); Dean Gloster, Comment, Abuse of Process and Attachment: Toward a Balance of Power, 30 UCLA L.Rev. 1218 (1983).

SECTION 3. CONSENT IN ADVANCE

D.H. Overmyer Co. v. Frick Co.

Supreme Court of the United States, 1972.
405 U.S. 174, 92 S.Ct. 775.

■ MR. JUSTICE BLACKMUN delivered the opinion of the Court.

This case presents the issue of the constitutionality, under the Due Process Clause of the Fourteenth Amendment, of the cognovit note authorized by Ohio Rev.Code § 2323.13.

The cognovit is the ancient legal device by which the debtor consents in advance to the holder's obtaining a judgment without notice or hearing, and possibly even with the appearance, on the debtor's behalf, of an attorney designated by the holder. It was known at least as far back as Blackstone's time. 3 W. Blackstone, Commentaries *397. In a case applying Ohio law, it was said that the purpose of the cognovit is "to permit the note holder to obtain judgment without a trial of possible defenses which the signers of the notes might assert." Hadden v. Rumsey Products, Inc., 196 F.2d 92, 96 (C.A.2 1952). And long ago the cognovit method was described by the Chief Justice of New Jersey as "the loosest way of binding a man's property that ever was devised in any civilized country." Alderman v. Diament, 7 N.J.L. 197, 198 (1824). Mr. Dickens noted it with obvious disfavor. Pickwick Papers, c. 47. The cognovit has been the subject of comment, much of it critical.

Statutory treatment varies widely. Some States specifically authorize the cognovit. Others disallow it. Some go so far as to make its employment a misdemeanor. The majority, however, regulate its use and many prohibit the device in small loans and consumer sales.

. . . .

The argument that a provision of this kind is offensive to current notions of Fourteenth Amendment due process is, at first glance, an appealing one. However, here, as in nearly every case, facts are important. [Overmyer was a warehousing enterprise with many warehouses in many states. It contracted with Frick for an automatic refrigeration system in a warehouse under construction in Ohio. Overmyer fell behind in its progress payments, and Frick stopped its work. After negotiations, the work resumed under new installment-payment terms and completed to Overmyer's then satisfaction. Later Overmyer requested additional time to make its installment payments. Negotiations finally resulted in a new agreement, which, unlike the earlier agreements, included the execution of a note with a cognovit provision. As the Supreme Court was later to observe, the execution and delivery of this note "were for an adequate consideration and were the product of negotiations carried on by corporate parties with the advice of competent counsel." Later Overmyer ceased to make the required monthly payments under the note, asserting a breach by Frick of the original contract. Frick caused judgment for the balance due on the note to be entered in an Ohio court without prior notice: an Ohio attorney, not known to Overmyer, appeared for Overmyer "by virtue of the warrant of attorney" in the note, and then waived service of process and confessed judgment. As required by Ohio law, the court clerk notified Overmyer of entry of judgment on the cognovit note. Overmyer moved to vacate judgment, and it tendered an answer and counterclaim. The Ohio court denied the motion, and the state appellate courts affirmed. Certiorari was granted.]

[Overmyer argues] that due process requires reasonable notice and an opportunity to be heard, citing Boddie v. Connecticut, 401 U.S. 371, 378, 91 S.Ct. 780, 786 (1971). It is acknowledged, however, that the question here is in a context of "contract waiver, before suit has been filed, before any dispute has arisen" and "whereby a party gives up in advance his constitutional right to defend any suit by the other, to notice and an opportunity to be heard, no matter what defenses he may have, and to be represented by counsel of his own choice."[9] In other words, Overmyer's position here specifically is that it is "unconstitutional to waive in advance the right to present a defense in an action on the note."[10] It is conceded that in Ohio a court has the power to open the judgment upon a proper showing. Bellows v. Bowlus, 83 Ohio App. 90, 93, 82 N.E.2d 429, 432 (1948). But it is claimed that such a move is discretionary and ordinarily will not be disturbed on appeal, and that it may not prevent execution before the debtor has notice, Griffin v. Griffin, 327 U.S. 220, 231–232, 66 S.Ct. 556, 561–562 (1946). Goldberg v. Kelly, 397 U.S. 254, 90 S.Ct. 1011 (1970), and Sniadach v. Family Finance Corp., 395 U.S. 337, 89 S.Ct. 1820 (1969), are cited.

---

9 Brief for Petitioners 16.

10 Trans. of Oral Arg. 17.

The due process rights to notice and hearing prior to a civil judgment are subject to waiver. In National Equipment Rental, Ltd. v. Szukhent, 375 U.S. 311, 84 S.Ct. 411 (1964), the Court observed:

> "[I]t is settled . . . that parties to a contract may agree in advance to submit to the jurisdiction of a given court, to permit notice to be served by the opposing party, or even to waive notice altogether." Id., at 315–316, 84 S.Ct., at 414.

And in Boddie v. Connecticut, supra, the Court acknowledged that "the hearing required by due process is subject to waiver." 401 U.S., at 378–379, 91 S.Ct., at 786.

This, of course, parallels the recognition of waiver in the criminal context where personal liberty, rather than a property right, is involved. Illinois v. Allen, 397 U.S. 337, 342–343, 90 S.Ct. 1057, 1060 (1970) (right to be present at trial); Miranda v. Arizona, 384 U.S. 436, 444, 86 S.Ct. 1602, 1612 (1966) (rights to counsel and against compulsory self-incrimination); Fay v. Noia, 372 U.S. 391, 439, 83 S.Ct. 822, 849 (1963) (habeas corpus); Rogers v. United States, 340 U.S. 367, 371, 71 S.Ct. 438, 440 (1951) (right against compulsory self-incrimination).

Even if, for present purposes, we assume that the standard for waiver in a corporate-property-right case of this kind is the same standard applicable to waiver in a criminal proceeding, that is, that it be voluntary, knowing, and intelligently made, Brady v. United States, 397 U.S. 742, 748, 90 S.Ct. 1463, 1468 (1970); Miranda v. Arizona, 384 U.S., at 444, 86 S.Ct., at 1612, or "an intentional relinquishment or abandonment of a known right or privilege," Johnson v. Zerbst, 304 U.S. 458, 464, 58 S.Ct. 1019, 1023 (1938); Fay v. Noia, 372 U.S., at 439, 83 S.Ct., at 849, and even if, as the Court has said in the civil area, "[w]e do not presume acquiescence in the loss of fundamental rights," Ohio Bell Tel. Co. v. Public Utilities Comm'n, 301 U.S. 292, 307, 57 S.Ct. 724, 731 (1937), that standard was fully satisfied here.

. . . .

We therefore hold that Overmyer, in its execution and delivery to Frick of the second installment note containing the cognovit provision, voluntarily, intelligently, and knowingly waived the rights it otherwise possessed to prejudgment notice and hearing, and that it did so with full awareness of the legal consequences.

. . . .

Some concluding comments are in order:

1. Our holding necessarily means that a cognovit clause is not, per se, violative of Fourteenth Amendment due process. Overmyer could prevail here only if the clause were constitutionally invalid. The facts of this case, as we observed above, are important, and those facts amply demonstrate that a cognovit provision may well serve a proper and useful purpose in the commercial world and at the same time not be vulnerable to constitutional attack.

2. Our holding, of course, is not controlling precedent for other facts of other cases. For example, where the contract is one of adhesion, where there is great disparity in bargaining power, and where the debtor receives nothing for the cognovit provision, other legal consequences may ensue.

3. Overmyer, merely because of its execution of the cognovit note, is not rendered defenseless. It concedes that in Ohio the judgment court may vacate its judgment upon a showing of a valid defense and, indeed, Overmyer had a post-judgment hearing in the Ohio court. If there were defenses such as prior payment or mistaken identity, those defenses could be asserted. And there is nothing we see that prevented Overmyer from pursuing its breach-of-contract claim against Frick in a proper forum. . . .

The judgment is affirmed.

■ [The concurring opinion of JUSTICE DOUGLAS, with whom Justice Marshall joined, is omitted. JUSTICES POWELL and REHNQUIST did not participate.]

Question: (7) Overmyer went bankrupt in 1973, so you can sense what is sometimes at stake here for the creditor. Yet the Overmyer case clearly suggests that a contractual waiver of notice and opportunity to be heard may sometimes be invalid in a consumer setting, as indeed the court held in Gonzalez v. County of Hidalgo, Texas, 489 F.2d 1043 (5th Cir.1973). As the attorney for a seller of consumer goods, how would you draft waiver provisions in a conditional sales contract so as to meet the requirements suggested by the Overmyer case? As the attorney for the buyer, what would you argue to establish the unconstitutionality of those provisions?

CHOICE OF LAW AND FORUM

As you have seen, the parties have significant powers to select the governing law and, of special interest here in this Part on authority to adjudicate, to select the forum. As indicated by the quotation in Overmyer from National Equipment Rental, Ltd. v. Szukhent, 375 U.S. 311, 315–16, 84 S.Ct. 411, 414 (1964), the defendant can in the proper circumstances waive in advance objections to territorial jurisdiction.

Questions: (8) Should the same principle be applied to venue, so that pursuant to waiver in advance an action may proceed in a place improper under the venue statute, or so that pursuant to agreement in advance an action may proceed only in a certain place despite the more permissive provisions of the venue statute? Compare The Bremen v. Zapata Off–Shore Co., 407 U.S. 1, 92 S.Ct. 1907 (1972) (generally yes), with Carnival Cruise Lines v. Shute, 499 U.S. 585, 111 S.Ct. 1522 (1991) (even more expansively enforcing agreement, seemingly recognizing as an exception only fraud in inclusion of clause or an unreasonably chosen forum). See generally Northwestern Nat'l Ins. Co. v. Donovan, 916 F.2d 372, 376 (7th Cir.1990) (Posner, J.) ("We are persuaded that the only good reason for treating a forum selection clause differently from any other contract (specifically, from the contract in which the clause appears) is the possibility of adverse effects on third parties.

Where that possibility is slight, the clause should be treated like any other contract. What is more, if any inconvenience to third parties can be cured by a change of venue under section 1404(a), that is the route to follow, rather than striking down the clause.").

(9) Should a similar principle be applied to subject-matter jurisdiction, so that pursuant to agreement in advance an action, which is not within exclusive federal jurisdiction, may proceed in state court but not in federal court? See Michael D. Moberly, Judicial Protection of Forum Selection: Agreements to Litigate in State Court, 1 Phoenix L.Rev. 1 (2008) (yes).

Thus, the parties may consent in advance to territorial jurisdiction not otherwise existing, and they may waive in advance the restrictions of venue and other doctrines of judicial self-restraint. Under modern law, courts will usually give effect to such "prorogation" agreements, apparently subject to ordinary contract law and the requirement that the forum not be an unconscionable one.

Conversely, the parties generally may, by a "derogation" agreement, restrict any potential litigation to one or more courts among the forums otherwise permissible under the law of territorial authority to adjudicate. That is, the law, in a further show of self-restraint, allows the parties themselves to restrict territorial authority to adjudicate.

The question remains open whether state law or federal law governs the enforceability and interpretation of forum selection clauses in federal court on state-created causes of action. See Preferred Capital, Inc. v. Sarasota Kennel Club, Inc., 489 F.3d 303 (6th Cir.2007).

Nevertheless, in federal court, 28 U.S.C. § 1404(a) can override any forum selection clause, allowing the agreed court to transfer to a court where the case might have been brought absent the clause. See Stewart Org. v. Ricoh Corp., 487 U.S. 22, 108 S.Ct. 2239 (1988). In international cases, a federal court may entertain the possibility that forum non conveniens can trump a forum selection clause agreeing on suit in that federal court.

If, conversely, the plaintiff lays federal venue in violation of the forum selection clause and the defendant protests under Federal Rule 12(b)(3), the court can transfer under 28 U.S.C. § 1406(a), making transferee law applicable. See Jackson v. West Telemktg. Corp. Outbound, 245 F.3d 518 (5th Cir.2001).

Overall, American courts have shifted with time from a view that territorial authority to adjudicate is largely a matter for the sovereign and not the parties to decide, through a grudging acceptance of party agreements, and toward a perhaps overly enthusiastic embrace of freedom of contract even in the face of uneven bargaining capabilities and powers. Where the optimum lies and where American law will end up are still matters of debate and evolution. In the meantime, international treaties giving effect to forum selection clauses are emerging.

Whatever the future holds, forum selection clauses are currently becoming more and more important. Good lawyers try increasingly by agreement to contract their clients' way around the morass of the law on territorial authority to adjudicate, and to do so in a way that advantages their clients. Lots of litigated cases, however, turn on how to interpret these clauses, most often as a result of the lawyers' failings. Office lawyers need to know a lot of law, including choice of law, to negotiate and write a forum selection clause effectively and clearly.

CUSTOMIZED LITIGATION

If, as Overmyer suggests, the parties can waive virtually all procedural protections by consent in advance, then they can likewise choose to customize their litigation, or at least do so up to some vaguely defined limits. In short, the normal rules of procedure and evidence are no more than default contractual rules, which the parties can modify through negotiation.

The parties could restrict joinder or discovery. They could alter the rules of evidence or waive jury trial. They could restrict or waive appeal. In fact, they could make litigation look a lot like a peculiarly effective brand of arbitration, or they might agree to abide by some set of transnationally "neutral" rules of procedure. See Michael L. Moffitt, Customized Litigation: The Case for Making Civil Procedure Negotiable, 75 Geo.Wash.L.Rev. 461 (2007) (post-dispute agreement); Henry S. Noyes, If You (Re)Build It, They Will Come: Contracts to Remake the Rules of Litigation in Arbitration's Image, 30 Harv.J.L. & Pub.Pol'y 579 (2007) (pre-dispute agreement). But perhaps that prospect should raise some caution flags, or perhaps not. Compare Elizabeth Thornburg, Designer Trials, 2006 J.Disp.Resol. 181, with Alon Klement & Daphna Kapeliuk, Contractualizing Procedure, http://ssrn.com/abstract=1323056 (Dec. 31, 2008).

PART FOUR

FORMER ADJUDICATION

TOPIC A

GENERAL OBSERVATIONS

We have already encountered a number of problems regarding rules designed to treat or prevent repetitious litigation. The purpose of this Part is to examine these problems systematically in a single place and to evaluate the policies that appear to mold decision. Our primary interest will be the centrally important doctrine of res judicata, which treats the effects of previously rendered adjudication on a subsequent action.

Res judicata, or res adjudicata by its older name, is a classic common-law doctrine. *First*, responding to felt needs, every legal system has produced a body of res judicata law. "The doctrine of res judicata is a principle of universal jurisprudence forming part of the legal systems of all civilized nations."[a] But each jurisdiction generates its own distinctive body of law, as has been done independently by each of the states, by the federal system, and by other countries. American res judicata is distinctively a good deal more expansive than res judicata law in other countries. *Second*, American res judicata is an almost entirely judge-made body of law. Courts responded to the needs they most acutely felt by formulating, revising, and complexifying a doctrine. It is true that constitutions, legislation, and rulemaking can override the judicial doctrine. The U.S. Constitution has a real albeit limited impact on res judicata doctrine. In many jurisdictions, statutes deal with small parts of the subject. Most court rules avoid most of the subject. The belief is that in general it is just too complex a subject for successful codification. *Third*, res judicata is policy-driven. Despite first impression, it comprises principles or standards as much as fixed rules and exceptions. As a result, it has been a surprisingly uncertain and contentious area of law. Some questions of res judicata have not been authoritatively resolved, and there is considerable dissatisfaction with some of the solutions that have been given. Indeed, there has been a certain uneasiness with the whole doctrine, even in the courts, as exemplified by Judge Clark's aphorism: "The defense of res judicata is universally respected, but actually not very well liked."[b] And there has long been strong advocacy of drastic change. Yet, as we shall see, the modern Supreme Court seems to have embraced res judicata with renewed affection.

Some basic propositions.—Res judicata's key propositions nevertheless can be simply stated. If a plaintiff sues and obtains a valid and final personal judgment in his favor, generally his claim is extinguished and merged in the judgment. He cannot relitigate the claim in hopes of winning

[a] 2 A.C. Freeman, A Treatise of the Law of Judgments § 627, at 1321 (5th ed. 1925).

[b] Riordan v. Ferguson, 147 F.2d 983, 988 (2d Cir.1945) (dissenting opinion).

a more favorable decision against the defendant, either in the same jurisdiction or elsewhere. The judgment is substituted for the claim, and it is only the judgment that he can then seek to enforce. (The plaintiff can get enforcement of the judgment where rendered. If necessary, he can sue upon the judgment in another jurisdiction and obtain a fresh judgment to enforce there. If he does so, the first judgment is not merged in the second. He can seek to enforce either or both, even in a third state by another action upon the judgment, but is of course limited to one satisfaction. See Moore v. Justices of the Mun. Court, 291 Mass. 504, 197 N.E. 487 (1935).)

Similarly, if a plaintiff sues but judgment goes against him, then generally his claim is extinguished and barred by the judgment. He cannot relitigate the same claim. (What is meant by these statements about "merger" and "bar"[c] is that if the plaintiff attempts relitigation of the same claim, the defendant may successfully plead res judicata. Here is another instance where rules of law are not self-executing. What happens when the defense of res judicata is not pleaded, and a second judgment inconsistent with the first is rendered, is considered later in this Part.)

How does the principle against relitigation apply to actions where the claims are different? Unlike the doctrines of merger and bar, which operate to preclude the whole claim without regard to what issues were in reality litigated in the first suit, an additional aspect of res judicata makes preclusive between the parties the prior determination of an issue, but only if the same issue was actually litigated and determined in the original action and, moreover, only if the determination of that issue was essential to the first judgment. This doctrine, applicable between different claims, is termed "collateral estoppel" by many courts and commentators. (If an exception to claim preclusion applies so that a claim may be relitigated, a doctrine identical to collateral estoppel acts to preclude relitigation of issues in any subsequent action on the same claim. This doctrine is termed "direct estoppel."[d])

For clarity of analysis it is useful to distinguish claim preclusion from issue preclusion, but courts too often in their thinking have lumped these doctrines together. Furthermore, courts have frequently confused the picture by using idiosyncratic terminology and categorization to subdivide the subject of res judicata; most confusingly, some courts persist in using the general term "res judicata" to encompass only claim preclusion and not issue preclusion too.

Rejecting the old muddle, the Restatement (Second) of Judgments § 17 (1982) presents its basic provision on res judicata this way, stating the general rules along with references to its more detailed provisions:

> A valid and final personal judgment is conclusive between the parties, except on appeal or other direct review, to the following extent:

[c] The two doctrines, merger and bar, now are collectively named "claim preclusion."

[d] The two doctrines, collateral and direct estoppel, now are collectively named "issue preclusion."

(1) If the judgment is in favor of the plaintiff, the claim is extinguished and merged in the judgment and a new claim may arise on the judgment (see § 18);

(2) If the judgment is in favor of the defendant, the claim is extinguished and the judgment bars a subsequent action on that claim (see § 19);

(3) A judgment in favor of either the plaintiff or the defendant is conclusive, in a subsequent action between them on the same or a different claim, with respect to any issue actually litigated and determined if its determination was essential to that judgment (see § 27).

We largely devote the rest of this Part to exploring the hidden depths of this basic provision on res judicata. But here, for orientation purposes, let us first take a preliminary look at some of the rather obvious implications of § 17—even though several of our tentative statements require later elaboration and qualification.

General context: second action.—The doctrine of res judicata specifies certain binding effects, in subsequent litigation, of a previously rendered judgment. Generally speaking, then, res judicata can apply only when an attempt is made in a second action to foreclose relitigation of a matter already adjudicated in a previous action. Res judicata therefore has no application to an attempt in the original action at correcting error in the judgment, as by motion for a new trial or by appeal.[e]

For example, compare Thompson v. Washington National Bank, 68 Wash. 42, 122 P. 606 (1912), with Louisville & Nashville Railroad v. Whitley County Court, infra p. 1437. In Thompson, the plaintiff sued for payment on a contract to lay a tile floor and lost on the ground that he had not substantially performed his contract, in that the tiled floor had been left in a discolored condition. Eight months after the judgment he sued again on the same contract, eager to show that after the first judgment the defendant had removed the discoloration at a cost of only $12 and that therefore the contract had been substantially performed. In Whitley, post-trial events similarly showed that the judgment was erroneous, and the aggrieved party moved for a new trial on the ground of newly discovered evidence. In Thompson, res judicata blocked suit; in Whitley, res judicata was not involved because the motion was made in the original action. Had Thompson promptly moved for a new trial instead of suing again, he could have avoided the application of res judicata.

First prerequisite: validity.—These rules of res judicata are applicable, as said in § 17, only to "valid" judgments. A judgment is treated as valid for this purpose if it is of sufficient quality to withstand any request for relief from judgment, such as a collateral attack launched in the second

[e] There is a doctrine called law of the case, which stands for the sensible proposition that a court, and courts coordinate with or inferior to it, will normally not depart from a ruling declared by it in a particular case if the point is again presented in the same case. However, this flexible and limited doctrine, although very similar to stare decisis, is distinguishable from res judicata. See generally 18B Wright, Miller & Cooper § 4478.

action. Generally speaking, a collateral attack lies on, and only on, the ground that the court rendering the prior judgment failed to satisfy the requirement of subject-matter jurisdiction, territorial jurisdiction, or opportunity to be heard.

On the one hand, if such a defect in competence, nexus, or notice can be shown, the judgment will normally be deemed not valid. Although those defects are rather rare, relief from judgment is available, even by collateral attack. Thus, the invocation of res judicata can be defeated.

On the other hand, the fact that the judgment may have been otherwise erroneous is usually immaterial with respect to res judicata. Mere error, as opposed to the three basic defects, does not affect a judgment's validity. Mere error can be corrected only on direct review. Indeed, the failure to honor an erroneous but valid judgment rendered by a court of another American jurisdiction is, in our federal system, an impermissible denial of full faith and credit.

Second prerequisite: finality.—These rules of res judicata are applicable, as we have also seen, only to "final" judgments. The law does not want to preclude on the basis of the tentative, contingent, or provisional. But what constitutes finality for this purpose? It is not precisely the same as "final" in the statute providing for appellate review of "final decisions of the district courts." 28 U.S.C. § 1291.

First, the rules of claim preclusion stick pretty closely to the traditional strict formulation of finality for appellate review: the court rendering the judgment must ordinarily have said its last word on the claim, except for award of costs and enforcement of judgment. Contrast Topic B of Part Nine, where it is shown how courts have stretched this strict concept of finality in the context of appealability so as to provide immediate review in situations where deemed necessary.

Second, when issue preclusion is involved, there is a cautious tendency to be somewhat more willing to find finality than in the case of claim preclusion. If the first court has firmly decided an issue after adequate hearing and full deliberation, a second court has discretion to give the decision preclusive effect despite its lack of finality in the strict sense. Of course, if the decision were avowedly tentative in the first court, it would not receive such effect. In Lummus Co. v. Commonwealth Oil Refining Co., 297 F.2d 80, 89 (2d Cir.1961), Judge Friendly put this discretionary relaxation of the finality standard in these words: " 'Finality' in the context here relevant may mean little more than that the litigation of a particular issue has reached such a stage that a court sees no really good reason for permitting it to be litigated again." In that case, the second court gave preclusive effect on an issue of fraud in the inducement of a contract to an earlier decision of the Court of Appeals for the First Circuit in litigation related to the same contract, by which decision the First Circuit had reversed a preliminary injunction staying arbitration between the parties. Restatement (Second) of Judgments § 13 (1982) adopts the view of the Lummus case, but in fact even this short description of Lummus reveals it to have been a peculiarly appropriate case for preclusion.

Questions: (1) For personal injuries in an automobile accident, *A* sues *B* in a jurisdiction where the issues as to liability are determined first, and the damage issues are heard later by another jury if liability is found. The jury goes for *A* on liability, by finding *B* negligent. Should this determination before the ultimate judgment, which would have to await the assessment of damages, now be controlling in a personal-injury action by *B* against *A*, wherein *A* pleads contributory negligence? Should this determination be controlling, by way of merger or otherwise, in another action by *A* against *B* on the same claim, now seeking property damages?

(2) Should your answers to the preceding question depend on whether the liability determination was immediately appealable, as had been the issue in Lummus? See Avondale Shipyards v. Insured Lloyd's, 786 F.2d 1265, 1269–72 (5th Cir.1986) (yes, although also generally disapproving modern relaxation of finality for issue preclusion).

Under the res judicata law of most American jurisdictions, a judgment otherwise final for res judicata purposes does not lose finality because time still exists for attack in the trial court, as by motion for a new trial, or because a party has actually made such an attack. Likewise, the fact that the time for appeal has not expired, or that an appeal has been taken and remains pending, does not prevent a judgment from being final for res judicata purposes.

More specifically as to appeal, Restatement of Judgments § 41 cmt. d (1942) considered loss of finality pending appeal in terms of whether taking the appeal "vacates" the judgment, as taking an appeal in equity did. That approach seems to have little relevance today. Restatement (Second) of Judgments § 13 cmt. f (1982) rejects it and says: "The better view is that a judgment otherwise final remains so despite the taking of an appeal unless what is called an appeal actually consists of a trial de novo . . . ." If there is to be a trial de novo in a higher court, the original decision does lose its finality pending the appeal.

In brief, claim preclusion and issue preclusion require a judgment's finality, but finality does not mean that direct review of the judgment is complete. Obviously, this early finality can present problems, and so sometimes needs a cure. If direct review eventually overturns the judgment, relief from a second judgment based upon it in the meantime under the doctrine of res judicata normally will be available by appropriate proceedings. See, e.g., Rule 60(b)(5).

Temporary focus: personal judgment.—For the moment, we are concerned only with the res judicata effects of ordinary judgments and indeed only with those effects between the parties thereto. Special rules for the effects of a judgment resting on jurisdiction over a thing are prescribed in Restatement (Second) of Judgments §§ 30, 32 (1982). Similarly, the effects of claim and issue preclusion on persons not parties to the prior judgment, and other special effects, are examined later in this Part.

Some closing thoughts.—Res judicata is a profoundly important doctrine. It is not merely a technical set of rules on the conduct of litigation. It fundamentally defines what a court has decided, what bundle of aspects constitute a judgment, what the product of the judicial branch is to be.

Strong policies underlie the scope of res judicata. Efficiency argues for avoiding wasteful litigation and possibly inconsistent adjudication, and also for achieving the certainty and stability of repose. Fairness looks to the burden on res judicata's invoker of conducting renewed litigation and to the opponent's fault in causing it, as well as to the reliance interests at stake. These policies deserve consideration in connection with both the instant case and the long run of cases. Substantive policies also demand consideration, sometimes adding to the arguments for broad res judicata.

Nevertheless, all those policies can cut the other way too. There are the "direct costs" of litigating about res judicata, while the possibility of future preclusion might produce overlitigation in the initial action. Also, there are the inefficient "error costs" of deciding to live with an incorrect judgment. By way of illustration of the possible harshness in the operation of res judicata, we shall summarize a much-cited case.

In Jacobson v. Mutual Benefit Health & Accident Association, 73 N.D. 108, 11 N.W.2d 442 (1943), the plaintiff had sued for $2000 on her husband's policy insuring against his accidental death. Part A of the policy entitled her to $2000 on the insured's accidental death; Part B provided that each year's renewal of the policy would add $200 to the death benefit, and there had been nine such renewals. That suit had resulted in judgment for the plaintiff for $2000. The plaintiff's lawyer apparently had neglected to read the policy's Part B.

Later, becoming aware of the error, Clara Jacobson, with the same lawyer, brought a new suit for the additional $1800. The defendant insurer pleaded the prior judgment as res judicata. The court held that the plaintiff was seeking improperly to split her cause of action; that there had been but one cause of action, in solido, for the $3800; that this cause of action had been extinguished by the prior judgment; and that the second action therefore could not be maintained.

The Jacobson result is not compelled by logic or by the nature of things, although it is one by which lawyers would not be surprised in the light of past decisions of the courts, and by which judicial economy is arguably served. Much can be said against exacting such a penalty from the plaintiff, and correspondingly giving such a windfall to the insurance company, because of counsel's failure to read the policy with care.

At any rate, returning from policy to doctrine, the Jacobson decision shows how essential it is in applying the principle that a cause of action is extinguished by a judgment to determine the precise dimensions of the thing that has been extinguished. So the question of the measure of "cause of action," or "claim" in modern usage, reappears in a new context. Why does the law say that a suit on the policy's Part A extinguishes rights under Part B? This question we shall examine in the next Topic.

TOPIC B

CLAIM PRECLUSION

SECTION 1. DIMENSIONS OF A CLAIM

Williamson v. Columbia Gas & Electric Corp.

United States Court of Appeals, Third Circuit, 1950.
186 F.2d 464, cert. denied, 341 U.S. 921, 71 S.Ct. 743 (1951).

■ Before GOODRICH, KALODNER and HASTIE, CIRCUIT JUDGES.

■ GOODRICH, CIRCUIT JUDGE. This case involves the application of the rules of res judicata to a civil suit brought by the plaintiff, through its trustee in bankruptcy, for injuries alleged to have been sustained because of the defendant's violation of the anti-trust laws.

This action, which we shall call action No. 1, was begun on February 14, 1938. It charged that the defendant, conspiring with certain other persons, had, in violation of the provisions of the anti-trust laws, inflicted great injury upon the plaintiff. But as the complaint was amended it sought recovery against Columbia Gas and Electric Corporation alone, although other parties were named as having conspired with Columbia in the various transactions of which complaint is made.

Subsequently, on September 16, 1938, the plaintiff brought in the same court (the United States District Court for the District of Delaware) another action against the defendant charging injury in violation of the anti-trust laws. This we shall call action No. 2. In this action the charge did not read in terms of conspiracy but alleged Columbia alone as the wrongdoer.

Thus we have two actions pending by the same plaintiff against the same defendant in the same court, each involving a suit for recovery of injuries alleged to have been sustained by action on the part of the defendant in violation of the anti-trust laws of the United States. Later to be examined is the identity, or substantial identity, of these suits.

The No. 2 action came to a conclusion first. On April 29, 1939, the court ordered "That the complaint in the . . . cause be and it hereby is dismissed. . . ."

The whole question with which we have to do in this case involves the effect of this judgment for the defendant upon the plaintiff's No. 1 action. In the District Court, the defendant moved [for summary judgment in] action No. 1 because of its victory in action No. 2. The motion was granted and the plaintiff appeals. Our discussion of the main question will be divided into consideration of the several issues presented.

Assume for the moment that the subject-matter of action No. 1 is identical with the subject-matter No. 2 so as to amount to the same "cause of action." Then we have two questions which may be disposed of first to clear the way for the most difficult thing about the case which is the assumption of identity just stated. The two questions are: (1) Does it matter for purposes of application of res judicata that the No. 2 action, later begun, was finished first? The answer to this question is no. The point is so well settled on authority that it is not a serious matter of contention in this case. (2) The second question is, what of the fact that the recital contained in the order of dismissal . . . mentioned a stipulation between the parties and the further fact that that stipulation had to do with the time in which the alleged cause of action accrued?

Here is what had occurred. Prior to the dismissal of action No. 2 the parties had entered into a stipulation. That stipulation provided that "The alleged right of action sued upon in this cause accrued not later than January 1, 1931." It was further agreed that if the court should consider the action barred by any applicable statute of limitations the pending motion to dismiss was to be granted. The plaintiff's theory at that time was that his action was not barred by the Delaware statute of limitations, and he evidently felt sufficiently confident of his position to enter into the stipulation which posed the legal issue of its correctness.

Subsequent events proved plaintiff's theory to be incorrect. Both the District Court and this Court held that the Delaware statute was applicable and the plaintiff's suit was begun too late.[5]

Does the fact that the judgment was entered for the defendant in action No. 2 on the basis that the action was barred by lapse of time preclude the application of res judicata to action No. 1, still assuming that the causes of action are identical? The answer to this question is likewise no. The adjudication in favor of the defendant operates as a bar to another suit on the same cause of action in the same jurisdiction.[6] The fact that the case was tried upon stipulation of fact does not make it any the less a final adjudication of the plaintiff's claim.

With these minor points out of the way we now get to the main question in the case which was hypothetically assumed in the discussion just preceding. That question is whether action 1 and action 2 are substantially identical. If they are the rule of law is clear enough. "Where a valid and final personal judgment is rendered on the merits in favor of the defendant, the plaintiff cannot thereafter maintain an action on the original cause of action."[7] The general principle is well known and undisputed. The difficulty comes in its application to varying sets of facts.

---

[5] Williamson v. Columbia Gas & Electric Corp., D.C.Del.1939, 27 F.Supp. 198, affirmed, 3 Cir.1939, 110 F.2d 15, certiorari denied, 1940, 310 U.S. 639, 60 S.Ct. 1087, 84 L.Ed. 1407. [See infra p. 1020.—Ed.]

[6] Restatement, Judgments § 49, comment a (1942) (note that it does not bar the action in another state). . . . [See Robert C. Casad & Kevin M. Clermont, Res Judicata 93–96 (2001).—Ed.]

[7] Restatement, Judgments § 48 (1942). Cromwell v. County of Sac, 1876, 94 U.S. 351, 352, 24 L.Ed. 195.

The best way to find out what is involved in the two actions is to look at the claims made by the plaintiff. Neither case went to trial on the facts so all we have is what the plaintiff charges, plus the supplementary affidavits, motions, and the like, which led up to the action of the Trial Judge dismissing plaintiff's action No. 1. The plaintiff alleges its organization and entry into the gas business. It says that the defendant, seeking to crush out a competitor, acquired the controlling shareholder interest in the plaintiff company and proceeded to manipulate its affairs to the disadvantage of the plaintiff and the advantage of the defendant. It says that after the plaintiff went into receivership the defendant named and controlled the receiver and the final result was that the plaintiff was forced into bankruptcy. . . .

The complaint in action No. 1 alleged that all this had been done as part of a continuing conspiracy in violation of Sections 1 and 2 of the Sherman Act, but, as amended, named only Columbia as defendant. The complaint in action No. 2, filed 7 months later, alleged that all that had transpired was in violation of Section 7 of the Clayton Act. The information set forth in the two complaints is substantially identical, plaintiff merely using words of conspiracy in the first action and replacing them with allegations that defendant did the same things on its own or through its agents in the second action. The wrongful acts alleged on the part of the defendant and the damages alleged to have been sustained by the plaintiff are practically identical in both suits. Indeed, the identity of the damage claims is almost startling, for except for a few figures with regard to interest the allegations of the particular items of damage are alike to the penny.

Nevertheless, plaintiff says the causes of action are different. We therefore proceed to examine the reasons stated to show the difference.

One alleged difference is that action No. 2 was a claim against Columbia as a sole tortfeasor and action No. 1 is a claim against Columbia as a conspirator. It is true that the complaint in No. 1 contains allegations of conspiracy and the complaint in action No. 2 did not. We do not think, however, that this constitutes a difference if the other elements alleged by the plaintiff are the same. Columbia was sought to be held as the party defendant in both suits. Whether Columbia is sought to be held as a sole tortfeasor or sued singly as one of several tortfeasors, assuming the injury is the same, does not matter. Several people getting together to do wrong to another do not commit a tort at the time they make their agreement, although they may commit a crime. The tort action arises when harm is done to the plaintiff. Then he may hold all the conspirators responsible for things done in pursuance of the conspiracy by any of them. But if he seeks to hold only one conspirator liable, as he may for the tort, since the liability is joint and several, he has not claimed anything substantially different from what he claims if he sues the sole conspirator as an individual tortfeasor. So we think, therefore, the presence of conspiracy allegations in action No. 1 and their absence in action No. 2 does not change the substance of the two claims.

Another difference claimed by the plaintiff in the two actions is that one suit is said to rest on the Sherman Act and the other on the Clayton Act. This argument carries no weight. While the rule may not have been clear at one time, we think it is now the law that the fact that different statutes are relied on does not render the claims different "causes of action" for purposes of res judicata. . . .

Also not in point, we think, are the cases cited by plaintiff in which the question involved was whether a plaintiff is required to state in separate counts claims based on the Sherman Act and the claims based on the Clayton Act. The purpose of the requirement of separate counts is to clarify the issues and simplify the trial, and thus the considerations in determining what are separate "causes of action" or claims for that purpose are not the same as those when the question is res judicata. As has often been said, the phrase "cause of action" means different things in different contexts.

Does action No. 1 differ from action No. 2 because the conspiracy charged in action No. 1 is alleged to be a continuing one? In a civil conspiracy suit each invasion of plaintiff's interest resulting from the conspiracy creates a new cause of action when the question is the application of the bar of the statute of limitations. This rule would be controlling if the issue here was whether the statute of limitations bars all or a part of the damages claimed by plaintiff as a result of a continuing conspiracy. But if the cause of action is the same, the principle of res judicata prevents our reaching that question, not because it was actually decided in action No. 2, but because the judgment is a final determination of not only what was actually in issue but what might have been in issue had it been raised. . . .

The purpose of the principle of res judicata is to end litigation. The theory is that parties should not have to litigate issues which they have already litigated or had a reasonable opportunity to litigate. A reading of the early cases as compared with recent ones makes it clear that the meaning of "cause of action" for res judicata purposes is much broader today than it was earlier. Formerly the whole aim in pleading, and in the elaborate system of writs, was to frame one single legal issue. That being the guiding principle, the phrase "cause of action" came to have a very narrow meaning. If the theory in the second suit was unavailable under the writ used in the first suit, the plaintiff had no opportunity to litigate it there and so plaintiff was not barred by res judicata. The force of the rule is still operative but the scope of its operation has been greatly limited by the modernization of our procedure. The principle which pervades the modern systems of pleading, especially the federal system, as exemplified by the free permissive joinder of claims, liberal amendment provisions, and compulsory counterclaims, is that the whole controversy between the parties may and often must be brought before the same court in the same action. The instant case presents an excellent example of one of the things these rules were designed to avoid. As pointed out above, the acts complained of and the demand for recovery are the same. The only thing that is different is the theory of recovery. The same witnesses and documents will be necessary in the trial in both cases. No material fact is alleged in action No.

1 that was not alleged in action No. 2, save the allegations of conspiracy. Everything that plaintiff was entitled to ask for from defendant was included in action No. 2.

Reference to the basic theory of tort liability substantiates the position taken here. To put it in rather elementary tort language, the basis of the plaintiff's recovery is liability-creating conduct on the part of defendant, the invasion of a legally protected interest of the plaintiff and the necessary causal connection between defendant's acts and plaintiff's injury. The plaintiff having alleged operative facts which state a cause of action because he tells of defendant's misconduct and his own harm has had his day in court. He does not get another day after the first lawsuit is concluded by giving a different reason than he gave in the first for recovery of damages for the same invasion of his rights. The problem of his rights against the defendant based upon the alleged wrongful acts is fully before the court whether all the reasons for recovery were stated to the court or not.

The points discussed here were all treated in the well-considered opinion of the District Judge. What we do is put in our own words our reason for thinking that he was right. The judgment will be affirmed.

Question: (1) There is a defense named "prior pending action." This defense will result in dismissal without prejudice if another action on the same claim between the same parties was pending in the same state, or in the same federal district, when the present action was commenced and if that other action is still pending. Why did the defendant in action No. 2 not plead immediately "prior pending action"?

SMITH v. KIRKPATRICK, 305 N.Y. 66, 111 N.E.2d 209 (1953). Plaintiff originally sued defendant in New York state court for money due him under an oral contract of employment. His complaint alleged that the contract required him to devote his full time to soliciting export accounts for defendant; that his remuneration was to be 50% of the income derived from the business procured by him; that he procured business from which defendant derived or would derive $26,000; and that defendant failed to pay him as agreed. Defendant obtained summary judgment for the reason that the agreement pleaded did not comply with the statute of frauds' requirement of a writing.

Plaintiff was granted leave to amend to quantum meruit. But he chose not to seek the modest recovery of that theory. Instead he set forth in his amended complaint two causes of action, in pursuit of an accounting and other relief. The first alleged an informal oral agreement terminable at will whereby plaintiff conducted some of his business through defendant's office, paying to defendant for such use of his office 50% of the gross profits of plaintiff's business so conducted. The second alleged an oral agreement of joint venture substantially to the same effect. A trial without jury was held, after which the trial judge dismissed the amended complaint on the merits because "plaintiff has failed to establish his causes of action by a fair preponderance of the credible evidence." The judge said: "It is clear to the court that the original position taken by the plaintiff correctly represented the relationship between the parties but, unfortunately for the plaintiff, that action was barred by the statute of frauds. . . . It ought to be stated, however, in fairness to the plaintiff, that the defendant was clearly guilty of overreaching the plaintiff, but the bar of the statute of frauds and the failure on the part of the plaintiff to proceed on the theory of quantum meruit have given to the defendant a windfall which in business morals and good conscience he is not entitled to."

Plaintiff took no appeal, or any other ameliorative procedural step. Instead he brought a second action, the present quantum meruit action seeking to recover the reasonable value of services rendered by him to defendant at defendant's request. The trial court denied a motion to dismiss on the ground of res judicata. The appellate division reversed and dismissed the complaint. The New York Court of Appeals in turn reversed the appellate division and affirmed the order of the trial court.

Judge Conway for the New York Court of Appeals conceded that deciding what constitutes the same or different causes of action is difficult. Quoting with approval earlier opinions holding that the number and variety of the facts alleged do not establish more than one cause of action so long as their result is the violation of but one right by a single legal wrong, he continued: "The two actions involve different 'rights' and 'wrongs'. The requisite elements of proof and hence the evidence necessary to sustain recovery vary materially. The causes of action are different and distinct and the rights and interests established by the previous adjudication will not be impaired by a recovery, if that be the outcome, in quantum meruit."[a]

---

[a] The court further held that plaintiff had not, by reason of the doctrine of election of remedies, lost his right to sue in quantum meruit by attempting and failing to succeed on the causes involved in the first action. The two types of remedies were not, said the court, so inconsistent or irreconcilable that the choice of the one precluded resort to the other.

What is this doctrine of election of remedies? Today much of the doctrine is substantive law. A person who originally had a choice of remedies may by his conduct before any action is brought disentitle himself to one or more of them. For instance, a defrauded person may lose the remedy of rescission, which involves a tender of return of the article purchased and a recovery of the purchase price: material alteration of the article after discovery of the fraud will confine the defrauded party to the remedy of damages in an action for deceit.

Sometimes it has been held that mere commencement of an action seeking a particular remedy is itself an election preventing resort to another remedy deemed to be inconsistent. Under the Federal Rules (and other modern procedural systems), however, such result should now be rare. As an example of today's procedural spirit, in federal court a party may pursue alternative and inconsistent remedies, subject always to the obligations of Rule 11, and may postpone the choice among them until a late stage of the action, even after findings of fact on the alternatives.

Question: (2) Is this case consistent with Williamson? Does it reach a desirable result, either as to res judicata doctrine or as to the merits?

O'BRIEN v. CITY OF SYRACUSE, 54 N.Y.2d 353, 429 N.E.2d 1158, 445 N.Y.S.2d 687 (1981). In 1973 plaintiffs sued defendants in New York state court for de facto appropriation, alleging that in the course of urban rehabilitation the defendant city authorities had so seriously interfered with plaintiffs' property rights as to constitute a de facto taking. A 1975 nonjury trial resulted in dismissal for failure to establish a de facto taking, which was affirmed on appeal. However, the appellate division did indicate that plaintiffs had suffered serious economic loss and that defendants' acts might have constituted trespass.

In 1978 plaintiffs brought a new suit against the same defendants for trespass to the same property at various times from 1967 to 1978. Defendants moved to dismiss on grounds of res judicata and failure to serve a timely notice of claim. The trial court denied the motion. The appellate division reversed, applying res judicata to dismiss the complaint. The New York Court of Appeals affirmed the appellate division on a somewhat different basis, as Chief Judge Cooke explained:

"In analyzing the complaint, plaintiffs' allegations fall into two categories: (1) those concerning activities underlying the 1973 litigation; and (2) those asserting trespass generally. Only the claims encompassed by the first category are definitely barred by res judicata.

"This State has adopted the transactional analysis approach in deciding res judicata issues (Matter of Reilly v. Reid, 45 N.Y.2d 24, 407 N.Y.S.2d 645, 379 N.E.2d 172). Under this address, once a claim is brought to a final conclusion, all other claims arising out of the same transaction or series of transactions are barred, even if based upon different theories or if seeking a different remedy (id., at pp. 29–30, 407 N.Y.S.2d 645, 648–49, 379 N.E.2d 172, 175–76). Here, all of defendants' conduct falling in the first category was also raised during the 1973 suit as the basis for that litigation. That proceeding having been brought to a final conclusion, no other claim may be predicated upon the same incidents.

"Plaintiffs, relying on Smith v. Kirkpatrick, 305 N.Y. 66, 111 N.E.2d 209, . . . urge that de facto appropriation and trespass are actions having different theoretical bases and requiring different evidentiary proof. This contention, however, erroneously characterizes the bases of the two causes. . . . [D]e facto appropriation, in the context of physical invasion, is based on showing that the government has intruded onto the citizen's property and interfered with the owner's property rights to such a degree that the conduct amounts to a constitutional taking requiring the government to purchase the property from the owner . . . . In effect, de facto appropria-

---

In any event, election of remedies, when properly viewed as a consequence of conduct, is distinguishable from res judicata, which is preclusion by judgment. See generally 18B Wright, Miller & Cooper § 4476.

tion may be characterized as an aggravated form of trespass. The pertinent evidence in both actions is the same. The basic distinction lies in the egregiousness of the trespass and whether it is of such intensity as to amount to a taking.

"In any event, even if it were assumed that the two actions involved materially different elements of proof, the second suit would be barred as to the claim predicated upon the first category allegations. When alternative theories are available to recover what is essentially the same relief for harm arising out of the same or related facts such as would constitute a single 'factual grouping' (Restatement, Judgments 2d, § 61 [Tent. Draft No. 5]), the circumstance that the theories involve materially different elements of proof will not justify presenting the claim by two different actions.[1] Consequently, plaintiffs' action is barred by the doctrine of res judicata insofar as the allegations in the first category are concerned.

"Finally, the second category of allegations—the general trespass allegations—are not barred by res judicata to the extent that they describe acts occurring after [commencement of] the 1973 lawsuit. They are, however, barred by reason of plaintiffs' failure to serve timely a notice of claim."

The court further explained that a condition precedent to bringing a tort claim against a municipality is a timely notice of claim providing information sufficient to permit investigation of the claim, and that the notice preceding the second suit had failed to mention any trespassory acts other than those underlying the 1973 lawsuit and so was ineffective with respect to the "claim" stemming from the second category of allegations.

Hennepin Paper Co. v. Fort Wayne Corrugated Paper Co.

United States Circuit Court of Appeals, Seventh Circuit, 1946.
153 F.2d 822.

[The plaintiff-seller first sued in the United States District Court for the Northern District of Indiana, alleging the defendant-buyer's failure to take and pay for 800 tons of corrugating material monthly. A written contract of July 1, 1941, provided: "Owner agrees to sell Customer, and Customer agrees to purchase, all of Customer's needs of .009 Corrugating Material that Customer will purchase monthly from the outside up to 600 tons, more or less." On the apparent assumption that this language was ambiguous and hence that evidence of contemporaneous negotiations would be admissible to clarify the meaning, plaintiff pleaded certain negotiations at about the time of the execution of the contract showing that the parties had intended a commitment to buy a minimum of 600 tons per month. Plaintiff also alleged that by oral agreement during October 1941 the parties had changed the minimum amount to 800 tons per month. On defendant's motion, the court struck out the allegations of the complaint

---

[1] To the extent Smith v. Kirkpatrick, 305 N.Y. 66, 111 N.E.2d 209, supra may be to the contrary, it is overruled.

regarding the negotiations contemporaneous with the written contract on the ground that the contract was unambiguous and parol evidence could not be used to vary its terms, and ruled that defendant was committed by the contract to buy only the amount it required. The case thus stood upon the written contract as allegedly modified by the oral agreement of October 1941. On this claim, defendant had verdict and judgment. Plaintiff took no appeal.

[Thereafter, plaintiff brought the present action in the United States District Court for the Northern District of Illinois to reform the written contract, so as to make it correspond with the "true intent and understanding of both parties," and to recover upon the contract as reformed. The alleged intent and understanding appeared from the negotiations contemporaneous with the written contract, i.e., a commitment to buy 600 tons monthly. The court granted defendant's motion for summary judgment, which was supported by affidavits setting forth the proceedings in the first action. Plaintiff appealed.]

■ Before EVANS and SPARKS, CIRCUIT JUDGES, and BALTZELL, DISTRICT JUDGE.

■ BALTZELL, DISTRICT JUDGE.

. . . .

Under the Federal Rules of Civil Procedure, and under the law of Indiana, the plaintiff had the right, in the first action, to, by proper pleading, ask that the written contract of July 1, 1941, be reformed and redrawn, as it is attempting to do in the second action. It certainly knew the same facts at the time the district court struck out paragraph 5 of the complaint in the first action [the allegations concerning the contemporaneous negotiations], as it knew at the time it drafted the complaint in the second action, and it should have filed either an amended complaint or an additional count or paragraph in that action so as to have presented all issues in the same action. This it could have done "regardless of consistency and whether based on legal or on equitable grounds or on both." Rule 8(e)(2) Federal Rules of Civil Procedure. The authority to thus have joined its claims is specifically provided for in Rule 18 of the Federal Rules of Civil Procedure, as follows, "(a) Joinder of Claims. The plaintiff in his complaint . . . may join either as independent or as alternate claims as many claims either legal or equitable or both as he may have against an opposing party."[b]. . .

. . . It made its election in the first action and it cannot now, in a separate action, assume an entirely different and inconsistent position in an effort to have the same written contract reformed. As heretofore observed, such effort, if it desired a reformation of the contract, should have been undertaken in the first action.

The Supreme Court of Indiana, in the case of Royal Insurance Co. v. Stewart, 190 Ind. 444, 129 N.E. 853, 857, said, "Where a party elects to sue upon a written contract as executed, and the action proceeds to trial and

---

[b] These were the texts of current Rules 8(d)(3) and 18(a) in force prior to July 1, 1966.

judgment, he cannot thereafter bring an action to reform the contract. 2 Black on Judgments, § 632" . . . . Again, in the case of Knight v. Electric Household Utilities Corp., 133 N.J.Eq. 87, 30 A.2d 585, 588, affirmed 134 N.J.Eq. 542, 36 A.2d 201, the court said, "Whether a plaintiff is precluded by the judgment, depends upon the extent to which legal and equitable remedies have been merged in the state where the judgment is rendered. Restatement—Judgments § 66. The judgment bars the suit for reformation if the plaintiff could have obtained reformation in his original action on the contract. Royal Ins. Co. v. Stewart, Inc., 190 Ind. 444, 129 N.E. 853. But where the law court cannot give equitable relief, the judgment is not a bar. Northern Assur. Co. v. Grand View Bldg. Ass'n, 203 U.S. 106, 27 S.Ct. 27, 51 L.Ed. 109." . . .

Not only under the Federal Rules of Civil Procedure, but under the law of Indiana, the plaintiff could have, in the first action, sought a reformation of the contract, and it was its duty to have done so if it desired to litigate that question. Not having done so, and having sought an entirely different and inconsistent remedy in that action, it cannot now maintain the second action. The district court properly granted the motion of defendant for a summary judgment.

The judgment of the district court is affirmed.

Questions: (3) Plaintiff brought an FELA action against a railroad and lost on the ground that he was not an employee of the railroad at the time of his injury. He now sues the railroad in the same court for the same injury, basing his claim on common-law negligence, a theory available only if he was not an employee. The railroad pleads bar. What decision on bar? (Reserve for later consideration the question of issue preclusion as to issues decided in the first action.) Compare Restatement (Second) of Judgments § 25 cmt. k (1982) (bar, thus counseling future litigants to plead in the alternative in the first suit), with People ex rel. Chicago & E. Ill. R.R. v. Fleming, 42 Ill.2d 231, 246 N.E.2d 275 (1969) (no bar, under older view of claim).

(4) Suppose a plaintiff sues in a state court for unfair competition, even though diversity of citizenship exists and more than the jurisdictional amount is at stake, but loses on the merits. She then alleges the same basic wrong in a federal-court action under the federal antitrust laws, an action over which the federal courts have exclusive jurisdiction. The defendant pleads bar. What judgment? (Assume that a generic law of res judicata applies here, so leaving for later consideration the choice of law on res judicata in an interjurisdictional setting.) See Cream Top Creamery v. Dean Milk Co., 383 F.2d 358 (6th Cir.1967) (no bar, because antitrust theory unavailable in state court and plaintiff not obliged to switch court systems).

(5) Reverse the situation in the preceding question, so that the first action was in the federal court under the federal antitrust laws, with no reference to the claim of unfair competition, and the second in the state court. Should the state-court action be barred by res judicata? Does the existence of diversity jurisdiction determine your answer? In the absence of diversity, what of supplemental jurisdiction? See Restatement (Second) of Judgments § 25 cmt. e (1982) (bar).

(6) Finally, assume that the plaintiff first sues in a state court for unfair competition, the suit is removed to federal court on the basis of diversity jurisdiction, and the plaintiff then loses on the merits, there never having been reference by amendment or otherwise to any federal antitrust claim. She later brings a second action in a federal court under the federal antitrust laws. Should the second action be barred by res judicata?

Sutcliffe Storage & Warehouse Co. v. United States

United States Circuit Court of Appeals, First Circuit, 1947.
162 F.2d 849.

■ Before CLARK,[1] MAHONEY and WOODBURY, CIRCUIT JUDGES.

■ CLARK, CIRCUIT JUDGE. The present four appeals were filed in four actions instituted in the district court on February 18, 25, 26, and 28, 1946, respectively, each claiming sums due, with interest, for the use and occupancy of the same realty in Boston, over different periods of time from June 15, 1942, to December 31, 1945. The first action covered the period from June 15, 1942, to June 30, 1943, the second and third each covered a succeeding year, and the fourth covered the final six months to the end in 1945. In all four the amounts claimed are computed at identical rates per square foot for the various parcels involved. In the latter three actions the district court has granted the defendant's motions to dismiss on the ground that they were brought for inseparable parts of the claim set forth in the first action. D.C.Mass., 68 F.Supp. 446. In the first action the defendant has made no motion and the court has entered no order.

Normally the district court would be acting quite within its discretion in taking steps to consolidate or otherwise avoid the duplication of such closely similar cases, whatever the substantive rights of the parties. Compare Rule 42(a), Federal Rules of Civil Procedure . . . . But the situation here is different because of the jurisdictional provisions of the Tucker Act. The first three actions claim amounts between eight and ten thousand dollars each; the last claims an amount in excess of four thousand dollars. The district court's jurisdiction of claims against the United States is limited to $10,000; for greater claims resort must be had to the Court of Claims in Washington. 28 U.S.C.A. § 41(20).[c] The plaintiff asserts a desire and right to sue for all amounts due in the courts of its own locality, asserting that the Tucker Act so permits and also relying on the facts alleged as showing four separate claims. And it is so entitled to sue if its contention is correct; otherwise it must either waive the excess or go to Washington to sue. The particular facts it relies upon are that on April 13, 1942, it executed a lease running until June 30, 1943, of certain premises it controlled to the United States Navy, and that this contract was renewed by separate renewal leases for periods identical with those covered by the last three actions. Plaintiff's contention—duly pleaded in each action—is

---

[1] Judge Clark of the Second Circuit, serving by designation.

[c] See present 28 U.S.C. § 1346(a)(2).

that beginning about June 15, 1942, the Navy occupied and used a greater area than was designated in the lease for the period in question and that therefore the plaintiff is entitled to the reasonable value of the use and occupancy of the additional area for each period.

The defendant, however, asserts that the general rule against "splitting causes of action" applies to the Government as defendant equally with all other litigants, and that the existence of separate renewal leases for the adjoining premises does not affect the nature of the plaintiff's claims, and, indeed, is important only in connection with the defendant's own defenses. For defendant has filed answers which both claim possession of the additional premises as being actually included in the leases and alternatively assert that if this is not the case the leases failed to include the additional premises by mistake and should now be reformed to include them. In the last three actions the answers also state as a separate defense the pendency of the first action. It was this defense, made the subject of a separate motion for preliminary hearing and adjudication, which was sustained by the court below.

As Professor Moore succinctly states, "The pendency of a prior pending action in the same federal court is ground for abatement of the second action." 1 Moore's Federal Practice 237; United States v. The Haytian Republic, 154 U.S. 118, 14 S.Ct. 992, 38 L.Ed. 930; [other citations omitted]. There is no reason why a court should be bothered or a litigant harassed with duplicating lawsuits on the same docket; it is enough if one complete adjudication of the controversy be had. As a matter of fact, it is often an advantage to the plaintiff to have the issue of double suits settled before he finds himself barred from full recovery by a partial but final judgment in one action. Thus here the plaintiff may count itself in luck to have the matter settled before a portion of its rights is irretrievably lost. For the test as ordinarily stated is whether the claims set up are legally the same so that judgment in one is a bar to the others. United States v. The Haytian Republic, supra, 154 U.S. 118, 129, 13 S.Ct. 992, 38 L.Ed. 930.

It is an ancient and well-settled legal principle that claims for amounts due on running accounts or as installment payments, such as rent under a lease, must include all amounts due at the time action is brought. [Citations omitted.] The same rule has been applied to claims for royalties under a patent, Buchanan v. General Motors Corp., 2 Cir., 158 F.2d 728, to claims affecting realty, as for continuing trespasses, Evans v. Durango Land & Coal Co., 8 Cir., 80 F. 433, 437, appeal dismissed Durango Land & Coal Co. v. Evans, 19 S.Ct. 875, 43 L.Ed. 1178, and to claims in quantum meruit for the occupancy of land, See v. See, 294 Mo. 495, 242 S.W. 949, 24 A.L.R. 880, with note collecting cases, 885–897. The doctrine is a salutary one in forcing the trial of identical matters together and affording a defendant once sued the protection of the doctrine of res judicata. Ordinarily there is no reason why a plaintiff cannot make all his claims on a running account at one time without piecemeal presentation. The fact that here involved are questions of federal jurisdiction is not a sufficient basis for departing from these usual rules as to the splitting of legal claims. The congressional policy is that all large claims must be presented in the one court in Washington, and in every practical sense there is here presented such a claim. Even though the plaintiff's own convenience might be served by adjudication in its vicinage, the congressional policy seems clearly opposed.

Nor can we see basis for varying the rule on the grounds urged by the plaintiff. There is no reason why the doctrine against splitting claims, which is thus only one application of the general doctrine of res judicata, should not apply to claims against the Government; and the cases so hold. . . .

Finally the particular facts urged by plaintiff do not vary the principle. That the plaintiff had separate leases for the adjoining property covering each fiscal year is not a sufficient basis to allow it to divide its claim for use and occupation of the particular premises here involved into four parts. In very truth its basic legal position depends upon its assertion that there were no leases covering these premises; once the existing leases are shown to affect them, the defendant has a solid basis for the assertion of its defenses. The plaintiff cannot in the same breath repudiate the leases and yet rely upon them as operating to separate its claim into parts.

The consequence of this conclusion is that there will be an affirmance of the dismissal of the latter three cases, Nos. 4238–4240 in this court. Since no action has been taken by the district court with reference to the earlier instituted action, No. 4241 in this court, there is nothing from which an appeal can be taken and we have no jurisdiction to consider it. [Citation omitted.] The plaintiff asks us, in the event of our affirmance of dismissal in the other three cases, to order dismissal also of this action to avoid what it terms its anomalous position in having one indivisible cause of action for an amount beyond the court's jurisdictional limit. But even if we had jurisdiction, no such action would be justified; for plaintiff has its own choice to make, whether it wishes to waive the greater amount and remain in the District Court for the District of Massachusetts, United States v. Johnson, 9 Cir., 153 F.2d 846, or now move that court for dismissal without prejudice under Rule 41(a)(2), F.R.C.P.[d] . . .

. . . .

OTHER WAYS TO SPLIT A CLAIM

Judge Charles Clark refers above to the "ancient and well-settled legal principle that claims for amounts due on running accounts . . . must include all amounts due at the time action is brought." Suppose *D* is *P*'s tenant under a lease calling for monthly payments. *P* sues for the May rent and obtains judgment. She cannot, because of the "ancient and well-settled legal principle," sue later for the earlier March or April rent.

---

[d] An additional option became available in 1960: transfer between the district court and the Court of Claims. See present 28 U.S.C. § 1631.

Question: (7) Does the punishment for splitting a claim fit the crime? Professor Cleary thought not. He would ordinarily have penalized the splitter by assessment of costs for trying to make two lawsuits do the work of one rather than by complete loss of the right of recovery. See Edward W. Cleary, Res Judicata Reexamined, 57 Yale L.J. 339, 349–50 (1948). But are costs a sufficient deterrent?

Change the facts and suppose that *D* gave *P* a series of promissory notes, one payable each month, for the rental under the lease. *P* obtains a judgment on a note falling due on May 1. May she sue thereafter on other notes in the series due on March 1 and April 1? Is this case different from the previous example? See Restatement (Second) of Judgments § 24 cmt. d (1982) (yes).

There is a conflict of authority as to whether the splitting rule precludes a person from bringing successive actions for property damage and for personal injury suffered in the same automobile accident. Compare Dearden v. Hey, 304 Mass. 659, 24 N.E.2d 644 (1939) (second action precluded), with Clancey v. McBride, 338 Ill. 35, 169 N.E. 729 (1929) (second action not precluded). Which is the preferable rule?

Much more difficult problems exist in this realm. For example, in the case of a toxic tort (such as exposure to asbestos), where the plaintiff has sued successfully for injury (from asbestosis) but chosen not to sue for considerably increased risk of injury (from cancer), can the plaintiff sue again when the risk later becomes reality? See Robert C. Casad & Kevin M. Clermont, Res Judicata 71–78 (2001).

Questions: (8) Judge Clark says that "the plaintiff may count itself in luck to have the matter settled before a portion of its rights is irretrievably lost." He apparently is suggesting that the attorney for the government might have let one of the four cases go to judgment and then have pleaded res judicata to the other three. Would this be an ethically permissible course of action by the government attorney? Would your answer be the same if it were done by a privately employed attorney? Indeed, would it be ethically permissible for a privately employed attorney not to use such a tactic if available?

(9) Can you make an argument that Judge Clark's suggested res judicata tactic ought not to be successful? See Todd v. Central Petroleum Co., 155 Kan. 249, 124 P.2d 704 (1942) (defendant's acquiescence in splitting).

RESTATEMENT OF JUDGMENTS

The traditional approach held that more than one "cause of action" could regularly arise out of the same transaction. Harking back to the days of the forms of action and the separation of law and equity, or to the days of code pleading, courts tended to equate a cause of action with a single theory or ground of recovery, to allow successive actions when the court concluded that different "rights" or "primary rights" had been simultaneously infringed, or otherwise to subdivide a transaction. See, e.g., Smith v. Kirkpatrick, supra p. 697, where the court strained to manipulate the terminology so as not to deny redress to a deserving plaintiff with misguided counsel.

Restatement of Judgments §§ 61–67 (1942) reflected this then-prevailing judicial attitude, but at the same time tried to set forth a series of black-letter rules that would bring order to a confused situation. The effort was not conspicuously successful.

Restatement (Second) of Judgments § 24 (1982) opts instead for a transactional view of "claim," providing that "the claim extinguished includes all rights of the plaintiff to remedies against the defendant with respect to all or any part of the transaction, or series of connected transactions, out of which the action arose" and also that the factual grouping constituting a "transaction" or a "series" is "to be determined pragmatically, giving weight to such considerations as whether the facts are related in time, space, origin, or motivation, whether they form a convenient trial unit, and whether their treatment as a unit conforms to the parties' expectations or business understanding or usage." The general rule of this section is exemplified in the Second Restatement's § 25 (along the lines of the Williamson, Hennepin, and Sutcliffe cases), but it is subject to the exceptions stated in § 26 (including the exceptions suggested by Cream Top Creamery v. Dean Milk Co., supra p. 701, and Todd v. Central Petroleum Co., supra p. 705).

This transactional approach of the Second Restatement puts pressure on the plaintiff not to overlook or withhold from his initial complaint any grievance he has relating to the transaction in question regardless of differences in "evidence," "grounds," "theories," "remedies," or "forms of relief." Should he err in the first instance, he will, given a modern procedural system, almost certainly have an opportunity to amend as the case unfolds. But failing that, he risks losing the unasserted portion of his claim.

Question: (10) Do you see any likely problems for counsel in applying the Second Restatement's definition of the factual grouping that constitutes a "transaction" or a "series"?

The Second Restatement is unarguably a work of high quality, although of course it is not perfect. It merits careful study because it manages to bring much order to the field and because it has so influenced the courts. It is thus worthy of debate. Here, it should be emphasized that although there is considerable and increasing case support for the Second Restatement's transactional approach, some courts still adhere to the older and narrower views.

COMMERCIAL BOX & LUMBER CO. v. UNIROYAL, INC., 623 F.2d 371 (5th Cir.1980). "On November 20, 1974, Commercial Box and Uniroyal entered into Purchase Contract No. 4–90145–2JB. The contract provided for Commercial Box to supply ammunition boxes to Uniroyal at the Joliet Army Ammunition Depot in Joliet, Illinois. . . . On July 21, 1975, after shipments began, Uniroyal notified Commercial Box of a change in destination. Uniroyal desired a change in its destination point from Joliet to the Kansas Army Ammunition Plant in Parsons, Kansas. Due to more rigid inspection procedures at the Kansas plant, a higher number of boxes were rejected. This required their transportation to Texarkana, Texas for correction of the defects. Upon re-delivery, they were accepted at the Kansas plant.

"After a breakdown in negotiations, Commercial Box filed a diversity suit in district court to recover its labor and lumber losses incurred in performing the contract arising out of the delivery and re-delivery of boxes to Kansas. A trial by jury resulted in a monetary judgment favorable to Commercial Box. The present suit arises out of the same purchase contract but involves a different issue. The [contract's] terms of payment allowed Uniroyal to deduct a discount if payment was made in ten days [from delivery]. . . .

"In the instant [diversity] suit, Commercial Box alleges a wrongful deduction of discounts from Uniroyal's payment prices for the period of November 1974 to January 1976. Commercial Box contends that Uniroyal had no right to the discounts since payments were made after the ten day period. Uniroyal filed a motion for summary judgment claiming that, in light of the allegations and decision in the first case, this case should be barred by res judicata . . . . The district court granted Uniroyal's motion . . . ."

After so stating the facts, the court of appeals reversed, explaining:

"The only dispute in this case as to the existence of the elements necessary to satisfy the federal res judicata rule is whether the present suit is based upon the same cause of action as the first. In comparing causes of action, the question is whether the prior right and duty and wrong are the same in each action. Kemp v. Birmingham News Company, 608 F.2d 1049, 1052 (5th Cir.1979). A second cause of action is the same if it refers to all grounds for relief arising out of the conduct complained of in the original action. Kilgoar v. Colbert County Board of Education, 578 F.2d [1033, 1035 (5th Cir.1978)].

"Based upon the foregoing discussion of the federal law on res judicata, it is clear that the present action does not arise out of conduct complained of in the first law suit. The first cause of action was based upon losses in labor and lumber which arose from Uniroyal's unilateral decision to change the destination point for the delivery of the ammunition boxes. That was the sole issue raised in the first action. There was no mention of Uniroyal's method of payment, the time period of its payments not [sic] its taking of discounts stemming from the payment price.[2] Not only were these issues

[2] Because the alleged wrongful discounting occurred both prior to and during Commercial Box' prior action, the district court held that the present issue could have been tried in the first cause of action. The district court thus found that Commercial Box' failure to litigate the present issue amounted to a lack of diligence. This court cannot agree. Commercial Box could have chosen to include the present issue in its first law suit under Rule 18(a). It was not required to do so, however. Commercial Box filed suit only on the labor losses it incurred

not raised but they are in no way germane or related to the challenge made in the first suit. The issue in the present suit is based upon a different cause of action than that alleged in the first suit. Likewise, the matter involved in the present case is not one that could have been litigated in the first case in light of that case's legal and factual bases. Since this court holds that the present issue is clearly a separate and distinct action from that raised in the first suit, the district court's granting of summary judgment based upon res judicata was clearly erroneous."

Question:(11) Does it matter whether a court proceeds (a) by defining "claim" narrowly so as to avoid claim preclusion or (b) by avoiding otherwise applicable claim preclusion through recognition of some exception thereto, such as defendant's agreement to claim-splitting?

Harrington v. Vandalia–Butler Board of Education

United States Court of Appeals, Sixth Circuit, 1981.
649 F.2d 434.

■ Before GEORGE CLIFTON EDWARDS, JR., CHIEF JUDGE, ENGEL and BOYCE F. MARTIN, JR., CIRCUIT JUDGES.

■ BOYCE F. MARTIN, JR., CIRCUIT JUDGE.

In 1974, Jeanne Harrington filed suit in the United States District Court for the Southern District of Ohio against the Vandalia–Butler Board of Education, alleging sex discrimination in [former] employment and seeking relief under Title VII of the Civil Rights Act of 1964, 42 U.S.C. § 2000e, et seq. After a bench trial in June, 1976, the court found that [by reason of inferior work facilities for the teaching of girls' physical education in junior high school] she had been discriminated against in violation of Title VII and awarded compensatory damages [of $6000] and attorney's fees [of $2000]. Harrington v. Vandalia–Butler Board of Education, 418 F.Supp. 603 (S.D.Ohio 1976). On appeal to this Court, the factual finding of discrimination was sustained. However, we reversed the judgment on the grounds that Title VII does not authorize compensatory damages and that the finding of discrimination, standing alone, did not support an award of attorney's fees. Harrington v. Vandalia–Butler Board of Education, 585 F.2d 192 (6th Cir.1978), cert. denied, 441 U.S. 932, 99 S.Ct. 2053, 60 L.Ed.2d 660 (1979).

---

related to the change in destination. The owner and general manager of Commercial Box, Robert Torrans, stated in his deposition that the fact that the first suit was confined to the issue of increased labor and lumber costs was due to representations by Uniroyal that if claims were made solely on those issues, there would be more likelihood of payment. When Uniroyal did not pay, Torrans believed that the prior law suit had better chances of success if it was confined to those issues. In light of such alleged representations by Uniroyal and since Commercial Box was never required to include the present issue in its first complaint, we refuse to accept the district court's finding of a lack of diligence.

In 1978, while Harrington's appeal was pending in this court, the Supreme Court decided Monell v. Department of Social Services, 436 U.S. 658, 98 S.Ct. 2018, 56 L.Ed.2d 611 (1978). That decision overruled Monroe v. Pape, 365 U.S. 167, 81 S.Ct. 473, 5 L.Ed.2d 492 (1961), insofar as the latter held that municipalities are not "persons" subject to liability under 42 U.S.C. § 1983. Immediately after Monell was decided, Harrington brought this action against the Board of Education, school principal Ralph Clay, and school superintendent Blutcher P. Gibson, alleging employment discrimination and seeking relief under § 1983.

The defendant Board of Education moved for summary judgment on the ground that the plaintiff's claim was barred by the doctrine of res judicata. On June 7, 1979, the District Court granted this motion, holding that the plaintiff had ample opportunity during the previous litigation to raise a claim for relief based on the alleged violation of § 1983.

. . . .

Harrington next contends that the defense of res judicata may not be invoked in this case because her present claim under § 1983 could not have been raised at the time the first suit was filed. She argues that the change in the law brought about by Monell precludes the availability of the defense. We disagree.

It is undisputed that appellant's earlier Title VII action and the present § 1983 suit are based on the same discriminatory acts. When two successive suits seek recovery for the same injury, "a judgment on the merits operates as a bar to the later suit, even though a different legal theory of recovery is advanced in the second suit." Cemer v. Marathon Oil Company, 583 F.2d 830, 832 (6th Cir.1978). [Other citations omitted.] This principle applies even if an intervening decision effects a change in the law which bears directly on the legal theory advanced in the second suit.

. . . Section 1983 was not "unavailable" to appellant when she filed her Title VII action. She was free to challenge the validity of Monroe v. Pape to the extent that it exempted municipalities from the ambit of § 1983. Moreover, it is clear that if she had brought the § 1983 claim initially and lost it on the basis of Monroe v. Pape, she would not be entitled to reassert the § 1983 claim in the aftermath of Monell. She would be bound by the prior judgment on the merits.[e] That prior judgment is no less binding against her here merely because she elected not to advance a § 1983 claim in her first action.

. . . .

In summary, the thrust of the decisions discussed above is this: generally, a judgment on the merits—even if erroneous—will be deprived of its conclusive effect only if it is vacated, reversed, or set aside on direct

[e] Congress has since provided for limited compensatory and punitive damages in Title VII actions for intentional discrimination. Civil Rights Act of 1991, Pub.L. No. 102–166, tit. I, § 102, 105 Stat. 1071, 1072. But likewise, Harrington would not be able to sue again under Title VII.

appeal. See Moitie v. Federated Department Stores, Inc., 611 F.2d 1267 (9th Cir.1980); 1B Moore's Federal Practice (2d Ed.) ¶ 0.416[2], p. 2231.

We are convinced, therefore, that the change in the law wrought by Monell, standing alone, does not preclude the application of res judicata to this case. That conclusion does not, however, end our inquiry, for "This court has held . . . that '[n]either collateral estoppel nor res judicata is rigidly applied. Both rules are qualified or rejected when their application would contravene an overriding public policy or result in manifest injustice.' Tipler v. E.I. du Pont de Nemours and Co., 443 F.2d 125, 128 (6th Cir.1971)." Bronson v. Board of Education, 525 F.2d 344 (6th Cir.1975), cert. denied, 425 U.S. 934, 96 S.Ct. 1665, 48 L.Ed.2d 175 (1976). See also United States v. LaFatch, 565 F.2d 81 (6th Cir.1977), cert. denied, 435 U.S. 971, 98 S.Ct. 1611, 56 L.Ed.2d 62 (1978); Ferguson v. Winn Parish Police Jury, 589 F.2d 173, 176 n. 6 (5th Cir.1979).

. . . .

In Bronson v. Board of Education, supra, we addressed the problem of res judicata in the context of school desegregation litigation. For our purposes in the present case, it is sufficient to recall our conclusion that the strong public policy against perpetuating racial segregation in public schools does not necessarily preclude the application of res judicata and collateral estoppel to school desegregation cases. 525 F.2d 349.

Finally, United States v. LaFatch, supra, involved an attempt by a corporation to recover $50,000.00 it had paid to Anthony LaFatch. According to the corporation, the money was paid in cooperation with the FBI and under its surveillance. The transaction had provided the basis for an extortion indictment against LaFatch. After the District Court dismissed the extortion charge at the close of the government's case, the corporation filed suit in an Ohio court to recover the $50,000.00. It obtained a verdict against LaFatch for only $15,000.00. The federal District Court, which had retained custody of the money, found that the Ohio court's judgment was res judicata as to the ownership of the money and granted LaFatch's motion asking for its return. We, however, held that res judicata should not be applied for reasons of overriding public policy. We said that if the corporation's claim that it made the payment in cooperation with the FBI were true, the application of res judicata would violate the public policy of encouraging cooperation with law enforcement authorities in thwarting attempts at bribery and extortion. 565 F.2d at 84.

. . . .

. . . The policy at issue here—the availability of compensatory damages for violations of Title VII rights—does not, in our view, rise to the degree of overall importance to our society which Bronson and LaFatch suggest is necessary to avoid the preclusive effect of judgments.

We realize that in the circumstances of this case the doctrine of res judicata seems to work an unfair result. Appellant has established that she was discriminated against; the defendant's "vindication" on the merits was attributable only to the remedial limits of Title VII. Compare Bronson, supra, at 349. When she filed her Title VII action, appellant had good reason to believe that she could not successfully sue a school board under § 1983, which permits the award of damages for violations of constitutional and statutory rights. Upon learning from Monell that a municipality is now considered a "person" for the purposes of § 1983, appellant filed another suit which raised the § 1983 claim for the first time. There is undoubtedly an element of injustice in the application of res judicata to preclude that claim. However, we believe that the decisions of the Supreme Court and of this circuit, together with the policies underlying the doctrine of res judicata, compel that result.

Manifest injustice of the type necessary to except a case from the application of the doctrine is simply not present here. A mere showing that the second litigation, if allowed to proceed, would produce a different result than the first is not a showing of manifest injustice. Because the doctrine of res judicata effects a balance between competing interests, a certain degree of inequity is inevitable. Res judicata ensures the finality of judicial decisions. It encourages reliance on those decisions, thereby establishing certainty in legal relations. It bars vexatious litigation and promotes economy of judicial time and effort. Brown v. [Felsen, 442 U.S. 127, 131, 99 S.Ct. 2205, 2209 (1979)]. If the Supreme Court had decided, subsequent to appellant's Title VII suit, that compensatory damages could indeed be awarded under that statute, appellant would nevertheless be barred from reasserting her Title VII claim to collect such damages. That result would be no more or less fair than the one achieved here. The injustice inherent in either result is a necessary by-product of the general rule that judgments are final. In our opinion, that general rule must prevail here.

. . . .

Questions: (12) Could the plaintiff have pressed a § 1983 count in her original suit without violating former Rule 11? Even if so, would the legal system have wanted to encourage her to do so? Did, then, her having originally "elected not to advance a § 1983 claim" really constitute a basis for the district court's application of res judicata?

(13) Similarly, did the Sixth Circuit mean to imply that claim preclusion would not apply if current Rule 11 had made a § 1983 count "unavailable"? Did, then, it matter whether she could have elected to advance a § 1983 claim?

(14) If she had brought a § 1983 count in her original suit and lost, then the Supreme Court changed the law in Monell, and so she sued again, the Sixth Circuit said the result would have been the same. Whether she had asserted a § 1983 count or had not, then, res judicata would have precluded a second suit. What, then, is this Harrington case's real rationale?

SECTION 2. ADJUDICATION NOT ON THE MERITS

Waterhouse v. Levine

Supreme Judicial Court of Massachusetts, 1903.
182 Mass. 407, 65 N.E. 822.

CONTRACT for goods sold and delivered. Writ in the Municipal Court of the City of Boston dated April 13, 1901.

On appeal to the Superior Court the case was tried before Sherman, J., without a jury. The defence pleaded and relied upon was a former judgment. The judge refused to rule that the judgment was a bar to this action, and made the ruling stated by the court, admitting evidence to show the issue tried in the former action. He found for the plaintiff[s] in the sum of $336.04; and the defendant alleged exceptions.

■ BARKER, J. The defendant contends that the plaintiffs cannot maintain this action because judgment was rendered for the defendant upon a trial in a previous action between the same parties and for the same cause of action. Evidence was admitted in this action against the defendant's exception that the former judgment was upon the ground that the first suit was prematurely brought, the goods for the price of which both suits were brought having been sold upon a credit which had not expired when the first action was begun. The judge found as a fact that the only issue decided in the former action was whether that action was prematurely brought, and that the former judgment was entered because the action was prematurely brought and for that reason alone.

The only answer in the former action was a general denial. But under that answer the defence that the goods were bought upon a credit not expired when the suit was begun was open. [Citations omitted.] Whether oral evidence would be admissible to show that a former judgment went solely upon an issue which strictly could not have been tried upon the pleadings as they stood, but was in fact tried with the assent of all parties, is a question upon which we express no opinion.

It is only when rendered upon the merits that a judgment constitutes an absolute bar to a subsequent action for the same cause and the parties are concluded upon all issues which might have been tried. . . .

. . . .

Exceptions overruled.

Questions: (15) To what extent, if any, should evidence extrinsic to the record be admissible to show that a prior judgment went solely on an issue that was not open on the pleadings but was tried by consent pursuant to Rule 15(b)(2)?

(16) If there was evidence at the first trial on each of two alternative issues and the trial judge's decision did not show upon which issue he decided, would his testimony on this point be admissible in the second action?

Keidatz v. Albany

Supreme Court of California, 1952.
39 Cal.2d 826, 249 P.2d 264.

■ TRAYNOR, JUSTICE. In this action to recover damages for fraud, plaintiffs alleged that they were induced to buy a newly-constructed home from defendants by certain false and fraudulent representations respecting the character of the construction of the house and its location on the described real property. They further alleged that the representations were known by defendants to be false and were made to induce plaintiffs to purchase the property and that the contract price of $6,500 exceeded the value of the property by $3,000. In their answer defendants denied the allegations of fraud and pleaded affirmatively that plaintiffs' action was barred by two former adjudications between the parties. Defendants then made a motion for summary judgment supported by affidavits setting out the following undisputed facts: In 1949, plaintiffs brought an action to rescind the contract for fraud and failure of consideration. A demurrer to the second amended complaint was sustained with leave to amend. Plaintiffs failed to amend within the time allowed, and judgment was entered for defendants for costs. Thereafter plaintiffs unsuccessfully sought relief from the judgment under section 473 of the Code of Civil Procedure. No appeal was taken, however, from the judgment or from the order denying relief under section 473. Approximately four months after the judgment in the rescission action was entered, plaintiff brought this action for damages for fraud. The trial court granted defendants' motion for summary judgment and plaintiffs have appealed.

Plaintiffs contend that their unsuccessful attempt to secure rescission of the contract does not bar their present action for damages for fraud. Defendants, on the other hand, contend that the former judgment is res judicata of all issues presented here. Since the former judgment was entered after a general demurrer had been sustained with leave to amend, it is necessary to determine the scope of the doctrine of res judicata in such circumstances. The procedural effect of such a judgment appears to be sui generis. It is a judgment on the merits to the extent that it adjudicates that the facts alleged do not constitute a cause of action, and will, accordingly, be a bar to a subsequent action alleging the same facts. [Citations omitted.] Moreover, even though different facts may be alleged in the second action, if the demurrer was sustained in the first action on a ground equally applicable to the second, the former judgment will also be a bar. [Citations omitted.] If, on the other hand, new or additional facts are alleged that cure the defects in the original pleading, it is settled that the former judgment is not a bar to the subsequent action whether or not plaintiff had an opportunity to amend his complaint. [Citations omitted]; Restatement, Judgments, § 50, Comments c and e.

In plaintiffs' first action they sought rescission of the contract. In addition to alleging certain fraudulent representations whereby they were induced to enter into the contract, they alleged that they had offered to restore everything of value they had received, and sought the return of the payments they had made. It appeared from the complaint, however, that the alleged defects in construction became apparent to plaintiffs over a year before they sought to rescind, and defendants successfully demurred on the ground that the action was barred by laches and by failure to rescind promptly. See, Civ.Code § 1691; Williams v. Marshall, 37 Cal.2d 445, 455–456, 235 P.2d 372. Whether or not the complaint stated a cause of action for rescission, the demurrer should have been overruled if a cause of action for damages was stated. [Citations omitted.] Plaintiffs' complaint did not, however, allege that the property was worth less than the price they agreed to pay for it, Civ.Code § 3343, and accordingly, it did not state a cause of action for damages for fraud. [Citations omitted.] In the present action, plaintiffs have added this allegation that was absent from their former complaint, and accordingly, under the rule hereinabove stated, the former judgment is not a bar to this action.

Defendants contend, however, that Wulfjen v. Dolton, 24 Cal.2d 891, 151 P.2d 846, establishes the rule that a party claiming to have been defrauded must seek all the relief to which he may be entitled in one action, and that he may not, after having failed in an action to rescind a contract for fraud, thereafter bring a second action for damages. In the Wulfjen case, however, the judgment in the rescission action had not been entered on demurrer, but had followed a full trial on the merits, and the court applied the rule that such a judgment is res judicata not only as to issues actually raised, but as to issues that could have been raised in support of the action. See, Sutphin v. Speik, 15 Cal.2d 195, 202, 99 P.2d 652, 101 P.2d 497. As has been pointed out above, however, it has been the settled rule in this state that a judgment entered on demurrer does not have such broad res judicata effect. [Justice Traynor analogized this rule to the plaintiff's former right to bring a new action after suffering an involuntary nonsuit. (This right was abrogated in 1947 by Cal.Code Civ. Proc. § 581c, providing that a judgment of nonsuit operates as an adjudication on the merits unless the court otherwise specifies.) He conceded that there are forceful arguments, in view of the liberal rules relating to amendments to the pleadings, for requiring the plaintiff to set forth in one action all the facts relating to his dispute.] On the other hand less prejudice is suffered by a defendant who has had only to attack the pleadings, than by one who has been forced to go to trial until a nonsuit is granted, and the hardship suffered by being forced to defend against a new action, instead of against an amended complaint, is not materially greater. See, Commercial Centre Realty Co. v. Superior Court, 7 Cal.2d 121, 129–130, 59 P.2d 978, 107 A.L.R. 714. We do not feel, however, that at this time we should reweigh the conflicting arguments over the wisdom of the rule we apply. Since it is a settled rule of procedure upon which parties are entitled to rely in conducting their litigation, any change therein should be made by the Legislature and not by this court.

. . . .

The judgment is reversed.

■ SCHAUER, J., concurs in the judgment.

DISMISSAL FOR INSUFFICIENCY OF COMPLAINT

The position of Restatement of Judgments § 50 (1942) was essentially as follows:

1. After judgment sustaining a demurrer on the ground that the facts stated were insufficient to constitute a cause of action, a new action on a complaint in which the defect has been corrected is not barred. It does not matter that the plaintiff failed in the first action to avail himself of permission to amend.

2. However, judgment sustaining a demurrer on such ground precludes a new action alleging the same, or virtually the same, facts as alleged in the first action. This was seen as an application of direct estoppel, which precludes repetitively litigating the same issue.

3. Also, judgment sustaining a demurrer precludes a new action where the defect in the first action was "an entire failure to state a cause of action" rather than "merely the omission of an essential allegation." If, for example, the plaintiff sued for invasion of privacy and the court dismissed on the ground that the state recognized no such right, a new action on the same cause is barred even if the state has meanwhile altered its views on the right of privacy.

Question: (17) Should this last rule be inexorably applied, or are there extraordinary situations where relitigation ought to be allowed? Suppose, for instance, that a board of education set up plans for reduction of the teaching force as part of a school desegregation program and that a group of African-American teachers brought an action seeking to enjoin the plans as racially discriminatory. On demurrer, the court upheld the plans and dismissed the action. There was no appeal. Subsequently, in an identical case arising in another state, the Supreme Court of the United States declares the plans to be unconstitutional. Should those original teachers be able to maintain a new action over the defendant's plea of res judicata? See Restatement (Second) of Judgments § 26(1)(d) (1982).

There persists limited support for the First Restatement's view. But some courts depart from it to the extent of also barring a new action if, after the demurrer was sustained in the first action, the plaintiff was expressly granted leave to amend and he neglected or refused to amend. E.g., Elfman v. Glaser, 313 Mass. 370, 47 N.E.2d 925 (1943). And other courts view even this revised version of the First Restatement's position as inconsistent with the modern rules of pleading and especially the freedom to amend, and hence as not going far enough toward embracing bar. See Osserman v. Jacobs, 369 Mass. 200, 339 N.E.2d 193 (1975) (Kaplan, J.);

Developments in the Law—Res Judicata, 65 Harv.L.Rev. 818, 836–37 (1952).

Therefore, Restatement (Second) of Judgments § 19 cmt. d (1982) abandons the position of the First Restatement, by providing in effect that a judgment for insufficiency of the complaint normally operates as a bar unless the rendering court otherwise specifies by order. Most states have followed suit. In this connection, consider the effect of a rule like Federal Rule 41(b), discussed in the following case and in 18A Wright, Miller & Cooper § 4435.

Rinehart v. Locke

United States Court of Appeals, Seventh Circuit, 1971.
454 F.2d 313

[Plaintiff, by his attorney, sued in 1969 under 42 U.S.C. § 1983, claiming that his arrest by the defendants—private detectives and police officers—deprived him of his constitutional rights. The Federal Rule 12(b)(6) dismissal by District Judge Julius J. Hoffman was based upon the failure to allege lack of probable cause. Plaintiff sought leave to amend to include such an allegation, but the judge denied leave, stating no reason. Plaintiff did not appeal.

[More than a year later (and nearly six years after the events in suit), plaintiff brought a second action based on the same arrest, the complaint being identical in substance to the first except that it included an allegation of lack of probable cause. The same district court, this time by Judge Joseph S. Perry, sustained the defense of res judicata and dismissed. Plaintiff appealed.]

■ Before SWYGERT, CHIEF JUDGE, and FAIRCHILD and STEVENS, CIRCUIT JUDGES.

■ FAIRCHILD, CIRCUIT JUDGE.

. . . .

Plaintiff contends that the May, 1969 dismissal did not establish that defendants were not liable to him under § 1983 on account of the 1964 arrest, but established only that he had no cause of action unless he was able to plead and prove lack of probable cause.

[The court stated that the traditional rule supported plaintiff's position, citing Gould v. Evansville & Crawfordsville R.R., 91 U.S. 526 (1876), and Restatement of Judgments § 50 cmt. c (1942).]

Arguably Rule 41(b), F.R.C.P., may have changed this rule where the earlier judgment, as in this case, was entered in a federal court. The Rule provides in part: "Unless the court in its order for dismissal otherwise specifies, a dismissal under this subdivision and any dismissal not provided for in this rule, other than a dismissal for lack of jurisdiction, for improper venue, or for failure to join a party under Rule 19, operates as an adjudication upon the merits."

It has been held that the list in Rule 41(b) of types of dismissal which are not presumptively adjudications on the merits is not exclusive, and that the situations where dismissals not provided for in Rule 41 are to operate as adjudication on the merits are those "in which the defendant must incur the inconvenience of preparing to meet the merits because there is no initial bar to the Court's reaching them."[2] The same decision indicates that a dismissal for failure to fulfill a "precondition" for consideration of the merits is not a decision on the merits.

With this gloss upon the Rule, the question remains a close one, but we are persuaded that under the Rule an order of a district court which dismisses a complaint for failure to state a claim, but which does not specify that the dismissal is without prejudice, is res judicata as to the then existing claim which it appears plaintiff was attempting to state. This view places upon a plaintiff in a case like the 1969 case in this instance the burden of persuading the district court either to include a specification that the dismissal is without prejudice or to permit an amendment. If plaintiff is unsuccessful, his recourse is to appeal. We think this view is consistent with the expedient purpose of the Rules.

[The other part of the opinion, to the effect that the action was also barred by the statute of limitations, is omitted.]

The judgment appealed from is affirmed.

Question: (18) May a district court specify that its dismissal for lack of jurisdiction is "with prejudice" or is "an adjudication upon the merits"? See Restatement (Second) of Judgments § 20 cmt. d (1982); 9 Wright & Miller § 2373.

DISMISSAL FOR FAILURE TO PROSECUTE OR TO OBEY A COURT ORDER OR RULE

Does a dismissal for failure to prosecute, or failure to obey a court order or rule, operate as an adjudication on the merits? In this situation, there has not been in a literal sense an adjudication on the merits—there usually has been no consideration whatever of the merits—but the dismissal nevertheless operates as a bar unless the rendering court otherwise specifies by order. Such is the result that is suggested by Rule 41(b), which has its counterpart in a majority of the states, and is more generally provided by Restatement (Second) of Judgments § 19 cmt. e (1982). The justification for the harsh result to the litigant deprived of a chance to

[2] Costello v. United States, 365 U.S. 265, 286, 81 S.Ct. 534, 545, 5 L.Ed.2d 551 (1961). [This case held that a dismissal of a denaturalization proceeding for failure to file a required affidavit of good cause with the complaint, where the dismissal order did not specify whether it was with or without prejudice, was not "an adjudication upon the merits" despite the wording of Rule 41(b). The Court reached this result by ruling that the Rule's term "lack of jurisdiction" is not to be read technically or narrowly, and that this dismissal was for "lack of jurisdiction."—Ed.]

establish his claim lies in the interests of his opponent and those of litigants generally in having the court effectively control its docket and enforce its procedure.

Dismissal on these grounds is reviewable on appeal for abuse of discretion. In most instances where abuse of discretion is the test, the appellate court strains to uphold the decision of the lower court. Here, however, appellate judges do not look with favor upon the sanction of dismissal. As the appellate court said in Industrial Building Materials, Inc. v. Interchemical Corp., 437 F.2d 1336, 1339 (9th Cir.1970): "Application of the remedy rests within the sound discretion of the court, but since it may severely punish a party not responsible for the alleged dereliction of his counsel, the rule should only be invoked in extreme circumstances. In reviewing the propriety of dismissal under Rule 41(b) we should, we think, look to see whether the court might have first adopted other, less drastic alternatives." See also Russell G. Vineyard, Note, Dismissal with Prejudice for Failure to Prosecute: Visiting the Sins of the Attorney upon the Client, 22 Ga.L.Rev. 195 (1987).

"ON THE MERITS"

Restatement of Judgments § 48 (1942) stated that a valid and final personal judgment for the defendant acts as a bar only if it was "on the merits." But, over time and in response to considerations of fairness and efficiency, the rule of bar has come to be applied more broadly, with judgments not passing directly on the substance of the claim acting as a bar.

Restatement (Second) of Judgments § 19 (1982) consequently omits the phrase "on the merits," and comment a thereto explains that this was done because the phrase is no longer descriptive of the many situations in which bar applies. But, of course, this omission does not mean that under the Second Restatement *any* valid and final personal judgment for the defendant acts as a bar: the remains of the on-the-merits condition became the set of not-on-the-merits exceptions laid out in § 20.

Restatement (Second) of Judgments

(1982).

§ 20. *Judgment for Defendant—Exceptions to the General Rule of Bar*

(1) A personal judgment for the defendant, although valid and final, does not bar another action by the plaintiff on the same claim:

(a) When the judgment is one of dismissal for lack of jurisdiction, for improper venue, or for nonjoinder or misjoinder of parties; or

(b) When the plaintiff agrees to or elects a nonsuit (or voluntary dismissal) without prejudice or the court directs that the plaintiff be nonsuited (or that the action be otherwise dismissed) without prejudice; or

(c) When by statute or rule of court the judgment does not operate as a bar to another action on the same claim, or does not so operate unless the court specifies, and no such specification is made.

(2) A valid and final personal judgment for the defendant, which rests on the prematurity of the action or on the plaintiff's failure to satisfy a precondition to suit, does not bar another action by the plaintiff instituted after the claim has matured, or the precondition has been satisfied, unless a second action is precluded by operation of the substantive law.

Question: (19) Should Restatement (Second) of Judgments § 20(2) (1982) apply to permit a second action even where the dismissal of the first action came not at the threshold but only after full-blown trial? Or instead should there be another exception to the exception, providing for bar where it would be "manifestly unfair" to subject the defendant to the second action? See John E. Eichhorst, Symposium Note, Res Judicata Effects of Involuntary Dismissals: When Involuntary Dismissals Based upon Prematurity or Failure to Satisfy a Precondition to Suit Should Bar a Second Action, 70 Cornell L.Rev. 667 (1985).

SECTION 3. COUNTERCLAIM

Counterclaim pleaded.—Once a defendant pleads a counterclaim, the principles of former adjudication generally apply to it just as they apply to an original claim in a complaint. See Restatement (Second) of Judgments §§ 21(1), 23 (1982).

The one exception to this rule applies when the defendant counterclaims, but the defendant cannot obtain full recovery because the action was brought in a court that was not empowered to give the defendant full recovery on his counterclaim (such as a court of limited jurisdiction with a ceiling on damages) and because no procedural devices were available by which the defendant might readily have obtained full recovery (such as transferring the entire case to another court in the same legal system). In this very narrow situation, the defendant's claim is not extinguished by the judgment, and he may seek recovery on the remainder of his claim by a subsequent action in a competent court. Cf. id. § 21(2).

Permissive counterclaim not pleaded.—Whenever applicable law permits a counterclaim to be asserted but does not make it compulsory, a defendant has the choice between responding to the plaintiff's claim with an answer that includes the counterclaim and reserving the subject matter of the potential counterclaim for an independent action.

This rule is usually straightforward enough, but complications ensue when the same facts constitute both a ground of defense to the plaintiff's claim and a basis for counterclaim. If these facts are not used as a defense, the main action may be lost, and therefore the defendant will almost certainly so use them. But suppose that the defendant nevertheless wishes to reserve his affirmative claim in order to bring it as an independent action, perhaps in another forum that is more convenient or might apply more favorable law. Should the defendant be free to rely on the common facts as a defense, without pleading a counterclaim, and still bring an independent action based on those same facts?

Schwabe v. Chantilly, Inc.

Supreme Court of Wisconsin, 1975.
67 Wis.2d 267, 226 N.W.2d 452.

■ WILKIE, CHIEF JUSTICE. This is a landlord-tenant case presenting a question of civil procedure. In a prior action, the landlord, Chantilly, Inc., sued the tenants, James and Mary Schwabe, for nonpayment of rent. The Schwabes set up the affirmative defense that they were fraudulently induced to sign the lease, but they did not counterclaim. Judgment was awarded to the Schwabes based upon this defense. Now in the present action they seek compensatory and punitive damages against Chantilly and Chantilly's managing officer, Abraham Wolinsky, based upon the fraud and upon malicious prosecution. Chantilly and Wolinsky moved to strike the causes of action based on fraud, arguing that by setting up the affirmative defense in the first action the Schwabes obliged themselves to also counterclaim in that action or else lose the claim completely. The trial court agreed and ordered the fraud causes of action struck from the complaint. The Schwabes appeal. We reverse.

. . . .

The sole question presented here is whether plaintiffs are barred from maintaining these causes of action for fraud because they raised fraud as an affirmative defense to the prior rent-collection action brought by Chantilly, one of the defendants here. This court considered a related problem in Wm. H. Heinemann Creameries v. Milwaukee Automobile Ins. Co.[3] arising from personal injury litigation following an auto collision between A and B. In the first action where A sued B, the suit was dismissed by court order upon stipulation of the parties. Then in a subsequent action, B sued A and one question raised on appeal was whether B's action was barred on principles of res judicata because B had not counterclaimed in the first suit. Relying on sec. 263.14(1), Stats., making all counterclaims permissive, and

[3] (1955), 270 Wis. 443, 71 N.W.2d 395, 72 N.W.2d 102.

sec. 58 of the Restatement of Judgments, the court held B's action not barred on this ground. Sec. 263.14(1), Stats., provides:

"A defendant *may* counterclaim any claim which he has against a plaintiff, upon which a judgment may be had in the action." (Emphasis supplied.)

Sec. 58 of the Restatement of Judgments provides, at page 230:

"Where the defendant does not interpose a counterclaim although he is entitled to do so, he is not precluded thereby from subsequently maintaining an action against the plaintiff on the cause of action which could have been set up as a counterclaim."

In discussing this section, the court in Heinemann particularly relied on comments b and f. However, comments c and d following this section apply to the facts in the instant case where plaintiffs set up an affirmative defense but not a counterclaim in the first action.

The comments distinguish between situations where the plaintiff in the second action lost in the first case and where he won. Where he loses in the first case, he is barred from commencing a new action. As comment c to sec. 58 provides:

"*Defense and counterclaim—Judgment for plaintiff—Collateral estoppel.* Where the same facts constitute a ground of defense to the plaintiff's claim and also a ground for a counterclaim, and the defendant alleges these facts as a defense but not as a counterclaim, and after litigation of the defense judgment is given for the plaintiff, the defendant is precluded from maintaining an action against the plaintiff based on these facts. This is in accordance with the rule as to collateral estoppel stated in sec. 68, that where a question of fact essential to a judgment is actually litigated and determined by the judgment, the determination is conclusive between the parties in a subsequent action on a different cause of action."

However, where the party wins in the first action, based on the affirmative defense, it is permissible then to start a new action. He is then not in the position of attacking facts previously established. As comment d indicates:

"*Defense and counterclaim—Judgment for defendant—Splitting Claims.* Where the same facts constitute a defense to the plaintiff's claim and also a ground for counterclaim, and the defendant sets up these facts as a defense but not as a counterclaim, and after litigation of the defense judgment is given for the defendant, the defendant is not precluded from maintaining a subsequent action against the plaintiff based upon these facts. In such a case he is not improperly splitting his cause of action (compare sec. 62), although he uses the same facts first as a defense to the plaintiff's claim and later as the basis of an action against the plaintiff. In the subsequent action, the judgment in the prior action is conclusive as to the facts actually litigated and determined in the first action (see sec. 68)."

. . . Because judgment was rendered for the Schwabes in the first case they may now sue for damages caused by the fraud. Their present action does not seek to upset the determination reached in the first case and, in fact, affirms it. If they had lost, however, in the first action, under comment c a different result would be reached.

Defendants argue that plaintiffs' action is barred based primarily upon . . . Vukelic v. Upper Third Street Savings & Loan Asso.[6] . . . .

In Vukelic, A sued B in a mortgage foreclosure action, and the court determined that approximately $15,000 was due under the mortgage. Then in a second action B sued A alleging as a "cause of action" that B had never received approximately $11,000 under the mortgage and that the amount due should be reduced accordingly. The court held B's action barred on the grounds that the first judgment was res judicata as to the amount due. For two reasons, however, Vukelic is not persuasive in the case at bar. First, the second action commenced by B really amounted to an attack on the first judgment. In the instant case the two actions involved are completely consistent. Second, although Vukelic contains language indicating that an unused counterclaim is lost unless it is a " 'distinct cause of action,' " "one having no connection with the matters involved in the former cause of action; one not involving the same subject matter," such is no longer the law. Vukelic was decided in 1936, and in 1943 this court adopted the present version of sec. 263.14(1), Stats., making all counterclaims optional. . . . The statement in Vukelic that the only unused counterclaims that survive are those with no connection to the subject matter of the first action is thus consistent with the federal rule, but not the present rule in Wisconsin.

. . . .

We conclude that the instant case seeking damages based on fraud is not barred . . . .

. . . .

Order reversed and cause remanded for further proceedings not inconsistent with this opinion.

Questions: (20) If the Schwabes had affirmatively sought in the first action to rescind the fraudulently induced lease, would their fraud causes of action for damages have been precluded? See Restatement (Second) of Judgments § 22 cmt. d, illus. 6 (1982) (indicating that claim preclusion would apply).

(21) Instead, if without provoking any objection the Schwabes had presented evidence in the first action of the extent of damages caused by the fraud, would their fraud causes of action for damages have been precluded? See Wickenhauser v. Lehtinen, 302 Wis.2d 41, 734 N.W.2d 855 (2007) (no, apparently unless parties and court formally treated the case as if a counterclaim were asserted).

Compulsory counterclaim not pleaded.—As conceded in Schwabe, there are two situations in which a defendant does not have a free choice between bringing a counterclaim and bringing an independent action.

[6] (1936), 222 Wis. 568, 269 N.W. 273.

Whenever one of these two important situations occurs, a defendant who could have but did not interpose his claim as a counterclaim will be barred from maintaining a subsequent action thereon.

1. One such situation occurs when the plaintiff's claim and the defendant's claim are related in such a way that if the defendant were to prevail on his claim in any subsequent action, the effect would be to nullify or undo the prior judgment. This "common-law compulsory counterclaim rule" applies whether or not the jurisdiction has a compulsory counterclaim statute or rule of court, and whether or not the prior judgment is by default. Indeed, it is this doctrine that makes default judgments mean something.

Perhaps the scope of this somewhat imprecisely stated doctrine can be best conveyed by example. On the one hand, Restatement (Second) of Judgments § 22(2)(b) cmt. f, illus. 9 (1982) offers this example: "A brings an action against B for failure to pay the contract price for goods sold and delivered and recovers judgment by default. After entry of final judgment and payment of the price, B brings an action against A to rescind the contract for mutual mistake, seeking restitution of the contract price and offering to return the goods. The action is precluded." On the other hand, *D* normally may default in *P*'s personal-injury action and then bring his own action against *P* for injuries sustained in the same accident, the idea being that a judgment for *D* would not "nullify" *P*'s prior judgment. The line lies somewhere between these two examples.

The doctrine's scope is also suggested by consideration of its genesis, which reveals the doctrine to be a specific aspect of a broad principle of claim preclusion: a valid and final personal judgment generally precludes the defendant from later asserting mere defenses to the claim. Therefore, the defendant cannot later pursue an action that is essentially a way to defend anew against an already adjudicated claim. See generally Kevin M. Clermont, Common–Law Compulsory Counterclaim Rule: Creating Effective and Elegant Res Judicata Doctrine, 79 Notre Dame L.Rev. 1745 (2004).

MENARD, INC. v. LITEWAY LIGHTING PRODUCTS, 282 Wis.2d 582, 698 N.W.2d 738 (2005). For six years Liteway sold lights to Menard. Often the buyer held money back for defective products it returned. But the relationship fizzled, with no more sales or returns after 1999 but with a persisting dispute over how much the buyer still owed. In 2000, Liteway sued Menard on the unpaid invoices and soon recovered about $355,000 by a default judgment.

Then, in 2001, Menard sued Liteway for failing to reimburse fully for the earlier returns. Liteway asserted claim preclusion as an affirmative defense and moved for summary judgment. The trial court denied the motion and, by nonjury trial, awarded Menard about $140,000. The court of appeals reversed. The Supreme Court of Wisconsin (5–2) affirmed that reversal, even though Wisconsin still has no compulsory counterclaim statute or rule of court, because "Menard's suit is merely an attempt to collaterally attack the original judgment by raising defenses and counterclaims to Liteway's original suit."

"Moreover, we conclude that Menard's claims fall under the common-law compulsory counterclaim rule because allowing Menard to proceed with its present suit would impair Liteway's rights as determined in the original action and would undermine the validity of the judgment Liteway obtained. Both suits involve the amount of money Menard owed Liteway, and Liteway could not have recovered the price of goods sold to Menard if those goods were defective."

---

2. The second situation occurs when the potential counterclaim falls within the express terms of a compulsory counterclaim statute or rule of court. After a case goes to judgment, a failure to have asserted an available counterclaim will preclude bringing a subsequent action thereon.

HORNE v. WOOLEVER, 170 Ohio St. 178, 163 N.E.2d 378 (1959), cert. denied, 362 U.S. 951, 80 S.Ct. 861 (1960). Woolever sued Horne in an Ohio court in February 1957, seeking $150,000 for personal injuries resulting from a collision between their two automobiles. Horne removed the action to the United States District Court for the Northern District of Ohio on diversity grounds, and he thereafter filed in the federal court an answer that was in effect a general denial. He did not plead a counterclaim.

Subsequently, in August 1957, while that federal action was pending, Horne sued Woolever in an Ohio court for $65,000 for his own injuries sustained in the same accident.

In March 1958, Horne paid Woolever $25,000 to settle the latter's claim in the first lawsuit. The attorneys filed a stipulation in the federal court for dismissal of Woolever's action with prejudice, and the federal judge so ordered.

Thereafter, Woolever used his federal judgment to defeat Horne's Ohio action. Ultimately, the Supreme Court of Ohio affirmed, holding the federal judgment to be a bar. Judge Taft explained that Rule 13(a) had required Horne to assert his own claim as a counterclaim in Woolever's action in the federal court, whether that action was originally instituted in that court or was removed from the state court, and even though Ohio has no statute or rule comparable to Rule 13(a). See Rule 81(c). He added: "To the extent to which a judgment of a federal court operates as res adjudicata in that court, it operates as res adjudicata in the courts of this state."

Question: (22) If the Horne case were decided the other way, would the Supreme Court of the United States have jurisdiction to review the final judgment of the Ohio court? (Of what, if any, relevance is the fact that Rule 13 is not an act of Congress but a rule of court promulgated pursuant to the Rules Enabling Act? Of what, if any, significance is the fact that the Rules Enabling Act provides that the Rules shall govern only procedural matters and not affect substantive rights?) If the Supreme Court of the United States were to hear this imagined case, how should it decide?

Dindo v. Whitney

United States Court of Appeals, First Circuit, 1971.
451 F.2d 1.

■ Before ALDRICH, CHIEF JUDGE, MCENTEE and COFFIN, CIRCUIT JUDGES.

■ ALDRICH, CHIEF JUDGE. Following remand of this case with our order vacating the district court's sustaining of the defense of the statute of limitations, 429 F.2d 25,[f] the defendant pleaded, successfully, that the action was barred by reason of plaintiff's having failed to assert it as a compulsory counterclaim, pursuant to F.R.Civ.P. 13(a), in a prior action. This question we had raised ourselves, but declined to resolve because of lack of briefing, and because of its possible complexity. In now granting defendant's motion to dismiss on this ground, the court had before it certain testimony by way of depositions to which it made reference in its opinion, 52 F.R.D. 194. We accordingly consider the case in terms of a motion for summary judgment. This, of course, requires accepting plaintiff's version of the facts, no matter how unlikely they may seem. See Coastwise Packet Co. v. United States, 1 Cir., 1968, 398 F.2d 77, 79, cert. denied 393 U.S. 937, 89 S.Ct. 300, 21 L.Ed.2d 274.

Briefly, plaintiff Dindo alleges that defendant Whitney was a passenger in a car belonging to Whitney, but driven by Dindo; that the car went off the road, severely injuring Dindo, and that the cause of the accident was Whitney's putting his hand through the steering wheel in reaching for a flashlight on the steering shaft. Suit was brought in the district court of New Hampshire on October 29, 1968, within the New Hampshire period for

---

[f] Vermont plaintiff-driver Dindo and New Hampshire defendant-owner-passenger Whitney, en route to a hunting trip in northern Maine, had an accident in the Province of Quebec. When suit was brought in the New Hampshire federal court, the Quebec statute of limitations had run but the New Hampshire statute (and the Vermont statute) had not. The district court dismissed. The court of appeals reversed, saying that the relation of the parties to Quebec was most fortuitous, and that the application of the Quebec statute would further no Quebec interest but would frustrate New Hampshire's interests to some degree.

In 1952 the New Hampshire Supreme Court on similar facts had applied the Quebec statute of limitations. However, in a 1966 case involving parties who had had an accident in Vermont on the way from their New Hampshire home to another part of New Hampshire, that court had applied New Hampshire law, which allowed a guest passenger to recover from a host driver for ordinary negligence, instead of Vermont law, which required gross negligence. The federal court of appeals concluded that the 1966 decision had implicitly overruled the 1952 case, and that the New Hampshire Supreme Court would have applied the New Hampshire statute of limitations in the instant case.

suit, the accident having occurred on October 30, 1965. Dindo and Whitney had long been friends, Dindo living in Vermont and Whitney in New Hampshire. In June, 1966 Whitney sued Dindo in the district court of Vermont. Dindo gave the papers to his insurance agent, who forwarded them to Whitney's insurer which, by virtue of a clause in the policy, insured Dindo as a driver of Whitney's car with Whitney's permission. The insurer retained counsel, but informed Dindo that he should retain his own counsel as well, as the ad damnum [$150,000] exceeded the coverage [$50,000]. Dindo did not do so. In March, 1967 [after an answer, including the defense of contributory negligence, was filed,] the insurer paid Whitney a sum within the policy limit in settlement [$45,000], and an entry was made on the court docket, "Settled and discontinued." The present action is defended by the same insurer, Whitney, as the car's owner, being covered by the policy that had included coverage of Dindo.

It is clear on the record that before insurance company counsel settled the case they conferred with Dindo on a number of occasions, and apparently saw no defense to the suit. All that was said is not entirely clear. The [N.H. district] court made findings of fact which may have been the most reasonable resolution, but which went beyond permissible bounds on a motion for summary judgment. It was proper for it to find that Dindo did not request counsel to file a counterclaim against Whitney, and that there had been time to do so, but we must accept Dindo's position that he did not realize, until he spoke with new counsel in September 1968, that he had a basis for so doing, namely, Whitney's conduct in reaching for the flashlight. Dindo, assertedly, had thought that because he was driving the car he could have no claim.

[The court here quoted from Rule 13(a).] The accident, by whomever caused, was obviously the same transaction or occurrence. Dindo claims, however, that the compulsory rule is inapplicable to him since the original case was settled, rather than pursued to final judgment on the merits. Alternatively, he says that it is inequitable to assert the rule against him when he had not realized he had a counterclaim until afterwards.

The bar arising out of Rule 13(a) has been characterized variously. Some courts have said that a judgment is res judicata of whatever could have been pleaded in a compulsory counterclaim. Dragor Shipping Corp. v. Union Tank Car Co., 9 Cir., 1967, 378 F.2d 241; United States v. Eastport S.S. Corp., 2 Cir., 1958, 255 F.2d 795. Other courts have viewed the rule not in terms of res judicata, but as creating an estoppel or waiver. Lawhorn v. Atlantic Refining Co., 5 Cir., 1962, 299 F.2d 353; Dow Chemical Co. v. Metlon Corp., 4 Cir., 1960, 281 F.2d 292. The latter approach seems more appropriate, at least when the case is settled rather than tried. The purposes of the rule are "to prevent multiplicity of actions and to achieve resolution in a single lawsuit of all disputes arising out of common matters." Southern Constr. Co. v. Pickard, 1962, 371 U.S. 57, 60, 83 S.Ct. 108, 110, 9 L.Ed.2d 31. If a case has been tried, protection both of the court and of the parties dictates that there should be no further directly related litigation. But if the case is settled, normally the court has not been greatly burdened, and the parties can protect themselves by demanding cross-releases. In such circumstances, absent a release, better-tailored justice seems obtainable by applying principles of equitable estoppel.

If, in the case at bar, Dindo, clearly having opportunity to assert it, cf. LaFollette v. Herron, D.C.Tenn., 1962, 211 F.Supp. 919, knew of the existence of a right to counterclaim, the fact that there was no final judgment on the merits should be immaterial, and a Rule 13(a) bar would be appropriate. His conscious inaction not only created the very additional litigation the rule was designed to prevent it exposed the insurer to double liability. We are not persuaded that a final judgment is a sine qua non to invocation of the bar; there is nothing in the rule limning the term "judgment."

However, on a motion for summary judgment this factual finding could not be made on the present record. We are not prepared to say at this time what lesser facts would compel a conclusion of estoppel as a matter of law. There should be a hearing on the merits, the facts to be found by the jury. United States ex rel. Westinghouse Electric v. James Stewart Co., 9 Cir., 1964, 336 F.2d 777, subject to instructions by the court, Home Indemnity Co. of New York v. Allen, 7 Cir., 1951, 190 F.2d 490. . . .

The judgment of the district court is vacated and the action remanded for further proceedings consistent herewith.

Question: (23) What did the court mean when it said that allowing this extra suit would expose the insurance company to "double liability"?

ESTOPPEL

Equitable estoppel, sometimes called estoppel in pais, generally provides that a party may not take a position in litigation when that position is inconsistent with earlier conduct and the change would unfairly burden another party who has detrimentally relied. For an example of when this many-faceted doctrine might apply, consider the situation of a party having recovered worker's compensation for an accident and then in subsequent tort litigation unfairly trying to deny that she was an employee. Obviously, this loose doctrine presents a risk of expanding to punish merely unseemly behavior. See generally 18B Wright, Miller & Cooper § 4477.

Contrasted with res judicata, the looser doctrine of equitable estoppel looks to the party's earlier out-of-court or in-court conduct, rather than to a prior judicial decision. Equitable estoppel can therefore play a role complementary to res judicata. For instance, failure to interpose a compulsory counterclaim in a proceeding that ended by a voluntary dismissal, rather than in an actual judgment, may nevertheless equitably estop the defendant from later pursuing the counterclaim.

Another doctrine that some people confuse with res judicata is judicial estoppel. This minor but controversial doctrine, which varies widely from jurisdiction to jurisdiction and which is even rejected outright in a good number of states, usually holds that a person cannot unfairly take factual positions in litigation that are directly inconsistent with positions previously taken by the person in a prior proceeding. See generally New Hampshire v. Maine, 532 U.S. 742, 121 S.Ct. 1808 (2001).

Judicial estoppel aims to prevent abuse of the judicial machinery. It differs from equitable estoppel in that it treats only in-court conduct but does not require detrimental reliance. It differs from the issue-precluding effect of res judicata in that it can estop a successful party and does not require the prior rendering of a judicial decision.

INSURER–INSURED CONFLICTS OF INTEREST

The Dindo case points up some of the numerous problems that exist when counsel for a liability insurance company represents its insured, as the interests of insurer and insured are likely not to be identical. A converse conflict of interest arises when the insured is interested in pressing a compulsory counterclaim, but the insurer has no interest in doing so. This kind of problem stimulated great criticism in Maine upon the adoption of a rule identical to Rule 13(a). After less than a year of experience under that rule, it was amended to except motor vehicle tort cases from its reach. See 1 Richard H. Field, Vincent L. McKusick & L. Kinvin Wroth, Maine Civil Practice 263–64 (2d ed. 1970).

Question: (24) Why should the whole doctrine of claim preclusion not be reduced to court rules similar to Rule 13(a) (and somewhat analogous to the compulsory party-joinder provisions of Rule 19)? See 18 Wright, Miller & Cooper § 4407, at 147–52.

TOPIC C

ISSUE PRECLUSION

SECTION 1. REQUIREMENTS OF THE RULE

Little v. Blue Goose Motor Coach Co.

Supreme Court of Illinois, 1931.
346 Ill. 266, 178 N.E. 496.

[Dr. Robert M. Little, while driving his automobile in East St. Louis, Illinois, collided with a bus owned and operated by Blue Goose Motor Coach Company. Blue Goose sued Dr. Little in a justice of the peace court for damage to its bus caused by the collision and, after nonjury trial, recovered judgment for $139.35. Dr. Little's appeal to the county court was dismissed for lack of prosecution on April 2, 1926.

[During the pendency of that suit before the justice of the peace, Dr. Little commenced an action against Blue Goose in the city court of East St. Louis for personal injuries suffered by him in the collision. Dr. Little died on May 25, 1926, and his wife as executrix was substituted as plaintiff. Her new declaration alleged in the first count that Dr. Little's death had been caused by the defendant's negligence, and in the second count that his death had been caused by the defendant's willful and wanton negligence. Blue Goose then set up as a defense the justice of the peace proceedings, contending that they constituted an "estoppel by verdict." Blue Goose introduced evidence, including testimony by the justice of the peace himself, bearing on what had occurred in the proceedings before the justice of the peace. The plaintiff had verdict and judgment for $5000.

[On appeal from the latter judgment to the Appellate Court of Illinois, that court reversed with the following finding of fact: "The Court finds that appellant sued Dr. Robert M. Little, appellee's testate, before a Justice of the Peace for damages to its bus in the collision which occurred on November 1, 1925, and recovered a judgment therefor in the sum of $139.35; that in the rendition of said judgment it was necessarily determined that the collision and damages occasioned to the bus were due to the negligence of Dr. Little and that immediately prior to his death he could not have maintained an action for personal injuries growing out of the same collision."]

■ PER CURIAM.

. . . .

The first question arises on the ruling of the Appellate Court invoking against the claim of plaintiff in error the doctrine of estoppel by verdict. It is argued on behalf of plaintiff in error that where a former adjudication is relied on as a bar to a subsequent action it is essential that there be identity both of the subject matter and of the parties, and that in the instant case the subject matter is not the same, as this is the action for death by wrongful act for the benefit of the widow and next of kin, while the former suit was a claim for damages for injury to personal property. The issue on which this case is bottomed was the issue of fact which lay at the base of the judgment recovered before the justice of the peace. The allegation of the special plea is that the issue there raised was one of negligence on the part of Dr. Little on one hand and the defendant in error on the other, and that issue having been determined against Dr. Little, the fact is forever settled between these parties or their privies. Estoppel by verdict arises when a material fact in any litigation has been determined in a former suit between the same parties or between parties with whom the parties to the subsequent suit are in privity, where the fact was also material to the issue. The Appellate Court found as a matter of fact that the issue tried before the justice of the peace was an issue of negligence and was the same issue, arising on the same facts as those relied upon in the action for the wrongful death of Dr. Little, and that the issue of negligence was necessarily determined in the suit by the defendant in error against Dr. Little. That question of fact was tried before the city court in this case, and on the evidence there adduced the Appellate Court made its finding of fact. That issue of fact therefore is not open here, and we are to proceed to further consideration of the cause under the established fact that the issue of negligence, at least under the first count of the declaration, is the same issue tried before the justice of the peace.

While on appeal to the county court the trial, had there been one, would have been de novo, yet when the appeal was dismissed and a procedendo was issued to the justice of the peace, the judgment of the justice of the peace became a final determination of that issue between the parties, and is conclusive not only upon the immediate parties to that suit but also upon all persons in privity with them, and cannot be litigated again between the parties to that case or their privies in any subsequent action in the same or other court where that question arises, whether upon the same or a different cause of action or whatever may have been the nature or purpose of the action in which the judgment was rendered or of that in which the estoppel is set up. [Citations omitted.] It follows that Dr. Little could not during his lifetime maintain the action filed by him against the defendant in error, and since plaintiff in error's right to recover damages under the Injuries Act depends upon Dr. Little's right, during his lifetime, to recover damages for injuries arising out of the same collision, plaintiff in error cannot recover here. [Citation omitted.] In a suit under the Injuries Act, the cause of action is the wrongful act and not merely the death itself. [Citations omitted.] Plaintiff in error therefore was not entitled to recover under the first count of her declaration, and the Appellate Court did not err in so holding.

It is contended, however, that as the second count of the declaration charges wanton and willful negligence on the part of defendant in error, contributory negligence on the part of Dr. Little is not a defense, and that the judgment of the city court was therefore right. Contributory negligence is not a defense to willful and wanton conduct, but it does not follow that the judgment of the city court was right because of that fact. In all cases charging willful and wanton negligence it is necessary to make proof of such negligence, and where there is no such proof no recovery under such charge can be had. [Citation omitted.] The finding of the Appellate Court that the collision was caused by the negligence of Dr. Little necessarily was a finding of fact on the willful negligence count as well as the general negligence count. Thus the rule that contributory negligence on the part of the plaintiff is not a defense to a charge of willful negligence does not apply. Whether Dr. Little or the bus driver was responsible for the accident was, as we have seen, settled. The judgment for $139.35 necessarily decided that the bus driver was not guilty of willful negligence.[a]

. . . .

Judgment affirmed.

Question: (1) In Illinois it was held that two causes of action arise when a negligent act causes a person to suffer both personal injury and property damage, so that a judgment for property damage did not preclude a later action for personal injury. Clancey v. McBride, supra p. 705. Suppose Dr. Little, and not Blue Goose, had brought suit in the justice of the peace court for property damage and, after trial, he had won judgment. What should be the effect of these proceedings in the later city court action by the executrix?

DIMENSIONS OF AN ISSUE

In applying the doctrine of issue preclusion, there predictably arises the difficult problem of defining the scope of the issue foreclosed. Restatement (Second) of Judgments § 27 cmt. c (1982) does not essay a precise definition of "issue," but instead proposes several factors to consider in resolving whether a matter to be presented in the second action and a matter presented in the first action constitute the same issue. Most notable among these factors is the degree of overlap, with respect to the two matters, between the evidence and legal argument advanced in the first action and that to be advanced in the second. This approach is then applied in illustrations 4 and 6:

"4. A brings an action against B to recover for personal injuries in an automobile accident. A seeks to establish that B was negligent in driving at an excessive rate of speed. After trial, verdict and judgment are given for B. In a subsequent action by B against A for injuries in the same accident, A is precluded from setting up B's negligence as a defense, whether or not the alleged negligence is based on an assertion of excessive speed. It is reason-

[a] Under then applicable Illinois law, the plaintiff in an ordinary negligence action had to plead and prove his own due care. See infra p. 1213.

able to require A to bring forward all evidence in support of the alleged negligence in the initial proceeding. (It is assumed in this Illustration that the forum has no applicable compulsory counterclaim rule. See § 22.)

"6. A brings an action against B to recover an installment payment due under a contract. B's sole defense is that the contract is unenforceable under the statute of frauds. After trial, judgment is given for A, the court ruling that an oral contract of the kind sued upon is enforceable. In a subsequent action by A against B to recover a second installment falling due after the first action was brought, B is precluded from raising the statute of frauds as a defense, whether or not on the basis of arguments made in the prior action, but is not precluded from asserting as a defense that the installment is not owing as a matter of law on any other ground."

Jacobson v. Miller

Supreme Court of Michigan, 1879.
41 Mich. 90, 1 N.W. 1013.

[Miller sued two persons in Michigan state court for installments of rent then due under a written lease. The general issue was pleaded, but there was no denial under oath of the execution of the lease as required by court rule if execution was to be disputed. Jacobson contended at the jury trial that he was not liable because the other defendant, and not he, had occupied the premises during the period for which rent was claimed. The plaintiff had verdict and judgment.

[Thereafter Miller sued for subsequent installments of rent now due under the same lease. Jacobson, by the requisite statement under oath, denied execution of the lease. The plaintiff offered the prior judgment as conclusive proof of execution, and the trial judge received it as such over the defendant's objection. The correctness of this ruling was the principal question on appeal from judgment for the plaintiff.]

■ COOLEY, J.

. . . .

It is not denied by the defendant that if the execution and delivery of the lease had been disputed in the first suit, the determination of the issue would have been conclusive upon the parties in any subsequent litigation involving the right to rents under the same lease. The case would then have been within the principle of Gardner v. Buckbee, 3 Cow. 120, where a question entirely similar in its legal aspects was considered and passed upon.

But the execution of the lease was not denied in the former suit. No issue was made upon it, and the defendant, by not denying it, suffered a default in respect to it which left it wholly outside the issue made and actually passed upon. Consequently it was not and could not have been considered by the court as a point which in that suit was open to controversy. The defendants, by their pleadings, made the actual existence of the lease an immaterial fact, and had the lease counted upon been a known forgery, the case must nevertheless have proceeded with its existence and genuineness admitted.

It is said, however, that the defendants in the first suit were at liberty to put the execution of the lease in issue, and that it was their duty to do so then if they proposed to contest it at all. This is upon the ground that public policy will not suffer the withholding of a defense with a view to further litigation, when a single suit might determine the whole controversy. This is no doubt true where the defense is sought to be made use of in the retrial of a dispute respecting the same subject matter of the former litigation. Pierce v. Kneeland, 9 Wis. 23, 31. The question now is, whether the proposition is applicable to a case where the subject matter of the second suit is different. In other words, where one is sued in respect to one subject matter, must he bring forward all his defenses, at the peril, if he fails to do so, of being debarred of them in any subsequent litigation which may involve the same questions, though relating to a different subject matter? We think not.

The precise point was before the Supreme Court of the United States in Cromwell v. County of Sac, 94 U.S. 351, 356, in which Mr. Justice Field, delivering the opinion of the court, says: "Various considerations, other than the actual merits, may govern a party in bringing forward grounds of recovery or defense in one action, which may not exist in another action upon a different demand, such as the smallness of the amount or the value of the property in controversy, the difficulty of obtaining the necessary evidence, the expense of the litigation, and his own situation at the time. A party acting upon considerations like these ought not to be precluded from contesting in a subsequent action other demands arising out of the same transaction. A judgment by default only admits for the purpose of the action the legality of the demand or claim in suit; it does not make the allegations of the declaration or complaint evidence in an action upon a different claim."

. . . .

The judgment must be reversed, with costs, and a new trial ordered.

■ [The concurring opinion of JUSTICE GRAVES is omitted.]

Questions: (2) What arguments may be made that the Jacobson decision was wrong? See Denio v. City of Huntington Beach, 74 Cal.App.2d 424, 168 P.2d 785 (1946) (suggesting preclusion of a more broadly defined issue); 18 Wright, Miller & Cooper § 4414, at 348–51 (arguing for preclusion of unlitigated defenses).

(3) As the realm of issue preclusion is allowed to expand to reach some matters not really considered in the prior action—which may be done by enlarging the dimensions of the "issue" or by relaxing the "actually litigated and determined" requirement—what differences, if any, remain between the doctrines of issue preclusion and claim preclusion? See 18 Wright, Miller & Cooper § 4406, at 139

("The distinction is one of emphasis and degree, no more."); id. § 4417, at 431 ("If different theories and consequences are to apply, care must be taken in seeking the most useful distinction possible."); cf. David P. Currie, Res Judicata: The Neglected Defense, 45 U.Chi.L.Rev. 317, 336–42 (1978).

(4) Assuming an issue has been properly raised, by the pleadings or otherwise, should it be deemed "actually litigated and determined" if it is disposed of via total absence of proof? judgment as a matter of law? summary judgment? demurrer? stipulation? admission? default?

RES JUDICATA AND THE MECHANICS OF SETTLEMENT

When a prospective defendant settles a claim by payment of an agreed sum before action is brought, it is routine practice for him to condition his payment upon the execution by the intending plaintiff of a release of the claim. If the plaintiff has already brought a suit, the defendant will still insist upon a release as part of the settlement, but there is the additional problem of disposing of the pending lawsuit. The defendant is likely to insist upon a disposition on the record that will protect him as fully as possible against further litigation on the claim. In that way, if the plaintiff does bring a later action on the same claim, the defendant may plead not only the release as a defense but also res judicata.

At common law a voluntary nonsuit or discontinuance by the plaintiff was not a bar to a new suit. However, there was a common-law device called a retraxit, a voluntary renunciation of the claim by the plaintiff in open court, which both terminated the particular action and barred relitigation of the same cause. It may be assumed that in usual practice the plaintiff made such a renunciation only after reaching a settlement.

Under present-day practice a mere voluntary dismissal is not a bar, nor is a dismissal by stipulation of the parties, unless the notice or order of dismissal or the stipulation states otherwise. See Rule 41(a). There is, however, some authority in state courts to the effect that a dismissal shown on its face to be by agreement is a bar to a new suit. E.g., Doan v. Bush, 130 Ark. 566, 198 S.W. 261 (1917).

Another way to dispose of a lawsuit that has been settled is to enter a consent judgment for the plaintiff in the agreed amount, with a further entry of "Judgment satisfied." But the parties who have adjusted their differences may prefer not to spread upon the record the details of their arrangement. They may therefore file a consent judgment for the plaintiff in a nominal amount, with a "Judgment satisfied" entry. Or the defendant may insist, as a condition of the settlement, that the entry be "Judgment for the defendant." All these forms of consent judgment terminate the pending action and normally preclude another suit upon the same claim.

A consent judgment is satisfactory enough when there is no possibility of an action upon a different claim involving the same issues. As just suggested, a consent judgment, like a judgment by default, has merger or bar effect so far as the same claim is concerned, even though nothing was in fact ever litigated. But when assertion of a different claim involving the same issues is possible, one must give attention to collateral estoppel.

The customary statement of the rule of collateral estoppel specifies that the issue must have been actually litigated and determined in order for there to be collateral estoppel effect. It is all very well to say conformably, as Professor Fleming James, Jr., convincingly did in Consent Judgments as Collateral Estoppel, 108 U.Pa.L.Rev. 173 (1959), that consent judgments ought not to have collateral estoppel effect. The fact remains that in some states, apparently a minority, the law is otherwise, as shown by Sheldon R. Shapiro, Annotation, Modern Views of State Courts as to Whether Consent Judgment Is Entitled to Res Judicata or Collateral Estoppel Effect, 91 A.L.R.3d 1170, 1183–91 (1979). The flawed theory of these states' approach is that the truth of all the facts alleged by the plaintiff and necessary to the recovery are raised by the plaintiff's pleading, and the defendant should not be able to escape the consequence of judgment by waiving the right to contest them.

Failure by counsel to take into account this risk involved in a consent judgment has produced unintended and serious consequences for the client in a later action. In Biggio v. Magee, 272 Mass. 185, 172 N.E. 336 (1930), for example, Magee's suit against Biggio for injuries from an automobile accident had been settled by Biggio's attorney, actually an attorney retained and paid by his liability insurer, with an entry on the court record of judgment for Magee in a substantial sum by agreement of the parties and with a further entry of judgment satisfied. When Biggio, this time represented by counsel of his own choosing, sued Magee for his own injuries, the court held him collaterally estopped by the consent judgment.[b]

How, then, should the parties effectuate their agreed settlement if they wish to avoid all risk of collateral estoppel? A consent judgment is in large part a contract of the parties, acknowledged in court and ordered to be recorded. The parties are free, unless a statute or rule of court otherwise provides, to include in this contract such terms as they wish. Just as they could efficaciously manifest their intention to wind up the entire controversy (i.e., give collateral estoppel effect to the judgment), see Restatement (Second) of Judgments § 27 cmt. e (1982), so can they provide that the agreement is to have no effect on any other claim.

Another approach is for the parties to agree on "Judgment for neither party, no further action to be brought on this claim." Such an entry should terminate the pending action and preclude a new suit by the plaintiff upon the same claim, but it should have no collateral estoppel effect. See Gendron v. Hovey, 98 Me. 139, 56 A. 583 (1903).

Question: (5) How would entry of a judgment for neither party have affected Horne v. Woolever? Might it therefore be better for courts to analyze consent

---

[b] Massachusetts promptly enacted a statute to undo the result of this decision in actions within that state's compulsory automobile insurance law, unless the settlement agreement was signed by the defendant himself. 1932 Mass.Acts ch. 130, § 1 (current version at Mass.Gen.Laws Ann. ch. 231, § 140A).

Incidentally, Massachusetts had no applicable compulsory counterclaim provision.

judgments exclusively in contractual terms, looking directly to the parties' intent and discarding the res judicata analysis?

Cambria v. Jeffery

Supreme Judicial Court of Massachusetts, 1940.
307 Mass. 49, 29 N.E.2d 555.

TORT. Writ in the First District Court of Eastern Middlesex dated April 4, 1938.

On removal to the Superior Court, the action was tried before Greenhalge, J. The finding of the judge of the District Court in the [earlier] action of Jeffery v. Cambria was as follows: "Defendant was clearly negligent. The only question is as to the due care of the plaintiff operator. Taking all the circumstances into consideration including the fact that Concord Avenue on which defendant was driving is the more important street, I find that Ernest Jeffery did not use due care in entering the intersection."

■ LUMMUS, J. Two automobiles, one owned by the plaintiff Cambria and operated by his servant, the other owned and operated by the defendant Jeffery, had a collision.

Jeffery brought in a District Court an action of tort for alleged negligence against Cambria to recover for bodily injury and damage to Jeffery's automobile. The judge found that the collision was caused by negligence of both operators, and therefore judgment was rendered in favor of the then defendant Cambria.

Afterwards the present action of tort, for alleged negligence of Jeffery causing damage to Cambria's automobile, was tried. The jury returned a verdict in favor of the plaintiff Cambria for $838.35; but the judge under leave reserved (G.L. [Ter.Ed.] c. 231, § 120) entered a verdict for the defendant Jeffery on the ground that the earlier judgment had adjudicated that the present plaintiff Cambria through his servant was guilty of contributory negligence, and reported the case.

A fact merely found in a case becomes adjudicated only when it is shown to have been a basis of the relief, denial of relief, or other ultimate right established by the judgment. [Citations omitted.]

The earlier judgment was in effect that Jeffery could not recover against Cambria. The sole basis for that judgment was the finding that Jeffery was guilty of contributory negligence. The further finding that Cambria's servant was negligent had no effect, and could have none, in producing that judgment. Therefore that judgment did not adjudicate that Cambria's servant was negligent.

Verdict under leave reserved set aside.

Judgment upon the verdict returned by the jury.

HOME OWNERS FEDERAL SAVINGS & LOAN ASS'N v. NORTHWESTERN FIRE & MARINE INSURANCE CO., 354 Mass. 448, 238 N.E.2d 55 (1968) (4–3 decision). On rather analogous facts, the Supreme Judicial Court modified the Cambria rule, making it more flexible in these words: "[O]ur holding expands the applicability of the doctrine to encompass certain findings not strictly essential to the final judgment in the prior action. Cf. Restatement, Judgments, § 68. Such findings may be relied upon if it is clear that the issues underlying them were treated as essential to the prior case by the court and the party to be bound. Stated another way, it is necessary that such findings be the product of full litigation and careful decision. Cf. Cambria v. Jeffery, 307 Mass. 49, 29 N.E.2d 555. This limited expansion of the class of findings within the ambit of the doctrine of collateral estoppel does no violence to the policies underlying the rule of the Cambria case, supra. See James, Civil Procedure, . . . at p. 583. We deem this limited extension of the rule warranted in view of the strong and oft-stated public policy of limiting each litigant to one opportunity to try his case on the merits."[c]

Questions: (6) *A* sues *B* for interest on a note. *B* alleges fraud in the execution of the note (a defense to both interest and principal obligations) and a later release of the obligation to pay any interest (a legally and factually distinct defense applicable only to interest obligations). Upon trial, *A* gets verdict and judgment. After maturity, *A* sues *B* for the note's principal. Is the prior judgment conclusive on the question of fraud?

(7) If instead there had been a general verdict and judgment for *B* in that first action, could *B* make effective use of the judgment in the subsequent action for the principal?

(8) What if *B*'s victory in the first action had come upon a special verdict and judgment for *B* on both issues? (Or, equivalently, if that result came in express findings after a bench trial?)

---

[c] A decade later, in Rudow v. Fogel, 376 Mass. 587, 382 N.E.2d 1046 (1978) (alternative holding) (Kaplan, J.), the Supreme Judicial Court unanimously returned to the unmodified Cambria rule.

ALTERNATIVE DETERMINATIONS

In the case of the preceding question, where a party prevails upon each of two issues and where either determination standing alone would be sufficient to support judgment in his favor, Restatement of Judgments § 68 cmt. n (1942) took the position that the judgment is binding on both issues. The judgment is not based on one issue more than on the other, so it must be said that it is conclusive as to both issues or as to neither. The comment continued: "It seems obvious that it should not be held that neither is material, and hence both should be held to be material."

Questions: (9) Why is it obvious?

(10) How is this situation different from Cambria v. Jeffery?

In Halpern v. Schwartz, 426 F.2d 102 (2d Cir.1970), Evelyn Halpern had been involuntarily adjudicated a bankrupt on each of three different grounds, only one of which had involved a finding of actual intent to hinder, delay, or defraud creditors. In a later proceeding Halpern sought a discharge in bankruptcy. The Bankruptcy Act provided that the court could not grant a discharge if it finds the bankrupt acted with that particular intent. The court denied Halpern her discharge on the ground that the prior determination of intent was preclusive. The court of appeals reversed, holding, contrary to the First Restatement, that a judgment resting on alternative grounds (here three) is not preclusive as to any of the grounds.

Questions: (11) What arguments can you make in support of this decision?

(12) Should there be, under the Halpern approach, a difference in result if there was an appeal in the prior case and the appellate court expressly affirmed on one of two alternative grounds? on both of the two alternative grounds?

Restatement (Second) of Judgments § 27 cmts. i, o (1982) likewise takes a position contrary to the First Restatement, by providing that neither determination is preclusive unless there was an appellate-court determination. The reporter's note thereon says that the question is a close and difficult one, but that the reasoning in Halpern v. Schwartz is highly persuasive.

Questions: (13) Assume that you as counsel have two alternative grounds of defense (or recovery) in each of which you have confidence. Assume further that you foresee the likelihood of later litigation involving one of the grounds and that the Halpern approach is recognized as governing authority. Accordingly, you perceive that you will be worse off winning on both grounds than on the one. What, then, should your tactics at trial be?

(14) *A* sues *B* for a note's principal in a Halpern jurisdiction. *B* alleges prematurity of the action and also fraud in the execution of the note. In the trial court, *B* gets judgment upon a special verdict favorable on both issues. There is no appeal. After maturity, *A* sues *B* again for the note's principal. Can *B* invoke claim preclusion based on the prior judgment? Compare Restatement (Second) of Judgments § 20 cmt. e (1982) (no bar), with Jo Desha Lucas, The Direct and Collateral Estoppel Effects of Alternative Holdings, 50 U.Chi.L.Rev. 701, 707–14 (1983) (bar).

Trying to chart a middle course in Malloy v. Trombley, 50 N.Y.2d 46, 52, 405 N.E.2d 213, 216, 427 N.Y.S.2d 969, 973 (1980) (4–3 decision), the New York Court of Appeals decided that the Halpern approach should not be applied rigidly and held "in this instance that the rule of issue preclusion is applicable notwithstanding that in a precise sense the issue precluded was the subject of only an alternative determination by the trial court. The issue was fully litigated, and the party precluded had full opportunity to be heard and was in no way, motivationally or procedurally, restricted or inhibited in the presentation of his position. Additionally, and critically in our view, the decision of the trial court gives significant internal evidence of the thorough and careful deliberation by that court, both in its consideration of the proof introduced and of the applicable law, and the determination made, although recognized to be an alternative, served a substantial operational purpose in the judicial process, thus negativing any conclusion that the trial court's resolution was casual or of any lesser quality than had the outcome of the trial depended solely on this issue."

Question: (15) *A* sues *B* for interest on a note. *B* alleges fraud in the execution of the note and a later release of the obligation to pay any interest. In the trial court, *B* gets judgment upon a special (or general) verdict favorable on both issues. There is no appeal. Later, *A* sues *B* for a subsequent installment of interest on the note. Can *B* invoke issue preclusion based on the prior judgment?

Noteworthily, the Halpern approach has received only limited acceptance in the courts, and even the Second Circuit has since backed away from it. After considering all these arguments pro and con, and the implications of and reactions to the Halpern rule regarding alternative determinations, what do you think? Might we be better off returning to the First Restatement rule, while trying to treat the relatively few cases of inappropriate collateral estoppel by means of exceptions to issue preclusion? See Monica Renee Brownewell, Note, Rethinking the Restatement View (Again!): Multiple Independent Holdings and the Doctrine of Issue Preclusion, 37 Val.U.L.Rev. 879 (2003).

INCONSISTENT JUDGMENTS

Question: (16) *A* sues *B* for interest on a note. *B* alleges a release of the obligation to pay any interest. Upon trial, *A* gets judgment. Later, *A* sues *B* for a subsequent installment of interest on the note. *B* alleges the release. Upon trial, *B* gets judgment on that ground. Later, *A* sues *B* yet again for another subsequent installment of interest on the note. *B* alleges the release. Are the prior judgments now conclusive on the question of release?

In Donald v. J.J. White Lumber Co., 68 F.2d 441 (5th Cir.1934), a taxpayer brought several successive tax actions, each action relating to a different tax year. The computation of the tax each year depended upon the determination of the depletion allowance for standing timber. This in turn depended upon the value as of March 1, 1913, the effective date of the first modern income tax law, of standing timber on land acquired by the taxpayer before that date. The higher that value was, the greater the depletion allowance and hence the lower the tax. In the first action, the Board of Tax Appeals valued the standing timber on March 1, 1913, at $5.34 per thousand feet—and the tax for the year in question was figured on that basis. In the second action, a federal district court adjudged the value on March 1, 1913, to be $7.00 per thousand feet—and the tax for the year involved was computed accordingly. No reference was made to the valuation of the timber in the prior action. There was no appeal from the decision in either case. In a third action, covering a third tax year, the government contended that the $5.34 valuation of the first action was binding, but the taxpayer contended that the $7.00 valuation of the second action controlled. The court of appeals held that the last judgment in time is controlling.

Question: (17) Why should the rule not be that neither determination is binding?

(18) Do the Federal Rules require a defendant relying upon the collateral estoppel effect of a prior judgment to set it up in her pleading? See Rule 8(c)(1). How about a plaintiff? See 18 Wright, Miller & Cooper § 4405, at 82–110.

Suppose, however, that judgments of different states are involved. The same last-in-time rule ordinarily prevails and, indeed, is compelled by the Full Faith and Credit Clause. But imagine: First, *A* wins on an issue against *B* in State *X*. Second, *A* later relies upon that judgment in a case involving the same issue in State *Y*, arguing the judgment is entitled to full faith and credit. The court of State *Y* wrongly rejects that argument and decides in favor of *B*. After appealing unsuccessfully in State *Y*, *A* seeks certiorari from the Supreme Court of the United States, but it is denied. Third, *A* then commences another case involving the same issue in State *X*, and *B* relies upon the State *Y* judgment as preclusive. Should the State *Y* judgment be controlling? See Restatement (Second) of Conflict of Laws § 114 cmt. b (1971); Ruth B. Ginsburg, Judgments in Search of Full Faith and Credit: The Last-in-Time Rule for Conflicting Judgments, 82 Harv. L.Rev. 798 (1969).

Berlitz Schools of Languages of America v. Everest House

United States Court of Appeals, Second Circuit, 1980.
619 F.2d 211.

[The facts, simplified to their essence, were as follows. Berlitz Schools and Berlitz Publications had sued certain defendants, including Charles Berlitz, in New York state court for unfair competition and trademark dilution under state law. In 1974 the court, although recognizing in accord with prior litigation that Charles Berlitz could not identify himself as author of language materials unless he made clear that he was not connected with the plaintiffs in any way, had found that the following book-cover disclaimer on his "Passport" series of language books sufficed to dispel confusion: "Charles Berlitz, world-famous linguist and author of more than 100 language teaching books, is the grandson of the founder of the Berlitz Schools. Since 1967, Mr. Berlitz has not been connected with the Berlitz Schools in any way." That state judgment had been affirmed on appeal.

[Later Charles Berlitz authored the new "Step–By–Step" series of language books, on the cover of which were his name and that disclaimer. Those same plaintiffs sued in the United States District Court for the Southern District of New York for trademark infringement and unfair competition under the Lanham Act, 15 U.S.C. §§ 1051–1127. The defendants' answer pleaded collateral estoppel. In 1979 the district court granted defendants' motion for summary judgment on the basis of collateral estoppel. Plaintiffs appealed.]

■ Before LUMBARD, MANSFIELD and NEWMAN, CIRCUIT JUDGES

■ LUMBARD, CIRCUIT JUDGE:

. . . .

. . . The question is whether the issues finally and necessarily determined in the state proceedings are identical to those presented to the district court for determination.

The sine qua non of an action for trademark infringement, dilution of a trademark or unfair competition, is a showing by the plaintiff of the likelihood of confusion as to the origin of the goods in issue at the consumer level. [Citations omitted.] Indeed, this is precisely the claim made by plaintiffs in the district court as well as in . . . the prior state proceedings.

. . . .

Plaintiffs' principal objection to the application of [collateral estoppel] is that the facts presented herein differ substantially from those before the state court in the prior proceedings. Thus, the principal question before us is: is the legend of Charles Berlitz's name and the disclaimer on the cover of the "Step–By–Step" language books substantially different from that which was given the blessing of the New York courts? This mixed question of fact and law was decided in favor of the defendants by the district court. We cannot say that the judgment of the district court was erroneous. On the contrary, the judgment is supported by the record and the applicable law.

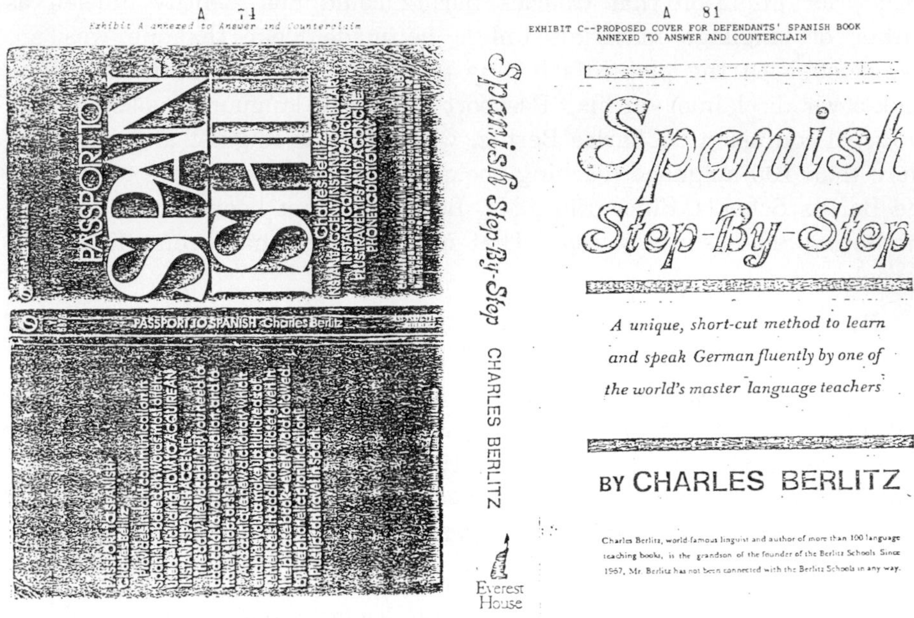

Reproductions of book covers—as submitted to the Second Circuit in Joint Appendix to the briefs and indistinctly showing the disclaimer at the bottom of each front cover

The appellants argue that on the "Step–By–Step" cover the name "Charles Berlitz" is larger in proportion to the disclaimer which consequently is less noticeable, and that these factual differences are sufficient to justify the relief they seek. We disagree.

It is true that the legend "Charles Berlitz" is slightly larger on the "Step–By–Step" volumes than it was on the "Passport" series, and that the disclaimer legend is slightly reduced in size. These proportional modifications are, however, so minuscule as to be hardly detectable on visual inspection. The differences are not so great as to warrant another judicial proceeding. Of course, substantially greater discrepancies in the presentation of the name "Charles Berlitz" and the disclaimer of his association with Berlitz schools may give rise to claims which might not be barred by principles of res judicata and collateral estoppel.

. . . .

Regarding plaintiffs' assertion that they are entitled to de novo determination of their federally created Lanham Act rights in a federal court [because they did not assert those rights in the state proceedings], it is enough to say that their state and federal claims all involved the issue of the likelihood of confusion. The state courts have concurrent jurisdiction to determine those claims, and having determined them adversely to the plaintiffs, that is the end of the matter. . . .

Accordingly, . . . the judgment which dismissed the complaint is affirmed.

Question: (19) Given such differences in circumstances between two actions, is the proper question in the second action (a) whether the same issue of law-application is involved or (b) whether the different circumstances should trigger an exception to otherwise applicable issue preclusion? Does this distinction have any significance?

SECTION 2. EXCEPTIONS TO THE RULE

United States v. Moser

Supreme Court of the United States, 1924.
266 U.S. 236, 45 S.Ct. 66.

[Moser was a cadet at the Naval Academy during the Civil War. Upon retirement forty years later, he sued in the Court of Claims for the difference between the pay of a captain and a rear admiral pursuant to a statute of the United States providing that "any officer of the Navy, with a creditable record, who served during the civil war shall, when retired, be retired with the rank and three-fourths the sea pay of the next higher grade." The government contended that service at the Naval Academy did not constitute service during the Civil War within the meaning of the statute, but the Court of Claims rejected the contention and decided in Moser's favor.

[Later in a suit by another claimant similarly situated, one Jasper, the Court of Claims had its attention called to another retirement statute, previously overlooked, and by reference to that statute denied Jasper recovery.

[In two subsequent actions by Moser for later installments of salary, the Court of Claims declined to follow the Jasper case, holding that by reason of its decision in the first Moser case the question was concluded as to Moser. In the present (fourth) action by Moser, the Court of Claims again held for him on the same ground. It ruled, alternatively, that its decision in the Jasper case was unsound as a matter of statutory interpretation and should be abandoned.]

■ MR. JUSTICE SUTHERLAND delivered the opinion of the Court.

. . . .

We find it unnecessary to consider the latter ruling, since we are of opinion that the court was clearly right in its application of the doctrine of res judicata.

. . . .

. . . The question expressly and definitely presented in this suit is the same as that definitely and actually litigated and adjudged in favor of the claimant in the three preceding suits, viz.: whether he occupied the status of an officer who had served during the civil war.

The contention of the Government seems to be that the doctrine of res judicata does not apply to questions of law; and, in a sense, that is true. It does not apply to unmixed questions of law. Where, for example, a court in deciding a case has enunciated a rule of law, the parties in a subsequent action upon a different demand are not estopped from insisting that the law is otherwise, merely because the parties are the same in both cases. But a *fact, question* or *right* distinctly adjudged in the original action cannot be disputed in a subsequent action, even though the determination was reached upon an erroneous view or by an erroneous application of the law. That would be to affirm the principle in respect of the thing adjudged but, at the same time, deny it all efficacy by sustaining a challenge to the grounds upon which the judgment was based. [Citations omitted.] A determination in respect of the status of an individual upon which his right to recover depends is as conclusive as a decision upon any other matter. [Citations omitted.]

Affirmed.

MONTANA v. UNITED STATES, 440 U.S. 147, 99 S.Ct. 970 (1979). Montana imposed a 1% gross-receipts tax upon contractors on public, but not private, construction projects in Montana. The United States had been involved in launching a state-court challenge to the tax on the ground that it discriminated against the United States in violation of the Federal Constitution. The Montana Supreme Court ultimately upheld the tax in 1973 ("Kiewit I"), and further appeal was abandoned.

Asserting a new claim that arose in connection with similar federal contracts, the United States challenged the Montana tax anew in the United States District Court for the District of Montana. The United States prevailed below. But the Supreme Court of the United States reversed, as Justice Marshall explained for the Court:

"A fundamental precept of common-law adjudication, embodied in the related doctrines of collateral estoppel and res judicata, is that a 'right, question or fact distinctly put in issue and directly determined by a court of competent jurisdiction . . . cannot be disputed in a subsequent suit between the same parties or their privies . . . .' Southern Pacific R. Co. v. United States, 168 U.S. 1, 48–49, 18 S.Ct. 18, 27 (1897). Under res judicata, a final judgment on the merits bars further claims by parties or their privies based on the same cause of action. Cromwell v. County of Sac, 94 U.S. 351, 352 (1877); Lawlor v. National Screen Service Corp., 349 U.S. 322, 326, 75 S.Ct. 865, 867 (1955); 1B J. Moore, Federal Practice ¶ 0.405[1], pp. 621–624 (2d ed. 1974) (hereinafter 1B Moore); Restatement (Second) of Judgments § 47 (Tent. Draft No. 1, Mar. 28, 1973) (merger); id., § 48 (bar).

Under collateral estoppel, once an issue is actually and necessarily determined by a court of competent jurisdiction, that determination is conclusive in subsequent suits based on a different cause of action involving a party to the prior litigation. Parklane Hosiery Co. v. Shore, 439 U.S. 322, 326 n. 5, 99 S.Ct. 645, 649 n. 5 (1979); Scott, Collateral Estoppel by Judgment, 56 Harv.L.Rev. 1, 2–3 (1942); Restatement (Second) of Judgments § 68 (Tent. Draft No. 4, Apr. 15, 1977) (issue preclusion). Application of both doctrines is central to the purpose for which civil courts have been established, the conclusive resolution of disputes within their jurisdictions. Southern Pacific R. Co., supra, 168 U.S., at 49, 18 S.Ct., at 27; Hart Steel Co. v. Railroad Supply Co., 244 U.S. 294, 299, 37 S.Ct. 506, 507 (1917). To preclude parties from contesting matters that they have had a full and fair opportunity to litigate protects their adversaries from the expense and vexation attending multiple lawsuits, conserves judicial resources, and fosters reliance on judicial action by minimizing the possibility of inconsistent decisions.

. . . .

"To determine the appropriate application of collateral estoppel in the instant case necessitates three further inquiries: first, whether the issues presented by this litigation are in substance the same as those resolved against the United States in Kiewit I; second, whether controlling facts or legal principles have changed significantly since the state-court judgment; and finally, whether other special circumstances warrant an exception to the normal rules of preclusion.

A

"A review of the record in Kiewit I dispels any doubt that the plaintiff there raised and the Montana Supreme Court there decided the precise constitutional [challenges advanced here]. . . .

. . . .

"Thus, the 'question expressly and definitely presented in this suit is the same as that definitely and actually litigated and adjudged' adversely to the Government in state court. United States v. Moser, 266 U.S. 236, 242, 45 S.Ct. 66, 67 (1924). Absent significant changes in controlling facts or legal principles since Kiewit I, or other special circumstances, the Montana Supreme Court's resolution of these issues is conclusive here.

B

"Relying on Commissioner of Internal Revenue v. Sunnen, 333 U.S. 591, 68 S.Ct. 715 (1948), the United States argues that collateral estoppel extends only to contexts in which 'the controlling facts and applicable legal rules remain unchanged.' Id., at 600, 68 S.Ct., at 720. In the Government's view, factual stasis is missing here because the contract at issue in Kiewit I contained a critical provision which the contracts involved in the instant litigation do not.

[The Court concluded that the Montana Supreme Court's opinion in Kiewit I had not been essentially predicated on the existence of that particular contractual provision and that therefore the change in facts did not suffice to avoid issue preclusion.]

"Thus, unless there have been major changes in the law governing intergovernmental tax immunity since Kiewit I, the Government's reliance on Commissioner of Internal Revenue v. Sunnen, 333 U.S. 591, 68 S.Ct. 715 (1948), is misplaced. Sunnen involved the tax status of certain income generated by a license agreement during a particular tax period. Although previous litigation had settled the status of income from the same agreement during earlier tax years, the Court declined to give collateral estoppel effect to the prior judgment because there had been a significant 'change in the legal climate.' Id., at 606, 68 S.Ct., at 723. Underlying the Sunnen decision was a concern that modifications in 'controlling legal principles,' id., at 599, 68 S.Ct., at 720, could render a previous determination inconsistent with prevailing doctrine, and that

> '[i]f such a determination is then perpetuated each succeeding year as to the taxpayer involved in the original litigation, he is accorded a tax treatment different from that given to other taxpayers of the same class. As a result, there are inequalities in the administration of the revenue laws, discriminatory distinctions in tax liability, and a fertile basis for litigious confusion. [Collateral estoppel] is not meant to create vested rights in decisions that have become obsolete or erroneous with time, thereby causing inequities among taxpayers.' Ibid. (citations omitted).

No such considerations obtain here. The Government does not contend and the District Court did not find that a change in controlling legal principles had occurred between Kiewit I and the instant suit. That the Government's amended complaint in this action replicates in substance the legal argument advanced by the . . . complaint in Kiewit I further suggests the absence of any major doctrinal shifts since the Montana Supreme Court's decision.

"Because the factual and legal context in which the issues of this case arise has not materially altered since Kiewit I, normal rules of preclusion should operate to relieve the parties of 'redundant litigation [over] the identical question of the statute's application to the taxpayer's status.' Tait v. Western Maryland R. Co., 289 U.S. 620, 624, 53 S.Ct. 706, 707 (1933). See United States v. Russell Mfg. Co., 349 F.2d 13, 18–19 (C.A.2 1965).

C

"The sole remaining question is whether the particular circumstances of this case justify an exception to general principles of estoppel. Of possible relevance is the exception which obtains for 'unmixed questions of law' in successive actions involving substantially unrelated claims. United States v. Moser, 266 U.S. 236, 242, 45 S.Ct. 66, 67 (1924). . . . Thus, when issues of law arise in successive actions involving unrelated subject matter, preclusion may be inappropriate. See Restatement (Second) of Judgments § 68.1, Reporter's Note, pp. 43–44 (Tent. Draft No. 4, Apr. 15, 1977); 1B Moore ¶ 0.448, p. 4235; Scott, 56 Harv.L.Rev., at 10. This exception is of particular importance in constitutional adjudication. Unreflective invocation of collateral estoppel against parties with an ongoing interest in constitutional issues could freeze doctrine in areas of the law where responsiveness to changing patterns of conduct or social mores is critical. To be sure, the scope of the Moser exception may be difficult to delineate, particularly where there is partial congruence in the subject matter of successive disputes. But the instant case poses no such conceptual difficulties. Rather, as the preceding discussion indicates, the legal 'demands' of this litigation are closely aligned in time and subject matter to those in Kiewit I.

. . . .

"Finally, the Government has not alleged unfairness or inadequacy in the state procedures to which it voluntarily submitted.[11] We must conclude therefore that it had a full and fair opportunity to press its constitutional challenges in Kiewit I. Accordingly, the Government is estopped from seeking a contrary resolution of those issues here."

Justice Rehnquist concurred in "the Court's opinion on the customary understanding that its references to . . . drafts or finally adopted versions of the Restatement of Judgments are not intended to bind the Court to the views expressed therein on issues not presented by the facts of this case."

Justice White dissented on the grounds that the change in facts sufficed to avoid issue preclusion and that the tax was unconstitutional.

Questions: (20) In an action to recover customs duties from Importer *A* Corp., the court determines that the articles in question fall within a classification that makes them duty-free. In a later action involving Importer *B* Corp., the court determines that articles of the same kind fall within a classification requiring payment of a substantial duty. Then *A* imports additional articles of the same kind. Is the judgment in the first action preclusive on the issue of classification? See United States v. Stone & Downer Co., 274 U.S. 225, 47 S.Ct. 616 (1927) (suggesting no).

(21) Ex-cadet Moser continued for life to have his pension fixed at the higher rate dictated by the result of United States v. Moser. Ex-cadet Jasper continued for life to have his pension fixed at the lower rate, despite an ingenious effort by his administrator to alter the result by a retroactive appointment to a higher rank. Was the continued disparity of treatment of Moser and Jasper more justifiable than allowing *A* in the preceding question a permanent built-in competitive advantage over *B*?

(22) If Jasper had again sued the United States to get later installments at the higher rate, could he have avoided the rule of collateral estoppel by invoking the Sunnen exception based on intervening legal change?

---

[11] Redetermination of issues is warranted if there is reason to doubt the quality, extensiveness, or fairness of procedures followed in prior litigation. See Restatement (Second) of Judgments § 68.1(c) (Tent. Draft No. 4, Apr. 15, 1977); [other citations omitted].

COURTS OF LIMITED JURISDICTION

It frequently happens that issue preclusion is asserted in an action that would be outside the jurisdiction of the court that rendered the prior judgment. Should issue preclusion effect extend to such a situation? The decisions are widely divergent. Consider the illustrative cases set forth below, which are designed to suggest that a flat answer either way is an unduly rigid approach.

1. *A* sues *B* for negligently inflicted property damage in a county court with jurisdiction limited to $5000. Should a judgment holding *B* negligent and *A* in the exercise of due care receive collateral estoppel effect from a court of general jurisdiction, in *B*'s action against *A* for $100,000 damages sustained in the same accident? See Gollner v. Cram, 258 Minn. 8, 102 N.W.2d 521 (1960) (giving preclusive effect).

2. Same as the preceding case, except that the first court is a small-claims court that has a $1000 limit and operates informally without counsel, pleadings, or strict rules of evidence. Does this make a difference? See Sanderson v. Niemann, 17 Cal.2d 563, 110 P.2d 1025 (1941) (denying preclusive effect); cf. N.Y. City Civ.Ct.Act § 1808 ("A judgment obtained under this [small-claims] article may be pleaded as res judicata only as to the amount involved in the particular action and shall not otherwise be deemed an adjudication of any fact at issue or found therein in any other action or court.").

3. A surrogate's court—the jurisdiction of which is limited to wills, administration of estates, guardianship, and the like—decides in favor of an attorney claiming sizable fees against an estate, with the court necessarily determining that he did not commit a certain alleged fraud while administering the estate. Should this determination receive collateral estoppel effect from a court of general jurisdiction, in a suit for damages for the fraud brought against the attorney by an adverse party to the prior proceeding? See United States v. Silliman, 167 F.2d 607 (3d Cir.1948) (giving preclusive effect).

4. A family court—the jurisdiction of which is limited to support, custody, and the like—denies a woman's support petition on the ground that the parties are not legally married. Should this determination receive collateral estoppel effect from a court of general jurisdiction with exclusive jurisdiction over divorce and the like, in the woman's suit to declare the parties' marital status? See Loomis v. Loomis, 288 N.Y. 222, 42 N.E.2d 495 (1942) (denying preclusive effect, because of legislative intent); cf. Vanderveer v. Erie Malleable Iron Co., 238 F.2d 510 (3d Cir.1956) (giving preclusive effect to state-court adjudication of patent issues).

UNFORESEEABILITY OF FUTURE LITIGATION

In Evergreens v. Nunan, 141 F.2d 927, 929 (2d Cir.1944), Judge Learned Hand said: "Were the law to be recast, it would . . . be a pertinent inquiry whether the conclusiveness . . . of facts decided in the first [suit] might not properly be limited to future controversies which could be thought reasonably in prospect when the first suit was tried. . . . Logical relevance is of infinite possibility; there is no conceivable limit which can be put to it. Defeat in one suit might entail results beyond all calculation by either party; a trivial controversy might bring utter disaster in its train." However, Judge Hand did not feel free to recast the law in this way. Instead, in an attempt to place a reasonable restriction upon the extent to which a determination in the first suit precluded its relitigation in a second, Judge Hand drew a distinction between "ultimate facts" and "mediate data" at issue in the second suit: only ultimate facts in the second suit could be conclusively established by prior determination; mediate data, being merely premises from which the ultimate facts could be inferred, were beyond the reach of issue preclusion. Hand's distinction has received some support.

The distinction between ultimate facts and mediate data is, however, vague and difficult to apply. It has been criticized by several commentators, who have suggested that truer hazards lie in making conclusive henceforth a determination that was not seriously contested or in imposing the risk of completely unforeseeable consequences. See, e.g., Fleming James, Jr., Geoffrey C. Hazard, Jr. & John Leubsdorf, Civil Procedure 707–08 (5th ed. 2001). This alternative of recasting the law in terms of foreseeability has also received some judicial support. In an early and prominent example, Hyman v. Regenstein, 258 F.2d 502, 511 (5th Cir.1958) (dictum), the court said that "collateral estoppel by judgment is applicable only when it is evident from the pleadings and record that determination of the fact in question was necessary to the final judgment and it was foreseeable that the fact would be of importance in possible future litigation."

It seems, indeed, that Judge Hand's actual decision in Evergreens has proven less influential than his dictum concerning foreseeability. Today, a typical court will not apply issue preclusion if such application was unforeseeable at the time of the initial action and such unforeseeability may have affected the effort therein by the party sought to be precluded. But such exceptional cases should be rare, and relitigation should follow only a clear and convincing showing of need. An example of where this constrained exception for unforeseeability would apply: the tax court's prior adjudication of the value of specific property would not be preclusive if it were to acquire tremendously greater financial significance for the taxpayer's future returns because of an amendment to the tax code's depletion provisions. The exception is necessary because there is no other way to escape inappropriate issue preclusion—the change in circumstances has not created a different issue, and this purely *factual* issue falls outside the Sunnen exception designed to avoid persons' unequal treatment on a more *legal* issue after an intervening change in the "legal climate."

Question: (23) Although unforeseeability creates a limitation under today's law, should foreseeability have the effect of extending collateral estoppel beyond essential issues actually litigated and determined, as in cases like Jacobson v. Miller where the prospect of future litigation was apparent at the time of the first action? See Developments in the Law—Res Judicata, 65 Harv.L.Rev. 818, 841 (1952).

Spilker v. Hankin

United States Court of Appeals, District of Columbia Circuit, 1951.
188 F.2d 35.

[Spilker gave her attorney Hankin a series of seven notes in payment for legal services in a matrimonial action. The first was a demand note for $500; and the others, each in the amount of $250, became due at three-month intervals thereafter. Spilker paid the demand note. When she failed to pay the second note, Hankin sued thereon in the Municipal Court for the District of Columbia. Spilker pleaded duress, alleged that the note in suit was for an exorbitant and unconscionable fee, and further alleged that she had already overpaid Hankin. She also filed a counterclaim seeking a determination that the amount already paid was to be considered full payment for his services and asking that the remaining notes be declared void. In a trial without jury, Hankin won judgment on the note and also prevailed against the counterclaim, without specific findings or conclusions. There was no appeal.

[Later Hankin brought the present action in the same court on the five remaining notes, all of which had now become due. Spilker's chief defense was misrepresentation in inducing execution of the notes, and she again urged that she had paid Hankin all his professional services were worth. The plaintiff's motion for summary judgment on the ground that the prior judgment precluded the defendant was denied by the same judge who had rendered the prior judgment. There was a jury trial leading to a verdict and judgment for the defendant. The Municipal Court of Appeals reversed and ordered judgment for the plaintiff. The defendant appealed.]

■ Before CLARK, FAHY and WASHINGTON, CIRCUIT JUDGES.

■ WASHINGTON, CIRCUIT JUDGE.

. . . .

We agree with much that the learned Municipal Court of Appeals has said with regard to the principles of res judicata. We agree, for example, that in successive suits on a series of notes, defenses failing in the first suit ordinarily are foreclosed to the defendant in subsequent litigation. Restatement, Judgments § 68, Comments c, m, Illustration 5. But, with all respect to that court, we consider that weight should have been given to a factor not mentioned in its discussion of the case, that is, the fiduciary relationship of attorney and client which existed between the parties. In a very real sense attorneys are officers of the courts in which they practice; and clients are wards of the court in regard to their relationship with their attorneys. This factor is one of high significance in the present context.

The doctrine of res judicata is but the technical formulation of the "Public policy . . . that there be an end of litigation; that those who have contested an issue shall be bound by the result of the contest; and that matters once tried shall be considered forever settled as between the parties." Baldwin v. Iowa State Traveling Men's Ass'n, 283 U.S. 522, 525, 51 S.Ct. 517, 518, 75 L.Ed. 1244. This policy has long been a tenet of the common law, and even finds expression in the Constitution of the United States, in the full faith and credit clause. Experience has taught that as a general rule there is no reason why the doctrine of res judicata "should not apply in every case where one voluntarily appears, presents his case and is fully heard . . . ." [Id.] But rules and policies such as these must be weighed against competing necessities: situations may arise which call for exceptions. . . .

. . . [R]es judicata, as the embodiment of a public policy, must, at times, on occasion, yield to other policies.

Fee contracts between attorney and client are a subject of special interest and concern to the courts. They are not to be enforced upon the same basis as ordinary commercial contracts. Especially is this true where, as in this case, a contract beneficial to the attorney is executed long after the attorney-client relationship has commenced, when the position of trust is well established, and the litigation involved is reaching its culmination. . . . When he seeks to enforce such a note the attorney cannot rely upon the usual commercial principles relative to negotiable instruments; he must rely upon the same basic considerations as if he were asking the court to enforce a fee arrangement not reflected in a note or notes.

Ordinarily the matter of a fee will be litigated but once, and the first determination will be conclusive. Were this merely a suit upon the original judgment we would, of course, consider res judicata to be applicable. But here we have a series of notes, one brought into litigation prior to the others. The original suit was for a much smaller amount, and some of the issues here in question were only indirectly involved in it. And it is the attorney who seeks further court aid with regard to his fee. The fee arrangement in question was reduced to promissory notes shortly before the termination of the litigation in which the attorney acted for the client, and appears to have been required by the attorney as a condition of his remaining in the case. While we do not mean to imply that an attorney can never protect himself with regard to his fee by making an arrangement of this sort, we consider that when under such circumstances the attorney twice brings the matter into court, the requirements of justice are better served by permitting reexamination of the merits than by treating the prior suit as foreclosing the matter. We think that the client should be permitted to make any legal or equitable defense to the remaining notes which appeals to the conscience of the court.

. . . .

Reversed . . . .

Restatement (Second) of Judgments

(1982).

§ 28. *Exceptions to the General Rule of Issue Preclusion*

Although an issue is actually litigated and determined by a valid and final judgment, and the determination is essential to the judgment, relitigation of the issue in a subsequent action between the parties is not precluded in the following circumstances:

(1) The party against whom preclusion is sought could not, as a matter of law, have obtained review of the judgment in the initial action; or

(2) The issue is one of law and (a) the two actions involve claims that are substantially unrelated, or (b) a new determination is warranted in order to take account of an intervening change in the applicable legal context or otherwise to avoid inequitable administration of the laws; or

(3) A new determination of the issue is warranted by differences in the quality or extensiveness of the procedures followed in the two courts or by factors relating to the allocation of jurisdiction between them; or

(4) The party against whom preclusion is sought had a significantly heavier burden of persuasion with respect to the issue in the initial action than in the subsequent action; the burden has shifted to his adversary; or the adversary has a significantly heavier burden than he had in the first action; or

(5) There is a clear and convincing need for a new determination of the issue (a) because of the potential adverse impact of the determination on the public interest or the interests of persons not themselves parties in the initial action, (b) because it was not sufficiently foreseeable at the time of the initial action that the issue would arise in the context of a subsequent action, or (c) because the party sought to be precluded, as a result of the conduct of his adversary or other special circumstances, did not have an adequate opportunity or incentive to obtain a full and fair adjudication in the initial action.

Question: (24) Should the general rule of issue preclusion be applied more flexibly, with a greater willingness to recognize exceptions, than the general rule of claim preclusion?

FEDERATED DEPARTMENT STORES v. MOITIE, 452 U.S. 394, 101 S.Ct. 2424 (1981). A number of plaintiffs each brought similar price-fixing actions against certain department stores. Treating the actions together, the district court dismissed for failure to state a claim. Plaintiffs in five of the actions appealed. But the plaintiff in another action instead chose to bring a new action with a complaint based on a different theory; the same district court dismissed on the ground of claim preclusion; and that plaintiff appealed.

The court of appeals then reversed in the five suits, indicating that they had stated a claim under the antitrust laws as interpreted by an intervening Supreme Court decision. Later the court of appeals reversed in the other case as well, ruling "that non-appealing parties may benefit from a reversal when their position is closely interwoven with that of appealing parties" and that the otherwise applicable claim preclusion must give way to simple justice and public policy.

On certiorari in the latter case, the Supreme Court reversed. Justice Rehnquist for the Court rejected any "interwoven" exception to claim preclusion. He further explained, in an opinion that seemed to use "res judicata" as a synonym for claim preclusion:

"The Court of Appeals also rested its opinion in part on what it viewed as 'simple justice.' But we do not see the grave injustice which would be done by the application of accepted principles of res judicata. 'Simple justice' is achieved when a complex body of law developed over a period of years is evenhandedly applied. The doctrine of res judicata serves vital public interests beyond any individual judge's ad hoc determination of the equities in a particular case. There is simply 'no principle of law or equity which sanctions the rejection by a federal court of the salutary principle of res judicata.' Heiser v. Woodruff, 327 U.S. 726, 733, 66 S.Ct. 853, 856 (1946). The Court of Appeals' reliance on 'public policy' is similarly misplaced. This Court has long recognized that '[p]ublic policy dictates that there be an end of litigation; that those who have contested an issue shall be bound by the result of the contest, and that matters once tried shall be considered forever settled as between the parties.' Baldwin v. Traveling Men's Association, 283 U.S. 522, 525, 51 S.Ct. 517, 518 (1931). We have stressed that '[the] doctrine of res judicata is not a mere matter of practice or procedure inherited from a more technical time than ours. It is a rule of fundamental and substantial justice, "of public policy and of private peace," which should be cordially regarded and enforced by the courts . . . .' Hart Steel Co. v. Railroad Supply Co., 244 U.S. 294, 299, 37 S.Ct. 506, 507 (1917). The language used by this Court half a century ago is even more compelling in view of today's crowded dockets:

> 'The predicament in which respondent finds himself is of his own making . . . . [W]e cannot be expected, for his sole relief, to upset the general and well-established doctrine of res judicata, conceived in the light of the maxim that the interest of the state requires that there be an end to litigation—a maxim which comports with common sense as well as public policy. And the mischief which would follow the establishment of precedent for so disregarding the salutary doctrine against prolonging strife would be greater than the benefit which would result

from relieving some case of individual hardship.' Reed v. Allen, [286 U.S. 191, 198–99, 52 S.Ct. 532, 533 (1932)]."

Justice Blackmun, joined by Justice Marshall, concurred in the judgment. Justice Brennan dissented on other grounds.

EXCEPTIONS BASED ON POSTURE OF PARTY

A party does not always come within the reach of the rules of claim and issue preclusion that we have studied so far. A party may find himself in a special posture in the litigation so that he does not have a full and fair opportunity to litigate certain aspects of the case, and so that to a certain extent the application of res judicata would be inappropriate. It could be said that, to such extent, the person will be deemed to have been a nonparty.

For example, Restatement (Second) of Judgments § 36(2) (1982) provides: "A party appearing in an action in one capacity, individual or representative, is not thereby bound by or entitled to the benefits of the rules of res judicata in a subsequent action in which he appears in another capacity." Thus, an individual will not normally be precluded by determinations in a prior action that she litigates as a trustee. This exception frees the fiduciary to litigate that first action without the influence of personal interest.

On a somewhat different point, the rules of res judicata that we have studied so far do not normally apply between parties who were not on opposite sides of the relevant claim—although issue preclusion can apply if they in actuality did litigate the issue fully and fairly as adversaries to each other. See id. § 38.

Questions: (25) *W*, administratrix of *H*'s estate, sues *D* for wrongful death of *H* in an automobile accident wherein *H* and *D* were drivers. *D* wins, with the court finding that *D* was not negligent. *W* then sues *D* for her own personal injuries sustained in the same accident as a passenger. May *D* invoke res judicata?

(26) An automobile passenger sues Driver *A* and Driver *B*, and she recovers against both. Then Driver *A* sues Driver *B*, who pleads contributory negligence. Is the prior judgment controlling on the issues of the two drivers' negligence? See Schwartz v. Public Administrator, 24 N.Y.2d 65, 246 N.E.2d 725, 298 N.Y.S.2d 955 (1969) (issue preclusion applies). Why?

TOPIC D

EFFECTS ON PERSONS NOT PARTIES

SECTION 1. PERSONS BOUND BY PRIOR JUDGMENT

A judgment not only will preclude the parties thereto in the various ways already considered, but also will have similar effects upon persons who are not parties but who stand in a relation of "privity" to them. "Privity" is a term of art, and it does not necessarily follow that a person who is a privy of a party for another purpose is a privy for the purpose of res judicata. Indeed, Restatement of Judgments § 83 cmt. a (1942) called the word "privity" in this context "a short method of stating that under the circumstances and for the purpose of the case at hand [a nonparty] is bound by and entitled to the benefits of all or some of the rules of res judicata."

By contrast, the Second Restatement does not use the term "privity" and, instead, treats in more than twenty separate sections the specific classes of nonparties falling to some degree within the reach of the binding rules of res judicata, classifying them (1) as persons having substantive legal relationships with parties justifying preclusion, (2) as persons whose conduct justifies preclusion, or (3) as persons represented by parties. Nevertheless, if the word "privity" is clearly recognized as being conclusory, it remains useful as a general descriptive term.

The premise in common to all findings of privity is that there was some substantial reason to bind a nonparty. Conventionally, privies include among others the following:

1. *Successors in interest to a party's property involved in an action.* For example, *A* brings an action to quiet title to Blackacre against an assertion by *B* that *B* holds a mortgage on the land. Judgment goes for *B*, adjudging the mortgage to be good. *A* conveys to *C* after judgment. The judgment is binding in a later attempt by *C* to quiet title, given that *A* in a sense represented *C*. Incidentally, if judgment had been for *A* in the first action, *C* would similarly have been entitled to benefit from the judgment.

2. *Nonparties who control the prosecution or defense of an action.* Such a person is bound by issue preclusion as if he were himself the party whose position he espouses. For example, *A* brings an action against *B* for infringement of *A*'s patent in connection with *B*'s manufacturing certain goods. *B* has a license from *O* to manufacture the goods under *O*'s patent. *O* controls the defense of the *A* versus *B* action. If *A* gets a judgment of infringement against *B*, that determination will be preclusive in a later

action between *A* and *O*. By contrast, one who participates as an amicus curiae is neither a party nor a controlling nonparty, and is not thereby bound by any res judicata effects of the judgment.

3. *Persons who are actually represented by a party to an action.* For example, beneficiaries of an express trust will normally be bound by a judgment in an action to which the trustee, in her character as trustee, was a party. This principle is not limited to formal trusts or to fiduciary relationships such as that between administrator and beneficiaries of an estate, but extends to situations of representation in the nature of principal-agent.

Restatement (Second) of Judgments

(1982).

§ 52. *Bailee and Bailor*

(1) A judgment in an action by either bailee or bailor against a third party for interference with ownership or destruction of or damage to property that is the subject of a bailment precludes a subsequent action by either, except that:

(a) Where the claim is limited to the claimant's own loss in the property it does not preclude an action by the other for his loss;

(b) If the action is by the bailee it does not preclude an action by the bailor if the judgment was based on a defense not available against the bailor;

(c) An action by the bailee against the third party for claims arising out of the transaction in which the loss occurred does not preclude an action by the bailor for his loss if the third party was on notice that the bailee's action did not seek recovery for the bailor's interest.

(2) The determination of issues in an action by either bailee or bailor is not preclusive against the other of them in a subsequent action between the latter and the third party.

INDEMNITY

There are numerous situations where either by contract or by operation of law a person is entitled to indemnity from another source against loss. The most familiar illustration of indemnity by contract, which figured in the Dindo case, is the liability insurance contract: the insurer undertakes to pay certain kinds of judgments against its insured and his attendant expenses, up to specified policy limits. (Under the typical policy, the insurer also undertakes to defend at its own expense claims made against the insured, and the insured obligates himself to give prompt notice of any accident and to cooperate in the defense.) An instance of indemnity by operation of law, already dealt with supra p. 244, is that of an employee whose negligent conduct in carrying out her employer's business is the sole basis of the employer's liability to a third person: the employee is legally bound to indemnify the employer for its loss. (In an ordinary automobile accident in which liability insurance protects the employer, the protection of the policy extends to the employee as well, pursuant to a standard policy provision covering, in addition to the named insured, any person operating a motor vehicle with the owner's express or implied consent.)

When either type of indemnity prevails, the indemnitee who is sued may "vouch in" the indemnitor, a still-available common-law device whereby the indemnitee gives the indemnitor simple notice of the action and offers it control of the defense. Once so vouched in, whether or not it accepts control of the defense, the indemnitor normally will be bound by the judgment on the questions of the indemnitee's liability. However, the indemnitor normally remains free to litigate in a later action whether and to what extent it is obligated by contract or by operation of law to indemnify that liability.

Instead of vouching in the indemnitor and so making it a privy, the indemnitee may, in a federal court or in a state court with a rule like Rule 14, go further by invoking impleader to make the indemnitor an actual party. This course allows the indemnitee to retain control of the defense and also to bring the indemnitor into the action and so obtain a judgment against it. The effectiveness of impleader is limited, however, by the requirement of service—whereas, according to the better view, a vouched-in entity need not be within the reach of the court's process.

If the indemnitee neither vouches in nor impleads the indemnitor, he does not thereby lose his right to indemnity. He must, however, establish his claim all over again without reference to the prior judgment, unless a contract provides otherwise. In the second action, the indemnitee would have to offer practically the same proof relied upon by the injured person in establishing the case against the indemnitee. This may leave the indemnitee the loser because of differing views of the evidence by the two fact-finders, and in any event it is a needless expense to him.

SHOW–WORLD CENTER v. WALSH, 438 F.Supp. 642 (S.D.N.Y.1977). A landlord (303 Corp.) unsuccessfully sued New York City officials twice in state court to challenge a safety order and later an eviction order that was enforced against only one of its many tenants, a sex shop. The landlord alleged that the orders were unconstitutional parts of a campaign to ban sex-oriented activity from the Times Square area.

Next the tenant (Show–World) sued New York City officials in federal court to challenge the eviction on similar grounds under 42 U.S.C. § 1983. District Judge Motley rejected the application of res judicata for this reason:

"During all of these proceedings . . . 303 Corp. was represented by Ralph J. Schwarz, Jr. (Schwarz) who is also general counsel to Show–World. When Schwarz perceived that the Buildings Department was acting solely against Show–World, he decided that Show–World should be separately represented and called in outside counsel on its behalf. Mr. Herald Price Fahringer has since represented Show–World.

. . . .

"A threshold issue of critical importance to disposition of the preliminary questions in this case . . . is the nature of the relationship between Show–World, the plaintiff in this action, and 303 Corp., the plaintiff in the two State court proceedings. The only clear, undisputed facts on this issue are that Show–World was a tenant of 303 Corp., and that both corporations have had dealings with one attorney, Ralph Schwarz. Mr. Schwarz has been General Counsel to Show–World since 1974, when he handled that entity's incorporation and negotiated its lease with 303 Corp. During the lease negotiation, 303 Corp. was represented in the main by its President and sole shareholder, Wallace Katz, who looked to another lawyer for legal advice on that occasion. Mr. Katz owns no part of Show–World and 303 Corp. owns no part of Show–World.

"During the State court proceedings, Mr. Schwarz represented only 303 Corp. although, on two occasions in the State court, he did identify himself as being also the attorney for Show–World, allegedly to provide support for his assertion of personal knowledge of some of the facts there in issue. He admitted at the hearing in the instant case that he kept his client, Show–World, informed as to the course of the [administrative] proceedings . . . . However, he made clear in this court that he at no time represented Show–World *as a party* in the State courts.

"On the basis of these facts adduced at the hearings thus far in the case, the court finds no privity between Show–World and 303 Corp. such as to equate the interests of the two entities in the State proceedings, and, thereby, to preclude the litigation by Show–World in this court.

"Assuming, without deciding, that Show–World might have had standing to intervene in either or both of the State proceedings to date, that fact alone would not be sufficient to bar this action. The fact that a party has a right to intervene, which it chooses not to exercise, is not enough to make it bound by a judgment in the proceeding in which it possessed such a right. Brown v. Wright, 137 F.2d 484, 487 (4th Cir.1943); Western Union Telegraph Company v. Foster, 247 U.S. 105, 38 S.Ct. 438, 62 L.Ed. 1006 (1918).

"Moreover, the mere existence of a landlord-tenant (lessor-lessee) relationship is insufficient to bind the tenant to the adjudication in the prior litigation to which the landlord only was a party. While there is language in the two cases cited to the court by defendants which would tend to indicate that under some circumstances, the 'privity of estate' between landlord and tenant may cause the latter to be bound by prior judgments to which the landlord only was a party, Kruger & Birch, Inc. v.

DuBoyce, 241 F.2d 849, 854 (3d Cir.1957); Fouke v. Schenewerk, 197 F.2d 234, 236 (5th Cir.1952) (dictum), those cases appear to involve only disputes relating to either title to, or right to possession of, real property. See 50 C.J.S. Judgments § 801 and cases cited therein; [other citations omitted]. Certainly this court has been cited no authority for the proposition that a landlord's derivative assertion of his tenant's constitutional rights in a proceeding to which the tenant was not a party should bind the tenant in a later proceeding in which the tenant seeks to raise those important rights directly. In view of the possible conflict of interest between landlord and tenant, whose rights a landlord might, at least hypothetically, be willing to sacrifice, there appears to be no basis for binding the tenant to the former adjudication on the basis of its relation to the landlord qua landlord.

"Finally, and most clearly, privity is not established from the mere fact that Show–World may happen to be 'interested' in the same question at issue in the earlier proceedings in the New York courts, whether by way of establishing a proposition of law, or by proving or disproving some state of facts. Sodak Distributing Co. v. Wayne, 77 S.D. 496, 93 N.W.2d 791, 795 (1958); Howard v. Fairmont Machinery Co., Inc., 101 F.Supp. 778, 779 (E.D.Ky.1951). Nor does the fact that the prior decision might affect Show–World's action in this court as a favorable or unfavorable judicial precedent cause Show–World to be considered a privy to 303 Corp. in the earlier proceeding. Bigelow v. Old Dominion Copper Mining & Smelting Co., 225 U.S. 111, 32 S.Ct. 641, 56 L.Ed. 1009 (1912)."

TAYLOR v. STURGELL, ___ U.S. ___, 128 S.Ct. 2161 (2008), rev'g Taylor v. Blakey, 490 F.3d 965 (D.C.Cir.2007). By this case, the Supreme Court conformed to the suggestion in Show–World's last paragraph and so pretty much killed off virtual representation as a route to privity. The court of appeals had described the case this way:

"Brent Taylor requested certain documents from the Federal Aviation Administration under the Freedom of Information Act. The FAA denied his request and Taylor sued to compel disclosure. The district court dismissed the case, holding res judicata barred Taylor's claim because Greg Herrick, a 'close associate' of Taylor's, had been his 'virtual representative' in a prior FOIA case Herrick had brought unsuccessfully seeking the same documents. We affirm that judgment.

"Herrick, a member of the Antique Aircraft Association (AAA) and the owner of an F–45 aircraft manufactured by a predecessor of the Fairchild Corporation, filed a request under the FOIA seeking the plans and specifications for the F–45. Herrick v. Garvey, 298 F.3d 1184, 1188 (10th Cir.2002). After conferring with Fairchild, the FAA determined the requested material was a trade secret and withheld the information pursuant to Exemption 4 of the FOIA. See 5 U.S.C. § 552(b)(4). Herrick challenged the FAA's determination, pointing to a 1955 letter from Fairchild's predecessor authorizing the government to disclose the information to the public. Kruger & Birch, Inc. v. DuBoyce, 241 F.2d 849, 854 (3d Cir.1957). The United States District Court for the District of Wyoming granted summary judgment to the FAA. The Tenth Circuit Court of Appeals, affirming, id. at 1194–95, opined that Fairchild's letter authorizing disclosure had deprived the F–45 documents of their status as a trade secret but, because Herrick had not challenged on appeal the district court's assumption that Fairchild's later revocation of that authorization restored their status as a trade secret, the Tenth Circuit assumed without deciding that revocation would have such an effect. Id. at 1194 n. 10.

"Approximately one month after the Tenth Circuit issued its decision in Herrick, Taylor, the executive director of the AAA, filed a FOIA request for the same documents relating to the F–45 that Herrick had sought. . . . Taylor, represented by the lawyer who had represented Herrick in his litigation, . . . argu[ed] the trade secret status of the F–45 documents, having long been abandoned, could not be restored. . . .

. . . .

". . . [Taylor] added that he did not know of Herrick's FOIA request until after the Tenth Circuit's decision. Also, he said Herrick and Taylor sought the information for different reasons—Herrick to restore his F–45 and Taylor more generally 'for the public and in the interest of the preservation of antique aircraft heritage.' "

The court of appeals then explained its approach to virtual representation this way: "An appropriate test for virtual representation must consider and balance competing interests in due process and efficiency. Too readily to find virtual representation risks infringing upon the nonparty's right to due process of law and departs from our 'deep-rooted historic tradition that everyone should have his own day in court.' Richards [v. Jefferson County, 517 U.S. 793, 798, 116 S.Ct. 1761, 1766 (1996)]. To find virtual representation under only very narrow circumstances, on the other hand, would expose defendants to the burden of relitigation, raise the possibility of inconsistent results, and compromise the public interest in judicial economy. [Citations omitted.] We believe these competing concerns can best be addressed by considering five factors . . . . [W]e believe identity of interests and adequate representation are necessary conditions. We do not, however, believe they are sufficient . . . . We therefore require in addition a showing of at least one of the other factors . . . : a close relationship between the present party and his putative representative, or substantial participation by the present party in the first case, or tactical maneuvering on the part of the present party to avoid preclusion by the prior judgment. As this approach clarifies, there can be no virtual representation absent an affirmative link between the later litigant and either the prior party or the prior case."

The court of appeals eventually concluded that "there is record evidence that: (1) Taylor and Herrick had identical interests, even when viewed in terms of incentives, and (2) Taylor's interest was adequately represented in Herrick, in addition to which (3) Herrick and Taylor had a close working relationship relative to these successive cases. There is no countervailing evidence. We therefore conclude Herrick served as Taylor's virtual representative in the litigation for the F–45 documents."

The Supreme Court unanimously vacated the court of appeals' judgment, and remanded for further proceedings on whether Taylor was in fact acting as Herrick's undisclosed agent in relitigating. Justice Ginsburg explained that the background rule is that nonparties are not bound—subject to quite limited and relatively rigid extensions of privity. Virtual representation was not to be one of those extensions under the federal common law of res judicata.

As to the recognized extensions resting on adequate representation, she said that they required certain protections at least "grounded in due process": "A party's representation of a nonparty is 'adequate' for preclusion purposes only if, at a minimum: (1) the interests of the nonparty and her representative are aligned, see Hansberry [v. Lee, 311 U.S. 32, 43, 61 S.Ct. 115, 119 (1940)]; and (2) either the party understood herself to be acting in a representative capacity or the original court took care to protect the interests of the nonparty, see Richards, 517 U.S., at 801–802, 116 S.Ct. 1761 . . . . In addition, adequate representation sometimes requires (3) notice of the original suit to the persons alleged to have been represented, see Richards, 517 U.S., at 801, 116 S.Ct. 1761. In the class-action context, these limitations are implemented by the procedural safeguards contained in Federal Rule of Civil Procedure 23."

Furthermore she warned against framing extensions in the loose terms of a balancing approach: "Preclusion doctrine, it should be recalled, is intended to reduce the burden of litigation on courts and parties. [Citation omitted.] 'In this area of the law,' we agree, ' "crisp rules with sharp corners" are preferable to a round-about doctrine of opaque standards.' Bittinger v. Tecumseh Products Co., 123 F.3d 877, 881 (C.A.6 1997)."

NEENAN v. WOODSIDE ASTORIA TRANSPORTATION CO., 261 N.Y. 159, 184 N.E. 744 (1933). Judge Crane, for the court, said in part:

"On February 7, 1929, at the corner of Seventeenth avenue and Jamaica avenue, in the borough of Queens, New York City, a collision occurred between the automobile owned and operated by John J. Huppmann and a bus of the Woodside Astoria Transportation Co., Inc. Huppmann sued the transportation company for damages [in New York state court] and proved that the collision was due solely to the negligence of its driver to which no carelessness on his part contributed. He recovered a judgment of $2,153.75 against the company.

"Later, a passenger in the bus, Mary Neenan, sued both Huppmann and the Woodside Astoria Transportation Co., Inc., for the damages due to personal injuries received in the collision and, strange as it may seem, recovered a judgment of $1,500 against both defendants. Huppmann sought to introduce the judgment roll in his action against the transportation company, but of course it was not res judicata as to the passenger, Mary Neenan, as she was not a party to that action. She was free to prove that Huppmann was also negligent. If this were not so a responsible party might by collusion shift the liability upon an irresponsible person who cared little about a judgment against him. A plaintiff may hold all joint tort feasors. There was no error in excluding the judgment roll in the action of Mary Neenan."

Questions: (1) Would a holding that Mary Neenan was bound by the prior judgment be consistent with due process of law?

(2) NYCPA § 211–a, in force at the time of the Neenan case, provided that a defendant who had paid more than his pro rata share of a judgment (i.e., the amount of the judgment divided by the number of defendants jointly liable under the judgment) could obtain contribution to the extent of the excess from the other defendants. If Woodside satisfied Mary Neenan's judgment in full and sued Huppmann for contribution, what if any effect should be given to the judgment in the prior action of Huppmann v. Woodside?

(3) Would your answer to the preceding question be different under New York's new contribution statute, NYCPLR art. 14, enacted in 1974 (the year before New York adopted comparative negligence between plaintiff and defendant)? It provides that a defendant who has paid more than his equitable share of a judgment (i.e., a share determined in accordance with his culpability relative to that of the other persons subject to liability for the injury) can obtain contribution to the extent of the excess from those other persons. The defendant can assert the contribution claim either by crossclaim or impleader or by separate action.

SECTION 2. PERSONS BENEFITED BY PRIOR JUDGMENT

Prevalence of mutual estoppel.—By definition, only parties and their privies are bound by a prior judgment, although of course the categories of "privies" are susceptible to stretching. Sound policy does not countenance binding other nonparties, who may be termed "strangers." Parties and their privies may also benefit from a prior judgment under the rules of res judicata. But may strangers benefit from the judgment, even though they are not bound?

First of all, collateral estoppel holds the greatest promise of benefits for such a person not a party or a privy. Involvement of strangers implies a different claim. Usually, then, only parties and their privies may obtain the benefits of the other rules of res judicata, as in the example already given of a successor in interest who could invoke bar based on her predecessor's successful quiet-title action against a rival claimant.

So let us first think in terms of a stranger's use of collateral estoppel. The traditional approach to collateral estoppel derived from the general rule that estoppels must be mutual—that because a stranger to a prior judgment could not be bound by it, letting the stranger benefit from it would be unfair. The Restatement of Judgments (1942) followed the generally prevailing case law in taking this narrow approach, but tempered it with exceptions to meet exigent situations. The result was a rather grudging retreat from mutuality of estoppel, which ignored a growing body of decisions espousing broader exceptions.

Mutuality's exceptions.—For an example that is critically important to understanding this whole area, consider once more the above-described employment-indemnity problem: Imagine that a servant *S*, driving her master *M*'s car on *M*'s business, is in a collision with a car owned and driven by *T*. The master-servant relation makes *M* liable to *T* for *S*'s negligence, if any; as between *M* and *S*, *S* is obliged (in theory at least) to make good to *M* any loss *M* suffers by *S*'s negligence. Assume that *T* sues *S*, and *S* wins. Next *T* sues *M*, relitigating the issues of *S*'s negligence and *T*'s due care, and this time *T* recovers. On the one hand, if *M* can now get indemnity from *S*, *S* must pay as a result of a trial to which she was not a party, when she has already achieved exoneration from liability in a trial to which she was a party. On the other hand, if *M* cannot recover from *S*, *M* has lost his right of indemnity as a result of a trial to which he was not a party.

The natural way around this dilemma would have been to allow *M* to plead res judicata against *T* based on the prior judgment for *S*. But if *T* had won against *S*, *T* could not have used the judgment against *M*, who had never had his day in court. The mutuality rule therefore prohibited that natural solution. This purity was too much for the First Restatement. Thus, an exception to the mutuality rule was created to the extent necessary to protect both *S*'s victory and *M*'s right of indemnity: *M*, the indemnitee, was allowed to use the judgment in favor of *S*, the indemnitor, as a defense to a second suit by *T*. See Restatement of Judgments §§ 96–97 (1942). (The First Restatement provided for the same result whether *S* had won the first suit as defendant or plaintiff, and so did the case law, e.g., Good Health Dairy Prods. Corp. v. Emery, 275 N.Y. 14, 9 N.E.2d 758 (1937).[a] However, the First Restatement, but not all courts, refused to allow the invoker of nonmutual preclusion to use it offensively as a plaintiff in the second suit, rather than defensively as a defendant.)

But what if *T*'s first suit was against *M* for *S*'s negligence, and *M* won? Because it was *S* who was obliged to indemnify *M* and not the other way around, the right of indemnity was not in the mix when *T* next sued *S* and so posed no dilemma. Here the First Restatement stuck with the mutuality requirement and refused to let *S* take advantage of the first judgment. The result was to give *T* a second chance on the same issues by merely shifting

[a] Similarly, a judgment for *T* against *S* for $200 fixed that as the maximum liability of *M* if *T*, not having satisfied his judgment against *S*, sued *M*. See Pinnix v. Griffin, 221 N.C. 348, 20 S.E.2d 366 (1942).

adversaries. Yet there was already authority contrary to the First Restatement's position, e.g., Giedrewicz v. Donovan, 277 Mass. 563, 179 N.E. 246 (1932), and much more thereafter.

Question: (4) What would the Massachusetts court do, in the light of Giedrewicz v. Donovan, if *T* successfully sued *M* for *S*'s negligence (with *T* winning after a trial at which *S* testified as a witness for *M*) and then *S* sued *T* for her own injuries? See Pesce v. Brecher, 302 Mass. 211, 19 N.E.2d 36 (1939) (no res judicata). Why?

Nevertheless, Restatement of Judgments § 99 (1942) recognized another breach in the wall of mutuality, which went beyond the narrow indemnity exception and which seemed to go beyond the demands of compelling need. This broader exception is illustrated by American Button Co. v. Warsaw Button Co., 31 N.Y.S.2d 395 (Sup.Ct.1941) (alternative holding), aff'd mem., 265 A.D. 905, 38 N.Y.S.2d 570 (1942). In a prior action *A* had sued *B* for breach of contract, and had lost. Then *A* sued *W* for inducing *B* to breach that contract with *A*. The court held the prior judgment to preclude *A* from recovering against *W*. The First Restatement generalized the result: a judgment in favor of a person charged with commission of a tort or with breach of a contract normally precluded recovery by the same plaintiff against another defendant who was responsible for the conduct of the former defendant.

For years almost all courts avoided a frontal attack on mutuality, living instead within its framework by an increasing recognition of such exceptions to mutuality (or extensions to preclusion), whose coverage eventually reached all the permutations of these secondary-liability cases. When the frontal attack finally came, it precipitated great controversy and great change in the law in most jurisdictions, a process that is still not fully played out.

COCA–COLA CO. v. PEPSI–COLA CO., 36 Del. 124, 172 A. 260 (Super.Ct.1934). Pepsi–Cola offered a $10,000 reward for information leading to the detection of any dealer substituting Pepsi–Cola for any other five-cent drink. Coca–Cola sued Pepsi–Cola, claiming the reward and alleging that it had made known to Pepsi–Cola instances where certain dealers had substituted Pepsi–Cola for Coca–Cola, a five-cent drink. Pepsi–Cola pleaded res judicata, asserting that the identical issues had been decided against Coca–Cola in prior actions brought by Coca–Cola against the dealers in Delaware state court. Coca–Cola demurred to this plea. The court considered res judicata to be universally applicable against any prior plaintiff, saying: "[W]e are of the opinion that a plaintiff who deliberately selects his forum and there unsuccessfully presents his proofs, is bound by such adverse judgment in a second suit involving all the identical issues already decided. The requirement of mutuality must yield to public policy."

Bernhard v. Bank of America National Trust & Savings Association

Supreme Court of California, 1942.
19 Cal.2d 807, 122 P.2d 892.

[Sather authorized Cook to deposit money for her in the defendant bank. Cook did so, but later withdrew it, deposited it in his name, and used it for his own purposes. Sather died, appointing Cook her executor. In Cook's final accounting to the probate court, no mention was made of this money. Helen Bernhard and other beneficiaries under Sather's will filed objections to Cook's account, claiming that Cook had embezzled the money from Sather. The probate court after a hearing found that Sather in her lifetime had made a gift to Cook of the money in question, and so it allowed Cook's account and discharged him as executor.

[Thereafter Helen Bernhard was appointed administratrix with the will annexed. She brought this suit against the bank, seeking to recover the deposit for the estate on the ground that Sather had never authorized its withdrawal. The bank pleaded that the fact that it had paid the money to Cook with the consent of Sather was res judicata by virtue of the finding of the probate court that she had made a gift of it to Cook. The trial court gave judgment for the defendant on this ground. The plaintiff appealed.]

■ TRAYNOR, J.

. . . .

Plaintiff contends that the doctrine of res judicata does not apply because the defendant who is asserting the plea was not a party to the previous action nor in privity with a party to that action and because there is no mutuality of estoppel.

. . . .

Many courts have stated the facile formula that the plea of res judicata is available only when there is privity and mutuality of estoppel. [Citations omitted.] Under the requirement of privity, only parties to the former judgment or their privies may take advantage of or be bound by it. . . . The estoppel is mutual if the one taking advantage of the earlier adjudication would have been bound by it, had it gone against him. [Citations omitted.]

The criteria for determining who may assert a plea of res judicata differ fundamentally from the criteria for determining against whom a plea of res judicata may be asserted. The requirements of due process of law forbid the assertion of a plea of res judicata against a party unless he was bound by the earlier litigation in which the matter was decided. [Citations omitted.] He is bound by that litigation only if he has been a party thereto or in privity with a party thereto. [Citation omitted.] There is no compelling reason, however, for requiring that the party asserting the plea of res judicata must have been a party, or in privity with a party, to the earlier litigation.

No satisfactory rationalization has been advanced for the requirement of mutuality. Just why a party who was not bound by a previous action should be precluded from asserting it as res judicata against a party who was bound by it is difficult to comprehend. (See 7 Bentham's Works (Bowring's ed.) 171.[b]) Many courts have abandoned the requirement of mutuality and confined the requirement of privity to the party against whom the plea of res judicata is asserted. (Coca–Cola Co. v. Pepsi–Cola Co., [36 Del. 124, 172 A. 260 (Super.Ct.1934)]; Liberty Mutual Ins. Co. v. George Colon & Co., 260 N.Y. 305, 183 N.E. 506; Atkinson v. White, 60 Me. 396;[c] Eagle, etc., Ins. Co. v. Heller, 149 Va. 82, 140 S.E. 314, 57 A.L.R. 490; Jenkins v. Atlantic Coast Line R. Co., 89 S.C. 408, 71 S.E. 1010; United States v. Wexler, 8 F.2d 880. See Good Health Dairy Food Products Corp. v. Emery, 275 N.Y. 14, 9 N.E.2d 758, 112 A.L.R. 401.) The commentators are almost unanimously in accord. (35 Yale L.J. 607; 9 Va.L.Reg.,N.S., 241; 29 Ill.L.Rev. 93; 18 N.Y.U.L.Q.R. 565, 570; 12 Corn.L.Q. 92.) The courts of most jurisdictions have in effect accomplished the same result by recognizing a broad exception to the requirements of mutuality and privity, namely, that they are not necessary where the liability of the defendant asserting the plea of res judicata is dependent upon or derived from the liability of one who was exonerated in an earlier suit brought by the same plaintiff upon the same facts. [Citations omitted.] Typical examples of such derivative liability are master and servant, principal and agent, and indemnitor and indemnitee. Thus, if a plaintiff sues a servant for injuries caused by the servant's alleged negligence within the scope of his employment, a judgment against the plaintiff on the grounds that the servant was not negligent can be pleaded by the master as res judicata if he is subsequently sued by the same plaintiff for the same injuries. Conversely, if the plaintiff first sues the master, a judgment against the plaintiff on the grounds that the servant was not negligent can be pleaded by the servant as res judicata if he is subsequently sued by the plaintiff. In each of these situations the party asserting the plea of res judicata was not a party to the previous action nor in privity with such a party under the accepted definition of a privy . . . . Likewise, the estoppel is not mutual since the party asserting the plea, not having been a party or in privity with a party to the former action, would not have been bound by it had it been decided the other way. The cases justify this exception on the ground that it would be unjust to

[b] Bentham there attacked the rule of mutuality as "a maxim which one would suppose to have found its way from the gaming-table to the bench." But see Note, A Probabilistic Analysis of the Doctrine of Mutuality of Collateral Estoppel, 76 Mich.L.Rev. 612, 616 n.15 (1978) (Bentham's book was proposing use of judgments as evidence, not preclusion); Michael J. Waggoner, Fifty Years of Bernhard v. Bank of America Is Enough: Collateral Estoppel Should Require Mutuality but Res Judicata Should Not, 12 Rev.Litig. 391, 430–31 (1993) (words were not Bentham's but his editor's, a very young John Stuart Mill).

[c] In this 1872 case the court said, 60 Me. at 399: "That law [that estoppels must be mutual] was adopted when parties could not be witnesses, and from a very tender care of suitors, lest by possibility injustice might be done. For it is said, and this appears to be the only reason on which the law is founded, that 'if the adverse party was not also a party to the judgment offered in evidence, it may have been obtained upon his own testimony; in which case, to allow him to derive benefit from it would be unjust.' "

permit one who has had his day in court to reopen identical issues by merely switching adversaries.

In determining the validity of a plea of res judicata three questions are pertinent: Was the issue decided in the prior adjudication identical with the one presented in the action in question? Was there a final judgment on the merits? Was the party against whom the plea is asserted a party or in privity with a party to the prior adjudication? In re Estate of Smead, 219 Cal. 572, 28 P.2d 348; Silva v. Hawkins, 152 Cal. 138, 92 P. 72, and People v. Rodgers, 118 Cal. 393, 46 P. 740, 50 P. 668, to the extent that they are inconsistent with this opinion, are overruled.

In the present case, therefore, the defendant is not precluded by lack of privity or of mutuality of estoppel from asserting the plea of res judicata against the plaintiff. Since the issue as to the ownership of the money is identical with the issue raised in the probate proceeding, and since the order of the probate court settling the executor's account was a final adjudication of this issue on the merits [citations omitted], it remains only to determine whether the plaintiff in the present action was a party or in privity with a party to the earlier proceeding. The plaintiff has brought the present action in the capacity of administratrix of the estate. In this capacity she represents the very same persons and interests that were represented in the earlier hearing on the executor's account. In that proceeding plaintiff and the other legatees who objected to the executor's account represented the estate of the decedent. They were seeking not a personal recovery but, like the plaintiff in the present action, as administratrix, a recovery for the benefit of the legatees and creditors of the estate, all of whom were bound by the order settling the account. (Prob.Code, sec. 931. See cases cited in 12 Cal.Jur. 62, 63.) The plea of res judicata is therefore available against plaintiff as a party to the former proceeding, despite her formal change of capacity. . . .

The judgment is affirmed.

Rise of nonmutual estoppel.—The immediate impact of Justice Traynor's root-and-branch demolition of mutuality was not significant. But later it came to have widespread repercussions in many states, thanks in no small part to an influential article by Professor Brainerd Currie, Mutuality of Collateral Estoppel: Limits of the Bernhard Doctrine, 9 Stan.L.Rev. 281 (1957). The notion that a party ought not to enjoy the luxury of a second trial on an issue he has already litigated and lost had growing appeal in days of crowded dockets and increased costs of maintaining the judicial system.

Nonetheless, the litigation-saving aspect of the Bernhard rule is not as obvious as it superficially appears. If courts completely abrogate mutuality, an adverse judgment will preclude a party on every litigated and determined issue essential to the judgment with respect to *all* persons. A prudent litigant may consequently feel bound to fight a case to the utmost in both trial and appellate courts, even though he would treat the case or a particular issue more casually if its sole effects regarded the immediate adversaries and their privies. The effect on the volume of litigation is thus not susceptible of clear proof. Moreover, there are concerns of basic fairness cutting both ways, as we soon shall show. See also James Wm. Moore & Thomas S. Currier, Mutuality and Conclusiveness of Judgments, 35 Tul. L.Rev. 301 (1961), which gives a stout defense of the doctrine of mutuality with "certain dispensing exceptions shown to be sound by theory and experience."

So, how far to go with Bernhard's disputable approach? Most of the courts influenced by Bernhard have stopped short of accepting the full sweep of Justice Traynor's dictum. There has, however, been a contrariety of views as to where the proper stopping point is. To explore this question, the four possible patterns in which the question arises deserve separate consideration. (For convenience, *P* = plaintiff in first action; *D* = defendant in first action; *NP* = new plaintiff, not a party or privy to first action; and *ND* = new defendant, not a party or privy to first action.)

1. *P* sues *D*, *D* wins. Then loser *P* sues *ND*. Can *ND* use collateral estoppel?

This is the strongest case for collateral estoppel. *P* chose the court and the adversary in the first action. (How important is this?) *P* now tries again against a new adversary, who wants to use the prior judgment defensively. This category includes Coca–Cola Co. v. Pepsi–Cola Co.

Question: (5) Is it fair to Coca–Cola to use against it in an action against Pepsi–Cola its defeat in a suit against a small dealer, who would presumably have had the fact-finder's sympathy? When a party has had a day in court, is it relevant to ask, "A day in court against whom?" Indeed, because traditionally an adjudication is an often close decision of a specific dispute involving particular litigants, where special factors off the merits may influence the outcome, could not one say generally that fairness requires a day in court against the present opponent? Or instead should adjudication yield a free-floating truth?

2. *P* sues *D*, *P* wins. Then loser *D* sues *ND*. Can *ND* use collateral estoppel?

This situation also involves a defensive use of collateral estoppel, the difference being that here the party to the prior action did not have the initiative and so did not choose the court or the adversary in that action.

Question: (6) Driver's car collides with a car driven by *T*. A passenger in Driver's car sues *T* and wins (*T* negligent). Then *T* sues Driver. Is it just to preclude *T* on the issue of her negligence? What of the jury's likely sympathy for the first plaintiff, or indeed for most plaintiffs?

3. *P* sues *D*, *D* wins. Then *NP* sues loser *P*. Can *NP* use collateral estoppel?

This is offensive use of collateral estoppel. (Is the difference between using a prior judgment as a sword rather than as a shield significant?) Note that *P*, the party against whom collateral estoppel is invoked, chose the court and the adversary in the first action.

Question: (7) *T* sues Driver and loses (*T* contributorily negligent). Then a passenger in Driver's car sues *T*. Is it just to preclude *T* on the issue of her negligence? Is this a harder case than the preceding situation to justify the use of collateral estoppel?

4. *P* sues *D*, *P* wins. Then *NP* sues loser *D*. Can *NP* use collateral estoppel?

This is the hardest case of all for collateral estoppel. *NP*wants to use the prior judgment offensively, and here the party to the prior action did not choose the court or the adversary in that action. This situation encompasses the favorite classroom hypothetical case called by Professor Currie the multiple-claimant anomaly. Assume there are forty passengers injured in a bus accident. If *P–1* sues the bus company and loses, presumably no other passenger can be bound by the result (see the Neenan case). So if *P–2, P–3,* and *P–4* all also sue and lose, but *P–5* has the good fortune to win, does this mean that *P–6* through *P–40* can win by collateral estoppel? If so, bear in mind that plaintiffs who might normally join in a single action would have strong incentive to hang back and hope for a case with a favorable result. Bear in mind also the likely tactic of planning the first suit to be on behalf of the most appealing of the potential plaintiffs.

Question: (8) Is there a practical way to take care of this anomaly? What of denying collateral estoppel effect to a later plaintiff if the bus company has prevailed in any of the prior actions? That seems to be a good but incomplete approach. To handle the situation where *P–1* won, should the law also deny collateral estoppel effect if there has been only one plaintiff victory so far? See Aaron Gershonowitz, Issue Preclusion: The Return of the Multiple Claimant Anomaly, 14 U.Balt.L.Rev. 227 (1985).

Nonmutuality's exceptions.—Even Justice Traynor balked at giving unrestricted effect to his own dictum. There have to be exceptions.

In the case of Taylor v. Hawkinson, 47 Cal.2d 893, 306 P.2d 797 (1957), Mr. Taylor obtained a verdict of $63.06 for property damage, the driver of his car won $65.00 for personal injuries, and Mrs. Taylor won $371.94 for personal injuries. Only Mrs. Taylor moved for a new trial for insufficiency of damages, and she succeeded on her motion. Thereafter the judgment for the other plaintiffs became final. Mrs. Taylor then sought to limit her retrial to damages, on the ground that the Bernhard rule precluded the issue of liability. Nevertheless, the trial court submitted all issues to the jury, which returned a verdict for the defendant. The judgment thereon was affirmed. Justice Traynor, for the court, said: "There is ample evidence to support the trial court's implied finding that the verdicts following the first trial were compromise verdicts and that the jury did not determine the issue of liability." Justice Carter, alone in dissent, said: "It is no answer to say that the judgment is not res judicata because being based on a compromise verdict the issue of liability was not determined. [Citation omitted.] If the jury did not decide that issue, it decided nothing, and the judgment entered on its verdict would not be binding on the parties thereto. To say it did not decide the issue is to ignore the pleadings, verdict and judgment, and to permit a collateral attack on the judgment which is not permitted."

Questions: (9) Does the Taylor holding mean that in any case the first trial is subject to reexamination to see whether the verdict appears to have been a compromise?

(10) There has been some tendency to draw the line between defensive and offensive use of collateral estoppel, allowing only the former. E.g., Albernaz v. City of Fall River, 346 Mass. 336, 191 N.E.2d 771 (1963). Is such a rule a more desirable solution than the flexibility implicit in Taylor?

Blonder–Tongue Laboratories v. University of Illinois Foundation

Supreme Court of the United States, 1971.
402 U.S. 313, 91 S.Ct. 1434.

[The rule in patent infringement cases in the federal courts had been, ever since Triplett v. Lowell, 297 U.S. 638, 56 S.Ct. 645 (1936), that a determination of invalidity of a patent in an action by the patentee against an alleged infringer did not preclude the patentee in a second action against another alleged infringer. Triplett was decided late in the heyday of the mutuality doctrine.

[In the present case, the lower courts followed Triplett to permit the Foundation, as patentee, to maintain and win a second action after losing its first action. But, on certiorari, the Supreme Court took it upon itself to reexamine Triplett.]

■ JUSTICE WHITE, speaking for a unanimous Court, said, after an extensive review of the doctrine:]

The cases and authorities discussed above connect erosion of the mutuality requirement to the goal of limiting relitigation of issues where that can be achieved without compromising fairness in particular cases. The courts have often discarded the rule while commenting on crowded dockets and long delays preceding trial. Authorities differ on whether the public interest in efficient judicial administration is a sufficient ground in and of itself for abandoning mutuality, but it is clear that more than crowded dockets is involved. The broader question is whether it is any longer tenable to afford a litigant more than one full and fair opportunity for judicial resolution of the same issue. The question in these terms includes as part of the calculus the effect on judicial administration, but it also encompasses the concern exemplified by Bentham's reference to the gaming table in his attack on the principle of mutuality of estoppel. In any lawsuit where a defendant, because of the mutuality principle, is forced to present a complete defense on the merits to a claim which the plaintiff has fully litigated and lost in a prior action, there is an arguable misallocation of resources. To the extent the defendant in the second suit may not win by asserting, without contradiction, that the plaintiff had fully and fairly, but unsuccessfully, litigated the same claim in the prior suit, the defendant's time and money are diverted from alternative uses—productive or otherwise—to relitigation of a decided issue. And, still assuming that the issue was resolved correctly in the first suit, there is reason to be concerned about the plaintiff's allocation of resources. Permitting repeated litigation of the same issue as long as the supply of unrelated defendants holds out reflects either the aura of the gaming table or "a lack of discipline and of disinterestedness on the part of the lower courts, hardly a worthy or wise basis for fashioning rules of procedure." Kerotest Mfg. Co. v. C–O–Two Co., 342 U.S. 180, 185, 72 S.Ct. 219, 222 (1952). Although neither judges, the parties, nor the adversary system performs perfectly in all cases, the requirement of determining whether the party against whom an estoppel is asserted had a full and fair opportunity to litigate is a most significant safeguard.

Some litigants—those who never appeared in a prior action—may not be collaterally estopped without litigating the issue. They have never had a chance to present their evidence and arguments on the claim. Due process prohibits estopping them despite one or more existing adjudications of the identical issue which stand squarely against their position. See Hansberry v. Lee, 311 U.S. 32, 40, 61 S.Ct. 115, 117 (1940); Bernhard, [19 Cal.2d 807, 811, 122 P.2d 892, 894 (1942)]. Also, the authorities have been more willing to permit a defendant in a second suit to invoke an estoppel against a plaintiff who lost on the same claim in an earlier suit than they have been to allow a plaintiff in the second suit to use offensively a judgment obtained by a different plaintiff in a prior suit against the same defendant. But the case before us involves neither due process nor "offensive use" questions. Rather, it depends on the considerations weighing for and against permitting a patent holder to sue on his patent after it has once been held invalid following opportunity for full and fair trial.

[The Court concluded (1) that the Triplett rule was not essential to effectuate the purposes of the patent system; (2) that the economic costs of continuing adherence to Triplett were substantial in terms of (a) costs to both sides of repetitive litigation and (b) economic disruption flowing from the multiple opportunities for holders of invalid patents to exact licensing agreements from alleged infringers, who will often pay royalties under a license rather than bear the costly burden of challenging the patent; and (3) that although any burden placed on the judiciary by Triplett was an incidental matter in comparison to the other economic costs of following Triplett, its abrogation would save some judicial time, if collateral estoppel fairly disposed of even a few relatively lengthy patent suits. The Court also stated:]

Moreover, we do not suggest, without legislative guidance, that a plea of estoppel by an infringement or royalty suit defendant must automatically be accepted once the defendant in support of his plea identifies the issue in suit as the identical question finally decided against the patentee or one of his privies in previous litigation. Rather, the patentee-plaintiff must be permitted to demonstrate, if he can, that he did not have "a fair opportunity procedurally, substantively and evidentially to pursue his claim the first time." Eisel v. Columbia Packing Co., 181 F.Supp. 298, 301 (Mass.1960). This element in the estoppel decision will comprehend, we believe, the important concerns about the complexity of patent litigation and the posited hazard that the prior proceedings were seriously defective.

Determining whether a patentee has had a full and fair chance to litigate the validity of his patent in an earlier case is of necessity not a simple matter. In addition to the considerations of choice of forum and incentive to litigate . . . , certain other factors immediately emerge. For example, . . . appropriate inquiries would be . . . whether the opinions filed by the District Court and the reviewing court, if any, indicate that the prior case was one of those relatively rare instances where the courts wholly failed to grasp the technical subject matter and issues in suit; and whether without fault of his own the patentee was deprived of crucial evidence or witnesses in the first litigation. But as so often is the case, no one set of facts, no one collection of words or phrases, will provide an automatic formula for proper rulings on estoppel pleas. In the end, decision will necessarily rest on the trial courts' sense of justice and equity.

. . . .

It is clear that judicial decisions have tended to depart from the rigid requirements of mutuality. In accordance with this trend, there has been a corresponding development of the lower courts' ability and facility in dealing with questions of when it is appropriate and fair to impose an estoppel against a party who has already litigated an issue once and lost. As one commentator has stated:

> "Under the tests of time and subsequent developments, the Bernhard decision has proved its merit and the mettle of its author. The abrasive action of new factual configurations and of actual human controversies, disposed of in the common-law tradition by competent courts, far more than the commentaries of academicians, leaves the decision revealed for what it is, as it was written: a shining landmark of progress in justice and law administration." Currie, [Civil Procedure: The Tempest Brews, 53 Cal.L.Rev. 25, 37 (1965)].

. . . [I]t is apparent that the uncritical acceptance of the principle of mutuality of estoppel expressed in Triplett v. Lowell is today out of place. Thus, we conclude that Triplett should be overruled to the extent it forecloses a plea of estoppel by one facing a charge of infringement of a patent that has once been declared invalid.

. . . .

Res judicata and collateral estoppel are affirmative defenses that must be pleaded. Fed.Rule Civ.Proc. 8(c). The purpose of such pleading is to give the opposing party notice of the plea of estoppel and a chance to argue, if he can, why the imposition of an estoppel would be inappropriate. Because of Triplett v. Lowell, petitioner did not plead estoppel and [the Foundation] never had an opportunity to challenge the appropriateness of such a plea on the grounds [that the patentee did not have "a full and fair chance to litigate the validity of his patent" in the prior case]. Therefore, given the partial overruling of Triplett, we remand the case. Petitioner should be allowed to amend its pleadings in the District Court to assert a plea of estoppel. [The Foundation] must then be permitted to . . . supplement the record with any evidence showing why an estoppel should not be imposed in this case. If necessary, petitioner may also supplement the record. In taking this action, we intimate no views on the other issues presented in this case. The judgment of the Court of Appeals is vacated and the cause is remanded to the District Court for further proceedings consistent with this opinion.[d]

Parklane Hosiery Co. v. Shore

Supreme Court of the United States, 1979.
439 U.S. 322, 99 S.Ct. 645.

■ MR. JUSTICE STEWART delivered the opinion of the Court.

This case presents the question whether a party who has had issues of fact adjudicated adversely to it in an equitable action may be collaterally estopped from relitigating the same issues before a jury in a subsequent legal action brought against it by a new party.

The respondent brought this stockholder's class action against the petitioners in a federal district court. The complaint alleged that the petitioners, Parklane Hosiery Company, Inc. (Parklane) and 12 of its officers, directors, and stockholders, had issued a materially false and misleading proxy statement in connection with a merger. The proxy statement, according to the complaint, had violated [various federal securities laws]. The complaint sought damages, rescission of the merger, and recovery of costs.

Before this action came to trial, the SEC filed suit against the same defendants in a federal district court, alleging that the proxy statement that had been issued by Parklane was materially false and misleading in essentially the same respects as those that had been alleged in the respondent's complaint. Injunctive relief was requested. After a four-day trial, the District Court found that the proxy statement was materially false and misleading in the respects alleged, and entered a declaratory judgment to that effect. Securities and Exchange Commission v. Parklane Hosiery Co., 422 F.Supp. 477. The Court of Appeals for the Second Circuit affirmed this judgment. 558 F.2d 1083.

The respondent in the present case then moved for partial summary judgment against the petitioners, asserting that the petitioners were collaterally estopped from relitigating the issues that had been resolved against them in the action brought by the SEC.[2] The District Court denied the

---

[d] Upon remand, the district court found that the Foundation failed to make the requisite showing to escape the defense of estoppel and entered summary judgment for the defendant, 334 F.Supp. 47 (N.D.Ill.1971) (Hoffman, J.), aff'd per curiam, 465 F.2d 380 (7th Cir.), cert. denied, 409 U.S. 1061, 93 S.Ct. 559 (1972).

[2] A private plaintiff in an action under the proxy rules is not entitled to relief simply by demonstrating that the proxy solicitation was materially false and misleading. The plaintiff

motion on the ground that such an application of collateral estoppel would deny the petitioners their Seventh Amendment right to a jury trial. The Court of Appeals for the Second Circuit reversed, holding that a party who has had issues of fact determined against him after a full and fair opportunity to litigate in a nonjury trial is collaterally estopped from obtaining a subsequent jury trial of these same issues of fact. 565 F.2d 815. The appellate court concluded that "the Seventh Amendment preserves the right to jury trial only with respect to issues of fact, [and] once those issues have been fully and fairly adjudicated in a prior proceeding, nothing remains for trial, either with or without a jury." Id., at 819. Because of an intercircuit conflict, we granted certiorari. 435 U.S. 1006, 98 S.Ct. 1875.

I

The threshold question to be considered is whether, quite apart from the right to a jury trial under the Seventh Amendment, the petitioners can be precluded from relitigating facts resolved adversely to them in a prior equitable proceeding with another party under the general law of collateral estoppel. Specifically, we must determine whether a litigant who was not a party to a prior judgment may nevertheless use that judgment "offensively" to prevent a defendant from relitigating issues resolved in the earlier proceeding.

A

[The Court here reviewed the rejection of the mutuality requirement by the Blonder–Tongue decision.]

B

The Blonder–Tongue case involved defensive use of collateral estoppel—a plaintiff was estopped from asserting a claim that the plaintiff had previously litigated and lost against another defendant. The present case, by contrast, involves offensive use of collateral estoppel—a plaintiff is seeking to estop a defendant from relitigating the issues which the defendant previously litigated and lost against another plaintiff. In both the offensive and defensive use situations, the party against whom estoppel is asserted has litigated and lost in an earlier action. Nevertheless, several reasons have been advanced why the two situations should be treated differently.

First, offensive use of collateral estoppel does not promote judicial economy in the same manner as defensive use does. Defensive use of collateral estoppel precludes a plaintiff from relitigating identical issues by merely "switching adversaries." Bernhard v. Bank of America Nat. Trust & Savings Assn., 19 Cal.2d 807, 813, 122 P.2d 892, 895 (1942). Thus defensive collateral estoppel gives a plaintiff a strong incentive to join all potential

---

must also show that he was injured and prove damages. [Citation omitted.] Since the SEC action was limited to a determination of whether the proxy statements contained materially false and misleading statements, the respondent conceded that he would still have to prove these other elements of his prima facie case in the private action. The petitioners' right to a jury trial on those remaining issues is not contested.

defendants in the first action if possible. Offensive use of collateral estoppel, on the other hand, creates precisely the opposite incentive. Since a plaintiff will be able to rely on a previous judgment against a defendant but will not be bound by that judgment if the defendant wins, the plaintiff has every incentive to adopt a "wait and see" attitude, in the hope that the first action by another plaintiff will result in a favorable judgment. [Citations omitted.] Thus offensive use of collateral estoppel will likely increase rather than decrease the total amount of litigation, since potential plaintiffs will have everything to gain and nothing to lose by not intervening in the first action.

A second argument against offensive use of collateral estoppel is that it may be unfair to a defendant. If a defendant in the first action is sued for small or nominal damages, he may have little incentive to defend vigorously, particularly if future suits are not foreseeable. Evergreens v. Nunan, 141 F.2d 927, 929; cf. Berner v. British Commonwealth Pac. Airlines, 346 F.2d 532 (application of offensive collateral estoppel denied where defendant did not appeal an adverse judgment awarding damages of $35,000 and defendant was later sued for over $7 million). Allowing offensive collateral estoppel may also be unfair to a defendant if the judgment relied upon as a basis for the estoppel is itself inconsistent with one or more previous judgments in favor of the defendant. Still another situation where it might be unfair to apply offensive estoppel is where the second action affords the defendant procedural opportunities unavailable in the first action that could readily cause a different result.[15]

C

We have concluded that the preferable approach for dealing with these problems in the federal courts is not to preclude the use of offensive collateral estoppel, but to grant trial courts broad discretion to determine when it should be applied. The general rule should be that in cases where a plaintiff could easily have joined in the earlier action or where, either for the reasons discussed above or for other reasons, the application of offensive estoppel would be unfair to a defendant, a trial judge should not allow the use of offensive collateral estoppel.

In the present case, however, none of the circumstances that might justify reluctance to allow the offensive use of collateral estoppel is present. The application of offensive collateral estoppel will not here reward a private plaintiff who could have joined in the previous action, since the respondent probably could not have joined in the injunctive action brought

---

[15] If, for example, the defendant in the first action was forced to defend in an inconvenient forum and therefore was unable to engage in full scale discovery or call witnesses, application of offensive collateral estoppel may be unwarranted. Indeed, differences in available procedures may sometimes justify not allowing a prior judgment to have estoppel effect in a subsequent action even between the same parties, or where defensive estoppel is asserted against a plaintiff who has litigated and lost. The problem of unfairness is particularly acute in cases of offensive estoppel, however, because the defendant against whom estoppel is asserted typically will not have chosen the forum in the first action. See Restatement (Second) of Judgments (Tent. Draft No. 2, 1975) § 88(2) and Comment d.

by the SEC even had he so desired.[17] Similarly, there is no unfairness to the petitioners in applying offensive collateral estoppel in this case. First, in light of the serious allegations made in the SEC's complaint against the petitioners, as well as the foreseeability of subsequent private suits that typically follow a successful government judgment, the petitioners had every incentive to litigate the SEC lawsuit fully and vigorously. Second, the judgment in the Commission action was not inconsistent with any previous decision. Finally, there will in the respondent's action be no procedural opportunities available to the petitioners that were unavailable in the first action of a kind that might be likely to cause a different result.[19]

We conclude, therefore, that none of the considerations that would justify a refusal to allow the use of offensive collateral estoppel is present in this case. Since the petitioners received a "full and fair" opportunity to litigate their claims in the SEC action, the contemporary law of collateral estoppel leads inescapably to the conclusion that the petitioners are collaterally estopped from relitigating the question of whether the proxy statements were materially false and misleading.

II

The question that remains is whether, notwithstanding the law of collateral estoppel, the use of offensive collateral estoppel in this case would violate the petitioners' Seventh Amendment right to a jury trial.

[The Court here rejected the petitioners' argument and affirmed the court of appeals. The Court ruled that because in 1791 an equitable determination could have collateral estoppel effect in a subsequent legal action, such estoppel by itself entails no violation of the Seventh Amendment. And even though the common law in 1791 permitted collateral estoppel only when there was mutuality, collateral estoppel is permissible in the circumstances of this case because the Seventh Amendment's protection of the fundamental elements of the jury right did not mandate the exact procedural incidents and details associated with jury trial in 1791 and so did not inhibit the subsequent evolution of collateral estoppel.]

■ [The decision drew a passionate dissent from JUSTICE REHNQUIST. He argued that the majority was condoning a violation of the Seventh Amendment by permitting nonmutual collateral estoppel to destroy a jury right. Moreover, he argued that simply as a matter of res judicata law, collateral estoppel should be denied here because it "runs counter to the strong federal policy favoring jury trials" and because "the opportunity for a jury

---

17 Securities and Exchange Commission v. Everest Management Corp., 475 F.2d 1236, 1240 ("the complicating effect of the additional issues and the additional parties outweighs any advantage of a single disposition of the common issues"). Moreover, consolidation of a private action with one brought by the SEC without its consent is prohibited by statute. 15 U.S.C. § 78u(g).

19 It is true, of course, that the petitioners in the present action would be entitled to a jury trial of the issues bearing on whether the proxy statement was materially false and misleading had the SEC action never been brought—a matter to be discussed in Part II of this opinion. [And the petitioners did not have a right to a jury trial in the equitable suit brought by the SEC.—Ed.] But the presence or absence of a jury as factfinder is basically neutral, quite unlike, for example, the necessity of defending the first lawsuit in an inconvenient forum.

trial in the second action could easily lead to a different result from that obtained in the first action before the court and therefore . . . it is unfair to estop petitioners from relitigating the issues before a jury." He closed by observing:]

The ultimate irony of today's decision is that its potential for significantly conserving the resources of either the litigants or the judiciary is doubtful at best. . . . It is . . . probable that today's decision will have the result of coercing defendants to agree to consent orders or settlements in agency enforcement action in order to preserve their right to jury trial in the private actions. In that event, the Court, for no compelling reason, will have simply added a powerful club to the administrative agencies' arsenals that even Congress was unwilling to provide them.[e]

Question: (11) What would have happened if the district court had invoked its "discretion" to determine that collateral estoppel should not apply, on the ground that the petitioners had not had a full and fair opportunity to litigate, instead of resting on the jury right? That is, what should be the scope of the trial court's discretion in this context? See 18A Wright, Miller & Cooper § 4465, at 732–33 (appellate courts differ).

SECOND RESTATEMENT'S APPROACH

Restatement (Second) of Judgments § 29 (1982) provides that issue preclusion, subject to all its usual requirements and exceptions, may be invoked by a nonparty against a party to the prior action, "unless the fact that he lacked full and fair opportunity to litigate the issue in the first action or other circumstances justify affording him an opportunity to relitigate the issue." The section goes on to mention some of the numerous such circumstances that should be considered as factors, including whether the nonparty could have joined in the prior action, whether the prior determination is itself inconsistent with some other determination of the same issue, whether relationships among the parties to the first action that are absent in the second seem to have affected the prior determination, and whether preclusion may complicate the second action or prejudice another party thereto. Indeed, the final sentence of the reporter's note thereon states: "The ultimate question is whether there is good reason, all things considered, to allow the party to relitigate the issue."

Questions: (12) Is the purpose of res judicata in putting an end to litigation defeated by such an approach? Might one argue that we would be better off with the bare minimum of preclusion than with a flexible doctrine of res judicata? See generally Maurice J. Holland, Modernizing Res Judicata: Reflections on the Parklane Doctrine, 55 Ind.L.J. 615 (1980).

---

[e] For the background story of the Parklane case, see Lewis A. Grossman, "The Story of Parklane: The 'Litigation Crisis' and the Efficiency Imperative," in Civil Procedure Stories 405 (Kevin M. Clermont ed., 2d ed. 2008).

(13) More specifically, was not the mutuality rule with a few defined extensions of preclusion (such as in the secondary-liability circumstances) preferable in terms of workability to the Second Restatement's more extensive preclusion that requires fuzzy exceptions entailing case-by-case inquiry into fairness and efficiency? Cf. Janet S. Ellis, Note, Nonmutuality: Taking the Fairness out of Collateral Estoppel, 13 Ind.L.Rev. 563, 596 (1980) ("Perhaps all nonmutuality runs too great a risk of unfairness because fairness cannot be unerringly determined. If fairness is the prime concern of courts, then requiring mutuality may be the best method of meeting this concern. Mutuality guarantees fairness to the party by restricting the effect of the judgment to parties with whom the original party has actually litigated. A nonparty who has not litigated has lost nothing when he is denied the use of a judgment for lack of mutuality.").

UNITED STATES v. MENDOZA, 464 U.S. 154, 104 S.Ct. 568 (1984). By a 1975 decision of the District Court for the Northern District of California, a number of Filipino war veterans established that the United States had denied them due process by its administration of the statute regarding the naturalization in the Philippines in 1945 and 1946 of noncitizens who had served in the American armed forces during World War II, a decision the United States did not appeal.

In 1978, another Filipino war veteran petitioned for naturalization. Sergio Mendoza was now an elderly resident of the U.S. subject to deportation, but he had served as an army doctor until he was captured by the Japanese, and he had then survived their notorious Bataan Death March. The District Court for the Central District of California and the Court of Appeals for the Ninth Circuit held that the prior decision collaterally estopped the United States on the constitutional issue. On certiorari, a unanimous Supreme Court reversed, holding that "nonmutual offensive collateral estoppel is not to be extended to the United States." Justice Rehnquist explained for the Court:

"We have long recognized that 'the Government is not in a position identical to that of a private litigant,' INS v. Hibi, 414 U.S. 5, 8, 94 S.Ct. 19, 21 (1973) (per curiam), both because of the geographic breadth of government litigation and also, most importantly, because of the nature of the issues the government litigates. It is not open to serious dispute that the government is a party to a far greater number of cases on a nationwide basis than even the most litigious private entity; in 1982, the United States was a party to more than 75,000 of the 206,193 [civil] filings in the United States District Courts. Administrative Office of the United States Courts, Annual Report of the Director 98 (1982). In the same year the United States was a party to just under 30% of the civil cases appealed from the District Courts to the Court of Appeals. Id., at 79, 82. Government litigation frequently involves legal questions of substantial public importance; indeed, because the proscriptions of the United States Constitution are so generally directed at governmental action, many constitutional questions can arise only in the context of litigation to which the government is a party. Because of those facts the government is more likely than any private party to be involved in lawsuits against different parties which nonetheless involve the same legal issues.

"A rule allowing nonmutual collateral estoppel against the government in such cases would substantially thwart the development of important questions of law by freezing the first final decision rendered on a particular legal issue. Allowing only one final adjudication would deprive this Court of the benefit it receives from permitting several courts of appeals to explore a difficult question before this Court grants certiorari. [Citations omitted.] Indeed, if nonmutual estoppel were routinely applied against the government, this Court would have to revise its practice of waiting for a conflict to develop before granting the government's petitions for certiorari. See Sup.Ct.R. [10].

"The Solicitor General's policy for determining when to appeal an adverse decision would also require substantial revision. The Court of Appeals faulted the government in this case for failing to appeal a decision that it now contends is erroneous. . . . But the government's litigation conduct in a case is apt to differ from that of a private litigant. Unlike a private litigant who generally does not forego an appeal if he believes that he can prevail, the Solicitor General considers a variety of factors, such as the limited resources of the government and the crowded dockets of the courts, before authorizing an appeal. Brief for the United States, at 30–31. The application of nonmutual estoppel against the government would force the Solicitor General to abandon those prudential concerns and to appeal every adverse decision in order to avoid foreclosing further review.

"In addition to those institutional concerns traditionally considered by the Solicitor General, the panoply of important public issues raised in governmental litigation may quite properly lead successive Administrations of the Executive Branch to take differing positions with respect to the resolution of a particular issue. While the Executive Branch must of course defer to the Judicial Branch for final resolution of questions of constitutional law, the former nonetheless controls the progress of government litigation through the federal courts. It would be idle to pretend that the conduct of government litigation in all its myriad features, from the decision to file a complaint in the United States District Court to the decision to petition for certiorari to review a judgment of the Court of Appeals, is a wholly mechanical procedure which involves no policy choices whatever.

. . . .

"The Court of Appeals did not endorse a routine application of nonmutual collateral estoppel against the government, because it recognized that the government does litigate issues of far-reaching national significance which in some cases, it concluded, might warrant relitigation. But in this case it found no 'record evidence' indicating that there was a 'crucial need' in the administration of the immigration laws for a redetermination of the due process question decided in [the 1975 case] and presented again in this case. . . . The Court of Appeals did not make clear what sort of 'record evidence' would have satisfied it that there *was* a 'crucial need' for redetermination of the question in this case, but we pretermit further discussion of that approach; we believe that the standard announced by the Court of Appeals for determining when relitigation of a legal issue is to be permitted is so wholly subjective that it affords no guidance to the courts or to the government. Such a standard leaves the government at sea because it can not possibly anticipate, in determining whether or not to appeal an adverse decision, whether a court will bar relitigation of the issue in a later case. . . .

"We hold, therefore, that nonmutual offensive collateral estoppel simply does not apply against the government in such a way as to preclude relitigation of issues such as those involved in this case. The conduct of government litigation in the courts of the United States is sufficiently different from the conduct of private civil litigation in those courts so that what might otherwise be economy interests underlying a broad application of collateral estoppel are outweighed by the constraints which peculiarly affect the government. We think that our conclusion will better allow thorough development of legal doctrine by allowing litigation in multiple forums. Indeed, a contrary result might disserve the economy interests in whose name estoppel is advanced by requiring the government to abandon virtually any exercise of discretion in seeking to review judgments unfavorable to it. . . .

"Our holding in this case is consistent with each of our prior holdings to which the parties have called our attention, and which we reaffirm. Today in a companion case we hold that the government may be estopped under certain circumstances from relitigating a question when the parties to the two lawsuits are the same. United States v. Stauffer Chemical Co., 464 U.S. 165, 104 S.Ct. 575 (1984); see also Montana v. United States, [440 U.S. 147, 99 S.Ct. 970 (1979)]; United States v. Moser, 266 U.S. 236, 45 S.Ct. 66 (1924). . . .

"The concerns underlying our disapproval of collateral estoppel against the government are for the most part inapplicable where mutuality is present, as in Stauffer Chemical, Montana, and Moser. The application of an estoppel when the government is litigating the same issue with the same party avoids the problem of freezing the development of the law because the government is still free to litigate that issue in the future with some other party. And, where the parties are the same, estopping the government spares a party that has already prevailed once from having to relitigate—a function it would not serve in the present circumstances. We accordingly hold that the Court of Appeals was wrong in applying nonmutual collateral estoppel against the government in this case."

Question: (14) Congress can get involved. On the one hand, six years later it bestowed citizenship on the Filipino war veterans directly. On the other hand, and with a totally different point, some versions of the proposed Federal Product Liability Act, which would have supplanted state law, provided that there shall be no preclusion on issues of fact between different claimants' product liability actions "unless both actions were based on harm caused by the same event in which two or more persons were harmed." E.g., S. 2631, 97th Cong., 2d Sess. § 4(d) (1982). What do you think of that proposal? See Michael D. Green, The Inability of Offensive Collateral Estoppel to Fulfill Its Promise: An Examination of Estoppel in Asbestos Litigation, 70 Iowa L.Rev. 141 (1984).

Note, A Probabilistic Analysis of the Doctrine of Mutuality of Collateral Estoppel

76 Mich.L.Rev. 612, 619, 622–24, 640–43, 645, 679 (1978).

Using probability theory as an aid to analysis, this Note will demonstrate that the mutuality doctrine is designed to allocate trial risks in a manner consistent with the burden of persuasion in civil litigation. Thus, the abandonment of mutuality strikes at the heart of the trial process. Where a single party (hereinafter the "common party") faces multiple opponents on a common question, the abandonment of mutuality can significantly alter the common party's probability of success. Bernhard thus amounts to little more than an instruction to the trier of fact to find against the common party simply because he is the common party, a fact entirely unrelated to the merits of the case.

. . . .

. . . [T]he burden of persuasion in civil litigation embodies a strategy designed to minimize the number of erroneous verdicts. . . . Whether the relief sought is compensatory or equitable, civil litigation is essentially a matter of loss shifting. A loss has been or will be incurred; the question is simply who should bear it. Absent some peculiar and cognizable virtue inhering in one of the parties, there is no reason to prefer an error in one direction over an error in the other. Consequently, the preponderance-of-the-evidence test instructs the factfinder to follow the error-minimizing strategy to choose the verdict most likely to be the truth. . . . The burden of persuasion is thus not merely a rule of convenience to be discarded or modified lightly. It embodies the fundamental assumption of civil litigation that, without regard to the merits, neither party is the more deserving of a favorable judgment.

. . . .

The central theme of mutuality is the fair apportionment of trial risks. By potentially precluding either party (if both would have been bound) or neither party (if either party would not have been bound), mutuality allows litigation risks to reflect only the merits of the cases. The abandonment of mutuality alters the litigation risks by forcing only one party to face the potential of preclusion in subsequent litigation, thus shifting additional risks to that party. In addition to altering the distribution of risks between the parties, the Bernhard doctrine affects the measure of trial efficacy by generally increasing the error rate.

To see more clearly and to what extent mutuality and Bernhard affect the allocation of litigation risks, consider the result in two hypothetical multiple litigation situations that differ only with respect to the presence or absence of the mutuality requirement. Because Currie initially suggested that Bernhard produces no objectionable results when the common party is the protagonist, as have other commentators, it will be assumed in both hypotheticals that a common party plaintiff seeks to assert related claims[80] against a series of defendants. As will become apparent, this assumption does not affect the alteration of trial risks produced by Bernhard.

Assume also that the plaintiff has a fifty percent probability of winning his case, that is, that if the case were tried indefinitely, the plaintiff would be successful fifty per cent of the time. . . . It is assumed that the plaintiff has ten claims, each liquidated in the amount of $100. . . .

. . . .

Finally, assume that no defendant is in privity with any other defendant, so that under the traditional mutuality doctrine, as well as under Bernhard, the common party plaintiff will not be able to use a favorable judgment against one defendant to preclude any other defendant from relitigating the common issue. Given this set of assumptions, if each case is tried separately and preclusive effect is denied for lack of mutuality, all ten cases will be litigated. By hypothesis, the plaintiff can expect to win fifty percent of his cases for a total expected recovery of $500. This result is illustrated in the mutuality column of Table I.

TABLE I

		Mutuality			Bernhard		
Trial	Recovery if win trial	Probability of winning trial	Expected Recovery	Cumulative Expected Recovery	Probability of winning trial	Expected Recovery	Cumulative Expected Recovery
1	$100	.5	$50	$50	.500	$50.00	$50.00
2	$100	.5	$50	$100	.250	$25.00	$75.00
3	$100	.5	$50	$150	.125	$12.50	$87.50
4	$100	.5	$50	$200	.063	$6.30	$93.80
5	$100	.5	$50	$250	.031	$3.10	$96.90
6	$100	.5	$50	$300	.016	$1.60	$98.50
7	$100	.5	$50	$350	.008	$.80	$99.30
8	$100	.5	$50	$400	.004	$.40	$99.70
9	$100	.5	$50	$450	.002	$.20	$99.90
10	$100	.5	$50	$500	.001	$.10	$100.00
Total expected recovery			$500			$100.00	

On the other hand, under Bernhard, once the plaintiff loses one case, he will be precluded from litigating the remaining cases. While the probability of winning any single case that is litigated is still fifty percent, the preclusive effect of a single loss makes the probability of ever litigating a case dependent upon the outcome of previous cases. This cumulative effect reduces the common party's expected recovery from $500 to $100, as illustrated in the Bernhard column of Table I.

80 "Related claims" denotes claims with a sufficient common basis to create a collateral estoppel problem. For the sake of simplicity, it is assumed that the common questions are dispositive of each case.

When the probability of winning a single case is initially assumed to be fifty percent, each successive claim under Bernhard is worth only half as much to the plaintiff as its predecessor because it is that much less likely that he will be able to recover. The presence of the preceding claims decreases the probability that the common party will recover on succeeding claims. The impact of the Bernhard doctrine is dramatic and can be evaluated in terms of expected recovery rather than mere conjecture.

. . . .

The argument advanced by one commentator—that the result produced by Bernhard is no worse than forcing a common party to litigate all claims at once so that any recovery is dependent upon that single outcome[91]—is, as Professor Currie argued, incorrect. If, in the hypotheticals, all defendants were joined in a single suit so that each would be bound by an adverse judgment as well as benefitted by a favorable one, the plaintiff's expected recovery would be $500. Thus, the expected recovery when all of the defendants are joined in a single action is the same as it would be if the suits were tried separately under mutuality, but it is not the same as it would be if they were tried under Bernhard. There is a vast difference between compelling a litigant to accept an all-or-nothing bet with even odds, as joinder rules do, and weighting the odds heavily in favor of his opponent, as the Bernhard doctrine does.

. . . .

This Note began by demonstrating, with the aid of probability theory, that the burden of persuasion in civil litigation embodies a strategy designed to minimize the total number of erroneous judgments and that this strategy is based on the various disutilities society attaches to the different possible outcomes of litigation. This Note then established that the abandonment of mutuality causes a statistically certain decrease in the recovery of a party facing multiple opponents on related claims. This effect of Bernhard is of concern to more than just the common party, for the mutuality doctrine is designed to allocate trial risks in a manner consistent with the burden of persuasion, that is, in a manner designed to minimize the total number of errors. Thus, the abandonment of mutuality harms the system of civil sanctions by weakening the causal link between culpable conduct and trial outcome. This Note also demonstrated [in omitted passages] that the objections to the abandonment of a mutuality requirement are not met by a requirement that the common party be precluded only if he has previously enjoyed a full and fair opportunity to litigate. Both the full and fair opportunity test and the mutuality requirement should be satisfied before the common party is precluded.

Finally, it was demonstrated [in other omitted passages] that the traditional [extensions of preclusion, such as in all the secondary-liability circumstances,] are entirely consistent with an error minimizing strategy.

---

[91] See Comment, [Privity and Mutuality in the Doctrine of Res Judicata, 35 Yale L.J. 607, 610–11 (1926)].

Questions: (15) Evaluate the argument that "the major shortcoming with the breakdown of mutuality is that it does not go far enough to relieve court congestion and operates as a one-way street to the serious disadvantage of parties to litigation." Thus, the argument runs, there should be "a return to mutuality, but a new kind of mutuality" under which collateral estoppel expands to bind as well as benefit strangers. Michael A. Berch, A Proposal to Permit Collateral Estoppel of Nonparties Seeking Affirmative Relief, 1979 Ariz.St.L.J. 511, 530–31. This change could be achieved by stretching the categories of privies or, more frankly, by abandoning the requirement of privity. Due process would be satisfied by looking to the stranger's earlier failure to intervene or, more aptly albeit shakily, by looking retrospectively to a party's adequate representation of the stranger. Apparent excesses could be controlled by delimiting the rule of preclusion or, similarly, by developing exceptions thereto. Taken to its logical conclusion, the new regime would give effects by collateral estoppel analogous to those of a class action. See Lawrence C. George, Sweet Uses of Adversity: Parklane Hosiery and the Collateral Class Action, 32 Stan.L.Rev. 655 (1980); cf. Robert G. Bone, Rethinking the "Day in Court" Ideal and Nonparty Preclusion, 67 N.Y.U.L.Rev. 193 (1992). Note that this argument runs along lines similar to how the less binding stare decisis already works. See EEOC v. Trabucco, 791 F.2d 1 (1st Cir.1986); cf. Amy Coney Barrett, Stare Decisis and Due Process, 74 U.Colo.L.Rev. 1011 (2003).

(16) Evaluate the argument that the most mainstream alternative to achieve nonmutuality's aim of eliminating relitigation would be to expand mandatory joinder of all the concerned persons. This route would efficiently dispose of common matters in one shot, but in a fair shot. The joined parties would be bound, but only after being heard. Their common opponent would be bound if it lost, but if it won it would win against all the joined parties. By so equating the parties' litigating risk, this procedural technique would restore procedural neutrality. Nevertheless, society has chosen, after balancing benefits and costs, to follow this mandatory joinder route no further than society has gone in such provisions as Federal Rule 19 on compulsory joinder. Because society has in fact chosen not to pursue this joinder alternative or any other alternative, the choice by the courts to adopt on their own the inferior reform of nonmutuality looks even more questionable. See generally Elinor P. Schroeder, Relitigation of Common Issues: The Failure of Nonparty Preclusion and an Alternative Proposal, 67 Iowa L.Rev. 917 (1982).

SPECIAL TYPES OF PROCEEDINGS

After trial, *A* is convicted of arson for having intentionally destroyed his own property by fire. Thereafter, he sues the *B* Fire Insurance Co. on its policy covering the property. Should the criminal conviction preclude *A* in the civil action?

The reason usually given for the traditional answer of denying preclusion was lack of mutuality: the parties in the two actions were not the same. While recognizing that the customary answer to this question was in the negative, Eagle, Star & British Dominions Insurance Co. v. Heller, 149 Va. 82, 140 S.E. 314 (1927), nevertheless held that there should be preclusion, saying that the contrary result "would be a reproach to the administration of justice." The retreat from mutuality heralded by Bernhard has led many more courts to give conclusive effect to a conviction, subject to the usual requirements and exceptions of issue preclusion. E.g., Teitelbaum Furs, Inc. v. Dominion Ins. Co., 58 Cal.2d 601, 375 P.2d 439, 25 Cal.Rptr. 559 (1962). See generally Jonathan C. Thau, Collateral Estoppel and the Reliability of Criminal Determinations: Theoretical, Practical, and Strategic Implications for Criminal and Civil Litigation, 70 Geo.L.J. 1079 (1982).

Where a criminal conviction does not so receive conclusive effect in a subsequent civil action, one might ask whether it is admissible therein as probative evidence on a common issue. As a general matter, a judgment either has conclusive effect under the rules of res judicata or has no effect at all, being inadmissible on hearsay grounds as a prior statement offered for its truth. See generally Hiroshi Motomura, Using Judgments as Evidence, 70 Minn.L.Rev. 979 (1986).

Accordingly, the normal rule has been that when the court had denied res judicata effect, the admission of evidence of a prior criminal conviction was reversible error. E.g., Silva v. Silva, 297 Mass. 217, 7 N.E.2d 601 (1937). But the heavier burden of proof and other protections in criminal cases would seem to make it reasonable to give a conviction at least some effect in a civil case. As a result, a number of states have adopted a half-way rule making a conviction admissible but not conclusive evidence, even against strangers, although there has been a tendency in those states to limit admissibility to convictions for serious offenses. Federal Evidence Rule 803(22) makes admissible in federal court proof of conviction of a felony, demonstrating the same doubt concerning the reliability of convictions for lesser offenses. The Advisory Committee's note thereto explains that this hearsay exception is to have no effect on the operation of res judicata.

Questions: (17) Should a conviction upon a guilty plea be conclusive in a subsequent civil action? See David L. Shapiro, Should a Guilty Plea Have Preclusive Effect?, 70 Iowa L.Rev. 27 (1984). Should such a conviction be admissible as evidence? See McCormick on Evidence §§ 257, 298 (Kenneth S. Broun gen. ed., 6th ed. 2006).

(18) Should an acquittal in a criminal case be conclusive in a subsequent civil action? Should an acquittal be admissible as evidence?

Allen v. McCurry

Supreme Court of the United States, 1980.
449 U.S. 90, 101 S.Ct. 411.

■ JUSTICE STEWART delivered the opinion of the Court.

At a hearing before his criminal trial in a Missouri court, the respondent, Willie McCurry, invoked the Fourth and Fourteenth Amendments to suppress evidence that had been seized by the police. The trial court denied the suppression motion in part, and McCurry was subsequently convicted after a jury trial. The conviction was later affirmed on appeal. State v.

McCurry, 587 S.W.2d 337 (Mo.Ct.App.). Because he did not assert that the state courts had denied him a "full and fair opportunity" to litigate his search and seizure claim, McCurry was barred by this Court's decision in Stone v. Powell, 428 U.S. 465, 96 S.Ct. 3037, from seeking a writ of habeas corpus in a federal district court. Nevertheless, he sought federal court redress for the alleged constitutional violation by bringing a damage suit under 42 U.S.C. § 1983 against the officers who had entered his home and seized the evidence in question. We granted certiorari to consider whether the unavailability of federal habeas corpus prevented the police officers from raising the state courts' partial rejection of McCurry's constitutional claim as a collateral estoppel defense to the § 1983 suit against them for damages. 444 U.S. 1070, 100 S.Ct. 1012.

I

In April 1977, several undercover police officers, following an informant's tip that McCurry was dealing in heroin, went to his house in St. Louis, Mo., to attempt a purchase. Two officers, petitioners Allen and Jacobsmeyer, knocked on the front door, while the other officers hid nearby. When McCurry opened the door, the two officers asked to buy some heroin "caps." McCurry went back into the house and returned soon thereafter, firing a pistol at and seriously wounding Allen and Jacobsmeyer. After a gun battle with the other officers and their reinforcements, McCurry retreated into the house; he emerged again when the police demanded that he surrender. Several officers then entered the house without a warrant, purportedly to search for other persons inside. One of the officers seized drugs and other contraband that lay in plain view, as well as additional contraband he found in dresser drawers and in auto tires on the porch.

McCurry was charged with possession of heroin and assault with intent to kill. At the pretrial suppression hearing, the trial judge excluded the evidence seized from the dresser drawers and tires, but denied suppression of the evidence found in plain view. McCurry was convicted of both the heroin and assault offenses.

McCurry subsequently filed the present § 1983 action for $1 million in damages against petitioners Allen and Jacobsmeyer [and other police]. The complaint alleged a conspiracy to violate McCurry's Fourth Amendment rights, an unconstitutional search and seizure of his house, and an assault on him by unknown police officers after he had been arrested and handcuffed. The petitioners moved for summary judgment. The District Court apparently understood the gist of the complaint to be the allegedly unconstitutional search and seizure and granted summary judgment, holding that collateral estoppel prevented McCurry from relitigating the search and seizure question already decided against him in the state courts. McCurry v. Allen, 466 F.Supp. 514 (E.D.Mo.1978).[2]

---

[2] The merits of the Fourth Amendment claim are discussed in the opinion of the Missouri Court of Appeals. State v. McCurry, 587 S.W.2d 337 (Mo.Ct.App.). The state courts upheld the entry of the house as a reasonable response to emergency circumstances, but held illegal the

The Court of Appeals reversed the judgment and remanded the case for trial. McCurry v. Allen, 606 F.2d 795 (C.A.8 1979).[3] The appellate court said it was not holding that collateral estoppel was generally inapplicable in a § 1983 suit raising issues determined against the federal plaintiff in a state criminal trial. Id., at 798. But noting that Stone v. Powell, supra, barred McCurry from federal habeas corpus relief, and invoking "the special role of the federal courts in protecting civil rights," id., at 799, the court concluded that the § 1983 suit was McCurry's only route to a federal forum for his constitutional claim and directed the trial court to allow him to proceed to trial unencumbered by collateral estoppel.

II

The federal courts have traditionally adhered to the related doctrines of res judicata and collateral estoppel. Under res judicata, a final judgment on the merits of an action precludes the parties or their privies from relitigating issues that were or could have been raised in that action. Cromwell v. County of Sac, 94 U.S. 351, 352. Under collateral estoppel, once a court has decided an issue of fact or law necessary to its judgment, that decision may preclude relitigation of the issue in a suit on a different cause of action involving a party to the first case. Montana v. United States, 440 U.S. 147, 153, 99 S.Ct. 970, 973.[5] As this Court and other courts have often recognized, res judicata and collateral estoppel relieve parties of the cost and vexation of multiple lawsuits, conserve judicial resources, and, by preventing inconsistent decisions, encourage reliance on adjudication. Id., at 153–154, 99 S.Ct., at 973–974.

In recent years, this Court has reaffirmed the benefits of collateral estoppel in particular, finding the policies underlying it to apply in contexts not formerly recognized at common law. Thus, the Court has eliminated the requirement of mutuality in applying collateral estoppel to bar relitigation of issues decided earlier in federal court suits, Blonder–Tongue Laboratories, Inc. v. University of Illinois Foundation, 402 U.S. 313, 91 S.Ct. 1434,

---

seizure of any evidence discovered as a result of that entry except what was in plain view. Id., at 340. McCurry therefore argues here that even if the doctrine of collateral estoppel generally applies to this case, he should be able to proceed to trial to obtain damages for the part of the seizure declared illegal by the state courts. The petitioners contend, on the other hand, that the complaint alleged essentially an illegal entry, adding that only the entry could possibly justify the $1 million prayer. Since the state courts upheld the entry, the petitioners argue that if collateral estoppel applies here at all, it removes from trial all issues except the alleged assault. The United States Court of Appeals, however, addressed only the broad question of the applicability of collateral estoppel to § 1983 suits brought by plaintiffs in McCurry's circumstances, and questions as to the scope of collateral estoppel with respect to the particular issues in this case are not now before us.

[3] Beyond holding that collateral estoppel does not apply in this case, the Court of Appeals noted that the District Court had overlooked the conspiracy and assault charges. 606 F.2d, at 797, and n. 1.

[5] The Restatement of Judgments now speaks of res judicata as "claim preclusion" and collateral estoppel as "issue preclusion." Restatement of Judgments (Second) § 74 (Tent. Draft No. 3, 1976). Some courts and commentators use "res judicata" as generally meaning both forms of preclusion. . . . [The Supreme Court soon came to adopt the Restatement's modern terminology. See Migra v. Warren City Sch. Dist. Bd. of Educ., 465 U.S. 75, 77 n.1, 104 S.Ct. 892, 894 n.1 (1984).—Ed.]

and has allowed a litigant who was not a party to a federal case to use collateral estoppel "offensively" in a new federal suit against the party who lost on the decided issue in the first case, Parklane Hosiery Co. v. Shore, 439 U.S. 322, 99 S.Ct. 645.[6] But one general limitation the Court has repeatedly recognized is that the concept of collateral estoppel cannot apply when the party against whom the earlier decision is asserted did not have a "full and fair opportunity" to litigate that issue in the earlier case. Montana v. United States, supra, 440 U.S., at 153, 99 S.Ct., at 973; Blonder–Tongue Laboratories, Inc. v. University of Illinois Foundation, supra, 402 U.S., at 328–329, 91 S.Ct., at 1443.[7]

The federal courts generally have also consistently accorded preclusive effect to issues decided by state courts. E.g., Montana v. United States, supra; Angel v. Bullington, 330 U.S. 183, 67 S.Ct. 657. Thus, res judicata and collateral estoppel not only reduce unnecessary litigation and foster reliance on adjudication, but also promote the comity between state and federal courts that has been recognized as a bulwark of the federal system. See Younger v. Harris, 401 U.S. 37, 43–45, 91 S.Ct. 746, 750–51.

Indeed, though the federal courts may look to the common law or to the policies supporting res judicata and collateral estoppel in assessing the preclusive effect of decisions of other federal courts, Congress has specifically required all federal courts to give preclusive effect to state-court judgments whenever the courts of the State from which the judgments emerged would do so . . . . 28 U.S.C. § 1738 . . . ; [citations omitted]. It is against this background that we examine the relationship of § 1983 and collateral estoppel, and the decision of the Court of Appeals in this case.

III

This Court has never directly decided whether the rules of res judicata and collateral estoppel are generally applicable to § 1983 actions. But in Preiser v. Rodriguez, 411 U.S. 475, 497, 93 S.Ct. 1827, 1840, the Court noted with implicit approval the view of other federal courts that res judicata principles fully apply to civil rights suits brought under that statute. [Citations omitted.] And the virtually unanimous view of the Courts of Appeals since Preiser has been that § 1983 presents no categorical bar to the application of res judicata and collateral estoppel concepts. These federal appellate court decisions have spoken with little explanation or citation in assuming the compatibility of § 1983 and rules of preclusion,

---

[6] In Blonder–Tongue the Court noted other trends in the state and federal courts expanding the preclusive effects of judgments, such as the broadened definition of "claim" in the context of res judicata and the greater preclusive effect given criminal judgments in subsequent civil cases. Blonder–Tongue Laboratories, Inc. v. University of Illinois Foundation, 402 U.S. 313, 326, 91 S.Ct. 1434, 1441.

[7] Other factors, of course, may require an exception to the normal rules of collateral estoppel in particular cases. E.g., Montana v. United States, 440 U.S. 147, 162, 99 S.Ct. 970, 978 (unmixed questions of law in successive actions between the same parties on unrelated claims).

. . . It must be emphasized that the question whether any exceptions or qualifications within the bounds of that doctrine might ultimately defeat a collateral estoppel defense in this case is not before us. See n. 2, supra.

but the statute and its legislative history clearly support the courts' decisions.

Because the requirement of mutuality of estoppel was still alive in the federal courts until well into this century, see Blonder–Tongue Laboratories, Inc. v. University of Illinois Foundation, supra, 402 U.S., at 322–323, 91 S.Ct., at 1439–1440, the drafters of the 1871 Civil Rights Act, of which § 1983 is a part, may have had less reason to concern themselves with rules of preclusion than a modern Congress would. Nevertheless, in 1871 res judicata and collateral estoppel could certainly have applied in federal suits following state-court litigation between the same parties or their privies, and nothing in the language of § 1983 remotely expresses any congressional intent to contravene the common-law rules of preclusion or to repeal the express statutory requirements of . . . 28 U.S.C. § 1738 . . . . Section 1983 creates a new federal cause of action. It says nothing about the preclusive effect of state-court judgments.[12]

Moreover, the legislative history of § 1983 does not in any clear way suggest that Congress intended to repeal or restrict the traditional doctrines of preclusion. The main goal of the Act was to override the corrupting influence of the Ku Klux Klan and its sympathizers on the governments and law enforcement agencies of the Southern States, see Monroe v. Pape, 365 U.S. 167, 174, 81 S.Ct. 473, 477, and of course the debates show that one strong motive behind its enactment was grave congressional concern that the state courts had been deficient in protecting federal rights, Mitchum v. Foster, 407 U.S. 225, 241–242, 92 S.Ct. 2151, 2161–2162; Monroe v. Pape, supra, 365 U.S., at 180, 81 S.Ct., at 480. But in the context of the legislative history as a whole, this congressional concern lends only the most equivocal support to any argument that, in cases where the state courts have recognized the constitutional claims asserted and provided fair procedures for determining them, Congress intended to override § 1738 or the common-law rules of collateral estoppel and res judicata. Since repeals by implication are disfavored, Radzanower v. Touche Ross & Co., 426 U.S. 148, 154, 96 S.Ct. 1989, 1993, much clearer support than this would be

[12] By contrast, the roughly contemporaneous statute extending the federal writ of habeas corpus to state prisoners expressly rendered "null and void" any state-court proceeding inconsistent with the decision of a federal habeas court, Act of Feb. 5, 1867, ch. 28, § 1, 14 Stat. 385, 386 (1867) (current version at 28 U.S.C. § 2254), and the modern habeas statute also expressly adverts to the effect of state-court criminal judgments by requiring the applicant for the writ to exhaust his state-court remedies, 28 U.S.C. § 2254(b), and by presuming a state court resolution of a factual issue to be correct except in eight specific circumstances, id., § 2254(d). In any event, the traditional exception to res judicata for habeas corpus review, see Preiser v. Rodriguez, supra, 411 U.S., at 497, 93 S.Ct., at 1840, provides no analogy to § 1983 cases, since that exception finds its source in the unique purpose of habeas corpus—to release the applicant for the writ from unlawful confinement. Sanders v. United States, 373 U.S. 1, 8, 83 S.Ct. 1068, 1073.

[Although res judicata supposedly does not apply in habeas corpus proceedings, the Supreme Court of late has further pursued similar policies in developing such doctrines as "abuse of the writ," which blocks repetitive petitions. See, e.g., McCleskey v. Zant, 499 U.S. 467, 111 S.Ct. 1454 (1991). Similarly, Congress has further tightened the habeas statute to reduce repetitive litigation. Antiterrorism and Effective Death Penalty Act of 1996, Pub.L. No. 104–132, tit. I, §§ 104, 106, 110 Stat. 1214, 1218, 1220.—Ed.]

required to hold that § 1738 and the traditional rules of preclusion are not applicable to § 1983 suits.

As the Court has understood the history of the legislation, Congress realized that in enacting § 1983 it was altering the balance of judicial power between the state and federal courts. See Mitchum v. Foster, supra, 407 U.S., at 241, 92 S.Ct., at 2161. But in doing so, Congress was adding to the jurisdiction of the federal courts, not subtracting from that of the state courts. See Monroe v. Pape, supra, 365 U.S., at 183, 81 S.Ct., at 481 ("The federal remedy is supplementary to the state remedy . . . ."). The debates contain several references to the concurrent jurisdiction of the state courts over federal questions, and numerous suggestions that the state courts would retain their established jurisdiction so that they could, when the then current political passions abated, demonstrate a new sensitivity to federal rights.

To the extent that it did intend to change the balance of power over federal questions between the state and federal courts, the 42d Congress was acting in a way thoroughly consistent with the doctrines of preclusion. In reviewing the legislative history of § 1983 in Monroe v. Pape, supra, the Court inferred that Congress had intended a federal remedy [inter alia] . . . where state procedural law was inadequate to allow full litigation of a constitutional claim, and where state procedural law, though adequate in theory, was inadequate in practice. 365 U.S., at 173–174, 81 S.Ct., at 476–477. In short, the federal courts could step in where the state courts were unable or unwilling to protect federal rights. Id., at 176, 81 S.Ct., at 478. This understanding of § 1983 might well support an exception to res judicata and collateral estoppel where state law did not provide fair procedures for the litigation of constitutional claims, or where a state court failed to even acknowledge the existence of the constitutional principle on which a litigant based his claim. Such an exception, however, would be essentially the same as the important general limit on rules of preclusion that already exists: Collateral estoppel does not apply where the party against whom an earlier court decision is asserted did not have a full and fair opportunity to litigate the claim or issue decided by the first court. . . . But the Court's view of § 1983 in Monroe lends no strength to any argument that Congress intended to allow relitigation of federal issues decided after a full and fair hearing in a state court simply because the state court's decision may have been erroneous.

. . . The Court of Appeals . . . concluded that since Stone v. Powell had removed McCurry's right to a hearing of his Fourth Amendment claim in federal habeas corpus, collateral estoppel should not deprive him of a federal judicial hearing of that claim in a § 1983 suit.

Stone v. Powell does not provide a logical doctrinal source for the court's ruling. This Court in Stone assessed the costs and benefits of the judge-made exclusionary rule within the boundaries of the federal courts' statutory power to issue writs of habeas corpus, and decided that the incremental deterrent effect that the issuance of the writ in Fourth Amendment cases might have on police conduct did not justify the cost the writ imposed upon the fair administration of criminal justice. 428 U.S., at 489–496, 96 S.Ct., at 3050–3053. The Stone decision concerns only the prudent exercise of federal court jurisdiction under 28 U.S.C. § 2254. It has no bearing on § 1983 suits or on the question of the preclusive effect of state-court judgments.

The actual basis of the Court of Appeals' holding appears to be a generally framed principle that every person asserting a federal right is entitled to one unencumbered opportunity to litigate that right in a federal district court, regardless of the legal posture in which the federal claim arises. But the authority for this principle is difficult to discern. It cannot lie in the Constitution, which makes no such guarantee, but leaves the scope of the jurisdiction of the federal district courts to the wisdom of Congress. And no such authority is to be found in § 1983 itself. For reasons already discussed at length, nothing in the language or legislative history of § 1983 proves any congressional intent to deny binding effect to a state-court judgment or decision when the state court, acting within its proper jurisdiction, has given the parties a full and fair opportunity to litigate federal claims, and thereby has shown itself willing and able to protect federal rights. And nothing in the legislative history of § 1983 reveals any purpose to afford less deference to judgments in state criminal proceedings than to those in state civil proceedings. There is, in short, no reason to believe that Congress intended to provide a person claiming a federal right an unrestricted opportunity to relitigate an issue already decided in state court simply because the issue arose in a state proceeding in which he would rather not have been engaged at all.[23]

Through § 1983, the 42d Congress intended to afford an opportunity for legal and equitable relief in a federal court for certain types of injuries. It is difficult to believe that the drafters of that Act considered it a substitute for a federal writ of habeas corpus, the purpose of which is not to redress civil injury, but to release the applicant from unlawful physical confinement, Preiser v. Rodriguez, supra, 411 U.S., at 484, 93 S.Ct., at 1833; Fay v. Noia, 372 U.S. 391, 399, n. 5, 83 S.Ct. 822, 827, n. 5,[24] particularly in light of the extremely narrow scope of federal habeas relief for state prisoners in 1871.

The only other conceivable basis for finding a universal right to litigate a federal claim in a federal district court is hardly a legal basis at all, but rather a general distrust of the capacity of the state courts to render correct decisions on constitutional issues. It is ironic that Stone v. Powell provided the occasion for the expression of such an attitude in the present litigation, in view of this Court's emphatic reaffirmation in that case of the

---

[23] The Court of Appeals did not suggest that the prospect of collateral estoppel in a § 1983 suit would deter a defendant in a state criminal case from raising Fourth Amendment claims, and it is difficult to imagine a defendant risking conviction and imprisonment because he hoped to win a later civil judgment based upon an allegedly illegal search and seizure.

[24] Under the modern statute, federal habeas corpus is bounded by a requirement of exhaustion of state remedies and by special procedural rules, 28 U.S.C. § 2254, which have no counterparts in § 1983, and which therefore demonstrate the continuing illogic of treating federal habeas and § 1983 suits as fungible remedies for constitutional violations.

constitutional obligation of the state courts to uphold federal law, and its expression of confidence in their ability to do so. [Citations omitted.]

The Court of Appeals erred in holding that McCurry's inability to obtain federal habeas corpus relief upon his Fourth Amendment claim renders the doctrine of collateral estoppel inapplicable to his § 1983 suit. Accordingly, the judgment is reversed, and the case is remanded to the Court of Appeals for proceedings consistent with this opinion.

It is so ordered.[f]

■ JUSTICE BLACKMUN, with whom JUSTICE BRENNAN and JUSTICE MARSHALL join, dissenting.

The legal principles with which the Court is concerned in this civil case obviously far transcend the ugly facts of respondent's criminal convictions in the courts of Missouri for heroin possession and assault.

The Court today holds that notions of collateral estoppel apply with full force to this suit brought under 42 U.S.C. § 1983. In my view, the Court, in so ruling, ignores the clear import of the legislative history of that statute and disregards the important federal policies that underlie its enforcement. It also shows itself insensitive both to the significant differences between the § 1983 remedy and the exclusionary rule, and to the pressures upon a criminal defendant that make a free choice of forum illusory. I do not doubt that principles of preclusion are to be given such effect as is appropriate in a § 1983 action. In many cases, the denial of res judicata or collateral estoppel effect would serve no purpose and would harm relations between federal and state tribunals. Nonetheless, the Court's analysis in this particular case is unacceptable to me. It works injustice on this § 1983 plaintiff, and it makes more difficult the consistent protection of constitutional rights, a consideration that was at the core of the enacters' intent. Accordingly, I dissent.

. . . .

. . . Although the legislators of the 42d Congress did not expressly state whether the then-existing common-law doctrine of preclusion would survive enactment of § 1983, they plainly anticipated more than the creation of a federal statutory remedy to be administered indifferently by either a state or a federal court. The legislative intent, as expressed by supporters and understood by opponents, was to restructure relations between the state and federal courts. Congress deliberately opened the federal courts to individual citizens in response to the States' failure to provide justice in their own courts. Contrary to the view presently expressed by the Court, the 42d Congress was not concerned solely with procedural regularity. Even where there was procedural regularity, which

[f] After remand and the appropriate application of collateral estoppel, and upon trial of the remaining issues, the judge directed a verdict against McCurry on his claim, and the jury rendered a $105,000 verdict against him on Jacobsmeyer's counterclaim for battery. The judgment was affirmed, 688 F.2d 581 (8th Cir.1982). Incidentally, McCurry made a bid to use collateral estoppel for establishing that part of the seizure had been illegal, but he failed on the ground that the defendants were strangers to the state proceedings.

the Court today so stresses, Congress believed that substantive justice was unobtainable. The availability of the federal forum was not meant to turn on whether, in an individual case, the state procedures were adequate. Assessing the state of affairs as a whole, Congress specifically made a determination that federal oversight of constitutional determinations through the federal courts was necessary to ensure the effective enforcement of constitutional rights.

That the new federal jurisdiction was conceived of as concurrent with state jurisdiction does not alter the significance of Congress' opening the federal courts to these claims. Congress consciously acted in the broadest possible manner. The legislators perceived that justice was not being done in the States then dominated by the Klan, and it seems senseless to suppose that they would have intended the federal courts to give full preclusive effect to prior state adjudications. That supposition would contradict their obvious aim to right the wrongs perpetuated in those same courts.

. . . .

. . . [M]y understanding of the policies underlying § 1983 would lead me to consider all relevant factors in each case before concluding that preclusion was warranted.

In this case, the police officers seek to prevent a criminal defendant from relitigating the constitutionality of their conduct in searching his house, after the state trial court had found that conduct in part violative of the defendant's Fourth Amendment rights and in part justified by the circumstances. I doubt that the police officers, now defendants in this § 1983 action, can be considered to have been in privity with the State in its role as prosecutor. Therefore, only "issue preclusion" is at stake.

The following factors persuade me to conclude that this respondent should not be precluded from asserting his claim in federal court. . . .

. . . [T]he process of deciding in a state criminal trial whether to exclude or admit evidence is not at all the equivalent of a § 1983 proceeding. The remedy sought in the latter is utterly different. In bringing the civil suit the criminal defendant does not seek to challenge his conviction collaterally. At most, he wins damages. In contrast, the exclusion of evidence may prevent a criminal conviction. A trial court, faced with the decision whether to exclude relevant evidence, confronts institutional pressures that may cause it to give a different shape to the Fourth Amendment right from what would result in civil litigation of a damages claim. Also, the issue whether to exclude evidence is subsidiary to the purpose of a criminal trial, which is to determine the guilt or innocence of the defendant, and a trial court, at least subconsciously, must weigh the potential damage to the truth-seeking process caused by excluding relevant evidence. See Stone v. Powell, 428 U.S. 465, 489–495, 96 S.Ct. 3037, 3050–3052 (1976). Cf. Bivens v. Six Unknown Federal Narcotics Agents, 403 U.S. 388, 411–424, 91 S.Ct. 1999, 2012–2018 (1971) (dissenting opinion).

A state criminal defendant cannot be held to have chosen "voluntarily" to litigate his Fourth Amendment claim in the state court. The risk of conviction puts pressure upon him to raise all possible defenses. . . . To hold that a criminal defendant who raises a Fourth Amendment claim at his criminal trial "freely and without reservation submits his federal claims for decision by the state courts," see England v. Medical Examiners, [375 U.S. 411, 419, 84 S.Ct. 461, 466 (1964)], is to deny reality. The criminal defendant is an involuntary litigant in the state tribunal, and against him all the forces of the State are arrayed. To force him to a choice between forgoing either a potential defense or a federal forum for hearing his constitutional civil claim is fundamentally unfair.

I would affirm the judgment of the Court of Appeals.

Question: (19) An African–American venireperson is the subject of a peremptory challenge by the prosecution in a state criminal case. The defendant objects, arguing that the prosecution based the challenge on race, thereby violating the venireperson's equal protection rights, which the defendant has third-party standing to assert. The prosecution responds that it had nondiscriminatory grounds for the challenge. The judge rules that there was no constitutional violation. The eventually convicted defendant loses a full appeal. If the would-be juror then brings a federal § 1983 action, will she be precluded from relitigating whether her civil rights were violated? See Shaw v. Hahn, 56 F.3d 1128 (9th Cir.1995) (yes).

Beyond collateral estoppel.—As already explained, usually parties and their privies are the only ones who can benefit from the rules of res judicata other than collateral estoppel, because for a stranger a different claim is necessarily involved. There remains the question of the unusual: when can a stranger use the other rules of res judicata?

Sometimes a stranger can use a former party's victory on a claim to bar a new assertion of the opposing party's claim against the stranger. A ready example lies in the old indemnitor-indemnitee situation. If the injured person litigates with the employee and loses—the employee being found not negligent—everyone agrees that the employer can invoke nonmutual collateral estoppel in the injured person's later action against the employer. But what if the injured party lost the prior action by failure to prosecute? The same indemnity dilemma argues for allowing the employer to use the prior judgment, even though this use would be an instance of nonmutual claim preclusion.

But how far should the law go with this new idea?

Fagnan v. Great Central Insurance Co.

United States Court of Appeals, Seventh Circuit, 1978.
577 F.2d 418, cert. denied, 439 U.S. 1004, 99 S.Ct. 615 (1978).

■ Before TONE and BAUER, CIRCUIT JUDGES, and CAMPBELL, SENIOR DISTRICT JUDGE.*

■ TONE, CIRCUIT JUDGE.

The issue presented is whether the federal compulsory counterclaim rule, Rule 13(a), Fed.R.Civ.P., precludes an action against an insurance company under the Wisconsin direct action statute, when an action directly against the insured would be barred by the rule. The District Court answered this question in the negative and entered judgment against the insurance company. We reverse.

The collision of two automobiles in Wisconsin resulted in the death of one of the drivers, Robert Thompson, and injuries to his passenger, David Harness [of California]. The driver of the other automobile, Duane Fagnan [of Wisconsin], was also injured.

Harness, Thompson's passenger, brought an action against the administrator of Thompson's estate [with Minnesota citizenship] in the United States District Court for the District of Minnesota. The administrator filed a third party claim for contribution against Fagnan, who filed an answer to that claim. Later Harness filed a claim under Rule 14(a) against Fagnan, which Fagnan also answered. In addition, Fagnan cross-claimed against the administrator for contribution. The case was settled without a trial, and the court dismissed the action. Under the last sentence of Rule 41(b), Fed.R.Civ.P., the dismissal operated as an adjudication upon the merits.[1]

A few months after the action in Minnesota was dismissed, Duane Fagnan and his father, Raymond Fagnan, sued in a Wisconsin state court against Thompson's insurer, Great Central Insurance Company, under the Wisconsin direct action statute. Raymond Fagnan's claim was for medical expenses and care of his minor child incurred as a result of the [collision].[2] Also named as a defendant was Thompson's father, Darrold Thompson. The defendants removed the case to the United States District Court for the Western District of Wisconsin, where a trial before a jury resulted in a directed verdict in favor of Darrold Thompson, from which no appeal is

---

* The Honorable William J. Campbell, Senior District Judge of the United States District Court for the Northern District of Illinois, is sitting by designation.

1 The court's order of dismissal recited that the court had been reliably informed that the case had been settled but the attorneys had "been negligent for some time in getting a stipulation of dismissal signed and filed." The court, therefore, sua sponte dismissed the action, retaining jurisdiction for 10 days, within which the parties could move to vacate. A stipulation to dismiss with prejudice had already been signed, the record before us shows, although it was apparently never filed with the court. The order of dismissal became final at the expiration of the 10 days and fell within the final category, "any dismissal not provided for in this rule," of Rule 41(b) and as such operated as an adjudication upon the merits.

2 Under Wisconsin law a parent's liability for the medical expense and care of his minor child are separate causes of action from the child's personal injury claims and can only be asserted by the parent. Sulkowski v. Schaefer, 31 Wis.2d 600, 143 N.W.2d 512, 515 (1966).

taken, and verdicts [finding Thompson 100% negligent] in favor of both Duane Fagnan and Raymond Fagnan against the insurer, who appeals.

Relying on Rule 13(a), the insurer argues that any claim of Duane Fagnan against Robert Thompson's estate was disposed of by the judgment in the Minnesota action. The insurer now concedes that the award to Raymond Fagnan of damages for the medical expenses and care of Duane Fagnan cannot properly be challenged, since Raymond Fagnan was not a party to the Minnesota action. Accordingly, the judgment in his favor is not subject to attack.

I.

At the time of the accident in this case, Wisconsin's direct action statutes were Wis.Stat. §§ 204.30(4) and 260.11(1). Section 204.30(4) was substantive and created "direct liability between the in[j]ured third person and the insurer," while § 260.11(1) provided the procedural vehicle by which the insurer could be made a party defendant. [Citations omitted.] However,

> [t]he fact that a third party can sue an insurer of a motor vehicle direct . . . without first recovering a judgment against the insured defendant does not enlarge the coverage afforded by such policy or determine the insure[r]'s liability thereunder. The third party can only recover from the insurer by virtue of the contract existing between it and its insured.

Nichols v. U.S.F. & Guaranty Co., 13 Wis.2d 491, 109 N.W.2d 131, 136 (1961).

Therefore, an insurance company's liability under the Wisconsin direct action statute is derivative, i.e., the "insurer is not liable unless the assured is." Hunt v. Dollar, 224 Wis. 48, 271 N.W. 405, 409 (1937). Thus the insurer is liable in this action only if the insured, Robert Thompson's administrator, is liable.

II.

[The court here quoted Rule 13(a).] A compulsory counterclaim that is not asserted is barred by the judgment. Baker v. Gold Seal Liquors, Inc., 417 U.S. 467, 469 n. 1, 94 S.Ct. 2504, 41 L.Ed.2d 243 (1974); Pipeliners Local Union No. 798, Tulsa, Okl. v. Ellerd, 503 F.2d 1193, 1198 (10th Cir.1974).

Duane Fagnan's claim against Robert Thompson's administrator existed at the time the pleadings were served in the Minnesota action,[5] arose out of the same transaction or occurrence that was the subject of that action, and did not require for its adjudication the presence of third parties.

[5] Duane Fagnan also could have asserted his direct action against the insurer, which Minnesota law permitted him to do in view of the existence of the Wisconsin direct action statute. Myers v. Government Employees' Insurance Company, 302 Minn. 359, 225 N.W.2d 238 (1974).

It was therefore a compulsory counterclaim and was extinguished by the judgment in that action.

Because Duane Fagnan's claim against the administrator is barred, his claim against the insurer is also barred. The judgment in favor of Duane Fagnan against Great Central must therefore be reversed.

Affirmed in part and reversed in part. Each side will bear its own costs.

Michael J. Waggoner, Fifty Years of Bernhard v. Bank of America Is Enough: Collateral Estoppel Should Require Mutuality but Res Judicata Should Not

12 Rev.Litig. 391, 396, 440 (1993).

These ancient [secondary-liability] exceptions to the mutuality requirement should be extended to produce a general rule that mutuality is not required for [claim preclusion]. Res judicata should be a defense, not only to claims against the defendant in the prior case, but also to claims against persons who could have been made defendants in that case, if the other requirements for res judicata are met. A person having claims arising from the same transaction against both agent and principal, or against alternative defendants, should be required to proceed against all at once, or forego the claims against those omitted. . . .

. . . .

Nonmutual [claim preclusion] should be implemented because it is both fair and efficient. Nonmutual collateral estoppel in civil cases should be rejected, because even where it might be fair and efficient nonmutual [claim preclusion] is more so, and because in other areas it is unfair. The authority in favor of nonmutual collateral estoppel is, upon careful examination, far weaker than it might initially appear, so weak that even at this late date reconsideration of the question whether to require mutuality for collateral estoppel should still be open.

A COMPARATIVE GLANCE

U.S. res judicata law is distinctively a good deal more expansive than the res judicata law of other countries, including civil-law countries. We can take a quick look at France, which is a prototypical civil-law country in most respects,[g] including its civil procedure.[h]

[g] See generally John Bell, French Legal Cultures (2001); John Bell, Sophie Boyron & Simon Whittaker, Principles of French Law (2d ed. 2008); Walter Cairns & Robert McKeon, Introduction to French Law (1995); Christian Dadomo & Susan Farran, The French Legal System (2d ed. 1996); Christel de Noblet, French Legal Methodology (2004); Brice Dickson, Introduction to French Law (1994); Catherine Elliott, Carole Geirnaert & Florence Houssais, French Legal System and Legal Language (1998); Catherine Elliott, Catherine Vernon & Eric Jeanpierre, French Legal System (2d ed. 2006); Introduction to French Law (George A.

In France, res judicata (authority of *la chose jugée*, or the thing adjudged) finds embodiment in *Code civil* article 1351, which appears in the part of the code treating presumptions. That is to say, French res judicata proceeds upon a presumption of correctness: when raised by a party, a prior judgment is presumed to be correct and should not be contradicted in a subsequent suit. By virtue of the prior contestation and decision, the judgment has established what the law will treat as truth, if the judgment is final and valid.

A final judgment on the merits acquires the authority of res judicata immediately upon rendition, according to *Code de procédure civile* articles 480 and 482. But a direct attack such as an appeal suspends its res judicata effect. A reversal will deprive a judgment of its res judicata effect, while an affirmance will render stronger the presumptive force of res judicata. The judgment becomes irrebuttable when the means of direct attack have expired.

A French court today will treat a prior judgment, even a foreign judgment, as valid if it did not entail violation of either international standards for jurisdiction or French exclusive jurisdiction or violation of either fundamental procedural fairness or basic public policy. Formerly, France gave foreign judgments much more suspicious treatment.

In general, as to a French judgment, only issues advanced in contested *conclusions* (the issues that the parties submit as necessary to decision, such as the existence of some right) and definitively decided by the court will have res judicata effect in a subsequent suit. A defendant must advance *conclusions* in the nature of a declaratory counterclaim on necessarily involved issues in order to get res judicata effect on other than the plaintiff's *conclusions*. Consequently, res judicata effect attaches only to the

---

Bermann & Etienne Picard eds., 2008); Eva Steiner, French Legal Method (2002); François Terré, Introduction générale au droit (1991); Andrew West, Yvon Desdevises, Alain Fenet, Dominique Gaurier & Marie-Clet Heussaff, The French Legal System (2d ed. 1998); Martin Weston, An English Reader's Guide to the French Legal System (1991); Konrad Zweigert & Hein Kötz, Introduction to Comparative Law 74–131 (Tony Weir trans., 3d ed. 1998); Claire M. Germain, French Law Guide (July 2004), http://www.lawschool.cornell.edu/library/encyclopedia/countries/france. A good source for actual French law, in French and English, appears at http://www.legifrance.gouv.fr/.

[h] See generally Gérard Couchez, Procédure civile (12th ed. 2002); 2 European Civil Practice 139–77 (Alexander Layton & Hugh Mercer gen. eds., 2d ed. 2004); European Traditions in Civil Procedure 25–68 (C.H. van Rhee ed., 2005); Serge Guinchard & Frédérique Ferrand, Procédure civile: droit interne et droit communautaire (28th ed. 2006); Peter Herzog & Martha Weser, Civil Procedure in France (1967); Thierry Bernard & Hedwige Vlasto, "France," in 2 Transnational Litigation: A Practitioner's Guide (John Fellas gen. ed., 2004); Robert W. Byrd & Christian Bouckaert, "Trial and Court Procedures in France," in Trial and Court Procedures Worldwide 138 (Charles Platto ed., 1990); Kevin M. Clermont & Emily Sherwin, A Comparative View of Standards of Proof, 50 Am.J.Comp.L. 243, 247–51 (2002); J.A. Jolowicz, "Civil Procedure in the Common and Civil Law," in Law and Legal Culture in Comparative Perspective 26 (Guenther Doeker-Mach & Klaus A. Ziegert eds., 2004); Christine Lécuyer-Thieffry, "France," in International Civil Procedures 241 (Christian T. Campbell ed., 1995); Raymond Martin & Jacques Martin, "France," in 1 International Encyclopaedia of Laws: Civil Procedure (Piet Taelman ed., 2005); Renée Y. Nauta & Gerard J. Meijer, "French Civil Procedure," in Access to Civil Procedure Abroad 131 (Henk J. Snijders ed. & Benjamin Ruijsenaars trans., 1996); Xavier Vahramian & Eric Wallenbrock, "France," in International Civil Procedure 213 (Shelby R. Grubbs ed., 2003).

judgment's decretal portion accepting or rejecting the *conclusions* of the parties (*le dispositif*), and not to its briefly stated rationale portion (*les motifs*).

As to the scope of res judicata, take an actual look at that article 1351:

> *L'autorité de la chose jugée n'a lieu qu'à l'égard de ce qui a fait l'objet du jugement. Il faut que la chose demandée soit la même; que la demande soit fondée sur la même cause; que la demande soit entre les mêmes parties, et formée par elles et contre elles en la même qualité.* [The authority of res judicata extends only to what was the subject matter of the judgment. The thing claimed must be the same; the action must be based on the same ground; the action must be between the same parties, and brought by and against them in the same capacities.]

It requires three identities between the successive lawsuits: of the parties, of the object demanded, and of the *cause*:

1. Identity of parties requires not physical identity but identity of quality, or legal capacity. Thus, privies represented in the prior suit have the same identities as the parties, but the same person who later sues in a different capacity does not.

2. The second required identity is the identity of object demanded, or the end the action has in view. This difficult concept means that the suits must involve generally the same juridical right sought as to the same matter. For close but contrary examples, a person who has lost an action in which he claimed title to a building may later sue freely for a life estate, but a person who has unsuccessfully claimed a debt owing cannot later sue for interest thereon.

3. The last required identity, and probably even more troublesome, is the identity of *cause*. On the one hand, it is generally accepted that this concept of *cause* is broader than the old common-law concept of cause of action, or theory of recovery. *Cause*refers to the ultimate facts and legal principle upon which the action is grounded, such that collection on a loan is a *cause*. On the other hand, all agree that the concept of *cause* remains more restrictive than the new common-law transactional view of a claim. For French examples, a party who has unsuccessfully attacked a will for a defect of form may renew the attack for lack of testamentary capacity, but that party cannot raise different formal defects in successive actions.

If these three identities are present, res judicata attaches, both preventing the losing party from asserting new evidence or theories to change the outcome and also preventing the winning party from relitigating. See Peter Herzog & Martha Weser, Civil Procedure in France 554–55 (1967).

The French tend to speak of their res judicata as a kind of claim preclusion, and they do not employ collateral estoppel. But, unlike common-law claim preclusion, which extends to extinguishing previously unasserted causes and defenses in the name of efficiency, the traditional French concept of res judicata sought only to avoid undoing decisions: more specifically, the required identities together suggested that France dealt in a brand of issue preclusion like direct estoppel. In certain recent cases, however, the French courts might be broadening the range of preclusion and so acting more in the spirit of claim preclusion.

By a different path to a similarly restrained scope in another civil-law country, Japanese res judicata law more overtly comprises a variant of claim preclusion applicable only to narrow claims actually asserted. See Minsohō [Code of Civil Procedure], arts. 114–115 (Japan); Takaaki Hattori & Dan Fenno Henderson, Civil Procedure in Japan § 7.06[8] (Yasuhei Taniguchi, Pauline C. Reich & Hiroto Miyake eds., 2d ed. 2004); Robert C. Casad, Issue Preclusion and Foreign Country Judgments: Whose Law?, 70 Iowa L.Rev. 53, 66–67 (1984); cf. J. Mark Ramseyer & Minoru Nakazato, Japanese Law: An Economic Approach 144–45 (1999) (attributing the narrowness of Japanese preclusion law to the low cost of proving anew in a system that relies on documentary evidence and operates without juries). In some recent cases, however, the Japanese courts seem to be introducing notions of issue preclusion.

Most interestingly, in order to affect other causes of action as well as other persons, civil-law countries broadly allow an evidential use of prior judgments, rather than expand their preclusive doctrine of res judicata. One could argue that the United States should have relaxed its hearsay rule in order to follow the same evidential route as the civilians, and so could have avoided its battles over scope of claim and nonmutuality of estoppel. Following that evidential route in this country would entail giving to all rulings a persuasive effect similar to the effect that stare decisis gives to legal rulings. However, there are arguments against extending evidential weight to factual findings: first, that combining a past decision with new evidence, especially new oral evidence, is a bit like combining apples and oranges; second, that our juries especially would have trouble in weighing a past decision; and, third, that the evidential approach lacks res judicata's advantage of altogether avoiding trial, an especially burdensome procedural stage in our system. Therefore, the United States has in the main rejected this civilian solution.

TOPIC E

CREDIT DUE TO VALID AND FINAL JUDGMENTS

SECTION 1. JUDGMENTS OF U.S. ADJUDICATORS

Fauntleroy v. Lum

Supreme Court of the United States, 1908.
210 U.S. 230, 28 S.Ct. 641.

[Fauntleroy brought action in a state court of Mississippi upon a Missouri judgment. The defendant pleaded that the original controversy arose in Mississippi out of a speculative transaction in cotton futures between two Mississippi citizens, which was illegal under Mississippi law;[a] that the parties submitted the controversy to arbitration in Mississippi, the question of illegality not being included in the submission, and the plaintiff won an award against the defendant; and that the plaintiff brought suit on the award in a Missouri state court, serving the defendant with process while he was temporarily in Missouri, but the Missouri trial court did not allow the defendant to show the nature of the transaction, and hence its illegality under Mississippi law, and eventually entered verdict and judgment for the plaintiff. On demurrer, the Mississippi trial court ordered judgment for the plaintiff. The Mississippi Supreme Court reversed, ruling that the Missouri judgment was not entitled to full faith and credit. The case came to the Supreme Court of the United States on a writ of error.]

■ MR. JUSTICE HOLMES delivered the opinion of the court.

. . . .

The doctrine laid down by Chief Justice Marshall was "that the judgment of a state court should have the same credit, validity, and effect in every other court in the United States which it had in the state where it was pronounced, and that whatever pleas would be good to a suit thereon in such state, and none others, could be pleaded in any other court in the United States." Hampton v. M'Connel, 3 Wheat. 234 [(1818) (discussing what is now 28 U.S.C. § 1738, on which see supra p. 509)]. . . .

. . . .

. . . Whether the award would or would not have been conclusive, and whether the ruling of the Missouri court upon that matter was right or wrong, there can be no question that the judgment was conclusive in

[a] The statutes of Mississippi made dealing in futures a misdemeanor and provided that such a contract "shall not be enforced by any court."

Missouri on the validity of the cause of action. Pitts v. Fugate, 41 Mo. 405; State ex rel. Hudson v. Trammel, 106 Mo. 510, 17 S.W. 502; Re Copenhaver, 118 Mo. 377, 40 Am.St.Rep. 382, 24 S.W. 161. A judgment is conclusive as to all the media concludendi (United States v. California & O. Land Co., 192 U.S. 355, 24 S.Ct. 266); and it needs no authority to show that it cannot be impeached either in or out of the state by showing that it was based upon a mistake of law. Of course, a want of jurisdiction over either the person or the subject-matter might be shown. Andrews v. Andrews, 188 U.S. 14, 23 S.Ct. 237; Clarke v. Clarke, 178 U.S. 186, 20 S.Ct. 873. But, as the jurisdiction of the Missouri court is not open to dispute, the judgment cannot be impeached in Mississippi even if it went upon a misapprehension of the Mississippi law. [Citations omitted.]

We feel no apprehensions that painful or humiliating consequences will follow upon our decision. No court would give judgment for a plaintiff unless it believed that the facts were a cause of action by the law determining their effect. Mistakes will be rare. In this case the Missouri court no doubt supposed that the award was binding by the law of Mississippi. If it was mistaken, it made a natural mistake. The validity of its judgment, even in Mississippi, is, as we believe, the result of the Constitution as it always has been understood, and is not a matter to arouse the susceptibilities of the states, all of which are equally concerned in the question and equally on both sides.

Judgment reversed.

■ [The dissenting opinion of JUSTICE WHITE, with whom Justices Harlan, McKenna, and Day joined, is omitted.]

Question: (1) Would the Supreme Court of the United States have had jurisdiction to review the Missouri judgment? If so, and the Supreme Court had heard the case, how should it have been decided?

JAMES v. GRAND TRUNK WESTERN RAILROAD, 14 Ill.2d 356, 152 N.E.2d 858, cert. denied, 358 U.S. 915, 79 S.Ct. 288 (1958). The plaintiff administratrix sued the railroad in an Illinois court under the Michigan Wrongful Death Act. Thereafter a state court of Michigan, where the plaintiff in the Illinois action resided, granted the railroad an injunction restraining the plaintiff from prosecuting the Illinois action;[b] the plaintiff

[b] The Illinois court was to say that "the Michigan injunction was apparently issued pursuant to the policy of the State embodied in a Michigan venue statute restricting venue in suits against railroads to the county in which plaintiff resides, if the railroad lines traverse that county."

On the limited propriety of issuing such interstate injunctions in the first place, see Edward Dumbauld, Judicial Interference with Litigation in Other Courts, 74 Dick.L.Rev. 369 (1970); James P. George, Parallel Litigation, 51 Baylor L.Rev. 769 (1999). Problems increase

did not appeal. Instead, she sought in Illinois a counter-injunction enjoining the railroad from enforcing the Michigan injunction. After denial of relief in the lower courts and an appeal by the plaintiff, the Illinois Supreme Court, in a 4–3 decision, restrained the enforcement of the Michigan injunction. It held that the Illinois court, having acquired jurisdiction first, was free not only to disregard an out-of-state injunction but also to protect its jurisdiction from usurpation by issuance of a counter-injunction, and that neither full faith and credit nor rules of comity precluded this result. The dissenters, while agreeing that the Michigan injunction was not entitled to full faith and credit, took the view that just as the first injunction sired the second, so the second might sire a third, and so forth, and that therefore the counter-injunction should be denied.

In fact, the U.S. Supreme Court has approved only rare and narrow exceptions where recognition or enforcement would so grossly and improperly interfere with the second state's important interests as to create a national interest against such recognition or enforcement and hence to create an exception to full faith and credit: where the rendering state has purported directly to transfer title to land in the second state or, as here, has enjoined litigation in the second state's courts. See Baker v. General Motors Corp., 522 U.S. 222, 235–36, 118 S.Ct. 657, 665 (1998).

Questions: (2) Would the Supreme Court of the United States have jurisdiction to review the Illinois decree granting the injunction against the railroad? If so, and the Supreme Court were to hear the case, how should it be decided? See Restatement (Second) of Conflict of Laws § 103 cmt. b (1971) (amended 1988).

(3) Suppose instead that the railroad initiates contempt proceedings in Michigan when the plaintiff continues to prosecute the Illinois action. What should the Michigan court do? See id. § 113 (1971).

KREMER v. CHEMICAL CONSTRUCTION CORP., 456 U.S. 461, 102 S.Ct. 1883 (1982). In this case, the Supreme Court decided that "a federal court in a Title VII case should give preclusive effect to a decision of a [New York] state court upholding a state administrative agency's rejection of an employment discrimination claim as meritless when the state court's decision would be [preclusive] in the state's own courts."

After overcoming a number of the plaintiff's arguments, Justice White for the Court observed:

"The more serious contention is that even though administrative proceedings and judicial review are legally sufficient to be given preclusive effect in New York, they should be deemed so fundamentally flawed as to be denied recognition under § 1738. We have previously recognized that

in the federal-state setting, as is suggested by the existence of 28 U.S.C. § 2283. See generally Charles A. Wright & Mary Kay Kane, Law of Federal Courts §§ 46–47 (6th ed. 2002).

the judicially created doctrine of collateral estoppel does not apply when the party against whom the earlier decision is asserted did not have a 'full and fair opportunity' to litigate the claim or issue . . . .

"Our previous decisions have not specified the source or defined the content of the requirement that the first adjudication offer a full and fair opportunity to litigate. But for present purposes, where we are bound by the statutory directive of § 1738, state proceedings need do no more than satisfy the minimum procedural requirements of the Fourteenth Amendment's Due Process Clause in order to qualify for the full faith and credit guaranteed by federal law. It has long been established that § 1738 does not allow federal courts to employ their own rules of res judicata in determining the effect of state judgments. Rather, it goes beyond the common law and commands a federal court to accept the rules chosen by the State from which the judgment is taken . . . .

"The State must, however, satisfy the applicable requirements of the Due Process Clause. A State may not grant preclusive effect in its own courts to a constitutionally infirm judgment, and other state and federal courts are not required to accord full faith and credit to such a judgment. Section 1738 does not suggest otherwise; other state and federal courts would still be providing a state court judgment with the 'same' preclusive effect as the courts of the State from which the judgment emerged. In such a case, there could be no constitutionally recognizable preclusion at all.

". . . We must bear in mind that no single model of procedural fairness, let alone a particular form of procedure, is dictated by the Due Process Clause. . . .

. . . .

"In our system of jurisprudence the usual rule is that merits of a legal claim once decided in a court of competent jurisdiction are not subject to redetermination in another forum. Such a fundamental departure from traditional rules of preclusion, enacted into federal law, can be justified only if plainly stated by Congress. Because there is no 'affirmative showing' of a 'clear and manifest' legislative purpose in Title VII to deny res judicata or collateral estoppel effect [in federal court] to a state court judgment affirming that a claim of employment discrimination is unproved, and because the procedures provided in New York for the determination of such claims offer a full and fair opportunity to litigate the merits, the judgment of the Court of Appeals is affirmed."

Justice Blackmun, with whom Justices Brennan and Marshall joined, and Justice Stevens dissented. They argued that Congress had intended mere judicial review of this sort to be nonpreclusive in this setting.

The Supreme Court later applied the Kremer majority's approach in an antitrust case, Marrese v. American Academy of Orthopaedic Surgeons, 470 U.S. 373, 105 S.Ct. 1327 (1985), and in a securities case, Matsushita Electrical Industrial Co. v. Epstein, 516 U.S. 367, 116 S.Ct. 873 (1996), both of which are within exclusive federal jurisdiction. Thus, in considering the preclusive effects of an earlier state judgment on a state claim, the federal court must apply the state res judicata law even though a state court could not have heard the federal claim.

Question: (4) Evaluate this position: A federal court in determining the effects of a state-court judgment must normally apply the preclusion law that the rendering state would apply, which includes some federal law such as the transsubstantive dictates of due process; this retroverse approach is, however, subject to rare and primarily congressional exceptions to § 1738 providing in substance-specific settings for less (or conceivably, by statute, more) credit to the state-court judgment in federal court. Does this position represent what the cases require or policy suggests, or both or neither?

UNIVERSITY OF TENNESSEE v. ELLIOTT, 478 U.S. 788, 106 S.Ct. 3220 (1986). In this case, the Supreme Court had to decide whether a federal court in a Title VII and § 1983 action should give preclusive effect to a state administrative adjudicatory finding that racial prejudice had not motivated the firing.

Justice White for the Court premised: "Title 28 U.S.C. § 1738 governs the preclusive effect to be given the judgments and records of state courts, and is not applicable to the unreviewed state administrative factfinding at issue in this case. However, we have frequently fashioned federal common-law rules of preclusion in the absence of a governing statute." (Here his cited cases included Parklane Hosiery and Blonder–Tongue. However, he did not cite McDonald v. City of West Branch, Michigan, 466 U.S. 284, 104 S.Ct. 1799 (1984), which had held that unreviewed state arbitration proceedings were not within § 1738 and, under the federal common law of preclusion, did not preclude a § 1983 action.)

As to the Title VII claim, he found by the statute's language and legislative history that Congress had impliedly intended unreviewed state administrative proceedings to have no preclusive effect on a Title VII claim in federal court, regardless of state preclusion law.

As to the § 1983 claim, he found no such intent. In formulating the consequently applicable federal common law, he observed, first, that giving issue preclusion effect to federal or state administrative factfinding serves the value of repose and, second: "Having federal courts give preclusive effect to the factfinding of state administrative tribunals also serves the value of federalism. Significantly, all of the opinions in Thomas v. Washington Gas Light Co., 448 U.S. 261, 100 S.Ct. 2647 (1980), express the view that the Full Faith and Credit Clause compels the States to give preclusive effect to the factfindings of an administrative tribunal in a sister State. . . . The Full Faith and Credit Clause is of course not binding on federal courts, but we can certainly look to the policies underlying the Clause in fashioning federal common-law rules of preclusion. 'Perhaps the major purpose of the Full Faith and Credit Clause is to act as a nationally unifying force,' id., at 289, 100 S.Ct., at 2664 (White, J., concurring in judgment), and this purpose is served by giving preclusive effect to state administrative factfinding rather than leaving the courts of a second forum, state or federal, free to reach conflicting results. Accordingly, we hold that when a state agency 'acting in a judicial capacity . . . resolves disputed issues of fact properly before it which the parties have had an adequate opportunity to litigate,' [United States v. Utah Constr. & Mining Co., 384 U.S. 394, 422, 86 S.Ct. 1545, 1560 (1966)], federal courts must give the agency's factfinding the same preclusive effect to which it would be entitled in the State's courts."

Justice Stevens, with whom Justices Brennan and Blackmun joined, dissented from authorizing preclusion on the § 1983 claim. See also Daan Braveman & Richard Goldsmith, Rules of Preclusion and Challenges to Official Action: An Essay on Finality, Fairness, and Federalism, All Gone Awry, 39 Syracuse L.Rev. 599 (1988). Justice Marshall did not participate.

Unlike its cases under § 1738 such as Kremer, the Court's opinion in Elliott did not indicate that its rationale would apply to authorize claim preclusion as well as issue preclusion. Indeed, most lower courts have since ruled that, under the federal common law of preclusion, unreviewed state administrative proceedings do not have claim preclusion effect on a § 1983 action. E.g., Gjellum v. City of Birmingham, Ala., 829 F.2d 1056 (11th Cir.1987).

Hart

Supreme Court of New York, New York County, 1969.
61 Misc.2d 41, 304 N.Y.S.2d 810.

■ HARRY B. FRANK, JUSTICE. Defendant American Airlines moves pursuant to CPLR, Section 602(a), for an order directing that all issues of liability in the death actions brought by plaintiffs Landano and Kirchstein be joined for trial with the 20 other American Airlines cases subject to joint trial under an order of the Appellate Division dated November 10, 1967. (See 28 A.D.2d 986 [including the Hart case].)

The actions all arise out of the crash, in Kentucky on November 8, 1965, of an American Airlines aircraft while the plane was en route from La Guardia Airport, New York to an airport in Covington, Kentucky. The crash resulted in the death of 58 out of the 62 persons aboard and, in addition to the multiple actions pending in this court, comparable actions have been instituted in other states and in various United States District Courts.

Of the various actions instituted as a result of the crash, the first case to be tried to conclusion was that brought in the United States District

Court, Northern District of Texas (Creasy v. American Airlines, Inc.), which resulted in a [$175,000] verdict in favor of the plaintiff therein against the defendant American Airlines. On a prior motion brought in the Hart case herein, the opinion of Mr. Justice Quinn, dated May 15, 1968, noted that in the Creasy trial, which lasted some 19 days, the Texas court applied the Kentucky wrongful death statute and submitted the question of American Airlines' liability on the basis of the substantive law of Kentucky relating to negligence. Reference to the pleadings in the two actions here sought to be joined for trial indicates that the basis for the recovery sought against defendant American Airlines is similarly predicated, and it is undisputable from the pleadings and papers herein that the issue of defendant airline's liability in these cases is identical to the issue in that regard determined in the Texas action.

In light of the Texas result which has now been affirmed on appeal, plaintiffs Landano and Kirchstein oppose defendant's motion for a joint trial by cross-moving for summary judgment on the issue of liability which, if granted, would obviate a trial on such issue and necessarily require a denial of defendant's motion.

Plaintiffs contend that while, concededly, they were not parties to the Texas action, nevertheless the determination in that action of defendant's liability for the plane crash of November 8, 1965 is, under the doctrine of collateral estoppel, conclusive on the issue of defendant's liability for such crash in the actions brought by these plaintiffs.

In its recent decision in Schwartz v. Public Administrator, 24 N.Y.2d 65, 298 N.Y.S.2d 955, 246 N.E.2d 725, our Court of Appeals definitively crystalized the controlling considerations governing the doctrine of collateral estoppel in this State and "arrived at a modern and stable statement of the law of res judicata" grounded on "the sound principle that, where it can be fairly said that a party has had a full opportunity to litigate a particular issue, he cannot reasonably demand a second one". . . . "There must be an identity of issue which has necessarily been decided in the prior action and is decisive of the present action, and, second, there must have been a full and fair opportunity to contest the decision now said to be controlling."

No extended discussion is necessary to demonstrate that such requirements are amply met in the instant cases. As already indicated, the issue of defendant airline's liability for the crash in which plaintiffs' decedents perished is identical to the issue of liability litigated in the Texas action where defendant was similarly charged with responsibility for that same accident. Indeed, in an airplane crash there are absent any of the problems with respect to "identity of issue" on liability which might arise in other types of accidents involving multiple participants such as automobile accident cases. With respect to the second requirement, it is in no way disputed that defendant had a full and fair opportunity to contest the issue of its liability in the course of the 19 day trial in the Texas action, and in order to defeat collateral estoppel on this ground the burden rests on the defendant to show that it had no such opportunity.

While defendant presents various arguments as to why the finding on liability should not be applied in these cases, it relies most heavily upon the prior decision of Mr. Justice Quinn in the Hart matter,[c] hereinbefore referred to, which was affirmed without opinion by the Appellate Division, 31 A.D.2d 896, 297 N.Y.S.2d 587. Although defendant concedes that such decision is not "in a strict sense" the law of the case here, it nevertheless contends that such decision compels a denial of plaintiffs' motion for summary judgment. This court disagrees. Contrary to defendant's assertions, the controlling factor in the Hart decision was the non-domiciliary status of the plaintiffs therein involved and the unwillingness of the court to apply the New York law of collateral estoppel with respect to a Texas determination on behalf of "non-domiciliary dependents of a deceased non-domiciliary 'bread winner' " having no significant contacts with New York. While such result will undoubtedly be effective to discourage possible "forum shopping" by non-residents, it does not, as defendant argues, preclude the application of the New York doctrine of collateral estoppel in an action brought by New York dependents of deceased New York residents. As was pointed out in Kilberg v. Northeast Airlines, 9 N.Y.2d 34, 39, 211 N.Y.S.2d 133, 135, 172 N.E.2d 526, 527–528, which involved a death action arising out of an airplane crash where decedent had been a New York resident, "The place of injury becomes entirely fortuitous. Our courts should if possible provide protection for our own State's people against unfair and anachronistic treatment of the lawsuits which result from these disasters." The state of Texas has no legitimate interest in imposing its rules on collateral estoppel upon these New York residents and a holding that permits such result would indeed constitute the "anachronistic treatment" warned against in Kilberg. The fact that the plaintiffs herein involved are New York domiciliaries, as were their decedents, sufficiently establishes this state's superior interest in the issue of collateral estoppel. It may be observed that these plaintiffs occupy much the same relationship to the state of Texas as the non-resident Hart plaintiffs do to New York, and the unavailability of the New York rule on collateral estoppel to the Hart plaintiffs is equally relevant in holding the instant resident plaintiffs outside the scope of the Texas rule on that issue.

Defendant's reliance on "full faith and credit" to defeat the application of collateral estoppel herein is misplaced. This is not a situation where the judgment, as such, of the Texas court is sought to be enforced. What is here involved is a policy determination by our courts that " 'One who has had his day in court should not be permitted to litigate the question anew' " (B.R. DeWitt, Inc. v. Hall, 19 N.Y.2d 141, 144, 278 N.Y.S.2d 596, 599, 225 N.E.2d 195, 197 . . .), and, further, refusal "to tolerate a condition where, on relatively the same set of facts, one fact-finder, be it court or jury" may find a party liable while another exonerates him leading to the "inconsistent results which are always a blemish on a judicial system" (Schwartz v.

[c] Unlike the cases of Landano and Kirchstein, this companion case involved only nonresidents. Justice Quinn there refused to extend collateral estoppel in favor of the New Jersey and Connecticut plaintiffs, looking to the state law of Texas which then followed the rule of mutuality of estoppel. N.Y.L.J., May 20, 1968, at 2, col. 6, excerpted in 36 U.S.L.W. 2736.

Public Administrator, 24 N.Y.2d 65, 74, 298 N.Y.S.2d 955, 962, 246 N.E.2d 725, 730, supra). It is in order to carry out these policy determinations in the disposition of cases in this jurisdiction that . . . use is being made of a particular issue determination made in the Texas action.

. . . .

Accordingly, plaintiffs' cross motion for summary judgment is granted and defendant's motion for a joint trial is denied. Settle order providing for an assessment of damages.

Questions: (5) Should the law that the rendering court would apply or the law of the forum court govern the basic res judicata effects of a prior judgment? See Restatement (Second) of Conflict of Laws §§ 94–95 (1971) (amended 1988) (rendering court).

(6) Should the Full Faith and Credit Clause and statute be read to prohibit a state from giving a sister state's judgment *more* credit than it would be given where rendered? Is the giving of more credit fair to the party to be burdened? See Farmland Dairies v. Barber, 65 N.Y.2d 51, 478 N.E.2d 1314, 489 N.Y.S.2d 713 (1985) (same credit).

(7) Should federal law or state law govern the res judicata effects of a prior judgment rendered by a federal court sitting in diversity, such as the Creasy judgment?

Semtek International Inc. v. Lockheed Martin Corp.

Supreme Court of the United States, 2001.
531 U.S. 497, 121 S.Ct. 1021.

■ JUSTICE SCALIA delivered the opinion of the Court.

This case presents the question whether the claim-preclusive effect of a federal judgment dismissing a diversity action on statute-of-limitations grounds is determined by the law of the State in which the federal court sits.

I

Petitioner filed a complaint against respondent in California state court, alleging breach of contract and various business torts. Respondent [a Maryland citizen] removed the case to the United States District Court for the Central District of California on the basis of diversity of citizenship . . . , and successfully moved to dismiss petitioner's claims as barred by California's 2–year statute of limitations. In its order of dismissal, the District Court, adopting language suggested by respondent, dismissed petitioner's claims "in [their] entirety on the merits and with prejudice." . . . Without contesting the District Court's designation of its dismissal as "on the merits," petitioner appealed to the Court of Appeals for the Ninth

Circuit, which affirmed the District Court's order. 168 F.3d 501 (1999) (table). Petitioner also brought suit against respondent in the State Circuit Court for Baltimore City, Maryland, alleging the same causes of action, which were not time barred under Maryland's 3–year statute of limitations. . . . Following a hearing, the Maryland state court granted respondent's motion to dismiss on the ground of res judicata. . . . The Court of Special Appeals affirmed, holding that, regardless of whether California would have accorded claim-preclusive effect to a statute-of-limitations dismissal by one of its own courts, the dismissal by the California federal court barred the complaint filed in Maryland, since the res judicata effect of federal diversity judgments is prescribed by federal law, under which the earlier dismissal was on the merits and claim preclusive. 128 Md.App. 39, 736 A.2d 1104 (1999). After the Maryland Court of Appeals declined to review the case, we granted certiorari. 530 U.S. 1260, 120 S.Ct. 2715 (2000).

II

Petitioner contends that the outcome of this case is controlled by Dupasseur v. Rochereau, 21 Wall. 130, 135 (1875), which held that the res judicata effect of a federal diversity judgment "is such as would belong to judgments of the State courts rendered under similar circumstances," and may not be accorded any "higher sanctity or effect." Since, petitioner argues, the dismissal of an action on statute-of-limitations grounds by a California state court would not be claim preclusive, it follows that the similar dismissal of this diversity action by the California federal court cannot be claim preclusive. While we agree that this would be the result demanded by Dupasseur, the case is not dispositive because it was decided under the Conformity Act of 1872, 17 Stat. 196, which required federal courts to apply the procedural law of the forum State in nonequity cases. That arguably affected the outcome of the case. [Citations omitted.]

Respondent, for its part, contends that the outcome of this case is controlled by Federal Rule of Civil Procedure 41(b) . . . .

. . . .

In short, it is no longer true that a judgment "on the merits" is necessarily a judgment entitled to claim-preclusive effect; and there are a number of reasons for believing that the phrase "adjudication upon the merits" does not bear that meaning in Rule 41(b). To begin with, Rule 41(b) sets forth nothing more than a default rule for determining the import of a dismissal (a dismissal is "upon the merits," with the three stated exceptions, unless the court "otherwise specifies"). This would be a highly peculiar context in which to announce a federally prescribed rule on the complex question of claim preclusion, saying in effect, "All federal dismissals (with three specified exceptions) preclude suit elsewhere, unless the court otherwise specifies."

And even apart from the purely default character of Rule 41(b), it would be peculiar to find a rule governing the effect that must be accorded federal judgments by other courts ensconced in rules governing the internal procedures of the rendering court itself. Indeed, such a rule would arguably violate the jurisdictional limitation of the Rules Enabling Act: that the Rules "shall not abridge, enlarge or modify any substantive right," 28 U.S.C. § 2072(b). Cf. Ortiz v. Fibreboard Corp., 527 U.S. 815, 842, 119 S.Ct. 2295 (1999) (adopting a "limiting construction" of Federal Rule of Civil Procedure 23(b)(1)(B) in order to "minimiz[e] potential conflict with the Rules Enabling Act, and [to] avoi[d] serious constitutional concerns"). In the present case, for example, if California law left petitioner free to sue on this claim in Maryland even after the California statute of limitations had expired, the federal court's extinguishment of that right (through Rule 41(b)'s mandated claim-preclusive effect of its judgment) would seem to violate this limitation.

Moreover, as so interpreted, the Rule would in many cases violate the federalism principle of Erie R. Co. v. Tompkins, 304 U.S. 64, 78–80, 58 S.Ct. 817 (1938), by engendering " 'substantial' variations [in outcomes] between state and federal litigation" which would "[l]ikely . . . influence the choice of a forum," Hanna v. Plumer, 380 U.S. 460, 467–468, 85 S.Ct. 1136 (1965). See also Guaranty Trust Co. v. York, 326 U.S. 99, 108–110, 65 S.Ct. 1464 (1945). Cf. Walker v. Armco Steel Corp., 446 U.S. 740, 748–753, 100 S.Ct. 1978 (1980). With regard to the claim-preclusion issue involved in the present case, for example, the traditional rule is that expiration of the applicable statute of limitations merely bars the remedy and does not extinguish the substantive right, so that dismissal on that ground does not have claim-preclusive effect in other jurisdictions with longer, unexpired limitation periods. See Restatement (Second) of Conflict of Laws §§ 142(2), 143 (1969); Restatement of Judgments § 49, Comment a (1942). Out-of-state defendants sued on stale claims in California and in other States adhering to this traditional rule would systematically remove state-law suits brought against them to federal court—where, unless otherwise specified, a statute-of-limitations dismissal would bar suit everywhere.

Finally, if Rule 41(b) did mean what respondent suggests, we would surely have relied upon it in our cases recognizing the claim-preclusive effect of federal judgments in federal-question cases. Yet for over half a century since the promulgation of Rule 41(b), we have not once done so. [Citations omitted.]

. . . .

We think, then, that the effect of the "adjudication upon the merits" default provision of Rule 41(b)—and, presumably, of the explicit order in the present case that used the language of that default provision—is simply that, unlike a dismissal "without prejudice," the dismissal in the present case barred refiling of the same claim in the United States District Court for the Central District of California. That is undoubtedly a necessary condition, but it is not a sufficient one, for claim-preclusive effect in other courts.

III

Having concluded that the claim-preclusive effect, in Maryland, of this California federal diversity judgment is dictated neither by Dupasseur v.

Rochereau, as petitioner contends, nor by Rule 41(b), as respondent contends, we turn to consideration of what determines the issue. Neither the Full Faith and Credit Clause, U.S. Const., Art. IV, § 1, nor the full faith and credit statute, 28 U.S.C. § 1738, addresses the question. By their terms they govern the effects to be given only to state-court judgments (and, in the case of the statute, to judgments by courts of territories and possessions). And no other federal textual provision, neither of the Constitution nor of any statute, addresses the claim-preclusive effect of a judgment in a federal diversity action.

It is also true, however, that no federal textual provision addresses the claim-preclusive effect of a federal-court judgment in a federal-question case, yet we have long held that States cannot give those judgments merely whatever effect they would give their own judgments, but must accord them the effect that this Court prescribes. See Stoll v. Gottlieb, 305 U.S. 165, 171–172, 59 S.Ct. 134 (1938); Gunter v. Atlantic Coast Line R. Co., 200 U.S. 273, 290–291, 26 S.Ct. 252 (1906); Deposit Bank v. Frankfort, 191 U.S. 499, 514–515, 24 S.Ct. 154 (1903). The reasoning of that line of cases suggests, moreover, that even when States are allowed to give federal judgments (notably, judgments in diversity cases) no more than the effect accorded to state judgments, that disposition is by direction of this Court, which has the last word on the claim-preclusive effect of all federal judgments . . . .

. . . In short, federal common law governs the claim-preclusive effect of a dismissal by a federal court sitting in diversity. See generally R. Fallon, D. Meltzer, & D. Shapiro, Hart and Wechsler's The Federal Courts and the Federal System 1473 (4th ed. 1996); Degnan, Federalized Res Judicata, 85 Yale L.J. 741 (1976).

It is left to us, then, to determine the appropriate federal rule. And despite the sea change that has occurred in the background law since Dupasseur was decided—not only repeal of the Conformity Act but also the watershed decision of this Court in Erie—we think the result decreed by Dupasseur continues to be correct for diversity cases. Since state, rather than federal, substantive law is at issue there is no need for a uniform federal rule. And indeed, nationwide uniformity in the substance of the matter is better served by having the same claim-preclusive rule (the state rule) apply whether the dismissal has been ordered by a state or a federal court. This is, it seems to us, a classic case for adopting, as the federally prescribed rule of decision, the law that would be applied by state courts in the State in which the federal diversity court sits. [Citations omitted.] As we have alluded to above, any other rule would produce the sort of "forum-shopping . . . and . . . inequitable administration of the laws" that Erie seeks to avoid, Hanna, 380 U.S., at 468, 85 S.Ct. 1136, since filing in, or removing to, federal court would be encouraged by the divergent effects that the litigants would anticipate from likely grounds of dismissal. See Guaranty Trust Co. v. York, 326 U.S., at 109–110, 65 S.Ct. 1464.

This federal reference to state law will not obtain, of course, in situations in which the state law is incompatible with federal interests. If, for example, state law did not accord claim-preclusive effect to dismissals for willful violation of discovery orders, federal courts' interest in the integrity of their own processes might justify a contrary federal rule. No such conflict with potential federal interests exists in the present case. Dismissal of this state cause of action was decreed by the California federal court only because the California statute of limitations so required; and there is no conceivable federal interest in giving that time bar more effect in other courts than the California courts themselves would impose.

* * *

Because the claim-preclusive effect of the California federal court's dismissal "upon the merits" of petitioner's action on statute-of-limitations grounds is governed by a federal rule that in turn incorporates California's law of claim preclusion (the content of which we do not pass upon today), the Maryland Court of Special Appeals erred in holding that the dismissal necessarily precluded the bringing of this action in the Maryland courts. The judgment is reversed, and the case remanded for further proceedings not inconsistent with this opinion.

It is so ordered.[d]

Q INTERNATIONAL COURIER, INC. v. SMOAK, 441 F.3d 214 (4th Cir.2006). "Glenn Smoak filed an action in Virginia state court ('the first action') against Q International Courier, Inc. ('Quick') seeking a declaration that Quick used an improper basis appraising the value of Smoak's stock after Smoak exercised his option requiring Quick to purchase his stock. Quick removed this first action to federal district court in the Eastern District of Virginia based on diversity jurisdiction. Quick also filed a counterclaim against Smoak, alleging that Smoak used an improper basis for his stock appraisal and breached the parties' stock option agreement. After a bench trial, the district court entered judgment substantially in favor of Quick." However, the court, for lack of proof, denied Quick the damages it sought for Smoak's suing rather than following the stock appraisal method specified in the parties' stock option agreement.

Four months after the first action concluded, Quick filed "the second action" in the same federal district court, seeking damages against Smoak, his lawyer, and his other advisors for their conspiracy not to follow that specified stock appraisal method. The district court, by a different district judge, dismissed the second action based on the federal law of res judicata. In its ruling from the bench, the district court stated: "I think the record is clear that there was a common core of operative facts that were fully litigated in that first case that [Quick] is trying to essentially relitigate in this case."

---

[d] On remand, the court denied the res judicata defense and then proceeded to the merits, 2002 WL 32500569 (Md.Cir.Ct. Mar. 20, 2002).

The court of appeals said: "Quick now appeals, asserting that the district court erred in applying the federal law of res judicata rather than the Virginia law of res judicata, and that its claims are not subject to dismissal under the Virginia law of res judicata. For the following reasons, we reverse and remand."

The court of appeals ruled that Semtek required looking to Virginia res judicata law. While leaving the details to the district court on remand, the appellate court indicated that the answer lay in the compulsory counterclaim rule: "Although the parties agree [on the broad outlines of] the Virginia law of res judicata, neither party has argued that Virginia also has a specific res judicata rule for cases—like the instant one—in which the first action was litigated in federal district court. In such a circumstance, the initial question under Virginia law is whether the claims filed in the second action would have been considered compulsory counterclaims in the first action under Federal Rule of Civil Procedure 13(a). See Nottingham v. Weld, 237 Va. 416, 377 S.E.2d 621, 623 (1989) ('[W]e look to the federal courts' constructions of the preclusive effect of a failure to file a compulsory counterclaim in the federal court'). If the claims asserted in the second action would have been considered compulsory counterclaims under Rule 13(a) in the first action, the claims will be precluded in the second action. See id."

Question: (8) In what sense, if any, is the court of appeals applying Virginia res judicata law? Was the court in Horne, supra p. 724, applying Ohio res judicata law?

(9) Did the court of appeals in Fagnan, supra p. 795, properly handle the initial choice-of-res-judicata-law question?

SECTION 2. JUDGMENTS FROM FOREIGN NATIONS

Hilton v. Guyot

Supreme Court of the United States, 1895.
159 U.S. 113, 16 S.Ct. 139.[e]

[French plaintiffs sued United States citizens in a circuit court of the United States in New York upon a French judgment. The defendants denied any indebtedness and contended that the merits of the case should be examined, because the French courts would do so in a suit in France upon an American judgment against a French national. The circuit court entered judgment for the French plaintiffs without examining the merits.]

---

[e] This case, covering 122 pages in the U.S. Reports, has been very drastically edited. For the background story of the Hilton case, see Louise Ellen Teitz, "The Story of Hilton: From Gloves to Globalization," in Civil Procedure Stories 445 (Kevin M. Clermont ed., 2d ed. 2008).

■ MR. JUSTICE GRAY, after stating the case, delivered the opinion of the court.

. . . .

The most certain guide, no doubt, for the decision of such questions is a treaty or a statute of this country. But when, as is the case here, there is no written law upon the subject, the duty still rests upon the judicial tribunals of ascertaining and declaring what the law is, whenever it becomes necessary to do so, in order to determine the rights of parties to suits regularly brought before them. In doing this, the courts must obtain such aid as they can from judicial decisions, from the works of jurists and commentators, and from the acts and usages of civilized nations. [Citations omitted.]

No law has any effect, of its own force, beyond the limits of the sovereignty from which its authority is derived. The extent to which the law of one nation, as put in force within its territory, whether by executive order, by legislative act, or by judicial decree, shall be allowed to operate within the dominion of another nation, depends upon what our greatest jurists have been content to call "the comity of nations." Although the phrase has been often criticised, no satisfactory substitute has been suggested.

"Comity," in the legal sense, is neither a matter of absolute obligation, on the one hand, nor of mere courtesy and good will, upon the other. But it is the recognition which one nation allows within its territory to the legislative, executive or judicial acts of another nation, having due regard both to international duty and convenience, and to the rights of its own citizens or of other persons who are under the protection of its laws.

. . . .

In view of all the authorities upon the subject, and of the trend of judicial opinion in this country and in England, following the lead of Kent and Story, we are satisfied that, where there has been opportunity for a full and fair trial abroad before a court of competent jurisdiction, conducting the trial upon regular proceedings, after due citation or voluntary appearance of the defendant, and under a system of jurisprudence likely to secure an impartial administration of justice between the citizens of its own country and those of other countries, and there is nothing to show either prejudice in the court, or in the system of laws under which it was sitting, or fraud in procuring the judgment, or any other special reason why the comity of this nation should not allow it full effect, the merits of the case should not, in an action brought in this country upon the judgment, be tried afresh, as on a new trial or an appeal, upon the mere assertion of the party that the judgment was erroneous in law or in fact. The defendants, therefore, cannot be permitted, upon that general ground, to contest the validity or the effect of the judgment sued on.

. . . .

It is next objected that in [the French] courts one of the plaintiffs was permitted to testify not under oath, and was not subjected to cross-examination by the opposite party, and that the defendants were, therefore, deprived of safeguards which are by our law considered essential to secure honesty and to detect fraud in a witness; and also that documents and papers were admitted in evidence, with which the defendants had no connection, and which would not be admissible under our own system of jurisprudence. But it having been shown by the plaintiffs, and hardly denied by the defendants, that the practice followed and the method of examining witnesses were according to the laws of France, we are not prepared to hold that the fact that the procedure in these respects differed from that of our own courts is, of itself, a sufficient ground for impeaching the foreign judgment.

[The Court next discussed whether a foreign judgment may be impeached on the ground that it rested on fraud, and the Court cited English cases holding that it may be so impeached.]

But whether those decisions can be followed in regard to foreign judgments, consistently with our own decisions as to impeaching domestic judgments for fraud, it is unnecessary in this case to determine, because there is a distinct and independent ground upon which we are satisfied that the comity of our nation does not require us to give conclusive effect to the judgments of the courts of France; and that ground is, the want of reciprocity, on the part of France, as to the effect to be given to the judgments of this and other foreign countries.

[An extended review of the law of many countries as to the recognition of foreign judgments is omitted.]

The reasonable, if not the necessary, conclusion appears to us to be that judgments rendered in France, or in any other foreign country, by the laws of which our own judgments are reviewable upon the merits, are not entitled to full credit and conclusive effect when sued upon in this country, but are prima facie evidence only of the justice of the plaintiffs' claim [which means that a plaintiff seeking enforcement can introduce a valid and final foreign judgment to show there is presumptively a judgment debt, but the defendant can then induce full and free reexamination of the merits of the claim].

In holding such a judgment, for want of reciprocity, not to be conclusive evidence of the merits of the claim, we do not proceed upon any theory of retaliation upon one person by reason of injustice done to another; but upon the broad ground that international law is founded upon mutuality and reciprocity, and that by the principles of international law recognized in most civilized nations, and by the comity of our own country, which it is our judicial duty to know and to declare, the judgment is not entitled to be considered conclusive.

■ [The judgment was reversed. The dissenting opinion of CHIEF JUSTICE FULLER, with whom Justices Harlan, Brewer, and Jackson joined, is omitted.]

Questions: (10) Should a state court, in considering whether to give conclusive effect to a French judgment in a case like Hilton v. Guyot, regard the questions as ones of federal law? See John Norton Moore, Federalism and Foreign Relations, 1965 Duke L.J. 248, 265.

(11) The New York courts, like those of most states, have given conclusive effect to judgments of foreign nations without regard to any question of reciprocity, thus rejecting the Hilton rule. Johnston v. Compagnie Générale Transatlantique, 242 N.Y. 381, 152 N.E. 121 (1926). In a diversity action upon a foreign judgment in a federal court in New York, like Hilton but commenced after Erie R.R. v. Tompkins, must the New York rule be followed? See Bank of Montreal v. Kough, 612 F.2d 467 (9th Cir.1980) (yes). But see John D. Brummett, Jr., Note, The Preclusive Effect of Foreign Country Judgments in the United States and Federal Choice of Law: The Role of the Erie Doctrine Reassessed, 33 N.Y.L.Sch.L.Rev. 83 (1988).

UNIFORM ACT

New York, long the preeminent state in matters of enforcing foreign judgments, codified its liberal law in 1970 by enacting NYCPLR art. 53 on recognition and enforcement of foreign judgments. It did so primarily to provide a ready means of demonstrating its liberality to any reciprocity-minded foreign court contemplating a New York judgment. The codification proceeded through enacting, as most other states have done, a version of the Uniform Foreign–Country Money Judgments Recognition Act.

The National Conference of Commissioners on Uniform State Laws had approved the Uniform Act in 1962 and clarified it by revision in 2005. It covers foreign-country court judgments granting or denying "recovery of a sum of money," other than judgments for taxes, a fine or other penalty, or support in domestic relations matters. Although the Uniform Act's application is thus to certain money judgments only, many states look to it for guidance in treating nonmonetary judgments as well. Indeed, the Restatement (Third) of Foreign Relations Law of the United States §§ 481–482 (1987) builds on the Uniform Act's approach by applying it to more kinds of judgments.

The Uniform Act now requires recognition in a subsequent lawsuit of a foreign money judgment that is "final, conclusive, and enforceable" under the rendering country's law. Recognition means that the judgment is "conclusive between the parties to the same extent as the judgment of a sister state entitled to full faith and credit in this state would be conclusive"; the comment to this section explains: "This means that the foreign-country judgment generally will be given the same effect in the forum state that it has in the foreign country where it was rendered." The section further provides that the judgment is "enforceable in the same manner and to the same extent as a judgment rendered in this state."

Section 4 of the Uniform Act specifies mandatory and discretionary grounds for nonrecognition, on which the resisting party has the burden of proof:

(b) A court of this state may not recognize a foreign-country judgment if:

(1) the foreign-country judgment was rendered under a judicial system that does not provide impartial tribunals or procedures compatible with the requirements of due process of law;

(2) the foreign court did not have personal jurisdiction over the defendant; or

(3) the foreign court did not have jurisdiction over the subject matter.

(c) A court of this state need not recognize a foreign-country judgment if:

(1) the defendant in the proceeding in the foreign court did not receive notice of the proceeding in sufficient time to enable the defendant to defend;

(2) the foreign-country judgment was obtained by fraud that deprived the losing party of an adequate opportunity to present its case;

(3) the foreign-country judgment or the [cause of action] [claim for relief] on which the foreign-country judgment is based is repugnant to the public policy of this state or of the United States;

(4) the foreign-country judgment conflicts with another final and conclusive judgment;

(5) the proceeding in the foreign court was contrary to an agreement between the parties under which the dispute in question was to be determined otherwise than by proceedings in that foreign court;

(6) in the case of jurisdiction based only on personal service, the foreign court was a seriously inconvenient forum for the trial of the action;

(7) the foreign-country judgment was rendered in circumstances that raise substantial doubt about the integrity of the rendering court with respect to the foreign-country judgment; or

(8) the specific proceeding in the foreign court leading to the foreign-country judgment was not compatible with the requirements of due process of law.

The brackets suggest to state legislatures a choice in the form of words to conform to state usage.

Section 5 restricts the especially important testing of personal jurisdiction, by essentially spelling out when the U.S. standards of substantive due process must be deemed satisfied:

(a) A foreign-country judgment may not be refused recognition for lack of personal jurisdiction if:

(1) the defendant was served with process personally in the foreign country;

(2) the defendant voluntarily appeared in the proceeding, other than for the purpose of protecting property seized or threatened with seizure in the proceeding or of contesting the jurisdiction of the court over the defendant;

(3) the defendant, before the commencement of the proceeding, had agreed to submit to the jurisdiction of the foreign court with respect to the subject matter involved;

(4) the defendant was domiciled in the foreign country when the proceeding was instituted or was a corporation or other form of business organization that had its principal place of business in, or was organized under the laws of, the foreign country;

(5) the defendant had a business office in the foreign country and the proceeding in the foreign court involved a [cause of action] [claim for relief] arising out of business done by the defendant through that office in the foreign country; or

(6) the defendant operated a motor vehicle or airplane in the foreign country and the proceeding involved a [cause of action] [claim for relief] arising out of that operation.

(b) The list of bases for personal jurisdiction in subsection (a) is not exclusive, and the courts of this state may recognize other bases of personal jurisdiction as sufficient to support a foreign-country judgment.

SOCIETY OF LLOYD'S v. ASHENDEN, 233 F.3d 473 (7th Cir.2000). Plaintiff in this diversity action invoked the Illinois version of the Uniform Act to collect on big money judgments obtained in England. The defendants collaterally attacked on the ground that the judgments rested on two contractual clauses so onerous as to deny due process, but the United States District Court for the Northern District of Illinois granted summary judgment to the plaintiff. The Seventh Circuit affirmed, per Judge Posner, in whose view "the key question is not the fairness of Lloyd's [contractual] measures but the fairness of the English court":

"The defendants . . . asked the district court not to recognize the English judgments as being enforceable in Illinois. They argued that those judgments had denied them due process of law and therefore were not enforceable under the foreign money-judgments recognition act, which makes a judgment rendered by a court outside the United States unenforceable in Illinois if 'the judgment was rendered under a *system* which does not provide impartial tribunals or procedures compatible with the requirements of due process of law.' . . .

"We have italicized the word that defeats the defendants' argument. The judgments about which they complain were rendered by the Queen's Bench Division of England's High Court, which corresponds to our federal district courts; they were affirmed by the Court of Appeal, which corresponds to the federal courts of appeals; and the Appellate Committee of the House of Lords, which corresponds to the U.S. Supreme Court, denied the defendants' petition for review. Any suggestion that this system of courts 'does not provide impartial tribunals or procedures compatible with the requirements of due process of law' borders on the risible. . . .

"Not that the English concept of fair procedure is identical to ours; but we cannot believe that the Illinois statute is intended to bar the enforcement of all judgments of any foreign legal system that does not conform its procedural doctrines to the latest twist and turn of our courts regarding, for example, the circumstances under which due process requires an opportunity for a hearing in advance of the deprivation of a substantive right rather than afterwards. See Hilton v. Guyot, 159 U.S. 113, 205, 16 S.Ct. 139, 40 L.Ed. 95 (1895); Ingersoll Milling Machine Co. v. Granger, 833 F.2d 680, 687–88 (7th Cir.1987). It is a fair guess that no foreign nation has decided to incorporate our due process doctrines into its own procedural law; and so we interpret 'due process' in the Illinois statute (which, remember, is a uniform act, not one intended to reflect the idiosyncratic jurisprudence of a particular state) to refer to a concept of fair procedure simple and basic enough to describe the judicial processes of civilized nations, our peers. The statute requires only that the foreign procedure be '*compatible* with the requirements of due process of law,' and we have interpreted this to mean that the foreign procedures are 'fundamentally fair' and do not offend against 'basic fairness.' Id. at 687–88; see also Hilton v. Guyot, supra, 159 U.S. at 202–03, 16 S.Ct. 139; [other citations omitted].

"We'll call this the 'international concept of due process' to distinguish it from the complex concept that has emerged from American case law. . . .

"It is true that no evidence was presented in the district court on whether England *has* a civilized legal system, but that is because the question is not open to doubt. We need not consider what kind of evidence would suffice to show that a foreign legal system 'does not provide impartial tribunals or procedures compatible with the requirements of due process of law' if the challenged judgment had been rendered by Cuba, North Korea, Iran, Iraq, Congo, or some other nation whose adherence to the rule of law and commitment to the norm of due process are open to serious question, [citations omitted], as England's are not. It is anyway not a question of fact. It is not, strictly speaking, a question of law either, but it is a question about the law of a foreign nation, and in answering such questions a federal court is not limited to the consideration of evidence that would be admissible under the Federal Rules of Evidence; any relevant material or source may be consulted. Fed.R.Civ.P. 44.1; [other citations omitted]."

Questions: (12) If Fauntleroy v. Lum had been an action to enforce a judgment of a foreign nation, rather than that of a sister state, how should the case have been decided (assuming no problem of lack of reciprocity)? See Restatement (Second) of Conflict of Laws § 117 cmt. c (1971).

(13) Assuming that the required circumstances exist for recognizing a judgment from a foreign nation, what is the extent of recognition? That is, should the res judicata effects of the prior judgment be governed by the foreign law, by the usual res judicata rules of domestic law, or by some special set of res judicata rules for international judgments? Is it significant that res judicata rules in American legal systems generally are considerably broader in effect than those elsewhere? See Robert C. Casad, Issue Preclusion and Foreign Country Judgment: Whose Law?, 70 Iowa L.Rev. 53 (1984).

GENERAL APPROACH

Current Law.—International law itself plays no real role in U.S. treatment of foreign judgments, except to the extent that the U.S. approach is already a manifestation of any generally recognized principles that constitute part of international law. The United States has not a single treaty on the subject. So, for foreign judgments, no binding law comparable to full faith and credit exists to take them out of the normal background rule: the acts of foreign governments have no effect within another government's territory, unless the latter government *chooses* to give them effect.

Yet U.S. courts at the federal and state level do give respect to foreign judgments, not only because finality is a fair and efficient policy even as to foreign judgments, but also because U.S. courts hope to encourage abroad similar respect for their own judgments. That is, freed from constitutional, statutory, and treaty obligations but motivated by similar policies, U.S. courts generally respect foreign judgments that are valid and final under the foreign law. Accordingly, the foreign res judicata law should be applicable, and the foreign judgment should be enforceable, in the United States.

The U.S. courts' approach to foreign judgments can still be somewhat flexible, precisely because their respect flows from "comity" rather than from external legal obligation. A closer look at the actual holdings and opinions suggests that U.S. courts apply somewhat different standards to judgments of foreign nations, as compared to those they apply to domestic, state, or federal judgments. The principal reason for the difference is that a U.S. court has no guarantee that a foreign judgment, although comporting with the basic requirements of the foreign nation, is minimally acceptable to Americans. The foreign laws concerning validity vary widely. Moreover, the Due Process Clause and the rest of the U.S. Constitution do not control foreign sovereigns, of course, and so the workings of the foreign legal system could be too foreign to tolerate.

From this realistic insight follow four corollaries. First, while a U.S. court will ask whether jurisdiction existed under the foreign law, the U.S. court more importantly may examine whether the foreign assertion of jurisdiction satisfied the U.S. tests of substantive due process. A U.S. court, for example, would disregard a French judgment for which personal jurisdiction was based solely on the plaintiff's French nationality. Second, a U.S. court will give no respect to a foreign judgment that it views as repugnantly unfair. A U.S. court will not recognize or enforce a foreign judgment resulting from proceedings that failed to meet the basic notions of U.S. procedural due process, such as adequate notice, and so prevented the parties from having a fair day in court. Third, a U.S. court might apply other limitations, such as refusing recognition or enforcement if the prior judgment resulted from fraud extrinsic to the merits or if the original claim is directly contrary to strong local public policy. For a procedural example of those limitations, a foreign default judgment rendered contrary to a forum selection clause's derogation might fall within the public policy exception, even where Uniform Act § 4(c)(5) is not in force. For a substantive example, a U.S. court would reject an English judgment for defamation that impinges on U.S. principles of free speech, and also U.S. courts would generally not regard judgments of foreign countries imposing tax obligations or penal sanctions as entitled to recognition or enforcement. Fourth, in principle not often applied in actual practice, a U.S. court may require reciprocity. In sum, U.S. courts treat judgments of foreign nations pretty much like U.S. judgments, but not quite.

This U.S. behavior is nevertheless fairly generous compared to most other nations'. Most other nations appear to demonstrate a relatively heightened notion of sovereignty in this regard. Even if the U.S. judgment passes the foreign court's jurisdictional reexamination, which very well might involve meeting all the standards of the foreign jurisdictional law, the foreign court tends to reexamine the merits to ensure that the applied law conformed to local policy. And as to the extent of any recognition, the foreign court tends to apply its own, narrower res judicata law. See generally Samuel P. Baumgartner, How Well Do U.S. Judgments Fare in Europe?, 40 Geo.Wash.Int'l L.Rev. 173 (2008).

Treaty Possibilities.—European countries appear ahead of the United States on the treatment of foreign judgments or, rather, on their treatment of European judgments. As already explained, the European Union has an enlightened, albeit far from perfect, jurisdiction-and-judgments system. By that so-called Brussels Regulation, the member states must provide virtually automatic recognition and enforcement of the judgments of the other member states, if rendered on specified jurisdictional bases.

The European Union does not appear superior in all regards, however. It discriminates against outsiders in matters of jurisdiction. The virtually automatic recognition and enforcement does not extend to judgments rendered by countries that are not member states. The European countries, in fact, have traditionally been and continue to be rather stingy in extending respect to foreign judgments not covered by treaty, such as U.S. judgments. In brief, Americans are being whipsawed by the European Union approach. Not only are they still subject (in theory) to the far-reaching jurisdiction of European courts and the wide recognition and enforceability of their resulting judgments, but also U.S. judgments tend (in practice) to receive short shrift in European courts.

The overall international situation, as exacerbated by the Brussels Regulation, is unacceptable in the long run for the United States. Therefore, in 1992 the United States initiated a push to conclude a worldwide convention on jurisdiction and judgments, naturally choosing to work through the Hague Conference on Private International Law. Drafting and agreeing on a multilateral convention could yield great returns for the United States. A convention would rationalize both jurisdiction law and judgments law on an international level. A convention would also resolve the whipsawing predicament in which Americans today find themselves regarding exercise of jurisdiction as well as treatment of judgments. As to the jurisdictional side, a convention would require nations to renounce their own exorbitant jurisdiction. It also could substantively improve U.S. jurisdiction law in international cases. In the specific matter of treatment of foreign judgments, a convention would more unarguably be desirable for the United States. It would mean that the United States could get returns for the respect the United States is already according other nations' judgments.

Will such a convention—as opposed to narrower conventions treating important but special problem areas (such as judgments resulting from business-to-business contracts containing choice-of-court agreements that select forums for disputes to the exclusion of other forums, on which see Ronald A. Brand & Paul Herrup, The 2005 Hague Convention on Choice of Court Agreements (2008))—come into existence? Not in the near future. The United States has little bargaining power under the current regime. It needs a convention, while the Europeans have little to gain over their presently favorable situation. Consequently, the general talks at The Hague broke down after a decade of effort.

Further because of the imbalance of power, any convention of general scope, if ever agreed upon, would turn out very similar to the Brussels Regulation. This prediction means that the United States would abandon—on the international level, but not necessarily with respect to its courts' actions against its own habitual residents—attachment jurisdiction (other than for security or enforcement), tag jurisdiction (a relic of the power theory), doing business (as a basis for general jurisdiction), and much of forum non conveniens (too discretionary). The Europeans' objection is to the U.S. proclivity to base general jurisdiction on rather thin contacts, namely, allowing any and all causes of action to be brought on the basis of the defendant's property ownership, physical presence, or doing business in the forum. They do not object to specific jurisdiction, as long as a rules-based approach makes its application nondiscretionary. Thus, jurisdiction under a general convention would exist at the unconsenting defendant's habitual residence or where a specific part of the events in suit occurred, but would not extend to the broader bases of jurisdiction now authorized by U.S. law. In sum, a general convention would agree on certain bases of territorial jurisdiction, but chiefly those palatable to the Europeans—and judgments based thereon would then receive virtually automatic recognition and enforcement in other signatory countries (except those judgments that the Europeans consider too generous or punitive).

Regardless of ultimate outcome, however, the fruits of negotiation to date have definitely been worth the effort. Merely negotiating a draft Hague Convention taught all sides a lot about jurisdiction. For example, exorbitant jurisdiction looks different when viewed through foreign eyes. In particular, the effort has revealed to the United States the possibility of untangling its jurisdictional law for domestic cases on its own.

SECTION 3. VALIDITY VERSUS FINALITY

As just suggested once again, a judgment must be deemed "valid" in order to have any res judicata effects. To be so treated, the judgment must be of sufficient quality to withstand any attack in the form of a request for relief from judgment.

GROUNDS FOR ATTACK

Generally, relief from judgment, which could come by various procedures in subsequent litigation outside the ordinary course of review in the trial and appellate courts, will lie on grounds set by the judgment-rendering sovereign. Of course, that sovereign's law is subject to any applicable external restraints, an example being where due process and other federal provisions are imposed on and become part of state law.

So in, say, an action to enforce a default judgment of a state court, that state's law governs the grounds for attack. At least traditionally, the common formulation of state law provided that the judgment was not valid in these circumstances if and only if the rendering court had failed to satisfy the requirement of (1) subject-matter jurisdiction, (2) territorial jurisdiction, or (3) opportunity to be heard.

If, instead, the defaulting party had proceeded promptly to the rendering court to move for relief from judgment, the list of grounds would have been slightly longer. Relief then would have lain in a situation of extraordinary injustice, such as in cases of certain kinds of fraud.

There have been some inroads on this traditional doctrine, and hence on its relative certainty. Among some theorists and in some cases, relief from judgment should turn more expressly on a discretionary balancing of equities. Various factors would determine the availability of relief: (1) the nature and importance of the judgment's alleged infirmity; (2) the procedural technique of relief from judgment employed, this factor being based on the view that such techniques form a spectrum and that the list of available grounds for relief should contract as the mode, place, and time of attack become more distant from the initial action; (3) the impact of the relief requested; and (4) the position of the parties, including diligence in seeking relief and reliance on the judgment.

This fluid approach approximates the traditional doctrine. But there are divergences. Sometimes and for some purposes, taking into account the fluid factors, judgments not meeting the three requirements of competence and nexus and notice nevertheless would have effect (even on motion in the rendering court, as in Gschwind v. Cessna Aircraft Co., 232 F.3d 1342 (10th Cir.2000) (disallowing Federal Rule 60(b)(4) motion despite a jurisdictional defect under the diversity statute)), and other judgments meeting those requirements would have no effect (even in an out-of-state action upon the judgment, as in Lee v. Carroll, 146 So.2d 242 (La.Ct.App.1962) (allowing collateral attack on an extrinsic fraud ground)).

Consider how well the traditional and fluid approaches explain the next three cases.

Bank of Montreal v. Olafsson

United States Court of Appeals, Sixth Circuit, 1981.
648 F.2d 1078, cert. denied, 454 U.S. 1084, 102 S.Ct. 641 (1981).

■ Before ENGEL and MERRITT, CIRCUIT JUDGES and PHILLIPS, SENIOR CIRCUIT JUDGE

■ PER CURIAM.

The plaintiff is a Canadian corporation, and the defendant a citizen of Iceland. The issue here is whether the trial court erred in setting aside a default judgment it had entered more than a year earlier. The ground for setting it aside was that it had no subject matter jurisdiction because the requisite diversity of citizenship was lacking.

The Bank of Montreal filed suit March 2, 1978 [in the Eastern District of Michigan] against Thorhallur G. Olafsson to recover $34,572 due it through promissory notes and an overdraft. On May 31, 1978 the District Court granted a default judgment. The Bank then filed liens on Michigan realty held in the name of Olafsson's wife, and the property was sold to the Bank in satisfaction of its judgment. On June 7, 1979 Olafsson moved to set aside the judgment on two grounds: (1) because he was never personally served with a copy of the complaint, and (2) because he had filed for bankruptcy in Canada on March 28, 1978,[2] and under Canada law it is illegal to pursue claims while bankruptcy proceedings are pending.

In argument on the motion, Olafsson raised the diversity question. The district court rendered its opinion from the bench, finding that the bank was a Canadian corporation and that Olafsson was not a citizen of the United States either. It stated that the Bank knew or should have known of the citizenship of Olafsson. It recognized that the Bank had taken action in

---

[2] In that proceeding the Bank was named as a creditor.

reliance on the default but found the policy against granting judgments in cases in which the court has no jurisdiction to be overriding. It noted that it had never before addressed the jurisdictional question and concluded that the default judgment should be vacated under Fed.R.Civ.P. 60(b)(4) or 60(b)(6) because it was entered "in excess of the power of this court." The court set aside the default judgment and "all liens, writs of levy and execution, and sheriff's sales," and dismissed the suit.

The grant of motions made under rule 60(b) is a matter of discretion for the district court, and its decision is to be set aside only if it constitutes an abuse of discretion. Wright & Miller, Federal Practice and Procedure: Civil § 2872; 7 Moore's Federal Practice ¶ 60.19. The competing values implicated in the decision are on the one hand the interest in finality of judgments and on the other the interest in maintaining federal constitutional jurisdictional limitations.

[Feeling that voidness under Rule 60(b)(4) was merely "arguable," the court of appeals decided to rely on Rule 60(b)(6).] The district court also relied on rule 60(b)(6), which allows for a weighing of equities, in setting aside the judgment. See Wright & Miller, § 2864; 7 Moore's ¶ 60.27[2]. It discounted the Bank's reliance interest because of its finding that the Bank "knew or reasonably should have known" of Olafsson's citizenship. Olafsson's stated reason for not responding to the Bank's suit was that he had forwarded the complaint to his bankruptcy trustee with the understanding that he would take care of it.

. . . .

Given the lack of federal jurisdiction in the case, and considering the equities of the case under rule 60(b), we agree with the district court that the default judgment should be set aside and the case dismissed for lack of subject matter jurisdiction. The dispute between the parties over the promissory notes, overdraft, and liens can be more fairly and completely adjudicated in the Canadian bankruptcy court, in the country where the loan was made, the bank is located and Olafsson's bankruptcy is pending.

Accordingly, the judgment of the district court is affirmed.

Marshall v. Lockhead

Court of Civil Appeals of Texas, 1952.
245 S.W.2d 307, writ of error refused n.r.e.

■ HALE, JUSTICE.

Appellant sued appellee [in the 134th Judicial District Court of Dallas County] to set aside a prior judgment rendered in a former suit for the collection of delinquent taxes and to recover the title and possession of a certain lot sold and conveyed to appellee under an order of sale issued on the judgment in the prior tax suit. The present case was tried before the court below without a jury and resulted in judgment that appellant take nothing.

Appellant says the judgment in the tax suit was invalid and void in so far as he is concerned, because he was not served with citation and did not enter any appearance in the former suit, and hence he insists the Court did not acquire jurisdiction over his person. On the other hand, appellee says the judgment was not void and hence is not subject to collateral attack in this suit, and that appellant, by accepting the benefits accruing to him under the same, is estopped from asserting in this suit that such judgment is void or invalid.

The record before us discloses that on May 10, 1945, a final judgment was rendered in the 44th Judicial District Court of Dallas County, whereby the court found the amount of delinquent taxes, penalties and interest due and owing to the State of Texas and certain of its political subdivisions by reason of the ownership of the two lots therein described, being hereafter referred to as Lots 6 and 18. The judgment recites that defendants, C.B. Marshall and wife, Isabelle Marshall, had been duly cited in terms of law to appear but had wholly made default. The court found the amount of taxes, penalties and interest due against each of the two lots, decreed a foreclosure of the tax lien on each lot as against the defendants and directed that an order of sale be issued for each lot.

In pursuance of an order of sale issued on the above judgment, the sheriff of Dallas County sold Lot 6 to one George A. Harnack on July 3, 1945 for the sum of $1160.00. Of this amount the sum of $530.59 was paid to the State of Texas and others in satisfaction of the taxes due on Lot 6, and the balance thereof in the sum of $626.41 was paid into the registry of the court for the former owner of said lot. Thereafter, on April 6, 1948, C.B. (Bruce) Marshall, the appellant herein, applied to the 44th Judicial District Court for an order granting him permission to withdraw such excess money from the registry of the court as the former owner of Lot 6. The court granted the application, appellant withdrew said sum of $626.41 from the registry of the court, appropriated the same to his own use and benefit, and he has not returned or offered to return the same, or any part thereof, into court. In pursuance of another order of sale issued on the above judgment, the sheriff of Dallas County sold and conveyed Lot 18 to appellee and it is this lot which appellant seeks to recover in the present suit.

. . . .

. . . [I]t is generally held upon sound principles of equity that one who accepts and retains the fruits of a judgment is estopped thereafter to assert its invalidity. 31 Am.Jur. 92, Sec. 432; 49 C.J.S., Judgments, § 453, p. 884; 17 T.J. p. 135, Sec. 7. This just rule applies to cases where the asserted invalidity arises from a lack of jurisdiction of the court over the person of a party to the suit. Therefore, even though the C.B. Marshall who was served with citation in the tax suit here involved was not in fact the same person as the appellant in this cause, nevertheless it appears to us that the appellant herein, by reason of his conduct in procuring and retaining the sum of $626.41 paid into the registry of the court under the judgment rendered in the tax suit, conclusively estopped himself from successfully asserting in this suit that the tax judgment or either of the sales emanating therefrom was void or invalid. [Citations omitted.]

Consequently, all of appellant's points of error are overruled and the judgment appealed from is affirmed.

Britton v. Gannon

Supreme Court of Oklahoma, 1955.
285 P.2d 407, cert. denied, 350 U.S. 886, 76 S.Ct. 140 (1955).

■ ARNOLD, JUSTICE.

Mark Gannon brought this action in the District Court of Pontotoc County against W.R. Britton on a foreign judgment rendered in favor of said Gannon against Britton in the Circuit Court of Fayette County, Illinois, in the sum of $18,000.

Defendant filed answer consisting of a general denial and allegations to the effect that Mark Gannon was only a nominal party; that the real party in interest was Roy or "Spike" Gannon, brother of Mark Gannon; that said "Spike" Gannon had advised defendant that he was filing suit to recover certain personal property owned by him and defendant which had been sold pursuant to mortgage foreclosure proceedings and that Britton was a necessary defendant, but that no judgment would be taken against him, and relying on these representations, although served with summons, Britton made no effort to defend such suit and did not know that judgment had been taken against him until the instant suit was filed. Upon motion of plaintiff and over the objections and exceptions of defendant all allegations of defendant's answer except his general denial were stricken.

[At trial, plaintiff proved his claim, but defendant's evidence was not admitted.]

The court found that under the full faith and credit clause of the Constitution of the United States, art. 4, § 1, it had no right to hear and determine the validity of the defendant's defense . . . and entered judgment in favor of plaintiff for the amount prayed for.

Defendant contends that the court erred in refusing to allow him to present evidence to the effect that the judgment in Illinois, the basis of the present suit, was procured by extrinsic fraud and therefore not entitled to full faith and credit in Oklahoma.

The general rule is that a state court is not required to recognize the judgment of a court of another state, territory, or country subject to the jurisdiction of the United States, where the court rendering the judgment was without jurisdiction or judgment was obtained by extrinsic fraud. Stephens v. Thomasson, 63 Ariz. 187, 160 P.2d 338, and cases therein cited. Whatever plea would be good in the state in which the judgment was rendered may be pleaded in suit on the judgment in any other court in the

United States. Ibid. Extrinsic fraud has been defined as any fraudulent conduct of the successful party which was practiced outside of an actual adversary trial directly and affirmatively on the defeated party whereby he was prevented from presenting fully and fairly his side of the cause. Included in such definition are false representations that the defeated party is merely a nominal party against whom no relief is sought, false promises of compromise, concealment of the suit, kidnapping of witnesses, and the like. Calkin v. Wolcott, 182 Okl. 278, 77 P.2d 96. In such cases a court of equity had power to annul the decree so obtained. Ibid. See also American Ry. Express Co. v. Murphy, 234 Ill.App. 346, Village of Hartford v. First National Bank of Wood River, 307 Ill.App. 447, 30 N.E.2d 524. Some cases, as United States v. Throckmorton, 98 U.S. 61, 25 L.Ed. 93, put this on the ground that in such cases there has never been a real contest in the hearing of the case; others, such as Williams v. State of North Carolina, 325 U.S. 226, 65 S.Ct. 1092, 89 L.Ed. 1577, cited as authority in Stephens v. Thomasson, supra, on the ground that such conduct on the part of the successful party prevented the court from having jurisdiction to render the judgment which was rendered. Others, such as Levin v. Gladstein, 142 N.C. 482, 55 S.E. 371, 32 L.R.A.,N.S., 905, put it on the ground that a foreign court is not required to give greater faith and credit to the judgment than it is entitled to at home, and when the state in which the judgment was rendered would enjoin the enforcement of such judgment because of the circumstances under which it was obtained, the sister state may do likewise.

Regardless of the reason assigned for the rule, the weight of authority is overwhelming that a defense of extrinsic fraud of the nature here sought to be plead and proved may be interposed in a suit on a foreign judgment, not for the purpose of reviewing, setting aside, modifying, or annulling the judgment of the sister state, but to prevent its enforcement in the collateral court. [Citations omitted.] The trial court erred in refusing the proffered evidence of extrinsic fraud.

Reversed and remanded for a new trial.[f]

PROCEDURES FOR ATTACK

Three primary techniques lead to relief from judgment:

1. A party or privy may attack the judgment in the rendering court by a motion for relief from judgment. Bank of Montreal v. Olafsson provides an example, which involves Federal Rule 60(b). Such a motion is technically a continuation of the initial action. Nevertheless, it lies only in fairly extraordinary situations of injustice, designedly not serving as a cure for

---

[f] In a different enforcement action, before the Oklahoma judgment became final, relief from the same Illinois judgment was denied. Gannon v. American Airlines, 251 F.2d 476, 482 (10th Cir.1957) (2–1 decision) (judgment "not open to collateral attack in this proceeding upon the ground of fraud not going to the jurisdiction of the court"), vacated per stipulation, 251 F.2d 486 (10th Cir.1958).

carelessness. See generally 11 Wright, Miller & Kane §§ 2857–2866. In appropriate cases, however, it is the preferred means of giving relief from judgment, being the most direct and orderly technique.

2. If adequate relief from judgment is unavailable by motion because of any applicable limitations on use of such motion, a person may properly bring an independent suit against the judgment-holder to nullify or to enjoin the enforcement of the judgment. The essence here is a separate claim, but one aimed directly at the prior judgment. The suit is preferably, but not necessarily, brought in the rendering court. An example, which shows the difficulty of definition, comes when Britton alleges extrinsic fraud to obtain relief from judgment by equitable counterclaim or defense—given the ground for relief, this would probably equate to an independent suit under the traditional classification, according to Restatement (Second) of Judgments § 80 cmt. a, reporter's note (1982).

3. If someone in a subsequent action relies on a prior judgment as a basis for claim or defense (as where the plaintiff sues upon the judgment to enforce it or where the defendant pleads res judicata), and if adequate relief from judgment is not available and more convenient by another procedural technique, then the other party may properly launch a collateral attack on the prior judgment to prevent its use. The term "collateral attack" is used in distinction to a "direct attack," which comes as a challenge to a judgment in a proceeding brought specially for that purpose. A tricky example is Bruce Marshall's unsuccessful attack upon Lockhead's use of the prior judgment as a defense against recovery of land—given the main objective of the subsequent action, this would probably be a collateral attack in traditional terms, according to id. ch. 5 introductory note, at 141–42.

In brief, direct attacks in the form of motions and independent suits for relief from judgment have traditionally been limited to cases of extraordinary injustice, although not quite as limited as collateral attack with its focus on jurisdiction and opportunity to be heard.

Notice that all three of the preceding illustrative cases involved an attack on a default judgment. In nondefault situations, res judicata (and waiver) may work to foreclose attack by any of these techniques. Such concerns are the focus of the next Section.

SECTION 4. "JURISDICTION TO DETERMINE JURISDICTION"—JURISDICTIONAL FINDINGS AS RES JUDICATA

Affirmative rulings on jurisdiction can preclude the parties from attacking the resultant judgment on that ground in subsequent litigation. The impact of this so-called jurisdiction to determine jurisdiction doctrine is a bit shocking upon first impression. After all, seemingly implicit in the concept of due process embodied in the Fifth and Fourteenth Amendments of the U.S. Constitution is the principle that one cannot be bound by a judgment of a court that lacked jurisdiction. This principle would seem to imply both that such a judgment cannot be entered against the person or the person's property and also that the judgment will not be enforced or recognized as a valid judgment would be. The fact is, however, that such a validity principle does not exist.

Baldwin v. Iowa State Traveling Men's Association

Supreme Court of the United States, 1931.
283 U.S. 522, 51 S.Ct. 517.

■ MR. JUSTICE ROBERTS delivered the opinion of the Court.

A writ of certiorari was granted herein to review the affirmance by the Circuit Court of Appeals of a judgment for respondent rendered by the District Court for Southern Iowa. The action was upon the record of a judgment rendered in favor of the petitioner against the respondent in the United States District Court for Western Missouri.[g]

The defense was lack of jurisdiction of the person of the respondent in the court which entered the judgment. After hearing, in which a jury was waived, this defense was sustained and the action dismissed. The first suit was begun in a Missouri state court and removed to the District Court. Respondent appeared specially and moved to quash and dismiss for want of service. The court quashed the service, but refused to dismiss. An alias summons was issued and returned served, whereupon it again appeared specially, moved to set aside the service, quash the return, and dismiss the case for want of jurisdiction of its person. After a hearing on affidavits and briefs, the motion was overruled, with leave to plead within thirty days. No plea having been filed within that period, the cause proceeded and judgment was entered for the amount claimed. Respondent did not move to set aside the judgment nor sue out a writ of error.

The ground of the motion made in the first suit is the same as that relied on as a defense to this one, namely, that the respondent is an Iowa corporation, that it never was present in Missouri, and that the person served with process in the latter State was not such an agent that service on him constituted a service on the corporation. The petitioner objected to proof of these matters, asserting that the defense constituted a collateral attack and a retrial of an issue settled in the first suit. The overruling of this objection and the resulting judgment for respondent are assigned as error.

The petitioner suggests that Article IV, Section 1 of the Constitution forbade the retrial of the question determined on respondent's motion in the Missouri District Court; but the full faith and credit required by that

---

[g] On the option of registration of federal judgments, which became available in 1948, see supra p. 510.

clause is not involved, since neither of the courts concerned was a state court. (Compare Cooper v. Newell, 173 U.S. 555, 567,[h] 19 S.Ct. 506; Supreme Lodge, Knights of Pythias v. Meyer, 265 U.S. 30, 33,[i] 44 S.Ct. 432.) The respondent, on the other hand, insists that to deprive it of the defense which it made in the court below, of lack of jurisdiction over it by the Missouri District Court, would be to deny the due process guaranteed by the Fourteenth Amendment; but there is involved in that doctrine no right to litigate the same question twice (Chicago Life Ins. Co. v. Cherry, 244 U.S. 25, 37 S.Ct. 492; compare York v. Texas, 137 U.S. 15, 11 S.Ct. 9).

The substantial matter for determination is whether the judgment amounts to res judicata on the question of the jurisdiction of the court which rendered it over the person of the respondent. It is of no moment that the appearance was a special one expressly saving any submission to such jurisdiction. That fact would be important upon appeal from the judgment, and would save the question of the propriety of the court's decision on the matter even though after the motion had been overruled the respondent had proceeded, subject to a reserved objection and exception, to a trial on the merits. Harkness v. Hyde, 98 U.S. 476; [other citations omitted]. The special appearance gives point to the fact that the respondent entered the Missouri court for the very purpose of litigating the question of jurisdiction over its person. It had the election not to appear at all. If, in the absence of appearance, the court had proceeded to judgment and the present suit had been brought thereon, respondent could have raised and tried out the issue in the present action, because it would never have had its day in court with respect to jurisdiction. Thompson v. Whitman, 18 Wall. 457; Pennoyer v. Neff, 95 U.S. 714; Hart v. Sansom, 110 U.S. 151, 3 S.Ct. 586; Wetmore v. Karrick, 205 U.S. 141, 27 S.Ct. 434; Bigelow v. Old Dominion Copper Co., 225 U.S. 111, 32 S.Ct. 641; McDonald v. Mabee, 243 U.S. 90, 37 S.Ct. 343. It had also the right to appeal from the decision of the Missouri District Court, as is shown by Harkness v. Hyde, supra, and the other authorities cited. It elected to follow neither of those courses, but, after having been defeated upon full hearing in its contention as to jurisdiction, it took no further steps, and the judgment in question resulted.

Public policy dictates that there be an end of litigation; that those who have contested an issue shall be bound by the result of the contest, and that matters once tried shall be considered forever settled as between the parties. We see no reason why this doctrine should not apply in every case where one voluntarily appears, presents his case and is fully heard, and why he should not, in the absence of fraud, be thereafter concluded by the judgment of the tribunal to which he has submitted his cause.

---

[h] "And the courts of the United States are bound to give to the judgments of the state courts the same faith and credit that the courts of one State are bound to give to the judgments of the courts of her sister States."

[i] "While the judicial proceedings of the federal courts are not within the terms of the constitutional provision, such proceedings, nevertheless, must be accorded the same full faith and credit by state courts as would be required in respect of the judicial proceedings of another State."

. . . .

Reversed [and remanded].

Questions: (14) Would the result have been different if the prior judgment against the respondent had been entered after a general appearance and the issue of personal jurisdiction had not been raised, litigated, or determined?

(15) Should the law that the rendering court would apply or the law of the forum court govern the res judicata effects of jurisdictional findings? What if the prior judgment came from a foreign nation? See Nippon Emo–Trans Co. v. Emo–Trans, Inc., 744 F.Supp. 1215, 1227 (E.D.N.Y.1990) ("the determination of a foreign court as to jurisdiction is to be treated with circumspection").

(16) In a second action a party launches a collateral attack for lack of personal jurisdiction in the first action, and the court sustains or rejects the attack. If in a third action the same question of personal jurisdiction again arises on collateral attack on the first judgment, what result and why? See Arecibo Radio Corp. v. Puerto Rico, 825 F.2d 589 (1st Cir.1987) (second decision has normal issue preclusion effect).

Chicot County Drainage District v. Baxter State Bank

Supreme Court of the United States, 1940.
308 U.S. 371, 60 S.Ct. 317.

■ MR. CHIEF JUSTICE HUGHES delivered the opinion of the Court.

Respondents brought this suit [on July 24, 1937] in the United States District Court for the Western Division of the Eastern District of Arkansas to recover on fourteen bonds of $1,000 each, which had been issued in 1924 by the petitioner, Chicot County Drainage District, organized under statutes of Arkansas, and had been in default since 1932.

In its answer, petitioner pleaded a decree of the same District Court in a proceeding instituted by petitioner to effect a plan of readjustment of its indebtedness under the Act of May 24, 1934, providing for "Municipal–Debt Readjustments". The decree recited that a plan of readjustment had been accepted by the holders of more than two-thirds of the outstanding indebtedness and was fair and equitable; that to consummate the plan and with the approval of the court petitioner had issued and sold new serial bonds to the Reconstruction Finance Corporation in the amount of $193,500 and that these new bonds were valid obligations; that, also with the approval of the court, the Reconstruction Finance Corporation had purchased outstanding obligations of petitioner to the amount of $705,087.06 which had been delivered in exchange for new bonds and canceled; that certain proceeds had been turned over to the clerk of the court and that the disbursing agent had filed his report showing that the Reconstruction Finance Corporation had purchased all the old bonds of petitioner other than the amount of $57,449.30. The decree provided for the application of the amount paid into court to the remaining old obligations of petitioner, that such obligations might be presented within one year, and that unless so presented they should be forever barred from participating in the plan of readjustment or in the fund paid into court. Except for the provision for such presentation, the decree canceled the old bonds and the holders were enjoined from thereafter asserting any claim thereon.

Petitioner pleaded this decree, which was entered in March, 1936, as res judicata. Respondents demurred to the answer. Thereupon the parties stipulated for trial without a jury.

The evidence showed respondents' ownership of the bonds in suit and that respondents had notice of the proceeding for debt readjustment. The record of that proceeding, including the final decree, was introduced. The District Court ruled in favor of respondents and the Circuit Court of Appeals affirmed. 8 Cir., 103 F.2d 847. The decision was placed upon the ground that the decree was void because, subsequent to its entry, this Court in a proceeding relating to a municipal district in Texas had declared the statute under which the District Court had acted to be unconstitutional. Ashton v. Cameron County District, 298 U.S. 513, 56 S.Ct. 892 [(1936)]. In view of the importance of the question we granted certiorari. October 9, 1939. 308 U.S. 532, 60 S.Ct. 84.

. . . .

First. Apart from the contention as to the effect of the later decision as to constitutionality, all the elements necessary to constitute the defense of res judicata are present. It appears that the proceedings in the District Court to bring about a plan of readjustment were conducted in complete conformity to the statute. The Circuit Court of Appeals observed that no question had been raised as to the regularity of the court's action. The answer in the present suit alleged that the plaintiffs (respondents here) had notice of the proceeding and were parties, and the evidence was to the same effect, showing compliance with the statute in that respect. As parties, these bondholders had full opportunity to present any objections to the proceeding, not only as to its regularity, or the fairness of the proposed plan of readjustment, or the propriety of the terms of the decree, but also as to the validity of the statute under which the proceeding was brought and the plan put into effect.[j] Apparently no question of validity was raised and the cause proceeded to decree on the assumption by all parties and the court itself that the statute was valid. There was no attempt to review the decree. If the general principles governing the defense of res judicata are applicable, these bondholders, having the opportunity to raise the question of invalidity, were not the less bound by the decree because they failed to raise it. Cromwell v. County of Sac, 94 U.S. 351, 352; Case v. Beauregard, 101 U.S. 688, 692; Baltimore Steamship Co. v. Phillips, 274 U.S. 316, 319,

[j] The briefs in this case indicate that while other bondholders did appear in the bankruptcy proceeding, the respondents themselves never appeared in person or by attorney. The court below likewise observed this fact, 103 F.2d at 848.

325, 47 S.Ct. 600, 601, 604; Grubb v. Public Utilities Commission, 281 U.S. 470, 479, 50 S.Ct. 374, 378.

Second. The argument is pressed that the District Court was sitting as a court of bankruptcy, with the limited jurisdiction conferred by statute, and that, as the statute was later declared to be invalid, the District Court was without jurisdiction to entertain the proceeding and hence its decree is open to collateral attack. We think the argument untenable. The lower federal courts are all courts of limited jurisdiction, that is, with only the jurisdiction which Congress has prescribed. But none the less they are courts with authority, when parties are brought before them in accordance with the requirements of due process, to determine whether or not they have jurisdiction to entertain the cause and for this purpose to construe and apply the statute under which they are asked to act. Their determinations of such questions, while open to direct review, may not be assailed collaterally.

. . . This rule applies equally to the decrees of the District Court sitting in bankruptcy, that is, purporting to act under a statute of Congress passed in the exercise of the bankruptcy power. The court has the authority to pass upon its own jurisdiction and its decree sustaining jurisdiction against attack, while open to direct review, is res judicata in a collateral action. Stoll v. Gottlieb, 305 U.S. 165, 171, 172, 59 S.Ct. 134, 137.

Whatever the contention as to jurisdiction may be, whether it is that the boundaries of a valid statute have been transgressed, or that the statute itself is invalid, the question of jurisdiction is still one for judicial determination. If the contention is one as to validity, the question is to be considered in the light of the standing of the party who seeks to raise the question and of its particular application. In the present instance it is suggested that the situation of petitioner, Chicot County Drainage District, is different from that of the municipal district before the court in the Ashton case. Petitioner contends that it is not a political subdivision of the State of Arkansas but an agent of the property owners within the District. See Drainage District No. 7 of Poinsett County v. Hutchins, 184 Ark. 521, 42 S.W.2d 996. We do not refer to that phase of the case as now determinative but merely as illustrating the sort of question which the District Court might have been called upon to resolve had the validity of the Act of Congress in the present application been raised. As the question of validity was one which had to be determined by a judicial decision, if determined at all, no reason appears why it should not be regarded as determinable by the District Court like any other question affecting its jurisdiction. There can be no doubt that if the question of the constitutionality of the statute had actually been raised and decided by the District Court in the proceeding to effect a plan of debt readjustment in accordance with the statute, that determination would have been final save as it was open to direct review upon appeal. Stoll v. Gottlieb, supra.

The remaining question is simply whether respondents, having failed to raise the question in the proceeding to which they were parties and in which they could have raised it and had it finally determined, were privileged to remain quiet and raise it in a subsequent suit. Such a view is contrary to the well-settled principle that res judicata may be pleaded as a bar, not only as respects matters actually presented to sustain or defeat the right asserted in the earlier proceeding, "but also as respects any other available matter which might have been presented to that end". Grubb v. Public Utilities Commission, supra; Cromwell v. County of Sac, supra.

The judgment is reversed and the cause is remanded to the District Court with direction to dismiss the complaint.

Reversed.

Questions: (17) Would the rule of Chicot—that lack of subject-matter jurisdiction generally cannot be raised on collateral attack even though it was not actually litigated in the prior action—apply if a prior judgment were invoked merely for issue preclusion purposes as to a litigated and determined issue involved in the merits?

(18) Would the rule of Chicot apply if a prior judgment were based on a complete default by all defendants? See Restatement (Second) of Judgments § 12 cmt. f (1982) (no).

(19) A federal statute provides that during the pendency of bankruptcy proceedings in a federal court, the state courts shall have no jurisdiction to foreclose a mortgage on the land of a farmer. In a contested state-court proceeding, at a time when federal bankruptcy proceedings are pending, the state court erroneously assumes, or decides, that it has jurisdiction and decrees foreclosure of the mortgage of *K*'s farm. The property is sold to the mortgagee at a sheriff's foreclosure sale, and the sheriff evicts *K*. In a new action in the same state court, *K* sues the mortgagee-purchaser for cancellation of the sheriff's deed and restoration of possession. Is the foreclosure decree subject to attack in this new proceeding? See Kalb v. Feuerstein, 308 U.S. 433, 60 S.Ct. 343 (1940) (yes), which is generalized by Restatement (Second) of Judgments § 12 (1982) (providing exceptions when "(1) The subject matter of the action was so plainly beyond the court's jurisdiction that its entertaining the action was a manifest abuse of authority; or (2) Allowing the judgment to stand would substantially infringe the authority of another tribunal or agency of government; or (3) The judgment was rendered by a court lacking capability to make an adequately informed determination of a question concerning its own jurisdiction and as a matter of procedural fairness the party seeking to avoid the judgment should have opportunity belatedly to attack the court's subject matter jurisdiction."), which in turn is criticized by Karen Nelson Moore, Collateral Attack on Subject Matter Jurisdiction: A Critique of the Restatement (Second) of Judgments, 66 Cornell L.Rev. 534 (1981).

DURFEE v. DUKE, 375 U.S. 106, 84 S.Ct. 242 (1963). Durfee, a Nebraska citizen, sued Duke, a Missouri citizen, in a Nebraska state court to quiet title to certain bottom land situated on the Missouri River, the main channel of which forms the boundary between Nebraska and Missouri. The Nebraska court had jurisdiction only if the land in question was in Nebraska; whether the land was Nebraska land depended entirely upon the factual question of whether a shift in the river's course had been caused by avulsion or accretion; when the change in the channel of a river is sudden (avulsion), the state boundary remains as before, but when the change is gradual (accretion), the boundary moves with the channel. Duke appeared in the Nebraska court and fully litigated the issues, explicitly contesting the court's jurisdiction. The court found the land to be in Nebraska by application of the rule of avulsion, and it ordered that title to the land be quieted in Durfee. On appeal, the Supreme Court of Nebraska affirmed. Duke did not petition for certiorari.

Two months later Duke sued in a Missouri state court to quiet title to the same land, alleging it to be in Missouri. Durfee removed to the federal district court by reason of diversity of citizenship. The district court, although expressing the view that on the evidence the land was in Missouri, found for Durfee on the ground that the Nebraska judgment was entitled to full faith and credit. On appeal, the Eighth Circuit reversed. The Supreme Court of the United States granted certiorari.

The Supreme Court in turn reversed the court of appeals, holding that the Nebraska judgment was entitled to full faith and credit when the jurisdictional issue had been fully and fairly litigated by the parties and finally determined in the Nebraska courts and when Nebraska would therefore not permit collateral attack. Justice Stewart, for the Court, said that the general rule of finality of litigated jurisdictional determinations, unambiguously established in the Baldwin case with respect to jurisdiction over the person, was "no different when the claim is made that the original forum did not have jurisdiction over the subject matter."

Questions: (20) Did this case really involve a question of subject-matter jurisdiction? Compare Restatement (Second) of Judgments §§ 10, 12 (1982), with Restatement (Second) of Conflict of Laws §§ 96–97 (1971) (amended 1988).

(21) In what circumstances should lack of opportunity to be heard survive as a ground for collateral attack?

(22) If the Nebraska court had dismissed for lack of jurisdiction because it had found the land to be in Missouri, could Duke have used this finding against Durfee in the later action in Missouri? See Michael J. Edney, Comment, Preclusive Abstention: Issue Preclusion and Jurisdictional Dismissals After Ruhrgas, 68 U.Chi. L.Rev. 193 (2001) (a finding of no jurisdiction does not produce a valid judgment and so should not be binding in another action, except to defeat jurisdiction in any attempt to sue again in a court where the very same jurisdictional issue arises).

SECTION 5. "JURISDICTION TO DETERMINE JURISDICTION"—POWER TO PUNISH DISOBEDIENCE OF IMPROPER COURT ORDER

The other side of the collateral attack coin is the so-called collateral bar rule, which holds that in subsequent litigation one cannot correct errors in a valid judgment, no matter how important or obvious the error. But surely, in the tradition of civil disobedience, one can violate any seriously improper court order, and still avoid punishment if one proves to have been in the right? No. Although for centuries one could argue fundamental error in the order when the court tried later to punish disobedience, today that is no longer allowed.

United States v. United Mine Workers

Supreme Court of the United States, 1947.
330 U.S. 258, 67 S.Ct. 677.

[In October 1946 the United States was in possession of, and operating, most of the nation's bituminous coal mines pursuant to an Executive Order of the President issued upon his determination that labor disputes were interrupting the production of coal necessary for the operation of the economy during the transition from war to peace. Terms and conditions of employment were controlled by an agreement between Secretary of the Interior Krug, as Coal Mines Administrator, and John L. Lewis, as president of the United Mine Workers. A dispute arose as to the union's power to terminate the Krug–Lewis agreement, and Lewis gave notice to Krug on November 15 of termination as of November 20, circulating to the mine workers a copy of his letter to Krug for their "official information."

[On November 18 the United States, contending that Lewis and the union had no power unilaterally to terminate the agreement, filed a complaint against them in the United States District Court for the District of Columbia, seeking a declaratory judgment to that effect and a temporary restraining order and preliminary injunction enjoining the defendants from encouraging the mine workers to strike and from taking any action that would interfere with the court's jurisdiction and its determination of the case. Jurisdiction was based on 28 U.S.C. § 1345. The court immediately issued without notice a temporary restraining order, to expire on November 27 when it would hold the hearing on a preliminary injunction. The complaint and restraining order were served on the defendants on November 18. A gradual walkout by the miners commenced that same day, and by midnight of November 20, consistent with the miners' "no contract, no work" policy, a full-blown strike was in progress. Mines furnishing most of the nation's bituminous coal were idle.

[On November 21 the United States, alleging a willful violation of the restraining order, filed a petition for a rule to show cause why the defendants should not be punished for contempt. The rule issued. On November 25, its return date, the defendants denied the "jurisdiction" of the court to issue the restraining order and subsequently moved to discharge the rule to show cause. They contended that the Norris–LaGuardia Act prohibited the granting of injunctive relief. Section 4 of the Act, 29 U.S.C. § 104, provided that "[n]o court of the United States shall have jurisdiction to issue any restraining order or temporary or permanent injunction in any case involving or growing out of any labor dispute" against various specified acts, including what the defendants had done. It seemed apparent that the Act would apply if the dispute were between the defendants and a private employer, but the United States urged that the Act did not apply to the government as employer. On November 27 the district judge extended the restraining order, and on November 29 he overruled the motion to discharge the rule and held that the restraining order was not affected by the Norris–LaGuardia Act. The bench trial for contempt proceeded, and both defendants were found guilty of both criminal and civil contempt. On December 4 Lewis was fined $10,000 and the union $3,500,000, without any apportionment between criminal and civil contempt. On the same day the judge issued a preliminary injunction in terms similar to those of the restraining order, effective until termination of the case.

[On December 5 Lewis sent the miners back to work. On the same day the defendants appealed to the court of appeals, and the judgments of contempt were stayed pending appeal. The United States asked for certiorari under 28 U.S.C. § 1254(1), which allows either party to do so prior to judgment in the court of appeals, and next the defendants also sought certiorari. Certiorari was granted, "[p]rompt settlement of this case being in the public interest." The Supreme Court rendered decision on March 6, 1947.]

■ MR. CHIEF JUSTICE VINSON delivered the opinion of the Court.

[Part I of the opinion held that the Norris–LaGuardia Act did not apply to a labor dispute with the government.]

II.

Although we have held that the Norris–LaGuardia Act did not render injunctive relief beyond the jurisdiction of the District Court, there are alternative grounds which support the power of the District Court to punish violations of its orders as criminal contempt.

. . . .

In the case before us, the District Court had the power to preserve existing conditions while it was determining its own authority to grant injunctive relief. The defendants, in making their private determination of the law, acted at their peril. Their disobedience is punishable as criminal contempt.

Although a different result would follow were the question of jurisdiction frivolous and not substantial, such contention would be idle here. The applicability of the Norris–LaGuardia Act to the United States in a case such as this had not previously received judicial consideration, and both the language of the Act and its legislative history indicated the substantial nature of the problem with which the District Court was faced.

Proceeding further, we find impressive authority for the proposition that an order issued by a court with jurisdiction over the subject matter and person must be obeyed by the parties until it is reversed by orderly and proper proceedings. This is true without regard even for the constitutionality of the Act under which the order is issued. In Howat v. Kansas, 258 U.S. 181, 189–90, 42 S.Ct. 277, 280–81 (1922), this Court said:

> "An injunction duly issuing out of a court of general jurisdiction with equity powers upon pleadings properly invoking its action, and served upon persons made parties therein and within the jurisdiction, must be obeyed by them however erroneous the action of the court may be, even if the error be in the assumption of the validity of a seeming but void law going to the merits of the case. It is for the court of first instance to determine the question of the validity of the law, and until its decision is reversed for error by orderly review, either by itself or by a higher court, its orders based on its decision are to be respected, and disobedience of them is contempt of its lawful authority, to be punished."

Violations of an order are punishable as criminal contempt even though the order is set aside on appeal, Worden v. Searls, 121 U.S. 14, 7 S.Ct. 814 (1887), or though the basic action has become moot, Gompers v. Buck's Stove & Range Co., 221 U.S. 418, 31 S.Ct. 492 (1911).

We insist upon the same duty of obedience where, as here, the subject matter of the suit, as well as the parties, was properly before the court; where the elements of federal jurisdiction were clearly shown; and where the authority of the court of first instance to issue an order ancillary to the main suit depended upon a statute, the scope and applicability of which were subject to substantial doubt. The District Court on November 29 affirmatively decided that the Norris–LaGuardia Act was of no force in this case and that injunctive relief was therefore authorized. Orders outstanding or issued after that date were to be obeyed until they expired or were set aside by appropriate proceedings, appellate or otherwise. Convictions for criminal contempt intervening before that time may stand.

It does not follow, of course, that simply because a defendant may be punished for criminal contempt for disobedience of an order later set aside on appeal, that the plaintiff in the action may profit by way of a fine imposed in a simultaneous proceeding for civil contempt based upon a violation of the same order. The right to remedial relief falls with an injunction which events prove was erroneously issued, [citations omitted]; and a fortiori when the injunction or restraining order was beyond the jurisdiction of the court. . . . If the Norris–LaGuardia Act were applicable in this case, the conviction for civil contempt would be reversed in its entirety.

[The Court then rejected the contention that procedural errors required reversal of the contempt judgments. The defendants urged that the criminal and civil contempts should not have been heard together, and that they had been deprived of their rights under Federal Rule of Criminal Procedure 42. The Court found that the defendants had been accorded all the rights owing to defendants in criminal contempt proceedings. The Court conceded that it might be "the better practice" to try criminal contempt alone, but found no substantial prejudice requiring reversal.

[Finally, the Court ordered the $10,000 fine imposed on Lewis to stand as punishment for criminal contempt, but found that $3,500,000 was excessive as to the union and instead imposed a $700,000 fine for criminal contempt with the balance of $2,800,000 for civil contempt being conditioned on the defendant's failure to purge itself within five days by publicly withdrawing its notice of termination.]

■ [Only Justices Reed and Burton concurred fully in the Chief Justice's opinion. Professor Chafee called this case "a masterpiece of judicial logrolling." Zechariah Chafee, Jr., Some Problems of Equity 366 (1950). The various separate opinions are omitted.

[JUSTICES FRANKFURTER and JACKSON separately believed that the Norris–LaGuardia Act applied to the government and forbade the injunction. But they acquiesced in part II of the opinion, justifying the reduced punishment by criminal contempt for violation of an order made to preserve the status quo while the court was determining its own jurisdiction to grant injunctive relief. This made a shaky majority of five for resort to criminal contempt, which the Chief Justice plainly wanted.

[For the ultimate combination of a sanction partly criminal and partly civil, the Chief Justice needed the support of JUSTICES BLACK and DOUGLAS. Those two agreed that the Norris–LaGuardia Act was inapplicable and that civil contempt sanctions in the full amounts were therefore authorized. But feeling that a criminal contempt sanction here was inconsistent with the principle that in contempt proceedings courts should never exercise more than "the least possible power adequate to the end proposed," they found it unnecessary to deal with the problems of part II.

[JUSTICES MURPHY and RUTLEDGE in separate opinions dissented all the way, noting that the rule of part II authorizing punishment for disobedience of orders issued in excess of "jurisdiction" was contrary to the long-settled course of decision. The several opinions took up 128 pages of the U.S. Reports.]

Question: (23) As counsel for John L. Lewis, how would you have advised him before this decision? How would you have advised him if the substance of this decision were already on the books?

Walker v. City of Birmingham

Supreme Court of the United States, 1967.
388 U.S. 307, 87 S.Ct. 1824.

[In the Easter season of 1963, Rev. Martin Luther King, Jr., and a group of Birmingham, Alabama, ministers organized a campaign featuring peaceful parades and picketing to protest racial segregation. A Birmingham ordinance required that public demonstrations be licensed by the city commission, which could refuse to grant a permit only if "in its judgment the public welfare, peace, safety, health, decency, good order, morals or convenience" so required. Two attempts to obtain a permit from Commissioner "Bull" Connor were rebuffed,[k] on April 3 and April 5, but no formal written application was submitted to the full three-person commission as the ordinance stipulated.

[On Wednesday, April 10, city officials sought and obtained from a state circuit court an ex parte temporary injunction enjoining Dr. King and specified others from participating in or encouraging further mass protests without a permit. Dr. King and others who had been served with copies of the writ of injunction held a press conference the next day, declaring their intention to disobey the injunction because it was "raw tyranny under the guise of maintaining law and order."

[On Good Friday, April 12, Dr. King and his followers defied the injunction by holding a parade of about 50 or 60 persons with a crowd of 1000 to 1500 onlookers standing by, clapping and shouting. On Easter Sunday, a crowd of 1500 to 2000 congregated. A group of about 50 started down the sidewalk two abreast. Some 300 or 400 of the onlookers followed in a crowd that occupied the entire width of the street and overflowed onto the sidewalks. Violence occurred. Members of the crowd threw rocks, which injured a newspaperman and damaged a police motorcycle.

[A week later Dr. King and other leaders were convicted by the state circuit court of criminal contempt and given the statutory maximum sentence of five days in jail and a $50 fine. The judge refused to consider contentions that the injunction and the ordinance were unconstitutional and that the ordinance had previously been administered in an arbitrary and discriminatory manner, ruling that because there had been no motion to dissolve the injunction, and no attempt to comply by applying for a permit, the only issues were whether there was jurisdiction to issue the injunction and whether the defendants had knowingly violated it. The Supreme Court of Alabama affirmed, citing Howat v. Kansas, 258 U.S. 181, 42 S.Ct. 277 (1922). The Supreme Court of the United States granted certiorari.]

■ MR. JUSTICE STEWART delivered the opinion of the Court.

[The opinion quoted the same passage from Howat v. Kansas as did the Court in the United Mine Workers case, and continued:]

The rule of state law accepted and approved in Howat v. Kansas is consistent with the rule of law followed by the federal courts.[5]

---

[k] A witness at the contempt hearing testified that Commissioner Connor said: "No, you will not get a permit in Birmingham, Alabama, to picket. I will picket you over to the City Jail." For a full treatment of the factual background of this case, see Alan F. Westin & Barry Mahoney, The Trial of Martin Luther King (1974); David Benjamin Oppenheimer, Martin Luther King, Walker v. City of Birmingham, and the Letter from Birmingham Jail, 26 U.C.Davis L.Rev. 791 (1993).

[5] [In a footnote here, after citing a number of cases, the majority made its lone citation to the United Mine Workers case.—Ed.]

In the present case, however, we are asked to hold that this rule of law, upon which the Alabama courts relied, was constitutionally impermissible. We are asked to say that the Constitution compelled Alabama to allow the petitioners to violate this injunction, to organize and engage in these mass street parades and demonstrations, without any previous effort on their part to have the injunction dissolved or modified, or any attempt to secure a parade permit in accordance with its terms. Whatever the limits of Howat v. Kansas,[6] we cannot accept the petitioners' contentions in the circumstances of this case.

Without question the state court that issued the injunction had, as a court of equity, jurisdiction over the petitioners and over the subject matter of the controversy. And this is not a case where the injunction was transparently invalid or had only a frivolous pretense to validity. We have consistently recognized the strong interest of state and local governments in regulating the use of their streets and other public places. Cox v. New Hampshire, 312 U.S. 569, 61 S.Ct. 762; Poulos v. New Hampshire, 345 U.S. 395, 73 S.Ct. 760. [Other citations omitted.] When protest takes the form of mass demonstrations, parades, or picketing on public streets and sidewalks, the free passage of traffic and the prevention of public disorder and violence become important objects of legitimate state concern. . . .

The generality of the language contained in the Birmingham parade ordinance upon which the injunction was based would unquestionably raise substantial constitutional issues concerning some of its provisions. [Citations omitted.] The petitioners, however, did not even attempt to apply to the Alabama courts for an authoritative construction of the ordinance. Had they done so, those courts might have given the licensing authority granted in the ordinance a narrow and precise scope, as did the New Hampshire courts in Cox v. New Hampshire and Poulos v. New Hampshire, both supra. [Other citations omitted.] Here, just as in Cox and Poulos, it could not be assumed that this ordinance was void on its face.

The breadth and vagueness of the injunction itself would also unquestionably be subject to substantial constitutional question. But the way to raise that question was to apply to the Alabama courts to have the injunction modified or dissolved. The injunction in all events clearly prohibited mass parading without a permit, and the evidence shows that the petitioners fully understood that prohibition when they violated it.

The petitioners also claim that they were free to disobey the injunction because the parade ordinance on which it was based had been administered

[6] In In re Green, 369 U.S. 689, 82 S.Ct. 1114 [(1962)], the petitioner was convicted of criminal contempt for violating a labor injunction issued by an Ohio court. Relying on the preemptive command of the federal labor law, the Court held that the state courts were required to hear Green's claim that the state court was *without jurisdiction* to issue the injunction. The petitioner in Green, unlike the petitioners here, had attempted to challenge the validity of the injunction *before* violating it by promptly applying to the issuing court for an order vacating the injunction. The petitioner in Green had further offered to prove that the court issuing the injunction had agreed to its violation as an appropriate means of testing its validity. [13D Wright, Miller, Cooper & Freer § 3537, at 22, observes that the briefs in Green made the point that state law did not permit appellate review of this temporary injunction.—Ed.]

in the past in an arbitrary and discriminatory fashion. In support of this claim they sought to introduce evidence that, a few days before the injunction issued, requests for permits to picket had been made to a member of the city commission. One request had been rudely rebuffed, and this same official had later made clear that he was without power to grant the permit alone, since the issuance of such permits was the responsibility of the entire city commission. Assuming the truth of this proffered evidence, it does not follow that the parade ordinance was void on its face. The petitioners, moreover, did not apply for a permit either to the commission itself or to any commissioner after the injunction issued. Had they done so, and had the permit been refused, it is clear that their claim of arbitrary or discriminatory administration of the ordinance would have been considered by the state circuit court upon a motion to dissolve the injunction.

This case would arise in quite a different constitutional posture if the petitioners, before disobeying the injunction, had challenged it in the Alabama courts, and had been met with delay or frustration of their constitutional claims. But there is no showing that such would have been the fate of a timely motion to modify or dissolve the injunction. There was an interim of two days between the issuance of the injunction and the Good Friday march. The petitioners gave absolutely no explanation of why they did not make some application to the state court during that period. The injunction had issued ex parte; if the court had been presented with the petitioners' contentions, it might well have dissolved or at least modified its order in some respects. If it had not done so, Alabama procedure would have provided for an expedited process of appellate review. It cannot be presumed that the Alabama courts would have ignored the petitioners' constitutional claims. Indeed, these contentions were accepted in another case by an Alabama appellate court that struck down on direct review the conviction under this very ordinance of one of these same petitioners.[13]

. . . .

The rule of law that Alabama followed in this case reflects a belief that in the fair administration of justice no man can be judge in his own case, however exalted his station, however righteous his motives, and irrespective of his race, color, politics, or religion. This Court cannot hold that the petitioners were constitutionally free to ignore all the procedures of the law and carry their battle to the streets. One may sympathize with the petitioners' impatient commitment to their cause. But respect for judicial process is a small price to pay for the civilizing hand of law, which alone can give abiding meaning to constitutional freedom.

Affirmed.

. . . .

■ MR. CHIEF JUSTICE WARREN, whom MR. JUSTICE BRENNAN and MR. JUSTICE FORTAS join, dissenting.

---

[13] Shuttlesworth v. City of Birmingham, 43 Ala.App. 68, 180 So.2d 114. The case is presently pending on certiorari review in the Alabama Supreme Court.

. . . .

These facts lend no support to the court's charges that petitioners were presuming to act as judges in their own case, or that they had a disregard for the judicial process. They did not flee the jurisdiction or refuse to appear in the Alabama courts. Having violated the injunction, they promptly submitted themselves to the courts to test the constitutionality of the injunction and the ordinance it parroted. They were in essentially the same position as persons who challenge the constitutionality of a statute by violating it, and then defend the ensuing criminal prosecution on constitutional grounds. It has never been thought that violation of a statute indicated such a disrespect for the legislature that the violator always must be punished even if the statute was unconstitutional. On the contrary, some cases have required that persons seeking to challenge the constitutionality of a statute first violate it to establish their standing to sue. Indeed, it shows no disrespect for law to violate a statute on the ground that it is unconstitutional and then to submit one's case to the courts with the willingness to accept the penalty if the statute is held to be valid.

The Court concedes that "[t]he generality of the language contained in the Birmingham parade ordinance upon which the injunction was based would unquestionably raise substantial constitutional issues concerning some of its provisions." . . . That concession is well-founded but minimal. I believe it is patently unconstitutional on its face. Our decisions have consistently held that picketing and parading are means of expression protected by the First Amendment, and that the right to picket or parade may not be subjected to the unfettered discretion of local officials. . . . The unconstitutionality of the ordinance is compounded, of course, when there is convincing evidence that the officials have in fact used their power to deny permits to organizations whose views they dislike. . . . The only circumstance that the court can find to justify anything other than a per curiam reversal is that Commissioner Connor had the foresight to have the unconstitutional ordinance included in an ex parte injunction issued without notice or hearing or any showing that it was impossible to have notice or a hearing . . . . This injunction was such potent magic that it transformed the command of an unconstitutional statute into an impregnable barrier, challengeable only in what likely would have been protracted legal proceedings and entirely superior in the meantime even to the United States Constitution.

I do not believe that giving this Court's seal of approval to such a gross misuse of the judicial process is likely to lead to greater respect for the law any more than it is likely to lead to greater protection for First Amendment freedoms. The ex parte temporary injunction has a long and odious history in this country, and its susceptibility to misuse is all too apparent from the facts of the case. As a weapon against strikes, it proved so effective in the hands of judges friendly to employers that Congress was forced to take the drastic step of removing from federal district courts the jurisdiction to issue injunctions in labor disputes. The labor injunction fell into disrepute largely because it was abused in precisely the same way that the injunctive power was abused in this case. Judges who were not sympathetic to the union cause commonly issued, without notice or hearing, broad restraining orders addressed to large numbers of persons and forbidding them to engage in acts that were either legally permissible or, if illegal, that could better have been left to the regular course of criminal prosecution. The injunctions might later be dissolved, but in the meantime strikes would be crippled because the occasion on which concerted activity might have been effective had passed. Such injunctions, so long discredited as weapons against concerted labor activities, have now been given new life by this Court as weapons against the exercise of First Amendment freedoms. Respect for the courts and for judicial process was not increased by the history of the labor injunction.

. . . .

It is not necessary to question the continuing validity of the holding in Howat v. Kansas, however, to demonstrate that neither it nor the Mine Workers case supports the holding of the majority in this case. In Howat the subpoena and injunction were issued to enable the Kansas Court of Industrial Relations to determine an underlying labor dispute. In the Mine Workers case, the District Court issued a temporary anti-strike injunction to preserve existing conditions during the time it took to decide whether it had authority to grant the Government relief in a complex and difficult action of enormous importance to the national economy. In both cases the orders were of questionable legality, but in both cases they were reasonably necessary to enable the court or administrative tribunal to decide an underlying controversy of considerable importance before it at the time. This case involves an entirely different situation. The Alabama Circuit Court did not issue this temporary injunction to preserve existing conditions while it proceeded to decide some underlying dispute. There was no underlying dispute before it, and the court in practical effect merely added a judicial signature to a preexisting criminal ordinance. Just as the court had no need to issue the injunction to preserve its ability to decide some underlying dispute, the city had no need of an injunction to impose a criminal penalty for demonstrating on the streets without a permit. The ordinance already accomplished that. In point of fact, there is only one apparent reason why the city sought this injunction and why the court issued it: to make it possible to punish petitioners for contempt rather than for violating the ordinance, and thus to immunize the unconstitutional statute and its unconstitutional application from any attack. I regret that this strategy has been so successful.

It is not necessary in this case to decide precisely what limits should be set to the Mine Workers doctrine in cases involving violations of the First Amendment. Whatever the scope of that doctrine, it plainly was not intended to give a State the power to nullify the United States Constitution by the simple process of incorporating its unconstitutional criminal statutes into judicial decrees. I respectfully dissent.

■ [The dissenting opinions of JUSTICES DOUGLAS and BRENNAN, each joined in by all of the dissenting Justices, are omitted.]

Martin Luther King, Jr., in the Birmingham jail, serving the contempt sentence in early November of 1967—photographed by Wyatt Tee Walker, his cellmate and one of the jailed ministers (AP/Wide World Photos)

SHUTTLESWORTH v. CITY OF BIRMINGHAM, 394 U.S. 147, 89 S.Ct. 935 (1969). Rev. Fred L. Shuttlesworth, one of the ministers accompanying Dr. King in the demonstrations described in Walker v. City of Birmingham and later one of the petitioners in that case, was arrested and convicted upon jury trial of violating the ordinance there involved by leading the march on April 12, 1963. The state circuit judge sentenced him to 90 days' imprisonment at hard labor, and to an additional 48 days in default of payment of a $75 fine and $24 costs.

The Alabama Court of Appeals overturned the conviction, but the Supreme Court of Alabama later reinstated it. The latter court rejected the contention that the ordinance was an unconstitutional censorship or prior restraint upon the exercise of First Amendment freedoms. The court did so by construing the ordinance so as to limit the applicability of its broad language to protection of the public safety and convenience in the use of the streets, and thus to save it from being unconstitutional on its face. The court also ruled that there was nothing in the record tending to show that the ordinance had been applied in other than a fair and nondiscriminatory fashion.

The Supreme Court of the United States granted certiorari. Then, in an opinion by Justice Stewart, who had written the majority opinion in Walker v. City of Birmingham, the Court unanimously reversed, holding that the ordinance "as it was written" was unconstitutional and that a person could ignore it with impunity. In light of past understanding of and practice under the ordinance, it could not be saved by narrow and precise construction. He called the Alabama court's construction "a remarkable job of plastic surgery upon the face of the ordinance" and said that it "would have taken extraordinary clairvoyance for anyone to perceive that this language meant what the Supreme Court of Alabama was destined to find that it meant more than four years later."

UNITED STATES v. RYAN, 402 U.S. 530, 91 S.Ct. 1580 (1971). This was a case holding, in accordance with Cobbledick v. United States, infra p. 1264, that denial of a motion to quash a subpoena duces tecum commanding production of documents before a federal grand jury is not appealable.

In the course of decision, the Court pointed out that one who claims a subpoena is unduly burdensome or otherwise unlawful may refuse to comply, and then litigate those questions in the event contempt proceedings are brought against him: if his contentions are rejected in the trial court, they will then be ripe for appellate review; if on appeal his contentions are upheld, any contempt adjudication will then fall. At this point in the opinion the Court dropped the following footnote: "Walker v. Birmingham . . . is not to the contrary. Our holding that the claims there sought to be asserted were not open on review of petitioners' contempt convictions was based upon the availability of review of those claims at an earlier stage."

Question: (24) Imagine a trial court has imposed criminal and civil contempt sanctions on someone for disobedience of what it believed to be its proper order. On appeal, the reasonably contestable question of the propriety of the order comes before the appellate court. That court finds the order to be beyond the trial court's power, but the circumstances are such that the criminal contempt punishment could stand under the collateral bar rule—that is, under the UMW–Walker approach that the Court explained in Ryan. Should the appellate court remand for reconsideration of the punishment in light of the finding of the order's impropriety? See Donovan v. City of Dallas, 377 U.S. 408, 84 S.Ct. 1579 (yes), on remand sub nom. City of Dallas v. Brown, 384 S.W.2d 724 (Tex.Civ.App.1964).

MANESS v. MEYERS, 419 U.S. 449, 95 S.Ct. 584 (1975). This was a case holding that a lawyer may not be held in criminal contempt for advising his client, a defendant in a state civil case, not to comply with a subpoena duces tecum that the court refused to quash, or with the court's follow-up order to comply, when the lawyer believed reasonably and in good faith that compliance might tend to incriminate his client in violation of the Fifth Amendment.

In the course of decision, the Court discussed the duty of the client to obey court orders. It began with the "basic proposition" that the "orderly and expeditious administration of justice by the courts requires" the client to comply with all court orders and then pursue review thereof. "Remedies for judicial error may be cumbersome but the injury flowing from an error generally is not irreparable . . . . When a court during trial orders a witness to reveal information, however, a different situation may be presented. Compliance could cause irreparable injury because appellate courts cannot always 'unring the bell' once the information has been released. Subsequent appellate vindication does not necessarily have its ordinary consequence of totally repairing the error." So here, although eventual review of the Fifth Amendment contention might be possible, there was no regular opportunity for review before compliance. And compliance constituted irreparable injury. Thus, the client could refuse to comply, and then raise his constitutional contention in any consequent contempt proceedings: if his contention were eventually upheld, any contempt adjudication would then fall.

Questions: (25) How should the courts construe this "irreparable injury" limitation to requiring pursuit of further review? If irreparable injury means merely feared infringement of a right for some time, the limitation would devour the requirement. So it must mean at least that temporary obedience would permanently and substantially impair a significant right, as subjectively anticipated by the violator and later objectively found on review. But how does that translate into practical application? What would have happened if Dr. King had litigated to the hilt in the Alabama courts until Good Friday, having no success but meeting no "delay or frustration" either, and then he decided that the critical moment had come for the movement and he therefore marched without completing the full course of review? Could he then rely on Maness? Or must he rely solely on the court's mercy in not pursuing and punishing disobedience of an arguably improper court order when the violator had acted with adequate excuse?

(26) In summary, this line of cases authorizes punishment by criminal contempt for the violation of any court order even though that order is judicially determined to have been erroneous, no matter how serious the error, including a constitutional violation or even lack of subject-matter jurisdiction—unless either (a) the violator lacked opportunity to pursue full review of the improper order or lacked such opportunity without incurring "irreparable injury" or (b) the order were subject to collateral attack for lack of personal jurisdiction or notice. Should there be additional exceptions to this power to punish? For example, would it matter if the order were crazy enough to be "transparently invalid"—can the violator ignore such an order with impunity? See In re Providence Journal Co., 820 F.2d 1354 (1st Cir.1987) (en banc, per curiam) (no), cert. dismissed, 485 U.S. 693, 108 S.Ct. 1502 (1988).

PART FIVE

PARTIES

TOPIC A

JOINDER ALTERNATIVES IN COMPLEX LITIGATION

How should society resolve disputes arising from mass torts and other such complex matters? Fixing the bounds on this question is almost as difficult as answering the question. Many fundamentally different kinds of disputes and matters constitute the problem. Nevertheless, the best way to begin may involve contemplating an example of the problem, albeit an extreme example—consider asbestos litigation as described in Alvin B. Rubin, Mass Torts and Litigation Disasters, 20 Ga.L.Rev. 429, 429–30 (1986):

"Asbestos has been used since the fifth century B.C. It is basically indestructable and is remarkably resistant to heat. More than 3000 products commonly used in the home and at work contain asbestos. Today, however, it is regarded as 'one of the most dangerous of all natural materials.' Inhalation of asbestos fibers may cause not only bronchial problems but also asbestosis, mesothelioma, and pulmonary bronchogenic cancer. Since the beginning of World War II, more than 11,000,000 workers have been exposed to asbestos, and uncounted millions of others have lived in homes, attended schools, or worked in buildings insulated with it. Various studies estimate that each year at least 8500 and perhaps as many as 67,000 persons die from asbestos-related causes. The number of deaths is not expected to decrease until 1990 because precautions against its dangers were not implemented until the 1960's and producers were slow in introducing substitute products. More than 30,000 suits against asbestos manufacturers have already been filed; about one-third of these suits are in federal court. This number includes class actions by public agencies seeking to recover the costs of removing asbestos insulation from public buildings, litigation concerning insurance coverage, and, of course, thousands of individual plaintiff suits. Additional suits are being filed at the rate of 500 a month.

"Asbestos litigation has resulted in far more expense than in recovery of damages for injured persons. A Rand Corporation study estimated that injured persons receive less than thirty-seven percent of the total amount spent on litigation."

Accordingly, the American Law Institute launched a study of complex litigation in 1985. The resulting publication, ALI Complex Litigation (1994), defined the problem in terms of multiforum and multiparty litigation causing "claim dispersion" across place and over time. Note that its definition does not reach common forms of complicatedness in nondispersed claims, but nevertheless sweeps more broadly than "mass torts" or some narrower definition that is perhaps more susceptible to feasible and effective reform. Cf. Jay Tidmarsh & Roger H. Trangsrud, Complex Litigation 2 (2002) (" 'Complex cases' are cases in which the procedural system that we have established does not function well to resolve a dispute."). The ALI specified the fallout from its kind of complex litigation thus: "Repeated relitigation of the common issues in a complex case unduly expends the resources of attorney and client, burdens already overcrowded dockets, delays recompense for those in need, results in disparate treatment for persons harmed by essentially identical or similar conduct, and contributes to the negative image many people have of the legal system." ALI Complex Litigation 7 (1994).

As to solution, the ALI naturally inclined to bypass substantive solutions, such as reshaping particular legal rights and remedies, perhaps by limiting damages in exchange for streamlined compensation. Although the narrowed focus on procedure may have been clearly necessary for its project, even clearer is the ultimate necessity of some substance-specific approaches to the problem. For an update on attempts to resolve the asbestos crisis by legislation, see Christopher J. O'Malley, Note, Breaking Asbestos Litigation's Chokehold on the American Judiciary, 2008 U.Ill. L.Rev. 1101 (incidentally making the preceding summary of the asbestos crisis laughably modest, as the number of filed claims has exceeded 850,000 and is still growing mightily).

Also, the ALI put beyond its project's scope both the development of alternative dispute resolution techniques, such as mediation or claims commissions or an administrative process, and also the development of alternative compensation systems, such as workers' compensation or social insurance or legislative compensation. The consequent reliance on courts helped to focus the analysis, but it does close some of the more promising avenues to solution of the most intractable matters. See generally Thomas F. Burke, Lawyers, Lawsuits, and Legal Rights (2002).

In the familiar setting of the courts, then, the ALI study of complex litigation began by cataloguing current procedural approaches to ameliorating claim dispersion. The arsenal is diverse but still inadequate.

Some currently existing devices may not immediately spring to mind. The example of bankruptcy is apt, because asbestos producer Johns–Manville utilized it to create a limited fund for distribution to the claimants. The ALI, however, observed that this device is available in only a few situations and that the bankruptcy system is basically maladapted to handling complex litigation. But see Douglas G. Smith, Resolution of Mass Tort Claims in the Bankruptcy System, 41 U.C.Davis L.Rev. 1613 (2008).

Other procedural devices will be better known to you. Consider what ALI Complex Litigation 24–35 (1994) had to say about the major devices to be studied in this Part Five:

"*Party joinder under Federal Rules 19 and 20.* The federal party joinder rules may be used to bring additional parties into a lawsuit and to promote unitary adjudication of an entire controversy. Neither device, however, is particularly helpful in actions involving large numbers of widely dispersed parties.

"There are two types of party joinder in the federal courts: compulsory and permissive. Compulsory joinder under Rule 19 requires that persons whose participation is necessary for a 'just adjudication' be joined if 'feasible.' Persons generally will be considered necessary for a just adjudication if complete relief cannot be afforded in their absence, or if either the absent person or one or more of those already before the court might be prejudiced by a determination of the action without joinder. When joinder is not 'feasible'—either because the absent party is not subject to the court's personal jurisdiction or because joinder would defeat the court's subject-matter jurisdiction over the action—the judge must determine whether the potential for prejudice is great enough to justify dismissing the suit. The Rule sets out some of the criteria to be considered. See Fed. R.Civ.P. 19(b). Courts frequently conclude that although the absentees should be joined to adjudicate the dispute completely, if their joinder is impossible, the suit may proceed without them. For example, most courts have held that there is no compulsory joinder for joint tortfeasors or injured parties, even when the tort claims derive from the same incident. For this reason, in cases in which potential plaintiffs or defendants are dispersed widely and do not want to combine their actions, the operation of Rule 19 often does not result in consolidation.

"The permissive joinder provision, Rule 20, authorizes multiple party suits when the persons to be joined assert or have asserted against them some right to relief arising out of the same transaction or occurrence or series of transactions or occurrences that form the basis of the litigation. Rule 20 also requires that there be one or more common questions of law or fact tying together the claims held by the parties. These standards are broad enough to encompass the degree of commonality present in most complex litigation. However, joinder generally is sought only in relatively small-scale suits because each new party must be joined separately and is expected to appear personally in the action. In cases involving large numbers of parties, the utility of Rule 20 joinder ordinarily is superseded by the class action device. The utility of permissive joinder also is limited by the fact that each party must satisfy jurisdiction and venue requirements. . . . Finally, because permissive joinder is left to the parties' initiative, the presence of all persons necessary to a unitary adjudication cannot be ensured because there often are tactical reasons to omit certain potential parties."

Question: (1) Are you as pessimistic as the ALI about generating a solution from the general joinder provisions? What of rewriting Rule 19 more broadly to require joinder in appropriate situations of complex litigation? See John C. McCoid, A Single Package for Multiparty Disputes, 28 Stan.L.Rev. 707 (1976) (suggesting such reform).

"*Class actions under Federal Rule 23.* Rule 23 provides for the adjudication of the claims or defenses of an entire class of similarly situated parties in a single action. The Federal Rule is intended to eliminate or reduce the threat of repetitive litigation, to prevent inconsistent resolution of similar cases, and to provide an effective means of redress for individuals whose claims are too small to make it economically viable to pursue them in independent actions. Despite Rule 23's ambitious goals, multiparty, multiforum cases often are not certified for class treatment because its requirements have been read quite restrictively by some federal courts. Large-scale tort actions involving personal injuries rarely are certified. In the past, this may have been due primarily to the federal courts' reliance on the statement in the 1966 Advisory Committee Note that

> [a] 'mass accident' resulting in injuries to numerous persons is ordinarily not appropriate for a class action because of the likelihood that significant questions, not only of damages but also of liability and defenses to liability, would be present, affecting the individuals in different ways. In these circumstances, an action conducted nominally as a class action would degenerate in practice into multiple lawsuits separately tried.

. . . Although this reasoning may be criticized as shortsighted, it nonetheless has been influential. In addition, concerns about how to handle individual issues and large numbers of claimants have served to restrict class certification in nationwide products liability cases, as well as in consumer, securities, and antitrust actions. Recent years, however, have seen some weakening in the resistance to the certification of mass tort class actions. [Citations omitted.] Nonetheless, the full procedural advantages of class actions have not been realized.

"An additional hurdle for damage class actions under Rule 23(b)(3)—the category best suited for most complex litigation—is that the text of the Rule guarantees class members individual notice, which can result in prohibitive costs, and the right to 'opt out' of the class and prosecute their actions individually. . . . If the right to opt out is exercised by those individual class members who have relatively large claims or by large numbers of class members, consolidation of related actions is impeded and the promise of repose that is so important to defendants is undermined.

"Rule 23 does not require individual notice or provide a right to opt out for actions brought under either subdivision (b)(1) or subdivision (b)(2). Thus, in an effort to minimize the notice and opt-out problems, some parties in damage class actions have attempted to utilize Rule 23(b)(1)(B), which authorizes class treatment when the prosecution of individual lawsuits would create a risk that those individual adjudications would be dispositive 'as a practical matter' of the interests of the other class members. It has been argued in the mass tort and nationwide products liability cases, for example, that the total of the class members' individual claims may exceed a defendant's resources so that class certification is necessary to avoid the risk that early victories by some individuals will deplete the funds available for later claimants. These limited fund tort class suits generally have found little favor in the courts, however, and have been permitted only in those cases in which there is clear proof that the defendant's assets are so limited.

"One relatively simple way to reduce some of these restrictions would be to expand the current perimeter of class action practice to embrace a wider range of complex litigation situations. This expansion might be accomplished, for example, by eliminating some of the inhibitions to certifying plaintiff classes in mass tort actions created by the Advisory Committee Note, such as by relaxing the Rule's notice requirements, or possibly by adding a new category of class action to the Rule either specifically identifying certain subject-matter areas in which class treatment seems well suited or identifying other dimensional criteria such as the number of parties or dispersed cases that should be the basis for class action certification. Each of these changes would streamline and make more attractive the class action approach for litigants, but success in achieving optimal consolidation would depend on the parties' willingness to take advantage of them. A more effective means of assuring consolidation and preventing claim dispersion would be by authorizing the greater use of mandatory classes under existing Rule 23(b)(1)(B). Although the elimination of the right to opt out might increase systemic efficiency greatly, other considerations must be weighed carefully. Even if the opt-out right is not constitutionally protected, it may not always be desirable as a matter of policy to force litigants to sacrifice control of their own actions, possibly depriving them of a meaningful individual day in court. In sum, merely altering the current class action rule, although it would ensure some improvements, falls short of achieving the maximum consolidation and coordination that is possible and desirable.

"Nonetheless, some aspects of current class action practice serve as excellent models for the development of a more complete remedy. In particular, Rule 23(c)(4) [and (5)] authorizes the use of partial class suits. Utilizing this provision, courts can allow common issues to be adjudicated as to the class, with individual issues being determined in separate proceedings, sometimes in separate courts. The formation of subclasses, for example, can permit class treatment of an issue even when different class members have conflicting interests or positions with respect to other matters. Similarly, the ability to limit class action treatment to only certain issues or parties offers a means of resolving the tension between the desire for collective adjudication of common issues and the need to resolve individual questions separately. Thus, experience with this device provides important data for similar approaches under a more expansive complex litigation statute."

Question: (2) Are you as pessimistic about the potential of the class-action route? See Linda S. Mullenix, Class Resolution of the Mass–Tort Case: A Proposed Federal Procedure Act, 64 Tex.L.Rev. 1039 (1986).

"*Intervention under Federal Rule 24.* Intervention occasionally is useful in aggregating parties to a complex dispute. In addition to those federal statutes specifically providing for intervention, Federal Rule 24 authorizes permissive intervention at the discretion of the trial court when the potential intervenor's claim or defense and the main action present a common question of law or fact. The rule further provides for intervention as of right when the potential intervenor has an interest in the property or transaction that is the subject matter of the action, the disposition of the action in the absence of the intervenor is likely to impair that person's ability to protect that interest, and the existing parties cannot adequately protect the potential intervenor's interests.

"As is true of the other existing party joinder devices, intervention ordinarily is too narrow to be helpful in the type of large-scale actions that lie at the core of the complex litigation problem. Intervention as of right frequently is denied because the interests of the outsider are not sufficiently intertwined with those of the parties to merit enlarging the lawsuit, or because the outsider is deemed adequately represented under Rule 24. Permissive intervention, although allowable under the rule's requirements, effectively is limited to the joinder of those parties who will not destroy diversity or who are asserting federal claims. One possibility for increasing the power of intervention is suggested in a Supreme Court dictum in Provident Tradesmens Bank & Trust Company v. Patterson, 390 U.S. 102, 114 (1968), which intimated that outsiders who have notice of and an opportunity to intervene in an action, but fail to do so, may be precluded from relitigating issues adjudicated in the action. The suggestion has not been pursued in subsequent cases, however, and at the present time intervention operates very much on the periphery of the complex litigation world."

Question: (3) Are you as pessimistic about creating a duty to intervene? See Louis Touton, Note, Preclusion of Absent Disputants to Compel Intervention, 79 Colum.L.Rev. 1551 (1979).

"*Interpleader.* Interpleader is an ancient equitable procedure that allows a 'stakeholder'—a holder of property that has become subject to two or more inconsistent claims—to bring together all the potential claimants in a single action. Because the claimants might file individual suits against the stakeholder, interpleader condenses several potential actions into one and prevents a race for judgment among the claimants. In the federal courts, interpleader may be invoked by using either Federal Rule 22 or the Federal Interpleader Act, 28 U.S.C. § 1335. In both function and effect, interpleader resembles the limited fund class action under Federal Rule 23(b)(1)(B), which authorizes a class suit if the absentees otherwise might be prejudiced if each proceeded individually because defendant's assets might be exhausted before all were able to obtain relief. One notable difference, however, is that the stakeholder, who ordinarily would be the defendant in a class action, is able to initiate the lawsuit. (A stakeholder who has been sued by one party and anticipates additional claims may invoke interpleader defensively.) See Grubbs v. General Electric Credit Corporation, 405 U.S. 699 (1972). Statutory interpleader also offers one further advantage over class suits; the statute specifically authorizes courts to issue injunctions restraining other proceedings relating to the property in question. 28 U.S.C. § 2361. Anti-suit injunctions are not available in class actions, so that courts must rely on the claimants' desire to consolidate the litigation in one proceeding.

"Despite these advantages, interpleader generally is limited to claims to specific property and does not operate on a sufficiently large scale to be important in most complex multiparty, multiforum actions. It is not a representative action because all of the claimants are expected to appear as parties. Thus, the device generally is less suitable than the class action for suits involving large numbers of claimants."

Question: (4) Are you as pessimistic about the interpleader route? See Paula J. McDermott, Comment, Can Statutory Interpleader Be Used as a Remedy by the Tortfeasor in Mass Tort Litigation?, 90 Dick.L.Rev. 439 (1985).

The ALI instead found a more promising, but stunted, model in 28 U.S.C. § 1407. Congress had enacted this statute in 1968 to allow the combined handling of dispersed but related claims, such as certain antitrust actions. The seven-judge Judicial Panel on Multidistrict Litigation, created by the statute, may transfer lawsuits pending in different federal district courts to one appropriate district judge "for coordinated or consolidated pretrial proceedings," including discovery. The Panel so acts—upon its own initiative or any party's motion, and after notice and hearing—when the actions involve "one or more common questions of fact" and when transfer "will be for the convenience of parties and witnesses and will promote the just and efficient conduct of such actions." See generally David F. Herr, Multidistrict Litigation (1986).

Although in theory this transfer is only for pretrial proceedings, in reality the judge rarely sends cases back to transferor courts. Under current practice most cases previously terminate, usually by settlement but sometimes by dispositive pretrial decision. A few go to trial in the transferee court, either with the parties' consent or waiver or as a result of a full transfer of venue *by the transferor court* within the more demanding terms of 28 U.S.C. § 1404(a). Such trials usually follow a consolidation order under Rule 42(a).

The ALI suggested that Congress should integrate and expand this transfer-and-consolidation model. Accordingly, Congress should expand § 1407 to authorize transfer for trial. It should adjust jurisdiction to reach cases pending in state courts. And it should regulate subsidiary matters, as by simplifying choice of law and enhancing res judicata.

In weighing such a proposal, numerous issues present themselves. See, e.g., Richard A. Epstein, The Consolidation of Complex Litigation: A Critical Evaluation of the ALI Proposal, 10 J.L. & Com. 1 (1990). Most fundamental, however, is the basic desirability—the fairness and the efficiency—of aggregated treatment. Here follow some views on individualization versus collectivization.

Roger H. Trangsrud, Joinder Alternatives in Mass Tort Litigation

70 Cornell L.Rev. 779, 779–80, 782–83, 815–16, 820–25, 829–30, 848 (1985).

Managing complex mass tort litigation fairly and efficiently poses a number of intractable procedural problems. The root cause of these problems is the inescapable tension between the interest of individual litigants in preserving individual control of claims and procedural fairness, on the one hand, and the interest of the judicial system in the efficient joinder of related claims, on the other. This tension forces courts to choose among a variety of joinder techniques for balancing these basic interests. The choice is important because our justice system relies almost exclusively on private litigation to compensate mass tort victims.

. . . .

The balancing of efficiency versus fairness leads to the conclusion that the substantial damage claims of mass tort victims deserve an uncompromised due process. Our judicial system should treat the claims of the many victims of a major airplane crash or hotel fire with as much care and sensitivity as it does the claim of the lone victim of an automobile accident. The practice of ordering the joint trial of common issues in mass tort cases involving substantial personal injuries or wrongful death claims should cease because it cannot be reconciled with this principle. Although joint *discovery* on common issues is desirable in most mass tort cases, the joint *trial* of such issues requires severing the common and noncommon issues, the use of special verdict forms, and the use of trial counsel selected by the court rather than by individual plaintiffs. These procedures constitute substantial departures from those usually followed in simple tort cases and adversely affect the fairness of the entire adjudicative process. The common question class action can be a desirable joinder device in some mass tort cases, however, for the limited purposes of structuring pretrial settlements and separately managing punitive damage claims. If carefully used, this type of joinder can facilitate global settlements and the fair determination and equitable distribution of punitive damage awards. Joinder in these circumstances facilitates the efficient management of mass tort cases in a way that is fair to all litigants.

. . . .

. . . [T]he limited fund class action is a proper joinder device in only a very small number of cases because most mass tort defendants have substantial assets and insurance coverage. In those few cases where a limited fund class action is proper, however, the court should certify a class action. Otherwise, there is a reasonable likelihood that plaintiffs losing the "race to the courthouse" will be unable to obtain fair compensation for their injuries. This prospect justifies the use of a limited fund class action because the interest of each class member in receiving a fair share of the limited fund outweighs his interest in individual control of his claim. The standard proposed here for certifying limited fund mass tort class actions would restrict them to cases where there is a reasonable danger that the plaintiffs' claims will exceed the defendant's available assets. In these special circumstances mandatory participation in the class action by all plaintiffs is proper and desirable.

. . . .

In a mass tort case several factors affect the plaintiff's interest in individual control over his personal injury or wrongful death claim. First, the individual plaintiff may perceive a number of tactical advantages in proceeding alone. Because significant differences in likely jury awards for particular injuries are perceived to exist between judicial districts, an individual plaintiff will probably file his case in the most convenient, high-award district that the applicable venue and jurisdictional rules permit. Defendants have a very heavy burden to overcome when trying to disturb the plaintiff's choice of forum in individual cases. In a mass tort case, however, if a class action is requested, or the transfer of the related claims to a single forum proposed, the deciding court is much less likely to defer to the forum preferences of individual litigants. The court will more likely site the litigation in the forum most convenient to witnesses or where most or all of the injuries occurred. The individual plaintiff may thus find himself before an unfamiliar jury in a district where jury awards tend to be less generous than those generally granted in the original forum. A plaintiff's right to have his damages evaluated by a jury familiar with his actual costs and economic situation is a substantial interest worthy of protection in most mass tort cases.

Second, if a class action is certified, the individual plaintiff may find that the state law applied by the forum court is not as favorable as the law which would have been applied had he been able to choose his own forum. The individual plaintiff also runs the risk that the representative plaintiffs in a class action will elect to proceed on liability theories better suited for class treatment at the expense of theories especially favorable to the individual plaintiff. These important considerations may not be highlighted during the certification process because named representatives and attorneys for the putative class have strong personal or financial interests in securing certification and will down-play possible conflicts of interest within the class.

Third, class members lack the direct control that an individual tort litigant can exercise over his own personal lawyer. The class action plaintiff cannot easily influence or control the handling of his claim. Even named plaintiffs exercise little control over class counsel. Class counsel proceeds based upon his estimation of what the interests of the class as a whole are, rather than those of individual plaintiffs, because no internal procedures exist by which a class can make decisions. Class counsel can thus easily ignore or poorly serve the interests of individual class members. Moreover, some courts exacerbate this problem by placing restrictions on the freedom of class counsel to communicate with absent class members without court approval.

In summary, given the traditional respect afforded an individual tort litigant's right to control the prosecution of a substantial personal injury or wrongful death claim, and that the plaintiff loses much of this individual control when the court certifies a class action, courts should avoid using this joinder device to try these cases.[244]

The consolidation for pretrial purposes of related mass tort claims in a common venue by the MDL Panel can also adversely affect the ability of an individual litigant to retain control over the development of his claim. The MDL Panel may consolidate related tort actions before a single judge over the objection of individual plaintiffs, and an individual plaintiff has no right to opt out of the consolidated proceedings. Although theoretically the individual plaintiff continues to be represented by a lawyer of his own choice, in reality the court often selects a small committee of lawyers to represent the plaintiffs for purposes of most pretrial motions and discovery on issues relating to liability. The court may select the lawyers committee over the objection of individual plaintiffs who wish to have their own lawyers conduct the discovery. Individual plaintiffs can thus lose control over the development of a case's common issue because the legal committee will operate under internal constraints making it inevitable that the interests of individual plaintiffs will be ignored or submerged in decisions concerning tactics and discovery affecting the entire plaintiff group.

. . . .

When consolidation goes beyond discovery to *trial,* . . . the individual plaintiff's position approximates that of the absent class member in a class action. At trial, he lacks effective control over the venue, the lawyers representing him, the legal theories relied upon, and the strategy and tactics employed. Further, he cannot opt out of the consolidated trial without court approval. For the same reasons that courts reject common question class actions in mass tort cases, they should also reject the unauthorized practice of allowing transferee judges to order the joint trial of mass tort claims. The concern for the individual claimant's loss of control makes both practices undesirable.

---

[244] It is no answer to this to assert that because individual plaintiffs may opt out of a common question class action their interest in individual control is fully protected. . . . This view ignores several important points. First, the certification and later decertification of a class action disrupt the normal progress of the litigation, result in the expenditure of substantial sums to provide notice to the class, can cause delay in the settlement of claims, and so can result in substantial costs and inefficiencies. A substantial number of opt-outs is often likely in mass tort cases. In the Federal Skywalk Cases, for example, 374 plaintiffs opted out of the federal common question class action leaving only 24 persons in the class. See Morris & See, The Hyatt Skywalks Litigation: The Plaintiffs' Perspective, 52 UMKC L.Rev. 246, 270 (1984). Since the number of opt-outs may later cause decertification of the class, the court should weigh the likelihood of opt-outs in deciding whether to certify a tort common question class action in the first place.

Second, a court should not certify a common question class action when other alternatives exist for better managing the litigation. . . . Moreover, the supposed gains in efficiency made possible by the class action may be largely illusory in many mass tort cases if a significant number of the liability, as well as the damage, issues must be tried on an individual instead of a common basis.

. . . .

In a class action or a consolidated action, the plaintiffs' various claims may be tried jointly only if the common factual issues are identical as to all plaintiffs. While attempting to achieve efficiency in mass tort cases, courts should not abridge the substantive rights of defendants [in violation of the Rules Enabling Act] by trying an issue, such as proximate causation, on a joint basis when pertinent factual differences exist among plaintiffs relating to that issue. Otherwise, the defendant's ability to offer evidence and to cross-examine witnesses relating to an individual plaintiff's particular situation may be impaired or foreclosed altogether.

. . . .

. . . But when factual differences between mass tort plaintiffs require that some liability issues be tried jointly and others separately, the litigant's right to trial by jury may be affected. For example, submitting the issue of a manufacturer's negligence in labelling a product to one jury and the affirmative defense of an individual consumer's assumption of the risk to another jury might run afoul of the [Seventh Amendment] rule that interwoven issues not be submitted to different juries. Other liability issues, such as scope of employment or questions of causation, may be sufficiently distinct from the remaining liability issues that severance is constitutionally permissible. Even where constitutionally allowed, severance of common liability issues from noncommon issues may prove undesirable when it might alter the jury's disposition of the issues or require that different juries decide the severed issues.

. . . .

The possible efficiencies of joinder in mass tort cases must be weighed against the imperative of preserving fairness in the trial of substantial personal injury or wrongful death claims. Whatever merit relaxed notions of due process may have when otherwise nonviable claims are jointly tried, these notions have no place in mass tort cases where the usually substantial compensatory damage claims of mass tort victims deserve an uncompromised due process. Although more efficient adjudication of liability issues in mass tort cases would be desirable, it is improper to seek this end through consolidation or common question class actions leading to the joint trial of the issues common to the related claims. In substantial personal injury or wrongful death cases, the joint trial of common issues adversely affects the traditional right of tort litigants to control the individual prosecution of their liability claims and unpredictably skews the fairness of the trial process. Moreover, the presence of noncommon liability and damage issues which must be severe for separate trial offset the modest, if not ephemeral, gains in efficiency made possible by the joint trial of common issues.

David Rosenberg, Class Actions for Mass Torts: Doing Individual Justice by Collective Means

62 Ind.L.J. 561, 561–67, 593–95 (1987).

From the perspective of the common law tradition of individual justice, class actions are a necessary evil, but an evil nonetheless. That tradition projects the private law adjudicatory ideal: the norms of right, duty, and remedy are applied according to the specific, relevant circumstances of the particular parties in the given case. It promises the parties not only their own day in court, but a good deal of control over what is said and decided on that day.

Class actions loom as a subversive element in this context because they import the processes of bureaucratic justice—a mode of decision-making associated with administrative agencies, which lacks the common law's traditional commitment to party control and focus on the discrete merits of each claim. In contrast to the party initiated and orchestrated common law trial, bureaucratic justice gives decisionmakers the controlling hand over the issue agenda as well as over the type and extent of evidence considered. But bureaucratic justice is most strikingly antithetical to notions of individual justice because it legitimates the aggregation and averaging of circumstances and interests of affected individuals in pursuit of the collective benefits from process efficiency, outcome consistency, and the maximum production of substantive goods. These goals are implemented through "public law" procedures which combine claims for uniform and summary treatment according to classifications based on a set of salient, if partial, common variables relating to the individuals involved.

Nowhere do class actions seem a more alien force than in the torts system, which epitomizes the individual justice tradition. . . .

In mass tort cases involving claims for personal injury, which pose daunting problems of causation and remedy, the price of individual justice is notoriously high. . . .

The case-by-case mode of adjudication magnifies this burden by requiring the parties and courts to reinvent the wheel for each claim. The merits of each case are determined de novo even though the major liability issues are common to every claim arising from the mass tort accident, and even though they may have been previously determined several times by full and fair trials. These costs exclude many mass tort victims from the system and sharply reduce the recovery for those who gain access. Win or lose, the system's private law process exacts a punishing surcharge from defendant firms as well as plaintiffs.

These costs of litigation, which are borne directly by the parties, also cast a broad array of shadow prices that have widespread indirect effects. The redundant adjudication of mass tort claims thus consumes vast quantities of public resources, raising the price of access for other, sporadic, types of tort claims. Moreover, even though most of the claims arising from mass accidents are eventually settled on the basis of recovery patterns projected from relatively few trials, the settlement calculus will reflect the costs of redundant, de novo, particularized adjudication, as well as the incentives of each party to increase the litigation expenses for the other. These conditions generally disadvantage claimants. Because defendant firms are in a position to spread the litigation costs over the entire class of mass accident claims, while plaintiffs, being deprived of the economies of scale afforded by class actions, can not, the result will usually be that the firms will escape the full loss they have caused and, after deducting their attorneys' shares, the victims will receive a relatively small proportion of any recovery as compensation.[15] As a consequence, the tort system's primary objectives of compensation and deterrence are seriously jeopardized.

. . . .

Individual justice critiques of class actions have little power when the primary purpose of tort liability is taken to be the utilitarian objective of maximizing welfare by deterring socially inappropriate risk-taking. The aggregation and averaging techniques of bureaucratic justice are not only consistent with the social welfare justification for tort liability—at least, when defendant firms are not on the whole under or overcharged—but they also produce the positive benefits of lower administrative costs. When, however, tort liability serves to vindicate rights to personal security transgressed by a defendant's wrongful conduct, the individual justice arguments against class actions may, depending on the normative content of the rights posited, suggest the location of certain outside limitations on the use of class actions in mass tort cases.[25] But, as I will explain below, these individual justice arguments are exaggerated. They ignore not only the realities of claimant dependency and powerlessness in individual actions, but they also fail to recognize the existence of collectivizing forces operating

[15] Some recent commentary urges courts and Congress to consider developing and expanding the scope of class action alternatives, particularly test-case, pattern settlements, and transjurisdiction consolidation of state and federal claims. [Omitted citations include Professor Trangsrud's article.] These commentators fail to recognize the inadequacy of such alternatives in the toxic tort context where information, cost barriers, and the long latency periods of diseases such as cancer prevent the initiation and actual (even if informal) joinder of many claims.

More generally, when the *sole* alternative to case-by-case adjudication consists of procedures, such as pattern settlements and consolidation, which curtail redundancy and spread litigation expenses only partially or not at all among all benefited claimants, the costs of that residual degree of inefficiency will be deducted from the settlement offered to each claimant. The availability of a class action alternative to case-by-case adjudication is necessary if there is to be any substantial reduction of individualizing litigation costs and their bite from the compensation received by victims. . . .

[25] Generally, rights-based limits would be reached when, as measured by the relevant entitlements baseline, collectively averaged treatment redistributes to one class of claimants the welfare of another class, which receives no offsetting benefits. Redistribution would not of itself warrant affording the disadvantaged claimants individually particularized treatment, unless the process of separate actions presented a less pronounced danger of redistribution than the class action. As such, process is merely an instrument for doing distributional justice. It is possible, of course, to conceive of process as having intrinsic participatory value, which should then be incorporated in the entitlements baseline. See Michelman, The Supreme Court and Litigation Access Fees: The Right to Protect One's Rights, 1973 Duke L.J. 1153, 1193–97. But, it would be incorrect to equate the participatory value with the notion of individual control. The participatory value could just as easily be expressed in terms of the group solidarity promoted by the collective processes of class actions.

. . . .

in the mass accident context, particularly the class-wide nature of the risk ex ante, which exerts a unifying influence over the security interests (deterrence) and protective responses (insurance) of the potential accident victims. A major aim of this paper is to demonstrate that, given such ex ante conditions, bureaucratic justice implemented through class actions provides better opportunities for achieving individual justice than does the tort system's private law, disaggregative processes.

. . . .

. . . Although such elements as mandatory class treatment [i.e., mandatory in the usual sense of not allowing opting out and also even in the sense of compelling class treatment on the court's initiative] and damage scheduling [i.e., awarding compensation equal to the average loss across subclass or class] make tort liability extremely potent, I have shown that the fears expressed by some commentators that this will only exacerbate the system's potential for overdeterring technological innovation have little basis in reality. Indeed, the "public law" approach represented by class actions minimizes the incentives for inefficiency and irrationality that have justifiably raised concerns about whether the tort system is a sensible mode of regulating the risks of advanced technology.

. . . By eliminating the inefficiencies of separate actions, mass accident class actions promise very substantial increases in compensation for victims. In addition, by assuring access to the system for relatively low value claims—claims that would not be marketable to competent plaintiff attorneys as separate actions—not only are those claimants compensated for their losses, but also the probability of incompensable loss is greatly reduced for all potential victims.

When the aggregative and averaging methods of bureaucratic justice are extended to noncommon questions raised by otherwise marketable claims—claims which do not require class treatment to gain access to the system—a danger of redistribution from higher to lower value claimants arises. In addition, regardless of the value of the classed claims, the class attorney has incentives to make a collusive settlement with the defendant, trading a significant amount of class recovery for a higher or certain attorney fee. These problems are not unique to class actions; the settlement of separate actions involves similar dangers of redistribution and attorney disloyalty. Moreover, careful analysis indicates that there is less warrant for concern about these dangers in the class action than in the separate action context. The greater stakes for the class attorney, combined with the possibility for effective judicial oversight of settlements and fees minimizes the risks of redistribution and class attorney disaffection. Judicial policing is not perfect nor are its costs negligible. Therefore, a market-type of approach should be adopted in certain cases—where the risks of redistribution and class attorney disloyalty and the costs of detecting them are high—to allow exit (opting out) from the class action's aggregative and averaged resolution of noncommon questions, particularly damages. To counter the more serious danger of plaintiff attorneys opposing class actions to protect their fees rather than their client's interests, permission to opt out should be conditioned on payment of the opt-out claimant's share of the costs incurred in preparing the common questions and of the costs represented by the public resources consumed by the individual damage trials. This compromise of bureaucratic justice is consistent with the instrumental conception of process embodied in the "public law" model of the tort system, which seeks not purity of form but simply to maximize substantive productivity.

The most ambitious thrust of this paper is to show that in certain contexts, even when there exist neither cost nor information barriers preventing access to the tort system, the aggregation and averaging of bureaucratic justice better serves individual justice than the system's traditional disaggregative process. Generally, this appears to be the case in mass accident situations because the ex ante risk of injury experienced by the population of exposed victims results in uniform and collective distributional consequences which are likely to be ignored in assessing liability and awarding compensation ex post in the system's traditional process. In contrast to the probabilistic and class-wide perspectives engendered by the bureaucratic justice of class actions, the traditional disaggregative process tends to seek linear, determinate, and particularized determinations of liability and compensable loss. Necessarily such a disaggregative process will fail to capture collective and statistically averaged responses to ex ante risk, even though these responses have demonstrable distributive consequences for the class of potential victims—consequences which are substantively relevant to prevailing liability and compensation norms.

The paper sketches two examples indicating the differences in distributive outcomes under the bureaucratic justice of class actions and the system's private law, disaggregative processes. First, I show that the disaggregative approach undermines the collective interest of potential class victims in rights-based deterrence. Unless the aggregate class-wide risk of an activity is compared to the defendant's safety investment, courts are likely to deny liability in cases involving low value claims. At a certain point, especially in cases where the choices among levels of care-taking are discontinuous, the removal of such claims from the threat of liability may sharply reduce the defendant's safety incentives. By thus increasing the risk of incompensable loss, the system's disaggregative process effectively devalues the security entitlements of the at-risk population.

Second, stimulated by conditions of ex ante risk, potential victims will purchase insurance. When the risk is randomly distributed among the population of potential victims, so that none has a distinctive chance of being injured, then insurance will be purchased to cover the average risk borne by the population as a whole. Where the risk arises in a contractual setting, for example consumer product injuries, the insurance will be purchased by the potential victim as part of the product price. Because each consumer pays an identical amount of the price as insurance premium, regardless of the economic status each victim suffering the same physical harm should receive compensation in equal shares computed at the average level. Ex post particularization ignores the ex ante uniformity of insurance response, and operates as a regressive tax against low-income consumers. A similar uniform insurance response arises in non-contract settings, for example when a population is subject to an environmental risk of disease from toxic substance exposure. If members of the population cannot affect the chance of injury, then each will purchase insurance based on the average probability for the population as a whole. The insurance they purchase will be supplementary, covering gaps in compensation provided by the tort system. However, if the ex post determinations are particularistic, then a large number of victims who receive below average (including zero) compensation from the tort system will not be made whole by their supplementary insurance. In order to assure that all victims are made whole by the combination of tort and private insurance, tort compensation must be provided to all victims on an average basis.

OTHER SOLUTIONS

The conservative route would be to side-step the fundamental issue of individualization versus collectivization, seeking to reduce the overall costs of current approaches without significantly diminishing individual control. For example, John C. Coffee, Jr., The Regulation of Entrepreneurial Litigation: Balancing Fairness and Efficiency in the Large Class Action, 54 U.Chi.L.Rev. 877, 936 (1987), argues for restructuring the fee for the opting-out attorney into a percentage of the amount by which the client's recovery exceeds the class's pro rata recovery, thus manipulating incentives to ensure that claimants opt out only when this move is in the client's better interests as opposed to the attorney's. Professor Coffee concludes:

"Candor requires the admission that the preference expressed in this article for retention of a greater measure of individualized justice than recent proponents of 'bureaucratic justice' have urged may prove very costly. The efficiency justifications for restricting duplicative litigation may prove to outweigh the fairness values underlying a broad right to opt out. In related contexts [such as collective bargaining], Congress has sometimes explicitly subordinated the interests of one sub-class to another in order to make the overall system work. Yet, we should recognize the consequences of such a decision: not only do we subordinate the goal of compensation to the goal of deterrence, but we risk converting private litigation into a system for judicially mandated wealth transfers. In some contexts, this may be justified; in others, not. Accordingly, considerable care and attention should be given both to defining the context narrowly and to making certain that the claimed efficiency gains cannot be realized almost as well by less restrictive alternatives. Before our system of private law accepts mandatory classing, damage averaging, or crude majoritarian rule, less drastic means—such as fee incentives, consolidation procedures, and even the use of alternative forums such as the bankruptcy court—need to be better explored. Individualized justice may be less costly than we think, because those with unmarketable claims should not opt out."

Contrariwise, other viable proposals to minimize costs plunge us not only into the issue of individualization versus collectivization, but also into different issues that are difficult and hot. For example, an article by Thomas D. Rowe, Jr. & Kenneth D. Sibley, Beyond Diversity: Federal Multiparty, Multiforum Jurisdiction, 135 U.Pa.L.Rev. 7, 49–58 (1986), confronted important questions of federalism in proposing a complex-litigation solution dependent on a new head of jurisdiction. The authors included a detailed draft of a federal statute, which received considerable attention in Congress over the years and finally enactment in a rather sloppy and limited form as the Multiparty, Multiforum Trial Jurisdiction Act of 2002, § 11020, Pub.L. No. 107–273, 116 Stat. 1758, 1826. Read 28 U.S.C. § 1369 ("original jurisdiction of any civil action involving minimal diversity between adverse parties that arises from a single accident, where at least 75 natural persons have died in the accident at a discrete location" with dispersed defendants or events), § 1391(g) (venue "in any district in which any defendant resides or in which a substantial part of the accident giving rise to the action took place"), § 1441(e) (removal), § 1697 (nationwide process), and § 1785 (nationwide subpoenas).

From among this array of proposals along the spectrum of turbulent change—proposals already made or to be made—further reform for complex litigation must and will come.

TOPIC B

GENERAL JOINDER PROVISIONS

SECTION 1. SETTING

Recall Part One's treatment of the general Rules regarding joinder of parties, including Rules 19, 20, 21, and 42. We shall now take a closer look at permissive and required joinder of parties.

PROPER PARTIES

In particular, recall that Rule 20 establishes an outer limit on whom the claimant may join as "proper" parties. Two other provisions in the Rules impose separate and further limits thereon, and so contribute to the definition of proper parties. The first is Rule 17(b) and (c) treating capacity to sue or be sued, which comprises the personal qualifications legally needed by a person to litigate. The other such provision is Rule 17(a), which deserves special attention.

Rule 17(a)(1) requires that every action be prosecuted by the real party in interest. To the student not aided by the perspective of history, the requirement may well seem either obvious or meaningless. At common law, an action had to be brought in the name of the person holding legal title to the right sued upon: so, for example, the assignee of a nonnegotiable chose in action controlled the lawsuit but had to sue in the name of his assignor. A similar example comes from the doctrine of subrogation, whereby a person who has paid another's debt can then assert the other's related rights: but at common law, for example, an insurer who had paid a loss and was therefore subrogated to the rights of his insured still had to sue in the latter's name. In equity, however, a person with a beneficial or equitable interest could sue in his own name. The Field Code in merging law and equity changed the common-law rule by requiring that all actions be brought by the real party in interest, by which was meant the person who under the substantive law is entitled to enforce the right sued upon, whether or not that person is the one who would actually enjoy the benefits of victory.

Most but not all states adopted provisions similar to the Field Code's, and so Federal Rule 17(a) followed suit, thus allowing and requiring assignees and subrogees to sue in their own names. Where an assignment is total or a subrogee has paid the full amount of the loss, the only real party in interest and hence the only proper plaintiff is the assignee or subrogee. If suit is brought in the name of some other person, the defendant may seasonably challenge that person's right to sue. If the defect appears on the face of the complaint, the defendant may move to dismiss. If it does not so appear, as is more likely, she may raise the point by including in her answer a defense invoking Rule 17(a) and then moving for summary judgment supported by affidavits or other proof of the facts.

Question: (1) Why might the real party in interest prefer to sue in another's name? Why might the defendant want to object?

If the defendant's challenge is sustained, the defect may be corrected by substitution of the real party in interest. The present Rule 17(a)(3), codifying the result in Link Aviation, Inc. v. Downs, 325 F.2d 613 (D.C.Cir. 1963), provides that the substitution relates back to the date of commencement of the action. See the original form of Rule 17, and the Advisory Committee's reasons for amending it in 1966, in the Rules booklet.

Question: (2) Plaintiff is injured by a hit-and-run driver, unidentified except that the person was driving a black Toyota with an attached trailer. An investigator at a later date observes such a car passing the scene of the accident and makes note of the license-plate number. Before the limitations period expires, plaintiff's lawyer institutes suit against the owner of the observed car. After the statute has run, plaintiff's lawyer learns the identity of the true offender and moves to amend by substituting her as defendant. Should the motion be granted? Was the attorney's conduct consistent with the obligations of Rule 11?

If a subrogee has paid only part of the loss (or an assignment is partial), the subrogee is still a real party in interest, but not the only one. If either the subrogee or his creditor sues alone, the defendant may by motion seek joinder of the other. Each is a person needed for just adjudication under Rule 19(a).

Question: (3) What if such joinder is not feasible because the absentee is not subject to service of process or his joinder would destroy subject-matter jurisdiction?

It should be noted that in diversity cases, state substantive law is controlling as to who is entitled to enforce the right. It is only after you so determine the identity of the real party in interest that Rule 17(a) comes into play, telling you that suit must be brought in his name. See, e.g., McNeil Constr. Co. v. Livingston State Bank, 300 F.2d 88 (9th Cir.1962). When the case is ripe for its use, Rule 17(a) is purely procedural, applying in federal court regardless of any procedural provisions the state has concerning the name in which suit is to be brought.

Finally, there are those who have advocated abolition of the real-party-in-interest rule. See Thomas E. Atkinson, The Real Party in Interest Rule: A Plea for Its Abolition, 32 N.Y.U.L.Rev. 926 (1957); John E. Kennedy, Federal Rule 17(a): Will the Real Party in Interest Please Stand?, 51 Minn.L.Rev. 675 (1967); June F. Entman, More Reasons for Abolishing Federal Rule of Civil Procedure 17(a): The Problem of the Proper Plaintiff and Insurance Subrogation, 68 N.C.L.Rev. 893 (1990). The argument is that the only function of a rule such as Rule 17(a), now that the common-law approach has been definitely put behind us, is to mislead. All that is correct in Rule 17(a) would still follow in its absence by the application of the remaining body of procedural and substantive law. But Rule 17(a)'s wording creates many difficulties—for one example among the many, the uninformed might not guess that Rule 17(a)(1)'s second sentence merely gives illustrations of some usually, *but not universally*, correct applications of its first sentence. Pertinent is that New York, where the rule originated, has heeded the plea and dropped it. See 3 Jack B. Weinstein, Harold L. Korn & Arthur R. Miller, New York Civil Practice: CPLR ¶ 1004.01 (2d ed. 2007).

SHIELDS v. BARROW, 58 U.S. (17 How.) 130 (1855). Robert Barrow, a citizen of Louisiana, in 1836 sold his plantations in Louisiana to Thomas Shields, a citizen of Louisiana, for $227,000 payable in installments, the obligations being evidenced by notes. Six persons, of whom four were citizens of Louisiana and two were citizens of Mississippi, each guaranteed the notes. Payment up to $107,000 was made, but the rest was defaulted. In 1842 Barrow, Shields, and the six guarantors agreed to a compromise under which the original transaction was to be undone with the plantations being returned to Barrow, Barrow was to retain the $107,000 paid, and the six guarantors were to execute notes in varying amounts aggregating $32,000. (A tough proposition for the debtors: the Panic of 1837 had intervened.) This compromise proceeded to the point where Barrow went into possession of the plantations and discontinued litigation previously begun, and the guarantors executed the new notes.

Barrow now claimed that he had been induced to enter the compromise by fraud. He commenced the instant suit in the United States Circuit Court for the Eastern District of Louisiana against only the two Mississippi citizens, Victoire Shields and William Bisland, seeking rescission of the compromise and recovery on the defendants' original obligations as guarantors.

The question in the Supreme Court was whether he could maintain the suit in the absence of the other interested persons, whose joinder would destroy diversity. The Court, reversing the circuit court, ordered the case dismissed for nonjoinder of Thomas Shields and the Louisiana guarantors, whose presence the Court deemed indispensable. Justice Curtis, in a passage endlessly repeated in later cases, wrote for the Court:

"The court [in Russell v. Clark's Executors, 11 U.S. (7 Cranch) 69, 98 (1812),] points out three classes of parties to a bill in equity. They are: 1. Formal parties. 2. Persons having an interest in the controversy, and who ought to be made parties, in order that the court may act on that rule which requires it to decide on, and finally determine the entire controversy, and do complete justice, by adjusting all the rights involved in it. These persons are commonly termed necessary parties; but if their interests are separable from those of the parties before the court, so that the court can proceed to a decree, and do complete and final justice, without affecting other persons not before the court, the latter are not indispensable parties. 3. Persons who not only have an interest in the controversy, but an interest of such a nature that a final decree cannot be made without either affecting that interest, or leaving the controversy in such a condition that its final termination may be wholly inconsistent with equity and good conscience.

"A bill to rescind a contract affords an example of this kind. For, if only a part of those interested in the contract are before the court, a decree of rescission must either destroy the rights of those who are absent, or leave the contract in full force as respects them; while it is set aside, and the contracting parties restored to their former condition, as to the others. We do not say that no case can arise in which this may be done; but it must be a case in which the rights of those before the court are completely separable from the rights of those absent, otherwise the latter are indispensable parties.

"Now it will be perceived, that in Russell . . . this court, after considering the embarrassments which attend the exercise of the equity jurisdiction of the circuit courts of the United States, advanced as far as this: They declared that formal parties may be dispensed with when they cannot be reached; that persons having rights which must be affected by a decree, cannot be dispensed with; and they express a doubt concerning the other class of parties. This doubt is solved in favor of the jurisdiction in subsequent cases, but without infringing upon what was held in Russell . . . concerning the incapacity of the court to give relief, when that relief necessarily involves the rights of absent persons."

Questions: (4) Does "affect" in the quoted passage mean *legally* or *practically* affected? Could it originally have meant something else altogether?

(5) Try to work out the practical consequences of going ahead with only the present parties and reaching (a) a decree on the merits against Barrow or (b) a decree for Barrow, the joined defendants being good for the total amount due to Barrow under the original agreement.

(6) What arguments could the joined defendants fairly make on their own behalf against the maintenance of this suit? on behalf of the absentees? on behalf of the public interest in a sound litigation system? With this suit dismissed for nonjoinder, did Barrow have recourse to any other court where all interested persons could be joined?

BACKGROUND OF RULE 19

The best background readings on the subject of compulsory joinder are Geoffrey C. Hazard, Jr., Indispensable Party: The Historical Origin of a Procedural Phantom, 61 Colum.L.Rev. 1254 (1961); John W. Reed, Compulsory Joinder of Parties in Civil Actions (pts. 1–2), 55 Mich.L.Rev. 327, 483 (1957); and Robert G. Bone, Mapping the Boundaries of a Dispute: Conceptions of Ideal Lawsuit Structure from the Field Code to the Federal Rules, 89 Colum.L.Rev. 1 (1989).

The ancient doctrine in this area largely evolved in equity, where multiparty problems were most acute and where judges were freer to innovate. In tracing the early developments, Professor Hazard contends "that until about 1780 the Court of Chancery had adhered with substantial consistency to what is presently known as the necessary party rule: all persons interested in a controversy should be made parties unless joinder is impossible or inconvenient." He says the "indispensable party rule," invented thereafter, "rests on the principle that a court should do 'complete' justice or none at all," a principle that is, in his opinion, "impossible to follow in any workable system of judicial administration." 61 Colum.L.Rev. at 1271.

Professor Reed speaks of the course of decision in this country thus, 55 Mich.L.Rev. at 355–56: "The result of Shields v. Barrow was to embed in American procedural law the now familiar division of required parties into categories (necessary and indispensable)—a classification not inherently bad—and a shoddy and unimaginative method of its application to individual cases. It is not surprising that other courts in picking up that classification have adopted also the Supreme Court's separability-of-rights terminology. It is one thing to determine that in the absence of some persons a case may not proceed ('indispensable' parties) and in the unavoidable absence of others a case may proceed ('necessary' parties). It is quite another to believe that certain persons, depending on the nature of their rights ('common,' 'joint,' 'united in interest'), are automatically and for all time relegated to one class or the other. That simply is not so, but it is the kind of result which the Shields v. Barrow process invites. Similarly, there is an assumption, possibly due to heavy reliance on the necessary-indispensable terminology, that a court has discretion to proceed or not to proceed in one category ('necessary') and no discretion in the other ('indispensable'). Although true when applied to a party to which the court has attached one of these labels, the assumption is basically false in failing to recognize that there is initially a broad discretion in assigning a party to the one category or other. Also, it is hard to understand, except by reference to Shields v. Barrow's misleading silence on the point, why so few courts have been aware of the availability of a less-than-absolute decree to avoid a termination of litigation without a chance to explore the merits." Nevertheless, the author's analysis of the decisions showed no landslide accumulation of obvious mistakes. Many of the cases reduced to standard types with the results reasonably defensible. Courts had, however, a tendency to shove cases into categories without attention to their differentia, to their specific facts. This tendency frustrated criticism of some cases because the opinions, concerned with opaque terms such as "joint" and "separable," were unrevealing as to the facts.

Professor Bone argues that the old rules and approaches resulted, and derived definition, from the prevailing normative framework. The nineteenth century generally had seen procedure's role as effectuating the appropriate remedy for the natural right involved. As the framework evolved toward being more pragmatic, however, joinder law changed or at least became more confused. In the twentieth century, the normative framework became strongly and openly pragmatic, with procedure seen as serving more diverse process values as well as serving a substantive law that was societally based. This new outlook exposed the old joinder law to intense criticism.

The rulemakers totally overhauled party joinder in 1966. Look at Rule 19 in its original form and the Advisory Committee's note on the 1966 amendment in the Rules booklet. Observe the use in original Rule 19 of the terms "joint interest" and "indispensable" to mark the boundaries of the two categories of persons falling within the compulsory joinder doctrine; the original provision seemed to be a confused retention of an old approach that no longer worked and that clashed with the advances in the rest of the Rules. The Advisory Committee in 1966 drew heavily upon the findings of Hazard and Reed in its discussion of the defects in the original Rule; it thought that the old Rule encouraged overemphasis on labels, which directed the attention of the courts to technical concepts at the expense of the pragmatic considerations that should be controlling. Thus, the new provision superseded a text that had operated at a high level of abstraction, and it implemented an approach that would lay more stress on tracing out the practical consequences of nonjoinder and making the critical elections in that light.

Questions: (7) In abandoning the old jurisprudence of labels in Rule 19, were the rulemakers justified in adopting a "non-rule" that in part just lists relevant considerations rather than drawing a precise and specific rule that would offer certainty and hence predictability and workability?

(8) So, when all is said and done, would the result in Shields be the same under the present Rule 19? See Benjamin Kaplan, Continuing Work of the Civil Committee: 1966 Amendments of the Federal Rules of Civil Procedure (I), 81 Harv.L.Rev. 356, 360–62 (1967).

Provident Tradesmens Bank & Trust Co. v. Patterson

Supreme Court of the United States, 1968.
390 U.S. 102, 88 S.Ct. 733.

■ MR. JUSTICE HARLAN delivered the opinion of the Court.

This controversy, involving in its present posture the dismissal of a declaratory judgment action for nonjoinder of an "indispensable" party, began nearly 10 years ago with a traffic accident [in Pennsylvania]. An automobile owned by Edward Dutcher, who was not present when the accident occurred, was being driven by Donald Cionci, to whom Dutcher had given the keys. John Lynch and John Harris were passengers. The automobile crossed the median strip of the highway and collided with a truck being driven by Thomas Smith. Cionci, Lynch, and Smith were killed and Harris was severely injured.

Three tort actions were brought. Provident Tradesmens Bank, the administrator of the estate of passenger Lynch and petitioner here, sued the estate of the driver, Cionci, in a diversity action. The administrator of Smith, and Harris in person, each brought a state-court action against the estate of Cionci, Dutcher the owner, and the estate of Lynch [on the theory that Lynch had been in "control" of Cionci]. These Smith and Harris actions, for unknown reasons, have never gone to trial and are still pending. The Lynch action against Cionci's estate was settled for $50,000, which the estate of Cionci, being penniless, has never paid.

Dutcher, the owner of the automobile and a defendant in the as yet untried tort actions, had an automobile liability insurance policy with Lumbermens Mutual Casualty Company, respondent here. That policy had an upper limit of $100,000 for all claims arising out of a single accident. This fund was potentially subject to two different sorts of claims by the tort plaintiffs. First, Dutcher himself might be held vicariously liable as Cionci's "principal"; the likelihood of such a judgment against Dutcher is a matter of considerable doubt and dispute. Second, the policy by its terms covered the direct liability of any person driving Dutcher's car with Dutcher's "permission."

The insurance company had declined, after notice, to defend the estate of Lynch's tort action against the estate of Cionci, believing that Cionci had not had permission and hence was not covered by the policy. The facts allegedly were that Dutcher had entrusted his car to Cionci, but that Cionci had made a detour from the errand for which Dutcher allowed his car to be taken. The estate of Lynch, armed with its $50,000 liquidated claim against the estate of Cionci, brought the present diversity action [in the Eastern District of Pennsylvania] for a declaration that Cionci's use of the car had been "with permission" of Dutcher. The only named defendants were the company and the estate of Cionci [administered by Patterson]. The other two tort plaintiffs were joined as plaintiffs [on Lumbermens' motion]. Dutcher, a resident of the State of Pennsylvania as were all the plaintiffs, was not joined either as plaintiff or defendant. The failure to join him was not adverted to at the trial level.

The major question of law contested at trial was a state-law question. The District Court had ruled that, as a matter of the applicable (Pennsylvania) law, the driver of an automobile is presumed to have the permission of the owner. Hence, unless contrary evidence could be introduced, the tort plaintiffs, now declaratory judgment plaintiffs, would be entitled to a directed verdict against the insurance company. The only possible contrary evidence was testimony by Dutcher as to restrictions he had imposed on Cionci's use of the automobile. The two estate plaintiffs claimed, however, that under the Pennsylvania "Dead Man Rule" Dutcher was incompetent to testify on this matter as against them. The District Court upheld this claim. It ruled that under Pennsylvania law Dutcher was incompetent to testify against an estate if he had an "adverse" interest to that of the estate. It found such adversity in Dutcher's potential need to call upon the insurance fund to pay judgments against himself, and his consequent interest in not having part or all of the fund used to pay judgments against Cionci. The District Court, therefore, directed verdicts in favor of the two estates. Dutcher was, however, allowed to testify as against the live plaintiff, Harris. The jury, nonetheless, found that Cionci had had permission, and hence awarded a verdict to Harris also.

Lumbermens appealed the judgment to the Court of Appeals for the Third Circuit, raising various state-law questions.[1] The Court of Appeals did not reach any of these issues. Instead, after reargument en banc, it decided, 5–2, to reverse on two alternative grounds neither of which had been raised in the District Court or by the appellant.

The first of these grounds was that Dutcher was an indispensable party. The court held that the "adverse interests" that had rendered Dutcher incompetent to testify under the Pennsylvania Dead Man Rule also required him to be made a party. The court did not consider whether the fact that a verdict had already been rendered, without objection to the nonjoinder of Dutcher, affected the matter. Nor did it follow the provision of Rule 19 of the Federal Rules of Civil Procedure that findings of "indispensability" must be based on stated pragmatic considerations. It held, to the contrary, that the right of a person who "may be affected" by the judgment to be joined is a "substantive" right, unaffected by the federal rules; that a trial court "may not proceed" in the absence of such a person; and that since Dutcher could not be joined as a defendant without destroying diversity jurisdiction the action had to be dismissed.

Since this ruling presented a serious challenge to the scope of the newly amended Rule 19, we granted certiorari. 386 U.S. 940, 87 S.Ct. 972. Concluding that the inflexible approach adopted by the Court of Appeals in this case exemplifies the kind of reasoning that the Rule was designed to avoid, we reverse.

I.

[The Court here quoted Rule 19(a) and (b).]

We may assume, at the outset, that Dutcher falls within the category of persons who, under § (a), should be "joined if feasible." The action was for an adjudication of the validity of certain claims against a fund. Dutcher, faced with the possibility of judgments against him, had an interest in having the fund preserved to cover that potential liability. Hence there existed, when this case went to trial, at least the possibility that a judgment might impede Dutcher's ability to protect his interest, or lead to later relitigation by him.

The optimum solution, an adjudication of the permission question that would be binding on all interested persons, was not "feasible," however, for Dutcher could not be made a defendant without destroying diversity. Hence the problem was the one to which Rule 19(b) appears to address itself: in the absence of a person who "should be joined if feasible," should the court dismiss the action or proceed without him? Since this problem emerged for

[1] Appellants challenged the District Court's ruling on the Dead Man issue, the fairness of submitting the question as to Harris to a jury that had been directed to find in favor of the two estates whose position was factually indistinguishable, and certain instructions.

the first time in the Court of Appeals, there were also two subsidiary questions. First, what was the effect, if any, of the failure of the defendants to raise the matter in the District Court? Second, what was the importance, if any, of the fact that a judgment, binding on the parties although not binding on Dutcher, had already been reached after extensive litigation? The three questions prove, on examination, to be interwoven.

We conclude, upon consideration of the record and applying the "equity and good conscience" test of Rule 19(b), that the Court of Appeals erred in not allowing the judgment to stand.

Rule 19(b) suggests four "interests" that must be examined in each case to determine whether, in equity and good conscience, the court should proceed without a party whose absence from the litigation is compelled. Each of these interests must, in this case, be viewed entirely from an appellate perspective since the matter of joinder was not considered in the trial court. First, the plaintiff has an interest in having a forum. Before the trial, the strength of this interest obviously depends upon whether a satisfactory alternative forum exists. On appeal, if the plaintiff has won, he has a strong additional interest in preserving his judgment. Second, the defendant may properly wish to avoid multiple litigation, or inconsistent relief, or sole responsibility for a liability he shares with another. After trial, however, if the defendant has failed to assert this interest, it is quite proper to consider it foreclosed.

Third, there is the interest of the outsider whom it would have been desirable to join. Of course, since the outsider is not before the court, he cannot be bound by the judgment rendered. This means, however, only that a judgment is not res judicata as to, or legally enforceable against, a nonparty. It obviously does not mean either (a) that a court may never issue a judgment that, in practice, affects a nonparty or (b) that (to the contrary) a court may always proceed without considering the potential effect on nonparties simply because they are not "bound" in the technical sense. Instead, as Rule 19(a) expresses it, the court must consider the extent to which the judgment may "as a practical matter impair or impede his ability to protect" his interest in the subject matter. When a case has reached the appeal stage the matter is more complex. The judgment appealed from may not in fact affect the interest of any outsider even though there existed, before trial, a possibility that a judgment affecting his interest would be rendered. When necessary, however, a court of appeals should, on its own initiative, take steps to protect the absent party, who of course had no opportunity to plead and prove his interest below.

Fourth, there remains the interest of the courts and the public in complete, consistent, and efficient settlement of controversies. We read the Rule's third criterion, whether the judgment issued in the absence of the nonjoined person will be "adequate," to refer to this public stake in settling disputes by wholes, whenever possible, for clearly the plaintiff, who himself chose both the forum and the parties defendant, will not be heard to complain about the sufficiency of the relief obtainable against them. After trial, considerations of efficiency of course include the fact that the time and expense of a trial have already been spent.

Rule 19(b) also directs a district court to consider the possibility of shaping relief to accommodate these four interests. Commentators had argued that greater attention should be paid to this potential solution to a joinder stymie, and the Rule now makes it explicit that a court should consider modification of a judgment as an alternative to dismissal. Needless to say, a court of appeals may also properly require suitable modification as a condition of affirmance.

Had the Court of Appeals applied Rule 19's criteria to the facts of the present case, it could hardly have reached the conclusion it did. We begin with the plaintiffs' viewpoint. It is difficult to decide at this stage whether they would have had an "adequate" remedy had the action been dismissed before trial for nonjoinder: we cannot here determine whether the plaintiffs could have brought the same action, against the same parties plus Dutcher, in a state court. After trial, however, the "adequacy" of this hypothetical alternative, from the plaintiffs' point of view, was obviously greatly diminished. Their interest in preserving a fully litigated judgment should be overborne only by rather greater opposing considerations than would be required at an earlier stage when the plaintiffs' only concern was for a federal rather than a state forum.

Opposing considerations in this case are hard to find. The defendants had no stake, either asserted or real, in the joinder of Dutcher. They showed no interest in joinder until the Court of Appeals took the matter into its own hands. This properly forecloses any interest of theirs, but for purposes of clarity we note that the insurance company, whose liability was limited to $100,000, had or will have full opportunity to litigate each claim on that fund against the claimant involved. Its only concern with the absence of Dutcher was and is to obtain a windfall escape from its defeat at trial.

The interest of the outsider, Dutcher, is more difficult to reckon. The Court of Appeals, concluding that it should not follow Rule 19's command to determine whether, as a practical matter, the judgment impaired the nonparty's ability to protect his rights, simply quoted the District Court's reasoning on the Dead Man issue as proof that Dutcher had a "right" to be joined . . . . There is a logical error in the Court of Appeals' appropriation of this reasoning for its own quite different purposes: Dutcher had an "adverse" interest (sufficient to invoke the Dead Man Rule) because he would have been *benefited*) by a ruling *in favor of* the insurance company; the question before the Court of Appeals, however, was whether Dutcher was *harmed* by the judgment *against* the insurance company.

The two questions are not the same. If the three plaintiffs had lost to the insurance company on the permission issue, that loss would have ended the matter favorably to Dutcher. If, as has happened, the three plaintiffs obtain a judgment against the insurance company on the permission issue, Dutcher may still claim that as a nonparty he is not estopped by that judgment from relitigating the issue. At that point it might be argued that

Dutcher should be bound by the previous decision because, although technically a nonparty, he had purposely bypassed an adequate opportunity to intervene. We do not now decide whether such an argument would be correct under the circumstances of this case. If, however, Dutcher is properly foreclosed by his failure to intervene in the present litigation, then the joinder issue considered in the Court of Appeals vanishes, for any rights of Dutcher's have been lost by his own inaction.

If Dutcher is not foreclosed by his failure to intervene below, then he is not "bound" by the judgment against the insurance company and, in theory, he has not been harmed. There remains, however, the practical question whether Dutcher is likely to have any need, and if so will have any opportunity, to relitigate. The only possible threat to him is that if the fund is used to pay judgments against Cionci the money may in fact have disappeared before Dutcher has an opportunity to assert his interest. Upon examination, we find this supposed threat neither large nor unavoidable.

The state-court actions against Dutcher had lain dormant for years at the pleading stage by the time the Court of Appeals acted. Petitioners assert here that under the applicable Pennsylvania vicarious liability law they have virtually no chance of recovery against Dutcher. We do not accept this assertion as fact, but the matter could have been explored below. Furthermore, even in the event of tort judgments against Dutcher, it is unlikely that he will be prejudiced by the outcome here. The potential claimants against Dutcher himself are identical with the potential claimants against Cionci's estate. Should the claimants seek to collect from Dutcher personally, he may be able to raise the permission issue defensively, making it irrelevant that the actual monies paid from the fund may have disappeared: Dutcher can assert that Cionci did not have his permission and that therefore the payments made on Cionci's behalf out of Dutcher's insurance policy should properly be credited against Dutcher's own liability. Of course, when Dutcher raises this defense he may lose, either on the merits of the permission issue or on the ground that the issue is foreclosed by Dutcher's failure to intervene in the present case, but Dutcher will not have been prejudiced by the failure of the District Court here to order him joined.

If the Court of Appeals was unconvinced that the threat to Dutcher was trivial, it could nevertheless have avoided all difficulties by proper phrasing of the decree. The District Court, for unspecified reasons, had refused to order immediate payment on the Cionci judgments. Payment could have been withheld pending the suits against Dutcher and relitigation (if that became necessary) by him. In this Court, furthermore, counsel for petitioners represented orally that they, the tort plaintiffs, would accept a limitation of all claims to the amount of the insurance policy. Obviously such a compromise could have been reached below had the Court of Appeals been willing to abandon its rigid approach and seek ways to preserve what was, as to the parties, subject to the appellant's other contentions, a perfectly valid judgment.

The suggestion of potential relitigation of the question of "permission" raises the fourth "interest" at stake in joinder cases—efficiency. It might have been preferable, at the trial level, if there were a forum available in which both the company and Dutcher could have been made defendants, to dismiss the action and force the plaintiffs to go elsewhere. Even this preference would have been highly problematical, however, for the actual threat of relitigation by Dutcher depended on there being judgments against him and on the amount of the fund, which was not revealed to the District Court. By the time the case reached the Court of Appeals, however, the problematical preference on efficiency grounds had entirely disappeared: there was no reason then to throw away a valid judgment just because it did not theoretically settle the whole controversy.

II.

Application of Rule 19(b)'s "equity and good conscience" test for determining whether to proceed or dismiss would doubtless have led to a contrary result below. The Court of Appeals' reasons for disregarding the Rule remain to be examined.[12] The majority of the court concluded that the Rule was inapplicable because "substantive" rights are involved, and substantive rights are not affected by the Federal Rules. Although the court did not articulate exactly what the substantive rights are, or what law determines them, we take it to have been making the following argument: (1) there is a category of persons called "indispensable parties"; (2) that category is defined by substantive law and the definition cannot be modified by rule; (3) the right of a person falling within that category to participate in the lawsuit in question is also a substantive matter, and is absolute.

With this we may contrast the position that is reflected in Rule 19. Whether a person is "indispensable," that is, whether a particular lawsuit

[12] Rule 19 was completely rewritten subsequent to the proceedings in the District Court in this case. There is, however, no occasion for separate consideration of the question whether the action of the Court of Appeals would have been proper under the old version of the Rule. The new version was adopted on July 1, 1966, while the appeal, in which the joinder question first arose, was pending. The majority in the Court of Appeals did not purport to rely on the older version, but on its conclusion that the Rule, in either form, had no application to this case. The dissent below found the Rule applicable, and concluded that the District Court should not be reversed on the basis of either version.

The new text of the Rule was not intended as a change in principles. Rather, the Committee found that the old text "was defective in its phrasing and did not point clearly to the proper basis of decision." This Court, having the ultimate rule-making authority subject to congressional veto, approved the Committee's suggestions. Where the new version emphasizes the pragmatic consideration of the effects of the alternatives of proceeding or dismissing, the older version tended to emphasize classification of parties as "necessary" or "indispensable." Although the two approaches should come to the same point, since the only reason for asking whether a person is "necessary" or "indispensable" is in order to decide whether to proceed or dismiss in his absence and since that decision must be made on the basis of practical considerations, Shaughnessy v. Pedreiro, 349 U.S. 48, 75 S.Ct. 591, and not by "prescribed formula," Niles–Bement–Pond Co. v. Iron Moulders' Union, 254 U.S. 77, 41 S.Ct. 39, the Committee concluded, without directly criticizing the outcome of any particular case, that there had at times been "undue preoccupation with abstract classifications of rights or obligations, as against consideration of the particular consequences of proceeding with the action and the ways by which these consequences might be ameliorated by the shaping of final relief or other precautions." . . .

must be dismissed in the absence of that person, can only be determined in the context of particular litigation. There is a large category, whose limits are not presently in question, of persons who, in the Rule's terminology, should be "joined if feasible," and who, in the older terminology, were called either necessary or indispensable parties. Assuming the existence of a person who should be joined if feasible, the only further question arises when joinder is not possible and the court must decide whether to dismiss or to proceed without him. To use the familiar but confusing terminology, the decision to proceed is a decision that the absent person is merely "necessary" while the decision to dismiss is a decision that he is "indispensable." The decision whether to dismiss (i.e., the decision whether the person missing is "indispensable") must be based on factors varying with the different cases, some such factors being substantive, some procedural, some compelling by themselves, and some subject to balancing against opposing interests. Rule 19 does not prevent the assertion of compelling substantive interests; it merely commands the courts to examine each controversy to make certain that the interests really exist. To say that a court "must" dismiss in the absence of an indispensable party and that it "cannot proceed" without him puts the matter the wrong way around: a court does not know whether a particular person is "indispensable" until it has examined the situation to determine whether it can proceed without him.

The Court of Appeals concluded, although it was the first court to hold, that the 19th century joinder cases in this Court created a federal, common-law, substantive right in a certain class of persons to be joined in the corresponding lawsuits.[16] . . .

[The Court here analyzed Elmendorf v. Taylor, 23 U.S. (10 Wheat.) 152 (1825); Mallow v. Hinde, 25 U.S. (12 Wheat.) 193 (1827); Northern Indiana Railroad v. Michigan Central Railroad, 56 U.S. (15 How.) 233 (1853); and Shields v. Barrow, 58 U.S. (17 How.) 130 (1855). After quoting the famous definitions from the Shields case, the Court said:]

These generalizations are still valid today, and they are consistent with the requirements of Rule 19, but they are not a substitute for the analysis required by that Rule. Indeed, the . . . Shields definition [of indispensability] states, in rather different fashion, the criteria for decision announced in Rule 19(b). One basis for dismissal is prejudice to the rights of an absent party that *"cannot"* be avoided in issuance of a final decree. Alternatively, if the decree can be so written that it protects the interests of the absent persons, but as so written it leaves the controversy so situated that the outcome may be inconsistent with "equity and good conscience," the suit should be dismissed.

---

[16] Numerous cases in the lower federal courts have dealt with compulsory joinder, and the Court of Appeals concluded that principles enunciated in those cases required dismissal here. However, none of the cases cited here or below presented a factual situation resembling this case: the error made by the Court of Appeals was precisely its reliance on formulas extracted from their contexts rather than on pragmatic analysis. . . .

. . . .

The majority of the Court of Appeals read Shields v. Barrow to say that a person whose interests "may be affected" by the decree of the court is an indispensable party, and that all indispensable parties have a "substantive right" to have suits dismissed in their absence. We are unable to read Shields as saying either. It dealt only with persons whose interests must, unavoidably, be affected by a decree and it said nothing about substantive rights.[22] Rule 19(b), which the Court of Appeals dismissed as an ineffective attempt to change the substantive rights stated in Shields, is, on the contrary, a valid statement of the criteria for determining whether to proceed or dismiss in the forced absence of an interested person. It takes, for aught that now appears, adequate account of the very real, very substantive claims to fairness on the part of outsiders that may arise in some cases. This, however, simply is not such a case.

III.

[The Court here rejected the court of appeals' second alternative ground, namely, that the district court, in the exercise of discretion, should have declined jurisdiction over this action for a declaratory judgment because supposedly the Smith and Harris actions pending in state court were presenting contemporaneously the same disputed issue.]

We think it clear that the judgment below cannot stand. The judgment is vacated and the case is remanded to the Court of Appeals for consideration of those issues raised on appeal that have not been considered, and, should the Court of Appeals affirm the District Court as to those issues, for appropriate disposition preserving the judgment of the District Court and protecting the interests of nonjoined persons.

It is so ordered.[a]

---

[22] Indeed, for example, it has been clear that in a diversity case the question of joinder is one of federal law. E.g., De Korwin v. First Nat. Bank, 156 F.2d 858, 860 (C.A.7th Cir.), citing Shields. To be sure, state-law questions may arise in determining what interest the outsider actually has, e.g., Kroese v. General Steel Castings Corp., 179 F.2d 760 (C.A.3d Cir.), but the ultimate question whether, given those state-defined interests, a federal court may proceed without the outsider is a federal matter.

[a] On remand, the estate plaintiffs urged that collateral estoppel now precluded the defendant insurance company. The argument was that the issue of permission had been settled by the verdict and judgment for Harris, against whom Dutcher had testified, and that, even if it was error not to have let him testify against the estate plaintiffs, the insurance company was not entitled to another trial of that issue. This was offensive use against a prior defendant.

The majority of the court of appeals' panel held that collateral estoppel applied, 411 F.2d 88 (3d Cir.1969). The majority went on to reject the other grounds urged by the insurance company for upsetting the district court's judgment. The opinion closed by remanding "the case to the district court for further proceedings. The district court should afford plaintiffs an opportunity to agree to the limitation to the policy limit of all their claims against the policy, whether arising out of judgments against Cionci or against Dutcher. If no such limitation is fixed, the district court should expressly stay any execution by virtue of the declaratory judgment decree until Dutcher shall have had a full opportunity either in the court below or in the state courts to present any claims he may have to the protection of Lumbermens' policy if any judgment is rendered against him in any of the now pending state court actions."

Question: (9) What would have been the effect on federal rulemaking if the Supreme Court had adopted the Third Circuit's view that the participatory right of a person who may be affected by the judgment is a "substantive right" unaffected by the Federal Rules?

SECTION 2. APPLICATION

With that background behind us, we are now ready to examine the joinder provisions in practice, with a continued focus on Rule 19.

INVOLUNTARY PLAINTIFF

Both the original and the present versions of Rule 19(a) say that a person who should join as a plaintiff but refuses to do so may be made a defendant or, in a proper case, an involuntary plaintiff. Therefore, all parties joined under Rule 19 normally come in as defendants. A "proper case" to the contrary is one in which the recalcitrant party as a defendant would not be subject to service of process, but equitable considerations require such party to permit the use of his name as a plaintiff. The involuntary plaintiff provision is thus a narrow means of circumventing the requirement of serving process.

The Advisory Committee's note on the original Rule cited Independent Wireless Telegraph Co. v. RCA, 269 U.S. 459, 46 S.Ct. 166 (1926), as a "proper case." There RCA, exclusive licensee of a patent, wanted to bring an infringement action. Under the authorities the patentee was an indispensable party to such an action. RCA requested the patentee to join as co-plaintiff, but the patentee refused. It could not be joined as a defendant because it was not within the reach of the personal jurisdiction of the court. Thereupon RCA brought the action naming the patentee as a plaintiff without its consent and giving it notice of the suit. The Supreme Court sanctioned this procedure. In Ferrara v. Rodale Press, 54 F.R.D. 3 (E.D.Pa. 1972), the district court permitted the same procedure in similar circumstances involving copyright infringement. In practice this provision of the Rule has generally been confined to such circumstances arising in patent and copyright cases, but the suggestion has been made that its use might appropriately be extended. See 4 Moore § 19.04[4][b].

Questions: (10) Can you suggest a situation where such extension would be appropriate?

(11) Two Texas lawyers bring a diversity action in Texas against a Delaware defendant to recover $82,500 in owed legal fees. The defendant moves to dismiss for nonjoinder of the plaintiffs' former partner, also a Texan, who has asserted that the defendant owes him part of those fees. The court determines that the former partner should come in as a defendant under Rule 19(a). Should the court now

dismiss for want of subject-matter jurisdiction? See Eikel v. States Marine Lines, 473 F.2d 959 (5th Cir.1973) (no). Why not?

Haas v. Jefferson National Bank

United States Court of Appeals, Fifth Circuit, 1971.
442 F.2d 394.

■ Before GEWIN, AINSWORTH and ALDISERT,* Circuit Judges.

■ ALDISERT, CIRCUIT JUDGE. Following a pre-trial conference, the district court entered an order finding that Charles H. Glueck was an "indispensable party" under Fed.R.Civ.Pro. 19, and dismissing the action on the ground that Glueck's presence in the case "violates the requirements of complete diversity." We must determine whether the court's action was appropriate at a pre-trial stage, and, if so, whether it abused its discretion in dismissing the action instead of proceeding without Glueck.

Invoking jurisdiction on the basis of diversity of citizenship, 28 U.S.C. § 1332, Haas, a citizen of Ohio, sought a mandatory injunction from the district court [for the Southern District of Florida] directing the Jefferson National Bank, a citizen of Florida, to issue to him 169½ shares of its common stock. Alternatively, he asked for damages reflecting the stock's value. He alleged a 1963 agreement with Glueck, also an Ohio citizen, under which they were to jointly purchase 250 shares of the bank's stock; the certificates were to issue in the name of Glueck but Haas was to have a one-half ownership of the shares. He also pleaded a similar 1966 agreement with Glueck to purchase 34 additional shares. According to Haas, he paid Glueck amounts representing one-half ownership, the bank had knowledge of his ownership interest, and the certificates and subsequent dividends were issued to Glueck.

Haas contends, however, that in 1967 he requested Glueck to order the bank to issue certificates in Haas' name, reflecting his ownership of 169½ shares, and that pursuant to this request Glueck presented to the bank properly endorsed certificates for 250 shares with instructions to reissue 170 shares to Haas and the balance to Glueck.

In its answer, the Bank explained that it had refused to make the assignment because at the time of the transfer request Glueck was indebted to it under the terms of a promissory note which required that Glueck pledge, assign, and transfer to the bank property of any kind owned by Glueck and coming into the possession of the Bank. The Bank averred that Glueck withdrew the transfer request and instead pledged the stock certificates with a second bank [in the Southern District of Florida] as collateral for a loan there.

---

* Of the Third Circuit, sitting by designation.

With these contentions forming the backdrop of the pre-trial conference, the parties stipulated to the questions of fact which remained to be litigated at trial:

(a) Did the Bank have knowledge of Haas' claimed ownership of the stock prior to Glueck's 1967 transfer request?

(b) Did Glueck withdraw the 1967 transfer request?

(c) What was the status of Glueck's obligation to the bank as represented by the promissory note?

(d) Did the second bank have possession of the stock in controversy at the time Haas filed the action?

(e) Did Haas in fact own 169½ shares of the bank stock?

Following the pre-trial conference and the entry of these stipulations, the district court entered an order directing Haas to amend his complaint to join Glueck as a party. The court then denied his motion to dismiss Glueck as a party, and granted the Bank's motion to dismiss the amended complaint on the jurisdictional ground of incomplete diversity.[1]

[The court had no difficulty in finding that the district court did not enter its joinder order prematurely and that, if it did not err in ordering the joinder of Glueck, it was obviously correct in finding the jurisdictional defect of incomplete diversity. In approaching the question whether Rule 19 required the joinder of Glueck, the court gave the classic quotation from Shields v. Barrow, referred to the Provident Tradesmens case, and set forth Rule 19.]

The Rule thus commands that we address ourselves to two broad questions: (1) Was Glueck a party "to be joined if feasible" under section (a)? If so, (2) was the court correct, under section (b), in dismissing the action or should it have proceeded without the additional party?

It is readily apparent that Glueck "falls within the category of persons who, under § (a), should be 'joined if feasible,' " Provident Tradesmens Bank & Trust Co. v. Patterson, supra, 390 U.S. at 108, 88 S.Ct. at 737, 19 L.Ed.2d 936, for his presence is critical to the disposition of the important issues in the litigation. His evidence will either support the complaint or bolster the defense: it will affirm or refute Haas' claim to half ownership of the stock; it will substantiate or undercut Haas' contention that the Bank had knowledge of his alleged ownership interest; it will corroborate or compromise the Bank's contention that Glueck rescinded the transfer order; and it will be crucial to the determination of Glueck's obligation to the Bank under the promissory note. The essence of Haas' action against the Bank is that it "unlawfully and recklessly seized, detained, [and] exercised improper dominion" over his shares in transferring and delivering them to the second bank as collateral for Glueck's loan. Thus, Glueck becomes more than a key witness whose testimony would be of inestimable

[1] Service of process was not properly effectuated because the attempted service in Ohio was beyond the territorial limits of the district court in Florida. . . .

value. Instead he emerges as an active participant in the alleged conversion of Haas' stock.

Applying the criterion of Rule 19(a)[(1)(B)(ii)], we believe that Glueck's absence would expose the defendant Bank "to a substantial risk of incurring double, multiple, or otherwise inconsistent obligations by reason of his claimed interest." If Haas prevailed in this litigation in the absence of Glueck and were adjudicated owner of half of the stock, Glueck, not being bound by res adjudicata, could theoretically succeed in later litigation against the Bank in asserting ownership of the whole. In addition, a favorable resolution of Haas' claim against the Bank could, under [19(a)(1)(B)(i)], "as a practical matter impair or impede [the absent party's] ability to protect [his] interest" in all of the shares—an interest that is at least apparent since all of the stock was issued in Glueck's name.

Because Glueck cannot be made a party without destroying diversity, however, it remains to be decided whether, under Rule 19(b), his presence is so vital that "in equity and good conscience the action . . . should be dismissed, the absent person being thus regarded as indispensable." This decision is always a matter of judgment and must be exercised with sufficient knowledge of the facts in order to evaluate the exact role of the absentees. . . .

We turn now to the specific factors enumerated in Rule 19(b), as applied to the facts before us. In our view the first factor tracks the considerations of 19(a)[(1)(B)(ii)] discussed above: "to what extent a judgment rendered in the person's absence might be prejudicial to him or those already parties." And based on the reasoning previously set forth, we believe this factor supplies weighty reason for a finding of indispensability.

The second factor directs the court to consider the extent to which the shaping of relief might avoid or lessen the prejudice to existing or absent parties. Because the title to the stock certificates, although not the immediate issue in this litigation, assumes such commanding importance, it is difficult to conceptualize a form of relief or protective provisions which would not require as a preliminary matter the determination of the question of title with all the resulting potential for prejudice.

In analyzing the third factor, "whether a judgment rendered in the person's absence will be adequate," . . . [i]t seems evident to us that the absence of Glueck in this litigation would, of necessity, result in less than a complete settlement of this controversy. For reasons already discussed, there is no semblance of a guarantee that a judgment on Haas' terms would settle the whole dispute generated by the facts here.

Finally Rule 19(b) requires us to consider whether the plaintiff will have an avenue for relief if the district court's dismissal for nonjoinder is affirmed. Clearly, the state courts of Ohio afford plaintiff Haas an opportunity to adjudicate his rights against Glueck.[9] They provide a ready forum to settle the question of title to the stock. Moreover assuming the disposition

---

[9] In response to the court's inquiry at oral argument, Haas' counsel reported that a state action between Haas and Glueck is now pending.

of the preliminary question of title in the Ohio courts, it is not difficult to conceptualize circumstances permitting the possibility of a second action against the Bank in which the problem of nonjoinder will not be so acute.

Accordingly, applying Rule 19(b)'s "equity and good conscience test", we hold that the district court did not abuse its discretion in concluding that Glueck was an indispensable party and in dismissing this action.

Affirmed.

Question: (12) The Kansas comparative negligence statute (a) provides that each tortfeasor is liable only in such proportion as that person's fault bears to total fault and (b) requires that, on motion of defendant, any absent person whose causal negligence is claimed to have contributed to the injury shall be joined as an additional defendant if feasible. Plaintiff, a Kansas citizen, was seriously injured as a bystander by an allegedly defective paint-sprayer manufactured by defendant, an out-of-state corporation. Plaintiff sued defendant in the Kansas federal court. Defendant moved to join the owner and the operator of the sprayer, who are insolvent Kansas citizens; and defendant also moved to dismiss, because the additional parties would destroy diversity of citizenship. What rulings?

WESTERN UNION TELEGRAPH CO. v. PENNSYLVANIA, 368 U.S. 71, 82 S.Ct. 199 (1961). Western Union, a New York corporation doing business throughout the United States and in foreign countries, carries on a telegraphic money-order business. The procedure is for the sender to pay Western Union the sum to be transmitted and the charge for doing so. If the payee is not located or fails to call for the money, the sending office tries to give a refund to the sender. Sometimes Western Union can neither make payment to the payee nor make a refund to the sender, and sometimes neither one cashes the draft issued by Western Union in payment or refund. Pennsylvania law provides that "any real or personal property within or subject to the control of this Commonwealth . . . shall escheat to the Commonwealth" whenever it "shall be without a lawful owner" or "remain unclaimed for the period of seven successive years" or whenever "the whereabouts of such owner . . . shall be and remain unknown for the period of seven successive years."

In this Pennsylvania state-court action, Pennsylvania managed under the statute to escheat the accumulation of undisbursed money held by Western Union arising out of money orders bought in Pennsylvania. Western Union did not claim the money for itself but challenged Pennsylvania's right to the money, urging that a judgment of escheat would not protect it from multiple liability in Pennsylvania or elsewhere. Western Union insisted that there was no "res" in Pennsylvania and that service by publication did not satisfy due process. Apparently, New York had already escheated part of the very funds claimed by Pennsylvania.

The U.S. Supreme Court, in an opinion by Justice Black, reversed on the ground that Pennsylvania had no power to escheat the money, saying:

"We find it unnecessary to decide any of Western Union's contentions as to the adequacy of notice to and validity of service on the individual claimants by publication. For as we view these proceedings, there is a far more important question raised by this record—whether Pennsylvania had power at all to render a judgment of escheat which would bar New York or any other state from escheating this same property.

"Pennsylvania does not claim and could not claim that the same debts or demands could be escheated by two states. See Standard Oil Co. v. New Jersey, 341 U.S. 428, 443, 71 S.Ct. 822, 831. And our prior opinions have recognized that when a state court's jurisdiction purports to be based, as here, on the presence of property within the State, the holder of such property is deprived of due process of law if he is compelled to relinquish it without assurance that he will not be held liable again in another jurisdiction or in a suit brought by a claimant who is not bound by the first judgment. Anderson National Bank v. Luckett, 321 U.S. 233, 242–243, 64 S.Ct. 599, 604; Security Savings Bank v. California, 263 U.S. 282, 286–290, 44 S.Ct. 108, 110–111. Applying that principle, there can be no doubt that Western Union has been denied due process by the Pennsylvania judgment here unless the Pennsylvania courts had power to protect Western Union from any other claim, including the claim of the State of New York that these obligations are property 'within' New York and are therefore subject to escheat under its laws. But New York was not a party to this proceeding and could not have been made a party, and, of course, New York's claims could not be cut off where New York was not heard as a party. Moreover, the potential multi-state claims to the 'property' which is the subject of this escheat make it not unlikely that various States will claim in rem jurisdiction over it. Therefore, Western Union was not protected by the Pennsylvania judgment, for a state court judgment need not be given full faith and credit by other states as to parties or property not subject to the jurisdiction of the court that rendered it. Pennoyer v. Neff, 95 U.S. 714; Riley v. New York Trust Co., 315 U.S. 343, 62 S.Ct. 608."[b]

CARL TOBIAS, RULE 19 AND THE PUBLIC RIGHTS EXCEPTION TO PARTY JOINDER, 65 N.C.L.Rev. 745, 745–47, 792 (1987). "Federal courts increasingly confront a difficult question of party joinder when 'public interest litigants,' such as the National Wildlife Federation, sue the government over administrative agency activity. These public interest litigants challenge an activity, like leasing of the public lands, but fail to join entities, such as major oil companies, holding oil and gas leases on the

[b] In Texas v. New Jersey, 379 U.S. 674, 85 S.Ct. 626 (1965), the Court exercising its original jurisdiction developed a federal rule for escheat cases, holding generally that intangible property is subject to escheat only by the state of the last known address of the creditor, as shown by the debtor's books and records.

public lands. The entities have interests that may be adversely affected by a determination on the merits favorable to the plaintiff. The party joinder issue that these suits present is whether Rule 19 of the Federal Rules of Civil Procedure requires that the plaintiff's case be dismissed, whether absentees must be joined because joinder is feasible, or whether the litigation can continue without joinder of such absentees. Numerous judges have treated this question by creating a 'public rights exception,' which permits the plaintiff's suit to proceed in the absence of entities that could be prejudiced should the litigation continue without them. But no court has clearly articulated, analyzed, or substantiated the exception. Moreover, most of these judges, out of apparent concern that plaintiffs have a forum in which to contest agency activity and vindicate public rights, have evinced little express solicitude for interests of others, particularly absentees. Furthermore, the plethora of varying factual contexts in which courts have been asked to apply the public rights exception are difficult to generalize. The history of recent public rights litigation, however, illustrates the problems that can attend invocation of the public rights exception.

"In recent public rights litigation, trial judges have not required joinder of a large number of geographically dispersed absentees that have spent millions of dollars exploring for, and developing, natural resources in reliance on government leases of public lands. When public interest litigants have successfully challenged the propriety of government activity relating to lease issuance, trial judges essentially have discontinued absentee exploration and development pursuant to the leases. Thus, the absentees have had to spend considerable time, money, and effort participating in prolonged litigation. Indeed, the absentees even could lose the substantial investments committed to exploration and development, should the federal judiciary ultimately reject their contentions, because the absentees cannot secure satisfactory relief against the government under existing compensation schemes. In short, trial judges have not ordered joinder of absentees, despite the apparent significance of the absentees' interests.

. . . .

". . . Indeed, solicitude for plaintiffs has been excessive and lack of concern for other interests inappropriate. Moreover, doubts about rule 19 have been ungrounded. Application of the rule and additional measures available to courts, litigants, absentees, and counsel will permit judges to facilitate plaintiffs' vindication of public rights and better serve others, namely absentees. Therefore, courts should rely on rule 19 and other available mechanisms, rather than engage in cryptic, unclear, and strained analysis to support an exception the application of which has engendered protracted litigation, wasted resources, and even eroded judicial credibility."

TOPIC C

CLASS ACTIONS

SECTION 1. REPRESENTATIVE LITIGATION

The class action's longer roots seemingly trace from the twelfth century and the origins of medieval group litigation, by which communities and other social groups in England naturally litigated at law through their leaders. Shorter roots trace more directly from the eighteenth century and English equity's troubled recognition of modern group litigation, whereby groups of persons merely with common objectives could sometimes litigate through representatives with congruent objectives. From such beginnings slowly evolved, by a convoluted and fitful legal process reflecting various social pressures, the limited but recognized device of representative proceedings (as they are called in England) or class suits.[a]

In such a class suit, certain absent persons were no longer deemed necessary parties, but were nevertheless bound by judgment, thus allowing one suit where otherwise many actions would be brought or where no individual action could practicably be brought. Given the somewhat confused blessing of Story, e.g., Joseph Story, Commentaries on Equity Pleadings § 97 (Boston 1838), the class suit became an accepted, albeit obscure, part of American jurisprudence at an early date.

A leading case was Smith v. Swormstedt, 57 U.S. (16 How.) 288 (1853). The Methodist Episcopal Church had split over the slavery issue. Six plaintiffs representing 1500 traveling preachers of the Methodist Episcopal Church South sued in federal court against three defendants as representatives of 3800 traveling preachers of the Methodist Episcopal Church North, seeking a division of church property. On objection for want of parties, the Court held that the plaintiffs could maintain the bill and indicated that the decree would bind all. The Court cited Story, who thought class-suit decrees to be ordinarily binding on absentees; but curiously the Court did

---

[a] On the historical evolution, see Stephen C. Yeazell, From Medieval Group Litigation to the Modern Class Action (1987), critically reviewed by Robert G. Bone, Personal and Impersonal Litigative Forms: Reconceiving the History of Adjudicative Representation, 70 B.U.L.Rev. 213 (1990). For a comparative perspective, see Edward F. Sherman, Group Litigation Under Foreign Legal Systems: Variations and Alternatives to American Class Actions, 52 DePaul L.Rev. 401 (2002); Symposium, Debates Over Group Litigation in Comparative Perspective: What Can We Learn from Each Other?, 11 Duke J.Comp. & Int'l L. 157 (2001).

not cite Federal Equity Rule 48, 42 U.S. (1 How.) lvi (1842), which authorized class suits while perplexingly saying that "the decree shall be without prejudice to the rights and claims of all the absent parties."

Later, Federal Equity Rule 38, 226 U.S. 659, 33 S.Ct. xxix (1912), omitted the quoted qualification. The Court in Supreme Tribe of Ben–Hur v. Cauble, 255 U.S. 356, 41 S.Ct. 338 (1921), took note of the omission. That case involved a previous federal suit by a group of Class A certificate holders in the Supreme Tribe, a fraternal benefit association, with the complainants purporting to sue on behalf of the more than 70,000 Class A holders and seeking to overturn a reorganization plan that had reclassified the certificates; but the Supreme Tribe as defendant had prevailed on the merits. Later, when another group of Class A holders tried to raise the same issue, the Court refused to permit this, firmly saying: "The parties bringing the suit truly represented the interested class. If the decree is to be effective and conflicting judgments are to be avoided all of the class must be concluded by the decree."

See the original form of Rule 23 in the Rules booklet, as well as the Advisory Committee's note on the 1966 amendment explaining the original Rule's inadequacy as a guide to the proper extent of a class-action judgment. Observe particularly the three subdivisions of original Rule 23(a), which set up three kinds of class actions known familiarly as "true," "hybrid," and "spurious." (Smith v. Swormstedt and the Supreme Tribe case were examples of "true" class actions under old Rule 23(a)(1).) The most striking point about this highly conceptual classification was that although "true" and "hybrid" class actions had binding effects on all members of the class, it was generally thought that "spurious" class actions bound only the parties actually before the court and thus operated largely as a rather ordinary permissive joinder device.

(a) CONSTITUTIONAL REQUIREMENT

Hansberry v. Lee

Supreme Court of the United States, 1940.
311 U.S. 32, 61 S.Ct. 115.

[Twenty-seven blocks in Chicago were subject to a restrictive agreement that none of the property should be sold to, leased to, or permitted to be occupied by blacks, the agreement to become effective when signed by owners of 95 percent of the frontage. Such agreements were very common in Chicago, which had highly segregated housing. Moreover, such agreements, running with the land, were judicially enforceable until the decision in Shelley v. Kraemer, 334 U.S. 1, 68 S.Ct. 836 (1948). Nevertheless, changed economic and social conditions in the 1930s, especially the inability of white sellers to find white buyers, were putting some such neighborhood agreements under significant erosive pressures. For the background story of the Hansberry case, see Jay Tidmarsh, "The Story of Hansberry: The Rise of the Modern Class Action," in Civil Procedure Stories 233 (Kevin M. Clermont ed., 2d ed. 2008).

[One of the owners had sued in an Illinois state court to enforce the agreement against four defendants involved in leasing an apartment to a black man. The action (Burke v. Kleiman) was stated to be brought on behalf of all similarly situated. The parties stipulated that owners of the requisite 95 percent had signed the agreement, and the court found the stipulated fact to be true. The only issue raised at the trial was that of change of neighborhood. The plaintiff succeeded in the action, and the court issued an injunction.

[A few years later, other property owners brought the instant non-class suit in an Illinois state court to enforce the agreement against other defendants in respect to another house. The defendants included the husband of the plaintiff in the Burke action and also the black purchasers, who incidentally were the parents of a little girl, Lorraine Hansberry, who would go on to write a celebrated play drawing on her family's ugly Chicago experience, A Raisin in the Sun (1959). The defendants tried to defend on the ground that owners of 95 percent in truth had not signed. Though the court found as a fact that owners of only 54 percent had signed, it felt obliged on principles of res judicata to hold the defense to be unavailable. An injunction followed. A divided Illinois Supreme Court affirmed, viewing the present defendants as members of the plaintiff class in the first action or successors in interest, and thus bound in the absence of fraud or collusion.[b] Certiorari was granted.]

■ MR. JUSTICE STONE delivered the opinion of the Court.

The question is whether the Supreme Court of Illinois, by its adjudication that petitioners in this case are bound by a judgment rendered in an earlier litigation to which they were not parties, has deprived them of the due process of law guaranteed by the Fourteenth Amendment.

---

[b] The trial court in Action #2 had found the stipulation in Action #1 to be false, fraudulent, and collusive, but it nevertheless had held res judicata to be applicable. The Illinois Supreme Court found the stipulation to be false but not fraudulent or collusive.

Lorraine Hansberry
1930–1965

". . . That fight also required that our family occupy the disputed property in a hellishly hostile 'white neighborhood' in which, literally, howling mobs surrounded our house. One of their missiles almost took the life of the then eight-year-old signer of this letter. . . ."

—Lorraine Hansberry, To Be Young, Gifted and Black 20–21 (Robert Nemiroff adapter, 1969)

(Photo: Courtesy Robert Nemiroff)

. . . .

State courts are free to attach such descriptive labels to litigations before them as they may choose and to attribute to them such consequences as they think appropriate under state constitutions and laws, subject only to the requirements of the Constitution of the United States. But when the judgment of a state court, ascribing to the judgment of another court the binding force and effect of res judicata, is challenged for want of due process it becomes the duty of this Court to examine the course of procedure in both litigations to ascertain whether the litigant whose rights have thus been adjudicated has been afforded such notice and opportunity to be heard as are requisite to the due process which the Constitution prescribes. Western Life Indem. Co. v. Rupp, 235 U.S. 261, 273, 35 S.Ct. 37, 40.

It is a principle of general application in Anglo–American jurisprudence that one is not bound by a judgment in personam in a litigation in which he is not designated as a party or to which he has not been made a party by service of process. Pennoyer v. Neff, 95 U.S. 714; 1 Freeman on Judgments, 5th ed., § 407. A judgment rendered in such circumstances is not entitled to the full faith and credit which the Constitution and statute of the United States, Rev.Stat. § 905, 28 U.S.C. § 687,[c] prescribe, [citations omitted]; and judicial action enforcing it against the person or property of the absent party is not that due process which the Fifth and Fourteenth Amendments require. [Citations omitted.]

To these general rules there is a recognized exception that, to an extent not precisely defined by judicial opinion, the judgment in a "class" or "representative" suit, to which some members of the class are parties, may bind members of the class or those represented who were not made parties to it. Smith v. Swormstedt, 16 How. (57 U.S.) 288; Supreme Council of the Royal Arcanum v. Green, 237 U.S. 531, 35 S.Ct. 724; Hartford Life Ins. Co. v. Ibs, 237 U.S. 662, 35 S.Ct. 692; Hartford Life Ins. Co. v. Barber, 245 U.S. 146, 38 S.Ct. 54; Supreme Tribe of Ben–Hur v. Cauble, 255 U.S. 356, 41 S.Ct. 338; cf. Christopher v. Brusselback, 302 U.S. 500, 58 S.Ct. 350.

The class suit was an invention of equity to enable it to proceed to a decree in suits where the number of those interested in the subject of the litigation is so great that their joinder as parties in conformity to the usual rules of procedure is impracticable. Courts are not infrequently called upon to proceed with causes in which the number of those interested in the litigation is so great as to make difficult or impossible the joinder of all because some are not within the jurisdiction or because their whereabouts is unknown or where if all were made parties to the suit its continued abatement by the death of some would prevent or unduly delay a decree. In such cases where the interests of those not joined are of the same class as the interests of those who are, and where it is considered that the latter fairly represent the former in the prosecution of the litigation of the issues

[c] Now 28 U.S.C. § 1738.

in which all have a common interest, the court will proceed to a decree. Brown v. Vermuden, Ch.Cas. 272, 22 Eng.Rep. 796; London v. Richmond, 2 Vern. 421, 23 Eng.Rep. 870; Cockburn v. Thompson, 16 Ves.Jr. 321, 33 Eng.Rep. 1005; West v. Randall, C.C., 2 Mason 181, Fed.Cas. No. 17,424; Beatty v. Kurtz, 2 Pet. (27 U.S.) 566; Smith v. Swormstedt, supra; Supreme Tribe of Ben–Hur v. Cauble, supra; Story, Equity Pleadings, 2d ed., § 98.

It is evident that the considerations which may induce a court thus to proceed, despite a technical defect of parties, may differ from those which must be taken into account in determining whether the absent parties are bound by the decree or, if it is adjudged that they are, in ascertaining whether such an adjudication satisfies the requirements of due process and of full faith and credit. Nevertheless there is scope within the framework of the Constitution for holding in appropriate cases that a judgment rendered in a class suit is res judicata as to members of the class who are not formal parties to the suit. Here, as elsewhere, the Fourteenth Amendment does not compel state courts or legislatures to adopt any particular rule for establishing the conclusiveness of judgments in class suits; [citations omitted], nor does it compel the adoption of the particular rules thought by this Court to be appropriate for the federal courts. With a proper regard for divergent local institutions and interests, [citation omitted], this Court is justified in saying that there has been a failure of due process only in those cases where it cannot be said that the procedure adopted, fairly insures the protection of the interests of absent parties who are to be bound by it. [Citation omitted.]

It is familiar doctrine of the federal courts that members of a class not present as parties to the litigation may be bound by the judgment where they are in fact adequately represented by parties who are present, or where they actually participate in the conduct of the litigation in which members of the class are present as parties, Plumb v. Goodnow (Plumb v. Crane), 123 U.S. 560, 8 S.Ct. 216; Confectioners' Machinery & Mfg. Co. v. Racine Engine & Machinery Co., 7 Cir., 163 F. 914; Id., 7 Cir., 170 F. 1021; Bryant Electric Co. v. Marshall, C.C., 169 F. 426, or where the interest of the members of the class, some of whom are present as parties, is joint, or where for any other reason the relationship between the parties present and those who are absent is such as legally to entitle the former to stand in judgment for the latter. Smith v. Swormstedt, supra; cf. Christopher v. Brusselback, supra, 302 U.S. at 503–04, 58 S.Ct. at 352, and cases cited.

In all such cases, so far as it can be said that the members of the class who are present are, by generally recognized rules of law, entitled to stand in judgment for those who are not, we may assume for the present purposes that such procedure affords a protection to the parties who are represented, though absent, which would satisfy the requirements of due process and full faith and credit. See Bernheimer v. Converse, 206 U.S. 516, 27 S.Ct. 755; Marin v. Augedahl, 247 U.S. 142, 38 S.Ct. 452; Chandler v. Peketz, 297 U.S. 609, 56 S.Ct. 602. Nor do we find it necessary for the decision of this case to say that, when the only circumstance defining the class is that the determination of the rights of its members turns upon a single issue of fact or law, a state could not constitutionally adopt a procedure whereby some of the members of the class could stand in judgment for all, provided that the procedure were so devised and applied as to insure that those present are of the same class as those absent and that the litigation is so conducted as to insure the full and fair consideration of the common issue. Compare New England Divisions Case, 261 U.S. 184, 197, 43 S.Ct. 270, 275; Taggart v. Bremner, 7 Cir., 236 F. 544. We decide only that the procedure and the course of litigation sustained here by the plea of res judicata do not satisfy these requirements.

The restrictive agreement did not purport to create a joint obligation or liability. If valid and effective its promises were the several obligations of the signers and those claiming under them. The promises ran severally to every other signer. It is plain that in such circumstances all those alleged to be bound by the agreement would not constitute a single class in any litigation brought to enforce it. Those who sought to secure its benefits by enforcing it could not be said to be in the same class with or represent those whose interest was in resisting performance, for the agreement by its terms imposes obligations and confers rights on the owner of each plot of land who signs it. If those who thus seek to secure the benefits of the agreement were rightly regarded by the state Supreme Court as constituting a class, it is evident that those signers or their successors who are interested in challenging the validity of the agreement and resisting its performance are not of the same class in the sense that their interests are identical so that any group who had elected to enforce rights conferred by the agreement could be said to be acting in the interest of any others who were free to deny its obligation.

Because of the dual and potentially conflicting interests of those who are putative parties to the agreement in compelling or resisting its performance, it is impossible to say, solely because they are parties to it, that any two of them are of the same class. Nor without more, and with the due regard for the protection of the rights of absent parties which due process exacts, can some be permitted to stand in judgment for all.

It is one thing to say that some members of a class may represent other members in a litigation where the sole and common interest of the class in the litigation is either to assert a common right or to challenge an asserted obligation. Smith v. Swormstedt, supra; Supreme Tribe of Ben–Hur v. Cauble, supra; Groves v. Farmers State Bank, 368 Ill. 35, 12 N.E.2d 618. It is quite another to hold that all those who are free alternatively either to assert rights or to challenge them are of a single class, so that any group, merely because it is of the class so constituted, may be deemed adequately to represent any others of the class in litigating their interests in either alternative. Such a selection of representatives for purposes of litigation, whose substantial interests are not necessarily or even probably the same as those whom they are deemed to represent, does not afford that protection to absent parties which due process requires. The doctrine of representation of absent parties in a class suit has not hitherto been thought to go so far. [Citations omitted.] Apart from the opportunities it would afford for the fraudulent and collusive sacrifice of the rights of absent parties, we think that the representation in this case no more satisfies the requirements of due process than a trial by a judicial officer who is in such situation that he may have an interest in the outcome of the litigation in conflict with that of the litigants. Tumey v. Ohio, 273 U.S. 510, 47 S.Ct. 437.

The plaintiffs in the Burke case sought to compel performance of the agreement in behalf of themselves and all others similarly situated. They did not designate the defendants in the suit as a class or seek any injunction or other relief against others than the named defendants, and the decree which was entered did not purport to bind others. In seeking to enforce the agreement the plaintiffs in that suit were not representing the petitioners here whose substantial interest is in resisting performance. The defendants in the first suit were not treated by the pleadings or decree as representing others or as foreclosing by their defense the rights of others; and, even though nominal defendants, it does not appear that their interest in defeating the contract outweighed their interest in establishing its validity. For a court in this situation to ascribe to either the plaintiffs or defendants the performance of such functions on behalf of petitioners here, is to attribute to them a power that it cannot be said that they had assumed to exercise, and a responsibility which, in view of their dual interests it does not appear that they could rightly discharge.

Reversed.

■ MR. JUSTICE MCREYNOLDS, MR. JUSTICE ROBERTS and MR. JUSTICE REED concur in the result.

Questions: (1) Where would Hansberry v. Lee fit in the tripartite classification of the 1938 formulation of Rule 23?

(2) Was Justice Stone intimating that the infirmities found in Action #1 could have been cured by either (a) some effective form of notice to all the land owners or (b) designation of the defendants in that action as representatives of a class of dissidents? See Developments in the Law—Class Actions, 89 Harv.L.Rev. 1318, 1471–75, 1481–82 (1976). What, then, was the critical defect?

(3) Due process thus establishes a justificatory prerequisite for class actions, a floor that restricts class actions to constitutionally acceptable costs and so justifies our pursuit of some of the benefits of class actions. This prerequisite is termed "adequate representation." But does "adequate representation" mean that, (a) presumptively or (b) actually, the represented persons in the purported class agree with the objectives of the representative parties, who vigorously and competently pursue those objectives? And does it mean something additional, such as that (a) the absentees share common substantive interests with their representatives or (b) the former have somehow consented to representation by the latter?

RICHARDS v. JEFFERSON COUNTY, ALABAMA, 517 U.S. 793, 116 S.Ct. 1761 (1996). Jason Richards and Fannie Hill brought this class action in Alabama state court on behalf of all nonfederal employees subject to the county's occupation tax, which they claimed was unconstitutional. The county moved for summary judgment on the ground of res judicata, looking to a prior action, Bedingfield v. Jefferson County, 527 So.2d 1270 (Ala. 1988), in which three taxpayers and a Birmingham city official unsuccessfully attacked the tax. The trial court granted the motion, and the Alabama Supreme Court affirmed.

Justice Stevens delivered the opinion for a unanimous Court:

"In Hansberry v. Lee, 311 U.S. 32, 37, 61 S.Ct. 115, 116 (1940), we held that it would violate the Due Process Clause of the Fourteenth Amendment to bind litigants to a judgment rendered in an earlier litigation to which they were not parties and in which they were not adequately represented. The decision of the Supreme Court of Alabama that we review today presents us with the same basic question in a somewhat different context.

. . . .

"We begin by noting that the parties to the Bedingfield case failed to provide petitioners with any notice that a suit was pending which would conclusively resolve their legal rights. That failure is troubling because, as we explained in Mullane v. Central Hanover Bank & Trust Co., 339 U.S. 306, 70 S.Ct. 652 (1950), the right to be heard ensured by the guarantee of due process 'has little reality or worth unless one is informed that the matter is pending and can choose for himself whether to appear or default, acquiesce or contest.' Id., at 314, 70 S.Ct., at 657; Phillips Petroleum Co. v. Shutts, 472 U.S. 797, 812, 105 S.Ct. 2965, 2974–2975 (1985); Schroeder v. City of New York, 371 U.S. 208, 212–213, 83 S.Ct. 279, 282–283 (1962). Nevertheless, respondents ask us to excuse the lack of notice on the ground that petitioners, as the Alabama Supreme Court concluded, were adequately represented in Bedingfield.[5]

. . . .

"Even assuming that our opinion in Hansberry may be read to leave open the possibility that in some class suits adequate representation might cure a lack of notice, but cf. [311 U.S.], at 40, 61 S.Ct., at 117; Eisen v. Carlisle & Jacquelin, 417 U.S. 156, 177, 94 S.Ct. 2140, 2152 (1974); Mullane v. Central Hanover Bank & Trust Co., 339 U.S., at 319, 70 S.Ct., at 659–660, it may not be read to permit the application of res judicata here. Our opinion explained that a prior proceeding, to have binding effect on absent parties, would at least have to be 'so devised and applied as to insure that those present are of the same class as those absent and that the

[5] Of course, mere notice may not suffice to preserve one's right to be heard in a case such as the one before us. The general rule is that "[t]he law does not impose upon any person absolutely entitled to a hearing the burden of voluntary intervention in a suit to which he is a stranger." Chase Nat. Bank v. Norwalk, 291 U.S. 431, 441, 54 S.Ct. 475, 479 (1934); but cf. Penn–Central Merger and N & W Inclusion Cases, 389 U.S. 486, 505, n. 4, 88 S.Ct. 602, 612, n. 4 (1968) (noting that absent parties were invited to intervene by the court).

litigation is so conducted as to insure the full and fair consideration of the common issue.' 311 U.S., at 43, 61 S.Ct., at 119; cf. Phillips Petroleum Co. v. Shutts, 472 U.S., at 811–812, 105 S.Ct., at 2974. It is plain that the Bedingfield action, like the prior proceeding in Hansberry itself, does not fit such a description.

"The Alabama Supreme Court concluded that the '*taxpayers* in the Bedingfield action adequately represented the interests of the taxpayers here,' 662 So.2d, at 1130 (emphasis added), but the three county taxpayers who were parties in Bedingfield did not sue on behalf of a class; their pleadings did not purport to assert any claim against or on behalf of any nonparties; and the judgment they received did not purport to bind any county taxpayers who were nonparties. That the acting director of finance for the city of Birmingham also sued in his capacity as both an individual taxpayer and a public official does not change the analysis. Even if we were to assume, as the Alabama Supreme Court did not, that by suing in his official capacity, the finance director intended to represent the pecuniary interests of all city taxpayers, and not simply the corporate interests of the city itself, he did not purport to represent the pecuniary interests of *county* taxpayers like petitioners.

"As a result, there is no reason to suppose that the Bedingfield court took care to protect the interests of petitioners in the manner suggested in Hansberry. Nor is there any reason to suppose that the individual taxpayers in Bedingfield understood their suit to be on behalf of absent county taxpayers. Thus, to contend that the plaintiffs in Bedingfield somehow represented petitioners, let alone represented them in a constitutionally adequate manner, would be 'to attribute to them a power that it cannot be said that they had assumed to exercise.' Hansberry, 311 U.S., at 46, 61 S.Ct., at 120.

"Because petitioners and the Bedingfield litigants are best described as mere 'strangers' to one another, Martin v. Wilks, 490 U.S. [755,] 762, 109 S.Ct. [2180,] 2184–2185 [(1989)], we are unable to conclude that the Bedingfield plaintiffs provided representation sufficient to make up for the fact that petitioners neither participated in, see Montana v. United States, 440 U.S. 147, 154, 99 S.Ct. 970, 974 (1979), nor had the opportunity to participate in, the Bedingfield action. Accordingly, due process prevents the former from being bound by the latter's judgment."

Question: (4) If any person has received constitutionally adequate representation, why should the judgment not bind as well as benefit that person, whether or not a class-action judgment was rendered? In other words, why not generally treat adjudication as legislation or administration? Is the answer any more complicated than that by a cost-benefit analysis the rulemakers have chosen to give a certain scope to Rule 23 and thus marked out how far we shall permit the binding of nonparties?

INTERNATIONAL UNION, UAW v. BROCK, 477 U.S. 274, 106 S.Ct. 2523 (1986). The union sued the Secretary of Labor to invalidate, as inconsistent with statute, certain of his guidelines that impeded its members in receiving federal unemployment benefits through state officials. The district court gave judgment for the union. The court of appeals reversed, saying that the union did not have standing to litigate on behalf of its injured members.

On certiorari the Supreme Court reversed. Disagreeing with the Secretary's position, Justice Marshall for the Court ruled that the union met the three-pronged test for associational standing: (1) its members would otherwise have standing to sue in their own right; (2) the interests it seeks to protect are germane to the organization's purpose; and (3) neither the claim asserted nor the relief requested requires the participation of individual members in the lawsuit.

The Secretary had also argued against the very idea of associational standing, contending that the doctrine served the same function as Rule 23 but lacked the Rule's safeguards to ensure adequate representation. Here the Court countered:

"The Secretary's presentation, however, fails to recognize the special features, advantageous both to the individuals represented and to the judicial system as a whole, that distinguish suits by associations on behalf of their members from class actions. While a class action creates an ad hoc union of injured plaintiffs who may be linked only by their common claims, an association suing to vindicate the interests of its members can draw upon a pre-existing reservoir of expertise and capital. . . . These resources can assist both courts and plaintiffs. . . .

"In addition, the doctrine of associational standing recognizes that the primary reason people join an organization is often to create an effective vehicle for vindicating interests that they share with others. . . . The very forces that cause individuals to band together in an association will thus provide some guarantee that the association will work to promote their interests.

"We are not prepared to dismiss out of hand the Secretary's concern that associations . . . will not always be able to represent adequately the interests of all their injured members. Should an association be deficient in this regard, a judgment won against it might not preclude subsequent claims by the association's members without offending due process principles. And were we presented with evidence that such a problem existed either here or in cases of this type, we would have to consider how it might be alleviated. However, the Secretary has given us absolutely no reason to doubt the ability of the [union] to proceed here on behalf of its aggrieved members, and his presentation has fallen far short of meeting the heavy burden of persuading us to abandon settled principles of associational standing."

Justice White, joined by Chief Justice Burger and Justice Rehnquist, dissented on a jurisdictional ground. Justice Powell dissented on the ground that the union should have had to establish the number of its injured members, that number having to be substantial enough to ensure adequate representation.

(b) RULE REQUIREMENTS

Rule 23 as originally written precipitated a considerable volume of litigation, apparently by directing the attention of lawyers to a hitherto unfamiliar procedural device. The issues became increasingly complex and the results highly uncertain, in good part because of the difficulties in the Rule. Professor Chafee was led to remark: "The situation is so tangled and bewildering that I sometimes wonder whether the world would be any the worse off if the class-suit device had been left buried in the learned obscurity of Calvert on Parties to Suits in Equity." Zechariah Chafee, Jr., Some Problems of Equity 200 (1950).

The 1966 revision of the Rule aimed to resolve the doubts about the binding effect of the resulting judgments, to broaden the usefulness of the class-action device, and to improve the procedural management of these complex actions. It abandoned the attempt to define class actions by technical reference to the abstract character of the rights involved and tried to describe in more homely and pragmatic terms the situations in which class actions would be available. There is unanimity on the fact that it has witnessed a torrent of class litigation, albeit with an ebb and flow, but certainly much heavier than the volume its predecessors had experienced. But there is no unanimity about the degree of success of the new Rule. It has suffered from the excessive enthusiasm of its friends and the calumny of its enemies. The material that follows is aimed to give a flavor of the problems and to furnish some basis for a tentative judgment about the propriety and efficacy of the Rule.

Gonzales v. Cassidy

United States Court of Appeals, Fifth Circuit, 1973.
474 F.2d 67.

■ Before DYER, CIRCUIT JUDGE, SKELTON, JUDGE,* and INGRAHAM, CIRCUIT JUDGE.

■ INGRAHAM, CIRCUIT JUDGE. The question in this appeal is whether plaintiff-appellant Gonzales and the class he seeks to represent are bound by the res judicata effect of a prior class suit involving the same class (represented by a different named plaintiff), the same defendants and the same issues. We agree with Gonzales that the class was inadequately represented when the class representative in the prior suit failed to appeal from the trial court's judgment. We reverse and remand.

---

* Hon. Byron G. Skelton, of the U.S. Court of Claims, sitting by designation.

The prior suit began in May 1969. Antonio Gaytan filed suit as a class action against Clifton Cassidy, Chairman of the Texas Department of Public Safety, in the United States District Court for the Western District of Texas, seeking a declaratory judgment that the Texas Safety Responsibility Act[2] was unconstitutional and an injunction against its enforcement. Gayton, an uninsured motorist, had been involved in an automobile accident in Texas, and pursuant to §§ 4, 5(a), 5(b) and 7 of the Act his driver's license and the registration receipt on his vehicle were suspended without a hearing on liability or fault because he did not post security—as required by the Act—for the damages claimed by the adverse party. A three-judge court was convened . . . and denied Gaytan and his class any relief by its holding that the Act was constitutional. On direct appeal to the Supreme Court, 28 U.S.C. § 1253, the district court's judgment was vacated, and the case was remanded for reconsideration in light of Bell v. Burson, 402 U.S. 535, 91 S.Ct. 1586, 29 L.Ed.2d 90 (1971), which was decided after the three-judge court's decision.

In Bell the Supreme Court held the [similar] Georgia Motor Vehicle Safety Responsibility Act unconstitutional as violative of procedural due process. . . .

On remand the three-judge court accordingly held the Texas Act unconstitutional. But, regarding the scope of relief to which Gaytan and his class were entitled, the court held:

> "This order shall apply retroactively to the Plaintiff ANTONIO R. GAYTAN, and prospectively from June 30, 1971, to all members of the class represented by said Plaintiff."[6]

Having obtained full relief for himself, Gaytan did not appeal the court's denial of retroactive relief to the other members of his class.

The present action began in the Northern District of Texas on June 24, 1971, after the Supreme Court vacated the first Gaytan decision, but before the case was heard on remand. Pedro Gonzales filed a class action against Cassidy, the defendant in Gaytan, seeking the same relief as had been sought by Gaytan in his suit. On July 1, 1971, the Gonzales court entered a temporary restraining order in favor of Gonzales and the other named plaintiffs in his action, prohibiting the defendant from suspending their licenses and vehicle registration receipts. This was before the amended order in Gaytan was rendered but only one day after the first order denying retroactive relief to all of the class except Gaytan was entered. On August 19, 1971, the Gaytan court entered its amended and final order. Then on August 25, 1971, the Gonzales court ordered a show cause hearing as to why its temporary restraining order of July 1 should not be made permanent. This hearing was held on September 28 and the court reasoned that, because Gaytan v. Cassidy was a class action and because Gonzales and the

---

[2] Tex.Rev.Civ.Stat.Ann., Art. 6701h (1969).

[6] Gaytan v. Cassidy, No. SA69CA153 (W.D.Tex., June 30, 1971, amended August 19, 1971). The amended order clarified the original order by explaining that it granted relief only to those persons whose effective date of suspension occurred after June 30, 1971, and to Gaytan whose suspensions occurred prior to June 30.

class he sought to represent were members of the Gaytan class, the principles of res judicata foreclosed their claims.[8] Gonzales appeals claiming that Gaytan's failure to appeal the final three-judge order in Gaytan v. Cassidy rendered his representation of the class inadequate, therefore precluding res judicata from attaching to that judgment.

To answer the question whether the class representative adequately represented the class so that the judgment in the class suit will bind the absent members of the class requires a two-pronged inquiry: (1) Did the trial court in the first suit correctly determine, initially, that the representative would adequately represent the class? and (2) Does it appear, after the termination of the suit, that the class representative adequately protected the interest of the class? The first question involves us in a collateral review of the Gaytan trial court's determination to permit the suit to proceed as a class action with Gaytan as the representative, while the second involves a review of the class representative's conduct of the entire suit—an inquiry which is not required to be made by the trial court but which is appropriate in a collateral attack on the judgment such as we have here. Our discussion will treat each question separately.

. . . .

The primary contention in this appeal is that Gaytan did not meet the requirements of 23(a)(4). Remembering that at this point we are only concerned with the court's initial determination that Gaytan would be an adequate representative, we look to the criteria on which the decision should be based. There are two: (1) the representative must have common interests with the unnamed members of the class; and (2) it must appear that the representative will vigorously prosecute the interests of the class through qualified counsel.[10] We have little difficulty in concluding that Antonio Gaytan met both of these requirements when he filed his suit in May of 1969. He was an uninsured motorist as were the members of his class; he had an automobile accident in Texas and had failed to post the necessary security under the Act as had the members of his class; his license and registration receipt were suspended without a hearing on liability or fault just as occurred to the members of his class. Likewise, he had the same basic interests in not having his license suspended or in having the suspension revoked as did the other members of his class. It is clear then that Gaytan had common interests which coincided with those of

---

[8] Since Gonzales and the other named plaintiffs fell within the group to whom only prospective relief had been granted by the Gaytan court, in that their licenses had been suspended prior to June 30, 1971, they were denied relief by the application of res judicata. Plaintiff Louanner H. Edwards was granted relief, for the reason that his license had not been suspended prior to June 30. At this time the court also denied the request that the Gonzales suit be maintained as a class action.

[10] . . . In Eisen v. Carlisle and Jacquelin, 391 F.2d 555, 562 (2d Cir., 1968), the court also noted:

"[A]n essential concomitant of adequate representation is that the party's attorney be qualified, experienced and generally able to conduct the proposed litigation. Additionally, it is necessary to eliminate so far as possible the likelihood that the litigants are involved in a collusive suit or that plaintiff has interests antagonistic to those of the remainder of the class."

the class he sought to represent. Furthermore, there are no allegations that Gaytan's attorney was not fully qualified to handle the case, or that, initially at least, he would not vigorously prosecute the action. The fact that Gaytan's counsel appealed to the Supreme Court after the three-judge court's adverse decision and subsequently won a reversal of that decision points significantly to counsel's qualification to handle the litigation. Therefore we cannot refuse to give res judicata effect to the judgment in Gaytan v. Cassidy on the basis that the trial court in that case erroneously determined that Gaytan would be an adequate representative of the class.

The second question is whether Gaytan's conduct of the entire suit was such that due process would not be violated by giving res judicata effect to the judgment in that suit. This is the crucial issue when the judgment in a class action is under collateral attack. Our first step, however, is to examine subdivisions (b) and (c) of Rule 23 in order to establish the proper context in which to make this inquiry.

. . . Gaytan v. Cassidy obviously fits within (b)(2)—thus, to be specific, we are dealing with the res judicata effect of the judgment in a (b)(2) type of class action.[12] Subdivision (c)(3) provides: "The judgment in an action maintained as a class action under subdivision . . . (b)(2), whether or not favorable to the class, shall include and describe those whom the court finds to be members of the class . . . ." Although the Gaytan court's opinion, neither originally nor on remand, describes the class it considered Gaytan to be representing, we agree with the lower court here that Gonzales and the class he seeks to represent were members of the Gaytan class and would at first blush appear bound by the Gaytan decision. But our inquiry into the binding effect of Gaytan does not end with Rule 23 for, "although thus declaring that the judgment in a class action includes the class, as defined, subdivision (c)(3) does not disturb the recognized principle that the court conducting the action cannot predetermine the res judicata effect of the judgment; this can be tested only in subsequent action. See Restatement, Judgments § 86, comment (h), § 116 (1942)." Advisory Committee's Notes to Rule 23 F.R.C.P., 28 U.S.C.A. at 301; Moore ¶ 23.60 at 1203. As a general rule though, a judgment in a class action will bind the absent members of the class. The exception to this general rule is grounded in due process. Due process of law would be violated for the judgment in a class suit to be res judicata to the absent members of a class unless the court applying res judicata can conclude that the class was adequately represented in the first suit. Hansberry v. Lee, 311 U.S. 32, 61 S.Ct. 115, 85 L.Ed. 22 [(1940)]. See Sam Fox Publishing Co. v. United States, 366 U.S. 683, 691, 81 S.Ct. 1309, 6 L.Ed.2d 604 (1961); Dierks v. Thompson, 414 F.2d 453 (1st Cir., 1969); Eisen v. Carlisle and Jacquelin, 391 F.2d 555 (2d

---

[12] One distinction between members of a class in a (b)(1), (b)(2), or (b)(3) action is that absent (b)(1) and (b)(2) members do not have the privilege of opting out of the suit that is accorded to class members in a (b)(3) suit. [Citations omitted.] Also, the mandatory notice requirements of 23(c)(2) do not apply to (b)(1) and (b)(2) actions even though the discretionary notice provisions of (d)[(1)(B)] are applicable. As a result of these distinctions class members in (b)(1) and (b)(2) actions must necessarily rely on the representative to protect their interests.

Cir., 1968); Mersay v. First Rep. Corp. of America, 43 F.R.D. 465 (S.D.N.Y., 1968).

The 1966 amendments to Rule 23 eliminated the distinctions between true, hybrid and spurious class actions and the differing res judicata effect of each type of action, thus broadening the effect of res judicata under the amended rule. It follows then that a court—whether it be the trial court making its initial 23(a)(4) determination, or a subsequent court considering a collateral attack on the judgment in a class action—must stringently apply the requirement of adequate representation. Judge Frankel has noted:

> "There are, of course, some obvious limitations in any case upon the extent to which absent parties will be concluded. For one thing, as the Advisory Committee observed, such parties have a clear right in some later litigation to attack the judgment which purports to bind them. In such a later case, at least the basic considerations going to the fairness of holding them bound will be open for reexamination. Factors which were not brought to the attention of the first court—including, most centrally, the adequacy of representation in the first suit; [citing Hansberry v. Lee, supra]—may lead to a changed perspective."

M. Frankel, Some Preliminary Observations Concerning Civil Rule 23, 43 F.R.D. 39 (1967). And, as Justice Harlan observed: "The judgment in a class action will bind only those members of the class whose interests have been adequately represented by existing parties to the litigation." Sam Fox Publishing Co. v. United States, supra, 366 U.S. at 691, 81 S.Ct. at 1314. Our inquiry then into the adequacy of class representation for purposes of res judicata is made with the understanding that generally the class will be bound unless the party attacking the judgment can show that the class was inadequately represented.

What standards should determine whether Gaytan adequately represented the class in Gaytan v. Cassidy? In Mersay v. First Republic Corp. of America, supra, the trial court was making the 23(a)(4) determination of whether the named plaintiff would adequately represent the class when it said, "the primary criterion is the forthrightness and vigor with which the representative party can be expected to assert and defend the interests of the members of the class, so as to insure them due process." Id. 43 F.R.D. at 470. This precept is equally applicable to the determination which must be made by a court when a class action judgment is under collateral attack. We hold that the primary criterion for determining whether the class representative has adequately represented his class for purposes of res judicata is whether the representative, through qualified counsel, vigorously and tenaciously protected the interests of the class. A court must view the representative's conduct of the entire litigation with this criterion as its guidepost.

We have previously recognized that Gaytan's representation was more than adequate up to the time the three-judge court entered its final order on remand. The narrow question, therefore, is whether Gaytan's failure to appeal this order, which denied retroactive relief to all members of the class except Gaytan, constitutes inadequate representation of the class so that they are not bound by the judgment. We are compelled to hold that Gaytan's failure to prosecute an appeal on behalf of the other members of his class rendered his representation of them inadequate. For this reason, the judgment in Gaytan v. Cassidy cannot be res judicata to the class.

Gaytan, through his attorney, vigorously represented the class until he obtained individual relief. The problem is that he was representing approximately 150,000 persons, who, although having had their licenses and registration receipts suspended without due process, were denied any relief by the three-judge court's prospective only application of its decision. So long as an appeal from this decision could not be characterized as patently meritless or frivolous, Gaytan should have prosecuted an appeal. Otherwise, it cannot be said that he vigorously and tenaciously protected the interests of the class he was purporting to represent, or that all members of the class had been afforded due process of law by having a full day in court. It is axiomatic that an appeal is a significant element in the judicial process. Gaytan's failure to prosecute an appeal deprived the members of his class, whose rights were not vindicated by the three-judge court's decision, of full participation in this process.

Appellees do not meet the argument that Gaytan's failure to appeal rendered him an inadequate representative of the class. Instead, they advance an estoppel-type argument to support the proposition that Gonzales cannot raise the inadequate representation issue. Their position is that since counsel for Gonzales was aware that on remand the Gaytan court denied retroactive relief by his June 30, 1971 order, and finally denied such relief in its amended order of August 19, Gonzales is estopped to attack the judgment collaterally because he should have intervened in Gaytan for the purposes of appeal. We reject this contention.

First, as the 1966 amendments to Rule 23 clearly illustrate, the purpose of a class action is to allow as few as one member of a class to prosecute an action for the benefit of the class if the requirements of 23(a) and (b) are met. This is one reason why the requirement of 23(a)(4) is stringently applied. The purpose of Rule 23 would be subverted by requiring a class member who learns of a pending suit involving a class of which he is a part to monitor that litigation to make certain that his interests are being protected; this is not his responsibility—it is the responsibility of the class representative to protect the interests of all class members.

Secondly, it would simply be inequitable to foreclose Gonzales from attacking the Gaytan judgment on the facts of our case. [The court here explained that the above-described chronology of events in the two actions was such as to discourage intervention.]

On remand there will be at least two issues. The first will be whether this action may be maintained as a class action. The district court denied Gonzales's motion to allow this suit to proceed as a class action. In light of our decision and for reasons of judicial economy, we think the district court should reexamine this decision, and if it concludes that Gonzales meets the prerequisites of 23(a) and (b), it would seem appropriate to allow a class action. The second issue will be the retroactivity question. We express no views on the resolution of this issue.

Reversed and remanded.

Question: (5) Should Gonzales be able to collaterally attack on the ground of erroneous certification respecting Rule 23(a)(4), in addition to the ground of constitutionally inadequate representation? What precisely should be the possible grounds for an absentee's collateral attack on a class-action judgment?

COLLATERAL ATTACK

A critical first step in specifying the appropriate grounds for challenging class treatment is to realize that the law of class actions and res judicata does not extend nearly as far toward binding absentees as the Constitution would permit. The Constitution is rather permissive. Some Supreme Court decisions that expressed a day-in-court theme may seem demanding, but they were interpreting statutes or rules or subconstitutional doctrine, not the Due Process Clause itself. Arguably, all that due process guarantees is a full and fair day in court enjoyed in person *or through a representative*: in this context, an adequately represented person was one in actual agreement generally, although not necessarily as to all details, with the objectives on the merits of the representative, who vigorously and competently pursued those objectives. That is, the "reasonable" due process test allows binding many more nonparties than most people assume: a judicial judgment could bind all persons whose interests received adequate representation—binding them not only through the flexible doctrine of stare decisis, as a judgment already does, but also through the strictures of res judicata, as a judgment could.

Nonetheless, society has chosen to authorize only certain class actions, screening out cases that the Constitution would permit. Federal Rule 23 and state equivalents impose this additional screen on class actions, and res judicata's definition of privity respects that screen. The helpful image here is of a due process hurdle that is quite low. Above it, in provisions like Rule 23(a) and (b) and the relevant caselaw, the lawmakers have built a screen that allows through only a select set of cases that satisfy society's policy desires. That is, this pragmatic screening device lets through all the cases for which class-action treatment is clearly appropriate on a cost-benefit basis—those cases that generously realize the goal of efficiency or the rulemakers' rather limited substantive goals and that also amply satisfy fairness concerns—but only those cases. By this screening, the law tries to ensure, with a comfortable margin, the adequacy of representation.

The law ensures adequacy of representation by imposing a demanding class-certification process at the outset of a class action. But does it also allow testing after the conclusion of a class action? When the class-action judgment is invoked in subsequent litigation, it is subject to attack on the usual limited grounds of jurisdiction and procedural due process. Should the law also allow the absentee to challenge validity on adequacy or other grounds when determining the res judicata effect of the class judgment? Three views exist and contest.

1. Restatement (Second) of Judgments § 42(1) (1982) reflected scanty caselaw that seemed to allow attack on the broad grounds of failure to comply with the applicable class-action rule. It provided for attack if, inter alia: "(a) Notice concerning the representation was required to be given to the represented person, or others who might act to protect his interest, and there was no substantial compliance with the requirement; or . . . (d) With respect to the representative of a class, there was such a substantial divergence of interest between him and the members of the class, or a group within the class, that he could not fairly represent them with respect to the matters as to which the judgment is subsequently invoked . . . ."

2. A few cases and commentators argued that this approach was too permissive. "An unlimited and ill-defined scope of collateral review threatens the finality of class action judgments and the usefulness of the class action device, reversing a century-long trend in the development of the class action rule." Note, Collateral Attack on the Binding Effect of Class Action Judgments, 87 Harv.L.Rev. 589, 606 (1974). Thus, the absentee should be able to raise due process on collateral attack, but not mere procedural failures.

3. Epstein v. MCA, Inc., 179 F.3d 641, 648 (9th Cir.1999) (2–1 decision), took the final step by foreclosing attack on judgment even for a constitutional defect, at least if the due process point was fully and fairly litigated in the course of the settled class action. "Due process requires that an absent class member's right to adequate representation be protected by the adoption of the appropriate procedures by the certifying court and by the courts that review its determinations; due process does not require collateral second-guessing of those determinations and that review." The American Law Institute, wandering back into the thicket by launching a whole new project, now leaned toward embracing Epstein. See ALI Principles of the Law of Aggregate Litigation §§ 2.07, 3.14 (Proposed Final Draft 2009).

Controversy in the law reviews has ensued. And in the famous Agent Orange case of Stephenson v. Dow Chemical Co., 273 F.3d 249 (2d Cir. 2001), the court of appeals rejected Epstein and adopted the second approach, thus creating a conflict of circuits. The issue there was whether the 1984 class-action settlement, which purported to settle all future claims, precluded a 1999 lawsuit brought by a person who had suffered exposure to the chemical defoliant in the Vietnam War, but had not fallen ill until after the close out of the settlement in 1994. The appellate court reversed the district court, citing Gonzales and saying that the future-injured could collaterally attack the judgment for inadequate representation. It concluded that the class representation had indeed violated due process by failing to provide any payments for the future-injured.

The thinking in support of Stephenson's *via media* is that an absent class member should be able to attack the judgment's binding effect by raising the question of constitutionally inadequate representation of the absentee's interests, as that representation actually played out in the course of the class action and produced an actual outcome. This ground falls partly within the usual ground for attack called procedural due process, as well as within its spirit of undoing fundamental defects in fairness but only those defects. The ground would, however, additionally require looking at the substantive outcome, at least for unconscionability, to shed light on the adequacy question. See David A. Dana, Adequacy of Representation After Stephenson: A Rawlsian/Behavioral Economics Approach to Class Action Settlements, 55 Emory L.J. 279 (2006) (arguing for allowing attack on a settlement that the absentee would not conceivably have accepted).

On the one hand, the absentee should not be able to collaterally attack on a ground like erroneous class-certification, as opposed to the ground of constitutionally inadequate representation. Considerations relevant to application of Rule 23—such as class certification, typicality, notice, and consent, as well as the monitored procedural activities of all litigants, attorneys, and judges and the required substantive interests—should be deemed to be constitutional requirements only insofar as needed to provide the essential assurance of adequacy of representation. Allowing attacks beyond the due process ground would permit absentees to escape a basically fair judgment, by means of a sort of post-judgment opt-out that would be unfair to the class's opponent and that would also discourage settlement in the first place.

On the other hand, not allowing any attack for inadequacy reflects an exaggerated devotion to finality and an unrealistic trust in careful class-action procedure. Fundamental fairness—due process—would seem to call for allowing attack on this core ground. Experience has shown that parties reach and courts approve grossly unfair settlements, giving some absentees no recovery or, rarely, even a negative recovery through assessment of costs and fees, because of a variety of reasons ranging from outright collusion between class counsel and the defendant down to mere inattention to the interests of some portion of the class. Allowing attack on the due process ground will encourage the court, and the defendant for that matter, to be serious in observance of Rule 23's limits and protections during the class action itself. Finally, there would be something odd, although admittedly not unthinkable, in any approach that precluded an absentee from challenging adequacy of representation because the class-action court had explicitly or implicitly determined adequacy in a case litigated by the allegedly inadequate representative. see Debra Lyn Bassett, Constructing Class Action Reality, 2006 BYU L.Rev. 1415 (arguing that shift from a "representative" metaphor to an "aggregate" metaphor represents a shift from fairness to efficiency, or an abandonment of the justificatory prerequisite for class actions in favor of an undue emphasis on claim disposal and deference to defendants).

So, the U.S. Supreme Court granted certiorari in Stephenson to resolve the circuit split. It affirmed the Second Circuit, but it did so by the equally divided vote of 4–4, which deprived the affirmance of precedential effect. Dow Chem. Co. v. Stephenson, 539 U.S. 111, 123 S.Ct. 2161 (2003) (per curiam). The question therefore remains an open one.

Question: (6) In a (b)(3) class action, an absent class member has a right to opt out of the class and thus to avoid any binding effect. If an absentee opts out and the class ultimately prevails (and given the demise of the doctrine of mutuality of estoppel described in Section 2 of Topic D of Part Four), may this absentee later use the class judgment as res judicata against the former adversary of the class? Compare Premier Elec. Constr. Co. v. National Elec. Contractors Ass'n, 814 F.2d 358 (7th Cir.1987) (no), with Roger Furman, Note, Offensive Assertion of Collateral Estoppel by Persons Opting Out of a Class Action, 31 Hastings L.J. 1189 (1980) (yes, for absentee with strong individual interest in controlling own litigation).

SECTION 2. SCOPE OF RULE 23

(a) RULE 23(a)

The new Rule 23(a) states some of the prerequisites for maintaining any class action. As already explained in Part One, all of the requirements of Rule 23(a)—numerosity, commonality, typicality, and adequacy—must be satisfied.

Numerosity is the sole requirement of Rule 23(a) that does not bear on adequate representation. It instead serves the critical function of determining whether a class action, as opposed to the traditional joinder studied in the preceding Topic, is appropriate practically. The Rule permits a class action only when the class is so numerous as to make ordinary joinder impracticable. It thus tries to ensure that class-action treatment will yield considerable benefits, while its other requirements aim at ensuring that a class action will impose only acceptable costs.

Factors that courts use in assessing whether or not the class is sufficiently numerous include the geographic diversity of class members, the ability of individual claimants to institute their own actions, and the seeking of injunctive or declaratory relief, according to Haley v. Medtronic, Inc., 169 F.R.D. 643, 647 (C.D.Cal.1996). Haley involved a product liability class action by patients against the manufacturer of leads for pacemakers. Approximately 66,166 of the defective leads had been implanted, and the patients were dispersed throughout the country (but they were easily identifiable, thus not running afoul of the implicit requirement that the class membership be "ascertainable"). For many of them, damages were not that great. In addition, the court considered the other twenty-five pending lawsuits and the large number of potential future lawsuits as a factor in favor of a class action. The court determined that numerosity was indeed satisfied, noting that " 'impracticability' does not mean 'impossibility.' " Nevertheless, the court ultimately denied class certification for failure to satisfy Rule 23(b).

General Telephone Co. v. Falcon

Supreme Court of the United States, 1982.
457 U.S. 147, 102 S.Ct. 2364.

■ JUSTICE STEVENS delivered the opinion of the Court.

The question presented is whether respondent Falcon, who complained that petitioner did not promote him because he is a Mexican–American, was properly permitted to maintain a class action on behalf of Mexican–American applicants for employment whom petitioner did not hire.

I

In 1969 petitioner initiated a special recruitment and training program for minorities. Through that program, respondent Falcon was hired in July 1969 as a groundman, and within a year he was twice promoted, first to lineman and then to lineman-in-charge. He subsequently refused a promotion to installer-repairman. In October 1972 he applied for the job of field inspector; his application was denied even though the promotion was granted several white employees with less seniority.

Falcon thereupon filed a charge with the Equal Employment Opportunity Commission stating his belief that he had been passed over for promotion because of his national origin and that petitioner's promotion policy operated against Mexican–Americans as a class. . . . In due course he received a right to sue letter from the Commission and, in April 1975, he commenced this action under Title VII of the Civil Rights Act of 1964, 74 Stat. 253, as amended, 42 U.S.C. § 2000e et seq., in the United States District Court for the Northern District of Texas. His complaint alleged that petitioner maintained "a policy, practice, custom, or usage of: (a) discriminating against [Mexican–Americans] because of national origin and with respect to compensation, terms, conditions, and privileges of employment, and (b) . . . subjecting [Mexican–Americans] to continuous employment discrimination." Respondent claimed that as a result of this policy whites with less qualification and experience and lower evaluation scores than respondent had been promoted more rapidly. The complaint contained no factual allegations concerning petitioner's hiring practices.

Respondent brought the action "on his own behalf and on behalf of other persons similarly situated, pursuant to Rule 23(b)(2) of the Federal Rules of Civil Procedure." The class identified in the complaint was "composed of Mexican–American persons who are employed, or who might be employed, by GENERAL TELEPHONE COMPANY at its place of business located in Irving, Texas, who have been and who continue to be or might be adversely affected by the practices complained of herein."[3]

After responding to petitioner's written interrogatories,[4] respondent filed a memorandum in favor of certification of "the class of all hourly Mexican–American employees who have been employed, are employed, or may in the future be employed and all those Mexican–Americans who have applied or would have applied for employment had the Defendant not practiced racial discrimination in its employment practices." App. 46–47. His position was supported by the ruling of the United States Court of Appeals for the Fifth Circuit in Johnson v. Georgia Highway Express, Inc., 417 F.2d 1122 (1969), that any victim of racial discrimination in employment may maintain an "across the board" attack on all unequal employment practices alleged to have been committed by the employer pursuant to a policy of racial discrimination. Without conducting an evidentiary hearing, the District Court certified a class including Mexican–American employees and Mexican–American applicants for employment who had not been hired.

Following trial of the liability issues, the District Court entered separate findings of fact and conclusions of law with respect first to respondent and then to the class. The District Court found that petitioner had not discriminated against respondent in hiring, but that it did discriminate against him in its promotion practices. App. to Pet. for Cert. 35a, 37a. The court reached converse conclusions about the class, finding no discrimination in promotion practices, but concluding that petitioner had discriminated against Mexican–Americans at its Irving facility in its hiring practices. Id., at 39a–40a.[6]

After various post-trial proceedings, the District Court ordered petitioner to furnish respondent with a list of all Mexican–Americans who had

---

[3] App. 13–14. The paragraph of the complaint in which respondent alleged conformance with the requirements of Rule 23 continued:

"There are common questions of law and fact affecting the rights of the members of this class who are, and who continue to be, limited, classified, and discriminated against in ways which deprive and/or tend to deprive them of equal employment opportunities and which otherwise adversely affect their status as employees because of national origin. These persons are so numerous that joinder of all members is impracticable. A common relief is sought. The interests of said class are adequately represented by Plaintiff. Defendant has acted or refused to act on grounds generally applicable to the Plaintiff." Id., at 14.

[4] Petitioner's Interrogatory No. 8 stated:

"Identify the common questions of law and fact which affect the rights of the members of the purported class." Id., at 26.

Respondent answered that interrogatory as follows:

"The facts which affect the rights of the members of the class are the facts of their employment, the ways in which evaluations are made, the subjective rather than objective manner in which recommendations for raises and transfers and promotions are handled, and all of the facts surrounding the employment of Mexican–American persons by General Telephone Company. The questions of law specified in Interrogatory No. 8 call for a conclusion on the part of the Plaintiff." Id., at 34.

[6] The District Court ordered petitioner to accelerate its affirmative action plan by taking specified steps to more actively recruit and promote Mexican–Americans at its Irving facility. See id., at 41a–45a.

applied for employment at the Irving facility during the period between January 1, 1973, and October 18, 1976. Respondent was then ordered to give notice to those persons advising them that they might be entitled to some form of recovery. Evidence was taken concerning the applicants who responded to the notice and backpay was ultimately awarded to 13 persons, in addition to respondent Falcon. The total recovery by respondent and the entire class amounted to $67,925.49, plus costs and interest.

Both parties appealed. The Court of Appeals rejected respondent's contention that the class should have encompassed all of petitioner's operations in Texas, New Mexico, Oklahoma, and Arkansas. On the other hand, the court also rejected petitioner's argument that the class had been defined too broadly. For, under the Fifth Circuit's across-the-board rule, it is permissible for "an employee complaining of one employment practice to represent another complaining of another practice, if the plaintiff and the members of the class suffer from essentially the same injury. In this case, all of the claims are based on discrimination because of national origin." . . .

On the merits, the Court of Appeals [remanded for reconsideration of the rulings that petitioner was liable. The Supreme Court] granted certiorari to decide whether the class action was properly maintained on behalf of both employees who were denied promotion and applicants who were denied employment.

II

The class-action device was designed as "an exception to the usual rule that litigation is conducted by and on behalf of the individual named parties only." Califano v. Yamasaki, 442 U.S. 682, 700–701, 99 S.Ct. 2545, 2557–2558. Class relief is "peculiarly appropriate" when the "issues involved are common to the class as a whole" and when they "turn on questions of law applicable in the same manner to each member of the class." Id., at 701, 99 S.Ct., at 2557. For in such cases, "the class-action device saves the resources of both the courts and the parties by permitting an issue potentially affecting every [class member] to be litigated in an economical fashion under Rule 23." Ibid.

Title VII of the Civil Rights Act of 1964, as amended, authorizes the Equal Employment Opportunity Commission to sue in its own name to secure relief for individuals aggrieved by discriminatory practices forbidden by the Act. See 42 U.S.C. § 2000e–5(f)(1). In exercising this enforcement power, the Commission may seek relief for groups of employees or applicants for employment without complying with the strictures of Rule 23. General Telephone Co. v. EEOC, 446 U.S. 318, 100 S.Ct. 1698. Title VII, however, contains no special authorization for class suits maintained by private parties. An individual litigant seeking to maintain a class action under Title VII must meet "the prerequisites of numerosity, commonality, typicality, and adequacy of representation" specified in Rule 23(a). Id., at 330, 100 S.Ct., at 1706. These requirements effectively "limit the class claims to those fairly encompassed by the named plaintiff's claims." Ibid.

We have repeatedly held that "a class representative must be part of the class and 'possess the same interest and suffer the same injury' as the class members." East Texas Motor Freight System, Inc. v. Rodriguez, 431 U.S. 395, 403, 97 S.Ct. 1891, 1896 (quoting Schlesinger v. Reservists Committee to Stop the War, 418 U.S. 208, 216, 94 S.Ct. 2925, 2929–2930). In East Texas Motor Freight, a Title VII action brought by three Mexican–American city drivers, the Fifth Circuit certified a class consisting of the trucking company's black and Mexican–American city drivers allegedly denied on racial or ethnic grounds transfers to more desirable line-driver jobs. We held that the Court of Appeals had "plainly erred in declaring a class action." 431 U.S., at 403, 97 S.Ct., at 1896. Because at the time the class was certified it was clear that the named plaintiffs were not qualified for line-driver positions, "they could have suffered no injury as a result of the allegedly discriminatory practices, and they were, therefore, simply not eligible to represent a class of persons who did allegedly suffer injury." Id., at 403–404, 97 S.Ct., at 1897.

Our holding in East Texas Motor Freight was limited; we noted that "a different case would be presented if the District Court had certified a class and only later had it appeared that the named plaintiffs were not class members or were otherwise inappropriate class representatives." Id., at 406, n. 12, 97 S.Ct., at 1898, n. 12. . . .

We cannot disagree with the proposition underlying the across-the-board rule—that racial discrimination is by definition class discrimination. But the allegation that such discrimination has occurred neither determines whether a class action may be maintained in accordance with Rule 23 nor defines the class that may be certified. Conceptually, there is a wide gap between (a) an individual's claim that he has been denied a promotion on discriminatory grounds, and his otherwise unsupported allegation that the company has a policy of discrimination, and (b) the existence of a class of persons who have suffered the same injury as that individual, such that the individual's claim and the class claims will share common questions of law or fact and that the individual's claim will be typical of the class claims.[13] For respondent to bridge that gap, he must prove much more than the validity of his own claim. Even though evidence that he was passed over for promotion when several less deserving whites were advanced may

[13] The commonality and typicality requirements of Rule 23(a) tend to merge. Both serve as guideposts for determining whether under the particular circumstances maintenance of a class action is economical and whether the named plaintiff's claim and the class claims are so interrelated that the interests of the class members will be fairly and adequately protected in their absence. Those requirements therefore also tend to merge with the adequacy-of-representation requirement, although the latter requirement also raises concerns about the competency of class counsel and conflicts of interest. In this case, we need not address petitioner's argument that there is a conflict of interest between respondent and the class of rejected applicants because an enlargement of the pool of Mexican–American employees will decrease respondent's chances for promotion. See General Telephone Co. v. EEOC, 446 U.S. 318, 331, 100 S.Ct. 1698, 1706–1707 ("In employment discrimination litigation, conflicts might arise, for example, between employees and applicants who were denied employment and who will, if granted relief, compete with employees for fringe benefits or seniority. Under Rule 23, the same plaintiff could not represent these classes."); see also East Texas Motor Freight System, Inc. v. Rodriguez, 431 U.S. 395, 404–405, 97 S.Ct. 1891, 1897–1898.

support the conclusion that respondent was denied the promotion because of his national origin, such evidence would not necessarily justify the additional inferences (1) that this discriminatory treatment is typical of petitioner's promotion practices, (2) that petitioner's promotion practices are motivated by a policy of ethnic discrimination that pervades petitioner's Irving division, or (3) that this policy of ethnic discrimination is reflected in petitioner's other employment practices, such as hiring, in the same way it is manifested in the promotion practices. These additional inferences demonstrate the tenuous character of any presumption that the class claims are "fairly encompassed" within respondent's claim.

Respondent's complaint provided an insufficient basis for concluding that the adjudication of his claim of discrimination in promotion would require the decision of any common question concerning the failure of petitioner to hire more Mexican–Americans. Without any specific presentation identifying the questions of law or fact that were common to the claims of respondent and of the members of the class he sought to represent, it was error for the District Court to presume that respondent's claim was typical of other claims against petitioner by Mexican–American employees and applicants. If one allegation of specific discriminatory treatment were sufficient to support an across-the-board attack, every Title VII case would be a potential company-wide class action. We find nothing in the statute to indicate that Congress intended to authorize such a wholesale expansion of class-action litigation.[15]

The trial of this class action followed a predictable course. Instead of raising common questions of law or fact, respondent's evidentiary approaches to the individual and class claims were entirely different. He attempted to sustain his individual claim by proving intentional discrimination. He tried to prove the class claims through statistical evidence of disparate impact. Ironically, the District Court rejected the class claim of promotion discrimination, which conceptually might have borne a closer typicality and commonality relationship with respondent's individual claim, but sustained the class claim of hiring discrimination. As the District Court's bifurcated findings on liability demonstrate, the individual and class claims might as well have been tried separately. It is clear that the maintenance of respondent's action as a class action did not advance "the efficiency and economy of litigation which is a principal purpose of the procedure." American Pipe & Construction Co. v. Utah, 414 U.S. 538, 553, 94 S.Ct. 756, 766.

---

[15] If petitioner used a biased testing procedure to evaluate both applicants for employment and incumbent employees, a class action on behalf of every applicant or employee who might have been prejudiced by the test clearly would satisfy the commonality and typicality requirements of Rule 23(a). Significant proof that an employer operated under a general policy of discrimination conceivably could justify a class of both applicants and employees if the discrimination manifested itself in hiring and promotion practices in the same general fashion, such as through entirely subjective decisionmaking processes. In this regard it is noteworthy that Title VII prohibits discriminatory employment *practices*, not an abstract policy of discrimination. The mere fact that an aggrieved private plaintiff is a member of an identifiable class of persons of the same race or national origin is insufficient to establish his standing to litigate on their behalf all possible claims of discrimination against a common employer.

We do not, of course, judge the propriety of a class certification by hindsight. The District Court's error in this case, and the error inherent in the across-the-board rule, is the failure to evaluate carefully the legitimacy of the named plaintiff's plea that he is a proper class representative under Rule 23(a). As we noted in Coopers & Lybrand v. Livesay, 437 U.S. 463, 98 S.Ct. 2454, "the class determination generally involves considerations that are 'enmeshed in the factual and legal issues comprising the plaintiff's cause of action.'" Id., at 469, 98 S.Ct., at 2458 (quoting Mercantile Nat. Bank v. Langdeau, 371 U.S. 555, 558, 83 S.Ct. 520, 522). Sometimes the issues are plain enough from the pleadings to determine whether the interests of the absent parties are fairly encompassed within the named plaintiff's claim, and sometimes it may be necessary for the court to probe behind the pleadings before coming to rest on the certification question. Even after a certification order is entered, the judge remains free to modify it in the light of subsequent developments in the litigation. For such an order, particularly during the period before any notice is sent to members of the class, "is inherently tentative." 437 U.S., at 469, n. 11, 98 S.Ct., at 2458, n. 11. This flexibility enhances the usefulness of the class-action device; actual, not presumed, conformance with Rule 23(a) remains, however, indispensable.

III

The need to carefully apply the requirements of Rule 23(a) to Title VII class actions was noticed by a member of the Fifth Circuit panel that announced the across-the-board rule. In a specially concurring opinion in Johnson v. Georgia Highway Express, Inc., supra, at 1125–1127, Judge Godbold emphasized the need for "more precise pleadings," id., at 1125, for "without reasonable specificity the court cannot define the class, cannot determine whether the representation is adequate, and the employer does not know how to defend," id., at 1126. He termed as "most significant" the potential unfairness to the class members bound by the judgment if the framing of the class is overbroad. Ibid. And he pointed out the error of the "tacit assumption" underlying the across-the-board rule that "all will be well for surely the plaintiff will win and manna will fall on all members of the class." Id., at 1127. With the same concerns in mind, we reiterate today that a Title VII class action, like any other class action, may only be certified if the trial court is satisfied, after a rigorous analysis, that the prerequisites of Rule 23(a) have been satisfied.

The judgment of the Court of Appeals affirming the certification order is reversed and the case is remanded for further proceedings consistent with this opinion.

It is so ordered.[d]

[d] On remand, the district court allowed one of the 13 claimants to intervene as representative for the hiring class, but both those class claims and Falcon's individual promotion claim failed on the merits, 611 F.Supp. 707 (N.D.Tex.1985), aff'd, 815 F.2d 317 (5th Cir.1987).

■ [The opinion of CHIEF JUSTICE BURGER, concurring in part and dissenting in part, is omitted.]

Question: (7) "Class action procedures assist courts in giving full realization to substantive policies in two ways. First, to the extent that they open courts to claims not ordinarily litigated, class actions enable courts to enforce policies underlying causes of action in circumstances where those policies might not otherwise be effectuated. Second, to the extent that they enable courts to see the full implications of recognizing rights or remedies, class action procedures assist courts in judging precisely what outcomes of litigation would best serve the policies underlying causes of action." Developments in the Law—Class Actions, 89 Harv.L.Rev. 1318, 1353 (1976). Does not General Telephone Co. v. Falcon indicate at the least that courts in interpreting Rule 23, and possibly that the rulemakers in writing and revising Rule 23 as well, should give no consideration to any effect on substantive policies more particularized than these two general effects? But compare Robert M. Covert, For James Wm. Moore: Some Reflections on a Reading of the Rules, 84 Yale L.J. 718, 732–39 (1975) (arguing that a court should read even a "trans-substantive" rule of general application with some attention to particularized effect on substantive policies in the particular case, and so Rule 23 can be expansively read in appropriate cases), with Martin H. Redish, Wholesale Justice: Constitutional Democracy and the Problem of the Class Action Lawsuit (2009) (arguing that because the courts have improperly utilized the procedure of Rule 23 to graft a qui tam provision onto various substantive laws, the rulemakers should amend to prevent use of class actions as a lawyer-driven bounty-hunting device that the appropriate lawmakers never adopted).

(b) RULE 23(b)

Rule 23(a) states some of the prerequisites for maintaining any class action, and these go considerably beyond the constitutional prerequisite. But it is not enough that the tests of Rule 23(a) are satisfied. A class action must also come within one of the subdivisions of Rule 23(b).

Rule 23(b)(1) did not occasion much difficulty, at least in the early years. The rulemakers had cautiously divided it into two clauses, one looking to the effect on the party opposing the class and the other looking to the risk of prejudice to the interests of absent members of the class. Often a case will come within both of these clauses, the Supreme Tribe case offering an example. Nothing turns, however, upon which provision is controlling, because actions under these two clauses are treated the same for purposes of other parts of the Rule.

Rule 23(b)(2) was designed to reach civil rights actions, such as General Telephone Co. v. Falcon, many of which had been maintained as class actions under the original Rule, e.g., Potts v. Flax, 313 F.2d 284 (5th Cir.1963). It is not, however, limited to such cases. It covers situations where the defendant opposing the class has acted or refused to act on grounds generally applicable to the class, although perhaps the defendant's behavior was immediately directed to only a few. It looks to final relief by way of injunction or corresponding declaratory judgment. A monetary award incidental to or as an element of the equitable remedy, when the primary relief is injunctive or declaratory, is permissible under this subdivision. But it does not extend to cases in which the appropriate final relief is exclusively or predominantly money damages. Courts have had a lot of difficulty patrolling this line.

Rule 23(b)(3) has been the source of many of the problems with and much of the controversy over the new Rule, but by no means all. If a class action truly meets the standards of (b)(1) or (2) and also (b)(3), the court should certify it under the former rather than under (b)(3). Then the special procedural provisions for (b)(3) actions will not apply. But this possibility of escaping procedural burdens has induced all participants to strive for certification under (b)(1) or (2), to the absentees' detriment. The result is that such "mandatory class actions" have become much more common and controversial over the years.

Question: (8) A patentee brings an action against a defendant as representative of a class of alleged infringers of one or more of five patents. Should the action be allowed to be maintained as a class action under Rule 23(b)(1)(A) or (B) or (b)(2)? What bearing does the holding of Blonder–Tongue Laboratories v. University of Illinois Foundation, supra p. 770, have upon this question?

The bounds of Rule 23(a) and (b) do not completely define the scope of the class-action device. Further limiting its use are jurisdictional restrictions as well as the practical hurdles of having to comply with the procedural protections dictated by the rest of Rule 23, which we shall soon consider in greater detail.

Amchem Products, Inc. v. Windsor

Supreme Court of the United States, 1997.
521 U.S. 591, 117 S.Ct. 2231.

■ JUSTICE GINSBURG delivered the opinion of the Court.

This case concerns the legitimacy under Rule 23 of the Federal Rules of Civil Procedure of a class-action certification sought to achieve global settlement of current and future asbestos-related claims. The class proposed for certification potentially encompasses hundreds of thousands, perhaps millions, of individuals tied together by this commonality: each was, or some day may be, adversely affected by past exposure to asbestos products manufactured by one or more of 20 companies. Those companies, defendants in the lower courts, are petitioners here.

. . . .

I

A

The settlement-class certification we confront evolved in response to an asbestos-litigation crisis. . . .

In the face of legislative inaction, the federal courts—lacking authority to replace state tort systems with a national toxic tort compensation regime—endeavored to work with the procedural tools available to improve management of federal asbestos litigation. Eight federal judges, experienced in the superintendence of asbestos cases, urged the Judicial Panel on Multidistrict Litigation (MDL Panel), to consolidate in a single district all asbestos complaints then pending in federal courts. Accepting the recommendation, the MDL Panel transferred all asbestos cases then filed, but not yet on trial in federal courts to a single district, the United States District Court for the Eastern District of Pennsylvania . . . [where] the collected cases were consolidated for pretrial proceedings . . . . The [transfer] order aggregated pending cases only; no authority resides in the MDL Panel to license for consolidated proceedings claims not yet filed.

B

After the consolidation, attorneys for plaintiffs and defendants formed separate steering committees and began settlement negotiations. . . .

. . . .

[The first round of negotiations broke down, but counsel for the Center for Claims Resolution (CCR), a consortium of the twenty former asbestos manufacturers] approached the lawyers who had headed the Plaintiffs' Steering Committee in the unsuccessful negotiations, and a new round of negotiations began; that round yielded the mass settlement agreement now in controversy. At the time, the former heads of the Plaintiffs' Steering Committee represented thousands of plaintiffs with then-pending asbestos-related claims—claimants the parties to this suit call "inventory" plaintiffs. CCR indicated in these discussions that it would resist settlement of inventory cases absent "some kind of protection for the future." [Georgine v. Amchem Products, Inc., 157 F.R.D. 246, 294 (E.D.Pa.1994); other citation omitted.]

Settlement talks thus concentrated on devising an administrative scheme for disposition of asbestos claims not yet in litigation. In these negotiations, counsel for masses of inventory plaintiffs endeavored to represent the interests of the anticipated future claimants, although those lawyers then had no attorney-client relationship with such claimants.

Once negotiations seemed likely to produce an agreement purporting to bind potential plaintiffs, CCR agreed to settle, through separate agreements, the claims of plaintiffs who had already filed asbestos-related lawsuits. In one such agreement, CCR defendants promised to pay more than $200 million to gain release of the claims of numerous inventory plaintiffs. After settling the inventory claims, CCR, together with the plaintiffs' lawyers CCR had approached, launched this case, exclusively involving persons outside the MDL Panel's province—plaintiffs without already pending lawsuits.

C

The class action thus instituted was not intended to be litigated. Rather, within the space of a single day, January 15, 1993, the settling parties—CCR defendants and the representatives of the plaintiff class described below—presented to the District Court a complaint, an answer, a proposed settlement agreement, and a joint motion for conditional class certification.

The complaint identified nine lead plaintiffs, designating them and members of their families as representatives of a class comprising all persons who had not filed an asbestos-related lawsuit against a CCR defendant as of the date the class action commenced, but who (1) had been exposed—occupationally or through the occupational exposure of a spouse or household member—to asbestos or products containing asbestos attributable to a CCR defendant, or (2) whose spouse or family member had been so exposed. Untold numbers of individuals may fall within this description. All named plaintiffs alleged that they or a member of their family had been exposed to asbestos-containing products of CCR defendants. More than half of the named plaintiffs alleged that they or their family members had already suffered various physical injuries as a result of the exposure. The others alleged that they had not yet manifested any asbestos-related condition. The complaint delineated no subclasses; all named plaintiffs were designated as representatives of the class as a whole.

The complaint invoked the District Court's diversity jurisdiction and asserted various state-law claims for relief . . . . Each plaintiff requested unspecified damages in excess of $100,000. CCR defendants' answer denied the principal allegations of the complaint and asserted 11 affirmative defenses.

A stipulation of settlement accompanied the pleadings; it proposed to settle, and to preclude nearly all class members from litigating against CCR companies, all claims not filed before January 15, 1993, involving compensation for present and future asbestos-related personal injury or death. An exhaustive document exceeding 100 pages, the stipulation presents in detail an administrative mechanism and a schedule of payments to compensate class members who meet defined asbestos-exposure and medical requirements. The stipulation describes four categories of compensable disease: mesothelioma; lung cancer; certain "other cancers" (colon-rectal, laryngeal, esophageal, and stomach cancer); and "non-malignant conditions" (asbestosis and bilateral pleural thickening). Persons with "exceptional" medical claims—claims that do not fall within the four described diagnostic categories—may in some instances qualify for compensation, but the settlement caps the number of "exceptional" claims CCR must cover.

For each qualifying disease category, the stipulation specifies the range of damages CCR will pay to qualifying claimants. Payments under the settlement are not adjustable for inflation. Mesothelioma claimants—the most highly compensated category—are scheduled to receive between $20,000 and $200,000. The stipulation provides that CCR is to propose the level of compensation within the prescribed ranges; it also establishes procedures to resolve disputes over medical diagnoses and levels of compensation.

Compensation above the fixed ranges may be obtained for "extraordinary" claims. But the settlement places both numerical caps and dollar limits on such claims. The settlement also imposes "case flow maximums," which cap the number of claims payable for each disease in a given year.

Class members are to receive no compensation for certain kinds of claims, even if otherwise applicable state law recognizes such claims. Claims that garner no compensation under the settlement include claims by family members of asbestos-exposed individuals for loss of consortium, and claims by so-called "exposure-only" plaintiffs for increased risk of cancer, fear of future asbestos-related injury, and medical monitoring. "Pleural" claims, which might be asserted by persons with asbestos-related plaques on their lungs but no accompanying physical impairment, are also excluded. Although not entitled to present compensation, exposure-only claimants and pleural claimants may qualify for benefits when and if they develop a compensable disease and meet the relevant exposure and medical criteria. Defendants forgo defenses to liability, including statute of limitations pleas.

Class members, in the main, are bound by the settlement in perpetuity, while CCR defendants may choose to withdraw from the settlement after ten years. A small number of class members—only a few per year—may reject the settlement and pursue their claims in court. Those permitted to exercise this option, however, may not assert any punitive damages claim or any claim for increased risk of cancer. Aspects of the administration of the settlement are to be monitored by the AFL–CIO and class counsel. Class counsel are to receive attorneys' fees in an amount to be approved by the District Court.

D

On January 29, 1993, as requested by the settling parties, the District Court conditionally certified, under Federal Rule of Civil Procedure 23(b)(3), an encompassing opt-out class. . . .

[Preliminarily, the district court held that it had subject-matter jurisdiction. Court-approved notice was then given to the class. Recipients were told they had three months to opt-out of the class, if they wished. Objectors were permitted to participate in the proceedings to determine the propriety of the class certification and the fairness of the settlement.

[Objectors challenged both the adequacy of representation and the fairness of the settlement. They maintained that those with manifested injuries and those whose injuries had not yet become manifest should not be in the same class or have the same counsel. Moreover, the same lawyers should not represent both the inventory plaintiffs and the new class. The settlement was unfair, they urged, because it ignored inflation and new developments in medical understanding, set much lower awards than those received by the inventory plaintiffs or in other tort litigation, and failed to cover certain claims.

[After lengthy hearings, the court on August 16, 1994, rejected these objections and found that the class certification was proper under Rule 23(a) and (b)(3) and that the settlement was fair. Later,] the District Court preliminarily enjoined all class members from commencing any asbestos-related suit against the CCR defendants in any state or federal court. See Georgine v. Amchem Products, Inc., 878 F.Supp. 716, 726–727 (E.D.Pa. 1994).

The objectors appealed [under 28 U.S.C. § 1292(a)(1) and pendent appellate jurisdiction]. The United States Court of Appeals for the Third Circuit vacated the certification, holding that the requirements of Rule 23 had not been satisfied. See Georgine v. Amchem Products, Inc., 83 F.3d 610 (1996).

E

. . . .

On class-action prerequisites, the Court of Appeals referred to an earlier Third Circuit decision, In re General Motors Corp. Pick–Up Truck Fuel Tank Products Liability Litigation, 55 F.3d 768 (C.A.3), cert. denied, 516 U.S. 824, 116 S.Ct. 88 (1995) (hereinafter GM Trucks), which held that although a class action may be certified for settlement purposes only, Rule 23(a)'s requirements must be satisfied as if the case were going to be litigated. 55 F.3d, at 799–800. The same rule should apply, the Third Circuit said, to class certification under Rule 23(b)(3). See 83 F.3d, at 625. But cf. In re Asbestos Litigation, 90 F.3d 963, 975–976, and n. 8 (C.A.5 1996), cert. pending, Nos. 96–1379, 96–1394.[e] . . .

[The court of appeals found that questions common to the class did not predominate over other questions, as required by Rule 23(b)(3). The court also found that serious intraclass conflicts meant that the representation of the class was not adequate. Nor were the named plaintiffs typical of the class. Finally, the court determined that the class action was not superior to other methods of adjudication.]

The Third Circuit, after intensive review, ultimately ordered decertification of the class and vacation of the District Court's anti-suit injunction. . . .

We granted certiorari, 519 U.S. 957, 117 S.Ct. 379 (1996), and now affirm.

II

Objectors assert in this Court, as they did in the District Court and Court of Appeals, an array of jurisdictional barriers. Most fundamentally, they maintain that the settlement proceeding instituted by class counsel and CCR is not a justiciable case or controversy within the confines of Article III of the Federal Constitution. In the main, they say, the proceed-

---

[e] After being remanded to the Fifth Circuit for further consideration in light of Amchem, this case ultimately returned to the Supreme Court as Ortiz v. Fibreboard Corp., which appears as the next case in this book.

ing is a nonadversarial endeavor to impose on countless individuals without currently ripe claims an administrative compensation regime binding on those individuals if and when they manifest injuries.

Furthermore, objectors urge that exposure-only claimants lack standing to sue: Either they have not yet sustained any cognizable injury or, to the extent the complaint states claims and demands relief for emotional distress, enhanced risk of disease, and medical monitoring, the settlement provides no redress. Objectors also argue that exposure-only claimants did not meet the then-current amount-in-controversy requirement (in excess of $50,000) specified for federal-court jurisdiction based upon diversity of citizenship. See 28 U.S.C. § 1332(a).

. . . [T]he Third Circuit declined to reach these issues because they "would not exist but for the [class action] certification." 83 F.3d, at 623. We agree that "[t]he class certification issues are dispositive," ibid.; because their resolution here is logically antecedent to the existence of any Article III issues, it is appropriate to reach them first, cf. Arizonans for Official English v. Arizona, 520 U.S. 43, 66–67, 117 S.Ct. 1055, 1068–1069 (1997) (declining to resolve definitively question whether petitioners had standing because mootness issue was dispositive of the case). We therefore follow the path taken by the Court of Appeals, mindful that Rule 23's requirements must be interpreted in keeping with Article III constraints, and with the Rules Enabling Act, which instructs that rules of procedure "shall not abridge, enlarge or modify any substantive right," 28 U.S.C. § 2072(b). See also Fed.Rule Civ.Proc. 82 ("rules shall not be construed to extend . . . the [subject matter] jurisdiction of the United States district courts").

III

. . . .

Among current applications of Rule 23(b)(3), the "settlement only" class has become a stock device. [Citation omitted.] Although all Federal Circuits recognize the utility of Rule 23(b)(3) settlement classes, courts have divided on the extent to which a proffered settlement affects court surveillance under Rule 23's certification criteria.

. . . [T]he Third Circuit [has] held that a class cannot be certified for settlement when certification for trial would be unwarranted. Other courts have held that settlement obviates or reduces the need to measure a proposed class against the enumerated Rule 23 requirements. [Citations omitted.]

. . . .

IV

We granted review to decide the role settlement may play, under existing Rule 23, in determining the propriety of class certification. The Third Circuit's opinion stated that each of the requirements of Rule 23(a) and (b)(3) "must be satisfied without taking into account the settlement."

83 F.3d, at 626 (quoting GM Trucks, 55 F.3d, at 799). That statement, petitioners urge, is incorrect.

We agree with petitioners to this limited extent: settlement is relevant to a class certification. The Third Circuit's opinion bears modification in that respect. But . . . the Court of Appeals in fact did not ignore the settlement; instead, that court homed in on settlement terms in explaining why it found the absentees' interests inadequately represented. See 83 F.3d, at 630–631. The Third Circuit's close inspection of the settlement in that regard was altogether proper.

Confronted with a request for settlement-only class certification, a district court need not inquire whether the case, if tried, would present intractable management problems, see Fed.Rule Civ.Proc. 23(b)(3)(D), for the proposal is that there be no trial. But other specifications of the rule—those designed to protect absentees by blocking unwarranted or overbroad class definitions—demand undiluted, even heightened, attention in the settlement context. Such attention is of vital importance, for a court asked to certify a settlement class will lack the opportunity, present when a case is litigated, to adjust the class, informed by the proceedings as they unfold. See Fed.Rule Civ.Proc. 23(c), (d).

And, of overriding importance, courts must be mindful that the Rule as now composed sets the requirements they are bound to enforce. Federal Rules take effect after an extensive deliberative process involving many reviewers: a Rules Advisory Committee, public commenters, the Judicial Conference, this Court, the Congress. See 28 U.S.C. §§ 2073, 2074. The text of a rule thus proposed and reviewed limits judicial inventiveness. Courts are not free to amend a rule outside the process Congress ordered, a process properly tuned to the instruction that rules of procedure "shall not abridge . . . any substantive right." § 2072(b).

Rule 23(e), on settlement of class actions, . . . was designed to function as an additional requirement, not a superseding direction, for the "class action" to which Rule 23(e) refers is one qualified for certification under Rule 23(a) and (b). [Citation omitted.] Subdivisions (a) and (b) focus court attention on whether a proposed class has sufficient unity so that absent members can fairly be bound by decisions of class representatives. That dominant concern persists when settlement, rather than trial, is proposed.

The safeguards provided by the Rule 23(a) and (b) class-qualifying criteria, we emphasize, are not impractical impediments—checks shorn of utility—in the settlement class context. First, the standards set for the protection of absent class members serve to inhibit appraisals of the chancellor's foot kind—class certifications dependent upon the court's gestalt judgment or overarching impression of the settlement's fairness.

Second, if a fairness inquiry under Rule 23(e) controlled certification, eclipsing Rule 23(a) and (b), and permitting class designation despite the impossibility of litigation, both class counsel and court would be disarmed. Class counsel confined to settlement negotiations could not use the threat of litigation to press for a better offer, [citation omitted], and the court would face a bargain proffered for its approval without benefit of adversarial investigation, see, e.g., Kamilewicz v. Bank of Boston Corp., 100 F.3d 1348, 1352 (C.A.7 1996) (Easterbrook, J., dissenting from denial of rehearing en banc) (parties "may even put one over on the court, in a staged performance"), cert. denied, 520 U.S. 1204, 117 S.Ct. 1569 (1997).

Federal courts, in any case, lack authority to substitute for Rule 23's certification criteria a standard never adopted—that if a settlement is "fair," then certification is proper. Applying to this case criteria the rulemakers set, we conclude that the Third Circuit's appraisal is essentially correct. Although that court should have acknowledged that settlement is a factor in the calculus, a remand is not warranted on that account. The Court of Appeals' opinion amply demonstrates why—with or without a settlement on the table—the sprawling class the District Court certified does not satisfy Rule 23's requirements.

A

We address first the requirement of Rule 23(b)(3) that "[common] questions of law or fact . . . predominate over any questions affecting only individual members." The District Court concluded that predominance was satisfied based on two factors: class members' shared experience of asbestos exposure and their common "interest in receiving prompt and fair compensation for their claims, while minimizing the risks and transaction costs inherent in the asbestos litigation process as it occurs presently in the tort system." 157 F.R.D., at 316. The settling parties also contend that the settlement's fairness is a common question, predominating over disparate legal issues that might be pivotal in litigation but become irrelevant under the settlement.

The predominance requirement stated in Rule 23(b)(3), we hold, is not met by the factors on which the District Court relied. The benefits asbestos-exposed persons might gain from the establishment of a grand-scale compensation scheme is a matter fit for legislative consideration, . . . but it is not pertinent to the predominance inquiry. That inquiry trains on the legal or factual questions that qualify each class member's case as a genuine controversy, questions that preexist any settlement.[18]

The Rule 23(b)(3) predominance inquiry tests whether proposed classes are sufficiently cohesive to warrant adjudication by representation. [Citation omitted.] The inquiry appropriate under Rule 23(e), on the other hand, protects unnamed class members "from unjust or unfair settlements affecting their rights when the representatives become fainthearted before the action is adjudicated or are able to secure satisfaction of their individual claims by a compromise." See 7B Wright, Miller, & Kane § 1797, at 340–

[18] In this respect, the predominance requirement of Rule 23(b)(3) is similar to the requirement of Rule 23(a)(3) that "claims or defenses" of the named representatives must be "typical of the claims or defenses of the class." The words "claims or defenses" in this context—just as in the context of Rule 24(b)[(1)(B)] governing permissive intervention—"manifestly refer to the kinds of claims or defenses that can be raised in courts of law as part of an actual or impending law suit." Diamond v. Charles, 476 U.S. 54, 76–77, 106 S.Ct. 1697, 1711 (1986) (O'Connor, J., concurring in part and concurring in judgment).

341. But it is not the mission of Rule 23(e) to assure the class cohesion that legitimizes representative action in the first place. If a common interest in a fair compromise could satisfy the predominance requirement of Rule 23(b)(3), that vital prescription would be stripped of any meaning in the settlement context.

The District Court also relied upon this commonality: "The members of the class have all been exposed to asbestos products supplied by the defendants . . . ." 157 F.R.D., at 316. Even if Rule 23(a)'s commonality requirement may be satisfied by that shared experience, the predominance criterion is far more demanding. See 83 F.3d, at 626–627. Given the greater number of questions peculiar to the several categories of class members, and to individuals within each category, and the significance of those uncommon questions, any overarching dispute about the health consequences of asbestos exposure cannot satisfy the Rule 23(b)(3) predominance standard.

The Third Circuit highlighted the disparate questions undermining class cohesion in this case:

> "Class members were exposed to different asbestos-containing products, for different amounts of time, in different ways, and over different periods. Some class members suffer no physical injury or have only asymptomatic pleural changes, while others suffer from lung cancer, disabling asbestosis, or from mesothelioma . . . . Each has a different history of cigarette smoking, a factor that complicates the causation inquiry.
>
> "The [exposure-only] plaintiffs especially share little in common, either with each other or with the presently injured class members. It is unclear whether they will contract asbestos-related disease and, if so, what disease each will suffer. They will also incur different medical expenses because their monitoring and treatment will depend on singular circumstances and individual medical histories." Id., at 626.

Differences in state law, the Court of Appeals observed, compound these disparities. See id., at 627 (citing Phillips Petroleum Co. v. Shutts, 472 U.S. 797, 823, 105 S.Ct. 2965, 2980 (1985)[f]).

No settlement class called to our attention is as sprawling as this one. [Citation omitted.] Predominance is a test readily met in certain cases alleging consumer or securities fraud or violations of the antitrust laws. See Adv. Comm. Notes, 28 U.S.C.App., p. 697 . . . . Even mass tort cases arising from a common cause or disaster may, depending upon the circumstances, satisfy the predominance requirement. The Advisory Committee

---

[f] In this state plaintiff-class action seeking money damages for claimants from all over the country and abroad, the U.S. Supreme Court ruled that the Kansas court could not apply Kansas law to class members' claims unrelated to Kansas. By its opinion with uncertain reverberations, the Court also held that absent class members need not otherwise be subject to effective service of process, as long as they received notice and had a right to participate and a right to opt out. But if a constitutionally adequate connection between the sovereign and an absent class member exists without any such resorting to implied consent, as normally would be true for Americans in federal court, then arguably neither territorial jurisdiction nor this latter Phillips holding should be of further concern with respect to that member.

for the 1966 revision of Rule 23, it is true, noted that "mass accident" cases are likely to present "significant questions, not only of damages but of liability and defenses of liability, . . . affecting the individuals in different ways." Ibid. And the Committee advised that such cases are "ordinarily not appropriate" for class treatment. Ibid. But the text of the Rule does not categorically exclude mass tort cases from class certification, and district courts, since the late 1970s, have been certifying such cases in increasing number. [Citation omitted.] The Committee's warning, however, continues to call for caution when individual stakes are high and disparities among class members great. As the Third Circuit's opinion makes plain, the certification in this case does not follow the counsel of caution. That certification cannot be upheld, for it rests on a conception of Rule 23(b)(3)'s predominance requirement irreconcilable with the Rule's design.

B

Nor can the class approved by the District Court satisfy Rule 23(a)(4)'s requirement that the named parties "will fairly and adequately protect the interests of the class." The adequacy inquiry under Rule 23(a)(4) serves to uncover conflicts of interest between named parties and the class they seek to represent. See General Telephone Co. of Southwest v. Falcon, 457 U.S. 147, 157–158, n. 13, 102 S.Ct. 2364, 2370–2371, n. 13 (1982). . . .

As the Third Circuit pointed out, named parties with diverse medical conditions sought to act on behalf of a single giant class rather than on behalf of discrete subclasses. In significant respects, the interests of those within the single class are not aligned. Most saliently, for the currently injured, the critical goal is generous immediate payments. That goal tugs against the interest of exposure-only plaintiffs in ensuring an ample, inflation-protected fund for the future. [Citation omitted.]

The disparity between the currently injured and exposure-only categories of plaintiffs, and the diversity within each category are not made insignificant by the District Court's finding that petitioners' assets suffice to pay claims under the settlement. See 157 F.R.D., at 291. Although this is not a "limited fund" case certified under Rule 23(b)(1)(B), the terms of the settlement reflect essential allocation decisions designed to confine compensation and to limit defendants' liability. For example, as earlier described, . . . the settlement includes no adjustment for inflation; only a few claimants per year can opt out at the back end; and loss-of-consortium claims are extinguished with no compensation.

The settling parties, in sum, achieved a global compromise with no structural assurance of fair and adequate representation for the diverse groups and individuals affected. Although the named parties alleged a range of complaints, each served generally as representative for the whole, not for a separate constituency. . . . The Third Circuit found no assurance here—either in the terms of the settlement or in the structure of the negotiations—that the named plaintiffs operated under a proper understanding of their representational responsibilities. See 83 F.3d, at 630–631. That assessment, we conclude, is on the mark.

C

Impediments to the provision of adequate notice, the Third Circuit emphasized, rendered highly problematic any endeavor to tie to a settlement class persons with no perceptible asbestos-related disease at the time of the settlement. Id., at 633; [other citation omitted]. Many persons in the exposure-only category, the Court of Appeals stressed, may not even know of their exposure, or realize the extent of the harm they may incur. Even if they fully appreciate the significance of class notice, those without current afflictions may not have the information or foresight needed to decide, intelligently, whether to stay in or opt out.

Family members of asbestos-exposed individuals may themselves fall prey to disease or may ultimately have ripe claims for loss of consortium. Yet large numbers of people in this category—future spouses and children of asbestos victims—could not be alerted to their class membership. And current spouses and children of the occupationally exposed may know nothing of that exposure.

Because we have concluded that the class in this case cannot satisfy the requirements of common issue predominance and adequacy of representation, we need not rule, definitively, on the notice given here. In accord with the Third Circuit, however, see 83 F.3d, at 633–634, we recognize the gravity of the question whether class action notice sufficient under the Constitution and Rule 23 could ever be given to legions so unselfconscious and amorphous.

V

The argument is sensibly made that a nationwide administrative claims processing regime would provide the most secure, fair, and efficient means of compensating victims of asbestos exposure. Congress, however, has not adopted such a solution. And Rule 23, which must be interpreted with fidelity to the Rules Enabling Act and applied with the interests of absent class members in close view, cannot carry the large load CCR, class counsel, and the District Court heaped upon it. As this case exemplifies, the rulemakers' prescriptions for class actions may be endangered by "those who embrace [Rule 23] too enthusiastically just as [they are by] those who approach [the Rule] with distaste." C. Wright, Law of Federal Courts 508 (5th ed. 1994); cf. 83 F.3d, at 634 (suggesting resort to less bold aggregation techniques, including more narrowly defined class certifications).

* * *

For the reasons stated, the judgment of the Court of Appeals for the Third Circuit is

Affirmed.

■ JUSTICE O'CONNOR took no part in the consideration or decision of this case.

■ JUSTICE BREYER, with whom JUSTICE STEVENS joins, concurring in part and dissenting in part.

Although I agree with the Court's basic holding that "settlement is relevant to a class certification," . . . I find several problems in its approach that lead me to a different conclusion. First, I believe that the need for settlement in this mass tort case, with hundreds of thousands of lawsuits, is greater than the Court's opinion suggests. Second, I would give more weight than would the majority to settlement-related issues for purposes of determining whether common issues predominate. Third, I am uncertain about the Court's determination of adequacy of representation, and do not believe it appropriate for this Court to second-guess the District Court on the matter without first having the Court of Appeals consider it [with the correct standard in mind]. Fourth, I am uncertain about the tenor of an opinion that seems to suggest the settlement is unfair. And fifth, in the absence of further review by the Court of Appeals, I cannot accept the majority's suggestions that "notice" is inadequate.

These difficulties flow from the majority's review of what are highly fact-based, complex, and difficult matters, matters that are inappropriate for initial review before this Court. The law gives broad leeway to district courts in making class certification decisions, and their judgments are to be reviewed by the Court of Appeals only for abuse of discretion. [Citation omitted.] Indeed, the District Court's certification decision rests upon more than 300 findings of fact reached after five weeks of comprehensive hearings. Accordingly, I do not believe that we should in effect set aside the findings of the District Court. That court is far more familiar with the issues and litigants than is a court of appeals or are we, and therefore has "broad power and discretion . . . with respect to matters involving the certification" of class actions. Reiter v. Sonotone Corp., 442 U.S. 330, 345, 99 S.Ct. 2326, 2334 (1979); cf. Cooter & Gell v. Hartmarx Corp., 496 U.S. 384, 402, 110 S.Ct. 2447, 2459 (1990) (district court better situated to make fact-dependent legal determinations in Rule 11 context).

I do not believe that we can rely upon the Court of Appeals' review of the District Court record, for that review, and its ultimate conclusions, are infected by a legal error. E.g., Georgine v. Amchem Products, Inc., 83 F.3d 610, 626 (C.A.3 1996) (holding that "*considered as a litigation class*," the class cannot meet Rule 23's requirements) (emphasis added). There is no evidence that the Court of Appeals at any point considered the settlement as something that would help the class meet Rule 23. I find, moreover, the fact-related issues presented here sufficiently close to warrant further detailed appellate court review under the correct legal standard. [Citation omitted.] . . .

. . . .

Question: (9) If a defendant is going to be bound by a settlement, it is in the defendant's interest to have the plaintiff-class members bound as well. If adequate representation of absent class members is a ground for collateral attack on the settlement, does not the defendant then have an interest in bringing defects in class representation to the court's attention? What self-interested litigation strategies might limit the defendant's effectiveness in raising those defects in class representation? Could the fact that the Amchem defendants did not oppose class certification have helped create the problems that lead the Court to upend the settlement? See Debra Lyn Bassett, The Defendant's Obligation to Ensure Adequate Representation in Class Actions, 74 UMKC L.Rev. 511 (2006).

ORTIZ v. FIBREBOARD CORP., 527 U.S. 815, 119 S.Ct. 2295 (1999). "Like Amchem . . . , this case is a class action prompted by the elephantine mass of asbestos cases, and our discussion in Amchem will suffice to show how this litigation defies customary judicial administration and calls for national legislation." This case again presented the Supreme Court with an attempted "global settlement" of future asbestos claims—this time, against Fibreboard and its two insurance carriers by a class action that would avoid Rule 23(b)(3)'s opt-out provision and that fell outside the reach of the MDL consolidation order.

Facing more than a billion dollars of settlement obligations in pending cases and ongoing fights over insurance coverage, Fibreboard and the insurance companies negotiated a complicated arrangement meant to bring "total peace" with lawyers representing thousands of plaintiffs; "talks focused on the feasibility of a mandatory class action, one binding all potential plaintiffs and giving none of them any choice to opt out of the certified class." Ultimately, Fibreboard and the carriers agreed to establish a trust to process and pay future claims. "Claimants seeking compensation would be required to try to settle with the trust. If initial settlement attempts failed, claimants would have to proceed to mediation, arbitration, and a mandatory settlement conference. Only after exhausting that process could claimants go to court against the trust, subject to a limit of $500,000 per claim, with punitive damages and prejudgment interest barred." As this deal on future claims was being struck, the parties settled "an inventory of some 45,000 pending claims, being substantially all those filed by one of the plaintiffs' firms negotiating the global settlement. The settlement amounts per claim were higher than average, with one-half due on closing and the remaining contingent upon either a global settlement or Fibreboard's success in the coverage litigation. This agreement provided the model for settling inventory claims of other firms."

Per the global settlement agreement, "a group of named plaintiffs filed an action in the United States District Court for the Eastern District of Texas, seeking certification for settlement purposes of a mandatory class" comprising future claimants against Fibreboard, but excluding anyone who had a claim pending before the date of the settlement. The district court certified the action as a Rule 23(b)(1)(B) "limited fund" class. Judge Robert Parker "found both the 'disputed insurance asset liquidated by the $1.535 billion Global Settlement,' and, alternatively, 'the sum of the value of Fibreboard plus the value of its insurance coverage,' as measured by the insurance funds' settlement value, to be relevant 'limited funds.'" Additionally, the judge found the settlement to be fair, pursuant to Rule 23(e). The Fifth Circuit affirmed. Shortly thereafter, the Supreme Court decided Amchem, vacated the Fifth Circuit's judgment, and remanded for consideration in light of Amchem. On remand, the Fifth Circuit again affirmed, distinguishing Amchem because it was a Rule 23(b)(3) class, while this was a Rule 23(b)(1)(B) class, and because awards in the present case were not allocated according to the nature of the injury. The Supreme Court granted certiorari and reversed.

The Court, in an opinion by Justice Souter, reviewed the historical antecedents of the limited fund class action and concluded as follows:

"The cases forming this pedigree of the limited fund class action as understood by the drafters of Rule 23 have a number of common characteristics, despite the variety of circumstances from which they arose. . . .

"The first and most distinctive characteristic is that the totals of the aggregated liquidated claims and the fund available for satisfying them, set definitely at their maximums, demonstrate the inadequacy of the fund to pay all the claims. The concept driving this type of suit was insufficiency, which alone justified the limit on an early feast to avoid a later famine. [Citations omitted.] The equity of the limitation is its necessity.

"Second, the whole of the inadequate fund was to be devoted to the overwhelming claims. [Citations omitted.] It went without saying that the defendant or estate or constructive trustee with the inadequate assets had no opportunity to benefit himself or claimants of lower priority by holding back on the amount distributed to the class. The limited fund cases thus ensured that the class as a whole was given the best deal; they did not give a defendant a better deal than seriatim litigation would have produced.

"Third, the claimants identified by a common theory of recovery were treated equitably among themselves. The cases assume that the class will comprise everyone who might state a claim on a single or repeated set of facts, invoking a common theory of recovery, to be satisfied from the limited fund as the source of payment. . . . Once the represented classes were so identified, there was no question of omitting anyone whose claim shared the common theory of liability and would contribute to the calculated shortfall of recovery. . . . Once all similar claims were brought directly or by representation before the court, these antecedents of the mandatory class action presented straightforward models of equitable treatment, with the simple equity of a pro rata distribution providing the required fairness, [citation omitted].

"In sum, mandatory class treatment through representative actions on a limited fund theory was justified with reference to a 'fund' with a definitely ascertained limit, all of which would be distributed to satisfy all those with liquidated claims based on a common theory of liability, by an equitable, pro rata distribution."

The Court then faced the question of how much of this precedent was codified in the Rule when it was amended in 1966. The Court decided to treat the three characteristics as presumptively necessary to satisfy the limited fund Rule. "At the least, the burden of justification rests on the proponent of any departure from the traditional norm."

Turning to the settlement before it, the Court found that it failed to meet any of the requirements of a limited fund class action. The Court first concluded that there was insufficient independent evidence on which to base a finding that the fund was indeed limited. "The 'fund' in this case comprised both the general assets of Fibreboard and the insurance assets provided by the two policies . . . ." Fibreboard had a then-current sale value of $235 million, according to the lower courts. As to the insurance assets, the Court said: "One may take a settlement amount as good evidence of the maximum available if one can assume that parties of equal knowledge and negotiating skill agreed upon the figure through arms-length bargaining, unhindered by any considerations tugging against the interests of the parties ostensibly represented in the negotiation. But no such assumption may be indulged in this case, or probably in any class action settlement with the potential for gigantic fees. In this case, certainly, any assumption that plaintiffs' counsel could be of a mind to do their simple best in bargaining for the benefit of the settlement class is patently at odds with the fact that at least some of the same lawyers representing plaintiffs and the class had also negotiated the separate settlement of 45,000 pending claims, . . . the full payment of which was contingent on a successful global settlement agreement or the successful resolution of the insurance coverage dispute . . . . Class counsel thus had great incentive to reach any agreement in the global settlement negotiations that they thought might survive a Rule 23(e) fairness hearing, rather than the best possible arrangement for the substantially unidentified global settlement class."

Next, the Court found the required equity among class members to be lacking. "As for the settled inventory claims, their plaintiffs appeared to have obtained better terms than the class members." Moreover, there were serious intraclass conflicts, so that "even ostensible parity between settling nonclass plaintiffs and class members would be insufficient to overcome the failure to provide the structural protection of independent representation as for subclasses with conflicting interests."

Finally, the Court noted that the entire fund was not to be distributed; "most notably, Fibreboard was allowed to retain virtually its entire net worth." The Court added, however, that "[g]iven our treatment of the two preceding deficiencies of the certification, there is of course no need to decide whether this feature of the agreement would alone be fatal to the Global Settlement Agreement. To ignore it entirely, however, would be so misleading that we have decided simply to identify the issue it raises, without purporting to resolve it at this time."

Justice Rehnquist concurred in this opinion, but wrote a separate opinion, joined by Justices Scalia and Kennedy, stressing the need for legislative action.

Justice Breyer, joined by Justice Stevens, dissented. He stressed the magnitude of this litigation and urged that deference be given to the trial judge's ruling. He remarked, "The judiciary cannot treat the problem as entirely one of legislative failure, as if it were caused, say, by a poorly drafted statute. Thus . . . , judges can and should search aggressively for ways, within the framework of existing law, to avoid delay and expense so great as to bring about a massive denial of justice."

Moreover, Justice Breyer maintained that the majority's test for a Rule 23(b)(1)(B) limited fund had been met. Whatever the assets were, he first noted, they were less than the total of claims, and the fund was thus "limited." Next, he pointed out that the district court had found, after hearing, that the class members were treated equitably, and the Fifth Circuit had affirmed. Finally, he took a more flexible approach to Rule 23(b)(1)(B) and concluded that it does not require the entire fund to be depleted, "where there is no doubt that 'the class as a whole was given the best deal.' " And, he averred, "[t]here is no doubt in this case that the settlement made far more money available to satisfy asbestos claims than was likely to occur in its absence." He added: "And, of course, not only is it better for the injured plaintiffs, it is far better for Fibreboard, its employees, its creditors, and the communities where it is located for Fibreboard to remain a working enterprise, rather than slowly forcing it into bankruptcy while most of its money is spent on asbestos lawyers and expert witnesses. I would consequently find substantial compliance with the majority's third condition."

Question: (10) Is there and should there be provision for a compulsory class action, as where a corporation faces an endless queue of individual actions against it and wishes that they be brought together despite the unwillingness of every plaintiff, or is this and should this be the exclusive domain of Rule 19 dealing with compulsory joinder?

SECTION 3. LITIGATING CLASS ACTIONS

(a) RULE 23(c)

Class actions, in the course of their litigation, pose major management problems for the courts. So, after Rule 23(a) and (b) sets the limits on the scope of the class-action device, the Rule turns to this subject of management.

Rule 23(c) treats a variety of threshold matters. In particular, Rule 23(c)(1) provides that soon after commencement of a proposed class action, the court must determine whether the requirements of Rule 23(a) and (b) are met and then enter an order either granting or denying certification as a class action.

In theory, the opponent will oppose the class representative's motion for certification and raise various potential defects for the court to consider. In reality, as we have seen, defendants may have negotiated with plaintiffs to produce a global settlement, and thereby reduce liability while providing generous fees. Therefore, a judge may face two sides who support certification and are unwilling to raise any defects.

Settlement negotiations sometimes fall apart later, though. Therefore, defendants who strategically supported class certification may unexpectedly face litigation and want to oppose certification by now raising defects. One court has ruled, however, that judicial estoppel can block defendants from so reversing their position on certification. Carnegie v. Household Int'l, Inc., 376 F.3d 656 (7th Cir.2004) (Posner, J.).

For certification, the class representative must show by a preponderance that the case satisfies the requirements for class treatment. "The evidence and arguments a district court considers in the class certification decision call for rigorous analysis," observed the appellate court in In re Hydrogen Peroxide Antitrust Litigation, 552 F.3d 305, 316–18 (3d Cir. 2008), adding: "An overlap between a class certification requirement and the merits of a claim is no reason to decline to resolve relevant disputes when necessary to determine whether a class certification requirement is met." These views conform to the usual approach, and indeed more courts are getting into the merits as a way to screen out class actions at the certification stage. See Steig D. Olson, "Chipping Away": The Misguided Trend Toward Resolving Merits Disputes as Part of the Class Certification Calculus, 43 U.S.F.L.Rev. 935 (2009). But the Third Circuit continued into unsupported pronouncement, when it mustered this comforting dictum: "Although the district court's findings for the purpose of class certification are conclusive on that topic, they do not bind the fact-finder on the merits."

Manual for Complex Litigation, Fourth

(2004).

SAMPLE CLASS ACTION ORDERS

§ 40.41 *Order Certifying Class*

[caption]

Order No. ______

In accordance with the findings and conclusions contained in the Opinion [omitted] filed concurrently with this order, it is, ORDERED:

1. **Class Certification.** Civil Action No. ______, styled ______ shall be maintained as a class action on behalf of the following class of plaintiffs:

[Describe class in objective terms to the extent possible. For example, "All persons and entities throughout the United States and its territories (other than widget manufacturers and entities owned or controlled by them) that, since [date], have purchased widgets directly from any of the defendants or from any other widget manufacturer."]

with respect to the following cause(s) of action:

[Describe class claims as precisely as possible. For example, "Any claims for damages or injunctive relief under federal antitrust laws premised upon an alleged conspiracy among the defendants and other widget manufacturers to restrict competition in the manufacture, distribution, and sale of widgets by setting the minimum prices charged for widgets after [date]."]

2. **Class Representative; Class Counsel.** Subject to further order of the court, [A.B. Co.] is designated as class representative and [X.Y.] is designated as counsel for the class.

3. **Notice.**

(a) Class counsel shall by [date], cause to be mailed in the name of the clerk by first class mail, postage prepaid, to all class members who can be identified through reasonable efforts, a notice written in plain language and approved by the court. For illustrative examples of the form of such notices, see the Federal Judicial Center's Web site (www.fjc.gov) and go to the "Class Action Notices" page. In addition to class members identified through an examination of defendants' records, this notice will also be mailed to persons who are members of [National Widget Dealers Trade Association].

(b) Class counsel shall cause to be published in the ______ by [date], a notice in substantially the same style and format as the illustrative summary notices posted on the "Class Action Notices" page of the Federal Judicial Center's Web site (www.fjc.gov).

4. **Exclusion.** The notice to class members must inform them as to how they may exclude themselves from the class.

5. **List of Class Members.** Class counsel will file with the clerk by [date], an affidavit identifying the persons to whom notice has been mailed and who have not timely requested exclusion.

Dated: ______

____
United States District Judge

Eisen v. Carlisle & Jacquelin

Supreme Court of the United States, 1974.
417 U.S. 156, 94 S.Ct. 2140.

■ MR. JUSTICE POWELL delivered the opinion of the Court.

On May 2, 1966, petitioner filed a class action on behalf of himself and all other odd-lot[1] traders on the New York Stock Exchange (the Exchange).

The complaint charged respondents with violations of the antitrust and securities laws and demanded damages for petitioner and his class. Eight years have elapsed, but there has been no trial on the merits of these claims. Both the parties and the courts are still wrestling with the complex questions surrounding petitioner's attempt to maintain his suit as a class action under Fed.Rule Civ.Proc. 23. We granted certiorari to resolve some of these difficulties. 414 U.S. 908, 94 S.Ct. 235 (1973).

I

Petitioner brought this class action in the United States District Court for the Southern District of New York. Originally, he sued on behalf of all buyers and sellers of odd lots on the Exchange, but subsequently the class was limited to those who traded in odd lots during the period from May 1, 1962, through June 30, 1966. 52 F.R.D. 253, 261 (1971). Throughout this period odd-lot trading was not part of the Exchange's regular auction market but was handled exclusively by special odd-lot dealers, who bought and sold for their own accounts as principals. Respondent brokerage firms Carlisle & Jacquelin and DeCoppet & Doremus together handled 99% of the Exchange's odd-lot business. S.E.C., Report of Special Study of Securities Markets, H.R.Doc. No. 95, pt. 2, 88th Cong., 1st Sess., 172 (1963). They were compensated by the odd-lot differential, a surcharge imposed on the odd-lot investor in addition to the standard brokerage commission applicable to round-lot transactions. For the period in question the differential was ⅛ of a point (12½¢) per share on stocks trading below $40 per share and ¼ of a point (25¢) per share on stocks trading at or above $40 per share.

Petitioner charged that respondent brokerage firms had monopolized odd-lot trading and set the differential at an excessive level in violation of §§ 1 and 2 of the Sherman Act, 15 U.S.C. §§ 1 and 2, and he demanded treble damages for the amount of the overcharge. Petitioner also demanded unspecified money damages from the Exchange for its alleged failure to regulate the differential for the protection of investors in violation of §§ 6 and 19 of the Securities Exchange Act of 1934, 15 U.S.C. §§ 78f and 78s. Finally, he requested attorneys' fees and injunctive prohibition of future excessive charges.

A critical fact in this litigation is that petitioner's individual stake in the damages award he seeks is only $70. No competent attorney would undertake this complex antitrust action to recover so inconsequential an amount. Economic reality dictates that petitioner's suit proceed as a class action or not at all. Opposing counsel have therefore engaged in prolonged combat over the various requirements of Rule 23. The result has been an exceedingly complicated series of decisions by both the District Court and the Court of Appeals for the Second Circuit. . . .

---

[1] Odd lots are shares traded in lots of fewer than a hundred. Shares traded in units of a hundred or multiples thereof are round-lots.

. . . .

Eisen I

As we have seen, petitioner began this action in May 1966. In September of that year [Judge Tyler of] the District Court dismissed the suit as a class action. 41 F.R.D. 147. Following denial of his motion for interlocutory review under 28 U.S.C. § 1292(b), petitioner took an appeal as of right under § 1291. Respondents then moved to dismiss on the ground that the order appealed from was not final. In Eisen I, the Court of Appeals held that the denial of class action status in this case was appealable as a final order under § 1291. 370 F.2d 119 (1966), cert. denied, 386 U.S. 1035, 87 S.Ct. 1487 (1967). This was so because, as a practical matter, the dismissal of the class action aspect of petitioner's suit was a "death knell" for the entire action . . . .[g]

Eisen II

Nearly 18 months later the Court of Appeals reversed the dismissal of the class action in a decision known as Eisen II. 391 F.2d 555 (1968). In reaching this result the court undertook an exhaustive but ultimately inconclusive analysis of Rule 23. Subdivision (a) of the Rule sets forth four prerequisites to the maintenance of any suit as a class action . . . . The

[g] Eisen I posed the question of whether an order dismissing a class action, but permitting the named plaintiff to litigate his individual claim, was appealable. Did it fall within the small class of collateral orders recognized as appealable in Cohen v. Beneficial Industrial Loan Corp., infra p. 1543, being "too important to be denied review and too independent of the cause itself to require that appellate consideration be deferred until the whole case is adjudicated"? Was it appealable under Gillespie v. United States Steel Corp., infra p. 1547, because "the danger of denying justice by delay" outweighed "the inconvenience and costs of piecemeal review"? The Second Circuit held it appealable as a final order, citing Cohen and Gillespie and saying that immediate review should be allowed where "a district court's order, if not reviewed, is the death knell of the action."

The Supreme Court, however, has since considered the appealability of an order denying class-action status. In Coopers & Lybrand v. Livesay, 437 U.S. 463, 98 S.Ct. 2454 (1978), the Court ruled that such an order is not appealable under 28 U.S.C. § 1291, the collateral order exception being inapplicable, Gillespie being limited to its facts, and the "death knell" rationale being here invalid. In dicta the Court observed that orders granting class certification are likewise interlocutory. On the same day it decided Coopers & Lybrand, the Supreme Court rejected an attempt to stretch 28 U.S.C. § 1292(a)(1) to cover an order on class-action status in a suit seeking class-wide permanent injunctive relief. Gardner v. Westinghouse Broadcasting Co., 437 U.S. 478, 98 S.Ct. 2451 (1978).

As usual, § 1292(b) offered only a slim possibility of interlocutory review of a class-action determination. Mandamus was rarely invoked successfully here. An additional discretionary route to immediate review of an order denying class-action status lay in Rule 54(b), but the Rule's applicability to this kind of order was particularly questionable. See Joyce E. Margulies, Comment, Appealability of Class Action Determinations, 44 Fordham L.Rev. 548, 561–65, 568–74 (1975).

On December 1, 1998, Rule 23(f) became effective, clarifying the appealability of a district court's order denying or granting class–action status. Now, a court of appeals may in its unfettered discretion permit an appeal from such an order as long as the application is made within fourteen days after entry of the order.

The alternative to interlocutory appeal is to await a final decision. Practically risky is the route whereby the disappointed named plaintiff accelerates a final decision by inviting a dismissal with prejudice. See Albert F. Cacozza, Jr., Comment, Rule 41(b) Dismissal as a Route to Appellate Review of an Adverse Class Determination, 48 U.Chi.L.Rev. 912 (1981).

District Court had experienced little difficulty in finding that petitioner satisfied the first three prerequisites but had concluded that petitioner might not "fairly and adequately protect the interests of the class" as required by Rule 23(a)(4). The Court of Appeals indicated its disagreement with the reasoning behind the latter conclusion and directed the District Court to reconsider the point.

In addition to meeting the four conjunctive requirements of 23(a), a class action must also qualify under one of the three subdivisions of 23(b). Petitioner argued that the suit was maintainable as a class action under all three subdivisions. The Court of Appeals held the first two subdivisions inapplicable to this suit[4] and therefore turned its attention to the third subdivision, (b)(3) . . . After a detailed review . . . , the Court of Appeals concluded that the only potential barrier to maintenance of this suit as a class action was the Rule 23(b)(3)(D) directive that a court evaluate "the difficulties likely to be encountered in the management of a class action." Commonly referred to as "manageability," this consideration encompasses the whole range of practical problems that may render the class action format inappropriate for a particular suit. With reference to this litigation, the Court of Appeals noted that the difficulties of distributing any ultimate recovery to the class members would be formidable, though not necessarily insuperable, and commented that it was "reluctant to permit actions to proceed where they are not likely to benefit anyone but the lawyers who bring them." 391 F.2d, at 567. The Court therefore directed the District Court to conduct "a further inquiry . . . in order to consider the mechanics involved in the administration of the present action." Ibid.

Finally, the Court of Appeals turned to the most imposing obstacle to this class action—the notice requirement of Rule 23(c)(2). The District Court had held that both the Rule and the Due Process Clause of the Fifth Amendment required individual notice to all class members who could be identified. 41 F.R.D., at 151. Petitioner objected that mailed notice to the entire class would be prohibitively expensive and argued that some form of publication notice would suffice. The Court of Appeals declined to settle this issue, noting that "[o]n the record before us we cannot arrive at any rational and satisfactory conclusion on the propriety of resorting to some form of publication as a means of giving the necessary notice to all members of the class on behalf of whom the action is stated to be commenced and maintained." 391 F.2d, at 569.

The outcome of Eisen II was a remand for an evidentiary hearing on the questions of notice, manageability, adequacy of representation, and "any other matters which the District Court may consider pertinent and proper." Id., at 570. And in a ruling that aroused later controversy, the

---

[4] Before the Court of Appeals, petitioner dropped the contention that the suit qualified under subdivision (b)(1)(B). The court held subdivision (b)(1)(A) inapplicable on the ground that the prospective class consisted entirely of small claimants, none of whom could afford to litigate this action in order to recover his individual claim and that consequently there was little chance of "inconsistent or varying adjudications with respect to individual members of the class which would establish incompatible standards of conduct for the party opposing the class . . . ." Subdivision (b)(2) was held to apply only to actions exclusively or predominantly for injunctive or declaratory relief. Advisory Committee's Note, Proposed Rules of Civil Procedure, 28 U.S.C.App., p. 7766.

Court of Appeals expressly purported to retain appellate jurisdiction while the case was heard on remand.

Eisen III

After it held the evidentiary hearing on remand, which together with affidavits and stipulations provided the basis for extensive findings of fact, the District Court issued an opinion and order holding the suit maintainable as a class action. 52 F.R.D. 253 (1971) [(Tyler, J.)]. The court first noted that petitioner satisfied the criteria identified by the Court of Appeals for determining adequacy of representation under Rule 23(a)(4). Then it turned to the more difficult question of manageability. Under this general rubric the court dealt with problems of the computation of damages, the mechanics of administering this suit as a class action, and the distribution of any eventual recovery. The last-named problem had most troubled the Court of Appeals, prompting its remark that if "class members are not likely ever to share in an eventual judgment, we would probably not permit the class action to continue." 391 F.2d, at 567. The District Court attempted to resolve this difficulty by embracing the idea of a "fluid class" recovery whereby damages would be distributed to future odd-lot traders rather than to the specific class members who were actually injured. The court suggested that "a fund equivalent to the amount of unclaimed damages might be established and the odd-lot differential reduced in an amount determined reasonable by the court until such time as the fund is depleted." 52 F.R.D., at 265. The need to resort to this expedient of recovery by the "next best class" arose from the prohibitively high cost of computing and awarding multitudinous small damages claims on an individual basis.

Finally, the District Court took up the problem of notice. The court found that the prospective class included some six million individuals, institutions, and intermediaries of various sorts; that with reasonable effort some two million of these odd-lot investors could be identified by name and address;[5] and that the names and addresses of an additional 250,000 persons who had participated in special investment programs involving odd-lot trading[6] could also be identified with reasonable effort. Using the then current first-class postage rate of six cents, the court determined that stuffing and mailing each individual notice form would cost 10 cents. Thus individual notice to all identifiable class members would cost $225,000, and additional expense would be incurred for suitable publication notice designed to reach the other four million class members.

The District Court concluded, however, that neither Rule 23(c)(2) nor the Due Process Clause required so substantial an expenditure at the

[5] These two million traders dealt with brokerage firms who transmitted their odd-lot transactions to respondents Carlisle & Jacquelin and DeCoppet & Doremus via teletype. By comparing the odd-lot firms' computerized records of these teletype transactions and the general-services brokerage firms' computerized records of all customer names and addresses, the names and addresses of these two million odd-lot traders can be obtained.

[6] In the period from May 1962 through June 1968, 100,000 individuals had odd-lot transactions through participation in the Monthly Investment Plan operated by the Exchange and 150,000 persons traded in odd lots through participation in a number of payroll deduction plans operated by Merrill Lynch, Pierce, Fenner & Smith.

outset of this litigation. Instead, it proposed a notification scheme consisting of four elements: (1) individual notice to all member firms of the Exchange and to commercial banks with large trust departments; (2) individual notice to the approximately 2,000 identifiable class members with 10 or more odd-lot transactions during the relevant period; (3) individual notice to an additional 5,000 class members selected at random; and (4) prominent publication notice in the Wall Street Journal and in other newspapers in New York and California. The court calculated that this package would cost approximately $21,720.

The only issue not resolved by the District Court in its first opinion on remand from Eisen II was who should bear the cost of notice. Because petitioner understandably declined to pay $21,720 in order to litigate an action involving an individual stake of only $70, this question presented something of a dilemma:

> "If the expense of notice is placed upon [petitioner], it would be the end of a possibly meritorious suit, frustrating both the policy behind private antitrust actions and the admonition that the new Rule 23 is to be given a liberal rather than a restrictive interpretation, Eisen II at 563. On the other hand, if costs were arbitrarily placed upon [respondents] at this point, the result might be the imposition of an unfair burden founded upon a groundless claim. In addition to the probability of encouraging frivolous class actions, such a step might also result in [respondents'] passing on to their customers, including many of the class members in this case, the expenses of defending these actions." 52 F.R.D., at 269.

Analogizing to the laws of preliminary injunctions, the court decided to impose the notice cost on respondents if petitioner could show a strong likelihood of success on the merits, and it scheduled a preliminary hearing on the merits to facilitate this determination. After this hearing the District Court issued an opinion and order ruling that petitioner was "more than likely" to prevail at trial and that respondents should bear 90% of the cost of notice, or $19,548. 54 F.R.D. 565, 567 (1972) [(Tyler, J.)].

Relying on the purported retention of jurisdiction by the Court of Appeals after Eisen II, respondents on May 1, 1972, obtained an order directing the clerk of the District Court to certify and transmit the record for appellate review. Subsequently, respondents also filed a notice of appeal under 28 U.S.C. § 1291. Petitioner's motion to dismiss on the ground that the appeal had not been taken from a final order was denied by the Court of Appeals on June 29, 1972.

On May 1, 1973, the Court of Appeals issued Eisen III [by the same panel that issued Eisen II]. 479 F.2d 1005. The majority disapproved the District Court's partial reliance on publication notice, holding that Rule 23(c)(2) required individual notice to all identifiable class members. The majority further ruled that the District Court had no authority to conduct a preliminary hearing on the merits for the purpose of allocating costs and that the entire expense of notice necessarily fell on petitioner as representative plaintiff. Finally, the Court of Appeals rejected the expedient of a fluid-class recovery and concluded that the proposed class action was unmanageable under Rule 23(b)(3)(D).[h] For all of these reasons the Court of Appeals ordered the suit dismissed as a class action. One judge concurred in the result solely on the ground that the District Court had erred in imposing 90% of the notice costs on respondents. Petitioner's requests for rehearing and rehearing en banc were denied. 479 F.2d, at 1020.

Thus, after six and one-half years and three published decisions, the Court of Appeals endorsed the conclusion reached by the District Court in its original order in 1966—that petitioner's suit could not proceed as a class action. In its procedural history, at least, this litigation has lived up to Judge Lumbard's characterization of it as a "Frankenstein monster posing as a class action." Eisen II, 391 F.2d, at 572.

II

At the outset we must decide whether the Court of Appeals in Eisen III had jurisdiction to review the District Court's orders permitting the suit to

---

h The court of appeals said in part:

"As soon as the evidence on the remand disclosed the true extent of the membership of the class and the fact that Eisen would not pay for individual notice to the members of the class who could be identified, and the evidence further disclosed that the class membership was of such diversity and was so dispersed that no notice by publication could be devised by the ingenuity of man that could reasonably be expected to notify more than a relatively small proportion of the class, a ruling should have been made forthwith dismissing the case as a class action. This dismissal could have saved several years of hard work by the judge and the lawyers and wholly unnecessary expense running into large figures. The fact that the cost of obtaining proofs of claim by individual members of the class and processing such claims was such as to make it clear that the amounts payable to individual claimants would be so low as to be negligible also should have been enough of itself to warrant dismissal as a class action. Other cases involving millions of diverse and unidentifiable members of an alleged class had been dismissed as unmanageable or altered in composition. And so even Eisen and his counsel conceded that the class was not manageable unless the 'fluid recovery' procedures were adopted.

. . . .

"Even if amended Rule 23 could be read so as to permit any such fantastic procedure, the courts would have to reject it as an unconstitutional violation of the requirement of due process of law. But as it now reads amended Rule 23 contemplates and provides for no such procedure. Nor can amended Rule 23 be construed or interpreted in such fashion as to permit such procedure. We hold the 'fluid recovery' concept and practice to be illegal, inadmissible as a solution of the manageability problems of class actions and wholly improper."

Fluid recovery means class-wide calculation of damages that are distributed by an individual proof-of-claim procedure plus some mechanism for indirectly applying the residue to the benefit of the class. On the subject of fluid recovery, it has been said that the holding of Eisen III "can be criticized as representing a mechanical and unsympathetic reading of Rule 23 and one that completely ignores the courts' discretion to fashion relief." 7AA Wright, Miller & Kane § 1784, at 337–38. The court of appeals' unexplained but often repeated dictum that fluid recovery violates due process has likewise been criticized. See, e.g., Developments in the Law—Class Actions, 89 Harv.L.Rev. 1318, 1523–25 (1976). So, the desirability of fluid recovery comes front and center. But can one even address desirability without first resolving the more fundamental question of whether the purpose of class actions such as Eisen should be compensating injured plaintiffs or sanctioning transgressive defendants? Compare Kenneth E. Scott, Two Models of the Civil Process, 27 Stan.L.Rev. 937 (1975), quoted supra p. 276, with Kenneth W. Dam, Class Actions: Efficiency, Compensation, Deterrence, and Conflict of Interest, 4 J.Legal Stud. 47 (1975). Consider also ALI Principles of the Law of Aggregate Litigation § 3.07 (Proposed Final Draft 2009) (arguing that a greater judicial power exists to approve such "cy pres" settlements than exists to order such relief by a contested judgment).

proceed as a class action and allocating the cost of notice. [The Supreme Court here held that the rulings concerning notice were appealable under the collateral order doctrine. The Court reached no other questions of appealability. Moreover, the Court observed that in view of its ultimate disposition of the notice issues, it had "no occasion to consider whether the Court of Appeals correctly resolved the issues of manageability and fluid-class recovery."]

III

Turning to the merits of the case, we find that the District Court's resolution of the notice problems was erroneous in two respects. First, it failed to comply with the notice requirements of Rule 23(c)(2), and second, it imposed part of the cost of notice on respondents.

A

Rule 23(c)(2) provides that, in any class action maintained under subdivision (b)(3), each class member shall be advised that he has the right to exclude himself from the action on request or to enter an appearance through counsel, and further that the judgment, whether favorable or not, will bind all class members not requesting exclusion. To this end, the court is required to direct to class members "the best notice practicable under the circumstances, *including individual notice to all members who can be identified through reasonable effort.*" We think the import of this language is unmistakable. Individual notice must be sent to all class members whose names and addresses may be ascertained through reasonable effort.

The Advisory Committee's Note to Rule 23 reinforces this conclusion. See 28 U.S.C.App., p. 7765. The Advisory Committee described subdivision (c)(2) as "not merely discretionary" and added that the "mandatory notice pursuant to subdivision (c)(2) . . . is designed to fulfill requirements of due process to which the class action procedure is of course subject." Id., at 7768. The Committee explicated its incorporation of due process standards by citation to Mullane v. Central Hanover Bank & Trust Co., 339 U.S. 306, 70 S.Ct. 652 (1950), and like cases.

In Mullane the Court addressed the constitutional sufficiency of publication notice rather than mailed individual notice to known beneficiaries of a common trust fund as part of a judicial settlement of accounts. The Court observed that notice and an opportunity to be heard were fundamental requisites of the constitutional guarantee of procedural due process. It further stated that notice must be "reasonably calculated, under all the circumstances, to apprise interested parties of the pendency of the action and afford them an opportunity to present their objections." Id., at 314, 70 S.Ct., at 657. The Court continued:

> "But when notice is a person's due, process which is a mere gesture is not due process. The means employed must be such as one desirous of actually informing the absentee might reasonably adopt to accomplish it. The reasonableness and hence the constitutional validity of any chosen method may be defended on the ground that it is in itself

reasonably certain to inform those affected." Id., at 315, 70 S.Ct., at 657.

The Court then held that publication notice could not satisfy due process where the names and addresses of the beneficiaries were known. In such cases, "the reasons disappear for resort to means less likely than the mails to apprise them of [an action's] pendency." Id., at 318, 70 S.Ct., at 659.

In Schroeder v. City of New York, 371 U.S. 208, 83 S.Ct. 279 (1962), decided prior to the promulgation of amended Rule 23, the Court explained that Mullane required rejection of notice by publication where the name and address of the affected person were available. The Court stated that the "general rule" is that "notice by publication is not enough with respect to a person whose name and address are known or very easily ascertainable . . . ." Id., at 212–213, 83 S.Ct., at 282. The Court also noted that notice by publication had long been recognized as a poor substitute for actual notice and that its justification was " 'difficult at best.' " Id., at 213, 83 S.Ct., at 283.

Viewed in this context, the express language and intent of Rule 23(c)(2) leave no doubt that individual notice must be provided to those class members who are identifiable through reasonable effort. In the present case, the names and addresses of 2,250,000 class members are easily ascertainable, and there is nothing to show that individual notice cannot be mailed to each. For these class members, individual notice is clearly the "best notice practicable" within the meaning of Rule 23(c)(2) and our prior decisions.

Petitioner contends, however, that we should dispense with the requirement of individual notice in this case, and he advances two reasons for our doing so. First, the prohibitively high cost of providing individual notice to 2,250,000 class members would end this suit as a class action and effectively frustrate petitioner's attempt to vindicate the policies underlying the antitrust and securities laws. Second, petitioner contends that individual notice is unnecessary in this case, because no prospective class member has a large enough stake in the matter to justify separate litigation of his individual claim. Hence, class members lack any incentive to opt out of the class action even if notified.

The short answer to these arguments is that individual notice to identifiable class members is not a discretionary consideration to be waived in a particular case. It is, rather, an unambiguous requirement of Rule 23. As the Advisory Committee's Note explained, the Rule was intended to insure that the judgment, whether favorable or not, would bind all class members who did not request exclusion from the suit. 28 U.S.C.App., pp. 7765, 7768. Accordingly, each class member who can be identified through reasonable effort must be notified that he may request exclusion from the action and thereby preserve his opportunity to press his claim separately or that he may remain in the class and perhaps participate in the management of the action. There is nothing in Rule 23 to suggest that the notice requirements can be tailored to fit the pocketbooks of particular plaintiffs.[13]

Petitioner further contends that adequate representation, rather than notice, is the touchstone of due process in a class action and therefore satisfies Rule 23. We think this view has little to commend it. To begin with, Rule 23 speaks to notice as well as to adequacy of representation and requires that both be provided. Moreover, petitioner's argument proves too much, for it quickly leads to the conclusion that no notice at all, published or otherwise, would be required in the present case. This cannot be so, for quite apart from what due process may require, the command of Rule 23 is clearly to the contrary. We therefore conclude that Rule 23(c)(2) requires that individual notice be sent to all class members who can be identified with reasonable effort.[14]

B

We also agree with the Court of Appeals that petitioner must bear the cost of notice to the members of his class. . . .

We find nothing in either the language or history of Rule 23 that gives a court any authority to conduct a preliminary inquiry into the merits of a suit in order to determine whether it may be maintained as a class action. Indeed, such a procedure contravenes the Rule by allowing a representative plaintiff to secure the benefits of a class action without first satisfying the requirements for it. He is thereby allowed to obtain a determination on the merits of the claims advanced on behalf of the class without any assurance that a class action may be maintained. This procedure is directly contrary to the command of subdivision (c)(1) that the court determine whether a suit denominated a class action may be maintained as such "[a]s soon as practicable after the commencement of [the] action . . . ." In short, we agree with Judge Wisdom's conclusion in Miller v. Mackey International, 452 F.2d 424 (C.A.5 1971), where the court rejected a preliminary inquiry into the merits of a proposed class action:

> "In determining the propriety of a class action, the question is not whether the plaintiff or plaintiffs have stated a cause of action or will prevail on the merits, but rather whether the requirements of Rule 23 are met." Id., at 427.

Additionally, we might note that a preliminary determination of the merits may result in substantial prejudice to a defendant, since of necessity it is

---

[13] Petitioner also argues that class members will not opt out because the statute of limitations has long since run out on the claims of all class members other than petitioner. This contention is disposed of by our recent decision in American Pipe & Construction Co. v. Utah, 414 U.S. 538, 94 S.Ct. 756 (1974), which established that commencement of a class action tolls the applicable statute of limitations as to all members of the class. [See 7B Wright, Miller & Kane § 1795; William A. Jonason, Note, The American Pipe Dream: Class Actions and Statutes of Limitations, 67 Iowa L.Rev. 743 (1982).—Ed.]

[14] We are concerned here only with the notice requirements of subdivision (c)(2), which are applicable to class actions maintained under subdivision (b)(3). By its terms subdivision (c)(2) is inapplicable to class actions for injunctive or declaratory relief maintained under subdivision (b)(2). Petitioner's effort to qualify his suit as a class action under subdivisions (b)(1) and (b)(2) was rejected by the Court of Appeals. See n. 4, supra.

not accompanied by the traditional rules and procedures applicable to civil trials. The court's tentative findings, made in the absence of established safeguards, may color the subsequent proceedings and place an unfair burden on the defendant.

In the absence of any support under Rule 23, petitioner's effort to impose the cost of notice on respondents must fail. The usual rule is that a plaintiff must initially bear the cost of notice to the class. The exceptions cited by the District Court related to situations where a fiduciary duty pre-existed between the plaintiff and defendant, as in a shareholder derivative suit.[15] Where, as here, the relationship between the parties is truly adversary, the plaintiff must pay for the cost of notice as part of the ordinary burden of financing his own suit.

Petitioner has consistently maintained, however, that he will not bear the cost of notice under subdivision (c)(2) to members of the class as defined in his original complaint. See 479 F.2d, at 1008; 52 F.R.D., at 269. We therefore remand the cause with instructions to dismiss the class action as so defined.[16]

The judgment of the Court of Appeals is vacated and the cause remanded for proceedings consistent with this opinion.

It is so ordered.

■ MR. JUSTICE DOUGLAS, with whom MR. JUSTICE BRENNAN and MR. JUSTICE MARSHALL concur, dissenting in part.

While I am in general agreement with the phases of this case touched on by the Court, I add a few words because its opinion does not fully explore the issues which will be dispositive of this case on remand to the District Court.

[Justice Douglas here explained that the subclass approach would, in his view, be highly appropriate on remand.]

I agree with Professor Chafee that a class action serves not only the convenience of the parties but also prompt, efficient judicial administration.[7] I think in our society that is growing in complexity there are bound to be innumerable people in common disasters, calamities, or ventures who would go begging for justice without the class action but who could with all regard to due process be protected by it. Some of these are consumers whose claims may seem de minimis but who alone have no practical

---

15 See, e.g., Dolgow v. Anderson, 43 F.R.D. 472, 498–500 (E.D.N.Y.1968). We, of course, express no opinion on the proper allocation of the cost of notice in such cases.

16 The record does not reveal whether a smaller class of odd-lot traders could be defined, and if so, whether petitioner would be willing to pay the cost of notice to members of such a class. We intimate no view on whether any such subclass would satisfy the requirements of Rule 23. We do note, however, that our dismissal of the class action as originally defined is without prejudice to any efforts petitioner may make to redefine his class either under Rule 23(c)([5]) or Fed.Rule Civ.Proc. 15. [The case disappears on remand. But for more on the idea of subdividing the class, see 7AA Wright, Miller & Kane § 1790; Scott Dodson, Subclassing, 27 Cardozo L.Rev. 2351 (2006); Note, Certifying Classes and Subclasses in Title VII Suits, 99 Harv.L.Rev. 619 (1986).—Ed.]

7 Z. Chafee, Some Problems of Equity 149 (1950).

recourse for either remuneration or injunctive relief. Some may be environmentalists who have no photographic development plant about to be ruined because of air pollution by radiation but who suffer perceptibly by smoke, noxious gases, or radiation. Or the unnamed individual may be only a ratepayer being excessively charged by a utility, or a homeowner whose assessment is slowly rising beyond his ability to pay.

The class action is one of the few legal remedies the small claimant has against those who command the status quo. I would strengthen his hand with the view of creating a system of law that dispenses justice to the lowly as well as to those liberally endowed with power and wealth.

Questions: (11) Does the notice requirement in a (b)(3) class action like Eisen arise from the Due Process Clause or just from Rule 23(c)(2)? Is there really no notice requirement for (b)(1) and (b)(2) actions?

(12) Why is it in Rule 23(b)(3) that there is a duty to exert only "reasonable effort" in identifying members of the class, but there is an absolute duty to give individual notice to those so identified?

(b) RULE 23(d)

Rule 23(d) authorizes a variety of appropriate management orders, thus confirming the court's authority to take an active role in running the case. In particular, Rule 23(d)(1)(B) authorizes the court in any class action discretionarily to order notice to class members advising them of any step in the action or any right they may have.

Oppenheimer Fund v. Sanders

Supreme Court of the United States, 1978.
437 U.S. 340, 98 S.Ct. 2380.

■ MR. JUSTICE POWELL delivered the opinion of the Court.

Respondents are the representative plaintiffs in a class action brought under Fed.Rule Civ.Proc. 23(b)(3). They sought to require petitioners, the defendants below, to help compile a list of the names and addresses of the members of the plaintiff class from records kept by the transfer agent for one of petitioners so that the individual notice required by Rule 23(c)(2) could be sent. The Court of Appeals for the Second Circuit held that the federal discovery rules, Fed.Rules Civ.Proc. 26–37, authorize the District Court to order petitioners to assist in compiling the list and to bear the $16,000 expense incident thereto. . . .

[This was a class action brought on behalf of about 121,000 purchasers of shares in the Oppenheimer Fund between 1968 and 1970, alleging violation of the federal securities laws and seeking damages that averaged about $15 per class member. The district court first held that the suit met the requirements for class-action treatment. It then imposed the task and the cost of "culling out the list of class members" on the defendants, but it put the responsibility of preparing and mailing notice to them on the plaintiffs.

[Upon defendants' appeal of this order concerning notice, the Second Circuit en banc ultimately affirmed, 558 F.2d 636, 646 (2d Cir.1976), deeming the Supreme Court's Eisen decision ("Eisen IV") to be not controlling. It thus brought itself into conflict with the Fifth Circuit's ruling in In re Nissan Motor Corp. Antitrust Litigation, 552 F.2d 1088 (5th Cir.1977). The Supreme Court granted certiorari in the instant case.]

A

Although respondents' request resembles discovery in that it seeks to obtain information, we are convinced that it more properly is handled under Rule 23(d). The critical point is that the information is sought to facilitate the sending of notice rather than to define or clarify issues in the case.

[The Court explained that Rule 26(b)(1) limits the scope of discovery to "matter that bears on, or that reasonably could lead to other matter that could bear on, any issue that is or may be in the case." Accordingly, "discovery is not limited to issues raised by the pleadings, for discovery itself is designed to help define and clarify the issues. [Citation omitted.] Nor is discovery limited to the merits of a case, for a variety of fact-oriented issues may arise during litigation that are not related to the merits. [Footnote, referring to jurisdictional discovery, omitted.]" Thus, "discovery often has been used to illuminate issues upon which a district court must pass in deciding whether a suit should proceed as a class action under Rule 23, such as numerosity, common questions, and adequacy of representation." But discovery was unavailable here where "respondents do not seek information because it may bear on some issue which the District Court must decide, but only for the purpose of sending notice."]

Rule 23, on the other hand, deals comprehensively with class actions, and thus is the natural place to look for authority for orders regulating the sending of notice. It is clear that Rule 23(d) vests power in the district court to order one of the parties to perform the tasks necessary to send notice.[21] Moreover, district courts sometimes have found it appropriate to

---

[21] Although Rule 23(c)(2) states that "the court shall direct" notice to class members, it commonly is agreed that the court should order one of the parties to perform the necessary tasks. See Frankel, Some Preliminary Observations Concerning Civil Rule 23, 43 F.R.D. 39, 44 (1967); Kaplan, Continuing Work of the Civil Committee: 1966 Amendments of the Federal Rules of Civil Procedure (I), 81 Harv.L.Rev. 356, 398 n. 157 (1967). Rule 23(d) provides that in the conduct of a class action, "the court may make appropriate orders: . . . (2) requiring, for the protection of the members of the class or otherwise for the fair conduct of the action, that notice be given in such manner as the court may direct . . . ; [and] (5) dealing with similar procedural matters." The Advisory Committee apparently contemplated that the court would make orders drawing on the authority of either Rule 23(d)(2) or 23(d)(5) in order to provide the notice required by Rule 23(c)(2), for its note to Rule 23(d)(2) states, "under subdivision (c)(2), notice must *be ordered* . . . ." Advisory Committee's Notes to Fed.Rule Civ.Proc. 23, 28 U.S.C. App., p. 7768 (emphasis supplied).

order a defendant, rather than a representative plaintiff, to perform tasks other than identification that are necessary to the sending of notice.[22] Since identification simply is another task that must be performed in order to send notice, we agree with the Court of Appeals for the Fifth Circuit that Rule 23(d) also authorizes a district court in appropriate circumstances to require a defendant's cooperation in identifying the class members to whom notice must be sent. We therefore turn to a consideration of the circumstances in which such an order is appropriate and of how the cost of the defendant's complying with such an order should be allocated.

B

. . . .

The first question that a district court must consider under Rule 23(d) is which party should perform particular tasks necessary to send the class notice. The general rule must be that the representative plaintiff should perform the tasks, for it is he who seeks to maintain the suit as a class action and to represent other members of his class. In Eisen IV we noted the general principle that a party must bear the "burden of financing his own suit," 417 U.S., at 179, 94 S.Ct., at 2153. Thus ordinarily there is no warrant for shifting the cost of the representative plaintiff's performance of these tasks to the defendant.

In some instances, however, the defendant may be able to perform a necessary task with less difficulty or expense than could the representative plaintiff. In such cases, we think that the District Court properly may exercise its discretion under Rule 23(d) to order the defendant to perform the task in question. As the Nissan court recognized, in identifying the instances in which such an order may be appropriate, a rough analogy might usefully be drawn to practice under Rule 33([d]) of the discovery rules. Under that rule, when one party directs an interrogatory to another party which can be answered by examination of the responding party's business records, "it is a sufficient answer to such interrogatory to specify the records from which the answer may be derived or ascertained and to afford the party serving the interrogatory reasonable opportunity to" examine and copy the records, if the burden of deriving the answer would be "substantially the same" for either party. Not unlike Eisen IV, this provision is intended to place the "burden of discovery upon its potential benefitee."[25] The holding of Nissan represents application of a similar principle, for when the court concluded that the representative plaintiffs could derive the names and addresses of the class members from the defendants' records with substantially the same effort as the defendants, it required the representative plaintiffs to perform this task and hence to bear the cost. . . . But where the burden of deriving the answer would not

[22] Thus, a number of courts have required defendants in Rule 23(b)(3) class actions to enclose class notices in their own periodic mailings to class members in order to reduce the expense of sending the notice . . . .

[25] Advisory Committee's Notes to Fed.Rule Civ.Proc. 33([d]), 28 U.S.C. App., p. 7793, quoting D. Louisell, Modern California Discovery 125 (1963).

be "substantially the same," and the task could be performed more efficiently by the responding party, the discovery rules normally require the responding party to derive the answer itself.

In those cases where a district court properly decides under Rule 23(d) that a defendant rather than the representative plaintiff should perform a task necessary to send the class notice, the question that then will arise is which party should bear the expense. On one hand, it may be argued that this should be borne by the defendant because a party ordinarily must bear the expense of complying with orders properly issued by the District Court; but Eisen IV strongly suggests that the representative plaintiff should bear this expense because it is he who seeks to maintain this suit as a class action. In this situation, the District Court must exercise its discretion in deciding whether to leave the cost of complying with its order where it falls, on the defendant, or place it on the party that benefits, the representative plaintiff. Once again, a rough analogy might usefully be drawn to practice under the discovery rules. Under those rules, the presumption is that the responding party must bear the expense of complying with discovery requests, but he may invoke the District Court's discretion under Rule 26(c) to grant orders protecting him from "undue burden or expense" in doing so, including orders conditioning discovery on the requesting party's payment of the costs of discovery. The analogy necessarily is imperfect, however, because in the Rule 23(d) context, the defendant's own case rarely will be advanced by his having performed the tasks. . . . Thus, one of the reasons for declining to shift costs under Rule 26(c) usually will be absent in the Rule 23(d) context. For this reason, a district court exercising its discretion under Rule 23(d) should be considerably more ready to place the cost of the defendant's performing an ordered task on the representative plaintiff, who derives the benefit, than under Rule 26(c). In the usual case, the test should be whether the expense is substantial, rather than, as under Rule 26(c), whether it is "undue."

Nevertheless, in some instances, the expense involved may be so insubstantial as not to warrant the effort required to calculate it and shift it to the representative plaintiff. In Nissan, for example, the court did not find it necessary to direct the representative plaintiffs to reimburse the defendants for the expense of producing their files for inspection. In other cases, it may be appropriate to leave the cost where it falls because the task ordered is one that the defendant must perform in any event in the ordinary course of its business.[28] Although we do not attempt to catalogue the instances in which a district court might be justified in placing the expense on the defendant, we caution that courts must not stray too far from the principle underlying Eisen IV that the representative plaintiff should bear all costs relating to the sending of notice because it is he who seeks to maintain the suit as a class action.

---

[28] Thus, where defendants have been directed to enclose class notices in their own periodic mailings and the additional expense has not been substantial, representative plaintiffs have not been required to reimburse the defendants for envelopes or postage. [Citations omitted.]

C

In this case, we think the District Court abused its discretion in requiring petitioners to bear the expense of identifying class members. The records containing the needed information are kept by the transfer agent, not petitioners. Since petitioners apparently have the right to control these records and since the class members can be identified only by reference to them, the District Court acted within its authority under Rule 23(d) in ordering petitioners to direct the transfer agent to make the records available to respondents. The preparation of the desired list requires . . . the manual sorting out of names and addresses from old records maintained on paper, the keypunching of up to 300,000 computer cards, and the creation of new computer programs for use with extant tapes and tapes that would have to be created from the paper records. It appears that neither petitioners nor respondents can perform these tasks, for both sides assume that the list can be generated only by hiring the services of a third party, the transfer agent, for a sum exceeding $16,000. As the expense of hiring the transfer agent would be no greater for respondents, who seek the information, than for petitioners, respondents should bear the expense. See Nissan, supra, at 1102–1103.

[The Supreme Court considered special circumstances that were suggested as reasons why the petitioners should pay the transfer agent. To the argument that $16,000 was a "relatively modest" amount, the Court said: "Although in some circumstances the ability of a party to bear a burden may be a consideration, the test in this respect normally should be whether the cost is substantial; not whether it is 'modest' in relation to ability to pay." To the argument that respondents had alleged petitioners to have breached a fiduciary duty to them and their class, the Court said: "A bare allegation of wrongdoing, whether by breach of fiduciary duty or otherwise, is not a fair reason for requiring a defendant to undertake financial burdens and risks to further a plaintiff's case." All other such arguments the Court likewise rejected.]

Given that respondents can obtain the information sought here by paying the transfer agent the same amount that petitioners would have to pay, that the information must be obtained to comply with respondents' obligation to provide notice to their class, and that no special circumstances have been shown to warrant requiring petitioners to bear the expense, we hold that the District Court abused its discretion in not requiring respondents to pay the transfer agent to identify the members of their own class. The judgment of the Court of Appeals is reversed, and the case is remanded for further proceedings consistent with this opinion.

It is so ordered.

Question: (13) To "manage" a (b)(3) class action by means of Rule 23(d), can the district court require the absentees to opt-in by an affirmative act at an early stage of the suit if they wish to be members of the class? See 7AA Wright, Miller &

Kane § 1787, at 522–25 (concluding likely not); see also John Bronsteen, Class Action Settlements: An Opt-in Proposal, 2005 U.Ill.L.Rev. 903 (arguing in favor of opt-in for class settlements but not for class adjudications, in order to discourage both parties' collusion and frivolous suits); cf. Hoffmann–La Roche Inc. v. Sperling, 493 U.S. 165, 110 S.Ct. 482 (1989) (treating the statutory opt-in scheme for so-called collective actions under the Fair Labor Standards Act and the Age Discrimination in Employment Act, which provide an informative contrast to ordinary class actions).

SECTION 4. TERMINATING CLASS ACTIONS

(a) RULE 23(e)

If a class action survives all these preliminary maneuvers, settlement is by far the most likely outcome. That is, although few filed class actions get certified, with most of the others ending after little court activity in a voluntary dismissal perhaps with a payoff, a certified class action almost always culminates in a class settlement. However, special dangers attend settlement of class actions.

Accordingly, the settlement process in certified class actions, unlike that in ordinary litigation, is a regulated one. Rule 23(e) attempts to protect the interests of the class members, whom the named parties or the class counsel may be abandoning in favor of self-interest. Notice of the proposed settlement must be given to all class members who would be bound; and the court must pass on the fairness, reasonableness, and adequacy of the proposed settlement, after a hearing where disgruntled class members may speak. All this means that the parties' agreement to settle may mark only the beginning of the procedural struggles.

Consider this comment from the student-written Developments in the Law—Class Actions, 89 Harv.L.Rev. 1318, 1536–37 (1976): "Negotiation presents a serious threat to the attainment of a major purpose of class litigation—full realization of substantive policies—unless privately controlled decisions are harmonized with public interests. Even when negotiations are completely in good faith, the outcome may not reflect the range of substantive concerns underlying the regulatory statute pursuant to which suit has been brought, because the parties may not share such a broad range of interests."

Consider also this comment by an attorney experienced in class-action litigation and highly critical of the operation of the Rule in (b)(3) actions, from William Simon, Class Actions—Useful Tool or Engine of Destruction, 55 F.R.D. 375, 389–90 (1973): "The principal impetus for settlement comes from the atomic dynamics of large user class actions. When a firm with assets of, say, a billion dollars is sued in a class action with a class of several million and potential liability of, say, $2 billion, it faces the possibility of destruction. A settlement offer may then be made of $20 million—or 1% of possible exposure; with plaintiff's counsel asking $5 million in fees for himself while his clients receive minuscule recoveries. What defense lawyer can tell his client that his probable success in any jury case is better than 100 to 1; no matter how little merit there is in plaintiff's claim? This situation is not hypothetical; it happens frequently in our Federal Courts. The potential exposure in broad class actions frequently exceeds the net worth of the defendants, and corporate management naturally tends to seek insurance against whatever slight chance of success plaintiffs may have. Such insurance is usually available for a comparatively modest premium in the form of a settlement with the attorney who initiated the litigation and who purports to speak for vast numbers of people who have not retained him."

Consider finally this comment by a law professor, from Christopher R. Leslie, The Significance of Silence: Collective Action Problems and Class Action Settlements, 59 Fla.L.Rev. 71, 72 (2007): "When the Federal Rules of Civil Procedure first provided for a class action vehicle, hopes were high that individuals would be able to act collectively to hold corporations liable for small injuries imposed upon large numbers of victims. But after almost forty years of operation, hope has transformed into suspicion and cynicism. Class action litigation often seems to be a mechanism for greedy class counsel and shrewd defendants to negotiate settlements that undermine the interests of the class. Anticipating the risk of such shady deals, the Federal Rules of Civil Procedure required that any settlement of a class action be approved by the district court judge in charge of the case. However, any optimism about this safety valve has waned, as judges routinely approve class action settlements that often make the class worse off than no settlement at all. No rational class members would want a settlement that eliminated their right to sue while giving them little or nothing of value in exchange. But judges approve such settlements with disheartening regularity. This Article argues that one of the primary reasons judges approve fundamentally flawed settlements in class action litigation is because judges consistently misread the response of the class to the proposed settlement. In particular, judges misinterpret the significance of silence."

Grunin v. International House of Pancakes

United States Court of Appeals, Eighth Circuit, 1975.
513 F.2d 114, cert. denied, 423 U.S. 864, 96 S.Ct. 124 (1975).

■ Before VOGEL, SENIOR CIRCUIT JUDGE, and LAY and STEPHENSON, CIRCUIT JUDGES.

■ STEPHENSON, CIRCUIT JUDGE. These consolidated appeals arise out of the district court's approval of a proposed settlement, pursuant to Rule 23(e) of the Federal Rules of Civil Procedure, of a private antitrust national class action brought by International House of Pancakes (IHOP) franchisees against their franchisor, a division of International Industries, Inc. . . .

. . . .

On August 23, 1971, the Judicial Panel on Multi–District Litigation transferred to the Western District of Missouri nine pending actions that had been instituted by current or former franchisees of IHOP against the franchisor. In re International House of Pancakes Franchise Litigation, 331 F.Supp. 556 (Jud.Pan.Mult.Lit.1971). On October 26, 1971, the district court ordered that these actions be maintained as a class action pursuant to Fed.R.Civ.P. 23. In accordance with that order, two categories of plaintiffs were created—a class composed of current franchisees and a subclass of former franchisees. Original notice of the class action was mailed to all prospective class members on November 19, 1971. Subsequently a similar notice was sent to those parties qualifying for subclass membership.

The class action sought injunctive relief, treble damages, and attorneys' fees from IHOP on the basis that the franchise agreements and equipment leases executed between franchisor and franchisee violated the Sherman Act, 15 U.S.C. §§ 1 & 2 (1970), and the Clayton Act, 15 U.S.C. § 14 (1970). Specifically the franchisees alleged that IHOP illegally tied to the acquisition of a standard 15–or 20–year restaurant franchise the requirement that the franchisee lease or purchase a wide variety of essential products and services from IHOP or an IHOP-approved supplier. Among these "tied" items were restaurant furniture and equipment, dining room supplies, menus, food items, insurance, advertising, training, management counseling and bookkeeping services. The franchisees sought additional damages on the theory that these goods and services had been supplied at a price greatly in excess of fair market value[4] and on the grounds that the IHOP prohibition against selling any non-IHOP approved and priced food items deprived them of the opportunity to increase their individual profits.

Following the appointment of counsel for the class, extensive discovery was undertaken by the parties.[5] Within a short time serious settlement negotiations began. On April 24, 1973, a proposed settlement agreement was forwarded to the class and subclass members along with notice of a hearing to be held on June 1, 1973, in Kansas City. The agreement provided for a damage fund of $4.025 million (less attorneys' fees of $1.11 million) but did not amend the equipment leases in any material respect. This factor was the major subject of the objections voiced at the June hearing by a group of dissatisfied franchisees.

The district court, in a memorandum and order issued on July 12, 1973, rejected the proposed settlement. In re International House of Pancakes Litigation, 1973–2 Trade Cases ¶ 74,616 (W.D.Mo.), aff'd, 487 F.2d 303 (8th Cir.1973). The court acknowledged that the "precarious financial condition" of IHOP caused plaintiffs' counsel to conclude that

---

[4] For example, the pancake mix which the agreement required the franchisees to purchase from IHOP was sold to them at a markup of 100% over raw costs.

[5] According to counsel for International Industries, Inc., 20,000 pages of depositions were taken in this case and approximately 100,000 documents were produced for inspection by the parties.

"any substantial monetary judgment that might be recovered would be uncollectible, and would only result in the bankruptcy of the defendant." Nonetheless, the court stated that approval of the settlement would continue those franchise and lease provisions which allegedly violated antitrust laws, would bar class members from seeking further injunctive relief, and would provide insignificant monetary damage relief to the franchisees. The court concluded: "Certainly, they [the franchisees] are entitled to their day in court on this vital issue, and this Court will not foreclose them by approval of this settlement." The rejection was subsequently affirmed by this court in In re International House of Pancakes Franchise Litigation, 487 F.2d 303 (8th Cir.1973).

On November 7, 1973, a second settlement proposal was submitted to the court for its approval. This agreement differed from the first in that it gave each class member the option to purchase his own equipment at a rate lower than the terms of the lease or to continue to lease at a reduced rate. In addition, the settlement amended the franchise agreement in that IHOP would require its franchisees to purchase from it only their pancake flour (at a lesser markup) and coffee. The agreement also expanded and made specific the services to be provided by IHOP in exchange for the management fee and granted other concessions. Finally, the settlement created a fund of $500,000 to be shared by the subclass of former franchisees and provided for the payment of up to $1.25 million in attorneys' fees at the court's direction. Notice was sent out on November 8, 1973, and a hearing on the proposal began on November 28, 1973. In contrast to the June hearing, there were no formal objections filed with the court regarding the new proposal. However, counsel for appellant Grunin participated in the hearing and voiced his objections through cross-examination.[6] At the close of the hearings the district court approved the settlement stating simply that it was "fair, reasonable, and adequate as to said class and sub-class plaintiffs." Another order was entered on February 1, 1974, awarding attorneys' fees to respective claimants. Appeals were taken from the entry of each order.

I.

The initial claim set forth by appellant Grunin is that the notice sent to class and subclass members in November regarding the second proposed settlement was so inadequate as to timing, content, and means of transmission that it violated the requirements of Rule 23 and the dictates of due process. We disagree.

By virtue of the fact that an action maintained as a class suit under Rule 23 has res judicata effect on all members of the class, due process requires that notice of a proposed settlement be given to the class. See Eisen v. Carlisle & Jacquelin, 417 U.S. 156, 172–77, 94 S.Ct. 2140, 40 L.Ed.2d 732 (1974); [other citations omitted].

---

[6] Appearing as amici curiae before this court are nine IHOP franchisees who object to the settlement. . . . Even if we add these nine individuals to the list of objectors, the record reveals that most IHOP franchisees favored the settlement.

The notice given must be "reasonably calculated, under all of the circumstances, to apprise interested parties of the pendency of the action and afford them an opportunity to present their objections." Mullane v. Central Hanover Bank & Trust Co., 339 U.S. 306, 314, 70 S.Ct. 652, 657, 94 L.Ed. 865 (1950). In addition, the notice must "[be of such nature as] reasonably to convey the required information . . . and it must afford a reasonable time for those interested to make their appearance." Id. . . . However, Rule 23(e) provides that notice be given "in such manner as the court directs." Thus, the mechanics of the notice process are left to the discretion of the court subject only to the broad "reasonableness" standards imposed by due process. See 7A C. Wright and A. Miller, Federal Practice and Procedure, Civil § 1797 at 237 (1972).

[The court here found the notice to be adequate as to timing.]

Appellant Grunin next contends that the method of notice used in this case—mailing notice to the last known addresses of class and subclass members—was constitutionally insufficient and therefore an abuse of discretion by the district court. Relying on Lamb v. United Security Life Co., 59 F.R.D. 25 (S.D.Iowa 1972), appellant urges that, since approximately one-third of the class members were not reached by the mailing, supplemental notice by means of publication should have been ordered by the court.

We are satisfied, however, that notice by publication was unnecessary in this case for due process purposes and probably would have been of little value in alerting members of the class and subclass that were previously uninformed. In Eisen v. Carlisle & Jacquelin, 417 U.S. 156, 174–77, 94 S.Ct. 2140, 40 L.Ed.2d 732 (1974), the Supreme Court specifically held that individualized notice by mail to the last known address was the "best notice practicable" in a class action contest. The Court also reiterated its dissatisfaction with notice by publication. . . . Since the 90 to 100 class and subclass members who did not receive mailed notices were, according to their last addresses, scattered throughout the nation, the publication of notice in three or four newspapers as suggested in Lamb would have been fruitless. Under the circumstances the court properly made use of the "last known address" method and was not required to expend further time and money on less productive notice efforts.

[The court here found the content of the notice to be a fair and neutral summary of the proposed settlement's terms. The notice had also advised class members how they could obtain a copy of the settlement agreement.]

II.

The second major contention set forth by appellant Grunin is that the district court abused its discretion in approving a settlement that was not fair, reasonable, and adequate. Specifically it is alleged . . . that the benefits of the settlement to the class are illusory . . . .

Under Rule 23(e) the district court acts as a fiduciary who must serve as a guardian of the rights of absent class members. [Citations omitted.]

The court cannot accept a settlement that the proponents have not shown to be fair, reasonable, and adequate. See, e.g., City of Detroit v. Grinnell Corp., 495 F.2d 448, 455 (2d Cir.1974); [other citations omitted].

Our review of the settlement approved by the district court in this case is guided by the principle that:

> Such a determination is committed to the sound discretion of the trial judge. Great weight is accorded his views because he is exposed to the litigants, and their strategies, positions and proofs. He is aware of the expense and possible legal bars to success. Simply stated, he is on the firing line and can evaluate the action accordingly.

Ace Heating & Plumbing Co. v. Crane Co., 453 F.2d 30, 34 (3d Cir.1971). Only upon a clear showing that the district court abused its discretion will this court intervene to set aside a judicially approved class action settlement. In re International House of Pancakes Franchise Litigation, 487 F.2d 303, 304 (8th Cir.1973). See also City of Detroit, 495 F.2d at 455. With these precepts in mind we turn to appellant's charges of error.

. . . .

The charge that the benefits of the settlement to the class are illusory calls into question the overall adequacy of the settlement. In making such an assessment "[t]he most important factor is the strength of the case for plaintiffs on the merits, balanced against the amount offered in the settlement." West Virginia v. Chas. Pfizer & Co., [440 F.2d 1079 (2d Cir.), cert. denied, 404 U.S. 871, 92 S.Ct. 81 (1971). Other citations omitted.] In addition, the court should consider such factors as the defendant's overall financial condition and ability to pay; the complexity, length and expense of further litigation; and the amount of opposition to the settlement. See City of Detroit, 495 F.2d at 463. Our evaluation of the settlement in light of these factors reveals that the agreement provided substantial benefits to the class.

. . . [T]he franchisees' probability of complete success in their suit against IHOP was by no means certain. There is evidence to suggest that a total victory, including a voiding of the equipment leases and an award of damages, would have been financially disastrous if not fatal to IHOP. Nonetheless, the district court in rejecting the first settlement proposal indicated that some revision in the equipment lease was essential. Given the court's directive and IHOP's cash flow difficulties, the parties worked out a settlement which gave valuable concessions to the franchisees yet maintained IHOP's corporate viability. It is estimated that the equipment lease options provided in the settlement were worth at least $131,000 to each class member with the total value to the class exceeding $12.5 million. Given the additional fact that any compromise involves some give and take by both sides, we feel that the district court's approval of this settlement was justified.

. . . .

III.

The final group of issues to be decided in this appeal relates to the district court's allocation of the $1.25 million in attorneys' fees provided for in the settlement agreement. The three appeals from the award of fees assert that the trial court erred in denying fees to attorney Fichtner, in failing to compensate attorney Shapiro for his efforts in opposing the June proposal, and in employing improper standards in making the award [of $325,000] to attorney Berger and his firm. . . .

The district court's award of attorneys' fees in a class action settlement will be set aside by this court only upon a showing that the action amounted to an abuse of discretion. See City of Detroit, 495 F.2d at 468–75; Merola v. Atlantic Richfield Co., 493 F.2d 292, 295 (3d Cir.1974); Lindy Brothers Builders, Inc. v. American Radiator & Standard Sanitary Corp., 487 F.2d 161, 166 (3d Cir.1973); [other citations omitted]. We hold that the district court's denial of all or part of the fee requests made by appellants Fichtner and Shapiro was consistent with the sound exercise of that discretion. However, we feel that the award to Berger and his firm was made on the basis of insufficient specific evidence regarding the time spent on this litigation and should be remanded to the district court for reevaluation in light of the standards set forth in City of Detroit v. Grinnell Corp., supra, and related cases.

. . . .

The formulation adopted by the Third Circuit in Lindy Brothers and reiterated in Merola provides a typical example of the factors that courts have been instructed to consider in establishing fee awards:

a) the number of hours spent in various legal activities by the individual attorneys,

b) the reasonable hourly rate for the individual attorneys.

c) the contingent nature of success, and

d) the quality of the attorneys' work.

[Citations omitted.] However, as the Second Circuit recognized in City of Detroit, the "only legitimate starting point" in establishing fees is "by merely multiplying attorney's hours and typical hourly rates. . . . It is only after such a calculation that other, less objective, factors can be introduced into the calculus." 495 F.2d at 471.

In order to insure that all necessary data is before the court, attorneys are generally required to submit detailed affidavits which itemize and explain their fee claims. Also, many courts have required that an evidentiary hearing be held at which each claimant is subject to cross-examination. See City of Detroit, 495 F.2d at 471–74. The district court in this case held such a hearing following the submission of affidavits. The record reveals that all of the attorneys involved, except Mr. Berger, furnished the court with detailed information concerning the total number of hours spent, how the time was used (e.g., research, negotiations), by whom (e.g., senior partners, associates), and what standard hourly rate was charged by each category of attorney for each type of work. At no time did Mr. Berger supply the court with *any* information relating to standard hourly rates for himself or his firm. Nor did he furnish a complete breakdown of who spent time in what endeavors. We see no reason for applying one standard to Berger and another to all other attorneys involved.

. . . .

This case is affirmed in all respects except for the award of attorneys' fees to David Berger and David Berger, P.A. On that issue we remand for reconsideration by the district court in accordance with this opinion.

Question: (14) The matter of attorney's fees obviously raises a host of difficult questions. Compare Gisbrecht v. Barnhart, 535 U.S. 789, 122 S.Ct. 1817 (2002) (giving percentage of recovery in Social Security action), with City of Burlington v. Dague, 505 U.S. 557, 112 S.Ct. 2638 (1992) (giving unenhanced lodestar under fee-shifting environmental statutes). See generally 7B Wright, Miller & Kane §§ 1803–1803.2. For example, assuming a court has accepted the lodestar approach and has calculated the "lodestar" as reasonable hours times a reasonable rate, just how should the court go about adjusting the lodestar by "multipliers" to reflect other factors such as risk and quality of representation?

UNITED STATES DISTRICT COURT
DISTRICT OF CONNECTICUT

In re CUISINART FOOD PROCESSOR ANTITRUST LITIGATION — M.D.L. 447

NOTICE OF CLASS ACTION AND PROPOSED SETTLEMENT, PROOF OF CLAIM

TO: ALL PURCHASERS WHO, DURING THE PERIOD FROM JANUARY 1, 1973 THROUGH AND INCLUDING DECEMBER 31, 1981, PURCHASED ONE OR MORE CUISINART FOOD PROCESSORS FROM A RETAIL STORE OR OUTLET.

PLEASE READ THIS ENTIRE NOTICE CAREFULLY. YOUR RIGHTS MAY BE AFFECTED BY LAWSUITS NOW PENDING IN THIS COURT.

This is a notice of a settlement of a class action lawsuit brought on behalf of purchasers of Cuisinart food processors. If you:

—purchased a Cuisinart food processor between January 1, 1973 and December 31, 1981 and

—want an opportunity to participate in the settlement and to receive a coupon entitling you to purchase designated Cuisinart products at a 50% discount from the suggested retail price,

then you must file a proof of claim on the form at the end of this notice. Read the terms of this notice carefully.

Pursuant to Rule 23 of the Federal Rules of Civil Procedure, 15 U.S.C. 15(c) and an order of the United States District Court for the District of Connecticut:

YOU ARE HEREBY NOTIFIED that there are now pending in this Court class actions for alleged violations of the antitrust laws with respect to the sale of Cuisinart food processors. The "national consumer actions" commenced by plaintiffs Archer, Blum, Cohn and Eisenberger are being prosecuted on behalf of a national consumer class consisting of all purchasers who, during the period from January 1, 1973 through and including December 31, 1981, purchased one or more Cuisinart food processors from a retail store or outlet (hereafter "the Class").

There are also pending in this Court *parens patriae* actions commenced by the respective Attorneys General of the State of New Jersey and the Commonwealth of Massachusetts (hereinafter "the States"), which are lawsuits on behalf of natural persons residing therein alleging materially the same violations as the national consumer class actions. The alleged violations are described below. The national consumer actions and the States' actions are hereafter collectively referred to as "the Settling Actions." The defendants in the Settling Actions are Cuisinarts, Inc., Carl G. Sontheimer, Shirley M. Sontheimer, and Federated Department Stores, Inc. ("Settling Defendants").

Nature of Allegations

Plaintiffs in the Settling Actions allege that the defendants violated the antitrust laws by combining and conspiring with one another and with others during the period from and after January 1, 1973 in unreasonable restraint of trade and commerce, to fix, raise, stabilize and maintain the retail prices of Cuisinart food processors. It is alleged that, as a result of this alleged conspiracy, the retail prices of Cuisinart food processors were fixed at artificially high levels by the defendants and that competition in the sale of those food processors was restrained, diminished and restricted. Recovery of treble damages and other relief is sought together with reimbursement of costs and an award of attorneys' fees. Defendants deny all these allegations, deny any violation of law, and deny that any alleged class member is entitled to any damages.

Pertinent Procedural History

In the national consumer actions, plaintiffs have moved the Court for an order permitting those actions to proceed as class actions, defendants have opposed these motions and the Court has not yet ruled on plaintiffs' motions. Additionally, there is pending before the Court a motion to dismiss the claims of all consumers who purchased Cuisinart food processors prior to September 17, 1976. If the settlement described in this notice is not effected, the Court will be required to determine whether these actions will be permitted to proceed as class actions and whether the claims based on pre-September 17, 1976 purchases will be dismissed. The plaintiffs in the national consumer actions, through their attorneys, and the States in the *parens patriae* actions, through their Attorneys General, on their own behalf and on behalf of all persons they represent, have made an investigation of the facts and circumstances underlying the issues raised in the Settling Actions and the applicable law. They and the defendants have concluded that further conduct of the Settling Actions will be protracted and no party can have an assurance of success. Accordingly, they have determined it is in the best interests of the parties to settle and terminate the Settling Actions. After extensive negotiations, the parties to the Settling Actions have agreed to the proposed settlement described in this notice, subject to the approval of the Court. The settlement of the *parens patriae* actions is to be administered jointly with and as a part of the settlement of the national consumer actions, with the consideration for settlement to each person whom the States claim to represent in the *parens patriae* actions being the consideration for the settlement to each Class member in the national consumer actions.

This notice is directed to you because you may be a member of the Class on whose behalf these suits are pending, and your rights therefore may be affected by these lawsuits and the proposed settlement described herein. The District Court has not passed on any contentions of the parties as to the merits and therefore no implications regarding the merits of the litigation should be drawn from the issuance of this notice.

The purpose of this notice is to inform you of the litigation and the proposed settlement and of the steps you may take with respect to these actions.

THE PROPOSED SETTLEMENT

The terms and conditions of the settlement are summarized in this notice. The complete settlement stipulations, including exhibits, are on file at the office of the Clerk of the U.S. District Court for the District of Connecticut, U.S. Courthouse, 450 Main Street, Hartford, Connecticut. They may be examined and copied during regular office hours.

In summary, the proposed settlement provides for the following:

One coupon will be issued by defendant Cuisinarts to (a) each person who filed a warranty card prior to January 31, 1982 with respect to each Cuisinart food processor purchased during the period January 1, 1973 through and including December 31, 1981 whose name and address appears on the warranty records maintained by Cuisinarts in the ordinary course of business, and (b) any person who files a valid proof of claim in response to this notice in the form printed below. No more than one coupon will be issued for any one food processor.

The coupons will be mailed to those persons entitled to receive them only if the proposed settlement is approved and only if the settlement becomes final and effective as provided in the settlement stipulations in the Settling Actions. Accordingly, the date of issuance of the coupons is not presently determinable.

Each coupon will entitle its owner to purchase directly from Cuisinarts one item from a list of Cuisinart products ("the product list") at a discount of 50% from the suggested retail price in effect on the date of issuance of the coupon. Alternatively, the coupon may be used to purchase more than one item on the product list at 50% of suggested retail price for each such item if the total discount for all purchased items does not exceed in the aggregate of $20. The product list will be distributed with the coupon. The product list includes accessories for Cuisinart food processors, cookware and cutlery having current suggested retail prices not exceeding $200; no food processors are included on the product list.

The coupons may be sold or transferred by the Class member, but may be redeemed only by an individual consumer acting on his, her or its own behalf, and not for purposes of resale, and not on behalf of a retail store or outlet, wholesaler or other distributing entity. Coupons must be mailed for redemption within 120 days of the date of issuance, which date will appear on the face of the coupons. Redemption of the coupons is subject to certain other terms and conditions which will be stated clearly on the coupons. A form of the coupon is included as an exhibit to the settlement stipulations on file at the office of the Clerk of the Court.

As provided in the settlement stipulations, the defendants can elect to terminate the proposed settlement upon the occurrence or non-occurrence of certain specified events, before or after final judicial approval.

Defendants have paid $700,000 into an interest-bearing escrow account for the reimbursement of expenses incurred in the prosecution of the national consumer actions by the plaintiffs' counsel and for the award of reasonable attorneys' fees to plaintiffs' counsel. Defendants also have paid $75,000 into an interest-bearing escrow account for the reimbursement of expenses incurred in the prosecution of the *parens patriae* actions by the Attorneys General of the States and for the award of reasonable attorneys' fees. Plaintiffs' counsel and the Attorneys General who intend to apply to the Court for reimbursement of such expenses and for an award of attorneys' fees in the full amount of this fund are listed below. Any attorneys' fees or costs paid out of this fund first must be approved by the Court as fair and reasonable. No such fees or costs shall be paid to any plaintiffs' counsel or Attorneys General until the order of approval of the settlement becomes final and effective, as provided in the Settlement Stipulations in the Settling Actions.

RELEASE OF DEFENDANTS AND INJUNCTION

Approval by the Court of the proposed settlement and the settlement becoming effective will result in dismissal of the Settling Actions on the merits and with prejudice to the plaintiffs and the members of the Class. This shall constitute a release by plaintiffs and all Class members, except those who individually file valid written elections of exclusion from the Class, of all claims which have been or might have been asserted, including but not limited to, all claims under federal antitrust laws and under the antitrust and unfair business practice laws of all States and territories of the United States, arising out of or related to the matters, transactions, events, facts, circumstances and occurrences set forth in the pleadings of the plaintiffs and the Attorneys General in the Settling Actions against each of the Settling Defendants identified above, or any retailer from whom you have purchased, their predecessors, successors, subsidiaries, affiliates, heirs, assigns and present or former officers, directors, employees and agents.

Approval by the Court of the proposed settlement will also result in the issuance of an injunction permanently barring and enjoining all Class members, their officers, agents, servants, employees and attorneys, and all persons in active concert or participation with them who receive actual notice of the injunction by personal service or otherwise, except those individual members of the Class who have individually filed valid written elections of exclusion, from instituting or continuing to prosecute, in this or any other jurisdiction, any individual or class claims which have been or might have been asserted in this action, including but not limited to, all claims under federal antitrust laws and under the antitrust and unfair business practice laws of all states and territories, arising out of or related to the matters, transactions, facts, circumstances, occurrences and events alleged by the plaintiffs and the Attorneys General in the Settling Actions.

In addition to the Settling Actions, there are certain other class actions pending in which antitrust violations are also alleged in connection with the sale at retail of Cuisinart food processors, which allegations set forth materially the same violations as the Settling Actions. In each of such other actions, the plaintiffs therein claim to represent persons who are also members of the Class in the national consumer actions being settled as described in this notice. If you are a member of the Class in the national consumer actions, you are entitled to participate in the settlement described in this notice and to receive its benefits even if you fall within the alleged class definitions in the other pending actions. The other actions are: Harwood v. Federated Department Stores, Inc. (pending in the United States District Court, District of Connecticut), in which plaintiff Harwood claims to represent persons who purchased a Cuisinart food processor from retail stores owned, operated or controlled by Federated Department Stores, Inc. during the period 1974 to at least August 1979; Gayer v. Cusinarts, Inc. (pending in the United States District Court, District of Connecticut), in which plaintiff Gayer claims to represent individuals who purchased a Cuisinart food processor at retail in California during the period 1974 to at least August 1980; Louie v. Cuisinarts, Inc., et al. and Reynolds v. Cuisinarts, Inc., et al. (consolidated actions pending in the California Superior Court, San

Francisco County), in which plaintiffs have obtained certification of a class consisting of "all current California residents who purchased any model of a Cuisinart brand food processor for a purpose other than for resale from a retail store located in California during the period from September 18, 1976 to October 1, 1980, inclusive." These other actions are not being settled under the settlement described in this notice. But under the terms of the proposed settlement, Class members who do not individually file valid written elections of exclusion from the Class will be bound by the orders and judgments entered by the Court in the Settling Actions and you will be barred upon the entry of such orders and judgments from prosecuting or recovering on claims asserted on your behalf in the other pending actions.

You may not both participate in the settlement described in this notice and continue to assert claims in the other pending actions. As provided in the settlement stipulations in the Settling Actions, should the proposed settlement become final and effective, there will have been a dismissal final beyond further appeal of the pending class action allegations of the Gayer, Harwood, Louie and Reynolds actions, or a modification final beyond further appeal of the class definitions in the Louie and Reynolds actions so as to include only Cuisinart food processor purchasers who have individually filed valid written elections of exclusion from the Class and who are within the class in Louie and Reynolds or entry of an order final beyond further appeal granting partial summary judgment in the Louie and Reynolds actions, or other relief, with the effect of dismissing with prejudice, on *res judicata* grounds or otherwise, the claims of all Class members who are within the class in Louie and Reynolds except those who have individually filed valid written elections of exclusion from the Class. An injunction against those actions continuing on behalf of Class members who have not individually filed valid written elections of exclusion from this Class will be issued as part of the final judgment in the Settling Actions.

IF YOU ARE A MEMBER OF THE CLASS AND HAVE NOT RECEIVED NOTICE BY MAIL, YOU ARE ENTITLED TO RECEIVE THE COUPON IF YOU TIMELY FILE A VALID PROOF OF CLAIM IN THE FORM PRINTED BELOW AND IF THE SETTLEMENT DESCRIBED ABOVE IS APPROVED BY THE COURT AND BECOMES FINAL AND EFFECTIVE. YOU WILL BE BOUND BY ALL ORDERS AND JUDGMENTS OF THE COURT IN THE SETTLING ACTIONS EVEN IF YOU RECEIVE THE COUPON DESCRIBED ABOVE AND IT IS NOT REDEEMED. IN ANY EVENT, YOU WILL BE BOUND BY ALL ORDERS AND JUDGMENTS OF THE COURT IN THE SETTLING ACTIONS, UNLESS YOU EXCLUDE YOURSELF FROM THE CLASS IN THE MANNER PRESCRIBED BELOW.

YOU ARE HEREBY NOTIFIED:

1. You must file a proof of claim in the form printed below and mail it to the Clerk of the Court at the address printed on the form, postmarked not later than October

14, 1983 if you have not received notice by mail of this proposed settlement and you wish to receive the coupon. If you do not mail a properly completed proof of claim on or before October 14, 1983, you will not receive the coupon and you will not receive any further notices with respect to this litigation. You will, however, be bound by the results of the litigation unless you timely mail a request to be excluded from the Class. If the proof of claim form has previously been removed from this notice and you wish to file a proof of claim, please write to the Clerk of the Court, United States District Court for the District of Connecticut, P.O. Box 31498, Hartford, Connecticut 06103–1498 and request that a proof of claim be sent to you.

Exclusion from class. If you desire to be excluded from the Class, you must file a written request for Exclusion with the Clerk of the United States District Court for the District of Connecticut, P.O. Box 31498, Hartford, Connecticut 06103–1498, no later than August 12, 1983. Such written request for exclusion shall include a statement certifying you are a member of the Class and elect to be excluded therefrom and forego the benefit of this settlement. If you exclude yourself from the Class, you will not be bound by any decision or judgment relating to this settlement, you will not be entitled to participate in the settlement and you will remain free to pursue whatever legal rights you may have.

3. Settlement Hearing. A hearing will be held in the courtroom of the Honorable José A. Cabranes, United States District Judge for the District of Connecticut, at the U.S. Courthouse, 450 Main Street, Hartford, Connecticut, on September 13, 1983 at 10:00 a.m. for the purpose of determining whether the proposed settlement is fair, reasonable and adequate and whether the proposed settlement should be approved by the Court. If you are satisfied with the proposed settlement, you need not appear at this hearing or take any other action at this time. If the Court approves the proposed settlement, all claims against the defendants, which claims are covered by this notice, will be dismissed with prejudice, except with respect to those class members who exclude themselves from the settlement class in the manner described above. In the event this settlement is not finally approved, the plaintiffs in the national consumer actions will retain all their rights to litigate all class action issues arising in these cases under Rule 23 of the Federal Rules of Civil Procedure. The hearing may be adjourned from time to time without any further notice to the class.

4. Appearance by Counsel. If you decide to remain a member of the Class you may but need not, enter an appearance through an attorney of your choice by having your attorney mail a Notice of Appearance to the Clerk of the Court for the United States District Court for the District of Connecticut, U.S. Courthouse, 450 Main Street, Hartford, Connecticut 06103. If you remain in the Class and do not enter an appearance through your own counsel, your interests will be represented by the attorneys of record for the plaintiffs listed below.

5. Objections to Settlement Must Be Filed and Served on Coun-

sel. Any Class member who desires to do so may appear at the hearing, in person or by counsel, and show cause, if any, why the proposed settlement should not be approved by the Court and why the terms of the settlement should not be found to be fair, reasonable and adequate. No such person will be heard at the hearing and no papers and briefs submitted by any such person shall be received and considered unless on or before August 15, 1983, written objections to the settlement together with any additional papers or briefs are filed with the Clerk of the Court, U.S. District Court for the District of Connecticut, 450 Main Street, Hartford, Connecticut 06103, with a certificate stating that copies of the written objections and any additional papers or briefs were mailed on or before August 15, 1983 to:

H. Laddie Montague, Jr., Esquire BERGER & MONTAGUE, P.C. 1622 Locust Street Philadelphia, Pennsylvania 19103 Liaison Counsel for Plaintiffs

Laurel A. Price, Esquire Deputy Attorney General Antitrust Section Division of Criminal Justice Richard J. Hughes Justice Complex CN–85 Trenton, New Jersey 08625 Counsel for Plaintiff State of New Jersey (with respect only to residents of New Jersey)

Alan L. Kovacs, Esquire Assistant Attorney General Chief, Antitrust Division One Ashburton Place, Rm. 1902 Boston, Massachusetts 02108 Counsel for Plaintiff Commonwealth of Massachusetts (with respect only to residents of Massachusetts)

Arthur M. Handler, Esquire GOLENBOCK AND BARELL 645 Fifth Avenue New York, New York 10022 Liaison Counsel for Defendants

6. Waiver of Objections. Any person who fails to comply with the requirements of paragraph 5 shall be deemed to have waived and shall be forever foreclosed from raising any objection to the proposed settlement in any forum. The filing of an objection to the proposed settlement shall not exclude the objector from any judgment entered in the Settling Actions.

7. Document Title. All documents which you file should be entitled "In re Cuisinart Food Processor Antitrust Litigation, M.D.L. 447", as shown in this Notice. The postmark on the envelope will determine whether any documents you may file have been filed timely.

ADDITIONAL INFORMATION

If you have any questions which you want to raise concerning the Settling Actions or the matters dealt with in this notice, please direct your inquiries in writing to:

Clerk of the Court
U.S. District Court for the
District of Connecticut
P.O. Box 31498
Hartford, Connecticut 06103–1498

The pleadings and other public records in this litigation, including papers in support of the proposed settlement, may be examined and copied at any time during regular office hours at the Office of the Clerk, United States District Court for the District of Connecticut, U.S.

Courthouse, 450 Main Street, Hartford, Connecticut.

Principal counsel for the plaintiffs who will be petitioning the Court for payment of attorneys' fees and reimbursement of the costs of this litigation are:

BERGER & MONTAGUE, P.C., 1622 Locust Street, Philadelphia, PA 19103, Attorneys for Plaintiff Frederic Blum; KOHN, MILSTEIN, COHEN & HAUSFELD, 1776 K Street, N.W., Washington, D.C. 20006, Co–Counsel for Plaintiff Frederic Blum; JEROME S. WAGSHAL, P.C., 3256 N Street, N.W., Washington, D.C. 20007, Attorney for Plaintiff Yvonne S. Archer; PHILLIPS, NIZER, BENJAMIN, KRIM & BALLON, 40 West 57th Street, New York, NY 10019, Attorneys for Plaintiff Fred Cohn; GLAZER, SEELIG & GLAZER, 30 Oak Street, Stamford, CT 06901, Co–Counsel for Plaintiff Fred Cohn; KAPLAN, KILSHEIMER & FOLEY, 122 East 42nd Street, New York, NY 10168, Attorneys for Plaintiff Agnes Eisenberger; Attorney General, State of New Jersey, Richard J. Hughes Justice Complex, CN–85, Trenton, NJ 08625, Attorney for Plaintiff State of New Jersey; Attorney General, Commonwealth of Massachusetts, One Ashburton Place, Rm. 1902, Boston, MA 02108, Attorney for Plaintiff Commonwealth of Massachusetts.

Date: Hartford, Connecticut
April 20, 1983

BY ORDER OF
HON. JOSÉ A.
CABRANES
s/John K.
Henderson, Jr.
Deputy Clerk–
In–Charge

Clerk of the Court
United States District Court
District of Connecticut
P.O. Box 31498
Hartford, Connecticut 06103–1498

Re: In re Cuisinart Food Processor Antitrust Litigation (M.D.L. 447)

Instructions for Filing Claim

1. This proof of claim must be completed, signed, dated and mailed to the Clerk at the address indicated above by October 14, 1983.

2. If you purchased more than one Cuisinart food processor during the period January 1, 1973 through December 31, 1981, you must supply the required information for each such Cuisinart food processor.

PROOF OF CLAIM

Your Name and Address

____

____

____

I purchased the Cuisinart food processor(s) indicated below during the period January 1, 1973 through December 31, 1981 from a retail store or outlet, as follows:

Quantity of Cuisinart Food Processors Purchased from January 1, 1973 Through December 31, 1981: ______

Date of Each Purchase: ______

Name and Location of Retail Store or Outlet from which Each Cuisinart Food Processor was Purchased: ____________

Serial No. of Each Cuisinart Food Processor Purchased from January 1, 1973 Through December 31, 1981: ____________

If you cannot locate serial nos., fill out the other information and attach to this form a legible copy of a receipt(s) showing payment for the Cuisinart food processor(s) or other proof of purchase.

I certify under penalty of perjury under the laws of the United States of America that all of the foregoing information is true and correct to the best of my knowledge and belief.

____
Signature

____
Date

Special Instruction Regarding Gifts

If you gave the Cuisinart food processor(s) you purchased to someone as a gift, please provide the name(s) and address(es) of such person(s).

____
Name of Gift Recipient

____
Address

I hereby authorize the gift recipient to receive the coupon described in this notice. I understand that, upon signing below, I will not receive the coupon.

____
Signature

Question: (15) Does this notice, published in both People and Cuisine magazines, follow the rules elaborated in this Topic? In struggling to handle unique and difficult cases, should a judge have to follow generalized rules? Note that Consumer Rep., Oct. 1983, at 513, opined:

> Philadelphia attorney H. Laddie Montague, who acted as lead counsel for the consumers, considers the settlement fair. We don't. A manufacturer's "suggested retail price" is not a true market price. Cuisinart products, like many other hard goods, are widely discounted; a 50–percent-off-list coupon may not be that much of a bargain. Further, to share in the settlement, consumers must spend more money—on a product they may not need or want. The option of a cash settlement might well have satisfied more purchasers.

Nevertheless, after a minuscule response rate from consumers, then District Judge Cabranes by a careful opinion of October 24, 1983, approved the settlement, which included certification of the class for purposes of the settlement.

(b) TRIAL

Trials in class actions are rarities. One reason is that manageability problems force the trial judge to reconceptualize trial itself. Performing that task encounters challenges under the Rules Enabling Act and the Constitution.

For example, in one of those asbestos class actions that remained in the Eastern District of Texas, District Judge Parker came up with the idea, with the plaintiffs' consent, of proving damages for about 3000 members of a Rule 23(b)(3) class by trying a small sample of the complex cases and then extrapolating by means of expert and statistical evidence. Ultimately the Fifth Circuit blocked such a scheme by invoking the defendant's Seventh Amendment right to jury trial of the distinct issue of damages suffered by each claimant, and so did not have to face whether sampling squared with the Due Process Clause. Cimino v. Raymark Indus., Inc., 151 F.3d 297 (5th Cir.1998).

If a class action can get through trial to a judgment, the court will have also had to face in a new context the recurrent problem of representativeness. This is true whether the case involves big money or exemplifies public law litigation.

PETTWAY v. AMERICAN CAST IRON PIPE CO., 576 F.2d 1157 (5th Cir.1978), cert. denied, 439 U.S. 1115, 99 S.Ct. 1020 (1979). This was a very complex (b)(2) class action brought by black employees against their employer for employment discrimination in violation of Title VII of the Civil Rights Act of 1964. The suit had been pending since 1966 and produced numerous opinions both before and after this one.

In 1974, after the previous remand by the court of appeals, the district court encouraged the litigants to engage in settlement negotiations. The district judge played an active role in the extensive negotiations that ensued. Agreement was never really reached, and ultimately in 1975 the judge issued an injunctive decree largely based on the defendant's final offer.

In the final stages of this process, the three named plaintiffs and almost a third of the over two thousand other class members asked the class attorney (Adams) to appeal, but he declined on the grounds that the decree was fair and that an appeal would only delay implementation. They retained a new attorney (Wiggins), but the district court denied a motion to substitute him as class counsel. A final judgment was entered. This appeal by the named plaintiffs followed.

Rejecting appellants' contention, the court of appeals first decided that Rule 23(e) did not apply:

"The role of an appellate court in reviewing a decree in a class action suit varies greatly depending on whether the decree was reached through a settlement by the litigants or whether the decree represents the judgment of the court. [Citations omitted.] These differing modes of review reflect a recognition of the different character of the two types of judicial resolution. The standard of review appropriate to a court judgment is premised on the requirement that the trial judge, following adversary presentation of the facts and law, exercise his *independent* judgment on each of the issues presented for decision. His ruling must be based on findings of fact supported by evidence in the record and on conclusions of law. The role of the trial court in arriving at an independent judgment closely parallels its more traditional role in the non-class action context. Consequently, review of class action judgments is patterned after the conventional modes of review. The appellate court can review the trial court's findings of fact to ensure that they are supported by the record and are not clearly erroneous, while giving appropriate deference to the trial judge's superior ability to assess demeanor and credibility. The reviewing court is also particularly well suited to make an independent assessment of the law as applied to the facts, again giving deference to the lower court where the law affords some measure of latitude and discretion.

"Different problems are posed by class action settlements. Lacking a fully developed evidentiary record, both the trial court and the appellate court would be incapable of making the independent assessment of the facts and law required in the adjudicatory context. Moreover, a definitive judicial determination of the facts and law would be inappropriate because compromise of legal rights is intrinsic to the settlement process. Because of the limited control exercised by any particular class member over the decision to engage in these compromises, however, the settlement process is more susceptible than adversarial adjudications to certain types of abuse. The interests of lawyer and class may diverge, as may the interest of different members of the class, and certain interests may be wrongfully compromised, betrayed, or 'sold out' without drawing the attention of the court. For this reason, in addition to requiring that the trial court evaluate whether a class action settlement is 'fair, adequate and reasonable and is not the product of collusion between the parties', Cotton v. Hinton, [559 F.2d 1326, 1330 (5th Cir.1977)], the law accords special protections, primarily procedural in nature, to individual class members whose interests may be compromised in the settlement process. These protections include notice, ensuring that class members know when their rights are being compromised, and an opportunity to voice objections to the settlement.

"We recognize that this neat dichotomy is in some respects oversimple. In the class action context, some of the abuses generally associated with settlements may insinuate themselves into litigation resulting in the court's own judgment. For example, in framing litigation strategy in a complex suit the class attorney and named plaintiffs might concentrate on relief for certain members of the class while ignoring the interests of others. Nevertheless, because the potential for abuse is much greater when class actions are resolved through a settlement, the procedural protections applicable to settlements are not utilized in the judgment context.[5]"

The court of appeals conceded: "Settlements and court judgments are distinguished not by different platonic essences, but by the processes of their creation." A careful examination of the record led to the conclusion that this was a court judgment.

Turning then to the defendant's contention that the named plaintiffs and Wiggins could not appeal on behalf of the class, the court said:

"In the context of individual-plaintiff litigation the roles of the attorney and the client are well defined. The A.B.A. Code of Professional Responsibility envisions the attorney as an advocate of the interests of the client. American Bar Ass'n, Code of Professional Responsibility, EC 7–1 [hereinafter cited as ABA Code]. Although the lawyer has some freedom to make tactical choices during litigation without consulting his client, the lawyer is expected to defer to the client's wishes on major litigation decisions. See ABA Code EC 7–1, EC 7–7, EC 7–9. Unfortunately, it remains unclear whether this model can be carried over to the class action context, as no clear concept of the allocation of decision-making responsibility between the attorney and the class members has yet emerged. [Citation omitted.] Certainly it is inappropriate to import the traditional understanding of the attorney-client relationship into the class action context by simply substituting the named plaintiffs as the client. The interests of the named plaintiffs and those of other class members may diverge, and a core requirement for preventing abuse of the class action device is some means of ensuring that the interests and rights of each class member receive consideration by the court. Were the class attorney to treat the named plaintiff as the exclusive client, the interests of other class members might go unnoticed and unrepresented. See Gonzales v. Cassidy, 474 F.2d 67, 69–71, 76 (5th Cir.1973); Developments in the Law, Class Actions, 89 Harv. L.Rev. 1318, 1592–95 (1976). Thus, when a potential conflict arises between the named plaintiffs and the rest of the class, the class attorney must not allow decisions on behalf of the class to rest exclusively with the named plaintiffs. In such a situation, the attorney's duty to the class requires him to point out conflicts to the court so that the court may take appropriate steps to protect the interests of absentee class members.

"This does not mean, however, that the class attorney may ignore the wishes of the class representatives in making fundamental litigation decisions. As one court has stated, 'An attorney who prosecutes a class action with unfettered discretion becomes, in fact, the representative of the class. This is an unacceptable situation because of the possible conflicts of interest involved.' Leib v. 20th Century Corp., 61 F.R.D. 592 (M.D.Pa. 1974). In the context of a shareholders' derivative action, Saylor v. Lindsley, 456 F.2d 896 (2d Cir.1972), Judge Friendly has stressed that courts should not 'accept the view that the attorney for the plaintiff is the dominus litis and the plaintiff only a key to the courthouse door dispensable once entry has been effected':

[5] This is not to say, however, that courts should not be conscious of the possibility of similar abuses in the judgment context. . . .

> There can be no blinking at the fact that the interests of the plaintiff in a stockholder's derivative suit and of his attorney are by no means congruent. While, in a general sense, both are interested in maximizing the recovery this is only a half-truth. Even apart from special considerations which . . . may cause divergence of interest in cases where extremely large amounts are at stake, there is a difference in every case. The plaintiff's financial interest is in his share of the total recovery less what may be awarded to counsel, simpliciter; counsel's financial interest is in the amount of the award to him less the time and effort needed to produce it. A relatively small settlement may well produce an allowance bearing a higher ratio to the cost of the work than a much larger recovery obtained only after extensive discovery, a long trial and appeal. We say this not in criticism but in simple recognition of the facts of class action life.

456 F.2d at 900–01. The same considerations may cause a class attorney who has been awarded a substantial fee by the court to conclude that an appeal of the court's judgment might result in personally unremunerative litigation or a substantial and undesirable delay in the receipt of the fee award. When the possibility that counsel's own fervor may have been exhausted by an apparently endless legal battle is added to the equation, the potential conflict between the interests of the class and those of its attorney in an appeal cannot be ignored.

"It is, therefore, clear that the decision to appeal cannot rest entirely with either the named plaintiffs or with class counsel. Nonetheless, the Rule 23(a)(4) requirement that the trial court determine whether 'the representative parties will fairly and adequately protect the interests of the class' contemplates that the named plaintiffs will undertake a major role in the prosecution of a class action. The requirement also provides an important guarantee of a coincidence of interest between the named plaintiffs and the class.

". . . Implicit in our discussion and holding in Gonzales was the conviction that, at least under the circumstances of that case, the class plaintiff and not the class attorney, was responsible for deciding whether to appeal.

"The foregoing considerations convince us that, at least as an initial matter, the decision to appeal a class action judgment must rest with the class plaintiffs. If in making that decision the class plaintiffs arguably fail to adequately represent the interests of the class, the class attorney should point out potential inadequacies or conflicts of interest to the trial judge. Where the named plaintiffs wish to appeal, but the class attorney concludes that an appeal is not in the best interest of the class, the district court must exercise its discretion in deciding whether to substitute class counsel to allow the named plaintiffs to maintain the appeal on behalf of the class.[19] The proper exercise of the district court's discretion will depend on the facts and circumstances of each case. Among the factors that should be considered by the court are (1) the adequacy of representation of the named

[19] Distinctive problems may be presented where the named plaintiffs refuse to undertake an appeal which the class attorney believes to be in the best interests of the class or where

plaintiffs, including any apparent or potential conflicts of interest they might have with the remainder of the class, (2) the extent to which other class members support or oppose the appeal, and the extent to which an appeal may be necessary to protect the interests of absent class members, (3) the adequacy of representation provided by the class attorney and any conflicts of interest between the class attorney and the class, and (4) the reasonableness of the decision to appeal, including an assessment of the possibility of success on the merits.

. . . .

"In conclusion, we hold that under the circumstances of this case the trial judge abused his discretion by not granting appellants' motion to substitute class counsel for purposes of appealing the court's judgment. The decision to appeal rested as an initial matter with the named plaintiffs. These representatives chose to appeal, and an analysis of the factors considered above demonstrates that their choice should have been honored. The named plaintiffs have provided excellent representation in the past, and there is no indication in the record that their decision to appeal was based on any considerations other than the interests of the class. The decision received widespread support among the class. . . . While we do not question the sincerity of Mr. Adams' belief that an appeal of the injunctive decree is not in the class' interest, nothing in the record convinces us that the named plaintiffs' conclusion on this question was unreasonable. . . . Finally, the issues raised on appeal are neither frivolous nor insubstantial. We therefore shall treat this appeal of the . . . district court's decree as an appeal on behalf of the class."

The court of appeals went on to reverse and remand in an opinion of sixty-six pages, observing that they " 'would not substitute one hour of efficiency for one moment of justice.' " In essence, the court required yet greater efforts by the district judge "to remedy past employment discrimination by restructuring the multi-faceted employment practices of a large industrial concern."

SECTION 5. OVERVIEW, REVIEW, AND PREVIEW

Frank M. Coffin, The Frontier of Remedies: A Call for Exploration

67 Cal.L.Rev. 983, 988–89 (1979).

What seems to be emerging and enduring is a kind of lawsuit that differs in many facets from conventional adjudication . . . . Here is my

both the named plaintiffs and the class attorney decide not to appeal. If no appeal is taken and the failure to pursue an appeal constitutes inadequate representation, other members of the class may certainly pursue relief in a collateral proceeding. Gonzales v. Cassidy, supra. Whether, and how, a direct appeal may be taken absent the participation of the original named plaintiffs, or the participation of both the named plaintiffs and the class attorney, are issues we need not resolve for purposes of this appeal.

catalogue of differences:[11]

	Conventional Adjudication	*New Model*
The Issue	Likely to be of private rights and duties. If public body involved, issue likely to be procedural.	Likely to involve substantive rights and means of compelling a public body to effectuate those rights.
Parties	Likely to be one "person" suing another.	Likely to be a class of individuals suing a class of officials, public institutions, and political entities.
Critical facts	Historical (what has happened) and adjudicative (relevant to rights and liabilities of the two parties).	Predictive (situation as it is likely to exist during life of decree) and legislative (relevant to continuing decree).
Governing Principle	Legal precedents.	Strategy, tactics, and potential outcomes not informed by legal precedent.
Taking of evidence	Adversary hearing and rules of evidence.	Wide participation, relaxed standards, more expert opinions.
Relief sought	Declaration, negative injunction, damages; normally narrow, closely tied to legal injury.	Affirmative injunction, affecting many beyond parties; potentially broad.
Framing of decree	Imposed by court after hearing evidence.	Large amount of negotiation.
Impact	Confined to parties.	Affects a large segment of society.
Duration of court involvement	One-time judgment.	Continuing decree; subject to reopening and amendment.
Role of Judge	Passive: adjudicative in resolving dispute between two parties in a one time, normally self-executing, judgment.	Active: legislative in framing criteria; executive in implementing decree.
Review	Abuse of discretion and error of law; sufficiency of evidence and legal precedents important.	Contribution of appellate court to policy, strategy, and tactics more important than monitoring fact findings or legal principles.

These add up to a significant qualitative difference between conventional adjudication and the new model of litigation. New model litigation generally is brought by a broad class that enjoys wide-ranging discovery and seeks affirmative injunctive relief from public officials and institutions; under these circumstances the judge must play not only an adjudicative role, but legislative and executive roles as well.

Deborah L. Rhode, Class Conflicts in Class Actions

34 Stan.L.Rev. 1183, 1183–86, 1191–94, 1196–97, 1202, 1221, 1247, 1261–62 (1982).

A fundamental premise of American adjudicative structures is that clients, not their counsel, define litigation objectives. Thus, the American Bar Association's current and proposed ethical codes both emphasize that an attorney must defer to the client's wishes on matters affecting the

[11] For a number of these perceptions, I am indebted to Abram Chayes and his article, The Role of the Judge in Public Law Litigation, 89 Harv.L.Rev. 1281, 1302 (1976). [See supra p. 301.—Ed.]

merits of legal action. However, by presupposing an individual client with clearly identifiable views, these codes elide a frequent and fundamental difficulty in class action proceedings. In many such cases, the lawyer represents an aggregation of litigants with unstable, inchoate, or conflicting preferences. The more diffuse and divided the class, the greater the problems in defining its objectives.

This article examines those problems in one selected context: plaintiff class actions seeking structural reforms in public and private institutions. Such cases merit special attention on two grounds. First, the often indeterminate quality of relief available makes conflicts within plaintiff classes particularly likely. Most school desegregation, employment discrimination, prison reform, and related cases present no obvious single solution flowing ineluctably from the nature of the violation. Nor will all class members alleging unlawful conduct agree on what should be done about it. Moreover, the prominence of institutional reform litigation vests these intra-class cleavages with particular significance. Such cases account for a high percentage of all class suits and an even greater proportion of legal claims attracting widespread societal concern. Thus, institutional reform litigation provides a useful paradigm for analyzing some of the most vexing issues in class representation.

In exploring these issues, this article takes one central proposition for granted. On the whole, institutional reform class actions have made and continue to make an enormous contribution to the realization of fundamental constitutional values—a contribution that no other governmental construct has proven able to duplicate. That contention has been defended at length elsewhere, and the arguments need not be recounted here. Thus, the following discussion should not be taken to suggest that institutional reform class actions are misused or misconceived, or that there are preferable alternatives. The point, rather, is that the framework in which such actions proceed could benefit from both conceptual and mechanical refurbishing.

Much of the renovation required concerns our concept of class representation. In particular, we need a more coherent theory of class interests and of the role plaintiff preferences should play in defining class objectives. As a first cut at reconceptualization, this article posits a theory of representation mandating full disclosure of, although not necessarily deference to, class sentiment. A central premise is that the class as an entity has interests that may not be coextensive with the preferences of its current membership. Often those able to register views will be insufficiently disinterested or informed to speak for the entire constituency of present and future class members who will be affected by the court's decree. Nonetheless, preferences matter, not because they are conclusive of class interests, but because their disclosure is critical to the efficacy and legitimacy of judicial intervention.

. . . .

For those seeking structural reforms, class actions afford a number of obvious advantages over suits involving individual plaintiffs. By definition, class proceedings force focus on institutional practices rather than isolated grievances. Also, if a variety of allegedly unlawful practices are at issue, it can be cumbersome to seek out separate plaintiffs with standing to challenge each violation. Representing individual plaintiffs also entails some risk of mootness. School children graduate, prison inmates obtain transfers or paroles, and individual employees are subject to temptation by generous settlement offers. By contrast, once the court certifies a suit as a class action, the proceedings can continue despite the termination of individual claims, and any settlement must obtain judicial approval.[9] Thus, class representation obviates the continual need to substitute plaintiffs, and minimizes the allure of proposed settlements benefitting only named litigants. Moreover, compared with individual suits, class litigation may promise counsel greater bargaining leverage, larger attorneys' fees, and enhanced access to funding sources.

Yet by the same token, class status can also generate substantial problems in accommodating divergent client interests. . . .

. . . .

Prevailing legal doctrine offers strikingly little guidance to courts and counsel who confront intra-class schisms. Rule 23 of the Federal Rules of Civil Procedure, which governs most actions seeking structural relief, is singularly laconic. In pertinent part, the Rule requires only that "the claims or defenses of the representative parties" be "typical" of those of the class, and that the "representative parties will fairly and adequately protect the interests of the class." Once the court certifies a class, all members will be bound by the final judgment; they have no right to opt out of the action or even to receive notice of its pendency, although the court may order notice at its own discretion, and must do so before approving any pretrial settlement. At any time after certification, dissenting class members, opposing parties, or the court, sua sponte, may subsequently challenge the adequacy of the named plaintiffs' representation. If successful, such challenges can result in decertification of the class, restriction of the decree's res judicata effect, or some form of separate representation for plaintiffs with conflicting interests.

Given the binding consequences that attach to class status, Rule 23's mandate of adequate representation is of constitutional dimension. In essence, this requirement embodies a fundamental tenet of due process: that judicial procedure fairly protect "the interest of absent parties who are to be bound by it."[32] Yet despite the centrality of the concept to class action theory and practice, judicial pronouncements on the subject have been notably unilluminating.

The Advisory Committee that drafted Rule 23 provided no amplification of the terms "adequately protect" or "interests," and judges applying the standard have done little to fill the void. Among the primary questions

---

[9] Fed.R.Civ.P. 23(e); see United States Parole Comm'n v. Geraghty, 445 U.S. 388 (1980); Goodman v. Schlesinger, 584 F.2d 1325, 1332–33 (4th Cir.1978).

[32] Hansberry v. Lee, 311 U.S. 32, 42 (1940). . . .

left unaddressed is whether interest ever means more than preference and, if so, when and what. Do the named representative and counsel serve primarily as "instructed delegates," pursuing objectives to which a majority of class members subscribe? If so, how are those objectives to be identified, particularly if the class comprises a diffuse and changing constituency of past, present, and future claimants? Alternatively, does the representative role track Edmund Burke's notion of an "enlightened trustee," who makes an independent assessment of class concerns? Under that advocacy model, what recourse is available to individuals who do not share their trustee's vision?

. . . On the rare occasions where courts have confronted the issue, they have done little more than acknowledge the absence of any "clear principles governing the allocation of decisionmaking authority between the attorney and the class."[38] Such principles are unlikely to emerge given the constricted framework in which representation issues are currently analyzed. In general, courts have insisted only that attorneys be competent and that the claims of the named representatives be "similar," "common," or "not antagonistic" to those of the membership generally. Since few judges are inclined to engage in public ad hominems, the inquiry concerning counsel's competence is rarely a meaningful exercise. And application of the common claims requirement has yielded no coherent principles for coping with divergent preferences.

. . . .[41]

Bailey v. Ryan Stevedoring Co.[51] is a case in point. There the district court denied class certification because almost all members of a black union had opposed the named plaintiffs' efforts to force integration with a white union. Opposition rested primarily on fears that minorities would lose certain beneficial employment arrangements under a consolidated structure. Plaintiffs nevertheless pursued the claim in a private suit and succeeded in obtaining merger of the unions. In contexts like Bailey, those who disagree with named plaintiffs' remedial proposals may have even less opportunity for notice and participation if the case proceeds as an individual rather than collective action. Thus, denying class certification would hardly secure, and could well impede, the protection of all interests affected by judicial decree.

---

38 Pettway v. American Cast Iron Pipe Co., 576 F.2d 1157 (5th Cir.1978), cert. denied, 439 U.S. 1115 (1979).

41 [Professor Rhode here dealt with a recent case:] Although in General Telephone Co. v. Falcon, 50 U.S.L.W. 4638, 4641 (U.S. Apr. 26, 1982), the Supreme Court made clear that named plaintiffs must specifically identify common questions of law or fact, the decision provides little authoritative guidance on the implications of conflict for purposes of certification. In essence, the Court held that a Mexican–American employee claiming discrimination in promotion had failed to allege facts in common with possible victims of discriminatory hiring. That holding made it unnecessary to resolve issues regarding potential conflicts of interest within the class. However, the Court did cite dictum from a prior case suggesting that the same plaintiff should not represent applicants and employees who would compete for the same fringe benefits or seniority. Id. at 4640 (citing General Telephone v. EEOC, 446 U.S. 318, 331 (1980)).

51 528 F.2d 551 (5th Cir.1976), cert. denied, 429 U.S. 1052 (1977).

On that reasoning, a federal district judge in Evans v. Buchanan[53] rejected the claim that named plaintiffs in a school desegregation case inadequately represented class members who favored different relief. Since any judicial decree would "of necessity . . . be determinative of the rights of all," the court viewed the issue as not whether interests were antagonistic but whether there had been "a full and fair presentation of all possible views on the matter." From a due process perspective, the Evans analysis makes eminent sense. In structural relief cases involving intra-class conflict, the preferable strategy is to grant certification and create sufficient procedural safeguards to ensure adequate disclosure of dissenting views.

. . . .

Formal mandates governing class adjudication assign responsibility for ensuring adequate representation to three quarters: the named plaintiffs, their attorneys, and the court. In practice, opposing parties and dissenting class members also play a role in exposing conflict. Frequently, however, none of these participants has sufficient incentive or information to respond adequately to class schisms.

. . . .

Confronted with the kinds of conflicts discussed above, courts and counsel have responded with two, not mutually exclusive, strategies. A pluralist approach is to have separate factions speak through separate representatives. A majoritarian alternative is to create opportunities for class members to express their preferences directly, through polls or public hearings.

Although useful in many instances, neither of these strategies provides anything approaching a full solution to class schisms. A generic weakness stems from the information and incentive structures discussed above. If neither the parties nor the courts are equipped or disposed to explore conflicts, then the theoretical availability of such alternatives is irrelevant. Moreover, each strategy has certain practical limitations that further impair its value in addressing conflicts.

. . . .

In addressing these problems, courts and legislatures should consider two sorts of reform. One set of strategies should focus on information and incentive structures. Through amendment or interpretation of Rule 23 mandates, efforts should be made to increase judicial awareness of class schisms at an earlier stage in litigation. A second set of strategies should be directed toward improving techniques for coping with intra-class conflicts once their significance becomes apparent.

[Professor Rhode's proposals included, on the one hand, requiring the trial judge to make a factual record concerning decisions on notice and concerning the finding of adequate representation and, on the other hand, calling for more sensitive judicial attention to intervention, amici presenta-

[53] 416 F.Supp. 328 (D.Del.), appeal dismissed, 429 U.S. 973 (1976).

tions, use of oversight committees of class members, and appointment of neutral advisors as experts or masters.]

To be sure, none of the proposals outlined here can guarantee better results in [every case]. But that conclusion, if disconcerting, is not necessarily damning. Given the values at issue in institutional reform cases, conflicts are an ineradicable feature of the legal landscape. Virtually all of the pluralist and majoritarian deficiencies that impede judicial management of such conflicts would arise with equal force if the underlying issues were addressed in legislative or bureaucratic settings. Indeed, one of the strongest justifications for those governance structures is equally available to class actions: While we cannot depend on disinterested and informed judgment by any single group of decisionmakers, we can at least create sufficient procedural checks and balances to prevent the worst abuses.

Moreover, to acknowledge that the formal mandates governing class actions promise far more than they deliver is not to condemn the pretense. No hypothesized procedures can insure that all class interests will be "adequately represented" or that counsel will singlemindedly pursue his "client's" objectives. But the risks of abandoning either fiction may be too great.

No matter how faulty the enforcement mechanism, such mandates serve important legitimating functions. Broad injunctions concerning client autonomy and adequate representation allow us to affirm the individual's right to be heard without in fact paying the entire price. Giving overly fixed content to those terms could propel us toward some generic prescription that raises more difficulties than it resolves. An unqualified embrace of pluralism would entail problems of increased expense and diminished effectiveness. To totter towards majoritarianism would require confrontation with the awkward fact that paternalism is often offensive in principle but desirable in practice. Like other "white lies" of the law,[297] those governing class adjudication have spared us such discomfitting choices by masking certain "weak spots in our intellectual structure."[298] But shoring up is generally preferable to papering over. And no durable renovation can proceed without more searching scrutiny of what adequate representation means in instances of conflict, and what mechanisms we might devise to nudge reality somewhat closer to fiction.

Abram Chayes, The Supreme Court, 1981 Term—Foreword: Public Law Litigation and the Burger Court

96 Harv.L.Rev. 4, 26–29, 32, 34–37 (1982).

For classical legal theory, the main problem posed by the class action was that the judgment determined the rights of absent members of the

[297] L. Fuller, Legal Fictions 5 (1967) (quoting R. von Ihering).

[298] Id. at 52.

class who had not had their day in court. Today, there is a more pragmatic engagement over whether and how the class action device is to be shaped as an instrument for the vindication of group interests when they are infringed by the action of government or corporate bureaucracies. In 1966 the Federal Rules of Civil Procedure were amended, in part with a view toward improving the capacity of the class action to serve this end. The revisions coincided almost exactly with the invention of "public interest law" in the late 1960's and with the general surge of reformist zeal into the courts.

The class action seemed perfectly adapted to the social, political, and even stylistic objectives of the reformist litigators, whether in school desegregation, civil rights, apportionment, environmental, consumer, or other lawsuits challenging far-reaching government or corporate actions. Indeed, in many of these cases—for example, school desegregation or environmental suits—it is hard to conceive of individual relief apart from class relief. And in many more, the only practical way of getting into court is by way of class action. The effect of the conduct under attack on any single individual is too small to justify a traditional lawsuit seeking compensation. But in the aggregate the impact is substantial enough to be a target for redress, whether the underlying justification is compensatory, deterrent, or punitive.

The availability of the class action, in my view, had not a little to do with the burgeoning of theories about groups (as opposed to individuals) as right bearers. In any case, it emphasized the vision enunciated in NAACP v. Button[137] of the lawsuit as a form of political expression and a vehicle for vindicating political and social rights. And the class action device confirmed the self-image of public interest lawyers as spokesmen for large groupings toward which they had duties and responsibilities different from those of the ordinary lawyer-client relationship.

The traditional justification for the class action stresses the potential economies to be achieved when numerous individual claims with similar factual or legal issues can be litigated in a single proceeding. But the class can also be seen as a single jural entity capable of suing and being sued, not unlike the more familiar organizational litigants—corporations, unions, government departments—save that it is constructed ad hoc for the very purpose of conducting a particular litigation and that its principal or only unifying characteristic is often the legal relationship or grievance in controversy.

In its encounters with class actions, the Burger Court has clung to the first conception of the class action as a congeries of individual claims loosely bundled together for purposes of judicial efficiency. For such purposes as amount in controversy, notice, [and] representative authority, . . . the Court's decisions tend to treat class representatives and members as classical individual claimants. The combined effect of these decisions has

[137] 371 U.S. 415, 429–30 (1963).

been to constrict arbitrarily . . . the operation of the class action as a device for the enforcement of statutory and constitutional policies.

. . . .

The foregoing pattern is best displayed by the Court's decisions concerning small claims class actions. The relevant provision is rule 23(b)(3) of the Federal Rules, which authorizes class treatment of claims linked by any common question of law or fact. Such actions can bring together hundreds, thousands, or even millions of persons damaged by corporate action allegedly in violation of antitrust, securities, or consumer legislation. The claims of the individual class members may be minuscule, but when aggregated they have generated enormous ad damnums, running to hundreds of millions—even billions—of dollars. Plaintiffs' lawyers in these cases have cast themselves as private attorneys general enforcing norms of conduct plainly established by statutes or common law, norms that the defendants would otherwise escape. Defense attorneys have replied that such class actions are no more than legalized blackmail.

The Court has never directly addressed the controversy over the function and operation of the small claims class action. Instead, it has disposed of the procedural problems it has faced by means of a variety of seemingly unrelated doctrines, each anchored in the classical conception of the lawsuit and each having the effect, in one way or another, of limiting the effectiveness of the class action as an enforcement device.

. . . .

Eisen is thus a triumph of form over substance. The reason for the notification requirement is to ensure that an absentee's claim is not foreclosed by litigation of which the absent party is not aware. But the precise effect of the Eisen decision is to foreclose the absentee along with all other class members in small claims cases; if the claimants cannot band together as a class, they will be unable to proceed at all.

[Professor Chayes also criticizes the Court's cases on calculating the jurisdictional amount in class actions.]

It is not clear what the actual impact of these class action decisions has been. On the one hand, federal judicial statistics have begun to show a reduction in class action filings. The breakdown of these figures is not fine enough to locate the decline in the rule 23(b)(3) category, but it seems plausible that the decline reflects the less hospitable climate for these actions generated by the Court's rulings.

On the other hand, lower courts have found a number of ways around the stringency of the [Court's] requirements. Costs have been sharply reduced by permitting plaintiffs to stuff the required notice in defendants' regular mailings to class members. . . . In addition, plaintiffs have shown a good deal of ingenuity in converting rule 23(b)(3) actions into (b)(1) or (b)(2) actions. . . .

The variety of expedients employed by the lower courts suggests that the judiciary is responding to felt pressures for the use of the class action device and that the Supreme Court has failed to address the underlying realities that are the source of those pressures. . . . [T]he perspective of public law litigation brings significant issues into focus that are obscured or ignored in the Court's concentration on notice and other requirements drawn from the classical model.

The small claims class action enables strict enforcement of a range of what may be called consumer protection norms, violation of which has individually small but widely diffused impacts. The basic difficulty is that all of the norms invoked are not necessarily appropriate for strict enforcement. . . . [T]he Court must determine the appropriate scope of private enforcement of public norms.

In pursuing this inquiry, the Court should obviously draw whatever light it can from relevant statutory language and history. In most cases, however, these guides will be silent. The dominant consideration will be that to permit strict enforcement through the small claims class action is to elevate deterrent and punitive objectives over compensatory ones. Because individual damage claims are by definition very small, the interest in punishing the violation becomes stronger than the desire to compensate the victims. A nice concern for the distribution of damages in exact conformity to the harm suffered by each claimant gives way to the overriding objective of stripping the defendant of the profits of its unlawful act. In what circumstances is such a shift in emphasis appropriate? It may be possible to approach an answer to that question through careful analysis of the expectations generated by the norm the claimants seek to enforce, the clarity with which that norm is stated, and the importance of the substantive policies involved in the particular case.

. . . [T]his proposed approach is unlikely to generate dispositive criteria. But a focus on considerations that should inform the discretionary decision to certify a class under rule 23(b)(3) is far more consistent with the philosophy of the rule than is the Court's creation of rigid and arbitrary limitations on the availability of the device.

Question: (16) In determining how the class-action device is to be shaped, the legitimacy (from the points of view of jurisprudence, separation of powers, federalism, and due process) and the desirability (also from a variety of viewpoints, including the politics) of public law litigation both must be considered. But, again, in dealing with a Federal Rule, is there not an additional question on the extent to which substantive policies can be written or read into Rule 23?

Linda S. Mullenix, Resolving Aggregate Mass Tort Litigation: The New Private Law Dispute Resolution Paradigm

33 Val.U.L.Rev. 413, 414–15, 431 (1999).

Professor Chayes's article [The Role of the Judge in Public Law Litigation (1976)] had such impact and lasting influence because his article described a paradigm shift in American jurisprudence away from the traditional, two-party lawsuit into the modern, sprawling complex litigation.

Nearly two decades later, Professor Chayes's public law model has been embraced as the conceptual model for explaining and resolving mass tort litigation. Yet, just as Professor Chayes's public law model was dated even at the time he described it, the public law model also fails to capture the dynamics of modern mass tort litigation. Thus, the public law model is not only *not* descriptive of modern mass tort litigation, but this model also fails as a prescriptive basis for resolving these cases.

If it is true that Professor Chayes's great insight was to capture a significant paradigm shift in the litigation landscape of the 1950s and 1960s, then a new descriptive model is necessary to capture the litigation landscape of two subsequent decades since Professor Chayes wrote, that is, the 1980s and the 1990s. Although the types of complex litigation that Professor Chayes identified have remained a fixture in the federal courts, these two subsequent decades have been the era of mass tort litigation, a type of litigation that had not truly emerged at the time Professor Chayes formulated his thesis.

Accurately characterizing modern mass tort litigation is important because this litigation has generated a new, hybrid form of dispute resolution that shares attributes of both the private law and public law models. . . .

In American jurisprudence, the end of the twentieth century has been the great era of aggregate private dispute resolution, a paradigm that shares some attributes of the public law model, but it also differs from the public law model in significant respects. This form of aggregate private dispute resolution has stretched the boundaries of the judicial function, arrogating to private parties and an array of judicial surrogates vast powers for resolving aggregate claims. This aggregative private dispute resolution paradigm resembles nothing so much as private legislation with wide-reaching effects, carrying the imprimatur of judicial oversight and approval, but frequently accompanied by troubling questions about fairness, adequate representation, and the subtle merger of legislative, administrative, and judicial functions.

. . . .

. . . What is confusing is that this litigation *looks as though* it is resolved through traditional judicial auspices, but in reality little of mass tort litigation actually is filtered through judicial process.

The modern mass tort paradigm instead involves the wholesale resolution of aggregate private claims through private auspices without the significant involvement of the very people whose claims are being resolved in wholesale fashion. Thus, the mass tort paradigm resembles more closely private legislation implemented through private administrative means but still sanctioned with a judicial imprimatur.

Mass tort litigation and late twentieth-century small claims consumer class actions support the thesis that we have moved to a model of the privatization of aggregate claim resolution.

CLASS–ACTION BILL

A sweeping reform of the current class-action procedures under Federal Rule 23(b)(3) emerged in 1977 from the Office for Improvements in the Administration of Justice, an office in the Justice Department then headed by Assistant Attorney General Daniel J. Meador. It reached Congress as S. 3475, 95th Cong., 2d Sess. (1978), a bill introduced in the Senate by Senator DeConcini of Arizona and cosponsored by Senator Kennedy of Massachusetts. See generally Stephen Berry, Ending Substance's Indenture to Procedure: The Imperative for Comprehensive Revision of the Class Damage Action, 80 Colum.L.Rev. 299 (1980) (explaining and approving bill).

Senator DeConcini's statement introducing his bill, found at 124 Cong.Rec. 27,859 (1978), summarized this unenacted attempt to alleviate the problems of pursuing, defending, and managing class actions:

"Mr. President, on behalf of Senator Kennedy and myself, I am introducing legislation to revise and reform the rules and procedures under which class actions are litigated in the Federal courts. Dissatisfaction with the current situation is widespread, and I believe the need for change is compelling. The proposal we are introducing, which was drafted in close consultation with the Department of Justice, contains some interesting and challenging departures from present practice. If implemented, it may go far toward rationalizing class action litigation. At the same time, I recognize that this is a subject matter of great complexity and great interest to many diverse groups. While this bill was prepared in consultation with a wide variety of interests, it is only a first step, not the last. Neither Senator Kennedy nor I are wedded to its provisions. The Subcommittee on Improvements in Judicial Machinery plans extensive hearings on the measure beginning this fall and continuing into the 96th Congress. Those hearings will focus on the broader questions associated with class actions. The need for revision of the class action rule; the legitimate purposes which class action litigation should serve; the extent to which our society should devote judicial resources to class actions; and the actual and potential abuses of this instrument.

"The bill which I am introducing repeals Federal rule 23(b)(3) and replaces it with two new procedures: First, a public action for redress of small monetary injuries (less than $300), and second, a class compensatory action for substantial monetary injuries (more than $300). In addition, the bill provides the courts with new tools to make cases under both procedures more manageable.

"The statute created by this bill reflects the recognition that there are, in fact, two distinct types of class suits which are presently litigated under rule 23(b)(3). One type arises where the economic injury is small but widespread. In these cases, it is not economically feasible for the injured parties to initiate individual actions. Nevertheless, where there has been a violation of the law, the public has a strong interest in seeing that the wrongdoer does not profit from his illegal conduct. Thus, the primary purpose of bringing suit in these cases is to prevent unjust enrichment and to deter illegal conduct rather than to compensate the injured parties. In contrast, the second type of suit arises from situations where the economic injury is more substantial and it is assumed that the parties will have sufficient incentive to form a class and secure adequate and representative counsel to assert their claims. In these cases, compensation of the parties remains the primary focus of the litigation.

"The public action created by this bill vests a single claim in the United States against a wrongdoer where, first, 200 persons have each sustained injury less than $300; second, the combined damages exceed $60,000; and third, the injuries arise out of the same transaction or occurrence and present a substantial common question of law or fact. The policy behind the public action is, as I mentioned earlier, the public interest in preventing unjust enrichment and deterring unlawful conduct.

"The public action can be brought by the United States, or on its behalf, by one or more injured persons, thereby providing a role for private enforcement of the public interest. If an action is brought by a private person, he must promptly serve notice on the Attorney General and the local U.S. attorney and provide them with all evidence in his possession supporting the claim. The United States may then either assume control of the action, permit the action to be prosecuted by the private party, refer the action to a State attorney general, or recommend to the court that the public interest would not be served by allowing the action to continue as a public action. If the United States assumes control of and prevails in an action brought initially by a private party, the party is entitled to an incentive fee. The public action thus accommodates public and private interests.

"The public action procedure also provides for a preliminary hearing, after strictly controlled discovery, within 4 months from the filing of the complaint. The court, at that time, decides if the prerequisites of the public action have been met and makes a preliminary assessment of the merits of the case. The preliminary hearing thus serves to protect all parties from open-ended discovery fishing expeditions and to screen out frivolous strike suits. It will also give the plaintiff a preliminary indication of his chances of prevailing before he invests substantial resources in pursuing the action. If a defendant is found liable, the judgment is calculated in an amount equal to either the total benefits realized by the defendant by this illegal conduct or the total damages caused by the defendant. This calculation can be made by any reasonable means.

"Judgments in public actions will be transferred to the Administrative Office of the U.S. Courts where they will be deposited into a public recovery fund. The Administrative Office is charged with the responsibility of giving notice of the judgment, processing claims and distributing the fund. A claim must be greater than $15 and submitted within 1 year. The transfer of this responsibility from the courts to the Administrative Office serves to conserve judicial resources.

"The compensatory action created by this bill is patterned on the present rule, but includes significant changes which are intended to increase the fairness of the procedure and to make it less expensive and time consuming. The compensatory action is to be used where 40 persons suffer injury exceeding $300 and the injuries arise out of the same transaction or occurrence and present a substantial common question of law or fact. The theory here is that persons injured in excess of $300 will have sufficient incentive to form a class and vindicate their claims.

"As in the public action, the trial judge in a compensatory action must hold a preliminary hearing, after strictly controlled discovery, within 4 months of the filing of the complaint. At this hearing, the court decides whether the class requirements have been met, makes a preliminary assessment of the merits, and also decides the content and the means of giving notice to the class. Where notice and proof of individual damage will be difficult and time-consuming, the court is given discretion to try the issues of liability and damage separately. If the defendant is found liable, then the cost of notice will shift to him. This provision, like many others in the bill, allows the court to divide complex cases into more manageable steps.

"Both the public action and the compensatory action would be subject to new management techniques which are intended to promote stronger judicial stewardship of these actions. For example, the bill provides for, first, the regulation of settlements; second, supervision by the circuit judicial councils of over-delayed district court rulings; and third, a precise method for computing an award of attorney fees based on hourly rates, but with provision for risk adjustments.

"This bill is by no means perfect. However, it does address in an innovative manner the problems inherent in present practice. And, unless we begin to act, the basic credibility of our justice system and access to our Federal courts will be called into question. To arbitrarily close the doors of the courts on class action claims gives the appearance of condoning illegal conduct. As Vice President Mondale has pointed out:

> Nothing is more destructive to a sense of justice than the widespread belief that it is much more risky for an ordinary citizen to take five dollars from one person at the point of a gun than it is for a corporation to take five dollars each from a million customers at the point of a pen.

"At the same time, however, we must protect honest and legitimate business interests from unwarranted attacks. The challenge is there, and I look forward to developing and further exploring the potential of the new concepts embodied in this legislation."

Arthur R. Miller, Of Frankenstein Monsters and Shining Knights: Myth, Reality, and the "Class Action Problem"

92 Harv.L.Rev. 664, 666–69, 676–77, 682, 684, 693–94 (1979).

The available information suggests that much of the [long and hot class-action] debate has been based on erroneous assumptions. It indicates that rule 23 is achieving some of its intended purposes and may well be providing systemwide economies in several contexts, even though small-claim, large-class damage cases have proven extremely resistant to expeditious processing. Although there have been instances of undesirable or unprofessional conduct, abuse does not appear to have been widespread. Stories about a few questionable occurrences have been repeated so often at professional meetings that they have created the impression that evils are commonplace in class action practice. The empirical evidence also implies that in settled class actions, particularly in the securities and treble damage antitrust contexts, the great bulk of the money received from the defendants actually is distributed to class members, in contrast to the widely held notion that the fund is either devoured by avaricious attorneys or consumed by administrative expenses.

. . . .

It is important in understanding the class action debate to realize that the "big case" phenomenon transcends the class action. The "big case" is an inevitable byproduct of the mass character of contemporary American society and the complexity of today's substantive regulations. It is a problem that would confront us whether or not rule 23 existed. Indeed, it is becoming increasingly obvious that the traditional notion of civil litigation as merely bilateral private dispute resolution is outmoded. Since our conception of the roles of judges and advocates is based on this traditional view, the ferocious attack on the class action may reflect anxiety over the growing challenge to the model's immutability.

This apprehension should be stated even more broadly. In my judgment, Federal Rule 23 is being used as a convenient scapegoat for grievances against our civil litigation system and trends in our society whose roots lie far deeper than the procedural aspects of practice under that rule. Our preoccupation with the so-called "class action problem" represents a misdirection of attention and energy, which might be better expended recalibrating the structure of litigation in light of contemporary conditions. Accordingly, the thesis of this essay is that drastic revision of class action practice at this time, either by legislation or rulemaking, would be tantamount to attempting a cure by treating one symptom of an ailment rather than dealing with its underlying cause. Any attempt at modification now not only runs the risk of being an overreaction to the argumentative din of the past few years, but seems particularly ill timed because, as will be developed below, class action practice under the existing rule appears to be stabilizing.

I. The 1966 Revision of Rule 23—Unjustly Accused

. . . .

The Advisory Committee's objectives in rewriting the rule were rather clear. It had few, if any, revolutionary notions about its work product. Although it was expected that the revision would operate to assist small claimants, the draftsmen conceived the procedure's primary function to be providing a mechanism for securing private remedies, rather than deterring public wrongs or enforcing broad social policies. . . .

. . . .

. . . The emergence of a vigorous body of class action litigators . . . does not lend credence to the oft-heard barb that rule 23 has modified "substantive rights" by permitting actions to be brought that either never could have or never would have been brought before. A more accurate formulation may be that because litigation resources exist today that were not hitherto available and a portion of them have been generated by an increased consciousness about various societal problems, more litigation—often class actions—is being instituted.

. . . .

II. Class Action Practice—Retrospective and Prospective

. . . .

Even in its current elaborated form, rule 23 really must be thought of as a procedural skeleton requiring fleshing out by judges and lawyers experimenting with it in an ever-increasing range of circumstances and in a variety of innovative ways. The Reporter to the Advisory Committee on Civil Rules that drafted the revision, Professor Benjamin Kaplan (now a Justice of the Massachusetts Supreme Judicial Court), has remarked that it would probably take at least a full generation (1) to discover the problems with the rule's text, (2) to understand its various components, and (3) to develop an image of how it actually functions. Although the rule provides guidance on a number of matters and expressly authorizes various kinds of judicial activity, its basic operation ultimately depends on the ingenuity of district judges working cooperatively with counsel to engineer the management of complicated lawsuits. Patience has been and continues to be the watchword; it probably will take the full generation that Professor Kaplan envisioned to achieve anything approaching a common understanding of the scope, utility, and application of rule 23.

[Professor Miller divided the history of the administration of the amended Rule into three phases. During the first phase, lasting until 1969, the legal community exhibited both euphoria over the Rule's potential and lack of technical attention to the prerequisites for class-action treatment.

The resultant overuse and misuse by plaintiffs induced the reactionary second phase, which was characterized by widespread criticism of class actions, defendants' intransigence, and judicial resistance as in Eisen. Around 1973 or 1974, the third phase set in. It was marked by increasing sophistication, restraint, and stabilization in class-action practice. Plaintiffs were becoming more reasonable and careful, and defendants less intransigent. Judges were becoming more effective, especially in their use of the powers set out in Rule 23(c), (d), and (e).]

Thus, there is reason to be optimistic. The effect of this continuing maturation should be better administration of class actions by making certain that issues worthy of group adjudication are accorded it, that the class is adequately represented, and that class members are divided into workable subclasses that avoid internecine conflicts. This could well lead to a reduction in the transaction costs of class actions and, in the long run, to a more realistic utilization of rule 23.

III. Proposals for Change

[Professor Miller criticized current proposals for change and, in particular, the class-action bill. He found troublesome the governmental involvement in the proposed "public action," which he otherwise found generally attractive from the viewpoints of social justice and efficiency. More strongly, he believed the "compensatory action" proposal to be too detailed in expression and too narrow in scope, and he saw this aspect of the bill as a legislative intrusion unnecessarily debilitating judicial rulemaking.

[However, Professor Miller noted that the Advisory Committee in 1977 had decided that any modification in class-action practice should come from Congress, a decision approved by the Judicial Conference in 1978. The Committee thought that the big issues involved were best dealt with in the political arena. Also, the Committee apparently had concluded that its mandate under the Rules Enabling Act did not give enough breadth for effective treatment. Finally, the Committee apparently had reached no consensus as to what to amend in Rule 23.]

IV. Conclusion

Given the emotional tone and misdirection of the class action debate during recent years, the ideological orientation of some of the proposals, and the indications of increased stabilization in the field, this is an inopportune time to attempt a major revision of class action practice. A few more years of experience under rule 23 should give us a better understanding of how well the class action can function and perhaps produce some movement toward consensus regarding the appropriate utilization of the federal courts for purposes of deterrence, public law enforcement, and small claim rectification.[i]

---

[i] In a later interview, in Third Branch, Nov. 1986, at 1, 10–11, Professor Miller had this to say:

Stephen N. Subrin & Margaret Y.K. Woo, Litigating in America

205–06 (2006).

By the end of the 1970s, the use of class actions had substantially decreased in the federal courts, and this trend continued through the 1980s.

But the 1990s brought a fourth development. There was a remarkable revival in the 23(b)(3) damages class action, with its previous detractors (defendants and the defense bar) reversing to become its staunchest advocates. . . . Asbestos litigation brought by thousands injured by exposure to the chemical is perhaps the most obvious example of the proliferation of mass tort cases brought as class actions. . . .

In the midst of this "litigation crisis," some of those who have been antagonistic to the class action in the past, including members of the judiciary, the defense bar, and corporate executives in companies faced with such suits, have in recent years embraced rather than rejected the class action. If large numbers of potential plaintiffs can gain from a class action, why couldn't large numbers of potential plaintiffs also be barred by a class action settlement? In other words, if the defendant can buy, as it has been called, "global peace" with class actions, then the class action has become a friend rather than an enemy for defendants. In some instances, settlements are first negotiated, and then class actions are subsequently brought in order to bind current and potential litigants in the future. This kind of a "settlement class action" proved controversial because it is brought for the sole purpose of having a judge certify the class or classes and approve the settlement in a way that binds all class members, past and future plaintiffs. In such a way, the defendant has limited its liability dramatically.[j]

CLASS–ACTION RULE AMENDMENTS

In 1991 the Advisory Committee began the revisit to Rule 23. The drafting process followed the usual course as a radically ambitious overhaul[k] distilled down to a few proposed changes, which were published for

---

"I think it is time [for the Advisory Committee] to go back to rule 23. Rule 23 has been like a religious war for many, many years. . . . I think a lot of the hysteria about the rule has quieted down. And I think it is time to lift the moratorium, and go back to rule 23 and take the more than 20 years' experience we have had under it and see if we can't build a better mousetrap. I think there are ways of improving the rule in terms of the notice requirement, in terms of describing what are proper class actions, improving descriptions of subclassing and the judicial powers in class actions. . . . I think we have now hit the point where we can make a reasonable reevaluation of class actions."

[j] The authors go on, in their book, to fear the possibility of a fifth, and final, stage of class-action development, marked by an upswing in courts' refusing to certify class actions for mass torts and in corporations' forcing contractual waiver of class actions on potential plaintiffs. They cite Myriam Gilles, Opting Out of Liability: The Forthcoming, Near–Total Demise of the Modern Class Action, 104 Mich.L.Rev. 373 (2005).

[k] See Section of Litigation, ABA, Report and Recommendations of the Special Committee on Class Action Improvements (1985), reprinted in 110 F.R.D. 195 (1986).

comment in 1996. The significant changes would have been the addition to Rule 23 of subdivisions (b)(4) and (f).

The latter change invoked the new rulemaking power in 28 U.S.C. § 1292(e) to provide a method of permissive interlocutory appeal from class-certification decisions. Rule 23(f) went into effect in 1998.

The addition of (b)(4) would have blessed and expanded the disputed practice of certifying class actions just for settlement, via a new category applicable when:

> (4) the parties to a settlement request certification under subdivision (b)(3) for purposes of settlement, even though the requirements of subdivision (b)(3) might not be met for purposes of trial.

This was a much more controversial proposal.

The Chair of the Advisory Committee explained in his transmittal memorandum: "New subdivision (b)(4) authorizes certification of a (b)(3) class for purposes of settlement. It requires that all of the subdivision (a) prerequisites for class certification be met, and that the predominance and superiority requirements of (b)(3) also be met. But it authorizes evaluation of these prerequisites and requirements from the perspective of settlement. A settlement class may be certified even though the same class would not be certified for purposes of litigation [because of, for example, choice-of-law or case-management difficulties]. Although (b)(4) is set out as a separate paragraph, the class is certified under (b)(3) and is subject to the rights of notice and exclusion that apply to all (b)(3) classes. Certification is permitted only on motion by parties to a settlement agreement already reached. The separate subdivision (e) requirements for notice of settlement and court approval continue to apply." The Advisory Committee note elaborated that settlement classes have great benefits, including that "settlement may prove far superior to litigation in devising comprehensive solutions to large-scale problems that defy ready disposition by traditional adversary litigation." The note conceded that settlement classes pose special risks, but relied on notice, opt-out, and judicial oversight to control those risks.

Evidence of controversy appeared in Richard B. Schmitt, Plan for Class–Action Settlements Is Dividing Judges, Law Professors, Wall St.J., June 6, 1996, at B10, which covered an unusual letter to the rulemakers from 144 law professors concerned with civil procedure and disturbed by the proposed (b)(4). The letter contended: "This provision is flawed for three reasons: first, it contains no limiting principles, standards or guidelines, except the basic requirements of 23(a), to help trial judges decide when a settlement class is desirable and what form the class should take; second, it raises serious constitutional and statutory questions [under the Case or Controversy and Due Process Clauses and the Rules Enabling Act] that have not been adequately addressed by the Advisory Committee; and third, it lends official approval to an extremely controversial practice, one plagued by serious agency problems and risks of collusion, and threatens to make those problems worse by insisting that all settlements in settlement classes be negotiated before class certification is sought or approved by a court." The letter elaborated the last concern by noting that the "proposed Rule 23(b)(4) arguably licenses a regime under which plaintiffs' lawyers are encouraged to compete to sell-out the claims of people in order to gain the defendant's acquiescence to a (b)(4) class. The plaintiffs' lawyers cannot leverage the defendant into settling by threatening trial: by definition (b)(4) actions need not be triable. Thus, [we get the] lawyers most willing to collude with the defendant in exchange for an award of class counsel fees. . . . Given that a court's fairness judgment is so dependent on the joint petition of class counsel and the defendant and that objectors are rare and have limited information, to encourage such collusion only undermines the ability of courts to assess what it is they are being asked to approve in fairness hearings that are rarely true adversary proceedings."

In the wake of the Supreme Court's intervening Amchem decision, as distinguished from the professorial plea, the Advisory Committee abandoned its proposal for a new Rule 23(b)(4) settlement class.

The Advisory Committee next did nothing with Rule 23 for several years, allowing a body of class-action caselaw to develop through the immediate appeals of certification rulings under the new Rule 23(f). Then, the Committee again took up the task of drafting amendments to Rule 23. The Committee recommended the adoption of several modest amendments to Rule 23, which became effective in 2003.

The focus of these new amendments was the correction of perceived abuses in class-action practice, such as settlements that provide little of value to absent class members and attorney's fees that are unreasonably out of proportion to the benefit received by the class. As to settlements, the amendments to Rule 23(e) gave the court more control of the process. For example, the court has to make detailed findings that a settlement is "fair, reasonable, and adequate." In addition, express provision was made for the court's permitting (b)(3) class members to opt out of the settlement.

As to class counsel, new Rule 23(g) sets out appointment procedures, expressly requiring that counsel "fairly and adequately represent the interests of the class." New Rule 23(h) details procedures for the awarding of "reasonable" attorney's fees. These changes reflect the shift from a public law model to a big money paradigm.

In addition, Rule 23(c)(1)(A), which governs the court's decision to certify a class action, underwent amendment. The rulemakers felt some of these decisions were made too hastily and thus changed the required certification from "as soon as practicable" to "an early practicable time," so the court would take the time needed to make an informed decision on the question. Rule 23(c)(2), covering notice, was amended to require the notice to be in "plain, easily understood language."

CLASS–ACTION STATUTES

Surprisingly, several of these modest proposals generated loud debate. One concern, expressed primarily by defense counsel, was that as the federal courts tighten up class-action procedure, more class actions will be filed in the state courts where settlements and large fee awards may be easier to obtain. It was Congress that addressed this concern.

In 1998, Congress enacted the Securities Litigation Uniform Standards Act (SLUSA), Pub.L. No. 105–353, 112 Stat. 3227 (codified in scattered sections of 15 U.S.C.), to deal with similar class-action problems in a specialized area. See generally 7B Wright, Miller & Kane § 1806.

Then, Congress enacted the Class Action Fairness Act of 2005 (CAFA), Pub.L. No. 109–2, 119 Stat. 4 (codified in scattered sections of 28 U.S.C.), with a broader scope covering interstate class actions and the expressed intent of defeating plaintiff lawyers' manipulation of state courts. This major statute reaches widely enough to cover many of the cases within Rule 23. The statute's primary purpose was to adjust federal jurisdictional rules in order to funnel more class actions away from the state courts and into the federal courts. When President George W. Bush signed it into law on February 18, 2005, he declared that it "marks a critical step toward ending the lawsuit culture in our country." However, neither the cause of any malady nor the effectiveness of this cure is beyond debate. See generally 7A Wright, Miller & Kane § 1756.2.

The 2005 Act contained a few minor provisions aimed at curbing certain class-action abuses. Notably, by what is now 28 U.S.C. § 1712, Congress ratcheted up the judicial scrutiny to be applied to settlement terms, while limiting fee awards, in connection with settlements that provide for a recovery of discount coupons by class members. Much more important, however, was the Act's expansion of federal subject-matter jurisdiction for class actions.

In 28 U.S.C. § 1332(d), Congress bestowed original jurisdiction on the federal district courts for sizable multistate class actions, generally if there is minimal diversity between any plaintiff member of the class and any defendant and if the plaintiff class contains at least 100 members and their claims aggregated together exceed $5 million. By a complicated qualification, this jurisdiction does not extend to a class action in which two-thirds or more of the plaintiff members are citizens of the state where the action was filed and the primary defendants are also local citizens, or the case has certain other markers of a local controversy. If that fraction falls between one-third and two-thirds, and if the primary defendants are citizens of the state where the action was filed, the district court may discretionarily decline jurisdiction over what it sees as an essentially local case.

In 28 U.S.C. § 1453, Congress further provided that any defendant can remove a class action from state court to the local federal district court—only if the action would be within the original federal jurisdiction of § 1332(d), as one presumes in accordance with the clear legislative history but not with the statute's wording. The statute went on to provide that the removing defendant can be a local citizen and need not seek the consent of the other defendants.

All sorts of legal skirmishes and interpretive problems lay ahead for the parties and the courts: what is the meaning of "primary defendants" and the related formulations? how will the one-third and two-thirds numerical tests work, especially for ill-defined classes? See Symposium, Fairness to Whom? Perspectives on the Class Action Fairness Act of 2005, 156 U.Pa.L.Rev.1439 (2008). But consider the following illustrative problem that the Act did not address.

As already suggested, one of CAFA's central purposes was to get state class actions into federal court, where federal judges would supposedly take a more disciplined approach to class certification. Thus, the statute provides for removal to federal court of certain cases filed as class actions in state court under the state procedures. But what happens if, after removal, the federal judge does indeed deny class certification under Federal Rule 23: does the case stay in federal court or does that court dismiss for lack of federal jurisdiction?

Apparently, the denial of certification will not oust jurisdiction, because the court reached a determination that the case was a class action for jurisdictional purposes under a different and lower standard of proof than the determination that the case was not a class action for certification purposes. Some might find it illogical to apply a different meaning of "class action" for jurisdiction and for certification. But the logical fog dissipates upon expressing the difference in the required showings. For jurisdiction, the court may demand merely a good-faith allegation of a class action. For certification, the plaintiff must show by a preponderance that the case satisfies Federal Rule 23's requirements. Accordingly, the removed but uncertified case will normally stay in the federal court as an individual action until someone ushers it out, as by a voluntary dismissal.

And if the plaintiff refiles the case as a class action in state court, it is again subject to removal to federal court, where preclusion will presumably apply to both jurisdiction and certification issues. The bottom line, which is consonant with the drafters' purposes, is that an action within the statute's coverage that previously could have gone forward in state court as a class action can no longer proceed as a class action, even in state court, unless it meets federal certification requirements.[1]

---

[1] Interestingly, previous drafts of the Act had treated this problem, but the enacted version omitted that provision as part of a final compromise. For example, CAFA's 2003 bill, S. 274, 108th Cong. § 4(a)(2) (2003), discussed in S.Rep. No. 108–123 (2003), had provided:

"(A) A district court shall dismiss any civil action that is subject to the jurisdiction of the court solely under this subsection if the court determines the action may not proceed as a class action based on a failure to satisfy the requirements of rule 23 of the Federal Rules of Civil Procedure.

"(B) Nothing in subparagraph (A) shall prohibit plaintiffs from filing an amended class action in Federal court or filing an action in State court, except that any such action filed in State court may be removed to the appropriate district court if it is an action of which the district courts of the United States have original jurisdiction."

TOPIC D

INTERVENTION

In addition to these ways of joining parties or litigating on behalf of nonparties, there is the possibility that an outsider might want to join himself to a pending lawsuit. Intervention allows but again does not compel certain persons not named as a party to enter an existing lawsuit, coming in on the appropriate side of the litigation. But which persons should be able so to complicate or even commandeer a lawsuit of others? Alternatively viewed, when should those already litigants be allowed to litigate in the absence of persons who could be affected?

Part One introduced you to Rule 24's (a) intervention of right and (b) permissive intervention. The former is where the outsider's right most obviously clashes with an insider's. So, to begin, take a look at Rule 24(a) in substantially its original form and the Advisory Committee's note on the 1966 amendment in the Rules booklet. First, the former Rule allowed intervention of right to one whose representation by existing parties might be inadequate and who might be bound by the judgment. In Sam Fox Publishing Co. v. United States, 366 U.S. 683, 81 S.Ct. 1309 (1961), the Court held that this meant "legally bound" but that no one could be so bound if not "adequately represented," citing Hansberry v. Lee, supra p. 891. By thus making the dual requirements mutually contradictory, the Court's decision tended to nullify this portion of the Rule. Second, the former Rule allowed intervention of right to one who was so situated as to be adversely affected by a disposition of property subject to the control of the court. Surprisingly, courts interpreted this clause so broadly as to disregard the wording of the Rule. See, e.g., Formulabs, Inc. v. Hartley Pen Co., 275 F.2d 52 (9th Cir.1960).[a]

The rulemakers amended Rule 24(a) in 1966 to remedy these apparent problems. The amendment put a single test in place of those two former grounds for intervention of right. The change in the Rule paralleled the simultaneous revision of Rules 19 and 23. Indeed, the new language in Rule 24(a)(2) defining a person who may intervene of right, unless the person's interest is adequately represented, now appears in substantially the same words where Rule 19(a)(1)(B)(i) describes certain persons to be joined if feasible. Although they are not necessarily interpreted identically, both of these Rules emphasize the same pragmatic approach. Under the new Rule

[a] Both the former and the amended Rule allow intervention of right, under Rule 24(a)(1), when a federal statute confers an unconditional right to intervene. There are not many such statutes. The most significant one is 28 U.S.C. § 2403, which gives the United States or a state the right to intervene in a federal action wherein the constitutionality of one of its statutes is questioned.

24(a)(2), then, intervention of right lies where one claims an *interest* relating to the subject of the action and is so situated that disposition of the action may *as a practical matter impair* one's ability to protect that interest, and one's interest is *not adequately represented* by existing parties.

The new pragmatic approach to intervention of right has created considerable uncertainty as to the nature of the interest required. Soon after the amended Rule became effective, the Supreme Court gave it an expansive reading in Cascade Natural Gas Corp. v. El Paso Natural Gas Co., 386 U.S. 129, 87 S.Ct. 932 (1967). The Court had previously ordered divestiture of Pacific Northwest Pipeline Corporation by El Paso, after it had found that El Paso had acquired Pacific Northwest in violation of the antitrust laws. After remand to the district court, the Attorney General negotiated an agreement of settlement with those companies. Cascade, a distributor of natural gas that was solely supplied by Pacific Northwest, feared for the continuance of its supply under the settlement plan and sought to intervene for the purpose of contending that the plan did not comply with the Court's earlier mandate. The district court denied intervention and approved the settlement, but on appeal the Supreme Court held that Cascade had an interest entitling it to intervene of right. It was manifest that a majority of the Court was dissatisfied with the settlement negotiated by the Attorney General in carrying out the divestiture mandate, and the only way it could get at the issue, given that all the parties were content, was to allow intervention. Justice Stewart, joined in dissent by Justice Harlan, thought that the Court had "rushed headlong into a jurisprudential quagmire" by allowing persons to intervene whose interest was far too general and indefinite, and by upsetting the long-established body of decisions denying intervention in government antitrust litigation.

Subsequent cases have avoided that quagmire. They have given Cascade the familiar alternative to overruling: a statement that the case must be limited to its facts. And the Supreme Court itself, in Donaldson v. United States, 400 U.S. 517, 91 S.Ct. 534 (1971), held, without citing Cascade, that a taxpayer being investigated by the Internal Revenue Service was not entitled to intervene of right in proceedings to enforce subpoenas against his former employer and its accountant, saying that Rule 24(a)(2) obviously requires "a significantly protectable interest." Yet subsequent cases have limited Donaldson to its facts too.

Because the lower federal court cases have not exhibited any sense of clear direction either, they offer no unequivocal guidance for interpreting the term "interest." Courts probably should approach this term flexibly in light of the functions of intervention and in conjunction with the impairment and representation requirements. See, e.g., Smuck v. Hobson, 408 F.2d 175, 180 (D.C.Cir.1969) ("If barriers are needed to limit extension of the right to intervene, the criteria of practical harm to the applicant and the adequacy of representation by others are better suited to the task. If those requirements are met, the nature of his 'interest' may play a role in determining the sort of intervention which should be allowed—whether, for example, he should be permitted to contest all issues, and whether he should enjoy all the prerogatives of a party litigant.").

The required extent of "practical impairment" of the interest also remains unclear, although there has been some tendency to apply this requirement rather leniently. For example, can the stare decisis effect of a decision in the action be a sufficient impairment to warrant intervention of right? Atlantis Development Corp. v. United States, 379 F.2d 818 (5th Cir.1967), gave an affirmative answer to this question, but the case was qualified by the fact that the would-be intervenor claimed a very direct interest in the property and transaction that was the subject of the main action, viz., control over the outer continental shelf.

Finally, the requirement as to "inadequacy of representation" is a relatively lenient one. In Trbovich v. United Mine Workers, 404 U.S. 528, 92 S.Ct. 630 (1972), the Court allowed a union member to intervene of right in an action by the Secretary of Labor to set aside a union election, saying that "the [amended] Rule is satisfied if the applicant shows that representation of his interest 'may be' inadequate; and the burden of making that showing should be treated as minimal." As the Secretary must represent the public interest in free union elections as well as protect the rights of the union member, "the union member may have a valid complaint about the performance of 'his lawyer.' " Nevertheless, in appropriate circumstances this third requirement can block nonstatutory intervention of right.

Questions: (1) What is the relationship between Rule 24(a) and the other party Rules, especially Rules 19 and 23? See Atlantis Dev. Corp. v. United States, supra. And what is the relationship between Rule 24(b) and the other party Rules, especially Rules 20 and 23? Indeed, what is the relationship of Rule 24(a) to Rule 24(b)? Should the existence of Rule 24(b) affect the reading of Rule 24(a)?

(2) What is the extent of an intervenor's right of participation? May the intervenor assert additional claims within the court's jurisdiction, engage in discovery, examine witnesses, appeal from an adverse decision? Does it matter whether the intervention is permissive under Rule 24(b) or of right under Rule 24(a)? Does the question always have to be answered the same way without regard to the circumstances of the particular case? See David L. Shapiro, Some Thoughts on Intervention Before Courts, Agencies, and Arbitrators, 81 Harv.L.Rev. 721 (1968).

(3) What is the extent of an intervenor's exposure? May the intervenor be subject to additional counterclaims and crossclaims within the court's jurisdiction or to full discovery like a party? May the intervenor be liable for the attorney's fees of an opponent? See Independent Fed'n of Flight Attendants v. Zipes, 491 U.S. 754, 109 S.Ct. 2732 (1989) (usually not liable for fees).

Emma Coleman Jones, Litigation Without Representation: The Need for Intervention to Affirm Affirmative Action

14 Harv.C.R.-C.L.L.Rev. 31, 31–34, 38–40, 42–44, 86–87 (1979).

When Allan Bakke went to court to challenge affirmative action and to secure an order for his admission to the University of California at Davis Medical School, no party in the suit directly represented the interests of minority applicants, who would be most affected by an unsuccessful defense of the University's race-conscious admission program. The University chose to defend its voluntary program as designed to serve general societal purposes without reference to its own arguably discriminatory practices. As a result, significant minority interests were imperiled.

The lack of minority participation in Regents of the University of California v. Bakke[, 438 U.S. 265, 98 S.Ct. 2733 (1978),] does not reflect a conscious effort by the University to exclude minorities from the litigation, but it does reflect a notable structural deficiency inherent in virtually all affirmative action litigation. . . .

. . . .

Intervention was sought [unsuccessfully by the NAACP in Bakke]. Although, due to narrow application, traditional notions of intervention have thus far failed to protect minority interests, intervention retains great potential for safeguarding those interests in affirmative action litigation. However, full realization of this potential requires recognition of liberalized intervention standards in this context. The intervention question in Bakke arose under a state provision; this Article, however, will focus on current intervention doctrine in the federal courts, as developed under rule 24 of the Federal Rules of Civil Procedure. . . .

. . . .

Intervention, a relatively recent development in our civil procedure,[24] runs counter to the traditional Anglo–American view of private law litigation. In part, this tradition assumed that litigation typically consisted of two individuals asserting directly opposed interests. Moreover, the plaintiff, as the "master of his suit," was largely allowed to control who would be included in the litigation. Hence, intervention was seldom available, and where it was granted it was simply a method to augment, on either side of the controversy, what remained essentially two antagonistic interests.

. . . .

Suits which challenge affirmative action programs do not fit the traditional private litigation model. The Bakke case illustrates this proposi-

[24] In early equity practice intervention not governed by statute was allowed. See Moore & Levi, Federal Intervention: I. The Right to Intervene and Reorganization, 45 Yale L.J. 565, 570–72 (1936). Moore and Levi describe the device of an examination pro interesse suo, which was granted to any third party claiming an interest in property under the control of the court. This procedure was the only method whereby such a party could secure protection during the pendency of the dispute.

tion all too clearly. Although Allan Bakke sued as an individual and named only the Regents of the University of California as defendants, many present and future applicants to the Davis Medical School were directly affected by the results of the suit. Other persons, such as minority men and women unable to obtain proper medical care, were similarly affected by the litigation. Far more than an individual's claim to admission was at stake; the case signified a major challenge to all affirmative action programs. Constitutional and statutory provisions of vital significance were debated and interpreted in Bakke in the light of overriding public policies and constitutional principles. . . .

. . . .

Although the policies underlying intervention vary, they may be summarized as follows. First, intervention serves the goal of judicial economy by the consolidation of related issues into a single suit. Intervenors are welcomed into a pending lawsuit when to do so would prevent proliferation of similar litigation or discourage piecemeal adjudication. Of course, the possibility of increased complexity resulting from intervention may undercut the potential for real judicial economy. Second, intervention can prevent injury to nonparties whose interests bear a sufficiently close connection to the matter being litigated. Although protecting the interests of outsiders was a major theme underlying the early grants of intervention, it has become even more important today. In public law litigation, with its frequent objective of reordering prominent social policies and institutions, nonparties must be protected from the ever-widening impact of such lawsuits. Finally, intervention often expands the information available to a court in its search for an equitable adjudication of the merits of the lawsuit. In particular, this third rationale would seem to justify expansive participation in the efforts to shape a suitable remedy. These reasons for permitting intervention are more compatible with public law litigation than with the private law model; accordingly, intervention should be viewed more liberally in the public law context.

Most of the current wave of challenges to affirmative action have been litigated as though they were private controversies. In the usual scenario, minority interests are excluded by default. The typical "reverse discrimination" plaintiff has no interest in pursuing the suit as a group action, preferring instead to challenge the program by asserting an individual right to the benefit in question. More important, the typical defendants are in a position of ethical and legal conflict and have no incentive to broaden the controversy. If the program was voluntarily instituted, its defense, it is reasoned, must be a defense of the right to continue such voluntary remediation of a general societal problem. To bring in minority representatives would only raise the issue of the defendant's prior discrimination with attendant embarrassment and potential liability. Finally, with both parties content to portray the dispute as a limited, private one, judges are conditioned by neither training nor experience to search for powers, which they may indeed possess, to ensure that the entire spectrum of interests affected by the action are duly represented. Paradoxically, then, an examination into the adequacy of the representation of all the interests in this type of litigation only begins when a volunteer with sufficient resources seeks to intervene. In effect, the parties are litigating a de facto class action without any of its procedural safeguards.

[Professor Jones (now Jordan) argues at length that in the circumstances of the Bakke case a minority applicant for admission to the medical school, or an organization representing such applicants, should henceforth be deemed to come within the terms of Rule 24(a)(2). In particular, she identifies three impaired and inadequately represented interests: (1) the interest in competing for every available admissions slot, (2) the interest in securing corrective measures to remedy past or present discrimination by the university, and (3) the interest in keeping alive the concept of voluntary affirmative action.]

Minorities must have direct representation in affirmative action litigation, and nonstatutory intervention of right under rule 24(a)(2) can serve as the vehicle by which such representation can be achieved. There are still unanswered questions: How can the representativeness of self-appointed minority intervenors be insured? Which minority groups should be represented? If intervention is permitted, should the intervenors be granted full participation rights or given a limited role? While these are important and perplexing questions, it is reasonable to expect that courts will find workable answers to them by experimentation in future cases. The fundamental message should not be obscured in the search for those answers: procedural barriers must not be erected that frustrate minorities' legitimate expectation that they will be able to participate in litigation which affects their basic interests.

What has been proposed will hopefully lay the foundation for a solution which serves as a call to bring intervention practice and theory into line with present day exigencies. Burgeoning public law litigation demands pluralistic participation in the formulation of judicial decisions on issues which affect large numbers of citizens and concern fundamental legal and political rights. What remains to be seen is whether the courts will respond appropriately to end litigation without representation.

Jack H. Friedenthal, Increased Participation by Non–Parties: The Need for Limitations and Conditions

13 U.C.Davis L.Rev. 259, 261–63 (1980).

[After observing that an expansive approach to intervention would be difficult to confine to any particular kinds of cases and that expansion of permissive intervention would seem the sounder course, Professor Friedenthal considers expanding the application of Rule 24(a)(2) in affirmative action suits:]

If new, broader rules of participation are to be adopted, more emphasis should be placed on how they are to be limited, rather than on when they should automatically apply. Just because a case is of great interest in the community, broad intervention is not justified. Only when it is clear that the rights of persons outside the case are directly at stake should the action be expanded to include them. Courts that go beyond that narrow compass are in danger of becoming quasi-legislative bodies, a development which raises a myriad of theoretical and practical questions.

Are the courts in such cases to hold "town meetings"? How can any interested citizen be excluded from presenting his or her point of view, or even from calling witnesses? . . .

The Bakke case . . . is a good example of an action in which a broad expansion could have caused serious difficulties. Virtually every applicant to medical school, regardless of his or her race, had an interest in the outcome of that suit. Indeed, every applicant or potential applicant to law school or other professional school had an important interest. In a sense, every citizen of California or even of the United States had a stake in the result.

As Professor Jones has noted, the interests of minority applicants were not represented. As her excellent article points out, their intervention would not have been proper under existing rules. But the interests of non-minority applicants were also unrepresented. Certainly Allan Bakke did not have any intention to provide such representation. From his perspective the result was ideal, but that is far from true from the perspective of other non-minority professional school applicants.

If Professor Jones is correct that minority applicants should have been permitted to intervene, wouldn't the judge also have been required to permit intervention by non-minorities? Where is the line to be drawn? Who is to be precluded from making argument or offering what he or she considers to be "vital" evidence?

The Bakke case is a particularly important example because the decision is not as broad as advertised, and does not necessarily preclude minority applicants from arguing in favor of affirmative action plans in future suits. The issue most discussed in regard to lack of representation is that of past discrimination on the part of the University of California. Bakke had no reason to raise the issue as it could only have worked against him, and the University was obviously not going to admit that it engaged in any such improper activity. So that issue, on which the decision might well have turned, was never presented.

But so what? The next person who brings a similar suit—for example a minority student who challenges rejection of his or her medical school application—can raise the issue of past discrimination and, if it is proven, can prevail regardless of Bakke. Only to the extent that issues cannot subsequently be raised, or when the result of the case will necessarily lead the parties to actions that will not be subject to subsequent challenge, should new broad rules of non-party participation be applicable.

Finally, the courts must pay careful attention to the rights of the original litigants before deciding to allow outsiders into the suit. An individual, such as Bakke, who merely wants to be accepted to medical school, and is not out to set a precedent or vindicate the rights of anyone else through use of a class action, should be given every fair chance to control his own lawsuit.

Such an individual will often have limited resources. As a result, he may enter into a number of stipulations just to reduce the potential costs and allow him to concentrate on key issues that will provide the relief he seeks. But what appears to be a very good chance of victory may be swept away if the court then allows all sorts of interested outsiders to enter the case and raise not only the issues as to which stipulations were made, but a host of others as well. The original party may have insufficient funds to engage in additional discovery, hire necessary experts, and search for evidence to meet these new issues.

It would therefore seem appropriate as an integral part of any new statute or rule allowing broad participation of non-parties to require those who enter the case to pay the additional costs and attorney fees reasonably necessary for the original parties to deal with such new issues. Not only would such a provision protect the original parties' interests, it would also help to assure that those who enter a case will not do so frivolously.

Questions: (4) To what extent, if any, does the Due Process Clause dictate a right to intervene?

(5) Recall the suggestion, made but not passed on by the Supreme Court in the Provident Tradesmens case, supra p. 879, that Dutcher might be bound by the decision because he had purposely bypassed an adequate opportunity to intervene. Recall also the appellees' argument in Gonzales v. Cassidy, supra p. 906, that Gonzales should be estopped by his failure to intervene in the earlier class action. When, if ever, should the opportunity to intervene be treated as a duty? Is this the solution that will satisfy our desire to handle a mass tort in a single proceeding? See Martin v. Wilks, 490 U.S. 755, 109 S.Ct. 2180 (1989) (no duty exists, in Title VII suit); cf. Restatement (Second) of Judgments § 62 (1982).

Civil Rights Act of 1991

Pub.L. No. 102–166, tit. I, § 108, 105 Stat. 1071, 1076.

Section 703 [of Title VII] of the Civil Rights Act of 1964 (42 U.S.C. 2000e–2) (as amended by sections 105, 106, and 107 of this title) is further amended by adding at the end the following new subsection:

"(n)(1)(A) Notwithstanding any other provision of law, and except as provided in paragraph (2), an employment practice that implements and is within the scope of a litigated or consent judgment or order that resolves a claim of employment discrimination under the Constitution or Federal civil rights laws may not be challenged under the circumstances described in subparagraph (B).

"(B) A practice described in subparagraph (A) may not be challenged in a claim under the Constitution or Federal civil rights laws—

"(i) by a person who, prior to the entry of the judgment or order described in subparagraph (A), had—

"(I) actual notice of the proposed judgment or order sufficient to apprise such person that such judgment or order might adversely affect the interests and legal rights of such person and that an opportunity was available to present objections to such judgment or order by a future date certain; and

"(II) a reasonable opportunity to present objections to such judgment or order; or

"(ii) by a person whose interests were adequately represented by another person who had previously challenged the judgment or order on the same legal grounds and with a similar factual situation, unless there has been an intervening change in law or fact.

"(2) Nothing in this subsection shall be construed to—

"(A) alter the standards for intervention under rule 24 of the Federal Rules of Civil Procedure or apply to the rights of parties who have successfully intervened pursuant to such rule in the proceeding in which the parties intervened;

"(B) apply to the rights of parties to the action in which a litigated or consent judgment or order was entered, or of members of a class represented or sought to be represented in such action, or of members of a group on whose behalf relief was sought in such action by the Federal Government;

"(C) prevent challenges to a litigated or consent judgment or order on the ground that such judgment or order was obtained through collusion or fraud, or is transparently invalid or was entered by a court lacking subject matter jurisdiction; or

"(D) authorize or permit the denial to any person of the due process of law required by the Constitution.

"(3) Any action not precluded under this sub that challenges an employment consent judgment or order described in paragraph (1) shall be brought in the court, and if possible before the judge, that entered such judgment or order. Nothing in this subsection shall preclude a transfer of such action pursuant to section 1404 of title 28, United States Code.".

MCI v. Logan Group, Inc.

United States District Court, Northern District of Texas, 1994.
848 F.Supp. 86.

■ MAHON, DISTRICT JUDGE.

. . . .

MCI Telecommunications Corporation ("MCI") filed this action in August 1991. The complaint alleged that defendants, The Logan Group, Inc. and Communication Specialties, Inc. ("CSI"), had failed to pay for telephone services MCI provided. Defendants counterclaimed, alleging that MCI had erred in its billing of the services provided. In addition, defendants asserted that MCI had willfully failed to pay money collected by MCI and owed to defendant CSI on a separate "900 Service," as a result of which CSI's business suffered consequential damages. In response, MCI denied billing defendants improperly and alleged that the "900 Service" addressed in the counterclaim was governed by a contract requiring arbitration of any disputes arising out of the "900 Service."

In February 1993, Fidelity filed an unopposed motion for leave to intervene in the action to assert claims against MCI. Fidelity alleged that it had been assigned certain of CSI's accounts receivable on the "900 Service" and had informed MCI of the assignment. Fidelity further alleged that prior to purchasing a particular account receivable, it requested and received verification from MCI that the account was owing and would be paid, yet MCI subsequently refused to pay the account on the ground that an unrelated party, Technical Resources, Inc., owed MCI money. Based on these facts, Fidelity asserted claims for fraud and breach of contract. Fidelity's brief in support of the motion to intervene stated that it was entitled to intervention of right under Fed.R.Civ.P. 24(a) because it would not be able to protect its interest in the account receivable unless it intervened in this action. Although the Court was not persuaded that Fidelity met the requirements of intervention of right, since the parties did not oppose the intervention and it appeared that Fidelity's claim had at least one question of fact in common with the main action, the Court permitted Fidelity to intervene.

In January 1994, Fidelity moved for leave to file an amended complaint in intervention. In reviewing the original and proposed amended complaints, the Court noted that Fidelity's only asserted basis of jurisdiction was 28 U.S.C. § 1331, the federal question statute. Fidelity's claims were based on state law, however. In addition, although the pleadings established that MCI and defendants were diverse in citizenship, Fidelity did not allege its state of incorporation, but only its principal place of business. The Court therefore ordered Fidelity to show a proper basis for federal jurisdiction over its claims in intervention.

. . . .

Fidelity admits there is no diversity between MCI and itself because both are incorporated in Delaware. . . .

Nevertheless, Fidelity contends that the Court has supplemental jurisdiction over its claims pursuant to 28 U.S.C. § 1367. [The court here quoted § 1367.] Fidelity argues that its claims against MCI are sufficiently related to those in the original action to bring it within the terms of subsection (a). Further, while it is undisputed that the Court has original jurisdiction over this action based solely on diversity, Fidelity claims it is not an intervening plaintiff excluded from supplemental jurisdiction by subsection (b), but instead has intervened as a defendant.

Fidelity bases its position that it is an intervening defendant rather than plaintiff on the practice, followed by courts in reviewing diversity jurisdiction, of aligning parties according to their side of the dispute. [Citation omitted.] See also Zurn Industries, Inc. v. Acton Construction Co., 847 F.2d 234, 236 (5th Cir.1988). Because Fidelity's claims arise out of an account receivable assigned to it by CSI, a defendant, Fidelity argues that it must be considered a defendant, asserting a defense that would otherwise belong to CSI. Fidelity also suggests that jurisdiction exists for its claims because it is an intervenor as of right.

Fidelity's arguments are in error in several respects. Initially, as Zurn makes clear, realignment of parties for diversity purposes is done only with respect to the "primary and controlling matter in dispute" and does not include counterclaims of the defendants. Id. at 237. Only after diversity jurisdiction is found on the primary claim does a court examine other claims in the action to determine if they are supported by ancillary (now supplemental) jurisdiction or by an independent basis of jurisdiction. Id. Here, MCI's original claim was to collect money for telephone services provided to the defendants. Fidelity did not receive those services, had no responsibility for paying for them and has not disputed those services in this case. Therefore, even under the realignment procedure upon which it relies, Fidelity cannot be characterized as a defendant with respect to the primary claim in this action.

Moreover, the Court is of the opinion that whether Fidelity is an intervening plaintiff for purposes of supplemental jurisdiction must be determined not by the alignment principles of diversity, but by examining why section 1367(b) excludes intervening plaintiffs from supplemental jurisdiction when the sole basis of original jurisdiction is diversity of citizenship. Traditionally, ancillary jurisdiction was exercised when the original claims in an action were supported solely by diversity jurisdiction, to adjudicate related state law claims "by a defending party haled into court against his will, or by another person whose rights might be irretrievably lost unless he could assert them in an ongoing action in a federal court." Owen Equip. & Erection Co. v. Kroger, 437 U.S. 365, 376, 98 S.Ct. 2396, 2404, 57 L.Ed.2d 274 (1978). However, parties who chose a federal rather than a state forum to assert state law claims were not permitted to use ancillary jurisdiction to circumvent the requirement of complete diversity. Id. at 376–77, 98 S.Ct. at 2403–04. Thus, while named plaintiffs were barred from relying on ancillary jurisdiction, so too were parties such as permissive intervenors who, like plaintiffs, voluntarily chose to litigate their claims in the federal forum. See, e.g., Mothersill D.I.S.C. Corp. v. Petroleos Mexicanos, S.A., 831 F.2d 59, 61–63 (5th Cir.1987); Blake v. Pallan, 554 F.2d 947, 955–56 (9th Cir.1977).

While there are no cases addressing this exact issue, section 1367(b), enacted on December 1, 1990, appears intended to continue these previously established rules. [Citation omitted.] Accordingly, the Court concludes that an intervening "plaintiff" within the terms of section 1367(b) is a party who voluntarily chooses to intervene in an ongoing federal action to assert its own affirmative claims. By contrast, non-plaintiff intervenors entitled to supplemental jurisdiction for their claims are those who must intervene to defend or protect interests put in issue by the federal action and likely to be lost without the party's intervention.[2]

Applying these principles, it appears that Fidelity is a plaintiff with regard to its intervention. That is, Fidelity's complaint in intervention consists of affirmative claims for monetary relief that could have been brought just as easily in a separate state court action. Further, despite Fidelity's conclusory contention that it must intervene in this case to protect its rights in the account receivable it purchased from CSI, the Court can see no way in which the outcome of the original parties' claims will have a binding effect on Fidelity or otherwise prejudice its rights.

Fidelity's claims are based not on its derivative rights arising from the assignment of CSI's account receivable, but on independent interactions that occurred between MCI and Fidelity. Specifically, Fidelity alleges that (1) there was a contract between MCI and itself requiring payment by MCI and (2) MCI fraudulently misrepresented that it would pay Fidelity a certain account receivable. Fidelity's proposed amended complaint amplifies upon its relationship with MCI, adding claims of promissory estoppel and equitable estoppel based on MCI's alleged representation that it would pay Fidelity for the account receivable at issue. These claims are unrelated to MCI's claim against defendants. More specifically, Fidelity's claims are not, as it suggests, defenses to MCI's claim. Nor are Fidelity's claims related to or contingent upon Defendant CSI's counterclaim against MCI. Instead, Fidelity's claims are entirely independent of the other claims in this action, requiring the determination of other facts and relying on different legal precepts. Resolution of MCI's and defendants' claims and counterclaims will have no bearing on the claims asserted by Fidelity in this case. Under these circumstances, the Court concludes that Fidelity is in effect a cross-plaintiff for purposes of its intervention. As such, Fidelity is excluded from supplemental jurisdiction under section 1367(b).

For the same reasons, the Court also concludes Fidelity is not . . . an intervenor of right. . . .

---

[2] Fidelity argues that if asserting affirmative claims makes an intervening party a plaintiff, then all intervenors would be plaintiffs excluded from supplemental jurisdiction by section 1367(b), and section 1367(a)'s reference to supplemental jurisdiction over intervenors would be meaningless. A review of cases where intervention of right has been granted, however, shows that parties may intervene for purposes other than asserting affirmative claims. For example, in Ceres Gulf v. Cooper, 957 F.2d 1199 (5th Cir.1992), the Director, Office of Workers' Compensation Programs, intervened in an action regarding benefits under the Longshore and Harbor Workers' Compensation Act in order to protect his administrative jurisdiction over claims under the Act and his ability to interpret the relevant law. In Thurman v. FDIC, 889 F.2d 1441 (5th Cir.1989), an action by borrowers challenging the validity of two promissory notes, the FDIC in its corporate capacity was permitted to intervene in order to defend the notes, which it had acquired subsequent to the commencement of the action, against allegations of fraud and usury.

The Court regrets that its resolution of the jurisdictional issue has come only after Fidelity has incurred time and expense in this action. It was Fidelity's choice, however, to voluntarily intervene in this case . . . . Accordingly, only after the Court examined the parties' claims more carefully did the jurisdictional problem emerge.

. . . DISMISSED without prejudice. . . .

Questions: (6) To the prevailing view that supplemental jurisdiction extends to defendant intervenors of right, there is "one long-established exception": for an intervenor within Rule 24(a) who is otherwise an indispensable party under Rule 19(b), "the ancillary concept cannot be invoked." 7C Wright, Miller & Kane § 1917, at 597–98; see also 7 id. § 1610. Does this exception make any sense? See Richard D. Freer, Rethinking Compulsory Joinder: A Proposal to Restructure Federal Rule 19, 60 N.Y.U.L.Rev. 1061, 1087 n.126 (1985).

(7) If in a plaintiff-class action a member of the class intervenes under Rule 24, should she be required to show independent jurisdictional grounds? See 7A Wright, Miller & Kane § 1755 (no by policy, but yes by words of § 1367(b)).

TOPIC E

INTERPLEADER

Part One explained that interpleader allows a person to avoid the risk of multiple liability by requiring two or more persons with actual or prospective claims against him to assert their respective adverse claims in a single action. How else might that person proceed?

Questions: (1) Bank has a deposit account in the name of *X*. *Y* says *X* has assigned the whole account to her and calls for payment. May Bank safely disregard *Y*'s claim? (Consider this set of questions to arise in the absence of banking regulation. In fact, there is considerable legislation and administration on the duties of banks in these situations.)

(2) *Y* instead says the account consists of money that *X* embezzled from her (e.g., the fruit of the embezzlement was a check from *Y* to *X*, deposited in Bank by *X*). May Bank safely disregard *Y*'s claim?

(3) Suppose in Case #1 or Case #2 that Bank investigates with due care and pays out to *X*, ignoring *Y*. May Bank defend successfully on that basis when sued by *Y*?

(4) Suppose that Bank awaits an action by *Y*. *Y* wins, and Bank pays *Y*. May Bank successfully assert this payment if *X* later demands payment?

(5) When *Y* sues, may Bank implead *X*? Instead, if Bank notifies *X* and offers *X* control of the defense, will *X* then be bound by the result of the action by *Y* versus Bank?

(6) In an action by *Y* versus Bank, may Bank successfully move to join *X* as a party needed for just adjudication?

(7) After *Y* makes demand, may Bank join *X* and *Y* in an action for declaratory judgment to determine which is entitled to the account? Upon an action by *Y* versus Bank, may Bank counterclaim, joining *X* and seeking a declaration?

(8) In an action by *Y* versus Bank, may *Y* join *X* as an additional party defendant?

(9) May *Y* commence an action for interpleader, joining Bank and *X*?

(10) After *Y* makes demand, Bank tries to commence an interpleader action in a state court. Suppose *Y* is a resident, but *X* is not. May Bank proceed?

New York Life Insurance Co. v. Dunlevy

Supreme Court of the United States, 1916.
241 U.S. 518, 36 S.Ct. 613.

■ MR. JUSTICE MCREYNOLDS delivered the opinion of the court.

Respondent, Effie J. Gould Dunlevy, instituted this suit in the Superior Court, Marin County, California, January 14, 1910, against petitioner and

Joseph W. Gould, her father, to recover $2,479.70, the surrender value of a policy on his life which she claimed had been assigned to her in 1893, and both were duly served with process while in that State. It was removed to the United States District Court, February 16, 1910, and there tried by the judge in May, 1912, a jury having been expressly waived. Judgment for amount claimed was affirmed by the Circuit Court of Appeals. 204 F. 670, 214 F. 1.

The insurance company by an amended answer filed December 7, 1911, set up in defense (1) that no valid assignment had been made, and (2) that Mrs. Dunlevy was concluded by certain judicial proceedings in Pennsylvania wherein it had been garnished and the policy had been adjudged to be the property of Gould. Invalidity of the assignment is not now urged; but it is earnestly insisted that the Pennsylvania proceedings constituted a bar.

In 1907 Boggs & Buhl recovered a valid personal judgment by default, after domiciliary service, against Mrs. Dunlevy, in the Common Pleas Court at Pittsburgh, where she then resided. During 1909, "the tontine dividend period" of the life policy having expired, the insurance company became liable for $2,479.70 and this sum was claimed both by Gould, a citizen of Pennsylvania, and his daughter, who had removed to California. In November, 1909, Boggs & Buhl caused issue of an execution attachment on their judgment and both the insurance company and Gould were summoned as garnishees. He appeared, denied assignment of the policy and claimed the full amount due thereon. On February 5, 1910,—after this suit was begun in California—the company answered, admitted its indebtedness, set up the conflicting claims to the fund and prayed to be advised as to its rights. At the same time it filed a petition asking for a rule upon the claimants to show cause why they should not interplead and thereby ascertain who was lawfully entitled to the proceeds and further that it might be allowed to pay amount due into court for benefit of proper party. An order granted the requested rule and directed that notice be given to Mrs. Dunlevy in California. This was done, but she made no answer and did not appear. Later the insurance company filed a second petition, and, upon leave obtained thereunder, paid $2,479.70 into court, March 21, 1910. All parties except Mrs. Dunlevy having appeared, a feigned issue was framed and tried to determine validity of alleged transfer of the policy. The jury found, October 1, 1910, there was no valid assignment and thereupon under an order of court the fund was paid over to Gould.

Beyond doubt, without the necessity of further personal service of process upon Mrs. Dunlevy, the Court of Common Pleas at Pittsburgh had ample power through garnishment proceedings to inquire whether she held a valid claim against the insurance company and if found to exist then to condemn and appropriate it so far as necessary to discharge the original judgment. Although herself outside the limits of the State such disposition of the property would have been binding on her. Chicago, R.I. & P. Ry. v. Sturm, 174 U.S. 710, 19 S.Ct. 797; Harris v. Balk, 198 U.S. 215, 226, 227,

25 S.Ct. 625, 628; Louisville & Nashville R.R. v. Deer, 200 U.S. 176, 26 S.Ct. 207; Baltimore & Ohio R.R. v. Hostetter, 240 U.S. 620, 36 S.Ct. 475; Shinn on Attachment and Garnishment, § 707. See Brigham v. Fayerweather, 140 Mass. 411, 413. But the interpleader initiated by the company was an altogether different matter. This was an attempt to bring about a final and conclusive adjudication of her personal rights, not merely to discover property and apply it to debts. And unless in contemplation of law she was before the court and required to respond to that issue, its orders and judgments in respect thereto were not binding on her. Pennoyer v. Neff, 95 U.S. 714; Shinn on Attachment and Garnishment, § 674. See Cross v. Armstrong, 44 Oh.St. 613, 623, 625.

[The Court held that in these circumstances there was no continuing jurisdiction over Mrs. Dunlevy based on the concluded 1907 action.]

It has been affirmatively held in Pennsylvania that a judgment debtor is not a party to a garnishment proceeding to condemn a claim due him from a third person and is not bound by a judgment discharging the garnishee (Ruff v. Ruff, 85 Pa. 333); and this is the generally accepted doctrine. Shinn on Attachment and Garnishment, § 725. Former opinions of this court uphold validity of such proceedings upon the theory that jurisdiction to condemn is acquired by service of effective process upon the garnishee.

The established general rule is that any personal judgment which a state court may render against one who did not voluntarily submit to its jurisdiction, and who is not a citizen of the State, nor served with process within its borders, no matter what the mode of service, is void, because the court had no jurisdiction over his person. Pennoyer v. Neff, supra; Freeman on Judgments, 4th ed., § 120a; Black on Judgments, 2d ed., §§ 904 and 905.

We are of opinion that the proceedings in the Pennsylvania court constituted no bar to the action in California and the judgment below is accordingly

Affirmed.

Question: (11) Would Dunlevy be decided in the same way today? That is, could Pennsylvania exercise jurisdiction either quasi in rem or in personam?

FEDERAL LEGISLATION

The Dunlevy decision, emphasizing the narrow limits on the power of state courts to deal with out-of-state claimants, gave impetus to federal interpleader legislation. The first federal act, applicable only to claims against insurance companies and aimed simply to cure the immediate Dunlevy problem, came a year after the decision. The culmination, largely the work of Professor Zechariah Chafee,[a] was the Federal Interpleader Act of 1936, ch. 13, 49 Stat. 1096. That statute, with some minor changes, is now distributed in title 28 of the United States Code. Read §§ 1335, 1397, and 2361.

Also reexamine Rule 22(a). This provision was not intended to change the rules of jurisdiction and venue, but rather to preserve and liberalize the old equitable remedy of interpleader as a supplement to statutory interpleader in the federal courts. See Rule 22(b).

State Farm Fire & Casualty Co. v. Tashire

Supreme Court of the United States, 1967.
386 U.S. 523, 87 S.Ct. 1199.

■ MR. JUSTICE FORTAS delivered the opinion of the Court.

Early one September morning in 1964, a Greyhound bus proceeding northward through Shasta County, California, collided with a southbound pickup truck. Two of the passengers aboard the bus were killed. Thirty-three others were injured, as were the bus driver, the driver of the truck and its lone passenger. One of the dead and 10 of the injured passengers were Canadians; the rest of the individuals involved were citizens of five American States. The ensuing litigation led to the present case, which raises important questions concerning administration of the interpleader remedy in the federal courts.

The litigation began when four of the injured passengers filed suit in California state courts, seeking damages in excess of $1,000,000. Named as defendants were Greyhound Lines, Inc., a California corporation; Theron Nauta, the bus driver; Ellis Clark, who drove the truck; and Kenneth Glasgow, the passenger in the truck who was apparently its owner as well. Each of the individual defendants was a citizen and resident of Oregon. Before these cases could come to trial and before other suits were filed in California or elsewhere, petitioner, State Farm Fire & Casualty Company, an Illinois corporation, brought this action in the nature of interpleader in the United States District Court for the District of Oregon.

In its complaint State Farm asserted that at the time of the Shasta County collision it had in force an insurance policy with respect to Ellis Clark, driver of the truck, providing for bodily injury liability up to $10,000 per person and $20,000 per occurrence and for legal representation of Clark in actions covered by the policy. It asserted that actions already filed in California and others which it anticipated would be filed far exceeded in

---

[a] The classic writings on interpleader are by Professor Chafee: Modernizing Interpleader, 30 Yale L.J. 814 (1921); Interstate Interpleader, 33 Yale L.J. 685 (1924); Interpleader in the United States Courts (pts. 1–2), 41 Yale L.J. 1134 (1932), 42 Yale L.J. 41 (1932); The Federal Interpleader Act of 1936 (pts. 1–2), 45 Yale L.J. 963, 1161 (1936); Federal Interpleader Since the Act of 1936, 49 Yale L.J. 377 (1940); Broadening the Second Stage of Interpleader, 56 Harv.L.Rev. 541 (1943); Broadening the Second Stage of Federal Interpleader, 56 Harv.L.Rev. 929 (1943).

aggregate damages sought the amount of its maximum liability under the policy. Accordingly, it paid into court the sum of $20,000 and asked the court (1) to require all claimants to establish their claims against Clark and his insurer in this single proceeding and in no other, and (2) to discharge State Farm from all further obligations under its policy—including its duty to defend Clark in lawsuits arising from the accident. Alternatively, State Farm expressed its conviction that the policy issued to Clark excluded from coverage accidents resulting from his operation of a truck which belonged to another and was being used in the business of another. The complaint, therefore, requested that the court decree that the insurer owed no duty to Clark and was not liable on the policy, and it asked the court to refund the $20,000 deposit.

Joined as defendants were Clark, Glasgow, Nauta, Greyhound Lines, and each of the prospective claimants. Jurisdiction was predicated upon 28 U.S.C. § 1335, the federal interpleader statute, and upon general diversity of citizenship, there being diversity between two or more of the claimants to the fund and between State Farm and all of the named defendants.

An order issued, requiring each of the defendants to show cause why it should not be restrained from filing or prosecuting "any proceeding in any state or United States Court affecting the property or obligation involved in this interpleader action, and specifically against the plaintiff and the defendant Ellis D. Clark." Personal service was effected on each of the American defendants, and registered mail was employed to reach the 11 Canadian claimants. Defendants Nauta, Greyhound, and several of the injured passengers responded, contending that the policy did cover this accident and advancing various arguments for the position that interpleader was either impermissible or inappropriate in the present circumstances. Greyhound, however, soon switched sides and moved that the court broaden any injunction to include Nauta and Greyhound among those who could not be sued except within the confines of the interpleader proceeding.

When a temporary injunction along the lines sought by State Farm was issued by the United States District Court for the District of Oregon, the present respondents moved to dismiss the action and, in the alternative, for a change of venue—to the Northern District of California, in which district the collision had occurred. After a hearing, the court declined to dissolve the temporary injunction, but continued the motion for a change of venue. The injunction was later broadened to include the protection sought by Greyhound, but modified to permit the filing—although not the prosecution—of suits. The injunction, therefore, provided that all suits against Clark, State Farm, Greyhound, and Nauta be prosecuted in the interpleader proceeding.

On interlocutory appeal,[2] the Court of Appeals for the Ninth Circuit reversed, 363 F.2d 7. The court found it unnecessary to reach respondents' contentions relating to service of process and the scope of the injunction, for it concluded that interpleader was not available in the circumstances of

[2] 28 U.S.C. § 1292(a)(1).

this case. It held that in States like Oregon which do not permit "direct action" suits against the insurance company until judgments are obtained against the insured, the insurance company may not invoke federal interpleader until the claims against the insured, the alleged tortfeasor, have been reduced to judgment. Until that is done, said the court, claimants with unliquidated tort claims are not "claimants" within the meaning of § 1335, nor are they "[p]ersons having claims against the plaintiff" within the meaning of Rule 22 of the Federal Rules of Civil Procedure.[3] Id., at 10. In accord with that view, it directed dissolution of the temporary injunction and dismissal of the action. Because the Court of Appeals' decision on this point conflicts with those of other federal courts, and concerns a matter of significance to the administration of federal interpleader, we granted certiorari. 385 U.S. 811, 87 S.Ct. 90 (1966). Although we reverse the decision of the Court of Appeals upon the jurisdictional question, we direct a substantial modification of the District Court's injunction for reasons which will appear.

I.

Before considering the issues presented by the petition for certiorari, we find it necessary to dispose of a question neither raised by the parties nor passed upon by the courts below. Since the matter concerns our jurisdiction, we raise it on our own motion. Treinies v. Sunshine Mining Co., 308 U.S. 66, 70, 60 S.Ct. 44, 47 (1939). The interpleader statute, 28 U.S.C. § 1335, applies where there are "Two or more adverse claimants, of diverse citizenship . . . ." This provision has been uniformly construed to require only "minimal diversity," that is, diversity of citizenship between two or more claimants, without regard to the circumstance that other rival claimants may be co-citizens. The language of the statute, the legislative purpose broadly to remedy the problems posed by multiple claimants to a single fund, and the consistent judicial interpretation tacitly accepted by Congress, persuade us that the statute requires no more. There remains, however, the question whether such a statutory construction is consistent with Article III of our Constitution, which extends the federal judicial power to "Controversies . . . between Citizens of different States . . . and between a State, or the Citizens thereof, and foreign States, Citizens or Subjects." In Strawbridge v. Curtiss, 3 Cranch 267 (1806), this Court held that the diversity of citizenship statute required "complete diversity": where co-citizens appeared on both sides of a dispute, jurisdiction was lost. But Chief Justice Marshall there purported to construe only "The words of the act of congress," not the Constitution itself. And in a variety of contexts this Court and the lower courts have concluded that Article III poses no obstacle to the legislative extension of federal jurisdiction, founded on diversity, so long as any two adverse parties are not co-citizens.[7]

---

[3] We need not pass upon the Court of Appeals' conclusions with respect to the interpretation of interpleader under Rule 22 . . . . State Farm could not have invoked it in light of venue and service of process limitations. . . .

[7] . . . We note that the American Law Institute's proposals for revision of the Judicial Code to deal with the problem of multiparty, multijurisdiction litigation are predicated upon the permissibility of "minimal diversity" as a jurisdictional basis.

Accordingly, we conclude that the present case is properly in the federal courts.

II.

We do not agree with the Court of Appeals that, in the absence of a state law or contractual provision for "direct action" suits against the insurance company, the company must wait until persons asserting claims against its insured have reduced those claims to judgment before seeking to invoke the benefits of federal interpleader. That may have been a tenable position under the 1926 and 1936 interpleader statutes. These statutes did not carry forward the language in the 1917 Act authorizing interpleader where adverse claimants "may claim" benefits as well as where they "are claiming" them.[10] In 1948, however, in the revision of the Judicial Code, the "may claim" language was restored.[11] Until the decision below, every court confronted by the question has concluded that the 1948 revision removed whatever requirement there might previously have been that the insurance company wait until at least two claimants reduced their claims to judgments. The commentators are in accord.

Considerations of judicial administration demonstrate the soundness of this view which, in any event, seems compelled by the language of the present statute, which is remedial and to be liberally construed. Were an insurance company required to await reduction of claims to judgment, the first claimant to obtain such a judgment or to negotiate a settlement might appropriate all or a disproportionate slice of the fund before his fellow claimants were able to establish their claims. The difficulties such a race to judgment pose for the insurer, and the unfairness which may result to some claimants, were among the principal evils the interpleader device was intended to remedy.[15]

III.

The fact that State Farm had properly invoked the interpleader jurisdiction under § 1335 did not, however, entitle it to an order both enjoining prosecution of suits against it outside the confines of the interpleader

[10] 39 Stat. 929 (1917). See Klaber v. Maryland Cas. Co., 69 F.2d 934, 938–939 (C.A.8th Cir.1934), which held that the omission in the 1926 Act of the earlier statute's "may claim" language required the denial of interpleader in the face of unliquidated claims (alternative holding).

[11] Although the Reviser's Note did not refer to the statutory change or its purpose, we have it on good authority that it was the omission in the Note rather than the statutory change which was inadvertent. See 3 Moore, Fed.Prac. ¶ 22.08, at 3025–3026, n. 13. And it was widely assumed that restoration of the "may claim" language would have the effect of overruling the holding in Klaber, supra, that one may not invoke interpleader to protect against unliquidated claims. See, e.g., Chafee, 45 Yale L.J., at 1163–1167; Chafee, Federal Interpleader Since the Act of 1936, 49 Yale L.J. 377, 418–420 (1940). In circumstances like these, the 1948 revision of the Judicial Code worked substantive changes. Ex parte Collett, 337 U.S. 55, 69 S.Ct. 944 (1949).

[15] The insurance problem envisioned at the time was that of an insurer faced with conflicting but mutually exclusive claims to a policy, rather than an insurer confronted with the problem of allocating a fund among various claimants whose independent claims may exceed the amount of the fund. S.Rep. No. 558, 74th Cong., 1st Sess., 2–3, 7, 8 (1935); Chafee, Modernizing Interpleader, 30 Yale L.J. 814, 818–819 (1921).

proceeding and also extending such protection to its insured, the alleged tortfeasor. Still less was Greyhound Lines entitled to have that order expanded so as to protect itself and its driver, also alleged to be tortfeasors, from suits brought by its passengers in various state or federal courts. Here, the scope of the litigation, in terms of parties and claims, was vastly more extensive than the confines of the "fund," the deposited proceeds of the insurance policy. In these circumstances, the mere existence of such a fund cannot, by use of interpleader, be employed to accomplish purposes that exceed the needs of orderly contest with respect to the fund.

There are situations, of a type not present here, where the effect of interpleader is to confine the total litigation to a single forum and proceeding. One such case is where a stakeholder, faced with rival claims to the fund itself, acknowledges—or denies—his liability to one or the other of the claimants.[16] In this situation, the fund itself is the target of the claimants. It marks the outer limits of the controversy. It is, therefore, reasonable and sensible that interpleader, in discharge of its office to protect the fund, should also protect the stakeholder from vexatious and multiple litigation. In this context, the suits sought to be enjoined are squarely within the language of 28 U.S.C. § 2361, which provides in part:

> "In any civil action of interpleader or in the nature of interpleader under section 1335 of this title, a district court may issue its process for all claimants and enter its order restraining them from instituting or prosecuting *any proceeding* in any State or United States court *affecting the property, instrument or obligation involved in the interpleader action* . . . ." (Emphasis added.)

But the present case is another matter. Here, an accident has happened. Thirty-five passengers or their representatives have claims which they wish to press against a variety of defendants: the bus company, its driver, the owner of the truck, and the truck driver. The circumstance that one of the prospective defendants happens to have an insurance policy is a fortuitous event which should not of itself shape the nature of the ensuing litigation. For example, a resident of California, injured in California aboard a bus owned by a California corporation should not be forced to sue that corporation anywhere but in California simply because another prospective defendant carried an insurance policy. And an insurance company whose maximum interest in the case cannot exceed $20,000 and who in fact asserts that it has no interest at all, should not be allowed to determine that dozens of tort plaintiffs must be compelled to press their claims—even those claims which are not against the insured and which in no event could be satisfied out of the meager insurance fund—in a single forum of the insurance company's choosing. There is nothing in the statutory scheme, and very little in the judicial and academic commentary upon that scheme, which requires that the tail be allowed to wag the dog in this fashion.

16 This was the classic situation envisioned by the sponsors of interpleader. See n. 15, supra.

State Farm's interest in this case, which is the fulcrum of the interpleader procedure, is confined to its $20,000 fund. That interest receives full vindication when the court restrains claimants from seeking to enforce against the insurance company any judgment obtained against its insured, except in the interpleader proceeding itself. To the extent that the District Court sought to control claimants' lawsuits against the insured and other alleged tortfeasors, it exceeded the powers granted to it by the statutory scheme.

We recognize, of course, that our view of interpleader means that it cannot be used to solve all the vexing problems of multiparty litigation arising out of a mass tort. But interpleader was never intended to perform such a function, to be an all-purpose "bill of peace."[17] Had it been so intended, careful provision would necessarily have been made to insure that a party with little or no interest in the outcome of a complex controversy should not strip truly interested parties of substantial rights—such as the right to choose the forum in which to establish their claims, subject to generally applicable rules of jurisdiction, venue, service of process, removal, and change of venue. None of the legislative and academic sponsors of a modern federal interpleader device viewed their accomplishment as a "bill of peace," capable of sweeping dozens of lawsuits out of the various state and federal courts in which they were brought and into a single interpleader proceeding. . . .

In light of the evidence that federal interpleader was not intended to serve the function of a "bill of peace" in the context of multiparty litigation arising out of a mass tort, of the anomalous power which such a construction of the statute would give the stakeholder, and of the thrust of the statute and the purpose it was intended to serve, we hold that the interpleader statute did not authorize the injunction entered in the present case. Upon remand, the injunction is to be modified consistently with this opinion.[18]

---

[17] There is not a word in the legislative history suggesting such a purpose. See S.Rep. No. 558, 74th Cong., 1st Sess. (1935). And Professor Chafee, upon whose work the Congress heavily depended, has written that little thought was given to the scope of the "second stage" of interpleader, to just what would be adjudicated by the interpleader court. See Chafee, Broadening the Second Stage of Federal Interpleader, 56 Harv.L.Rev. 929, 944–945 (1943). We note that in Professor Chafee's own study of the bill of peace as a device for dealing with the problem of multiparty litigation, he fails even to mention interpleader. See Chafee, Some Problems of Equity 149–198 (1950). In his writing on interpleader, Chafee assumed that the interpleader court would allocate the fund "among all the claimants who get judgment within a reasonable time . . . ." Chafee, The Federal Interpleader Act of 1936: II, 45 Yale L.J. 1161, 1165–1166 (1936). See also Chafee, 49 Yale L.J., at 420–421.

[18] We find it unnecessary to pass upon respondents' contention, raised in the courts below but not passed upon by the Court of Appeals, that interpleader should have been dismissed on the ground that the 11 Canadian claimants are "indispensable parties" who have not been properly served. The argument is that 28 U.S.C. § 2361 provides the exclusive mode of effecting service of process in statutory interpleader and that § 2361—which authorizes a district court to "issue its process for all claimants" but subsequently refers to service of "such process" by marshals "for the respective districts where the claimants reside or may be found"—does not permit service of process beyond the Nation's borders. Since our decision will require basic reconsideration of the litigation by the parties as well as the lower courts, there appears neither need nor necessity to determine this question at this time. We intimate no view as to the exclusivity of § 2361, whether it authorizes service of process in foreign

IV.

The judgment of the Court of Appeals is reversed, and the case is remanded to the United States District Court for proceedings consistent with this opinion.

It is so ordered.

■ [The dissenting opinion of JUSTICE DOUGLAS is omitted. He agreed with the Court on parts I and III of its opinion, but he did not regard the victims as "claimants" to the fund in the statutory sense until their claims against the insured were reduced to judgment.]

FIRST STAGE

The requirements of jurisdiction, venue, and service.—Given these threshold requirements, particular actions can be brought under Rule 22(a), under the federal interpleader statute, or under both. Recall that Rule 22(a) actions must look to the general statutes on subject-matter jurisdiction and venue and to the Federal Rules for service of process, whereas the interpleader statute has its own provisions on these matters.

Questions: (12) *A* Life Insurance Co., incorporated and having its principal place of business in State *X*, issued a life insurance policy to *B* that excluded death by suicide within the period before the policy became incontestable. *B* died within that period, and both *C* and *D* have claimed the proceeds of the policy as sole beneficiary. *A* Co. wants to defend on the ground of suicide and to determine which claimant can recover if that defense fails. Is interpleader available to *A* Co.? In what factual circumstances could *A* Co. proceed under the Rule? under the statute? under both?

(13) If interpleader could be invoked—as far as subject-matter jurisdiction, service, and venue are concerned—under both the Rule and the statute, what other factors would influence a stakeholder's choice between the two devices? Compare 4 Moore § 22.04[5] (power to enjoin other proceedings exists for both devices), with id. § 22.04[6] (deposit in court registry is permissive under Rule 67(a) but obligatory under § 1335(a)(2)).

(14) Could the defendant bank in the Haas case, supra p. 884, have interpleaded by counterclaim, thus allowing Haas and Glueck to fight it out in the Florida federal court? Consider the application of supplemental jurisdiction for statutory interpleader, or of quasi in rem jurisdiction for Rule interpleader. See 7 Wright, Miller & Kane §§ 1710–1712; cf. 13F Wright, Miller & Cooper § 3636, at 372.

The classic limits on interpleader.—According to 4 John N. Pomeroy, Equity Jurisprudence § 1322 (5th ed. 1941): "[F]rom the whole course of authorities, it is clear that the equitable remedy of interpleader, independent of statutory regulations, depends upon and requires the existence of

---

lands, whether in light of the limitations we have imposed on the interpleader court's injunctive powers the Canadian claimants are in fact "indispensable parties" to the interpleader proceeding itself, or whether they render themselves amenable to service of process under § 2361 when they come into an American jurisdiction to establish their rights with respect either to the alleged tortfeasors or to the insurance fund. See 2 Moore, Fed.Prac. ¶ 4.20, at 1091–1105.

the four following elements, which may be regarded as its essential conditions: 1. The same thing, debt, or duty must be claimed by both or all the parties against whom the relief is demanded; 2. All their adverse titles or claims must be dependent, or be derived from a common source; 3. The person asking the relief—the plaintiff—must not have nor claim any interest in the subject-matter; 4. He must have incurred no independent liability to either of the claimants; that is, he must stand perfectly indifferent between them, in the position merely of a stakeholder."[b]

Question: (15) The student should consider which of Pomeroy's "classic limits" are intrinsic to interpleader and which, in Chafee's phrase, were merely obstacles to just relief. Also, which of the classic limits were abolished by the federal interpleader statute? by Rule 22(a)?

Neither the statute nor the Rule expressly does away with the requirement that the plaintiff must have incurred no independent liability to either of the claimants, i.e., that the plaintiff must not have rendered himself liable to one claimant without reference to his possible liability to the other, as by a subsequent contract concerning the stake. It is probable that Professor Chafee, the draftsman of the statute, considered the independent-liability restriction to be only an aspect of the requirement that the claims be of common origin. Cf. Ex parte Mersey Docks & Harbour Board, [1899] 1 Q.B. 546 (C.A.). A conflict, however, developed. Compare Poland v. Atlantis Credit Corp., 179 F.Supp. 863 (S.D.N.Y.1960) (restriction still exists), with Knoll v. Socony Mobil Oil Co., 369 F.2d 425 (10th Cir.1966) (restriction no longer a bar). The ALI Study of the Division of Jurisdiction Between State and Federal Courts § 2361(b) commentary at 420–21 (1969) recommended resolution of this conflict by adding at the end of current § 1335(b) the words "or although the plaintiff may be independently liable to one or more of the claimants." A similar amendment of Rule 22(a) is probably desirable, although increasingly the cases under both the statute and the Rule are, without the benefit of amendment, reaching the conclusion that the independent-liability restriction no longer exists. See 7 Wright, Miller & Kane § 1706.

SECOND STAGE

The addition of claims in federal court.—Once it is determined that interpleader has been properly instituted (the so-called first stage of interpleader), the parties or some of them may discover that they have further claims against one another, either connected or unconnected with the subject of the interpleader. When must or may such claims be asserted in

[b] On the origins of the classic limits, see the biting and highly interesting account by Geoffrey C. Hazard, Jr. & Myron Moskovitz, An Historical and Critical Analysis of Interpleader, 52 Cal.L.Rev. 706 (1964). In addition to strict interpleader as described by Professor Pomeroy, equity permitted "a bill in the nature of a bill of interpleader" when the stakeholder was not disinterested, but the stakeholder had to have some ground for equitable relief other than the assertion of conflicting claims against him. See Killian v. Ebbinghaus, 110 U.S. 568, 4 S.Ct. 232 (1884).

the interpleader action? What requirements, if any, of subject-matter jurisdiction, venue, and service will have to be satisfied? The answers to such questions define the scope of the so-called second stage of interpleader.

Questions: (16) Assume that a bank of State *X* brings statutory interpleader in a federal court in State *X* to resolve conflicting claims to a bank deposit of $15,000 made by *A* of State *Y* with provision that it could be withdrawn by *B* of State *X* upon satisfactory completion of *A*'s rental of a boat. Service is made upon *A* in State *Y* under 28 U.S.C. § 2361, effective personal service on *A* not being otherwise possible. *A* does not appear to claim the deposit. *B* serves and files a crossclaim against *A* for $105,000 damages allegedly arising out of *A*'s negligence in connection with operating the boat. Is there jurisdiction over *A*'s person for purposes of the crossclaim? See 7 Wright, Miller & Kane § 1715, at 641–45.

(17) In the preceding question, should it matter how closely related the crossclaim issues are to those in the interpleader? See Rubinbaum LLP v. Related Corporate Partners V, L.P., 154 F.Supp.2d 481, 488–90 (S.D.N.Y.2001) (yes). Should it matter whether *A* has appeared to claim the deposit? See Restatement (Second) of Judgments § 9 (1982) (yes). What if the interpleader action were under Rule 22(a) rather than the statute?

The law applied in federal interpleader.—Obviously, in the first stage of interpleader the governing law should be federal. In the second stage, however, some problems of choice of law crop up.

Question: (18) Who should have the burden of proof on the claims to the deposit? See Phoenix Mut. Life Ins. Co. v. Reich, 75 F.Supp. 886 (W.D.Pa.1948) (each claimant).

It will be recalled that the Supreme Court in Klaxon Co. v. Stentor Electric Manufacturing Co., supra p. 353, directed the lower federal court hearing that diversity case to follow the rules for conflict of laws of the state in which it sat. On that same day the Supreme Court decided Griffin v. McCoach, 313 U.S. 498, 61 S.Ct. 1023 (1941), and there directed like obedience to the rules for conflict of laws of the forum state in a federal statutory interpleader action.

Many think that whatever the merits of the Klaxon rule in the ordinary diversity action, those merits are much attenuated when it comes to federal statutory interpleader. Why so? The American Law Institute proposed an amendment to the federal interpleader statute, which would declare: "Whenever State law supplies the rule of decision on an issue, the district court may make its own determination as to which State rule of decision is applicable." ALI Study of the Division of Jurisdiction Between State and Federal Courts § 2363(c) (1969).

PART SIX

THE UNITARY CIVIL ACTION

TOPIC A

INTRODUCTION

WILLIAMSON v. COLUMBIA GAS & ELECTRIC CORP., 110 F.2d 15 (3d Cir.1939), cert. denied, 310 U.S. 639, 60 S.Ct. 1087 (1940). On September 16, 1938, one Williamson, as trustee in bankruptcy of Inland Gas Corporation, commenced an action in the United States District Court for the District of Delaware against Columbia Gas & Electric Corporation. He charged in his complaint that Columbia had injured Inland by committing various acts in violation of § 7 of the Clayton Act, 15 U.S.C. § 18, which then provided in part: "No corporation engaged in commerce shall acquire . . . the whole or any part of the stock . . . of another corporation engaged also in commerce, where the effect of such acquisition may be to substantially lessen competition between the corporation whose stock is so acquired and the corporation making the acquisition." He demanded treble damages in accordance with § 4 of the Clayton Act, 15 U.S.C. § 15.

Columbia presented by motion under Rule 12(b)(6) the defense that the complaint failed to state a claim upon which relief could be granted, contending that plaintiff's claim was barred by the applicable statute of limitations. The parties entered into a stipulation, which accompanied the motion, to the effect that the right of action "accrued not later than January 1, 1931."

As there was no act of Congress fixing a period of limitations for commencing actions under the Clayton Act, the district court resorted to the laws of Delaware to find the applicable period. A Delaware statute provided in part: "No action of trespass, no action of replevin, no action of detinue, no action of debt not found upon a record or specialty, no action of account, no action of assumpsit, and no action upon the case shall be brought after the expiration of three years from the accruing of the cause of such action."[a] Plaintiff contended that his action was in the nature of an action of "debt on a specialty,"[b] which the quoted Delaware statute did not cover, and as to which the Delaware courts had said that the only limitation was the backup presumption of satisfaction after twenty years.

---

[a] The specific, as opposed to the general, problem of this case could not arise today in Delaware for two reasons. First, with the effectiveness in 1948 of the Delaware Rules of Civil Procedure, including a rule corresponding to Federal Rule 2, the Delaware statute of limitations was amended to eliminate references to the forms of action. See Del.Code Ann. tit. 10, § 8106. Second, as of 1956, Congress added a four-year period of limitations for actions arising under the antitrust laws. See 15 U.S.C. § 15b.

[b] This was a variant form of debt that lay to enforce a grant of a fixed sum of money, if made in a sealed instrument. Delaware had stretched this form to cover a fixed sum owing by statute.

Defendant contended that the action was one on the "case,"[c] which the statute therefore barred.

The district court granted the motion, and the circuit court of appeals affirmed. The opinion of the circuit court of appeals went at some length into the differences among the ancient forms of action mentioned in the Delaware statute, citing not only Delaware cases but also English cases and treatises, and concluded that the action was one on the "case."

In an alternative bid for the twenty-year presumption, plaintiff had contended that "since the 'civil action' provided for by the Federal Rules of Civil Procedure . . . has abolished all distinctions in the forms of actions the state statutes of limitations based upon differences in forms of action no longer apply." Answering this contention, the appellate court per Judge Maris, joined by Judges Biddle and Jones, said:

"Exactly the same contention was made in England, after the abolition of forms of action by the Judicature Act of 1873. In Gibbs v. Guild, 1882, 9 Q.B.D. 59, page 67, Brett, L.J., said: 'It was said that inasmuch as the names of actions are altered, and there is no longer an action on the case, or an action of trespass, the Statute of Limitations did no longer apply; but I am of opinion that the Judicature Act, 1873, did not alter or touch the Statute of Limitations at all, and that the statute still applies to the circumstances which constituted the actions named in it, that is to say, that if the circumstances would have constituted an action on the case or an action of trespass, although the action which involves the remedy sought would not now be called an action on the case or an action of trespass, yet, notwithstanding the Statute of Limitations applies to it, if the facts are such as would have supported an action on the case or an action of trespass.'

"In Kirkman v. Philips' Heirs, 54 Tenn. 222 [(1872)], the limitation period for tort actions was three years, for contract actions six years. The court analyzed the pleadings to determine which cause of action was involved. The court said: 'This right is not interfered with by the provisions of the Code abolishing the distinctions in the forms of actions. The statute of limitations applicable to the cause depends upon the nature and character of the action, and not upon its form.'

"We fully agree with the views expressed by the Circuit Court of Appeals of the Fifth Circuit, in City of El Paso v. West et al., 104 F.2d 96, 97 [(1939)], in which that court disposed of a similar argument with the statement 'Even under the new rules, when limitation depends on the State law and that law refers to a form of action as determinative, it will be necessary to ascertain what sort of case the pleader is presenting.' We find no evidence in the Federal Rules of Civil Procedure or in the notes thereto of an intent to cover the field of limitations of actions. . . .

"In order to apply a statute of limitations, such as that of Delaware, which reads in terms of common law actions, to a civil action brought in a

[c] This late-developing form of action evolved from trespass to fill some of the lacunae in torts under the writ system.

district court, it is necessary for the court through a consideration of the nature of the cause of action disclosed in the complaint to determine the form of action which would have been brought upon it at common law. It is evident that the complaint in the case before us discloses a cause of action which, under the common law of Delaware, would be enforceable in an action on the case and not in an action of debt on a specialty. The district court, therefore, properly held that the action was barred by the Delaware statute of limitations."

FEDERAL RULE 2

What, then, is the meaning of Federal Rule 2, which provides that there is "one form of action" to be known as a "civil action"?

A large number of states have statutes or rules of court substantially to the same effect. Section 103(a) of New York Civil Practice Law and Rules is somewhat more explicit than Rule 2. It provides: "*One form of civil action.* There is only one form of civil action. The distinctions between actions at law and suits in equity, and the forms of those actions and suits, have been abolished." This language, stemming from the famous New York Code of Procedure of 1848 associated with the name of David Dudley Field, suggests that there was once a distinction between "actions at law" and "suits in equity" and further that there were various "forms" at least of those actions; that the distinction and the forms have been abolished; and that consequently there is only one form of civil action.

The following passages from the great English legal historian Frederic Maitland (1850–1906) shed more light on what the one form of civil action entails. He contrasts the position in England during the eighteenth-century time of Blackstone (1723–1780) with the position after the English legislation of 1873 finally adopting the concept of the unitary civil action.

F.W. Maitland, The Forms of Action at Common Law

2–5, 8–9 (1936).[d]

The forms of action we have buried, but they still rule us from their graves. Let us then for awhile place ourselves in Blackstone's day, or, for this matters not, some seventy years later in 1830, and let us look for a moment at English civil procedure.

---

[d] This book consists of a course of seven lectures given by Maitland at Cambridge around the turn of the century. He is addressing himself chiefly to the forms of action at law and their abolition. He does not here consider at any length the English erasure of the dividing line between actions at law and suits in equity.

In the United States, a constitutional barrier prevents the complete procedural merger of law and equity. What is that barrier?

Let it be granted that one man has been wronged by another; the first thing that he or his advisers have to consider is what form of action he shall bring. It is not enough that in some way or another he should compel his adversary to appear in court and should then state in the words that naturally occur to him the facts on which he relies and the remedy to which he thinks himself entitled. No, English law knows a certain number of forms of action, each with its own uncouth name, a writ of right, an assize of novel disseisin or of mort d'ancestor, . . . an action of covenant, debt, detinue, replevin, trespass, assumpsit, ejectment, case. This choice is not merely a choice between a number of queer technical terms, it is a choice between methods of procedure adapted to cases of different kinds. Let us notice some of the many points that are implied in it.

(i) There is the competence of the court. For very many of the ordinary civil cases each of the three courts which have grown out of the king's court of early days, the King's Bench, Common Pleas and Exchequer is equally competent, though it is only by means of elaborate and curious fictions that the King's Bench and the Exchequer can entertain these matters, and the Common Pleas still retains a monopoly of those actions which are known as real.

(ii) A court chosen, one must make one's adversary appear; but what is the first step towards this end? In some actions one ought to begin by having him summoned, in others one can at once have him attached, he can be compelled to find gage and pledge for his appearance. In the assize of novel disseisin it is enough to attach his bailiff.

(iii) Suppose him contumacious, what can one do? Can one have his body seized? If he can not be found, can one have him outlawed? This stringent procedure has been extending itself from one form of action to another. Again, can one have the thing in dispute seized? This is possible in some actions, impossible in others.

(iv) Can one obtain a judgment by default, obtain what one wants though the adversary continues in his contumacy? Yes in some forms, no in others.

(v) It comes to pleading, and here each form of action has some rules of its own. For instance the person attacked—the tenant he is called in some cases, the defendant in others—wishes to oppose the attacker—the demandant he is called in some actions, the plaintiff in others—by a mere general denial, casting upon him the burden of proving his own case, what is he to say? In other words, what is the general issue appropriate to this action? In one form it is *Nihil debet,* in another *Non assumpsit,* in another "Not guilty," in others, *Nul tort, nul disseisin.*

(vi) There is to be a trial; but what mode of trial? Very generally of course a trial by jury. But it may be trial by a grand or petty assize, which is not quite the same thing as trial by jury; or in Blackstone's day it may still conceivably be a trial by battle. Again in some forms of action the defendant may betake himself to the world-old process of compurgation or wager of law. Again there are a few issues which are tried without a jury by the judges who hear witnesses.

(vii) Judgment goes against the defendant, what is the appropriate form of execution? Can one be put into possession of the thing that has been in dispute? Can one imprison the defendant? Can one have him made an outlaw? or can he merely be distrained?

(viii) Judgment goes against the defendant. It is not enough that he should satisfy the plaintiff's just demand; he must also be punished for his breach of the law—such at all events is the theory. What form shall this punishment take? Will an amercement suffice, or shall there be fine or imprisonment? Here also there have been differences.

(ix) Some actions are much more dilatory than others; the dilatory ones have gone out of use, but still they exist. In these oldest forms—forms invented when as yet the parties had to appear in person and could only appoint attorneys by the king's special leave—the action may drag on for years, for the parties enjoy a power of sending essoins, that is, excuses for non-appearance. The medieval law of essoins is vast in bulk; time is allowed for almost every kind of excuse for non-appearance—a short essoin *de malo veniendi,* a long essoin *de malo lecti.* Now-a-days all is regulated by general rules with a wide discretion left in the Court. In the Middle Ages discretion is entirely excluded; all is to be fixed by iron rules. This question of essoins has been very important—in some forms, the oldest and solemnest, a party may betake himself to his bed and remain there for year and day and meanwhile the action is suspended.

These remarks may be enough to show that the differences between the several forms of action have been of very great practical importance—"a form of action" has implied a particular original process, a particular mesne process [pronounced like mean and covering all writs or orders between the original writ and the writ of execution], a particular final process, a particular mode of pleading, of trial, of judgment. But further to a very considerable degree the substantive law administered in a given form of action has grown up independently of the law administered in other forms. Each procedural pigeon-hole contains its own rules of substantive law, and it is with great caution that we may argue from what is found in one to what will probably be found in another; each has its own precedents. It is quite possible that a litigant will find that his case will fit some two or three of these pigeon-holes. If that be so he will have a choice, which will often be a choice between the old, cumbrous, costly, on the one hand, the modern, rapid, cheap, on the other. Or again he may make a bad choice, fail in his action, and take such comfort as he can from the hints of the judges that another form of action might have been more successful.[e] The plaintiff's choice is irrevocable; he must play the rules of the game that he has

[e] A judgment for the defendant solely on the ground that the plaintiff had selected the wrong form of action terminated that lawsuit and made the losing plaintiff liable for costs. Because the judgment was not an adjudication on the merits, the principle of res judicata did not come into play. The plaintiff could therefore commence a new action under the proper form, unless the period of limitations had run meanwhile.

chosen. Lastly, he may find that, plausible as his case may seem, it just will not fit any one of the receptacles provided by the courts and he may take to himself the lesson that where there is no remedy there is no wrong.

The key-note of the form of action is struck by the original writ, the writ whereby the action is begun. . . .

. . . .

The final blow was struck by the Judicature Act of 1873 and the rules made thereunder, which came into force in 1875. This did much more than finally abolish the forms of actions known to the common law for it provided that equity and law should be administered concurrently. Since that time we have had what might fairly be called a Code of Civil Procedure. Of course we can not here speak of the details of that Code; but you will not misunderstand me if I say that the procedure which it enjoins is comparatively formless. Of course there are rules, many rules.

We can not say that whatever be the nature of the plaintiff's claim the action will always take the same course and pass through the same stages. For instance, when the plaintiff's claim falls within one of certain classes he can adopt a procedure whereby when he has sworn positively to the truth of his claim the defendant can be shut out from defending the action at all unless he first makes oath to some good defence. So again there are cases in which either party can insist that the questions of fact, if any, shall be tried by jury; there are other cases in which there will be no trial by jury. Again, I must not allow you to think that a lawyer can not do his client a great deal of harm by advising a bad or inappropriate course of procedure, though it is true that he can not bring about a total shipwreck of a good cause so easily as he might have done some years ago. The great change gradually brought about and consummated by the Judicature Acts is that the whole course of procedure in an action is not determined for good and all by the first step, by the original writ. It can no longer be said, as it might have been said in 1830 that we have about 72 forms of action, or as it might have been said in 1874 that we have about 12 forms of action. This is a different thing from saying that our English law no longer attempts to classify *causes* of action, on the contrary a rational, modern classification of causes of action is what we are gradually obtaining—but the forms of action belong to the past.

Since the Judicature Acts there are, of course, differences of procedure arising out of the character of the various actions, whether for divorce, probate of a will, specific performance of a contract: such differences there must be, but they can now be regarded as mere variations of one general theme—procedure in an action in the High Court of Justice.

EFFECTS OF THE UNITARY CIVIL ACTION

As Maitland makes obvious, the unitary civil action signifies a tremendous change in procedural law. Our system went from many procedures to basically one procedure. Study of the old procedures truly is the study of the *past*.

Of course, the study of older procedures will illuminate the understanding of modern procedure in the *present*. Even more so, legal history helps in the understanding of current substantive law. For example, as the Williamson case proves, Rule 2, like the rest of the Federal Rules of Civil Procedure, did not directly alter substantive law. The older substantive law survived. Indeed, the substantive law of the present perpetuates much of the old writ system. "Nobody will gainsay the importance to an understanding of our common-law system of a knowledge of the essentials of the forms of action at common law, for as Maitland has truly said, 'The forms of action we have buried, but they still rule us from their graves.' They rule us, however, not as procedure but as substantive law . . . ." Arthur T. Vanderbilt, Cases and Other Materials on Modern Procedure and Judicial Administration 7 (1952). And as to law and equity: "It was evidently the intention of the legislature, in framing the code, not to destroy, but to mingle, common law and equitable actions, in so far as form is concerned, but the substance of each remains unchanged and wholly unchangeable, and cannot be united, fused or commingled into one by any human legislation." T.A. Green, A General Treatise on Pleading and Practice in Civil Proceedings at Law and in Equity Under the Code System 51–52 (St. Louis, W.J. Gilbert 1879).

Studying the sweep of history prepares the student for the *future* of not only substantive law but also procedural law. The grand theme of the historical development, which is the emergence of the unitary civil action, underlies the three hottest topics in civil procedure today: (1) case management, (2) tracking, and (3) substance-specific procedures.

The cause and effect might run like this: The old system generated a revulsion that pushed the reform of unification perhaps too far, thereby causing the ills of modern procedure that require renewed reform. A need to differentiate among cases persists—whether by the questionable means of (1) intensifying the ad hoc method of case management by judges, (2) elaborating tracking schemes ranging from alternative dispute-resolution mechanisms to forms of complex litigation that pigeonhole cases according to their procedural nature, or (3) tailoring procedural law overtly to particular substantive fields. Indeed, today's dissatisfaction is escalating toward the level prevailing at the overthrow of the old regime. "The present espousal of such devices as case management and alternative dispute resolution is both a sign of and a reaction to a procedural regime that is in question and in decline, if not in its death throes." Stephen N. Subrin, David Dudley Field and the Field Code: A Historical Analysis of an Earlier Procedural Vision, 6 Law & Hist.Rev. 311, 311 (1988).

Thus, among the questions of civil procedure most in need of basic research are: "[S]hould the drive toward a unitary procedure be abated, should special procedures be set up that are better accommodated to the intrinsic qualities of the problems presented? I suggest that we need to think less about 'procedure' eo nomine and more about the particular social matrix; we should go from the problem in its setting to the appropriate procedure; whether or how the courts or any other dispute-resolving mechanisms are to be invoked will be conditioned by the other material solutions." Benjamin Kaplan, An American Lawyer in the Queen's Courts: Impressions of English Civil Procedure, 69 Mich.L.Rev. 821, 845 (1971). This article goes on to note: "With regard to variations on a standard procedure, recall that the English are not as much attached to unitary procedure as we have been; a number of variant procedures are today in use in the High Court, but whether the particular variations are justified functionally may be doubted."

JUDITH RESNIK, FAILING FAITH: ADJUDICATORY PROCEDURE IN DECLINE, 53 U.Chi.L.Rev. 494, 495, 526–27, 547–48 (1986). A basic premise of the original Federal Rules, "one trans-substantive set of rules for all kinds of cases," already "has been silently undermined—de jure and de facto. At a formal level, the Court has promulgated special rules for the litigation of prisoners' habeas corpus cases. In addition, the recently revised Manual for Complex Litigation has created a distinct set of rules for cases with multiple parties or complex issues. At an informal level, the emergence of managerial judging and the approval of that phenomenon in the 1983 amendments to Rule 16 (governing pretrial procedures) exemplify ad hoc efforts to tailor rules to individual cases. . . .

. . . .

"Given the problems of contemporary litigation, the Rules need reworking in several respects. First, the trans-substantive premise of the Rules has proved unworkable. We must face that, whatever the horrors of forms of action, we need to determine what subsets of cases require special kinds of rules, and write rules for those kinds of cases. Thus, a plea for contextualism.

. . . .

"Moving to a process point, the trans-substantive Rules could be contextualized in one of two fashions—through ad hoc decisionmaking by individual judges or districts, or through comprehensive rulemaking. . . . I am deeply skeptical of the capacity of individual judges to craft rules on a case-by-case basis. Federal judges tell us repeatedly that they are overwhelmed by their caseloads. I do not believe that these judges can perform their adjudicatory tasks and still have sufficient time to ascertain which mode of procedure is best suited to each individual case. Moreover, I have substantial reservations about the propriety of such an ad hoc judicial enterprise. Deciding how to mold procedures to a given case may well involve a judge so deeply in managerial and adversarial events that it undermines the ability of the judge to adjudicate—should that become necessary. Therefore, I suggest that federal judges participate in the effort to review the Rules, rather than in the design of specific procedures for each case."

GEOFFREY C. HAZARD, JR., FORMS OF ACTION UNDER THE FEDERAL RULES OF CIVIL PROCEDURE, 63 Notre Dame L.Rev. 628, 636 (1988). "The need . . . to impose order on complicated issues has forced reliance on a control mechanism that is not in the form of rules. This mechanism is judicial management through exercise of judicial discretion. The managerial technique is susceptible of overuse or abuse, and the risks of such abuse have invited reconsideration of whether cases ought to be allowed to become as complicated as they now can be. Correlatively, the question arises whether different kinds of procedures can be devised for different kinds of cases.

". . . At least two general remedial strategies are possible. The first is to impose restrictions on the substantive legal contentions that can be made when a transaction is drawn into litigation. The second is to restrict the kinds of evidence that can be pursued.

. . . .

"Such a set of limitations would of course re-create the common law forms of action, or at least their more lenient Field Code derivative."

EFFECTS OF PROCEDURE ON SUBSTANCE

Procedure has already moved in the direction of the "new forms of action." It could go much farther. For example, tracking is now in place implicitly, even becoming a fashionable buzzword. But tracking could turn much more serious.

Thus, it has been argued that the Federal Rules' notions of minimal pleading, liberal joinder, and wide discovery have "produced a nightmare" when applied to smaller cases. "We need a less-expansive process. Otherwise, ordinary disputes will continue to blossom into Federal cases." Stephen N. Subrin, The Law and the Rules, N.Y. Times, Nov. 10, 1979, at 23. According to Mark C. Weber, The Federal Civil Rules Amendments of 1993 and Complex Litigation: A Comment on Transsubstantivity and Special Rules for Large and Small Federal Cases, 14 Rev.Litig. 113, 114 (1994): "New contributions to efficiency in the operation of the federal courts might be obtained by departing from the transsubstantivity and insensitivity to size that is characteristic of the current Federal Rules, but not by the creation of special rules for various kinds of complex litigation. Instead, the federal courts would more likely benefit from special rules for small cases of the types that are commonly found on the federal civil docket: collections of federally guaranteed debt, lower-damages diversity suits, Federal Employers Liability Act (FELA) suits, and other cases in which litigation costs are most likely to rise out of proportion to the amount in controversy [except civil rights cases]." See also Inst. for the Advancement of the Am. Legal System, The Federal Simplified Procedure Project: A History (2009).

The significant insight offered by considering changes such as tracking concerns the effects of procedure on substance. One has a tendency to think of the two as separate realms, involving separate values and susceptible to separate reform. The thought is that society can rework the procedural regime in pursuit of the supposedly neutral values of fairness, economy, and accuracy independently of substantive values. But the reality is that changes in the procedural law inevitably entail effects, albeit indirect effects, on the substantive law. See Thomas O. Main, The Procedural Foundation of Substantive Law, 87 Wash.U.L.Rev. ___ (2010). Indeed, the best reason for studying the development of the unitary civil action is to uncover this interaction between procedure and substance.

As the great legal historians have phrased the situation under the old English regime, procedure preceded substance, and later shaped the emerging substantive law. The primary question for a lawyer was what court to sue in and then what form of action to utilize. Each body of substantive law independently grew up within a particular writ, substance so being "secreted in the interstices of procedure" and being nonexistent outside the writs. A neat piece of evidence of the interaction is that legal commentators did not recognize a distinction between procedural and substantive law until the late eighteenth century.

In the early nineteenth century, first in the United States and then in England, the common law began to transform. It reorganized around coherent substantive doctrines. The contemporaneous institution of the modern procedural regime helped to shove substance radically to the foreground, leaving procedure well in the background. Most obviously, this shift from "writs to rights" led to gap-filling in the substantive law, which logically extended to cover situations formerly falling between writs. Among countless more subtle changes, the supposedly neutral shift from multitudinous forms to one form of action disadvantaged small plaintiffs with small grievances, thereby generating suggestions for a new tracking scheme.

The hottest of all debates in civil procedure today centers on whether procedural reformers should not only acknowledge the effects of procedure on substance but actually enhance them, rather than vainly try to avoid them. Should reformers, for example, create detailed intervention rules to serve substantive values, so that interested groups have a duty to intervene in civil rights cases? Should Congress enact special pleading and joinder rules for securities fraud actions? In other words, should reformers abandon the ideal of transsubstantive rules of procedure that govern all sorts of cases and instead shape substance-specific rules—creating what truly would be the new forms of action?

The classic critique of the Federal Rules' ideal came from Robert M. Covert, For James Wm. Moore: Some Reflections on a Reading of the Rules,

84 Yale L.J. 718, 718 (1975), who wrote: "We have become so transfixed by the achievement of . . . creating, nurturing, expounding and annotating a great trans-substantive code of procedure that we often miss the persistent and inevitable tension between procedure generalized across substantive lines and procedure applied to implement a particular substantive end. There are, indeed, trans-substantive values which may be expressed, and to some extent served, by a code of procedure. But there are also demands of particular substantive objectives which cannot be served except through the purposeful shaping, indeed, the manipulation, of process to a case or to an area of law."

But now the end of the debate is in sight, according to Robert G. Bone, Making Effective Rules: The Need for Procedure Theory, 61 Okla.L.Rev. 319, 333–34 (2008), who concludes that "we must bury, once and for all, the thoroughly misguided idea that trans-substantivity is an independent value or ideal for the Federal Rules. The Federal Rule drafters were committed to trans-substantive rules because they assumed that procedural rules could be justified without reference to substantive values. But this is just plain wrong. The fact that substantive policy is always a part of procedural justification means that trans-substantivity as an independent value or ideal makes no sense at all. This does not imply, of course, that all procedural rules should be substance-specific. What it means is that the optimal level of generality should be determined not by reference to some trans-substantive ideal, but by balancing the costs and benefits of general versus more specific rules."

JAY TIDMARSH, POUND'S CENTURY, AND OURS, 81 Notre Dame L.Rev. 513, 514–17, 570–71 (2006). "In England (and eventually America), procedure had dominated substance for much of the time since the eleventh century. . . . The energy devoted to constructing a procedural system yielded dozens of technical terms—such as the praecipe quod reddat, the capias ad respondendum, the demurrer, the general issue, the plea in avoidance, the traverse, and the wager of law—whose meanings would have been clear to lawyers one hundred years ago, and whose intricacies often determined the outcome of cases."

Reform came, through the efforts of people like Dean Roscoe Pound. "But we never fully integrated procedure and substance. Instead, we now have a system in which the importance of substance and procedure has been inverted. Substance now dominates procedure." In other words: "When we ask what rule we should use to declare a design defect in a product, or what the level of scienter should be for corporate wrongdoing, or what rule should apply to affirmative action programs, we do not stop to ask how we propose to enforce the rights under consideration. Instead, those who argue about the terms of substantive law assume procedural enforcement is possible. At best, difficulties of enforcement are secondary considerations. Today in the academy, procedure is often a second-class subject, thought to be a practically oriented matter devoid of insight and unworthy of sustained thought. We take for granted that cases will be, or at least ought to be, decided on their merits. How that is accomplished is a matter of mere practice and detail."

Professor Tidmarsh proclaims that "it is again time to consider bold reforms to our procedural system. Today our system faces pressures and challenges across numerous fronts, and modest tweaking of this rule or that doctrine cannot address the system's fundamental crisis. . . . The time for clear-eyed critique and for imagination about the next procedural moment is now. To be successful, however, we must recover a sense of the importance of procedure . . . ."

He follows with many criticisms and a few suggestions, including: "Procedural law is undertheorized. When I talk about undertheorization, I do not necessarily mean the lack of connection to the fanciest metaphysical construction or the most recent interdisciplinary insight that is removed by several levels of abstraction from the concerns of everyday litigators. Instead, I mean a connection to ideas that are deeper than the rules themselves. These ideas are guideposts that determine the skeleton of the procedural system; they are specific enough that, through the use of practical reason, they can help to put some flesh on the bones as well. As Pound would have appreciated, they spring from philosophy, political theory, economics, history, sociology, and other disciplines, as well as from lived experience. They provide a sense of purpose and direction for the rules we use; they have predictive force for how we should handle new procedural contexts; hopefully they exercise a moral suasion that make us believe that this approach is what we ought to be pursuing. Ideally, they connect to the ideas that drive the substantive law. Such ideas are not the sole determinants of a procedural system; they interact with history, tradition, and culture in a struggle for the dominant role in determining procedural rules."

WHY BOTHER?

The usual law student, who finds more than enough challenge in mastering the current law, naturally questions whether to bother with extending the field of study to include the past. Also, at first impression, the complex legal system operating in old England seems of questionable relevance to learning the system of modern America, a system that has repealed most of the old complexities while introducing new and unimagined complexities. Nevertheless, the practical reasons for studying what came before should already be emerging. Let us here try to collect just those practical reasons.

First, in thinking of *what law has been*, think how a modern course in civil procedure illuminates the study of the rest of current law as well as enabling practice in any field of law. Just so, a look at history helps one to deal with old cases, which are after all still part of the law. In their studies and research, the student and the practicing lawyer regularly come across pre-reform American cases and, less frequently, hoary English cases. The ability to understand the substantive import of these older cases often depends upon comprehension of the then prevailing procedure. Without a working knowledge of the vocabulary and a grasp of the rules and doctrines of past procedural systems—such as Maitland tried to provide—one may well misread such cases, never having the slightest inkling of error. The same goes for old legal materials other than cases.

Second, as to *what law is*, much of the law of today still feels the influence of its origins, and truly to learn current law the student must study its history. The right of trial by jury, for an extreme example, turns in part on whether the particular issue would have arisen in 1791 as part of an action at law or a suit in equity. Another ready example of current law directly incorporating legal history is a statute of limitations that classifies actions by common-law names and that so requires a sensitive appreciation of history in order to associate modern claims with their analogues among the forms of action. In its less direct or merely ancestral role, history explains and illuminates countless other aspects of procedure. Examples abound from pleadings to appeals, and this book draws such examples in all its Parts. Think of the modern procedural implications of the ancient elements of a cause of action. Moreover, as that thinking should reveal, budding proceduralists are not alone in benefiting from a knowledge of procedural history. Substantive law evolved within the structure of procedure, and so procedure has profoundly shaped the substantive law that comes down to today. To understand today's substance, one must know yesterday's procedure. An ahistorical approach to law, and especially to the laws of torts, property, and contracts, permits at best only partial mastery.

Third, and perhaps most important, think of *what law tends to become*. A good lawyer has a sense for the law as a developing organism. Too often lawyers see only the pattern of things immediately before them, pondering neither the past nor the future. Yet some critical problems of the law, such as the relationship of procedure and substance, defy even detection of the problem without the lawyer's appreciating that law has a time dimension. Historical study will not only reveal certain ageless problems but also deepen practical understanding and possibly lead to true reform. The future matters too. Every lawyer who has enjoyed a career of some length has left a legal system fundamentally different from the one in which that lawyer received training. There is no reason to expect legal development to reach its destination soon, and in fact there is every reason to anticipate legal change to accelerate. An intelligent view of the future of this living institution of law requires a broad perspective, which knowledge of the past can further extend. Thereby, for example, we can better perceive and comprehend the emergence, in pursuit of values both procedural and substantive, of the new forms of action.

To sum up, we recall that Justice Holmes went on to explain his aphorism that "[t]he life of the law has not been logic: it has been experience." O.W. Holmes, Jr., The Common Law 1 (1881). Part of that explanation was this: "The law embodies the story of a nation's development through many centuries, and it cannot be dealt with as if it contained only the axioms and corollaries of a book of mathematics. In order to know what it is, we must know what it has been, and what it tends to become."

TOPIC B

EVOLUTION OF COMMON LAW

SECTION 1. COMMON-LAW ROOTS

The roots of common law extend back well more than a millennium. One can be rather indefinite about the length of these roots because of the surprising legal continuity over the centuries—from the Anglo-Saxon invasions in the 400s, which wiped Roman law clean from the Briton slate, until the latter 1100s, when England's common law began to flower.

Even the Norman Conquest in 1066, while traumatic politically and socially, was a small deal legally. William the Conqueror claimed a lawful right to the English throne, by a succession promised by his relative Edward the Confessor. Although William came to a governmental and legal system basically similar to that of Normandy, he kept England and Normandy separate. One of his first acts after the Conquest was to promise the English that they could keep their laws, pronouncing that "you be worthy of all the laws that you were worthy of in the time of King Edward."

Thus, we could pick any period in those long centuries as representative. Let us take that of King Canute (or Cnut), who reigned before the Norman Conquest from 1016 to 1035. Although Danes had raided and settled in England for a couple of hundred years, he was the first Dane to be crowned king of England. He ascended the throne at the age of twenty-two, and he became the most commanding figure of his time, being later King of Denmark and Norway as well as of England. His dream of a Northern Empire might have changed the face of the world and the course of history, had he not died at forty. He began as a ruthless and effective king, early on rather cruel; but later he became more measured, transforming himself into a good and beneficent ruler.

The Oxford Book of Royal Anecdotes 35–36 (Elizabeth Longford ed., 1989) recounts the most celebrated story of Canute, in which he tries to teach his sycophants a lesson "when at the summit of his power, he ordered a seat to be placed for him on the sea-shore when the tide was coming in; thus seated, he shouted to the flowing sea, 'Thou, too, art subject to my command, as the land on which I am seated is mine; and no one has ever resisted my commands with impunity. I command you, then, not to flow over my land, nor presume to wet the feet and the robe of your lord.' The tide, however, continuing to rise as usual, dashed over his feet and legs without respect to his royal person. Then the King leapt backwards, saying: 'Let all men know how empty and worthless is the power of kings, for there is none worthy of the name, but He whom heaven, earth, and sea obey by eternal laws.' From thenceforth King Canute never wore his crown of gold, but placed it for a lasting memorial on the image of Our Lord affixed to a cross, to the honour of God the almighty King: through whose mercy may the soul of Canute, the King, enjoy everlasting rest."

(a) PROCEDURE

In the time of Canute, various institutions served the function of courts. Some of these embodied centralized royal authority. Far more important, at that time, were the local authorities. The early story of procedure is in large part the story of the eventual displacement of local by royal authority. So let us begin at the local level, where there were communal and feudal courts.

Local courts.—As to communal courts, the basic organizational unit was the hundred, notionally containing one hundred families of freemen. Once a month, each hundred held a moot, or assembly, at which the freemen would discuss local business, both administrative and judicial. This body was fully competent in matters criminal and civil. It is quite a stretch, however, to call this body a court. There were no trained judges or lawyers applying the law or keeping any records; instead, these moots were public meetings transacting public business in accordance with local custom. The hundred's assembly handled the more judicial matters not by reasoned decisionmaking, but by pushing settlement or by appealing to the supernatural. The simple purpose was to channel and discourage the urge toward violent self-help and blood feud.

The shires, or counties, contained an arbitrary number of hundreds. Twice a year the shire's royally appointed chief official, at first the ealdorman and later the reeve (shire-reeve or sheriff), convened an assembly of the more important freemen. It proceeded in the same manner as the hundred. Indeed, it had no hierarchical relationship with the hundred, although presumably it handled more important disputes. Similarly, a confusing welter of decentralized and nonspecialized local authorities, such as borough assemblies, acting more as meetings than as courts, helped dispose of the nation's judicial business.

The feudal courts were a natural outgrowth of the prevailing feudal system, although they grew in importance after the Conquest. At a time when violence was rife, the smaller had to seek protection from the greater, in the exchange becoming tenants of the latter. Land was all-important then, being not only necessary for subsistence but also the chief determinant of status. The lord handled civil disputes between his tenants in so-called seignorial courts. The lord might also exercise criminal jurisdiction, by special grant from the king, in so-called franchise courts. These private feudal courts dispensed a brand of justice that involved the individual lord's view of the case, unlike the communal courts' purer resort to customary law.

Such was the legal system of those days. It might seem undeveloped to our eyes, but imagine the conditions. England was a rough and wild land, with a small dispersed population. Travel was difficult, with roads long unrepaired and most rivers unbridged. Agriculture was the chief activity, and little trade went on. Disputes centered on land, with injuries to person and property being a growing concern, but with contract disputes being few and simple. A primitive legal system sufficed.

Royal courts.—Compared to other European kings of that time, the English king was not an insignificant figure, as Alfred the Great had converted a bunch of tribes into almost a real kingdom in part of England way back in the 800s. But the king had less power than we today are apt to imagine, and he had to remain constantly on the move throughout the kingdom to preserve it. So English government remained quite decentralized.

Writ of Henry I

Nevertheless, the king had begun to concern himself with justice, and indeed to appear as its fountainhead. He precociously used written orders, called writs, to define or confer jurisdiction. Canute used them, but given the verbal worth of an available picture, we shall reproduce as an example a writ of Henry I, the youngest and brightest son of William the Conqueror, from around 1113. It reads: "Henry, king of the English, to Almod, the archdeacon, greeting. Restore to the abbot of Thorney his manor of Sawbridge, stocked as you received it, that I hear no complaint of default of right as to this matter. Witness: Geoffrey, son of Wimund. Unless you do it, Ralf Basset [the county justiciar] shall do it. Witness: the same. At Westminster."[a] It seems that Almod had come into possession of an estate

[a] This writ, reprinted from the Burghley House series, appears in 4 Publications of the Northamptonshire Record Society: Facsimiles of Early Charters from Northamptonshire Collections plate III(b) (F.M. Stenton ed., 1930), along with its original Latin text and a rough translation.

owned by the Thorney abbey at Sawbridge in Warwickshire, during a vacancy in the abbacy, and now Almod was refusing to return the estate. So the king tells him to do right, or else. This predecessor of the so-called praecipe writ was not judicialized as yet, although Henry was threatening to involve his official, and so this technique held obvious promise for eventually drawing cases into the royal courts. This particular writ is six inches wide and an inch-and-a-half along its left side. Two strips of parchment were cut at the bottom: the king's seal in wax, showing the king enthroned, was attached to the upper strip, and the other narrower strip was used to wrap around the writ after folding.

The seed of royal courts existed in the king's council of wise men, or the witan as it was then called. First, the witan served as a feudal court for tenants-in-chief. Second, it acted on occasion as a court of last resort for ordinary litigants in cases of failure of justice, as II Laws of Canute ch. 17 provided that "no-one shall appeal to the king, unless he fails to obtain justice within his hundred." Third, the witan concerned itself with the steadily lengthening list of matters of special interest to the king, namely, the criminal pleas of the crown described by F.W. Maitland, The Constitutional History of England 107–09 (1908):

"Already before the Conquest we find that there are certain criminal cases in which the king is conceived to have a special interest. Thus in the Laws of Canute [chs. 12–15] it is said 'These are the rights which the king has over all men . . . —*mund-bryce*, *ham-socne*, *forstal*, *flymena-fyrmde* and *fyrd-wite*.' Apparently in case of any of these crimes no lord may presume to exercise jurisdiction—unless it has been expressly granted to him; such cases must come before the king, or his officer the sheriff, and the consequent forfeitures are specially the king's. A word as to the nature of these crimes:—*mund-bryce* is breach of the king's special peace or protection, this as we shall soon see becomes a matter of the utmost moment; *ham-socne* is housebreaking, the seeking of a man in his house; *forstal* seems to mean ambush; *flymena-fyrmde* the receipt of outlaws; *fyrd-wite* the fine for neglecting the summons to the army. In these cases, it is conceived there is something more than ordinary crime, e.g. homicide or theft, there is some injury to the king, some attack upon his own peculiar rights.

. . . .

Why Latin? After the Conquest, England was truly a trilingual culture, using French, English, and Latin. The chancellor and the royal courts used Latin in most of their written work because it was the universal scholarly language of certainty and elegance, and because the clerks of Chancery and of the courts were clerics (whence the term "clerk") who knew Latin. That language's later use in written common-law pleadings persisted until Parliament abrogated it in 1731.

Before abrogation, lawyers had problems aplenty in using a dead language. They engaged in all kinds of gymnastics just to handle the problem of modern words, because they could not plead in English and would suffer defeat if they made any mistake in their Latin. After abrogation, they had all sorts of other problems as they became cut off from their precedents. They tended repeatedly to use literal translations of pleadings to play it safe. See generally David Mellinkoff, The Language of the Law (1963).

"There is one term, however, which . . . can be so extended as to cover a very large space—that is the *mund-bryce* of Canute's laws . . . . Let us go back a little. The idea of law is from the first very closely connected with the idea of peace—he who breaks the peace, puts himself outside the law, he is outlaw. But besides the general peace which exists at all times and in all places, and which according to ancient ideas is the peace of the nation rather than of the king, every man has his own special peace and if you break that you injure him. Thus if you slay *A* in *B*'s house, not only must you pay *A*'s price or wergild to his kinsfolk, but you have broken *B*'s peace and you will owe *B* a sum of money, the amount of which will vary with *B*'s rank—you have broken *B*'s peace or *mund*; the *mund* of an archbishop is worth so much, that of an ealdorman so much, and so forth. Like other men the king has his peace. In course of time, we may say, the king's peace devours all other peaces—but that has not been effected until near the end of the twelfth century. In . . . the law of the first half of the [twelfth] century, the king's peace covers but certain times, places, and persons. *Pax Regis multiplex est*—the king's peace is manifold. First there is that which he gives with his own hand. Then there is the peace of his coronation day, and this extends eight days. Then the peace of the three great festivals, Christmas, Easter, Pentecost: each endures for eight days. Then there is the peace of the four great highways—the four ancient Roman roads which run through England. To commit a crime in one of these peaces is to offend directly against the king.

"Before the end of the [twelfth] century there has been a great change, a great simplification; apparently it has been effected thus:—the king's justices seem to have allowed any . . . use of the words 'in the king's peace' . . . and did not allow the [defendant] to take exception to these words—did not allow him to urge that though he might have committed theft or homicide still he had not broken the king's peace, since the deed was not done against a person, or at a time or place which was covered by the king's peace. Fictions of this kind are very common in our legal history, they are the means whereby the courts amplify their jurisdiction. Any deed of violence then, any use of criminal force, can be converted into a breach of the king's peace and be brought within the cognizance of the king's own court."

(b) SUBSTANCE

The law of Canute's time was mainly diverse customs made into customary law. The references above to the "Laws of Canute" could therefore have been misleading. Although kings had compiled dooms, or codes, these were quite limited in effect. They were incomplete, which presented no practical or theoretical problem because customary law underlay them. Much of what was in the codes consisted of homilies. The codes might regulate administration of justice and sometimes treat novel matters, and they did fix the amount of money payable as "bot" for various offenses. But the rest of their substance declared and clarified bits of local custom rather than displaced it wholesale. Although the codes thus did provide a little uniformity, lots of practical and theoretical room for variation persisted in the communal traditions.

The point here is that, in any real sense, there was no legislation and no king's law. Law was customary. With that in mind, consider further Canute's code. There follow the first five of the eighty-four chapters of the secular part of the Laws of Canute from around 1027, reprinted from a collection of the early kings' codes. His was one of the most important, as it represented for the Norman conquerors the last record of Anglo–Saxon law. But Canute did not write it (a certain archbishop probably wrote it). It hops about in coverage, making no pretense of completeness. Some of its homilies are quite modern in tone, but their impression weakens by proximity to sections treating wizards. It is very unoriginal, being largely drawn verbatim from earlier codes—but remember that unoriginality was a virtue here.

The Laws of the Kings of England from Edmund to Henry I

175, 177 (A.J. Robertson ed. & trans., 1925).

This is further the secular ordinance which, by the advice of my councillors, I desire should be observed over all England.

1. The first provision is, that I desire that justice be promoted and every injustice zealously suppressed, that every illegality be rooted up and eradicated from this land with the utmost diligence, and the law of God promoted.

> § 1. And henceforth all men, both poor and rich, shall be regarded as entitled to the benefit of the law, and just decisions shall be pronounced on their behalf.

2. And we enjoin that, even if anyone sins and commits grievous crime, the punishment shall be ordered as shall be justifiable in the sight of God and acceptable in the eyes of men.

2a. And he who has authority to give judgment shall consider very earnestly what he himself desires when he says thus: "And forgive us our trespasses as we forgive [them that trespass against us]."

> § 1. And we forbid the practice of condemning Christian people to death for very trivial offences. On the contrary, merciful punishments shall be determined upon for the public good, and the handiwork of God and the purchase which he made at a great price shall not be destroyed for trivial offences.

3. We forbid the all too prevalent practice of selling Christian people out of the country, and especially of conveying them into heathen lands, but care shall be zealously taken that the souls which Christ bought with his own life be not destroyed.

4. And we enjoin that the purification of the land in every part shall be diligently undertaken, and that evil deeds shall everywhere be put an end to.

4a. Wizards.

If wizards or sorcerers, those who secretly compass death, or prostitutes be met with anywhere in the land, they shall be zealously driven out of this land or utterly destroyed in the land, unless they cease from their wickedness and make amends to the utmost of their ability.

§ 1. We enjoin that apostates and those who are cast out from the fellowship of God and of men shall depart from the land, unless they submit and make amends to the utmost of their ability.

§ 2. And thieves and robbers shall forthwith be made an end of, unless they desist.

5. Concerning heathen practices.

We earnestly forbid all heathen practices.

§ 1. Namely, the worship of idols, heathen gods, and the sun or the moon, fire or water, springs or stones or any kind of forest trees, or indulgence in witchcraft, or the compassing of death in any way, either by sacrifice or by divination or by the practice of any such delusions.

SECTION 2. COMMON-LAW MATURATION

Once those long roots were in place, England's common law—in the sense of law common to all of England rather than local customary law—developed rapidly. The great leap upward occurred under Henry II, who reigned from 1154 to 1189. He was the son of the Count of Anjou and Henry I's daughter, with two decades of debilitating civil war necessary for him to reach the throne and thus to found the Plantagenet dynasty. He succeeded in shoring up royal authority at home. Abroad, through warfare and marriage to Eleanor of Aquitaine—which were seemingly not that different—he extended his rule from Ireland to the Pyrenees.

His greatest and most lasting contribution, however, was to the law. He did not intend to displace or absorb the local courts, but that was the consequence of his actions. He acted to limit the power of the sheriffs and the lords. He sought the money that came from administering courts. But also he wished to promote order in his realm and especially to provide justice. He took seriously his role as the fountainhead of justice.

The outcome of his initiatives was that by 1300 the royal courts and their common law had triumphed as the superior jurisdiction, even though the local courts continued to conduct much judicial business for decades to come. The kings did not manage this triumph by fiat. The elite who used the courts wanted a new system. Suitors preferred the royal courts' brand of justice, and thus these courts quickly became the origin for almost all litigation. Indeed, the triumph was decisive enough that the common law was already showing signs of closing off and some rigidity by 1300.

Henry II was able to play such a key part because he was an exceptional person. He was a man of action and learning, impetuous and charming, of splendid physique and overwhelming will. However, his temper and other negative aspects of his temperament got him involved in the 1170 murder in the cathedral of his chancellor and archbishop, Thomas à Becket. These two old friends had fallen out in a dispute over jurisdiction, namely, whether royal or ecclesiastical courts would try "criminous clerks," or clergy accused of crime.

That infamous and disastrous event brings to the fore the relation of the common law to canon and Roman law. The renewed canon law systematized by the monk Gratian, and the academic revival of Roman law upon the rediscovery of Justinian's Digest, swept from Italy through Europe in the 1100s and 1200s. These developments had undeniably significant effects in England too, but they did not overwhelm the common law. Why not? Because the common law had gotten such an early and strong start under Henry II. He thereby immunized his island's precocious legal system from foreign invasion. And so by "a breath-taking twist of fate," as phrased in the book giving the best overview of the whole subject, today our considerable part of the world lives under the common law, not the civil law. J.H. Baker, An Introduction to English Legal History 28 (4th ed. 2002).

(a) Procedure

Writs.—In the jurisdictional contest between the local courts and the royal courts, the latter were exercising what was in theory exceptional jurisdiction. Therefore, the litigant had to kickstart a king's court into action, doing so by getting the king to grant specially the favor of royal justice. This grant usually came in the shape of a writ. The officer in charge of writs was the chancellor, who was the handler of the king's written business and the keeper of the Great Seal of England. The plaintiff went to the chancellor to seek the particular writ that fit his case. The chancellor's staff, or Chancery, issued the writ for a fee. In the writ, the king ordered the local sheriff to get things going. The sheriff noted his action on the writ itself, and then he returned it to the court. The action was then rolling in a royal court.

The irony was that these writs, developed for very practical jurisdictional reasons, became the intellectual framework of the law. Within the confines of each type of writ the substantive law grew up to create a form of action, growing independently of the substantive law within every other type of writ and its associated form of action. The substantive law grew as the royal courts' rulings on pleadings, deciding whether a remedy lay but with no great substantive scheme in mind, slowly specified elements and defenses for the particular form of action.

The prominent role of the royal writs as the common law's framework is shown by a glance at England's very first legal treatise. It dates from around 1188 and is attributed to Ranulf de Glanvill, the chief justiciar under Henry II. Already the royal courts were busy enough to justify a treatise based solely on their workings. More tellingly, this treatise's organization was predominantly a compilation, albeit in Latin, of about fifty writs and the associated procedures peculiar to each. Here is how begins The Treatise on the Laws and Customs of the Realm of England Commonly Called Glanvill (G.D.G. Hall ed. & trans., 1965):

"Not only must royal power be furnished with arms against rebels and nations which rise up against the king and the realm, but it is also fitting that it should be adorned with laws for the governance of subject and peaceful peoples; so that in time of both peace and war our glorious king may so successfully perform his office that, crushing the pride of the unbridled and ungovernable with the right hand of strength and tempering justice for the humble and meek with the rod of equity, he may both be always victorious in wars with his enemies and also show himself continually impartial in dealing with his subjects.

"No-one doubts how finely, how vigorously, how skillfully our most excellent king has practiced armed warfare against the malice of his enemies in time of hostilities, for now his praise has gone out to all the earth and his mighty works to all the borders of the world. Nor is there any dispute how justly and how mercifully, how prudently he, who is the author and lover of peace, has behaved toward his subjects in time of peace, for his Highness's court is so impartial that no judge there is so shameless or audacious as to presume to turn aside at all from the path of justice or to digress in any respect from the way of truth. For there, indeed, a poor man is not oppressed by the power of his adversary, nor does favor or partiality drive any man away from the threshold of judgment. For truly he does not scorn to be guided by the laws and customs of the realm which had their origin in reason and have long prevailed; and, what is more, he is even guided by those of his subjects most learned in the laws and customs of the realm whom he knows to excel all others in sobriety, wisdom and eloquence, and whom he has found to be most prompt and clear-sighted in deciding cases on the basis of justice and in settling disputes, acting now with severity and now with leniency as seems expedient to them.

"Although the laws of England are not written, it does not seem absurd to call them laws—those, that is, which are known to have been promulgated about problems settled in council on the advice of the magnates and with the supporting authority of the prince—for this also is a law, that 'what pleases the prince has the force of law.' For if, merely for lack of writing, they were not deemed to be laws, then surely writing would seem to supply to written laws a force of greater authority than either the justice of him who decrees them or the reason of him who establishes them.

"It is, however, utterly impossible for the laws and legal rules of the realm to be wholly reduced to writing in our time, both because of the ignorance of scribes and because of the confused multiplicity of those same laws and rules. But there are some general rules frequently observed in court which it does not seem to me presumptuous to commit to writing, but rather very useful for most people and highly necessary to aid the memory. I have decided to put into writing at least a small part of these general rules . . . ."

Those general rules centered on procedure. Procedure was what a man who was learned in law had learned. And procedure centered on writs. The writs that operated as a pass into a royal court, and thereby originated the proceeding, were called original writs. Under Henry II, two general sorts of original writ came to exist for civil matters.

First, the oldest writs were merely executive commands, often to the sheriff, to take some specified action. From them developed the praecipe writs, which told the sheriff to command (*praecipe*) someone to do right as demanded or else come into the king's court to explain the refusal. This approach built on the king's special interest in rectifying contempt of his precepts. The prototype—the so-called writ of right—lay for invoking royal oversight of feudal courts' decisions on title to land. As such writs dealt with matters of eternal "right," such as ownership, the common law handled them solemnly and slowly.

Second, Henry II developed the possessory assizes, such as novel disseisin and mort d'ancestor, to deal with the wrong of dispossession of one's land by one's lord without due process. Later, but from similar roots, the ostensurus quare writs emerged to tell the sheriff directly to make the defendant appear in the king's court and show why (*ostensurus quare*) he had committed an alleged wrongdoing of some other sort. This general approach built on the king's peace idea that had already conquered all important criminal cases. These writs dealt with a mere "wrong," or past events generically called trespasses on the civil side, so the common law handled them a good deal more expeditiously. Of course, plaintiffs preferred the more expeditious writs. F.W. Maitland, The Constitutional History of England 112–14 (1908), continued his narrative thus:

"Henry II . . . took seisin . . . under his special protection . . . . This protection . . . is, I think, closely connected with that extension of the king's peace which we have been watching. He who takes upon himself to eject another from his freehold, breaks the peace, and the peace is the king's. This possessory procedure the king keeps in his own hands—it is a royal matter, the feudal courts have nothing to do with it. Thus there grows up a large class of actions (the possessory assizes) relating to land, which are beyond the cognizance of any but the king's justices, and these justices take good care that the limits of these actions shall not be narrow . . . .

"[The pleas of the crown had come to include] pleas touching the contempt of his writs or precepts. Now here is an idea of which great use can be made: *B* detains from *A* lands or goods or owes *A* a debt; this may not be a case for the royal jurisdiction—but suppose that the king issues a writ or precept ordering *B* to give up the land or goods or to pay the debt, and *B* disobeys this order, then at once the royal jurisdiction is attracted to the case. The king's chancellor begins to issue such writs with a liberal hand. A writ is sent to the sheriff in such words as these: Command *B* (*Praecipe B*) that justly and without delay he give up to *A* the land or the chattel or the money which, as *A* says, he unjustly detains from him, and if he will not do so command him to be before our court on such a day to answer why he hath not done it. Thus the dispute between *A* and *B* is brought within the sphere of the king's justice; if *B* is in the wrong he has been guilty of contemning the king's writ. Such writs in Henry II's time are freely sold to litigants: but this is somewhat too high-handed a proceeding to be stood, for in the case of land being thus demanded, the manorial courts are deprived of their legitimate jurisdiction. So we find that one of the concessions extorted from John by Magna Carta is this: The writ called *Praecipe* shall not be issued for the future, so as to deprive a free man of his court, i.e., so as to deprive the lord of the manor of cases which ought to come to his court, his court being one of his sources of income. To a certain extent in cases of land this puts a check on the acquisitiveness of the royal court. But even as regards land, it is evaded in many different ways, in particular, by an extension of the possessory actions which make them serve the purpose of proprietary actions. As regards chattels and debts the king has a freer hand.

"The notion of the king's peace is by no means exhausted when it has comprehended the whole field of criminal law: mere civil wrongs, 'torts' as we call them, can be brought within it—a mere wrongful step upon your land, a mere wrongful touch to your goods or to your person can be regarded as a breach of the peace; any wrongful application of force, however slight, can be said to be made *vi et armis et contra pacem domini Regis*: in such cases there may be no felony and no intention to do what is wrong—I may believe the goods to be mine when they are yours, and carry them off in that belief; still this may be called a breach of the peace. Hence in the thirteenth century a large class of writs grows up known as writs of trespass; for a long time the procedure is regarded as half-civil, half-criminal: the vanquished defendant has not only to pay damages to the plaintiff, he has to pay a fine to the king for the breach of the peace. Gradually (but this is not until the end of the Middle Ages) the fine becomes an unreality: actions of trespass are regarded as purely civil actions—and in course of time this form of action and forms derived out of it are made to do duty instead of all, or almost all, the other forms.

. . . .

"But the king's court could not have succeeded in thus extending the sphere of its activity if it had not been able to offer to suitors advantages which they could not get elsewhere. Royal justice was a good article—that is to say, a masterful thing not to be resisted."

As new needs emerged, the chancellor drafted new types of original writ. In the 1200s, however, the lords managed to put constraints on the chancellor's inventiveness. The resulting closed set of forms of action constituted the common law, although the courts over the centuries were to give rather elastic treatment to the existing writs' fairly fixed wording.

Courts.—Early on, the Norman successor to the witan, called the Curia Regis, handled the royal judicial work while traveling about with the king. As that workload increased, the natural innovation was division of labor and specialization, a development encouraged by the king's frequent journeys abroad to tend to the empire. So, the Curia Regis spawned a knot of trained jurists and later a set of royal courts, just as its successor, the King's Council, would later produce all the other branches and organs of government.

The royal treasury provided an initial display of this tendency to spin off departments. The impracticality of the treasury following the king was evident by the beginning of the 1100s. The barons who managed the treasury therefore settled into a large palace just west of London near a monastery, or minster. At Westminster Palace they did their accounting on a large checkered tablecloth, which served as a money counting board. Their department consequently became known as the Exchequer.

Meanwhile, Henry II played an active judicial role, often sitting as a judge in his traveling court. But especially often he was absent from the realm, producing an acute problem for the administration of justice. So in 1178, he detached five judges from his entourage to hear cases regularly in the banquet hall of Westminster Palace. To this group, litigants could at any time bring their disputes against other subjects, these being called common pleas as opposed to actions involving the king.

When King John, the youngest son of Henry II, tried to bring all litigation before his traveling court once again, those who had come to enjoy the advantages of a stationary court protested strongly. The result was the provision in chapter 17 of Magna Carta in 1215 by which King John promised to maintain hearing of common pleas in a certain place: "Common Pleas shall not follow our court, but shall be held in some certain place."

With its existence assured, the judicial delegation for hearing common pleas slowly evolved into a recognizable court. It began to keep separate records in 1234, and it acquired a chief justice in 1272. This first court—eventually known variously as the Bench, the Place, the Common Bench, or the Court of Common Pleas—made most of the common law. It had considerable collateral impact as well. First, a small corps of professional advocates developed, expert in the art of pleading. They soon generated standards governing how others might acquire their title of serjeant-at-law and thus gain admission to their restricted ranks. The serjeants were truly officers of the court, appearing to assist the judges even when the serjeant himself had no cases being heard. Second, the office of judge changed. The early judges tended to be knights, but more often clerics later on, because knights came from the king's entourage and because clerics could read and write. Still later the king appointed judges from the ranks of serjeants. Third, this professional bench and bar helped to complexify the legal system. That complexity necessitated study prior to admission to the bar. Thus emerged medieval law students in the form of legal apprentices.

The Curia Regis still handled a fair amount of judicial business. But this ever increasingly specialized business required specialists as decision-makers. A court separate from the Curia Regis began to form to meet this need. It kept its own records from 1234, and it received a chief justice as early as 1268. It did not always follow the king, although it did retain a close association with him. By a slow formation process, the King's Bench became an independent court and settled in Westminster. It long showed its roots in its official name, "The Justices of our Lord the King Assigned to Hold Pleas before the King Himself," and in the form of its writs, fictionally returnable "before the lord king wheresoever he should be in England." It eventually showed its grandeur in its chief justice's holding the title of Chief Justice of England—and in its conducting some of the most famous trials in English history, such as the one in 1535 condemning Henry VIII's chancellor Thomas More to death for refusing to recognize royal supremacy over the church. It had jurisdiction over criminal cases. On the civil side, the King's Bench at first handled actions involving the king, but by various maneuvers over the centuries it tremendously expanded its jurisdiction to hear personal common pleas, although not the real or mixed actions for the specific recovery of property. Such fee-driven jurisdictional competition among the royal courts impelled some of the key procedural and substantive changes over the centuries. And, finally, the King's Bench ended up the busiest by far of the common law's courts.

Lastly, the Exchequer, as the department of the treasury, had always had exclusive jurisdiction to decide revenue questions in the course of its functions. But it found ways to handle more ordinary cases. For instance, the writ of quo minus allowed a creditor to invoke its jurisdiction to enforce a mere private debt, on the ground that the king had an interest in any unpaid debt by which the creditor was less (*quo minus*) able to satisfy his tax liabilities to the king. By such clever maneuvers, the Exchequer of Pleas augmented its judicial business until it became a true court exercising a jurisdiction that extended to personal common pleas. It attained coequal status with the two other courts by act of Queen Elizabeth I in 1579. However, the Court of Exchequer retained its peculiarities—its judges were even called barons—so that it never played quite the role of the other two courts.

Westminster Hall

Westminster Hall, the palace banquet hall, was the home of the three courts until they moved to the Royal Courts of Justice on the Strand in 1882. This magnificent hall, built by the year 1099 and remodeled in the late 1300s, was a then unbelievable 239.25 feet long, 67.5 feet wide, and 92 feet high. Being a center of political life, it hosted such events as the coronation banquets, at which the King's Champion would ride his horse into the hall and symbolically challenge anyone to dispute the succession. It was the venue for state trials, including the trial of Sir Thomas More. Most gloriously, it was the forum where the common law developed. Today it remains a wonder, attached to the Houses of Parliament and still in occasional use.

As in the reprinted drawing from the year 1738, one entered Westminster Hall by the great north door. On the left of the far wall you can see the Court of King's Bench, separated by a flight of stairs from the Court of Chancery. On the near right wall, you can see the Court of Common Pleas. Each court was about 25 feet square. Nearer still on that wall was a passageway to a large chamber where the Court of Exchequer sat. A "bar," at which counsel stood, separated each court from the greater room. Inside the bar was a large table covered with a green cloth (or a checkered cloth in the Exchequer), at which the court officials kept records. The judges sat on a high bench against the wall, under tapestries bearing the royal arms. The courts remained here throughout the tumultuous course of English history. Indeed, one Chief Justice of Common Pleas supposedly refused to move his court a few feet back from the drafty north door, because he viewed any move from the "certain place" as violative of Magna Carta.

On both sides of the hall were shops rented to booksellers and clothiers. Food vendors circulated noisily among the milling populace. The result was a racket mixed confusingly with court proceedings. A visitor, around the time of the drawing, reported being "surprised to see in the same place, men on the one side with baubles and toys, and the other taken up with the fear of judgement, on which depends their inevitable destiny. In this shop are sold ribbons and gloves, towels and commodes by word of mouth; in another shop lands and tenements are disposed of by decree. On your left hand you hear a nimble-tongued painted seamstress, with her charming treble invite you to buy some of her nicknacks; and on your right a deep-mouthed cryer demanding impossibilities: that silence be kept among women and lawyers." Patrick Cormack, Westminster Palace & Parliament 18 (1981).

Of course, royal justice could not completely localize its operation at Westminster. All litigants and jurors could not travel there. So, the royal courts relied on a scheme of itinerant justice. From the Conquest the Norman kings regularly sent out high commissioners, later called the eyre, to inquire into the administration of the counties and to hear cases, their visitations becoming normalized under Henry II. Between eyres, more ad hoc judicial commissions traveled the country, taking over the task of itinerant justice with the end of the unpopular eyre in the early 1300s. With time, the commissioner was more and more likely to be a judge from any one of the three common-law courts.

The central courts integrated those itinerant institutions into royal justice by developing the nisi prius system. The nisi prius system entailed commencing an action at Westminster. A writ would then order the sheriff of the county where the action arose to send jurors to Westminster, unless before (*nisi prius*) the rather distant trial date a traveling judge appeared in order to hold court in that county. As he always arrived in time, the judge would conduct the trial locally and report the outcome to Westminster for entry of judgment. Thus, the king's justice became available throughout the realm, in increasingly regularized fashion.

Proofs.—A major reason for suitors' preferring the royal courts was that those courts employed a superior method of proof. The story here is the development of jury trial.

The local courts had long used trial by ordeal or by oath. The plaintiff had to establish a prima facie case, albeit merely by oaths in very general terms. The defendant next swore the truth of his position, again in very general terms. The court did not dissect the oaths, and of course there was no cross-examination. Normally the court, when faced with unresolved contradiction, would instead require the defendant either to undergo an ordeal or to bring in oath-helpers in support of his oath.

Trial by ordeal was an ancient mode of trial, coming from the Franks, used in criminal cases. A fair number of types of ordeal existed, but in England most involved fire or water. The precise ordeal depended on the defendant's status and the alleged offense. For example, freemen usually underwent the ordeal of hot iron. The accused fasted and prayed for three days. At the most solemn moment of a mass, the priest exhorted the accused to confess if guilty. The recalcitrant accused had to carry one or three pounds of burning iron in the form of a bar over a distance of three or nine feet, depending on the offense. Bandages went on the hand for three days. Finally, inspection: if the hand was clean, the accused was innocent, but if infected, guilty. The ordeal of hot water was similar, but involved the defendant's removing a stone from a cauldron of boiling water. The ordeal of cold water entailed dunking the bound defendant in a pond: the guilty floated, but the water received the innocent (who was promptly pulled out). Obviously, trial by ordeal heavily involved the Church. This involvement led to disquiet and eventually to the discredit of trial by ordeal. Finally, in 1215, the Lateran Council forbade clergy from participating in ordeals and thus completed their official demise.

Trial by oath, or so-called wager of law, was the principal form of proof in civil cases, as well as in some criminal cases. The defendant had to bring in eleven of his neighbors to swear that his oath was "clean." These oath-helpers, or compurgators, swore as to the defendant's general credibility, not as to the specific facts of the case. They had to recite precisely, "The oath that [defendant] hath sworn is true, so help me God and the saints." The outcome lay solely with the compurgators. Under this method the local courts never had to go behind the oaths and get into the facts, nor did they have to develop and refine a substantive law. The royal courts temporarily adopted the old modes of proof, but used this one regularly in certain of the older forms of action until about 1600 (formal abolition of wager of law awaited 1833), and thus contributed to the unpopularity among suitors of those older forms of action. This method surely worked better during religious times in small communities than during later years at Westminster where the defendant could rent compurgators at a modest rate.

Additionally, the Normans, it seems, introduced into England trial by battle, for use in some civil and criminal cases. The battle determined the case's outcome, so the court served only as umpire. In civil cases, champions, who in fiction were contradictory witnesses but in fact were hired, fought to the point of exhausted submission. In criminal cases, accuser and accused fought, usually to the death. Never too common or trusted, trial by battle fell off in use almost completely during the 1200s.

These methods of conflict-resolution seem primitive to us, but establishment of any method represented a step forward in terms of fairness. And remember their context. Early on, they served more the purposes of religious and social resolution by which God gave judgment, rather than establishing facts en route to finding truth. But even as truth-finding mechanisms, they may have worked better than we would guess. The participants were God-fearing persons with local knowledge who fully expected a sign from above and who would not lightly risk damnation by lying. Less obviously, but perhaps more importantly, the adjudicator likely chose and manipulated the mode of proof to facilitate the right outcome. So, the system was not wholly irrational. As already suggested, however, these methods kept the courts from working with the facts or with the substantive law. For those courts, procedure was all.

The various inadequacies of the old modes of proof left the royal courts and their litigants yearning for a new way. The obvious alternative was closed because judges were not willing to accept responsibility for performing the divine role of giving judgment. Instead, the new way—trial by jury—drew on ancient antecedents from throughout northern Europe and perhaps well beyond. In England the jury was at first a group of local people summoned by a public official to give upon oath their true word, or verdict, on some question put to them. That question might be a matter of administration, or it might have arisen in litigation. It might involve naming the landowners in the district, such as the inquests contributing to the historic Domesday Book compiled under William the Conqueror to ascertain title to land on the grand scale of the whole realm. Or it might involve identifying the suspects of crime, this accusation or presentment jury evolving into our grand jury. Or it might involve deciding who had the greater right to a disputed piece of land, as with the so-called assize used in the possessory assizes under Henry II. This new method of trial was fundamentally innovative, in that it actually passed on the merits. But the twelve men only "recognized" the facts on the basis of what they knew or could find out on their own.

The trial jury, or recognition jury, was thus on its way to displace the older modes of proof. As its use increased, spreading to the criminal law and then to the new family of trespass writs during the 1200s, its character changed. In the 1300s, rules of sequestration and unanimity arose: from the moment of the jurors' oath until their verdict, the jury was shielded from outside contact; decision became a collective adjudication, no longer permitted by majority vote. In the 1400s, the jury was ceasing to be a group of self-informing witnesses and beginning to develop into a representative and impartial group to hear evidence. Now the royal courts, with their nisi prius system to try cases locally, were effectively employing modern trial by jury.

The consequences of the rise of jury trial were profound. Its existence kept common-law procedure from developing in the directions of civil-law procedure. Moreover, the jury's existence shaped England's substantive law. Its existence forced the separation of questions of fact from questions of law. And in order to pose precisely the questions of fact to the jurors, pleading became the fine art lying at the core of the lawyers' job. Pleading also produced questions of law for the judges, such as which circumstances must exist to constitute a trespass. The result was the development of the substantive law.

(b) SUBSTANCE

Writ of Trespass

[From Anthony Fitz–Herbert, Natura Brevium 86 I (9th ed., London, J. Butterworth 1794)].

The King to the Sheriff, &c. If A. shall make you secure, &c. then put by gages and safe pledges B. that he be before us on the morrow of All Souls, wheresoever we shall then be in England, to show wherefore with force and arms he made an assault upon him the said A. at N. and beat, wounded and ill treated him, so that his life was despaired of, and other enormous things to him did, to the great damage of him the said A. and against our peace: and have there the names of the pledges and this writ. Witness, &c.

Questions: (1) Does the language of the writ provide any apparent confirmation of our account of the growth of royal civil jurisdiction?

(2) Which court will handle this case?

DEVELOPMENT OF TORT REMEDIES

Trespass originally meant any wrong, as in "forgive us our trespasses." The royal courts began to handle certain wrongs, especially those committed with force and arms against the king's peace. They first handled crimes of that sort, and then during the 1200s they utilized the ostensurus quare type of writ to give the civil remedy of damages for substantial wrongs committed with force and arms against the king's peace. Trespass thus acquired its specialized meaning of those wrongs that were within the reach of royal justice.

Trespass came to include direct and unauthorized interference with land, chattel, or person. There were variant forms of the writ of trespass, including forms for entry upon real property (trespass quare clausum fregit, or q.c.f.), injury to personal property, carrying away of personal property (trespass de bonis asportatis, or d.b.a.), and false imprisonment. A medieval affray might have involved all these wrongs, and more besides, but a single writ could be used to cover the whole affray.

As to property, the law conceived of trespass as a form of action protecting possession, rather than as a means to remedy a consequential injury to a mere right to possession. This distinction led to much fine discrimination by the courts. But to use a fairly simple illustration, imagine that *A* owned a chattel. *B* wrongfully took it from *A*. *C* wrongfully took it from *B*. *A* could maintain trespass against *B*. *B*, although himself a wrongdoer, could maintain trespass against *C*. But classically, *A* could not maintain trespass against *C*.

As the years went by, and after the royal courts had triumphed in the jurisdictional war, the writ of trespass became more and more obviously concerned with wholly private wrongs. The courts reacted during the 1300s by treating the key allegations of a royal interest—with force and arms against the king's peace—as fictions.[b]

Anonymous

Court of Common Pleas, 1304.
Y.B.Trin. 32 & 33 Edw. (Rolls Series) 258–59.

One R. brought his writ against J. and others &c., and said that they tortiously came with force and arms, and his wood cut and carried away &c. The defendants said that they were not guilty.—THE INQUEST came and said that they did cut his trees, but not with force and arms. Therefore it was adjudged by BEREFORD[c] that he should recover his damages &c.; and that the defendants should be taken notwithstanding they did not come with force or arms.

In the 1360s, the courts began to cease requiring the fictitious allegations in the writ, as long as the writ went on to describe the wrong in detail by laying out a so-called special case. This practice opened the door to a great expansion of the royal courts' jurisdiction. If the grievance did not fall within the scope of wrongs formerly treated under the trespass formulae, which were generalized versions of forcible breaches of peace without detailed allegations, the writ would tell a full story of wrong. That story might involve consequential harm, or the damaging results of the plaintiff's voluntary submission to the defendant's services, or even a wrong by omission.

Writ of Trespass on the Case or Action on the Case

[From Anthony Fitz-Herbert, Natura Brevium 92 F (9th ed., London, J. Butterworth 1794)].

The King to the Sheriff, &c. [Continue as in Trespass], to show wherefore he fixed piles across the water of Plim, along which, between the

[b] Fiction is a common first route to reform. The nature and role of fictions in the law are analyzed in Lon L. Fuller, Legal Fictions (1967).

Ejectment, another form of action deriving from trespass, showed perhaps the greatest proliferation of fiction. See the description infra p. 1112. Ejectment was ultimately generalized as a means of recovering the possession of real property, superseding the ancient real actions.

[c] Much exciting research keeps appearing in the field of legal history. The purpose of this summary of the common law is not consistent with citations to all that work. But perhaps an account of the judge rendering our book's earliest decision warrants an exception. See Thomas Lund, Activist Judges of the Early Fourteenth Century, 2008 Utah L. Rev. 471, 471 ("As the dominant figure within the formative years of the early common law, Chief Justice Bereford played a role comparable to that of Chief Justice Marshall in early American law.").

Humber and Gaunt, there is a common passage for ships and boats, whereby a certain ship, with thirty quarters of malt of him the said W. was sunk under water, and twenty perished; and other wrongs, &c. [continue as in Trespass].

Except for the wording of the writs, trespass and case were very similar.[d] But in the 1600s lawyers and judges tried to draw a distinction. After all, one had to choose the right writ, and one could not join different forms of action. So what constituted trespass and what constituted case? In the 1700s, the legal mind focused on immediate injury versus consequential injury.

REYNOLDS v. CLARKE, 93 Eng.Rep. 747 (K.B.1726). "Trespass for entering the plaintiff's yard, and fixing a spout there, *per quod* the water came into the yard and rotted the walls of the plaintiff's house. The defendant justifies, that before the trespass John Fountain was seised in fee of the plaintiff's house and yard, and two other houses adjoining, and demised the plaintiff's house and yard to one Tyler, except the free use of the yard and privy for the tenants of the other two houses jointly with the tenant of the plaintiff's house: then he shews how the house of the defendant, which was one of the two houses, came to him, and that he entered the yard and fixed the spout for his necessary use, to carry off the rain, *prout ei bene licuit* [as is well permitted to him]." Plaintiff demurred. Held, judgment for defendant.

Lord Raymond, C.J., said: "We must keep up the boundaries of actions, otherwise we shall introduce the utmost confusion: if the act in the first instance be unlawful, trespass will lie; but if the act is prima facie lawful (as it was in this case) and the prejudice to another is not immediate, but consequential, it must be an action upon the case; and this is the distinction."

Fortescue, J., said: "[I]f a man throws a log into the highway, and in that act hits me, I may maintain trespass, because it is an immediate wrong; but if as it lies there I tumble over it, and receive an injury, I must bring an action upon the case; because it is only prejudicial in consequence, for which originally I could have no action at all."

---

[d] In trespass and in case, the successful plaintiff recovered only damages. Suppose *B* wrongfully took a chattel from *A*. Was there any way in which *A* could recover the chattel in specie? By the old personal form of action known as replevin—originally a remedy only for wrongful "distress," or the taking of a chattel as security, but later extended to other wrongful takings or detentions—the plaintiff could compel such recovery. Indeed, seizure of the chattel by the sheriff and its return to the plaintiff were interlocutory steps in the action.

Scott, an Infant, by His Next Friend v. Shepherd, an Infant, by Guardian

Court of Common Pleas, 1773.
96 Eng.Rep. 525.

Trespass and assault for throwing, casting, and tossing a lighted squib at and against the plaintiff, and striking him therewith on the face, and so burning one of his eyes, that he lost the sight of it, whereby, &c. On not guilty pleaded, the cause came on to be tried before Nares, J., last Summer Assizes, at Bridgwater, when the jury found a verdict for the plaintiff with 100*l.* damages, subject to the opinion of the Court on this case:—On the evening of the fairday at Milborne Port, 29th October, 1770, the defendant threw a *lighted squib*, made of gun-powder, &c. from the street into the market-house, which is a covered building, supported by arches, and enclosed at one end, but open at the other and both the sides, where a large concourse of people were assembled; which lighted squib, so thrown by the defendant, fell upon the standing of one Yates, who sold gingerbread, &c. That one Willis instantly, and to prevent injury to himself and the said wares of the said Yates, took up the said lighted squib from off the said standing, and then threw it *across* the said market-house, when it fell upon another standing there of one Ryal, who sold the same sort of wares, who instantly, and to save his own goods from being injured, took up the said lighted squib from off the said standing, and then threw it to another part of the said market-house, and, in so throwing it, struck the plaintiff then in the said market-house in the face therewith, and the combustible matter then bursting, put out one of the plaintiff's eyes. *Qu.* If this action be maintainable?

This case was argued last term by *Glyn*, for the plaintiff, and *Burland*, for the defendant: and this term, the Court, being divided in their judgment, delivered their opinions seriatim.

■ NARES, J., was of opinion, that trespass would well lie in the present case. That the natural and probable consequence of the act done by the defendant was injury to somebody, and therefore the act was illegal at common law. And the throwing of squibs has by Statute W. 3 [1697], been since made a nuisance. Being therefore unlawful, the defendant was liable to answer for the consequences, be the injury *mediate* or *immediate* . . . . The principle I go upon is what is laid down in Reynolds and Clarke, Stra. 634, that if the act in the first instance be unlawful, trespass will lie for the consequences of it. . . . I do not think it necessary, to maintain trespass, that the defendant should personally touch the plaintiff; if he does it by a mean it is sufficient.—*Qui facit per aliud facit per se* [he who acts through another thing acts himself]. He is the person, who, in the present case, gave the mischievous faculty to the squib. That mischievous faculty remained in it till the explosion. No new power of doing mischief was communicated to it by Willis or Ryal. It is like the case of a mad ox turned loose in a crowd. The person who turns him loose is answerable in trespass for whatever mischief he may do. The intermediate acts of Willis and Ryal will not purge the original tort in the defendant. But he who does the first wrong is answerable for all the consequential damages. [Citations omitted.] And it was declared by this Court, in Slater and Baker, M. 8 Geo. 3, 2 Wils. 359, that they would not look with eagle's eyes to see whether the evidence applies exactly or not to the case: but if the plaintiff has obtained a verdict for such damages as he deserves, they will establish it if possible.

■ BLACKSTONE, J., was of opinion, that an action of *trespass* did not lie for Scott against Shepherd upon this case. He took the settled distinction to be, that where the injury is *immediate*, an action of *trespass* will lie; where it is only *consequential*, it must be an action on the *case*: Reynolds and Clarke, Lord Raym. 1401. Stra. 634; [other citations omitted]. The *lawfulness* or *unlawfulness* of the original act is not the criterion; though something of that sort is put into Lord Raymond's mouth in Stra. 635, where it can only mean, that if the act then in question, of erecting a spout, had been in itself unlawful, trespass might have lain; but as it was a lawful act (upon the defendant's own ground), and the injury to the plaintiff only consequential, it must be an action on the case. But this cannot be the general rule; for it is held by the Court in the same case, that if I throw a log of timber into the highway (which is an unlawful act), and another man tumbles over it, and is hurt, an action on the case only lies, it being a *consequential* damage; but if in throwing it I hit another man, he may bring trespass, because it is an *immediate* wrong. Trespass may sometimes lie for the consequences of a lawful act. If in lopping my own trees a bough accidentally falls on my neighbour's ground, and I go thereon to fetch it, trespass lies. This is the case cited from 6 Edw. 4, 7. But then the entry is of itself an immediate wrong. And case will sometimes lie for the consequence of an unlawful act. If by false imprisonment I have a special damage, as if I forfeit my recognizance thereby, I shall have an action on the case; *per* Powell, J., 11 Mod. 180. Yet here the original act was unlawful, and in the nature of trespass. So that *lawful* or *unlawful* is quite out of the case; the solid distinction is between *direct* or *immediate* injuries on the one hand, and *mediate* or *consequential* on the other. And trespass never lay for the latter. If this be so, the only question will be, whether the injury which the plaintiff suffered was *immediate*, or *consequential* only; and I hold it to be the latter. The original act was, as against Yates, a trespass; not as against Ryal, or Scott. The tortious act was complete when the squib lay at rest upon Yates' stall. He, or any bystander, had, I allow, a right to protect themselves by removing the squib, but should have taken care to do it in such a manner as not to endamage others. But Shepherd, I think, is not answerable in an action of trespass and assault for the mischief done by the squib in the new motion impressed upon it, and the new direction given it, by either Willis or Ryal; who both were free agents, and acted upon their own judgment. This differs it from the cases put of turning loose a wild beast or a madman. They are only instruments in the hand of the first agent. Nor is it like diverting the course of an enraged ox, or of a stone thrown, or an arrow glancing against a tree; because there the original motion, the *vis impressa*, is continued, though diverted. Here the instrument of mischief was at rest, till a new *impetus* and a new direction are given it, not once only, but by two successive rational agents. But it is said that the act is not complete, nor the squib at rest, till after it is spent or exploded. It certainly has a power of doing fresh mischief, and so has a stone that has been thrown against my windows, and now lies still. Yet if any person gives that stone a new motion, and does farther mischief with it, trespass will not lie for that against the original thrower. No doubt but Yates may maintain trespass against Shepherd. And, according to the doctrine contended for, so may Ryal and Scott. Three actions for one single act! nay, it may be extended *in infinitum*. If a man tosses a football into the street, and after being kicked about by one hundred people, it at last breaks a tradesman's windows; shall he have *trespass* against the man who first produced it? Surely only against the man who gave it that mischievous direction. But it is said, if Scott has no action against Shepherd, against whom must he seek his remedy? I give no opinion whether *case* would lie against Shepherd for the *consequential* damage; though, as at present advised, I think, upon the circumstances, it would. But I think, in strictness of law, trespass would lie against Ryal, the immediate actor in this unhappy business. Both he and Willis have exceeded the bounds of self-defence, and not used sufficient circumspection in removing the danger from themselves. The throwing it *across* the market-house, instead of brushing it down, or throwing [it] out of the open sides into the street (if it was not meant to continue the sport, as it is called), was at least an unnecessary and incautious act. Not even menaces from others are sufficient to justify a trespass against a third person; much less a fear of danger to either his goods or his person;—nothing but inevitable necessity; [citations omitted]. So in the case put by Brian, J., and assented to by Littleton and Cheke, C.J., and relied on in Raym. 467,—"If a man assaults me, so that I cannot avoid him, and I lift up my staff to defend myself, and, in lifting it up, undesignedly hit another who is behind me, an action lies by that person against me; and yet I did a lawful act in endeavouring to defend myself." But none of these great lawyers ever thought that trespass would lie, by the person struck, against him who first assaulted the striker. . . . Slater and Baker was first a motion for a new trial after verdict. In our case the verdict is suspended till the determination of the Court. And though after verdict the Court will not look with eagle's eyes to spy out a variance, yet, when a question is put by the jury upon such a variance, and it is made the very point of the cause, the Court will not wink against the light, and say that evidence, which at most is only applicable to an action on the case, will maintain an action of trespass. 2. It was an action on the case that was brought, and the Court held the special case laid to be fully proved. So that the present question could not arise upon that action. 3. The same evidence that will maintain *trespass*, may also frequently maintain *case*, but not *e converso*. Every action of trespass with a "*per quod*" includes an action on the case. I may bring trespass for the immediate injury, and subjoin a "*per quod*" for the consequential damages;—or may bring case for the consequential damages, and pass over the immediate injury, as in the case from 11 Mod. 180, before cited. But if I bring trespass for an immediate injury, and prove at most only a consequential damage, judgment must be for the defendant; Gates and Bailey, Tr. 6 Geo. 3, 2 Wils. 313. It is said by Lord

Raymond, and very justly, in Reynolds and Clarke, "we must keep up the boundaries of actions, otherwise we shall introduce the utmost confusion." As I therefore think no immediate injury passed from the defendant to the plaintiff (and without such immediate injury no action of trespass can be maintained), I am of opinion, that in this action judgment ought to be for the defendant.

■ GOULD, J., was of the same opinion with Nares, J., that this action was well maintainable.—The whole difficulty lies in the form of the action, and not in the substance of the remedy. The line is very nice between case and trespass upon these occasions: I am persuaded there are many instances wherein both or either will lie. . . . I think the defendant may be considered in the same view as if he himself had personally thrown the squib in the plaintiff's face. . . . [A]ctions of trespass will lie for the mischievous consequences of another's act, whether lawful or unlawful . . . .

■ DE GREY, C.J.—This case is one of those wherein the line drawn by the law between actions on the case and actions of trespass is very nice and delicate. Trespass is an injury accompanied with force, for which an action of trespass *vi et armis* lies against the person from whom it is received. The question here is, whether the injury received by the plaintiff arises from the force of the original act of the defendant, or from a new force by a third person. I agree with my brother Blackstone as to the principles he has laid down, but not in his application of those principles to the present case. The real question certainly does not turn upon the lawfulness or unlawfulness of the original act . . . . But the true question is, whether the injury is the direct and immediate act of the defendant; and I am of opinion, that in this case it is. The throwing the squib was an act unlawful and tending to affright the bystanders. So far, mischief was originally intended; not any particular mischief, but mischief indiscriminate and wanton. Whatever mischief therefore follows, he is the author of it . . . . And though criminal cases are no rule for civil ones, yet in trespass I think there is an analogy. Every one who does an unlawful act is considered as the doer of all that follows; if done with a deliberate intent, the consequence may amount to murder; if incautiously, to manslaughter; Fost. 261. So too, in 1 Ventr. 295, a person breaking a horse in Lincoln's Inn Fields hurt a man; held, that trespass lay: and, 2 Lev. 172, that it need not be laid *scienter.* I look upon all that was done subsequent to the original throwing as a continuation of the first force and first act, which will continue till the squib was spent by bursting. And I think that any innocent person removing the danger from himself to another is justifiable; the blame lights upon the first thrower. The new direction and new force flow out of the first force, and are not a new trespass. The writ in the Register, 95a. for trespass in maliciously cutting down a head of water, which thereupon flowed down to and overwhelmed another's pond, shews that the immediate act need not be instantaneous, but that a chain of effects connected together will be sufficient. It has been urged, that the intervention of a free agent will make a difference: but I do not consider Willis and Ryal as free agents in the present case, but acting under a compulsive necessity for their own safety and self-preservation. On these reasons I concur with Brothers Gould and Nares, that the present action is maintainable.

[Judgment] to the plaintiff.

Soon pressure in the opposite direction grew, as suitors sought in some instances to utilize case rather than trespass, despite trespass's often preferable pleading and proof features, because case was broader and more flexible in scope and more favorable as to award of costs and statute of limitations. Lawyers started invoking case in a series of running-down suits, alleging negligence. The courts struggled with this tactic, ruling first that trespass was the sole remedy if the injury had been immediate, but later that case was permissible as long as the act had been unintentional. Then in Williams v. Holland, 131 Eng.Rep. 848 (C.P.1833), the court held that for immediate injury by unintentional act, the plaintiff could elect trespass or case. That is, the plaintiff could waive the trespass and sue for negligence in case. Earlier, such flexibility would have been unthinkable, and indeed such flexibility sounded the death knell of the system of the forms of action. But even after Williams, only trespass would lie for immediate injury by intentional act, and only case would lie for consequential injury from negligence.

So, by this process of logic-chopping, which proceeded in remarkably similar ways in England and in the United States, the courts worked with these two writs to develop the distinctively separate substantive laws of intentional and negligent torts. Because trespass included intentional and direct wrongs, the courts developed the relevant substantive law within that writ. Because case would not lie for an intentional act's direct harm but would lie for any actionable negligence, the courts utilized actions on the case to flesh out the law of negligence—expanding liability toward and beyond any injury caused by the defendant's breach of the duty to exercise reasonable care, but always requiring the plaintiff to plead and prove fault and harm.

You are probably familiar with that story of the tort law, but you may not have focused on the impact of procedure on that substance. For an illustration, the shift from trespass to case allowed the courts to get more involved in lawmaking. In trespass, given its very general formulae, the blameworthiness of the conduct was not alleged but instead liability was left to the jury. In case, the detailed allegations included blameworthiness, generating questions of law that allowed the courts to expand and to limit that law.

Of course, the common law was extending its reach to many other sorts of torts. Another instructive example is the development from detinue to trover.

Writ of Debt or Detinue

[From Anthony Fitz-Herbert, Natura Brevium 119
L, I (9th ed., London, J. Butterworth 1794)].

The King to the Sheriff of Surrey, greeting: Command A. that justly and without delay he render to B. one hundred shillings, which he owes to him, and unjustly detains, as it is said (or, render to B. a certain book, or a certain cup, or a certain horse, or two lambs of the price of, &c. which he unjustly detains from him, &c.); and unless he will do it, and the aforesaid B. shall make you secure to prosecute his claim, then summon by good summons the aforesaid A. that he be before our justices at Westminster [on such a day] to show wherefore he hath not done it. And have there the summoners and this writ.

Question: (3) Does the language of this Common Pleas writ provide any apparent confirmation of our account of the growth of royal civil jurisdiction?

As the wording of this ancient writ suggests, detinue was at first quite indistinguishable from debt, but in the 1200s it differentiated from debt and lay for specific chattels. A bailor could use it against a bailee who wrongfully detained, or withheld, the bailed chattel. Through alterations in the set language of the declaration sanctioned by the courts, detinue extended to cover a number of situations, outside the bailment field, where someone withheld a chattel from the person entitled to its possession. Thus detinue would lie by the owner against a finder who refused on demand to return the found article.

Question: (4) Construct an example where detinue and trespass de bonis asportatis were available as alternative remedies.

In detinue, as in debt, the old method of trial by wager of law, rather than trial by jury, was available to the defendant. From the plaintiff's point of view, this was a serious objection to the use of that form. As a consequence of the procedure, the substantive law of bailment and related areas remained stunted. Moreover, the defeated defendant could satisfy a judgment in detinue, at his option, either by returning the chattel to the plaintiff or by keeping it and paying damages. Where the defendant had injured the chattel, he could satisfy the judgment by returning it in its injured condition.

For these reasons, pleaders began to cast about for a better remedy. The courts commenced to entertain actions on the case analogous to detinue, and during the 1500s trover appeared as a differentiated form of action. At first, the courts debated whether trover would lie in situations where detinue would lie or whether trover instead existed only to supplement detinue. But the pressures were such that trover quickly replaced detinue. In trover, trial was by jury, and the successful plaintiff recovered damages. The language of the writ, which the plaintiff tracked in the declaration, soon became set and ran as follows.

Writ of Trespass on the Case in Trover

[From Henry J. Stephen, Pleading 18 (London, J. Butterworth 1824)].

The King to the Sheriff, &c. [Continue as in Trespass], to show for that whereas the said A.B. heretofore, to wit, on the ______ day of ______ in the year of our Lord ______ at ______ in the county of ______ was lawfully possessed, as of his own property, of certain goods and chattels, to wit, twenty tables and twenty chairs of great value, to wit, of the value of ______ pounds, of lawful money of Great Britain; and being so possessed thereof, he, the said A.B., afterwards, to wit, on the day and year aforesaid, at ______ aforesaid, in the county aforesaid, casually lost the said goods and chattels out of his possession; and the same afterwards, to wit, on the day and year aforesaid, at ______ aforesaid, in the county aforesaid, came to the possession of the said C.D. by finding; Yet the said C.D., well knowing the said goods and chattels to be the property of the said A.B., and of right to belong and appertain to him, but contriving and fraudulently intending, craftily and subtilly, to deceive and defraud the said A.B. in this behalf, hath not as yet delivered the said goods and chattels, or any part thereof, to the said A.B. (although often requested so to do); but so to do hath hitherto wholly refused, and still refuses; and afterwards, to wit on the ______ day of ______ in the year ______ at ______ aforesaid, in the county aforesaid, converted and disposed of the said goods and chattels to his, the said C.D.'s own use, to the damage of the said A.B. of ______ pounds, as it is said; and have you there the names of the pledges, and this writ. Witness, &c.

The use of trover extended to a great many situations other than cases of finding. The method was not to change the set form of the writ and declaration, but rather to dispense with the need of proving what was alleged. In time virtually none of these required allegations had to be proved. Lord Mansfield frankly said of trover: "In form it is a fiction: in substance a remedy to recover the value of personal chattels wrongfully converted by another to his own use." Cooper v. Chitty, 97 Eng.Rep. 166, 172 (K.B.1756). Plaintiff need not have lost the goods, nor need defendant have found them: "a trover and conversion well lies, although [the defendant] came to them by a lawful delivery, and not by trover." Ratcliff v. Davies, 79 Eng.Rep. 210, 210 (K.B.1611). The courts took the allegations "lawfully possessed" and "as of his own property" in a highly qualified sense, so that a finder could bring trover against a subsequent converter. Request and refusal to deliver did not need to be shown, at least in many instances. Not only was the plaintiff not required to establish the truth of these atrophied allegations, the defendant was not allowed to prove their falsity.

Speaking very generally, trover could be maintained by the person entitled to possession of personal property for any conversion thereof by the defendant: the chief problem became one of defining what was meant by conversion. Professors Scott and Kent say that the act of conversion could be "a wrongful taking of possession of the chattel, a wrongful user of a chattel in the defendant's possession, a wrongful sale by the defendant of a chattel in his possession, or a wrongful detention." Austin W. Scott & Robert B. Kent, Cases and Other Materials on Civil Procedure 40 (1967). Trover thus had become both a tortious and a proprietary action, sometimes lying against a wholly blameless person.

Questions: (5) Did trover cover all the ground covered by trespass d.b.a.? See Johnson v. Weedman, 5 Ill. 495 (1843) (Abraham Lincoln successfully argued for defendant that someone tending a horse did not convert it by merely taking it on a fifteen-mile ride without the intent to keep it and therefore was not liable for the value of the horse).

(6) Did it cover all the ground of trespass for injury to personal property? See Intel Corp. v. Hamidi, 30 Cal.4th 1342, 71 P.3d 296, 1 Cal.Rptr.3d 32 (2003) (mass e-mailing to corporate employees could constitute trespass, if it damaged computers).

Imagine that *B* stole goods from *A* and sold them for a fair price to *C*, who knew nothing of the theft.

Questions: (7) Could *A* bring trespass against *B*?

(8) Could *A* bring trover against *B*?

(9) Could *A* bring trespass against *C*?

(10) Could *A* bring trover against *C*?

DEVELOPMENT OF CONTRACT REMEDIES

1. *Debt and covenant and their deficiencies.—B* struck *A* and injured him ten pounds' worth. Debt would not lie for the £10, although in a sense *B* "owed" *A* the money. The early conception of debt appears to have been quite different. "The conception [as in the writ of right for land] was that the debtor was holding back something which he had granted, and which therefore actually belonged, to the creditor, not that he was merely under an obligation to pay money." Edmund M. Morgan, Introduction to the Study of Law 92–93 (2d ed. 1948). Debt was a proprietary action. Examine again the wording of the writ of debt.

A and *B* orally agreed, *A* to deliver the horse Dobbin, *B* then to pay £10. *A* delivered Dobbin, but *B* did not pay. Debt would lie by *A* against *B* to recover the promised price.[e] This was an instance of "simple debt." One

[e] Detinue would also lie against *B* to recover Dobbin or the value of Dobbin. But here the value came to be equated to the promised price. Hence, this remedy had no usefulness to *A*

could rationalize the result with the thought that by the agreement and upon the delivery of Dobbin, *B* had granted and *A* had acquired the £10. An action could be brought not on *B*'s promise to perform, but on the half-completed transaction that created *A*'s property right. The horse having been given, debt lay to recover the definite, fixed sum that remained owing. But the object that was given need not have been an article of personal property. It might be money lent, work performed, or the like. So long as a fixed sum was owed for something by agreement, simple debt lay to recover the sum.

A variant form of debt, "debt on a specialty," lay to enforce a grant of a fixed sum of money, if made in a sealed instrument. Other variants of debt were "debt on a record" (i.e., a judgment) and "debt on a statute" (e.g., a statute prescribing a penalty recoverable by private suit).

By contrast, the ancient form of action called covenant, which did lie for breach of promise, was originally a comprehensive remedy. Such promises to do something in the future should be contrasted with a grant, which transfers an immediate right or interest to the grantee. In the 1300s, however, covenant narrowed so that it could be brought only for breach of a promise under seal. Moreover, covenant came to work only to recover damages for failure to perform, not to get specific performance or compensation for misperformance.

This array of forms suffered from at least two grave sorts of deficiencies. In the first place, as has already been noted, wager of law was often open to the defendant as the method of trial. In the second place, some important kinds of defaults in elementary commercial transactions were at this stage beyond the range of debt and covenant, being thus left to the local courts.

Question: (11) Imagine examples illustrating the last statement.

By adroit manipulation of specialty instruments and other maneuvers, commercial transactions could be and were rigged so as to provide easy access to the established forms of action in the royal courts of law. There was, however, a lengthy development by which new forms of action were devised to supply the omissions of debt and covenant, and in the course of which the substantive law of contract was shaped.

2. *Rise of special assumpsit to fill lacunae left by debt and covenant.*— A germinal situation in this development was one where defendant negligently injured a chattel entrusted to his care. An action on the case would lie. This form of action shifted the judicial focus from an old proprietary framework to a new tortious construct.

Question: (12) What of detinue? trespass?

The pleader in the action on the case would take care to allege in his declaration that defendant undertook (*assumpsit*) to care for the goods properly. Why the allegation of *assumpsit*? It has been surmised that this

---

beyond that of simple debt. Similarly, the later development of trover did not alter the available measure of damages.

part of the allegation of wrongdoing served to distinguish the situation from that of trespass for forcible breach of peace. And similarly *assumpsit* appeared in actions on the case for negligence of barbers, surgeons, and others.

The *assumpsit* then began to live a life of its own, so that in time the defendant in an action on the case in assumpsit might be held liable for breaking a promise (1) even where he had not been negligent and (2) even where his violation of the promise had consisted of his not doing anything at all. There was at work also a nontechnical notion of deceit, especially so where defendant had received value and then misperformed his promise or failed to perform it and where plaintiff had relied to his detriment.

The following report shows action on the case in assumpsit at midpassage. The judges are concerned over the failure of the plaintiff to allege what in later days would be termed consideration for the defendant's promise not under seal, and also over the failure to allege a misfeasance as distinguished from a nonfeasance. (For "trespass" in this report, read "trespass on the case." "Covenant" is used in some places in the report as the equivalent of an agreement or promise, in others as signifying the action of covenant.)

Watkins' Case

Court of Common Pleas, 1425.
Y.B.Hil. 3 Hen. 6, f. 36, pl. 33.[f]

A writ of Trespass was brought by one W.B. against Watkins of London, mill-maker. And he counted by *Strangeways sur ce cas*, that is to say, that on such a day and year in London in such a ward he took upon himself (*emprist sur luy*) to make a mill for the said plaintiff; and he showed that the mill was to be all ready and built by the following Christmas, but that by this time the mill was not built, *à tort* and to the damage of the plaintiff ten marks.

---

[f] The translation from Law French is by C.H.S. Fifoot, History and Sources of the Common Law 341–43 (1949), as corrected by J.H. Baker & S.F.C. Milsom, Sources of English Legal History 380–83 (1986).

Why French? That is not easy to explain. Of course, French had been the language of the early ruling class and the lay elite. Henry II had spoken at best broken English. But later, as French and Latin were losing out to English on many levels, the law courts more firmly embraced the losing languages. Perhaps there lies the law's reason, because continuing to use French and Latin was a way to create mystery, status, and monopoly.

What was Law French? The law courts developed a peculiar derivative of Norman French. An example might best make the point: Church v. Brownewick, 82 Eng.Rep. 1140, 1140 (K.B.1667) (per curiam), approved a general pleading "*pur avoid le stuffing del rolls ove multiplicity de matter*." The courts used Law French in most oral proceedings and the records of those proceedings into the 1500s. A modern relic of that use is the tendency of legal language toward redundancy. This comes from the times when lawyers played it safe and sound by coupling an English word with a French word, as in breaking and entering, had and received, goods and chattels, fit and proper, or free and clear.

Rolfe: Judgment of the writ: for by the writ it is supposed that the defendant should make a mill, and he has not declared for certain how much he should have for the making.

Strangeways: Since you have said nothing, we ask judgment and pray our damages.[g]

■ BABINGTON, C.J. If I bring a writ of Deceit against one, for that the defendant was my attorney and that by his negligence I have lost my land, etc., in this case I must declare how he was retained by me, or else the writ shall be abated. So here.

■ MARTIN, J. I do not know that I have seen in the Law that a writ *sur tiel mattere* lies, where no tort is alleged in the writ, but only that the defendant has promised to do something and he has not done it: for in such case a good writ of Covenant lies, supposing that he has a specialty. But if he had made a mill which was not good but altogether badly made, then a good writ of Trespass would lie. Suppose we put the case that a farrier makes a covenant with me to shoe my horse, and by his negligence he lames my horse, on this matter shewn a good writ of Trespass lies, for notwithstanding that in the rehearsal of the matter a covenant is supposed, I say that, inasmuch as he has done badly what he had covenanted to do, the covenant is thereby changed and made into a tort, for which a good writ of Trespass lies. But in the case at bar there is no such thing; for no tort is alleged in the writ by any feasance, but only a nonfeasance, which sounds only in covenant.

■ BABINGTON, C.J. I think the contrary. Put the case that one makes a covenant with me to roof my hall [in] a certain house by a certain time, and within this time he does not roof it, so that by default of the roofing the furniture of the house is all damaged by the rain; in this case I say that I shall have a good writ of Trespass *sur le mattere monstré* against him who made the covenant with me. So too I shall recover damages because I have suffered loss by the not making the [roof. Likewise here, the plaintiff is damaged by the nonfeasance of the] mill.

■ COKAYNE, J. To the same intent. As to the first argument, that he should have declared that he made the covenant with him for a sum certain, it seems to me, Sir, that he has thus declared in effect. For it is not to be supposed that he should make the mill for nothing, and so it is all one as if he had expressly said so in his pleading, and on the matter shown the writ is well enough. And put the case that one makes a covenant to repair certain ditches on my land, and he does not do so, so that by his default the water which should run into the ditches floods my land and destroys my corn; I say that I shall have a good writ of Trespass for this nonfeasance. So here.

. . . .

[g] "A young barrister had been talking for about four hours to a jury who, when he had finished, felt somewhat exhausted. His opponent then arose and, looking sweetly at the judge, said: My lord, I will follow the example of my friend who has just finished and submit the case without argument." Richard Fountain, The Wit of the Wig 110 (1968). But see Peter Hay, The Book of Legal Anecdotes 171 (1989) (attributing the same to a nineteenth-century American).

■ MARTIN, J. . . . But truly, as it seems to me, if this action be maintainable *sur cette mattere*, for every broken covenant in the world a man shall have an action of Trespass.

■ BABINGTON, C.J. All our talk is vain; for as yet they have not demurred in law.

Wherefore he said to *Strangeways* and *Rolfe*, Plead and say what you will, or demur; and then there can be debate and dispute enough.

Wherefore *Rolfe* pleaded over, and said that, long after the time when it was supposed that he made the covenant, that is to say, on such a day, etc., the defendant came to the plaintiff in such a ward and said to him that the mill was quite ready [to be] built, and asked him when he would have the mill, and discharged himself completely of the mill [when the plaintiff said he did not want to have the mill]. And so we demand judgment if the action lies.

Strangeways: He did not discharge himself.

Issue joined.

Quaere de l'opinion de MARTIN.[h]

In the 1500s the action called special assumpsit became a differentiated form of action. The plaintiff had to plead specifics of the agreement, and the judicial analysis turned from the tortious to the contractual. It was said broadly in Strangborough v. Warner, 74 Eng.Rep. 686 (K.B.1589), that "a promise against a promise will maintain an action upon the case, as in consideration that you do give me £10 on such a day, I promise to give you £10 such a day after."

Question: (13) That quotation represents the whole report. Whom does the reporter in the Strangborough case envisage as plaintiff, *you* (lender) or *I* (borrower)? What would be the measure of damages?

Declaration in Special Assumpsit

[From 2 Joseph Chitty, Pleading 99–100 (London, J. Butterworth 1809)].

In the Common Pleas.

[h] This last expression of disagreement is a note by the reporter. That might seem odd—except in the context of the Yearbooks. These annual anthologies reported oral proceedings in Common Pleas from before 1300 to about 1560. Their authorship is unknown, as they were really evolving sets of communal notes compiled with a pedagogic purpose. They seldom related a cases's outcome after trial, but instead reported the legal discussion in court that was of interest to lawyers and students. Thus, in Watkins' Case, we read a transcript of the preliminary interaction between serjeants and justices. The Yearbooks were replaced by more formal reports, eventually reprinted as the English Reports, that progressively comprised nearly complete texts as in Scott v. Shepherd, albeit texts of decisions that were still compiled by individuals as privately published reporters until 1865.

Hilary Term, 47 Geo. 3, Middlesex, (to wit) C.D. was attached to answer A.B. of a plea of trespass on the case, &c. and thereupon the said A.B. by E.F. his attorney, complains, For that whereas heretofore, to wit, on, &c. at, &c. the said A.B. at the special instance and request of the said C.D. bargained with the said C.D. to buy of him the said C.D. and the said C.D. then and there sold to the said A.B. a large quantity, to wit, ten loads of wheat at the rate or price of £ ______ for each and every load thereof, to be delivered by the said C.D. to the said A.B. in a week then next following, at ______, and to be paid for by the said A.B. to the said C.D. on the delivery thereof as aforesaid; and in consideration thereof, and that the said A.B. at the like special, &c. had then and there undertaken and faithfully promised the said C.D. to accept and receive the said wheat, and to pay him for the same at the rate or price aforesaid; he the said C.D. undertook, &c. to deliver the said wheat to him the said A.B., as aforesaid; and although the said time for the delivery of the said wheat, as aforesaid, hath long since elapsed, and the said A.B. hath always been ready and willing to accept and receive the said wheat, and to pay for the same at the rate or price aforesaid, to wit, at, &c. aforesaid; yet the said C.D. not regarding, &c. but contriving, &c. to deceive and defraud the said A.B. in this behalf, did not nor would within the time aforesaid, or at any time afterwards, deliver the said wheat, or any part thereof for the said A.B. at, &c. aforesaid, or elsewhere, but wholly neglected and refused so to do, whereby the said A.B. hath lost and been deprived of divers great gains and profits, which might and otherwise would have arisen and accrued to him from the delivery of the said wheat to him the said A.B., as aforesaid, to wit, at, &c. aforesaid. Wherefore the said A.B. saith that he is injured, and hath sustained damages to the value of £ ______, and therefore he brings his suit, &c.

To return to the case of the horse Dobbin: special assumpsit now lay by *B* to recover damages in the event of *A*'s nondelivery of the horse. But if instead *B* failed to pay after *A* had delivered, *A* could not maintain special assumpsit to recover the agreed price. Here the remedy remained simple debt, with its attendant wager of law. The notion seems to have been that *B*'s promise to pay was "merged" in the owed debt, so that it afforded no ground for special assumpsit.

3. Assumpsit engulfs simple debt.—Now came a movement by which assumpsit became a remedy alternative to simple debt.

The first step. Suppose *B*, being indebted for Dobbin, made a *fresh* promise to pay (*indebitatus assumpsit*) for nominal consideration. It was held that special assumpsit would lie for damages from reliance on the fresh promise. The pleading did not have to contain specifics on how the original debt accrued because the plaintiff was suing on the fresh promise.

The second step. Then in Slade's Case, 76 Eng.Rep. 1072 (K.B.1602), the court held after much deliberation that even if *B* had not actually made a subsequent promise to pay, special assumpsit would nevertheless lie if the plaintiff pleaded specifics concerning the original debt. The court found a promise to pay implicit in the original bargain. The fact that another form of action was available no longer interposed a barrier.

The third step. In the years immediately following Slade's Case, a new variant of assumpsit, called general assumpsit, came to be accepted as an alternative to simple debt for money owed. The averment of a fresh promise to pay had to appear in the declaration, but the courts now recognized it as fictitious: no proof was necessary. The plaintiff had to plead some information about the original debt, but specifics were now unnecessary: a general rather than a special pleading sufficed. As a consequence of freeing the plaintiff from the need of pleading specifically the original debt and of proving a subsequent promise, the path to expansion of the form of action was open wide.

The replacement of simple debt by assumpsit, and the consequential move from wager of law to trial by jury, shifted the risk of loss by perjury from plaintiffs to defendants. The direct result was Parliament's 1677 passage of the Statute of Frauds, and its descendants still require certain kinds of contracts to be in writing.

4. Extension of general assumpsit beyond the range of simple debt.—In the sweep of time, general assumpsit extended far beyond the province of simple debt. It was no objection to the maintenance of general assumpsit that the amount involved was not fixed. A common situation for general assumpsit was where plaintiff had delivered goods or done work for defendant without agreement as to the amount of compensation; if plaintiff was successful, he recovered a judgment for the reasonable value, as determined in the action.

A series of simple, stylized forms of declaration evolved within general assumpsit. These "common counts" may be classed as follows: (1) the indebitatus counts, including the money counts (money lent; money paid; money had and received; and money due upon an account stated) and including other counts (goods sold and delivered; goods bargained and sold; and work, labor, and materials provided); and (2) the value counts (quantum meruit, for the reasonable value of work done; and quantum valebant, for the reasonable value of goods supplied). Here follows a form of declaration in general assumpsit for goods sold and delivered.

Declaration in General Assumpsit

[From Henry J. Stephen, Pleading 47–48 (London, J. Butterworth 1824)].

In the King's Bench.

______ Term, in the ______ year of the reign of King George the Fourth.

______ to wit, C.D. was attached to answer A.B. of a plea of trespass on the case; and thereupon the said A.B., by ______ his attorney, complains: For that, whereas the said C.D. heretofore, to wit, on the ______ day of ______ in the year of our Lord ______ at ______ in the county of ______ was indebted to the said A.B. in the sum of ______ pounds, of lawful money of Great Britain, for divers goods, wares and merchandizes, by the said A.B. before that time sold and delivered to the said C.D. at his special instance and request; and being so indebted he the said C.D., in consideration thereof, afterwards to wit, on the day and year aforesaid, at ______ aforesaid, in the county aforesaid, undertook and faithfully promised the said A.B. to pay him the said sum of money when he the said C.D. should be thereto afterwards requested. Yet the said C.D. not regarding his said promise and undertaking, but contriving and fraudulently intending craftily and subtilly to deceive and defraud the said A.B. in this behalf, hath not yet paid the said sum of money, or any part thereof, to the said A.B. (although oftentimes afterwards requested). But the said C.D., to pay the same, or any part thereof, hath hitherto wholly refused, and still refuses, to the damage of the said A.B. of ______ pounds; and therefore he brings his suit, &c.

Consider now the case of Lamine v. Dorrell, 92 Eng.Rep. 303 (K.B. 1705). A man died intestate owning certain Irish debentures. Defendant wrongfully procured his own appointment as administrator and wrongfully sold the debentures, apparently representing them to be his own. Estate administration was then granted to plaintiff, who sued to recover the price received by defendant, using general assumpsit "for money received by the defendant to the use of the plaintiff as administrator." It was held that the action could be maintained.

Question: (14) Could any argument be made that simple debt would lie, and hence general assumpsit?

(15) To what extent must the language of the declaration in general assumpsit be fictionalized in order to bring a situation like Lamine v. Dorrell within the scope of the declaration?

If the Lamine case could be maintained in general assumpsit, it was plain that the way was open for the use of that form of action as a remedy for a wide variety of cases of unjust enrichment.

Note that trover could have been brought for the conversion of the debentures. Justice Powell said in the Lamine case: "But the plaintiff may dispense with the wrong, and suppose the sale made by his consent, and bring an action for the money they were sold for, as money received to his use." Here is the germ of a powerful idea. You will now begin to understand what is meant by the lawyer's phrase, "waiving the tort and suing in (general) assumpsit" for the proceeds of the tort.

The classic justification for these new uses of general assumpsit was by Lord Mansfield in Moses v. Macferlan, 97 Eng.Rep. 676, 678 (K.B.1760):

"The 1st objection is, 'that an action of debt would not lie here; and no *assumpsit* will lie, where an action of debt may not be brought:' some sayings at *nisi prius*, reported by note takers who did not understand the force of what was said, are quoted in support of that proposition. But there is no foundation for it.

"It is much more plausible to say, 'that where debt lies, an action upon the case ought not to be brought.' And that was the point relied upon in Slade's case: but the rule then settled and followed ever since is, 'that an action of *assumpsit* will lie in many cases where debt lies, and in many where it does not lie.'

"A main inducement, originally, for encouraging actions of *assumpsit* was, 'to take away the wager of law:' and that might give rise to loose expressions, as if the action was confined to cases only where that reason held.

"2d objection.—'That no assumpsit lies, except upon an express or implied contract: but here it is impossible to presume any contract to refund money . . . .'

"Answer. If the defendant be under an obligation, from the ties of natural justice, to refund; the law implies a debt, and gives this action, founded in the equity of the plaintiff's case, as it were upon a contract ('quasi ex contractu,' as the Roman law expresses it)."

General assumpsit thus became a flexible means to fill the gaps in the substantive law. But the bounds on this idea of unjust enrichment were difficult to fix. From a formal point of view, one might be tempted to agree with Holt v. Markham, [1923] 1 K.B. 504, 513 (C.A.1922) (Scrutton, L.J.), that ever since Lord Mansfield, "the whole history of this particular form of action has been what I may call a history of well-meaning sloppiness of thought."

5. *Relation between special and general assumpsit.*—General assumpsit thus would lie as an alternative to simple debt, as a means for recovery of reasonable value under contracts implied in fact, and as a remedy for unjust enrichment. Speaking perhaps too simply, special assumpsit came to be a remedy for breach of any express promise not under seal.

It is evident that this scheme involved considerable overlap among writs. To round out our account, we return again to the case of the horse Dobbin. We have seen that debt would lie by *A* for the promised price after delivery of the horse. When the common-law development was over, general and special assumpsit would also lie for the price.

Some of the subtler relations among the forms of action for breach of promise, at the close of the entire development that has just been reviewed, will be brought out by considering the following problem cases.

Question: (16) *X* and *Y* contract orally, or in an instrument not under seal, *X* to perform work over a period of time, *Y* to pay a stated sum upon completion of the work. When *X* has performed in part, *Y* wrongfully discharges him from the job. What forms of action were available to *X* against *Y*, and how would the court figure recovery in each instance?

(17) *B* promises to pay *A* an agreed price, *A* then to deliver Dobbin. *B* pays, but *A* fails to deliver. What forms of action were available to *B* against *A*? Will *B*'s choice of a form of action depend on what he thinks he can prove to be the reasonable value of the horse?

(18) *A* is to deliver Dobbin, and *B* is then to pay an agreed price. If *B* receives the horse and fails to pay the price, may *A* use general assumpsit to recover not the agreed price, but the reasonable value of the horse, if that value exceeds the price? See Restatement (Second) of Contracts § 373(2) (1979) (no).

(19) Defendant put up at auction a certain cow and 400 pounds of hay, which was then in a bay with other hay. Plaintiff bid off the cow and the hay for one gross sum of $17, which he paid at the time. He received the cow and afterwards made demand for the hay, which was refused by defendant, who had used it. What forms of action were available to plaintiff, and what would be his recovery under each? See Miner v. Bradley, 39 Mass. (22 Pick.) 457, 457–58 (1839) (Morton, J.) ("We cannot break down the well known distinctions between different modes of declaring, without endangering the principles of justice upon which they are founded.").

A significant substantive consequence of this procedural history is that our law of contracts is, for the most part, a broad law based on general principles of liability. In contrast, our law of torts remains a pigeonholed system of separate and named torts. The contrast is not inevitable, as the civil-law systems treat both contractual and noncontractual liability by general principles. Moreover, the contrast is not without consequence. The common law sometimes fails to draw necessary distinctions between different contract claims, even though debt collection is obviously very different from a warranty claim. Nominate torts arguably keep our law from spinning out of control but also prevent it from performing some functions of systematic social control. Do you see any reasons, other than tradition, for the common law's contrast between contract and tort?

SECTION 3. COMMON-LAW PLEADING

Pleading was the critical link between procedure and substance. The techniques of pleading changed with time. Early on, pleading was oral and tentative, as in Watkins' Case. The lawyers told their story in a "counte" and a defense, tentatively feeling their way toward joinder of issue with the advice of the judges. But in the 1400s pleadings became written, in the 1500s binding, and in the 1600s highly technical.

Pleading in theory worked for the good. "[P]leading is the honorable, commendable and profitable part of the law, and by good desert it is so. For cases arise by chance, and are many times intricate, confused and obscured, and are cast into form, and made evident, clear and easie, both to Judge and jury (which are the arbitrators of all causes) by good and fair pleading. So that this is the principal art of law, for pleading is not talking; and therefore it is required that pleading be true; that is, the goodness and virtue of pleading; and that it be certain and single, and that is the beauty and grace of pleading." Slade v. Drake, 80 Eng.Rep. 439, 440 (C.P.1618) (Hobart, C.J.). Nevertheless, pleading in practice degenerated into a baleful game of skill.

Because the nineteenth-century reform movement that swept away the forms of action at law also aimed, almost as a corollary, at the amelioration of the common-law system of pleading, it is convenient at this point to examine briefly that pleading system in its mature state. In the interests of simplicity, the following account generally omits mention of various divergences in the pleading techniques among the several forms of action.

The fundamental notion of common-law pleading—or at least its somewhat mythical ideal, which intensified with the centuries before it began to unravel—was that the parties should, by as extensive an interchange of statements of position as necessary, wind up with a single issue of law or of fact upon whose resolution the controversy would depend. We shall review briefly the moves and countermoves by which this result was supposed to be achieved.

1. **Declaration.**—After determining the proper form of action and obtaining the appropriate writ, the plaintiff's first step toward the production of an issue was to prepare a *declaration*. The declaration had to conform to the writ, and it had to contain a statement of the cause's elements sufficient in law to sustain the action. Declarations under most of the forms of action took on set and rigid forms. Some of them, notably the declaration in trover, contained loads of fictitious allegations frequently giving the defendant no hint of what the plaintiff would later seek to prove. They also varied greatly in the specificity of allegation that was required. The declaration on the common counts in general assumpsit, for example, was generalized, while the declaration in special assumpsit was pretty detailed albeit with some fictitious allegations. Samples appeared just above in the contract materials.

2. **Responses to declaration.**—The defendant, in order to prevent the entry of judgment against him, had to make a choice among three types of countermoves:

a. The defendant might *demur*.—Demurrers were of two kinds, *general* and *special*. The former attacked defects of substance, the latter defects in form. For the moment we shall confine our attention to the general demurrer. A general demurrer was appropriate when, supposing the assertions in the declaration to be true, the defendant believed that the plaintiff was not entitled to the redress he sought. Thus the parties were at issue immediately, the plaintiff affirming and the defendant denying the sufficiency in law of the declaration. This question of law was resolved by the court on argument. In England the hearing on such an issue of law was before the full bench of the court sitting at Westminster. There was no occasion for a trial of the facts because for purposes of the demurrer the allegations of the declaration stood as admitted. Originally, a judgment on demurrer ended the case, but eventually leave to plead over came to be given as a matter of course.

b. The defendant might interpose a *dilatory plea.*—Such a plea did not dispute the justice of the plaintiff's claim on the merits, and its aim was simply to show that the particular suit could not be maintained in that court at that time. If successful, it defeated the particular action, but it did not preclude the plaintiff from starting afresh if he could cure the defect. One such plea was a *plea to the jurisdiction*, by which the defendant challenged the jurisdiction of the court to entertain the action. Another, and more common, class of dilatory plea was a *plea in abatement*, by which several kinds of defect could be attacked, including lack of capacity of the plaintiff to sue or of the defendant to be sued, misjoinder (too many) or nonjoinder (too few) of plaintiffs or defendants, and pendency of another action between the same parties for the same cause. Successive pleas in abatement could be made in the same action, but there was a set order that had to be followed. Any matter in abatement was treated as waived if it was preceded by or combined with another matter that, according to the prescribed order, was supposed to come after it. Courts looked with disfavor on pleas in abatement and required them to be framed with great exactness. It was necessary for the defendant to point out the defect with particularity so that the plaintiff could correct it in a new action. For example, if the basis of the plea was the nonjoinder of a necessary party defendant, the missing defendant had to be named.

c. The defendant might interpose a *plea in bar.*—If the declaration was sufficient in law and there was no basis for a dilatory plea, the defendant had to meet the plaintiff's case on the merits by a plea in bar. Such a plea might be (i) by way of *traverse* or (ii) by way of *confession and avoidance.*

A traverse was the denial of a material allegation of the plaintiff's declaration. With time, the insistence upon the singleness of issue became so strong that in some circumstances only one such allegation could be denied, even though several were untrue. We shall refer below to the subsequent relaxation of this restriction. A denial produced an issue of fact, the plaintiff affirming and the defendant denying the truth of the allegation. This closed the pleadings, and the action was ripe for trial. In England the trial of an issue of fact ordinarily took place not at Westminster but at nisi prius, i.e., before a judge on circuit sitting with a local jury.

When the declaration was true in fact, the defendant might be able to resort to a plea in confession and avoidance. As the name implies, such a plea confessed the truth of the declaration but asserted further matter thought to be sufficient to avoid a judgment. The confession was an essential part of the plea, that is, the defendant had to confess before he could set up new matter in avoidance. The avoidance might show some justification or excuse for the matters alleged in the declaration, as where in an action for trespass to the person the defendant admitted striking the plaintiff but asserted that he had acted in self-defense. Or the avoidance might show the release or discharge of an obligation that had once existed, as by payment; release; accord and satisfaction; or the running of the statute of limitations.

3. Replication and later pleadings.—If the defendant's plea was in confession and avoidance, no issue emerged and the pleading process continued. The next move was up to the plaintiff. If he believed that the matter asserted in avoidance was insufficient in law, he could demur to the plea. Otherwise he filed a *replication*. Like the defendant's plea in bar, the replication might either (a) deny a material allegation in the plea or (b) admit the truth of the plea but set forth new matter by way of confession and avoidance. For an example of the latter, if the defendant pleaded his infancy as a defense to an action of assumpsit for goods sold and delivered, the plaintiff might in his replication admit the defendant's infancy but assert that the goods were necessaries. (As a matter of substantive law, infants were chargeable in assumpsit for necessaries.)

If the replication was in the nature of denial, an issue of fact was created and a trial of that issue followed. If, however, the replication contained new matter by way of avoidance, no issue was reached and it was again the defendant's turn to plead. He might demur to the replication, or he might file a *rejoinder*, either denying the new matter in the replication or confessing it and pleading further matter in avoidance. If he took the latter course, still another round of pleading was required from the plaintiff. This process continued until either a demurrer created an issue of law or a denial created an issue of fact. The succeeding pleadings were called respectively the *surrejoinder*, the *rebutter*, and the *surrebutter*. Subsequent rounds after the surrebutter were theoretically possible, but they were of such rarity that no names existed for them. Indeed, it was an unusual case that would not wind up at issue well before the named pleadings were exhausted.

a. Demurrer *searches the record*.—When a line of pleadings ended with a demurrer, the demurrer not only challenged the validity of the immediately prior pleading, but "opened the record." Thus, if the declaration was found to be deficient in substance, judgment on the demurrer went against the plaintiff even though there had been no demurrer to the declaration. This was equally true whether the demurrer was interposed by the defendant (for example, to the plaintiff's replication) or by the plaintiff (for example, to the defendant's rejoinder). Similarly, if the declaration was sufficient and the defendant's plea insufficient, judgment on the demurrer went against the defendant. A concomitant of this rule was the proposition that certain deficiencies in a pleading might be cured by a later pleading. For example, let us assume a declaration omitted an essential allegation. At this point a demurrer by the defendant would have succeeded. Instead of demurring, however, the defendant answered to the merits and in his plea supplied the missing allegation. Upon a demurrer to the plea or to any later pleading, the defect in the declaration was disregarded. In other words, judgment on a demurrer went against the party who made the first uncorrected pleading error.

b. There could be no *departure*.—In his later rounds of pleading, a party could not desert his ground of complaint or defense and rely upon another. The replication had to support the declaration; the rejoinder had to support the plea; and so on through the later stages of pleading on both sides. Otherwise the pleader was guilty of a departure, and his new pleading was demurrable. To illustrate, if the plaintiff alleged one cause of action in his declaration and in his replication introduced a new cause of action, this would be a departure. Similarly, a defendant asserting infancy as a defense in his plea would be guilty of a departure if he responded to a replication of necessaries with a rejoinder alleging payment. It should be noted that a departure, although demurrable, was "cured" by verdict; that is, the objection had to be raised at an early stage and was not available after rendition of a verdict.

4. **Motions in arrest and n.o.v.**—The demurrer was not the only device for challenging the legal sufficiency of pleadings. If an issue of fact was made on the pleadings, a trial held, and a verdict rendered for the plaintiff, the defendant could file a *motion in arrest of judgment.* This was in essence a delayed demurrer, raising an uncured question of law that would have been open on demurrer. A similar delayed attack could be made by the plaintiff after a verdict for the defendant by a *motion for judgment notwithstanding the verdict* (non obstante veredicto). If successful, it resulted in a judgment for the plaintiff despite the verdict for the defendant, for the verdict would have been rendered on an insufficient defense.

These devices did allow the parties to join issue on the facts and also, after trial, to litigate a legal point before the court in banc. Accordingly, these procedures were quite popular. Much of the substantive law resulted from proceedings on these motions.

5. **Joinder of causes of action.**—The plaintiff could combine under a single writ as many separate causes of action as he might have against the defendant so long as they fell within the same form of action. Each cause would then in effect be separately pleaded in the same action. It was no objection to joinder that such causes were entirely unrelated to each other. Thus the plaintiff could combine in an action on the case (a) a cause that the defendant negligently ran him down in May and (b) a cause that the defendant obstructed his right of way over Blackacre in October. Without going into the antique learning, it may be said that for this purpose a form of action included its variants. Thus separate causes under all the varieties of debt could be joined in a declaration, and so could causes in special and general assumpsit. Debt and detinue were joinable, as were case and trover.

If the same street affray included both blows and slanderous words, however, the aggrieved plaintiff could not join (a) the cause of action for trespass to the person with (b) the cause for slander. That was a fatal misjoinder.

There was some possibility of relief from the effects of the restrictions on joinder of causes. Matter not joinable when made the subject of an separate cause, because it would require a different form of action, might sometimes be shown in aggravation of the damages. In an action for trespass quare clausum fregit, the damages might be increased by proof of the taking of goods, a personal assault, seduction of the plaintiff's wife or daughter, and even slander. Such matters in aggravation, called consequential damages, had to be set forth specifically in the declaration introduced by a *per quod* (whereby). But if the plaintiff failed to establish his main claim of trespass q.c.f., it did him no good to prove matters in aggravation, as there was nothing to aggravate. If, however, causes of action were properly joined, the failure to establish any one of them would have no effect upon the others.

6. Subsidiary rules of pleading.—There were various subsidiary rules of pleading, most of them calculated to foster producing a single, clear-cut, and definite issue. Many were highly technical, and some to the modern eye appear to be flatly absurd. Some of the rules, on the other hand, enunciated principles of pleading that remain sound today (even though the consequences of error are mitigated in modern practice). We shall mention a few of the guiding ideas.

Duplicity was a cardinal sin of common-law pleading. A declaration, for instance, could not ask for the same relief on two distinct grounds. Nor could a plea or any later pleading contain more than one distinct answer to the pleading that preceded it. The reason for the rule was to preserve the singleness of issue. Illustrative of the same principle was the proposition that a party could not simultaneously plead and demur to the same matter. That is, he could not in effect say, "Your pleading is untrue, but even if it were true it is insufficient in law."

There were also numerous rules designed to produce precision and particularity in the issue. Thus a pleading might be fatally defective for *uncertainty* if facts were not pleaded distinctly and explicitly in detail. There were, in addition, rules designed to prevent confusion or obscurity. Naturally, if a pleading was unintelligible or, in the language of the common law, *insensible*, the defect was fatal. Further, if a pleading was inconsistent within itself, it was demurrable as being *repugnant*.

Hypothetical and *alternative* pleadings were also forbidden by the common-law rules. Both the "if" and "either-or" forms of allegation were bad for uncertainty and also as violating the principle of singleness of issue.

Another pleading fault was *ambiguity*. Pursuant to the general principle that pleadings were construed against the pleader, the court adopted the construction of an ambiguous pleading that was the most unfavorable to the pleader. An illustration of ambiguity was the *negative pregnant*, a form of negative statement implying within itself an affirmative. If the plaintiff alleged that the defendant had "struck and kicked" the plaintiff and if the defendant denied that he had "struck and kicked" him, the denial that the defendant had done both of these things would be taken impliedly to admit that he had done one or the other. Because either one would be sufficient to establish the defendant's liability, such a plea raised no defense, and on a demurrer to the plea the plaintiff would be entitled to judgment.

Nor could pleadings be *argumentative*. The rule against argumentativeness required that a denial be negative in form as well as substance. For instance, if the plaintiff alleged that *X* was dead and if the defendant pleaded that *X* was alive, this was argumentative. The proper form of pleading would be to allege that *X* was not dead.

REFORMS UP TO THE 1830s

The stringency of these pleading requirements produced sporadic pressures over the years for reform. We shall here tell something of this story up to the 1830s.

Originally, many purely formal defects were open to challenge at any stage in the case, even after verdict, with the result that the fruits of victory were frequently snatched away from a litigant for pleading flaws. The first step in the reform was a statute in the time of Queen Elizabeth I, namely, 27 Eliz. 1, ch. 5, § 1 (1585), supplemented by 4 Anne, ch. 16, § 1 (1705). The aim of this statute was to require defects in form to be challenged promptly by a *special demurrer* specifying the particular fault. Any merely formal defect not so challenged was waived, and the judges were to give judgment, in the words of the statute, "according as the very right of the cause and matter in law shall appear unto them." Thus a defect in the form of the pleading could still be fatal to the pleader's case, but only if it was timely challenged with particularity. The distinction between defects in form and defects of substance was not found easy to draw, but the former category included such things as duplicity and argumentativeness.

The onerous principle of singleness of issue was doomed eventually to break down. From the 1600s the plaintiff could avoid its rigors by declaring in separate *counts*. A plaintiff with several separate causes of action falling within the same form of action could always declare in separate counts for each of them. Why should not the same device be available to a plaintiff who had only a single cause but was uncertain as to what in law he had to prove or what in fact he would be able to prove? In fact, it was available. Although the plaintiff was required to make the elaborate pretense that separate causes were involved, he indeed could state the same cause of action in various ways in separate counts. He thus gained by indirection the benefit of pleading in the alternative. For example, the plaintiff frequently pleaded a common count as an additional count in an action of special assumpsit for fear that the proof would fail to show a binding express contract but would nevertheless reveal the necessary elements of an implied undertaking to pay the reasonable value of a benefit conferred upon the defendant.

The plaintiff frequently used counts in order to lessen the possibility of a fatal *variance*. A variance occurred when the matters proved did not correspond to the allegations of the pleading. Most kinds of allegations were subject to the requirement of conforming proof, making any such variance fatal. Even a minor such variance was fatal to a count, until the nineteenth century when a statute empowered the judge to allow an amendment at trial to correct a variance immaterial to the merits of the case. 3 & 4 Will. 4, ch. 42, § 23 (1833).

While the plaintiff could avoid the singleness requirement by using separate counts, the defendant had no comparable opportunity. For any particular count, he might have several possible defenses but be forced to select one of them and abandon the others. If he chanced to lose on the defense he selected, the fact that he might have succeeded on another defense would do him no good. By statute in 1705, however, a defendant could, with leave of court, be permitted to interpose *several pleas* in bar to the same count. 4 Anne, ch. 16, § 4 (1705). There was no requirement that these several pleas be consistent with each other: an admission of an allegation in one plea did not prevent its denial in another plea. This reform did not extend to the replication or later pleadings, so there still could be only as many issues as there were pleas.

Another step toward breaking down the requirement of singleness was more broadly to allow the defendant to enter a plea in bar called the *general issue*—"nil debet" in debt, "not guilty" in trespass and case, and so on. This not only constituted a blanket denial of the plaintiff's allegations, but also came to allow proof of some matters in avoidance, the matters varying from one form to another. A plea of the general issue thus permitted a certain freedom in interposing defenses, but at the same time it left the plaintiff in the dark as to the exact grounds of defense that the defendant would urge. A similar type of blanket denial known as the *replication de injuria* was available to the plaintiff in certain situations.

The demand to eliminate such uncertainty of pleading culminated in 1834 in a reform embodied in rules of court denominated the Hilary Rules. To illustrate, the Hilary Rules sharply restricted the scope of the general issue. Before the Hilary Rules, a defendant under the general issue in trover ("not guilty") could show not only that he had not converted the goods, but almost any matter in justification, excuse, or discharge (but not release or the statute of limitations, which had to be specially pleaded). After the Hilary Rules, the general issue amounted only to a denial of the conversion. It is generally conceded that the Hilary Rules were unsuccessful, as they had the effect of placing even more emphasis on niceties of pleading.

In appraising the merits and demerits of the common-law system, it is worth bearing in mind that there was no device available at law comparable to the modern discovery devices (although in some situations discovery was obtainable by a bill in equity in aid of the action at law), nor was any device available at law comparable to the modern motion for summary judgment. We shall renew examination of the difficulties in procedures at law in Topic D of this Part.

TOPIC C

COMPLEMENTARY SYSTEM OF EQUITY

SECTION 1. EQUITY DEVELOPING

The law courts showed considerable ingenuity in accommodating the forms of action to changing needs. Nevertheless the formulary system was essentially a rigid one, and it is a question, and an intrinsically unanswerable question, whether it would not have collapsed under the pressures of a vastly ramified and complexified society if it had stood alone to meet the hammer blows of time. That the formulary system continued well into the 1800s seems attributable in part to the coexistence and side-by-side growth of a complementary system of justice known as equity, generated and administered principally by a separate Court of Chancery. This system was not pinned to any forms of action and had its own distinctive procedures.

George B. Adams, The Origin of English Equity

16 Colum.L.Rev. 87, 94–97 (1916).

When we go into the thirteenth century, we pass into a time when the older system of law and courts was rapidly falling into insignificance before the advance of the newer system, and when this latter, the Common Law system, was coming to be looked upon as the normal and prevailing law of the community. It is a time also when differentiation was slowly but steadily taking place in the judicial system. [The three superior common-law courts emerged.] The natural effect of these developments was to bring forward as never before, probably not into very clear consciousness but as a practical matter, the question of jurisdiction, of boundary lines and fields of action.

As parallel to this tendency there must also be noticed another affecting the history of the writ. It is the increasing attitude of suspicion from before the middle of the century which the community at large adopted towards the growing number of writs and the power of Chancery to make new writs at will. Growing out of this are various attempts at the middle of the century and later to regulate and limit the issue of writs. If we recall the principle which had been early established in the Common Law that the action as developed before the court must not be different from that foreshadowed in the writ, and the consequent fact that the multiplication of writs which characterized the first century of the Common Law was a process of the multiplying and classifying of actions, it will be clear that a limitation upon the making of new writs was a marking out of the field of Common Law to a certain extent and a setting of boundaries to it.

The effect of both these tendencies to mark out for the courts the boundaries of their jurisdiction and also the boundaries of the law which they applied, was the same. The Common Law was becoming a hard and fast system with certain clearly defined things which it could not do. I do not intend to assert that this point in the development was reached at the end of the thirteenth century. It is very evident that it was not, though considerable approach had been made towards it. When the fourteenth century opened, boundary lines still seem now and then vague, fields overlap, content is still variable, the same body will do things that are later regarded as quite distinct, two different bodies will do the same thing, but as compared with the beginning of the thirteenth century great progress had been made towards definition and exclusion. . . .

It is in this situation, as carried on into the fourteenth century, that we must find the origin of Equity as a separate system and by which we must account for its late origin as compared with the Common Law. So long as the Common Law remained a flexible system, its field undefined, its power of inclusion unlimited, its organs undifferentiated, there was no reason for distinguishing between it and Equity, and all that was later done by Equity could still be done in the field of the Common Law. Such a distinction between them was indeed impossible. All acts of the king in opening his prerogative procedure to the community were alike in the teeth of the existing system, furnishing unusual remedies, and founded upon his duty to secure justice to all. There was no ground upon which they could be divided into two great classes by the later tests which distinguished Equity and the Common Law. It is only as the Common Law became a hard and fast system, as men began to ask themselves about boundaries of action and limitations upon the new, that a new field must be found for the action of the royal prerogative in securing general justice not specially provided for in the ordinary way, for this duty and this function still remained to the king.

The seat of this action was found in a place where it had always existed, in an organ which had come to be more and more recognized, as definition and differentiation increased, as being the special organ of the king's prerogative, in the Council.

Early petitions were "often couched in piteous terms." F.W. Maitland, Equity 5 (1909). The petitioner related that by reason of his poverty or illness, or the wealth and power of his adversary, he was unable to get a remedy in the ordinary course of law. Petitioners were not complaining, or not so much complaining, about the substantive rules of the common law, but rather about the defects in its procedures or its officials. Later petitions more obviously complained about the woodenness of the common law's substantive law. The petitioner sought to avoid the law's tendency to suffer hardship in his case rather than create an exception to its rule.

At first, the petitions were addressed to the King's Council for action, with the chancellor shepherding the petitions along. But the Council was ever busier, so that around 1350 it took to referring the more routine petitions to the chancellor for action, with instructions that increasingly comprised only the simple directive to proceed appropriately. By 1400, petitions were addressing directly the chancellor, who soon thereafter started issuing decrees in his own name. Here were the makings of a new court.

Why did this jurisdiction fall to the chancellor? The answer lies in administrative convenience. He was a more and more important official on the Council, as well as the one most constantly in attendance. He was usually both a cleric and a lawyer. Moreover, he was already associated with the administration of justice. He had a large and well-organized staff of clerks, who had lots of experience issuing original and other writs, and who would have to get involved anyway in issuing any remedies in response to the petition. Chancery indeed already exercised a common-law jurisdiction—called its Latin side because of its record-keeping language—a jurisdiction consisting largely of cases based on the king's feudal rights and duties.

How did the chancellor handle the petitions within his new extraordinary jurisdiction—the so-called English side of Chancery? The procedure began as informal and streamlined.

After examining the petition, the chancellor might issue a writ of subpoena ordering the adversary to appear and answer. These pleadings initially were oral, but eventually almost everything was in writing. The written answer would respond to each of the particular charges of the bill. The chancellor would then interrogate the witnesses in writing under oath, and he would seek discovery of other evidence. On this dossier, the chancellor, not a jury, would decide. This procedure allowed evaluation of each party's conscience. Any remedy would operate personally, such as by a decree of injunction or specific performance. The chancellor's individualized decision emerged from the facts and from conscience, rather than from any new general rule. The court did not keep records of most of its decisions.

Godemond's Case

[From C.H.S. Fifoot, History and Sources of the Common Law 324 (1949)].

Petition (1480).

To the right reverend Fader in god and my gode lorde the Bisshope of Lyncoln Chauncellar of Englonde:

Mekely besecheth your gode and gracious lordshipp your Poure Oratour Roger Godemond, that where he [years ago] was bounde to one Alice

Reme, Wedowe, by his syngle Obligacion [under seal] in 10 marke sterlyng paiable at a certeyn day in the said Obligacion specified, and afterward [Alice named John Hale and one Thomas Plane as her executors and died, after which Roger truly paid the executors his debt, trusting by that payment to be discharged of the said Obligation, and left the Obligation in the hands of the executors, trusting that they would deliver it whenever requested; and afterward John Hale died, after whose death Thomas Plane as Alice's executor, notwithstanding the payment, brought an action in debt before Common Pleas, not dreading God nor the offense of his own conscience, intending to recover the debt,] because the seid payment can make no barr at the comen lawe, and so to be twys satisfied upon the same Obligacion for one dewte, contrary to all reason and gode conscience, whereof your seid besecher is withoute remedy be the Comen lawe without your gode and gracious lordshipp to him be shewed in this behalf:

Please it therfor your gode and gracious lordshipp the premysses tenderly to consyder and to graunte a writte Suppena to be directe to the seid Thomas Plane, comaundyng hym bi the same to appere afore the kyng in his Court of Chauncerie at a certeyn day and upon a certeyn peyn by your lordshipp to be lemette, there to answer to the premysses and to bryng afore your seid lordshipp the seid Obligacion to be cancelled, and ferthermore that he may [be enjoined] no further to procede in the seid accion at Comen lawe till your seid lordshipp have examyned the premysses and sett such rewle and direction in the same as shall accorde with reason and gode consciens, and this for the love of god and in the Wey of Charite.

Pledges for petitioner: Ricardus Somer de London, Gentilman. Thomas Mey de London, Gent'.

Answer to the Petition.

This is the answere of Thomas Plane oon of the executours of Alice Reme, Wedowe, to the bill of complaynt of Roger Godmond:

The seid Thomas Plane by protestacon sayeth that the mater conteigned in the bill of compleynt of the seid Roger is not sufficient in lawe to put hym to answere to the same; for plee [he says that Roger did not pay any part of the debt to him or to John Hale in the manner and form alleged by Roger]; all whiche maters the seid Thomas Plane is redy to averre as this court will award, and askith juggement and prayeth to be dysmyssed out of this court wyth his resonable costys and expenses for his wrongfull hurte and vexacon in that behalf don, had or susteyned.[a]

---

[a] "What the ultimate finding of fact [in Godemond's Case] was, we have no means of knowing; but there is small doubt that if the complainant could prove the truth of his bill, the chancellor would order the obligation to be cancelled." W.T. Barbour, "The History of Contract in Early English Equity," in 4 Oxford Studies in Social and Legal History 1, 88 (Paul Vinogradoff ed., 1914). In fact, by endorsement on the petition, the chancellor had enjoined Plane's attorney from proceeding at law until the chancellor could rule in the matter.

To understand Godemond's Case, you need to realize that the common law did not have some absurd rule that the debtor had to pay twice or that the creditor was free to defraud, but instead held that a sealed obligation was incontrovertible proof of the debt. The law's rule worked nicely in the overwhelming majority of cases. And the law would not subvert its rule to aid a fool. But it had no objection to the fool's seeking relief from an obvious wrong in Chancery, which exercised a jurisprudence based on the fair exception.

This arrangement meant that a defendant in a law action might be obliged to "go across the hall" for an injunction staying the action, doing so where he had some matter that ought to defeat the action and that would be recognized by the chancellor but not by law. Nevertheless, the chancellor was not acting in conflict with the law, but instead was facilitating and hence reinforcing its operation. The law court could strictly adhere to its rules without having to worry about the hard cases. Moreover, the chancellor's case-focused process ensured that he was not creating rules in contradiction of the common law.

Analogously, a plaintiff desiring both legal and equitable remedies would have to bring separate actions. These two systems of justice were indeed separate, and so legal and equitable causes were not joinable.

Question: (1) Do you see any administrative or other advantage in such a bifurcated procedure?

The chancellor was as yet for the most part dealing with matters cognizable by the law courts, acting when the common law was supposedly inadequate. His occasional arrogance in such matters was objected to by the law courts and Parliament. "And so the Chancellor is warned off the field of common law . . . . But then just at this time it is becoming plain that the Chancellor is doing some convenient and useful works that could not be done, or could not easily be done by the courts of common law. He has taken to enforcing uses or trusts." F.W. Maitland, Equity 6 (1909).

USES

What was a use? Let us take the date 1500 to examine the question.

A owned land in fee simple. When *A* died and the land passed to his heir—we speak now of a time when the power to transfer land by will was very limited—certain feudal dues or taxes became payable to *A*'s overlord. However, the old feudal justifications for these taxes had disappeared, or were at least not felt as creating a strong moral obligation.

To increase freedom to devise and to minimize these exactions, *A* during his lifetime might convey the land in fee simple to *B*, *C*, and *D*, jointly, "to the use of" *A* during his lifetime and thereafter to *A*'s eventual designate, *X*. This meant that *B*, *C*, and *D* were thenceforth the technical owners of the land (the holders of the title "at law"), but they were bound in conscience and confidence to recognize that the substantial benefits of ownership belonged to the use-holder, *A*. For instance, they would be expected to pay over any income of the property to the use-holder. Thus *B*, *C*, and *D* were the "feoffees to uses" (trustees), and *A* the "cestui que use" (beneficiary).

The law courts acted largely as if they were oblivious of the purpose of this maneuver. They considered *B*, *C*, and *D* as the owners of the land and largely disregarded the existence of the use. No feudal taxes were due when *A* died, for he was not the legal owner. Nor were the taxes due when *B* died, leaving *C* and *D* surviving, for as *B*, *C*, and *D* were joint legal owners the law dealt with them as a kind of unit. It was only when the last survivor of *B*, *C*, and *D* died that the taxes would become due. But the last survivor might again in his lifetime convey to *E*, *F*, and *G* to the same uses.

There was a difficulty with this arrangement. What would happen if the trustees should at any point become faithless, deny the use, and violate the confidence reposed in them? Suppose they began to collect the income for themselves and refused to pay over to the beneficiary? The common-law courts could not be looked to for relief. Instead, it was the Court of Chancery that came to the aid of the beneficiary by ordering the trustees to carry out their trust. In this way a large class of cases passed into the domain of the chancellor.

Observe that when the Court of Chancery gave relief in the use case, it did not do so according to the style or manner of an ordinary law judgment. You will recall that the law judgment for money was that plaintiff do recover so much from defendant; and even in ejectment the judgment was that plaintiff do recover possession of the land. The sheriff was prepared to execute on defendant's property and sell it to satisfy the judgment for money; and he was prepared to eject defendant to satisfy the judgment in ejectment. Yet neither judgment was in the form of a command to defendant. Chancery's decree was typically just such a command. In the use case, the decree ordered the trustees to behave according to the use, on pain of going to jail if they did not. Dean Ames was especially insistent on this point. He said: "[T]ime has strengthened the conviction of the present writer that the principle 'Equity acts upon the person' is, and always has been, the key to the mastery of equity. The difference between the judgment at law and the decree in equity goes to the root of the matter. The law regards chiefly the right of the plaintiff, and gives judgment that he recover the land, debt, or damages because they are his. Equity lays stress upon the duty of the defendant, and decrees that he do or refrain from doing a certain thing because he ought to act or forbear. It is because of this emphasis upon the defendant's duty that equity is so much more ethical than law." James Barr Ames, "The Origin of Uses," in Lectures on Legal History and Miscellaneous Legal Essays 233, 233–34 (1913).

Especially because of the form of the decree, it could plausibly, if not altogether convincingly, be argued that equity had not acted in derogation of law. For nothing had been done to disturb the legal title. That was still in the trustees, and the law courts still continued to regard them as essentially the sole owners.

This example of the use thus helps you to understand the frequent pronouncements (1) that equity acts in personam and (2) that equity does not act in opposition to law. You should appreciate these ideas, even if they were not entirely or in all cases accurately descriptive of how equity acted. This oversimplified story of the use also introduces you to the potent concept of the separation of the "legal" from the "beneficial" (we are now prepared to say "equitable") ownership.

We, however, do not pause to give you in full depth the reasons for the emergence of the use device. Nor shall we describe its tortuous development or the attempts over the years to combat it, of which the most notable effort was the Statute of Uses in 1536. These matters are dealt with in the courses in Property and Trusts. Suffice it to say that the familiar familial and commercial trusts of today are lineal descendants of the old use—and that ideas developed in equity were capable of being fictionalized. Suppose a person acquired property by unjust means and was thereby unjustly enriched. Was it not possible to say that he held the legal title impressed with a trust in favor of the person justly entitled, a "constructive trust"? Take even the case of mistake: "Owing to a mutual mistake of fact, say as to the existence of a debt, Doe delivers to Roe in payment of the supposed debt a horse. What are Doe's rights? They may possibly be at least: (1) A right to rescind as in the case of personal property obtained by fraud, and so to sue in trover or statutory replevin after a demand for return or perhaps without demand; (2) assumpsit for goods sold and delivered; (3) bill in equity for specific restitution." Walter W. Cook, The Place of Equity in Our Legal System, 37 A.B.A.Rep. 997, 1007 (1912).

By 1600 the Court of Chancery had become a very busy institution, a major court. It had ceased dealing only with extraordinary matters, but instead had acquired a usual jurisdiction now called equity. One can classify under five main heads the matters then dealt with by the Court of Chancery, as did 1 William S. Holdsworth, A History of English Law 454–59 (7th ed. 1956). They were:

"Firstly, the recognition, protection and development of uses and trusts."

"Secondly, the court of Chancery interfered to enforce contracts on principles very different from any known to the common lawyers." While the law courts were painfully evolving remedies for breach of promise, the chancellors are said to have "enforced agreements, just as they enforced trusts, whenever they thought that in the interests of good faith and honest dealing they ought to be enforced." As the law courts perfected their remedies, Chancery tended to withdraw from the field. Yet all that the law courts would usually give by way of relief was damages. Chancery could give specific performance (that is, order the defendant to perform his promise). "But in this period it was not settled what cases did, and what did not entitle a plaintiff to specific relief."

"Thirdly, the Chancellor interfered in a class of cases where, owing to the rigidity of the law, the enforcement of the strict legal right was clearly contrary to equity. Fraud, forgery and duress were some of the chief grounds of his interference." Mistake and accident were further grounds.

"Fourthly, the procedure of the court enabled the Chancellor to give remedies in cases where the common law either could not act at all, or could not act with effect." The injunction is an instance in point. Chancery could examine the parties, and it could compel discovery (that is, production and examination) of documents even in aid of proceedings in the law courts.

"Fifthly, the organization of the court of Chancery made it a tribunal much more efficient than the courts of common law for the investigation of matters of account." The administration of estates became for this reason an important part of equity jurisdiction.

The rest of the story of equity was not always a pretty one. In the 1600s there were titanic struggles with the common law and Parliament. The spirit of their attack on equity and the Crown can be partly sensed in the sneer of lawyer and historian John Selden around 1650 that "Equity is a Roguish thing: for Law we have a measure, know what to trust to; Equity is according to the Conscience of him that is Chancellor, and as that is larger or narrower, so is Equity. 'Tis all one as if they should make the Standard for the measure we call a Foot, a Chancellor's Foot; what an uncertain Measure would be this." See Table Talk of John Selden 43 (Frederick Pollock ed., 1927).

Chancery prevailed in those struggles. But to do so, it surrendered its rationale of exercising the royal prerogative. Equity no longer simply "did equity," but instead acted only within its fixed jurisdictional bounds. And it recognized an obligation to treat like cases alike. It was no longer the king's delegate extraordinarily dispensing justice case-by-case, but a regular court of constant resort separately applying its general principles called maxims and even applying rules that it largely adopted from the common law. As a consequence, Chancery received a flood of cases. To embody the output, a reporting system started up. Equity was even following stare decisis by 1700.

So, in the 1800s, equity exhibited all the rigidities of a mature judicial system. The distance traveled was unwittingly revealed by Lord Chancellor Eldon: "Nothing would inflict on me greater pain, in quitting this place, than the recollection that I had done any thing to justify the reproach that the equity of this Court varies like the Chancellor's foot." Gee v. Pritchard, 36 Eng.Rep. 670, 674 (Ch.1818). Matters in Chancery were by then out of hand. The delay, expense, inefficiency, and corruption had become legendary. The imperfect meshing of equity and law had turned very troublesome. Reform was a pressing need. But before reviewing the reform, we shall view equity in its mature state, be it during yesteryear or today.

SECTION 2. EQUITY MATURED

(a) SCOPE OF EQUITY JURISDICTION

In opening his series of lectures on equity, Maitland observed that "we are driven to say that Equity now is that body of rules administered by our English courts of justice which, were it not for the operation of the Judicature Acts [the legislation effective in 1875], would be administered only by those courts which would be known as Courts of Equity." He added: "This, you may well say, is but a poor thing to call a definition. . . . Still I fear that nothing better than this is possible." F.W. Maitland, Equity 1 (1909).

Judge Phelps attempted, on the basis of a previous attempt by Professor Venable, to write a catalogue of the heads of equity jurisdiction. This appears in Charles E. Phelps, Juridical Equity Abridged 222–24 (Baltimore, M. Curlander 1894):

"*Principal heads of equity jurisdiction.* The *heads* of equity jurisdiction have been long established, and cover all possible cases which may properly be brought within the cognizance of courts of equity. Those of most frequent occurrence in practice are as follows: ACCIDENT, MISTAKE, FRAUD, TRUST, specific performance, account, administration, mortgages and liens, partnerships, creditors' bills, partition, injunctions, receivers, interpleader, bills of peace, quia timet, divorce, alimony, infants, persons of unsound mind, married women.

"More particularly, equity has jurisdiction: to relieve against a class of unforeseen and injurious occurrences, not attributable to mistake, neglect or misconduct—(ACCIDENT, and herein of *re-execution*); to relieve against acts, or contracts, done, or made, from ignorance of fact, forgetfulness or inadvertence—(MISTAKE, and herein of *reformation* and *rescission*); to set aside, correct, annul, or prevent advantage being taken of, instruments and acts induced by FRAUD, (and herein of *cancellation*); to enforce a beneficial interest in property against the holder of the legal title—(TRUST, and herein of trusts, *active* and *passive*, *express* and *implied*, the latter including *constructive* and *resulting* trusts); to compel *specific performance* of contracts; to adjust accounts between co-owners, partners, principal and agent, principal and surety, debtor and creditor, &c.—(*account*, and herein of *set-off*, *contribution*, *exoneration*, *subrogation* and *marshalling* of assets and securities); to superintend, in certain cases, the settlement of decedent's estates—(*administration*, and herein of *election*, *conversion*, *satisfaction* and *performance*); to establish the true *construction of wills*; to enforce *mortgages* by foreclosure, or to extinguish them by redemption; to enforce *liens* generally; to provide for the dissolution and settlement of *partnerships*; to entertain applications to charge the real property of deceased owners, or the real and personal property of living owners, beyond the reach of ordinary legal process, with their debts—(*creditors' bills*); among co-owners to make *partition*; to prevent persons from enforcing judgments, prosecuting suits, or setting up defences, in a court of law, where the claim or defence is inequitable, and to prevent the performance of acts which, if performed, would inflict an injury on a person, for which he would have no adequate remedy—(*injunction*); to secure property in dispute pending litigation—(*receiver*); to prevent vexatious litigation by protecting a party liable to the suit of two or more conflicting claimants (*interpleader*), or of a numerous class insisting upon the same adverse right, or of the same party repeating an unsuccessful claim (*bills of peace*); to preserve the means by which existing rights may be secured from impending violations (*quia timet*); to dissolve, either partially or absolutely, the marriage relation, with incidental provision for *pendente lite*, or permanent, support (*divorce alimony*); to guard and administer the estates of *infants*, persons of *unsound mind*, and *married women*; and to compel a party to a suit at law to disclose facts and produce documents within his knowledge and control—(*discovery*)."

There was a great expansion of the field of equity in the United States during the past century. Perhaps one would better speak of a filling-in of an already existing outline. Thus the simple "receiver" of the Phelps list foreshadowed the complex corporate receiverships of the Twenties and Thirties. But perhaps new paths were being blazed. The reference to "injunction" only dimly suggested the interpolation of the courts as the ultimate enforcer of elaborate schemes of governmental controls and as the last line of defense of citizens seeking protection against governmental abuses. The involvement of the courts in effectuating social change in such areas as legislative reapportionment, civil rights, and environmental protection carried equity to a point far beyond what Judge Phelps could have envisaged. Indeed, the "weight of important business of the courts today (the bias of contemporary legal education notwithstanding) seems to have shifted toward the equity side." Louise Weinberg, The New Meaning of Equity, 28 J.Legal Educ. 532, 532 (1977).

Today the pendulum may be swinging back. Growing concerns about "judicial activism" and growing disrepute for structural reform injunctions have had an impact on equity's vitality. Nevertheless, in the following pages we examine briefly some characteristic and still current equitable doctrines and attitudes.

(b) EQUITABLE RELIEF AGAINST PENALTIES

The form of the old "penal bond" was that the obligor promised to pay a sum to the obligee on a stated day, but this penalty was to be void and of no effect if the obligor had done thus-and-so on a previous day. There was often a great disproportion between the penal sum of the bond and the value of the obligor's performance: in loan transactions the penal sum might be twice the amount of the actual loan, repayment of which appeared as the condition for voiding the penalty. The law courts enforced these bonds according to their terms, a result not surprising if you consider the importance that they attached to the seal and the fact that even fraud in the inducement was not a defense to an action on a sealed instrument.

Equity, however, seems first to have given relief when through accident the obligor had not performed the condition on the due date. Later it intervened to prevent collection of penalties without even the pretext of accident. For example, in the loan cases it would stay the action at law or enjoin collection of the law judgment and confine the recovery to the amount borrowed with interest. In the study of Contracts you will see the spread of the idea of penalty, study the distinction between "penalty" and "liquidated damages," and examine to what extent the common law absorbed equitable ideas.

A similar development took place in mortgage cases where the intervention of equity was necessary to protect the mortgagor who had defaulted on the mortgage loan. The initial excuse of accident as a basis for the chancellor's action gave way to routine, with the end result being complex foreclosure proceedings involving sale of the property, payment of the loan out of the proceeds, and establishment of any deficiency against the mortgagor or payment of any surplus to the mortgagor. This falls within the boundaries of Property courses.

(c) EQUITABLE RELIEF ON CONTRACTS

Inadequacy of legal relief.—In the 1700s, equity's enforcement of contracts crystallized around the idea that it would give specific performance only if the law's remedy was "inadequate." An enormous gloss was written on this idea of inadequacy.

Suppose *V* and *P* contract in writing for the sale by *V* and the purchase by *P* of a parcel of real property, the payment and conveyance to take place at a future date. On that day *V* defaults. Of course, *P* may go to law and recover the difference between the price and the value of the land. But does *P* have the option to go to equity and get a decree ordering *V* to convey the land (conditioned on *P*'s paying the price—note that an equity decree, unlike a judgment at law, may be, and often is, cast in conditional form)? This option in theory turns on whether law damages are an inadequate remedy. It is easy to say that damages are inadequate if the land has a dwelling house on it and *P* wants the place as a residence. But is the case the same if the land is vacant and there is a similar adjacent parcel, which is available for purchase by *P* with the proceeds of his law judgment plus the original agreed price? Even in the latter case it is held that *P* is entitled to specific performance, on the ground that land is intrinsically unique.

What of the case where the purchaser of the land defaults in making payment: may the vendor get specific performance? The answer is yes. But how are damages at law inadequate? There have been some rather ingenious explanations. It does seem, however, that for sales of interests in land, the inadequacy formula has become somewhat detached from the facts.

It may be said generally that outside the land cases, the plaintiff must make some real showing of the inadequacy of law damages in order to obtain specific performance of a contract.

Question: (2) May specific performance be had of a promise to deliver a quantity of bales of cotton, where there is a free and fair market for the commodity? What of a promise to deliver a hundred shares of Microsoft stock? or shares of a close corporation not previously traded in? or an heirloom? What of a promise to supply at a fixed price all the output of a mine until it is exhausted an indefinite number of years hence?

Imagine that *V*, having contracted to sell to *P* property of such a type that *P* would have a right to specific performance against *V*, breaches by conveying the property to *X*. What are *P*'s rights against *X*? Equity considers that *P* has a kind of beneficial ownership in the property from the date of the contract, based on his right to specific performance against *V*, so that *V* is in a sense a trustee for *P*. *X* did indeed obtain the legal title from *V*. But what of *P*'s equitable interest? If *X* knew of the contract between *V* and *P* (and in the case of land, if the *V–P* contract had been publicly recorded, *X* would not be heard to say that he did not have knowledge), *X*'s legal title is subject to *P*'s equity, which means that *P* can compel *X* to convey to him (*P* paying the agreed price to *X*). The same result follows if *X* did not know of the contract between *V* and *P* but received the property from *V* by way of gift. But if *X* paid a fair price to *V* without knowledge of the *V–P* contract (that is, if *X* was a "bona fide purchaser for value without notice"), *P*'s equitable interest is extinguished: he cannot secure specific performance or, indeed, any other kind of relief against *X*, and he is left only with rights against *V*.

Question: (3) Suppose *P* contracted to buy Blackacre from *V* for $10,000, and *V* then sold to *X*, a bona fide purchaser without notice, for $15,000. If *P* does not believe that he can establish the fair market value to be as much as $15,000 (the fact that *X* paid $15,000 would not be decisive on the question of value), what recourse should *P* have against *V*, and on what theories?

Difficulty of administering equitable relief.—Thus far we have spoken of contracts respecting the sale of property. What other types of contract are specifically enforceable? The test of inadequacy of the law remedy is still to the fore, but additional factors may enter.

Assume that *X* Construction Company undertakes to build a house for *Y* but fails to perform its promise. May *Y* get specific performance? Ordinarily the law remedy is adequate, in that *Y* may arrange otherwise to build the house and recover from *X* the difference between the new cost and the old contract price. But suppose *Y* has bought from *X* one of the lots in a real estate development, and *X* has agreed to put in roads and sewers on *X*'s own land. Here the remedy at law is inadequate, in that *Y* cannot have the work done himself. But there is a contrary argument, successfully made in many situations, that specific performance should not be decreed because of the difficulties of enforcing and supervising the execution of the decree. The modern tendency is to weigh the difficulties of administration against the importance to the plaintiff of the equitable relief sought. Here is an instance of the balancing of interests by an equity court to determine whether to grant or withhold relief.

How about a contract for personal services? A shoe clerk refuses to perform his contract to work in a department store, or Kathleen Battle refuses to sing for the Metropolitan Opera in New York. Plainly the Metropolitan has a better case for specific performance than the department store, but is it good enough? No, equity will not command Battle to sing. Why not?

In some situations, equity may grant a negative decree that forbids Battle from singing for others for some time. Should it matter whether the promise to sing for no one else was an express term of the contract or was rather an implied term? whether Battle now seeks to sing for a company in New York or one in San Francisco? Compare Lon L. Fuller, The Forms and Limits of Adjudication, 92 Harv.L.Rev. 353, 404–05 (1978), with Restatement (Second) of Contracts § 367 (1979). Would not damages, which would compensate the plaintiff for lost business and deprive the defendant of unfair profit, be a fairly good substitute for a negative decree? and are the objections to an affirmative decree really obviated by a negative decree? See Lumley v. Wagner, 42 Eng.Rep. 687 (Ch.1852) ("I disclaim doing indirectly what I cannot do directly.").

Discretionary character of equitable relief.—More generally, courts of equity have traditionally taken the view that even when specific performance is available because damages at law are inadequate, the grant of the equitable remedy still lies in the sound judicial discretion of the court. Thus the court may deny equitable relief because the plaintiff drove an unconscionable bargain; because the contract was induced by misrepresentation, concealment, nondisclosure, or mistake; or because specific enforcement would cause undue hardship to the defendant or third persons or cause detriment to the public interest.

Question: (4) *A* is the owner of Blackacre. *B* is a manufacturer who intends to locate a factory in the town where Blackacre lies. *B* does not disclose her intentions to *A*. In consideration of $100 in cash, *A* contracts to sell his land to *B* at the latter's option for $10,000 if paid within three months. The latter amount is a fair purchase price at existing market prices. Later *B*'s intentions become generally known, prices of land rise immediately, and *A* repudiates his contract. *B* sues for specific performance within the three months and pays $10,000 into court. What should be the result? See Restatement (Second) of Contracts § 364 cmt. a, illus. 2 (1979).

Usually the reason that prevents the plaintiff from getting specific performance would equally defeat him at law. In other cases this is not so, so that the plaintiff will be denied equitable relief but will be remitted to his legal remedy.

Question: (5) Do you approve this double standard? Should a contract that is too unfair to be specifically enforced nevertheless furnish the basis for an action for damages? See Emily L. Sherwin, Law and Equity in Contract Enforcement, 50 Md.L.Rev. 253 (1991).

Carmen v. Fox Film Corp.

United States Circuit Court of Appeals, Second Circuit, 1920.
269 F. 928, cert. denied, 255 U.S. 569, 41 S.Ct. 323 (1921).

[Jewel Carmen, a twenty-year-old moving-picture actress, made contracts with two Fox companies, which would run for several years if Fox chose to exercise its options, with a salary starting at $125 a week and gradually increasing to $250. Several months later, while still a minor, she made a contract for her exclusive services with Keeney Corporation at a starting salary of $450 a week, which would increase to $1000. Keeney was ignorant of the Fox contracts. Shortly afterward, she came of age and repudiated her Fox contracts on the ground of her prior infancy. Fox threatened Keeney with suit if Keeney employed her, and thereafter Keeney refused to do so.

[Carmen sued for an injunction restraining Fox from interfering with her contractual relations with Keeney and for damages. The district court entered a decree in her favor, and Fox appealed.]

■ Before WARD, ROGERS, and HOUGH, CIRCUIT JUDGES.

■ ROGERS, CIRCUIT JUDGE.

. . . .

. . . [T]he conduct of the plaintiff has been such as entitles her to no relief in this court. According to her own allegations in her complaint, she was a minor when she entered into the contract with Keeney, and she misled him into making the contract by representing that she was free to make it, when in fact she was morally not free to make the contract, and there was doubt whether she was legally free to make it. If the contracts with defendants were valid, she was under a legal and moral obligation not to make the contract with the Keeney corporation. And if the contracts were voidable because of her infancy, then, while she was under no legal obligation to recognize them, she was under a moral obligation to abide by them, and good faith required her to continue to render the services she had agreed to give. In either case her action in repudiating her pledged word was misconduct of which no person of honor and conscience would have been guilty. That no action could be brought against her at law because of what she did does not alter the moral character of her act. And when she comes into a court of conscience and asks its affirmative aid to assist her in carrying into effect the inequitable arrangement into which she unfaithfully entered, the appeal falls on deaf ears. One who comes into equity must come with clean hands, and her hands are not clean. The testimony discloses that reliance cannot be placed upon her agreements which the law does not oblige her to keep, and that for a money gain to herself she unscrupulously disregarded her express contracts.

. . . .

The maxim that one who comes into equity must come with clean hands expresses rather a principle of inaction than one of action.[b] It means

[b] "I propose to show that the clean hands doctrine does not definitely govern anything, that it is a rather recent growth, that it ought not to be called a maxim of equity because it is by no means confined to equity, that its supposed unity is very tenuous and it is really a bundle of rules relating to quite diverse subjects, that insofar as it is a principle it is not very helpful but is at times capable of causing considerable harm." Zechariah Chafee, Jr., Some Problems of Equity 2 (1950). More broadly, this and the other maxims of equity may perhaps give some sense of how the conscience of the chancellor works, but on the whole they probably

that equity will refuse its aid in any manner to one seeking its active interposition if he has been guilty either of unlawful or inequitable conduct respecting the subject-matter of the litigation.

An illustration of the maxim is found in the attitude of courts of equity in the matter of specific performance. A court of equity always refuses specific performance of a contract which has been obtained by the plaintiff by sharp and unscrupulous practices, by overreaching, by concealment of important facts, even though not actually fraudulent. The contract may be a legal one, against which no defense could be set up at law, and one which a court of equity would not cancel. But if it has been procured by unconscientious means a court of equity refuses specific performance. Pomeroy's Equity Jurisprudence (3d Ed.) vol. 1, § 400.

The right which one seeks to enforce in a court of equity must be one which in and of itself appeals to the conscience of a chancellor. Mr. Justice Brewer, speaking for the court in Deweese v. Reinhard, 165 U.S. 386, 390, 17 Sup.Ct. 340, 341 (41 L.Ed. 757), said:

"A court of equity acts only when and as conscience commands, and if the conduct of the plaintiff be offensive to the dictates of natural justice, then, whatever may be the rights he possesses and whatever use he may make of them in a court of law, he will be held remediless in a court of equity."

. . . .

The fact that a contract has been dishonestly or dishonorably obtained is a bar to relief in equity.

Decree reversed.

Professor Chafee said of this case: "Of course, the ancient doctrine of 'infantile paralysis,' designed to protect children from improvident bargains, becomes absurd when applied to annul a contract entitling the minor to over $6,500 a year. The remedy is to change the doctrine by statute, as California has since done, and not to call the minor immoral. Furthermore, if her contract right was not worth protecting in equity, it should not have been worth protecting at law against this sort of interference. Yet the jury in a New York state court made Fox pay Jewel over $60,000. What did she care that Judge Rogers called her unethical, so long as she brought home the bacon?" Zechariah Chafee, Jr., Some Problems of Equity 98 (1950). On the other hand, how many of you had previously heard of Jewel Carmen (née Florence Quick)? Her fast-rising career never recovered, and she died in obscurity in 1984.

Flexible character of equitable relief.—Concomitantly, the flexibility of equity decrees is in striking contrast to the rigidity of a judgment

---

confuse more than they clarify. See Henry L. McClintock, Handbook of the Principles of Equity §§ 24–25 (2d ed. 1948).

for damages at law. Not only will equity order a defendant to do or refrain from doing specified things, but it will also cast its decree in a conditional mold when justice so requires. See Thomas O. Main, Judicial Discretion to Condition, 79 Temp.L.Rev. 1075 (2006).

A typical instance already mentioned is the decree that *V* shall convey certain land on condition that *P* pay the agreed price. On occasion, equity will even condition its relief upon the doing by the plaintiff of an act he was not legally bound to do. "He who seeks equity must do equity," as the maxim runs. For instance, a plaintiff seeking specific performance may in the interests of fairness have to accept some modification of his contract as a condition of obtaining equitable relief. If he does not consent, he will be left to his legal remedy on the contract as made.

Question: (6) In 1854, *P* leased a Washington hotel from *D* for a ten-year term with an option to buy for $22,500. After (a) the Civil War had made property values in Washington much higher, (b) Congress had enacted legislation making greenbacks legal tender (previously only gold had been legal tender), and (c) greenbacks had depreciated to slightly more than half their gold equivalent, *P* tendered $22,500 in greenbacks and demanded a conveyance pursuant to the option. *D* refused. Should *P* have been able to get specific performance? See Willard v. Tayloe, 75 U.S. (8 Wall.) 557 (1870).

A decree, moreover, is subject to modification on the initiative of any party in the light of changing conditions. Indeed, a decree may be frankly of an experimental, "let's-see-how-it-works" type. The prime example of flexibility in an equity decree is Brown v. Board of Education, 349 U.S. 294, 75 S.Ct. 753 (1955), where the Supreme Court, having declared in 1954 the fundamental principle that racial discrimination in public education is unconstitutional and that all provisions of federal, state, or local law requiring or permitting such discrimination must yield to this principle, decided to leave the matter of relief to the district courts. The Court directed the district courts to be guided by equitable principles. Traditional equity was characterized "by a practical flexibility in shaping its remedies and by a facility for adjusting and reconciling public and private needs." The Court added, perhaps unwisely, that the district courts were to proceed "with all deliberate speed." See also Board of Education v. Dowell, 498 U.S. 237, 111 S.Ct. 630 (1991) (standard for dissolving desegregation decree).

Mutuality of remedy.—A word is in order about the supposed rule of "mutuality of remedy." This rule took two forms: one, affirmative ("you have a right to specific performance, so your opponent also should have one"); the other, negative ("you must give up your right to specific performance, because your opponent has none"). The former, sometimes used as a justification for granting the vendor of land a right to specific performance for the price, was relatively harmless. Usually in the situations where it was applied, there was some other sound basis for equitable relief. If not, no great injustice was done by compelling the defendant to perform his contract, instead of breaking it and becoming liable for damages. The negative aspect of the rule, on the other hand, often resulted in obvious injustice. The negative aspect has now been either flatly repudiated or largely nullified by exceptions. See Restatement (Second) of Contracts

§ 363 cmt. c (1979) ("[T]he fact that specific performance or an injunction is not available to one party is not a sufficient reason for refusing it to the other party.").

There is, however, one related doctrine, akin to but distinguishable from "negative mutuality," that courts of equity generally follow. It can be illustrated by the following situation. *V* agrees to convey Whiteacre to *P* on May 1, 2010, *P* agreeing to pay the purchase price in five annual installments thereafter. Should *P* be able to get specific performance if *V* refuses to convey? In this case, unlike those where the conveyance and the payment are to be concurrent, a court of equity cannot be certain that *P* will perform when the time comes. True, this risk of nonperformance was inherent in *V*'s bargain, but equity is reluctant specifically to impose it upon him. Ames put it thus: "Equity will not compel specific performance by a defendant, if after performance the common law remedy of damages would be his sole security for the performance of the plaintiff's side of the contract." J.B. Ames, Mutuality in Specific Performance, 3 Colum.L.Rev. 1, 12 (1903).

Question: (7) Do you see any way in which equity might grant relief in this case of *P* v. *V* without violating the rule laid down by Ames? See Van Scoten v. Albright, 5 N.J.Eq. 467 (1846); Edgar N. Durfee, Mutuality in Specific Performance, 20 Mich.L.Rev. 289, 298–305 (1922).

Closing thought.—As all the foregoing suggests, specific performance of contracts has for some time been regarded as being available only in the exceptional case. There are signs that courts are now becoming more liberal in granting this kind of relief.

Question: (8) What reasons can you suggest for this change of attitude? See Gene R. Shreve, The Premature Burial of the Irreparable Injury Rule, 70 Tex. L.Rev. 1063 (1992) (reviewing Douglas Laycock, The Death of the Irreparable Injury Rule (1991)); Jeffrey J. Rachlinski & Forest Jourden, Remedies and the Psychology of Ownership, 51 Vand.L.Rev. 1541 (1998) (questioning law-and-economics approach).

(d) EQUITABLE RELIEF IN DEBTOR-CREDITOR RELATIONSHIPS

Beneficiaries may call upon their trustees to account for their management of the trust. Similarly, where there is a fiduciary relationship, although not strictly a trust, as in the case of partners or of principal and factor, an accounting might be compelled in equity. Even where the relationship was not considered "fiduciary," but was that of creditor-debtor, resort might sometimes be had to equity to compel an accounting if the job was likely to be too complicated for the law court with its adjunct, the jury. Accountings, particularly in the case of trusts, might involve elements of continuous administration.

We have already mentioned the receiver, appointed to preserve or care for property during the pendency of an equity suit. American courts, especially the federal courts, developed the receivership idea as a means of superintending the operations of corporations in financial trouble and preventing their being disemboweled at the suit of particular creditors before some final arrangement could be made, often a reorganization of financial structure. Here equity took on very large tasks of administration. See also Morgan v. McDonough, 540 F.2d 527 (1st Cir.1976) (affirming appointment of receiver for Boston high school as part of desegregation effort), cert. denied, 429 U.S. 1042, 97 S.Ct. 743 (1977), on remand, 456 F.Supp. 1113 (D.Mass.1978); Morgan v. Gittens, 915 F.Supp. 457 (D.Mass. 1996) (same receivership, still ongoing).

More mundanely, a creditor who obtained a judgment at law might require aid in equity to obtain satisfaction of the judgment, for example, to force disclosure of concealed assets or to set aside fraudulent conveyances made by the debtor. See Rule 18(b). He might also use such a creditor's bill to reach assets of the debtor not subject to execution at law, for example, property interests of an equitable as distinguished from a legal type.

(e) Equitable Relief for Misconduct and Mistake

Fraud.—We take fraud as an example of the many kinds of misconduct against which equity undertook to give relief. Particularly through the action on the case for deceit, the action of general assumpsit (as broadly conceived), and the allowance of fraud as a defense in an action for relief on a simple contract, the law courts in the 1800s were able to deal effectively with a large number of fraud cases. Equity, which had largely pioneered the field, seems to have retained a concurrent jurisdiction with law over some of these cases. And there were many situations where it was only in equity that a fully satisfactory remedy could be had. Equity's distinctive procedures and powers were especially needed where the fraudulent transaction had been executed and hence had to be undone (rescinded) or changed (reformed). Equity's reach extended, of course, to the cancellation or reformation of documents delivered in consummation of the transaction.[c]

Suppose *P* has induced *V* by fraud to enter into a contract to sell Whiteacre to *P* for $5000, and they have actually carried out the transaction, *V* signing and delivering a deed with intent to pass title. At law *V* can recover damages for the fraud, but surely he ought to be able to recover Whiteacre in specie from *P*. In equity he can get this relief under a conditional decree of rescission, by which the court orders *P* to reconvey to *V* if *V* repays the price he received.

Question: (9) What remedies are available to *V* when *P*, the fraudulent buyer, has resold the property to *X*?

---

[c] The bill quia timet ("because he fears") may be mentioned at this point. Suppose *A* had signed a negotiable instrument in *B*'s favor. Because the giving of the instrument had been induced by *B*'s fraud, or for some other reason, the instrument was voidable while in *B*'s hands. Yet if *B* should negotiate it to *C*, a bona fide purchaser for value without notice, and if *C* should sue *A*, *A* would have no defense. To forestall this possibility, *A* could bring a bill quia timet against *B* and get the instrument canceled. Equity extended this principle to certain other cases where a person feared future injury and an action at law could not relieve the fear. The bill to remove a cloud on title to property proceeded on a similar principle. In these situations, and in many others, equity granted preventive relief, while law did not. In a sense, the bill quia timet was a forerunner of the modern declaratory judgment.

What is the meaning of "fraud" in equity? Should innocent misrepresentation be dealt with on the same footing as fraud, or in some other way? See Henry L. McClintock, Handbook of the Principles of Equity §§ 79–80 (2d ed. 1948). These and many other questions we must pass over.

Mistake.—By a mutual mistake, *V* conveys to *P* a larger amount of land than they actually bargained for. Both parties thought the conveyance described just the property that the parties had in mind, but in truth it extended to additional property owned by *V*. The effect at law of the transaction is to vest *P* with legal title in accordance with the conveyance. A judgment at law for damages would hardly do full justice. But the chancellor may direct *P* to reconvey the surplus property, or he may direct *P* to give up the deed and *V* to deliver a fresh deed in proper form.

In the case imagined, there is an anterior agreement of the parties to which the court may conform the transaction. Imagine instead a case where both parties were mistaken, but the relief fairly called for is to restore the parties to their condition before they entered into their deal and so to undo the transaction completely, rather than to rectify it. Rescission, rather than reformation, would be the appropriate remedy.

Is mistake of law to be treated differently from mistake of fact, and can "law" and "fact" be satisfactorily distinguished in the context of mistake? Should the chancellor treat unilateral mistake differently from mutual mistake? Should it make any difference whether the plaintiff delays in seeking equitable relief after discovery of the mistake (or misconduct)?

(f) EQUITABLE RELIEF AGAINST TORTS

Recaption or protection of personal property.—The form of action called replevin might fail of its object because the defendant could put the chattel beyond the reach of the sheriff or could destroy it before the sheriff was able to reach it. If the chattel was "unique," there was reason for equity to use its compulsive procedures against the tortfeasor to compel him to deliver it, and equity did so in proper cases. In a variety of cases, also, equity used its injunctive process to prevent threatened injury to tangible personal property.

Trespass.—Suppose *B*, without right and claiming no right, commits continuing or repeated acts of trespass on land owned and possessed by *A*, and he threatens to continue his tortious behavior. After early hesitation to deal with trespass, equity began to grant injunctions in such cases, for *A* would otherwise have to bring a series of actions at law for the damages.[d]

[d] The notion that equity may prevent a multiplicity of actions was at the heart of the so-called bill of peace. When a large number of persons with similar but separate grievances sued or threatened to sue one or more defendants, the latter might resort to a bill of peace, the effect of which was to prevent the maintenance of separate actions and to allow all the grievances to be heard as a single suit. Similarly, an intending plaintiff might avoid multiplicity of actions by bringing a bill of peace against a large number of defendants when he had separate grievances against them that involved one or more common questions. Often in these cases the basic dispute was one appropriate for a law court, but the common law so restricted the joinder of parties and claims as to require separate individual actions. The only reason for

Where *B*'s acts resulted in permanent injury, the case for an injunction would appear to be even clearer.

If the plaintiff establishes wilful trespass and the remedy at law is inadequate to prevent its continuance or repetition, should a court of equity consider the degree of hardship to the defendant in relation to the value of the plaintiff's right and perhaps exercise its discretion against granting relief?

Questions: (10) *B* owned valuable mining property and also owned water rights, without use of which the mine could not be operated. Between the mine and the water, however, was a strip of barren, rocky, unusable land owned by *A*. *B*'s negotiations for a right of way across the strip failed. *B* then dug a trench across the strip, laid a pipeline, replaced the soil, and employed a force of armed men to patrol the pipeline and prevent *A*'s interference with it. The mine employed several hundred men and yielded a large and highly profitable output. "The laying of the pipeline across this barren, valueless land caused no appreciable injury" to *A*. Ejectment being unavailable because *A* was still in possession, *A* seeks an injunction against the maintenance of the pipeline. What arguments would you make for *A*? for *B*? What do you think the result should be? See Crescent Mining Co. v. Silver King Mining Co., 17 Utah 444, 54 P. 244 (1898) (In addition to the above-quoted sentence, the court said: "No peculiar, present, speculative, or other value is attached to the land crossed by the line." Do you agree with this statement?).

(11) If the court denies an injunction, remitting *A* to his right to damages at law, what should the measure of *A*'s legal relief be? See Restatement (Second) of Torts §§ 929–930 (1977); Charles T. McCormick, Damages for Anticipated Injury to Land, 37 Harv.L.Rev. 574 (1924).

(12) If, after failing to get an injunction, *A* employs a larger force of armed men who expel *B*'s men, should *B* be able to get injunctive relief to prevent *A* from digging up the pipeline?

When the title to land was genuinely in dispute, equity approached the question of enjoining acts of trespass in a gingerly way, for trial of title to real estate was the historic preserve of the law courts. At first it seems that equity would not touch the case at all, at least if the title turned on a question of fact. Later equity might go so far as to grant a temporary injunction, remitting the plaintiff to an action at law to try the title, after which the injunction was accordingly made permanent or dissolved. See Edgar N. Durfee, Trial of Legal Issues in Injunction Against Tort, 57 Mich.L.Rev. 539 (1959).

Suppose *A*, out of possession but claiming title and the right to possession of land, wants to prevent *B*, in possession and also claiming title and the right to possession, from cutting the timber and extracting the minerals. *A*'s remedy at law would be an action of ejectment. This would eventually restore the land to him if he succeeded in establishing his claim, but it would not give him damages for what *B* had done up to then. *A*

---

coming into equity, then, was to avoid litigating the same question over and over again. We do not attempt to catalogue the other situations in which a bill of peace could be maintained. See Zechariah Chafee, Jr., Bills of Peace with Multiple Parties, 45 Harv.L.Rev. 1297 (1932), reprinted with slight revisions in Zechariah Chafee, Jr., Some Problems of Equity 149–98 (1950).

would have to bring a second action at law in "trespass for mesne profits" to collect those damages. Here again, because title was in dispute, there was trouble in getting equity to intervene, but in later years some courts would grant a temporary injunction against those acts of *B* going beyond normal use of the land until the title could be tried at law. Conceivably, equity could even install a receiver to manage and exploit the property during the interval, holding the avails for the party ultimately deemed entitled.

Nuisance.—A landowner allows smoke to escape from his factory, causing injury to an adjacent property owner. The noxious odors from a piggery cause annoyance to nearby residents. A tannery pollutes the water of a stream, damaging the crops of a lower riparian owner. These are examples of nuisances, the continuance of which a court of equity may in appropriate circumstances enjoin.

Is a nuisance case a proper one for the consideration of such discretionary factors as relative hardship to the parties and third persons, the public interest, and the like? Should it make any difference whether it is possible for the defendant to install protective devices that would eliminate the nuisance and still enable it to conduct its business? Are the considerations any different from those in the case of wilful trespass, which we just discussed?

Question: (13) A factory supplying the city of Pittsburgh with light and power emitted smoke and soot that damaged an adjoining nursery. The installation of the latest devices reduced but could not eliminate the nuisance. The nursery sought an injunction. What arguments might be made in support of and against equitable relief? What, if any, additional facts would it be useful for each of the parties to show? See Elliott Nursery Co. v. Duquesne Light Co., 281 Pa. 166, 126 A. 345 (1924).

Other types of injunctions.—Equity intervenes not only to protect tangible property, personal and real, from tortious conduct, but also to protect intangible property interests. Injunctions against infringements of patents and copyrights are familiar. Trademarks and trade secrets receive similar protection. Equity courts have enjoined a large array of miscellaneous wrongs to business interests, usually collected under the head of unfair competition.

Injunctions in labor disputes forbidding various kinds of conduct by striking employees have gone on the ground of protecting tangible or intangible property interests of the employers. The question of what conduct may be enjoined has been a difficult one. One of the claimed judicial abuses in the past was breaking strikes by the issuance of broad temporary injunctions ex parte, that is, without notice to the defendant unions or employees affected. In federal courts the availability of injunctions in labor disputes has been controversial and now is dealt with by special legislation, referred to in Rule 65(e)(1). There are similar state statutes.

The extent to which equity will make use of its injunctive power to protect or vindicate citizens' claims of right is far from static. Our examination of typical equitable remedies has so far involved protection of property interests. But what of interests of "personality" more or less unconnected with property interests? Is there, for instance, a right of privacy—a right to be let alone—that equity will protect by injunction? May a libel ever be enjoined?

The attempt of the United States in 1971 to enjoin publication of a classified study entitled "History of U.S. Decision–Making Process on Viet Nam Policy," popularly called the Pentagon Papers, could serve as a case study in modern equity. The district-court hearing was on June 18, and its decision came on June 19. The court of appeals heard the appeal on June 22 and decided on June 23. The petition for certiorari and motion for accelerated consideration thereof were filed in the Supreme Court on June 24. Certiorari was granted and the record was filed on June 25. The briefs were received less than two hours before argument on June 26. The case was decided on June 30. Each Justice wrote a separate opinion. The outcome illustrates the proposition that " '[a]ny system of prior restraints of expression comes to this Court bearing a heavy presumption against its constitutional validity.' " The majority of the Court held that the government had not met the " '. . . heavy burden of showing justification for the imposition of such a restraint.' " New York Times Co. v. United States, 403 U.S. 713, 91 S.Ct. 2140 (1971). The three dissenters, Chief Justice Burger and Justices Harlan and Blackmun, recognized the constitutional limitations on prior restraint of expression. All of them objected to the "frenetic haste" in which the case had been conducted and the dealing with rights of great magnitude without an adequate record and without time for adequate consideration. The Chief Justice did not address the merits but would have remanded for development of the issues—the district court, meanwhile, continuing the restraint on publication. Justices Harlan and Blackmun, "forced" to reach the merits, dissented thereon.

The modern model of American public law litigation—exemplified by reapportionment and desegregation cases—entails heavy reliance on the injunctive remedy. "One of the most striking procedural developments of this century is the increasing importance of equitable relief." Abram Chayes, The Role of the Judge in Public Law Litigation, 89 Harv.L.Rev. 1281, 1292 (1976). But this model looks to no ordinary injunction. "The traditional prohibitory injunction contained large discretionary elements: deciding whether to grant equitable relief, balancing the equities of the case and the interests of the often numerous parties, and shaping the exact contours of the decree. But in contemporary affirmative orders, especially structural injunctions—decrees establishing an ongoing regime governing the institution that is the real target of the lawsuit—the discretionary component is dramatically enhanced. To be sure, the purpose of the decree is to rectify a course of conduct that has been found to abridge rights asserted by the plaintiffs. But the trial judge has broad discretion to elaborate remedial arrangements in response to the particular characteristics of the situation and parties before him. This discretion makes it impossible to identify a unique remedial regime that follows ineluctably from and is measured by the determination of substantive liability." Abram

Chayes, The Supreme Court, 1981 Term—Foreword: Public Law Litigation and the Burger Court, 96 Harv.L.Rev. 4, 46 (1982). See also Owen M. Fiss, The Civil Rights Injunction (1978).

(g) COMPLICATED LITIGATION

An action at law was basically a contest between two and only two adversary sides (although there might be more than one party on each side), in which one side would eventually get a single judgment against the other. Even at a relatively late date, law narrowly restricted the types of setoffs and counterclaims that it would allow in an action.

Equity could and did deal with litigation of a much more complex character. It not only was more liberal in allowing setoffs and counterclaims, but also allowed multi-sided controversies (interpleader, for example, is an equity contrivance) and considerable complication of the party-structure of the suit. Where a number of parties were before it, equity would grant whatever relief inter se appeared necessary; for example, one plaintiff might emerge with a decree against a coplaintiff. Many of the modern statutes and rules regulating complex litigation are traceable to equity practice.

(h) DISCOVERY

In an action at law a party had no effective way to prove facts within the exclusive knowledge of his adversary. Parties were not permitted to testify, and there was no process for compelling the production of documents in an opponent's possession.

In a suit in equity the position was quite different. To remedy the defective procedures at law, equity assumed an auxiliary jurisdiction and permitted bills of discovery in aid of a law action. By such a bill a party could ascertain the facts necessary for success in the legal action. The remedy was, however, hedged in by such restrictive requirements that its use was much less general than one might expect. Still, the bill of discovery was the precursor of modern discovery devices, illustrated by Rules 26 to 37.

(i) THE "CLEAN-UP" DOCTRINE

When separate law and equity courts were operating side by side, there were frequent occasions when equity took jurisdiction of a claim for an equitable remedy and then retained it—at least if the plaintiff so wished—to clean up the entire controversy by granting "legal" relief in addition to or in lieu of "equitable" relief. The plaintiff could thereby save the inconvenience, expense, and delay of beginning a new action in a court of law and, in some instances, avoid the statute of limitations. However, the precise extent to which an English equity court would thus act was not wholly clear, nor were the pre-merger precedents in the American courts.

A typical example of legal relief *in addition to* equitable relief was when equity took jurisdiction to grant specific performance of a contract and also gave damages for delay in performance or past breach. The equitable clean-up doctrine has also frequently applied in suits to enjoin a tort, where the plaintiff seeks compensation for the injury already suffered as well as an injunction. For instance, *P* successfully shows that *D* has damaged him by means of unfair competition, so that the equity court enjoins *D* from continuing the conduct complained of and also assesses damages for the past wrongs.

As an example of legal relief *in lieu of* equitable relief, consider the situation where *P* sued *V* to compel the conveyance of Whiteacre pursuant to a contract of sale but learned at trial that, while the suit was pending, *V* had conveyed the land to *X*, a bona fide purchaser for value without notice. This wrongful act of the defendant made specific performance impossible, but equity would normally retain the case and award damages to *P*. The same result ordinarily followed when *V*'s act was prior to the commencement of suit but *P* did not know of it.

In *P* v. *V*, if the plaintiff knew the facts precluding equitable relief when he brought suit in an equity court, should the equity court retain the case and give legal relief? Should it make any difference if, knowing the facts, the plaintiff mistakenly but in good faith believed that he was entitled to equitable relief?

Now suppose that the case is one where specific performance is denied as a discretionary matter because of difficulties in supervising enforcement of a decree or because specific relief would be contrary to the public interest. Should a court denying equitable relief that the plaintiff might reasonably have expected to be granted retain the case for assessment of damages? Or suppose that the plaintiff, like Jewel Carmen, is denied specific enforcement because of conduct on her part so unconscionable that it offends the conscience of the chancellor, although the contract would be enforceable in a law court. Should the equity court give legal damages?

Bear in mind that the defendant's right to jury trial turned on all this. The extent to which the clean-up doctrine has survived the merger of law and equity into the unitary action will be examined later in its bearing on the present-day American right to trial by jury. See Topic E of Part Eight.

(j) ENFORCEMENT OF EQUITY DECREES

The classical method of enforcing an equitable decree was through imprisonment for contempt. The object of the imprisonment was to coerce the defendant into doing what the court had ordered him to do. When he tired of imprisonment and complied with the decree, he was released. Thus he was said to "carry the keys to his prison in his own pocket." A defendant might, and sometimes did, remain recalcitrant and frustrate the plaintiff's relief simply by staying in jail. This state of affairs, in theory at least, might continue indefinitely.

Fines conditional on continued noncompliance could also be imposed through contempt proceedings in order to coerce obedience. And contempt proceedings might be supplemented by the coercive measure of seizure of property under a writ of sequestration.

In addition to a sanction for contempt to coerce obedience, which was civil in nature, there was also criminal contempt, the object of which was to vindicate the dignity of the court by punishing wilful disobedience of its orders. A fixed prison term or an unconditional fine was the form of punishment.

The same conduct might lead to proceedings for either civil or criminal contempt, or both, and attempts to distinguish between the two have frequently caused difficulties. See International Union, UMW v. Bagwell, 512 U.S. 821, 114 S.Ct. 2552 (1994); Ronald L. Goldfarb, The Contempt Power 49–67 (1963).

Constitutional or statutory provisions against imprisonment for debt may, in some circumstances, prevent enforcement of a simple decree for the payment of money by imprisonment for contempt. Although courts have upheld such imprisonment, e.g., Reeves v. Crownshield, 274 N.Y. 74, 8 N.E.2d 283 (1937) ("To compel the judgment debtor to obey the order of the court is not imprisonment for debt, but only imprisonment for disobedience of an order with which he is able to comply."), such imprisonment would apparently be impermissible if the order were not reasonably within the defendant's means, see Hicks ex rel. Feiock v. Feiock, 485 U.S. 624, 108 S.Ct. 1423 (1988). See generally Richard E. James, Note, Putting Fear Back into the Law and Debtors Back into Prison: Reforming the Debtors' Prison System, 42 Washburn L.J. 143 (2002).

So, under later practice, equity came to secure satisfaction of simple money decrees by the same method of execution that law courts used. See Rule 69(a)(1). Also, under modern statutes, a decree for the conveyance of real estate may be made self-executing, so that the decree itself is given by statute the effect of a deed. An alternative statutory approach is to authorize an officer of the court to execute a deed on behalf of the defendant, the statute giving such deed full effect. See Rule 70. Receivership is another effective device for enforcement. See Rule 66. Where applicable, these devices furnish relief to the plaintiff by means other than coercing the defendant.

(k) EQUITY IN THE INFANT UNITED STATES

In the early colonial period in this country, conditions of life were simple as compared to those in England. There was no real need for a sophisticated legal system, and there were very few lawyers to make such a system work if there had been one. The unitary colonial courts administered a sort of homespun justice, presumably neither knowing nor caring whether they were doing the work of a chancellor or any one of the common-law courts in the mother country, where the division of labor had long lost most of its rationale. In addition, the lingering identification of equity courts with the Crown impeded their development.

Thus, Chancery almost missed being transplanted altogether. At first, the colonial officials administered a sort of layman's equity. As judicial equity slowly came to develop, it did so in greatly varying ways in the several colonies, and likewise after the colonies became states. In 1789, while some states had separate courts of equity and other states had courts with separate law and equity sides, there were several states where equity jurisdiction was either in a very primitive form or truly nonexistent. For an extreme example, Massachusetts courts did not have full equity jurisdiction until 1877. But the states' equity jurisdiction did grow with time, raising problems like England's that demanded reform.

One result of these disparities among the states was that a federal act conforming equity procedure to state practice was not feasible, and so Congress made federal equity uniform from the start. The first Congress in a stop-gap fashion and the second Congress in a permanent formulation, which lasted until the merger of the federal courts' law and equity sides in 1938, provided for modes of equity proceedings "according to the principles, rules and usages which belong to courts of equity" but with the vital additional provision that these rules could be altered "as the supreme court of the United States shall think proper from time to time by rule to prescribe." Act of May 8, 1792, ch. 36, § 2, 1 Stat. 275, 276, amending Act of September 29, 1789, ch. 21, § 2, 1 Stat. 93, 93–94. This rulemaking authority, later confirmed in more specific and sweeping language, was first exercised in 1822, when the Court prescribed equity rules for the lower federal courts.

Grupo Mexicano de Desarrollo v. Alliance Bond Fund

Supreme Court of the United States, 1999.
527 U.S. 308, 119 S.Ct. 1961.

■ JUSTICE SCALIA delivered the opinion of the Court.

This case presents the question whether, in an action for money damages, a United States District Court has the power to issue a preliminary injunction preventing the defendant from transferring assets in which no lien or equitable interest is claimed.

[A Mexican holding company (GMD) issued $250 million of unsecured notes in 1994. Certain investment funds purchased $75 million of the notes.

[Economic problems in Mexico led the company into serious financial trouble in 1997. It defaulted on interest payments. Negotiations to restructure its debt failed. The investment funds sued for $81 million due in the United States District Court for the Southern District of New York, where GMD had consented to personal jurisdiction.

[The plaintiffs requested a preliminary injunction restraining GMD and its subsidiaries from dissipating its assets or preferring its Mexican creditors. The district court granted that relief upon the plaintiffs' showing irreparable harm and "almost certain" success on the merits and their posting of a $50,000 bond. The Second Circuit affirmed. The Supreme Court granted certiorari.]

We turn, then, to the merits question whether the District Court had authority to issue the preliminary injunction in this case pursuant to Federal Rule of Civil Procedure 65.[3] The Judiciary Act of 1789 conferred on the federal courts jurisdiction over "all suits . . . in equity." 1 Stat. 78. We have long held that "[t]he 'jurisdiction' thus conferred . . . is an authority to administer in equity suits the principles of the system of judicial remedies which had been devised and was being administered by the English Court of Chancery at the time of the separation of the two countries." Atlas Life Ins. Co. v. W.I. Southern, Inc., 306 U.S. 563, 568, 59 S.Ct. 657 (1939). . . . We must ask, therefore, whether the relief respondents requested here was traditionally accorded by courts of equity.

. . . .

Respondents do not even argue this point. The United States as amicus curiae, however, contends that the preliminary injunction issued in this case is analogous to the relief obtained in the equitable action known as a "creditor's bill." This remedy was used (among other purposes) to permit a judgment creditor to discover the debtor's assets, to reach equitable interests not subject to execution at law, and to set aside fraudulent conveyances. [Citations omitted.] It was well established, however, that, as a general rule, a creditor's bill could be brought only by a creditor who had already obtained a judgment establishing the debt. [Citations omitted]; F. Wait, Fraudulent Conveyances and Creditors' Bills § 73, pp. 110–111 (1884). The rule requiring a judgment was a product, not just of the procedural requirement that remedies at law had to be exhausted before equitable remedies could be pursued, but also of the substantive rule that a general creditor (one without a judgment) had no cognizable interest, either at law or in equity, in the property of his debtor, and therefore could not interfere with the debtor's use of that property. As stated by Chancellor Kent: "The reason of the rule seems to be, that until the creditor has established his title, he has no right to interfere, and it would lead to an unnecessary, and, perhaps, a fruitless and oppressive interruption of the exercise of the debtor's rights." Wiggins v. Armstrong, 2 Johns. Ch. 144, 145–146 (N.Y.1816). [Citations omitted.]

. . . .

---

3 Although this is a diversity case, respondents' complaint sought the injunction pursuant to Rule 65, and the Second Circuit's decision was based on that rule and on federal equity principles. Petitioners argue for the first time before this Court that under Erie R. Co. v. Tompkins, 304 U.S. 64, 58 S.Ct. 817 (1938), the availability of this injunction under Rule 65 should be determined by the law of the forum State (in this case New York). Because this argument was neither raised nor considered below, we decline to consider it.

The dissent concedes that federal equity courts have traditionally rejected the type of provisional relief granted in this case. . . . It invokes, however, "the grand aims of equity," and asserts a general power to grant relief whenever legal remedies are not "practical and efficient," unless there is a statute to the contrary. Post . . . . This expansive view of equity must be rejected. Joseph Story's famous treatise reflects what we consider the proper rule, both with regard to the general role of equity in our "government of laws, not of men," and with regard to its application in the very case before us: "Mr. Justice Blackstone has taken considerable pains to refute this doctrine. 'It is said,' he remarks, 'that it is the business of a Court of Equity, in England, to abate the rigor of the common law. But no such power is contended for. Hard was the case of bond creditors, whose debtor devised away his real estate . . . . But a Court of Equity can give no relief . . . .' And illustrations of the same character may be found in every state of the Union. . . . In many [States], if not in all, a debtor may prefer one creditor to another, in discharging his debts, whose assets are wholly insufficient to pay all the debts." 1 Commentaries on Equity Jurisprudence § 12, pp. 14–15 (1836). . . . We do not question the proposition that equity is flexible; but in the federal system, at least, that flexibility is confined within the broad boundaries of traditional equitable relief. . . . When there are indeed new conditions that might call for a wrenching departure from past practice, Congress is in a much better position than we both to perceive them and to design the appropriate remedy. Despite the dissent's allusion to the "increasing complexities of modern business relations," post . . ., and to the bygone "age of slow-moving capital and comparatively immobile wealth," . . . we suspect there is absolutely nothing new about debtors' trying to avoid paying their debts, or seeking to favor some creditors over others—or even about their seeking to achieve these ends through "sophisticated . . . strategies" . . . . The law of fraudulent conveyances and bankruptcy was developed to prevent such conduct; an equitable power to restrict a debtor's use of his unencumbered property before judgment was not.

Respondents argue (supported by the United States) that the merger of law and equity changed the rule that a general creditor could not interfere with the debtor's use of his property. But the merger did not alter substantive rights. "Notwithstanding the fusion of law and equity by the Rules of Civil Procedure, the substantive principles of Courts of Chancery remain unaffected." Stainback [v. Mo Hock Ke Lok Po, 336 U.S. 368, 382 n. 26, 69 S.Ct. 606, 614 n. 26 (1949)]. Even in the absence of historical support, we would not be inclined to believe that it is merely a question of procedure whether a person's unencumbered assets can be frozen by general-creditor claimants before their claims have been vindicated by judgment. It seems to us that question goes to the substantive rights of all property owners. In any event it appears, as we have observed, that the rule requiring a judgment was historically regarded as serving, not merely the procedural end of assuring exhaustion of legal remedies (which the merger of law and equity could render irrelevant), but also the substantive end of giving the creditor an interest in the property which equity could then act upon. . . .

[The Court distinguished earlier cases upholding preliminary injunctions of the requested sort, by characterizing them either as preserving the status quo in aid of a cognizable claim to final equitable relief with respect to specific assets or as involving a plaintiff's pursuing the public rather than merely private interests.]

As further support for the proposition that the relief accorded here was unknown to traditional equity practice, it is instructive that the English Court of Chancery, from which the First Congress borrowed in conferring equitable powers on the federal courts, did not provide an injunctive remedy such as this until 1975. In that year, the Court of Appeal decided Mareva Compania Naviera S.A. v. International Bulkcarriers S.A., 2 Lloyd's Rep. 509. Mareva, although acknowledging that the prior case of Lister & Co. v. Stubbs, [1890] 45 Ch.D. 1 (C.A.), said that a court has no power to protect a creditor before he gets judgment, relied on a statute giving courts the authority to grant an interlocutory injunction " 'in all cases in which it shall appear to the court to be just or convenient,' " 2 Lloyd's Rep., at 510 (quoting Judicature Act of 1925, Law Reports 1925(2), 15 & 16 Geo. V, ch. 49, § 45). It held (in the words of Lord Denning) that "[i]f it appears that the debt is due and owing—and there is a danger that the debtor may dispose of his assets so as to defeat it before judgment—the Court has jurisdiction in a proper case to grant an interlocutory judgment so as to prevent him [sic] disposing of those assets." 2 Lloyd's Rep., at 510. The Mareva injunction has now been confirmed by statute. See Supreme Court Act of 1981, § 37, 11 Halsbury's Statutes 966, 1001 (4th ed. 1985).

Commentators have emphasized that the adoption of Mareva injunctions was a dramatic departure from prior practice. . . . The Mareva injunction has been recognized as a powerful tool for general creditors; indeed, it has been called the "nuclear weapo[n] of the law." R. Ough & W. Flenley, The Mareva Injunction and Anton Piller Order: Practice and Precedents xi (2d ed. 1993).

The parties debate whether Mareva was based on statutory authority or on inherent equitable power. See Brief for Petitioners 17, n. 8; Brief for Respondents 35–36. Regardless of the answer to this question, it is indisputable that the English courts of equity did not actually exercise this power until 1975, and that federal courts in this country have traditionally applied the principle that courts of equity will not, as a general matter, interfere with the debtor's disposition of his property at the instance of a nonjudgment creditor. We think it incompatible with our traditionally cautious approach to equitable powers, which leaves any substantial expansion of past practice to Congress, to decree the elimination of this significant protection for debtors.

. . . .

The parties and amici discuss various arguments for and against creating the preliminary injunctive remedy at issue in this case. The United

States suggests that the factors supporting such a remedy include "simplicity and uniformity of procedure; preservation of the court's ability to render a judgment that will prove enforceable; prevention of inequitable conduct on the part of defendants; avoiding disparities between defendants that have assets within the jurisdiction (which would be subject to prejudgment attachment 'at law') and those that do not; avoiding the necessity for plaintiffs to locate a forum in which the defendant has substantial assets; and, in an age of easy global mobility of capital, preserving the attractiveness of the United States as a center for financial transactions." Brief for United States as Amicus Curiae 16.

But there are weighty considerations on the other side as well, the most significant of which is the historical principle that before judgment (or its equivalent) an unsecured creditor has no rights at law or in equity in the property of his debtor. As one treatise writer explained: "A rule of procedure which allowed any prowling creditor, before his claim was definitely established by judgment, and without reference to the character of his demand, to file a bill to discover assets, or to impeach transfers, or interfere with the business affairs of the alleged debtor, would manifestly be susceptible of the grossest abuse. A more powerful weapon of oppression could not be placed at the disposal of unscrupulous litigants." Wait, Fraudulent Conveyances, § 73, at 110–111. The requirement that the creditor obtain a prior judgment is a fundamental protection in debtor-creditor law—rendered all the more important in our federal system by the debtor's right to a jury trial on the legal claim. There are other factors which likewise give us pause: The remedy sought here could render Federal Rule of Civil Procedure 64, which authorizes use of state prejudgment remedies, a virtual irrelevance. Why go through the trouble of complying with local attachment and garnishment statutes when this all-purpose prejudgment injunction is available?[e] More importantly, by adding, through judicial fiat, a new and powerful weapon to the creditor's arsenal, the new rule could radically alter the balance between debtor's and creditor's rights which has been developed over centuries through many laws—including those relating to bankruptcy, fraudulent conveyances, and preferences. Because any rational creditor would want to protect his investment, such a remedy might induce creditors to engage in a "race to the courthouse" in cases involving insolvent or near-insolvent debtors, which might prove financially fatal to the struggling debtor. . . . It is significant that, in England, use of the Mareva injunction has expanded rapidly. . . .

We do not decide which side has the better of these arguments. We set them forth only to demonstrate that resolving them in this forum is incompatible with the democratic and self-deprecating judgment we have long since made: that the equitable powers conferred by the Judiciary Act of 1789 did not include the power to create remedies previously unknown to equity jurisprudence. Even when sitting as a court in equity, we have no authority to craft a "nuclear weapon" of the law like the one advocated

---

[e] In this case, at least, the creditor could not have utilized Rule 64 to get a freeze order because New York law did not authorize injunctive relief in these circumstances.

here. Joseph Story made the point many years ago: "If, indeed, a Court of Equity in England did possess the unbounded jurisdiction, which has been thus generally ascribed to it, of correcting, controlling, moderating, and even superceding the law, and of enforcing all the rights, as well as the charities, arising from natural law and justice, and of freeing itself from all regard to former rules and precedents, it would be the most gigantic in its sway, and the most formidable instrument of arbitrary power, that could well be devised. It would literally place the whole rights and property of the community under the arbitrary will of the Judge, acting, if you please, *arbitrio boni judicis*, and it may be, *ex aequo et bono*, according to his own notions and conscience; but still acting with a despotic and sovereign authority. . . ." 1 Commentaries on Equity Jurisprudence § 19, at 21. The debate concerning this formidable power over debtors should be conducted and resolved where such issues belong in our democracy: in the Congress.

* * *

Because such a remedy was historically unavailable from a court of equity, we hold that the District Court had no authority to issue a preliminary injunction preventing petitioners from disposing of their assets pending adjudication of respondents' contract claim for money damages. We reverse the judgment of the Second Circuit and remand the case for further proceedings consistent with this opinion.

It is so ordered.

■ JUSTICE GINSBURG, with whom JUSTICE STEVENS, JUSTICE SOUTER, and JUSTICE BREYER join, dissenting.

. . . .

The Judiciary Act of 1789 gave the lower federal courts jurisdiction over "all suits . . . in equity." § 11, 1 Stat. 78. We have consistently interpreted this jurisdictional grant to confer on the district courts "authority to administer . . . the principles of the system of judicial remedies which had been devised and was being administered" by the English High Court of Chancery at the time of the founding. Atlas Life Ins. Co. v. W.I. Southern, Inc., 306 U.S. 563, 568, 59 S.Ct. 657 (1939).

As I see it, the preliminary injunction ordered by the District Court was consistent with these principles. We long ago recognized that district courts properly exercise their equitable jurisdiction where "the remedy in equity could alone furnish relief, and . . . the ends of justice requir[e] the injunction to be issued." Watson v. Sutherland, 5 Wall. 74, 79 (1867). Particularly, district courts enjoy the "historic federal judicial discretion to preserve the situation [through provisional relief] pending the outcome of a case lodged in court." 11A Charles Alan Wright, Arthur R. Miller, & Mary Kay Kane, Federal Practice and Procedure § 2943, p. 79 (1995). . . .

. . . In my view, the Court relies on an unjustifiably static conception of equity jurisdiction. From the beginning, we have defined the scope of federal equity in relation to the principles of equity existing at the separation of this country from England, see, e.g., Payne v. Hook, 7 Wall. 425, 430

(1869); Gordon v. Washington, 295 U.S. 30, 36, 55 S.Ct. 584 (1935); we have never limited federal equity jurisdiction to the specific practices and remedies of the pre-Revolutionary Chancellor.

Since our earliest cases, we have valued the adaptable character of federal equitable power. [Citations omitted.] We have also recognized that equity must evolve over time, "in order to meet the requirements of every case, and to satisfy the needs of a progressive social condition in which new primary rights and duties are constantly arising and new kinds of wrongs are constantly committed." Union Pacific R. Co. v. Chicago, R.I. & P.R. Co., 163 U.S. 564, 601, 16 S.Ct. 1173 (1896) (internal quotation marks omitted); see also 1 J. Pomeroy, Equity Jurisprudence § 67, p. 89 (S. Symons 5th ed. 1941) (the "American system of equity is preserved and maintained . . . to render the national jurisprudence as a whole adequate to the social needs. . . . [I]t possesses an inherent capacity of expansion, so as to keep abreast of each succeeding generation and age."). A dynamic equity jurisprudence is of special importance in the commercial law context. As we observed more than a century ago: "It must not be forgotten that in the increasing complexities of modern business relations equitable remedies have necessarily and steadily been expanded, and no inflexible rule has been permitted to circumscribe them." Union Pacific R. Co., 163 U.S., at 600–601, 16 S.Ct. 1173. On this understanding of equity's character, we have upheld diverse injunctions that would have been beyond the contemplation of the eighteenth century Chancellor.[4]

Compared to many contemporary adaptations of equitable remedies, the preliminary injunction Alliance sought in this case was a modest measure. In operation, moreover, the preliminary injunction to freeze assets pendente lite may be a less heavy-handed remedy than prejudgment attachment, which deprives the defendant of possession and use of the seized property. See Wasserman, Equity Renewed: Preliminary Injunctions to Secure Potential Money Judgments, 67 Wash.L.Rev. 257, 281–282, 323–324 (1992). Taking account of the office of equity, the facts of this case, and the moderate, status quo preserving provisional remedy, I am persuaded that the District Court acted appropriately.[5]

. . . .

Contrary to the Court's suggestion, . . . this case involves no judicial usurpation of Congress' authority. Congress, of course, can instruct the federal courts to issue preliminary injunctions freezing assets pending final

---

[4] In a series of cases implementing the desegregation mandate of Brown v. Board of Education, 347 U.S. 483, 74 S.Ct. 686 (1954), for example, we recognized the need for district courts to draw on their equitable jurisdiction to supervise various aspects of local school administration. [Citation omitted.] Similarly, courts enforcing the antitrust laws have superintended intricate programs of corporate dissolution or divestiture. [Citations omitted.]

[5] The Court suggests that a "debtor's right to a jury trial on [a] legal claim" counsels against the exercise of equity power here. Ante . . . . But the decision to award provisional relief—whether equitable or legal—always rests with the judge. Moreover, the merits of any legal claim will be resolved by a jury, if there is any material issue of fact for trial, and findings made at the preliminary stage do not bind the jury. See Wasserman, 67 Wash.L.Rev., at 322–323.

judgment, or instruct them not to, and the courts must heed Congress' command. See Guaranty Trust Co. v. York, 326 U.S. 99, 105, 65 S.Ct. 1464 (1945) ("Congressional curtailment of equity powers must be respected."). Indeed, Congress has restricted the equity jurisdiction of federal courts in a variety of contexts. See Yakus v. United States, 321 U.S. 414, 442, n. 8, 64 S.Ct. 660 (1944) (cataloging statutes regulating federal equity power).

The Legislature, however, has said nothing about preliminary freeze orders. The relevant question, therefore, is whether, absent congressional direction, the general equitable powers of the federal courts permit relief of the kind fashioned by the District Court. I would find the default rule in the grand aims of equity. Where, as here, legal remedies are not "practical and efficient," Payne, 7 Wall., at 431, the federal courts must rely on their "flexible jurisdiction in equity . . . to protect all rights and do justice to all concerned," Rubber Co. v. Goodyear, 9 Wall. 805, 807 (1870). No countervailing precedent or principle holds the federal courts powerless to prevent a defendant from dissipating assets, to the destruction of a plaintiff's claim, during the course of judicial proceedings. Accordingly, I would affirm the judgment of the Court of Appeals and uphold the District Court's preliminary injunction.

TOPIC D

REFORM

SECTION 1. THE CONDITION OF CIVIL PROCEDURE IN THE 1830S

Charles S. Bowen, "Progress in the Administration of Justice During the Victorian Period"

1 Select Essays in Anglo-American Legal History 516, 517–28 (1907).

The ancient barrier which separated the several Courts of the Common Law from the Court of Chancery still subsisted in the year 1837 [accession of Queen Victoria]. Two systems of judicature, in many respects at variance with each other, flourished side by side under the famous roof of Westminster Hall. The principle of a division of labour by which distinct machinery can be accommodated to special subject-matter is based upon reason and convenience. A large portion of the law business of the country is made up of litigation in the result of which no one is directly interested but the rival combatants. But there are many matters of which the law takes cognisance that necessitate a special and a more complicated mechanism for their adjustment. The property of infants, for example, requires to be protected—trusts to be managed day by day during a long period of years—the estates of deceased persons to be dealt with for the benefit of creditors, the assets to be collected and distributed, accounts to be taken, directions to be given, questions to be settled once for all that affect the interests of many. It is desirable that special tribunals should be armed with the particular organization requisite for purposes such as these. The distinction between law and equity went, however, far beyond what was needed to carry out this natural division of labour. The two jurisdictions had no common historical origin, and the principles on which they administered justice were unlike. The remedies they afforded to the suitor were different; their procedure was irreconcilable; they applied diverse rules of right and wrong to the same matters. The common law treated as untenable claims and defences which equity allowed, and one side of Westminster Hall gave judgments which the other restrained a successful party from enforcing. The law had always cherished as its central principle the idea that all questions of fact could best be decided by a jury. Except in cases relating to the possession of land, the relief it gave took, as a rule, the shape of money compensation, in the nature either of debt or of damages. The procedure of the Court of Chancery, on the other hand, was little adapted for the determination of controverted issues of fact, and it was constantly compelled to have recourse for that purpose to the assistance of a court of law. The common law had no jurisdiction to prevent a threatened injury; could issue no injunctions to hinder it; was incompetent to preserve property intact until the litigation which involved the right to it was decided; had no power of compelling litigants to disclose what documents in their possession threw a light upon the dispute, or to answer interrogatories before the trial. In all such cases the suitor was driven into equity to assist him in the prosecution even of a legal claim. The Court of Chancery, in its turn, sent parties to the Law Courts whenever a legal right was to be established [such as title to land], when a decision on the construction of an Act of Parliament was to be obtained, a mercantile contract construed, a point of commercial law discussed. Suits in Chancery were lost if it turned out at the hearing that the plaintiff, instead of filing his bill in equity, might have had redress in a law court; just as plaintiffs were nonsuited at law because they should have rather sued in equity, or because some partnership or trust appeared unexpectedly on the evidence when all was ripe for judgment. Thus the bewildered litigant was driven backwards and forwards from law to equity, from equity to law. The conflict between the two systems, and their respective modes of redress, was one which, if it had not been popularly supposed to derive a sanction from the wisdom of our forefathers, might well have been deemed by an impartial observer to be expressly devised for the purpose of producing delay, uncertainty, and untold expense.

The common law tribunals of Westminster Hall consisted of three great courts, each with a different history and originally different functions. In the growth of time, and by dint of repeated legislation, all, so far as the bulk of the litigation of the country was concerned, had acquired equal jurisdiction, and no practical necessity was left for the maintenance side by side of three independent channels of justice, in each of which the streams ran in a similar fashion and performed the same kind of work. First came the Queen's Bench, composed of a chief justice and four puisne [pronounced like puny] judges. Its authority was supreme over all tribunals of inferior jurisdiction. It took sovereign cognisance of civil and criminal causes alike—kept the Ecclesiastical Courts and the Admiralty within bounds, controlled magistrates and justices, supervised the proceedings of civil corporations, repressed and corrected all usurpations, all encroachments upon common right. It wielded two great weapons of justice over public bodies; mandamus, whereby, when no other remedy appeared available, it compelled them to fulfil the law; prohibition, by means of which it confined all inferior authorities strictly to their respective provinces and powers. The Court of Common Pleas, historically the most ancient of the three, which had retained, with no particular benefit to society, supervision over the few ancient forms of real actions that still survived, exercised also a general authority over personal actions. It was directed by a chief justice and four puisne justices. It laboured, however, under the disadvantage that, as far as the general bar of England was concerned, it was a "champ clos." Serjeants-at-law had exclusive audience in it during term time, and it was not till 1847 that this vexatious and injurious monopoly was finally abolished. The Court of Exchequer had been from early years the special tribunal for dealing with matters in which the king's revenue was interested. It still retained in revenue cases and some other matters a particular jurisdiction, though clothed by this time (like the Queen's Bench and the Common Pleas) with power over all actions that were personal. Besides these functions, it was also a Court of Equity, and took part from time to time in the Chancery business of the realm. A chief baron was at the head, assisted by four puisne barons . . . .

The procedure at the common law, as compared with the wants of the country, had become antiquated, technical, and obscure. In old days the courts at Westminster were easily able to despatch, during four short terms of three weeks each, . . . the mass of the business brought before them. But, from the beginning of the century, the population, the wealth, the commerce of the country had been advancing by great strides, and the ancient bottles were but imperfectly adapted to hold the new wine. At a moment when the pecuniary enterprises of the kingdom were covering the world, when railways at home and steam upon the seas were creating everywhere new centres of industrial and commercial life, the Common Law courts of the realm seemed constantly occupied in the discussion of the merest legal conundrums, which bore no relation to the merits of any controversies except those of pedants, and in the direction of a machinery that belonged already to the past. Frivolous and vexatious defences upon paper delayed the trial of a litigant's cause. Merchants were hindered for months and years from recovering their just dues upon their bills of exchange. Causes of action had become classified, as if they were so many Aristotelian categories—a system which secured learning and precision, but at the risk of encouraging technicality; and two causes of complaint could not be prosecuted in one and the same action unless they belonged to the same metaphysical "form." An action on a bond could not be joined with a claim upon a bill of exchange. A man who had been assaulted and accused of theft in the market-place of his town was obliged, if he wished redress for the double wrong, to issue two writs and to begin two litigations, which wound their course through distinct pleadings to two separate trials. If surprise occurred at Nisi Prius or the assizes, the court was unable to adjourn the proceedings beyond a single day. Old fictions still survived, invented in bygone ages to assist justice—with no particular harm left in them, it is true, but which were well fitted to encourage the popular delusion that English law was a mass of ancient absurdity. In order to recover possession of any piece of land, the claimant began his action by delivering to the defendant a written statement narrating the fictitious adventures of two wholly imaginary characters called John Doe and Richard Roe, personages who had in reality no more existence than Gog and Magog. The true owner of the land, it was averred, had given John Doe a lease of the property in question, but John Doe had been forcibly and wrongly ejected by Richard Roe, and had in consequence begun an action of trespass and ejectment against him. Richard Roe, meanwhile, being a "casual ejector" only, advised the real defendant to appear in court and procure himself to be made defendant in the place of the indifferent and unconcerned Richard Roe, otherwise the defendant would infallibly find himself turned out of possession. Till [1852], this tissue of invention of unreal persons and of non-existent leases preceded every investigation of the claim to possession of land. Nor was the trial itself of a common law cause productive of certain justice. Right was liable to be defeated by mistakes in pleading, by variances between the case as previously stated upon paper and the case as it stood ultimately upon the evidence, or by the fact that the right party to the suit had not been nominally joined, or that some wrong party had been accidentally joined with him. Perhaps the most serious blemish of all consisted in the established law of evidence, which excluded from giving testimony all witnesses who had even the minutest interest in the result, and, as a crowning paradox, even the parties to the suit themselves. "The evidence of interested witnesses," it was said, "can never induce any rational belief." The merchant whose name was forged to a bill of exchange had to sit by, silent and unheard, while his acquaintances were called to offer conjectures and beliefs as to the authenticity of the disputed signature from what they knew of his other writings. If a farmer in his gig ran over a foot-passenger in the road, the two persons whom the law singled out to prohibit from becoming witnesses were the farmer and the foot-passenger. In spite of the vigorous efforts of Lord Denman and others, to which the country owes so much, this final absurdity, which closed in court the mouths of those who knew most about the matter, was not removed till the year 1851.

In a strictly limited number of cases the decisions of the three courts could be reviewed [after 1830] in the Exchequer Chamber—a shifting body composed of alternate combinations of the judges, and so arranged that selected members from two of the courts always sat to consider such causes as came to them by writ of error from the third. The House of Lords, in its turn, was the appointed Court of Error from the Exchequer Chamber. The modern system of appeal, rendered necessary in our day by the weakening of the Courts in Banc and the development of what has been called the single-judge system, had not yet come into existence. Nor, in truth, on the common law side of Westminster Hall was there any great necessity for it. The Queen's Bench, the Common Pleas, and the Exchequer—whatever the imperfection of the procedure—were great and powerful tribunals. In each of them sat a chief of mark, with [throughout most of history] three puisnes to assist him, and the weight of authority of four judges, amongst whom there could not well fail to be present one or more men of the first rank of intellect and experience, was sufficient as a rule to secure sound law and to satisfy the public. The prestige, again, of the Exchequer Chamber in such cases as were allowed to reach it upon error was of the highest order. But the principle upon which appeals were allowed by the law in some matters, and refused in others, was full of anomalies. Only matters of "error" which were apparent on the record could be the subject of a hearing in the Exchequer Chamber. No appeal lay on subjects so important as a motion for a new trial or to enter a verdict or a nonsuit—motions which proceeded on the assumption of miscarriages in law by the judge or the jury who tried the cause. If the aggrieved party had not succeeded in complying at the trial with the difficult formalities of the rule as to bills of exceptions—an old-fashioned and often impracticable method of challenging the direction of a judge—no review of it was possible. Error lay from a special verdict, where the parties had arranged, or the judge directed at the trial, a special statement of the facts. No error lay upon a special case framed without a trial by consent. That is to say, no appeal was permitted unless the expensive preliminary of a useless trial had first been thrown away.

The technicalities which encumbered the procedure of the courts furnished one reason, no doubt, for the arrears which loaded the lists at the accession of her Majesty. . . .

The Court of Chancery was both a judicial tribunal and an executive department of justice for the protection and administration of property, but the machinery that it employed for the two purposes was, unfortunately, not kept distinct. Its procedure in contentious business served as the basis of its administrative operations, and persons between whom there was no dispute of fact at all found themselves involved in the delays and the embarrassments of a needless lawsuit. In its judicial capacity the Court of Chancery gave effect to rights beyond the reach of the common law, corrected the evils that flowed from the imperfect jurisdiction and remedies of the Common Law Courts, and dealt with whole classes of transactions over which it had acquired a special cognisance. The code of ethics which it administered was searching and precise—academical, perhaps, rather than worldly, the growth of the brains of great masters of learning and of subtlety, whose maxims and refinements had crystallised into a system. But its practice was as dilatory and vexatious as its standard of right and wrong was noble and accurate. For deciding matters of conflicting testimony it was but little fitted. It tossed about as hopelessly in such cases as a ship in the trough of the sea, for want of oral testimony—a simple and elementary method of arriving at the truth, which no acuteness can replace. It had no effective machinery at all for the examination or the cross-examination of witnesses, and (as we have seen) fell back upon the Common Law Courts whenever questions of pure law were raised, or as soon as depositions and affidavits became hopelessly irreconcilable. Oral evidence had always been at common law the basis of the entire system, although the common law perversely excluded from the witness-box the parties to the cause who naturally knew most about the truth. The Court of Chancery, on the other hand, allowed a plaintiff to search the conscience of the defendants, and the defendants, by a cross bill, to perform a similar operation upon their antagonist, but only permitted the inquiry to be on paper. A bill in a Chancery suit was a marvellous document, which stated the plaintiff's case at full length and three times over. There was first the part in which the story was circumstantially set forth. Then came the part which "charged" its truth against the defendant—or, in other words, which set it forth all over again in an aggrieved tone. Lastly came the interrogating part, which converted the original allegations into a chain of subtly framed inquiries addressed to the defendant, minutely dovetailed and circuitously arranged so as to surround a slippery conscience and to stop up every earth. No layman, however intelligent, could compose the "answer" without professional aid. It was inevitably so elaborate and so long, that the responsibility for the accuracy of the story shifted, during its telling, from the conscience of the defendant to that of his solicitor and counsel, and truth found no difficulty in disappearing during the operation. Unless the defendant lived within twenty miles of London, a special commission was next directed to solicitors to attest the oath upon which the lengthy answer was sworn, and the answer was then forwarded by sworn messenger to London. Its form often rendered necessary a restatement of the plaintiff's whole position, in which case an amended bill was drawn requiring another answer, until at last the voluminous pleadings were completed and the cause was at issue. By a system which to lawyers in 1887 appears to savour of the Middle Ages, the evidence for the hearing was thereupon taken by interrogatories written down beforehand upon paper and administered to the witnesses in private before an examiner or commissioner. At this meeting none of the parties were allowed to be present, either by themselves or their agents, and the examiner himself was sworn to secrecy. If cross-examined at all (for cross-examination under such conditions was of necessity somewhat of a farce), the witnesses could only be cross-examined upon written inquiries prepared equally in advance by a counsel who had never had the opportunity of knowing what had been said during the examination-in-chief. If the examination was in the country, it took place at some inn before the commissioner and his clerk, the process seldom costing less than £60 or £70. It often lasted for days or weeks, at the end of which its mysterious product was sealed up and forwarded to London. On the day of the publication of the depositions copies were furnished to the parties at their own expense; but, from that moment, no further evidence was admissible, nor could any slip in the proofs be repaired, except by special permission of the court, when, if such leave was granted, a fresh commission was executed with the same formalities and in the same secret manner as before. The expense of the pleadings, of the preparation for the hearing, and of the other stages of the litigation may be imagined, when we recollect that it was a necessary maxim of the Court of Chancery that all parties interested in the result must be parties to the suit. If, for example, relief was sought against a breach of trust, all who were interested in the trust estate had to be joined, as well as all who had been privy to the breach of trust itself. During the winding journey of the cause towards its termination, whenever any death occurred, bills of review or supplemental suits became necessary to reconstitute the charmed circle of litigants which had been broken. On every such catastrophe the plaintiff had again to begin wearily to weave his web, liable on any new death to find it unravelled and undone. It was satirically observed that a suit to which fifty defendants were necessary parties (a perfectly possible contingency) could never hope to end at all, since the yearly average of deaths in England was one in fifty, and a death, as a rule, threw over the plaintiff's bill for at least a year. The hearing in many cases could not terminate the cause. Often inquiries or accounts were necessary, and had still to be taken under the supervision of a master. Possibly some issue upon the disputed facts required to be sent for trial at the assizes, or a point of law submitted to a common law court. In such cases, the verdict of the jury, or the opinions of the court so taken, in no way concluded the conscience of the Court of Chancery. It resumed charge of the cause again, when the intermediate expedition to the common law was over, and had the power, if it saw fit, to send the same issue to a new trial, or to disregard altogether what had been the result. In a case which was heard in February 1830, there had been seven trials, three before judges and four before the Chancellor, at the close of which the suit found its way upwards to the House of Lords. When a cause had reached its final stage—when all inquiries had been made, all parties represented, all accounts taken, all issues tried—justice was done with vigour and exactitude. Few frauds ever in the end successfully ran the gauntlet of the Court of Chancery. But the honest suitor emerged from the ordeal victorious rather than triumphant, for too often he had been ruined by the way. Courts where ultimate justice is achieved, but where delay and expense reign supreme, become at last a happy hunting-ground for the fraudulent. The hour for reform has struck when the law can be made an instrument of abuse. . . . With all its distinction and excellence, the Court of Equity was thus practically closed to the poor. The middle classes were alarmed at its very name, for it swallowed up smaller fortunes with its delays, its fees, its interminable paper processes. The application of such a procedure to the large class of transactions, where no fact was in dispute, and only the careful administration of an estate required, was a cruel burden upon property. . . .

The judges of the court were the Lord High Chancellor (who then, as now, was a political officer and changed with every change of Ministry); the Master of the Rolls stood next in dignity; last came the Vice–Chancellor of England—a judge who in 1813 had been created to relieve the pressure. Some equity work was also done by the Chief Baron, or, in his stead, a puisne baron sitting on the equity side of the Exchequer; but this could only be during a limited portion of the year. The appellate system was defective in the extreme. The Chancellor sat singly on appeals from the Vice–Chancellor of England and from the Master of the Rolls (whose inferior in the science of equity he easily might be), and presided in the House of Lords over the hearing of appeals from himself—a position the less satisfactory inasmuch as, owing to the imperfect constitution of that August tribunal, the Chancellor was very often its ruling spirit. These appellate functions left him not too much time to bestow on his own duties as a Chancery judge of first instance. To a court so loaded with procedure and so undermanned in its judicial strength, the Chancery business of this kingdom, contentious or non-contentious, metropolitan or provincial, all flowed. A formidable list of arrears naturally blocked the entrance of the Temple of Equity.

THE SITUATION IN THE UNITED STATES IN THE 1830s

The situation in the United States can be appreciated from a nineteenth-century lawyer's summary of the vices in civil procedure. According to him, the underlying problem was "an inveterate incongruity between our law of procedure and our substantive law. The former had early lost the power of developing along with the substantive law. It had petrified while our modern substantive law was still in its budding growth. But the chief grounds of complaint which were urged against common law pleading were more specific. They related to the wall of separation between legal and equitable relief; to the labyrinth of arbitrary forms of action at law; to the artificial restrictions of the common law as to joining parties and as to joining causes of action; to the concealment of the real facts of a case through the verbiage or the vagueness of common law pleading." Charles M. Hepburn, The Historical Development of Code Pleading 18–19 (Cincinnati, W.H. Anderson 1897). A statement in greater detail by David Dudley Field, who was chiefly responsible for the New York Code of Procedure of 1848, appeared in his 1847 essay, "What Shall Be Done with the Practice of the Courts?," in 1 Speeches, Arguments, and Miscellaneous Papers of David Dudley Field 226 (A.P. Sprague ed., New York, D. Appleton 1884).

SECTION 2. THE REFORM MOVEMENT

Consider the following well-known passage from Sir Henry Maine: "A general proposition of some value may be advanced with respect to the agencies by which Law is brought into harmony with society. These instrumentalities seem to me to be three in number, Legal Fictions [changing the rule while pretending not to], Equity [changing the rule by creating fair exceptions], and Legislation [changing the rule directly by means of authority]. Their historical order is that in which I have placed them. Sometimes two of them will be seen operating together, and there are legal systems which have escaped the influence of one or other of them. But I know of no instance in which the order of their appearance has been changed or inverted." Henry S. Maine, Ancient Law 24–25 (London, J. Murray 1861).

Filled with revulsion at Blackstone's parochial and self-satisfied laudation of the common law, Jeremy Bentham (1748–1832), a law-trained philosopher, sustained for many years a brilliant and bitter attack on English law both substantive and procedural. His ideas attracted a group of able and influential supporters, including in this country Edward Livingston in Louisiana and the powerful figure of David Dudley Field in New York. The movement entailed a reaction against case-made law and in favor of legislative codification. Although the movement got its initial impetus from Englishmen, Field achieved the greatest early success in procedural reform with New York's Code of Procedure of 1848. This success in turn encouraged the effort in England.

The English movement counted among its adherents some practicing lawyers and judges, but Professor Sunderland concluded thus: "England has just completed a century of struggle for procedural reform, and it is to the energy and determination of the public, and not to the leadership of the bar, that the credit for the present English practice is due." Edson R. Sunderland, The English Struggle for Procedural Reform, 39 Harv.L.Rev. 725, 727 (1926). And Field similarly observed that credit for the American reforms must be given principally to nonlawyers. This rather sad record of the legal profession in cleaning its own house is relieved by the story of the more recent procedural reform movement that culminated in the Federal Rules and has not yet spent its force. Here the American legal profession may claim to have made a very solid contribution.

(a) ENGLISH ADVANCES

In England, reform on a substantial scale began in the 1830s. Most of the real and mixed forms of action at law died by legislation of 1833 and 1860, leaving in their place a few statutory actions. In 1832, a statute made process in the personal forms of action substantially uniform. Advances toward abolishing the personal forms of action appeared in an act of 1852, but the final dissolution of the forms awaited the Judicature Act of 1873.

Certain changes in pleading at law came in the Hilary Rules of 1834, written by the judges under legislative authority. As we have noted, these rules proved largely abortive. More effective reforms in pleading both at law and in equity lay in legislation from the 1850s onward.

Parties became competent to testify at law by legislation dating from 1851. Legislation also accomplished the reform of Chancery practice in large part, although practice orders issued by several chancellors played a part. Among many reforms in equity was the allowance in 1852 of oral testimony in open court in lieu of the cumbersome depositions. The result was to transform radically the outlandish procedures lampooned by Dickens in Bleak House. See Thomas Alexander Fyfe, Charles Dickens and the Law (1910). Dickens had earlier done much the same lampooning of the common law in The Pickwick Papers, whose legal case is abstracted in Bardell v. Pickwick: The Most Famous Fictional Trial in the English Language (Edward J. Bander ed., 2004).

The steps by which law and equity were fused or merged in England will not be recounted here. Complete fusion came through the Judicature Act of 1873—law and equity were now to be "administered concurrently," to use Maitland's phrase, and although there remained "differences of procedure arising out of the character of the various actions, . . . they can now be regarded as mere variations of one general theme—procedure in an action in the High Court of Justice."

These reforms called for a reconstitution of the courts, which the Judicature Act and later legislation effected. At present there are the Senior Courts of England and Wales into which have been merged the three superior courts of law, the Court of Chancery, the Court of Exchequer Chamber, and certain other courts. The Senior Courts have a general branch, the High Court of Justice (in turn divided administratively into three divisions: Queen's Bench Division, Chancery Division, and Family Division); a special criminal branch, the Crown Court; and an appellate branch, the Court of Appeal. The court of highest appeal was the House of Lords, but its jurisdiction shifted in 2009 to a new Supreme Court of the United Kingdom.

A significant feature of the Judicature Act remains to be mentioned. It gave the judges wide rulemaking powers over procedure. Either House of Parliament could secure an annulment of a rule by resolution, and Parliament of course could enact any procedural legislation on its own initiative. Rulemaking remains vibrant. Indeed, the so-called Woolf Reforms, called for by the Civil Practice Act of 1997 and comprising the Civil Procedure Rules of 1998, completely overhauled and somewhat simplified English procedure to foster case management, institute tracking, and lessen adversariness. See Penny Darbyshire, Darbyshire on the English Legal System (9th ed. 2008).

(b) FIELD CODE

In the United States the bellwether of reform, as we have suggested, was the Field Code. Its major provisions, basic to all others, were these:[a]

> § 69. The distinction between actions at law and suits in equity, and the forms of all such actions and suits, heretofore existing, are abolished; and, there shall be in this state, hereafter, but one form of action, for the enforcement or protection of private rights and the redress of private wrongs, which shall be denominated a civil action.[b]
>
> § 142. The complaint shall contain:
>
> 1. The title of the cause, specifying the name of the court in which the action is brought, the name of the county in which the plaintiff desires the trial to be had, and the names of the parties to the action, plaintiff and defendant;
>
> 2. A plain and concise statement of the facts constituting a cause of action without unnecessary repetition;[c]

---

[a] Quotations in the text are from the Code of Procedure as it stood in 1851, the Act of 1848 (1848 N.Y.Laws ch. 379) being but a partial code and so having been amended in 1849 and again in 1851 (1849 id. ch. 438; 1851 id. ch. 479).

Over the years Field's Code, which was notably brief and simple, received unsympathetic treatment by the New York courts, and the legislature persisted in amending and enlarging it until it became a structure with incredible detail. The same thing happened to a number of state codes modeled on the Field Code. All this increased the need for renewed reform.

[b] Section 1 divided remedies in courts into "actions" and "special proceedings." Section 2 defined an "action" as "an ordinary proceeding in a court of justice, by which a party prosecutes another party for the enforcement or protection of a right, the redress or prevention of a wrong, or the punishment of a public offence." Actions were then classified as either civil or criminal (§§ 4–6). "Every other remedy is a special proceeding" (§ 3).

[c] In the 1848 Act, § 120(2) had read as follows: "A statement of the facts constituting the cause of action, in ordinary and concise language, without repetition, and in such manner as to enable a person of common understanding to know what is intended."

The New York lawyer-diarist George Templeton Strong made this sardonic entry on September 28, 1847: "Report of the Commissioners on Practice and Pleading indicating the

3. A demand of the relief, to which the plaintiff supposes himself entitled. If the recovery of money be demanded, the amount thereof shall be stated.

The precept of § 142(2) was carried forward through other sections of the Code. For instance, the provision dealing with the answer declared:

§ 149. The answer of the defendant must contain:

1. A specific denial of each material allegation of the complaint controverted by the defendant, according to his knowledge, information or belief, or of any knowledge or information thereof sufficient to form a belief.

2. A plain and concise statement of any new matter constituting a defence or set-off without unnecessary repetition.

Question: (1) What significant differences do you observe between § 142 and Federal Rule 8(a)?

The New York Code embodied a number of other changes and reforms. It required verification of most pleadings; cut down the number of permissible pleadings by the parties to complaint, answer, reply, and demurrers; limited the use of demurrers; revised the old rules on joinder of causes of action; altered and made somewhat more pliant the rules as to joinder of, and relief against, parties in an action; reformed the rules governing permissible counterclaims (this came into the Code by an amendment in 1852); slightly liberalized the granting of amendments and softened the consequences of variances between pleading and proof; set out a flexible system of provisional remedies; authorized limited discovery procedures; extended the jury right, but facilitated the waiver of jury trial; modernized the procedures on execution and simplified proceedings supplementary to execution; and made the parties to some extent competent as witnesses. The New York Constitution had previously been amended to provide that "the testimony in equity cases shall be taken in like manner as in cases at law."

---

course of their intended reformation, which is to be root and branch work, all existing law and usage to be swept away and a new system created *in vacuo* by these enlightened and modest jurists. Rather like their plan. I shall know as much law as Daniel Lord the moment it's adopted, or rather I shall know more, for I won't have so much to forget. And with such a bench as we're likely soon to have, this reduction of legal practice to a . . . standard of simplicity and despatch is indispensable. Being ignorant, our elected judges will be thereby preserved from blunders; being inclined to be mischievous, they'll not be protected in partisan decisions and wilful injustice by mysteries and formalities unintelligible to the public at large. *Vive la République* and *à bas* the Common money counts! To the Lantern with John Doe and Richard Roe, and let there be a *noyade* and a *fusillade* and a general extermination done upon all extant reporters and writers of treatises." 1 The Diary of George Templeton Strong 301 (Allan Nevins & Milton H. Thomas eds., 1952).

Field brothers: Cyrus W. Field, Henry Martyn Field, Matthew Dickinson Field, David Dudley Field (leading lawyer, who was principal drafter of the Field Code), Jonathan Edwards Field, and Stephen J. Field (Supreme Court Justice, who authored Pennoyer v. Neff)—photographed by Mathew Brady in 1867 (Courtesy Eagle Publishing Company, Pittsfield, MA) (See generally The Fields and the Law (1986).)

The New York code system promptly induced copying in many states including California, and the California version became itself the basis of codes in several western states. The Field Code still constitutes the basis of the procedural law in a good number of states, especially the populous ones. The Federal Rules owe a great deal to the Field Code model, as naturally do the rules of the great many states now patterned upon the Federal Rules. There remain only a handful of states—and the number is ever dwindling—that can be said still to show noticeable allegiance to the common-law practice, and these bear little resemblance to the pristine form of the classic common law. In the few states where law and equity have not been merged in a unitary action, the consequences have been softened by provisions for easy transfer from one division of the court system to the other.

The mode of more recent reform in the majority of states has been through legislation confiding rulemaking power in some form to the courts, most often by statutes similar to the Federal Rules Enabling Act. Some states, however, still choose to proceed directly by the enactment of a code by the legislature; and a few states make rules under only the inherent power of the courts.

SUBRIN ON FIELD

The Field Code was probably the single most important procedural reform in Anglo–American history. Varieties of it govern in about half of American lawsuits at present. Its experience continues to influence strongly any reform projected for the future. Therefore, the context of its adoption merits a closer look, especially in the hope that its social and intellectual history might illuminate the context of the preceding and succeeding systems of procedure.

In the interest of space, we will focus on the principal drafter of the Code, David Dudley Field, to give a glimmering of the relevant social and intellectual themes. Our guide will be Professor Subrin, a pioneer of this type of study. See, e.g., Stephen N. Subrin, David Dudley Field and the Field Code: A Historical Analysis of an Earlier Procedural Vision, 6 Law & Hist.Rev. 311 (1988).

Who was this man Field? He lived from 1805 to 1894, while America transformed from an agrarian and maritime society into a complex industrialized one. He was born in Connecticut to a remarkable family, which soon moved to Stockbridge, Massachusetts. His mother, named Submit Dickinson, and his father, a Congregational minister, had nine children after him including Stephen, who was to be a Supreme Court Justice; Emelia, wife of the missionary who introduced European education to Turkey and mother to David Brewer, who would join his uncle on the Supreme Court; Matthew, builder of the longest suspension bridge of his time; Jonathan, a leader of the Massachusetts legislature; Cyrus, the famous financier who laid the first transatlantic cable; and Henry, clergyman, author, and newspaperman. David Dudley Field attended Williams College, where he loved the certainty of math but, after being suspended for "rebellion or opposition to the faculty," refused to return. Instead, he began his law apprenticeship in Albany, and then completed it in New York City. He there became a prominent trial lawyer, probably the best paid lawyer in the country. He came to represent mainly the wealthy, such as

Boss Tweed, as well as Jim Fisk and Jay Gould in their notorious battles to control the Erie Railroad. His clients needed a predictable legal system to enforce the newly overhauled and favorably limited substantive law.

What kind of person was Field? He was driven and determined, competitive and argumentative, individualistic and cantankerous. His diary entry on his twentieth birthday pledged: "If it please God to continue to me my life and health twenty years more, *my name shall be known*." His obituary observed: "Mr. Field was not a popular man in any sense. He was even unpopular among the members of the bar. He had few personal qualities that appealed to the sympathies of the masses or that attracted the affection of his legal brethren." Basically, he had wanted to succeed under known rules, and otherwise be left alone.

What was Field's value system? He had an unshakable belief that each person should be able to compete with equal opportunity but through individual effort. The government's role should not extend much beyond protecting the fruits of one's labor and preventing others from interfering with one's rights, which derived from natural law. Although politically progressive as to international peace, feminism, and abolitionism, he was Social Darwinist and laissez-faire at his core. He wanted rewards and punishments based on concrete and fixed rules in a fixed environment, independent of the whims of anyone.

Given then that his profession, personality, and values pushed him toward certainty, what did he try to change about the law? He devoted himself to scientific law reform through codification. He wrote: "Without [legal science] there could be no civilization and no order. Where there is no law, there can be no order, since order is but another name for regularity, or conformity to rule. Without order, society would relapse into barbarism." He became one of New York's three commissioners for law reform, which produced various codes including 1848's "An Act To Simplify and Abridge the Practice, Pleadings and Proceedings of the Courts of This State." This procedural code swept away the fictions and technicalities of the common law. But his aim was not anarchy. He had no desire to eliminate the need for lawyers. He took pleadings seriously, expecting them to lay out the facts clearly for objective application of the correct law to get consistent vindication of rights. Procedure would thus serve substance. And he would limit the unpredictable flexibility of judicial discretion. In his words: "It may be first observed, that flexibility, in its ordinary sense, is one of the worst qualities which a law can have, or rather that it is inconsistent with the idea of law." "[F]lexibility is uncertainty, and of course, inflexibility is certainty, which, so far from being a fault, is, to my way of thinking a merit of the highest value."

The significant point here is that the New York Code of Procedure was the embodiment of a set of process and outcome values that reflected David Dudley Field's world view.

(c) FEDERAL REFORM

Recall that Article III, Section 2 of the Constitution of the United States says that the judicial power shall extend to "all Cases, in Law and Equity" falling into described categories; and the Seventh Amendment provides that in "suits at common law," where the value in controversy is more than twenty dollars, the right of trial by jury shall be preserved. Do these provisions prevent a merger of law and equity? The federal constitutional situation is not materially different from the situation of those states that have similar guarantees of jury trial written into their several constitutions but that nevertheless merged their law and equity. With "in Law and Equity" read as merely an emphatic repetition of "all," these provisions do not prevent a merger, although of course any merger may not abridge the guaranteed right of jury trial.

Pre-merger.—Until 1938, however, law and equity were kept separate in the lower federal courts. In these courts the same judges administered the two systems of jurisprudence not "concurrently," but in separate law and equity sides and according to separate procedures.

In actions at law, the procedure in the federal district courts was, pursuant to the Conformity Act, a reflection of procedure for like actions in the forum state, subject always to particular federal statutes regulating procedure and to various intractable elements deriving from the very nature of the federal judicial power. Thus there was no uniformity of procedure in the district courts on the law side.

On the equity side, Congress had authorized the Supreme Court to regulate procedure by rules, and under this rulemaking power the Supreme Court laid down a uniform equity procedure for the district courts. Incidentally, it was not until the adoption of the Equity Rules of 1912 that the Court assimilated the method of taking testimony in federal equity cases to the method at law. Up to that time, the parties had to use depositions in much the English way described above by Lord Bowen. See Richard L. Marcus, Completing Equity's Conquest? Reflections on the Future of Trial Under the Federal Rules of Civil Procedure, 50 U.Pitt.L.Rev. 725, 731–35 (1989).

Separation of law from equity was of course not so complete as in the English heyday. For example, Congress enacted the following sections in 1915:[d]

> § 397. *Amendments to pleadings.* In case any United States court shall find that a suit at law should have been brought in equity or a suit in equity should have been brought at law, the court shall order any amendments to the pleadings which may be necessary to conform them to the proper practice. Any party to the suit shall have the right, at any stage of the cause, to amend his pleadings so as to obviate the objection that his suit was not brought on the right side of the court.

[d] Quotations in the text are from the sections' former codification in title 28, but they have since been repealed.

The cause shall proceed and be determined upon such amended pleadings. All testimony taken before such amendment, if preserved, shall stand as testimony in the cause with like effect as if the pleadings had been originally in the amended form.

§ 398. *Equitable defenses and equitable relief in actions at law.* In all actions at law equitable defenses may be interposed by answer, plea, or replication without the necessity of filing a bill on the equity side of the court. The defendant shall have the same rights in such case as if he had filed a bill embodying the defense or seeking the relief prayed for in such answer or plea. Equitable relief respecting the subject matter of the suit may thus be obtained by answer or plea. In case affirmative relief is prayed in such answer or plea, the plaintiff shall file a replication. Review of the judgment or decree entered in such case shall be regulated by rule of court. Whether such review be sought by writ of error or by appeal the appellate court shall have full power to render such judgment upon the records as law and justice shall require.[e]

A lawyer practicing in the state court and the United States District Court of a particular locality must thus have mastered three systems of procedure: the state procedure (which might be unmerged and therefore comprise two procedures); the federal law-procedure (which was the state procedure in law actions but with a federal overlay); and the federal equity-procedure. A lawyer practicing in federal courts throughout the country (as a government lawyer, for example, might well do) had to beware of the state procedure at law (as modified by the federal overlay) for each state in which the lawyer appeared.

Post-merger.—The movement for reform of the procedures of the lower federal courts has a history dating back to the nineteenth century. It culminated in 1934 in the Rules Enabling Act and in 1938 in the Federal Rules of Civil Procedure. The story of these developments, and the continuing series of amendments and the Federal Rules of Evidence, has already been told.[f]

The key figure in drafting the original Federal Rules was Charles E. Clark, Yale Law School Dean and later Second Circuit Judge, who detested procedural rigidity as an impediment to like-minded judges' ability to work social reform. See Stephen N. Subrin, "Charles E. Clark and His Procedur-

---

[e] Statutes that allow so-called equitable defenses to be interposed in actions at law (presupposing that law and equity are otherwise to be kept distinct) have given rise to some intricate questions. It was perhaps easiest to deal with a case where the equitable matter would under the classical practice have entitled the defendant to an unconditional decree enjoining the plaintiff from prosecuting the action. But suppose the equitable matter would have resulted in a conditional decree or a decree of reformation? This type of relief was quite foreign to law, and notwithstanding the statutes some law courts declined to entertain equitable matter that envisioned such relief. Would the situation be clarified by broadening the statutes to cover so-called equitable counterclaims? Many jurisdictions so broadened their statutes.

[f] See especially supra pp. 21–22.

al Outlook: The Disciplined Champion of Undisciplined Rules,'' in Judge Charles Edward Clark 115 (Peninah Petruck ed., 1991).

John Leubsdorf, ''The Myth of Civil Procedure Reform''

Civil Justice in Crisis 53, 53–54 (Adrian A.S. Zuckerman ed., 1999).

Most lawyers in the United States emerge from law school in the grip of a myth. In the beginning, the myth runs, there was common law pleading, and it was very bad. Parties exchanged almost interminable series of pleadings—from declaration to surrebutter and beyond—in expensive and unsuccessful attempts to filter out invalid claims and defences without holding trials. Plaintiffs could not join related claims; defendants could not assert more than one defence; and advocates argued about how to fit claims into an incoherent medieval system of forms of action.

After this had gone on for 500 years, God said, ''let Bentham be'' and all was light. Over the opposition of greedy conservative lawyers, an enlightened English public won legislation culminating in the Judicature Acts of 1873 and 1875. In the United States, the Field Code of 1848 initiated similar reforms, which the Federal Rules of Civil Procedure of 1938 consummated. As a result, cases were decided on their merits, without wasteful technicalities, and justice was done until 1975, when civil litigation somehow became even more expensive and time-consuming than under the common law.

Even today, many first-year law students find much of this story in their books or hear it in their civil procedure classes. Most teachers realize that it is an oversimplification, but it furnishes too useful an organizing perspective to discard. Indeed, it is hard to survey common law procedure and its replacements at all without students hearing this as a narrative of progress. Most never learn or soon forget most of the necessary qualifications, bringing the myth into their lives as lawyers and judges. The forms of action we have buried, but we keep on digging them up to show how rotten they were.

The myth of past reform impedes present reform. If we believe that we have already emerged from darkness into light, we are less likely to seek further illumination. The historical narrative that structures our understanding of civil procedure functions as a justification for the status quo.

How false is the myth? I do not know, and doubt that anyone else does either.

SECTION 3. THE FUTURE

The judicial rulemaking machinery is currently very much under attack and reconsideration. Its contribution has been great, but some argue for radical change. From the 1970s onward, Congress has been reasserting its authority in the procedural arena. Legislation rewriting the Rules Enabling Act in 1988 helped to move the rulemaking machinery out into public view. Persisting concerns center on process (e.g., lack of participatory process), institutional structure (e.g., supersession clause of the Rules Enabling Act that allows Rules to override statutes), and scope (e.g., dealing with subjects too important for rulemaking). See Winifred R. Brown, Federal Rulemaking: Problems and Possibilities (1981). But see Paul D. Carrington, The New Order in Judicial Rulemaking, 75 Judicature 161 (1991); cf. Robert G. Bone, The Process of Making Process: Court Rulemaking, Democratic Legitimacy, and Procedural Efficacy, 87 Geo.L.J. 887, 955 (1999) (justifying rulemaking as akin to common-law reasoning, as long as rulemaking centers on "inferring general principles from existing practice and choosing rules that implement those principles well in light of practice realities").

Inevitably, debate also persists about the rulemaking machinery's output. One dominant theme of both praise and criticism has been the open-textured nature of the Federal Rules. The Rules' generality, simplicity, and brevity have generated three subthemes.

First, the Rules' open-textured nature permitted their hearty embrace of the universal model: one set of uniform rules for all types, procedural and substantive, of cases. This problematic pursuit was generally discussed in Topic A of this Part (and was specifically examined in Part Five's study of class actions). For now, recall the debates on case management, tracking, and substance-specificity. These debates led us to the realization that procedural changes inevitably affect substantive law. Procedural reforms affect substantive values, perhaps in unintended ways but perhaps in intentionally systematic ways. In either event, these effects cannot remain politically neutral.

JUDITH RESNIK, THE DOMAIN OF COURTS, 137 U.Pa.L.Rev. 2219, 2219–20 (1989). "[A] remarkable aspect of this conference [on the Rules' fiftieth anniversary] has been the repeated references to the 'political' aspects of the Federal Rules of Civil Procedure. From a variety of perspectives, many of the speakers have made comments about the political implications of various Rules. Others, seeming to accept the political content of the Rules, have warned that 'we' (that is, all litigants) are safer when the facade, if not the reality, is maintained that 'neutral' Rules are applied to 'anonymous' (that is, not identifiable in advance) plaintiffs and defendants. I believe we cannot and should not ignore the political content and consequences of procedural rules. Over the last decade, a variety of powerful 'repeat players' have sought, sometimes openly, to influence 'court reform' efforts. By and large, that work has been done not by letters written to the Advisory Committee on Civil Rules, but rather by lobbying efforts directed towards legislatures and the public, by well-financed media campaigns, and by support for conferences and meetings to address and describe the 'litigation crisis.' However appealing might be the notion that writing the Rules . . . is a 'neutral' task with diverse consequences on anonymous and interchangeable civil plaintiffs and defendants, that description is no longer available. 'Tort reform,' among other events of the last decade, has denied us the refuge of a comforting image."

JUDITH RESNIK, FAILING FAITH: ADJUDICATORY PROCEDURE IN DECLINE, 53 U.Chi.L.Rev. 494, 541–42, 555–56 (1986). "A . . . possibility is that no one ever cares about adjudicatory procedure per se. It is always a means to an end—a technique for establishing another agenda. The 'procedure' cases of the nineteen-fifties, sixties, and early seventies could all be understood as not really about process but as efforts to use procedure to achieve results the Court believed appropriate. The contemporary 'procedure' cases simply exemplify the agenda of a new majority. Similarly, one could understand the rulemaking activities as prompted by goals other than procedural reform. In the nineteen-thirties, lawyers and judges saw the possibility of improving their lot by restructuring the ways in which they worked, so they advocated a series of rule reforms which enhanced their professional lives and which advanced the interests of their clients. Today, a new generation of lawyers and judges struggles to rid itself of the conditions found oppressive. Bored with the tedium of writing, answering, and ruling upon discovery requests, fearful of public criticism of the waste and inefficiencies of their work, lawyers and judges once again propose new reforms to protect self-interest. Lawyers seek new arenas in which to work; now the training sessions encompass information about the role of the lawyer in alternative dispute resolution. Judges, facing an increasingly bureaucratic task, are searching for means by which to rise above that anonymous role.

. . . .

"As we sit in contemplation of the enormously powerful work of the drafters of the Federal Rules of Civil Procedure, we must be careful and thoughtful in our examination of the decisions made fifty years ago. We must understand that conversations about procedure are often used as vehicles for many other conversations that are difficult to have in a straightforward manner. Proposals for 'tort reform' that include caps on liability emanate from those who have to pay damage awards, as well as from disinterested social scientists, concerned about the impact of liability rules and the utility of reliance upon tort litigation for risk-spreading and for deterrence. Desires to abolish appeal-as-of-right come not only from those interested in decreasing litigation costs but also from those who wish to give greater power to first-tier decisionmakers and to restrict individuals' abilities to challenge judicial wrongdoing. In short, some of the current vogue for complaining about overuse of the courts and of procedural excesses masks an important, value-laden debate about individual rights and the role of the judiciary in this society. In the current surge of concern about procedural innovation, we must sort out which suggestions are put forth in an effort to limit judicial power and which are made in an effort to enhance the judicial function."

Second, the Rules' open-textured nature also permitted full pursuit of the goal of rules uniform across the nation. But it simultaneously undermined that goal by stimulating the proliferation of local rules. The district courts now have over 6000 local rules, not to mention thousands of standing orders issued by individual district judges. Many local rules deal in surprising ways with important matters. Some seem inconsistent with the Federal Rules, or at least with their permissive spirit. Others seem to be exceeding the limit of "procedure." The unsatisfactory role of local rules led to the amendment of Rule 83 in 1985 and again in 1995 and to the amendment of 28 U.S.C. § 2071 by the aforementioned legislation of 1988. See generally Carl Tobias, Local Federal Civil Procedure for the Twenty-first Century, 77 Notre Dame L.Rev. 533 (2002).

Third, to the extent that the Federal Rules' system relies on particularized procedural decisionmaking to meet the foregoing potential problems of ignoring case individuality and of stimulating local rulemaking, the system intensifies the third and deeper difficulty. The generality and simplicity of the Rules did allow writing a concise body of rules that apply to case after case throughout the nation. The cases' undeniably considerable and varied procedural needs could not be so broadly ignored, however, and were intended to be met usually by ad hoc judicial decisionmaking. "It is not an exaggeration to say that the keystone to the effective functioning of the federal rules is the discretion given to the trial court." 4 Wright & Miller § 1029, at 154. But this heavy reliance on judicial discretion, the freedom of the judge to choose the procedure applicable to the case, can be troubling. Such concerns escalate in a procedural system that is fundamentally permissive. Is there today too much discretion?

Stephen N. Subrin, How Equity Conquered Common Law: The Federal Rules of Civil Procedure in Historical Perspective

135 U.Pa.L.Rev. 909, 912, 914, 922–25, 983, 988, 1000–02 (1987).

[T]his Article concentrates . . . on the inherent nature of the Federal Rules and on the basic choice of procedural form made by their promulgators. It advances two theses. First, an historical examination of the evolution of the Federal Rules reveals that rules of equity prevailed over common law procedure. Second, this conquest represents a major contributing factor to many of the most pressing problems in contemporary civil procedure. . . .

. . . .

. . . The more formalized common law procedure has been so ridiculed that we tend to ignore its development to meet important needs, some of which still endure, and that many of its underlying purposes still make sense. Conversely, especially during this century, equity has been touted in ways that obscure the underlying drawbacks to its use as the procedural model.

. . . .

. . . The underlying philosophy of, and procedural choices embodied in, the Federal Rules were almost universally drawn from equity rather than common law. The expansive and flexible aspects of equity are all implicit in the Federal Rules. Before the Rules, equity procedure and jurisprudence historically had applied to only a small percentage of the totality of litigation. Thus the drafters made an enormous change: in effect the tail of historic adjudication was now wagging the dog. Moreover, the Federal Rules went beyond equity's flexibility and permissiveness in pleading, joinder, and discovery.

. . . The result is played out in the Federal Rules in a number of different but interrelated ways: ease of pleading; broad joinder; expansive discovery; greater judicial power and discretion;[76] flexible remedies; latitude for lawyers; control over juries; reliance on professional experts; reliance on documentation; and disengagement of substance, procedure, and remedy. . . . The norms and attitudes borrowed from equity define our current legal landscape: expansion of legal theories, law suits, and, consequently, litigation departments; enormous litigation costs; enlarged judicial discretion; and decreased jury power.

. . . .

. . . It was the search for human perfection, trying to cover everybody and everything, combined with lawyer abuse, that caused the delay, expense, and endless fog in [Dickens' Bleak House] and that helps account for the same conditions under the Federal Rules. Equity has no boundaries, and, when standing alone without law, presents a largely lawless system. Maitland warned that "[e]quity was not a self-sufficient system, at every point it presupposed the existence of common law . . . . [If] the legislature said, 'Common Law is hereby abolished,' this decree if obeyed would have meant anarchy . . . . Equity without common law would have been a castle in the air, an impossibility."

. . . .

At common law, procedure joined with substance in order to achieve law application and rights vindication. As Pound suggested, form is the essence of procedure. A procedural system based on equity, however, no longer provides that form, and consequently no longer provides the defini-

---

[76] . . . Examples of Federal Rules of Civil Procedure that lend themselves to, or specifically provide for, judicial discretion include: 1, 8(a), ([d]), 11, 12(e), 13, 14, 15, 16, 19(b), 20, 23, 26(b)([2]), (c), (d), 35(a), 37(a)([5]), (b)(2), 39(b), 41(a)(2), 42(a), (b), 49, 50(a), (b), 53(b), 54(b), 54(c), 55(c), 56(c), 59(a)(1), [60](b)(1), 60(b)(6), 61, 62(b), 65(c). . . .

tion, confinement, and focus that aid in law application and rights vindication. . . .

. . . .

The major change in American civil procedure over the centuries is that equity procedures have swallowed those of common law. Common law procedure represented, among other things, an attempt to confine and define disputes so that the law could be applied to relatively few issues by lay juries. Field and the Code Commissioners, in the mid-nineteenth century, moved in the direction of equity practice, but continually emphasized the restrictions of procedure. . . .

The movement toward equity procedures reached fruition in the Federal Rules of Civil Procedure and structural change cases that take advantage of a procedural mentality based in equity. The Field Code was born in the political, social, and economic climates of the nineteenth century. It was grounded first in liberalism and then in laissez faire economics and Social Darwinism. Similarly, the Federal Rules represented a conservative impulse to empower judges as a bulwark against progressive attacks, which was joined later by a legal realist, anti-formalist, pro-regulatory, New Deal mentality. . . .

. . . The answer of proceduralists [in conceiving and drafting the Federal Rules] was to rely on expertise and judicial discretion. Give judges all the facts and a litigation package that includes every possible theory and every possibly interested party, and the judges—largely on an ad hoc basis—will figure out what the law and remedy should be.

As Dickens and others had known for centuries, equity procedure is slow and cumbersome, and has a high potential for arbitrariness. Over the years, those who have both stressed individual rights and liberties, and distrusted centralized power, have also criticized unbridled equity power. One has to be very careful here, for equity also had the admirable ability to act with a conscience and to create new rights. Such new rights, over time, tended to become defined and part of the more rigorous common law. Maitland and others warned that although equity and law worked well complementing each other, equity without common law had the capacity to be unwieldy or chaotic.

The modern procedural experience bears out this prophecy. Common law procedure, of course, had its own burdens. It is also obvious that many factors other than procedure have contributed to unwieldy litigation and undefined law. The point is that equity practice standing alone also has extreme burdens, and many of the complaints about modern law and contemporary court processes are related to equity's engorgement of common law practice.

Our infatuation with equity has helped us to forget the historic purpose of adjudication. Courts exist not only to resolve disputes, but to resolve them in a way that takes law seriously by trying to apply legal principles to the events that brought the parties to court. The total victory of equity process has caused us to forget the essence of civil adjudication:

enabling citizens to have their legitimate expectancies and rights fulfilled. We are good at using equity process and thought to create new legal rights. We have, however, largely failed at defining rights and providing methods for their efficient vindication. The effort to defeat formalism so that society could move forward toward new ideas of social justice neglected the benefits of formalism once new rights had been created. The momentum toward case management, settlement, and alternative dispute resolution represents, for the most part, a continued failure to use predefined procedures in a manner that will try, however imperfectly, to deliver predefined law and rights.

We need judges who judge as well as judges who manage. We need oral testimony, oral argument, and juries to balance documents, judges, and magistrates. This is not a plea for arid formalism that over-emphasizes the value of form. Nor is it a plea for uncontrolled juries. This is a reminder that there is another rich tradition to draw upon, that the common law virtues of form and focus are necessary to help us develop methods that can realize our rights. It is a reminder that law and equity developed as companions, and that equity set adrift without the common law may in fact be Maitland's "castle in the air." The cure for our uncontrolled system does not require the elimination of equity. It does require that we revisit our common law heritage.

Question: (2) On the descriptive side, putting any overstatements aside, Professor Subrin is correct that equity has prevailed over common law, is he not? But is he describing anything more than the most recent oscillation of a pendulum that has swung from customary law over to common law, back to equity, then to the Field Code, and certainly not finally back to the Federal Rules?

Thomas O. Main, Traditional Equity and Contemporary Procedure

78 Wash.L.Rev. 429, 429–37 (2003).

Much of the grand history of Anglo–American law could be characterized as an epic struggle between the regimes of law and equity. The roots of this conflict run deep and straight—to Aristotle, who recognized that universal laws could promote injustice as well as justice, and thus fashioned a notion of juridical equity to temper the strict application of laws. Equity moderates the rigid and uniform application of law by incorporating standards of fairness and morality into the judicial process. Equity assures just results in each application of strict law and eliminates the need for elaborate legislative drafting to contemplate all conceivable applications. Naturally, there exists some tension between the two regimes: law ensures strict uniformity and predictability, while equity tempers law to offer relief from hardship. Yet although there is tension between the two regimes, they are also complementary, and for centuries separate systems of law and equity combined to administer the laws with both certainty and discretion.

. . . .

This Article argues that in merging the regimes of law and equity, reformers may have swept away part of the wisdom that had guided the development and operation of dual systems. One virtue of an autonomous system of equity was its authority to act in opposition to the strict law when the unique circumstances of a particular case demanded intervention. The architects of the merger took great pains to sustain this virtue by preserving the substantive principles of both law and equity; only the procedure was modified, they insisted. But even assuming that the antagonistic substantive regimes of law and equity can co-exist and be applied contemporaneously within a single unified procedural system, a fundamental flaw inheres in the procedural infrastructure of a merged system. In denying equity any structural autonomy, there remains no relief from the procedures of the merged system itself when the modes of proceeding in that system are inadequate. Indeed, the jurisdiction of equity is impaired if equity cannot operate as a check upon the "strict law" that is codified in the procedures of the merged system.

. . . .

. . . A merged system offers no recourse from insufficiency created by the procedural apparatus of the merged system. The argument for institutional autonomy is compelling even though unified Federal Rules of Civil Procedure incorporated much of the philosophy and practices of equity procedure. First, the Federal Rules have not been immune to the complication, trivialization and ossification pathogens that have plagued earlier procedural systems. Second, procedural rules featuring discretion and flexibility within a unified system cannot replicate the administration of justice pursuant to a separate system of equity. The Federal Rules, like any codification, are unavoidably a product of experience developed by reason, and reason tested by experience. Yet generalizations in laws cannot always be completely general, and human calculations are imperfect. Indeed, the unimaginable is inevitable and, when the unexpected occurs, some authority must stand in the breach and supply that which prevents the general rules from meeting the immediate necessity. A separate system of equity viewed each lawsuit from the standpoint of the "wrong" presented. The powers of that court were as vast, and its processes and procedure as elastic, as all the changing emergencies of increasingly complex relations could demand. By contrast, the common law system viewed every lawsuit as a test of the existence and scope of the alleged "right." Whether by design or by unfortunate evolution, the procedural infrastructure of the unified system today increasingly resembles the latter vision, compromising fair and just results at the behest of formalism.[g]

---

[g] On the one hand, Thomas O. Main, Judicial Discretion to Condition, 79 Temp.L.Rev. 1075, 1120–21 (2006), gave examples: "federal judges may not fashion new forms of equitable relief without express congressional permission, and, even when permission has been granted, that authority must be read narrowly by judges. . . . And judges are unable to invoke equity

. . . .

In the current system, the procedural rules typically are applied as drafted, and the response to the procedural mischief is to amend the rules specifically to address that problem. But amendment, if any, may come too late for the problem that occasioned the amendment. Furthermore, the amended language itself may become the "strict law" that, in turn, creates the insufficiency for the next generation . . . .

Finally, . . . I offer a proposal to resurrect the curative purpose of equity in circumstances when the procedural apparatus of our merged system fails to provide plain, adequate and complete relief. I urge judges to use and credit equity as a source of authority to avoid applications of the Federal Rules that, although achieving technical compliance, result in inequitable outcomes in violation of the spirit of the Rules. Also, I urge procedural rulemakers to draft amendments to the Federal Rules that better accommodate the enduring jurisprudence of equity.

Question: (3) On the normative side, is Professor Subrin correct in maintaining that equity's triumph should be set right? Can this megatheme of prescription versus discretion—a megatheme of history, law, and reform that might be phrased as workable certainty versus individualized precision, or law versus equity—resolve itself consistently across the whole breadth of civil procedure? If not, where then is Professor Subrin correct and where is Professor Main correct? Compare Richard L. Marcus, Slouching Toward Discretion, 78 Notre Dame L.Rev. 1561 (2003), with Robert G. Bone, Who Decides? A Critical Look at Procedural Discretion, 28 Cardozo L.Rev.1961 (2007).

---

or equitable principles to supplant or override existing procedural rules: summary jury trials, mandatory alternative dispute resolution ("ADR"), settlement class actions, . . . and creative contempt sanctions are among the many judicial innovations once held to be beyond the proper exercise of judicial authority."

On the other hand, Thomas O. Main, ADR: The New Equity, 74 U.Cin.L.Rev. 329, 330 (2005), saw the reincarnation of equity in ADR: "ADR offers an alternative system for relief from the hardship created by the substantive and procedural law of formal adjudication. Moreover, the freedom, elasticity, and luminance of ADR bear a striking resemblance to traditional Equity, offering relaxed rules of evidence and procedure, tailored remedies, a simpler and less legalistic structure, improved access to justice, and a casual relationship with the substantive law. Alas, the dark side of ADR is also reminiscent of Equity: unaccountability, secrecy, an inability to extend its jurisdictional reach beyond the parties immediately before it, and a certain vulnerability to capture by special interests."

PART SEVEN

PRETRIAL

TOPIC A

PLEADINGS

SECTION 1. GENERAL OBSERVATIONS

(a) THE OBJECTIVES OF MODERN PLEADING

The aim of the Federal Rules, as stated in Rule 1, is "to secure the just, speedy, and inexpensive determination of every action." Any procedural system should aspire to this goal. See generally Pre-trial and Pre-hearing Procedures Worldwide (Charles Platto ed., 1990). However, one must also measure the efficacy of a procedural system in part by the court's power to enforce the rules in the face of resistance by parties and counsel.

In the adversary system of litigation, the initiative for taking procedural steps rests primarily on parties whose interest in attaining justice in the particular case is ordinarily less than their interest in victory. The person against whom a claimant seeks a remedy, usually having no interest in a speedy determination of the action, will likely embrace any open opportunity for delay; and even the claimant may find benefits in delay. Making litigation as expensive as possible for the opponent is a tactic as old as the adversary system itself. Moreover, although we may sometimes deplore it, we must recognize the fact that we cannot count upon counsel to cooperate fully in achieving the objectives of the procedural rules when it appears to be to their clients' advantage to thwart them.

Accordingly, in appraising the role of pleading in the judicial process, we must consider not only its legitimate part in advancing a lawsuit to the point when the court can properly try or otherwise conclude the case, but also its susceptibility to misuse despite judicial sanctions. A relevant question is how the parties and counsel will respond to the assignment of tasks. It may be taken as a fair working hypothesis that each well-advised party to a lawsuit wants to find out as much as possible about his adversary's case and to disclose as little as possible about his own, at least in the pleadings; among other reasons, the tactical advantage of being able to present testimony at the trial that an opponent is unprepared to meet is obvious. Equally obvious is the advantage of using such weapons as the rules provide to limit the opponent's area of offense or defense and, where possible, to expose the barrenness of the opponent's claim or defense so as to avoid a trial entirely. A party's pleading moves will often spring from these strategic considerations. And whatever their other purposes, attacks on pleadings entail delay and expense for the opponent, and it will sometimes seem apparent that this was the attacker's goal.

To address the central question with all this in mind, what ideally should pleading accomplish? Immediately, however, you should see that in coming to a judgment as to what we should expect of pleading, it is only good sense to consider the extent to which other devices can better carry the burdens traditionally assigned to pleading. Thus, a principal task of this Part will be to put pleading in its proper perspective as one, but not the sole, method of pretrial interchange among the parties. And so the initial question morphs. What should be accomplished prior to trial, either by pleading or by some other means?

EDWARD W. CLEARY, THE USES OF PLEADING, 40 Ky.L.J. 46, 46 (1951). "Regardless of the means employed to achieve them, these factors seem to inhere inescapably in the concept of an orderly judicial process:

1. Notice to the opponent which is adequate to enable him to prepare and present his side of the case effectively;

2. Determination of the elements which are relevant to the ultimate decision and allocating between the parties the responsibility for bringing them into the litigation;

3. Isolation of the area of actual controversy;

4. Ascertaining the governing substantive principles.

"Without them, litigation has no apparent origin or discernible destination."

CHARLES E. CLARK, SIMPLIFIED PLEADING, 2 F.R.D. 456, 456–57 (1943). Judge Clark, principal drafter of the Federal Rules, made this further observation as to the minimum that can be expected of pleadings: "They must sufficiently differentiate the situation of fact which is being litigated from all other situations to allow of the application of the doctrine of res judicata, whereby final adjudication of this particular case will end the controversy forever. As a natural corollary, they will also show the type of case brought, so that it may be assigned to the proper form of trial, whether by the jury in negligence or contract, or to a court, referee, or master, as in foreclosure, divorce, accounting, and so on."

Overemphasis on the niceties of pleading did sometimes defeat or impede justice in the distant past. Pleading had become the center of legal attention, ended up all too often mired down in battles over technicalities, and so provided the vehicle for monumental abuse. It thereby generated resentment against the system and eventually actuated procedural reform in England and the United States.

As narrated in Part Six, the elaborate "issue pleading" of the common law gave way to the "fact pleading" of the codes. But this substitution did not obviate the preliminary skirmishes, so often sham battles, over pleading points. The framers of the Federal Rules believed that the trouble lay in seeking to accomplish too much through the pleading process. Their solution therefore was to subordinate the role of pleading still further and to place increased emphasis upon discovery, pretrial conferences, summary judgment, and the like as preliminary steps to narrow the issues and reveal the facts.

Interpreters of the Federal Rules eventually settled on "notice pleading" as the way to effectuate that vision of the framers and better deliver a proper decision on the merits. The 1957 Conley case, digested and quoted in Part One, stands as the preeminent statement of that approach, under which the main task of pleadings is to give the adversary (and the court and the public) fair notice of the pleader's contentions. The consequence was to discourage spending time and money toiling or skirmishing over pleadings. Indeed, academics pushed for paring pleadings down further to only the notice function.

Yet perhaps the Federal Rules had gone too far in subordinating the role of pleading. Calls for requiring more factual detail in pleadings punctuated the Federal Rules' era. Then in 2007 came the thunderbolt of Twombly, also digested and quoted in Part One. It invented "nonconclusory-and-plausible pleading," which claimed to forswear fact pleading while requiring a showing of convincingness that went well beyond notice pleading.

ROBERT G. BONE, TWOMBLY, PLEADING RULES, AND THE REGULATION OF COURT ACCESS, 94 Iowa L. Rev. 873, 876 (2009). Professor Bone "views Twombly not so much as a pleading decision but rather as a court access decision, one that addresses a general problem of institutional design: how best to prevent undesirable lawsuits from entering the court system. From this broader perspective, screening more aggressively at the front door by demanding more from the complaint is just one approach, with its own costs and benefits, and should be evaluated relative to other alternatives. It makes no sense, for example, to strengthen pleading requirements if the same result can be achieved much better by bolstering Rule 11 sanctions, placing stricter limits on discovery in complex cases, shifting fees, or allowing truncated summary judgment determinations based on targeted and phased discovery."

When pleading serves a gatekeeping function, a few contextual considerations become more relevant. For example, integral to the problem of what tasks to assign specifically to pleading is the modern freedom of amendment. Its result is that a challenge to a pleading, whether successful or not, is most often not dispositive of the case in the trial court.

Indeed, under some procedural systems a ruling on the sufficiency of a pleading may be subject to immediate review on appeal, thus causing further delay and expense and often still not ending the case. (Shall we conclude that interlocutory appeal on pleading matters ought to be wholly prohibited? On the one hand, speedy and inexpensive justice is not achieved by forcing a defendant to go through what may be a long and costly trial on a claim that the appellate court eventually says is insufficient. On the other hand, delay of the plaintiff's trial by what turns out to be a fruitless appeal is equally a denial of speedy and inexpensive justice. Yet we cannot be certain who is aggrieved until the appellate court speaks.) The availability or nonavailability of interlocutory appeal will affect the judicial handling of pleading problems in the trial court.

(b) THE RELATION OF PLEADING TO PROOF

Professor James Bradley Thayer listed as one of the few "great, fundamental rules which are said to govern the production of testimony" that "evidence must be relevant to what is alleged in pleading," or that "the evidence must correspond with the allegations and be confined to the point in issue." James B. Thayer, A Preliminary Treatise on Evidence at the Common Law 484–85 (1898).

1. If the pleadings determine the elements upon which the ultimate decision depends, it readily follows that evidence not relevant to the allegations in the pleadings serves no proper purpose. Successful objections to evidence on this ground are a commonplace in the trial of cases. So, suppose at the trial a party objects to proffered evidence as "not within the pleadings." The first question for the judge is whether the evidence bears on some proposition that is in issue under the pleadings. Is this always apparent from an inspection of the language of the pleadings, or are other problems involved? Will it make any difference in decision whether the pleadings are particularized or general?

2. Assume that the court finds the proffered evidence to be not within the pleadings. The next question is what the court should then do. Should the evidence be excluded? Should it be admitted then and there, the pleadings being amended to correspond to the proof? When will it be the proper course to allow an amendment at trial and let the evidence come in under it, but only after a continuance? When evidence not within the pleadings is offered, will a voluntary dismissal ever be allowed or a mistrial declared, with leave to amend the pleadings and retry the case?

3. If the trial court does exclude the evidence upon objection as not being within the pleadings, and if the appellate court later holds that it was error so to exclude it, the result may well be a new trial if the evidence might have changed the outcome of the trial had it been received. But suppose instead that the trial court erroneously admits the evidence over

the objection that it is outside the pleadings. What then should be the consequences on appeal?

4. Additional problems arise when evidence not within the pleadings comes in at trial without any objection. To what extent can the nonobjecting party later invoke the pleadings to complain of the variance caused by absent allegations?

You see that it is not enough to require that the proof conform to the pleading, whatever that means. The further question is what consequences should attach to such a discrepancy—commonly called a variance. And again it is worth asking whether a court's attitude toward variance should be affected by the devices available in the jurisdiction for disclosure and discovery and for pretrial conferences, or by pleading amendments and interlocutory appeals, and the extent to which those devices were employed in the particular case.

Manning v. Loew

Supreme Judicial Court of Massachusetts, 1943.
313 Mass. 252, 46 N.E.2d 1022.

■ LUMMUS, J. In this action of contract the plaintiff was the only witness on the question of liability. Her testimony tended to prove the following facts. The defendant lives in Boston, but the parties met in January, 1941, in a restaurant in Miami, Florida, where the plaintiff was employed as a waitress. The defendant owned a chain of moving picture theatres in New England, and also had such a theatre in Miami, where he gave the plaintiff employment. Later, at the invitation of the defendant, the plaintiff came to Boston, where the defendant met her. She later went to New York, but returned to Boston on request of the defendant.

When the plaintiff got back to Boston, the defendant met her, and told her, to use her words, that "if I would stay here in Boston, and not go back to New York, and be like a daughter to him, accompany him to his home and on trips and see him any time that he wanted to see me, and be a companion and daughter to him, that he would then put me in the movies; he would get me a screen test. He would see that I got this screen test; if I couldn't that he would produce a picture himself, he would star me in it." It could be found that the plaintiff accepted this offer and agreed to perform its terms.

Subsequently the plaintiff accompanied the defendant to his house, to eating places, to New York and other cities, and on a yachting trip. The defendant was living apart from his wife. In December, 1941, the defendant told the plaintiff that he was through with her and that he was not serious about the alleged agreement. The plaintiff then consulted a lawyer, and this action was begun. At the trial a verdict was directed for the defendant, subject to the plaintiff's exception.

The declaration set forth as the consideration for the defendant's promise that the plaintiff agreed "that she would devote herself at all times required by him [the defendant] to the companionship and service of the defendant and to accompany him to such places as he should designate." Nothing was said in the declaration about being a daughter, or like a daughter, to him, though that was an essential part of the contract according to the plaintiff's testimony, by which she is bound. There was therefore a variance between the declaration and the proof. The action of the judge in directing a verdict for the defendant was not error, even though there was no express statement that the ruling was made with the pleadings in mind. Ferris v. Boston & Maine Railroad, 291 Mass. 529, 533, 197 N.E. 506.

But if we consider the merits without regard to the pleadings, the direction of a verdict for the defendant was not error. Not only did the plaintiff admit that she had sexual intercourse at various times with the defendant [citation omitted], but she also admitted that she had been in bed with another man, and had gone to resorts with that man after the defendant had left her at her hotel for the night, as he thought. Her admitted conduct was not consistent with her promise to act as a daughter to the defendant.

Exceptions overruled.

Questions: (1) Might the plaintiff have avoided the hazard of variance by pleading differently? Suppose she had merely alleged that the defendant had promised for "a valuable consideration"? Would a court hold this sufficient under a typical code? Compare California Packing Corp. v. Kelly Storage & Distrib. Co., 228 N.Y. 49, 126 N.E. 269 (1920) (yes), with Foley v. Cowan, 80 Cal.App.2d 70, 181 P.2d 410 (1947) (no). Should a court hold it sufficient under the Federal Rules?

(2) If such a generalized statement is acceptable and if Doris Manning has so pleaded, what can Elias Loew's lawyer do, under a procedural system like the Federal Rules, to expedite a decision of the case if in fact the consideration for the promise was illegal? Cf. Richardson v. Gregory, 219 App.Div. 211, 219 N.Y.S. 397 (1927).

VARIANCE

There were various ways in which a variance might occur, but to generalize, they all revolved around the general rule that a claim or defense could succeed only if it was both pleaded in full *and* proved in conformity therewith.

Variance was heavily penalized at common law. The same was true in some states long after ameliorative provisions had been introduced by statute in England.[a] So, a plaintiff who offered evidence of all the necessary elements to prove a cause of action might nevertheless lose the chance for a jury verdict if in some particular his proof failed to conform to the allegations in his declaration.

Illustrative of the extremes to which this doctrine went was Spangler v. Pugh, 21 Ill. 85 (1859). There the plaintiff declared upon a promissory note for $2579.57. The note offered in evidence, and received over the defendant's objection, was for $2579.57½. The appellate court reversed the lower court's judgment for the plaintiff on account of this variance and remanded the cause with leave to amend, saying: "However much courts may regret that a slip in pleading should delay the party in the administration of justice, the rules of law must be observed. If the rule were relaxed in this case, it would be to sanction a looseness in practice that might eventually be productive of more injury than benefit."

Benjamin J. Shipman, Handbook of Common–Law Pleading 515–16 (3d ed. 1923), provided a different illustration: "The harsh rule by which the courts punish a party who pleads immaterial facts by compelling him to prove them literally as alleged, although they need never have been set out to state the cause of action, is shockingly illustrated in negligence cases. New trials have frequently been granted for want of proof of wholly unnecessary allegations. The pleader has to steer his course between Scylla and Charybdis, and is driven to state his case in a confusing variety of counts, which multiply and complicate the issues. He has to learn just how general he may make his allegations, avoiding all unnecessary detail, on the one hand, and the danger of stating mere conclusions of law or fact, on the other. By unnecessary particularity in a descriptive statement, he binds himself to prove this surplusage in addition to the essential facts of the case."

In application, this Shipman rule proved complicated. It dealt with pleaded matter that was "descriptive" of what was essential to the case. If instead the unnecessary matter pleaded was wholly foreign or irrelevant, the court would ignore it or on motion strike it out, and the matter would not vitiate the pleading or require conforming proof.

As Shipman suggested and as we further described in Section 3 of Topic B of Part Six, even at common law the harshness of the rule against variance was mitigated by the possibility of stating the same cause of action in various ways in different counts. If, for example, in a negligence action the plaintiff was uncertain what the proof would show, he could plead several specifications of negligence. There was no penalty for such over-pleading. If the proof supported any one of the specifications, a verdict for

[a] 3 & 4 Will. 4, ch. 42, § 23 (1833). This statute gave the nisi prius judge power to amend at trial in order to cure a variance between pleading and proof that was "not material to the merits of the case," upon reasonable terms as to costs and continuance. Previously, no amendment could be allowed except by the full bench of the court sitting at Westminster, which could provide the old statutory remedies for purely formal defects in pleadings. For a chronological list of these "Statutes of Jeofails and Amendments," commencing in 1340, see Charles E. Clark & Ruth A. Yerion, Amendment and Aider of Pleadings, 12 Minn.L.Rev. 97, 125 (1928).

the plaintiff would stand. Today there are in most states statutes or rules that provide less cumbersome and more general antidotes.

CALIFORNIA CODE OF CIVIL PROCEDURE

§ 469. No variance between the allegation in a pleading and the proof is to be deemed material, unless it has actually misled the adverse party to his prejudice in maintaining his action or defense upon the merits. Whenever it appears that a party has been so misled, the Court may order the pleading to be amended, upon such terms as may be just.

§ 470. Where the variance is not material, as provided in Section 469 the court may direct the fact to be found according to the evidence, or may order an immediate amendment, without costs.

§ 471. Where, however, the allegation of the claim or defense to which the proof is directed, is unproved, not in some particular or particulars only, but in its general scope and meaning, it is not to be deemed a case of variance, within the meaning of Sections 469 and 470, but a failure of proof.

Question: (3) California treats the three kinds of variance. How do the Federal Rules solve the middle one, that is, the problem of a lack of conforming proof with respect to wholly unnecessary allegations?

Wasik v. Borg

United States Court of Appeals, Second Circuit, 1970.
423 F.2d 44.

■ Before LUMBARD, CHIEF JUDGE, and FRIENDLY and FEINBERG, CIRCUIT JUDGES.

■ FEINBERG, CIRCUIT JUDGE. While driving his station wagon in Rutland, Vermont, Robert W. Borg rammed into the rear of a vehicle operated by appellee Albert J. Wasik, injuring both Wasik and his automobile. Wasik sued Borg, a resident of Maryland, in the United States District Court for the District of Vermont, basing jurisdiction on diversity of citizenship. Borg served a third-party complaint on appellant Ford Motor Company, alleging that the accident was due to a dangerous defect in the design or manufacture of the automobile, which had caused it to accelerate suddenly. Ford answered, denying Borg's claims and alleging his contributory negligence. Ford also filed an answer to Wasik's original complaint, denying knowledge of the facts of the accident. Trial was held in the summer of 1969 before the late Ernest W. Gibson, J., and a jury, which found that Ford—but not Borg—was liable to Wasik. Damages were assessed at $8,700, and judgment was entered in that amount. On Ford's appeal, we affirm.

The jury indicated by its verdict that it believed that Borg was free from negligence, and that the accident was caused exclusively by a defect in the design or manufacture of his vehicle. Ford contends that it was improper to hold it directly liable to Wasik because Ford was a mere third-party defendant whose liability was contingent on the liability of Borg, for whom the jury found. In another age this argument might have been persuasive, but appellant has ignored two vital factors which we consider dispositive—the course of the proceedings below and the Federal Rules of Civil Procedure. While it would doubtless have been better if appellee Wasik had amended his complaint to include a claim against Ford once it became obvious that a major theory of recovery was to be Ford's liability as manufacturer of a defective product, Wasik's failure to do so does not require reversal.

Rule 14(a) specifically contemplates that

> The plaintiff may assert any claim against the third-party defendant arising out of the transaction or occurrence that is the subject matter of the plaintiff's claim against the third-party plaintiff . . . .

and Rule 15(b) provides:

> When issues not raised by the pleadings are tried by express or implied consent of the parties, they shall be treated in all respects as if they had been raised in the pleadings. Such amendment of the pleadings as may be necessary to cause them to conform to the evidence and to raise these issues may be made upon motion of any party at any time, even after judgment; but failure so to amend does not affect the result of the trial of these issues. . . .

Borg's complaint put Ford on notice that it would be called to account for alleged defects in its product leading to the accident. Throughout the trial, Ford was apparently treated by counsel and the trial judge as a defendant subject to direct liability. The trial record makes it clear that Ford had the opportunity to, and did, litigate all the factual issues essential to the jury verdict, particularly Borg's claim that the throttle cable on his Ford vehicle was in a "runaway condition." All the issues were raised, either by Wasik's pleadings or by Borg's. And it is also evident that counsel for Wasik early sought the benefit of Borg's theory of the accident. Borg was cross-examined as part of Wasik's main case; Wasik's counsel encouraged Borg to describe his non-negligent operation of the vehicle both before and after its sudden "take off." Appellant cross-examined both Wasik and Borg during this early stage of the trial. Had the parties not understood that Ford could be held directly liable to appellee, this tactic of Wasik would hardly be explicable; if the jury were to find, as it ultimately did, that Borg had not been negligent and that the vehicle had been defective, appellee could recover only from Ford, if at all. We see no reason to treat issues which were fully litigated as if they had not been litigated, where no prejudice to appellant has been suggested or is apparent from the record.[1] Under these

---

[1] It is undisputed that Wasik never formally sought to amend his complaint prior to or during trial to assert a claim directly against Ford. Such a formal motion was made in this court, and if it were necessary to rule upon it, we would grant it.

circumstances, we do not think it was error for the trial judge to treat appellant as a defendant potentially subject to primary liability. See Falls Industries, Inc. v. Consolidated Chemical Industries, Inc., 258 F.2d 277, 283–287 (5th Cir.1958); 3 J. Moore, Federal Practice ¶ 15.13.

[Discussion of other alleged errors is omitted.]

Judgment affirmed.

Robbins v. Jordan

United States Court of Appeals, District of Columbia Circuit, 1950.
181 F.2d 793.

■ Before EDGERTON, [Bennett] CLARK and FAHY, CIRCUIT JUDGES.

■ CLARK, CIRCUIT JUDGE. The court below directed a verdict in favor of the defendant at the close of the plaintiffs' case. The plaintiffs have prosecuted this appeal to test the validity of that judgment.

The action sounds in tort for malpractice. The plaintiffs claim negligence on the part of Dr. Jordan in that he failed to take pelvic measurements of Mrs. Robbins at the proper time and as a result a normal birth was attempted when timely measurements would have indicated to a practitioner of average skill and knowledge in this locality that a Caesarean operation was necessary. The husband asks damages for loss of services and consortium while Mrs. Robbins asks compensation for certain resulting injuries including pain and suffering.

The principal error assigned by the appellants to the proceedings below involves the failure of the trial judge to allow them to amend their pleadings in order to introduce evidence to the effect that the defendant held himself out to them as a specialist in obstetrics.

The complaint alleged that the defendant was a "duly licensed physician practicing medicine in the District of Columbia and holding himself out to the general public, including the plaintiffs, as a practicing physician, and a doctor of medicine, and one well qualified in the treatment of disorders and diseases of women." But the court ruled that these allegations were not broad enough to permit proof that the defendant had represented himself to the plaintiffs as an obstetrician. After this ruling the appellants sought permission to amend their complaint so as to enable them to introduce the evidence, but the court again ruled against them and disallowed the amendment.

There can be no question that the plaintiffs were prejudiced by these rulings. Instead of being able to proceed on the theory that the defendant was a specialist and was therefore held to a standard of care and skill normally exercised by such specialists, they were compelled to try their case on the theory that the duty owed them by the defendant was to be measured by that standard of skill and knowledge required of a general practitioner. That the standard of care and skill required of the specialist in obstetrics is stricter than that required of the general practitioner is demonstrable from the record. Take for example the testimony of the roentgenologist who examined Mrs. Robbins with reference to the anticipated delivery of her second child.[1] He stated on cross-examination that in his experience, since 1930, no general practitioner had resorted to the use of pelvimetry.[2] And yet since he testified that he had made a great many thousand of such measurements, it is reasonable to suppose that they were made at the behest of specialists.

Having found that the court's refusal to grant the plaintiffs leave to amend their complaint worked to their prejudice, the only other problem for us to decide,[3] therefore, is whether or not the learned trial judge exceeded the limits of his discretion in so refusing. Rule 15(b) . . . provides in part: ". . . If evidence is objected to at the trial on the ground that it is not within the issues made by the pleadings, the court may allow the pleadings to be amended and shall do so freely when the presentation of the merits of the action will be subserved thereby and the objecting party fails to satisfy the court that the admission of such evidence would prejudice him in maintaining his action or defense on the merits. The court may grant a continuance to enable the objecting party to meet such evidence."

As was said in International Ladies' Garment Workers' Union v. Donnelly Garment Co., 8 Cir., 1941, 121 F.2d 561, 563: "The Supreme Court of the United States has fixed the limits of permissible amendments with increasing liberality and has ruled that a change of the legal theory of the action is no longer accepted as a test of the propriety of a proposed amendment. . . . Rule 15 of the Rules of Civil Procedure . . . expresses the same liberality with respect to the amendment of pleadings."

. . . .

In the instant case the amendment proposed by the plaintiffs did not state a new cause of action. It simply altered the theory of their case. The only reason for denying the proposed amendment was stated by the lower court in the following discussion which was had at the beginning of the trial.

"The Court: Well, I think that would come too late, because that prejudices the defendant in his defense.

"Mr. Quimby: The case has not started.

"The Court: I know, but I am assuming that, being the type of lawyer that I know Mr. Daily is, he has prepared his defense. If the plaintiff is going to change his theory of the case, then he is in a position where he ought to be protected from going forward on a change of theory."

---

[1] The second child was delivered by Caesarean section.

[2] The measurement of the female pelvis by X-ray.

[3] Although we do not necessarily mean to imply that we agree with the trial judge that the allegations of the complaint are not broad enough to permit in proof that the defendant held himself out as a specialist in obstetrics, we prefer to decide this case on other grounds.

There can be no question that a defendant should be protected from surprise resulting from a change of theory; but it is our opinion that the court erred in the method it chose to protect him. The proper procedure would have been to grant the defendant a continuance in order to meet the new evidence. But it was beyond the limits of its judicial discretion to refuse to allow the amendment.

. . . .

Reversed and remanded.

Questions: (4) The court in Robbins v. Jordan said the proper procedure would have been to grant the defendant a continuance. How might a continuance have been helpful to him?

(5) Suppose testimony to the effect that the defendant had represented himself to the plaintiffs as an obstetrician had been admitted without objection. What would you expect the subsequent course of the proceedings to have been?

(6) Suppose the specified testimony had been admitted over objection by the defendant, and there had been a verdict for the plaintiffs. Should the plaintiffs be able to hold their verdict on appeal if the appellate court believes that the objection ought to have been sustained? Should it make any difference whether the defendant, after the overruling of his objection, had requested a continuance? Should it make any difference if the defendant, after the overruling of his objection, had either tried to discredit the testimony by cross-examination or presented evidence of his own to discredit it?

COX v. FREMONT COUNTY PUBLIC BUILDING AUTHORITY, 415 F.2d 882 (10th Cir.1969). This was an action against a building contractor and his surety for breach of contract for construction of a courthouse. Leaking and breaking of glass in a skylight in the courthouse roof were the center of the controversy. The trial judge refused to charge on the defense that the skylight problem resulted from defective design, stating that the assertion of this theory was outside the pleadings and was untimely. In affirming a judgment for the plaintiff, the appellate court said:

"Appellants say that since proof on the defective design theory was admitted without objection, any contention that the issue was not pleaded was waived. Objection was made when the principal testimony on the theory was offered. The trial court stated that the proof was admitted because of its relevance to the separate issue of whether a lack of maintenance caused the skylight problem. We conclude that the defective design issue was not tried by consent. It was not raised in the answers filed or in the pretrial order fixing the issues. Refusal of the instruction was not error. Miller v. Brazel, 300 F.2d 283 (10th Cir.1962). Complaint is also made of denial of a motion to amend during the trial to include the defense of a defective design. The circumstances show no abuse of the trial court's discretion by denying the motion. Heilig v. Studebaker Corporation, 347 F.2d 686 (10th Cir.1965)."

SECTION 2. THE COMPLAINT

(a) STATING THE CLAIM

The pleader draws the essential elements of a cause of action or claim for relief from the substantive law. The form of statement required of a complaint, however, is a matter of procedure.

We make no attempt here to explore the substantive requirements, but the following generalizations, from Fleming James, Jr., Geoffrey C. Hazard, Jr. & John Leubsdorf, Civil Procedure 218, 225 (5th ed. 2001), on the elements of negligence and breach of contract claims may be helpful examples for use in studying the upcoming pages:

"The elements of a cause of action or claim for negligence are as follows: (1) a duty to use care must be owed by defendant to plaintiff; (2) there must be a breach of that duty; (3) that breach must be a proximate cause of (4) injury to plaintiff. In general, the plaintiff must include each of these elements in the complaint. . . .

"The elements of a cause of action or claim for breach of contract are as follows: (1) a contract or agreement involving a quid pro quo (or the presence of some other factor that under substantive law makes an agreement binding), (2) performance by plaintiff of all conditions precedent, and (3) breach of the contract by defendant. Actual damage caused by breach of contract may not be an essential element of a claim . . . ."

Fact pleading.—As to the procedure on pleading, a major problem is the degree of detail or specificity required. The fact pleading approach introduced by the Field Code remains important, because it still prevails in a number of the most prominent states and because courts and commentators are clamoring for federal pleading to relearn and apply the key precepts of fact pleading.

Section 142 of the Field Code, which appears supra p. 1119, instituted fact pleading and remains typical of the provisions still prevailing in code jurisdictions. It calls for a statement of the facts constituting a cause of action. How best to understand that requirement? Probably by contrast to the federal model with which you are most familiar.

Garcia v. Hilton Hotels International, Inc., 97 F.Supp. 5 (D.P.R.1951), illustrates the difference between a permissible federal complaint and the customary code requirements. A former employee alleged that he "was violently discharged by the defendant, being falsely and slanderously accused[b] of being engaged in bringing women from outside the Hotel and

---

[b] The introduction of an allegation by the participial phrase "being . . . accused" would have made it subject to special demurrer at common law. This is an illustration of "recital

introducing them into the rooms thereof for the purpose of developing prostitution in the Hotel." This would be demurrable under the typical code provision, just as it would have been at common law.[c] Publication of a defamation was and is a necessary substantive element of the cause of action, failure of proof of which is fatal, so the code pleader would have to state the underlying facts. In Garcia, the federal court agreed that the complaint failed to state "in so many words" a publication, but nevertheless upheld the complaint as stating a claim upon which relief could be granted. The court explained its result thus: "While in a technical sense, this language states a conclusion, it is clear that plaintiff used it intending to charge publication of the slanderous utterance and it would be unrealistic for defendant to claim that it does not so understand the allegations. [Citation omitted.] Clearly, under such allegations it reasonably may be conceived that plaintiff, upon trial, could adduce evidence tending to prove a publication. If the provisions of rule 8(a) are not to be negatived by recourse to rule 12(b), the statement in . . . the complaint must be deemed sufficient."

If the pleader's failure lies in the statement of claim as distinguished from the existence of an actionable claim, as is very often the case, the expensive paper battle as to formal sufficiency causes delay, takes up valuable judicial time, and may end merely in giving plaintiff's counsel a lesson in pleading. It will not, however, finally dispose of the action because of the freedom in obtaining leave to amend. The federal system supposes it can better handle a lack of clarity in the complaint via Rule 12(e) or, better yet, by disclosure and discovery or a pretrial conference.

---

pleading." Its vice is that it assumes facts instead of alleging facts. Other types of recital pleading were allegations commencing with "whereas" or "notwithstanding the fact that."

Some decisions in code states have even held such pleading insufficient against a general demurrer. E.g., Malott v. Sample, 164 Ind. 645, 74 N.E. 245 (1905); Thompson v. Read, 63 Misc. 235, 118 N.Y.S. 452 (1909) (holding "The foregoing words being spoken in the presence of . . ." to be an insufficient allegation of publication in a slander action).

How would you answer the contention that recital pleading is prohibited by Federal Rule 8(d)(1)'s admonition that each allegation be "simple, concise, and direct"? Whether forbidden or not, recital pleading is not artistic pleading under the Federal Rules or in code-pleading states.

[c] Slander was one of those disfavored actions as to which the common-law pleading requirements were extremely strict. After setting forth the essentials of a declaration in slander, Shipman characterizes them as "an elaborate and absurd jargon of recitals and explanations which obscure the real issues to be tried almost as effectually as if the pleadings were still drawn in Latin." He then quotes Odgers in his work on libel and slander as follows: "Again, in Ball v. Roane (1593) Cro.Eliz. 308, the words were: 'There was never a robbery committed within forty miles of Wellingborough but thou hadst thy part in it.' After a verdict for the plaintiff, the court arrested judgment, 'because it was not averred there was any robbery committed within forty miles, etc., for otherwise it is no slander.' So in Foster v. Browning (1625) Cro.Jac. 688, where the words were, 'Thou art as arrant a thief as any is in England,' the court arrested judgment 'because the plaintiff had not averred that there was any thief in England.' But the climax was reached in a case cited in Dacy v. Clinch (1661) 1 Sid. 53, where the defendant had said to the plaintiff, 'As sure as God governs the world, or King James this kingdom, you are a thief.' After verdict for the plaintiff, the defendant moved in arrest of judgment, on the ground that there was no averment on the record that God did govern the world, or King James this kingdom. But here the court drew the line, and held that 'these things were so apparent' that neither of them need be averred." Benjamin J. Shipman, Handbook of Common–Law Pleading 219–20 (3d ed. 1923).

In the relatively rare case where the real problem is inability to state a good claim because there is not one in fact, devices other than pleading challenges make it possible to expose the situation without a trial. For example, if publication were genuinely a problem in Garcia, the defendant could raise the point by a motion for summary judgment under Rule 56, showing by affidavit or otherwise that there was no publication.

PLEADING FACTS NECESSARY TO CONSTITUTE CAUSE OF ACTION: PROS AND CONS

The contrast presented thus appears to disadvantage code pleading. So what are some of the arguments of the adherents to the code requirement of pleading the facts necessary to constitute a cause of action?

1. The code pleader must think through his case, evolving a tenable theory and ascertaining what facts are necessary to support that theory. This process may satisfy him that his client has no valid claim, whereas the sloppiness permitted under notice pleading does not necessitate this disciplined thinking and hence leads to unfounded lawsuits.

2. The imprecision of notice pleading creates a needless uncertainty as to the issues and a resultant risk of surprise at trial. To guard against this hazard the litigant has to undertake extensive discovery, expending time and money that could be saved by maintaining the code-pleading requirements.

3. The clarification of issues required under code pleading not only puts outer limits on permitted discovery but also facilitates summary judgment motions.

4. The trial is likely to take longer under the Federal Rules. The trial judge will let in doubtful evidence because it will not be clear, especially in the early stages of the case, what the bounds of relevance are going to be. It is the course of safety not to risk reversal by excluding testimony the significance of which may become apparent as the case develops.

5. The clarification of issues required under code pleading facilitates the application of the doctrine of res judicata.

Although the number of states with a rule patterned on Federal Rule 8(a)(2) is considerable, the adherents of the code formulation have successfully held the line in many states. In modernizing the procedure of New Jersey by comprehensive rules of court in 1948, the New Jersey Supreme Court followed the Federal Rules to a substantial extent but did not accept Federal Rule 8(a)(2). The parallel New Jersey Court Rule 4:5–2 reads as follows: "Except as may be more specifically provided by these rules in respect of specific actions, a pleading which sets forth a claim for relief, whether an original claim, counter-claim, cross-claim or third-party claim, shall contain a statement of the facts on which the claim is based, showing that the pleader is entitled to relief . . . ."

There have also been guerrilla attacks on the Federal Rule itself. Upon reports and discussion that appear at 13 F.R.D. 253 (1953), the 1952 Judicial Conference of the Ninth Circuit adopted a resolution recommending the amendment of Rule 8(a)(2) to read substantially as follows: "a short and plain statement of the claim showing that the pleader is entitled to relief, which statement shall contain the facts constituting a cause of action." But the Federal Rules' Advisory Committee, in a 1955 report proposing numerous other amendments, resisted the pressure to change Rule 8(a)(2), with the following explanation:

"*Note.* Rule 8(a)(2) is retained in its present form. This Note is appended to it in answer to various criticisms and suggestions for amendment which have been presented to the Committee.

"The criticisms appear to be based on the view that the rule does not require the averment of any information as to what has actually happened. That Rule 8(a) envisages the statement of circumstances, occurrences, and events in support of the claim presented is clearly indicated not only by the forms appended to the rules showing what should be considered as sufficient compliance with the rule, but also by other intermeshing rules; see, inter alia, Rules 8(c) and ([d]), 9(b)–(g), 10(b), 12(b)(6), 12(h), 15(c), 20, and 54(b). Rule 12(e), providing for a motion for a more definite statement, also shows that the complaint must disclose information with sufficient definiteness. The intent and effect of the rules is to permit the claim to be stated in general terms; the rules are designed to discourage battles over mere form of statement and to sweep away the needless controversies which the codes permitted that served either to delay trial on the merits or to prevent a party from having a trial because of mistakes in statement. The decision in Dioguardi v. Durning, 139 F.2d 774 (2d Cir.1944), to which proponents of an amendment to Rule 8(a) have especially referred, was not based on any holding that a pleader is not required to supply information disclosing a ground for relief. The complaint in that case stated a plethora of facts and the court so construed them as to sustain the validity of the pleading.

"While there has been some minority criticism, the consensus favors the rule and the reported cases indicate that it has worked satisfactorily and has advanced the administration of justice in the district courts. The rule has been adopted verbatim by a number of states in framing their own rules of court procedure. This circumstance appears to the Committee to confirm its view that no change in the rule is required or justified.

"It is accordingly the opinion of the Advisory Committee that, as it stands, the rule adequately sets forth the characteristics of good pleading; does away with the confusion resulting from the use of 'facts' and 'cause of action'; and requires the pleader to disclose adequate information as the basis of his claim for relief as distinguished from a bare averment that he wants relief and is entitled to it."

PLEADING EVIDENCE, ULTIMATE FACTS, AND CONCLUSIONS: HOPELESS DISTINCTIONS

There was a beguiling appearance of simplicity in the requirement adopted by the framers of the codes that a pleader should give a "plain and concise statement of the facts constituting a cause of action." The codifiers would probably be amazed to see the vast accumulation of cases interpreting this simple-sounding mandate. Scanning the West digest system under Pleading nos. 8, 11 will disclose the volume of litigation but will not reveal clear guidelines for decision.

Where did the code framers go astray? A big difficulty was their apparent failure to realize that every statement of fact is generalized to some degree, and that the appropriate degree depends upon the objectives. Any statement of fact about a given situation necessarily involves a process of selection and rejection. The pleader was not to "plead his evidence," for that was being too specific; nor was he to "plead conclusions of law," for that was being too general; he was to plead the "ultimate facts."[d]

One can scarcely imagine a lawyer asking her client for a "plain and concise statement of the facts" and finding a transcript of that statement to be a suitable pleading. The lawyer's training and experience supposedly enable her to cull from a client's story the facts relevant to her purpose and to couch them in terms neither too specific nor too general. Suppose the lawyer knows the substantive rule of contract law into which she hopes to fit her client's cause. Does she plead a contract by reciting that "*A* said this, *B* said that, and so on" or by reciting that "*A* and *B* mutually agreed such and such"? Is this mere evidence? Is "*A* converted to *A*'s own use" a proper statement of ultimate fact or bad as a conclusion? (See Federal Form 15.) How about "*A* negligently drove a motor vehicle against *B*"? (See Federal Form 11.)

Another difficulty unacknowledged by the codifiers was the impossibility of separating facts from law cleanly. Are "*A* is the owner of Blackacre" and "*A* is the wife of *B*" proper statements of fact, even though either may involve one or more intricate matters of law?

From what source does today's pleader learn how to steer between "mere evidence" and "legal conclusion"? Surely not from the sterile statement of the code itself. Under a typical code the object should perhaps be, as Judge Charles E. Clark suggested in Handbook of the Law of Code Pleading 232 (2d ed. 1947), "fair notice of each material fact of the pleader's cause," but the pleader may find that this is merely a restatement of the problem rather than a solution. Should the required particularity of

---

[d] Compare the former English requirement in Rules of the Supreme Court, O. 18, r. 7(1), which provided that "every pleading must contain, and contain only, a statement in a summary form of the material facts on which the party pleading relies for his claim or defence, as the case may be, but not the evidence by which those facts are to be proved, and the statement must be as brief as the nature of the case admits." After the 1998 Woolf Reforms, England by Civil Procedure Rule 16.4(1)(a) now requires in the statement of case only "a concise statement of the facts on which the claimant relies."

statement depend on whether the allegation is likely to be in serious dispute in the litigation?

About all that the pleader has to go on is precedent and analogy. Courts of the code states have by now dealt with most of the common pleading problems (although frequently with results varying from state to state and inconsistencies within a single state), so the careful lawyer is likely to find a related precedent with judicial blessing. Many states have provided officially approved forms for common types of action, and unofficial practice books with forms are numerous.

In New York, NYCPLR § 3013 tries to avoid the morass of the mere-evidence/ultimate-fact/legal-conclusion distinctions. It reads: "Statements in a pleading shall be sufficiently particular to give the court and parties notice of the transactions, occurrences, or series of transactions or occurrences, intended to be proved and the material elements of each cause of action or defense." See Foley v. D'Agostino, 21 A.D.2d 60, 248 N.Y.S.2d 121 (1964), in which the court gave this section a liberal construction that substantially equates it to the federal "claim for relief." In discouraging time-consuming attacks on pleadings, the court also relied upon NYCPLR § 3026, which provides: "Pleadings shall be liberally construed. Defects shall be ignored if a substantial right of a party is not prejudiced."

A leading commentator made this wry comment on Federal Rule 8(a)(2): "You will notice the words 'cause of action' do not appear; neither does the word 'fact'. The reason for that is, nobody knows what 'facts' are; courts have been trying for five hundred years to find 'facts' and nobody has ever been able to draw a line between what were and what were not 'facts.' Since the word 'facts' has given a great deal of trouble the suggestion was, Why not eliminate it? Since the phrase 'cause of action' has given trouble, eliminate that also. Whether this will do any good is very doubtful, for both terms are embedded in the literature of the law and in the vocabulary of the profession." Edson R. Sunderland, The New Federal Rules, 45 W.Va.L.Q. 5, 12 (1938).

Question: (7) The Colorado Rules, patterned on the Federal Rules, add this sentence to its rule 8: "Pleadings otherwise meeting the requirements of these rules shall not be considered objectionable for failure to state ultimate facts as distinguished from conclusions of law." Is this provision necessary? Is it wise? See 5 Wright & Miller § 1218.

Notice pleading.—How far does tolerance for imprecision in a complaint extend in federal practice? Remember what Justice Black had to say on the subject in Conley back in Part One. The Supreme Court there made clear that the required precision depends upon the objectives of pleading. Its opinion also made it sound settled that the primary purpose of federal pleading is to give the adversary (and the court and the public) fair notice of the pleader's contentions.

In Conley, the Court discussed the need for *factual detail* in the complaint: "all the Rules require is 'a short and plain statement of the claim' that will give the defendant fair notice of what the plaintiff's claim is and the grounds upon which it rests." This purpose implies that there is little need for detailed statement in the pleadings. The pleader should indicate the elements of his claims or defenses by giving a somewhat particularized mention of their factual circumstances, but particularized only enough to give fair notice. The complaint need not allege facts that constitute each of the substantive elements of a recognizable legal claim, as long as all those elements are reasonably inferrable from the mention of some of the circumstances of the transaction on which the claim is based. There is no call for pleading evidence.

Question: (8) *P* alleges a contract claim with no reference to consideration. Assuming that a gratuitous promise is as a matter of substantive law not enforceable on the given facts, should a motion to dismiss be granted? If not, what might *D* do?

Conley also set out a very loose test of *legal sufficiency* of the complaint, looking to see if any legal claim existed that would be consistent with the words of the complaint. This test implies that there is no need for expressly legal content in the pleadings. A complaint need not identify any issues likely to be in dispute, as long as it encompasses a legal claim and does not contain allegations that actually defeat the plaintiff's claim.

AMERICAN NURSES' ASSOCIATION v. ILLINOIS, 783 F.2d 716 (7th Cir.1986). Employees in predominantly female jobs sued the state as an employer for sex discrimination. The district court dismissed under Rule 12(b)(6), ruling that the complaint pleaded a failure to pay employees in accordance with comparable worth and that this did not violate antidiscrimination law. On appeal, the Seventh Circuit reversed, ruling that the complaint might also have sketchily and secondarily pleaded intentional discrimination. Judge Posner explained in part:

"So if all that the plaintiffs in this case are complaining about is the State of Illinois' failure to implement a comparable worth study, they have no case and it was properly dismissed. We must therefore consider what precisely they are complaining about. Our task would be easier if the complaint had been drafted with the brevity that the Federal Rules of Civil Procedure envisage though do not require. . . .

"The idea of 'a plain and short statement of the claim' has not caught on. Few complaints follow the models in the Appendix of Forms. Plaintiffs' lawyers, knowing that some judges read a complaint as soon as it is filed in order to get a sense of the suit, hope by pleading facts to 'educate' (that is to say, influence) the judge with regard to the nature and probable merits of the case, and also hope to set the stage for an advantageous settlement by showing the defendant what a powerful case they intend to prove. The pleading of facts is well illustrated by the present case. The complaint is twenty pages long and has a hundred page appendix (the comparable worth study).

"A plaintiff who files a long and detailed complaint may plead himself out of court by including factual allegations which if true show that his legal rights were not invaded. . . .

. . . .

". . . But the court is not to pounce on the plaintiff and by a crabbed and literal reading of the complaint strain to find that he has pleaded facts which show that his claim is not actionable, and then dismiss the complaint on the merits so that the plaintiff cannot replead. . . . The district judge did not quite do that here, because this complaint can easily be read to allege a departure from the principles of comparable worth, and no more. But that reading is not inevitable, and the fact that it is logical and unstrained is not enough to warrant dismissal. In the system created by the Federal Rules [Conley governs. Its] language, repeated though it has been in countless later cases (see, e.g., Hishon v. King & Spalding, 467 U.S. 69, 104 S.Ct. 2229, 2233, 81 L.Ed.2d 59 (1984)), should not be taken literally; for taken literally it would permit dismissal only in frivolous cases. As we said earlier, if the plaintiff, though not required to do so, pleads facts, and the facts show that he is entitled to no relief, the complaint should be dismissed. There would be no point in allowing such a lawsuit to go any further; its doom is foretold. But this is not such a case."

Question: (9) *P*, asserting that he was a guest passenger in *D*'s automobile, states a personal-injury claim in language drawn from Form 11 to the effect that *D* drove her motor vehicle negligently. Assuming that as a matter of substantive law gross negligence is an essential element of a guest passenger's case (as is the law in many states), should a motion to dismiss be granted? If so, what might *P* do?

KIRKSEY v. R.J. REYNOLDS TOBACCO CO., 168 F.3d 1039 (7th Cir.1999). "The plaintiff appeals from the dismissal, on the defendants' motion under Fed.R.Civ.P. 12(b)(6), of a personal-injury suit that she brought against two cigarette manufacturers as the executor of the estate of her husband, who, she alleges, smoked cigarettes manufactured by the defendants. The complaint, captioned 'complaint for damages for wrongful death and emotional distress,' charges that the defendants accelerated Mr. Kirksey's death from lung cancer by falsely advertising that their cigarettes were not addictive and by adding addicting agents to their cigarettes without informing him either that they were doing this or that cigarettes (with or without such agents) are addictive. Had it not been for these acts or omissions, the complaint alleges, Kirksey would have smoked less and lived longer.

"The motion to dismiss claimed that the facts alleged in the complaint do not add up to a tort under Illinois law, which supplies the substantive law governing this diversity case. The motion characterized the plaintiff's claim as one of products liability or false advertising and argued that it was either preempted by federal law or barred by the cases interpreting Illinois' tort law. . . . The plaintiff says that she was not 'required at this stage of the litigation to specifically characterize or identify the legal basis of the claims in the complaint. . . . Rather, what Plaintiff is required to do at the initial pleading stage, and what Plaintiff has done, is to assert a colorable claim that has some factual support.' . . . The plaintiff's essential contention is that in requiring her to specify the legal theory underlying her complaint, the judge violated Fed.R.Civ.P. 8(a)(2), which requires only that the complaint contain 'a short and plain statement of the [plaintiff's] claim showing that the [plaintiff] is entitled to relief'—not a long-winded statement of legal theories replete with citations to cases or statutes. To require more, the plaintiff argues, would be inconsistent with the 'notice pleading' philosophy of the civil rules.

"Her characterization of Rule 8(a)(2) is correct. All that's required to state a claim in a complaint filed in a federal court is a short statement, in plain (that is, ordinary, nonlegalistic) English, of the legal claim. . . .

"Where the plaintiff has gone astray is in supposing that a complaint which complies with Rule 8(a)(2) is immune from a motion to dismiss. This confuses form with substance. Rule 8(a)(2) specifies the conditions of the formal adequacy of a pleading. It does not specify the conditions of its substantive adequacy, that is, its legal merit. Suppose the complaint had alleged that the defendants had violated Illinois or federal law by failing to obtain a license to manufacture cigarettes. The complaint would comply with Rule 8(a)(2), but, assuming no such license is required, it would be highly vulnerable to dismissal under Rule 12(b)(6). If the defendants filed a motion to dismiss in which they pointed out that there was no such licensing requirement, it would not be responsive of the plaintiff to say that she was not 'required at this stage of the litigation to specifically characterize or identify the legal basis of the claims in the complaint.' The defendants would have given reasons for dismissing the complaint despite its formal beauties, and she would have to give reasons against. Our system of justice is adversarial, and our judges are busy people. If they are given plausible reasons for dismissing a complaint, they are not going to do the plaintiff's research and try to discover whether there might be something to say against the defendants' reasoning. An unresponsive response is no response. In effect the plaintiff was defaulted for refusing to respond to the motion to dismiss. And rightly so. [Citations omitted.]"

And so Judge Posner, writing for the court, affirmed.

ACADEMIC PROPOSAL

When writing the Federal Rules, Judge Clark would have favored eliminating battles over pleadings and relying instead on summary judgment, but the more conservative views of others prevailed. See Michael E. Smith, Judge Charles E. Clark and the Federal Rules of Civil Procedure, 85 Yale L.J. 914, 917–19, 927–31 (1976). Perhaps Clark was right. As a thought experiment, let us formulate a proposal based on his view, theorizing that now the time has come to go farther than Conley toward pure notice pleading. More precisely, one could propose abrogating the Rule 12(b)(6) motion, as well as the Rule 12(c) motion for judgment on the pleadings and the Rule 12(f) motion to strike an insufficient defense.

The argument in support would focus first on pleading motions that end up accomplishing nothing. It seems that this describes a solid majority of such motions, even many of those made in good faith. Apparently, many pleaders are quite capable of adequately stating an unfounded claim or defense, while others with a well-founded position might fail initially to follow the pleading Rules but with instruction can do so by amendment. Abolishing pleading battles would eliminate the abuse and waste involved in pointless motions.

Now focus on pleading motions that succeed in doing something but should not. Abolition would naturally cure this problem too. Rule 12 motions are an open invitation to force pleadings to perform functions that are more efficiently and fairly handled by the later stages of discovery, pretrial conferences, and summary judgment. In particular, abolition would keep judges from subversively reviving fact pleading—whether they are doing so in order substantively to disfavor certain kinds of claims or litigants or simply to speed the process up, and whether they do so by demanding greater particularity or even by requiring pleaders to proffer evidence—and also keep them from actually deciding factual disputes without suitable procedures and at a premature point.

Lastly the focus falls on pleading motions that serve a good function. Here other procedural devices can step in to deliver at least the same benefits as motions to dismiss on the pleadings. First, if the purpose served is notice, then Rule 12(e) is there. It lies only where really needed, and it works without the cumbersomeness of dismissal and amendment. Better yet, disclosure and discovery or a pretrial conference can provide the needed clarity. Second, if the function to be served is cutting off discovery by frivolous litigants, then a court could use a Rule 26(c) protective order to limit discovery. Perhaps big complex cases present a generic threat, but then a Rule amendment would be the preferred way to impose special pleading requirements, or directly to restrict early discovery, in certain kinds of cases. Finding such a cure in the words of Rule 8(a) is a poor idea. Third, if the purpose to be served is disposition on the merits, then Rule 56 is better tailored to ask the right questions and produce the right answers. It lies in simple form where the pleadings present an issue of law, and it continues to work even where an issue fades into one of the facts underlying the pleadings.

In sum, abolishing pleading battles would finally pare pleading down to the sole proper function of giving fair notice of the pleader's contentions to the adversary and to the court. Litigants should not be allowed to fight over, say, whether a contract complaint must state consideration, especially when there is freedom to amend and when there is a superior procedural mechanism for exploring both the legal need for proving consideration and its basis in actual fact—let them fight over the adequacy of the actual claim, not the adequacy of its statement.

Moreover, removing the redundancy of Rule 12(b)(6), (c), and (f) would clean up the Federal Rules, which has its own rewards of fairness and efficiency. Probably summary judgment should undergo amendment to facilitate challenges, on the law or on the facts and in whole or in part, as to whether a need for trial exists. Indeed, summary judgment, which is examined in Topic D, should perhaps undergo reconception as "summary adjudication," or a broadened alternative to full-blown procedure. We do need a more effective way to test the *merits* of claims and defenses, but we can live henceforth without testing the *pleadings*.

Questions: (10) Do you agree? See generally Yoichiro Hamabe, Functions of Rule 12(b)(6) in the Federal Rules of Civil Procedure: A Categorization Approach, 15 Campbell L.Rev. 119 (1993).

(11) After such a reform, should a defendant's motion for summary judgment extend the time to answer?

Yet undeniably, out in the real world, a desire abides that federal pleadings do more than give notice, as evidenced by the courts' still entertaining pleading-motion contests on the law and on the facts. A tort complaint may suggest that the plaintiff is intending to seek recovery not on some traditional theory conceivably within the general allegations but on some innovative theory that goes beyond the law's current extent given the facts. The defendant naturally wants to nip the case in the bud, and the court might be inclined to go along with the effort in order to clear the docket. Or a pleading might suggest an absence of basis for claim or defense—perhaps by omission of some expected allegation—but does not actually defeat itself. The defendant and the court therefore want more facts in the complaint.

Indeed, the courts went in the opposite direction from the academics, especially in regard to the pleadings' factual content. The courts argued that Rule 8(a) sometimes calls for "heightened pleading."

RICHARD L. MARCUS, THE REVIVAL OF FACT PLEADING UNDER THE FEDERAL RULES OF CIVIL PROCEDURE, 86 Colum.L.Rev. 433, 434–37 (1986). "One seeming impact of Conley v. Gibson was that commentators lost interest in pleading. For years before and after the adoption of the Federal Rules in 1938, pleading had been the subject of intense academic discussion. After the decision, this discussion stopped abruptly. Perhaps that was because some viewed the battle about detailed pleadings as irretrievably over, or because they understood that Conley authorized a 'fishing expedition' to determine whether plaintiff actually had a claim. Whatever the reason, for more than twenty years after Conley, there was virtually no academic recognition that pleading practice had not vanished; defendants continued to make motions to dismiss and courts continued to grant them. Only recently have commentators begun to acknowledge this reality.

"Not only has pleading practice survived, but fact pleading, the bête noir of the codes, seems to be enjoying a revival in a number of areas in which courts refuse to accept 'conclusory' allegations as sufficient under the Federal Rules. . . . Although they rarely acknowledge the shift, federal courts are insisting on detailed factual allegations more and more often, particularly in securities fraud and civil rights cases.

". . . The new fact pleading is an effort to cope with the pressures of the litigation boom, itself caused in part by the innovations of the Federal Rules. Contrary to the conventional wisdom that the sole purpose of pleadings is to give notice, this Article suggests that their role should be to enable courts to decide cases on their merits. The important question then is how pleading rules can be used to accomplish that purpose. Unfortunately, operating in the shadow of Conley v. Gibson and caught up in the vocabulary of notice pleading, the courts have not given that question much attention.

"This Article finds that the answer is to look for cases in which the plaintiff's legal conclusions can be profitably evaluated. It identifies two broad categories of such cases—those in which more specificity is likely to disclose a fatal defect in a plaintiff's case, and those in which sufficient detail will enable the court to make a reliable determination that the defendant did not violate the plaintiff's rights. Used in this fashion, pleading practice is an important tool, but not a panacea. In other kinds of cases, whether purportedly justified as providing 'notice' or otherwise, pleading motions are largely a waste of time.

"The new fact pleading does not stop with these two kinds of cases, however. Courts now regularly use it . . . to probe and reject plaintiff's factual conclusions. Although this practice is understandable in view of the breadth of modern discovery and the limits on summary judgment, it does not provide a reliable method for determining whether a defendant has violated the plaintiff's rights because it requires the plaintiff to marshall evidence before conducting discovery. Neither can it be justified as a special way of handling certain 'suspicious' claims or as a step toward discretionary dismissals. Instead, the preferable route for probing plaintiff's factual conclusions should be to rely on more flexible use of summary judgment. Under this approach, the principal focus would often be on the amount of discovery to be allowed a plaintiff under Rule 56(f) before ruling on summary judgment, thereby controlling the risk of abuse of discovery. Such flexible use of summary judgment would be particularly effective if done in conjunction with more active case management by judges. Combined with selective cost-shifting in cases of proven litigation abuse, this evidentiary scrutiny would provide a better system for pretrial disposition."

Swierkiewicz v. Sorema N.A.

Supreme Court of the United States, 2002.
534 U.S. 506, 122 S.Ct. 992.

■ JUSTICE THOMAS delivered the opinion of the Court.

This case presents the question whether a complaint in an employment discrimination lawsuit must contain specific facts establishing a prima facie case of discrimination under the framework set forth by this Court in McDonnell Douglas Corp. v. Green, 411 U.S. 792, 93 S.Ct. 1817 (1973). We hold that an employment discrimination complaint need not include such facts and instead must contain only "a short and plain statement of the claim showing that the pleader is entitled to relief." Fed.Rule Civ.Proc. 8(a)(2).

I

Petitioner Akos Swierkiewicz is a native of Hungary, who at the time of his complaint was 53 years old.[1] In April 1989, petitioner began working for respondent Sorema N.A., a reinsurance company headquartered in New York and principally owned and controlled by a French parent corporation. Petitioner was initially employed in the position of senior vice president and chief underwriting officer (CUO). Nearly six years later, François M. Chavel, respondent's Chief Executive Officer, demoted petitioner to a marketing and services position and transferred the bulk of his underwriting responsibilities to Nicholas Papadopoulo, a 32-year-old who, like Mr. Chavel, is a French national. About a year later, Mr. Chavel stated that he wanted to "energize" the underwriting department and appointed Mr. Papadopoulo as CUO. Petitioner claims that Mr. Papadopoulo had only one year of underwriting experience at the time he was promoted, and therefore was less experienced and less qualified to be CUO than he, since at that point he had 26 years of experience in the insurance industry.

Following his demotion, petitioner contends that he "was isolated by Mr. Chavel . . . excluded from business decisions and meetings and denied the opportunity to reach his true potential at SOREMA." App. 26. Petitioner unsuccessfully attempted to meet with Mr. Chavel to discuss his discontent. Finally, in April 1997, petitioner sent a memo to Mr. Chavel outlining his grievances and requesting a severance package. Two weeks later, respondent's general counsel presented petitioner with two options: He could either resign without a severance package or be dismissed. Mr. Chavel fired petitioner after he refused to resign.

Petitioner filed a lawsuit alleging that he had been terminated on account of his national origin in violation of Title VII of the Civil Rights Act of 1964, 78 Stat. 253, as amended, 42 U.S.C. § 2000e et seq. (1994 ed. and Supp. V), and on account of his age in violation of the Age Discrimination in Employment Act of 1967 (ADEA), 81 Stat. 602, as amended, 29 U.S.C. § 621 et seq. (1994 ed. and Supp. V). App. 28. The United States

---

[1] Because we review here a decision granting respondent's motion to dismiss, we must accept as true all of the factual allegations contained in the complaint. [Citation omitted.]

District Court for the Southern District of New York dismissed petitioner's complaint because it found that he "ha[d] not adequately alleged a prima facie case, in that he ha[d] not adequately alleged circumstances that support an inference of discrimination." Id., at 42. The United States Court of Appeals for the Second Circuit affirmed the dismissal . . . . 5 Fed.Appx. 63, 65 (C.A.2 2001). We granted certiorari, 533 U.S. 976, 122 S.Ct. 23 (2001), to resolve a split among the Courts of Appeals concerning the proper pleading standard for employment discrimination cases, and now reverse.

II

Applying Circuit precedent, the Court of Appeals required petitioner to plead a prima facie case of discrimination in order to survive respondent's motion to dismiss. See 5 Fed.Appx., at 64–65. In the Court of Appeals' view, petitioner was thus required to allege in his complaint: (1) membership in a protected group; (2) qualification for the job in question; (3) an adverse employment action; and (4) circumstances that support an inference of discrimination. Ibid.; cf. McDonnell Douglas, 411 U. S., at 802, 93 S.Ct. 1817; Texas Dept. of Community Affairs v. Burdine, 450 U.S. 248, 253–254, n. 6, 101 S.Ct. 1089 (1981).

The prima facie case under McDonnell Douglas, however, is an evidentiary standard, not a pleading requirement. In McDonnell Douglas, this Court made clear that "[t]he critical issue before us concern[ed] the order and allocation *of proof* in a private, non-class action challenging employment discrimination." 411 U. S., at 800, 93 S.Ct. 1817 (emphasis added). In subsequent cases, this Court has reiterated that the prima facie case relates to the employee's burden of presenting evidence that raises an inference of discrimination. [Citations omitted.]

This Court has never indicated that the requirements for establishing a prima facie case under McDonnell Douglas also apply to the pleading standard that plaintiffs must satisfy in order to survive a motion to dismiss. For instance, we have rejected the argument that a Title VII complaint requires greater "particularity," because this would "too narrowly constric[t] the role of the pleadings." McDonald v. Santa Fe Trail Transp. Co., 427 U.S. 273, 283, n. 11, 96 S.Ct. 2574 (1976). Consequently, the ordinary rules for assessing the sufficiency of a complaint apply. See, e.g., Scheuer v. Rhodes, 416 U.S. 232, 236, 94 S.Ct. 1683 (1974) ("When a federal court reviews the sufficiency of a complaint, before the reception of any evidence either by affidavit or admissions, its task is necessarily a limited one. The issue is not whether a plaintiff will ultimately prevail but whether the claimant is entitled to offer evidence to support the claims.").

. . . .

Moreover, the precise requirements of a prima facie case can vary depending on the context and were "never intended to be rigid, mechanized, or ritualistic." Furnco Constr. Corp. v. Waters, 438 U.S. 567, 577, 98 S.Ct. 2943 (1978); [other citations omitted]. Before discovery has unearthed relevant facts and evidence, it may be difficult to define the precise formulation of the required prima facie case in a particular case. Given that the prima facie case operates as a flexible evidentiary standard, it should not be transposed into a rigid pleading standard for discrimination cases.

Furthermore, imposing the Court of Appeals' heightened pleading standard in employment discrimination cases conflicts with Federal Rule of Civil Procedure 8(a)(2), which provides that a complaint must include only "a short and plain statement of the claim showing that the pleader is entitled to relief." Such a statement must simply "give the defendant fair notice of what the plaintiff's claim is and the grounds upon which it rests." Conley v. Gibson, 355 U.S. 41, 47, 78 S.Ct. 99 (1957). This simplified notice pleading standard relies on liberal discovery rules and summary judgment motions to define disputed facts and issues and to dispose of unmeritorious claims. See id., at 47–48, 78 S.Ct. 99; Leatherman v. Tarrant County Narcotics Intelligence and Coordination Unit, 507 U.S. 163, 168–169, 113 S.Ct. 1160 (1993). "The provisions for discovery are so flexible and the provisions for pretrial procedure and summary judgment so effective, that attempted surprise in federal practice is aborted very easily, synthetic issues detected, and the gravamen of the dispute brought frankly into the open for the inspection of the court." 5 C. Wright & A. Miller, Federal Practice and Procedure § 1202, p. 76 (2d ed. 1990).

Rule 8(a)'s simplified pleading standard applies to all civil actions, with limited exceptions. Rule 9(b), for example, provides for greater particularity in all averments of fraud or mistake. This Court, however, has declined to extend such exceptions to other contexts. In Leatherman we stated: "[T]he Federal Rules do address in Rule 9(b) the question of the need for greater particularity in pleading certain actions, but do not include among the enumerated actions any reference to complaints alleging municipal liability under § 1983. *Expressio unius est exclusio alterius*." 507 U. S., at 168, 113 S.Ct. 1160. Just as Rule 9(b) makes no mention of municipal liability under Rev. Stat. § 1979, 42 U.S.C. § 1983 (1994 ed., Supp. V), neither does it refer to employment discrimination. Thus, complaints in these cases, as in most others, must satisfy only the simple requirements of Rule 8(a).[4]

Other provisions of the Federal Rules of Civil Procedure are inextricably linked to Rule 8(a)'s simplified notice pleading standard. Rule 8([d])(1) states that "[n]o technical forms of pleading or motions are required," and Rule 8([e]) provides that "[a]ll pleadings shall be so construed as to do substantial justice." . . . If a pleading fails to specify the allegations in a manner that provides sufficient notice, a defendant can move for a more definite statement under Rule 12(e) before responding. Moreover, claims lacking merit may be dealt with through summary judgment under Rule 56. The liberal notice pleading of Rule 8(a) is the starting point of a

[4] These requirements are exemplified by the Federal Rules of Civil Procedure Forms, which "are sufficient under the rules and are intended to indicate the simplicity and brevity of statement which the rules contemplate." Fed.Rule Civ.Proc. 84. For example, Form [11] sets forth a complaint for negligence in which plaintiff simply states in relevant part: "On June 1, 1936, in a public highway called Boylston Street in Boston, Massachusetts, defendant negligently drove a motor vehicle against plaintiff who was then crossing said highway."

simplified pleading system, which was adopted to focus litigation on the merits of a claim. [Citation omitted.]

Applying the relevant standard, petitioner's complaint easily satisfies the requirements of Rule 8(a) because it gives respondent fair notice of the basis for petitioner's claims. Petitioner alleged that he had been terminated on account of his national origin in violation of Title VII and on account of his age in violation of the ADEA. App. 28. His complaint detailed the events leading to his termination, provided relevant dates, and included the ages and nationalities of at least some of the relevant persons involved with his termination. Id., at 24–28. These allegations give respondent fair notice of what petitioner's claims are and the grounds upon which they rest. See Conley, supra, at 47, 78 S.Ct. 99. In addition, they state claims upon which relief could be granted under Title VII and the ADEA.

Respondent argues that allowing lawsuits based on conclusory allegations of discrimination to go forward will burden the courts and encourage disgruntled employees to bring unsubstantiated suits. Brief for Respondent 34–40. Whatever the practical merits of this argument, the Federal Rules do not contain a heightened pleading standard for employment discrimination suits. A requirement of greater specificity for particular claims is a result that "must be obtained by the process of amending the Federal Rules, and not by judicial interpretation." Leatherman, supra, at 168, 113 S.Ct. 1160. Furthermore, Rule 8(a) establishes a pleading standard without regard to whether a claim will succeed on the merits. "Indeed it may appear on the face of the pleadings that a recovery is very remote and unlikely but that is not the test." Scheuer, 416 U. S., at 236, 94 S.Ct. 1683.

For the foregoing reasons, we hold that an employment discrimination plaintiff need not plead a prima facie case of discrimination and that petitioner's complaint is sufficient to survive respondent's motion to dismiss. Accordingly, the judgment of the Court of Appeals is reversed, and the case is remanded for further proceedings consistent with this opinion.

It is so ordered.

Nonconclusory-and-plausible pleading.—Recall that in Twombly the Court required a complaint to be sufficiently convincing to pass the new test of nonconclusory plausibility. In doing so, it expressly preserved the Swierkiewicz (pronounced SVAIR-ke-vich) case's rejection of heightened pleading in the absence of a special Rule or statutory provision. The Twombly case said that "we do not require heightened fact pleading of specifics, but only enough facts to state a claim to relief that is plausible on its face."

Nevertheless, the Twombly Court was adding a requirement, just for claimants, above and beyond their having to give notice. The Court had unearthed, in Rule 8(a)(2)'s required "showing," the requirement that at the pleading stage the plaintiff must establish by nonconclusory allegations the complaint's plausibility on the merits. Although much puzzlement persists, pleading apparently works this way now for complaints.

First, as to *legal sufficiency*, the judge would decide any pure issues of law in the traditional way for a Rule 12(b)(6) motion. Practically, however, the plaintiff must now do more to identify the complaint's legal theories, doing so well enough for the judge to weigh their factual sufficiency.

Second, as to *factual sufficiency*, the plaintiff practically must plead a lot of facts, so that the product will not look much different from a complaint in a fact-pleading regime. The plaintiff should give a particularized mention of the factual circumstances of each element of the claim. The plaintiff who needs discovery to learn the required factual particulars is the person whom the Court has newly put in jeopardy. The degree of particularization should be sufficient to make an inference of liability plausible, or reasonably possible. The judge performs the decisional task by ignoring any conclusory allegation that an element exists, and then, after accepting the remaining allegations as true, by weighing the plausibility of the liability inference in light of his judicial experience and common sense as applied to the case's particular context.

Ashcroft v. Iqbal

Supreme Court of the United States, 2009.
___ U.S. ___, 129 S.Ct. 1937.

■ JUSTICE KENNEDY delivered the opinion of the Court.

Respondent Javaid Iqbal is a citizen of Pakistan and a Muslim. In the wake of the September 11, 2001, terrorist attacks he was arrested in the United States on criminal charges and detained by federal officials. Respondent claims he was deprived of various constitutional protections while in federal custody. To redress the alleged deprivations, respondent filed a complaint against numerous federal officials, including John Ashcroft, the former Attorney General of the United States, and Robert Mueller, the Director of the Federal Bureau of Investigation (FBI). Ashcroft and Mueller are the petitioners in the case now before us. As to these two petitioners, the complaint alleges that they adopted an unconstitutional policy that subjected respondent to harsh conditions of confinement on account of his race, religion, or national origin.

In the District Court petitioners raised the defense of qualified immunity [in the course of moving] to dismiss the suit, contending the complaint was not sufficient to state a claim against them. The District Court denied the motion to dismiss, concluding the complaint was sufficient to state a claim despite petitioners' official status at the times in question. Petitioners brought an interlocutory appeal in the Court of Appeals for the Second Circuit. The court . . . affirmed the District Court's decision.

Respondent's account of his prison ordeal could, if proved, demonstrate unconstitutional misconduct by some governmental actors. But the allegations and pleadings with respect to these actors are not before us here. This case instead turns on a narrower question: Did respondent, as the plaintiff in the District Court, plead factual matter that, if taken as true, states a claim that petitioners deprived him of his clearly established constitutional rights. We hold respondent's pleadings are insufficient.

. . . .

. . . The complaint contends that petitioners designated respondent a person of high interest on account of his race, religion, or national origin, in contravention of the First and Fifth Amendments to the Constitution. The complaint alleges that "the [FBI], under the direction of Defendant MUELLER, arrested and detained thousands of Arab Muslim men . . . as part of its investigation of the events of September 11." [Complaint], ¶ 47, at 164a. It further alleges that "[t]he policy of holding post–September–11th detainees in highly restrictive conditions of confinement until they were 'cleared' by the FBI was approved by Defendants ASHCROFT and MUELLER in discussions in the weeks after September 11, 2001." Id., ¶ 69, at 168a. Lastly, the complaint posits that petitioners "each knew of, condoned, and willfully and maliciously agreed to subject" respondent to harsh conditions of confinement "as a matter of policy, solely on account of [his] religion, race, and/or national origin and for no legitimate penological interest." Id., ¶ 96, at 172a–173a. The pleading names Ashcroft as the "principal architect" of the policy, id., ¶ 10, at 157a, and identifies Mueller as "instrumental in [its] adoption, promulgation, and implementation." Id., ¶ 11, at 157a.

[The Court ruled that, for liability under the substantive law, the defendants had to have acted with discriminatory purpose through their own individual actions, i.e., that the Attorney General and the FBI Director subjected the plaintiff to harsh confinement *because of* his race, religion, or national origin and not for a neutral investigative reason.]

To survive a motion to dismiss, a complaint must contain sufficient factual matter, accepted as true, to "state a claim to relief that is plausible on its face." [Bell Atlantic Corp. v. Twombly, 550 U.S. 544, 570, 127 S.Ct. 1955, 1974 (2007).] A claim has facial plausibility when the plaintiff pleads factual content that allows the court to draw the reasonable inference that the defendant is liable for the misconduct alleged. Id., at 556, 127 S.Ct. 1955. The plausibility standard is not akin to a "probability requirement," but it asks for more than a sheer possibility that a defendant has acted unlawfully. Ibid. . . .

Two working principles underlie our decision in Twombly. First, the tenet that a court must accept as true all of the allegations contained in a complaint is inapplicable to legal conclusions. Threadbare recitals of the elements of a cause of action, supported by mere conclusory statements, do not suffice. Id., at 555, 127 S.Ct. 1955 (Although for the purposes of a motion to dismiss we must take all of the factual allegations in the complaint as true, we "are not bound to accept as true a legal conclusion couched as a factual allegation" (internal quotation marks omitted)). Rule 8 marks a notable and generous departure from the hyper-technical, code-pleading regime of a prior era, but it does not unlock the doors of discovery for a plaintiff armed with nothing more than conclusions. Second, only a complaint that states a plausible claim for relief survives a motion to dismiss. Id., at 556, 127 S.Ct. 1955. Determining whether a complaint states a plausible claim for relief will, as the Court of Appeals observed, be a context-specific task that requires the reviewing court to draw on its judicial experience and common sense. 490 F.3d, at 157–158. But where the well-pleaded facts do not permit the court to infer more than the mere possibility of misconduct, the complaint has alleged—but it has not "show[n]"—"that the pleader is entitled to relief." Fed. Rule Civ. Proc. 8(a)(2).

In keeping with these principles a court considering a motion to dismiss can choose to begin by identifying pleadings that, because they are no more than conclusions, are not entitled to the assumption of truth. While legal conclusions can provide the framework of a complaint, they must be supported by factual allegations. When there are well-pleaded factual allegations, a court should assume their veracity and then determine whether they plausibly give rise to an entitlement to relief.

. . . .

We begin our analysis by identifying the allegations in the complaint that are not entitled to the assumption of truth. Respondent pleads that petitioners "knew of, condoned, and willfully and maliciously agreed to subject [him]" to harsh conditions of confinement "as a matter of policy, solely on account of [his] religion, race, and/or national origin and for no legitimate penological interest." Complaint ¶ 96, App. to Pet. for Cert. 173a–174a. The complaint alleges that Ashcroft was the "principal architect" of this invidious policy, id., ¶ 10, at 157a, and that Mueller was "instrumental" in adopting and executing it, id., ¶ 11, at 157a. These bare assertions, much like the pleading of conspiracy in Twombly, amount to nothing more than a "formulaic recitation of the elements" of a constitutional discrimination claim, 550 U.S., at 555, 127 S.Ct. 1955 . . . . As such, the allegations are conclusory and not entitled to be assumed true. Twombly, supra, 550 U.S., at 554–555, 127 S.Ct. 1955. To be clear, we do not reject these bald allegations on the ground that they are unrealistic or nonsensical. We do not so characterize them any more than the Court in Twombly rejected the plaintiffs' express allegation of a " 'contract, combination or conspiracy to prevent competitive entry,' " id., at 551, 127 S.Ct. 1955, because it thought that claim too chimerical to be maintained. It is the conclusory nature of respondent's allegations, rather than their extravagantly fanciful nature, that disentitles them to the presumption of truth.

We next consider the factual allegations in respondent's complaint to determine if they plausibly suggest an entitlement to relief. The complaint alleges that "the [FBI], under the direction of Defendant MUELLER, arrested and detained thousands of Arab Muslim men . . . as part of its investigation of the events of September 11." Complaint ¶ 47, App. to Pet. for Cert. 164a. It further claims that "[t]he policy of holding post–September–11th detainees in highly restrictive conditions of confinement until they were 'cleared' by the FBI was approved by Defendants ASHCROFT and MUELLER in discussions in the weeks after September 11, 2001." Id., ¶ 69, at 168a. Taken as true, these allegations are consistent with petitioners' purposefully designating detainees "of high interest" because of their race, religion, or national origin. But given more likely explanations, they do not plausibly establish this purpose.

. . . .

This the complaint fails to do. Though respondent alleges that various other defendants, who are not before us, may have labeled him a person of "of high interest" for impermissible reasons, his only factual allegation against petitioners accuses them of adopting a policy approving "restrictive conditions of confinement" for post–September–11 detainees until they were " 'cleared' by the FBI." Ibid. Accepting the truth of that allegation, the complaint does not show, or even intimate, that petitioners purposefully housed detainees in the [maximum security unit] due to their race, religion, or national origin. All it plausibly suggests is that the Nation's top law enforcement officers, in the aftermath of a devastating terrorist attack, sought to keep suspected terrorists in the most secure conditions available until the suspects could be cleared of terrorist activity. Respondent does not argue, nor can he, that such a motive would violate petitioners' constitutional obligations. He would need to allege more by way of factual content to "nudg[e]" his claim of purposeful discrimination "across the line from conceivable to plausible." Twombly, 550 U.S., at 570, 127 S.Ct. 1955.

. . . .

Respondent [next] says that our decision in Twombly should be limited to pleadings made in the context of an antitrust dispute. Iqbal Brief 37–38. This argument is not supported by Twombly and is incompatible with the Federal Rules of Civil Procedure. Though Twombly determined the sufficiency of a complaint sounding in antitrust, the decision was based on our interpretation and application of Rule 8. 550 U.S., at 554, 127 S.Ct. 1955. That Rule in turn governs the pleading standard "in all civil actions and proceedings in the United States district courts." Fed. Rule Civ. Proc. 1. Our decision in Twombly expounded the pleading standard for "all civil actions," ibid., and it applies to antitrust and discrimination suits alike. See 550 U.S., at 555–556, and n. 3, 127 S.Ct. 1955.

. . . .

Respondent finally maintains that the Federal Rules expressly allow him to allege petitioners' discriminatory intent "generally," which he equates with a conclusory allegation. . . .

It is true that Rule 9(b) requires particularity when pleading "fraud or mistake," while allowing "[m]alice, intent, knowledge, and other conditions of a person's mind [to] be alleged generally." But "generally" is a relative term. In the context of Rule 9, it is to be compared to the particularity requirement applicable to fraud or mistake. Rule 9 merely excuses a party from pleading discriminatory intent under an elevated pleading standard. It does not give him license to evade the less rigid—though still operative—strictures of Rule 8. . . .

We hold that respondent's complaint fails to plead sufficient facts to state a claim for purposeful and unlawful discrimination against petitioners. The Court of Appeals should decide in the first instance whether to remand to the District Court so that respondent can seek leave to amend his deficient complaint.

The judgment of the Court of Appeals is reversed, and the case is remanded for further proceedings consistent with this opinion.

It is so ordered.

■ [The dissenting opinions of JUSTICE SOUTER, with whom Justices Stevens, Ginsburg, and Breyer joined, and of JUSTICE BREYER are omitted. Justice Souter, who had authored Twombly, agreed that nonconclusory allegations are to be taken as true, unless they "are sufficiently fantastic to defy reality as we know it: claims about little green men, or the plaintiff's recent trip to Pluto, or experiences in time travel"; yet he disagreed with the majority's classifying the key allegations here as conclusory. Justice Breyer would have also relied on the lower court's using case-management tools to structure minimally intrusive discovery in anticipation of a summary judgment motion; but the majority expressly rejected such a route in lieu of dismissal.]

PLEADING THE COMMON COUNTS

The widespread practice of pleading by the common counts is among the many practice areas potentially affected by the new pleading regime.

The common counts in general assumpsit were brief and stylized statements giving the defendant notice of no more than that the plaintiff was seeking to recover on a money claim of one of several generalized types. Topic B of Part Six described their evolution, and also their many eventual uses. First, they were used in lieu of simple debt. Second, they were used where there was no express contract to pay a stated price but where the circumstances were such as to give rise to a mutual understanding of the parties as to making payment of the reasonable value of the goods, services, or the like. Third, the common counts came to be used for a wide variety of claims now called quasi contracts, both in "waiver-of-the-tort" situations and, more broadly, where the "ties of natural justice" imposed an implied legal obligation to make payment although there was in fact no intention to pay.

The question naturally arose whether the summary form of statement used in the common counts was permissible under the "facts" requirement of code pleading. Some early commentators thought not, because the common counts tended to conceal rather than to disclose the facts. But the common counts were so convenient, and the bar so favorably regarded them, that most states sanctioned their use, at least for contracts express or implied in fact.

Question: (12) Should a complaint like a common count be sufficient under a typical code in a "waiver-of-the-tort" case? in a case where the obligation to pay rests only on the "ties of natural justice"?

Where the common counts are now used, the old requirement of stating a fictitious promise to pay has usually been abandoned. See, e.g., New York Official Form 11, which runs as follows:

> Defendant owes plaintiff twenty thousand dollars for money had and received from one G.H. on June 1, 1965, to be paid by defendant to plaintiff.
>
> Wherefore plaintiff demands judgment against defendant for the sum of twenty thousand dollars, interest from June 1, 1965, and costs and disbursements.

Questions: (13) To what extent are pleadings like the common counts now permissible under the Federal Rules? See Federal Forms 4 to 10.

(14) A plaintiff suing in federal court on a complaint similar to a common count for money had and received offers evidence that G.H. paid money to the defendant under a contract obtained by fraud. The defendant objects to the evidence as not within the pleadings. Should the court sustain the objection? Does Rule 9(b) have any bearing? See 5 Wright & Miller § 1222.

Special pleading.—As suggested, a special Rule or statutory provision can impose additional pleading requirements. Two prominent examples involve, first, the pleading of fraud and, second, a frivolity test meant to serve an intensified gatekeeping function. In Iqbal, Justice Kennedy referred directly to the former example, while Justice Souter invoked the latter when referring to "little green men."

WILLIAM M. RICHMAN, DONALD E. LIVELY & PATRICIA MELL, THE PLEADING OF FRAUD: RHYMES WITHOUT REASON, 60 S.Cal. L.Rev. 959, 971 (1987). "Rule 9(b) should not be construed to require a return to the detailed 'fact' pleading required under the codes. Rather, it should be read in light of the purpose of Rule 8(a)(2)—to give defendant notice of plaintiff's claim. To the extent a fraud claim may be more vague than others, greater particularity may be necessary to ensure the kind of notice contemplated by Rule 8(a)(2).

"Enlightened pleading policy is defeated, however, when specificity is mandated merely because an action is denominated as fraud. Its subversion is particularly evident when securities fraud actions, pursuant to modern regulatory schemes, are subject to ancient practice guides. Rules designed to govern disfavored claims may hold captive actions which are legislatively and judicially favored. Regulatory goals thus may become vulnerable to the treacherous process of determining what constitutes sufficient particularity."

STEPHEN N. SUBRIN, HOW EQUITY CONQUERED COMMON LAW: THE FEDERAL RULES OF CIVIL PROCEDURE IN HISTORICAL PERSPECTIVE, 135 U.Pa.L.Rev. 909, 985 (1987). "Although [recent] developments reveal an awareness of some of the problems inherent in [the Federal Rules] system, they do not sufficiently address the underlying issue: how to achieve a reasonable measure of constancy and predictability in law application. Amended Rule 11, making the attorney's signature a certificate that the pleading is 'well grounded in fact' and 'warranted by existing law or a good faith argument for the extension, modification, or reversal of existing law,' illustrates the point. This rule seems to look backward to the Field Code's pleading requirement of 'facts constituting a cause of action.' But the pleading rules themselves remain untouched, and the lawyer is not given concrete guidance about how much she must know or plead in advance to bring a specific kind of case. . . .

"A more logical approach to pleading and signature requirements would require reconsideration of several different tenets that underlie the Federal Rules. Providing more guidance for lawyers and their clients would necessitate inroads on trans-substantive procedure. . . . Perhaps there should be different procedural rules for different types of cases. But this also means confronting the demons of technicality, line-drawing, and definition. The honing of procedure to fit and confine substance and the use of categories will begin to look more like the common law mentality. Moreover, one cannot discuss what procedure should go with what substantive areas without acknowledging that the choices will deeply affect the substantive law and influence which cases are brought and won. This suggests a more active role for legislators in procedural rulemaking."

PSLRA

As Professor Subrin suggests, inroads on transsubstantivity call for greater legislative involvement. See generally David Marcus, The Past, Present, and Future of Trans–Substantivity in Federal Civil Procedure, 59 DePaul L.Rev. ___ (2010). In the Private Securities Litigation Reform Act of 1995, Congress heightened the pleading requirements for federal securities fraud actions, in order to curtail the filing of abusive lawsuits:

(1) MISLEADING STATEMENTS AND OMISSIONS.—In any private action arising under this title in which the plaintiff alleges that the defendant—

(A) made an untrue statement of a material fact; or

(B) omitted to state a material fact necessary in order to make the statements made, in the light of the circumstances in which they were made, not misleading;

the complaint shall specify each statement alleged to have been misleading, the reason or reasons why the statement is misleading, and, if an allegation regarding the statement or omission is made on information and belief, the complaint shall state with particularity all facts on which that belief is formed.

(2) REQUIRED STATE OF MIND.—In any private action arising under this title in which the plaintiff may recover money damages only on proof that the defendant acted with a particular state of mind, the complaint shall, with respect to each act or omission alleged to violate this title, state with particularity facts giving rise to a strong inference that the defendant acted with the required state of mind.

Pub.L. No. 104–67, tit. I, § 101(b), 109 Stat. 737, 747 (1995) (codified at 15 U.S.C. § 78u–4(b)). In Tellabs, Inc. v. Makor Issues & Rights, Ltd., 551 U.S. 308, 127 S.Ct. 2499 (2007), the Court construed "strong inference" to mean that the plaintiff's allegations must make the inference of scienter more than merely plausible or reasonable, and instead make it cogent and at least as compelling as any opposing inference of nonfraudulent intent.

In the same Act, Congress reinforced Rule 11 just for federal securities actions. 15 U.S.C. § 78u–4(c). In every such action, the district court now must make specific findings as to all parties' and attorneys' compliance with Rule 11(b) on pleadings and dispositive motions. The district court also must impose sanctions for any such violation found. See generally Symposium, The Implications of the Private Securities Litigation Reform Act, 76 Wash.U.L.Q. 447 (1998).

NEITZKE v. WILLIAMS, 490 U.S. 319, 109 S.Ct. 1827 (1989). A prisoner brought a pro se, in forma pauperis civil rights action, alleging that denial of medical treatment violated his constitutional rights. The district court dismissed the complaint sua sponte as frivolous under 28 U.S.C. § 1915(d) (now § 1915(e)(2)(B)(i)), for the reason that the prisoner had failed to state a claim under Rule 12(b)(6). The Seventh Circuit reversed.

On certiorari, the Supreme Court affirmed the circuit court. Justice Marshall for a unanimous Court wrote that a complaint "is frivolous where it lacks an arguable basis either in law or in fact," a standard not automatically satisfied by a failure to state a claim:

"Rule 12(b)(6) authorizes a court to dismiss a claim on the basis of a dispositive issue of law. Hishon v. King & Spalding, 467 U.S. 69, 73, 104 S.Ct. 2229, 2232 (1984); Conley v. Gibson, 355 U.S. 41, 45–46, 78 S.Ct. 99, 101–02 (1957). This procedure, operating on the assumption that the factual allegations in the complaint are true, streamlines litigation by dispensing with needless discovery and factfinding. Nothing in Rule 12(b)(6) confines its sweep to claims of law which are obviously insupportable. On the contrary, [an inadequate] claim must be dismissed, without regard to whether it is based on an outlandish legal theory or on a close but ultimately unavailing one. . . .

"Section 1915(d) has a separate function, one which molds rather differently the power to dismiss which it confers. Section 1915(d) is designed largely to discourage the filing of, and waste of judicial and private resources upon, baseless lawsuits that paying litigants generally do not initiate because of the costs of bringing suit and because of the threat of sanctions for bringing vexatious suits under Federal Rule of Civil Procedure 11. To this end, the statute accords judges not only the authority to dismiss a claim based on an indisputably meritless legal theory, but also the unusual power to pierce the veil of the complaint's factual allegations and dismiss those claims whose factual contentions are clearly baseless. Examples of the former class are claims against which it is clear that the defendants are immune from suit, see, e.g., Williams v. Goldsmith, 701 F.2d 603 (C.A.7 1983), and claims of infringement of a legal interest which clearly does not exist . . . . Examples of the latter class are claims describing fantastic or delusional scenarios, claims with which federal district judges are all too familiar.

"To the extent that a complaint filed in forma pauperis which fails to state a claim lacks even an arguable basis in law, Rule 12(b)(6) and § 1915(d) both counsel dismissal. But the considerable common ground between these standards does not mean that the one invariably encompasses the other. When a complaint raises an arguable question of law which the district court ultimately finds is correctly resolved against the plaintiff, dismissal on Rule 12(b)(6) grounds is appropriate, but dismissal on the basis of frivolousness is not. This conclusion follows naturally from § 1915(d)'s role of replicating the function of screening out inarguable claims which is played in the realm of paid cases by financial considerations. The cost of bringing suit and the fear of financial sanctions doubtless deter most inarguable paid claims, but such deterrence presumably screens out far less frequently those arguably meritorious legal theories whose ultimate failure is not apparent at the outset."

Justice Marshall also explained that § 1915 was designed to ensure equal consideration for all litigants. To conflate the standards of decision would defeat this goal, given the difference in procedures: "Dismissals [under § 1915(d)] are often made sua sponte prior to the issuance of process, so as to spare prospective defendants the inconvenience and expense of answering such complaints. See Franklin v. Murphy, 745 F.2d 1221, 1226 (C.A.9 1984)." He continued: "Under Rule 12(b)(6), a plaintiff with an arguable claim is ordinarily accorded notice of a pending motion to dismiss for failure to state a claim and an opportunity to amend the complaint before the motion is ruled upon. These procedures alert him to the legal theory underlying the defendant's challenge, and enable him meaningfully to respond by opposing the motion to dismiss on legal grounds or by clarifying his factual allegations so as to conform with the requirements of a valid legal cause of action. This adversarial process also crystallizes the pertinent issues and facilitates appellate review of a trial court dismissal by creating a more complete record of the case. [Citation omitted.] By contrast, the sua sponte dismissals permitted by and frequently employed under § 1915(d), necessary though they may sometimes be to shield defendants from vexatious lawsuits, involve no such procedural protections."

Worth noting is that the 1996 statute that renumbered § 1915(d) also added § 1915A. It requires the district court at the very outset to screen prisoners' actions against the government before docketing, with dismissal not only for frivolity but also for mere failure to state a claim.

DENTON v. HERNANDEZ, 504 U.S. 25, 112 S.Ct. 1728 (1992). A prisoner brought a number of pro se, in forma pauperis civil rights actions, alleging that in prison he repeatedly was first drugged and then raped by various inmates and prison officials. The district court dismissed the complaints as factually frivolous under 28 U.S.C. § 1915(d), for the reason that the pattern of allegations appeared wholly fanciful, even though the plaintiff had submitted two supporting affidavits by fellow inmates. The Ninth Circuit reviewed the dismissals de novo and reversed, ruling that dismissal was proper only if allegations conflicted with judicially noticeable facts.

On certiorari, the Supreme Court vacated the circuit court's decision. Justice O'Connor for the Court explained the standards to be applied on remand:

"As we stated in Neitzke, a court may dismiss a claim as factually frivolous only if the facts alleged are 'clearly baseless,' 490 U.S., at 327, 109 S.Ct., at 1833, a category encompassing allegations that are 'fanciful,' id., at 325, 109 S.Ct., at 1831, 'fantastic,' id., at 328, 109 S.Ct., at 1833, and 'delusional,' ibid. As those words suggest, a finding of factual frivolousness is appropriate when the facts alleged rise to the level of the irrational or the wholly incredible, whether or not there are judicially noticeable facts available to contradict them. An in forma pauperis complaint may not be dismissed, however, simply because the court finds the plaintiff's allegations unlikely. Some improbable allegations might properly be disposed of on summary judgment, but to dismiss them as frivolous without any factual development is to disregard the age-old insight that many allegations might be 'strange, but true; for truth is always strange, Stranger than fiction.' Lord Byron, Don Juan, canto XIV, stanza 101 (T. Steffan, E. Steffan & W. Pratt eds. 1977).

"Although Hernandez urges that we define the 'clearly baseless' guidepost with more precision, we are confident that the district courts, who are 'all too familiar' with factually frivolous claims, Neitzke, supra, at 328, 109

S.Ct., at 1833, are in the best position to determine which cases fall into this category. . . .

"Because the frivolousness determination is a discretionary one, we further hold that a § 1915(d) dismissal is properly reviewed for an abuse of that discretion, and that it was error for the Court of Appeals to review the dismissal of Hernandez's claims de novo."

Justice Stevens, joined by Justice Blackmun, dissented. They agreed with the majority's standards, but felt that the circuit court's decision was consistent therewith.

(b) DRAFTING THE COMPLAINT

ALLEGATIONS OF TIME AND PLACE

Common-law pleading required certainty in pleadings, including certainty of time and place. Somewhat paradoxically, although the pleader thus had to make specific allegations of time and place, else the pleading would be defective, the common law generally considered these allegations as exceptions to the rule forbidding variance and therefore did not require them to be proved as alleged. For instance, the allegation of one time and the proof of another would not be a fatal variance. Furthermore, the allegation of time so being regarded as wholly irrelevant, a declaration seeming to show on its face that the action was barred by the statute of limitations was not demurrable. This rule, formalistic in its origin, was later rationalized on the ground that if the defendant could raise the defense of limitations by demurrer, the plaintiff would lose his chance to assert in his replication to the limitations defense that special circumstances, such as conduct of the defendant constituting estoppel or waiver, avoided the statute.

Some of the codes specifically provide for a demurrer, or its equivalent, when the complaint shows that the action is barred by the statute of limitations. In the absence of such codified guidance, there has been diversity of opinion as to when a demurrer will put the timeliness of suit in issue. See Thomas E. Atkinson, Pleading the Statute of Limitations, 36 Yale L.J. 914 (1927).

Federal Rule 9(f), in making allegations of time and place material for the purpose of testing the sufficiency of a pleading, departs from the earlier practice. It is silent as to the necessity of such allegations, but simply states their materiality if made.

Questions: (15) In the light of Rule 9(f), should a court dismiss a federal action on motion under Rule 12(b)(6) if the complaint on its face shows that it is time-barred? Does Rule 8(c)(1), listing the statute of limitations as an affirmative defense, have any bearing on your answer? See 5 Wright & Miller § 1277.

(16) If a federal complaint makes no allegation as to time or place, what remedy should be open to the defendant? See 5A id. § 1309.

DEFENSIVE MATTER IN THE COMPLAINT

Suppose the plaintiff alleges a good cause of action and goes on to allege further facts constituting a good defense. At common law one can find statements that a matter of defense set forth in a declaration is surplusage and should be disregarded on demurrer. But these statements usually appear in cases where the plaintiff after anticipating a defense proceeded to avoid it. The common-law approach was to disregard both the defense and the avoidance, and thus to hold the declaration good against a demurrer.

The usual code approach is to sustain a demurrer if the complaint discloses a defense and does not avoid it, but to hold that a good avoidance of the defense saves the complaint. Nevertheless, there is some code support for the common-law view. For instance, in Trotter v. Mutual Reserve Fund Life Ass'n, 9 S.D. 596, 70 N.W. 843 (1897), the plaintiff sued on a life insurance policy. In his complaint he anticipated the defense of a release but alleged that it was procured by fraud. The court overruled the defendant's demurrer on the theory that both the defense and the avoidance were surplusage.

This difference in approach becomes especially important at the next step in pleading. Consider what the defendant should next do on the facts of the Trotter case. Because it cannot demur, it must answer. Suppose it pleads the release and ignores the fraud, and the plaintiff demurs to the answer or moves for judgment on the pleadings. Following the common-law view, Canfield v. Tobias, 21 Cal. 349 (1863), held that on these facts the plaintiff's motion for judgment on the pleadings would not lie. The court reasoned that only material allegations were admitted if not denied and that the defendant had properly disregarded the pure surplusage of the plaintiff's allegations of release and fraud. On the more usual code approach, however, the plaintiff's complaint would have been defective if he had alleged a defense without avoiding it. Accordingly the allegation of fraud, being necessary to save the complaint, was material. Being material, it had to be denied in the answer or be taken as admitted. Hence the plaintiff's motion would lie. This latter analysis is generally regarded as more in harmony with the code objectives.

Question: (17) How would this problem of what the defendant should plead be treated under the Federal Rules? Does Rule 8(b)(6) shed any light on the point?

Leggett v. Montgomery Ward & Co.

United States Court of Appeals, Tenth Circuit, 1949.
178 F.2d 436.

[Plaintiff, seeking damages for malicious prosecution, alleged in his amended complaint that defendant, through an authorized agent, maliciously and without probable cause filed with a justice of the peace in Wyoming a criminal complaint charging plaintiff with the crime of embezzlement; that plaintiff was arrested and required to furnish bail; that on advice of counsel he waived preliminary hearing (for tactical reasons that the complaint went on to explain); that plaintiff was tried on such charge and acquitted; and that he was damaged. Defendant filed a motion to dismiss the action on the ground that it appeared from the face of the amended complaint that plaintiff waived preliminary hearing upon the charge; that by reason of such waiver there was prima facie evidence of probable cause to believe that plaintiff was guilty of the offense charged in the criminal complaint; and that therefore the allegation of want of probable cause contained in the amended complaint was insufficient to state a claim against defendant upon which relief could be granted. The court dismissed the action. Plaintiff appealed.]

■ Before BRATTON and HUXMAN, CIRCUIT JUDGES, and RICE, DISTRICT JUDGE.

■ BRATTON, CIRCUIT JUDGE.

. . . .

The motion to dismiss the action for failure of the amended complaint to state a cause of action for which relief could be granted admitted all facts well pleaded in the amended complaint. But whether the facts thus pleaded and admitted constituted a cause of action for which relief could be granted in the form of damages for malicious prosecution was a question to be determined by the law of Wyoming. Van Sant v. American Express Co., 3 Cir., 158 F.2d 924.

[The court held that Wyoming law, as enunciated in Penton v. Canning, 57 Wyo. 390, 118 P.2d 1002 (1941), treated waiver of preliminary hearing and binding over for trial as equivalent in law to a hearing and a finding of probable cause and that, in the absence of allegation and proof that defendant procured the binding over by perjury, false testimony, or other improper means, plaintiff could not maintain an action like this for malicious prosecution.]

Apparently in an effort to avoid the impact of Penton v. Canning, supra, plaintiff argues in effect that the question whether the amended complaint stated a cause of action for which relief could be granted must be determined by the rules of pleading applicable to the United States District Courts, and that under such rules the amended complaint was not fatally defective. . . . It is the general rule of pleading that where a complaint alleges facts constituting a cause of action and also alleges facts which constitute a valid defense, unless it alleges further facts avoiding such defense, it may be attacked by demurrer or motion to dismiss. St. Louis, Kennett and Southeastern Railroad Company v. United States, 267 U.S. 346, 45 S.Ct. 245, 69 L.Ed. 649; [other citations from Indiana and Georgia omitted]. Alleging that the criminal complaint was filed, that plaintiff waived preliminary examination, and that he was bound over to the district court; and failing to allege that the action of the justice of the peace in binding plaintiff over to the district court was procured by perjury, false testimony, or other improper means on the part of defendant, the pleading did not state a claim for which relief could be granted under the law of Wyoming. Sheffield v. Cantwell, 7 Cir., 101 F.2d 351.

[The court also held that it did not appear that the trial court abused its discretion in the denial of the application further to amend.]

The judgment is affirmed.

■ RICE, DISTRICT JUDGE (dissenting). . . . Apparently the test of the sufficiency of a complaint in federal court, under the majority opinion, now is—would the complaint if filed as a petition in the state court be sustained when attacked by a general demurrer? . . .

Questions: (18) Would you expect a court to decide this case differently under current Erie doctrine?

(19) How should a court decide the same point in a federal question case? See Kozlowski v. Ferrara, 117 F.Supp. 650, 652 (S.D.N.Y.1954) (under federal law, "waiver of a hearing by the present plaintiff and his detention until he raised bail was not of itself tantamount to a finding of probable cause").

JUDICIAL NOTICE OF FACT AND LAW

Judicial notice of fact.—We have discussed judicial notice as a means of dispensing with ordinary testimony, in Part One's coverage of evidence law. The doctrine also has its place in pleading. First, a pleader need not allege a proposition of which the court takes judicial notice, however material to the pleader's case it may be. The court reads the attacked pleading as if any material propositions judicially noticed were added. Second, a court disregards an allegation in a pleading that contradicts a proposition judicially noticed. The court reads the attacked pleading as if such untenable allegations were omitted, so that a demurrer or motion to dismiss does not admit any allegation in the attacked pleading running counter to the court's judicial knowledge. The classic illustrative case at common law was Cole v. Maunder, 2 Rolle's Abr. 548 (K.B.1635), where an allegation that stones were thrown "*molliter et molli manu*" ("gently and with a gentle hand") was held not to be admitted by demurrer, "for the judges say that one cannot throw stones *molliter.*" In Southern Ry. Co. v. Covenia, 100 Ga. 46, 29 S.E. 219 (1896), the court took judicial notice that a child under two years of age was unable to have any earning capacity and held on demurrer that an allegation that such a child performed valuable services did not stand as admitted.

State courts and judicial notice of law.—The courts of a state take judicial notice of local law, common and statutory, and of the United States Constitution and other federal law. This is done without pleading or proof. But counsel will naturally call attention to the appropriate sources so that the judge's actual knowledge will match what the judge judicially "knows." However, neither the trial nor the appellate courts are limited to the sources called to their attention.

State courts traditionally treated the law of sister states and of foreign countries as a matter of "fact" to be pleaded and proved, although relief from failure to do so sometimes came by a presumption that such foreign law was the same as the forum's. The "fact" characterization often went to the extreme of leaving the determination to the jury if there was a dispute, and it considerably complicated the process of appellate review of the findings on foreign-law issues. On the one hand, this whole tradition of law as "fact" is now approaching extinction as a result of the Uniform Judicial Notice of Foreign Law Act—approved by the National Conference of Commissioners on Uniform State Laws in 1936 and adopted by a good number of the states—and of similar reform statutes providing for the extension of judicial notice to the law of other states. The Act further provides that to enable a party to ask for judicial notice of another state's law, the party shall give reasonable notice either in the pleadings or otherwise. There has been a conflict of decisions as to whether the Act thereby dispenses with pre-existing pleading requirements. In Litsinger Sign Co. v. American Sign Co., 11 Ohio St.2d 1, 227 N.E.2d 609 (1967), the court held that it could judicially notice the unpleaded law of a sister state so long as the reasonable-notice provision of the Act was satisfied. In Scott v. Scott, 153 Neb. 906, 46 N.W.2d 627 (1951), the court held that the Act related to proof only and so refused to take judicial notice of the unpleaded sister state's law, but instead resorted to the presumption that the sister state's law was the same as Nebraska's. As a consequence, some state statutes or court rules specifically negate the need of pleading foreign law. On the other hand, the Uniform Judicial Notice of Foreign Law Act does not cover the law of foreign countries, other than in a section providing that an issue of such law is for the court rather than for the jury. But some of the similar state reform statutes cover the law of foreign countries too. See John G. Sprankling & George R. Lanyi, Pleading and Proof of Foreign Law in American Courts, 19 Stan.J.Int'l L. 3 (1983). For a comparative perspective, see Sofie Geeroms, Foreign Law in Civil Litigation (2004).

Federal courts and treatment of law.—Lower federal courts, and the Supreme Court on review of their decisions, take judicial notice of federal law and of the law of all the states. Moreover, a federal court sitting in Nebraska in a diversity case has taken judicial notice of the law of another state despite the fact that it was not pleaded, thus refusing to follow the state law referred to above. Simmons v. Continental Cas. Co., 410 F.2d 881 (8th Cir.1969). But on review of a case from a state court, the Supreme Court judicially notices only such law as the state court would notice. See Hanley v. Donoghue, 116 U.S. 1, 6 S.Ct. 242 (1885).

Traditionally, lower federal courts treated the law of foreign countries as a matter of "fact." Rule 44.1, adopted by amendment in 1966, changed that practice. Also, there had been uncertainty in the federal courts as to whether a party had to plead the law of a foreign country under Rule 8.

Courts have held that Rule 44.1 eliminated that uncertainty, just as the Advisory Committee had asserted, by requiring reasonable written notice of the intention to raise an issue concerning foreign law in the pleadings or otherwise. Nevertheless, when the relevance of the law of a foreign country is apparent from the outset, the easy and sensible way of complying with the notice requirement of Rule 44.1 is to give in the pleading notice of the intention to raise the foreign-law issue.

Indeed, Rule 44.1 represents a new approach to the problems of handling the law of foreign countries. The Rule does not use the term "judicial notice." It so renders obsolete much of the old learning about judicial notice and should simplify litigation involving nondomestic law. See Arthur R. Miller, Federal Rule 44.1 and the "Fact" Approach to Determining Foreign Law: Death Knell for a Die–Hard Doctrine, 65 Mich.L.Rev. 613 (1967), which deals thoroughly with the entire problem. See also Doug M. Keller, Comment, Interpreting Foreign Law Through an Erie Lens: A Critical Look at United States v. McNab, 40 Tex.Int'l L.J. 157 (2004) (arguing that the federal court should determine uncertain foreign country law just as it decides the content of uncertain state law, by surmising what the other sovereign's highest court would say). The Uniform Interstate and International Procedure Act—which was intended to supersede the Uniform Judicial Notice of Foreign Law Act, was approved by the National Conference of Commissioners on Uniform State Laws in 1962 but withdrawn for other reasons in 1977, and was adopted by a number of states—takes the same approach as Rule 44.1, and it applies to the law of sister states as well as of foreign countries.

COMPLYING WITH FORMALITY RULES

In O'Donnell v. Elgin, Joliet & Eastern Railway, 338 U.S. 384, 70 S.Ct. 200 (1949), the plaintiff, seeking recovery for a death resulting from the breaking of a coupler, had joined in a single count (1) a claim under the Safety Appliance Act, 45 U.S.C. § 2, for which negligence need not be shown, with (2) an FELA claim for negligence. The trial court had indiscriminately submitted the whole to the jury as a negligence case. Judgment for the defendant, affirmed by the Seventh Circuit, was reversed by the Supreme Court because the trial court had failed to give a peremptory instruction that equipping a car with a coupler that broke in a switching operation was a violation of the Safety Appliance Act, thus rendering the defendant liable without a showing of negligence. Justice Jackson for the Court observed in passing:

"We no longer insist upon technical rules of pleading, but it will ever be difficult in a jury trial to segregate issues which counsel do not separate in their pleading, preparation or thinking. We think the unfortunately prolonged course of this litigation is in no small part due to the failure to heed the admonition well stated by the Court of Appeals of the Seventh Circuit in a similar case: 'Of course, it is not proper to plead different theories in the same paragraph, but it is not necessarily fatal especially when the adversary makes no objection.' Vigor v. Chesapeake & Ohio R. Co., 101 F.2d 865, 869 (1939). Pleadings will serve the purpose of sharpening and limiting the issues only if claims based on negligence are set forth separately from those based on violation of the appliance acts.[6]"

Questions: (20) Was the plaintiff's pleading actually inconsistent with Rule 10(b)? with Rule 8(d)(2)? with any other provision of the Rules? By what procedure might the defendant have sought to enforce any violated pleading Rules?

(21) In what other ways might "the unfortunately prolonged course of this litigation" have been shortened?

(22) After *P* set forth in the same paragraph of a single count alternative allegations of wilfulness and negligence in an automobile collision, the court dismissed the action for failure to state separately these allegations, although it granted leave to amend. Sherman v. Renth, 22 F.R.D. 59 (E.D.Ill.1957) (separate paragraphs required and separate counts desirable). Was the decision correct?

(23) How would you rewrite Rule 10(b)?

COMPLETING THE COMPLAINT

Rule 8(a)(1) requires the federal plaintiff to set forth the grounds upon which subject-matter jurisdiction depends. See Form 7. This requirement stems from the limited jurisdiction of the federal courts, and so it generally does not exist in state practice. See also 28 U.S.C. § 1653.

Question: (24) In federal court plaintiff alleges that she is not a citizen of Texas and defendant is a citizen of Texas, and that the matter in controversy exceeds the jurisdictional amount exclusive of interest and costs. Defendant moves under Rule 12(b)(1). What decision? Compare Bryant v. Harrelson, 187 F.Supp. 738 (S.D.Tex.1960) (suggesting dismissal), with Kiser v. General Elec. Corp., 831 F.2d 423 (3d Cir.1987) (liberal amendment).

Rule 8(a)(3) requires a demand for judgment. This requirement is common in state practice, but there are a few states in which no demand for a specific sum is required, as under Fla.R.Civ.P. 1.110(b), or in which such a specific demand is expressly forbidden, N.J.Ct.R. 4:5–2. Incidentally, a majority of the states, although requiring or permitting a specific demand, do allow recovery of damages in excess of those demanded, except in default cases, either because of a provision adopted from the Field Code or because of a rule modeled on Federal Rule 54(c). A tiny minority of states do not allow recovery in excess of the amount demanded, but in such states

---

[6] This, after all, is the command of Rule 10(b), Federal Rules of Civil Procedure, which provides: "All averments of claim or defense shall be made in numbered paragraphs, the contents of each of which shall be limited as far as practicable to a statement of a single set of circumstances . . . ."

Professor Moore, in discussing this Rule with reference to claims based upon both common law and statutory grounds, states: "Separate statement by way of counts is not required; separate paragraphing in setting out the grounds in the above actions is desirable and required." 2 Moore's Federal Practice, 2006–2007 (2d ed. 1948).

the court is likely to permit an amendment of the ad damnum clause, even after verdict.

Question: (25) 28 U.S.C. § 1441 generally confines the right of removal to actions over which the federal court has original jurisdiction. Assume that the defendant wishes to remove a state-court damages action in which the plaintiff has demanded no specific sum. What problems does the defendant have in establishing that the matter in controversy exceeds the jurisdictional amount? See ALI Study of the Division of Jurisdiction Between State and Federal Courts § 1381(c)(2) commentary at 344–48 (1969).

Burlington Transp. Co. v. Josephson

United States Circuit Court of Appeals, Eighth Circuit, 1946.
153 F.2d 372.

[Plaintiff sued for false arrest and imprisonment at Rapid City, South Dakota, and obtained judgment on a jury verdict in the amount of $19,500, with costs in the sum of $44.50. Defendants appealed.

[Several errors were assigned, but only those relating to damages are included here. The allegations in the complaint as to damages were these: "III. Plaintiff was thereby damaged and injured in his character, good name and reputation; he has suffered intense embarrassment, humiliation and mental anguish; he was compelled to incur and pay attorneys fees and costs in a large amount to obtain his release from said arrest and confinement; he was thereby necessarily compelled to be away from his business and suffered a large consequent loss, all to his damage in the sum of $100,000.00."]

■ Before SANBORN, THOMAS, and RIDDICK, CIRCUIT JUDGES.

■ THOMAS, CIRCUIT JUDGE.

. . . .

Josephson testified in his own behalf saying that he resides in New York City; that his business or profession is that of a physician engaged in the specialized practice relating to the eye, ear, nose and throat . . . .

. . . .

On the question of damages he testified that he was worried and anxious and quite a bit embarrassed by the arrest; and that his attorney's fees and costs for his release were approximately $500.

Over the objection of counsel for the defendants he testified that due to his delay in returning to New York occasioned by his remaining in Rapid City for his trial he sustained large losses in connection with the remodeling of a building which he had recently purchased; that because of the delay he missed a conference with a contractor with whom he was negotiating for the remodeling, and the delay resulted in a loss of rentals and increased cost of material and labor.

. . . .

The gist of defendants' [appeal] is that damages, if sustained by reason of remodeling a building in New York, are special and not general damages, and that recovery for such damages could not be had because they were not pleaded and because they are speculative.

[The court here quoted Rule 9(g).]

In the case of Simmons v. Leighton, 60 S.D. 524, 244 N.W. 883, 884, the Supreme Court of South Dakota said: "The distinction between general and special damages and the necessity of a special allegation to permit proof and recovery of damages is well settled. Special, as distinguished from general, damages are those which are the natural but not the necessary consequence of the act complained of. 17 C.J. 715. The plaintiff under a general allegation of damages may recover all such damages as are the natural and necessary result of such injuries as are alleged for the law implies their sequence. 2 Sutherland on Damages (4th Ed.) § 418. Not every loss which may result from an injury is a natural and necessary result of the injury. To permit recovery of other or special damages, there must be allegation of the specific facts showing such damages to apprise the defendant of the nature of the claim against him."

This distinction between general and special damages prevails generally. C.J.S., Damages, § 2; 15 Am.Jur., Damages, § 10. General compensatory damages only were claimed in this case. In other words, only such damages were alleged in the complaint as are the natural consequence of the false arrest and false imprisonment, such as humiliation, embarrassment and the costs incident to obtaining a release from detention. In the federal courts an indispensable allegation in a demand for special damages is a statement "of the special circumstances giving rise to the special damages." Huyler's v. Ritz–Carlton Restaurant & Hotel Co., D.C., 6 F.2d 404, 406, 407.

But the plaintiff claims that the pleading was sufficient to entitle him to special damages. Such claim is unwarranted. . . . His proof showed that he is a professional, not a business, man. The allegation that "he was thereby necessarily compelled to be away from his business" specifies only loss of time in the practice of his profession. The rule is well settled that "In the case of a professional man the proper measure for damages for loss of time is the amount he would have earned by the practice of his profession." 15 Am.Jur., Damages, § 97. No loss of professional earnings whatever was shown.

The damages, if any, arising out of the remodeling of the apartment building in New York were special damages, and the court erred . . . in admitting the objectionable evidence, and in permitting recovery under the instructions. . . .

. . . .

For the errors pointed out the judgment appealed from is reversed and the case remanded with instructions to grant a new trial.

SPECIAL DAMAGES

The requirement of Rule 9(g) that the pleader specifically state special damages reflects the traditional doctrine. The line between general and special damages is not, however, clearly drawn by the cases, nor is the degree of specificity called for by Rule 9(g) settled. See generally Note, The Definition and Pleading of Special Damage Under the Federal Rules of Civil Procedure, 55 Va.L.Rev. 542 (1969).

On the one hand, the specific pleading requirement aims to protect the defendant from surprise at trial when the plaintiff seeks special damages in addition to general damages. This gives a handle on what kind of damages should be deemed special. Moreover, this sheds light on the required specificity, because great detail is not necessary to give notice. The defendant alerted to a claim for special damages may resort to a motion for a more definite statement if he cannot frame a responsive pleading, and he may pursue discovery in order to prepare for trial.

On the other hand, special damages are an essential element of the plaintiff's claim for relief in certain types of cases. That is, if the plaintiff does not plead special damages, the complaint is subject to dismissal for failure to state a claim. This requirement exists primarily in "disfavored causes of action," such as defamation where the words are not actionable per se, disparagement of property, and trade libel. Here the court may require considerable particularity of allegation.

Questions: (26) In a diversity of citizenship case, to what extent is state law controlling with respect to special damages and to what extent federal law?

(27) What, if any, relationship is there between the pleading requirement as to special damages and the reasoning of Hadley v. Baxendale, 156 Eng.Rep. 145 (Ex.1854), to the effect that damages not within the contemplation of the defendant at the time of contracting are not recoverable?

(28) In Niedland v. United States, 338 F.2d 254 (3d Cir.1964), the operator of an Arthur Murray School of Dancing sued the United States under the Federal Tort Claims Act, 28 U.S.C. § 1346(b), for personal injuries sustained in a collision between his car and a Post Office vehicle. Plaintiff offered testimony at trial to prove that by reason of his injuries, it had been necessary for him to employ a full-time assistant at a certain salary. There was no objection to this testimony, and the government did not request a continuance to meet this evidence. Government counsel cross-examined plaintiff and plaintiff's medical witness on the need for an assistant, and also questioned the defense medical witnesses on this point. At the close of the testimony, government counsel objected to any argument respecting the cost of hiring an assistant because plaintiff had not specially pleaded this matter. The court overruled this objection. On appeal from a judgment for plaintiff, the government asserted error with respect to the damage award. The appellate court said: "It is clear that even under the more generalized notice pleadings of the Federal Civil Rules, special damages must be specifically pleaded. . . . It is equally clear that expenditures for the hiring of a substitute are special damages, under both federal and state law." Having reached this conclusion, should the court sustain the government's claim of error?

(c) SIGNING THE PLEADING

VERIFICATION OF PLEADINGS

Rule 11(a) requires a pleading to be verified or supported by affidavit only when a federal rule or statute specifically so requires. Such provisions lie in Rules 23.1, 27(a), and 65(b) and, inferentially, in Rule 66 because the historical practice in the federal courts required verification of a complaint seeking appointment of a receiver. A few federal statutes, cited and summarized in 5A Wright & Miller § 1339, also require verification. As to the form of verification, see 28 U.S.C. § 1746.

Question: (29) The District of Colorado formerly required, by local rule, that pro se prisoners verify their civil rights complaints. Was such a local rule valid under Federal Rule 83(a)?

There are extensive statutory provisions for verification in some states, as for example NYCPLR § 3020(a):

"*Generally*. A verification is a statement under oath that the pleading is true to the knowledge of the deponent, except as to matters alleged on information and belief, and that as to those matters he believes it to be true. Unless otherwise specified by law, where a pleading is verified, each subsequent pleading shall also be verified, except the answer of an infant and except as to matter in the pleading concerning which the party would be privileged from testifying as a witness. Where the complaint is not verified, a counterclaim, cross-claim or third-party claim in the answer may be separately verified in the same manner and with the same effect as if it were a separate pleading."

Question: (30) If the plaintiff files a verified complaint in a diversity action in the Southern District of New York, must the answer be verified? Cf. Follenfant v. Rogers, 359 F.2d 30 (5th Cir.1966) (indicating no).

Surowitz v. Hilton Hotels Corp.

Supreme Court of the United States, 1966.
383 U.S. 363, 86 S.Ct. 845.

[Plaintiff, a Polish immigrant with a very limited English vocabulary and practically no formal education, saved several thousand dollars from her work as a seamstress and invested it in stocks on the advice of her son-in-law, Irving Brilliant, a professional investment adviser who was a graduate of the Harvard Law School and possessed a master's degree in economics from Columbia University—"and in addition to his degrees and his financial acumen, he wore a Phi Beta Kappa key." Among these investments was stock in Hilton Hotels Corporation, for which she paid over $2000 in 1957. The plaintiff sought her son-in-law's advice in 1962 about a mailed notice from Hilton announcing its plan to purchase a large amount of its own stock, and in 1963 about Hilton's failure to pay its usual dividend. He and a lawyer friend named Rockler investigated and concluded that Hilton's management had wrongfully damaged the corporation by a fraudulent scheme. Brilliant advised her to bring suit, and she agreed. Rockler prepared the complaint for a shareholders' derivative action. The plaintiff verified it as required by Rule 23(b), now Rule 23.1, stating that some of the allegations were true and "on information and belief" she thought that all the other allegations were true. In reality, she did this not on the basis of her own knowledge, but on faith in her son-in-law's advice and his explanation of the complaint to her.

[The district court, over her counsel's objection, allowed the defendants before answer to take the oral deposition of the plaintiff. In the deposition the plaintiff showed that she did not understand the complaint at all and that in signing it she had relied upon her son-in-law. Thereupon defendants moved to dismiss the complaint, alleging that the pleading was a sham. Rockler filed two affidavits about the extensive investigation preceding the commencement of the action. The court, holding that the plaintiff's verification was "false" and hence a "sham," dismissed the case "with prejudice." The court of appeals affirmed. The Supreme Court granted certiorari.]

■ MR. JUSTICE BLACK delivered the opinion of the Court.

. . . .

We assume it may be possible that there can be circumstances under which a district court could stop all proceedings in a derivative cause of action, relieve the defendants from filing an answer to charges of fraud, and conduct a pre-trial investigation to determine whether the plaintiff had falsely sworn that the facts alleged in the complaint were either true or that he had information which led him to believe they were true. And conceivably such a pre-trial investigation might possibly reveal facts surrounding the verification of the complaint which could justify dismissal of the complaint with prejudice. However, here we need not consider the question of whether, if ever, Federal Rule 23(b) might call for such summary action. Certainly it cannot justify the court's summary dismissal in this case. Rule 23(b) was not written in order to bar derivative suits. Unquestionably it was originally adopted and has served since in part as a means to discourage "strike suits" by people who might be interested in getting quick dollars by making charges without regard to their truth so as to coerce corporate managers to settle worthless claims in order to get rid of them. On the other hand, however, derivative suits have played a rather important role in protecting shareholders of corporations from the designing schemes and wiles of insiders who are willing to betray their company's interest in order to enrich themselves. And it is not easy to conceive of anyone more in need of protection against such schemes than little investors like Mrs. Surowitz.

When the record of this case is reviewed in the light of the purpose of Rule 23(b)'s verification requirement, there emerges the plain, inescapable fact that this is not a strike suit or anything akin to it. Mrs. Surowitz was not interested in anything but her own investment made with her own money. Moreover, there is not one iota of evidence that Mr. Brilliant, her son-in-law and counselor, sought to do the corporation any injury in this litigation. In fact his purchases for the benefit of his family of more than $50,000 of securities in the corporation, including a $10,000 debenture, all made years before this suit was brought, manifest confidence in the corporation, not a desire to harm it in any way. The Court of Appeals in affirming the District Court's dismissal, however, indicated that whether Mrs. Surowitz and her counselors acted in good faith and whether the charges they made were truthful were irrelevant once Mrs. Surowitz demonstrated in her oral testimony that she knew nothing about the content of the suit. . . . In fact the opinion of the Court of Appeals indicates in several places that a woman like Mrs. Surowitz, who is uneducated generally and illiterate in economic matters, could never under any circumstances be a plaintiff in a derivative suit brought in the federal courts to protect her stock interests.

We cannot construe Rule 23 or any other one of the Federal Rules as compelling courts to summarily dismiss, without any answer or argument at all, cases like this where grave charges of fraud are shown by the record to be based on reasonable beliefs growing out of careful investigation. The basic purpose of the Federal Rules is to administer justice through fair trials, not through summary dismissals as necessary as they may be on occasion. These rules were designed in large part to get away from some of the old procedural booby traps which common-law pleaders could set to prevent unsophisticated litigants from ever having their day in court. If rules of procedure work as they should in an honest and fair judicial system, they not only permit, but should as nearly as possible guarantee that bona fide complaints be carried to an adjudication on the merits. Rule 23(b), like the other civil rules, was written to further, not defeat the ends of justice. The serious fraud charged here, which of course has not been proven, is clearly in that class of deceitful conduct which the federal securities laws were largely passed to prohibit and protect against. There is, moreover, not one word or one line of actual evidence in this record indicating that there has been any collusive conduct or trickery by those who filed this suit except through intimations and insinuations without any support from anything any witness has said. The dismissal of this case was error. It has now been practically three years since the complaint was filed and as yet not one of the defendants has even been compelled to admit or deny the wrongdoings charged. They should be. The cause is reversed and remanded to the District Court for trial on the merits.

Reversed and remanded.[e]

■ [CHIEF JUSTICE WARREN and JUSTICE FORTAS did not participate.]

■ MR. JUSTICE HARLAN, concurring.

Rule 23(b) directs that in a derivative suit "the complaint shall be verified by oath" but nothing dictates that the verification be that of the plaintiff shareholder. See Bosc v. 39 Broadway, Inc., D.C., 80 F.Supp. 825.

---

[e] The directors of Hilton Hotels then settled. They agreed to pay $825,000 to the corporation over six and one half years but did not admit wrongdoing. The corporation stated to its shareholders that the suit was "without merit" but was settled to avoid the expenses and burden of litigation. See N.Y. Times, Nov. 17, 1966, at 69.

In the present circumstances, it seems to me the affidavit of Walter J. Rockler, counsel for Mrs. Surowitz, amounts to an adequate verification by counsel, which I think is permitted by a reasonable interpretation of the Rule at least in cases such as this. On this premise, I agree with the decision of the Court.

CERTIFICATION OF PLEADINGS

The original Rule 11 had been a weak and ineffective provision. A 1983 amendment gave it teeth, converting it into a powerful and significant Rule that generated much litigation and controversy. Courts eventually took to applying its sanctions with such enthusiasm as to generate raging concerns about the possible undermining of notice pleading, the risk of uncivil harassment and satellite litigation, and the fear of a chilling effect on certain kinds of claims or litigants and other deleterious effects on the attorney-client relationship.

The 1993 amendment attempted to refine the Rule while reducing the volume of litigation. See generally Carl Tobias, The 1993 Revision of Federal Rule 11, 70 Ind.L.J. 171, 171 (1994) (calling the 1983 amendment "the most controversial amendment in the long history of the Federal Rules," and explaining and in general favorably evaluating the 1993 amendment); Theodore C. Hirt, A Second Look at Amended Rule 11, 48 Am.U.L.Rev. 1007 (1999). On the one hand, the 1993 version of the Rule somewhat broadens the scope of obligation under Rule 11. For example, the person's obligation now is a continuing duty. According to Rule 11(b), the certification is renewed whenever the person presents the paper to the court anew, as by later advocating its position. On the other hand, the new Rule seriously tries to reduce the burdens of Rule 11 practice. For example, according to Rule 11(c)(1), the court no longer "shall" but merely "may" impose an appropriate sanction. A more obvious attempt along these lines is the new 21–day "safe harbor" provision of Rule 11(c)(2).

Although some critics would have revised Rule 11 back to its pre–1983 condition of permissiveness, others had proposed making Rule 11 more draconian. Indeed, Justice Scalia, joined by Justice Thomas, dissented from the Supreme Court's order promulgating the new Rule 11 on the ground that the "revision would render the Rule toothless." Order of April 22, 1993, 507 U.S. 1089, 1096–97. But defenders of the new Rule have replied: "Rule 11 has not been rendered toothless. Rather, it has been defanged and only the poisonous elements that reduced civility and chilled advocacy have been removed." Jerold Solovy, Laura Kaster & Kenneth Wittenberg, Curbing Frivolity in the Courts: Updated Cure, Nat'l L.J., May 2, 1994, at A19.

How does this amended Rule, a product of a very modern spirit, tie in to the old but enduring themes under consideration in this Topic on pleadings? Professor Subrin, supra p. 1170, observed that Rule 11 leaves the pleading rules "untouched" as a legal matter. But consider the following observations from Note, Plausible Pleadings: Developing Standards for

Rule 11 Sanctions, 100 Harv.L.Rev. 630, 631, 633–35 (1987): "The clauses requiring that papers be grounded in fact and warranted by law threaten to undermine the liberal standard of pleading when they are interpreted to demand pleading with greater particularity and with an earlier commitment to a legal theory than the federal rules system otherwise requires. Courts have also read these clauses in ways that risk deterring novel claims that the original rules sought to encourage. The prefiling inquiry and improper purpose clauses similarly threaten to undermine liberal pleading to the extent that courts rely exclusively on the content of pleadings to infer violations of these clauses."

The note indeed argued that the "amendments to rule 11 have altered the standard for sufficient pleading. Although they do not explicitly change that standard, the amendments articulate a standard for avoiding sanctions that requires a complaint to specify legal and factual bases to a fuller extent than that necessary to survive a motion to dismiss. Lawyers must meet this new standard unless they are prepared to suffer the imposition of sanctions for their work. The amendments thereby effectively compel lawyers to file papers aimed at meeting the rule 11 standard rather than the liberal standard of pleading."

While lamenting this development, and arguing that in the absence of explicit change Rule 11 should be read more narrowly so as to restore compatibility with the established procedural scheme, the notewriter also sounded a specific warning: "Responses to the litigation explosion, including the amendment of rule 11, reflect a widely held view that increased use of the courts is a negative development. And judges' willingness to grant rule 11 sanctions in particular categories of cases suggests the degree to which they view those cases as especially contributing to overuse and misuse of the federal courts. Although almost every major lawsuit now includes at least the threat of a rule 11 motion, sanctions are more likely to be imposed in public interest litigation, such as civil rights and employment discrimination cases, than in other types of federal litigation." See Danielle Kie Hart, Still Chilling After All These Years: Rule 11 of the Federal Rules of Civil Procedure and Its Impact on Federal Civil Rights Plaintiffs After the 1993 Amendments, 37 Val.U.L.Rev. 1 (2002).

Question: (31) Since that notewriter sounded the alarm, nonconclusory-and-plausible pleading has come along to close the gap between Rules 8 and 11—but it does so by upping the demands of the pleading rules, for claimants at least. Ironically, however, Rule 11(b)(3) may offer a way out of nonconclusory-and-plausible pleading by allowing a claimant to make factual allegations that, "if specifically so identified, will likely have evidentiary support after a reasonable opportunity for further investigation or discovery." What if Mr. Twombly had alleged some suspected details of the time, place, and persons involved in the alleged conspiracy, with a certification of likely getting evidentiary support through discovery? Would this satisfy the pleading requirements, although exposing Twombly to a Rule 11 motion instead?

Heimbaugh v. City & County of San Francisco

United States District Court, Northern District of California, 1984.
591 F.Supp. 1573.

■ SCHWARZER, DISTRICT JUDGE.

Plaintiff, Robert Heimbaugh, appearing on his own behalf, complains that defendants, the City and County of San Francisco and its elected officials and employees, are interfering with plaintiff's softball playing at Golden Gate Park. As a consequence, plaintiff alleges that he has been deprived of his rights under the First, Fourth and Fourteenth Amendments. Plaintiff seeks both declaratory and injunctive relief as well as damages for a number of alleged torts suffered by him. The Court will treat the complaint as brought under the First, Fourth and Fourteenth Amendments pursuant to § 1983. Defendants now move for summary judgment. Defendants also seek attorneys fees pursuant to Rule 11.

The motion for summary judgment is granted. First, plaintiff does not allege any facts suggesting communicative expression or symbolic conduct sufficient to fall within the scope of the First Amendment. Second, even if plaintiff's softball playing were symbolic speech protected by the First Amendment, expression, whether oral, written or symbolized by conduct, is subject to reasonable time, place and manner restrictions. Third, plaintiff cannot claim that the City's classification of baseball players and softball players violates the equal protection clause because the classification is rationally related to a legitimate government interest [in safety]. Fourth, plaintiff's complaint fails to allege any facts to support his Fourth Amendment claim. Finally, plaintiff cannot state a claim against the City and County of San Francisco for the various torts allegedly committed against him because § 1983 imposes liability for violation of rights protected by the Constitution, not for violations of duties arising out of tort law. Baker v. McCollan, 443 U.S. 137, 99 S.Ct. 2689, 61 L.Ed.2d 433 (1979). Redress for defendants' alleged tortious conduct would lie only in state court under traditional tort law principles, if it lies anywhere.

FACTS

The following facts are undisputed. On September 4, 1982, plaintiff was playing softball in an area of Golden Gate Park posted under Article 6, § 3.02 of the San Francisco Park Code as prohibited for softball playing. Officers of the San Francisco Police Department informed plaintiff he was in violation of Park Code § 3.02 and that he could not play in the [hardball] area. Plaintiff refused to leave and stated he wished to be cited. The officers informed plaintiff of the law and the citation procedure. Following plaintiff's repeated request, the police issued him a citation. Plaintiff was then arrested following his refusal to sign the citation.

DISCUSSION

On defendants' motion for summary judgment the evidence is construed in the light most favorable to plaintiff and plaintiff is given the benefit of all favorable inferences. Adickes v. S.H. Kress & Co., 398 U.S. 144, 90 S.Ct. 1598, 26 L.Ed.2d 142 (1970).

It is well settled that a message may be conveyed by symbolic conduct that is intended to be communicative and that, in context, would reasonably be understood by the viewer to be communicative. [Citations omitted.] Plaintiff claims that by playing softball "they [plaintiff and his friends] are making a statement about the right to democracy in recreation as opposed to elitism." Although the Supreme Court has not provided explicit standards to evaluate whether conduct is sufficiently communicative to fall within the ambit of the First Amendment, Spence v. Washington, [418 U.S. 405, 94 S.Ct. 2727 (1974)], lists several factors relevant to the evaluation: the nature of the activity; the context and environment in which the activity was undertaken; whether there was an intent to convey a message; and whether, under the circumstances, there was a likelihood that the message would be understood by those who viewed it.

Plaintiff's softball playing, in the context, has not been shown to have been intended to convey a message. Even if it was so intended, there is no indication that persons observing plaintiff playing softball in Golden Gate Park would understand his conduct to be a message "about the right to democracy in recreation as opposed to elitism."

[The court similarly expanded on its other four points listed above, and then quoted from the then-current Rule 11.]

Plaintiff's claim is entirely unwarranted by existing law or a good faith argument for modification or extension of existing law. It is frivolous on its face.

While plaintiff appears in pro per, he is schooled in the law, having recently completed law school and taken the bar examination. There is every reason to hold him to the certification he made by signing the pleadings he has filed in this action.

The motion for summary judgment is granted. Taking into consideration plaintiff's economic situation and inexperience, he is ordered to pay defendants on account of their reasonable expenses incurred in making this motion the amount of $50.00.

It is so ordered.

Question: (32) In connection with the 1993 amendment to Rule 11 that required a continuing certification of evidentiary support, the Advisory Committee's note thereon observed: "That summary judgment is rendered against a party does not necessarily mean, for purposes of this certification, that it had no evidentiary support for its position." But is not Rule 56's standard of no genuine issue of fact the same as Rule 11's standard of no evidentiary support? Yet if it is, would not every grant of summary judgment on factual grounds result in finding a violation of Rule 11?

Chambers v. NASCO, Inc.

Supreme Court of the United States, 1991.
501 U.S. 32, 111 S.Ct. 2123.

■ JUSTICE WHITE delivered the opinion of the Court.

This case requires us to explore the scope of the inherent power of a federal court to sanction a litigant for bad-faith conduct. Specifically, we are asked to determine whether the District Court, sitting in diversity, properly invoked its inherent power in assessing as a sanction for a party's bad-faith conduct attorney's fees and related expenses paid by the party's opponent to its attorneys. We hold that the District Court acted within its discretion, and we therefore affirm the judgment of the Court of Appeals.

I

This case began as a simple action for specific performance of a contract, but it did not remain so. Petitioner G. Russell Chambers was the sole shareholder and director of Calcasieu Television and Radio, Inc. (CTR), which operated television station KPLC–TV in Lake Charles, Louisiana. On August 9, 1983, Chambers, acting both in his individual capacity and on behalf of CTR, entered into a purchase agreement to sell the station's facilities and broadcast license to respondent NASCO, Inc., for a purchase price of $18 million. The agreement was not recorded in the parishes in which the two properties housing the station's facilities were located. Consummation of the agreement was subject to the approval of the Federal Communications Commission (FCC); both parties were obligated to file the necessary documents with the FCC no later than September 23, 1983. By late August, however, Chambers had changed his mind and tried to talk NASCO out of consummating the sale. NASCO refused. On September 23, Chambers, through counsel, informed NASCO that he would not file the necessary papers with the FCC.

NASCO decided to take legal action. On Friday, October 14, 1983, NASCO's counsel informed counsel for Chambers and CTR that NASCO would file suit the following Monday in the United States District Court for the Western District of Louisiana, seeking specific performance of the agreement, as well as a temporary restraining order (TRO) to prevent the alienation or encumbrance of the properties at issue. NASCO provided this notice in accordance with Federal Rule of Civil Procedure 65 and Rule 11 of the District Court's Local Rules (now Rule 10), both of which are designed to give a defendant in a TRO application notice of the hearing and an opportunity to be heard.

The reaction of Chambers and his attorney, A.J. Gray III, was later described by the District Court as having "emasculated and frustrated the purposes of these rules and the powers of [the District] Court by utilizing this notice to prevent NASCO's access to the remedy of specific performance." NASCO, Inc. v. Calcasieu Television & Radio, Inc., 623 F.Supp. 1372, 1383 (W.D.La.1985). On Sunday, October 16, 1983, the pair acted to place the properties at issue beyond the reach of the District Court by means of the Louisiana Public Records Doctrine. Because the purchase agreement had never been recorded, they determined that if the properties were sold to a third party, and if the deeds were recorded before the issuance of a TRO, the District Court would lack jurisdiction over the properties.

To this end, Chambers and Gray created a trust, with Chambers' sister as trustee and Chambers' three adult children as beneficiaries. The pair then directed the president of CTR, who later became Chambers' wife, to execute warranty deeds conveying the two tracts at issue to the trust for a recited consideration of $1.4 million. Early Monday morning, the deeds were recorded. The trustee, as purchaser, had not signed the deeds; none of the consideration had been paid; and CTR remained in possession of the properties. Later that morning, NASCO's counsel appeared in the District Court to file the complaint and seek the TRO. With NASCO's counsel present, the District Judge telephoned Gray. Despite the judge's queries concerning the possibility that CTR was negotiating to sell the properties to a third person, Gray made no mention of the recordation of the deeds earlier that morning. NASCO, Inc. v. Calcasieu Television & Radio, Inc., 124 F.R.D. 120, 126, n. 8 (W.D.La.1989). That afternoon, Chambers met with his sister and had her sign the trust documents and a $1.4 million note to CTR. The next morning, Gray informed the District Court by letter of the recordation of the deeds the day before, and admitted that he had intentionally withheld the information from the court.

Within the next few days, Chambers' attorneys prepared a leaseback agreement from the trustee to CTR, so that CTR could remain in possession of the properties and continue to operate the station. The following week, the District Court granted a preliminary injunction against Chambers and CTR and entered a second TRO to prevent the trustee from alienating or encumbering the properties. At that hearing, the District Judge warned that Gray's and Chambers' conduct had been unethical.

Despite this early warning, Chambers, often acting through his attorneys, continued to abuse the judicial process. In November 1983, in defiance of the preliminary injunction, he refused to allow NASCO to inspect CTR's corporate records. The ensuing civil contempt proceedings resulted in the assessment of a $25,000 fine against Chambers personally. NASCO, Inc. v. Calcasieu Television & Radio, Inc., 583 F.Supp. 115 (W.D.La.1984). Two subsequent appeals from the contempt order were dismissed for lack of a final judgment. See NASCO, Inc. v. Calcasieu Television & Radio, Inc., No. 84–9037 (CA5, May 29, 1984); NASCO, Inc. v. Calcasieu Television & Radio, Inc., 752 F.2d 157 (C.A.5 1985).

Undeterred, Chambers proceeded with "a series of meritless motions and pleadings and delaying actions." 124 F.R.D., at 127. These actions triggered further warnings from the court. At one point, acting sua sponte, the District Judge called a status conference to find out why bankers were being deposed. When informed by Chambers' counsel that the purpose was to learn whether NASCO could afford to pay for the station, the court canceled the depositions consistent with its authority under Federal Rule of Civil Procedure 26(g).

At the status conference nine days before the April 1985 trial date, the District Judge again warned counsel that further misconduct would not be tolerated. Finally, on the eve of trial, Chambers and CTR stipulated that the purchase agreement was enforceable and that Chambers had breached the agreement on September 23, 1983, by failing to file the necessary papers with the FCC. At trial, the only defense presented by Chambers was the Public Records Doctrine.

In the interlude between the trial and the entry of judgment during which the District Court prepared its opinion, Chambers sought to render the purchase agreement meaningless by seeking permission from the FCC to build a new transmission tower for the station and to relocate the transmission facilities to that site, which was not covered by the agreement. Only after NASCO sought contempt sanctions did Chambers withdraw the application.

The District Court entered judgment on the merits in NASCO's favor, finding that the transfer of the properties to the trust was a simulated sale and that the deeds purporting to convey the property were "null, void, and of no effect." 623 F.Supp., at 1385. Chambers' motions, filed in the District Court, the Court of Appeals, and this Court, to stay the judgment pending appeal were denied. Undeterred, Chambers convinced CTR officials to file formal oppositions to NASCO's pending application for FCC approval of the transfer of the station's license, in contravention of both the District Court's injunctive orders and its judgment on the merits. NASCO then sought contempt sanctions for a third time, and the oppositions were withdrawn.

When Chambers refused to prepare to close the sale, NASCO again sought the court's help. A hearing was set for July 16, 1986, to determine whether certain equipment was to be included in the sale. At the beginning of the hearing, the court informed Chambers' new attorney, Edwin A. McCabe, that further sanctionable conduct would not be tolerated. When the hearing was recessed for several days, Chambers, without notice to the court or NASCO, removed from service at the station all of the equipment at issue, forcing the District Court to order that the equipment be returned to service.

Immediately following oral argument on Chambers' appeal from the District Court's judgment on the merits, the Court of Appeals, ruling from the bench, found the appeal frivolous. The court imposed appellate sanctions in the form of attorney's fees and double costs, pursuant to Federal Rule of Appellate Procedure 38, and remanded the case to the District Court with orders to fix the amount of appellate sanctions and to determine whether further sanctions should be imposed for the manner in which the litigation had been conducted. NASCO, Inc. v. Calcasieu Television & Radio, Inc., 797 F.2d 975 (C.A.5 1986) (per curiam) (unpublished order).

On remand, NASCO moved for sanctions, invoking the District Court's inherent power, Fed.Rule Civ.Proc. 11, and 28 U.S.C. § 1927. After full briefing and a hearing, see 124 F.R.D., at 141, n. 11, the District Court determined that sanctions were appropriate "for the manner in which this proceeding was conducted in the district court from October 14, 1983, the time that plaintiff gave notice of its intention to file suit to this date." Id., at 123. At the end of an extensive opinion recounting what it deemed to have been sanctionable conduct during this period, the court imposed sanctions against Chambers in the form of attorney's fees and expenses totaling $996,644.65, which represented the entire amount of NASCO's litigation costs paid to its attorneys.[5] In so doing, the court rejected Chambers' argument that he had merely followed the advice of counsel, labeling him "the strategist" . . . .

In imposing the sanctions, the District Court first considered Federal Rule of Civil Procedure 11. It noted that the alleged sanctionable conduct was that Chambers and the other defendants had "(1) attempted to deprive this Court of jurisdiction by acts of fraud, nearly all of which were performed outside the confines of this Court, (2) filed false and frivolous pleadings, and (3) attempted, by other tactics of delay, oppression, harassment and massive expense to reduce plaintiff to exhausted compliance." Id., at 138. The court recognized that the conduct in the first and third categories could not be reached by Rule 11, which governs only papers filed with a court. As for the second category, the court explained that the falsity of the pleadings at issue did not become apparent until after the trial on the merits, so that it would have been impossible to assess sanctions at the time the papers were filed. Id., at 138–139. Consequently, the District Court deemed Rule 11 "insufficient" for its purposes. Id., at 139. The court likewise declined to impose sanctions under § 1927, both because the statute applies only to attorneys, and therefore would not reach Chambers, and because the statute was not broad enough to reach "acts which degrade the judicial system," including "attempts to deprive the Court of jurisdiction, fraud, misleading and lying to the Court." Ibid. The court therefore relied on its inherent power in imposing sanctions, stressing that "[t]he wielding of that inherent power is particularly appropriate when the offending parties have practiced a fraud upon the court." Ibid.

The Court of Appeals affirmed. NASCO, Inc. v. Calcasieu Television & Radio, Inc., 894 F.2d 696 (C.A.5 1990). The court rejected Chambers'

[5] In calculating the award, the District Court deducted the amounts previously awarded as compensatory damages for contempt, as well as the amount awarded as appellate sanctions. 124 F.R.D., at 133–134.

The court also sanctioned other individuals, who are not parties to the action in this Court. Chambers' sister, the trustee, was sanctioned by a reprimand; attorney Gray was disbarred and prohibited from seeking readmission for three years; attorney Richard A. Curry, who represented the trustee, was suspended from practice before the court for six months; and attorney McCabe was suspended for five years. Id., at 144–146. Although these sanctions did not affect the bank accounts of these individuals, they were nevertheless substantial sanctions and were as proportionate to the conduct at issue as was the monetary sanction imposed on Chambers. Indeed, in the case of the disbarment of attorney Gray, the court recognized that the penalty was among the harshest possible sanctions and one which derived from its authority to supervise those admitted to practice before it. See id., at 140–141.

argument that a federal court sitting in diversity must look to state law, not the court's inherent power, to assess attorney's fees as a sanction for bad-faith conduct in litigation. The court further found that neither 28 U.S.C. § 1927 nor Federal Rule of Civil Procedure 11 limits a court's inherent authority to sanction bad-faith conduct "when the party's conduct is not within the reach of the rule or the statute." 894 F.2d, at 702–703. Although observing that the inherent power "is not a broad reservoir of power, ready at an imperial hand, but a limited source; an implied power squeezed from the need to make the court function," id., at 702, the court also concluded that the District Court did not abuse its discretion in awarding to NASCO the fees and litigation costs paid to its attorneys. Because of the importance of these issues, we granted certiorari, 498 U.S. 807, 111 S.Ct. 38 (1990).

II

Chambers maintains that 28 U.S.C. § 1927 and the various sanctioning provisions in the Federal Rules of Civil Procedure[8] reflect a legislative intent to displace the inherent power. At least, he argues that they obviate or foreclose resort to the inherent power in this case. We agree with the Court of Appeals that neither proposition is persuasive.

A

It has long been understood that "[c]ertain implied powers must necessarily result to our Courts of justice from the nature of their institution," powers "which cannot be dispensed with in a Court, because they are necessary to the exercise of all others." United States v. Hudson, 7 Cranch 32, 34 (1812); see also Roadway Express, Inc. v. Piper, 447 U.S. 752, 764, 100 S.Ct. 2455, 2463 (1980) (citing Hudson). For this reason, "Courts of justice are universally acknowledged to be vested, by their very creation, with power to impose silence, respect, and decorum, in their presence, and submission to their lawful mandates." Anderson v. Dunn, 6 Wheat. 204, 227 (1821); see also Ex parte Robinson, 19 Wall. 505, 510 (1874). These powers are "governed not by rule or statute but by the control necessarily vested in courts to manage their own affairs so as to achieve the orderly and expeditious disposition of cases." Link v. Wabash R. Co., 370 U.S. 626, 630–631, 82 S.Ct. 1386, 1388–1389 (1962).

Prior cases have outlined the scope of the inherent power of the federal courts. For example, the Court has held that a federal court has the power

[8] A number of the rules provide for the imposition of attorney's fees as a sanction. See Fed.Rule Civ.Proc. 11 (certification requirement for papers), 16(f) (pretrial conferences), 26(g) (certification requirement for discovery requests), 30(g) (oral depositions), 37 (sanctions for failure to cooperate with discovery), 56(g) (affidavits accompanying summary judgment motions). In some instances, the assessment of fees is one of a range of possible sanctions, see, e.g., Fed.Rule Civ.Proc. 11, while in others, the court must award fees, see, e.g., Fed.Rule Civ.Proc. 16(f). In each case, the fees that may be assessed are limited to those incurred as a result of the rule violation. In the case of Rule 11, however, a violation could conceivably warrant an imposition of fees covering the entire litigation, if, for example, a complaint or answer was filed in violation of the rule. The court generally may act sua sponte in imposing sanctions under the rules.

to control admission to its bar and to discipline attorneys who appear before it. See Ex parte Burr, 9 Wheat. 529, 531 (1824). While this power "ought to be exercised with great caution," it is nevertheless "incidental to all Courts." Ibid.

In addition, it is firmly established that "[t]he power to punish for contempts is inherent in all courts." Robinson, supra, at 510. This power reaches both conduct before the court and that beyond the court's confines, for "[t]he underlying concern that gave rise to the contempt power was not . . . merely the disruption of court proceedings. Rather, it was disobedience to the orders of the Judiciary, regardless of whether such disobedience interfered with the conduct of trial." Young v. United States ex rel. Vuitton et Fils S.A., 481 U.S. 787, 798, 107 S.Ct. 2124, 2132 (1987) (citations omitted).

Of particular relevance here, the inherent power also allows a federal court to vacate its own judgment upon proof that a fraud has been perpetrated upon the court. See Hazel–Atlas Glass Co. v. Hartford–Empire Co., 322 U.S. 238, 64 S.Ct. 997 (1944); Universal Oil Products Co. v. Root Refining Co., 328 U.S. 575, 580, 66 S.Ct. 1176, 1179 (1946). This "historic power of equity to set aside fraudulently begotten judgments," Hazel–Atlas, 322 U.S., at 245, 64 S.Ct., at 1001, is necessary to the integrity of the courts, for "tampering with the administration of justice in [this] manner . . . involves far more than an injury to a single litigant. It is a wrong against the institutions set up to protect and safeguard the public." Id., at 246, 64 S.Ct., at 1001. Moreover, a court has the power to conduct an independent investigation in order to determine whether it has been the victim of fraud. Universal Oil, supra, 328 U.S., at 580, 66 S.Ct., at 1179.

There are other facets to a federal court's inherent power. The court may bar from the courtroom a criminal defendant who disrupts a trial. Illinois v. Allen, 397 U.S. 337, 90 S.Ct. 1057 (1970). It may dismiss an action on grounds of forum non conveniens, Gulf Oil Corp. v. Gilbert, 330 U.S. 501, 507–508, 67 S.Ct. 839, 842–843 (1947); and it may act sua sponte to dismiss a suit for failure to prosecute, Link, supra, 370 U.S., at 630–631, 82 S.Ct., at 1388–1389.

Because of their very potency, inherent powers must be exercised with restraint and discretion. See Roadway Express, supra, 447 U.S., at 764, 100 S.Ct., at 2463. A primary aspect of that discretion is the ability to fashion an appropriate sanction for conduct which abuses the judicial process. As we recognized in Roadway Express, outright dismissal of a lawsuit, which we had upheld in Link, is a particularly severe sanction, yet is within the court's discretion. 447 U.S., at 765, 100 S.Ct., at 2463. Consequently, the "less severe sanction" of an assessment of attorney's fees is undoubtedly within a court's inherent power as well. Ibid. See also Hutto v. Finney, 437 U.S. 678, 689, n. 14, 98 S.Ct. 2565, 2573, n. 14 (1978).

Indeed, "[t]here are ample grounds for recognizing . . . that in narrowly defined circumstances federal courts have inherent power to assess attorney's fees against counsel," Roadway Express, supra, 447 U.S., at 765, 100 S.Ct., at 2463, even though the so-called "American Rule" prohibits fee-shifting in most cases. See Alyeska Pipeline Service Co. v. Wilderness Society, 421 U.S. 240, 259, 95 S.Ct. 1612, 1622 (1975). As we explained in Alyeska, these exceptions fall into three categories. The first, known as the "common fund exception," derives not from a court's power to control litigants, but from its historic equity jurisdiction, see Sprague v. Ticonic National Bank, 307 U.S. 161, 164, 59 S.Ct. 777, 778 (1939), and allows a court to award attorney's fees to a party whose litigation efforts directly benefit others. Alyeska, 421 U.S., at 257–258, 95 S.Ct., at 1621–1622. Second, a court may assess attorney's fees as a sanction for the " 'willful disobedience of a court order.' " Id., at 258, 95 S.Ct., at 1622 (quoting Fleischmann Distilling Corp. v. Maier Brewing Co., 386 U.S. 714, 718, 87 S.Ct. 1404, 1407 (1967)). Thus, a court's discretion to determine "[t]he degree of punishment for contempt" permits the court to impose as part of the fine attorney's fees representing the entire cost of the litigation. Toledo Scale Co. v. Computing Scale Co., 261 U.S. 399, 428, 43 S.Ct. 458, 466 (1923).

Third, and most relevant here, a court may assess attorney's fees when a party has " 'acted in bad faith, vexatiously, wantonly, or for oppressive reasons.' " Alyeska, supra, 421 U.S., at 258–259, 95 S.Ct., at 1622–1623 (quoting F.D. Rich Co. v. United States ex rel. Industrial Lumber Co., 417 U.S. 116, 129, 94 S.Ct. 2157, 2165 (1974)). [Other citations omitted.] In this regard, if a court finds "that fraud has been practiced upon it, or that the very temple of justice has been defiled," it may assess attorney's fees against the responsible party, Universal Oil, supra, 328 U.S., at 580, 66 S.Ct., at 1179, as it may when a party "shows bad faith by delaying or disrupting the litigation or by hampering enforcement of a court order,"[10] Hutto, 437 U.S., at 689, n. 14, 98 S.Ct., at 2573, n. 14. The imposition of sanctions in this instance transcends a court's equitable power concerning relations between the parties and reaches a court's inherent power to police itself, thus serving the dual purpose of "vindicat[ing] judicial authority without resort to the more drastic sanctions available for contempt of court and mak[ing] the prevailing party whole for expenses caused by his opponent's obstinacy." Ibid.

B

We discern no basis for holding that the sanctioning scheme of the statute and the rules displaces the inherent power to impose sanctions for the bad-faith conduct described above. These other mechanisms, taken alone or together, are not substitutes for the inherent power, for that power is both broader and narrower than other means of imposing sanctions. First, whereas each of the other mechanisms reaches only certain individuals or conduct, the inherent power extends to a full range of litigation abuses. At the very least, the inherent power must continue to exist to fill in the interstices. Even the dissent so concedes. . . . Second,

---

[10] In this regard, the bad-faith exception resembles the third prong of Rule 11's certification requirement, which mandates that a signer of a paper filed with the court warrant that the paper "is not interposed for any improper purpose, such as to harass or to cause unnecessary delay or needless increase in the cost of litigation."

while the narrow exceptions to the American Rule effectively limit a court's inherent power to impose attorney's fees as a sanction to cases in which a litigant has engaged in bad-faith conduct or willful disobedience of a court's orders, many of the other mechanisms permit a court to impose attorney's fees as a sanction for conduct which merely fails to meet a reasonableness standard. Rule 11, for example, imposes an objective standard of reasonable inquiry which does not mandate a finding of bad faith.[11] See Business Guides, Inc. v. Chromatic Communications Enterprises, Inc., 498 U.S. 533, 548–549, 111 S.Ct. 922, 931–932 (1991).

It is true that the exercise of the inherent power of lower federal courts can be limited by statute and rule, for "[t]hese courts were created by act of Congress." Robinson, 19 Wall., at 511. Nevertheless, "we do not lightly assume that Congress has intended to depart from established principles" such as the scope of a court's inherent power. Weinberger v. Romero–Barcelo, 456 U.S. 305, 313, 102 S.Ct. 1798, 1803 (1982); see also Link, 370 U.S., at 631–632, 82 S.Ct., at 1389–1390. In Alyeska we determined that "Congress ha[d] not repudiated the judicially fashioned exceptions" to the American Rule, which were founded in the inherent power of the courts. 421 U.S., at 260, 95 S.Ct., at 1623. Nothing since then has changed that assessment, and we have thus reaffirmed the scope and the existence of the exceptions since the most recent amendments to § 1927 and Rule 11, the other sanctioning mechanisms invoked by NASCO here. See Pennsylvania v. Delaware Valley Citizens' Council for Clean Air, 478 U.S. 546, 561–562, and n. 6, 106 S.Ct. 3088, 3096–3097, and n. 6 (1986). As the Court of Appeals recognized, 894 F.2d, at 702, the amendment to § 1927 allowing an assessment of fees against an attorney says nothing about a court's power to assess fees against a party. Likewise, the Advisory Committee Notes on the 1983 Amendment to Rule 11, 28 U.S.C.App., p. 575, declare that the Rule "build[s] upon and expand[s] the equitable doctrine permitting the court to award expenses, including attorney's fees, to a litigant whose opponent acts in bad faith in instituting or conducting litigation" . . . . Thus, as the Court of Appeals for the Ninth Circuit has recognized, Rule 11 "does not repeal or modify existing authority of federal courts to deal with abuses . . . under the court's inherent power." Zaldivar v. Los Angeles, 780 F.2d 823, 830 (C.A.9 1986).

The Court's prior cases have indicated that the inherent power of a court can be invoked even if procedural rules exist which sanction the same conduct. In Link, it was recognized that a federal district court has the inherent power to dismiss a case sua sponte for failure to prosecute, even though the language of Federal Rule of Civil Procedure 41(b) appeared to require a motion from a party:

---

[11] Indeed, Rule 11 was amended in 1983 precisely because the subjective bad-faith standard was difficult to establish and courts were therefore reluctant to invoke it as a means of imposing sanctions. See Advisory Committee Notes on the 1983 Amendment to Rule 11, 28 U.S.C.App., pp. 575–576. Consequently, there is little risk that courts will invoke their inherent power "to chill the advocacy of litigants attempting to vindicate all other important federal rights." See [dissent]. To the extent that such a risk does exist, it is no less present when a court invokes Rule 11. See Cooter & Gell v. Hartmarx Corp., 496 U.S. 384, 393, 110 S.Ct. 2447, 2454 (1990).

> "The authority of a court to dismiss sua sponte for lack of prosecution has generally been considered an 'inherent power,' governed not by rule or statute but by the control necessarily vested in courts to manage their own affairs so as to achieve the orderly and expeditious disposition of cases. That it has long gone unquestioned is apparent not only from the many state court decisions sustaining such dismissals, but even from language in this Court's opinion in Redfield v. Ystalyfera Iron Co., 110 U.S. 174, 176[, 3 S.Ct. 570, 571 (1884)]. It also has the sanction of wide usage among the District Courts. It would require a much clearer expression of purpose than Rule 41(b) provides for us to assume that it was intended to abrogate so well-acknowledged a proposition." 370 U.S., at 630–632, 82 S.Ct., at 1388–1390 (footnotes omitted).

. . . .

There is, therefore, nothing in the other sanctioning mechanisms or prior cases interpreting them that warrants a conclusion that a federal court may not, as a matter of law, resort to its inherent power to impose attorney's fees as a sanction for bad-faith conduct. This is plainly the case where the conduct at issue is not covered by one of the other sanctioning provisions. But neither is a federal court forbidden to sanction bad-faith conduct by means of the inherent power simply because that conduct could also be sanctioned under the statute or the rules. A court must, of course, exercise caution in invoking its inherent power, and it must comply with the mandates of due process, both in determining that the requisite bad faith exists and in assessing fees, see Roadway Express, supra, at 767, 100 S.Ct., at 2464. Furthermore, when there is bad-faith conduct in the course of litigation that could be adequately sanctioned under the rules, the court ordinarily should rely on the rules rather than the inherent power. But if in the informed discretion of the court, neither the statute nor the rules are up to the task, the court may safely rely on its inherent power.

Like the Court of Appeals, we find no abuse of discretion in resorting to the inherent power in the circumstances of this case. It is true that the District Court could have employed Rule 11 to sanction Chambers for filing "false and frivolous pleadings," 124 F.R.D., at 138, and that some of the other conduct might have been reached through other rules. Much of the bad-faith conduct by Chambers, however, was beyond the reach of the rules, his entire course of conduct throughout the lawsuit evidenced bad faith and an attempt to perpetrate a fraud on the court, and the conduct sanctionable under the rules was intertwined within conduct that only the inherent power could address. In circumstances such as these in which all of a litigant's conduct is deemed sanctionable, requiring a court first to apply rules and statutes containing sanctioning provisions to discrete occurrences before invoking inherent power to address remaining instances of sanctionable conduct would serve only to foster extensive and needless satellite litigation, which is contrary to the aim of the rules themselves. See, e.g., Advisory Committee Notes on the 1983 Amendment to Rule 11, 28 U.S.C.App., pp. 575–576.

. . . .

III

Chambers asserts that even if federal courts can use their inherent power to assess attorney's fees as a sanction in some cases, they are not free to do so when they sit in diversity, unless the applicable state law recognizes the "bad-faith" exception to the general rule against fee shifting. He relies on footnote 31 in Alyeska, in which we stated with regard to the exceptions to the American Rule that "[a] very different situation is presented when a federal court sits in a diversity case. '[I]n an ordinary diversity case where the state law does not run counter to a valid federal statute or rule of court, and usually it will not, state law denying the right to attorney's fees or giving a right thereto, which reflects a substantial policy of the state, should be followed.' 6 J. Moore, Federal Practice ¶ 54.77[2], pp. 1712–1713 (2d ed. 1974) (footnotes omitted)." 421 U.S., at 259, n. 31, 95 S.Ct., at 1622, n. 31.

We agree with NASCO that Chambers has misinterpreted footnote 31. The limitation on a court's inherent power described there applies only to fee-shifting rules that embody a substantive policy, such as a statute which permits a prevailing party in certain classes of litigation to recover fees. That was precisely the issue in People of Sioux County v. National Surety Co., 276 U.S. 238, 48 S.Ct. 239 (1928), the only case cited in footnote 31. There, a state statute mandated that in actions to enforce an insurance policy, the court was to award the plaintiff a reasonable attorney's fee. . . . In enforcing the statute, the Court treated the provision as part of a statutory liability which created a substantive right. . . . Indeed, Alyeska itself concerned the substantive nature of the public policy choices involved in deciding whether vindication of the rights afforded by a particular statute is important enough to warrant the award of fees. See 421 U.S., at 260–263, 95 S.Ct., at 1623–1625.

Only when there is a conflict between state and federal substantive law are the concerns of Erie R. Co. v. Tompkins, 304 U.S. 64, 58 S.Ct. 817 (1938), at issue. As we explained in Hanna v. Plumer, 380 U.S. 460, 85 S.Ct. 1136 (1965), the "outcome determinative" test of Erie and Guaranty Trust Co. v. York, 326 U.S. 99, 65 S.Ct. 1464 (1945), "cannot be read without reference to the twin aims of the Erie rule: discouragement of forum-shopping and avoidance of inequitable administration of the laws." 380 U.S., at 468, 85 S.Ct., at 1142. Despite Chambers' protestations to the contrary, neither of these twin aims is implicated by the assessment of attorney's fees as a sanction for bad-faith conduct before the court which involved disobedience of the court's orders and the attempt to defraud the court itself. In our recent decision in Business Guides, Inc. v. Chromatic Communications Enterprises, Inc., 498 U.S., at 553, 111 S.Ct., at 934, we stated, "Rule 11 sanctions do not constitute the kind of fee shifting at issue in Alyeska [because they] are not tied to the outcome of litigation; the relevant inquiry is whether a specific filing was, if not successful, at least well founded." Likewise, the imposition of sanctions under the bad-faith exception depends not on which party wins the lawsuit, but on how the parties conduct themselves during the litigation. Consequently, there is no risk that the exception will lead to forum-shopping. Nor is it inequitable to apply the exception to citizens and noncitizens alike, when the party, by controlling his or her conduct in litigation, has the power to determine whether sanctions will be assessed. As the Court of Appeals expressed it, "Erie guarantees a litigant that if he takes his state law cause of action to federal court, and abides by the rules of the court, the result in his case will be the same as if he had brought it in state court. It does not allow him to waste the court's time and resources with cantankerous conduct, even in the unlikely event a state court would allow him to do so." 894 F.2d, at 706.

. . . .

Chambers argues that because the primary purpose of the sanction is punitive, assessing attorney's fees violates the State's prohibition on punitive damages. Under Louisiana law, there can be no punitive damages for breach of contract, even when a party has acted in bad faith in breaching the agreement. Lancaster v. Petroleum Corp. of Delaware, 491 So.2d 768, 779 (La.App.1986). Cf. La.Civ.Code Ann., Art. 1995 (West 1987). Indeed, "as a general rule attorney's fees are not allowed a successful litigant in Louisiana except where authorized by statute or by contract." Rutherford v. Impson, 366 So.2d 944, 947 (La.App.1978). It is clear, though, that this general rule focuses on the award of attorney's fees because of a party's success on the underlying claim. . . . This substantive state policy is not implicated here, where sanctions were imposed for conduct during the litigation.

Here the District Court did not attempt to sanction petitioner for breach of contract, but rather imposed sanctions for the fraud he perpetrated on the court and the bad faith he displayed toward both his adversary and the court throughout the course of the litigation. See 124 F.R.D., at 123, 143. We agree with the Court of Appeals that "[w]e do not see how the district court's inherent power to tax fees for that conduct can be made subservient to any state policy without transgressing the boundaries set out in Erie, Guaranty Trust Co., and Hanna," for "[f]ee-shifting here is not a matter of substantive remedy, but of vindicating judicial authority." 894 F.2d, at 705.

IV

We review a court's imposition of sanctions under its inherent power for abuse of discretion. Link, 370 U.S., at 633, 82 S.Ct., at 1390; see also Cooter & Gell v. Hartmarx Corp., 496 U.S. 384, 405, 110 S.Ct. 2447, 2460–2461 (1990) (Rule 11). Based on the circumstances of this case, we find that the District Court acted within its discretion in assessing as a sanction for Chambers' bad-faith conduct the entire amount of NASCO's attorney's fees.

. . . .

For the foregoing reasons, the judgment of the Court of Appeals for the Fifth Circuit is

Affirmed.

■ JUSTICE SCALIA, dissenting.

[Justice Scalia generally agreed with the majority's view of the law, but agreed with Justice Kennedy] that the District Court here had no power to impose any sanctions for petitioner's flagrant, bad-faith breach of contract; and I agree with him that it appears to have done so. For that reason, I dissent.

■ JUSTICE KENNEDY, with whom THE CHIEF JUSTICE and JUSTICE SOUTER join, dissenting.

Today's decision effects a vast expansion of the power of federal courts, unauthorized by rule or statute. I have no doubt petitioner engaged in sanctionable conduct that warrants severe corrective measures. But our outrage at his conduct should not obscure the boundaries of settled legal categories.

With all respect, I submit the Court commits two fundamental errors. First, it permits the exercise of inherent sanctioning powers without prior recourse to controlling rules and statutes, thereby abrogating to federal courts Congress' power to regulate fees and costs. Second, the Court upholds the wholesale shift of respondent's attorney's fees to petitioner, even though the District Court opinion reveals that petitioner was sanctioned at least in part for his so-called bad faith breach of contract. The extension of inherent authority to sanction a party's prelitigation conduct subverts the American Rule and turns the Erie doctrine upside down by punishing petitioner's primary conduct contrary to Louisiana law. Because I believe the proper exercise of inherent powers requires exhaustion of express sanctioning provisions and much greater caution in their application to redress prelitigation conduct, I dissent.

I

. . . .

. . . By allowing courts to ignore express Rules and statutes on point, . . . the Court treats inherent powers as the norm and textual bases of authority as the exception. . . .

The Court has the presumption backwards. Inherent powers are the exception, not the rule, and their assertion requires special justification in each case. Like all applications of inherent power, the authority to sanction bad faith litigation practices can be exercised only when necessary to preserve the authority of the court. [Citations omitted.]

. . . Inherent powers can be exercised only when necessary, and there is no necessity if a rule or statute provides a basis for sanctions. It follows that a district court should rely on text-based authority derived from Congress rather than inherent power in every case where the text-based authority applies.

. . . .

Upon a finding of bad faith, courts may now ignore any and all textual limitations on sanctioning power. By inviting district courts to rely on inherent authority as a substitute for attention to the careful distinctions contained in the rules and statutes, today's decision will render these sources of authority superfluous in many instances. A number of pernicious practical effects will follow.

The Federal Rules establish explicit standards for, and explicit checks against, the exercise of judicial authority. Rule 11 provides a useful illustration. . . .

By contrast, courts apply inherent powers without specific definitional or procedural limits. True, if a district court wishes to shift attorney's fees as a sanction, it must make a finding of bad faith to circumvent the American Rule. But today's decision demonstrates how little guidance or limitation the undefined bad faith predicate provides. The Court states without elaboration that courts must "comply with the mandates of due process . . . in determining that the requisite bad faith exists," ante, . . . but the Court's bad-faith standard, at least without adequate definition, thwarts the first requirement of due process, namely, that "[a]ll are entitled to be informed as to what the State commands or forbids." Lanzetta v. New Jersey, 306 U.S. 451, 453, 59 S.Ct. 618, 619 (1939). This standardless exercise of judicial power may appear innocuous in this litigation between commercial actors. But the same unchecked power also can be applied to chill the advocacy of litigants attempting to vindicate all other important federal rights.

In addition, the scope of sanctionable conduct under the bad-faith rule appears unlimited. As the Court boasts, "whereas each of the other mechanisms [in Rules and statutes] reaches only certain individuals or conduct, the inherent power extends to a full range of litigation abuses." . . . By allowing exclusive resort to inherent authority whenever "conduct sanctionable under the rules was intertwined within conduct that only the inherent power could address," . . . the Court encourages all courts in the federal system to find bad faith misconduct in order to eliminate the need to rely on specific textual provisions. This will ensure the uncertain development of the meaning and scope of these express sanctioning provisions by encouraging their disuse, and will defeat, at least in the area of sanctions, Congress' central goal in enacting the Federal Rules—" 'uniformity in the federal courts.' " Hanna v. Plumer, 380 U.S. 460, 472, 85 S.Ct. 1136, 1145 (1965). Finally, as Part IV of the Court's opinion demonstrates, the lack of any legal requirement other than the talismanic recitation of the phrase "bad faith" will foreclose meaningful review of sanctions based on inherent authority. [Citation omitted.]

. . . .

II

. . . .

The District Court's own candid and extensive opinion reveals that the bad faith for which petitioner was sanctioned extended beyond the litigation tactics and comprised as well what the District Court considered to be bad faith in refusing to perform the underlying contract three weeks before the lawsuit began. The Court made explicit reference, for instance, to "this massive and absolutely unnecessary lawsuit forced on NASCO by Chambers' arbitrary and arrogant refusal to honor and perform this perfectly legal and enforceable contract." 124 F.R.D., at 136. See also id., at 143 ("Chambers arbitrarily and without legal cause refused to perform, forcing NASCO to bring its suit for specific performance"); ibid. ("Chambers, knowing that NASCO had a good and valid contract, hired Gray to find a defense and arbitrarily refused to perform, thereby forcing NASCO to bring its suit for specific performance and injunctive relief"); id., at 125 (petitioner's "unjustified and arbitrary refusal to file" the FCC application "was in absolute bad faith"). The District Court makes the open and express concession that it is sanctioning petitioner for his breach of contract:

> "[T]he balance of . . . fees and expenses included in the sanctions, would not have been incurred by NASCO if Chambers had not defaulted and forced NASCO to bring this suit. There is absolutely no reason why Chambers should not reimburse in full all attorney's fees and expenses that NASCO, by Chambers' action, was forced to pay." Id., at 143.

The trial court also explained that "[t]he attorney's fees and expenses charged to NASCO by its attorneys . . . *flowed from and were a direct result of this suit.* We shall include them in the attorney's fees sanctions." Id., at 142 (emphasis added).

. . . .

SECTION 3. THE RESPONSE

(a) PARRIES

MOTION FOR A MORE DEFINITE STATEMENT

Clarification of the complaint may be sought under the codes by a motion for a more definite statement or a motion for a bill of particulars. In some jurisdictions the two have become substantially interchangeable, but in others a distinction is made. A motion for a more definite statement is appropriate when the moving party requires further details in order to frame a responsive pleading. A bill of particulars enables the moving party to prepare for trial, and especially to protect against surprise and to limit the issues at trial. Originally used in connection with declarations in general assumpsit under the common counts, the bill of particulars has in a number of code states come to be available, at the discretion of the court, in any kind of action. When there is no provision for discovery comparable to that obtainable under Federal Rules 26 to 37, the value of bills of particulars is obvious.

Originally, Federal Rule 12(e) allowed both types of motion. After a few years of actual operation, Rule 12(e) had generated more judicial rulings than any other part of the Rules. In a large percentage of the cases the rulings were adverse to the moving party, but motions under Rule 12(e) were nevertheless productive of considerable waste and confusion. The original Rule accordingly received much criticism from commentators, judges, and lawyers, who pointed out that as an aid in preparation for trial it was superfluous in the light of the more effective provisions for discovery.

In 1948, the rulemakers amended Rule 12(e) by eliminating the bill of particulars entirely and permitting a motion for a more definite statement only when the moving party shows that the pleading is so vague or ambiguous that the party cannot reasonably frame a responsive pleading. Cases where the motion should be granted today are rare. Indeed, the motion has even been characterized as "superfluous and unnecessary." Stefan F. Tucker, Comment, Federal Rule 12(e): Motion for More Definite Statement—History, Operation and Efficacy, 61 Mich.L.Rev. 1126, 1138 (1963).

Curiously, however, there has been some recent talk of reviving Rule 12(e)'s function as a bill of particulars. The thought was that it could serve on a case-by-case basis to relieve the increasing pressure for heightened-pleading requirements.

MOTION TO STRIKE

The motion to strike may be used to eliminate "any redundant, immaterial, impertinent, or scandalous matter." Federal Rule 12(f). This use is uncommon and rarely successful.

On the one hand, we have seen the adjurations against "pleading evidence." But suppose the pleader does so plead. Obviously, saying too much is less of a sin than saying too little, and the needless pleading of evidence ordinarily does the adversary no harm. There is not much point in seeking to prune harmless evidentiary matter from pleadings, and the court will most often deny a motion to strike if it is made. See, e.g., Mitchell v. Hart, 41 F.R.D. 138 (S.D.N.Y.1966).

On the other hand, a statement of the claim that is neither short nor plain, because of flagrant violation of Rule 8(d)(1)'s mandate that the averments of a pleading be "simple, concise, and direct," can be stricken on motion even in the absence of other prejudice. See, e.g., Johns–Manville Sales Corp. v. Chicago Title & Trust Co., 261 F.Supp. 905 (N.D.Ill.1966) (single count ran to 69 paragraphs covering 39 pages, including numerous exhibits containing evidentiary material, some of it extraneous to any issue). More frequently, the court will strike matter that it finds to be prejudicial in other ways. See, e.g., Bernstein v. N.V. Nederlandsche–Amerikaansche Stoomvaart–Maatschappij, 7 F.R.D. 63 (S.D.N.Y.1946) (allegations concerning general attitude of Nazis toward Jews and defendant's knowledge that plaintiff was Jewish and at mercy of Nazis stricken from complaint for money had and received), appeal dismissed, 161 F.2d 733 (2d Cir.1947); Hughes v. Kaiser Jeep Corp., 40 F.R.D. 89 (D.S.C.1966) (allegations characterizing automobile manufactured by defendant as "death trap" stricken from complaint in death action).

Whether there is in fact prejudice usually turns on whether the pleadings are read or shown to the jury. There is a great variation in the rules of practice or custom on this point, in both state and federal courts. Some jurisdictions espouse the very strict rule that it is reversible error for the court or counsel to read or comment upon any pleading, except where a particular pleading is admissible in evidence and has in fact been introduced. See Louisville & N.R.R. v. Hull, 113 Ky. 561, 68 S.W. 433 (1902). But a substantial number of jurisdictions allow counsel to read the pleadings upon which the parties go to trial, whether or not such pleadings have been or could be introduced in evidence. In Woodworth v. Fuller, 235 Mass. 443, 446, 126 N.E. 781, 782 (1920), the court stated: "In this Commonwealth from time immemorial, in opening, the pleadings have been read to the jury. [Citations omitted.] At the close of trial, the writ and declaration and answers in their final form customarily go to the jury. [Citation omitted.] It is not necessary to consider whether this practice is founded on right rather than upon discretionary authority." Between these two extreme positions, the increasingly common practice today is routinely to keep the jury from hearing of or seeing pleadings not introduced in evidence, or at least to do so in any case where they contain prejudicial matter. See H.E. Miller Oil Co. v. Socony–Vacuum Oil Co., 37 F.Supp. 831 (E.D.Mo.1941) (pleadings are not evidence and may not be read to jury over objection).

Questions: (33) Even in Massachusetts, where the jury may hear and see the pleadings, some judges except a specific ad damnum clause from this practice. Assume, however, you are a plaintiff before a judge who allows reading such an ad damnum to the jury. Would doing so be tactically wise if the demand were low? if it were very inflated? See John J. McNaught & Martin L. Aronson, Trial Without Error—Plaintiff's Presentation, 57 Mass.L.Q. 171, 172–73 (1972).

(34) Plaintiff, suing in a federal court for her husband's wrongful death, prays in her complaint for damages "in the sum of $2,000,000.00." Defendant moves to strike from the complaint this portion of the prayer, contending that it is prejudicial for the jury to be informed of the amount plaintiff is seeking. Defendant points to psychology studies that show an anchoring effect whereby big demands generate higher awards. Plaintiff points to Rule 8(a)(3). What action should the court take on the motion? See 5 Wright & Miller § 1259.

Drewett v. Aetna Casualty & Surety Co.

United States District Court, Western District of Louisiana, 1975.
405 F.Supp. 877.

[Plaintiffs sued insurers to recover on flood insurance policies issued under the National Flood Insurance Act of 1968, 42 U.S.C. §§ 4001–4127, and also demanded penalties and attorney's fees under the state insurance law.]

■ NAUMAN, S. SCOTT, DISTRICT JUDGE. Defendants . . . have moved the Court to strike plaintiffs' demands for penalties and attorneys fees.

Federal Rules of Civil Procedure, Rule 12(f) provides that the motion to strike is directed toward any insufficient defense[f] or redundant, immaterial, impertinent or scandalous matter. Defendants' motion to strike herein is directed toward a specific allegation in the complaint; that is, plaintiffs' demand for penalties and attorneys fees theoretically provided for by Louisiana Revised Statutes 22:658. It is clear that this specific allegation of the complaint constitutes neither an insufficient defense nor a redundant, immaterial, impertinent or scandalous allegation such as covered by the motion to strike. Therefore, that particular procedural device is inappropriate in this case. Wright & Miller, Federal Practice and Procedure, Section 1380.

On the other hand, the subject matter of this motion may be properly presented to the Court by means of a motion directed to the failure to state a claim upon which relief can be granted. F.R.C.P. 12(b)(6). Authorities indicate that this motion may be used to challenge the sufficiency of part of a pleading such as a single count or claim for relief. Wright & Miller, Federal Practice and Procedure, Section 1358. . . .

. . . .

. . . We think it clear that Congress intended only Federal law to apply to claims arising under the National Flood Insurance Act.

In light of the above considerations, defendants' motion to dismiss the demand for penalties and attorneys fees for failure to state a claim upon which relief can be granted is hereby granted.

CONSEQUENCES OF MOTION TO DISMISS FOR FAILURE TO STATE A CLAIM

One study of motions to dismiss found in 1988 that the percentage of federal cases involving one or more Rule 12(b)(6) motions was 13% of the sample; the court decided such a motion in 10%, and granted it in 6%, of all cases in the sample; and grant of the motion resulted in termination of 3% of the sample. See Thomas E. Willging, Use of Rule 12(b)(6) in Two Federal District Courts 8–9 (1989); cf. Inst. for the Advancement of the Am. Legal System, Civil Case Processing in the Federal District Courts 47–49 (2009)

[f] The motion to strike an insufficient defense appeared in Rule 12(f) by a rather clumsy amendment in 1948. The plaintiff can use it to challenge the legal sufficiency of a defense. Such a motion to strike, if granted, will dispose of a question of law in advance of trial and may significantly simplify the trial. But courts show reluctance to strike a defense as insufficient. If the defense presents a question of law that the court can better determine in the context of facts proved at trial, the court plainly should not strike it. Yet there are many cases involving a purely legal question where the court strangely says that its function on a motion to strike is not to determine disputed questions of law.

(finding that 15% of federal cases in 2005 involved one or more motions to dismiss of any kind, of which 54% were granted in whole or part).

Consider a motion under Rule 12(b)(6) that the defendant aims at the whole complaint. Under Rule 15(a)(1)(B) the plaintiff may amend once as of right during the first twenty-one days that the motion to dismiss pends. Thus the plaintiff may render the motion moot by filing an amended complaint.

Now let us assume that the court *grants* the motion to dismiss. Although the right to amend as a matter of course at any time before service of a responsive pleading should be subject to the qualification that this right ceases with dismissal for failure to state a claim,[g] the order for dismissal itself will often expressly provide for leave to amend. Counsel will be well advised to request such a provision if there is room for amendment. In view of the admonition of Rule 15(a)(2) that the court should freely give leave to amend "when justice so requires," any refusal to allow leave is likely to constitute an abuse of discretion in the appellate court's eyes. See Britton v. Atlantic Coast Line R.R., 303 F.2d 274 (5th Cir.1962). But denial of leave to amend may sometimes be a proper exercise of discretion, especially if the plaintiff has made several unsuccessful efforts to state a claim and subsequent success seems unlikely. See Shall v. Henry, 211 F.2d 226 (7th Cir.1954) (after four amended complaints, no abuse of discretion to deny further opportunity to amend). If the trial court enters judgment of dismissal without leave to amend, it can later allow amendment only if the plaintiff moves for relief under Rule 59(e) within the time limit of twenty-eight days there provided, or perhaps under Rule 60(b) if the plaintiff can satisfy its requirements. See Keene Lumber Co. v. Leventhal, 165 F.2d 815 (1st Cir.1948).

On the one hand, if the plaintiff amends, the question may arise whether he thereby waives any subsequent chance to argue that the dismissal was erroneous. The more reasonable approach would reject waiver, so that the appellate court will reverse an adverse judgment on the amended complaint if the plaintiff can show that his defeat is directly traceable to the alteration of his case made necessary by the erroneous dismissal of his original complaint. Although the plaintiff who pleads over naturally cannot thereafter argue any claimed error in the dismissal for technical defects, he should still be able to argue the substantive validity of his original claim for relief and that the dismissal "struck a vital blow to a substantial part of plaintiff's cause of action." Williamson v. Liverpool & London & Globe Ins. Co., 141 F. 54, 57 (8th Cir.1905); see Blazer v. Black, 196 F.2d 139 (10th Cir.1952).[h]

---

[g] A few courts have refused to recognize this qualification and have indicated that amendment may be made as of right even after dismissal. E.g., Camp v. Gregory, 67 F.3d 1286 (7th Cir.1995). At the least, it would seem that any such amendment must come within a reasonable time after dismissal. See 6 Wright, Miller & Kane § 1483.

[h] In a few courts, it appears that there is such a waiver. E.g., Loux v. Rhay, 375 F.2d 55 (9th Cir.1967).

On the other hand, if the plaintiff stands on his pleading and appeals from the judgment of dismissal, the trial court no longer has jurisdiction to allow an amendment without leave of the appellate court. See Thompson v. Harry C. Erb, Inc., 240 F.2d 452 (3d Cir.1957). A reversal by the appellate court will reinstate the complaint, and naturally the defendant may then answer. But what if the appellate court agrees that the complaint was insufficient and affirms the judgment? The appellate court may in the interest of justice include in its mandate express leave to amend or to apply to the trial court for such relief. See 28 U.S.C. § 2106. If the mandate does not grant such leave, it seems that the trial court, at least in ordinary circumstances, lacks power to allow an amendment. See Tkaczyk v. Gallagher, 265 F.Supp. 791 (D.Conn.1967).

Next let us assume instead that the trial court *denies* the motion to dismiss. After denial the defendant may answer. Suppose she does, and then she loses at trial. May she on appeal from judgment for the plaintiff urge again the legal insufficiency of the plaintiff's claim, or has she forgone that opportunity by answering?

Question: (35) How is this question different from the question of the plaintiff's waiver by amending the complaint after the court grants a motion to dismiss?

On the one hand, if the defendant answers, it may be that the appellate court will treat the point as waived and so will not reexamine the action of the trial court in denying the motion to dismiss. But a legal-sufficiency question may reappear in a different guise. For example, at trial the defendant might move for judgment as a matter of law, contending that the plaintiff's proof does not constitute a claim for relief; the trial court's denial of that motion can be preserved for review on appeal from the final judgment; thus the appellate court may in effect be passing on one of the same questions that confronted the trial judge on the motion to dismiss the complaint, inasmuch as the legal-sufficiency question will be the same when the proof has established the allegations of the complaint and nothing more.

On the other hand, if the defendant declines to answer, the trial court will enter judgment for the plaintiff. If the appellate court reverses the judgment because of the complaint's insufficiency, the plaintiff ought to have leave to replead. But if the appellate court affirms the judgment, we have the question whether the judgment for the plaintiff should stand without more, or whether the appellate court should ever exercise its power to provide the defendant with leave to answer. Consider again the applicability of 28 U.S.C. § 2106.

Finally, note that we have set the foregoing discussion with respect to the consequences of both a grant and a denial of a motion to dismiss in the context of federal practice, with limited rights of interlocutory appeal. In jurisdictions that freely allow interlocutory appeals from rulings on such motions, the considerations are obviously different.

Question: (36) Is it fair to say that allowance of a right to replead after a party has stood on a pleading, appealed, and lost is tantamount to allowing an interlocutory appeal in derogation of the final decision rule? What bearing, if any, does 28 U.S.C. § 1292(b) have on the problem?

DENIALS

The common-law plea of the general issue, a means of making a blanket denial of all the plaintiff's allegations, has its analogue under the codes called the general denial. There was dispute as to whether use of the general denial conformed to the spirit of code pleading. It was forbidden in a few states, but its convenience was appealing and it has generally been allowed.

Note, however, that where the code in terms allows use of the general denial only when the defendant "intends in good faith to controvert all the allegations," as is true in many codes, the general denial is technically unavailable in most cases. The traditions of the bar in many states, however, are such that lawyers habitually file routine general denials when they should not. Neither published criticisms[i] nor ethical pronouncements[j] nor attempted regulation in the form of statutory imposition of costs for unfair use of the general denial[k] has been significantly effective. See Charles E. Clark, Handbook of the Law of Code Pleading 582 (2d ed. 1947). In explanation, if not justification, of the indiscriminate use of the general denial, one may say that typically it involves neither deception nor the intent to deceive. Counsel look upon this form of pleading as merely an easy way to satisfy a formal requirement, and they recognize that later developments will clarify what is actually in controversy.

Question: (37) Does this practice, and the attitude of the bar toward it, suggest the wisdom of abolishing the requirement of a responsive pleading, at least in some constantly recurring types of cases? But see State Farm Mut. Auto. Ins. Co. v. Riley, 199 F.R.D. 276 (N.D.Ill.2001) (laying out the judge's intention to apply Rule 8 strictly to answers).

Federal Rule 8(b)(3) preserves the general denial. However, it is available in theory even less frequently than under the codes.

Question: (38) Why do we say that it is less available in theory? What sanctions are available under the Federal Rules for abuse of the general denial? See United States v. Long, 10 F.R.D. 443 (D.Neb.1950); cf. American Auto Ass'n v. Rothman, 104 F.Supp. 655 (E.D.N.Y.1952).

Rule 8(b) also authorizes the "qualified general denial," which denies everything not expressly admitted; the "specific denial," which denies designated portions of the complaint; and the denial based on lack of "knowledge or information."

---

[i] E.g., Wilfred Bolster, The Municipal Court, 134 Boston B.Bull. 3, 7–8 (1938), reprinted in the first edition of this book at p. 418.

[j] E.g., N.Y.S.B.A. Comm. on Professional Ethics, Op. 469 (1977).

[k] E.g., Conn.Gen.Stat. § 52–99.

In addition to these forms of denial set forth in Rule 8(b), the federal courts allow a party without firsthand knowledge but with sufficient information to form a belief as to the truth of an allegation to deny it "upon information and belief." This form of denial has been generally permissible under state codes. The provision of Rule 11(b) that the signature to a pleading certifies "knowledge, information, and belief" lends support for the federal use of this form of denial. Indeed, Rule 11(b)(4) now authorizes denials that, "if specifically so identified, are reasonably based on belief or a lack of information." Such a pleading would be appropriate when the pleader has sufficient information to form a belief as to the questionable truth of the opponent's position, but does not feel comfortable asserting that the negative is true. See Boykin v. v. KeyCorp, 521 F.3d 202, 215 (2d Cir.2008). For an example, the defendant might have a reasonable basis for thinking that the plaintiff will not be able to prove her case.

Questions: (39) In the light of these rules, consider how in each of the following situations the defendant's attorney should plead in response to the plaintiff's assertion in the federal complaint of a fact upon which the plaintiff has the burden of proof:

(a) Neither the defendant nor his attorney knows whether the fact is true, but it involves a matter of public record easily verifiable.

(b) The defendant tells his attorney that he thinks the fact to be likely true but does not think the plaintiff can prove it.

(c) The only person with firsthand knowledge of the fact is *W*, an apparently disinterested witness. The defendant's attorney interviews *W*, who says the fact is true. The attorney is impressed by her seeming candor and believes that she is telling the truth.

(d) The attorney is unimpressed by *W* and believes that she may well be lying or mistaken.

(40) *P*'s complaint includes allegations that, if true, would establish that *D* was guilty of a crime. *D* in his answer refuses to respond to these allegations upon the ground that a response might tend to incriminate him. *P* moves for judgment on the pleadings. What decision? See National Acceptance Co. of Am. v. Bathalter, 705 F.2d 924 (7th Cir.1983) (deny motion).

AFFIRMATIVE DEFENSES

Federal Rule 8(c)(1) enumerates multiple affirmative defenses, but the list is not exhaustive, as the defendant must plead affirmatively any other matter constituting an avoidance or affirmative defense. One example of an unlisted affirmative defense is "prior pending action," which we have encountered several times. For another example, in Schmidtke v. Conesa, 141 F.2d 634 (1st Cir.1944), the plaintiff sued for overtime pay under the Fair Labor Standards Act, 29 U.S.C. § 216(b). After nonjury trial the district court dismissed his complaint on the ground that his employment had been in a professional capacity and hence was exempt under § 213(a)(1) of the Act, even though this matter had not been specifically pleaded or tried. The court of appeals reversed, holding that exemption was a matter of defense that the defendant had to have raised under Rule 8(c)(1), although not specifically enumerated there.

The pleader thus may have difficulty in determining whether a particular matter is an affirmative defense or instead is one that the parties can litigate under a denial. There is no sure test. But statutes, precedents, and form books will often provide the answer. If not, one must look to considerations of history and apparent logic and of convenience, fairness, and good policy, similar to those that govern allocation of the burden of proof and that Topic A of Part Eight will explain further.

In fact, the allocation of the burden of allegation customarily parallels the allocation of the burden of proof, but this is not invariably so. Indeed, as Part Two observed, the Supreme Court of the United States has indicated that Rule 8(c) governs pleading in federal court even though burden of proof must under Erie follow state law.

Questions: (41) *P* sues *D* for damage to his growing crops by reason of *D*'s negligent failure to keep open a drainage ditch. *D*'s answer is a general denial. Should evidence be admissible that the flooding of *P*'s property was caused by a rain so unprecedented as to be regarded an act of God and not by any fault of *D*? See Chesapeake & O. Ry. Co. v. Carmichael, 298 Ky. 769, 184 S.W.2d 91 (1944) (yes).

(42) *P* sues *D* for breach of contract. *D*'s answer is a general denial. Should evidence be admissible that the alleged offer and acceptance were made in jest? See Good v. Chiles, 57 S.W.2d 1100 (Tex.Comm'n App.1933) (no).

Still another example of an affirmative defense not listed in Federal Rule 8(c)(1) is the defense of truth in actions for libel or slander. Although the plaintiff must allege falsity in the complaint, truth is nevertheless an affirmative defense that the defendant must plead and prove. The defendant cannot offer evidence of truth under a general denial.

Question: (43) The plaintiff suing on an obligation to pay money must allege nonpayment in the complaint, but payment is nevertheless an affirmative defense. See FDIC v. Siraco, 174 F.2d 360 (2d Cir.1949). Under the Federal Rules, should a specific denial of the plaintiff's allegation of nonpayment be sufficient to raise the defense of payment?

NYCPLR § 3018(b) provides: "*Affirmative defenses.* A party shall plead all matters which if not pleaded would be likely to take the adverse party by surprise or would raise issues of fact not appearing on the face of a prior pleading such as [here are listed twelve affirmative defenses generally corresponding to those in Federal Rule 8(c)(1), not mentioning some on the federal list but including comparative negligence]. The application of this subdivision shall not be confined to the instances enumerated."

Question: (44) Does this New York provision make easier or harder the task of an attorney trying to decide whether to treat a matter as an affirmative defense?

PLEADING PLAINTIFF'S NEGLIGENCE

We have intermittently discussed the pleading and proof of contributory negligence, as in Part One, supra pp. 37, 159, because it often provides a good and simple illustration. It nevertheless can present some complications. See generally Fleming James, Jr., Geoffrey C. Hazard, Jr. & John Leubsdorf, Civil Procedure 198–204, 220–21, 420–23 (5th ed. 2001); W. Page Keeton, Dan B. Dobbs, Robert E. Keeton & David G. Owen, Prosser and Keeton on the Law of Torts 451 (5th ed. 1984).

Over time, there have been various views with respect to the pleading and proof of contributory negligence, including the following:

1. The plaintiff must plead and prove his own due care.

2. The plaintiff must prove his due care, but need not in terms allege it, the allegation that the defendant's negligence caused the injury being sufficient.

3. The defendant must plead and prove contributory negligence. (This became the most common view.)

4. The defendant must prove contributory negligence, but may do so under a denial that the defendant's negligence caused the injury.

A number of problems could arise in a federal court sitting in a state that took position (1), as Illinois did until 1981 when it converted to comparative negligence. First, Francis v. Humphrey, 25 F.Supp. 1 (E.D.Ill. 1938), coming after Erie and the adoption of the Federal Rules, held that an allegation of due care was necessary in order to state a claim. Should this be so? See Merit Ins. Co. v. Colao, 603 F.2d 654, 659 (7th Cir.1979) (no). Second, assuming that the plaintiff does allege his own due care, must the defendant still plead contributory negligence pursuant to Rule 8(c)(1) in order to have the issue in the case, or does a specific denial of the plaintiff's allegation of due care suffice? It does not seem that the defendant should have to plead contributory negligence. But the cautious defendant would be wise to heed the literal language of Rule 8(c)(1). Third, assuming that the defendant does allege contributory negligence, does she have to worry about the possible impact of certain state cases, e.g., Boyd v. Geary, 126 Conn. 396, 12 A.2d 644 (1940), holding that when a party needlessly assumes the burden of pleading a matter, that party thereby also assumes the burden of proving it? This doctrine has little to recommend it and is, moreover, pretty clearly a procedural matter that a federal court would not follow under Erie. The cautious defendant should make it plain, nevertheless, that she is not assuming the burden of proof.

Questions: (45) In a jurisdiction taking position (3), the plaintiff unnecessarily alleges his own due care. The answer specifically denies this allegation. Is the issue of contributory negligence in the case? See Rider v. Jarrard, 109 Ga.App. 645, 136 S.E.2d 920 (1964) (yes).

(46) Suppose instead that the answer is a general denial. Is the issue of contributory negligence in the case? Compare Wells v. Steinek, 49 Ga.App. 482, 176 S.E. 42 (1934) (yes), with Capps v. Beene, 162 S.W.2d 80, 82–83 (Mo.Ct.App.1942) (no).

(47) How does all this learning carry over to pleading under the now much more common regime of comparative negligence? See 4 Fowler V. Harper, Fleming James, Jr. & Oscar S. Gray, The Law of Torts § 22.11 (2d ed. 1986).

(b) COUNTERCLAIMS

Recoupment.—At common law there were narrowly confined situations where a defendant, by asserting a claim in the action, could reduce the recovery to which the plaintiff would otherwise get. A building contractor sues the owner for work done and materials furnished; in that action the owner might seek a recoupment on the ground that the contractor did not do the work well; and if the recoupment succeeded, any contractor's recovery would decrease accordingly.

Sedgwick says that "recoupment, in its original sense, was a mere right of deduction from the amount of the plaintiff's recovery, on the ground that his damages were not really as high as he alleged," but in time the sharpness of this definition diminished. 3 Theodore Sedgwick, Damages 2162 (9th ed. 1912). For instance, where the plaintiff sued on a promissory note given for the sale of his business, the defendant could recoup for the plaintiff's breach of an agreement not to compete with the business.

In summary, a recoupment could reduce the plaintiff's claim but could not result in an affirmative judgment in the action in the defendant's favor. It must have arisen out of the *same transaction* as the plaintiff's claim. However, to maintain a recoupment it was not necessary that the plaintiff's or the defendant's claim be liquidated or otherwise certain in amount.

Question: (48) Would recoupment be available to a defendant in a highway accident case where both plaintiff and defendant received injuries and each asserts that the other was solely to blame?

As the matter asserted by way of recoupment must have arisen out of the same transaction as plaintiff's claim, it would naturally follow in most cases that if plaintiff's action was not barred by the statute of limitations, the recoupment matter would not be barred if an independent action had been brought upon it on the date of commencement of plaintiff's action. In a small number of cases this would not be true. Moreover, defendant's recoupment might be barred as an independent action at the time defendant pleaded, even if timely on the date of commencement of plaintiff's action. It was laid down as a general rule, however, that if plaintiff's action was timely, defendant's recoupment was also timely.

Setoff.—Where the defendant's claim arose out of a different transaction, recoupment was unavailable. So, at early common law the defendant could secure adjudication of the defendant's claim only by bringing an independent action. Equity, however, borrowed the Roman and civil-law doctrine of compensation and allowed the setoff of mutual debts. See 3 Joseph Story, Commentaries on Equity Jurisprudence § 1881 (14th ed. 1918).

In the course of time this principle of equity carried over to the law courts. The first step was the statute of 4 Anne, ch. 17, § 11 (1705), which made setoff available at law in cases where the parties were mutually indebted and the plaintiff was insolvent. Then the statute of 2 Geo. 2, ch. 22, § 13 (1729), as amended by 8 Geo. 2, ch. 24, § 5 (1735), eliminated the requirement of insolvency and made setoff generally available wherever there were mutual debts.

In summary, this statutory setoff, like recoupment, could not provide affirmative relief, and so its only effect was to reduce the plaintiff's claim. Although it was not necessary that the claims arose from the same transaction, the plea of setoff lay only for *mutual debts certain in amount*, where the claims on both sides involved liquidated debts or debts that could be readily and without difficulty ascertained. (There were, however, some inroads on these English rules in the United States.)

Unlike recoupment, defendant's plea in setoff was not immune from the bar of the statute of limitations. But the crucial date was the day when plaintiff instituted his action. The setoff was therefore timely even though the statutory period for bringing an independent action upon it had expired between the commencement of plaintiff's action and the bringing of the claim in setoff. See Walker v. Clements, 117 Eng.Rep. 755 (Q.B.1850).

Counterclaim.—New York made provision by amendment to the Field Code in 1852 for counterclaims, which were materially broader than common-law recoupment or statutory setoff. Many code states soon followed New York's lead. The most striking change was to permit the defendant to recover an affirmative judgment. Thus the defendant whose claim exceeded that of the plaintiff could wind up with a money judgment in the defendant's favor, as could the defendant whose counterclaim succeeded when the plaintiff's claim failed. Nor did contract claims arising from different transactions have to be certain in amount, as their setoff ancestor required.

The New York provision allowed as a counterclaim: (1) "A cause of action arising out of the contract or transaction set forth in the complaint, as the foundation of the plaintiff's claim, or connected with the subject of the action"; or (2) "In an action arising on contract, any other cause of action arising also on contract, and existing at the commencement of the action." 1852 N.Y.Laws ch. 392, amending Code of Procedure § 150. Code provisions in other states were usually to the same effect.

Words like "transaction" give the usual troubles. The other restrictions also create obvious classification problems, such as whether an action in quasi contract is an action "on contract." Furthermore, a number of the codes provide expressly, or courts have construed them to mean, that the counterclaim must tend to diminish or defeat the plaintiff's recovery. This requirement may have a curiously restrictive effect. It has been held, for instance, that in a suit in equity for cancellation of a deed to real property, a counterclaim for a money judgment for expenditures made in the operation of the property is improper. Bandy v. Westover, 200 Cal. 222, 252 P. 593 (1927).

In modern times many states, including New York in its CPLR § 3019(a), have extended the scope of this *permissive* counterclaim provision in the same fashion as Federal Rule 13(b). A good many states, but not New York, have gone further to provide as well for *compulsory* counterclaims along the lines of Federal Rule 13(a).

STATUTE OF LIMITATIONS

Courts have had difficulty in dealing with the statute of limitations as applied to counterclaims. They have generally heeded the common-law precedents developed in recoupment and setoff cases. Accordingly, in the absence of a statute dictating a different result, the usual view is that the defendant may use a counterclaim of the old-fashioned types "defensively," that is, in reduction of the plaintiff's claim, no matter when the events giving rise to the counterclaim occurred—except the defendant cannot maintain a counterclaim if it arose from a different transaction and if an independent action upon it was barred when the plaintiff instituted his action.

In several states, statutes deal specifically with the problem of time limitations on counterclaims. Occasionally these statutes seem more restrictive than the common-law approach. For example, a former Wisconsin statute provided: "A cause of action upon which an action cannot be maintained, as prescribed in this chapter [on limitations of actions], cannot be effectually interposed as a defense, counterclaim or set-off." Wis.Stat. § 893.27 (1977) (repealed 1979).

Other jurisdictions take different and more permissive approaches, but all jurisdictions fall along a spectrum that we shall now sketch. Note for each situation whether the counterclaim merely relates back to the time of the complaint, whether there is a requirement of transactional relation, and whether only "defensive" relief is allowed. The task is to choose the optimal approach, which lies somewhere along the spectrum.

Questions: (49) Under a statute like that of Wisconsin, which we take as the first situation on our spectrum, a doctor sues a patient for professional services within the period of limitations for a contract action, but the patient is quite unhappy with those services. (a) After institution of suit but before answer, the shorter statute on malpractice actions runs. Can the patient set up "defensively" that the doctor negligently performed the services, a matter that was a basis for recoupment at common law? (b) Can the patient do so if the doctor's suit was brought after the malpractice statute had run? See Peterson v. Feyereisen, 203 Wis. 294, 234 N.W. 496 (1931) (indicating yes).

(50) On June 1, *A* sues *B* on a note for $1000. On June 15, *B* counterclaims on another note for $3000, upon which the limitations period expired on June 5. The counterclaim statute is like Federal Rule 13(b), and the statute of limitations contains no specific reference to counterclaims. *A* moves against the counterclaim. What result? Note that an English court in dealing with this problem followed setoff's Walker v. Clements to the extent of allowing the "defensive" use of the counterclaim, denying affirmative recovery because it was unknown in Walker's

time. Lowe v. Bentley, 44 T.L.R. 388 (K.B.1928). So, would you dismiss *B*'s counterclaim, follow Lowe v. Bentley, or allow *B* an affirmative recovery? Would your answer be different if both claims were contract claims for uncertain amounts, or if both were for unrelated torts?

Azada v. Carson

United States District Court, District of Hawaii, 1966.
252 F.Supp. 988.

■ TAVARES, DISTRICT JUDGE. On October 12, 1963, plaintiff Mariano Azada was driving a car which collided with a car driven by defendant Roger Carson. Plaintiff and his wife filed suit for personal injuries three days before the running of the two-year statute of limitations.

Defendant was not served with process until nearly three months after the complaint was filed; thus the counterclaim later filed by the defendant was filed more than two years following the date of the collision. Plaintiffs move to dismiss the counterclaim on the ground that it was filed after the statute of limitations had become a bar.

Jurisdiction here is based upon diversity of citizenship, and therefore this Court must apply Hawaii law. However, no Hawaii statute nor reported decision had been found that disposes of the question here.

Authorities outside of Hawaii are divided on the question. C.J.S. Limitations of Actions § 285, pp. 342–343, reports:

> "There is a conflict of opinion as to when a claim interposed as a set-off or counterclaim becomes barred by the statute of limitations. The weight of authority supports the rule, said to be the better rule, that, where defendant's claim, asserted in a set-off or counterclaim, was an existing debt not barred by the statute of limitations at the time plaintiff's action was begun, it will be a valid set-off or counterclaim, although the statutory period may have elapsed before the filing of the answer setting it up, provided, under some of the statutes, the counterclaim arose out of the same transaction as gave rise to the main action."

Plaintiff argues that most of the cases allowing a counterclaim, if it was not barred at the time the action was begun, involved contracts and not torts. But there seems to be no logical reason for making such a distinction. The same considerations of fair play and justice apply, whether the action is based upon contract or tort.

Statutes of limitation are statutes of repose—they are designed to bar stale claims. Where, as in this case, the counterclaim arises from the same incident as the complaint, the counterclaim is no more stale than the complaint.

Simple justice dictates that if the plaintiffs are given an opportunity to present a claim for relief based upon a particular automobile collision, the defendant should not be prevented from doing so by a mere technicality.

Without meaning to suggest in any way that the instant suit involves frivolous claims, the rule adopted by this Court will also have the beneficial effect of tending to discourage the filing of frivolous claims just before the running of the statute of limitations.

Therefore plaintiffs' motion to dismiss the counterclaim is hereby denied.

New York Civil Practice Law and Rules

§ 203. *Method of computing periods of limitation generally*

. . . .

(d) **Defense or counterclaim.** A defense or counterclaim is interposed when a pleading containing it is served. A defense or counterclaim is not barred if it was not barred at the time the claims asserted in the complaint were interposed, except that if the defense or counterclaim arose from the transactions, occurrences, or series of transactions or occurrences, upon which a claim asserted in the complaint depends, it is not barred to the extent of the demand in the complaint notwithstanding that it was barred at the time the claims asserted in the complaint were interposed.[1]

. . . .

Question: (51) The Federal Tort Claims Act provides in 28 U.S.C. § 2401(b) that a tort claim against the United States must be asserted within two years after such claim accrues. The United States sues for damage to a government-owned motor vehicle more than two years after the date of the accident but well within the applicable statute of limitations for motor vehicle torts. The defendant counterclaims for her own damage, seeking affirmative relief. Should the counterclaim be dismissed on the government's motion? Compare United States v. Capital Transit Co., 108 F.Supp. 348 (D.D.C.1952) (no), with United States v. Yellow Cab Co., 188 F.Supp. 660 (E.D.Pa.1960) (yes).

United States Code, Title 28

§ 2415. *Time for commencing actions brought by the United States*

. . . .

[1] Massachusetts, which now has a counterclaim rule modeled on Federal Rule 13, has a limitations statute to the same effect as this New York provision. Mass.Gen.Laws Ann. ch. 260, § 36. For the background of the Massachusetts statute, see Bose Corp. v. Consumers Union of United States, 367 Mass. 424, 326 N.E.2d 8 (1975) (Kaplan, J.).

(f) The provisions of this section shall not prevent the assertion, in an action against the United States or an officer or agency thereof, of any claim of the United States or an officer or agency thereof against an opposing party, a co-party, or a third party that arises out of the transaction or occurrence that is the subject matter of the opposing party's claim. A claim of the United States or an officer or agency thereof that does not arise out of the transaction or occurrence that is the subject matter of the opposing party's claim may, if time-barred, be asserted only by way of offset and may be allowed in an amount not to exceed the amount of the opposing party's recovery.

. . . .

Questions: (52) To close out the spectrum, imagine that *P* sues *D* for breach of contract within the applicable period of limitations but after the statute has run on *D*'s unrelated tort claim. Can any argument be made to allow *D* affirmative relief by way of counterclaim?

(53) For a slightly different problem, assume that a claim upon which the statute of limitations has otherwise run would have been saved under the applicable law in a federal-court action by one or another of the above-suggested approaches, if the defendant had pleaded it as a counterclaim in the answer. However, the defendant omitted it from the answer and only later added it by amendment. The plaintiff moves against the counterclaim. What result? See Diematic Mfg. Corp. v. Packaging Indus., 412 F.Supp. 1367 (S.D.N.Y.1976) (applying Rule 15(c)(2) to transactionally related counterclaim).

(c) REPLIES

In the absence of a counterclaim, to which the plaintiff must prepare a responsive pleading, the pleading process under the Federal Rules stops with the answer, save in the rare case where the court orders a reply.

The majority of codes, however, carry pleading somewhat further, although none of them adheres to the common-law scheme of continuing the pleadings until they terminate in an issue of fact or law. Typically, the codes forbid further pleadings after the reply (the common-law replication). But the codes vary in their provisions with respect to that reply. On the one hand, they frequently require a reply to new matter in the answer, else the new matter stands as admitted. On the other hand, New Jersey Court Rule 4:5–1(a) requires such a reply only if the plaintiff wishes to raise new matter in avoidance of the defense, and prohibits a reply simply to deny new matter in the answer.

The requirement of a reply to new matter creates pitfalls for the pleader that do not exist when permitted pleadings end with the answer. We have, for instance, already seen something of the difficulties in deciding whether the defendant can show a particular matter of defense under a general denial. If the defendant's answer unnecessarily includes matter that would be open to the defendant under a general denial, it is not "new matter" that stands as admitted if not denied in a reply. But the consequences of a wrong guess may be serious. Suppose the defendant in a case involving the facts of question (41) pleads that the plaintiff's loss was due to an act of God. The plaintiff's attorney does not reply, believing that this matter is provable under a general denial (as the Kentucky court in the cited Carmichael case held) and hence that no reply is necessary. The defendant moves for judgment on the pleadings. If the court takes a view opposed to the Carmichael case (as some courts have), then the plaintiff has unwittingly admitted the existence of a good defense to his claim.

A reply may also involve the hazards of departure. Just as at common law, a code plaintiff may not in his reply abandon the claim stated in his complaint and rely upon another. In Grobart v. Society for Establishing Useful Manufacturers, 2 N.J. 136, 65 A.2d 833 (1949), the court inveighed against permitting a pleader to shift his ground from pleading to pleading, as distinguished from allowing in the same pleading alternative or hypothetical or inconsistent positions. With the present-day freedom of amendment a plaintiff can ordinarily avoid a departure by simply amending his complaint when the need to do so becomes manifest. Some observers have indeed suggested that for this reason a rigid enforcement of the rule against departure would be inconsistent with the modern spirit of procedure. See Commentary, Departure in the Reply, 4 Fed.R.Serv. (Callaghan) 889 (1941). Nevertheless, as the following cases demonstrate, other parts of the old learning do carry over, even to the Federal Rules.

Gunder v. New York Times Co.

United States District Court, Southern District of New York, 1941.
37 F.Supp. 911.

■ CONGER, DISTRICT JUDGE. Plaintiff has moved for an order striking out all of the affirmative defenses in the answer as legally insufficient, and striking out specific paragraphs as irrelevant, etc.

Although opposing the motion on the merits, defendant has challenged the sufficiency of the complaint, and asks that it be dismissed. Both under the state and federal practice, the principle is well settled that a bad answer is good enough for a bad complaint. In Baxter v. McDonnell, 154 N.Y. 432, at page 436, 48 N.E. 816, at page 817, it is stated: "The rule is that, on demurrer to an answer for insufficiency, the defendant may attack the complaint on the ground that it does not state facts sufficient to constitute a cause of action. . . . A demurrer searches the record for the first fault in pleading, and reaches back to condemn the first pleading that is defective in substance, because he who does not so plead as to invite an issue cannot compel his adversary to so plead as to accept it. . . ." See also Gise v. Brooklyn Society for the Prevention of Cruelty to Children, 262 N.Y. 114, 186 N.E. 412. In Cheatham v. Wheeling & L.E. Ry. Co., D.C., 37 F.2d 593, 598, the court stated: "It is a settled, though oft-forgotten, rule that a plaintiff's demurrer to a defense tests his own pleading. . . . A motion to strike out pleadings or parts thereof as insufficient in law is the modern equivalent of a demurrer. Carmody, Pleading and Practice in New York, § 246. When addressed to a defense in the answer of a defendant or to a replication by a plaintiff, it opens up the whole record as a demurrer did of old.

"The rationale of this principle is that such an attack, whether by motion or demurrer, has to be based on, and necessarily presupposes, a sound pleading in behalf of the party making it. Otherwise, it would be futile to grant the relief, however great the infirmity of the pleading attacked might be." See also Gay v. E.H. Moore, Inc., D.C., 26 F.Supp. 749; Ashman v. Coleman, D.C., 25 F.Supp. 388.

The sound reasons underlying this rule are just as cogent since the advent of the new Federal Rules as they were before. A bad complaint tenders no issue and requires no answer. Thus it is necessary to examine into the sufficiency of the complaint at bar.

I am satisfied that no cause of action is stated in this complaint.

[A discussion of the substantive law of libel is omitted.]

Feeling as I do that the matter set forth in the complaint is clearly not libelous, I am constrained to dismiss the complaint. The motion, therefore, is denied, and plaintiff's complaint dismissed. Settle order on notice.

WATERTOWN MILK PRODUCERS' CO–OPERATIVE ASS'N v. VAN CAMP PACKING CO., 199 Wis. 379, 226 N.W. 378 (1929). After pointing out that an essential allegation was lacking in the complaint, the court said:

"A demurrer to the complaint would have been sustained. But there was no demurrer to the complaint. The defendants answered, and by their answers they supplied the substance of this essential allegation. A demurrer to the answer searches the record. It goes back to the complaint. If the complaint is bad the demurrer will be overruled, as a bad answer is considered good enough for a bad complaint. However, where the entire record reveals facts constituting a good cause of action, a demurrer to the answer will not be overruled on the ground that the complaint does not state facts sufficient to constitute a cause of action. Colwell Lead Co. v. Home Title Ins. Co., 154 App.Div. 83, 138 N.Y.S. 738; Sill v. Sill, 31 Kan. 248, 1 P. 556. While there are decisions holding that upon a demurrer to the answer the averments in the answer will not be permitted to supply a deficiency in the complaint, we find very little considerate discussion of the subject. . . .

". . . Upon mature consideration, it would seem that the cause of simplified procedure is illy served by a rule which ignores the allegations of the answer where the complaint is under scrutiny by virtue of a demurrer to the answer. Where in such case it appears that essential facts omitted in the complaint are supplied by the answer of the one who challenges the complaint, why should the litigants be required to retrace their steps and frame new pleadings all along the line?''

Whatever the procedural arrangement may be, there comes a point when no further pleading is proper and new matter in the last permitted pleading is taken as ''denied or avoided,'' as it is under Federal Rule 8(b)(6). This means that the pleadings may leave the parties in ignorance of the exact issues, with clarification coming, if at all, from any disclosure, discovery, and pretrial conference devices that may exist or from informal discussion between counsel.

TOPIC B

DISCOVERY

SECTION 1. SCOPE OF DISCOVERY

(a) WORK PRODUCT

Hickman v. Taylor

Supreme Court of the United States, 1947.
329 U.S. 495, 67 S.Ct. 385.

■ MR. JUSTICE MURPHY delivered the opinion of the Court.

This case presents an important problem under the Federal Rules of Civil Procedure as to the extent to which a party may inquire into oral and written statements of witnesses, or other information, secured by an adverse party's counsel in the course of preparation for possible litigation after a claim has arisen. Examination into a person's files and records, including those resulting from the professional activities of an attorney, must be judged with care. It is not without reason that various safeguards have been established to preclude unwarranted excursions into the privacy of a man's work. At the same time, public policy supports reasonable and necessary inquiries. Properly to balance these competing interests is a delicate and difficult task.

On February 7, 1943, the tug "J.M. Taylor" sank while engaged in helping to tow a car float of the Baltimore & Ohio Railroad across the Delaware River at Philadelphia. The accident was apparently unusual in nature, the cause of it still being unknown. Five of the nine crew members were drowned. Three days later the tug owners and the underwriters employed a law firm, of which respondent Fortenbaugh is a member, to defend them against potential suits by representatives of the deceased crew members and to sue the railroad for damages to the tug.

A public hearing was held on March 4, 1943, before the United States Steamboat Inspectors, at which the four survivors were examined. This testimony was recorded and made available to all interested parties. Shortly thereafter, Fortenbaugh privately interviewed the survivors and took statements from them with an eye toward the anticipated litigation; the survivors signed these statements on March 29. Fortenbaugh also interviewed other persons believed to have some information relating to the accident and in some cases he made memoranda of what they told him. At the time when Fortenbaugh secured the statements of the survivors, representatives of two of the deceased crew members had been in communication with him. Ultimately claims were presented by representatives of all five of the deceased; four of the claims, however, were settled without litigation. The fifth claimant, petitioner herein, brought suit in a federal court under the Jones Act on November 26, 1943, naming as defendants the two tug owners, individually and as partners, and the railroad.

One year later, petitioner filed 39 interrogatories directed to the tug owners. The 38th interrogatory read: "State whether any statements of the members of the crews of the Tugs 'J.M. Taylor' and 'Philadelphia' or of any other vessel were taken in connection with the towing of the car float and the sinking of the Tug 'John M. Taylor.' Attach hereto exact copies of all such statements if in writing, and if oral, set forth in detail the exact provisions of any such oral statements or reports."

Supplemental interrogatories asked whether any oral or written statements, records, reports or other memoranda had been made concerning any matter relative to the towing operation, the sinking of the tug, the salvaging and repair of the tug, and the death of the deceased. If the answer was in the affirmative, the tug owners were then requested to set forth the nature of all such records, reports, statements or other memoranda.

The tug owners, through Fortenbaugh, answered all of the interrogatories except No. 38 and the supplemental ones just described. While admitting that statements of the survivors had been taken, they declined to summarize or set forth the contents. They did so on the ground that such requests called "for privileged matter obtained in preparation for litigation" and constituted "an attempt to obtain indirectly counsel's private files." It was claimed that answering these requests "would involve practically turning over not only the complete files, but also the telephone records and, almost, the thoughts of counsel."

In connection with the hearing on these objections, Fortenbaugh made a written statement and gave an informal oral deposition explaining the circumstances under which he had taken the statements. But he was not expressly asked in the deposition to produce the statements. The District Court for the Eastern District of Pennsylvania, sitting en banc, held that the requested matters were not privileged. 4 F.R.D. 479. The court then decreed that the tug owners and Fortenbaugh, as counsel and agent for the tug owners, forthwith "answer Plaintiff's 38th interrogatory and supplementary interrogatories; produce all written statements of witnesses obtained by Mr. Fortenbaugh, as counsel and agent for Defendants; state in substance any fact concerning this case which Defendants learned through oral statements made by witnesses to Mr. Fortenbaugh whether or not included in his private memoranda and produce Mr. Fortenbaugh's memoranda containing statements of fact by witnesses or to submit these memoranda to the Court for determination of those portions which should be revealed to Plaintiff." Upon their refusal, the court adjudged them in contempt and ordered them imprisoned until they complied.

The Third Circuit Court of Appeals, also sitting en banc, reversed the judgment of the District Court. 153 F.2d 212. It held that the information here sought was part of the "work product of the lawyer" and hence privileged from discovery under the Federal Rules of Civil Procedure. The importance of the problem, which has engendered a great divergence of views among district courts, led us to grant certiorari. 328 U.S. 876, 66 S.Ct. 1337.

The pre-trial deposition-discovery mechanism established by Rules 26 to 37 is one of the most significant innovations of the Federal Rules of Civil Procedure. Under the prior federal practice, the pre-trial functions of notice-giving, issue-formulation and fact-revelation were performed primarily and inadequately by the pleadings. Inquiry into the issues and the facts before trial was narrowly confined and was often cumbersome in method. The new rules, however, restrict the pleadings to the task of general notice-giving and invest the deposition-discovery process with a vital role in the preparation for trial. The various instruments of discovery now serve (1) as a device, along with the pre-trial hearing under Rule 16, to narrow and clarify the basic issues between the parties, and (2) as a device for ascertaining the facts, or information as to the existence or whereabouts of facts, relative to those issues. Thus civil trials in the federal courts no longer need be carried on in the dark. The way is now clear, consistent with recognized privileges, for the parties to obtain the fullest possible knowledge of the issues and facts before trial.

[The Court here said that in using interrogatories to obtain documents the petitioner chose the wrong device, but the Court decided to overlook this procedural irregularity and reach the underlying problem of scope of discovery.]

In urging that he has a right to inquire into the materials secured and prepared by Fortenbaugh, petitioner emphasizes that the deposition-discovery portions of the Federal Rules of Civil Procedure are designed to enable the parties to discover the true facts and to compel their disclosure wherever they may be found. It is said that inquiry may be made under these rules, epitomized by Rule 26, as to any relevant matter which is not privileged; and since the discovery provisions are to be applied as broadly and liberally as possible, the privilege limitation must be restricted to its narrowest bounds. On the premise that the attorney-client privilege is the one involved in this case, petitioner argues that it must be strictly confined to confidential communications made by a client to his attorney. And since the materials here in issue were secured by Fortenbaugh from third persons rather than from his clients, the tug owners, the conclusion is reached that these materials are proper subjects for discovery under Rule 26.

As additional support for this result, petitioner claims that to prohibit discovery under these circumstances would give a corporate defendant a tremendous advantage in a suit by an individual plaintiff. Thus in a suit by an injured employee against a railroad or in a suit by an insured person against an insurance company the corporate defendant could pull a dark veil of secrecy over all the pertinent facts it can collect after the claim arises merely on the assertion that such facts were gathered by its large staff of attorneys and claim agents. At the same time, the individual plaintiff, who often has direct knowledge of the matter in issue and has no counsel until some time after his claim arises could be compelled to disclose all the intimate details of his case. By endowing with immunity from disclosure all that a lawyer discovers in the course of his duties, it is said, the rights of individual litigants in such cases are drained of vitality and the lawsuit becomes more of a battle of deception than a search for truth.

But framing the problem in terms of assisting individual plaintiffs in their suits against corporate defendants is unsatisfactory. Discovery concededly may work to the disadvantage as well as to the advantage of individual plaintiffs. Discovery, in other words, is not a one-way proposition. It is available in all types of cases at the behest of any party, individual or corporate, plaintiff or defendant. The problem thus far transcends the situation confronting this petitioner. And we must view that problem in light of the limitless situations where the particular kind of discovery sought by petitioner might be used.

We agree, of course, that the deposition-discovery rules are to be accorded a broad and liberal treatment. No longer can the time-honored cry of "fishing expedition" serve to preclude a party from inquiring into the facts underlying his opponent's case. Mutual knowledge of all the relevant facts gathered by both parties is essential to proper litigation. To that end, either party may compel the other to disgorge whatever facts he has in his possession. The deposition-discovery procedure simply advances the stage at which the disclosure can be compelled from the time of trial to the period preceding it, thus reducing the possibility of surprise. But discovery, like all matters of procedure, has ultimate and necessary boundaries. As indicated by Rules 30(b) and (d) and 31(d),[a] limitations inevitably arise when it can be shown that the examination is being conducted in bad faith or in such a manner as to annoy, embarrass or oppress the person subject to the inquiry. And as Rule 26(b) provides, further limitations come into existence when the inquiry touches upon the irrelevant or encroaches upon the recognized domains of privilege.

We also agree that the memoranda, statements and mental impressions in issue in this case fall outside the scope of the attorney-client privilege and hence are not protected from discovery on that basis. It is unnecessary here to delineate the content and scope of that privilege as recognized in the federal courts. For present purposes, it suffices to note that the protective cloak of this privilege does not extend to information which an attorney secures from a witness while acting for his client in anticipation of litigation. Nor does this privilege concern the memoranda, briefs, communications and other writings prepared by counsel for his own use in prosecuting his client's case; and it is equally unrelated to writings which reflect an attorney's mental impressions, conclusions, opinions or legal theories.

But the impropriety of invoking that privilege does not provide an answer to the problem before us. Petitioner has made more than an ordinary request for relevant, non-privileged facts in the possession of his

[a] Old Rules 30(b) and 31(d) now appear as Rule 26(c).

adversaries or their counsel. He has sought discovery as of right of oral and written statements of witnesses whose identity is well known and whose availability to petitioner appears unimpaired. He has sought production of these matters after making the most searching inquiries of his opponents as to the circumstances surrounding the fatal accident, which inquiries were sworn to have been answered to the best of their information and belief. Interrogatories were directed toward all the events prior to, during and subsequent to the sinking of the tug. Full and honest answers to such broad inquiries would necessarily have included all pertinent information gleaned by Fortenbaugh through his interviews with the witnesses. Petitioner makes no suggestion, and we cannot assume, that the tug owners or Fortenbaugh were incomplete or dishonest in the framing of their answers. In addition, petitioner was free to examine the public testimony of the witnesses taken before the United States Steamboat Inspectors. We are thus dealing with an attempt to secure the production of written statements and mental impressions contained in the files and the mind of the attorney Fortenbaugh without any showing of necessity or any indication or claim that denial of such production would unduly prejudice the preparation of petitioner's case or cause him any hardship or injustice. For aught that appears, the essence of what petitioner seeks either has been revealed to him already through the interrogatories or is readily available to him direct from the witnesses for the asking.

The District Court, after hearing objections to petitioner's request, commanded Fortenbaugh to produce all written statements of witnesses and to state in substance any facts learned through oral statements of witnesses to him. Fortenbaugh was to submit any memoranda he had made of the oral statements so that the court might determine what portions should be revealed to petitioner. All of this was ordered without any showing by petitioner, or any requirement that he make a proper showing, of the necessity for the production of any of this material or any demonstration that denial of production would cause hardship or injustice. The court simply ordered production on the theory that the facts sought were material and were not privileged as constituting attorney-client communications.

In our opinion, neither Rule 26 nor any other rule dealing with discovery contemplates production under such circumstances. That is not because the subject matter is privileged or irrelevant, as those concepts are used in these rules. Here is simply an attempt, without purported necessity or justification, to secure written statements, private memoranda and personal recollections prepared or formed by an adverse party's counsel in the course of his legal duties. As such, it falls outside the arena of discovery and contravenes the public policy underlying the orderly prosecution and defense of legal claims. Not even the most liberal of discovery theories can justify unwarranted inquiries into the files and the mental impressions of an attorney.

Historically, a lawyer is an officer of the court and is bound to work for the advancement of justice while faithfully protecting the rightful interests of his clients. In performing his various duties, however, it is essential that a lawyer work with a certain degree of privacy, free from unnecessary intrusion by opposing parties and their counsel. Proper preparation of a client's case demands that he assemble information, sift what he considers to be the relevant from the irrelevant facts, prepare his legal theories and plan his strategy without undue and needless interference. That is the historical and the necessary way in which lawyers act within the framework of our system of jurisprudence to promote justice and to protect their clients' interest. This work is reflected, of course, in interviews, statements, memoranda, correspondence, briefs, mental impressions, personal beliefs, and countless other tangible and intangible ways—aptly though roughly termed by the Circuit Court of Appeals in this case as the "work product of the lawyer." Were such materials open to opposing counsel on mere demand, much of what is now put down in writing would remain unwritten. An attorney's thoughts, heretofore inviolate, would not be his own. Inefficiency, unfairness and sharp practices would inevitably develop in the giving of legal advice and in the preparation of cases for trial. The effect on the legal profession would be demoralizing. And the interests of the clients and the cause of justice would be poorly served.

We do not mean to say that all written materials obtained or prepared by an adversary's counsel with an eye toward litigation are necessarily free from discovery in all cases. Where relevant and nonprivileged facts remain hidden in an attorney's file and where production of those facts is essential to the preparation of one's case, discovery may properly be had. Such written statements and documents might, under certain circumstances, be admissible in evidence or give clues as to the existence or location of relevant facts. Or they might be useful for purposes of impeachment or corroboration.[b] And production might be justified where the witnesses are no longer available or can be reached only with difficulty. Were production of written statements and documents to be precluded under such circumstances, the liberal ideals of the deposition-discovery portions of the Federal Rules of Civil Procedure would be stripped of much of their meaning. But the general policy against invading the privacy of an attorney's course of preparation is so well recognized and so essential to an orderly working of our system of legal procedure that a burden rests on the one who would invade that privacy to establish adequate reasons to justify production through a subpoena or court order. That burden, we believe, is necessarily implicit in the rules as now constituted.

Rule 30(b), as presently written, gives the trial judge the requisite discretion to make a judgment as to whether discovery should be allowed as to written statements secured from witnesses. But in the instant case there was no room for that discretion to operate in favor of the petitioner. No attempt was made to establish any reason why Fortenbaugh should be forced to produce the written statements. There was only a naked, general

[b] What differences do you perceive with respect to use at trial for impeachment purposes between (i) the signed statement of a witness and (ii) memoranda made by the attorney as to oral statements of the witness, whether made contemporaneously with the interview or later pursuant to a discovery order such as that of the district court in this case?

demand for these materials as of right and a finding by the District Court that no recognizable privilege was involved. That was insufficient to justify discovery under these circumstances and the court should have sustained the refusal of the tug owners and Fortenbaugh to produce.

But as to oral statements made by witnesses to Fortenbaugh, whether presently in the form of his mental impressions or memoranda, we do not believe that any showing of necessity can be made under the circumstances of this case so as to justify production. Under ordinary conditions, forcing an attorney to repeat or write out all that witnesses have told him and to deliver the account to his adversary gives rise to grave dangers of inaccuracy and untrustworthiness. No legitimate purpose is served by such production. The practice forces the attorney to testify as to what he remembers or what he saw fit to write down regarding witnesses' remarks. Such testimony could not qualify as evidence; and to use it for impeachment or corroborative purposes would make the attorney much less an officer of the court and much more an ordinary witness. The standards of the profession would thereby suffer.

Denial of production of this nature does not mean that any material, non-privileged facts can be hidden from the petitioner in this case. He need not be unduly hindered in the preparation of his case, in the discovery of facts or in his anticipation of his opponents' position. Searching interrogatories directed to Fortenbaugh and the tug owners, production of written documents and statements upon a proper showing and direct interviews with the witnesses themselves all serve to reveal the facts in Fortenbaugh's possession to the fullest possible extent consistent with public policy. Petitioner's counsel frankly admits that he wants the oral statements only to help prepare himself to examine witnesses and to make sure that he has overlooked nothing. That is insufficient under the circumstances to permit him an exception to the policy underlying the privacy of Fortenbaugh's professional activities. If there should be a rare situation justifying production of these matters, petitioner's case is not of that type.

We fully appreciate the wide-spread controversy among the members of the legal profession over the problem raised by this case. It is a problem that rests on what has been one of the most hazy frontiers of the discovery process. But until some rule or statute definitely prescribes otherwise, we are not justified in permitting discovery in a situation of this nature as a matter of unqualified right. When Rule 26 and the other discovery rules were adopted, this Court and the members of the bar in general certainly did not believe or contemplate that all the files and mental processes of lawyers were thereby opened to the free scrutiny of their adversaries. And we refuse to interpret the rules at this time so as to reach so harsh and unwarranted a result.

We therefore affirm the judgment of the Circuit Court of Appeals.

Affirmed.

■ MR. JUSTICE JACKSON, concurring.

. . . .

The primary effect of the practice advocated here would be on the legal profession itself. But it too often is overlooked that the lawyer and the law office are indispensable parts of our administration of justice. Law-abiding people can go nowhere else to learn the ever changing and constantly multiplying rules by which they must behave and to obtain redress for their wrongs. The welfare and tone of the legal profession is therefore of prime consequence to society, which would feel the consequences of such a practice as petitioner urges secondarily but certainly.

. . . .

To consider first the most extreme aspect of the requirement in litigation here, we find it calls upon counsel, if he has had any conversations with any of the crews of the vessels in question or of any other, to "set forth in detail the exact provision of any such oral statements or reports." Thus the demand is not for the production of a transcript in existence but calls for the creation of a written statement not in being. But the statement by counsel of what a witness told him is not evidence when written. Plaintiff could not introduce it to prove his case. What, then, is the purpose sought to be served by demanding this of adverse counsel?

Counsel for the petitioner candidly said on argument that he wanted this information to help prepare himself to examine witnesses, to make sure he overlooked nothing. He bases his claim to it in his brief on the view that the Rules were to do away with the old situation where a lawsuit developed into "a battle of wits between counsel." But a common law trial is and always should be an adversary proceeding. Discovery was hardly intended to enable a learned profession to perform its functions either without wits or on wits borrowed from the adversary.

The real purpose and the probable effect of the practice ordered by the district court would be to put trials on a level even lower than a "battle of wits." I can conceive of no practice more demoralizing to the Bar than to require a lawyer to write out and deliver to his adversary an account of what witnesses have told him. Even if his recollection were perfect, the statement would be his language, permeated with his inferences. Everyone who has tried it knows that it is almost impossible so fairly to record the expressions and emphasis of a witness that when he testifies in the environment of the court and under the influence of the leading question there will not be departures in some respects. Whenever the testimony of the witness would differ from the "exact" statement the lawyer had delivered, the lawyer's statement would be whipped out to impeach the witness. Counsel producing his adversary's "inexact" statement could lose nothing by saying, "Here is a contradiction, gentlemen of the jury. I do not know whether it is my adversary or his witness who is not telling the truth, but one is not." Of course, if this practice were adopted, that scene would be repeated over and over again. The lawyer who delivers such statements often would find himself branded a deceiver afraid to take the stand to support his own version of the witness's conversation with him, or else he will have to go on the stand to defend his own credibility—perhaps against that of his chief witness, or possibly even his client.

Every lawyer dislikes to take the witness stand and will do so only for grave reasons. This is partly because it is not his role; he is almost invariably a poor witness. But he steps out of professional character to do it. He regrets it; the profession discourages it. But the practice advocated here is one which would force him to be a witness, not as to what he has seen or done but as to other witnesses' stories, and not because he wants to do so but in self-defense.

And what is the lawyer to do who has interviewed one whom he believes to be a biased, lying or hostile witness to get his unfavorable statements and know what to meet? He must record and deliver such statements even though he would not vouch for the credibility of the witness by calling him. Perhaps the other side would not want to call him either, but the attorney is open to the charge of suppressing evidence at the trial if he fails to call such a hostile witness even though he never regarded him as reliable or truthful.

Having been supplied the names of the witnesses, petitioner's lawyer gives no reason why he cannot interview them himself. If an employee-witness refuses to tell his story, he, too, may be examined under the Rules. He may be compelled on discovery, as fully as on the trial, to disclose his version of the facts. But that is his own disclosure—it can be used to impeach him if he contradicts it and such a deposition is not useful to promote an unseemly disagreement between the witness and the counsel in the case.

. . . .

The question remains as to signed statements or those written by witnesses. Such statements are not evidence for the defendant. Palmer v. Hoffman, 318 U.S. 109, 63 S.Ct. 477. Nor should I think they ordinarily could be evidence for the plaintiff. But such a statement might be useful for impeachment of the witness who signed it, if he is called and if he departs from the statement. There might be circumstances, too, where impossibility or difficulty of access to the witness or his refusal to respond to requests for information or other facts would show that the interests of justice require that such statements be made available. [No sufficient showing was made in this case.]

I agree to the affirmance of the judgment of the Circuit Court of Appeals which reversed the district court.

■ MR. JUSTICE FRANKFURTER joins in this opinion.

LITIGATION–PREPARATION MATERIALS: BEFORE AND AFTER HICKMAN

Prior to the decision in Hickman v. Taylor,[c] the law in state courts had been unclear with respect to discovery of materials prepared in anticipation

[c] For the background story of the Hickman case, see Richard L. Marcus, "The Story of Hickman: Preserving Adversarial Incentives While Embracing Broad Discovery," in Civil Procedure Stories 323 (Kevin M. Clermont ed., 2d ed. 2008).

of litigation or for trial. There was authority that statements of third persons prepared for the lawyer's use were within the scope of professional privilege, just as were statements of the client's agents to the lawyer. There was some reliance on English precedents, themselves not entirely clear, giving a broad protection to materials gathered by or for the solicitor in connection with litigation.

Before the Federal Rules, decisions by the federal courts had been rare in this area. Under the Federal Rules but before the Hickman decision, some courts had denied discovery of witness statements on the ground of privilege, others simply on the broad ground that discovery "would penalize the diligent and place a premium on laziness." McCarthy v. Palmer, 29 F.Supp. 585, 586 (E.D.N.Y.1939). Still others, a minority, had rejected these objections and permitted discovery. See, e.g., Hoffman v. Palmer, 129 F.2d 976 (2d Cir.1942), aff'd on other grounds, 318 U.S. 109, 63 S.Ct. 477 (1943).

Nevertheless, federal courts generally held that discovery was freely available to learn the identity and location of persons having knowledge of discoverable matter. This information even in the hands of a party was not privileged and was often an essential starting point in the adversary's own investigation. The party was subject to interrogation under Rule 33 about such persons, and he could not refuse to answer on the ground that the information sought was solely within the knowledge of his attorney. A distinction existed, however, between revealing the witnesses to the events and revealing the witnesses whom the party planned to call at trial. The latter was usually not accessible at the discovery stage, although there were a few decisions to the contrary. It was plain, nonetheless, that at pretrial conference the party might have to reveal trial witnesses.

Question: (1) Why should there be any distinction between witnesses to the events and witnesses to be called at trial? Consider current Rule 26(a).

After the grant of certiorari in Hickman v. Taylor, the Advisory Committee submitted to the Supreme Court a large number of proposed amendments, including some that liberalized the scope of discovery and also the following provision on trial-preparation materials, which appears at 5 F.R.D. 433, 456–57 (1946): "The court shall not order the production or inspection of any writing obtained or prepared by the adverse party, his attorney, surety, indemnitor, or agent in anticipation of litigation or in preparation for trial unless satisfied that denial of production or inspection will unfairly prejudice the party seeking the production or inspection in preparing his claim or defense or will cause him undue hardship or injustice. The court shall not order the production or inspection of any part of the writing that reflects an attorney's mental impressions, conclusions, opinions, or legal theories, or, except as provided in Rule 35, the conclusions of an expert."

Then, after the oral argument in Hickman v. Taylor, the Court adopted most of the proposed amendments, but it did not adopt the quoted proposal.[d] It seems plain that the Court believed it preferable to leave the

[d] New Jersey adopted the Advisory Committee's proposal with minor changes in phrasing, and a good number of states followed its lead.

protection of trial-preparation materials to the processes of adjudication on a case-by-case basis.

Question: (2) What is the rationale of the Hickman decision? What matters did it definitively settle?

(3) To what extent were the policy determinations underlying the Hickman opinion in accord with those underlying the rejected 1946 proposal?

(4) Was it wise for the Supreme Court in 1947 to deal with the problem of work product[e] by judicial decision rather than by rule?

Whether it was right or wrong at the time to refrain from adopting a rule, the result was a welter of conflicting decisions. There was disagreement as to whether work-product protection should cover the preparatory work only of lawyers or should extend to preparatory work by lay investigators such as claim agents. Compare Alltmont v. United States, 177 F.2d 971 (3d Cir.1949) (protecting statements obtained by FBI agents for use of government counsel in a civil action), with Southern Ry. v. Campbell, 309 F.2d 569 (5th Cir.1962) (denying protection to statements taken by claim agents). The question was whether, as the Alltmont court put it, the rationale of Hickman "applies to all statements of prospective witnesses which a party has obtained for his trial counsel's use." There was apparently no dissent, however, from the proposition that materials assembled in the ordinary course of business or for purposes unrelated to litigation did not come within work-product protection. See, e.g., Goosman v. A. Duie Pyle, Inc., 320 F.2d 45 (4th Cir.1963) (statements made pursuant to ICC regulations).

Probably the most perplexing area of controversy centered on the showing necessary to overcome the qualified protection given to ordinary work product. Because Rule 34 then required "good cause" for the production of any document, there was difficulty in determining the relationship between the general "good cause" requirement of that Rule and the showing required under Hickman v. Taylor to obtain work product, which the lower courts often characterized as "good cause." (The Court in Hickman did not use the term "good cause," but referred to "adequate reasons," "necessity or justification," and failure to demonstrate "that denial of production would cause hardship or injustice.") It was confusing to have "good cause" mean one thing for obtaining routine documents and another for piercing work-product protection. Yet it was also confusing, as the Advisory Committee would point out in 1970, to have "two verbally distinct requirements of justification that the courts have been unable to distinguish clearly."

In cases not involving trial-preparation materials, courts commonly equated "good cause" under Rule 34 to relevance and the absence of privilege, and so required no more than a perfunctory showing of need. But in cases arguably involving trial-preparation materials, courts demanded a much more rigorous showing, even if the court held the materials not

[e] The label "work product" was used in the argument in the court of appeals and by that court in its opinion. Hickman v. Taylor, 153 F.2d 212, 223 (3d Cir.1945). Despite that court's expressed misgivings about adopting it, the phrase has stuck.

within work-product protection because they did not entail the work of a lawyer. In a much-cited case, Guilford National Bank v. Southern Railway, 297 F.2d 921 (4th Cir.1962), the court avoided passing upon the trial judge's ruling that statements taken by claim agents did not come within the protection of the Hickman doctrine, doing so by finding on the facts that the discovering party had not shown good cause under Rule 34. The same result would clearly have followed under the work-product test. In Southern Railway v. Lanham, 403 F.2d 119 (5th Cir.1968), the court upheld an order for production of statements taken by a claim agent, saying that "good cause" under Rule 34 "requires something more than relevance and something less than the demonstration required to overcome the work product immunity." On the facts of that case it seems likely that there was a sufficient showing to compel production even if a lawyer had taken the statements.

Thus, this variable standard for good cause offset the difference in holdings on the extent of the work-product doctrine. For trial-preparation materials, then, there was far less disparity in results reached than there was in verbalizations of the result's reasons.

TRIAL-PREPARATION MATERIALS: THE 1970 AMENDMENTS

The 1970 amendments to the discovery Rules did much to dispel the confusion engendered by the accumulation of lower-court decisions after Hickman v. Taylor. First, the elimination of the "good cause" requirement in Rule 34 made documents unconnected with trial preparation routinely discoverable. Second, the new Rule 26(b)(3) dealt expressly with the scope of discovery of work product, trying to resolve the uncertainties that had plagued the courts.

A careful examination of Rule 26(b)(3) is essential. Note that this new subdivision pertains to documents and tangible things otherwise discoverable under subdivision (b)(1). So, relevance is naturally still a requirement. Privileged matter continues to be undiscoverable, and the rules of privilege here referred to are the evidentiary rules applicable at trial. See Evidence Rules 1101(c) and 501.

Question: (5) What is the effect on the Hickman doctrine of the Rule's giving work-product protection to documents and tangible things prepared by or for another party or its representative (including the other party's attorney, consultant, surety, indemnitor, insurer, or agent)?

(6) Suppose that a witness dictates a statement to an attorney's secretary at the attorney's request but in the attorney's absence. Can the opposing party discover the statement without any special showing?

(7) What of a written statement of a witness obtained by a party himself on his own initiative and then turned over to his attorney?

(8) What of an unsolicited letter written to the attorney giving the writer's version of the events she observed?

Consider next the special showing required by the Rule in order to obtain discovery of ordinary work product. The party seeking discovery must show that he has substantial need of the materials and that he is unable without undue hardship to obtain their substantial equivalent by other means. The Advisory Committee noted that this provision conforms to the holdings of the prior cases when viewed in the light of their facts, as distinguished from the courts' explanations of the results reached under the "good cause" formulations.

But how should the new formulation work in practice? For example, a witness statement taken immediately after an accident is arguably "a catalyst of unique value in the development of the truth through the judicial process." De Bruce v. Pennsylvania R., 6 F.R.D. 403, 406 (E.D.Pa. 1947). In that light, of what significance are the words "substantial equivalent" in relation to production of a contemporaneous statement? It is arguable that courts should freely order production of a contemporaneous statement whenever there has been a considerable lapse of time between its taking and the interview of the witness by the party seeking discovery, and indeed there is case authority for this approach. E.g., Clower v. Walters, 51 F.R.D. 288 (S.D.Ala.1970). But see, e.g., Almaguer v. Chicago, R.I. & P.R.R., 55 F.R.D. 147 (D.Neb.1972).

Even for contemporaneous statements, the diligence or lack of diligence of the party seeking discovery might be material. For other statements, the Advisory Committee's note cited as factors lapse of memory of the witness or his reluctance or hostility. Should the discovering party be required first to take a deposition in order to demonstrate the need for discovery of a statement? Is great inequality of investigative resources a suitable consideration? The Rule does not provide categorical answers to these questions, and it is not feasible to devise rules that would answer them all. Rather this subdivision establishes guidelines within the framework of which the courts may decide on a discretionary case-by-case basis.

Despite the guidance it gives on these old questions, Rule 26(b)(3) creates new brands of confusion. For example, difficult and fundamental questions lurk in the relation between the Rule and Hickman, as the next few pages will suggest. And so this passage from Kevin M. Clermont, Surveying Work Product, 68 Cornell L.Rev. 755, 755 (1983), could stand as a summary of the state of the law both before and after the 1970 amendments: "Work product is the legal doctrine that central casting would send over. First, it boasts profundities, arising as it does from the colliding thrusts of our discovery and trial processes and from conflicting currents in our modified adversary system. Second, it will surface frequently, because the protected materials are commonly created by each side but uncommonly useful to the opponent. Third, it has generated a small mountain of lower-court case law, with the foothills forming a labyrinth of rules and wrinkles. In short, work product has for a couple of generations dramatically bewitched academics, bothered practitioners, and bewildered students."

As that quoted passage suggests, the persisting questions go much deeper than doctrinal confusion. Particular facets of the work-product doctrine are still under attack on the level of policy. Indeed, Professor Thornburg has called for the doctrine's wholesale elimination, arguing that it "is not needed to protect the adversary system or the legal profession" while it "hides relevant information, increases costs, and exaggerates the inequality of wealth and information of the parties to a lawsuit" by disadvantaging individual and "one-shot" litigants. Elizabeth Thornburg, Rethinking Work Product, 77 Va.L.Rev. 1515, 1517, 1583 (1991).

RACKERS v. SIEGFRIED, 54 F.R.D. 24 (W.D.Mo.1971). Plaintiff sued for his child's injuries from being hit by defendant's automobile. Plaintiff requested production of documents, including "any notes, measurements and diagrams made by Max Miller [an insurance adjuster] or anyone else on behalf of defendant within seven days after the accident which show the length of skidmarks left by defendant's automobile at the scene of said accident." Defendant objected, invoking Rule 26(b)(3). Plaintiff moved under Rule 37(a).

The court ruled: "The critical materiality of the measurement of the skid marks in the case at bar is apparent from the direct bearing the measurement may have on the issues of both negligence and injuries (causation). If one party were to have knowledge of the precise measurements and the other party were to be without such knowledge, a distinct trial advantage would accrue to the former party. Therefore, plaintiff has shown a substantial need for the discovery of the documents within the meaning of the applicable rule. Defendant, however, suggests two possible alternative sources: (1) the personal observation of plaintiff after the accident, and (2) the accident report of the highway patrol. With respect to the former, however, it is observable that plaintiff's observations after an accident in which his infant child was involved could in no way approximate the precision of the measurements made by an insurance adjuster 'on the spot' soon after the accident. It is not shown that plaintiff made any exact measurements and, under the circumstances appearing from the file, it is not presumable that he did. With respect to the accident report, plaintiff states that it is erroneous and this statement is not contradicted by defendant. But, assuming that there is presently a disagreement over the accuracy of the highway patrol report, plaintiff should, for that reason, have access to the notes, measurements and diagrams made by defendant's agent after the accident. In these circumstances the alternative source cannot be deemed sufficient."

Question: (9) Could plaintiff have discovered by interrogatory and without any special showing the length of the skid marks measured by defendant's representatives, instead of seeking the documents embodying that fact?

Duplan Corp. v. Moulinage et Retorderie de Chavanoz

United States Court of Appeals, Fourth Circuit, 1974.
509 F.2d 730, cert. denied, 420 U.S. 997, 95 S.Ct. 1438 (1975).

■ Before ADAMS,* FIELD and WIDENER, CIRCUIT JUDGES.

■ WIDENER, CIRCUIT JUDGE. This case presents the question whether an attorney's opinion work product material developed in prior terminated litigation may properly become the subject of discovery in connection with subsequent litigation. The issue involves the work product doctrine of Hickman v. Taylor, 329 U.S. 495, 67 S.Ct. 385, 91 L.Ed. 451 (1947), and the scope of the protection afforded a lawyer's "mental impressions, conclusions, opinions, or legal theories" by Rule 26(b)(3) of the Federal Rules of Civil Procedure.

We hold that such opinion work product material, as distinguished from material not containing mental impressions, conclusions, opinions, or legal theories, is immune from discovery although the litigation in which it was developed has been terminated. Thus, for reasons which follow, we vacate the judgment of the district court and remand.

This patent-antitrust litigation presently consists of 37 cases which have been consolidated in the district court. Duplan Corporation (the throwsters) brought this suit charging Moulinage et Retorderie de Chavanoz (Chavanoz) and others with violating Sections 1 and 2 of the Sherman Act by denying the throwsters a free and open market for the purchase of unlicensed royalty-free false twist machines.[f] Claiming patent misuse and inequitable conduct on the part of Chavanoz in dealing with the United States Patent Office, the throwsters also seek a declaratory judgment that 21 patents owned by Chavanoz are invalid, unenforceable, and not infringed.

In this context, the throwsters seek discovery of work product material developed by Chavanoz's attorneys and others relating to 1964 settlement agreements with Leesona Corporation,[2] and also relating to knowledge by Chavanoz of the state of the prior art involved in its patented process.[3]

---

* United States Court of Appeals for the Third Circuit; sitting by designation.

[f] These machines produce texturized yarn.

[2] In the early 1960's, Leesona Corporation claimed in a series of lawsuits that United States patents which it owned were infringed by the sale and operation of machines manufactured by a licensee of Chavanoz. These lawsuits were settled in 1964 by agreement between Leesona and Chavanoz.

[3] "In particular, the throwsters request that documents should be produced dealing with the following matters:

"(a) *Patent Procurement.* What knowledge did Chavanoz possess about prior 'false twist' art at the time that it filed and prosecuted each patent application in the U.S. Patent Office? Did the French patent agent, Leo Soep, disclose to the U.S. Patent Office the pertinent facts he knew about the prior art? Did the American patent attorneys Armitage and Mueller disclose to Chavanoz or to the U.S. Patent Office the pertinent facts they knew about the prior art? Were representations to the appropriate Patent Office officials accurate and candid? . . .

"(b) *Patent Enforcement.* When the patent owner and/or the exclusive U.S. use-licensee filed infringement suits against the defaulting sublicensee throwsters, did they know or have reason to know that they were attempting to enforce invalid or inapplicable patents? . . .

In an earlier appeal, Duplan Corp. v. Moulinage et Retorderie de Chavanoz, 487 F.2d 480 (4th Cir.1973), we held, "upon the narrow question whether upon the termination of litigation the work product documents prepared incident thereto lose the qualified immunity extended to them under Rule 26(b)(3), Federal Rules of Civil Procedure," they do not automatically "become freely discoverable in subsequent and unrelated litigation." Because we were not then confronted with any claim relating to opinion work product, we dealt solely with the first sentence of Rule 26(b)(3) as applied to factual materials contained in an attorney's files.

Upon remand, the district court separately reviewed the documents in question, and in an order dated December 21, 1973 directed Chavanoz to produce 105 of them. Fifty-eight of these 105 documents have been produced; the remaining 47 were the subject of a motion for reconsideration by Chavanoz. As to these, Chavanoz claimed they were protected from discovery under Rule 26(b)(3) since they contained mental impressions, conclusions, opinions, and legal theories of attorneys and other representatives of Chavanoz prepared in anticipation of litigation or for trial. Nevertheless, on February 5, 1974, the district court ordered production of 22 of the 47 documents, finding that as to each of these the throwsters had demonstrated "substantial need" and "undue hardship." And although it acknowledged that Rule 26(b)(3) accords an absolute privilege during pending litigation to opinion work product materials prepared incident thereto, the court held that immunity ceases and the protection becomes only "qualified" once the litigation for which they were prepared terminates.

. . . .

. . . The first sentence [of Rule 26(b)(3)] grants a qualified immunity to "documents and tangible things . . . prepared in anticipation of litigation." The second sentence, however, provides "[i]n ordering discovery of *such materials* . . . the court *shall* protect against disclosure of the mental impressions. . . ." [Emphasis added] By their terms, the two sentences are complementary. Thus, it is apparent that the clear command of the second sentence to "protect against disclosure" applies to all the materials referred to in the first sentence. In our view, no showing of relevance, substantial need or undue hardship should justify compelled disclosure of an attorney's mental impressions, conclusions, opinions or legal theories. This is made clear by the Rule's use of the term "shall" as opposed to "may."

The district court, however, reasoned that what was a mental impression, opinion, conclusion, or legal theory, although absolutely protected during the pendency of a lawsuit, may change to an "operative fact" in a subsequent case once the earlier lawsuit is terminated. And should this

---

"(c) *Termination of Patent Litigation*. . . . what facts were known by the Chavanoz/Deering Milliken Research Corporation Group about the alleged invalidity and inapplicability of Chavanoz' patents when entering the 1964 agreements with the Leesona/Permatwist Group? [What evidence is there] . . . about the alleged invalidity and inapplicability of Leesona patents . . . [involved in the same] settlement agreements . . ."[?] Opinion of district court, pp. 4–5.

happen, upon a proper showing of substantial need and undue hardship, the district court held that it might in its discretion order the production of opinions and conclusions where the denial of such production would frustrate the demands of justice and result in suffocation of the truth.

The district court then devised an operative fact exception to the otherwise absolute immunity accorded opinion work product by Rule 26(b)(3).[7] In our view, this construction fails to comport with the policies underlying Hickman v. Taylor and Rule 26(b)(3).

It seems clear from the whole tenor of the Hickman opinion that the court was concerned with protecting the thought processes of lawyers and thus the very adversary system. . . . Should an advocate's thoughts, theories, opinions, and impressions, collected and developed during pending litigation, become discoverable in connection with later litigation because they are thought to be relevant, our adversary system would clearly suffer. Its foundation would be undermined. . . .

. . . .

We are mindful that certain documents may contain both discoverable material and non-discoverable material. On remand, the district court may, providing the other prerequisites for discovery have been met, excise from such documents the mental impressions, conclusions, opinions, or legal theories of an attorney or other representative, and order the balance of the documents to be produced. See Note of the Advisory Committee, etc., 48 F.R.D. 457, 502; 8 Federal Practice and Procedure, Civil, Wright and Miller (1970), pp. 231–2. The district court also may require Chavanoz to abstract such documents for turning over to the throwsters, or may itself abstract the documents, in either case taking care to protect against disclosure of mental impressions, conclusions, opinion, or legal theories as directed by . . . F.R.C.P. 26(b)(3).

Reversed and remanded.

Question: (10) Instead of seeking the documents, could the throwsters have discovered by interrogatories or depositions the mental impressions, etc.?

---

[7] Because it was contended here that the 1964 settlement agreements between Leesona Corporation and the patent owner, Chavanoz, were in fact an antitrust conspiracy, the district court ordered production of certain opinion work product materials since "the mental impressions, opinions, conclusions, and legal theories of the attorney in the prior litigation are now operative facts as to the motive and intent of the parties at the time of the settlement." District court opinion at p. 16. As to the contentions that fraud was practiced on the U.S. Patent Office, the court ordered production of similar materials since "the mental impressions, opinions, conclusions, and legal theories of the attorneys prosecuting the patent applications for Chavanoz are now operative facts as to the motive and intent of the patent owner in its dealing with the Patent Office." District court opinion at p. 16.

PETERSON v. UNITED STATES, 52 F.R.D. 317 (S.D.Ill.1971). Plaintiffs sued for alleged overpayments of federal income taxes. Plaintiffs by interrogatories requested a detailed description of the contents of certain audit reports prepared by IRS agents concerning plaintiffs. The government objected, arguing that the reports were work product and also that they consisted entirely of mental impressions, conclusions, opinions, or legal theories.

The court observed: "The only things protected by rule 26(b)(3) are 'documents and tangible things.' It is clear to this court that discovery of a detailed description of the contents of documents through interrogatories is equivalent to the discovery of the documents themselves. The discovery sought by plaintiff through the interrogatories is therefore covered by rule 26(b)(3)." However, the court ultimately decided that the government had to respond to the interrogatories because the reports were not prepared in anticipation of litigation or for trial but were instead prepared in the assessment and review process of the IRS.

Question: (11) Rule 26(b)(3) "is an accurate codification of the doctrine announced in the Hickman case and developed in later cases in the lower courts. . . . Rule 26(b)(3) provides protection only for 'documents and tangible things.' There is a distinction . . . between documents that a party has assembled and the facts he has learned from those documents. The courts have consistently held that the work product concept furnishes no shield against discovery, by interrogatories or by deposition, of the facts that the adverse party's lawyer has learned . . . , even though the documents themselves may not be subject to discovery." 8 Wright & Miller § 2023, at 193–94 (first edition). Was the court in Peterson correct, then, in expanding the Rule as suggested in the passage quoted from its opinion?

(12) "It is to be noted that the 'work product' doctrine, as announced in Hickman, was not limited to documents, but applies with special force to discovery of the mental impressions of the attorney, as illustrated by the recollections of oral interviews with witnesses sought by the plaintiff in that case. Since Rule 26(b)(3) is limited in terms to the discovery of documents and other tangible things, it leaves the 'work product' doctrine unchanged in this regard." 4 Moore ¶ 26.64[1], at 26–414 (former version). "Thus, when discovery of 'work product' is sought through interrogatories or through questions propounded at the taking of depositions, the Rule has no application and one must revert to the principles enunciated in Hickman." Id. ¶ 26.64[4], at 26–451 (former version). Was the court in Peterson correct, then, in concluding that even mental impressions, etc., get protection only if formed in anticipation of litigation or for trial? See Minebea Co. v. Papst, 355 F.Supp.2d 526, 529–30 (D.D.C.2005) (yes).

FORD v. PHILIPS ELECTRONICS INSTRUMENTS CO., 82 F.R.D. 359 (E.D.Pa.1979). "Defendant's counsel subpoenaed Frederic J. Prior, who is not a party to this action, to appear for oral deposition. Because of objections raised by plaintiff's counsel during the course of the deposition, the deposition was suspended, and plaintiff has moved for an order limiting the scope of examination. Plaintiff, relying on Federal Rule of Civil Procedure 26(b)(3) and Hickman v. Taylor, 329 U.S. 495, 67 S.Ct. 385, 91 L.Ed. 451 (1947), contends that defendant's questioning impermissibly impinged upon protected work product of plaintiff's attorney.

"The dispute arose when defendant's counsel questioned Mr. Prior concerning a discussion between the witness and Mr. Feldman, plaintiff's counsel, that had occurred the morning of the deposition. Plaintiff interpreted this exchange as an attempt to reveal his counsel's mental impressions and legal theories concerning the present case."

The court observed that this dispute did not come within Rule 26(b)(3), which pertains only to documents and tangible things. However, that Rule in no way implies that mental impressions not embodied in documents are discoverable, which would fly in the face of Hickman's "general policy against invading the privacy of an attorney's course of preparation." Hence, the court ruled: "Insofar as defendant's question attempted to elicit from the witness the specific questions that plaintiff's counsel posed to him, or even the area of the case to which he directed the majority of his questions, it exceeds the permissible bounds of discovery and begins to infringe on plaintiff's counsel's evaluation of the case. However, insofar as it was directed to the substance of the witness' knowledge of relevant facts, it is clearly an acceptable line of inquiry." The court closed by observing that to the extent defendant was seeking to uncover the basis of plaintiff's claim in the form of contentions or opinions, Rules 33(a)(2) and 36(a)(1)(A) might provide more appropriate vehicles.

Question: (13) To what degree does Hickman protect against an interrogatory asking for the substance of a witness statement?

(14) Now how would you respond to Professor Shapiro's hypothetical interrogatory, supra p. 95?

UNITED STATES v. NOBLES, 422 U.S. 225, 95 S.Ct. 2160 (1975). In the course of ruling that the court in a federal criminal trial could condition admission of testimony from a defense investigator, who would use his interviews with prosecution witnesses to impeach them, on production by the defense of the relevant parts of the investigator's report, the Supreme Court stated:

"The work product doctrine, recognized by this Court in Hickman v. Taylor, 329 U.S. 495, 67 S.Ct. 385 (1947), reflects the strong 'public policy underlying the orderly prosecution and defense of legal claims.' . . .

"Although the work product doctrine most frequently is asserted as a bar to discovery in civil litigation, its role in assuring the proper functioning of the criminal justice system is even more vital. The interests of society and the accused in obtaining a fair and accurate resolution of the question of guilt or innocence demand that adequate safeguards assure the thorough preparation and presentation of each side of the case.

"At its core, the work product doctrine shelters the mental processes of the attorney, providing a privileged area within which he can analyze and prepare his client's case. But the doctrine is an intensely practical one, grounded in the realities of litigation in our adversary system. One of those realities is that attorneys often must rely on the assistance of investigators and other agents in the compilation of materials in preparation for trial. It is therefore necessary that the doctrine protect material prepared by agents for the attorney as well as those prepared by the attorney himself. Moreover, the concerns reflected in the work product doctrine do not disappear once trial has begun. Disclosure of an attorney's efforts at trial, as surely as disclosure during pretrial discovery, could disrupt the orderly development and presentation of his case. We need not, however, undertake here to delineate the scope of the doctrine at trial, for in this instance it is clear that the defense waived such right as may have existed to invoke its protections.

"The privilege derived from the work product doctrine is not absolute. Like other qualified privileges, it may be waived. Here respondent sought to adduce the testimony of the investigator and contrast his recollection of the contested statements with that of the prosecution's witnesses. Respondent, by electing to present the investigator as a witness, waived the privilege with respect to matters covered in his testimony.[14]"

Question: (15) As for a former party's work product not reduced to tangible form, to what degree does Hickman protect them in subsequent litigation to which she is not a party? What of tangible work product? Compare Special Project, The Work Product Doctrine, 68 Cornell L.Rev. 760, 861–64 (1983), with D. Christopher Wells, The Attorney Work Product Doctrine and Carry-over Immunity: An Assessment of Their Justifications, 47 U.Pitt.L.Rev. 675 (1986).

(b) Other Limitations and Extensions

PERSON'S OWN STATEMENT

A party may obtain upon request, without the showing generally required for discovery of statements of witnesses, his own previously made

[14] What constitutes a waiver with respect to work product materials depends, of course, upon the circumstances. . . . [See also Evidence Rule 502; Fred C. Zacharias, Who Owns Work Product?, 2006 U.Ill.L.Rev. 127. Incidentally, the throwsters in Duplan subsequently claimed—unsuccessfully—that production of some work product in the course of discovery had waived protection for other work product dealing with the same subject matter. Duplan Corp. v. Deering Milliken, Inc., 540 F.2d 1215 (4th Cir.1976) (throwsters also argued for exception to strict protection of any opinion work product prepared in furtherance of crime or fraud, but court ruled that if such exception existed it did not here apply); see Note, Protection of Opinion Work Product Under the Federal Rules of Civil Procedure, 64 Va. L. Rev. 333 (1978). However, the defendants ultimately lost on the merits. Duplan Corp. v. Deering Milliken Inc., 594 F.2d 979 (4th Cir.1979), cert. denied, 444 U.S. 1015, 100 S.Ct. 666 (1980), after remand sub nom. Burlington Indus. v. Milliken & Co., 690 F.2d 380 (4th Cir.1982), cert. denied, 461 U.S. 914, 103 S.Ct. 1893 (1983).—Ed.]

statement about the subject matter of the action. Rule 26(b)(3)(C). Note the definition therein of "previous statement."

The typical situation involves a personal-injury case where an attorney, insurance company investigator, or other claim agent interviews a prospective plaintiff before he has retained counsel and takes a signed statement from him. (It is impermissible under the rules of ethics to communicate directly with a person known to be represented by a lawyer without that lawyer's prior consent. See Model Rules of Professional Conduct Rule 4.2 (1983) (amended 1995).) Later the prospective plaintiff retains an attorney, who wants to obtain the statement. There had been conflicting cases in the federal courts and also in the state courts as to the discoverability of such statements. Compare Smith v. Central Linen Serv. Co., 39 F.R.D. 15 (D.Md.1966) (discovery allowed), with Safeway Stores v. Reynolds, 176 F.2d 476 (D.C.Cir.1949) (discovery denied).

In the Smith case, Chief Judge Thomsen (long a member of the Advisory Committee) said: "There is justification for a different treatment of the request of a party to obtain his own statement, and his request to obtain the statement of a witness."

Question: (16) What is that justification? What arguments are there against allowing routine discovery of a party's own statement?

Chief Judge Thomsen coupled the order for discovery with a ruling that the defendant could choose to take the plaintiff's deposition before making his statement available to him. The 1970 Advisory Committee's note on Rule 26(b)(3) stated that in appropriate cases the court could make a similar order.

Question: (17) What is the purpose of ordering a party's deposition before production of his statement?

A perceptive commentator has asserted that on the whole it would be better to deny special protection to all witness statements, making them discoverable as a matter of course but affording, as in the Smith case, an opportunity to depose the witness before producing his statement. Edward H. Cooper, Work Product of the Rulesmakers, 53 Minn.L.Rev. 1269, 1322–28 (1969).

Question: (18) Is this proposal a sound one? See Kathleen Waits, Work Product Protection for Witness Statements: Time for Abolition, 1985 Wis.L.Rev. 305 (arguing that such proposal does not go far enough).

Interestingly, Rule 26(b)(3)(C) goes partway toward routine discoverability of all witness statements by providing that a nonparty witness may obtain his own statement upon request without making the showing required of a party for ordinary work product. It is a fair assumption that in most cases a party to whom the witness is favorably disposed will instigate such a request and that the witness will then make the statement available to that party. A party may thus by indirection achieve a result that the party could not get directly. See Jack H. Friedenthal, The Rulemaking Power of the Supreme Court: A Contemporary Crisis, 27 Stan. L.Rev. 673, 681–82 (1975).

Question: (19) Could a party, by means of a subpoena duces tecum, compel even an unfriendly witness to obtain his statement under Rule 26(b)(3)(C) and then to produce it?

FOIA

There are, of course, means other than disclosure and discovery for obtaining information to prepare one's case. For example, since 1966 the Freedom of Information Act, 5 U.S.C. § 552, has provided a means of access to all federal agency records subject to certain exemptions—a means separate from disclosure and discovery in a lawsuit. See generally Janice Toran, Information Disclosure in Civil Actions: The Freedom of Information Act and the Federal Discovery Rules, 49 Geo.Wash.L.Rev. 843 (1981).

IMPEACHMENT EVIDENCE

There is no doubt about the propriety of using discovery to obtain information that will impeach an opposing witness. When, however, a party wants to discover what information the adversary has acquired to impeach the discovering party's witness, the considerations are different.

In the personal-injury action of Margeson v. Boston & Maine Railroad, 16 F.R.D. 200 (D.Mass.1954), the plaintiff made a voluminous demand for statements and records, including his own statement. Judge Aldrich denied the motion and said:

"The adoption of the Civil Procedure Rules was not a denial of the concept that the court is the forum and the trial the procedure best calculated to uncover the truth. The enthusiasm which greeted the discovery provisions of the Rules when carried, as it has been, to the extent here advocated, that 'the truth should be known before the trial, and nobody be surprised', seems calculated, however, to weaken the efficacy of ordinary trial procedure. There is a vast difference between surprise and unfair surprise. The one is as beneficial as the other is harmful. Not merely may too many rehearsals, in the form of too much discovery, take the bloom off the opening night, but this absence of freshness may make the performance sterile. A certain amount of surprise is often the catalyst which precipitates the truth. Alternatively it may serve as a medium by which the court or jury may gauge the accuracy of the account.

"If every witness consistently told the truth, and none cut his cloth to the wind, little possible harm and much good might come from maximum pretrial disclosure. Experience indicates, however, that there are facile witnesses whose interest in 'knowing the truth before trial' is prompted primarily by a desire to find the most plausible way to defeat the truth. For this, and other reasons, I believe the requirement of good cause for compulsory pretrial production should mean more than mere relevancy and competency, or ordinary desirability from the standpoint of the movant, and should be something in the nature of special circumstances.''

Although the Rules as amended in 1970 do date some of Judge Aldrich's statements (how so?), courts have much cited his words. Judge Dawson contemporaneously expressed somewhat comparable views in this single sentence: ''While it may be true that, in the language of the vernacular, a party involved in a lawsuit under the present Federal Rules may be required, when entering Court, to 'put all his cards upon the table', this is no basis for assuming that he must also put all his clothes upon the table.'' Service Liquor Distribs., Inc. v. Calvert Distillers Corp., 16 F.R.D. 344, 347 (S.D.N.Y.1954). These judges nicely raised the question whether, for discovery purposes, material that has value only for the responding party's impeachment of another party or a witness is different from other evidence.

A party or witness with advance knowledge of impeaching material may on that account refrain from giving false or distorted testimony, but the adversary will then lose the opportunity dramatically to unmask him before the fact-finder and thus discredit not only the impeached testimony but his general credibility as well. This type of surprise is a legitimate aid to ascertainment of the truth.

But one problem is that most evidence is not only impeaching but also relevant to the merits of the case. For example, evidence that a party in a negligence action was intoxicated is of major importance in establishing negligence or contributory negligence, as well as for impeachment. It would seem that such evidence should be as readily discoverable as any other substantive evidence tending to establish a claim or defense.

There is another problem with creating immunity from discovery. Even for purely impeaching evidence, the impeaching witness may in turn be subject to impeachment if the discovering party has an opportunity to investigate before trial. The same is true of nontestimonial impeaching material.

A final argument against shielding impeachment evidence is that we have moved toward much fuller discovery in general, thus changing the context of the policy argument. The remaining pockets of immunity from discovery do raise line-drawing difficulties. Moreover, full knowledge of all admissible evidence would help the parties to reach a fair settlement, as well as to prepare for trial.

Surveillance of a plaintiff in a personal-injury action and his prior medical history provide excellent examples of impeachment evidence. Suppose, for a specific instance, that witnesses have observed the plaintiff performing labor inconsistent with his claim of disability, or that an investigator has taken films showing the same thing.

Some courts, but not others, require production. Some state courts have forcefully put the case for requiring production, making the point that the impeaching evidence itself may be fraudulent and that the plaintiff should have a chance to investigate it. E.g., Zimmerman v. Superior Court,

98 Ariz. 85, 402 P.2d 212 (1965); Boldt v. Sanders, 261 Minn. 160, 111 N.W.2d 225 (1961). In the former case the Supreme Court of Arizona stressed the substantive import of this kind of evidence, over the strongly worded dissent of Vice Chief Justice Struckmeyer who said:

"The category of surveillance evidence, which is the only issue before the Court, has two obvious attributes: First, it pertains to facts which come into existence after an accident occurs. As such, it has nothing to do with the merits of the plaintiff's right of action. Second, it almost invariably concerns facts which are better known to the plaintiff than to the defendant, facts which in all fairness should be known equally to both parties but which, because of their nature, often are impossible for the defendant to discover with certainty. It is, therefore, a fertile field for fraud and magnification, and a field in which the parties are not on even terms. Because of the strong public policy against perjury and because the parties are often not on even terms in the presentation of evidence of the exact extent of a plaintiff's injuries, a defendant should not be required to disclose the results of his surveillance.

"This does not mean that there is embraced a 'sporting theory' of litigation for nothing is hidden from the plaintiff which he does not already know. Rather, I call it 'sporting' to take from a defendant the ability to surprise a dishonest witness thereby leaving the cause vulnerable to perjury. As has been aptly said, 'An honest witness cannot be discredited and a dishonest one ought to be.' "

Question: (20) What about not requiring production in the discovery process, but requiring submission of the impeachment evidence to the court in camera at pretrial conference for a discretionary ruling as to whether the party should then produce it? Cf. John P. Frank, Pretrial Conferences and Discovery—Disclosure or Surprise?, 1965 Ins.L.J. 661, 664–67.

(21) What about requiring production at a time shortly before trial, after the party with the impeachment evidence has had an opportunity to commit the other side by depositions to a final version of its position? See Edward H. Cooper, Work Product of the Rulesmakers, 53 Minn.L.Rev. 1269, 1314–18 (1969).

Some federal judges had refused to allow discovery of such impeachment evidence, including the identity of the witnesses or the existence of such evidence. E.g., Bogatay v. Montour R.R., 177 F.Supp. 269 (W.D.Pa. 1959); Stone v. Marine Transp. Lines, 23 F.R.D. 222 (D.Md.1959). In the latter case Chief Judge Thomsen said: "Ordinarily a party need not divulge facts necessarily known to his opponent where the only purpose of the interrogatory is to prevent effective cross-examination."

Since the 1970 amendments to the Rules, however, the trend in the federal courts is to allow discovery of impeachment evidence, e.g., Mason v. T.K. Stanley, Inc., 229 F.R.D. 533 (S.D.Miss.2005); Pro Billiards Tour Ass'n v. R.J. Reynolds Tobacco Co., 187 F.R.D. 229 (M.D.N.C.1999), while affording in occasional cases an appropriate opportunity to depose the adverse party or witness before production, e.g., Blount v. Wake Elec. Membership Corp., 162 F.R.D. 102 (E.D.N.C.1993); Snead v. American Export–Isbrandtsen Lines, 59 F.R.D. 148 (E.D.Pa.1973).

Question: (22) If a federal judge were inclined to establish some such special procedure for discovery of certain impeachment evidence, or for that matter if she were inclined to prohibit such discovery, where could she find authority in the current Federal Rules to do so?

RICHARDS OF ROCKFORD, INC. v. PACIFIC GAS & ELECTRIC CO., 71 F.R.D. 388 (N.D.Cal.1976). Plaintiff sued defendant utility seeking to recover payment for certain spray cooling modules. Defendant asserted that the modules did not adequately perform. A research assistant for a university professor had confidentially interviewed employees of defendant as part of a study of the manner in which utilities make environmental decisions, and the decision to install those modules had been one subject of inquiry. Plaintiff sought to depose the research assistant concerning those interviews. Upon meeting refusal to answer, plaintiff moved for an order compelling answers.

The court said that the discovery Rules required it to "balance the interests of the private litigant in obtaining the information sought against the costs of providing it." Here, the profound interest of society in the research of its scholars, the necessity of maintaining confidential relationships if they were to accomplish their research, and the rather tenuous relation of this research to this claim all argued against compelling discovery. And the court so ruled.

Question: (23) Plaintiffs sued defendants under Title VII for sex discrimination during training for state police. A doctoral candidate as part of her research on gender integration had been an observer throughout the training and had confidentially interviewed the participants. Plaintiffs sought to depose her. She moved for a protective order. What result? Compare Kennedy v. Connecticut Dep't of Pub. Safety, 115 F.R.D. 497 (D.Conn.1987) (discovery allowed, except for identity of confidential interviewees), with Rule 45(c)(3).

EXPERT INFORMATION

Before 1970 the cases disagreed concerning the discovery of facts known and opinions held by experts. Many decisions had denied discovery of expert information acquired or developed in anticipation of litigation or preparation for trial, doing so by holding the information to be privileged, or protected as work product, or shielded simply because the court deemed it unfair for a party to learn from discovery what the adversary had paid to acquire. Other cases, especially the more recent ones, had allowed discovery, doing so by rejecting the arguments of privilege and work product and by mitigating the unfairness through requiring the discovering party in appropriate cases to share the payment of the expert's fees and expenses.

In 1970, Rule 26(b)(4) sought to resolve that disagreement. Today it works in conjunction with disclosure's later-added Rule 26(a)(2).

Rule 26(a)(2) and (b)(4)(A) is favorable to disclosure and discovery of facts known and opinions held by experts whom the retaining party may call at trial. This enables the other parties to check the qualifications of the opposing experts and to prepare for cross-examination and rebuttal.

Question: (24) May a discovering party obtain documents prepared for the opponent by its expert expected to be called at trial? See Michael J. O'Hara & Graham Mitenko, Scope of Discovery of an Expert's Work Product, J.Legal Econ., Fall 2000, at 37; cf. Colindres v. Quietflex Mfg., 228 F.R.D. 567 (S.D.Tex.2005) (holding unprotected an unsolicited e-mail sent by defendants' expert to defense counsel). Note that an amendment to Rule 26(b)(4) proposed for effectiveness on December 1, 2010, would cut off most such discovery.

Rule 26(b)(4)(B), which will become 26(b)(4)(D) under the proposed amendment, deals separately with experts who are not expected to be called as witnesses and requires a showing of "exceptional circumstances" for discovery of facts known or opinions held by them.

Question: (25) What was the rationale behind this separate treatment?

(26) "As we read Rule 26(b)(4)(B), factual information, even when acquired [by an expert] in expectation of litigation, is shielded only if discovery is attempted from the expert, and not at all if the effort is to obtain it from a party or another sharing it." Marine Petroleum Co. v. Champlin Petroleum Co., 641 F.2d 984, 994 (D.C.Cir. 1979). Do you agree?

Apparently subject to ordinary discovery is expert information not acquired or developed in anticipation of litigation or preparation for trial, see Spaulding v. Denton, 68 F.R.D. 342 (D.Del.1975), including information acquired by an expert as an actor or viewer with respect to the events in suit, see Duke Gardens Found. v. Universal Restoration, Inc., 52 F.R.D. 365 (S.D.N.Y.1971). See generally David S. Day, The Ordinary Witness Doctrine: Discovery of the Pre–Retention Knowledge of a Nonwitness Expert Under Federal Rule 26(b)(4)(B), 38 Ark.L.Rev. 763 (1985). Courts also have held that the identity of an expert is freely discoverable under Rule 26(b)(1). See generally Note, Discovery of Retained Nontestifying Experts' Identities Under the Federal Rules of Civil Procedure, 80 Mich.L.Rev. 513 (1982).

Question: (27) May a party discover the facts known and opinions held by an expert who has acquired or developed her information in anticipation of litigation or preparation for trial, who is not expected to be called at trial, and who is a regular employee of the opposing party but is "retained or specially employed" for the case? See In re Shell Oil Ref., 132 F.R.D. 437, clarified, 134 F.R.D. 148 (E.D.La.1990) (such expert falls within Rule 26(b)(4)(B)).

(28) What of an expert not "retained or specially employed" by the opposing party but only "informally consulted" (the 1970 Advisory Committee's note used the latter phrase, although the Rule itself does not)? See 8 Wright, Miller & Marcus § 2033, at 455 ("neither the names of these persons nor their information should be subject to discovery"). What is the test for distinguishing between the two roles? Compare Ager v. Jane C. Stormont Hosp. & Training School for Nurses, 622 F.2d 496, 501–02 (10th Cir.1980), with Nemetz v. Aye, 63 F.R.D. 66, 68 (W.D.Pa.1974).

What happens if the informally consulted expert destroys in tests the only existing sample?

(29) As a practical matter, what should the attorney do when she has obtained a mildly unfavorable opinion from an expert whom she may or may not call, depending upon later developments in preparation for trial or at trial?

SECTION 2. SUPERVISION OF DISCOVERY

The discovery Rules reflect the desirability of having discovery carry on so far as practicable without the intervention of the court. Needless trips to court are costly and wasteful of time. It is necessary, however, to provide the opportunity for supervision of discovery by the trial court, to prescribe sanctions against misuse of and noncompliance with the discovery procedure, and perhaps to obtain further supervision from the appellate court. Today, such supervision, or rather its claimed inadequacy, has become the focus of controversy over discovery, and the locus of most of the recent, frequent amendments to the discovery Rules.

Discovery orders.—Federal Rule 26(c) sets up the ground rules for protective orders to prevent harassing and oppressive use of oral depositions and the other discovery devices by resort to the court before the discovery has begun. However, because the typical notice for taking an oral deposition does not even reveal the subject matter of the examination, often the need for protection does not become apparent before commencement of the examination. Rule 30(d) therefore provides for an order to check abuses developing during the examination. Suspension of the deposition, during the time necessary to go to court to seek the order, will follow upon demand of either the objecting party or the witness.

Alternatively, the witness may simply refuse to answer, doing this on his own to assert discovery's limitations or at the direction of another in some circumstances. The discovering party can then turn to Rule 37(a) for an order to compel answers from the balky deponent. Commonly, however, if the witness refuses to answer a question, the examiner continues with other lines of inquiry instead of rushing immediately into court. Unanswered questions may thus pile up until a convenient time for resort to court, and frequently later questioning leads the examiner to conclude that it is not worthwhile to pursue the resisted matters further.

Question: (30) Supervision may be invoked by the objecting party or the witness, under Rule 26(c) or 30(d), *or* by the discovering party, under Rule 37(a). Should the burden of proof depend on this difference?

Excessive resort to the court can plainly make a shambles out of a deposition, and the Rules attempt to forestall this by costs sanctions against parties, deponents, or counsel. It may be, however, that the theoretical protection of these Rules proves an insufficient protection against insistent abuse or stubborn recalcitrance. Even if the court administers them with sternness and vigor, delay and the consumption of the court's energy inevitably result. The court will often find it difficult to determine the propriety of the questioning when presented out of context, necessitating an extended inquiry that will constitute an added burden on a busy court and an added expense to the litigants.

Use of parajudges.—One approach to limiting the burden on district judges is the greatly increasing reliance on United States magistrate judges to play the judicial role in supervision of the discovery procedure. District judges may designate these salaried court officials so to act under 28 U.S.C. § 636(b) and may review their decisions under a "clearly erroneous or contrary to law" standard. See generally 12 Wright, Miller & Marcus §§ 3068–3069; Christopher E. Smith, United States Magistrates in the Federal Courts (1990).

Another approach is to appoint special masters under Rule 53 to supervise discovery closely in cases of considerable need, especially big cases. See, e.g., Eggleston v. Chicago Journeymen Plumbers' Local Union No. 130, 657 F.2d 890, 904 (7th Cir.1981); see also Wayne D. Brazil, Geoffrey C. Hazard, Jr. & Paul R. Rice, Managing Complex Litigation: A Practical Guide to the Use of Special Masters (1983). The special master differs from a magistrate judge in being normally an outsider, whose compensation is fixed by the court and paid by the parties upon court-directed terms. Rule 53 specifies the court's standard of review. See generally 9C Wright & Miller §§ 2601–2615; Jerome I. Braun, Special Masters in Federal Court, 161 F.R.D. 211 (1995).

To cut down on delay, some courts have even resorted to the use of a special master to preside at depositions with authority to rule on disputes on the spot, but that is especially expensive. See, e.g., Fisher v. Harris, Upham & Co., 61 F.R.D. 447 (S.D.N.Y.1973), appeal dismissed, 516 F.2d 896 (2d Cir.1975); cf. Rambus, Inc. v. Infineon Techs. AG, 222 F.R.D. 280 (E.D.Va.2004) (indicating that a magistrate judge can also play this role of presiding at deposition); Park–Tower Dev. Group v. Goldfeld, 87 F.R.D. 96 (S.D.N.Y.1980) (suggesting that the special master be available by telephone for ruling during depositions). In Hirsch v. Glidden Co., 79 F.Supp. 729 (S.D.N.Y.1948), the court authorized an appointment of a special master to supervise a deposition, but at the cost of the party requesting the appointment.

Shapiro v. Freeman, 38 F.R.D. 308 (S.D.N.Y.1965), flipped the Hirsch idea under unusual circumstances. The infant plaintiff's claim for personal injuries included permanent psychiatric shock resulting from the crash into her home of the defendant's private airplane. After her school teachers on instructions from the plaintiff's attorneys had declined to talk informally, the defendant took depositions of the teachers to obtain information about her pre-injury adjustment to everyday life. At the depositions, the plaintiff's lawyer objected to almost every question and successfully instructed the deponents not to answer, making the depositions a complete waste of time. On a motion to compel answers, the court, finding that the plaintiff's attorneys had acted "in the utmost bad faith," appointed a special master to preside at the depositions and rule on all objections and motions relating to discovery. The court ordered the fees and expenses of the master, as well as the defendant's expenses and counsel fees in bringing the motion, to be paid by the plaintiff's attorneys without reimbursement from their client.

Place of deposition.—An obvious and excellent illustration of the necessity and operation of discovery supervision arises from the possibilities for harassment and oppression through setting up oral depositions at inconvenient places in order to inflict costly travel and counsel fees. Parties may make burdensome and costly requests under the other discovery Rules. See, e.g., Niagara Duplicator Co. v. Shackleford, 160 F.2d 25 (D.C.Cir.1947) (holding that production of books and records for inspection and copying under Rule 34 should occur in San Francisco, where the defendant company kept its records, rather than in Washington, D.C., where the plaintiff had brought suit). But let us look at this particular abuse under Rule 30.

A party can compel a nonparty witness to appear for a deposition only by a subpoena and only within the geographical limits set by Rule 45. But a party need not serve a subpoena on another party in order to take his deposition. Even if the party is far beyond the reach of a subpoena, a simple notice served upon his attorney pursuant to Rule 5(b) suffices.

If the deponent-party wants protection from an inconvenient deposition, he must resort to a seasonal motion under Rule 26(c). What will the court do? Ordinarily a plaintiff must appear for a deposition in the district he selected for institution of his action, but the court is likely to show more solicitude to a defendant notified to appear in the forum district if it is distant from his home. Similarly, an individual party receives more solicitude than does a corporate party. Some district courts have bolstered Rule 26(c) by local rules providing that the court, as a condition of refusing to vacate a notice for taking a deposition, may order the discovering party to pay prior to the examination the expenses of the adverse party; other courts have ordered prepayment of expenses under Rule 26(c)'s general authority to protect a party from undue burden or expense or its special authority to put terms on discovery. The five cases summarized below further illustrate how flexibly courts have exercised discretion in an effort to achieve fairness in the use of the deposition machinery.

V.O. MACHINOIMPORT v. CLARK EQUIPMENT CO., 11 F.R.D. 55 (S.D.N.Y.1951). Plaintiff, a Soviet corporation not engaging in business in the United States, brought suit in the Southern District of New York against defendant, a Michigan corporation, seeking to recover about $2,500,000 for breach of contract. Defendant asserted a counterclaim. Plaintiff took rather extensive depositions of defendant's officers and employees, lasting over a period of four days. Then defendant served notice to take the deposition of plaintiff in New York, designating nine individuals, all residents of the U.S.S.R., as the persons to be examined. Plaintiff moved for a court order (1) that no oral examination proceed because only two of the named individuals were officers, directors, or managing agents of plaintiff and those two had not participated in any of the transactions at issue, (2) that written depositions treat only matters not previously covered by plaintiff's answers to Rule 33 interrogatories, (3) that those depositions take place in Russia, not New York, and (4) that defendant pay plaintiff's expenses and counsel fees incurred by reason of any order entered.

Plaintiff did not prevail. (1) The court ruled that because of the technical and complex problems involved, denial of oral examination would result in serious prejudice to defendant and so would be improper. It ordered examination of two of the named individuals, but held decision as to the rest in abeyance pending clarification of their status as officers, directors, or managing agents of plaintiff. (The examining party can designate only persons of such status in a notice of deposition of a corporate party. See Marlin M. Volz, Depositions of Organizations: The Designation Procedure Under the Federal Rules, 33 S.D.L.Rev. 236 (1988).) (2) The court denied the motion to limit the depositions to matters not covered by answers to interrogatories. (3) The court further ruled that the place of examination should be New York, saying: "The plaintiff experienced little difficulty in sending its representatives here when it sought to obtain the benefits of a contract and the know-how of American industry; it should have no trouble in sending the persons to be examined and the documents which may be required when it is seeking a very substantial recovery from the defendant." (4) The court finally denied plaintiff's request for expenses and counsel fees.

Thereafter, plaintiff did not comply with the order. The court then granted a motion by defendant under Rule 37(b)(2) for the dismissal of plaintiff's complaint with prejudice and the direction of a default judgment in defendant's favor on its counterclaim, the amount of damages to be determined by an inquest, 12 F.R.D. 191 (1951).

GROTRIAN, HELFFERICH, SCHULZ, TH. STEINWEG NACHF. v. STEINWAY & SONS, 54 F.R.D. 280 (S.D.N.Y.1971). In this case, without the 1951 cold war overtones of the prior case, plaintiff sought to take the oral deposition in Germany of one of its own executive officers. The court granted defendant's motion for a protective order that the deposition be taken in New York. It found a claim of hardship, because of the age (72) and the state of health of the witness, not to be established.

FARQUHAR v. SHELDEN, 116 F.R.D. 70 (E.D.Mich.1987). Plaintiff sought damages from defendant, a wealthy citizen and resident of the Netherlands, for sexually abusing him in Michigan a decade before. Plaintiff noticed a deposition of defendant in the forum district. With several criminal sexual conduct charges outstanding against him in Michigan, defendant moved to shift the deposition to Amsterdam. The magistrate so ordered, on condition that defendant advance to plaintiff all "costs" for the deposition, with these ultimately to be taxed as costs paid by the losing party in the litigation.

CONNELL v. BILTMORE SECURITY LIFE INSURANCE CO., 41 F.R.D. 136 (D.S.C.1966). A South Carolina plaintiff brought a tort action involving securities against defendant, an Arizona corporation, in South Carolina and sought to depose defendant's president in South Carolina. Defendant moved that the deposition be upon written questions or that the oral deposition take place in St. Paul, where the corporation had its principal place of business and where the president maintained his office and residence. The corporation kept some books and records in South Carolina. The court ordered that an oral deposition take place in South Carolina, that the parties share equally the deponent's travel expense, that plaintiff pay the deponent's living expenses on the days of his testimony, and that all "expenses" be taxed as costs paid by the losing party in the litigation.

DePETRO v. EXXON INC., 118 F.R.D. 523 (M.D.Ala.1988). Plaintiff, a resident of California, had brought a Title VII action in Alabama for employment discrimination allegedly sustained there. Defendants had served a notice to take her deposition in Montgomery, Alabama. Plaintiff was without funds. The court had granted a protective order. Defendants then sought to depose her in California. The court granted another protective order, because she did not have the funds to fly her Alabama attorney to California. The court suggested as alternatives a deposition by telephone, a written deposition, or an oral deposition just before trial when the plaintiff would be in Alabama, but "in order to fully protect the defendants' interest, the court hereby notifies DePetro that it may impose appropriate sanctions against her if the evidence later shows that she did not fully disclose information that is pertinent to this trial in whichever alternative discovery method the defendants choose to use and the defendants are prejudiced thereby. Of course, if the defendants still want a face-to-face deposition they can always pay for DePetro to travel to Montgomery or they can go to California and pay for DePetro's lawyer to travel there as well."

Question: (31) Here is an additional subdivision of Rule 30(b) proposed by Jeffrey S. Kinsler, Location of Party–Depositions Under Federal Rules of Civil Procedure, 37 Res Gestae 358, 362 (1994): "The party noticing a deposition of another party may choose any reasonable location to take the deposition. If the deponent is an individual defendant, the district in which he or she resides is presumed reasonable. If the deponent is an individual plaintiff or an officer, director or managing agent of an organizational plaintiff, the district in which the suit is pending is presumed reasonable. If the deponent is an officer, director or managing agent of an organizational defendant, the district in which the organization maintains its principal place of business is presumed reasonable. These presumptions may be rebutted by a showing of undue hardship or expense on the part of the deponent, and the expenses associated with the deposition may be allocated among the parties if justice requires. For purposes of this section, defendants who have filed cross-claims or permissive counterclaims are treated as plaintiffs." What do you think?

Public Citizen v. Liggett Group

United States Court of Appeals, First Circuit, 1988.
858 F.2d 775, cert. denied, 488 U.S. 1030, 109 S.Ct. 838 (1989).

[In 1983 a smoker's wife and mother brought this diversity action in the District of Massachusetts against a cigarette maker, Liggett, for the smoker's wrongful death from lung cancer. The complaint alleged Liggett's inadequate warnings.

[In 1985, over plaintiffs' opposition, the district court issued a protective order barring nonlitigatory use of the many documents, including research, that Liggett had turned over during discovery. Pursuant to local rule, the parties had not filed these documents with the court.

[In 1987 plaintiffs lost finally. Dismissal and judgment rested on the ground that the federal cigarette labeling statute preempted the claim.

[About three months later Public Citizen, which represented a group of public health organizations, moved to intervene and to modify the protective order, so as to allow free dissemination by the parties. The district court granted the motion, and Liggett appealed from that final decision.]

■ Before BOWNES and BREYER, CIRCUIT JUDGES, and CAFFREY,* SENIOR DISTRICT JUDGE.

■ BOWNES, CIRCUIT JUDGE.

. . . .

In assessing the claimed right of access in this case, it is helpful to begin by noting what is not being claimed. Unlike many prior litigants in this court and others,[13] Public Citizen has not claimed that it has—independent of the federal rules—a general common law or first amendment right to inspect the discovery materials. Such a claim has been largely foreclosed by the Supreme Court's decision in Seattle Times Co. v. Rhinehart, 467 U.S. 20, 104 S.Ct. 2199, 81 L.Ed.2d 17 (1984), which must serve as the background for any claimed right of access to discovery materials.

In Seattle Times, members of a religious group sued the Seattle Times in state court for defamation and invasion of privacy. As part of its defense of that case, the Seattle Times sought to discover information regarding membership in and donations to the religious group during the previous five years. When the group resisted, the trial court compelled production, but entered a protective order under the state analog of Federal Rule 26(c) prohibiting the Seattle Times from disseminating or using the information in any way except as necessary to prepare and try its case. The Seattle Times then challenged the protective order as a prior restraint on speech in violation of the first amendment.

The Supreme Court rejected the Seattle Times's claim and also rejected the suggestion that review of a protective order requires any heightened scrutiny under the first amendment. Although acknowledging that litigants do have limited first amendment rights concerning information obtained through discovery, the Court focused on the fact that discovery is "a matter of legislative grace" and that litigants gain access to discovery materials

---

* Of the District of Massachusetts, sitting by designation.

13 See, e.g., In re Alexander Grant & Co. Litigation, 820 F.2d 352, 354–55 (11th Cir.1987); Anderson v. Cryovac, Inc., 805 F.2d 1 (1st Cir.1986); In re San Juan Star Co., 662 F.2d 108 (1st Cir.1981); In re Halkin, 598 F.2d 176 (D.C.Cir.1979); Mokhiber v. Davis, 537 A.2d 1100, 1109 (D.C.1988) (collecting cases).

"only by virtue of the trial court's discovery processes." Id. at 31–32, 104 S.Ct. at 2207. Moreover, the Court said, protective orders "furthe[r] a substantial government interest unrelated to the suppression of expression." Id. at 34, 104 S.Ct. at 2208. Thus, where "a protective order is entered on a showing of good cause as required by Rule 26(c), is limited to the context of pretrial discovery, and does not restrict the dissemination of the information if gained from other sources, it does not offend the first amendment." Id. at 37, 104 S.Ct. at 2209–10.

As we said in Anderson v. Cryovac, Inc., 805 F.2d 1, 6–7 (1st Cir.1986), the Seattle Times decision has not completely eliminated the first amendment as a relevant consideration in reviewing protective orders. Seattle Times has, however, established that first amendment scrutiny of protective orders "must be made within the framework of Rule 26(c)'s requirement of good cause." Anderson, 805 F.2d at 7.

It is, therefore, very significant that Public Citizen has not asserted a common law or first amendment right of access independent of the federal rules. Rather, Public Citizen has based its claim *on* the federal rules, asserting that . . . the public has a presumptive right of access to discovery materials unless good cause for confidentiality is shown, and that no good cause exists here. Nothing in Seattle Times or Anderson precludes such a claim. Discovery is "a matter of legislative grace," 467 U.S. at 32, 104 S.Ct. at 2207, but Public Citizen asks for no more than compliance with the legislative scheme embodied in the federal rules.

In seeking to defeat Public Citizen's claim, Liggett and amici Product Liability Advisory Council, Inc., and Motor Vehicle Manufacturers Association of the United States, Inc., have pointed to some expansive language in Seattle Times, Anderson and similar cases to bolster their claim that the public should not be afforded access to discovery materials. See, e.g., Seattle Times, 467 U.S. at 33, 104 S.Ct. at 2207 ("pretrial depositions and interrogatories are not public components of a civil trial"); Mokhiber, 537 A.2d at 1110 ("there exists no common law tradition of access to discovery materials as such"). Liggett and amici have used these statements to launch broad-based "policy" arguments to the effect that litigants have legitimate privacy interests in discovery materials and that permitting public access would undermine these privacy interests and excessively disrupt the litigation process. We acknowledge that our own Anderson opinion seemingly lends some support to this contention. 805 F.2d at 12 (permitting public access to discovery might actually make the civil discovery process "more complicated and burdensome than it already is"); see also Marcus, Myth and Reality in Protective Order Litigation, 69 Cornell L.Rev. 1 (1983) (generally criticizing claimed rights of public access to discovery).

We think, however, that these arguments and authorities are misplaced here. All of the cases upon which Liggett and amici rely are cases where the claimed right of access was based not on the federal rules, but on the common law or the first amendment. They are cases where, in essence, litigants put forth common law and constitutional arguments in an effort to *trump* application of the federal rules standard for protective orders. In rejecting such arguments and adhering to the federal rules standard, courts sensibly have noted that a contrary result would lead to thwarting the interests of privacy and litigative efficiency which are embodied in the federal rules. But nothing in those opinions purported to elevate privacy and efficiency as factors to be considered over and above compliance with the federal rules. Rather, the point of the cases was that, because of privacy and efficiency concerns, the federal rules should be followed.

Thus, when in Anderson we noted that "[t]here was no tradition of public access to depositions before [passage of the federal rules in] 1938," we went on to say that now, under Rule 5(d), courts *may* require public filing of discovery requests and responses. 805 F.2d at 12. Likewise, in Alexander Grant & Co. Litigation, the Eleventh Circuit recognized that, on the one hand, "private litigants have protectable privacy interests in confidential information disclosed through discovery," but it added that the means for protecting that privacy interest is Rule 26(c), not judicial fiat. 820 F.2d at 355.

Liggett and amici would have us turn these cases on their heads by holding that privacy and litigative efficiency concerns ought to work independently of the federal rules, actually limiting a district court's ability to *deny* protection under Rule 26(c), even when no good cause is shown. We are not willing to do so. This case involves a claim of access to discovery materials under the federal rules and we believe that the merits of the claim must be judged by the text of the rules and the applicable cases interpreting the rules. The rules themselves seek to accommodate concerns of privacy and litigative efficiency, and we find no reason for imposing additional judge-made constraints on the district court's control of discovery. Accordingly, we turn to consideration of the relevant federal rules.

Centrally at issue is Rule 26(c), which permits a district court to issue protective orders covering discovery materials upon a showing of good cause [here the court quoted the Rule].

As the Second Circuit has noted,

> A plain reading of the language of Rule 26(c) demonstrates that the party seeking a protective order has the burden of showing that good cause exists for issuance of that order. It is equally apparent that the obverse also is true, i.e., if good cause is not shown, the discovery materials in question should not receive judicial protection and therefore would be open to the public for inspection. . . . Any other conclusion effectively would negate the good cause requirement of Rule 26(c): Unless the public has a presumptive right of access to discovery materials, the party seeking to protect the materials would have no need for a judicial order since the public would not be allowed to examine the materials in any event.

In re Agent Orange Product Liability Litigation, 821 F.2d 139, 145–46 (2d Cir.), cert. denied, 484 U.S. 953, 108 S.Ct. 344, 98 L.Ed.2d 370 (1987), aff'g 104 F.R.D. 559, 567 (E.D.N.Y.1985). Rule 26(c)'s good cause requirement means that, "[a]s a general proposition, pretrial discovery must take place in the public unless compelling reasons exist for denying the public access to the proceedings." American Telephone & Telegraph Co. v. Grady, 594 F.2d 594, 596 (7th Cir.1978), cert. denied, 440 U.S. 971, 99 S.Ct. 1533, 59 L.Ed.2d 787 (1979); [other citations omitted]. Rule 26(c) thus lends support to the right of access claimed by Public Citizen and found by the district court below.

We agree with the Second Circuit. It is implicit in Rule 26(c)'s "good cause" requirement that ordinarily (in the absence of good cause) a party receiving discovery materials might make them public. In this instance, Public Citizen wished to relieve the plaintiff[s] of the burden of an order that prevented [them] from making public previously obtained discovery materials. Given the fact that Public Citizen directly benefitted from modification of that order, . . . we conclude that it had standing to intervene in the case and to ask the court to modify its pre-existing protective order.

[The court found that the district court did not abuse its discretion in modifying the protective order and therefore affirmed that decision, making these observations:]

To begin with, the protective order modified by the district court was a blanket protective order, that is, it was an order extending broad protection to all documents produced by Liggett, without a showing of good cause for confidentiality as to any individual documents. Although such blanket protective orders may be useful in expediting the flow of pretrial discovery materials, they are by nature overinclusive and are, therefore, peculiarly subject to later modification. [Citations omitted.] Moreover, as the district court made clear . . . , the point of this protective order was to promote a fair trial, not to guarantee Liggett perpetual secrecy. . . . The dismissal of the case on the merits eliminated the possibility of trial and was, therefore, a significant change in circumstances calling into question the necessity of the protective order. . . .

It is argued that a protective order of this sort may lead a party to be more forthcoming in discovery. A protective order may induce a party, for example, to permit an opponent to go through its files, taking relevant material. The party would not insist upon screening the materials first because it would not fear that irrelevant or confidential material, protected by the order, would be made public. Insofar as a rationale of this sort underlay the original protective order, it would seem unfair later to remove that order's protection.

We do not accept this argument as controlling here, however, for one simple reason. As far as we can tell from this record, the particular documents that Public Citizen seeks are *not* documents that were irrelevant to the litigation nor do they contain trade secrets or other specially confidential material. Insofar as it applies to the documents they seek, the protective order did not rest upon the rationale just mentioned. Rather, the court initially protected those documents for a very different reason: namely, the court, believing that the documents would become public in any event during trial, wished to conduct that trial free of the pretrial publicity that might follow premature release of the documents. Liggett, of course, remained free, in respect to any particular document, to argue to the district court that the document in question either was irrelevant to the discovery request or should remain protected as a confidential document for some special reason (such as "trade secrets") that would have prevented its having been made public at trial.

. . . .

. . . [W]e find that under these facts the district court had the legal power to modify its prior protective order: the reasons underlying the initial promulgation of the order in respect to the particular document[s] sought no longer exist; and the district court made a reasoned determination that public interest considerations favored allowing counsel to make those particular documents public [because they concern an important public health issue].

. . . .

Enforcement of discovery orders.—The discovery procedure would not be effective without adequate machinery for its enforcement. Federal Rule 37(b) sets forth the wide-ranging choice of sanctions open to the court for failure to comply with a discovery order. And the discovery Rules enable the court to impose expenses on those who unjustifiably attempt either to prevent or to obtain discovery.

Although the Rules did not in terms so prescribe, the practice of the courts had long been to impose the lightest remedial sanction thought to be consistent with effective administration of the discovery procedure. See Sterry R. Waterman, An Appellate Judge's Approach When Reviewing District Court Sanctions Imposed for the Purpose of Insuring Compliance with Pretrial Orders, 29 F.R.D. 420 (1962). Indeed, the original Advisory Committee's note on Rule 37 had recognized that there were due process limitations upon the power of the court to order dismissal or default without giving the party an opportunity for hearing on the merits. The Supreme Court had said that "substantial constitutional questions" would arise if a court struck a pleading for noncompliance with a discovery order with which the party had made a good faith effort to comply. Société Internationale pour Participations Industrielles et Commerciales, S.A. v. Rogers, 357 U.S. 197, 210, 78 S.Ct. 1087, 1095 (1958) (holding unwarranted a dismissal with prejudice, for failure to comply with order under Rule 34 to produce Swiss banking records, when production would subject party to criminal sanctions in Switzerland); see also Keith Y. Cohan, Note, Need for a Refined Balancing Approach when American Discovery Orders Demand the Violation of Foreign Law, 87 Tex.L.Rev. 1009 (2009).

More recently, however, an appellate court has upheld the drastic sanction of entry of a default judgment for willful and deliberate disregard of discovery orders. TWA v. Hughes, 449 F.2d 51 (2d Cir.1971) (default entered upon Howard Hughes's failure to comply with order to appear for deposition, and judgment entered for over $145 million), rev'd on other grounds sub nom. Hughes Tool Co. v. TWA, 409 U.S. 363, 93 S.Ct. 647 (1973). And in language encouraging some degree of increased severity, the Supreme Court itself has approved dismissal of an action for bad faith failure to comply with discovery orders. National Hockey League v. Metropolitan Hockey Club, 427 U.S. 639, 96 S.Ct. 2778 (1976); see also Roadway Express, Inc. v. Piper, 447 U.S. 752, 100 S.Ct. 2455 (1980) (attorney's fees assessed against attorney).

Meanwhile, the 1970 amendments revised Rule 37 in order to tighten the sanctions for failure to cooperate in discovery (one revision was to change "refusal" to "failure" in the caption and at several places in the body of the Rule, thus negating the idea of a requirement of willfulness). See Cine Forty–Second St. Theatre Corp. v. Allied Artists Pictures Corp., 602 F.2d 1062, 1067 (2d Cir.1979) ("Negligent, no less than intentional, wrongs are fit subjects for general deterrence . . . ."). The new Advisory Committee's note reflected dissatisfaction with the reluctance of the courts to use their powers more vigorously. For instance, Rule 37(a)(5) now requires an award of expenses *unless* the non-prevailing person's position "was substantially justified." The former Rule provided for such an order *if* the person's position was "without substantial justification." It may be doubted whether this shifting of the burden will of itself often change the result. But the Advisory Committee pointed out that the change in language was intended to encourage judges to be more alert to abuses in the discovery process.

Then, in 1983, the Advisory Committee used even tougher talk. Referring to the "widespread recognition that there is a need for more aggressive judicial control and supervision," the Committee provided mandatory sanctions for violations of the new Rule 26(g), stressing the aim of deterrence. It may again be doubted whether this additional shift in emphasis from the remedial to the deterrent will have a dramatic impact on the actual practice of the courts. See Robert E. Rodes, Jr., Kenneth F. Ripple & Carol Mooney, Sanctions Imposable for Violations of the Federal Rules of Civil Procedure at 5–31 (1981). Yet many of the recent cases at least sound more aggressive.

In any event, an empirical study indicates that parties in fact do not use the compelling process of Rule 37(a) or the sanction process of Rule 37(b) very often, even though, when the discovering party does invoke Rule 37, the court usually grants the motion. Paul R. Connolly, Edith A. Holleman & Michael J. Kuhlman, Judicial Controls and the Civil Litigative Process: Discovery 18–26 (1978). So if the goal is case management, perhaps the district court cannot rely on party-initiative but must act on its own—a prospect considered in the next Topic.

———

Coca–Cola Bottling Co. v. Coca–Cola Co.

United States District Court, District of Delaware, 1986.
110 F.R.D. 363.

■ MURRAY M. SCHWARTZ, CHIEF JUDGE.

Two groups of bottlers of Coca–Cola products ("the Bottlers") have brought suit against the Coca–Cola Company ("the Company") under various theories, seeking declaratory judgments, injunctive relief, and damages. In brief, the Bottlers contend the Company is obligated to sell them the syrup used in the bottling of diet Coke under the terms of their existing contracts for Coca–Cola Bottler's Syrup. On August 20, 1985, this Court granted plaintiffs' motion to compel production of certain formulae . . . , subject to an agreed-upon protective order. See Coca–Cola Bottling Co. v. Coca–Cola Co., 107 F.R.D. 288 (D.Del.1985). . . .

[The court had ruled: "Except for a few privileged matters, nothing is sacred in civil litigation; even the legendary barriers erected by The Coca–Cola Company to keep its formulae from the world must fall if the formulae are needed to allow plaintiffs and the Court to determine the truth in these disputes." The formulae ordered produced were those of several of the Company's soft drinks, the formulae being deemed relevant to the Bottlers' contention that diet Coke syrup fell within the contractual term "Coca–Cola Bottler's Syrup" and discovery of these trade secrets being deemed necessary for a fair trial.]

By letter dated September 9, 1985, counsel for the Company informed the Court that the Company would not disclose its formulae, "[i]n light of the overriding commercial importance of the secrecy of formulae to the entire Coca–Cola system, . . . even under the terms of a stringent protective order. . . ." The Company acknowledged the Court "may order . . . a sanction" for that refusal, and requested an opportunity to be heard on the sanctions issue.

Plaintiffs moved for the entry of an order under Fed.R.Civ.P. 37(b)(2)[(A)(ii)] striking the Company's answer and entering judgment in favor of plaintiffs . . . . In addition, they moved for expenses and attorney's fees. Defendant contended a limited preclusion order is the proper sanction and argued the award of expenses and attorney's fees is unwarranted.

. . . .

. . . The Poulis court set out six specific factors to be considered by the district courts in determining whether default should be entered under Rule 37(b):

> (1) the extent of the *party*'s personal *responsibility*; (2) the *prejudice* to the adversary caused by the failure to meet scheduling orders and respond to discovery; (3) a *history* of dilatoriness; (4) whether the conduct of the party or the attorney was *willful* or in *bad faith*; (5) the effectiveness of sanctions other than dismissal, which entails an analy-

sis of *alternative sanctions*; and (6) the *meritoriousness* of the claim or defense.

[Poulis v. State Farm Fire & Cas. Co., 747 F.2d 863, 868 (3d Cir.1984) (emphasis in original); other citations omitted.]

Two important Poulis factors point forcefully in favor of entering a default judgment in this instance. The Company was fully responsible for the decision to disobey the order and its failure to comply was willful.

Other factors, however, counsel restraint. Defendant has raised facially meritorious defenses to plaintiffs' claims. Except for the delay associated with the instant matter, plaintiffs have not alleged a history of dilatoriness by defendant. Prejudice to plaintiffs due to defendant's noncompliance, while now substantial, can be remedied. Most importantly, effective alternative sanctions exist. . . .

. . . .

The Court's previous Opinion in this litigation noted an order to compel disclosure of the Company's secret formulae could be "a bludgeon in the hands of plaintiffs to force a favorable settlement." . . . 107 F.R.D. at 290. The Court now declines to wield on plaintiffs' behalf the ultimate bludgeon in this litigation, default judgment, when careful use of a scalpel is far more appropriate. In the accompanying Order, the Court will establish certain facts regarding the various formulae and strictly limit defendant's use of formulae evidence for the purposes of this litigation. In addition, the Court will order defendant to pay the reasonable expenses and attorney's fees incurred by plaintiffs in prosecuting the motion for sanctions. . . .

[After what was actually a rather long opinion, the court in its order established a large number of detailed facts for conclusive use at the Bottlers' option, but it did not foreclose the ultimate issue. The aim was to establish all favorable facts that could have been directly inferred from the formulae. For example, it established that the diet Coke syrup formula was within the range of formulae for syrups sold over the years as Coca–Cola Bottler's Syrup and that 99% of the ingredients in diet Coke and in old and/or new Coca–Cola were the same, but it did not establish that diet Coke syrup "is" Coca–Cola Bottler's Syrup. Thus, although hobbled, the Company could still litigate "product identity," conceivably by proving differences in taste, marketing, and consumer perceptions and even by stressing the dietetic/nondietetic distinction. Indeed, the Company ultimately prevailed on the merits, 988 F.2d 414 (3d Cir.), cert. denied, 510 U.S. 908, 114 S.Ct. 289 (1993).]

Rubenstein v. Kleven

United States District Court, District of Massachusetts, 1957.
150 F.Supp. 47.

■ ALDRICH, DISTRICT JUDGE. This is an action by an unmarried woman for breach of an alleged agreement to render companionship and other services to a married man. The defendant has answered that the agreement was against public policy. While this is not an express assertion of illegal consideration, viz., an illicit relationship, I would regard evidence of such admissible under this general allegation. The plaintiff has taken defendant's deposition, and has asked certain questions to which affirmative answers might indicate adultery. The defendant has refused to answer on the ground of incrimination. Plaintiff moves for an order compelling him to answer. . . .

Since it would be to plaintiff's disadvantage for defendant to testify to an illicit relationship, I inquired of her counsel why he was pressing for an answer. He replied that he was of opinion that the answers would, in fact, be in the negative, and that defendant, being unable to testify truthfully to anything of a criminal nature, was seeking to create the impression of such, to plaintiff's disfavor, by the inference which would attach to his refusal. The suggestion that the defendant is a sheep in wolf's clothing presents a novel reverse-English to the Fifth Amendment.[3] I do not, however, find it necessary to pursue it. Defendant can not work both sides of the street. Illegality is an affirmative defence. If he is going to assert it predicated upon criminal acts involving himself, to be established through the testimony of any witness, or even simply by inference, he cannot remain aloof, asking the jury to find that such acts occurred, and at the same time claim a privilege against incrimination on cross-examination. Since he refuses on his deposition to incriminate himself, I will assume, as the rule of the case, that equally he does not intend to prove criminality, through his own testimony or otherwise, at the trial. Unless within twenty days he notifies plaintiff that he proposes to answer the questions, plaintiff's motion will be denied and the issue of criminality foreclosed.[g]

Appellate review of discovery rulings.—A discovery order is in theory reviewable on appeal from a final judgment, if there ever is one. Yet then, if the trial court ordered discovery, there will be great difficulty in demonstrating prejudicial error in allowing too extensive discovery. Not only is the trial court's discretion so broad that an appellate court would

---

[3] Can the principle that unfavorable inferences may be drawn against the witness in a civil proceeding, Attorney General v. Pelletier, 240 Mass. 264, 134 N.E. 407, permit an inference of criminality where, because of the peculiar circumstances of the case, this is a favorable inference? This is like the question posed by the court in McLoughlin v. American Circular Loom Co., 1 Cir., 125 F. 203, 205, whether it may be held defamatory to call someone in a community of thieves an honest man.

[g] After this astonishing decision, the plaintiff on deposition testified that the defendant had paid her $1000 a month for over six years pursuant to the alleged agreement to make such payments for her life in exchange for her complete time and attention. The defendant, contending he had made no payments, filed a motion under Rule 34 for production of her bank records and her state and federal income tax returns for the period in question. The court ordered that she produce the bank records, and that she also produce the tax returns unless she admitted that there was nothing in them directly or indirectly relating to the alleged payments, 21 F.R.D. 183 (1957). The defendant eventually obtained summary judgment on his plea of the New York statute of frauds, 163 F.Supp. 237, aff'd, 261 F.2d 921 (1st Cir.1958).

seldom find abuse, but there is often no effective way to correct an erroneous order once the material has come out. If the trial court denied discovery, the appellant may somewhat more readily show prejudicial error. E.g., Mellon v. Cooper–Jarrett, Inc., 424 F.2d 499 (6th Cir.1970) (erroneous protection of plaintiff in automobile accident action from answering whether he had ever been convicted of a lesser criminal offense than a felony or of driving under the influence of alcohol or drugs); Edgar v. Finley, 312 F.2d 533 (8th Cir.1963) (erroneous refusal to order the divulging of identity of a witness given to plaintiff's attorney by another attorney "in confidence").

Nevertheless, and even though compliance with a discovery order can be very burdensome or harmful, there are serious obstacles to prompter review in the federal courts. A discovery order ordinarily is merely interlocutory and hence not appealable under the final decision rule of 28 U.S.C. § 1291. See New York v. United States Metals Ref. Co., 771 F.2d 796 (3d Cir.1985). This limited appealability has tremendous impact on actual discovery practice in the district courts. See Elizabeth G. Thornburg, Interlocutory Review of Discovery Orders: An Idea Whose Time Has Come, 44 Sw.L.J. 1045 (1990) (arguing that more liberal review would not create significant burdens or delays, but would produce more accurate and uniform rulings by limiting power of district judges).

However, as Part Nine will suggest, there is the possibility that an occasional discovery order will be appealable as a "collateral order," which is a final determination of an important question separable from the main litigation that requires review before final adjudication of the whole action. E.g., Nicholas v. Wyndham Int'l, Inc., 373 F.3d 537 (4th Cir.2004) (reviewing a denial of discovery from a nonparty by a district court not in the Third Circuit where the action was pending). But see Mohawk Indus., Inc. v. Carpenter, 130 S.Ct. ___ (2009) (declining to extend collateral order doctrine to allow review of a discovery order adverse to attorney-client privilege). And rarely a discovery order may come within some other judge-made exception to the normal final decision rule. E.g., United States v. Nixon, 418 U.S. 683, 94 S.Ct. 3090 (1974); Perlman v. United States, 247 U.S. 7, 38 S.Ct. 417 (1918).

As to interlocutory review, in O'Malley v. Chrysler Corp., 160 F.2d 35 (7th Cir.1947), Chrysler appealed from a discovery order compelling it to prepare extensive computations, which would require much additional time and expense over and above the 90 days and $10,000 spent in compliance with a prior order. Chrysler argued that the order was an interlocutory mandatory injunction under 28 U.S.C. § 1292(a)(1). The court of appeals dismissed the appeal for want of jurisdiction.

The chance of an interlocutory appeal under 28 U.S.C. § 1292(b) is rather remote, although use of this procedure has occasionally been successful. E.g., Garner v. Wolfinbarger, 430 F.2d 1093 (5th Cir.1970) (denial of attorney-client privilege claimed by a corporation against its stockhold-

Christie & Merritt v. LoBianco, 336 F.2d 969 (D.C.Cir.1964) (order in malpractice action requiring defendant partnership of doctors to produce for inspection and copying a letter to its liability insurer reporting about the events in suit—although the vigorous dissent called it "a garden variety discovery motion" and "a graphic illustration of the mischief that results when the Interlocutory Appeals Act is misused").

The likelihood of successful resort to the extraordinary writ of mandamus is also remote, but some discovery orders have undergone review by this means. E.g., Schlagenhauf v. Holder, infra p. 1570; Pfizer Inc. v. Lord, 456 F.2d 545 (8th Cir.1972) (denial of attorney-client privilege on ground of the crime-fraud exception, in complex case).

Assuming that a party is unable to get immediate review of a discovery order, there remains the question of what happens if the party violates the order. The resulting discovery sanction also encounters serious obstacles to prompt review in the federal courts. On the one hand, the cases indicate that even a decision adjudging a party to be in civil contempt is not final for purposes of review. See Fox v. Capital Co., 299 U.S. 105, 57 S.Ct. 57 (1936). On the other hand, if a court holds a party guilty of criminal contempt for failure to comply with a discovery order, the contempt judgment is final and hence immediately appealable, and on that appeal the court will review the propriety of the discovery order. See Hanley v. James McHugh Constr. Co., 419 F.2d 955 (7th Cir.1969). If an adjudication for contempt has both a civil and a criminal character, "the criminal feature of the order is dominant and fixes its character for purposes of review." Union Tool Co. v. Wilson, 259 U.S. 107, 110, 42 S.Ct. 427, 428 (1922).

If a person not a party to the action disobeys a discovery order and if the court holds him in either civil or criminal contempt, he can appeal from the contempt judgment. Because he could not appeal from the ultimately final judgment in the case, the contempt judgment is as to him final. This proposition derives from Cobbledick v. United States, 309 U.S. 323, 60 S.Ct. 540 (1940), where Cobbledick moved to quash a subpoena duces tecum to appear and produce documents before a federal grand jury and then appealed from denial of his motion. The decision was nonfinal, and the appeal therefore failed. The Court said that the subject of a subpoena may refuse to obey, contest its validity if he is cited for contempt, and then appeal if his contentions are rejected. The contempt, the Court pointed out, is "so severed from the main proceeding as to permit an appeal." United States v. Ryan, supra p. 848, affirmed the continuing validity of the Cobbledick rule in 1971.

Question: (32) Under this scheme, is a monetary discovery sanction against an attorney immediately appealable? See Cunningham v. Hamilton Co., Ohio, 527 U.S. 198, 119 S.Ct. 1915 (1999) (no); cf. David Simon, Mo' Money, Mo' Problems: Should Appellate Courts Have Non–Party Jurisdiction over Lawyers' Appeals from Non–Monetary Sanctions?, 78 U.Cin.L.Rev. ___ (2009) (discussing limits that exist even on reviewability).

The appellate review in Sibbach v. Wilson & Co., supra p. 6, is hard to account for under this scheme. The trial court ordered the plaintiff jailed until she submitted to the physical examination. This was plainly a civil contempt designed to coerce her into accepting the examination, rather than a criminal contempt designed to punish. The Supreme Court nevertheless decided the case without mention of any problem of appealability.

Similarly, in Hickman v. Taylor, supra p. 1223, no question of appealability was raised. The Third Circuit characterized the contempt as criminal. The Supreme Court did not label it as either civil or criminal, although its recital that "the court adjudged them in contempt and ordered them imprisoned until they complied" made it sound like a civil contempt proceeding "in which the defendant had the key to the jail house door." Southern Ry. v. Lanham, 408 F.2d 348, 350 n.2 (5th Cir.1969) (Brown, C.J., dissenting). But what of the presence of Fortenbaugh as an appellant?

SECTION 3. E–DISCOVERY

Today's big discovery problem, beyond doubt, involves the discovery of electronically stored information. "As a result, litigation battles often are fought on two fronts: the case on the merits and the EDD [electronic data discovery] game of 'gotcha,' wherein one side probes to see whether its adversary has preserved and produced all responsive electronic data." Stephen D. Whetstone & Michael S. Simon, The Stakes Have Never Been Higher, Nat'l L.J., July 17, 2006, at S1, S1. Electronic data discovery raises difficulties of both scope and supervision of discovery.

The 1938 discovery Rules quite naturally focused on paper-based information. The 1970 amendments gave the Rules' first attention to changing technology. They clarified Rule 34's description of "documents" to include "data compilations." The court could require the responding party to translate them into reasonably usable form. Often this would mean a print-out of computer data, but the court had flexible powers sufficient to assure the discovering party adequate information and at the same time to protect the responding party against undue burden or expense. Courts could adequately handle the problem of computer-based discovery under the discovery Rules as so written, until about 1995.

Then, the problem just exploded. Judicial efforts to cope became herculean, as did the lawyers' performances. Digital information certainly has its tricky facets, such as the dynamic and precarious form of its storage. But the central difficulty is simply its volume. Any statistic on volume will be hopelessly inaccurate tomorrow. Suffice it to say that already the vast majority of all information exists exclusively in digital form. Each day produces many billions of e-mails in this country alone.

The looming possibility of e-discovery has deeply affected business and personal practices. Appropriate here is mention of the increasingly common existence of "document retention policies." Finally, law practice has surely changed. Office lawyers as well as litigators spend much of their time anticipating, if not conducting, e-discovery.

Once litigation is on the horizon, efforts and expenses pick up. The nature and volume of computer-based information mean that it will hold the key to winning or losing numberless cases, ranging from divorce suits to corporate megasuits. Regardless of its content, its sheer volume means that the parties' discovery requests and responses will often entail crushing effort and expense. The lawyer must retain third-party computer experts, while taking steps to ensure the preservation of digital evidence by both the client and the opponent. Many specialized businesses have sprung up to supply e-discovery services to litigants.

Parties will engage in a fair amount of meeting and conferring, under Rules 26(f) and 16, about e-discovery. Discoverers will rely most heavily on Rule 33 to acquire the necessary knowledge of the respondent's computer system, and then on Rules 34 and 45 to get the actual computer-based information. See generally Sharon D. Nelson, Bruce A. Olson & John W. Simek, The Electronic Evidence and Discovery Handbook (2006) (providing many useful, and lengthy, forms). Finally, the courts must wade in, all too often.

Zubulake v. UBS Warburg LLC (Zubulake I)

United States District Court, Southern District of New York, May 13, 2003.
217 F.R.D. 309.

■ SCHEINDLIN, DISTRICT JUDGE.

The world was a far different place in 1849, when Henry David Thoreau opined (in an admittedly broader context) that "[t]he process of discovery is very simple."[1] That hopeful maxim has given way to rapid technological advances, requiring new solutions to old problems. The issue presented here is one such problem, recast in light of current technology: To what extent is inaccessible electronic data discoverable, and who should pay for its production?

I. INTRODUCTION

. . . The Rules contemplate a minimal burden to bringing a claim; that claim is then fleshed out through vigorous and expansive discovery.

In one context, however, the reliance on broad discovery has hit a roadblock. As individuals and corporations increasingly do business electronically—using computers to create and store documents, make deals, and exchange e-mails—the universe of discoverable material has expanded exponentially.[6] The more information there is to discover, the more expensive it is to discover all the relevant information . . . .

---

[1] Henry David Thoreau, A Week on the Concord and Merrimack Rivers (1849).

[6] Rowe Entm't, Inc. v. William Morris Agency, Inc., 205 F.R.D. 421, 429 (S.D.N.Y.2002) (explaining that electronic data is so voluminous because, unlike paper documents, "the costs

This case provides a textbook example of the difficulty of balancing the competing needs of broad discovery and manageable costs. Laura Zubulake is suing UBS Warburg LLC, UBS Warburg, and UBS AG (collectively, "UBS" or the "Firm") under Federal, State and City law for gender discrimination and illegal retaliation. Zubulake's case is certainly not frivolous[8] and if she prevails, her damages may be substantial.[9] She contends that key evidence is located in various e-mails exchanged among UBS employees that now exist only on backup tapes and perhaps other archived media. According to UBS, restoring those e-mails would cost approximately $175,000.00, exclusive of attorney time in reviewing the e-mails. Zubulake now moves for an order compelling UBS to produce those e-mails at its expense.

II. BACKGROUND

A. Zubulake's Lawsuit

UBS hired Zubulake on August 23, 1999, as a director and senior salesperson on its U.S. Asian Equities Sales Desk (the "Desk"), where she reported to Dominic Vail, the Desk's manager. At the time she was hired, Zubulake was told that she would be considered for Vail's position if and when it became vacant.

In December 2000, Vail indeed left his position to move to the Firm's London office. But Zubulake was not considered for his position, and the Firm instead hired Matthew Chapin as director of the Desk. Zubulake alleges that from the outset Chapin treated her differently than the other members of the Desk, all of whom were male [at that time, although Chapin later hired a number of females]. In particular, Chapin "undermined Ms. Zubulake's ability to perform her job by, inter alia: (a) ridiculing and belittling her in front of co-workers; (b) excluding her from work-related outings with male co-workers and clients; (c) making sexist remarks in her presence; and (d) isolating her from the other senior salespersons on the Desk by seating her apart from them." No such actions were taken against any of Zubulake's male co-workers.

Zubulake ultimately responded by filing a Charge of (gender) Discrimination with the EEOC on August 16, 2001. On October 9, 2001, Zubulake was fired with two weeks' notice. On February 15, 2002, Zubulake filed the instant action, suing for sex discrimination and retaliation under Title VII, the New York State Human Rights Law, and the Administrative Code of the City of New York. UBS timely answered on March 12, 2002, denying

---

of storage are virtually nil. Information is retained not because it is expected to be used, but because there is no compelling reason to discard it"), aff'd, 2002 WL 975713 (S.D.N.Y. May 9, 2002).

[8] Indeed, Zubulake has already produced a sort of "smoking gun": an e-mail suggesting that she be fired "ASAP" after her EEOC charge was filed, in part so that she would not be eligible for year-end bonuses . . . .

[9] At the time she was terminated, Zubulake's annual salary was approximately $500,000 [plus bonuses of about $150,000]. Were she to receive full back pay and front pay, Zubulake estimates that she may be entitled to as much as $13,000,000 in damages, not including any punitive damages or attorney's fees. . . .

the allegations. UBS's argument is, in essence, that Chapin's conduct was not unlawfully discriminatory because he treated everyone equally badly. . . .

B. The Discovery Dispute

Discovery in this action commenced on or about June 3, 2002, when Zubulake served UBS with her first document request. At issue here is request number twenty-eight, for "[a]ll documents concerning any communication by or between UBS employees concerning Plaintiff." The term document in Zubulake's request "includ[es], without limitation, electronic or computerized data compilations." On July 8, 2002, UBS responded by producing approximately 350 pages of documents, including approximately 100 pages of e-mails. UBS also objected to a substantial portion of Zubulake's requests.

On September 12, 2002—after an exchange of angry letters and a conference before United States Magistrate Judge Gabriel W. Gorenstein—the parties reached an agreement (the "9/12/02 Agreement"). With respect to document request twenty-eight, the parties reached the following agreement, in relevant part:

> Defendants will [] ask UBS about how to retrieve e-mails that are saved in the firm's computer system and will produce responsive e-mails if retrieval is possible and Plaintiff names a few individuals.

Pursuant to the 9/12/02 Agreement, UBS agreed unconditionally to produce responsive e-mails from the accounts of five individuals named by Zubulake: Matthew Chapin, Rose Tong (a human relations representation who was assigned to handle issues concerning Zubulake), Vinay Datta (a co-worker on the Desk), Andrew Clarke (another co-worker on the Desk), and Jeremy Hardisty (Chapin's supervisor and the individual to whom Zubulake originally complained about Chapin). UBS was to produce such e-mails sent between August 1999 (when Zubulake was hired) and December 2001 (one month after her termination), to the extent possible.

UBS, however, produced no additional e-mails and insisted that its initial production (the 100 pages of e-mails) was complete. As UBS's opposition to the instant motion makes clear—although it remains unsaid—UBS never searched for responsive e-mails on any of its backup tapes. To the contrary, UBS informed Zubulake that the cost of producing e-mails on backup tapes would be prohibitive (estimated at the time at approximately $300,000.00).

Zubulake, believing that the 9/12/02 Agreement included production of e-mails from backup tapes, objected to UBS's nonproduction. In fact, Zubulake knew that there were additional responsive e-mails that UBS had failed to produce because she herself had produced approximately 450 pages of e-mail correspondence. Clearly, numerous responsive e-mails had been created and deleted[19] at UBS, and Zubulake wanted them.

---

[19] The term "deleted" is sticky in the context of electronic data. " 'Deleting' a file does not actually erase that data from the computer's storage devices. Rather, it simply finds the

On December 2, 2002, the parties again appeared before Judge Gorenstein, who ordered UBS to produce for deposition a person with knowledge of UBS's e-mail retention policies in an effort to determine whether the backup tapes contained the deleted e-mails and the burden of producing them. In response, UBS produced Christopher Behny, Manager of Global Messaging, who was deposed on January 14, 2003. Mr. Behny testified to UBS's e-mail backup protocol, and also to the cost of restoring the relevant data.[h]

C. UBS's E–Mail Backup System

In the first instance, the parties agree that e-mail was an important means of communication at UBS during the relevant time period. Each salesperson, including the salespeople on the Desk, received approximately 200 e-mails each day. Given this volume, and because Securities and Exchange Commission regulations require it, UBS implemented extensive e-mail backup and preservation protocols. In particular, e-mails were backed up in two distinct ways: on backup tapes and on optical disks.

1. Backup Tape Storage

UBS employees used a program called HP OpenMail, manufactured by Hewlett–Packard, for all work-related e-mail communications. With limited exceptions, *all* e-mails sent or received by *any* UBS employee are stored onto backup tapes. To do so, UBS employs a program called Veritas NetBackup, which creates a "snapshot" of all e-mails that exist on a given server at the time the backup is taken. Except for scheduling the backups and physically inserting the tapes into the machines, the backup process is entirely automated.

. . . Using NetBackup, UBS backed up its e-mails at three intervals: (1) daily, at the end of each day, (2) weekly, on Friday nights, and (3) monthly, on the last business day of the month. Nightly backup tapes were kept for twenty working days, weekly tapes for one year, and monthly tapes for three years. After the relevant time period elapsed, the tapes were recycled.[25]

Once e-mails have been stored onto backup tapes, the restoration process is lengthy. Each backup tape routinely takes approximately five

---

data's entry in the disk directory and changes it to a 'not used' status—thus permitting the computer to write over the 'deleted' data. Until the computer writes over the 'deleted' data, however, it may be recovered by searching the disk itself rather than the disk's directory. Accordingly, many files are recoverable long after they have been deleted—even if neither the computer user nor the computer itself is aware of their existence. Such data is referred to as 'residual data.' " Shira A. Scheindlin & Jeffrey Rabkin, Electronic Discovery in Federal Civil Litigation: Is Rule 34 Up to the Task?, 41 B.C.L.Rev. 327, 337 (2000) (footnotes omitted). Deleted data may also exist because it was backed up before it was deleted. Thus, it may reside on backup tapes or similar media. Unless otherwise noted, I will use the term "deleted" data to mean residual data, and will refer to backed-up data as "backup tapes."

[h] The judge denied the plaintiff's motion to release Behny's confidential deposition to securities regulators, 230 F.R.D. 290 (S.D.N.Y. May 13, 2003) (Zubulake II).

[25] Of course, periodic backups such as UBS's necessarily entails the loss of certain e-mails. Because backups were conducted only intermittently, some e-mails that were deleted from the server were never backed up. For example, if a user both received *and* deleted an e-mail on the same day, it would not reside on any backup tape. . . .

days to restore, although resort to an outside vendor would speed up the process (at greatly enhanced costs, of course). Because each tape represents a snapshot of one server's hard drive in a given month, each server/month must be restored separately onto a hard drive. Then, a program called Double Mail is used to extract a particular individual's e-mail file. That mail file is then exported into a Microsoft Outlook data file, which in turn can be opened in Microsoft Outlook, a common e-mail application. A user could then browse through the mail file and sort the mail by recipient, date or subject, or search for key words in the body of the e-mail.

Fortunately, NetBackup also created indexes of each backup tape. Thus, Behny was able to search through the tapes from the relevant time period and determine that the e-mail files responsive to Zubulake's requests are contained on a total of ninety-four backup tapes.

2. Optical Disk Storage

In addition to the e-mail backup tapes, UBS also stored certain e-mails on optical disks. For certain "registered traders," probably including the members of the Desk, a copy of *all* e-mails sent to or received from outside sources (i.e., e-mails from a "registered trader" at UBS to someone at another entity, or vice versa) was simultaneously written onto a series of optical disks. Internal e-mails, however, were not stored on this system.

. . . Thus, UBS has *every* e-mail sent or received by registered traders (except internal e-mails) during the period of Zubulake's employment, even if the e-mail was deleted instantaneously on that trader's system.

The optical disks are easily searchable using a program called Tumbleweed. . . .

III. LEGAL STANDARD

Federal Rules of Civil Procedure 26 through 37 govern discovery in all civil actions. . . .

. . . Finally, "[u]nder [the discovery] rules, the presumption is that the responding party must bear the expense of complying with discovery requests, but [it] may invoke the district court's discretion under Rule 26(c) to grant orders protecting [it] from 'undue burden or expense' in doing so, including orders conditioning discovery on the requesting party's payment of the costs of discovery."[32]

The application of these various discovery rules is particularly complicated where electronic data is sought because otherwise discoverable evidence is often only available from expensive-to-restore backup media. That being so, courts have devised creative solutions for balancing the broad scope of discovery prescribed in Rule 26(b)(1) with the cost-consciousness of Rule 26(b)(2). By and large, the solution has been to consider cost-shifting: forcing the requesting party, rather than the answering party, to bear the cost of discovery.

---

[32] Oppenheimer Fund, Inc. v. Sanders, 437 U.S. 340, 358, 98 S.Ct. 2380, 57 L.Ed.2d 253 (1978).

By far, the most influential response to the problem of cost-shifting relating to the discovery of electronic data was given by United States Magistrate Judge James C. Francis IV of this district in Rowe Entertainment. Judge Francis utilized an eight-factor test to determine whether discovery costs should be shifted. Those eight factors are:

> (1) the specificity of the discovery requests; (2) the likelihood of discovering critical information; (3) the availability of such information from other sources; (4) the purposes for which the responding party maintains the requested data; (5) the relative benefits to the parties of obtaining the information; (6) the total cost associated with production; (7) the relative ability of each party to control costs and its incentive to do so; and (8) the resources available to each party.

Both Zubulake and UBS agree that the eight-factor Rowe test should be used to determine whether cost-shifting is appropriate.

IV. DISCUSSION

A. Should Discovery of UBS's Electronic Data Be Permitted?

Under Rule 34, a party may request discovery of any document, "including writings, drawings, graphs, charts, photographs, phonorecords, and other data compilations . . . ." . . . Thus, "[e]lectronic documents are no less subject to disclosure than paper records."[37] This is true not only of electronic documents that are currently in use, but also of documents that may have been deleted and now reside only on backup disks.

. . . .

Nonetheless, UBS argues that Zubulake is not entitled to any further discovery because it already produced all responsive documents, to wit, the 100 pages of e-mails. This argument is unpersuasive for two reasons. *First*, because of the way that UBS backs up its e-mail files, it clearly could not have searched all of its e-mails without restoring the ninety-four backup tapes (which UBS admits that it has not done). UBS therefore cannot represent that it has produced all responsive e-mails. *Second*, Zubulake herself has produced over 450 pages of relevant e-mails, including e-mails that would have been responsive to her discovery requests but were never produced by UBS. These two facts strongly suggest that there are e-mails that Zubulake has not received that reside on UBS's backup media.

B. Should Cost–Shifting Be Considered?

Because it apparently recognizes that Zubulake is entitled to the requested discovery, UBS expends most of its efforts urging the court to shift the cost of production to "protect [it] . . . from undue burden or expense." Faced with similar applications, courts generally engage in some sort of cost-shifting analysis, whether the refined eight-factor Rowe test or a cruder application of Rule 34's proportionality test, or something in between.

---

[37] Rowe, 205 F.R.D. at 428 (collecting cases).

The first question, however, is whether cost-shifting must be considered in every case involving the discovery of electronic data, which—in today's world—includes virtually all cases. In light of the accepted principle, stated above, that electronic evidence is no less discoverable than paper evidence, the answer is, "No." The Supreme Court has instructed that "the presumption is that the responding party must bear the expense of complying with discovery requests . . . ." Any principled approach to electronic evidence must respect this presumption.

Courts must remember that cost-shifting may effectively end discovery, especially when private parties are engaged in litigation with large corporations. As large companies increasingly move to entirely paper-free environments, the frequent use of cost-shifting will have the effect of crippling discovery in discrimination and retaliation cases. . . .

Thus, cost-shifting should be considered *only* when electronic discovery imposes an "undue burden or expense" on the responding party. The burden or expense of discovery is, in turn, "undue" when [under Rule 26(b)(2)(C)] it "outweighs its likely benefit, taking into account the needs of the case, the amount in controversy, the parties' resources, the importance of the issues at stake in the litigation, and the importance of the proposed discovery in resolving the issues."

Many courts have automatically assumed that an undue burden or expense may arise simply because electronic evidence is involved. This makes no sense. Electronic evidence is frequently cheaper and easier to produce than paper evidence because it can be searched automatically, key words can be run for privilege checks, and the production can be made in electronic form obviating the need for mass photocopying.

In fact, whether production of documents is unduly burdensome or expensive turns primarily on whether it is kept in an *accessible or inaccessible* format (a distinction that corresponds closely to the expense of production). In the world of paper documents, for example, a document is accessible if it is readily available in a usable format and reasonably indexed. Examples of inaccessible paper documents could include (a) documents in storage in a difficult to reach place; (b) documents converted to microfiche and not easily readable; or (c) documents kept haphazardly, with no indexing system, in quantities that make page-by-page searches impracticable. But in the world of electronic data, thanks to search engines, any data that is retained in a machine readable format is typically accessible.

Whether electronic data is accessible or inaccessible turns largely on the media on which it is stored. Five categories of data, listed in order from most accessible to least accessible, are described in the literature on electronic data storage:

1. *Active, online data:* . . . Examples of online data include hard drives.

2. *Near-line data:* . . . Examples include optical disks.

3. *Offline storage/archives:* . . . The principled difference between nearline data and offline data is that offline data [requires

manual intervention] and is, in the lingo, JBOD ("Just a Bunch Of Disks").

4. *Backup tapes:* [These resemble a tape recorder that linearly records compressed data.]

5. *Erased, fragmented or damaged data:* . . . .

Of these, the first three categories are typically identified as accessible, and the latter two as inaccessible. The difference between the two classes is easy to appreciate. Information deemed "accessible" is stored in a readily usable format. Although the time it takes to actually access the data ranges from milliseconds to days, the data does not need to be restored or otherwise manipulated to be usable. "Inaccessible" data, on the other hand, is not readily usable. Backup tapes must be restored using a process similar to that previously described, fragmented data must be de-fragmented, and erased data must be reconstructed, all before the data is usable. That makes such data inaccessible.[61]

The case at bar is a perfect illustration of the range of accessibility of electronic data. As explained above, UBS maintains e-mail files in three forms: (1) active user e-mail files; (2) archived e-mails on optical disks; and (3) backup data stored on tapes. The active (HP OpenMail) data is obviously the most accessible: it is online data that resides on an active server, and can be accessed immediately. The optical disk (Tumbleweed) data is only slightly less accessible, and falls into either the second or third category. The e-mails are on optical disks that need to be located and read with the correct hardware, but the system is configured to make searching the optical disks simple and automated once they are located. For these sources of e-mails—active mail files and e-mails stored on optical disks—it would be wholly inappropriate to even consider cost-shifting. UBS maintains the data in an accessible and usable format, and can respond to Zubulake's request cheaply and quickly. Like most typical discovery requests, therefore, the producing party should bear the cost of production.

E-mails stored on backup tapes (via NetBackup), however, are an entirely different matter. Although UBS has already identified the ninety-four potentially responsive backup tapes, those tapes are not currently accessible. In order to search the tapes for responsive e-mails, UBS would have to engage in the costly and time-consuming process detailed above. It is therefore appropriate to *consider* cost shifting.

C. What Is the Proper Cost–Shifting Analysis?

In the year since Rowe was decided, its eight factor test has unquestionably become the gold standard for courts resolving electronic discovery

[61] A report prepared by the Sedona Conference recently propounded "Best Practices" for electronic discovery. See The Sedona Conference, The Sedona Principles: Best Practices Recommendations & Principles for Addressing Electronic Document Production (March 2003), ("Sedona Principles"), available at http://www.thesedonaconference.org/publications_html. Although I do not endorse or indeed agree with all of the Sedona Principles, they do recognize the difference between "active data" and data stored on backup tapes or "deleted, shadowed, fragmented or residual data," see id. (Principles 8 and 9), a distinction very similar to the accessible/inaccessible test employed here.

disputes. But there is little doubt that the Rowe factors will generally favor cost-shifting. Indeed, of the handful of reported opinions that apply Rowe or some modification thereof, *all of them* have ordered the cost of discovery to be shifted to the requesting party.

In order to maintain the presumption that the responding party pays, the cost-shifting analysis must be neutral; close calls should be resolved in favor of the presumption. The Rowe factors, as applied, undercut that presumption for three reasons. *First*, the Rowe test is incomplete. *Second*, courts have given equal weight to all of the factors, when certain factors should predominate. *Third*, courts applying the Rowe test have not always developed a full factual record.

. . . .

Set forth below is a new seven-factor test based on the modifications to Rowe discussed in the preceding sections.

1. The extent to which the request is specifically tailored to discover relevant information;

2. The availability of such information from other sources;

3. The total cost of production, compared to the amount in controversy;

4. The total cost of production, compared to the resources available to each party;

5. The relative ability of each party to control costs and its incentive to do so;

6. The importance of the issues at stake in the litigation; and

7. The relative benefits to the parties of obtaining the information.

. . . .

Whenever a court applies a multi-factor test, there is a temptation to treat the factors as a check-list, resolving the issue in favor of whichever column has the most checks. . . . The seven-factor test articulated above provide some guidance in answering this question, but the test cannot be mechanically applied at the risk of losing sight of its purpose.

Weighting the factors in descending order of importance may solve the problem and avoid a mechanistic application of the test. The first two factors—comprising the marginal utility test—are the most important. . . .

The second group of factors addresses cost issues: "How expensive will this production be?" and, "Who can handle that expense?" [The court noted: "UBS, for example, reported net profits after tax of 942 million Swiss Francs (approximately $716 million) for the third quarter of 2002 alone."] . . . The third "group"—(6) the importance of the litigation itself—stands alone, and as noted earlier will only rarely come into play. But where it does, this factor has the potential to predominate over the others. [For example, if a case has the potential for broad public impact, then public policy weighs heavily in favor of permitting extensive discovery.

Cases of this ilk might include toxic tort class actions, environmental actions, so-called impact or social reform litigation, cases involving criminal conduct, or cases implicating important legal or constitutional questions.] . . . Finally, the last factor—(7) the relative benefits of production as between the requesting and producing parties—is the least important because it is fair to presume that the response to a discovery request generally benefits the requesting party. But in the unusual case where production will also provide a tangible or strategic benefit to the responding party, that fact may weigh *against* shifting costs.

D. A Factual Basis Is Required to Support the Analysis

Courts applying Rowe have uniformly favored cost-shifting largely because of assumptions made concerning the likelihood that relevant information will be found. . . . But such proof will rarely exist in advance of obtaining the requested discovery. The suggestion that a plaintiff must not only demonstrate that probative evidence exists, but also prove that electronic discovery will yield a "gold mine," is contrary to the plain language of Rule 26(b)(1), which permits discovery of "any matter" that is "relevant to [a] claim or defense."

. . . Requiring the responding party to restore and produce responsive documents from a small sample of backup tapes will inform the cost-shifting analysis laid out above. When based on an actual sample, the marginal utility test will not be an exercise in speculation—there will be tangible evidence of what the backup tapes may have to offer. There will also be tangible evidence of the time and cost required to restore the backup tapes, which in turn will inform the second group of cost-shifting factors. Thus, by requiring a sample restoration of backup tapes, the entire cost-shifting analysis can be grounded in fact rather than guesswork.

. . . .

Accordingly, UBS is ordered to produce *all* responsive e-mails that exist on its optical disks or on its active servers (i.e., in HP OpenMail files) at its own expense. UBS is also ordered to produce, at its expense, responsive e-mails from any *five* backups tapes selected *by Zubulake*. UBS should then prepare an affidavit detailing the results of its search, as well as the time and money spent. After reviewing the contents of the backup tapes and UBS's certification, the Court will conduct the appropriate cost-shifting analysis.

A conference is scheduled in Courtroom 12C at 4:30 p.m. on June 17, 2003.

ZUBULAKE v. UBS WARBURG LLC, 216 F.R.D. 280 (S.D.N.Y. 2003) (Zubulake III). "Having reviewed the results of this sample restoration, Laura Zubulake now moves for an order compelling UBS to produce all remaining backup e-mails at its expense. UBS argues that based on the sampling, the costs should be shifted to Zubulake."

UBS had hired Pinkerton Consulting & Investigations to restore the five tapes and search for the plaintiff's name or initials, a process that cost $11,524.63 and yielded 1075 e-mails. In reviewing these e-mails and producing about 600 of them (853 pages) as responsive, UBS had expended "$4,633 in attorney time for the document review (11.3 hours at $410 per hour) and $2,845.80 in paralegal time for tasks related to document production (16.74 hours at $170 per hour)." So UBS wanted to shift the cost ($165,954.67) of restoring and searching the remaining tapes, of which UBS now said there were only seventy-two, as well as to shift the cost ($107,694.72) of reviewing and producing the e-mails.

Judge Scheindlin refused to shift the latter costs, for two reasons:

"*First,* the producing party has the exclusive ability to control the cost of reviewing the documents. In this case, UBS decided—as is its right—to have a senior associate at a top New York City law firm conduct the privilege review at a cost of $410 per hour. But the job could just as easily have been done (while perhaps not as well) by a first-year associate or contract attorney at a far lower rate. UBS could similarly have obtained paralegal assistance for far less than $170 per hour.

"Moreover, the producing party unilaterally decides on the review protocol. When reviewing electronic data, that review may range from reading every word of every document to conducting a series of targeted key word searches. Indeed, many parties to document-intensive litigation enter into so-called 'claw-back' agreements that allow the parties to forego privilege review altogether in favor of an agreement to return inadvertently produced privileged documents. The parties here can still reach such an agreement with respect to the remaining seventy-two tapes and thereby avoid any cost of reviewing these tapes for privilege.

"*Second*, the argument that *all* costs related to the production of restored data should be shifted misapprehends the nature of the cost-shifting inquiry. Recalling that cost-shifting is only appropriate for inaccessible—*but otherwise discoverable*—data, it necessarily follows that once the data has been restored to an accessible format and responsive documents located, cost-shifting is no longer appropriate. Had it always been accessible, there is no question that UBS would have had to produce the data at its own cost. Indeed, this is precisely what I ordered in Zubulake I with respect to certain e-mails kept on UBS's optical disk system.

"Documents stored on backup tapes can be likened to paper records locked inside a sophisticated safe to which no one has the key or combination. The cost of accessing those documents may be onerous, and in some cases the parties should split the cost of breaking into the safe. But once the safe is opened, the production of the documents found inside is the sole responsibility of the responding party. The point is simple: technology may increasingly permit litigants to reconstruct lost or inaccessible information, but once restored to an accessible form, the usual rules of discovery apply."

As to shifting the costs of restoring and searching, the judge proceeded through her seven factors: (1) Zubulake felt that 68 of the 600 e-mails were highly relevant. The court agreed that these were relevant, although none provided direct evidence of discrimination. One example was "[a]n e-mail from Chapin to one of his employees on the Desk, Joy Kim, suggesting to her how to phrase a complaint against Zubulake. A few hours later, Joy Kim did in fact send an e-mail to Chapin complaining about Zubulake, using precisely the same words that Chapin had suggested. But at his deposition (taken before these e-mails were restored), Chapin claimed that he did not solicit the complaint." Together these e-mails told "a compelling story of the dysfunctional atmosphere" in that workplace, but not "that Chapin's dislike of Zubulake related to her gender." (2) Some of such information was available only from the backup tapes. Thus, "the marginal utility is *potentially* high." (3) The "case has the potential for a multi-million dollar recovery." (4) UBS had much greater resources than the unemployed Zubulake. (5) At this stage, neither side could do much to control these particular discovery costs. (6) "Although this case revolves around a weighty issue—discrimination in the workplace—it is hardly unique." (7) Surely, "Zubulake stands to gain far more than does UBS" from this discovery. To summarize: "Factors one through four tip against cost-shifting (although factor two only slightly so). Factors five and six are neutral, and factor seven favors cost-shifting."

"The next question is how much of the cost should be shifted. It is beyond cavil that the precise allocation is a matter of judgment and fairness rather than a mathematical consequence of the seven factors discussed above. Nonetheless, the analysis of those factors does inform the exercise of discretion. Because the seven factor test requires that UBS pay the lion's share, the percentage assigned to Zubulake must be less than fifty percent. A share that is too costly may chill the rights of litigants to pursue meritorious claims. However, because the success of this search is somewhat speculative, any cost that fairly can be assigned to Zubulake is appropriate and ensures that UBS's expenses will not be unduly burdensome. A twenty-five percent assignment to Zubulake meets these goals."

ZUBULAKE v. UBS WARBURG LLC, 220 F.R.D. 212 (S.D.N.Y. Oct. 22, 2003) (Zubulake IV). Considering the cost to her, the plaintiff chose to restore only sixteen backup tapes. At that point, the parties learned that several of those tapes were missing, apparently recycled through negligence or possibly recklessness. Zubulake sought sanctions against UBS for this failure, as well as for some of its employees' having deleted e-mails from their computers.

"Finding a suitable sanction for the destruction of evidence in civil cases has never been easy. Electronic evidence only complicates matters. As documents are increasingly maintained electronically, it has become easier to delete or tamper with evidence (both intentionally and inadvertently) and more difficult for litigants to craft policies that ensure all relevant documents are preserved. This opinion addresses both the scope of a litigant's duty to preserve electronic documents and the consequences of a failure to preserve documents that fall within the scope of that duty."

Judge Scheindlin explained: "Spoliation is 'the destruction or significant alteration of evidence, or the failure to preserve property for another's use as evidence in pending or reasonably foreseeable litigation.'[9] The spoliation of evidence germane 'to proof of an issue at trial can support an inference that the evidence would have been unfavorable to the party responsible for its destruction.'[10] However, '[t]he determination of an appropriate sanction for spoliation, if any, is confined to the sound discretion of the trial judge, and is assessed on a case-by-case basis.'[11] The authority to sanction litigants for spoliation arises jointly under the Federal Rules of Civil Procedure and the court's own inherent powers."

To justify a sanction, the judge had first to find a duty to preserve. "The obligation to preserve evidence arises when the party has notice that the evidence is relevant to litigation or when a party should have known that the evidence may be relevant to future litigation."[13] The judge concluded, from certain e-mails and deposition testimony, that the pertinent people at UBS had anticipated litigation as of April 2001. A duty then had arisen to preserve relevant evidence, which here included documents sent to and from the "key players." Moreover, "[o]nce a party reasonably anticipates litigation, it must suspend its routine document retention/destruction policy and put in place a 'litigation hold' to ensure the preservation of relevant documents."

UBS had breached this duty. But the judge refused Zubulake's request to reconsider cost-shifting. "Zubulake next argues that UBS's spoliation warrants an adverse inference instruction. Zubulake asks that the jury in this case be instructed that it can infer from the fact that UBS destroyed certain evidence that the evidence, if available, would have been favorable to Zubulake and harmful to UBS. In practice, an adverse inference instruction often ends litigation—it is too difficult a hurdle for the spoliator to overcome. . . . When a jury is instructed that it may 'infer that the party who destroyed potentially relevant evidence did so "out of a realization that the [evidence was] unfavorable," '[38] the party suffering this instruction will be hard-pressed to prevail on the merits. Accordingly, the adverse inference instruction is an extreme sanction and should not be given lightly." Because Zubulake could not show the spoliation to be willful, she had to show the judge that the missing evidence would have favored her, but could not do so given the nature of the previously discovered e-mails.

"Even though an adverse inference instruction is not warranted, there is no question that e-mails that UBS should have produced to Zubulake

---

9 West v. Goodyear Tire & Rubber Co., 167 F.3d 776, 779 (2d Cir.1999).

10 Kronisch v. United States, 150 F.3d 112, 126 (2d Cir.1998).

11 Fujitsu Ltd. v. Federal Express Corp., 247 F.3d 423, 436 (2d Cir.2001).

13 Fujitsu, 247 F.3d at 436 (citing Kronisch, 150 F.3d at 126). [Other citation omitted.]

38 Linnen v. A.H. Robins Co., No. 97–2307, 1999 WL 462015, at * 11 (Mass.Super. June 16, 1999) (alteration in original) (quoting Blinzler v. Marriott International, Inc., 81 F.3d 1148, 1158 (1st Cir.1996)).

were destroyed by UBS. That being so, UBS must bear Zubulake's costs for re-deposing certain witnesses for the limited purpose of inquiring into issues raised by the destruction of evidence and any newly discovered e-mails. In particular, UBS is ordered to pay the costs of re-deposing Chapin, Hardisty, Tong, and Josh Varsano (a human resources employee in charge of the Asian Equities Sales Desk and known to have been in contact with Tong during August 2001)."

Zubulake v. UBS Warburg LLC (Zubulake V)

United States District Court, Southern District of New York, July 20, 2004.
229 F.R.D. 422.

■ SCHEINDLIN, DISTRICT JUDGE.

. . . .

. . . Laura Zubulake is once again moving to sanction UBS for its failure to produce relevant information and for its tardy production of such material. . . .

This decision addresses counsel's obligation to ensure that relevant information is preserved by giving clear instructions to the client to preserve such information and, perhaps more importantly, a client's obligation to heed those instructions. Early on in this litigation, UBS's counsel—both in-house and outside—instructed UBS personnel to retain relevant electronic information. Notwithstanding these instructions, certain UBS employees deleted relevant e-mails. Other employees never produced relevant information to counsel. As a result, many discoverable e-mails were not produced to Zubulake until recently, even though they were responsive to a document request propounded on June 3, 2002. In addition, a number of e-mails responsive to that document request were deleted and have been lost altogether.

Counsel, in turn, failed to request retained information from one key employee and to give the litigation hold instructions to another. They also failed to adequately communicate with another employee about how she maintained her computer files. Counsel also failed to safeguard backup tapes that might have contained some of the deleted e-mails, and which would have mitigated the damage done by UBS's destruction of those e-mails.

. . . Because of this failure by both UBS and its counsel, Zubulake has been prejudiced. As a result, sanctions are warranted.

. . . .

Fully aware of their common law duty to preserve relevant evidence, UBS's in-house attorneys gave oral instructions in August 2001—immediately after Zubulake filed her EEOC charge—instructing employees not to destroy or delete material potentially relevant to Zubulake's claims, and in fact to segregate such material into separate files for the lawyers' eventual review. This warning pertained to both electronic and hard-copy files, but did *not* specifically pertain to so-called "backup tapes," maintained by UBS's information technology personnel. In particular, UBS's in-house counsel, Robert L. Salzberg, "advised relevant UBS employees to preserve and turn over to counsel all files, records or other written memoranda or documents concerning the allegations raised in the [EEOC] charge or any aspect of [Zubulake's] employment." Subsequently—but still in August 2001—UBS's outside counsel met with a number of the key players in the litigation and reiterated Mr. Salzberg's instructions, reminding them to preserve relevant documents, "including e-mails." Salzberg reduced these instructions to writing in e-mails dated February 22, 2002—immediately after Zubulake filed her complaint—and September 25, 2002. Finally, in August 2002, after Zubulake propounded a document request that specifically called for e-mails stored on backup tapes, UBS's outside counsel instructed UBS information technology personnel to stop recycling backup tapes. . . .

. . . .

The essence of the current dispute is that during the re-depositions . . . , Zubulake learned about more deleted e-mails and about the existence of e-mails preserved on UBS's active servers that were, to that point, never produced. In sum, Zubulake has now presented evidence that UBS personnel deleted relevant e-mails, some of which were subsequently recovered from backup tapes (or elsewhere) and thus produced to Zubulake long after her initial document requests, and some of which were lost altogether. Zubulake has also presented evidence that some UBS personnel did not produce responsive documents to counsel until recently, depriving Zubulake of the documents for almost two years.

. . . .

. . . A party's discovery obligations do not end with the implementation of a "litigation hold"—to the contrary, that's only the beginning. Counsel must oversee compliance with the litigation hold, monitoring the party's efforts to retain and produce the relevant documents. Proper communication between a party and her lawyer will ensure (1) that all relevant information (or at least all sources of relevant information) is discovered, (2) that relevant information is retained on a continuing basis; and (3) that relevant non-privileged material is produced to the opposing party.

1. Counsel's Duty to Locate Relevant Information

Once a "litigation hold" is in place, a party and her counsel must make certain that all sources of potentially relevant information are identified . . . . To do this, counsel must become fully familiar with her client's document retention policies, as well as the client's data retention architecture. This will invariably involve speaking with information technology personnel, who can explain system-wide backup procedures and the actual (as opposed to theoretical) implementation of the firm's recycling policy. It will also involve communicating with the "key players" in the litigation, in order to understand how they stored information. . . .

To the extent that it may not be feasible for counsel to speak with every key player, given the size of a company or the scope of the lawsuit, counsel must be more creative. . . .

In short, it is *not* sufficient to notify all employees of a litigation hold and expect that the party will then retain and produce all relevant information. Counsel must take affirmative steps to monitor compliance so that all sources of discoverable information are identified and searched. . . .

2. Counsel's Continuing Duty to Ensure Preservation

Once a party and her counsel have identified all of the sources of potentially relevant information, they are under a duty to retain that information . . . and to produce information responsive to the opposing party's requests. Rule 26 creates a "duty to supplement" those responses. . . .

. . . .

. . . A lawyer cannot be obliged to monitor her client like a parent watching a child. At some point, the client must bear responsibility for a failure to preserve. At the same time, counsel is more conscious of the contours of the preservation obligation; a party cannot reasonably be trusted to receive the "litigation hold" instruction once and to fully comply with it without the active supervision of counsel.

There are thus a number of steps that counsel should take to ensure compliance with the preservation obligation. While these precautions may not be enough (or may be too much) in some cases, they are designed to promote the continued preservation of potentially relevant information in the typical case.

First, counsel must issue a "litigation hold" at the outset of litigation or whenever litigation is reasonably anticipated. The litigation hold should be periodically re-issued so that new employees are aware of it, and so that it is fresh in the minds of all employees.

Second, counsel should communicate directly with the "key players" in the litigation, i.e., the people identified in a party's initial disclosure and any subsequent supplementation thereto. . . . As with the litigation hold, the key players should be periodically reminded that the preservation duty is still in place.

Finally, counsel should instruct all employees to produce electronic copies of their relevant active files. Counsel must also make sure that all backup media which the party is required to retain is identified and stored in a safe place. In cases involving a small number of relevant backup tapes, counsel might be advised to take physical possession of backup tapes. In other cases, it might make sense for relevant backup tapes to be segregated and placed in storage. Regardless of what particular arrangement counsel chooses to employ, the point is to separate relevant backup tapes from others. One of the primary reasons that electronic data is lost is ineffective communication with information technology personnel. By taking possession of, or otherwise safeguarding, all potentially relevant backup tapes, counsel eliminates the possibility that such tapes will be inadvertently recycled.

. . . .

UBS's counsel—both in-house and outside—repeatedly advised UBS of its discovery obligations. In fact, counsel came very close to taking the precautions laid out above. . . .

. . . .

. . . In this case, counsel failed to properly oversee UBS in a number of important ways, both in terms of its duty to locate relevant information and its duty to preserve and timely produce that information.

. . . .

At the end of the day, however, the duty to preserve and produce documents rests on the party. Once that duty is made clear to a party, either by court order or by instructions from counsel, that party is on notice of its obligations and acts at its own peril. Though more diligent action on the part of counsel would have mitigated some of the damage caused by UBS's deletion of e-mails, UBS deleted the e-mails in defiance of explicit instructions not to.

. . . .

I therefore conclude that UBS acted wilfully in destroying potentially relevant information, which resulted either in the absence of such information or its tardy production . . . . Because UBS's spoliation was willful, the lost information is presumed to be [favorable to Zubulake].

. . . .

. . . I now consider the full panoply of available sanctions. In doing so, I recognize that a major consideration in choosing an appropriate sanction—along with punishing UBS and deterring future misconduct—is to restore Zubulake to the position that she would have been in had UBS faithfully discharged its discovery obligations. That being so, I find that the following sanctions are warranted.

First, the jury empanelled to hear this case will be given an adverse inference instruction with respect to e-mails deleted after August 2001, and in particular, with respect to e-mails that were irretrievably lost when UBS's backup tapes were recycled. No one can ever know precisely what was on those tapes, but the content of e-mails recovered from other sources—along with the fact that UBS employees wilfully deleted e-mails—is sufficiently favorable to Zubulake that I am convinced that the contents of the lost tapes would have been similarly, if not more, favorable.[99]

---

[99] [Citations omitted.]

Second, Zubulake argues that the e-mails that *were* produced, albeit late, "are brand new and very significant to Ms. Zubulake's retaliation claim and would have affected [her] examination of every witness . . . in this case." . . . Accordingly, UBS is ordered to pay the costs of any depositions or re-depositions required by the late production.

Third, UBS is ordered to pay the costs of this motion.

. . . .[i]

2006 RULE AMENDMENTS

The federal rulemakers started their serious study of this new problem in 2000. Meanwhile, courts gave ever increasing attention to the problem. Amendments worked through the rulemaking process to emerge in 2006 as new provisions on e-disclosure and e-discovery. Rules 16, 26, 33, 34, 37, and 45, among others, underwent amendment to codify the formerly disparate practices ordained by case law and local rules, as the Advisory Committee notes explain. See also Richard L. Marcus, E–Discovery & Beyond: Toward Brave New World or 1984?, 25 Rev.Litig. 633 (2006).

The changes promoted the discovery of "electronically stored information" (ESI) to equal status with discovery of "documents" and "things," thereby lifting the necessity of conceptually squeezing the digital within the documentary. The changes also tried to refine the scope of e-discovery by encouraging the balancing of costs and benefits under Rules 33, 34, and 45.

Note that I am *not* sanctioning UBS for the loss of the tapes (which was negligent), but rather for its *willful* deletion of e-mails. Those e-mails happen to be lost forever because the tapes that might otherwise have contained them were lost.

[The judge said that she would give this instruction:

> You have heard that UBS failed to produce some of the e-mails sent or received by UBS personnel in August and September 2001. Plaintiff has argued that this evidence was in defendants' control and would have proven facts material to the matter in controversy.
>
> If you find that UBS could have produced this evidence, and that the evidence was within its control, and that the evidence would have been material in deciding facts in dispute in this case, you are permitted, but not required, to infer that the evidence would have been unfavorable to UBS.
>
> In deciding whether to draw this inference, you should consider whether the evidence not produced would merely have duplicated other evidence already before you. You may also consider whether you are satisfied that UBS's failure to produce this information was reasonable. Again, any inference you decide to draw should be based on all of the facts and circumstances in this case.]

[i] This Zubulake (pronounced ZOO-boo-lake) case produced two more reported opinions, 231 F.R.D. 159 (S.D.N.Y. Feb. 3, 2005) (denying as too late the defendants' motion to amend their answer to add an affirmative defense, they having allegedly learned that Zubulake on her job application had misrepresented two prior job terminations for performance problems as being voluntary departures), and 382 F.Supp.2d 536 (S.D.N.Y. Mar. 16, 2005) (making evidence rulings via motions in limine). Bloomberg.com reported that the case went to a three-week trial before a jury of six women and two men. Judge Scheindlin "instructed the jurors to assume that e-mails UBS discarded after Zubulake filed her EEOC complaint would have hurt the bank's case." The verdict in April 2005 awarded the plaintiff over $9 million in compensatory damages and over $20 million in punitive damages. The defendants moved for judgment as a matter of law or for a new trial. The parties settled the case in October 2005.

In particular, Rule 26(b)(2)(B) distinguishes digital material that is reasonably accessible from digital material that is not, with cost-shifting openly on the table for the latter. Incidentally, Rule 26(b)(5) provides a new procedure for asserting privilege and immunity after inadvertent production (and see the new Evidence Rule 502 on the distinguishable question of whether the production itself constituted waiver of protection). And the discovering party under Rule 34 or 45 can now designate the form of production, subject to the respondent's objection.

Meanwhile, changes to the conferencing procedures of Rules 26(f) and 16(b), by becoming information-technology sensitive, facilitate supervision of e-discovery by the court. Incidentally, while the Rules recognize the existence of a duty to preserve digital material imposed by common law, statute, regulation, or court order, Rule 37(e) creates a safe harbor for destruction of digital material as part of "the routine, good-faith operation of an electronic information system."

How does it all work? Steven Gensler, Some Thoughts on the Lawyer's E-volving Duties in Discovery, 36 N.Ky.L.Rev. 521, 521 (2009), gave this summary: "Are electronic records discoverable? Of course they are. [Rule 34(a)(1)(A).] Do parties have to search all of their possible sources of electronic records, even their hard-to-access back-up tapes or other disaster recovery systems? Not initially, but it can be ordered for good cause. [Rule 26(b)(2)(B).] Must parties produce their electronic records in their native format, or will printed-out pages of the information suffice? That's for the parties to work out, though the judge has the ultimate say. [Rule 34(b)(1)(C), (2)(E).] And for the love of all that is holy, who pays for it all? As with ordinary discovery, the responding party presumptively bears the expense of search and production, though the e-discovery amendments give a nod to cost-shifting for so-called inaccessible data. [Rule 26(b)(2) advisory committee's note (2006).]" On the more subtle level, he predicts that with e-discovery the process will become even more front-loaded, with the parties heavily investing in the case from its beginnings through Rule 26(f), and ever more dependent on the opposing lawyers' cooperation to operate. But he also fears that Rule 26(g) and cases like Zubulake V will undesirably impose on lawyers the task of intimate involvement in overseeing their clients' preservation, identification, and production of ESI.

Question: (33) How would the new Rules have affected the Zubulake litigation?

TOPIC C

PRETRIAL CONFERENCES

E. DONALD ELLIOTT, MANAGERIAL JUDGING AND THE EVOLUTION OF PROCEDURE, 53 U.Chi.L.Rev. 306, 319–21 (1986). "[T]he problem that managerial judging [as under Federal Rule 16] aims to solve is, at base, structural: it results from a fundamental imbalance in the Rules between the techniques available for developing and expanding issues and those for narrowing or resolving them prior to trial.

. . . .

". . . [A]s the framers envisioned their new system, the issue-narrowing function was to be performed not by pleading, but by discovery and summary judgment.

. . . .

". . . However, in general the combination of discovery and summary judgment has proved inadequate to narrow the issues in litigation prior to trial.

. . . .

"Ironically, our great reluctance to narrow issues prematurely on the merits has been a major factor in the evolution of managerial judging which may narrow issues capriciously. . . . Because . . . issue-narrowing tools available in the Rules are so difficult to use, issue-narrowing is increasingly being performed through managerial judging, without any formal procedures or safeguards for assessing the merit of the issues that are foreclosed. Litigants actually end up with less, not more, protection against arbitrariness. A further irony is that the use of managerial judging to narrow issues reintroduces two of the primary evils that the drafters of the Federal Rules were at pains to abolish—premature definition of issues, and outcomes based on preliminary procedural skirmishing rather than the legal merit of claims."

JAQUETTE v. BLACK HAWK COUNTY, IOWA, 710 F.2d 455 (8th Cir.1983). A terminated employee brought a civil rights action for violation of her First and Fourteenth Amendment rights. Eventually she settled for $1500. She then requested almost $93,000 in attorney's fees, for 1034.45 hours' work, under 42 U.S.C. § 1988. The district court awarded about $20,000, finding the time expended to be excessive. She appealed.

The court of appeals remanded for an evidentiary hearing on the reasons behind expending excessive hours and for consideration of sanctions against either side. The court added:

"This case, although not unusual on its facts, exemplifies not only society's concern, but the profession's acknowledgment that there exists excessive cost and delay in litigation. The direct effect is the denial of reasonable access to justice in our courts. The entire administration of justice is involved. The searching question is why. Assuming counsel for each side acted in good faith, and we have no reason at this stage to suggest otherwise, nonetheless the time, expense and delay involved in the litigation of a relatively simple claim demands full judicial attention. . . .

"In almost all cases the key to avoiding excessive costs and delay is early and stringent judicial management of the case. Sending counsel off into extended 'paper chases' in compliance with pretrial orders has now been demonstrated not to be the answer. See Peckham, The Federal Judge as a Case Manager: The New Role in Guiding a Case from Filing to Disposition, 69 Calif.L.Rev. 770 (1981); Pollack, Pretrial Procedures More Effectively Handled, 65 F.R.D. 475 (1975); Solomon, Techniques for Shortening Trials, 65 F.R.D. 485 (1975); Will, Judicial Responsibility for the Disposition of Litigation, 75 F.R.D. 117 (1978). The recognition of early judicial management, not by the clerk, not by the magistrate, but by the trial judge before whom the case will be tried is essential. Management conferences at the pleading stage, which simplify the extent of discovery as well as the issues involved, have proven successful. The newly adopted Federal Rule of Civil Procedure 16(b) contemplates such a practice.[19] We request each district judge to re-evaluate local rules with the view toward early case management. With such management procedure, we are confident that litigation such as this, extending almost three years in the district court, would be avoided. Excessive costs of litigation is as much the court's concern as it is of counsel and litigants. We fully recognize district judges are busy people; it has been argued that they do not have time for pretrial skirmishes because they are too busy in the 'adjudication' of cases (that is, the trial itself). However, it is time to recognize that the adjudication process begins at the time of the filing of the complaint and carries through to the last appeal. Lack of proper judicial supervision in the pretrial stage leads to excessive discovery, the development of complex and multiple issues, extended motion practice, and long and expensive trials. Conversely, time expended wisely by counsel and the district judge at the early stages will save many hours of unnecessary labor later in the process. We suggest that under the newly amended rules of civil procedure requiring early judicial supervision and management, the present litigation could have been resolved within six to nine months. The litigation should have terminated long before the plaintiff's counsel could have expended 1,000 hours. Early and ongoing judicial management is essential if the judicial process is to survive. It is now obvious that adversarial lawyers are unable

---

[19] [The court, deciding on June 27, 1983, here quoted the new Rule 16(b), promulgated by the Supreme Court on April 28 and due to become effective August 1.]

to achieve proper management alone. This new procedure may necessitate changes in the practice of many judges and attorneys, but unless we are willing to innovate and break away from our present conduct, excess costs and delays will geometrically multiply, and the result will be the denial of justice in our courts."

Steven Flanders, Case Management and Court Management in United States District Courts

ix–xi, 18–19, 35–37 (1977).

This volume reports the overall results of the District Court Studies Project, a long-range effort by the Federal Judicial Center to assist the work of the United States district courts. . . . Specifically, the project has been designed to determine what procedures are associated with the greatest possible speed and productivity, consistent with the highest standards of justice. A secondary goal is to determine precisely what some of the statistical measures in use actually measure. This report is based on visits to ten courts. It presents extensive data from the civil dockets of six of those courts. The visits included detailed discussions with judges and most supporting personnel, and observation of the widest possible variety of proceedings.

. . . .

The following factors primarily distinguish the fast and/or highly productive courts from the others:

An automatic procedure assures, for every civil case, that pleadings are strictly monitored, discovery begins quickly and is completed within a reasonable time, and a prompt trial follows if needed. These procedures are automatic in that they are invoked at the start of every case, subject only to a small number of necessary exceptions. Although all the courts visited have procedures designed to achieve early and effective control, most do not attain that goal. In slow courts, much of the time during which a typical case is pending is either unused or violates the time limits in the Federal Rules of Civil Procedure.

Procedures minimize or eliminate judges' investment of time through the early stages of a case, until discovery is complete. Docket control, attorney contacts, and most conferences are delegated, generally to the courtroom deputy clerk or a magistrate. A case comes to the judge's attention only when he is indispensable to resolve preliminary matters, handle dispositive motions, or plan the preparation of an exceptionally complex case.

The role of the court in settlement is minimized; judges are highly selective in initiating settlement negotiations, and normally do so only when a case is ready, or nearly ready, for trial. Some judges also arrange to raise the issue early in each case, or have a magistrate do so.

Relatively few written opinions are prepared for publication.

All proceedings that do not specifically require a confidential atmosphere are held in open court.

We recommend that widespread adoption of these approaches be considered. . . .

. . . .

The District Court Studies Project research revealed problems with some widely accepted opinions about speed and productivity, such as:

—"*It all comes down to strong case management.*" Most courts visited are characterized by "strong case management" in one form or another. The differences lie in the relative effectiveness of alternative forms of case management.

. . . .

—"*A comprehensive pretrial order is essential.*" None of the courts enforced this requirement fully in routine cases. The ones that enforced it most vigorously were not necessarily the speediest or most efficient.

—"*Get the lawyers in early and often.*" Our observations suggest that frequent conferences are a poor use of time.

. . . .

TABLE 5

Overall Disposition Times

Fiscal 1975

	All cases sampled	
	Median (days)	Number (cases)
FL/S	121	595
CA/C	166	541
MD	223	502
LA/E	313	494
PA/E	352	497
MA	500	468
Average	279	516

. . . Each court was visited in late 1975 or in 1976 to obtain data on approximately 500 randomly selected civil cases. A group of highly skilled researchers (most of them present or past law clerks to district judges) filled out a detailed form for each case, under the direction of Paul Connolly of the Federal Judicial Center staff. Cases were selected from a list of all cases terminated in the district in fiscal 1975, listed in order of their docket numbers (therefore also the order in which they were filed).

From a random starting point, every third, or fifth, or *n*th case was selected; the interval was chosen to yield approximately 500 cases from each court.

. . . .

TABLE 21

Scheduling Pretrials

	Initiation time *		Control time **		Overall time: answer until first pretrial[a]	
	Median (days)	Number (cases)	Median (days)	Number (settings)	Median (days)	Number (cases)
FL/S	18	250	49	401	94	77
CA/C	21	196	63	342	186	96
MD	82	145	33	266	71	169
LA/E	104	305	43	603	158	253
PA/E	175	122	42	203	192	193
MA	595	58	28	91	763	84
Average	165.8	179.3	43	317.7	244	145.3

* Time interval between the answer to the original complaint and the first date on which a pretrial date is set.
** Time interval between the date on which a pretrial date is set and the date pretrial is set for.

Some courts could save several months by asserting earlier control of civil cases. The controls asserted are fairly effective, once imposed.

. . . Table 21 shows the courts' pretrial conference scheduling practices. (. . . Maryland and Eastern Pennsylvania figures are affected by several judges' practice of holding pretrial conferences, no record of which appears in the file or on the docket sheet.)

The key variable seems to be the time interval between the answer to the original complaint and the date on which the first pretrial was scheduled. The range of differences here is extraordinarily large, from 18 and 21 days, respectively, in Southern Florida and Central California, up to 595 days (in a very small number of cases) in Massachusetts. This appears to be a crucial variable. Eastern Pennsylvania, for example, could possibly save four or five months of "dead time" in many cases by earlier scheduling of the first pretrial conference.

[Other data on the courts' setting of a discovery cutoff date generally showed a similar effectiveness of early control.]

---

[a] A later footnote explained: "It should be noted that these figures . . . are not additive. One cannot add the median initiation time to the median control time. Medians in general are not additive. Beyond that, different groups of cases are involved in the variables displayed in this table, and a time interval measured for one group is not necessarily applicable to another. The clearest instance is the three medians shown for Maryland. The median overall time is actually shorter than the median initiation time. It is much shorter than the sum of initiation plus control time."

The data on pretrials and discovery cutoffs, in summary, show great differences among the courts in the nature and extent of case management control—differences that appear to have a powerful impact on disposition time.

Mary L. Luskin, Building a Theory of Case Processing Time

62 Judicature 115, 117, 120–23 (1978).

Writing on court delay is voluminous, but much of it might simply be termed inspirational. Judges, administrators and prosecutors who feel that they have been successful in reducing delay in their own courts describe their actions and report "significant" reductions in delay or backlog. The authors assume the actions have caused the reduction in delay but make no attempt to actually separate the effect of the innovation from that of other potential causes nor to measure the size of the effect that can be attributed to the action taken by the court relative to other variables. In the absence of a theory of case processing time, these reports may be helpful to court administrators, judges and prosecutors looking for suggestions about how they might approach problems of court delay, but they contribute little or nothing to the development of a theory of case processing time.

More analytic works on court delay specify variables thought to affect case processing time and backlog and describe the relationships among them. The articles discussed below vary in the degree to which they do this, in appropriateness of the statistical models used to represent their theory, and, thus, in their contribution to a theory of case processing time. I have organized this work under four general headings: (1) inventories of causes, (2) experiments, (3) surveys, and (4) process models.

. . . .

Surveys are by far the most common research designs for studying court delay. In surveys, unlike experiments, the researcher does not manipulate the independent variables; both the independent and dependent variables vary naturally. The researcher observes variation in the dependent variable, hypothesizes causes for it, and seeks to sort out and estimate the effects produced by these causes.

This characteristic lack of control over the independent variables means that the causal ordering of the variables is more problematic in surveys than in experiments. . . . Lack of control over the independent variables also means that statistical techniques must be used to disentangle the effects of multiple causes of the dependent variable.

. . . .

Often, however, the theoretical and policy utility of court delay studies using survey designs has been limited by the inadequacy of the statistical models used to test the researcher's hypotheses. Most researchers hold, at least implicitly, theories of case processing time that are multivariate and asymmetric, that is, theories that say that variation in case processing time is produced by at least two independent variables and that influence flows *to* the dependent variable *from* these variables . . . . The analysis models many of these same researchers use, however, are bivariate (they examine the association between two variables only) and symmetric (the statistic estimates the degree to which the independent and dependent variable vary together, but not the change in the dependent variable produced by the change in the independent variable). If the theory is multivariate and asymmetric but the analysis model is bivariate and associational, the model is mis-specified.

. . . From a seriously mis-specified model (e.g., one that omits an important causal variable), one can develop neither satisfactory theory nor satisfactory policy recommendations.

Some examples will illustrate the shortcomings of a bivariate, symmetric model for analyzing case processing time. . . .

. . . Sovern and Rosenberg looked at the relationships between case characteristics and case processing time in civil cases.[13] They reported that the size of the claim has the single largest correlation with case processing time. Because they measure bivariate associations without having introduced controls for variables that affected the size of those associations, they did not rule out the alternative hypothesis that the association is spurious—that is, that some other variable produced the observed association between claim size and case processing time. Furthermore, if the relationship is real, do we want to know only that size of claim and case processing time vary together? Or do we want an estimate of the magnitude of the effect of size of claim given the presence of the other causes? If we believe that differences in the size of the claim cause differences in case processing time, a symmetric statistical model is inappropriate to our theory and does not yield the information we want.

. . . .

The District Court Studies Project . . . seeks to relate differences in speed and productivity to differences in the practices of courts. The project has two goals: to identify differences below "slow" courts and "fast" courts and to identify the ways in which current measures of speed and delay may be misleading. To accomplish these goals, [certain] metropolitan federal courts representing the extremes in speed and delay in the federal system were studied. Once again, the design looks at a small group of fast and slow courts that vary on many dimensions. Because of the small number of courts studied and the cross-sectional nature of the data, most of the analysis relies on informal observations of associations between various activities—opinion writing, for example—and measures of speed or productivity.

. . . .

In the reports on this project, the informal analysis model used, for the most part, is bivariate even though the implicit theoretical model is

---

[13] Michael I. Sovern and Maurice Rosenberg, Delay and the Dynamics of Personal Injury Litigation, 59 Colum.L.Rev. 1115 (1959).

multivariate. As a result, the authors cannot assess the relative importance of differences among courts in the speed of processing nor can they rule out the possibility that the relationships they observe are spurious. The District Court Studies Project can point to some variables that may be related to delay and may be susceptible to manipulation, but it cannot assess the size of the effects to be expected.

JOSEPH W. BARTLETT, THE LAW BUSINESS: A TIRED MONOPOLY 93–94 (1982). "In the course of implementing reforms, one must come to grips with the argument that the causes of delay in the court system are mysterious and complex, the efficacy of currently recommended solutions has not in many cases been supported by empirical data and further research is necessary. To give this view its due, it is certainly the fact that some of the current suggestions for slaying the dragon of delay have been off the mark—indeed some, like the pretrial conference, may even foster the opportunities for delay in certain instances. On the other hand, the lack of a study is not . . . a necessary or sufficient reason for delaying change that experience and common sense recommends. The business of studying delay in the courts has become an industry in itself. And, the product of those studies has been, in many instances, disappointing; the 'findings' too often reflect what is or should be obvious to any one with experience in the field.

. . . .

". . . The vice of interminable studies is that studies condition people who are already cautious by nature (as lawyers undoubtedly are) and who are protected by lifetime tenure (as judges generally are) to think in terms of 'more studies, more data' before acting. Moreover, studies usually don't uncover quirks in the system—actual practice does; systems can only be debugged in use."

KEVIN M. CLERMONT, LITIGATION REALITIES REDUX, 84 Notre Dame L.Rev. 1919, 1939, 1946–48 (2009). This survey article observes that for pretrial conference, just as for discovery, "Rule amendments over recent decades again have been frequent, but still reliant on guesswork. Despite some promising early empirical work, the system's continuing reliance on conferences has seen virtually nothing in the way of systematic empirical study." It then sounds a note of caution:

"Moreover, there are other good reasons to proceed with wariness before accepting the truth of either old maxims about delay or the potential of new reforms based merely on intuition. Both recent theoretical work and recent empirical study argue for such caution.

"Theoretical work contends that delay is not necessarily an evil. Delay is an unavoidable feature of life, and it is not an evil in itself. The only evil is excessive delay, where excessive means that the costs of delay outweigh its benefits. The costs of figuratively queuing to try a case tend to be exaggerated, because we overlook that the parties can engage in other pursuits while waiting. Meanwhile, queuing in fact has some benefits, such as lowering the demand for expensive trials.

"Another study,[152] both theoretical and empirical, shows that many obvious reforms simply have not worked and will not work to reduce delay. The basic insight is that any reduction in delay increases the incentives to litigate and reduces the parties' incentives to settle, with the consequent increase in caseload offsetting the reduction in delay. Therefore, most attempts at reform, such as heeding the constant call for adding judges, will only increase the number of dispositions, rather than decreasing the time to disposition. Adding judges to the system to reduce congestion is similar to expanding the number of lanes on a freeway, an improvement that would draw traffic off the side streets and from public transportation. More cases might flow into the system, and the lesser burden of litigating might reduce the subsequent incentives to settle rather than litigate, so the increased number of judges would be able to adjudicate basically the same percentage of cases. Indeed, the author of the study postulated a 'congestion equilibrium hypothesis': almost all reform attempts to accelerate litigation will be largely offset by increases in the amount of litigation.

"Pure empirical work in this area is rather rare because of the scarcity of data and the inherently complex nature of the relevant research questions. It is unclear even what to measure, no less how to measure in a controlled way. But the empirical work that exists, while suggesting that delay is neither that lengthy nor increasing recently, is otherwise consistently discouraging for the persistent reformer. One study used state data to demonstrate that particular processes, such as alternative dispute resolution (ADR), do not correlate with shortened disposition times—meanwhile, the factors that do so correlate, such as forum locale and case category, are beyond the reach of process-oriented reform.[155]"

Wayne D. Brazil, Improving Judicial Controls over the Pretrial Development of Civil Actions: Model Rules for Case Management and Sanctions

1981 Am.B.Found.Res.J. 873, 916–20.

[Based on extensive interviews with lawyers and judicial officers, then Professor and now Magistrate Judge Brazil develops his own comprehen-

---

[152] George L. Priest, Private Litigants and the Court Congestion Problem, 69 B.U.L.Rev. 527 (1989).

[155] Michael Heise, Justice Delayed?: An Empirical Analysis of Civil Case Disposition Time, 50 Case W.Res.L.Rev. 813, 848 (2000); see also Priest, supra note 152, at 535, 537 (forwarding the "congestion equilibrium hypothesis" while suggesting "that there is likely to be some equilibrium level of delay within any jurisdiction," but recognizing that procedure can be made more or less just at any given equilibrium level of delay and also acknowledging that certain reforms such as increasing court costs or altering the local legal culture could lower the equilibrium somewhat).

sive model rule for judicial pretrial management. Nevertheless, he approves the basic purposes and concepts of what would be the 1983 and 1993 revisions of Rule 16. He goes on to suggest further changes:]

Subdivision (a) of the revised rule would confer upon courts the power to convene pretrial conferences and would describe in general terms some of the major purposes such conferences could serve. . . .

Subdivision (a) also should acknowledge that responsibility to be alert to the need for or potential utility of an early pretrial conference is not confined to the court. One way to incorporate such an acknowledgment in the rule itself (as opposed to merely discussing it in accompanying notes) is to indicate that the litigants or their lawyers may file a motion requesting the court to convene a conference. It is not clear, however, that the court should be *obligated* to schedule a conference merely because a potential participant requests one. A rule that would give the parties or their attorneys an essentially unqualified right to compel the convening of these kinds of conferences might be abused to delay the movement of an action toward trial or to burden (e.g., economically) an opponent. This possibility, coupled with the notion that pretrial conferences should remain primarily *judges'* tools for case control, suggest that at least in the absence of the kinds of requirements [that would impose on the movant the duty to have first prepared proposed orders and sought agreement thereon with opponents], Rule 16(a) should leave the court with the discretion to deny a motion for any pretrial conference not required by the language of the federal rule itself or by a local rule adopted by a district court.

Subdivision (b) of the new rule would require the courts, except in categories of cases exempted by local rule, to consult at least informally (e.g., by telephone or correspondence) with counsel and unrepresented parties about the time requirements for joinder, amended pleadings, motions, and discovery, and then within [about the first hundred days] to issue an order fixing the dates for completion of these matters. Some matters 16(b) leaves optional for the court to include in a scheduling order should be moved to the mandatory list: at least the dates for the final pretrial conference and for the trial itself. As discussed above, the data produced by our interviews and by other studies indicate that fixing early and firm dates *for the completion of trial preparation and for the trial itself* is probably the single most effective device thus far developed for encouraging prompt and well-focused case development. There does not appear to be any consequential practical obstacle to setting these dates very shortly after an action is commenced. Several judges we interviewed reported that they routinely follow such a procedure and that it has had very beneficial effects. Other studies and commentaries have described the successful use of this approach in several federal courts.

As the description of my model rule for pretrial management should make clear, I believe there is a need for a more fundamental change in proposed 16(b). That subdivision (or some other part of Rule 16) should set forth criteria for identifying "potentially complex or protracted cases" or should require each district court to adopt a local rule that does so.

Thereafter, the rule should separately set forth additional requirements for managing actions that satisfy the criteria. For potentially complex or protracted cases, these additional requirements should convert the scheduling conference into a broader and more formal management session by expanding the list of mandatory subjects for consultation and incorporation in an order to include: (1) exploring, at least briefly, the possibility of settlement and various means to achieve it, (2) formulating and attempting to narrow the issues genuinely in dispute, (3) devising means to secure stipulations to as many matters as possible, (4) discussing possibilities for voluntary, informal exchanges of information, (5) deciding whether to hold a . . . discovery conference and, if not, estimating the amount and kinds of discovery the case will require and setting guidelines for the first round of discovery, (6) deciding whether to refer any pretrial matters to a magistrate or special master and, if so, specifying the scope of his authority as well as procedures for appealing his decisions and the standards to be applied on such appeals, and (7) fixing an early date and an agenda for the next pretrial or status conference.

It is particularly important that the federal rules assure that the courts take affirmative steps at the outset of each action to identify potentially complex cases. Clause [(2)(L)] of 16(c) of the proposed rule identifies four "illustrative" characteristics, any one of which, according to the note, makes "a case a strong candidate for special treatment." Because the discovery stage consumes such a significant percentage of the overall litigation time of complex actions and because of the great need for control during that stage, I recommend adding a fifth characteristic to the list . . . : "extensive discovery." This addition should encourage judges to focus on the potential for inefficiency and delay during discovery when they are deciding whether to adopt "special procedures for managing potentially difficult or protracted actions."

It also is important that the rules compel prompt and meaningful judicial involvement in assessing discovery needs and shaping and pacing discovery proceedings. . . . There is reason to question the potential effectiveness of any rule that . . . relies primarily on initiatives by counsel to involve the judiciary in case management. Even though most of the big case litigators we interviewed said they would favor, at least as an abstract proposition, "greater judicial involvement in the discovery stage of litigation," some of our respondents suggested that attorneys might feel considerable reluctance, in specific cases, to take steps that would foreseeably reduce the scope of their freedom to maneuver by vesting significant control over pretrial developments in a judicial officer. Widely shared beliefs that many judges and magistrates are not interested in discovery matters and, under current procedures, tend to be superficial or arbitrary in ruling on discovery disputes could intensify that reluctance. . . . In any event, one thing seems clear: prompt, close, and continuous judicial or parajudicial monitoring of the discovery process is too important in big cases to be left to chance. Either Rule 16 or Rule 26 should establish compulsory procedural machinery to secure that kind of monitoring in all potentially complex actions.

Rule 16(b) and (c) should also describe counsel's obligations with respect to both scheduling and pretrial conferences more clearly . . . . Responsibilities of participants in scheduling or pretrial conferences are mentioned in two places in the proposed rule. The first of these is [in] 16(c), which appears to relate only to pretrial conferences. It requires counsel to "have authority to enter into stipulations and to make admissions regarding all matters that the participants may reasonably anticipate may be discussed." The only other reference to the duties of parties and counsel is in 16(f), which is devoted to "Sanctions." That paragraph authorizes courts to impose sanctions if

> a party or party's attorney fails to obey a scheduling or pretrial order, or if no appearance is made on behalf of a party at a scheduling or pretrial conference, or if a party or party's attorney is substantially unprepared to participate in the conference, or if a party or party's attorney fails to participate in good faith.

Together, these passages in essence require counsel to "substantially" prepare for scheduling or pretrial conferences, to acquire authority to enter stipulations and make admissions during pretrial conferences (but not during scheduling conferences), and to appear (when ordered) and to participate in good faith in both kinds of conferences.

There are several ways in which these duty provisions could be improved. The rule would communicate much more clearly what counsels' obligations are if it described them in a separately lettered subdivision to precede the subdivision authorizing sanctions. The subdivision devoted to articulating the obligations the rule imposes should explicitly require the court to give counsel (and unrepresented parties) timely advance notice of any subjects the court expects to cover or tasks the court intends to accomplish that are not described with particularity in a standing order or local rule applying to the type of conference involved. The "duties" subdivision also should compel counsel, in advance of the scheduling conference or within 60 days after commencement of the action, to draft estimates of the amount of time required for joinder, amending pleadings, presenting Rule 12 motions, completing discovery, and preparing for the final pretrial conference. Such estimates are necessary to enable the judge to make the decisions required by 16(b). By failing to make the duty to prepare such estimates clear, the rule invites either irrational judicial decision making or delays while counsel scramble belatedly to respond to the court's initial effort at "consultation."

The duties section of Rule 16 also should have a separate subdivision setting forth additional obligations that counsel or parties involved in potentially complex cases must fulfill. That subdivision should require counsel, in advance of the first judicially hosted conference, (1) to draft and exchange statements of the major issues and narrative descriptions of the events or acts on which the lawsuit is based, (2) to explore the possibility of arranging for voluntary, informal exchanges of information, (3) to estimate the amount and kinds of discovery they will conduct, and (4) to discuss the advisability of referring matters to a magistrate or special master and, if appropriate, to exchange lists of names of acceptable masters.

[Professor Brazil would also tighten up the sanctions subdivision and recognize a right to compensation for violations.]

Judith Resnik, Managerial Judges

96 Harv.L.Rev. 374, 376–80, 388–90, 400–02, 422, 431–32, 444–45 (1982), reprinted in Rand R–3002–ICJ (1982).

Until recently, the American legal establishment embraced a classical view of the judicial role. Under this view, judges are not supposed to have an involvement or interest in the controversies they adjudicate. Disengagement and dispassion supposedly enable judges to decide cases fairly and impartially. . . .

Many federal judges have departed from their earlier attitudes; they have dropped the relatively disinterested pose to adopt a more active, "managerial" stance.[4] In growing numbers, judges are not only adjudicating the merits of issues presented to them by litigants, but also are meeting with parties in chambers to encourage settlement of disputes and to supervise case preparation. Both before and after the trial, judges are playing a critical role in shaping litigation and influencing results.

. . . .

. . . Judges have described their new tasks as "case management"—hence my term "managerial judges." As managers, judges learn more about cases much earlier than they did in the past. They negotiate with parties about the course, timing, and scope of both pretrial and posttrial litigation. These managerial responsibilities give judges greater power. Yet the restraints that formerly circumscribed judicial authority are conspicuously absent. Managerial judges frequently work beyond the public view, off the record, with no obligation to provide written, reasoned opinions, and out of reach of appellate review.

This new managerial role has emerged for several reasons. One is the creation of pretrial discovery rights. The 1938 Federal Rules of Civil Procedure embodied contradictory mandates: a discovery system ("give your opponent all information relevant to the litigation") was grafted onto American adversarial norms ("protect your client zealously" and therefore "withhold what you can"). In some cases, parties argued about their obligations under the discovery rules; such disputes generated a need for someone to decide pretrial conflicts. Trial judges accepted the assignment and have become mediators, negotiators, and planners—as well as adjudicators. Moreover, once involved in pretrial discovery, many judges became convinced that their presence at other points in a lawsuit's development

---

[4] I focus on changes in the federal courts, but similar changes are underway in many state courts. See P. Ebener, Court Efforts to Reduce Pretrial Delay (1981); L. Freedman, State Legislation on Dispute Resolution (1982).

would be beneficial; supervision of discovery became a conduit for judicial control over all phases of litigation and thus infused lawsuits with the continual presence of the judge-overseer.

Partly because of their new oversight role and partly because of increasing case loads, many judges have become concerned with the volume of their work. To reduce the pressure, judges have turned to efficiency experts who promise "calendar control." Under the experts' guidance, judges have begun to experiment with schemes for speeding the resolution of cases and for persuading litigants to settle rather than try cases whenever possible. During the past decade, enthusiasm for the "managerial movement" has become widespread; what began as an experiment is likely soon to become obligatory. Unless the Supreme Court and Congress reject proposed amendments to [rule 16], pretrial judicial management will be required in virtually all cases.

In the rush to conquer the mountain of work, no one—neither judges, court administrators, nor legal commentators—has assessed whether relying on trial judges for informal dispute resolution and for case management, either before or after trial, is good, bad, or neutral. Little empirical evidence supports the claim that judicial management "works" either to settle cases or to provide cheaper, quicker, or fairer dispositions.[21] Proponents of judicial management have also failed to consider the systemic effects of the shift in judicial role. Management is a new form of "judicial activism," a behavior that usually attracts substantial criticism. Moreover, judicial management may be teaching judges to value their statistics, such as the number of case dispositions, more than they value the quality of their dispositions. Finally, because managerial judging is less visible and usually unreviewable, it gives trial courts more authority and at the same time provides litigants with fewer procedural safeguards to protect them from abuse of that authority. In short, managerial judging may be redefining sub silentio our standards of what constitutes rational, fair, and impartial adjudication.

---

21 [Here Professor Resnik cross-refers to a later section where she points out the limits of currently available information and includes these observations:]

Commentators and rulemakers rely heavily on Flanders' work for the proposition that pretrial management techniques actually promote efficiency. Perhaps the most prominent example of this reliance is found in the Advisory Committee's notes to draft rule 16:

> Empirical studies reveal that when a trial judge intervenes personally at an early stage to assume judicial control over a case and to schedule dates for completion by the parties of the principal pretrial steps, the case is disposed of by settlement or trial more efficiently and with less cost and delay than when the parties are left to their own devices.

. . . Flanders, however, measured neither parties' costs nor court management costs.

Some commentators also rely on Flanders' data to assert that case management does not "necessarily" diminish quality. [Omitted citations include Professor Brazil's above-excerpted article.] But Flanders provides no measurement of quality; instead he assumes a "close positive relationship between speed and quality." . . . He concedes that "no staff member on this project could be considered qualified to attempt a comprehensive evaluation of the quality of justice rendered in the several courts we observed. That evaluation is a task well left to others . . . ."

[Professor Resnik constructs some hypothetical but realistic cases to demonstrate the ways in which the new managerial role influences litigation. For example:]

2. Paulson v. Danforth, Ltd.—On July 1, 1980, Sarah Paulson bought a "Zip," a car manufactured by the small British company Danforth, Ltd., from a dealer in Manhattan. She drove the car home to the state of Essex in the fall of 1980. On March 4, 1981, while driving at about fifty miles per hour on an interstate highway in Essex, Ms. Paulson lost control of the car and skidded into a side railing. The gas tank exploded immediately, and Ms. Paulson was badly burned. On January 4, 1982, Ms. Paulson's attorney, Robert Adams, filed Paulson v. Danforth, Ltd. in the United States District Court for the District of Essex. The complaint alleged that defective design had caused the gas tank to explode upon impact, and sought $750,000 in damages. The case was randomly assigned to Judge Edward Kinser.

Danforth's counsel in New York City received a copy of the complaint on January 15 and promptly telecopied it to Danforth's headquarters in London. Danforth retained Deborah Alford, an Essex City lawyer, on January 18. On February 4, Danforth filed a motion to dismiss the suit for lack of personal jurisdiction. Danforth claimed that, because its only business offices in the United States were in New York and California, it could not be sued in Essex. Ms. Paulson countered that Danforth was a commercial enterprise that voluntarily and deliberately did business with people coming from and going to Essex.

On June 10, Judge Kinser denied Danforth's motion to dismiss. On June 18, Danforth filed its answer denying liability. Thereafter, pursuant to rules 33 and 34 of the Federal Rules of Civil Procedure, Mr. Adams served a set of interrogatories and a notice to produce documents. Among the fifty interrogatories were the following:

> 13. From 1977 until 1982, did Danforth test the gas tank on the "Zip" to learn about the tank's durability and ability to withstand impact?
>
> 14. If the tests described in question 13 above were performed, list below the names of all personnel who had any responsibility for the tests.

Plaintiff also made several document requests, including this one:

> 8. Provide all data on the results of any tests performed on the "Zip" from January 1, 1977, through June 1, 1982.

Plaintiff served these discovery requests on Danforth's attorney on July 10, 1982. After the thirty days that the Federal Rules permit for response had passed, Mr. Adams reminded Ms. Alford of the discovery requests. She expressed reservations about the propriety of several questions. Aware of the local district court rule requiring counsel to negotiate discovery disputes "in good faith" before filing discovery motions, the lawyers discussed the questions for several minutes but could not resolve their differences.

Twenty days later, defendant moved for a protective order. Danforth asked Judge Kinser to rule that: (1) twenty-nine of the fifty interrogatories were vague, irrelevant, or overly burdensome, or requested privileged information, and therefore need not be answered; (2) Danforth need not produce crash test data for 1977–1979 and for 1981–1982, because such statistics were irrelevant; and (3) only plaintiff's attorney could see the information produced, because of its "commercial" nature. In opposition to the motion, Mr. Adams asserted the relevance of the information and the absence of any special reason to protect the disclosure. Claiming that Danforth had no legal basis for a protective motion, Mr. Adams requested that his client be awarded the costs and attorney's fees incurred in opposing the motion.

After Judge Kinser read the papers on the pending discovery motion, he decided that he did not know enough about plaintiff's theories to decide the questions presented. He called the attorneys to his chambers and asked them to explain more about the case. After listening for several minutes to the lawyers' posturing, Judge Kinser asked whether all these legal battles were really necessary: was not settlement the least expensive, quickest, and fairest resolution of most disputes? When the attorneys insisted upon pursuing their arguments, the judge asked whether the lawyers were acting in their clients' best interests. Had they thought about how costly the litigation would be? Did the clients know how risky trials were? That the loser would have to pay the victor's court costs? That discovery could take years and that he, the judge, had control over the schedule?

Judge Kinser then asked Mr. Adams to leave the room so that the judge could confer privately with defendant's lawyer. Judge Kinser explained to Ms. Alford that he had learned a bit about plaintiff's case and that it looked "sound" to him. Did Danforth understand that a jury would surely be sympathetic to an injured plaintiff? What harm would there be in giving this injured victim some money? Had the parties talked numbers? Perhaps she could tell her client that $250,000 seemed "about right" to the judge. And perhaps she could mention that his court looked with disfavor upon uncompromising litigants.

Judge Kinser then called in plaintiff's counsel for a private meeting. Did Mr. Adams know how hard it was to prove a products liability claim? Had he thought about how long it might take to get to trial? What numbers would his client "go for"? The judge thought that $250,000 "sounded right" and that the case looked like one that "should settle."

Summoning both attorneys before him once more, Judge Kinser concluded the conference by announcing that he would defer ruling on the discovery motion until the parties had had time to negotiate further. He set a date to hold another conference in six weeks.

. . . .

Under [rule 16's] new regime of judicial management, discovery disputes and efforts to promote settlement would not be the only occasions upon which Judge Kinser would become acquainted with the parties' attorneys and the details of lawsuits. Rather, by virtue of rule 16, he would be obliged to issue pretrial orders within 120 days of filing of a complaint.[b] To do so with any intelligence, he would need to learn a good deal about the lawsuits to which he was assigned.

"Replaying" Paulson v. Danforth, Ltd. as if proposed rule 16 were in effect illustrates that the grant of pretrial power to federal judges would be expansive. In the hypothetical, Ms. Paulson's attorney, Mr. Adams, filed the complaint on January 4, 1982. But suppose that, instead of promptly replying, defendant asked for an additional twenty days to respond. Plaintiff's counsel readily agreed, and the parties filed a stipulation to that effect. However, Judge Kinser refused to permit any extension beyond the time permitted by the Federal Rules—twenty days after receipt of service.

On May 14, Judge Kinser held a rule 16 pretrial conference. Although he had not yet decided Danforth's pending motion to dismiss for lack of personal jurisdiction, rule 16 required him to issue a pretrial order "in no event more than 120 days after filing of the complaint." Ms. Alford argued that it would be a substantial waste of time and money for her to present discovery plans, because (she believed) the case should be dismissed on the jurisdictional ground. Mr. Adams was reluctant to discuss the case at all; he explained to the judge that, because no answer had been filed, he did not know what defenses would be raised, and he certainly did not want to suggest any.

Judge Kinser agreed that the conference was premature. He decided to postpone issuing a pretrial order (although he was not sure that rule 16 permitted the postponement). But he told the lawyers that the case should be resolved "quickly." "Looking down the road," the judge would neither tolerate further requests for delay nor let discovery "get out of hand." This case, like most, should be settled. He instructed the parties to return to his chambers on June 30 prepared to "talk settlement" with "real numbers."

On June 10, Judge Kinser denied Danforth's motion to dismiss. On June 18, Danforth filed its answer denying liability. A week later the parties once again met with the judge in chambers. After the attorneys reported that they had no settlement proposals to offer, the judge responded by announcing his schedule for the lawsuit. He ordered each side to inform him, by August 16, of the names of their prospective deponents. He directed the parties to exchange their first interrogatories by July 15, to begin taking depositions by August 25, and to finish discovery by November 30. Both sides objected, but the judge issued a pretrial order with this timetable.

Subsequently, the parties requested and obtained changes in the original scheduling order. Experts for both sides were unavailable for most of the summer of 1982, and a shipment of documents disappeared in the mail and required several months to replace. At each of the three pretrial conferences that Judge Kinser has conducted to date, he has raised the issue of settlement, but with little success. As a result of his efforts,

[b] Rule 16(b) so provided from 1983 to 1993.

however, the parties have begun to discuss the same "ball park" settlement figures.

Although this description of Paulson was presented as though proposed rule 16 were in effect, the scenario is not futuristic: under current rule 16, many federal judges manage their cases much as Judge Kinser did in the revised hypothetical. As they gain more experience with such new procedures, judges are acting more forcefully. Indeed, not all judges are as circumspect as Judge Kinser. Some warn the parties that the judge would take a dim, and possibly hostile, view of either side's insistence on going to trial.

. . . .

In the preceding discussion, I have argued for reflection before we plunge headlong into judicial management. I do not mean to suggest, however, that adjudication must be frozen into earlier forms or that more efficient decisionmaking is an unworthy aim. Rather, as we reorient the judicial system to accommodate contemporary demands, I believe that we should preserve the core of adjudication. To help judges remain impartial, we should limit the flow of untested information. To ensure that judges have the time and patience for deliberation, we should refrain from giving them too many distracting new responsibilities. To hold judges accountable for the quality—not merely the quantity—of their actions, we should require judges to act in public and to state reasons for their decisions.

With these goals in mind, I outline below some alterations of and alternatives to judicial management. . . .

. . . .

Ideas about statutory timetables for litigation, diverse procedural rules for different categories of cases, alternative dispute resolution centers, curtailed discovery rights, state-controlled case preparation, limitations on court access, and penalties for those who do not settle lawsuits should give us pause, for these reforms would drastically alter the civil litigation world. But equally far-reaching changes, instituted by the judiciary itself and carried out in the name of increased efficiency, are already under way. Unfortunately, these changes are being carried out piecemeal and with little reflection on their cumulative implications for the adversarial system.

If, as many of their critics assert, the courts cannot meet the demands they face, revamping adjudication may well be appropriate. But if the time to reappraise the process of adjudication has arrived, the work should not be left to the judiciary, its support staff, a handful of academics, or a few American Bar Association committees. Rather, the hard questions about pace (how quickly should lawsuits proceed?), allocation of authority (should the pace be decided by judges, the parties, or Congress?), and the continued existence of the adversary process (who should be responsible for case investigation, preparation, and presentation?) should be subjected to a more searching and free-ranging public debate.

. . . .

In the debate over appropriate responses to the increasingly heavy work load of the federal courts, I am concerned about preserving the uniqueness of the judicial function. Seduced by controlled calendars, disposition statistics, and other trappings of the efficiency era and the high-tech age, managerial judges are changing the nature of their work. The old judiciary was doing something different from the modern managerial ideal, something quite out of step with the world of time and motion studies. Among all of our official decisionmakers, judges—and judges alone—are required to provide reasoned explanations for their decisions. Judges alone are supposed to rule without concern for the interests of particular constituencies. Judges alone are required to act with deliberation—a steady, slow, unhurried task.

I want to take away trial judges' roving commission and to bring back the blindfold. I want judges to balance the scales, not abandon them altogether in the press to dispose of cases quickly. No one has convincingly discredited the virtues of disinterest and disengagement, virtues that form the bases of the judiciary's authority. Our society has not yet openly and deliberately decided to discard the traditional adversarial model in favor of some version of the continental or inquisitorial model. Until we do so, federal judges should remain true to their ancestry and emulate the goddess Justicia. I fear that, as it moves closer to administration, adjudication may be in danger of ceasing to be.

BEARY v. CITY OF RYE, 601 F.2d 62 (2d Cir.1979). This diversity action alleged malicious prosecution for sex crimes.

"Appellant brought the instant suit in federal court on January 26, 1977. A pretrial order provided that

> [t]he parties shall, in order to prevent delay or interruption of the trial, have sufficient witnesses present at all times during the trial and shall perpetuate before trial the testimony of any essential witnesses, on direct and cross examination, . . . likely to be unavailable when required upon the trial.

The pretrial order also provided that failure to comply with any of its provisions 'may result in this court's imposing appropriate sanctions, including termination of the action.'

"Trial of the federal action commenced on Monday, November 27, 1978. Appellant's counsel had, on November 24, subpoenaed six witnesses to appear on Wednesday, November 29, one at 9:00 a.m. and five at 9:30 a.m. At the luncheon recess on the first day of the trial appellant's first witness, appellant himself, was still testifying; opposing counsel subjected him to a vigorous cross-examination which continued after the luncheon recess. After redirect examination of appellant, appellant then called two other witnesses . . . . At this point in the trial, which was 3:30 p.m., the following occurred:

Mr. Greenspan [counsel for plaintiff]: I have no further questions.

. . . .

Mr. Zawacki [counsel for defendant]: I have no questions.

The Court [Judge Lloyd MacMahon]: You are excused.

(Witness excused.)

The Court: Next witness.

Mr. Greenspan: I have no further witnesses today, your Honor. I request a continuance until tomorrow morning.

The Court: You rest.

Mr. Greenspan: No, sir, I do not rest.

The Court: Put in your defense.

Mr. Zawacki: The defendant moves to dismiss the complaint.

The Court: Granted. The jury may be excused.

(Jury leaves courtroom.)

The court did not give appellant time to explain, as he contends on appeal, that he had a number of depositions of witnesses taken for use at the trial or any opportunity to read those depositions into the record.

"Immediately after the jury left the courtroom the following occurred:

Mr. Greenspan: Your Honor, at this time—

The Court: Just a moment. Let the record reflect . . . .

Mr. Greenspan: If your Honor please, at this point I would move for a new trial.

The Court: Denied.

In the court's remarks above elided, the court referred to the pretrial order above quoted, stated that counsel came in 'without sufficient witnesses to complete the day' and went on to hold that the plaintiff had failed to make out a prima facie case. . . . The court went on to say that 'we cannot tolerate waste of time, interruption of trials and delays which have a ripple effect on our whole docket . . . .' "

The plaintiff appealed. The court of appeals reversed the judgment dismissing the complaint, explaining:

"This appeal is an example of a trial court's permitting its zeal for clearing its calendar to overcome the right of a party to a full and fair trial on the merits. . . .

"In striking the balance between alleviating court calendar congestion and protecting a party's right to due process and a fair chance to be heard, we have repeatedly given a great deal of latitude to the individual district judges laboring conscientiously in a day of ever-rising filings closely to control their dockets. [Citations omitted.] At the same time this court has always recognized that 'a court must not let its zeal for a tidy calendar overcome its duty to do justice.' Peterson v. Term Taxi, Inc., 429 F.2d 888, 891 (2d Cir.1970). . . .

. . . .

"In our view justice has been impaired by such a 'close inflexible attention to the docket.' [Id.] Here we have no flagrant or intentional disregard of the pretrial order but rather an understandable mistake of judgment in thinking that the examination of appellant, who had a criminal record and other habits and problems which would prompt a rather extensive cross-examination for impeachment as well as to show a diminished reputation, combined with the examination of two other witnesses, would probably consume the entire first day of trial. At least counsel could reasonably have thought that if they did not do so depositions would enable counsel to make valuable use of the court's and the jury's time. Counsel's belief was particularly reasonable because appellant was still on the stand at the luncheon recess. There was clearly no failure on appellant's part to prosecute his action. Here the plaintiff had obtained the necessary subpoenas for his witnesses, selected a jury, made his opening statement, and presented the testimony of three witnesses. We believe that the ordering of the plaintiff's rest, especially without giving him an opportunity to use the time alternatively, was an abuse of discretion under the circumstances.

"We direct a retrial to take place before a different judge."

STEVEN FLANDERS, BLIND UMPIRES—A RESPONSE TO PROFESSOR RESNIK, 35 Hastings L.J. 505, 507, 511–12 (1984). "In this Commentary, I wish to reassure Professor Resnik's readers, as well as others who are interested in the direction of the civil litigation system. Resnik exaggerates the extent of any judicial activity that is inconsistent with due process. More important, she confuses genuinely questionable approaches, which have long been understood to be questionable and thus are rare in practice, with established practices that are generally recognized as acceptable and even essential. By muddling almost every managerial technique that a trial judge might use with the special and well-understood concerns that attend an aggressive judicial insistence on settlement, Resnik does a disservice: she suggests that all judicial case management, however unexceptionable, is inconsistent with due process or with traditional images of justice. The corresponding service that she performs—focusing attention upon important changes in the roles and responsibilities of trial judges—is largely vitiated.

. . . .

"There is no evidence that the Paulson case reflects anything other than Professor Resnik's imagination, though I would not claim that it is so implausible that nothing like it could happen. When Resnik later addresses the issues generated from [this] model, she appears to have been blinded by concerns over potential abuse of judicial powers in efforts to encourage or to force settlements—a blindness incorporated in the model. Were the practices of federal trial judges in settlement matters even distantly related to Resnik's understanding of them, there might indeed be a serious problem. In fact, even the sources that she uses suggest a more reassuring picture. In general, federal judges are circumspect and selective in their discussions of settlement. It is my experience that virtually all are keenly aware of the dangers Resnik identifies, dangers that have been widely discussed and understood for many years.

"Most judges regard their primary role in the settlement process as that of an indirect facilitator."

JOSEPH L. EBERSOLE, "DISCOVERY AND PRETRIAL PROCEDURES," in The Improvement of the Administration of Justice 137, 138, 143–44 (Fannie J. Klein ed., 6th ed. 1981). In the 1970s, with the full flowering of the discovery and pretrial rules, judges clearly assumed new roles in addition to "the traditional role of umpire."

"*Case Manager.* This role is based on the premise that the flow of the court calendar should be controlled by the court, not by the attorneys. It recognizes the court has a responsibility for assuring just resolutions of disputes expeditiously and inexpensively. Effective case management requires a personal concern that a just, speedy and inexpensive determination be reached in every action and the belief that managing the flow of litigation in the pretrial phases is an essential and important part of the art of judging. Thus, attitude is all important as a necessary (although not sufficient) condition.

. . . .

"*Mediator.* This role is based on the premises that (1) in most cases the absolute result of a trial is not as high a quality of justice as is a freely negotiated settlement, (2) it is appropriate for a judge to function as a mediator, and (3) a judge who is familiar with a case can often be the most effective mediator for that case. It is normally not advisable for a judge to 'force' settlement discussions. Formal settlement conferences held on a routine basis tend not to be effective. However, where judges make it known they are available for settlement discussions and ask counsel when the opportunity occurs whether they wish to discuss settlement possibilities fruitful mediation often occurs.

"It should be recognized that judicial settlement of lawsuits is . . . an art and some judges may find it more comfortable to serve as mediators than others. Further, mediation of a nonjury case by the judge who will try the case if it is not settled is considered inadvisable by many judges and attorneys. Therefore, each court should have procedures under which a judge who will not try the case can serve the role of mediator."

Questions: (1) As the pretrial judge begins actively to adjudicate by formulation of the issues through eliminating frivolous claims or defenses and by disposition of pending motions, or even as the mediator role begins to look more like negotiation or arbitration when the judge pushes disposition by settlement, does this judicial role of case disposer come into conflict with that of case manager? That is, are there conflicts among the various roles that the modern pretrial conference gives the judge simultaneously? If so, does recognition of these conflicts inform the specific decision on whether pretrial conferences should be held in the courtroom or in chambers? with or without a court reporter? Would the ideal manager have trappings different from the ideal disposer's?

(2) Does either the role of case manager or that of case disposer conflict with the traditional role of umpire? Does the possibility of decoupling to avoid simultaneity of these roles resolve these conflicts?

CONGRESS AND CASE MANAGEMENT

Congress waded into the case management area in the Judicial Improvements Act of 1990, Pub.L. No. 101–650, tit. I, 104 Stat. 5089, 5089, which title was known as the Civil Justice Reform Act of 1990 and which was codified at 28 U.S.C. §§ 471–482. The legislation, based on a Brookings Institution study by a 36–member task force of lawyers and law professors, was swiftly enacted, despite considerable and distinguished opposition.

The Civil Justice Reform Act in § 471 required each district court to implement a civil justice expense and delay reduction plan. The purposes of each plan were "to facilitate deliberate adjudication of civil cases on the merits, monitor discovery, improve litigation management, and ensure just, speedy, and inexpensive resolutions of civil disputes." The districts had to consider the specific guidelines and techniques of litigation management and cost and delay reduction contained in § 473 of the Act.

The implemented plans widely varied among the districts. Generally, they favored tough judicial management and stressed mandatory disclosure and alternative dispute resolution. A tracking system for cases, categorized by complexity, was also a common feature. Despite the tremendous efforts expended, good reason existed to question the plans' effectiveness, or even to suggest their counterproductivity. Also, they raised several questions about rulemaking. Was it desirable for Congress, or local groups, to supplant the central judiciary in rulemaking? On this question, Carl Tobias, Civil Justice Reform and the Balkanization of Federal Civil Procedure, 24 Ariz.St.L.J. 1393, 1393, 1403 (1992), made these related observations:

"The recent civil war ripping apart Yugoslavia is a trenchant reminder of the horrors of balkanization. Without trivializing the Yugoslavian experience, the term balkanization usefully applies to developments in American federal civil procedure that now threaten the continued viability of a uniform, simple system of procedure. [The] federal courts' nascent implementation of the Civil Justice Reform Act (CJRA) of 1990 will exacerbate these developments . . . . This article cautions those responsible for maintaining an efficacious procedural system that they must slow balkanization, lest civil procedure become even more disuniform and complex.

. . . .

"Congress intentionally or inadvertently drafted the CJRA, and courts . . . practically implemented the statute, in numerous ways that will exacerbate balkanization. The potential for increased balkanization should not come as a surprise because Congress premised essential aspects of the CJRA on many of the earlier procedural developments, such as the expansion of managerial judging and the proliferation of local rules, that had already substantially increased fragmentation. Perhaps the most striking facets of the CJRA's enactment are congressional willingness to stamp its imprimatur on these general developments in procedure and to invoke those specific entities and procedures that have fostered balkanization while encouraging every one of the federal districts to employ the precise instrumentalities and procedures that have promoted disuniformity and complexity."

In any event, much of the Civil Justice Reform Act of 1990, including the requirements of § 473, expired by its own terms on December 1, 1997. However, the Judicial Conference of the United States reported to Congress that, before that date, the judiciary had "adopted most of the principles, guidelines and techniques in the Act." Judicial Conference of the United States, The Civil Justice Reform Act of 1990—Final Report, 175 F.R.D. 62, 67 (1997). Many of the districts continued their local plans. Also, the guidelines contained in § 473 dealing with pretrial conferences, discovery, disclosure, and case management were implemented through the 1993 amendments to Rules 16, 26, and 37.

Interestingly, after reviewing a study by the RAND Corporation, the Judicial Conference concluded on the use of alternative dispute resolution mechanisms: "Although many courts have found alternative dispute resolution (ADR) to be a benefit to litigants, the RAND analysis failed to discern a significant positive cost and delay impact associated with this principle. However, the Conference does believe that the positive attributes often associated with ADR argue for continued experimentation." 175 F.R.D. at 71. Congress responded with the Alternative Dispute Resolution Act of 1998, Pub.L. No. 105–315, 112 Stat. 2993, which provides at 28 U.S.C. § 652(a) that "each district court shall, by local rule adopted under section 2071(a), require that litigants in all civil cases consider the use of an alternative dispute resolution process at an appropriate stage in the litigation. Each district court shall provide litigants in all civil cases with at least one alternative dispute resolution process, including, but not limited to, mediation, early neutral evaluation, minitrial, and arbitration . . . ."

INSTITUTE FOR THE ADVANCEMENT OF THE AMERICAN LEGAL SYSTEM, CIVIL CASE PROCESSING IN THE FEDERAL DISTRICT

COURTS 9–10 (2009). An updated study, of a nature similar to the Flanders study, led to these recommendations for judges:

"1. Setting firm dates early in the pretrial process for the close of discovery, the filing of dispositive motions, and trial, and maintaining those dates except in rare and truly unusual circumstances;

2. Ruling expeditiously on motions, even when the motions are denied;

3. Limiting the number of extensions sought by the parties during any phase of the case;

4. Working to foster a local legal culture that accepts efficient case processing as the norm, and enforcing that culture through active judicial case management; and

5. Tracking the status of cases and motions through internal statistical reporting, and disseminating the results internally and externally as appropriate.

In the same vein, attorneys may also resolve cases more quickly for their clients by:

1. Agreeing to realistic deadlines early in the case and not seeking a deviation from those deadlines except under rare and truly unusual circumstances;

2. Commencing discovery early in the discovery period, so that any discovery disputes may be presented to the court and resolved well before the discovery deadline;

3. Filing dispositive motions as early as possible in the case; and

4. Working within the bar generally, and with opposing counsel specifically, to foster expectations of efficient case processing."

TOPIC D

Summary Judgment

Celotex Corp. v. Catrett

Supreme Court of the United States, 1986.
477 U.S. 317, 106 S.Ct. 2548.

■ Justice Rehnquist delivered the opinion of the Court.

The United States District Court for the District of Columbia granted the motion of petitioner Celotex Corporation for summary judgment against respondent Catrett because the latter was unable to produce evidence in support of her allegation in her wrongful-death complaint that the decedent had been exposed to petitioner's asbestos products. A divided panel of the Court of Appeals for the District of Columbia Circuit reversed, however, holding that petitioner's failure to support its motion with evidence tending to *negate* such exposure precluded the entry of summary judgment in its favor. Catrett v. Johns–Manville Sales Corp., 756 F.2d 181 (1985). [The Supreme Court granted certiorari to resolve a conflict among the circuits.]

Respondent commenced this lawsuit in September 1980, alleging that the death in 1979 of her husband, Louis H. Catrett, resulted from his exposure to products containing asbestos manufactured or distributed by 15 named corporations. Respondent's complaint sounded in negligence, breach of warranty, and strict liability. Two of the defendants filed motions challenging the District Court's in personam jurisdiction, and the remaining 13, including petitioner, filed motions for summary judgment. Petitioner's motion, which was first filed in September 1981, argued that summary judgment was proper because respondent had "failed to produce evidence that any [Celotex] product . . . was the proximate cause of the injuries alleged . . . ." In particular, petitioner noted that respondent had failed to identify, in answering interrogatories specifically requesting such information, any witnesses who could testify about the decedent's exposure to petitioner's asbestos products. In response to petitioner's summary judgment motion, respondent then produced three documents which she claimed "demonstrate that there is a genuine material factual dispute" as to whether the decedent had ever been exposed to petitioner's asbestos products. The three documents included a transcript of a deposition of the decedent, a letter from an official of one of the decedent's former employers whom petitioner planned to call as a trial witness, and a letter from an insurance company to respondent's attorney, all tending to establish that the decedent had been exposed to petitioner's asbestos products in Chicago during 1970–1971. Petitioner, in turn, argued that the three documents were inadmissible hearsay and thus could not be considered in opposition to the summary judgment motion.

In July 1982, almost two years after the commencement of the lawsuit, the District Court granted all of the motions filed by the various defendants. The court explained that it was granting petitioner's summary judgment motion because "there [was] no showing that the plaintiff was exposed to the defendant Celotex's product in the District of Columbia or elsewhere within the statutory period." App. 217. Respondent appealed only the grant of summary judgment in favor of petitioner, and a divided panel of the District of Columbia Circuit reversed. . . .

We think that the position taken by the majority of the Court of Appeals is inconsistent with the standard for summary judgment set forth in Rule 56(c) of the Federal Rules of Civil Procedure. Under Rule 56(c), summary judgment is proper "if the pleadings, depositions, answers to interrogatories, and admissions on file, together with the affidavits, if any, show that there is no genuine issue as to any material fact and that the moving party is entitled to a judgment as a matter of law." In our view, the plain language of Rule 56(c) mandates the entry of summary judgment, after adequate time for discovery and upon motion, against a party who fails to make a showing sufficient to establish the existence of an element essential to that party's case, and on which that party will bear the burden of proof at trial. In such a situation, there can be "no genuine issue as to any material fact," since a complete failure of proof concerning an essential element of the nonmoving party's case necessarily renders all other facts immaterial. The moving party is "entitled to a judgment as a matter of law" because the nonmoving party has failed to make a sufficient showing on an essential element of her case with respect to which she has the burden of proof. "[T]h[e] standard [for granting summary judgment] mirrors the standard for a directed verdict under Federal Rule of Civil Procedure 50(a) . . . ." Anderson v. Liberty Lobby, Inc., 477 U.S. 242, 250, 106 S.Ct. 2505, 2511 (1986).

Of course, a party seeking summary judgment always bears the initial responsibility of informing the district court of the basis for its motion, and identifying those portions of "the pleadings, depositions, answers to interrogatories, and admissions on file, together with the affidavits, if any," which it believes demonstrate the absence of a genuine issue of material fact. But unlike the Court of Appeals, we find no express or implied requirement in Rule 56 that the moving party support its motion with affidavits or other similar materials *negating* the opponent's claim. On the contrary, Rule 56(c), which refers to "the affidavits, *if any*" (emphasis added), suggests the absence of such a requirement. And if there were any doubt about the meaning of Rule 56(c) in this regard, such doubt is clearly removed by Rules 56(a) and (b), which provide that claimants and defendants, respectively, may move for summary judgment "*with or without supporting affidavits*" (emphasis added). The import of these subsections is that, regardless of whether the moving party accompanies its summary judgment motion with affidavits, the motion may, and should, be granted so long as whatever is before the district court demonstrates that the standard for the entry of summary judgment, as set forth in Rule 56(c), is satisfied. One of the principal purposes of the summary judgment rule is to isolate and dispose of factually unsupported claims or defenses, and we think it should be interpreted in a way that allows it to accomplish this purpose.

Respondent argues, however, that Rule 56(e), by its terms, places on the nonmoving party the burden of coming forward with rebuttal affidavits, or other specified kinds of materials, only in response to a motion for summary judgment "made and supported as provided in this rule." According to respondent's argument, since petitioner did not "support" its motion with affidavits, summary judgment was improper in this case. But as we have already explained, a motion for summary judgment may be made pursuant to Rule 56 "with or without supporting affidavits." In cases like the instant one, where the nonmoving party will bear the burden of proof at trial on a dispositive issue, a summary judgment motion may properly be made in reliance solely on the "pleadings, depositions, answers to interrogatories, and admissions on file." Such a motion, whether or not accompanied by affidavits, will be "made and supported as provided in this rule," and Rule 56(e) therefore requires the nonmoving party to go beyond the pleadings and by her own affidavits, or by the "depositions, answers to interrogatories, and admissions on file," designate "specific facts showing that there is a genuine issue for trial."

We do not mean that the nonmoving party must produce evidence in a form that would be admissible at trial in order to avoid summary judgment. Obviously, Rule 56 does not require the nonmoving party to depose her own witnesses. Rule 56(e) permits a proper summary judgment motion to be opposed by any of the kinds of evidentiary materials listed in Rule 56(c), except the mere pleadings themselves, and it is from this list that one would normally expect the nonmoving party to make the showing to which we have referred.

. . . [A]s we have explained, the burden on the moving party may be discharged by "showing"—that is, pointing out to the district court—that there is an absence of evidence to support the nonmoving party's [affirmative] case.

. . . .

Our conclusion is bolstered by the fact that district courts are widely acknowledged to possess the power to enter summary judgments sua sponte, so long as the losing party was on notice that she had to come forward with all of her evidence. See 756 F.2d, at 189 (Bork, J., dissenting); 10A C. Wright, A. Miller & M. Kane, Federal Practice and Procedure § 2720, pp. 28–29 (1983). It would surely defy common sense to hold that the District Court could have entered summary judgment sua sponte in favor of petitioner in the instant case, but that petitioner's filing of a motion requesting such a disposition precluded the District Court from ordering it.

Respondent commenced this action in September 1980, and petitioner's motion was filed in September 1981. The parties had conducted discovery, and no serious claim can be made that respondent was in any sense "railroaded" by a premature motion for summary judgment. Any potential problem with such premature motions can be adequately dealt with under Rule 56(f), which allows a summary judgment motion to be denied, or the hearing on the motion to be continued, if the nonmoving party has not had an opportunity to make full discovery.

In this Court, respondent's brief and oral argument have been devoted as much to the proposition that an adequate showing of exposure to petitioner's asbestos products was made as to the proposition that no such showing should have been required. But the Court of Appeals declined to address either the adequacy of the showing made by respondent in opposition to petitioner's motion for summary judgment, or the question whether such a showing, if reduced to admissible evidence, would be sufficient to carry respondent's burden of proof at trial. We think the Court of Appeals with its superior knowledge of local law is better suited than we are to make these determinations in the first instance.

The Federal Rules of Civil Procedure have for almost 50 years authorized motions for summary judgment upon proper showings of the lack of a genuine, triable issue of material fact. Summary judgment procedure is properly regarded not as a disfavored procedural shortcut, but rather as an integral part of the Federal Rules as a whole, which are designed "to secure the just, speedy and inexpensive determination of every action." Fed.Rule Civ.Proc. 1; see Schwarzer, Summary Judgment Under the Federal Rules: Defining Genuine Issues of Material Fact, 99 F.R.D. 465, 467 (1984). Before the shift to "notice pleading" accomplished by the Federal Rules, motions to dismiss a complaint or to strike a defense were the principal tools by which factually insufficient claims or defenses could be isolated and prevented from going to trial with the attendant unwarranted consumption of public and private resources. But with the advent of "notice pleading," the motion to dismiss seldom fulfills this function any more, and its place has been taken by the motion for summary judgment. Rule 56 must be construed with due regard not only for the rights of persons asserting claims and defenses that are adequately based in fact to have those claims and defenses tried to a jury, but also for the rights of persons opposing such claims and defenses to demonstrate in the manner provided by the Rule, prior to trial, that the claims and defenses have no factual basis.

The judgment of the Court of Appeals is accordingly reversed, and the case is remanded for further proceedings consistent with this opinion.

It is so ordered.

■ [The concurring opinion of JUSTICE WHITE is omitted.]

■ JUSTICE BRENNAN, with whom THE CHIEF JUSTICE [BURGER] and JUSTICE BLACKMUN join, dissenting.

This case requires the Court to determine whether Celotex satisfied its initial burden of production in moving for summary judgment on the ground that the plaintiff lacked evidence to establish an essential element of her case at trial. I do not disagree with the Court's legal analysis. The Court clearly rejects the ruling of the Court of Appeals that the defendant must provide affirmative evidence disproving the plaintiff's case. Beyond this, however, the Court has not clearly explained what is required of a moving party seeking summary judgment on the ground that the nonmoving party cannot prove its case. This lack of clarity is unfortunate: district courts must routinely decide summary judgment motions, and the Court's opinion will very likely create confusion. For this reason, even if I agreed with the Court's result, I would have written separately to explain more clearly the law in this area. However, because I believe that Celotex did not meet its burden of production under Federal Rule of Civil Procedure 56, I respectfully dissent from the Court's judgment.

I

Summary judgment is appropriate where the court is satisfied "that there is no genuine issue as to any material fact and that the moving party is entitled to a judgment as a matter of law." Fed.Rule Civ.Proc. 56(c). The burden of establishing the nonexistence of a "genuine issue" is on the party moving for summary judgment. 10A C. Wright, A. Miller & M. Kane, Federal Practice and Procedure § 2727, p. 121 (2d ed. 1983) . . . (citing cases); 6 J. Moore, W. Taggart & J. Wicker, Moore's Federal Practice ¶ 56.15[3] (2d ed. 1985) . . . (citing cases). . . . This burden has two distinct components: an initial burden of production, which shifts to the nonmoving party if satisfied by the moving party; and an ultimate burden of persuasion, which always remains on the moving party.[a] See 10A Wright, Miller & Kane § 2727. The court need not decide whether the moving party has satisfied its ultimate burden of persuasion[2] unless and until the court finds that the moving party has discharged its initial burden of production. Adickes v. S.H. Kress & Co., 398 U.S. 144, 157–161, 90 S.Ct. 1598, 1608–1610 (1970); 1963 Advisory Committee's Notes on Fed.Rule Civ.Proc. 56(e), 28 U.S.C.App., p. 626.

The burden of production imposed by Rule 56 requires the moving party to make a prima facie showing that it is entitled to summary

[a] See infra p. 1328.

[2] The burden of persuasion imposed on a moving party by Rule 56 is a stringent one. 6 Moore ¶ 56.15[3], p. 56–466; 10A Wright, Miller & Kane § 2727, p. 124. Summary judgment should not be granted unless it is clear that a trial is unnecessary, Anderson v. Liberty Lobby, Inc., 477 U.S. 242, 255, 106 S.Ct. 2505, 2514 (1986), and any doubt as to the existence of a genuine issue for trial should be resolved against the moving party, Adickes v. S.H. Kress & Co., 398 U.S. 144, 158–159, 90 S.Ct. 1598, 1608–1609 (1970). In determining whether a moving party has met its burden of persuasion, the court is obliged to take account of the entire setting of the case and must consider all papers of record as well as any materials prepared for the motion. 10A Wright, Miller & Kane § 2721, p. 44; see, e.g., Stepanischen v. Merchants Despatch Transportation Corp., 722 F.2d 922, 930 (C.A.1 1983); Higgenbotham v. Ochsner Foundation Hospital, 607 F.2d 653, 656 (C.A.5 1979). As explained by the Court of Appeals for the Third Circuit in In re Japanese Electronic Products Antitrust Litigation, 723 F.2d 238 (1983), rev'd on other grounds sub nom. Matsushita Electric Industrial Co. v. Zenith Radio Corp., 475 U.S. 574, 106 S.Ct. 1348 (1986), "[i]f . . . there is any evidence in the record from any source from which a reasonable inference in the [nonmoving party's] favor may be drawn, the moving party simply cannot obtain a summary judgment . . . ." 723 F.2d, at 258.

judgment. 10A Wright, Miller & Kane § 2727. The manner in which this showing can be made depends upon which party will bear the burden of persuasion on the challenged claim at trial. If the *moving* party will bear the burden of persuasion at trial, that party must support its motion with credible evidence—using any of the materials specified in Rule 56(c)—that would entitle it to a directed verdict if not controverted at trial. Ibid. Such an affirmative showing shifts the burden of production to the party opposing the motion and requires that party either to produce evidentiary materials that demonstrate the existence of a "genuine issue" for trial or to submit an affidavit requesting additional time for discovery. Ibid.; Fed. Rules Civ.Proc. 56(e), (f).

If the burden of persuasion at trial would be on the *nonmoving* party, the party moving for summary judgment may satisfy Rule 56's burden of production in either of two ways. First, the moving party may submit affirmative evidence that negates an essential element of the nonmoving party's claim. Second, the moving party may demonstrate to the court that the nonmoving party's evidence is insufficient to establish an essential element of the nonmoving party's claim. See 10A Wright, Miller & Kane § 2727, pp. 130–131; Louis, Federal Summary Judgment Doctrine: A Critical Analysis, 83 Yale L.J. 745, 750 (1974) (hereinafter Louis). If the nonmoving party cannot muster sufficient evidence to make out its claim, a trial would be useless and the moving party is entitled to summary judgment as a matter of law. Anderson v. Liberty Lobby, Inc., 477 U.S. 242, 249, 106 S.Ct. 2505, 2510–2511 (1986).

Where the moving party adopts this second option and seeks summary judgment on the ground that the nonmoving party—who will bear the burden of persuasion at trial—has no evidence, the mechanics of discharging Rule 56's burden of production are somewhat trickier. Plainly, a conclusory assertion that the nonmoving party has no evidence is insufficient. . . . Such a "burden" of production is no burden at all and would simply permit summary judgment procedure to be converted into a tool for harassment. See Louis 750–751. Rather, as the Court confirms, a party who moves for summary judgment on the ground that the nonmoving party has no evidence must affirmatively show the absence of evidence in the record. . . . This may require the moving party to depose the nonmoving party's witnesses or to establish the inadequacy of documentary evidence. If there is literally no evidence in the record, the moving party may demonstrate this by reviewing for the court the admissions, interrogatories, and other exchanges between the parties that are in the record. Either way, however, the moving party must affirmatively demonstrate that there is no evidence in the record to support a judgment for the nonmoving party.

If the moving party has not fully discharged this initial burden of production, its motion for summary judgment must be denied, and the court need not consider whether the moving party has met its ultimate burden of persuasion. Accordingly, the nonmoving party may defeat a motion for summary judgment that asserts that the nonmoving party has no evidence by calling the court's attention to supporting evidence already in the record that was overlooked or ignored by the moving party. In that event, the moving party must respond by making an attempt to demonstrate the inadequacy of this evidence, for it is only by attacking all the record evidence allegedly supporting the nonmoving party that a party seeking summary judgment satisfies Rule 56's burden of production.[3] Thus, if the record disclosed that the moving party had overlooked a witness who would provide relevant testimony for the nonmoving party at trial, the court could not find that the moving party had discharged its initial burden of production unless the moving party sought to demonstrate the inadequacy of this witness' testimony. Absent such a demonstration, summary judgment would have to be denied on the ground that the moving party had failed to meet its burden of production under Rule 56.

. . . .

II

I do not read the Court's opinion to say anything inconsistent with or different than the preceding discussion. My disagreement with the Court concerns the application of these principles to the facts of this case.

Defendant Celotex sought summary judgment on the ground that plaintiff had "failed to produce" any evidence that her decedent had ever been exposed to Celotex asbestos. App. 170. Celotex supported this motion with a two-page "Statement of Material Facts as to Which There is No Genuine Issue" and a three-page "Memorandum of Points and Authorities" which asserted that the plaintiff had failed to identify any evidence in responding to two sets of interrogatories propounded by Celotex and that therefore the record was "totally devoid" of evidence to support plaintiff's claim. See id., at 171–176.

Approximately three months earlier, [in September 1981,] Celotex had filed an essentially identical motion. Plaintiff responded to this earlier motion by producing three pieces of evidence which she claimed "[a]t the very least . . . demonstrate that there is a genuine factual dispute for trial," id., at 143: (1) a letter from an insurance representative of another defendant describing asbestos products to which plaintiff's decedent had been exposed, id., at 160; (2) a letter from T.R. Hoff, a former supervisor of decedent, describing asbestos products to which decedent had been exposed, id., at 162; and (3) a copy of decedent's deposition from earlier workmen's compensation proceedings, id., at 164. Plaintiff also apparently indicated at

---

[3] Once the moving party has attacked whatever record evidence—if any—the nonmoving party purports to rely upon, the burden of production shifts to the nonmoving party, who must either (1) rehabilitate the evidence attacked in the moving party's papers, (2) produce additional evidence showing the existence of a genuine issue for trial as provided in Rule 56(e), or (3) submit an affidavit explaining why further discovery is necessary as provided in Rule 56(f). See 10A Wright, Miller & Kane § 2727, pp. 138–143. Summary judgment should be granted if the nonmoving party fails to respond in one or more of these ways, or if, after the nonmoving party responds, the court determines that the moving party has met its ultimate burden of persuading the court that there is no genuine issue of material fact for trial. See, e.g., First National Bank of Arizona v. Cities Service Co., 391 U.S. 253, 289, 88 S.Ct. 1575, 1592 (1968).

that time that she intended to call Mr. Hoff as a witness at trial. Tr. of Oral Arg. 6–7, 27–29.

Celotex subsequently withdrew its first motion for summary judgment. See App. 167. However, as a result of this motion, when Celotex filed its second summary judgment motion, the record *did* contain evidence—including at least one witness—supporting plaintiff's claim. Indeed, counsel for Celotex admitted to this Court at oral argument that Celotex was aware of this evidence and of plaintiff's intention to call Mr. Hoff as a witness at trial when the second summary judgment motion was filed. Tr. of Oral Arg. 5–7. Moreover, plaintiff's response to Celotex' second motion pointed to this evidence—noting that it had already been provided to counsel for Celotex in connection with the first motion—and argued that Celotex had failed to "meet its burden of proving that there is no genuine factual dispute for trial." App. 188.[b]

On these facts, there is simply no question that Celotex failed to discharge its initial burden of production. Having chosen to base its motion on the argument that there was no evidence in the record to support plaintiff's claim, Celotex was not free to ignore supporting evidence that the record clearly contained. Rather, Celotex was required, as an initial matter, to attack the adequacy of this evidence. Celotex' failure to fulfill this simple requirement constituted a failure to discharge its initial burden of production under Rule 56, and thereby rendered summary judgment improper.

. . . .

■ [The opinion of JUSTICE STEVENS, dissenting on other grounds, is omitted.]

Oral Argument

April 1, 1986.

CHIEF JUSTICE BURGER: Mr. Van Koten, I think you may proceed whenever you're ready.

MR. VAN KOTEN [for petitioner]: Thank you, Mr. Chief Justice, and may it please the Court.

. . . .

QUESTION: How about that letter from Mr.—what is it, Mr. Hoff?

MR. VAN KOTEN: The letter from Mr. Hoff, Your Honor, certainly did not purport to be made on personal knowledge. It was not under oath. It also, I think, from reading the letter, pretty clearly indicates that it was not on personal knowledge. . . .

. . . .

[b] Soon after that second response, but before hearing and decision, plaintiff more officially listed Mr. Hoff as a trial witness in supplemental answers to defendant's earlier interrogatories.

QUESTION: It seems to me that it might be just a question if his letter really was a meaningful letter, was unambiguous, it might be just a question of who had to go take his deposition.

MR. VAN KOTEN: That may be correct, Justice White. I—

QUESTION: Who do you think would have to—if this letter was a straightforward letter that really did give some credence to the Plaintiff's case, do you think, to make your motion, do you think you would have to go take his deposition?

MR. VAN KOTEN: Had I been trial counsel for Celotex, if the letter indicated that Mr. Hoff really knew something, I would have certainly been there taking the deposition in Chicago in any event.

. . . .

I think it is interesting, though, that trial counsel for the Plaintiff didn't request additional time to put this evidence in admissible form, and even after the district court had granted the motion for summary judgment and had thrown the Plaintiff out of court against Celotex, never filed a motion for reconsideration with an affidavit showing that Mr. Hoff really in fact knew anything about the facts of this case. . . .

. . . .

QUESTION: That would have—if they had obtained an affidavit from Hoff, for example, and he stated it on his own knowledge that there was exposure in Illinois, that would have satisfied the Plaintiff's requirement in your view, I suppose.

MR. VAN KOTEN: I think that—I think that's correct. . . . There are instances where I have seen where defense counsel will raise affirmative defenses, for example, of a decedent's contributory negligence without any evidence produced in the course of discovery that the defendant—that the decedent—that the plaintiff's decedent was contributorily negligent. The rule that we are urging would not be a rule that would just help defendants, it would help trial courts in that instance narrow down the real focus of the case to what were the real issues which were supported by the real evidence in the case.

I think that that is the importance of this case. We have—my office has been involved in over 1000 asbestos cases in Maryland and the District of Columbia. It's by definition impossible to prove, for a defendant to prove that the plaintiff cannot possibly produce evidence of exposure or proximate causation. The best that the defense can ever do in any of these cases is say that simply at this point the plaintiff has not done so. And that's true in many other respects, in many products liability cases and other cases as well.

What—the holding that we would urge would allow trial judges to control their dockets, to get rid of frivolous cases before putting not only the parties but the judicial system to the burden of a needless trial, and to whittle the issues down to what are in fact the real issues in the cases.

. . . .

MR. SMITH [for respondent]: . . . .

. . . .

. . . At the summary judgment stage the defendant has to do something affirmative to undermine the plaintiff's listed evidence. If she has a witness, the plaintiff—the defendant has to take the deposition.

. . . .

QUESTION: And you suggest that your obligation, if you had any, was to, is just to list the witness, and you don't need to get an affidavit from him and present it in opposition to any motion, and you don't need to take his deposition?

MR. SMITH: What this case is about is when a party opposing summary judgment incurs that further duty not just to list a witness but to present an affidavit from that witness, and the rule is clear that you have that further duty only where the motion itself is supported in some way other than by the lawyer's mere assertions. Here the motion was essentially unsupported because it relied entirely on the existing record, and that record . . . didn't by any means suggest that the Plaintiff lacked a meritorious case; indeed, quite the contrary. So the motion was invalid on its face, and under our system, at that point the party opposing summary judgment—

QUESTION: And you think that once you listed that witness, if Celotex, if the Defendant was going to move for summary judgment, it had to deal with Mr. Hoff.

MR. SMITH: That's exactly right, Justice White. . . .

. . . .

Now, . . . it really is hard to understand the failure of Celotex to do anything else in this case to support its motion.

. . . .

QUESTION: Do you think you have to at least say what Mr. Hoff will, what your witness will testify to?

MR. SMITH: I think that's certainly something that the Defendant has a right to know. Here they had his letter . . . .

. . . .

The other point I would make about this requirement, not only is it pretty well established, but it's not merely a technicality that we are trotting out here to try to save the Plaintiff's case. The requirement that there be some support for an, for a summary judgment motion is a fundamental principle in our system of civil litigation. Under our system, a plaintiff who pleads a valid claim and can identify in discovery evidence that she plans to use at trial generally has a right to have that case tried. If the opponent wants to cut the process short prior to trial, he has to come up with something other than his own lawyer's assertions to suggest that the plaintiff lacks a meritorious case. He can do that either by attacking the plaintiff's evidence or denying the claim in an affidavit, but he has to do something, and it is only then that the plaintiff incurs the additional obligation of reducing her trial evidence to affidavit form and submitting it to the court prior to trial.

. . . .

QUESTION [during rebuttal]: Well, what if the—what if in answer to the interrogatory they had said we are going to call Mr. Hoff and here is what he will testify to, and—

MR. VAN KOTEN: And it had indeed shown exposure, Justice White?

QUESTION: Yes.

MR. VAN KOTEN: I believe in that case that at least unless Celotex took Mr. Hoff's deposition and demonstrated that he in fact was not in a position to—

QUESTION: So you agree that the—if the Plaintiff had answered that way, it would not have had to present an affidavit of Mr. Hoff or to go take his deposition.

MR. VAN KOTEN: At least not unless Celotex wished to go ahead and take his deposition.

. . . .

QUESTION: So it comes down to, this comes down to whether this listing Mr. Hoff's name and this letter, whether that's enough of a showing to trigger any obligation on Celotex's part.

. . . .

CHIEF JUSTICE BURGER: Thank you gentlemen. The case is submitted.

PLAINTIFF'S SHOWING

Here is the relevant part of the body of Hoff's letter of October 15, 1981, to O'Keefe, a representative of Hoff's company's insurer:

"I apologize for not getting back to your September 8, 1981 letter sooner.

"This letter will confirm our telephone conversation of yesterday. Mr. Catrett worked for us one calendar year ending, 12/22/71. His duties were to supervise and train crews in the application of Firebar Fireproofing. He worked only in new construction and traveled from district to district.

. . . .

"The material was manufactured by:

Carey–Canada Inc. & Carey–Canadian Asbestos

P.O. Box 190

East Broughton, Quebec Canada, G0N 1H0

Which is now owned by:

Celotex Corporation

a Jim Walters Corporation

P.O. Box 22601

Tampa, Florida 33622

"We understand that the Firebar product was manufactured by Carey–Canadian. . . .

"Please keep us informed."

And here is the relevant supplemental interrogatory answer, filed February 1, 1982, and signed by the plaintiff and her attorney:

"Comes now plaintiff, Myrtle Nell Catrett, Administratrix of the Estate of Louis H. Catrett, by and through counsel, and supplements its answers to the master set of interrogatories propounded by the defendant as follows:

"26. In regard to any person or persons having knowledge of facts relevant to the subject matter in this lawsuit:

. . . .

(b) Identify any other persons, i.e., other than workers, who have such knowledge.

(c) Identify those persons identified whom you intend to produce as witnesses in the trial in this action.

"26. *ANSWER:* (Supplemental)

. . . .

1(b) T.R. Hoff
Assistant Secretary
Anning–Johnson Company
1959 Anson Drive
Melrose Park, Illinois 60160

. . . .

(c) All of the above.

. . . .

"I do solemnly swear and affirm under the penalties of perjury that the contents of the foregoing document is true and correct to the best of my knowledge."

As to the other two items, the court of appeals on remand would say:

"We do not consider two items from the record: (1) Mr. Catrett's workmen's compensation testimony; and (2) the letter from Mr. O'Keefe to Mrs. Catrett's attorney. We believe it would be inappropriate to consider the first item. It is not unlikely that the evidence would be held inadmissible, see Fed.R.Evid. 804(b)(1); in addition, Celotex specifically objected before the District Court to its consideration . . . . The second item, the

O'Keefe letter, is not considered for a more basic reason. To paraphrase, liberally, Gertrude Stein's observation, there is nothing there to consider. The O'Keefe letter is merely a restatement of the contents of the Hoff letter and, as such, offers no independent evidence of a genuine issue of material fact."

ON REMAND

On remand, the same divided panel again held summary judgment improper. The majority, again by Judge Starr with Judge Wald, ruled that the district court could consider the Hoff letter, even if inadmissible, because it had not actually been objected to by the defendant and, anyway, was reducible to admissible form as trial testimony. Moreover, the pertinent evidentiary items—the Hoff letter and the supplemental interrogatory answer, plus some documents in the record linking Celotex to Firebar at Anning-Johnson—in the context of this case sufficed to avoid summary judgment, at least at this stage of the case's development. Catrett v. Johns-Manville Sales Corp., 826 F.2d 33 (D.C.Cir.1987), cert. denied, 484 U.S. 1066, 108 S.Ct. 1028 (1988).

Judge Bork was again in dissent. Although he agreed with the majority's statement that the Supreme Court "concluded that Celotex had met its initial burden of production and filed a proper summary judgment motion," he felt that Catrett had failed to carry her resultant burden. He argued, inter alia, that the plaintiff's showing was not specific enough as to Hoff's personal knowledge of asbestos exposure, with the majority thus in effect relying on evidence that only later might emerge.

For the background story of the Celotex case, one of the most cited cases of all time, see David L. Shapiro, "The Story of Celotex: The Role of Summary Judgment in the Administration of Civil Justice," in Civil Procedure Stories 359 (Kevin M. Clermont ed., 2d ed. 2008).

FRITO-LAY, INC. v. WILLOUGHBY, 863 F.2d 1029 (D.C.Cir.1988). In this action, brought to review an administrative decision, the plaintiff had the initial burden of production on the merits, but the defendant had the ultimate burden of persuasion. The defendant moved for summary judgment on the ground of absence of evidence, and the plaintiff essentially offered none in response. The district court granted summary judgment. The court of appeals, by Judge Sentelle with Judges Wald and Starr, affirmed, observing:

"Of course, in the Celotex case, the nonmoving party was to bear the ultimate burden of proof at trial, while, in the present case, the moving party (Willoughby) faced the ultimate burden of proof. Nonetheless, we conclude that the Celotex principle applies where a silent nonmoving party is to bear an *initial burden of production* at trial. . . . This is consistent with Celotex and is entirely logical: A party who bears an initial burden of production should not be permitted to waste the resources of its opponent and of the courts if it cannot show that it could possibly meet that burden.

. . . .

"Once the movant has discharged his duty, the onus shifts to the nonmovant, and, once it has, the need to respond with specific facts is well established. . . .

. . . .

"[This obligation] cannot be met by 'mere allegation or denial[ ],' but instead, require[s] a showing by 'affirmative evidence.' Anderson v. Liberty Lobby, 477 U.S. 242, 256–57, 106 S.Ct. 2505, 2514, 91 L.Ed.2d 202 (1986); see also First Nat'l Bank v. Cities Service, 391 U.S. 253, 290, 88 S.Ct. 1575, 1593, 20 L.Ed.2d 569 (plaintiff could not defeat the properly supported summary judgment motion without offering 'any significant probative evidence tending to support the complaint'); Matsushita Elec. Indus. Co. v. Zenith Radio Corp., 475 U.S. 574, 586–87, 106 S.Ct. 1348, 1355–56, 89 L.Ed.2d 538 (1986) (the nonmovant 'must do more than simply show that there is some metaphysical doubt as to the material facts . . . the nonmoving party must come forward with "specific facts showing that there is a genuine issue for trial" ' (citations and emphasis omitted)). Likewise in Laningham v. U.S. Navy, 813 F.2d 1236 (D.C.Cir.1987), we made clear that to survive the government's properly supported motion for summary judgment, plaintiff 'was required to provide evidence that would permit a reasonable jury to find' in his favor. . . .

"We similarly reject appellant's claim that the 'district court should have examined the entire record when considering Mr. Willoughby's summary judgment motion.' Br. for Appellant at 11 n. 4. Appellant's failure to designate and reference triable facts was, in light of the language of Rule 56(c) and governing precedent, fatal to its opposition."

JACK H. FRIEDENTHAL, CASES ON SUMMARY JUDGMENT: HAS THERE BEEN A MATERIAL CHANGE IN STANDARDS?, 63 Notre Dame L.Rev. 770, 771, 787 (1988). "It is important to see, whether, in an era of increasing litigation costs and the consequent maneuverings by parties which are more related to their assets than to the strength of their legal arguments, the legal system gives too little credence to a procedural device that has the potential for providing just results in many cases and which could leave judicial resources free to concentrate on those actions for which a trial is required.

. . . .

"On the whole, courts in the past have been reluctant to analyze sensitive aspects of summary judgment to determine when the granting of a motion is or is not appropriate. The result, in general, has been to deny summary judgment in cases where it should have been granted. The

Supreme Court in its opinions in Anderson and Matsushita, as well as in Celotex, has refocussed attention on summary judgment and has made a start on providing a logical framework for deciding how and when it can be used. Unfortunately, none of the decisions are as clear and precise as one would hope; nevertheless, the net effect should be the more widespread granting of summary judgment in those cases in which it is justified."

JEFFREY W. STEMPEL, A DISTORTED MIRROR: THE SUPREME COURT'S SHIMMERING VIEW OF SUMMARY JUDGMENT, DIRECTED VERDICT, AND THE ADJUDICATION PROCESS, 49 Ohio St.L.J. 95, 161, 171–73 (1988). "By making summary judgment easier to obtain, the Court implicitly bestowed a political favor (and greater judicial power) on litigants who can make most use of the motion. Defendants use the motion more than plaintiffs. Defendants are disproportionately comprised of society's 'haves': banks, insurance companies, railroads, business organizations, governments, and government agencies. Plaintiffs are disproportionately comprised of society's 'have nots': individuals, business sole proprietorships, and smaller entities. . . .

. . . .

"In changing rule 56, the Court implicitly has decided that the economic gains of the change are worth any reduced accuracy and justice to some claimants. My criticism of the Court stems in part from its failure to conduct this decision openly and upon a factual record rich enough to permit reasoned decision. In addition, suggestions that more widespread use and granting of summary judgment will lead to faster, less expensive adjudication (irrespective of the accuracy of outcome) overlook several considerations militating against such anticipated benefits.

"First, a summary judgment takes time to prepare and support. Although perhaps not so time consuming to counsel and client as trial preparation, the differences may not be particularly significant. Second, whatever the time and cost savings to litigants, the motion requires more judicial time than otherwise consumed by pretrial procedures. The judge deciding a summary judgment question must along with her law clerks read, research, reflect, hold a hearing, read and research some more, and often must draft, revise, and issue a lengthy written opinion as well. Although presiding over a jury trial takes time, it may not take any more of the judge's time than does consideration of the summary judgment motion. While jury trial proceeds, the law clerks are usually free to perform other tasks and the judge, although unlikely to admit it, may be reading orders, pleadings, motion papers, and draft opinions while on the bench. With the average cost of an hour of judicial time estimated at $600 per hour, one can argue that use of summary judgment may exact a higher total cost to the system than it saves the system and its participants.

"Third, and most obvious, the summary judgment usually saves time only when it is granted and terminates a case or is sufficiently partially granted to streamline trial of a case. Ordinarily, when the motion is denied, it has merely added more pretrial work without reducing the work required at and after trial. Even the suggestions that summary judgment motions serve to 'educate the judge' or increase the chances of a directed verdict at trial do not refute this essential truth. Until one has more facts, the claims that [the new] approach will save time and money are only claims and theory, not even compelling theory at that.

. . . .

"The Supreme Court's new attitude toward eased summary judgment also permits more case disposition based upon an incomplete, possibly inadequate, or sometimes fraudulent record. In the celebrated . . . Dalkon Shield cases, for example, defendants fared well initially. Subsequently, redoubled discovery efforts resulted in unearthing new evidence that ultimately carried the day for plaintiffs. In light of A.H. Robins', maker of the Dalkon Shield, shredding or concealing relevant documents requested by the opposition, the cases provide striking examples of the wisdom of refraining from a rush to judgment in the name of efficiency. Although avenues for attacking a wrongfully obtained judgment exist, they are not always effective and are frequently costly and cumbersome for the party who did nothing wrong.

"Even absent fraud or the need for additional time, a rule making summary judgment too easy adversely reduces the accuracy of court decisions. Inevitably, summary judgment is granted or denied based on a record less informative than that achieved through trial. Consequently, one should always be less confident in the result obtained through summary judgment than that obtained at later stages of trial."

PARTIAL SUMMARY ADJUDICATION

Obviously, a lot of doctrine adheres to Federal Rule 56. The authors Wright, Miller, and Kane devote over 850 pages to it, not counting their thick and steadily growing pocket parts. An illustrative and important set of problems under the Rule concerns the availability of summary judgment on part of a case. See generally 10B Wright, Miller & Kane §§ 2736–2737.

Can a plaintiff obtain partial relief on a claim? Rule 56(d)(2) authorizes a motion for an interlocutory order establishing liability but leaving damages for trial. But the question here is different. The question on partial relief is whether the plaintiff can get an actual judgment for part of the damages so as to permit collection from the defendant, as where the plaintiff sues for two months' salary and the defendant concedes that one month's salary is due. There might be good reason to allow a partial judgment, which would prevent the defendant from withholding the plaintiff's money during a prolonged lawsuit. Nevertheless, the courts say such partial relief is not within Rule 56, read as a whole but rather restrictively read to give the part-of-the-claim phrase in Rule 56(a) negligible effect. Thus, the plaintiff's sole avenue to partial relief is the appealability provision of Rule 54(b) for multiple claims or parties. See, e.g., In re Air Crash Disaster Near Warsaw, Poland on May 9, 1987, 979 F.Supp. 164

(E.D.N.Y.1997) (denying plaintiffs partial relief on their $3 million claim for the airline's wilful misconduct, even though the Montreal Agreement entitled them to $75,000 on strict liability).

A related question is whether one can get an interlocutory order under Rule 56(d)(1) as merely a means for narrowing the case's issues, much like the Rule 16 procedure. There might be good reason for paring the case down to genuine issues, as for example by fixing the amount of total damages if uncontroverted and thus removing that matter from trial. Nevertheless, the courts traditionally tended to frown on Rule 56(d)(1), seeing it as bypassing the normal pretrial process under Rule 16 (even though it is not clear how far or by what procedure Rule 16 permits this sort of "partial summary judgment").

Is a motion for partial summary judgment under Rule 56(d)(1) even proper? Not really, according to most courts. Rule 56(d)(1) apparently applies only as a procedure ancillary to an ordinary motion for summary judgment on a whole claim, or at least on liability, under Rule 56(a) or (b). Its purpose is to salvage something from the effort expended in denying an ordinary summary judgment motion.

In those situations where Rule 56(d)(1) does apply, is the judge obliged to make a partial summary judgment? Oddly enough, the answer is literally yes, if "practicable." This would open the door to a burdensome and even abusive practice. In reality, however, the judicial role is discretionary. The judge might indulge a disinclination to adjudicate by finding the motion to be not properly made, the adjudicatory task not practicable, the time not right under Rule 56(f), or the facts in genuine controversy. In any event, because a denial is normally nonappealable and nonreviewable, the trial judge's refusal to adjudicate on a partial and summary basis is normally not correctable.

Nevertheless, the judicial antagonism toward partial summary judgment appears now on the wane, as the device's net efficiency has become more accepted. See Edward J. Brunet & Martin H. Redish, Summary Judgment § 3.2 (3d ed. 2006). Interestingly, those authors find the authority for such a trend not in Rule 56(d) but in the specific reference to "part" of the claim in Rule 56(a) and (b).

Questions: (1) Currently there is a significant push to rationalize and codify summary judgment doctrine, and to increase the device's availability, by amending Rule 56. One failed proposal floated by the Advisory Committee in the past would have provided an elaborate discretionary pretrial mechanism for establishing individual matters of law or fact, with such mechanism invokable by a special motion or at a pretrial conference. Alternatively, how would you rewrite the Rule 56(d) provisions on partial summary judgment?

(2) More generally, how would you amend Rule 56? See, e.g., William W Schwarzer, Summary Judgment: A Proposed Revision of Rule 56, 110 F.R.D. 213 (1986). Note that an amendment to Rule 56 is proposed for effectiveness on December 1, 2010. While it would totally rewrite and rearrange the Rule's subdivisions, it tries principally to restate clearly the prevailing doctrine. Its major innovation is to authorize in Rule 56(a) the motion for partial summary judgment on any part of each claim or defense, but without specifying any procedural details for such motion.

PART EIGHT

TRIAL

TOPIC A Preliminary Questions About Forensic Proof

TOPIC B Judgment as a Matter of Law

TOPIC C Verdict

TOPIC D New Trial

TOPIC E Constitutional Right to Jury Trial

TOPIC A

PRELIMINARY QUESTIONS ABOUT FORENSIC PROOF

Trial is our system's method for determining contestable facts. Old England knew a variety of modes of trial. The common law eventually settled on trial by a jury, hearing mainly oral evidence.[a] The equity courts instead relied on trial by a judge, considering written evidence.[b] The United States, after the colonial period of informal and experimental procedures, drew on these two settled traditions of England to formulate trial methods that have remained fairly consistent for state and federal courts throughout the nation's history. The major change over time was the extension of the common law's orality to equitable procedure. More recently, a change of a different sort has been the loss of the trial's centrality to procedure, and even more recently the drastic drop in the percentage of cases that reach trial. See generally Ellen E. Sward, A History of the Civil Trial in the United States, 51 U.Kan.L.Rev. 347 (2003); cf. Trial and Court Procedures Worldwide (Charles Platto ed., 1990).

Anyway, today when a trial occurs, it involves a designated fact-finder making the determination, by crediting and weighing evidence put before that fact-finder through an adversary proceeding. A key question is how the fact-finder, within limits set by its overseers, combines that evaluated evidence and converts it into a finding of fact. Here lie the most profound problems of the law of evidence. See generally Terence Anderson, David Schum & William Twining, Analysis of Evidence (2d ed. 2005). We shall introduce those problems under the headings of burden and standard of proof.

SECTION 1. BURDEN OF PROOF

Professor John M. Maguire says in Evidence: Common Sense and Common Law 175–77 (1947):

"Under our law the term burden of proof has been used to express two rather different ideas, and as might be expected this usage has led to a jumble. Incisive thinkers have framed a more particularized vocabulary, duly segregating the ideas, but have not managed to get their vocabulary into universal use. Let us try to phrase the two ideas:

[a] See supra pp. 1047–49.

[b] See supra pp. 1114–16.

"During a trial the evidence concerning an issue of fact may become decisively one-sided. If no controlling counter-evidence is presented before the end of the trial, the judge must remove that issue from the jury's deliberations and cause it to be resolved in favor of the party whose contentions have thus overwhelmed opposition. When at the end of the trial an issue is more nearly in balance, so that it should be submitted to the jury for a deliberative verdict, the judge must decide which party has to make his contentions of fact prevail or suffer an adverse determination. If the issue is commonplace, there will be precedents for this decision; if it is unusual, the judge may find precedents or may have to decide the question as an original problem. Having decided, the judge transmits the effect of the decision to the jury, to prevent their verdict from being merely the chance result of unregulated discussion. He may do the transmitting in either of two ways. More commonly, perhaps, he simply states his decision for the jury's guidance. Alternatively he puts to the jury one or more questions, carefully but colloquially worded, the answers to which will show whether the party with the laboring oar has successfully wielded that implement.

"Both these situations are sometimes lumped under the term burden of proof. Careful verbalists therefore feel that we should have a brace of subordinate terms to keep the distinction clear. Speaking of the deliberative verdict, they say that the litigant in whose hands we have put the laboring oar has 'the burden of persuasion of the fact.' Verbalists who are *very* careful, noting that any litigant may derive useful evidence from the probative mischances of his opponent as well as from his own efforts, abandon the metaphors of oarsmanship and burden bearing in favor of 'risk of non-persuasion of the fact.' This last refinement has not gained much practical support. Careful phraseology about the other situation is that while opposition is overwhelmed, the opponent has 'the burden of producing evidence of the fact' in order to escape an adverse directed verdict rather than an adverse deliberative verdict.

"As to the self-same issue of fact, burden of persuasion may be on one party in case of ultimate submission to the jury, and burden of producing evidence, in the course of the case, now on him and now on his opponent as evidence or counter-evidence is called for to avoid a directed verdict."

Let us illustrate Professor Maguire's remarks with a simple case in which there is but one disputed issue of fact: the plaintiff asserts *A*, the defendant denies it, and the persuasion-burden is on the plaintiff.

Ordinarily, if the plaintiff offered no proof of *A*, the judge would grant judgment as a matter of law against him. Hence it may be said, in Professor Maguire's terms, that the plaintiff is "overwhelmed" at the moment when the trial commences. That is, the production-burden is upon him.

The plaintiff is, therefore, bound to go forward with his evidence until he satisfies the judge that the jury would be warranted in finding *A*. When the plaintiff has thus carried his production-burden, he is in the hands of the jury in the sense that if both parties rest at this point, the judge will submit the case to the jury for decision.

But the plaintiff realizes that the minimum amount of evidence needed to prevent an adverse judgment as a matter of law may not be enough to bring the minds of the jurors to the required degree of persuasion regarding *A*. That is, he may fail to sustain the persuasion-burden. Hence, he would go on with his evidence in order to strengthen his case with the jury.

Sometimes the plaintiff's evidence may be overwhelming, so that the judge would hold that no reasonable juror could fail to find *A*. If on this posture of the evidence both parties rest, the judge could grant judgment as a matter of law for plaintiff. At this stage, the production-burden has shifted to the defendant.

To avoid such a judgment for the plaintiff, the defendant is bound in her turn to go forward with such evidence that it would become reasonable for the jury to decline to find *A*. The judge will then submit the case to the jury for decision.

The defendant's evidence may do more than push the issue back into the area of doubt where the jury is the arbiter. It may be overwhelming, in which case the production-burden shifts to the plaintiff.

As a theoretical matter, the production-burden may thus shift several times with the pull and haul of the evidence. As a practical matter, however, such multiple shifting on a single issue of fact is very unlikely. The reason is that conflicting evidence on a single issue would in most realistic settings leave the matter in the realm where decision is properly for the jury: a reasonable jury could find *A* or decline to find *A*, and so the judge should not grant judgment as a matter of law. Thus the pull and haul of the evidence will result only in oscillation within the jury's realm.

A diagram adapted from 9 John H. Wigmore, Evidence § 2487 (James H. Chadbourn rev. 1981), should help you to visualize this process:

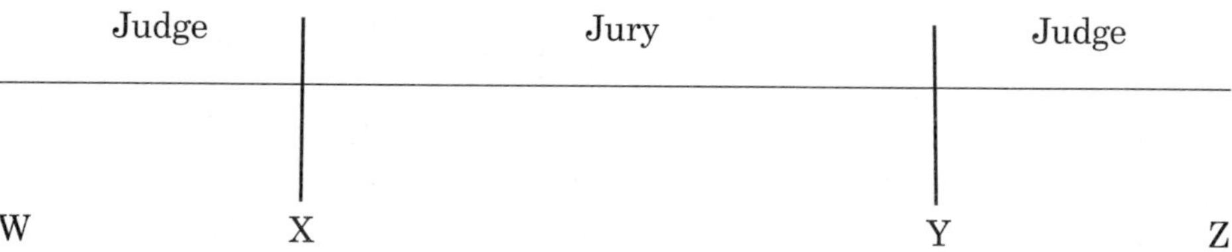

The plaintiff in our illustrative case starts at point W. He must get beyond point X to make a jury question of *A*, our assumed single issue of fact. If he gets beyond point Y, he is entitled to judgment as a matter of law in his favor unless the defendant comes forward with enough evidence to push the case back beyond point Y into the X–Y area. If the defendant succeeds in this, it is again a case for the jury. She may, however, be so successful that her evidence carries the case beyond point X into the W–X area. If so, the defendant becomes entitled to judgment as a matter of law unless the plaintiff in his turn comes forward with more evidence. But if, at the close of all the evidence, the case lies between points X and Y, it goes to the jury and the plaintiff has the persuasion-burden. He will lose if the jury is not persuaded of *A*.

Professor John T. McNaughton criticized the Wigmore diagram, and offered some interesting alternative diagrams, in Burden of Production of Evidence: A Function of a Burden of Persuasion, 68 Harv.L.Rev. 1382 (1955). He characterized the Wigmore diagram as misleading in its inaccurate implication that points X and Y represent respectively a certain small and a certain large probability of the existence of *A*. To appreciate his insight, you should realize that on specified evidence the judge could believe that the probability of *A* was very small indeed—and yet nevertheless the judge would properly deny judgment as a matter of law for the defendant because the judge believed that a reasonable jury, *crediting and weighing the evidence differently but still reasonably*, could find *A*. In other words, the judge should not be measuring the judge's own belief in *A* but instead be hypothesizing decision by a jury and determining the range of reasonable decision.

You can meet Professor McNaughton's criticism by visualizing precisely what point X or Y does represent. Do not think of point X as, say, the ten-percent line. Instead, the plaintiff's getting beyond point X means that although the judge might still disagree with a verdict for the plaintiff, the judge thinks a reasonable jury could find that the plaintiff sustained his persuasion-burden. For example, the judge might think that the jury could wrongly but reasonably believe all the plaintiff's evidence and disbelieve all the defendant's evidence. Therefore, the judge would hold that the plaintiff sustained his production-burden. By contrast, if the plaintiff does not get to point X, that means that the judge would so vehemently disagree with a verdict for the plaintiff as to consider the jury irrational. Point X thus represents the judge's view on the limit of rationality in the jury's finding for the plaintiff, rather than the judge's view of the evidential probability that *A* exists. More generally, the horizontal dimension in the refined Wigmore diagram represents the judge's disagreement with a potential verdict for the plaintiff, or the judge's view of probability of error in such a verdict, with disagreement or probability decreasing from left to right.

Where the case involves more than one disputed issue of fact, we can conveniently use a separate diagram for each such issue. In the typical case, the burden will rest upon the plaintiff on some issues and upon the defendant on others.

Question: (1) How must the foregoing description of burden of proof be altered to describe accurately the situation in trials by judge without jury? Cf. Rule 52(c).

As to the burden of persuasion, you may have had the reaction that it should not matter much. After all, in theory, it works only as a tiebreaker. But, in practice, lawyers and judges fight and suffer over it. Why? The reasons lie in psychology. First, how the law frames a question—whether the plaintiff or the defendant bears the risk of nonpersuasion of a fact—matters. The plaintiff may start from "zero," or the defendant may. An anchoring heuristic lowers the willingness of the fact-finder's determining that the burdened part has prevailed, because people fail to adjust fully from even an arbitrarily set starting point. Second, the zone of evidential ties is broader and fuzzier that point probabilities would suggest. The fact-finder will consider a range of showings indeterminate, not just perfect ties. Thus, the fact-finder will rely on the burden of persuasion more often than you would imagine. See generally Kevin M. Clermont, Procedure's Magical Number Three: Psychological Bases for Standards of Decision, 72 Cornell L.Rev. 1115 (1987).

This view of the burden of persuasion makes more sense of the burden of production too. At the trial's outset, the supposed perfect ignorance provides at best an evidential tie. The initial burden of production requires the burdened party to introduce a quantum of evidence sufficient to permit a reasonable fact-finder to break the tie and decide in that party's favor. Subsequent shifts in the burden of production impose an analogous requirement. The operation of the burden of production is important, as we shall see, in effectuating process and outcome values, as by facilitating early termination of very weak claims or defenses and safeguarding against irrational jury error.

ALLOCATION OF BURDENS

Whether one or the other of the parties has sustained or failed to sustain the production-burden is a matter for the judge to decide, and there is no occasion for the jury to hear anything about it. But as it is for the jury, when a case is submitted to it, to decide whether the party with the persuasion-burden on a particular issue of fact has sustained it, the judge must explain to the jury in the charge (1) upon whom this burden rests with regard to each issue that is left to the jury and (2) the degree of persuasion to which the minds of the jurors must be brought before they are warranted in finding that this burden has been carried with respect to the particular issue.

Problem (2) is reserved for Section 2 of this Topic. With respect to problem (1), Professor Edmund M. Morgan says in Some Observations Concerning Presumptions, 44 Harv.L.Rev. 906, 910–11 (1931):

"Inasmuch as under our adversary system of litigation the court conducts no independent investigation of its own, it must distribute between the litigants the burden of making the facts appear. In assigning to the plaintiff the burden of persuasion of the existence of *X,* it in substance notifies him that unless he makes *X* appear, the court will assume for the purposes of the litigation that *X* does not exist. In reaching its determination to put this burden upon plaintiff or defendant, it is influenced by substantially the same considerations as those which obtain in the determination of any question of substantive law. As in many branches of substantive law, precedents have developed rules of thumb, so here at least four a priori tests for placing this burden have emerged. These respectively make it fall upon (1) the party having the affirmative of the issue, (2) the party to whose case the fact in question is essential, (3) the party having peculiar means of knowing the fact, and (4) the party who has the burden of pleading it. Needless to say, these formulae are not self-executing; frequently to apply one is to repudiate another. Ordinarily the one selected is used only as a facile form of statement of the result. The real decision is made upon the judicial judgment based upon experience as to what is convenient, fair, and good policy; and some opinions frankly so declare."

Not only would it be erroneous to assume that the burden of persuasion is inevitably allocated between the parties in the same way as the burden of allegation, although this is typically the case,[c] but also it would be erroneous to assume that the burden of persuasion and the initial burden of production necessarily are allocated to the same party. A familiar illustration to the contrary from the criminal law is the matter of the defendant's insanity: in some states the defendant must plead and initially present some evidence of insanity, but the prosecution must ultimately persuade the jury that the defendant was sane.

Question: (2) What considerations of convenience, fairness, and good policy might dictate this allocation of the burdens as to insanity?

Thus, courts (or legislatures) allocate the burdens of allegation, production, and persuasion by similar thought processes, although not always with the same results for all three burdens. For each of the three a purposive approach that looks at many factors, reflecting substantive policies as well as procedural policies such as burdening the party with peculiar means of knowing the fact, appears preferable to the analytical approach suggested by the first two tests listed by Professor Morgan.

Accordingly, Professor Fleming James, Jr., in Burden of Proof, 47 Va.L.Rev. 51, 60–61 (1961), argues for putting the burden (1) "on the party having the readier access to knowledge about the fact in question," but noted that this factor could be overcome by (2) "the extent to which a party's contention departs from what would be expected in the light of ordinary human experience," (3) "a feeling that a charge of wrongdoing should in fairness be proven by the party making it," or (4) substantive considerations such as where "the law sometimes disfavors claims and defenses which it nevertheless allows."

Using law and economics, Professor Bruce L. Hay, in Allocating the Burden of Proof, 72 Ind.L.J. 651, 677 (1997), rather similarly concludes that the plaintiff should, and does, normally bear the burden on an issue because he is launching a claim that we have no reason to suppose is meritorious. But that burden can instead fall on the defendant if one or more of four factors is big enough to shift the balance of costs and benefits: (1) the plaintiff's relative expense of presenting evidence to support his position on the issue, (2) the plaintiff's likelihood of being correct on the issue, (3) the relative amount at stake for the plaintiff, and (4) the relative social cost of an erroneous decision against the plaintiff.

---

[c] See supra p. 1213, on pleading and proving contributory negligence.

Texas Department of Community Affairs v. Burdine

Supreme Court of the United States, 1981.
450 U.S. 248, 101 S.Ct. 1089.

■ JUSTICE POWELL delivered the opinion of the Court.

This case requires us to address again the nature of the evidentiary burden placed upon the defendant in an employment discrimination suit brought under Title VII of the Civil Rights Act of 1964, 42 U.S.C. § 2000e et seq. The narrow question presented is whether, after the plaintiff has proved a prima facie case of discriminatory treatment, the burden shifts to the defendant to persuade the court by a preponderance of the evidence that legitimate, nondiscriminatory reasons for the challenged employment action existed.

I

Petitioner, the Texas Department of Community Affairs (TDCA), hired respondent, a female, in January 1972, for the position of accounting clerk in the Public Service Careers Division (PSC). PSC provided training and employment opportunities in the public sector for unskilled workers. When hired, respondent possessed several years' experience in employment training. She was promoted to Field Services Coordinator in July 1972. Her supervisor resigned in November of that year, and respondent was assigned additional duties. Although she applied for the supervisor's position of Project Director, the position remained vacant for six months.

PSC was funded completely by the United States Department of Labor. The Department was seriously concerned about inefficiencies at PSC. In February 1973, the Department notified the Executive Director of TDCA, B.R. Fuller, that it would terminate PSC the following month. TDCA officials, assisted by respondent, persuaded the Department to continue funding the program, conditioned upon PSC's reforming its operations. Among the agreed conditions were the appointment of a permanent Project Director and a complete reorganization of the PSC staff.

After consulting with personnel within TDCA, Fuller hired a male [named Watts] from another division of the agency as Project Director. In reducing the PSC staff, he fired respondent along with two other employees, and retained another male, Walz, as the only professional employee in the division. It is undisputed that respondent had maintained her application for the position of Project Director and had requested to remain with TDCA. Respondent soon was rehired by TDCA and assigned to another division of the agency. She received the exact salary paid to the Project Director at PSC, and the subsequent promotions she has received have kept her salary and responsibility commensurate with what she would have received had she been appointed Project Director.

Respondent filed this suit in the United States District Court for the Western District of Texas. She alleged that the failure to promote and the subsequent decision to terminate her had been predicated on gender discrimination in violation of Title VII. After a bench trial, the District

Court held that neither decision was based on gender discrimination. The court relied on the testimony of Fuller that the employment decisions necessitated by the commands of the Department of Labor were based on consultation among trusted advisers and a nondiscriminatory evaluation of the relative qualifications of the individuals involved. He testified that the three individuals terminated did not work well together, and that TDCA thought that eliminating this problem would improve PSC's efficiency. The court accepted this explanation as rational and, in effect, found no evidence that the decisions not to promote and to terminate respondent were prompted by gender discrimination.

The Court of Appeals for the Fifth Circuit reversed in part. 608 F.2d 563 (1979). . . . [T]he court affirmed the District Court's finding that respondent was not discriminated against when she was not promoted. The Court of Appeals, however, reversed the District Court's finding that Fuller's testimony sufficiently had rebutted respondent's prima facie case of gender discrimination in the decision to terminate her employment at PSC. The court reaffirmed its previously announced views that the defendant in a Title VII case bears the burden of proving by a preponderance of the evidence the existence of legitimate nondiscriminatory reasons for the employment action . . . . It, therefore, reversed the judgment of the District Court and remanded the case for computation of backpay. Because the decision of the Court of Appeals as to the burden of proof borne by the defendant conflicts with interpretations of our precedents adopted by other Courts of Appeals, we granted certiorari. 447 U.S. 920, 100 S.Ct. 3009 (1980). We now vacate the Fifth Circuit's decision and remand for application of the correct standard.

II

In McDonnell Douglas Corp. v. Green, 411 U.S. 792, 93 S.Ct. 1817 (1973), we set forth the basic allocation of burdens and order of presentation of proof in a Title VII case alleging discriminatory treatment.[5] First, the plaintiff has the burden of proving by the preponderance of the evidence a prima facie case of discrimination. Second, if the plaintiff succeeds in proving the prima facie case, the burden shifts to the defendant "to articulate some legitimate, nondiscriminatory reason for the employee's rejection." Id., at 802, 93 S.Ct., at 1824. Third, should the defendant carry this burden, the plaintiff must then have an opportunity to prove by a preponderance of the evidence that the legitimate reasons offered by the defendant were not its true reasons, but were a pretext for discrimination. Id., at 804, 93 S.Ct., at 1825.

The nature of the burden that shifts to the defendant should be understood in light of the plaintiff's ultimate and intermediate burdens. The ultimate burden of persuading the trier of fact that the defendant intentionally discriminated against the plaintiff remains at all times with the plaintiff. See Board of Trustees of Keene State College v. Sweeney, 439

[5] We have recognized that the factual issues, and therefore the character of the evidence presented, differ when the plaintiff claims that a facially neutral employment policy has a discriminatory impact on protected classes. [Citations omitted.]

U.S. 24, 25, n. 2, 99 S.Ct. 295, 296, n. 2 (1978); id., at 29, 99 S.Ct., at 297 (Stevens, J., dissenting). See generally 9 J. Wigmore, Evidence § 2489 (3d ed. 1940) (the burden of persuasion "never shifts"). The McDonnell Douglas division of intermediate evidentiary burdens serves to bring the litigants and the court expeditiously and fairly to this ultimate question.

The burden of establishing a prima facie case of disparate treatment is not onerous. The plaintiff must prove by a preponderance of the evidence that she applied for an available position for which she was qualified, but was rejected under circumstances which give rise to an inference of unlawful discrimination.[6] The prima facie case serves an important function in the litigation: it eliminates the most common nondiscriminatory reasons for the plaintiff's rejection. See Teamsters v. United States, 431 U.S. 324, 358, and n. 44, 97 S.Ct. 1843, 1866, and n. 44 (1977). As the Court explained in Furnco Construction Corp. v. Waters, 438 U.S. 567, 577, 98 S.Ct. 2943, 2949 (1978), the prima facie case "raises an inference of discrimination only because we presume these acts, if otherwise unexplained, are more likely than not based on the consideration of impermissible factors." Establishment of the prima facie case in effect creates a presumption that the employer unlawfully discriminated against the employee. If the trier of fact believes the plaintiff's evidence, and if the employer is silent in the face of the presumption, the court must enter judgment for the plaintiff because no issue of fact remains in the case.[7]

The burden that shifts to the defendant, therefore, is to rebut the presumption of discrimination by producing evidence that the plaintiff was rejected, or someone else was preferred, for a legitimate, nondiscriminatory reason. The defendant need not persuade the court that it was actually motivated by the proffered reasons. See Sweeney, supra, at 25, 99 S.Ct., at 296. It is sufficient if the defendant's evidence raises a genuine issue of fact as to whether it discriminated against the plaintiff.[8] To accomplish this, the

---

[6] In McDonnell Douglas, supra, we described an appropriate model for a prima facie case of racial discrimination. The plaintiff must show:

"(i) that he belongs to a racial minority; (ii) that he applied and was qualified for a job for which the employer was seeking applicants; (iii) that, despite his qualifications, he was rejected; and (iv) that, after his rejection, the position remained open and the employer continued to seek applicants from persons of complainant's qualifications." 411 U.S., at 802, 93 S.Ct., at 1824.

We added, however, that this standard is not inflexible, as "[t]he facts necessarily will vary in Title VII cases, and the specification above of the prima facie proof required from respondent is not necessarily applicable in every respect in differing factual situations." Id., at 802, n. 13, 93 S.Ct., at 1824, n. 13.

In the instant case, it is not seriously contested that respondent has proved a prima facie case. She showed that she was a qualified woman who sought an available position, but the position was left open for several months before she finally was rejected in favor of a male, Walz, who had been under her supervision.

[7] The phrase "prima facie case" not only may denote the establishment of a legally mandatory, rebuttable presumption, but also may be used by courts to describe the plaintiff's burden of producing enough evidence to permit the trier of fact to infer the fact at issue. 9 J. Wigmore, Evidence § 2494 (3d ed. 1940). McDonnell Douglas should have made it apparent that in the Title VII context we use "prima facie case" in the former sense.

[8] This evidentiary relationship between the presumption created by a prima facie case and the consequential burden of production placed on the defendant, is a traditional feature of the

defendant must clearly set forth, through the introduction of admissible evidence, the reasons for the plaintiff's rejection.[9] The explanation provided must be legally sufficient to justify a judgment for the defendant. If the defendant carries this burden of production, the presumption raised by the prima facie case is rebutted,[10] and the factual inquiry proceeds to a new level of specificity. Placing this burden of production on the defendant thus serves simultaneously to meet the plaintiff's prima facie case by presenting a legitimate reason for the action and to frame the factual issue with sufficient clarity so that the plaintiff will have a full and fair opportunity to demonstrate pretext. The sufficiency of the defendant's evidence should be evaluated by the extent to which it fulfills these functions.

The plaintiff retains the burden of persuasion. She now must have the opportunity to demonstrate that the proffered reason was not the true reason for the employment decision. This burden now merges with the ultimate burden of persuading the court that she has been the victim of intentional discrimination. . . . See McDonnell Douglas, 411 U.S., at 804–805, 93 S.Ct., at 1825–1826.

III

. . . .

The Court of Appeals has misconstrued the nature of the burden that McDonnell Douglas and its progeny place on the defendant. . . . It is plain that the Court of Appeals required much more: it placed on the defendant the burden of persuading the court that it had convincing, objective reasons for preferring the chosen applicant above the plaintiff.[11]

---

common law. "The word 'presumption' properly used refers only to a device for allocating the production burden." F. James & G. Hazard, Civil Procedure § 7.9, p. 255 (2d ed. 1977) (footnote omitted). See Fed.Rule Evid. 301. See generally 9 J. Wigmore, Evidence § 2491 (3d ed. 1940). Cf. J. Maguire, Evidence, Common Sense and Common Law 185–186 (1947). Usually, assessing the burden of production helps the judge determine whether the litigants have created an issue of fact to be decided by the jury. In a Title VII case, the allocation of burdens and the creation of a presumption by the establishment of a prima facie case is intended progressively to sharpen the inquiry into the elusive factual question of intentional discrimination.

9 An articulation not admitted into evidence will not suffice. Thus, the defendant cannot meet its burden merely through an answer to the complaint or by argument of counsel.

10 See generally J. Thayer, Preliminary Treatise on Evidence 346 (1898). In saying that the presumption drops from the case, we do not imply that the trier of fact no longer may consider evidence previously introduced by the plaintiff to establish a prima facie case. A satisfactory explanation by the defendant destroys the legally mandatory inference of discrimination arising from the plaintiff's initial evidence. Nonetheless, this evidence and inferences properly drawn therefrom may be considered by the trier of fact on the issue of whether the defendant's explanation is pretextual. Indeed, there may be some cases where the plaintiff's initial evidence, combined with effective cross-examination of the defendant, will suffice to discredit the defendant's explanation [and so prove discrimination].

11 The court reviewed the defendant's evidence and explained its deficiency:

"Defendant failed to introduce comparative factual data concerning Burdine and Walz. Fuller merely testified that he discharged and retained personnel in the spring shakeup at TDCA primarily on the recommendations of subordinates and that he considered Walz qualified for the position he was retained to do. Fuller failed to specify any objective criteria on which he based the decision to discharge Burdine and retain Walz. He stated only that the action was in the best interest of the program and that there had been some friction within

The Court of Appeals distinguished Sweeney on the ground that the case held only that the defendant did not have the burden of proving the absence of discriminatory intent. But this distinction slights the rationale of Sweeney and of our other cases. We have stated consistently that the employee's prima facie case of discrimination will be rebutted if the employer articulates lawful reasons for the action; that is, to satisfy this intermediate burden, the employer need only produce admissible evidence which would allow the trier of fact rationally to conclude that the employment decision had not been motivated by discriminatory animus. The Court of Appeals would require the defendant to introduce evidence which, in the absence of any evidence of pretext, would *persuade* the trier of fact that the employment action was lawful. This exceeds what properly can be demanded to satisfy a burden of production.

The court placed the burden of persuasion on the defendant apparently because it feared that "[i]f an employer need only *articulate*—not prove—a legitimate, nondiscriminatory reason for his action, he may compose fictitious, but legitimate, reasons for his actions." Turner v. Texas Instruments, Inc., [555 F.2d 1251, 1255 (5th Cir.1977)] (emphasis in original). We do not believe, however, that limiting the defendant's evidentiary obligation to a burden of production will unduly hinder the plaintiff. First, as noted above, the defendant's explanation of its legitimate reasons must be clear and reasonably specific. [Citations omitted.] This obligation arises both from the necessity of rebutting the inference of discrimination arising from the prima facie case and from the requirement that the plaintiff be afforded "a full and fair opportunity" to demonstrate pretext. Second, although the defendant does not bear a formal burden of persuasion, the defendant nevertheless retains an incentive to persuade the trier of fact that the employment decision was lawful. Thus, the defendant normally will attempt to prove the factual basis for its explanation. Third, the liberal discovery rules applicable to any civil suit in federal court are supplemented in a Title VII suit by the plaintiff's access to the Equal Employment Opportunity Commission's investigatory files concerning her complaint. See EEOC v. Associated Dry Goods Corp., 449 U.S. 590, 101 S.Ct. 817 (1981). Given these factors, we are unpersuaded that the plaintiff will find it particularly difficult to prove that a proffered explanation lacking a factual basis is a pretext. We remain confident that the McDonnell Douglas framework permits the plaintiff meriting relief to demonstrate intentional discrimination.

. . . .[d]

---

the department that might be alleviated by Burdine's discharge. Nothing in the record indicates whether he examined Walz' ability to work well with others. This court in [a previous case] found such unsubstantiated assertions of 'qualification' and 'prior work record' insufficient absent data that will allow a true *comparison* of the individuals hired and rejected." 608 F.2d, at 568.

[d] On remand the court of appeals affirmed the district court's judgment against the plaintiff, 647 F.2d 513 (5th Cir.1981). See Leonardo J. Raznovich, A Comparative Review of

PRESUMPTIONS

A full-dress treatment of burden of proof would involve us deeply in "presumptions," all the intricacies of which cannot be explored here. The word has, as Professor Maguire says in Evidence: Common Sense and Common Law 183 (1947), suffered badly from rough and careless handling.

1. To the layperson its most common use is doubtless the "presumption of innocence" in criminal cases. This is not really a presumption at all, but rather another way of saying that the prosecution must prove its case beyond a reasonable doubt, that there is to be no inference against the defendant because of his arrest, indictment, and presence in the dock, and so on. In instructions to the jury the phrase does, however, have a satisfying ring to defense counsel, and the judge's refusal to use it may be reversible error, no matter how accurately and meticulously the judge tells the jury in other words what it means. See Taylor v. Kentucky, 436 U.S. 478, 98 S.Ct. 1930 (1978).

2. Another use of the word is in the phrase "conclusive presumption." This is not a presumption in any useful sense, but a rule of law that so equates one fact (the basic fact) to another (the presumed fact) that no one will be heard to say the latter does not exist if the former is proved. For instance, the statement in a workers' compensation act that the children under sixteen living in a worker's household at the time of his or her death are conclusively presumed to be dependent upon him or her really means that the law is not concerned with dependency in fact so long as the prescribed circumstances exist.

3. The word is also loosely used, by lawyers as well as laypersons, as a synonym for inference ("Dr. Livingstone, I presume"), a matter of logic and experience and not of law. All circumstantial evidence is a matter of inference, and the use of presumption terminology in this context can only be confusing. Nevertheless, "permissive presumption" is sometimes used to describe certain inferences that by law the jury is authorized but not required to draw. According to most courts, this is the situation in res ipsa loquitur cases. Permissive presumptions are usually *reasonable* based on probabilities (e.g., presuming negligence from the fact of damage in certain circumstances, such as a piano falling on the plaintiff's head), but are occasionally *arbitrary* in the sense that the rule authorizing the particular inference may be based instead on policy concerns (e.g., presuming negligence from the fact of damage by certain defendants, such as railroads). If the jury is authorized to find the existence of the presumed fact from proof of the basic fact when the raw probabilities alone would not justify the finding, the judge may so instruct the jury without violation of the common

---

the Socio–Legal Implication of Burden of Proof and Presumptions to Deal with Factual Uncertainty, 32 Am.J.Trial Advoc. 57 (2008) (discussing how some other countries have adhered to the court of appeals' initial approach of shifting the burden of persuasion); Jarrett Haskovec, Note, A Beast of a Burden? The New EU Burden-of-Proof Arrangement in Cases of Employment Discrimination Compared to Existing U.S. Law, 14 Transnat'l L. & Contemp.Probs. 1069 (2005).

ban in state practice against comment on the evidence. It can be argued that this is as much a rule of law as that about to be discussed.

4. We finally come to the more general view, held by Thayer, Wigmore, Morgan, Maguire, and other commentators and illustrated recurringly in common and statutory law, that the word "presumption" should be used only to denote the convention that when a designated basic fact exists, a certain presumed fact *must* be taken to exist *in the absence of adequate rebuttal*.[e] It is in this sense that we shall use it hereafter.

For convenience in the discussion that follows, we shall designate the basic fact as *B* and the presumed fact as *P*. Assume that the single disputed issue of fact in a civil case is *P*, the plaintiff asserts the affirmative and initially has the production-burden and the persuasion-burden thereon, and there is a common-law or statutory presumption that when *B* exists *P* is presumed to exist. Assume further that the presumption is grounded upon reasonable probabilities; that is, proof of *B* would have sufficient evidentiary value to warrant the jury in finding *P* if there were no presumption. (We shall refer in a moment to the less common presumptions that are arbitrary; that is, apart from such a presumption, proof of the basic fact would not be sufficient to warrant the jury's finding the presumed fact.)

Suppose, first, that the plaintiff offers overwhelming evidence of *B*, and there is no other evidence bearing on *B* or *P*. The judge will grant judgment as a matter of law for the plaintiff. But suppose, second, that the defendant introduces evidence of non-*B* to the point where the jury could reasonably find either way as to *B*'s existence, and there is still no other evidence bearing on *P*. The presumption compels the judge to instruct the jury: "If, but only if, you find *B*, you are bound to find *P*." There is no advantage in more expressly mentioning the presumption to the jury in the charge.

Questions: (3) How does the action of the judge in these two situations differ from what it would be in the absence of the presumption?

(4) When there are other disputed issues in addition to *P*, how does the judge instruct the jury if the evidence as to *B* is overwhelming and there is no other evidence bearing on *P* ? if the evidence as to *B* is conflicting and there is no other evidence bearing on *P* ?

So long as all the evidence relates only to *B*, the basic fact, the courts are in universal agreement that when *B* is established, *P*, the presumed fact, must be taken as true. But when evidence of non-*P* is introduced, that unanimity disappears and the decisions are in what Wigmore termed a state of "variegated inconsistency." There is little point in running down these inconsistencies, which were reflected in the deliberations of the American Law Institute in drawing up its Model Code of Evidence, promulgated in 1942.[f] But the major approaches deserve attention.

---

[e] "This careful, particularized use of the word presumption, by the way, is getting more and more consistent acceptance in the courts; nobody has ever succeeded in making consistent the legislative use of this or any other important word." John M. Maguire, Evidence: Common Sense and Common Law 183–84 (1947).

[f] 18 A.L.I. Proc. 197–226 (1941). Professor Morgan lists eight different views exhibited in judicial opinions. Edmund M. Morgan, Basic Problems of State and Federal Evidence 28–30

a. The Institute, over the opposition of its Reporter, Professor Morgan, wound up adopting what is often called the Thayer approach because of the distinguished early pioneering in the field by Professor James B. Thayer. The Institute generalized as follows: when the basic fact has been established, the presumed fact must be assumed until other evidence has been introduced that would warrant a finding of the presumed fact's nonexistence; when such evidence has been introduced, the existence or nonexistence of the presumed fact is to be determined exactly as if no presumption had ever been applicable.[g] In other words, the presumption affects the production-burden only; when other evidence warranting a finding of the nonexistence of the presumed fact appears, the presumption has spent itself like a "bursting bubble." If the presumption was grounded upon the reasonable probability that *P* exists when *B* is shown, that probability remains for the jury to consider against the evidence to the contrary, but without any artificial weight by reason of the presumption. There is no occasion for the judge to mention the presumption in charging the jury.

b. The original Uniform Rules of Evidence, approved by the National Conference of Commissioners on Uniform State Laws in 1953, took a very different tack.[h] Adopting the view of Professor Morgan, the Uniform Rules provided that if the basic fact has any probative value as evidence of the existence of the presumed fact, the presumption continues and the burden of proof (that is, the burden of persuasion) as to the nonexistence of the presumed fact is upon the party against whom the presumption operates. The traditional dogma of Wigmore that the burden of persuasion never shifts is thus violated. A plaintiff who starts out with the burden of proving *P* has the benefit, once he proves *B,* of placing the burden of proving non-*P* on the defendant.

However, the 1953 Uniform Rules gave less procedural effect to presumptions where the basic fact has no probative value with respect to the fact presumed. When such probative value is lacking, the Uniform Rules provided that only the burden of production is affected. Thus, the presumption disappears when other evidence is offered that would warrant a finding that the presumed fact does not exist. (The drafters of the Uniform Rules were frightened off by Western & Atlantic Railroad v. Henderson, 279 U.S. 639, 49 S.Ct. 445 (1929). There a Georgia statute provided that a railroad company would be liable for damage from its locomotive unless the company made it appear that it had exercised due care, the presumption in all cases being against the company. The Court held the statute unconstitu-

---

(Jack B. Weinstein ed., 5th ed. 1976). He also observes: "Every writer of sufficient intelligence to appreciate the difficulties of the subject-matter has approached the topic of presumptions with a sense of hopelessness and has left with a feeling of despair." Edmund M. Morgan, Presumptions, 12 Wash.L.Rev. & St.B.J. 255, 255 (1937).

[g] Model Code of Evidence Rule 704 (1942). This Thayer approach had attracted considerable judicial support prior to the Model Code and still does. A majority of states follow the Thayer–Model Code approach today. It is doubtful whether the Code itself was of significant influence in this development. The Code was not very well received by the bench and bar. Its proposed relaxation of the rules as to admission of hearsay evidence, for example, was widely thought to be dangerously radical.

[h] Unif.R.Evid. 14 (1953 version).

tional because it shifted the burden of persuasion when the basic fact, damage, had no probative value in establishing the presumed fact, negligence. The Supreme Court distinguished Mobile, Jackson & Kansas City Railroad Co. v. Turnipseed, 219 U.S. 35, 31 S.Ct. 136 (1910), in which a somewhat similar Mississippi statute had been construed to affect only the burden of production and had been upheld.) The effect of the 1953 Uniform Rules, then, was to treat nonprobative presumptions in precisely the same way that the Thayer–Model Code approach treated all presumptions.

c. The Federal Rules of Evidence, as originally *proposed* by the Supreme Court in 1972 but not as eventually enacted, treated all presumptions in exactly the same way that the 1953 Uniform Rules treated probative presumptions. Once the plaintiff proves *B,* the defendant must produce evidence and must ultimately persuade the jury of non-*P*. That is, the proposed Federal Rules provided that a presumption imposes on the party against whom it is directed the burden of persuasion of the nonexistence of the presumed fact, as well as the usual burden of production. The rationale for this approach is that the reasons giving rise to presumptions are too important to permit them to disappear entirely like bursting bubbles. Shifting the burden of persuasion gives presumptions lasting effect without hopelessly confusing the jury.[i]

Under the proposed Federal Rules, moreover, no distinction was drawn between reasonable and arbitrary presumptions. It was thought that the social policies behind arbitrary presumptions might be no less important than the evidentiary value underlying reasonable presumptions and, indeed, might be more in need of special procedural treatment. (The drafters found no constitutional infirmity in this view, believing that the Court would not follow the Henderson case today.) Still, there is no occasion for the judge to mention the presumption in charging the jury.[j]

---

[i] Such a shift in the burden of persuasion also occurs under various substantive doctrines, without any direct reference to evidence law. The substantive law might provide that if the plaintiff proves *B*, then the defendant is liable, unless the defendant proves non-*P*.

For example, the Supreme Court later supplemented the Burdine framework. Price Waterhouse v. Hopkins, 490 U.S. 228, 109 S.Ct. 1775 (1989), presented a disparate treatment case under Title VII involving an employer's "mixed motives" in passing a woman over for partnership. The divided Court held if the plaintiff manages to show that an unlawful consideration such as gender was at least a motivating factor in the adverse employment decision, then to escape liability the defendant must prove that the other, legitimate considerations would have generated the same decision anyway. Here, then, the burden of persuasion shifted, in that the defendant now had to establish in effect an affirmative defense of noneffect.

Dissatisfied with the Court's decision in Price Waterhouse as not going far enough, Congress overturned it by the Civil Rights Act of 1991, Pub.L. No. 102–166, tit. I, § 107, 105 Stat. 1071, 1075. The statute provides that if an employer proves other, legitimate considerations would have generated the same employment decision anyway, the employer does not thereby escape liability but merely limits the remedies available to the plaintiff to the more prospective kinds.

More recently, the Court has backed away from Price Waterhouse burden-shifting, by declining to extend it to related contexts. See Gross v. FBL Fin. Servs. Inc., 129 S.Ct. 2343 (2009) (age discrimination).

[j] The new Uniform Rules of Evidence, approved by the National Conference of Commissioners on Uniform State Laws in 1974 to supersede the 1953 Uniform Rules, and revised in 1999, follow the approach of the proposed Federal Rules. Unif.R.Evid. 302(a) (1999 version).

Question: (5) The distinction between reasonable and arbitrary presumptions is complicated by the fact that different jurisdictions may take different views as to whether a particular presumption falls within one category or the other. For instance, State *X* may regard proof of employment as warranting a finding that the employee was acting within the scope of his employment on a given occasion; State *Y* may not. In other words, in an action in State *X*, proof of employment will take the issue of scope of employment to the jury; in State *Y*, proof of employment alone will not suffice to prevent judgment as a matter of law. Now superimpose a presumption of scope from the fact of employment on the law of each state. In a case where the plaintiff has the burden of proving scope and where the only evidence bearing on scope is overwhelming evidence of employment, what would be the effect of the presumption in State *X* and State *Y* respectively under (a) the Thayer–Model Code approach, (b) the 1953 Uniform Rules, and (c) the proposed Federal Rules? If the defendant were to introduce other evidence warranting a finding that the employee was not acting within the scope of his employment, what would then be the effect of the presumption in those two states respectively under these three approaches?

d. The Federal Rules of Evidence, as ultimately *enacted* into law in 1975 by congressional statute, appear to have reverted in Evidence Rule 301 to the Thayer–Model Code approach, unless an act of Congress otherwise provides. Evidence Rule 302 provides that state law is controlling as to the effect of a presumption respecting a fact which is an element of a claim or defense itself governed by state law, and this deference naturally cuts down the impact of Evidence Rule 301. This deference also accords with the Erie result that the initial burden of production and the burden of persuasion are matters for state law on state claims and defenses.

With those different approaches in mind, one should note that some states give varying procedural effect to different presumptions, depending upon the nature and force of the reasons giving rise to each. See Alfred L. Gausewitz, Presumptions in a One–Rule World, 5 Vand.L.Rev. 324 (1952). The Federal Rules of Evidence, preferring the greater ease of administration, treat all presumptions alike in civil cases. However, the proposed Federal Rules had included a special provision covering presumptions in criminal cases. Congress omitted this provision with the intention of treating the matter in subsequent legislation. Evidence Rules 301 and 302 are thus left extending only to the civil side.[k]

Questions: (6) How are the constitutional questions as to presumptions different in a criminal case? See 21B Wright & Graham § 5148.

(7) How must the foregoing description of presumptions be altered to describe accurately the situation in trials by judge without jury?

Finally, it could be argued that all these rarefied logical constructions of burdens and presumptions hurt more than they help (or at the least these doctrines suffer from redundancy) and that they derive mainly from

---

[k] The Model Code generally treated all presumptions alike, there being only a minor exception. Model Code of Evidence Rule 703 (1942). Putting aside the distinction based on probative value, one could say the same for the original Uniform Rules. Unif.R.Evid. 16 (1953 version). The new Uniform Rules followed the approach of the proposed Federal Rules, distinguishing between civil and criminal cases but treating both. Unif.R.Evid. 303 (1999 version).

judges' distrust of juries and appellate courts' distrust of trial courts. See Wells v. Colorado Department of Transportation, 325 F.3d 1205, 1221 (10th Cir.2003) (concurring opinion) (arguing that the Burdine "framework only creates confusion and distracts courts from 'the ultimate question of discrimination vel non.' United States Postal Serv. Bd. of Governors v. Aikens, 460 U.S. 711, 714, 103 S.Ct. 1478 (1983)"); Ronald J. Allen & Craig R. Callen, The Juridical Management of Factual Uncertainty, 7 Int'l J.Evidence & Proof 1 (2003). But do the doctrines not help to understand the following old chestnut of a case?

SUMMERS v. TICE, 33 Cal.2d 80, 199 P.2d 1 (1948). The plaintiff and two defendants were hunting quail. In the course of hunting, the plaintiff went ahead. One of the defendants flushed a quail, and both defendants fired simultaneously in the direction of the plaintiff. One shot struck the plaintiff in the eye. Both defendants were using 12–gauge shotguns with shells containing 7½–size shot, making it substantially impossible to determine from which gun the shot causing the damage came. The trial judge sitting without a jury found that the plaintiff's injury was the "direct result of the shooting by the defendants," that both defendants were negligent in so shooting, and that the plaintiff was not contributorily negligent. Judgment was entered against both defendants. On appeal, judgment was affirmed. The appellate court said:

"When we consider the relative position of the parties and the results that would flow if plaintiff was required to pin the injury on one of the defendants only, a requirement that the burden of proof on that subject be shifted to defendants becomes manifest. They are both wrongdoers—both negligent toward plaintiff. They brought about a situation where the negligence of one of them injured the plaintiff, hence it should rest with them each to absolve himself if he can. The injured party has been placed by defendants in the unfair position of pointing to which defendant caused the harm. If one can escape the other may also and plaintiff is remediless."

SECTION 2. STANDARD OF PROOF

The principal task of the law's actors is decisionmaking, and decisionmaking takes place in the real world, where everything is uncertain. A legal decisionmaker therefore needs to know not only the issue but also how certain one must be to decide it in a particular way.

Much of procedure aims at facilitating optimal decisionmaking in the face of uncertainty. A central and critical task of procedure, then, is to specify the level of certainty required to support a particular decision. Whatever psychological path the legal decisionmaker follows in evaluating likelihood or degree of certainty, the law tells the decisionmaker next to compare this evaluation to that legally established standard of decision. More specifically, the type of standard of decision called the standard of proof specifies the degree of certainty required for finding that a contested fact exists.

Degrees of belief.—As our attention turns from burden of proof to standard of proof, our focus more obviously moves inside the fact-finder's mind. How does the fact-finder reach a decision?

No one knows. It is clear that humans do not naturally use perfectly "rational" techniques like Bayes' theorem, but instead use less accurate "intuitive" techniques. Social scientists have tried to model the cognitive black box by experimentally comparing inputs and outputs. A result is the model called information integration theory. Although only one of several contesting theories, and a relatively optimistic one at that, information integration theory has suggestive powers. We describe it also because it serves to highlight that many critical but unstated psychological assumptions underlie this whole area of procedure.

Information integration theory tries to describe how humans naturally combine information to produce judgment. According to the theory, the human decisionmaker who has to make a finding on a fact's existence would begin with an initial impression, or predisposition, and then would process additional pieces of information. Each of these, including the initial impression, would receive a scale value, which is a measure of the likelihood of the fact's existence. Each would also receive a weighting factor, which is a measure of evidential importance that takes into account both directness and credibility. The decisionmaker would then combine these into a weighted average. The following thus represents the judged likelihood based on k pieces of information:

$$J = \frac{\Sigma W_k S_k}{\Sigma W_k}$$

See Martin F. Kaplan, Cognitive Processes in the Individual Juror, in The Psychology of the Courtroom 197 (Norbert L. Kerr & Robert M. Bray eds., 1982). But see, e.g., Jennifer Groscup & Jennifer Tallon, Theoretical Models of Jury Decision–Making, in Jury Psychology 41 (Joel D. Lieberman & Daniel A. Krauss eds., 2009) (sketching some contesting models).

In actuality, performance of any such cognitive process would usually be nonquantitative and vague. Moreover, the judged likelihood would usually find expression in terms of a limited set of broad and fuzzy categories such as more likely than not, high probability, and almost certainty.

Significantly, the law today seems to limit its choice to no more than three standards of proof—preponderance, clearly convincing, and beyond a reasonable doubt—from among the infinite range of probabilities stretching from slightly probable to virtual certainty. The law did not always recognize this limitation, but with time the law acknowledged that the conceivable spectrum of standards had coalesced irresistibly into three. See, e.g., J.P. McBaine, Burden of Proof: Degrees of Belief, 32 Cal.L.Rev. 242 (1944) (arguing that, for standards of proof, only three levels of strictness exist). Why?

Well, the cognitive psychology literature suggests that limited, step-like standards accord with how humans naturally process information. Studies of humans' absolute judgment, short-term memory, and use of biased heuristics all support the "bounded rationality" of humankind. In particular, our cognitive limitations leave us able only weakly to judge probabilities. Judged likelihood usually finds expression in terms of that very small set of broad and fuzzy categories. Perhaps the law has optimized by conforming to the coarsely gradated scale of probability already in people's customary use. If so, this legal development represents the law's intuitive but wise reconciliation with humans' cognitive limitations.

Formulating standards.—How, more precisely, does the law formulate the various standards of proof?

In Livanovitch v. Livanovitch, 99 Vt. 327, 131 A. 799 (1926), the trial court gave the following charge: "If . . . you are more inclined to believe from the evidence that he did so deliver the bonds to the defendant, even though your belief is only *the slightest degree* greater than that he did not, your verdict should be for the plaintiff." The appellate court said: "The instruction was not erroneous. It was but another way of saying that the slightest preponderance of the evidence in his favor entitled the plaintiff to a verdict. . . . All that is required in a civil case of one who has the burden of proof is that he establish his claim by a preponderance of the evidence. . . . When the equilibrium of proof is destroyed, and the beam inclines toward him who has the burden, however slightly, he has satisfied the requirement of the law, and is entitled to the verdict. 'A bare preponderance is sufficient, though the scales drop but a feather's weight.' This rule accords with the practice in this State as remembered by the Justices of this Court, and is well supported by the authorities."

In Lampe v. Franklin American Trust Co., 339 Mo. 361, 96 S.W.2d 710 (1936), one of the defendant's contentions was that the note in suit had been altered after it had been signed by the defendant's decedent. The trial court refused the defendant's request for an instruction that the jury should find that the instrument was not the decedent's note "if you find and believe that it is *more probable* that such changes or alterations have been made in the instrument after it was signed by the deceased and without his knowledge and consent, than it is that such alterations and changes were made at or about the time that the deceased signed the instrument and under his direction and with his knowledge and consent." Holding the refusal to have been proper, the appellate court said: "The trouble with this statement is that a verdict must be based upon what the jury finds to be facts rather than what they find to be 'more probable.' "

These two cases are an almost random sampling of the contrariety of views on a subject that has long plagued trial judges and appellate courts. The problem is present in every charge to a jury.

If the trial judge meets it by resorting to the conventional language of "preponderance of the evidence," does the judge convey any meaningful concept to the ordinary juror? In replies of 843 former jurors in Ohio to a questionnaire submitted by Judge Walter B. Wanamaker, 232 thought that this phrase was the most difficult to understand. ("Proximate cause" was runner-up with 203 votes.) Trial by Jury, 11 U.Cin.L.Rev. 119, 192 (1937). And in replies of 173 former jurors in the District of Columbia to a questionnaire asking them to pick the most accurate definition of preponderance of the evidence from (1) one party's evidence is stronger than the other's, (2) a slow and careful pondering of the evidence, and (3) looking at the exhibits in the jury room, 76 chose one of the latter two. Kathleen F. O'Reilly, Why Some Juries Fail, D.C.B.J., Jan.–June 1974, at 69.

The use of pattern jury instructions has developed in recent years. In some jurisdictions their use where applicable is mandatory. See, e.g., Ill.Sup.Ct.R. 239(a). More often they are available for the trial judge to use in the judge's discretion. For example, the New York pattern instruction on burden of proof, prepared by a panel of New York judges, is as follows: "The burden of proof rests on the plaintiff. That means that it must be established by a fair preponderance of the credible evidence that the claim plaintiff makes is true. The credible evidence means the testimony or exhibits that you find to be worthy to be believed. A preponderance of the evidence means the greater part of such evidence. That does not mean the greater number of witnesses or the greater length of time taken by either side. The phrase refers to the quality of the evidence, that is, its convincing quality, the weight and the effect that it has on your minds. The law requires that in order for the plaintiff to prevail on a claim, the evidence that supports (his, her) claim must appeal to you as more nearly representing what took place than the evidence opposed to (his, her) claim. If it does not, or if it weighs so evenly that you are unable to say that there is a preponderance on either side, then you must decide the question in favor of the defendant. It is only if the evidence favoring the plaintiff's claim outweighs the evidence opposed to it that you can find in favor of plaintiff." New York Pattern Jury Instructions 1:23 (3d ed. 2006).

In attacking a similar pattern instruction as "gobbledygook," Professor Mellinkoff argues that the "judge would have done his job much better telling the jury: Jones brought this case to court and it is his job to satisfy you that Smith hit him." David Mellinkoff, The Language of the Law 433–34 (1963).

Is there a feasible means of avoiding this confusion? Professor Morgan has this suggestion: "If the trial judge tells the jury that the burden is upon a party to prove a specified fact by a preponderance of the evidence, he should explain that this means only that they must find that the fact does not exist unless the evidence convinces them that its existence is more probable than its non-existence. Indeed, there is no need for him to talk of burden of proof or of preponderance of evidence. He may well confine his instruction on this matter to a specification of the disputed propositions of fact and a direction as to which party must fail on each proposition unless the jury is convinced by the evidence that the truth of that proposition is more probable than its falsity." Edmund M. Morgan, Instructing the Jury upon Presumptions and Burden of Proof, 47 Harv.L.Rev. 59, 66–67 (1933). See generally Amiram Elwork, Bruce D. Sales & James J. Alfini, Making Jury Instructions Understandable (1982).

Optimizing standards.—Let us put aside questions of form and get back to the substance of preponderance of the evidence as the standard of proof in civil cases. In setting the standard at more likely than not, the law has overcome the appealing but unsound lay intuition that outcome should not swing from no recovery to full recovery on the basis of a slight shift in the weight of evidence. Instead, the law pursues an error-minimizing strategy by routinely applying a standard of more likely than not, rather than some higher standard. The argument for this approach is strong, because the low standard is optimal given two conditions that are very plausible. The first condition is that an error in favor of the plaintiff is neither more undesirable nor less undesirable than an error in favor of the defendant, or that a dollar mistakenly paid by the defendant (a false positive) is just as costly to society as a dollar mistakenly uncompensated to the plaintiff (a false negative). The second condition is that the goal is to minimize the sum of expected costs from these two types of error, that is, the system wants to keep the amounts suffered mistakenly to a minimum. Under these conditions, which generally prevail outside the criminal law, the preponderance standard performs better than any other nonvariable standard of proof.

By so deciding in accordance with apparent probabilities, the legal system in the long run makes fewer errors than, for example, the many false negatives that a virtual-certainty standard would impose. Formal proofs indeed show that the preponderance standard minimizes not only the expected number of erroneous decisions but also the expected sum of wrongful amounts of damages, while it optimizes the incentives for primary conduct. If you want an idea of one proof, let p be the apparent probability that the defendant is liable (for D dollars). If $p>\frac{1}{2}$, call it p_1; and if $p\leq\frac{1}{2}$, call it p_2. On the one hand, under the preponderance standard, the expected sum of false positives and false negatives over the run of cases is $\Sigma[(1-p_1)D + p_2D]$. On the other hand, under a very high standard that eliminates false positives, the analogous sum is $\Sigma[p_1D + p_2D]$. Because $(1-p_1)$ is less than p_1, the preponderance standard lowers the system's expected error costs. See generally D.H. Kaye, The Error of Equal Error Rates, 1 Law, Probability & Risk 3 (2002).

It might be that if we knew more about the realities of the type of case or the particular case itself, we would adjust the standard of proof. For example, a variable standard of proof, set on a case-by-case basis by the ideal judge, could serve accuracy by offsetting the unavailability or inadmissibility of evidence in the particular case. More generally, in an ideal world, one could argue that the standard of proof should slightly vary issue by issue in response to the expected value of each outcome. But the path of the law in the real world has not been toward variable standards of proof—except for making gross adjustments as to whole categories of issues when substantive considerations, such as the high social cost of criminally convicting the innocent, invalidate the first condition stated above.

Thus, on certain issues in civil cases some courts have imposed a stricter standard than preponderance of the evidence. See, e.g., Johnson v. Johnson, 172 N.C. 530, 90 S.E. 516 (1916) (fraud and undue influence). In certain kinds of civil cases this stricter standard applies generally to all the issues involved. See, e.g., Santosky v. Kramer, 455 U.S. 745, 102 S.Ct. 1388 (1982) (termination of parental rights). This standard is usually expressed by such synonyms as "clear and convincing" or "clear, precise, and indubitable." For other issues and cases as to which this stricter standard may apply, see 9 John H. Wigmore, Evidence § 2498 (James H. Chadbourn rev. 1981).

In criminal cases the degree of persuasion must be beyond a reasonable doubt, a concept that has also been a source of confusion. One of the best-known formulations of reasonable doubt is that of Chief Justice Shaw: "It is not mere possible doubt; because every thing relating to human affairs, and depending on moral evidence, is open to some possible or imaginary doubt. It is that state of the case, which, after the entire comparison and consideration of all the evidence, leaves the minds of jurors in that condition that they cannot say they feel an abiding conviction, to a moral certainty, of the truth of the charge." Commonwealth v. Webster, 59 Mass. (5 Cush.) 295, 320 (1850). There are holdings that whenever in a civil case a criminal act is charged, proof of the act must be beyond a reasonable doubt. An example would be proof of forgery in a proceeding to set aside an allegedly forged deed. This view has not been widely adopted in common-law countries. See McCormick on Evidence § 341 (Kenneth S. Broun gen. ed., 6th ed. 2006). But strangely, applying the high criminal standard on all issues in civil cases is the norm in civil-law countries. See Kevin M. Clermont, Standards of Proof Revisited, 33 Vt.L.Rev. 469 (2009).

Professor Morgan, following the quotation with respect to preponderance of the evidence above set forth, goes on to deal with the stricter standards as follows: "In like manner, if he charges that the burden is upon a party to prove a proposition by clear and convincing evidence, or by clear, satisfactory and convincing evidence, he should interpret this by saying that it requires the jury to be convinced not only that the truth of this proposition is more probable than its falsity, but also that its truth is much more probable than its falsity, though it is not necessary that the preponderance of probability of its truth shall be so great as to dissipate all reasonable doubt. Here too it is entirely unnecessary to use the orthodox phraseology, though it can do no harm if elucidated. As to issues which must be proved beyond reasonable doubt, there is no necessity for abandoning the familiar formula though there could be no rational objection to charging, instead, that the preponderance of probability must be so great as to banish all reasonable doubts."

Question: (8) In a diversity case, would the required degree of persuasion be governed by federal or state law?

Reid v. San Pedro, Los Angeles & Salt Lake Railroad Co.

Supreme Court of Utah, 1911.
39 Utah 617, 118 P. 1009.

[The plaintiff's first cause of action was for the death of a three-year-old heifer, which strayed onto the defendant's right of way and was killed by a train. There was no evidence of negligence on the part of the train crew. On the one hand, a Utah statute absolved the railroad from liability in such a case if the cow got onto the track through an open privately owned gate. On the other hand, if the cow entered through the fence inclosing the railroad's right of way at a point where the fence was out of repair, the railroad might be held liable. There was evidence that part of the fence between the pasture and the right of way was down and out of repair. There was also evidence that a gate into the pasture had been left open almost continuously prior to the accident. Verdict and judgment were for the plaintiff. The defendant appealed.]

■ McCARTY, J.

. . . .

There is no direct evidence as to where the cow got onto the right of way. It is conceded, however, that she was killed in the immediate vicinity of the gate mentioned, and, as shown by the evidence, about one mile from the point where the fence inclosing the right of way was down and out of repair. The inference, therefore, is just as strong, if not stronger, that she entered upon the right of way through the open gate as it is that she entered through the fence at the point where it was out of repair. The plaintiff held the affirmative, and the burden was on her to establish the liability of the defendant by a preponderance of the evidence. It is a familiar rule that where the undisputed evidence of the plaintiff, from which the existence of an essential fact is sought to be inferred, points with equal force to two things, one of which renders the defendant liable and the other not, the plaintiff must fail. So in this case, in order to entitle respondent to recover, it was essential for her to show by a preponderance of the evidence that the cow entered upon the right of way through the broken down fence. This the respondent failed to do.

We are of the opinion that the verdict rendered on the first cause of action is not supported by the evidence, and that the trial court should have directed a verdict for appellant on that cause of action in accordance with appellant's request. [Citations omitted.]

. . . .

Questions: (9) Should the verdict have been upheld if the cow had been killed at a point in the immediate vicinity of the break in the fence?

(10) If the cow had been killed at the equidistant point between the break in the fence and the gate, should the case have been submitted to the jury upon a showing that the break in the fence was twice as wide as the open gate? ten times as wide? What if it were also shown that the barn was closer to the gate than to the break?

(11) Is there a real difference between saying that because all the evidence points with equal force to opposite inferences a reasonable jury could not decide either way and saying that because different evidence of equal force supports each of opposite inferences a reasonable jury could decide either way? Compare Chaney v. Smithkline Beckman Corp., 764 F.2d 527 (8th Cir.1985), with Wratchford v. S.J. Groves & Sons Co., 405 F.2d 1061 (4th Cir.1969).

SARGENT v. MASSACHUSETTS ACCIDENT CO., 307 Mass. 246, 29 N.E.2d 825 (1940). This was an action to recover on an accident insurance policy. The insured, a young man of twenty-one, had attempted to go down the perilous Nottaway River to James Bay in a kayak. He was never heard from again, nor was his body recovered, but his paddle and a part of the kayak were found downstream. Perhaps he died by accidental injury or drowning. But perhaps he did not die or he died by disease or starvation, which would not be covered by the policy.

The question was whether there was evidence on which the jury might find death by accident within the terms of the policy or whether the court should say that it was a case where the plaintiff must fail because "the evidence tended equally to support two inconsistent propositions as to what happened" and consequently neither could be found to be true. The trial judge directed a verdict for the defendant insurance company. In reversing, Justice Lummus said:

"The burden of proof that is on the plaintiff in this case does not require him to establish beyond all doubt, or beyond a reasonable doubt, that the insured died from [accident]. He must prove that by a preponderance of the evidence. It has been held not enough that mathematically the chances somewhat favor a proposition to be proved; for example, the fact that colored automobiles made in the current year outnumber black ones would not warrant a finding that an undescribed automobile of the current year is colored and not black, nor would the fact that only a minority of men die of cancer warrant a finding that a particular man did not die of cancer. [Citations omitted.] Compare Commonwealth v. Clark, 292 Mass. 409, 415, 198 N.E. 641. The weight or ponderance of evidence is its power to convince the tribunal which has the determination of the fact, of the actual truth of the proposition to be proved. After the evidence has been weighed, that proposition is proved by a preponderance of the evidence if it is made to appear more likely or probable in the sense that actual belief in its truth, derived from the evidence, exists in the mind or minds of the tribunal notwithstanding any doubts that may still linger there."

SECTION 3. APPLYING THE BURDEN AND STANDARD OF PROOF

The reference by Justice Lummus to mathematical chances in the Sargent case was in no way necessary to the decision. No effort had been made to resort to mathematical proof. The question was simply whether the inference of accidental death could reasonably be drawn from the evidence. The use of mathematics as a tool of decisionmaking has, however, been much discussed in recent years, and the Lummus passage has been frequently quoted. The large volume of writing in the field reflects, on the one hand, the desire to enhance the objectivity and precision of judicial proof and, on the other hand, the costs of misusing and perhaps of merely using mathematical tools.[1]

The hazards of improper use of mathematics are illustrated in People v. Collins, 68 Cal.2d 319, 438 P.2d 33, 66 Cal.Rptr. 497 (1968). There the perpetrators of a robbery in Los Angeles were described as a white woman with her blond hair in a ponytail and a black man with moustache and beard, who were said to flee in a partly yellow automobile. The defendants, who seemed to match these descriptions, were arrested later. At trial the identification evidence was weak. So, the prosecutor tried to bolster it through the testimony of a mathematics instructor designed to show that there was but one chance in twelve million that a couple chosen at random would possess the described characteristics. The prosecutor argued to the jury in effect that there was therefore only one chance in twelve million that the defendants were innocent. The California Supreme Court reversed the conviction, holding that the mathematical testimony was inadmissible and the prosecutor's argument improper.

The hazards become more apparent upon a closer inspection of Collins. The mathematician testified to the "product rule," which states that the

[1] To get into the widely and hotly divergent literature on this subject, one should read in order Vaughn C. Ball, The Moment of Truth: Probability Theory and Standards of Proof, 14 Vand.L.Rev. 807 (1961); Laurence H. Tribe, Trial by Mathematics: Precision and Ritual in the Legal Process, 84 Harv.L.Rev. 1329 (1971); Michael J. Saks & Robert F. Kidd, Human Information Processing and Adjudication: Trial by Heuristics, 15 Law & Soc'y Rev. 123 (1981); David Kaye, The Limits of the Preponderance of the Evidence Standard: Justifiably Naked Statistical Evidence and Multiple Causation, 1982 Am.B.Found.Res.J. 487; Charles Nesson, The Evidence or the Event? On Judicial Proof and the Acceptability of Verdicts, 98 Harv. L.Rev. 1357 (1985); and Jonathan J. Koehler & Daniel N. Shaviro, Vertical Verdicts: Increasing Verdict Accuracy Through the Use of Overtly Probabilistic Evidence and Methods, 75 Cornell L.Rev. 247 (1990). See generally Probability and Inference in the Law of Evidence, 66 B.U.L.Rev. 377 (1986) (a six-hundred-page symposium); Decision and Inference in Litigation, 13 Cardozo L.Rev. 247 (1991) (an eight-hundred-page symposium).

probability of the joint occurrence of a number of mutually independent events is the product of the probabilities of each event. Then the prosecutor suggested probabilities for the various characteristics at issue: partly yellow automobile, 1/10; man with moustache, 1/4; woman with ponytail, 1/10; woman with blond hair, 1/3; black man with beard, 1/10; and interracial couple in car, 1/1000. The product rule yielded the one-in-twelve-million figure. The most obvious error in all this was that the prosecutor picked out of the air specific probability factors for each of the specified characteristics and asked the witness and jury to assume their accuracy without any supporting evidence. The court went on, however, to point out three additional flaws in the mathematical evidence that would be fatal even if each of the assumed probabilities was correct: there was no proof of statistical independence of the six factors; the mathematical approach hid the fact that the characteristics of the true perpetrators might not have been accurately established; and, all other errors aside, a one-in-twelve-million chance that a random couple would have the specified characteristics can be proven, by complicated mathematics, to mean that there was a better than forty-percent chance of the existence of a couple in the Los Angeles area other than the Collinses who also had those same characteristics. The court concluded that "under the circumstances the 'trial by mathematics' so distorted the role of the jury and so disadvantaged counsel for the defense, as to constitute in itself a miscarriage of justice."

Yet even where the mathematics have not been the subject of misunderstanding, courts seem to frown upon their use in decisionmaking. And this is so even in civil cases.

Questions: (12) A jet plane bearing U.S. Air Force markings flies low over a field that *P* is plowing with his mule Emma. Emma, frightened by the buzzing plane, bolts. *P* is injured. *P* sues the United States under the Federal Tort Claims Act. It is shown that there is a base twenty miles away, from which the Air Force planes are piloted by both Air Force and National Guard pilots. As a matter of substantive law, the United States is liable for negligence of the former but not of the latter. Sawyer v. United States, 148 F.Supp. 877 (M.D.Ga.1956).

(a) If there is no better evidence of the pilot's identity, would proof that 60 percent of the pilots flying out of the base were Air Force personnel be enough to warrant a finding of operation by a servant of the United States? 85 percent? 99 percent? Compare Guenther v. Armstrong Rubber Co., 406 F.2d 1315, 1318 (3d Cir.1969) (plaintiff injured by exploding tire; dictum that 75–to–80–percent chance it came from defendant manufacturer not enough for case to go to jury), with Kramer v. Weedhopper of Utah, Inc., 141 Ill.App.3d 217, 490 N.E.2d 104 (1986) (plaintiff injured in crash of ultralight aircraft; implication that 90–percent chance defective bolt came from defendant manufacturer enough for case to go to jury).

(b) A criminal defendant seeking a change of venue offers testimony of a pollster that, using standard scientific techniques, she has taken a sampling of public opinion in the district where the case is pending and the sampling shows a widespread prejudice against the defendant. Should the pollster's evidence be admitted? Should it, if believed, be enough to support a grant of the motion for change of venue? What, if any, difference is there between this case and that of the Air Force plane?

(c) Should the cooperation or lack of cooperation of the United States in seeking to identify the pilot have any bearing upon your answer to the question regarding the Air Force plane?

(d) Should it matter whether *P* could reasonably have produced more evidence of the pilot's identity?

(e) Should the sufficiency of *P*'s evidence be measured differently if his claim was for $100 instead of $100,000?

(f) Assume a case, plainly an extremely rare one, where there is virtually no possibility of discovering any evidence except a showing of mathematical chances, but this naked statistical evidence is extremely sound and directly relevant. What if the mathematical chances of the single disputed fact being true are 60 percent? 85 percent? 99 percent? Should the jury ever be allowed to decide the case on its view of these odds or should there always be judgment as a matter of law for one party or the other?

(13) If there were some nonstatistical evidence identifying the pilot as an Air Force pilot, should evidence of the proportion of Air Force pilots flying out of the base be admissible in supplementary support of such identification?

(14) The issue in a workers' compensation case is whether the employee's death from cancer was causally related to an injury sustained in the course of his employment when he fell off a truck. The only medical evidence supporting causation is from a specialist in internal medicine who had not treated the employee and whose testimony is based upon the medical records. He expresses the opinion that the force of the fall directly affected the pre-existent cancerous tissue of the pancreas and thereby hastened the metastatic spread of the cancer to other parts of the employee's body, thus hastening his death. On cross-examination, the doctor concedes that there was no clinical evidence of pre-existing cancer or of disturbance of cancerous tissue by the accident. It would, he admits, be conceivable that the cancer of the pancreas originated after the accident, but he says: "This would be unusual in view of the widespread metastasis; the size and the spread indicate it has probably been present for years." He adds: "I answer in terms of likelihood." Does this testimony support a finding of causal relation? Does the quoted statement of Justice Lummus in Sargent v. Massachusetts Accident Co. have any bearing on your answer? See King's Case, 352 Mass. 488, 225 N.E.2d 900 (1967).

Why, then, is there this resistance to statistical evidence? Does the resistance to mathematical tools derive from an unreasonable distaste, or do valid reasons justify a preference for nonmathematical proof? To progress we should get behind us the matters on which most people agree.

First, we can meaningfully speak in terms of probability even about a past event, although admittedly debate persists about how precisely we should think about those probabilities. Many theorists would speak in terms of so-called subjective probability, which measures how sure a person feels that the event occurred.

Second, no real difference exists between statistical evidence and nonstatistical evidence, between evidence that 60 percent of the pilots are Air Force personnel and eyewitness identification of an Air Force pilot by someone who happens to have a 60-percent chance of testifying accurately. Evidence may be more or less overtly numerical, rather than verbal. Evidence may be more or less general in relation to the case, rather than particularistic. Any such characteristic of evidence is a matter of degree on a spectrum, a spectrum that ideally has no bearing on the pure determination of the fact's existence.

Third, resisting something characterized as statistical evidence, in pursuit of some benefit, will entail offsetting costs. For example, raising the standard of proof significantly above 50 percent for the civil proponent relying on statistical evidence would push toward increasing overall error costs (incidentally, "proponent" here means the party having the burden of proof).

Nevertheless, there is a widely assumed and admitted resistance among judges to statistical evidence. So, again, why? Writers justifying the resistance operate on a variety of planes ranging from the mystical to the pragmatic, with less or more convincing force. Illustrative arguments include: (1) Statistical evidence moves society away from intuition and ritual and thus tends to dehumanize justice. (2) Statistical evidence tends to yield decisions less acceptable and final in the eyes of the public and the parties. (3) We simply want to encourage the use of nonstatistical proof because it meshes more smoothly and safely with the rest of our legal system and especially with our jury system.

Perhaps the more expansive explanations are unnecessary, and indeed prove too much. Surely courts should worry about and struggle against mishandling of statistical proof, and in fact judges try to use evidentiary and procedural mechanisms such as Evidence Rule 403 and jury instructions to mitigate mishandling. That is not a surprising caution, even when the caution sometimes becomes excessive.

Surely, too, courts should want to encourage the introduction of more evidence than mere statistics. So it is that most, if not all, of the mysterious judicial resistance to statistical evidence manifests itself in connection with the burden of production. Courts say that the proponent cannot rely only on statistical evidence, but can use it to supplement nonstatistical evidence. To justify this position, less dramatic explanations might suffice.

The apparent resistance to judgment as a matter of law *for* a proponent relying heavily on statistical evidence seems appropriate in a straightforward way. After all, rationally converting the statistical evidence into a final measure of subjective probability represents a substantial task, at least in all but the most fanciful cases. The evidence may have to be connected up with the issue in the individualized case by a series of permissible but uncertain inferences; the evidence may have to be discounted for defects in believability; the probability may have to be adjusted in light of the probative value of the absence of other proof, an effect most often cutting against the proponent. These are all jobs for the jury, within the bounds of rationality. Fixing those bounds of rationality is a daunting task because it involves consideration of such matters as the relevance and reliability of the statistics as well as the justifications for relying so heavily thereon. Hence, it should come as no surprise that the judge is reluctant to take the case from the jury by giving judgment for the proponent as a matter of law.

More difficult to explain is the supposed willingness to grant judgment as a matter of law *against* a proponent who has to rely solely on, say, a good 60–percent showing of identity by statistical evidence. Perhaps here the judge is trying to protect the notion of burden of production. After all, any plaintiff could introduce merely some numerical evidence of a general nature, such as that 60 percent of like plaintiffs win, in the hope that the jury might give a verdict for this plaintiff. Perhaps the judge harbors a special fear of the jury's handling of statistical evidence when undiluted by other admitted evidence—fear of an unreasoned verdict for the proponent based either on prejudice without regard to the evidence or, less likely, on undue deference to the statistics. To avoid such an outcome, and to ensure that the burden of production means something, the judge would require sufficient evidence of certain kinds, which must be nonnumerical and particularistic, at least in the absence of very special circumstances. Once the proponent clears that hurdle, the tribunal should give the proponent's statistical evidence its full effect.

In sum, the courts' only special rule for statistics seems to be that statistical evidence will not work to carry the proponent's burden of production. Limited and crude though this rule be, it appears to be the approach that courts actually employ. Also, this approach has the incidental advantage of defusing, albeit arbitrarily, most of the discomfiting paradoxes of hypothetical cases built on statistical evidence.

STIMPSON v. HUNTER, 234 Mass. 61, 125 N.E. 155 (1919). *P* sued *D* for dental services rendered to *D*'s minor son. *D* rested at the close of *P*'s case. Despite the absence of evidence thereon, the trial judge put to the jury the special question: "Was the work done by the plaintiff [on the son] authorized or ratified by the defendant?" The jury answered in the affirmative and thereupon, by order of the judge, found for *P*. *D*'s exceptions were sustained, the Supreme Judicial Court holding that the evidence did not warrant submission of the question to the jury and saying: "The failure of the defendant and of his son to testify although present in court was not equivalent to affirmative proof of facts necessary to maintain the action. The defendant was not bound to offer any evidence unless and until evidence was offered by the plaintiff warranting the submission of the case to the jury."

Question: (15) If there had been a case for the jury and the defendant had not testified, would it have been proper argument on behalf of the plaintiff that the defendant's failure to testify justified an inference against him? See Mitchell v. Silverstein, 323 Mass. 239, 81 N.E.2d 364 (1948) (yes). What if the defendant's failure to testify had been premised on the privilege against self-incrimination? Cf. Baxter v. Palmigiano, 425 U.S. 308, 96 S.Ct. 1551 (1976) (suggesting same result).

Cruzan v. New York Central & Hudson River Railroad Co.

Supreme Judicial Court of Massachusetts, 1917.
227 Mass. 594, 116 N.E. 879.

[The deceased, a brakeman on a freight train that was backing into a siding, was coming down a ladder on the side of one of the cars to set a switch when he was struck by the locomotive of a passenger express train going about sixty miles per hour on the other main track. The plaintiff sued under the FELA to recover for the death of her intestate. The judge refused to rule that there was no evidence of the railroad's negligence. The jury returned a verdict for the plaintiff, and the defendant alleged exceptions.]

■ RUGG, C.J.

. . . .

The only negligence alleged in the case at bar is that of the fireman and engineer of the passenger express train. We are of the opinion that there is no evidence of negligence on the part of either. There is nothing to indicate that it was their duty to be observant of the movements of brakemen upon other trains in the position in which Cruzan was. The only rule pertinent in this connection was this: "Firemen and Helpers. . . . They must keep a constant lookout ahead (except as to firemen when engaged in firing), and give instant notice to the engineman or motorman of any danger signals or obstructions on the track." It is manifest that this rule relates only to the safety of the train on which they are at work. It imposes no duty to be on the watch for other employees on other tracks and trains. The duty of exercising care for their own safety was placed by explicit rule upon such other employees. There can be no negligence in the ordinary case when no duty has been violated. It is manifest that the danger of Cruzan was momentary. So long as he kept close to the car even coming down the ladder on its side, he was in a safe place. It was only for the instant when he swung out from the body of the car as he was on the point of jumping to the ground that he came within the sweep of the rapidly moving express train. It may be assumed that, if the fireman or engineer of the passenger express train had seen him, there would have been evidence of their negligence. But there was no evidence that either the engineer or fireman saw Cruzan in time to give him any warning. Both testified that they did not see him earlier than an instant before he was struck. Mere disbelief of denials of facts which must be proved is not the equivalent of affirmative evidence in support of those facts. Wakefield v. American Surety Co., 209 Mass. 173, 177, 95 N.E. 350; Southern Ry. v. Gray, 241 U.S. 333, 337, 36 S.Ct. 558.

. . . .

It becomes unnecessary to consider the other questions raised. The request that a verdict be ordered for the defendant should have been granted. In accordance with St.1909, c. 236, judgment may be entered for the defendant.

So ordered.[m]

GUINAN v. FAMOUS PLAYERS–LASKY CORP., 267 Mass. 501, 167 N.E. 235 (1929). The plaintiff was injured by ignition of scrap film given to one Shirley by Doherty, the defendant's agent. Shirley had carried it away in a burlap bag, in which it had been stuffed in the presence of Doherty. The bag caught fire when Shirley set it against a heater in a subway car. The issue was whether Doherty had been acting in the scope of his employment. Doherty testified that he had authority to dispose of scrap film only by delivering it to the Film Transfer Company, which was paid to carry it away, and that he had forgotten that limitation when he gave the film to Shirley. It was held that this testimony created an issue of fact for the jury on scope of employment. In overruling exceptions to the plaintiff's judgment, the Supreme Judicial Court said: "Although mere disbelief of testimony is not proof of facts of an opposite nature or tendency, [citations omitted], the jury might have believed that part of Doherty's testimony that related to his authority to dispose of the scrap film, and disbelieved the alleged limitation of his authority to dispose of it only to the Film Transfer Company."

Question: (16) Does the Guinan decision suggest a possible basis for a different result in the Cruzan case?

DYER v. MacDOUGALL, 201 F.2d 265 (2d Cir.1952). The plaintiff brought an action for slander, based on alleged defamatory statements by the defendants to a Mr. Almirall and a Mrs. Hope. The defendants moved for summary judgment, supporting their motion by affidavits of the defendants and Mr. Almirall and by a deposition of Mrs. Hope previously taken by the plaintiff, in which the defendants unequivocally denied utterance of the slanders attributed to them, and in which Mr. Almirall and Mrs. Hope denied hearing utterance of the statements. When the motion came on for decision, the court offered the plaintiff an opportunity to take the depositions of the defendants and Mr. Almirall and a further deposition of Mrs.

[m] This decision is representative of many cases. In Moore v. Chesapeake & Ohio Railway, 340 U.S. 573, 71 S.Ct. 428 (1951) (FELA case where plaintiff's theory was that engineer's sudden stop threw decedent off train; engineer, the sole eyewitness, testified that he saw decedent brakeman fall from car and that he then made emergency stop), the Court said: "True, it is the jury's function to credit or discredit all or part of the testimony. But disbelief of the engineer's testimony would not supply a want of proof." In Clairmont v. Cilley, 85 N.H. 1, 7, 153 A. 465, 468 (1931), the court made the point thus: "Falsity of testimony is no proof of what is true, and disbelief does not supply the need of proof. [Citation omitted.] Otherwise any fact might be proved by discrediting testimony to the contrary. While the falsehood of testimony may add to the weight to be given evidence to the contrary, the testimony by itself does not go far enough to establish the fact it denies."

Hope. After a continuance for this purpose, the plaintiff told the court that he did not wish to take the depositions. Thereafter the court granted summary judgment on the ground that the plaintiff would have no evidence to offer in support of the slanders except the testimony of witnesses all of whom would deny their utterance.

On appeal, the court of appeals affirmed. Judge Learned Hand for the court said: "The question is whether, in view of the defendants' affidavits and Mrs. Hope's deposition, there was any 'genuine issue' under Rule 56(c) as to the utterance of the slanders. The defendants had the burden of proving that there was no such issue; on the other hand, at a trial the plaintiff would have the burden of proving the utterances; and therefore, if the defendants on the motion succeeded in proving that the plaintiff would not have enough evidence to go to the jury on the issue, the judgment was right. As the plaintiff has refused to avail himself of the privilege under Rule 56(f) of examining by deposition the witnesses whom the defendants proposed to call at the trial, we must assume that what they said in their affidavits they would have repeated in their depositions; and that what they would have said in their depositions, they would say at a trial, with one possible exception, the consideration of which we will postpone for the time being."

Judge Hand observed that the only witnesses by whom the plaintiff could prove the slanders would deny that they had been uttered, and on this showing the plaintiff could not escape a directed verdict. He conceded that the demeanor of a witness was part of the evidence and might satisfy the tribunal not only that the witness's testimony was not true, but that the truth was the opposite of the witness's story. The opinion continued as follows:

"Nevertheless, although it is therefore true that in strict theory a party having the affirmative might succeed in convincing a jury of the truth of his allegations in spite of the fact that all the witnesses denied them, we think it plain that a verdict would nevertheless have to be directed against him. This is owing to the fact that otherwise in such cases there could not be an effective appeal from the judge's disposition of a motion for a directed verdict. . . . It may be argued that such a ruling may deprive a party of a possibly rational verdict and indeed that is theoretically true, although the occasions must be to the last degree rare in which the chance so denied is more than fanciful. Nevertheless we do not hesitate to set against the chance so lost, the protection of a review of the judge's decision.

"There remains the second point which we reserved for separate discussion: i.e. whether by an examination in open court the plaintiff might extract from the four witnesses admissions which he would not have got on the depositions that he refused. Although this is also at best a tenuous possibility, we need not say that there could never be situations in which it might justify denying summary judgment. It might appear for example that upon a deposition a witness had been recalcitrant, or crafty, or defiant, or evasive, so that the immediate presence of a judge in a court-room was likely to make him tell more. That would be another matter; and it might be enough. But the plaintiff is in no position to invoke such a possibility for he has refused to try out these witnesses upon deposition, where he might discover whether there was any basis for supposing that awe of a judge was necessary to make them more amenable. A priori we will not assume that that is true. The course of procedural reform has all indeed been towards bringing witnesses before the tribunal when it is possible; but that is not so much because more testimony can be got out of them as because only so can the 'demeanor' evidence be brought before the tribunal."

RELATION OF SUMMARY JUDGMENT TO JUDGMENT AS A MATTER OF LAW

A party moving for summary judgment in federal court has the burden of establishing that there is no genuine issue of material fact and that the movant is then entitled to judgment as a matter of law. See Topic D of Part Seven. But where the plaintiff will have the burden of proof on an essential issue at trial, the defendant may successfully move for summary judgment by showing that the defendant would be entitled to judgment as a matter of law at trial if the plaintiff presented nothing more than was before the court at the hearing on the motion. Plaintiff has the opportunity to adduce evidence—by affidavit, deposition, and the like—that would justify submission of his claim to a jury. He cannot choose to hold back his evidence until the time of trial and nevertheless escape summary judgment by the mere assertion that he may or will then produce evidence. Here is no battle of affidavits, which would of course be improper on a summary judgment motion. The plaintiff fails simply for lack of proof.

Nevertheless, even though the two standards thus are theoretically the same, denial of summary judgment does not necessarily rule out the possibility of granting judgment as a matter of law at trial. That is, despite the fact that the standards for the judge to *grant* the motions may be the same, the judge can discretionarily choose to *deny* (or to decline to grant at this time) the earlier motion. This difference in the standards to deny makes the later motion easier to obtain in actual practice.

But are the standards to grant really the same? The motion for judgment as a matter of law comes at a later stage in the litigation with lesser worry of prematurely interceding and thereby triggering an appeal, and arguably it is decided upon a more complete and effective airing of the evidence. Perhaps a court could more readily impose the rarely imposed rationality limit on credibility determinations when deciding judgment as a matter of law. The result might be a practical difference in standards to grant, with summary judgment being slightly harder to get. See 9B Wright & Miller § 2532; 10A Wright, Miller & Kane § 2713.1. Contrariwise, granting an early summary judgment better serves the movant's interests and the court's docket interests than granting a later judgment as a matter of law. So the judge may look at the paper record and tend to see no genuine issue impeding summary judgment. The result of these contrary factors might be a practical difference in standards to grant, with summary judgment being slightly easier to get. That is, the policies all together seem to offset each other.

In the past, some courts have been especially cautious about granting a motion for summary judgment in certain kinds of cases. For example, they may have been reluctant so to act in cases requiring determination of a state of mind; there they might prefer to give an opportunity to see and hear the witnesses during direct and cross-examination, even though it may then appear that there was no genuine issue as to a material fact. See, e.g., Croley v. Matson Navigation Co., 434 F.2d 73 (5th Cir.1970). Similarly, there have been cases to the effect that when the facts are within the personal knowledge of the movant, the opponent is entitled to a trial at which the movant may be examined, with demeanor observed and credibility evaluated. See, e.g., Subin v. Goldsmith, 224 F.2d 753 (2d Cir.1955).

This caution still left the plaintiff in a difficult position if, as in Dyer v. MacDougall, he must prove his case exclusively through the adverse party or hostile witnesses. It would be unfair to render summary judgment against him on the basis of their affidavits negating his claim without an opportunity to test their stories by deposition. If, given the opportunity to take the deposition of an affiant, he elects not to do so, he normally cannot maintain that summary judgment should be denied because he hopes to break the affiant down on examination at trial. If he pursues full discovery but fails to unearth evidence sufficient to suggest a genuine issue of material fact, most courts will likewise grant summary judgment. See, e.g., Jones v. Borden Co., 430 F.2d 568 (5th Cir.1970). It is not, however, a wholly satisfactory answer to say that the plaintiff's opportunity to examine on deposition is the equivalent of an opportunity to do so at trial. And the examination on deposition necessary to prevent summary judgment may well give a crafty witness a lesson in how to perform that will make examination at trial less likely to be effective.

This difficulty may have accounted for the outright refusal of some courts to grant summary judgment in cases where questions of state of mind or personal knowledge were involved. See, e.g., Arnstein v. Porter, 154 F.2d 464 (2d Cir.1946). In that case, which involved a claim of plagiarism against Cole Porter, defendant moved for summary judgment. In his deposition defendant had denied copying, and plaintiff had little evidence to support his contention to the contrary. The court of appeals, speaking through Judge Frank, an obdurate opponent of summary judgment, especially in state-of-mind and personal-knowledge cases, reversed a grant of the motion on the ground that plaintiff should have the opportunity to discredit defendant's denial by cross-examination in a jury trial. Judge Clark strongly dissented, saying that the majority opinion was "a novel method of amending rules of procedure" and that it gave impetus to strike suits. In fact, the jury returned a verdict for defendant after a long trial. The Second Circuit, by a panel including Judge Frank but not Judge Clark, affirmed per curiam but stated that there was undoubtedly enough evidence to make a jury issue, 158 F.2d 795 (2d Cir.1946), cert. denied, 330 U.S. 851, 67 S.Ct. 1096 (1947).

Nevertheless, the Supreme Court has more recently undertaken, with possible success, to encourage the granting of summary judgments under Rule 56. The leading case of Anderson v. Liberty Lobby, Inc., 477 U.S. 242, 106 S.Ct. 2505 (1986)—indeed, Anderson is the most judicially cited Supreme Court case in history—is indicative. First, the Anderson Court settled that essentially the same standard applies on motions for summary judgment and for judgment as a matter of law. Second, the Court clarified that on those motions the judge must hypothesize a reasonable jury measuring the evidence against the applicable standard of proof, whether it be preponderance of the evidence or clear and convincing evidence or proof beyond a reasonable doubt; so, for example, the defendants in the instant case could somewhat more easily obtain summary judgment because the plaintiffs would have to prove their libel case by clear and convincing evidence. Third, the Court seemed to reject any special standard for state-of-mind or personal-knowledge cases.

It appears then that the legal standards for granting summary judgment and judgment as a matter of law are now effectively identical. Moreover, it could be that any practical difference between the two standards, attributable to the judge's discretion to deny early motions, is disappearing. See, e.g., Jeffreys v. City of New York, 426 F.3d 549 (2d Cir.2005). In that case, the plaintiff brought a civil rights action against police officers for allegedly beating him and throwing him out a third-floor window during an arrest. The defendants moved for summary judgment. The court granted it because the plaintiff's largely unsubstantiated and strongly contradicted account was "so replete with inconsistencies and improbabilities" that no reasonable juror could believe it. The court of appeals unanimously affirmed.

PROBLEM OF CONJUNCTION

Professor Charles Nesson in The Evidence or the Event? On Judicial Proof and the Acceptability of Verdicts, 98 Harv.L.Rev. 1357, 1385–90 (1985), describes the problem this way:

"We purport to decide civil cases according to a more-probable-than-not standard of proof. We would expect this standard to take into account the rule of conjunction, which states that the probability of two independent events occurring together is the product of the probability of each event occurring separately. The rule of conjunction dictates that in a case comprised of two independent elements the plaintiff must prove each element to a much greater degree than 50%: only then will the plaintiff have shown that the probability that the two elements occurred together exceeds 50%. Suppose, for example, that a plaintiff must prove both causation and fault and that these two elements are independent. If the plaintiff shows that causation is 60% probable and fault is 60% probable, then he apparently would have failed to satisfy the civil standard of proof because the probability that the defendant *both* acted negligently and caused injury is only 36%.

"In our legal system, however, jurors do not consider whether it is more probable than not that all elements occurred in conjunction. Judges instruct jurors to decide civil cases element by element, with each element decided on a more-probable-than-not basis. Once jurors have decided that an element is probable, they are to consider the element established, repress any remaining doubts about it, and proceed to consider the next element. If the plaintiff proves each element by a preponderance of the evidence, the jury will find in his favor. . . . Thus, jurors may find a defendant liable even if it is highly unlikely that he acted negligently, that is, the conjoined probability of the elements is much less than 50%. In such cases, the verdict fails to reflect a probable account of what happened and thus fails to minimize the cost of judicial errors. . . .

. . . .

". . . Although courts direct juries to consider and decide each element seriatim, juries do not consider each item of evidence seriatim when deciding whether a given element is proved. The jury must decide each element by looking at all of the evidence bearing on proof of that element. Thus, although the jury does not assess the conjunction of the elements of a case, it does decide each element by assessing the conjunction of the evidence for it."

Assuming the law to be as described, you should realize that the implications are profound but boggling. For example, ponder the persistent criticality of how exactly the ancients (and moderns) divided our causes of action and defenses into elements: the more subdivisions, the lower the standard of proof applied to the conjunction. See James A. Henderson, Jr., Fred Bertram & Michael J. Tõke, Optimal Issue Separation in Modern Products Liability Litigation, 73 Tex.L.Rev. 1653, 1655–59, 1667–75 (1995). And yet: "Anyone who has ever litigated a real case knows the exact opposite of the conjunction paradox is true: the more disputed elements the plaintiff has to prove, the *less* likely the plaintiff is to prevail. . . . [A]lthough it is possible that a particular plaintiff could obtain an unjust verdict in a case with several disputed elements, [there is an increased] probability that the jury will find at least one element to be less likely than not." David A. Moran, Jury Uncertainty, Elemental Independence and the Conjunction Paradox: A Response to Allen and Jehl, 2003 Mich.St.L.Rev. 945, 946–47, 950.

Even more interesting is the reason for the law's approach to conjunction. Professor Nesson sees the approach as illustrating his broad thesis that the law's process of proof aims at generating acceptable statements about past events and thus at projecting behavioral norms to the public, rather than at reaching probable conclusions in a search for truth: "Application of the more-probable-than-not test to each element produces the most acceptable conclusion as to that element. The conjunction of these conclusions constitutes a story that is more probable than any other story about the same elements. Suppose, for example, that the elements of a story are *A* and *B*, and *A* (70%) is more probable than not-*A* (30%), and *B* (60%) is more probable than not-*B* (40%). The conjunction (*A* & *B*) (42%) may not be more probable than its negation (not-(*A* & *B*)) (58%). But the conjunction (*A* & *B*) (42%) is more probable than any other version: (*A* & (not-*B*)) (28%), ((not-*A*) & *B*) (18%), or ((not-*A*) & (not-*B*)) (12%). The application of the more-probable-than-not standard of proof on an element-by-element basis will produce the single most probable story."

Many psychologists agree with a notion that fact-finders naturally construct such "stories," although perhaps not in such a systematic manner. Consider the story model of decisionmaking, as described in Jeffrey T. Frederick, The Psychology of the American Jury 296–97 (1987) (omitted citations include Reid Hastie, Steven Penrod & Nancy Pennington, Inside the Jury (1983)):

"Several authors have recently proposed a model for juror decisionmaking based on the concept of a story as an organizing and interpreting schema. The story model attempts to explain how jurors organize and interpret the vast amount of information they encounter at trial and apply the appropriate decision criteria. . . .

" . . . The jurors construct a story adequately describing what happened. At the conclusion of the trial, they construct the verdict categories based on the instructions given by the judge. The individual juror arrives at his decision by determining the best match between his story and the available verdict categories. The task of the jury in deliberations then becomes one of selecting a story from among those offered by the jurors and fitting it to the available verdict options.

" . . . The story model . . . provides a plausible explanation of how jurors make decisions in the complex situation they face, both in terms of information processing and decisionmaking. This model is relatively new and has not received the empirical examination necessary to evaluate its potential more fully. There is some evidence, however, that jurors may indeed use stories in arriving at their verdicts. Analysis of jury deliberations has shown that descriptions equivalent to stories are used by jurors in communicating their verdict preferences to other jurors. In addition, one study has shown that the presence of multiple stories in deliberations supporting one side affects jury decisionmaking. Even though the multiple stories favored the same verdict, their presence increased the complexity of the task and increased the probability of a hung jury."

If a juror constructs a story for the whole case, or otherwise cognitively processes the entirety while the trial progresses, and then the judge instructs on standard of proof, it may be that actually the jurors apply the standard to the whole claim or defense and hence to the conjoined elements. It may also be that, being human, a judge when acting as fact-finder proceeds in essentially the same manner, testing whether the conjunction is more likely than not. If so, in practice the law ends up following the preferred strategy of minimizing error costs.

Indeed, by providing for obscure instructions only at the end of oral trials, the law seems determined to encourage overall consideration and to discourage applying the standard of proof element by element. Although the judge does instruct in literal element-by-element terms, this may work largely to encourage the jurors' detailed evaluation of the evidence and to stress the requirement of a story containing all of a series of elements. Likewise, many of the evidence rules may work to brake any undesirable tendency of the fact-finder to rush toward creating a story.

Sometimes, however, the law does impose the element-by-element theory and thereby impedes the holistic practice. An apparent example would be when the judge requires a special verdict that asks the jury to find each element by a preponderance—assuming that a special verdict actually changes the jury's decisionmaking practice. See Elizabeth G. Thornburg, The Power and the Process: Instructions and the Civil Jury, 66 Fordham L.Rev. 1837 (1998). Nonetheless, these legal intrusions, uncommon to begin with, only rarely would serve to sustain a showing that did not conjoinedly meet the standard of proof.

All this does not justify the "errors" that follow from element-by-element application of the standard of proof. But perhaps instead of supporting risky assertions on the law's nontruth purposes, here the smallness of the practical impact of the law's subtle illogic on conjunction may simply have failed to generate reform.

Question: (17) If there is to be reform, what shape should it take? See generally Ronald J. Allen & Sarah A. Jehl, Burdens of Persuasion in Civil Cases: Algorithms v. Explanations, 2003 Mich.St.L.Rev. 893, 929–43.

TOPIC B

JUDGMENT AS A MATTER OF LAW

SECTION 1. GENERAL OBSERVATIONS

Attrition of the right of voluntary dismissal.—The plaintiff had the right at common law voluntarily to abandon his action at any time before the verdict. He could and frequently did take this course in order to forestall either the direction of a verdict against him or an expected adverse verdict from the jury. The result was a nonsuit, which ended the case and made the plaintiff liable for costs but did not preclude a new action on the same cause.

There have been substantial inroads upon this common-law doctrine, some by statute or rule of court and others by judicial decision. The inroads vary widely as to when the plaintiff loses the right to abandon his case without precluding a new action. The critical point may be, for example, the commencement of the trial, the opening of the defendant's case, the beginning of argument to the jury, the close of argument, the submission to the jury, or the time when the jury is ready to give its verdict.

The federal rulemakers in Rule 41(a)(1) more aggressively limited the unqualified right to voluntary dismissal without prejudice to the period prior to service of the answer or a motion for summary judgment (not a motion to dismiss for failure to state a claim). When this right exists, the filing of a notice of dismissal results in ending the case. The court has no occasion to pass upon it and is without power to impose terms or conditions on the dismissal.

Under Rule 41(a)(1)(B), the right to voluntary dismissal by notice of dismissal is subject to the "two-dismissal" rule. Cf. 8 Moore § 41.33[7][b] (arguing that both dismissals must be by notice of dismissal for rule to apply).

Questions: (1) Plaintiff voluntarily dismisses a state-court action, then sues on the same claim in federal court and dismisses that diversity action by notice of dismissal. Is a third action in a federal court barred by reason of Rule 41(a)(1)(B)? in a state court that has no comparable rule?

(2) Plaintiff voluntarily dismisses a federal-court action, then sues on the same claim in state court and dismisses that action by notice of dismissal. Is a third action in a federal court barred by reason of Rule 41(a)(1)(B)?

Once the grace period is over, unilateral voluntary dismissal requires a motion and court order, which may be on terms that the court considers proper, according to Rule 41(a)(2). After some early authority that the right to voluntary dismissal without prejudice remained absolute as at common law, with the court's discretion relating only to the terms of dismissal, it has been settled that the whole matter rests in the court's discretion, which is reviewable only for abuse when reviewable at all. See Grivas v. Parmelee Transp. Co., 207 F.2d 334 (7th Cir.1953), overruling Bolten v. General Motors Corp., 180 F.2d 379 (7th Cir.1950). Courts in exercising this discretion typically adhere to the principle of allowing dismissal without prejudice unless the defendant will suffer disadvantage other than the prospect of having to defend another action. See Hyde v. Hoffmann–La Roche, Inc., 511 F.3d 506 (5th Cir.2007) (reversing dismissal, where defendants would lose a limitations defense if plaintiff were allowed to sue in another state), on remand, 2008 WL 4191529 (N.D.Tex. 2008) (granting summary judgment to defendants). The terms ordinarily include a requirement that the plaintiff pay court costs, and sometimes that he pay attorney's fees. However, the plaintiff is normally free to reject the terms and conditions and so to proceed with the lawsuit.

Question: (3) Suppose the plaintiff is willing to accept a voluntary dismissal with prejudice, which will bar further action. Should the court have discretion to refuse dismissal at the behest of a defendant who wants the vindication of a trial? See Smoot v. Fox, 340 F.2d 301 (6th Cir.1964) (plaintiff, a television and radio broadcaster, sues the League of Women Voters for libel, the action stirring a great deal of public interest; the judge refuses to dismiss with prejudice; plaintiff obtains mandamus to force dismissal).

Rule 41(d), dealing with costs of previously dismissed actions and arguably including attorney's fees, has its counterpart in many state statutes. This type of provision gives inadequate protection to a defendant harassed by repeated actions, as where the plaintiff takes voluntary dismissals at a stage in proceedings early enough under the applicable rules to avoid costs and not to foreclose a new action on the same claim. Does the defendant have any effective remedy against such tactics? In Steinberg v. McKay, 295 Mass. 139, 3 N.E.2d 23 (1936), the plaintiff successfully sought equitable relief in the nature of a bill of peace[a] to enjoin the defendant from instituting repeated groundless actions for false arrest. In Renfroe v. Johnson, 142 Tex. 251, 177 S.W.2d 600 (1944), the plaintiff sued twice on the same promissory notes, taking a nonsuit each time after the defendants pleaded the statute of limitations. The plaintiff's counsel announced in open court, at the time of the first nonsuit, his intention to file a new suit against the defendants at every term of court in the future. The defendants filed a cross-action in the second suit for an injunction to prevent the filing of any more suits on these notes. The court granted the requested relief. See Restatement (Second) of Torts § 679 (1977); see also id. § 681 (damages). See generally John W. Wade, On Frivolous Litigation: A Study of Tort Liability and Procedural Sanctions, 14 Hofstra L.Rev. 433 (1986).

A formerly unsettled question had involved the court's power to impose Rule 11 sanctions after a voluntary dismissal under Rule 41(a). The Supreme Court settled the question by endorsing the clear trend in the lower courts. Cooter & Gell v. Hartmarx Corp., 496 U.S. 384, 110 S.Ct. 2447 (1990) (8–1 decision), held that the district court could impose a

[a] See supra p. 1095 note d.

sizable Rule 11 monetary sanction on the plaintiff and its lawyers for inadequate prefiling inquiry, even when the court acted after a dismissal by notice of dismissal. A voluntary dismissal does not deprive the district court of jurisdiction to consider collateral matters, such as sanctioning a prior filing violation. This resolution, wrote Justice O'Connor for the Court, gives effect to Rule 11's "central goal of deterrence" while avoiding conflict with Rule 41(a)'s purpose.

In Willy v. Coastal Corp., 503 U.S. 131, 112 S.Ct. 1076 (1992), the Court upheld imposition of Rule 11 sanctions even in a case dismissed for lack of subject-matter jurisdiction. There the sanctions had been imposed against the plaintiff and his attorney for irresponsible filings in a removed case eventually dismissed for lack of subject-matter jurisdiction.

Nevertheless, the 1993 amendment to Rule 11 makes the court's broad power largely theoretical. The "safe harbor" provision of Rule 11(c)(2) seems to protect the offender from the opponent's motion. Monetary sanctions even on the court's own initiative may become unavailable by Rule 11(c)(5)(B). So the court still has wide power, but will not often get to use it.

Preventing unreasonable verdicts by midtrial motions.—The demurrer to the evidence (to be sharply distinguished from a demurrer to pleadings) was the earliest means of withdrawing a case from the jury in the course of trial, before verdict. A defendant would demur to the evidence where at the close of plaintiff's case it appeared that plaintiff's evidence was insufficient to warrant a verdict for plaintiff even if the evidence was taken as true and construed as strongly as possible in plaintiff's favor. The device was a cumbersome one, for the demurrer had to contain a statement of the evidence demurred to and (in later years) a distinct admission of every fact that plaintiff's evidence tended to prove.[b] It was hazardous as well as cumbersome, because defendant's tacit or direct admission was final, not provisional. If the demurrer was sustained, judgment went for defendant, terminating the action and barring a later action on the same cause. But if the demurrer was overruled, judgment went for plaintiff; that is, defendant could not offer evidence of his own, nor could the case go to the jury with argument that plaintiff's evidence should not be believed. Only in instances where plaintiff's evidence was very plainly insufficient would a defendant take this risk. See generally Comment, Trial Practice—Demurrer upon Evidence as a Device for Taking a Case from the Jury, 44 Mich.L.Rev. 468 (1945).

The compulsory nonsuit on motion of the defendant was another means of preventing a case from reaching the jury. It seems that the compulsory nonsuit for failure of proof was unknown at common law, but in many American jurisdictions the practice developed of nonsuiting the plaintiff involuntarily. The defendant would move for a nonsuit when the plaintiff rested. If the motion was granted, judgment would go for the

[b] Gibson v. Hunter, 126 Eng.Rep. 499 (H.L.1793), spelling out the latter requirement, meant the end of the demurrer to the evidence in England. The device was little used in the United States, except where the requirement of Gibson v. Hunter was not adopted.

defendant, but this was not a bar to a new action on the same cause. See Restatement (Second) of Judgments § 20 cmt. g (1982). If the motion was denied, the defendant could proceed with his own evidence as though no motion had been made. In doing so the defendant might supply the deficiency in the plaintiff's proof, and his exception to the denial of his motion would later be unavailing. See Gagnon v. Dana, 69 N.H. 264, 39 A. 982 (1898). Indeed, even if the defendant's evidence did not supply the deficiency in the plaintiff's proof, the exception to denial of the nonsuit at the close of the plaintiff's case was unavailing, so that the defendant had to make an appropriate motion at the close of all the evidence in order to have the court scrutinize the whole record to determine the sufficiency of the evidence. See Spencer v. State, 187 N.Y. 484, 80 N.E. 375 (1907).

Finally, going well beyond any common-law roots, there is the motion for a directed verdict. A party makes the motion at the close of his opponent's case.[c] If such a motion is granted, the judgment entered thereon has the same preclusive effect as a judgment entered on a verdict of the jury. Thus, a judgment on a directed verdict is a bar to a new action on the same cause.

Some states follow the old rule that a directed verdict can be sought by a party only by immediately resting his own case; that is, the price of making the motion is that the moving party forgoes his chance to offer any evidence thereafter. Even if the motion is denied, however, he may still have a chance for a favorable verdict from the jury on the basis of the plaintiff's evidence, which would be subject to disbelief and which would include any material developed in cross-examination of the plaintiff's witnesses.

Therefore, in jurisdictions that still recognize the compulsory nonsuit and also exact the price of waiver by a motion for a directed verdict, a defendant may be put to a choice at the close of the plaintiff's case: (1) He can move for a nonsuit with no serious consequences if the motion is denied; but if the motion is granted, he faces the possibility of a second action on the same cause. (2) If he wants protection against a second action, he must choose a directed verdict; but then he must rest his own case and lose the opportunity to put in his own proof. (3) When the defendant has evidence that he thinks will be persuasive with the jury, he may well prefer not to make any motion at the close of the plaintiff's case and instead go ahead with his own evidence and then move for a directed verdict at the close of all the evidence; if this motion is denied, he still has a chance for a jury verdict based on all the evidence, including his own.

The Federal Rules ease that choice by providing a means for a party to test the sufficiency of the opponent's evidence before he decides whether to

---

[c] A word of warning about terminology: in some states what is in practical effect a motion for a directed verdict, as here described, is called a demurrer to the evidence, but it has no kinship with the old common-law device of that name. In Virginia, where a statute forbids the trial court to direct a verdict, the same result can be achieved by a "demurrer to the evidence" or "motion to strike out the evidence." See Va.Code § 8.01–378; Davis v. Rodgers, 139 Va. 618, 124 S.E. 408 (1924).

offer evidence of his own. So, in an action tried to a jury, the defendant may move under Rule 50(a) for judgment as a matter of law after the plaintiff has been full heard, a motion formerly called a motion for a directed verdict. Incidentally, in an action tried without a jury, he may move for judgment on partial findings under Rule 52(c) after the plaintiff has been full heard (this Rule permits the judge, who will be the eventual fact-finder anyway, to evaluate the evidence objectively and order judgment at this point if, in the judge's view, the plaintiff has failed to carry the burden of persuasion—even though enough evidence has been adduced to have prevented judgment as a matter of law in a jury case). If a motion under either Rule is denied, the defendant may proceed with his own evidence, as he could have done under the prior practice after denial of a motion for a compulsory nonsuit.

Question: (4) In what way were the consequences of the grant of a compulsory nonsuit different from those of the grant of a Rule 50(a) or a Rule 52(c) judgment?

Just as was true for the compulsory nonsuit, the defendant in federal court traditionally could not on appeal rely upon any error in the denial of his motion for judgment as a matter of law at the close of the plaintiff's case if he goes forward with his own evidence. That is, he could not argue that he was technically entitled to victory because at midtrial the plaintiff's case really had been too weak to survive, even though the plaintiff's case later became strong enough. As Judge Magruder said in Home Ins. Co. v. Davila, 212 F.2d 731, 733 (1st Cir.1954): "It is well-settled that if a motion under Rule 50(a) . . . at the close of the plaintiff's case is denied, and the defendant thereupon presents his own evidence, this constitutes a waiver of the motion; unless a renewed motion for [judgment as a matter of law is made on the basis] of all the evidence, the defendant is precluded from questioning on appeal the sufficiency of the evidence to take the case to the jury." Likewise, if the defendant presents evidence after denial of his Rule 52(c) motion on the ground of insufficiency of the evidence, he cannot on appeal rely upon any error in its denial. It does seem appropriate that the midtrial state of the evidence should not be reviewable, does it not?

Question: (5) Should a pretrial denial of summary judgment, made on the ground of insufficiency of the evidence, be reviewable on appeal after trial? See Varghese v. Honeywell Int'l, Inc., 424 F.3d 411 (4th Cir.2005) (no, even for motion made on purely legal ground).

Preventing unreasonable verdicts by motions at the close of all the evidence.—The appropriate device here is the motion for judgment as a matter of law under Rule 50(a). If a party feels that the judge should take only a part of the case from the jury, this motion can take the form of a request for a peremptory, or binding, instruction.

But how has all this historical evolution proceeded consistently with the Seventh Amendment? Recall that the Constitution provides that in "suits at common law, where the value in controversy shall exceed twenty dollars,[d] the right of trial by jury shall be preserved." On issues that the

---

[d] On the now rightly forgotten monetary clause, see Note, The Twenty Dollars Clause, 118 Harv.L.Rev. 1665 (2005).

jury decided in common-law cases, the jury must still decide. However, federal courts have read this Trial-by-Jury Clause rather loosely—preserving the wide array of procedural incidents of jury trial at common law, such as the number of jurors, only to the extent necessary to preserve the essence rather than the form of common-law trial by jury. Thus, the modern federal jury need only operate substantially the same as the common-law jury. Accordingly, the Supreme Court upheld the constitutionality of the directed verdict in Galloway v. United States, 319 U.S. 372, 390, 394, 63 S.Ct. 1077, 1087, 1089 (1943) (holding that the Seventh "Amendment did not bind the federal courts to the exact procedural incidents or details of jury trial according to the common law in 1791" but only to what was "essential"). Cf. Walker v. New Mexico & S. Pac. R.R. Co., 165 U.S. 593, 596 17 S.Ct. 421, 422 (1897) (upholding constitutionality of general verdict with answers to written questions, because the Seventh Amendment's "aim is not to preserve mere matters of form and procedure, but substance of right"); Fidelity & Deposit Co. v. United States, 187 U.S. 315, 23 S.Ct. 120 (1902) (upholding constitutionality of summary judgment).

Revising improper verdicts after rendition.—Perhaps the most venerable device for controlling the jury was the attaint. When it was claimed that the verdict was "false," a jury of twenty-four was summoned to reexamine the issue on the same evidence; if they found the verdict to be false, it would be reversed and the first jury might be severely punished. The attaint may have been tolerable when the jury was a body of witnesses drawn from the vicinage who decided issues on their own knowledge. It could not survive as the trial of issues came to rest upon evidence offered in open court. In Bushell's Case, 124 Eng.Rep. 1006 (C.P.1670), jurors who had failed to find William Penn guilty of unlawful assembly and who had been fined and imprisoned for their verdict were released on habeas corpus. Although it was a ground of this decision that the jurors had not been proceeded against by the ancient method of attaint, it was understood that that method was already obsolete. The decision "therefore amounted to a declaration of the irresponsibility of the jury." Theodore F. Plucknett, A Concise History of the Common Law 134 (5th ed. 1956).

Meanwhile, the practice of granting new trials for misconduct of jurors and for improper verdicts was being elaborated. Eventually, the motion for judgment n.o.v. also developed into a tool for revising unreasonable verdicts, today called the motion for judgment as a matter of law under Rule 50(b). We shall deal with these matters in Topic D of this Part, along with the restraints imposed by the rest of the Seventh Amendment. For now, recall that its Re-examination Clause goes on to provide that "no fact tried by a jury, shall be otherwise re-examined in any Court of the United States, than according to the rules of the common law." This clause means that federal courts today must find a historical antecedent to authorize any review, at the trial or appellate level, of a jury's fact-finding. But if an antecedent existed, then its procedural incidents could change as long as they preserved the essence or substance of common-law trial by jury.

SECTION 2. JUDGMENT AGAINST PARTY WITH BURDEN OF PROOF

What is the proper standard to be applied by the court upon a motion for judgment as a matter of law against the party with the burden of proof? This is a question to which courts give different answers.

Professor McBaine stated that there were two possible tests: (1) if the judge looking at all the evidence, both favorable and unfavorable to the proponent (by "proponent" is meant the party having the burden of proof), determines that he would be duty bound to set aside a verdict for the proponent because it would be against the weight of the evidence, he may grant judgment as a matter of law; and (2) if the judge considering only the evidence favorable to the proponent, and completely disregarding all unfavorable evidence, determines that a reasonable jury, viewing that evidence in the light most favorable to the proponent, could find every essential fact in the proponent's favor, he may not grant judgment as a matter of law. The two tests are often termed for convenience the "set aside" and the "most favorable evidence" tests. Professor McBaine confusingly added: "In each test the judge must determine what a reasonable jury can conclude. The first test involves passing upon credibility of witness; the second does not." J.P. McBaine, Trial Practice: Directed Verdicts; Federal Rule, 31 Cal.L.Rev. 454, 460–61 (1943).

By contrast, in Pedrick v. Peoria & Eastern Railroad Co., 37 Ill.2d 494, 229 N.E.2d 504 (1967), the court reviewed the standards for a directed verdict prevailing in other states as indicated in their recent decisions, reexamined its own standards, and concluded: "In our judgment verdicts ought to be directed and judgments n.o.v. entered only in those cases in which all of the evidence, when viewed in its aspect most favorable to the opponent, so overwhelmingly favors movant that no contrary verdict based on that evidence could ever stand." The only allegation of the railroad's negligence submitted to the jury was that the electrically operated red-flasher warning signals that protected the crossing where the train-automobile collision occurred were not working. The testimony of the two plaintiffs and their passenger that the flashers were not operating was weak, highly equivocal, and of "dubious probative value," the court said, when considered in the light of unequivocal testimony by two disinterested witnesses that they saw the flashers working, the corroborative testimony of four of the train crew, and the testimony of the signal maintenance man that the flashers were working a few days before and two-and-a-half hours after the accident. The court held that a verdict should have been directed for the defendant.

In fact, there are more disparities in the language of the formulation than in the results of the cases. Professors James, Hazard, and Leubsdorf refer to these expressions of doctrinal differences as largely battles of words and suggest that, despite some shadings in application, there is now a pretty uniform test of the sufficiency of the evidence to withstand a directed verdict motion. Whatever the nomenclature, they say, there is "a fairly uniform reluctance to go very far in taking matters of credibility from the jury." Fleming James, Jr., Geoffrey C. Hazard, Jr. & John Leubsdorf, Civil Procedure 450 (5th ed. 2001). As for equating the directed verdict test to that for setting aside a verdict and granting a new trial, they concede that the equation is more nearly valid in some jurisdictions than in others but argue that the differences are rather because of variations in the new trial test than because of any variation in the directed verdict test.

So let us try to pin down the standard for granting judgment as a matter of law against the party with the burden of proof. In the interest of clarity we shall speak of the party with the burden of proof as the "plaintiff," instead of as the "proponent." (In the typical case it is the defendant who moves for judgment on the ground that the plaintiff has not sustained the burden of proof. At times, however, as when the sole issue is one on which the defendant has the burden of proof, the plaintiff might move for such a judgment as a matter of law.) In the interest of precision we should specify that here by "burden of proof" we mean burden of persuasion, except that when little or no evidence on the relevant issue has been introduced we mean the initial burden of production.

In pinning down the standard for directing a verdict, we may, without major theoretical difficulty, dispose of a few matters not involving possible differences in standards. First, if there is literally no evidence on an element of the plaintiff's case, the court naturally will direct a verdict against the plaintiff. Second, the same is true if, looking only at the evidence favorable to the plaintiff, the court is satisfied that no properly functioning jury could find for the plaintiff (except perhaps in Alabama, which still professes to follow the almost universally discredited "scintilla" rule). Such a situation in which a jury could not reasonably find for the plaintiff may result from unquestionable uncertainty of the plaintiff's facts, leaving the case within the realm of conjecture or speculation, or from the failure of facts fully known to measure up to the requirements set by the court to establish, for example, negligence on the part of the defendant. All this is not to say that applying the standard in some such cases will not be difficult, or that some courts will not push or manipulate the standard. E.g., Denman v. Spain, 242 Miss. 431, 135 So.2d 195 (1961) (no issue for jury when plaintiff's evidence showed that defendant was negligent in speeding just before head-on automobile collision in rain and fog, because no evidence existed as to which driver caused the accident or in which lane the collision occurred). But differences among courts do not rest on differences as to the applicable standard.

Next, we come to the somewhat trickier course of rejecting otherwise adequate evidence on the ground that it is simply unbelievable. Any court will consider incredible as a matter of law testimony flatly contrary to the laws of nature. E.g., Seiwell v. Hines, 273 Pa. 259, 116 A. 919 (1922) (no issue for jury on plaintiff's testimony that his stationary automobile on an upward grade with the brakes on was drawn by suction into the rear wheels of the locomotive of a passing train). Some courts may extend the concept of incredibility as a matter of law beyond the area of what is judicially recognized to be in defiance of natural laws, allowing them to disregard evidence asserted to be contrary to the physical facts or in other ways incredible and making this another area in which we shall see there is some room for pushing and manipulation. But still it is an accepted generalization to say that testimony that is not incredible when viewed by itself does not become incredible as a matter of law merely because a number of witnesses have told a diametrically different story.

Finally, this brings us to the more difficult questions that arise where there is evidence that, standing alone, would warrant a finding for the plaintiff but where there is overwhelming evidence to the contrary.

Pennsylvania Railroad Co. v. Chamberlain

Supreme Court of the United States, 1933.
288 U.S. 333, 53 S.Ct. 391.

■ MR. JUSTICE SUTHERLAND delivered the opinion of the Court.

This is an [FELA] action brought by respondent against petitioner to recover for the death of a brakeman, alleged to have been caused by petitioner's negligence. The complaint alleges that the deceased, at the time of the accident resulting in his death, was assisting in the yard work of breaking up and making up trains and in the classifying and assorting of cars operating in interstate commerce; that in pursuance of such work, while riding a cut of cars, other cars ridden by fellow employees were negligently caused to be brought into violent contact with those upon which deceased was riding, with the result that he was thrown therefrom to the railroad track and run over by a car or cars, inflicting injuries from which he died.

At the conclusion of the evidence, the trial court directed the jury to find a verdict in favor of petitioner. Judgment upon a verdict so found was reversed by the court of appeals, Judge Swan dissenting. 59 F.2d 986.

That part of the yard in which the accident occurred contained a lead track and a large number of switching tracks branching therefrom. The lead track crossed a "hump," and the work of car distribution consisted of pushing a train of cars by means of a locomotive to the top of the "hump," and then allowing the cars, in separate strings, to descend by gravity, under the control of hand brakes, to their respective destinations in the various branch tracks. Deceased had charge of a string of two gondola cars, which he was piloting to track 14. Immediately ahead of him was a string of seven cars, and behind him a string of nine cars, both also destined for track 14. Soon after the cars ridden by deceased had passed to track 14, his body was found on that track some distance beyond the switch. He had evidently fallen onto the track and been run over by a car or cars.

The case for respondent rests wholly upon the claim that the fall of deceased was caused by a violent collision of the string of nine cars with the string ridden by deceased. Three employees, riding the nine-car string, testified positively that no such collision occurred. They were corroborated by every other employee in a position to see, all testifying that there was no contact between the nine-car string and that of the deceased. The testimony of these witnesses, if believed, establishes beyond doubt that there was no collision between these two strings of cars, and that the nine-car string contributed in no way to the accident. The only witness who testified for the respondent was one Bainbridge; and it is upon his testimony alone that respondent's right to recover is sought to be upheld. His testimony is concisely stated, in its most favorable light for respondent, in the prevailing opinion below by Judge Learned Hand, as follows:

"The plaintiff's only witness to the event, one Bainbridge, then employed by the road, stood close to the yardmaster's office, near the 'hump.' He professed to have paid little attention to what went on, but he did see the deceased riding at the rear of his cars, whose speed when they passed him he took to be about eight or ten miles. Shortly thereafter a second string passed which was shunted into another track and this was followed by the nine, which, according to the plaintiff's theory, collided with the deceased's. After the nine cars had passed at a somewhat greater speed than the deceased's, Bainbridge paid no more attention to either string for awhile, but looked again when the deceased, who was still standing in his place, had passed the switch and onto the assorting track where he was bound. At that time his speed had been checked to about three miles, but the speed of the following nine cars had increased. They were just passing the switch, about four or five cars behind the deceased. Bainbridge looked away again and soon heard what he described as a 'loud crash,' not however an unusual event in a switching yard. Apparently this did not cause him at once to turn, but he did so shortly thereafter, and saw the two strings together, still moving, and the deceased no longer in sight. Later still his attention was attracted by shouts and he went to the spot and saw the deceased between the rails. Until he left to go to the accident, he had stood fifty feet to the north of the track where the accident happened, and about nine hundred feet from where the body was found."

The court, although regarding Bainbridge's testimony as not only "somewhat suspicious in itself, but its contradiction . . . so manifold as to leave little doubt," held, nevertheless, that the question was one of fact depending upon the credibility of the witnesses, and that it was for the jury to determine, as between the one witness and the many, where the truth lay. The dissenting opinion of Judge Swan proceeds upon the theory that Bainbridge did not testify that in fact a collision had taken place, but inferred it because he heard a crash, and because thereafter the two strings of cars appeared to him to be moving together. It is correctly pointed out in that opinion, however, that the crash might have come from elsewhere in the busy yard and that Bainbridge was in no position to see whether the two strings of cars were actually together; that Bainbridge repeatedly said he was paying no particular attention; and that his position was such, being

900 feet from the place where the body was found and less than 50 feet from the side of the track in question, that he necessarily saw the strings of cars at such an acute angle that it would be physically impossible even for an attentive observer to tell whether the forward end of the nine-car cut was actually in contact with the rear end of the two-car cut. The dissenting opinion further points out that all the witnesses who were in a position to see testified that there was no collision; that respondent's evidence was wholly circumstantial, and the inferences which might otherwise be drawn from it were shown to be utterly erroneous unless all of petitioner's witnesses were willful perjurers. "This is not a case," the opinion proceeds, "where direct testimony to an essential fact is contradicted by direct testimony of other witnesses, though even there it is conceded a directed verdict might be proper in some circumstances. Here, when all the testimony was in, the circumstantial evidence in support of negligence was thought by the trial judge to be so insubstantial and insufficient that it did not justify submission to the jury."

We thus summarize and quote from the prevailing and dissenting opinions, because they present the divergent views to be considered in reaching a correct determination of the question involved. It, of course, is true, generally, that where there is a direct conflict of testimony upon a matter of fact, the question must be left to the jury to determine, without regard to the number of witnesses upon either side. But here there really is no conflict in the testimony as to the facts. The witnesses for petitioner flatly testified that there was no collision between the nine-car and the two-car strings. Bainbridge did not say there was such a collision. What he said was that he heard a "loud crash," which did not cause him at once to turn, but that shortly thereafter he did turn and saw the two strings of cars moving together with the deceased no longer in sight; that there was nothing unusual about the crash of cars—it happened every day; that there was nothing about this crash to attract his attention except that it was extra loud; that he paid no attention to it; that it was not sufficient to attract his attention. The record shows that there was a continuous movement of cars over and down the "hump," which were distributed among a large number of branch tracks within the yard, and that any two strings of these cars moving upon the same track might have come together and caused the crash which Bainbridge heard. There is no direct evidence that *in fact* the crash was occasioned by a collision of the two strings in question; and it is perfectly clear that no such fact was brought to Bainbridge's attention as a perception of the physical sense of sight or of hearing. At most there was an inference to that effect drawn from observed facts which gave equal support to the opposite inference that the crash was occasioned by the coming together of other strings of cars entirely away from the scene of the accident, or of the two-car string ridden by deceased and the seven-car string immediately ahead of it.

We, therefore, have a case belonging to that class of cases where proven facts give equal support to each of two inconsistent inferences; in which event, neither of them being established, judgment, as a matter of law, must go against the party upon whom rests the necessity of sustaining one of these inferences as against the other, before he is entitled to recover. United States F. & G. Co. v. Des Moines Nat. Bank, 145 F. 273, 279–280, and cases cited; [other citations omitted].

. . . .

That Bainbridge concluded from what he himself observed that the crash was due to a collision between the two strings of cars in question is sufficiently indicated by his statements. But this, of course, proves nothing, since it is not allowable for a witness to resolve the doubt as to which of two equally justifiable inferences shall be adopted by drawing a conclusion, which, if accepted, will result in a purely gratuitous award in favor of the party who has failed to sustain the burden of proof cast upon him by the law.

And the desired inference is precluded for the further reason that respondent's right of recovery depends upon the existence of a particular fact which must be inferred from proven facts, and this is not permissible in the face of the positive and otherwise uncontradicted testimony of unimpeached witnesses consistent with the facts actually proved, from which testimony it affirmatively appears that the fact sought to be inferred did not exist. This conclusion results from a consideration of many decisions, of which the following are examples: Wabash R. Co. v. De Tar, 141 F. 932, 935; [other citations omitted]. A rebuttable inference of fact, as said by the court in the Wabash Railroad case, "must necessarily yield to credible evidence of the actual occurrence." And, as stated by the court in George v. Missouri Pac. R. Co., [213 Mo.App. 668, 674, 251 S.W. 729, 732 (1923)], "It is well settled that where plaintiff's case is based upon an inference or inferences, that the case must fail upon proof of undisputed facts inconsistent with such inferences." Compare Fresh v. Gilson, 16 Pet. 327, 330–331. In Southern Ry. Co. v. Walters, [284 U.S. 190, 52 S.Ct. 58 (1931)], the negligence charged was failure to stop a train and flag a crossing before proceeding over it. The court concluded that the only support for the charge was an inference sought to be drawn from certain facts proved. In rejecting the inference, this court said:

"It is argued that it may be inferred from the speed of the train when some of the witnesses observed it crossing other streets as well as Bond Avenue, and from such a guess of the engineer as to the time required to get up such speed after a full stop, that none could have been made at Bond Avenue. But the argument amounts to mere speculation in view of the limited scope of the witnesses' observation, the down grade of the railway tracks at the point, and the time element involved. (Compare Chicago, M. & St.P.R. Co. v. Coogan, 271 U.S. 472, 46 S.Ct. 564.) Five witnesses for defendant [employees] testified that a full stop was made and the crossing flagged, and that no one was hit by the rear of the tender, which was the front of the train.

"An examination of the record requires the conclusion that the evidence on the issue whether the train was stopped before crossing Bond Avenue was so insubstantial and insufficient that it did not justify a submission of that issue to the jury."

Not only is Bainbridge's testimony considered as a whole suspicious, insubstantial and insufficient, but his statement that when he turned shortly after hearing the crash the two strings were moving together is simply incredible, if he meant thereby to be understood as saying that he saw the two in contact; and if he meant by the words "moving together" simply that they were moving at the same time in the same direction but not in contact, the statement becomes immaterial. As we have already seen he was paying slight and only occasional attention to what was going on. The cars were eight or nine hundred feet from where he stood and moving almost directly away from him, his angle of vision being only 3° 33′ from a straight line. At that sharp angle and from that distance, near dusk of a misty evening (as the proof shows), the practical impossibility of the witness being able to see whether the front of the nine-car string was in contact with the back of the two-car string is apparent. And, certainly, in the light of these conditions, no verdict based upon a statement so unbelievable reasonably could be sustained as against the positive testimony to the contrary of unimpeached witnesses, all in a position to see, as this witness was not, the precise relations of the cars to one another.[e] The fact that these witnesses were employees of the petitioner, under the circumstances here disclosed, does not impair this conclusion. Chesapeake & Ohio Ry. v. Martin, 283 U.S. 209, 216–220, 51 S.Ct. 453.

We think, therefore, that the trial court was right in withdrawing the case from the jury. It repeatedly has been held by this court that before evidence may be left to the jury, "there is a preliminary question for the judge, not whether there is literally no evidence, but whether there is any upon which a jury can properly proceed to find a verdict for the party producing it, upon whom the onus of proof is imposed." Pleasants v. Fant, 22 Wall. 116, 120–121. And where the evidence is "so overwhelmingly on one side as to leave no room to doubt what the fact is, the court should give a peremptory instruction to the jury." Gunning v. Cooley, 281 U.S. 90, 94, 50 S.Ct. 231, 233; Patton v. Texas & Pacific Ry. Co., 179 U.S. 658, 660, 21 S.Ct. 275. The rule is settled for the federal courts, and for many of the state courts, that whenever in the trial of a civil case the evidence is clearly such that if a verdict were rendered for one of the parties the other would be entitled to a new trial, it is the duty of the judge to direct the jury to find according to the views of the court. Such a practice, this court has said, not only saves time and expense, but "gives scientific certainty to the law in its application to the facts and promotes the ends of justice." Bowditch v. Boston, 101 U.S. 16, 18; [other citations omitted]. The scintilla rule has been definitely and repeatedly rejected so far as the federal courts are concerned. [Citations omitted.]

---

[e] To get beyond disparities in phrasing and see what a court is really doing, one must grapple with all the facts and thus see what the court's formulation means in action. But there are facts, and then there are facts. The Brief for Respondent at 5–6 correctly pointed out that one of the railroad's employee-witnesses who was riding the seven-car string, Jetter, had been impeached by testimony of the decedent's family to the effect that he had told them a markedly different story shortly after the accident. In interpreting the Court's holding, however, we should look to the facts as stated by Justice Sutherland, should we not?

Leaving out of consideration, then, the inference relied upon, the case for respondent is left without any substantial support in the evidence, and a verdict in her favor would have rested upon mere speculation and conjecture. This, of course, is inadmissible. [Citations omitted.]

The judgment of the Circuit Court of Appeals is reversed and that of the District Court is affirmed.

■ MR. JUSTICE STONE and MR. JUSTICE CARDOZO concur in the result.

Question: (6) Would, and should, the direction of verdict for the defendant have been upheld (a) if Bainbridge had been the only witness on the issue of negligence or (b) if Bainbridge, standing 900 feet away and at an angle making accurate observation difficult but not "physically impossible," had testified that he "saw the two strings collide" and if the testimony of the seven other witnesses had been as summarized in the opinion?

LAVENDER v. KURN, 327 U.S. 645, 66 S.Ct. 740 (1946). In this FELA case, Haney, the decedent, was found unconscious on the ground near the railroad track with a skull fracture from which he died. There were no eyewitnesses. Plaintiff's theory was that Haney was struck by the curled end of a mail hook that extended from a mail car. Defendant contended that plaintiff's theory was practically a physical impossibility and that in fact Haney was probably murdered by one of the hoboes shown to frequent the area at night. Hence, death by hook or by crook? The examining doctor testified that the fatal blow might have come from an object attached to a moving train, but also admitted that it might have resulted from a pipe or club wielded by an individual. The Missouri Supreme Court overturned a verdict for the plaintiff, saying the case should not have gone to the jury over objection. On certiorari, the Supreme Court of the United States reversed, with Justice Murphy's opinion for the Court saying: "It is no answer to say that the jury's verdict involved speculation and conjecture. Whenever facts are in dispute or the evidence is such that fair-minded men may draw different inferences, a measure of speculation and conjecture is required on the part of those whose duty it is to settle the dispute by choosing what seems to them to be the most reasonable inference. Only when there is a complete absence of probative facts to support the conclusion reached does a reversible error appear." Chief Justice Stone and Justice Frankfurter concurred in the result. Justice Jackson did not participate. Justice Reed dissented.

WILKERSON v. McCARTHY, 336 U.S. 53, 69 S.Ct. 413 (1949). In this FELA case, Wilkerson, the plaintiff, was injured when he fell from a narrow board stretching across a deep work pit in the railroad yard. The central issue in determining the defendant's negligence was whether its employees habitually used the plank as a walkway. On this there was conflicting evidence, with the plaintiff and another employee testifying that such practice was an established one but with strong testimony to the contrary from other employees. The Utah Supreme Court affirmed a directed verdict for the defendant. On certiorari, the Supreme Court of the United States reversed. In the course of his opinion for the Court, Justice Black said: "It is the established rule that in passing upon whether there is sufficient evidence to submit an issue to the jury we need look only to the evidence and reasonable inferences which tend to support the case of a litigant against whom a peremptory instruction has been given." Justice Frankfurter, concurring in the opinion, put the standard this way: "When a plaintiff claims that an injury which he has suffered is attributable to a defendant's negligence—want of care in the discharge of a duty which the defendant owed to him—it is the trial judge's function to determine whether the evidence in its entirety would rationally support a verdict for the plaintiff, assuming that the jury took, as it would be entitled to take, a view of the evidence most favorable to the plaintiff." Justices Black and Frankfurter agreed that there was enough evidence here to go to the jury. Chief Justice Vinson and Justice Jackson dissented.

Questions: (7) What, if any, significant difference is there between these two formulations in Wilkerson?

(8) Should the result in Pennsylvania Railroad Co. v. Chamberlain be different under Justice Black's formulation? under Justice Frankfurter's formulation?

(9) In Reid v. Nelson, 154 F.2d 724 (5th Cir.1946), plaintiff sued husband and wife for injuries allegedly caused by their dog. Plaintiff's only evidence tending to show the essential fact of ownership in the wife was that she had referred to "our dog." If the wife had rested at the close of the plaintiff's case and moved for judgment as a matter of law, should the motion have been granted? In fact, the defendants went on to offer uncontradicted and unimpeached direct evidence of the husband's sole ownership. Should the wife's motion for judgment as a matter of law now be granted?

STANDARD IN FELA ACTIONS

The pro-plaintiff tilt of the FELA itself may have led to what seemed to have become an especially lenient standard for avoiding judgment as a matter of law in cases brought under that Act. The test of a jury case thereunder has been expressed as "whether the proofs justify with reason the conclusion that employer negligence played any part, even the slightest, in producing the injury or death for which damages are sought." Rogers v. Missouri Pac. R.R. Co., 352 U.S. 500, 506, 77 S.Ct. 443, 448 (1957). This test has been held to require submission to the jury of cases that some lower courts have regarded as based on conjecture or speculation. Indeed, the states' Conference of Chief Justices in 1966, reflecting its dissatisfaction with the reversals by the Supreme Court of state-court decisions in FELA cases, adopted a resolution that these actions should by amendment to the statute be placed exclusively within federal jurisdiction.

Perhaps the seemingly lenient FELA practice in sending cases to the jury reflected merely this tilt in the substantive law, or perhaps there was indeed a difference in kind between the standard in FELA cases and the standard in other federal actions. This was the subject of much dispute. Compare Boeing Co. v. Shipman, 411 F.2d 365 (5th Cir.1969) (en banc) (likening the FELA test to the long-rejected scintilla test, and holding it to be not controlling in other federal cases), with Wratchford v. S.J. Groves & Sons Co., 405 F.2d 1061 (4th Cir.1969) (holding that FELA decisions control in other federal cases).

There was nothing in Justice Black's opinion in Wilkerson v. McCarthy, nor in Justice Frankfurter's concurrence, to indicate a difference between FELA cases and other federal actions with respect to the standard for granting judgment as a matter of law. And it may be that the dampening oscillation of the common-law method was bringing the courts in the FELA cases to the same point at which they were arriving in other types of federal actions. In any event, today's Rule 50 makes no special provision for FELA cases.

O'Connor v. Pennsylvania Railroad Co.

United States Court of Appeals, Second Circuit, 1962.
308 F.2d 911.

[Plaintiff slipped on the terrace of Pennsylvania Station in New York City during a snowstorm on February 16, 1958. Plaintiff brought suit in New York state court, but defendant removed the case on the basis of diversity of citizenship. (It was not an FELA case.) Defendant was liable only if the ice on which plaintiff had allegedly slipped had persisted from earlier snowfalls. The issue on appeal, arising from the grant of defendant's motion for judgment n.o.v., was whether there was sufficient evidence for plaintiff to reach the jury.]

■ Before LUMBARD, CHIEF JUDGE, and FRIENDLY and KAUFMAN, CIRCUIT JUDGES.

■ KAUFMAN, CIRCUIT JUDGE.

. . . .

. . . The plaintiff . . . fell . . . on what he described as a "rugged" patch of ice "roughly two by four feet". The usual conflict of testimony as to the condition of the premises was present here as in most negligence suits. There was testimony on behalf of the plaintiff that the center of the terrace floor was almost completely clear of snow while there was an accumulation of snow along the edges. The plaintiff testified that the ice on which he slipped was dirty gray and that all the irregular bits and patches of ice on the stone terrace floor were dirty. He further said that he did not remember whether the falling snow was being blown and whipped. The defendant submitted testimony to the effect that there was an accumulation of approximately two inches of wet snow on the terrace floor and that a gale was blowing the snow onto the terrace, which showed no traces of ice.

[United States Weather Bureau records indicated that in the preceding week only unmeasurably small amounts ("traces") of snow had fallen or remained on the ground, and that in the snowstorm of February 15 and 16 nine inches of snow fell, with drifts of two feet and with strong winds gusting to 54 miles per hour.]

All of these factors, supported by unquestioned documentary evidence, tend strongly to contradict the evidence offered on behalf of the plaintiff. Even if it could reasonably be assumed that some traces of snow from the earlier February snowfalls might possibly have persisted on the terrace floor through some negligence of the defendant, the evidence overwhelmingly supports the inference that the snow or ice upon which O'Connor fell at 7:20 a.m. on February 16 was a product of the snowfall raging at the time. To warrant submitting this case to the jury, it was incumbent upon the plaintiff to offer other evidence which could more convincingly overcome the proven physical facts offered on behalf of the defendant.

[The court avoided the Erie question by observing that the federal and state standards for reaching the jury were "substantially similar."]

"The propriety of granting or denying a motion for a directed verdict [or for judgment non obstante veredicto] is tested both in the trial court and on appeal by the same rule. The trial court must view the evidence and all inferences most favorably to the party against whom the motion is made. The reviewing court must do the same with respect to a judgment entered on a directed verdict or the denial of a motion for a directed verdict or a judgment entered notwithstanding the verdict." 2B Barron & Holtzoff, Federal Practice and Procedure, § 1075 at 378 (1961). In granting such a motion for a judgment notwithstanding the verdict, and in affirming it on appeal, the function of the jury is not usurped. The jury is simply not being permitted to make unreasonable findings of fact. The case is withdrawn from them "as a matter of law" because no jury could reasonably bring in a verdict for the opponent of the moving party. To decide upon the propriety of granting this motion, the court looks to the substantial evidence tending to bolster the case of the non-moving party and draws all reasonable inferences therefrom. But the evidence cannot properly be deemed substantial nor the inferences reasonable if they are contrary to proven physical facts. The inferences which may be drawn must be within the range of reasonable probability, Ford Motor Co. v. McDavid, 259 F.2d 261 (4th Cir.), cert. denied, 358 U.S. 908, 79 S.Ct. 234, 3 L.Ed.2d 229 (1958) and must not be at war with undisputed facts.

This is not a case where two competing versions of the facts, depending upon the credibility of oral testimony, are to be resolved but instead one where the uncontested documentary evidence of weather conditions at the time in question overwhelms the plaintiff's testimony so as to render the inference sought to be drawn unreasonable. Here, the documentary evidence reveals that the snowfall of February 15 and 16 was so severe that it would be grossly unreasonable to find that the plaintiff's icy nemesis was the result of the traces of snow falling several days earlier and of ground precipitation too small to measure, rather than of the snowfall in progress. Since the weather records so overwhelmingly outweigh the oral testimony offered in behalf of the plaintiff, [citations omitted], it would have been improper to permit the jury's verdict to stand.

Affirmed.

SECTION 3. JUDGMENT FOR PARTY WITH BURDEN OF PROOF

The refusal to grant judgment as a matter of law against the party with the burden of proof even though a verdict in his favor would be contrary to the weight of the evidence is explainable by the unwillingness to invade the jury's province of assessing the credibility of witnesses. The grant of judgment as a matter of law in favor of the party with the burden of proof involves passing on credibility in almost every case. Does it follow then that the court can never grant judgment as a matter of law for such a party on the basis of oral testimony, because the jury might not accept the testimony as true? Only a few states reach this conclusion.[f]

Chesapeake & Ohio Railway v. Martin

Supreme Court of the United States, 1931.
283 U.S. 209, 51 S.Ct. 453.

[The respondents sued in a Virginia state court for misdelivery of a carload of potatoes transported from Michigan to Richmond, Virginia, on a through bill of lading. The bill of lading required claim for loss or injury to be made within six months after a reasonable time for delivery had elapsed. This claim was made six months and twenty days after shipment from Michigan. The railroad's freight agent at Richmond, qualified to speak by twenty years' experience, testified that a reasonable time for delivery to the consignee in Richmond would be about eight days and that any longer time

[f] In Giles v. Giles, 204 Mass. 383, 90 N.E. 595 (1910), the direction of a verdict in favor of the party with the burden of proof was held to have been erroneous, the court saying: "We know of no case in this Commonwealth in which it has been determined that a jury can be directed to return a verdict, upon the oral testimony of witnesses, in favor of a party who has the burden of proving the facts to which they have testified." No such Massachusetts case has since been found, although a direction in favor of the burdened party is possible if his case does not depend on the credibility of witnesses, e.g., where his case is documentary and there is no question about the genuineness of the documents, as in Goldstein v. D'Arcy, 201 Mass. 312, 87 N.E. 584 (1909).

would be considered a delayed movement. There was no evidence to the contrary. The railroad demurred to the evidence[g] on the ground that the claim was barred by the provision of the bill of lading. The demurrer was overruled, and judgment was entered upon a verdict against the railroad. The judgment was affirmed on appeal. The railroad's petition for certiorari was granted to review the federal question of compliance with a provision in a bill of lading authorized by the Interstate Commerce Act.]

■ MR. JUSTICE SUTHERLAND delivered the opinion of the Court.

. . . .

Not only is the estimate of the agent reasonable upon its face and in accordance with probability; and not only is it wholly unchallenged by other evidence or circumstances; but it is so completely corroborated by the undisputed facts in respect of this very shipment as to put it beyond the reach of a fair doubt. The movement of the car from the point of origin to the yards of petitioner in Richmond actually was made in six days; and, if there be added full forty-eight hours thereafter for completing delivery to the Bowman warehouse, the testimony of the agent as to time stands verified by indubitable test. [The evidence was that the shipment was mistakenly delivered by the railroad not to the Bowman warehouse, as directed by the respondents, but to the Harwood warehouse, where it was eventually located by the respondents in a spoiled condition.] In the face of this record, the conclusion of the court that it was still open for the jury to say that not eight days merely, but twenty days, fell short of being a reasonable time for delivery, is so clearly erroneous as to cause the ruling of the court, in effect, to rest upon nothing more substantial than the power of a jury arbitrarily to disregard established facts.

We recognize the general rule, of course, as stated by both courts below, that the question of the credibility of witnesses is one for the jury alone; but this does not mean that the jury is at liberty, under the guise of passing upon the credibility of a witness, to disregard his testimony, when from no reasonable point of view is it open to doubt. The complete testimony of the agent in this case appears in the record. A reading of it discloses no lack of candor on his part. It was not shaken by cross-examination; indeed, upon this point, there was no cross-examination. Its accuracy was not controverted by proof or circumstance, directly or inferentially; and it is difficult to see why, if inaccurate, it readily could not have been shown to be so. The witness was not impeached; and there is nothing in the record which reflects unfavorably upon his credibility. The only possible ground for submitting the question to the jury as one of fact was that the witness was an employee of the petitioner. In the circumstances above detailed, we are of opinion that this was not enough to take the question to the jury, and that the court should have so held.

It is true that numerous expressions are to be found in the decisions to the effect that the credibility of an interested witness always must be

---

[g] This is the equivalent under Virginia practice of a motion for a directed verdict. See supra p. 1369 note c.

submitted to the jury, and that that body is at liberty to reject his testimony upon the sole ground of his interest. But these broad generalizations cannot be accepted without qualification. Such a variety of differing facts, however, is disclosed by the cases that no useful purpose would be served by an attempt to review them. In many, if not most, of them, there were circumstances tending to cast suspicion upon the testimony or upon the witness, apart from the fact that he was interested. We have been unable to find any decision enforcing such a rule where the facts and circumstances were comparable to those here disclosed. . . .

. . . .

Judgment reversed.

Simblest v. Maynard

United States Court of Appeals, Second Circuit, 1970.
427 F.2d 1.

[A car driven by plaintiff collided with a fire engine, a 500–gallon pumper driven by defendant, at the intersection of Main Street and South Willard Street, Burlington, Vermont, during the electric power blackout that left most of New England in darkness on the night of November 9, 1965. Both parties were experienced drivers thoroughly familiar with the intersection. Plaintiff was driving west on Main Street and defendant, responding to a fire alarm, was driving south on South Willard Street as they approached the intersection, at which there was an overhead traffic light. The neighborhood was partly business, partly residential. It was dark, the traffic was light, and the weather was clear. Defendant struck plaintiff's car on the front right side. Plaintiff was knocked unconscious for about a minute.

[Plaintiff testified that the traffic light was green in his favor as he entered the intersection, but that when he was partway through it the power failure extinguished all lights, including the traffic light. All other witnesses for both sides testified that the power failure occurred at least 10 to 15 minutes earlier. Plaintiff testified that he was going 12 to 15 miles per hour as he approached the intersection, that he did not look to the right before he entered, that he looked to his right for the first time when he was one-half to three-quarters of the way through the intersection and then saw the fire engine within 12 feet of him, and that he did not hear the fire engine's siren or see the flashing lights or any other lights on the engine. Plaintiff further testified that his vision was obstructed to the right as he entered the intersection by traffic signs, trees, and an information booth. All of the evidence, including photographs, demonstrated that he could have seen the engine if he had looked between the obstructions or after he passed the information booth; one of plaintiff's witnesses testified that he might have seen the fire truck "maybe five to ten seconds" before he was struck.

[Defendant testified that he approached the intersection at 20 to 25 miles per hour (the highest estimate of speed was 30 to 35 miles per hour from another witness) and that the following warning devices were in operation on the fire engine: the penetrator making a wailing sound, the usual fire siren, a flashing red light attached to the dome of the fire engine, two red lights on either side of the cab, and the usual headlights. He saw plaintiff's car before it passed the information booth and next as it entered the intersection. He testified that he applied his brakes and turned to his right in an attempt to avoid the collision. He estimated his speed at 15 to 20 miles per hour at the time of impact.

[Other witnesses virtually bracketed the intersection from various vantage points. The two called by plaintiff saw the flashing lights of the engine, and one of those two also heard the siren. The two called by defendant both heard the warning signals and saw the flashing lights.

[Defendant's motion for a directed verdict at the close of all the evidence was denied, the jury returned a verdict for plaintiff, and the trial judge granted defendant's motion for judgment n.o.v. The plaintiff appealed.]

■ Before KAUFMAN and FEINBERG, CIRCUIT JUDGES, and TIMBERS, DISTRICT JUDGE.

■ TIMBERS, DISTRICT JUDGE.

. . . .

In determining whether the motion for judgment n.o.v. should have been granted, a threshold question is presented as to the correct standard to be applied. This standard has been expressed in various ways. Simply stated, it is whether the evidence is such that, without weighing the credibility of the witnesses or otherwise considering the weight of the evidence, there can be but one conclusion as to the verdict that reasonable men could have reached. See, e.g., Brady v. Southern Railway Company, 320 U.S. 476, 479–80 (1943); O'Connor v. Pennsylvania Railroad Company, 308 F.2d 911, 914–15 (2 Cir.1962). See also 5 Moore's Federal Practice ¶ 50.02[1], at 2320–23 (2d ed. 1968); Wright, Law of Federal Courts § 95, at 425 (2d ed. 1970). On a motion for judgment n.o.v., the evidence must be viewed in the light most favorable to the party against whom the motion is made and he must be given the benefit of all reasonable inferences which may be drawn in his favor from that evidence. O'Connor v. Pennsylvania Railroad Company, supra, at 914–15; 5 Moore, supra, at 2325; Wright, supra, at 425.

We acknowledge that it has not been settled in a diversity action whether, in considering the evidence in the light most favorable to the party against whom the motion is made, the court may consider all the evidence or only the evidence favorable to such party and the uncontradicted, unimpeached evidence unfavorable to him. Under Vermont law, all the evidence may be considered. Kremer v. Fortin, 119 Vt. 1, 117 A.2d 245 (1955) (intersection collision between fire engine and passenger car). Plaintiff here urges that under the federal standard only evidence favorable to him should have been considered, citing Wilkerson v. McCarthy, 336 U.S. 53, 57 (1949). As plaintiff reads that case, the court below should not have considered anything else, not even the uncontradicted, unimpeached evidence unfavorable to him. However, we are committed to a contrary view in a diversity case. O'Connor v. Pennsylvania Railroad Company, supra.

The Supreme Court at least twice has declined to decide whether the state or federal standard as to the sufficiency of the evidence is controlling on such motions in diversity cases. Mercer v. Theriot, 377 U.S. 152, 156 (1964) (per curiam); Dick v. New York Life Insurance Company, 359 U.S. 437, 444–45 (1959). Our Court likewise has declined to decide this issue in recent cases. [Citations omitted.][3]

Our careful review of the record in the instant case leaves us with the firm conviction that, under either the Vermont standard or the more restrictive federal standard, plaintiff was contributorily negligent as a matter of law; and that Chief Judge Leddy correctly set aside the verdict and entered judgment for defendant n.o.v. [Citations omitted.]

Under the Vermont standard which permits all the evidence to be considered, Kremer v. Fortin, supra, plaintiff was so clearly guilty of contributory negligence that no further dilation is required.

Under the more restrictive federal standard—i.e., considering only the evidence favorable to plaintiff and the uncontradicted, unimpeached evidence unfavorable to him—while a closer question is presented than under the Vermont standard, we nevertheless hold that plaintiff was guilty of contributory negligence as a matter of law.

In our view, applying the federal standard, the critical issue in the case is whether the fire engine was sounding a siren or displaying a red light as it approached the intersection immediately before the collision. Upon this critical issue, Chief Judge Leddy accurately and succinctly summarized the evidence as follows:

> "All witnesses to the accident, except the plaintiff, testified that the fire truck was sounding a siren or displaying a flashing red light. All of the witnesses except Miss Burgess and the plaintiff testified that the fire truck was sounding its siren and displaying a flashing red light."

---

[3] Assuming that the federal standard were controlling, plaintiff's contention that under that standard evidence introduced by the moving party may not be considered is open to question. Plaintiff relies on Wilkerson v. McCarthy, 336 U.S. 53, 57 (1949). But most Courts of Appeals have held that evidence introduced by the moving party may be considered, distinguishing Wilkerson on the ground that FELA cases are sui generis. 5 Moore, supra, at 2329.

See especially the comprehensive opinion of the Fifth Circuit in Boeing Company v. Shipman, 411 F.2d 365 (5 Cir.1969) (en banc), holding (1) that in diversity cases a federal rather than state standard should be applied in testing the sufficiency of the evidence in connection with motions for a directed verdict and for judgment n.o.v.; (2) that the FELA standard for testing the sufficiency of the evidence on such motions is not applicable in diversity cases; and (3) that the federal standard to be applied in diversity cases requires the court to consider "all of the evidence—not just that evidence which supports the nonmover's case—but in the light and with all reasonable inferences most favorable to the party opposed to the motion." 411 F.2d at 374.

The reason such evidence is critical is that under Vermont law, 23 V.S.A. § 1033, upon the approach of a fire department vehicle which is sounding a siren or displaying a red light, or both, all other vehicles are required to pull over to the right lane of traffic and come to a complete stop until the emergency vehicle has passed.[5] Since the emergency provision of this statute supersedes the general right of way statute regarding intersections controlled by traffic lights, 23 V.S.A. § 1054, the lone testimony of plaintiff that the traffic light was green in his favor as he approached and entered the intersection is of no moment. And since the emergency provision of 23 V.S.A. § 1033 becomes operative if *either* the siren is sounding *or* a red light is displayed on an approaching fire engine, we focus upon plaintiff's own testimony that he did not see the fire engine's flashing light, all other witnesses having testified that the red light was flashing.

As stated above, plaintiff testified that he first saw the fire engine when he was one-half to three-quarters of the way through the intersection and when the fire engine was within 12 feet of his car. At the speed at which the fire engine was traveling, plaintiff had approximately one-third of a second in which to observe the fire engine prior to the collision. Accepting plaintiff's testimony that his eyesight was excellent, and assuming that the fire engine's flashing red light was revolving as rapidly as 60 revolutions per minute, plaintiff's one-third of a second observation does not support an inference that the light was not operating, much less does it constitute competent direct evidence to that effect. Opportunity to observe is a necessary ingredient of the competency of eyewitness evidence. Plaintiff's opportunity to observe, accepting his own testimony, simply was too short for his testimony on the operation of the light to be of any probative value whatsoever.

Plaintiff's testimony that he did not see the fire engine's flashing red light, in the teeth of the proven physical facts, we hold is tantamount to no proof at all on that issue. O'Connor v. Pennsylvania Railroad Company, supra, at 915. As one commentator has put it, " . . . the question of the total absence of proof quickly merges into the question whether the proof adduced is so insignificant as to be treated as the equivalent of the absence of proof." 5 Moore, supra, at 2320. . . .

. . . .

Affirmed.

Questions: (10) Would the judgment for defendant have been upheld if the n.o.v. standard were to look only at the evidence favorable to plaintiff?

(11) Assume instead that the standard allows the judge to look also at the unquestionable evidence favorable to defendant. What result if plaintiff had had enough time to make accurate observation difficult but not physically impossible

---

[5] . . . Violation of this statute under Vermont law constitutes prima facie evidence of negligence. Dashnow v. Myers, 121 Vt. 273, 155 A.2d 859 (1959).

and if the testimony of all the other witnesses had been as summarized in the opinion? What if there were additionally twenty witnesses testifying that they saw the flashing red light? What if the twenty were bishops? What if it were two hundred bishops so testifying? What if there were also videotape of the accident showing the flashing red light?

REEVES v. SANDERSON PLUMBING PRODUCTS, INC., 530 U.S. 133, 120 S.Ct. 2097 (2000). "This case concerns the kind and amount of evidence necessary to sustain a jury's verdict that an employer unlawfully discriminated on the basis of age. Specifically, we must resolve whether a defendant is entitled to judgment as a matter of law when the plaintiff's case consists exclusively of a prima facie case of discrimination and sufficient evidence for the trier of fact to disbelieve the defendant's legitimate, nondiscriminatory explanation for its action." Deciding in the negative, Justice O'Connor for a unanimous Court explained some basics:

"The Courts of Appeals have articulated differing formulations as to what evidence a court is to consider in ruling on a Rule 50 motion. [Citation omitted.] Some decisions have stated that review is limited to that evidence favorable to the nonmoving party, [citations omitted], while most have held that review extends to the entire record, drawing all reasonable inferences in favor of the nonmovant, [citations omitted].

"On closer examination, this conflict seems more semantic than real. Those decisions holding that review under Rule 50 should be limited to evidence favorable to the nonmovant appear to have their genesis in Wilkerson v. McCarthy, 336 U.S. 53, 69 S.Ct. 413 (1949). See 9A C. Wright & A. Miller, Federal Practice and Procedure §§ 2529, pp. 297–301 (2d ed. 1995). In Wilkerson, we stated that 'in passing upon whether there is sufficient evidence to submit an issue to the jury we need look only to the evidence and reasonable inferences which tend to support the case of' the nonmoving party. 336 U.S., at 57, 69 S.Ct. 413. But subsequent decisions have clarified that this passage was referring to the evidence to which the trial court should *give credence*, not the evidence that the court should *review*. In the analogous context of summary judgment under Rule 56, we have stated that the court must review the record 'taken as a whole.' Matsushita Elec. Industrial Co. v. Zenith Radio Corp., 475 U.S. 574, 587, 106 S.Ct. 1348 (1986). And the standard for granting summary judgment 'mirrors' the standard for judgment as a matter of law, such that 'the inquiry under each is the same.' Anderson v. Liberty Lobby, Inc., 477 U.S. 242, 250–251, 106 S.Ct. 2505 (1986); see also Celotex Corp. v. Catrett, 477 U.S. 317, 323, 106 S.Ct. 2548 (1986). It therefore follows that, in entertaining a motion for judgment as a matter of law, the court should review all of the evidence in the record.

"In doing so, however, the court must draw all reasonable inferences in favor of the nonmoving party, and it may not make credibility determinations or weigh the evidence. [Citations omitted.] 'Credibility determinations, the weighing of the evidence, and the drawing of legitimate inferences from the facts are jury functions, not those of a judge.' Liberty Lobby, supra, at 255, 106 S.Ct. 2505. Thus, although the court should review the record as a whole, it must disregard all evidence favorable to the moving party that the jury is not required to believe. See Wright & Miller 299. That is, the court should give credence to the evidence favoring the nonmovant as well as that 'evidence supporting the moving party that is uncontradicted and unimpeached, at least to the extent that that evidence comes from disinterested witnesses.' Id., at 300."

Question: (12) The federal standard, one could argue, tells the judge to look at the evidence favorable to the nonmovant, except any evidence that a reasonable jury could not believe, and also to consider other evidence that a reasonable jury could not disbelieve. If that is so, does this whole string of cases add anything, other than meaningful illustration, to our starting idea that a federal judge can give judgment as a matter of law if a reasonable jury could not find for the nonmovant?

STANDARD IN DIVERSITY ACTIONS

Generally, diversity of citizenship actions are controlled by state law as to the substantive elements of the case, and we have also seen that under the command of Erie the allocation of the burden of proof, as well as the standard of proof, in such actions is governed by state law. But the Supreme Court has never decided whether or not the quantum of evidence necessary to take a diversity case to the jury is state controlled. The assertion by Chief Judge Parker in Davis Frozen Foods, Inc. v. Norfolk Southern Ry., 204 F.2d 839, 842 (4th Cir.1953), that the applicability of federal law "is too well settled to admit of argument," appears to have been an overstatement. However, there has been a definite trend toward applying federal law, as was done in Boeing Co. v. Shipman, 411 F.2d 365 (5th Cir.1969), and Wratchford v. S.J. Groves & Sons Co., 405 F.2d 1061 (4th Cir.1969).

Although the Supreme Court's decision in Gasperini v. Center for Humanities, Inc., supra p. 383, might have put that trend in doubt, the rulemakers' articulation of the standard in Rule 50(a)(1) by its 1991 amendment had already added a strong argument in favor of applying federal law. See Ellis v. Weasler Eng'g Inc., 258 F.3d 326, amended, 274 F.3d 881 (5th Cir.2001); Steven Alan Childress, Judicial Review and Diversity Jurisdiction: Solving an Irrepressible Erie Mystery?, 47 SMU L.Rev. 271 (1994). Some circuits are holding out, but the federal-law trend remains strong. See 9B Wright & Miller § 2525.

Questions: (13) Should it matter whether the state law is more or less lenient than the federal law in allowing the case to go to the jury?

(14) Should state law control on permissive-inference doctrines, such as res ipsa loquitur?

SERVICE AUTO SUPPLY CO. v. HARTE & CO., 533 F.2d 23 (1st Cir.1976). Plaintiff wholesaler from Puerto Rico sued defendant manufacturer from New York for breach of contract, alleging delivery of defective car mats. Three witnesses "sympathetic" to plaintiff testified. For defendant only its president testified, but he failed to contradict and in part corroborated the testimony of plaintiff's witnesses as to the condition of the delivered goods. At the close of all the evidence, the district court granted plaintiff's motion for a directed verdict as to liability. A verdict and judgment for almost $90,000 followed. On defendant's appeal, the court of appeals said:

"The most troublesome issue lies in the direction of the verdict for plaintiff on liability. While such a direction in favor of the party having the burden of proof is rare, it is permitted where that party 'has established his case by testimony that the jury is not at liberty to disbelieve.'[2] But the standard of proof to be met is a strict one. The Supreme Court in Brady v. Southern Ry. Co., 320 U.S. 476, 479, 64 S.Ct. 232, 234, 88 L.Ed. 239, 243 (1943), has defined the evidence meriting such a sudden death result as 'such that without weighing the credibility of the witnesses there can be but one reasonable conclusion as to the verdict.' . . .

"In ordinary cases, such as this one, where the issues are factual, oral testimony is dominant, and the testimony from each side is likely to be given by witnesses who are committed in their views to one party or the other, whether or not legally 'interested', the making of a motion for directed verdict by a party having the burden is a long shot gamble. In the generality of cases, it saves perhaps a few hours of jury time but nothing else. Affirmance requires the most detailed combing of the record and exposition by the appellate court. Reversal means an entire new trial and possibly another appeal. Perhaps its only merit is that if made and refused, the motion preserves, for a plaintiff, the issue of sufficiency of defendant's evidence in the event of a verdict for defendant. While counsel may feel obligated to make the motion, we advise caution on the part of the court.

. . . .

". . . We conclude, though not without travail and antipathy for this kind of analysis, that a jury could not have found for the defendant on the issue of liability. The directed verdict on this issue may stand."

---

[2] 9 Wright and Miller, Federal Practice and Procedure, 591. See authorities gathered in § 2535.

Questions: (15) In an action on a fidelity bond designed to protect an employer from loss through defalcation by its employees, the plaintiff employer offers in evidence against the defendant surety company the testimony of *W*, an employee, that he stole the money and used it for his own purposes. There is no other evidence bearing upon the issue of loss. Should the plaintiff's motion for a directed verdict be granted? See Nanty–Glo Boro. v. American Sur. Co., 309 Pa. 236, 163 A. 523 (1932) (no).

(16) In an action on a note, plaintiff seeks to recover the principal without interest, although previously he tried to collect with interest. Defendant pleads a material alteration of the note after delivery to plaintiff (a complete affirmative defense, on which defendant has the burden of proof). At trial, plaintiff introduces the note, which has the words "with interest" inserted and erased, and then rests. Defendant's testimony as to the added words and as to plaintiff's out-of-court admission to adding those words is such that if it were not true, plaintiff could and would deny it of his own knowledge. Plaintiff does not testify, and no explanation is offered for his failure to do so, but defendant does not call him either. Should defendant's motion for judgment as a matter of law be granted? See Scribner v. Cyr, 148 Me. 329, 93 A.2d 126 (1952) (yes). (The actual motion in Scribner was for a new trial after verdict for plaintiff, but in Maine, contrary to the prevailing view, the standard for granting this motion was as high as Maine's standard for directing a verdict, which conformed to the prevailing view. See 1 Richard H. Field, Vincent L. McKusick & L. Kinvin Wroth, Maine Civil Practice 664 (2d ed. 1970). Indeed, the court explained: "The unexplained failure of a party to testify with respect to material facts within his own knowledge, or to take the stand and deny the existence of material facts testified to by the adverse party, has long been recognized as proper matter for the consideration of the jury. . . . There may be cases, however, where the unexplained failure of a party to take the witness stand and testify as to facts within his own knowledge, or to deny facts testified to by his adversary is of such importance and so significant in connection with the other facts in the case that a jury can reasonably reach but one conclusion with respect thereto. This is such a case.")

TOPIC C

VERDICT

SECTION 1. DIVISION OF FUNCTIONS BETWEEN JUDGE AND JURY

The statement that questions of law are for the judge and questions of fact are for the jury has been reiterated over the centuries, but "this conventional brocard cannot be taken as a trustworthy guide to the solution of any particular controversy on the subject." 9 John H. Wigmore, Evidence § 2549 (John H. Chadbourn rev. 1981); see Ronald J. Allen & Michael S. Pardo, The Myth of the Law–Fact Distinction, 97 Nw.U.L.Rev. 1769 (2003).

Judges have always decided questions of fact, even in jury trials. For example, threshold matters such as jurisdictional challenges often involve questions of fact, but these matters are normally decided by the judge. The admissibility of evidence likewise may turn on preliminary questions of fact, which are routinely decided by the judge. See Federal Evidence Rule 104(a) and (c). And Judge Madden said in Wunderlich v. United States, 117 Ct.Cl. 92, 212 (1950), rev'd on other grounds, 342 U.S. 98, 72 S.Ct. 154 (1951): "We are, of course, aware that questions of the interpretation of written documents are not, speaking with analytical accuracy, in most cases questions of law in the sense that a lawyer or a judge has the special skill needed to answer them. They may be questions of agriculture, or engineering, or finance, or medicine, or law. In the division of judicial functions between the judge and the lay jury which only by accident would have the requisite skill in a particular case, the judge reserved this function to himself, presumably as being more competent than the jury. And judges and lawyers began to call the questions 'questions of law,' as a short way of saying that they should be decided by the judge. This method of expression, though analytically inaccurate was, so far as we know, quite universal."

Among the questions of "fact" assigned to the jury, there may be two types of questions: (1) determining what happened, that is, what the parties did and what the circumstances were; and (2) evaluating those facts in terms of their legal consequences, for instance, whether the conduct of the defendant in the circumstances was not that of a reasonable person. But the court always sets the outside limits within which the jury may perform its function. Sometimes such judicial interceding invokes only the rationality limit on the jury's function that was the concern of the two preceding Topics, but at other times what the court is actually doing is specifically formulating a substantive rule of law. For example, with respect to the latter type of question the Court, in Railroad Co. v. Stout, 84 U.S.

(17 Wall.) 657, 663 (1874), said: "So if a coach-driver intentionally drives within a few inches of a precipice, and an accident happens, negligence may be ruled as a question of law. On the other hand, if he had placed a suitable distance between his coach and the precipice, but by the breaking of a rein or an axle, which could not have been anticipated, an injury occurred, it might be ruled as a question of law that there was no negligence and no liability." The court is saying that in certain circumstances there is or is not liability.

Question: (1) Note that the lawmaker could formulate the law in such a detailed fashion as to reduce greatly the role of the jury. It is said that considerations of policy will often determine whether the lawmaker will specifically formulate the law or leave the task to the jury. Fleming James, Jr., Geoffrey C. Hazard, Jr. & John Leubsdorf, Civil Procedure 433–35, 451 (5th ed. 2001). Thus, the prevailing approach today in negligence cases commits to the jury the application of the objective community standard of what the reasonably prudent person would do in the circumstances, but the judge tends to play a much bigger role in actions for malicious prosecution. What are the considerations of policy that explain this difference?

Although the line between what is law for the court and what is fact for the jury is not always bright and clear, reversals are not uncommon for leaving to the jury questions that the judge should have decided or for committing the converse error. In Savannah, F. & W. Ry. v. Daniels, 90 Ga. 608, 17 S.E. 647 (1892), a statute prescribed a speed limit for a train crossing "any drawbridge over a stream." In a negligence action the trial judge left it to the jury whether the term included the trestles and approaches or only the bridge proper, of which the "draw" or movable section forms a part. This was held to be error. But suppose the action were one on a written contract to paint a certain "drawbridge." Does it necessarily follow that in an action for breach of contract the meaning of the term is for the court? It may be that extrinsic evidence is necessary to determine what the parties meant or to resolve an ambiguity. Or it may be contended that the parties contracted in the light of a trade usage giving words other than their natural meaning. If the proffered evidence does not run afoul of the parol evidence rule, it is for the jury to resolve conflicts in the evidence on such matters, these situations being recognized as exceptions to the general rule that interpretation of writings is for the judge. See Western Petroleum Co. v. Tidal Gasoline Co., 284 F. 82 (7th Cir.1922) ("tank wagon price").

Question: (2) Does the Seventh Amendment restrict the division of functions here? Or is the lawmaker free to redefine the law/fact line and so move toward ousting the jury, say, in libel cases or in complex actions? Compare Colleen P. Murphy, Integrating the Constitutional Authority of Civil and Criminal Juries, 61 Geo.Wash.L.Rev. 723, 754 (1993) (arguing that by text, precedent, and policy, Seventh Amendment's role here is to preserve the "essence" or "substance" of the jury), with Paul F. Kirgis, The Right to a Jury Decision on Questions of Fact Under the Seventh Amendment, 64 Ohio St.L.J. 1125, 1125 (2003) (looking to history to argue that under the Seventh Amendment "questions requiring inductive inferences about the transactions or occurrences in dispute are 'fact' questions, which must be decided by the jury in appropriate cases"). Note that any law/fact line could be a restraint separate from the Seventh Amendment's loose procedural-incident preservation that we have been applying until here in this Part, but also separate from the demands of the law/equity line that we shall study later in this Part.

Markman v. Westview Instruments, Inc.

Supreme Court of the United States, 1996.
517 U.S. 370, 116 S.Ct. 1384.

■ JUSTICE SOUTER delivered the opinion of the Court.

The question here is whether the interpretation of a so-called patent claim, the portion of the patent document that defines the scope of the patentee's rights, is a matter of law reserved entirely for the court, or subject to a Seventh Amendment guarantee that a jury will determine the meaning of any disputed term of art about which expert testimony is offered. We hold that the construction of a patent, including terms of art within its claim, is exclusively within the province of the court.

I

. . . It has long been understood that a patent must describe the exact scope of an invention and its manufacture to "secure to [the patentee] all to which he is entitled, [and] to apprise the public of what is still open to them." McClain v. Ortmayer, 141 U.S. 419, 424, 12 S.Ct. 76, 77 (1891). Under the modern American system, these objectives are served by two distinct elements of a patent document. First, it contains a specification describing the invention "in such full, clear, concise, and exact terms as to enable any person skilled in the art . . . to make and use the same." 35 U.S.C. § 112; see also 3 E. Lipscomb, Walker on Patents § 10:1, pp. 183–184 (3d ed. 1985) (Lipscomb) (listing the requirements for a specification). Second, a patent includes one or more "claims," which "particularly poin[t] out and distinctly clai[m] the subject matter which the applicant regards as his invention." 35 U.S.C. § 112. . . .

. . . .

Petitioner in this infringement suit, Markman, owns United States Reissue Patent No. 33,054 for his "Inventory Control and Reporting System for Drycleaning Stores." The patent describes a system that can monitor and report the status, location, and movement of clothing in a dry-cleaning establishment. The Markman system consists of a keyboard and data processor to generate written records for each transaction, including a bar code readable by optical detectors operated by employees, who log the progress of clothing through the dry-cleaning process. Respondent Westview's product also includes a keyboard and processor, and it lists charges for the dry-cleaning services on bar-coded tickets that can be read by portable optical detectors.

Markman brought an infringement suit against Westview and Althon Enterprises, an operator of dry-cleaning establishments using Westview's products (collectively, Westview). Westview responded that Markman's patent is not infringed by its system because the latter functions merely to record an inventory of receivables by tracking invoices and transaction totals, rather than to record and track an inventory of articles of clothing. Part of the dispute hinged upon the meaning of the word "inventory," a term found in Markman's independent claim 1, which states that Markman's product can "maintain an inventory total" and "detect and localize spurious additions to inventory." The case was tried before a jury, which heard, among others, a witness produced by Markman who testified about the meaning of the claim language.

After the jury compared the patent to Westview's device, it found an infringement . . . . The District Court nevertheless granted Westview's deferred motion for judgment as a matter of law, one of its reasons being that the term "inventory" in Markman's patent encompasses "both cash inventory and the actual physical inventory of articles of clothing." 772 F.Supp. 1535, 1537–1538 (E.D.Pa.1991). Under the trial court's construction of the patent, the production, sale, or use of a tracking system for dry cleaners would not infringe Markman's patent unless the product was capable of tracking articles of clothing throughout the cleaning process and generating reports about their status and location. Since Westview's system cannot do these things, the District Court directed a verdict on the ground that Westview's device does not have the "means to maintain an inventory total" and thus cannot "detect and localize spurious additions to inventory as well as spurious deletions therefrom," as required by claim 1. Id., at 1537.

Markman appealed, arguing it was error for the District Court to substitute its construction of the disputed claim term "inventory" for the construction the jury had presumably given it. The United States Court of Appeals for the Federal Circuit affirmed, holding the interpretation of claim terms to be the exclusive province of the court and the Seventh Amendment to be consistent with that conclusion. 52 F.3d 967 (1995). Markman sought our review on each point, and we granted certiorari. 116 S.Ct. 40 (1995). We now affirm.

II

The Seventh Amendment provides that "[i]n Suits at common law, where the value in controversy shall exceed twenty dollars, the right of trial by jury shall be preserved. . . ." U.S. Const., Amdt. 7. Since Justice Story's day, United States v. Wonson, 28 F.Cas. 745, 750 (No. 16,750) (CC Mass.1812), we have understood that "[t]he right of trial by jury thus preserved is the right which existed under the English common law when the Amendment was adopted." Baltimore & Carolina Line, Inc. v. Redman, 295 U.S. 654, 657, 55 S.Ct. 890, 891 (1935). In keeping with our long-standing adherence to this "historical test," Wolfram, The Constitutional History of the Seventh Amendment, 57 Minn.L.Rev. 639, 640–643 (1973), we ask, first, whether we are dealing with a cause of action that either was tried at law at the time of the Founding or is at least analogous to one that was, see, e.g., Tull v. United States, 481 U.S. 412, 417, 107 S.Ct. 1831, 1835 (1987). If the action in question belongs in the law category, we then ask whether the particular trial decision must fall to the jury in order to preserve the substance of the common-law right as it existed in 1791. . . .

A

As to the first issue, going to the character of the cause of action, "[t]he form of our analysis is familiar. 'First we compare the statutory action to 18th-century actions brought in the courts of England prior to the merger of the courts of law and equity.' " Granfinanciera, S.A. v. Nordberg, 492 U.S. 33, 42, 109 S.Ct. 2782, 2790 (1989) (citation omitted). Equally familiar is the descent of today's patent infringement action from the infringement actions tried at law in the 18th century, and there is no dispute that infringement cases today must be tried to a jury, as their predecessors were more than two centuries ago. See, e.g., Bramah v. Hardcastle, 1 Carp. P.C. 168 (K.B.1789).

B

This conclusion raises the second question, whether a particular issue occurring within a jury trial (here the construction of a patent claim) is itself necessarily a jury issue, the guarantee being essential to preserve the right to a jury's resolution of the ultimate dispute. In some instances the answer to this second question may be easy because of clear historical evidence that the very subsidiary question was so regarded under the English practice of leaving the issue for a jury. But when, as here, the old practice provides no clear answer, . . . we are forced to make a judgment about the scope of the Seventh Amendment guarantee without the benefit of any foolproof test.

The Court has repeatedly said that the answer to the second question "must depend on whether the jury must shoulder this responsibility *as necessary to preserve the 'substance of the common-law right of trial by jury.'* " Tull v. United States, supra, at 426, 107 S.Ct., at 1840 (emphasis added) (quoting Colgrove v. Battin, 413 U.S. 149, 156, 93 S.Ct. 2448, 2452 (1973)); see also Baltimore & Carolina Line, supra, at 657, 55 S.Ct., at 891. " 'Only those incidents which are regarded as fundamental, as inherent in and of the essence of the system of trial by jury, are placed beyond the reach of the legislature.' " Tull v. United States, supra, at 426, 107 S.Ct., at 1840 (citations omitted); see also Galloway v. United States, 319 U.S. 372, 392, 63 S.Ct. 1077, 1088 (1943).

The "substance of the common-law right" is, however, a pretty blunt instrument for drawing distinctions. We have tried to sharpen it, to be sure, by reference to the distinction between substance and procedure. See Baltimore & Carolina Line, supra, at 657, 55 S.Ct., at 891; see also Galloway v. United States, supra, at 390–391, 63 S.Ct., at 1087–1088; Ex parte Peterson, 253 U.S. 300, 309, 40 S.Ct. 543, 546 (1920); Walker v. New Mexico & Southern Pacific R. Co., 165 U.S. 593, 596, 17 S.Ct. 421, 422 (1897); but see Sun Oil Co. v. Wortman, 486 U.S. 717, 727, 108 S.Ct. 2117,

2124 (1988). We have also spoken of the line as one between issues of fact and law. See Baltimore & Carolina Line, supra, at 657, 55 S.Ct., at 891; see also Ex parte Peterson, supra, at 310, 40 S.Ct., at 546; Walker v. New Mexico & Southern Pacific R. Co., supra, at 597, 17 S.Ct., at 422; but see Pullman–Standard v. Swint, 456 U.S. 273, 288, 102 S.Ct. 1781, 1789 (1982).

But the sounder course, when available, is to classify a mongrel practice (like construing a term of art following receipt of evidence) by using the historical method, much as we do in characterizing the suits and actions within which they arise. Where there is no exact antecedent, the best hope lies in comparing the modern practice to earlier ones whose allocation to court or jury we do know, cf. Baltimore & Carolina Line, supra, at 659, 660, 55 S.Ct., at 892, 893; Dimick v. Schiedt, 293 U.S. 474, 477, 482, 55 S.Ct. 296, 297 (1935), seeking the best analogy we can draw between an old and the new, see Tull v. United States, supra, at 420–421, 107 S.Ct., at 1836–1837 (we must search the English common law for "appropriate analogies" rather than a "precisely analogous common-law cause of action").

C

"Prior to 1790 nothing in the nature of a claim had appeared either in British patent practice or in that of the American states," Lutz, Evolution of the Claims of U.S. Patents, 20 J.Pat.Off.Soc. 134 (1938), and we have accordingly found no direct antecedent of modern claim construction in the historical source. . . .

. . . .

The closest 18th-century analogue of modern claim construction seems, then, to have been the construction of specifications, and as to that function the mere smattering of patent cases that we have from this period shows no established jury practice sufficient to support an argument by analogy that today's construction of a claim should be a guaranteed jury issue. Few of the case reports even touch upon the proper interpretation of disputed terms in the specifications at issue, [citations omitted], and none demonstrates that the definition of such a term was determined by the jury. This absence of an established practice should not surprise us, given the primitive state of jury patent practice at the end of the 18th century, when juries were still new to the field. . . .

. . . There is no more reason to infer that juries supplied plenary interpretation of written instruments in patent litigation than in other cases implicating the meaning of documentary terms, and we do know that in other kinds of cases during this period judges, not juries, ordinarily construed written documents. The probability that the judges were doing the same thing in the patent litigation of the time is confirmed by the fact that as soon as the English reports did begin to describe the construction of patent documents, they show the judges construing the terms of the specifications. [Citations omitted.] This evidence is in fact buttressed by cases from this Court; when they first reveal actual practice, the practice revealed is of the judge construing the patent. See, e.g. Winans v. New York

& Erie R. Co., 21 How. 88, 100 (1859); Winans v. Denmead, 15 How. 330, 338 (1854); Hogg v. Emerson, 6 How. 437, 484 (1848); cf. Parker v. Hulme, 18 F.Cas. 1138 (No. 10,740) (CC ED Pa.1849). These indications of our patent practice are the more impressive for being all of a piece with what we know about the analogous contemporary practice of interpreting terms within a land patent, where it fell to the judge, not the jury, to construe the words.

. . . .

III

Since evidence of common law practice at the time of the Framing does not entail application of the Seventh Amendment's jury guarantee to the construction of the claim document, we must look elsewhere to characterize this determination of meaning in order to allocate it as between court or jury. We accordingly consult existing precedent[10] and consider both the relative interpretive skills of judges and juries and the statutory policies that ought to be furthered by the allocation.

A

The two elements of a simple patent case, construing the patent and determining whether infringement occurred, were characterized by the former patent practitioner, Justice Curtis. "The first is a question of law, to be determined by the court, construing the letters-patent, and the description of the invention and specification of claim annexed to them. The second is a question of fact, to be submitted to a jury." Winans v. Denmead, 15 How., at 338; see Winans v. New York & Erie R. Co., 21 How., at 100; Hogg v. Emerson, supra, at 484; cf. Parker v. Hulme, supra, at 1140.

. . . .

B

Where history and precedent provide no clear answers, functional considerations also play their part in the choice between judge and jury to define terms of art. We said in Miller v. Fenton, 474 U.S. 104, 114, 106 S.Ct. 445, 451 (1985), that when an issue "falls somewhere between a pristine legal standard and a simple historical fact, the fact/law distinction at times has turned on a determination that, as a matter of the sound administration of justice, one judicial actor is better positioned than another to decide the issue in question." So it turns out here, for judges, not juries, are the better suited to find the acquired meaning of patent terms.

The construction of written instruments is one of those things that judges often do and are likely to do better than jurors unburdened by

---

10 Because we conclude that our precedent supports classifying the question as one for the court, we need not decide either the extent to which the Seventh Amendment can be said to have crystallized a law/fact distinction, cf. Ex parte Peterson, 253 U.S. 300, 310, 40 S.Ct. 543, 546 (1920); Walker v. New Mexico & Southern Pacific R. Co., 165 U.S. 593, 597, 17 S.Ct. 421, 422 (1897), or whether post–1791 precedent classifying an issue as one of fact would trigger the protections of the Seventh Amendment if (unlike this case) there were no more specific reason for decision.

training in exegesis. Patent construction in particular "is a special occupation, requiring, like all others, special training and practice. The judge, from his training and discipline, is more likely to give a proper interpretation to such instruments than a jury; and he is, therefore, more likely to be right, in performing such a duty, than a jury can be expected to be." Parker v. Hulme, 18 F.Cas., at 1140. Such was the understanding nearly a century and a half ago, and there is no reason to weigh the respective strengths of judge and jury differently in relation to the modern claim; quite the contrary, for "the claims of patents have become highly technical in many respects as the result of special doctrines relating to the proper form and scope of claims that have been developed by the courts and the Patent Office." Woodward, Definiteness and Particularity in Patent Claims, 46 Mich.L.Rev. 755, 765 (1948).

Markman would trump these considerations with his argument that a jury should decide a question of meaning peculiar to a trade or profession simply because the question is a subject of testimony requiring credibility determinations, which are the jury's forte. It is, of course, true that credibility judgments have to be made about the experts who testify in patent cases, and in theory there could be a case in which a simple credibility judgment would suffice to choose between experts whose testimony was equally consistent with a patent's internal logic. But our own experience with document construction leaves us doubtful that trial courts will run into many cases like that. In the main, we expect, any credibility determinations will be subsumed within the necessarily sophisticated analysis of the whole document, required by the standard construction rule that a term can be defined only in a way that comports with the instrument as a whole. [Citations omitted.] Thus, in these cases a jury's capabilities to evaluate demeanor, cf. Miller, supra, at 114, 117, 106 S.Ct., at 451, 453, to sense the "mainsprings of human conduct," Commissioner v. Duberstein, 363 U.S. 278, 289, 80 S.Ct. 1190, 1198 (1960), or to reflect community standards, United States v. McConney, 728 F.2d 1195, 1204 (C.A.9 1984) (en banc), are much less significant than a trained ability to evaluate the testimony in relation to the overall structure of the patent. The decisionmaker vested with the task of construing the patent is in the better position to ascertain whether an expert's proposed definition fully comports with the specification and claims and so will preserve the patent's internal coherence. We accordingly think there is sufficient reason to treat construction of terms of art like many other responsibilities that we cede to a judge in the normal course of trial, notwithstanding its evidentiary underpinnings.

C

Finally, we see the importance of uniformity in the treatment of a given patent as an independent reason to allocate all issues of construction to the court. . . .

Uniformity would, however, be ill served by submitting issues of document construction to juries. . . . [T]reating interpretive issues as purely legal will promote (though it will not guarantee) intrajurisdictional certainty through the application of stare decisis on those questions not yet subject to interjurisdictional uniformity under the authority of the single appeals court.

* * *

Accordingly, we hold that the interpretation of the word "inventory" in this case is an issue for the judge, not the jury, and affirm the decision of the Court of Appeals for the Federal Circuit.

It is so ordered.

SECTION 2. INSTRUCTIONS BY JUDGE

General approaches.—At common law the trial judge was under a duty to instruct the jury on the law, whether or not the parties made any requests to charge. He would commonly sum up the evidence, indicating how the rules of law should be applied to the findings of fact the jury might make. He could also comment on the credibility of the witnesses and the weight of the evidence, giving his own opinion on these matters, provided he made clear to the jurors that the ultimate decision was theirs. The instructions came following the arguments of counsel and before the jury retired to deliberate.

The federal courts and some state courts still adhere in large part to the common-law tradition, but many states have departed from it in various ways, primarily as part of an old popular movement to diminish the role of the judge and increase that of the jury. In several states, the charge must precede the arguments of counsel. There are provisions in the majority of states, some of them in state constitutions, forbidding comment on the evidence. A good many states do not even allow the judge to sum up the evidence. Some do not require instructions on the law governing the case generally but only upon points covered by specific requests. All these rules are considered procedural matters as to which state law is not controlling in federal court.

Delivering the instructions.—The differences from state to state are so great that generalizations on framing instructions to the jury are difficult. See generally Fleming James, Jr., Geoffrey C. Hazard, Jr. & John Leubsdorf, Civil Procedure 451–57 (5th ed. 2001). Following are a few guiding ideas widely, but not universally, applied. These generalizations do accord with the federal approach. See generally 1 Kevin F. O'Malley, Jay E. Grenig & William C. Lee, Federal Jury Practice and Instructions 455–531 (5th ed. 2000).

1. The trial judge must tell the jury what questions of fact it has to decide. The judge typically instructs the jury, even in the absence of requests, on the rules of law applicable generally to the case and necessary

to the jury's task. The judge may instruct the jurors on how practically they should proceed with their task. For an illustration of the difficulties in framing the law for the jury, see Catherine T. Struve, Constitutional Decision Rules for Juries, 37 Colum.Hum.Rts.L.Rev. 659 (2006).

2. It is error to give an instruction that assumes as true a disputed proposition of fact. To illustrate, in Barnett v. H.L. Green Co., 233 Ala. 453, 171 So. 911 (1936), the charge in an assault case was: "I charge you, gentlemen of the jury, if you believe from the evidence that the defendant . . . used no more force than was necessary to repel the attack, your verdict cannot be for the plaintiff." There had been a sharp conflict in the evidence as to whether the plaintiff did attack the defendant. The charge was held to be error.

Questions: (3) How should the instruction on this point have been framed?

(4) A Nebraska statute provided that "the fact that the plaintiff may have been guilty of contributory negligence shall not bar a recovery when the contributory negligence of the plaintiff was slight and the negligence . . . of the defendant was gross in comparison." The trial judge instructed the jury as follows: "If you find negligence on the part of the plaintiff but that such negligence of the plaintiff was slight in comparison with the gross negligence of the defendant, then you will find for the plaintiff." In what way was the instruction erroneous? How should it have been framed? See Pratt v. Western Bridge & Constr. Co., 116 Neb. 553, 218 N.W. 397 (1928).

3. The correctness of a particular statement is not to be determined from the isolated language. The charge is to be taken as a whole in the light of the evidence.

4. The trial judge need not charge the jury in the precise language of any request even though it is a proper and correct statement of the law. A party has no vested right to the party's own carefully couched form of words. If the judge gives the substance of the request, there is no basis for complaint.

5. The trial judge must give specific instructions on the party's theory of the case if there is evidence to support it and if the party made timely request. The fact that the request is not strictly accurate in form or content should not be fatal. If the meaning is reasonably apparent and sufficiently calls the court's attention to the point, the court should instruct the jury with reference to it.

6. The trial judge is not required, however, to single out a part of all the evidence and give an instruction upon that part. The combinations of facts that the jury may find are likely to be so numerous that instructions cannot reasonably cover the legal effect of every fragment of the evidence upon which the jury might rest a finding. There is also the danger that singling out a particular fact and instructing upon it will lead the jury to believe it to be of greater weight than other unmentioned facts. Such undue emphasis may even constitute reversible error. (The obvious difficulties in application of this principle, in conjunction with that of the preceding generalization, are discussed in Barnes v. Berkshire Street Railway, 281 Mass. 47, 183 N.E. 416 (1932)).

7. The charge is delivered orally in open court. The trial judge may in his discretion also submit a copy of his instructions to the jury, but many judges do not do so. The charge may not be formally and completely written out in advance, and to await a stenographic transcript might cause delay. Moreover, there is danger that jurors might pick passages out of context and give them a distorted effect. If during deliberations the jury is in doubt about the instructions given, it may request the judge to repeat a portion of the charge or give a supplemental charge.

Questions: (5) What do you think of giving the retiring jury a tape recording of the charge? See United States v. Watson, 669 F.2d 1374, 1385–87 (11th Cir.1982) (not reversible error).

(6) What of giving specific instructions at the outset and periodically throughout the trial? See Janice C. Goldberg, Comment, Memory, Magic, and Myth: The Timing of Jury Instructions, 59 Or.L.Rev. 451 (1981).

(7) What of advising the jurors that they may take notes during the trial? See Leonard B. Sand & Steven A. Reiss, A Report on Seven Experiments Conducted by District Court Judges in the Second Circuit, 60 N.Y.U.L.Rev. 423, 446–53 (1985).

(8) What of permitting the jurors to discuss the evidence among themselves during the trial? See Jessica L. Bregant, Note, Let's Give Them Something to Talk About: An Empirical Evaluation of Predeliberation Discussions, 2009 U.Ill.L.Rev. 1213.

(9) What of letting the jurors ask questions of the trial judge and, through the judge, of witnesses and counsel? See Shari Seidman Diamond, Mary R. Rose, Beth Murphy & Sven Smith, Juror Questions During Trial: A Window into Juror Thinking, 59 Vand.L.Rev. 1925 (2006). But see Richard S. Walinski, The ABA's New Vision of the Jury's Function: An Opposing View, Litigation, Spring 2006, at 5 (arguing that this reform would fundamentally change trial from a test of the parties' evidence into an unguided search for truth; for example, it is incompatible with the notion of burden of proof, because jurors may expect answers from the unburdened party).

(10) How else could the scheme for giving instructions be improved? See generally Joel D. Lieberman, The Psychology of the Jury Instruction Process, in Jury Psychology 129 (Joel D. Lieberman & Daniel A. Krauss eds., 2009). Apparently, federal judges have considerable discretion in these matters, but most of the above-suggested changes have not been widely implemented or encouraged. Why not? Because the benefits are negligible? Or because the costs outweigh the benefits? Or is it because the need for reform is unperceived? Or because we do not want to perceive the need? See generally Nancy S. Marder, Bringing Jury Instructions into the Twenty-first Century, 81 Notre Dame L.Rev. 449 (2006).

Commenting on the evidence.—At common law and now where comment is permitted, it must be fair: the judge must not assume the advocate's role. Reversals for prejudicial comments do occur. Compare Virginian Ry. v. Armentrout, 166 F.2d 400 (4th Cir.1948) (reversal for "an argumentative presentation of the case which must necessarily have prejudiced defendant's cause"), with Trezza v. Dame, 370 F.2d 1006 (5th Cir.1967) (comments leaving no doubt of judge's conclusion that defendant was negligent "came dangerously close to usurping the function of the jury" and "would have been better left unsaid," but were not prejudicial in light of the strong evidence and the instruction that jury was free to disagree with judge). See generally Jack B. Weinstein, The Power and Duty of Federal Judges to Marshall and Comment on the Evidence in Jury Trials and Some Suggestions on Charging Juries, 118 F.R.D. 161 (1988).

In Commonwealth v. Barry, 91 Mass. (9 Allen) 276 (1864), the defendant's counsel in his argument to the jury made adverse comments as to the testimony of policemen. The judge told the jury that the same rules were applicable to policemen as to other witnesses in determining their credibility, adding that policemen had testified in many cases tried during that term of court and he thought the jury would agree with him that in these cases they had manifested great intelligence and testified with apparent candor and impartiality. The Supreme Judicial Court reversed for comment on the evidence, which Massachusetts does not permit.

It should be noted that the Barry judge could have achieved much the same effect by a generalized statement that the jury is entitled to consider as to all witnesses their interest or lack of it in the outcome, their training and experience in observation, and the like. Furthermore, a judge could, if so disposed, convey views to the jury by a tone of voice or gesture that a stenographic transcript does not reveal. See Note, Judges' Nonverbal Behavior in Jury Trials: A Threat to Judicial Impartiality, 61 Va.L.Rev. 1266 (1975).

Question: (11) What do you think of requiring a videotape of the charge to be made part of the record on appeal?

Many judges in jurisdictions where the power to comment on the evidence exists exercise it only infrequently. The existence of the power to comment then serves mainly as a shield against reversal when the trial judge, perhaps inadvertently, says something that may be construed as a comment on credibility or weight.

Judicial efforts to induce unanimity.—Until recently it was accepted without question that the jury right preserved by the Seventh Amendment entitled a party in a federal civil case to a unanimous verdict of twelve jurors. As we have seen, however, the number of twelve jurors is no longer sacrosanct. So far there has been no federal authority for dispensing with the unanimity requirement other than by stipulation of the parties pursuant to Rule 48(b), but well more than half of the states permit a less than unanimous verdict in a civil case.

Question: (12) What effect would you expect this disparity between state and federal courts to have on the choice of forum, either originally or by removal?

Provisions for a nonunanimous verdict reflect an awareness of the hazard of frustration of a trial by a minority of the jurors persistently holding out. Sometimes use of the judge's power to comment on the evidence may help to achieve unanimity. Another and more obvious means is by a supplemental charge after it appears that a disagreement is imminent.

In Railway Express Agency v. Mackay, 181 F.2d 257 (8th Cir.1950), after lengthy deliberation, a rereading of the original charge, and still further deliberation, the trial judge gave the following additional instruction: "This is an important case. The trial has been long and expensive. Your failure to agree upon a verdict will necessitate another trial equally as expensive. The Court is of the opinion that the case cannot be again tried better or more exhaustively than it has been on either side. It is therefore very desirable that you should agree upon a verdict. The Court does not desire that any juror should surrender his or her conscientious convictions. On the other hand, each juror should perform his or her duty conscientiously and honestly according to the law and the evidence. And although the verdict to which a juror agrees must, of course, be his or her own verdict, the result of his or her own convictions and not a mere acquiescence in the conclusions of his or her fellows, yet in order to bring twelve minds to a unanimous result you must examine the questions submitted to you with candor and with a proper regard and deference to the opinions of each other. You should consider that the case must at some time be decided, that you are selected in the same manner and from the same source from which any future jury must be, and there is no reason to suppose that the case will ever be submitted to twelve men and women more intelligent, more impartial or more competent to decide it; or that more or clearer evidence will be produced on one side or the other. You may conduct your deliberations as you choose, but I suggest you now retire and carefully consider again the evidence in this case." The appellate court rejected the objection to this instruction as being coercive in character.

This type of charge, often termed the "Allen charge" because of the approval of its use in Allen v. United States, 164 U.S. 492, 17 S.Ct. 154 (1896), and sometimes the "dynamite charge," the "hammer charge," the "third-degree instruction," or the "shotgun instruction," has been used much more frequently in criminal than in civil cases. It has come under heavy criticism on the criminal side and has indeed been banned for such purpose in some jurisdictions. See 2A Wright § 502. However, "[t]he noisy controversy that arose a number of years ago about the use of the charge upheld in Allen v. United States in criminal cases has not reached the civil side of the docket." 9C Wright & Miller § 2556, at 135. The Fifth Circuit reapproved the Allen charge in civil cases "if it makes clear to members of the jury that (1) they are duty bound to adhere to honest opinions; (2) they are doing nothing improper by maintaining a good faith opinion even though a mistrial may result." Brooks v. Bay State Abrasive Prods., Inc., 516 F.2d 1003, 1004 (5th Cir.1975).

Questions: (13) After protracted deliberations in a personal-injury action, the trial judge gives a supplemental charge that includes the following: "And now if a jury is unable to reach a verdict that is satisfactory, it seems to me that that constitutes a black eye on our system of Government. It is really an encouragement to the Communists and the other people who would like to overthrow our system of Government." Is this reversible error? See Weinell v. McKeesport Connecting R.R. Co., 411 F.2d 510 (3d Cir.1969) (yes).

A trial judge trying to produce jury unanimity and anxious to avoid reversal is likely to quote verbatim an Allen charge that has been sustained by the appellate court, even though that court may have conceded that the charge approached the limits of propriety.

Questions: (14) An instruction like that in Railway Express Agency v. Mackay is given to a jury that has already deliberated for fifty hours in a personal-injury action. After twenty hours more, the jury returns a verdict for the plaintiff. Should the defendant's objection to the instruction and to the action of the court in holding the jury together for the additional hours be sustained on appeal? See Clemens v. Chicago, R.I. & P. Ry., 163 Iowa 499, 144 N.W. 354 (1913) (yes). What if instead of waiting twenty hours the judge had simply given the supplemental Allen charge a second time after a few hours, and the jury then went for the plaintiff?

(15) After protracted deliberations in a personal-injury action, the trial judge for the first time uses her power to comment on the evidence. Is this reversible error? See People v. Cook, 33 Cal.3d 400, 658 P.2d 86, 189 Cal.Rptr. 159 (1983) (yes, in criminal case), overruled, People v. Rodriguez, 42 Cal.3d 730, 726 P.2d 113, 230 Cal.Rptr. 667 (1986).

PLAIN ERROR

Normally, in order to preserve alleged error for appellate review, objection must be made promptly to the giving of an instruction or the failure to give one. In some states, the party must still take a formal "exception." In the federal courts and the states following the federal pattern, a specific objection is sufficient, but the party must state "distinctly" the objection and the grounds for it. Rule 51(c)(1); see Rule 46.

The purpose of requiring the objection, which the party makes out of the hearing of the jury, is to give the judge a fair opportunity to correct any error he may have made. It follows that a general objection "to the refusals to charge as requested" does not serve the intended purpose and is ordinarily insufficient to present any question for review. See Rogers v. Long Island R.R. Co., 29 A.D.2d 47, 285 N.Y.S.2d 803 (1967), aff'd, 22 N.Y.2d 918, 242 N.E.2d 84, 295 N.Y.S.2d 47 (1968). It is a questionable game, and one not likely to succeed, for counsel to try to make the objection specific enough to preserve error but still not so specific as to alert the judge to his error.

Nevertheless, appellate courts reserve the right in the interest of justice—more in the public's interest than in the party's forfeited interest—to reverse for "plain error" in instructions that affected substantial rights, even though no objection was made. Rule 51(d)(2). The plain error doctrine is invoked most often in connection with faulty instructions, but sometimes for other errors.

The power to reverse for plain error is an exception to the adversary principle of party-presentation, which sticks a party with a formulation or application of the law to which it fails to object. Although any such power could reflect appellate whim and so be difficult to restrain, the cases suggest that this power is very sparingly exercised and normally will be invoked only to correct an obvious error that caused a miscarriage of justice. See, e.g., Nimrod v. Sylvester, 369 F.2d 870, 873 (1st Cir.1966) (finding no plain error).

In sum, the plain error doctrine, as applied, requires a clear and convincing showing of reversible error as well as of the error's net harm to the public interest if left uncorrected. Although in applying it a court will often stress the harm to the appellant, the court in effect does so only in measuring the harm to the system. But the court will apply the doctrine only to the appellant's earlier "forfeiture" by omitting timely assertion of a right, rather than a "waiver" by voluntary and intentional relinquishment of a known right.

Question: (16) In an action on a life insurance policy, the judge instructs the jury that to establish a defense the insurer must show by a "fair preponderance of the credible evidence" that the insured's statements in applying for the policy were fraudulent. In fact, the controlling law requires "clear, precise, and indubitable" evidence. No specific objection is made to the charge as given. The jury finds that the statements were fraudulent. Should the error be considered on appeal? See Ratay v. Lincoln Nat'l Life Ins. Co., 378 F.2d 209 (3d Cir.1967) (yes).

SECTION 3. DELIBERATIONS BY JURY

J. Alexander Tanford, An Introduction to Trial Law

51 Mo.L.Rev. 623, 700 (1986).

Perhaps more surprising than the discovery that jurors are not routinely allowed to take all exhibits with them [into the jury room] is the discovery that they are not permitted to use their own personal experiences as a basis for decision. Jurors are encouraged to use *common* experience, but are prohibited from becoming a kind of "expert witness" and telling other jurors about their own unique experiences, making the assumption that it was similar to what happened in the case being tried. For example, a juror may not properly discuss how severe his own back pain was in evaluating how severe the plaintiff's pain is; nor bring expertise from his or her employment into the deliberations. This injects information into the case that is not part of the evidence, and is usually considered error. It also is undoubtedly one of the most frequently violated rules of trial procedure, and one of the most difficult violations to detect.

Jeffrey T. Frederick, The Psychology of the American Jury

278–81, 285–87 (1987).

Stages of deliberations. If you have ever had the opportunity to hear a jury deliberate (ethically, not in a real trial) you are likely to come away from it with the impression that these deliberations represent a random exchange of opinions among jurors. However, juries, like other small groups, follow a pattern in their discussions which is composed of four different phases. The first phase of the deliberations is the *orientation phase,* where jurors elect the foreman, set out the task at hand, and provide their tentative positions on the issues. This phase is characterized by statements made by the jurors which reveal their personal opinions and preferences. Once these initial preferences are presented and differences are revealed, the jury proceeds to the *open conflict phase* of deliberations. In this phase jurors become aware of which jurors or groups of jurors disagree with them and they direct their comments to these jurors. This phase is characterized by relatively rigid statements aimed at convincing opposing jurors of the incorrectness of their positions.

The third phase is the *conflict resolution phase.* If the jury is going to come to a decision, the jurors eventually begin to realize which verdict possibilities are more likely to yield agreement. Jurors' comments shift from firm position statements to more open and less rigid statements, reflecting the potential for change toward the dominant verdict preference. Finally, provided that an agreement will be reached (or if agreement is impossible but animosity has not reached high levels), deliberations enter the *reconciliation phase.* In this phase, jurors' comments are directed toward mutual support and consensus. Attempts will be made to heal the wounds produced in the conflict and group solidarity is emphasized.

. . . .

Informational and normative influence. In considering the process by which jurors arrive at a verdict it is necessary to address two major influences which operate in group decisionmaking: informational influence and normative influence. Informational influence refers to the changing of an opinion as a result of the exchange of information in the group. Through deliberation, jurors become aware of information that they may have forgotten or not have given the same weight as did other members of the jury. Normative influence, on the other hand, refers to the change in opinion as a result of conforming to the desires or preferences of other members of the group. Research on conformity has indicated that majorities can exert strong pressures on individuals to adopt the majority view, even when the majority position is obviously incorrect. Thus, through deliberations, the majority of jurors can also exert pressure on minority members to change their opinions in order to conform to the majority view.

Both informational and normative influences have been found to be present in jury deliberations. In terms of relative dominance, informational influence has received greater support in its impact on jury decisions. That is, the exchange of information and arguments in favor of the majority position appear to exert a greater influence on decisions than simply a minority's desire not to be seen as deviant. However, to view informational and normative influences as competitive is misleading. The communication from the majority to the minority contains both types of influence. Not only do majority members state their positions (normative influence) but they also provide information and arguments as to why their position is "correct" (informational influence).

Finally, one point should be made regarding normative influence. Normative influences would be expected to achieve their greatest impact when the minority consists of one juror. As indicated in the extensive research on conformity, the presence of just one other minority member (even if there is disagreement between them) drastically reduces the pressure to conform.

. . . .

A final consideration regarding deliberations is their outcome. While the process and outcome of deliberations are closely tied together, there are two general findings which are directly concerned with deliberation outcomes. These findings involve the topics of group polarization and majority effects.

Group polarization. One finding that has been prevalent in the area of group decisionmaking is the tendency for group decisions to be more extreme than individual decisions. This finding has been labeled polarization because of the tendency of individuals to shift to more extreme decisions as a result of group discussion. If a decision is considered to be on a single bipolar continuum, with one endpoint representing one extreme (e.g., absolute certainty of guilt or harsh punishment) and the other endpoint representing the other extreme (e.g., absolute certainty of innocence or lenient punishment) with the midpoint reflecting a neutral opinion (or moderate treatment), when the opinions of members of the group fall on one side or the other of the neutral/midpoint, group discussions tend to shift the group and the individuals' final decisions toward the more extreme end of the decision continuum. The group polarization effect has been found to operate in jury decisionmaking as well. When cases are predominantly against the defendant, jurors have been found to ascribe greater guilt, favor greater punishment, and to convict the defendant of a more serious offense as a result of deliberations. . . .

. . . It appears that the group polarization effect as reflected in jury decisionmaking is a function of information exchanged in deliberations. When juries are predominantly on one side or the other on the issue of guilt, the information exchanged is predominantly one-sided in these discussions that serve to reinforce the individual's verdict preference. . . .

Majority effect. In addition to the general finding of a group polarization effect with deliberations, research has indicated that the final decision can be predicted fairly accurately by knowing the initial distribution of verdict preferences at the start of deliberations. Kalven and Zeisel noted that, based on post-trial interviews of actual jurors, the initial majority on the first ballot is determinative of the final verdict [even under a unanimous decision rule]. This finding led them to postulate their radical hunch: "The deliberation process might well be likened to what the developer does for an exposed film: it brings out the picture, but the outcome is predetermined."[159]

---

[159] See H. Kalven and H. Zeisel, The American Jury (1966).

SECTION 4. VALIDITY OF VERDICT

Jorgensen v. York Ice Machinery Corp.

United States Circuit Court of Appeals, Second Circuit, 1947.
160 F.2d 432, cert. denied, 332 U.S. 764, 68 S.Ct. 69 (1947).

■ Before L. HAND, AUGUSTUS N. HAND and CLARK, CIRCUIT JUDGES.

■ L. HAND, CIRCUIT JUDGE. The plaintiff appeals from a judgment, entered on the verdict of a jury, dismissing his complaint in an action for personal injuries caused by the defendant's negligence; he also brings up an order denying his motion for a new trial. . . .

. . . .

On the motion for a new trial based . . . upon the misconduct of the jury, the following appeared by affidavits. One, Murphy, was foreman of the jury, and, on the morning of the last day of the trial before the summations, he received word at his home that his son, a lieutenant in the Navy, had been killed in action. He applied to the clerk of the court to have the trial postponed for a day, but the clerk told him that this could not be done; and neither counsel nor the court learned of the occurrence and the jury was sent out. Murphy and one other of the panel swore that during their deliberations the jury stood seven to five for the defendant and that this vote never changed. All the jurors learned of the death of Murphy's son and of his wish to rejoin his family as soon as possible; and, as they thought it likely that there would be a deadlock, one or more of them wished to announce to the judge their inability to agree. However, since others thought that this would only result in their being sent back, someone suggested that, as seven were for the defendant and only five for the plaintiff, they should return a verdict for the defendant. This they did; it was a compromise to avoid further discussion and to let the foreman return to his home. Murphy's affidavit also declared that he was "much upset mentally" at the time, that he thought the plaintiff should have a verdict, and that he consented to a verdict for the defendant because he felt that he ought to return home as soon as possible. The plaintiff's attorney added an affidavit saying that another of the jurors confirmed these facts to him. The judge considered the motion on its merits, but decided that the affidavits contained nothing which would justify setting aside the verdict.

. . . .

There remains the only question on the appeal which has any substance: the order denying a new trial because of the supposed misconduct of the jury. Such an order, though discretionary, is indeed at times appealable,[3] although the occasions are extremely rare.[4] The whole subject has been obscured, apparently beyond hope of clarification, by Lord Mansfield's

[3] Mattox v. United States, 146 U.S. 140, 13 S.Ct. 50, 36 L.Ed. 917.

[4] McDonald v. Pless, 238 U.S. 264, 35 S.Ct. 783, 59 L.Ed. 1300.

often quoted language in Vaise v. Delaval,[5] that no evidence of misconduct was competent which came from the jurors themselves, although, as judges have repeatedly pointed out, it is impossible to see from what source better evidence could be obtained.[6] On the other hand, it would be impracticable to impose the counsel of absolute perfection that no verdict shall stand, unless every juror has been entirely without bias, and has based his vote only upon evidence he has heard in court. It is doubtful whether more than one in a hundred verdicts would stand such a test; and although absolute justice may require as much, the impossibility of achieving it has induced judges to take a middle course, for they have recognized that the institution could not survive otherwise; they would become Penelopes, forever engaged in unravelling the webs they wove. Like much else in human affairs, its defects are so deeply enmeshed in the system that wholly to disentangle them would quite kill it. The discussion of Lamar, J., in McDonald v. Pless, supra, well states the necessary compromise . . . .

All this has, however, nothing to do with what evidence shall be competent to prove the facts when the facts do require the verdict to be set aside, as concededly some facts do. The two decisions of the Supreme Court which we have cited, as well as its approach in United States v. Reid[8] and Hyde v. United States,[9] suggest it as not improbable that when the question arises in the future, the testimony of the jurors may be held competent, and that we shall no longer hear that they may not "impeach their verdict," when it is "impeachable" if what they say is true. Maybe not; judges again and again repeat the consecrated rubric which has confused the subject; it offers an easy escape from embarrassing choices. In the case at bar at any rate we shall not dispose of the appeal in that way; we shall accept what the affidavits said, as did the judge, and like him we shall decide whether it requires the relief asked. Drunkenness, bribery, receiving incompetent documents, or privately interviewing a party, do require it; but there are many irregularities, which, however proved, do not, and among them is an agreement to abide by the vote of the majority.[10] Indeed, that is a no greater impropriety than a "quotient" verdict which the Supreme Court sustained in McDonald v. Pless, supra, and the Eighth Circuit in Manhattan Oil Co. v. Mosby.[11] Not only ought we not upset the

---

5 1 Term Rep. 11 [(K.B.1785). On a motion for a rule to set aside a verdict "upon an affidavit of two jurors, who swore that the jury, being divided in their opinion, tossed up, and that the plaintiff's friends won," the rule was refused. Chief Justice Mansfield said: "The Court cannot receive such an affidavit from any of the jurymen themselves, in all of whom such conduct is a very high misdemeanor: but in every such case the Court must derive their knowledge from some other source: such as from persons having seen the transaction through a window, or by some such other means."—Ed.]

6 Wigmore § 2353.

8 12 How. 361, 366, 13 L.Ed. 1023.

9 225 U.S. 347, 383, 32 S.Ct. 793, 56 L.Ed. 1114, Ann.Cas. 1914A, 614.

10 Fabris v. General Foods Corporation, 2 Cir., 152 F.2d 660.

11 72 F.2d 840. [The quotient method is one by which each juror indicates the damages award he favors, these amounts are totaled, and this total is divided by the number of jurors to yield the award reported out of the jury room. The point decided in the McDonald and

judge's discretion in refusing to grant a new trial for such a reason; but, had he granted the motion, and had his order been in some unknown way appealable, we should not have sustained it.

Judgment affirmed.

If there is a rigorous rule like that in Vaise v. Delaval excluding jurors' testimony to impeach their verdict, as there still is in some jurisdictions, then what is usually the one potential source of testimony is closed. And a hard question is ducked. However, it is true that the testimony of an eavesdropper as to jury misconduct can be received, as can physical evidence such as documents left in the jury room.

However, there is a growing trend in various jurisdictions to allow some juror testimony of misconduct. Neither the flat rule of Vaise v. Delaval nor allowance of unlimited inquiry of jurors—which would supposedly impede free discussion in the jury room, invite jury tampering and harassment, endanger every verdict even after judgment, and demean the jury system—appears satisfactory.

Authorities are in virtually total accord in excluding evidence of mental operations of jurors. As to objective misconduct, the line has frequently been drawn between misconduct inside the jury room (e.g., the toss of a coin; the advance agreement for a quotient verdict or a majority vote) and misconduct outside the jury room (e.g., taking an unauthorized view of the scene of an accident; talking with a party or counsel), with juror testimony as to the latter being admissible.

Federal Evidence Rule 606(b) instead draws the line between testimony as to mental and deliberative processes, on the one hand, and testimony as to improper intrusion of extraneous prejudicial information or outside influence, on the other hand, without regard to whether the happening is within or without the jury room. The Rule, as amended in 2006, also permits juror testimony that the verdict reported was the result of a clerical mistake, but the Advisory Committee's note says that this permission does not extend to juror misunderstandings of the law.

Question: (17) Under Evidence Rule 606(b), could a juror testify to the drunken condition of a fellow juror? That is, is alcohol an "outside influence"? See Tanner v. United States, 483 U.S. 107, 107 S.Ct. 2739 (1987) (no). Could a juror testify to another juror's discussion in the jury room of her personal experience as a victim of sex abuse? That is, does this constitute "extraneous prejudicial information"? See Lopez v. Aramark Uniform & Career Apparel, Inc., 417 F.Supp.2d 1062 (N.D.Iowa 2006) (no). Could a juror testify on the role played by the racial prejudice of a fellow juror? See 3 Christopher B. Mueller & Laird C. Kirkpatrick, Federal Evidence § 6:17, at 91–92 (3d ed. 2007) (probably not).

Manhattan Oil cases was that the jurors would not be allowed to impeach their verdict by giving evidence that they had used the quotient method.—Ed.]

The original Advisory Committee's note to Evidence Rule 606(b) stated: "This rule does not purport to specify the substantive grounds for setting aside verdicts for irregularity; it deals only with the competency of jurors to testify concerning those grounds."

By the way, as an alternative to excluding evidence from jurors or limiting the substantive grounds for relief, a different and popular approach is judicial exhortation, or even an order or local rule, aimed at preventing disclosure of jurors' deliberations in the first place. See Note, Public Disclosures of Jury Deliberations, 96 Harv.L.Rev. 886 (1983).

FREID v. McGRATH, 135 F.2d 833 (D.C.Cir.1943). A general verdict in a personal-injury action awarded plaintiff $425 against one defendant and $425 against the other defendant. The jurors expressly confirmed their verdict in open court. After entry of judgment, plaintiff moved to correct the verdict, offering affidavits and testimony from almost all the jurors to the effect that they intended plaintiff to recover $850. However, cross-examination revealed that they had not focused or agreed on the extent of each defendant's liability beyond $425.

On that motion, the court of appeals (2–1) gave this guidance for the remand: "The rules of law which will govern the exercise of the District Court's discretion may be stated, briefly, as follows: Where the jury's error is patent on the face of the verdict, the court should so amend the verdict as to make it conform to correct legal principles. But where the mistake is latent in and not apparent on the face of the verdict, it is sometimes proper to receive the affidavits of the jurors to ascertain their true verdict. Although great caution should be exercised in the use of such affidavits, there is no inflexible rule against their use, especially when they are offered, not for impeachment of the verdict, but rather for ascertainment of the true verdict. . . . If the jury actually found a verdict in the amount of $850.00, but mistakenly apportioned that amount between two defendants, the District Court, if properly convinced of that fact, would have power to correct the verdict accordingly; so that it would express the conclusion actually reached, and finally agreed upon by the jury—but mistakenly reported to the court."

CONTINENTAL CASUALTY CO. v. HOWARD, 775 F.2d 876 (7th Cir.1985), cert. denied, 475 U.S. 1122, 106 S.Ct. 1641 (1986). Days after a jury award of $9500 against an insurance company and a collective polling of the jury, the trial judge excluded the foreman's affidavit that the jury had meant not only to "award" the amount claimed on a policy covering a truck destroyed by fire but also to "entitle" the claimant to $369,500 claimed in the lawsuit on another policy with the same company covering a factory destroyed in the same suspicious fire.

The appellate court unanimously affirmed, suggesting the result might have differed if the juror testimony had been to the effect that a separate verdict form had gone astray: "Rule 606(b) does not bar testimony by a juror that all jurors agree that through inadvertence, oversight or mistake the verdict announced was not the verdict on which agreement had been reached." But this affidavit was "an attempt to testify about the jury's thought processes . . . . Because the affidavit seeks to introduce new evidence barred by Rule 606(b), the trial court properly ordered it stricken."

THE PROBLEM OF SURPLUSAGE

To what extent, if any, may the trial judge properly disregard as surplusage part of what the jury has included in its verdict or in a statement appended thereto? The problem is again illustrated by the not uncommon attempt of the jurors to apportion the verdict between two defendants despite proper instructions that a verdict for the plaintiff should be for the full amount of her damages against each defendant found liable. Suppose the jury returns this verdict: "We find for the plaintiff in the sum of $20,000, $15,000 to be paid by defendant *A* and $5000 to be paid by defendant *B*." Is it proper for the trial judge to disregard the apportionment as surplusage and order judgment for $20,000 against both defendants?

Questions: (18) Would the case be different if the jury had simply returned the verdict: "We find for the plaintiff against defendant *A* in the sum of $15,000 and against defendant *B* in the sum of $5000"? What should the trial judge do? See City of Fort Worth v. Williams, 55 Tex.Civ.App. 289, 298, 119 S.W. 137, 142 (1909) ("According to one line of cases, the plaintiff may elect his best damages and have judgment entered for that amount against all of the defendants found guilty jointly. According to another, he may select which of the defendants he will take judgment against for the sum assessed against him."). Is the plaintiff entitled to a new trial, if wished?

(19) In an action against agents to recover a secret profit, the jury, after much obvious trouble in reaching agreement, brought in a plaintiff's verdict for the several thousand dollars demanded. Appended to the verdict was a statement signed by all the jurors: "We, the jurors, recommend that the sum of $2300.00 claimed to be recovered by this suit be donated to the American Red Cross." What, if any, action should the trial court take? See Robyn v. White, 153 Minn. 76, 189 N.W. 577 (1922) (approved striking as surplusage, but would have preferred further deliberation).

THE IMPOSSIBLE VERDICT

Assume an action on a $1000 note. The jury returns a verdict for $500. The judge knows, without piercing the privacy of the jury room, that the jury has acted improperly. There is no inadmissible-evidence rule to hide behind. The problem appears on the face of the verdict. The only possible verdicts were for the plaintiff for $1000 or for the defendant. Plainly the plaintiff can complain and get a new trial (if the judge has not resolved the difficulty by sending the jury out again with further instructions). But can the defendant complain? What of the argument that the defendant is not harmed because the verdict is lower than it should have been? See Martin Realty Co. v. Garver, 116 Kan. 689, 229 P. 70 (1924) (giving new trial to defendant).

How is the case different if the damages are not liquidated? In Simmons v. Fish, 210 Mass. 563, 97 N.E. 102 (1912), the jury returned a $200 verdict for loss of an eye in an accident. Should the plaintiff be able to get a new trial? (Would the strength of the plaintiff's evidence on liability matter?) Should the defendant be able to get a new trial? (Would the defendant want a new trial?)

But courts will not jump to the conclusion of an impossible verdict. If further deliberation is no longer feasible, courts tend to let the verdict stand if a rational jury could possibly have reached it. E.g, United States Football League v. National Football League, 644 F.Supp. 1040 (S.D.N.Y. 1986) (after excluding juror testimony of confusion and compromise, court upheld verdict that had found antitrust violation and awarded one dollar, viewing it as permissible award of nominal damages), aff'd, 842 F.2d 1335 (2d Cir.1988), after remand, 887 F.2d 408 (2d Cir.1989) (approving $5.5 million in attorney's fees to plaintiff), cert. denied, 493 U.S. 1071, 110 S.Ct. 1116 (1990). See generally Shaun P. Martin, Rationalizing the Irrational: The Treatment of Untenable Federal Civil Jury Verdicts, 28 Creighton L.Rev. 683 (1995) (arguing that courts should take a more activist approach to overturning verdicts).

Questions: (20) Should failure to object to an irregularity apparent on the verdict's face constitute a waiver once the judge discharges the jury? Would not this approach obviate most such problems, albeit in a sometimes arbitrary manner? See Diamond Shamrock Corp. v. Zinke & Trumbo, Ltd., 791 F.2d 1416, 1422–24 (10th Cir.1986) (dictum) (waiver).

(21) But what if a verdict, covering multiple parties or claims, is only later seen to be so ambiguous as to obscure its meaning? Is this a situation that calls for the judge's allowing jurors to explain their verdict, despite Evidence Rule 606(b)? See E.F. Hutton & Co. v. Arnebergh, 775 F.2d 1061 (9th Cir.1985) (jurors' explanation allowed, but with parties' consent).

THE SEALED VERDICT

The modern practice commonly allows the jury to deliver its verdict in a sealed envelope to the court officer in charge and to disperse, instead of remaining together until the judge receives the verdict.[a] The sealed verdict

[a] "And it has been held, that if the jurors do not agree in their verdict before the judges are about to leave the town, though they are not to be threatened or imprisoned, the judges

is opened in the presence of the jurors when the court next sits. As usual, a party may demand a poll of the individual jurors before their discharge. See Federal Rule 48(c).

In theory the verdict is not truly a verdict when sealed but only when opened.[b] All is well if the jurors then agree, but if a juror dissents, even though he admits that he agreed with the others when the verdict was sealed, the verdict cannot stand. The judge is then faced with the choice of sending the jury back for further deliberation or declaring a mistrial. Some courts hold that the latter is the lesser evil because of the hazard of improper influence or coercion. E.g., Kramer v. Kister, 187 Pa. 227, 40 A. 1008 (1898). Others quiz the jurors as to whether they have discussed the case with outsiders and may require further deliberation upon receiving appropriate answers. E.g., Dziegiel v. Town of Westford, 274 Mass. 291, 174 N.E. 495 (1931).

Questions: (22) The jury returned a verdict for the defendant. The clerk polled the jurors. When he asked Juror No. 11 if that was her verdict, she replied: "Yes, only insofar as it had to be unanimous." The judge asked the juror to explain her statement, and she said: "The verdict, as I understand, had to be one hundred per cent in favor and we had to present one statement. I was, I think, the only one that held out and there was no possibility of any change and because of that I did." Should the verdict for the defendant have been recorded? See Grace Lines v. Motley, 439 F.2d 1028 (2d Cir.1971) (yes, although preferable to interrogate juror further or to send jury back for further deliberation).

(23) With respect to allowing further deliberation by the jury, should it matter whether (a) the jury reports a disagreement upon the opening of a sealed verdict or (b) the verdict contains surplusage or is on its face an impossible one?

SECTION 5. TYPE OF VERDICT

Federal Rule 49, in providing for both special verdicts and general verdicts with answers to written questions, adopted procedural devices of respectable historical origin.[c] The theoretical merits of these alternatives to a general verdict can be easily expressed. These special devices could guide the jurors' deliberations and help restrict the jury to its proper function.

---

are not bound to wait for them, but may carry them round the circuit from town to town in a cart." 3 William Blackstone, Commentaries *376.

[b] In Rich v. Finley, 325 Mass. 99, 89 N.E.2d 213 (1949), a juror died after the verdict was sealed and before it was opened. The eleven remaining jurors assented to the verdict. It was held to have been error to record the "verdict" over objection, because it lacked the final concurrence of the twelve jurors.

[c] Edith Guild Henderson in The Background of the Seventh Amendment, 80 Harv.L.Rev. 289 (1966), points out the wide use of the special verdict in England long before our Revolution, and in the colonies as well, although there were changes over time in whether the jury, judge, or parties got to choose the type of verdict. The general verdict with answers to written questions also has a long, but thinner, history, as related by Edmund M. Morgan in A Brief History of Special Verdicts and Special Interrogatories, 32 Yale L.J. 575, 591–92 (1923).

By contrast, a general verdict may mask the jurors' misunderstanding or willful disregard of the evidence or of the judge's instructions. Also, the way a general verdict veils the jurors' decisionmaking process often makes it hard to determine the effect of an error in, say, the judge's instructions. General verdicts are no doubt often set aside for misdirection when, if the truth could be known, the jurors' decision properly turned on a point wholly unrelated to the judge's error. For example, in Pacific Greyhound Lines v. Zane, 160 F.2d 731 (9th Cir.1947), an action for personal injuries, the judge charged correctly on so-called actual fraud in securing a release that had been pleaded as a defense and incorrectly on so-called constructive fraud. There was a general verdict for the plaintiff, signifying that the jury had found one or the other kind of fraud. The circuit court of appeals felt obliged to reverse the judgment because of the erroneous instruction, even though there was enough evidence to go to the jury on either kind of fraud. The court remarked that had a special verdict or a general verdict with answers to written questions been employed, a reversal might have been avoided.

Question: (24) What bearing does the type of verdict have on questions of issue preclusion?

Judges have nonetheless taken divergent views of the value of the special devices. In dissenting from the submission to Congress of the 1963 amendments to the Federal Rules of Civil Procedure, which included inconsequential changes in Rule 49(b), Justices Black and Douglas expressed the view that Rule 49 should be repealed, not amplified. It was, they said, "but another means utilized by courts to weaken the constitutional power of juries and to vest judges with more power to decide cases according to their own judgments." Order of January 21, 1963, 374 U.S. 865, 868, 83 S.Ct. 43, 45. For another illustration, Judge Charles Clark in Morris v. Pennsylvania R., 187 F.2d 837 (2d Cir.1951), where a general verdict with answers to written questions had been taken, cautioned that trial judges should use the device with discrimination and foresight. He favored it when the issues could be clearly and sharply differentiated, so as "to save on appeal at least that portion [of the verdict] which cannot be questioned," but he disfavored it in "a relatively simple factual situation."

Judge Frank, concurring in that Morris case, disagreed. He quoted an earlier opinion of Judge Learned Hand in his support: "I should like to subject a verdict, as narrowly as was practical, to a review which should make it in fact, what we very elaborately pretend that it should be: a decision based upon laws." See also Jerome Frank, Courts on Trial 141–43 (1949).

Professor Moore stated his views thus, formerly in 5A Moore ¶ 49.05, at 2235–36: "Also the general verdict, at times, achieves a triumph of justice over law. The jury is not, nor should it become, a scientific fact finding body. Its chief value is that it applies the 'law,' oftentimes a body of technical and refined theoretical principles and sometimes edged with harshness, in an earthy fashion that comports with 'justice' as conceived by the masses, for whom after all the law is mainly meant to serve. The general verdict is the answer from the man in the street. If on occasion the trial judge thinks the jury should be quizzed about its overall judgment as evidenced by the general verdict, this can be done by interrogatories accompanying the general verdict. But if there is sufficient evidence to get by a motion for directed verdict, then the problem is usually best solved by an overall, common judgment of the jurors—the general verdict."

Question: (25) If the jurors return what is indisputably a compromise verdict, as in Simmons v. Fish, should the judge accept this answer from the "man in the street"? Would it matter whether strongly differing jurors compromised liability and damages or whether all the jurors agreed in ignoring the law? Is there not a risk that instead of representing rough justice, the verdict rested on jury misunderstanding, malfunctioning, or prejudice? To any such verdict finally rendered, if the judge cannot reason away the impossibility, is not the proper response for the civil system to enforce its decisional rules by his ordering a new trial, while its lawmaker pursues changing any unjust substantive laws? But see Fleming James, Jr., Geoffrey C. Hazard, Jr. & John Leubsdorf, Civil Procedure 479–80 (5th ed. 2001).

It is to be noted that today under Rule 49, and as a matter of general practice in the states, the use of a special verdict or a general verdict with answers to written questions is discretionary with the court. It no longer requires the consent of the jury, nor the consent of the parties, if it ever did. There appears to have been no case where a trial judge was reversed for abuse of discretion in deciding whether to resort to Rule 49.

All that be as it may, neither part of the Federal Rule has been very extensively used—except by the federal courts in Texas, Wisconsin, and North Carolina, where special verdicts[d] were firmly embedded in state practice prior to the adoption of the Federal Rules. In federal court this is, nevertheless, strictly a federal matter not controlled by state law.

Special verdict.—By a special verdict at common law, the jury at nisi prius would find the facts in detail; the findings would be entered of record; and the record would go on to recite: "That they are ignorant in point of law on which side they ought upon those facts to find the issue, but if upon the whole matter the Court shall be of opinion that the issue is proved for the Plaintiff, they find for the Plaintiff accordingly, and assess the damages at such and such a sum, but if the Court are of an opposite opinion then they find for the Defendant." Upon the record so made, the court in banc would enter the judgment that it thought appropriate.[e]

Questions: (26) Although the circuits are in conflict, the Seventh Circuit has said that it is error for the judge in instructions to inform the jurors of the legal consequences of their answers to special questions. Gullett v. St. Paul Fire & Marine Ins. Co., 446 F.2d 1100, 1105 (7th Cir.1971). Appraise this position.

(27) What if, in a district court in the Seventh Circuit, counsel in closing argument expressly or by clear implication tells the jury what answers she wants it

[d] These are called special issues in Texas, where they are used in virtually every jury case. See 9B Wright & Miller § 2501.

[e] Ralph Sutton, Personal Actions at Common Law 128 (1929). The special verdict device is to be distinguished from the so-called special case, or case stated, at common law. This entailed an agreed statement of facts—a special case—on which the court would render judgment, without substantial participation by the jury.

to give? How can she argue effectively without doing this? See 9B Wright & Miller § 2509.

Special verdict practice has continued in modern times. The lawyers usually drew it up in the form of questions or alternative findings, often in the heat of trial with little opportunity for reflection or care in wording. As the judgment had to be supported by the very findings embodied in the verdict, an inadvertent omission or an irregularity or ambiguity in the verdict might vitiate the judgment. The difficulties in the use of the device were summed up by Professor Edson R. Sunderland, Verdicts, General and Special, 29 Yale L.J. 253, 261 (1920), in this way:

"The chief substantial objection which can be taken to the common use of the special verdict is that in practice it is difficult and hazardous to deal with. The risks are: (1) Immaterial matters may be included; (2) material matters may be omitted; (3) conclusions of law instead of facts may be found; (4) evidentiary instead of ultimate facts may be found; (5) questions may be put to the jury in such form as to be uncertain, misleading or prejudicial.

"These are very serious risks, and a historical survey of the practice relating to special verdicts will disclose a rocky road strewn with innumerable wrecks."

Rule 49(a) sought to correct defects in the special verdict technique as manifested in the cases both ancient and modern.

Question: (28) By what means does Rule 49(a) deal with the problem of omitted issues?

Columbia Horse & Mule Commission Co. v. American Ins. Co.

United States Court of Appeals, Sixth Circuit, 1949.
173 F.2d 773.

■ Before ALLEN, MARTIN, and MCALLISTER, CIRCUIT JUDGES.

■ ALLEN, CIRCUIT JUDGE. This action seeks recovery under an insurance policy for the loss of 43 mules destroyed in a fire near Dickson, Tennessee. By agreement of counsel the case was submitted to the jury for special verdict upon [a question on damages and upon these two] issues:

No. 1:

"Was the fire that destroyed the barns rented by Plaintiff John Dodd caused by his own act for the purpose of collecting on the insurance policy in question?"

No. 2:

"How many mules were destroyed when plaintiff's barns burned on April 11, 1945?"

The jury found for the appellants on Issue No. 1, and on Issue No. 2 it found the number of mules destroyed to be 34.

Appellant John Dodd, in an affidavit accompanying the proof of loss and in his testimony at the trial, asserted that the number of mules lost was 43. The jury's finding that 34 mules were destroyed is based upon the testimony of several witnesses who examined the premises immediately after the fire, and is not questioned here. The court considered that the proof of loss and affidavit claiming recovery for 43 mules constituted a willful and material misrepresentation and a false swearing in violation of the policy of insurance, which contained the usual provision that the policy should be void if the insured concealed or misrepresented any material fact or circumstance concerning the insurance or the interest of the insured in the property. Upon this ground . . . the court dismissed the action.[f]

Appellants' principal contention is that the court erred in not submitting to the jury the question whether or not Dodd's sworn statement was willfully false and fraudulent, and that the court erred in deciding as a matter of law that a false statement in the affidavit as to the property destroyed by fire voided the policy. They urge that Dossett v. First National Fire Ins. Co., 138 Tenn. 551, 198 S.W. 889, a decision of the Supreme Court of Tennessee relied upon by the District Court as supporting its decision herein, was an equity case and is not controlling in this action at law. Appellants also urge that innocent or mere mistaken misrepresentation of value, sworn to in a proof of loss, will not avoid an insurance policy. Dossett v. First National Fire Ins. Co., supra, 138 Tenn. at page 554, 198 S.W. 889. They rely upon the established rule that false statements, innocently or inadvertently made, do not constitute fraud or false swearing within the forfeiture clause of the usual policy, nor result in its avoidance. Sundquist v. Camden Fire Ins. Ass'n, 7 Cir., 119 F.2d 955, 957. Hence they maintain that an issue whether Dodd willfully or fraudulently misrepresented the number of mules lost should have been submitted to the jury. [Citations omitted.]

Assuming, but not deciding, that these questions might have been resolved in favor of the appellants if they had been presented free from procedural complications, we think the case is governed squarely by Rule 49(a) of the Federal Rules [which the court here quoted].

The two issues submitted were framed after conference between court and counsel, and after ample notice. The issue now raised, namely, whether appellant Dodd's representation as to the number of mules lost was willfully or innocently false, was omitted from the special issues submitted to the jury. Under Rule 49(a), each party, including appellants, waived the right to a jury trial upon the issue omitted. Waiver on appellants' part is

[f] The briefs suggest that the parties and the trial court proceeded on the assumption that falsity, willful or innocent, constituted a defense, as implied by the insurance contract and as pleaded by the defendant and as established by the jury's second finding. The first mention of willfulness came as a finding by the judge in his judgment, prepared by the defendant's counsel and entered two weeks after the verdict. The plaintiffs then objected by motion for a new trial, which the judge denied.

emphasized by the fact that the court in its preliminary charge submitting the issues to the jury, asked counsel for further requests, and later repeated the invitation to submit further requests at the close of the general charge. Appellants did not avail themselves of this opportunity.

No demand was made by either party that a question whether Dodd's misrepresentation was innocent or willful and fraudulent be submitted to the jury before its retirement. It follows that under Rule 49(a) the court was empowered to make a finding on that issue.

The judgment entered in accordance with the finding is not erroneous, and is affirmed.

Questions: (29) What if the trial judge had made no express finding whether the plaintiffs' misrepresentation was willfully false and fraudulent or was innocent and merely mistaken, but had entered judgment for the defendant on the special verdict? What if the judge had made no finding on the issue because he erroneously believed that it was legally immaterial whether the misrepresentation was willful or innocent? (Yet a jury could have accepted the defense by a general verdict for the defendant, without specific findings and largely safe from review, could it not? So perhaps Rule 49(a)(3) authorizes the trial judge to act on the omitted issue as a jury would, with all its usual obscurity.)

(30) Did Rule 49(a) mean to cover an omitted issue as basic and ignored as the one in Columbia Horse? Or does that case's result simply follow from adversary principles of party-presentation, in that the plaintiffs had accepted innocent misrepresentation to be a defense? (More pointedly, was the trial judge free to find under Rule 49(a) that the misrepresentation had in fact been innocent, thus rejecting rather than accepting the defense on grounds never really tried? If not, then Rule 49(a) was not really at work.)

(31) Should every failure to object to an irregularity in the special verdict, such as even a subtle inconsistency, constitute a waiver once the judge discharges the jury, as is argued in Donald Olander, Note, Resolving Inconsistencies in Federal Special Verdicts, 53 Fordham L.Rev. 1089 (1985)? (The judicial practice of reconciling inconsistent findings whenever rationally possible is almost the functional equivalent of waiver, is it not?)

General verdict with answers to written questions.—The practice of submitting a case to the jury for a general verdict but at the same time submitting written questions on one or more issues of fact was, in this country, originally identified with New England but later copied elsewhere.

Questions: (32) What practical differences do you perceive between the operation of Rule 49(a) and that of Rule 49(b)?

(33) What, if any, is the difference in the purposes of the two procedures?

(34) Rule 49(b) presents the trial judge with a number of permissible courses of conduct when any of a variety of inconsistencies appears in the action taken by the jury. What factors should guide discretion in making the choice?

Mayer v. Petzelt

United States Court of Appeals, Seventh Circuit, 1962.
311 F.2d 601, cert. denied, 373 U.S. 936, 83 S.Ct. 1538 (1963).

■ Before HASTINGS, CHIEF JUDGE, and DUFFY and KILEY, CIRCUIT JUDGES.

■ KILEY, CIRCUIT JUDGE. This is an appeal by plaintiff following the second trial of a diversity personal injury action against a Crystal Lake, Illinois, policeman. The first trial resulted in a $25,000 verdict for plaintiff, but a new trial was granted defendant. At the second trial on liability alone, the jury returned a general verdict for plaintiff with a special interrogatory against him on the question of due care. The District Court [for the Northern District of Illinois], notwithstanding the verdict for plaintiff, entered judgment for defendant.

While driving at night in Crystal Lake, plaintiff violated a traffic law. He then drove into a dark alley behind his hotel, and defendant followed on his police department motorcycle. While defendant was attempting to arrest plaintiff, the latter ran, fell in the alley, and was injured.

. . . .

The most favorable view of the evidence for plaintiff is: On the night of his injury, plaintiff had illegally crossed the center line in making a wide right turn. Afterward he drove into the dark alley behind his hotel, parked and turned out the car lights. He then recognized, standing by his car, defendant, who had, about a month before, pursued plaintiff for "telling a lie," caught him and dragged him back to the police station ripping his shirt off in the process.[8] Defendant, then a man of 27 who weighed 190 pounds, said to plaintiff, a man of 64, "You ___ ___ ___ ___, now I got you where I want you, and you come out of that car and you are going to get it." Defendant did not have his flashlight or ticket book with him at the time. While "hollering" and shaking plaintiff's car, defendant tried to open the locked doors. When defendant went to the right side, plaintiff got out the left, ran down the alley and was injured. Defendant later told a fellow officer that he ". . . must have scared hell out of him because he started to run from me."

We think the jury could on this evidence draw a reasonable inference that defendant should have foreseen, as a reasonably prudent man, that his conduct on the night in question, in view of the incident the previous month, would probably cause plaintiff, in fear for his safety, to leave the automobile, run away in the dark alley and be injured while running. This inference would support the finding of negligence. Karas v. Snell, 11 Ill.2d 233, 142 N.E.2d 46, 56 (1957), Hood v. Brinson, 30 Ill.App.2d 498, 175 N.E.2d 300 (1961).

. . . .

---

[8] The evidence of the prior incident was excluded at the trial. We think the ruling was erroneous because it has a bearing on plaintiff's mental state on the night of June 23. Smith v. Cornell, 59 Ill. 66 (1871), Jennings v. Murphy, 194 F.2d 35, 37 (7th Cir.1952), 2 Jones Evidence, 1149 (2d ed. 1926), 18 Illinois Law & Practice, Evidence, § 61, pp. 193–194.

Implicit in the general verdict for plaintiff is a finding of absence of contributory negligence. Theurer v. Holland Furnace Co., 124 F.2d 494, 497 (10th Cir.1941). But a special interrogatory answered in the negative the question: "Did the plaintiff use ordinary care and caution for his own safety on the occasion in question?" This interrogatory is not inconsistent with the general verdict because, even though the jury might believe plaintiff was guilty of lack of due care, it might also believe that plaintiff's actions were not the proximate cause of his injury.[10] Furthermore, the District Court would not be justified in deciding that plaintiff's conduct proximately caused the injury, and entering judgment on the interrogatory.[g] . . .

We hold that the District Court erred in entering judgment notwithstanding the verdict. . . . For the reasons given, the judgment is reversed, and the cause is remanded for trial upon the issue of damages only.

Questions: (35) Is not the effect of the foregoing judicial approach under Rule 49(b) to treat the verdict as a general verdict if there were any issues omitted from the questions or if there is any other way to save the general verdict logically, but otherwise, and only then, to treat the answers as virtually a special verdict?

(36) In an action by the beneficiary on a life insurance policy, the insurance company offers inconsistent evidence (a) that the insured committed suicide and (b) that the insured was murdered by the beneficiary, proof of either of which would defeat recovery. The unanimous jury returns a general verdict for the defendant and answers "yes" to each of two accompanying written questions asking (a) whether the insured committed suicide and (b) whether the beneficiary murdered her. What should the trial judge do? What effect does Rule 49(b) have on your answer? Is the proper course to order further deliberation if possible, but otherwise to order a new trial unless it is realistic to find waiver by the plaintiff's failure to object before the jury's discharge? See Austin v. Paramount Parks, Inc., 195 F.3d 715, 725–26 (4th Cir.1999) (adopting waiver approach, although other circuits require new trial).

(37) If among the many possible situations encompassed by the preceding question the jury believed that suicide was a 40–per-cent likelihood and that murder was a 30–per-cent likelihood, how should it have responded to the questions? Should the judge have posed those separate questions?

---

[10] "It is plain that the general verdict must yield when it is so clearly at variance with one or more of the [special interrogatory] answers that the two are irreconcilable in a legal sense. But every reasonable intendment in favor of the general verdict should be indulged in an effort to harmonize the two. The answers override the general verdict and warrant the entry of judgment in disregard of the latter only where the conflict on a material question is beyond reconciliation on any reasonable theory consistent with the evidence and its fair inferences." Theurer v. Holland Furnace Co., 124 F.2d 494, 498 (10th Cir.1941).

[g] In a similar case, the Seventh Circuit later ruled that if the jury's answer to an interrogatory found lack of due care and found proximate causation of injury, then the judge could enter judgment for the defendants. Elston v. Morgan, 440 F.2d 47 (7th Cir.1971).

Arkansas Midland Railway v. Canman

Supreme Court of Arkansas, 1890.
52 Ark. 517, 13 S.W. 280.

[The plaintiff sued for personal injuries caused by the derailment of the defendant's railway coach in which he was a passenger. The trial resulted in a verdict and judgment for the plaintiff, from which the defendant appealed. The portion of the opinion holding that the judgment must be reversed because of errors in the instructions to the jury is omitted.]

■ BATTLE, J.

. . . .

Another question is presented for our consideration. The statutes of this State provide that the court may require the jury, "in any case in which they render a general verdict, to find specially upon particular questions of facts to be stated in writing," and that "when the special finding of facts is inconsistent with the general verdict the former controls the latter, and the court may give judgment accordingly." (Mansf.Dig., secs. 5142, 5143.) In pursuance of these statutes the court propounded interrogatories and gave instructions to the jury, on motion of the appellant, as follows:

"1. Was the derailment of the coach in which plaintiff was a passenger caused by the insufficient skill and care of the defendant in constructing its road-bed?

"2. Was the derailment of the coach in which plaintiff was a passenger caused by the want of skill and prudence of defendant in maintaining its road-bed?

"3. Was such derailment caused by the defect in the rolling stock in the defendant's train or any of its appliances?

"4. Was such derailment caused by any negligence in operating such train?

"5. If the jury find negligence in either case, they will state in what said negligence consisted.

"6. If the jury find that after the derailment of the car the track was torn up and the ties broken, they will state whether the tearing up of the track and the breaking of the ties contributed to the injury of the plaintiff, and if so, in what way and to what extent."

And against the objection of the defendant, instructed the jury as follows:

"If the jury find negligence and cannot agree what the particular negligence was which caused the derailment of the car, they may so state.

"If the jury find that the derailment was caused by a bent rail or spreading of the track, say so."

To each of the interrogatories the jury responded: "We fail to agree," and further said: "We find negligence on the part of the defendant, but fail to agree as to what particular neglect caused the derailment of the train."

The appellant contends that the court erred in instructing the jury that if they found that the appellant had been guilty of negligence, and could not agree as to what the negligence which caused the derailment was, they might so state; and insists, that before a verdict could have been legally returned against it, there must have been an agreement of the minds of the twelve jurors as to the existence of some particular fact constituting negligence, and that they must have agreed on an affirmative answer to one of the interrogatories. The correctness of this contention depends on the evidence. It is not necessary that a jury, in order to find a verdict, should, in all cases, concur in a single view of a transaction or occurrence disclosed by the evidence. If the verdict is sustained by any one of two or more interpretations of the evidence, it cannot be impeached by showing that a part of the jury proceeded upon one interpretation and a part upon the others. Murray v. New York Life Ins. Co., 96 N.Y. 614; Chicago & N.W.R. Co. v. Dunleavy, 22 N.E. 15. But if they must necessarily agree upon the answer to any particular question before they can find a verdict, they would be guilty of a violation of duty if they returned a general verdict without doing so. Ebersole v. Northern Central Railroad Co., 23 Hun 114. If they should reply to such a question, to the effect they cannot agree, the court ought not to receive their verdict, as the reply and verdict, in that case, would be in irreconcilable conflict. As to the consistency of the verdict, and the answers of the jury to the interrogatories in this case, we express no opinion.[h]

. . . .

SPLIT TRIAL

A local rule for the Northern District of Illinois, whence came Mayer v. Petzelt, provided that the court could order, on motion of a party or on the court's own motion, a separate trial of the issues of liability, to be followed if necessary by a trial on damages, before the same or a different jury as appropriate. Professor Charles Alan Wright in Procedural Reform: Its

---

[h] See Stewart Jay, Juror Agreement on the Basis of Negligence, 8 Rev.Litig. 119 (1989); Hayden J. Trubitt, Patchwork Verdicts, Different–Jurors Verdicts, and American Jury Theory: Whether Verdicts Are Invalidated by Juror Disagreement on Issues, 36 Okla.L.Rev. 473 (1983); Ruth B. Ginsburg, Special Findings and Jury Unanimity in the Federal Courts, 65 Colum.L.Rev. 256 (1965). There appears to be no federal civil case squarely facing the fundamental problem presented by the Arkansas Midland case. Cf. Jazzabi v. Allstate Ins. Co., 278 F.3d 979 (9th Cir.2002) (unanimity must exist as to each element).

On a distinguishable matter, courts are now tending to hold that under a nonunanimous decision rule, different jurors can provide the support for independent parts of the verdict. See, e.g., Williams v. James, 113 N.J. 619, 552 A.2d 153 (1989); cf. Jonathan Remy Nash, A Context–Sensitive Voting Protocol Paradigm for Multimember Courts, 56 Stan.L.Rev. 75 (2003) (appellate analogy).

Limitations and Its Future, 1 Ga.L.Rev. 563, 569–70 (1967), had this to say about the split trial pursuant to such a rule:

"In the last few years some courts have adopted rules providing that the issue of liability may be tried first in a negligence case, and a second trial on damages is held only if plaintiff prevails on liability. This has had marvelous results in terms of saving court time. A competent study has been made of experience with such a procedure. That study concludes that cases handled in this fashion take 20 percent less time than do cases tried routinely, with the liability and damage issues submitted simultaneously to the jury.[11] A saving of 20% in trial time of negligence cases would be an important gain for the courts. The same data show, however, that while defendants win in 42% of the cases tried routinely, they win in 79% of the cases in which the liability issue is submitted alone. This certainly suggests that juries are moved by sympathy when they have heard evidence as to the extent of plaintiff's injuries, and that this influences their decision on the liability issue. Quite possibly this is a bad thing—certainly orthodox theory supposes that it is. But when it is seen that the split trial reduces by more than half the cases in which personal injury plaintiffs are successful, it is apparent that the new procedure has made a substantial change in the nature of jury trial itself."

However, bear in mind, on the one hand, that the cases being tried in the two different ways (split or unitary) were two different sets of cases, and their different case characteristics may have accounted in part for the different win rates. See Steven S. Gensler, Bifurcation Unbound, 75 Wash. L.Rev. 705 (2000). Also bear in mind, on the other hand, that even the shorter trial times are uncertain in effect, as lower costs will increase the number of lawsuits and of trials, and hence augment the aggregate cost of litigation. See William M. Landes, Sequential Versus Unitary Trials: An Economic Analysis, 22 J.Legal Stud. 99 (1993). More recent experimental research suggests that though split-trial defendants do indeed win more on liability, they pay bigger awards when they lose. Stephan Landsman, Shari Diamond, Linda Dimitropoulos & Michael J. Saks, Be Careful What You Wish for: The Paradoxical Effects of Bifurcating Claims for Punitive Damages, 1998 Wis. L. Rev. 297.

Questions: (38) Is the local rule consistent with the Seventh Amendment? See Hosie v. Chicago & Nw. Ry., 282 F.2d 639 (7th Cir.1960) (yes); Eunice A. Eichelberger, Annotation, Propriety of Ordering Separate Trials as to Liability and Damages, Under Rule 42(b) of Federal Rules of Civil Procedure, in Actions Involving Personal Injury, Death, or Property Damage, 78 A.L.R.Fed. 890 (1986). Is it a desirable rule?

(39) In a motor-vehicle tort case, who would be more likely to seek a separate trial of the liability issues, plaintiff or defendant? Does your answer depend upon the expected nature of the evidence on liability? on damages? upon whether comparative negligence is the governing substantive scheme?

The American Bar Association, in its Principles for Juries & Jury Trials princ. 13(H) (2005), concludes: "In civil cases the court should seek a

[11] Zeisel & Callahan, Split Trials and Time Saving: A Statistical Analysis, 76 Harv.L.Rev. 1606, 1619 (1963).

single, unitary trial of all issues in dispute before the same jury, unless bifurcation or severance of issues or parties is required by law or is necessary to prevent unfairness or prejudice." But see Drury Stevenson, Reverse Bifurcation, 75 U.Cin.L.Rev. 213 (2006) (arguing for trying damages before liability, to facilitate settlement).

Pamela J. Stephens, Controlling the Civil Jury: Towards a Functional Model of Justification

76 Ky.L.J. 81, 82–83, 153–54, 159, 165 (1988).

Ambivalence toward the right to a jury trial in civil cases has been a feature of our judicial system from the outset. The jury has been hailed as the very essence of our freedom and contemporaneously attacked as inept and "lawless." Since the origin of the jury, the common law has devised various ways of controlling the power of that institution; currently, federal rules of procedure embody many of these jury control devices. Those assessing the usefulness and constitutional validity of these procedural devices often have found them in conflict with the jury-trial right. This apparent conflict results, at least in part, because those assessing control devices have relied upon excessively narrow and incomplete theoretical models of the civil-jury-trial right. Generally, these prior models describe and circumscribe a role for the civil jury without giving adequate consideration to the dynamics of a judge/jury system or without giving a convincing justification for power allocation within that system. . . .

Traditional models describing the role of the civil jury rest primarily upon historical, legal, and political grounds. Historical models define the jury's role under the seventh amendment's mandate to follow common law practices. Legal models focus on the law/fact distinction and limit the jury's role to consideration of those matters defined as factual. Political models emphasize the democratizing influence of juries in an otherwise antimajoritarian judicial system and describe the necessity of jury participation. While each of these models explains some aspect of the jury's role, none of them systematically explores the limits of what that role is or should be. . . .

. . . .

None of the models presented offers a wholly satisfactory justification for controlling the civil jury. Each affords some basis for rejecting the concept of a broad, freely available civil-jury-trial right subject to few if any controls. What is lacking is any principled way of distinguishing valid from invalid jury control devices. Therefore, use of certain devices creates apparent conflicts with the scope of the jury right. The model that comes the closest to grappling with that problem is the legal model. . . .

I suggest that one may look beyond the law-fact labels to identify valued facets of judge and jury decision making. Then, one may evaluate the current jury control devices in light of the extent to which they encourage or discourage performance of the valued functions. . . .

. . . .

Three categories of valued jury functions suggest themselves: (1) special competency, (2) public acceptance, and (3) equity functions. . . .

. . . .

Valued judge functions fall into two broad categories: (1) those involving the special competency of judges and (2) those involving the supervisory functions of judges. . . .

. . . .

. . . Framing the justification in functional terms provides the basis for discussing these control issues in a context amenable to further development. As research progresses into the actual, as opposed to the perceived, value of the respective functions of the judge and the jury, balancing those functions will promote theorizing about the extent to which control of the civil jury is appropriate.

TOPIC D

NEW TRIAL

In the present Topic a few problems under the vast rubric of "New Trial" have been selected for study. Much of this Topic relates back to questions already touched on. We have already seen many instances of motions for a new trial, and of reversals by appellate courts that in the ordinary course would need to be followed by new trials.

Federal Rule 59(a)(1), without undertaking to give a catalogue of all imaginable grounds for a new trial, refers to the reasons for which new trials have heretofore been granted in actions at law in federal courts and, in respect to actions tried without a jury, refers to the reasons for which rehearings have heretofore been granted in suits in equity in such courts.

Question: (1) California has enacted a catalogue of grounds for a new trial. Cal.Civ.Proc.Code § 657. Is this preferable to Rule 59(a)(1), with its reference to what has been done "heretofore"?

SECTION 1. ERROR IN COURSE OF TRIAL

Many of the grounds for a new trial involve errors committed by the trial judge in the admission or exclusion of evidence, in giving or refusing instructions to the jury, and the like. Ordinarily, the aggrieved party must duly object when the error is committed in order successfully to complain of it later.

The aggrieved party may renew the objection after verdict by a motion for a new trial. If a party moves for a new trial relying upon such an error, the trial judge has an opportunity to reconsider his ruling, which was initially made in the heat of trial and which upon reflection and study he may conclude to have been erroneous. Not to allow him to grant a new trial but instead to require the aggrieved party to appeal would be wasteful of time and money.

However, in federal court the aggrieved party is not required so to renew the objection by motion. If due objection was made at the time of the ruling, there is no necessity to assert the alleged error again as the basis for a motion for a new trial in order to preserve the point for appellate review. See Kiernan v. Van Schaik, 347 F.2d 775 (3d Cir.1965). By contrast, there are some jurisdictions where the point is lost unless incorporated in a new trial motion, although it is often hard to say whether the motion then is simply doing service as a kind of assignment of the errors that will be relied upon on appeal instead of being really intended to give the trial judge a chance to correct his error.

Many other sorts of error in the course of trial call for a new trial, such as misconduct by participants other than the judge. A prompt objection ordinarily remains necessary. However, if an error does not come to light until after verdict—for example, it is disclosed that a party or her counsel communicated improperly with a juror or that a juror made an unauthorized private investigation during the trial—a motion after verdict is the earliest and mandatory means of raising the question.

Question: (2) If it were shown that the party claiming to be aggrieved knew of the episode of juror misconduct before the case was submitted to the jury but deferred raising the question until after suffering an adverse verdict, should he be able to upset the verdict? See Stampofski v. Steffens, 79 Ill. 303 (1875) (no).

HARMLESS ERROR

Not every error duly objected to during the course of trial—even if inadequately cured and properly renewed—requires a new trial (or reversal on appeal). After unearthing error, the court normally must decide whether the error failed to change the outcome. See Rule 61 and 28 U.S.C. § 2111; see also Evidence Rule 103(a).

The question of what error in the admission or exclusion of evidence is deemed prejudicial was long a matter of controversy in the English courts. One attitude is illustrated in the remarks of Chief Justice Tindal of the Court of Common Pleas in Doe dem. Lord Teynham v. Tyler, 130 Eng.Rep. 1397, 1398 (C.P.1830) (a case where questionable evidence had been admitted and where verdict went for defendant): "But the Court will not close their eyes to the rest of the evidence; and if they see that there is enough, not merely to make the scales hang even, but greatly to preponderate in favour of the Defendant, they will not send the cause to a jury again." The second attitude, originating in the Court of Exchequer, is illustrated by the statement of Baron Parke in Crease v. Barrett, 149 Eng.Rep. 1353, 1359 (Ex.1835) (a case where evidence had been erroneously excluded and where verdict went for plaintiff): "We cannot say, however strong our opinion may be on the propriety of the present verdict, that, if the lease had been received, it would have had no effect with the jury; nor that it is clear beyond all doubt, if the verdict had been for the defendant, that it would have been set aside as improper; and therefore we think that there must be a new trial." The Court of King's Bench sided with the Court of Exchequer in Frederick v. Farr, 111 Eng.Rep. 707 (K.B.1835) (erroneous admission). Eventually a middle course was seemingly followed by rules of court issued under the Supreme Court of Judicature Act, 1875, 38 & 39 Vict., ch. 77, sched. 1, O. 39, r. 3, which called for overlooking evidence errors unless they occasioned some substantial wrong or miscarriage.

In America too a mere technical mistake not affecting a substantial right is harmless error. Alternatively phrased, error should be reversible unless "the appellate court believes it highly probable that the error did not affect the judgment . . . . Any test less stringent entails too great a risk of affirming a judgment that was influenced by an error. Moreover, a less stringent test may fail to deter an appellate judge from focusing his inquiry on the correctness of the result and then holding an error harmless whenever he equated the result with his own predilections. . . . Like all too easy affirmance, all too ready reversal is also inimical to the judicial process. Again, nothing is gained from such an extreme, and much is lost. Reversal for error, regardless of its effect on the judgment, encourages litigants to abuse the judicial process and bestirs the public to ridicule it." Roger J. Traynor, The Riddle of Harmless Error 35, 50 (1970).

This standard—requiring the nonaggrieved party to show the noneffect of error on outcome to be highly probable—has commonly applied in civil cases. E.g., McQueeney v. Wilmington Trust Co., 779 F.2d 916, 928 (3d Cir.1985). Note, however, that the Supreme Court has recently indicated that in a civil case it is the aggrieved party's burden to show effect—which would rephrase the usual standard to require that the aggrieved party show a substantial possibility of the error's effect on outcome. See Shinseki v. Sanders, 129 S.Ct. 1696 (2009).

Courts often mask the standard in idiosyncratic terminology or in a vague test like "substantial justice." Note further that palpably different standards sometimes do apply, in certain circumstances or in certain jurisdictions. Most notably, with respect to an error on a constitutional matter, the court might require the nonaggrieved party to show harmlessness beyond a reasonable doubt.

Kotteakos v. United States, 328 U.S. 750, 761–62, 66 S.Ct. 1239, 1246 (1946), observed in the criminal law context: "Easier was the [harmless error] command to make than it has been always to observe. This, in part because it is general; but in part also because the discrimination it requires is one of judgment transcending confinement by formula or precise rule. [Citation omitted.] That faculty cannot ever be wholly imprisoned in words, much less upon such a criterion as what are only technical, what substantial rights; and what really affects the latter hurtfully." Nevertheless, it concluded: "All this hardly needs to be said again. But it must be comprehended and administered every day. The task is not simple, although the admonition is. Neither is it impossible. By its very nature no standard of perfection can be attained. But one of fair approximation can be achieved. Essentially the matter is one for experience to work out. For, as with all lines which must be drawn between positive and negative fields of law, the precise border may be indistinct, but case by case determination of particular points adds up in time to discernible direction. In the final analysis judgment in each case must be influenced by conviction resulting from examination of the proceedings in their entirety, tempered but not governed in any rigid sense of stare decisis by what has been done in similar situations."

Questions: (3) What doctrinal differences exist between harmless error and plain error, which was discussed supra p. 1406?

(4) Should the often rather vague doctrine of harmless error (or the even vaguer doctrine of plain error, which requires a strong showing of error and harm) be pinned down or be left to the we-know-it-when-we-see-it approach?

Rojas v. Richardson

United States Court of Appeals, Fifth Circuit, 1983.
703 F.2d 186, vacated, 713 F.2d 116 (5th Cir.1983).

■ Before RUBIN, JOHNSON and WILLIAMS, CIRCUIT JUDGES.

■ JERRE S. WILLIAMS, CIRCUIT JUDGE.

[Plaintiff worked as a ranch hand for defendants. After being thrown by a horse and severely injured, he sued them for negligence and breach of contract in the Eastern District of Texas. During closing argument the defense counsel referred to plaintiff as an "illegal alien," to which plaintiff failed to object. After verdict and judgment for defendants, plaintiff appealed.]

Even if Rojas has waived his right to appeal the use of the phrase "illegal alien," however, this Court is not precluded from reviewing the use of the phrase at trial. Fed.R.Evid. 103(d) provides: "Nothing in this rule [requiring objection to preserve appealability] precludes taking notice of plain errors affecting substantial rights although they were not brought to the attention of the court." Our authority to review, we note, is limited to "plain errors," and the errors must affect "substantial rights." We find that allegations unsupported by the record that Rojas was an illegal alien might well have a serious and negative effect on his substantial right to an impartial jury. The only serious issue is whether the allegations rise to the level of "plain error."

The plain error rule is "not a run-of-the-mill remedy." United States v. Gerald, 624 F.2d 1291, 1299 (5th Cir.1980), cert. denied, 450 U.S. 920, 101 S.Ct. 1369, 67 L.Ed.2d 348 (1981). It is invoked "only in exceptional circumstances to avoid a miscarriage of justice." Eaton v. United States, 398 F.2d 485, 486 (5th Cir.), cert. denied, 393 U.S. 937, 89 S.Ct. 299, 21 L.Ed.2d 273 (1968). The exact delineation of plain error is difficult to articulate. We have defined plain error as error which is "both obvious and substantial." United States v. Gerald, 624 F.2d at 1299; Sykes v. United States, 373 F.2d 607, 612 (5th Cir.1966), cert. denied, 386 U.S. 977, 87 S.Ct. 1172, 18 L.Ed.2d 138 (1967). But such elegant phraseology yields little guidance. The determination still rests ultimately on the facts of each case.

Perhaps the most telling guidelines were laid down by Justice Stone in 1936, when he wrote:

> In exceptional circumstances, especially in criminal cases, appellate courts, in the public interest, may, of their motion, notice errors to which no exception has been taken, if the errors are obvious, or if they otherwise seriously affect the *fairness, integrity, or public reputation of judicial proceedings.*

United States v. Atkinson, 297 U.S. 157, 160, 56 S.Ct. 391, 392, 80 L.Ed. 555 (1936) (emphasis added). Following the clarion call of Justice Stone's words, we must hold that the "fairness, integrity, or public reputation" of the proceedings in this case were adversely affected by the closing jury argument of defense counsel. The closing remarks included this paragraph:

> I hope—I hope—that you don't, because Mr. Rojas is an alien, give him any more benefit than you would any United States citizen who comes in this Court. If the situation were reversed and you or I were in Mexico—were illegal aliens in Mexico—I would hope Mexico would open up their Courts, would open up their job market, would open up their public schools, would open up their State hospitals, as we have in this country for Mr. Rojas. Certainly he is—I'm not saying we shouldn't do those things, but he shouldn't be entitled to any extra benefits because he is an illegal alien in this country than would any other citizen of the United States be entitled.

These remarks prejudiced the jury on two counts. First, by introducing irrelevant and unproven allegations that Rojas was an illegal alien, the defense clearly was appealing to the prejudice and bias of members of the jury on the basis of national origin. Although there was justification for presenting Rojas' Mexican citizenship to the jury to establish diversity jurisdiction, 28 U.S.C. § 1332(a)(2), his status as an "illegal" alien was completely irrelevant to the negligence claims the jury was to evaluate. Furthermore, the closing reference to "illegal alien" could have placed a prejudicial gloss on the many references throughout trial to Rojas as an "alien." Having laid a strong foundation through use of the term "alien" throughout trial, even counsel's single reference to the incendiary, derogatory expression "illegal alien" is prejudicial. Finally, the allegation that Rojas was in the country illegally is unsupported in the record.

. . . .

Second, these remarks were an impermissible invocation of the "golden rule" argument. As we recently explained,

> What every lawyer should know is that a plea to the jury that they "should put themselves in the shoes of the plaintiff and do unto him as they would have done unto them under similar circumstances. . . . [is] improper because it encourages the jury to depart from neutrality and to decide the case on the basis of personal interest and bias rather than on the evidence."

Loose v. Offshore Navigation, Inc., 670 F.2d 493, 496 (5th Cir.1982), quoting Ivy v. Security Barge Lines, Inc., 585 F.2d 732, 741 (5th Cir.1978), rev'd on other grounds, 606 F.2d 524 (5th Cir.1979) (en banc), cert. denied, 446 U.S. 956, 100 S.Ct. 2927, 64 L.Ed.2d 815 (1980). [Other citations omitted.] The fact that the statement in this case was an inverse incantation of this golden rule is insufficient to validate the partiality inherent in the argument. Loose, supra. The "golden rule" argument, while not plain error, is normally ground for new trial. Id.

The closing remarks of defense counsel were highly prejudicial and a blatant appeal to jury bias. Although the district court gave a jury instruction emphasizing equal access to justice, even this instruction was ambiguous. The jury was instructed:

> You are instructed that all persons are equal before the law, and this case should be considered and decided by you as an action between persons of equal standing in the community, of equal worth, and holding the same or similar stations in life. The law is no respector of persons. All persons, including partnerships, and other lawful organizations, stand equal before the law, and are to be dealt with as equals in a Court of Justice.

While its wording might have been adequate to indicate that aliens must be treated equally, it was not adequate to tell the jury that "illegal aliens" are "equal before the law." A jury could readily conclude that someone who is "illegal" is not "equal before the law" to law abiding citizens and jurors. We are not convinced that the jury instruction could rebuild the "fairness, integrity, or public reputation of jury proceedings" that Justice Stone admonished us to protect, see Atkinson, 297 U.S. at 160, 56 S.Ct. at 392. As we first noted in Dunn v. United States, 307 F.2d 883, 887 (5th Cir.1962), "if you throw a skunk into the jury box, you can't instruct the jury not to smell it." Some references are so prejudicial that it is difficult for curative instructions to resuscitate fairness. [Citation omitted.] Even assuming that a proper jury instruction could have cured prejudice, this instruction did not do so.

. . . .

We have examined other exceptions to the manner in which the trial was conducted and find no further grounds for reversal. There is substantial evidence to support the jury verdict in this case. However, on the basis of the defendants' closing references to Rojas as an "illegal alien" and their appeal to jury prejudice, we must reverse the judgment of the district court and remand for new trial.

Reversed and remanded.[a]

Questions: (5) In his closing argument, the plaintiff's counsel said: "I do not ask for a verdict for my client because he is a poor man, nor because the city [defendant] is rich and powerful. I only ask for a verdict if he is entitled to one

[a] See Janelle L. Davis, Comment, Sticks and Stones May Break My Bones, But Names Could Get Me a Mistrial: An Examination of Name–Calling in Closing Argument in Civil Cases, 42 Gonz.L.Rev. 133 (2006). But on rehearing of the Rojas decision before the same panel, a defendant supplemented the record with the transcript of the proceedings on voir dire, which showed that for tactical reasons the plaintiff's attorney had then made known to prospective jurors the plaintiff's status as an "illegal alien." In view of the jury's knowledge, the court could no longer conclude that the defense counsel's "highly prejudicial" reference to Rojas' status in the closing argument was "so prejudicial as to be plain error, even when coupled with the Golden Rule argument." Therefore, the court set aside its earlier decision and affirmed the district court's judgment, 713 F.2d 116 (5th Cir.1983).

under the law and the evidence." After objection by the defendant and then verdict for the plaintiff, is a new trial warranted? See Gilman v. City of Laconia, 71 N.H. 212, 51 A. 631 (1902) (no, the "disproportion in power and resource being already before the jury"); cf. Timothy J. Conner, What You May Not Say to the Jury, Litigation, Spring 2001, at 36.

(6) Should incompetence of counsel, as distinguished from misconduct, be a ground for a new trial in a civil action? Compare Everett v. Everett, 319 Mich. 475, 29 N.W.2d 919 (1947) (apparently unaware of the Dead Man's Act and of the best evidence rule, counsel was blocked on the first day of trial by objections on these grounds, and on opening of court the next day he consented to a dismissal of the action with prejudice; new trial motion denied), with Community Dental Servs. v. Tani, 282 F.3d 1164 (9th Cir.2002) (counsel virtually abandoned client in failing to proceed with the defense; relief from default judgment granted under Rule 60(b)(6) for such "gross" negligence, as opposed to "ordinary" negligence).

EVIDENCE RULINGS IN NONJURY CASES

Errors in the admission or exclusion of evidence in trials without a jury are viewed in a unique light. See McCormick on Evidence § 60 (Kenneth S. Broun gen. ed., 6th ed. 2006).

Consider the remarks of the court in Builders Steel Co. v. Commissioner, 179 F.2d 377, 379 (8th Cir.1950): "In the trial of a nonjury case, it is virtually impossible for a trial judge to commit reversible error by receiving incompetent evidence, whether objected to or not. An appellate court will not reverse a judgment in a nonjury case because of the admission of incompetent evidence, unless all of the competent evidence is insufficient to support the judgment or unless it affirmatively appears that the incompetent evidence induced the court to make an essential finding which would not otherwise have been made. Thompson v. Carley, 8 Cir., 140 F.2d 656, 660; Doering v. Buechler, 8 Cir., 146 F.2d 784, 786; Grandin Grain & Seed Co. v. United States, 8 Cir., 170 F.2d 425, 427. On the other hand, a trial judge who, in the trial of a nonjury case, attempts to make strict rulings on the admissibility of evidence, can easily get his decision reversed by excluding evidence which is objected to, but which, on review, the appellate court believes should have been admitted. In the case of Donnelly Garment Co. v. National Labor Relations Board, 8 Cir., 123 F.2d 215, 224, we stated our views upon this subject as follows: '. . . We think that experience has demonstrated that in a trial or hearing where no jury is present, more time is ordinarily lost in listening to arguments as to the admissibility of evidence and in considering offers of proof than would be consumed in taking the evidence proffered, and that, even if the trier of facts, by making close rulings upon the admissibility of evidence, does save himself some time, that saving will be more than offset by the time consumed by the reviewing court in considering the propriety of his rulings and by the consequent delay in the final determination of the controversy. One who is capable of ruling accurately upon the admissibility of evidence is equally capable of sifting it accurately after it has been received, and, since he will base his findings upon the evidence which he regards as competent, material and convincing, he cannot be injured by the presence in the record of testimony which he does not consider competent or material. Lawyers and judges frequently differ as to the admissibility of evidence, and it occasionally happens that a reviewing court regards as admissible evidence which was rejected by the judge, special master, or trial examiner. If the record on review contains not only all evidence which was clearly admissible, but also all evidence of doubtful admissibility, the court which is called upon to review the case can usually make an end of it, whereas if evidence was excluded which that court regards as having been admissible, a new trial or rehearing cannot be avoided. We say this in the hope of preventing a repetition of what occurred in the case now before us, and to obviate any misunderstanding as to what the attitude of this Court is with respect to the taking of evidence in a hearing before a special master or a trial examiner.' "

SECTION 2. NEWLY DISCOVERED EVIDENCE

In Marshall's U.S. Auto Supply v. Cashman, 111 F.2d 140, 142 (10th Cir.1940), the court said: "A motion for new trial on the ground of newly discovered evidence must show that the evidence was discovered since the trial; must show facts from which the court may infer reasonable diligence on the part of the movant; must show that the evidence is not merely cumulative or impeaching; must show that it is material; and must show that it is of such character that on a new trial such evidence will probably produce a different result." The requirements set forth in this case, along with the implicit requirement that the evidence must pertain to facts existing at the time of trial, generally prevail in both federal and state courts.

See Rules 59(b) and 60(c)(1) respectively for the twenty-eight-day and one-year time limits on asking for a new trial based on newly discovered evidence. A motion under Rule 59(a)(1) suspends the running of the time for appeal, but a motion under Rule 60(b)(2) does not affect the finality of the judgment for purposes of appeal. The same standard for relief on the ground of newly discovered evidence generally applies under both Rules, although the passage of time does decrease the likelihood of relief.

The requirement that the evidence must be newly discovered (after the trial) is an obvious one, and the necessity of a showing of reasonable diligence by the moving party is no less so. It would be intolerable to let a party be casual and careless in his preparation for trial and then, after he has lost, grant him a new trial on the basis of post-trial effort that he could readily have made before.

Question: (7) Should a motion for a new trial be denied for lack of diligence upon a showing that the moving party could have ascertained the substance of the testimony of an opponent's witness, which surprised him at trial, if he had made full use of discovery procedures? Cf. Krock v. Electric Motor & Repair Co., 339 F.2d 73 (1st Cir.1964).

Many cases hold that a new trial should not be granted if the newly discovered evidence is merely cumulative, e.g., Johnson v. United States, 270 F.2d 488 (9th Cir.1959), or impeaching, e.g., Davis v. Yellow Cab Co., 220 F.2d 790 (5th Cir.1955), or is not material, e.g., Kodekey Elecs., Inc. v. Mechanex Corp., 486 F.2d 449 (10th Cir.1973).

Questions: (8) Assume that the only witnesses at the trial of an automobile negligence case were the plaintiff and the defendant, who told diametrically different stories. Is the newly discovered evidence of a disinterested witness supporting the testimony of one of the parties "merely cumulative or impeaching" for the purposes of a new trial motion?

(9) At the trial of a personal-injury action, the defendant put in evidence films ostensibly showing the plaintiff doing manual labor inconsistent with the claim of disability. After verdict for the plaintiff, should a new trial motion be granted on the basis of additional film taken after the trial that showed the plaintiff engaged in heavy lifting and other types of laborious work? See Great Am. Indem. Co. v. Brown, 307 F.2d 306 (5th Cir.1962) (no).

The mere fact that the new evidence would justify a different verdict is commonly not considered enough. The probability that the new trial would produce a different result is emphasized in the cases. As a practical matter, the motion is usually denied unless the trial judge has an abiding feeling that injustice has resulted.

In Wagner v. Loup River Public Power District, 150 Neb. 7, 33 N.W.2d 300 (1948), an unsuccessful action to recover damages to riparian lands from the diversion of water by the defendant, a defense expert had testified as to his opinion that the ground water level would restore itself in the future. As the basis for a new trial on the ground of newly discovered evidence, the plaintiff relied upon subsequent events proving the expert wrong. The trial judge granted the new trial motion, and the appellate court reversed for abuse of discretion.

In Louisville & Nashville Railroad Co. v. Whitley County Court, 100 Ky. 413, 38 S.W. 678 (1897), the governmental plaintiff recovered a $10,000 judgment against the railroad for a sliding of earth away from a highway, allegedly caused by the location of a railroad bed on the side of a hill below the highway. Evidence at trial had been to the effect that the sliding could not be stopped without the expenditure of at least that amount. The railroad moved for a new trial on a showing that after the trial the plaintiff had actually cured the situation by an expenditure of $200 or $300 for laying pipes under the highway so as to conduct away the water of a spring previously hidden. The trial court denied the motion, saying that the evidence was not "newly discovered evidence." On appeal, the denial was reversed as an abuse of discretion.

Questions: (10) What differences do you perceive between the two cases? Do they justify different results? Cf. Rule 60(b)(5) and (6).

(11) Drawing the usual line at facts existing at the time of trial, the Wagner appellate court invoked "a policy that is intended to secure care and vigilance and prevent parties from coming forward subsequently with claims of new evidence which tend to prolong litigation unduly. A failure of justice in a particular instance is ofttimes not so great an evil as that there should be no certain end to litigation. In any but a very extraordinary case in which an utter failure of justice will unequivocally result, a verdict on the evidence at the trial will not be set aside and a new trial granted on the basis of evidence of facts occurring subsequent to such trial." Does not this reasoning go further to suggest abolishing, as a basis for a new trial motion, newly discovered evidence even regarding facts existing at the time of trial?

In both of these last two cases, the action of the trial judge was upset for abuse of discretion. It should be emphasized, however, that the trial judge's discretion is broad and reversals for abuse are rare on motions for a new trial on the ground of newly discovered evidence.

SECTION 3. ERROR IN JURY'S WEIGHING EVIDENCE

Assuming that the state of the evidence is such as to survive a motion for judgment as a matter of law, however named and whatever be the standard in the particular jurisdiction, a party may still seek to have the resulting verdict set aside as against the weight of the evidence. The standards for the exercise of the trial judge's discretion in passing upon a motion for a new trial on this ground are not uniform across jurisdictions.

In the federal courts the federal formulation, from a much-cited opinion by Judge Parker, Garrison v. United States, 62 F.2d 41, 42 (4th Cir.1932), is as follows: "Where there is substantial evidence in support of plaintiff's case, the judge may not direct a verdict against him, even though he may not believe his evidence or may think that the weight of the evidence is on the other side; for, under the constitutional guaranty of trial by jury, it is for the jury to weigh the evidence and pass upon its credibility. He may, however, set aside a verdict supported by substantial evidence where in his opinion it is contrary to the clear weight of the evidence, or is based upon evidence which is false; for, even though the evidence be sufficient to preclude the direction of a verdict, it is still his duty to exercise his power over the proceedings before him to prevent a miscarriage of justice. [Citation omitted.] Verdict can be directed only where there is no substantial evidence to support recovery by the party against whom it is directed or where the evidence is all against him or so overwhelmingly so as to leave no room to doubt what the fact is. [Citation omitted.] Verdict may be set aside and new trial granted when the verdict is contrary to the clear weight of the evidence, or whenever in the exercise of a sound discretion the trial judge thinks this action necessary to prevent a miscarriage of justice."

The federal test as thus stated is followed in substance by most state courts. But there are two other basic patterns, put thus in Fleming James, Jr. & Geoffrey C. Hazard, Jr., Civil Procedure 385–86 (3d ed. 1985) (former version, with similar viewpoint currently expressed in Fleming James, Jr., Geoffrey C. Hazard, Jr. & John Leubsdorf, Civil Procedure 473–74 (5th ed. 2001)): "(1) In some states, the trial court has a genuine and well-nigh unfettered discretion which will not be deemed abused 'where there is any evidence which would support a judgment in favor of the moving party.' Here the trial court is indeed invited to act as a 'thirteenth juror.' (2) In some states, the trial court is forbidden to set aside a verdict if 'on the evidence as presented and under the pleadings, the jury could reasonably have found in accordance with the verdict as rendered.' Even these jurisdictions say the trial judge has discretion to order a new trial but it is clear that if the term has any meaning here at all it is a far narrower discretion than that of the trial judge in the first group of states described. The test for new trial is phrased and administered in such a way that it very nearly approaches the test for directed verdict, though the two are perhaps not exactly equated."

AMOUNT OF DAMAGES

In addition to the case where a new trial is proper because of prejudicial error in the instructions on damages, parties frequently challenge verdicts as being against the weight of the evidence on the issue of the amount of damages. The trial judge has discretion to grant a new trial because of either the excessiveness or the inadequacy of the verdict. The practice of granting new trials on the ground of excessiveness of the verdict goes far back in the common law. See, e.g., Wood v. Gunston, 82 Eng.Rep. 864 (K.B.1655). New trials because of inadequacy of the verdict were a later development in England, but the power to grant a new trial on this ground has long been settled both in England and in this country. See Donald R. Wilson, The Motion for New Trial Based on Inadequacy of Damages Awarded, 39 Neb.L.Rev. 694 (1960).

When the damages are unliquidated, as in the typical action in tort for personal injuries, the question is raised as to how (1) to formulate the standard that the trial judge should apply in reviewing the decision of the jury in fixing the damages, as is also the question, discussed in the two following cases, of what the trial judge may do (2) to limit the scope of a new trial or (3) to eliminate the need for a new trial altogether.

As to that question (1), the standard for damages is, in theory, the same test as is applied on whether a liability verdict is against the weight of the evidence. But courts, including the Supreme Court in Gasperini v. Center for Humanities, Inc., supra p. 385, often rephrase the damages test as whether the award "shocks the conscience." This phrasing might lead in effect to a more hands-off irrationality test, as suggested by the trial judge's saying in Coward v. Ruckert, 381 Pa. 388, 392–93, 113 A.2d 287, 290

(1955): "When the jury's verdict, at the time of its rendition, causes the trial judge to lose his breath, temporarily, and causes him to almost fall from the bench, then it is truly 'shocking to the judicial conscience'. That is the effect the jury's verdict had on the trial judge in the present case, and we can truly say it was the first such shock so experienced in almost ten years of trial experience on the bench." But, in actual practice, judges have not been shy about stepping in to control large awards.

GASOLINE PRODUCTS CO. v. CHAMPLIN REFINING CO., 283 U.S. 494, 51 S.Ct. 513 (1931). In an action in the District of Maine brought to recover royalties due on a license to use certain "cross cracking units," defendant counterclaimed for breach by plaintiff of a contract to construct a "cross vapor treating tower" for treatment of the gasoline produced by the cracking units. The jury returned a verdict for the plaintiff on its claim and a smaller one for the defendant on its counterclaim. On appeal by defendant attacking the disposition of the counterclaim, the First Circuit reversed because of errors in the court's charge on the measure of damages on the counterclaim, and it directed a new trial limited to the amount of those damages.

The Supreme Court granted certiorari, on plaintiff's petition, to review the question whether the court below erred in thus limiting the new trial. Regarding the constitutional problem, the Court by Justice Stone said:

"It is true that at common law there was no practice of setting aside a verdict in part. If the verdict was erroneous with respect to any issue, a new trial was directed as to all. This continued to be the rule in some states after the adoption of the Constitution; but in many it has not been followed, notwithstanding the presence in their constitutions of provisions preserving trial by jury. The Massachusetts courts early modified it to permit a new trial of less than all the issues of fact when they were clearly separable. Bicknell v. Dorion, 16 Pick. 478; see Simmons v. Fish, 210 Mass. 563, 565, 97 N.E. 102. The rule as thus modified has been generally accepted in the New England states, see Zaleski v. Clark, 45 Conn. 397, 404; McKay v. New England Dredging Co., 93 Maine 201, 44 A. 614; Lisbon v. Lyman, 49 N.H. 553, 582 et seq.; Clark v. New York, N.H. & H.R. Co., 33 R.I. 83, 80 A. 406; Parizo v. Wilson, 101 Vt. 514, 144 A. 856, and consistently followed by the Court of Appeals for the First Circuit.

"Lord Mansfield, in applying the common law rule where the verdict, correct as to one issue, was erroneous as to another, said: '. . . for form's sake, we must set aside the whole verdict . . . .' Edie v. East India Co., 1 W.Bl. 295, 298. But we are not now concerned with the form of the ancient rule. It is the Constitution which we are to interpret; and the Constitution is concerned, not with form, but with substance. All of vital significance in trial by jury is that issues of fact be submitted for determination with such instructions and guidance by the court as will afford opportunity for that consideration by the jury which was secured by the rules governing trials at common law. See Herron v. Southern Pacific Co., [283 U.S. 91, 51 S.Ct. 383 (1931)]. Beyond this, the Seventh Amendment does not exact the retention of old forms of procedure. See Walker v. New Mexico & Southern Pacific R. Co., 165 U.S. 593, 596, 17 S.Ct. 421. It does not prohibit the introduction of new methods for ascertaining what facts are in issue, see Ex parte Peterson, 253 U.S. 300, 309, 40 S.Ct. 543, or require that an issue once correctly determined, in accordance with the constitutional command, be tried a second time, even though justice demands that another distinct issue, because erroneously determined, must again be passed on by a jury.

"If, in the present case, the jury has found, in accordance with the applicable legal rules, the amount due to petitioner on the contract for royalties and all the elements fixing its liability on the treating plant contract, there is no constitutional requirement that those issues should again be sent to a jury, merely because the exigencies of the litigation require that a separable issue be tried again."

However, the Court warned: "Where the practice permits a partial new trial, it may not properly be resorted to unless it clearly appears that the issue to be retried is so distinct and separable from the others that the trial of it alone may be had without injustice." As the record showed a dispute regarding the extent of the plaintiff's obligation under the contract that was the subject of the counterclaim, as well as on the defendant's duty to minimize damages, the Court concluded that "the question of damages on the counterclaim is so interwoven with that of liability that the former cannot be submitted to the jury independently of the latter without confusion and uncertainty, which would amount to a denial of a fair trial. [Citation omitted.] There should be a new trial of all the issues raised by the counterclaim."

Questions: (12) Is it appropriate to limit the grant of a new trial because of an excessive verdict to the issue of damages alone (a) if there was error in the instructions on damages? (b) if the instructions on damages were proper?

(13) Would your answers be different if a new trial is granted because of inadequate damages? Compare Rosa v. City of Chester, 278 F.2d 876 (3d Cir.1960), with Simmons v. Fish, 210 Mass. 563, 97 N.E. 102 (1912). Assuming proper instructions, are your answers in terms of the probable reason for erroneous damages? How would you explain Spell v. McDaniel, 824 F.2d 1380, 1400 (4th Cir.1987) (after criminal brought civil rights action based on police brutality and obtained $1000 verdict for ruptured testicle, court granted new trial for inadequate damages but limited retrial to damages alone; new trial yields $900,000 verdict, which is upheld on appeal)?

Dimick v. Schiedt

Supreme Court of the United States, 1935.
293 U.S. 474, 55 S.Ct. 296.

■ MR. JUSTICE SUTHERLAND delivered the opinion of the Court.

This is an action brought by respondent (plaintiff) against petitioner (defendant) in the federal district court for the district of Massachusetts to recover damages for a personal injury resulting from the alleged negligent operation of an automobile on a public highway in Massachusetts. The jury returned a verdict in favor of respondent for the sum of $500. Respondent moved for a new trial on the grounds that the verdict was contrary to the weight of the evidence, that it was a compromise verdict, and that the damages allowed were inadequate. The trial court ordered a new trial upon the last named ground, unless petitioner would consent to an increase of the damages to the sum of $1500. Respondent's consent was neither required nor given. Petitioner, however, consented to the increase, and in accordance with the order of the court a denial of the motion for new trial automatically followed. Respondent appealed to the circuit court of appeals, where the judgment was reversed, the court holding that the conditional order violated the Seventh Amendment of the Federal Constitution in respect of the right of trial by jury. . . .

[The Court here quoted the Seventh Amendment and the statutory predecessor of Rule 59(a)(1)(A).]

In order to ascertain the scope and meaning of the Seventh Amendment, resort must be had to the appropriate rules of the common law established at the time of the adoption of that constitutional provision in 1791. Thompson v. Utah, 170 U.S. 343, 350, 18 S.Ct. 620; Patton v. United States, 281 U.S. 276, 288, 50 S.Ct. 253. A careful examination of the English reports prior to that time fails to disclose any authoritative decision sustaining the power of an English court to increase, either absolutely or conditionally, the amount fixed by the verdict of a jury in an action at law, with certain exceptions [such as in ancient actions for mayhem].

[The Court's discussion of the English cases is omitted.]

From the foregoing and from many other English authorities which we have examined but deem it unnecessary to cite, we conclude that, while there was some practice to the contrary in respect of *decreasing* damages, the established practice and the rule of the common law, as it existed in England at the time of the adoption of the Constitution, forbade the court to *increase* the amount of damages awarded by a jury in actions such as that here under consideration.

We could well rest this opinion upon that conclusion, were it not for the contention that our federal courts from a very early day have upheld the authority of a trial court to deny a motion for new trial because damages were found to be excessive, if plaintiff would consent to remit the excessive amount, and that this holding requires us to recognize a similar rule in respect of increasing damages found to be grossly inadequate. There is a decision by Mr. Justice Story, sitting on circuit, authorizing such a remittitur, as early as 1822. Blunt v. Little, Fed.Cas. No. 1,578, 3 Mason 102. There, the jury returned a verdict for $2,000 damages, suffered as a result of a malicious arrest. Defendant moved for a new trial on the ground that the damages were excessive. The court asserted its power to grant a new trial upon that ground, but directed that the cause should be submitted to another jury unless plaintiff was willing to remit $500 of the damages. This view of the matter was accepted by this Court in Northern Pacific R. Co. v. Herbert, 116 U.S. 642, 646–7, 6 S.Ct. 590, and has been many times reiterated. [Citations omitted.]

Since the decision of Mr. Justice Story in 1822, this court has never expressed doubt in respect of the rule, and it has been uniformly applied by the lower federal courts. It is, however, remarkable that in none of these cases was there any real attempt to ascertain the common law rule on the subject. . . .

. . . .

In the last analysis, the sole support for the decisions of this court and that of Mr. Justice Story, so far as they are pertinent to cases like that now in hand, must rest upon the practice of some of the English judges—a practice which has been condemned as opposed to the principles of the common law by every reasoned English decision, both before and after the adoption of the Federal Constitution, which we have been able to find.

In the light reflected by the foregoing review of the English decisions and commentators, it, therefore, may be that if the question of remittitur were now before us for the first time, it would be decided otherwise. But, first announced by Mr. Justice Story in 1822, the doctrine has been accepted as the law for more than a hundred years and uniformly applied in the federal courts during that time. And, as it finds some support in the practice of the English courts prior to the adoption of the Constitution, we may assume that in a case involving a remittitur, which this case does not, the doctrine would not be reconsidered or disturbed at this late day.

Nevertheless, this court in a very special sense is charged with the duty of construing and upholding the Constitution; and in the discharge of that important duty, it ever must be alert to see that a doubtful precedent be not extended by mere analogy to a different case if the result will be to weaken or subvert what it conceives to be a principle of the fundamental law of the land. Compare Judson v. Gray, 11 N.Y. 408, 412.

. . . .

The controlling distinction between the power of the court and that of the jury is that the former is the power to determine the law and the latter to determine the facts. In dealing with questions like the one now under consideration, that distinction must be borne steadily in mind. Where the verdict returned by a jury is palpably and grossly inadequate or excessive, it should not be permitted to stand; but in that event, both parties remain entitled, as they were entitled in the first instance, to have a jury properly determine the question of liability and the extent of the injury by an assessment of damages. Both are questions of fact. Where the verdict is excessive, the practice of substituting a remission of the excess for a new trial is not without plausible support in the view that what remains is included in the verdict along with the unlawful excess—in that sense that it has been found by the jury—and that the remittitur has the effect of merely lopping off an excrescence. But where the verdict is too small, an increase by the court is a bald addition of something which in no sense can be said to be included in the verdict. When, therefore, the trial court here found that the damages awarded by the jury were so inadequate as to entitle plaintiff to a new trial, how can it be held, with any semblance of reason, that the court, with the consent of the defendant only, may, by assessing an additional amount of damages, bring the constitutional right of the plaintiff to a jury trial to an end in respect of a matter of fact which no jury has ever passed upon either explicitly or by implication? To so hold is obviously to compel the plaintiff to forego his constitutional right to the verdict of a jury and accept "an assessment partly made by a jury which has acted improperly, and partly by a tribunal which has no power to assess."[b]

It is said that the common law is susceptible of growth and adaptation to new circumstances and situations, and that the courts have power to declare and effectuate what is the present rule in respect of a given subject without regard to the old rule; and some attempt is made to apply that principle here. The common law is not immutable, but flexible, and upon its own principles adapts itself to varying conditions. Funk v. United States, 290 U.S. 371, 54 S.Ct. 212. But here, we are dealing with a constitutional provision which has in effect adopted the rules of the common law, in respect of trial by jury, as these rules existed in 1791. To effectuate any change in these rules is not to deal with the common law, qua common law, but to alter the Constitution. The distinction is fundamental, and has been clearly pointed out by Judge Cooley in 1 Const.Limitations, 8th ed., 124.

It is worthy of note that while for more than a century the federal courts have followed the approved practice of conditioning the allowance of a new trial on the consent of plaintiff to remit excessive damages, no federal court, so far as we can discover, has ever undertaken similarly to increase the damages, although there are numerous cases where motions for new trial have been made and granted on the ground that the verdict was inadequate. [Citations omitted.] This, it is true, is but negative evidence; but it is negative evidence of more than ordinary value. For, when we consider that during the great length of time mentioned, the federal courts were constantly applying the rule in respect of the remission of excessive damages, the circumstance that the practice here in question in respect of inadequate damages was never followed or, apparently, its approval even suggested, seems highly significant as indicating a lack of judicial belief in the existence of the power.

State decisions in respect of the matter have been brought to our attention and have received consideration. They embody rulings both ways. A review of them we think would serve no useful purpose.

Judgment affirmed.

---

[b] The Court was here repeating a quotation from Lionel Barber & Co. v. Deutsche Bank, [1919] A.C. 304, 335, which was set forth in the omitted portion of the opinion.

■ MR. JUSTICE STONE, dissenting.

I think the judgment should be reversed.

What the trial court has done is to deny a motion for a new trial, for what seemed to it a good reason: that the defendant had given his binding consent to an increased recovery, which the court thought to be adequate, and thus to remove any substantial ground for awarding a new trial. . . .

. . . .

The decision of the Court is rested on the ground that the Constitution prohibits the trial judge from adopting the practice. Accordingly, I address myself to the question of power without stopping to comment on the generally recognized advantages of the practice as a means of securing substantial justice and bringing the litigation to a more speedy and economical conclusion than would be possible by a new trial to a jury, or the extent to which that or analogous practice has been adopted and found useful in the courts of the several states. See Correction of Damage Verdicts by Remittitur and Additur, 44 Yale Law J. 318. The question is a narrow one: whether there is anything in the Seventh Amendment or in the rules of the common law, as it had developed before the adoption of the Amendment, which would require a federal appellate court to set aside the denial of the motion merely because the particular reasons which moved the trial judge to deny it are not shown to have similarly moved any English judge before 1791.

The Seventh Amendment commands that "in suits at common law," the right to trial by jury shall be preserved and that "no fact tried by a jury shall be otherwise re-examined by any court of the United States, than according to the rules of the common law." Such a provision of a great instrument of government, intended to endure for unnumbered generations, is concerned with substance and not with form. There is nothing in its history or language to suggest that the Amendment had any purpose but to preserve the essentials of the jury trial as it was known to the common law before the adoption of the Constitution. For that reason this Court has often refused to construe it as intended to perpetuate in changeless form the minutiae of trial practice as it existed in the English courts in 1791. From the beginning, its language has been regarded as but subservient to the single purpose of the Amendment, to preserve the essentials of the jury trial in actions at law, serving to distinguish them from suits in equity and admiralty, see Parsons v. Bedford, 3 Pet. 433, 446, and to safeguard the jury's function from any encroachment which the common law did not permit.

Thus interpreted, the Seventh Amendment guarantees that suitors in actions at law shall have the benefits of trial of issues of fact by a jury, but it does not prescribe any particular procedure by which these benefits shall be obtained, or forbid any which does not curtail the function of the jury to decide questions of fact as it did before the adoption of the Amendment. It does not restrict the court's control of the jury's verdict, as it had previously been exercised, and it does not confine the trial judge, in determining what issues are for the jury and what for the court, to the particular forms of trial practice in vogue in 1791.

Thus this Court has held that a federal court, without the consent of the parties, may constitutionally appoint auditors to hear testimony, examine books and accounts and frame and report upon issues of fact, as an aid to the jury in arriving at its verdict, Ex parte Peterson, 253 U.S. 300, 40 S.Ct. 543; it may require both a general and a special verdict and set aside the general verdict for the plaintiff and direct a verdict for the defendant on the basis of the facts specially found, Walker v. New Mexico & Southern Pacific R. Co., 165 U.S. 593, 17 S.Ct. 421; and it may accept so much of the verdict as declares that the plaintiff is entitled to recover, and set aside so much of it as fixes the amount of the damages, and order a new trial of that issue alone, Gasoline Products Co. v. Champlin Refining Co., 283 U.S. 494, 51 S.Ct. 513. Yet none of these procedures was known to the common law. In fact, the very practice, so firmly imbedded in federal procedure, of making a motion for a new trial directly to the trial judge, instead of to the court en banc, was never adopted by the common law. But this Court has found in the Seventh Amendment no bar to the adoption by the federal courts of these novel methods of dealing with the verdict of a jury, for they left unimpaired the function of the jury, to decide issues of fact, which it had exercised before the adoption of the Amendment. Compare Nashville, C. & St.L.R. Co. v. Wallace, 288 U.S. 249, 264, 53 S.Ct. 345.

If we apply that test to the present case it is evident that the jury's function has not been curtailed. After the issues of fact had been submitted to the jury, and its verdict taken, the trial judge was authorized to entertain a motion to set aside the verdict and, as an incident, to determine the legal limits of a proper verdict. A denial of the motion out of hand, however inadequate the verdict, was not an encroachment upon the province of the jury as the common law defined it. It would seem not to be any the more so here because the exercise of the judge's discretion was affected by his knowledge of the fact that a proper recovery had been assured to the plaintiff by the consent of the defendant. Thus the plaintiff has suffered no infringement of a right by the denial of his motion. The defendant has suffered none because he has consented to the increased recovery, of which he does not complain.

. . . .

. . . The fact that in one case the recovery is less than the amount of the verdict [remittitur], and that in the other it is greater [additur], would seem to be without significance. For in neither does the jury return a verdict for the amount actually recovered, and in both the amount of recovery was fixed, not by the verdict but by the consent of the party resisting the motion for a new trial.

. . . .

If our only guide is to be this scant record of the practice [in 1791] of controlling the jury's verdict, however fragmentary the state of its development at this period, and if we must deny any possibility of change, development or improvement, then it must be admitted that search of the legal scrap heap of a century and a half ago may commit us to the incongruous position in which we are left by the present decision: a federal trial court may deny a motion for a new trial where the plaintiff consents to decrease the judgment to a proper amount, but it is powerless to deny the motion if its judgment is influenced by the defendant's consent to a comparable increase in the recovery.

But I cannot agree that we are circumscribed by so narrow and rigid a conception of the common law. The Judiciary Act of 1789, c. 20, 1 Stat. 73, which impliedly adopted the common law rules of evidence for criminal trials in federal courts, and which gave to the federal courts jurisdiction of equity as it had then been developed in England, and the state constitutions which adopted the common law as affording rules for judicial decision, have never been construed as accepting only those rules which could then be found in the English precedents. When the Constitution was adopted, the common law was something more than a miscellaneous collection of precedents. It was a system, then a growth of some five centuries, to guide judicial decision. One of its principles, certainly as important as any other, and that which assured the possibility of the continuing vitality and usefulness of the system, was its capacity for growth and development, and its adaptability to every new situation to which it might be needful to apply it. "This flexibility and capacity for growth and adaptation is," as the Court declared in Hurtado v. California, 110 U.S. 516, 530, 4 S.Ct. 111, "the peculiar boast and excellence of the common law." [Citations omitted.]

. . . .

■ THE CHIEF JUSTICE [HUGHES], MR. JUSTICE BRANDEIS and MR. JUSTICE CARDOZO concur [in dissent].

REMITTITUR

Remittitur gets heavy use in the federal courts. Moreover, once the judge offers remittitur, the overwhelming majority of plaintiffs bow to it, rather than insist on a new trial. This remittitur practice has its academic critics. See Suja A. Thomas, Re-examining the Constitutionality of Remittitur Under the Seventh Amendment, 64 Ohio St.L.J. 731 (2003) (arguing unconstitutionality of remittitur, using a fairly strict historical test under the Re-examination Clause); Irene Deaville Sann, Remittiturs (and Additurs) in the Federal Courts: An Evaluation with Suggested Alternatives, 38 Case W.Res.L.Rev. 157 (1987) (criticizing federal courts' use of remittitur, before suggesting its elimination).

Remittitur is an almost universal feature of practice in the state courts. Some states also recognize additur. Of course, Dimick is not controlling in the interpretation of state constitutions and laws. See, e.g., Freeman v. Wood, 379 Mass. 777, 401 N.E.2d 108 (1980) (Kaplan, J.).

Question: (14) Remittitur would seem to be an improper course if excessive damages result from juror (or other) misconduct rather than from only jury error in weighing the evidence. But how should the two be distinguished? See, e.g., Wells v. Dallas Indep. School Dist., 793 F.2d 679 (5th Cir.1986) (disapproving remittitur in civil rights action from $1,900,000 to $250,000, and saying proportionally big reduction indicated jury passion or prejudice for which new trial is proper remedy).

The most difficult question of remittitur practice regards how the trial judge should determine the actual amount of the remittitur. The answer to this question is not often spelled out in the cases, and the courts that have faced it have not all taken the same view.

In Earl v. Bouchard Transportation Co., 917 F.2d 1320, 1330 (2d Cir.1990), the court held that reduction of the verdict by remittitur should be "only to the maximum amount that would be upheld by the district court as not excessive." Professors Wright, Miller, and Kane, as well as the majority of courts, favor this "maximum recovery" rule. 11 Wright, Miller & Kane § 2815.

In Rosa v. American Oil Co., 129 Conn. 585, 30 A.2d 385 (1943), the trial judge ordered a remittitur of $2350 from a verdict of $6000. He said: "In my judgment, a fair verdict in this case would have been $2,500, and one of $3,650 the limit of legitimate generosity." On appeal, the Connecticut Supreme Court of Errors held that the remittitur should have been $3500, saying that "in fixing the amount a court should be just rather than generous." Similarly, Cal.Civ.Proc.Code § 662.5(b) provides for remittitur in the amount that "the court in its independent judgment determines from the evidence to be fair and reasonable." Professor Moore favored this approach. 6A Moore ¶ 59.08[7] (former version) (citing inter alia Raske v. Raske, 92 F.Supp. 348, 352 (D.Minn.1950)).

In Meissner v. Papas, 35 F.Supp. 676 (E.D.Wis.1940), aff'd, 124 F.2d 720 (7th Cir.1941), the court adopted the standard that the remittitur should reduce the verdict to the lowest amount that could properly be found by the jury. Does not this neglected "minimum recovery" rule—or, to reformulate, remitting on the defendant's new trial motion to the lowest amount that could withstand a new trial motion by the plaintiff—have the most to be said for it? Does it not seem fairest to both parties (by offering the *plaintiff* the choice of a new trial or a recovery rather favorable to the *defendant*), most effective in encouraging the parties to settle for a just amount (otherwise the defendant has little bargaining power, so that the plaintiff will settle only for more than a just amount), and actually least intrusive on the parties' jury rights (the plaintiff should not have veto power over the defendant's right to a properly functioning jury)? See also Durant v. Surety Homes Corp., 582 F.2d 1081 (7th Cir.1978).

AKERMANIS v. SEA-LAND SERVICE, INC., 688 F.2d 898 (2d Cir. 1982), cert. denied, 461 U.S. 927, 103 S.Ct. 2087 (1983). An injured seaman sued the shipowner under the Jones Act. By special verdict, the jury found that defendant had been negligent, its negligence had been a proximate cause of the accident, plaintiff had suffered $528,000 in damages, and plaintiff had been contributorily negligent to the extent of four-percent responsibility. On defendant's motion, the trial judge found that this percentage was against the weight of the evidence and "that the lowest contributory negligence factor the evidence would support was 25 percent. He therefore ordered a new trial on liability issues, but with the condition that the defendant's motion for new trial would be denied if the plaintiff would accept a 'remittitur' of damages based on an increase of the contributory negligence factor from four to 25 percent. The plaintiff accepted, and judgment was entered in favor of the plaintiff for 75% of the jury's determination of the total amount of damages suffered." Defendant appealed, and plaintiff cross-appealed.

The court of appeals found this use of remittitur to be unconstitutional under Dimick. It then remanded the case for the trial judge's reconsideration of the new trial motion because it was not clear that he had applied the correct standard, and the court of appeals also indicated that a new trial could be limited to the existence and extent of contributory negligence.

CORPUS v. BENNETT, 430 F.3d 912 (8th Cir.2005). An arrestee, who got in a scuffle with a jailer, brought a § 1983 civil rights action for use of excessive force. The jury by special verdict found that he had suffered no direct injury but awarded nominal damages for deprivation of constitutional rights—doing so in the amount of $75,000 despite the judge's instruction that in the absence of direct injury they "may return a verdict for plaintiff in some nominal sum such as one dollar." The district judge reduced the verdict to $1 and entered judgment. The plaintiff appealed.

The court of appeals affirmed (2–1). It viewed the reduction as the correction of an error of law.

PUNITIVE DAMAGES

Today the common-law remedy of punitive damages works to punish or deter by making an example of the defendant, a sort of largely private fine designed not to compensate but rather to express moral condemnation.

Question: (15) Given a civil rights verdict for a prisoner in the amount of $95,000 in compensatory damages and $900,000 in punitive damages, can the district judge remit the award of punitive damages down to zero? See Hill v. Marshall, 962 F.2d 1209 (6th Cir.1992) (no, as such a "remittitur" is really a grant of judgment as a matter of law and must be reviewed as such).

The applicable substantive law specifies the considerations involved in, and the limits imposed on, fixing punitive damages. The amount might turn on factors such as the character of the defendant's conduct, the defendant's motives and assets, and the need for deterrence. The tort reform movement has of late had some success in tightening the restrictions on punitive damages and even in capping them. See Developments in the Law—The Civil Jury, 110 Harv.L.Rev. 1408, 1513–36 (1997). Due process also imposes some restrictions on the law of punitive damages, such as prohibiting any amount to punish the defendant directly for harms inflicted on nonparties. See Philip Morris USA v. Williams, 549 U.S. 346, 127 S.Ct. 1057 (2007).

As to procedure, fixing the award under that substantive law is at least somewhat a fact-sensitive task, and so normally it has been and is for the jury to perform. In performing it, the jury is subject to all the usual rules and review. Recently, however, the U.S. Supreme Court has imposed a new level of review. Concerned with the absence of the protections of criminal procedure and with the unguided discretion of the jury, the Court found in the Due Process Clause a prohibition on "grossly excessive" punitive damages, empowering itself to strike down the relatively rare case in which the system goes overboard. BMW of N. Am., Inc. v. Gore, 517 U.S. 559, 562, 116 S.Ct. 1589, 1592 (1996); see State Farm Mut. Auto. Ins. Co. v. Campbell, 538 U.S. 408, 123 S.Ct. 1513 (2003). The Court explained that the due process ceiling depends on three factors: the degree of the defendant's reprehensibility in harming the plaintiff; the ratio, which State Farm specified should seldom if ever exceed nine-to-one, between the punitive damages award and the compensated harm to the plaintiff; and the civil penalties imposable in cases of similar misconduct.

The Supreme Court has specified the applicable procedure as well. In Cooper Industries, Inc. v. Leatherman Tool Group, Inc., 532 U.S. 424, 121 S.Ct. 1678 (2001), its language was a bit confusing, but its message was fairly clear. In reviewing the jury award, the trial judge is to apply those three imprecise factors, applying them as a matter of law independently of the jury. Such application of the legal ceiling is not a re-examination of a fact tried by a jury, said the Court, but instead is an ordinary kind of application of law to a jury verdict as allowed by the Seventh Amendment. Then, when reviewing the trial judge's application of the three factors to the facts of the case, the appellate court is to act "de novo." Apparently, the appellate court itself can just cut an excessive award, setting it at the maximum amount that the jury could have awarded consistently with due process.

Thus, in that particular case, Leatherman had sued Cooper in federal court for passing off Leatherman's "pocket survival tool" as Cooper's own. The jury had awarded $50,000 in compensatory damages and $4,500,000 in punitive damages. The district judge had let that award stand. The court of appeals had affirmed, applying the typical abuse-of-discretion standard of review. The Supreme Court reversed, saying that the court of appeals should on its own consider the due process ceiling. On remand, the court of appeals considered the three factors and then rather arbitrarily set $500,000 as "the maximum award of punitive damages consistent with due process on the facts of this case," 285 F.3d 1146, 1152 (9th Cir.2002).

Of course, the due process ceiling also applies to state court awards. Moreover, state supreme courts are holding that the accompanying procedure for review is mandatory in state courts, under the Supremacy Clause. See Cynthia L. Blackwell, Note, Did Cooper v. Leatherman Require State Appellate Courts to Apply a De Novo Standard of Review for Determining the Constitutional Excessiveness of Punitive Damages Claims? Aken v. Plains Electric Generation & Transmission Cooperative, Inc., 34 N.M.L.Rev. 405 (2004).

SECTION 4. APPELLATE REVIEW OF GRANT OR DENIAL OF NEW TRIAL

Fairmount Glass Works v. Cub Fork Coal Co.

Supreme Court of the United States, 1933.
287 U.S. 474, 53 S.Ct. 252.

■ MR. JUSTICE BRANDEIS delivered the opinion of the Court.

Cub Fork Coal Company and Paragon Colliery Company brought this action in the federal court for southern Indiana to recover from Fairmount Glass Works $32,417, with interest, as damages for breach of a contract to purchase 17,500 tons of coal, at $6.50 per ton f.o.b. mines, deliverable in twelve monthly installments beginning June, 1920. Jurisdiction of the federal court was invoked on the ground of diversity of citizenship. The Glass Works pleaded in bar several defenses; and it also set up a counterclaim in the sum of $2,000 as damages for failure to make delivery as provided by the contract. [During the early months of the contract, the market price was above the contract price and the plaintiffs-sellers delivered less than the contract installments, ostensibly because of inability to arrange for railroad cars. Later, the market price fell below the contract price and the defendant-buyer refused to accept deliveries after December 4, 1920.] Three trials before a jury were had. At each of the first two the verdict was for the defendant; and each time the judgment entered thereupon was reversed by the Circuit Court of Appeals [for errors of law] with a general direction for a new trial, 19 F.2d 273; 33 F.2d 420. On the third trial the plaintiffs recovered a verdict for $1; and, after further proceedings, judgment was entered thereon with costs.

The plaintiffs appealed [the denial of their motion for a new trial. The circuit court of appeals reversed, on the ground that the minimum amount recoverable was ascertainable as $18,250 by known market prices. Certiorari was granted.]

First. . . .

. . . Under certain circumstances the appellate court may inquire into the action of the trial court on a motion for a new trial. Thus, its denial may be reviewed if the trial court erroneously excluded from consideration matters which were appropriate to a decision on the motion, Mattox v. United States, 146 U.S. 140, 13 S.Ct. 50; Ogden v. United States, 112 F. 523; or if it acted on the mistaken view that there was no jurisdiction to grant it, or that there was no authority to grant it on the ground advanced, Felton v. Spiro, 78 F. 576, 581; Dwyer v. United States, 170 F. 160, 165; Paine v. St. Paul Union Stockyards Co., 35 F.2d 624, 626–628. It becomes necessary, therefore, to determine whether the circumstances of the case at bar justify an enquiry into the trial court's refusal to set aside the verdict.

Second. It is urged that the motion for a new trial presented an issue of law. The argument is that on the motion or on the court's own initiative the verdict should have been set aside as inconsistent on its face, since if the plaintiffs were entitled to recover at all they were entitled to substantial, not merely nominal, damages. The case, it is contended, is comparable to one in which the award of damages exceeded a statutory limit, see Southern Ry. Co. v. Bennett, 233 U.S. 80, 34 S.Ct. 566; or was less than an amount undisputed, Glenwood Irrig. Co. v. Vallery, 248 F. 483; Stetson v. Stindt, 279 F. 209; or was in pursuance of erroneous instructions on the measure of damages, Chesapeake & O. Ry. Co. v. Gainey, 241 U.S. 494, 496, 36 S.Ct. 633; or was in clear contravention of the instructions of the trial court, United Press Ass'ns v. National Newspapers Ass'n, 254 F. 284; compare American R.R. Co. v. Santiago, 9 F.2d 753, 757–758.

To regard the verdict as inconsistent on its face is to assume that the jury found for the plaintiff and failed to perform its task of assessing damages. The trial judge was not obliged so to regard the verdict. The defendant had insisted upon several defenses and had set up a counterclaim. The plaintiffs were not entitled to a directed verdict. The evidence was voluminous; and, on some issues at least, conflicting. The instructions left the contested issues of liability to the jury. The verdict may have represented a finding for the defendant on those issues; the reason for the award of nominal damages may have been that the jury wished the costs to be taxed against the defendant. The defendant did not complain of the verdict. The record before us does not contain any explanation by the trial court of the refusal to grant a new trial, or any interpretation by it of the jury's verdict. In the absence of such expressions by the trial court in the case at bar, the refusal to grant a new trial cannot be held erroneous as a matter of law. Appellate courts should be slow to impute to juries a disregard of their duties, and to trial courts a want of diligence or perspicacity in appraising the jury's conduct. Compare Union Pacific R.R. Co. v. Hadley, 246 U.S. 330, 334, 38 S.Ct. 318; Dunn v. United States, 284 U.S. 390, 394, 52 S.Ct. 189.

Third. It is urged that the refusal to set aside the verdict was an abuse of the trial court's discretion, and hence reviewable. The Court of Appeals has not declared that the trial judge abused his discretion. Clearly the mere refusal to grant a new trial where nominal damages were awarded is not an abuse of discretion. This Court has frequently refrained from disturbing the trial court's approval of an award of damages which seemed excessive or inadequate, and the circuit courts of appeals have generally followed a similar policy. Whether refusal to set aside a verdict for failure to award substantial damages may ever be reviewed on the ground that the trial judge abused his discretion, we have no occasion to determine.

. . . .

The judgment of the Circuit Court of Appeals is reversed and that of the District Court is affirmed.

■ MR. JUSTICE STONE and MR. JUSTICE CARDOZO, dissenting.

A verdict found in contravention of the instructions of the court may be reversed on appeal as contrary to law.

So much the prevailing opinion apparently concedes.

The verdict of $1 returned by the jury upon the trial of this cause may not be squared with their instructions and hence was properly annulled.

By the instructions of the trial judge they were required, if they found that the defendant had broken its contract, to award to the plaintiffs the difference between the contract price of the coal and its market value, after allowance for the defendant's counterclaim. The evidence most favorable to the defendant, both as to claim and counterclaim, made it necessary, if there was any breach, to return a substantial verdict, the minimum being capable of accurate computation. The distinction is not to be ignored between this case of a breach of contract and [tort] cases . . . . There the discretion of the jury was not subject to tests so determinate and exact. . . . Enough for present purposes that in the circumstances of the case at hand the verdict of $1 is a finding that the contract had been broken, and this irrespective of the motive that caused the verdict to be given. What the motive was we cannot know from anything disclosed to us by the record. Nothing there disclosed lays a basis for a holding that the nominal verdict for the plaintiffs was designed to save them from the costs which the law would have charged against them if there had been a verdict for defendant. The jury were not instructed as to the liability for costs, and for all that appears had no knowledge on the subject. Nor would such a motive, if there were reason to ascribe it, rescue them from the reproach of disobedience and error. It would merely substitute one form of misconduct for another. It would do this, moreover, in contradiction of the record. By no process of mere construction can a verdict that nominal loss has resulted from a breach be turned into a verdict that there had been no breach at all. On the face of the record, the jury found there was a wrong, and then, in contravention of instructions, refused, either through misunderstanding or through wilfulness, to assess the damages ensuing.

Justice is not promoted in its orderly administration when such conduct is condoned.

PETTINGILL v. FULLER, 107 F.2d 933 (2d Cir.1939), cert. denied, 309 U.S. 669, 60 S.Ct. 609 (1940). The jury in a personal-injury case returned a verdict for the defendant. On the plaintiff's motion, the judge set the verdict aside for misconduct by the defendant's counsel during the cross-examination of a witness: in arguing an evidentiary point in the presence of the jury, counsel had said that the witness had been convicted of negligent driving in connection with the events in suit. A second trial followed at which the plaintiff won verdict and judgment. The defendant appealed, claiming as error the setting aside of the first verdict in his favor and seeking to reinstate that verdict.

The court of appeals found that it had been an abuse of discretion to set that verdict aside, in view of the nature of the misconduct and the plaintiff's failure to request a curative instruction. Judge Augustus Hand, joined by Learned Hand and Charles Clark, continued:

"The question remains whether on an appeal from the final judgment for the plaintiff we may review the interlocutory order setting aside the verdict rendered at the first trial and order that verdict reinstated.

"In spite of the fact that the courts of the United States have been most loath to review orders granting or denying motions to set aside verdicts, it is implicit in the opinion of Justice Brandeis in Fairmount Glass Works v. Cub Fork Coal Co., 287 U.S. 474, 483–486, 53 S.Ct. 252, that they may do so in certain cases, one of which would seem to be an abuse of the trial judge's discretion. 287 U.S. at p. 485, 53 S.Ct. 252. There a review was declined because there was no explanation by the trial judge of his refusal to set the verdict aside and the record did not show that the verdict was clearly erroneous and arbitrary. The question whether an order granting or denying a motion for a new trial may be reviewed on appeal when not followed by a final judgment entered after a new trial is not involved in the case at bar. Here we are reviewing an interlocutory order after final judgment in the action. An attempt to review an order setting aside a verdict has rarely been made under such circumstances; indeed never within our knowledge. That such an order may be reviewed on an appeal from a final judgment is undoubted unless the exercise of judicial discretion involved in making it is beyond the correcting hand of a court of appeal, no matter how arbitrary it was. . . .

"The refusal to review the denial of a motion for a new trial on newly discovered evidence may stand on a different footing. Here the error of the trial court was in the course of one trial. It was not in declining to open the record where no fraud was shown and the case so far as the trial court was concerned had come to an end.

"The judgment for the plaintiff on the second trial is reversed with costs, the order setting aside the verdict for the defendant is reversed, the verdict for the defendant is ordered reinstated and final judgment thereon shall be entered for the defendant."[c]

---

[c] A similar standard of abuse of discretion was applied in City of Cleveland v. Peter Kiewit Sons' Co., 624 F.2d 749 (6th Cir.1980) (reversing *denial* of new trial based on misconduct of counsel).

Question: (16) Why did not the defendant appeal immediately after the first verdict was set aside?

Grunenthal v. Long Island Rail Road

Supreme Court of the United States, 1968.
393 U.S. 156, 89 S.Ct. 331.

■ MR. JUSTICE BRENNAN delivered the opinion of the Court.

Petitioner was working for respondent as foreman of a track gang when a 300–pound railroad tie being lifted by the gang fell and severely crushed his right foot. He sued respondent for damages under the Federal Employers' Liability Act, 45 U.S.C. § 51 et seq., and a jury in the District Court for the Southern District of New York awarded him $305,000.[1] The trial judge denied the railroad's motion to set the award aside as excessive. The railroad appealed the denial to the Court of Appeals for the Second Circuit, and that court, one judge dissenting, ordered the District Court to grant the railroad a new trial unless the petitioner would agree to remit $105,000 of the award. 388 F.2d 480 (1968). We granted certiorari, 392 U.S. 902, 88 S.Ct. 1651 (1968). We reverse.

Petitioner argues that the Court of Appeals exceeded its appellate powers in reviewing the denial of the railroad's motion, either because such review is constitutionally precluded by the provision of the Seventh Amendment that "no fact tried by a jury, shall be otherwise reexamined in any Court of the United States, than according to the rules of the common law,"[3] or because such review is prohibited by the Federal Employers' Liability Act itself. We have no occasion in this case to consider that argument, for assuming, without deciding, that the Court of Appeals was empowered to review the denial and invoked the correct standard of review, the action of the trial judge, as we view the evidence, should not have been disturbed. See Neese v. Southern R. Co., 350 U.S. 77, 76 S.Ct. 131 (1955).

[The Court's summary of the trial judge's opinion, 292 F.Supp. 813 (S.D.N.Y.1967), is omitted.]

The Court of Appeals regarded its inquiry as limited to determining whether the trial judge abused his discretion in denying the railroad's motion. Its guide for that determination, the court stated, was the standard of review announced in its earlier decision in Dagnello v. Long Island R. Co., 289 F.2d 797, 806 (1961): "[W]e appellate judges [are] not to decide

---

[1] Petitioner's complaint sought damages of $250,000. This was amended with leave of the trial judge to $305,000 after the jury returned its verdict in that amount.

[3] All 11 Courts of Appeals have held that nothing in the Seventh Amendment precludes appellate review of the trial judge's denial of a motion to set aside an award as excessive. [Citations from each circuit omitted. The Supreme Court finally agreed with them, by so holding in Gasperini v. Center for Humanities, Inc., supra p. 391. Cassandra Burke Robertson, Judging Jury Verdicts, 83 Tul.L.Rev. 157, 213–15 (2008), goes further to argue that appellate courts should change their practice of reviewing denial of new trial more deferentially than grant of new trial.—Ed.]

whether we would have set aside the verdict if we were presiding at the trial, but whether the amount is so high that it would be a denial of justice to permit it to stand. We must give the benefit of every doubt to the judgment of the trial judge; but surely there must be an upper limit, and whether that has been surpassed is not a question of fact with respect to which reasonable men may differ, but a question of law."[4]

We read Dagnello, however, as requiring the Court of Appeals in applying this standard to make a detailed appraisal of the evidence bearing on damages. Indeed this re-examination led to the conclusion in Dagnello that it was not a denial of justice to permit the jury's award to stand. If the Court of Appeals made a similar appraisal of the evidence in this case, the details are not disclosed in the majority opinion. Beyond attaching unexplained significance to petitioner's failure in his complaint "to ask for damages in such a large sum as $305,000," the relevant discussion is limited to the bald statement that "giving Grunenthal the benefit of every doubt, and weighing the evidence precisely in the same manner as we did in Dagnello . . . we cannot in any rational manner consistent with the evidence arrive at a sum in excess of $200,000." 388 F.2d, at 484. We have therefore made our own independent appraisal of the evidence. We conclude that the trial judge did not abuse his discretion in finding "nothing untoward, inordinate, unreasonable or outrageous—nothing indicative of a runaway jury or one that lost its head."

[The Court's appraisal of the evidence is omitted.]

The judgment of the Court of Appeals is reversed and the case is remanded to that court with direction to enter a judgment affirming the judgment of the District Court.

It is so ordered.

■ [The dissenting opinions of JUSTICES HARLAN and STEWART are omitted.]

TAYLOR v. WASHINGTON TERMINAL CO., 409 F.2d 145 (D.C.Cir.), cert. denied, 396 U.S. 835, 90 S.Ct. 93 (1969). An injured fireman sued the railroad for negligence under the FELA. The plaintiff won a verdict of $80,000. The defendant moved for a new trial based on excessive damages. The trial court granted the motion conditioned on a remittitur of $60,000. The plaintiff refused, and on retrial he received a verdict and judgment for $25,000. The plaintiff appealed.

The court of appeals ultimately set aside the lower court's new trial order and reinstated the original verdict. But first it had to fix the standard of review. It began by referring to the by-then generally accepted learning that new trial orders based on the weight of the evidence could be reversed, but only in rare cases:

[4] The standard has been variously phrased: "Common phrases are such as: 'grossly excessive,' 'inordinate,' 'shocking to the judicial conscience,' 'outrageously excessive,' 'so large as to shock the conscience of the court,' 'monstrous,' and many others." Dagnello v. Long Island R. Co., supra, 289 F.2d, at 802.

"This learning has largely arisen from consideration of cases in which motions for new trial—especially on the ground of excessive verdict—have been *denied.* Two factors unite to favor very restricted review of such orders. The first of these is the deference due the trial judge, who has had the opportunity to observe the witnesses and to consider the evidence in the context of a living trial rather than upon a cold record. The second factor is the deference properly given to the jury's determination of such matters of fact as the weight of the evidence and the quantum of damages. This second factor is further weighted by the constitutional allocation to the jury of questions of fact.

"Where the jury finds a particular quantum of damages and the trial judge refuses to disturb its finding on the motion for a new trial, the two factors press in the same direction, and an appellate court should be certain indeed that the award is contrary to all reason before it orders a remittitur or a new trial. However, where, as here, the jury as primary fact-finder fixes a quantum, and the trial judge indicates his view that it is excessive by granting a remittitur, the two factors oppose each other. The judge's unique opportunity to consider the evidence in the living courtroom context must be respected. But against his judgment we must consider that the agency to whom the Constitution allocates the fact-finding function in the first instance—the jury—has evaluated the facts differently.[13]

"In this jurisdiction particularly, District Court judges have given great weight to jury verdicts. They have stated that a new trial motion will not be granted unless the 'verdict is so unreasonably high as to result in a miscarriage of justice,'[14] or, most recently, unless the verdict is 'so inordinately large as obviously to exceed the maximum limit of a reasonable range within which the jury may properly operate.'[15]

"At the appellate level, in reviewing a trial judge's grant of a new trial for excessive verdict, we should not apply the same standard. The trial judge's view that a verdict is outside the proper range deserves considerable deference. His exercise of discretion in granting the motion is reviewable only for abuse. Thus we will reverse the grant of a new trial for excessive verdict only where the quantum of damages found by the jury was *clearly* within 'the maximum limit of a reasonable range.' "

---

[13] In taking this approach, we follow the lead taken by the Third Circuit en banc in a similar case. In Lind v. Schenley Industries, Inc., 278 F.2d 79, cert. denied, 364 U.S. 835, 81 S.Ct. 58, 5 L.Ed.2d 60 (1960), that court reversed a trial court's grant of a new trial because the verdict was against the weight of the evidence. The court distinguished between cases where a new trial is granted because of some legal error and cases in which the trial judge simply reweighed evidence already submitted to a jury. In cases of the latter sort (in which grants of new trials for excessive general damages must be included), "the [trial] judge takes over, if he does not usurp, the prime function of the jury as the trier of the facts. It then becomes the duty of the appellate tribunal to exercise a closer degree of scrutiny and supervision than is the case where a new trial is granted because of some undesirable or pernicious influence obtruding into the trial. Such a close scrutiny is required in order to protect the litigants' right to jury trial." 278 F.2d at 90.

[14] Frank v. Atlantic Greyhound Corp., D.D.C., 172 F.Supp. 190, 191 (1959).

[15] Graling v. Reilly, D.D.C., 214 F.Supp. 234, 235 (1963).

Donovan v. Penn Shipping Co.

Supreme Court of the United States, 1977.
429 U.S. 648, 97 S.Ct. 835.

■ PER CURIAM.

The petitioner, while employed by the respondents as a seaman on the SS Penn–Sailor, slipped on wet paint, injuring his right wrist and elbow. He sued the respondents under the Jones Act, 46 U.S.C. § 688, and obtained a $90,000 verdict at his jury trial. The respondents moved to set aside the verdict as excessive. Fed.Rules Civ.Proc. 50, 59. The District Court granted the motion, and ordered a new trial on damages unless the petitioner agreed to remit $25,000 of the $90,000 award.

After some time the petitioner submitted to the District Court a proposed order stating that he accepted "under protest" the reduced verdict of $65,000, but reserving nonetheless "his right to appeal therefrom." This language was adopted by the District Court in entering a judgment for the petitioner in the amount of $65,000.

The petitioner sought appellate review of the District Court's decision to order a conditional new trial. In so doing he asked the Court of Appeals for the Second Circuit to discard the settled rule that a plaintiff who has accepted a remittitur may not appeal to seek reinstatement of the original verdict. The Court of Appeals refused the petitioner's invitation, and dismissed the appeal. 536 F.2d 536.

. . . .

The proper role of the trial and appellate courts in the federal system in reviewing the size of jury verdicts is . . . a matter of federal law, see Hanna v. Plumer, 380 U.S. 460, 466–469, 85 S.Ct. 1136, 1141–1142 (1965); Byrd v. Blue Ridge Rural Electric Co–op., 356 U.S. 525, 78 S.Ct. 893 (1958), and that law has always prohibited appeals in the situation at bar. The Court of Appeals for the Second Circuit correctly adhered to the consistent rule established by this Court's decisions. In order to clarify whatever uncertainty might exist, we now reaffirm the longstanding rule that a plaintiff in federal court, whether prosecuting a state or federal cause of action, may not appeal from a remittitur order he has accepted.

The petition for a writ of certiorari is granted, and the judgment is affirmed.

■ THE CHIEF JUSTICE [BURGER] and MR. JUSTICE BLACKMUN would grant the petition for certiorari but would have the case argued and given plenary consideration rather than disposed of summarily.

KEVIN M. CLERMONT, PROCEDURE'S MAGICAL NUMBER THREE: PSYCHOLOGICAL BASES FOR STANDARDS OF DECISION,

72 Cornell L.Rev. 1115, 1155–56 (1987). "I submit that a definite improvement would flow from recognizing only three review standards for decisions on new-trial motions. At one extreme, all issues currently classified as matters of law should still undergo review as such, with the appellate court asking whether it simply disagrees with the trial judge's decision and thus reversing only if it thinks error to be more likely than not. At the other extreme, on factual reconsideration the appellate court should reverse a denial of a motion on the ground that the verdict was against the weight of the evidence or that the verdict was excessive or inadequate only if it is almost certain that the trial judge erred. All other reviewable new-trial issues should receive customary middle-level scrutiny, by which the appellate court looks for clear or highly probable error.

"This formulation of three standards roughly conforms to the present state of the doctrine, and likely even more closely to what most courts do as opposed to what they say. It covers the same range as the current standards, but reduces potentially infinite gradations to the three discrete standards of probable, highly probable, and almost certain error. This easy formulation would improve comprehension and application by the courts, as well as better control them. Moreover, quantum leaps adequately serve the policies behind variable deference on review; indeed, because the limited choice of standards illuminates the policy question, courts may be able more soundly to effectuate those policies, once three and only three discrete standards of new-trial review come to be recognized."

APPELLATE REVIEW OF FACTS IN NONJURY CASES

Rule 52(a) requires the judge in a nonjury trial to make specific findings of fact. It further provides that those findings will stand unless "clearly erroneous." See generally Charles Alan Wright & Mary Kay Kane, Law of Federal Courts § 96 (6th ed. 2002) (treating judge trial).

The findings must be sufficiently comprehensive to indicate to the appellate court the factual basis of the ultimate judgment and thus to permit appropriate review. The nature of the requirement is illustrated in Dearborn Nat. Casualty Co. v. Consumers Petroleum Co., 164 F.2d 332 (7th Cir.1947). Insurer brought this action against insured for a declaratory judgment of nonliability on an insurance policy that required notice of an accident "as soon as practicable." The notice had been given 94 days after the accident, but only 10 days after the injured party had brought a suit against the insured, who contended that this suit was his first knowledge of the accident. The trial court found simply that notice was given "as soon as practicable." The appellate court remanded for further findings because it could not tell whether the trial court meant that a delay of 94 days, unexplained, was "as soon as practicable" within the meaning of the policy or whether it found that the insured, until sued, lacked knowledge of the accident. On remand, the trial judge made detailed findings that the insured had no knowledge of any accident that would suggest any liability until suit was brought. Upon these findings, the judgment in favor of the insured was affirmed, 178 F.2d 277 (7th Cir.1949).

Imposing the clearly erroneous standard of review struck a compromise between the highly deferential approach to factual review at common law, where jury trial had dominated, and the nondeferential review in old equity, where all evidence had come in written form. Of the clearly erroneous standard the Supreme Court said in United States v. United States Gypsum Co., 333 U.S. 364, 395, 68 S.Ct. 525, 542 (1948), that a judge's finding "is 'clearly erroneous' when although there is evidence to support it, the reviewing court on the entire evidence is left with the definite and firm conviction that a mistake has been committed."

What bounds should be placed on the application of this relatively insulating standard of review?

Kind of evidence.—In Orvis v. Higgins, 180 F.2d 537, 539–40 (2d Cir.1950), Judge Frank had particularized as follows: "Where a trial judge sits without a jury, the rule varies with the character of the evidence: (a) If he decides a fact issue on written evidence alone, we are as able as he to determine credibility, and so we may disregard his finding. (b) Where the evidence is partly oral and the balance is written or deals with undisputed facts, then we may ignore the trial judge's finding and substitute our own, (1) if the written evidence or some undisputed fact renders the credibility of the oral testimony extremely doubtful, or (2) if the trial judge's finding must rest exclusively on the written evidence or the undisputed facts, so that his evaluation of credibility has no significance. (c) But where the evidence supporting his finding as to any fact issue is entirely oral testimony, we may disturb that finding only in the most unusual circumstances."

Compare the original note of the Advisory Committee on Rule 52(a): "[The clearly erroneous test] is applicable to all classes of findings in cases tried without a jury whether the finding is of a fact concerning which there was conflict of testimony, or of a fact deduced or inferred from uncontradicted testimony."

On March 19, 1985, the Supreme Court decided Anderson v. City of Bessemer City, North Carolina, 470 U.S. 564, 105 S.Ct. 1504 (1985), which expressly rejected the view of Orvis v. Higgins. The Court explained that because fact-finding is the job of the trial judge and because active appellate review would be ineffective and burdensome, the clearly erroneous standard applies even when findings rest on physical or documentary evidence or inferences from other facts. And on April 29, 1985, the Supreme Court promulgated the Advisory Committee's previously proposed amendment to Rule 52(a), which became effective August 1, 1985, and added the phrase reprinted in italics: "Findings of fact, *whether based on oral or documentary evidence,* shall not be set aside unless clearly erroneous, and due regard shall be given to the opportunity of the trial court to judge of the credibility of the witnesses." The Advisory Committee had explained that more active review "would tend to undermine the legitimacy of the district courts in the eyes of litigants, multiply appeals by encouraging appellate retrial of some factual issues, and needlessly reallocate judicial authority."

Interestingly, the Anderson Court further ruled: "When findings are based on determinations regarding the credibility of witnesses, Rule 52(a) demands even greater deference to the trial court's findings; for only the trial judge can be aware of the variations in demeanor and tone of voice that bear so heavily on the listener's understanding of and belief in what is said. . . . [W]hen a trial judge's finding is based on his decision to credit the testimony of one of two or more witnesses, each of whom has told a coherent and facially plausible story that is not contradicted by extrinsic evidence, that finding, if not internally inconsistent, can virtually never be clear error."

Law/fact line.—In United States v. General Motors Corp., 384 U.S. 127, 141 n.16, 86 S.Ct. 1321, 1328 n.16 (1966), the Court tried to articulate a distinction between "law" and "fact" but had a hard time of it. Consider now a passage from its opinion: "We note that, as in United States v. Parke, Davis & Co., 362 U.S. 29, 44–45, 80 S.Ct. 503, 511–512, the ultimate conclusion by the trial judge, that the defendants' conduct did not constitute a combination or conspiracy in violation of the Sherman Act, is not to be shielded by the 'clearly erroneous' test embodied in Rule 52(a) . . . . As in Parke, Davis, supra, the question here is not one of 'fact,' but consists rather of the legal standard required to be applied to the undisputed facts of the case."

Compare Commissioner v. Duberstein, 363 U.S. 278, 289, 80 S.Ct. 1190, 1198 (1960), which defined "fact" to include any finding "based ultimately on the application of the fact-finding tribunal's experience with the mainsprings of human conduct." Accordingly, the Supreme Court has shown some tendency to counteract perceived appellate-court intrusion by classifying mixed questions as "fact." E.g., Pullman–Standard v. Swint, 456 U.S. 273, 102 S.Ct. 1781 (1982) (discriminatory intent under civil rights statute is question of fact), discussed in Evan Tsen Lee, Principled Decision Making and the Proper Role of Federal Appellate Courts: The Mixed Questions Conflict, 64 S.Cal.L.Rev. 235 (1991).

Thus, Rule 52(a) requires separating legal matters from facts. But how to distinguish in the gray cases? See Randall H. Warner, All Mixed Up About Mixed Questions, 7 J.App.Prac. & Process 101 (2005). The sound approach would involve breaking a decision on a mixed question into its components, and then applying to each the standard of review for law or fact as function dictates, so that the trial and appellate courts each end up deciding the issues they should. On components right in the middle, involving the purest matters of applying law to fact, the appellate court would classify them as law or fact in accordance with the importance of having been present on the trial court scene, where one could hear evidence and such. The result would be that the ultimate determination of an antitrust conspiracy in restraint of trade might be a question of law for purposes of appeal, while discriminatory intent might be a question of fact insulated from review. Indeed, once classified as a question of law, and given the judge's specific findings of fact, the existence of an antitrust conspiracy could receive a rather searching review from the appellate court.

Question: (17) How does this law/fact line compare to the division of functions between judge and jury, which was discussed supra pp. 1393–95? Compare Martin B. Louis, Allocating Adjudicative Decision Making Authority Between the Trial and Appellate Levels: A Unified View of the Scope of Review, the Judge/Jury Question, and Procedural Discretion, 64 N.C.L.Rev. 993, 996–97, 1003–04, 1027–29 (1986) (asserting the lines are basically the same), with 1 Steven Alan Childress & Martha S. Davis, Federal Standards of Review § 3.09 (3d ed. 1999) (noting differences).

Kind of fact.—In Bose Corp. v. Consumers Union of United States, 466 U.S. 485, 104 S.Ct. 1949 (1984), the Court decreed nondeferential review of a federal judge's finding of actual malice in a product-disparagement action, citing First Amendment concerns. Indeed, the Court later held, in Harte–Hanks Communications, Inc. v. Connaughton, 491 U.S. 657, 109 S.Ct. 2678 (1989), that this vaguely defined exception for "constitutional fact" requires nondeferential review by trial and appellate judges of such a right-endangering finding by a federal *jury* in a libel case. See David L. Faigman, Constitutional Fictions: A Unified Theory of Constitutional Facts (2008).

And in Lockhart v. McCree, 476 U.S. 162, 168 n.3, 106 S.Ct. 1758, 1762 n.3 (1986), the Court indicated that there would be nondeferential review for "legislative fact," such as in reconsidering social-science studies relied upon in judicial lawmaking. Cf. Caitlin E. Borgmann, Rethinking Judicial Deference to Legislative Fact–Finding, 84 Ind.L.J. 1 (2009) (treating the distinguishable doctrine of judicial deference to the legislative branch).

Thus, there might be still other exceptions to the "clearly erroneous" standard based not so much on the kind of evidence or on the issue's supposedly legal nature as on the kind of fact involved. Consider this passage from Martin M. Shapiro, Courts: A Comparative and Political Analysis 41 (1981): "In the United States the distinction between questions of fact and questions of law which is supposed to be the key to the limits of appellate jurisdiction, is a notoriously slippery one. It is so slippery that a whole new category, 'mixed questions of fact and law,' has been invented. In reality that category [includes] the huge number of instances in which appellate courts have refused to accept trial court findings of fact and substituted their own fact-finding under the guise of law finding. As we have noted, the Supreme Court has long held that it will make its own findings of 'constitutional fact.' But constitutional facts are often the same routine facts that the trial court has already decided. For instance, let us suppose a trial court has determined that a given speech did incite a riot and so convicts a speaker of incitement to riot. The Supreme Court will, under the constitutional fact doctrine, redetermine exactly the same factual question. For it will decide the constitutional issue of whether the speech constituted such a clear and present danger of serious social evil that its repression might be justified in the face of the First Amendment's guarantees of free speech." See also Bryan L. Adamson, Federal Rule of Civil Procedure 52(a) as an Ideological Weapon?, 34 Fla.St.U.L.Rev. 1025 (2007).

SECTION 5. INTERPLAY OF NEW TRIAL MOTION WITH RULE 50

Suppose the trial judge grants a motion for judgment as a matter of law and accordingly withdraws the case from the jury before verdict. If, on appeal from the judgment, the appellate court holds that the trial judge committed error in granting the motion, the consequence is ordinarily a reversal of the judgment with an order for a new trial.

But suppose the trial judge denies a motion for judgment as a matter of law at the close of all the evidence and accordingly submits the case to the jury, and the jury brings in a verdict against the party who made the motion. If the judge's denial of the motion was erroneous—if on the evidence the judge should have granted judgment in favor of the moving party—what ought the consequence to be? It may seem natural and obvious that when the error becomes manifest, the consequence should be the entry of a judgment in favor of the movant. There are in fact a number of state statutes that allow the *trial* court to correct its own error by granting a contrary judgment and that alternatively allow the *appellate* court to correct the trial court's error by ordering the entry of such a judgment. Some of these statutes required the aggrieved party to have renewed its motion for a directed verdict by making a motion for judgment notwithstanding the verdict.

Before the promulgation of the Federal Rules, and while the Conformity Act applied generally to procedure in actions at law in the federal courts, the question arose whether a state statute along these lines could be constitutionally applied in the federal courts. That is, imagine that a motion for a directed verdict at the close of all the evidence had been denied by the trial court. After a jury verdict against the party who had made the motion, the trial court denied that party's motion for judgment notwithstanding the verdict and entered judgment on the verdict. On appeal, the circuit court of appeals, holding that the motion for a directed verdict had been erroneously denied, reversed the judgment for the appellee entered on the verdict and ordered the entry of judgment for the appellant. On certiorari, the Supreme Court, agreeing that the directed verdict had been erroneously denied, held that the judgment entered on the verdict must indeed be reversed, but the Court held further that the circuit court of appeals could not order the entry of the opposite judgment and that the most it could do was to order a new trial. Slocum v. New York Life Ins. Co., 228 U.S. 364, 33 S.Ct. 523 (1913) (5–4 decision). The Court thought the Re-examination Clause of the Seventh Amendment to forbid the federal courts from following the practice authorized by the state statute. Measuring the requirements of the Seventh Amendment largely by the condition of common-law procedures in 1791, the Court had found no precedent in the English courts of the proper historical vintage that would support the practice in question.[d]

---

[d] The court rejected as analogies, inter alia, the old-style motions in arrest of judgment and for judgment n.o.v., which when granted had the effect of putting the previous jury verdict to naught and resulted in judgment for the moving party. See supra p. 1073.

Comment on the Slocum case was generally adverse. State courts continued to follow their statutory practice, finding it consonant with state guarantees of the right to trial by jury. See, e.g., Bothwell v. Boston Elevated Ry., 215 Mass. 467, 102 N.E. 665 (1913).

Twenty-three years later the Supreme Court found a way to overcome the Slocum decision. In olden times an English judge trying a case at nisi prius as a kind of delegate of one of the central courts at Westminster might, while submitting the case to the jury, reserve for decision by the court in banc a point of pure law that had arisen during the trial.[e] The point of law might be dispositive of the case, and there were occasions when the court upon deciding the point would go on to order judgment for the party who had lost the verdict. Even though the court in banc was not operating as an appellate court in the modern sense, here was a stretchable analogy that could be used to advantage. In Baltimore & Carolina Line v. Redman, 295 U.S. 654, 55 S.Ct. 890 (1935), the Court in effect sanctioned the following practice in federal courts operating under the Conformity Act: if the trial judge, while denying a motion for a directed verdict and submitting the case to the jury, reserved the point whether the directed verdict should have been granted, the judge could thereafter grant a motion for judgment n.o.v. on being persuaded that the motion for a directed verdict should have been granted; or the appellate court, on review of a judgment entered on the verdict, might similarly act on the reserved point and order judgment n.o.v. to be entered.

It remained only to reduce to fiction the reservation of the point of law. This was accomplished by the original Rule 50(b), which the Court blessed in Berry v. United States, 312 U.S. 450, 453, 61 S.Ct. 633, 638 (1941). On the one hand, when in 1946 the Advisory Committee recommended the elimination of the language of fiction from Rule 50(b), the Supreme Court declined to adopt the recommendation. On the other hand, the rulemakers in 2006 changed the prerequisite motion, the one that would be deemed a reservation, from a motion made at the close of all the evidence to a motion made at any time under Rule 50(a).

Questions: (18) Does this persisting requirement—that a party must have moved at or sometime before the close of all the evidence for judgment as a matter of law in order effectively to move after the verdict for judgment as a matter of law—have any practical justification today? Do we not want to require objection early enough to permit cure, as by warning the nonmovant to introduce further evidence in order to cure a defect in proof, and early enough to allow the judge to streamline the case, as by withdrawing some issues from the jury?

(19) Under the new Rule 50, if the defendant moves for judgment as a matter of law at the close of the plaintiff's case, the judge denies the motion, and the defendant goes forward with her own evidence, what is the question put to the court when the defendant renews that motion after verdict for the plaintiff? Does the judge consider whether the plaintiff's case was strong enough at midtrial even if the plaintiff or defendant later cured any deficiency in the plaintiff's proof, or does the judge consider the evidence as a whole even if the defendant failed to move at

[e] See, e.g., Scott v. Shepherd, supra p. 1053.

the close of all the evidence? See Connie Alt, Note, Preservation of Judgment n.o.v. Motion Under Rule 50(b): Renewal of Directed Verdict Motion, 70 Iowa L.Rev. 269, 283 (1984).

Thus, the basis was laid for making, after the verdict, a renewed motion for judgment as a matter of law as well as a motion for a new trial. However, the interplay of these two motions generated much confusion. Montgomery Ward & Co. v. Duncan, which follows immediately below, revolutionized this post-verdict practice. When the Court decided it in 1940, Rule 50(b) was similar to the present Rule 50(b), but there were no subsequent subsections in Rule 50 until they were added by the 1963 amendments. The opinion of Justice Roberts, much of which was unnecessary to the decision, provided the lower courts and lawyers, as doubtless it was intended to do, with much the same kind of guidance for nearly a quarter of a century that an amendment to the Rule would have done.[f]

Montgomery Ward & Co. v. Duncan

Supreme Court of the United States, 1940.
311 U.S. 243, 61 S.Ct. 189.

[The plaintiff sued for personal injuries. At the close of all the evidence the defendant moved for a directed verdict. The motion was denied, and there was a verdict for the plaintiff upon which judgment was entered. Promptly the defendant moved for judgment notwithstanding the verdict and "for a new trial in the alternative," the latter request being on the grounds that the verdict was against the weight of the evidence and was excessive and that the court erred in rulings on the evidence and the instructions. The motion concluded with a prayer that the verdict and judgment be set aside and judgment rendered for the defendant, and with the further prayer "that in the event the Court refuses" to enter judgment for the defendant, the court set aside the verdict and judgment and grant the defendant a new trial. The trial court held that there was no evidence of negligence and ordered judgment for the defendant. The plaintiff filed a motion praying that "in order that the judgment of the appellate court may be final," the motion for a new trial be overruled. The court, however, merely entered a judgment for the defendant notwithstanding the verdict.

[On appeal by the plaintiff, it was held that the trial court erred in holding the evidence insufficient to make a case for the jury. The circuit court of appeals reversed and remanded with instructions to enter judgment on the verdict for the plaintiff. It overruled the defendant's conten-

[f] In reading this opinion, the student may well have difficulty with the terminology. Justice Roberts, infra p. 1468 & n.12, says that an order denying a new trial is not "appealable" save in most exceptional circumstances. Further, infra p. 1468 & n.15, he says that the granting of a motion for a new trial would not ordinarily be "reviewable." "Appealable order" properly relates to the kind of order from which an appeal may be taken, a matter of the timing of the appeal, as distinguished from "reviewable order," the kind of order the propriety of which the appellate court will consider when an appeal (typically from a final judgment) is before it. It is not clear that Justice Roberts has this distinction in mind.

tion that the case should be remanded with leave to the trial court to dispose of the motion for a new trial. Its reasoning was that the defendant had asked for a new trial only "in the event" judgment notwithstanding the verdict was denied, a condition that did not come into existence. "The order sustaining the motion for judgment notwithstanding the verdict," said the court, "was equivalent to a denial of the motion for a new trial; and the latter motion passed out of the case upon the entry of the order." The Supreme Court granted certiorari.]

■ MR. JUSTICE ROBERTS delivered the opinion of the Court.

In this case we are called upon to determine the appropriate procedure under Rule 50(b) of the Federal Rules of Civil Procedure.

. . . .

The defendant contends that the rule continues the existing practice respecting granting of new trials, and also regulates the procedure for rendering judgment notwithstanding a verdict; that the provision for an alternative motion for a new trial would be meaningless and nugatory if the granting of the motion for judgment operated automatically to dismiss it, since the bases of the two motions are, or may be, different, and orderly procedure requires that the court first rule on the motion for judgment, the granting of which renders unnecessary a ruling upon the motion for a new trial, which should be reserved until final disposition of the former.

The plaintiff insists that the trial court is limited to a choice of action on one motion or the other, but cannot rule upon the motion for judgment and leave that for a new trial to be disposed of only if judgment notwithstanding the verdict is denied. . . .

. . . .

. . . We come then to the substantial question which moved us to issue the writ, namely, whether under Rule 50(b) the District Court's grant of the motion for judgment effected an automatic denial of the alternative motion for a new trial. We hold that it did not.

The rule was adopted for the purpose of speeding litigation and preventing unnecessary retrials. . . .

. . . It adds nothing of substance to rights of litigants heretofore existing and available through a more cumbersome procedure.

A motion for judgment notwithstanding the verdict did not, at common law, preclude a motion for a new trial. And the latter motion might be, and often was, presented after the former had been denied. The rule was not intended to alter the existing right to move for a new trial theretofore recognized and confirmed by statute. It permits the filing of a motion for judgment in the absence of a motion for a new trial or the filing of both motions jointly or a motion for a new trial in the alternative.

Each motion, as the rule recognizes, has its own office. The motion for judgment cannot be granted unless, as matter of law, the opponent of the movant failed to make a case and, therefore, a verdict in movant's favor should have been directed. The motion for a new trial may invoke the discretion of the court in so far as it is bottomed on the claim that the verdict is against the weight of the evidence, that the damages are excessive, or that, for other reasons, the trial was not fair to the party moving; and may raise questions of law arising out of alleged substantial errors in admission or rejection of evidence or instructions to the jury.

We are of opinion that the provision of the rule,—"A motion for a new trial may be joined with this motion, or a new trial may be prayed for in the alternative"—does not confine the trial judge to an initial choice of disposing of either motion, the exercise of which choice precludes consideration of the remaining motion. We hold that the phrase "in the alternative" means that the things to which it refers are to be taken not together but one in the place of the other.[10]

The rule contemplates that either party to the action is entitled to the trial judge's decision on both motions, if both are presented. A decision in favor of the moving party upon the motion for judgment ends the litigation and often makes it possible for an appellate court to dispose of the case without remanding it for a new trial. If, however, as in the present instance, the trial court erred in granting the motion the party against whom the verdict went is entitled to have his motion for a new trial considered in respect of asserted substantial trial errors and matters appealing to the discretion of the judge. In this case the reasons assigned in support of the motion for a new trial were in both categories. The grounds assigned for a new trial have not been considered by the court. In the circumstances here disclosed the uniform practice in state appellate courts has been to remand the case to the trial court with leave to pass upon the motion for new trial.

The plaintiff urges that, whereas the rule was intended to expedite litigation, to prevent unnecessary trials, and to save the time of courts and litigants, the course urged by the defendant tends to extend the duration of litigation, to create unnecessary hardship, and to defeat the purpose of the rule.

We are of opinion that the position is untenable. This case well illustrates the efficacy of the procedure sanctioned by the rule. In view of the trial judge's conclusion that the plaintiff failed to make out a case for the jury he would, under the earlier practice, simply have granted a new trial. Upon the new trial, the judge, if his view as to the law remained unchanged, would have directed a verdict for the defendant. The only recourse of the plaintiff would have been an appeal from this second judgment. If the appellate court had been of the view it here expressed, it would have reversed that judgment and remanded the cause for a third trial. Upon such third trial, if the trial court had ruled upon the evidence and given the instructions to which the defendant objects a judgment for the plaintiff would have been the subject of a third appeal and, if the defendant's position were sustained by the appellate court, the cause would

10 The word "alternative" may be used properly in this sense. See Webster's International Dictionary, Second Edition.

be remanded for a fourth trial at which proper rulings would be rendered and proper instructions given.

Much of the delay formerly encountered may be avoided by pursuing the course for which the defendant contends. But the courts should so administer the rule as to accomplish all that is permissible under its terms. Is it necessary, if the trial judge's order for judgment be reversed on appeal, that only thereafter he deal with the alternative motion? If so, and he then refuses to set aside the original judgment, a second appeal will lie,—not from his order denying a new trial, for that order, save in most exceptional circumstances, is not appealable,[12] but from the judgment entered on the verdict, for errors of law committed on the trial. Can such a second appeal be avoided in the interest of speeding litigation? We think so.

If alternative prayers or motions are presented, as here, we hold that the trial judge should rule on the motion for judgment. Whatever his ruling thereon he should also rule on the motion for a new trial, indicating the grounds of his decision. If he denies a judgment n.o.v. and also denies a new trial the judgment on the verdict stands, and the losing party may appeal from the judgment entered upon it, assigning as error both the refusal of judgment n.o.v. and errors of law in the trial, as heretofore. The appellate court may reverse the former action and itself enter judgment n.o.v. or it may reverse and remand for a new trial for errors of law. If the trial judge, as he did here, grants judgment n.o.v. and denies the motion for a new trial, the party who obtained the verdict may, as he did here, appeal from that judgment. Essentially, since his action is subject to review, the trial judge's order is an order nisi. The judgment on the verdict may still stand, because the appellate court may reverse the trial judge's action. This being so, we see no reason why the appellee may not, and should not, cross-assign error, in the appellant's appeal, to rulings of law at the trial, so that if the appellate court reverses the order for judgment n.o.v., it may pass on the errors of law which the appellee asserts nullify the judgment on the verdict.

Should the trial judge enter judgment n.o.v. and, in the alternative, grant a new trial on any of the grounds assigned therefor, his disposition of the motion for a new trial would not ordinarily be reviewable,[15] and only his action in entering judgment would be ground of appeal. If the judgment were reversed, the case, on remand, would be governed by the trial judge's award of a new trial.

. . . .

In the circumstances, we think the failure of the District Court to rule in the alternative on both matters can be cured without depriving the defendant of opportunity to have its motion for a new trial heard and decided by the trial court, by modifying the judgment below to provide that

[12] See Fairmount Glass Works v. Cub Fork Coal Co., 287 U.S. 474, 481–85, 53 S.Ct. 252, 254–55.

[15] United States v. Young, 94 U.S. 258; Young v. United States, 95 U.S. 641; Phillips v. Negley, 117 U.S. 665, 671, 6 S.Ct. 901, 903; Hume v. Bowie, 148 U.S. 245, 13 S.Ct. 582; Fairmount Glass Works v. Cub Fork Coal Co., supra.

the cause be remanded to the District Court to hear and rule upon that motion.

Modified.

Questions: (20) Assume that after losing a Rule 50(a) motion and the verdict, the party has moved for judgment as a matter of law and in the alternative for a new trial, the latter request being on the sole ground that the court erred in ruling on the instructions. Construct four hypothetical cases demonstrating that each of the four conceivable dispositions—grant or denial of each of the two motions—can properly be made by the trial judge. Now do the same assuming instead that the motion for a new trial is on the sole ground that the verdict was against the weight of the evidence.

(21) In Momand v. Universal Film Exchange, 72 F.Supp. 469 (D.Mass.1947), aff'd, 172 F.2d 37 (1st Cir.1948), Judge Wyzanski, after granting defendants' motion for judgment n.o.v., said, in passing upon defendants' accompanying motion for a new trial: "It is doubtful whether the draftsmen of the rules and the Justices who participated in the Montgomery Ward case realized in what a dilemma their rule might in some cases place a trial judge and what foresight, abnegation and stultification it might require of him." Do you see the nature of the dilemma in which a trial judge may be placed?

Marsh v. Illinois Cent. R.

United States Court of Appeals, Fifth Circuit, 1949.
175 F.2d 498.

■ Before HUTCHESON, SIBLEY and WALLER, CIRCUIT JUDGES.

■ SIBLEY, CIRCUIT JUDGE. Marsh, called herein appellant, a fireman on a switch engine, sued for a personal injury alleged to have been caused by negligence in maintaining the switching track and the apron covering the coupling between the engine and tender, on which apron he stood in firing. At the conclusion of the evidence the defendant's motion for an instructed verdict was denied, and a verdict for plaintiff was returned. The defendant then moved for a judgment notwithstanding the verdict, or . . . for a new trial on the ground, among others, that the verdict was against the overwhelming weight of the evidence. The judge held: "The weight of the evidence is so overwhelmingly against the plaintiff that as a matter of law it becomes the duty of the court to withdraw the case from the jury and enter a judgment for the defendant. The motion . . . for a judgment notwithstanding the verdict of the jury will be entered for the reason that the motion for a directed verdict should have been sustained. . . . It is my judgment that the evidence was insufficient to go to the jury, but if I am wrong in that, then I do not think a new trial should be granted as there were no other errors of law." Appeal is taken by plaintiff from the judgment notwithstanding the verdict, and a cross-appeal by the defendant from the refusal of a new trial.

1. . . . A motion for a directed verdict, or for a judgment notwithstanding the verdict under Rule of Civil Procedure 50, 28 U.S.C.A., raises a question of law only: Whether there is any evidence which, if believed, would authorize a verdict against movant. The trial judge in considering those motions does not exercise discretion, but makes a ruling of law, and if he errs the appellate court may reverse. A motion for new trial is addressed to the trial judge's discretion. He may grant a new trial if he thinks he has committed error; and he may grant one (and he alone can) because he thinks the verdict is wrong, though supported by some evidence. The exercise of his discretion is not ordinarily reviewable on appeal, though a failure to exercise discretion, or an abuse of it, may be corrected. The motion for a new trial is entirely independent of the other two motions and is governed by different principles, and has a different result. It never supersedes the jury, but as its name states, it results in another jury trial, perhaps with different evidence produced. But the motion for directed verdict or for judgment notwithstanding the verdict if granted, ends the case.

Rule of Civil Procedure 50, while altering the procedure in federal courts, did not alter the nature and effect of these motions, and each is entitled to be decided according to the principles applicable to it without confusing them. Montgomery Ward & Co. v. Duncan, 311 U.S. 243, 61 S.Ct. 189, 85 L.Ed. 147.

2. While it is not our function to weigh the evidence, we do agree with the trial judge's first expressed opinion that the weight of the evidence is "overwhelmingly against the plaintiff". But we do not agree that the grant of a judgment notwithstanding the verdict was therefore justified. There was evidence of the appellant, not very explicit or positive, which if believed might authorize a jury to conclude he was hurt in the manner he claims. Because the trial judge does not believe it, because of appellant's own contradictions and conduct and of opposing evidence which seem to overwhelm it, is not ground for a judgment notwithstanding the verdict, and we must reverse that judgment. Howard v. Louisiana & A.R. Co., 5 Cir., 49 F.2d 571.

3. But it is ground for the trial judge to grant a new trial, though the trial was free of other error. He has in strong terms disapproved the verdict as contrary to the evidence, so much as to warrant setting the verdict aside and entering judgment for the defendant. We have reversed the entering of a final judgment, but it is evident that the new trial ought to be granted and would have been except for the misconception that absence of other error prevented it. The full discretion vested in the trial judge not having been exercised, we will remand the case with direction to the judge to grant a new trial instead of a judgment notwithstanding the verdict if he continues to think the verdict to be against the overwhelming weight of the evidence.

The judgment is reversed on both appeals and the cause remanded for further proceedings not inconsistent with this opinion. Reversed.

Questions: (22) Consider what the court of appeals may do in each of the situations discussed by Justice Roberts in the Montgomery Ward case, taking into account the possibility that each of the alternative rulings may have been either correct or incorrect: (a) both n.o.v. and new trial denied; (b) n.o.v. granted and new trial denied; and (c) both n.o.v. and new trial granted.

(23) What of the situation omitted by Justice Roberts—denial of n.o.v. and grant of new trial? Why did Justice Roberts omit it? Imagine that *P* sues *D* for breach of contract. *D*'s motion for judgment as a matter of law at the close of all the evidence is denied. The jury returns a verdict for *P* for $120,000. *D* renews the motion for judgment as a matter of law and also moves for a new trial, urging that there was too little evidence to justify a finding of breach of contract. *D*'s renewed motion for judgment is denied, but her motion for a new trial is granted. On retrial, there is a verdict and judgment for *P* for $130,000 after a trial admittedly free of error. *D* appeals, contending that there was error in denial of the renewed motion for judgment after the first trial. What position should *P* take on the appeal, if *P* believes that the court of appeals would find such error? What disposition should the court of appeals make, if indeed it believes there was such error? Is Pettingill v. Fuller, supra p. 1453, controlling? Compare Basciano v. Reinecke, 313 F.2d 542 (2d Cir.1963), with Ford Motor Co. v. Busam Motor Sales, 185 F.2d 531 (6th Cir.1950).

Cone v. West Virginia Pulp & Paper Co.

Supreme Court of the United States, 1947.
330 U.S. 212, 67 S.Ct. 752.

■ MR. JUSTICE BLACK delivered the opinion of the Court.

The petitioner brought this action in a South Carolina state court. Upon motion of respondent, it was removed to the Federal District Court because of diversity of citizenship of the parties. The complaint claimed $25,000 damages upon allegations that the respondent's agents had trespassed upon and cut timber from lands owned by and in the possession of the petitioner. Respondent's answer denied that the petitioner had title or possession of the lands and timber. Both title and possession became crucial issues in the trial. The burden of proving them rested on the petitioner.[1] When all the evidence of both parties had been introduced, the respondent moved for a directed verdict in its favor on the ground that the petitioner had failed to prove that he either owned or was in possession of the land. This motion was denied. The jury returned a verdict for petitioner for $15,000, and the court entered judgment on the verdict. The respondent moved for a new trial on the ground of newly discovered evidence. The motion was denied. Respondent did not move for judgment notwithstanding the verdict as it might have done under Rule 50(b) of the Federal Rules of Civil Procedure . . . .

---

[1] Under governing South Carolina law an action such as this is not one to try title but "to recover damages for trespass to property of which the plaintiff was in possession." [Citation omitted.] But possession may be presumed from proof of legal title. [Citations omitted.] Petitioner here undertook to prove possession both by showing that he had legal title and by showing that he had openly and notoriously exercised acts of dominion, possession, and ownership over a long period of years.

The Circuit Court of Appeals decided that the admission of certain evidence offered by the petitioner to prove legal title was prejudicial error. It held that without this improperly admitted evidence petitioner's proof was not sufficient to submit the question of title to the jury. That court also held that petitioner's evidence showing possession was insufficient to go to the jury. It therefore reversed the case. But instead of remanding it to the District Court for a new trial, the Circuit Court of Appeals directed that judgment be entered for respondent. 153 F.2d 576. That court has thus construed Rule 50(b) as authorizing an appellate court to direct a judgment notwithstanding the verdict, even though no motion for such a judgment had been made in the District Court . . . .

The petition for certiorari challenged the power of an appellate court to direct entry of a judgment notwithstanding the verdict where timely motion for such a judgment had not been made in the District Court. On three previous occasions we have granted certiorari to consider this point but failed to reach it because, upon examination of the evidence, we found it sufficient to justify submission of all three cases to the jury. Conway v. O'Brien, 312 U.S. 492, 61 S.Ct. 634; Berry v. United States, 312 U.S. 450, 61 S.Ct. 637; Halliday v. United States, 315 U.S. 94, 62 S.Ct. 438. In this case we granted certiorari "limited to the questions of federal procedure raised by the petition for the writ." 329 U.S. 701. The point we had in mind was whether a party's failure to make a motion in the District Court for judgment notwithstanding the verdict, as permitted in Rule 50(b), precludes an appellate court from directing entry of such a judgment. Other questions have been discussed here, but we do not consider them. Consequently, we accept, without approving or disapproving, the Circuit Court of Appeals' holding that there was prejudicial error in the admission of evidence and in the submission of the case to the jury.

Rule 50(b) contains no language which absolutely requires a trial court to enter judgment notwithstanding the verdict even though that court is persuaded that it erred in failing to direct a verdict for the losing party. The rule provides that the trial court "may reopen the judgment and either order a new trial or direct the entry of judgment as if the requested verdict had been directed." This "either-or" language means what it seems to mean, namely, that there are circumstances which might lead the trial court to believe that a new trial rather than a final termination of the trial stage of the controversy would better serve the ends of justice. In short, the rule does not compel a trial judge to enter a judgment notwithstanding the verdict instead of ordering a new trial; it permits him to exercise a discretion to choose between the two alternatives. See Berry v. United States, supra, 312 U.S. at 452–453, 61 S.Ct. at 638. And he can exercise this discretion with a fresh personal knowledge of the issues involved, the kind of evidence given, and the impression made by witnesses. His appraisal of the bona fides of the claims asserted by the litigants is of great value in reaching a conclusion as to whether a new trial should be granted. Determination of whether a new trial should be granted or a judgment entered under Rule 50(b) calls for the judgment in the first instance of the judge who saw and heard the witnesses and has the feel of the case which no appellate printed transcript can impart. [Citations omitted.] Exercise of this discretion presents to the trial judge an opportunity, after all his rulings have been made and all the evidence has been evaluated, to view the proceedings in a perspective peculiarly available to him alone. He is thus afforded "a last chance to correct his own errors without the delay, expense or other hardships of an appeal." See Greer v. Carpenter, 323 Mo. 878, 882, 19 S.W.2d 1046, 1047. Cf. United States v. Johnson, 327 U.S. 106, 112, 66 S.Ct. 464, 466.

There are other practical reasons why a litigant should not have his right to a new trial foreclosed without having had the benefit of the trial court's judgment on the question. Take the case where a trial court is about to direct a verdict because of failure of proof in a certain aspect of the case. At that time a litigant might know or have reason to believe that he could fill the crucial gap in the evidence. Traditionally, a plaintiff in such a dilemma has had an unqualified right, upon payments of costs, to take a nonsuit in order to file a new action after further preparation, unless the defendant would suffer some plain legal prejudice other than the mere prospect of a second lawsuit. Pleasants v. Fant, 22 Wall. 116, 122; Jones v. S.E.C., 298 U.S. 1, 19–20, 56 S.Ct. 654, 659, and cases cited. Rule 41(a)(1) preserves this unqualified right of the plaintiff to a dismissal without prejudice prior to the filing of defendant's answer. And after the filing of an answer, Rule 41(a)(2) still permits a trial court to grant a dismissal without prejudice "upon such terms and conditions as the court deems proper."

In this case had respondents made a timely motion for judgment notwithstanding the verdict, the petitioner could have either presented reasons to show why he should have a new trial, or at least asked the court for permission to dismiss. If satisfied from the knowledge acquired from the trial and because of the reasons urged that the ends of justice would best be served by allowing petitioner another chance, the judge could have so provided in his discretion. The respondent failed to submit a motion for judgment notwithstanding the verdict to the trial judge in order that he might exercise his discretionary power to determine whether there should be such a judgment, a dismissal or a new trial. In the absence of such a motion, we think the appellate court was without power to direct the District Court to enter judgment contrary to the one it had permitted to stand.

It has been suggested that the petitioner could have presented affidavits to the Circuit Court of Appeals to support his claim for a new trial, and that that court could thereupon have remanded the question to the District Court to pass upon it. Such a circuitous method of determining the question cannot be approved. For Rule 50(b) specifically prescribes a period of ten days for making a motion for judgment notwithstanding the verdict. Yet the method here suggested would enable litigants to extend indefinitely the prescribed ten-day period simply by adoption of the expedient of an appeal. Furthermore, it would present the question initially to the appellate court when the primary discretionary responsibility for its decision rests on the District Court.

Reversed.[g]

Questions: (24) Johnson sued the railroad in district court under the Jones Act for the wrongful death of her husband. When all the evidence was in, the railroad moved for a directed verdict in its favor on the ground that no negligence of the railroad had been shown and that the deceased had been responsible for his own death. The court reserved decision on the motion and submitted the case to the jury, which returned a verdict for the plaintiff on which judgment was entered. Within twenty-eight days the railroad moved to set aside the verdict and judgment as excessive and contrary to the law, to the evidence, and to the weight of the evidence. It did not expressly move for judgment n.o.v. The court denied the motion to set aside the verdict and judgment and, at the same time, denied the motion for a directed verdict on which it had reserved decision. Holding that the motion for a directed verdict should have been granted, the court of appeals directed the entry of judgment for the railroad. Was this action by the court of appeals proper? See Johnson v. New York, New Haven & Hartford R.R. Co., 344 U.S. 48, 73 S.Ct. 125 (1952) (Rule "forbids the trial judge or an appellate court to enter such a judgment").

(25) Assume that the railroad had instead moved for judgment n.o.v. but not for a new trial. The trial court denied the motion. Holding that the verdict was against the weight of the evidence, the court of appeals ordered a new trial. Was this action by the court of appeals proper? Cf. Kain v. Winslow Mfg., Inc., 736 F.2d 606 (10th Cir.1984) (suggesting that neither the trial judge nor an appellate court could so act, unless the trial judge was acting pursuant to Rule 59(d), because the railroad had not timely raised the issue of weight of the evidence).

(26) Assume instead that the railroad had moved neither for judgment n.o.v. nor for a new trial. If Johnson's case had been very weak, but the trial judge did not act under Rule 59(d), what action could the court of appeals (or the trial judge) properly take? See Unitherm Food Sys. v. Swift–Eckrich, Inc., 546 U.S. 394, 126 S.Ct. 980 (2006) (none, because the directed verdict motion alone did not preserve the issue of insufficiency of the evidence); Nitco Holding Corp. v. Boujikian, 491 F.3d 1086 (9th Cir.2007) ("Unitherm precludes even plain error review").

NEELY v. MARTIN K. EBY CONSTRUCTION CO., 386 U.S. 317, 87 S.Ct. 1072 (1967). Plaintiff brought a diversity action claiming that defendant's negligence caused her decedent's death. Defendant's motion for a directed verdict at the close of all the evidence was denied. After a verdict for plaintiff, defendant moved for judgment n.o.v. and in the alternative for a new trial. Both motions were denied, and judgment was entered for plaintiff.

---

[g] On remand, the district court interpreted the Supreme Court's opinion to require a new trial, at which the defendant ultimately prevailed by means of judgment n.o.v. This outcome was affirmed, 170 F.2d 770 (4th Cir.1948), cert. denied, 337 U.S. 920, 69 S.Ct. 1149 (1949). Incidentally, the ten-day period changed to twenty-eight days in 2009.

Defendant appealed. The court of appeals held that the evidence was insufficient to go to the jury and reversed "with instructions to dismiss the action."

Without seeking a rehearing in the court of appeals, plaintiff sought and obtained certiorari, presenting the question whether the court of appeals could—consistent with the Seventh Amendment, with 28 U.S.C. § 2106, and with the Federal Rules (principally Rule 50, which at the time said no more than that the court of appeals could order a new trial or direct the trial court to determine whether a new trial should be granted)—direct the trial court to dismiss the action. The Supreme Court, in an opinion by Justice White, affirmed, holding that the court of appeals had the power to order final judgment.

Only Justice Black dissented on this point. Justices Douglas and Fortas agreed with the Court's construction of Rule 50, but they believed, as did also Justice Black, that the evidence was sufficient to go to the jury.

Questions: (27) Is Neely consistent with Cone v. West Virginia Pulp & Paper Co.? See Weisgram v. Marley Co., 528 U.S. 440, 120 S.Ct. 1011 (2000) (adhering unanimously to Neely). In the fact situation of Neely, what may the court of appeals do if it decides that the ruling below on the motion for judgment n.o.v. was erroneous? Cf. 28 U.S.C. § 2106. What factors should influence its exercise of discretion?

(28) Plaintiff brought a diversity action for her husband's death, claiming that defendant had negligently designed a "skip hoist." Defendant's motion for a directed verdict at the close of all the evidence was denied. By special verdict the jury found negligent design; but being asked, if it found negligent design, to "please indicate" which, if any, of five specified design aspects of the hoist had been found unsafe, the jury answered "yes" to one and left the other four unanswered. The trial judge ordered judgment for plaintiff on the verdict and denied defendant's motion for judgment n.o.v. The court of appeals reversed, holding that the evidence did not warrant the jury's finding of negligence in the aspect of design it had found unsafe. Upon plaintiff's petition for rehearing, what disposition should it then have made of the case? See Iacurci v. Lummus Co., 387 U.S. 86, 87 S.Ct. 1423 (1967) (remand to trial judge to decide whether plaintiff is entitled to new trial).

O'HARE v. MERCK & CO., 381 F.2d 286 (8th Cir.1967). In this product liability case, after the denial of defendant's motion for a directed verdict at the close of all the evidence and then a verdict for plaintiff, the trial judge granted defendant's motion for judgment n.o.v. because of insufficient proof of negligence. The court of appeals affirmed, and it later denied plaintiff's petition for rehearing without explanation.

In dissent, Judge Lay would have remanded to the district court for decision on plaintiff's motion for a new trial, made in her petition for rehearing and based on allegedly erroneous jury instructions, or at least would have fully considered the motion at the appellate level.

Judge Lay first faced the argument that plaintiff had waived the point by not moving in the trial court under Rule 50(d). After quoting the 1963 Advisory Committee's note thereon and the Neely case, he said: "Therefore, it is clear that appellant has not waived any rights by failing to [move] for new trial in the court below. There are practical and cogent reasons for this rule of non-waiver, in that a verdict-winner appealing from a judgment n.o.v. primarily desires a review of that judgment and a reinstatement of the verdict. He is generally not interested in pursuing an immediate new trial order, which, if granted by the trial court, could supersede the appealable judgment. If a new trial would be granted the verdict-winner is left with no opportunity to obtain review of his original judgment. Of course, the trial court could enter a conditional order of a new trial as well as granting the n.o.v., under Fed.R.Civ.P. 50(b) and (c), but even under these circumstances the plaintiff may be reluctant to move for a new trial because of the uncertainty that the order will be conditional."

Judge Lay's dissent further concluded that plaintiff did not have to raise the issue of a new trial in her original appellate brief. It said: "Until the court of appeals has finally ruled on the granting of defendant's motion for judgment n.o.v., the verdict-holder's single purpose is to reinstate the verdict he obtained below from the jury. Until he sees finality in the judgment invalidating that verdict, again, he is not interested in even suggesting a new trial. In fact, in the court of appeals in many instances his argument that the jury verdict was proper under the record could be vitiated by his simultaneous emphasis on errors in the trial. Inconsistent pleas and alternative motions in his original briefs would add to his already heavy burden of persuasion. This would, of course, not always be true since frequently similar grounds could underlie both his appeal and his motion for new trial."

Question: (29) Under Rule 50 as amended, what may each party do in the trial court and in the court of appeals in order fully to protect his position against all contingencies?

TOPIC E

CONSTITUTIONAL RIGHT TO JURY TRIAL

SECTION 1. CONSTITUTIONAL, STATUTORY, AND RULE FRAMEWORK

In federal court, there can be trial by jury on those issues: (1) that are triable of right by a jury under the Seventh Amendment to the Federal Constitution; (2) that are triable of right by a jury under some federal statute, such as the Jones Act covering certain actions by seamen, as provided in Rule 38(a); or (3) on which the court, in its discretion with the express or implicit consent of both parties, orders a trial by jury under Federal Rule 39(c)(2).

Even if an issue does fall within one of these three categories, it may nonetheless be tried by the judge as the result of any of three rules: (1) There is a waiver of a constitutional or statutory right to trial by jury if neither party makes a timely written demand for trial by jury on the issue as provided in Rule 38(b)–(d), although the court in its discretion upon motion may, but sparingly does, relieve such waiver as provided in Rule 39(b). (2) The parties may consent to withdraw a demand for jury trial, as Rules 38(d) and 39(a)(1) provide. (3) The parties have agreed to nonjury trial, as by contract in advance.

In sum, there are constitutional and statutory rights in the federal structure, as well as the equivalent possibility of jury trial by consent. But these rights can be surrendered. Note that allowance of trial by jury is determined on an issue-by-issue basis.

NEW YORK CONSTITUTION art. I § 2 (1938): "Trial by jury in all cases in which it has heretofore been guaranteed by constitutional provision shall remain inviolate forever;[a] but a jury trial may be waived by the parties in all civil cases in the manner to be prescribed by law. . . ."

[a] This means that there is a constitutional right to trial by jury "in all cases in which it has been heretofore used," as stated in the Constitution of 1894, which was the last in a series of New York constitutions that so provided. (The first was the Constitution of 1777, which protected the jury right "in all cases in which it hath heretofore been used in the Colony of New York.") Thus, 1894 is the critical date of historical reference in New York under its current constitution.

NEW YORK CIVIL PRACTICE LAW AND RULES § 4101: "In the following actions, the issues of fact shall be tried by a jury unless a jury trial is waived or a reference is directed under section 4317 [trial by a referee], except that equitable defenses and equitable counterclaims shall be tried by the court:

1. an action in which a party demands and sets forth facts which would permit a judgment for a sum of money only;

2. an action of ejectment; for dower; for waste; for abatement of and damages for a nuisance; to recover a chattel; or for determination of a claim to real property under article fifteen of the real property actions and proceedings law; and

3. any other action in which a party is entitled by the constitution or by express provision of law to a trial by jury."[b]

CONNECTICUT CONSTITUTION art. I § 19 (1965): "The right of trial by jury shall remain inviolate[c] . . . ."

CONNECTICUT GENERAL STATUTES: ". . . The following-named classes of cases shall be entered in the docket as jury cases upon the written request of either party made to the clerk within thirty days after the return day: Appeals from probate involving the validity of a will or paper purporting to be such, appeals from the actions of commissioners on insolvent estates, and, except as hereinafter provided, civil actions involving such an issue of fact as, prior to January 1, 1880, would not present a question properly cognizable in equity, except that there shall be no right to trial by jury in civil actions in which the amount, legal interest or property in demand does not exceed two hundred fifty dollars or in a summary process case. . . . All issues of fact in any such case shall be tried by the jury, provided the issues agreed by the parties to be tried by the court may be so tried. . . ."[d]

Questions: (1) Are there any significant differences between the foregoing New York and Connecticut provisions? How do they compare with the Seventh Amendment to the United States Constitution and Federal Rule 38(a)?

(2) On the federal level, is there any constitutional right to trial without a jury? See Note, The Right to a Nonjury Trial, 74 Harv.L.Rev. 1176 (1961).

---

[b] Cf. NYCPLR § 4102 (demand and waiver of trial by jury), most of which has more recent origins than § 4101.

[c] This provision first appeared in the Constitution of 1818. As a constitutional matter, 1818 is interpreted still to be the critical date of historical reference in Connecticut.

[d] The substance of this statute dates back to the Practice Act of 1879, which merged law and equity in Connecticut and which became effective January 1, 1880.

ADVISORY JURY

Rule 39(c)(1) preserves the power of the court, in actions not being tried by a jury, upon motion or of its own initiative, to try an issue with the assistance of an advisory jury. See Matthew L. Zabel, Advisory Juries and Their Use and Misuse in Federal Tort Claims Act Cases, 2003 BYU L.Rev. 185 (criticizing courts' use of advisory juries in the face of the FTCA's expressly confirming that actions against the United States are to be tried without a jury, which Congress could do because the Seventh Amendment does not apply to actions against the sovereign).

This discretionary power has nothing to do with the right to jury trial. It dates back to the power of the chancellor in classical equity to send an issue for trial before a law court for the purpose of enlightening his conscience. In order to create a matter litigable in a common-law court, a wager was "feigned" over the disputed issue. A jury could then decide, by resolving the issue, whether a debt was owing on the bet. Having been so enlightened, the chancellor might proceed to make his own findings contrary to those of the jury, the advisory verdict in theory being nonbinding. The advisory jury and the use of the "feigned issue" procedure were incorporated in American practice from the earliest days. See Richard E. Guggenheim, A Note on the Advisory Jury in Federal Courts, 8 Fed.B.J. 200 (1947).

Under modern practice, of course, there is no need to shuttle a case from court to court. The trial judge can in a merged system simply impanel an advisory jury and submit such issues to it as the judge wishes. See Note, Practice and Potential of the Advisory Jury, 100 Harv.L.Rev. 1363 (1987).

Rule 52(a)(1) provides that in all actions tried with an advisory jury the court shall find the facts specially. This is particularly important if the judge proposes to enter a judgment contrary to the findings of the advisory jury. The appellate court has the same power of review of the facts in a case with an advisory jury as in any nonjury case.

Question: (3) Suppose a trial judge, uncertain as to whether a jury right exists, impanels a jury, takes its verdict, and then treats it as advisory and makes her own findings inconsistent with the verdict. On appeal from a judgment entered on the findings, can the court of appeals order judgment on the verdict if it finds that there was a constitutional right to jury trial? Compare Hildebrand v. Board of Trustees, 607 F.2d 705, 712 (6th Cir.1979) ("This case presents a procedural nightmare worthy of inclusion in a first year of law school civil procedure examination authored by the most cunning of professors."), with Bereda v. Pickering Creek Indus. Park, Inc., 865 F.2d 49 (3d Cir.1989).

SECTION 2. "HISTORICAL TEST"

A constitutional provision that the right of trial by jury shall be preserved as at common law, or remain inviolate, suggests that the question of the jury right should involve resort to the situation prevailing at the time the provision was adopted, either in 1791 when the Seventh Amendment was adopted or, in the case of the states, at the date of the relevant state constitution. At least as an initial inquiry, we arguably should ask whether a factual issue arises in what would have been a common-law case.[e]

Some difficulty in applying any such historical test is inevitable. The line of demarcation between law and equity was never a clear one. There was a continuing process of change. The law courts came to deal with matters formerly cognizable only in equity, and equity courts came to try issues that had previously been left exclusively to law. It is often very hard and sometimes impossible to determine precisely when such takeovers came to pass, even for the few scholars who still master the old learning.

Inaptness and artificiality are also inevitable in applying any such historical test. The judges of 1791 could not know that their allocation of cases between the courts of law and equity would two centuries later be determinative of the right to trial by jury in a judicial system where law and equity have merged and where very different procedures govern. The old line dividing law and equity was to a large degree the product of historical and political influences wholly unrelated to procedural concerns.

---

[e] The English right of trial by jury in civil cases is a prized common-law heritage. See World Jury Systems (Neil Vidmar ed., 2000). But the English themselves have curtailed it in the High Court of Justice almost to the vanishing point. "Against the obsolescence of the English civil jury, which has come about quite casually, with a minimum of soul-searching, is to be set the robust survival of the American jury." Benjamin Kaplan, An American Lawyer in the Queen's Courts: Impressions of English Civil Procedure, 69 Mich.L.Rev. 821, 830 (1971).

England's big step was the Juries Act of 1918, which was enacted during World War I when manpower was short and which limited the jury right to cases alleging fraud, libel, malicious prosecution, and the like—cases involving reputation and not merely money. Except for the years 1925 to 1933, this pattern has been continued by later legislation. Today, it is put this way by the Supreme Court Act, 1981, ch. 54, § 69(1)–(4):

"(1) Where, on the application of any party to an action to be tried in the Queen's Bench Division, the court is satisfied that there is in issue—

(a) a charge of fraud against that party; or

(b) a claim in respect of libel, slander, malicious prosecution or false imprisonment; or

(c) any question or issue of a kind prescribed for the purposes of this paragraph,

the action shall be tried with a jury, unless the court is of opinion that the trial requires any prolonged examination of documents or accounts or any scientific or local investigation which cannot conveniently be made with a jury.

"(2) An application under subsection (1) must be made not later than such time before the trial as may be prescribed.

"(3) An action to be tried in the Queen's Bench Division which does not by virtue of subsection (1) fall to be tried with a jury shall be tried without a jury unless the court in its discretion orders it to be tried with a jury.

"(4) Nothing in subsections (1) to (3) shall affect the power of the court to order, in accordance with rules of court, that different questions of fact arising in any action be tried by different modes of trial; and where any such order is made, subsection (1) shall have effect only as respects questions relating to any such charge, claim, question or issue as is mentioned in that subsection."

See also Civil Procedure Rule 26.11. Discretionary orders for trial by jury are in fact rarely made. See Terence Ingman, The English Legal System 225–29 (10th ed. 2004).

Moreover, because the right to jury trial is the one significant aspect of the law/equity allocation to survive merger, it is easy to forget that the jury right was but one of many procedural concerns that affected the allocation of jurisdiction between law and equity courts in pre-merger days. On the one hand, equity made available types of specific relief and means of handling multiple parties unknown in courts of law and, in addition, the testimony of parties was permitted and could be compelled in equity at a time long before this was possible at law. On the other hand, the testimony of witnesses at law was oral and subject to cross-examination, and their demeanor was observable by the trier of fact, whereas in equity such evidence came by written depositions. Obviously, the parties' exercise of any choice of courts was a many-factored decision. "To put it colloquially, jury trial (or court trial) was often merely the tail of the dog under a system in which you had to take the whole dog." Fleming James, Jr., Geoffrey C. Hazard, Jr. & John Leubsdorf, Civil Procedure 499 (5th ed. 2001).

Beyond all this confusion in application, sharp disagreements exist as to the basic meaning of the historical test. Professor Redish argues for a very narrow reading of the Seventh Amendment that would protect only the jury right that actually existed in 1791, ignoring as far as possible all changed conditions and excluding any new developments. Martin H. Redish, Seventh Amendment Right to Jury Trial: A Study in the Irrationality of Rational Decision Making, 70 Nw.U.L.Rev. 486 (1975). The range of disagreement will perhaps be suggested by contrasting the view of Professor Wolfram.

Charles W. Wolfram, The Constitutional History of the Seventh Amendment

57 Minn.L.Rev. 639, 736, 738, 744–45 (1973).

Nor does the term "common law" necessarily require a static reference. Even if one is confined to the meaning of that phrase as understood in 1791, by that time a commonly understood concept of "common law" had become that of a process characterized by occasional flexibility and capacity for growth in order to respond to changing social pressures, rather than that of a fixed and immutable body of unchanging rules. . . .

If "common law" in 1791 was understood by the framers of the seventh amendment as a process, rather than as a set of perpetually static rules, then one must ask whether, with the passage of time, the historical test has caused the amendment to diverge from the original conception. . . . During the centuries of their coexistence, the jurisdictions of the law courts and the chancellor, until they were merged, were subject to an unstatic process of accretion and erosion. . . . What remains constant over the history of this process, however, is the tendency toward expansion and enrichment of the remedies provided by the law courts. While the law courts in recent centuries never attempted directly to warn the chancellor off territory that had been claimed for the law courts, it seems rather certain that between the two the equity court was destined to have its powers circumscribed. . . .

. . . .

The most appealing view of the political settlement achieved by the seventh amendment is the version suggested by the argument that the term "common law" in the seventh amendment was probably intended to refer to a process of legal development, rather than to an immutable and changeless state of the law. If that was a widely shared understanding of the nature of the "common law" at the time of the adoption of the seventh amendment, then the future development of the "common law" should also be regarded as part of the political bargain that was struck. If future development was contemplated—and if it is correct to view that development as largely one of the expansion of the remedies available at "common law"—then it would seem to follow that the "common law" of the seventh amendment was intended to have a changing meaning over time. While the day might then have been some distance in the future, it would not have been unintended to have the right extend at some future point in time to the trial by jury of what in 1791 would have been termed "equity" or "admiralty" cases.

I wish to suggest, therefore, that the seventh amendment two centuries after its adoption could justifiably be read to refer neither to the law of England nor to the law of any of the states and certainly not to an arbitrary point in time, but rather to the distinctive common-law process of adjudication and lawmaking that then and now, in England and in the United States, was recognized as flexible and changing. Principally because this process cannot with fidelity be locked into any particular point in time and in order to emphasize its characteristics as a process, this may fittingly be called the "dynamic" reading of the seventh amendment.

---

1. **New cause of action.**—There are, to be sure, many rights and remedies created since the adoption of the federal and state constitutions.

Sometimes a statute creating a new cause of action specifies trial by jury, as in the Jones Act; sometimes it is silent as to mode of trial, but a jury right may be inferred from the statute, as under the FELA. In general, whether expressly or impliedly, the legislature not only may resolve any historical doubts by choosing in favor of a jury right, but also clearly can expand historical jury rights. See Rule 38(a).

By contrast, the generally accepted view, even though there is some room for innovative counterargument, is that the legislature cannot cut back on the jury right otherwise protected by the constitutional provision. See Granfinanciera, S.A. v. Nordberg, 492 U.S. 33, 109 S.Ct. 2782 (1989) (bankruptcy trustee's separate action to recover fraudulent monetary transfer; jury required by Seventh Amendment, notwithstanding federal statute); Pernell v. Southall Realty, 416 U.S. 363, 94 S.Ct. 1723 (1974) (by implication) (repossession of real property; jury required by Seventh Amendment). Thus, a negative legislative view does not affect the outcome of the constitutional test. Nevertheless, this view does not leave the legislature's hands completely tied.

First, the legislature has some freedom to formulate a new cause of action so that it looks sufficiently foreign to the common law and hence falls on the nonjury side of the constitutional test. Cf. Luria v. United States, 231 U.S. 9, 34 S.Ct. 10 (1913) (in statutory proceedings to cancel a certificate of citizenship, there was no jury right because right and remedy were essentially equitable). The legislature may even abolish a common-law cause of action and replace it with something new of this sort that does not involve a jury trial. Cf. Mountain Timber Co. v. Washington, 243 U.S. 219, 37 S.Ct. 260 (1917) (when the employee's right of action against the employer for negligence was replaced by statutes setting up a system of compensation for industrial injuries without regard to fault, with a commission to adjudicate factual disputes, those statutes would not violate the Seventh Amendment when they act to block any federal court action for such injuries).

Second, where policy so motivates, the legislature may entrust adjudicatory matters to an administrative agency or legislative court for nonjury adjudication—but, at least on the federal level, only those matters involving public rights, which would extend to statutory rights that are closely intertwined with a public regulatory scheme. See Atlas Roofing Co. v. Occupational Safety & Health Review Comm'n, 430 U.S. 442, 97 S.Ct. 1261 (1977) (government claim, before administrative agency, seeking civil penalties for employer's violation of OSHA; no jury required). This second exception is similar to the first, but by itself it represents an extremely important facilitation of the modern administrative state.

In any event, if the legislature is silent, the courts have traditionally resorted to historical analogy in determining the jury right.

Curtis v. Loether

Supreme Court of the United States, 1974.
415 U.S. 189, 94 S.Ct. 1005.

■ MR. JUSTICE MARSHALL delivered the opinion of the Court.

Section 812 of the Civil Rights Act of 1968, 82 Stat. 88, 42 U.S.C. § 3612, authorizes private plaintiffs to bring civil actions to redress violations of Title VIII, the fair housing provisions of the Act, and provides that "[t]he court may grant as relief, as it deems appropriate, any permanent or temporary injunction, temporary restraining order, or other order, and may award to the plaintiff actual damages and not more than $1,000 punitive damages, together with court costs and reasonable attorney fees . . . ."

The question presented in this case is whether the Civil Rights Act or the Seventh Amendment requires a jury trial upon demand by one of the parties in an action . . . under this section.

Petitioner, a Negro woman, brought this action under § 812, claiming that respondents, who are white, had refused to rent an apartment to her because of her race, in violation of § 804(a) of the Act, 42 U.S.C. § 3604(a). [She sought] actual and punitive damages.

Respondents made a timely demand for jury trial in their answer. The District Court, however, held that jury trial was neither authorized by Title VIII nor required by the Seventh Amendment, and denied the jury request. Rogers v. Loether, 312 F.Supp. 1008 (E.D.Wis.1970). After trial on the merits, the District Judge found that respondents had in fact discriminated against petitioner on account of her race. Although he found no actual damages, . . . he awarded $250 in punitive damages, denying petitioner's request for attorney's fees and court costs.

The Court of Appeals reversed on the jury trial issue. Rogers v. Loether, 467 F.2d 1110 (C.A.7 1972). . . . In view of the importance of the jury trial issue in the administration and enforcement of Title VIII and the diversity of views in the lower courts on the question, we granted certiorari, 412 U.S. 937, 93 S.Ct. 2770 (1973). We affirm.

The legislative history on the jury trial question is sparse, and what little is available is ambiguous. . . . Both petitioner and respondents have presented plausible arguments from the wording and construction of § 812. We see no point to giving extended consideration to these arguments, however, for we think it is clear that the Seventh Amendment entitles either party to demand a jury trial in an action for damages in the federal courts under § 812.

The Seventh Amendment provides that "[i]n suits at common law, where the value in controversy shall exceed twenty dollars, the right of trial by jury shall be preserved." Although the thrust of the Amendment was to preserve the right to jury trial as it existed in 1791, it has long been settled that the right extends beyond the common-law forms of action recognized at that time. Mr. Justice Story established the basic principle in 1830:

> "The phrase 'common law,' found in this clause, is used in contradistinction to equity, and admiralty, and maritime jurisprudence. . . . By *common law,* [the Framers of the Amendment] meant . . . not merely suits, which the *common* law recognized among its old and settled proceedings, but suits in which *legal* rights were to be ascertained and determined, in contradistinction to those where equitable rights alone were recognized, and equitable remedies were administered . . . . In a just sense, the amendment then may well be construed to embrace all suits which are not of equity and admiralty jurisdiction, whatever might be the peculiar form which they may assume to settle legal rights." Parsons v. Bedford, 3 Pet. 433, 446–447 (1830) (emphasis in original).

Petitioner nevertheless argues that the Amendment is inapplicable to new causes of action created by congressional enactment. . . . The Seventh Amendment does apply to actions enforcing statutory rights, and requires a jury trial upon demand, if the statute creates legal rights and remedies, enforceable in an action for damages in the ordinary courts of law.

NLRB v. Jones & Laughlin Steel Corp., 301 U.S. 1, 57 S.Ct. 615 (1937), relied on by petitioner, lends no support to her statutory-rights argument. The Court there upheld the award of back pay without jury trial in an NLRB unfair labor practice proceeding, rejecting a Seventh Amendment claim on the ground that the case involved a "statutory proceeding" and "not a suit at common law or in the nature of such a suit." Id., at 48, 57 S.Ct., at 629. Jones & Laughlin merely stands for the proposition that the Seventh Amendment is generally inapplicable in administrative proceedings, where jury trials would be incompatible with the whole concept of administrative adjudication and would substantially interfere with the NLRB's role in the statutory scheme. . . . But when Congress provides for enforcement of statutory rights in an ordinary civil action in the district courts, where there is obviously no functional justification for denying the jury trial right, a jury trial must be available if the action involves rights and remedies of the sort typically enforced in an action at law.

We think it is clear that a damages action under § 812 is an action to enforce "legal rights" within the meaning of our Seventh Amendment decisions. [Citations omitted.] A damages action under the statute sounds basically in tort—the statute merely defines a new legal duty, and authorizes the courts to compensate a plaintiff for the injury caused by the defendant's wrongful breach. As the Court of Appeals noted, this cause of action is analogous to a number of tort actions recognized at common law.[10] More important, the relief sought here—actual and punitive damages—is the traditional form of relief offered in the courts of law.

We need not, and do not, go so far as to say that any award of monetary relief must necessarily be "legal" relief. See, e.g., Mitchell v. Robert DeMario Jewelry, Inc., 361 U.S. 288, 80 S.Ct. 332 (1960); Porter v. Warner Holding Co., 328 U.S. 395, 66 S.Ct. 1086 (1946). A comparison of Title VIII with Title VII of the Civil Rights Act of 1964, where the courts of appeals have held that jury trial is not required in an action for reinstatement and back pay, is instructive, although we of course express no view on the jury trial issue in that context. In Title VII cases the courts of appeals have characterized back pay as an integral part of an equitable remedy, a form of restitution. But the statutory language on which this characterization is based—

---

[10] For example, the Court of Appeals recognized that Title VIII could be viewed as an extension of the common-law duty of innkeepers not to refuse temporary lodging to a traveler without justification, a duty enforceable in a damages action triable to a jury, to those who rent apartments on a long-term basis. See 467 F.2d at 1117. An action to redress racial discrimination may also be likened to an action for defamation or intentional infliction of mental distress. Indeed, the contours of the latter tort are still developing, and it has been suggested that "under the logic of the common law development of a law of insult and indignity, racial discrimination might be treated as a dignitary tort." C. Gregory & H. Kalven, Cases and Materials on Torts 961 (2d ed. 1969).

> "[T]he court may enjoin the respondent from engaging in such unlawful employment practice, and order such affirmative action as may be appropriate, which may include, but is not limited to, reinstatement or hiring of employees, with or without back pay . . . , or any other equitable relief as the court deems appropriate," 42 U.S.C. § 2000e–5(g) (1970 ed., Supp. II)—

contrasts sharply with § 812's simple authorization of an action for actual and punitive damages. In Title VII cases, also, the courts have relied on the fact that the decision whether to award back pay is committed to the discretion of the trial judge. There is no comparable discretion here: if a plaintiff proves unlawful discrimination and actual damages, he is entitled to judgment for that amount. Nor is there any sense in which the award here can be viewed as requiring the defendant to disgorge funds wrongfully withheld from the plaintiff. Whatever may be the merit of the "equitable" characterization in Title VII cases, there is surely no basis for characterizing the award of compensatory and punitive damages here as equitable relief.[f]

We are not oblivious to the force of petitioner's policy arguments. Jury trials may delay to some extent the disposition of Title VIII damages actions. But Title VIII actions seeking only equitable relief will be unaffected, and preliminary injunctive relief remains available without a jury trial even in damages actions. Dairy Queen, Inc. v. Wood, [369 U.S. 469, 479 n.20, 82 S.Ct. 894, 901 n.20 (1962)]. Moreover, the statutory requirement of expedition of § 812 actions, 42 U.S.C. § 3614 (1970), applies equally to jury and nonjury trials.[g] We recognize, too, the possibility that jury prejudice may deprive a victim of discrimination of the verdict to which he or she is entitled. Of course, the trial judge's power to direct a verdict, to grant judgment notwithstanding the verdict, or to grant a new trial provides substantial protection against this risk, and respondents' suggestion that jury trials will expose a broader segment of the populace to the example of the federal civil rights laws in operation has some force. More fundamentally, however, these considerations are insufficient to overcome the clear command of the Seventh Amendment.[15] The decision of the Court of Appeals must be affirmed.

---

[f] With the passage of the Civil Rights Act of 1991, Pub.L. No. 102–166, tit. I, § 102, 105 Stat. 1071, 1072, some limited legal remedies became available for intentional discrimination claims brought under Title VII. When compensatory or punitive damages are sought thereunder, either party may now demand a jury trial.

[g] See 28 U.S.C. § 1657, which repealed 42 U.S.C. § 3614 in 1984.

[15] Although petitioner has emphasized that the policies underlying the Fair Housing Act are derived from the Thirteenth and Fourteenth Amendments, she expressly "does not maintain that these constitutional considerations could prevent a jury trial if a jury were otherwise required by the Seventh Amendment." Brief for Petitioner 7. Moreover, although the legislative history of Title VIII with respect to jury trials is ambiguous, there is surely no indication that Congress intended to override the requirements of the Seventh Amendment if it mandates that jury trials be provided in § 812 damage actions. We therefore have no occasion to consider in this case any question of the scope of congressional power to enforce § 2 of the Thirteenth Amendment or § 5 of the Fourteenth Amendment.

Affirmed.

---

2. **Joinder of legal and equitable causes.**—The historical test is relatively easy to apply when dealing with an action involving a single claim for relief as to which an ancient analogue can be found. More serious difficulties arise in some of the more complicated actions brought under today's procedure, requiring an attempt to fit them into historical pigeonholes. What is to be the mode of trial when a party includes both legal and equitable issues in the same complaint, or when a legal complaint is met by an equitable defense or counterclaim (or vice versa)? There is another, separate problem. If, as under Rule 38, the jury right goes by issues, not by cases, what approach should govern the order of trial when a factual issue is common to a legal claim or defense and an equitable claim or defense?

The cases now to be set out show these difficulties in applying the historical test, while even showing in certain respects the possible irrelevance of history. Let us begin by assuming that, after merger of law and equity, the plaintiff seeks legal and equitable relief, where both are available cumulatively. Does the plaintiff have a right to trial by jury on the legal issues? Does the defendant?

FARRELL v. CITY OF ONTARIO, 39 Cal.App. 351, 178 P. 740 (1919). Plaintiff sued defendant for diverting storm waters upon his land. The prayer was for damages and for an injunction. Plaintiff claimed a right to trial by jury on the legal issues. The court said: "According to the allegations of his complaint, plaintiff had two rights of action and was entitled to two remedies, of which he might pursue either or both at his election, the legal remedy of damages for past injuries suffered and the equitable remedy of injunction to prevent their recurrence in the future. He might have prosecuted separate actions for these two remedies concurrently. In that case the facts alleged in the two actions would have been the same, except that in the action at law he would have alleged the money value of the injuries suffered and in the suit in equity he would have alleged the facts showing a threat of future repetitions thereof. Under those circumstances it will be conceded that the plaintiff would have been entitled as of right to a trial by jury of the legal issues . . . . Instead of doing this, he accepted the invitation held out to him by our laws and joined his two actions in one. He should not be held to have thereby forfeited his right to a jury trial of the legal issues . . . ."

The court then referred to the clean-up doctrine, which had allowed the chancellor (if the plaintiff so wished) to decide all aspects of a suit wherein compensatory damages were sought as incidental to an injunction.[h] The court observed that this doctrine had no bearing on the plaintiff's jury right. But this observation led the court to an alternative ground for decision, narrower than the one given in the above-quoted passage:

"The doctrine that equity, once having taken jurisdiction, will retain it for the purpose of disposing of the entire case was limited and safeguarded in its application under the former procedure by another rule, equally well established, namely, that where the title of the plaintiff is doubtful or the violation of his right by the defendant is not clear, he will be required to first establish his title, his right, and the violation thereof, in an action at law, before equity will entertain his application for extraordinary relief.[i] High on Injunctions, § 8; 29 Cyc. 1228, and cases cited. Under this rule, if the plaintiff had filed in a court of purely equitable jurisdiction the complaint upon which this action is based and the defendant had made answer thereto, as it did here, denying plaintiff's title to the land alleged to have been injured, denying the diversion of waters, and denying the alleged injuries to the land, the court would have said to the plaintiff, in effect:

'You must first go into a court of law and there establish these disputed claims of right upon which you are basing your claims for relief; if you succeed in establishing there your legal rights, we will then entertain and consider your petition for equitable relief.'

"And, of course, in such action at law the parties would have been entitled to a jury . . . ."

IMPERIAL SHALE BRICK CO. v. JEWETT, 169 N.Y. 143, 62 N.E. 167 (1901). An "inland marine certificate of insurance" issued to plaintiff covered a cargo of bricks shipped by plaintiff from Cleveland, Ohio, to "Waukegan, Mich." The cargo became a total loss and did not reach its destination. Plaintiff sued defendants, as joint insurers, to reform the certificate to read "Waukegan, Illinois" (there being no Waukegan, Michigan) and to recover on the certificate as reformed.[j] After disposing of various defenses, the court said:

"The defendants complain that against their objection and exception the action was tried at the Equity Term instead of before a jury. . . . The plaintiff properly asked in its complaint to have the certificate corrected in this respect. If the defendants had admitted by their answer the statement of facts alleged in this behalf in the complaint, as they did upon the trial, the equitable issue would not have arisen, but they did not, but interposed a denial, and thus the case properly came on for trial at the Equity Term.

"The complaint does not contain separate equitable and legal causes of action, but it asks such relief in equity as would, if granted, permit a recovery, as at common law. But the complaint stated no common-law

[h] See supra p. 1099.

[i] See supra p. 1096.

[j] See supra p. 1095.

cause of action, except as conditioned upon the equitable relief, and hence the right to recovery rested primarily upon equitable grounds. The court having obtained jurisdiction in equity, may, if it grant the equitable relief, retain jurisdiction and render that further judgment which properly follows thereon."

Question: (4) Is the ruling in this case compatible with the New York statute (which was at the time of decision the same as its current statute quoted above, for all purposes here relevant)?

PARTIES' MUTUALITY

The plaintiff who joins legal and equitable causes thus has a jury right on the legal issues. Moreover, the plaintiff historically had the power—to the extent of the clean-up doctrine—to preclude the defendant's jury right.

Question: (5) Should this lack of equality, or of mutuality, affect the "chancellor's" discretion in granting clean-up relief today?

Previously, state courts pursued other routes to alleviate the lack of mutuality. In Cogswell v. New York, New Haven & Hartford Railroad Co., 105 N.Y. 319, 11 N.E. 518 (1887), plaintiff, complaining of a nuisance, sought damages, abatement, and an injunction. Her demand for a jury was granted below as a matter of right, but on appeal this was held to be error. At common law, said the appellate court, the remedies of damages and abatement were available in a legal action known as an assize of nuisance, but the law court could not grant an injunction. This, then, is not a case that as a whole "was triable by jury at the adoption of the Constitution, nor is it one where, under the present system, the plaintiff is compelled to unite her claims for both equitable and legal relief in the same action." But as plaintiff chose to bring "an action for both legal and equitable relief in respect to the same cause of action," she "submits to have the issues tried by the court, or by the court with the aid of a jury, as the court in its discretion may determine, according to the practice in equity cases." (This waiver rule has been limited by NYCPLR § 4102(c), which provides that there is no waiver by joining legal and equitable claims based upon separate transactions. See Tanenbaum v. Anchor Sav. Bank, 95 A.D.2d 827, 464 N.Y.S.2d 19 (1983) (still waiver if same transaction, apparently despite the evolution toward the transactional view for claim preclusion).)

A somewhat more direct route toward equalizing plaintiff's and defendant's jury rights—also by cutting back the jury right—was charted in Koeper v. Town of Louisville, 109 Minn. 519, 124 N.W. 218 (1910), where plaintiff sought the same three heads of relief. The court said there was a clear distinction between a case where "two causes of action, one legal and the other equitable, are united in the same action" and a case where "the cause of action is an equitable one, in which equitable relief is sought, and also legal relief as an incident to the equitable cause of action." The present case was of the latter type, and it followed that neither party was entitled to the constitutional jury.

---

3. **Order of trial.**—Still assume that, after merger, the plaintiff seeks cumulatively legal and equitable relief. Once you have decided that a party has a jury right, there remains the separate question of whether the right will be protected by an appropriate order of trial when a factual issue is common to the legal and the equitable relief.

The historical resolution was simple. If the plaintiff prior to merger had the right to seek cumulatively both legal and equitable relief and if there was an issue common to both types of relief, the plaintiff generally had the choice whether to bring the legal or the equitable action first. And the first judgment determining the common issue would bind the parties in the second action. See Brady v. Daly, 175 U.S. 148, 20 S.Ct. 62 (1899). Hence the plaintiff could choose the mode of trial of the common issue.

Under a merged system, the plaintiff may or must seek all his relief in a single action. Fidelity to history would call for letting the plaintiff preserve the substance of his option by simply claiming or not claiming a jury on the common issue in the single action. If the teachings of history were to be followed, the defendant would have no choice as to mode of trial.

BRUCKMAN v. HOLLZER, 152 F.2d 730 (9th Cir.1946). Harold Lloyd Corporation, claiming copyright infringement of its photoplay, sued in separate counts, Count 1 asking damages from the three defendants for the infringement and Count 2 asking that one of the defendants, Universal Pictures Corporation, be enjoined from future infringement. (Formerly, the legal and equitable causes could have been brought separately, and either could have been brought before the other.) The plaintiff demanded a trial by jury on the first count, and the defendants moved to strike the demand. The trial court denied the motion to strike and indicated that the equitable issues would be tried by the court without a jury simultaneously with the damages claim "to the extent practicable."

The defendants then brought a mandamus petition in the circuit court of appeals to compel the district judge to strike the demand. The defendants conceded that the claim for damages, if sued on separately, would be triable before a jury, but they contended that the plaintiff by combining the damages claim with a claim for equitable relief had waived its right to jury trial. The mandamus petition was denied, the court completely rejecting the waiver theory. Judge Denman for the court of appeals pointed out that the issue of infringement, common to the legal and equitable claims for relief, might conceivably be decided on conflicting evidence one way by the jury and the opposite way by the judge, but the first judgment would be binding. Hence, he concluded, the judge could preserve the right to trial by jury as declared by the Seventh Amendment only by trying the common issue so that judgment would be rendered on the verdict before the equitable claim was decided.

JUDGE'S DISCRETION

The plaintiff thus generally could control the mode of trial on the common issue. There were, however, two historical exceptions to this rule. In certain kinds of actions, represented by the Imperial Shale case, the equitable issues had to be tried first; neither the parties nor the court had any choice as to this. In certain other kinds of actions, represented by the Farrell case, the legal issues had to be tried first; again, there was no choice.

As a historical matter, both in the general situation and in the two exceptional situations, the court had no discretion as to the mode of trial on the common issue. Yet a number of cases held that judicial discretion with respect to order of trial could be invoked in a way that would dictate mode of trial. See, e.g., Orenstein v. United States, 191 F.2d 184 (1st Cir.1951). This position had no historical support.

RALPH BLECHMAN, INC. v. I.B. KLEINERT RUBBER CO., 98 F.Supp. 1005 (S.D.N.Y.1951). The plaintiffs sued under the antitrust laws for treble damages and injunctive relief. (Formerly, a claim for treble damages for violation of the antitrust laws could not be joined with a claim for equitable relief, because equity could not award damages penal in character. Hence separate actions at law and in equity were necessary, and either could be brought before the other.) The defendants moved to strike the plaintiffs' jury demand on the ground that the action was essentially equitable in nature. The court denied the motion, saying that where the same claim is made the basis for both legal and equitable relief, it is of little aid to determine whether the issues are essentially legal or essentially equitable in their nature. The court also said: "Whether or not this question [of the plaintiffs' right of the to injunctive relief] should be separately tried by the court, and, if so, whether or not it should be tried before the legal issues, are questions not presented by the instant motion, and are matters within the discretion of the trial judge."

---

4. **Alternative remedies.**—Now assume that, after merger, the plaintiff seeks legal and equitable remedies that are available only alternatively. What happens to the jury right?

Fraser v. Geist, 1 F.R.D. 267 (E.D.Pa.1940), can provide an example. Fraser, an expert golfer, sued the executors of the estate of Geist, a wealthy golf devotee, alleging that Geist "induced" plaintiff to leave high school prior to graduation to become his golf companion by promising to set up a trust fund of at least $100,000 for plaintiff in his will. The complaint further alleged that Fraser performed his part of the arrangement for more than five years until Geist's death, that Geist made no provision in his will for the promised trust fund, and that the executors of his estate refused to recognize any obligation. Plaintiff prayed that the executors be ordered either (1) to set up a $100,000 trust fund and pay the income to plaintiff for life or (2) to pay plaintiff a lump sum in lieu thereof as damages. Defendants denied the making of the contract. The plaintiff demanded a jury trial. The defendants moved to strike the demand on the ground that the plaintiff's claim was cognizable only in equity. Judge Kalodner avoided the difficulties by concluding that the complaint stated no claim for legal relief because of the "uncertainty as to the computation of damages," and hence he struck the plaintiff's demand for jury trial. He expressed regret that Rule 39 precluded "a more desirable solution—one in which the court could try the case with a jury and, in the event that equitable relief should be granted, could treat the verdict of the jury as merely advisory; but, in the event that legal relief is appropriate, could treat the jury's verdict as binding"—his thought here being "that Rule 39 makes it incumbent upon the court to decide from the pleadings and prior to trial whether or not the action is one at law or in equity."

The question of how to resolve the jury claim, where the complaint really can stand on both of the alternative grounds, has been a favorite subject for commentators.

Professor Moore believed that Judge Kalodner's "more desirable solution" is not precluded by Rule 39. See 5 Moore ¶ 38.18, at 38–172 n.5 (second edition). Professor Moore's own solution, however, was to deny the plaintiff a jury because the preferred theory of a plaintiff who requests equitable relief makes the case one for the court. See 3 Moore 3018 (first edition). But is the equitable remedy necessarily preferred?

Professor Morris characterized Judge Kalodner's ruling that the complaint stated no claim for legal relief as "dubious substantive law." Professor Morris's solution required the plaintiff to specify at the outset which remedy he prefers, and the court to treat the jury right accordingly. See Clarence Morris, Jury Trial Under the Federal Fusion of Law and Equity, 20 Tex.L.Rev. 427, 435–36 (1942).

Curiously, Professor McCoid's solution required the plaintiff to take a position at the outset on trial by jury, and the court to treat the corresponding remedy as preferred. See John C. McCoid, II, Right to Jury Trial in the Federal Courts, 45 Iowa L.Rev. 726, 731–34 (1960).

Questions: (6) What could the plaintiff have done under the practice prior to the Federal Rules? Does this suggest that Professor Morris's approach is historically superior, even if it clashes with the Rules' policy to allow the pursuit of alternative remedies?

(7) Under the Morris approach, if the plaintiff indicates that he prefers the equitable remedy but this request for relief fails on "purely equitable" grounds, is there a jury right on the remaining legal issues? Can Judge Kalodner's "more desirable solution" be utilized to meet this contingency?

(8) Employing the Morris approach in tandem with Kalodner's "more desirable solution," can you construct a decision-tree that would accurately reconstruct historical choices in a modern procedural system?

(9) In light of Rule 54(c), is not the Fraser v. Geist problem present in every action?

5. Equitable device.—Assume that, after merger, the plaintiff uses a traditionally equitable device for getting into court in order to press what is otherwise a legal claim. Examples of such devices include class action, shareholders' derivative action, intervention, interpleader, and declaratory judgment. Is there a jury right on the legal-type issues?

For one example, in Rankin v. Frebank Co., 47 Cal.App.3d 75, 121 Cal.Rptr. 348 (1975), two minority stockholders brought a derivative action, seeking recovery of "secret profits" alleged to have been wrongfully diverted by two of the corporation's officers. The plaintiffs demanded a jury trial, but the trial court refused. This was affirmed on appeal, the court saying there was no right to jury trial in a shareholders' derivative action under the "historically based approach" followed in California.

6. Equitable defense to legal claim.—Assume that, after merger, the plaintiff brings a purely legal claim and the defendant interposes a defense, such as mutual mistake, that was formerly cognizable only in equity. What happens to the jury right?

As a historical matter, the law-defendant here would have immediately gone into equity to seek relief, such as reformation or rescission, based on mutual mistake. The equity court would as a matter of course have temporarily enjoined the law action. The equitable issues would then have been tried to the court. If these issues were decided in favor of the law-defendant, the law action would be defeated. If not, the law action would then proceed. See Liberty Oil Co. v. Condon Nat'l Bank, 260 U.S. 235, 43 S.Ct. 118 (1922); cf. City of Morgantown v. Royal Ins. Co., 169 F.2d 713 (4th Cir.1948), aff'd on other grounds, 337 U.S. 254, 69 S.Ct. 1067 (1949).

Question: (10) How can this history be replicated in a modern procedural system?

7. Dueling legal and equitable claims.—Finally assume that, after merger, the plaintiff brings a purely legal claim and the defendant seeks to defeat it on some ground, such as fraud, that was formerly cognizable as a defense at law and also as a claim in equity. Or assume that these parties sue in the reverse order. What happens to the jury right? What of common factual issues?

This problem of the jury right under merged procedure, when one party presents in his pleading a legal claim and the other a potentially equitable claim and when there is a substantial question of fact common to the two, is well illustrated by life insurance cases in which the insurance company seeks to establish that the policy was obtained by fraud of the insured. Additionally, consideration of these cases is relevant to an understanding of the implications of the landmark Beacon Theatres, Inc. v. Westover, which begins the next Section.

Tactically, the beneficiary will almost always prefer a jury determination of the common issue of fraud, and the insurer will prefer a court determination. Whether a jury be thought actually "outcome determinative" or not in the Erie–Guaranty–Byrd sense, the popular view of the probabilities is that the bereaved spouse and children contesting with the big insurance company are likely to fare better with a jury than with a judge.

First, assume that the insurer uncovers evidence of fraud while the insured is still alive. The insurer does not have to wait until the insured dies and then try to prove fraud, but instead may sue immediately to cancel the policy by rescission. The lapse of time otherwise might be extremely prejudicial. This is especially true when the policy contains, as most life insurance policies do by statutory requirement, an "incontestability clause" providing that after a prescribed period, commonly two years, the policy cannot be cancelled for any reason except nonpayment of premiums; because the running of the time period is fatal to the claim of fraud, the insurer must be able to protect itself by suing for cancellation before the policy becomes incontestable.

Questions: (11) Would the insured have a right to trial by jury on the issue of fraud in such an action? See Connecticut Gen. Life Ins. Co. v. Candimat Co., 83 F.Supp. 1 (D.Md.1949) (no).

(12) Would there be a right to jury trial if the insured brought an action for a declaratory judgment that the policy was valid?

Second, assume that the insured dies while the policy is still contestable for fraud. Then the beneficiary or the insurer could sue, but whoever sues first will likely generate a compulsory counterclaim. If the beneficiary brings an action to recover on the policy and if the insurer counterclaims for cancellation, should the fraud issue be determined by the jury or the judge? Alternatively, if the insurer is the first to sue for cancellation and if the beneficiary counterclaims for recovery on the policy, should the issue of fraud be for the judge or the jury?

A possible but unattractive solution would be to have the question of the right to a jury on the issue of fraud, common to the claim and the counterclaim, turn simply upon which party wins the race to the courthouse. See Prudential Ins. Co. of Am. v. Saxe, 134 F.2d 16 (D.C.Cir.1943) (rejecting the approach that would allow a first-suing insurer to avoid a jury trial).

So, what does resort to history in this situation suggest? Originally, fraud in the procurement of insurance was cognizable only in equity as a suit for cancellation; such fraud could not be shown in defense of an action at law to recover on the policy. In the relatively recent course of time, however, fraud worked from equity over to law and came to be recognized as a law defense triable to a jury; but, in appropriate circumstances, cancellation could still be decreed in equity. See Ettelson v. Metropolitan

Life Ins. Co., 137 F.2d 62 (3d Cir.1943). Things still depended somewhat on who sued first.

On the one hand, the insurer might be first to sue, bringing a bill in equity to cancel the policy and to restrain the beneficiary from bringing an action on the policy until the disposition of the suit. The beneficiary might soon thereafter institute a law action on the policy, before any injunction issued, and the beneficiary might then contend that the insurer's remedy at law was adequate because of the availability of the defense of fraud in the legal action. However, equity jurisdiction was commonly determined as of the date of institution of the suit, continuing even though the remedy at law later became adequate. Moreover, given an incontestability clause and the former permissiveness as to voluntary dismissal, the beneficiary might sue within the period of contestability, take a voluntary dismissal after the insurer had responded and the incontestability period had run, and then, still within the statute of limitations, bring another action. So, the equity court might hold the case on its docket until the action on the policy was actually tried to a jury, or it might enjoin prosecution of the law action and decide the fraud issue for itself. Professor James said: "Where *A* seeks equitable relief principally to defeat an action at law by *B* against him on grounds cognizable as a defense at law, and where *B* interposes the law action by way of counterclaim, fidelity to the historical pattern would usually require that the order of trial sequence be left to the trial court's discretion, to be guided by the kind of factors enumerated in American Life Insurance Co. v. Stewart.[k] This, it should be noted, is the only type of situation in which history warrants the use of discretion for this purpose."[l]

On the other hand, if the beneficiary first sued on the policy, the insurer could similarly bring a bill in equity and seek to restrain the further prosecution of the law action. And a similar historical analysis then applies. Here, however, equity would most often refuse to enjoin the law action in order to decide about fraud, on the view that the remedy at law was adequate.

SECTION 3. BREAKING WITH HISTORY

Beacon Theatres, Inc. v. Westover

Supreme Court of the United States, 1959.
359 U.S. 500, 79 S.Ct. 948.

■ MR. JUSTICE BLACK delivered the opinion of the Court.

[k] 300 U.S. 203, 57 S.Ct. 377 (1937). Insurer's bill in equity to cancel for fraud was followed by beneficiaries' action at law on the policy. The Court, in discussing the appropriate factors to be taken into account for the exercise of equitable jurisdiction, said: "There would be many circumstances to be weighed, as, for instance, the condition of the court calendar, whether the insurer had been precipitate or its adversaries dilatory, as well as other factors. In the end, benefit and hardship would have to be set off, the one against the other, and a balance ascertained."

[l] Fleming James, Jr., Civil Procedure 371 (1965) (first edition).

Petitioner, Beacon Theatres, Inc., sought by mandamus to require a district judge in the Southern District of California to vacate certain orders alleged to deprive it of a jury trial of issues arising in a suit brought against it by Fox West Coast Theatres, Inc. The Court of Appeals for the Ninth Circuit refused the writ, holding that the trial judge had acted within his proper discretion in denying petitioner's request for a jury. 252 F.2d 864. We granted certiorari, 356 U.S. 956, 78 S.Ct. 996, because "Maintenance of the jury as a fact-finding body is of such importance and occupies so firm a place in our history and jurisprudence that any seeming curtailment of the right to a jury trial should be scrutinized with the utmost care." Dimick v. Schiedt, 293 U.S. 474, 486, 55 S.Ct. 296, 301.

Fox had asked for declaratory relief against Beacon alleging a controversy arising under the Sherman Antitrust Act, 26 Stat. 209, as amended, 15 U.S.C. §§ 1, 2, and under the Clayton Act, 38 Stat. 731, 15 U.S.C. § 15, which authorizes suits for treble damages against Sherman Act violators. According to the complaint Fox operates a movie theatre in San Bernardino, California, and has long been exhibiting films under contracts with movie distributors. These contracts grant it the exclusive right to show "first run" pictures in the "San Bernardino competitive area" and provide for "clearance"—a period of time during which no other theatre can exhibit the same pictures. After building a drive-in theatre about 11 miles from San Bernardino, Beacon notified Fox that it considered contracts barring simultaneous exhibitions of first-run films in the two theatres to be overt acts in violation of the antitrust laws.[1] Fox's complaint alleged that this notification, together with threats of treble damage suits against Fox and its distributors, gave rise to "duress and coercion" which deprived Fox of a valuable property right, the right to negotiate for exclusive first-run contracts. Unless Beacon was restrained, the complaint continued, irreparable harm would result. Accordingly, while its pleading was styled a "Complaint for Declaratory Relief," Fox prayed both for a declaration that a grant of clearance between the Fox and Beacon theatres is reasonable and not in violation of the antitrust laws, and for an injunction, pending final resolution of the litigation, to prevent Beacon from instituting any action under the antitrust laws against Fox and its distributors arising out of the controversy alleged in the complaint. Beacon filed an answer, a counterclaim against Fox, and a cross-claim against an exhibitor who had intervened. These denied the threats and asserted that there was no substantial competition between the two theatres, that the clearances granted were therefore unreasonable, and that a conspiracy existed between Fox and its distributors to manipulate contracts and clearances so as to restrain trade

[1] Beacon allegedly stated that the clearances granted violated both the antitrust laws and the decrees issued in United States v. Paramount Pictures, Inc., D.C., 66 F.Supp. 323, 70 F.Supp. 53, affirmed in part and reversed in part, 334 U.S. 131, 68 S.Ct. 915, subsequent proceedings in the District Court, 85 F.Supp. 881. The decrees in that case set limits on what clearances could be given when theatres were in competition with each other and held that there should be no clearances between theatres not in substantial competition. Neither Beacon nor Fox, however, appears to have been a party to those decrees. Their relevance, therefore, seems to be only that of significant precedents.

and monopolize first-run pictures in violation of the antitrust laws. Treble damages were asked.

Beacon demanded a jury trial of the factual issues in the case as provided by Federal Rule of Civil Procedure 38(b). The District Court, however, viewed the issues raised by the "Complaint for Declaratory Relief," including the question of competition between the two theatres, as essentially equitable. Acting under the purported authority of Rules 42(b) and 57, it directed that these issues be tried to the court before jury determination of the validity of the charges of antitrust violations made in the counterclaim and cross-claim. A common issue of the "Complaint for Declaratory Relief," the counterclaim, and the cross-claim was the reasonableness of the clearances granted to Fox, which depended, in part, on the existence of competition between the two theatres. Thus the effect of the action of the District Court could be, as the Court of Appeals believed, "to limit the petitioner's opportunity fully to try to a jury every issue which has a bearing upon its treble damage suit," for determination of the issue of clearances by the judge might "operate either by way of res judicata or collateral estoppel so as to conclude both parties with respect thereto at the subsequent trial of the treble damage claim." 252 F.2d at page 874.

The District Court's finding that the Complaint for Declaratory Relief presented basically equitable issues draws no support from the Declaratory Judgment Act, 28 U.S.C. §§ 2201, 2202; Fed.Rules Civ.Proc., 57. See also 48 Stat. 955, 28 U.S.C. (1940 ed.) § 400. That statute, while allowing prospective defendants to sue to establish their nonliability, specifically preserves the right to jury trial for both parties. It follows that if Beacon would have been entitled to a jury trial in a treble damage suit against Fox it cannot be deprived of that right merely because Fox took advantage of the availability of declaratory relief to sue Beacon first. Since the right to trial by jury applies to treble damage suits under the antitrust laws, and is, in fact, an essential part of the congressional plan for making competition rather than monopoly the rule of trade, see Fleitmann v. Welsbach Street Lighting Co., 240 U.S. 27, 29, 36 S.Ct. 233, 234, the Sherman and Clayton Act issues on which Fox sought a declaration were essentially jury questions.

Nevertheless the Court of Appeals refused to upset the order of the district judge. It held that the question of whether a right to jury trial existed was to be judged by Fox's complaint read as a whole. In addition to seeking a declaratory judgment, the court said, Fox's complaint can be read as making out a valid plea for injunctive relief, thus stating a claim traditionally cognizable in equity. A party who is entitled to maintain a suit in equity for an injunction, said the court, may have all the issues in his suit determined by the judge without a jury regardless of whether legal rights are involved. The court then rejected the argument that equitable relief, traditionally available only when legal remedies are inadequate, was rendered unnecessary in this case by the filing of the counterclaim and cross-claim which presented all the issues necessary to a determination of the right to injunctive relief. Relying on American Life Ins. Co. v. Stewart,

300 U.S. 203, 215, 57 S.Ct. 377, 380, decided before the enactment of the Federal Rules of Civil Procedure, it invoked the principle that a court sitting in equity could retain jurisdiction even though later a legal remedy became available. In such instances the equity court had discretion to enjoin the later lawsuit in order to allow the whole dispute to be determined in one case in one court. Reasoning by analogy, the Court of Appeals held it was not an abuse of discretion for the district judge, acting under Federal Rule of Civil Procedure 42(b), to try the equitable cause first even though this might, through collateral estoppel, prevent a full jury trial of the counterclaim and cross-claim which were as effectively stopped as by an equity injunction.

Beacon takes issue with the holding of the Court of Appeals that the complaint stated a claim upon which equitable relief could be granted. As initially filed the complaint alleged that threats of lawsuits by petitioner against Fox and its distributors were causing irreparable harm to Fox's business relationships. The prayer for relief, however, made no mention of the threats but asked only that pending litigation of the claim for declaratory judgment, Beacon be enjoined from beginning any lawsuits under the antitrust laws against Fox and its distributors arising out of the controversy alleged in the complaint. Evidently of the opinion that this prayer did not state a good claim for equitable relief, the Court of Appeals construed it to include a request for an injunction against threats of lawsuits. This liberal construction of a pleading is in line with Rule 8 of the Federal Rules of Civil Procedure. See Conley v. Gibson, 355 U.S. 41, 47–48, 78 S.Ct. 99, 102–103. But this fact does not solve our problem. Assuming that the pleadings can be construed to support such a request and assuming additionally that the complaint can be read as alleging the kind of harassment by a multiplicity of lawsuits which would *traditionally* have justified equity to take jurisdiction and settle the case in one suit, we are nevertheless of the opinion that, under the Declaratory Judgment Act and the Federal Rules of Civil Procedure, neither claim can justify denying Beacon a trial by jury of all the issues in the antitrust controversy.

The basis of injunctive relief in the federal courts has always been irreparable harm and inadequacy of legal remedies. At least as much is required to justify a trial court in using its discretion under the Federal Rules to allow claims of equitable origins to be tried ahead of legal ones, since this has the same effect as an equitable injunction of the legal claims. And it is immaterial, in judging if that discretion is properly employed, that before the Federal Rules and the Declaratory Judgment Act were passed, courts of equity, exercising a jurisdiction separate from courts of law, were, in some cases, allowed to enjoin subsequent legal actions between the same parties involving the same controversy. This was because the subsequent legal action, though providing an opportunity to try the case to a jury, might not protect the right of the equity plaintiff to a fair and orderly adjudication of the controversy. See, e.g., New York Life Ins. Co. v. Seymour, 6 Cir., 45 F.2d 47. Under such circumstances the legal remedy could quite naturally be deemed inadequate. Inadequacy of remedy and irreparable harm are practical terms, however. As such their existence today must be determined, not by precedents decided under discarded procedures, but in the light of the remedies now made available by the Declaratory Judgment Act and the Federal Rules.

Viewed in this manner, the use of discretion by the trial court under Rule 42(b) to deprive Beacon of a full jury trial on its counterclaim and cross-claim, as well as on Fox's plea for declaratory relief, cannot be justified. Under the Federal Rules the same court may try both legal and equitable causes in the same action. Fed.Rules Civ.Proc., 1, 2, 18. Thus any defenses, equitable or legal, Fox may have to charges of antitrust violations can be raised either in its suit for declaratory relief or in answer to Beacon's counterclaim. On proper showing, harassment by threats of other suits, or other suits actually brought, involving the issues being tried in this case, could be temporarily enjoined pending the outcome of this litigation. Whatever permanent injunctive relief Fox might be entitled to on the basis of the decision in this case could, of course, be given by the court after the jury renders its verdict. In this way the issues between these parties could be settled in one suit giving Beacon a full jury trial of every antitrust issue. Cf. Ring v. Spina, 2 Cir., 166 F.2d 546. By contrast, the holding of the court below while granting Fox no additional protection unless the avoidance of jury trial be considered as such, would compel Beacon to split his antitrust case, trying part to a judge and part to a jury.[10] Such a result, which involves the postponement and subordination of Fox's own legal claim for declaratory relief as well as of the counterclaim which Beacon was compelled by the Federal Rules to bring, is not permissible.

Our decision is consistent with the plan of the Federal Rules and the Declaratory Judgment Act to effect substantial procedural reform while retaining a distinction between jury and nonjury issues and leaving substantive rights unchanged. Since in the federal courts equity has always acted only when legal remedies were inadequate, the expansion of adequate legal remedies provided by the Declaratory Judgment Act and the Federal Rules necessarily affects the scope of equity. Thus, the justification for equity's deciding legal issues once it obtains jurisdiction, and refusing to dismiss a case, merely because subsequently a legal remedy becomes available, must be re-evaluated in the light of the liberal joinder provisions of the Federal Rules which allow legal and equitable causes to be brought and resolved in one civil action. Similarly the need for, and therefore, the availability of such equitable remedies as Bills of Peace, Quia Timet and Injunction must be reconsidered in view of the existence of the Declaratory Judgment Act as well as the liberal joinder provision of the Rules. This is not only in accord with the spirit of the Rules and the Act but is required by the provision in the Rules that "[t]he right of trial by jury as declared by the Seventh Amendment to the Constitution or as given by a statute of the United States shall be preserved . . . inviolate."

---

[10] Since the issue of violation of the antitrust laws often turns on the reasonableness of a restraint on trade in the light of all the facts, see, e.g., Standard Oil Co. of New Jersey v. United States, 221 U.S. 1, 60, 31 S.Ct. 502, 515, it is particularly undesirable to have some of the relevant considerations tried by one fact finder and some by another.

If there should be cases where the availability of declaratory judgment or joinder in one suit of legal and equitable causes would not in all respects protect the plaintiff seeking equitable relief from irreparable harm while affording a jury trial in the legal cause, the trial court will necessarily have to use its discretion in deciding whether the legal or equitable cause should be tried first. Since the right to jury trial is a constitutional one, however, while no similar requirement protects trials by the court,[17] that discretion is very narrowly limited and must, wherever possible, be exercised to preserve jury trial. As this Court said in Scott v. Neely, 140 U.S. 106, 109–110, 11 S.Ct. 712, 714: "In the Federal courts this [jury] right cannot be dispensed with, except by the assent of the parties entitled to it; nor can it be impaired by any blending with a claim, properly cognizable at law, of a demand for equitable relief in aid of the legal action or during its pendency." This long-standing principle of equity dictates that only under the most imperative circumstances, circumstances which in view of the flexible procedures of the Federal Rules we cannot now anticipate, can the right to a jury trial of legal issues be lost through prior determination of equitable claims. See Leimer v. Woods, 8 Cir., 196 F.2d 828, 833–836. As we have shown, this is far from being such a case.

Respondent claims mandamus is not available under the All Writs Act, 28 U.S.C. § 1651. Whatever differences of opinion there may be in other types of cases, we think the right to grant mandamus to require jury trial where it has been improperly denied is settled.

The judgment of the Court of Appeals is reversed.

■ MR. JUSTICE FRANKFURTER took no part in the consideration or decision of this case.

■ MR. JUSTICE STEWART, with whom MR. JUSTICE HARLAN and MR. JUSTICE WHITTAKER concur, dissenting.

. . . .

Assuming the existence of a factual issue common both to the plaintiff's original action and the defendant's counterclaim for damages, I cannot agree that the District Court must be compelled to try the counterclaim first. It is, of course, a matter of no great moment in what order the issues between the parties in the present litigation are tried. What is disturbing is the process by which the Court arrives at its decision—a process which appears to disregard the historic relationship between equity and law.

I.

The Court suggests that "the expansion of adequate legal remedies provided by the Declaratory Judgment Act . . . necessarily affects the scope of equity." Does the Court mean to say that the mere availability of an action for a declaratory judgment operates to furnish "an adequate remedy at law" so as to deprive a court of equity of the power to act? That novel

---

[17] See Hurwitz v. Hurwitz, 78 U.S.App.D.C. 66, 136 F.2d 796, 798–799; cf. The Propeller Genesee Chief v. Fitzhugh, 12 How. 443, 459–460.

line of reasoning is at least implied in the Court's opinion. But the Declaratory Judgment Act did not "expand" the substantive law. That Act merely provided a new statutory remedy, neither legal nor equitable, but available in the areas of both equity and law. When declaratory relief is sought, the right to trial by jury depends upon the basic context in which the issues are presented. See Moore's Federal Practice (2d ed.) §§ 38.29, 57.30; Borchard, Declaratory Judgments (2d ed.), 399–404. If the basic issues in an action for declaratory relief are of a kind traditionally cognizable in equity, e.g., a suit for cancellation of a written instrument, the declaratory judgment is not a "remedy at law." If, on the other hand, the issues arise in a context traditionally cognizable at common law, the right to a jury trial of course remains unimpaired, even though the only relief demanded is a declaratory judgment.

Thus, if in this case the complaint had asked merely for a judgment declaring that the plaintiff's specified manner of business dealings with distributors and other exhibitors did not render it liable to Beacon under the antitrust laws, this would have been simply a "juxtaposition of parties" case in which Beacon could have demanded a jury trial.[7] But the complaint in the present case, as the Court recognizes, presented issues of exclusively equitable cognizance, going well beyond a mere defense to any subsequent action at law. Fox sought from the court protection against Beacon's allegedly unlawful interference with its business relationships—protection which this Court seems to recognize might not have been afforded by a declaratory judgment, unsupplemented by equitable relief. The availability of a declaratory judgment did not, therefore, operate to confer upon Beacon the right to trial by jury with respect to the issues raised by the complaint.

II.

The Court's opinion does not, of course, hold or even suggest that a court of equity may never determine "legal rights." For indeed it is precisely such rights which the Chancellor, when his jurisdiction has been properly invoked, has often been called upon to decide. Issues of fact are rarely either "legal" or "equitable." All depends upon the context in which they arise. The examples cited by Chief Judge Pope in his thorough opinion in the Court of Appeals in this case are illustrative: ". . . In a suit for specific performance of a contract, the court may determine the making, validity and the terms of the contract involved. . . ." 252 F.2d 864, 874.

Though apparently not disputing these principles, the Court holds, quite apart from its reliance upon the Declaratory Judgment Act, that Beacon by filing its counterclaim and cross-claim acquired a right to trial by jury of issues which otherwise would have been properly triable to the court. Support for this position is found in the principle that, "in the federal courts equity has always acted only when legal remedies were

[7] Moore's Federal Practice (2d ed.) § 57.31[2]. "Transposition of parties" would perhaps be a more accurate description. A typical such case is one in which a plaintiff uses the declaratory judgment procedure to seek a determination of nonliability to a legal claim asserted by the defendant. The defendant in such a case is, of course, entitled to a jury trial.

inadequate. . . ." Yet that principle is not employed in its traditional sense as a limitation upon the exercise of power by a court of equity. This is apparent in the Court's recognition that the allegations of the complaint entitled Fox to equitable relief—relief to which Fox would not have been entitled if it had had an adequate remedy at law. Instead, the principle is employed today to mean that because it is possible under the counterclaim to have a jury trial of the factual issue of substantial competition, that issue must be tried by a jury, even though the issue was primarily presented in the original claim for equitable relief. This is a marked departure from long-settled principles.

It has been an established rule "that equitable jurisdiction existing at the filing of a bill is not destroyed because an adequate legal remedy may have become available thereafter." American Life Ins. Co. v. Stewart, 300 U.S. 203, 215, 57 S.Ct. 377, 380. See Dawson v. Kentucky Distilleries & Warehouse Co., 255 U.S. 288, 296, 41 S.Ct. 272, 275. It has also been long settled that the District Court in its discretion may order the trial of a suit in equity in advance of an action at law between the same parties, even if there is a factual issue common to both. In the words of Mr. Justice Cardozo, writing for a unanimous Court in American Life Ins. Co. v. Stewart, supra:

> "A court has control over its own docket. . . . In the exercise of a sound discretion it may hold one lawsuit in abeyance to abide the outcome of another, especially where the parties and the issues are the same. . . . If request had been made by the respondents to suspend the suits in equity till the other causes were disposed of, the District Court could have considered whether justice would not be done by pursuing such a course, the remedy in equity being exceptional and the outcome of necessity. . . . There would be many circumstances to be weighed, as, for instance, the condition of the court calendar, whether the insurer had been precipitate or its adversaries dilatory, as well as other factors. In the end, benefit and hardship would have to be set off, the one against the other, and a balance ascertained." 300 U.S. 203, 215–216, 57 S.Ct. 377, 380.[9]

III.

The Court today sweeps away these basic principles as "precedents decided under discarded procedures." It suggests that the Federal Rules of Civil Procedure have somehow worked an "expansion of adequate legal remedies" so as to oust the District Courts of equitable jurisdiction, as well as to deprive them of their traditional power to control their own dockets. But obviously the Federal Rules could not and did not "expand" the substantive law one whit.

Like the Declaratory Judgment Act, the Federal Rules preserve inviolate the right to trial by jury in actions historically cognizable at common

[9] It is arguable that if a case factually similar to American Life Ins. Co. v. Stewart were to arise under the Declaratory Judgment Act, the defendant would be entitled to a jury trial. See footnote 7. But cf. 5 Moore's Federal Practice (2d ed.), p. 158.

law, as under the Constitution they must. They do not create a right of trial by jury where that right "does not exist under the Constitution or statutes of the United States." Rule 39(a). Since Beacon's counterclaim was compulsory under the Rules, see Rule 13(a), it is apparent that by filing it Beacon could not be held to have waived its jury rights. Compare American Mills Co. v. American Surety Co., 260 U.S. 360, 43 S.Ct. 149. But neither can the counterclaim be held to have transformed Fox's original complaint into an action at law. See Bendix Aviation Corp. v. Glass, D.C., 81 F.Supp. 645.

The Rules make possible the trial of legal and equitable claims in the same proceeding, but they expressly affirm the power of a trial judge to determine the order in which claims shall be heard. Rule 42(b). Certainly the Federal Rules were not intended to undermine the basic structure of equity jurisprudence, developed over the centuries and explicitly recognized in the United States Constitution.

For these reasons I think the petition for a writ of mandamus should have been dismissed.

Dairy Queen, Inc. v. Wood

Supreme Court of the United States, 1962.
369 U.S. 469, 82 S.Ct. 894.

■ MR. JUSTICE BLACK delivered the opinion of the Court.

The United States District Court for the Eastern District of Pennsylvania granted a motion to strike petitioner's demand for a trial by jury in an action now pending before it on the alternative grounds that either the action was "purely equitable" or, if not purely equitable, whatever legal issues that were raised were "incidental" to equitable issues, and, in either case, no right to trial by jury existed. The petitioner then sought mandamus in the Court of Appeals for the Third Circuit to compel the district judge to vacate this order. When that court denied this request without opinion, we granted certiorari because the action of the Court of Appeals seemed inconsistent with protections already clearly recognized for the important constitutional right to trial by jury in our previous decisions.

At the outset, we may dispose of one of the grounds upon which the trial court acted in striking the demand for trial by jury—that based upon the view that the right to trial by jury may be lost as to legal issues where those issues are characterized as "incidental" to equitable issues—for our previous decisions make it plain that no such rule may be applied in the federal courts. In Scott v. Neely, decided in 1891, this Court held that a court of equity could not even take jurisdiction of a suit "in which a claim properly cognizable only at law is united in the same pleadings with a claim for equitable relief."[3] That holding, which was based upon both the

[3] 140 U.S. 106, 117, 11 S.Ct. 712, 716. [This was a suit in equity in which the plaintiffs sought to establish a debt of the defendant to them and to set aside as fraudulent his

historical separation between law and equity and the duty of the Court to insure "that the right to a trial by a jury in the legal action may be preserved intact,"[4] created considerable inconvenience in that it necessitated two separate trials in the same case whenever that case contained both legal and equitable claims. Consequently, when the procedure in the federal courts was modernized by the adoption of the Federal Rules of Civil Procedure in 1938, it was deemed advisable to abandon that part of the holding of Scott v. Neely which rested upon the separation of law and equity and to permit the joinder of legal and equitable claims in a single action. [The Court here quoted Rule 18.]

The Federal Rules did not, however, purport to change the basic holding of Scott v. Neely that the right to trial by jury of legal claims must be preserved. Quite the contrary, Rule 38(a) expressly reaffirms that constitutional principle . . . . Nonetheless, after the adoption of the Federal Rules, attempts were made indirectly to undercut that right by having federal courts in which cases involving both legal and equitable claims were filed decide the equitable claim first. The result of this procedure in those cases in which it was followed was that any issue common to both the legal and equitable claims was finally determined by the court and the party seeking trial by jury on the legal claim was deprived of that right as to these common issues. This procedure finally came before us in Beacon Theatres, Inc. v. Westover, a case which, like this one, arose from the denial of a petition for mandamus to compel a district judge to vacate his order striking a demand for trial by jury.

Our decision reversing that case not only emphasizes the responsibility of the Federal Courts of Appeals to grant mandamus where necessary to protect the constitutional right to trial by jury but also limits the issues open for determination here by defining the protection to which that right is entitled in cases involving both legal and equitable claims. The holding in Beacon Theatres was that where both legal and equitable issues are presented in a single case, "only under the most imperative circumstances, circumstances which in view of the flexible procedures of the Federal Rules we cannot now anticipate, can the right to a jury trial of legal issues be lost through prior determination of equitable claims." That holding, of course, applies whether the trial judge chooses to characterize the legal issues presented as "incidental" to equitable issues or not.[8] Consequently, in a case such as this where there cannot even be a contention of such "imperative circumstances," Beacon Theatres requires that any legal issues

---

conveyance of land to his codefendant in order to subject it to the payment of the debt. The Court held that an action at law on the debt must precede a suit in equity to set aside the conveyance and ordered the bill in equity dismissed. The Court further held that the defendant was entitled to trial by jury on the debt claim.—Ed.]

[4] Id., 140 U.S. at 110, 11 S.Ct. at 714.

[8] "It is therefore immaterial that the case at bar contains a stronger basis for equitable relief than was present in Beacon Theatres. It would make no difference if the equitable cause clearly outweighed the legal cause so that the basic issue of the case taken as a whole is equitable. As long as any legal cause is involved the jury rights it creates control. This is the teaching of Beacon Theatres, as we construe it." Thermo–Stitch, Inc. v. Chemi–Cord Processing Corp., 5 Cir., 294 F.2d 486, 491.

for which a trial by jury is timely and properly demanded be submitted to a jury. There being no question of the timeliness or correctness of the demand involved here, the sole question which we must decide is whether the action now pending before the District Court contains legal issues.

The District Court proceeding arises out of a controversy between petitioner and the respondent owners of the trademark "DAIRY QUEEN"[m] with regard to a written licensing contract made by them in December 1949, under which petitioner agreed to pay some $150,000 for the exclusive right to use that trademark in certain portions of Pennsylvania. The terms of the contract provided for a small initial payment with the remaining payments to be made at the rate of 50% of all amounts received by petitioner on sales and franchises to deal with the trademark and, in order to make certain that the $150,000 payment would be completed within a specified period of time, further provided for minimum annual payments regardless of petitioner's receipts. In August 1960, the respondents wrote petitioner a letter in which they claimed that petitioner had committed "a material breach of that contract" by defaulting on the contract's payment provisions and notified petitioner of the termination of the contract and the cancellation of petitioner's right to use the trademark unless this claimed default was remedied immediately. When petitioner continued to deal with the trademark despite the notice of termination, the respondents brought an action based upon their view that a material breach of contract had occurred.

The complaint filed in the District Court alleged, among other things, that petitioner had "ceased paying . . . as required in the contract;" that the default "under the said contract . . . [was] in excess of $60,000.00;" that this default constituted a "material breach" of that contract; that petitioner had been notified by letter that its failure to pay as alleged made it guilty of a material breach of contract which if not "cured" would result in an immediate cancellation of the contract; that the breach had not been cured but that petitioner was contesting the cancellation and continuing to conduct business as an authorized dealer; that to continue such business after the cancellation of the contract constituted an infringement of the respondents' trademark; that petitioner's financial condition was unstable; and that because of the foregoing allegations, respondents were threatened with irreparable injury for which they had no adequate remedy at law. The complaint then prayed for both temporary and permanent relief, including: (1) temporary and permanent injunctions to restrain petitioner from any future use of or dealing in the franchise and the trademark; (2) an accounting to determine the exact amount of money owing by petitioner and a judgment for that amount; and (3) an injunction pending accounting to prevent petitioner from collecting any money from "Dairy Queen" stores in the territory.

---

[m] H.A. McCullough and H.F. McCullough, doing business as McCullough's Dairy Queen, were the owners of the trademark, plaintiffs in this action, and respondents (in addition to the district judge) in the Supreme Court.

In its answer to this complaint, petitioner raised a number of defenses, including: (1) a denial that there had been any breach of contract, apparently based chiefly upon its allegation that in January 1955 the parties had entered into an oral agreement modifying the original written contract by removing the provision requiring minimum annual payments regardless of petitioner's receipts thus leaving petitioner's only obligation that of turning over 50% of all its receipts; (2) laches and estoppel arising from respondents' failure to assert their claim promptly, thus permitting petitioner to expend large amounts of money in the development of its right to use the trademark; and (3) alleged violations of the antitrust laws by respondents in connection with their dealings with the trademark. Petitioner indorsed upon this answer a demand for trial by jury in accordance with Rule 38(b) of the Federal Rules of Civil Procedure.

Petitioner's contention, as set forth in its petition for mandamus to the Court of Appeals and reiterated in its briefs before this Court, is that insofar as the complaint requests a money judgment it presents a claim which is unquestionably legal. We agree with that contention. The most natural construction of the respondents' claim for a money judgment would seem to be that it is a claim that they are entitled to recover whatever was owed them under the contract as of the date of its purported termination plus damages for infringement of their trademark since that date. Alternatively, the complaint could be construed to set forth a full claim based upon both of these theories—that is, a claim that the respondents were entitled to recover both the debt due under the contract and damages for trademark infringement for the entire period of the alleged breach including that before the termination of the contract. Or it might possibly be construed to set forth a claim for recovery based completely on either one of these two theories—that is, a claim based solely upon the contract for the entire period both before and after the attempted termination on the theory that the termination, having been ignored, was of no consequence, or a claim based solely upon the charge of infringement on the theory that the contract, having been breached, could not be used as a defense to an infringement action even for the period prior to its termination. We find it unnecessary to resolve this ambiguity in the respondents' complaint because we think it plain that their claim for a money judgment is a claim wholly legal in its nature however the complaint is construed. As an action on a debt allegedly due under a contract, it would be difficult to conceive of an action of a more traditionally legal character. And as an action for damages based upon a charge of trademark infringement, it would be no less subject to cognizance by a court of law.

The respondents' contention that this money claim is "purely equitable" is based primarily upon the fact that their complaint is cast in terms of an "accounting," rather than in terms of an action for "debt" or "damages." But the constitutional right to trial by jury cannot be made to depend upon the choice of words used in the pleadings. The necessary prerequisite to the right to maintain a suit for an equitable accounting, like all other equitable remedies, is, as we pointed out in Beacon Theatres, the absence of an adequate remedy at law. Consequently, in order to maintain such a suit on a cause of action cognizable at law, as this one is, the plaintiff must be able to show that the "accounts between the parties" are of such a "complicated nature" that only a court of equity can satisfactorily unravel them. In view of the powers given to District Courts by Federal Rule of Civil Procedure 53(b) to appoint masters to assist the jury in those exceptional cases where the legal issues are too complicated for the jury adequately to handle alone,[18] the burden of such a showing is considerably increased and it will indeed be a rare case in which it can be met. But be that as it may, this is certainly not such a case. A jury, under proper instructions from the court, could readily determine the recovery, if any, to be had here, whether the theory finally settled upon is that of breach of contract, that of trademark infringement, or any combination of the two. The legal remedy cannot be characterized as inadequate merely because the measure of damages may necessitate a look into petitioner's business records.

Nor is the legal claim here rendered "purely equitable" by the nature of the defenses interposed by petitioner. Petitioner's primary defense to the charge of breach of contract—that is, that the contract was modified by a subsequent oral agreement—presents a purely legal question having nothing whatever to do either with novation, as the district judge suggested, or reformation, as suggested by the respondents here. Such a defense goes to the question of just what, under the law, the contract between the respondents and petitioner is and, in an action to collect a debt for breach of a contract between these parties, petitioner has a right to have the jury determine not only whether the contract has been breached and the extent of the damages if any but also just what the contract is.

We conclude therefore that the district judge erred in refusing to grant petitioner's demand for a trial by jury on the factual issues related to the question of whether there has been a breach of contract. Since these issues are common with those upon which respondents' claim to equitable relief is based, the legal claims involved in the action must be determined prior to any final court determination of respondents' equitable claims.[20] The Court of Appeals should have corrected the error of the district judge by granting the petition for mandamus. The judgment is therefore reversed and the cause remanded for further proceedings consistent with this opinion.

Reversed and remanded.

■ MR. JUSTICE STEWART concurs in the result.

■ MR. JUSTICE FRANKFURTER took no part in the decision of this case.

■ MR. JUSTICE WHITE took no part in the consideration or decision of this case.

■ MR. JUSTICE HARLAN, whom MR. JUSTICE DOUGLAS joins, concurring.

---

18 Even this limited inroad upon the right to trial by jury " 'should seldom be made, and if at all only when unusual circumstances exist.' " La Buy v. Howes Leather Co., 352 U.S. 249, 258, 77 S.Ct. 309, 314. See also In re Watkins, 5 Cir., 271 F.2d 771.

20 This does not, of course, interfere with the District Court's power to grant temporary relief pending a final adjudication on the merits. . . .

I am disposed to accept the view, strongly pressed at the bar, that this complaint seeks an accounting for alleged trademark infringement, rather than contract damages. Even though this leaves the complaint as formally asking only for equitable relief, this does not end the inquiry. The fact that an "accounting" is sought is not of itself dispositive of the jury trial issue. To render this aspect of the complaint truly "equitable" it must appear that the substantive claim is one cognizable only in equity or that the "accounts between the parties" are of such a "complicated nature" that they can be satisfactorily unraveled only by a court of equity. Kirby v. Lake Shore & Michigan Southern R. Co., 120 U.S. 130, 134, 7 S.Ct. 430, 432. See 5 Moore, Federal Practice (1951), 198–202. It is manifest from the face of the complaint that the "accounting" sought in this instance is not of either variety. A jury, under proper instructions from the court, could readily calculate the damages flowing from this alleged trademark infringement, just as courts of law often do in copyright and patent cases. Cf., e.g., Hartell v. Tilghman, 99 U.S. 547, 555; Arnstein v. Porter, 2 Cir., 154 F.2d 464; Bruckman v. Hollzer, 9 Cir., 152 F.2d 730.

Consequently what is involved in this case is nothing more than a joinder in one complaint of prayers for both legal and equitable relief. In such circumstances, under principles long since established, Scott v. Neely, 140 U.S. 106, 110, 11 S.Ct. 712, 714, the petitioner cannot be deprived of his constitutional right to a jury trial on the "legal" claim contained in the complaint.

On this basis I concur in the judgment of the Court.

Question: (13) If there is a jurisdictional challenge that involves factual issues also involved in the merits of the claim, which is legal in nature, may the judge decide the jurisdictional challenge on her own and at the outset of the action? See Kevin M. Clermont, Jurisdictional Fact, 91 Cornell L.Rev. 973, 990–91 (2006) (yes, but the decision will not bind the fact-finder on the merits because a lesser standard of proof applies to overlapping jurisdictional issues).

SIMLER v. CONNER, 372 U.S. 221, 83 S.Ct. 609 (1963). The plaintiff brought a diversity action in the Western District of Oklahoma for a declaratory judgment as to the extent of his liability to the defendant, an attorney, for legal services in a will contest. There was originally a written contract for a "reasonable" attorney's fee. Two months later the parties again discussed fees, and the plaintiff wrote a confirmatory letter to the defendant agreeing that the reasonable fee was to be contingent upon recovery and fixed on the basis of specified percentages of any recovery. The defendant's work in the will action resulted in a substantial recovery for the plaintiff, and under the terms of the letter the defendant would get 50 percent thereof. Now the plaintiff contended that the letter was the product of fraud and overreaching by the lawyer.

The district court denied the plaintiff's demand for a jury trial and later rendered summary judgment to the effect that the defendant was entitled to the 50 percent fee. The court of appeals reversed the summary judgment and remanded for a jury trial on the question whether the contingent fee contract was just, equitable, and free from fraud and, if it was not, then also on the question of a reasonable fee.

The Supreme Court per curiam, without citing Byrd v. Blue Ridge Rural Electric Cooperative, supra p. 364, and with Chief Justice Warren and Justices Black and Douglas dissenting, granted certiorari and summarily remanded the case for reconsideration in the light of an Oklahoma decision that held, where the cancellation of a contingent fee contract is the basic relief sought and is necessary before any other relief can be granted, the suit is a purely equitable matter as to which neither party is entitled to a jury. Thereupon, the court of appeals on reconsideration remanded for a trial without jury.

But certiorari was again granted. The Supreme Court now unanimously held, after argument but by a unanimous per curiam opinion, that the right to a jury trial in the federal courts is to be determined as a matter of federal law in diversity as well as other actions and that, although the substantive dimension of the claim is established by state law, its characterization as legal or equitable for purposes of the right to jury must be by recourse to federal law. The fact that the action was in form a declaratory judgment case should not, the Court said, obscure the essentially legal nature of this action to determine the fee owing. The questions involved were "traditional common-law issues," which should go to a jury. The Court then said: "Accordingly, the courts below erred in denying petitioner the jury trial guaranteed him by the Seventh Amendment and the judgment is reversed."

Question: (14) In a federal diversity action, should there be a right to jury trial on an issue of a kind that state law would give to the jury but that in a federal court would normally be decided by the judge?

INDIANHEAD TRUCK LINE v. HVIDSTEN TRANSPORT, INC., 268 Minn. 176, 128 N.W.2d 334 (1964). Plaintiff sued for specific performance of an agreement for the sale and transfer by the defendant trucking company of certain operating rights, equipment, real estate, and other property and, in addition, for monetary damages for the period between the time that performance was due and the time of trial. A jury was impanelled on defendant's demand, but at the close of the evidence the trial judge dismissed the jury on the ground that neither of the parties was entitled to a jury trial as a matter of right. The judge then decreed specific performance and awarded damages for the delayed performance.

On appeal, defendant asserted a violation of its right to trial by jury. But the court affirmed the judgment, with a modification not here relevant. The court said that the award of interim damages was not to be classed as an award of damages for breach of contract, and added, quoting from J.E. Macy, Annotation, Specific Performance: Compensation or Damages Awarded Purchaser for Delay in Conveyance of Land, 7 A.L.R.2d 1204, 1206 (1949):

"The compensation awarded as incident to a decree for specific performance is not for breach of contract and is therefore not legal damages. The complainant affirms the contract as being still in force and asks that it be performed. He cannot have it both ways, performed and broken. The situation is simply that, if the court orders it to be performed, the decree must as nearly as possible order it to be performed according to its terms, and one of those terms is the date fixed by it for its completion. This date having passed, the court, in order to relate the performance back to it, equalizes any losses occasioned by the delay by offsetting them with money payments. Often the result is more like an accounting between the parties than like an assessment of damages."

Question: (15) The Indianhead court referred to federal decisions cited by the defendant and said that they "arose under constitutional . . . provisions different from those of Minnesota and therefore appear to have no bearing upon the scope of a jury trial in this state." The Minnesota Constitution provides: "The right of trial by jury shall remain inviolate, and shall extend to all cases at law without regard to the amount in controversy." What result would you expect if the case came before a federal court? (Consider Dairy Queen, Inc. v. Wood, but also reconsider the discussion in Curtis v. Loether, supra pp. 1485–86, concerning the reinstatement and back-pay remedy under Title VII.)

FEDERAL DOCTRINE IN STATE COURTS

Federal jury law sometimes applies of its own force in state court under the reverse-Erie doctrine, as held in Dice v. Akron, Canton & Youngstown Railroad Co., supra p. 405. But have the Supreme Court's revised views on the jury right influenced the state courts indirectly, by altering the state courts' interpretation of state jury law itself?

In fact, the federal developments that broke with history, beginning with the Beacon Theatres decision, have not had a pronounced effect upon state-court decisions dealing with their jury right when legal and equitable elements appear in the same case. The federal decisions have been infrequently cited and less frequently followed. See Gregory Gelfand, Smith v. University of Detroit: Is There a Viable Alternative to Beacon Theatres?, 45 Wash. & Lee L.Rev. 159 (1988). So the old learning on the jury right's historical test still matters!

For example, the New York Court of Appeals had for decision another of those life insurance cases. Phoenix Mut. Life Ins. Co. v. Conway, 11 N.Y.2d 367, 183 N.E.2d 754, 229 N.Y.S.2d 740 (1962). The policy, taken out in October 1959, contained a two-year incontestability clause. The insured died in July 1960, and in September 1960 the insurer notified the beneficiaries that it was rescinding the policy for fraud and tendered return of the premiums. Finally the insurer sued to cancel and the beneficiaries were served with process, seven months after notice of the alleged fraud and eighteen months after issuance of the policy. The beneficiaries then counterclaimed for recovery under the policy and moved for a prior jury trial on the fraud issue. The Court of Appeals unanimously affirmed denial of the motion, holding that the beneficiaries were not entitled as a matter of law to their claimed jury trial, that the question was one of discretion, and that the timing of the events justified the conclusion that the beneficiaries were seeking to outmaneuver the insurer. It relied upon American Life Insurance Co. v. Stewart and then added, somewhat enigmatically, "cf. Beacon Theatres v. Westover."

Reconsider also Rankin v. Frebank Co., which denied a jury trial in a shareholders' derivative action and which expressly noted that the following case's rereading of "the historical underpinnings of the Seventh Amendment" was not binding on California.

Ross v. Bernhard

Supreme Court of the United States, 1970.
396 U.S. 531, 90 S.Ct. 733.

[Shareholders brought a derivative suit in federal court against the directors of their closed-end investment company, the Lehman Corporation, and against its broker, Lehman Brothers, contending that the broker controlled the corporation through an illegally large representation on its board of directors in violation of the Investment Company Act of 1940, 15 U.S.C. §§ 80a–1 to –52, and used this control to extract excessive brokerage fees from the corporation. The plaintiffs demanded a jury on the claims that they were asserting derivatively. The district court refused to strike the jury demand. On interlocutory appeal under 28 U.S.C. § 1292(b), the Court of Appeals for the Second Circuit reversed, holding that a derivative action was entirely equitable in nature with no jury right as to any part of it. The Supreme Court granted certiorari to resolve a conflict of circuits.]

■ MR. JUSTICE WHITE delivered the opinion of the Court.

. . . .

We reverse the holding of the Court of Appeals that in no event does the right to a jury trial preserved by the Seventh Amendment extend to derivative actions brought by the stockholders of a corporation. We hold that the right to jury trial attaches to those issues in derivative actions as to which the corporation, if it had been suing in its own right, would have been entitled to a jury.

. . . .

The common law refused . . . to permit stockholders to call corporate managers to account in actions at law. The possibilities for abuse, thus presented, were not ignored by corporate officers and directors. Early in the 19th century, equity provided relief both in this country and in England. Without detailing these developments, it suffices to say that the remedy in this country, first dealt with by this Court in Dodge v. Woolsey, 18 How. 331 (1856), provided redress not only against faithless officers and directors but also against third parties who had damaged or threatened the corporate properties and whom the corporation through its managers refused to pursue. The remedy made available in equity was the derivative suit, viewed in this country as a suit to enforce a *corporate* cause of action against officers, directors, and third parties. As elaborated in the cases, one precondition for the suit was a valid claim on which the corporation could have sued; another was that the corporation itself had refused to proceed after suitable demand, unless excused by extraordinary conditions. Thus the dual nature of the stockholder's action: first, the plaintiff's right to sue on behalf of the corporation and, second, the merits of the corporation's claim itself.

Derivative suits posed no Seventh Amendment problems where the action against the directors and third parties would have been by a bill in equity had the corporation brought the suit. Our concern is with cases based upon a legal claim of the corporation against directors or third parties. Does the trial of such claims at the suit of a stockholder and without a jury violate the Seventh Amendment?

. . . .

. . . What can be gleaned from this Court's opinions is not inconsistent with the general understanding, reflected by the state court decisions and secondary sources, that equity could properly resolve corporate claims of any kind without a jury when properly pleaded in derivative suits complying with the equity rules.

Such was the prevailing opinion when the Federal Rules of Civil Procedure were adopted in 1938. It continued until 1963 when the Court of Appeals for the Ninth Circuit, relying on the Federal Rules as construed and applied in Beacon Theatres, Inc. v. Westover, 359 U.S. 500, 79 S.Ct. 948 (1959), and Dairy Queen, Inc. v. Wood, 369 U.S. 469, 82 S.Ct. 894 (1962), required the legal issues in a derivative suit to be tried to a jury. DePinto v. Provident Security Life Ins. Co., 323 F.2d 826. It was this decision that the District Court followed in the case before us and that the Court of Appeals rejected.

Beacon and Dairy Queen presaged DePinto. Under those cases, where equitable and legal claims are joined in the same action, there is a right to jury trial on the legal claims which must not be infringed either by trying the legal issues as incidental to the equitable ones or by a court trial of a common issue existing between the claims. The Seventh Amendment question depends on the nature of the issue to be tried rather than the character of the overall action.[10] See Simler v. Conner, 372 U.S. 221, 83 S.Ct. 609 (1963). The principle of these cases bears heavily on derivative actions.

We have noted that the derivative suit has dual aspects: first, the stockholder's right to sue on behalf of the corporation, historically an equitable matter; second, the claim of the corporation against directors or third parties on which, if the corporation had sued and the claim presented legal issues, the company could demand a jury trial. . . . [L]egal claims are not magically converted into equitable issues by their presentation to a court of equity in a derivative suit. The claim pressed by the stockholder against directors or third parties "is not his own but the corporation's." Koster v. Lumbermens Mut. Cas. Co., 330 U.S. 518, 522, 67 S.Ct. 828, 831 (1947). The corporation is a necessary party to the action; without it the case cannot proceed. Although named a defendant, it is the real party in interest, the stockholder being at best the nominal plaintiff. The proceeds of the action belong to the corporation and it is bound by the result of the suit. The heart of the action is the corporate claim. If it presents a legal issue, one entitling the corporation to a jury trial under the Seventh Amendment, the right to a jury is not forfeited merely because the stockholder's right to sue must first be adjudicated as an equitable issue triable to the court. Beacon and Dairy Queen require no less.

If under older procedures, now discarded, a court of equity could properly try the legal claims of the corporation presented in a derivative suit, it was because irreparable injury was threatened and no remedy at law existed as long as the stockholder was without standing to sue and the corporation itself refused to pursue its own remedies. Indeed, from 1789 until 1938, the judicial code expressly forbade courts of equity from entertaining any suit for which there was an adequate remedy at law. This provision served "to guard the right of trial by jury preserved by the Seventh Amendment and to that end it should be liberally construed." Schoenthal v. Irving Trust Co., 287 U.S. 92, 94, 53 S.Ct. 50, 51 (1932). If, before 1938, the law had borrowed from equity, as it borrowed other things, the idea that stockholders could litigate for their recalcitrant corporation, the corporate claim, if legal, would undoubtedly have been tried to a jury.

Of course, this did not occur, but the Federal Rules had a similar impact. Actions are no longer brought as actions at law or suits in equity. Under the Rules there is only one action—a "civil action"—in which all claims may be joined and all remedies are available. Purely procedural impediments to the presentation of any issue by any party, based on the difference between law and equity, were destroyed. In a civil action presenting a stockholder's derivative claim, the court after passing upon the

---

[10] As our cases indicate, the "legal" nature of an issue is determined by considering, first, the pre-merger custom with reference to such questions; second, the remedy sought; and, third, the practical abilities and limitations of juries. Of these factors, the first, requiring extensive and possibly abstruse historical inquiry, is obviously the most difficult to apply. See James, Right to a Jury Trial in Civil Actions, 72 Yale L.J. 655 (1963).

plaintiff's right to sue on behalf of the corporation is now able to try the corporate claim for damages with the aid of a jury. Separable claims may be tried separately, Fed.Rule Civ.Proc. 42(b), or legal and equitable issues may be handled in the same trial. Fanchon & Marco, Inc. v. Paramount Pictures, Inc., 202 F.2d 731 (C.A.2d Cir. 1953). The historical rule preventing a court of law from entertaining a shareholder's suit on behalf of the corporation is obsolete; it is no longer tenable for a district court, administering both law and equity in the same action, to deny legal remedies to a corporation, merely because the corporation's spokesmen are its shareholders rather than its directors. Under the rules, law and equity are procedurally combined; nothing turns now upon the form of the action or the procedural devices by which the parties happen to come before the court. The "expansion of adequate legal remedies provided by . . . the Federal Rules necessarily affects the scope of equity." Beacon Theatres, Inc. v. Westover, 359 U.S., at 509, 79 S.Ct., at 956.

Thus, for example, before-merger class actions were largely a device of equity, and there was no right to a jury even on issues that might, under other circumstances, have been tried to a jury. 5 J. Moore, Federal Practice ¶ 38.38[2] (2d ed. 1969); 3B id., ¶ 23.02[1]. Although at least one post-merger court held that the device was not available to try legal issues, it now seems settled in the lower federal courts that class action plaintiffs may obtain a jury trial on any legal issues they present. [Citations omitted.]

Derivative suits have been described as one kind of "true" class action. [2 William W. Barron & Alexander Holtzoff, Federal Practice and Procedure § 562.1 (Charles A. Wright ed., 1961).] We are inclined to agree with the description, at least to the extent it recognizes that the derivative suit and the class action were both ways of allowing parties to be heard in equity who could not speak at law.[15] 3B J. Moore, Federal Practice ¶¶ 23.02[1], 23.1.16[1] (2d ed. 1969). After adoption of the rules there is no longer any procedural obstacle to the assertion of legal rights before juries, however the party may have acquired standing to assert those rights. Given the availability in a derivative action of both legal and equitable remedies, we think the Seventh Amendment preserves to the parties in a stockholder's suit the same right to a jury trial that historically belonged to the corporation and to those against whom the corporation pressed its legal claims.

In the instant case we have no doubt that the corporation's claim is, at least in part, a legal one. The relief sought is money damages. There are allegations in the complaint of a breach of fiduciary duty, but there are also allegations of ordinary breach of contract and gross negligence. The corporation, had it sued on its own behalf, would have been entitled to a jury's determination, at a minimum, of its damages against its broker under the brokerage contract and of its rights against its own directors because of

[15] Other equitable devices are used under the rules without depriving the parties employing them of the right to a jury trial on legal issues. [The Court here cited lower court cases allowing a jury right on common-law issues to intervenors under Rule 24 and in interpleader actions.]

their negligence. Under these circumstances it is unnecessary to decide whether the corporation's other claims are also properly triable to a jury. Dairy Queen, Inc. v. Wood, 369 U.S. 469, 82 S.Ct. 894 (1962). The decision of the Court of Appeals is reversed.

It is so ordered.

■ MR. JUSTICE STEWART, with whom THE CHIEF JUSTICE [BURGER] and MR. JUSTICE HARLAN join, dissenting.

In holding as it does that the plaintiff in a shareholder's derivative suit is constitutionally entitled to a jury trial, the Court today seems to rely upon some sort of ill-defined combination of the Seventh Amendment and the Federal Rules of Civil Procedure. Somehow the Amendment and the Rules magically interact to do what each separately was expressly intended not to do, namely, to enlarge the right to a jury trial in civil actions brought in the courts of the United States.

The Seventh Amendment, by its terms, does not extend, but merely *preserves* the right to a jury trial "[i]n Suits at common law." All agree that this means the reach of the Amendment is limited to those actions that were tried to the jury in 1791 when the Amendment was adopted.[1] Suits in equity, which were historically tried to the court, were therefore unaffected by it. Similarly, Rule 38 of the Federal Rules has no bearing on the right to a jury trial in suits in equity, for it simply preserves inviolate "[t]he right of trial by jury as declared by the Seventh Amendment." Thus this Rule, like the Amendment itself, neither restricts nor enlarges the right to jury trial. Indeed nothing in the Federal Rules can rightly be construed to enlarge the right of jury trial, for in the legislation authorizing the Rules, Congress expressly provided that they "shall neither abridge, enlarge, nor modify the substantive rights of any litigant." 48 Stat. 1064. See 28 U.S.C. § 2072. I take this plain, simple, and straightforward language to mean that after the promulgation of the Federal Rules, as before, the constitutional right to a jury trial attaches only to suits at common law. So, apparently, has every federal court that has discussed the issue. Since, as the Court concedes, a shareholder's derivative suit could be brought only in equity, it would seem to me to follow by the most elementary logic that in such suits there is no constitutional right to a trial by jury. Today the Court tosses aside history, logic, and over 100 years of firm precedent to hold that the plaintiff in a shareholder's derivative suit does indeed have a constitutional right to a trial by jury. This holding has a questionable basis in policy[5] and no basis whatever in the Constitution.

---

[1] Where a new cause of action is created by Congress, and nothing is said about how it is to be tried, the jury trial issue is determined by fitting the cause into its nearest historical analogy. Luria v. United States, 231 U.S. 9, 34 S.Ct. 10; see James, Right to a Jury Trial in Civil Actions, 72 Yale L.J. 655.

[5] See, e.g., J. Frank, Courts on Trial 110–111 (1949). Certainly there is no consensus among commentators on the desirability of jury trials in civil actions generally. Particularly where the issues in the case are complex—as they are likely to be in a derivative suit—much can be said for allowing the court discretion to try the case itself. See discussion in 5 J. Moore, Federal Practice ¶ 38.02[1].

The Court begins by assuming the "dual nature" of the shareholder's action. While the plaintiff's right to get into court at all is conceded to be equitable, once he is there the Court says his claim is to be viewed as though it were the claim of the corporation itself. If the corporation would have been entitled to a jury trial on such a claim, then, it is said, so would the shareholder. This conceptualization is without any historical basis. For the fact is that a shareholder's suit was not originally viewed in this country, or in England, as a suit to enforce a *corporate* cause of action. Rather, the shareholder's suit was initially permitted only against the managers of the corporation—not third parties—and it was conceived of as an equitable action to enforce the right of a beneficiary against his trustee. The shareholder was not, therefore, in court to enforce indirectly the corporate right of action, but to enforce directly his own equitable right of action against an unfaithful fiduciary. Later the rights of the shareholder were enlarged to encompass suits against third parties harming the corporation, but "the postulated 'corporate cause of action' has never been thought to describe an actual historical class of suit which was recognized by courts of law."[7] Indeed the commentators . . . recognize that historically the suit has in practice always been treated as a single cause tried exclusively in equity. They agree that there is therefore no constitutional right to a jury trial even where there might have been one had the corporation itself brought the suit.

[A discussion of prior decisions is omitted.]

These pre–1938 cases, then, firmly establish the unitary, equitable basis of shareholders' derivative suits and in no way support the Court's holding here. But, the Court says, whatever the situation may have been before 1938, the Federal Rules of Civil Procedure of that year, at least as construed in our decisions more than 20 years later in Beacon Theatres, Inc. v. Westover, 359 U.S. 500, 79 S.Ct. 948, and Dairy Queen, Inc. v. Wood, 369 U.S. 469, 82 S.Ct. 894, in any event require the conclusion reached today. I can find nothing in either of these cases that leads to that conclusion.

. . . .

It is true that in Beacon Theatres it was stated that the 1938 Rules did diminish the scope of federal equity jurisdiction in certain particulars. But the Court's effort to force the facts of this case into the mold of Beacon Theatres and Dairy Queen simply does not succeed. Those cases involved a combination of historically separable suits, one in law and one in equity. Their facts fit the pattern of cases where, before the Rules, the equity court would have disposed of the equitable claim and would then have either retained jurisdiction over the suit, despite the availability of adequate legal remedies, or enjoined a subsequent legal action between the same parties involving the same controversy.

---

7 Note, The Right to a Jury Trial in a Stockholder's Derivative Action, 74 Yale L.J. 725, 730.

But the present case is not one involving traditionally equitable claims by one party, and traditionally legal claims by the other. Nor is it a suit in which the plaintiff is asserting a combination of legal and equitable claims. For, as we have seen, a derivative suit has always been conceived of as a single, unitary, equitable cause of action. It is for this reason, and not because of "procedural impediments," that the courts of equity did not transfer derivative suits to the law side. In short, the cause of action is wholly a creature of equity. And whatever else can be said of Beacon Theatres and Dairy Queen, they did not cast aside altogether the historic division between equity and law.

If history is to be so cavalierly dismissed, the derivative suit can, of course, be artificially broken down into separable elements. But so then can any traditionally equitable cause of action, and the logic of the Court's position would lead to the virtual elimination of all equity jurisdiction. An equitable suit for an injunction, for instance, often involves issues of fact which, if damages had been sought, would have been triable to a jury. Does this mean that in a suit asking only for injunctive relief these factual issues *must* be tried to the jury, with the judge left to decide only whether, given the jury's findings, an injunction is the appropriate remedy? Certainly the Federal Rules make it *possible* to try a suit for an injunction in that way, but even more certainly they were not intended to have any such effect. Yet the Court's approach, it seems, would require that if any "legal issue" procedurally *could* be tried to a jury, it constitutionally *must* be tried to a jury.

The fact is, of course, that there are, for the most part, no such things as inherently "legal issues" or inherently "equitable issues." There are only factual issues, and, "like chameleons [they] take their color from surrounding circumstances."[12] Thus the Court's "nature of the issue" approach is hardly meaningful.

. . . .

The Court's decision today can perhaps be explained as a reflection of an unarticulated but apparently overpowering bias in favor of jury trials in civil actions. It certainly cannot be explained in terms of either the Federal Rules or the Constitution.

JOHNS HOPKINS UNIVERSITY v. HUTTON, 488 F.2d 912 (4th Cir.1973), cert. denied, 416 U.S. 916, 94 S.Ct. 1622, 1623 (1974). The university sued under the antifraud provisions of the securities laws, asking damages. The court on its own explored the possibility of the equitable remedy of rescission. In response to the court's inquiry, the plaintiff by letter said that it was "primarily seeking rescission" and asking damages "only if [it] is not entitled to rescission." The complaint was later amended to add a request for rescission. The trial court ruled that the defendant was

[12] James, supra, n. 1, at 692. . . .

"entitled to a jury trial in connection with any and all triable fact issues" that were common to the legal and equitable remedies or that related only to the legal remedy "so long as Hopkins continues to hold in reserve, in the event Hopkins is held not entitled to rescission, its claim for damages." Later, however, the trial court granted summary judgment that the plaintiff was entitled to rescission. The court of appeals reversed the summary judgment, remanding for trial. However, the court of appeals agreed with the trial judge as to the jury right, simply stating that this followed from the rationale of Ross, Dairy Queen, and Beacon Theatres.

SECTION 4. NEW DIRECTIONS

In re Boise Cascade Securities Litigation

United States District Court, Western District of Washington, 1976.
420 F.Supp. 99.

■ MORELL E. SHARP, DISTRICT JUDGE. Before the Court are defendants' motions to strike plaintiffs' jury demands in this securities fraud litigation. The question before the Court is whether these jury demands may be stricken without conflicting with the Seventh Amendment. The Court is of the opinion that the answer is in the affirmative.

[In part I of its opinion, the court explained that the five consolidated cases before it arose from the acquisition of two companies by Boise Cascade. When the deals went sour, former stockholders brought these actions against Boise, its officers and directors, and its accountant for various alleged violations of federal and state securities laws. Extensive discovery ensued. Thus far more than 50,000 lawyer-hours had been expended and more than 900,000 documents produced.

[In part II, the court described in detail the highly complex issues of financial accounting and the problems of proof presented by this litigation.]

In sum, it appears to this Court that the scope of the problems presented by this case is immense. The factual issues, the complexity of the evidence that will be required to explore those issues, and the time required to do so leads to the conclusion that a jury would not be a rational and capable fact finder.

III

There can be no doubt that jury trials are favored in civil litigation in this country. The combination of the Seventh Amendment and the merger of actions at law and in equity into a single civil action under the Federal Rules of Civil Procedure encourages the use of juries to determine facts. See Ross v. Bernhard, 396 U.S. 531, 539–40, 90 S.Ct. 733, 24 L.Ed.2d 729 and Opinion of Stewart, J., dissenting, see also 28 U.S.C.A. § 1861 and

Redish, Seventh Amendment Right to Jury Trial: A Study in the Irrationality of Rational Decision Making, 70 Nw.U.L.Rev. 486, 490–98.

However broad this policy may be, the Supreme Court has recognized that the use of juries is not without limits. In Ross v. Bernhard, supra, the Court set forth three factors which determine the susceptibility of a claim to trial by jury:

> [F]irst, the pre-merger custom with reference to such questions; second the remedy sought; and third, the practical abilities and limitations of juries. Id. at 538 n. 10, 90 S.Ct. at 738.

No authority was cited for these three factors. As for the first two, Supreme Court precedent appears so clear as to be obvious. See e.g., Parsons v. Bedford, 28 U.S. (3 Pet.) 433, 447, 7 L.Ed. 732 (1830) (Story, J.). The third part is not explicit from previous opinions.

The procedural safeguards inherent in our legal system provide the impression and fact of fairness to the litigants and society. This is necessary in order to assure obedience to judgments and resort to the legal system as the only sanctioned means of settling disputes in a complex civilized society. Indeed, under the Fifth and Fourteenth Amendments, the legitimacy of government action is measured in terms of fairness.

Central to the fairness which must attend the resolution of a civil action is an impartial and capable fact finder. A properly selected panel of veniremen must generally be presumed to yield an impartial and capable jury. However, at some point, it must be recognized that the complexity of a case may exceed the ability of a jury to decide the facts in an informed and capable manner. When that occurs, the question arises as to whether the right and necessity of fairness is defeated by relegating fact finding to a body not qualified to determine the facts. The third part of the analysis in footnote 10 to the majority opinion in Ross v. Bernhard, supra, directly recognizes this. See also Kirkham, Complex Civil Litigation—Have Good Intentions Gone Awry? 70 F.R.D. 199, 208 (1976).

Of course, the point at which a jury's limitations exceed its abilities is not precise nor is it easy of definition. No single factor alone can dictate that a jury should not hear a case. As in this case, a number of factors must combine to convince the Court that a jury would be incapable of fairly deciding the case.

IV

It must be apparent that any jury chosen to hear this case will not be a fair cross section of the community at large because of the estimated trial time of four to six months. It would not be unreasonable to excuse prospective jurors from serving in this civil case if they believe that service for that period of time would impair their employment. At the outset, then, the availability of employed persons to serve on this jury is limited. This suggests that at least the appearance of fairness would be diminished, if not eliminated, when a lengthy civil action involving millions of dollars in potential damages in a commercial setting would be heard by jurors who have not had exposure to a contemporary commercial or business environment. This should not be taken to mean that a non-employed person is somehow less able to determine facts. Rather, a basic purpose of the jury, the determination of facts by impartial minds of diverse backgrounds, is defeated if a sizable and significant portion of the community must be excluded from service.

Pointing out the limits of a jury to hear an extended civil action does not answer the problems presented by a particular case unless it can be shown that trial to the Court would be superior.

In addition to the Court's experience in presiding over other complicated cases involving commercial matters, the Court has available to it tools that are unwieldy in the possession of a jury. Among these tools are review of daily transcripts; admission of depositions into evidence instead of reading relevant portions aloud; review of selected portions of testimony from the reporter's notes and flexibility in scheduling trial activities. In addition, the Court is able to study exhibits in depth and carry on colloquies with witnesses, expert and non-expert alike, in an orderly and systematic manner. Of course, this is in addition to the Court's knowledge of the litigation resulting from its review of the record since the cases were filed.

In the light of the limitation of a jury to determine the facts in an informed manner and the ability of the Court to hear and review the evidence in an efficient and effective manner, the Court believes that it would be more capable of fairly deciding the facts.

V

The Court is of the opinion that the third part to footnote 10 in Ross v. Bernhard, supra, is of constitutional dimensions. It must be seen as a limitation to or interpretation of the Seventh Amendment. Furthermore, the Court is of the opinion that there is no conflict in this case with any statutory policy favoring trial by jury, 28 U.S.C.A. § 1861, or the Federal Rules of Civil Procedure.

The explosion of litigation in the past two decades in terms both of number of filings and the complexity and scope of many of those cases has led thoughtful minds to wonder whether the judicial system as we now know it can cope with some of these cases. See e.g., Rifkind, Are We Asking Too Much of Our Courts? 70 F.R.D. 96 (1976).

Similarly, thoughtful minds have questioned the expansion of the right to jury trial in complex commercial civil actions. See Redish, supra, at 514–530. It has been observed that:

> Any close question—and sometimes one that is not so close—is resolved in favor of the jury trial right without serious analysis of history, precedent, or policy. Shapiro and Coquillette, The Fetish of Jury Trial in Civil Cases: A Comment on Rachal v. Hill, 85 Harv.L.Rev. 442 (1971).

While it is true that the Supreme Court has favored jury trial in the cases where it has reviewed the issue, the opinions are not totally consistent. Compare Ross v. Bernard, supra, with Katchen v. Landy, 382 U.S. 323, 339, 86 S.Ct. 467, 15 L.Ed.2d 391 (1966).

With these thoughts in mind, the necessity for the appearance and fact of fairness dictate that the motions now before the Court be granted.

. . . .

Valerie P. Hans & Neil Vidmar, Judging the Jury

245–47, 249, 251 (1986).

Critics have charged that the jury falls short on three main grounds: it is incompetent, it is prejudiced, and it wages war with the law. However, when hard facts rather than anecdote and opinion are considered, the charges do not appear warranted. Juries are generally competent fact finders. Our best evidence suggests that in four cases out of five, juries reach the same verdict that the judge would have reached. In the remaining case, the verdict can usually be ascribed not to a failure to understand the evidence but rather to a different sense of justice.

. . . .

While trial by jury is not perfect, calls for abolition of the jury seem draconian in light of the fact that it displays competence and fairmindedness in the overwhelming majority of criminal and civil cases. In instances where the jury falls short, jury performance could be improved by modification of existing legal procedures: through developing more coherent legal instructions, allowing jurors to take notes or to ask questions, or providing some directions at the beginning of the trial.

. . . .

In judging the jury there are some other issues to consider. The first concerns the alternatives to the jury. . . . [I]n most instances those who advocate abolition of the jury propose that the jury's work should be done by a judge. The question then becomes, are judges really superior to juries? Unfortunately, we have little data about the competence of judges . . . . To be sure, judges have training in law, and perhaps, as Judge Frank claimed, they attempt to be more scientific in their approach to the evidence. On the other hand, many knowledgeable legal commentators have argued that judges are not necessarily better triers of fact. A jury which contains one or more persons proficient in automobile repair might be far better at assessing evidence in a products liability case involving a car manufacturer than a judge whose experience with things mechanical is limited to changing a spare tire. Even if one argues that the average judge is smarter in discerning legal facts than the average juror, is the judge as smart as twelve jurors?

. . . .

In brief, political functions of the jury are not to be ignored. They coexist with the fact-finding functions and should be considered in judging the jury's role in society.

. . . .

Proponents of the civil jury have pointed out that there is no evidence that juries are incompetent in complex cases, at least no more incompetent than judges. Moreover, there are less drastic alternatives to abolishing the jury. For example, in some complicated cases, neutral experts are used to interpret and explain data to judges; such experts could be used to assist the jury about difficult evidence. In addition, some extremely complex factual issues could be decided by the judge, while leaving the central issues to the jury. Others argue against a complexity exception on the basis of the political function of the jury. Some civil matters involving giant corporations could have greater effects on society than criminal matters, and, thus, the people should have a say in them. A complexity exception would also ignore the important symbolic and legitimating functions of the jury. Additionally, it is argued that there are no Constitutional precedents for restricting Seventh Amendment rights.

. . . .

Our final judgment on the jury system is a positive one. Despite some flaws, it serves the cause of justice very well. For over 700 years it has weathered criticism and attack, always to survive and to be cherished by the peoples who own it. Adaptability has been the key to its survival. It should remain open to experimentation and modification, but those who would wish to curtail its powers or abolish it should bear the burden of proof. Defenders of the jury clearly have the weight of the evidence on their side.

IN RE U.S. FINANCIAL SECURITIES LITIGATION, 609 F.2d 411 (9th Cir.1979) (2–1 decision), cert. denied, 446 U.S. 929, 100 S.Ct. 1866 (1980). In this mass of consolidated cases, plaintiffs sought damages under the securities laws and for common-law fraud and negligence. The factual and legal issues were highly complex, and they would apparently have required the fact-finder to decipher many financial statements and to read over 100,000 pages ("which would be the equivalent of reading the first 90 volumes of the Federal Reporter, 2d Series") during a trial lasting at least two years. The trial judge struck the demands by some plaintiffs and some defendants for jury trial. On interlocutory appeal under 28 U.S.C. § 1292(b), the court of appeals reversed, rejecting any "complexity exception" to the Seventh Amendment. First, with little explanation, the appellate court ruled that complexity did not serve to transform this action into the "narrow and little-used" equitable suit for an accounting. Second, it held that the famous Ross footnote should not be read as introducing some new "functional" interpretation of the Seventh Amendment. Third, it concluded that trial by jury in a complex case does not deny due process.

An intelligent procedural approach can greatly reduce complexity, and even in a complex case jurors are as competent as a judge in fact-finding. Moreover, the judge's power to grant a new trial or judgment n.o.v. protects litigants from an "irrational" verdict. In sum, "the Seventh Amendment requires a jury trial in even the most complex cases at law."

IN RE JAPANESE ELECTRONIC PRODUCTS ANTITRUST LITIGATION, 631 F.2d 1069 (3d Cir.1980) (2–1 decision). These complex consolidated cases essentially involved U.S. television manufacturers suing their Japanese counterparts for treble damages under the antitrust laws. The trial judge refused to strike plaintiffs' demands for jury trial, rejecting any complexity exception to the Seventh Amendment. On interlocutory appeal under 28 U.S.C. § 1292(b), the court of appeals reversed. The appellate court ruled that in 1791 mere complexity did not make an action equitable, noting in particular that an equitable suit for an accounting required some relationship between the parties greater than that between an ordinary tortfeasor and victim. It also conceded that the Ross footnote is too weak a foundation on which to build a new interpretation of the Seventh Amendment. It concluded, however, that trial by jury of a case too complex for jurors to decide by rational means, with a fair and reasonable understanding of the evidence and applicable law, violates the Due Process Clause of the Fifth Amendment, which thus overrides the Seventh Amendment. Accordingly, the court of appeals remanded this case for careful consideration of its complexity, cautioning nevertheless that "[d]ue process should allow denials of jury trials only in exceptional cases." Judge Gibbons in dissent concluded "that the majority has substituted for an express guarantee in the Bill of Rights a rule of district court discretion that in practice will be virtually unreviewable, and therefore largely unfettered."[n]

---

[n] On remand, then United States District Judge Edward R. Becker never reached the point of having to consider the case's complexity in relation to the question of trial by jury. Instead, he disposed of the plaintiffs' claims by granting summary judgment in favor of the defendants, which was eventually upheld on appeal. See Matsushita Elec. Indus. Co. v. Zenith Radio Corp., 475 U.S. 574, 106 S.Ct. 1348 ("the published [district-court opinions in this case] alone would fill an entire volume of the Federal Supplement"; "the parties have filed a forty-volume appendix in this Court that is said to contain the essence of the evidence"), on remand sub nom. In re Japanese Elec. Prods. Antitrust Litig., 807 F.2d 44 (3d Cir.1986), cert. denied, 481 U.S. 1029, 107 S.Ct. 1955 (1987).

Indeed, no federal appellate court has ever prescribed an actual jury denial on the ground of complexity, and the flurry of case and commentary on complexity's bearing on the law/equity question has ebbed. See, e.g., SRI Int'l v. Matsushita Elec. Corp. of Am., 775 F.2d 1107, 1128–29 (Fed.Cir.1985) (separate opinion):

"However some may view what they see as a 'better system,' and however one may weigh its effect on the due process clauses of the Fifth and Fourteenth Amendments, judges are nowhere authorized to exercise their personal predilection by revising or repealing the Seventh Amendment. . . . To permit a judicial interpretation of a constitutional provision that destroys another constitutional provision is to place at risk the entire Constitution."

Tull v. United States

Supreme Court of the United States, 1987.
481 U.S. 412, 107 S.Ct. 1831.

[The government sought a civil penalty in excess of twenty million dollars under the Clean Water Act, 33 U.S.C. § 1319(d), against a person alleged to have dumped fill on certain wetlands. The defendant, contesting such critical facts as whether the property in question constituted "wetlands," demanded a jury. The district court denied the jury demand and eventually assessed a $325,000 penalty. The Fourth Circuit affirmed, viewing the suit as equitable. The Supreme Court granted certiorari.]

■ JUSTICE BRENNAN delivered the opinion of the Court.

[Following Curtis v. Loether, the Court historically analogized this action to a law action in debt. The Court laid special stress on the legal form of relief, here civil penalties, to find a constitutional right to jury trial. Thus, a jury right would henceforth exist if any plausible legal analogue exists and the remedy is ordinary compensatory damages.

[However, the Court seemed not to draw any inference from Ross or otherwise as to a new "functional" reading of the Seventh Amendment, whether for expanding or contracting the common law's realm relative to equity's. The Court instead construed the Ross footnote toward oblivion, apparently reading its third factor as referring only to the congressional power to entrust matters to administrative agencies.

[The Court then turned to the issue of whether the jury would assess the amount of the penalty. Here Congress had broken its silence to provide for nonjury trial.] We must decide therefore whether Congress can, consistent with the Seventh Amendment, authorize judges to assess civil penalties.

The Seventh Amendment is silent on the question whether a jury must determine the remedy in a trial in which it must determine liability.[9] The answer must depend on whether the jury must shoulder this responsibility as necessary to preserve the "substance of the common-law right of trial by jury." Colgrove v. Battin, 413 U.S. 149, 157, 93 S.Ct. 2448, 2452 (1973). Is a jury role necessary for that purpose? We do not think so. " 'Only those incidents which are regarded as fundamental, as inherent in and of the essence of the system of trial by jury, are placed beyond the reach of the legislature.' " Id., at 156, n. 11, 93 S.Ct., at 2452, n. 11 (quoting Scott, Trial by Jury and the Reform of Civil Procedure, 31 Harv.L.Rev. 669, 671 (1918)). See also Galloway v. United States, 319 U.S. 372, 392, 63 S.Ct.

---

[9] Nothing in the Amendment's language suggests that the right to a jury trial extends to the remedy phase of a civil trial. Instead, the language "defines the kind of cases for which jury trial is preserved, namely, 'suits at common law.' " Colgrove v. Battin, 413 U.S. 149, 152, 93 S.Ct. 2448, 2450 (1973). Although " '[w]e have almost no direct evidence concerning the intention of the framers of the seventh amendment itself,' the historical setting in which the Seventh Amendment was adopted highlighted a controversy that was generated . . . by fear that the civil jury itself would be abolished." Id., at 152, 93 S.Ct., at 2450 (footnote and citation omitted). We have been presented with no evidence that the Framers meant to extend the right to a jury to the remedy phase of a civil trial.

1077, 1088 (1943) ("the Amendment was designed to preserve the basic institution of jury trial in only its most fundamental elements"). The assessment of a civil penalty is not one of the "most fundamental elements." Congress' authority to fix the penalty by statute has not been questioned, and it was also the British practice, see, e.g., Atcheson v. Everitt, 1 Cowper 382, 98 Eng.Rep. 1142 (K.B.1776). In the United States, the action to recover civil penalties usually seeks the amount fixed by the Congress. [Citations omitted.] The assessment of civil penalties thus cannot be said to involve the "substance of a common-law right to a trial by jury," nor a "fundamental element of a jury trial."

Congress' assignment of the determination of the amount of civil penalties to trial judges therefore does not infringe on the constitutional right to a jury trial. Since Congress itself may fix the civil penalties, it may delegate that determination to trial judges. In this case, highly discretionary calculations that take into account multiple factors are necessary in order to set civil penalties under the Clean Water Act. These are the kinds of calculations traditionally performed by judges. [Citation omitted.] We therefore hold that a determination of a civil penalty is not an essential function of a jury trial, and that the Seventh Amendment does not require a jury trial for that purpose in a civil action.

[The Court therefore reversed and remanded for jury trial on liability.]

■ [JUSTICE SCALIA, joined by Justice Stevens, dissented in part. He agreed that a jury right existed but argued that it should extend to the assessment of penalty. "I can recall no precedent for judgment of civil liability by jury but assessment of amount by the court."]

TENTATIVE CLOSING NOTE ON THE SEVENTH AMENDMENT'S TRIAL-BY-JURY CLAUSE

Although judicial developments on the law/equity front thus seemed to be slowing and stabilizing, no signs appeared that the academic debates were subsiding. We already noted that theorists had championed various historical tests all along the spectrum from a dividing line frozen at what was existing as common law in 1791 to a common law hypothetically growing and contracting with time. On a more fundamental level, argument persists across another whole spectrum on whether the Seventh Amendment imposed any historical test at all. Some maintain that the courts have basically erred in looking to history. See, e.g., Stanton D. Krauss, The Original Understanding of the Seventh Amendment Right to Jury Trial, 33 U.Rich.L.Rev. 407 (1999) (arguing that Congress has plenary control). At the opposite extreme, other scholars would apply an unprecedentedly strict historical test both to the right of jury trial on facts and to the jury's procedural incidents. See, e.g., Suja A. Thomas, Why Summary Judgment Is Unconstitutional, 93 Va.L.Rev. 139 (2007).

Currently, the courts seem indeed to have settled down as to law/equity, doing so around the middle of the academic debates' ranges. Subsequent cases on the law/equity question have confirmed Tull's historical approach, which laid special stress on the form of relief. See Chauffeurs, Local No. 391 v. Terry, 494 U.S. 558, 110 S.Ct. 1339 (1990) (holding in favor of jury trial in fair-representation claim for compensatory damages, but putting ever heavier emphasis on the form of relief in the decisional process); Wooddell v. International Bhd. of Elec. Workers, Local 71, 502 U.S. 93, 112 S.Ct. 494 (1991) (same); cf. Pereira v. Farace, 413 F.3d 330 (2d Cir.2005) (holding in favor of jury trial in bankruptcy trustee's claim for compensatory damages against the bankrupt corporation's officials for breach of fiduciary duty, ruling that the legal nature of the relief overcame the equitable nature of the historical analogue because the form-of-relief step is more important than the analogue step). That is, the Supreme Court appears to have accepted that its precedents from the preceding pro-jury expansionist era locked it into a formally historical approach, albeit one leaving it still free to play with history and thereby shape a loose and simpler historical test. Thus, the federal jury right will likely remain expansive, now extended beyond the clearly common-law realm to reach many new causes of action that give legal relief and reach the merged procedure's various gray areas on the frontier between law and equity, but go no further.

Nevertheless, anti-jury sentiment continues to exert pressures on courts, and so the Court has found other outlets for those pressures. Early on, this sentiment found an outlet in the Court's lenient and functional approach toward preserving the procedural incidents of jury trial, such as the number of jurors. More recently, it emerged in a separate effort to demark the law/fact line, as in Tull's treatment of penalty assessment and in Tull's progeny, including Markman v. Westview Instruments, Inc., supra p. 1395.

It is important to recall the location of this latter line. The answer to the law/equity question means that presumptively the jury will decide all the issues in the case that trace from common-law actions, as opposed to equitable suits. The law/fact question then looks at those issues and asks the second, backup question of whether those issues are sufficiently legal, as opposed to factual, that the judge should decide them even in a common-law case. In Markman, we saw that the court's answer involved a historical-functional inquiry. This inquiry will not always give an answer displacing the jury. See Feltner v. Columbia Pictures Television, Inc., 523 U.S. 340, 118 S.Ct. 1279 (1998) (stressing history to give statutory damages under the Copyright Act to the jury); City of Monterey v. Del Monte Dunes, Ltd., 526 U.S. 687, 119 S.Ct. 1624 (1999) (stressing function to give takings issue to the jury). But because the inquiry comes after and in addition to the law/equity question, its effect will be to cut back on the federal jury right. Concomitantly, functionality has a renewed role in fixing the scope of that right.

In retrospect, then, the Supreme Court played with history in Beacon Theatres, Dairy Queen, and Ross in order to accommodate the Seventh Amendment to the modern procedural system, doing so in a clever way that protected the jury. But playing with history has its risks. So, in the longer run, the jury right might have lost the protection offered by a more wooden historical approach. It is true that the jury right, in facing the law/equity question, appears today to have dodged Ross's ahistorical bullet. Still, the risk of a ricochet remains for the jury, coming from the direction of either pushing the law/fact line or further reforming procedural incidents. See Joan E. Schaffner, The Seventh Amendment Right to Civil Jury Trial: The Supreme Court Giveth and the Supreme Court Taketh Away, 31 U.Balt.L.Rev. 225 (2002).

PART NINE

APPEAL

TOPIC A General Observations

TOPIC B Appeal of Final Decisions

TOPIC C Appeal of Interlocutory Decisions

TOPIC D Mandamus

TOPIC E Theory on Appeal

TOPIC A

GENERAL OBSERVATIONS

SECTION 1. RATIONALE

Paul D. Carrington, Daniel J. Meador & Maurice Rosenberg, Justice on Appeal

2–4 (1976).

In the received tradition, the functions of appellate adjudication are two-fold. One is to "review for correctness." It is probably true for most legal systems, and is emphatically true for this country's, that appellate courts serve as the instrument of accountability for those who make the basic decisions in trial courts and administrative agencies. The traditional appeal calls for an examination of the rulings below to assure that they are correct, or at least within the range of error the law for sufficient reasons allows the primary decision-maker. The availability of the appellate process assures the decision-makers at the first level that their correct judgments will not be, or appear to be, the unconnected actions of isolated individuals, but will have the concerted support of the legal system; and it assures litigants that the decision in their case is not prey to the failings of whichever mortal happened to render it, but bears the institutional imprimatur and approval of the whole social order as represented by its legal system. Thus, the review for correctness serves to reinforce the dignity, authority, and acceptability of the trial, and to control the adverse effects of any personal shortcomings of the basic decision-makers.

The second function in the traditional tandem is sometimes described as "institutional" review. Trial courts working independently have no self-regulating capacity to promote uniformity among their decisions. Without appellate review, such great divergences in practices and variations in results would arise between trial courts in the same system that they would jeopardize the belief that legal principles are a vital force in their decisions or provide a basis for predicting the application of official power. Accordingly, appellate courts are needed to announce, clarify, and harmonize the rules of decision employed by the legal system in which they serve. Until recent decades, it was customary to conceal, even from ourselves, the creative and political aspects of this function; we were given to proclaiming that judges do not make law. Today, such comment is seldom heard; it is widely understood that the judges who enunciate legal principles are engaged in a creative activity which can have significant social, economic, and political consequences. On the other hand, it is still true that rampant judicial free-wheeling in law-declaring may threaten the democratic ideal that representative government is designed to foster. Few would deny that there are appropriate limits to the judges' assumption of responsibility for the full range of social, economic and political ills which might conceivably be subjected to the judicial power.

Recognizing traditional duality in the functions of appellate adjudication is unquestionably helpful to understanding. It serves to illumine the contrast in both the concerns and the affects of appellate justice. On the one hand, appellate justice is preoccupied with the impact of decisions on particular litigants, but on the other it is concerned with the general principles which govern the affairs of persons other than those who are party to the cases decided. While appellate justice has impact on the realities of situations, it also affects the appearances and symbols which pervade the government. An appellate system which is unduly preoccupied with one of these functions to the neglect of the other, is inadequate to advance the purposes which appellate courts should serve.

The dual function analysis has served as the basis for several developments of recent decades, beginning at least as early as the Federal Judiciary Act of 1925, which conferred on the Supreme Court of the United States the power to refuse to hear many of the appeals which it had formerly been required to hear. It was the premise of that reform that the highest Court would continue to hear the cases which are of institutional importance, but would decline to hear cases which are of importance only to the individuals affected, thus leaving the function of review of district court decisions for correctness to the intermediate courts, the . . . Courts of Appeal. Many states now have intermediate court structures comparable to that of the federal system, and most have established, at least in some degree, a difference of function for the two levels of appellate courts, based on this duality.

Question: (1) Do we unthinkingly accept uniformity of law as a judicial goal? Amanda Frost, Overvaluing Uniformity, 94 Va.L.Rev. 1567 (2008), thinks so. Besides arguing that disuniformity is not so deleterious after all, she argues that the main goal of federal courts is to ensure the supremacy of federal law and that Congress is better positioned to ensure the uniformity of federal law by legislating away courts' disagreements. Do you agree?

(2) Do we suffer costs from the Supreme Court's coming to focus primarily on *institutional review* through discretionary jurisdiction? The next-excerpted article argues that (a) decision by a "volunteer" lessens acceptability, (b) discretionary jurisdiction diminishes judicial attention to case specifics and concern for individual fates, although oddly we still make the litigants finance this adjudication of public importance, (c) institutional review both blurs the justificatory distinction between the Court and the avowedly political organs of government and also contributes to public and scholarly cynicism about law, and (d) less effective oversight by the Court has allowed the courts of appeals to emulate the Supreme Court and neglect correctness review. Do you agree? Are there other costs?

Paul D. Carrington, The Function of the Civil Appeal: A Late–Century View

38 S.C.L.Rev. 411, 432 (1987).

If we continue on the present course, it would seem likely that the formal appeal of right in civil cases will be abandoned, even though that would be of little benefit to overcrowded appellate dockets. The courts of appeals seem likely to be forced to increase the range and depth of delegation to staff, perhaps increasingly to mature lawyers reporting to the court at large rather than individual judges. The courts of appeals seem likely to become increasingly selective about the cases in which they hear oral argument, confer, or explain themselves. In short, appellate courts are likely to become even more faceless to the lawyers and district judges. If so, their work will be increasingly disconnected from the realities of the district courts and the work of trial lawyers, who will give declining attention to the circuit courts. The utterances of the courts of appeals will be longer and more numerous, and less significant.

As the courts of appeals become less connected to the realities of the trial court, the Supreme Court must become less connected as well. . . .

One must acknowledge that this may not be a malign event. Humane and professional district judges may use their growing freedom and discretion to the greater advantage of litigants than could have been achieved through a more tightly textured judicial system that more rigorously said what it meant and meant what it said. These judges might work in the tradition of the great Chancellors.

Question: (3) Do we realize the benefits of the federal courts of appeals' supposedly primary focus on *correctness review*? The above-excerpted article argues that (a) intermediate appellate judges prefer and overplay the role of lawmaker, (b) the increasing caseload has critically eroded appellate procedure, as by restricting oral arguments and downplaying the opinion-writing task in routine cases, and (c) the influence of the appellate courts has lessened in the daily work of the district courts. In light of this reality-based argument, which reveals some illusions of theory, should we frankly eliminate the statutory right of appeal in civil cases and embrace appeal by leave of the court of appeals? See William M. Richman & William L. Reynolds, Elitism, Expediency, and the New Certiorari: Requiem for the Learned Hand Tradition, 81 Cornell L.Rev. 273 (1996) (instead recommending a radical increase in the size of the federal appellate judiciary).

Harlon Leigh Dalton, Taking the Right to Appeal (More or Less) Seriously

95 Yale L.J. 62, 65, 84, 92–93 (1985).

[This article first argues that the error-correction rationale for appeal of right cannot "withstand close scrutiny." The rationale rests on the questionable assumption that appellate courts are better positioned to decide correctly than are trial judges. Of the four possible outcomes of appeals, the only one that could justify allowing appeals would be reversal of a wrong decision. The actual distribution of appeals and their outcomes (which includes an affirmance rate of 80% in federal civil appeals) does not suggest that this one type of outcome predominates sufficiently to offset the costs of the other three outcomes. "A distribution that produces positive outcomes is improbable because: even true affirmances are negative [in benefits, because of the redundant process]; false affirmances are virtually guaranteed, given the considerable pressure to uphold judgments that seem reasonable; and false reversals (which are inevitable, given the fallibility of real-world appellate judges) exert an even stronger downward pull."

[So, the article turns to the possibility that "appeal of right is not so much a mechanism for correcting errors as it is a means of ensuring that such errors are not made in the first place," and then discounts this possibility too:]

Thus, on several counts there is reason to question the intuitively appealing notion that the threat of reversal induces trial judges to self-correct. Some judges just don't take the threat seriously, because the ratio of reversals to total cases is so small, because they view reversals as inevitable or arbitrary, or because they think it inappropriate to concern themselves with what might happen on appeal. For others, appellate review is a pressing concern, but their response to it may have little to do with improving case outcomes. Where the name of the game is to avoid reversal by toeing the appellate court line, victory will bring juster justice only if the appellate court has drawn the line in the right place, and if there is no better place that the trial judge might happen upon if left to her own devices. Where the trial judge fends off the higher court by insulating her opinion from review, the world is better off only if she has reached a better result than that dictated by the appellate court's teachings and has protected that result in a manner that does not itself produce offsetting injustice. In those happy cases where the trial judge responds to the pressure of Big Brother by taking a sober second look at her handiwork, justice is enhanced only if she has the capacity to self-correct and has rightly determined when she should and should not follow the appellate court's lead.

Finally, and most importantly, even if appeal of right does promote self-correction by trial judges, any consequent gain in accuracy may be more than offset by harm done to the trial court as an institution. The more we underscore the fact that trial courts are hierarchically inferior to appellate courts, the more we feed the notion that they are inferior in other ways as well. Furthermore, the specter of appeal induces passivity in some judges, blunts or misdirects the creativity of others, distorts fact-finding and law-choosing, undermines common law doctrinal development, promotes doctrinal vagueness, encourages jurisprudential sleight of hand, imperils candor, imposes on the parties (as well as the system) additional costs and delays, and imposes on the losing party psychic costs whenever negative facts about her are embellished by the trial judge in an effort to render the opinion appeal-proof.

Question: (4) Do we unthinkingly accept correction of any sort of error as an appellate goal? Chad M. Oldfather, Error Correction, 85 Ind.L.J. ___ (2010), thinks so. Discounting errors as to the merits, he would limit the corrective task to resolving second-order disputes between the parties concerning the propriety of the way the trial court handled the case. Do you agree?

Section 2. A Review of Reviewability

Fleming James, Jr., Geoffrey C. Hazard, Jr. & John Leubsdorf, Civil Procedure

766–68 (5th ed. 2001).

Appellate review is not a retrial of the case, but rather a review of the trial court's determination to discern whether prejudicial error occurred. The rules on scope of review are discussed below.

Error in the record. Review is limited to considering errors revealed in the record. An appellate court will not consider matter that may have been received in the trial court unless it is included in the record on appeal. Ordinarily the appellate court will also refuse to receive evidence of events outside the proceedings below—for example, evidence of jury misconduct that was not presented to the trial court through a vehicle such as a motion for a new trial. The main exception is evidence that a case has become moot. This limitation on the evidentiary matter that an appellate court may consider is one reason why application for relief in the trial court is usually an essential precondition to seeking relief by way of appeal.

Asserted at trial. Apart from the evidentiary problem just considered, the general rule is that a party may not complain to an appellate court of an occurrence in the trial court unless it had objected in the trial court at or promptly after the time of the occurrence. Failure to raise the issue with the trial court precludes any review except for the most manifest error.[a] The underlying concept is that a party should take measures in the trial court that will avoid the commission or consequences of an error so that an appeal will be necessary only insofar as such measures have failed. Arguments raised in a lower court in a perfunctory or underdeveloped manner similarly may be lost on appeal. . . .

---

[a] On this plain error exception, which requires a clear and convincing showing of reversible error as well as of the error's net harm to the private and especially the public interests if left uncorrected, see supra pp. 1406–07, 1432–34.

Asserted on appeal. The principle of adversarial presentation applies in appellate review as well as in trial court proceedings. Accordingly, an appellate court will not ordinarily consider errors not presented in the appeal or arguments belatedly raised after appellee has filed its brief. It usually will not on its own initiative search the record for error. Issues or claims presented in the trial court that are unargued or not raised on appeal will be considered waived or abandoned.

. . . .

Prejudicial error. Even when the error is clear, erroneous determinations in the trial court do not warrant reversal unless the appellate court concludes that they materially affected the outcome or involved an important issue of procedural justice. This harmless error principle, like other barriers to appellate reversal, tends to increase the power of trial judges at the expense of appellate judges, or (from a different perspective) to protect the latter from too many appeals. In general, the task of the appellate court is to determine whether the judgment can justly be allowed to stand, despite error. . . .

Invited error. A party may not raise on appeal an error that the party invited or provoked the court or the opposite party to commit. Known as the doctrine of "invited error," this has been applied to a wide range of conduct . . . . Thus, a plaintiff who "invited" witnesses to make references to inadmissible evidence was not allowed to complain on appeal that the evidence should have been excluded.

STANDARDS OF REVIEW

Appellate courts simply will not review certain issues. For example, a federal plaintiff gets no review of a remittitur that he has accepted. Donovan v. Penn Shipping Co., 429 U.S. 648, 97 S.Ct. 835 (1977).

When considering a reviewable issue, the appellate court unavoidably must apply a standard of review. Such a standard specifies how certain the reviewer must be of error by the original decisionmaker in order to overturn the original decision. This degree of appellate scrutiny is indeed the most important feature of reviewability doctrine. Accordingly, the parties must specifically state in their briefs the applicable standard of review for each issue on appeal, as required by Federal Rule of Appellate Procedure 28(a)(9)(B), (b)(5). See generally Steven Alan Childress & Martha S. Davis, Federal Standards of Review (3d ed. 1999).

For a particular reviewable issue, the appellate courts' selection of a standard of review rests on a complex balancing of the needs for appellate review of the issue (such as controlling possible abuses of power by the trial judge and maintaining uniformity of the law) against the policies that favor limited review (such as conserving judicial resources and enhancing the appellate court's effective functioning, as well as augmenting the trial court's sense of responsibility and image of legitimacy). Consider how these factors bear on the standards of review for new trial decisions in jury cases and for findings and conclusions in nonjury trials, both of which were discussed in Section 4 of Topic D of Part Eight.

The available choices among standards of review conceivably constitute a sliding scale of infinite gradations. A contrary view holds that only three standards do, can, and should exist—and the three are nondeferential, middle-tier, and highly restricted review. Kevin M. Clermont, Procedure's Magical Number Three: Psychological Bases for Standards of Decision, 72 Cornell L.Rev. 1115, 1128–30 (1987):

"On so-called issues of law, the appellate court normally engages in plenary review, employing a virtually de novo approach, but reversing only if it disagrees with the trial judge's resolution and so thinks error in ascertainment of the correct law to be more likely than not. On issues of judge-found fact, the appellate court normally defers to the trial court's view, reversing only if that view is clearly erroneous and thus generates 'the definite and firm conviction that a mistake has been committed.' In performing certain functions, however, the appellate court will intrude only in the most extreme circumstances. For instance, the appellate court will grant a petition for mandamus only if the trial judge has clearly and indisputably committed reversible error; if the trial error alleged is abuse of discretion, then this threshold test means at least 'clear abuse of discretion,' which seems to be equivalent to almost certain error.

"Appellate courts do employ other formulations, such as an abuse-of-discretion standard of review for certain applications of law to fact. To illustrate, the core decision on a motion for a new trial on the ground of misconduct of counsel lies within the trial judge's discretion, and the appellate court will reverse only if there was an abuse of that discretion. How such a standard correlates with the tripartite scale of the preceding paragraph is not immediately apparent. 'Abuse of discretion is thus a nebulous concept which remains essentially undefined.' In the usual situation, most observers would say 'that only if an appellate court is convinced that the court below was clearly wrong will it reverse.' In other situations, however, the appellate court might be more willing or more reluctant to intercede, given stronger or weaker reasons for review rather than deference. This variety of meanings justifies a generalization: 'Discretionary decisions fall into three categories, with corresponding limitations on appellate review.' Thus, review of discretionary decisions seems to replicate in parallel the traditionally tripartite standards of appellate review."

Section 3. A Preview of Appealability

A "reviewable" issue is one that the appellate court will consider on an appeal from a trial judge's decision, whenever that appeal occurs. An "appealable" decision is one that can receive immediate appellate review.

Hence, appealability is the law on when an appeal can occur. Appealability turns out to be an intensely practical subject for the competent litigator, who works with the possibility of review by the court of appeals constantly in mind. It is of immense theoretical importance too, because appealability defines appellate subject-matter jurisdiction. It therefore proved, over the course of history, to be the determinative feature of the federal appellate system.

OLD MODES OF REVIEW

In actions at law instituted in any of the three superior courts in England, attacks on the pleadings prior to trial—for instance, demurrers—were heard and ruled on by the court in banc. A ruling at this stage might dispose of the case and result in judgment for one of the parties.

Where the pleadings eventuated in an issue of fact, a single judge and jury at nisi prius typically tried the issue. In the course of the trial, the judge made rulings on points of evidence and finally charged the jury, which rendered a verdict. Thereupon the record, including the jury verdict, was returned to the central court. In due time, barring other steps by the party who had lost the verdict, judgment would be entered in accordance with the verdict.

After the trial but prior to the entry of the judgment, the party who had lost the verdict might apply to the court in banc for relief. Technically this application might take the form of a request for the service of a rule on the opponent to show cause why an order should not be made by the court in favor of the applicant. These applications and the orders sought were of various kinds. First, plaintiff or defendant who had lost the verdict might apply for a new trial on the ground that the nisi prius judge had ruled erroneously on a point of evidence or had charged the jury incorrectly or on the ground that the verdict was against the weight of the evidence. Here the notes of the trial judge would be available to the court in banc. If the application was successful, the verdict would be set aside and a new trial ordered. Second, a losing defendant might move in arrest of judgment on the ground that the pleadings were not sufficient in law to support a judgment for plaintiff. Third, a losing plaintiff might move for judgment notwithstanding the verdict on the ground that the plea in confession and avoidance, on which the jury had given a verdict in defendant's favor, was not sufficient in law.[b]

Such applications to the court in banc served in some cases as a means of securing reexamination of the actions of the trial judge, but they did not involve review by a higher court. The trial judge had acted as a kind of agent of the court in trying the case at nisi prius. The court was examining and, if necessary, correcting the actions of one of its own members or at least its agent, not those of a judge of an inferior court.

[b] See supra p. 1073.

It was only after the court entered judgment, by one route or another, that proceedings in error by another court, the court of error, could be instituted.[c] The plaintiff-in-error (the party against whom judgment had gone below) would sue a writ of error out of the Chancery. This was an original writ directed to the court that had entered the judgment, directing it to send the record to the court of error in order that the claimed error might be there corrected. The return to the writ was the record.

It is important to bear in mind of what this record consisted, because the scope of review was naturally determined by what was laid before the court of error. The record comprised the process, the pleadings (together with rulings on the pleadings[d]), the clerk's minutes, the verdict,[e] and the judgment. In no event did the record contain the proceedings on a motion for a new trial made to the original court in banc, and accordingly the ruling on such a motion, whether granted or denied, was not reviewable on writ of error. Indeed, except where a bill of exceptions (described below) had been employed, the record did not contain a word of the testimony given at the trial, nor did it contain the trial judge's rulings on matters of evidence or his charge to the jury.

After the Statute of Westminster II, 1285, 13 Edw., ch. 31, the plaintiff-in-error could bring alleged errors of the trial judge before the court of error by bill of exceptions, but only as an alternative to a motion for a new trial. A party claiming error in the trial judge's rulings on points of evidence or in his charge to the jury reduced to writing the substance of the rulings or the parts of the charge excepted to. This bill of exceptions then formed a part of the record. The original court took no further notice of it. But after judgment and upon writ of error, the court of error was thereby able to review the errors of law allegedly committed at the trial. "The advantage of this method of proceeding, instead of moving for a new trial, was that a bill of exceptions was taken to the Court of Error, . . . whereas the motion for a new trial was . . . made to the Court in which the case was started, of which court the Judge, whose ruling was objected to, might be a member, and there was no appeal from the judgment of such court to a Court of Error on a motion for a new trial." Ralph Sutton, Personal Actions at Common Law 126 (1929).

---

[c] In the old days, the scheme was a confused one: speaking generally, the King's Bench was the court of error for the Court of Common Pleas, the House of Lords was the court of error for the King's Bench, and a special court called the Exchequer Chamber was the court of error for the Court of Exchequer. After 1830, the court of error for all three superior courts was a new Court of Exchequer Chamber, which consisted of the judges of the two superior courts that had not been involved in the action under review. Further review, as always, could be had in the House of Lords.

[d] These included rulings on demurrer, motion in arrest of judgment, and motion for judgment n.o.v. A ruling on demurrer to the evidence, see supra p. 1368, would also appear in the record.

[e] This included a so-called special verdict, but not a so-called special case. See supra pp. 1418–19. The former device resulted in jury findings being entered of record, but the latter device's agreed statement of facts did not become part of the record and hence could not figure in proceedings in error.

Review by another court in actions at law thus was confined substantially to claimed errors of law appearing on a bare record, and it took place only after judgment.

Carleton M. Crick, The Final Judgment as a Basis for Appeal

41 Yale L.J. 539, 545–48 (1932).

A complete picture of appellate processes in England in past years cannot be obtained merely by consideration of the common law courts. Much of the business now handled by our courts of general jurisdiction was taken care of in England by chancery, and we must, therefore, consider the procedure in those types of cases.

Taking Blackstone's time as a convenient point of departure, we find that the course of litigation in a simple case in equity went something as follows.

The pleadings having been filed and the parties at issue upon the facts, the evidence was taken down in writing and the case set for hearing before the chancellor or Master of the Rolls. There the evidence was read and such orders made from time to time as might be necessary. When everything had been heard the decree was pronounced. Generally it was merely interlocutory, but eventually the final decree was made and the rights of the parties completely adjudicated.

We see, then, that there were three types of pronouncements made during the course of a case. First, orders, second, interlocutory decrees, and third, final decrees. Unlike the common law, however, which as we have seen, required a case to go to final judgment before the decisions of the court might be questioned, equity gave relief from all three types of pronouncements. If a party was dissatisfied by an order made during the course of the proceedings his remedy was by way of rehearing by petition to the Lord Chancellor, whether the cause had been heard before that dignitary or the Master of the Rolls. On this rehearing the evidence is reread and any additional evidence presented. From the decision on this rehearing an appeal lay to the House of Lords.

An interlocutory decree differed from an order in that it had to be signed by the chancellor before it could be enrolled, and prior to his signing it had only the force of an order. Therefore, prior to signing relief was the same as in the case of an order, namely, petition for a rehearing before the chancellor, and from there appeal to the House of Lords. After a decree was signed and enrolled, whether it was interlocutory or final, relief could be had only by bill of review for an error in judgment appearing on the face of the decree, or by special leave of the chancellor upon the discovery of new evidence. From a decision on this bill appeal might be taken to the House of Lords.

Appeal to the House of Lords, whether from an order or from an interlocutory or final decree, was by petition to that body, which, if it consented to hear the case, considered all the documents and not merely the enrolled decree.

Thus we see that equity practice never knew the rule of the common law that only final judgments were appealable. Not only could interlocutory decrees be taken to the House of Lords, but also those decisions which had not even attained the dignity of decrees, that is, orders. As to the reason for this, we may tentatively assign two factors. First, appeals to the House of Lords from the Lord Chancellor were established comparatively late in legal history. The chancery had come to be regarded as a court as early as the 14th or 15th Century, but appeals to the House of Lords did not become established until the latter half of the 17th Century. During the intervening centuries, therefore, a given case had its beginning and ending in the same court, and the only method by which a decision could be altered was by rehearing before the chancellor. That he reviewed all interlocutory decrees and orders made by masters in the chancery may be explained historically, as originally the chancellor was the sole judge in chancery, and the masters were regarded as mere clerks rather than judges. Even in Blackstone's time a decree was a decree of the chancellor and not of the master who really gave it, since before it could become effective as a decree it had to be signed by the chancellor.

When the House of Lords finally asserted appellate jurisdiction over proceedings in chancery, therefore, it found a system whereby the chancellor passed on all decrees issued, as well as on interlocutory orders, and we need not be surprised that appeals were taken to the Lords from interlocutory decrees because in chancery there was no particular magic in a final decree. All were, so as to speak, of equal dignity. We might expect, however, that while appeals from all decrees would be heard, there might be some doubt as to the appealability of mere orders. This supposition is borne out by Spence, who says that it was not until 1726 that appellate jurisdiction was established over interlocutory orders.

Second, when we consider the character of litigation handled in chancery we see how much more convenient it was to review intermediate decisions as the case progressed. Equity cases were those of which the chancellor had taken cognizance because there was no adequate remedy at law. Consequently much of its litigation was of a complicated type unsuited to the more simple common law forms of action. There was a much greater use of subordinate officials than in the common law courts, and the requirement of documentation of evidence introduced difficulties unknown to the King's courts. In equity, judgments were not compelled to follow stereotyped forms, and this made possible dealing with the case by as many orders, decrees, and modifications of the same as were necessary in the particular case. Thus, equity had a more elastic procedure, and also required a less rigid practice on appeal to review the many and varied steps taken below.

Mary Sarah Bilder, The Origin of the Appeal in America

48 Hastings L.J. 913, 914–15 (1997).

Almost every legal system develops procedures to address grievances about initial judicial determinations.[f] However, as familiar as the word "appeal" is to us today, the appeal was a surprising procedure for the American colonists to have adopted. Three hundred years ago, the term "appeal" referred to a legal procedure which was available only in the separate system of English courts governed by canon and civil law—and not in the common law system with which the Puritan settlers were so enamored. The legal procedure known as "the appeal" did not refer to what we now think of as an "appeal"—the correction by a higher court of errors of law made by a lower court. Instead, the "appeal" referred to a procedure under which a higher tribunal could completely and broadly rehear and redecide not only the law, but also the entire facts of a case. Moreover, the legal procedure called "the appeal" represented a substantive theory of justice, emphasizing the importance of equity and a particular attitude towards the hierarchy of authority. It was this more liberal system of redress that eight of the colonies initially adopted, including Massachusetts and Rhode Island.

. . . .

Over time, many of these American colonies would replace or combine the appeal [of equity] with the more traditional review procedures of the common law: the writ of error and the writ of certiorari. And by the eighteenth and nineteenth centuries, these more common-law-like procedures had significantly narrowed the possibilities of review—for example, courts only permitted redress for errors of law shown in the written record of the case, similar to procedures in England. Yet the word "appeal" and arguably some of its broader jurisprudential connotations never completely vanished from the American legal system.

The appeal and the writ of error thus were two separate paths, and although our modern appellate system seems to owe more today to the narrow theory of redress represented by the writ of error, the fact that we stubbornly continue to use the word "appeal" suggests that some part of the original substantive theory of the appeal remains with us. In a legal world often obsessed with a static view of the rule of law, with a mechanical distinction between law and facts, and with one-bite-at-the-apple theories of review, perhaps the word still survives because we still remember, perhaps still continue to believe in, this early, broader and more flexible and equitable notion of appeal.

---

[f] Scholars have done very little comparative work on appeal. But even a quick look suggests that what different countries mean by "appeal" varies greatly. See Sophie M.F. Geeroms, Comparative Law and Legal Translation: Why the Terms Cassation, Revision and Appeal Should Not Be Translated . . . , 50 Am.J.Comp.L. 201 (2002). The whole notion of appeal, over space as well as over time, turns out to be highly contingent. See Civil Appeal Procedures Worldwide (Charles Platto ed., 1992); Oscar G. Chase, Helen Hershkoff, Linda Silberman, Yasuhei Taniguchi, Vincenzo Varano & Adrian Zuckerman, Civil Litigation in Comparative Context ch. 7 (2007).

TOPIC B

APPEAL OF FINAL DECISIONS

Note, Appealability in the Federal Courts

75 Harv.L.Rev. 351, 351–53 (1961).

Any judicial system that affords a right to appellate review must ensure that appeal does not come too late to be effective. At the same time—especially when the amount of litigation is substantial—the system must be designed to promote the efficient disposition of judicial business. The balance is almost universally struck by a general rule allowing appeal only from final judgment, with exceptions for circumscribed classes of interlocutory orders. In regulating appeals from the district courts the federal system has followed this pattern since the original Judiciary Act of 1789. Although both the courts and the Congress have adopted exceptions for defined classes of orders, these have proved inadequate. Until [1948] the extraordinary writs were the only means for providing additional flexibility in the review of interlocutory orders. At that time an amendment to the Federal Rules of Civil Procedure conferred discretion on the district courts to permit appeal from an order terminating fewer than all claims in a multiclaim litigation. And in 1958 the Judicial Code was amended to allow appeal from a broad group of interlocutory orders at the discretion of both the trial and the appellate courts. [Since then, 28 U.S.C. § 1292(e), added in 1992, authorized the Supreme Court to prescribe Federal Rules that would allow immediate appeal of types of interlocutory decisions. So far, the Supreme Court has promulgated only Federal Rule of Civil Procedure 23(f) in 1998, by which the court of appeals in its discretion may permit an immediate appeal from an order granting or denying class certification.] . . .

The basic rationale of the finality rule is conservation of judicial resources. Constant interruption of trial would follow from a general practice of interlocutory appeals and would consume trial court time, forestall the ultimate resolution of the case, and facilitate the harassment of one party by his opponent. Since substantial time elapses before appellate determination,[1] it would be necessary for the trial court to spend extra hours refamiliarizing itself with the case and perhaps to select a new jury

[1] The median time interval from filing notice of appeal to final disposition by the court of appeals is 8.3 months [for 2681appeals. See 1960 Dir. Admin. Office U.S. Courts] Ann.Rep. 221. [Table B–4's comparable measurement was 12.7 months for 29,608 appeals in fiscal 2008.—Ed.] This span may be considerably shortened in individual cases. See Shawe v. Wendy Wilson, Inc., 25 F.R.D. 1 (S.D.N.Y.), rev'd sub nom. Jaftex Corp. v. Randolph Mills, Inc., 282 F.2d 508 (2d Cir.1960). But interlocutory appeals will on the average still require several months for appellate consideration. See Ann.Rep. 73.

and begin anew. A single appeal consolidating all alleged errors also minimizes the appellate court burden by eliminating more than one set of records, briefs, and arguments in an individual case. And if the prejudiced party is the ultimate victor, if parties settle, or if the trial court later corrects its own error, appellate review will prove unnecessary. The requirement of finality also helps to ensure the correct disposition of the merits. After the proceedings below are complete, the appellate court is in position to assess the wisdom of particular interlocutory orders with heightened perspective; the lower court is apt to consider its orders with greater care, for errors not requiring reversal will never be corrected and those that warrant reversal will compel a complete retrial. Finally, to allow an appeal from every order to which an objection is lodged might reduce respect for the authority of the trial judge.

But there are frequent situations in which prompt review is urgent. Reversal of some interlocutory orders will terminate litigation or preclude subsequent retrial, thereby eliminating needless proceedings in the lower court. Fairness demands swift appeal in cases where delayed review will be of little or no avail. Certain types of frequently recurring orders, such as discovery orders, seldom require reversal and hence may never be reviewed; the absence of appellate guidance may result in inconsistent treatment by the lower courts. Finally there must be some means for immediately restraining a district judge in the rare case where his conduct exceeds all bounds of judicial propriety.

Of particular importance is the method for distinguishing those interlocutory orders that should be appealable from those that should not. A statute granting appeal as of right from a rigidly defined class of interlocutory orders obviates the need for preliminary judicial determination of the right to appeal. But the application of a statutory definition often gives rise to substantial litigation before the appellate tribunal, and sometimes permits appeal where it is not needed or, still worse, prevents appeal when immediate review is warranted. To permit appeal in the latter cases, tortuous constructions of finality have often been adopted. The consequent uncertainty as to the right to appeal is particularly undesirable, for a mistaken party may forfeit his right to review. An alternative approach is to establish broad statutory guidelines and condition the appeal of an interlocutory order upon the consent of either the trial or appellate court. Although such an approach imposes the additional burden of preliminary consideration of the desirability of appeal, it affords greater flexibility, confines appeal to appropriate cases, and avoids uncertainty as to the right of appeal.

Cohen v. Beneficial Industrial Loan Corp.

Supreme Court of the United States, 1949.
337 U.S. 541, 69 S.Ct. 1221.

[A digest of the facts appears supra p. 358. Essentially, the district court had denied the corporate defendant's motion to require security under the state statute. The court of appeals entertained an appeal and reversed. The case reached the Supreme Court on certiorari.]

■ MR. JUSTICE JACKSON delivered the opinion of the Court.

. . . .

At the threshold we are met with the question whether the District Court's order refusing to apply the statute was an appealable one. Title 28 U.S.C. § 1291 provides, as did its predecessors, for appeal only "from all final decisions of the district courts," except when direct appeal to this Court is provided. Section 1292 allows appeals also from certain interlocutory orders, decrees and judgments, not material to this case except as they indicate the purpose to allow appeals from orders other than final judgments when they have a final and irreparable effect on the rights of the parties. It is obvious that, if Congress had allowed appeals only from those final judgments which terminate an action, this order would not be appealable.

The effect of the statute is to disallow appeal from any decision which is tentative, informal or incomplete. Appeal gives the upper court a power of review, not one of intervention. So long as the matter remains open, unfinished or inconclusive, there may be no intrusion by appeal. But the District Court's action upon the application was concluded and closed and its decision final in that sense before the appeal was taken.

Nor does the statute permit appeals, even from fully consummated decisions, where they are but steps towards final judgment in which they will merge. The purpose is to combine in one review all stages of the proceeding that effectively may be reviewed and corrected if and when final judgment results. But this order of the District Court did not make any step toward final disposition of the merits of the case and will not be merged in final judgment. When that time comes, it will be too late effectively to review the present order, and the rights conferred by the statute, if it is applicable, will have been lost, probably irreparably. We conclude that the matters embraced in the decision appealed from are not of such an interlocutory nature as to affect, or to be affected by, decision of the merits of this case.

This decision appears to fall in that small class which finally determine claims of right separable from, and collateral to, rights asserted in the action, too important to be denied review and too independent of the cause itself to require that appellate consideration be deferred until the whole case is adjudicated. The Court has long given this provision of the statute this practical rather than a technical construction. Bank of Columbia v. Sweeny, 1 Pet. 567, 569; United States v. River Rouge Improvement Co., 269 U.S. 411, 414, 46 S.Ct. 144, 145; Cobbledick v. United States, 309 U.S. 323, 328, 60 S.Ct. 540, 542.

We hold this order appealable because it is a final disposition of a claimed right which is not an ingredient of the cause of action and does not require consideration with it. But we do not mean that every order fixing security is subject to appeal. Here it is the right to security that presents a serious and unsettled question. If the right were admitted or clear and the order involved only an exercise of discretion as to the amount of security, a matter the statute makes subject to reconsideration from time to time, appealability would present a different question.

[The remainder of the opinion, dealing with the merits, is omitted.]

■ [The dissenting opinions of JUSTICE DOUGLAS, with whom Justice Frankfurter joined, and of JUSTICE RUTLEDGE did not discuss appealability and are also omitted.]

FIRESTONE TIRE & RUBBER CO. v. RISJORD, 449 U.S. 368, 101 S.Ct. 669 (1981). This case held that under 28 U.S.C. § 1291, no immediate appeal lies in a civil case from a district court order denying a motion to disqualify opponent's counsel for conflict of interest. Quoting Coopers & Lybrand v. Livesay, 437 U.S. 463, 468, 98 S.Ct. 2454, 2458 (1978), the Court specified the requirements of the collateral order doctrine in these terms: " '[T]he order must conclusively determine the disputed question, resolve an important issue completely separate from the merits of the action, and be effectively unreviewable on appeal from a final judgment.' " An order refusing disqualification fails the third requirement, because such an order is "indeed reviewable on appeal after final judgment."

Later the Supreme Court extended this rule against immediate appeal to an order granting a motion to disqualify opponent's counsel for misconduct, largely because disqualification orders in general "are not sufficiently separable from the merits." Richardson–Merrell, Inc. v. Koller, 472 U.S. 424, 105 S.Ct. 2757 (1985). Still, Cohen's fourth requirement of a "serious and unsettled question" seemed no longer to exist.

DIGITAL EQUIPMENT CORP. v. DESKTOP DIRECT, INC., 511 U.S. 863, 114 S.Ct. 1992 (1994). This case held that under 28 U.S.C. § 1291, no immediate appeal lies in a trademark case from an order refusing to enforce a settlement agreement. The Court generalized:

"The collateral order doctrine is best understood not as an exception to the 'final decision' rule laid down by Congress in § 1291, but as a 'practical construction' of it [citing Cohen and Coopers & Lybrand]. We have repeatedly held that the statute entitles a party to appeal not only from a district court decision that 'ends the litigation on the merits and leaves nothing more for the court to do but execute the judgment,' Catlin v. United States, 324 U.S. 229, 233, 65 S.Ct. 631, 633 (1945), but also from a narrow class of decisions that do not terminate the litigation, but must, in the interest of 'achieving a healthy legal system,' cf. Cobbledick v. United States, 309 U.S. 323, 326, 60 S.Ct. 540, 541 (1940), nonetheless be treated as 'final.' The latter category comprises only those district court decisions that are conclusive, that resolve important questions completely separate from the merits, and that would render such important questions effectively unreviewable on appeal from final judgment in the underlying action. See generally Coopers & Lybrand, supra. Immediate appeals from such orders, we have explained, do not go against the grain of § 1291, with its object of efficient administration of justice in the federal courts, see generally Richardson–Merrell, Inc. v. Koller, 472 U.S. 424, 105 S.Ct. 2757 (1985).

"But we have also repeatedly stressed that the 'narrow' exception should stay that way and never be allowed to swallow the general rule, id., at 436, 105 S.Ct., at 2763–2764, that a party is entitled to a single appeal, to be deferred until final judgment has been entered, in which claims of district court error at any stage of the litigation may be ventilated [citation omitted]. We have accordingly described the conditions for collateral order appeal as stringent, see, e.g., Midland Asphalt Corp. v. United States, 489 U.S. 794, 799, 109 S.Ct. 1494, 1498 (1989), and have warned that the issue of appealability under § 1291 is to be determined for the entire category to which a claim belongs, without regard to the chance that the litigation at hand might be speeded, or a 'particular injustic[e]' averted, Van Cauwenberghe v. Biard, 486 U.S. 517, 529, 108 S.Ct. 1945, 1953 (1988), by a prompt appellate court decision. See also Richardson–Merrell, supra, 472 U.S., at 439, 105 S.Ct., at 2764 (this Court 'has expressly rejected efforts to reduce the finality requirement of § 1291 to a case-by-case [appealability] determination'); Carroll v. United States, 354 U.S. 394, 405, 77 S.Ct. 1332, 1339 (1957)."

The order in this case failed the third requirement of the collateral order doctrine ("that the decision on an 'important' question be 'effectively unreviewable' upon final judgment"), rejecting the argument that the private interest in avoiding a possibly improper trial suffices to justify immediate appeal. Later the Supreme Court applied this rule against immediate appeal to an order denying a defense motion for judgment on the pleadings premised on a defense in the nature of claim preclusion. Will v. Hallock, 546 U.S. 345, 126 S.Ct. 952 (2006) (emphasizing that the important question must impact a substantial public interest), distinguishing Mitchell v. Forsyth, 472 U.S. 511, 105 S.Ct. 2806 (1985) (allowing immediate appeal of public officials' denied immunity-from-suit defense as a collateral order).

Questions: (1) In a class action for damages, does an appeal lie from an order disapproving a proposed settlement? Does the threat of irreparable harm to a claimed "important" right mean that delayed review will come "too late effectively to review the present order"? To what degree is that claim of right "separable from, and collateral to," and "independent of the cause itself"? Indeed, did the order "finally determine" the claim of right? See Seigal v. Merrick, 590 F.2d 35 (2d Cir.1978) (nonappealable). But see Norman v. McKee, 431 F.2d 769 (9th Cir.1970) (appealable).

(2) If in Cohen the district court had granted security in the requested amount, would an appeal have lain? Was the question collateral? How grave was the threatened harm of delayed review? See 15A Wright, Miller & Cooper § 3914.2.

APPEALABILITY OF CONTEMPT ORDERS

There are several doctrines, other than the collateral order doctrine, that can also be classified as judicial attempts at creating rigidly defined categorical exceptions to the normal finality standard. See generally id. §§ 3910 (orders transferring property), 3912 (death knell orders); 15B id. § 3917 (contempt orders). As a general matter, the various exceptions are cumulative, in the sense that an appeal lies if any exception applies.

Among the categorical exceptions is the set of rules concerning the appealability of contempt orders, which rules were discussed in the discovery setting supra p. 1264. Essentially, all definitive contempt sanctions, except an order sanctioning a *party* adjudged to be in purely *civil* contempt, are considered final and hence appealable.

Questions: (3) For a party who has been jailed until she complies with a discovery order requiring surrender of material claimed to be privileged, no appeal is ordinarily allowed under these rules. What arguments can you make against this result? See generally Thomas J. André, Jr., The Final Judgment Rule and Party Appeals of Civil Contempt Orders: Time for a Change, 55 N.Y.U.L.Rev. 1041 (1980). Alternatively, could you argue sometimes that an appeal from such a contempt sanction will lie under the collateral order doctrine, or that the discovery order itself is an appealable collateral order? See United States v. Philip Morris Inc., 314 F.3d 612, 620–21 (D.C.Cir.2003) (yes).

(4) Might one argue that, in defining what is in effect an exception to the finality standard, one is inevitably forced to choose between the certainty (ensuring predictability and workability) of a categorical definition and the accuracy (permitting appeal if and only if needed) of a discretionary definition, unless one wants only the drawbacks of both? In the appealability context, which is the more practicably attainable goal?

Gillespie v. United States Steel Corp.

Supreme Court of the United States, 1964.
379 U.S. 148, 85 S.Ct. 308.

■ MR. JUSTICE BLACK delivered the opinion of the Court.

The petitioner, administratrix of the estate of her son Daniel Gillespie, brought this action in federal court against the respondent shipowner-employer to recover damages for Gillespie's death, which was alleged to have occurred when he fell and was drowned while working as a seaman on respondent's ship docked in Ohio. She claimed a right to recover for the benefit of herself and of the decedent's dependent brother and sisters under the Jones Act, which subjects employers to liability if by negligence they cause a seaman's injury or death. She also claimed a right of recovery under the Ohio wrongful death statute because the vessel allegedly was not seaworthy as required by the "general maritime law." The complaint in addition sought damages for Gillespie's pain and suffering before he died, based on the Jones Act and the general maritime law, causes of action which petitioner said survived Gillespie's death by force of the Jones Act itself and the Ohio survival statute, respectively. The District Judge, holding that the Jones Act supplied the exclusive remedy, on motion of respondent struck all parts of the complaint which referred to the Ohio statutes or to unseaworthiness. He also struck all reference to recovery for the benefit of the brother and sisters of the decedent, who respondent had argued were not beneficiaries entitled to recovery under the Jones Act while their mother was living.

Petitioner immediately appealed to the Court of Appeals. Respondent moved to dismiss the appeal on the ground that the ruling appealed from was not a "final" decision of the District Court as required by 28 U.S.C. § 1291 (1958 ed.). . . . Without definitely deciding . . . the "close" question of appealability, the Court of Appeals proceeded to determine the controversy "on the merits as though it were submitted on an appeal"; this the court said it felt free to do since its resolution of the merits did not prejudice respondent in any way, because it sustained respondent's contentions by . . . affirming the District Court's order. 321 F.2d 518. Petitioner brought the case here, and we granted certiorari. 375 U.S. 962, 84 S.Ct. 487.

. . . .

In this Court respondent joins petitioner in urging us to hold that 28 U.S.C. § 1291 (1958 ed.) does not require us to dismiss this case and that we can and should decide the validity of the District Court's order to strike. We agree. Under § 1291 an appeal may be taken from any "final" order of a district court. But as this Court often has pointed out, a decision "final" within the meaning of § 1291 does not necessarily mean the last order possible to be made in a case. Cohen v. Beneficial Industrial Loan Corp., 337 U.S. 541, 545, 69 S.Ct. 1221, 1225. And our cases long have recognized that whether a ruling is "final" within the meaning of § 1291 is frequently so close a question that decision of that issue either way can be supported with equally forceful arguments, and that it is impossible to devise a formula to resolve all marginal cases coming within what might well be called the "twilight zone" of finality. Because of this difficulty this Court has held that the requirement of finality is to be given a "practical rather than a technical construction." Cohen v. Beneficial Industrial Loan Corp., supra, 337 U.S., at 546, 69 S.Ct., at 1226. [Citations omitted.] Dickinson v. Petroleum Conversion Corp., 338 U.S. 507, 511, 70 S.Ct. 322, 324, pointed out that in deciding the question of finality the most important competing considerations are "the inconvenience and costs of piecemeal review on the one hand and the danger of denying justice by delay on the other." Such competing considerations are shown by the record in the case before us. It is true that the review of this case by the Court of Appeals could be called "piecemeal"; but it does not appear that the inconvenience and cost of trying this case will be greater because the Court of Appeals decided the issues raised instead of compelling the parties to go to trial with them unanswered. We cannot say that the Court of Appeals chose wrongly under the circumstances. And it seems clear now that the case is before us that the eventual costs, as all the parties recognize, will certainly be less if we now pass on the questions presented here rather than send the case back with those issues undecided. Moreover, delay of perhaps a number of years in having the brother's and sisters' rights determined might work a great injustice on them, since the claims for recovery for their benefit have been effectively cut off so long as the District Judge's ruling stands. And while their claims are not formally severable so as to make the court's order unquestionably appealable as to them, cf. Dickinson v. Petroleum Conversion Corp., supra, there certainly is ample reason to view their claims as severable in deciding the issue of finality . . . . Furthermore, in United States v. General Motors Corp., 323 U.S. 373, 377, 65 S.Ct. 357, 359, [which was not a case involving appealability,] this Court contrary to its usual practice reviewed a trial court's refusal to permit proof of certain items of damages in a case not yet fully tried, because the ruling was "fundamental to the further conduct of the case." . . . We think that the questions presented here are equally "fundamental to the further conduct of the case." It is true that if the District Judge had certified the case to the Court of Appeals under 28 U.S.C. § 1292(b) (1958 ed.), the appeal unquestionably would have been proper; in light of the circumstances we believe that the Court of Appeals properly implemented the same policy Congress sought to promote in § 1292(b) by treating this obviously marginal case as final and appealable under 28 U.S.C. § 1291 (1958 ed.). We therefore proceed to consider the correctness of the Court of Appeals' judgment.

[The Supreme Court went on to affirm on the merits in all major respects.]

■ [The dissenting opinion of JUSTICE GOLDBERG, who agreed with the majority on appealability but disagreed on the merits, is omitted. Also omitted is the dissenting opinion of JUSTICE HARLAN, stoutly defending the finality standard and arguing that it was not met in this case. JUSTICE STEWART agreed with Justice Harlan on appealability and with the majority on the merits.][a]

APPEALABILITY IN MULTI-CLAIM AND MULTI-PARTY LITIGATION

Before the Federal Rules, a judgment generally had to make final disposition with regard to all claims and all parties in the action in order to

[a] In Coopers & Lybrand v. Livesay, 437 U.S. 463, 477 n.30, 98 S.Ct. 2454, 2462 n.30 (1978), the Court noted: "If Gillespie were extended beyond the unique facts of that case, § 1291 would be stripped of all significance." Nevertheless, the Court has since used Gillespie to uphold appealability, but only once and on peculiar facts in American Export Lines v. Alvez, 446 U.S. 274, 279, 100 S.Ct. 1673, 1676 (1980) (reviewing a state court decision that upheld a maritime complaint). At any rate, the courts of appeals have made only sparing use of the Gillespie approach. See, e.g., Utah v. Kennecott Corp., 14 F.3d 1489, 1495–96 (10th Cir.1994) (holding nonappealable an order that disapproved a proposed settlement).

qualify as appealable under the final decision rule. As a result of great expansion of the potential size of a lawsuit through the liberal joinder provisions of the Federal Rules, it became desirable to permit appeal from orders finally disposing of some but fewer than all of the claims or parties before the entire action was terminated. It was even more important that a litigant should know just when such an order became appealable, or otherwise the litigant might take a wasteful premature appeal or even forfeit the right to review by neglecting to appeal in time from an order disposing of some claims or parties.

Scope of the Rule.—The rulemakers intended Rule 54(b) to take care of this situation, but they had to amend it twice before accomplishing their purpose. The original Rule, which appears with the Advisory Committee's notes in the Rules booklet, failed to provide a reliable guide for determining precisely which orders would be considered final. The first amendment, in 1948, reduced this uncertainty by overtly relying on the trial court's discretion and by requiring a clear statement of the trial court's intention regarding finality. After that amendment, the Rule read substantially the same as the present Rule except that the reference to multiple parties, as distinguished from multiple claims, did not appear. The second amendment, in 1961, added the party language in order to overcome some resistance in the cases. Thus, the present rule permits the trial court to "direct entry of a final judgment" as to fewer than all the claims or parties, but only when in its discretion it makes an express determination that "there is no just reason for delay."[b]

In short, under Rule 54(b) the trial judge acts as a dispatching agent: the trial judge can refuse to allow an appeal or, within specified guidelines, can decide to allow an appeal. This approach differs from rigidly defined categorical exceptions to the normal finality standard, in that it relies on discretion. This approach also differs from Gillespie, in that it relies on the discretion of the "dispatcher" and not on the discretion of the "receiver." This approach thus promises accuracy by relying on the informed discretion of the trial judge, who is familiar with the case and the desirability of an immediate appeal. But this approach also promises certainty, as the trial judge can readily pick out and label appropriate rulings for appeal.

If the trial judge refuses to certify an appeal, a litigant is safe not to appeal before termination of the entire action. Any immediate appeal of the underlying order will be dismissed, unless the order is appealable under some other doctrine or provision. Appellate review of the refusal to certify under Rule 54(b) itself should be unavailable However, there is some weak authority for using mandamus to force a recalcitrant district judge to certify an appeal, reaching refusals coming from either bad motives or seriously bad judgment.

If the trial judge certifies an appeal, a litigant is put on notice that the time for appeal has begun to run. Systemically, a risk exists that the lower

[b] The Rule 54(b) judgment will have collateral effects. It will allow enforcement, it will accrue interest, and it will have res judicata effects. So not only the would-be appellant but also the victor might seek such a judgment. The district court can also act sua sponte.

court will be too willing to send cases up, either shirking judicial duties or giving inadequate weight to the appellate court's interests. But appellate review of the Rule 54(b) certification itself is available, albeit of narrow scope, and this review will result in dismissal of an immediate appeal (1) if there was no final disposition of some but fewer than all of the claims or parties, (2) if only a single claim for relief with two or more variants was involved, or (3) if the trial court abused its discretion under the Rule. Indeed, to ensure carefulness and to facilitate review, some appellate courts require the district judge to articulate the reasons for certification. Nevertheless, the risk of too readily certifying will persist to some extent. Perhaps, it would be well to recognize that whoever determines appealability might be wrong occasionally, and here it might be better to hear an appeal than to expend energy on second-guessing allowance of appeal.

Questions: (5) What meaning should be given the term "claim for relief" in Rule 54(b)? See 10 Wright, Miller & Kane § 2657.

(6) Could not the rulemakers eliminate most such definitional problems by broadening the applicability of Rule 54(b), so that the trial judge could certify for immediate appeal any nonfinal order when there is no just reason for delay? Is there any impediment to the rulemakers' doing so?

Authority to make a Rule.—There was controversy over the interpretation and validity of the part of Rule 54(b) that made an order appealable by reason of the trial judge's certification when it would not have been regarded as final before the Rules. The questions were how the Rule was to be read with 28 U.S.C. § 1291 and whether it went beyond the Rules Enabling Act or the Constitution. Had the Court meant to override § 1291? Could the Court regulate appellate jurisdiction?

These issues were settled, or ducked, by the Supreme Court in Sears, Roebuck & Co. v. Mackey, 351 U.S. 427, 76 S.Ct. 895 (1956), where Justice Burton said: "[Rule 54(b)] does not supersede any statute controlling appellate jurisdiction. It scrupulously recognizes the statutory requirement of a 'final decision' under § 1291 as a basic requirement for an appeal to the Court of Appeals. It merely administers that requirement in a practical manner in multiple claims actions and does so by rule instead of by judicial decision."

Then the Judicial Improvements Act of 1990, Pub.L. No. 101–650, tit. III, § 315, 104 Stat. 5089, 5115, added 28 U.S.C. § 2072(c) to the Rules Enabling Act. The statute at least confirms the Sears, Roebuck rulemaking authority to interpret the meaning of finality, as H.R.Rep. No. 101–734 explained that this provision gives the Court authority to promulgate rules that "clarify the scope of a final decision" under § 1291.

Finally the Federal Courts Administration Act of 1992, Pub.L. No. 102–572, tit. I, § 101, 106 Stat. 4506, 4506, added 28 U.S.C. § 1292(e) to the interlocutory appeals statute. H.R.Rep. No. 102–1006 explained that this broad provision gives the Court rulemaking authority "to expand the appealability of interlocutory determinations by the courts of appeals."

These two statutes were based on earlier recommendations that had come from the Federal Courts Study Committee. This blue-ribbon panel of members of Congress, judges, and lawyers had been established by Congress in 1988 and appointed by the Chief Justice. It had conducted a comprehensive examination of the federal court system. In 1990 and 1992 Congress acted to adopt the so-called noncontroversial proposals of the Committee. Its appealability proposal appeared, together with its explanation, in Federal Courts Study Committee, Report 95–96 (1990):

> **To deal with difficulties arising from definitions of an appealable order, Congress should consider delegating to the Supreme Court the authority under the Rules Enabling Act to define what constitutes a final decision for purposes of 28 U.S.C. § 1291, and to define circumstances in which orders and actions of district courts not otherwise subject to appeal under acts of Congress may be appealed to the courts of appeals.**
>
> The state of the law on when a district court ruling is appealable because it is "final," or is an appealable interlocutory action, strikes many observers as unsatisfactory in several respects. The area has produced much purely procedural litigation. Courts of appeals often dismiss appeals as premature. Litigants sometimes face the possibility of waiving their right to appeal when they fail to seek timely review because it is unclear when a decision is "final" and the time for appeal begins to run. Decisional doctrines—such as "practical finality" and especially the "collateral order" rule—blur the edges of the finality principle, require repeated attention from the Supreme Court, and may in some circumstances restrict too sharply the opportunity for interlocutory review.
>
> We propose that Congress consider permitting the rulemaking process to refine and supplement definitions of appellate jurisdiction under the Rules Enabling Act, 28 U.S.C. § 2072, which, we emphasize, includes the constraint that "[s]uch rules shall not abridge, enlarge or modify any substantive right." Congress has given admirable attention to many technical issues in the Judicial Code in recent years, but the area of appellate jurisdiction might profit as well from the specialized focus of those responsible for the Federal Rules of Appellate Procedure. The rulemaking authority under this proposal would include authority both to change (by broadening, narrowing, or systematizing) decisional results under the finality rule of 28 U.S.C. § 1291 and to add to—but not subtract from—the list of categories of interlocutory appeal permitted by Congress in 28 U.S.C. § 1292. Favorable experience under this limited rulemaking authority over appellate jurisdiction might later support a broader delegation of power to treat the entire area of appealability from federal district courts by rule rather than statute.

APPEALABILITY OF STATE DECISIONS

State decision to higher federal court.—With respect to review of state judgments and decrees by the Supreme Court of the United States, 28 U.S.C. § 1257 imposes a finality rule. Surprisingly enough, this has been interpreted in a manner similar to that hammered out in the cases under § 1291. Indeed, the cases under the two statutes are often cited interchangeably.

Question: (7) Why could one properly term this similarity "surprising"? Would you have expected the § 1257 standard to be more or less hospitable to appeal than that of § 1291? See Note, The Finality Rule for Supreme Court Review of State Court Orders, 91 Harv.L.Rev. 1004 (1978).

State decision to higher state court.—With respect to review of state decisions by a higher state court, there was a tendency in the young states to depart from the old English system with its insistence on a final judgment rule at law and its freedom of interlocutory appeals in equity. Often the state legislation required finality both at law and in equity. The merger of law and equity under the codes, and the emergence of the codes' one form of action, seemed to accentuate the trend. But a finality rule worked serious hardship in long and complicated equity litigation, and the result was a series of attempts to engraft exceptions upon the statutory rule.

Modern state statutes reflect both the force of the old law tradition and the dissatisfactions engendered by its strict application. Very common is the theme that the trial court must have rendered a final adjudication winding up the case before review becomes available, but very often a countertheme appears in the way of statutory exceptions. Moreover, the words of the statutes cannot be taken at face value, as judicial decision sometimes belies the statutory language.

1. In some states, the statute authorizes appeals only from "final judgments and orders," but it goes on to define final orders in such a way as to include orders that fall far short of the common-law concept of finality. Judicial constructions of finality vary too, of course.

2. Elsewhere, the statutes define in generalized terms the kinds of interlocutory orders from which appeals may be taken, such as "any intermediate order involving the merits and necessarily affecting the judgment" or "any order affecting a substantial right which determines the action and prevents a judgment." These phrases do not receive uniform construction and may be either a narrow or a broad avenue to appeal. For example, courts often hold the quoted language not to authorize an appeal from an order sustaining or overruling a demurrer or other motion to dismiss for insufficiency of statement, with the result that the aggrieved party must stand on his pleading and submit to a judgment in order to obtain immediate appellate review of the ruling.

3. A number of legislatures have sought to avoid some of these uncertainties arising under general definitions by specifying particular interlocutory orders as appealable, such as orders granting or (less fre-

quently) denying a new trial and orders sustaining or overruling a demurrer. The list could be short or very long. But even such specificity may be frustrated by judicial decisions invoking what the judges think are first principles. For instance, although Iowa had long authorized an appeal from an "order which . . . sustains or overrules a demurrer," Iowa Code § 12823 (1927), it was held in Devoe v. Dusey, 205 Iowa 1262, 217 N.W. 625 (1928), that "a party may not appeal from an adverse ruling on a demurrer unless he elects to stand upon his pleading or suffers judgment for want of pleading or of amendment to his pleading." The court went on to say: "The reason for such a rule is manifest. . . . To allow an appeal from a mere ruling by the trial court in settling the issues would open the door to endless appeals to this court from rulings that lack finality."

4. Other state approaches are to permit interlocutory appeals in the discretion of either the appellate court or the trial court.

5. Full appreciation of the appeal system in any state must take account of the possibilities of review by means of extraordinary writs instead of appeal.

In sum, taking into account the several states' statutes and the decisions interpreting them, we find a range from a pretty strict insistence on finality, beyond the lines of the federal model, to an extreme liberality in permitting interlocutory appeals, as has been traditional in New York.

TOPIC C

Appeal of Interlocutory Decisions

Carson v. American Brands, Inc.

Supreme Court of the United States, 1981.
450 U.S. 79, 101 S.Ct. 993.

■ Justice Brennan delivered the opinion of the Court.

The question presented in this Title VII class action is whether an interlocutory order of the District Court denying a joint motion of the parties to enter a consent decree containing injunctive relief is an appealable order.

I

Petitioners, representing a class of present and former black seasonal employees and applicants for employment at the Richmond Leaf Department of the American Tobacco Company, brought this suit in the United States District Court for the Eastern District of Virginia under 42 U.S.C. § 1981 and Title VII of the Civil Rights Act of 1964, 42 U.S.C. § 2000e et seq. Alleging that respondents[1] had discriminated against them in hiring, promotion, transfer, and training opportunities, petitioners sought a declaratory judgment, preliminary and permanent injunctive relief, and money damages.

After extensive discovery had been conducted and the plaintiff class had been certified,[2] the parties negotiated a settlement and jointly moved the District Court to approve and enter their proposed consent decree. See Fed.Rules Civ.Proc. 23(e). The decree would have required respondents to give hiring and seniority preferences to black employees and to fill one-third of all supervisory positions in the Richmond Leaf Department with qualified blacks. While agreeing to the terms of the decree, respondents "expressly den[ied] any violation of . . . any . . . equal employment law, regulation, or order." Jt.App., at 25a.

---

1 Respondents in this case are: American Brands, Inc., which operates the Richmond Leaf Department of the American Tobacco Company; Local 182 of the Tobacco Workers International Union, the exclusive bargaining agent for all hourly paid production unit employees of the Richmond Leaf Department; and the International Union.

2 The class was certified pursuant to Fed.Rule Civ.Proc. 23(b)(2). It consisted of black persons who were employed as seasonal employees at the Richmond Leaf Department on or after September 9, 1972, and black persons who applied for seasonal employment at the Department on or after that date.

The District Court denied the motion to enter the proposed decree. Carson v. American Brands, Inc., 446 F.Supp. 780 (E.D.Va.1977). Concluding that preferential treatment on the basis of race violated Title VII and the Constitution absent a showing of past or present discrimination, and that the facts submitted in support of the decree demonstrated no "vestiges of racial discrimination," id., at 790, the court held that the proposed decree illegally granted racial preferences to the petitioner class. It further declared that even if present or past discrimination had been shown, the decree would be illegal in that it would extend relief to *all* present and future black employees of the Richmond Leaf Department, not just to *actual* victims of the alleged discrimination. Id., at 789.

The United States Court of Appeals for the Fourth Circuit, sitting en banc, dismissed petitioners' appeal for want of jurisdiction. Carson v. American Brands, Inc., 606 F.2d 420 (C.A.4 1979). It held that the District Court's refusal to enter the consent decree was neither a "collateral order" under 28 U.S.C. § 1291, nor an interlocutory order "refusing" an "injunctio[n]" under 28 U.S.C. § 1292(a)(1). Three judges dissented, concluding that the order refusing to approve the consent decree was appealable under 28 U.S.C. § 1292(a)(1).

Noting a conflict in the circuits,[6] we granted certiorari. 447 U.S. 920, 100 S.Ct. 3009 (1980). We hold that the order is appealable under 28 U.S.C. § 1292(a)(1), and accordingly reverse the Court of Appeals.[7]

II

The First Judiciary Act of 1789, 1 Stat. 73, established the general principle that only *final* decisions of the Federal District Courts would be reviewable on appeal. 28 U.S.C. § 1291. [Citations omitted.] Because rigid application of this principle was found to create undue hardship in some cases, however, Congress created certain exceptions to it. [Citation omitted.] One of these exceptions, 28 U.S.C. § 1292(a)(1), [dates from 1891 and now] permits appeal as of right from "[i]nterlocutory orders of the district courts . . . granting, continuing, modifying, *refusing* or dissolving *injunctions* . . . ." (Emphasis added.)

Although the District Court's order declining to enter the proposed consent decree did not in terms "refus[e]" an "injunctio[n]," it nonetheless had the practical effect of doing so. Cf. General Electric Co. v. Marvel Rare Metals Co., 287 U.S. 430, 433, 53 S.Ct. 202, 203 (1932). This is because the proposed decree would have permanently enjoined respondents from dis-

[6] Compare Norman v. McKee, 431 F.2d 769 (C.A.9 1970), cert. denied, 401 U.S. 912, 91 S.Ct. 879 (1971) (refusal to enter consent decree appealable under § 1291), and United States v. City of Alexandria, 614 F.2d 1358 (C.A.5 1980) (refusal to enter consent decree appealable under § 1292(a)(1)), with Seigal v. Merrick, . . . 590 F.2d 35 [(2d Cir.1978)] (not appealable under § 1291), and Carson v. American Brands, Inc., 606 F.2d 420 (C.A.4 1979) (not appealable under § 1291 or § 1292(a)(1)). See also In re International House of Pancakes Franchise Litigation, 487 F.2d 303 (C.A.8 1973) (refusal to enter proposed settlement agreement appealable; no discussion of jurisdictional question).

[7] We therefore need not decide whether the order is also appealable under 28 U.S.C. § 1291.

criminating against black employees at the Richmond Leaf Department, and would have directed changes in seniority and benefit systems, established hiring goals for qualified blacks in certain supervisory positions, and granted job bidding preferences for seasonal employees. Indeed, prospective relief was at the very core of the disapproved settlement.

For an interlocutory order to be immediately appealable under § 1292(a)(1), however, a litigant must show more than that the order has the practical effect of refusing an injunction. Because § 1292(a)(1) was intended to carve out only a limited exception to the final judgment rule, we have construed the statute narrowly to ensure that appeal as of right under § 1292(a)(1) will be available only in circumstances where an appeal will further the statutory purpose of "permit[ting] litigants to effectually challenge interlocutory orders of serious, perhaps irreparable, consequence." Baltimore Contractors, Inc. v. Bodinger, [348 U.S. 176, 181, 75 S.Ct. 249, 252 (1955)]. Unless a litigant can show that an interlocutory order of the District Court might have "serious, perhaps irreparable, consequence," and that the order can be "effectually challenged" only by immediate appeal, the general congressional policy against piecemeal review will preclude interlocutory appeal.

In Switzerland Cheese Association, Inc. v. E. Horne's Market, Inc., 385 U.S. 23, 87 S.Ct. 193 (1966), for example, petitioners contended that the District Court's denial of their motion for summary judgment was appealable under § 1292(a)(1) simply because its practical effect was to deny them the permanent injunction sought in their summary judgment motion. Although the District Court order seemed to fit within the statutory language of § 1292(a)(1), petitioners' contention was rejected because they did not show that the order might cause them irreparable consequences if not immediately reviewed. The motion for summary judgment sought permanent and not preliminary injunctive relief and petitioners did not argue that a denial of summary judgment would cause them irreparable harm pendente lite. Since permanent injunctive relief might have been obtained after trial, the interlocutory order lacked the "serious, perhaps irreparable, consequence" that is a prerequisite to appealability under § 1292(a)(1).

Similarly, in Gardner v. Westinghouse Broadcasting Co., 437 U.S. 478, 98 S.Ct. 2451 (1978), petitioner in a Title VII sex discrimination suit sought a permanent injunction against her prospective employer on behalf of herself and her putative class. After the District Court denied petitioner's motion for class certification, petitioner filed an appeal under § 1292(a)(1). She contended that since her complaint had requested injunctive relief, the court's order denying class certification had the effect of limiting the breadth of the available relief, and therefore of "refus[ing] a substantial portion of the injunctive relief requested in the complaint." 437 U.S., at 480, 98 S.Ct., at 2453.

As in Switzerland Cheese, petitioner in Gardner had not filed a motion for a preliminary injunction and had not alleged that a denial of her motion would cause irreparable harm. The District Court order thus had "no direct or irreparable impact on the merits of the controversy." Id., at 482, 98 S.Ct., at 2454. Because the denial of class certification was conditional, Fed.Rules Civ.Proc. 23(c)(1), and because it could be effectively reviewed on appeal from final judgment, petitioner could still obtain the full permanent injunctive relief she requested and a delayed review of the District Court order would therefore cause no serious or irreparable harm. As Gardner stated:

> "The order denying class certification in this case did not have any such 'irreparable' effect. It could be reviewed both prior to and after final judgment; it did not affect the merits of petitioner's own claim; and it did not pass on the legal sufficiency of any claims for injunctive relief." 437 U.S., at 480–481, 98 S.Ct., at 2453–2454 (footnotes omitted).[11]

III

In the instant case, unless the District Court order denying the motion to enter the consent decree is immediately appealable, petitioners will lose their opportunity to "effectually challenge" an interlocutory order that denies them injunctive relief and that plainly has "serious, perhaps irreparable, consequence." First, petitioners might lose their opportunity to settle their case on the negotiated terms. . . . Settlement agreements may . . . be predicated on an express or implied condition that the parties would, by their agreement, be able to avoid the costs and uncertainties of litigation. In this case, that condition of settlement has been radically affected by the District Court. By refusing to enter the proposed consent decree, the District Court effectively ordered the parties to proceed to trial and to have their respective rights and liabilities established within limits laid down by that court. Because a party to a pending settlement might be legally justified in withdrawing its consent to the agreement once trial is held and final judgment entered, the District Court's order might thus have the "serious, perhaps irreparable, consequence" of denying the parties their right to compromise their dispute on mutually agreeable terms.[14]

---

[11] By contrast, General Electric Co. v. Marvel Rare Metals Co., 287 U.S. 430, 53 S.Ct. 202 (1932), a case in which respondents sought to appeal the District Court's dismissal of their counterclaim for injunctive relief on jurisdictional grounds, concluded that the District Court's order *did* have serious, perhaps irreparable, consequence and that it could not be effectually challenged unless an appeal were immediately taken. The Court noted that the District Court "necessarily decided that upon the facts alleged in the counterclaim defendants were not entitled to an injunction," 287 U.S., at 433, 53 S.Ct., at 204, and that this decision resolved "the very question that, among others, would have been presented to the court upon formal application for an interlocutory injunction." Ibid.

[14] Furthermore, such an order would also undermine one of the policies underlying Title VII. In enacting Title VII, Congress expressed a strong preference for encouraging voluntary settlement of employment discrimination claims. . . .

Moreover, post-judgment review of a District Court's refusal to enter a proposed consent decree raises additional problems. Not only might review come after the prevailing party has sought to withdraw its consent to the agreement, but even if the parties continued to support their decree, the Court of Appeals might be placed in the difficult position of having to choose between ordering the agreed-upon relief or affirming the relief granted by the trial court even when such relief rested on different facts or different judgments with respect to the parties' ultimate liability.

There is a second "serious, perhaps irreparable, consequence" of the District Court order that justifies our conclusion that the order is immediately appealable under § 1292(a)(1). In seeking entry of the proposed consent decree, petitioners sought an immediate restructuring of respondents' transfer and promotional policies. They asserted in their complaint that they would suffer irreparable injury unless they obtained that injunctive relief at the earliest opportunity. Because petitioners cannot obtain that relief until the proposed consent decree is entered, any further delay in reviewing the propriety of the District Court's refusal to enter the decree might cause them serious or irreparable harm.

In sum, in refusing to approve the parties' negotiated consent decree, the District Court denied petitioners the opportunity to compromise their claim and to obtain the injunctive benefits of the settlement agreement they negotiated. These constitute "serious, perhaps irreparable, consequences" that petitioners can "effectually challenge" only by an immediate appeal. It follows that the order is an order "refusing" an "injunctio[n]" and is therefore appealable under § 1292(a)(1).

Reversed.[a]

Questions: (1) In a class action for damages, does an appeal under § 1292(a)(1) lie from an order disapproving a proposed settlement that includes an injunctive provision simply forbidding the defendant from violating particular federal laws? See New York v. Dairylea Co–op., 698 F.2d 567, 570–71 (2d Cir.1983) (suggesting no). In a Title VII class action for an injunction, does disapproving a proposed settlement that includes an injunctive provision necessarily entail a consequence sufficiently serious to satisfy Carson? See Grant v. Local 638, 373 F.3d 104, 108–09 (2d Cir.2004) (suggesting no).

(2) Where a decision of a district court is interlocutory, but appealable under § 1292(a)(1), and the party aggrieved does not appeal from the decision, is she legally foreclosed from any review of it by the court of appeals later in the case? See 19 Moore § 203.10[7][a] (normally no). More generally, where a mid-civil-case decision of a district court is appealable under some doctrine or provision, and the party aggrieved does not appeal from the decision, is she legally foreclosed from subsequent review? See 15A Wright, Miller & Cooper § 3905.1, at 261–62 (distin-

---

In addition, delaying appellate review until after final judgment would adversely affect the Court of Appeals' ability fairly to evaluate the propriety of the District Court's order. Courts judge the fairness of a proposed compromise by weighing the plaintiff's likelihood of success on the merits against the amount and form of the relief offered in the settlement. See Protective Comm. for Independent Stockholders v. Anderson, 390 U.S. 414, 424–425, 88 S.Ct. 1157, 1163–1164 (1968). They do not decide the merits of the case or resolve unsettled legal questions. Since the likely outcome of a trial is best evaluated in light of the state of facts and perceptions that existed when the proposed consent decree was considered, appellate review would be more effective if held prior to the trial court's factfinding rather than after final judgment when the rights and liabilities of the parties have been established.

[a] On remand, the court of appeals ruled in a short opinion that the district court had abused its discretion by refusing to enter the consent decree, 654 F.2d 300 (4th Cir.1981) (in banc) (per curiam).

guishing Rule 54(b), for which immediate appeal is mandatory, from other doctrines and provisions).

North Supply Co. v. Greater Development & Services Corp.

United States Court of Appeals, Sixth Circuit, 1984.
728 F.2d 363.

[North Supply contracted with GDSC for the latter to represent the former in an attempt to sell telephone equipment to the Nigerian military. The deal with Nigeria ultimately fell through under unusual circumstances. Strangely, however, the agency contract, which had an arbitration clause covering disputes under the contract, seemed to entitle GDSC to a commission. So North Supply brought this action to reform the contract, rather than paying. Then GDSC instituted arbitration proceedings.

[GDSC moved to *stay the court proceedings*s pending arbitration. The district court denied the motion, ruling that reformation was a matter for court determination. The court of appeals dismissed GDSC's appeal as not involving an "injunction" within 28 U.S.C. § 1292(a)(1), the order below relating only to the conduct or progress of litigation before the district court.

[Also, North Supply had moved to *stay the arbitration proceedings* pending litigation. The district court had denied this motion too. Now, on a cross-appeal, the court of appeals faced the issue of appealability under § 1292(a)(1) of refusals to stay arbitration.]

■ Before KENNEDY and JONES, CIRCUIT JUDGES, and GILMORE, DISTRICT JUDGE.

■ NATHANIEL R. JONES, CIRCUIT JUDGE.

. . . .

. . . This issue is one which has evoked widespread disagreement among the various circuits in which it has been considered. In fact, not only have these circuits disagreed on the appealability of such orders, but the rationale for allowing or denying an appeal in such cases varies from circuit to circuit.

The Ninth Circuit was apparently the first to consider this issue. In A. & E. Plastik Pak Co. v. Monsanto Co., 396 F.2d 710, 713 (9th Cir.1968), that circuit held that orders granting or denying stays of arbitration were a "classic form of injunction" and, hence, appealable under § 1292(a)(1):

> Here the court was asked . . . affirmatively to interfere with proceedings in another forum; to exercise its equity powers to halt action of its litigants outside of its own court proceedings—the classic form of injunction.

The Ninth Circuit has since affirmed this position with no further analysis or rationale. Power Replacements, Inc. v. Air Preheater Co., 426 F.2d 980, 982 (9th Cir.1970).

On the opposite side of the ledger the Second Circuit has held that orders granting or denying stays of arbitration are not injunctions within the meaning of § 1292(a). Greater Continental Corp. v. Schechter, 422 F.2d 1100, 1102–3 (2d Cir.1970). Finding also that such orders were not final orders under § 1291, the Second Circuit held that they were simply nonappealable. Id. The Second Circuit reasoned that § 1292(a) was specifically intended to allow appeals from some orders which, although not final, have serious and perhaps irreparable consequences. Id. at 1103. That court believed that a denial of a stay of arbitration would not cause irreparable consequences because arbitration does not produce an enforceable result absent further judicial action where the arbitral decision can be reviewed. Therefore, in the Second Circuit's view, § 1292(a) could not have been intended to apply to orders granting or denying stays of arbitration. Id.

. . . .

The First Circuit has adopted a hybrid approach to the issue, finding that while orders granting a stay of arbitration are appealable, those denying a stay are not. New England Power Co. v. Asiatic Petroleum Corp., 456 F.2d 183 (1st Cir.1972). That court . . . admitted that the orders were injunctions, but found . . . various policy reasons for not simply resorting to the plain language of § 1292(a) to resolve the issue. The New England Power court reasoned that the important central policies behind the federal arbitration act and the various Supreme Court cases presumptively favoring arbitration in all cases, mandated its hybrid approach. The court addressed and rejected both the Second and Ninth Circuits' approaches, favoring their own intermediate stance:

> Without caviling at the correctness of the label, we are of the opinion that whether an injunction is "classic" or not does not resolve the question when strong countervailing policies are involved. It is one thing to hold as we have, that an order enjoining arbitration is appealable, but quite another to hold that a refusal to so order may be immediately reviewed on motion of one of the parties. A decision to stay impending arbitration may well be an injunction in the "classic" sense since it effectively deprives at least one of the parties to the dispute of one of the principal objects for which he has contracted—that is, a relatively expeditious and inexpensive preliminary resolution of any controversy. A refusal to stay arbitration, on the other hand, has no such potentially adverse impact on the ultimate rights of the parties. The effect of a refusal to intervene is either to permit arbitration to run its course, with the mutual—albeit reluctant—consent of the parties, or if one of the parties persists in refusing to submit to arbitration, to require the party favoring arbitration to move under 9 U.S.C. § 4 for court order compelling the objecting party to go to arbitration.

456 F.2d at 186 (citations omitted). The First Circuit reasoned that its approach would ensure the ultimate protection of the policies embodied in the federal arbitration act in all possible instances.

Though the precise issue before the Court today has not been addressed by this Circuit, this Circuit has addressed the question of the appealability of an order *granting* a stay of arbitration. In Buffler v. Electronic Computer Programming Institute, Inc., 466 F.2d 694 (6th Cir. 1972), a panel of this Court held that an order granting a preliminary injunction against arbitration is appealable under § 1292(a)(1) as an interlocutory order granting an injunction. . . . [T]he decision in that case specifically left open the question of whether or not an order denying a stay of arbitration was also appealable under § 1292(a)(1) . . . . The effective result of the opinion then is to, absent overruling that opinion, give this Court only one of two options: to follow the First Circuit's hybrid approach or to adopt the blanket appealability rule of the Ninth Circuit. Because of the strong federal policies in favor of arbitration and against interlocutory piecemeal appeals, we believe the First Circuit's approach embodies the better view. Accordingly, we hold that the district court's order denying the motion for a stay of arbitration is non-appealable and therefore dismiss the appeal for lack of jurisdiction.[5]

■ CORNELIA G. KENNEDY, CIRCUIT JUDGE, dissenting.

. . . As I read § 1292(a)(1), inquiry is properly directed to the nature of the relief sought rather than to whether the relief was granted or refused.

In Buffler v. Electronic Computer Programming Institute, Inc., 466 F.2d 694 (6th Cir.1972), this Circuit addressed the question of the appealability of an order *granting* a preliminary injunction against arbitration. Dismissing the public policy concerns which led the Second Circuit to prohibit appeals from either denials or grants of stays of arbitration, this Court concluded that not only is it unlikely that arbitration proceedings will be delayed by the appeal from an order denying the stay (because presumably the arbitration would go forth untouched unless an injunction against arbitration pending appeal is issued), but "[i]f there are delays in arbitration which may accompany an appeal from an order denying a stay of arbitration, they do not appear to be as significant as the delays in arbitration which can result from the inability to appeal from an order *granting* a stay of arbitration." Id. at 698 (emphasis in original).

As § 1292(a)(1) mandates that orders granting and refusing injunctions be equally appealable or non-appealable, I cannot support the majority's hybrid position. Whether an order regarding arbitration takes the form of an order refusing to stay arbitration or an order compelling it will often depend upon which party takes the initiative to have arbitrability determined. If a party refuses to arbitrate, the opposite party must secure an order compelling arbitration. That order is appealable. However, if the party opposing arbitration asks the same court to stay or enjoin arbitration from proceeding on the same basis on which the order compelling arbitra-

[5] In dismissing the appeal, we decline North Supply's invitation to issue a writ of mandamus directed to the district court as an alternative to assuming jurisdiction. Although the district court's orders will result in some duplication, we do not feel that such duplication warrants the extraordinary remedy of mandamus relief.

tion was resisted, the order is not appealable under the majority's holding. Appealability should not rest on such a tenuous distinction.

Because arbitration may well be concluded before an appeal is disposed of, the right to appeal orders denying a stay of arbitration may be illusory. However, the right is accorded by statute. Accordingly, I would hold that interlocutory orders granting or denying stays of arbitration are appealable by right under § 1292(a)(1).[b]

SAUDI BASIC INDUSTRIES CORP. v. EXXON CORP., 364 F.3d 106 (3d Cir.2004). In a dispute between joint venture participants over ownership rights in patented technology, the district court ordered SABIC, in accordance with the participants' agreement, not to practice the technology until ownership rights were determined. SABIC immediately appealed. In upholding appellate jurisdiction before vacating the lower court's order, the court of appeals explained:

"An order need not have the 'literal characterization' of an injunction for § 1292(a)(1) to apply, as long as it has the same practical effect. Hershey Foods Corp. v. Hershey Creamery Co., 945 F.2d 1272, 1276 (3d Cir.1991). We have previously defined an injunctive order as one that is '[1] directed to a party, [2] enforceable by contempt, and [3] designed to accord or protect "some or all of the substantive relief sought by a complaint" in more than a temporary fashion.' Cohen v. Bd. of Trs. of the Univ. of Med. & Dentistry of N.J., 867 F.2d 1455, 1465 n. 9 (3d Cir.1989) (en banc) (quoting 16 Wright, Miller & Cooper, et al., Federal Practice and Procedure § 3922 (1977)) . . . . In contrast, '[o]rders that in no way touch on the merits of the claim but only relate to pretrial procedures' are not interlocu-

---

[b] In 1988 Congress addressed this particular area by enacting 9 U.S.C. § 16, which now provides:

"(a) An appeal may be taken from—

(1) an order—

(A) refusing a stay of any action under section 3 of this title,

(B) denying a petition under section 4 of this title to order arbitration to proceed,

(C) denying an application under section 206 of this title to compel arbitration [pursuant to an international agreement],

(D) confirming or denying confirmation of an award or partial award, or

(E) modifying, correcting, or vacating an award;

(2) an interlocutory order granting, continuing, or modifying an injunction against an arbitration that is subject to this title; or

(3) a final decision with respect to an arbitration that is subject to this title.

"(b) Except as otherwise provided in section 1292(b) of title 28, an appeal may not be taken from an interlocutory order—

(1) granting a stay of any action under section 3 of this title;

(2) directing arbitration to proceed under section 4 of this title;

(3) compelling arbitration under section 206 of this title; or

(4) refusing to enjoin an arbitration that is subject to this title."

tory injunctions within the meaning of § 1292(a)(1). Hershey Foods, 945 F.2d at 1277 (citing Switzerland Cheese Ass'n v. E. Horne's Market, Inc., 385 U.S. 23, 87 S.Ct. 193, 17 L.Ed.2d 23 (1966)).

"We conclude that the June 2002 Order satisfies the three Cohen factors for an effective injunction appealable under 28 U.S.C. § 1292(a)(1). . . .

"Finally, we reject ExxonMobil's argument that SABIC must demonstrate "serious, perhaps irreparable consequences' from the June 2002 Order in order to sustain an appeal. ExxonMobil points to Carson v. American Brands, Inc., 450 U.S. 79, 101 S.Ct. 993, 67 L.Ed.2d 59 (1981), in which the Supreme Court stated that '[u]nless a litigant can show that an interlocutory order of the district court might have a "serious, perhaps irreparable, consequence," and that the order can be "effectually challenged" only by immediate appeal, the general congressional policy against piecemeal review will preclude interlocutory appeal.' Id. at 84, (citing Baltimore Contractors v. Bodinger, 348 U.S. 176, 181, 75 S.Ct. 249, 99 L.Ed. 233 (1955)). But we have since recognized that Carson required the showing of a 'serious, perhaps irreparable consequence' in the context of determining the appealability of an order denying injunctive relief. Cohen, 867 F.2d at 1467. We have consistently refused to require such a showing of an enjoined party appealing an order granting an injunction. See Casey v. Planned Parenthood of S.E. Pa., 14 F.3d 848, 855 (3d Cir.1994) ('Unlike a denial, a grant of injunctive relief subjects the losing party to contempt, and provides some or all of the relief sought by the claimant, two of the key features we identified in Cohen as justifying an interlocutory appeal.'); [other citations omitted]. Thus, because the June 2002 Order granted injunctive relief, SABIC need not show 'serious, perhaps irreparable consequence' to sustain its appeal."

Question: (3) When a district court decision comes up under § 1292(a)(1), to what extent should the appellate court consider matters that go beyond the propriety of granting or refusing the injunction? For example, in reviewing an order that stays certain other judicial or administrative proceedings, should the court of appeals review another order that declines to stay the district court's own proceedings in the same case? See 16 Wright, Miller & Cooper § 3921.1. More generally, when a district court decision on an issue comes up mid-civil-case under some doctrine or provision, to what extent could and should the appellate court consider matters that go beyond the issue? See Joan Steinman, The Scope of Appellate Jurisdiction: Pendent Appellate Jurisdiction Before and After Swint, 49 Hastings L.J. 1337 (1998).

FRED WEBER, INC. v. SHELL OIL CO., 566 F.2d 602 (8th Cir.1977), cert. denied, 436 U.S. 905, 98 S.Ct. 2235 (1978). While allowing a collateral order appeal on a denied disqualification of counsel for conflicting prior representation (an appeal that would not be allowed today under Firestone), the court noted: "Although often phrased as injunctions against further participation in a suit, the disqualification of counsel is not considered an injunction in determining appealability. [Citations omitted.] Appeal under § 1292(b), discretionary with the district and appellate courts, is uncertain in result and not generally used."

Question: (4) Section 1292(b) deals expressly with the matter of staying lower court proceedings while the interlocutory appeal is pending. More generally, while a mid-civil-case district court decision on an issue is up on immediate appeal under some doctrine or provision, to what extent could and should the district court exercise continuing jurisdiction over the rest of the case? See Allan Ides, The Authority of a Federal District Court to Proceed After a Notice of Appeal Has Been Filed, 143 F.R.D. 307 (1993); cf. Federal Rule 62.1.

Kraus v. Board of County Road Commissioners

United States Court of Appeals, Sixth Circuit, 1966.
364 F.2d 919.

[Kraus sued the Board for wrongful death of her intestate in an automobile accident, upon the theory that the Board had failed to keep the roads where the accident occurred in reasonable repair. One of the defenses asserted was the failure to give written notice of claim within sixty days of the date of the accident as provided by a Michigan statute. The district court overruled a defense motion for summary judgment based on this defense, ruling that the statute did not apply to an action for wrongful death, but the court inserted in its order a certification for immediate appeal under 28 U.S.C. § 1292(b).]

■ Before PHILLIPS, EDWARDS and CELEBREZZE, CIRCUIT JUDGES.

■ PHILLIPS, CIRCUIT JUDGE.

. . . .

Section 1292(b) was enacted in 1958, following a study by a committee of the Judicial Conference of the United States, and was endorsed by the Judicial Conference. The purpose of this legislation was explained in the report of the committee, of which the late Judge Shackelford Miller, Jr., of this court was a member, as follows:

> "[W]e have given consideration to the action taken by the circuit conferences and have reached the conclusion that provision should be made for the allowance of appeals from the interlocutory orders in those exceptional cases where it is desirable that this be done to avoid unnecessary delay and expense and that the danger of opening the door to groundless appeals and piecemeal litigation can be avoided by proper limitations to be included in the amendatory statute . . . .

> "Your Committee is of the view that the appeal from interlocutory orders thus provided should and will be used only in exceptional cases where a decision of the appeal may avoid protracted and expensive litigation, as in antitrust and similar protracted cases, where a question which would be dispositive of the litigation is raised and there is serious doubt as to how it should be decided, as in the recent case of Austrian v. Williams (2 Cir., 198 F.2d 697). It is not thought that district judges would grant the certificate in ordinary litigation which could otherwise be promptly disposed of or that mere question as to the correctness of the ruling would prompt the granting of the certificate. The right of appeal given by the amendatory statute is limited both by the requirement of the certificate of the trial judge, who is familiar with the litigation and will not be disposed to countenance dilatory tactics, and by the resting of final discretion in the matter in the court of appeals, which will not permit its docket to be crowded with piecemeal or minor litigation."

. . . .

Although it is not incumbent upon this court to express our reasons for granting or denying an application for permission to take an interlocutory appeal, we do so in the present case. We conclude that this case is not within the class of interlocutory appeals contemplated by the statute . . . .

The granting of an interlocutory appeal in the present case would not "materially advance the ultimate termination of the litigation." Many months would be required before the case would be reached for argument on the congested docket of this court. If we grant the appeal and then should affirm the order of the district court based upon the opinion published in 236 F.Supp. 677, the case then would be remanded to the district court for trial on its merits.

On the other hand, it would appear that only a few days would be required for a jury trial and final disposition of the case in the district court. This procedure, which would avoid a piecemeal appeal, is preferable except in the extraordinary type of case contemplated by § 1292(b).

The application for leave to appeal is denied.

SHURANCE v. PLANNING CONTROL INTERNATIONAL, INC., 839 F.2d 1347 (9th Cir.1988). Defendant moved to disqualify opponent's counsel for ethical misconduct in obtaining privileged information. The district court denied the motion, but certified an appeal under 28 U.S.C. § 1292(b). The court of appeals then denied the petition for leave to appeal. It explained that this was not a "controlling" issue because defendant could still block the plaintiff's use of the information. Moreover, an immediate appeal would not "materially advance the ultimate termination of the litigation" because of the time an appeal would consume. At any rate, this court of appeals in its discretion would reject an appeal so as not to encourage the tactical use of disqualification motions.

Questions: (5) District court certificates under § 1292(b) are rare, and the courts of appeals allow interlocutory appeal on those certificates more rarely still, so that such appeals comprise well fewer than one percent of all appeals. What situations can you suggest in which a § 1292(b) appeal would be appropriate?

(a) Imagine a nonjury action with a long trial in prospect in which, at the start of the testimony, the district judge sustains defendant's objection that an important line of evidence offered by plaintiff is inadmissible. Consider whether appeal under § 1292(b) should be permitted from the judge's ruling.

(b) Imagine a complex action in which, at the pretrial stage, the district judge makes what she sees as a close call in her discretion and stays proceedings on one of the damages counts of the federal complaint until the rather distant completion of a related state court action. Consider whether the judge's ruling fits within the criteria specified in § 1292(b). Are any other avenues of appeal open to the plaintiff? See Note, Appellate Review of Stay Orders in the Federal Courts, 72 Colum.L.Rev. 518, 525–36 (1972) (discussing stay of whole action and so omitting discussion of Rule 54(b)); compare Gulfstream Aerospace Corp. v. Mayacamas Corp., 485 U.S. 271, 108 S.Ct. 1133 (1988) (holding that denial of motion to stay or dismiss the federal action for damages in favor of a similar state action is not a collateral order or denial of an injunction), with Quackenbush v. Allstate Ins. Co., 517 U.S. 706, 116 S.Ct. 1712 (1996) (indicating that grant of a stay of the whole federal action can be an appealable collateral order).

(6) Evaluate the argument that all the foregoing exceptions to the finality standard should be scrapped, and in their place should operate a statute patterned on the "dispatcher" idea of Rule 54(b) but much more broadly applicable: for any nonfinal order the trial judge, familiar with the litigation and the desirability of an interlocutory appeal, could decide to refuse an immediate appeal or, as long as he respects the statutory guidelines enforced by the appellate court's oversight, could decide to allow an immediate appeal. What should those statutory guidelines say? Cf. Timothy P. Glynn, Discontent and Indiscretion: Discretionary Review of Interlocutory Orders, 77 Notre Dame L.Rev. 175 (2001) (proposing categories of appealable orders, plus dispatcher scheme). How, under a dispatcher scheme that aims at both accuracy and certainty, could one deal with the problem of a recalcitrant trial judge who refuses an interlocutory appeal for which there is a real need? See Topic D.

TOPIC D

MANDAMUS

ROCHE v. EVAPORATED MILK ASS'N, 319 U.S. 21, 63 S.Ct. 938 (1943). "The question for decision is whether the Circuit Court of Appeals below rightly issued its writ of mandamus to the district court to correct that court's alleged error in striking respondent's pleas in abatement to a criminal indictment." In deciding in the negative, the Supreme Court noted:

"As the jurisdiction of the circuit court of appeals is exclusively appellate, its authority to issue writs of mandamus is restricted by statute to those cases in which the writ is in aid of that jurisdiction. [28 U.S.C. § 1651(a).] Its authority is not confined to the issuance of writs in aid of a jurisdiction already acquired by appeal but extends to those cases which are within its appellate jurisdiction although no appeal has been perfected. Otherwise the appellate jurisdiction could be defeated and the purpose of the statute authorizing the writ thwarted by unauthorized action of the district court obstructing the appeal. [Citations omitted.]

"The common-law writs, like equitable remedies, may be granted or withheld in the sound discretion of the court. [Citations omitted.] Hence the question presented on this record is not whether the court below had power to grant the writ but whether in the light of all the circumstances the case was an appropriate one for the exercise of that power. In determining what is appropriate we look to those principles which should guide judicial discretion in the use of an extraordinary remedy rather than to formal rules rigorously controlling judicial action. Considerations of importance to our answer here are that the trial court, in striking the pleas in abatement, acted within its jurisdiction as a district court; that no action or omission on its part has thwarted or tends to thwart appellate review of the ruling; and that while a function of mandamus in aid of appellate jurisdiction is to remove obstacles to appeal, it may not appropriately be used merely as a substitute for the appeal procedure prescribed by the statute.

"The traditional use of the writ in aid of appellate jurisdiction both at common law and in the federal courts has been to confine an inferior court to a lawful exercise of its prescribed jurisdiction or to compel it to exercise its authority when it is its duty to do so."

LA BUY v. HOWES LEATHER CO., 352 U.S. 249, 77 S.Ct. 309 (1957). This decision came in a large antitrust case brought in the overcrowded

circumstances and in light of the authorities, the Court of Appeals had such power.

The petitioner, however, also alleged that, even if Rule 35 gives a district court power to order mental and physical examinations of a defendant in an appropriate case, the District Court here exceeded that power in ordering examinations when petitioner's mental and physical condition was not "in controversy" and no "good cause" was shown, both as expressly required by Rule 35. As we read its opinion, the Court of Appeals reached the "in controversy" issue and determined it adversely to petitioner. 321 F.2d, at 51. It did not, however, reach the issue of "good cause," apparently considering that it was not appropriate to do so on a petition for mandamus. Ibid.

We recognize that in the ordinary situation where the sole issue presented is the district court's determination that "good cause" has been shown for an examination, mandamus is not an appropriate remedy, absent, of course, a clear abuse of discretion. See Bankers Life & Casualty Co. v. Holland, supra, 346 U.S., at 383, 74 S.Ct., at 148. Here, however, the petition was properly before the court on a substantial allegation of usurpation of power in ordering any examination of a defendant, an issue of first impression that called for the construction and application of Rule 35 in a new context. The meaning of Rule 35's requirements of "in controversy" and "good cause" also raised issues of first impression. In our view, the Court of Appeals should have also, under these special circumstances, determined the "good cause" issue, so as to avoid piecemeal litigation and to settle new and important problems.

Thus we believe that the Court of Appeals had power to determine all of the issues presented by the petition for mandamus.[8] Normally, wise judicial administration would counsel remand of the cause to the Court of Appeals to reconsider this issue of "good cause." However, in this instance the issue concerns the construction and application of the Federal Rules of Civil Procedure. It is thus appropriate for us to determine on the merits the issues presented and to formulate the necessary guidelines in this area. See Van Dusen v. Barrack, 376 U.S. 612, 84 S.Ct. 805. As this Court stated in Los Angeles Brush Mfg. Corp. v. James, 272 U.S. 701, 706, 47 S.Ct. 286, 288:

> "[W]e think it clear that where the subject concerns the enforcement of the . . . Rules which by law it is the duty of this Court to formulate and put in force . . . it may . . . deal directly with the District Court . . . ."

See McCullough v. Cosgrave, 309 U.S. 634, 60 S.Ct. 703.

This is not to say, however, that, following the setting of guidelines in this opinion, any future allegation that the District Court was in error in

[8] It is not necessary to determine whether or not a refusal by the Court of Appeals to issue the writ, after consideration of the good-cause issue, would have been reversible error. The issuance of this extraordinary writ is itself generally a matter of discretion. See La Buy v. Howes Leather Co., 352 U.S. 249, 260, 77 S.Ct. 309, 315–316; Bankers Life & Casualty Co. v. Holland, supra; 6 Moore, Federal Practice, ¶ 54.10[4] (1953 ed.).

applying these guidelines to a particular case makes mandamus an appropriate remedy. The writ of mandamus is not to be used when "the most that could be claimed is that the district courts have erred in ruling on matters within their jurisdiction." Parr v. United States, 351 U.S. 513, 520, 76 S.Ct. 912, 917; see Bankers Life & Casualty Co. v. Holland, supra, 346 U.S., at 382, 74 S.Ct., at 147.

[Proceeding to the merits, the Supreme Court ultimately vacated and remanded.]

■ [The dissenting opinions of JUSTICE BLACK, with whom Justice Clark joined, and of JUSTICE DOUGLAS did not discuss the propriety of mandamus and are omitted.]

■ MR. JUSTICE HARLAN, dissenting.

In my view the Court's holding that mandamus lies in this case cannot be squared with the course of decisions to which the majority at the threshold pays lip service. . . . As the Court recognizes, mandamus, like the other extraordinary writs, is available to correct only those decisions of inferior courts which involve a "usurpation of judicial power" or, what is tantamount thereto, "a clear abuse of discretion"; such a writ "is not to be used as a substitute for appeal." . . .

Mandamus is found to be an appropriate remedy in this instance, however, because (1) petitioner's challenge was based on an asserted lack of power in the District Court to issue the examination order, and (2) that being so, the Court of Appeals had the right also to inquire into the application of the "in controversy" and "good cause" requirements of Rule 35(a), particularly since those issues, like the question of "power," were matters of "first impression" which in "these special circumstances" should be determined by the Court of Appeals "so as to avoid piecemeal litigation and to settle new and important problems." . . .

For me this reasoning is unacceptable. Of course a court of appeals when confronted with a substantial challenge to the power of a district court to act in the premises may proceed to examine that question without awaiting its embodiment in a final judgment, as the Court of Appeals did here by issuing an order to show cause why a writ of mandamus should not issue. But once it is determined that the challenged power did exist, and that the district court acted within the limit of that power, an extraordinary writ should be denied. I know of no case which suggests that a court of appeals' right to consider such a question at an interlocutory stage of the litigation also draws to the court the right to consider other questions—here the "in controversy" and "good cause" issues—which otherwise would not be examinable upon a petition for an extraordinary writ. . . . And, as the Court correctly states, the fact that "hardship may result from delay and perhaps unnecessary trial," . . . is not a factor that makes for the issuance of such a writ.

Manifestly, today's procedural holding, when stripped of its sugar-coating, is born of the Court's belief that the petitioner should not be exposed to the rigors of these examinations before the proper "guidelines" have been established by this tribunal. Understandable as that point of view may be, it can only be indulged at the expense of making a deep inroad into the firmly established federal policy which, with narrow exceptions, permits appellate review only of the final judgments of district courts. To be sure the Court is at pains to warn that what is done today puts an end to future "interlocutory" review of Rule 35 questions. . . . Nevertheless, I find it hard to escape the conclusion that this decision may open the door to the extraordinary writs being used to test any question of "first impression," if it can be geared to an alleged lack of "power" in the district court. . . .

The Court of Appeals having correctly concluded, as this Court now holds and as I agree, that the District Court had power to order the physical and mental examinations of this petitioner, and since I believe that there was no clear abuse of discretion in its so acting, I think the lower court was quite right in denying mandamus, and I would affirm its judgment on that basis.

Will v. United States

Supreme Court of the United States, 1967.
389 U.S. 90, 88 S.Ct. 269.

[Judge Will, a United States District Judge for the Northern District of Illinois, in a pretrial order in a criminal tax-evasion case directed the government to respond to a bill of particulars through which the defendant sought information concerning any of his oral statements relied upon by the prosecution, including identification of the persons to whom they were made, whether those persons were government agents, whether the government had transcripts or memoranda of the statements, and the substance of any of the statements made to government agents. The government refused to comply and, facing dismissal of the indictment, sought a writ of mandamus to compel the judge to vacate his order. The Court of Appeals for the Seventh Circuit at first denied the writ, but on reconsideration reversed itself and issued the writ without opinion. Judge Will's petition for certiorari was granted "because of the wide implications of the decision below for the orderly administration of criminal justice in the federal courts."]

■ MR. CHIEF JUSTICE WARREN delivered the opinion of the Court.

. . . .

Both parties have devoted substantial argument in this Court to the propriety of petitioner's order. In our view of the case, however, it is unnecessary to reach this question.[4] The peremptory writ of mandamus has

---

[4] It is likewise unnecessary for us to reach the question whether the writ in the circumstances of this case may be said to issue in aid of an exercise of the Court of Appeals' appellate jurisdiction. See 28 U.S.C. § 1651; Roche v. Evaporated Milk Assn., 319 U.S. 21, 25, 63 S.Ct. 938, 941 (1943). Compare In re United States, 348 F.2d 624 (1st Cir.1965), with

traditionally been used in the federal courts only "to confine an inferior court to a lawful exercise of its prescribed jurisdiction or to compel it to exercise its authority when it is its duty to do so." Roche v. Evaporated Milk Assn., 319 U.S. 21, 26, 63 S.Ct. 938, 941 (1943). While the courts have never confined themselves to an arbitrary and technical definition of "jurisdiction," it is clear that only exceptional circumstances amounting to a judicial "usurpation of power" will justify the invocation of this extraordinary remedy. De Beers Consol. Mines, Ltd. v. United States, 325 U.S. 212, 217, 65 S.Ct. 1130, 1132 (1945). Thus the writ has been invoked where unwarranted judicial action threatened "to embarrass the executive arm of the government in conducting foreign relations," Ex parte Peru, 318 U.S. 578, 588, 63 S.Ct. 793, 799 (1943), where it was the only means of forestalling intrusion by the federal judiciary on a delicate area of federal-state relations, Maryland v. Soper, 270 U.S. 9, 46 S.Ct. 185 (1926), where it was necessary to confine a lower court to the terms of an appellate tribunal's mandate, United States v. United States Dist. Court, 334 U.S. 258, 68 S.Ct. 1035 (1948), and where a district judge displayed a persistent disregard of the Rules of Civil Procedure promulgated by this Court, La Buy v. Howes Leather Co., 352 U.S. 249, 77 S.Ct. 309 (1957); [other citations omitted]. And the party seeking mandamus has "the burden of showing that its right to issuance of the writ is 'clear and indisputable.'" Bankers Life & Cas. Co. v. Holland, 346 U.S. 379, 384, 74 S.Ct. 145, 148 (1953); [other citation omitted].

We also approach this case with an awareness of additional considerations which flow from the fact that the underlying proceeding is a criminal prosecution. . . . This general policy against piecemeal appeals takes on added weight in criminal cases . . . . It is enough to note that we approach the decision in this case with an awareness of the constitutional precepts that a man is entitled to a speedy trial and that he may not be placed twice in jeopardy for the same offense.

In light of these considerations and criteria, neither the record before us nor the cryptic order of the Court of Appeals justifies the invocation of the extraordinary writ in this case.

We do not understand the Government to argue that petitioner was in any sense without "jurisdiction" to order it to file a bill of particulars.[6] . . .

United States v. Bondy, 171 F.2d 642 (2d Cir.1948). In our view, even assuming that the possible future appeal in this case would support the Court of Appeals' mandamus jurisdiction, it was an abuse of discretion for the court to act as it did in the circumstances of this case.

[6] Nor do we understand the Government to argue that a judge has no "power" to enter an erroneous order. Acceptance of this semantic fallacy would undermine the settled limitations upon the power of an appellate court to review interlocutory orders. Neither "jurisdiction" nor "power" can be said to "run the gauntlet of reversible errors." Bankers Life & Cas. Co. v. Holland, 346 U.S. 379, 382, 74 S.Ct. 145, 147 (1953). Courts faced with petitions for the peremptory writs must be careful lest they suffer themselves to be misled by labels such as "abuse of discretion" and "want of power" into interlocutory review of nonappealable orders on the mere ground that they may be erroneous. "Certainly Congress knew that some interlocutory orders might be erroneous when it chose to make them nonreviewable." De Beers Consol. Mines, Ltd. v. United States, 325 U.S. 212, 223, 225, 65 S.Ct. 1130, 1136 (1945) (dissenting opinion of Mr. Justice Douglas).

The Government seeks instead to justify the employment of the writ in this instance on the ground that petitioner's conduct displays a "pattern of manifest noncompliance with the rules governing federal criminal trials." . . .

The action of the Court of Appeals cannot, on the record before us, bear the weight of this justification. There is absolutely no foundation in this record for the Government's assertions concerning petitioner's practice. . . .

. . . .

Even more important in our view, however, than these deficiencies in the record is the failure of the Court of Appeals to attempt to supply any reasoned justification of its action. Had the Government in fact shown that petitioner adopted a policy in deliberate disregard of the criminal discovery rules and that this policy had proved seriously disruptive of the efficient administration of criminal justice in the Northern District of Illinois, it would have raised serious questions under this Court's decision in La Buy v. Howes Leather Co., 352 U.S. 249, 77 S.Ct. 309 (1957).[14] . . .

. . . .

Mandamus is not a punitive remedy. The entire thrust of the Government's justification for mandamus in this case, moreover, is that the writ serves a vital corrective and didactic function. While these aims lay at the core of this Court's decisions in La Buy and Schlagenhauf v. Holder, 379 U.S. 104, 85 S.Ct. 234 (1964), we fail to see how they can be served here without findings of fact by the issuing court and some statement of the court's legal reasoning. A mandamus from the blue without rationale is tantamount to an abdication of the very expository and supervisory functions of an appellate court upon which the Government rests its attempt to justify the action below.

The peremptory common-law writs are among the most potent weapons in the judicial arsenal. "As extraordinary remedies, they are reserved for really extraordinary causes." Ex parte Fahey, 332 U.S. 258, 260, 67 S.Ct. 1558, 1559 (1947). There is nothing in the record here to demonstrate that this case falls into that category, and thus the judgment below cannot stand. What might be the proper decision upon a more complete record, supplemented by the findings and conclusions of the Court of Appeals, we cannot and do not say. Hence the writ is vacated and the cause is remanded to the Court of Appeals for the Seventh Circuit for further proceedings not inconsistent with this opinion.

---

14 The Government also places reliance on Schlagenhauf v. Holder, 379 U.S. 104, 85 S.Ct. 234 (1964), arguing that it "reaffirmed" La Buy. Insofar as it did so, the case does not help the Government here, since we have no quarrel with La Buy, which is simply inapposite where there is no showing of a persistent disregard of the federal rules. And it cannot be contended that Schlagenhauf on its facts supports an invocation of mandamus in this case. The Court there did note that the various questions concerning the construction of Rule 35 were new and substantial, but it rested the existence of mandamus jurisdiction squarely on the fact that there was real doubt whether the District Court had any power at all to order a defendant to submit to a physical examination.

It is so ordered.

■ MR. JUSTICE MARSHALL took no part in the consideration or decision of this case.

■ [The concurring opinion of JUSTICE BLACK is omitted.]

WILL v. CALVERT FIRE INSURANCE CO., 437 U.S. 655, 98 S.Ct. 2552 (1978). The same Judge Will stayed in large part a federal civil action until the completion of previously commenced and substantially identical proceedings in state court. He refused to certify an interlocutory appeal pursuant to 28 U.S.C. § 1292(b).

Calvert, the plaintiff, then petitioned for a writ of mandamus. The Court of Appeals for the Seventh Circuit granted the writ, directing Judge Will to proceed with the federal action. On certiorari, the Supreme Court reversed.

On the one hand, the question of whether the district court had the power to stay the federal action in these particular circumstances seriously split the Supreme Court. In the plurality opinion, Justice Rehnquist ruled that the abstention order was a matter committed to the discretion of the district judge.

On the other hand, there seemed to be little disagreement on the standard for the court of appeals' granting mandamus. On this Justice Rehnquist wrote:

"The correct disposition of this case hinges in large part on the appropriate standard of inquiry to be employed by a court of appeals in determining whether to issue a writ of mandamus to a district court. On direct appeal, a court of appeals has broad authority to 'modify, vacate, set aside or reverse' an order of a district court, and it may direct such further action on remand 'as may be just under the circumstances.' 28 U.S.C. § 2106. By contrast, under the All Writs Act, 28 U.S.C. § 1651(a), courts of appeals may issue a writ of mandamus only when 'necessary or appropriate in aid of their respective jurisdictions.' Whereas a simple showing of error may suffice to obtain a reversal on direct appeal, to issue a writ of mandamus under such circumstances 'would undermine the settled limitations upon the power of an appellate court to review interlocutory orders.' Will v. United States, 389 U.S. 90, 98 n. 6, 88 S.Ct. 269, 275 n. 6 (1967).

"As we have repeatedly reaffirmed in cases such as Kerr v. United States District Court, 426 U.S. 394, 402, 96 S.Ct. 2119, 2123 (1976), and Bankers Life & Cas. Co. v. Holland, 346 U.S. 379, 382, 74 S.Ct. 145, 147 (1953), the 'traditional use of the writ in aid of appellate jurisdiction both at common law and in the federal courts has been to confine an inferior court to a lawful exercise of its prescribed jurisdiction or to compel it to exercise its authority when it is its duty to do so.' Roche v. Evaporated Milk Assn., 319 U.S. 21, 26, 63 S.Ct. 938, 941 (1943). Calvert makes no contention that petitioner has exceeded the bounds of his jurisdiction.

Rather, it contends that the District Court, in entering the stay order, has refused 'to exercise its authority when it is its duty to do so.' Ibid. There can be no doubt that, where a district court persistently and without reason refuses to adjudicate a case properly before it, the Court of Appeals may issue the writ 'in order that [it] may exercise the jurisdiction of review given by law.' Knickerbocker Insurance Co. v. Comstock, 16 Wall. 258, 270 (1873). 'Otherwise the appellate jurisdiction could be defeated and the purpose of the statute authorizing the writ thwarted by unauthorized action of the district court obstructing the appeal.' Roche, supra, 319 U.S., at 25, 63 S.Ct., at 941.

"To say that a court of appeals has the power to direct a district court to proceed to judgment in a pending case 'when it is its duty to do so,' id., at 26, 63 S.Ct., at 941, states the standard but does not decide this or any other particular case. It is essential that the moving party satisfy 'the burden of showing that its right to issuance of the writ is "clear and indisputable."' Bankers Life & Cas. Co., supra, 346 U.S., at 384, 74 S.Ct., at 148, quoting United States v. Duell, 172 U.S. 576, 582, 19 S.Ct. 286, 287 (1899). Judge Will urges that Calvert does not have a 'clear and indisputable' right to the adjudication of its claims in the District Court without regard to the concurrent state proceedings."

Justice Rehnquist then explained his view that the stay was a discretionary matter for the district court. Finally returning to the standard for granting mandamus, he concluded: "Although the District Court's exercise of its discretion may be subject to review and modification in a proper interlocutory appeal, [citation omitted], we are convinced that it ought not to be overridden by a writ of mandamus.[7] Where a matter is committed to the discretion of a district court, it cannot be said that a litigant's right to a particular result is 'clear and indisputable.'"

Justice Blackmun wrote a cryptic opinion concurring in the judgment, but shedding no light on the subject of mandamus.

Justice Brennan, writing for a group of four dissenters, concluded that the district court had no authority to issue its stay order. On mandamus Justice Brennan wrote: "Whether evaluated under the 'clear abuse of

---

[7] Although in at least one instance we approved the issuance of the writ upon a mere showing of abuse of discretion, La Buy v. Howes Leather Co., 352 U.S. 249, 257, 77 S.Ct. 309, 314 (1957), we warned soon thereafter against the dangers of such a practice. "Courts faced with petitions for the peremptory writs must be careful lest they suffer themselves to be misled by labels such as 'abuse of discretion' and 'want of power' into interlocutory review of nonappealable orders on the mere ground that they may be erroneous." Will, supra, 389 U.S., at 98 n. 6, 88 S.Ct., at 275 n. 6.

Beacon Theatres, Inc. v. Westover, 359 U.S. 500, 79 S.Ct. 948 (1959), is not to the contrary. Both the Court and the dissenters agreed that mandamus should issue to protect a clear right to a jury trial. Id., at 511, 79 S.Ct., at 957; ibid. (Stewart, J., dissenting). The Court simply concluded that it was "not permissible," id., at 508, 79 S.Ct., at 955, for the District Court to postpone a jury trial until after most of the relevant issues had been settled in an equitable action before the court. Here, we have repeatedly recognized that it is permissible for a district court to defer to the concurrent jurisdiction of a state court. [For an approving account of the recent waning of the special willingness to grant mandamus to protect the jury right, see Nathan A. Forrester, Comment, Mandamus as a Remedy for the Denial of Jury Trial, 58 U.Chi.L.Rev. 769 (1991).—Ed.]

discretion' standard set forth in La Buy v. Howes Leather Co., 352 U.S. 249, 257, 77 S.Ct. 309, 314 (1957), or under the prong of Will v. United States, 389 U.S. 90, 95, 88 S.Ct. 269, 273 (1967), and Roche v. Evaporated Milk Assn., 319 U.S. 21, 26, 63 S.Ct. 938, 941 (1943), that permits the use of mandamus 'to compel [an inferior court] to exercise its authority when it is its duty to do so,' the issuance of the writ of mandamus by the Court of Appeals was proper . . . ."

Question: (1) Adopting Justice Rehnquist's rationale in Will v. Calvert Fire Insurance Co., the Supreme Court summarily reversed the court of appeals' issuance of a writ of mandamus overturning the trial judge's grant of a new trial in Allied Chemical Corp. v. Daiflon, Inc., 449 U.S. 33, 101 S.Ct. 188 (1980) (per curiam) ("In short, our cases have answered the question as to the availability of mandamus in situations such as this with the refrain: 'What never? Well, *hardly* ever!' "). In what circumstances would granting a new trial warrant mandamus? See Central Microfilm Serv. Corp. v. Basic/Four Corp., 688 F.2d 1206, 1212 (8th Cir.1982) (issuing mandamus to overturn grant of new trial and observing that "a district court's action generally must be 'blatantly wrong' to justify mandamus relief").

IN RE AMERICAN CABLE PUBLICATIONS, INC., 768 F.2d 1194 (10th Cir.1985). The district court in this civil case granted a motion to disqualify opponent's counsel for conflict of interest, on the ground that a lawyer-litigant cannot be represented by his or her law partner. The court of appeals granted mandamus, with the writ justified by the "exceptional circumstances" that the district court's legal position was clearly wrong, the petitioner had no adequate remedy other than mandamus, and the point of law was an important general one.

Questions: (2) Mandamus is available under these Supreme Court decisions in certain circumstances, that is, where two requirements are met: (a) the case ultimately could be within the court of appeals' jurisdiction, but the petitioner has no other means to get adequate relief, and (b) the petition passes the threshold screening test of a clear and indisputable showing that the district court has committed reversible error by usurping power, disregarding a duty to exercise power, or perhaps just abusing its discretion. Given those circumstances that generate appellate power to grant mandamus, what considerations should then influence the court of appeals' discretion in whether actually to issue the writ? Should they be the benefits and costs of immediate review, such as whether pursuing instead a regular appeal would result in irreparable harm? Do they include considering the supervisory and advisory functions suggested, respectively, by La Buy and Schlagenhauf?

(3) Will not the discretionary considerations on mandamus affect the threshold decision on appellate power to issue the writ? If so, will not the standard for

mandamus inevitably become one that requires only a clear and indisputable showing of the desirability of immediate review? See Cheney v. U.S. Dist. Court, 542 U.S. 367, 382, 124 S.Ct. 2576, 2588 (2004) (after relating the usual rules, the Court indicated the availability of mandamus to review a discovery order against the Vice President thus: "Accepted mandamus standards are broad enough to allow a court of appeals to prevent a lower court from interfering with a coequal branch's ability to discharge its constitutional responsibilities.").

FREQUENCY OF MANDAMUS

Observe that mandamus was used in the following Supreme Court cases referred to earlier in this casebook: Colgrove v. Battin, p. 144; Carnegie–Mellon University v. Cohill, p. 472; Hoffman v. Blaski, p. 638; Van Dusen v. Barrack, p. 641; Beacon Theatres, Inc. v. Westover, p. 1495; Dairy Queen, Inc. v. Wood, p. 1503. Lower-court cases in which mandamus was used include: Reserve Mining Co. v. Lord, p. 297; Webster Eisenlohr, Inc. v. Kalodner, p. 298; Executive Software North America, Inc. v. United States District Court, p. 448; Borough of West Mifflin v. Lancaster, p. 472; Smoot v. Fox, p. 1367; Bruckman v. Hollzer, p. 1490.

Nevertheless, according to the statistics of the Administrative Office of the United States Courts, only 1.2% of all appeals terminated in fiscal year 2000 were mandamus proceedings, and of those few petitions the courts of appeals granted only 2.3%—or 1⅓ petitions granted per circuit each year. Thus, 16 Wright, Miller, Cooper & Gressman § 3934, at 241 (first edition, with similar viewpoints being expressed in the current 16 Wright, Miller & Cooper §§ 3934.1 & 3935.7), could observe that "stern admonitions that the writs remain reserved for extraordinary situations have been effective in preventing a debilitating rush of petitioners. Substantial benefits have been obtained at seemingly acceptable costs. With considerable luck, this may always be so."

TOPIC E

THEORY ON APPEAL

Change of theory in the pleadings.—In the nineteenth century, many judges were reluctant to pull away too far from the comforting rigidities of the common law's forms of action. Justice Grier of the Supreme Court of the United States expressed the feeling this way: "The distinction between the different forms of action for different wrongs, requiring different remedies, lies in the nature of things; it is absolutely inseparable from the correct administration of justice in common-law courts." McFaul v. Ramsey, 61 U.S. (20 How.) 523, 525 (1858).

That statement came a decade after the Field Code. The code provision requiring the pleader merely to make "a plain and concise statement of the facts constituting a cause of action" had seemed to such judges to countenance, indeed to encourage, an undisciplined approach to pleading wholly at odds with the system that they had known all their professional lives, which they believed to be not only right but eternally so. Consequently, in some states there developed under the early codes a "theory of the pleadings" doctrine. A leading case espousing the doctrine's requirement was Supervisors of Kewaunee County v. Decker, 30 Wis. 624, 629–30, 632–33 (1872), in which Chief Justice Dixon said:

"It thus appears that the authorities relied upon do not sanction the position, that a complaint in the first instance and where challenged by demurrer, may be uncertain and ambulatory, purposely so made, now presenting one face to the court and now another, at the mere will of the pleader, so that it may be regarded as one in tort, or one on contract, or in equity as he is pleased to name it and the necessities of argument require, and if discovered to be good in any of the turns or phases which it may thus be made to assume, that it must be upheld in that aspect, as a proper and sufficient pleading by the court. As already observed, the opinion of the court is quite to the contrary. We have often held that the inherent and essential differences and peculiar properties of actions have not been destroyed, and from their very nature cannot be. Howland v. Needham, 10 Wis. 495, 498. These distinctions continuing, they must be regarded by the courts now as formerly, and now no more than then . . . can any one complaint or count be made to subserve the purposes of two or more distinct and dissimilar causes of action at the option of the party presenting it. It cannot be 'fish, flesh or fowl' according to the appetite of the attorney preparing the dish set before the court. If counsel disagree as to the nature of the action or purpose of the pleading, it is the province of the court to settle the dispute. It is a question when properly raised which cannot be left in doubt, and the court must determine with precision and certainty upon inspection of the pleading to what class of actions it belongs or was intended, whether of tort, upon contract, or in equity, and, if necessary or material, even the exact kind of it within the class must also be determined. [Citations omitted.]

. . . .

" . . . And this we take to be the true rule, that the court must in the first instance decide with certainty what the specific cause of action counted and relied upon is, and, having decided that, it must next determine whether the complaint contains a sufficient statement of such cause, and if it does not, the demurrer must be sustained."

The question posed by this doctrine was not whether the plaintiff must have a theory. He would always be well advised not to institute an action if his analysis disclosed none. The real and recurring problem arose when he wanted to shift his position and embrace a new theory. Was the plaintiff stuck with the originally chosen theory of action, just as the common-law plaintiff had been stuck in his chosen form of action?

We can illustrate the application of the theory of the pleadings requirement by the following case. *P*'s complaint alleges that *D* owned a gray mare, represented by him to be worth $100, which he offered to exchange for *P*'s horse, worth $100; that *P* relying on *D*'s representations left his horse at an agreed place, where *D* picked it up; that *D* failed to leave his gray mare there as agreed, but instead left a bay mare of no value, which later died; that *P* promptly notified *D* of his dissatisfaction with the bay mare; that *D* did not have the gray mare in his possession and did not intend to deliver it as agreed, but falsely represented to *P* that he would do so and thereby induced *P* to part with his horse; and that *D* made his statements knowing them to be false with intent to defraud *P*. The complaint asks for $100 damages. The answer denies the material allegations of the complaint. The court finds the facts as alleged by *P*, except that *D* did not knowingly make false statements to induce *P* to part with his horse and that the value of the gray mare promised by *D* was $30. *D* argues, in true theory of the pleadings fashion, that *P*'s theory was fraud and that, not having proved fraud, *P* must fail. *P* argues that, without proof of fraud, he has nevertheless alleged and proved all the elements of breach of contract. What result?

The court in the case from which we drew the illustration, Knapp v. Walker, 73 Conn. 459, 47 A. 655 (1900), accepted *P*'s argument and allowed recovery. The Wisconsin court of Chief Justice Dixon's day, and later, would not. Indeed, that court would not even allow an amendment changing the theory before trial. See Supervisors of Kewaunee County v. Decker, 34 Wis. 378 (1874) (a second appeal); Klipstein v. Raschein, 117 Wis. 248, 94 N.W. 63 (1903). Wisconsin did a complete turnabout, however, and by 1911 the theory of the pleadings doctrine was dead in that state. The change may be observed in Bieri v. Fonger, 139 Wis. 150, 120 N.W. 862 (1909); Bruheim v. Stratton, 145 Wis. 271, 129 N.W. 1092 (1911); and Frechette v. Ravn, 145 Wis. 589, 130 N.W. 453 (1911).

In some code states, theory of the pleadings philosophy seems never to have exerted much influence. Other states, like Wisconsin, were at one time attracted to it but have since abandoned it. In very few jurisdictions must litigants still to some degree reckon with it as a factor at the trial level.

Question: (1) As a plaintiff's lawyer operating under the theory of the pleadings doctrine, how could you seek to avoid its pitfalls? Would such stratagem undermine any justifiable rationale of the doctrine?

In 1931, the following proposal was advanced in New York: "A party shall no longer be permitted to plead several causes of action or counterclaims arising out of a single transaction or connected set of facts, but shall be required to make a single statement of the transaction or facts, followed by a statement of the various legal theories upon which he claims to be entitled to recover under those facts. He may demand one or more kinds of relief warranted by the facts and legal theories pleaded, whether legal or equitable or both. He shall not be required to elect as between the various theories, but a verdict shall be rendered upon each separate claim, unless the court shall dismiss the action or direct a verdict as to such claim. If there are different measures of damage for the various legal theories pleaded, he shall be entitled to recover the highest measure of damages on any of the theories proven." Comm. on Law Reform of the Ass'n of the Bar of the City of N.Y., Tentative Proposals for Changes in Civil Procedure and Practice 14 (1931). This proposal precisely corresponded to a method of pleading that had long been followed in Scotland, where each party was "required to append to his unitary statement of facts a 'concise note of the legal propositions' upon which he rests his claim or defense," a correspondence pointed out by Robert Wyness Millar, Civil Procedure of the Trial Court in Historical Perspective 196 (1952). See Elizabeth G. Thornburg, Detailed Fact Pleading: The Lessons of Scottish Civil Procedure, 36 Int'l Law. 1185 (2002).

Question: (2) Was the New York proposal a meritorious one? If it were adopted, to what extent should a party be bound by his statement of legal theory?

It was undoubtedly the intent of the framers of the Federal Rules in 1938 to do away with the theory of the pleadings doctrine, and the decided cases show that a great measure of success has been achieved. "The Federal Rules, drafted in the midst of the realist movement, drew on a newly emerging understanding of law. . . . The realist perception of doctrine as dynamic supported the rejection of any reference to 'causes of action' in the new Federal Rules system: if the law springs from the facts and adapts to changing circumstances, then pleading should not be confined to the immutable versions of legal arguments that the established causes of action represented. . . . The drafters believed that decisions about legal validity must be informed by the factual context of the asserted claim. . . . The role of discovery in the Federal Rules scheme supports the realist emphasis on factually informed decisionmaking." Note, Plausible Pleadings: Developing Standards for Rule 11 Sanctions, 100 Harv.L.Rev. 630, 646–47 (1987).

Question: (3) Which provisions of the Rules can be said to have outlawed the theory of the pleadings doctrine in federal practice? Which can be said to preserve some of its spirit? See 5 Wright & Miller § 1219.

Change of theory on appeal.—So, the theory of the pleadings doctrine has by now been buried: consequently, in the trial court the federal rule is that one may change one's grounds as the case evolves, subject to exceptions. But considerations on appeal differ from those in the trial court: accordingly, the general rule remains today that one cannot change even one's theories on appeal, subject to exceptions.

The question posed here is not simply whether a party can introduce a bald-faced new issue on appeal. On the one hand, for good reasons both of history and of policy, the law forecloses most new issues. The ordinary rules of reviewability limit appellate review to asserted errors appearing in the record, subject to the special solicitude for raising subject-matter jurisdiction and subject to the narrowly drawn plain error exception. So, a party generally cannot raise new grounds for appeal. On the other hand, the party can freely refine arguments on appeal. We would surely want to encourage the parties to exercise that freedom. So, a party can forward different legal authority on appeal.

An interesting problem arises in the middle, when the party wants to shift his position and embrace a new theory on a preserved error. For example, can the plaintiff, on appeal from dismissal of the claim, forward a new theory of liability? Carryover policies dictate that the general rule still works here to limit the plaintiff's freedom. But the plaintiff will enjoy somewhat greater freedom than the plain error doctrine alone would provide. That is, the general rule against new issues sees more exceptions in this middle area.

Apex Smelting Co. v. Burns

United States Court of Appeals, Seventh Circuit, 1949.
175 F.2d 978, cert. denied, 338 U.S. 911, 70 S.Ct. 350 (1950).

■ Before MAJOR, CHIEF JUDGE, KERNER and DUFFY, CIRCUIT JUDGES.

■ MAJOR, CHIEF JUDGE. This is an appeal from a judgment in defendants' favor, entered September 14, 1948, following a directed verdict, allowed on defendants' motion, at the conclusion of plaintiff's case.

Plaintiff filed its complaint against the defendants, alleging that it was the owner and in possession of certain described premises located in the city of Chicago, Illinois, and was in the exercise of due care and caution for the preservation of such premises from injury and harm, and was active in the conduct and operation of a large and commodious manufacturing plant. That its plant might have care and protection from sabotage and other interruption of efficient operation, plaintiff and defendants on February 2, 1943, entered into a certain written agreement, which is set forth verbatim in the complaint, the salient portions of which are as follows: The defendants agreed to furnish a uniformed armed guard service consisting of five armed guards or more as might be agreed upon from time to time between the parties for the protection of the property. Such guards were to be guided by a set of general rules and written instructions issued by the plaintiff through its designated representatives. Defendants agreed to pay the expense of equipping the guards, as well as social security, unemployment taxes and employers' liability insurance. Supervision of the guards was made the responsibility of defendants, who in turn were to be responsible to and receive instructions from the plaintiff. The guards were charged with the function of guarding plaintiff's plant in the manner best suited, depending upon the circumstances. It was agreed that the wishes of the plaintiff would be honored at all times consistent with good judgment in replacing guards who in its opinion did not fill the requirements of the service as outlined. The agreement set forth the compensation to be paid defendants by the plaintiff for the services thus rendered and provided that the supervisor in charge of the guard force was to be responsible at all times for the proper functioning of the operation. The service provided was to begin on Monday, February 15, 1943, at 6 a.m., and was to remain in force until the expiration of thirty days' written notice by either or both of the parties to the agreement.

The complaint alleged that the defendants entered upon the performance of the agreement at the time and in the manner provided and that among the armed guards furnished by the defendants was one Harry Frontczak, who on or about the 8th of September, 1946, "while active in his duties, as the servant of the defendants, in, upon and about the premises of the plaintiff, and coincident therewith, from infirmity of temper, and under the influence of passion aroused by real or fancied grievance, did, wilfully and with intent to wreak vengeance upon the plaintiff, cause combustion to take place within the premises of the plaintiff and a conflagration to ensue thereon, to the harm and injury of said premises and to the contents therein." The complaint concluded by alleging that as a result of the combustion caused by the servant of the defendants, plaintiff's premises and contents were damaged by the fire and that it expended large sums of money in the restoration and repair of the same and was damaged by the interruption of operation and delayed production in the amount of $20,000.00 for which judgment against the defendants was sought.

Defendants filed a motion to strike the complaint as insufficient in law and to dismiss the action, specifying the following grounds as reason therefor: (1) the complaint did not charge any act of negligence against the defendants nor that any damage was suffered by the plaintiff through the negligence of or as a direct and proximate result of any negligence on the part of the defendants; (2) the complaint did not charge any breach of contract on the part of the defendants, and (3) the complaint did not charge that the alleged damage was caused as a direct and proximate result of any negligence or breach of contract by any of the defendants' agents, servants or employees, acting within the scope of their authority or employment.

The court took the motion to dismiss under advisement and briefs were filed by the respective parties upon the issues raised by defendants' motion to dismiss. Subsequently the court denied such motion, "without prejudice to the right of the defendants to renew said motion on the same grounds at the end of the plaintiff's case." Thereupon, the defendants by their answer admitted the execution of the agreement with the plaintiff and that they entered upon the performance of the same, as alleged in the complaint. Also, defendants admitted that Harry Frontczak was one of the guards employed by the defendants and assigned to plaintiff's plant, but denied that the acts complained of and committed by him were within the scope of his employment or that such acts were committed while performing any act incident to his employment, and that plaintiff's damage was not sustained as a result of any of defendants' agents or servants acting within the scope of their employment. Defendants' answer, as its motion to dismiss, specifically averred that the complaint did not charge any acts of negligence against the defendants or that any damage was suffered as a result of such negligence, and that the complaint did not charge a breach of contract on the part of the defendants.

In the view which we take of the situation before us, there appears no occasion to narrate plaintiff's testimony in detail. . . .

. . . .

We agree with the lower court that there was no basis for recovery upon the theory of negligence. Plaintiff's evidence showed that Frontczak had been employed by the government in various capacities, in handling its mail, finances, records and personnel during the time of war. Under such circumstances, we think there was no negligence in his employment by defendants. More than that, plaintiff had an equal opportunity to observe his conduct, as well as that of all other guards, and it did not complain or request his removal. We also agree that in setting the fires he was not acting within the scope of his employment or in furtherance of the master's business. [Citations omitted.]

We need not pursue this negligence theory further, however, because it is no longer relied upon. Here, for the first time, plaintiff advances the theory that defendants were liable for breach of contract. As already noted, no such breach was alleged in the complaint and the record is plain that such a theory was not relied upon below. Neither is the liberalized rule which permits the amendment of a pleading to conform to the proof of any benefit to plaintiff. No such amendment was proposed, but even if it had been we doubt if it could have been properly permitted in view of plaintiff's proof. . . .

. . . .

Finally, if we were impressed with the theory of liability argued before this court, which we are not, we would not be justified in reversing the judgment because the case was neither tried nor decided below on such theory. As was said in Helvering v. Rubinstein, 8 Cir., 124 F.2d 969, 972:

"The rule that an appellate court will not ordinarily consider questions not tried below is an important rule of appellate procedure and one which is usually not unjust to litigants. It requires them to deal fairly and frankly with each other and with the trial tribunal with respect to their controversies. It prevents the trial of cases piecemeal or in installments. It tends to put an end to litigation."

And as said by this court in Maloney v. Brandt, 7 Cir., 123 F.2d 779, 782:

"It has long been a rule of practice that a reviewing Court will not consider assignments of error not called to the attention of the trial court where such matters do not concern the jurisdiction of the court. It would manifestly be unfair to hold that the trial court had erred in a matter it had not considered. Litigants are not entitled to hide a point in an obscure pleading and present it for the first time on review, but should fully and fairly acquaint the trial court with all matters relied upon."

. . . In fact, the cases are legion where the same or a similar rule has been announced and followed. [Citations omitted.]

True, there are cases which, while recognizing the general rule, have held that where an injustice will result owing to the particular circumstances of the case, a reviewing court may consider questions which have not been pressed below. See Hormel v. Helvering, 312 U.S. 552, 556–557, 61 S.Ct. 719, 85 L.Ed. 1037. In Lambur v. Yates, 8 Cir., 148 F.2d 137, 138, the reviewing court in noticing an error not raised on the record stated, "This power is and should be sparingly exercised only for the purpose of preventing a miscarriage of justice and in cases in which the public interest is directly and substantially involved." And the exception to the general rule was followed in Schaff v. Claxton, Inc., 79 U.S.App.D.C. 207, 144 F.2d 532, 533, because a decision rendered subsequent to the trial below had changed the law as it was thought to be at the time of trial.

Plaintiff tried its case below on the negligence theory of liability and lost, and we discern nothing in the situation which would justify this court in reversing that decision so that plaintiff may again try its case on a different theory of liability. If the instant plaintiff be permitted to do that, it would seem that the losing party could do it in any case, and the general rule against such procedure would soon become an empty gesture.

The judgment appealed from is affirmed.

■ KERNER, CIRCUIT JUDGE, dissenting.

SEARS, ROEBUCK & CO. v. MARHENKE, 121 F.2d 598 (9th Cir. 1941). Infant *P* was scalded by hot water leaking from a hot water bag purchased from *D*. *P* sued for the resulting injuries. The court tried the case without a jury. *P* obtained a judgment based upon a finding that *D* had been negligent.

P's brief on appeal relied solely upon the theory of negligence. *D* briefed and argued the question of implied warranty, contending it was not involved, and *P* agreed that the real question was one of negligence and not warranty. The circuit court of appeals on oral argument directed the parties' attention to the state statute on implied warranty, and they filed additional briefs on the question.[a] *P* at this point contended "that the allegations of the complaint were sufficient to sustain the judgment upon the ground of a breach of the warranty implied by statute."

The appellate court held the evidence insufficient to sustain a finding of negligence. The court further ruled that to recover under the warranty statute a plaintiff must plead and prove (1) that the buyer informed the seller of the particular purpose for which the goods were required and (2) that the buyer relied upon the seller's skill and judgment. "But," said the court, "the complaint failed to allege [the first] of these essential facts and the trial court made no finding as to the other." It found the pleadings and findings "altogether inconsistent with the theory of liability for breach of an implied warranty advanced in the supplementary brief." Nor was this a case, according to the court, where issues not raised by the pleadings were tried by express or implied consent, so Rule 15(b)(2) had no application. The judgment was reversed, but "without prejudice to the right of plaintiff" to amend.[b]

Judge Healy dissented. He thought that breach of warranty was sufficiently alleged, that *D* was apprised of the essential facts relied upon, that these facts were fully established by the evidence, and that *D* was not prejudiced by *P*'s "insistence on the theory of negligence." He pointed out that *D* made no claim of surprise and could not well do so because a substantial portion of its opening brief on appeal was devoted to a discussion of the warranty theory. He would have affirmed using the warranty theory.

WALL v. BRIM, 138 F.2d 478 (5th Cir.1943), after remand, 145 F.2d 492 (5th Cir.1944), cert. denied, 324 U.S. 857, 65 S.Ct. 858 (1945). Patient

---

[a] A problem distinguishable from the one before us is the sua sponte power of the court to inject a new issue in the case without notice to the parties or against the will of all parties. Presumably, because there are additional reasons not to act, the sua sponte power would exist in a subset of the situations in which the court would allow a party to raise a new issue. See Barry A. Miller, Sua Sponte Appellate Rulings: When Courts Deprive Litigants of an Opportunity to Be Heard, 39 San Diego L. Rev. 1253 (2002).

[b] A similar last-ditch argument was made by the plaintiff in the Sierocinski case, supra p. 41. The case had been pleaded and tried on the ground of negligence, and on appeal *P* attempted to sustain his judgment on the basis of breach of warranty. The court rejected the argument and reversed, ordering final judgment for the defendant. Unlike Marhenke, the reversal was not without prejudice to *P*'s right to amend, very likely because the court thought there was no merit in the breach of warranty theory.

That is to say, the appellate court may in the interest of justice include in its mandate express leave to amend or to apply to the trial court for such relief. See 28 U.S.C. § 2106. This route gives the appellate court, if it inclines toward entertaining a new issue, a significant means to reduce the unfairness to the opposing party.

P sued Dr. *D* for malpractice, claiming negligence in removal of a cyst from *P*'s neck and proving serious facial injury. *D*'s motion for a directed verdict was denied, as was his motion for judgment n.o.v. after a verdict for *P*.

On *D*'s appeal from the ensuing judgment, the circuit court of appeals held that there was no evidence of negligence, because *P* had failed to present any expert evidence. It noted, however, the undisputed evidence from both sides showing how *D* had discovered after making his incision that the operation would not be the simple one he had secured *P*'s consent to perform ("simply pull it out like hulling a pea out of a pod") and that instead it would be a serious and difficult one, and showing that *D* nevertheless went ahead without disclosing these difficulties to the plaintiff, who was still conscious, and without obtaining a new consent. This, the court said, would amount to a battery or trespass for which *D* would be liable. Hence the court did not order judgment for *D*. Nor was the court willing to affirm the judgment for *P*, because the issue as to battery or trespass had not been developed and tried below as it should have been. The cause was remanded for a new trial "with full right to the parties to amend their pleadings."

On remand, the case was tried again on amended pleadings asserting a claim for trespass. This time *D* testified that he told *P* of the unexpected conditions he had found and that she consented to his going ahead. *P* testified that there was no such warning or consent. On this conflicting evidence the jury returned a verdict for *P*.

D again appealed the ensuing judgment. The most strongly argued point on appeal was *D*'s contention that a new cause of action had been introduced by the amendment more than two years after it arose and therefore the two-year statute of limitations was a bar. The court rejected this contention, saying: "As was pointed out in the reversing opinion on the former appeal, the evidence on that trial definitely presented this ground for recovery and, under Federal Rules of Civil Procedure, rule 15(b), . . . it could then have been submitted to the jury if requested, though no formal amendment had been made. Under these circumstances, it would be a sticking in the bark of pure technicality to say that when the pleadings were later formally amended to conform to the evidence, the claim was then first presented. If, therefore, we could agree that the claim on which the verdict and judgment appealed from were based did present a new cause of action, it is quite clear that the introduction of that claim into the case long antedated the filing of the amended pleading." The court added that it could not agree that the claim on which recovery was based constituted a new cause of action, so that Rule 15(c) provided an additional reason to reject *D*'s statute of limitations argument. The judgment was affirmed.

UNIVERSE TANKSHIPS, INC. v. UNITED STATES, 528 F.2d 73 (3d Cir.1975). On appeal from a judgment for defendant in a negligence action tried without a jury, plaintiff attempted to invoke res ipsa loquitur. The court of appeals rebuffed the attempt and affirmed the judgment, explaining that a "different theory of recovery may not be urged on appeal where prejudice would result to the other party. The test for prejudice in this context is whether the other party 'had a fair opportunity to defend and whether it could offer any additional evidence on the different theory.' Jurinko v. Edwin L. Wiegand Co., 477 F.2d 1038, 1045 (3d Cir.), vacated on other grounds, 414 U.S. 970, 94 S.Ct. 293, 38 L.Ed.2d 214 (1973); [other citations omitted].[3]" This case did not fit in the exception:

"We feel that consideration of plaintiff's argument in the nature of res ipsa loquitur would be prejudicial to the government. At the very least, if the government had been aware of this theory at trial it might have been more contentious about the facts of the accident. The government stipulated to several facts . . . and . . . relied primarily on the plaintiff's burden of proving the government negligent rather than offering its own version of the accident. Accordingly, we decline the invitation to reverse the district court on the theory in the nature of res ipsa loquitur, which was not raised in the district court."

ALTMAN v. ALTMAN, 653 F.2d 755 (3d Cir.1981). Sydney sued his brother Ashley to dissolve their partnerships. Defendant alleged that plaintiff's retirement had dissolved the partnerships years earlier, which would change the financial picture considerably. The court by a nonjury trial gave judgment for plaintiff, finding no retirement.

On appeal, defendant contended that plaintiff was estopped from denying retirement by his sworn contrary statements in his Florida divorce proceedings. The court of appeals rejected that contention and affirmed the judgment, explaining:

"Our review of the record reveals that Ashley did not raise this issue in the district court. He did not plead judicial estoppel or argue to the court that Sydney should be estopped from denying he had retired by his statements in the Florida proceedings.[1] We have emphasized that 'absent

---

[3] We recognize that, in Jurinko, we considered the different theory on appeal. There, however, we found no prejudice to the defendant. Moreover, the theory was advanced to affirm the judgment of the district court, rather than to reverse it. . . . [To affirm the plaintiff's judgment after nonjury trial in that employment discrimination case, the court of appeals allowed the theory to shift from discrimination against married women to discrimination against women, saying that the facts disclosed by the proof supported this theory.—Ed.]

[1] Ashley notes that he confronted Sydney with his Florida statements at trial and argued to the court that in light of those statements Sydney's testimony that he had not retired should not be "believed." As a result, Ashley maintains that the "facts" supporting judicial estoppel were presented to the district court, and that any failure to use the term estoppel was merely a technical omission. However, under the estoppel theory now espoused by Ashley, Sydney's statements in the Florida proceedings would be deemed to have conclusively established the fact of his retirement in this litigation. Thus, Ashley's failure to use the term estoppel in the district court cannot be said to be a mere technical omission. Cf. Fed.R.Civ.P. 8(c) (estoppel must be pled as affirmative defense).

exceptional circumstances, an issue not raised in the district court will not be heard on appeal.' Franki Foundation Co. v. Alger–Rau & Associates, Inc., 513 F.2d 581, 586 (3d Cir.1975). Exceptional circumstances have been recognized when the public interest requires that the issue be heard or when manifest injustice would result from the failure to consider the new issue. Id.; see Princeton Community Phone Book, Inc. v. Bate, 582 F.2d 706, 708 n. 1 (3d Cir.), cert. denied, 439 U.S. 966, 99 S.Ct. 454, 58 L.Ed.2d 424 (1978) (first amendment issue not raised in district court considered on appeal because of great public interest); Richerson v. Jones, 572 F.2d 89, 97 (3d Cir.1978) (public interest served by hearing on appeal issue concerning exhaustion of administrative remedies under title VII). In addition, we have considered the merits of an issue raised for the first time on appeal when the new theory was advanced to affirm the district court and prejudice would not result to the other party.[2] See Jurinko v. Edwin L. Wiegand Co., 477 F.2d 1038 (3d Cir.), vacated on other grounds, 414 U.S. 970, 94 S.Ct. 293, 38 L.Ed.2d 214 (1973); cf. Walker v. Sinclair Refining Co., 320 F.2d 302, 305 (3d Cir.1963) (district court should not be reversed on grounds not argued before it).

"We find no exceptional circumstances in this case that would allow Ashley to raise judicial estoppel on appeal. No great public interest would be advanced by consideration of this issue. Moreover, Ashley offers no explanation for his failure to raise judicial estoppel in the district court, and we are not aware of any obstacles that prevented him from doing so. Cf. Princeton Community Phone Book, 582 F.2d at 708 n.1 (first amendment issue heard for first time on appeal because controlling Supreme Court case decided after district court's decision). Therefore, no manifest injustice to Ashley would result if we do not consider this issue. In addition, the new issue raised on appeal is presented as a ground for reversing the district court. As a result, we find that the rule barring a party from raising new issues on appeal precludes our consideration of Ashley's judicial estoppel argument."

PEGUES v. MOREHOUSE PARISH SCHOOL BOARD, 706 F.2d 735 (5th Cir.1983). This was a prolonged and unsuccessful civil rights action, brought by an African–American football coach whom the board had passed over for the position of head coach.

["In short, there are many ways in which a case may present what Singleton describes as 'issues not passed upon below.' Singleton [v. Wulff, 428 U.S. 106, 120, 96 S.Ct. 2868, 2877 (1976)]. One is a bald-faced new issue. Another is a situation where a litigant changes to a new theory on appeal that falls under the same general category as an argument presented at trial. A third is a theory that was discussed in a vague and ambiguous way. A fourth is issues that were raised and then abandoned pre-trial. A fifth is an issue raised for the first time in an untimely motion. These are all different aspects of the same principle that issues not passed upon below will not be considered on appeal." Lyons v. Jefferson Bank & Trust, 994 F.2d 716, 722 (10th Cir.1993).—Ed.]

2 We do not read Universe Tankships, Inc. v. United States, 528 F.2d 73 (3d Cir.1975), as creating a rule that an issue may be raised for the first time on appeal solely because prejudice to the other party would not occur.

On this second appeal in the nonjury case, the plaintiff-appellant contended "for the first time . . . that the district court was bound by principles of res judicata and the law of the case to adhere to the panel's determination in [his earlier appeal], and that his rights accruing thereunder had been violated." The court of appeals responded: "It is axiomatic that an issue not raised in the trial court will not be considered on appeal unless it involves a pure question of law, and our refusal to address it would result in a miscarriage of justice. Coastal States Marketing, Inc. v. Hunt, 694 F.2d 1358 (5th Cir.1983). Recognizing that '[t]he matter of what questions may be taken up and resolved for the first time on appeal . . . .' is committed to the discretion of the courts of appeals the Supreme Court remarked: 'there are circumstances in which a federal appellate court is justified in resolving an issue not passed on below, as where the proper resolution is beyond any doubt . . . or where "injustice might otherwise result".' Singleton v. Wulff, 428 U.S. 106, 121, 96 S.Ct. 2868, 2877, 49 L.Ed.2d 826 (1976). Because the preclusive effect of the law of the case and res judicata doctrines presents a pure legal question, and being satisfied that no prejudice will accrue to the defendants, see Payne v. McLemore's Wholesale & Retail Stores, 654 F.2d 1130 (5th Cir.1981), cert. denied, 455 U.S. 1000, 102 S.Ct. 1630, 71 L.Ed.2d 866 (1982), we exercise our discretion and address the question."

Nevertheless, the court of appeals affirmed, after easily deciding that neither res judicata nor law of the case applied. Res judicata applies only in a subsequent action, and "the law of the case doctrine does not encompass issues presented for decision but left unanswered by the appellate court."

DIEMER v. DIEMER, 8 N.Y.2d 206, 168 N.E.2d 654, 203 N.Y.S.2d 829 (1960). This was a separation action. The complaint alleged that *H*, a Protestant, and *W*, a Catholic, were married, *W* agreeing to take up *H*'s faith. After a child was born, religious conflict revolved around the child. Finally *W* told *H* that they were not married in the eyes of her church, and that there would be no more sexual relations until there was a second ceremony in the Catholic Church. *H* refused such a ceremony, and *W* refused further sexual relations. On these facts, *H* sought a separation, characterizing *W*'s conduct as "cruel and inhuman treatment." *W* counterclaimed for a separation, but neither in her answer nor at the trial did she deny the essentials of *H*'s story. After making findings of fact, the trial court denied a separation to either spouse, saying that cruel and inhuman treatment was not established. The appellate division affirmed.

The New York Court of Appeals reversed (5–2), awarding *H* a separation and holding that the facts alleged and proved had established *H*'s right to separation on the ground of abandonment. Judge Fuld, for the majority, rejected the argument that *H* must fail because he did not denominate *W*'s conduct as "abandonment." He said: "Surely, we have advanced far beyond that hypertechnical period when form was all-important and a pleader had to attach the correct label to his complaint, at the risk of having it dismissed. It is enough now that a pleader states the facts making out a cause of action, and it matters not whether he gives a name to the cause of action at all or even that he gives it a wrong name."

Chief Judge Desmond, dissenting, quoted earlier opinions by the court: "Pleadings and a distinct issue are essential to every system of jurisprudence . . . . It is fundamental that in civil actions the plaintiff must recover on the facts stated in his complaint, or not at all. In case a complaint proceeds on a definite, clear and certain theory, it will not support or permit another theory because it contains isolated or subsidiary statements consistent therewith." He added: "For no reason at all we are making a precipitous retreat from the good old rule that the parties to a private lawsuit fix the theory of suit and that no appellate court can present the losing side with a new theory."

Question: (4) When all this is said and done, in which categories of situations—besides those involving subject-matter jurisdiction and those within the plain error doctrine—do the federal courts of appeals appear to allow a party to forward an actually new theory on appeal? They do so if the new theory allows them to affirm, without inflicting "prejudice" on the appellant. Are there really any other exceptions that make sense?

NATIONAL ASS'N OF SOCIAL WORKERS v. HARWOOD, 69 F.3d 622 (1st Cir.1995). Lobbyists brought this civil rights action against Rhode Island legislators for banning them, and them alone, from the floor while the legislature was in session. The defendants denied the allegations. The plaintiffs prevailed by a bench trial.

On appeal, the defendants' new counsel raised the defense of legislative immunity, which the defendants had, as the court put it, "inexplicably neglected" to raise below "for some unfathomable reason." The court nevertheless entertained the defense, thereby reversing the judgment.

"It is very late in the day to bring a new argument to the fore. Ordinarily, an appellant who has not proffered a particular claim or defense in the district court 'may not unveil it in the court of appeals.' United States v. Slade, 980 F.2d 27, 30 (1st Cir.1992). This rule is deeply embedded in our jurisprudence, [citation omitted], and we have invoked it with a near-religious fervor, [citation omitted]. Nor can this variant of the raise-or-waive principle be dismissed as a pettifogging technicality or a trap for the indolent; the rule is founded upon important considerations of fairness, judicial economy, and practical wisdom. [Citations omitted.] Thus, parties must speak clearly in the trial court, on pain that, if they forget their lines, they will likely be bound forever to hold their peace. This is as it should be:

the rule fosters worthwhile systemic ends and courts will be the losers if they permit it to be too easily evaded.

"But foolish consistency is reputedly the hobgoblin of little minds, see Ralph Waldo Emerson, 'Self Reliance,' in Essays: First Series (1841), and in the last analysis, this articulation of the raise-or-waive principle, though important, is a matter of discretion. [Citations omitted.] Thus, this rule (like most rules) admits of an occasional exception. 'Occasional' is the key word. Since exceptions must be few and far between, an appellate court's discretion should not be affirmatively exercised unless the equities heavily preponderate in favor of such a step."

The court decided to invoke an exception here by considering the circuit's established list of relevant, albeit not necessary, factors: (1) "the omitted issue is purely legal in nature, and lends itself to satisfactory resolution on the existing record without further development of the facts"; (2) it "raises an issue of constitutional magnitude"; (3) it is "highly persuasive" and threatens "a miscarriage of justice [involving] a discernible public interest"; (4) "we see no special prejudice or inequity to the plaintiffs"; (5) "the omission seems entirely inadvertent rather than deliberate" and "yielded no tactical advantage to the defendants"; and most saliently in this case (6) "the omitted issue implicates matters of great public moment, and touches upon policies as basic as federalism, comity, and respect for the independence of democratic institutions."

Judge Lynch dissented. She felt the defendants had forfeited the defense. She also forcefully argued that legislative immunity did not reach this far.

Question: (5) In this realm, then, the cases replay the eternal struggle between certainty and accuracy. In the end, the federal courts of appeals can do what they want as to entertaining new issues, and some acknowledge this openly. Do you find such a discretionary approach more acceptable for this undertheorized subject of reviewability than it proved for the overworked subject of appealability?

INDEX

References are to Pages

†